Special thanks to 115,000 CAMRA members who carried out research for the pubs; Rick Pickup and Steve Westby for advising on new breweries; the Campaign's Regional Directors and Area Organisers, who co-ordinated the pub entries; Paul Moorhouse for assembling the beer tasting notes; Geoff Brandwood for writing the Pub Heritage feature; Michael Slaughter for checking pubs on the National Inventory; Colin Valentine for compiling the list of beer festivals; the publicans who kindly contributed their photographs; and CAMRA's National Executive for their support.

Thanks also to the following at CAMRA head office: Chief Executive Mike Benner; Marketing and Public Affairs: Louise Ashworth, Tarli Cable, John McCann; Kim Carvey, Jon Howard, Tony Jerome, Iain Loe, Jonathan Mail, Emily Ryans; What's Brewing: Claire-Michelle Pearson, Tom Stainer; Administration: Gillian Dale, Cressida Feiler, Robert Ferguson, Gary Ranson, Nicky Shipp; Membership Services: Caroline Clerembeaux, John Cottrell, Catrin Davies, Gary Fowler. Finance and Branch support: Anita Gibson, Liz McGlynn, Malcolm Harding. Warehouse: Neil Cox, Steve Powell, Barnaby Smith, Ron Stocks.

Photo credits: [Key: t = top; b = bottom; l = left; r = right] Front cover: John Morrison/Alamy; p8: Roger Protz; pp10–11: Roger Protz; p12: Phillip Gill (l); pp14-15: Cath Harries; p18: Graham Percy (b); p20: Roger Protz (t); p21: National Brewery Centre; pp22–24: Cath Harries; pp26–27: Cath Harries; p29: Hawkshead Brewery (bl); p30: Black Isle Brewery (tr); p873: Lothian Buses; p874: Neil Lloyd (l), Warren Wordsworth (r); p877: James Taylor (r); p881: Mick Slaughter (t); p886: Apple Inc.

Production: Cover design: Dale Tomlinson; colour section design: Keith Holmes, Thames Street Studio; database, typesetting and beers index: AMA Dataset, Preston, Lancs; maps David and Morag Perrot, PerroCarto, Machnylleth, Wales.

Printed and bound in the UK by William Clowes, Beccles, Suffolk.

Published by the Campaign for Real Ale Ltd, 230 Hatfield Road, St Albans, Herts, AL1 4LW. www.camra.org.uk

ISBN 978-1-85249-272-4

All of the papers used in this book are recyclable and made from wood grown in managed, sustainable forests. They are manufactured at mills certified to ISO 14001 and/or EMAS.

About the Good Beer Guide

Democracy at work

For 38 years, the *Good Beer Guide* has been underlining CAMRA's work by championing real ale pubs. But it's more than a pub guide: the Breweries section makes it a unique publication, listing every brewery in the country and keeping pace with their beers and plans for expansion.

The manner in which the Guide is compiled is made possible only by CAMRA's members. Every brewery has a liaison officer appointed by the Campaign, a volunteer who meets his or her brewery on a regular basis to discuss the company's plans and beer range.

The Pubs section of the Guide is compiled in an equally grass-roots fashion. Unlike most pub guides, where entries are chosen by a small editorial team or are sent in, unchecked, by members of the public, every pub in this guide is the result of regular inspection by CAMRA members, often on a weekly basis. The Guide is unique in offering only full entries, with no unchecked 'lucky dip' sections of pubs sent in at random. The Campaign comprises several hundred branches. Each branch surveys the pubs in its area and monitors not only the quality of the cask beer in each one but also watches out for change of ownership or management that could affect the range of ales on offer.

Democracy rules when CAMRA members meet to choose their pubs for each edition of the Guide. Short lists are drawn up and votes are taken to reduce the list to the required number to meet each branch's allocation. The branches do not relax once they have chosen their entries. They continue to monitor their pubs and if one needs to be replaced – for such reasons as closure, change of ownership or poor beer quality – then it will be de-listed on both the CAMRA website and in the members' newspaper, *What's Brewing*.

Beer quality, above all, determines the choice of pubs. The *Good Beer Guide* is concerned about the history and the architecture of pubs and such important creature comforts as food, family and disabled facilities, gardens, special events and even the standard of the toilets. But it has always been our belief that if a publican looks after the real ales in the cellar – a task that requires a degree of skill and even passion – then the quality of the other facilities should be of an equally high standard.

The Guide has moved with the times: 38 years ago, entries tended to be terse; of the 'busy street-corner pub' variety. Today, the pub has to meet both the competition of high street restaurant chains and a growing tendency to stay at home and watch multi-channel television. As a result, such important matters as pub food need to be detailed. But we remain committed to the belief that the aroma and flavour of the beer in the glass is our prime consideration.

The Guide also offers a wide cross-section of pubs in all parts of the country. In these pages you will find many delightful pubs in villages and small market towns. We are committed to helping rural pubs survive and CAMRA has argued that such pubs need special support, such as rate relief, to keep them in business. But most people live in towns and cities or visit them for a variety of reasons and we list scores of pubs in such vital hubs of communities. We happen to believe that when one so-called pub guide offers no main entries for Leeds, it's both a dereliction of duty and an insult to the people of that city.

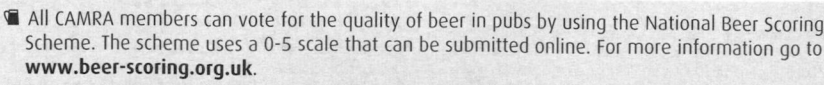

- All CAMRA members can vote for the quality of beer in pubs by using the National Beer Scoring Scheme. The scheme uses a 0-5 scale that can be submitted online. For more information go to **www.beer-scoring.org.uk**.
- You can keep you copy of the Guide up to date by visiting the CAMRA website **www.camra.org.uk**. Click on 'Good Beer Guide' then 'Updates to GBG 2011' where you will find information about changes to pubs and breweries.
- The Guide is keen to hear from readers. If you wish to recommend a pub or feel that one you have visited fell below expectations, then we would like to know. Please use the Readers' Recommendations and Have Your Say forms at the back of the book.

GOOD BEER GUIDE 2011

Edited by Roger Protz

Project Co-ordinator **Emma Haines**

Assistant Editors **Ione Brown, Katie Hunt, Simon Tuite**

Head of Publishing **Simon Hall**

CAMRA BOOKS

Campaign for Real Ale Ltd

Contents

CAMRA at 40

We're not resting on our laurels

The Campaign for Real Ale is 40 years old in 2011 but it will not be resting on its laurels. As this edition of the *Good Beer Guide* makes clear, there is still much work to be done to protect the interests of beer drinkers.

Demonstration in London in the early days of CAMRA against the planned closure of the Courage Brewery in Reading.

The beer world has changed out of all recognition since CAMRA was founded in the monochrome days of the early 1970s. Then, the Campaign's major opponents were known as the 'Big Six' national brewers, all British-owned and British-based. Compared to the global brewers and giant pub companies that bestride the modern brewing industry and pub trade, the Big Six of yesteryear were pussycats. Most had some commitment to cask beer. It was their determination to concentrate on keg beer and such national brands as Watneys Red, Double Diamond and Worthington E that encouraged a small group of beer lovers to set up the Campaign for the Revitalisation of Ale in 1971, which rapidly became the more manageable Campaign for Real Ale.

It was a pre-lager time. Those dreadful, risible keg beers have long since disappeared. But in one important respect, little has changed. In order to concentrate on keg beer, the Big Six closed regional breweries and axed local ales to promote their national brands. The global brewers follow the same well-trod path. Heineken has closed its Tyneside brewery while Carlsberg will pull down the shutters on the Tetley plant in Leeds during 2011. A-B InBev, the world's biggest brewer, plans to sell off Draught Bass, Boddingtons and Flowers.

But there is a lot to celebrate during CAMRA's fortieth year. There are twice as many breweries operating today than when the Campaign was founded. Many are tiny but, as this section of the Guide shows, others are growing and expanding at a fast rate due to the demand for their ales. Choice for beer drinkers has never been greater – and that is cause for celebration. The anniversary will be marked at CAMRA beer festivals during the course of the year, culminating in the Great British Beer Festival in London in August. For further information, see **www.camra.org.uk**.

The best way for readers and users of the Guide to mark the anniversary is to join the Campaign. The strength of the real ale revival is shown by CAMRA's membership, which now stands at 115,000. The figure has more than doubled in a decade and proves the enormous support for Britain's unique beer style and pubs.

The Campaign is now listened to with respect by the British and European parliaments and enjoys the status of a Special Complainant with the Office of Fair Trading. But strength lies in numbers and your membership and your voice will increase our ability to fight for beer drinkers' interests. There's a membership form at the back of the Guide.

CAMRA's Chief Executive, Mike Benner (left) took part in a debate in parliament in 2010 on 'Who will save the pub?' with Greg Mulholland MP (right) and Gerry Sutcliffe MP.

Introduction

Bitter taste for beer drinkers

Craft brewers prosper, despite an economy in the doldrums. But the multi-nationals turn their backs on real ale, supermarkets continue to sell cut-price drink and a VAT increase will place a further burden on pubs.

The yawning gap between craft and global brewers has widened since the last edition of the *Good Beer Guide* appeared. As the Breweries section of this edition shows, the craft sector continues to grow and that growth is driven by real ale. There's a mantra running through the section: 'installed new equipment due to increasing demand... moved to bigger premises... beers now more widely available'. Cask beer is the only successful sector of an otherwise stagnant brewing industry but the message seems to be lost on the giant producers of mass lager and keg beer brands.

The Guide in pages 18-20 reports on some of the remarkable success stories of small, medium and regional-size brewers. We could have filled the entire editorial section with similar reports. As the country emerges from a deep recession and pubs continue to close, brewers of quality beers nevertheless prosper. In spite of all the problems facing the economy and the almost crippling burden of tax levied on beer, some 88 new breweries came on stream in the past year, adding to the astonishing variety of beers now available.

Draught Bass and Boddington's - put up for sale by beer giant A-B InBev.

Giants' sell-out

The message is lost on the global producers. In the summer of 2010, A-B InBev, the world's biggest brewer, announced it was putting up for sale Boddingtons Bitter, Draught Bass and Flower's Original and IPA. The asking price is £15 million. Draught Bass at its peak accounted for two million barrels a year. Under-promoted and clearly unloved by its new owner, production has fallen to 60,000 barrels. That's still more than the combined annual production of three or four craft brewers. But A-B InBev, obsessed with mass volume lager brands, can't be bothered to breathe life back into one of Britain's best-loved ales.

Carlsberg will close the Tetley Brewery in Leeds in 2011, a move that has angered and dismayed legions of beer lovers in Yorkshire. In an astonishing example of cack-handed decision-making, Carlsberg has decided that the keg version of Tetley's Bitter will continue to be brewed in Yorkshire by John Smith's but the cask-conditioned beer will move to Banks's Brewery in Wolverhampton. Do the Danish owners of Carlsberg, locked in their Copenhagen redoubt, seriously think that beer lovers in God's Own County will accept iconic Tyke ale trunked up from the West Midlands? To add insult to injury, Carlsberg announced it was bringing back the famous Huntsman logo for Tetley cask at the very moment it decided to close the Leeds brewery. If the Danes thought this would appease drinkers, they should read the volumes of deserved abuse they have received in the Yorkshire media.

Heineken UK, which now owns the former Scottish & Newcastle breweries and brands, closed its Gateshead factory in 2010 and announced it would transfer production of Newcastle Brown Ale to that repository of lost beer souls, John Smith's. The Dutch, in common with their Danish colleagues, need a crash course in

Tetley's Huntsman - the famous Yorkshire image brought back as Carlsberg plans to brew the bitter in... the West Midlands.

both British geography and local pride. A Geordie beer brewed in Yorkshire is likely to sink like a lead parachute.

The state of the global brewers' sector of the industry was brought into sharp focus in 2010 when Molson Coors, the Canadian-American giant that owns the former Bass breweries in Burton-on-Trent, announced it was making only one penny in profit from each pint of beer it makes – mainly Carling lager. This is voodoo economics. It's driven by the global giants' Faustian pact with supermarket chains, who demand such deep discounts on beer that it's sold at little more than cost price. Molson Coors' answer to this absurd state of affairs was not to tackle the greed of the supermarkets but to increase the price of draught beer it sells to pubs. So once again, poor, hard-pressed pub-goers pay the price for the frightening power that high-street retailers exercise over their beer suppliers.

The price of a pint has been a dominant theme of the past year. The last Labour government increased beer duty by 25 per cent in two years. The decision by the new coalition government to freeze duty in its emergency budget in June 2010 brought some relief to a battered brewing industry and pub trade, but that was offset by the decision to increase Value Added Tax in January 2011. When the VAT increase kicks in, it will mean that for the first time ever the tax element – duty and VAT – of the price of a pint will constitute more than £1. Is it any wonder that pubs close as customers rush for the comfort blanket of cheap booze in supermarkets?

When VAT is increased in January 2011, tax will account for £1.00 of the price of a pint.

Crocodile tears

Government ministers, regardless of party, fail to realise that making and selling beer is one of Britain's last remaining major industries, providing jobs for close to one million people. Yet successive governments regard beer as a convenient milch cow and then weep crocodile tears when pubs close. The problem is compounded by the abject failure of past and present governments to tackle the power of the supermarkets whose cost-cutting leads to pub closures.

This edition of the Guide, in The Battered Pub feature, devotes space to the plight of the pub and how it can be helped. Greg Mulholland MP's Save the Pub parliamentary group is helping to spotlight the problem and, with CAMRA, is putting forward sensible ideas, such as rate relief, an end to restrictive covenants and weakening the power of the major pub companies. Real ale also has a vital role to play in preventing pub closures. All the evidence – including data from Cask Marque and the annual Cask Ale Report – indicates that pubs that promote real ale, offer a wide choice and stage innovative events such as regular beer festivals can see their business grow.

Data from the annual Cask Ale Report indicates that pubs that promote real ale and stage innovative events such as regular beer festivals can see their business grow.

The heartening revival of real ale has once again put it centre stage in pubs. The commitment and the passion for the product among brewers as well as drinkers deserve special recognition. Britain is the only major country that continues to produce a beer style that comes to fruition in its cask in the pub cellar. It's a style that deserves special support. The *Good Beer Guide* urges the government to support CAMRA's call for the European Union to redraft the tax rules to enable member states to levy lower rates of duty on beer sold in pubs. Such a move would encourage more drinkers to switch to cask ale. It would mean increased business for the beleaguered pub trade and would bring even greater choice and diversity as new breweries start up.

In short, Back British Beer!

The Battered Pub

Why CAMRA supports the family brewers' tie

Giant companies must give publicans more freedom to buy beer – but small brewers have to keep the tie in order to stay in business

Tied pubs are the bedrock of family brewers and the Campaign for Real Ale is determined to protect their right to run their own estates. CAMRA's Chief Executive, Mike Benner, makes it clear that the Campaign differentiates itself from groups that demand the total abolition of the tie – a demand they have taken to both the British and European parliaments.

'Without the right to tie pubs, family brewers wouldn't bother to bring their beers to the bar,' Benner says. 'Closures among small brewers would be inevitable. The tie is a viable way for them to run their pubs.'

CAMRA's criticism of the tie has been directed at the giant pub companies, or pubcos, that dominate the supply of beer. 'The business model isn't working,' Benner argues. 'The partnership between pubcos and their tenants and leaseholders needs to be rebalanced. While the pubcos make profits, some tenants have incomes of just £15,000 a year or work for less than the minimum wage. They can't invest in their pubs while beer prices and pub rents continue to rise.'

Rents and beer prices

In 2009, CAMRA, which has the status of a Super Complainant, took its campaign against the pubcos to the Office of Fair Trading. The Campaign complained about the rents and beer prices charged by the pub companies and sought a referral to the Competition Commission. CAMRA's evidence said that the pubcos charged wholesale beer prices to its estates that worked out at around 50 pence a pint more than in the free trade.

The OFT turned down CAMRA's complaint but the Campaign appealed against the decision. The OFT's response had not been received when the Guide went to press but Mike Benner makes it clear that even if the appeal is rejected it will pursue its campaign to force the pubcos to charge lower prices for its beers.

'The OFT must stand up for the consumer,' he says, 'and pubcos should offer their tenants both guest beers and the right to buy beers outside of the tie.'

There has been some movement on the part of two of the giant pubcos, Enterprise Inns and Punch Taverns. They are revising their leases with a 'rent for discount option' and also a 'free of the tie' price option. The options would mean that tenants would have to pay increased rents but would have some freedom to buy beers outside of the tie and could also have a say on the level of discounts offered by the pub companies.

'Rents are a major problem,' Benner says. 'A review by the Royal Institute of Chartered Surveyors is looking at the way in which pub rents are set and we're hoping that could lead to fairer rents for tenants. We expect the regulators to take action against the anti-competitive nature of the way pubcos runs their estates.'

CAMRA also wants action against supermarkets and the enormous discounts the high-street multiples demand of beer suppliers. 'The price differential between supermarkets and pubs is now seven to one,' Benner says. 'The supermarkets tell their suppliers to absorb increases in beer duty but publicans are unable to do the same, which puts them at an enormous disadvantage. When excise duty goes up or there are special events like the 2010 World Cup, the price gap between pubs and supermarkets widens.'

The new coalition government says it will appoint an Ombudsman for supermarkets and CAMRA will call on the government to make a similar appointment for pubs.

'Well-run pubs are essential to society,' Mike Benner says. 'They are vital hubs of local communities.'

The Swan Inn in Kettelshulme, Cheshire, dates from the 15th century. In 2004, when the owner threatened to turn it into a private house, locals raised £425,000 to buy the inn. A committee ran it for three years and the inn was then handed over to tenants.

Run your local pub

CAMRA welcomed the call in July 2010 by Prime Minister David Cameron for pubs threatened with closure to be taken over by local communities. The Campaign's own polling research shows that 43 per cent of people would be willing to join efforts to save their local pub. Among regular pub-goers, this figure rises to 63 per cent.

The Campaign wrote to the government, seeking assurances that adequate resources will be allocated to provide business, legal and financial advice to communities that wish to save their local pubs by running them as mutuals, cooperatives or social enterprises. There are currently 30 community-owned pubs in Britain.

Break up the giant pubcos

Radical call by Greg Mulholland MP

Britain's giant pub companies must be broken up and handed back to tenants and customers – that's the radical call from Greg Mulholland MP, chairman of the All-Party Parliamentary Save the Pub Group. The Leeds North-West Liberal Democrat MP says a ceiling should be placed on how many outlets a pub company can own.

'The pub trade has lost its way,' Mulholland says. 'Pubs are about serving communities, not boosting the fortunes of companies whose only interest is in maximising rents.'

Greg Mulholland set up the Save the Pub Group during the time of the last Labour government. He will put pressure on the new coalition government to change the law in order that pubs can be saved for their communities.

'We have to recognise the cultural, historical and social importance of the pub to the nation,' Mulholland adds. 'Instead of closing pubs, we have to promote pubs and get young people going to them.'

He feels strongly that the pub trade is controlled by a few large groups who are incapable of reforming themselves. 'We need government action and we need a referral to the Competition Commission. I want a "Beer Orders II" to put right the mistakes of the original Beer Orders.'

Beer Orders 'a disaster'

The Beer Orders in the early 1990s – described by Mulholland as a 'disaster and a tragedy' – flowed from an investigation by the Monopolies & Mergers Commission into the supply of beer to the pub trade. It found that the then 'Big Six' national brewers acted as a cartel and fixed prices. As a result, a ceiling was put on the number of tied pubs a brewery could own.

Most of the Big Six decided to leave brewing rather than give up the tie. Their pubs were bought by the new wave of pub companies – pubcos – that don't own breweries. The big three pubcos – Enterprise, Punch and Mitchells & Butlers – own far more pubs today than the Big Six of yesteryear.

'Pubs are closing not only as a result of the recession but also because the giant pubcos charge exorbitant rents to their tenants and charge them top dollar for beer', Greg Mulholland says. He argues that if the pubcos are forced by law to divest themselves of thousands of pubs, they could be run by smaller pub companies or by local communities.

Greg Mulholland MP and Lord Bilston of the All-Party Parliamentary Save the Pub Group.

'Pubs are more than businesses,' Mulholland says. 'They're part of their communities and they often do valuable charity work. They need greater recognition and they need to pay lower rates to help them survive.

'Any threat to close a community pub must lead to a viability study and genuine consultation with local people. The biggest scandal is that profitable, viable pubs are being closed against the wishes of their communities and at present people are powerless to stop it.'

Mulholland argues for a major overhaul of planning laws to stop pubs being converted to flats and shops. He also wants restrictive covenants to be outlawed.

The chairman of the Save the Pub Group also wants government action to prevent supermarkets selling beer at cost price or as lost leaders. 'It's socially irresponsible and makes it difficult for pubs to compete,' he says. 'It should be outlawed. Of course, people should be able to drink at home but we must stop irresponsible drinking, caused by cheap supermarket packaged lagers and alcopops.'

Mulholland says the case for minimum pricing of alcohol, which the Scottish government has considered, is one possible way of tackling cheap drink in supermarkets, but he believes more research needs to be done in this area.

But he's convinced that increasing excise duty and other taxes on drink is not the way to tackle irresponsible drinking by a minority. 'Raising duty doesn't tackle binge drinking,' he says. 'We want to encourage people – young people in particular – to drink in the controlled environment of the pub'.

The pub fights back

A record number of pubs have closed in recent years as a result of the recession, cut-price alcohol in supermarkets and the smoking ban. But pubs can thrive if they attract customers with a wide range of cask ales and regular beer festivals.

Casks of beer behind the bar of the Dove Street Inn in Ipswich bore the label 'Sold Out'. But plenty more ale was available. A bleary-eyed Ady Smith, who runs the pub with his partner, Karen Beaumont, said, 'We had a fantastic night last night.' It looked like being a fantastic Saturday as well, as drinkers started to fill up the two bars and a large marquee at the back.

The Dove, Ipswich, with a marquee where beer festivals are staged.

It was the 2010 Spring bank holiday, one of three occasions during the year when the Dove stages beer festivals. Ady and Karen have 12 years' experience of running beer festivals and have used that experience and their enthusiasm to breathe life back into the Dove.

'Wet sales' – draught beer – account for 84 per cent of the Dove's business. That's an astonishingly high proportion for a pub in the 21st century but it's beer that is driving the Dove's success. Cask ales are keenly priced, with an average of £2.80 a pint, and regular drinkers can join a loyalty scheme that gives discounts on beer.

'There's a Wetherspoon's nearby – it makes you price aware,' Ady admits. 'We're getting a lot of young people drinking real ale and 40 per cent of those real ale drinkers are women.'

The Dove is a small pub but Ady and Karen pack in as many as 66 ales during a festival, some on handpump, the rest straight from the cask. They have 80 suppliers, many of them small brewers keen to get their beers on the bar.

'Our website is constantly updated to show the beers available and how much of each beer is left,' Ady says. 'Tickers can see if they can get here before their favourite beer runs out.'

As well as guest ales from small craft breweries throughout Britain, the Dove has regular beers. Crouch Vale's Brewers Gold is the biggest seller, followed by Hop Back Summer Lightning and Fuller's London Pride. Such East Anglian favourites as Adnams Broadside, Mauldon's Black Adder and Woodforde's Wherry are also usually on tap.

Ady Smith and Karen Beaumont of the Dove, Ipswich, plan to build a micro-brewery in the town.

Beer from the wood

Ady is keen to develop 'beer from the wood' in order that drinkers can see how real ale varies when it's served from both wooden and metal containers. Black Adder was served from the wood during the May beer festival. Ady sends wooden pins and firkins – 4.5 and 9-gallon casks – to selected brewers and Theakston's Old Peculier was due to be the next ale to get the wood treatment.

The success of the Dove – it sold 7,500 pints during the Spring bank holiday festival – is all the more remarkable as the pub was sold by its previous owner, the giant pub company Enterprise Inns. The street-corner inn dates from the early 18th century and has wood beams, bare floors and an impressive inglenook in the small back bar. The recent addition of a conservatory houses a kitchen for Karen during beer festivals, with the marquee latched on at the back.

Dove Street Inn, St Helens Street, Ipswich
01473 211270
www.dovestreetinn.co.uk

Mark Frazer in his marquee behind the Blacksmiths.

Enterprise declared the Dove to be unviable and planned to close it in 2003. Ady and Karen snapped it up and have turned it into a thriving business.

Ady gives a wry smile. 'Now, seven years later and seeing what we've achieved, Enterprise wants to buy it back.'

The pubco will be disappointed, for Ady and Karen will not only hold on to the Dove but also plan to expand. 'Ipswich is a desert for beer choice,' he says, 'and we're helping to fund a new micro-brewery on the waterfront. Drinkers want local beers and we intend to supply them.'

Blacksmiths finds new feet

The Blacksmiths Arms in St Albans sold more cask beer than lager in May 2010. It's a remarkable statistic, as even the most successful real ale publican would be satisfied if the split were 40 cask to 60 lager. Manager Mark Frazer is convinced the growth of real ale in the pub is due to staging monthly beer festivals and serving a wide range of ales from regional and craft breweries sourced from all over the country.

The pub has Tudor and Georgian features with 20th-century additions. Part of the complex was once stables and, centuries ago, the inn may have brewed for St Peter's Church a few yards away. Until 2000, the Blacksmiths was a Whitbread tied house and then became a specialist Hogshead pub run by Laurel Inns, with a good range of real ales. But when Laurel altered Hogshead to Hogs Head, a minor change of branding became a disaster for cask beer. Only one handpump was left as Laurel chased the local youth market, assuming that the large number of students in and around St Albans would drink only lager.

The Blacksmiths, St Albans, attracts young drinkers with cask ale.

Real ale in favour

The solitary cask beer was Wells' Bombardier, an excellent ale but not uncommon in the city, with a Charles Wells' pub a few hundred yards away. The Blacksmiths became a virtual no-go area for real ale drinkers until Laurel went into administration. It was rescued in 2008 by a large injection of capital by property tycoon Robert Tchenguiz, who split the company into two, with Town & City running specialist pubs.

The Blacksmiths has blossomed under Town & City. The company gives managers like Mark Frazer considerable freedom to choose beers. Mark uses specialist wholesalers and the Society of Independent Brewers (SIBA) delivery scheme to source beers from all over Britain. He hails from the North East, speaks fondly of the ales from the region, and assiduously reads the trade press, CAMRA journals and websites to monitor new breweries.

Mark now has eight handpumps on the bar in the spacious two-level pub. He has done the unthinkable and removed one T-bar font serving keg beers and lagers to make way for cask beer and he plans to install two additional beer engines. Bombardier remains and has been joined by Timothy Taylor's Landlord, Courage Directors, Crouch Vale Brewers Gold and Oakham Inferno, with local ales from Buntingford and Red Squirrel. There are always six guest ales.

The range is augmented by a vast array of ales during beer festivals. A large car park behind the pub has been turned in to a sunny garden with a marquee where beers are served straight from the cask during festivals. Several of the festivals are themed: July 2010, for example, was devoted to a 1980s Punk revival, while August went back two decades earlier with Flower Power, which featured beers with a floral hop character.

Mark Frazer also attracts large crowds with a policy of regular live music, featuring local groups. The pub and garden are packed and the customers are mainly young, disproving Laurel Inns' belief that students and young people in general won't drink cask beer.

Blacksmiths Arms,
56 St Peter's Street, St Albans, Herts
01727 868845

Jollydarity wins the day

The Jolly Anglers in Kennetside, Reading, a popular riverside pub, has been saved as a result of a vigorous campaign by locals and CAMRA members, backed by the All-Party Parliamentary Save the Pub Group. The pub was owned by Enterprise Inns, which announced in June 2009 that it was unviable. The manager of the pub was given just one day's notice of the plan to close it and sell the site. A 'restricted covenant' was slapped on the pub, which meant that new owners would be unable to re-open it as a pub. Campaigners are convinced the closure had more to do with Enterprise Inn's cash-flow problems than the alleged lack of viability of the Jolly Anglers and wanted a quick sale for the site.

Within days, a group called Jollydarity was formed to save the pub. It was made up of local residents, CAMRA members and local politicians from all parties. The group was given media coverage by the press and BBC in the region and it received a message of support from the All-Party Parliamentary Save the Pub Group.

Behind the scenes, Jollydarity went into negotiations with Enterprise Inns, urging the pub company to remove the restrictive covenant on the pub. Jollydarity stressed that it was nonsense to claim the pub was not viable. It stands on the Kennet river, close to its junction with the Thames and is also close to the Kennet & Avon Canal. As a result of this prime location, the pub is popular with all those who use the area for walking, boating and angling. The group also persuaded the new owners of the property – a private couple – to allow the site to re-open as a pub and to apply for a new licence, as the previous licence had expired.

John Westendorp... pulling pints again.

The campaign was successful. The covenant was removed, a licence was granted and the owners agreed to re-open the Jolly Anglers in March 2010. Life has come full circle for landlord John Westendorp. He was running the pub when he was told by Enterprise it was closing. Now he's manning the handpumps again.

The house beer is called Jolly Angry from the local Loddon Brewery and other craft brewers are well represented. Art Brew was the first to deliver and others include Ascot Ales, Andwell, Cottage, Hammerpot, Triple fff and Two Bridges. There's no Guinness on sale but there's always a cask stout. And if you ask for Stella, you'll meet the resident black labrador who answers to the name.

Jolly Anglers, 313 Kennetside, Reading
0872 1077077

A growing number of entries in the Guide refer to pubs supporting the LocAle system. This was devised by CAMRA members in Nottingham and is now in widespread use in England, Wales, Scotland and Northern Ireland.

The aim is to encourage publicans to stock at least one cask beer that comes from a local brewery – the distance between pub and brewery varies but is now generally accepted to be not more than 30 miles. The scheme also encourages publicans to use the Direct Delivery Scheme run by SIBA, the Society of Independent Brewers. SIBA members deliver direct to pubs in their localities rather than going through the central warehouses of pub-owning companies.

The overall aim of LocAle is to cut down on 'beer miles'. Research by CAMRA shows that food and drink transport accounts for 25 per cent of all HGV vehicle miles in Britain. Taking into account the miles that ingredients have travelled on top of distribution journeys, an imported lager produced by a multinational brewery could have notched up more than 24,000 'beer miles' by the time it reaches a pub.

Pubs that support the LocAle scheme receive a special window sticker. For more information, see the CAMRA website **www.camra.org.uk** and type 'locale' into the search window.

Pub of the Year

Historic victory for Sheffield tavern

The Kelham Island Tavern in Sheffield was named National Pub of the Year for the second year in succession in 2010 – the first time a pub has won the coveted prize two years running.

The CAMRA competition analyses all the criteria that make a good pub, including the quality of the beer, atmosphere, decor, customer service and all-round value of the visit. The competition is overseen by the Campaign's 115,000-strong membership. Look out for the 🏆 symbol against pub entries in the Guide and see the 'Award winning pubs' listing on pages 874-7.

The Kelham Island Tavern has held the title of CAMRA Yorkshire Regional Pub of the Year on four occasions. Praising the pub for its historic achievement, Julian Hough, CAMRA's Pubs Director, said: 'The Kelham Island Tavern holds a remarkable record in CAMRA's pub competitions, bearing in mind the pub only opened in 2002. With so many fantastic community pubs in Sheffield, it's difficult enough to be crowned the best in Steel City, let alone the whole of the UK. The pub's success is thoroughly deserved due to its high attention to detail, service to the surrounding community and quality in all areas, not least the beer.'

Trevor Wraith, owner of the tavern, said: 'We are once again overwhelmed at the judges' results and delighted to be awarded CAMRA's top prize for the second year running. It's a truly great achievement and something we never dreamt of when we first opened. Winning last year only made us work harder to meet and beat people's expectations, with drinkers travelling from all over the country to visit us. With this award, our aim is that we maintain our high standards and continue to fulfil people's high hopes of our pub.'

Trevor Wraith with his second National Pub of the Year award.

The runners-up were:

Central Southern

Royal Oak Inn, Wantage, Oxfordshire.

The judges said: 'Photos of ships bearing the pub's name adorn the walls in this street-corner pub. The lounge bar features a wrought-iron trelliswork, largely hidden by more than 300 pump clips. The smaller public bar attracts a younger crowd. A Mecca for discerning drinkers, the pub is a primary outlet for Pitstop and West Berks ales – two beers carry the landlord's name.'

Greater Manchester

Crown Hotel, Worthington.

The judges said: 'Local CAMRA Pub of the Year in 2006 and 2008, this country inn offers eight cask beers and two scrumpy ciders and acts as the brewery tap for Prospect beers. High quality home-cooked food is sold in the bar and conservatory restaurant, while a large decked sun terrace at the rear has patio heaters for cooler evenings. Mini beer festivals are held four times a year.'

Surrey & Sussex

Royal Oak, Friday Street, West Sussex.

The judges said: 'A lovely, isolated, low-beamed, narrow free house that's well worth finding, with seven handpumps for real ale, three for cider and two for perry. Ales are from local micro-breweries and are constantly changing. The pub was also CAMRA National Pub of the Year runner-up in 2009. This is a real gem.'

Cask Marque

The demanding life of a pub landlord

It's what goes on in the pub cellar that determines whether or not your pint is in perfect condition. Publicans are helped and tested by Cask Marque to make sure their real ale is always on top form.

Chris Cochran of the Victoria, Paddington, pulls another perfect pint.

There's a lot more to running a pub than opening the doors and inviting drinkers in. In these difficult times, pubs need to serve consistently good pints of cask beer and as most people are aware – 46 per cent of cask ale drinkers, according to an National Opinion Poll survey – Cask Marque's prime remit is to improve beer quality in pubs. In 2010 Cask Marque carried out 16,000 visits, undertaken by some 45 qualified assessors, mostly brewers. But we rely heavily on the pub landlord to do his or her job correctly.

Landlords undertake the final part of the brewing process – the second fermentation in the cask. This requires:

- A temperature-controlled cellar set at between 11 - 13°C
- Allowing 48 hours for secondary fermentation and settling before the beer is ready for sale
- Checking on delivery that the beer is well within its sell-by date
- Placing each cask on a stillage (rack) and venting the cask with a soft peg to allow the excess CO^2 to escape. The gas is generated as a bi-product of the conversion of sugars to alcohol by the live yeast in the cask. This will normally take 24 hours to complete
- Tapping the cask and allowing the yeast to settle at the bottom of the cask

Before connecting the cask to the beer line to the bar the landlord must:

- Test the beer by sampling directly from the cask to see it is clear in appearance – all yeast has settled – and tastes true to type
- Ensure beer lines are cleaned every seven days to avoid a build up of yeast
- Ideally, use line cooling from cellar to bar, including lagged cylinder jackets on the beer engines operated by handpumps to control temperture
- Test the temperature of the beer in the glass every day to ensure it hits the correct temperature of 10 - 14°C
- Renovate glassware on a regular basis. This is a process where all glasses have a deep clean to remove a yeast film that develops and which is not removed by the normal glass-washing process. If no action is taken, the film can lead to a flat pint

You may think that is more than enough to deliver the perfect pint – but it does not stop there:

- Cask ale must be sold within three days of going on sale. It's a live product, so stockholding and range are important. Ordering too many different beers could lead to poor throughputs
- The cellar must be kept spotless, as contaminated air can quickly infect beer. Normally a cellar is spring cleaned the day before a delivery
- Training is important for new licensees and bar staff. The industry has developed a Cellar Management Qualification and Cask Marque runs more than 200 one-day courses per year throughout the country. We have also written an online training programme for bar staff that explains legal and customer responsibilities, and also how to serve a perfect pint. Visit **www.barexcellence.co.uk**.

Promoting excellence

When landlords get it right and serve excellent cask beer, they need to share it with their customers. Gaining recognition in the *Good Beer Guide* is very important to their business. Also, Cask Marque accreditation is an independent endorsement of their cellar management skills and ability to serve great beer.

The *Good Beer Guide* and Cask Marque create awareness of great pubs – hence our sponsorship of the Guide. Every Cask Marque-accredited pub in the Guide is shown by a ✔ symbol. We also list all pubs with the Cask Marque Award (nearly 7,000) on our website, where regional guides can be downloaded. Visit **www.cask-marque.co.uk**.

Our future is in the hands of landlords to do their job with enthusiasm and passion. Do congratulate them if their beer delights you, as it is always good to receive a pat on the back for a job well done. To ensure standards, we rely on feedback from customers. If you find that beer in a Cask Marque pub does not meet expectations, please talk to the landlord and also notify us either by email **info@cask-marque.co.uk** or phone **01206 752212**. We make unannounced visits twice a year but feedback is always welcome.

Cask beer is attracting a new audience, so let's not disappoint them!

A Cask Marque assessor checks beer temperature.

Cask Marque joins the digital age

To find the nearest Cask Marque pubs to a postcode or town, you can use our text service or download from the Cask Marque website our free sat-nav programme.

By Sat Nav	By Text
1. Visit our website: **www.cask-marque.co.uk**	1. Text **Cask**
2. Click on **Free Sat Nav** page	2. Followed by a **Full Stop.**
3. Follow the instructions depending on your type of navigation system	3. Then **where** (town or full/part postcode) e.g. **Cask.HP18 1PH**
4. View the pubs under **Points of Interest** heading on your sat nav, absolutely free!	4. Send to **60300**
	5. You will receive back the **2** nearest outlets

Users download Sat Nav info at their own risk. Texts cost 25p plus your standard operator rate. To stop, text Cask stop to 60300 at anytime. Numbers will be retained for future Cask Marque announcements. E&OE

Also, we have available a new mobile-phone app, Caskfinder, which can be downloaded from the iTunes App Store and the Android Market.

What is on Caskfinder?

- Details of Cask Marque pubs and beers stocked
- Beer descriptions using Cyclops descriptors
- Brewers and details of their beers
- Beer festivals throughout the country
- Pete Brown's beer blog

To download free of charge, go to the iTunes App Store or the Android Market and search for 'Caskfinder'

National Cask Ale Week

Cask Marque works with CAMRA, the Society of Independent Brewers (SIBA) and regional brewers to promote this event to raise awareness of Britain's national drink and encourage new drinkers to discover cask ale.

NATIONAL Cask Ale WEEK

The 2010 event saw:

- 7,257 pubs promoting the event
- 26 brewers providing merchandising kits
- 3,700 people visiting the Cask Ale Week website on one day
- 16 page supplement on beer in *The Independent*
- On-line competition
- The launch of the Cask Marque iPhone application which within a month had 3,738 downloads and was used 18,449 sessions.

Look out for Cask Ale Week 2011 and enjoy a great pint.

Beer Festivals & Key Events

THE CAMPAIGN FOR REAL ALE'S BEER FESTIVALS are magnificent shop windows for cask ale and they give drinkers the opportunity to sample beers from independent brewers rare to particular localities. Beer festivals are enormous fun: many offer good food and live entertainment, and – where possible – facilities for families. Some seasonal festivals specialise in spring, summer, autumn and winter ales. Festivals range in size from small local events to large regional ones. CAMRA holds two national festivals, the National Winter Ales Festival in January, and the Great British Beer Festival in August; the latter features around 500 beers.

The festivals listed are those planned for 2010. For up-to-date information, visit the CAMRA website **www.camra.org.uk** and click on 'CAMRA Near You'. By joining CAMRA – there's a form on page 888 – you will receive the Campaign's monthly newspaper *What's Brewing*, which lists every festival on a month-by-month basis. Dates listed are liable to change: check with the website or *What's Brewing*.

JANUARY

NATIONAL WINTER ALES (MANCHESTER)

Atherton – Bent & Bongs Beer Bash
Cambridge – Winter
Colchester – Winter
Ely – Elysian
Exeter – Winter
Ipswich – Winter
Redditch
Salisbury – Winter

FEBRUARY

Battersea
Chappel – Winter
Chelmsford – Winter
Chesterfield
Derby – Winter
Dorchester
Dover – White Cliffs Winter
Fleetwood
Gosport – Winter
Liverpool
Luton
Pendle
Stockton – Ale & Arty
Tewkesbury – Winter

MARCH

Bradford
Bristol
Burton – Spring
Coventry
Darlington – Spring
Hitchin
Hove – Sussex
Leeds
Leicester
London Drinker
Loughborough
Oldham
Overton (Hampshire)
St Neots
Walsall
Whitehaven
Wigan
Winchester (provisional)

APRIL

Bexley
Bury St Edmunds – East Anglian
Chippenham
Doncaster
Farnham
Glenrothes – Kingdom of Fife
Larbert – Falkirk
Maldon
Mansfield
Newcastle-upon-Tyne
Paisley
Thanet

MAY

Banbury
Cambridge
Colchester
Halifax
Lincoln
Macclesfield
Newark
Newark & Notts Show
Newport (Gwent)
Northampton – Delapre Abbey
Reading
Rugby
Stourbridge
Stratford-Upon-Avon
Yapton

JUNE

Aberdeen
Braintree
Cardiff – Great Welsh
Chappel – Winter
Edinburgh – Scottish
Ely – Elysian (provisional)
Ely – Winter
Gibberd Garden – Harlow
Harpenden
Kingston
Lewes – South Downs
Southampton
St Ives (Cornwall)
Skipton
Stockport
Tenterden – Kent & East Sussex Railway
Thurrock
Wolverhampton
Woodchurch – Rare Breeds

JULY

Ardingly
Bishops Stortford
Bromsgrove
Canterbury – Kent

Chelmsford
Ealing
Derby
Devizes
Hereford – Beer on the Wye
Plymouth
Stafford
Stowmarket
Winchcombe – Cotswold
Woodcote – Steam Fair
Northwich
Rochford – Cider
Shrewsbury
Southport
St Albans
St Ives (Cambs) – Booze on the Ouse
Tamworth
Ulverston
York
Sawbridgeworth
Sheffield
Solihull
Stoke-on-Trent – Potteries
Sunderland
Swindon
Troon – Ayrshire
Wallington
Weymouth
Worthing

AUGUST

GREAT BRITISH, LONDON
Barnstaple
Clacton
Grantham
Harbury
Peterborough
Swansea
Watnall – Moorgreen
Worcester

SEPTEMBER

Ascot
Bridgnorth – Severn Valley
Burton
Chappel
Darlington – Rhythm 'N' Brews
Durham
Faversham – Hop
Hinckley
Ipswich
Jersey
Keighley
Letchworth
Lytham
Melton Mowbray
Minehead
Nantwich
Newton Abbot
North Cotswolds – Moreton-in-Marsh

OCTOBER

Alloa
Barnsley
Basingstoke
Bath
Bedford
Birkenhead
Birmingham
Cambridge – Octoberfest
Carlisle
Chester
Chesterfield – Market
Eastbourne
Egremont, Cumbria – (provisional)
Falmouth
Gainsborough
Heathrow
Huddersfield – Oktoberfest
Kendal
Long Eaton (provisional)
Louth
Milton Keynes
Norwich
Nottingham
Oxford
Poole
Quorn Octoberfest
Redhill
Richmond (N Yorks.)
St Helens

NOVEMBER

Bury
Dudley
Rochford
Saltburn
Wakefield
Wantage
Watford
Whitchurch (Hampshire)
Woking

DECEMBER

Harwich
London – Pig's Ear

Good Beer Bounces Back

Brewing up a storm

Real ale continues to grow despite the economic downturn and pub closures. The *Good Beer Guide* traces the success stories of just some of the craft breweries that are investing in new plant and recording remarkable growth in their sales.

In the summer of 2010, Castle Rock Brewery in Nottingham faced the dreadful prospect summed up by that famous Australian ditty: 'There's nothing so lonesome, so morbid or drear than to stand at the bar of a pub with no beer'. Supplies of Castle Rock's best-selling brand, Harvest Pale, had run so low that the brewery was rationing supplies to free trade customers and had none left over for its own pubs.

Fortunately, help was at hand in the shape of an impressive new brewery being built alongside the original plant next door to the Vat & Fiddle pub. The new site came on stream in July 2010 and Harvest Pale was once again available and in greater volumes.

'Demand has been phenomenal,' Castle Rock owner Chris Holmes says. He sells Harvest Pale to Punch Taverns and to the free trade via the Society of Independent Brewers' (SIBA) direct delivery scheme and 'they both just want more and more.'

Holmes was national chairman of CAMRA in the 1970s and went on to own several pubs in the Nottingham area before launching Castle Rock Brewery in 1998. He produced 30 barrels a week at first, then upgraded to 70 barrels in 2005 with additional fermenting vessels. The new plant, in a spacious former probationer officers' building close to Nottingham railway station, will allow Castle Rock to produce 20,000 barrels a year.

The Castle Rock team (left to right): Adrian Redgrove, Colin Wilde, Chris Holmes and Neil Kellett.

Chris Holmes and his team are bringing brewing pride back to a city that has lost such famous names as Hardy & Hanson, Home and Shipstones. The new brewery, which is based on the traditional English system of mash tun and copper, cost £600,000, a considerable sum at a time when the country is coming out of recession. But there are no signs of economic downturn at Castle Rock, which owns 22 pubs and supplies the free trade as far as York and Lincoln. The brewery also does 'beer swaps' with other producers, which is why its ales can be found, for example, in some Fuller's pubs in London.

Harvest Pale, which accounts for 50 per cent of production, has won prestigious awards for Castle Rock from both CAMRA and SIBA. But the brewery has an impressive range of other beers, including a dark Mild and an India Pale Ale. A new beer is produced every month to support Nottinghamshire Wildlife Fund: Chris Holmes believes in putting something back in to the locality.

He is equally committed to brewing beers of the highest quality, which accounts for the substantial investment in the new brewery. 'Quality is essential to grow the business,' he says.

Remarkable success

One of the most remarkable, rags-to-riches, success stories among craft brewers comes from Dark Star in Sussex. It began life in 1994 in the cellar of a renowned cask beer pub in Brighton, the Evening Star, on kit scarcely bigger than the equipment used by home brewers. The tiny brewery was run by Rob Jones, who had earned his spurs at the Pitfield Brewery in London, where he won the Champion Beer of Britain competition in 1987 for Dark Star.

His hoppy Brighton beers proved so popular that in 2001 Dark Star relocated to Ansty Green with new equipment that could produce 15 barrels at a time. But the demand for Dark Star's beer was insatiable and in January 2010 the company moved yet again to a custom-built site at Partridge Green near Hayward's Heath. The company is on a sound business footing. Chairman Peter Halliday and managing director Paul Reed have expertise in finance and marketing. As well as the brewery, they own three pubs, the Evening Star in Brighton, the Stand Up Inn in Lindfield and the Duke of

Wellington in Shoreham. They have invested £250,000 in the brewing kit at Partridge Green.

Rob Jones is also a director but has handed over day-to-day brewing to Mark Tranter, who has a Hungarian-built brew house that uses the Continental system of mash mixer, separate filtration vessel and brew kettle for the boil with hops. The system allows more brews per day to be processed than the conventional British one and also gives Tranter scope to produce a wide variety of beer styles. He uses English, European, American and Australasian malts and hops. His American Pale Ale, bursting with citrus hop notes, walked away with the Golden Ale award in the 2009 Champion Beer of Britain competition. Other regular beers include the flagship Hophead and Dark Star Original while the flexibility of the brew house enables him to make such seasonals as a German *Weiss*, or wheat beer, a Belgian *Saison*, a smoked porter, India Pale Ale and a stunningly bitter Six Hop Ale.

In total, Dark Star now produces 20,000 barrels a year. Demand for its beers from pubs throughout the South East has seen the brewery come a long way from its humble origins in a Brighton pub cellar.

Brilliant interpretations

In London, the innovative Meantime Brewery has moved to a new site near the Blackwall Tunnel to increase a portfolio of beers that includes brilliant interpretations of India Pale Ale and London Porter as well as Belgian and German styles. But brewmaster Alastair Hook, who trained in Germany as well as Britain, is not content with just one new brewery. He has also built a micro plant in the Old Naval College in Greenwich, close to the Cutty Sark. In the 18th century, the college had a small brewery where Porter was brewed for sick and dying sailors. Hook has re-created the college's Porter and uses a 'wild' yeast strain known as *Brettanomyces* that gives the beer its characteristic note of lactic sourness. He plans to recreate even older beer styles dating back to Tudor times. Visitors can see the brewery in operation.

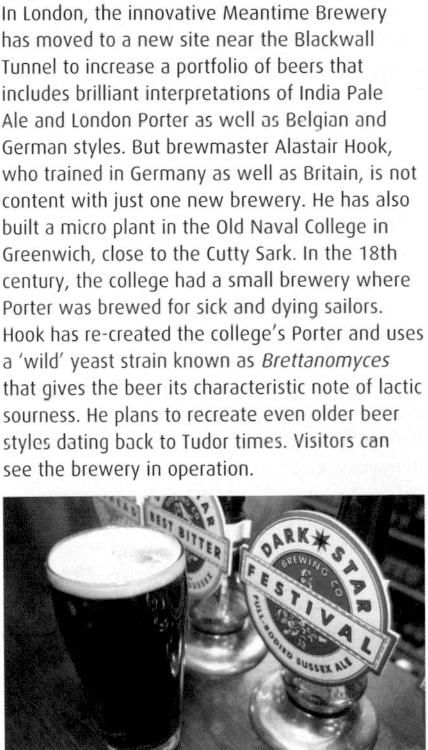

Dark Star: from pub cellar to new Euro plant.

Brewery tun around

With his eye for history, Alastair Hook would be delighted to know that a brewery that opened soon after the end of the Tudor period has been saved from closure. The Three Tuns Brewery in the small Shropshire town of Bishop's Castle dates from 1642 and supplied ale to the Three Tuns coaching inn next door. In the late 19th century, a new brewery was built on the site by John Roberts. The Grade II-listed building was designed along the 'tower brewery' model that was popular in Victorian Britain, with the brewing process flowing from floor to floor without the need for mechanical pumps.

Meantime's micro plant in the Old Naval College, Greenwich, has brought back London Porter.

In the 1990s, both pub and brewery were bought by a small consortium that planned to develop the inn but close the brewery and turn it into holiday flats. The plans met fierce local resistance and in 2003 the brewery was bought by Bill Bainbridge, Samantha Edwards and John Russell, who raised the considerable sum of £1 million to renovate and restore the site. As a result of the building being listed, great care had to be taken to avoid damaging the structure. The roof, rotting floors and brickwork needed to be replaced. Windows had to be taken out to allow new hot and cold water tanks to be installed, along with additional fermenting vessels. One hundred tons of steel were inserted to stop the entire structure, built on a slope, from falling over. In a major operation, a new copper was lowered in to place through old louvered windows.

The brewery closed for a year and a half while renovations were under way. Bill Bainbridge, a lawyer by trade and a long-standing CAMRA member, went to the Brewer's Laboratory in Sunderland to learn the brewing skills and develop a wider range of beers at the Three Tuns. The brewery, which reopened in June 2010, now has a considerably increased capacity of 140 barrels a week and, as well as supplying the pub next door, it delivers to around 300 outlets in the Midlands, the North West and the Welsh borders. The core

Three Tuns Brewery.

brand, XXX, which dates from John Roberts' time in the 19th century, has been joined by1642, Cleric's Cure and such seasonal beers as Solstice for summer and Old Scrooge in winter. Most importantly, a fascinating, working example of Britain's brewing history has been saved for future generations to enjoy.

Acorn grows

In Yorkshire, another piece of brewing history, in the shape of Barnsley Bitter, has been restored. The Barnsley Brewery in Oakwell was taken over and closed by John Smith's of Tadcaster in the 1970s and its much-loved Barnsley Bitter disappeared. The brand was briefly restored in the 1990s but disappeared again when the company producing it went out of business. It was revived in 2003 when Dave Hughes and his wife Judi launched Acorn Brewery in the Barnsley suburb of Wombwell. They were able to use both the name Barnsley Bitter and also the original yeast culture. Brewing started on plant bought from a former Firkin brew-pub but such was the demand for the beer that the Hughes' moved to a new site in 2007 with a major investment in a 20-barrel plant. Today, Dave Hughes and head brewer Steve Bunting have expanded to a 100-barrel plant and even that figure will grow when new fermenting vessels are installed.

As well as the legendary Bitter, Acorn produces Barnsley Gold, Old Moore Porter and Gorlovka Imperial Stout. Gorlovka is Barnsley's twin town in Ukraine and the beer – on draught and also bottle-fermented – recalls the hey-day of Porter and Stout brewing in England, when strong versions of the dark beers were exported to Russia and the Baltic States.

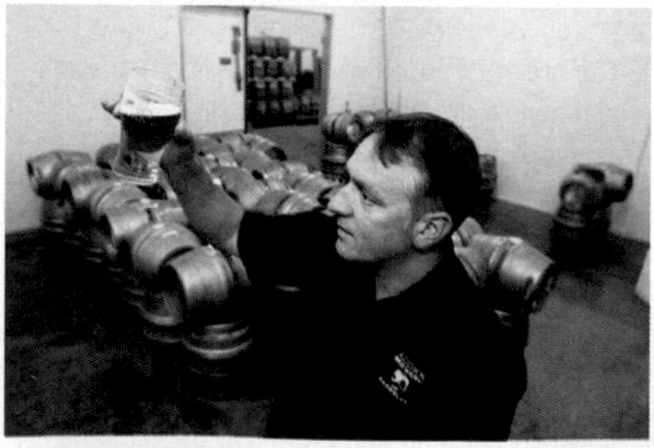

Dave Hughes checks beer clarity at Acorn.

Many breweries produce interpretations of 19th-century India Pale Ale but none can match Acorn's numerous versions of the style. Dave Hughes to date has brewed 36 different IPAs and wonders if that's a world record. All the beers have a strength of 5% but each brew uses different hops, ranging from Amarillo, Cascade and Liberty from the United States, Hallertau Mittelfruh from Germany, Bobek from Slovenia and English Bramling Cross, Challenger, First Gold and Fuggles. 'When we used Amarillo, with its intense citrus character, the aroma could be smelt for miles around,' Dave Hughes says. The entire Acorn range is sold to 300 outlets, using the Society of Independent Brewers' (SIBA) direct delivery scheme.

Masham flourishes

Two further Yorkshire breweries prove that expansion is not confined to craft breweries. In the famous brewing town of Masham in North Yorkshire, both Black Sheep and Theakston's are flourishing. Theakston's dates from 1827 and was family-owned until it was taken over by Scottish & Newcastle in 1987. It returned to the family in 2003 and six years later started to brew its main brand, Best Bitter, at Masham once more. New fermenting vessels have been installed and production has boomed. The company doesn't reveal its volumes but as it doesn't qualify for Progressive Beer Duty it's producing well in excess of 30,000 barrels a year. A few yards away, the rival Black Sheep Brewery, run by Paul Theakston – who left the family brewery at the time of the S&N takeover – brews 80,000 barrels a year and there are plans to expand.

Truman returns

Another historic name has been restored to brewing in London. James Morgan and Michael-George Hemus have negotiated the right to bring back the Truman's name. Truman, Hanbury & Buxton was a major force in London and Essex from 1666 but had the misfortune to be taken over by Grand Metropolitan in the 1970s and was eventually merged with Watneys. The historic Truman's Brewery in Brick Lane, Whitechapel, closed. In a strange case of pass the parcel, the Truman's brand name went to Courage, S&N and finally Heineken UK. Now Morgan and Hemus have brought back the name. Their first beer, Truman's Runner, is brewed for them by Nethergate in Essex but they hope eventually to open their own brewery in the East End of London.

The success stories outlined here are just the tip of a brewing iceberg. Throughout Britain, craft and regional brewers are bucking the economic hard times and are producing ever greater volumes of the country's favourite beer, cask ale.

Burton is back in business

Local campaign re-opens visitor centre in Midlands 'Beer Town'

Britain once again has a museum dedicated to the country's unique beer styles. The National Brewery Centre in Burton-on-Trent is on the site of the former Bass Museum, which closed in 2008 but has been saved as a result of a vigorous campaign by beer lovers.

The museum passed to Coors Brewers in 2001 when Bass left brewing. Seven years later, Molson Coors, as the group had become, announced it would close the museum as a result of poor attendances. At its peak, the museum attracted 120,000 visitors a year. But, under-promoted, the crowds dwindled and Molson Coors said it could no longer sustain losses of around £1 million a year.

Actors in 19th-century dress welcome visitors.

There was an immediate reaction to the news of closure. The local MP, Janet Dean, convened a meeting in Burton attended by the local Civic Society and Chamber of Commerce, the borough and county councils, Staffordshire Arts and Museums, CAMRA and the British Guild of Beer Writers. There was a united determination to save the museum and maintain it as a focal point in the Midlands, with its rich brewing tradition of Burton Ale in the 18th century and India Pale Ale and pale ale in the 19th. A task group was set up to look into several options for the museum, including turning it in to a trust that could apply for National Heritage Lottery Funding.

Feelings were running high in Burton and neighbouring Derby. The *Burton Mail* highlighted the campaign to save the museum while a 400-strong demonstration through Burton won considerable media coverage. In far away Boulder, Colorado, Coors was horrified by the bad publicity. Executives flew to Britain and the local management was told to sort out the problem. At a meeting of the museum task group in November 2009, the members were startled

Traditional horse-drawn dray used to deliver beer.

but delighted to learn that Molson Coors had reached an agreement with Planning Solutions to take over the site. Molson Coors made an initial donation of £200,000 to the new centre and will add an annual contribution of £100,000. Planning Solutions has a good track record of running visitor attractions, including Conkers in the National Forest and an interest in Vinopolis, the wine centre in London.

The new National Brewery Centre opened in May 2010. It's based in a three-storey, Grade II-listed Bass Joiners' Shop, the centre of the old museum. As well as static displays, there are also modern interactive ones, both tracing the history of brewing in Burton.

Beer will be the heart-beat of the centre. Bass master brewer Steve Wellington, who has run the White Shield micro-plant on the site for several years, was due to move into the visitor centre in 2010 with new equipment that will enable him to produce 100 barrels of beer a week. The brewery will be open to view and its beers will include the new premium Red Shield.

There are restaurants and bars on site and there also facilities for conferences, meetings and seminars. And within the complex, visitors are able to see and admire steam locomotives from the 19th century that moved Bass beers around Britain, while the much-loved Bass dray horses have returned to their stables.

The success and viability of the centre rests with beer lovers. Burton-on-Trent transformed brewing on a world scale in the 19th century. The town is reviving thanks to both the visitor centre and craft brewers active in the town. It's now up to beer drinkers to ensure the centre survives.

National Brewery Centre, Burton-on-Trent
£8.95 full ticket; family tickets; off-peak rates; 20% discount for CAMRA members or visitors showing a copy of the *Good Beer Guide.*
01283 532880
www.nationalbrewerycentre.co.uk

Perfect pub crawl

Derby has an unrivalled choice of ancient and modern pubs – including one that is matching real ale and food

The Brunswick Inn: matches beer and food.

The **Brunswick Inn** in Derby doesn't rank as a gastro pub. It's a down-to-earth, street-corner boozer. Brilliant beer is brewed on the premises and manager Graham Yates and his chefs Ralph Edge and John Chamberlain have started to match their ales with food. Beer and food evenings, dubbed Upstairs at the Brunswick, have been a great success, helped by the fact that you can enjoy four courses for £18 – not exactly gastro-pub prices.

It's a remarkable pub, first built in 1842 as part of a row of cottages donated by a grateful railway company to its workers. The inn stands at the end of the row, a red-brick, wedge-shaped building with imposing chimneys and a large pub sign offering 'a true ale house and brewery'. A central corridor and bar has several small rooms leading off, with open fires, old station furniture and lamps, and a plethora of railway photographs from the age of steam. There's a small brewery at the end of the corridor where Graham and his team fashion a large range of fine ales.

The Brunswick was in danger of demolition in the 1980s but a campaign led by the local Civic Trust, Derbyshire Railway Trust and CAMRA saved it. It was taken on by Trevor Harris in 1987 and he added the brewery four years later. When Everards of Leicester bought the pub in 2002, Trevor moved on to launch his Derby Brewing Company and Graham Yates has been in situ ever since.

Graham says the idea of food and beer events was the result of a passing conversation he had with Ralph Edge: Ralph, as well as being head cook, is also an active member of the local CAMRA branch. He was preparing a curry for the pub's specials board and Graham suggested one of the house beers, Triple Hop, would go well with it. It was a suggestion that spawned the idea of staging dinners with each course matched by a Brunswick ale. There have been several events, held in the spacious room above the inn, with Burn's Night and Valentine's Night proving especially popular.

Finding beers to match four courses is not difficult. The Brunswick brews three Milds – Midnight Express, Father Mike's and Black Sabbath – along with a Porter, and pale, gold and copper beers. Triple Hop is one of the best-selling brews and has a pronounced citrus hop character that's ideal for curries, while Second Brew has a powerful bitterness that will marry well with rich dishes.

A few sample dishes from the beer dinners include: pork fillet with a Stilton, leek and walnut sauce with Old Accidental, a fruity and malty beer; pan-fried Gressingham duck breast with a Porter and chestnut mushroom sauce, parsnip and celeriac rosti with Railway Porter; tomato fettucine with black olives and pancetta with Triple Hop; sticky rum-soaked raisin pudding with Rambo strong winter ale; homemade thyme crème brûlée and shortbread with Black Sabbath mild; rhubarb and almond frangipane with homemade custard, accompanied by Triple Hop; and a selection of English cheeses with Father Mikes, Black Sabbath or Rambo. There are always vegetarian alternatives for main courses.

The Brunswick is a couple of hundred yards from Derby station and is a good first and last stop for a pub crawl of the city.

The Brunswick Inn: Graham Yates says hoppy beers go well with food .

The Royal Standard was saved from demolition.

The **Royal Standard** takes its name from a visit to Derby by Queen Victoria when buildings were allowed to fly the royal flag. In common with the Brunswick, this is another street-corner pub that was almost demolished to make way for houses in a gentrified area of the city. It was saved by Trevor Harris, late of the Brunswick, who opened his Derby Brewing Company in 2004 and was keen to have a shop window for his beers.

The pub, which is also known as the Brewery Tap, is a clever blend of old and new. Inside the Victorian shell there's a large open-plan, bare-brick main room with a large curved bar serving Trevor's own brews, true European lagers such as Budvar, German wheat beers, and a good range of bottled Belgian beers. An upstairs room is used for beer and wine tastings events, while a balcony has good views of the River Derwent.

The house beers include Triple Hop – as Trevor designed the beer at the Brunswick, he's allowed to keep the name – Hop Till You Drop, Business as Usual, Dashingly Dark, Double Mash, Penny's Porter, Old Intentional and seasonal brews. The pub is run by Trevor's son Paul Harris and the menus suggest beer matches, such as Quilmes Argentinian Lager with chicken stir-fry; Hop Till You Drop with chicken Caesar salad; Schneider Weisse German wheat beer with mushroom burger; and Budweiser Budvar with fish and chips. The last-named is not as odd as it sounds, as carp and golden lager is a popular dish in the Czech Republic.

Ye Olde Dolphin Inne is rich in history.

Nobody would dare lay a finger on the **Olde Dolphin Inne**. This creakingly ancient inn, heavy with history and beams, dates from 1530 and is just a few feet from the looming Gothic tower of the cathedral. Inside there are several small, snug rooms with bare boards and settles. Even the smoking area in the back garden has a mock-Tudor air. The back lounge is not to be missed: packed with just six people, it exudes so much history you feel you have been transported back to the 16th century. But in spite of the history, the Olde Dolphin is now owned by a very modern pub company and the emphasis is on major cask brands such as Adnams, Black Sheep, Caledonian Deuchars, Greene King Abbot and Marston's Pedigree. But you will find pumps for that now rare but still delectable offering, Draught Bass.

The inn is supposedly haunted. A ghoulish lady is said to walk through the walls and nobody enters the cellar on their own: in the 18th century, a doctor dissected bodies delivered by the local hangman. The doctor allegedly went mad when one body he was about to carve sat up and spoke to him. Stay in the bar and enjoy the Bass. Good pub grub is served and there's an upstairs steak restaurant. A beer festival is held every July.

The Flower Pot: beer festival every day.

The **Flower Pot** is a few minutes' walk from the Olde Dolphin and is a daily beer festival. The cliché 'a Tardis-like building' applies here, for the small frontage doesn't prepare visitors for the size of the interior. A small front bar leads to bigger back rooms, one of which houses an impressive ground-floor 'cellar' with a glass front. Behind are rows of temperature-controlled beer casks: at weekends, as many as 25 ales are served. You may find Oakham and Whim beers and many, many more. The range includes beers from the tiny in-house brewery, Headless, a 10-barrel plant set up in 2007 at the back of the pub. The beers include King Street Ale, First Bloom and Five Gates. This is a lively pub, catering for music lovers as well as beer drinkers: yet another room has a stage for live bands.

Temperature-controlled casks in the Flower Pot.

It's hard to believe the **Falstaff** was once a coaching inn, as it's now almost lost in the side streets of the Normanton suburb of Derby. It's a good 20 minutes' walk from the city centre but it's worth the hike. Known locally as the Folly, it was once owned by Ind Coope of Burton. It became an Allied Breweries' pub when the national giant swallowed Ind Coope and it then passed to a pub company when Allied gave up the ghost. It was rescued by Jim Hallows and Steph Briggs who have lovingly restored it, with open fires, comfortable seating, several rooms and masses of brewery memorabilia.

The lounge is a shrine to the much-missed Derby brewery Offiler's, that once stood close to the Falstaff. Offiler's was bought by the London brewer Charrington in 1965 and was closed a year later when Bass of Burton took over Charrington. The lounge has Offiler's advertising, pump clips and jugs by the yard.

The Falstaff also has its own 10-barrel brewery, producing Fist Full of Hops, Phoenix, Smiling Assassin and seasonal brews. The pub is haunted but run the risk: stay in one of the bars and sup both the marvellous ales and the Offiler's shrine: this is a pub about Derby's proud brewing past and vibrant present.

The Falstaff is a shrine to Derby beer.

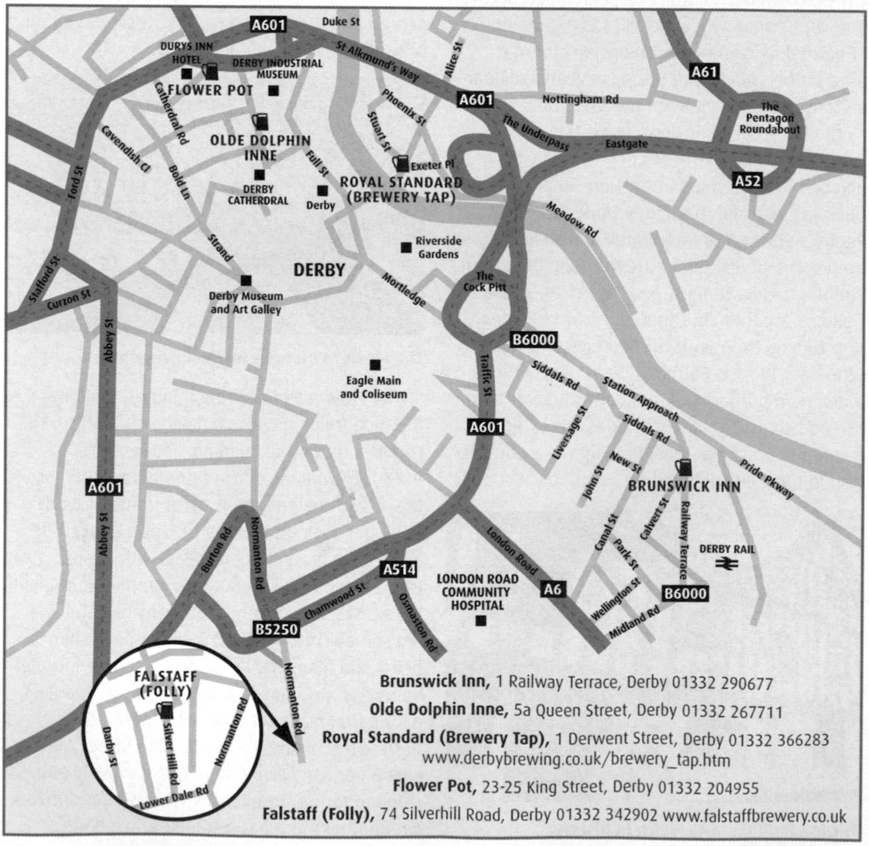

Brunswick Inn, 1 Railway Terrace, Derby 01332 290677

Olde Dolphin Inne, 5a Queen Street, Derby 01332 267711

Royal Standard (Brewery Tap), 1 Derwent Street, Derby 01332 366283 www.derbybrewing.co.uk/brewery_tap.htm

Flower Pot, 23-25 King Street, Derby 01332 204955

Falstaff (Folly), 74 Silverhill Road, Derby 01332 342902 www.falstaffbrewery.co.uk

Real Ale
The jewel in the beer crown

Real ale is a beer style that has deep roots in Britain. Small amounts of cask-conditioned beer can be found in the United States, Australia and New Zealand, while Belgium has many beers that re-ferment in the bottle. But only in Britain are large volumes of cask beer found in thousands of pubs throughout the country.

While most beers, including lager, leave their breweries in finished form – usually filtered and pasteurised and then pumped to the bar by applied carbon dioxide or mixed gas – real ale leaves the brewery unfinished and reaches maturity in the pub cellar.

On the following two pages the *Good Beer Guide* follows the brewing process in Harveys Brewery. No two breweries are the same and no two beer recipes are the same but the Harveys traditional system is one, with variations, that's used by most regional and craft breweries in Britain. The essential difference between real ale and both keg beer and industrial lager is that cask beer is made by a natural method using the finest malted grain and the best hops. Cask beer brewers may use wheat or other grains alongside barley malt for flavour and colour. But they avoid the cheaper adjuncts, such as rice, corn, syrup and hop oils, favoured by bigger brewers in order to cut production costs.

The growth of the real ale sector in Britain is caused by many factors. But it's the insistence on quality ingredients that appeals to a growing number of consumers who want to enjoy food and drink made naturally from locally-grown ingredients. Legally, you can make something called beer from rice, maize and corn syrup and flavoured with green juice extracted from pulverised hops. But cask beer is the result of a simple, natural process that involves malted grain with hops plucked from the field, not a crushing machine.

The major dividing line between real ale and other types of beer is drawn at the brewery gates. Keg beer and lager are finished in the brewery. Cask beer, as the name implies, has yet to finish its journey.

In the brewery, additional hops and malt sugar may be added to casks to encourage a second fermentation and to increase hop aroma. In the pub cellar, each cask is 'stillaged' on its belly on a cradle. A tap is knocked through the bung at the flat end of the cask while a spile or peg is driven into the shive hole on top. The peg, made of porous wood, allows excess carbon dioxide to escape as the beer enjoys a secondary fermentation: as the beer has not been filtered, it retains yeast that attacks the remaining sugars in the beer. After 24 hours, the porous peg is replaced by a hard one that keeps the remaining carbon dioxide inside the cask to give the finished beer a natural sparkle in the glass.

At the same time, isinglass finings added in the brewery begin a natural chemical process that draws yeast cells and protein to the foot of the cask. When the publican is satisfied – by drawing off a sample from the cask – that the beer has 'dropped bright', plastic tubes called lines are attached to the tap in the bung and the beer is ready to be served. The famous 'policeman's truncheon', the handpump on the bar, operates a beer engine or suction pump that draws the beer from cellar to bar.

Real ale should be served cool: 'warm British beer' is a myth. While keg beer and mass lager are often served at a near freezing temperature to mask their lack of finesse and taste, cask beer should be delivered to the glass at a cellar temperature of 11 – 13°C. Some summer beers and golden ales are served cooler, at 9 – 10°C. The result should be a beer rich in malt and hop aroma and flavour, naturally made and naturally served – the Champagne of the beer world.

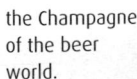

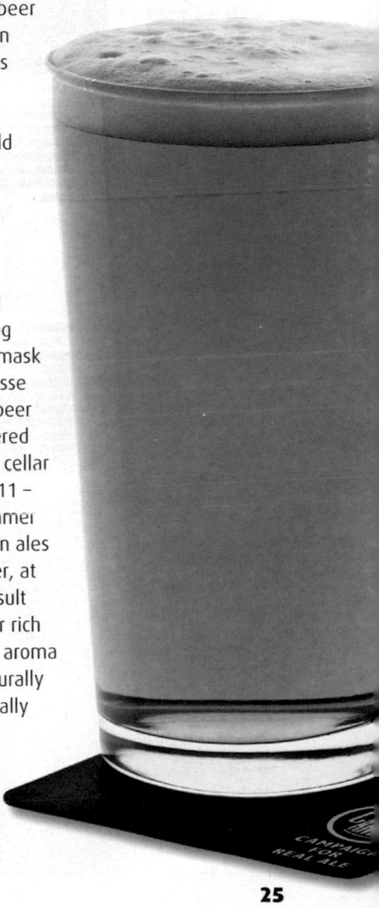

In the beginning is the wort...

The real-ale brewing process from mash tun to bar

Before you can raise a pint in the pub, enormous skill and the finest natural ingredients come together in the brewery to turn barley malt, hops, yeast and water into beer. Here, the *Good Beer Guide* follows the brewing skills at Harveys.

Harveys' classic tower brewery in Lewes, where the brewing process flows from floor to floor.

❸ Pure water, known as 'liquor', has percolated through the chalk downs of Sussex before reaching the brewery. Hot liquor is mixed in the mash tun with the malt grist. ▶ ▶ ▶

❹ Head brewer Miles Jenner checks the temperature of the mash as brewing gets under way. Temperature is crucial to allow malt starch to turn into fermentable sugar. ▶ ▶ ▶

❼ The hop store: Harveys uses traditional hop varieties from farmers in Sussex and surrounding counties. ▶ ▶ ▶

❽ The copper, where wort is vigorously boiled with hops: the boil extracts acids and tannins from the hops that add aroma and bitterness to the beer. ▶ ▶ ▶

⓫ To keep the yeast working busily, turning malt sugar into alcohol, the fermenting beer is roused or oxygenated from time to time. ▶ ▶ ▶

⓬ Beer is racked into casks in preparation for the final destination: the pub cellar where it enjoys a vigorous second fermentation. ▶ ▶ ▶

❶ Malt – partially germinated barley – is stored at the top of the brewery. Harveys uses the classic Maris Otter variety. ◀◀◀

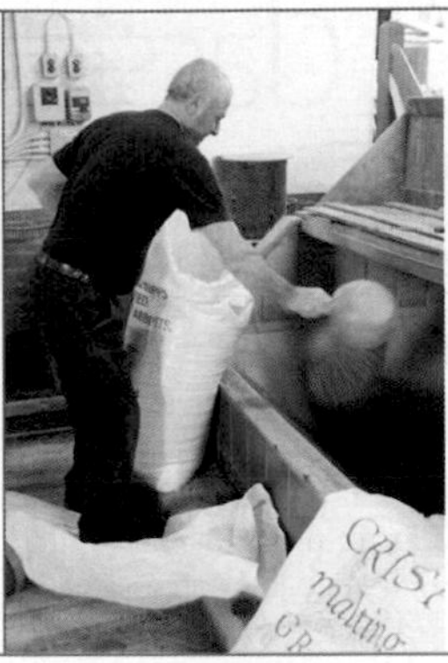

❷ Malt is added to a hopper ready to be ground into grist. The grist is then dropped into the mash tun to start the brewing process. ◀◀◀

❺ At the end of the mash, the grain is 'sparged' or sprinkled with hot liquor to wash out remaining malt sugars. ◀◀◀

❻ The wort or sugary extract runs out of the mash tun into a receiving vessel where it is checked en route to the copper. ◀◀◀

❾ Some of the hops are added late in the boil for additional aroma and flavour. 'Late hopping' restores any aroma lost earlier during the boil. ◀◀◀

❿ After the boil the hopped wort is cooled and transfered to a fermenting vessel. Yeast is 'pitched' or blended into the wort to start fermentation. ◀◀◀

⓭ In the racking hall, finings are added that will clear the beer of yeast and protein in the pub cellar. ◀◀◀

⓮ And finally... checking the quality of the finished beer in the pub. Another perfect pint is poured! ◀◀◀

Britain's Classic Beer Styles

THE GOOD BEER GUIDE helps you deepen your appreciation of cask ale by detailing the styles listed in the Breweries section. This year we single out two styles – golden ales and Porter & Stout – that represent modern innovation and a style from the past.

MILD

Mild was once the most popular style of beer but was overtaken by Bitter from the 1950s. It was developed in the 18th and 19th centuries as a less aggressively bitter style of beer than Porter and Stout. Early Milds were much stronger that modern interpretations, which tend to fall in the 3% to 3.5% category, though there are stronger versions, such as Sarah Hughes' Dark Ruby. Mild ale is usually dark brown in colour, due to the use of well-roasted malts or roasted barley, but there are paler versions, such as Banks's Original, Timothy Taylor's Golden Best and McMullen's AK. Look for rich malty aromas and flavours with hints of dark fruit, chocolate, coffee and caramel and a gentle underpinning of hop bitterness.

OLD ALE

Old ale recalls the type of beer brewed before the Industrial Revolution, stored for months or even years in unlined wooden vessels known as tuns. The beer would pick up some lactic sourness as a result of wild yeasts, lactobacilli and tannins in the wood. The result was a beer dubbed 'stale' by drinkers: it was one of the components of the early, blended Porters. The style has re-emerged in recent years, due primarily to the fame of Theakston's Old Peculier and Gale's Prize Old Ale. Old ales, contrary to expectation, do not have to be especially strong: they can be no more than 4% alcohol, though the Gale's version is considerably stronger. Neither do they have to be dark: old ale can be pale and burst with lush sappy malt, tart fruit and spicy hop notes. Darker versions will have a more profound malt character with powerful hints of roasted grain, dark fruit, polished leather and fresh tobacco. The hallmark of the style remains a lengthy period of maturation, often in bottle rather than bulk vessels. Greene King's bottled Strong Suffolk Ale is a fascinating example of a 'stale beer'. It's a blend of two beers, one of which, Old 5X, is stored for a year in unlined wooden vessels and is then blended with Best Pale Ale. The beer is filtered and beer lovers should encourage Greene King to produce it in bottle-conditioned form.

BITTER

Towards the end of the 19th century, brewers built large estates of tied pubs. They moved away from vatted beers stored for many months and developed 'running beers' that could be served after a few days' storage in pub cellars. Draught Mild was a 'running beer' along with a new type that was dubbed 'Bitter' by drinkers. Bitter grew out of pale ale but was generally deep bronze to copper in colour due to the use of slightly darker malts such as crystal that give the beer fullness of palate. Best is a stronger version of Bitter but there is considerable crossover. Bitter falls into the 3.4% to 3.9% band, with Best Bitter 4% upwards, but a number of brewers label their ordinary Bitters 'Best'. A further development of Bitter comes in the shape of Extra or Special Strong Bitters of 5% or more: familiar examples of this style include Fuller's ESB and Greene King Abbot. With ordinary Bitter, look for a spicy, peppery and grassy hop character, a powerful bitterness, tangy fruit and juicy and nutty malt. With Best and Strong Bitters, malt and fruit character will tend to dominate but hop aroma and bitterness are still crucial to the style, often achieved by 'late hopping' in the brewery or adding hops to casks as they leave for pubs.

GOLDEN ALE

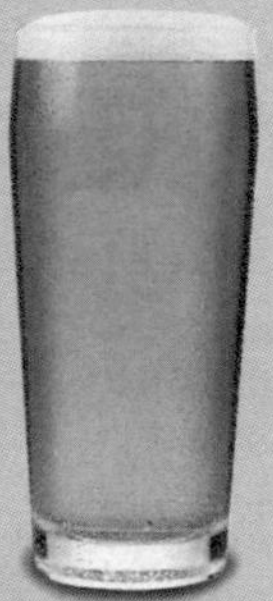

Golden ales are a phenomenon – they have become so popular, with many brewers of all sizes producing them, that they now have their own category in the Champion Beer of Britain competition. Two beers from South-West England, Exmoor Gold and Hop Back Summer Lightning, launched the trend in the early 1990s and the success of the beers prompted other brewers to follow in their footsteps. Exmoor Gold was not meant to be a regular beer: it was produced to celebrate Exmoor's 1,000th brew. Similarly, as the name Summer Lightning suggests, the Hop Back beer was launched as a summer refresher. But sales of both beers turned them into regular members of the companies' portfolios.

Golden ales pre-date the revival of cask beer's fortunes in recent years. In the early 1990s, real ale was struggling and it seemed the rise of lager was unstoppable. Craft brewers, who lacked the necessary cash to invest in lager-making equipment, were desperate to attract young drinkers to cask beer and they launched golden ales as an alternative.

One key question is: how do golden ales differ from pale ale? Pale ale is an older style, dating from the 19th century. The success of India Pale Ale (IPA) prompted many brewers to produce similar beers for the domestic market but with lower levels of alcohol and hop bitterness. Although they are called pale ale, they tend to be darker than golden ales: many have small amounts of darker malt such as crystal and are less aggressively hopped than golden ales.

Some golden ales use extremely pale malt to get the desired colour. Crouch Vale Brewers Gold, for example – twice Champion Beer of Britain – uses lager malt and the only hop is a German one, Brewers Gold, normally used for lager production. As a result, the beer has a toasted malt and pungent citrus/grapefruit hop aroma and palate that is radically different from a conventional pale ale.

The beauty of golden ales is that they give full expression to hops. As they lack the characteristics given to beer by darker malts – burnt fruit, roasted coffee and chocolate, for example – hops are allowed free rein to demonstrate their resinous, piny, spicy, peppery and citrus aromas and flavours. Pale malt balances the hops with a biscuity, juicy and sappy character that helps make golden ales wonderfully quenching.

While British pale ales tend to use traditional English hop varieties such as Fuggles and Goldings, many producers of golden ales look abroad for inspiration. The extreme citrus character of such American hop varieties as Cascade, Chinook and Willamette enables brewers to offer golden ales with hop palates radically different to conventional British Bitters and pale ales. Hops from mainland Europe are also popular with brewers of golden ales. The floral and fruity notes of Styrian Goldings from Slovenia have become familiar to British drinkers and, as Crouch Vale shows with Brewers Gold, 'noble hops' from the vast Bavarian Hallertau region are also finding favour.

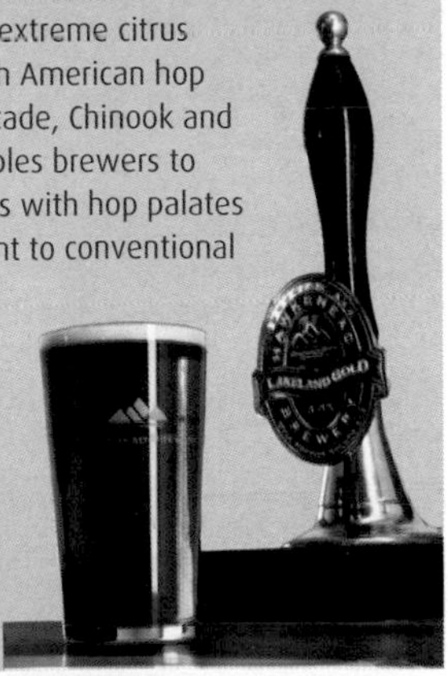

Golden ales offer a new and exciting drinking experience. They are often served colder than draught bitter and some brewers, such as Fuller's, have installed special cooling devices attached to beer engines to ensure the beer reaches the glass at an acceptably refreshing temperature.

Golden ales are no longer the small brewers' alternative to lager. They are a major part of the modern brewing scene and deliver a range of aromas and flavours rarely if ever experienced in mainstream lager brands.

GOLDEN ALES TO TRY

ADNAMS EXPLORER
CASTLE ROCK HARVEST PALE
BRAINS SA GOLD
ELLAND BEYOND THE PALE
HAWKSHEAD LAKELAND GOLD

PALE ALE

The success of IPA in the colonial trade led to a demand in Britain for beer of a similar colour – the new style coincided with commercial glass-blowing and drinkers preferred a pale, clear beer to darker Porters and Stouts. But IPA, with its heavy level of hopping, was considered to be too strong for the domestic market and the brewers developed a beer dubbed simply 'pale ale' that was lower in both levels of alcohol and hops.

Pale ale was known as 'the beer of the railway age', carried around the country from Burton-on-Trent by the new railway system. Brewers from London, Liverpool and Manchester built breweries in Burton to make use of the Trent waters.

Until the arrival of Bitter at the turn of the 19th century, pale ale was a dominant form of draught beer. But Bitter's popularity led to pale ale becoming mainly a bottled version. London brewers such as Watney and Whitbread grew their fame and fortune on the quality of their bottled pale ales. Today the style is overshadowed by Bitter but a true pale ale should be different, as pale as an IPA and brewed without the addition of coloured malts. It should have a spicy, resinous aroma and palate, with biscuity malt and tart citrus fruit. Marston's Pedigree, although dubbed a Bitter, is a fine example of a true Burton-style pale ale.

IPA

India Pale Ale changed the face of brewing early in the 19th century. The new technologies of the Industrial Revolution enabled brewers to use pale malts to fashion beers that were genuinely golden or pale bronze in colour. First brewed in London and Burton-on-Trent for the colonial market, IPAs were strong in alcohol and high in hops: the preservative character of the hops helped keep the beers in good condition during long sea journeys. IPA's life span was brief, driven out of the colonies by German lager, brewed with the aid of ice-making machines. But the style has made a spirited recovery in recent years, brewed with great passion by many craft brewers in both Britain and the United States. In Chicago, Goose Island's IPA is arguably the finest American interpretation of the style while in Britain, Marston's Old Empire and Meantime's IPA — rich in juicy malt and peppery hop character – are just two modern versions of the style arousing new interest.

PORTER & STOUT

Porter was a London beer style that created the first mass commercial brewing industry in the world. Early in the 18th century there was enormous demand in London for a beer known as 'three threads', a mixture of pale, brown and stale ales. Stale meant a beer matured in wooden vessels for a year or more, where it picked up an acetic or stale character.

A brewer called Ralph Harwood in East London developed a version of the beer that was served from just one cask, making it unnecessary to mix each pint from three separate casks. He called his beer Entire Butt as it came from just one large wooden butt or cask. But both three threads and Entire Butt became so popular with the large army of porters working in the streets, markets and docks of London that it acquired the nickname of Porter. At the time, the strongest – or stoutest – beer from a brewery was called Stout and the stronger versions of Porter were branded Stout Porter, later shortened to just Stout.

The demand for Porter and Stout was so enormous that brewers switched to producing just that style. Harwood was soon eclipsed by the likes of Samuel Whitbread in London's Barbican, whose brewery harnessed the power of new steam engines to produce vast amounts of Porter.

The style at first was a brown beer but it became darker in the early 19th century as a result of the invention of malt roasting machines, similar to coffee roasters, which enabled black and chocolate malts to be produced. Porter and Stout were exported from London to all parts of Great Britain and the colonies: George Washington, first president of the United States, was partial to Porter but, following the War of Independence, preferred to brew his own version at home rather than import it from Britain. Extra strong versions of Porter and Stout were exported to the Baltic States and Russia and became known as Imperial Porter and Stout.

In Dublin, an ale brewer called Arthur Guinness saw so much London Porter and Stout pouring in to the city that he decided to brew the style himself – with some success. His son, Arthur Guinness II, blended some un-malted roasted barley in to the beer and developed a style that became known as Dry Irish Stout. Guinness was followed by the Cork brewers Beamish & Crawford and Murphy. Irish Stout came to dominate production of the style early in the 20th century. The British government banned brewers from using heavily-roasted malts during World War One as the energy created by coal, gas and electricity was needed for the armaments industry. As a result, production of Porter and Stout all but disappeared from Britain and the Irish were given a free hand to develop their sector of the market.

But in the past 20 years there has been a remarkable revival of interest in the style in both Britain and the United States. There are several hundred interpretations of the style now available, and many brewers have researched the archives to produce faithful recreations of Porter and Stout from the 18th and 19th centuries.

Look for a jet-black colour with – when the glass is held to the light – a ruby edge. Expect a profound dark and roasted malt character, with raisin and sultana fruit, espresso or cappuccino coffee, liquorice and molasses. The beer should have a deep hop bitterness to balance the richness of malt and fruit.

PORTERS AND STOUTS TO TRY

- ACORN GORLOVKA IMPERIAL STOUT
- BLACK ISLE ORGANIC PORTER
- HARVEY'S IMPERIAL EXTRA DOUBLE STOUT
- MEANTIME LONDON PORTER
- NETHERGATE OLD GROWLER
- THORNBRIDGE SAINT PETERSBURG IMPERIAL RUSSIAN STOUT

BARLEY WINE

Barley wine is a style that dates from the 18th and 19th centuries when England was often at war with France and it was the duty of patriots, usually from the upper classes, to drink ale rather than Claret. Barley wine had to be strong – often between 10% and 12% – and was stored for prodigious periods of as long as 18 months or two years. When country houses had their own small breweries, it was often the task of the butler to brew ale that was drunk from cut-glass goblets at the dining table. The biggest-selling barley wine for years was Whitbread's 10.9% Gold Label, now available only in cans. Bass's No 1 Barley Wine (10.5%) is occasionally brewed in Burton-on-Trent, stored in cask for 12 months and made available to CAMRA beer festivals. Fuller's Vintage Ale (8.5%) is a bottle-conditioned version of its Golden Pride and is brewed with different varieties of malts and hops every year. Expect massive sweet malt and ripe fruit of the pear drop, orange and lemon type, with darker fruits, chocolate and coffee if darker malts are used. Hop rates are generous and produce bitterness and peppery, grassy and floral notes.

SCOTTISH BEERS

Historically, Scottish beers tend to be darker, sweeter and less heavily hopped than English and Welsh ales: a colder climate demands warming beers. But many of the new craft breweries produce beers lighter in colour and with generous hop rates. The traditional, classic styles are Light, low in strength and so-called even when dark in colour, also known as 60/-; Heavy or 70/-; Export or 80/-; and a strong Wee Heavy, similar to a barley wine and also labelled 90/-. In the 19th century, beers were invoiced according to strength, using the now defunct currency of the shilling.

Only accept perfect pints

Remember, you're the consumer, forking out a high price for beer, so don't be afraid to take your pint back to the bar if:

- It's either too cold or too warm. Cask beer should be cool, not cold – but bear in mind that some golden ales are meant to be served at a lower temperature than Milds and Bitters. At the other end of the spectrum, it's a myth that real ale should be served at room temperature. Warm beer tastes bad, as the temperature creates unpleasant off flavours. If your beer smells of acetone, vinegar or stale bread, take it back.
- The pint has no head, is totally flat and out of condition.
- It's not only flat but hazy and has yeast particles or protein floating in the liquid.

If you get the response 'Real ale is meant to be warm and cloudy', invite the publican to join the 21st century. If the offending pub has a Cask Marque plaque, get in touch with Cask Marque. Otherwise, let us know at the *Good Beer Guide* **camragbgeditor@camra.org.uk**.

And please go back to the bar if you are served a short measure – less than a pint of liquid in the glass. Drinkers lose millions of pounds a year as a result of short measure. It's an outrageous rip-off. CAMRA beer festivals serve beer in over-size glasses that ensure drinkers always get a full pint. Most pub owners refuse to use over-size glasses, preferring brim-measure glasses that allow them consistently to serve short measure. It's a scandal. Don't put up with it.

CAMRA's Beers of the Year

THE BEERS LISTED BELOW are CAMRA'S Beers of the Year. They were short-listed for the Champion Beer of Britain competition in August 2010 and the Champion Winter Beer of Britain competition in January that year. The August competition judged Dark & Light Milds; Bitters; Best Bitters; Strong Bitters; Golden Ales; Speciality Beers; and Real Ale in a Bottle. The winter competition judged Old Ales & Strong Milds; Porters & Stouts; and Barley Wines. Each beer was found by a panel of trained CAMRA judges to be consistently outstanding in its category and they all receive a 'full tankard' [■] in the Breweries section.

DARK & LIGHT MILDS

Beckstones Black Gun Dog Freddy Mild
Brains Dark
Church End Gravediggers Mild
Golcar Dark Mild
Greene King XX Mild
Highland Dark Munro
Nottingham Rock Ale Mild
St Austell Black Prince
Surrey Hills Hammer Mild

BITTERS

Belhaven 70/-
Brimstage Trappers Hat Bitter
Elgood's Cambridge Bitter
Facer's Flintshire Bitter
Fuller's Chiswick Bitter
Great Oakley Wot's Occurring
Hadrian & Border Gladiator
Holden's Black Country Bitter
Moor Revival
Orkney Raven
Purity Pure Gold
Purple Moose Snowdonia Ale
RCH PG Steam
Spire Overture
Triple fff Alton's Pride
Woodforde's Wherry
Yates Bitter
York Guzzler

BEST BITTERS

Atlas Three Sisters
Bowman Quiver Bitter
Breconshire Cribyn
Derby Brewing Triple Hop
Evan Evans Cwrw
George Wright Pipe Dream
Great Oakley Gobble
Hobsons Town Crier
Keswick Thirst Quencher
Kinver Edge
McMullen Country Bitter
Milton Pegasus
Mordue Workie Ticket
Orkney Red MacGregor
Rother Valley Level Best
Skinner's Betty Stogs
St Austell Tribute
Timothy Taylor Landlord

STRONG BITTERS

Beckstones Rev Bob
Fuller's Gales HSB
Highland Orkney Blast
Hobsons Old Henry
Mordue Radgie Gadgie
Otley OG
South Hams Eddystone
Thornbridge Jaipur IPA
Woodforde's Admiral's Reserve

GOLDEN ALES

Castle Rock Harvest Pale
Celt Experience Golden Ale
Dark Star Hophead
Farmer's Ales Pucks Folly
Inveralmond Ossian
Marble Manchester Bitter
Ossett Silver King
Salopian Shropshire Gold
St Austell Proper Job

OLD ALES & STRONG MILDS

Beartown Black Bear
Breconshire Ramblers Ruin
Country Life Country Bumpkin
Dark Star Original
Leeds Midnight Belle
Stewart 80/-
Wolf Woild Moild

PORTERS & STOUTS

Acorn Gorlovka Imperial Stout
Beowulf Dragon Smoke Stout
Church End Pews Porter
Derby Brewing Penny's Porter
Elland 1872 Porter
Hop Back Entire Stout
Humpty Dumpty Porter
Mauldon's Black Adder
Milton Marcus Aurelius
O'Hanlon's Dry Stout
Orkney Dragonhead
RCH Old Slug Porter
Sulwath Black Galloway
Vale Black Beauty Porter
Wapping Stout

BARLEY WINES

Abbeydale Last Rites
Burton Bridge Old Expensive
Kinver Over the Edge
Moor JJJ IPA
Orkney Skullsplitter
Otley O8
Robinson's Old Tom
Yates' (Isle of Wight) Yule Be Sorry

SPECIALITY BEERS

Amber Ales Chocolate Orange Stout
Bob's Brewing Chardonnayle
Breconshire Ysbrid Y Ddraig
Dark Star Espresso Stout
Fox Grizzly Beer
O'Hanlon's Original Port Stout
Sulwath Mist
Titanic Iceberg
Yates Sun Goddess

REAL ALE IN A BOTTLE

Acorn Gorlovka Imperial Stout
Breconshire Night Beacon
Dark Star Imperial Stout
Fuller's Vintage (2008)
Great Gable Yewbarrow
Great Oakley Delapre Dark
Hesket Newmarket Catbells Pale Ale
Islay Black Rock Ale
Little Valley Ginger Pale Ale
Molson Coors Worthington's White Shield
Otley O-Garden
Pitfield 1850 London Porter
Red Squirrel Conservation Bitter
Spire Sgt Pepper Stout
St Austell Admiral's Ale
St Austell Clouded Yellow
Tryst Brockville Dark
Wye Valley Dorothy Goodbody's Golden Ale

CHAMPION WINTER BEER OF BRITAIN
Elland 1872 Porter

CHAMPION BEER OF BRITAIN 2010
Castle Rock Harvest Pale

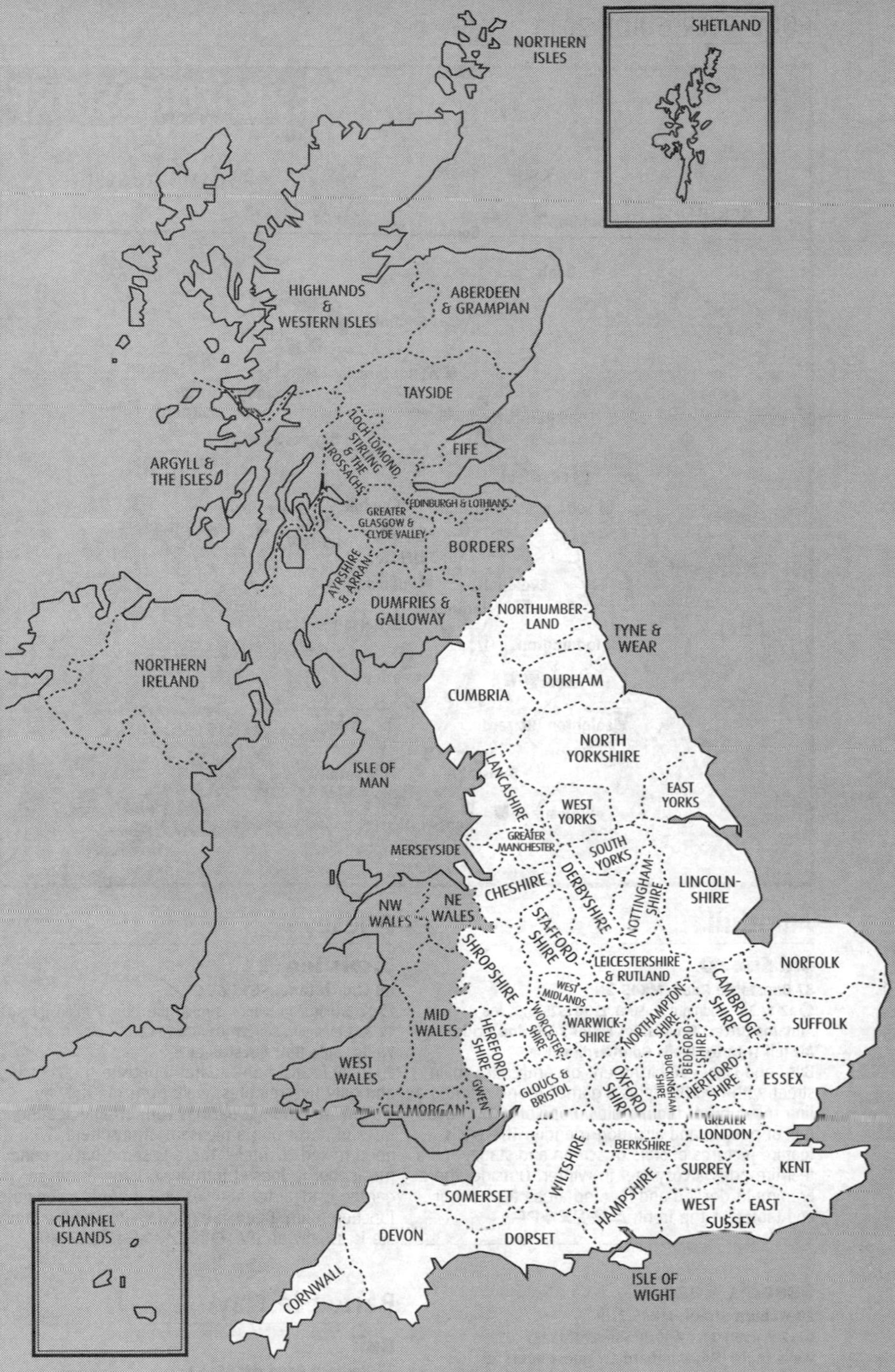

SHETLAND
NORTHERN ISLES
HIGHLANDS & WESTERN ISLES
ABERDEEN & GRAMPIAN
TAYSIDE
LOCH LOMOND, STIRLING & THE TROSSACHS
FIFE
ARGYLL & THE ISLES
EDINBURGH & LOTHIANS
GREATER GLASGOW & CLYDE VALLEY
BORDERS
AYRSHIRE & ARRAN
DUMFRIES & GALLOWAY
NORTHUMBER-LAND
TYNE & WEAR
NORTHERN IRELAND
DURHAM
CUMBRIA
NORTH YORKSHIRE
ISLE OF MAN
LANCASHIRE
EAST YORKS
WEST YORKS
GREATER MANCHESTER
SOUTH YORKS
MERSEYSIDE
CHESHIRE
DERBYSHIRE
NOTTINGHAM-SHIRE
LINCOLN-SHIRE
NW WALES
NE WALES
STAFFORD-SHIRE
SHROPSHIRE
LEICESTERSHIRE & RUTLAND
NORFOLK
WEST MIDLANDS
CAMBRIDGE-SHIRE
NORTHAMPTON-SHIRE
WARWICK-SHIRE
WORCESTER-SHIRE
HEREFORD-SHIRE
MID WALES
SUFFOLK
BEDFORD-SHIRE
BUCKINGHAM-SHIRE
HERTFORD-SHIRE
ESSEX
WEST WALES
GWENT
GLOUCS & BRISTOL
OXFORD-SHIRE
GLAMORGAN
GREATER LONDON
BERKSHIRE
WILTSHIRE
SURREY
KENT
SOMERSET
HAMPSHIRE
WEST SUSSEX
EAST SUSSEX
CHANNEL ISLANDS
DEVON
DORSET
ISLE OF WIGHT
CORNWALL

England

BEDFORDSHIRE

Ampthill

Old Sun ✔

87 Dunstable Road, MK45 2NQ

12-11.30 (midnight Fri-Sun) ☎ (01525) 405466

Adnams Bitter, Broadside; Fuller's London Pride; St Austell Tribute; Wells Bombardier Ⓗ

Busy and cosy establishment on Ampthill's main street with two bars plus a games room, offering a fine selection of regular ales. Popular with a good mix of people and also dog-friendly. The walls feature pictures of stars of screen and stage, and a real fire adds a cosy feel in winter. Outside, there are ample decked and lawned areas to the rear and tables to the front. ♣P

Queen's Head

20 Woburn Street, MK45 2HP

12 (11 Sat)-11; 12-10.30 Sun ☎ (01525) 405016

Wells Eagle IPA, Bombardier; guest beers Ⓗ

Truly charming 18th-century tavern in historic Ampthill close to the park and the Greensand Ridge Walk. Inside is a low-beamed saloon bar, lounge and a further room available for private functions. Irregular beer festivals are held throughout the year and the occasional real cider is offered. Bar snacks are served all day. The Queen's Head is the focus for an interesting array of the town's more unusual events. The pub's name refers to Henry VIII's first wife, Catherine of Aragon, who was imprisoned in Ampthill Castle. ♣

Arlesey

Vicars Inn

68 Church Lane, SG15 6UX

12-3 (not Mon & Tue), 5-midnight; 12-4, 7-midnight Sat; 12-3, 7-midnight Sun ☎ (01462) 731215

Wells Eagle IPA; guest beer Ⓗ

Friendly locals' pub situated opposite the church and only five minutes' walk from the railway station. The lounge bar has comfortable seating, tasteful decor and a pleasant atmosphere, with a good mixed clientele. There is some background music, but it doesn't intrude. A large enclosed garden is ideal for families and there is a separate function room. Beers are good value and the guest ale is usually an IPA. Q(M2,E7)♣P

Barton-le-Clay

Bull

77 Bedford Road, MK45 4LL

12-2.30, 6-midnight (2am Fri); 12-2am Sat; 12-midnight Sun ☎ (01582) 705070

Adnams Broadside; Sharp's Doom Bar; guest beers Ⓗ

INDEPENDENT BREWERIES

B&T Shefford
Potton Potton
Wells & Young's Bedford
White Park Cranfield

This low-beamed, traditional, olde-worlde coaching inn offers a friendly public bar with extensive seating areas for dining. Two consistent and regular real ales are served in addition to two ever-changing guests. A pub since the 1740s, the main part of the building dates from 1600. Ask the landlord about the pub's history and painted beams. Lunchtime and evening meals are served daily except Saturday. Pool and darts are played in the main bar area. 🛏❀◐◑♿🚌♣P⚡

Bedford

Bedford Arms

2 Bromham Road, MK40 2QA (opp HM Prison)
⏲ 12-11 (midnight Thu-Sat) ☎ (01234) 214656
Courage Best Bitter; Wells Bombardier; Young's Bitter, Special; guest beers Ⓗ
Following an extensive rebuild, the Bedford Arms has reopened as a Charles Wells Speciality Ale House. Wood panelling dominates and the wooden floor makes for interesting acoustics. A changing range of guest beers adds choice to the four regular Wells & Young's ales. Bar meals are available daily, with a roast on Sunday. There is a quiz on Monday, a poetry club on Thursday and live music on Tuesday, Friday and all day Sunday from 1pm. Nearby street parking is limited. ❀◐◑⇌🚌⚡

Cricketers Arms

35 Goldington Road, MK40 3LH (on A4280 near rugby ground)
⏲ 5 (7 Sun)-11 ☎ (01234) 303958 🌐 cricketersarms.co.uk
Adnams Bitter; guest beers Ⓗ
Small, friendly, one-bar pub near Bedford Blues rugby ground, popular with fans of the game and very busy on match days. It opens at noon on Saturdays for Blues home games. Live rugby is shown and the pub also opens early for live Six Nations games. Guest beers are from Punch Taverns' finest cask selection. There is a covered, heated courtyard for smokers and drinkers. No food is available Sunday and Monday, or Saturday when the rugby is on. ❀◑🚌(5)⚡

Devonshire Arms ✔

32 Dudley Street, MK40 3TB (1 mile E of town centre S of A428)
⏲ 5.30 (2 Fri)-11; 12-11 Sat & Sun ☎ (01234) 359329
Wells Eagle IPA, Bombardier; guest beers Ⓗ
Pleasant two-bar local in a quiet residential area east of the town centre near Russell Park and the Embankment. The landlady previously worked for the Charles Wells brewery so knows the trade well. An annual beer festival is hosted in May. Good wine is served by the jug. The garden has a covered space with heating and lighting for smokers as well as a non-smoking area. Hanging baskets adorn the exterior in summer and there is a grapevine in the garden. ❀🖵🚌(4)♣⚡

Three Cups

45 Newnham Street, MK40 3JR (200m S of A4280 near rugby ground)
⏲ 11-11; 12-10.30 Sun ☎ (01234) 352153
Greene King XX Mild, IPA, Abbot; guest beers Ⓗ
Just five minutes from the town centre and close to the rugby ground, this 1770s pub with old-style wood panelling feels more like a welcoming village pub. A popular lunchtime menu is available with a wide range of food served in generous portions and a roast on Sunday. The pleasant garden has a heated smoking shelter. Dogs are welcome in the public bar and garden. Quiz night is a highlight on Tuesday. Local CAMRA Pub of the Year 2009. ❀◐🖵♿🚌(5,7)♣P⚡

Wellington Arms 🏆 ✔

40-42 Wellington Street, MK40 2JX (off A6 N of town centre)
⏲ 12-11 (10.30 Sun) ☎ (01234) 308033
Adnams Bitter; B&T Two Brewers; guest beers Ⓗ
Award-winning, street-corner B&T local offering a wide range of regional and micro-brewery beers, plus real cider and perry from 14 handpumps. A good selection of draught and bottled Belgian and imported beers is also available. Filled rolls are served at lunchtimes (not Sun). The courtyard is partly covered for drinkers and smokers. Street parking is limited, but why would you want to drive here? A friendly pub with an interesting, mixed clientele. Local CAMRA Pub of the Year 2010. ❀🍎⚡

White Horse ✔

84 Newnham Avenue, MK41 9PX (on A5140 just S of A4280)
⏲ 11 (12 Sun)-11 ☎ (01234) 409306
🌐 whitehorsebedford.co.uk
Wells Eagle IPA, Bombardier; guest beers Ⓗ
Large, suburban pub a mile east of the town centre with a central bar. Good value food is available, with a Sunday roast and occasional themed evenings. Quiz nights are Sunday and Tuesday, while Monday is 'open-mike' night. The pub has won several brewery and local business awards. A May Day weekend local beer, food and talent festival and a November beer and banger festival are hosted annually. Check the website for monthly events highlights. ❀◐◑♿🚌(4)P⚡

Biggleswade

Golden Pheasant ✔

71 High Street, SG18 0JH
⏲ 11-11 (1am Fri & Sat) ☎ (01767) 313653
🌐 goldenpheasantpub.co.uk
Wells Eagle IPA; guest beers Ⓗ
Mid-19th-century ale house with many original features including oak beams and a low ceiling. The five guest handpumps offer beers from Wells & Young's plus a variety of micro-brews, usually including a stout or porter. Located near the market place and a short walk from both railway and bus stations, the pub hosts quiz and chess evenings, plus an autumn beer festival. Soft background music plays but there is no fruit machine, TV or pool table. Local CAMRA Pub of the Year 2009. ❀⇌🚌⚡

Stratton House Hotel ✔

London Road, SG18 8ED
⏲ 11-11 (midnight Fri & Sat) ☎ (01767) 312442
🌐 strattonhouse-hotel.com
Wells Eagle IPA, Bombardier; guest beers Ⓗ
Former council offices located at the top of the High Street, converted into a large hotel in 1981. Facilities include 32 bedrooms, a function room and a spacious restaurant, open daily. Meals can also be taken in the main bar area, which is bright and airy with tasteful decor and comfortable seating. Popular with all age groups, the bar can get very busy at the weekend. Two Charles Wells' ales are supplemented by two ever-changing guest beers. 🛏◐◑♿⇌🚌P⚡

Blunham

Salutation

20 High Street, MK44 3NL

◎ 11-3, 5-midnight (1am Fri & Sat); 11-10.30 Sun

☎ (01767) 640620 ⊕ thesalutationblunham.co.uk

Greene King IPA; guest beers Ⓗ

Situated in the centre of Blunham village, the pub's frontage dates from the early 17th century, although the rest is later. Inside, there is a large bar with table skittles and a small games room with pool table. Behind the bar is a function room/restaurant. There are five handpumps, three serving Greene King beers and two guest ales, free of tie. The pub hosts beer festivals twice a year at Easter and August bank holiday.

🏛️❀◐&➡(E3)♣●P⁵⁻

Bolnhurst

Plough ✅

Kimbolton Road, MK44 2EX (on B660 at S end of village)

◎ 12-3, 6.30-11; closed Mon; 12-3 Sun ☎ (01234) 376274

⊕ bolnhurst.com

Beer range varies Ⓗ

This award-winning pub restaurant can trace its roots back to Tudor times. It offers excellent food and good service. The main bar features a modern open fireplace with a view through to the kitchen. A second room is set aside for diners. Outside is a large drinking area alongside the car park. There are three handpumps dispensing a range of beers, often from local micro-breweries. The pub is closed from Christmas until the second week of the new year. 🏛️Q❀◐&P

Clophill

Stone Jug

10 Back Street, MK45 4BY (off A6 at N end of village)

◎ 12-3, 6-11; 12-11 Fri & Sat; 12-10.30 Sun

☎ (01525) 860526

B&T Shefford Bitter; Batemans XB; Wadworth 6X; guest beers Ⓗ

Originally three 16th-century cottages, this popular village local has an L-shaped bar that serves two drinking areas and a family/function room. Excellent home-made lunches are available Tuesday to Saturday. There are picnic benches at the front and a rear patio garden for outdoor drinking in fine weather. Parking can be difficult at busy times. Bedfordshire CAMRA Pub of the Year 2006. Q🍂❀◐➡(S1,X44)♣●P⁵⁻

Dunstable

Globe 🍷

43 Winfield Street, LU6 1LS

◎ 12-11 (midnight Fri & Sat); 12-10.30 Sun

☎ (01582) 512300

B&T Two Brewers, Shefford Bitter, Black Dragon Mild, Dunstable Giant, Edwin Taylor's Extra Stout; guest beers Ⓗ

Popular local and beer destination pub decorated with breweriana and disordered pump clips. It serves 11 real ales including Everards Tiger plus real cider and Westons Herefordshire Country Perry. The Dunstable Giant is named after the late landlord, Mel Hall. Beer festivals are hosted twice yearly with 50 micro-brews, and an ever-changing range of guest beers is always on offer for the discerning traveller. Folk night is Tuesday and dogs are always welcome. Local CAMRA Pub of the Year 2007-10 and county winner 2009. Q❀&♣●⁵⁻

Star & Garter

147 High Street South, LU6 3SQ

◎ 12-midnight; 11-1am Fri & Sat; 12-10.30 Sun

☎ (01582) 529465

Courage Directors; Sharp's Doom Bar; Wadworth 6X; Young's Special; guest beer Ⓗ

Traditional two-bar, street-corner local. Friendly and well run, there is a TV showing sporting events as well as pool, darts, dominoes and crib. Quiz night is Thursday. Freshly-made sandwiches are available all day (to 9pm Fri & Sat). Smokers may use the covered rear courtyard area. ❀🍴&♣⁵⁻

Victoria

69 West Street, LU6 1ST

◎ 11-12.30am (1am Fri & Sat); 12-midnight Sun

☎ (01582) 662682

Beer range varies Ⓗ

Popular town-centre pub that usually offers four ales including a house beer, Victoria Bitter, from Tring Brewery. The varying guest ales are from micro and regional breweries. Good value food is available until early evening Monday-Friday, and Saturday and Sunday lunchtimes. Darts and dominoes are popular and televised sport features in the bar. Quarterly beer festivals are held. There is no admittance after 11pm. ❀◐➡(61)♣⁵⁻

Eversholt

Green Man

Church End, MK17 9DU SP984325

◎ 12-2.30 (not Mon), 6-11; 5-11 Fri; 12-11 Sat; 12-7 Sun

☎ (01525) 288111 ⊕ greenmaneversholt.com

Fuller's London Pride; guest beers Ⓗ

Conveniently located near the tourist attractions of Woburn, this is an early Victorian building with a recently refurbished interior featuring a modern flagstone floor and exposed fireplaces in the main bar area. Good food is served in a separate restaurant area. Outside is a large patio and garden. This is a genuine, privately-owned free house with two guest ales – usually one from a local brewery. An annual beer festival is held over the May bank holiday weekend. 🏛️Q❀◐&♣P⁵⁻

Flitton

Jolly Coopers

Wardhedges, MK45 5ED

◎ 12-3 (not Mon), 5.30-11.30; 12-midnight Sat; 12-11 Sun

☎ (01525) 860626

Wells Eagle IPA; guest beers Ⓗ

A charming and welcoming proper village pub with a traditional flagstone-floored bar and a restaurant to the rear. Two varying guest beers are sourced from a variety of brewers. The pub is the hub of the little community of Wardhedges and is home to various local interest groups and games teams. Hearty, home-cooked meals are served daily in the bar and Tuesday to Sunday in the restaurant. 🏛️❀◐&♣P⁵⁻

Great Barford

Anchor Inn ✅

High Street, MK44 3LF (by river bridge 1 mile S of village centre)

12-3, 6 (5.30 Fri)-11; 12-11 Sat; 12-4, 6.30-10.30 Sun
☎ (01234) 870364
Young's Bitter; guest beers Ⓗ
Busy local pub situated next to the church, overlooking the Great Ouse. At least two guest beers are usually available from an extensive range. Good home-cooked food is served in the bar and restaurant, as well as a fine selection of wines. The pub is popular with river users in the summer. Occasional themed nights are hosted, mainly during the winter months. Q⇌◑◗♿P⁄–

Harlington

Old Sun

34 Sundon Road, LU5 6LS
12-midnight (1am Fri & Sat) ☎ (01525) 877330
theoldsunharlington.com
Adnams Bitter; St Austell Tribute; Taylor Landlord; guest beers Ⓗ
A traditional half-timbered pub situated in a popular commuter village. The new licensees have shown great dedication to real ale and plan to add more to their range. Regular beer festivals are held. With two separate bars and outdoor seating, this charming pub dates back to 1785 and the building to the 1740s. ⩕Q❀⊟⇌⊟(X42)♣P⁄–

Henlow

Crown

2 High Street, SG16 6BS
11-11; 12-10.30 Sun ☎ (01462) 812433
crownpub.co.uk
Greene King IPA; Wells Bombardier; guest beer Ⓗ
Large 18th-century inn, now operating as a family business. Although mainly open plan, there are plenty of secluded seating areas full of wooden beams and panelling, decorated with brasses, pictures and historical artefacts. The large restaurant offers a comprehensive menu with a mix of British and continental cuisine. The garden is a popular haven for summertime drinkers.
⩕❀◑◗♿⇌(Arlesey)⊟(82,M1)P⁄–

Engineers Arms ✔

68 High Street, SG16 6AA
12-midnight (1am Fri & Sat) ☎ (01462) 812284
engineersarms.co.uk
Beer range varies Ⓗ
Popular freehouse with a mixed clientele, offering up to 10 beers on handpump, as well as three real ciders and a perry. Located in the middle of the High Street, this is the place for sports enthusiasts and music lovers. The vibrant pub hosts live bands, discos and games nights, and the October beer festival with pig roast is an annual highlight. Winner of many branch and county CAMRA awards in recent years. ⩕❀⊟♿⅄⊟(82,M1)♣●⁄–

Kempston

Duke

Woburn Road, MK42 7QA
12-11 (midnight Fri & Sat) ☎ (01234) 857201
Wells Eagle IPA, Bombardier; guest beers Ⓗ
This large community pub can be found just south of the main shopping street and close to a residential area. An L-shaped bar separates the large lounge from a games area with a pool table and there is a beer garden at the rear of the pub.
❀◑◗♿⊟(1,2)P⁄–

Half Moon ✔

108 High Street, MK42 7BN
12-3, 6 (5 Fri)-11.30; 12-4, 7-11 Sat & Sun
☎ (01234) 852464
Courage Best Bitter; Wells Eagle IPA Ⓗ
Well-supported community pub with a comfortable lounge bar and a public bar with games, now including the new Wii bowling. The pub hosts a number of games teams playing in local leagues. The large garden, which includes a children's play area, is well used in good weather. The Great Ouse a short distance away offers popular riverside walks. Lunches are served Monday to Saturday.
⩕❀◑◗⊟♿⊟(1,2)♣P⁄–

Kensworth

Farmers Boy ✔

216 Common Road, LU6 2PJ
12-2, 5-11; 12-midnight Fri & Sat; 12-11 Sun
☎ (01582) 872207 thefarmersboykensworth.co.uk
Fuller's London Pride, ESB; Gale's Seafarers; guest beer Ⓗ
There is a warm welcome at this village local with several bar areas where you can take the weight off your feet and enjoy an open fire and a good chat. This pub is ideally placed to visit Whipsnade Zoo or to explore the Bedfordshire Chilterns. It's one of a very few pubs to practise Dwyle Flonking. Good pub food is served daily lunchtimes and evenings, with a carvery 12-5pm Sunday.
⩕Q❀◑◗⊟(X31)♣P⁄–

Leighton Buzzard

Golden Bell ✔

4-6 Church Square, LU7 1AE
10-11 (midnight Fri & Sat); 11-11 Sun ☎ (01525) 373330
St Austell Tribute; Tetley Bitter; guest beers Ⓗ
Welcoming and friendly pub originally built for stonemasons erecting the nearby 13th-century church. The two regular ales are complemented by two changing guests dispensed either by handpump or gravity from the cellar on request. Traditional pub food includes home-made pies and roasts with all the trimmings on Tuesday market days. The single bar has an original low-beamed ceiling and a comfy area with sofas. Live sporting events are shown on large TVs. ◑◗⊟⁄–

Luton

Black Horse

23 Hastings Street, LU1 5BE
2 (1 Sat)-11; 1-10.30 Sun ☎ (01582) 450994
Beer range varies Ⓗ
This one-room pub is popular with football fans and opens at noon on Saturday when Luton Town are playing at home. The number of beers varies during the week, with up to four at weekends. The ales are mainly from micro-breweries and Westons Old Rosie cider is also available. The jukebox features a wide range of music including local bands but appears to have no low volume setting. Occasional live bands play and a beer festival is held every November. The pool table is popular here. Well-behaved dogs are welcome. ⩕❀⊟●⁄–

Bricklayers Arms ✔

16-18 High Town Road, LU2 0DD
12-11 Mon; 12-2.30, 5-11 Tue-Thu; 12-midnight Fri & Sat; 12-10.30 Sun ☎ (01582) 611017

Everards Beacon, Tiger; guest beers Ⓗ
Tucked away behind Luton station, this somewhat quirky town pub has been run by the same landlady for more than 23 years. On average, 10 guest ales are served per week, mainly from micro-breweries. Forthcoming ales are temptingly displayed on a noticeboard by the bar. Popular with Hatters fans, the pub's two TVs mainly show football. Monday is quiz night. There are three draught Belgian beers and a selection of foreign bottled beers. Pub lunches are served 12-2pm Monday to Friday. ❀◐⇌(Luton)♣P⚊

English Rose
46 Old Bedford Road, LU2 7PA
❂ 12-11 ☎ (01582) 723889 🌐 englishroseluton.co.uk
Beer range varies Ⓗ
Friendly street-corner community local. Four frequently-changing guest beers are on offer from a range of breweries nationwide, with more than 500 served in 2009. Food is served Tuesday to Friday lunchtime and until early evening on Saturday, with a takeaway service. The quiz on Tuesday evening is a highlight. The garden, one of the best pub gardens in the town centre, accommodates both smokers and non-smokers in four specially designed heated huts. An annual beer festival is held. ❀◐♿⇌⊟(24,25)⚊

Globe
26 Union Street, LU1 3AN
❂ 11 (12 Sun)-midnight ☎ (01582) 728681
Caledonian Deuchars IPA; Greene King IPA; guest beers Ⓗ
Popular one-room street-corner local, just out of the town centre. The Caledonian Deuchars is often replaced by Black Sheep Best Bitter or Sharp's Doom Bar. A frequently changing guest ale is also on offer, generally of a premium strength from a micro or regional brewery. Occasional beer festivals are staged. Impromptu acoustic music sessions often feature on Thursday evenings. Sport is shown on TV and good value food is served Monday to Saturday lunchtimes. A large patio and heated smoking shelter can be accessed from the bar. ❀◐♣P⚊

Odell

Bell
Horsefair Lane, MK43 7AU
❂ 11.30-3 (12-4 Sat), 6-11.30; 12-4, 7-10.30 Sun
☎ (01234) 720254 🌐 thebellinodell.co.uk
Greene King IPA, Abbot; guest beers Ⓗ
Handsome thatched village pub with a large garden near the River Great Ouse. With the Harrold-Odell Country Park just down the lane, this is a popular stop for walkers. Sympathetic refurbishment and a series of linked but distinct seating areas help retain a traditional pub atmosphere. Good quality and value food includes a Sunday roast, with small portions available at lunchtime. ♨Q❀◐◑⊟(125)P⚊

Potton

Rising Sun 🏆 ✔
11 Everton Road, SG19 2PA
❂ 12-2.30, 6-11 (midnight Fri); 12-midnight Sat; 12-11 Sun
☎ (01767) 260231
St Austell Tribute; Wells Eagle IPA; guest beers Ⓗ
Large community-based pub with an upstairs function room and rooftop terrace available for birthday and wedding parties. Downstairs, the wood-beamed lounge bar features a covered well. Meals are popular, served daily until 9.30pm. Behind the bar, there are four guest ales from across the nation – some from micro-breweries. The spring beer festival provides further opportunity to explore a wider range of ales. ❀◐◑⊟(E1,E2)♣P⚊

Pulloxhill

Cross Keys ✔
13 High Street, MK45 5HB
❂ 12-3, 6-11; 12-10.30 Sun ☎ (01525) 712442
Adnams Broadside; Wells Eagle IPA; guest beer Ⓗ
This old oak-beamed inn in the middle of the village is a popular venue for dining thanks to the good home-made specials. Its large restaurant area can also be used for private functions. Run by the same landlord and lady for more than 39 years, the pub is well known locally for its jazz offering on a Sunday evening. Extensive grounds include a children's play area next to the car park and another area where the local archery group practises. Q❀◐◑♿⛺⊟♣P⚊

Renhold

Polhill Arms
25 Wilden Road, MK41 0JP (at Salph End)
❂ 12-3, 5-11; 12-11 Fri & Sat; 12-10.30 Sun
☎ (01234) 771398 🌐 polhillarms.co.uk
Greene King IPA, Old Speckled Hen; guest beers Ⓗ
One-bar family-friendly village local with a welcoming atmosphere and large garden, play area and restaurant. An interesting collection of pub and brewery artefacts is on view. Traditional pub food is served as well as fish and chips and a choice of pizzas (not Sun eve). Live entertainment and quiz nights feature regularly, and darts and skittles are played. At least one guest beer is usually available. ♨❀◐◑⊟(151)♣P⚊

Riseley

Fox & Hounds ✔
High Street, MK44 1DT
❂ 11.30-2.30, 6.30-11; 12-3, 7-10.30 Sun ☎ (01234) 708240
Wells Eagle IPA, Bombardier; guest beers Ⓗ
Old village inn, originally two 16th-century cottages complete with a priest's hiding hole and resident ghosts. It has a reputation for good food, with charcoal-grilled steak a speciality. Roast lunch is available on Sundays. The dining room can be reserved for parties, but there is no need to book for bar meals – relax over a pint while your food is cooked. The large lawned garden includes a covered patio with heaters. Q❀◐◑⊟(152)P⚊

Salford

Red Lion Hotel
Wavendon Road, MK17 8AZ (2 miles N of M1 J13)
❂ 11-2.30, 6.30-11; 12-2.30, 6.30-10.30 Sun
☎ (01908) 583117 🌐 redlionhotel.eu
Wells Eagle IPA, Bombardier Ⓗ
A traditional country hotel serving a fine choice of home-cooked food in the bar and restaurant. The cosy bar is heated by an open fire in winter and offers a selection of interesting board games. The

large garden includes a covered area and a secure children's playground. Overnight accommodation includes six rooms, some with four-poster beds. ♨Q❀⇌◐⊟♿P⅛

Sandy

Queen's Head

244 Cambridge Road, SG19 1JE

⏲ 11.30 (12 Sun)-11 ☎ (01767) 681115

Greene King IPA, Abbot; guest beers Ⓗ

Dating back to the 1700s and situated near the market square, this old inn has wooden beams and many original features, contributing to a cosy atmosphere. A large open fire warms the main bar area and separate dining room. Lunches are served every day with the Sunday roast especially popular. An ideal venue for playing darts and other pub games. The railway station is a 10-minute walk. ♨Q❀◐♿⇄⊟P

Sir William Peel ✔

39 High Street, SG19 1AG (opp church)

⏲ 12 (11 Sat)-midnight; 12-10.30 Sun ☎ (01767) 680607

Beer range varies Ⓗ

This freehouse was known as the Lord Nelson until 1994 when it changed name to immortalise a local entrepreneur. Four ales are available, with beers from Tring Brewery often featuring, and the spring beer festival is very popular. No meals are served, although customers are welcome to bring in food from nearby takeaways. The evenings may include a quiz or a disco – the more adventurous can join in with the 'open mike' sets. ❀♿⇄⊟(178)P⅛

Shefford

Brewery Tap

14 North Bridge Street, SG17 5DH

⏲ 11.30-11; 12-10.30 Sun ☎ (01462) 628448

B&T Shefford Bitter, Dunstable Giant, Dragonslayer; Everards Tiger; guest beers Ⓗ

A short walk from the B&T brewery, the Tap was rescued and renamed by B&T in 1996. Primarily a drinkers' pub, it offers four regular and one guest beer. The open-plan interior, featuring a display of breweriana, is divided into two distinct areas plus a family room to the rear, all served from a single bar. Pies and filled rolls are available at lunchtime. The rear patio garden is heated on cool evenings. Car park access is through an archway next to the pub. ☋❀⊟(M1,M2)♣P⅛

Souldrop

Bedford Arms

High Street, MK44 1EY SP987616

⏲ Closed Mon; 12-3, 6-11; 12-midnight Fri & Sat; 12-11 Sun ☎ (01234) 781384

Black Sheep Best Bitter; Greene King IPA; guest beers Ⓗ

Large village pub dating from the 17th century in parts, when it was a hop house and ale house. Guest beers are often from local micro-breweries. The welcoming restaurant has a central, open fireplace and serves traditional pub favourites prepared to order, with daily specials and a roast lunch on Sunday (no food Sun eve). A large games room with skittles runs off the main bar. The spacious garden and play area are popular with families in summer. ♨❀◐⊟(125)♣P⅛

> A fine beer may be judged with only a sip, but it's better to be thoroughly sure.
> **Czech proverb**

Stotfold

Stag

35 Brook Street, SG5 4LA

⏲ 12-11 (midnight Fri & Sat) ☎ (01462) 730261

🌐 thestag-stotfold.co.uk

Adnams Bitter; Fuller's London Pride; guest beers Ⓗ

Friendly pub with a horseshoe-shaped bar and a separate dining room, where food is served daily except for Monday evening. Try the weekday offer of two main meals for £10 or the Sunday carvery (until 5.30pm). Two guest ales often come from micro-breweries and a real cider is available, usually from Westons. Regular events include the Wednesday quiz and Sunday meat raffle, plus a beer festival on the late spring bank holiday weekend. ♨❀◐♿⊟(97)♣●P⅛

Streatley

Chequers

171 Sharpenhoe Road, LU3 3PS (next to Church)

⏲ 12-11.30 (10.30 Sun) ☎ (01582) 882072

🌐 thechequers-streatley.co.nr

Greene King IPA, Morland Original, Old Speckled Hen, Abbot; guest beers Ⓗ

Village pub of Georgian origin on the green next to the church. It usually has five real ales on handpump and is one of the few hostelries in the region to use oversized, lined pint glasses. Attracting locals and visitors alike, the pub is especially popular in good weather due to the large patio area. Quiz night is Tuesday and traditional jazz plays on the first Sunday afternoon of the month. The AONB Sharpenhoe Clappers is nearby. ♨❀⇌◐♿♣P⅛⊔

Sutton

John O' Gaunt Inn

30 High Street, SG19 2NE

⏲ 12-2.30, 7-11; 12-10.30 Sun ☎ (01767) 260377

Black Sheep Best Bitter; Fuller's London Pride; Greene King Abbot; Woodforde's Wherry Ⓗ

This popular community-oriented two-bar pub has featured regularly in the Guide for many years. Here you can enjoy good home-cooked food and choose from four regular ales, or a cider from the Westons range. Try your hand at Northamptonshire skittles in the public bar or take part in the impromptu folk music evenings. In the large garden you can relax with a game of petanque or sit back and watch visiting morris men. ♨Q❀◐⊟⊟♣●P

Tebworth

Queen's Head

The Lane, LU7 9QB

⏲ 12-3 (not Mon-Wed), 6 (7 Sat)-11 ☎ (01525) 874101

Adnams Broadside; Courage Directors Ⓖ; **Wells Eagle IPA** Ⓗ; **guest beer** Ⓖ

Traditional two-bar village local with a public bar, popular for darts and dominoes, and a lounge where live music plays on Fridays. The beers are served directly from the cask (except for Eagle IPA).

The pub has featured in the Guide for more than 25 years under the present landlord who also has a career as an actor. ♨❀⊟♣P⅟

Toddington

Oddfellows Arms

2 Conger Lane, LU5 6BP

☉ 5-11 (midnight Fri); 12-midnight Sat; 12-11 Sun

☎ (01525) 872021

Adnams Broadside; Fuller's London Pride; guest beers Ⓗ

Attractive 15th-century pub facing the village green with a heavily-beamed and brassed bar featuring a vast collection of pump clips and a games room with a pool table. Westons Old Rosie, and often a guest cider or perry, are available as well as a good range of bottled ciders. Beer festivals are held in the spring and autumn. The patio garden is popular in summer and has shelter for smokers. ♨❀⊟♣●⅟

Sow & Pigs

14 Church Street, LU5 6AA

☉ 4.30-11; 12-midnight Sat; 12-11 Sun ☎ (01525) 873089

⊕ sowandpigs.co.uk

Greene King IPA; guest beers Ⓗ

The Sow is a 19th-century inn with a long, narrow and dog-friendly bar heated by open fires. Two guest beers are usually available, one from the Greene King stable and one from the local White Park Brewery. At present only Sunday lunches are served but this is due to change – check the pub website for details. There is a monthly curry night and banquets can be booked by larger groups. There is also a pleasant garden to the rear. ♨Q❀⊟♣P⅟

Whipsnade

Old Hunters Lodge

The Crossroads, LU6 2LN

☉ 11:30-2pm (3pm Sat) & 6-11; 12-11 Sun

☎ (01582) 872228 ⊕ old-hunters.com

Greene King IPA, Abbot; guest beer Ⓗ

Set on the edge of Whipsnade common, this is one of the oldest houses in the village. Thatched with reed in the Norfolk style, the building is said to date from the 15th century. Nearby, discover the glorious scenery of Dunstable Downs, Whipsnade tree cathedral and the world-renowned Whipsnade Zoo, famous for breeding rare species. There are five guest rooms and a large dining area providing food all week (until 7pm Sun).
♨Q❀⊏◑⊟(X31)P

Wingfield

Plough

Tebworth Road, LU7 9QH

☉ 12-3, 5.30-midnight; 12-midnight Sat; 12-11 Sun

☎ (01525) 873077 ⊕ theploughinn.com

Fuller's London Pride, ESB; Gale's HSB; guest beers Ⓗ

Charming, thatched village inn dating from the 17th century, decorated with paintings of rural scenes and ploughs. Beware the low beams! Two guest beers are offered – one the Fuller's seasonal offering, the other usually from elsewhere. Good food is served daily except Sunday evening when the weekly quiz is held. Food tends to dominate until later at weekends. There are tables outside at the front – to the rear is a conservatory and prize-winning garden illuminated at night in the summer. Heated umbrellas are provided for smokers. ♨❀◑P⅟

Farmers Boy, Kensworth (Photo: Ed Button)

A Beer a Day

Jeff Evans

"This book of good pints and bottles is a friendly source of trivia that will help you through any pub quiz... Expert beer writer Jeff Evans finds an event (Battle of Hastings, Brunel's birthday, the last episode of 'Blackadder') for each day of the year and chooses an appropriate tipple with which to celebrate." Time Out magazine.

Written by leading beer writer Jeff Evans, **A Beer a Day** is a beer lover's almanac, crammed with beers from around the world to enjoy on every day and in every season, and celebrating beer's connections with history, sport, music film and television. Whether it's Christmas Eve, Midsummer's Day, Bonfire Night, or just a wet Wednesday in the middle of October, **A Beer a Day** has just the beer for you to savour and enjoy.

£9.00 ISBN 978-1-85249-235-9 CAMRA members' price £8.00 384 pages

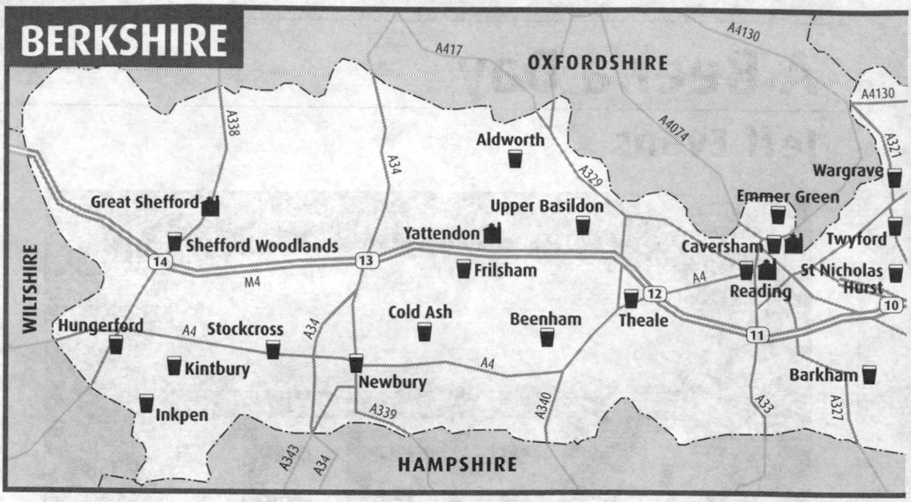

Aldworth

Bell 🏆 ☆

Bell Lane, RG8 9SE (in centre of village, off B4009) SU555796

✪ 11-3, 6-11; closed Mon; 12-3, 7-10.30 Sun

☎ (01635) 578272

Arkell's 3B, Kingsdown; West Berkshire Maggs Mild, Good Old Boy, seasonal beers Ⓗ

In the same family for 200 years, this traditional country pub is a real gem. The ageless interior includes a one-handed grandfather clock and an unusual glass-walled bar. The pub's location makes it popular with walkers as well as locals and real ale enthusiasts. Delicious filled rolls and tasty desserts complement the excellent beers and award-winning Upton cider. ⚑Q❀◘♣●P▯

Barkham

Bull ✔

Barkham Road, RG41 4TL (on B3349, 2 miles W of Wokingham)

✪ 11.30-3, 5.30-11; 12-4 ☎ (0118) 9760324

🌐 thebullatbarkham.com

Adnams Bitter, Broadside; Courage Best; Fuller's ESB Ⓗ

Formerly a brewhouse for Sparks Farm, then from 1728 to 1982 this was a forge with a working smithy. The original building is now the restaurant and Grade II listed. The menu features local produce including Barkham Bull Bangers – hand-made sausages using local pork, sage and award-winning Barkham Blue Cheese. These are also available to take home. The bar has an inglenook fireplace. Outside is a pleasant garden and an area for alfresco dining. No children permitted under 10. ⚑❀◐◑♿🚌(144)P

Beenham

Six Bells

The Green, RG7 5NX (at Bucklebury end of main road through village) SU585688

✪ 12-2.30 (not Mon & Tue), 6-11; 12-3, 6.30-11 Sat; 12-3, 6.30-10.30 Sun ☎ (01189) 713368 🌐 thesixbells.co.uk

Fuller's London Pride Ⓖ**; guest beers** Ⓗ

This popular village pub was voted local CAMRA Pub of the Year in 2008 for its commitment to the local community, beer quality, atmosphere and high standard of service. In addition to Fuller's London Pride it offers two guest beers, usually from small local breweries, to be enjoyed in either of the two comfortable bars. High quality home-cooked food is served in the bars, conservatory or separate restaurant, which also acts as a function room. The lovely garden overlooks open fields. ⚑❀🛏◐◑◘♿🚌(104)♣P

Binfield

Jack o' Newbury 🏆

Terrace Road North, RG42 5PH (NE of village, towards church) SU845718

✪ 11-3, 5.30-11; 12-3, 7-10.30 ☎ (01344) 454881

🌐 jackofnewbury.co.uk

Loddon Hoppit; West Berkshire Good Old Boy; guest beers Ⓗ

Victorian free house of considerable character and tradition with a strong local following but welcoming to all, situated on the outskirts of the village and featuring a separate skittle alley. A large selection of tankards and bells hang from the beams. It has been recently refurbished to expose the original beams and floor, giving the pub a light and airy feel. The house beer, Binfield Best, is of unknown origin – see if you can get the friendly landlord to reveal it. ⚑Q❀◐◑🚌(152)♣P⌐

Victoria Arms ✔

Terrace Road North, RG42 5JA SU842713

✪ 11.30-11 (midnight Fri & Sat); 12-11 Sun

☎ (01344) 483856

Fuller's Discovery, London Pride, ESB, seasonal beer; Gale's ESB Ⓗ

Longest standing Guide entry in the area, local CAMRA Branch Pub of the Year 2009 and Fuller's

INDEPENDENT BREWERIES

Butts Great Shefford
Two Bridges Caversham (NEW)
West Berkshire Yattendon
Windsor & Eton Windsor (NEW)
Zerodegrees Reading

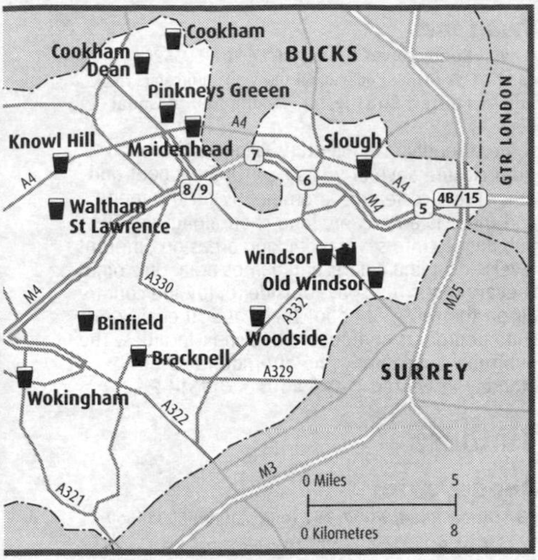

Best Country Village Pub 2009. This delightful and friendly Victorian pub is popular with locals and visitors alike. Two large TVs screen major sporting fixtures and Sunday night is quiz night. A pretty garden with heated decked area is in use all year round. The pub is a big supporter of charities and is well-known for its excellent fund-raising.
♨❀◑♿🚌(53,153)P⌐

Bracknell

Bull

High Street, RG12 1DP
⏲ 8-11 (2am Fri & Sat); 11-5 Sun ☎ (01344) 566858
🌐 thebullbracknell.com
Fuller's London Pride; Skinner's Betty Stogs Ⓗ
This recently refurbished 16th-century pub is a welcome addition to the real ale outlets in Bracknell town centre. The interior divides into a bar with a real fire on one side and a restaurant on the other. Live entertainment is a regular feature. Outside, there are drinking and smoking areas front and back. The pub opens early to serve breakfast (Mon-Sat). There is limited parking at the back.
♨❀◑♿⇌P⌐

Old Manor ✔

Church Road, Grenville Place, RG12 1BP (on inner ring road)
⏲ 9am-midnight ☎ (01344) 304490
Greene King Ruddles Best Bitter, Abbot; Marston's Pedigree; guest beers Ⓗ
This Tudor manor house was in private hands until the 1930s. Now a small free house, by Wetherspoon's standards, it has two larger bars and further individual seating areas. Outside there is a courtyard and garden seating. The guest ales change regularly. A room is available for private functions. Usual Wetherspoon keen pricing and acceptable pub grub. Q❀◑♿⇌🚌●P⌐

Caversham

Baron Cadogan ✔

22-24 Prospect Street, RG4 8JG
⏲ 9-11 (midnight Fri & Sat) ☎ (0118) 947 0626
Greene King Ruddles Best Bitter, Abbot; guest beers Ⓗ
Named after Baron William Cadogan (a one-time Commander-in-Chief of the British Army), this is a Wetherspoon at the more intimate end of the chain's spectrum with a pleasant 'local' feel. Up to six cask ales are available including a local ale from the nearby Loddon Brewery. Guest beers are occasionally available on gravity. The house beer, Cadogan's Gold, is Ferryman's Gold rebadged. Food is served 9am-10pm all week. Children are welcome during the day. There is full disabled access with a level entrance from the rear car park.
Q◑♿🚌(2,22,24)●⌐

Cold Ash

Castle Inn ✔

Cold Ash Hill, RG18 9PS SU511697
⏲ 11.30-3, 5.30-11.30; 11.30-midnight Fri & Sat; 12-11 Sun
☎ (01635) 863232 🌐 thecastleatcoldash.co.uk
Courage Best Bitter; Fuller's London Pride; guest beers Ⓗ
This warm and welcoming 19th-century pub has been in the same family for the last 15 years and is at the heart of the local community, with a meat raffle on Friday night, local music monthly and regular charity events. Monday is quiz night when no evening meals are served. Booking for lunchtimes is advised as the pub offers a popular pensioners' menu during the week. One of the guest beers is always a local ale in this dog-friendly pub. ♨❀◑🚌(101)♣P⌐

Cookham

Bounty

Riverside, SL8 5RG (footpath from station car park, across bridge, along towpath) SU907880
⏲ 12-10.30 (winter 12-dusk Sat & Sun; closed Mon-Fri)
☎ (01628) 520056
Rebellion IPA, Mutiny; guest beer Ⓗ
Quirky riverside pub that can only be reached on foot (the beer is delivered by boat). Dogs, walkers with muddy boots and children are made welcome and, as a result, summer weekends can be very busy. The boat-shaped bar is packed with nautical knick-knacks and daft jokes. Bar billiards can be played while listening to an eclectic mix of music on the jukebox. Books and cards are sold in aid of an African orphanage. Note the winter opening times. ♨♉❀◐⛺⇌(Bourne End)♣

Cookham Dean

Jolly Farmer

Church Road, SL6 9PD
⏲ 11.30-11 (11.45 Fri); 12-10.30 Sun ☎ (01628) 482905
🌐 jollyfarmercookhamdean.co.uk
Brakspear Bitter; Courage Best Bitter; Young's Bitter; guest beers Ⓗ
Situated opposite the church, this pub is owned by the village and accommodates the local post office. The adults-only Jolly bar is cosy with a tiled floor and low beams. The larger Dean bar accommodates families, diners and drinkers and features a log fire in winter. There is a small formal dining area (no meals Sun or Mon eve in winter) which is used for the pub's St George's Day and Halloween beer festivals. The large garden has a children's play area. ♨Q❀◑P

Emmer Green

Black Horse

16 Kidmore End Road, RG4 8SE
11 (12 Sun)-11 (0118) 947 4111
Caledonian Deuchars IPA; Courage Best Bitter; guest beer H
Traditional in design and layout, this CAMRA-friendly pub is easily reached by bus from Reading station. Choose from the public bar on the right with pool table and sports TV, or the quieter lounge bar on the left with a real fire. No food, just good beer and conversation. A decked patio at the rear gives extra drinking options in summer. Don't confuse this with the White Horse over the road. (23)

Frilsham

Pot Kiln

Bucklebury Road, RG18 0XX (on the Yattendon to Bucklebury road) SU552732
12-3, 6-11 (closed Tue); 12-11 Sat; 12-11 (6 winter) Sun
(01635) 201366 potkiln.org
West Berkshire Mr Chubb's Lunchtime Bitter, Brick Kiln Bitter, Maggs Mild; guest beers H
Originally an ale house for the kiln workers, this rural gem now attracts a more upmarket clientele who come for the excellent and extensive restaurant, specialising in game. However, the pub retains a small traditional bar, supplied by West Berkshire Brewery which first started brewing in the grounds of this pub. Great walking country, surrounded by hills, meadows and woods, and not far from Pangbourne Valley. Dogs are welcome. Q P

Hungerford

Downgate

13 Down View, Park Street, RG17 0ED (edge of Hungerford Common) SU341683
11-11 (01488) 682708 the-downgate.co.uk
Arkell's 3B; guest beers H
Friendly local on the eastern edge of town where tables outside offer rural views across the common and Kennet Valley. This one-room pub contains collections of suspended model aircraft and blowtorches. A cosy lower room houses a real fire and Sid, the caged parrot. Guest beers include 2B and Moonlight from Arkell's or a Donnington ale. Traditional home-cooked pub food is served. P

Inkpen

Crown & Garter

Inkpen Common, RG17 9QR SU378639
12-3 (not Mon & Tue), 5.30-11; 12-5, 7-10.30 Sun
(01488) 668325 crownandgarter.co.uk
Arkell's Moonlight; Ramsbury Gold; West Berkshire Mr Chubb's Lunchtime Bitter, Good Old Boy H
A well-maintained, wood-beamed, 17th-century inn handily placed for country rambles and close to Combe Gibbet. Food service, using fresh ingredients from local suppliers, leads the way but drinkers are welcome in the bar area with large tables, an enormous settle and an enclosed stove. Outside is a heated, covered, smoking shelter and a large garden with tables around an old oak tree. Accommodation is in eight purpose-built en-suite bedrooms. (13) P

Swan Inn

Craven Road, Lower Green, RG17 9DX SU359644
12-11 (01488) 668326 theswaninn-organics.co.uk
Adnams Bitter; Butts Jester, Traditional, seasonal beers H
Large, friendly, 17th-century village pub, saved from closure several years ago. Organic beef and other produce feature prominently on the menu, and there is an organic food shop alongside. The pub divides into several drinking areas on different levels, including a darts and games area. Quiz night is every other Thursday. Outside, enjoy the country air on the terraced patio. There are 10 quality en-suite bedrooms and good wheelchair facilities. The pub may close during the afternoon and on Monday in winter. Q (13) P

Kintbury

Dundas Arms

53 Station Road, RG17 9UT (opp station) SU385669
11-2.30, 6-11; 12-2.30 Sun (01488) 658263
dundasarms.co.uk
Adnams Bitter; Ramsbury Gold; West Berkshire Good Old Boy; guest beer H
Voted local CAMRA Pub of the Year in 2009, this 18th-century inn is set in an area of outstanding natural beauty on the banks of the River Kennet and Kennet & Avon Canal. The pub promotes beers from local breweries and there is always at least one guest ale available. Where possible the food, available to eat in the bar or separate restaurant, is locally sourced (not served Sun lunch or Mon eve). Q (13) P

Knowl Hill

Bird in Hand

Bath Road, RG10 9UP (on bend of A4 next to garage) SU820792
11-11; 12-10.30 Sun (01628) 826622
birdinhand.co.uk
Beer range varies H
Two or three beer festivals are held each year. There is always a LocAle and usually a dark beer among the rapidly-changing selection. The bar serves a comprehensive range of home-cooked food to eat in the comfortably furnished wood-panelled lounge, with even more choice in the restaurant. The real cider is in the cellar, just ask. Q (127,239) P

Maidenhead

Greyhound

92-96 Queen Street, SL6 1HZ
9am-midnight (1am Fri & Sat) (01628) 779410
Greene King Ruddles Best Bitter, Abbot; Marston's Pedigree; guest beers H
This large Wetherspoon (Lloyds No 1) near the station is LocAle accredited and stocks Loddon and Rebellion beers among its four guests. Westons Old Rosie and Vintage cider are available on handpump. The pub's open plan area has a family section. A smaller room is quiet except for music at weekends. There is a small smoking area at the rear.

Maidenhead Conservative Club

32 York Road, SL6 1SF
11-11 (11.45 Fri & Sat); 12-11 Sun (01628) 620579
maidenheadconclub.co.uk

Fuller's London Pride, seasonal beers; Gale's Seafarers Ale; guest beers H
Friendly real ale outlet close to the station voted CAMRA Regional Club of the Year 2009. Two guests from independent breweries are available, along with bottle-conditioned beers. Monday is crib night, Tuesday and Wednesday darts. Hot meals are available (Mon-Fri lunchtime). Parking is limited, but a public car park is 100 metres away. This Guide or a CAMRA membership card allows entry for a minimal fee. ♨ᗑᗩ✦P↳

Newbury

Lock, Stock & Barrel ✓

104 Northbrook Street, RG14 1AA (tucked down alley near canal bridge) SU471672
✪ 11-11 (midnight Fri & Sat); 12-10.30 Sun
☎ (01635) 580550
Fuller's Discovery, London Pride, seasonal beers H
This single bar, town-centre pub is welcoming and comfortable. Adjacent to the Kennet & Avon Canal, outside seating and a rooftop terrace offer fine views south, towards Newbury Lock and St Nicolas Church. Live jazz plays every Sunday afternoon with rock/blues on alternate Friday evenings. Meals are freshly prepared and available all day until 9pm (10pm Mon-Wed). Dog are welcome and there is free Wi-Fi and newspapers. ❀◑ᗑ✦↳

Old Windsor

Jolly Gardeners ✓

92-94 St Luke's Road, SL4 2QJ
✪ 12-11 (midnight Thu-Sat); 12-10.30 Sun
☎ (01753) 830215 ⊕ jollygardeners.com
Courage Best Bitter; Wells Bombardier H
Friendly, welcoming local close to the village shops, with a U-shaped bar divided into three areas, one with a large TV and dartboard. It offers good-value home-made food (12-3pm Thu-Sat). The Sunday roasts are popular. The well-tended garden is large enough to house a marquee for events. Reasonably-priced B&B is available. ❀⊨◑P↳

Pinkneys Green

Stag & Hounds

1 Lee Lane, SL6 6NU
✪ 11-3, 5.30-11; 11-11 Sat; 12-10.30 Sun ☎ (01628) 630268
Rebellion seasonal beer; guest beers H
The new landlord has maintained the standards of his predecessor, serving four ales from independent brewers plus the monthly offering from Rebellion. Thatchers cider is generally available. The lounge bar has a real fire and tables for dining. The large garden is popular in summer and a function room houses a carvery for Sunday lunches, making the pub family friendly. There is a heated shelter for the smoking fraternity. Regular beer festivals are held. Well-behaved dogs are welcome. ♨Q❀◑⊞✦P↳

Reading

Allied Arms

57 St Marys Butts, RG1 2LG
✪ 12 (6 Mon)-11; closed Sun ☎ (0118) 958 3323
⊕ allied-arms.co.uk
Fuller's London Pride; Loddon Hullabaloo; guest beers H

An ancient-looking pub whose small frontage belies the space inside – a cobbled side passage opens into two cosy rooms with exposed beams. The large, sheltered, patio-style garden is an ideal place to chill out after a busy shopping spree. Family-run with friendly staff, it can get quite busy at times. Quiz night is every other Wednesday in aid of the local air ambulance. Outdoor darts and table football are available. ❀≒⊞✦●↳

Butler

85-91 Chatham Street, RG1 7DS
✪ 3-11.30; 12-midnight Fri & Sat; 12-11 Sun
☎ (0118) 959 5500 ⊕ thebutlerreading.co.uk
Fuller's Chiswick Bitter, London Pride, ESB, seasonal beer; guest beer H
Originally Butler's Wine Merchants, the building was bought by Fuller's and turned into a pub in the 1970s. Close to the town centre, it is an active hostelry, supportive of local bands and frequently hosting music evenings. There is a pool table and poker evenings are held regularly. ♨❀≒⊞(17)P↳

Eldon Arms

19 Eldon Terrace, RG1 4DX (15 mins from station via Kings Road)
✪ 11-3, 5.30-11.30 (midnight Fri); 11-3, 7-midnight Sat; 12-3, 7-11.30 Sun ☎ (0118) 957 3857
Wadworth IPA, 6X, Bishop's Tipple, seasonal beers H
An unspoilt back-street local just out of town in a conservation area. The pub is divided into a lounge bar and public bar with some nice glasswork on the doors. The licensees have been in charge for an impressive 35 years and counting. Pub games are played and regular quiz nights are held. Westons Scrumpy features at the bar. ♨❀◑⊞(9,17)✦●↳

Hobgoblin

2 Broad Street, RG1 2BH
✪ 11-11; 12-10.30 Sun ☎ (0118) 950 8119
Beer range varies H
An unexpected survivor in the bustling town centre. This is a simple building with a small interior not to be missed as every available surface is covered with pump clips. Don't expect lots of space and comfortable seating (although there are several booths out the back). Do expect an ever-changing selection of good quality real ales from micro-breweries across the country. Three West Berkshire Brewery ales are complemented by five guests. No food here – beer is king. ≒⊞●↳

Lyndhurst

88 Queens Road, RG1 4DG (10-15 mins from station via Kings Road)
✪ 12-11 (10.30 Sun) ☎ (0118) 957 4615
⊕ spirit-house.co.uk/lyndhurst
Beer range varies H
A short walk from the Oracle for those wanting to escape the bustle of the town centre. The Lyndhurst is run by a small local pub group that is enthusiastic about real ale. You can just pop in for a drink or enjoy something from its interesting menu with your pint – food is of a higher standard than the usual pub grub. Aimed at the younger drinker, it's often busy in the early evening with students and office workers. ◑⊞(9,17)✦↳

Monks Retreat ✓

163 Friar Street, RG1 1HE
✪ 9am-midnight (1am Fri & Sat) ☎ (0118) 950 7592

Greene King Ruddles Best Bitter, Abbot; guest beers Ⓗ
Located opposite the old red-brick town hall, this was Wetherspoon's first pub in Reading – opened in 1994, and is beginning to show its age. Nevertheless, the ales are of exceptional quality and the Monks is now LocAle accredited. The name of the pub, and the street it is in, recall the Franciscan monks who came to Reading in the 13th century and inhabited the Abbey nearby – watch out for the monk dangling from the ceiling of the pub in homage! Q◑≉🚌●⌐

Nag's Head

5 Russell Street, RG1 7XD (10 mins from station via Oxford Road)
⏲ 12-11; 11-midnight Sat ☎ (0118) 957 4649
🌐 nagsheadreading.com
Beer range varies Ⓗ
A change of ownership transformed this pub from an ailing, ale-less local boozer into a destination venue for real ale drinkers, winning local CAMRA Pub of the Year in 2009. Twelve handpumps provide a varied selection – mild on the right, rising in gravity to stouts and strong ales on the left. Darts, crib and assorted table games are available. Food is served lunchtimes and early evenings. ♨❀◑≉(Reading West)🚌(17)♣●P⌐

Retreat

8 St John's Street, RG1 4EH (15 mins from station via Kings Road)
⏲ 4.30-11; 12-11.30 Fri & Sat; 12-11 Sun ☎ (0118) 957 1593
🌐 retreatpub.co.uk
Loddon Ferryman's Gold; Ringwood Best Bitter; guest beers Ⓗ
A fine example of a Victorian terraced pub, nestled among the back streets in a conservation area off Eldon Road. Sit and chat or read the paper in the front bar, or go into the back to play pool or listen to the live musicians (see website for the gig list). Proud holder of the CAMRA Central Southern Cider Pub of the Year in 2008 and 2009. The Retreat is also well known for its selection of foreign bottled beers. 🚌(9,17)♣●⌐

Zerodegrees

9 Bridge Street, RG1 2LR
⏲ 12-midnight (11 Sun) ☎ (0118) 959 7959
🌐 zerodegrees.co.uk/location-reading.html
Zerodegrees Wheat Ale, Pale Ale, Black Lager, Pilsner, seasonal beers Ⓗ
Restaurant and bar combined in harmony – this is real ale continental style, brewed on-site. The stainless steel brewing plant, visible from the bar, is very much a feature of the establishment. Beer is served unfiltered, unpasteurised and chilled – direct from conditioning tanks. Fruit beers and seasonal specialities are often available. The large wood-fired oven bakes 24 types of pizza. Salads, pasta dishes and gourmet sausages are also on the Italian-based menu. ◑♿≉🚌⌐

St Nicholas Hurst

Wheelwrights Arms ✔

Davis Way, RG10 0TR (opp entrance to Dinton Pastures)
⏲ 11-3, 5.30-11; 11.30-11 Sat; 12-10.30 Sun
☎ (0118) 934 4100
Wadworth IPA, Horizon, 6X, JCB, seasonal beers; guest beers Ⓟ
This delightful 18th-century pub was originally a wheelwright's shop. It has two main bars with dining areas, one with an open fire, and a separate restaurant/function room with a sign advising: 'No children after 8.30pm – they take too long to cook!' The eight handpumps activate electric pumps and dispense regular ales, two guests and a real cider. Monday is quiz night and there is an active golf society. Good pub food is served (not Sun eve). ♨❀◑♿≉(Winnersh)🚌●P⌐

Shefford Woodlands

Pheasant Inn

Ermin Street, RG17 7AA (exit M4 J14 N, left onto B4000) SU362733
⏲ 11-12.30am (1am Fri & Sat); 11-midnight Sun
☎ (01488) 648284 🌐 thepheasant-inn.co.uk
Loddon Hoppit, Ferryman's Gold; Wadworth 6X Ⓗ
A large rural pub, said by some to be the highest in Berkshire, comes complete with a range of en-suite accommodation and fine views across the Berkshire Downs. The traditional bar has a rare bottle glass screen and offers pub games including ring the bull. Much favoured by racegoers to Newbury, it provides fine dining in the comfortable restaurant as well as a welcome stop-off from the nearby M4. ♨❀🛏◑🚌(90)♣P⌐

Slough

Moon & Spoon ✔

86 High Street, SL1 1EL
⏲ 9am-midnight ☎ (01753) 531650
Greene King Ruddles Best Bitter, Abbot; Marston's Pedigree; guest beers Ⓗ
A large Wetherspoon shop conversion that's popular with a wide cross section of the community. It has a modern, bright interior with one long central bar connecting various spacious areas and many private booths. A family dining area offers a separate children's menu. Regular steak, curry and ale nights are hosted, with a 20 per cent main meal discount for CAMRA members. Three guest ales are usually on offer. Real cider, often from Westons, is kept in a box in the fridge. ◑≉🚌●

Rose & Crown

312 High Street, SL1 1NB (E end of High St)
⏲ 11-midnight; 12-12.30am Sun ☎ (01753) 521114
Beer range varies Ⓗ
This attractive Grade II-listed Regency inn is the oldest pub on the High Street and makes a pleasant contrast to its more modern surroundings. Two small bars display an impressive range of pump clips reflecting the landlord's passion for real ale and the variety of beers that has been served. Two ales are usually available along with a real cider. Entertainment includes regular quiz nights and three TV screens. The pub hosts the annual Slough conker championship in October. ❀⊟≉🚌♣●⌐

Stockcross

Rising Sun

Ermin Street, RG20 8LG
⏲ 12-3, 5.30-11.30; 12-11.30 Sat; 12-11 Sun
☎ (01488) 608131
West Berkshire Waltham St Lawrence No 1, Maggs Mild, Good Old Boy, Dr Hexter's Healer Ⓗ
West Berkshire Brewery's only tied house lies three miles outside Newbury on the Lambourn road, handy for both the A34 and M4 (junction 13). There

are three drinking areas, including a snug, divided by a central passageway. This dog-friendly village local holds regular live music and occasional beer festivals. Locally-sourced and free-range food is served until 9pm each day. Tutts Clump Cider and Westons Country Perry are also available. ♕Q❀◑⊟(4)♣●P

Theale

Crown

2 Church Street, RG7 5BT
✪ 11-11; 12-10.30 Sun ☎ (07798) 771817
Taylor Landlord; Wells Bombardier; West Berkshire Good Old Boy Ⓗ
The Crown dates from the coaching era when Church Street was part of the main London to Bath coaching route. A single bar area is divided into three parts, each with its own character, but with an open feel. Outside is a large and peaceful garden area. Food from the Chinese takeaway – based in the Crown's kitchen – can be eaten on the premises. ❀◑⇌⊟(1,N26)♣P⊁

Twyford

Waggon & Horses

61 High Street, RG10 9AJ (W from the town centre crossroads)
✪ 12-midnight (5.30 Mon) ☎ (0118) 934 0376
guest beer; Courage Best Bitter; Fuller's London Pride Ⓗ
The Waggon & Horses blends country pub ambience (flagstone floor, low wooden beams, large well-kept garden with an aviary and wendy house) with community pub features (large TV for sport, darts and crib). The pub's darts team recently claimed the world record for the longest continuous darts match. Hearty cooked food is served lunchtimes and evenings. Closed Monday afternoon. ❀◐◑⇌⊟(127,129)♣P⊁

Upper Basildon

Red Lion

Aldworth Road, RG8 8NG SU597761
✪ 11-3, 5-11; 12-10.30 Sun ☎ (01491) 671234
🌐 red-lion-upper-basildon.co.uk
Brakspear Bitter; Otter Ale; West Berkshire Good Old Boy; guest beer Ⓗ
Following the speculative closure of a nearby pub, the former restaurant extension has been opened out during a recent makeover, reinvigorating what was originally a small beer house. Thankfully, the distinctive mural in the ladies' has been retained – viewings can be arranged for those of the opposite gender. Full meals are served during all sessions and at least up to an hour before closing, while individual courses can be ordered as snacks. ♕❀◐◑⊟(133)♣P

Waltham St Lawrence

Bell

The Street, RG10 0JJ (opp church in centre of village) SU830769
✪ 12-3, 5-11; 12-11 Sat; 12-10.30 Sun ☎ (0118) 934 1788
🌐 thebellinn.biz
West Berkshire Waltham St Lawrence No 1 Brew; guest beers Ⓗ
Dating from circa 1400, this free house was bequeathed for the benefit of the parish in 1608. The two cosy bars have log fires as well as many historic and interesting features. There is a separate dining room with a popular range of food. Five ales are on offer, usually including a house beer from West Berkshire Brewery. Walkers, children and dogs are welcome. Real ciders and a perry are usually available. ♕Q❀◐◑⊟(4)●

Star

Broadmoor Road, RG10 0HY (on B3024, E end of village) SU834766
✪ 12-11 (6 Sun) ☎ (0118) 934 3486 🌐 thestar-inn.co.uk
Wadworth IPA, 6X, seasonal beer Ⓗ
Large and friendly, with beamed ceilings and a big garden. Quality food is served daily in the bar and separate dining area. A genuine community pub, it hosts a quiz night on Monday, open mike on Wednesday and live music nights. Following the closure of the local Post Office, a PO counter is open in the pub on Wednesday lunchtimes, helping to keep the village alive. The pub is dog-friendly and reputedly haunted, although the landlord is yet to see the ghost. ♕❀◐◑⊟(4)♣P⊁

Wargrave

Wargrave & District Snooker Club

Woodclyffe Hostel, Church Street, RG10 8EP
✪ 7-11; closed Sat & Sun ☎ (0118) 940 3537
Beer range varies Ⓗ
Friendly club situated in a Victorian hostel. Staffed by volunteers, the bar is dominated by two handpumps (only one in use). A wide range of snacks is available. Games include darts, chess, crib and dominoes. Show this Guide for entry (guest fee to play on the snooker tables). New members are welcome. Recent winner of several local CAMRA and regional Club of the Year awards. ⇌⊟(850)♣

Windsor

Carpenters Arms 🏆 ✔

4 Market Street, SL4 1PB
✪ 11-11 (midnight Fri & Sat) ☎ (01753) 755961
Beer range varies Ⓗ
Situated in a narrow cobbled street between Windsor Castle and the Guildhall, this split-level Nicholson's pub has an excellent reputation for the quality and range of its reasonably priced ales. The entrance to a series of tunnels in the lower drinking area reputedly link it to the Castle. Mosaic floors in the entrance porches are a reminder of the long defunct Ashby's Brewery. It's the winner of various CAMRA awards. Pub grub includes an excellent range of pies. ❀◐◑⇌(Central)⊟

Duke of Connaught ✔

165 Arthur Road, SL4 1RZ
✪ 10-midnight (1am Fri & Sat); 12-11.30 Sun
☎ (01753) 840748 🌐 thedukeofconnaught.co.uk
Greene King IPA, Abbot; guest beers Ⓗ
Originally No 1 Connaught Cottages, this pub was the home of Charles Wilkins, a beer retailer in 1895. Today it is a friendly, stylish street-corner tavern. It shows sport on TV and hosts live music most weekends. The interior has bare floorboards and the walls are decorated with old film photos. The food is recommended and the landord makes full use of the Greene King guest ale list. ♕❀◐◑⇌(Central)⊟⊁

King & Castle

15-16 Thames Street, SL4 1PL

9am midnight (2am Fri & Sat) ☎ (01753) 625120

Greene King Abbot; Marston's Pedigree; guest beers H

Spacious multi-floored Wetherspoon pub situated directly opposite Windsor Castle. A wide open street level bar leads to a variety of more intimate areas. Stairs lead down to a lower bar containing a small dance floor, which attracts a younger crowd later in the evening when a dress code applies. The large patio is popular during the summer and is partially heated during cooler weather.
❀ ≥(Central)

Two Brewers

34 Park Street, SL4 1LB

11.30-11 (11.30 Fri & Sat); 12-10.30 Sun
☎ (01753) 855426

Adnams Bitter; Fuller's London Pride; Wadworth 6X H

Grade II-listed 17th-century building, once part of the Crown Estate. At one time it was reputedly a brothel and drinking house on what was then the main London-Windsor road. The frontage was replaced after a fire in the 19th century. The interior has a cosy feel – the ideal place for a drink after completing the Long Walk through Windsor Great Park. Food is very popular, served daily except Sunday evening and Friday (booking is advisable). ❀ ≥(Central)

Vansittart Arms

105 Vansittart Road, SL4 5DD

12-11 (11.30 Thu; midnight Fri & Sat) ☎ (01753) 865988
vansittartarms.co.uk

Fuller's Discovery, London Pride, ESB, seasonal beers H

Situated in a residential area a short walk from the town centre, this consistently good Fuller's pub was originally the site of cottages housing workers from Windsor Castle. The two main bar areas have recesses and real fires. Special events are held in the large garden in summer and there is a covered, heated area for smokers. Sport is keenly followed, with rugby taking priority on the TV screens. To the rear is a pool room with comfy sofas. No food Sunday evening. ❀ ≥(Central)

Windsor Castle

98 Kings Road, SL4 2AP

12-11 ☎ (01753) 830766

Brakspear Bitter; Courage Best Bitter; Fuller's London Pride; Harveys Sussex Best Bitter H

Single-bar pub situated adjacent to the Long Walk that leads up to the real Windsor Castle. The large windows afford a fine view of the park. It has a strong local following but also welcomes visitors – the decked seating area outside is perfect for those long summer evenings. Sports fans are well catered for, with a large TV in the main bar area, which makes for a tight squeeze on rugby match days. Food is recommended. ❀ P

Wokingham

Broad Street Tavern

29 Broad Street, RG40 1AU

12-11 (midnight Thu-Sat, but no entry after 11); 12-10.30 (11 July & Aug) Sun ☎ (0118) 977 3706
broadstreettavern.co.uk

Wadworth Henry's Original IPA, Horizon, 6X, JCB, Bishops Tipple, seasonal beers H

Neatly pointed walls and metal railings mark the entrance to this town-centre pub. There are wood-panelled rooms on either side, a corridor with a bar on one side and 'local loo scheme' toilets on the other. This leads to a large seating area and the biggest beer garden in the whole of Wokingham. Food is served all day (steak night on Monday). Newspapers are available. ❀ ≥

Olde Leathern Bottel

221 Barkham Road, RG41 4BY (SW from Wokingham station, just over 1 mile along B3349 Barkham Road)

11-11 (11.30 Fri & Sat); 12-10.30 Sun ☎ (0118) 978 4222

Adnams Broadside; Sharp's Doom Bar; Wells Bombardier H

While retaining its traditional 17th-century origins, the pub has a spacious and contemporary feel – a recent refurbishment has helped to open up the interior. It now appeals to broad tastes, with low wood beams complementing the modern decor. Food is served all day. Friendly, helpful bar staff and a pleasant atmosphere help to make this Chef & Brewer pub a worthwhile visit.
❀ (144)P

Queen's Head

23 The Terrace, RG40 1BP

12-11 (10.30 Sun) ☎ (0118) 978 1221

Greene King IPA, Morland Original, Abbot H

This late 16th-century cruck-framed inn is situated on a charming terrace at the edge of the town centre. In the summer months, locals and visitors alike bask on the terrace or rear garden, while in the winter, the fire offers solace to drinkers, chatting freely in the absence of piped muisc and other electronic distractions. Simple platters of meat and cheese provide a good accompaniment for the beer. ❀≥

Ship Inn

104 Peach Street, RG40 1XH (on A329)

12-11 (midnight Thu-Sat) ☎ (0118) 978 0389

Fuller's Discovery, London Pride, ESB, seasonal beers H

This Grade II-listed, 17th-century former coaching inn provides a warm welcome. The two main bars, side bar for darts and refurbished former stables make for a lively and entertaining atmosphere. Sports are shown on flat screen TVs and there is a covered, heated patio area. Home-cooked food is available daily 12-9.30pm (9pm Sun). The London Porter is not real ale. Wi-Fi available. A weekly quiz night and other events are hosted. ❀ ≥P

Woodside

Duke of Edinburgh

Woodside Road, SL4 2DP (200m off A332 Ascot-Windsor road, signed Woodside) SU927709

11-11; 12-6.30 Sun ☎ (01344) 882736
thedukeofedinburgh.org.uk

Arkell's 2B, 3B, Kingsdown, seasonal beers H

A welcome return to the Guide for this friendly country pub, handy for both Ascot Racecourse and Legoland. The licensees are in their 12th year at the pub and were recently given a long service award from the local CAMRA branch. Food of a high standard is served in the bar and restaurant from 12-2pm and 6.15-9pm (no food Sun eves, restaurant closed Sun and Mon). The landlord is a huge Chelsea FC fan and often hosts evenings with Chelsea legends. ❀ P

BUCKINGHAMSHIRE

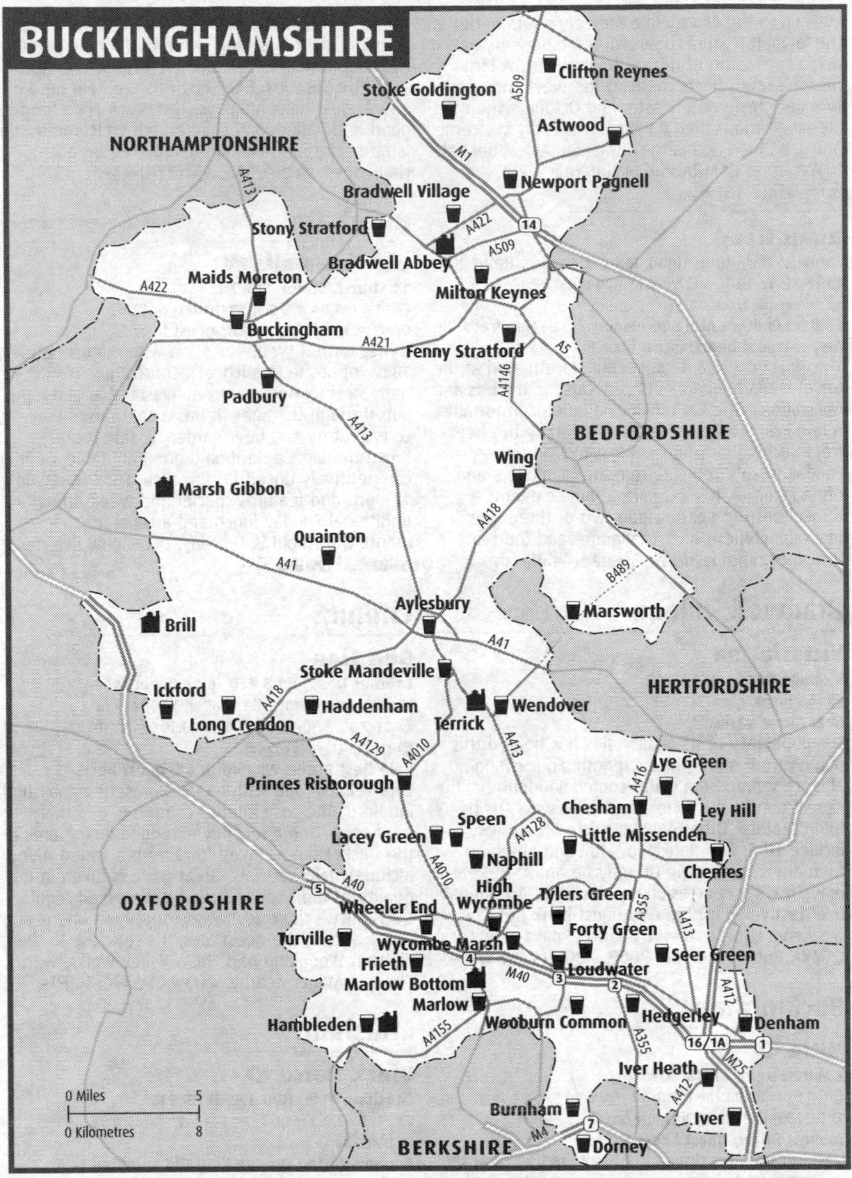

Astwood

Old Swan

8 Main Road, MK16 9JS (off A422)

❂ closed Mon; 11-3, 6-11; 12-3 Sun ☎ (01234) 391351

🌐 oldswanastwood.co.uk

Beer range varies 🄷

Seventeenth-century free house in a village just off the northern Milton Keynes-Bedford road. The pub has a superb reputation for high-quality food, with fresh fish a speciality on the menu (booking is a must). A large blue china collection and an impressive display of water jugs adorn the walls and ceiling. Up to three changing beers are on handpump, with regulars from Fuller's or Wells & Young's. More than 100 different ales were dispensed in 2009. ⌂Q❀◐♿🚌(1C)P🚭

Aylesbury

Hop Pole

83 Bicester Road, HP19 9AZ

❂ 12-11 (midnight Fri & Sat) ☎ (01296) 482129

Vale Best Bitter, VPA, seasonal beers; guest beers 🄷

The pub boasts that it is 'Aylesbury's Permanent Beer Festival' and with 10 handpumps it easily

INDEPENDENT BREWERIES

Chiltern Terrick
Concrete Cow Bradwell Abbey
Old Luxters Hambleden
Oxfordshire Ales Marsh Gibbon
Rebellion Marlow Bottom
Vale Brill

lives up to the claim. Vale Brewery's sole outlet in the town, it features beers from the brewery plus a myriad selection of micro-brewery ales. A large function room hosts music at the weekends and two beer festivals in Easter and October when the ale range more than doubles. A friendly welcome and good food add to the attraction. Aylesbury Vale & Wycombe CAMRA Pub of the Year 2008.
❀⇄◐▣(2,16)●

Kings Head

Farmers' Bar, Kings Head, Market Square, HP20 2RW
✪ 11-11; 12-10.30 Sun ☎ (01296) 718812
🌐 farmersbar.co.uk
Chiltern Chiltern Ale, Beechwood, Three Hundreds Old Ale, seasonal beers; guest beer Ⓗ
The oldest courtyard inn in England, situated at the top of Market Square, and very close to the bus and rail stations. The bar provides a quiet, comfortable, relaxed environment in which to enjoy the beer from Buckinghamshire's oldest micro-brewery. Food is freshly sourced from local suppliers and often incorporates local ales. Various events throughout the year include two or three beer festivals, Chiltern beer challenges and food and beer matching sessions. Q❀◐♿⇌▣⊱

Bradwell Village

Victoria Inn

Vicarage Road, MK13 9AQ
✪ 11.30-midnight; 12-11 Sun ☎ (01908) 316355
Beer range varies Ⓗ
The popularity of its quality ales has helped this pub go from strength to strength. Four changing ales are served from water-cooled handpumps. The closest pub to the Concrete Cow brewery, its beers often feature. Other popular micro-breweries include Tring and Bank Top, although anything from anywhere in the UK may be on offer. Real draught cider is occasionally available. An annual beer festival is hosted on August bank holiday weekend. Lunches are served weekdays only. Local CAMRA Pub of the Year 2009. ❀◐▣(12)♣●P⊱

Buckingham

Mitre ✔

2 Mitre Street, MK18 1DW
✪ 5-11 (midnight Thu & Fri); 12-midnight Sat; 12-10.30 Sun
☎ (01280) 813080 🌐 themitre.org.uk
Young's Bitter; guest beers Ⓗ
Nestling under a disused railway viaduct near the university, this free house has been extensively renovated by the present owners, but the unspoilt interior retains the feel of a village inn. Three handpumps dispense a variety of beers, usually including a LocAle, with another dedicated to Biddenden cider. Look out for Cotswold Lager and Wheat Beer, which might change your ideas about lager. Taller customers be aware of the low entrance door! Live music is held monthly. Parking can be tricky. ♨❀♿▣♣●⊱

Woolpack ✔

57 Well Street, MK18 1EP
✪ 5-11; 12-midnight Fri & Sat; 12-10.30 Sun
☎ (01280) 817972 🌐 buckinghamwoolpack.co.uk
Black Sheep Best Bitter; St Austell Tribute; guest beers Ⓗ
This busy, attractively modernised pub, with a garden backing onto the River Ouse near the town centre, upholds the market town tradition of early opening. Its four pumps serve two regular beers and, depending on the season, one or two guests from the SIBA list. Beer festivals are held on Whit and August bank holidays. The Woolpack's food is good and varied, and children are welcome in the large back room. Parking nearby can be a challenge. ♨☕❀◐⊟♿▣(32A)♣⊱

Burnham

Old Five Bells ✔

14 Church Street, SL1 7HZ
✪ 11-11; 12-10.30 Sun ☎ (01628) 604276
Greene King IPA, Abbot; guest beer Ⓗ
Large, former Wethered's inn with origins before 1822, opposite St Michael's Church, just off the High Street. Photographs above the bar show the pub through the ages. It has a spacious, sunny conservatory and beer garden. A side room accommodates a dartboard and pool table. Beer is competitively priced for the area. Food is served 12-9pm and features special mid-week offers, a traditional Sunday lunch and a separate children's menu. Quiz night is Tuesday. Occasional live music is hosted. ❀◐♿▣⊱

Chenies

Red Lion

Latimer Road, WD3 6ED (off A404 between Chorleywood and Little Chalfont) TQ021980
✪ 11-2.30, 5.30-11; 12-3, 6.30-10.30 Sun ☎ (01923) 282722
🌐 redlionchenies.co.uk
Vale Best Bitter; Wadworth 6X; guest beers Ⓗ
Ever-reliable pub with an ever-present established landlord. The cosy interior comprises a homely front room and a recently extended dining area at the back. Home-cooked food from a varied menu includes daily specials. Great pride is taken in the quality of the beer and food. A deserved regular GBG entry – there is always something interesting to try among the guest ales. It's set close to the Chiltern Woodland and Chess Valley walks, with Chenies Manor nearby. ♨Q❀◐♿▣(336)P⊱

Chesham

Black Horse ✔

Chesham Vale, HP5 3NS SP964046
✪ 11-3, 5.30-11; 12-4, 7-11 Sun ☎ (01494) 784656
🌐 black-horse-inn.co.uk
Adnams Bitter; Greene King Old Speckled Hen; Wadworth 6X Ⓗ
Set in a beautiful valley, this traditional 500-year-old pub is ideal for enjoying a relaxed beer without electronic games or music. There are always at least three real ales. In winter there are roaring log fires to take the chill off those who may spot one of the resident ghosts. Outside is a large garden and patio area for drinkers and diners. Ample parking is provided. Dogs are welcome. Internet access for laptops is free. ♨Q❀◐♿P

Queens Head ✔

120 Church Street, HP5 1JD
✪ 12-11 (midnight Thu-Sat); 11-10.30 Sun
☎ (01494) 778690
Brakspear Bitter; Fuller's London Pride, ESB; guest beer Ⓗ
Traditional old town pub with two bars and a Thai restaurant upstairs. The public bar is a classic with

noteworthy fittings and old local cricketing photos on the walls. The saloon boasts a large original Fuller's mirror and other pub memorabilia. Thai food is also served in both bars. The pub organises a local cycle ride called Tour de Pednor, which takes place evey summer. Quiz night is Thursday and there is also a monthly Saturday night music quiz. Mini beer and cider festivals are held throughout the year. ⌂Q❀◐⊟♿⊖⊟(T1)♣P⁴–

Clifton Reynes

Robin Hood

Church Road, MK46 5DR (off A509 Milton Keynes-Olney road) SP903512

⏲ 12-3, 6.30-11; closed Mon; 12-4 Sun (11 summer)
☎ (01234) 711574 🌐 therobinhoodpub.co.uk

Greene King IPA, Abbot; guest beer ⊞

A past local CAMRA Pub of the Year, the Robin Hood is all you could wish for in a country pub. Landlords can be traced back as far as 1577. Food features highly, with dishes ranging from traditional fare to the more unusual. Ringing mobile phones will cost a £1 donation to charity. Northants skittles is played, and bands play occasionally in the garden. The Three Shires Way passes the door, popular with walkers and horse riders. The pub is motorbike-friendly.
⌂Q❀◐⊟♿⊟(42)♣●P⁴–

Denham

Falcon Inn ✔

Village Road, UB9 5BE

⏲ 11-3, 5-11; 11-11 Fri-Sun ☎ (01895) 832125
🌐 falcondenham.com

Brakspear Bitter; Taylor Landlord; Wells Bombardier ⊞

Overlooking the village green, the inn dates from the 16th-century. The bar retains old world charm, with timber beams and open hearths. Steps lead down to a back room and delightful garden. The brasserie features a varied menu. Parking can be difficult in the village but there is easy access to Denham station via a footpath. A community bus operates three times a day on Monday-Saturday from Uxbridge, and will drop you right outside. Attractive en-suite rooms are available.
Q☕❀⊭◐⇌⊟⁴–

Dorney

Palmer Arms

Village Road, SL4 6QW

⏲ 11-midnight; 12-10.30 Sun ☎ (01628) 666612
🌐 thepalmerarms.co.uk

Greene King IPA, Old Speckled Hen, Abbot ⊞

Smart, stylishly-decorated open-plan pub, with friendly staff helping to create a relaxed atmosphere. The emphasis is on food here, but there is a dedicated drinking area with comfy chairs and sofas. The large, attractive garden has a children's play area and free range chickens, making it popular with families. Its location, in a conservation village close to the Jubilee River, makes it ideal for walkers. Food is served all day and is recommended. Try the hand-cut chunky chips. ❀◐♿P⁴–

Fenny Stratford

Chequers

48 Watling Street, MK2 2BY

⏲ 11-11; 12-10.30 Sun ☎ (01908) 365197

Vale Wychert, Gravitas, seasonal beers ⊞

Tightly packed into a terrace, its 19th-century facade masks the pub's ancient history. Records go back to 1662, when it was named the Bell. Inside, its original fireplace is still in situ, together with low ceilings and black beams. A small, cosy one-bar local with a comfy settee and easy chairs, it is Vale Brewery's only outlet in Milton Keynes. It has a TV and big screen, and holds occasional karaoke evenings. MK Dons football stadium is a 15-minute walk. ⊭⇌(Fenny Stratford)⊟(5,7)♣P–

Red Lion 🏆

11 Lock View Lane, MK1 1BA (off Simpson Road)

⏲ 12-11 (midnight Fri & Sat); 12-10.30 Sun
☎ (01908) 372317

Beer range varies ⊞

The Grade II-listed exterior reflects this small lock-side pub's canal history. It is a gem of a local, renowned for friendly conversation and regularly-changing seasonal ales, contrasting in strength and style. The smaller of the two bars may be reserved for club meetings. TV screens show sports. The garden is the perfect place to sit and watch the efforts of narrowboat crew negotiating the lock. MK Dons football stadium is less than a mile away.
⌂❀♿⇌⊟(5, 7)♣●P⁴–

Forty Green

Royal Standard of England

Forty Green Road, HP9 1XT (off Beaconsfield to Penn Road at Knotty Green) SU 923919

⏲ 11-11; 12-10.30 Sun ☎ (01494) 673382 🌐 rsoe.co.uk

Brakspear Bitter; Chiltern Ale; Marston's Pedigree; Rebellion Mild, IPA; guest beer ⊞

This historic hostelry with its fascinating pedigree is well worth a detour. A barrel-shaped wooden partition wall leads to rooms warmed by log fires or cast iron stoves. Architecture and furniture is mixed rustic, with hops adorning the bar areas. The food is of exemplary standard and bottled beers are sourced from craft breweries. Orchard Pig Farm pressed cider is also available. Bekonscot Model Village is close to Beaconsfield railway station. This area is a walkers' paradise. ⌂Q❀◐●P⁴–

Frieth

Prince Albert

Fingest Road, RG9 6PY

⏲ 11-11; 12-10.30 Sun ☎ (01494) 881683

Brakspear Bitter; Wychwood Hobgoblin ⊞

A friendly welcome awaits you at this charming Brakspear country local. Sited a stone's throw from Frieth village, this pub is well worth seeking out for its cosy aura. The small bar area boasts a log fire in winter and leads either way to further rooms and seating. The beer garden offers secluded summer family drinking. It's a classic example of a quaint rural inn, in good rambling territory for hikers. Evening meals are served Friday and Saturday only.
⌂Q❀◐P⁴–

Haddenham

Green Dragon ✓

8 Churchway, HP17 8AA SP 742082
12-11 (10.30 Sun) ☎ (01844) 291403
greendragon.co.uk
Sharp's Doom Bar; guest beers H
This Grade II-listed 18th-century building, close to the church and duck pond, reopened in July 2008 as a classic country pub. With its welcoming atmosphere, it is proving to be popular with locals and visitors alike. Enjoy three excellent ales in front of two open log fires. The two guests change monthly, with local SIBA breweries preferred. Excellent food is served every day (no food Sun eve), the pub boasting a Michelin Bib Gourmand.
Q(280)P

Hambleden

Stag & Huntsman

RG9 6RP (opp churchyard)
11-2.30, 6-11; 11-11 Fri & Sat; 12-3, 7-10.30 Sun
☎ (01491) 571227 stagandhuntsman.co.uk
Loddon Hoppit; Rebellion IPA; Wadworth 6X; guest beer H
Utopian and traditional country inn, situated in a dreamy, brick and flint National Trust village. Popular all year round, locals and visitors enjoy the rural charm that this rustic gem offers. Food is served throughout the three bars and dining room. The Wadworth 6X is drawn from wooden casks and the guest beer often hails from a south-west independent. An annual beer festival is held the first weekend in September. Thatchers cider is available on handpump during the summer months. P

Hedgerley

White Horse

Village Lane, SL2 3UY (in old village, near the church)
11-2.30, 5-11; 11-11 Sat; 12-10.30 Sun ☎ (01753) 643225
Rebellion IPA; guest beers G
A regular GBG entry, this picturesque, genuine family-run free house comprises two bars, an enclosed, covered patio seating area and a large garden. One regular ale is supplemented by seven ever-changing guests, mostly from micros all over the UK. Three real ciders and a foreign draught beer are stocked, and good home-cooked lunches are served every day. A 100-plus barrel annual beer festival is held in May, and smaller ones at Easter and August bank holiday. QP

High Wycombe

Belle Vue

45 Gordon Road, HP13 6EQ (100m from train station)
12-11 (midnight Fri; 1am Sat; 10.30 Sun)
☎ (01494) 524728
Beer range varies H
Purpose-built street-corner local on the other side of the railway tracks from the town centre and near the station. There seems to be no explanation for the pub's name. There are five ales on offer from the Punch portfolio, and the cider is from Westons. Regular live music is hosted including open jam sessions. The pub is popular with Wasps rugby fans.
(31,33)

Half Moon

103-105 Dashwood Avenue, HP12 3DZ (500m from A40, W of town centre)
12-midnight (1am Fri & Sat; 10.30 Sun) ☎ (01494) 441558
Shepherd Neame Spitfire; Taylor Landlord; guest beers H
Stylish and comfortable edge-of-town establishment run by the same licensees for more than 20 years. There are four TV screens showing Sky Sports, ESPN and music. Interactive online multi-game and pub quiz machines await the aficionados. Activities include pool and darts teams, Friday-night karaoke, various entertainments on Saturday plus disco/quiz/card games on Sunday evening. Sunday roast lunch is served 1-5pm, with all food home-cooked. The guest beers are chosen by customers.
(32,33)P

Ickford

Rising Sun ✓

36 Worminghall Road, HP18 9JD
12-2.30, 5-11; 12-11 Sat; 12-10.30 Sun ☎ (01844) 339238
Adnams Bitter, Broadside; Black Sheep Best Bitter; Flowers IPA H
After a disastrous fire early in 2006, the pub was rebuilt, rethatched, totally refurbished and reopened in April 2007. This classic local has since become the hub of the village. Dating from the 15th century, with many oak beams and a welcoming open fire, it hosts local events and games including crib, darts, quizzes and Aunt Sally. Four ales are always available and basic pub food is served most sessions. Close to the Oxford Way, it attracts many ramblers and cyclists. Families and dogs on leads are welcome.
Q(261)P

Iver

Bull ✓

7 High Street, SL0 9ND
12-midnight (1am Fri & Sat); 12-10.30 Sun
☎ (01753) 651115
Adnams Bitter; Fuller's London Pride; Wadworth 6X; guest beer H
This traditional two-bar pub was rebuilt in 1817. A sign of the pub's age is the bull motifs in the leaded windows, and the saloon features old-fashioned Victorian panelling. Pool and darts are played in the public bar. Guest ales come from Punch's Finest Cask range. Quiz nights and occasional live music evenings are held. A heated, covered smoking area is provided outside. The food is well-priced and tasty. No food on Sunday. Three reasonably-priced letting rooms are available.
(58,459)P

Iver Heath

Black Horse

95 Slough Road, SL0 0DH (corner of Slough Rd A4007 and Bangors Rd)
11-11; 12-10.30 Sun ☎ (01753) 652631
Badger First Gold, Tanglefoot, seasonal beers H
Recently refurbished by Hall & Woodhouse, this large pub/diner has a country house feel with oak panelling and shelving packed with interesting books. The separate drinking area has comfortable leather armchairs. A green oak timber conservatory restaurant opens on to a patio and garden. Meals

and snacks, including vegetarian, are served all day. The Uxbridge to Slough bus stops outside (no service on Sun). ⛰❀◐♿🚌(58)P⅟

Lacey Green

Black Horse

Main Road, HP27 0QU

⊙ 11-3 (not Mon), 5-11; 11-11 Thu; 11-midnight Fri; 12-midnight Sat; 12-11 Sun ☎ (01844) 345195

🌐 blackhorse-pub.co.uk

Brakspear Bitter; guest beers Ⓗ

A real village pub offering a cosy, friendly atmosphere, located in the heart of the village opposite the village hall. Excellent home-cooked, freshly-prepared food includes traditional Sunday lunch (children under six eat free). A good selection of draught and bottled beers is stocked including four real ales, three changing every month. Quiz night is on the last Sunday of the month. Children are welcome and there is a children's play area. A full English breakfast is served Tuesday-Saturday from 9am. Wi-Fi hot spot. ◐♿🚌(300)♣P

Whip

Pink Road, HP27 0PG

⊙ 11-11; 12-10.30 Sun ☎ (01844) 344060 🌐 whipinn.co.uk

Beer range varies Ⓗ

Local CAMRA Pub of the Year 2009, this is a real ale gem and now serves in excess of 800 different ales annually from its five handpumps. The beer variety is exceptional and beer festivals are held each year, including the alternative Oktoberfest. High in the Chilterns with an attractive enclosed garden, the pub enjoys splendid views, including the Lacey Green smock mill, and is a popular destination for ramblers. Good food includes fish freshly landed from Devon. Real cider is available.

⛰Q❀◐🚌(300)♣🍎⅟

Ley Hill

Swan ✔

Ley Hill Common, HP5 1UT (opp cricket pitch) SP990018

⊙ 12-3, 5.30-11; 12-10.30 Sun ☎ (01494) 783075

🌐 swanleyhill.com

Adnams Bitter; Brakspear Bitter; Fuller's London Pride; Taylor Landlord; guest beer Ⓗ

Step back in time upon entering this timber-beamed free house formed from an old row of cottages, said to have been visited by James Stewart, Clark Gable and Glenn Miller during WWII. A large open fire and a cosy old snug are focal points, and there is a newer but characterful restaurant to the rear. Separate bar, children's and à la carte menus are available (no eve meals Sun and Mon). Outside, picnic tables to the front overlook the cricket pitch, beacon and golf course. There is further seating in the side and rear gardens. An annual beer and music festival is hosted. No dogs. ⛰Q❀◐🚌(4)P⅟

Little Missenden

Crown

HP7 0RD (off A413, between Amersham and Gt Missenden) SU924989

⊙ 11-2.30, 6-11; 12-3, 7-11 Sun ☎ (01494) 862571

🌐 the-crown-little-missenden.co.uk

Adnams Bitter; Hook Norton Hooky Bitter; St Austell Tribute; guest beer Ⓗ

Run by the same family for almost a century, this village pub has been refurbished to include bed and breakfast accommodation and a bigger bar, but retains a cosy, friendly atmosphere. Good pub food, served at lunchtime, is simple and generous. Popular with walkers, the large and attractive garden is a great place to relax and enjoy a peaceful pint. A regular in the Guide for more than 30 years. ⛰Q❀🛏◐⛺♣🍎P⅟

Long Crendon

Eight Bells 🏆 ✔

51 High Street, HP18 9AL

⊙ 12-3 (not Mon), 5.30-11 (midnight Fri); 12-11 Sat & Sun ☎ (01844) 208244 🌐 eightbellspub.com

Ringwood Hells Bells Best Bitter; Wadworth Henry's IPA Ⓗ**; guest beers** Ⓖ

This traditional local, in a picturesque village, is just over 400 years old and is popular with both drinkers and diners. A finalist local CAMRA Branch Pub of the Year in 2009, it usually serves five real ales – with three ever-changing guests dispensed by gravity from a purpose-built stillage behind the bar. The unspoilt interior features some original tiled flooring and beams, and an alcove dedicated to the village morris men. The extensive garden hosts two beer festivals every year. Local CAMRA Pub of the Year 2010. ⛰❀◐🚌(261)♣P⅟

Loudwater

Derehams Inn

5 Derehams Lane, HP10 9RH (off London Road)

⊙ 11.30-3.30, 6-11; 11-midnight Fri & Sat; 12-10.30 Sun ☎ (01494) 530965 🌐 derehamsinn.co.uk

Brakspear Bitter; Fuller's London Pride; Young's Bitter; guest beers Ⓗ

Wonderful, friendly locals' pub situated just off London Road, offering three regular real ales plus three ever-changing guests, often from local breweries. Traditional pub games are very much alive here, including darts, crib and dominoes. Quiz nights and regular themed evenings provide entertainment for all. An annual beer festival is held the first weekend of July in the impressive garden. The pub's website keeps customers up to date with what is happening. Traditional pub food includes regular specials from the landlady. It's a dog-friendly pub. ⛰❀◐♿🚌♣P⅟

Lye Green

Black Cat ✔

Lycrome Road, HP5 3LF (off A416 2 miles from centre of Chesham)

⊙ 11-2.30, 5-11; 11-11 Sat; 12-10.30 Sun ☎ (01494) 773966

🌐 blackcatchesham.co.uk

Taylor Landlord; Young's Bitter; guest beer Ⓗ

A fine example of hard work paying dividends. Run by a family who pride themselves on an honest, welcoming approach, the pub thrives on high standards while keeping its feet on the gound. The atmosphere is cosy and relaxed, with a mixed clientele. Thursday's quiz and Sunday's roast dinner are legendary. Good food comes in generous portions. Families and dogs are welcome. A real traditional pub. ⛰Q❀◐🚌(52)♣P⅟

Maids Moreton

Wheatsheaf

Main Street, MK18 1QR (off A413, Buckingham-Towcester road)

⏲ 12-3, 6-11 (not Sun eve) ☎ (01280) 815433

Beer range varies 🄷

Ancient, atmospheric, thatched village pub on the fringe of Buckingham, sympathetically extended with a modern dining conservatory where children are welcome. Full of nooks and crannies and old world charm, it was local CAMRA Branch Autumn Pub of the Season in 2009. Cask breathers may be used on some ales – ask at the bar. Close to National Trust Stowe Landscape Gardens and Silverstone Circuit. No food Monday evenings, booking advised at other times.
♨Q❀◐◑🚌(32A)P⌐

Marlow

Duke of Cambridge

19 Queens Road, SL7 2PS

⏲ 11-11 (midnight Fri & Sat); 10-midnight Sun
☎ (01628) 488555

Beer range varies 🄷

Prominent locals' local, offering the discerning drinker the most adventurous choice of ales in town. Local breweries are well represented as well as far-flung independents and micros, and you'll often find a mild, porter and stout. This single-roomed pub is frequented by a diverse clientele. Occasional themed evenings and regular catering contests are popular. Food highlights include Sunday roasts and steak night on the first Saturday of the month. A summer solstice weekend beer festival is now an annual event.
♨❀◐◑♿≋🚌(800,850)♣⌐

Three Horseshoes

Burroughs Grove Hill, SL7 3RA (on High Wycombe-Marlow Bottom road)

⏲ 11.30-3, 5-11; 11.30-11 Fri & Sat; 12-5, 7-10.30 Sun
☎ (01628) 483109

Rebellion Mild, IPA, Smuggler, Mutiny, seasonal beers 🄷

Rebellion's tap house with six of its beers, half a mile uphill from the brewery, and a former CAMRA local branch Pub of the Year. The pub is renowned for very generous food portions from extensive chalkboard menus. The interior comprises three distinct areas, and the rear garden is popular with drinkers and families in the summer months. Darts is played on Sunday evenings. Frequented by walkers using nearby trekking routes, two log fires keep out the winter chill. ♨Q❀◐◑🚌(800,850)P

Marsworth

Red Lion ✔

90 Vicarage Road, HP23 4LU (off B489, by canal bridge)

⏲ 11-3, 5 (6 Sat)-11; 12-3, 7-10.30 Sun ☎ (01296) 668366

Fuller's London Pride; guest beers 🄷

Fine 17th-century classic village pub close by the Grand Union Canal. The lounge has comfortable sofas and a small restaurant, while the public bar's open fire and separate games area includes darts, bar billiards and shove ha'penny. Children are allowed in the games area only; dogs are welcome. There is rear door wheelchair access. Some of the beers are local.
♨Q❀◐◑🀄♿🚌(61)♣●P⌐

Milton Keynes

Wetherspoons ✔

201 Midsummer Boulevard, MK9 1EA

⏲ 9-midnight (1am Fri & Sat) ☎ (01908) 606074

Greene King Ruddles Best Bitter, Abbot; guest beers 🄷

This pub is a long-standing entry in the Guide. Guest beers are sourced directly from micros such as Concrete Cow, Great Oakley and Potton, and are promoted with meal deals, such as the Tuesday grills and Thursday curries. The pub wholeheartedly participates in company beer festivals. Staff will remove sparklers if asked. Westons cider is also served. There is a covered, heated patio for smokers. Q❀◐◑♿≋(Central)🚌●⌐

Naphill

Wheel

100 Main Road, HP14 4QA

⏲ 12.30-2.30 (not Mon), 4.30-11; 12-midnight Fri & Sat; 12-10.30 Sun ☎ (01494) 562210 🌐 thewheelnaphill.com

Greene King Ruddles Best Bitter; guest beers 🄷

Situated in the heart of Chilterns red kite country, the Wheel is both a community local and a welcome stopping-off point for hikers in this splendid walking country – even muddy boots are welcome. The cosy, traditional pub, dating from the 1700s, has two distinct bar areas and extensive provision for smokers in the rear garden. Popular with families, there is a children's play area in the large, enclosed front garden. Two beer festivals are held every year. ♨❀◐◑🀄🚌(300)♣P⌐

Newport Pagnell

Cannon

50 High Street, MK16 8AQ

⏲ 11-11 (midnight Fri & Sat); 12-11 Sun ☎ (01908) 211495

Banks's Bitter; Brakspear Bitter; Marston's Pedigree; guest beers 🄷

Now in its 15th consecutive year in the Guide, the Cannon deserves its reputation for well-kept, keenly-priced real ale. Very much a drinkers' pub, its four pumps dispense Marston's beers and local ales. Look out for military memorabilia and intriguing bric-a-brac in display cases above the bar and on the walls. There are two heated smoking areas outside, and a function room for hire. Access to the car park is from Union Street behind the pub.
♨Q❀🚌(1,2)P⌐

Padbury

New Inn ✔

Winslow Road, MK18 2AW (on A413 Buckingham-Aylesbury road)

⏲ 5-11; closed Wed; 12-2.30, 5-midnight Fri; 11-midnight Sat; 11-10 Sun ☎ (01280) 813173

Beer range varies 🄷

This pub, owned and run by the third generation of the same family, is an object lesson on how to modernise an old building sensitively. It combines three small interconnected bars, where old and new blend beautifully, with a compact modern dining room. Three handpumps serve a changing choice of often local ales. The bar doubles as a village shop, so you can buy cornflakes or marmalade with your pint! There is a pleasant garden and seating area outside.
♨Q❀◐◑🀄♿🚌(60)♣P⌐

Princes Risborough

Bird in Hand

47 Station Road, HP27 9DE

⏲ 11 (3 Mon)-11; 11-midnight Fri & Sat; 12-11 Sun

☎ (01844) 345602

Greene King IPA, H&H Olde Trip; guest beers ⊞

Popular, friendly community pub in a Victorian terrace close to the railway station about half a mile from the town centre. It has an L-shaped drinking area offering four real ales from the Greene King range. The hostelry supports many pub games and sports teams including darts, dominoes, crib and Aunt Sally. Outside is a pleasant part-paved garden, with extensive shelter for smokers. A member of Greene King's Head Brewers club. ⛼◑⇌🚌(300)♣⚐

Quainton

George & Dragon

The Green, HP22 4AR

⏲ 12-11 (midnight Fri & Sat); 12-2.30, 5-11 winter

☎ (01296) 655436

Hook Norton Hooky Bitter; Marston's Pedigree; Vale Best Bitter; guest beers ⊞

Two-bar local on the village green overlooked by a restored windmill, which provides flour for the pub. An extensive menu of value for money food includes vegetarian and children's options. There are meal deals for older customers on Tuesdays and steak specials on Tuesday evenings. Post office facilities are in the bar on Wednesday afternoons (2-4pm). The pub was voted Best Village Pub in Aylesbury Vale for 2009 by the district council. The Buckinghamshire Steam Railway Centre is close by. ⛼Q❀◑⊟🚌(16)♣●P⚐

Seer Green

Jolly Cricketers ✔

24 Chalfont Road, HP9 2YG

⏲ 12-11.30 (midnight Fri & Sat); 12-10.30 Sun

☎ (01494) 676308

Chiltern Beechwood; Rebellion IPA; Tring Jack O' Legs; guest beer ⊞

In just two years the pub's first-time landlords have turned an average village local into a thriving, something-for-everyone, busy focal point. Winner of CAMRA Chiltern District Pub of the Year 2009, it offers four beers, mainly local, and two beer festivals are hosted in spring and summer. A wide choice of extremely good food is served. The pub attracts a mixed clientele of all ages and local clubs meet here. Quiz night is weekly on a Sunday. A fine example of hard work and listening to what people want has paid off – a total success story. ⛼Q❀◑♣●P⚐

Speen

King William IV

Hampden Road, HP27 0RU

⏲ closed Mon; 12-3, 6-10 (11 Fri); 12-3, 5-11 Sat; 12-2 (closed eve) Sun ☎ (01494) 488329

🌐 thekingwilliamivspeen.co.uk

Loddon Ferryman's Gold; Rebellion IPA; guest beer ⊞

Built as a farm in 1668 and obtaining its first liquor licence in 1827, three years before King William IV ascended the throne, this lively family pub/restaurant is situated in the heart of the Chilterns. It reopened in 2008 as a free house after total refurbishment, offering three changing real ales from local breweries. Traditional food is also sourced locally including Beechdean ice cream served in the ice cream parlour. Pub games include skittles and darts. ⛼☕◑♿♣P⚐

Stoke Goldington

Lamb

16-20 High Street, MK16 8NR

⏲ 12-2.30 (not Mon), 5-11; 12-11 Sat; 12-7 Sun

☎ (01908) 551233 🌐 thelambstokegoldington.com

Beer range varies ⊞

This excellent village free house is very much the hub of the local community. Five handpumps offer ales from micros such as Frog Island and Tring, as well as a Westons cider. Northamptonshire skittles and darts teams are based here. Run by the Porritts since 2000, the pub hosts occasional live music events and, in September, a jazz and blues festival. Good genuinely home-cooked food is available; popular Sunday lunches run until 5pm. Local CAMRA Pub of the Year 2008. ⛼❀◑⊟🚌(1B)♣●P⚐

Stoke Mandeville

Bull

5 Risborough Road, HP22 5UP

⏲ 12-3, 5.30-11; 12-11 Fri & Sat; 12-10.30 Sun

☎ (01296) 613632

Adnams Bitter; Fuller's London Pride; Tetley Bitter ⊞

Small two-bar village pub, situated on a main road, well served by buses and trains. The public bar at the front is popular with locals, especially those who gather to watch football and horse racing on TV. The comfortable lounge bar at the back tends to be quieter, leading on to the large secure garden behind the pub. The garden is a big attraction, especially in summer. Q❀⊟⇌🚌(300)♣P⚐

Stony Stratford

White Horse

49 High Street, MK11 1AA

⏲ 12-midnight (11 Sun) ☎ (01908) 567082

🌐 rockinghorsenights.com

Beer range varies ⊞

Said to be the oldest pub in the town, with records dating back to 1540, this is a no-frills venue with live football on TV and darts played in the back room. Live music also features, with blues or folk on Thursday nights, and rock on Saturday nights. Two beers are served: one handpump is home to either Shepherd Neame Spitfire or Wadworth 6X, while the other dispenses ales from local micros such as B&T, Great Oakley, Nobby's and Vale. 🛏♿🚌(4,14)♣P

Turville

Bull & Butcher

RG9 6QU (off M40 jct 5 through Ibstone to Turville)

⏲ 11-11; 12-10.30 Sun ☎ (01491) 638283

🌐 thebullandbutcher.com

Brakspear Bitter, Oxford Gold, seasonal beers; Hook Norton Hooky Dark ⊞

This very popular pub is set in an unspoilt village in a valley in the beautiful Chiltern countryside. The 16th-century timbered pub has open log fires and a bar extension that incorporates a table above a 50ft well. An excellent food menu is reasonably priced and often includes local game (booking is recommended). A function room is available for meetings; walkers and dogs are welcome. The picturesque pub and church regularly feature in films and TV series. ♨Q❀◑♿P

Tylers Green

Horse & Jockey ✔

Church Road, HP10 8EG (left at church at top of Hammersley Lane)

⏲ 12-3, 5-11; 12-midnight Fri & Sat; 12-10.30 Sun

☎ (01494) 815963 🌐 horseandjockeytylersgreen.co.uk

Adnams Bitter, Broadside; Brakspear Bitter; Fuller's London Pride; Greene King Abbot; guest beer Ⓗ

This picturesque local, a Guide regular, was converted to a pub in 1821. The single U-shaped room has a games area on the right and an area on the left available for drinkers and diners. There are tasting notes for ales above the bar. Food is served all week, lunchtimes and evenings, with special nights a feature. A quiz night is held on the first Thursday of the month. The main parking area is across the road from the pub. ♨Q❀◑🚌♣P⁄

Wendover

Pack Horse

29 Tring Road, HP22 6NR

⏲ 12-11 (midnight Fri & Sat); 12-10.30 Sun

☎ (01296) 622075

Fuller's London Pride, seasonal beers; Gale's Seafarers Ale; guest beer Ⓗ

Small, friendly village pub dating from 1769 and situated at the end of a terrace known as the Anne Boleyn cottages. On the Ridgeway path, it has been owned by the same family for 47 years. The wall above the bar is decorated with RAF squadron badges, denoting connections with nearby RAF Halton. The pub runs men's and women's darts, dominoes and cribbage. ⇌🚌(50)♣⁄

Wheeler End

Chequers Inn ✔

Bullocks Farm Lane, HP14 3NH (Lane End Road towards Sands, turn left over M40) SU807926

⏲ 12-3, 6-11; 6-10.30 Mon; 12-5 (closed eve) Sun

☎ (01494) 883070

Fuller's London Pride, ESB, seasonal beers; Gale's Seafarers Ale, HSB Ⓗ

This popular pub, which dates back to the 17th century, faces Wheeler End Common in a very pleasant part of the Chilterns. In earlier times it was a small establishment, but has been considerably enlarged over the years and now includes a dining room and a much larger bar area. Three ales are usually available. Families and well-behaved dogs are welcome. No meals are served on Mondays or Sunday evenings. ♨Q❀◑♣P

Wing

Queens Head ✔

9 High Street, LU7 0NS

⏲ 11-3, 5.30-11; 11.30-11 Fri & Sat; 12-10.30 Sun

☎ (01296) 688268 🌐 thequeensheadwing.co.uk

Courage Directors; Wells Bombardier; Young's Bitter; guest beers Ⓗ

This is Aylesbury Vale Council's Village Pub of the Year in 2007. A village local with an increasing number of real ales, the 16th-century building features open log fires in the restaurant and main bar. Make yourself comfortable on a cosy sofa in the snug, and enjoy a range of board games. The food is excellent and sensibly-priced. Fish dishes are a speciality together with regular favourites and other daily and lunchtime specials. Outside is a large attractive garden and patio.
♨❀◑⊟🚌(150)♣P

Wooburn Common

Royal Standard

Wooburn Common Road, HP10 0JS (follow signs to Odds Farm) SU923876

⏲ 12-11 (10.30 Sun) ☎ (01628) 521121

Caledonian Deuchars IPA; Hop Back Summer Lightning; St Austell Tribute; guest beers Ⓗ

Consequential, semi-rural, single-bar drinkers' haven patronised by locals and real ale connoisseurs alike. Ten ales, half on gravity dispense and half hand-pumped, grace the bar, which also boasts real cider. A dark beer is usually available and an annual beer festival is staged on August bank holiday weekend. Lively banter is openly encouraged among the regulars. The pub also attracts diners, especially on Sundays and during the summer months. A former CAMRA Branch Pub of the Year. ♨Q❀◑♿●P⁄

Wycombe Marsh

General Havelock

114 Kingsmead Road, HP11 1HZ (N of M40)

⏲ 12-2.30, 5.30-11; 12-11 Fri & Sat; 12-10.30 Sun

☎ (01494) 520391

Fuller's London Pride, ESB, seasonal beers; Gale's Seafarers Ale; guest beer Ⓗ

A regular entry in the Guide, this imposing building was converted from three farmyard cottages. A warm, friendly, local pub with an open fire, it sits between the Kingsmead playing fields and the site of the old dry ski slope. There are six ales always available. Food is served every lunchtime except Saturday. The garden is a peaceful haven in the summer. ♨❀◐🚌(35)♣P⁄

Drunken primates

Brehm asserts that the natives of north-eastern Africa catch the wild baboons by exposing vessels with strong beer, by which they are made drunk. On the following morning they (the baboons) were very cross and dismal; they held their aching heads with both hands, and wore a most pitiable expression: when beer was offered them, they turned away in disgust.

Charles Darwin, The Origin of Species, 1859

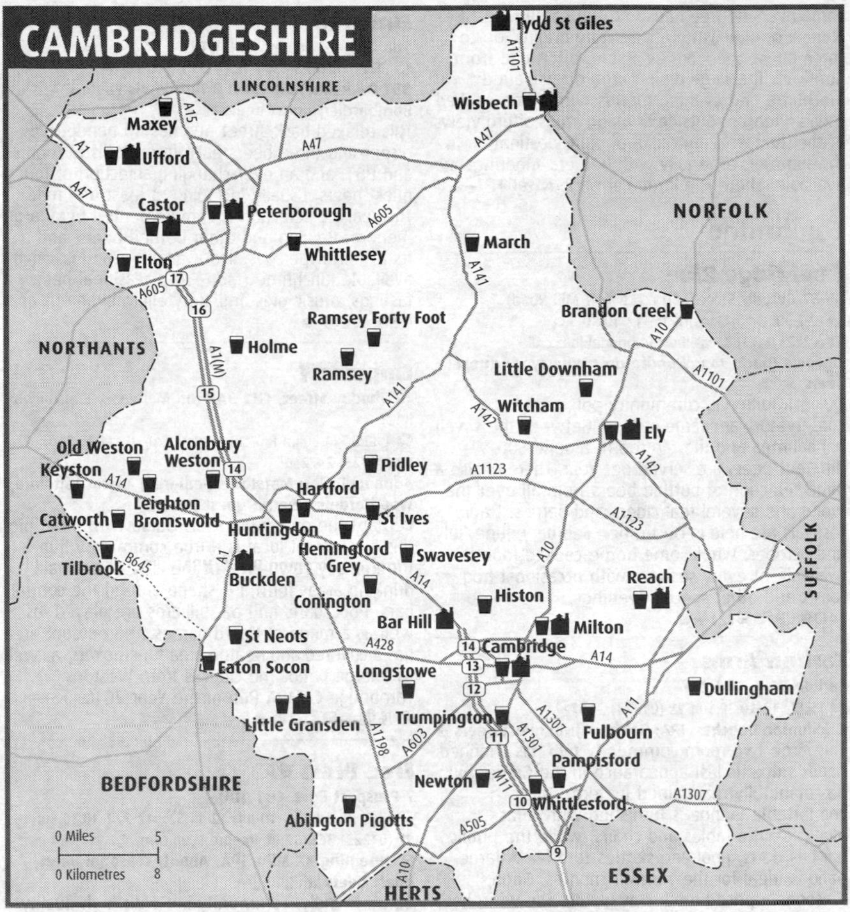

Abington Pigotts

Pig & Abbot

High Street, SG8 0SD (off A505 through Litlington)
TL306444
⏲ 12-3, 6-11; 12-11 Sat; 12-10.30 Sun ☎ (01763) 853515
🌐 pigandabbot.co.uk
Adnams Bitter; Fuller's London Pride; guest beers Ⓗ
Located in a remote part of the countryside, this Queen Anne period pub offers a warm welcome. The interior has exposed oak beams and a large inglenook featuring a wood-burning stove. A comfortable restaurant offers home-made traditional pub food and specialises in Thai curry. Two guest beers are stocked, often including a beer from Woodforde's or Timothy Taylor. ⩩Q❀◐P

Alconbury Weston

White Hart

2 Vinegar Hill, PE28 4JA
⏲ 12-2.30 (4 Sat), 5.30 (6.30 Sat)-11; 12-5.30 Sun
☎ (01480) 890331
Adnams Bitter; Courage Directors; guest beers Ⓗ
Welcoming former coaching inn on the old Great North Road. An open plan, two-tiered layout provides different drinking sections and a darts area. Outside there is a pleasant garden and petanque pitch. Two guest beers are stocked and changed regularly. Locally sourced, home-cooked food is served lunchtimes and evenings, including Sunday lunches. International dining theme nights are a feature and there is occasional live music. ❀◐🚌(46)♣P⌐

Brandon Creek

Ship

Brandon Creek Bridge, PE38 0PP (just off A10 on Cambridgeshire/Norfolk border)
⏲ 12-3, 6-midnight (closed winter Mon); 12-11 (12-4, 6-10.30 winter) Sun ☎ (01353) 676228
Adnams Bitter; guest beers Ⓗ

INDEPENDENT BREWERIES

Cambridge Moonshine Cambridge
Castor Castor (NEW)
Devil's Dyke Reach
Draycott Buckden (NEW)
Elgood's Wisbech
Hereward Ely
Lord Conrad's Bar Hill (NEW)
Milton Milton
Oakham Peterborough
Son of Sid Little Gransden
Tydd Steam Tydd Saint Giles
Ufford Ufford

Large riverside free house on the Cambridgeshire/Norfolk border with 16th-century origins. Up to three guest beers are available, often one from Cornwall. The large dining area offers varied lunchtime and evening menus with home-cooked meals. Pleasant outside drinking areas afford views of the river, making this a popular destination in the summer, especially with boaters. Moorings are available. There is a large car park. ⛫❀◑P⚋

Cambridge

Cambridge Blue

85-87 Gwydir Street, CB1 2LG (off Mill Road)
🕐 12-2.30, 5-11 Mon; 12-11; 12-10.30 Sun
☎ (01223) 471680 🌐 the-cambridgeblue.co.uk
Elgood's Black Dog; Woodforde's Wherry [H]**; guest beers** [H]/[G]
Quiet, traditional, community pub with a conservatory and large garden. Between the seven handpumps and the tap room, around 600 different beers are served per year. There is also a large selection of bottled beers from all over the world and several real ciders and perries. Beer festivals are held in December, February, June/July and October. Wholesome home-cooked food is available at every session, with occasional hog roasts and other special evenings.
⛫Q❀◑⇌🚌(2)♣●

Carlton Arms

Carlton Way, CB4 2BY
🕐 11-11; 12-10.30 Sun ☎ (01223) 355717
Caledonian Deuchars IPA; Oakham JHB; guest beers [H]
This large two-room community pub has changed hands since its last appearance in the Guide, but has thankfully maintained its form. The comfortable lounge is furnished with sofas alongside the tables and chairs, while the public bar has darts, pool and skittles to offer. A large patio is ideal for the warmer months. Good, reasonably priced food is available. The wide beer range will almost always include a mild. A real cider from Westons is kept. ❀◑⊟🚌(C1)♣●P

Castle Inn

38 Castle Street, CB3 0AJ
🕐 11.30-3, 5-11; 11.30-11.30 Fri & Sat; 12-11 Sun
☎ (01223) 353194
Adnams Bitter, Explorer, Broadside; Taylor Landlord; guest beers [H]
Adnams' most westerly tied house, offering a great selection of its beers including seasonals, plus changing guests from all over the country. There is a wide choice of drinking areas on two floors and the sun-trap garden is a delight. Excellent food is served at every session. The landlord was Barry Wom in the Rutles. ⛫❀◑

Champion of the Thames

68 King Street, CB1 1LN
🕐 11-11 (midnight Fri & Sat) (hours may vary in winter); 11-10.30 Sun ☎ (01223) 352043
Greene King IPA, Abbot; guest beers [H]
This small two-room, city-centre pub has a truly friendly atmosphere. It is one of the four remaining pubs on the infamous King Street Run pub crawl, which historically visited all of the eight pubs on this street. The oarsmen in the pub's name are also commemorated on the fine etched glazing in the exterior windows. The wood-panelled interior is filled with sturdy furniture and leather upholstered seats. ⛫Q❀⊟🚌♣⚋

Elm Tree

16a Orchard Street, CB1 1JT
🕐 11-11; 12-10.30 Sun ☎ (01223) 502632
B&T Dark Mild, Shefford Bitter; Wells Eagle IPA, Bombardier; guest beers [H]
This relaxed back-street pub has 10 handpumps dispensing three beers each from Wells & Young's and B&T, and an ever-changing selection of four guest beers, usually including at least one mild. The real ale selection is complemented by a large menu of Belgian and other bottled beers, and a real cider or perry is also available. Food is available lunchtime (Mon-Fri). Occasional beer tastings, music gigs and storytelling evenings are held. ❀♿♣●

Empress 🏆

72 Thoday Street, CB1 3AX (off Mill Road, E of railway line)
🕐 4-11.30 (1.30am Fri); 12-1.30am Sat; 12-11.30 Sun
☎ (01223) 247236
Adnams Bitter; Marston's Pedigree; Taylor Landlord; Woodforde's Wherry; guest beers [H]
Perhaps the only pub in this Guide with a pet pig, this back-street local is a true community hub in the Romsey Town area of the city. Three main drinking areas form a U-shape around the central bars. Pool, darts and bar billiards are played, as well as a range of board games. The outdoor area has a covered and heated area for smokers, as well as a large patio. The cider is from Westons. Cambridge CAMRA Pub of the Year 2010.
❀◑⊟⇌🚌(C2)♣●⚋

Free Press ✔

7 Prospect Row, CB1 1DU
🕐 12-2.30, 6 (4.30 Fri)-11; 12-11 Sat; 12-3, 7-10.30 Sun
☎ (01223) 368337 🌐 freepresspub.com
Greene King XX Mild, IPA, Abbot, seasonal beers; guest beers [H]
Quiet, friendly, community inn with high-quality food and Greene King seasonals and guests. A pub for more than 120 years, the traditional interior includes a tiny snug, which is a popular feature. No mobile phones are permitted. Well-supervised children and dogs are welcome. Outside is a small, sheltered garden. ⛫Q❀◑🚌♣⚋▯

Geldart

1 Ainsworth Street, CB1 2PF
🕐 closed Mon; 5-11.30 Tue-Thu; 12-3, 5-1am Fri; 12-1am Sat; 12-11.30 Sun ☎ (01223) 314264 🌐 the-geldart.co.uk
Caledonian Deuchars IPA; Courage Directors; Young's Special [H]
Fairly large back-street corner pub with two separate bar areas. Three changing guest ales come from Punch Taverns' Finest Cask list. The landlord has recently moved from Good Beer Guide regular Kingston Arms. Home-made food includes hot rocks – where diners cook their own meat on a volcanic stone. Free internet is available with Wi-Fi access. Live music from folk to jazz-tango plays on the first Saturday of each month (see the website for details). Functions can be catered for. The real ale bar also includes a good selection of malt whiskies and rums. ⛫❀◑⊟⇌⚋

Kingston Arms ✔

33 Kingston Street, CB1 2NU (off Mill Rd)
🕐 5-11; 12-midnight Fri & Sat; 12-11 Sun ☎ (01223) 319414
🌐 kingston-arms.co.uk

Crouch Vale Brewers Gold; Elgood's Black Dog; Hop Back Entire Stout, Summer Lightning; Oakham JHB; Taylor Landlord; guest beers Ⓗ
A classic pub, free of any keg products, with four changing guest beers and one cider in addition to those listed. Simply furnished, with table space often at a premium. Award-winning food is served lunchtimes and evenings. Free internet, Wi-Fi access and newspapers are available for customers. The walled garden has canopies and heaters and is popular all year round.
♨Q❀◐◑≑🚌(2)🍎⚡

Live & Let Live
40 Mawson Road, CB1 2EA
⏲ 11.30-2.30, 5.30 (6 Sat)-11; 12-3, 7-11 Sun
☎ (01223) 460261
Nethergate Umbel Ale; Tring Jack O'Legs; guest beers Ⓗ
Wood panelling and railway and beer memorabilia add to the atmosphere at this modest street-corner local. Seven handpumps present an array of both regular and ever-changing guest ales, ranging from a session bitter to a stronger ale, and always a dark beer. The eighth handpump dispenses locally produced Cassels cider. A fine selection of bottled Belgian beer, a guest Belgian beer on draught, and a wide choice of rums complete the impressive range. Q◐◑≑🚌(2)♣🍎🍷

Maypole ✔
20a Portugal Place, CB5 8AF
⏲ 11.30-midnight (2am Fri & Sat); 12-midnight Sun
☎ (01223) 352999
Crouch Vale Brewers Gold; Hop Back Summer Lightning; Woodforde's Wherry; guest beers Ⓗ
The family who have run this city centre pub for the last 28 years bought it from Punch Taverns in 2009. Since then, the beer range has widened and now regularly includes guests from local breweries. The two rooms are either side of the bar, and an upstairs room is also available. A large patio provides covered space for smokers and a pleasant sun trap. Food focuses on home-cooked Italian dishes. ❀◐◑♿🚌⚡

Mitre ✔
17 Bridge Street, CB2 1UF
⏲ 11-11 (midnight Thu; 1am Fri & Sat) ☎ (01223) 358403
Adnams Broadside; Fuller's London Pride; Greene King IPA; Shepherd Neame Spitfire; Taylor Landlord; guest beers Ⓗ
Standing on the site of two former inns, the pub has been known as the Mitre since 1881. The interior is smart café-bar style with cream and salmon-pink walls, parquet flooring and large windows. The stone-flagged floor in the lower area is a remnant of a previous ale house design. Three changing guest beers come from regionals or larger micros. Beer and food sampling nights are held on Tuesdays plus regular Meet the Brewer sessions. Good value food is available 11am-10.30pm. ◐◑🚌

Salisbury Arms ✔
76 Tenison Road, CB1 2DW (off Mill Road)
⏲ 12-2, 5-11 (midnight Fri); 6-midnight Sat; 12-2, 7-10.30 Sun ☎ (01223) 576363
Adnams Broadside; St Austell Tribute; Wells Eagle IPA, Bombardier; guest beers Ⓗ
Large Victorian pub with a good selection of beers on eight handpumps plus Crones organic cider. The decor includes an impressive collection of old folk festival and beer festival posters. No food is served Saturday and Sunday evenings. A traditional hook and ring pub game is a popular feature.
❀◐◑≑🚌(2)♣🍎⚡

St Radegund
129 King Street, CB1 1LD
⏲ 12-3, 5-11; 12-11 Sat & Sun ☎ (01223) 311794
🌐 radegund.org.uk/
Beer range varies Ⓗ
The smallest pub in Cambridge, this unique freehouse is very traditional, with a selection of up to seven real ales mostly from local breweries including several from the Milton Brewery, along with a real cider and perry. The interior is packed with mementos, from steam railway photos to local sporting memorabilia. The pub is also the base of the infamous Hash House Harriers and has its own sports teams, including rowing and cricket. Occasional background music is not intrusive.
Q🚌🍎

Castor

Prince of Wales Feathers
38 Peterborough Road, PE5 7AL
⏲ 12-11.30 (1am Fri, Sat); 12-midnight Sun
☎ (01733) 380222 🌐 princeofwalesfeathers.co.uk
Adnams Bitter; John Smith's Bitter; Woodforde's Wherry; guest beers Ⓗ
This small 300-year-old stone-built pub with stained glass windows has been sympathetically refurbished. The single room layout is divided into different areas to cater for a mixed clientele. Live music plays on alternate Saturdays and a quiz is hosted on Sundays. Lunches are served daily. The patio is popular in summer. The pub is the unofficial brewery tap for locally-brewed Castor Ales, one of which is usually available. An annual beer festival is held in May. Lined glasses are available on request. ♨❀◐♿🚌(402,404)♣🍎⚡🍷

Catworth

Fox
Fox Road, PE28 0PW (off A14, near B660 exit)
⏲ 11-11; 12-10.30 Sun ☎ (01832) 710363
🌐 thefoxcatworth.co.uk
Beer range varies Ⓗ
A traditional family run pub with an open-plan interior with a bar in the centre. Outside is a patio with a garden and children's play area. The beer range regularly includes ales from local micro-breweries such as Digfield and Grainstore. Meals are available all day every day – there is an extensive blackboard menu. The real cider is Westons Old Rosie. ♨Q👶❀◐◑🍎P🍷

Conington

White Swan
High Street, CB23 4LN
⏲ 12-3, 6-11.30 (midnight Fri & Sat); 12-3, 6-11 Sun
☎ (01954) 267251 🌐 whiteswanconington.co.uk
Greene King XX Mild, IPA, Old Speckled Hen Ⓗ**, Abbot** Ⓖ**; guest beer** Ⓗ
Imposing mid-19th century building in Tudoresque style. Many old features remain, notably the fireplace in the main bar and the floor tiling. Several motorcycle and car clubs meet here. Good, unfussy food is served every session (no food Sun eve) and can be enjoyed in the conservatory-style

dining room with its fine views. The huge garden is well-equipped for younger customers. Bar billiards is played. ⛪❀◖◗⊟⊡(8)♣P⚟

Dullingham

Boot

18 Brinkley Road, CB8 9UW

⏲ 11-2.30, 5-11; 11-11 Sat; 12-3, 7-11 Sun
☎ (01638) 507327

Adnams Bitter, Broadside; guest beers Ⓗ

Basic village inn brought to life by the friendly atmosphere generated by the locals. Saved from closure a few years ago, it has since become a Cambridge CAMRA Pub of the Year. Sport is high on the agenda, especially horse-racing, and many community events are based around the pub. Children are permitted until 8pm. No meals served Sunday lunchtime. ⛪❀◖≠♣P⚟

Eaton Socon

Rivermill Tavern

School Lane, PE19 8GW

⏲ 12-11 (midnight Fri) ☎ (01480) 219612

Adnams Broadside; Greene King IPA, St Edmunds; guest beers Ⓗ

This popular riverside pub was converted from a flour mill and has a galleried area above the bar. There is an extensive, varied menu, served all day on Saturday and Sunday. Live music plays on Tuesday and Friday evenings and a quiz is hosted on Sunday evening. Up to two guest beers are stocked from independent breweries. The patio offers splendid views of the river and marina. ❀◖◗⊡(X5)♣P⚟

Elton

Black Horse

14 Overend Road, PE8 6RU

⏲ 12-midnight (6 Sun) ☎ (01832) 280240
🌐 theblackhorseelton.co.uk

Adnams Bitter; Digfield Barnwell Bitter; Everards Tiger; Oakham JHB Ⓗ

Once the village jail, the original 400-year-old wall runs through the middle of the pub and the pool room has the old prison door. Harry Kirk, the hangman, was a previous landlord and is now said to haunt the pub. A food-oriented pub, it offers a large menu. Occasional live music plays. The beer garden is huge. It's an Oakham Ales' Oakademy of Excellence member. ⛪Q❀◖◗⊡●P⚟

Crown ✔

8 Duck Street, PE8 6RQ

⏲ 12 (5 Mon)-11; 12-10.30 Sun ☎ (01832) 280232
🌐 thecrowninn.org

Greene King IPA; Oakham JHB; guest beer Ⓗ

This is a listed building rebuilt in 1985 in stone with a thatched roof after a major fire. The bar has a beamed ceiling and inglenook fireplace, and there is a separate snug and orangery restaurant. Four to six real ales are usually available. The house beer, Golden Crown Bitter, is supplied by the Tydd Steam Brewery. A beer festival is hosted on the early May bank holiday. 'Open mike' night is the third Monday of each month. No food is served Sunday evening or Monday.
⛪Q❀◖◗⊟♿⊡(X4,24)♣P⚟

Ely

Prince Albert

62 Silver Street, CB7 4JF (opp cathedral car park)

⏲ 11 (12 Sun)-midnight ☎ (01353) 663494

Greene King XX Mild, IPA, Abbot; guest beers Ⓗ

A change in landlord has not seen alterations to this great little back-street local, only a lick of paint! This is a rare outlet for XX Mild, plus three guest beers from the Greene King portfolio. Enjoy the pleasant bar-room banter and, in warmer weather, the suntrap garden. Secondhand books and regular quiz nights help fundraise for local good causes. Food is served until 9pm. No music or gaming machines. Q❀◖◗⚟

West End House 🏆 ✔

16 West End, CB6 3AY (100m from St Mary's St jct)

⏲ 12.30-3, 6-11; 12-midnight Fri & Sat; 12-4, 7-11 Sun
☎ (01353) 669718 🌐 westendhouseely.co.uk

Adnams Bitter; Shepherd Neame Spitfire; guest beers Ⓗ

A warm and cosy pub with low ceiling beams, located away from the city centre and a short walk from Oliver Cromwell's house. Up to four guest beers are available, including a local regional brew and occasionally a locally-produced cider. The pub is split into four distinct areas and has a pleasant snug room. Outside is an enclosed patio area with a marquee and heating for smoking and drinking. Light snacks are served at lunchtime. Well-behaved children are allowed until 8pm. ⛪❀◖⚟

Fulbourn

Six Bells

9 High Street, CB21 5DH

⏲ 11.30-3, 6-midnight; 11.30-midnight Fri-Sun
☎ (01223) 880244 🌐 thesixbellsfulbourn.com

Adnams Bitter; Woodforde's Wherry; guest beers Ⓗ

A former coaching inn with thatched roof and low ceilings, this classic two-bar village pub serves home-cooked, locally-sourced food in the bar and dining room (not Sun and Mon eves). Trad jazz features in the function room on the first and third Wednesdays of the month. Quiz night is Thursday. The comfortable patio and sprawling garden to the rear are popular in summer. Real cider is Westons Old Rosie. CAMRA local Pub of the Year 2008.
⛪❀◖◗⊟♿⊡(1)♣●P

Hartford

King of the Belgians

27 Main Street, PE29 1XU

⏲ 11-11 (midnight Fri & Sat); 12-10.30 Sun ☎ (01480) 52030

Beer range varies Ⓗ

Sixteenth-century pub comprising a bar and dining area, in a picturesque village setting. It offers a constantly-changing range of three real ales and good value food (no food Mon eve) including the traditional Sunday roast until 4pm. It is believed that Oliver Cromwell used to drop in and that the pub is haunted – possibly by an ex-serviceman from one of the squadrons whose stickers cover the bar ceiling. ❀◖◗⊟⊡(55)P

Hemingford Grey

Cock

47 High Street, PE28 9BJ (off A14, SE of Huntingdon)

🕘 11.30-3, 6-11; 12-4, 6.30-10.30 Sun ☎ (01480) 463609
🌐 cambscuisine.com
Nethergate IPA; Wolf Golden Jackal; guest beers Ⓗ
This is an award-winning pub and restaurant not far from the River Great Ouse. The pub area is a cosy place to enjoy one of the well-kept locally sourced beers, as well as real Cromwell cider produced in the village. Accessed via a separate door, the restaurant features an extensive fish board, meat, game, and excellent home-made sausages (booking essential at all times). During the summer, occasional beer festivals are held in the beer garden. ♨Q❀◐◑⊟⅄🚌(5)●P⁓

Histon

Red Lion

27 High Street, CB24 9JD
🕘 10.30-11 (midnight Fri); 12-11 Sun ☎ (01223) 564437
Everards Tiger; Mighty Oak Oscar Wilde Mild; Oakham Bishops Farewell; Theakston Best Bitter; Tring Blonde; guest beers Ⓗ
The two bars of this free house are adorned with a wonderful collection of breweriana. Two changing guest beers and three Belgian beers on draught are complemented by a huge range of bottled Belgian and German beers. Food is served every lunchtime and monthly themed food nights are popular. Two beer festivals are held each year – an Easter aperitif, then the main event in September.
♨❀◐◑⊟🚌(7,104,110)♣●P

Holme

Admiral Wells

41 Station Road, PE7 3PH (jct of B660 & Yaxley Rd)
🕘 12-2.30, 5-11; 12-11 Sat; 12-10.30 Sun ☎ (01487) 831214
Nethergate Augustinian Ale; Shepherd Neame Spitfire; Woodforde's Wherry; guest beers Ⓗ
Victorian pub next to the Holme Fen nature reserve. The interior comprises two drinking areas with real fires, a lounge and restaurant overlooking the large garden and play area. The pub has a reputation for good food and offers up to six real ales and a cider. It partakes in the LocAle scheme. A function room is available for hire.
♨❀◐◑♣●P⁓

Huntingdon

Market Inn

Market Hill, PE29 3NG (near bus station)
🕘 11-11 (1am Fri & Sat); 12-11 Sun ☎ (01480) 431183
Young's Bitter; guest beers Ⓗ
A 400-year-old traditional pub down an alley off the market square, it was once a series of tied cottages serving the former Fountain Hotel Brewery. The front bar has an unspoilt wood-panelled decor and stained glass windows. Live music, karaoke on Saturday and a quiz on the first Wednesday of the month are popular. Two guest beers are on offer and tea, coffee, pies and pasties are always available. ⊟⇌🚌♣⁓

Old Bridge Hotel ✔

1 High Street, PE29 3TQ (S end of High St on ring road, by river)
🕘 11-11; 12-10.30 Sun ☎ (01480) 424300
🌐 huntsbridge.com
Adnams Bitter; City of Cambridge Hobson's Choice; guest beer Ⓗ
Handsome hotel in an 18th-century former private bank enjoying a prominent position on the banks of the River Great Ouse in the town of Oliver Cromwell's birth. Imaginative, high-quality food is served on the covered terrace and drinkers can relax in the bar or lounge area. Winner of the 2010 AA Guide award for the best restaurant wine list. The Old Bridge Wine Shop offers wine tasting as a diversion. The bus station is a short walk away.
♨Q❀🛏◐◑⇌🚌P

Victoria

52 Ouse Walk, PE29 3QW (via Montagu St or Euston St)
🕘 4-11; 11-midnight Fri & Sat; 12-10 Sun ☎ (01480) 453899
Woodforde's Wherry; guest beers Ⓗ
A traditional community local, formerly two houses, tucked away in Victoria Square, a quiet residential area just off the town centre near the fire station. The beer garden is a popular feature in the summer when the opening hours are extended. Darts and pool are played and the pub hosts poker on Monday evening, a quiz night on Wednesday and live music on Saturday. Two guest beers are served. ♨❀🛏♣P⁓

Keyston

Pheasant

Village Loop, PE28 0RE (on B663, 1 mile S of A14, E of Thrapston)
🕘 12-11; closed Mon; 12-2.30 Sun ☎ (01832) 710241
🌐 thepheasant-keyston.co.uk
Adnams Bitter; guest beers Ⓗ
The village is named after Ketil's Stone, probably an Anglo-Saxon boundary marker. Created from a row of thatched cottages in an idyllic setting, the pub offers high-quality food, fine wines and well-kept cask ales. There is a splendid lounge bar and three dining areas include the Garden Room in a rear extension overlooking a herb garden. Three regularly-changing guest beers are offered – local micro-breweries usually feature. Food is served 12-2.30pm and 6-9.30pm. ♨Q❦❀◐◑P

Leighton Bromswold

Green Man

37 The Avenue, PE28 5AW (1 mile N of A14, W of Huntingdon) TL113754
🕘 12-2, 7-11; closed Mon; 12-5 Sun ☎ (01480) 890238
🌐 greenmanpub.org
Beer range varies Ⓗ
Delightful local in a charming village on a ridge near the Northamptonshire border. The pub provides a congenial focus for a small village community and attracts visitors from a wide area. The range of real ales often includes beers from Nethergate, Young's, Digfield, Oakham and Buntingford. Good food is served 12-2pm, 7-9.30pm Tuesday to Saturday and 12-3pm Sunday. Hood skittles is popular, and there is a petanque court. A real fire adds atmosphere in winter.
♨❦❀◐◑♣P⁓

Little Downham

Plough

106 Main Street, CB6 2SX (W end of village)
🕘 12-3 (not Mon), 6-11; 12-midnight Fri & Sat; 12-3, 6-10.30 Sun ☎ (01353) 698297
Greene King IPA; guest beers Ⓗ

Grade II-listed corner pub retaining much of its early-Victorian charm. Up to three guest beers are available, often from regional breweries, plus an occasional local real cider. Thai food is served and can be ordered to take away. This is a popular spot for local customs, including folk dancing and dwyle flunking. Children are welcome up to 9pm but no dogs are allowed except guide dogs. ⛼❀◑♣●⚟

Little Gransden

Chequers 🏆

71 Main Road, SG19 3DW

✪ 12-2, 7-11; 12-11 Fri & Sat; 12-6, 7-10.30 Sun
☎ (01767) 677348

Beer range varies Ⓗ

Village inn, owned and run by the same family for 60 years. The unspoilt middle bar, with its wooden bench seating and roaring fire, is a favourite spot to pick up on the local gossip. The pub's Son of Sid brewhouse brews for the pub and provides ale for occasional beer festivals. Fish and chips is a highlight on Friday night (booking essential). Real cider is available occasionally. Winner of numerous local CAMRA awards. ⛼Q❀⊟🚌(18A)♣P⚟

Longstowe

Red House

134 Old North Road, CB23 2UT

✪ closed Mon; 12-3, 5.30-11.30 (midnight Sat); 12-10.30 Sun
☎ (01954) 718480

Beer range varies Ⓗ

Former coaching inn on the Old North Road in a peaceful rural location, not far from the National Trust's Wimpole Hall. Four handpumps offer a changing selection of ales, often from local breweries. Adjoining the pub is a barn converted into a restaurant area with a good reputation for food. A local artist painted the sporting murals and the decor features many eccentric touches. ⛼♉❀◑♣P

March

Rose & Crown

41 St Peters Road, PE15 9NA

✪ 12-11 (midnight Fri & Sat) ☎ (01354) 652077

Oakham JHB; guest beers Ⓗ

This 150-year-old building is a local community pub offering a warm welcome to ale lovers prepared to walk away from the town centre. The low-beamed main bar offers up to six ales and a real cider. A smaller bar has a pool table. Live music plays on the last Saturday of the month. Good quality food is available until 9pm. A beer festival is held at Easter which has become very popular. Keen supporter of CAMRA's LocAle scheme. ⛼Q❀◑🚌(X9)●P⚟

Maxey

Blue Bell ✔

39-41 High Street, PE6 9EE

✪ 5.30 (1 Sat)-midnight; 12-4.30, 7.30-11 (12-11 summer) Sun ☎ (01778) 348182 🌐 maxey.co.uk/bluebell.htm

Abbeydale Absolution; Fuller's London Pride; Oakham JHB; guest beers Ⓗ

Busy free house converted from a barn dating back to 1645. Seven real ales are usually available. A pub that is at the hub of the village, it is used as a meeting place by several groups including birdwatchers and golfers. The interior features stuffed game birds and fishing photographs on the walls. Awarded Community Pub of the Year 2007 as well as Peterborough CAMRA Pub of the Year 2006. ⛼Q❀🚌(413)♣P

Milton

Waggon & Horses

39 High Street, CB24 6DF

✪ 12-2.30, 5-11 (midnight Fri); 12-3, 6-11.30 Sat; 12-3, 7-10.30 Sun ☎ (01223) 860313

Elgood's Black Dog, Cambridge Bitter, Golden Newt; guest beers Ⓗ

Imposing mock Tudor one-room pub, adorned with a large collection of hats. The Elgood's beers are dispensed via cylinderless handpumps, and there is always a guest beer from Milton Brewery. The real cider comes from local producer Cassels. Meals are good value, and baltis are a speciality on Thursday evening. There is a challenging quiz on Wednesday evenings, and bar billiards is a mainstay. Dogs on leads are welcome. ⛼❀◑🚌(9,C2)♣●P⚟🗑

Newton

Queen's Head

Fowlmere Road, CB22 7PG

✪ 11.30-2.30, 6-11; 12-2.30, 7-10.30 Sun ☎ (01223) 870436

Adnams Bitter, Broadside, seasonal beers Ⓖ

One of just a few pubs to have appeared in every edition of the Guide, this two-room village local has had just 18 landlords since 1729. Simple but excellent food centres on soup and sandwiches at lunchtime. Beer is served from casks behind the bar. The cosy lounge has a welcoming fire. The public bar is simply furnished with an eclectic range of fixtures. ⛼Q◑⊟⛺🚌(31,139)♣●P

Old Weston

Swan

Main Street, PE28 5LL (on B660, N of A14)

✪ 12-2.30 (not Mon-Fri), 6.30 (7 Sat)-11; 12-3.30, 7-10.30 Sun ☎ (01832) 293400

Greene King Abbot; Taylor Landlord; guest beer Ⓗ

Dating from the 16th century, this oak-beamed inn has evolved from two private houses over the years. At the end of the 19th century the pub had its own brewery. There is a central bar with a large inglenook, a dining area and a games section offering hood skittles and pool. At weekends a varied menu of traditional pub food is available, including home-made puddings. ⛼Q♉◑♣P

Pampisford

Chequers ✔

1 Town Lane, CB22 3ER

✪ 11-11 (10.30 Sun) ☎ (01223) 833220
🌐 chequerspampisford.com

Greene King IPA; Woodforde's Wherry; guest beers Ⓗ

A warm welcome and friendly atmosphere await you at this archetypal country pub. The character of the place stems from the wealth of exposed timbers and split-level interior – tables divided into separate berths at the lower end offer privacy while the more open top end lends itself to convivial dining. Speciality food nights are a regular feature and the Sunday quiz is very popular. There is an attention to detail that sets this pub apart and ensures customers will return. ❀◑♿🚌(7)♣P⚟

Peterborough

Brewery Tap
80 Westgate, PE1 2AA
12-11 (until late Fri & Sat) ☎ (01733) 358500
oakhamales.com/btwelcome
Oakham JHB, White Dwarf, Inferno, Bishops Farewell; guest beers Ⓗ
Converted from an employment exchange, this spacious pub opened in 1998 and is the home of a recently installed custom-made specialist brew plant for Oakham Ales, which can be viewed through a glass wall. Twelve real ales are on handpump complemented by a selection of bottled Belgian beers. Excellent, good value Thai food is served. Seating areas mix comfortable leather sofas and low tables with tables and chairs for dining. A function room is available and there is regular weekend entertainment. ◑⇌⊟

Charters
Town Bridge, PE1 1EH
12-11 (until late Fri & Sat); 12-10.30 Sun
☎ (01733) 315700 oakhamales.com/charters
Oakham JHB, White Dwarf, Inferno, Bishops Farewell; guest beers Ⓗ/Ⓖ
Large Dutch barge called the Leendert-R built in 1907 and now moored on the River Nene by Town Bridge. Twelve real ales are usually available plus Belgian bottled beers. The upper deck houses a fine Oriental restaurant and food is also available in the bar at lunchtime 12-2.30pm. Poetry night is the second Wednesday of the month. The large beer garden has a marquee and landing stage for boats. The footpath from the garden leads to the Nene Valley Railway. Very busy on football match days. ❀◑⇌⊟♣P

Coalheavers Arms
5 Park Street, Woodston, PE2 9BH
12-2 Thu only, 5-11; 12-11 Fri & Sat; 12-10.30 Sun
☎ (01733) 565664 individualpubs.co.uk/coalheavers
Beer range varies Ⓗ
Friendly one-room back-street boozer not to be missed, with nine handpumps featuring beers from Milton Brewery and ever-changing guest ales. Real cider is always available along with a good range of Belgian bottled beers, single malt whiskies and an unpasteurised lager. The large enclosed garden is popular in summer and hosts beer festivals in May and September. The only pub in Peterborough to be bombed during WWII, an exclusive Milton beer named Bomber's Drop is usually available. Q❀⊟(6,7)♣

Drapers Arms ✔
29-31 Cowgate, PE1 1LZ
9-midnight (1am Fri & Sat) ☎ (01733) 847570
Beer range varies Ⓗ
This city centre Wetherspoon started life in 1899 as Armstrong's drapers and opened as the Draper's Arms in 2005. The interior is split into intimate spaces by wood-panelled dividers featuring pictures of bygone days in the city. Good value food is available all day. Ten handpumps serve the regular beers plus a constantly-changing selection of guest ales, often from local breweries. Traditional cider is also stocked and regular beer and wine festivals are hosted. Quiz night is Wednesday. Peterborough CAMRA Pub of the Year 2007. Q◑♿⇌⊟

Hand & Heart ★
12 Highbury Street, Millfield, PE1 3BE
3 (11 Fri & Sat)-11; 12-10.30 Sun ☎ (01733) 564653
Beer range varies Ⓗ
Unspoilt 1930s back-street community local run by an active CAMRA member. It retains many original features including the windows and bar, smoke room and drinking corridor. This is one of England's Real Heritage Pubs. Beer festivals are held three times a year. Crib, darts and dominoes are played and a cheese club meets here on the last Thursday of the month. A choice of five real ales changes constantly and the pub supports CAMRA's LocAle scheme. Occasional live music plays.
♔Q❀⊟(1)♣

Ostrich
17 North Street, PE1 2RA (off Westgate)
12-11 (2am Thu-Sat) ☎ (01733) 752255
Beer range varies Ⓗ
Once the Ostrich, then a home brew shop, the pub reopened in August 2009. Up to three regularly-changing real ales are available, mainly from local breweries. Live music plays every Friday and Saturday night, quiz night is Wednesday and karaoke night Sunday. Pub games include bar billiards. Outside is a small, enclosed patio area at the rear. Food is served 12-3pm. ❀◑♿⇌⊟♣

Palmerston Arms
82 Oundle Road, PE2 9PA
3 (12 Sat)-11 (midnight Fri & Sat); 3-11 Sun
☎ (01733) 565865 palmerston-arms.co.uk
Batemans Dark Mild, XXXB; guest beers Ⓖ
Owned by Batemans Brewery, this is a 400-year-old listed stone-built locals pub. It usually stocks three Batemans beers and up to nine more real ales at weekends – beers from Oakham, Newby Wyke, Church End, Abbeydale and Hop Back regularly feature. Traditional ciders and perries and bottled beers are always available. There are no handpumps – all beers are served straight from the casks in the cellar. Busy on match days, live music is hosted once a month. ❀⊟(1)♣

Swiss Cottage
2 Grove Street, PE2 9AG (100m from A605 Oundle Rd)
12-midnight (1am Fri & Sat) ☎ (01733) 568734
Beer range varies Ⓗ/Ⓖ
Back-street local, built in the style of an alpine chalet, this small, friendly and lively Irish-themed pub is especially busy on match days due to its close proximity to the football ground. Up to three regularly-changing real ales are available, usually including a Roosters beer on handpump, with some served direct from the cask. Live music features every Friday night. Sky Sports and a pool table provide entertainment for the mixed clientele. A separate function room at the rear is used for meetings. ❀⊟(1)♣

Woolpack
29 North Street, Stanground, PE2 8HR
12-11.30 (11 Sun) ☎ (01733) 753544
Taylor Landlord; Woodforde's Wherry; guest beers Ⓗ
Friendly back-street pub very popular with the locals, this is a mid 18th-century building on an older site. The single L-shaped bar offers up to four ales. The walls feature a collection of old photos and militaria. Outside, the large garden leads to the old River Nene. Charity events are held throughout the year including an annual conker championship. ❀◑⊟(3)

Pidley

Mad Cat

High Street, PE28 3BX

⏲ 12-midnight (11 Sun) ☎ (01487) 842245

Beer range varies Ⓗ

Community local on the edge of the fens. Two regularly-changing cask beers, often from local brewers, are always available. A sociable bar has a welcoming open fire, crib and dominoes. The dining room is popular with villagers and visitors, especially for the Sunday lunchtime carvery. There is a large garden with a decked patio. The village is the home of the Pidley Mountain Rescue Team, a charity supporting local disabled people. ⛫❀◐▲🚌(35)♣P⅄–

Ramsey

Jolly Sailor ✔

43 Great Whyte, PE26 1HH

⏲ 11 (12 Sun)-midnight ☎ (01487) 813388

Black Sheep Best Bitter; Fuller's London Pride; Greene King Abbot; Wells Bombardier; guest beers Ⓗ

This Grade II-listed building has been a pub for 400 years. The three linked rooms feature wooden beams and pictures while paintings of old Ramsey adorn the walls. A welcoming, friendly pub, it attracts a mixed age clientele and holds charity nights throughout the year. The guest beer is only available at the weekend. No music or food here. ⛫Q❀♿🚌(31)♣P⅄–

Ramsey Forty Foot

George Inn

1 Ramsey Road, PE26 2XN (at jct of B1096)

⏲ 12-3, 5.30-11.30; 11.30-3, 5.30-12.30am Fri & Sat; 12-11 Sun ☎ (01487) 812775

Greene King IPA; guest beers Ⓗ

A true local Fenland community pub. Three ales are on offer, usually including one from Oakham Brewery. The three-roomed inn is split into two levels – a small restaurant is separate from the main bar area with a higher level bar. Good-quality food is served daily (no food Mon and Tue). It is possible to reach the pub by boat via the nearby Fenland drain. Many artefacts from old Fenland life adorn the walls. Q❀◐🚌(31)♣P⅄–

Reach

Dyke's End

8 Fair Green, CB25 0JD

⏲ 12-3 (not Mon), 6-11; 12-3, 7-10.30 Sun

☎ (01638) 743816 ⊕ dykesend.co.uk

Adnams Bitter; Dyke's End Mild, Bitter, Pale, Victorian; Woodforde's Wherry; guest beers Ⓗ

Quintessential country pub now privately owned by a villager with a passion for good beer and real food. A family-run micro-brewery to the rear produces the Dyke's End beer range. The interior comprises a food-free tap room, bar and attractive, cosy restaurant serving freshly-prepared, home-cooked meals (no food Sun eve or Mon). Photographs and art of local interest adorn the walls inside, while the idyllic garden overlooks the village green. ⛫Q❀◐♿▲🚌(10)♣P

St Ives

Oliver Cromwell

13 Wellington Street, PE27 5AZ

⏲ 11-11 (11.30 Thu; 12.30am Fri & Sat); 12-11 Sun

☎ (01480) 465601

Adnams Bitter, Broadside; Oakham JHB; Woodforde's Wherry; guest beers Ⓗ

Cosy wood-panelled bar near the old St Ives river quay. There are two or three guest beers, real local Cromwell Cider, a warm lively atmosphere and an imaginative lunch menu. Entertainment includes live music every Thursday evening and occasional Sunday afternoons. Sports are screened on TV on special occasions. Families are welcome until 8pm. ❀◐🚌●⅄–

St Neots

Pig n Falcon

9 New Street, PE19 1AE (behind Barretts)

⏲ 11am-midnight; 10am-2am Fri & Sat ☎ (07951) 785678

⊕ pignfalcon.co.uk

Greene King IPA; Potbelly Best Ⓗ**; guest beers** Ⓖ

Local CAMRA's most improved pub for 2010, this small one-bar hostelry offers at least eight real ales and two ciders. There is a focus on local micro-breweries and unusual beers including milds, porters, stouts and barley wines. Regular mini beer festivals are held throughout the year. Live jazz, blues and rock nights, including 'open mike' sessions, are hosted on Wednesdays, Fridays and Saturdays. Outside is a large, imaginative, covered and heated beer garden. ❀🚌●⅄–▯

Swavesey

White Horse

Market Street, CB24 4QG

⏲ 12-2.30 (not Mon), 6-11 (12.30am Fri); 11.30-12.30am Sat; 12-11 Sun ☎ (01954) 232470 ⊕ whitehorseswavesey.com

Hall & Woodhouse K&B Sussex Bitter; Ringwood Best Bitter; guest beer Ⓗ

A fine old inn in the former market area of the village. The public bar is the oldest room and looks the part with polished floor tiles and wood panelling. In later years the pub expanded into adjoining buildings, adding a lounge bar with dining area, pool room and function room. An annual regional pinball meet is hosted and the public bar boasts its own vintage machine. A beer festival is held every May bank holiday. Occasional musical entertainment features and sports are screened. The large beer garden has play equipment for children. ⛫❀◐⊟🚌(15)♣⅄–

Tilbrook

White Horse ✔

High Street, PE28 0JP

⏲ 12 (5.30 Mon)-11 ☎ (01480) 860764 ⊕ twht.co.uk

Wells Eagle IPA; Young's Bitter; guest beer Ⓗ

Two-roomed village pub dating back in parts to 1735, surrounded by large gardens and open fields. The public bar is furnished with sofas and bar stools and offers a dartboard and hood skittles. There is a large lounge and bright conservatory with further seating. Traditional locally-sourced food is served (12-9pm Tue-Sat, 12-3pm Sun). The garden has swings and slides for children plus a petting zoo featuring ducks, chickens, goats and a goose. ♘❀◐⊟🚌♣P⅄–▯

Trumpington

Unicorn

22 Church Lane, CB2 9LA

❂ 12-11.30 ☎ (01223) 845102 🌐 the-unicorninn.co.uk

Shepherd Neame Spitfire; Wells Bombardier; guest beers 🄷

Remnants of old walls and varied floor levels serve to break up the heavily timbered main bar area into more intimate sections. The back bar doubles as a lounge and meeting room. Good value meals and snacks are generally available. There are regular music evenings, events in the large garden, and a quiz on Monday evening. The new accommodation block is in keeping with the older building. ♨ℬ❀🛏◐◑♿🚌♣🍎P⌐

Ufford

White Hart

Main Street, PE9 3BH

❂ 12-11 (midnight Fri & Sat); 12-9 (6 winter) Sun ☎ (01780) 740250 🌐 whitehartufford.co.uk

Ufford White Hart, seasonal beers; guest beers 🄷

Restored 16th-century stone-built village local. The interior comprises a public bar with woodburner, bar/restaurant and orangery for diners. Outside, there are large gardens, a patio area and seating. Ufford Ales brewery is located in the rear car park; its seasonal beers are available in addition to guest beers. There is also a function room and six letting bedrooms, all named after Ufford Ales beers. ♨❀🛏◐◑⊟♿🚌♣🍎P

Whittlesey

Boat

2 Ramsey Road, PE7 1DR

❂ 11-midnight ☎ (01733) 202488 🌐 theboatuk.com

Elgood's Black Dog, Cambridge Bitter, Golden Newt, seasonal beers; guest beers 🄶

This 11th-century inn is popular with locals, anglers and visitors. The lounge has an unusual boat-shaped bar. Up to five traditional ciders and perries supplement the real ales, which are all served direct from the cask. A good selection of malt whiskies is also on offer. Bar billiards is played and there is a petanque terrain. Live music features on Saturday evenings. The pub has a reputation for good value accommodation. Qℬ❀🛏⊟♿⇌🚌(31,32,33)♣🍎P⌐

Bricklayers Arms

9 Station Road, PE7 1UA

❂ 11-12.30am (1.30am Fri); 11-midnight Sun ☎ (01733) 202593

Elgood's Cambridge Bitter; John Smith's Bitter; Oakham JHB; guest beers 🄷

Popular town local with a very friendly atmosphere. The interior comprises a spacious, simply furnished bar and a smaller, cosy lounge. The large garden is popular in summer and boat moorings are available close by. The pub is the official headquarters for the Whittlesey Straw Bear Festival, held in January. ♨ℬ❀⊟▲⇌🚌(31,32,33)♣P⌐

Letter B ✔

53-57 Church Street, PE7 1DE

❂ 5 (12 Fri & Sat)-11; 12-10.30 Sun ☎ (01733) 206975 🌐 letterbpublichouse.com

Adnams Bitter; Fox Huran; Oakham Bishops Farewell; Tydd Steam Barn Ale; guest beers 🄷

This 200-year-old local community pub near the town centre offers a warm welcome to all visitors. It was called the Bee for a while, but is now the Letter B again – so called because there were once so many pubs in Whittlesey that they ran out of names. There was also a Letter A and a Letter C. An annual beer festival is held in the spring around St George's Day. Q❀🛏⊟⇌🚌(31,32,33)♣🍎⌐

Whittlesford

Bees In The Wall

36 North Road, CB22 4NZ

❂ 12-2.30, 6-11; 12-2.30, 7-10.30 Sun ☎ (01223) 834289

Taylor Landlord; guest beers 🄷

Situated on the village's northern edge, this pub really does have bees in one wall. The public bar oozes atmosphere, especially with the fire blazing, and tends to be where the locals gather. Diners favour the long split-level lounge which opens on to a patio, huge paddock-style garden and the pub's own wood. Two guest beers are always stocked. Evening meals are served Wednesday to Saturday only. The pub may stay open all day during the summer. ♨Q❀◐◑⊟♣P

Wisbech

Red Lion

32 North Brink, PE13 1JR

❂ 11.30-2.30, 6-11; 11.30-2.30, 7-11.30 Sat; 12-3, 7-11 Sun ☎ (01945) 582022

Elgood's Black Dog, Cambridge Bitter, Golden Newt; guest beer 🄷

This is the nearest Elgood's pub to the brewery. It has a pleasant atmosphere and is very comfortable. Both drinkers and diners are well catered for, with quality ales and excellent food served seven days a week in the refurbished split-level restaurant. The outdoor drinking area is popular on sunny days. Wheelchair access is from the rear. Q❀◐◑♿🚌(X1)P⌐

Witcham

White Horse

7 Silver Street, CB6 2LF (1 mile from A142 jct)

❂ closed Mon; 5-11 (midnight Fri); 12-midnight Sat; 12-11 Sun ☎ (01353) 778298

Beer range varies 🄷

The only pub in the village, set in an attractive area. Three ever-changing guest beers come from regional and local breweries and occasional seasonal beer festivals are hosted. There is a pleasant lounge and dining area offering a varied home-cooked menu, available evenings till 9pm plus weekend lunchtimes. The public bar area is more basic with darts and a pool table. During WWII the pub was frequented by New Zealanders based at the local Mepal airfield and many veterans continue to revisit today. Q❀◐◑🚌(106)♣

Give my people plenty of beer, good beer and cheap beer, and you will have no revolution among them. **Queen Victoria**

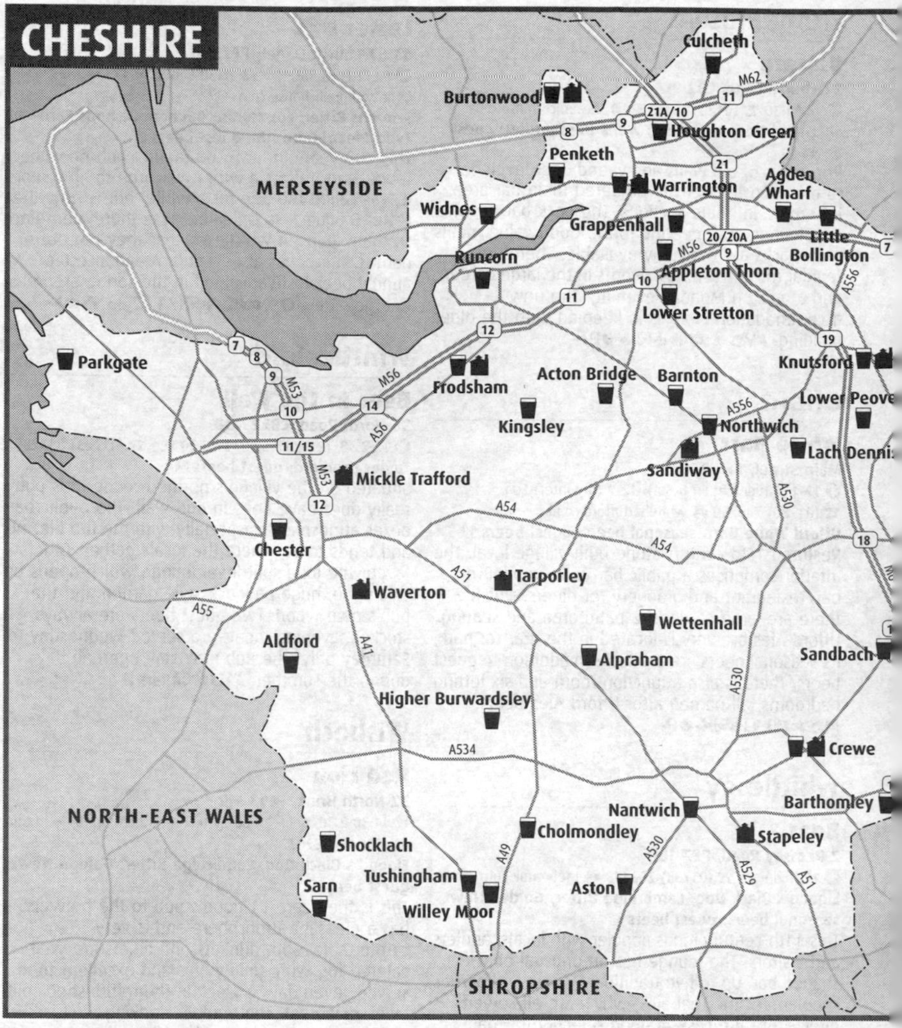

Acton Bridge

Hazel Pear Inn

1 Hill Top Road, CW8 3RA (opp railway station) SJ598746
12-11 (10.30 Sun) ☎ (01606) 853195
thehazelpearinn.co.uk
Marston's Pedigree; Taylor Landlord; Tetley Bitter; guest beers H
This pub features a mini-farm at the rear with goats, rabbits, a pig, owls, ducks and chickens. Eggs from their chickens and ducks are served with meals (12-2, 5.30-9 Mon-Sat, 12.30-8.30 Sun and holidays). They are also available for sale to take away. Recently introduced are lunchtime credit crunch meals for just £1. The bowling green is well-used, with nine different leagues. Guest beer is from the Punch list. (48)♣P

Agden Wharf

Barn Owl

Warrington Lane, WA13 0SW (off A56) SJ707872
11-11; 12-10.30 Sun ☎ (01925) 752020
thebarnowlinn.co.uk
Marston's Burton Bitter, Pedigree; guest beers H
Large single room pub alongside the Bridgewater Canal, with farmland views to the front and rear. An outside area caters for drinkers and diners. The friendly pub is popular with a mixed clientele of all ages, from walkers, cyclists and boaters looking for sustenance to others who just want a nice quiet drink. A multi-award-winner for both food and drink, five guest ales are available from micro-brewers. ♣P

Aldford

Grosvenor Arms

Chester Road, CH3 6HJ (on B5130)
11.30-11; 12-10.30 Sun ☎ (01244) 620228
grosvenorarms-aldford.co.uk
Brunning & Price Original Bitter; Weetwood Cheshire Cat; guest beers H
Large and stylish Victorian free house with a lively open-plan bar and several well-furnished quieter areas. A pleasant conservatory leads to an outdoor

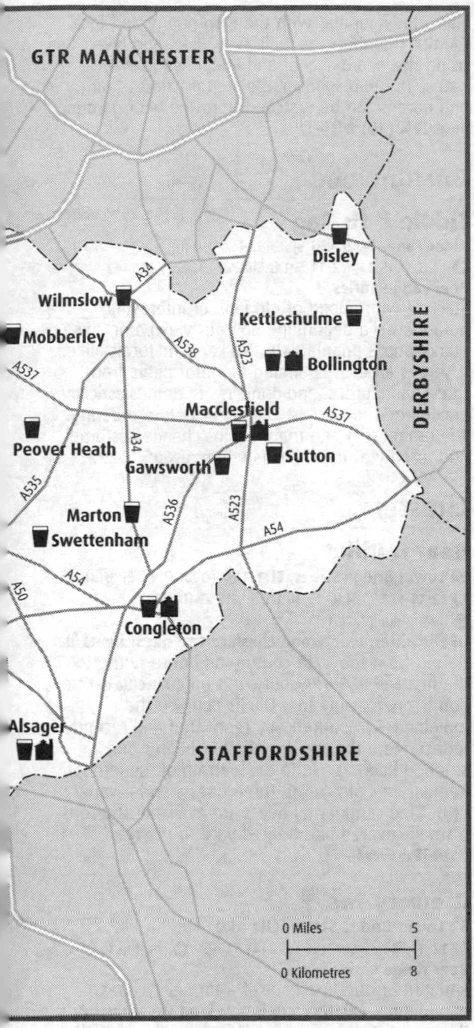

terrace and lawn with picnic tables. The range of regularly changing ales is complemented by an extensive wine list and a good range of whiskies. Imaginative food is extremely popular with diners. Families are welcome, as are dogs on leads away from dining areas. ⌂Q❀◑♿🚌(C56)P

Alpraham

Travellers Rest ★

Chester Road, CW6 9JA (on A51 at N end of village) SJ578598

◷ 6.30-11; 12-4, 6-11 Sat; 12-3, 7-10.30 Sun

☎ (01829) 260523

Weetwood Eastgate; Tetley Bitter Ⓗ

Close to the Shropshire Union Canal, this genuine rural free house has been owned and run by the same family for more than 100 years. A former local CAMRA Pub of the Year, the cosy inn is always a delight to visit. The four rooms and their furnishings reflect an era when people had time to sit, sup, talk and relax. Visitors – locals, walkers, cyclists, boaters and passing motorists – are always made to feel at home. Q❀🚌(84)♣P⁵–

Alsager

Lodge

88 Crewe Road, ST7 2LX

◷ 4-11; 1-midnight Fri & Sat; 1-11 Sun ☎ (01270) 873669

Beer range varies Ⓗ

A revitalised and renovated pub, the Lodge offers an ever-changing range of ales, often sourced from micro-breweries. Three draught ciders and a selection of bottled beers are also available. An on-site brewery is planned. Tapas-style snacks are available at all times. The garden is popular in summer. Well-served by public transport, there is a public car park to the rear. ⌂❀◑♿⇌🚌(20)●

Appleton Thorn

Appleton Thorn Village Hall

Stretton Road, WA4 4RT SJ637838

◷ closed Mon-Wed; 7.30-11; 1-4, 7.30-10.30 Sun

☎ (01925) 261187 🌐 appletonthornvillagehall.co.uk

Beer range varies Ⓗ

CAMRA National Club of the Year 2008, the Village Hall was Super-Regional winner and also North Cheshire Cider and Perry winner for 2009. Seven regularly changing beers from regionals and micro-breweries are offered alongside up to seven ciders and perries. The quiet lounge complements the bar/function room where regular live music sessions and quizzes are held, as well as an annual October beer festival. Buses serve the club on Friday and Saturday evenings only.
Q❀♿🚌(8,8X,9)♣●P☐

Aston

Bhurtpore Inn 🏆

Wrenbury Road, CW5 8DQ (¼ mile from A530 Nantwich-Whitchurch road) SJ610469

◷ 12-2.30, 6.30-11.30; 12-midnight Fri & Sat; 12-11 Sun

☎ (01270) 780917 🌐 bhurtpore.co.uk

Beer range varies Ⓗ

This multi-award-winning free house, twice CAMRA Regional Pub of the Year, offers an exceptional range of beer as well as locally sourced food. Twelve handpumps serve 11 frequently changing real ales from micros, some LocAle and others further afield, as well as a cider, often from a smaller producer. Genuine continental lagers, bottled Belgian beers and malt whiskies are an added attraction. The pub is known for serving quality home-made, locally sourced food, with curries a speciality. Beer festivals are held in July and November.
⌂Q❀◑♿Ā⇌(Wrenbury)🚌(72)♣●P

Barnton

Barnton Cricket Club

Broomsedge, Townfield Lane, CW8 4QL (200m from A533 via Stoneheyes Lane) SJ631757

◷ 6.30 (12 Sat)-midnight; 12-11 Sun ☎ (01606) 77702

🌐 barntoncc.co.uk

Boddingtons Bitter; Hydes Dark Mild, 1863; Theakston Best Bitter; guest beers Ⓗ

Sports feature heavily here, with three resident cricket teams, four junior cricket teams, six squash teams and 10 bowling teams. Monday night is poker night, and darts, dominoes and pool are also played. The club has recently gained Clubmark accreditation from the England & Wales Cricket Board. Three guest beers usually sourced from

micro-breweries are available at any time. The club hosts a popular beer festival in November.
❀◑♿🚌(4)♣P⁵–

Barthomley

White Lion ★ ✔

Audley Road, CW2 5PG (jct of Audley Road and Radway Green Road) SJ767524
✪ 11.30-11; 12-10.30 Sun ☎ (01270) 882242
Jennings Snecklifter; Marston's Burton Bitter; guest beers Ⓗ
Cosy, welcoming thatched pub, dating from 1614, in a small village, popular with locals and visitors alike. The main bar has a quarry tile floor, 17th-century wood panelling and exposed beams. A smaller, simpler room, up two steps, also panelled, features a fine example of a winged settle. A third room at the back has a solid fuel burner. The River Waldron (formerly Wulvern) borders the pub, named in memory of the last wolf in England, supposedly killed in Barthomley Woods.
♨Q❀◐P⁵–

Bollington

Cock & Pheasant ✔

15 Bollington Road, SK10 5EJ
✪ 11.30-11 (midnight Fri & Sat); 12-11 Sun
☎ (01625) 573289
Copper Dragon Golden Pippin; Storm Brewing Bosley Cloud; guest beer Ⓗ
Large, popular pub dating from 1756 on the main road entering Bollington from Macclesfield. Low ceilings and a stone-flagged floor make for a cosy bar with a separate secluded dining area. The conservatory, patio and children's play area caters for all tastes. An ideal pub to enjoy well-kept cask ales and good food, it offers a well-balanced menu every day until 9pm and beers from local brewer Storm Brewing. It's home to an active dominoes team. The bus stops outside the front door.
🐴❀◑🚌(10)♣P⁵–

Poachers Inn 🏆

95 Ingersley Road, SK10 5RE
✪ 12-2 (not Mon), 5.30-11; 12-midnight Fri & Sat Apr-Oct; 12-11 Sun ☎ (01625) 572086 🌐 thepoachers.org
Storm Brewing Desert Storm; Weetwood Old Dog; guest beer Ⓗ
Friendly and welcoming family-run free house on the Gritstone Way, converted from five stone-built terraced cottages. It has a lovely sun-trap garden in summer and coal fire in winter. Two house beers, including one from Storm Brewing, and three guests come from local and distant breweries. Twenty Belgian beers are available in bottles. The pub is well regarded for its good value, home-prepared food. Monthly quiz nights are held for local charities. ♨❀◑🚌(10)P⁵–

Vale Inn

29-31 Adlington Road, SK10 5JT
✪ 12-2.30, 5-11; 12-11 Sat; 12-10.30 Sun ☎ (01625) 575147
🌐 valeinn.co.uk
Beer range varies Ⓗ
Dating from the 1860s, this single-room family-run free house is the brewery tap for the nearby Bollington Brewing Company. It usually offers three to five beers from Bollington and one or two beers from micro-breweries, and hosts seasonal beer festivals. Excellent home-cooked food is served. The pub is popular with the community and local CAMRA members, as well as walkers and bikers using the nearby canal and Middlewood Way paths. The pub sponsors Bollington cricket team and games can be watched from the beer garden.
♨❀◑🚌(10)●P⁵–⊟

Burtonwood

Fiddle i' th Bag

Alder Lane, WA5 4BJ SJ584929
✪ 12-3, 4.45-11; 12-11 Sat & Sun ☎ (01925) 225442
Beer range varies Ⓗ
Stacked with a load of old junk or interesting paraphernalia depending on your viewpoint, this quirky pub is popular with walkers and locals alike. It serves an ever-changing range of beers from three handpumps, and drinkers are enthusiastically encouraged to sample each beer before ordering. The orangutans and mannequins change costumes and activity at mine host's whim. ❀◑🚌(329)P

Chester

Bear & Billet

94 Lower Bridge Street, CH1 1RU (near Old Dee Bridge)
✪ 12-11 (11.30 Thu, 12.30 Fri & Sat) ☎ (01244) 311886
🌐 bearandbillet.com
Okells Bitter; Weetwood Cheshire Cat; guest beers Ⓗ
Dating from the 17th-century and once home to the first Earl of Shrewsbury, this popular city-centre pub is one of only four Okells pubs on the mainland. Sympathetically renovated and recently redecorated, the real fire, timber beams and stripped flooring add to the warmth of the interior. Regular ales plus up to three guests and a variety of bottled continental beers are available. There is a small covered and heated yard to the rear.
♨❀◑♿🚌●⁵–

Brewery Tap 🏆

52 Lower Bridge Street, CH1 1RU
✪ 12-11 (10.30 Sun) ☎ (01244) 340999 🌐 the-tap.co.uk
Beer range varies Ⓗ
Situated on the first floor of a former Jacobean banqueting hall, the pub is accessed via steps from the street. The large room has stone floors, high ceilings and tapestries, creating a terrific ambience. A comprehensive, frequently changing list of real ales from micros, many local, complements the Spitting Feathers house beers, giving drinkers a wide, balanced choice. The real cider is usually Westons Traditional Scrumpy. Inventive, freshly prepared food is served. An unmissable gem.
Q◑🚌●

INDEPENDENT BREWERIES

Beartown Congleton
Bollington Bollington
Borough Arms Crewe
Burtonwood Burtonwood
Coach House Warrington
Frodsham Frodsham
Goodall's Alsager (NEW)
Northern Sandiway
Spitting Feathers Waverton
Storm Macclesfield
Tatton Knutsford (NEW)
WC Mickle Trafford
Weetwood Tarporley
Woodlands Stapeley

Bridge Inn
111 Tarvin Road, CH3 5EF (on A51)
⌚ 12-midnight (1am Fri & Sat); 12-11 Sun
☎ (01244) 316299 🌐 bridgeinnchester.co.uk
Beer range varies Ⓗ
Splendidly revitalised by the current owners, this canal-side inn is now a vibrant community pub popular with both locals and students from the nearby law college. Five handpumps dispense a changing range of ales primarily from independent breweries. Real cider is also available. The pub hosts quiz nights and live music at the weekend, and sports fans are catered for with two large-screen TVs. Excellent value home-cooked food is available lunchtimes and evenings. Parking is limited. ♨❀◑♿🚌(10,21,84)♣🍎P⅟

Mill Hotel
Milton Street, CH1 3NF
⌚ 12-midnight (10.30 Sun) ☎ (01244) 350035
🌐 millhotel.com
Coach House Mill Premium; Phoenix Cornmill; Weetwood Best Ⓗ
This city-centre hotel adjacent to the Shropshire Union Canal is housed in a former corn mill dating from 1830. It boasts Chester's largest choice of cask beers, with over a dozen on handpump including a guest mild and real cider. The hotel serves a range of food from bar snacks to full restaurant fare. Sports fans are catered for with three large TV screens. Alternatively, you can simply sit on the patio and watch the narrowboats pass by.
❀🛏◑🚌♿⇌🍎P⅟

Old Harkers Arms
1 Russell Street, CH3 5AL (down steps off City Road to canal towpath) SJ412666
⌚ 11.30-11; 12-10.30 Sun ☎ (01244) 344525
🌐 harkersarms-chester.co.uk
Brunning & Price Original; Weetwood Cheshire Cat; guest beers Ⓗ
This pub was converted from the run-down basement of a former Victorian warehouse situated alongside the Shropshire Union Canal where it passes under City Road. Wooden floors and wood panelled walls decorated with prints create a drawing room feel – an ambience reinforced by bookcases with real books. Four or more ever-changing guest beers plus two regulars provide plenty of choice. The pub can be very busy evenings and weekends. Parking is difficult.
Q◑⇌🚌🍎

Telford's Warehouse
Tower Wharf, CH1 4EZ
⌚ 12-11 (1am Wed; 12.30am Thu; 2am Fri & Sat); 12-1am Sun ☎ (01244) 390090 🌐 telfordswarehousechester.com
Thwaites Original; Weetwood Cheshire Cat; guest beers Ⓗ
Converted warehouse overlooking the Shropshire Union Canal. Three guest ales are always available from local micros and independents, as well as a small selection of bottled beers from around the world, and seasonal beers. There is an outdoor drinking area next to the canal. Food is served in the bar and a separate restaurant. A popular venue for live music, an admission fee may be charged at times, particularly after 10pm on Friday and Saturday. ❀◑🚌P⅟

Cholmondeley

Cholmondeley Arms
SY14 8HN (jct A49 and Wrenbury Road)
⌚ 10-11 ☎ (01829) 720300 🌐 cholmondeleyarms.co.uk
Beer range varies Ⓗ
Built in 1862 as a village school, it closed in 1982 and the old schoolhouse was later converted into a pub. The interior retains many of the original features and is a charming and characterful place to visit. Four real ales are usually available, often including a LocAle, to complement the award-winning food. On the edge of the Cholmondeley Estate, there is good walking in the local hills and on the Sandstone Trail. Dogs are welcome.
♨🛏◑P

Congleton

Beartown Tap
18 Willow Street, CW12 1RL
⌚ 12-2, 4-11; 12-11 Fri & Sat; 12-10.30 Sun
☎ (01260) 270990 🌐 beartownbrewery.co.uk/tap.htm
Beartown Kodiak Gold, Bearskinful, Polar Eclipse, Black Bear, Ursa Major; guest beer Ⓗ
This is the brewery tap for Congleton's Beartown Brewery, just across the road. Probably the town's best-known pub, it has been twice winner of the Regional CAMRA Pub of the Year award. The Tap offers a selection from the full range of Beartown beers and a regularly changing guest ale from a micro-brewery. Real cider is also available.
♨Q❀⇌🚌♣🍎⅟

Congleton Leisure Centre
Worrall Street, CW12 1DT (off A54 Mountbatten Way)
⌚ 7-10.30 (11 Thu Sep-Apr); closed Sat; 8-10.30 Sun
☎ (01270) 529502
Beer range varies Ⓗ
Municipal leisure centre bar open to all, not just those participating in sporting activities. The walls are decorated with posters and pump clips, helping to create a genuine pub atmosphere. Beers usually include one from Copper Dragon's range plus one or two from micro-breweries. Regular beer festivals are held in March and October with around 20 ales plus a couple of real ciders. Five minutes walk from Congleton bus station. ♿🚌P🍷

Lord Mountbatten
70 Mill Street, CW12 1AG (off Mountbatten Way)
⌚ 4 (12 Fri-Sun)-midnight ☎ (07811) 199902
Beer range varies Ⓗ
Reopened in 2009, this pub is a rising star, with four to six real ales plus draught cider, all from from local brewers including Storm, Bollington, Wincle and Titanic. At this town-centre drinking tavern you will meet real people enjoying real ale and playing pool or darts. Bringing a bag of coal will endear you to the landlord and get you the job of stoker for the night. On the local bus route but distant from Congleton railway station.
♨❀♿🚌♣🍎P⅟

Queens Head Hotel
Park Lane, CW12 3DE (next to Congleton station)
⌚ 11 (4 Mon)-11; 11-midnight Fri & Sat; 12-midnight Sun
☎ (01260) 272546 🌐 queensheadhotel.org.uk
Black Sheep Best Bitter; Greene King Abbot; Wells Bombardier; guest beer Ⓗ
Great town pub that continues to evolve and expand its range of ales, with the regular beers complemented by guests from local breweries

including Storm, Bollington and Titanic. Good bar food is a recent addition, available lunchtimes and evenings. The B&B facilities are popular with train travellers and canal boat owners looking for a dry berth. Live music plays once a month.
❀🛏◐◑ ⊟♿⇌🚌(9,99)♣●P⚟

Crewe

Borough Arms
33 Earle Street, CW1 2BG (on Earle Street Bridge)
⏲ 5 (12 Fri & Sat)-11; 12-10.30 Sun ☎ (01270) 254999
🌐 borougharmscrewe.co.uk
Beer range varies Ⓗ
Town-centre free house with an extensive range of real ales dispensed from nine handpumps. The majority of the beers are from micro-brewers with paler hoppy beers predominating, plus a good Belgian beer range. Conversation is the main entertainment thanks to the absence of gaming machines, music and pool. The open-plan ground floor has three distinct seating areas, there is another large room downstairs and outside a sheltered beer garden. The building is home to Borough Arms Brewery. Q♉❀🚌(14)♣⚟▯

British Lion
Nantwich Road, CW2 6AL (from station turn right along Nantwich road for aprox 300m)
⏲ 12-3, 7-11; Fri & Sat 11-midnight; 12-10.30 Sun
☎ (01477) 532033
Tetley Mild, Bitter Ⓗ
Country-style pub in a town. Wood carvings of the British Lion stand over the coal fireplace in the front part of this one-roomed main road pub, which has a small cubby corner to the rear of the main room, a central bar, and an outside drinking and smoking area to the rear of the pub. Many traditional pub games, like darts and dominoes, are played here, and the venue is home to the local golf society. There is a regular changing guest ale.
♨Q❀♿⇌🚌♣P⚟

Hops
8-10 Prince Albert Street, CW1 2DF
⏲ 11 (5 Mon)-11.30; 12-11.30 Sun ☎ (01270) 211100
Beer range varies Ⓗ
Welcoming, family-run free house close to the town centre. It has a café-bar style interior at ground level and a large additional room upstairs. The beers are mainly from micro-brewers and frequently LocAle. There is no pool, TV or bandits to distract from interesting conversations. An excellent range of Belgian beers is stocked in bottle and on tap. There are generous discounts on real ales Monday nights for CAMRA members. It's baby friendly too. Food is served 12-2.30pm Monday to Saturday. Q❀◐♿♣●

Culcheth

Cherry Tree ✔
35 Common Lane, WA3 4EX (on B5207, 400m from A574) SJ653952
⏲ 11-11 (midnight Fri & Sat) ☎ (01925) 762624
Greene King Abbot; Tetley Bitter; guest beers Ⓗ
Large open-plan pub with a strong emphasis on dining, with regular meal deals available. Food is served until 9.30pm (9pm Sun). Three changing guest beers are on offer, usually two from local breweries. Quiz night is Wednesday, a disco is hosted on Friday and karaoke on Saturday. Outside is a large, impressive smokers' area with a tree growing out of the middle. Free Wi-Fi is available.
❀◐◑♿🚌(19,28,28A)⚟

Disley

White Lion ✔
135 Buxton Road, SK12 2HA
⏲ 11.30 (6.30 Mon)-11 (12.30am Fri & Sat); 12-11 Sun
☎ (01663) 762800 🌐 whitelion-disley.co.uk
Jennings Cumberland Ale; Theakston Best Bitter; guest beers Ⓗ
Large white pub on the A6 towards the easterly end of the village. It offers eight real ales, six of which are constantly changing beers from SIBA member micro-breweries. The contemporary interior is largely open-plan but with a separate 'dog room' offering blankets, water bowls and canine dinners. A comprehensive and varied menu is on offer with food served all day (except Mon) until 9pm. Quiz night is Thursday and live entertainment is hosted on the last Saturday of the month. A short walk from Peak Forest Canal.
♨❀◐◑⇌🚌(199)P

Frodsham

Helter Skelter
31 Church Street, WA6 6RW SJ518777
⏲ 11-11 (11.30 Sat); 12-10.30 Sun ☎ (01928) 733361
🌐 helterskelter-frodsham.co.uk
Weetwood Best Cask; guest beers Ⓗ
A stalwart of real ale choice in the town, this single-roomed bar continues to thrive. There is a choice of seating, with a raised decked area toward the back. The local Weetwood beer is always available and ales from other Cheshire breweries are often among the guests. A changing real cider is also stocked. Food is served in the bar and an upstairs restaurant. ◐◑⇌🚌(48)●

Gawsworth

Harrington Arms ☆
Church Lane, SK11 9RR (off A536)
⏲ 12-3, 5-11.30 (midnight Thu-Sat); 12-4, 7-11 Sun
☎ (01260) 223325
Robinson's Hatters Mild, Unicorn, seasonal beer Ⓗ
A former working farmhouse/inn, this Grade II listed building is a superb example of a largely unspoilt country pub, and features on CAMRA's National Inventory. The interior comprises a number of small rooms with simple wooden tables, chairs and open fires in winter. Home-cooked food is on offer lunchtimes and evenings, made with locally sourced products where possible. The bus stop is just 100 metres from the pub. Local CAMRA Branch Pub of the Year 2008.
♨Q❀◐◑⊟♿🚌(38)♣⚟

Grappenhall

Bellhouse Club
Bellhouse Farm, Bellhouse Lane, WA4 2SG (200m off A50) SJ642862
⏲ 5 (7 Mon & Tue)-11.30; 12-11.30 Sun ☎ (01925) 268633
🌐 grappenhall.com
Beer range varies Ⓗ
Part of the Community Centre, the Bellhouse Club is near the cobbled Grappenhall village and handy for the Bridgewater Canal. Regularly changing beers, mainly from micros and regionals, are served from

the main bar, which services a lounge area and games room. The club is home to traditional games such as darts and dominoes, a quiz on Wednesday and live football fixtures shown on a big screen. A beer festival is held in May. CAMRA members are welcome. Q❀♿🚌(6,7)♣P⚟−▯

Higher Burwardsley

Pheasant Inn

Barracks Lane, CH3 9PF (access from A534 or A41) SJ523566

⏲ 12-11 (10.30 Sun) ☎ (01829) 770434

🌐 thepheasantinn.co.uk

Weetwood Best, Eastgate, Old Dog; guest beers Ⓗ

Delightful country inn high in the Peckforton Hills with glorious views across the Cheshire Plain to the Clwydian mountains and handy for ramblers walking the nearby Sandstone Trail. The Pheasant is popular for its wholesome meals prepared from fresh locally-sourced produce (no food Mon afternoon). Weetwood Cheshire Cat replaces Old Dog in summer. The guest beer is usually from a local micro. Accommodation is in 12 en-suite rooms housed in old Cheshire sandstone buildings. ♨❀🛏◐◑♿P

Houghton Green

Millhouse

Ballater Drive, WA2 0LX SJ623915

⏲ 12-11 (11.30 Tue & Thu; midnight Fri & Sat)

☎ (01925) 831189

Holts Mild, Bitter, seasonal beers Ⓗ

Built in the 1980s to cater for the expanding new estates of North Warrington, this large two-roomed open-plan pub is a popular community local. It has a spacious bar/games room with darts and pool and a large lounge where quizzes take place on Tuesday and Thursday nights, and live music on Saturday. Food is served until 9pm (6pm Sun). The monthly guest beer is from Holts.

❀◐◑⊟♿🚌(23,26)♣P⚟

Plough ✔

Mill Lane, WA2 0SU (off Delph Lane) SJ622918

⏲ 11.30-11 (11.30 Thu & Sat; midnight Fri); 12-11 Sun

☎ (01925) 815409

Weetwood Best Cask, Cheshire Cat; Wells Bombardier; guest beers Ⓗ

Set between the M62 and the estates of North Warrington, this CAMRA North Cheshire Pub of the Year 2009 grows increasingly popular. It now offers up to five ever-changing cask beers alongside the three regulars. The modern open-plan interior complements the pub's 1774 origins. A food-focused operation, regular meal deals ensure the pub is always busy. Food is served until 9pm seven days a week. Quiz night on Thursday is popular.

❀◐◑♿🚌(23,26)P⚟

Kettleshulme

Swan

Macclesfield Road, SK23 7QU (on B5470)

⏲ 12 (5.30 Mon)-11; 12-10.30 Sun ☎ (01663) 732943

🌐 the-swan-kettleshulme.co.uk

Marston's Burton Bitter; guest beers Ⓗ

Small, idyllic 15th-century whitewashed stone building with a quaint interior featuring timber beams, stone fireplaces and a real fire. Two or three changing guest beers, usually from quality micros, are always available, and a small beer festival takes place in autumn. Food is of high quality from an interesting, ever-changing menu (booking advisable). Situated in the Peak District National Park surrounded by good walking country, families and walkers are welcome. Outside there are two patios for warmer weather.

♨❀🛏◐◑🚌(60,64)P

Kingsley

Red Bull 🏆

The Brow, WA6 8AN (100m from B5153) SJ522748

⏲ 12-2.30, 5.30-11 (11.30 Fri & Sat); 12-3, 7-11 Sun

☎ (01928) 788097 🌐 redbullpub.co.uk

Rudgate Ruby Mild; Thwaites Best Bitter; guest beers Ⓗ

Located in the village centre, just off the main road, this recent local CAMRA Pub of the Year winner offers four cask ales. First mentioned in records in 1771, the original thatched building was replaced by the present inn in 1906. Inside, it has the atmosphere of a typical English village pub, and outside there are lovely gardens. Award-winning home-cooked food is available at all sessions (no food Sun eve). Home to regular village activities, with a pint and a curry on Wednesday.

♨Q❀◐◑🚌(48)♣P▯

Knutsford

Cross Keys Hotel

52 King Street, WA16 6DT

⏲ 11.30-3, 5.30-11; 11.30-midnight Fri & Sat; 11.30-midnight Sun ☎ (01565) 750404 🌐 crosskeysknutsford.com

Caledonian Deuchars IPA; Jennings Cumberland; Taylor Landlord; guest beer Ⓗ

This former 18th-century coaching inn is now a friendly and lively town-centre pub with modern accommodation. It has a lounge and vault separated by an unusual wood and glass partition, and a dining area, reached via stairs from the lounge, converted from the old cellar. Food is served Tuesday to Sunday, with a wide choice of bar meals at lunchtime. Two or three guest beers are usually available, at least one from an independent brewery. ♉❀🛏◐◑⊟⇌🚌(300)♣P

Lord Eldon

27 Tatton Street, WA16 6AD

⏲ 11-11 (midnight Thu-Sat); 12-10.30 Sun

☎ (01565) 652261

Tetley Bitter; guest beer Ⓗ

The interior of this 300-year-old pub is surprisingly spacious, comprising a large bar area with a real fire and three further rooms leading from it. The decor includes many horse brasses and pictures, often of old Knutsford. At the rear is a pleasant beer garden. Live music features twice a week – 'open mike' on Thursday and live bands on Saturday. One of the guest ales is usually from a local brewery. ♨Q❀⇌🚌(300)♣⚟

Lach Dennis

Duke of Portland

Penny's Lane, CW9 7SY SJ704720

⏲ 12-3, 5.30-11; 12-11 Fri-Sun ☎ (01606) 46264

🌐 dukeofportland.com

Banks's Mild; guest beers Ⓗ

The Duke has recently undergone a programme of refurbishment inside and out. This relaxed, civilised dining pub is always inviting for a meal and a pint or two of the four ales on offer. The interior with its lofty ceilings creates quite a sense of occasion while retaining a pub feel, albeit an upmarket one. A good selection of ales is on offer from this Marston's tied pub. Outside, the neat terrace has uninterrupted views of the Cheshire countryside. Q❀◑◗♿P⚟

Little Bollington

Swan With Two Nicks

Park Lane, WA14 4TJ (off A56) SJ730871
✪ 12-11 (10.30 Sun) ☎ (0161) 928 2914
Dunham Massey Dark Mild, Big Tree Bitter, Stamford Bitter; Green King Abbot; Taylor Landlord Ⓗ
A classic country pub near the National Trust's Dunham Park and convenient for boaters on the Bridgewater Canal. The cosy front rooms are welcoming to drinkers, with real fires, beams and brasses. Quiet background music plays but there are no TVs or games machines. The spacious restaurant at the rear serves meals all day. There are usually seven cask ales available including three from the local Dunham Massey Brewery and the house beer from nearby Coach House. Dogs are welcome. ♨Q❀◑◗🚌P

Lower Peover

Crown

Crown Lane, WA16 9QB (on B5081 off A50 S of Knutsford) SJ737735
✪ 11.30-3, 5.30-11; 12-10.30 Sun ☎ (01565) 722074
Caledonian Deuchars IPA; Flowers IPA; Taylor Landlord; Tetley Bitter; guest beers Ⓗ
Homely 17th-century country inn with good friendly service, low ceilings and beams creating a cosy atmosphere. The stone-flagged bar has a well-used dartboard. The front room is used mainly by diners enjoying the home-cooked meals. Among the good selection of ales is, pleasingly, always a cask mild. A gooseberry competition is held in July. With easy access from the M6, you really must try this pub if you are nearby. ♨Q◑◗♿♣P

Lower Stretton

Ring o' Bells

Northwich Road, WA4 4NZ (on A559 just off jct 10 M56) SJ622818
✪ 12-2.30 (not Mon), 5.30-11; 12-11 Thu; 12-3, 5.30-midnight Fri; 12-2, 7-11 Sat; 12-10.30 Sun
☎ (01925) 730556
Fuller's London Pride; Tetley Bitter; guest beer Ⓗ
This pub's exterior exhibits more campaigning material than CAMRA. A traditional village local, the focal point is the main bar room. Good banter and conversation dominate, but two small side rooms provide refuge for a more peaceful drink. It hosts a twice-monthly Monday quiz night (go early to get a seat) and boules is played outside on the pitch next to the car park. A previous CAMRA Branch Pub of the Year winner.
♨Q❀🚌(45,46)P⚟

Macclesfield

Dolphin

76 Windmill Street, SK11 7HS (off A523 Mill Lane)
✪ 12-2.30, 5-11; 12-11 Sat; 12-10.30 Sun ☎ (01625) 616179
Robinson's Hatters Mild, Dizzy Blonde, Unicorn, seasonal beers Ⓗ
Friendly, family-run local with separate public and lounge bars and a real fire in winter. Traditional pub sports are popular here and the pub is home to several local teams. Four beers are on handpump throughout the year, with Old Tom added in winter. A good range of malt whiskies is available. Home-cooked food is served Friday and Saturday lunchtimes only. Local CAMRA Branch Autumn Pub of the Season. ♨Q◑⊟♿🚌♣

Old Ship Inn

61-63 Beech Lane, SK10 2DS
✪ 4 (3 Fri)-11; 12-11 Sat & Sun ☎ (01625) 261909
Storm Brewing Bosley Cloud, Ale Force; Worthington Bitter; guest beer Ⓗ
Friendly and welcoming pub with two blazing open hearth fires in winter. A 15-minute walk from the town centre, it is well-worth seeking out as it is a premier outlet for Macclesfield based Storm Brewing, with up to three of its beers on pump. Behind the bar is another room with a pool table. The pub caters for a mixed clientele of all ages, making it a true hub of the community.
♨❀⇌🚌(10)♣P⚟

Railway View

1 Byrons Lane, SK11 7JW
✪ 5 (12 Sat & Sun)-11 ☎ (01625) 423657
Skinner's Betty Stogs; Taylor Landlord; guest beer Ⓗ
Attractive local free house with stone-flagged floors and real fires during the winter months. It serves a good selection of up to eight cask-conditioned beers, at least one from a local micro, with prices reduced on Monday night. Seasonal beer festivals are held. Entertainment includes live music on Friday and a quiz on Sunday. The pub is home to local dominoes, crib, darts, bar skittles, pool and football teams. ♨❀🚌(9,14)♣⚟

Society Rooms ✔

Park Green, SK11 7NA
✪ 9-midnight (11 Jan); 9-1am (midnight Jan) Fri & Sat
☎ (01625) 507320
Greene King Ruddles Best Bitter, Abbot; Marston's Pedigree; guest beer Ⓗ
Large, centrally located stone-built Wetherspoon conversion of an 18th-century vicarage and college – hence the name. Divided internally into two large areas, the pub is popular with shoppers and families enjoying good value food and drinks. Staff favour cask ale and regular beer festivals often showcase regional micro-breweries. The range of five guest beers often includes a local ale.
☕❀◑◗♿⇌🚌●P⚟

Waters Green Tavern

96 Waters Green, SK11 6LH
✪ 12-3, 5.30-11; 11-3, 7-11 Sat; 12-3, 7-10.30 Sun
☎ (01625) 422653
Beer range varies Ⓗ
Close to rail and bus stations, this pub is in a convenient location and so good that visitors may be tempted to linger and catch a later train. It has been so successful that the award-winning licensees have now bought it and made it a genuine free house. Up to seven ever-changing cask beers are sourced from Phoenix, Thornbridge, York and Oakham among others. Great value home-cooked food is served at lunchtime.
♨◑⇌🚌♣●⚟

Marton

Davenport

Congleton Road, SK11 9HF (on A34)
☼ 11.45-3 (not Mon), 6-11; 12-11 Fri-Sun ☎ (01260) 224269
🌐 thedavenportarms.co.uk
Courage Directors; Theakston Black Bull; guest beer Ⓗ
Popular pub restaurant north of Congleton forging a good reputation for beer and food. The separate bar area means that drinkers are made as welcome as diners. Guest beers are typically from Cheshire breweries with Beartown and Storm featuring regularly. Food is freshly prepared, made with local and seasonal produce. Booking is advised for the restaurant at weekends. Bar meals are also served (no food on Mon). There is a large garden and patio area to the rear. ♛☕❀◐♿P

Mobberley

Roebuck ✔

Mill Lane, WA16 7HX (off Alderley Road, B5085)
☼ 12-3, 5-11; 12-11 Sat; 12-10.30 Sun ☎ (01565) 873322
🌐 theroebuck.com
Black Sheep Best Bitter; Taylor Landlord; Tetley Bitter; guest beer Ⓗ
Tucked away in a tranquil part of Cheshire, this fashionable pub restaurant has a modern farmhouse-style interior. Three open rooms have timber and tiled floors and scrubbed wooden tables. The emphasis here is on food, with an adventurous menu of home-cooked local produce. However the quality of the beer is not forgotten either, with three house beers and a guest from a local brewery. A private function room is available. ♛Q❀◐🚌(88)P⚐

Nantwich

Black Lion

29 Welsh Row, CW5 5ED
☼ 11-3 (not Mon), 5-11; 11-11 Fri & Sat; 12-10.30 Sun ☎ (01270) 628711
Weetwood Best Bitter, Cheshire Cat Ⓗ
This 350-year-old black and white timbered pub has a tranquil, relaxed atmosphere and is conveniently situated on the fringe of the main shopping area. The pub has a front room with a roaring fire, a conservatory to the side and an upstairs lounge. Guest beers tend to come from local north-west breweries. Excellent home-cooked food is available daily (no food Mon). ♛Q❀◐⇌🚌(45,84)⚐

Crown Hotel

24 High Street, CW5 5AS
☼ 11-11 ☎ (01270) 625283 🌐 crownhotelnantwich.com
Beer range varies Ⓗ
This Grade II-listed building was burnt down in the Great Fire of Nantwich in 1583 and quickly rebuilt by Queen Elizabeth I. Uneven floors throughout add to the character. The traditional bar offers a beer range including three guests (usually LocAle, often Salopian or Storm) and a house ale brewed by a local micro. Attached to the bar is an Italian restaurant. Entertainment includes a monthly film night. Live music often plays upstairs and the pub hosts an annual jazz and blues festival. ♛🛏◐⇌🚌P

Globe

100 Audlem Road, CW5 7EA
☼ 12-11 ☎ (01270) 623374
Woodlands Light Oak, Oak Beauty, Midnight Stout, Bitter, Bees Knees, Redwood Ⓗ
This traditional pub is local brewery Woodlands' first tied house, acquired and renovated in 2007, and usually offers up to nine of its beers. Seasonal ales complement the regular choices and draught cider is available at times. Home-cooked food is served until 9pm (8pm Sunday). Conversation dominates the comfortable open-plan interior. The pub supports a wide range of social activities including its own football team and a summer beer festival. ♛❀◐⇌🚌(73)●P⚐▯

Northwich

Penny Black ✔

110 Witton Street, CW9 5AB SJ661740
☼ 9am-midnight (1am Fri & Sat) ☎ (01606) 42029
Greene King Abbot; Marston's Pedigree; Tetley Bitter; guest beers Ⓗ
Dating from 1914, Wetherspoon has done an excellent job bringing this Grade II listed former post office back to life. Large and mainly open plan, TVs screen news channels with subtitles throughout the day. LocAle accredited, Cheshire-brewed beers are often to be found on the bar as well as at least one darker beer (mild, stout or porter). The car park is behind the pub off Meadow Street immediately after the new Royal Mail sorting office. Q☕❀◐♿⇌🚌(1,45,289)●P⚐

Parkgate

Boat House

1 The Parade, CH64 6RN
☼ 11.30-11; 12-10.30 Sun ☎ (0151) 336 4187
🌐 theboathouseparkgate.co.uk
Caledonian Deuchars IPA; Greene King Old Speckled Hen; Weetwood Eastgate Ale; guest beer Ⓗ
Attractive half-timbered building on the Dee Estuary overlooking an RSPB nature reserve. Beware the occasional high tides that lap right up to the pub walls. The pub supports local breweries and offers changing guest ales. A folk club meets upstairs on the last Thursday of the month and a jazz group plays on Tuesday evening. Freshly prepared food is served until 9.30pm (9pm Sun), with fish the speciality. A haven for nature lovers, good beer and food fans alike. ❀◐♿🚌(487)P⚐

Penketh

Ferry Tavern

Station Road, WA5 2UJ SJ563866
☼ 12-3.30 (not Fri), 5.30-11 (11.30 Fri); 12-11.30 Sat; 12-10.30 Sun ☎ (01925) 791117 🌐 theferrytavern.com
Greene King Abbot; Lees Bitter; Ruddles County; guest beers Ⓗ
First park your car in the car park at the end of Station Road. Go through the gate and cross the railway line, then navigate across a narrow footbridge over the St Helens Canal before turning right to walk to the pub alongside the banks of the River Mersey. Hopefully the river won't be in flood – markers on the bar indicate the height of recent floods. Six real ales and 300 whiskies await you. ♛❀◐P⚐

Peover Heath

Dog Inn

Wellbank Lane, WA16 8UP (off A50 at Whipping Stocks Inn)

⊛ 11.30 (12 Sun)-11 ☎ (01625) 861421
⊕ doginn-overpeover.co.uk

Hydes Original; Weetwood Best Cask, Old Dog ⊞

This picturesque pub has a tap room for pool and darts, a comfortable lounge bar with a real fire and an extensive restaurant. There is an attractive heated patio at the front with cover for smokers and a small beer garden next to the car park. Popular quizzes are held on Thursday and Sunday. Live music plays once a month on Friday. A beer festival is held at the end of July.

⋈⊛⋈⊕⊞⅄⊞(27A)♣P⅄

Runcorn

Ferry Boat ✓

10 Church Street, WA7 1LR

⊛ 9-midnight (1am Fri & Sat) ☎ (01928) 583380

Greene King Ruddles Best, Abbot; Marston's Pedigree; guest beers ⊞

Located in the centre of the old town, this Wetherspoon shop conversion takes its name from the 12th-century ferry service that once linked Runcorn with Widnes. An attractive, spacious, open-plan pub, it is a welcome find in the real ale desert that is the old town. The interior is divided into several distinct seating areas and food is served all day. ⊕⅄⊞⅄

Sandbach

Lower Chequer

Crown Bank, CW11 1FW

⊛ 12 (6 Mon-Wed)-11; 12-10.30 Sun ☎ (01270) 762569

Beer range varies ⊞

This friendly local run by award-winning licensees is situated close to the Saxon Crosses at the rear of the Cobbles. Dating back to 1570, it is said to be the oldest building in the town. It offers a varying range of six free-of-tie real ales sourced from Cheshire, Manchester and Shropshire breweries, including one dark beer. There are two rooms either side of the central bar and more seating outside. Q⊛⊞⅄

Sarn

Queen's Head

Sarn Road, SY14 7LN SJ440447

⊛ closed Mon; 6 (12 Sun)-midnight ☎ (01948) 770244

Marston's Burton Bitter; Taylor Golden Best; guest beer ⊞

A small, unchanging village local, The Sarn, as it is known locally, is just a few metres from the Welsh border and is well-known for its home-made locally sourced food. The dining area is next to the homely lounge and pool can be played in the small games room. Outside, the covered patio is next to a converted water mill on Wych Brook, the national boundary. The guest beer is usually from a local micro-brewery and the pub provides a rare outlet for Taylor's light mild. ⋈Q⊛⊕⊞▲♣P⅄

Shocklach

Bull

SY14 7BL (off A534, 4 miles S of Farndon)

⊛ 12-3, 5-11; 12-11 Fri & Sat; 12-10.30 Sun
☎ (01829) 250239 ⊕ thebullshocklach.com

Stonehouse Station Bitter; guest beers ⊞

Old, recently refurbished country pub that combines good beer, excellent food and community activities. It has a single bar divided into three distinct areas plus a curtained-off dining room for private parties and busy times. Note the patchwork-tiled floor. The enthusiastic owners keep five real ales, with at least one from a local brewer. Beer festivals are held and brewery tours organised. ⋈Q⊛⊕⅃⅄P⅄

Sutton

Church House ✓

Church Lane, SK11 0DS

⊛ 12-midnight ☎ (01260) 252436

Banks's Bitter; Robinson's Unicorn; guest beer ⊞

A popular, brick-built local pub at the four-way junction on the Macclesfield/Langley Road. The bar has a choice of two house beers and one or two guest ales. Good food is served lunchtimes and evenings Monday to Friday and all day Saturday and Sunday. The interior has three seating areas with a real fire and there is also a large outdoor drinking area. Crib and dominoes are played and a pub team plays in the local quiz league.

⋈Q⊛⊕⊞(14)♣P⅄

Sutton Hall

Bullocks Lane, SK11 0HE

⊛ 11.30-11; 12-10.30 Sun ☎ (01260) 253211
⊕ suttonhall.co.uk

Thwaites Original; Weetwood Cheshire Cat; guest beer ⊞

Splendid 480-year-old manor house set in its own grounds, close to the Macclesfield Canal. Tastefully refurbished by Brunning & Price, it is notable for many nooks and crannies including a snug, library and seven dining areas. There is a strong food focus here with an excellent menu, but this is a proper pub too and drinkers are always welcome. There are five real ales to enjoy, often from local breweries. Complemented by lovely gardens, Sutton Hall is a real gem. ⋈Q⊛⊕⅃⅄⊞P⅄

Swettenham

Swettenham Arms ✓

CW12 2LF

⊛ 11.30-3, 6-11.30; 11.30-11 Sun ☎ (01477) 571284
⊕ swettenhamarms.co.uk

Beartown Kodiak Gold; Hydes Original; Sharp's Doom Bar; guest beer ⊞

This established country pub is set in the Dane Valley, an area of outstanding natural beauty. Dating from the 16th-century, the pub was once a nunnery. A winner of local and national awards for its quality food, it has a bar, restaurant and function room. The beer range changes regularly, with a minimum of three real ales on at any time. At the rear of the pub is a two-acre lavender and sunflower meadow, superb in summer.
⋈Q⊛⊕⅃P⅄

Tushingham

Blue Bell Inn

SY13 4QS (signed Bell o' t' Hill from A41)

⊛ 12-3 (not Mon), 6-11 (midnight Fri & Sat); 12-3, 7-11 Sun
☎ (01948) 662172 ⊕ bluebellinn.net

Oakham JHB; Salopian Shropshire Gold; guest beers Ⓗ
Wonderful black and white timber-framed 17th-century pub with plenty of atmosphere. A cobbled front leads to an ancient front door. The main bar is popular and visitors are sure to be drawn into the enlightened conversation at the bar. One of the walls in the dining room reveals part of the pub's original wattle and daub. Real cider is available in summer only. Well-behaved dogs are welcome.

Warrington

Albion

94 Battersby Lane, WA2 7EG (200m N of A57/A49 jct)
12 (10 Sat)-midnight; 12-1am Fri & Sat; 12-11 Sun
☎ (01925) 231820
Beer range varies Ⓗ
The first winner of CAMRA Champion Pub of Cheshire in 2010, this large, multi-roomed community pub is on the edge of the town centre. The rooms all have a character of their own, including the reading room, and the pub supports a variety of sports teams and community activities. Regular live music plays on Saturday night. Beer festivals are held in May, August and over the Christmas period. Lunchtime snacks and light meals are available daily (no food Mon) and 5-8pm Tuesday-Friday evenings. Sunday roasts are a highlight (served 12-5pm).
(Central)

Lower Angel

27 Buttermarket Street, WA1 2LY
11-11 (midnight Sat); 12-8 Sun ☎ (01925) 653326
Tetley Bitter; Theakston Dark Mild; guest beers Ⓗ
A fine, friendly, two-roomed town-centre local with a tap room and smarter lounge served by a central bar. Walker's Brewery memorabilia features throughout, including a magnificent window at the front. Eight ales are on handpump, with up to six guests from both regional and micro-breweries. The pub has plans for its own one-barrel brewery. Central railway station and the bus interchange are only five minutes' walk away.
(Central)

Porter's Ale House

78 Buttermarket Street, WA1 2NN
11-midnight; 12-2am Fri & Sat; 1-midnight Sun
☎ (01925) 632885 myspace.com/portersalehouse
Beer range varies Ⓗ
Long single-roomed town-centre local with six handpumps. Music and drinking predominate in the bar, which also has a pool table. Outside, there is a covered drinking area. There is free pool and jukebox Monday and Tuesday, quiz night on Wednesday, karaoke on Thursday and live/DJ classic rock music Friday and Saturday. Sunday is acoustic night. Five minutes' walk to the station and bus interchange. (Central)

Tavern

25 Church Street, WA1 2SS
2-11; 12-11.30 Fri & Sat; 12-11 Sun ☎ (01925) 577990
Beer range varies Ⓗ
Warrington town centre's oldest true free house, featuring an ever-changing range of up to eight beers. The single main room has a wood floor and furnishings. TV screens show sport and the pub gets busy when Rugby League is on, or Wolves are playing at home. Smokers also have a TV in the rear covered courtyard. A range of Scotch and Irish whiskies is available. Ten minutes' walk from Central railway station and the bus station.
(Central)

Wettenhall

Little Man

Winsford Road, CW7 4DL SJ625605
12.30-4 (not Tue), 7 (7.30 Tue)-11; 12.30-4, 7.30-10.30 Sun ☎ (01270) 528203
Beer range varies Ⓗ
Believed to be named after a 19th-century local character, this rural inn serves the local farming communities. One side of the pub has a public bar feel, with televised sport, the other opens out into a comfortable lounge/dining area, traditionally decorated, with a welcoming open fire. Five real ales are usually available, sourced from the length and breadth of the country, including local brews. The management is passionately devoted to real ale and good value food.

Widnes

Premier

93-96 Albert Road, WA8 6JS
9-midnight (12.30am Fri & Sat) ☎ (0151) 422 4920
Greene King IPA, Abbot; Marston's Pedigree Ⓗ
Originally the Premier cinema, which closed in the 1960s, this is a typical open-plan Wetherspoon pub with a separate family dining area. Outside there is a raised patio area. The pub is five minutes' walk from Widnes Shopping Centre and main bus stops. There is no car park.

Willey Moor

Willey Moor Lock Tavern

Tarporley Road, SY13 4HF (300m from A49) SJ534452
12-2.30 (3 summer), 6-11; 12-2.30 (3 summer), 7 (6 summer)-10.30 Sun ☎ (01948) 663274
Theakston Best Bitter; guest beers Ⓗ
Reached by a footbridge over the Llangollen Canal, the Willey Moor is a former lock keeper's cottage and is popular with canal boaters and walkers on the nearby Sandstone Trail. This genuine free house always has an interesting range of up to six beers on offer. The interior is comfortably furnished with padded wall seats, and decorated with local watercolour paintings and a collection of teapots. Real fires warm in the winter months and an outside terrace plus enclosed beer garden are ideal for families in summer. P

Wilmslow

Bollin Fee

6-12 Swan Street, SK9 1HE
9-midnight (1am Thu; 2am Fri & Sat) ☎ (01625) 441850
Greene King Ruddles Best Bitter, Abbot; guest beer Ⓗ
Smart, modern Wetherspoon Lloyds No 1 bar in the town centre attracting a mixed clientele. It has an open-plan layout including family and dining areas with Sky TV, and two beer gardens, as well as a smoking area at the front. Weekend nights are very busy. The guest beers change regularly and a beer festival is hosted on the first week of the month, promoting local ales. Q (88,130,378)

CORNWALL

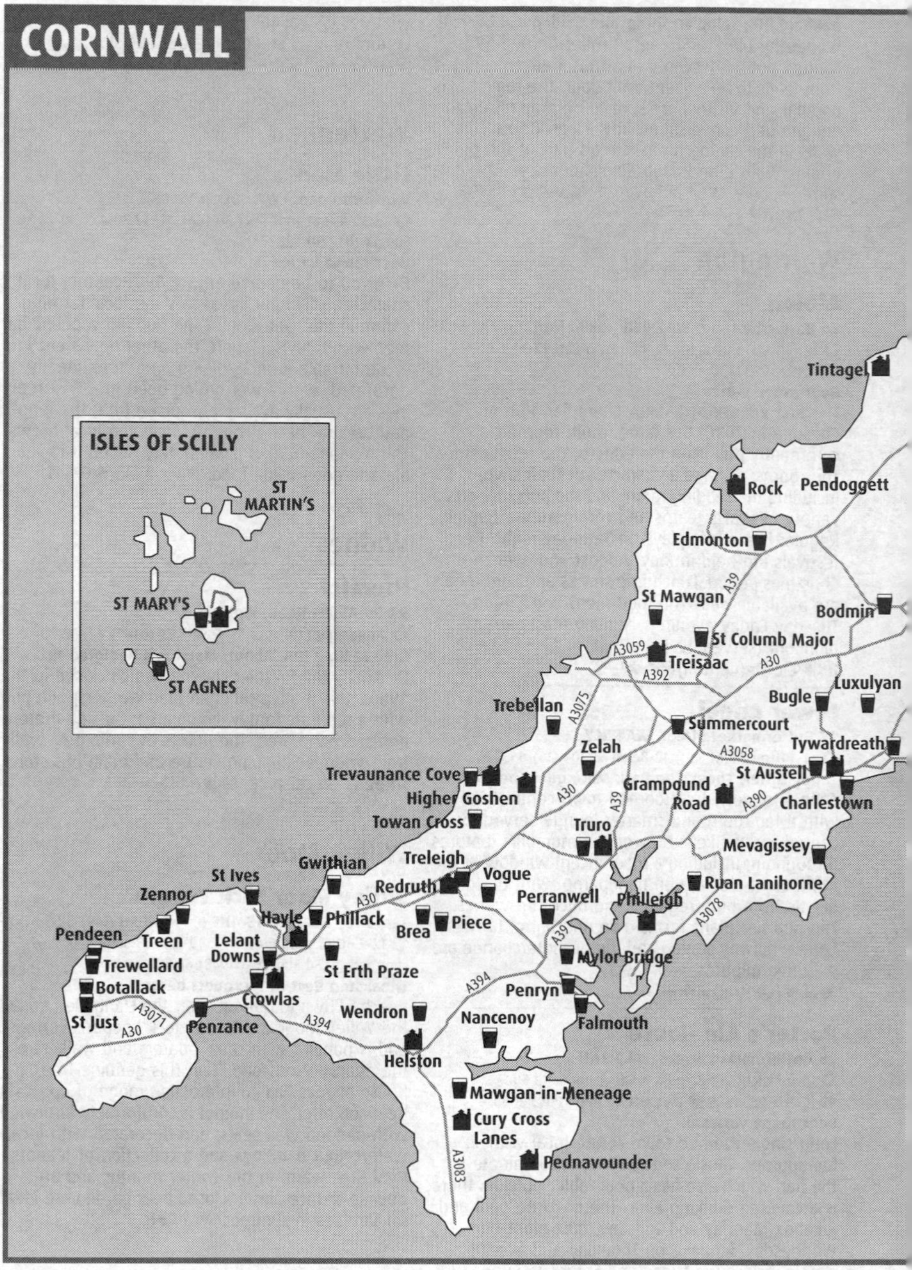

Blisland

Blisland Inn

The Green, PL30 4JF (off A30) SX100733

⚙ 11.30-11; 12-10.30 Sun ☎ (01208) 850739

🌐 bodminmoor.co.uk/blislandinn

Beer range varies Ⓗ/Ⓖ

The Blisland is set in an idyllic moorland location by the village green, the only one in Cornwall. This granite community pub is well worth seeking out for its friendly, warm and welcoming atmosphere. The decor includes numerous barometers, toby jugs, beer mats and pump clips. The bar menu features a range of good home-cooked food. Up to six varying real ales are available, and draught cider, often imaginatively sourced.

♨Q☋❀◁🚌(Corlink)♣●P⚡–

Bodmin

Bodmin Jail

Berrycoombe Road, PL31 2NR (bottom of town near Camel Trail) SX066673

⚙ 11-11; 12-10.30 Sun ☎ (01208) 76292

Brains SA, The Rev James; guest beer Ⓗ

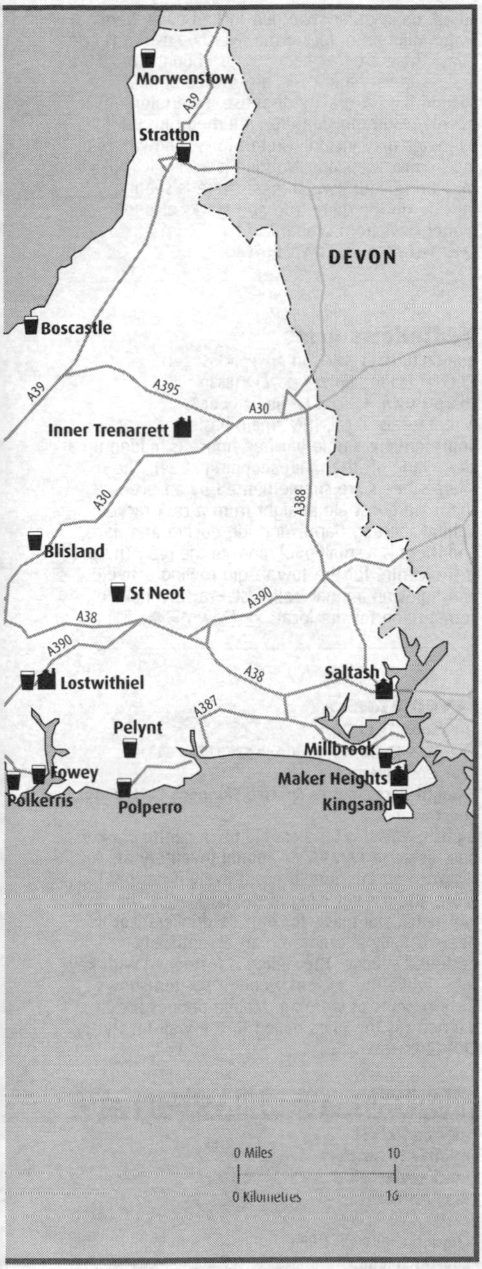

Situated on the outskirts of Bodmin, the Jail is a former 18th-century county prison. Now primarily a restaurant, it boasts a comfortable lounge bar, with at least two well-kept ales. Good bar snacks are available and the attached restaurant offers good-quality meals. The Jail is easy to find – it's one of the largest buildings in Bodmin and dominated by a bell tower. The building itself is of great interest and contains a visitor centre. ⛰Q❀◑◐🚌P⁴–

> I never drink water. I'm afraid it will become habit-forming. **W C Fields**

Boscastle

Napoleon Inn ✔

High Street, PL35 0BD (at top of village)

11-2.30 (3 summer), 5.30-11; 11-11 Sat summer; 12-10.30 Sun ☎ (01840) 250204 🌐 napoleoninn.co.uk

St Austell Tinners, Tribute, HSD G

Comfortable 16th-century inn at the top of Boscastle, set back from the road. The two bars are set at right angles, the smaller simply furnished and home to the dartboard. The larger lounge has three separate drinking areas and a restaurant, while the decor is a mix of drinking pots and assorted bric-a-brac. The pub has a colourful history – it was once a 'recruiting centre' for press gangs during the Napoleonic wars, and enjoyed a reputation as a bawdy house. ⛰Q❀◑◐🚌(594,595)P⁴–

Botallack

Queens Arms

TR19 7QG (off B3306) SW368328

12 (11 summer)-11; 12-3, 6.30-10.30 Sun ☎ (01736) 788318

Sharp's Doom Bar; Skinner's Heligan Honey H

Pleasant, traditional granite-built village local, not far from Land's End and the coastal path. Although a single bar, it has several distinct drinking areas including a separate family room, and there is a spacious beer garden outside. Mining pictures around the walls reflect the once-dominant local industry. Skinner's brew the house beer, Tallack Tipple, as well as the Press Gang cider also on handpump. Known for its imaginative and good-quality food, the pub also holds a popular beer festival in September. A good bus service stops outside. ⛰Q❀◑◐▲🚌(17,507)●P

Brea

Brea Inn

Higher Brea, TR14 9DA (off Four Lanes-Pool road) SW666404

12-3, 6.30-midnight; 12-3, 7-11 Sun ☎ (01209) 713706

Sharp's Doom Bar; guest beers H

Small, split-level, cottage-style pub, with the bar on the lower level and a drinking/dining area on the higher. Dating from the 18th century and set in the former copper mining district of Camborne, the pub was once a mine captain's residence before becoming a miners' ale house. It has been attractively modernised and displays an interesting collection of old mining, farming and other artefacts on the walls and shelves. The two guest ales are mainly Cornish brews. A noisy blue macaw lives behind the Gents. Q❀◑◐🚌(342)P

Bugle

Bugle Inn ✔

57 Fore Street, PL26 8PB (on A391)

10-midnight (10.30 Sun) ☎ (01726) 850307

🌐 bugleinn.co.uk

St Austell IPA, Dartmoor Best, Tribute H

Named after the sound of the horn of passing stagecoaches of yesteryear, this village-centre pub is lively and welcoming. Situated in the heart of the china clay district, the family-friendly pub with five en-suite rooms is an ideal base for touring Cornwall or visiting the nearby Eden Project. The comfortable interior has a large Z-shaped bar displaying an interesting collection of carved coconuts and witch effigies. Meals including breakfast are served all day. Live music plays most Sunday evenings. ⛫❀⇌◑⇌⊟(529)♣P⚊

Charlestown

Harbourside Inn ✔

Charlestown Road, PL25 3NJ (on harbour front)
SX029516
⏲ 11-11 (midnight Fri & Sat); 12-11 Sun ☎ (01726) 76955
🌐 pierhousehotel.com/harbourside_inn_in_cornwall.htm
Draught Bass; St Austell Tribute; Sharp's Doom Bar, Special; Skinner's Betty Stogs, Cornish Knocker Ⓗ

Former harbourside warehouse, stylishly converted to a lively sports-oriented modern pub. Attached to the Pier House Hotel, its glass frontage affords views of the tall ships normally moored in Charlestown's historic harbour. The charming single-bar interior features exposed stonework, wood flooring and wooden furnishings throughout. Up to seven real ales are often available on the beer menu. Good value food is served throughout the day. Popular sporting events are screened and there is usually live entertainment on Saturday evenings. ❀⇌◑♿⛺⊟(25B,525)●⚊

Crowlas

Star Inn

TR20 8DX (on A30 just E of Penzance)
⏲ 11.30-11; 12-10.30 Sun ☎ (01736) 740375
Penzance Crowlas Bitter, Potion No 9; guest beers Ⓗ

A Mecca for Cornwall's real ale aficionados, this friendly free house with its own micro-brewery is a beer lovers' paradise – here the emphasis is firmly on beer quality and presentation. Local CAMRA Pub of the Year in 2007 and 2008, this is a quiet pub where conversation flourishes. The attractive single bar interior features a raised seating area, wooden partitions and wood and slate furnishings. Up to four house beers feature on the ever-changing beer menu, with guest ales generally from micros. No food is served. Q❀⊟(17,18,X18)P⚊

Edmonton

Quarryman Inn

PL27 7JA (off A39 near Royal Cornwall Showground)
SW965727
⏲ 12-10.30 (11 Fri & Sat) winter; 12-11 summer; 12-10.30 Sun ☎ (01208) 816444
Beer range varies Ⓗ

An ever-popular gem of a pub situated near the county showground, well worth a diversionary visit. Conversation thrives in this characterful and convivial free house, where mobile phone usage is prohibited. The interior divides into a public bar and a lounge with dining area, their eclectic decor generating a cosy ambience. An ever-changing beer menu includes one Skinner's brew and one or two guest beers from micros, and a beer from the Sharp's range is added in summer. Excellent food uses local produce.
⛫Q❀⇌◑⊟⛺⊟(555,594)♣●P⚊

Falmouth

Front

Custom House Quay, TR11 3JT
⏲ 10 (12 winter)-midnight ☎ (01326) 212168
Beer range varies Ⓗ/Ⓖ

Small, dark, cellar-style pub tucked away beneath Trago Mills store, facing the river by Custom House quay. There are four handpumps, though not all are always in use, and casks are racked behind a second bar for gravity dispense. Entertainment is mainly a summer feature – themed musical evenings may include Breton folk, songwriters or 'open mike' sessions. No food is available, but you may bring your own snacks. There is seating outside on the quay. The pub stocks alcoholic ginger beer from Wheal Maiden.
Q❀⇌(Falmouth Town)⊟♣●

Oddfellows Arms

Quay Hill, TR11 3HG (off Arwenack Street)
⏲ 12-11 (10.30 Sun) ☎ (01326) 318530
Sharp's Own, Special Ⓗ**; guest beer** Ⓖ

A real locals' local, this small, basic and unpretentious single-bar free house is hidden up a steep lane off the main shopping street. The Sharp's beers are supplemented by an ever-changing guest ale straight from a cask racked behind the bar. Games include euchre and darts, and there is a small pool room to the rear. The pub is the centre for the town's gig rowing activities, and holds an annual 'cakefest' – a cake-baking competition for the locals. ⇌(Town)⊟♣

Seven Stars ★

The Moor, TR11 3QA
⏲ 11-3, 6-11; 12-3, 7-10.30 Sun ☎ (01326) 312111
🌐 sevenstarsfalmouth.co.uk
Draught Bass; Sharp's Special; Skinner's Betty Stogs; guest beer Ⓖ

A priest runs this timeless old town-centre drinkers' pub, listed in CAMRA's National Inventory of Historic Pub Interiors. It has a lively if narrow tap room and a quiet snug at the back – the 'bottle & jug' hatch still exists for outside drinkers. Local beers usually alternate on an eccentrically-designed stillage. The ceiling is festooned with key fobs, while the ancient wooden bar top shows distinct signs of warping. Mobile phones are banned (as the ones nailed to the wall testify!).
Q❀⊟⇌(Town)⊟

INDEPENDENT BREWERIES

Ales of Scilly St Mary's
Atlantic Treisaac
Blackawton Saltash
Blue Anchor Helston
Castle Lostwithiel
Chough Cury Cross Lanes
Coastal Redruth
Driftwood Trevaunance Cove
Forgotten Corner Maker Heights
Hogswood Higher Goshen (NEW)
Keltek Redruth
Lizard Pednavounder
Paradise Hayle (NEW)
Penpont Inner Trenarrett
Penzance Crowlas
Roseland Philleigh
Sharp's Rock
Skinner's Truro
St Austell St Austell
Tintagel Tintagel
Wooden Hand Grampound Road

Fowey

Galleon Inn

12 Fore Street, PL23 1AQ
⌚ 10 (12 Sun)-11 (midnight summer) ☎ (01726) 833014
🌐 galleon-inn.co.uk
Sharp's Cornish Coaster, Doom Bar; guest beers 🄷
Riverside pub in the town centre dating back 400 years, reached through a glass-covered corridor off Fore Street with a colourful marine life mural. The only free house in Fowey, it features mainly Cornish real ales and boasts delightful harbour views from the modernised main bar and conservatory dining area. Tables outside overlook the water and there is a heated, sheltered courtyard. A wide range of meals is available daily. Accommodation is en-suite, some with river views. ♨Q❀⇌◑♿🚌(25,524)⚐

Gwithian

Red River Inn

1 Prosper Hill, TR27 5BW SW586411
⌚ closed Mon; 12-3 (not Tue), 5.30-11; 12-11 Sat; 12-10.30 Sun ☎ (01736) 753223 🌐 red-river-inn.co.uk
Sharp's Doom Bar; guest beers 🄷
Family-friendly and convivial family-run free house beside the towans (sands) of St Ives Bay. The quiet single bar room has wood flooring, wooden furnishings including chapel seating and wood panels, warmed by a wood-burning stove. The ever-changing beer range provides up to six ales depending on season. There are separate dining areas where quality freshly-cooked meals made with local produce are served. Barbecues are offered on summer evenings, and the pub holds two successful beer festivals a year. Accessible by public transport in the daytime, it is well worth a visit. ♨Q❀◑⛺🚌(501,515)P⚐

Kingsand

Rising Sun Inn

The Green, PL10 1NH (off B3247) SX435505
⌚ 12-11 (closed winter Mon); 12-10.30 Sun
☎ (01752) 822840
Courage Best Bitter; Sharp's Doom Bar; Skinner's Heligan Honey 🄷
This welcoming 18th-century inn, popular yet peaceful, was once the customs & excise house in this coastal village of narrow streets. The pub has a single, spacious bar room carpeted throughout, wood-panelled walls decorated with nautical prints and photos of old Kingsand, and an interesting collection of large toby jug characters gazing down from a shelf. Access by car is difficult, especially in summer, with parking limited – the village public car park is advised. Live entertainment is hosted some Thursday and Saturday evenings. ♨❀◑P

Lelant Downs

Watermill Inn

Old Coach Road, TR27 6LQ (off A3074, on secondary St Ives road) SW541364
⌚ 12-11 ☎ (01736) 757912
🌐 thewatermillinncornwall.co.uk
Sharp's Doom Bar; Skinner's Betty Stogs; guest beer 🄷
Standing in beautiful surroundings, this family-friendly, two-storey free house is a former 18th-century mill house close to Lelant Saltings Station. Downstairs is a comfortable, traditionally-styled, single-bar pub; upstairs, in the former mill loft, is a stylish evenings-only restaurant specialising in local seafood. The original working waterwheel, complete with millstones, extends into the bar, which is divided into drinking and dining areas. Outside, an expansive beer garden surrounds the mill stream. The Skinner's beer varies; beer festivals are held in June.
♨Q❀◑⇌(Lelant Saltings)🚌(14,17)P⚐

Lostwithiel

Globe Inn

3 North Street, PL22 0EG (close to railway station, over bridge)
⌚ 12-2.30, 6-11 (5-midnight Fri); 12-midnight Sat & summer; 12-11.30 Sun ☎ (01208) 872501 🌐 globeinn.com
Sharp's Doom Bar; Skinner's Betty Stogs; guest beers 🄷
Cosy 13th-century pub nestling in the narrow streets of this ancient stannary town. A somewhat rambling old building, it features a comfortable single bar encompassing several drinking and dining areas. A stylish restaurant and sun-trap patio lie to the rear. Fish and game are specialities on an extensive menu of home-cooked food. A second guest ale is added to the beer range during the summer months. The pub name commemorates the 19th-century warship on which a former owner's relative was killed in battle.
♨Q❀⇌◑♿⛺⇌♣⚐

Luxulyan

King's Arms ✓

Bridges, PL30 5EF (7km N of St Austell) SX048580
⌚ 10-midnight; 12-11 Sun ☎ (01726) 850202
St Austell Tinners, Tribute, HSD 🄷
On the Atlantic Coast Line Rail Ale Trail, this granite village pub, locally known as 'Bridges', offers a friendly, no-nonsense welcome to all, including children and dogs. Tastefully refurbished, the spacious room is still partially divided into two sections by an archway – the former bar area is mainly for drinking, the lounge mainly for food. The pub can be reached via the beautiful Luxulyan Valley, with its many remnants of the area's industrial past. The Eden Project is nearby.
♨Q❀◑♿⛺⇌🚌(523)♣P⚐

Mawgan-in-Meneage

Ship Inn

TR12 6AD (off B3293) SW709250
⌚ 12-2.30 (not Mon-Wed), 5-11 winter; 12-3, 5-11 summer; 12-3, 6-11 Sun ☎ (01326) 221240 🌐 ship-inn-mawgan.co.uk
Beer range varies 🄷
Located down a steep leafy lane off the Helston-St Keverne road, this welcoming family-friendly free house is well worth seeking out. Full of character and charm, the stylish interior features a single bar, snug and raised dining area. Attractively furnished throughout, the decor is distinctly rural with wood-burning stoves creating a cosy ambience. The varying beer menu features only Cornish brews, and the good-value food menu uses local produce. The bus stop is at the top of the hill.
♨Q❀◑🚌(32,35)●P⚐

Mevagissey

Fountain Inn ✔
3 Cliff Street, PL26 6QH
⏲ 12-midnight ☎ (01726) 842320
St Austell Tinners, HSD ⊞
Friendly, two-bar, 15th-century inn with slate floors, stone walls, historic photographs and low ceilings – the tunnel to the side door is particularly low. The Smugglers Bar features signs of the pilchard press that was once housed here, a glass plate in the floor covering the pit where the oil was caught, which also doubled as a store for contraband. The meat was compressed to feed Nelson's navy. Buses run to St Austell and the Lost Gardens of Heligan. ♔Q⇌◐⊟⊟(26,526)

Millbrook

Devon & Cornwall ✔
West Street, PL10 1AA (near B3247) SX422520
⏲ 12 (3 Mon-Wed)-11; 12-10.30 Sun ☎ (01752) 822320
Courage Best Bitter, Directors; Otter Ale ⊞
Convivial single-bar local in the centre of the village. The seating area at one end of the L-shaped bar is furnished comfortably with sofas and wing chairs, presided over by a piano. At the other end, a partially-screened area is available for more private dining and drinking. Essentially a locals' pub, visitors are nonetheless warmly welcomed, with conversation the main entertainment. Cooked meals are available as well as filled rolls at the bar. Q✿⇌◐Å⊟(81)♣⚋

Morwenstow

Bush Inn ✔
Cross Town, EX23 9SR (5km off A39 N of Kilkhampton) SS209150
⏲ 11-midnight ☎ (01288) 331242
🌐 bushinn-morwenstow.co.uk
St Austell Tribute, HSD; Skinner's Betty Stogs ⊞
This pub is an ancient former chapel dating in parts from 950AD. Unassuming externally, it is a gem inside, its two bar rooms simply furnished with slate floors, granite walls and exposed beams, one room divided into distinct drinking areas. Conversation is the main entertainment here. There is a smokers' area in the courtyard at the front of the pub, and a large garden at the back offering outstanding views over the valley and out to sea. ♔Q✿⇌◐⊟Å⊟(319)♣P⚋

Mylor Bridge

Lemon Arms ✔
Lemon Hill, TR11 5NA (off A393 at Penryn) SW804362
⏲ 11-3, 6.30-11; 12-3, 7-11 Sun ☎ (01326) 373666
St Austell Tinners, Tribute, HSD ⊞
There has been an inn on this site since 1765. Once called the Griffin Inn, it became the Red Lion in 1829 and took its present name in 1837. A friendly, one-bar pub in the centre of the village, it is home to local sports teams. Good home-cooked food is available (booking for the popular Sunday lunches is advisable). Families with children are made most welcome. Daytime buses run from Falmouth and Truro during the week. ♔✿◐⊟(500)♣P⚋

Nancenoy

Trengilly Wartha Inn
TR11 5RP (off B329) SW732283
⏲ 11-3, 6.30-11; 12-3, 7-10.30 Sun ☎ (01326) 340332
🌐 trengilly.co.uk
Beer range varies ⊞
Well-organised, versatile inn situated in a steeply-wooded valley near the village of Constantine. Converted from a farmhouse, it has a bar, snug and restaurant, with a later conservatory extension serving as a family room. Up to three real ales are offered from Cornish breweries. Winner of many awards, the Trengilly's main emphasis is on fresh food. It offers a wide-ranging and imaginative menu prepared where possible with Cornish produce. Accommodation is above the pub or in garden rooms nearby. ♔Q♉✿⇌◐♣P

Pelynt

Jubilee Inn ✔
Jubilee Hill, PL13 2JZ (on B3359) SX205547
⏲ 11-11; 12-10.30 Sun ☎ (01503) 220312
🌐 jubilee-inn.co.uk
St Austell Tribute; guest beer ⊞
Historic village inn, carefully extended and refurbished, with low beamed ceilings, exposed stonework and period furniture giving the two bar areas a welcoming feel. Guest beers are from the St Austell range, and a wide menu makes use of locally-sourced ingredients. The inn was renamed to commemorate Queen Victoria's Diamond Jubilee and the decor features souvenirs of several other royal jubilees. Outside at the back are a part-covered patio and large enclosed beer garden. ♔Q✿⇌◐⊟♿Å⊟(573)P⚋

Pendeen

North Inn ✔
TR19 7DN (on B3306) SW382344
⏲ 12-midnight (1am Fri & Sat); 12-11 Sun ☎ (01736) 788417
St Austell IPA, Tinners, Tribute ⊞
Welcoming village inn, a former Cornwall CAMRA Pub of the Year, in an area of outstanding natural beauty, close to the coastal path, moors and Geevor tin mining museum. Pictures and artefacts from the tin mining industry decorate the large single bar room. The St Austell real ales vary according to seasonal demand, while quality home-cooked food is served daily – the landlord's curries are locally famous. There is a small overflow restaurant upstairs. B&B and camping are available. ♔Q✿⇌◐Å⊟(17A,507)♣P⚋

Pendoggett

Cornish Arms
PL30 3HH (on B3314) SX024794
⏲ 11-2.30, 6-11; 11-11 Fri-Sun ☎ (01208) 880263
🌐 cornisharms.com
Sharp's Doom Bar; guest beer ⊞
Picturesque coaching inn, full of charm and character. The family-friendly and welcoming interior accommodates a main bar, snug, two drinking and dining areas and a restaurant. The flagstoned floors, open beams, wood-panelled walls, partitions and furnishings reflect the pub's 16th-century origins. Quiet and cosy, its open fires add to the ambience. The rural decor includes caricatures of locals adorning the walls and

handbells over the bar. Locally-sourced quality food with daily specials is available, and Thai banquets are held monthly (booking advised).
⛫Q❀⇆◑♣●P⁄

Penryn

Seven Stars

73 The Terrace, TR10 8EL

✪ 11 (12 Sun)-11 ☎ (01326) 373573

Blue Anchor Spingo Middle; Skinner's Betty Stogs, Heligan Honey, Cornish Knocker, Figgy's Brew Ⓗ

The nearest thing Penryn has to an ale house, this single-bar town pub is run by a jovial Dutchman. Decorated with foreign cash, postcards and beer-related clippings, the spacious interior has a raised and comfortably-furnished drinking annexe at the rear, dominated by a huge ship's wheel. The pub is home to the Penryn Community Theatre, who entertain with plays and pantos. A piano is available for competent pianists and occasional live music is performed. The Skinner's beer selection may vary. ⛫❀⇌(Penryn)⊟⁄

Penzance

Crown Inn

Victoria Square, TR18 2EP SW474305

✪ 12-midnight (12.30am Fri & Sat) ☎ (01736) 351070

⊕ thecrownpenzance.co.uk

Otter Ale; Skinner's Betty Stogs; guest beer Ⓗ

Close to the bus and railway stations, this small community local has a relaxing atmosphere. Tucked away behind the main shopping street, the pub has a tidily-furnished single bar and a small back room which has an open fire and provides extra dining space when needed. Two regular real ales, one from a Cornish micro-brewery, are complemented by a varying guest ale. Soup and sandwiches are available daily, with quality home-cooked meals served on Friday, Saturday and Sunday lunchtime. ⛫Q❀◑⛺⇌⊟♣⁄

First & Last Inn

24 Alverton Road, TR18 4TN

✪ 10.30-11; 12-10.30 Sun ☎ (01736) 364095

Beer range varies Ⓗ

This traditional Cornish inn was in Victorian times known as Mr Tonkin's Beer House, and once served as a staging post for the Royal Mail in the Land's End area. The small public bar has a wooden floor, wood-panelled walls and a beamed ceiling, and offers three ever-changing real ales, one of which is from a Cornish micro-brewery; Draught Bass often also appears. The lounge has a small bar and carpeted dining area. Quality home-cooked food is served lunchtimes (no food Mon).
Q❀◐⊟⇌(Penzance)⊟(5, 6, 512)♣⁄

Pirate Inn

Alverton Road, TR18 4PS

✪ 10.30 (12 winter)-11.30; 12-10.30 Sun ☎ (01736) 366094

⊕ thepirateinnpenzance.co.uk

Greene King Abbot; Sharp's Doom Bar; Skinner's Betty Stogs Ⓗ

Former 17th-century granite farmhouse, now a family-friendly Cornish country pub situated near the edge of town, although the well-stocked, capacious gardens create a rural air. The welcoming, quiet interior has large public and lounge bars, the latter with a raised dining area and impressive stone fireplace. Carpeted throughout, the comfortable furnishings and relaxing decor contribute to a homely atmosphere. An annual beer festival is held to coincide with town festivities, and numerous charity events are staged. Buses stop directly outside.
⛫Q❀◑⊟♿⊟(5,6)♣●P⁄

Perranwell

Royal Oak

TR3 7PX

✪ 11-3, 6-11; 12-3, 7-10.30 Sun ☎ (01872) 863175

Skinner's Betty Stogs; guest beers Ⓗ

Small and friendly 18th-century cottage-style village community pub where the emphasis is on good ale and food. Most of the tables are set for meals, so drinkers congregate around the bar. Booking for meals is advisable as the pub often gets busy. At least one of the two guest beers is Cornish. Bus services connecting with Truro and Helston stop outside; the railway station is 15 minutes' walk away. Q❀◑⇌⊟(47,82,82A)●P

Phillack

Bucket of Blood ✔

14 Churchtown Road, TR27 5AE SW563383

✪ 11.30-2 (not Mon-Wed winter), 6-11 (midnight Fri); 11.30-3, 6-midnight Sat; 12-4, 7-11 Sun ☎ (01736) 752378

St Austell Dartmoor Best Bitter, Black Prince, HSD Ⓗ

Gory legend (involving a well with a body at the bottom of it) explains the name of this old pub near the dunes of Hayle Towans. Tastefully refurbished, the single bar room houses a pool table at one end and a cosy drinking and dining area at the other with settles and an old fireplace. A mural depicting St Ives Bay overlooks the pool table. 'Familiarity breeds contempt' written on one of the unusually low beams offers a valuable warning! The St Austell beers vary occasionally. No food is served during the winter. ⛫Q❀◑⛺♣P⁄

Piece

Countryman Inn

TR16 6SG (on Four Lanes-Pool road) SW679398

✪ 11-11 (midnight Sat); 12-11 Sun ☎ (01209) 215960

Greene King Old Speckled Hen; Skinner's Betty Stogs, Heligan Honey; Theakston Old Peculier; guest beers Ⓗ

Lively, welcoming country pub, once a miners' grocery shop, set high among the copper mines near the prominent landmark of Carn Brea. The larger bar hosts entertainment most nights, and on Sunday lunchtime there is a charity raffle. Wednesday is 'pub night', when conversation and cards take the floor. Within the range of nine ales, there are generally two brews from Sharp's and Skinner's. The house beer, brewed by Sharp's, is called No-Name because it has never acquired one! Good value food is available all day.
⛫❀◑⊟⛺⊟(342)♣P⁄

Polkerris

Rashleigh Inn

PL24 2TL (off A3082 Par-Fowey road) SX094522

✪ 11-11; 12-10.30 Sun ☎ (01726) 813991

⊕ therashleighinnpolkerris.co.uk

Otter Bitter; Sharp's Doom Bar; Skinner's Cornish Knocker; Taylor Landlord; guest beers Ⓗ

Former 18th-century pilchard boathouse, now an excellent family-run free house. Beside a secluded beach near the Saints Way footpath and popular with coastal walkers, this cosy, atmospheric pub features stonework, beamed ceilings, open fires, comfortable furnishings and a splendid slate-topped bar. A sheltered terrace boasts panoramic views of St Austell Bay and the setting sun. First-rate food is served in the bar and split-level restaurant. The Skinner's and Otter brews vary, and guest ales are added in summer. Piano-accompanied singalongs are a highlight on Saturday evening. ⛫Q❀◐▲♣●P⊱

Polperro

Blue Peter Inn

Quay Road, PL13 2QZ SX210509

⚙ 11-11; 12-10.30 Sun ☎ (01503) 272743

🌐 thebluepeterinn.co.uk

St Austell Tribute; Sharp's Doom Bar; guest beers Ⓗ

Named after the naval flag, this friendly inn is close to the outer harbour, boasting the only sea view from any Polperro pub. It offers up to four guest ales in summer, and an enticing menu using locally-sourced ingredients. Cider comes from nearby Cornish Orchards. On two levels, it has wooden floors, low beams and snug corners, decorated with unusual souvenirs, foreign breweriana and work by local artists. The pub is popular with visitors, locals, fishermen – and their dogs. ⛫☋◐▲⊟(573)♣●⊱

Crumplehorn Inn

The Old Mill, PL13 2RJ (at end of A387) SX205515

⚙ 11-11; 12-10.30 Sun ☎ (01503) 272348

🌐 crumplehorn-inn.co.uk

St Austell Tribute; Skinner's Betty Stogs; guest beer Ⓗ

Once a corn mill and mentioned in the Domesday Book, this 14th-century inn at the village entrance has a working waterwheel outside. Inside, there are three comfortable drinking and dining areas on split levels – two bars and a restaurant. Guest beers are Cornish and a wide menu includes locally-caught fish dishes. A large outdoor patio by the millstream is sheltered by sunshades. B&B and self-catering accommodation is available. In summer catch a converted milk float down to the village centre! ⛫Q❀⛟◐▲⊟(573)♣

Ruan Lanihorne

King's Head Inn

TR2 5NX (off A3078 at Tregony) SW895420

⚙ 12-2.30, 6-11 (closed Mon winter); 12-2.30, 6-10.30 (12-4 winter) Sun ☎ (01872) 501263 🌐 kingsheadruan.co.uk

Skinner's Betty Stogs, Cornish Knocker Ⓗ

Renowned locally for quality ales and superb locally-sourced food, this delightful family-run free house nestles in the Fal estuary on the Roseland Peninsula. Quiet and traditional, the homely interior accommodates a single bar and two dining areas. Comfortable furnishings and open fires generate a cosy ambience. Full of character, the decor reflects traditional country life. A sun terrace and quaint sunken garden cater for alfresco drinking and dining. Up to four ales are available from the Skinner's range – the house beer is called Kings Ruan. ⛫Q❀◐P⊱

St Agnes: Isles of Scilly

Turk's Head

TR22 0PL

⚙ 11-4.30, 7-11 (11-11 Jul & Aug; restricted hours winter); 12-4.30, 7-10.30 (12-11 Jul & Aug; restricted hours winter) Sun ☎ (01720) 422434

St Austell Tribute; guest beers Ⓗ

The only pub on the island, well-loved by locals and visitors, with an outdoor drinking area unrivalled for its scenic beauty. Opening hours vary somewhat according to boat times – the jetty is only a couple of minutes walk away and you can watch your boat approaching from the bar. Evening boat trips run from St Mary's in summer to sample the ale and food. The Tribute is sold as the house beer Turk's Ale. Order lunchtime pasties early! ☋❀◐▲

St Austell

Rann Wartha ✔

9 Biddick's Court, PL25 5EW

⚙ 9am-midnight (1am Fri & Sat) ☎ (01726) 222940

Greene King Ruddles Best Bitter, Abbot; Marston's Pedigree; guest beer Ⓗ

Busy and popular town centre Wetherspoon's, appealing to all ages and families, offering an imaginative selection of up to four varying guest beers. The bar is L-shaped with cosy alcoves, the walls decorated with pictures of local landscapes and prominent people. Parking is in the adjacent bar-level public car park at the rear – access from the street at the front is via steps or a lift. The pub's name means Higher Quarter, relating to its position in the town. ⛫❀◐♿⇌⊟⊱

St Columb Major

Ring O' Bells

3 Bank Street, TR9 6AT

⚙ 5-11; 12-3, 7-10.30 Sun ☎ (01637) 880259

Sharp's Doom Bar, Own Ⓗ**; guest beer** Ⓖ

The narrow frontage of this charming 15th-century free house belies its capacious interior. A former brewhouse built to commemorate the parish church tower, this is the oldest pub in town. Its interior comprises three bars and a restaurant, formerly the brewery. Each bar has its own character and clientele, with open beams, slate floors and wooden furnishings creating a traditional atmosphere. A fine cosmopolitan menu is served in the restaurant and rear bar. A guest ale is available in summer.
⛫Q❀◐⊡▲⊟(593,594)♣●⊱

St Erth Praze

Smugglers Inn

3 Calais Road, TR27 6EG (on B3302, 3km from Hayle) SW576352

⚙ 12-11 ☎ (01736) 850280

Skinner's Betty Stogs; guest beers Ⓗ

Families and dogs are welcome at this spacious roadside hostelry. The entrance corridor leads to a good-sized bar room with an enormous fire in winter, a smaller games room, a light, airy restaurant and a function room. Outside is a large garden and plenty of parking space. Food is available all day on Sunday. Occasional live entertainment includes visiting jazz bands, which play on Sunday lunchtimes. The two guest ales may be sourced from national or local breweries. ⛫❀⛟◐P⊱

St Ives

Golden Lion ✔

Market Place, TR26 1RZ

11.15-midnight ☎ (01736) 793679

Beer range varies Ⓗ

A former coaching inn, this popular town-centre two-bar locals' pub is located near the church. Inside, at the front is a small horseshoe-shaped lounge where conversation reigns supreme, to the rear is the longer public bar with pool table which is more boisterous and favoured by younger drinkers. Generally brews from both Sharp's and Skinner's feature in a frequently-changing beer menu of three real ales. The home-cooked food using local produce is of good quality and value. Q

St Just

Star Inn ✔

1 Fore Street, TR19 7LL

11-11; 12-10.30 Sun ☎ (01736) 788767

thestarinn-stjust.co.uk

St Austell Tinners, Dartmoor Best Bitter, Tribute, Proper Job, seasonal beer Ⓗ

Located close to the Square, this 18th-century inn is reputedly the oldest pub in St Just. Conversation and singing are the main entertainment in this proper drinkers' pub. Full of tradition and character, its single bar displays pictures and artefacts reflecting its long association with mining and the sea. A separate snug also serves as a family room. Up to five ales are available from the St Austell brewery range. Monday is Fiddly-Dee night, Saturday night features live music.

Q(17,504)

St Mary's: Isles of Scilly

Old Town Inn

Old Town, TR21 0NN

12-11 summer; 5-11 winter; 12-3 Sat; 12-10.30 Sun ☎ (01720) 422301

Ales of Scilly Scuppered; Sharp's Doom Bar; guest beer Ⓗ

This modern and roomy pub lies just below the airport, a 20 minute stroll from Hugh Town. Wood panelling and flooring dominate the two bars. The front bar is for day-to-day drinking; the bar to the rear is a dual-purpose dining and function room. Offering occasional live entertainment, the pub is home to the Islands Folk Club. Food is served daily and includes takeaway pizzas and curries. A beer festival is held twice yearly, in June and September. P

St Mawgan

Falcon Inn ✔

TR8 4EP (near airport) SW873658

12-3, 6-11 (midnight Fri & Sat); 12-11 Sun ☎ (01637) 860225 thefalconinn-stmawgan.co.uk

St Austell Tinners, Tribute, HSD; guest beer Ⓗ

Though close to Newquay airport, this charming, family-friendly, 16th-century pub is quietly situated in the unspoilt, idyllic Lanherne Valley. Central to the picturesque village, the pub is the hub of local activities. The quiet single-bar interior has a cosy, relaxed atmosphere with decor reflecting country life. Excellent home-cooked meals are available in the bar and separate dining room. Outside, the surroundings of the extensive well-kept gardens are ideal for alfresco drinking and dining. Good quality accommodation is available.

Q(556)P

St Neot

London Inn

PL14 6NG (off A38) SX186678

12-midnight summer; 12-3, 6-11 winter; 12-midnight Fri & Sat; 12-11 Sun ☎ (01579) 320263

Sharp's Doom Bar; guest beer Ⓗ

This popular, lively village local near Colliford Lake is the focal point for village activities. A former 16th-century coaching inn, it has an open-beamed, flagstoned interior accommodating a single bar, restaurant and traditional skittle alley. Welcoming and family-friendly, its wood furnishings, open fires and rustic decor generate a cosy ambience. Quality beer is the main focus but good pub grub and an evening à la carte menu are also on offer. A second guest beer appears in summer, with occasional beer festivals held in support of local cricket. QP

Stratton

King's Arms ✔

Howells Road, EX23 9BX SS228065

12-11 ☎ (01288) 352396

Exmoor Ale; Otter Ale; Sharp's Doom Bar; guest beer Ⓗ

This locals' local is a 17th-century coaching inn in the heart of an ancient market town. The town's name reflects its loyalties after the Civil War – the battle of Stamford Hill took place nearby in 1643. The pub has many original features including two simply-furnished bars with well-worn Delabole slate flagstone and wooden floors. During renovation of a large open fireplace, a small bread oven was exposed. Draught cider is served in summer. Four letting rooms are available.

Q(X9,128,519)P

Summercourt

London Inn

1 School Road, TR8 5EA (off A30) SW888561

12-2 (not Mon-Thu winter), 5 (6 Sat)-midnight; 12-2, 7-11 Sun ☎ (01872) 510281

Beer range varies Ⓗ

On the old London road, this former 17th-century coaching inn is central to the annual village fair celebrations in September. A lively, family-friendly free house, it is full of bonhomie and banter – a warm welcome is assured. The spacious single bar is divided by wooden screens into drinking and dining areas, with an eclectic decor featuring wooden furnishings, coach lamp lighting and Laurel and Hardy figurines. Quality is guaranteed on an ever-changing beer menu and traditional home-cooked food is served. Buses stop nearby.

Q(527,597)P

Towan Cross

Victory Inn

TR4 8BN SW706484

12 (4 Tue winter)-midnight ☎ (01209) 890359

thevictoryinncornwall.co.uk

Sharp's Doom Bar; Skinner's Betty Stogs; guest beer Ⓗ

High on the cliff tops above Porthtowan, this large and convivial family-run free house boasts extensive sea views. A real traditional local, the quiet, comfortable, single-bar interior is open plan with separate dining areas. The adjoining conservatory doubles as a family or dining room. The house beer, brewed by Skinner's, is called Kiss Me Harder, and local brews feature on the guest list. An interesting, good-quality menu is on offer lunchtimes and evenings. Families are welcome. Outside is a large beer garden, ample parking and camping facilities. ❀◑♿⛺🚌(304)♣P⅃

Trebellan

Smugglers' Den Inn

TR8 5PY (off Cubert road from A3075) SW783574
🕐 11-11; 12-3, 6-11 Thu-Sat winter; 12-11 Sun
☎ (01637) 830209 🌐 thesmugglersden.co.uk
St Austell Tribute, Proper Job; Sharp's Doom Bar Ⓗ
This thatched former farmhouse down a steep and narrow country lane is a popular venue for food and drink. Oak beams, paved yards and open fires all add to its charm. Beers are locally brewed with four usually on offer – the house beer, brewed by Skinner's, is called Smugglers Ale. An ale and pie festival is held over the May Day weekend, and jazz or folk evenings are hosted occasionally. The pub is convenient for nearby caravan sites, and local buses stop at the top of the lane.
⛫Q❀◑⛺🚌(585,587)P⅃

Treen

Gurnard's Head

TR26 3DE (on B3306 north coast road) SW436376
🕐 10-11.30 ☎ (01736) 796928 🌐 gurnardshead.co.uk
St Austell Tribute; Skinner's Ginger Tosser, Betty Stogs Ⓗ
Named after the nearby headland, this impressive free house enjoys a growing reputation for fine ales and excellent food. Situated close to the coastal path, it draws custom from near and far. The pub is community-oriented, and holds weekly Cornish song and poetry evenings and monthly folk events. The expansive wood-floored interior accommodates a spacious single bar, cosy snug and stylish dining room. Wooden furnishings, comfy sofas and open fires create a relaxed atmosphere. The attractive decor features local art.
⛫Q❀🛏◑🚌(507,508)P⅃

Treleigh

Treleigh Arms

TR16 4AY (beside old Redruth bypass) SW703436
🕐 11-3, 5-11; 11-11 Fri-Sun ☎ (01209) 315095
Draught Bass; Keltek Golden Lance; Sharp's Doom Bar; Skinner's Betty Stogs; guest beer Ⓗ
Popular free house with friendly service offering beer, cider and good food. This cosy pub features a wood-burning fire and comfortable seating includes sofas for relaxing. Or you can sit at the bar and chat with the regulars in 'Old Codgers Corner'. There are no intrusive machines, music or TV. Regular highlights include themed meal nights and the popular Tuesday quiz. The pub is also HQ for the Royle Treleigh Yacht Club. Outside are a patio and floodlit petanque pitch. Dogs are welcome.
⛫Q❀◑🚌(45)♣●P⅃

Trevaunance Cove

Driftwood Spars 🏆 ✔

Quay Road, TR5 0RT (signed from St Agnes Peterville) SW721513
🕐 11-11 (1am Fri & Sat) ☎ (01872) 552428
🌐 driftwoodspars.com
Driftwood Blue Hills Bitter; St Austell Tinners; Sharp's Doom Bar; Skinner's Betty Stogs; guest beers Ⓗ
Cornwall CAMRA Pub of the Year 2009, this outstanding coastal free house is popular and vibrant. The nautical-themed interior of the historic granite building accommodates three bars, a sea view dining room and sun terrace. Up to seven varying local beers are on offer, and annual beer festivals are held in March and May. Quality meals using local produce are served, and entertainment includes live music and occasional live theatre. Outside there are two separate beer gardens.
⛫Q❀🛏◑⊟♿⛺🚌(85,315)●P⅃

Trewellard

Trewellard Arms

Trewellard Road, TR19 7TA (on B3318/B3306 jct) SW377338
🕐 12-11 (midnight Sat & Sun) ☎ (01736) 788634
Sharp's Doom Bar; Skinner's Betty Stogs; guest beers Ⓗ
Thriving, welcoming, family-run free house, near Geevor Mine, family-friendly and popular with locals and tourists alike. Formerly the mine owner's house, the cosy interior accommodates a large open-beamed single bar, pleasant restaurant and cellar seating area. Comfortably furnished throughout, it generates a homely atmosphere, open fires adding to the warmth. Two guest ales, up to four in summer, are served on an ever-changing beer menu. Good value home-cooked food is also offered. Outside are a patio beer garden and ample parking. Regular buses pass by.
⛫Q❀🛏◑⛺🚌(17A,507)P⅃

Truro

City Inn ✔

Pydar Street, TR1 3SP (N side of city centre, through railway arch) SW822452
🕐 12-11.30; 11-12.30am Sat ☎ (01872) 272623
Courage Best Bitter; Sharp's Doom Bar; Skinner's Betty Stogs; guest beers Ⓗ
Close to the city centre, near the railway viaduct, this community-focused two-bar pub has the feel of a village local. The interior has a comfortable lounge with several drinking areas and is decorated with an impressive collection of water jugs; the more functional back bar is sports-oriented. Up to four guest beers change regularly, and good pub grub is available. The beer garden is an excellent sun trap in summer. Regular charity events include the annual conker championships. A beer festival is held at Easter. ⛫Q❀🛏◑⊟⇌🚌⅃

White Hart (Crab & Ale House) ✔

25 New Bridge Street, TR1 2AA
🕐 11-11 (1am Fri & Sat); 12-10.30 Sun ☎ (01872) 277294
Greene King IPA, Old Speckled Hen; St Austell Tribute; Sharp's Doom Bar; guest beer Ⓗ
Opened originally as the White Hart in 1802, this hostelry is now known as the Crab & Ale House. It is one of the few remaining pubs close to the main shopping area of the city – many have been converted into shops. A comfortable town pub,

popular with the locals, it is decorated with nautical bric-a-brac. The guest ale changes weekly and is often Cornish. Bar meals are available 12-2.30pm daily. The bus station is nearby.

Tywardreath

New Inn

Fore Street, PL24 2QP SX086543
12-11 (01726) 813901
Draught Bass G; St Austell Tinners, Tribute, Proper Job H, seasonal beer G
Built in 1752 by local mine owners, this classic local is the hub of village life. Many functions are held in its large, secluded garden, with electronic amusements confined to the back room. Good conversation is the entertainment here, except on Cornish song nights. It sells the only gravity-dispensed Bass that remains in the St Austell estate and always offers a brewery seasonal beer. Look out for the brass token slot on the bar once used by miners. Bus services pass the door.
Q (Par) (25,524) P

Vogue

Star Inn

TR16 5NP SW724424
12-midnight (1am Fri & Sat); 12-11 Sun
(01209) 820242 starinnvogue.biz
Draught Bass G; Skinner's Betty Stogs; guest beers H
Plenty of local character is to be found in this old mining village inn, especially popular with sports enthusiasts. Converted cottages provide a multi-roomed interior for either quiet dining (Sunday lunch a speciality) or livelier drinking activities – big-screen sports, live music, quizzes, karaoke and pool. Outside, a boules pitch is frequently in use. Live entertainment is hosted at weekends. The Skinner's beer is varied, while other Cornish micros are well-represented. A beer festival – Bash Out The Back – is staged every St Day Feast in June.
(47) P

Wendron

New Inn

TR13 0EA (on B3297 Helston-Redruth road) SW310678
12-3, 6-11; 12-3, 7-10.30 Sun (01326) 572683
Beer range varies H
A welcoming and cosy village pub with a bar on the left of the entrance and dining room on the right, accessed from the main door or through the bar. The character has changed little over the years, with an interesting carving of the Four Horsemen of the Apocalypse above the fire. Three to four real ales are available and a 'Malt of the Moment' at a special price. Good food from an attractive specials menu is cooked by the landlady and her daughter.
(34,82A) P

Zelah

Hawkins Arms

High Road, TR4 9HU (off A30)
11.30-3, 6-11; 12-3, 6-10.30 Sun (01872) 540339
Beer range varies H
Easy to find off the A30 (follow the brown signs), this traditional village free house offers a friendly welcome to locals and visitors alike. Exposed stone walls, wood furnishings and an open fire in winter create a cosy ambience, and there are plenty of quiet, partitioned nooks and crannies in which to enjoy a beer. Excellent home-cooked meals promote local produce, with home-made pies a speciality. The beers are mainly from Cornish breweries. Daytime Newquay-Truro buses stop close by. Q (585,586) P

Zennor

Tinners Arms

TR26 3BY (off B3306 north coast road) SW454385
11.30 (11 Sat)-11 summer; 11.30-3, 6.30-11 winter; 11-11 Sat; 12-10.30 Sun (01736) 796927 tinnersarms.com
St Austell Tinners; Sharp's Own H
Reputedly dating from 1217, this ancient granite village pub stands near the windswept northern cliffs and granite moors of the Penwith peninsula. It is popular with walkers and tourists drawn by the local mermaid legend – hence the house beer, Zennor Mermaid, brewed by Sharp's. Families and dogs are welcome. The cosy, homely single bar interior with separate dining room exudes a timeless atmosphere. Quality food is served, but availability in winter varies – phone first. For fair-weather drinking the south-facing sheltered garden is perfect. Q (508,300) P

Blisland Inn, Blisland (Photo: Dave Kirkby)

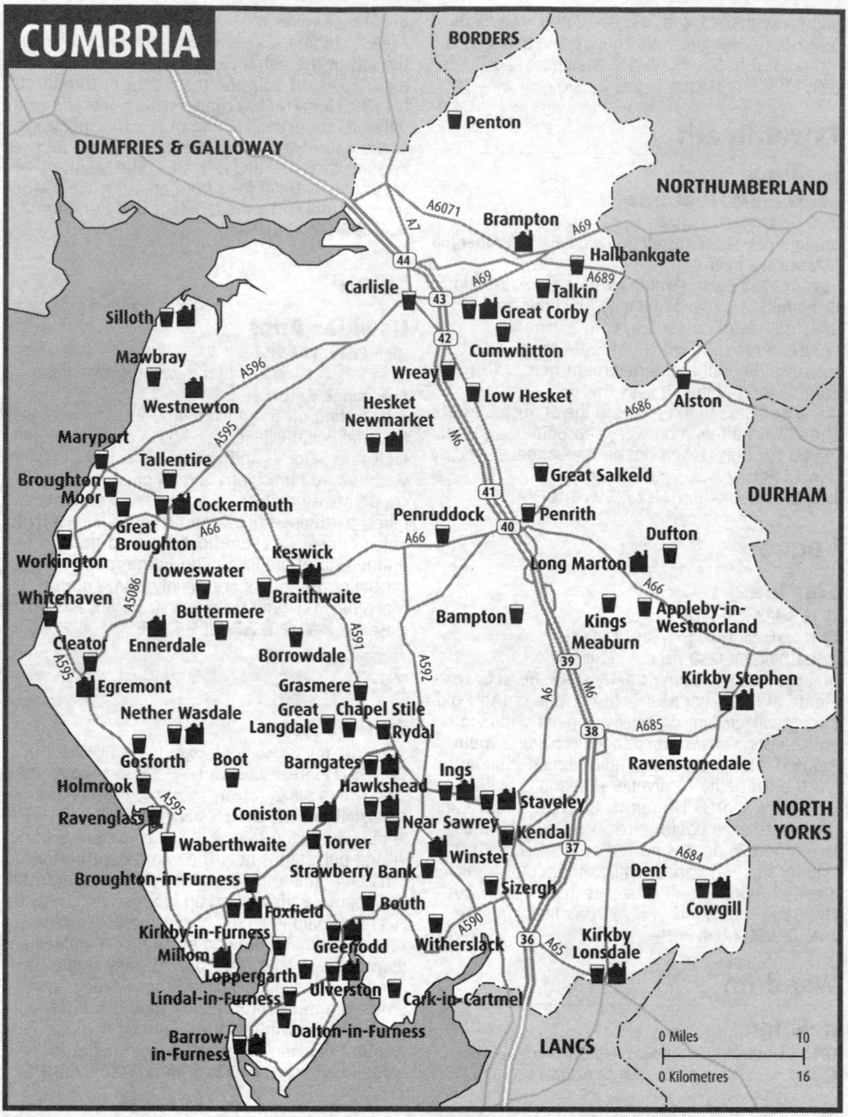

Alston

Cumberland Inn 🏆

Townfoot, CA9 3HX

12-11 ☎ (01434) 381875 alstoncumberlandhotel.co.uk

Yates Bitter; guest beers Ⓗ

Owned by CAMRA members, this family-run 19th-century inn overlooks the South Tyne River. Situated on the Coast-to-Coast cycle route and the Pennine Way, it is an ideal base to explore England's highest market town with its steep cobbled main street, South Tynedale Railway and the North Pennines. At least two Cumbrian beers are on handpump alongside a selection of Northumbrian ales and beers from further afield. Known as Alston's real cider venue, Westons Old Rosie and occasional Cumbrian ciders and perry are stocked. Food is served all day until 9pm. Local CAMRA Pub of the Year 2009 and 2010.
(680) P

Appleby-in-Westmorland

Golden Ball

4 High Wiend, CA16 6RD (off Boroughgate)

11 (12 Sun)-midnight ☎ (01768) 351493

Marston's Burton Bitter; guest beers Ⓗ

A traditional side-street pub which has changed little over recent decades. The simply furnished lounge to the left of the entrance, and the bar to the right with TV and games, are served from a central back-to-back bar counter. As well as a strong local following, the pub also attracts railway buffs using the Settle to Carlisle line. The patio has a large covered area which leads to a garden with a play area. (563)

Bampton

Mardale Inn ✔

CA10 2RQ NY514181

✪ 11-11 (10.30 Sun) ☎ (01931) 713244 🌐 mardaleinn.co.uk
Bampton Emergency; Coniston Bluebird; guest beers Ⓗ
Off the beaten track rustic pub, well situated for exploring the Far Eastern Fells and Haweswater. Underfloor-heated stone flags, an open fire, ceiling beams and agricultural implements make for a cosy bar area. The Bampton beer is brewed elsewhere until the brewery is operational. A reasonable two-course Farmers Meal is available until 5pm. 'Nails' from Austria is an unusual pub game. Dogs welcome in the bar. ♨Q❀⇌◑♣

Barngates

Drunken Duck Inn ✔

LA22 0NG NY351013
✪ 11.30-11 (10.30 Sun) ☎ (01539) 436347
🌐 drunkenduckinn.co.uk
Beer range varies Ⓗ
Home of Barngates Brewery, the Duck always serves four of the 10 beers brewed here and brewery tours can be arranged. The bar has been extensively renovated to create a pleasing mix of local and modern styles. Lunchtime bar meals and the a la carte menu available in the dining room in the evening are of an exceptionally high standard. The outside seating area at the front offers magnificent views of the fells to the north east.
♨Q❀⇌◑Ⲁ●P⁄–

Barrow-in-Furness

Cross Keys Hotel

Preston Street, LA14 1JZ (next to back door of Debenhams)
✪ 11-1.30am; 12-1am Sun ☎ (01229) 828447
Barngates Tag Lag; Marston's Pedigree; Theakston Best Bitter; guest beer Ⓗ
Typical back-street boozer with bags of character(s). There is one room with a horseshoe bar and a raised stage in the corner for the four-times-weekly karaoke and live acts. During the day the jukebox belts out classic rock and pop from the past 40 years. Simple sandwiches are available to soak up the very reasonably priced beers. A great place to rest your bones while someone else does the shopping. ⇌⇌▭♣

Duke of Edinburgh Hotel

Abbey Road, LA14 5QR
✪ 11-11.30 (midnight Fri & Sat); 11-11 Sun
☎ (01229) 821039 🌐 thedukehotelandbar.co.uk
Lancaster Amber, Gold, Red, Black; Thwaites Original; guest beers Ⓗ
Situated on the edge of the town centre near the station, the Duke doesn't get as noisy as similar large bars in the town. The bar has an airy feel with modern, comfortable furniture and a fine open fire. Paintings by local artists are displayed around the walls. Good quality, reasonably priced bar meals are available, including pizzas. Beers are mainly from Lancaster (owned by the same company) and Thwaites, with guest ales too.
♨⇌◑♿⇌▭

Boot

Brook House Inn 🏆

CA19 1TG
✪ 11 (12 Sun)-11 ☎ (01946) 723288
🌐 brookhouseinn.co.uk
Hawkshead Bitter; Taylor Landlord; guest beers Ⓗ
Just a step away from the nine-mile Ravenglass & Eskdale steam railway, in a delightful valley with lovely views of surrounding fells, this haven of top-quality food and ale – with up to eight beers and ciders – is owned by a dedicated family group of several generations. They instigated the June Boot Beer Festival, when the valley throngs with good-natured real ale lovers, morris dancers and walkers, enjoying up to 100 beers in Boot's three pubs. Log fires, stained glass, stuffed animals and old gin traps reflect historic country sports and farming. ♨Q♉❀⇌◑Ⲁ⇌(Dalegarth)●P⁄–

Borrowdale

Scafell Hotel

Rosthwaite, CA12 5XB
✪ 11-11; 12-10.30 Sun ☎ (01768) 777208 🌐 scafell.co.uk
Copper Dragon Golden Pippin; Jennings Bitter, Cumberland Ale; Theakston Old Peculier; guest beers Ⓗ
A pleasantly-situated country inn at the heart of one of the Lakes' most famous valleys. The Riverside Bar has a rustic stone-floored interior and a warming real open fire in winter months. In the summer there is the option of going into the delightful beer garden overlooking the river. There are several handpumps along the lengthy bar and plenty of seating for those who would like to dine or simply enjoy good ale in a cosy setting.
♨❀⇌◑Ⲁ▭♣P

Bouth

White Hart ✔

LA12 8JB (off A590, 6 miles NE of Ulverston)
✪ 12-11 (10.30 Sun) ☎ (01229) 861229
🌐 whitehart-lakedistrict.co.uk

INDEPENDENT BREWERIES

Abraham Thompson Barrow-in-Furness
Barngates Barngates
Beckstones Millom
Bitter End Cockermouth
Blackbeck Egremont
Coniston Coniston
Croglin Kirkby Stephen (NEW)
Cumberland Great Corby
Cumbrian Legendary Hawkshead
Dent Cowgill
Derwent Silloth
Foxfield Foxfield
Geltsdale Brampton
Great Gable Egremont
Greenodd Greenodd (NEW)
Hardknott Millom
Hawkshead Staveley
Hesket Newmarket Hesket Newmarket
Jennings (Marston's) Cockermouth
Keswick Keswick
Kirkby Lonsdale Kirkby Lonsdale
Strands Nether Wasdale
Stringers Ulverston
Tirril Long Marton
Ulverston Ulverston
Watermill Ings
Whitehaven Ennerdale
Winster Valley Winster (NEW)
Yates Westnewton

Black Sheep Best Bitter; Coniston Bluebird; Ulverston Another Fine Mess; guest beers ⊞
This 17th-century inn has everything you would expect from an old hostelry. Old farming and hunting implements adorn the walls, with horse brasses and hops on exposed beams. The slate-flagged floor and wood burning stove add to a welcoming atmosphere. The food is of a high standard, using locally-sourced ingredients, and can be eaten in the bar, upstairs dining area or on the terrace – the latter two giving splendid views of the sun setting behind Colton Fell. ⛫❀⇌◐◑P⊱⊟

Braithwaite

Middle Ruddings Country Inn

CA12 5RY (just off A66 at Braithwaite)
✪ 12-11 ☎ (01768) 778436 ⊕ middle-ruddings.co.uk
Beer range varies ⊞
This inn boasts three real ales and a draught cider. The landlord, who has a passion for real ale, sells only Cumbrian-brewed beers. He has hosted two well-attended Ale Lovers Dinners on behalf of Cumbrian CAMRA branches. There are two dining rooms and a bar sitting area which has a real fire. Locally-sourced produce is served. Close to the A66 just north of the main turning for Braithwaite village, there are great views across to the Skiddaw Massif. ⛫Q♉❀⇌◐◑⛺⊟(X5,74,74A)P⊱

Broughton Moor

Miners Arms

CA15 7RY
✪ 5-11; 12-midnight Sat & Sun ☎ (01900) 812760
Jennings Dark Mild, Bitter; Whitehaven Ennerdale Blonde, Darkest Ennerdale; guest beers ⊞
This pit pub stands at the crossroads of a former mining village – hence the name. Popular for functions, it also offers themed evening meals, quizzes, large TV screens and live entertainment. Although a free house, the licensees are supporters of Cumbrian micros and organise an annual beer festival in May. The regulars enjoy the local Jennings Bitter (and Dark Mild, a rare find and a gem) and the licensees organise trips to the brewery in Cockermouth to convert them off the lager! ⛫◑♿⊟(35)P

Broughton-in-Furness

Manor Arms

The Square, LA20 6HY
✪ 12-11.30 (midnight Fri & Sat); 12-11 Sun
☎ (01229) 716286 ⊕ manorarmsthesquare.co.uk
Copper Dragon Golden Pippin; Yates Bitter; guest beers ⊞
This outstanding pub, where the Varty family has celebrated over 20 years of ownership, flies the flag for real ale in this popular Cumbrian village. Winner of numerous CAMRA awards, it has made it to the latter stages of National Pub of the Year three times. The beer range promotes independent breweries and the eight handpumps are in themselves a mini beer festival. If you want to try real ale, this is the place. ⛫Q⇌⊟(X7,511)♣●⊟

Buttermere

Fish Hotel

CA13 9XA (9 miles SE of Cockermouth on B5289)
✪ 10.30-3, 6-11; 11-11 Sat & Sun; closed Jan
☎ (01768) 770287 ⊕ fish-hotel.co.uk
Jennings Bitter; guest beers ⊞
Run by the same family for 40 years, the Fish is situated between Buttermere and Crummock Water in the centre of the village. The hotel welcomes walkers. Good value bar meals are served in a family-friendly atmosphere along with six real ales from Lakeland breweries – including offerings from Keswick and Hesket Newmarket. A terrace outside provides good views of the local fells. Check opening hours out of season.
Q❀⇌◐◑⛺⊟(77,77A)♣P

Cark-in-Cartmel

Engine Inn

LA11 7NZ (3 miles W of Grange-over-Sands)
✪ 11.30 (12 Sun)-1.30am ☎ (01539) 558341
⊕ engineinn.co.uk
Beer range varies ⊞
Seventeenth-century family-run traditional inn, which took its name from the steam engines that used to service the local mills in Cark. Multi-roomed, it has a games room and restaurant area. Five en-suite letting rooms get booked very early for Cartmel Races and events at nearby Holker Hall. An extensive menu uses the finest locally sourced and produced ingredients. Beers from the Punch Taverns list are supplemented by one local brew. Will close earlier if quiet. Handy for the railway station. ⛫Q♉❀⇌◐◑⊟♿⛺⇌⊟(532)♣P⊱

Carlisle

Griffin ✔

Court Square, CA1 1QX (next to train station)
✪ 9-11 (midnight Fri & Sat); 10-midnight Sun
☎ (01228) 598941
Keswick Thirst Ascent; guest beers ⊞
This former Midland Bank building has been transformed by the John Barras chain into a two-storey pub. Several large screens show different sports for all tastes. Guest beers rotate on four handpumps. A separate area is available for private functions. Meals are served all day but no children are allowed. Situated next to the railway station, it's handy for travellers waiting for trains. It's used as an away supporters' pub when Carlisle United play at home. ◐◑♿⇌⊟⊱

Howard Arms

107 Lowther Street, CA3 8ED
✪ 11-midnight (1am Fri & Sat); 12-10.30 Sun
☎ (01228) 532926
Caledonian Deuchars IPA; Theakston Bitter; guest beers ⊞
A beautiful original tiled exterior from pre-State Management time welcomes visitors to this stalwart of the Guide. The landlord was awarded a certificate in recognition of 25 years of devotion to real ale by the local branch (no keg here). A collection of divided rooms surrounds the horseshoe-shaped bar. Pictures of the acts that performed at the now sadly demolished theatre opposite are a reminder of bygone years.
Q❀◐♿⇌⊟⊱

King's Head

Fisher Street, CA3 8RF (behind old town hall)
✪ 10-11 (midnight Fri); 11-midnight Sat; 12-11 Sun
☎ (01228) 533797 ⊕ kingsheadcarlisle.co.uk

Yates Bitter; guest beers Ⓗ
This CAMRA multi-award winning pub is one of the oldest in Carlisle. Pictures of old Carlisle adorn the walls inside, and outside is an explanation of why Carlisle is not in the Domesday Book. The Lanes shopping centre, castle and cathedral are nearby. Good value meals are served at lunchtime. Take-away beer cartons are available to enjoy later. The covered smoking area to the back has a large TV and barbecue for parties. No children allowed.
❀◐⇌🚌♣⚡

Linton Holme

82 Lindisfarne Street, CA1 2NB
✪ 5 (4 Fri; 12 Sat)-11; 12-10.30 Sun ☎ (01228) 532637
Yates Bitter; guest beer Ⓗ
Former hotel retaining many original features including tiled mosaic floors, etched windows and a wonderful marble pillar outside. Situated in a quiet residential area, it is well worth making the effort to seek out. Inside, a variety of rooms all open out to a bar area where there is a large pool table suitable for use by wheelchair users. The guest ale is frequently from a micro-brewery. TVs show sporting events, and regular darts, pool and quiz nights are held. Local CAMRA award winner.
⛼❀🚌(76)♣⚡

Spinners Arms

Cummersdale Road, Cummersdale, CA2 6BD (1 mile W of Carlisle off B5299)
✪ 6 (12 Sat & Sun)-midnight ☎ (01228) 532928
Ennerdale Blonde; guest beer Ⓗ
Refurbished and cosy family-friendly Redfern hostelry with unique animal-decorated gutters and a welcoming real fire. The pub is situated at the heart of the village, which is less than half a mile from the city of Carlisle's south western boundary. It is close to the Cumbrian Way and National Cycle Route 7 which run alongside the River Caldew. The landlord and locals ensure there is a good variety of guest ales mostly from local Cumbrian micro-breweries. Well-behaved dogs are welcome.
⛼❀♿🚌(75)♣⚡

Woodrow Wilson ✔

48 Botchergate, CA1 1QS
✪ 9am-midnight (12.30am Fri & Sat) ☎ (01228) 819942
Greene King Abbot; Marston's Pedigree; guest beers Ⓗ
Wetherspoon pub in a former Co-op building, offering the largest range of real ales in Carlisle and a regular outlet for local beers including Geltsdale and Derwent. Food is available all day till 10pm. At the rear there is a spacious heated patio for smokers. Children are welcome in some areas until 9pm. It's five minutes walk from the railway station and city centre. Q❀◐◑♿⇌🚌🍎P⚡

Chapel Stile

Wainwrights Inn ✔

LA22 9JH (on B5343 from Skelwith Bridge)
✪ 11.30 (12 Sun)-11 ☎ (01539) 438088 🌐 langdale.co.uk/dine/wainwrights
Banks's Original; Jennings Cumberland Ale, Sneck Lifter; guest beers Ⓗ
Built as a farmhouse, subsequently converted to the manager's house for the former gunpowder works (see wall-mounted display cabinet at the far end of the bar), this is now a well-regarded pub in the Langdale Valley. Three beers from the Marston's ranges are complemented by four changing guests, mainly sourced from smaller northern breweries. Dogs are welcome in the part-flagged, part-carpeted bar area. The separate dining area offers a good choice of meals.
⛼❀◐◑♿⛺🚌(516)P

Cleator

Brook

Trumpet Terrace, CA23 3DX (on A5086 between Cleator Moor and Egremont) NY021140
✪ 11-midnight (1am Fri & Sat) ☎ (01946) 811635
Taylor Landlord; Yates Golden Ale; guest beers Ⓗ
A popular community pub with a well-earned reputation for its cask ale, excellent food and welcoming candlelit atmosphere. Two frequently changing guest ales, sometimes from Salopian and Scottish breweries, complement the regular beers. Well worth a detour for walkers and cyclists on the Coast to Coast routes, live music and birthday parties can make the pub lively in the evenings but a quiet pint can be enjoyed during the day. Local CAMRA Pub of the Year runner-up in 2009.
⛼Q◐◑🚌(22)♣🍎⚡

Cockermouth

Swan

55 Kirkgate, CA13 9PH
✪ 6-11.30 (midnight Fri); 11-midnight Sat; 12-11 Sun
☎ (01900) 822425
Jennings Dark Mild, Bitter, Cumberland Ale Ⓗ
One of the oldest pubs in Cockermouth, situated on a cobbled Georgian square, this friendly pub has stone-flagged floors, low beams and, like the landlady, plenty of character. A 'talkers' pub – you'll always find someone to have a conversation with, plus there's no music or jukebox – it hosts quizzes and various community events. You can be sure of an excellent pint of Jennings Dark Mild here – a rare treat as it's hard to find in most Jennings pubs.
⛼Q♣

Coniston

Black Bull Inn ✔

Yewdale Road, LA21 8DU
✪ 11-11 (10.30 Sun) ☎ (01539) 441335
🌐 conistonbrewery.com
Coniston Olivers Light Ale, Bluebird Bitter, Bluebird XB, Oldman Ale, Special Oatmeal Stout, Blacksmiths Ale Ⓗ
This 16th-century coaching inn serves good food in traditional and comfortable surroundings and is the tap house for the on-site Coniston Brewing Company: an obvious place to sample its wares. Large and spacious, the bar and lounge, with beamed ceilings and tasteful decor, are always popular with tourists. The outside seating area is perfect for the summer months. Winner of numerous awards and accolades, this family-run pub is situated in the centre of the village.
⛼Q🏠❀🛏◐◑⛺🚌(X12,505)🍎P⚡

Sun Hotel

LA21 8HQ
✪ 12-11.30 ☎ (01539) 441248 🌐 thesunconiston.com
Coniston Bluebird; Copper Dragon Golden Pippin; Hawkshead Bitter; guest beers Ⓗ
Take the Walna Scar road up from Coniston village, or down from Coniston Old Man to visit this 16th-century pub and hotel. The recently refurbished

dual level bar area has atmosphere and character, with slate flooring and abundant exposed beams. The Brathay-slate topped bar, offering up to eight cask ales, is complemented by a large open fire range, especially welcome in winter. Quality dining facilities, conservatory and delightful views from the terrace complete the picture.
♔Q❀⇄◑⛺⊟(X12,505)P⚡–

Cowgill

Sportsman's Inn

LA10 5RG (off B6255 towards Dent) SD 767864
✪ 12-3 (not Mon), 7-11 ☎ (01539) 625282
Beer range varies Ⓗ
A fine example of a rural local at the heart of its community. The beer range, extended in summer, always includes one from the Dent range. Run by the same family for 22 years, it welcomes both locals and visitors who are often enjoying the great surrounding walking country. The Dales Way and Arten Gill viaduct are nearby and Dent station on the Settle to Carlisle line is up a steep climb about one mile distant. Notices advertising themed seasonal events are displayed. The local bus runs on Wednesday and Saturday.
♔Q❀⇄◑♿⛺⊟(564)♣P⚡–

Cumwhitton

Pheasant Inn ✔

CA8 9EX (4 miles SE of A69 at Warwick Bridge)
✪ closed Mon; 6-11 (midnight Sat); 6-10.30 Sun
☎ (01228) 560102
Geltsdale Pheasant Ale; guest beers Ⓗ
Formerly known as the Red Lion, the Pheasant was taken over in 2005 by a mother and daughter team and their infectious enthusiasm has turned it into one of the most popular pubs in the wider area. It's twice recent winner of the local CAMRA Pub of the Year. Excellent food is available in both the dining room and the bar where a flagged floor, exposed beams and a roaring fire in winter add to the atmosphere. ♔❀⇄◑⛺♣P

Dalton-in-Furness

Black Dog Inn 🏆

Holmes Green, Broughton Road, LA15 8JP (follow signs to South Lakes Animal Park from Dalton. Carry on for a further mile) SD233761
✪ closed Mon & Tue; 12-11; 12-10.30 Sun ☎ (01229) 462561
Beer range varies Ⓗ
A quiet unassuming country pub that's just a 20-minute walk from Dalton town centre. It hosts regular beer festivals throughout the year and serves up to six beers between times. In essence it's a one-roomed pub, with quarry tiled floor, beams and two real fires. The 'snug' in front of the bar provides a focal point for the locals, and visitors will invariably be drawn into the conversation. The pub is popular with diners as well as drinkers.
♔Q❀⇄◑P⚡–

Brown Cow

Goose Green, LA15 8LQ (just off A590)
✪ 11.30-midnight ☎ (01229) 462553
🌐 browncowinndalton.co.uk
Beer range varies Ⓗ
A warm and friendly atmosphere greets visitors to this 400-year-old coaching house which has retained many original features including beams, brasses, local prints and an open fire. A winner of many awards for its five real ales, the pub also serves excellent food from a full and varied menu. Meals can be enjoyed in the large dining room or on warmer days on the charming patio with heating and lighting. Well worth a visit.
♔Q❀⇄◑≹⊟P⚡–

Dent

George & Dragon ✔

Main Street, LA10 5QL
✪ 11-midnight ☎ (01539) 625256
🌐 thegeorgeanddragondent.co.uk
Beer range varies Ⓗ
The Dent Brewery tap showcases its own beers alongside guest ales. Set in the cobbled main street of this attractive village, it is a friendly two-bar local welcoming walkers, cyclists and dogs. Extensive mahogany panelling is adorned with brewery memorabilia and award certificates for both the pub and brewery. A games room with pool table is off the front bar and a large restaurant offering a good variety of meals is down a flight of stairs. Served by the local bus on Wednesday and Saturday. ♔Q♨❀⇄◑⊞⛺⊟(564)♣●P

Dufton

Stag Inn

CA16 6DB (3 miles NE of Appleby-in-Westmorland) NY689253
✪ 12-3 (not Mon), 6-11: 12-midnight Sat; 12-10.30 Sun
☎ (01768) 351608 🌐 thestagdufton.co.uk
Black Sheep Best Bitter; Hawkshead Bitter; guest beers Ⓗ
A genuine local beside the village green, the front door (which opens outwards) is approached across a paved patio. The bar has an operational kitchen range and a dining area. The rear lounge gives access to the garden and impressive fell views. Good value meals using local produce are served. A local beer festival is held in August. It's set in a good walking area, with the Pennine Way passing close by. ♔Q❀⇄◑⛺♣P⚡–

Foxfield

Prince of Wales

LA20 6BX (opp station)
✪ closed Mon & Tue; 2.45 (12 Fri & Sat)-11; 12-10.30 Sun
☎ (01229) 716238 🌐 princeofwalesfoxfield.co.uk
Beer range varies Ⓗ
This gem of a pub is testament to what can be achieved through passion and hard work. It has been newly extended without losing any of its charm, and in winter its two fires give a homely feel. The guest beers come from the pub's two house breweries – Foxfield and Tigertops – and breweries throughout the country. Beers will always include a mild. Frequent beer festivals throughout the year are an added bonus. A discount on B&B is offered to CAMRA members. Bus and rail stops outside.
♔Q❀⇄♿≹⊟(X7,511)♣●P⚡–🥛

Gosforth

Gosforth Hall Inn

CA20 1AZ (from A595 follow road signed Wasdale. Turn left at church) NY073036

3 (12 Fri-Sun)-midnight ☎ (01946) 725322
gosforthhallinn.co.uk
Yates Golden Ales; guest beers Ⓗ
Grade II-listed former 17th-century fortified farmhouse with priest hole and England's widest-spanning sandstone hearth. The adjacent St Mary's Church has a famous 15ft Viking cross. This dog-friendly pub has a boules pitch, large landscaped garden and hosts occasional medieval-themed evenings. Meals – including speciality home-made pies – are served weekend lunchtimes and every evening. Two interesting guest beers often come from Yates, Hawkshead and Keswick breweries.
Q♣P

Grasmere

Dale Lodge Hotel (Tweedies Bar) ✔

Langdale Road, LA22 9SW
12-11 (midnight Thu-Sun) ☎ (01539) 435300
dalelodgehotel.co.uk
Theakston Old Peculier; guest beers Ⓗ
The bar area has been enlarged by moving the bar counter back to include a former games room. The excellent choice of changing beers remains, and the wood burning winter stove still manages to keep drinkers warm. Above-average meals are served in both the bar and the slightly more formal adjoining dining room. The large lawned grounds have ample seating. The Grasmere Guzzler beer festival, including a hog roast, is held each September. Open top buses (599) run from Easter to October. (555,599)♣P

Great Broughton

Punchbowl Inn

19 Main Street, CA13 0YJ
12-4 (Fri & Sat), 7-11; 12-3, 7-11 Sun ☎ (01900) 824708
Jennings Bitter; guest beers Ⓗ
Built in the 17th century, this traditional village pub has beams, open fires and is full of character. Two well-kept ales include Jennings and a guest from anywhere in Britain, changing regularly. Winner of local CAMRA Pub of the Season Autumn 2009. The landlord is a keen supporter of local charities. The pub boasts a large collection of water jugs suspended from the ceiling above the bar.
Q(58)♣

Great Corby

Queen Inn

CA4 8LR (1 mile off A69 at Warwick Bridge)
closed Tue; 12-2 (Mon, Wed & Thu summer only), 5.30-11 (midnight Fri & Sat) ☎ (01228) 562088
thequeeninngreatcorby.co.uk
Cumberland Corby Bitter; guest beers Ⓗ
Situated at the heart of a picturesque village, this friendly pub is a true supporter of locally-brewed ales. Two pumps serve real ale from a range of local micro-breweries including the Cumberland Brewery just across the green. There is a spacious bar area with floor tiles, beams and open log fires at either end, plus an adjacent family room. Lunchtime and evening meals served in the bar and restaurant are made with best quality local produce. Regular speciality food events and seasonal mini beer festivals are hosted.
Q(Wetheral)♣P

Great Langdale

Old Dungeon Ghyll Hotel

LA22 9JY (over bridge at end of B5343)
11-11 (10.30 Sun) ☎ (01539) 437272 odg.co.uk
Black Sheep Best Bitter, Ale; Jennings Cumberland Ale; Theakston XB, Old Peculier; Yates Bitter; guest beers Ⓗ
The surrounding high fells make it difficult to imagine a more appropriate location for this bar. It specialises in the needs of serious rock climbers and walkers, thus wet clothing and muddy boots cause no distress to the hard bench seating or flooring. A fine range of beers is supplemented with hearty home-made pub grub. The paved patio area has uninterrupted mountain views. The bus along the Langdale Valley to Ambleside stops across the bridge at the end of the approach road.
Q(516)P

Great Salkeld

Highland Drove

CA11 9NA (off B6412 between A686 and Lazonby)
12-3 (not Mon), 6-midnight; 12-midnight Sat & Sun
☎ (01768) 898349 highland-drove.co.uk
John Smith's Bitter; Theakston Black Bull Bitter; guest beer Ⓗ
Carefully refurbished after the owners rescued it from oblivion some years ago, the meticulous attention to detail has transformed it into a popular hostelry. There is an award-winning upstairs restaurant known as Kyloes, a comfortable lounge offering a varying food selection, and a games room. The pub name derives from its location on an old cattle driving route from central Scotland to the markets in England. ♣P

Greenodd

Ship Inn

Main Street, LA12 7QZ
closed Mon; 6-11.30; 5-midnight Fri; 12-12.30am Sat; 12-10.30 Sun ☎ (07782) 655294
Lancaster Amber; guest beers Ⓗ
Traditional village pub, blending the old and the new. Beamed ceilings contrast with leather suites, and real fires enhance the ambience of the relaxing lounge and bar areas. A separate games room houses a pool table, dartboard and jukebox. Guest beers often come from local breweries. There is usually a good selection of cider and perry available. Phone to check food times. ♣P

Hallbankgate

Belted Will

CA8 2NJ (on A689 Alston road 4 miles E of Brampton)
12-2 (summer only), 5-midnight; 12-midnight Sat & Sun
☎ (01697) 746236 beltedwill.co.uk
Jennings Cumberland Ale; guest beers Ⓗ
Popular pub with three real ales on offer – at least one from a local brewery. Lunchtime meals are served weekends all year round and all week in summer. Located at the foot of the Northern Pennines, this is an ideal base for fans of all outdoor pursuits including walking and hiking, mountain biking and cycling, fishing, golfing, bird watching and pony trekking. The pub's unusual name refers to William Howard of nearby Naworth Castle whose nickname was mentioned in a poem by Sir Walter Scott. (680)♣

Hawkshead

King's Arms Hotel

The Square, LA22 0NZ

☼ 11-midnight ☎ (01539) 436372

⊕ kingsarmshawkshead.co.uk

Coniston Oldman Ale; Hawkshead Bitter; guest beers Ⓗ

This often-busy 500-year-old inn has an open fire and traditional beamed ceilings, one of which is held up by a hand-carved bearded king. A spacious dining room ensures that diners can usually find a table if the bar area is busy. On sunny days you can sit outside in the beer garden overlooking the village square. Guest beers are usually from local breweries. Good dogs and children are welcome. ⌂❀⇌◑⛺▣(505)♣

Hesket Newmarket

Old Crown ✔

Main Street, CA7 8JG

☼ 12-3 Fri-Sun only, 5.30-11 (10.30 Sun) ☎ (01697) 478288

⊕ theoldcrownpub.co.uk

Hesket Newmarket Great Cockup Porter, Blencathra Bitter, Skiddaw Special Bitter, Hellvellyn Gold, Doris's 90th Birthday Ale, Old Carrock Strong Ale Ⓗ

On the edge of the northern Lakeland fells, this pub is at the centre of village life. It is owned as a co-operative by the local community, who are dedicated to maintaining its original character. It offers the full range of Hesket Newmarket beers from the brewery located at the rear of the pub. Brewery tours are usually followed by samples, and a meal can be arranged by contacting the pub. A firm favourite of Prince Charles and Sir Chris Bonington, the hostelry is popular with visitors and locals. ⌂Q❀◑⊟⛺♣⁵–

Holmrook

Bridge Inn ✔

Santon Bridge, CA19 1UX (3 miles E of A595 at Holmrook) NY110016

☼ 11-midnight ☎ (01946) 726221 ⊕ santonbridgeinn.com

Jennings Bitter, Cumberland Ale, Cocker Hoop, Sneck Lifter; guest beers Ⓗ

Once a modest mail coach halt, now an award-winning country inn with creaking floors, low beams and warming fires. A comprehensive range of Jenning's beers and home-cooked food makes this a pub not to be missed. Guest beers come from the Marston's range. In summer relax outside by the river and take in the lovely mountain views. The pub hosts the immensely popular 'World's Biggest Liar' competition in November. ⌂Q☋❀⇌◑♿⛺♣P⁵–

Ings

Watermill Inn

LA8 9PY (turn off A591 by church)

☼ 12-11 (10.30 Sun) ☎ (01539) 821309

⊕ lakelandpub.co.uk

Coniston Bluebird; Hawkshead Bitter; Theakston Old Peculier; guest beers Ⓗ

The inn has deservedly won many awards during its 20-year history as a friendly, family-owned pub and brewery where the accent has always been on the range and quality of real ale and the ability to hold a conversation thanks to the absence of piped sound, TV, fruit machines or pool. Two bars, though separate, are served from a central counter. Viewing windows permit examination of both the cellar and brewery. A wide selection of meals is served every day until 9pm and dogs are provided with water and biscuits. ⌂Q❀⇌◑♿▣(555)♣●P⁵–⊓

Kendal

Alexanders

Castle Green Lane, LA9 6RG

☼ 12-11 ☎ (01539) 797017 ⊕ castlegreenhotel.co.uk

Beer range varies Ⓗ

Set in the grounds of the Castle Green Hotel (a former electricity board regional headquarters), Alexanders occupies an older barn/stable block and, as a free house, offers up to three ever-changing mainly north western beers. A large conservatory provides comfortable seating, dining facilities and fine views over the extensive pub and hotel grounds, Kendal castle ruins and the distant fells. Q❀⇌◑♿⇌♣P⁵–

Burgundy's Wine Bar

19 Lowther Street, LA9 4DH

☼ closed Mon; 11.30-3.30 (not Tue & Wed), 6.30-midnight; 11-midnight Sat; 7-11 Sun ☎ (01539) 733803

⊕ burgundyswinebar.co.uk

Beer range varies Ⓗ

Multi-level, town-centre bar with plans for expansion. It offers a fine selection of real ales – including Yates – in top condition, as well as an above-average range of continental lagers both draught and bottled. The street level bar area has bench seating, upstairs is a mezzanine floor with tables and chairs and access to a patio, downstairs is another room with access to the rear alleyway. The Cumbria Beer Challenge is hosted here prior to Easter each year. ❀⇌▣(41,555)●⁵–

Castle Inn

Castle Street, LA9 7AA

☼ 11.30-midnight (1am Sat); 12-11.30 Sun

☎ (01539) 729983

Black Sheep Best Bitter; Jennings Bitter; guest beers Ⓗ

Traditional two-room community local. A lounge to the left is served from a central counter and has a fish tank set into the wall. A larger bar to the right has TV and a framed former Duttons Brewery window pane. An adjoining games room up a step has pool and darts. Good value, promptly-served lunchtime meals are popular, especially when time is limited. The ruins of Kendal Castle are a short walk away. ❀◖⇌▣(42,43)♣⁵–

Miles Thompson ✔

Allhallows Lane, LA9 4JH

☼ 9-11 (midnight Fri & Sat) ☎ (01539) 815710

Coniston Bluebird Bitter; Greene King Ruddles Best Bitter, Abbot; guest beers Ⓗ

Originally a snuff factory, then a public baths/swimming pool, more recently local council offices and now a town centre Wetherspoon pub. Drinking and dining areas are spread over several levels; the upper space retains the original roof timbers and has wall-mounted prints of old Kendal. The venue is popular with early morning breakfasters and drinkers attracted by the range of ales, ciders and keen prices. Can be busy at peak times of an evening. ⌂Q☋❀◑♿⇌▣(44,48)●P⁵–

ENGLAND

Keswick

Dog & Gun ✔
2 Lake Road, CA12 5BT (off Market Place)
⌚ 12-11 ☎ (01768) 773463
Theakston Old Peculier; guest beers ⊞
Busy town-centre pub with a changing selection of six real ales, five of which come from Cumbrian breweries, always including two from the nearby Keswick Brewing Company. The pub retains much of its original character with stone floors, a low ceiling and the remains of a stone spiral staircase. Climbing memorabilia adorns the walls and the pub supports the Keswick Mountain Rescue Team. Bar meals are served all day until 9pm; well-behaved dogs welcome. ♛◑▲🚌(X4,X5,73)

Kings Meaburn

White Horse 🏆 ✔
CA10 3BU NY620211
⌚ 7 (6 Thu & Fri)-11; 12-2, 6-2am Sat; 12-midnight Sun
☎ (01931) 714256
Beer range varies ⊞
This cosy, single room local is the focal point of social life for residents of the village and the surrounding farming community. The ever-changing beers are often collected by the owner from breweries near and far. The Eden Valley beer festival is held under canvas in an adjoining field each July, and an in-house festival is hosted in March. Food is locally sourced wherever possible. Hours may extend in summer. ♛Q❀◑♿♣●P⚟

Kirkby Lonsdale

Orange Tree ✔
9 Fairbank, LA6 2BD
⌚ 12-11 (midnight Fri & Sat) ☎ (01524) 271716
⊕ theorangetreehotel.com
Kirkby Lonsdale Ruskin's Bitter, Radical Red, Monumental Blonde, Jubilee Stout; guest beer ⊞
Welcoming, oak-beamed, traditional hostelry at the end of the main street in this historic market town. The family-owned pub is proud to offer beers from its own brewery situated in the former Kirkby Lonsdale railway station goods yard. Hearty meals and themed evenings are a speciality. Note the framed sporting caricatures and other memorabilia that adorn the walls. An excellent base from which to explore the surrounding countryside. ⇔◑▲🚌(567)♣

Kirkby Stephen

Kings Arms Hotel
Market Street, CA17 4QN
⌚ 10 (11 winter)-midnight; 12-midnight Sun
☎ (01768) 371378 ⊕ kingsarmskirkbystephen.co.uk
Dent Aviator; guest beers ⊞
A 17th-century town-centre coaching inn with a bar and adjoining snug to the right and a dining/function room to the left. It is renowned for real ales – including a speciality 'Coast to Coast' from Dent Brewery – locally sourced home-cooked food, friendliness and conversation. The former railway station hosts an annual classic commercial vehicle rally, and the closed line to Warcop is being restored. Dogs welcome. ⇔◑🚌(563,564)♣P⚟

Kirkby-in-Furness

Burlington Inn
Askew Gate Brow, LA17 7TF (on A595) SD230824
⌚ 4-midnight; 2-1am Fri & Sat; 12-midnight Sun
☎ (01229) 889039
Beer range varies ⊞
Busy roadside inn on the crossroads at the centre of the village, named after the slate quarry, situated on the hills above and the reason for the village's existence. Three handpumps dispense a varied selection of ales, often local. Food is served Wednesday to Saturday evenings and Sunday lunchtime only. Several separate drinking areas make this a cosy atmospheric pub. The dining room at the rear has pleasant views over the Duddon Estuary to the fells beyond. No trains on Sunday. ♛☕❀⇔⇌🚌(X7)♣P⚟

Lindal-in-Furness

Railway Inn
London Road, LA12 0LL
⌚ 4 (3 Fri)-midnight; 12-midnight Sat; 12-11 Sun
☎ (01229) 462889
Ulverston Lonesome Pine; guest beers ⊞
A welcoming open-plan single room pub with a beamed ceiling and slate floor. At one end is a comfortable lounge area around the stone feature fireplace and open fire. Adding to the character is a centrally positioned bar made from old church pews, with up to four handpumps on offer. Food is served on candlelit tables Saturday and Sunday lunchtimes and every evening till 9pm – booking is advisable. Visitors are also welcome at the quiz night held every Thursday. ♛❀◑🚌(6,6A)⚟

Loppergarth

Wellington
Main Street, LA12 0JL (1 mile from A590 between Lindal and Pennington) SD260772
⌚ 6-midnight (1am Fri & Sat) ☎ (01229) 582388
Foxfield Dark Mild; guest beers ⊞
Family-run local in a picturesque hamlet. The central bar is surrounded by four distinct drinking areas, with a widescreen TV above a cosy fire. A separate games/family room with a warming stove features pool, darts, fruit machine and books for sale to raise playground funds. The pub hosts gents' and ladies' darts and pool teams, and holds a popular quiz on alternate Saturdays. Four handpumps feature mainly local beers, particularly from Ulverston and Stringers. No food. ♛☕❀♣●

Low Hesket

Rose & Crown
Low Hesket, CA4 0HG (next to A6 in village)
⌚ 6-11; 12-11.30 Sat; 12-10.30 Sun ☎ (01697) 473346
Jennings Dark Mild, Bitter, Cumberland Ale; guest beer ⊞
Eighteenth-century coaching inn with a definite transport feel. On the walls are pictures of various forms of transport and some of the seats are from a vintage bus. The theme continues into the dining room with railway memorabilia and model trains featuring the Royal Scot, which makes occasional journeys above diners' heads. Quiz nights and themed food evenings are sometimes hosted. No food on Monday. Local CAMRA Pub of the Season Winter 2009. ♛Q❀◑♿🚌(104,130,134)♣P⚟

Loweswater

Kirkstile Inn

CA13 0RU (signed off B5289) NY140210
⌚ 10-11 (10.30 Sun) ☎ (01900) 85219 🌐 kirkstile.com
Yates Bitter; guest beers Ⓗ
Award-winning 16th-century Lakeland inn with a spectacular setting between Loweswater and Crummock Water. Low ceilings, stone walls and an open fire add character to this deservedly popular pub, which can be very busy at peak times. It was formerly home to Loweswater Brewery, which has now moved to bigger premises. Now now part of Cumbrian Legendary Ales – expect four ales from the range on draught. Local CAMRA Pub of the Year 2003-2005, 2008 and 2009, it holds a beer festival in spring. ⛰Q🧸❀🛏◑♿P⊡

Maryport

Lifeboat Inn

Shipping Brow, CA15 6AB
⌚ 12-midnight ☎ (01900) 814636
Jennings Bitter, Cocker Hoop; Whitehaven Ennerdale Blonde, Darkest Ennerdale; guest beers Ⓗ
There has been a pub on this site, near the harbour at Maryport, since 1751. Re-opened in 2009 after a period of closure, the Lifeboat's owner wants it to be a Mecca for real ale and has four handpumps serving local beers. It is the venue for the 'Biggest Vegetable in the World' competition. There is a small but comfortable area and bar downstairs, a function room upstairs and 'the best fish and chips in the country'. Meals are home-cooked and popular. ⛰Q❀🛏◑♿▲⇌⊟P

Mawbray

Lowther Arms

CA15 6QT (off B5300, through village for ½ mile)
⌚ 12-midnight (closed 3-5.30 Mon-Thu Jan & Feb)
☎ (01900) 881337 🌐 lowtherarms.co.uk
Beer range varies Ⓗ
Traditional family-oriented 18th-century country pub catering for both holidaymakers and locals. The bar area has a stone floor and open fire. Local brewery Yates usually provides one of the ales dispensed from the two handpumps. There is a caravan park attached to the pub and accommodation is available. The pub holds a beer festival in May and a music festival in August. A fun quiz is held on a Monday evening.
⛰❀◑▲⊟(60)♣P

Near Sawrey

Tower Bank Arms

LA22 0LF (on B5285 6 miles S of Ambleside) SD370956
⌚ 11-11 (closed 2.30-5.30 Mon-Fri winter); 12-10.30 Sun
☎ (01539) 436334 🌐 towerbankarms.co.uk
Hawkshead Bitter; guest beers Ⓗ
All the features of a traditional 17th-century Lakeland inn are to be found here: slate floor, oak beams and a cooking range housing an open fire. Set in a beautiful rural location next to Hill Top, the former home of Beatrix Potter, which is open to the public, it can be very busy at holiday times. Food is served in the bar and restaurant. Beers are sourced locally. Children are welcome, as are dogs, but not in the restaurant. ⛰Q❀🛏◑♣P

Nether Wasdale

Strands

CA20 1ET NY125039
⌚ 12 (4 winter)-11; 12-10.30 Sun ☎ (01946) 726237
🌐 strandshotel.co.uk
Strands Brown Bitter, Errmmm..., Corrsberg; Stands Red Screes; Strands T'Errmmm-inator Ⓗ
One of two excellent pubs in this Lake District National Park hamlet, situated close to England's deepest lake and highest mountain – Wastwater and Scafell Pike – and official favourite view. A great location for ale lovers, walkers and climbers. Two bars have open log fires and there are separate games and dining rooms. The selection of Strands beers is ever changing and there are occasional guest ales. The pub takes pride in its food as well as its beer. Children and dogs are welcome. Local CAMRA Pub of the Year runner-up 2009. ⛰🧸❀🛏◑▲♣P⚟

Penrith

Agricultural Hotel

Castlegate, CA11 7JE
⌚ 11-11; 12-10.30 Sun ☎ (01768) 862622
🌐 the-agricultural-hotel.co.uk
Jennings Bitter, Cumberland Ale, Sneck Lifter; guest beers Ⓗ
The hotel is built from local sandstone and the bar and dining room are open plan with steps from one to the other. There is also a small reception area. The bar itself is a wonderfully made wooden structure, with four handpumps selling Jenning's beers. Food is served in the large dining area as well as the bar at quiet times.
⛰Q❀🛏◑♿⇌⊟♣P⚟

Cross Keys

Carleton, CA11 8TP (E off A66 on A686 towards Alston)
⌚ 12-midnight (11 Sun) ☎ (01768) 865588
Theakston Black Bull Bitter; Tirril 1823; guest beer Ⓗ
Formerly a pub then closed and used as a house for many years, the Cross Keys was converted back to a pub and reopened in late 2008. With a very modern feel, the bar, pool room, darts, dining area and upstairs restaurant are spread over several levels. Food is served all day until 9pm. The LocAle is from the nearby Tirril Brewery. The owners also run Kyloes restaurant at the nearby Highland Drove pub in Great Salkeld. ⛰❀◑⊡♿⊟(888)♣P⚟

Gloucester Arms

Great Dockray, CA11 7DE
⌚ 11-11; 12-10.30 Sun ☎ (01768) 863745
Hawkshead Bitter; guest beers Ⓗ
The oldest pub in Penrith, claiming links as far back as Richard III. It has a separate restaurant offering good home-cooked food and bar meals are also available throughout the pub. The main bar/lounge area has dark wood panels and is made cosy and welcoming with good lighting and a real fire. There is an outdoor heated smoking area to the rear. The main bus station is a short walk away.
⛰❀◑⇌♣⚟

Lowther Arms

3 Queen Street, CA11 7XD
⌚ 11-3, 6-11; 11-midnight Sat; 12-3, 6-10.30 Sun
☎ (01768) 862792
Caledonian Deuchars IPA; Fuller's London Pride; guest beers Ⓗ

Visitors are assured of a warm welcome at this coaching inn next to the A6 in a busy market town. A sympathetic extension has added more space without losing the character of the old building. Drinkers are spoiled for choice with a range of up to six real ales usually available. Good food is served and the pub can get busy at meal times. A past winner of awards from CAMRA and Britain in Bloom. ♔Q◑⇌▭

Penruddock

Herdwick Inn

CA11 0QU

⌚ 12-3, 5.30-11; 12-midnight Sat; 12-10.30 Sun

☎ (01768) 483007 🌐 herdwickinn.com

Jennings Bitter, Cumberland Ale; guest beer Ⓗ

This charming 18th-century pub is named after the hardy breed of Cumbrian sheep. Situated just north of the A66 between Penrith and Keswick, it is all that a traditional village pub should be and more. Original oak beams, open fireplaces and local stone walls add to the character of this local CAMRA award winner. The Herdwick includes a bar, games room, large garden and restaurant with excellent food. Close to the Coast-to-Coast cycle route, the inn has secure cycle storage. Accommodation is recommended. ♔❀⇋◑▲♣P⁄

Penton

Bridge Inn

CA6 5QB NY438764

⌚ 7-11 ☎ (01228) 577041

Marston's Pedigree; guest beers Ⓗ

The closest real ale pub to Scotland in the area, this quiet countryside drinking establishment is spread over three rooms. It is frequented by locals, and has several teams competing in darts and pool leagues. The regulars choose the guest ale from the list provided. Renowned base for fishing on the nearby River Esk. ♔Q❀⇋♣P⁄

Ravenglass

Ratty Arms

CA18 1SN (through main line station or village car park)

⌚ 11-midnight Sat & summer; 11-2.30, 5.30-midnight Mon-Fri winter; 12-10.30 Sun ☎ (01229) 717676

Greene King Ruddles Best Bitter; Jennings Cumberland Ale; Theakston Best Bitter; Yates Bitter Ⓗ

Railway-themed pub, deservedly popular with locals and tourists. It occupies the former station building at the junction of the main line and the 'La'al Ratty'. The narrow gauge steam train runs deep into the striking Upper Eskdale, with more good pubs, high fells and Roman remains to explore. Local attractions are Muncaster Castle, a Roman bathhouse and an impressive estuary rich in wildlife. Two guest beers are offered, usually from Keswick and Whitehaven breweries. Excellent good-value food is served all day.
♔Q❀◑♿▲⇌▭(6)♣P⁄

Ravenstonedale

Black Swan Inn ✔

CA17 4NG (village signed off A685)

⌚ 8.30am-11 (1am Fri & Sat); 11-midnight Sun

☎ (01539) 623204 🌐 blackswanhotel.com

Black Sheep Best Bitter, Ale; John Smith's Bitter; guest beers Ⓗ

A fine example of Pub is the Hub, combining a Cask Marque-accredited real ale outlet with a village shop offering local produce and household necessities. The bar has TV and darts while the lounge has adjoining well-appointed dining rooms. Across the road is an extensive, well maintained garden with a stream. Dogs are welcome.
♔Q❀⇋◑⊟♿▭(564,569)♣P

Rydal

Glen Rothay Hotel (Badger Bar)

LA22 9LR

⌚ 11-11 (10.30 Sun) ☎ (01539) 434500

🌐 theglenrothay.co.uk

Beer range varies Ⓗ

The roadside entrance leads into the bar area with its plinth-mounted handpumps serving beers from Cumbrian brewers only. The adjoining Oak Room has fine panelling and an elaborate fireplace with an impressive dated overmantle. The pub has won awards for environmental awareness – its fine wines come from European vintners and food ingredients from local suppliers. Badgers can often be seen in the grounds of an evening. The open top 599 bus passes the door in summer.
♔Q❀⇋◑▭(555,599)♣P⁄

Silloth

Albion

Eden Street, CA7 4AS

⌚ 3 (7 Mon; 4.30 winter)-midnight; 2-midnight Fri; 11-midnight Sat & Sun ☎ (01697) 331321

Derwent Parsons Pledge; Tetley Mild Ⓗ

Traditional one bar pub with a separate family room with pool table and TV, well supported by friendly locals and summer visitors. Pictures of old Silloth decorate the walls along with two models of whaling trawlers. There are also numerous photos celebrating the Isle of Man TT races alongside old motoring memorabilia. The pub serves as a meeting place for several local groups. The nearby Derwent Brewery often brings in new beers for trial periods. A holiday cottage is available next door. ♔ठ❀⇋▲▭(38,60)♣P⁄

Sizergh

Strickland Arms

LA8 8DZ (follow signs to Sizergh Castle off A590)

⌚ 11.30-3, 5.30-11; 11.30-11 Sat & summer; 12-10.30 Sun

☎ (01539) 561010 🌐 thestricklandarms.com

Coniston Bluebird Bitter; Dent Rambrau; Kirkby Lonsdale Ruskin's Bitter; Thwaites Lancaster Bomber Ⓗ

The handsome exterior of this road house just off the A6 is matched by the well-furnished, wood floored bar area on the ground floor. Upstairs are several equally well-furnished dining/meeting rooms. The beer range may vary. Good quality meals are available. The Sizergh Castle estate was passed to the National Trust by the Strickland family. Run by the same group that owns the Derby Arms in Witherslack. Dogs are welcome.
♔Q❀◑♿▲▭(X35,555)♣P⁄

Staveley

Beer Hall ✔

Mill Yard, LA8 9LR

12-5 (6 Wed-Sun) ☎ (01539) 825260
hawksheadbrewery.co.uk
Hawkshead Bitter, Red, Lakeland Gold, Brodie's Prime, seasonal beers H
This well-appointed tap to the brewery below, which can be viewed through large windows, has gained a deserved reputation for the quality of its Hawkshead beer offering. It also serves an important role as a judging venue and showcase for Society of Independent Brewers (North) category winners at two beer festivals held in February and November. Food can be brought in from the adjoining Wilf's Café. Q❀⇌🚌(555)P

Eagle & Child
Kendal Road, LA8 9LP
11-11; 12-10.30 Sun ☎ (01539) 821320
eaglechildinn.co.uk
Hawkshead Bitter; guest beers H
The central entrance leads to a U-shaped bar area with the bar counter on one side. A miscellany of tables, benches and chairs is matched by memorabilia on the shelves above. Guest beers are usually from smaller nearby brewers. Good value weekday lunches are very popular, as are the beer festivals held under canvas in the riverside garden across the road. There is a function/meeting room upstairs. ⋒❀⇋◑⇌🚌(555)●P⊱

Strawberry Bank

Masons Arms
Cartmel Fell, LA11 6NW SD413895
11.30-11; 12-10.30 Sun ☎ (01539) 568486
masonsarmsstrawberrybank.co.uk
Black Sheep Bitter; Hawkshead Bitter, Lakeland Gold; guest beers H
Owned by the Individual Inns group, this picturesque pub is set on a hillside with spectacular views across the Winster Valley. Two solid fuel ranges and three seating areas provide a cosy atmosphere in winter, while the outdoor seating and dining area is an idyllic location on a warm sunny day. Excellent quality meals are provided lunchtime and evening. Very popular with walkers and the local community alike. Shortlisted for Country Life magazine Country Pub of the Year 2009. ⋒Q❀⇋◑♣P⊱

Talkin

Blacksmith's Arms
CA8 1LE
12-3, 6-11 ☎ (01697) 73452 blacksmithstalkin.co.uk
Geltsdale Cold Fell, Brampton Bitter; Jennings Cumberland Ale; Yates Bitter H
The ever-popular Blackies, as it is known locally, continues to attract long-standing loyal customers as well as many visitors drawn by its reputation for a warm welcome and the host of outdoor attractions in the vicinity. These include a nearby golf course and country park, with Hadrian's Wall within easy reach. The well-stocked bar offers four real ales, and there are three further rooms including the Old Forge Restaurant.
⋒Q❀⇋◑⊟♿⛺♣P⊱

Tallentire

Bush Inn
CA13 0PT
closed Mon; 6-midnight; 12-2, 7-11.30 Sun
☎ (01900) 823707
Beer range varies H
Traditional Cumbrian village pub with simple decor, stone-flagged floors and low ceilings. The pub is at the centre of many village events, and hosts monthly folk music evenings. There are two changing guest beers, usually from northern and Scottish breweries – the house beer Old Tallentire is Robinsons Old Stockport. Meals are served in the separate restaurant, Thursday-Saturday evenings and Sunday lunchtime. Well behaved dogs are welcome in THE bar. A previous local CAMRA Pub of the Season and Pub of the Year runner-up.
Q❀🚌(58)♣P

Torver

Church House Inn
LA21 8AZ (2 miles SW of Coniston near jct of A593/A5084) SD285942
11-11 summer; 12-3, 5-11 winter ☎ (01539) 441282
churchhouseinntorver.com
Barngates Tag Lag; Hawkshead Bitter; guest beers H
Offering good quality food in the bar and dining room, and a friendly welcome, this unspoilt 14th-century inn features low beams, flagged floors and a magnificent open fire. A welcome sight whether you have just walked up Coniston Old Man or simply come in search of a fine pint (there are up to five to choose from) and a bit of craic with the locals. Occasional live folk music plays at weekends. The garden boasts a fine view of the surrounding fells. ⋒Q❀⇋◑♿⛺🚌(X12)♣P⊱

Ulverston

Devonshire Arms
Braddyll Terrace, Victoria Road, LA12 0DH (corner of Victoria Road and Conishead Road)
4-11; 3-midnight Fri; 12-midnight Sat; 12-11 Sun
☎ (01229) 582537
Lancaster seasonal beers; guest beers H
Situated away from the main town centre, 'The Dev' is handy for both the bus and train stations. The open plan layout is ideal for viewing the comprehensive coverage of TV sports, while seating closer to the bar provides a quieter area for conversation. Tables outside give additional space for those warmer days. Up to six real ales are on offer with ever-changing guests. There is also a May Day beer festival in support of local charities.
❀⛺⇌🚌♣P⊱

Stan Laurel Inn
The Ellers, LA12 0AB
7-midnight Mon; 12-2.30, 6-midnight Tue-Sat; 12-midnight Sun ☎ (01229) 582814 thestanlaurel.co.uk
Thwaites Original; Ulverston Lonesome Pine; guest beers H
Close to the town centre and named after the town's most famous son, this welcoming pub focuses on locally-produced beers – six handpulls are available in the main bar, which features a cosy log stove. Also popular for good value quality meals, booking is recommended (no food Mon). In summer drinks can be enjoyed outside at picnic tables. There is a separate darts/pool room and a smaller room for diners which can be used for functions or meetings. ⋒❀⇋◑⛺⇌🚌♣P⊱

Swan Inn
Swan Street, LA12 7JX
🕓 3.30-11; 12-midnight Fri & Sat; 12-11 Sun
☎ (01229) 582519
**Hawkshead Bitter, Lakeland Gold, Brodie's Prime;
Yates Bitter; guest beers** Ⓗ
On the edge of the town centre, this pub offers a wide selection of up to nine beers. An open fire serves a seating area to the right, with a darts area to the rear separated by a half wall. Events include a quiz night on Tuesday, jazz club on Thursday, and occasional live music and beer festivals including the regular Oktoberfest. The festivals are held in a marquee, with all beers on handpull. There is a large sunny beer garden at the back. Dogs are welcome. ♨️❀♿Å⇄🚃(6,6A,X35)♣♀ 🛏

Waberthwaite

Brown Cow
LA19 5YJ (on A595) SD 106932
🕓 11.30-1am; 12-midnight Sun ☎ (01229) 717243
🌐 thebrowncowinn.com
Hawkshead Bitter; guest beers Ⓗ
Popular 100-year-old local Cumbrian village pub offering three to six interesting and frequently changing real ales – often from Cumbrian and north Lancashire breweries – always including a mild and a Cumbrian cider. Meals use locally-sourced food, particularly from the village butcher (by Royal Command!). Occasional live music, regular quiz nights and an annual beer festival are hosted. The pub is situated close to the Western Fells, the coastline and Eskmeals Nature Reserve. The licensees previously ran a CAMRA award-winning pub in south Cumbria. ♨️🚲❀🚄◑♿Å🚃♣●P♀🛏

Whitehaven

Bransty Arch ✔
9 Bransty Row, CA28 7XE
🕓 9-midnight (1am Fri & Sat) ☎ (01946) 517640
Greene King Ruddles Best Bitter, Abbot; Jennings Cocker Hoop, Sneck Lifter; Yates Golden Ale; guest beers Ⓗ
A modern but elegant town-centre Wetherspoon pub. The large glass windows allow in plenty of light with good views of the busy streets outside. The interior is a mixture of carpeted, wooden and stone flooring. There is plenty of seating, though even the large bar area can become quite congested on busy nights. The pub has a policy of stocking certain 'core' real ales, with regularly rotating guest ales – these are often from local breweries but can come from further afield, especially at festival times. ◑♿⇄🚃(1,2,6)●

Candlestick
22 Tangier Street, CA28 7UX
🕓 12-midnight ☎ (01946) 599032
Robinsons Dizzy Blonde, Double Hop, seasonal beers Ⓗ
The Candlestick is a popular town pub with a friendly atmosphere and many regular customers. The bar has recently been refurbished and has new seating and bar stools. There is a widescreen TV for sport, karaoke every Sunday and live music in the middle of the month. The pub is convenient for the harbour, marina, bus stops and railway station, with a car park next door. A discount on real ale is offered to CAMRA members. Awarded local CAMRA Pub of the Season in December 2009. ♿⇄🚃

Globe
Main Street, Hensingham, CA28 8QX
🕓 5 (12 Fri-Sun)-midnight ☎ (01946) 590772
Beer range varies Ⓗ
A warm, friendly welcome awaits in this small, traditional Cumbrian free house, now a destination real ale outlet. The beers change frequently and are mainly from Cumbrian breweries. Sampling of the ales is encouraged. The food is home-cooked, with an ever-changing menu. The pub focuses on the community with many events taking place such as parties, charity fundraising and quizzes. ♨️❀◑🚃(30,31A)●♀

Witherslack

Derby Arms Hotel
LA11 6RN (just off A590)
🕓 12-3, 5.30-midnight; 12-midnight Sat & Sun
☎ (01539) 552207 🌐 thederbyarms.co.uk
Hawkshead Bitter; Thwaites Wainwright, Lancaster Bomber; guest beers Ⓗ
The hotel was rescued from closure by the Witherslack Community Land Trust and now being managed by the same company as the Strickland Arms at Sizergh. Furnished with the same high quality period pieces and comprising several rooms, including a village shop, it has restored the quality of life of the village, offering them and visitors a comfortable drinking, dining and social experience. ♨️Q❀🚲🚄◑♿🚃(X35)♣P♀

Workington

Henry Bessemer ✔
CA14 2NA
🕓 9-11 (midnight Thu-Sat) ☎ (01900) 734650
Greene King IPA, Ruddles Best Bitter, Abbot; Jennings Bitter; guest beers Ⓗ
This town-centre pub, opened as a Wetherspoon in 2001, is instantly recognisable as a former cinema —the decor has a 1930s feel. Although the interior is essentially one high-ceilinged room, there are separate seating areas and a couple of discrete alcoves. Up to 10 ales are offered and although the regulars are nationals, Cumbrian guests are eagerly sourced by the management. Inexpensive, reasonable meals are available at most times of the day, and it can get busy at weekends. ◑♿⇄🚃●

Wreay

Plough Inn
Wreay, CA4 0RL (5 miles S of Carlisle, W of A6)
🕓 closed Mon; 6-11 Tue; 12-2.30, 6-11 Wed-Fri; 12-11 Sat; 12-10.30 Sun ☎ (01697) 475770 🌐 wreayplough.co.uk
Cumberland Corby Ale; guest beers Ⓗ
Fully refurbished in 2006 after a previous owner nearly converted it into a house, the pub features an underfloor heated split-level, sandstone flagged floor, comfy sofas and a brick built central bar. Meals are freshly prepared from locally sourced ingredients and the pub is proud of supporting local producers and farmers. Booking for meals is recommended. ❀◑♿ÅP

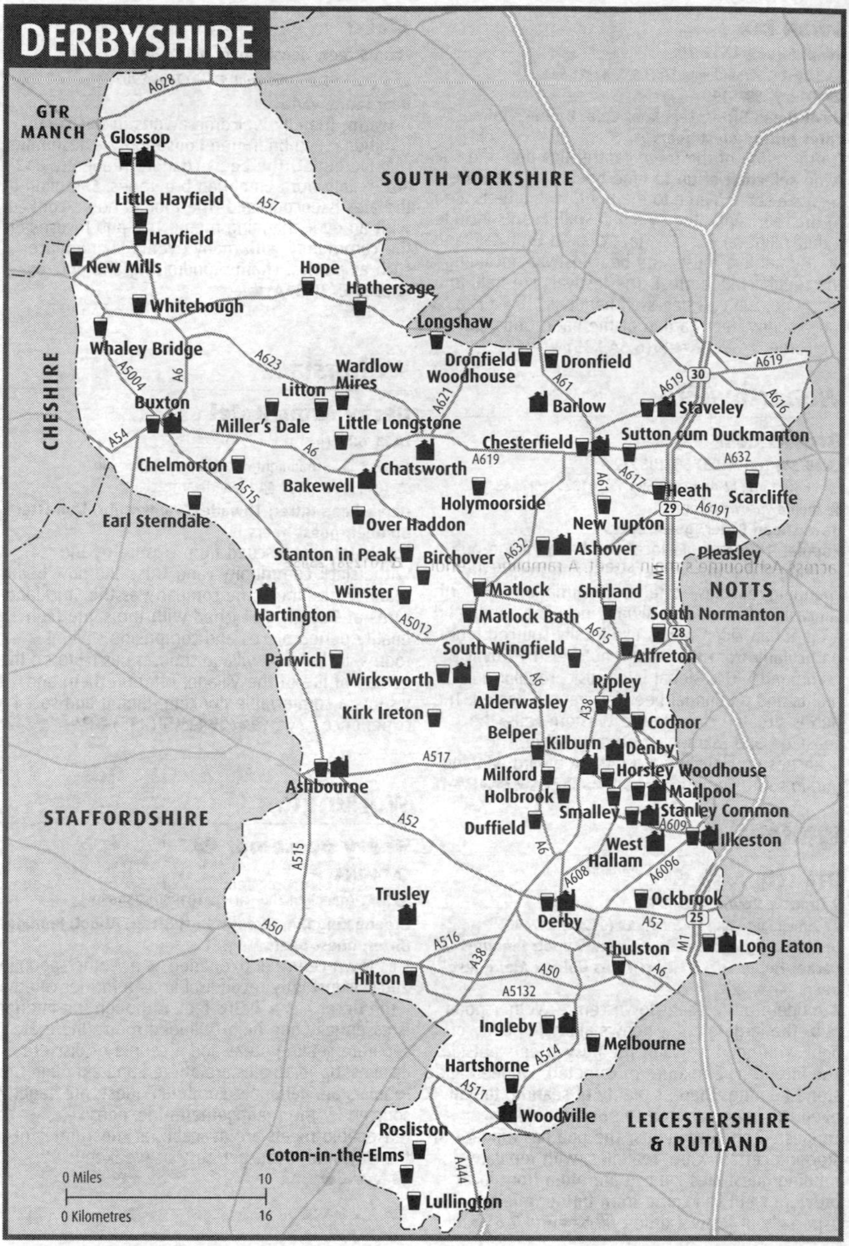

Alderwasley

Bear Inn & Hotel

DE56 2RD SK314527

✪ 12-midnight ☎ (01629) 822585 ⊕ bear-hotel.com

Draught Bass; Greene King Old Speckled Hen ⊞; Taylor Landlord ⓖ; Thornbridge Jaipur; Whim Hartington Bitter; guest beers ⊞

Originally a farmhouse, this pub opened as the Brown Bear Inn in 1735. There are three stone-framed hatchways form the bar, backed by paintings of bears. Rooms subdivided by settles lead off from the bar, filled with old curios, including many on the bear theme. Bear Hall occupies the other end of the inn, where a popular carvery is served on Sunday lunchtime. Three beers from the Thornbridge range are usually available. The garden offers panoramic views of Derbyshire countryside towards Crich Stand. ⌂Q❀⇌◑◐♣P

Alfreton

Waggon & Horses ✔

9 King Street, DE55 7AF

✪ 9-midnight (1am Fri & Sat) ☎ (01773) 545890

Greene King Ruddles Best Bitter, Abbot; guest beers ⊞

Centrally located, opposite the war memorial, this Wetherspoon house is deceptively large with an elongated bar and an open-plan layout with some cosy corners. The pub plays an active role in the local community and welcomes customer suggestions for real ales. Amber Ales, Derventio and Thornbridge are among the Derbyshire breweries featured and, accordingly, the pub is LocAle accredited. CAMRA members enjoy a 20 per cent discount on food with the exception of club deals. Q❀◐♿⇌🚌●⅟

Ashbourne

Green Man & Black's Head Royal Hotel

10 St John's Street, DE6 1GH

11-11 (midnight Thu; 1am Fri; 2am Sat); 12-11 Sun

☎ (01335) 345783 🌐 gmrh.com

Greene King Abbot; Leatherbritches Dr Johnson, seasonal beer; guest beers Ⓗ

Warmly praised by Boswell in his famous biography of Samuel Johnson, this 300-year-old former coaching inn still has its old gallows sign across Ashbourne's main street. A rambling interior hosts two contrasting sections, one traditional with real fires and wood panelling, the other trendier with music and modern decor. Leatherbritches brewery and shop are situated in outbuildings and an August bank holiday beer festival is held. A wide range of locally-sourced food is available.

♨❀🛏◐🀫🚌⅟

Ashover

Old Poets' Corner

Butts Road, S45 0EW (downhill from church)

12-11 ☎ (01246) 590888 🌐 oldpoets.co.uk

Ashover Light Rale, Poets Tipple; guest beers Ⓗ

The home of Ashover Brewery, this mock-Tudor building has a warm, welcoming atmosphere with open fires, candle-lit tables and hop-strewn beams. Choose from 10 handpumps, including three or four Ashover beers, along with a range of guest ales, six traditional ciders, draught and bottled Belgian beers and country wines. Winner of CAMRA national Cider Pub of the Year 2006 and local CAMRA Pub of the Year 2009. Entertainment includes live music, weekly quiz, folk evenings and three beer festivals a year. Dogs are welcome.

♨Q❀🛏◐◐♿⛺🚌(63,64)♣●P⅟

Belper

George & Dragon

117 Bridge Street, DE56 1BA

3 (11 Thu-Sat)-11.30; 12-10.30 Sun ☎ (01773) 880210

Draught Bass; Exmoor Gold; Greene King Abbot; Tower East Mill; guest beers Ⓗ

A fine Georgian roadside pub on the town's main thoroughfare, featuring an attractive portico. Formerly a coaching inn, it has an archway that now provides access to the car park. A deep open-plan pub, the unusual airline-style seating in the back area comes from the old Derby Rugby Club. Outside is a skittle alley. Belper Town Football Club, River Gardens and Derwent Valley Mills World Heritage Site visitors centre are all nearby. CAMRA members are offered a discount on beer.

♨❀🛏◐⇌🚌♣●P⅟

Birchover

Red Lion 🏆

Main Street, DE4 2BN

closed Mon; 12-2, 7 (6 Fri)-11; 12-11 Sat; 12-10.30 Sun

☎ (01629) 650363 🌐 birchoverredlion.com

Peak Ales seasonal beers; Peakstones Rock 9 Ladies Ale; guest beers Ⓗ

This traditional, gritstone-built free house is located in the centre of the village, close to the historic Stanton Moor and Nine Ladies stone circle (after which one of the pub's beers is named). Recently refurbished with log burning stoves in both rooms and an impressive outside seating area, and serving excellent food, it is popular with walkers, tourists and locals alike. It offers a minimum of three real ales – more in busy summer periods – usually sourced from local micros, plus real cider.

♨Q❀◐◐⛺🚌♣●P⅟

Buxton

Old Sun Inn

33 High Street, SK17 6HA

12-11 (11.30 Thu; midnight Fri & Sat); 12-11.30 Sun

☎ (01298) 23452

Marston's Burton Bitter, Pedigree; guest beers Ⓗ

Former coaching inn formed of six connected rooms with lots of nooks and crannies and a cosy, welcoming atmosphere. A folk jam session takes place on Tuesday and a quiz night on Sunday. In addition to the usual Marston's beers there are four guests selected from the Marston's range. Good food is served daily except Monday lunchtime. Outside is a small roadside-fronting garden area.

♨❀◐🀫⛺⇌🚌

Ramsey's Bar

Buckingham Hotel, 1 Burlington Road, SK17 9AS

6-midnight ☎ (01298) 70481 🌐 buckinghamhotel.co.uk

Howard Town Longdendale Light, Wrens Nest; guest beers Ⓗ

This large public bar and adjoining restaurant are part of the Buckingham Hotel. The name originates from No 1 Burlington Road, home and studio to local artist George Ramsey in the early part of the last century. With up to seven beers from micro-breweries, often including one from Thornbridge, the bar is very popular despite prices that are high for the area. A wide choice of food includes simple bar meals and a full restaurant menu.

❀🛏◐◐♿⛺⇌🚌P

Swan

40 High Street, SK17 6HB

11-1am ☎ (01298) 23278

Greene King Old Speckled Hen; Storm seasonal beer; Tetley Bitter; guest beers Ⓗ

This is a hostelry that prides itself on being a drinkers' pub, and has a friendly, welcoming atmosphere. Three rooms surround a central bar and major sports matches are shown on the TVs, otherwise background music plays. The tartan room is a former whisky bar. There is always a Storm beer from nearby Macclesfield on handpump and the pub has thriving darts and dominoes teams. Quiz night is Thursday and a small outdoor patio area is available. ❀🀫⇌🚌♣P

Chelmorton

Church Inn ✔

Main Street, SK17 9SL

⚙ 12-3.30, 6.30-11 ☎ (01298) 85319
Adnams Bitter; Marston's Burton Bitter, Pedigree; guest beers Ⓗ
Set in beautiful surroundings opposite the local church, this traditional village pub caters for both locals and walkers. The main room is laid out for dining and good home-cooked food is on offer, however a cosy pub atmosphere is maintained with a low ceiling and real fire. Guest beers are usually from local micros. Parking is available at the end of the road in front of pub and there is a patio area outside. Monday is quiz night.
♔Q❀⇌◑▲♣

Chesterfield

Chesterfield Arms 🏆
Newbold Road, S41 7PH
⚙ 12-11 ☎ (01246) 236634
Everards Tiger; Fuller's London Pride; Leatherbritches CAD, Bounder; guest beers Ⓗ
A real ale emporium. This family-run pub offers a friendly welcome and a selection of 10 real ales – mainly from micros – six ciders, bottled Belgian beers, and country wines. Oak-clad walls, open fires and hop-strewn beams create a relaxed atmosphere. A log burner warms the barn, open every Friday and Saturday and housing an extra selection of fine ales. Wednesday is quiz night, Thursday is curry night, and live music plays on the last Thursday of the month. Chesterfield CAMRA Pub of the Year 2010. ♔Q❀●P⊱

Derby Tup
387 Sheffield Road, Whittington Moor, S41 8LS
SK382735
⚙ 12-3, 5-11; 12-midnight Fri & Sat; 12-11 Sun
☎ (01246) 454316
Castle Rock Harvest Pale, Screech Owl; Taylor Landlord Ⓗ
This down-to-earth, much-loved traditional boozer has now been in the Guide for 27 years, which says it all really. A true drinkers' pub, with no music or other distractions, up to 10 real ales are offered, mainly from small breweries. Stouts and porters from local micros regularly feature. A wide range of gins and whiskies sit alongside traditional cider. Real fires enhance the snug and back room, as well as the main bar. Handily situated for the new Chesterfield football stadium.
♔Q◐⊟⊞(50,43)♣●

Grouse
136 Chatsworth Road, Brampton, S40 2AR (on A619 Chesterfield-Baslow)
⚙ 3-midnight; 12-1.30am Fri & Sat; 12-midnight Sun
☎ (01246) 279632
Brampton Best, seasonal beers; guest beers Ⓗ
Friendly, main road pub with one U-shaped room around a central bar area. Located very close to Brampton Brewery, it features its beers. The many TV screens make this pub a popular place for viewing sporting events, and live music plays regularly. To the rear of the building is a small beer garden. Fifteen minutes' walk from the town centre, there is also a frequent bus service.
❀♿⊞♣

Market
95 New Square, S40 1AH (N side of New Square market place)
⚙ 11-11; 7-10.30 Sun ☎ (01246) 273641
Greene King Abbot; Kelham Island Easy Rider; Taylor Landlord; Tetley Bitter; guest beers Ⓗ
This popular, town-centre local is run by enthusiastic young proprietors, serving good quality real ale and food. Several small beer festivals are held here and it is popular with locals and marketeers alike. There are occasional live music events and a quiz night is held on Thursday evening. A small patio to the rear is available for fair weather drinking. There are 10 handpumps on the bar: one is dedicated to a dark beer and at least one more to a local micro brewery.
❀◑⇌⊞♣●⊱

Peacock
412 Chatsworth Road, Brampton, S40 3BQ (on A619 Baslow road)
⚙ 12-11.30 ☎ (01246) 275115
Adnams Broadside; Black Sheep Best Bitter; Caledonian Deuchars IPA; guest beer Ⓗ
Situated on the main Baslow road, this popular, welcoming, friendly two-roomed pub has an open fire in the lounge. The central bar offers a selection of real ales including an ever-changing guest. To the rear it has a large garden, ideal for families in the summer months, with an additional seating area at the front. It hosts a quiz night on Monday, and games include darts and dominoes.
♔Q❀⊟⊞(25)♣⊱

Portland Hotel ✔
West Bars, S40 1AY (on New Square Market Place)
⚙ 9am-midnight (1am Fri & Sat) ☎ (01246) 245410
Greene King IPA, Abbot; Marston's Pedigree; guest beers Ⓗ
Built in 1899 to serve the former Lancashire, Derbyshire and East Coast Railway, this JD Wetherspoon hotel welcomes children in the dining areas. The big mock-Tudor building has an

INDEPENDENT BREWERIES

Amber Ripley
Ashover Ashover
Barlow Barlow (NEW)
Bottle Brook Kilburn
Brampton Chesterfield
Brunswick Derby
Buxton Buxton
Derby Derby
Derventio Trusley
Falstaff Derby: Normanton
Funfair Ilkeston
Globe Glossop
Haywood Bad Ram Ashbourne
Headless Derby
Howard Town Glossop
John Thompson Ingleby
Leadmill Denby
Leatherbritches Ashbourne
Marlpool Marlpool (NEW)
Mr Grundys Derby (NEW)
Muirhouse Long Eaton
Nutbrook Stanley Common/West Hallam
Peak Ales Chatsworth
Raw Staveley (NEW)
Rowditch Derby (NEW)
Spire Staveley
Thornbridge Bakewell
Tollgate Woodville
Townes Staveley
Whim Hartington
Wirksworth Wirksworth

ornate exterior and the spacious interior gets very busy due to the pub's location in the centre of town. The bar serves up to four guest ales and regularly features beers from Spire and Wentworth breweries. The hotel has 22 en-suite rooms.
❀🛏◐⇌🚌(25)P

Red Lion

570 Sheffield Road, Whittington Moor, S41 8LX
SK381737
12-11 (10.30 Sun) ☎ (01246) 450770
Old Mill Mild, Bitter, Bullion, seasonal beers Ⓗ
Traditional two-roomed pub with a central bar. The interior has some attractive stained glass and walls decorated with historic pictures. It is the only outlet for Old Mill's excellent beers in Chesterfield, and one of only a few that serve mild regularly. The public bar plays host to live bands occasionally and there is a widescreen TV. Charity events are held frequently supporting the Edale Mountain Rescue.
Q❀🚌(25,50)♣P

Rose & Crown

104 Old Road, Brampton, S40 2QT
12-11 (midnight Fri & Sat) ☎ (01246) 563750
roseandcrownbrampton.co.uk
Brampton Golden Bud, Best, Wasp Nest, seasonal beers; Everards Tiger; guest beers Ⓗ
Brampton Brewery's first tied house can be found just off the main A619 Baslow to Chatsworth road. A complete refurbishment provides warm, cosy surroundings and a traditional snug. There are five regular Brampton beers together with one Everards and two guest ales. Bar food features award-winning local produce, some spiced with Brampton ale. Quiz night is Tuesday, with a music quiz on the last Sunday of the month. A rear drinking area can be accessed through the pub. ❀◐🚌P

Royal Oak

Low Pavement, S40 1PX
10-6 (11 Thu & Fri; 11.30 Sat); 11-4 Sun
Brampton Golden Bud; Peak Ales Chatsworth Gold; Thornbridge Jaipur; guest beers Ⓗ
Nestling in the Shambles, off the Market Place, this two-roomed pub with its stained glass windows and high ceiling is the oldest in Chesterfield. It has been an inn since 1722, but the building has its origins in the 12th century. An imaginative menu, and dishes such as mussels and chips, make it busy at lunchtimes. Most of the eight beers available are from local breweries, such as Brampton, Thornbridge and Peak Ales. ◐⇌

Codnor

Poet & Castle

2 Alfreton Road, DE5 9QY
12-11 ☎ (01773) 744150 poetandcastle.co.uk
Ashover Golden Valley Ale, Poet's Tipple; Everards Original; Wells Bombardier; guest beers Ⓗ
Rescued from closure by Everards and run by the Ashover Brewery, the open plan layout is sub-divided into two areas with the low, beamed bar decorated with hops. Traditional cider, continental beers and fruit wines are available. Live acoustic music features on Thursday and bands play on Friday or Saturday. The upstairs function room becomes the Poet's Pantry Restaurant on Friday and Saturday evenings. Sunday is Takeaway Night: you provide the food, the pub supplies plates, cutlery and washing-up. No food Monday evening.
❀◐♿🚌(R1,H1)♣P

Coton-in-the-Elms

Black Horse

17 Burton Road, DE12 8HJ SK246152
4-11 (midnight Fri); 12-midnight Sat; 12-10.30 Sun
☎ (01283) 762947 theblackhorsesouthderbyshire.co.uk
Draught Bass; Marston's Pedigree; guest beer Ⓗ
This former Guide pub has been revived as a lively, convivial and increasingly popular free house after more than a decade of neglect. Tastefully renovated with extensive use of wood, the bright and airy main room is divided into bar and lounge areas by glass-topped wood partitions. There is also a separate small snug served through a hatch. The guest beer is often sourced from a local micro-brewery. Quiz night is Tuesday; occasional live music plays on Sunday. ❀🚌(22)♣P

Derby

Babington Arms ✔

11-13 Babington Lane, DE1 1TA
9-11 (midnight Fri & Sat) ☎ (01332) 383647
Greene King Ruddles Best, Abbot; Marston's Burton Bitter, Pedigree; Wyre Piddle Marcos King of the Watusi; guest beers Ⓗ
Probably the best Wetherspoon's in the country, it has won the company's prestigious Cask Ale Pub of the Year and local CAMRA City Pub of the Year twice. It showcases an amazing range of 18 beers on handpump, with permanent guest beers from Wyre Piddle and Falstaff breweries and regular themed brewery weekends. The pub stands in the former grounds of Babington House and the first performance of Bram Stoker's Dracula was given in the neighbouring Grand Theatre in 1924.
Q❀◐♿🚌

Brewery Tap – Derby's Royal Standard

1 Derwent Street, DE1 2ED (from Market Place head over Exeter bridge)
11-11 (midnight Thu; 1am Fri & Sat) ☎ (01332) 366283
derbybrewing.co.uk/brewery_tap
Derby Triple Hop, Business As Usual, Dashingly Dark, Double Mash, Old Intentional; guest beers Ⓗ
The stylish brewery tap for the Derby Brewing Company occupies a flat iron site, and has an open-plan interior, with a curved bar acting as a focal point for two distinct drinking areas. Exposed brickwork and wooden floors lend a contemporary feel. In fine weather the roof terrace affords a view across the River Derwent. Food is served until 8pm (5pm Sun). ❀◐♿🚌

Brunswick Inn

1 Railway Terrace, DE1 2RU
11-11; 12-10.30 Sun ☎ (01332) 290677
brunswickinn.co.uk
Brunswick White Feather, Triple Hop, Second Brew, Porter, Father Mike's Dark Rich Ruby Ⓗ/Ⓖ**; Everards Beacon; Taylor Landlord; guest beers** Ⓗ
Originally built in 1842 as the centrepiece of a railway village, the pub was closed in 1974 and fell into disrepair. Eventually rescued and restored, it opened as Derby's first multiple choice real ale house some 13 years later. The pub's photographs illustrate the transformation from dereliction to restoration. A purpose-built brewery was added, and it rapidly became one of the best known free houses in the country. It's now owned by Everards although the brewery is operated independently.
Q❀◐♿⇌🚌♣

Falstaff

74 Silverhill Road, DE23 6UJ

12-11 (midnight Fri & Sat) ☎ (01332) 342902

falstaffbrewery.co.uk

Falstaff Fistful of Hops, Phoenix, Smiling Assassin, seasonal beer [H]

A 10-minute walk from the city centre rewards you with this atmospheric and reputedly haunted free house. Originally a coaching inn before the surrounding area was built up, it is now the Falstaff brewery tap, making it the best real ale house in Normanton. The curved bar is flanked on one side by a small lounge exuding an air of timelessness, where Offilers Brewery memorabilia is displayed. Other collectables can be viewed throughout the games room and second bar room.

Flowerpot

23-25 King Street, DE1 3DZ

11-11 (midnight Fri & Sat); 12-11 Sun ☎ (01332) 204955

Headless KSA, First Bloom, seasonal beers [H]**; Oakham Bishop's Farewell; Whim Hartington IPA; guest beers** [H]/[G]

Dating from around 1800 but much expanded from its original premises, this pub reaches back from the small, roadside frontage and divides into several interlinking rooms. One room provides the stage for regular live bands and another has a glass cellar wall, revealing rows of stillaged firkins. The on-site Headless Brewery is at the rear. A real ale showcase, up to 25 beers are on offer every weekend. Local CAMRA Pub of the Year 2007. Q

Horse & Groom

48 Elms Street, DE1 3HN

12-11 ☎ (01332) 384775 horseandgroomderby.co.uk

Draught Bass; Marston's Pedigree; guest beers [H]

Situated in the city's old West End and dating from around 1850, the 'Horse' was rescued from almost certain closure when the current licensees purchased the inn from Punch in 2007. A complete refurbishment has restored the pub back to a thriving community local. The regular Bass and Pedigree are accompanied by two changing guests, often from Thornbridge. There is live music at weekends and jazz every Wednesday.

Mr Grundy's Tavern

32-34 Ashbourne Road, DE22 3AD

11 (12 Sat)-11; 12-10.30 Sun ☎ (01332) 340279

mrgrundystavern.info

Burton Bridge Golden Delicious; Falstaff seasonal beers; Hop Back Summer Lightning; Marston's Pedigree; guest beers [H]

The public bar within this Grade II-listed Georgian house hotel serves up to seven real ales. Wood-panelled throughout, it has open fires, low lighting and wooden bench seating. The bar area features hanging hops, breweriana, film memorabilia, an unusual collection of hats and an old red telephone box. Outdoors is a large covered area and beer garden. The pub supports LocAle, frequently featuring Falstaff, Blue Monkey and Derventio breweries, and is opening an on-site brewery. No evening meals on Sunday. (29)P

Old Silk Mill

19 Full Street, DE1 3AF

11-midnight; 12-11 Sun

Blue Monkey Cathedral Quarter [H]**; Draught Bass** [G]**; Purity Pure Gold, Mad Goose** [H]**; guest beers** [H]/[G]

An amazing transformation into a traditional ale house has returned the 'Mill' to prominence. Its nine real ales increase to 12 or more at weekends when the rear John Lombe Bar features beers straight from the cask. Dating from 1928, its two rooms both have real fires creating a warm and cosy atmosphere throughout. No food, but you can bring your own. Live music features on Thursday, with jazz on Sunday. Just metres away from the birthplace of the Industrial Revolution.

Olde Dolphin Inne ★ ✔

5a Queen Street, DE1 3DL

10.30-midnight; 12-11 Sun ☎ (01332) 267711

Adnams Bitter; Black Sheep Best Bitter; Caledonian Deuchars IPA; Draught Bass; Greene King Abbot; Nottingham Dolphin Ale [H]

The most picturesque and oldest surviving pub in the city centre, though the 'Tudor' facade dates from 1912. The warm, cosy and characterful interior comprises a bar, snug, and two lounges, plus an upstairs steak bar. More recently it has added an extensive outside patio to its street frontage, which is much used in fine weather and gives the pub a cafe-bar feel. The Dolphin's beer festivals, the largest of which follows Derby CAMRA's July festival, feature an extensive beer range. There is often a guest ale, too. Q

Rowditch Inn

246 Uttoxeter New Road, DE22 3LL

12-2 Sat & Sun only, 7-11 ☎ (01332) 343123

Marston's Pedigree; guest beers [H]

No-frills pub with first class beer – winner of local CAMRA City Pub of the Year in 2006. A plain fronted but warmly welcoming roadside hostelry, its unexpectedly deep interior divides into two drinking areas and a small snug. The long rear garden is a positive haven in warmer weather. Pump clips adorning the walls of the bar are evidence of myriad guest ales. A micro-brewery is set to open at the rear of the pub.

(Mb/Mr)

Smithfield

Meadow Road, DE1 2BH

11-11; 12-10.30 Sun ☎ (01332) 370429

thesmithfield.co.uk

Draught Bass; Headless seasonal beer; Oakham Bishop's Farewell; Whim Arbor Light, Hartington IPA; guest beers [H]

Out-of-the-way pub situated midway between the railway station and the market place and a short, pleasant walk from both. It has a long basic bar and small back lounge with settles. The rear patio overlooks the river. One of the city's two Headless pubs (the other is the Flowerpot), favourite guests include beers from Oakham, Whim and Enville. No food on Sunday. P

Station Inn ✔

12 Midland Road, DE1 2SN (left out of railway station, 100m on the right) SK359354

11.30-2.30, 5 (7 Sat)-11; 11.30-11 Fri; 12-3, 7-10.30 Sun

☎ (01332) 608014

Caledonian Deuchars IPA [H]**; Draught Bass** [G]**; Wells Bombardier; Wychwood Hobgoblin; guest beer** [H]

Narrow but deep pub rebuilt by Charrington (see signs on frontage) shortly before it withdrew to London. The extended front bar and adjacent pool room obscure the huge function room and dining area to the rear (well-used by Derby CAMRA). The landlord heads up the Derby Pub Watch scheme and is renowned for his immaculate award-winning cellar. The Bass, served from a jug, is a benchmark for the city. Saturday opening hours can vary depending on whether Derby County are playing home or away. ⊟≋⊟(41,44,45)♣⊱

Dronfield

Coach & Horses 🏆

Sheffield Road, S18 2GD

⏲ 5-10 Mon; 12-11 (midnight Fri & Sat); 12-10.30 Sun

☎ (01246) 413269

Thornbridge Jaipur, seasonal beers ⊞

Roadside pub north of the town centre, with one comfortably furnished open-plan room. It is owned by Sheffield FC, the world's oldest football club, founded in 1857, whose ground is adjacent. There are up to five Thornbridge beers available on a rotating basis, usually including the latest specials. Good home-cooked food is made with locally sourced ingredients where possible, and served in a friendly, relaxed atmosphere. Evening meals are available to 8.30pm, but no food Sunday evening or Monday. Q❀◐⊳≋⊟(43,44)♣P⊱

Dronfield Woodhouse

Jolly Farmer ✔

Pentland Road, S18 8ZQ

⏲ 12-midnight (1am Fri & Sat) ☎ (01246) 418018

Black Sheep Best Bitter; Taylor Landlord; Tetley Bitter; guest beers ⊞

Community pub built on a large housing estate in 1976 by Shipstones, and turned into a themed ale house in the 1990s. The cask beers are stillaged in a glass-fronted cellar behind the bar, which is free of the usual ostentatious lager pumps. The pub is open plan but has distinct areas including a tap room with pool table and a raised dining area. Two guest beers feature, usually from small independents, and a beer festival is held in November. Q❀◐⊟♿⊟(43,89)♣P⊱

Duffield

Pattenmakers Arms ✔

4 Crown Street, DE56 4EY

⏲ 12-2, 5-midnight; 12-midnight Fri & Sat; 12-4, 7-midnight Sun ☎ (01332) 842844

Draught Bass ⊡**; Marston's Pedigree; Taylor Landlord; guest beer** ⊞

Pleasant late 19th-century inn, tucked away behind the main road. The pub is open plan, with a central horseshoe bar. This lively, family-friendly pub offers a warm welcome to all, and runs skittles, darts and dominoes teams, as well as quizzes and meat raffles. Older architectural features survive, including quarry tiled and parquet floors, and stained glass and etched windows. Simple, nourishing lunchtime meals are served all week 12-2pm. From April 2011 the Duffield to Wirksworth heritage railway will be operational. ❀◐≋⊟♣P⊱

Earl Sterndale

Quiet Woman

SK17 0BU (off B5053)

⏲ 12-3, 7-11 ☎ (01298) 83211

Coach House Gray's Mild; Marston's Burton Bitter, Pedigree; guest beer ⊞

This unspoilt local set in the heart of the Peak District National Park is opposite the church and village green. Inside, a low-beamed room has a real fire on the left and a small bar to the right. There is a separate games room with a pool table. Local fresh eggs and traditional pork pies can be purchased at the bar. The pub offers its own selection of naturally conditioned bottled beers brewed by Leek Brewery. ♨Q⊵❀⛺⊟(442)♣P

Glossop

Crown Inn ★

142 Victoria Street, SK13 8JF (on Hayfield Road out of town centre)

⏲ 5 (11.30 Fri & Sat)-11; 12-10.30 Sun ☎ (01457) 862824

Samuel Smith OBB ⊞

This end-of-terrace local, a few minutes from the town centre and Glossop station, was built in 1846 and has been the only Smith's house in the High Peak area since 1977. An attractive curved bar serves two side snugs, each with real fires in winter, and a pool/games room. Old pictures of Glossop's past add to the traditional character. Prices are very keen and Smith's bottled beers are also available. An enclosed outdoor drinking area is provided in the rear yard. ♨Q❀♿≋⊟♣⊱

Globe

144 High Street West, SK13 8HJ

⏲ 5-1am (2am Fri & Sat); closed Tue; 1-midnight Sun

☎ (01457) 852417 🌐 globemusic.org

Globe Amber, Porter, Comet, Blondie; guest beers ⊞

A cosy local, at the lower end of the High Street, with its own brewery. Broad Oak Perry and Bristol Port Cider are available on handpump in addition to the range of beers. A lively music scene includes folk night on Monday and live bands performing in the upstairs rear function room. The pub has built up a good reputation for good value vegan food. A well-kept rear walled garden area is popular in summer. ❀◐⊟≋⊟●⊱

Star Inn ✔

2 Howard Street, SK13 7DD (next to railway station)

⏲ 2 (4 Mon & Tue)-11 (midnight Fri & Sat); 12-10.30 Sun

☎ (01457) 853072

Black Sheep Best Bitter; guest beers ⊞

Often the first and last stop-off for visitors by public transport, as Glossop train station and bus stops are very close by. This highly-regarded local is currently run by long-standing CAMRA members. A range of six ales is on offer along with Old Rosie real cider – all on handpumps. Pictures of bygone Glossop, wood floors and a rear tap room served by a hatch add to the traditional atmosphere. ⇌≋⊟●P⊱

Hartshorne

Mill Wheel

31 Ticknall Road, DE11 7AS (on A514) SK326213

⏲ 12-3, 5.30-11; 12-11 Sat; 12-10.30 Sun ☎ (01283) 550335

🌐 themillwheel.co.uk

Greene King Abbot; Tollgate Bitter; guest beers ⊞

This attractive and comfortable free house incorporates a 24-foot diameter 19th-century iron water-wheel, visible from both the main open-plan bar area and the upstairs restaurant. Originally the site of a corn mill, various industrial uses followed, such as a furnace, screw mill and saw mill. Radical reconstruction saw the conversion into a pub in 1987, with further sensitive and extensive restoration work in 1999. Food is available all day Saturday and Sunday. Accommodation is in an attached cottage. (61)P

Hathersage

Millstone Inn

Sheffield Road, S32 1DA (on A6187 E of village)
11.30-11; 12-10.30 Sun ☎ (01433) 650258
millstoneinn.co.uk
Abbeydale Moonshine; Black Sheep Best Bitter; Fuller's Discovery; Taylor Landlord; guest beers Ⓗ
This pub originally served the nearby millstone quarry and is now popular with walkers and climbers. Although recently opened out, it retains two large, well-furnished seating and dining areas either side of the central bar. There is also an extensive outdoor area partly under cover. Guest beers are from local breweries. Quiz night is Friday. Meals are available all day every day. The traditional cider is Black Rat.
(272)♣P

Hayfield

Royal Hotel

Market Street, SK22 2EP
12-11 ☎ (01663) 742721 theroyalhayfield.co.uk
Hydes Original Bitter; guest beers Ⓗ
An imposing stone pub near the church, cricket ground and River Sett. The interior boasts original oak panels and pews that create a relaxing atmosphere, with real fires in winter. Several guest beers from local micros are usually available and an annual beer festival is hosted in October. A restaurant and function room complete the facilities. The village is the base for many leisure activities in the Dark Peak area and was also the birthplace of Arthur Lowe, the immortal Captain Mainwaring in Dad's Army. Q P

Heath

Elm Tree

Mansfield Road, S44 5SE SK446672
11-3, 5-midnight; 11.30-midnight Sat; 12-10.30 Sun
☎ (01246) 850490 theelmtreeheath.co.uk
Jennings Sneck Lifter; guest beers Ⓗ
The only pub in the village, the Elm Tree boasts a menu of fine home-cooked food as well as regular changing guest ales. Friendly and welcoming, there are two bars and a dining area. Well-maintained gardens surround the pub, with fine views overlooking the Derbyshire countryside. Only a mile from the M1. ♣P

Hilton

Old Talbot

1 Main Street, DE65 5FF
3.30-11.30; 3-12.30am Fri; 12.30-12.30am Sat; 12-11.30 Sun ☎ (01283) 733728 oldtalbot.co.uk
Draught Bass; Marston's Pedigree; guest beers Ⓗ
Grade II-listed, with a low beamed ceiling dating from the early 1500s. A malt drying kiln on the back of the main fireplace testifies to the existence of an ale house built on this site. Bass and Pedigree are joined by three changing guests and at least one LocAle. Social activities include regular live music, quiz nights and poker evenings, and an annual beer festival held in September.
Q(V1,V2)♣P

Holbrook

Dead Poets Inn

38 Chapel Street, DE56 0TQ
12-2.30, 5-11; 12-11 Fri & Sat; 12-10.30 Sun
☎ (01332) 780301
Greene King Abbot; Marston's Pedigree Ⓖ**; guest beers** Ⓗ
Built in 1800 and formerly known as the Cross Keys, the pub has undergone a remarkable transformation to create an inn with a real medieval feel within. There is a delightful snug and the main bar has high-backed pews, stone-flagged floors, a real fire and inglenook. Around 25 guest beers feature each week (six at any one time), usually including at least one from Abbeydale and Whim breweries. Winner of the local CAMRA Pub of the Year award in 2010. Q(71,138)P

Holymoorside

Lamb

16 Loads Road, S42 7EU SK339694
5 (4 Fri)-11; 12-3, 7-11 Sat & Sun ☎ (01246) 566167
Daleside Blonde; Taylor Landlord; Theakston Black Bull; guest beers Ⓗ
A locals' pub, unspoilt by progress, with a mixed clientele where all are welcome including dogs and walkers (but take your boots off before going in). The public bar (a valued survivor of the craze for one room pub conversions) is warmed by a real fire. The paved outdoor drinking area is ideal for warm, dry summer evenings and hosts a jazz session as part of the annual Holymoorside Festival. Frequent winner of local CAMRA awards.
Q(50,99)♣P

Hope

Cheshire Cheese

Edale Road, S33 6ZF SK170841
closed Mon; 12-3, 6.30-11.30; 12-11.30 Sat; 12-10.30 Sun
☎ (01433) 620381
Bradfield Farmers Blonde; Caledonian Deuchars IPA; Copper Dragon Best Bitter; guest beers Ⓗ
This cosy pub dating from 1578 has an open plan bar area and a smaller room at a lower level that was probably originally used to house animals but nowadays is used as a dining area. No evening meals are served on Sundays during the winter. The pub is situated in walking country but parking is limited and the road outside narrow. A holiday cottage is available. Q P

Horsley Woodhouse

Old Oak Inn

176 Main Street, DE7 6AW (on A609)
4 (3 Thu & Fri; 12 Sat & Sun)-midnight ☎ (01332) 882996
Bottle Brook seasonal beers; Leadmill seasonal beers; guest beers Ⓗ
Flagship of the Leadmill brewery, featuring a mouthwatering variety of its beers. This traditional pub boasts a variety of rooms ranging from cosy open-fired bars to a larger, more modern room where occasional live music is enjoyed. At weekends the RuRad Bar recreates the much lamented Stables Bar, which spotlights a large range of gravity dispensed micro-brewery beers alongside Leadmill and Bottle Brook offerings. Regional CAMRA Pub of the Year 2009.
Q(AMB)♣P

Ilkeston

Dewdrop

24 Station Street, DE7 5TE (50m from A6096)
12.30 (12 Fri & Sat)-11; 12-10.30 Sun (0115) 9329684
thedewdrop.co.uk
Castle Rock Harvest Pale; Oakham Bishops Farewell; Taylor Best Bitter; guest beers H
Built in 1884, and named for Lord Middleton, a local landowner, this traditional corner house served the old-time colliery and mill workers, and was a three storey hotel. Now named the Dewdrop, it still boasts its three-roomed format, and a grand lobby where a plaque hangs commemorating the wartime stay of Ripley-born Barnes Wallis, inventor of the 'bouncing bomb'. LocAle affiliated and winner of local CAMRA Pub of the Year 2009, there aren't many pubs like this left.
Q(27)

Good Old Days

93 Station Road, DE7 5LJ (on A6096)
12-3, 6-midnight; 12-1am Fri & Sat; 12-midnight Sun
(0115) 8751103
Beer range varies H
Situated alongside the Erewash Canal, this former local CAMRA Club of the Year is a perennial Guide entry that continues to champion the cause of real ale by stocking micro-brewery beers sourced from near and far, often showcasing ales from new brewers. Traditional pub games include snooker, and a pianist makes an occasional guest appearance. The large landscaped garden hosts live music performances and barbecues during the summer months and there are adjacent narrowboat moorings. (27,T1)

Needlemakers Arms

12 Kensington Street, DE7 5NY
5 (12 Fri & Sat)-11.30; 11-11.30 Sun (07853) 273174
Beer range varies H
Created by knocking two former workers' cottages into one, this popular ex-Shipstones local takes its name from the former needlemaking factory nearby. Set back from the road, inside it has a quiet lounge to one side of the central bar, and to the rear there is a pool room which hosts beer festivals. Darts, dominoes and quiz nights regularly feature. Owned by Punch, its listed beers plus those from the SIBA range are served.
Q(2,15)P

Spanish Bar

76 South Street, DE7 8QJ
10-11 (midnight Fri & Sat); 11-10.30 Sun
(0115) 9308666
Mallard Quacker Jack; Whim Hartington IPA; guest beers H
Bustling, friendly locals' pub with a cafe-bar style, frequented by all ages. Regular customers enjoy card and domino schools, and Tuesday is quiz night. The colourful main bar has comfy chairs surrouding a log burner, and a second room, open in the evenings, has a large screen TV showing important events. A pleasant rear garden features a heated skittle alley. There is a range of bottled continental beers and the guest beers are often sourced from micro-breweries.

Ingleby

John Thompson Inn

DE73 7HW (off A514)
11-2.30 (not Mon), 6-11; 11-11 Sat & Sun
(01332) 862469 johnthompsoninn.com
John Thompson JTS XXX, seasonal beers; guest beers H
John Thompson revived brewing in Derbyshire at his eponymous pub in 1977. Both brewery and pub are now run by his son Nick. With rural views over the River Trent, this delightful setting is enhanced by the carefully crafted interior, featuring works by the local Gresley family of artists. A modern extension offers TV and pool. Lunches are served Tuesday to Sunday. Accommodation is in six four-bed self-catering chalets in the grounds of the pub.
P

Kirk Ireton

Barley Mow ★

Main Street, DE6 3JP (off B5023)
12-2, 7-11; 12-2, 7-10.30 Sun (01335) 370306
Whim Hartington IPA; guest beers G
Set in a village overlooking the Ecclesbourne Valley, this gabled Jacobean building features a sundial dated 1683. Several interconnecting rooms of different size and character have low, beamed ceilings, mullioned windows, slate-topped tables, well-worn woodwork and open fires. A small serving hatch reveals a stillage with up to six beers dispensed straight from the cask. This pub is well worth a visit as there are not many rural gems like it left. Local CAMRA Pub of the Year 2008.
Q

Little Hayfield

Lantern Pike

45 Glossop Road, SK22 2NG
12 (5 Mon winter)-11 (01663) 747590
lanternpikeinn.co.uk
Taylor Landlord; guest beer H
Picturesque ivy-clad stone pub nestling in this small hamlet within the Dark Peak area. The comfortable traditional lounge bar, with a real fire in winter, connects to separate dining areas. Coronation Street originator Tony Warren once lived nearby and wrote some of the first episodes of the soap while in the pub (see photos and letter on display). There are superb views from the rear patio. The guest beer is usually either Black Sheep Best Bitter, Howard Town Longdendale Lights or Whim Hartington Bitter. (61)P

Little Longstone

Packhorse Inn

Main Street, DE45 1NN SK191718
12-3, 4.45-11.30; 12-11.30 Sat & Sun (01629) 640471
packhorselongstone.co.uk
Black Sheep Best Bitter; guest beers H
This small pub began life as two miners' cottages but has been welcoming drinkers since 1787. Situated just a short walk from stunning views of Monsal Head, dogs and walkers are welcome. Locally sourced food is a passion, an ethos also extending to the beers which include at least two from the nearby Thornbridge Brewery. To the rear is a large beer garden which features a barbecue in the summer months. (173)

Litton

Red Lion ✔

Church Lane, SK17 8QU SK163753
⏲ 12-11 (midnight Fri & Sat); 12-10.30 Sun
☎ (01298) 871458 🌐 theredlionlitton.co.uk
Abbeydale Absolution; Oakwell Barnsley Bitter; guest beers 🄷
Nestled on the green and the only pub in the village, the Red Lion is the focus of community life as well as a welcome refuge for visitors. There is a large fireplace that warms several rooms off a central passageway. The guest beers are often LocAle. Not to be missed is the annual Wakes Week at the end of June with events including well dressing on the village green. Food is available all day every day. ⛫Q❀◑⊟⊟(65,66)♣⸗

Long Eaton

Stumble Inn

37 Tamworth Road, NG10 1JF
⏲ 12-midnight ☎ (0115) 9724529
Greene King IPA; guest beers 🄷
Previously known as the Wheatsheaf, the Stumble is enjoying a phoenix-style rise from the ashes under the guidance of an enthusiastic landlord and landlady. Family run, with a broad mix of clientele, the pub has a large, open-plan room with two indoor sports areas, and a small snug with easy chairs, warmed by an open fire. Many local micro-breweries feature, together with beers from much further afield. ⛫⥶⊟(5,15)♣

Twitchel Inn ✔

Howitt Street, NG10 1ED (off main pedestrian area)
⏲ 9-midnight ☎ (0115) 9722197
Greene King Abbot; Marston's Pedigree; guest beers 🄷
Hidden down a side street, this Wetherspoon pub has a large, open-plan room with two distinct areas, one for meals, the other a general drinking area, partly raised and containing many small cubicles. Photographs of bygone Long Eaton adorn the walls. The familiar Wetherspoon beer range is augmented by a variety of micro-brewery offerings, one locally sourced. The pub is LocAle accredited and Marcle Hill traditional cider is available. ◑⥶⊟(5,15)●

Longshaw

Grouse Inn

S11 7TZ (on A625) SK258779
⏲ 12-11 ☎ (01433) 630423
Banks's Bitter; Caledonian Deuchars IPA; Marston's Pedigree; guest beer 🄷
In the same family since 1965, this free house stands in isolation on bleak moorland south west of Sheffield, and is deservedly popular with walkers and climbers. There are some fine photographs of nearby gritstone edges, as well as a collection of international bank notes on display. The comfortable lounge is situated at the front, with a smaller bar area to the rear separated by a conservatory. Lunch and evening meals are available (not Mon), with food served all day on Sunday. ⛫Q♨❀◑♣P⊟

Lullington

Colvile Arms

Main Street, DE12 8EG SK249131
⏲ 6-11; 12-3, 7-10.30 Sun ☎ (01827) 373212
Draught Bass; Marston's Pedigree; guest beer 🄷
Leased from the Lullington Estate, the seat of the Colvile family until the early 1900s, this popular 18th-century free house is at the heart of an attractive hamlet at the southern tip of the county. The public bar has an adjoining hallway and snug, each featuring high-backed settles with wood panelling. The bar and a comfortable lounge are situated on opposite sides of a central serving area. A second lounge/function room overlooks the beer garden and lawn. Quiz teams and the local cricket and football teams meet here. ❀⊟♣P⸗

Marlpool

Queens Head

1 Breach Road, DE75 7LX (1 km from Heanor on A6007)
⏲ 11-midnight ☎ (01773) 768015
Abbeydale Deception, Absolution; Castle Rock Black Gold; Oakham Tera, Bishops Farewell; guest beers 🄷
This beautifully restored ex-Shipstones house is an absolute delight. The multi-roomed interior is blissfully free of electronic accoutrements and each area is individually styled, with two open fires and a log burning stove to warm a winter's evening. A myriad guest beer range, frequently including ales from Thornbridge and Funfair, is complemented by a dozen traditional ciders, many from small producers. A perfect balance has been struck between contemporary and traditional, and there is even a fire in the outside smokers' area. Dog friendly. ⛫Q❀⊟⊟(23)●P⸗

Matlock

Thorn Tree

48 Jackson Road, DE4 3JQ (off Bank Rd) SK300608
⏲ 12-2, 6-11; 12-2.30, 6-midnight Fri; 12-midnight Sat; 12-11 Sun ☎ (01629) 580295
Black Sheep Best Bitter; Draught Bass; Greene King Ruddles Best Bitter; Taylor Landlord; guest beers 🄷
Situated on the top of Matlock Bank, the pub enjoys stunning views from the patio area over the Derwent Valley, Bonsall Moor and Matlock Town. The small, compact and lively two-roomed pub is popular with office workers at lunchtime and locals in the evening. Food is served Tuesday to Friday lunchtimes; Wednesday evening is the pub's famous pie night. Barbecues are served on the patio every Sunday throughout the summer. Q❀◑⊟♣⸗

Matlock Bath

Temple Hotel

Temple Walk, DE4 3PG (off A6)
⏲ 12-3, 6-11; 12-11 Sat; 12-10 Sun ☎ (01629) 583911
🌐 templehotel.co.uk
Beer range varies 🄷
Situated above the main riverside promenade of Matlock Bath, this Georgian hotel affords splendid views over the Derwent Valley. Tourist attractions close by include the cable car rides, lead mines and the Peak District Mining Museum. The hotel provides an ideal base for enjoying the excellent walking and history around the area. The keen landlord's preference is to present up to four locally

sourced ales in the public bar, with Amber Ales and Howard Town breweries often featuring.
⛫❀⇌◐♿⇶🚌(6)♣P

Melbourne

Alma Inn

59 Derby Road, DE73 8FE
⏲ 4-11 (12.30am Fri); 11-12.30am Sat & Sun
☎ (01332) 695200
Marston's Pedigree; guest beers Ⓗ
The delightful small town of Melbourne is best known for its Antipodean cousin, which actually took its name from the 2nd Viscount Melbourne whose family still live here. The pub gets its name from the Crimean War battle, so it is only to be expected that beers from Marston's are in winning form. The hostelry is usually lively, often catering for a younger clientele, and holds two beer festivals each year, which are free of tie.
⛫❀▲🚌(68)♣P⁄–

Milford

King William IV

The Bridge, DE56 0RR (on A6)
⏲ 5 (12 Sat)-11.30; 12.30-11 Sun ☎ (01332) 840842
Marston's Pedigree; Taylor Landlord; guest beers Ⓗ
Situated next to the bridge in the centre of a historic mill village, backed by sandstone cliffs. A small, narrow, single-roomed local, it has exposed interior stone walls, a welcoming fireplace, low-beamed ceiling, quarry tiled floor and wooden settles. The three guest beers usually include one from a local micro-brewery and there are beer festivals in April and September. An ideal base for exploring the Derwent Valley World Heritage site.
⛫⇌🚌♣●

Miller's Dale

Angler's Rest ✔

SK17 8SN (on B6049) SK142734
⏲ 12-3, 6.30-11; 12-11 Sat & Sun ☎ (01298) 871323
🌐 theanglersrest.co.uk
Storm Silk of Amnesia; Tetley Bitter; guest beers Ⓗ
This ivy-clad pub on the banks of the River Wye dates from 1753 and is well-placed for the spectacular walk along the Monsal Trail. A multi-room hostelry, it includes a cosy lounge with a real fire and a comfortable dining room. Walking boots and dogs are welcome in the hikers' bar. Good food is mostly home cooked – Thursday is pie night. Guest beers are usually LocAle. Accommodation is in a self-catering apartment.
⛫Q⇌◐⊟▲🚌(65,66)♣P

New Mills

Pack Horse Inn ✔

Mellor Road, SK22 4QQ
⏲ 12-3, 5-11; 12-midnight Sat; 12-10.30 Sun
☎ (01663) 742365 🌐 packhorseinn.co.uk
Phoenix Arizona; Tetley Bitter; guest beers Ⓗ
A much extended pub built from local stone, with a recent matching extension incorporating an elegant dining room and high-standard accommodation. The bar room interior, however, remains largely unaltered with its traditional style and open fire, plus a stove for the winter; sentimental picture lovers should look out for 'fireside joys'. Two regularly changing guest beers, usually from local micros, are available. Outside there are two stone patio areas, one imaginatively built into the hillside, the other offering sweeping Pennine views. ⛫Q❀⇌◐P⁄–

New Tupton

Britannia Inn

Ward Street, S42 6XP SK397661
⏲ 4-11; 3-midnight Fri; 11.30-midnight Sat; 12-10.30 Sun
☎ (01246) 861438 🌐 spirebrewery.co.uk/britannia
Beer range varies Ⓗ
A friendly community pub, this free house is the brewery tap for Spire Brewery. It features eight cask ales including a mild and a stout or porter, along with a selection of cider and perry, and locally produced Czech-style lager, Moravka. It is a big supporter of local CAMRA campaigns as well as local charities. Quiz night is Tuesday. Outdoors boasts a skittles alley. The pub is easily accessible by public transport. Q❀⊟🚌(51)♣●P⁄–▯

Ockbrook

Royal Oak

55 Green Lane, DE72 3SE
⏲ 11.30-2.30, 5.30-11 (11.30 Fri); 11.30-3, 5.30-11.30 Sat; 12-4, 7-11 (12-11 May-Oct) Sun ☎ (01332) 662378
Draught Bass; guest beers Ⓗ
A CAMRA regional Pub of the Year 2000, the Royal Oak has featured in this Guide since 1976. Run by the same family since Coronation year, it is little changed, with each of the six rooms preserving its own distinctive character and customers. Many community groups meet and various events are held in the function room as well as May and October beer festivals. Excellent home-cooked food is served every lunchtime, and Monday to Friday evenings (Tuesday is themed food night).
Q❀◐♿🚌(9)♣●P⁄–

Over Haddon

Lathkil Hotel

DE45 1JE (signed in village) SK206665
⏲ 11.30-3, 6-11; 11.30-11 Sat; 12-10.30 Sun
☎ (01629) 812501 🌐 lathkil.co.uk
Everards Tiger; Whim Hartington Bitter; guest beers Ⓗ
The pub overlooks a masterpiece of Peak District scenery, marvellous in any weather. Walking in, one side is an old-fashioned bar room with real fire and oak beams, while superb home-cooked meals are served in the larger room opposite. A covered beer garden is the perfect place to while away summer evenings with a pint. Well-equipped rooms are available for staying over; dogs are welcome in the bar and walkers should take off their boots at the door. ⛫Q❀⇌◐⊟▲🚌P⁄–▯

Parwich

Sycamore Inn

DE6 1QL
⏲ 12-2 (4 Sat), 7 (6 Thu & Fri)-11; 12-11 Sun
☎ (01335) 390212
Robinson's Double Hop, seasonal beers Ⓗ
Residing in a small, remote Peak District village, this inn, named after nearby cottages, is next to the village green, duck pond and church. The bar has a real fire and warm greetings from staff and locals. There are separate rooms for pool and darts, and dominoes is also played. Regular and seasonal

beers are from the Robinson's range and Old Tom is regularly featured in winter. The village shop is located in the pub and the licensee has a holiday cottage 200m away. ♛Q❀◐◑⊟▲♣P

Pleasley

Nags Head ✔

Chesterfield Road, NG19 7PA (400m off A617 at Pleasley)

⏲ 5 (4 Fri)-midnight; 12-midnight Sat & Sun
☎ (01623) 810235

Greene King XX Mild, H&H Bitter, Morland Original Bitter, seasonal beers Ⓗ

A friendly family-run pub that always has four real ales, including a draught mild, on offer. Locals still order their 'mixed' mild and bitter from the real ale-enthusiast landlord. Darts and dominoes are played and there is also a full-sized table tennis table. The local bus service runs past the door, until 11pm. ♛Q♉❀⊟⊟♣P⊬

Ripley

George Inn

20 Lowes Hill, DE5 3DW (fork left on Butterley Hill at Talbot Taphouse)

⏲ 6 (2.30 Fri, 1 Sat)-1am; 1-11 Sun ☎ (01773) 512041

Amber seasonal beers; guest beers Ⓗ

This former Bateman's pub is handily situated between the town centre and the Midland Railway heritage centre at Butterley. It is also equidistant between Amber Ales Brewery and the Talbot Taphouse, which is the brewery's flagship pub. Amber Ales are always available, along with those from Tollgate and other guests. Football, pool, dominoes and skittles teams are based here. Live bands feature most Saturday nights. Opening hours may vary. ⊟(9.2)♣P

Red Lion ✔

Market Place, DE5 3BS

⏲ 9-midnight (1am Fri & Sat) ☎ (01773) 512875

Greene King Ruddles Best Bitter, Abbot; Marston's Pedigree; guest beers Ⓗ

Dating from the 1960s, this former Home Brewery house is at the hub of a vibrant market town. The large, open-plan interior is frequently well patronised, especially on weekend evenings. Outside there is a pleasant patio area that overlooks the parish church. A comprehensive selection of six guest beers should satisfy the most ardent ale enthusiast, with Black Hole and Thornbridge prominent among the local micro-breweries featured. Q❀◐◑♿⊟●P⊬

Rosliston

Bull's Head 🏆

Burton Road, DE12 8JU (NW edge of village) SK242168

⏲ 12-3, 7-11 ☎ (01283) 761705

Draught Bass; Marston's Pedigree Ⓗ

Late 19th-century brick-built free house with a comfortable public bar and cosy lounge – both featuring open fires and beamed ceilings – plus a large function room in a converted stable block. A collection of china bulls is displayed behind the bar, and encased models of a Burton union brewing system can be found in both the public bar and the function room. The National Forest Forestry Centre is located about half a mile away.
♛◑⊟▲⊟(22)♣P

Scarcliffe

Horse & Groom

Rotherham Road, S44 6SU (B6417 Bolsover to Shirebrook road) SK490687

⏲ 12-midnight ☎ (01246) 823152

Black Sheep Best Bitter; Greene King Abbot; Stones Bitter; Wells Bombardier; guest beers Ⓗ

Now in the second generation of family ownership, this family-owned 500-year-old free house always has up to seven real ales on offer. The lounge is mobile free. The impressive array of CAMRA certificates reflects this family's long-standing commitment to the care of its real ales, and the pub has featured in the Guide for more than 12 years. No hot food is served. Three self catering cottages are available (booking essential).
♛Q♉❀⇄⊟♿▲⊟(53,82)♣P⊬

Shirland

Shoulder of Mutton

Hallfieldgate Lane, DE55 6AA (on B6013, Wessington-Shirland crossroad) SK393582

⏲ 12-11 (7 Tue); 12-10.30 Sun ☎ (01773) 834992

Beer range varies Ⓗ

Eclectic 16th-century traditional drinking den, nestling on the edge of Amber Valley. The beer garden offers spectacular views and sunsets. A true free house where real people enjoy real ale from small breweries. There is no beer list on the wall because the ales change daily. The regulars are drawn from far and wide, fuelling the unique, easy atmosphere created by the irrepressible landlord and landlady. Dogs and hikers are welcome. Check out the tea cups. ♛Q❀⊟▲♣P⊬

Smalley

Bell Inn ✔

35 Main Road, DE7 6EF (on A608) SK407445

⏲ 11.30-3, 5-11; 11.30-11 Fri-Sun ☎ (01332) 880635

Adnams Broadside; Marston's Pedigree; Oakham JHB; Whim Hartington Bitter, Hartington IPA; guest beers Ⓗ

Situated near Shipley Country Park, this mid-19th century inn has three rooms where brewing and other memorabilia adorn the walls, as well as a large, attractive garden. Excellent for food, with a good and varied menu with daily specials, it is also still a drinkers' pub, serving five regular beers plus guests. Accommodation is available in three apartments in converted stables. Weekday opening hours may be extended in the summer.
♛Q❀⇄◐◑⊟⊟(H1,AMB)P

South Normanton

Devonshire Arms 🏆

137 Market Street, DE55 2AA

⏲ 12-midnight ☎ (01773) 810748

🌐 the-devonshire-arms.co.uk

Sarah Hughes Dark Ruby; guest beers Ⓗ

Winner of numerous local CAMRA awards, this is a genuine free house offering four reasonably priced real ales and Westons traditional cider. Sky Sports and ESPN are shown on three large-screen TVs. Home-cooked meals are served every day except Sunday, when a very popular carvery is offered (booking advised). Vegetarians, vegans and coeliacs are all catered for, and daily specials are offered. ♉❀◐◑♿⊟♣●P⊬

South Wingfield

Old Yew Tree
51 Manor Road, DE55 7NH (on B5035)
✪ 12-2.30 (not Mon), 5-11 (midnight Fri & Sat); 12-11 Sun
☎ (01773) 833763 ● theoldyewtreeinn.co.uk
Marston's Pedigree; Whim Hartington Bitter ℍ
There is nothing paranormal about the beer in one of Britain's most haunted pubs, which is situated near the magnificent remains of the 15th-century Wingfield Manor, destroyed by Cromwell during the Civil War. A brace of guest beers augments the two regulars, and good home-cooked food, including excellent Sunday lunches, draws people from near and far. There is limited parking.
⚞Q☸◑&♣●P'—

Stanley Common

White Post Inn
237 Belper Road, DE7 6FT (on A609) SK412425
✪ 12-3 (not Mon), 6-11; 12-1am Fri & Sat; 12-11 Sun
☎ (0115) 9300194 ● myspace.com/thewhitepost
Beer range varies ℍ
This white-painted roadside inn is on the main road through Stanley Common. Three interlinking rooms are served by a central bar with up to five changing guests, including a LocAle usually from Funfair. Quality, locally sourced food is served at pub prices with daily chef's specials. There is a family-friendly dining area and a conservatory leading to a heated smoking area overlooking the large garden. The pub hosts live Saturday evening entertainment and regular beer festivals. ⚞☸◑▶🍴(59)♣P'—

Stanton in Peak

Flying Childers
Main Road, DE4 2LW (off B6056 Bakewell-Ashbourne Rd) SK240643
✪ 12-2 (not Mon & Tue), 7-11; 12-3, 7-11 Sat & Sun
☎ (01629) 636333
Wells Bombardier; guest beers ℍ
Unspoilt two-roomed village pub named after a famous 18th-century racehorse owned by the Duke of Devonshire. Located in the centre of the village near the historic Stanton Moor and Nine Ladies Stone circle, it is patronised by a good mix of locals, tourists and walkers – dogs are welcome. Two interesting guest beers are always on offer, usually from micros. Simple home-cooked food is available at lunchtimes. A monthly quiz is hosted and there are open acoustic and dominoes nights. The attractive beer garden behind the pub is a sun trap on a summer afternoon. ⚞Q☸🍴P

Staveley

Speedwell Inn
Lowgates, S43 3TT
✪ 6-11 (10.30 Sun) ☎ (01246) 474665
Townes Speedwell Bitter, Staveley Cross, IPA, Pynot Porter ℍ
This is the brewery tap for Townes beers, which have been brewed on the premises for the past 12 years. The core ales are supplemented by regular specials and the occasional guest beer from another micro. A small range of bottled and continental beers is also stocked. Open plan but with several distinct seating areas, the bar is the focal point for conversation. Q🍴♣

Sutton cum Duckmanton

Arkwright Arms
Chesterfield Road, S44 5JG (A632 between Chesterfield and Bolsover)
✪ 11-11 (12.30am Fri) ☎ (01246) 232053
● arkwrightarms.co.uk
Beer range varies ℍ
There is always a warm welcome at this mock Tudor-fronted free house. All three rooms are made cosy with open fires. An excellent range of ever-changing guest ales, many from local micros, is complemented by 10 ciders and two perries. Beer festivals are held at Easter and on bank holidays, with mini events throughout the year. Quality food is served lunchtimes and evenings. Winner of numerous CAMRA awards.
⚞☸◑🍴(81,82,83)♣●P'—

Thulston

Harrington Arms
4 Grove Close, DE72 3EY (off B5010)
✪ 11.30-3 (not Mon), 6-11; 11.30-11 Sat; 12-10.30 Sun
☎ (01332) 571798
Draught Bass ℍ/Ⓖ; Tollgate Earl's Ale; guest beers ℍ
Two former cottages, refronted to stand out and brightly lit after dark, have been smartly modernised without losing their cottage feel. This free house has low, beamed ceilings, wooden-clad interior walls and open fires in winter. Regular beer festivals are held and an adjoining restaurant serves good food. Elvaston Castle Country Park, former estate of the Earls of Harrington (hence the house beer's name) is close by. Bass is served on gravity by request. ⚞☸◑▲🍴●P'—

Wardlow Mires

Three Stags Heads ★
SK17 8RW (A623/B6465 jct) SK180756
✪ closed Mon-Thu; 7-11 Fri; 11-11 Sat; 12-10.30 Sun
☎ (01298) 872268
Abbeydale Deception, Absolution, Black Lurcher; guest beer ℍ
One of the few hostelries in the area on CAMRA's national inventory of unspoilt interiors, this quaint 300-year-old inn has two small rooms with stone-flagged floors and low ceilings. An ancient range warms the bar and the house dogs – the house beer, Black Lurcher, is named after a former resident. The food is locally sourced with game a speciality. A severe rebuke awaits those asking for draught lager – imported lagers are available in bottles. ⚞Q☸◑P

Whaley Bridge

Shepherd's Arms
7 Old Road, SK23 7HR
✪ 3 (12 Sat)-midnight; 2-midnight Sun ☎ (01663) 732384
Marston's Burton Bitter, Pedigree; guest beers ℍ
This attractive, whitewashed stone-built pub has been preserved unspoilt, conveying the feel of the farmhouse it once was. The unchanged tap room, the best for miles around, is a delight, with open fire, flagged floor and scrubbed-top tables. Additionally there is a comfortable lounge. Guest beers are selected from the Marston's range. A short walk from Whaley Bridge station, the pub is also on the Manchester Airport-Buxton and other bus routes. ⚞Q☸🍴(199)♣P'—

Whitehough

Old Hall Inn

SK23 6EJ (⅓ mile off B6062)
12-midnight (01663) 750529 old-hall-inn.co.uk
Marston's Burton Bitter; guest beers
Nestling in the attractive hamlet of Whitehough, near Chinley, this 16th-century inn offers a warm welcome. Food and drink focuses on local produce, including four or five beers from local micros, one always from Thornbridge Brewery. The adjacent 14th-century Whitehough Hall, with minstrels' gallery and mullioned windows, is used for dining and accessed directly from the inn. Popular beer festivals take place on the third weekend in September and the last weekend in February. Ten minutes' walk from Chinley station.
(Chinley) (189,190) **P**

Winster

Old Bowling Green

East Bank, DE4 2DS (25m from Market Hall)
closed Mon & Tue; 6-11 (midnight Fri & Sat); 12-11 Sun
(01629) 650219 peakparkpub.co.uk
Beer range varies
Dating from the 15th century, this attractive pub is located close to the National Trust-owned Market Hall at the centre of this historic Peak District village. A central bar serves a long main room with cosy log fire and two smaller rooms to the rear. Up to four ever-changing beers come from local micro-breweries, often Bradfield and Abbeydale. Food is served Sunday lunchtime and Thursday to Saturday evenings. Note limited opening hours.
Q (172) **P**

Wirksworth

Hope & Anchor

Market Place, DE4 4ET
12 (4 Mon & Wed)-midnight; 12-11 Sun
(01629) 823340 hopenanchor.co.uk
St Austell Tribute; Wirksworth seasonal beer; guest beers
This Grade II-listed building was once described as the governor's residence and retains some interesting original features. The corner lounge overlooking the market place has a magnificent carved wooden fireplace and a curious bow-fronted floor-to-ceiling cabinet containing a bureau. The bar is split between pool and seating, and there are tables outside on the gravel courtyard. This family-run pub provides home-cooked meals and hosts an annual beer festival in September as part of the Wirksworth Festival.
(6.1)

Royal Oak

North End, DE4 4FG (off B5035)
8-11.30 (midnight Fri & Sat); 12-3, 7.30-11 Sun
(01629) 823000
Draught Bass; Taylor Landlord; Whim Hartington IPA; guest beers
Excellent, small, ultra-traditional local in a stone terrace near the market place, highlighted at night by rows of fairy lights. The bar features old pictures of local interest and there is also a pool room and smoking grotto. The Oak enjoys a long-standing reputation for Draught Bass, and always has five ales to choose from including a LocAle. The Ecclesbourne Valley Railway Line visitor attraction is close by. **Q** (6.1)

Old Bowling Green, Winster (Photo: Nick Wheat)

Cider

Photography by Mark Bolton

Proper cider and perry – made with apples and pears and nothing but, is a wonderful drink – but there's so much more to it than that. **Cider** is a lavishly illustrated celebration of real cider, and its close cousin perry, for anyone who wants to learn more about Britain's oldest drink. With features on the UK's most interesting and characterful cider and perry makers, how to make your own cider, foreign ciders, and the best places to drink cider – including unique dedicated cider houses, award-winning pubs and year-round CAMRA festivals all over the country – **Cider** is the essential book for any cider or perry lover.

"This book, clearly a work of devotion by its authors, represents a tour de force of the world of cider, covering history, recipes, museums, and a compendium of sources for both drink and trees. Lovingly written (with several critiques of the abomination of carbonised cider), the chapters are compiled by different experts in clear, accessible prose. Mark Bolton's warm images capture the emotional involvement of those involved in its production." BBC Countryfile Magazine

£14.99 ISBN 978-1-85249-259-5 CAMRA members' price £12.99 192 pages

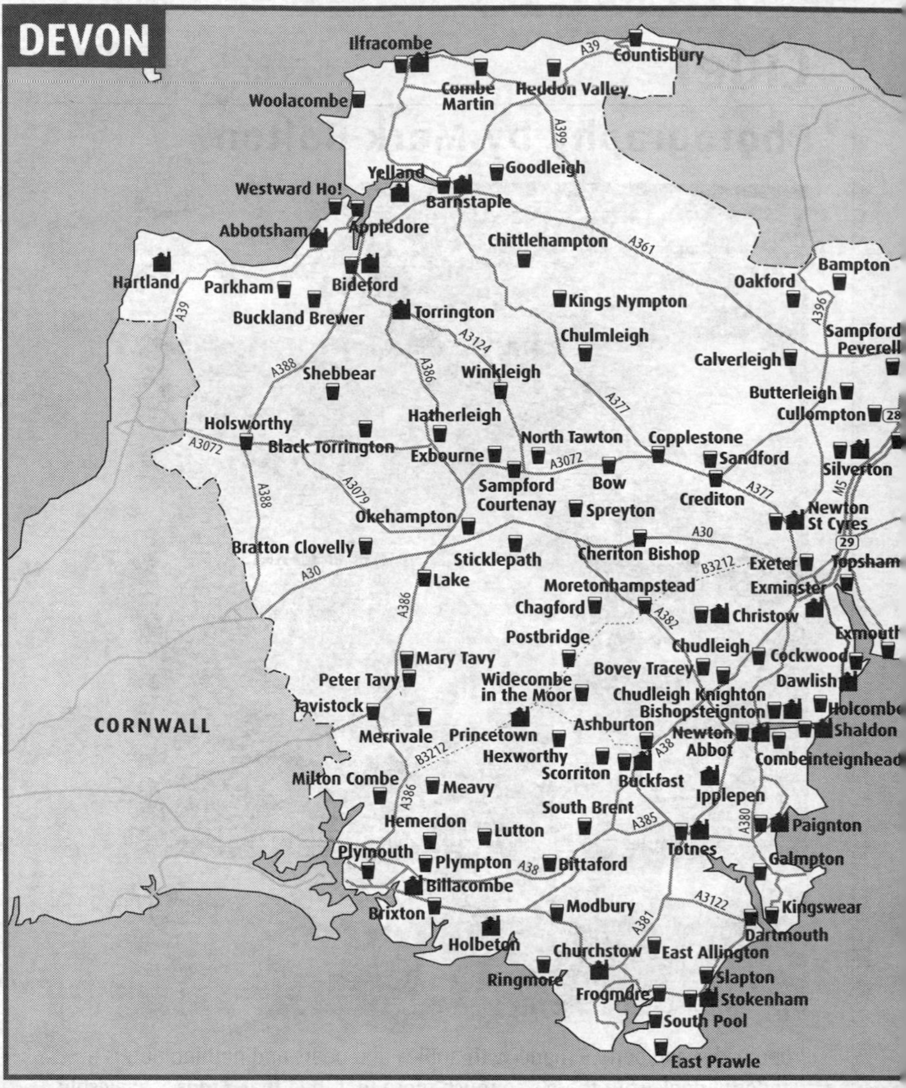

Appledore

Beaver Inn

2 Irsha Street, EX39 1RY SS462308

✪ 11-midnight; 11.30-10.30 Sun ☎ (01237) 474822

🌐 beaverinn.co.uk

St Austell Tribute; Sharp's Doom Bar; guest beers Ⓗ

Situated in a small fishing village, superb views of the Taw and Torridge estuaries can be enjoyed from the riverside patio. There are attractive walks along the sands and nearby quay towards Bideford and Westward Ho! The single bar has three handpumps plus Sam's cider from Winkleigh. Excellent locally-sourced food is served in the bar, restaurant or on the patio. Fresh fish is a speciality and the desserts are home-made. ❀◑⊟♣●

Ashburton

Dartmoor Lodge ✔

Peartree Cross, TQ13 7JW (just off A38 at Peartee jct)

✪ 11-11; 12-10.30 Sun ☎ (01364) 652232

🌐 dartmoorlodge.co.uk

Bays Gold; Dartmoor Jail Ale; Exmoor Ale; Sharp's Doom Bar; guest beers Ⓗ

A good selection of local real ales is served at this 24-bedroom roadside hotel on the edge of the Dartmoor National Park and the town of Ashburton. There is a friendly and comfortable atmosphere in the beamed bar and restaurant area which, in winter, has a welcoming log fire. Plenty of seating is available in the bar area where, in addition to the restaurant, good quality local food is served. Rooms are available for meetings and conferences. ⚔Q☕❀⇌◑♿⛺⊟(X38,88)P⁻

Exeter Inn

26 West Street, TQ13 7DU (on main road through Ashburton opp church)

✪ 11-2.30, 5-11 (midnight Fri & Sat); 12-3, 7-10.30 Sun ☎ (01364) 652013

Dartmoor IPA; guest beer Ⓗ

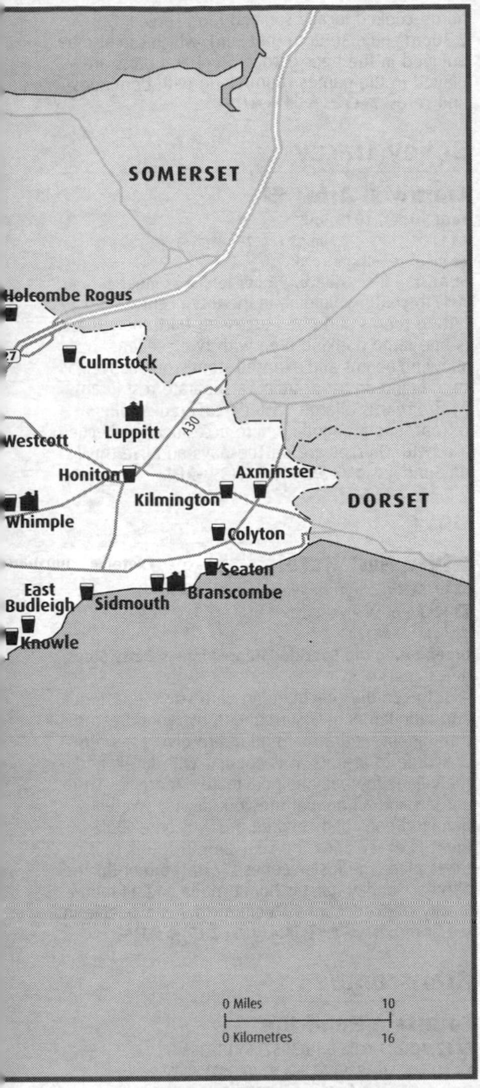

The oldest pub in Ashburton, built in 1131, with additions in the 17th century. This is a friendly local that originally housed the workers constructing the nearby church, and the inn was used by Sir Francis Drake on his journeys to London. The main bar has seated drinking areas either side of the entrance hallway and is L-shaped, rustic and wood-panelled, with a canopy. At the rear is a further bar served via a small hatch and counter.
Q❀◐🚌(X38,88)♣🍏⁵—

Axminster

Lamb Inn

Lyme Road, EX13 5BE
⌚ 11.30-midnight (1am Fri; 2am Sat); 12-10.30 Sun
☎ (01297) 33922
Branscombe Vale Branoc; guest beer Ⓗ
Traditional local half a mile from the town centre. The single room interior has a comfortable bar area for dining and playing pool, plus a large-screen TV that often shows sports. There is a spacious garden with two boule pistes, and a heated smokers' shelter. The landlady's pub fare is very good and exceptional value for money, with food served all day. No dogs please because the resident dog gets very jealous. ❀◐🚌(31)P⁵—

Bampton

Exeter Inn ✔

Tiverton Road, EX16 9DY (on A396 on roundabout jct with B3190)
⌚ 11-11 ☎ (01398) 331345 🌐 exeterinn.net
Exmoor Ale; Otter Ale; Sharp's Doom Bar; guest beers Ⓖ
A traditional Devon longhouse, with refurbished interlinking small rooms with logburners. All are served from a central bar displaying the six-barrel stillage as a focal point from which the ales are dispensed by gravity. Food is served 12-2pm and 6-9pm all week. The 11 bedrooms are all en-suite, with TV and Wi-Fi. Popular with walkers and tourists to Devon and Exmoor, this is a top-quality, friendly pub, and a great new addition to the pubs in the local CAMRA branch.
♨Q❀⛟◐▲🚌(398)P⁵—

Barnstaple

Panniers ✔

33-34 Boutport Street, EX31 1RX (opp the Queens Theatre)
⌚ 9-midnight (1am Fri & Sat) ☎ (01271) 329720
Greene King Ruddles Best Bitter, Abbot; Marston's Pedigree; Shepherd Neame Spitfire; guest beers Ⓗ
A popular town-centre Wetherspoon's with an unrivalled selection of real ales in the area, many coming from local micro-breweries, plus cider from Westons. Butchers Row opposite once had 33 butchers' shops and a vegetable market (now Pannier Market, hence the name). Regular beer

INDEPENDENT BREWERIES

Barum Barnstaple
Baskerville Yelland (NEW)
Bays Paignton
Beer Engine Newton St Cyres
Branscombe Vale Branscombe
Bridgetown Totnes
Clearwater Torrington
Country Life Abbotsham
Dartmoor Princetown
Dartmouth Newton Abbot (brewing suspended)
Devon Earth Buckfastleigh
Exe Valley Silverton
Exeter Exminster
Forge Hartland
Gidley's Christow
Hunter's Ipplepen
Isca Dawlish
Jollyboat Bideford
O'Hanlon's Whimple
Otter Luppitt
Quercus Churchstow
Red Rock Bishopsteignton
Ringmore Shaldon
South Hams Stokenham
Summerskills Billacombe
Teignworthy Newton Abbot
Union Holbeton
Wizard Ilfracombe

festivals, including one exclusive to Devon branches, offer discounted real ales. Competitively priced meals with a drink are offered on themed food days. The rear garden area offers covered seating for less clement weather. ☋❀◐♿⊟●⊱

Bideford

Lacey's Ale & Cider House

1-5 Bridge Street, EX39 2BU (50m uphill from A386)
⊙ 12-11 (1am Sat; 10.30 Sun) ☎ (01237) 425417
Country Life Old Appledore, Lacey's Best, Pot Wallop, Golden Pig, Black Boar, Country Bumpkin ⊞
The first venture into pub ownership by the owners of Country Life Brewery. The renovated premises includes the Tavern in the Port bar with log-burning stove (open at weekends), restaurant, split-level bar area and a function room with integral skittle alley. Most beers are from Country Life, with a range of up to two guest ales and four ciders. Good value, reasonably priced pub food is served (no food Wed or Sun eve). Well-behaved children and dogs are welcome. ♛◐⊟(1,85,315)♣●

Bishopsteignton

Bishop John de Grandisson

Clanage Street, TQ14 9QS
⊙ 12-2.30 (not Mon), 6-11 (midnight Fri & Sat); 12-11 Sun
☎ (01626) 775285
Greene King IPA; Otter Amber, Ale; guest beers ⊞
A traditional pub situated in the middle of the village. The public bar where the locals drink is L-shaped and preserves some original features. The smaller split-level lounge has a separate dining room serving home-cooked food (no food Mon or Tue lunch). The pub has darts teams, poker nights and a takeaway food night. At the rear is a good-sized car park and a seating area with an upper deck offering fine views of the Teign Estuary.
♛Q❀◐⊟♿⛺⊟♣P⊱

Bittaford

Horse & Groom

Exeter Road, PL21 0EL SX667569
⊙ 12-midnight (11 Sun) ☎ (01752) 892358
St Austell Dartmoor Best Bitter; guest beer ⊞
Previously sited on the opposite side of the main road, this 1930s community pub features one large bar, and is decorated with historic photos of the area taken from the former Moorhaven Hospital which overlooks the village. Two real ales and Thatchers cider are served. The licensee bought the pub in 2009, and now hosts seasonal events promoting beers from local breweries. There are separate areas for dining and games, with pool and televised sport available in the bar area.
♛❀◐⛺⊟(X38,X80)♣●P⊱

Black Torrington

Torridge Inn

Broad Street, EX21 5PT SS465056
⊙ 12-3 (not Tue), 6-11; 12-3, 6-10.30 Sun
☎ (01409) 231243 ⊕ thetorridgeinn.co.uk
Sharp's Doom Bar; guest beers ⊞
Village local near the River Torridge, the Tarka Trail and the National Cycle Network. A large log fire welcomes guests, and three handpumps dispense real ale (two in winter) with Sam's Cider from Winkleigh on the other. There is a good selection of home-cooked locally sourced food served 12-2.30pm and 6.30-9pm (not Sun), which can also be enjoyed in the beer garden. Pool and darts are played in the games room along with dominoes and cards. ♛Q☋❀◐♣●P⊱

Bovey Tracey

Cromwell Arms ✔

Fore Street, TQ13 9AE
⊙ 11-11; 12-10.30 Sun ☎ (01626) 833473
⊕ thecromwellarms.co.uk
St Austell IPA, Tribute, Proper Job, seasonal beers ⊞
A 17th-century building in the town centre with 12 letting rooms and good access to Dartmoor. There is one large drinking area with two sections showing beams and exposed stonework, as well as two dining areas including a separate restaurant. At the rear is a large wisteria-covered smokers' retreat, and a pagoda where occasional barbecues are held. Quizzes are on Tuesdays and live music on Sundays. ♛Q❀⛟◐♿⊟(39)♣P⊱

Bow

White Hart Hotel

EX17 6EN (Bottom of village on main A3072)
⊙ 12-3 (not Mon), 6-11; 12-11 Sat; 12-3, 6-10.30 Sun
☎ (01363) 881287
Greene King Old Speckled Hen; Skinners Betty Stogs; guest beers ⊞
A 16th-century coaching inn with stone flagstones and wooden panels surrounded by wood beams throughout, and a roaring log fire giving a warm welcome to visitors. It is popular with locals and the village football and pool teams. There is a large garden and an annual firework display. Well-behaved dogs and children are welcome. Quiz night is every third Thursday and Irish folk music takes place the first Wednesday of the month. The popular Sunday roast is home-made and all food is locally sourced. Sam's Medium cider is available in the summer. ♛☋❀◐⛺⊟(51,315)♣●P⊱

Branscombe

Fountain Head Inn

EX12 3BG (1 mile off A3052) SY187888
⊙ 11-3, 6-11; 12-10.30 Sun ☎ (01297) 680359
Branscombe Vale Branoc, BVB, Summa That; guest beers ⊞
Popular with walkers, this neat 500-year-old pub is at the west end of this long straggly village in a beautiful coastal valley. It retains wood-panelled walls and flagstoned floors with an inglenook fireplace. A beer festival is held in June on the nearest weekend to the longest day. The beers are all from the local Branscombe Vale Brewery and the cider is Cheddar Valley. Good food is served at reasonable prices. ♛Q☋❀◐⛺⊟(899)●P⊱

Bratton Clovelly

Clovelly Inn ✔

EX20 4JZ (between A30 and A3079) SX464919
⊙ 12-3, 6-midnight; 12-midnight Sat & Sun
☎ (01837) 871447
Beer range varies ⊞
Traditional village pub that is over 150 years old (although an oak fireplace lintel has 1789 inscribed) situated near Dartmoor National Park and Roadford Lake. The village also boasts a signed

three mile trail. The main bar has a large wood-burning stove with two separate dining areas and a games room. The pub is known for its food, and booking is advisable in the evenings. During the summer the three real ales are joined by Sam's Medium cider from Winkleigh. ⌂☕◑⛺♣●P⊬

Brixton

Foxhound

Kingsbridge Road, PL8 2AH
⏲ 11-11 (midnight Fri & Sat); 12-11 Sun ☎ (01752) 880271
🌐 foxhoundinn.co.uk
Courage Best Bitter; guest beers Ⓗ
A two-bar 18th-century inn in a small village just east of Plymouth, which continues to go from strength to strength. Up to four guest beers are always available, with the local Summerskills Brewery always featured. Rotating ciders are now also on handpump. The food is locally sourced and the menu often showcases classic English dishes that are frequently overlooked elsewhere. The pub hosts popular monthly quizzes, and the lounge bar features an interesting collection of toby jugs.
⌂Q◑◑⛺⛺🚌(93,94)♣●P⊬

Buckfast

Abbey Inn ✔

TQ11 0EA (off A38, follow signs to Buckfast Abbey)
⏲ 11-11 (11-3, 5-11 Mon-Thu winter); 12-10.30 Sun
☎ (01364) 642343 🌐 theabbeyinnbuckfast.co.uk
St Austell Dartmoor Best, Tribute, HSD Ⓗ
Situated in a beautiful setting next to the River Dart within Dartmoor National Park, close to the famous Buckfast Abbey. It has an outside terrace with seating and views overlooking the river, including glimpses of the Abbey. Inside, the warm and welcoming oak-panelled bar is spacious, with traditional furniture. The large dining room serves an excellent range of food and there any many visitor attractions within close vicinity of the pub.
⌂Q❀🛏◑⛺🚌(X38,88)P⊬

Buckland Brewer

Coach & Horses

EX39 5LU SS423206
⏲ 12-3; 5.30 (6.30 Sun)-11.30 ☎ (01237) 451395
Cotleigh Golden Seahawk; Otter Ale; St Austell Tribute Ⓗ
This 13th-century, low-beamed, thatched two-storey inn was reputedly used as a court room in the 17th century with the cellars as a gaol and an execution drop in the main bar. There is a woodburner with antique settle and a small back room where darts and pool are played. The skittle alley doubles as a function room. Quizzes are held three times a year and the frontage is used for drinking and dining al fresco. An old innkeeper's house is available to rent nearby.
⌂Q❀◑⛺🚌(372)P⊬

Butterleigh

Butterleigh Inn

The Green, EX15 1PN (opp church)
⏲ 12-2.30, 6-11 (midnight Fri & Sat); 12-2.30, 7-10.30 Sun (not Nov-Mar) ☎ (01884) 855407
Cotleigh Tawny Owl; O'Hanlon's Yellowhammer; guest beers Ⓗ

An excellent country pub in a small quaint village, this is a splendid 17th-century Devon cob building. Lunchtimes tend to be quiet. It is busier evenings and weekends, when a mix of generations creates a great atmosphere with diverse conversation. A choice of three real ales is always on offer, two of which are LocAle, and ciders. There is a main bar, lounge and a modern dining room. Drink inside or outside, with lovely surroundings either way.
⌂Q☕❀🛏◑⛺♿♣●P⊬

Calverleigh

Rose & Crown

EX16 8BA (on the old Rackenford Road)
⏲ 11.30 (12 Sun)-midnight ☎ (01884) 256301
Butcombe Bitter; Otter Ale; Taylor Landlord Ⓗ
A traditional 17th-century village pub, with beamed ceilings and exposed stone walls, just a mile from Tiverton town centre. It has a restaurant, beer garden and skittle alley that doubles as a function room. Excellent home-cooked food, made with local produce where possible, is available, together with local cider from Palmershayes across the road. Q❀◑♿♣●P

Chagford

Sandy Park Inn

Sandy Park, TQ13 8JW (on A382 Moretonhampstead-Whiddon Down road)
⏲ 12-11 ☎ (01647) 433267 🌐 sandyparkinn.co.uk
Dartmoor Jail Ale; O'Hanlon's Yellowhammer; Otter Bitter Ⓗ**; guest beer** Ⓗ/Ⓖ
Thatched free house, thought to be 17th century. The main bar has a large open fireplace, ancient beams, stone floor and high-backed wooden bench seating. A small snug is set around a large table. Another bar becomes an intimate restaurant at weekends serving home-cooked food. Castle Drogo (National Trust), Fingle Bridge and Chagford Village are nearby. A covered smoking den is next to the large garden, and there is a small car park at the front of the pub. ⌂❀🛏◑🚌♣P

Cheriton Bishop

Old Thatch Inn

EX6 6JH (¼ mile off the A30) SX775930
⏲ 11.30-3, 6-11 (not Sun eve) ☎ (01647) 24204
🌐 theoldthatchinn.com
O'Hanlon's Port Stout, Stormstay; Otter Ale; Sharp's T.O.T.I.'s Best Ⓗ
Totally and sympathetically refurbished throughout 2007 following a fire, this is a traditional Grade II-listed thatched free house, originally built as a coaching house. On the eastern edge of Dartmoor, it is popular with walkers and welcomes dogs. Four handpumps serve West Country ales. Exmoor Brewery supplied the popular third-pint glasses. The restaurant-style menu offers a good selection, and there is a specials board too, all using local produce, and a choice of two roasts on Sundays.
Q☕❀🛏◑⛺🚌(173,X30)♣P⊬

Chittlehampton

Bell Inn

The Square, EX37 9QL (opp church) SS636245
⏲ 11-3, 6-midnight; 11-midnight Sat; 12-11 Sun
☎ (01769) 540368 🌐 thebellatchittlehampton.co.uk
Beer range varies Ⓗ/Ⓖ

Situated in the main square since 1888 and owned by the same family for over 30 years, the pub is popular with locals and visitors alike. The landlord offers a range of West Country beer from three handpumps, with more occasionally available on gravity. Excellent value food using local produce is served 12-2pm and 6-9pm every day (6.30-9pm Sun). The attractive garden has a children's play area. Music jam nights are held on the second Monday of the month.

Christow

Teign House Inn

Teign Valley Road, EX6 7PL (on B3193)
12-3, 5-11.30; 12-11.30 Sat & Sun ☎ (01647) 252286
teignhouseinn.co.uk
Dartmoor Jail Ale; Otter Amber; guest beers H
Welcoming, atmospheric country pub, with beams and a warming log fire, enjoying strong local support. The sizeable garden attracts the families of locals and visitors alike, while an adjoining field has space for caravans and campers. An annual beer festival with up to 30 beers is held on the second weekend in July. Great pub food, all home-cooked, includes a separate gluten-free menu. Two guest beers are available, both from West Country breweries. Local CAMRA Branch Pub of the Year 2010. (360)P

Chudleigh

Bishop Lacy

52-53 Fore Street, TQ13 0HY
12-midnight (1am Fri & Sat) ☎ (01626) 854585
O'Hanlon's Stormstay; Sharp's Doom Bar; guest beers H
A regular Guide entry in a Grade II-listed building. A warm welcome is guaranteed from licensees of 16 years' standing. The public bar is dominated by a fireplace which incredibly is just half of its original size and retains the hooks for hanging hams. The pub is reputedly haunted by a white lady upstairs and a monk downstairs. There is strong emphasis on West Country beers and excellent home cooking. Sambucca the dog welcomes other hounds and well-behaved children.
Q(39,182)

Chudleigh Knighton

Anchor Inn

Plymouth Road, TQ13 0EN
12-11 (10.30 Sun) ☎ (01626) 853123
Butcombe Bitter; St Austell Tribute G
This 15th-century building on the old A38 was once a coaching inn, with the stables being the present day skittle alley. It is almost Tardis-like, starting with a gem of a largely unspoilt, low-beamed, public bar, through into a games area that was once a vet's surgery, then out into a smokers' gazebo in the large garden. Play equipment is available for children. The beers are served directly from a stillage at the side of the bar.
Q(39,182)

Chulmleigh

Old Court House

South Molton Street, EX18 7BW
11.30-midnight ☎ (01769) 580045
oldcourthouseinn.co.uk
St Austell Tribute; guest beers H
Grade II-listed thatched local where Charles I held court in 1634. A huge coat of arms commemorating the event dominates one of the bedrooms. Guest beers, mostly from the south-west area, change regularly, and the cider is from Thatchers. Thursday quiz night supports local charities and a folk night is held every second Tuesday of the month. The harvest festival includes a religious service held in the bar by the local vicar. Food is served all day until 9.30pm.
(377)

Cockwood

Anchor Inn

EX6 8RA (just off the A379, outside Starcross, next to Cockwood harbour) SX 976 807
11-11 (Sun 10.30) ☎ (01626) 890203 or 891203
anchorinncockwood.com
Otter Bitter, Ale; St Austell Tribute; Taylor Landlord; guest beers H
On picturesque Cockwood harbour, this 450 year-old-inn and former seaman's mission has many old settles, timber panelling, low beams and snugs, with old nautical memorabilia everywhere. Live music events feature at least three times a week. It has an award-winning, extensive seafood menu, especially mussels. Haunted by a friendly ghost and his dog, this is a really atmospheric Devon gem. It offers a free pick-up service within 20 miles for 8-14 people. Starcross station is a mile away.
Q(2)P

Colyton

Kingfisher Inn

Dolphin Street, EX24 6NA
11-3, 6-11 (midnight Fri & Sat); 12-3, 7-10.30 Sun
☎ (01297) 552476 kingfisherinn.co.uk
Bays Best; Sharp's Doom Bar; guest beers H
A traditional 16th-century stone and timber pub close to the centre of this delightful small town, with public car park nearby, and a tram that connects to the town of Seaton. A separate restaurant at the rear serves locally sourced good-value food. Themed food events take place once a month, and skittles, darts, crib and boules are regularly played at this friendly pub. Families and dogs are welcome. The guest beers are often Sharp's seasonal brews. No food Sunday evening.
(20,885)

Combe Martin

Castle Inn

High Street, EX34 0HS (opp church)
12-1.30am (midnight Sun) ☎ (01271) 883706
castleinn.info
Brains Rev James; guest beers H
Main-street pub with wood-panelled walls and a large purpose-built function room. There is an excellent range of ales, Winkleigh cider is available in summer, and there is a logburner for winter months. The rear garden overlooks the church and holds barbecues and hog roasts in summer. A beer festival is held during carnival week in August, and good value food is served all year round. Games include skittles, darts, table football and pool. Live music plays twice a month.
(3,30)P

Combeinteignhead

Wild Goose

TQ12 4RA (between Newton Abbot and Shaldon on S side of River Teign)

⚙ 11-3, 5.30-11; 12-3, 7-11 Sun ☎ (01626) 872241

Otter Bright; Sharp's Doom Bar; Skinner's Betty Stogs; guest beers Ⓗ

A 17th-century free house in the heart of the village near the Teign estuary. The beamed bar has two open fires, pews, bar billiards and up to seven different beers plus a real cider. The pleasant, large dining area overlooks the rural garden. Home-cooked food, including fresh fish and vegetarian meals, is complemented by a good wine list. Tastings using third-of-a-pint glasses are available at a fixed price. ♨Q❀◐◑♿♣●P⅄

Copplestone

Devonshire Dumpling

Morchard Road, EX17 5LP

⚙ 11.30 (12.30 Sat & Sun)-3, 5.30-11 ☎ (01363) 85102

🌐 devonshiredumpling.com

St Austell Tribute; Sharp's Doom Bar; guest beers Ⓗ

This family-run country inn situated in the heart of the countryside is a destination pub with the emphasis on dining. More than 100 years old, it was formerly called the Sturt Arms after a local family. It is well known for its fresh home-cooked food, offering quality produce from local suppliers. Children are welcome, and a play area is provided outside the conservatory restaurant. Three bedrooms are available for bed and breakfast. ❀🛏◐◑♿⛺⇌(Morchard Road)🚌(325,377)P⅄

Countisbury

Blue Ball Inn ✔

Countisbury Hill, EX35 6NE (1½ miles E of Lynmouth) SS747496

⚙ 9-11 ☎ (01598) 741263 🌐 blueballinn.com

St Austell Cousin Jack, Tribute; guest beers Ⓗ

Old coaching inn open every day of the year, with a large 13th-century inglenook fire near the bar. Three real ales are available including one guest, normally sourced from a local micro-brewery. Food is served from an extensive menu (12-9pm daily) in the spacious dining area. The pub rears its own pigs and pork is available 'from paddock to plate'. Ideally situated for exploring Exmoor, well-behaved children and dogs are welcome. ♨❀🛏◐◑🚌(300,401)P

Crediton

Crediton Inn

28A Mill Street, EX17 1EZ (near A377 and station)

⚙ 11-11; 12-3, 7-10.30 Sun ☎ (01363) 772882

🌐 crediton-inn.co.uk

Fuller's London Pride; Sharp's Doom Bar; guest beers Ⓗ

The framed deeds date this inn to 1878, with windows etched with the ancient town seal. This genuine free house is well supported by the locals. Following recent refurbishment, it now has eight handpumps, served by local breweries, with an ale festival in November. The skittle alley doubles as a function room, and good home-cooked food is served at weekends, with snacks available at other times. The bubbly owner is the longest serving landlady in Crediton, having been here for 30 years. ♨❀◐◑⇌🚌(50,51,315)♣P⅄

Cullompton

Pony & Trap

10 Exeter Hill, EX15 1DJ (on B3181 S of town)

⚙ 5-11; 11-midnight Sat; 12-11 Sun ☎ (01884) 34182

O'Hanlon's Yellowhammer; guest beers Ⓗ

A traditional local with a good atmosphere, which has been newly refurbished with a pleasant decor and open fires, making it cosy in winter. Flowers on the bar and ornaments give this pub a homely feel. There are always two real ales available. Food is only available Saturday breakfast-time and Sunday lunch. Darts and skittles are played. ♨Q❀◐🚌(1)♣

Culmstock

Culm Valley Inn

EX15 3JJ

⚙ 12-4, 6-11; 11-11 Fri & Sat; 12-10.30 Sun ☎ (01884) 840354

Beer range varies Ⓖ

A 300-year-old village inn by the River Culm, with at least six changing real ales from small breweries at any one time, rising to 10 at weekends, all served by gravity from the cellar. The car park was formerly the sidings of the Tiverton Light Railway. Local produce, often organic and free range, features on the menu, while Bollhayes and Tricky ciders are served from the cask. There is a beer festival every end of May bank holiday weekend. ♨Q❀🛏◐◑♣●P

Dartmouth

Cherub Inn

13 Higher Street, TQ6 9RB

⚙ 11-11 Fri, Sat & summer; 11-2.30, 5.30-11 winter; 11 (12 winter)-10.30 Sun ☎ (01803) 832571 🌐 the-cherub.co.uk

St Austell Tribute, Proper Job; Sharp's Doom Bar; guest beers Ⓗ

This Grade II-listed property, with a beautiful Tudor facade, is the oldest building in Dartmouth. It holds a small, quaint, beamed bar and has a cosy atmosphere. It was a merchant's house in the 12th century and has many original features, including some old ship's timbers and a lovely old staircase to the next two floors, which house the restaurant. Otter Ale or Bitter and a local guest ale supplement the three house beers. Q◐◑

Royal Castle Hotel

The Quay, TQ6 9PS

⚙ 9-11 ☎ (01803) 833033 🌐 royalcastle.co.uk

Bays Gold; Dartmoor Jail Ale; Sharp's Doom Bar Ⓗ

Large, imposing hotel situated close to the small harbour. It has two bars, one catering for a younger clientele, while the other is a cosy hotel bar decorated in a traditional manner, with oak panelling and wooden beams. Unlike many hotel bars this, surprisingly, has a pub-like feel and appeals to hotel residents, visitors to the town and local drinkers alike. The beers are predominantly from Devon and Cornwall breweries. The hotel has an excellent reputation for food. ♨🛏◐◑♿

East Allington

Fortescue Arms

TQ9 7RA

⏲ 12-2.30 (not Mon), 6-11; 12-3, 6-10.30 Sun
☎ (01548) 521215 🌐 fortescue-arms.co.uk
Butcombe Bitter; Dartmoor IPA; guest beers Ⓗ
A delightful old pub in the heart of the village. The L-shaped bar has a real fire and a beamed ceiling with ample seating and tables. The lovely restaurant serves very fine food and has a good wine list; look out for some Austrian specialities. Three beers are always available, with a beer from the local Quercus Brewery regularly among the guests. A most attractive flower garden to the rear complements the stone-built premises and makes a visit well worthwhile. ⛫Q❀⇄◑♿🚌P⅃

East Budleigh

Sir Walter Raleigh

22 High Street, EX9 7ED (off B3178 opp Hayes Lane)
⏲ 11-2.30, 6-11; 12-3, 7-10.30 Sun ☎ (01395) 442510
Otter Amber, Ale; guest beer Ⓖ
Pleasant 16th-century inn at the top of the village at the junction with Hayes Lane, which leads to the birthplace of Sir Walter Raleigh. A quiet, friendly pub, it is at its busiest lunchtime and early evening. No gaming machines or muzak, but dogs are welcome in the main bar. A varied selection of good food is available. There is a small public car park close by. Q❀◑🚌(157)P

East Prawle

Pig's Nose Inn

TQ7 2BY SX781365
⏲ 12-2.30, 7-11 (closed winter eves) ☎ (01548) 511209
🌐 pigsnoseinn.co.uk
Sharp's Doom Bar; South Hams Devon Pride Ⓖ**, Old Pedantic** Ⓗ**, Eddystone** Ⓖ
An old three-roomed smugglers' inn on the village green in an area that attracts birdwatchers and coastal walkers. Gravity beers are stored on a specially made rack behind the bar. Home-cooked, locally sourced food is served. Children and dogs are welcome and even have their own menus. The maritime-themed interior is cluttered with objects, children's games and knitting. For visitors, there are occasional performances of live music in a hall adjoining the pub. ⛫🛋❀◑⛺♣🍎⅃

Exbourne

Red Lion Inn ✔

High Street, EX20 3RY (200m N of jct with A386)
SS602017
⏲ 6 (4.30 Fri; 12 Sat & Sun)-midnight ☎ (01837) 851551
St Austell Tribute; Sharp's Doom Bar; guest beers Ⓖ
Village local with an L-shaped single bar. The adjacent cosy dining area includes an original low-beamed ceiling, log fire and a room offset with pool table and TV. Casks are set on the bar, along with Sam's Dry cider from Winkleigh. A new chef has enhanced the pub's reputation for high-quality locally sourced food, available evenings Monday-Friday in winter and all day weekends and summer. Thursday's themed steak night is proving very popular so book ahead. ⛫❀◑♣🍎P

Exeter

Fat Pig

2 John Street, EX1 1BL (near Corn Exchange)
⏲ 12-3 (not Mon & Tue), 5-11; 12-11 Sat & Sun
☎ (01392) 437217 🌐 fatpig-exeter.co.uk
O'Hanlon's Yellowhammer; guest beers Ⓗ
Breathing new life into an old back-street local, this small freehold pub was refurbished in 2007, and now has a more open feel to it. Two ales are available, often local, plus two real ciders, and sometimes a perry. Food is locally sourced. Expect a friendly welcome, with live music on Sunday afternoon. Well-behaved children and dogs are allowed daytimes only. There is a pay-and-display car park opposite, and local buses pass nearby. ⛫Q❀◑⇌(Central)🚌🍎

Great Western Hotel

St Davids Station Approach, EX4 4NU
⏲ 10-midnight (1am Fri & Sat) ☎ (01392) 274039
🌐 greatwesternhotel.co.uk
Branscombe Vale Branoc; Dartmoor Jail Ale; O'Hanlon's Yellowhammer, Port Stout; RCH Hewish IPA, Pitchfork Ⓗ
Traditional railway hotel built in 1847 close to St David's Station. A large range of mostly local ales is offered alongside guest beers from around the country, with beer festivals usually held over the bank holidays. It has a good community atmosphere, and easy disabled access. Well-priced meals, with a varied menu, are available in the bar and Brunel restaurant, including a Sunday roast, steak and curry nights.
⛫Q❀⇄◑♿⇌(Exeter St David's)🚌(H)

Imperial ✔

New North Road, EX4 4AH
⏲ 7am-midnight (1am Fri & Sat) ☎ (01392) 434050
Greene King Ruddles Best Bitter, Abbot; guest beers Ⓗ
A fine example of a Wetherspoon pub, originally the Imperial Hotel, set in large grounds with ample outdoor seating and its own car park. It is an architecturally interesting building, with two bars and three drinking areas, including the impressive orangery. There is a small bookable function room. The usual Wetherspoon's food is available, along with a varied range of guest ales, usually six or more from local and national breweries, plus two real ciders. Well worth a visit.
Q❀◑⊟♿⇌(St David's/Central)🚌🍎P⅃

Old Fire House

50 New North Road, EX4 4EP SX 923 930
⏲ 12-1am (2am Thu; 3am Fri & Sat) ☎ (01392) 277279
Otter Bitter, Amber, seasonal beers; guest beers Ⓖ
Close to the railway and bus stations, this popular city-centre pub serves good-value food lunchtimes and evenings, including late-night pizzas and Sunday roasts. Up to eight generally local ales are available on gravity and four real ciders adorn the bar. Regular ciders include Sam's, Green Valley, Sunnybrook, Sandford and Venton. The upper floor serves bottled ales due to the distance from the cellar. There is live music Friday and Saturday evenings, and beer festivals on bank holidays.
❀◑⇌(Central)🚌🍎⅃

Royal Oak ✔

79-81 Fore Street, Heavitree, EX1 2RN SX940924
⏲ 11.30-11 (midnight Fri & Sat); 12-4, 7-11 Sun
☎ (01392) 254121 🌐 royaloakex1.co.uk
Adnams Broadside; Otter Amber, Ale; Taylor Landlord; guest beers Ⓗ
This historic 1800s roadside, thatched, multi-room pub is on the B3183 through Heavitree. A relaxing lounge area is on the right, and the public bar on the left has several rooms and areas offering a

variety of seating options. Locally sourced produce used in home-made meals is displayed on the chalkboard and menu (£4-£11). Sunday roast is popular. Food is served lunchtimes and most evenings. Outside, there is a rear courtyard with benches. ☺❀🍴♿🚌♣🚬

Well House Tavern

16-17 Cathedral Yard, EX1 1HB (in city centre overlooking Cathedral Green) SX 921 926
11-11 (midnight Fri & Sat); 12-10.30 Sun
☎ (01392) 223611 michaelcaines.com/taverns/exeter
O'Hanlon's Yellowhammer; Otter Ale; Sharp's Doom Bar; guest beers Ⓗ
Overlooking historic Exeter Cathedral, this tavern is at the heart of the City. Part of the Royal Clarence Hotel (owned by two-star Michelin chef Michael Caines within the Abode Group), it stands alone as a place to drink and watch the world go by. There are regular beer and cider festivals, and live music on the last Sunday of the month. Several brewery trips are arranged each year and food is prepared in the hotel's kitchens. Cider is Rich's Farmhouse.
🍴♿≷(Central)🚌♣🍎

Exmouth

First & Last Inn

10 Church Street, EX8 1PE
11-11 (11.30 Sat); 12-10.30 Sun ☎ (01395) 263275
Courage Directors; Otter Ale Ⓗ**; guest beer** Ⓖ
Victorian pub near the town centre, with a public car park opposite, it's a genuine free house much enlarged by the present owners. It provides three distinct drinking areas, and an outside patio area with heated awnings. Games include pool and darts, and there is a skittle alley. Televised sport is prominent in the pub. Well-behaved dogs are welcome. The guest beer is usually from the West Country, and the cider is Thatchers Dry. The pub has air conditioning. ❀♿≷🚌♣🍎🚬

Holly Tree ✔

161 Withycombe Village Road, EX8 3AN (leave A376 at Gipsy Lane lights, then turn left)
11 (12 Sun)-midnight ☎ (01395) 273440
Draught Bass; Greene King Abbot; St Austell Proper Job, HSD; Wells Bombardier; guest beers Ⓗ
A substantial village pub a mile from the town centre, originally Victorian with extensions added perhaps 80 years ago, recently acquired by St Austell. Much supported by the local community, it is a place where beer and conversation predominate. League pool, darts and euchre are played, and Sunday is quiz night. Dogs are welcome at all times and families until 7pm. Guest beers tend to come from the St Austell range, or from local breweries. The cider is Taunton.
❀♿🚌(97)♣🍎P🚬

Frogmore

Globe Inn

TQ7 2NR
12-2.30 (not Mon), 6-11; 12-3, 6.30-10.30 Sun
☎ (01548) 531351 theglobeinn.co.uk
Otter Ale; Skinners Betty Stogs; South Hams Eddystone; guest beer Ⓗ
Accessible by car, bus or boat (the tidal Frogmore creek is being enhanced with a new pontoon) and very popular with locals and visitors, the pub has ample seating where West Country beers can be enjoyed. Full meals and light snacks are served (no food Mon). The restaurant area has room for families. There is folk music on the third Thursday of each month. Eight en-suite rooms are available.
⌂☺❀🛏🍴🚌(93)P▯

Galmpton

Manor Inn ✔

2 Stoke Gabriel Road, TQ5 0NL
11-11; 12-10.30 Sun ☎ (01803) 661101
manorinngalmpton.co.uk
Otter Ale; Sharp's Doom Bar; Skinner's Betty Stogs; St Austell Dartmoor Best Bitter; guest beers Ⓗ
Purpose built in the 19th century to replace a cider house that had been closed, this substantial stone building houses spacious accommodation, which includes a games room, function room, two bars and a dining area. The car park was once a cattle market and, for two decades, the pub has hosted the village Gooseberry Pie Fair on the first Sunday of July. A typical village pub providing the best of service, it is at the heart of all local activities.
Q☺❀🛏🍴♿≷(Churston Steam Railway)♣P🚬

Goodleigh

New Inn

EX32 7LX (on main road through village) SS599341
12-2.30 (not Tue-Thu Jan & Feb), 6-11; 12-3, 7-10.30 Sun
☎ (01271) 342488
Sharp's Cornish Jack, Special; guest beer Ⓗ
The rural setting of this traditional village inn is a pleasant contrast to the expanding area of nearby Barnstaple. A warm welcome awaits from the friendly licensees. The large bar is on two levels boasting an eclectic range of decor and furnishings, with a wood-burning fire and old beams. High quality, home-cooked, locally-sourced food is served, with the emphasis on meat, game and fish. Facilities include skittles and darts, with a beer garden for warmer months. Well-behaved dogs are welcome. ⌂Q❀🍴♿♣P🚬

Hatherleigh

Tally Ho!

14 Market Street, EX20 3JN (opp church)
12 (11 Tue)-11 ☎ (01837) 810306
tallyhohatherleigh.co.uk
Clearwater High Tide; St Austell Tribute; guest beers Ⓗ
A cosy 15th-century oak-beamed inn with a single bar and two wood-burning stoves. Three real ales are available with one changing guest, which are reduced in price 11-3pm on Tuesday market day. Sam's cider from Winkleigh is available all year. Good-quality food made with local produce is served. The rear garden provides seating, with a summer barbecue and a covered smoking area. The Tarka Trail for walkers passes nearby and fishing is available on the nearby River Torridge.
⌂❀🛏🍴🚌(51,86,118)♣🍎🚬

Heddon Valley

Hunters Inn

EX31 4PY (signed from A399) SS655483
10-11 ☎ (01598) 763230 thehuntersinn.net
Exmoor Ale, Hart, Gold, Stag, Beast; guest beers Ⓗ
Recently renovated North Devon CAMRA Pub of the Year 2009, near National Trust land, with peacocks

wandering freely in the grounds. There is a front seating area for dining and drinking outside, with more gardens to the rear. Food is served daily 12-3pm and 6-9pm. Sam's Medium cider from Winkleigh is now stocked. The pub attracts walkers, hikers, families with children and dog owners. A popular three-day beer festival takes place in early September. The addition of a micro-brewery is planned. ⛰Q❀⇌◐♿⛺♣●P

Hemerdon

Miners Arms

PL7 5BU

✪ 12-3, 5.30-midnight; 12-midnight Sun ☎ (01752) 336040

🌐 theminersarmspub.co.uk

Draught Bass; guest beers Ⓗ

There is a wishing well hidden in the snug, but visitors might feel they have already enjoyed good fortune if they happen upon this 18th-century establishment. The Garden Restaurant is in the conservatory, but the main bar, with a locally mined slate floor, retains the feel of a proper pub. There are fine views of Plymouth Sound from the dining area, patio and garden – the outdoor space making this a popular destination for those with children. ⛰Q♉❀◐⊟♿⊟(58,59)♣P⊱

Hexworthy

Forest Inn

PL20 6SD (on unclassified road linking Holne and B3357)

✪ 11-2.30, 6-11 ☎ (01364) 631211 🌐 theforestinn.co.uk

Teignworthy Reel Ale; guest beers Ⓗ

Agreeable country inn in Dartmoor Forest welcoming walkers, riders, fishermen, canoeists, dogs and children. One guest beer from the Teignworthy range is complemented by a second in the summer, often from a Devon brewery, and Countryman cider is also available. There is a comfortable bar area and lounge plus dining areas, with locally-sourced produce featuring on the menu and specials board. It is a good calling point on walks, with a variety of accommodation available, plus stabling and grazing.
⛰Q♉❀⇌◐⛺●P⊱

Holcombe

Smugglers Inn

27 Teignmouth Road, EX7 0LA (on A379 between Dawlish and Teignmouth)

✪ 11-11; 12-10.30 Sun ☎ (01626) 862301

🌐 thesmugglersinn.net

Draught Bass; Teignworthy Reel Ale; guest beers Ⓗ

With splendid coastal views, this roadside free house has an excellent reputation for food, the carvery being a particular attraction. The bar area has a wood-burning stove. There are two regular ales and one variable guest. The outside area is popular all seasons, with its separate smokers' canopy. A mini beer festival is held towards the end of January, usually featuring about 14 ales, and regular entertainment is hosted. There is a car park, and buses pass the door. ⛰❀◐♿⛺⊟(2)P⊱

Holcombe Rogus

Prince of Wales

TA21 0PN

✪ 12-3, 6-11.30; 11-11.30 Sat summer; 12-11 Sun

☎ (01823) 672070

Otter Bitter; Sharp's Doom Bar; guest beers Ⓗ

Seventeenth-century country pub near the Grand Western Canal and the Somerset border, an area popular with walkers and cyclists. Inside, the bar features unusual cash register handpumps. Home-cooked food is available, including vegetarian options and a carvery on Sunday, as well as regular curry nights. A large log-burning stove warms the pub in winter. There is a darts area, shove ha'penny and dominoes. A beer festival is held in September, and occasional live music. The walled garden is popular in summer. ⛰❀◐♿♣P⊱

Holsworthy

Old Market Inn 🏆 ✔

Chapel Street, EX22 6AY (on A388 S of town square)

✪ 11-midnight (1am Fri & Sat); 12-11 Sun

☎ (01409) 253941 🌐 oldmarketinn.co.uk

Bays Gold; Sharp's Doom Bar; Skinner's Betty Stogs; guest beers Ⓗ

Situated in the historic market town of Holsworthy, which is mentioned in the Domesday Book, this family-run inn and free house is known for the quality of its beer and food. There are usually five real ales available, along with Autumn Scrumpy cider from Winkleigh. Locally-sourced food is served in the restaurant which overlooks the outdoor decking area. Wednesday is very busy with a thriving livestock and food market. During St Peter's Fair week the pub holds a mini beer festival. ❀⇌◐♿⊟(X9,X90)♣●P⊱

Rydon Inn

Rydon Road, EX22 7HU (§ mile W of Holsworthy on A3072 Bude road)

✪ 11.30-3 Tue-Sat, 6-11; closed Mon winter; 12-3, 6-10.30 (not eve winter) Sun ☎ (01409) 259444 🌐 rydon-inn.com

Beer range varies Ⓗ

This free house and licensed wedding venue is ideally situated for the market town of Holsworthy and is just a few miles from the Cornish coast. A modern extention to an original Devon longhouse, the thatched bar has a high vaulted ceiling making it light and airy inside. There is a large conservatory restaurant serving high quality locally-sourced food and a spacious garden area, leading down to a small lake, with picturesque views of Holsworthy in the distance. Families with well-behaved children are welcome. Sam's Medium cider is available in winter. ⛰Q♉❀◐♿⛺⊟(X9,71,85)♣●P⊱

Honiton

Holt

178 High Street, EX14 1LA

✪ closed Sun & Mon; 11-3, 5.30-11 (midnight Sat)

☎ (01404) 47707 🌐 theholt-honiton.com

Otter Bitter, Amber, Bright, Ale, Head Ⓗ

The Otter Brewery tap, formerly a wine bar, has been converted to a pub with a cosy bar at street level. There is a dining area upstairs; both are smartly decorated, with plenty of exposed wood. The kitchen is in full view of the clientele. In addition to the restaurant there is a lunchtime menu, tapas, specials and smoked food available in the bar. Seasonal music festivals are held. Gastropub of the Year and winner of Taste of the West. ◐⇌⊟(20,52b,367)

Ilfracombe

Hele Billys

26 Watermouth Road, Hele, EX34 9QY (on A399, 1 mile E of Ilfracombe)
⏲ 11-midnight (4.30-midnight Tue winter); 12-11.30 Sun
☎ (01271) 866488 🌐 helebillys.com
St Austell Tribute; guest beer Ⓗ
Situated 250 metres from Hele Bay beach, this friendly, family-run pub with a welcoming atmosphere has been recently renovated and includes a log fire for winter. The regular ale is complemented by a varying guest beer, and a beer festival with 12 real ales is held once a year. The separate dining area serves excellent locally-sourced food at reasonable prices, with fresh fish featuring heavily on the menu. Food is not served Monday or Tuesday in winter. ♔❀◐▲♣⚡

Kilmington

New Inn ✔

The Hill, EX13 7SF (in village, S of A35)
⏲ 11.30-2.30 (3 Sat), 6-11; 12-3, 7-10.30 Sun
☎ (01297) 33376
Palmers Copper, IPA, seasonal beers Ⓗ
This thatched Devon longhouse, which became a pub in the early 1800s, has appeared in every edition of the Guide. After a major fire in 2004 it was sympathetically rebuilt by the owner, Palmers, with the toilets completely modernised to meet current disabled standards. Outside there is a large safe garden with aviaries. A skittle alley, quizzes and other events help maintain this pub at the heart of village life. Q❀◐♿🚌(380)♣P

Old Inn ✔

EX13 7RB
⏲ 11-3, 6-11; 12-3, 7-10.30 Sun ☎ (01297) 32096
🌐 oldinnkilmington.co.uk
Branscombe Vale Branoc, Monterey; Otter Bitter; guest beer Ⓗ
Thatched 16th-century inn on the A35. The public bar has a cricketing theme, the lounge has a log fire and restaurant area, and there is a patio and raised lawn. Food is sourced locally; the blackboard menu changes daily. A skittle alley can be made available for functions. There are regular theme nights, and a loyalty card allowing regular customers to obtain discounts on food and drink. On the last Saturday in May and August there is a beer festival/hog roast. ♔Q❀◐🀫🚌P⚡

Kings Nympton

Grove Inn

EX37 9ST SS684195
⏲ 12-3 (not Mon), 6-11; 12-3, 7-10.30 Sun
☎ (01769) 580406 🌐 thegroveinn.co.uk
Exmoor Ale; guest beers Ⓗ
Seventeenth-century, Grade II-listed thatched pub in a picturesque north Devon village. The bar has low beams, local historical information, and bookmarks hanging from the ceiling. Award-winning food is served in the dining area with open fire 12-2pm Tuesday-Sunday, 7-9pm Tuesday-Saturday. The cider is Sam's Dry from Winkleigh. A quiz night is held on the first Monday of each month. Well-behaved children and dogs are welcome. A self-catering cottage opposite is available for hire. ♔Q❀🛏◐♿♣●⚡

Kingswear

Ship Inn ✔

Higher Street, TQ6 0AG
⏲ 12-midnight (closed 3.30-6 Mon-Thu winter)
☎ (01803) 752348 🌐 theshipinnkingswear.co.uk
Adnams Bitter; Otter Bitter, Ale; guest beers Ⓗ
Situated up a short hill beside the village church, this 15th-century pub is welcoming, busy and full of nautical memorabilia. The horseshoe-shaped bar connects to the dining room, with beautiful views of the River Dart and Dartmouth. The patio, with a similar view, is a popular spot in the summer. The restaurant has a reputation for its fish dishes. In the winter there are log fires, weekly quizzes and music evenings. Four beers are always available. ♔Q❀◐⇌🚌⚡

Knowle

Dog & Donkey

24 Knowle Village, EX9 6AL (on B3178)
⏲ 12-3, 6-11.30 (10.30 Sun) ☎ (01395) 442021
🌐 thedoganddonkey.co.uk
Draught Bass; Otter Ale; guest beer Ⓖ
With a blazing log fire in the main bar, this traditional village pub has a separate public bar and spacious dining room. Quality real ales are served in a friendly and informal atmosphere, and excellent pub food is offered, including an extensive home-made speciality sausage menu. The pub hosts weekly quiz nights and occasional live music. Dogs are welcome in the main bar. The cider is Taunton Traditional, plus one guest. ♔Q❀◐🀫▲🚌(357,157)●P⚡

Lake

Bearslake Inn

EX20 4HQ (on A386 S of Sourton between Okehampton and Tavistock) SX528888
⏲ 11-3, 6-11; 12-4 Sun ☎ (01837) 861334
🌐 bearslakeinn.com
Otter Bitter; Teignworthy Springtide; guest beers Ⓗ/Ⓖ
Believed to date back to the 13th century and originally a working farm, the main building is a traditional, Grade II-listed thatched Devon longhouse. The single bar offers a range of primarily West Country ales - as many as four are available in summer. There is a lounge area with log fires where families are welcome. Views of Dartmoor can be appeciated from the large riverside garden, and a path to the Granite Way is close by. Excellent food is prepared from local ingredients with the menu changing daily. ♔Q☕❀🛏◐🚌(86)♣P⚡

Lutton

Mountain Inn

Old Chapel Road, PL21 9SA SX595594
⏲ 12 (4.30 Tue)-11 ☎ (01752) 837247
Dartmoor Jail Ale; guest beers Ⓗ
A traditional two-roomed pub with simple cob walls and real fires. The local favourite Dartmoor Jail Ale is accompanied by three wide-ranging guest ales, occasional draught ciders and up to eight bottled ciders. There is also an annual beer festival over the August bank holiday weekend. Simple home-made pub food is served daily (no food Tue). Although situated in the foothills of

Dartmoor, the pub's name is actually a corruption of Montain, the name of an old local landowner. Q (58,59) P

Mary Tavy

Elephant's Nest

Horndon, PL19 9LQ SX517800
12-3, 6.30-11 (10.30 Sun) (01822) 810273
elephantsnest.co.uk
Palmers Traditional Best Bitter; guest beers
Not many pubs can boast their own cricket ground, but this 16th-century pub has the space, and also a large garden that affords magnificent views over Dartmoor. Renamed from the New Inn in the 1950s by a corpulent landlord, the bar here remains traditional despite featuring many elephantine items, while the word 'elephant' is spelt out in many languages on the beams. Two further rooms off the bar are suitable for children. Locally produced real cider is available from Countryman. Q P

Meavy

Royal Oak

PL20 6PJ
12-3; 6-11; 12-11 Sat & Sun (01822) 852944
royaloakinn.org.uk
Dartmoor IPA, Jail Ale; guest beers
Marvellous two-roomed country inn in a quintessential English village with green, church and old oak tree (hence the name). Two guest beers feature alongside those from Dartmoor; two ciders from Westons are also available. Flagstoned floors and a fire maintain the atmosphere, while frequently changing menus and festivals (beer, cider and bean) ensure this pub receives many return visits, while maintaining its status as the focus of the community. The bus from Yelverton runs daytimes (not Sun and bank holidays). Q (56)

Merrivale

Dartmoor Inn

Merrivale Bridge, PL20 6ST
11.30-2.30, 6.30-11.30 (01822) 890340
Beer range varies
A 17th-century free house situated beneath an old quarry, near an ancient ritual site and adjacent to the B3357 Tavistock-Princetown road, this welcoming inn serves up to four West Country beers. Pleasantly fitted out with wood and red furnishings, and decorated with chamber pots, jugs and plates, the unobtrusive music and friendly staff ensure its popularity, as does the food, particularly for Sunday lunchtimes. There is no bus service on winter Sundays, and the pub closes for a fortnight in January. (98,272)P

Milton Combe

Who'd Have Thought It

PL20 6HP
12-3; 6-11 (12-11 Sat and summer); 12-3, 7-10.30 (12-10.30 summer) Sun (01822) 853313
whodhavethoughtitdevon.co.uk
Dartmoor Jail Ale; guest beers
Just down the road from the National Trust's Buckland Abbey, this delightful pub is located in a secluded Tamar Valley village. Dartmoor Jail Ale is served alongside a further three beers, usually from Devon or Cornwall, and an imaginative, good value menu features much local produce, including game. A woodburner keeps the bar area cosy; there are two further rooms and three outdoor drinking areas, one of which is covered. The bus from Yelverton stops outside weekdays and Saturday daytimes. Q (55)P

Modbury

Modbury Inn

Brownston Street, PL21 0RQ
11.30-2.30, 4.45-11; 11.30-11 Sat; 12-3, 7-11 Sun
(01548) 830275 modburyinn.co.uk
Courage Best Bitter; Draught Bass; Otter Ale
Multi-roomed 16th-century coaching inn featuring exposed beams and decorated with horse brasses, this friendly local sustains the world's first plastic bag free town. Food is served Tuesday to Saturday – meals can be taken in an airy, spacious dining room or outside on the Mediterranean-style garden terrace. The pub supports a euchre team, and occasionally hosts local musicians. The Mayflower Link Plymouth to Dartmouth bus stops just down the road until early evening, making this a convenient destination for visitors.
(93)

Moretonhampstead

Union Inn

10 Ford Street, TQ13 8LN
11 (12 Sun)-11 (01647) 440199 theunioninn.co.uk
Fuller's London Pride; Red Rock Lighthouse, Dark Ness, Breakwater
Sixteenth-century town-centre free house. The beamed bar displays old photographs of the town and has an adjoining pool room. The function room with its own bar and skittle alley is reached via a corridor displaying many artefacts relating to the inn's history. The Red Rock beers have house names. Gray's cider is available. Good food is home-cooked (served all day Sun). Outside, there is a seating area next to the small car park at the rear. P

Newton Abbot

Richard Hopkins

34-42 Queen Street, TQ12 2EW (400m from railway station)
9-midnight (01626) 323930
Greene King Ruddles Best Bitter, Abbot; guest beers
This busy Wetherspoon's has a long bar with 10 handpumps featuring up to eight different guest beers mainly selected from south-west breweries including Bays, Exmoor, O'Hanlons and Red Rock. The wood-panelled interior is divided into several seating areas. Illustrations depicting local people and historic events adorn the walls. Monday is quiz night and mini beer festivals are planned. Children are welcome up to 9pm and a covered terrace at the front accommodates smokers.

Union Inn

6 East Street, TQ12 1AF (opp magistrates court)
10-11 (midnight Fri & Sat) (01626) 354775
Draught Bass; St Austell Tribute; Sharp's Doom Bar; guest beers

A bustling town-centre local and refuge for shoppers. Guest beers usually include a local brew from Bays, Hunters or Gidleys. A good value home-cooked menu uses locally-sourced produce and features lunchtime roasts and daily specials. Excellent breakfasts are served from 8.30am. The pub supports darts, euchre and football teams. The big screen shows premiership football and rugby internationals. Other entertainment includes karaoke and quiz nights. ❀⇌◐≥⊟♣⁄

Newton St Cyres

Beer Engine

EX5 5AX (N of A377, next to station)
⏲ 11-11; 12-10.30 Sun ☎ (01392) 851282
🌐 thebeerengine.co.uk
Beer Engine Rail Ale, Silver Bullet, Piston Bitter, Sleeper Heavy, seasonal beer Ⓗ
Popular brew-pub on the Exeter to Barnstaple Tarka Line, two-thirds of a mile north of the A377, well-frequented by locals, visitors and the cricket team. The bar is adorned with dried hops and adjoins the busy restaurant which serves its own bread and locally sourced wholesome food. Well-behaved dogs and children are welcome. A railway theme is reflected in the ales, old pub signs and local village scenes in photographs. Overall, a thoroughly unspoilt pub. ♨Q❀◐♿≥⊟(50,51,315)♣P⁄–⊡

North Tawton

Railway Inn

Whiddon Down Road, EX20 2BE (1 mile S of town) SS666001
⏲ 12-3 (Fri & Sat only), 6-11; 12-3, 7-11 Sun
☎ (01837) 82789
Teignworthy Reel Ale; guest beers Ⓗ
This family-run single-bar local is part of a working farm. A translation of the landlord's Devon dialect is displayed in the bar area for the benefit of confused visitors! Situated next to the former North Tawton Railway Station (closed 1971), the bar decor includes railway memorabilia. The beer range changes regularly, normally West-Country based, as is the cider stocked in summer. The dining room is popular in the evening (no food Thu eve), with light meals served at lunchtime. ♨◐♣🍎P

Oakford

Red Lion Hotel

Rookery Hill, EX16 9ES
⏲ closed Mon; 12-2.30 (not Tue & Wed), 6-11; 12-3, 6-10.30 Sun ☎ (01398) 351219 🌐 theredlionhoteloakford.co.uk
Otter Bitter, Ale Ⓗ
Welcoming free house, set in a quiet village in undulating countryside, on the fringes of Exmoor. The area around Oakford is renowned for shooting, fishing and walking. The main bar features a large inglenook fireplace, and excellent value food is served in a separate dining room. Westons cider is available in summer months only. A small car park and garden area can be found across the road. Overnight accommodation comprises four comfortable en-suite rooms, including one with a four-poster bed. ♨Q☋❀⇌◐▲♣P

Okehampton

Plymouth Inn

26 West Street, EX20 1HH (W end of town near West Okement bridge)
⏲ 11-midnight (2 Fri & Sat) ☎ (01837) 53633
Beer range varies Ⓖ
Coaching inn and friendly village-style local dating from the 17th-century. The constantly changing ales are mainly from West Country brewers, with Green Valley cider from Exeter. Two popular beer festivals take place in the function room, one coinciding with the Ten Tors Challenge in May, and the other with the Baring Gould Folk Festival in October. Reasonably priced locally-sourced food is served, with special theme nights held every six weeks or so. Children and dogs are welcome. ☋❀◐⊟(X9,X90)♣🍎P⁄–

Paignton

Isaac Merritt ✔

54-58 Torquay Road, TQ3 3AA
⏲ 9am-midnight ☎ (01803) 556066
Bays Gold; Courage Directors; Greene King Ruddles Best Bitter, Abbot; guest beers Ⓗ
Popular town-centre Wetherspoon's pub themed on the inventor of the Singer sewing machine. It has a good reputation for its changing guest beers, augmented by mini beer festivals on Sundays and Mondays. Friendly surroundings with cosy alcoves and helpful staff make this hostelry appealing to all ages. Good value meals are served all day in this former local CAMRA Pub of the Year and Wetherspoon's award winner. There is easy access for wheelchair users with a designated ground-floor WC. ❀◐♿≥⊟(12)🍎⁄–

Parkham

Bell Inn

Rectory Lane, EX39 5PL (1 mile S of the A39 at Horns Cross) SS387212
⏲ 12-3, 5.30 (5 Fri)-11; 12-3, 6-10.30 Sun
☎ (01237) 451201 🌐 thebellinnparkham.co.uk
Greene King IPA; Sharp's Doom Bar; Skinner's Betty Stogs; guest beers Ⓗ
Historic 13th-century free house with oak beams, cob walls and open fires, all under a traditional thatched roof, which up until recently also housed the village store. The single bar normally has four real ales available, one of which will be a guest. A well-attended beer festival takes place around June, and summer spit roasts have become a popular feature. Locally produced food using traditional Devon recipes is served in the bar or the raised dining area. ♨❀◐♣P⁄–

Peter Tavy

Peter Tavy Inn

PL19 9NN
⏲ 12-3, 6-11; 12-3, 6.30-10.30 Sun ☎ (01822) 810348
🌐 petertavyinn.com
Dartmoor Jail Ale; guest beers Ⓗ
In a quiet village on the edge of Dartmoor, up to four guest beers from local breweries and a proper German lager can be found at the pub's small central bar. Traditionally decorated throughout, there are also two larger rooms, one for families. Outside, a patio and hidden garden are added attractions. The pub is highly regarded for its food

and situated on Route 27 of the National Cycle Network, with a caravan and campsite down the road. ♨Q☋❀◐◑ÅP

Plymouth

Artillery Arms

6 Pound Street, Stonehouse, PL1 3RH (opp RM barracks gate)

☼ 11 (12 Sun)-midnight ☎ (01752) 262515

Draught Bass; guest beers Ⓗ

Cracking back-street local tucked away in the old quarter of Stonehouse, close to the magnificent Grade I-listed Royal William Yard – this pub maintains the military connections of the area. Good home-cooked food is served (no food Sun); two guest beers and Thatchers Heritage cider are available to drink. An out-of-season beach party takes place the last weekend in February, and there are charity monkey-racing nights. Popular with hockey teams who use the nearby pitches, this place is a real find. ♨Q◐◑🚌(34)●

Blue Peter

68 Pomphlett Road, Plymstock, PL9 7BN

☼ 11-11; 12.30-10.30 Sun ☎ (01752) 402255

Beer range varies Ⓗ

Situated in Plymouth's south-east suburb and an oasis in an area where real ale availability can at best be described as variable, this friendly house has twice been local CAMRA Pub of the Year. Home-cooked food is available lunchtimes (no food Mon); the lounge bar doubles as the dining area. Two beer festivals are hosted, one around Easter and another in October, with barbecues in the summer. There are monthly quizzes and acoustic sessions, and pool and darts are popular. ♨Q❀◐⊟🚌♣P⁵

Boringdon Arms

13 Boringdon Terrace, Turnchapel, PL9 9TQ

☼ 11 (Sun)-midnight ☎ (01752) 402053 🌐 bori.co.uk

Butcombe Bitter; Draught Bass; RCH Pitchfork; guest beers Ⓗ

A former local CAMRA Pub of the Year, this waterside establishment is famed for its long-running bi-monthly beer festivals, held on the last weekend of odd numbered months. The Bori has an excellent reputation for home-made food in pleasant indoor and outdoor surroundings, with children and dogs welcome, and hosts a quiz on a Sunday night. Accessible by bus, or water taxi from the Barbican to Mount Batten, and a popular stop for Coast Path walkers. The accommodation has recently been refurbished.
♨Q☋❀⇌◐◑⊟🚌(2,17)♣⁵

Britannia ✓

1 Wolseley Road, Milehouse, PL2 3AA

☼ 9am-midnight (1am Fri & Sat) ☎ (01752) 607596

Greene King Ruddles Best Bitter, Abbot; Marston's Pedigree; guest beers Ⓗ

Large Edwardian Wetherspoon's which undoubtedly benefits from having always been a pub, situated opposite the Citybus depot and handy for Central Park and Plymouth Argyle FC's Home Park ground – the pub can be busy on match days. Numerous buses pass by from the city centre and railway station, and this is one of only a handful of pubs serving real ale in the western half of the city. In addition to the usual fare, draught Westons ciders and perry are available. ♨Q❀◐◑♿🚌●⁵

Clifton ✓

35 Clifton Street, Greenbank, PL4 8JB

☼ 2-11.30 (12.30am Fri), 12-12.30am Sat; 12-11.30 Sun

☎ (01752) 266563 🌐 cliftonpub.com

Draught Bass; Dartmoor Jail Ale; Summerskills Clifton Classic; guest beers Ⓗ

Clifton Classic is the house beer brewed by local brewery Summerskills for this back-street local between the city centre and Mutley, with a frequently-changing guest also supplied. A warm welcome awaits; there is also warmth outside on the large heated patio area. The pub is a second home to the local university Real Ale Society, with darts and pool teams also well supported; two large televisions ensure it is also busy for major sporting events, particularly Six Nations rugby matches. ❀≹🚌♣⁵

Clovelly Bay Inn

Boringdon Road, Turnchapel, PL9 9TB

☼ 11-3, 6-11; 12-4, 7-10.30 Sun ☎ (01752) 402765

🌐 clovellybayinn.co.uk

Beer range varies Ⓗ

This family-run free house now ensures that Turnchapel is a must-visit for anyone seeking real ale in Plymouth. Four beers, sourced from across the country, are available, with requests accommodated where possible. Ale & Pie and Cider & Sausage festivals are annual events, and a collection of over 30 malt whiskies is also offered. Hearty, locally-sourced food is extremely popular, and a free Wurlitzer vinyl jukebox adds to the warm ambience. ♨Q❀⇌◐◑♿🚌(2,17)♣

Dolphin Hotel

14 The Barbican, PL1 2LS

☼ 10-11 (midnight Fri & Sat); 11-11 Sun ☎ (01752) 660876

Draught Bass; St Austell Tribute; guest beers Ⓖ

A Plymouth institution, its fame ensured as the first stop for the returning Tolpuddle Martyrs, and more recently in the paintings of the late Beryl Cook, who was a regular. The Dolphin is unabashedly no frills and much the better for it – a stark contrast to many of the identikit establishments that increasingly clutter the historic Barbican area. The logo of Plymouth's old Octagon Brewery is visible on the windows – however, the panels above from Ansells are even older. ♨🚌(25)

Fawn Private Members Club

39 Prospect Street, Greenbank, PL4 8NY

☼ 2 (12 Sat)-11; 12-10.30 Sun ☎ (01752) 660540

St Austell Dartmoor Best, Proper Job; Sharp's Fawn Ale; guest beers Ⓗ

Fawn Ale is a blended beer produced by Sharp's for this unassuming street-corner club, named after the former HMS Fawn, which was decommissioned in 1991. CAMRA members are welcome with a membership card, but regular visitors will be required to join. The club is popular for rugby and other televised sports, and supports multiple darts and euchre teams. Two guest ales including a national brand are generally available, plus a rotating range of local cider. ≹🚌♣●⁵

Fishermans Arms ✓

31 Lambhay Street, PL1 2NN

☼ 12-3 (not Mon), 6-11; 12-11 Sun ☎ (01752) 661457

🌐 thefishermansarms.com

St Austell Tribute, Proper Job, HSD Ⓗ

Ambitiously refurbished by St Austell and the licensee two years ago, this is a completely different experience from before. Excellent dining

is to the fore (booking advisable) but certainly not to the exclusion of the beer – this is a pub with great food, not a gastro-pub. The stylish interior and real fire create a fine ambience. First-timers should turn right on leaving and head down the steps towards the Barbican – knowing this route saves much time for the inevitable return.
⛫◑◐🚌(25)

Fortescue 🏆 ✔

37 Mutley Plain, Mutley, PL4 6JQ
✪ 11-11 (midnight Fri & Sat); 12-10.30 Sun
☎ (01752) 660673 🌐 fortescueonline.co.uk
Butcombe Bitter; Dartmoor Jail Ale; Green King Abbot; Highgate Irish Whiskey Ale; Taylor Landlord; guest beers Ⓗ
Local CAMRA Branch Pub of the Year for the third year in a row, this lively local is frequented by a broad section of the community, with conversation flourishing. A perfect Sunday can be had here – a home-cooked roast, washed down with Spingo Special, and a brainteasing quiz in the evening. The patio beer garden draws crowds in the summer and is heated in winter. Cricket memorabilia features considerably. There are up to nine ales available; real cider is Thatchers Dry. ❀⇌🚌♣🍎⌐

Lounge

7 Stopford Place, Devonport, PL1 4QT
✪ 11.30-3 (not Mon), 6-11 (midnight Fri); 11.30-11 Sat; 12-11 Sun ☎ (01752) 561330
Draught Bass; guest beers Ⓗ
One of the few pubs to sell real ale in the western side of the city, and thus a haven for discerning drinkers. Nearby Stoke is crammed with promising-looking establishments but don't be fooled, make sure you head straight here. 'One weaker, one stronger' than the regular Bass is the rule for the guest beers, with lighter and darker brews also alternating. The wood-panelled bar is comfortable and relaxing, although may be busy if Plymouth Albion RFC are at home. Q❀◑⇌(Devonport)🚌⌐

Prince Maurice ✔

3 Church Hill, Eggbuckland, PL6 5RJ
✪ 11-3, 6-11; 11-11 Fri & Sat; 12-10.30 Sun
☎ (01752) 771515
Courage Best Bitter; Dartmoor Jail Ale; O'Hanlon's Stormstay; St Austell HSD; Sharp's Doom Bar; Summerskills Best Bitter Ⓗ
Although within the City of Plymouth, this is almost a rural village pub, from the inside at least. A cosy lounge bar is complemented by a lively public bar, and the trellis over the patio provides a further space in summer. The pub name comes from the Royalist General, the King's nephew, who had his headquarters here during the siege of Plymouth in the Civil War. The presence of Thatchers Cheddar Valley cider is not advertised. Food weekdays only.
⛫❀◑🀫🚌(28/A/B)♣🍎⌐

Thistle Park Brewhouse

32 Commercial Road, Coxside, PL4 0LE
✪ 12-1am (4am Fri & Sat) ☎ (01752) 204890
South Hams Devon Pride, XSB, Eddystone, seasonal beers Ⓗ
Flagship outlet for the South Hams Brewery which, as Sutton, was formerly located next door. There is a roof garden and Thai restaurant upstairs and biltong is available in the bar. Cheddar Valley cider and Dortmunder lager are on offer alongside four beers from the brewery's range. The pub can be accessed across the swing bridge from the Barbican (this shuts at 9.30pm), and from there is situated behind the National Marine Aquarium. Live music and extra-late opening feature at the weekend.
⛫❀◐♿🚌♣🍎⌐

Plympton

Foresters Arms

44 Fore Street, PL7 1NB
✪ 12.30-11 (10.30 Sun) ☎ (01752) 336018
Dartmoor Jail Ale; guest beers Ⓗ
Situated in the smart St Maurice area, this is an unfussy single-roomed pub, next door to the old Guildhall. The building features acanthus carvings under the eaves, and was formerly the holding cells when the Guildhall was used as a court – condemned men went to the gallows in what is now the ladies' toilet. Alongside Dartmoor Jail Ale guest beers are sourced primarily from the West Country, although others from further afield may be ordered on request. Dogs are welcome.
⛫❀🚌♣⌐

George Inn

191 Ridgeway, PL7 2HJ
✪ 11.30-11 (midnight Fri & Sat); 12-11 Sun
☎ (01752) 342674
Courage Best Bitter; Greene King Abbot; guest beer Ⓗ
Friendly 17th-century former coaching house by the side of the old Plymouth to Exeter road, popular with locals and visitors to this stannary town. The inn provides an extensive menu supplemented by blackboard specials, with booking advisable at weekends – food is served all day Sunday. In fine weather, meals can be taken on a florally-festooned patio outside. The flagstone floor bar has a warm atmosphere and a fire for chilly days. Newspapers are provided; dogs on leads are welcome. ⛫Q♉❀◑◐🀫♿🚌♣P

Postbridge

Warren House Inn

PL20 6TA (on B3212, 2 miles NE of Postbridge) SX674809
✪ 11-11 (5 Mon & Tue winter); 11-10.30 Sun
☎ (01822) 880208 🌐 warrenhouseinn.co.uk
Otter Ale; guest beers Ⓗ
This isolated, exposed inn which dates from 1845 is the third highest in England. The fire – reputed to have been burning continuously since the year the pub opened – is welcome, even in summer. Good home-cooked food uses locally-sourced produce, including Dartmoor beef and lamb, and a new dining room opened in 2009. Guest beers from around the country complement local brews, and mini beer festivals are planned. Real cider is from Countryman. The Transmoor Link bus is seasonal.
⛫Q♉❀◑◐🍎P⌐

Ringmore

Journey's End Inn

TQ7 4HL (car park is opp All Hallows Church 200m from village on road from St Anne's Chapel) SX650460
✪ closed Mon; 12-3, 6-11 (12-11 summer); 12-3, 6-10.30 (12-10.30 summer) Sun ☎ (01548) 810205
🌐 thejourneysendinn.co.uk
Sharp's Doom Bar; guest beers Ⓖ
Thirteenth-century inn named after R.C. Sherriff's famous play, which he started writing while staying here. Dogs are welcome at this cosy village pub, which is the hub of the local community. Beer

is served on gravity, with up to five ales available in summer and three in winter – one guest is from the Otter range. A winter ale festival is held in October. There is a separate lounge and dining room with a regular pub menu, daily specials and children's options. ᗑ☋❀⇋◑◗♣●P

Sampford Courtenay

New Inn

EX20 2TB (on A3072 Hatherleigh-Crediton Road)
SS633009
✪ 12-11 (11.30 Fri-Sun) ☎ (01837) 82247
Otter Ale; Skinner's Betty Stogs; guest beers Ⓖ
A 16th-century coaching house situated on the edge of the village built because coaches could not travel up the adjacent hill to the 'Old Inn' in winter. The comfy single bar has original low beams, plenty of seating and a large fireplace at each end. Good food is served daily 12-9pm. A spacious rear garden with benches and thatched smoking area has pleasant views of the village. Quiz nights, live music and fancy dress events are held regularly. ᗑQ☋❀◑◗♿⊟(51,51A)♣P⁼

Sampford Peverell

Globe Inn ✔

16 Lower Town, EX16 7BJ
✪ 8-midnight ☎ (01884) 821214 ⊕ the-globeinn.co.uk
Otter Bitter, Amber, Ale, Head Ⓗ
Situated in the heart of Sampford Peverell, this traditional Devon village inn is near Tiverton, backing on to the Grand Western Canal, which is popular with both walkers and cyclists. All food products are locally sourced and the meat farm-assured with full traceability. A carvery is available Friday, Saturday evening, all day Sunday and Monday lunch. There are two private function rooms and six bedrooms. Two beer festivals are held each year, in spring and autumn. Breakfast is served 8-10am daily.
ᗑ☋❀⇋◑◗♿▲⇚(Tiverton Parkway)⊟(1)♣P⁼

Sandford

Lamb Inn

The Square, EX17 4LW
✪ 9-midnight; 11-11 Sun ☎ (01363) 773676
⊕ lambinnsandford.co.uk
Cotleigh Tawny Ⓗ**; guest beers** Ⓗ/Ⓖ
Genuine 16th-century free house in the centre of the village with a traditional inviting atmosphere. Popular for both its beer and food (local produce dominates), it is well supported by both local and city folk. Skittles is played four nights a week in the alley and there are regular themed nights, including live music and open mike comedy evenings. Three rooms are now available for B&B accommodation. Sandford Orchards cider is stocked. ᗑQ❀⇋◑◗⊟(369)♣●⁼

Scorriton

Tradesmans Arms

Scorriton, TQ11 0JB (near Buckfastleigh, about 3 miles from A38) 704684
✪ 12-2.30, 6-11.30; 12-11 Sun ☎ (01364) 631206
⊕ thetradesmansarms.co.uk
Dartmoor IPA; Otter Bitter; guest beers Ⓗ
On the edge of Dartmoor, this pub reopened in early 2009 after it was bought by four locals who drank at the pub prior to its demise. It was renovated and updated, and has an L-shaped main bar with plenty of seating in a long alcove to one side, and a conservatory open to the pub at the other. There is a very friendly atmosphere and good local food is served together with a local real cider. Accommodation is available.
ᗑQ☋❀⇋◑◗♿▲♣●P

Seaton

Kings Arms

55 Fore Street, EX12 2AN
✪ 11-3, 6-midnight; 11-midnight Sat; 12-10.30 Sun
☎ (01297) 23431
Branscombe Vale Branoc; Teme Valley T'Other; guest beers Ⓗ
Busy local just outside the tourist area of Seaton. The pub has one large bar with very popular reasonably priced food available every weekday, lunchtime and evening. Sunday roast is offered all year, with food Sunday evenings in the summer only. There is a separate restaurant where children are welcome. A large garden at the rear, hidden from the road, affords good views over the River Axe estuary. ❀◑◗⊟♣⁼

Shaldon

Clifford Arms

34 Fore Street, TQ14 0DE
✪ 11-2.30, 5-11.30; 11.30-3, 5-11 (6-10.30 winter) Sun
☎ (01626) 872311
Dartmoor IPA; Ringmore Oarsome Ale; guest beers Ⓗ
Situated in the centre of a pretty coastal village, this pub has an attractive, modern interior and a warming log fire in winter. The guest and seasonal beers are sourced mainly from West Country breweries. The low-level restaurant area at the rear serves good quality food every day and leads out on to a sunny, decked patio. Special menus are available on modern jazz evening on Monday, monthly trad jazz sessions on Sunday lunchtime, and Thursday charity quiz nights. ᗑ❀◑◗⊟(32)●⁼

Shebbear

Devil's Stone Inn

Shebbear, EX21 5RU (in village square opp church)
SS438094
✪ 12-3, 6-11; 11-11 Fri-Sun ☎ (01409) 281210
⊕ devilsstoneinn.com
Beer range varies Ⓗ
This haunted 17th-century former coaching inn's name comes from the local tradition of turning the Devil's Stone annually on 5 November to keep the Devil away. The stone, which lies outside the church opposite the inn, apparently fell out of the Devil's pocket on his journey from Heaven to Hell. The single bar features flagstone floors, an open fire and comfortable armchairs. Winkleigh's Sam's cider is available in summer. There is a large garden, games room and separate dining room.
ᗑQ❀⇋◑◗♿⊟(72)♣●P⁼

Sidmouth

Swan Inn

37 York Street, EX10 8BY
✪ 11-2.30 (3 Sat), 5.30-11; 11-11 Fri; 12-3, 7-10.30 Sun
☎ (01395) 512849
Young's Bitter, Special, seasonal beers Ⓗ

A traditional and quiet back-street inn, established around 1770, that lies just off the centre of this quaint town, a short walk from the seafront and bus terminus. An old-style wood-panelled bar with an open fire attracts a strong local trade and leads to a dedicated dining area. Three beers, all from the Wells & Young's range, are normally available, and various sports teams are supported. Dogs, but not children, are welcome indoors. Find out about the King of Chit. ♨Q❀◐♿🚌(52,157)♣⁻

Silverton

Lamb Inn ✔

Fore Street, EX5 4HZ

⏲ 11.30-2.30, 6-11 (1am Thu; 2am Fri); 11.30-2am Sat; 12-11 Sun ☎ (01392) 860272

Dartmoor IPA; Exe Valley Dob's Best Bitter; Otter Ale; guest beers 🄶

Broadly popular family-run village pub with stone flooring, stripped timber and old pine furniture inside. It has a good-sized bar, with strong local trade. There is a minimum of three regular ales, plus various guests, served by gravity from a temperature-controlled stillage behind the bar. A multi-purpose function room plus skittle alley and bar is well used by local teams. Good value home-cooked food is served, together with popular Sunday roasts and a specials board that changes weekly. ♨❀◐♿🚌♣

Slapton

Queen's Arms

TQ7 2PN

⏲ 12-3, 6-11 (7-10.30 Sun) ☎ (01548) 580800

🌐 queensarmsslapton.co.uk

Otter Bitter, Bright; Teignworthy Reel Ale; guest beer 🄷

A large open fire welcomes you in the bar which has numerous photographs depicting the wartime evacuation. The large gardens and patios are filled with flowers, and children and dogs are made very welcome inside and out. A full menu is available with daily specials. The chef's home-made pies are a noted speciality. During the winter months, Sunday roasts are served (booking advised). A food takeaway service is also provided.
♨❀◐⛺🚌(93)♣P

South Brent

Royal Oak

Station Road, TQ10 9BE (near old railway station)

⏲ 12-2.30, 4.30-11; 12-midnight Fri & Sat; 12-11 Sun ☎ (01364) 72133 🌐 oakonline.net

Dartmoor Jail Ale; Teignworthy Reel Ale; guest beers 🄷

Busy village-centre pub on the edge of Dartmoor. The main wood-panelled, L-shaped bar is surrounded by a large open-plan area with plenty of seating. An excellent range of real ales is available. At the rear a restaurant serves good quality food, and a new function room can be found upstairs, which is available for meetings. There is a no-smoking courtyard outside and accommodation is offered. Occasional beer festivals are held with a discount on real ales for CAMRA members. Q❀🛏◐♿⛺

South Pool

Millbrook Inn

TQ7 2RW (off A379 at Frogmore; E of Kingsbridge) SX 774402

⏲ 12-11 (10.30 Sun) ☎ (01548) 531581

🌐 millbrookinnsouthpool.co.uk

Millbrook Pale Ale; Red Rock Red Rock; guest beers 🄷

Situated in the picturesque village of South Pool, most of the pub's summer trade comes from walkers and boaters using the tidal South Pool creek. The chef has built a good reputation with his award-winning food. Sunday roasts are served at 2.30pm (booking recommended) before a jazz band starts playing at 4pm. A summer barbecue is provided, mainly for use by the boating fraternity. Aylesbury ducks swim by the back terrace. The house beer is brewed by Red Rock. ♨Q🚸❀◐⁻

Spreyton

Tom Cobley Tavern 🏆

EX17 5AL (on A3124)

⏲ 12-3, 6-midnight (6.30-11 Mon); 12-3, 6-1am Fri & Sat; 12-4, 7-10.30 Sun ☎ (01647) 231314

Cotleigh Tawny; Cottage Broad Gauge; Dartmoor Jail Ale; Otter Ale; St Austell Tribute; Sharp's Doom Bar 🄷

Since winning National CAMRA Pub of the Year in 2006, this gem attracts visitors from afar who come to witness its remarkable turnover of up to 22 ales at any one time, mainly on gravity, with one cider also on gravity. The 16th-century village inn gives a warm welcome in the homely bar and spacious dining room. There is home-cooked food served 12-2pm and 7-9pm from an extensive menu; booking is advisable, especially for Sunday lunch. Dogs are allowed in the bar area only.
♨Q❀🛏◐●P⁻

Sticklepath

Taw River Inn

EX20 2NW (on main road, old A30, through village) SX641941

⏲ 12-midnight (11 Sun) ☎ (01837) 840377

🌐 tawriver.co.uk

Bays Best; Greene King Abbot; St Austell Tribute; Sharp's Doom Bar; guest beers 🄷

Oak-beamed pub in a village on the edge of Dartmoor which offers picturesque walks and historical attractions such as the Finch Foundry Museum (National Trust) opposite. The large single bar hosts numerous sports and pub games played by friendly locals. A range of real ales is available at very attractive prices, and good value pub food is served. Children and dogs are welcome, with an attractive beer garden at the back and outdoor seating at the front. ♨❀🛏◐♿🚌(X9,X90)♣P⁻

Stokenham

Tradesman's Arms

TQ7 2SL (just off A379 by village green)

⏲ 11-2.30, 6-11 ☎ (01548) 580996

🌐 thetradesmansarms.com

Otter Bitter; St Austell Tribute; South Hams Eddystone 🄷

Tucked away just off the main coastal road and by the village green, this traditional, turn of the 14th century, friendly pub is very welcoming. Black beams, bar stools and small tables and chairs resting in little alcoves greet you. A wood-burning stove keeps customers warm. Blackboard menus focusing on local produce show daily specials and desserts which can be enjoyed in the separate restaurant. The beer garden is next to the car park. In summer colourful hanging baskets adorn the exterior of this pretty inn. P

Tavistock

Trout & Tipple ✔

Parkwood Road, PL19 0JS

12-2.30 (not Tue), 6-11; 12-2.30, 6-10.30 (7-10.30 winter) Sun ☎ (01822) 618886 troutandtipple.co.uk

Dartmoor Jail Ale; guest beers H

A mile north of the town and unsurprisingly close to a trout fishery, this friendly roadside inn boasts a hop-draped bar with a collection of pump clips on the ceiling, with a large conservatory, games room and patio. Seasonal beers from Teignworthy and two changing ciders are served. Beer festivals in February and October are augmented by frequent single-brewery events. Children are permitted until 9pm and dogs welcome. Awarded local CAMRA Branch Country Pub of the Year in 2009. Q (118) P

Topsham

Bridge Inn ★

Bridge Hill, EX3 0QQ

12-2, 6-10.30 (11 Fri & Sat); 12-2, 7-10.30 Sun ☎ (01392) 873862 cheffers.co.uk

Branscombe Vale Branoc; guest beers G

A unique pub and local treasure – an ale house since the 16th century, and run by the same family for 113 years, now in its sixth generation. The Bridge offers up to nine beers, often featuring dark and strong ales, which are all dispensed by gravity from the cellar. The pub offers local as well as national beers, and qualifies as a LocAle hostelry. In 1998 the Queen paid a visit, her only official visit to a pub. Q (57) P

Exeter Inn

68 High Street, EX3 0DY

11-11 (midnight Fri & Sat); 12-10.30 Sun ☎ (01392) 873131

Teignworthy Beachcomber; guest beers H

Genuine community pub run by a welcoming and enthusiastic couple who are SIBA members. Originally a coaching house dating from the 17th-century, part of the building is thatched. The pub has a choice of five ales, four of which change regularly; these include both local and national beers. It qualifies as a LocAle pub. Traditional pub games are played, including euchre. There is a large screen for sporting events. The real cider comes from Green Valley. (57,T)

Globe Hotel

Fore Street, EX3 0HR (from station head down main street towards the Quay) SX966880

11-11 (midnight Fri & Sat); 12-11 Sun ☎ (01392) 873471 globehotel.com

Butcombe Bitter; Otter Ale; Sharp's Doom Bar; guest beers H

Historic 17th-century coaching house, retaining characterful wood panelling and beams. The family-owned hotel at the centre of the community offers a warm welcome. Up to five ales are served and, as a genuine free house, LocAle predominates. The hotel offers 19 en-suite rooms and period furnished rooms, and the restaurant serves good traditional English food made with local produce. On Sunday evening the Topsham Folk Club meets to add a touch of live music. The adjacent Malt House can be booked and is popular for skittles and parties. Q (57,T) P

Totnes

Bay Horse Inn

8 Cistern Street, TQ9 5SP

12-midnight ☎ (01803) 862088 bayhorsetotnes.com

Dartmoor Jail Ale; Otter Amber; guest beers H

Situated at the top of the medieval town of Totnes, this former 15th-century coaching inn continues to provide good service. It has a stone-flagged bar, snug and dining room. Three times a year, beer festivals are held in the attractive garden, which has a heated patio. Live music features frequently, with the After Eight Jazz Club every Sunday night. The four or five beers are from local breweries, with occasional forays further afield. Food is only available from Easter to the end of the summer. Q

Westcott

Merry Harriers

EX15 1SA (on B3181, 2 miles S of Cullompton)

12-3, 6-11 (midnight Fri & Sat); 12-10 Sun ☎ (01392) 881254 themerryharriers.co.uk

Cotleigh Tawny; O'Hanlon's Yellowhammer; guest beers H

Traditional Devon hostelry with a friendly atmosphere, a welcoming log fire, and the old ambience of oak beams. Families are welcome in the restaurant, which serves locally-sourced produce, cooked fresh to order. Guest beers are supplied by south-west regional breweries. The skittle alley can also double-up as a function room. There is ample car parking, with an overspill car park at the rear of the pub. Q P

Westward Ho!

Pig on the Hill

West Pusehill, Pusehill, EX39 5AH (turn off A39 to B3236, then signed) SS426282

12-3, 6.30-11; 12-4, 7-10.30 Sun ☎ (01237) 425889

Bays Gold; Country Life Golden Pig; St Austell HSD; Sharp's IPA; guest beers H

A converted farmhouse with a porcine theme and extensive grounds. Formerly the home of Country Life brewery, the landlord is a real ale enthusiast who stocks a wide range of mainly West Country beers and Winkleigh cider. The family and dog friendly pub serves high quality food in two dining areas. Outside is a sheltered patio and large garden with playground facilities for children. A petanque club is run from here with the pitch situated within the grounds. Q P

Whimple

New Fountain Inn

Church Road, EX5 2TA

12-2.30, 6.30-11 (7-10.30 Sun) ☎ (01404) 822350

Bays Gold; Teignworthy Reel Ale; guest beer G

Small, friendly two-bar local in a lovely village, converted from cottages around 1890, with new toilets added in 2009. A genuine free house, this pub has been owned by the current licensees for 20 years. The handpumps are not in use; ale is fetched from the cellar. Extremely good value home-cooked food is served daily (booking advisable for Sunday lunch). The village heritage centre in the car park was donated by the landlord and is well worth a visit. ♔Q◑⊟⇌⊟♣P

Widecombe in the Moor

Rugglestone Inn

TQ13 7TF (¼ mile from village centre) SX721760
✪ 11.30-3, 6-midnight; 11.30-midnight Sat; 12-11 Sun
☎ (01364) 621327 ⊕ rugglestone.co.uk
Butcombe Bitter; St Austell Dartmoor Best; guest beer Ⓖ
Unspoilt pub in a splendid Dartmoor setting. The stone-flagged bar area has seating, with beer served through a hatch in the passageway. An open fire warms the lounge. Across the stream is a large grassed seating area with a shelter for bad weather (and smokers). A wide selection of home-cooked food is available. The pub is named after a local logan stone. There is a good size car park close by. Blackawton beers are occasionally available. Local farm cider is sold.
♔Q⛟❀◑⊟⋀●P⁻

Winkleigh

Kings Arms

The Square, Fore Street, EX19 8HQ
✪ 11-11; 12-10.30 Sun ☎ (01837) 83384
⊕ thekingsarmswinkleigh.co.uk
Butcombe Bitter; Otter Bitter; Sharp's Doom Bar Ⓗ
Listed thatched pub in the centre of a picturesque village. The single bar has low beamed ceilings, a flagstone floor and a large welcoming log fire in the winter. There are several nooks and dining areas. A range of excellent food from sandwiches and snacks to substantial restaurant meals, using locally-sourced produce where possible, is served in one of the dining areas or in the bar. The cider is Sam's Medium from Winkleigh, situated just down the road. ♔Q❀◑⊟(315)♣●⁻

Woolacombe

Red Barn ✔

Barton Road, EX34 7DF (opp beach car park)
✪ 11-11 (midnight Fri); 9.30-midnight Sat; 9.30-11 Sun
☎ (01271) 870264
St Austell Tribute, HSD; guest beers Ⓗ
At the north end of Woolacombe beach with excellent sea views, particularly from the outside seating area. A welcoming establishment that serves good food, it can get extremely busy in the holiday season. At least two and up to four real ales are available, including regularly changing guests, normally from local West Country brewers. An ale and music festival is held in December and local live music is supported all year round.
❀◑⋀⊟(3B,303)♣⁻

Tom Cobley Tavern, Spreyton (Photo: Ian Packham)

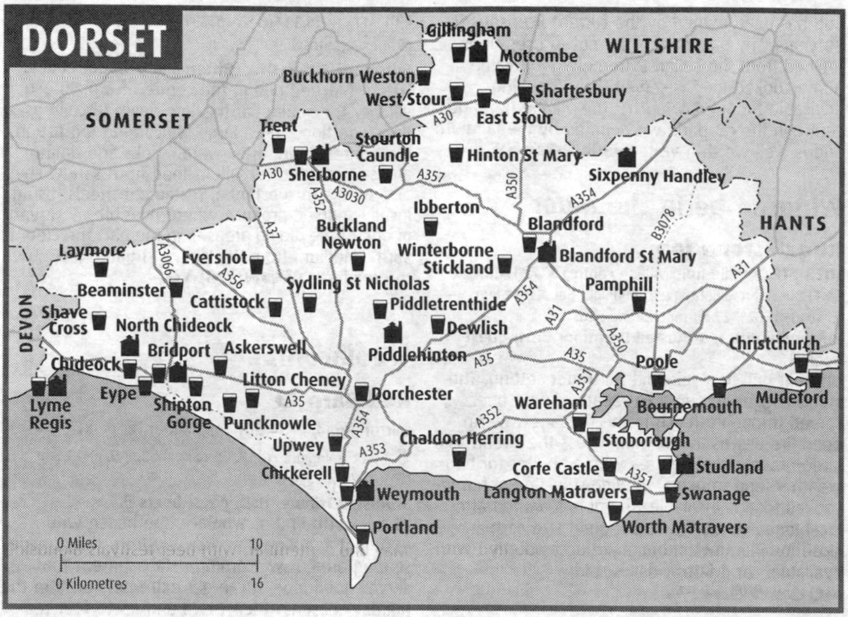

Askerswell

Spyway

DT2 9EP SY528933

✪ 12-3, 6-11 ☎ (01308) 485250 🌐 spyway-inn.co.uk

Otter Bitter, Ale; guest beer Ⓖ

This 16th-century smugglers' inn is perched on a hill outside Askerswell on the road to the ancient Eggardon Hill Fort. In summer there is usually a guest beer and a cask of cider. The small lounge bar has beams and a wood burner; a further bar is set for dining. The food menu features dishes made with locally-produced ingredients. Popular with locals and walkers, the sunny garden attracts families with a lovely view and a play area. Dogs are allowed only in the garden. ♨Q✿🛏◑▲P⅟

Beaminster

Knapp Inn

Clay Lane, DT8 3BU

✪ 12-2.30, 5-late Mon, Tue & Thu; 12-late Wed, Fri & Sat; 12-late (not winter) Sun ☎ (01308) 862408

Theakston Best Bitter; guest beers Ⓗ

A small, friendly free house on the edge of town, popular with the locals. Guest beers are usually from the West Country. Meals are served at the weekend only – the landlady's tasty bar snacks are made with local breads. Monthly live music, and the pub runs traditional games and supports the local cricket team. Several types of rye whisky are stocked. Dogs are welcome. ♨Q✿♿🚌♣🍎⅟

Blandford

Railway Hotel ✔

Oakfield Street, DT11 7EX (off B3082)

✪ 10-12.30am (1am Fri & Sat) ☎ (01258) 456374

🌐 railwayblandford.com

Palmers Best Bitter; Ringwood Best; guest beers Ⓗ

A lively community pub in the heart of Blandford, built in 1864 to serve the now defunct Blandford Station on the Somerset and Dorset line. This popular venue focuses on sport, with skittles, cribbage, shove ha'penny, darts and pool played and myriad TVs screening sports fixtures. Live music is hosted on Friday and Saturday evenings, food is served daily and an annual beer festival held over the May bank holiday weekend showcases West Country ales and ciders. ✿◑🚌(X8)♣🍎⅟

Bournemouth

Cricketers Arms 🏆

41 Windham Road, Springbourne, BH1 4RN

✪ 11-11; 12-10.30 Sun ☎ (01202) 551589

Fuller's London Pride; guest beers Ⓗ

This totally unspoilt Victorian pub is one of the oldest in Bournemouth and retains some lovely original features including stained glass internal windows. The vaulted lounge where the legendary boxer Freddie Mills once trained is now adorned with an eclectic range of historic rock posters. Two well chosen guest ales complement the regular beer. Dog friendly, the pub hosts occasional live music as well as quiz, folk and bingo nights. Sunday lunches are served. East Dorset CAMRA Pub of the Year 2009. ✿⊞♿⇌🚌♣P⅟

Goat & Tricycle ✔

27-29 West Hill Road, BH2 5PF

✪ 12-11 (11.30 Fri & Sat) ☎ (01202) 314220

Wadworth Henry's IPA, 6X, JCB, seasonal beers; guest beers Ⓗ

Originally two separate drinking establishments as the partially green-tiled frontage testifies, this pub has been modernised but not spoilt. The single bar serves several distinct areas and hosts 11 handpumps offering the complete Wadworth range, five guests and a cider. Home-made food is served lunchtimes and early evenings. There is a conference room and small pool room, comfortable seating areas and TVs. Sunday is quiz night. Outside is a heated and partially-covered patio garden. Disabled access is limited. ✿◑♿🚌♣🍎⅟

Porterhouse
113 Poole Road, Westbourne, BH4 9BG
11-11 (12 Fri & Sat); 12-11 Sun ☎ (01202) 768586
Ringwood Best, Fortyniner, Old Thumper, seasonal beers; guest beers H
Ringwood Brewery's only tied house in Bournemouth, it sells the full range of its award-winning ales. This is a pleasant, cosy, welcoming pub with wooden floors and panelled walls, with a strong local following. Truly a pub for all, bar games and conversation dominate in the music-free interior. Awarded East Dorset CAMRA Pub of the Year several times, Porterhouse is a true gem. Simple lunchtime food is available and dogs are welcome. Q(Branksome)

Royal Oak
Wimborne Road, Kinson, BH10 7BB
10.30-11; 12-6 Sun ☎ (01202) 572305
Sharp's Doom Bar; guest beers H
A popular community free house located in the oldest part of Bournemouth with a classic two-bar layout. The basic public bar has traditional pub games, including shove ha'penny and darts, while the more comfortable lounge bar is adorned with motor-racing prints and has an open log fire. Entertainment is provided most weekends when the landlord hosts a disco featuring his eclectic range of music. The bar now hosts five handpumps with an emphasis on local breweries including Isle of Purbeck and Piddle. P

Bridport

Tiger Inn
14-16 Barrack Street, DT6 3LY
12-11.30 (12.30am Fri & Sat) ☎ (01308) 427543
tigerinnbridport.co.uk
Otter Bitter, Ale; Sharp's Doom Bar; guest beers H
This bright and cheerful Victorian ale house offers a frequently-changing beer list from mainly West Country breweries, plus Thatchers cider. The single split level bar has TV for major sports events, plus pub games including table skittles. Dogs are allowed. There is a small, attractive restaurant, a pretty garden and a heated courtyard. Close to the town centre and shops, the Tiger is well worth seeking out if you like a traditional public house. A beer festival is held annually.
(31)

Woodman Inn
61 South Street, DT6 3NZ
11-midnight; 12-11 Sun ☎ (01308) 456455
Branscombe Vale BVB; guest beers H
A short stroll from the town centre, this small and attractive pub offers all the features a real ale enthusiast could want, including two West Country guest ales. The single bar has space for drinkers and diners to enjoy delicious home-cooked food. The skittle alley also acts as a family dining area although it can be rather cool in winter. Outside is a small garden next to the public car park. Regular live music is an added attraction. Dogs are permitted. Q(X53)

Buckhorn Weston

Stapleton Arms
Church Hill, SP8 5HS (between A303 and A30) ST757247
11-3, 6-11; 11-11 Sat & Sun ☎ (01963) 370396
thestapletonarms.com
Butcombe Bitter; Moor Revival; guest beers H
Imposing and stylish village pub with a relaxed, friendly atmosphere and a quiet, secluded garden. Inside is a single spacious bar and adjacent dining area. The guest beer range often reflects the season – milds in May, winter and summer ales – frequently from Moor Beer Company. Real ciders and a wide selection of draught and bottled foreign beers are always available. Excellent food is served including hand-made pork pies, scotch eggs and chutney. Children, dogs and muddy boots are welcome. Modern en-suite accommodation completes the Drink, Eat, Sleep motto.
QP

Buckland Newton

Gaggle of Geese
DT2 7BS SY050688
11.30-3, 6-11.30; 12-10.30 Sun ☎ (01300) 345249
thegaggle.co.uk
Ringwood Best; St Austell Tribute; guest beers H
Attractive pub down a back road in the village. The large garden accommodates two goose fairs in May and September, with beer festivals alongside. Chickens are kept in the pub orchard and goats and sheep in the paddock. Food is prepared with local ingredients such as pork, game and goat's cheese. Sunday meals are served 12-4pm and fish & chips and burgers are available to take away. Dorset cider and wines are stocked. Dogs welcome.
QP

Cattistock

Fox & Hounds Inn
Duck Street, DT2 0JH
12-3 (not Mon), 7-late; 12-late Sat & Sun summer
☎ (01300) 320444 foxandhoundsinn.com
Palmers Copper Ale, IPA, seasonal beer H
A warm welcome is assured in this delightful village pub set in picturesque countryside. It offers three well-kept Palmer's ales – Dorset Gold alternates with 200 – and Thatchers cider on handpump. Excellent home-cooked food is served from a daily-changing menu (booking advised). Steak night is Thursday and folk music night is the second Monday of the month. The pub is home to several teams and clubs from crib to cricket, and a function room is available. Dogs are very welcome – they can even enjoy their own bar snack. Taste of Dorset Pub of 2009.
Q(D11,212)

Chaldon Herring

Sailor's Return
DT2 8DN SY791834

INDEPENDENT BREWERIES

Art Brew North Chideock
Dorset (DBC) Weymouth
Dorset Piddle Piddlehinton
Hall & Woodhouse/Badger Blandford St Mary
Isle of Purbeck Studland
Palmers Bridport
Sherborne Sherborne
Small Paul's Gillingham
Town Mill Lyme Regis (NEW)
Wayland's Sixpenny Sixpenny Handley

12-3 (not Mon), 6-11; 12-midnight Fri & Sat; 11-11 Sun
☎ (01305) 854571
Hop Back GFB; Palmers Copper Ale; Ringwood Best; guest beers H
This thatched inn on the edge of a small village, also known as East Chaldon, provides a welcome stop for ramblers on the nearby coastal path. The original Purbeck-style layout is still intact, with a passageway to the bar and two adjacent rooms, although the bar is now in the room on the right. Up to six beers are available in high season, as well as real cider. Children and dogs are welcome.
Q❀◐♿♣P

Chickerell

Lugger
30 West Street, DT3 4DY (W end of village)
8am (8.30am Sun)-midnight ☎ (01305) 766611
theluggerinn.co.uk
Dorset Piddle Piddle; guest beers H
An attractive, family-friendly inn with a large split-level bar, a small room suitable for families and a separate dining room. It opens early for walk-in breakfasts until 11am then continues to serve good food all day from noon. The pub offers a choice of excellent ales from local breweries, including the house beer brewed by Dorset Brewing Company three miles away. Holiday cottages overlooking the garden can be booked through the pub, and beer-lovers breaks include brewery tours. Dogs are welcome in the bar (if the house cat allows!).
Q❀◐♿Λ(X53)♣P

Chideock

Clock House
Main Street, DT6 6JN
12-3, 6-11; 11-11 summer ☎ (01297) 489423
Art Tempest; Otter Bitter, Ale H
Thatched family-owned free house a mile from the sea. The comfortable bar has an adjoining spacious dining room. The local Art Brewery provides a changing guest beer, and Westons cider is on handpump. During the summer meals are served all day, plus takeaways. A dedicated games annexe is home to many local teams. Dogs and children are welcome. Community and national charities are well supported, assisted by a large charity library. Caravans are permitted at the camp site.
❀◐Λ(X53)♣P

Christchurch

Olde George Inn ✔
2A Castle Street, BH23 1DT
10.30-11 (midnight Fri & Sat) ☎ (01202) 479383
Dorset Piddle Jimmy Riddle, Piddle, Yogi Beer, Silent Slasher; guest beers H
Lovely old coaching inn, a short walk from the historic priory church. In earlier times the journey could be made by secret underground passage. The pub was the original tap for the Dorset Piddle brewery, and the full range is usually available plus two guests, often sourced locally. The heated courtyard provides a pleasant seating area and seasonal beer festivals are held in a marquee. Excellent food is available all day. The pub has won several CAMRA awards. Dog friendly.
❀◐♿≹(1b,1c)♣

Ship in Distress ✔
66 Stanpit, BH23 3NA (towards Mudeford off the B3059 at Purewell Cross) SZ172926
11-midnight (11 Sun) ☎ (01202) 485123
theshipindistress.com
Adnams Broadside; Dorset Brewing Company Jurassic; Ringwood Best; guest beers H
Formerly home to the smuggler John Streeter, a snuff factory and Avon Brewery before conversion to a pub in 1899, this attractive establishment is steeped in history. The original beams can still be viewed behind the bar and the walls are adorned with a mix of old photographs and seafaring memorabilia. With a quiet snug bar, a large comfortable lounge bar and an award-winning seafood restaurant, this pub has something for everyone. Q❀◐♿♣P

Corfe Castle

Greyhound Inn
The Square, BH20 5EZ
11(12 Sun)-11 ☎ (01929) 480205
greyhoundcorfe.co.uk
Ringwood Best; Sharp's Doom Bar; guest beers H
The most photographed pub in England is located in a picturesque village, below the imposing castle ruins. Seating is at wooden tables with an extensive menu and daily specials. The gardens provide fantastic views of the castle and steam railway, which is a short walk away. The pub hosts beer festivals in May and August plus themed food festivals. Live music is hosted regularly. Children, walkers, cyclists and dogs are all welcome, and free Wi-Fi is available. Real cider is served in summer. Q❀◐Λ≹(Swanage Railway)(40)♣

Royal British Legion Club
East Street, BH20 5EQ (on A351)
12-3, 6-11; 12-midnight Sat; 12-10.30 Sun
☎ (01929) 430591
Ringwood Best; Taylor Landlord; guest beer H
Built in Purbeck stone, this club has a small bar area with upholstered bench seating, wooden tables and chairs, and a lovely garden with access to the car park and clubhouse. Traditional sports include darts and shove ha'penny, plus a boules court outside. Filled rolls are available at the bar. Major sporting events are screened on TV. Occasionally there is live entertainment on Saturday evening. Entry is with a CAMRA membership card or a copy of this Guide.
❀≹(Swanage Railway)(40)♣P

Dewlish

Oak
DT2 7ND SY774981
11.30-2.30, 6-11; 12-3, 7-10.30 Sun ☎ (01258) 837352
Beer range varies H
Unpretentious village local with an ever-changing range of ales, mainly local. The horseshoe-shaped bar has a dining area and opens on to a patio and large garden. Home-cooked food includes Sunday roasts and real puddings. Dogs and children are welcome. B&B and self-catering accommodation is available in a converted coach house next door. Dewlish is of historical interest with its medieval settlement opposite the Oak, Roman villa and a fine Stuart mansion. Q◐♣

Dorchester

Blue Raddle

9 Church Street, DT1 1JN

11.30-3 (not Mon), 6.30-midnight; 12-3, 7-10.30 Sun

(01305) 267762

Butcombe Bitter; Otter Bitter; guest beers

Popular, genuine free house with friendly staff. The two-roomed town-centre pub offers up to three guest beers as well as the regulars, and a local cider. Good locally-sourced food is served lunchtimes (no food Mon) and Friday and Saturday evenings. The pub takes part in local events and hosts regular live music nights. Piped comedy and Private Eye are conveniently available in the conveniences. No children, but dogs allowed. Local CAMRA Pub of the Year 2009.

Q(South)

Colliton Club

Colliton House, Colliton Park, DT1 1XJ (opp county hall & crown court)

9-3, 6.30-11.30; 10-3.30 Sat; closed Sun & bank holidays

(01305) 224503

Greene King Old Speckled Hen, Abbot; St Austell Tribute; guest beers

Thriving club opposite County Council HQ with six real ales always available, if a little Greene King heavy. The club is housed in the mainly 17th-century Grade II-listed Colliton House and welcomes CAMRA members – just show your membership card. Busy in and out of office hours, this is a popular meeting place for a number of local associations. Evening snacks are served. Dogs and children are allowed. CAMRA Wessex Region Club of the Year 2008. Q(South/West)

Tom Brown's

47 High East Street, DT1 1LU

11-11 (2am Fri & Sat); 12-11 Sun (01305) 264020

Beer range varies

Previously home to the Goldfinch Brewery, this is now the Dorset Brewing Company tap. The full range of Goldfinch (now brewed by DBC), DBC and interesting guest ales rotate round the four handpumps. Refurbished but retaining the feel of a town centre ale house, the pub hosts mini beer festivals, live music and other events. It has a large garden, ideal for lazy pints in the sun. Bottled DBC beers and presentation packs are on sale. Local ciders include DBC's own pressing. Dog friendly.

Q(West/South)P

East Stour

King's Arms

East Stour Common, SP8 5NB (on A30, W of Shaftesbury)

12-3, 5.30-11; 12-midnight Sat; 12-10.30 Sun

(01747) 838325 thekingsarmsdorset.co.uk

St Austell Tribute; Wadworth 6X; guest beers

This imposing roadside pub is a multi-roomed establishment served by a single bar with many areas provided for diners. The bar is popular with locals, who have a say in the selection of the guest beers. The Scottish-influenced food is excellent, made with locally-sourced ingredients where possible, and the all-day Sunday carvery can be very busy. The patio and large enclosed garden are a welcome addition in the summer, and there is comfortable accommodation all year round. Dogs and muddy boots are welcome in the bar.

P

Evershot

Acorn

28 Fore Street, DT2 0JW

11-11 (01935) 83228 acorn-inn.co.uk

Otter Ale; guest beers

This attractive 16th-century small hotel in a pretty village has a fine pillared porch on the main street. A large flagstoned room at the back is known as the village bar, adorned with local photos and a wood burning stove – a smaller bar and AA-listed restaurant are at the front. There are always two ales available, and often a third, plus Somerset cider. This is the coaching inn that was mentioned in Thomas Hardy's Tess of the d'Urbervilles as 'The Sow & Acorn'. QP

Eype

New Inn

Mount Lane, DT6 6AP (off A35)

12-3 (not Mon), 6-11; 12-11 Sun (01308) 423254

new-inn-eype.co.uk

Palmers Copper, IPA, Dorset Gold, 200

An attractive pub that nestles at the top of a steep, leafy lane in a tiny village bordering the Jurassic coast. The open-plan bar is adjoined by a neat area for those dining on the home-cooked, sensibly-priced food. The beer garden must rank among Dorset's finest, with dramatic views across Lyme Bay. There is easy access to the coastal path from here. P

Gillingham

Phoenix Inn

The Square, SP8 4AY

10-2.30 (3 Sat), 7-11 (not Mon); 12-3, 7-10.30 Sun

(01747) 823277

Badger First Gold, seasonal beers

Popular town-centre pub built in the 15th century, originally a coaching inn complete with its own brewery. A cosy, one-bar hostelry, it is justifiably renowned for good-value home-cooked food, including magnificent breakfasts, served in the bar and a separate dining area. A Badger seasonal beer is always available. It has no games machines, just occasional background music. A small courtyard for drinking alfresco is next to the quaint town square.

Q

Hinton St Mary

White Horse

DT10 1NA (off B3092)

closed Mon; 12-3, 6-11; 12-3, 7-11 Sun (01258) 472723

Beer range varies

This 16th-century stone building is a genuine old-fashioned public house at the heart of the village community. With wooden beams throughout, the public bar features stone flooring and an open fire, while the lounge is comfortable, cosy and home to the resident ghost. A genuine and friendly welcome is extended to all including families and pets. No music, games machines or TV spoil the atmosphere. Two beers are usually available. Excellent home-prepared food is served throughout and there is a small but pretty garden.

Q(309)P

Ibberton

Crown

Church Lane, DT11 0EN ST 787077
⏲ closed Mon; 12-3, 6-11; 12-3, 7-10.30 Sun
☎ (01258) 817448
Palmers Copper Ale, Best Bitter; guest beer Ⓗ
Tranquil 16th-century inn located in the heart of a picturesque village in an area of outstanding natural beauty overlooking Blackmore Vale. Popular with locals and tourists alike, the pub retains many original features including flagstone floors, an inglenook fireplace and oak doors. In the summer the hillside garden is filled with walkers from the Wessex Ridgeway and visitors to the local church, dedicated to St Eustace, relaxing by the burbling stream with a pint or enjoying the excellent food. ♨Q☋❀◑P

Langton Matravers

Ship Inn

Coombe Hill, BH19 3EU
⏲ 12-3, 5.30-11; 12-11 Fri-Sun and summer
☎ (01929) 426910 🌐 shipinnlangton.co.uk
Isle of Purbeck Best Bitter, Fossil Fuel, Studland Bay Wrecked; guest beer Ⓗ
Originally a cottage known as Hill View, the inn was founded in 1765 and reopened in 2009. This increasingly popular village local now boasts good food, accommodation and step-free disabled access from the car park. Outside is a small garden and separate covered smoking areas. Local ales and a locally-brewed lager are stocked, with guest beers often from Bath Ales. Note the interesting conundra chalked above the bar to catalyse conversation. Q❀🛏◑♿🚌(40)♣P🚬

Laymore

Squirrel

TA20 4NT (on B3162 between Winsham and Drimpton)
⏲ 11-2.30 (3 Sat), 6.30-11; 12-10.30 Sun ☎ (01460) 30298
🌐 squirrelinn.co.uk
Branscombe Vale Best Bitter; Otter Bitter; guest beer Ⓗ
This is a 1952 brick reincarnation of an earlier stone pub in this hamlet. Inside is a long carpeted bar divided into nooks by wooden posts. The guest beer is usually from Yeovil or Cottage brewery. Well-cooked traditional pub food includes a popular steak night on Wednesday. There is a beer festival on the second weekend of August, and the local Ashen Faggot festival is held in January. Dogs and children are welcome. ♨❀🛏◑♿🚌(99)♣🍎P

Litton Cheney

White Horse ✔

DT2 9AT SY549900
⏲ 12-3 (not Mon), 5-11; 12-midnight Sat; 12-10 Sun
☎ (01308) 482539
Palmers Copper Ale, IPA, 200 Ⓗ
True country pub south west of the village, beside a stream and a YMCA, with friendly and helpful staff. The open-plan bar has a stone-flagged floor and wood-burning stove. Darts and dominoes are played and there is a boules pitch outside for the summer. A well-thought-out menu offers local freshly-cooked food. Disabled access is reasonable but the WC doors are narrow. Dog friendly. ♨Q☋❀◑♣P🚬

Lyme Regis

Nag's Head 🏆

32 Silver Street, DT7 3HS
⏲ 11-midnight ☎ (01297) 442312
Otter Ale; guest beers Ⓗ
CAMRA's Dorset Pub of the Year for 2010 is an old coaching inn with magnificent views along the Jurassic Coast. It offers a changing choice of ales in two linked bar areas, plus a games room. The house beer, Sark Lark, is brewed by Otter. No meals are available but regular barbecues are held in summer. Live music often plays on Saturday. The garden has a covered terrace heated by a woodburner in winter for smokers. Dogs are welcome. ♨❀🛏⛺🚌(31,X53)♣🚬

Volunteer

31 Broad Street, DT7 3QE
⏲ 11-11; 12-10.30 Sun ☎ (01297) 442214
Beer range varies Ⓗ
Historic two-room pub in the heart of this historic seaside town, a few steps from the seafront, with a lovely olde-worlde atmosphere. Popular with locals, the main bar buzzes with jolly banter and conversation. The house beer, Donegal, is Branscombe Vale Best and is stillaged behind the bar. A rotating choice of West Country ales is on offer. Dogs and well-behaved owners are allowed, and families are welcome in the lounge bar. ♨☋◐♿⛺🚌(31,X53)

Motcombe

Coppleridge Inn ✔

SP7 9HW (signed from village)
⏲ 12-3, 6-11; 12-11 Sun ☎ (01747) 851980
🌐 coppleridge.com
Butcombe Bitter; Greene King IPA; guest beer Ⓗ
Family-run country inn and restaurant – the main building is a converted farmhouse set in 15 acres of woodland, meadow and gardens. There is a cosy wood-panelled bar and a number of separate, discrete dining areas. A guest beer is offered, often quite unusual to the area. Local produce is sourced for the excellent meals and there are occasional themed nights. Accommodation is provided in converted stables around a courtyard. Function and conference facilities are available and the pub is licensed for weddings. ♨Q❀🛏◑♣P🚬

Mudeford

Nelson Tavern ✔

75 Mudeford, BH23 3NJ
⏲ 10-11.30 ☎ (01202) 485105 🌐 nelsontavern.com
Ringwood Best, Fortyniner; guest beers Ⓗ
Situated a short walk from Avon Beach and Mudeford Quay, you are assured of a warm welcome at this traditional single-bar village pub. Ales from Yeovil and Bowman breweries regularly feature on the guest list, with a third beer and real ciders available direct from the cellar. This popular pub hosts three beer festivals a year over the bank holiday weekends in the garden, and also features regular live music, excellent Thai cuisine and Sky Sports. Dogs are made welcome. ♨❀◑♿🚌(X12)🍎P🚬

Pamphill

Vine Inn ★

Vine Hill, BH21 4EE (off B3082) ST994003
⏲ 11 (12 Sun)-3, 7-10.30 ☎ (01202) 882259
Fuller's London Pride 🄷; guest beer 🄶
Listed on CAMRA's National Inventory of Historic Pub Interiors, this former bakehouse has been in the same family for three generations. Entrance to the tiny public and small lounge bars is via the beer garden – a sun trap in summer and popular with ramblers, dogs and cyclists all year round. A family room completes the interior. The guest beer is often from a local brewery such as Palmers. Sandwiches, toasties and ploughmans are available lunchtimes only. Handy for the nationally important Whitemill and Badbury Rings Hill Fort. Timeless. Q❀♣⚲–

Piddletrenthide

Piddle Inn ✔

DT2 7QF
⏲ 11.30 (12 Sun)-midnight ☎ (01300) 348468
🌐 piddleinn.co.uk
Dorset Piddle Piddle; St Austell Tribute; guest beer 🄶
Named after the river on whose banks it stands, this is the closest pub to the Dorset Piddle Brewery serving its ales. It has a large, cheery single bar, brightly decorated and carpeted throughout. Three ales are served straight from the cask, plus cider in summer. A large restaurant seats 50 with dining also available in the bar. Popular locally, it hosts regular events including live music. There is a sunny garden and riverside patio. AA 4-star rooms are available. Children and dogs are welcome. ❀♿(D13,323)♣P–

Poole

Angel

28 Market Street, BH15 1NF
⏲ 11-11 (11.30 Thu-Sat); 11-10.30 Sun ☎ (01202) 666431
Ringwood Best, Fortyniner, Old Thumper, seasonal beers; guest beers 🄷
This pub is tucked away in Poole old town beside the historic Guildhall, not far from the tourist bustle of the quay. The angelic staff serve Ringwood Brewery's full range, plus guests provided by Marston's, accompanied by fabulous food. The bright interior has a central bar with views of the cask ale cellar. The pub benefits from a heated patio area that is a sun trap in summer. Quiz night is every Tuesday and music night on Thursday. ❀♿≹♣–

Bermuda Triangle

10 Parr Street, Lower Parkstone, BH14 0JY
⏲ 12-2.30, 5-11 (midnight Fri); 12-midnight Sat; 12-11 Sun
☎ (01202) 748087
Beer range varies 🄷
Recently celebrating 20 years as a free house under the present owner, the Bermuda Triangle is a Guide regular. The interior of this single-room pub is themed on its name – a plane wing is suspended from the ceiling, one of the seating areas is boat-shaped, and the walls are crammed with eclectic paraphernalia. Four handpumps serve an ever-changing range of ales sourced from far and wide. There is a pavement drinking area at the front of the pub. A true gem.
❀≹(Parkstone)🚌(M1)

Blue Boar

29 Market Close, BH15 1NE
⏲ 12-11 (midnight Fri & Sat); 12-10.30 Sun
☎ (01202) 682247
Fuller's Discovery, London Pride, ESB, seasonal beer 🄷
A former merchant's house dating back to 1750, this is Poole's only Fuller's house and is situated a two-minute walk from the High Street in the old town. The large bar is comfortable, while the atmospheric cellar bar plays live jazz every Sunday night. Both bars are bedecked with nautical artefacts including photographs and a brief history. Pub food is served from a reasonably-priced bar menu. There are two TV screens, and upstairs is a large function room. A former local CAMRA Pub of the Year. Q❀≹–

Branksome Railway Hotel

429 Poole Road, Branksome, BH12 1DQ (opp train station)
⏲ 11-11 (midnight Fri & Sat); 12-10.30 Sun
☎ (01202) 769555 🌐 branksomerailwayhotel.co.uk
Otter Ale; Hop Back Summer Lightning; guest beer 🄷
Dating from 1894, this traditional Victorian station pub still serves the main rail link between London Waterloo and Weymouth. Essentially open plan, it is partitioned into two rooms served by a single bar. The front room houses a pool table, games machines and a small seating area. The rear area has comfortable seating, with views of the trains passing by, and a TV. A DJ and bands play at weekends. There is a function room that regularly hosts branch meetings. En-suite accommodation is available. ≹🚌♣P

Brewhouse

68 High Street, BH15 1DA
⏲ 11-11; 12-10.30 Sun ☎ (01202) 685288
🌐 milkstreetbrewery.co.uk
Milk Street Mermaid, Beer, seasonal beers; guest beers 🄷
This long, narrow off-street local serves beers from the Milk Street Brewery in Frome accompanied by interesting guest ales and occasional ciders. It has a hop-covered bar and a raised area at the rear which houses pool tables, darts, pinball and a jukebox. There is a patio area to the rear and seating at the front on the old high street – the perfect place to enjoy a pint and watch the world wander by. ❀≹♣–

Bricklayers Arms

41 Parr Street, Ashley Cross, BH14 0JX
⏲ 12-2.30, 5-11; 12-11 Sat & Sun ☎ (01202) 740304
Greene King Old Speckled Hen; Hop Back Summer Lightning; Ringwood Best, Fortyniner 🄷
Popular free house located in the affluent area of lower Parkstone. The single L-shaped bar serves a main area with an open fireplace and a further area with settles, tables and chairs. Outside is a large beer garden and Gents toilet. A raised, decked space at the front of the pub is a sun trap in summer and overlooks the local church. No food is served and no children under 14 are allowed in the bar. Q❀≹(Parkstone)🚌(M1)

Portland

Royal Portland Arms

40 Fortune's Well, DT5 1LZ
⏲ 11-11.50 (12.50am Fri & Sat); 12-11.30 Sun
☎ (01305) 862255

Beer range varies Ⓖ
Full of character, this Portland-stone pub stands alongside the main road, with public car parks nearby. More than 200 years old, George III is reputed to have stopped here for a drink and some Portland mutton on a visit to the island. Inside you will find basic, homely furnishings and a friendly welcome for all. It hosts regular live music and other locally-attended events. An ever-changing range of mainly West Country ales and ciders are served on gravity dispense. Bar snacks are available. Dogs welcome. Q🚌(1)♣🍎🛢

Puncknowle

Crown ✔
DT2 9BN
⏲ 12-3; 6-11; 12-11 (not eve winter) Sun ☎ (01308) 897711
Palmers Copper Ale, IPA, 200 Ⓗ
Lovely 16th-century thatched pub in the village – pronounced 'Punnel'. The bar has an open fire and books to read if you don't want to join in the conversation with the friendly staff and locals. Tally Ho! is added to the beer range when brewed. Locally-sourced home-cooked food is available from the bar and in the restaurant (no food winter Mon eve). There is a large garden at the back, and children and dogs are welcome.
⛰Q🏠❀🛏◐♿🚌(210)🍎

Shaftesbury

Mitre
23 High Street, SP7 8JE
⏲ 10.30-midnight; 12-11 Sun ☎ (01747) 853002
Wells Bombardier; Young's Bitter, Special, seasonal beers Ⓗ
Historic pub close to the town hall at the top of Gold Hill, with grand views overlooking the beautiful Blackmore Vale. Popular with younger drinkers but catering for all, an extensive food menu ranges from morning coffee to cream teas to good pub food. The Mitre runs crib and darts teams and hosts charity quizzes as well as occasional live music nights. Guest and seasonal beers change regularly. ⛰🏠❀◐♿🚌♣⊢

Shave Cross

Shave Cross Inn ✔
DT6 6HW (W of B3162 Bridport-Broadwindsor road) SY415980
⏲ closed Mon; 11-3, 6-1am; 12-3, 7-1am Sun
☎ (01308) 868358 🌐 theshavecrossinn.co.uk
Dorset Brewing Company Weymouth Bitter; guest beers Ⓗ
This 700-year-old rural inn, stone-built with a thatched roof, was rescued from oblivion by the local owners who have now added impressive accommodation next door. Historically a busy stop-off point for pilgrims and monastic visitors, now an award-winning free house with a small flagstoned bar offering a changing and interesting selection of real ales, and several ciders, including a local one. The restaurant serves Caribbean-influenced dishes. A remote rural idyll well worth the extra mileage, with an attractive and mature garden. Dog friendly.
⛰Q❀🛏◐🍎P

Sherborne

Digby Tap ✔
Cooks Lane, DT9 3NS
⏲ 11 (12 Sun)-11 ☎ (01935) 813148 🌐 digbytap.co.uk
Beer range varies Ⓗ
Sherborne's only free house and worth seeking out for the building alone which dates back to the 16th century – once the parish workhouse, many features of the original building remain. A supporter of West Country ales, beers come from Teignworthy, Sharp's and Dorset Brewing Company. There are benches on a paved area outside for summer drinking. Food is served lunchtimes, Monday to Saturday. Children and dogs allowed. ⛰Q🏠❀◑♿⇌🚌⊢

Shipton Gorge

New Inn ✔
Shipton Road, DT6 4LT SY498927
⏲ 11-3 (not Mon), 6-11 (not Mon winter); 12-3 Sun
☎ (01308) 897302
Palmers Copper Ale, IPA, 200 Ⓗ
Well-off the beaten track, this pub was saved from closure in 2006 by a group of local people. In the last two years it has become the focus for a range of village activities. The pub has a single bar serving three Palmer's ales, and an adjoining dining room. Those seeking food on Sunday to Tuesday evenings should telephone ahead; there is a good home-made vegetarian selection. A ramp from the car park gives access via the rear door. Dogs welcome. Q❀◐♿🚌(210)P

Stoborough

King's Arms
1-3 Corfe Road, BH20 5AB (adjacent to B3075)
⏲ 11-3, 5-11; 11-11 Fri-Sun and summer ☎ (01929) 552705
Black Sheep Best Bitter; Isle of Purbeck Fossil Fuel; Ringwood Best; guest beer Ⓗ
This 400-year-old listed thatched building played host to Cromwell's troops in 1642 at the time of the siege of Corfe Castle. The pub is renowned for its food, and holds popular themed evenings. A long, thin interior with a split-level bar, it has a dining area providing access for the disabled. The garden is always busy in summer. Up to four real ales and a traditional cider are available, with an annual beer festival held over Whitsun.
⛰Q🏠❀◐♿⛺🚌(40)🍎P⊢

Stourton Caundle

Trooper Inn
Golden Hill, DT10 2JW (1½ miles E of A357) ST715149
⏲ 12-2.30 (not Mon), 7 (6 Wed & Thu)-midnight; 12-3.30, 7-midnight Sun ☎ (01963) 362405
Otter Bitter; guest beers Ⓗ
Stone-built, single-room village centre pub with a separate function room housing a bar and skittle alley. Two large inglenook fireplaces have been converted to seating areas and there is a children's area next to the beer garden. Good food is available lunchtimes and early evenings including a popular Friday fish & chips night. There are usually two guest ales and the pub hosts an annual beer festival. Real cider is served throughout the summer. Dogs and walkers are welcome.
Q❀◑♿♣🍎P

Studland

Bankes Arms

Watery Lane, BH19 3AU

⊙ 11-11 ☎ (01929) 450225 ⊕ bankesarms.com

Isle of Purbeck Best Bitter, Fossil Fuel, Solar Power, Studland Bay Wrecked, IPA; guest beers Ⓗ

Built more than 200 years ago, owned by the National Trust and run by the same family for more than 26 years, this famous country inn is home to the Isle of Purbeck Brewery. Nine handpumps dispense the entire range plus guest ales. The huge beer garden with views across the bay hosts a beer festival every August. The pub has an adjacent car park (free after 5pm or in winter), and moorings for 12 boats. Local CAMRA Rural Pub of the Year 2008. ♨Q❀⇌◑▲🚌(50)●

Swanage

Red Lion

63 High Street, BH19 2LY

⊙ 11-11.30; 12-11 Sun ☎ (01929) 423533

⊕ redlionswanage.co.uk

Palmers Copper Ale; Ringwood Best; Sharps Doom Bar; Taylor Landlord Ⓗ**; guest beers** Ⓖ

This 17th-century hostelry retains many traditional features. It serves up to six real ales in the summer, often from local breweries, but what makes the pub special are the ciders – Westons' full range, plus a variety of bottled ciders and perry. The recently refurbished restaurant offers an extensive selection of food. Live music occasionally features. The garden is busy in the summer. Popular with locals and tourists, the pub is handy for the beach, Swanage steam railway and the south west coastal path.
❀⇌◑⊟⇌(Swanage Railway)🚌(50)♣●P⊱

White Swan

31 High Street, The Square, BH19 2LJ

⊙ 11-11 ☎ (01929) 423804 ⊕ whiteswanswanage.co.uk

Dorset Piddle Piddle; Ringwood Best; guest beer Ⓗ

Fifty yards from the sea and opposite the small town square, the pub is set on four levels and is a blend of old with modern touches, with a walled garden at the rear. It offers meals from pub grub to daily chef's specials including fresh fish. Guest beers are locally sourced. Live music plays on Friday and Saturday nights, and regular jazz, folk and blues festivals are hosted. A computer is available for customers' use. Accommodation is in en-suite rooms.
♉❀⇌◑⇌(Swanage Railway)🚌(50)♣P⊱

Sydling St Nicholas

Greyhound

26 High Street, DT2 9ED

⊙ 11-2.30, 6-11; 12-3 Sun ☎ (01300) 841303

Otter Bitter; guest beers Ⓗ

Sydling St Nicholas is hidden in the valley of the Sydling Water, a pretty river running past the Greyhound. The pub has a large bar, conservatory and a restaurant with a well in the centre. The house beer, Sydling Bitter, is brewed by Otter, and there are usually two guest ales. An excellent food menu is displayed on a blackboard, and features much local food. Dogs are allowed. Dorset Dining Pub of the Year in 2009. ♨❀⇌◑♿P

Trent

Rose & Crown

DT9 4SL 589185

⊙ closed Mon; 12-3, 6-11; 12-11 Sat; 12-10 Sun

☎ (01935) 850776 ⊕ roseandcrowntrent.co.uk

Wadworth Henry's IPA, 6X, seasonal beers; guest beer Ⓗ

Large 14th-century pub in the west end of the village near the church – Charles II hid here en route to France. The bar has flagstones and beams, and the lounge has an open fire. Wadworth Horizon and Bishop's Tipple alternate with seasonal and guest beers. The conservatory dining area has lovely views over the extensive garden and surrounding countryside. Excellent locally-sourced food includes home-made pork scratchings. Popular with familes, walkers and cyclists, dogs are welcome. ♨Q❀◑♿P⊱

Upwey

Old Ship Inn ✔

The Ridgeway, DT3 5QQ

⊙ 11.30-11.30 (midnight Fri & Sat); 12-11 Sun

☎ (01305) 812522

Dorset Brewing Company Jurassic; Ringwood Best; guest beer Ⓗ

This attractive 400-year-old Punch pub on an ancient track at the top of Upwey village is mentioned in two of Thomas Hardy's novels. The food menu is wide ranging and features local produce, including fish dishes and vegetarian meals. The dish of the day is always good value. Teas are also served. Live music plays and the pub hosts the annual Nurdling Tourney on New Year's Day. Children and dogs are welcome.
♨Q♉❀◑⇌🚌P

Wareham

Black Bear Hotel

14 South Street, BH20 4LT

⊙ 7.30am-midnight ☎ (01929) 553339

Ringwood Best, Fortyniner; Wychwood Hobgoblin Ⓗ

Dating from the 18th century, this coaching inn has a stone-floor corridor running through the centre, leading to a restaurant and a beer garden at the rear. The front two rooms feature some fine wood panelling, with the room on the right containing the bar. A cosy room with sofas can be found further down the corridor. A large black bear above the entrance makes the pub easily recognisable and a distinguishing feature on the town's high street. ♨Q❀⇌◑⊟♿⇌🚌(40,X53)⊱

Duke of Wellington ✔

7 East Street, BH20 4NN

⊙ 11-11 (11.30 Fri & Sat); 12-11 Sun ☎ (01929) 553015

Hop Back Summer Lightning; Isle of Purbeck Fossil Fuel; Ringwood Best; guest beers Ⓗ

Atmospheric 400-year-old town-centre pub with six handpumps dispensing a range of beers, some from local breweries – look out for the beer of the month. Photographs of Wareham of yesteryear adorn the wood-panelled walls and copper ornaments surround the open fire. An extensive menu is served in the bar and restaurant. At the rear is an attractive, enclosed pub garden that is heated during the winter months. Ideally situated for walking the Wareham Wall. Former local CAMRA Summer Pub of the Year.
♨Q❀⇌◑⇌🚌(40)♣⊱

Kings Arms ✓

41 North Street, BH20 4AD

11-11; 12-10.30 Sun ☎ (01929) 552503

Ringwood Best; guest beers H

Cosy town-centre thatched pub in a terrace with two rooms at the front and a dining area and beer garden at the rear. The original flagstone floor and warming open fire help preserve the pub's 15th-century heritage, while a frame in one of the walls reveals a section of the original clay wall behind. Traditional ciders and perries are always available. Quality bar meals are served at affordable prices. ♨Q❀◐◑⊟⇌⊟(40,X53)♣●P⚟

West Stour

Ship Inn

SP8 5RP (on A30)

12-3, 6-11; 12-11 Sun ☎ (01747) 838640

shipinn-dorset.com

Ringwood Best; guest beers H

Built in 1750 as a coaching inn, this popular roadside pub has fine views across the Blackmore Vale. The public bar features a flagstone floor and low ceiling; the lounge and restaurant area is light and airy with stripped oak floorboards and farmhouse furniture. There is a pretty patio and large garden to the rear. This family-friendly pub is renowned for superb home-cooked food (no meals Sun eve) and comfortable accommodation. Two guest beers are always available. Dogs are welcome in the bar. ♨Q❀⊟◐◑♣P⚟

Weymouth

Duke of Cornwall

St Edmund Street, DT4 8AS

10 (11 winter)-2am; 12-2am Sun ☎ (01305) 776594

Dartmoor Jail Ale; guest beers H

This popular local is close to the harbour and the registry office. Open all day, it is ideal for that quick drink before the wedding ceremony. The only pub in the area serving Dartmoor Jail Ale, the Duke has a mostly wooden interior with a large room at the back. Some fishing memorabilia and cartoons of local characters are displayed on the walls. Live music plays frequently and there is a lively atmosphere on weekend evenings, especially in summer. ♨⇌⊟

Weatherbury

7 Carlton Road North, DT4 7PX

12 midnight ☎ (01305) 786040

Fuller's London Pride; guest beers H

Down-to-earth free house in a residential part of the town. The single-bar interior is divided into different areas with a TV screen in each one. The London Pride is accompanied by frequently-changing guest beers. Outside there is a patio with a covered, heated area for smokers. Well-behaved children and dogs are welcome. Food may not be served on Sundays – phone to check. Q⊛❀⊟◐◑⇌⊟P⚟

Winterborne Stickland

Crown

North Street, DT11 0NJ (2 miles N of A354)

12- 3, 6-midnight; 12-midnight Sat & Sun

☎ (01258) 880838

Ringwood Best, Fortyniner, seasonal beers H

This 18th-century Grade II-listed inn is situated in the centre of the village surrounded by pleasant walking country. There is an outdoor seating area and garden complete with original well. Excellent home-cooked food is available and can be enjoyed in front of the inglenook fireplace or in the beamed dining room at the back. A local bus service is available Monday-Saturday from Blandford. ♨⊛❀◐◑♿⛺⊟(311)♣P

Worth Matravers

Square & Compass ★

BH19 3LF (off B3069) SY974777

12-3, 6-11; 12-11 summer; 12-11 Sun ☎ (01929) 439229

Palmers Copper Ale; guest beers G

This iconic inn boasts both a museum and a book detailing its fascinating history. Featuring in every edition of this Guide, its many awards are too numerous to list. The single serving hatch offers guest beers from near and far, plus a range of ciders including the landlord's own and Hecks. For the hungry there are pasties. The sea-facing beer garden features stone carvings from the annual Square Fair, and mutant pumpkins come autumn. In winter real fires draw walkers from the coast path. Truly a pub for all seasons. ♨Q❀⛺⊟(44)●P

Of Ale

Ale is made of malte and water, and they the which do put any other thynge to ale than is rehersed, except yest, barme or godisgood (other forms of yeast) do sofysticat (adulterate) theyr ale. Ale for an englysshe man is a natural drynke. Ale must have these propertyes, it must be freshe and cleare, it must not be ropy (cloudy) or smoky, nor it must have no welt nor tayle (sediment or dregs). Ale should not be dronke under V days olde. Newe ale is unholsome for all men. And soure ale and deade ale the which doth stande a tylt is good for no man. Barley malte maketh better ale then oten malte or any other corne doth, it doth engender grosse humoures, but yette it maketh a man stronge.

Of Bere

Bere is made of malte, of hoppes, and water, it is a natural drinke for a dutche man. And nowe of late dayes it is moche used in Englande to the detryment of many englysshe men, specyally it kylleth them the which be troubled with the colycke and the stone & strangulion (quinsy), for the drynke is a colde drynke: yet it doth make a man fat and doth inflate the bely, as it doth appere by the dutche mens faces & belyes. If the beer be well served and be fyned & not newe, it doth qualify ye heat of the lyver.

Andrew Boorde (c.1490-1549), A 'Compendyous Regyment' or 'a Dyetary of Helth', 1542

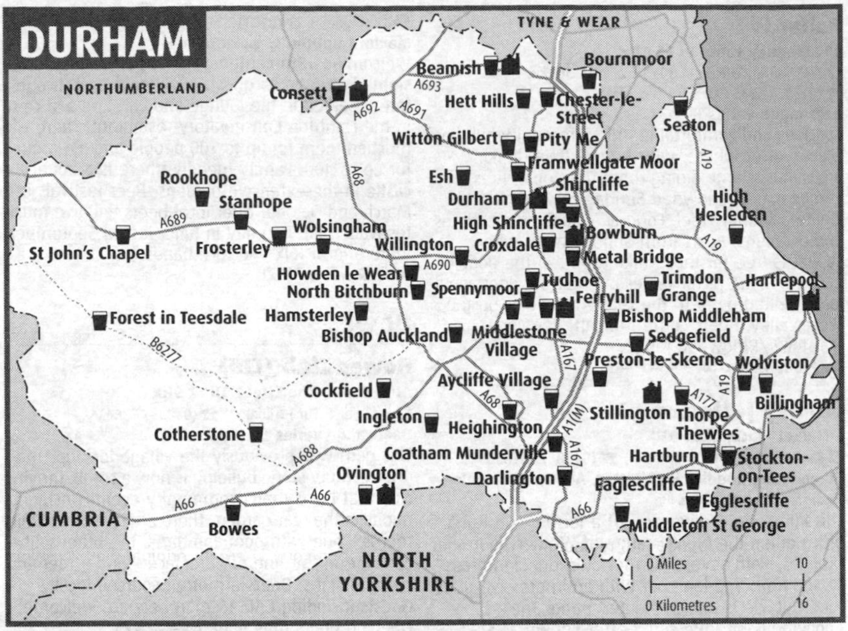

Co Durham incorporates part of the former county of Cleveland

Aycliffe Village

County

13 The Green, DL5 6LX

☼ 12-3, 6-11 ☎ (01325) 312273

🌐 thecountyaycliffevillage.com

Yard of Ale County Best Bitter; guest beers Ⓗ

Overlooking the award-winning green in a picturesque village, this attractive cream-coloured country free house was originally three 17th-century cottages. It is now open plan with the bar and three dining areas unified by bright modern decor, complemented by older beams and log fireplaces. The current owners took over in 2008 and have a passion to marry good food with excellent beers. The house beer is brewed by local micro Yard of Ale, and up to three guests come from northern micros. Sunday is quiz night. ♨Q❀⇔◐⊟P⁵–▯

Beamish

Shepherd & Shepherdess

DH9 0RS (follow signs for Beamish Museum)

☼ 11.30-11.30 (11 Sun) ☎ (0191) 370 0349

Black Sheep Best Bitter; guest beer Ⓗ

Friendly refurbished village pub full of interesting photos and pictures, many with a fox hunting theme. Note the outside sign depicting a shepherd and shepherdess, and a mural in oil behind the bar of old Durham County. Wednesday is quiz night. One guest ale is available in winter, two in summer. The pub serves generously-portioned meals offering good value for money. Baby-changing facilities are available and outside is a play area for children. Buses to Newcastle and Sunderland pass close to the pub. ❀◐♿⊟P⁵–▯

> Beer makes you feel the way you ought to feel without beer. **Henry Lawson**

Billingham

Catholic Club

37 Wolviston Road, TS23 2RU (on E side of old A19, just S of Roseberry Rd roundabout, next to bus stop)

☼ 7-11 (midnight Fri); 12-midnight Sat; 12-10.30 Sun ☎ (01642) 551137

Copper Dragon Best Bitter; guest beers Ⓗ

Described as Teesside's best-kept secret, this Victorian mansion and former school is now a thriving, friendly private members' club, where a genuine welcome to card-carrying CAMRA members is guaranteed. Dedicated and enthusiastic volunteers ensure that the club's reputation for serving fine real ales continues to grow. One regular and up to nine guest ales are supplemented by beer festivals held over a weekend or bank holiday. Weekly blues/R&B nights have become increasingly popular. ❀♿⊟(36)♣♠P⁵–

Bishop Auckland

Grand Hotel

Holdforth Crest, DL14 6DU (on A6072, near Asda car park)

☼ 6-11; 12-3 Sun ☎ (07891) 665792

Beer range varies Ⓗ

Well regarded throughout the region for its live music on Saturday nights, this imposing pub now also enthusiastically promotes local young talent on Thursdays and Fridays. There is a pool table in the bar and a large screen showing football in the function room, plus the usual pub games in evidence. The smoking area in the yard is covered and heated. It's a five-minute walk from the railway station, past Asda and under the railway bridge. Beer often comes from the Yard of Ale brewery. ❀♿⥈♣♠P⁵–

Pollards
104 Etherley Lane, DL14 6TW
⚙ 7-11 Mon; 12-2, 5-11.30; 12 2, 7-10.30 Sun
☎ (01388) 603539
Beer range varies Ⓗ
Spacious and comfortable, this community pub has a good atmosphere, with four distinct drinking areas plus a large dining room. Two open fires, pub games and a renowned Sunday carvery help to create a friendly feel. Food is available lunchtimes and evenings, apart from Sunday night when supper is free for those taking part in the popular quiz. There are picnic tables by the front door and a large heated patio to the rear with views up the Wear Valley. Beers come from the Jennings/ Marston's/Ringwood range.
♨Q❀◐◑⊟♿⇌🚌(94)♣P⁻⊡

Stanley Jefferson ✔
5 Market Place, DL14 7NJ
⚙ 9am-midnight (1am Fri & Sat) ☎ (01388) 452836
Greene King Ruddles Best Bitter, Abbot; Marston's Pedigree; guest beers Ⓗ
This interesting conversion of a former solicitors' office offers the typical range of Wetherspoon's facilities, with several comfortable drinking areas served from one long bar with an impressive glass roof. Outside is a large heated patio. The eponymous Mr Jefferson, better known as Stan Laurel, lived in the town and was schooled nearby. Ciders are Westons Old Rosie and Organic. Food is available all day and children are welcome if dining until 9pm. The Bishop of Durham's palace and park are nearby. ❀◐◑♿⇌🚌●⁻

Tut 'n' Shive
68 Newgate Street, DL14 7EQ
⚙ 11-11 (1am Thu-Sat); 12-11 Sun ☎ (01388) 603252
Beer range varies Ⓗ
Single-room pub with a popular jukebox and busy pool table, right in the heart of the town. It attracts a varied clientele thanks to its eclectic range of ales, mostly from independent and local breweries, preaching the cask gospel to younger drinkers. The cider is Old Rosie. Bagatelle and shove-ha'penny are played. The pub hosts a general knowledge quiz on Monday, music quiz on Thursday, karaoke on Friday, and regular live music. There is an outdoor drinking area next to the small car park.
❀⇌🚌♣●P⁻

Bishop Middleham

Cross Keys
9 High Street, DL17 9AR (1 mile from A177)
⚙ 12 (5 Mon)-11; 12-10.30 Sun ☎ (01740) 651231
Wells Bombardier; guest beer Ⓗ
Busy family-run village pub with a warm, friendly atmosphere and a good reputation for excellent meals. The spacious, open-plan lounge bar is complemented by a large restaurant/function room serving an extensive menu of freshly-prepared meals. Situated in excellent wildlife and walking country, a three-mile circular walk starts opposite. Quiz night is Tuesday, Teesside Tornadoes Bike Club meets on Wednesday and the pub has its own football team. ♨❀◐◑🚌

Bournmoor

Dun Cow
Primrose Hill, DH4 6DY
⚙ 12-midnight ☎ (0191) 385 2631
Maxim Lambton's; guest beer Ⓗ
Welcoming 18th-century country pub with an often sighted 'grey lady' ghost. Traditional English pub fare is served in the lounge and bar, and à la carte in the Lambton Conservatory restaurant. There is a function room for up to 100 people and a marquee for up to 400. Family friendly, there is a bouncy castle in the extensive gardens. Beer festivals in March and October offer local beers and live music festivals (first Saturday in June, last in September) feature local folk and rock bands.
♨❀◐◑♿🚌●P⁻⊡

Bowes

Bowes Club (CIU)
Arch House, The Street, DL12 9HR
⚙ 7 (3 Sat & Sun)-midnight ☎ (01833) 628431
Beer range varies Ⓗ
This gem was previously the village lock-up. The 18th-century stone building is now a small, thriving club that hosts many community events, including quoits in the rear garden. There are two downstairs rooms – one with pool and darts, the other with a cosy fire in the fine old fireplace – and a meeting room upstairs. Beers are often sourced locally. Guests including CAMRA members are welcome. Opening hours may vary. ♨❀⊟▲♣

Chester-le-Street

Butchers Arms
Middle Chare, DH3 3QD (on Front Street)
⚙ 11-11 (midnight Fri & Sat); 12-3, 7-11 Sun
☎ (0191) 386 3605
Jennings Cumberland Ale; Marston's Pedigree; guest beers Ⓗ
Acknowledged for the quality and quantity of its beers, this is the only traditional real ale pub left in the town. Joan Robinson, an employee of the pub for many years, is now the landlady and is planning to increase the beer range. The pub is also noted for its food, with home cooking a speciality – Sunday lunches are popular and good value for money. Teas and coffees are also served. Convenient for the railway station and all buses through the town. Accommodation is now available. Q🛏◐⇌🚌♣

Chester-le-Street Cricket Club ✔
Hawthorn Terrace, DH3 3PE
⚙ 11-11 (12.30am Fri & Sat); 11-midnight Sun
☎ (0191) 3883684
Cumberland Corby Ale; guest beer Ⓗ
A splendid club house with two main rooms downstairs and an area outside for warm-weather drinking – all with fine views over the cricket ground. Sandwiches and pies are available from the bar on most days. Functions for up to 100 people (including wheelchair users) can be

INDEPENDENT BREWERIES

Camerons Hartlepool
Consett Ale Works Consett
Durham Bowburn
Four Alls Ovington
Hill Island Durham City
Stables Beamish
Windlestone Stillington (NEW)
Yard of Ale Ferryhill

accommodated in the well-appointed function room on the first floor. Local CAMRA Club of the Year 2008/2009, and north east Club of the Year 2009. Shelter is provided outside for smokers. ❀♿⇌🚌P⁴–

Pelaw Grange Greyhound Stadium

Drum Road, DH3 2AF (signed from Barley Mow roundabout on A167)
⏲ 6.30-11 (closed Mon, Wed & Thu); 12-4 Sun
☎ (0191) 410 2141 🌐 pelawgrange.co.uk
Beer range varies ⊞
Managed by a CAMRA member, this is the only greyhound stadium in Britain with real ales. The large open bar, Panorama restaurant and a concert room all overlook the track. There is a lively atmosphere on race nights (Tue, Fri and Sat) when CAMRA members are admitted free. An annual beer festival is hosted on the Easter weekend and trips to local micro-breweries are organised. The trackside terrace is available for smokers. Children are welcome. Twice Durham CAMRA Branch Club of the Year. ❀◗♿🚌(21,22,50)P⁴–

Smiths Arms

Brecon Hill, Castle Dene, DH3 4HE NZ299507
⏲ 12 (4 Mon-Wed)-11; 12-10.30 Sun ☎ (0191) 3856915
Black Sheep Best Bitter; Jarrow Rivet Catcher, guest ale ⊞
A little off the beaten track, this traditional pub has a small, cosy bar with a log-burning stove, a room with a pool table and a larger lounge with an open fire. The Forge restaurant is once again operating Wednesday-Sunday and is well worth a visit (book ahead). The pub is reputed to be haunted.
♨Q◐◗⊟♣P

Coatham Mundeville

Foresters Arms

Brafferton Lane, DL1 3LU (on A167 ¼ mile S of A1M jct 59)
⏲ 12 (4 Mon)-midnight ☎ (01325) 320565
Taylor Landlord; Wells Bombardier; guest beer ⊞
You can be sure of a warm welcome from the landlady at this Grade II-listed historic stone-built roadside pub close to the A1. The interior comprises a main bar with an adjoining restaurant/ function room. A folk club meets on Monday, a quiz is held every Thursday and live entertainment is hosted at weekends. To the rear of the pub is a large car park and garden area which includes the Foresters Farm (chickens, ducks, sheep). Beware – the pub is reputedly haunted and mysterious happenings occur! ♨❀◐◗♿⛺🚌♣P⁴–

Cockfield

Queen's Head

106 Front Street, DL13 5AA
⏲ 1 (5 Mon & Tue)-11; 12-11 Sat & Sun ☎ (07792) 413352
Beer range varies ⊞
Popular, community-focused local towards the south end of the village, with two constantly-changing guest ales. The open plan interior is divided into various sections for drinking and dining. A good-value set meal is served on Thursday from 1.30pm. The historic Cockfield Fell is just out the back, and visitors to this interesting area will find a warm welcome here. There is seating outside the front door and a bus stop nearby. ❀◐🚌(8)♣P

Consett

Grey Horse ✔

115 Sherburn Terrace, DH8 6NE (off A692)
⏲ 12-12.30am ☎ (01207) 502585 🌐 thegreyhorse.co.uk
Consett Ale Works Steel Town Bitter, White Hot, Red Dust; guest beers ⊞
An oasis in a cask beer desert, this traditional pub dates back to 1848. With Consett Ale Works Brewery at the rear, the inn is one of a chain of four including the Beamish Mary in No Place and the White Swan in Stokesley that brews Captain Cook ales. The interior comprises a lounge and L-shaped bar, with a wood-beamed ceiling. Beer festivals are held twice a year, live entertainment hosted on Thursday and a quiz on Wednesday. Cider is Westons Old Rosie. The coast-to-coast cycle route is close by. ♨Q❀⊟♣●

Cotherstone

Red Lion

Main Street, DL12 9QE
⏲ 12-3 Sat only, 7-11; 12-4, 7-10.30 Sun ☎ (01833) 650236
Jennings Cumberland Ale; Caledonian Deuchars IPA; guest beer ⊞
Nestling in a terrace of stone buildings dating from around 1738, this traditional local has changed little since the 1960s. It has a long main room with a serving-hatch-style bar, and still has outside toilets. There is no TV or jukebox, just good beer and conversation. Local CAMRA Community Pub of the year 2008 and Pub of the Season 2009, the venue is used by various clubs. Children and dogs are welcome and there is a small beer garden. Guest beer comes from a local micro.
♨Q☕❀⛺🚌♣P

Croxdale

Daleside Arms

Front Street, DH6 5HY (on B6288, 3 miles S of Durham, off A167)
⏲ 3 (7 Tue)-11 (midnight Thu & Fri); 12-midnight Sat; 11-8 Sun ☎ (01388) 814165
Beer range varies ⊞
Up to two beers, usually from Yorkshire Dales Brewery, can be found in this comfortable roadside rural setting. Visitors are greeted by stunning award-winning floral displays. Sporting memorabilia adorns the cosy main bar. Food is served in the spacious lounge (booking is advised). A previous local CAMRA Pub of the Year winner, it remains an oasis in a village ideally situated for country walks but well served by public transport. Worth making the effort for the simple things done properly. Q☕❀🛏◐◗⊟♿🚌♣P⁴–

Darlington

Britannia

1 Archer Street, DL3 6LR (next to ring road W of town centre)
⏲ 11.30-3, 5.30-11; 11.30-11 Thu-Sat; 12-10.30 Sun
☎ (01325) 463787
Camerons Strongarm; John Smith's Bitter; guest beers ⊞
Warm, friendly, popular local CAMRA award-winning pub – a bastion of cask beer for more than 150 years. The pub retains much of the appearance and layout of the private house it once was – a modestly enlarged bar and small parlour (used for

meetings) sit either side of a central corridor. Prize-winning floral displays adorn the exterior in summer. Listed for its historical associations, it was the birthplace of teetotal 19th-century publisher JM Dent. Four countrywide guest beers are available. ❀⇌🚌♣P⁵–🗑

Darlington Snooker Club

1 Corporation Road, DL3 6AE (corner of Northgate)
⏲ 11-midnight (late Fri & Sat); 12-midnight Sun
☎ (01325) 241388
Beer range varies Ⓗ
This first floor, family-run and family-oriented private snooker club offers a warm, friendly welcome. Four guest beers from micros countrywide are on offer and a small range of real ales in a bottle is stocked. A small, comfortable TV lounge is available for those not playing on one of the 10 top-quality snooker tables. Twice yearly, the club plays host to a professional celebrity, and two beer festivals are held annually. Winner of CAMRA regional Club of the Year 2004-2008, it welcomes CAMRA members on production of a membership card or this Guide. ⇌(North Rd)🚌♣

Number Twenty 2 ✔

22 Coniscliffe Road, DL3 7RG
⏲ 12-11; closed Sun ☎ (01325) 354590
🌐 twenty2.villagebrewer.co.uk
Burton Bridge Bitter; Village Brewer White Boar, Seasonabull, Old Raby, Zetland; guest beers Ⓗ
Town-centre ale house with a passion for cask beer and winner of many CAMRA awards. Ales are dispensed from up to 13 handpumps, including a stout or porter, along with nine draught European beers. Huge curved windows, stained glass panels and a high ceiling give the interior an airy, spacious feel. To the rear The Canteen serves upmarket home-cooked lunches. The pub comes alive early evening as people pop in after work or shopping. This is the home of Village Brewer beers, commissioned from Hambleton by the licensee. Q◐♿⇌🚌🗑

Old Yard Tapas Bar

98 Bondgate, DL3 7JY
⏲ 10-11; 12-10.30 Sun ☎ (01325) 467385 🌐 tapasbar.co.uk
Theakston Old Peculier; guest beers Ⓗ
Interesting mixture of a town-centre bar and Mediterranean-style taverna offering a range of real ales alongside a fascinating blend of international wines and spirits in a friendly setting. Five guest beers from micros countrywide are stocked. Although this is a thriving restaurant, you are more than welcome to simply pop in for a pint – and maybe a tapa or two (Greek and Spanish). The excellent south-facing pavement café is popular in good weather. TV is for sport only. ❀◐⇌🚌⁵–

Quakerhouse 🏆

1-3 Mechanics Yard, DL3 7QF (off High Row)
⏲ 11-11 (midnight Fri & Sat); 12-11 Sun ☎ (07817) 108756
🌐 quakerhouse.net
Beer range varies Ⓗ
Seven times Town Pub of the Year, this bar is often the first point of call for CAMRA members visiting Darlington. The lively award-winning free house opened in 1998 in the former Quaker Coffee House in one of the old yards just off the pedestrianised town centre. It has the feel of a cellar bar, offering 10 guests from regional and micro-breweries countrywide. Live rock music features on Wednesday (there is a door charge after 7.30pm). An upstairs function room is available for hire. ❀♿⇌🚌♣●🗑

Tanners Hall ✔

63-64 Skinnergate, DL3 7LL
⏲ 9-midnight (1am Fri & Sat) ☎ (01325) 369939
Greene King Ruddles Best Bitter, Abbot; guest beers Ⓗ
A popular Wetherspoon town pub with a varied clientele, named after the leather trade that once dominated the town until the 18th century. Its 12 handpumps provide a good selection of real ales including up to six guests, often from local micros. Converted from a furniture shop in 1998, its spacious interior makes it an ideal venue for holding its own beer festivals as well as the chain's national events. Reasonably priced food is served until 10pm. It gets very busy at weekends, in fact occasionally boisterous. ❀◐♿⇌🚌⁵–

Durham

Bridge Hotel

40 North Road, DH1 4SE (200m from Durham rail station)
⏲ 11-11 ☎ (0191) 3868090 🌐 bridgehoteldurham.co.uk
Wells Bombardier; Greene King Old Speckled Hen; guest beer Ⓗ
Originally built in the 1850s as lodgings for the Irish navvies constructing the railway viaduct under which it sits, it evolved into a public house a few years after completion of the railway. Three immaculately kept ales are always available, one a weekly-changing guest. The comfortable dining area offers a diverse, high-quality menu of home-cooked food throughout the day at reasonable prices. It can get busier at the weekend, but you are always assured of a warm welcome and excellent service from the attentive staff. 🛏◐♿⇌🚌

Colpitts Hotel

Colpitts Terrace, DH1 4EL
⏲ 2 (12 Thu-Sat)-11; 12-10.30 Sun ☎ (0191) 386 9913
Samuel Smith OBB Ⓗ
An unspoilt gem, this late Victorian pub has changed little since it was first built. Occupying a corner site, the building has an unusual A shape with three rooms – a small lounge, a snug used as a pool room and the comfortable main bar partially divided by a fireplace. Like all Sam Smith's, the noise comes from conversation not jukebox or games machines. A must-visit hostelry for anyone who appreciates pubs as they used to be. 🔥Q❀🍺⇌🚌⁵–

Dun Cow ✔

37 Old Elvet, DH1 3HN (between Royal County Hotel & Durham Prison)
⏲ 11-11.30; 12-10.30 Sun ☎ (0191) 386 9219
Black Sheep Best Bitter; Camerons Castle Eden Ale; Jennings Cumberland Ale Ⓗ
In 995AD Lindisfarne monks were searching for a resting place for the body of St Cuthbert when they came across a milkmaid looking for her lost cow. She directed them to Dun Holm (Durham). This Grade II-listed pub, part of which dates back to the 16th century, is named after the historic animal. At the front of the building is a friendly snug and a larger lounge to the rear. The story of the monks' legendary journey is told on the wall of the corridor alongside the two rooms. Q◐🍺⇌🚌(20)⁵–

Half Moon ✔

86 New Elvet, DH1 3AQ (opp Royal County Hotel)
✪ 11-11 (midnight Fri & Sat); 12-11 Sun ☎ (0191) 383 6981
Draught Bass; Fuller's London Pride; Taylor Landlord; guest beer Ⓗ
A long-term regular in the Guide, this city-centre pub is named after the crescent-shaped bar that runs from the front room through to the lounge area. Run by the same landlord for 29 years, the interior is largely unchanged with traditional decor throughout and interesting photos of the pub at the beginning of the 20th century on the walls. Attracting a lively crowd on Friday and Saturday evenings, it has a large backyard next to the river which is popular in summer. The guest beer is from Durham Brewery. ❀⇌🚌(21)⚐–

Market Tavern

27 Market Place, DH1 3NJ
✪ 11-11 (midnight Thu; 1am Fri & Sat); 12-11 Sun
☎ (0191) 3862069
Beer range varies Ⓗ
Situated in Durham's historic market place, this single roomed, L-shaped bar offers an array of six ales from all over Britain. The management makes full use of its guest list and has featured Mordue, Hydes, Beartown and Oakleaf to name but a few. One of the most improved venues in town, it serves good food up to 9pm. Although the interior is of basic wooden ale house appearance, friendly staff provide a warm welcome to both the regular and casual visitor. ◑♿⇌

Olde Elm Tree ✔

12 Crossgate, DH1 4PS
✪ 12-11; 11-midnight Fri & Sat; 12-10.30 Sun
☎ (0191) 3864621
Caledonian Deuchars IPA; guest beers Ⓗ
One of Durham's oldest pubs, dating back to at least 1600, as befits its age it is reputed to have two ghosts. The interior comprises an L-shaped bar room and a top room linked by a set of stairs. A popular pub, it attracts a good mix including students, locals and bikers. Enjoy excellent home-cooked food, the Wednesday quiz (arrive early) and folk group on Monday and Tuesday. Ask the landlord for details of the next Elm beer festival. ❀⇌P⚐–

Shakespeare Tavern ★

63 Saddler Street, DH1 3NU (100m from Market Place)
✪ 11-1.30am ☎ (0191) 3843261
🌐 shakespearedurham.co.uk
Caledonian Deuchars IPA; Fuller's London Pride; guest beers Ⓗ
A CAMRA North East heritage pub in the city centre close to the Cathedral. The interior comprises a small bar with a recently spruced-up side snug and a back lounge which was enlarged in 2008. it was originally a haunt for 19th-century theatre actors and patrons, hence the name. Despite the recent alterations and other ill-judged attempts at change over the years, it has largely maintained its character, except in the eyes of the purists. Popular with locals and students. Q⊟⇌

Victoria Inn ★

86 Hallgarth Street, DH1 3AS
✪ 11.45-3, 6-11; 12-2, 7-10.30 Sun ☎ (0191) 386 5269
🌐 victoriainn-durhamcity.co.uk
Big Lamp Bitter; guest beers Ⓗ
This warm and welcoming, Grade II-listed, three-room Victorian pub remains almost unaltered since it was built in 1899. The quaint decor, coal fires, tiny snug and a genuine Victorian cash drawer help create an olde-worlde feel. Ales are mainly from local breweries and a wide selection of single malt whiskies is on display. No meals are served but toasties are available. Voted local CAMRA Pub of the Year for the sixth time in 2009. ♨Q🛏⊟⇌🚌(21)♣

Water House ✔

65 North Road, DH1 4SQ
✪ 9am-11.30 ☎ (0191) 370 6540
Greene King Ruddles Best Bitter, Abbot; guest beers Ⓗ
Situated in former water board offices and a short distance from the bus station, this pub is popular with young and old alike and extremely busy at weekends. A selection of beers from regional and micro-brewers awaits, with single brewery weekends now a feature. The modern decor is complemented by coal-effect open fires. Good value food is served. It's an excellent Wetherspoon's pub. ◑♿⇌🚌

Eaglescliffe

Cleveland Bay

718 Yarm Road, TS16 0JE (jct of A67 and A135)
✪ 11-1am ☎ (01642) 780275
Taylor Landlord; guest beers Ⓗ
Dating from the arrival of the world's first public railway, the Stockton & Darlington, the gate pillars from the goods yard now adorn the entrance to the car park. An ever-popular pub, you can be sure of a friendly and genuine welcome here. A previous local CAMRA Pub of the Season winner, its reputation for fine cask beers is now well established. The interior comprises a main bar with two sports TVs, lounge and large function room. ❀⊟🚌(7)P⚐–⊡

Egglescliffe

Pot & Glass

Church Road, TS16 9DQ (300m from A135, opp church)
✪ 12-2 (not Mon), 6-11 (5.30-midnight Fri; 6-midnight Sat); 12-11 Sun ☎ (01642) 651009
Draught Bass; Black Sheep Best Bitter; Caledonian Deuchars IPA; guest beers Ⓗ
A previous local CAMRA Pub of the Season winner, this classic and ever popular multi-roomed village local is situated in a quiet cul-de-sac opposite the parish church. Former licensee and cabinet maker Charlie Abbey, whose last resting place overlooks the pub, fashioned the ornate bar fronts from old country furniture. Tasting notes are available for the five handpumps, which include two guests. Outside is a large south-facing garden. Themed food evenings support the good value home-cooked menu. Q☕❀◑⊟🚌(7)P⚐–⊡

Esh

Cross Keys

Front Street, DH7 9QR (3 miles W of A691 via Langley Park) NZ197440
✪ 12-2, 5.30 (6 Sat)-11; 12-2, 7-10.30 Sun
☎ (0191) 373 1279
Black Sheep Best Bitter; guest beer Ⓗ
Pleasant 18th-century pub in a picturesque village offering a varied food menu including vegetarian and children's choices. A comfortable locals' bar is

complemented by a lounge/restaurant overlooking the Browney Valley. Delft racks display porcelain artefacts, some of which portray the old village. The village is commonly known as Old Esh to distinguish it from nearby Esh Winning.
Q❀◐⊟♿♣P⁄–

Ferryhill

Surtees Arms 🏆 ✔

Chilton Lane, DL17 0DH
⌚ 4-11; 12-midnight Sat; 12-11 Sun ☎ (01740) 655724
🌐 thesurteesarms.co.uk
Yard of Ale One Foot in the Yard, Black as Owt Stout; guest beers Ⓗ
Large multi-roomed traditional pub owned by CAMRA members. Guest beers are sourced from local and national breweries and the real cider also changes regularly. Annual beer festivals are held in the summer and at Halloween. Live music and charity nights are regular events. A function room is available for private gatherings. Lunches are served on Sunday only. The pub is also home to the Yard of Ale micro-brewery, established in 2008, and its beers are permanent in the pub.
♨Q❀◐⊟♿🚌♣●⁄–

Forest in Teesdale

Langdon Beck Hotel

DL12 0XP (on B6277, 8 miles NW of Middleton in Teesdale) NY853312
⌚ 11-10.30 (closed Mon Nov-Easter); 12-10.30 Sun
☎ (01833) 622267 🌐 langdonbeckhotel.com
Black Sheep Best Bitter; Jarrow Rivet Catcher; guest beer Ⓗ
Situated high in the Pennines, in some of the finest countryside in England, this welcoming inn has long been a destination for walkers, fishermen and those seeking tranquility. But visitors do not just come for the scenery – this gem also offers excellent food, two regular beers, and extra guest ales in the summer. A beer festival is held over the last weekend in May. The spectacular High Force and Cauldron Snout waterfalls are around three miles away and the Pennine Way passes close by.
♨Q❀⛽◐⊟♿P

Framwellgate Moor

Tap & Spile ✔

Front Street, DH1 5EE (off A167 bypass)
⌚ 12-3 (Fri & Sat only), 6 (5 Fri)-11; 12-3, 7-10.30 Sun
☎ (0191) 386 5451
Beer range varies Ⓗ
One of the last survivors of the old Cameron's chain, the pub has two front bars in traditional wood and stone and a larger back room, popular with families at the weekend. A regular local CAMRA award winner with a wide and varied selection of ales, the hostelry is well known in the area with drinkers of all ages. It hosts a quiz on Wednesday evening and the rear room is popular for meetings on Tuesday. The cider is Old Rosie.
Q⊟🚌(1A,21)●

Frosterley

Black Bull

Bridge End, DL13 2SL (100m S of A689 at W end of village, next to railway station)
⌚ closed Mon; 10.30-11; 10.30-5.30 Sun ☎ (01388) 527784
Beer range varies Ⓗ
Four ales from local breweries, plus up to four ciders and perries, set the tone for this unique pub. Step back in time on stone and bare wooden floors, sit by the kitchen range and piano in the bar, and savour the real old-fashioned pub ambience. High-quality food is from locally-sourced ingredients. There are tables outside the front door and a covered yard to the side. The only pub in the country to have its own peal of bells. Winter hours may vary.
♨Q❀◐⛺⇌(Weardale Railway)🚌(101)♣●P

Hamsterley

Cross Keys ✔

DL13 3PX (2 miles S of A68) NZ115311
⌚ 12-3, 5-11; 12-11 Sat & Sun ☎ (01388) 488457
🌐 thecrosskeyshamsterley.com
Beer range varies Ⓗ
Centrally located in the village near Hamsterley Forest, the Keys is a great combination of restaurant, tourist meeting place and, most importantly, real village local. Family run, it has a comfortable dining room, dog-friendly snug and a long lounge across the front of the building with a huge open fire. Very much part of the community, post can be collected here. Food is locally sourced, and a wine and cheese night is hosted on Tuesday. One of the three beers is chosen by the regulars.
♨Q❀◐⛺🚌(88)♣P⁄–

Hartburn

Parkwood Hotel ✔

64-66 Darlington Road, TS18 5ER (on Darlington Road)
⌚ 12-11 (midnight Fri & Sat) ☎ (01642) 587933
🌐 theparkwoodhotel.com
Adnams Broadside; Camerons Strongarm; Greene King Abbot; guest beer Ⓗ
This magnificent red brick Victorian building, with its imposing porch, tiled hallway, staircase and public rooms, is the former home of the Ropner family – shipbuilders, ship owners and civic benefactors. The licensee has been a real ale enthusiast for many years and is determined to keep the friendly bar for drinkers. The guest beer is usually a rarity for the area. Accommodation is in six high-quality en-suite bedrooms. Winner of local CAMRA 2009 Pub of the Season.
Q❀⛽◐🚌(20)P⁄–

Hartlepool

Brewery Tap

Stockton Street, TS24 7QS (on A689 in front of Camerons Brewery)
⌚ 11-4; closed Sun ☎ (01429) 868686
🌐 cameronsbrewery.com
Camerons Strongarm, seasonal beers Ⓗ
When Camerons discovered that it owned the next-door and somewhat derelict Stranton Inn, its future was secured when the brewery turned it into its visitor centre. Visitors to this award-winning development can sample Strongarm, the brewery's flagship brand, together with quarterly specials from the main brewery and Cameron's own Lions Den micro-brewery. The Tap also acts as the brewery shop, museum and starting point for brewery tours. Conferences, evening opening and other social events can be arranged.
Q♿⇌🚌(36)P🀫

Causeway

Vicarage Gardens, Stranton, TS24 7QT (beside Camerons Brewery) Hartlepool
⊛ 3-11 (11.30 Thu); 11-midnight Fri & Sat; 12-10.30 Sun
☎ (01429) 273954
Banks's Bitter; Camerons Strongarm; guest beers Ⓗ
This marvellous multi-roomed red-brick Victorian building has been Cameron's unofficial brewery tap for decades. Though owned by Marston's, the sales of Strongarm remain huge. This CAMRA multi-award-winning pub even gets a mention in Hansard for the quality of its Strongarm. The licensee, a keen musician, hosts an eclectic mix of live music most evenings. Good value home-cooked lunches are served Friday-Sunday. Three guest beers are always available. The covered walled beer garden is, not surprisingly, a smokers' paradise. ⚐☊❀◐♿⇌▣(36)♣⌐

Globe

26 Northgate, TS24 0LJ (Headland, towards fish quay)
⊛ 11-11 ☎ (01429) 860097
Camerons Strongarm Ⓗ
Family-run friendly community pub, under the stewardship of a licensee celebrating 25 years service to the trade. The price of the Strongarm now reflects the pub's new-found freehold status. It has a large main public bar and a smaller lounge which features a centrepiece Victorian fireplace and exposed brickwork. Once a thriving port, the area is best known nowadays for the legend of the hanging of the monkey – but be careful who you ask. ⚐Q☊❀⊟♿▣(7)♣⌐▯

Jackson's Arms ✔

Tower Street, TS24 7HH (100m S of railway/bus stations)
⊛ 12-midnight (2am Fri & Sat) ☎ (01429) 862413
Beer range varies Ⓗ
Close to the Grand Central and Northern Rail station, bus station, and Hartlepool United football ground, this warm, friendly street-corner local was once offered as the prize in a raffle. However, at £100 a ticket there weren't many takers. There are two busy bars, one for convivial conversation and one for pool and darts. An upstairs function room is available. Up to four premium beers are on offer, sourced from throughout the country. ⊟⇌▣

Rat Race Ale House

Station Approach, TS24 7ED (on platform 2 of railway station)
⊛ 12.02-2.15, 4.02-8.15; closed Sun ☎ (07889) 828648
⊕ ratracealehouse.co.uk
Beer range varies Ⓗ/Ⓖ
The railway station's former newsagents is now an ale lover's paradise. Opening and closing times coincide with the arrival/departure of the coast trains. No lager, no fizzy beer, no fizzy cider, no spirits, no alcopops, no food, no TV, no music, no jukebox, no one-arm-bandit, no quiz machine, no bar! Just four ever-changing real ales, real cider and real perry, all served at the correct temperature in over-sized lined glasses at reasonable prices. Takeaway containers are also available. Perfect! Q♿⇌▣♣●▯

Tall Ships

Mulberry Rise, Middle Warren, TS26 0BF (on A179, 3km NW of centre of town)
⊛ 10-11 (midnight Thu-Sat); 11-11 Sun ☎ (01429) 273515
John Smith's Bitter; guest beers Ⓗ
Aptly named in recognition of the town's Tall Ships Race Festival, this newly-built, out-of-town Ember Inns pub lets you embark on your own mini beer festival in a friendly and comfortable environment. Four guest beers are always available, while the regular ale is sold at a discounted price. Third-of-a-pint tasting racks come complete with tasting notes, and details of forthcoming beers are also listed. Quality, good value food is served all day, every day. Children are not permitted. ❀◐♿▣(6)P⌐

Heighington

Bay Horse

28 West Green, DL5 6PE
⊛ 11-11.30 (11.45 Fri & Sat); 12-10.30 Sun
☎ (01325) 312312
Black Sheep Best Bitter; Camerons Strongarm; Greene King Old Speckled Hen; Taylor Landlord; guest beer Ⓗ
Picturesque, historic, 300-year-old pub overlooking the village's largest green. Its exposed beams and stone walls offer traditional surroundings, partitioned into distinct drinking and dining areas, with a large restaurant extending from the lounge. Food plays a prominent role, with home-cooked meals available as well as bar snacks. The bar area gives drinkers the chance to enjoy the beer range in the evening, along with Old Rosie cider. ❀◐⊟♿▣●P

George & Dragon

4 East Green, DL5 6PP (behind church)
⊛ 12-3 (not Mon & Tue), 5-11; 12-midnight Fri & Sat; 12-11 Sun ☎ (01325) 313152
Black Sheep Best Bitter; Wells Bombardier; guest beers Ⓗ
Friendly village pub where locals warmly welcome visitors, situated in a fine position on the smaller green. An old coaching inn complete with stables, it has been refurbished in a modern style with a bar and spacious lounge. Excellent home-cooked food is served in the lounge and conservatory-style restaurant area. There are tables outside when the weather permits. The pub appeals to a wide spectrum of customers, with three guest ales (Wylam beers are regulars) helping ensure its popularity with lovers of good beer. ⚐Q❀◐⊟♿♣P

Locomotion Number One

Heighington Station, Heighington Lane, DL5 6QG
⊛ 11-11; 12-10.30 Sun ☎ (01325) 320132
⊕ thelocomotion1.co.uk
Beer range varies Ⓗ
This multi-roomed pub occupies the former stationmaster's house at Heighington Station, next to the level crossing where the first ever locomotive to haul a passenger train was hoisted on to the track in 1825. Four guest beers and a friendly atmosphere are enjoyed by locals and visitors alike. A terrace occupies the original platform with an additional courtyard for outside drinking. Home-made food is served in the pub or upstairs restaurant. Beware – the last train leaves early. ⚐Q❀◐♿⇌♣P⌐

Hett Hills

Moorings

DH2 3JU (off B6313) NZ240513

12-11.30 (10.30 Sun) ☎ (0191) 370 1597
themooringsdurham.co.uk
Taylor Landlord; guest beers H
Large, well-appointed, nautically-themed pub on two levels, recently extended by the addition of quality hotel accommodation – some rooms with hot tubs. The bar and bistro serve food all day, with a wide choice of traditional home-cooked English dishes. Upstairs, with splendid views, the Prime Rib restaurant offers quality food including seafood and fine cuts of local meats – ideal for special occasions. A smoking cabin is available outside. Wheelchair users can only access the ground floor. (28)P

High Hesleden

Ship Inn

TS27 4QD NZ453381
closed Mon; 12-3 (Fri & Sat only), 6-11; 12-9 Sun
☎ (01429) 836453 theshipinn.net
Beer range varies H
Neglected gem of a country free house in the east of the county near the coast. A nautical theme runs through the pub with pictures of warships in the bar and models of sailing ships in the lounge/restaurant. Up to seven ales, mainly from micro-breweries, are available and an award-winning selection of superb food is served. Adjacent to the large rear garden are six chalets plus a family apartment providing accommodation. There is ample parking and a good view of the sea on clear days. QP

High Shincliffe

Avenue Inn

Avenue Street, DH1 2PT (150m from A177)
12-11 ☎ (0191) 3865954 theavenue.biz
Black Sheep Best Bitter; guest beers H
A friendly out-of-town pub offering decent bed and breakfast facilities, providing a handy base for walkers exploring the attractive countryside. The Monday night quiz and Thursday night dominoes knockout are popular with customers. The evening menu offers quality food at modest prices and the pub serves traditional Sunday lunches. Regular bus services stop just outside, providing easy access to historic Durham City nearby. P

Howden le Wear

Green Tree

Bridge Street, DL15 8EX
3 (12 Sat & Sun)-11 ☎ (01388) 762743
Beer range varies H
Lively village pub with a single open-plan room across the front of the building, partitioned with a dining area and space for the pool table. Big on proper pub pastimes like darts, dominoes and pool, there is a quiz on Sunday, lively karaoke on Friday and live music on Saturday. Evening meals and Sunday lunches are available, and the two guest ales are usually local. A big screen shows sporting events. (1)P

Ingleton

Black Horse

Front Street, DL2 3HS
6 (7 Mon & Tue)-midnight; 12-3.30, 8-midnight Sun
☎ (01325) 730374
Jennings Cocker Hoop; guest beers H
Traditional, family-run village free house set back from the road with a large car park. A leaded glazed screen separates the dining area from the lounge bar. Run by the same landlord for more than 15 years, this is a popular community hostelry with a relaxed atmosphere. The two guest ales come from local micros. Excellent Thai food is served Wednesday to Saturday evenings, with traditional lunch on Sunday. A discounted taxi service is available for groups of four to eight people. The pub also serves as a basic village shop. Q(88)P

Metal Bridge

Old Mill Hotel

Thinford Road, DH6 5NX (off A1M jct 61, follow signs on A177 for 1¼ miles) NZ303351
12-11 (10.30 Sun) ☎ (01740) 652928
theoldmill.uk.com
Beer range varies H
Originally built as a paper mill in 1813, this spacious inn is now the venue of choice for discerning locals and visitors alike. Offering good-quality food and well-kept ales, three handpumps serve an ever-changing range, with the nearby Durham Brewery often supplying one of the beers. The food menu is extensive with daily specials written up on a board above the bar. Larger groups are welcome in the conservatory room. Accommodation is of a high standard, with all rooms en-suite. P

Middlestone Village

Ship Inn

Low Road, DL14 8AB (on B6287)
4 (12 Fri-Sun)-11 ☎ (01388) 810904
shipinnmiddlestone.co.uk
Beer range varies H
The epitome of a village pub, this bustling local is very much at the heart of the community, though regulars come from miles around to sample up to six beers. Entertainment includes darts and dominoes on Monday, a quiz on Thursday, plus regular themed nights and twice-yearly beer festivals. The open-plan bar has three drinking areas and there is an upstairs function room with two rooftop patios, providing spectacular views of the North Yorkshire moors. Food is served lunchtime and evening Friday-Sunday, evening only Monday-Thursday. (2,3)P

Middleton St George

Old Farmhouse

Yarm Road, DL2 1JZ
12-11 (10.30 Sun) ☎ (01325) 332191
Beer range varies H
A quiet, traditional pub on the outskirts of Darlington. Built over 250 years ago, it started life as an inn, then became a farmhouse, and more recently converted back to a pub. Operated by Mitchells & Butlers under the Vintage Inns brand, it offers up to three guest beers, often from Timothy Taylor, Harviestoun and Black Sheep. Food is served all day or you can just have a drink in front of the open fire in a welcoming atmosphere.
QP

North Bitchburn

Red Lion

North Bitchburn Terrace, DL15 8AL (just off A689)
⏲ 12-2 (not Mon), 6.30-11; 12-3, 6.30-11 Sun
☎ (01388) 763561
Black Sheep Best Bitter; Taylor Landlord; guest beers Ⓗ
Popular 250-year-old village pub with fine south-easterly views over the Wear Valley from the dining room. Originally a farm, it was also a stop-off for drovers on the way to Bishop Auckland market. The cheerful, refurbished interior is light and bright, with a comfortable bar room, small pool room and larger restaurant with a second dining area down a couple of steps. The pub has a well-deserved reputation for good food, available lunchtime and evening. Guest beers tend to come from smaller north-eastern breweries, with a monthly feature brewery such as Mordue or Jarrow. ❀◗🚌(1C)P

Ovington

Four Alls

The Green, DL11 7BP (2 miles S of Winston & A67)
⏲ 7 (6 Fri; 3 Sat)-11; 12-10.30 Sun ☎ (01833) 627302
🌐 thefouralls-teesdale.co.uk
Beer range varies Ⓗ
Friendly 18th-century inn opposite the village green in what is known as the 'maypole village'. A Victorian sign denotes the four alls: 'I govern all (queen), I fight for all (soldier), I pray for all (parson), I pay for all (farmer).' The pub has a bar, games room and restaurant serving excellent value food. Home of the Four Alls Brewery, this is the only place to sample its beers. Comfortable country-inn accommodation is available in seven rooms in a lovely setting. ♨Q☕❀🛏◗♿♣P⚡

Pity Me

Lambton Hounds

Front Street, DH1 5DE (100m from A167 bypass roundabout)
⏲ 4-11; 11-midnight Fri & Sat; 12-11 Sun ☎ (0191) 3864742
🌐 lambtonhoundsinn.com
Beer range varies Ⓗ
Situated on the Great North Road, this 250-year-old former coaching inn offers comfortable en-suite accommodation. It has a basic bar and a comfortable lounge with a small back room that is almost a snug. A slightly larger side room serves as the restaurant, but good home-made food is available throughout. The handpumps are in the lounge bar, where part of the counter is from the cocktail bar of the Titanic's sister ship the Olympic. Local brewers are usually well represented. Meals are not available on Sunday evening. ❀🛏◗⊟🚌(21)♣P⚡

Preston-le-Skerne

Blacksmiths Arms

Preston Lane, DL5 6JH (1 mile E of A167 at Gretna Green)
⏲ closed Mon; 11.30-2, 5.30 (6.30 winter)-11; 12-10.30 Sun
☎ (01325) 314873
Beer range varies Ⓗ
Welcoming free house known locally as 'The Hammers', situated in a rural location. A long corridor separates the bar, lounge and restaurant. The beamed lounge is furnished in farmhouse style. It has an excellent reputation for home-cooked food and up to three guest beers are available, sourced mainly from local micros. A former local CAMRA Rural Pub of the Year, it even has a helicopter landing pad. Pub of the Season 2008 & 2009. Q☕❀◗⊟♿♣P⚡

Rookhope

Rookhope Inn

Rear Hogarth Terrace, DL13 2BG
⏲ 12-midnight ☎ (01388) 517215
Beer range varies Ⓗ
Off the beaten track in the North Pennines, this Grade II-listed building dating from 1680 retains the original open fires and wood beams. A welcome rest stop on the coast-to-coast cycle route, this friendly community pub also offers accommodation and a function room. The big fire in the bar is welcome in the winter. Spectacular views of Upper Weardale can be enjoyed from the garden. Situated in a pretty former lead-mining village, the surrounding area provides ample opportunity for exploration. ♨Q❀🛏◗⊟♣P

St John's Chapel

Blue Bell ✔

12 Hood Street, DL13 1QJ
⏲ 5 (12 Sat & Sun)-1am ☎ (01388) 537256
Caledonian Deuchars IPA; guest beers Ⓗ
This small, homely village local is situated in beautiful Upper Weardale, and is very much at the heart of the community. The pub hosts ladies and gents darts and pool teams and runs a quiz on Sunday night. It also has a leek club which holds an annual show, and there is a small library for customers' use. The local angling club is based here and fishing licences are on sale at the bar. The guest beer often comes from the local Allendale Brewery. There is a covered and heated area outside. ♨❀🚌(101)♣●P⚡

Seaton

Seaton Lane Inn

Seaton Lane, SR7 0LP (on B1404 W of A19)
⏲ 11.30-12.30am (11.30 Sun) ☎ (0191) 581 2038
🌐 seatonlaneinn.co.uk
Caledonian Deuchars IPA; Taylor Landlord; guest beers Ⓗ
This roadside inn can trace its origins to an 18th-century blacksmith's – the basic stone-walled bar was the original building. A pictorial history is displayed on the walls. Behind this room is a recently refurbished lounge and restaurant. Quiz nights are Wednesday and Thursday. To the rear is an 18-room hotel, one room with disabled facilities. ♨Q❀🛏◗⊟♿🚌P⚡

Sedgefield

Ceddesfeld Hall

Sedgefield Community Association, Rectory Row, TS21 2AE
⏲ 7.30-10.30; 8-11 Fri & Sun; 9-11 Sat ☎ (01740) 620341
Beer range varies Ⓗ
Built in 1791 as the local parsonage, the hall comes complete with resident ghost 'the Pickled Parson'. Set in extensive grounds, ideal for a summer evening, this is a private club but CAMRA members

are most welcome. There is a bar, comfortable lounge and large function room. Run by volunteers from the Sedgefield Community Association, it is used by wide variety of groups. An annual beer festival is held on the first weekend in July with very reasonably-priced ale. Q❀⊟♿🚌P⚡–⊓

Nag's Head

8 West End, TS21 2BS
✪ 6 (5 Wed-Fri; 12 Sat)-midnight; 12-11 Sun
☎ (01740) 620234
Taylor Landlord; guest beers Ⓗ
Situated at the centre of the village, close to Sedgefield Racecourse, this free house is a traditional local attracting all age groups – families with well-behaved children are very welcome. There is a comfortable bar, a smaller lounge and a restaurant serving traditional Sunday lunch prepared with fresh local produce. Meals are also served in the bar (no food Sun and Mon eve). The landlord and landlady both come from the village. ❀◗⊟♿🚌♣P⚡–

Shincliffe

Seven Stars Inn

High Street North, DH1 2NU (on A177, S of Durham)
✪ 11-11 (10.30 Sun) ☎ (0191) 384 8454
🌐 sevenstarsinn.co.uk
Black Sheep Best Bitter; Durham Magus; guest beers Ⓗ
Dating from 1724, this small, cosy, beamed pub is situated on the edge of a pleasant village. Local country walks and the long Weardale Way pass nearby. Walkers are welcome in the bar - just make sure your boots are clean. Well-behaved dogs are also permitted. Meals are served in the bar and traditional restaurant. Comfortable accommodation makes the pub a great base for visiting the city and other attractions in the area. ❀🛏◖◗⊟🚌

Spennymoor

Frog & Ferret

Coulson Street, DL16 7RS
✪ 3 (12 Fri & Sat)-11; 12-10.30 Sun ☎ (01388) 818312
Beer range varies Ⓗ
This friendly family-run free house offers four constantly-changing real ales sourced from far and wide, with local and northern micro-breweries well represented. A welcoming atmosphere greets you on arrival at the three-sided bar in the comfortably furnished lounge, with brick, stone and wood cladding. Darts and dominoes are played and bar snacks are available. Well-behaved children are permitted until 4pm. A quiz is held on Sunday evening. ♛❀◖♿♣P⚡–

Stanhope

Grey Bull

17 West Terrace, DL13 2PB (on A689 at W end of town)
✪ 12-11 ☎ (01388) 526663 🌐 finepubs.co.uk/greybullstanhope/
Consett Ale Works White Hot; guest beer Ⓗ
At the foot of Crawleyside Bank, this lively local is run by a community trust. Quiz night on Wednesday, live music and film evenings complement the traditional pub games, with a cosy front bar across the front of the building and a snug to the rear with piano and internet access. A 40-seater function room completes the layout, and you can make your own music on Thursdays. Sandwiches are always available and hot food is served on games nights. Guest ales are usually local. Q❀◗▲♣P

Stockton-on-Tees

Sun Inn ✔

Knowles Street, TS18 1SU
✪ 11-11; 12-10.30 Sun ☎ (01642) 611461
Draught Bass Ⓗ
Popular town-centre drinkers' pub reputed to sell more Draught Bass than any other pub in the country. It was rescued from an uncertain future seven years ago by a regular at the pub who became the licensee, and who quickly increased sales of Bass to twelve 18-gallon casks a week – his son-in-law is the current licensee. The pub supports darts and football teams and charitable causes. On Monday evenings the function room is home to the famous Stockton Folk Club.
⇌(Stockton/Thornaby)🚌♣⚡–

Thomas Sheraton ✔

4 Bridge Road, TS18 1BH (at S end of High St)
✪ 9-midnight (1am Fri & Sat) ☎ (01642) 606134
Greene King Ruddles Best Bitter, Abbot; guest beers Ⓗ
This local CAMRA 2009 Pub of the Year winner is a fine Wetherspoon conversion of the Victorian law courts, and named after one of the country's great Georgian cabinet makers born in the town in 1751. It comprises several distinct dining and drinking areas downstairs, and a balcony and patio upstairs. Eight guest beers are available, several sourced locally. Regular beer festivals and occasional brewery trips are arranged. CAMRA members receive a 20 per cent discount off the regular menu. ☕❀◖◗♿⇌(Stockton/Thornaby)🚌●⚡–

Thorpe Thewles

Hamilton Russell Arms

Bank Terrace, TS21 3JW (100m off A177)
✪ 12-11 (10.30 Sun) ☎ (01740) 630757
🌐 hamiltonrussell.com
Marston's Pedigree; guest beers Ⓗ
Customers come from afar to this impressive and very popular village pub, where a genuine greeting is assured from the friendly staff. While the emphasis leans towards good-value top-quality food, served in abundance all day every day, real ale remains the licensee's lasting passion and drinkers are always made most welcome. The two weekly-changing guest beers are always premium or stronger bitters. The extensive south-facing patio areas are ideal for the warmer weather.
♛❀◖◗♿🚌(69)P

Trimdon Grange

Dovecote Inn

Salters Lane, TS29 6EP (on B1278)
✪ 7 (12 Fri-Sun)-11 ☎ (01429) 880967
Beer range varies Ⓗ
Hosts Susan and Stephen hail from Charles Wells country and their twin passions are Rugby Union and real ale. Situated on the outskirts of a former mining village, the free house dates back to at least 1820, growing an extra storey in 1927, resulting in the building's distinctive tall but narrow appearance. There used to be a dovecote on one

corner, hence the name. Inside, the single large room houses a popular pool table and dartboard. Quiz night is Tuesday. ♨🚌

Tudhoe

Black Horse Inn

4 Attwood Terrace, DL16 6TD (on B6288, 4 miles S of Durham)

⏲ 11.30-11 ☎ (01388) 420662

Caledonian Deuchars IPA; Courage Directors; guest beers Ⓗ

Once closed down by a pubco as unviable, this is now a busy, atmospheric and friendly free house, reopened by the current owners in 2008 after a period of closure. Two permanent and two regularly changing guest ales are always available. Excellent food is served lunchtimes and evenings in the restaurant and bar. Buses from Durham City pass the door. This family-friendly pub is well worth a visit. ❀◐◑♿🚌♣P⁄

Willington

Burn Inn

14 West End Terrace, DL15 0HW (jct of B6286 & A690 at W end of village)

⏲ 11-11 (midnight Sat); 12-11 Sun ☎ (01388) 746291

Beer range varies Ⓗ

This cosy establishment has become a first-class community pub, serving three ales from the Punch Taverns Finest Cask range. Various pub games are played here throughout the week and a quiz is held on Wednesday. It also has its own golf society, provides a meeting point for village junior football teams and acts as a venue for local Labour Party meetings. There is a heated outdoor area for smokers. ❀🚌♣P⁄

Witton Gilbert

Glendenning Arms ✔

Front Street, DH7 6SY (off A691 bypass, 3 miles from city centre)

⏲ 4-11; 3-midnight Fri; 12-midnight Sat; 12-11 Sun

☎ (0191) 371 0316

Black Sheep Best Bitter; guest beer Ⓗ

Typical village community local and Guide regular with a small, comfortable lounge and a lively and welcoming bar with the original Vaux 1970s red and white handpulls. The bar is attractively decorated in a contemporary style while the lounge remains more traditional. The pub runs darts, dominoes and football teams. Situated on the village's main road, there is ample car parking. ♨Q❀🍴🚌(15)♣P⁄

Travellers Rest

Front Street, DH7 6TQ (off A691 bypass 3 miles from city centre)

⏲ 11-11; 12-10.30 Sun ☎ (0191) 371 0458

Black Sheep Best Bitter; guest beers Ⓗ

Open-plan country-style pub, popular with diners. The bar area is split into three sections with a conservatory off to the side where families are welcome. There is also a more private dining room. Now owned by TR Leisure Partnership, an extensive food menu suits all tastes, with dining throughout the pub. The restaurant was redesigned two years ago and the kitchen upgraded to modern standards. Quiz nights are Tuesday and Sunday. Q👶❀◐◑♿🚌(15)P⁄

Wolsingham

Bay Horse Hotel

59 Uppertown, DL13 3EX (on B6296 to Tow Law) NZ078378

⏲ 11-midnight (11-3, 5-midnight Mon-Fri winter)

☎ (01388) 527220

Camerons Strongarm; guest beer Ⓗ

Large Camerons house on the north edge of the village, with interesting decor. Excellent quality, good value food is served in the bar and à la carte restaurant. The guest beer is usually from the Cameron's range. Quiz night is Sunday. Good quality B&B accommodation is available, providing an ideal base for exploring Weardale. ♨👶❀🛏◐◑🍴♿🚌(101)♣P⁄

Black Bull

27 Market Place, DL13 3AB

⏲ 12-11 (11.30 Sun) ☎ (01388) 527332

Caledonian Deuchars IPA; guest beer Ⓗ

Imposing hotel in the centre of the village, providing excellent food and accommodation. The pub runs various games nights and local Weight Watchers members enjoy the facilities after their meetings in the town hall opposite. It serves as headquarters for the village cricket team in the summer and hosts its social events. A good base for walkers and cyclists, it is also convenient for the Weardale Railway, which has a station in the village. The garden is a real surprise, especially in summer. ♨Q❀🛏◐◑🍴♿⛺🚂(Weardale Railway)🚌(101)♣⁄

Wolviston

Ship Inn

50 High Street, TS22 5JX (¼ mile E of A19/A689 jct, E end of village)

⏲ 12-3, 5-11; 12-3.30, 7-11 Sun ☎ (01740) 644420

🌐 theshipinnwolviston.co.uk

Beer range varies Ⓗ

Situated in a picturesque village, this impressive pub was rebuilt during the 19th century on the site of the old coaching inn – the full intriguing story of one-upmanship among competing breweries is featured on the pub's informative website. The licensee follows a vigorous real ale policy, with three handpumps providing a constantly-changing range of premium bitters, usually sourced from local north-east breweries. Only freshly-cooked, good-value, traditional pub food is served (no food Sun eve), including the Captain's Whopper Cod. Q❀◐◑P⁄

We would like to hear from you. If you think a pub not listed in the Guide is worthy of consideration, please let us know. Send us the name, full address and phone number (if known). If a pub in the Guide has given poor service, we would also like to know. Write to Good Beer Guide, CAMRA, 230 Hatfield Road, St Albans, Herts, AL1 4LW or email **gbgeditor@camra.org.uk**

Aingers Green

Royal Fusilier

Aingers Green Road, CO7 8NH
⏲ 11-1 (not Mon, Tue & Thu), 6-11; 11-11 Sat; 12-10.30 Sun
☎ (01206) 250001 🌐 theroyalfusilier.co.uk
Beer range varies Ⓗ
This tucked-away local is very friendly and continues to go from strength to strength. A varying choice of at least two real ales is always on offer. Starting life as a beer house more than 50 years ago, it retains a traditional appearance. The popular fish and chip supper from an award-winning shop in Brightlingsea is now a regular feature. Other themed evenings are also held. The pub supports a number of active pool and darts teams, and a beer festival is held annually. Well-behaved dogs are welcome.
⌂Q✿⊟⇌(Great Bentley)P⊢

Ashingdon

Victory Inn ✔

485 Ashingdon Road, SS4 3EU
⏲ 12-11 (10.30 Sun) ☎ (01702) 548440
Adnams Bitter; guest beers Ⓗ
A large and sometimes busy local pub situated on the main Rochford to Ashingdon road. Run by a long-standing landlord and landlady, it features a range of seasonal and guest cask ales, with informative tasting notes displayed at the bar. An extensive food menu is served all day until mid-evening. The pub attracts families in the daytime, especially in spring and summer. Live music events are held regularly, plus a very popular quiz night on Thursday evening. ☋✿◐◗⊟(7)P

INDEPENDENT BREWERIES

Brentwood South Weald
Crouch Vale South Woodham Ferrers
Famous Railway Tavern Brightlingsea
Farmer's Ales Maldon
Felstar Felsted
Hart of Stebbing Stebbing
Harwich Town Harwich
Mersea Island East Mersea
Mighty Oak Maldon
Nethergate Pentlow
Pitfield North Weald
Red Fox Coggeshall
Saffron Henham
Shalford Shalford
Sticklegs Elmstead Market
Wibblers Mayland

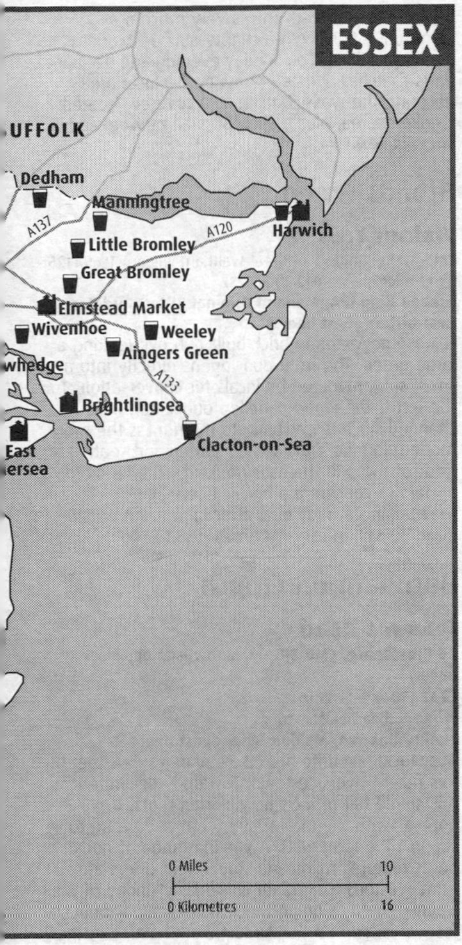

Aythorpe Roding

Axe & Compasses ✔

Dunmow Road, CM6 1PP (on B1845 5 miles SW of Dunmow) TL594154
⏲ 11-11 (midnight Fri & Sat); 12-10.30 Sun
☎ (01279) 876648 🌐 theaxeandcompasses.co.uk
Nethergate IPA Ⓗ**; Sharp's Doom Bar; guest beers** Ⓖ
Refurbished and reopened in 2007 after being closed for some time. It's a friendly thatched pub, frequented by many local drinkers, it provides both good beer and fine food, from lunchtime snacks to elegant dining in the separate restaurant. In winter there is an open fire and in summer a pleasant garden, with views over farmland to the nearby windmill and open countryside. Winner of the Best Traditional Pub 2010 sponsored by BBC Radio Essex. ♨Q❀◐◑●⁻

Ballards Gore (Stambridge)

Shepherd & Dog

Gore Road, SS4 2DA (between Rochford and Paglesham)
⏲ 12-3 (4 Sat), 6-11; 12-4, 6-10.30 Sun ☎ (01702) 258279
Beer range varies Ⓗ
This excellent cottage-style pub was a former local CAMRA Pub of the Year, and was Rural Pub of the Year in 2008. The restaurant serves excellent meals and a wide range of food is also available in the bar. The four changing real ales generally come from micro-breweries and are often unusual for the area. Cider is stocked in the summer, when the pub is open all day at weekends. Traditional pub games including shut-the-box are available. Walkers, cyclists and coach groups are welcome.
❀◐◑♿🚌(60)♣P

Basildon

Selex Sports & Leisure Club

Gardiners Way, SS14 3AP (small turning off Gardiners Lane, easily missed) TQ721908
⏲ 11-11; 12-10.30 Sun ☎ (01268) 523773
Beer range varies Ⓗ
Members' social club in an industrial estate area, two miles from Basildon town centre. Three changing, low-priced guest ales are available from local and distant brewers. The club has a quiet lounge bar and a separate games room with pool table and satellite TV. There is patio seating overlooking a park with football pitches. Bar snacks are available at most times during the week. The club has a covered smoking area. Card-carrying CAMRA members are welcome. Q❀◐◑⊟♣P⁻

Belchamp St Paul

Half Moon

Cole Green, CO10 7DP TL792423
⏲ 12-3, 7-11 ☎ (01787) 277402
Greene King XX Mild, IPA; guest beers Ⓗ
Beautiful thatched rural pub dating from about 1685 opposite the village green, with a cosy interior and an attentive landlord and landlady. The second pump alternates between Adnams, Black Sheep and Taylor Landlord, while the third pump varies. There is good local trade, and an excellent choice of bar and restaurant food. In the past the pub provided one of the locations for the Lovejoy television series. No meals Monday or Sunday evening. There's a smoking area under the thatch with a heat lamp. ♨❀◐◑♣P⁻

Billericay

Blue Boar ✔

39 High Street, CM12 9BA
⏲ 9am-11.30pm ☎ (01277) 655552
Courage Best Bitter, Directors; Greene King Abbot; Marston's Pedigree; Shepherd Neame Spitfire; guest beers Ⓗ
Popular Wetherspoon venue, especially at weekends, with the usual suspects on handpumps, plus guests from micro-breweries, often local, such as the Brentwood Brewing Co. The car park at the rear is pay and display but arriving here by public transport is easy, with the station and bus stops close by. Breakfast is available until noon, followed by main meals and snacks until 10pm. There is no music, but there are fruit machines and muted TVs, and an outside area at the rear for drinking and smoking. Q❀◐◑♿⇌🚌(100)●⁻

Coach & Horses

36 Chapel Street, CM12 9LU
⏲ 10-11; 12-10.30 Sun ☎ (01277) 622873
Adnams Bitter; Greene King Abbot; Mighty Oak IPA; guest beers Ⓗ
A popular one-bar pub, situated off the High Street, with a cosy welcoming ambience. Good quality

food is served Monday to Saturday, daytime and evening, from an extensive menu featuring home-made pies and food made with locally-sourced ingredients. The bar and food service is quick, efficient and friendly, enhancing the feel-good factor. The walls are adorned with prints and decorative plates, and there is a fine collection of ceramic and gleaming copper jugs.
Q❀◑⇌🚌(100)P

Black Notley

Vine Inn

105 Witham Road, CM77 8LQ TL767208
⏲ 12-2.30, 6.30-11; 12-4, 7-11 Sun ☎ (01376) 324269
Adnams Bitter; guest beers Ⓗ
Sixteenth-century open plan free house with a central bar, a drinking/lounge area to the left, a restaurant area to the right and log-burning stoves at both ends. An unusual feature is the six-person mezzanine above the lounge, accessible via a steep staircase. The two guest beers are usually of East-Anglian origin, one is often from Mighty Oak. Cressing railway station is a 15-minute walk away down country lanes. ⌂Q❀◑🚌(21)P🚬

Blackmore

Leather Bottle

Horsefayre Green, CM4 0RL
⏲ 11-11 (midnight Fri & Sat); 12-11 Sun ☎ (01277) 821891
🌐 theleatherbottle.net
Adnams Bitter, Broadside Ⓗ**; guest beers** Ⓗ/Ⓖ
Large village pub with a smallish flagstone-floored bar area. Most of the pub is taken up by a good quality restaurant. Two guest beers are generally available on handpump, with maybe a third on gravity at weekends in the summer; a beer of around 5% ABV or higher is usually on offer. Westons Old Rosie cider may be available in the summer. An annexe to the bar has a pool table, dartboard and silent fruit machine.
⌂❀◑🀫🚌(32)♣P

Braintree

Picture Palace ✔

Fairfield Road, CM7 3HA
⏲ 9-11 (midnight Fri-Sat) ☎ (01376) 550255
Greene King Ruddles Best Bitter, Abbot; guest beers Ⓗ
This spacious former cinema retains a gently-sloping floor down to the curved bar where the stage once stood. Above it is allegedly the largest screen in Essex, on which major sporting events are shown. The balcony remains, as do two large decor panels whose design is replicated in the carpet. Three guest beers include a local brew, and Westons cider is always available. Free Wi-Fi is among all the usual facilities of a Lloyds No 1 bar.
◑⇌🚌🍎

Brentwood

Rising Sun

144 Ongar Road, CM15 9DJ (on A128, at Western Rd jct)
⏲ 3 (12 Sat)-11.30 (midnight Fri & Sat); 12-10.30 Sun
☎ (01277) 213749
Brentwood Maple Mild; Fuller's London Pride; Taylor Landlord; Woodforde's Wherry; guest beers Ⓗ
Comfortable and friendly local with a good selection of real ales, in an area where beer choice can be fairly limited. This is very much a community pub, with a charity quiz on Monday evening, cribbage on Sunday evening and frequent darts matches. Framed prints of the local area decorate the walls. Outside is a covered, heated smokers' area, plus a shellfish stall at weekends.
⌂Q❀🀫🚌♣P🚬

Broads Green

Walnut Tree ✔

CM3 1DT (¾ mile S of Great Waltham village) TL694125
⏲ 12-midnight ☎ (01245) 360222
Greene King IPA, Morland Original Bitter, Ruddles Best Bitter; guest beer Ⓖ
Handsome Victorian brick-built pub overlooking a large green. The front door opens directly into a small snug favoured by locals for conversation. To the left is the wood-panelled public bar, little changed since it was built; to the right is the more modern lounge. Outside is a garden and seating in front of the pub. There is no food – the landlord prefers to concentrate on his beers and maintaining a traditional atmosphere. An outside gents' is still in use. ⌂Q❀🀫🚌(33,52)♣P

Burnham-on-Crouch

Queen's Head

26 Providence, CM0 8JU (in narrow lane opp clock tower)
⏲ 12 (5 Mon)-11 ☎ (01621) 784825
🌐 queensheadburnham.com
Mighty Oak IPA, Maldon Gold; guest beers Ⓗ
Busy local favourite tucked away in a side street of this quaint riverside town. Tastefully decorated, this single bar reflects its Victorian roots. It is popular with the local rugby team and proud to support the local RNLI. A varying range of guest beers features milds and stouts; real ciders are from Westons. Folk night is the last Sunday of the month, shanty singing the first Tuesday. A beer festival is held on the August bank holiday in the enclosed courtyard. Home-baked traditional Essex Huffers and the landlord's curried goat are a must.
⌂❀◐⇌🚌(31X)♣🍎🚬🍺

Canewdon

Chequers

High Street, SS4 3QA
⏲ 12-3, 7-11; 12-11.30 Sat; 12-10.30 Sun ☎ (01702) 258251
Fuller's London Pride; Greene King Abbot; Mighty Oak Maldon Gold; Nethergate IPA; guest beers Ⓗ
Spacious, comfortable and welcoming 17th-century village inn comprising several rooms and an outdoor paved drinking area. A CAMRA local award winner in 2010, it offers up to six beers including LocAles, and popular beer festivals are held twice a year. Good value home-made food is served lunchtimes and Friday and Saturday evenings. Traditional pub games include shut-the-box and shove-ha'penny. Regular quizzes and charity events reflect the community focus of this friendly pub. The number 60 bus from Southend/Rochford runs daytimes only (not Sun). Q❀◑🚌(60)♣P

Castle Hedingham

Bell 🏆

10 St James Street, CO9 3EJ (off A1017 signed Castle Hedingham)

⊙ 11.45-3, 6-11; 11.45-12.30am Fri; 12-11.30 Sat; 12-11 Sun
☎ (01787) 460350 ⊕ hedinghambell.co.uk
Adnams Bitter; Mighty Oak IPA, Maldon Gold; guest beers 🄶
A 15th-century coaching inn owned by Gray and Sons that is well worth a visit. There are small rooms for drinking and dining alongside the two main bars. Beers come direct from the cask. Summer and winter beer festivals are held. Live jazz plays on the last Sunday of every month; folk and pop on Friday evening, with a quiz on Sunday night. Local Delvin End Storm cider is usually available and often Mighty Oak Oscar Wilde at weekends. Local CAMRA Pub of the Year 2010. ♔Q☕❀◐◑⊞♿🚌♣●P⚞

Chelmsford

Endeavour

351 Springfield Road, CM2 6AW (on B1137)
⊙ 11 (12 Sun)-11 ☎ (01245) 257717
Greene King IPA, Abbot; Mighty Oak IPA, Maldon Gold; guest beer 🄷
A 15-minute walk from the town centre, this friendly pub has three rooms, one used for early evening dining on Friday (fish night) and Saturday (steak night) – there are no evening meals on other days. The guest beer comes from the wide-ranging Gray's list and Westons Bounds cider is stocked. Regular charity events are held, including a meat raffle on Sunday. Several bus routes pass by. ♔◐◑🚌♣●⚞

Ivory Peg ✔

3-7 New London Road, CM2 0SW
⊙ 7am-midnight (1am Fri & Sat) ☎ (01245) 253130
Greene King Ruddles Best Bitter, Abbot 🄷
Excavations prior to the building of this Wetherspoon pub on the site of an old department store revealed an ivory tuning peg from a medieval musical instrument, hence the name. The four to five guest ales often come from Brentwood and Nethergate, and there are occasional presentations by local brewers. Westons Marcle Hill cider is sold. Open from 7am-9am for breakfast and coffee only. Free Wi-Fi access. ◐◑♿⇌🚌●

Orange Tree

6 Lower Anchor Street, CM2 0AS
⊙ 12-11 (11.30 Fri & Sat) ☎ (01245) 262664 ⊕ the-ot.com
Mighty Oak Oscar Wilde, Maldon Gold; Sharp's Doom Bar 🄷**; guest beers** 🄷/🄶
The Orange Tree has established its place as one of the top real ale pubs in Chelmsford. There are usually six or seven beers on (often including a stout or porter), with two or three on gravity from casks behind the bar. The cider is from the Westons range. There is a charity quiz on Tuesday evening and Sunday lunch is very popular. Rock/blues bands play one Saturday a month.
Q❀◐⊞♿🚌♣●P⚞

Original Plough ✔

28 Duke Street, CM1 1HY
⊙ 11-11 (midnight Fri & Sat); 12-10.30 Sun
☎ (01245) 250145
Beer range varies 🄷
Busy pub opposite the bus station and next to Chelmsford railway station, split into three areas – a quieter comfortable area to the left, a wooden-floored area to the centre and a flat stone-laid area with larger tables. Rugby takes preference over football on the TV, which can dominate on match days. Six to eight beers are on offer, mainly from regionals and larger micros, with mild sometimes available, and other dark beers occasionally. There is a heated, partly-covered outdoor patio area.
❀◐◑⇌🚌P⚞

Queen's Head

30 Lower Anchor Street, CM2 0AS
⊙ 12-11 (11.30 Fri & Sat) ☎ (01245) 265181
⊕ queensheadchelmsford.co.uk
Crouch Vale Essex Boys Bitter, Brewer's Gold, Crouch Best, Amarillo; guest beers 🄷
Crouch Vale's only pub, the Queen's Head sells four of its beers, occasionally supplemented or replaced by a beer from its seasonal list. The four guest ales from far and wide always vary, and often include a stout or porter. The cider, not always available in the winter, is from the Westons range. This popular local can be busy when there is a cricket match nearby, or when clubs and societies, such as the Essex Beard Club, meet. ♔Q❀◐♿🚌♣●P

White Horse

25 Townfield Street, CM1 1QJ (opp multi-storey car park N of railway station)
⊙ 12-11 (midnight Fri & Sat); 12-10.30 Sun
☎ (01245) 269556
Beer range varies 🄷
A welcome return to the Guide for the White Horse, which is now under a new landlord. This games-oriented pub has one long narrow bar with a bar billiards table at one end, darts at the other, and several TV screens showing sport. The beer range generally includes one or two beers from Adnams, while Otter Bitter and Brains Dark are often also available. Lunches are served Monday to Friday.
◐⇌♣

Woolpack 🏆 ✔

23 Mildmay Road, CM2 0DN (S of main road into town)
⊙ 12-11 (midnight Fri & Sat) ☎ (01245) 259295
⊕ thewoolpackchelmsford.com
Greene King H&H Bitter, St Edmunds 🄷**, Abbot** 🄶**; guest beers** 🄷
Local CAMRA Pub of the Year 2010, the Woolpack has free-of-tie beers from all over the country on one pump, as well as seven Greene King guest ales. There are darts and pool in a small public bar, while the large main lounge leads to an annexe with a large-screen TV. There is a Tuesday quiz, monthly folk music, and beer festivals at Easter and in September. An ever-changing range of speciality sausages complements the food menu, which is available Monday to Friday and Sunday lunchtime.
❀◐◑⊞🚌♣●P⚞

Chrishall

Red Cow

11 High Street, SG8 8RN (2 miles N of B1039) TL445394
⊙ 12-3 (not Mon), 6-11; 12-10.30 Sun ☎ (01763) 838792
⊕ theredcow.com
Adnams Bitter; guest beers 🄷
Thatched 14th-century pub close to an old barn in a small village near the Cambridge and Hertfordshire borders. Guest beers are usually from East Anglia. The owners welcome visitors and many local groups including the cricket club (who run regular quizzes), the village book group, stall holders from the farmers' market and the WI. Special occasions can be celebrated with meals from the extensive menu, either in the tiled bar or in the restaurant separated by original open timbering. ♔❀◐◑P

Clacton-on-Sea

Moon & Starfish

1 Marine Parade East, CO15 1PU
9am-11 (midnight Thu-Sat) ☎ (01255) 222998
Courage Directors; Greene King Ruddles Best Bitter, Abbot; guest beers H
This spacious Wetherspoon pub occupies half the ground floor of the Royal Hotel and is directly opposite Clacton's well-known Pier. It has recently had a major internal facelift. The outside area in front of the pub offers excellent views of the Clacton Air Show in August. In common with other Wetherspoon outlets it holds two beer festivals each year.

Old Lifeboat House

39 Marine Parade East, CO15 6AD
11-11 (1am Fri & Sat); 12-10.30 Sun ☎ (01255) 476799
oldlifeboathouseclacton.co.uk
Greene King Old Speckled Hen; Shepherd Neame Spitfire; Taylor Landlord H
A former lifeboat station that changed ownership in early 2009 and is now owned by a local coastguard and his family. It is situated a short walk from the beach and pier. There is a large single bar with a darts area – the pub hosts six darts teams. A small adjoining room will be of interest to historians as it houses photographs of the building in its previous guise, as well as of the lifeboat crews of yesteryear. P

Coggeshall

Queens Head

Old Road, CO6 1RS (on A120, ½ mile E of Coggeshall)
12-11 (midnight Fri & Sat) ☎ (01376) 564999
Red Fox Fox and Hind Bitter, seasonal beers H
Rescued in 2008 with a major investment when derelict after many years closure, the Queens Head has a modern, light and airy restaurant and large bar. It retains the feeling of a real pub, with a woodburner in the bar. The restaurant offers an excellent menu Tuesday to Sunday, with a carvery daily from 12-2pm and 7-9pm (12-7pm Sun), and bar meals are also available. Offering a range of beers from the nearby Red Fox Brewery, it is well worth a visit. Q(70)P

Colchester

Bricklayers

27 Bergholt Road, CO4 5AA (jct A134/B1508 nr main station N of town)
11-3, 5.30-11; 11-midnight Fri; 11-11 Sat; 12-3, 7-11 (not winter eve) Sun ☎ (01206) 852008
Adnams Bitter, Explorer, Broadside, seasonal beers; Nethergate Suffolk County Best Bitter; guest beers H
Very close to the main station, north of the town and on a number of major bus routes, the 'Brick' is a lively, friendly pub used by locals and commuters. Run by a CAMRA award-winning family, it has between seven and nine ales, and real cider is always available. The food is very good – the Sunday roast is recommended. There is a busy public bar with darts and pool, and a lounge bar with a light, airy conservatory.
(65)P

British Grenadier

67 Military Road, CO1 2AP (½ mile SW of Colchester Town station)
12-2.30 (not Wed), 5-11.30; 11-midnight Sat; 12-3, 7-11.30 Sun ☎ (01206) 500933
Adnams Bitter, Broadside, seasonal beers; guest beers H
A warm welcome is guaranteed at this award-winning traditional local, saved from closure by the persistence of the landlord and landlady in 2009. The pub makes the most of Adnams' generous guest beer policy, as can be seen from the numerous pump clips around the walls, and the tempting 'beers to come' board. Darts is popular in the main bar, with pool played in a separate room. The pub hosts a quiz on Sunday. CAMRA Branch Pub of the Year 2008. (66)

Fat Cat

65 Butt Road, CO3 3BZ (on B1026, near police station)
12-11 (midnight Fri); 11-midnight Sat ☎ (01206) 577990
Crouch Vale Brewers Gold; Fat Cat Bitter, Honey Cat; Nethergate Mouse Ale; Woodforde's Wherry H**; guest beers** G
Offering up to 16 real ales, including the house beer Mouse Ale, this friendly free house is LocAle accredited and also features breweries from further afield. There is a full programme of events, including live music on Saturday night, quiz night on Sunday, and beer festivals on the May Day and August bank holiday weekends. The social side includes brewery trips and the golf society. Food is limited to lunchtimes, with a roast on Sunday. Takeaways can be ordered any night of the week.

Fox & Fiddler

1 St John's Street, CO2 7AA
12-11 (midnight Fri & Sat); 12-10.30 Sun
☎ (01206) 560520
Mighty Oak Oscar Wilde, English Oak; Young's Bitter; guest beers H
Friendly town-centre LocAle-accredited pub dating from 1420, with a deceptively small frontage disguising a long single bar and three separate heavily-timbered drinking and dining areas. Excellent home-cooked food using local produce is served Wednesday (steak night) to Sunday lunchtime; Sunday roasts offer particularly good value. With a relaxing atmosphere and comfortable seating, you can be sure the Mighty Oak beers, with guests from local breweries, will hit the spot. Weekend evenings can be lively, with occasional music on Saturday. (Town)P

Hole in the Wall

Balkerne Passage, CO1 1PT (opp Mercury Theatre)
12-11 (midnight Fri & Sat); 12-10.30 Sun
☎ (01206) 579897
Banks's Mild; Caledonian Deuchars IPA; St Austell Tribute; guest beers H
This multi-roomed split-level pub sits on top of Colchester's famous Roman wall like a Trappist monastery. Up to eight real ales are served on a changing basis, and the place is a rare local outlet for Lindisfarne Mead. Good-value food is served daily. The venue is handy for the Mercury Theatre, with ample parking in St Mary's multi-storey car park just over the footbridge on Balkerne Hill. There is occasional live music, and two beer festivals are held each year. (Town)

New Town Tavern

3-5 Kendall Road, CO1 2BN
4-11 (midnight Fri); 12-midnight Sat; 12-11 Sun
☎ (01206) 869490

Adnams Bitter; Wolf Golden Jackal; guest beers Ⓗ
A nice makeover for a traditional back-street local. The landlord has done a good job here, with a pub that went from being the Blue Boar, then the Pink Panther, and now a real ale treat in the heart of Colchester. The pub is quite large, with an outside drinking and smoking area. Five handpumps are featured, with Adnams Bitter plus guests, including Wolf beer. Darts and a pool table are available.
❀≋(Town)⊟♣⚐

Odd One Out 🏆

28 Mersea Road, CO2 7ET (on B1025)
⏲ 4.30 (12 Fri; 11 Sat)-11; 12-10.30 Sun ☎ (01206) 513958
Beer range varies Ⓗ
Twenty-five years ago John opened this pub and since then it has been ever-present in the Guide. In 2010 it was local CAMRA Pub of the Year, and in 2009 a National Cider Pub of the Year finalist. Five guest ales, usually including a dark beer, at least three ciders and a perry, are served from casks on the bar, and there are over 50 Scottish and Irish whiskies. With real fires and a no mobile phone policy, it is the ideal pub to just relax and chat in.
♔Q❀≋(Town)⊟(8A,67)●⚐

Colne Engaine

Five Bells

Mill Lane, CO6 2HY (2 miles E of Halstead) TL851303
⏲ 12-3, 6-midnight; 12-1am Fri-Sun ☎ (01787) 224166
🌐 fivebells.net
Beer range varies Ⓗ
A 16th-century free house with original beams set in a peaceful village where the enthusiastic landlord has transformed the pub. Selling more than 400 different ales each year, local breweries and micros are well represented. There are several small dining and drinking areas plus a separate restaurant, all serving quality locally-sourced food. The pub has pool and football teams, live music on Friday night, jazz on Sunday afternoon, plus a November beer festival. The smoking area is covered and heated. ♔Q♨❀◐⊟♿♣P⚐

Coxtie Green

White Horse

173 Coxtie Green Road, CM14 5PX (1 mile W of A128, at jct with Mores Lane) TQ564959
⏲ 11.30-11 (midnight Fri & Sat); 12-11 Sun
☎ (01277) 372410
Adnams Bitter; Fuller's London Pride; guest beers Ⓗ
Excellent country free house with a relaxed, friendly atmosphere. There is a comfy saloon bar, and a public bar with TV and dartboard. Six beers are usually on handpump, including a local beer from Brentwood Brewery. The Adnams alternates with Greene King IPA. The pub has a large garden at the rear which includes a children's play area and accommodates a beer festival each July, plus occasional small festivals. There is a limited bus service. ♔❀◑⊟♿⊟♣●P

Dedham

Sun Inn

High Street, CO7 6DF (on B1029, opp church)
⏲ 12-11 (6 Sun) ☎ (01206) 323351
🌐 thesuninndedham.com
Adnams Broadside; Crouch Vale Brewers Gold; guest beers Ⓗ
This 15th-century inn comprises a bar area, side lounge, restaurant and garden. The lounge, open to non-residents, has a range of comfortable furniture, and board games are available. Guest ales change frequently, featuring micros and local brewers. The restaurant serves an award-winning range of food and fine wines, with regular culinary lectures and tasting sessions (booking advised). One of the four well-appointed guest bedrooms has a four-poster bed for that romantic weekend.
♔Q❀⛿◐⊟♣P⚐

Duton Hill

Three Horseshoes

CM6 2DX (½ mile W of B184 Dunmow-Thaxted road) TL606268
⏲ 12-2.30 (not Mon-Wed; 3 Sat), 6-11; 12-3, 7-10.30 Sun
☎ (01371) 870681
Mighty Oak IPA; guest beers Ⓗ
Cosy village local with a garden, wildife pond and terrace overlooking the Chelmer Valley and farmland. The landlord hosts a weekend of open-air theatre in July. A millennium beacon in the garden, breweriana, and a remarkable collection of Butlins memorabilia are features. Two guest beers are offered. A beer festival is held on the late spring bank holiday in the Duton Hill Den. Look for the pub sign depicting a famous painting, The Blacksmith, by former local resident Sir George Clausen. ♔❀♿⊟(313)♣P

Elmdon

Elmdon Dial

Heydon Lane, CB11 4NH TL461397
⏲ closed Mon; 12-3, 6-11; 12-4, 6-10.30 Sun
☎ (01763) 837386 🌐 theelmdondial.co.uk
Adnams Bitter; Mighty Oak Oscar Wilde; Taylor Landlord; guest beers Ⓗ
CAMRA local Pub of the Year 2008, this friendly pub dating from 1450 is owned by a real ale enthusiast. Previously called the Kings Head, the pub was closed in 1998. After a seven-year planning battle and support from villagers and CAMRA, it was reopened with a new name and pub sign to commemorate a window sundial in the village church. The building was extended in 2006 to provide a modern kitchen and restaurant in addition to a tasteful bar. An a la carte menu is cooked fresh from local ingredients where possible and changes with the seasons. ♔Q❀◐♿⊟♣P⚐

Epping

Forest Gate

111 Bell Common, CM16 4DZ (opp Bell Hotel) TL450011
⏲ 10-2.30, 5-11; 12-3, 7-10.30 Sun ☎ (01992) 572312
Adnams Bitter, Broadside; Nethergate IPA Ⓗ**; guest beers** Ⓗ/Ⓖ
This 17th-century pub is a genuine free house and specialises in traditional ales. On the edge of Epping Forest and a short walk from Epping, it is popular with locals and hikers. It is free from TV and fruit machines. Food is usually available – the long-standing house speciality is turkey broth. A large lawn at the front is used for summer drinking – just look out for the geese! ♔Q❀⛿◐●P

Finchingfield

Red Lion

6 Church Hill, CM7 4NN (on B1053, opp church)
✪ 12-11 (midnight Fri & Sat) ☎ (01371) 810400
🌐 theredlionfinchingfield.com
Greene King IPA, Old Speckled Hen; guest beers Ⓗ
Friendly local with a warm atmosphere in a famously picturesque village, just up the hill from the pond. The 15th-century coaching inn has a heavily beamed interior with an open fire and separate restaurant. There is also a garden for better weather. Popular with cyclists, walkers and locals, families are welcome. Good value menus of home-cooked food along with an extensive wine selection are available at all times except Sunday evening. High-quality accommodation is offered.
♔Q❀⇌◐◑🚌P⁄

Fuller Street

Square & Compasses

Fairstead, CM3 2BB (1.5 miles E off the A131 at Gt Leighs, St Anne's Castle) TL748161
✪ 11.30-3, 5.30-11.30; 12-midnight Sat; 12-11 Sun
☎ (01245) 361477 🌐 thesquareandcompasses.co.uk
Nethergate Stoker's Ale; guest beers Ⓖ
Seventeenth-century three-roomed free house with a first-floor meeting/private dining room. Known locally as The Stokehole, it reopened in 2007 having been closed for two years. There are exposed beams throughout and two inglenook fireplaces, one housing a woodburner. Old local woodworking tools adorn the public bar. Up to four beers and Westons cider and perry are sold. Food is prepared from locally-sourced produce, including game from the surrounding estates (not available Sun eve or Mon). It hosts an August beer festival.
♔❀◐◑⊟●P

Fyfield

Queen's Head

Queen Street, CM5 0RY (off B184)
✪ 11-3.30, 6-11; 11-11 Sat; 12-10.30 Sun ☎ (01277) 899231
🌐 thequeensheadfyfield.co.uk
Adnams Bitter, Broadside; Crouch Vale Brewers Gold; guest beers Ⓗ
Although geared for dining, customers popping in just for a beer are made welcome. A lovely garden leading to the River Roding is very popular during summer months. Children and dogs are welcome in the garden, but not in the pub. Up to three guest beers from independent breweries are normally on offer. Note that this pub usually closes between Christmas and New Year. Q❀◐◑●P

Gestingthorpe

Pheasant

Church Street, CO9 3AU (off B1058 Castle Hedingham-Sudbury road) TL813375
✪ 12-3, 6-11 (not Sun & Mon eve) ☎ (01787) 461196
🌐 thepheasant.net
Beer range varies Ⓗ
Set in a tiny village, this traditional pub enjoys good local trade and a reputation for fine food, ale and cider. Recently refurbished, it has three separate rooms with two bars, and a large garden. Occasional quiz nights and music evenings make this pub an ideal venue for summer evenings and long winter nights. The house beer, Pleasant Pheasant, is brewed by Mauldons. Guest beers from local breweries frequently feature.
♔Q❀◐◑⊟●P⁄

Goldhanger

Chequers ✔

The Square, CM9 8AS (500m from B1026) TL904088
✪ 11-11; 12-10.30 Sun ☎ (01621) 788203
🌐 thechequersgoldhanger.co.uk
Caledonian Deuchars IPA; Marston's seasonal beers; St Austell Tribute; guest beers Ⓗ
Regular finalist and frequent winner of CAMRA local Pub of the Year awards, the Chequers guarantees a warm welcome and a great atmosphere. The inn dates from the 15th century and remains largely untouched, with two main bars and several smaller rooms, including a games room with bar billiards. Exceptional food is served, ranging from bar snacks to a full restaurant menu. There is a wide range of guest ales, with beer festivals in March and September. Frequent community events are held – see website for details. ♔Q❀◐◑⊟⛺🚌(95)♣P⁄

Grays

Theobald Arms

141 Argent Street, RM17 6HR (5 mins from Grays rail and bus stations down Kings Walk)
✪ 11-11 (midnight Fri & Sat); 12-11 Sun ☎ (01375) 372253
🌐 theobaldarms.com
Beer range varies Ⓗ
Genuine, traditional pub with a public bar that has an unusual hexagonal pool table. The changing selection of four guest beers features local independent breweries, and a range of British bottled beers is also stocked. Regular St George's weekend and summer beer festivals are held in the old stables and on the rear enclosed patio. Lunchtime meals are served 12-2pm Monday to Friday. Darts and cards are played. A former local CAMRA Branch Pub of the Year. ❀◐⊟♿⇌♣P⁄

White Hart ✔

Kings Walk, Argent Street, RM17 6HR (10 mins walk from Grays rail and bus stations)
✪ 12-11.30 (midnight Fri & Sat); 12-11 Sun
☎ (01375) 373319 🌐 whitehartgrays.co.uk
Crouch Vale Brewers Gold; Sharp's White Hart; guest beers Ⓗ
This traditional local just outside the town centre has been rejuvenated since 2006. Two regular ales, including the house beer White Hart, are supplemented by three guest beers and many bottled Belgian beers. There is a meeting/function room available and a beer garden. Pool is played and sport screened on TV. Live blues bands play on alternate Thursdays, and a beer festival is held in February. Local CAMRA Pub of the Year 2007, 2008 and 2009. ♔❀⇌◐⊟⇌🚌♣P⁄

Great Bromley

Cross Inn

Ardleigh Road, CO7 7TL (on B1029 between Great Bromley and Ardleigh)
✪ 12-2 (Fri & Sat only), 6.30-11; 12-3, 7-10.30 Sun
☎ (01206) 230282 🌐 bromleycrossinn.co.uk
Sticklegs Malt Shovel Mild, Old Forge Bitter; Wadworth Henry's Original IPA; Woodforde's Wherry; guest beers Ⓖ

Quiet, cosy free house where a warm welcome is assured, with a single bar with woodburner, fresh flowers and comfortable seating. The landlord has run previous pubs listed in the Guide. An annual beer festival is held in May. Very much a community pub, it hosts regular quiz evenings, folk music and charity events. Booking is advisable for meals and to check food availability. Outside is a large car park and enclosed beer garden featuring a heated smoking shelter. ⛬Q❀◐♣P⍀

Great Chesterford

Crown & Thistle

High Street, CB10 1PL (near B1383, close to M11/A11 jct)
✪ 12-3, 6-midnight; 12-3, 7-11 (not winter eve) Sun
☎ (01799) 530278
Adnams Bitter; Fuller's London Pride; guest beers Ⓗ
Popular inn in an interesting village, frequented by locals, including the cricket team. The pub, built in 1528 and called The Chequers, was renamed and extended in 1603 to serve as a coaching inn. According to legend, James I stopped here on his way to London for his coronation. The magnificent inglenook fireplace in the bar is the earliest example of its type in Essex. A patio has seating for outdoor drinking and eating, with a heated smoking area. ⛬Q❀◐Å⇌🚌P⍀

Great Easton

Swan

The Endway, CM6 2HG (3 miles N of Dunmow, off B184) TL606255
✪ 12-3, 6-11; 12-3, 7-10.30 (not winter eve) Sun
☎ (01371) 870359 🌐 swangreateaston.co.uk
Adnams Bitter; guest beers Ⓗ
A warm welcome is assured at this 15th-century free house in an attractive village. A log-burning stove, exposed beams and comfortable sofas feature in the lounge, while pool and darts are played in the public bar. Featuring in CAMRA's Good Pub Food Guide, all meals are prepared to order from fresh local produce, including the chips. The chef looks after the beers, chosen to complement the food. Accommodation is now available in four superb double rooms.
⛬Q❀🛏◐⊟♣P

Halstead

Dog Inn

37 Hedingham Road, CO9 2DB (on A1124)
✪ 4 (11 Sat)-11; 12-10.30 Sun ☎ (01787) 477774
🌐 innpubs.co.uk/thedoginn
Adnams Bitter, Broadside; guest beers Ⓗ
A quiet pub within easy walking distance of the town centre, which is well served by buses. In summer this hostelry provides a welcome stop for walkers, families and pets, where a pleasant time can be spent in the garden with its petanque court. It overlooks the Colne Valley, and en-suite accommodation is available. The pub hosts an annual beer festival (phone for details).
⛬Q🛝❀🛏⊟🚌♣●P⍀

Harlow

William Aylmer ✔

Aylmer House, Kitson Way, CM20 1DG
✪ 9am-midnight (1am Fri & Sat) ☎ (01279) 620630
Greene King Ruddles Best Bitter, Abbot; guest beers Ⓗ
Named after a local medical pioneer, this is a fairly typical Wetherspoon pub, located in the town centre. As well as the standard beers, at least three varied guest beers are available. During the week the hostelry attracts a varied clientele and, due to its location, gets very busy on weekend evenings. ◐♿⇌(Town)🚌●

Harwich

Hanover Inn

65 Church Street, CO12 3DR
✪ 3-midnight (1am Fri); 11-5, 7-11 Sat; 12-5, 7-11 Sun
☎ (01255) 502927 🌐 hanover-inn-harwich.co.uk
Thwaites Nutty Black, Original Ⓗ
A welcome return for this old favourite, situated next to the church. The pub comprises a public bar to the front and pool room to the rear; a small function room is also available upstairs. The regular beers are accompanied by Addlestones cider. With easy access from the rail and bus station, it is ideal for a short visit, or a great base for a stopover using the B&B upstairs. 🛏⊟⇌(Town)🚌♣●

New Bell Inn

Outpart Eastward, CO12 3EN
✪ 11-3, 7-11 (midnight Sat); 12-4, 7-11 (12-11 summer) Sun
☎ (01255) 503545
Greene King IPA; Mighty Oak Oscar Wilde; guest beers Ⓗ
Situated in the heart of Old Harwich, a short walk from the rail and bus stations, this pub is a favourite with locals and visitors alike. As well as the regular beers, a pair of handpumps feature ever-changing guest beers from near and far, with East Anglian breweries getting a good showing. Home-cooked food is available at lunchtime, including the famous soups and huffers. Three bar areas are complemented by a walled garden for warmer days. Q❀◐⊟⇌(Town)🚌P

Hatfield Broad Oak

Cock Inn

High Street, CM22 7HF TL546164
✪ 12-11 (12.30am Fri & Sat); 12-10.30 Sun
☎ (01279) 718306
Adnams Bitter; Woodforde's Wherry; Young's Bitter; guest beers Ⓗ
Village local in a Grade II-listed building, dating from the 16th century. In the main bar the hardwood floor and elegant but simple wooden tables and chairs emphasise the traditional pub atmosphere. Sensibly priced meals using local produce are served until 9pm daily (4pm Sun). A second bar has a dartboard and satellite sport, while a third room is normally quiet. In summer use the pavement-side seating to watch village life drift by. ⛬🛝◐🚌(5,347)♣P

Hawkwell

White Hart

274 Main Road, SS5 4NS
✪ 11-11; 12-10.30 Sun ☎ (01702) 203438
Beer range varies Ⓗ
A well-established friendly local, dating from the 18th century, facing the village green. The pub is community-oriented and supportive of local charities through its quiz nights and music events.

Two changing guest ales are served. Lunchtime food is available all week, including roasts on Sunday, with evening meals served Monday-Thursday. Sporting events are shown in a new function room. There is a large rear garden with seating and a patio area, plus picnic tables at the front. Q❀◑⇌(Hockley)⊟P

Hazeleigh

Royal Oak

Fambridge Road, CM9 6PE

✪ 12-11 ☎ (01621) 853249 🌐 royaloakmaldon.com

Adnams Bitter; Greene King IPA; guest beer Ⓗ

Early 19th-century road house one mile south of Maldon. Three handpumps offer two permanent ales and a guest beer chosen from the Gray's list. Several darts teams use this homely two-bar pub as their base. Themed and charity nights feature on a regular basis and a book club is hosted on the first Monday of the month. A daily menu of locally-sourced, home-cooked food is served until 7pm. Hardy souls may camp by prior arrangement but facilities are limited. ⌂❀◑⊟♿♣P⚟

Hempstead

Bluebell Inn

High Street, CB10 2PD (on B1054, between Saffron Walden and Haverhill)

✪ 12-3, 6-11; 12-11 Fri & Sat (winter hours vary); 12-10.30 Sun ☎ (01799) 599199

Adnams Bitter, Broadside; Woodforde's Wherry; guest beers Ⓗ

Late 16th-century village pub with 18th-century additions, reputed to be the birthplace of Dick Turpin; the bar displays posters about his life. Six beers are usually available. The restaurant serves excellent meals from an extensive menu and the large bar has a log fire. Ample seating is provided outside, plus a children's play area. A folk evening is hosted on a Tuesday. ⌂Q❀◑⊟♣P⚟

Heybridge

Maltsters Arms

Hall Road, CM9 4NJ (nr B1022)

✪ 12-midnight (1am Fri & Sat); 12-10.30 Sun

☎ (01621) 853880

Greene King IPA, Abbot; guest beers Ⓖ

Single-bar local, owned by Gray's, where a warm welcome is extended to all drinkers – and their dogs. The pub can be busy at lunchtimes with locals and ramblers. The pleasant atmosphere is enhanced by a collection of mirrors and some breweriana. Two guest beers are usually on offer, one from a local brewery. A selection of rolls is available. Occasional mini beer festivals are held. The rear patio overlooks the old course of the tidal river. Q❀⊟♣⚟

Horndon-on-the-Hill

Bell Inn

High Road, SS17 8LD (near B1007, almost opp the Woolmarket)

✪ 11-3, 5.30 (6 Sat)-11; 12-4, 7-10.30 Sun

☎ (01375) 642463 🌐 bell-inn.co.uk

Crouch Vale Brewers Gold Ⓗ**; Draught Bass** Ⓖ**; Greene King IPA; guest beers** Ⓗ

Busy 15th-century coaching inn, where the beamed bars feature wood panelling and carvings. Note the unusual hot cross bun collection – a bun is added every Good Friday. The hilltop village, much more peaceful since the bypass was completed, has a restored Woolmarket. Up to five guest ales are stocked, including beers from Essex breweries. The award-winning restaurant is open daily, lunchtimes and evenings, except bank holidays. Accommodation is in 16 bedrooms, including five honeymoon suites. ⌂Q❀⛌◑⊟⊟(11,374)P⚟

Lamarsh

Lamarsh Lion

Bures Road, CO8 5EP (1¼ miles NW of Bures) TL892355

✪ 12-11 (10.30 Sun) ☎ (01787) 227918

Greene King IPA; guest beers Ⓗ

This attractive 14th-century inn is situated in a quiet lane, with tables outside offering a wonderful view over the Stour Valley. Popular with locals and ramblers, the wealth of beams and roaring log fire in winter make this a genuinely welcoming free house. Four guest beers are normally on offer, including a dark beer and at least one on gravity, mainly from local micros. A full menu is available daily. Attached to the large single bar is a room with pool table and TV. ⌂Q❀◑♣●P⚟

Langenhoe

Langenhoe Lion

Mersea Road, Abberton, CO5 7LF

✪ 12-3, 5-11; 12-11 Sat & Sun ☎ (01206) 735263

Adnams Bitter; Mersea Island Skippers Bitter; Woodforde's Wherry; guest beers Ⓗ

The Lion is a friendly community pub with a restaurant, public bar, sun terrace and garden. As a free house it can sell the local Mersea Island ales. It is currently in the process of designing and building a cottage garden to supply fresh ingredients for the kitchen. Food is sourced locally, and new owner and chef Shaun, who has worked with Gary Rhodes and other renowned chefs, is showing his talent with a menu based on modern British and Mediterranean influences. ⌂Q❀◑⊟⊟(67)P⚟

Layer-de-la-Haye

Donkey & Buskins

Layer Road, CO2 0HU (on B1026 S of Colchester) TL974208

✪ 11.30-3, 6-11; 11.30-11.30 Sat; 12-11 Sun

☎ (01206) 734774

Adnams Bitter; Greene King IPA; guest beers Ⓗ

Friendly village local with a good reputation for fine beer. The two regular ales are supplemented by one or two guest beers, often from local micros. Good-quality home-cooked food is available daily, with a wide range of dishes. A large secluded garden is used for the July beer festival and for live bands. The Sunday quiz is very popular. Worth checking is the ancient Ind Coope price list on display in the front bar. ⌂Q⌂❀⛌◑♿⊟P⚟

Leigh-on-Sea

Crooked Billet ✔

51 High Street, SS9 2EP (½ mile E of Leigh railway station)

✪ 12-11 (midnight summer); 10-10.30 Sun

☎ (01702) 480289

Adnams Bitter; Caledonian Deuchars IPA; Fuller's London Pride; guest beers Ⓗ

This pub, in Old Leigh, dates from the 16th century. The two bars with their cosy nooks and snugs have bare floorboards, beamed ceilings and enjoy waterfront views from large bay windows. The walls are adorned with local fishing pictures. Up to three guest ales are available. Food is served daily until 10pm (9pm winter). A small garden to the side is complemented by a large waterside seating area which is shared with the local cockle shed. Popular in the summer. Q❀◑⇌⊢

Elms ✔

1060 London Road, SS9 3ND (on A13)

⌚ 9am-midnight (1am Fri & Sat) ☎ (01702) 474687

Greene King Ruddles Best, Abbot; Marston's Pedigree; guest beers 🄷

Old coaching inn converted by Wetherspoon into a large, open mock-Tudor pub decorated with old photos of the local area. Breakfast is available until noon, plus main meals and snacks until 10pm. Children are admitted until 9pm. Up to six changing guest ales and up to three Westons real ciders are served. There is no music but there are fruit machines and muted TVs. Outside is a paved, heated and covered area for smokers and a hedged front garden. ❀◑♿🚌♠P⊢

Little Bromley

Haywain 🏆

Bentley Road, CO11 2PL

⌚ closed Mon; 12-2.30, 6-10.30 Tue-Thu (6-10 Tue & Wed Oct-Feb); 12-2.30, 6-11 Fri & Sat; 12-5 Sun ☎ (01206) 390004

🌐 thehaywain.co.uk

Adnams Bitter; guest beers 🄷

Andy and Dawn, both CAMRA members, reopened this 18th-century pub, with its large function room, in 2007. Two years later it was awarded local CAMRA Pub of the Year. Dawn provides generous portions of home-made food, which is sourced locally whenever possible, while her father, Ernie, ensures the beers are in excellent condition. ♨❀◑♿🚌P⊢

Little Dunmow

Flitch of Bacon

The Street, CM6 3HT (850m S of B1256)

⌚ 12-3 (not Mon), 5.30 (6 Sat)-11; 12-10 Sun ☎ (01371) 820323

Fuller's London Pride; Greene King IPA; guest beers 🄷

A traditional country inn that is the focal point of this rural village. The sign depicts a side, or 'flitch' of bacon – the prize awarded to a happily married couple in an ancient contest still held every four years. Inside, there are exposed timbers, with an open fire in winter. Note the old signs advertising Bass and Worthington in bottles. A menu of locally-sourced food is available in the bar or the rear restaurant area (not Sun eve). ♨❀🛏◑🚌(16,133)

Little Thurrock

Traitor's Gate 🏆

40-42 Broadway, RM17 6EW (on A126, 1 mile E of Grays town centre)

⌚ 3 (1 Fri)-11; 12-11 Sat; 12-10.30 Sun ☎ (01375) 372628

Beer range varies 🄷

A variety of three guest beers is on offer, with forthcoming ales displayed on the blackboard above the bar, as well as two draught ciders and one draught perry. This is a friendly hostelry with a wide and varied clientele, mostly local, showing how a good pub attracts a good trade. Sport is shown most nights on large-screen TVs. The beer garden has won Thurrock in Bloom awards in recent years. Local CAMRA Branch Pub of the Year 2005 and 2010. ❀🚌(66)♣♠⊢

Little Totham

Swan

School Road, CM9 8LB (1 country mile SE of B1022) TL889117

⌚ 11-11; 12-10.30 Sun ☎ (01621) 892689

🌐 theswanpublichouse.co.uk

Crouch Vale Brewers Gold; Farmer's Ales Pucks Folly; Mighty Oak Oscar Wilde, Maldon Gold, Totham Parva; guest beers 🄶

Multi-award-winning pub, with the rare accolade of twice becoming National CAMRA Pub of the Year. It is the epitome of the traditional warm, welcoming village pub, with original beams and some exposed internal wattle and daub, roaring fires in winter and a walled garden for better weather. There is a wide range of guest ales and listed beers, including mild, plus cider and perry. Live music and morris dancing occasionally feature. The menu is varied, including basket meals and takeaways. ♨Q❀◑🀫♿⛺♣♠P⊢▯

Little Walden

Crown

High Street, CB10 1XA (on B1052)

⌚ 11.30-2.30 (3 Sat), 6-11; 12-10.30 Sun ☎ (01799) 522475

Adnams Broadside; Greene King IPA, Abbot; Woodforde's Wherry; guest beers 🄶

Charming 18th-century beamed pub in a quiet hamlet. A feature is a large walk-through fireplace. The pub is popular with diners, especially at weekends when booking is advisable. Evening meals are available Tuesday to Saturday. Racked cask stillage is used for dispensing an excellent range of beers. The pub is used for club meetings and hosts traditional jazz on Wednesday evenings. ♨Q❀◑🚌P

Littley Green

Compasses

CM3 1BU (turn off B1417 at former Ridley's Brewery, Hartford End) TL699172

⌚ 12-3, 5.30-midnight; 12-midnight Thu-Sun

☎ (01245) 362308 🌐 compasseslittleygreen.co.uk

Adnams Bitter; Woodforde's Wherry; guest beers 🄶

The former Ridley's Brewery tap is a picturesque country pub in a quiet hamlet. Beers are drawn direct from the cask in the half-cellar. The renowned huffers (giant baps), with a wide variety of fillings, are available lunchtimes and evenings. There are seats and tables outside and in the large gardens. There are no electronic games or piped music, but a folk evening is held monthly. Guest beers are from local breweries, and ciders and perries are available. ♨Q❀◑♣♠P

Loughton

Victoria Tavern ✔

165 Smarts Lane, IG10 4BP (off A121 at edge of forest)

⌚ 11-3, 5-11; 11-10.30 Sun ☎ (020) 8508 1779

Adnams Bitter; Greene King IPA; Taylor Landlord; guest beers 🄷

Traditional pub on the edge of Epping Forest with one large and one small interconnected dark wood-panelled bar. It is decorated with old photos of the West Ham United football team and the local area, bottles and a small display of barrel bushes. Generous portions of well-cooked pub fare are served daily. There is occasionally a real fire in the bar. The pub is popular with locals, enjoys a lively atmosphere, and has occasional quizzes and charity events. Q❀🛏◐♿⊖🚌(20,167)P⅃

Maldon

Blue Boar Hotel 🏆

Silver Street, CM9 4QE (opp All Saints church)
⌚11-11 ☎(01621) 855888 🌐 blueboarmaldon.co.uk
Adnams Bitter Ⓖ**; Farmer's Ales IPA** Ⓗ**, Drop of Nelson's Blood, Pucks Folly, Golden Boar, seasonal beers** Ⓖ
In the heart of the town, this is a 14th-century coaching inn. CAMRA Branch Pub of the Year for 2010, it is a friendly and popular place with young and old alike. Farmer's Ales are brewed on the premises, and the pub regularly features themed ales. There is a good-value bar menu with some old favourites, and it has a good-sized beer garden as well as a courtyard, accommodation and function room. Several local groups meet here. ♨Q❀🛏◐⊟🚌(31X)P⅃🥛

Queen Victoria

Spital Road, CM9 6EP
⌚11-midnight (1am Fri & Sat); 11.30-midnight Sun
☎(01621) 852923
Greene King IPA, Abbot; Mighty Oak Maldon Gold Ⓗ
Opened in 1845, this comfortable, welcoming Gray and Sons local offers well-kept beers, friendly service and excellent home-cooked food. The single bar provides separate areas for darts, dominoes, music, TV and quiet dining. The extensive food menu and ever-changing specials board provides good value for the heartiest appetite. Meals are served 12-9pm Monday-Saturday and 12-5pm Sunday. There is car park and beer garden to the side. Superb hanging flower baskets adorn the exterior. ❀◐⊟♿🚌(31X)♣P⅃

Queen's Head

The Hythe, CM9 5HN
⌚10-11 (midnight Fri & Sat); 10.30-10.30 Sun
☎(01621) 854112 🌐 thequeensheadmaldon.co.uk
Adnams Broadside; Farmer's Ales Pucks Folly; Greene King Abbot; Sharp's Doom Bar; Taylor Landlord; guest beers Ⓗ
This welcoming old pub is superbly situated on the River Blackwater adjacent to the town quay, with old Thames barges moored alongside. There is a spacious seating area overlooking the river. The small local front bar has a log fire in winter. The extensive food menu features fish and seafood, served in the restaurant or the bars. Children are allowed in the restaurant and until 6pm in the bar. Good disabled access and WC facilities. ♨Q❀◐⊟♿⅃

Manningtree

White Hart

High Street, CO11 1AG (directly opp main Post Office)
⌚11-11; 12-10.30 Sun ☎(01206) 392768
🌐 whitehartmanningtree.co.uk
Adnams Bitter; Greene King IPA; guest beers Ⓗ
A historic building in a medieval high street in the smallest town in England. Fine ceiling beams plus two interesting carved facial features in the uprights are on display in the tastefully modernised interior. The regular beers are complemented by an occasional guest from a local brewery. This is a popular pub with a loyal clientele. 🛏◐♿🚌⅃

Margaretting Tye

White Hart Inn

Swan Lane, CM4 9JX TL684011
⌚11.30-3, 6-midnight; 11.30-midnight Sat; 12-11 Sun
☎(01277) 840478 🌐 thewhitehart.uk.com
Adnams Bitter, Broadside; Mighty Oak IPA, Oscar Wilde; Red Fox Hunter's Gold; guest beers Ⓖ
Slightly off the beaten track but still accessible, this fine pub has origins in the 17th century. The recent sympathetic restoration created an atmosphere conducive to both diners and drinkers. Regular club meetings are held here for cyclists, car owners, ramblers and young farmers. Very much community-focused, a book stall raises money for charities and beer festivals are held in June and November. Local CAMRA Pub of the Year 2007 and 2008. Two rooms for accommodation were recently added. ♨Q☕❀🛏◐♿♣P⅃

Mill Green

Viper ☆

Mill Green Road, CM4 0PT TL641018
⌚12-3, 6-11; 12-11 Sat; 12-10.30 Sun ☎(01277) 352010
Mighty Oak Oscar Wilde; Viper Ales Jake the Snake, VIPA; guest beers Ⓗ
The only pub in the country with this name, the Viper is an isolated, unspoilt country pub with a lounge, public bar and wood-panelled snug. Jake the Snake is occasionally replaced by another Viper ale. Viper Ales are commissioned from Mighty Oak and Nethergate, who also sometimes supply the two guest beers, although these may come from anywhere. Good home-cooked food is served at lunchtime, and Westons cider is sold. Beer festivals are held at Easter and August bank holiday. ♨Q❀◐⊟♣●P⅃

Monk Street

Farmhouse Inn

CM6 2NR (off B184, 2 miles S of Thaxted) TL612287
⌚11-midnight ☎(01371) 830864 🌐 farmhouseinn.org
Greene King IPA; Mighty Oak Maldon Gold; guest beers Ⓗ
Built in the 16th century, this former Dunmow Brewery pub has been enlarged to incorporate a restaurant and accommodation; the bar is in the original part of the building. The quiet hamlet of Monk Street overlooks the Chelmer Valley, two miles from historic Thaxted. A disused well in the garden supplied the hamlet with water during WWII. The pub has a rear patio, front garden and 'top' field. Draught cider from Westons is usually sold in the summer. Q❀🛏◐🚌(313)●P⅃

Mount Bures

Thatchers Arms ✔

Hall Road, CO8 5AT (1½ mile S of Bures, 1½ mile N of Chappel) TL905319
⌚closed Mon; 12-3, 6-11; 12-11 Sat & Sun
☎(01787) 227460 🌐 thatchersarms.co.uk

Adnams Bitter; Crouch Vale Brewers Gold; guest beers Ⓗ
This family-friendly pub on the Essex-Suffolk border is popular with locals and visitors alike. Its two main bar areas and extensive garden overlook the Stour Valley. Up to five real ales are available, mainly from local micro-breweries, together with an extensive selection of British, Belgian and American bottled beers. Winter and spring beer festivals are held at the pub, which is also renowned for its quality food made with locally-sourced produce. ❀◑⛺P

Old Harlow

Queen's Head

26 Churchgate Street, CM17 0JT TL483114
⏲ 11.45-3, 5 (6 Sat)-11; 12-4 Sun ☎ (01279) 427266
Adnams Bitter, Broadside; Crouch Vale Brewers Gold; Nethergate IPA Ⓗ
The new town of Harlow seems a long way from this traditional village pub. It was originally built as two cottages in 1530, then joined together and converted into a pub in 1750. Wooden beams feature throughout and there is a welcoming open fire during the winter months. Guest beers are usually from East Anglian breweries. A full range of food is served. ♨Q❀◑🚌(7,59)P⁵–

Paglesham

Punch Bowl

Church End, SS4 2DP
⏲ 11.30-3, 6.30-11; 12-10.30 Sun ☎ (01702) 258376
Adnams Bitter; guest beers Ⓗ
White-painted, weatherboarded pub dating from the 16th century, facing south in a quiet one-street village. It has been an ale house since the mid-1800s, when it was reputedly frequented by smugglers. The low-beamed single bar displays a large collection of mugs, brassware and old local pictures. There is a small restaurant to one side serving excellent good-value food. There are picnic tables at the front and in the rear garden, and ample parking all round the pub. Q❀◑P

Pentlow

Pinkuah Arms

Pinkuah Lane, CO10 7JW (off B1064 in small lane, opp red phone box) TL816448
⏲ 12-midnight (7 Mon & Sun) ☎ (01787) 280857
🌐 pinkuaharms.co.uk
Nethergate seasonal beers; Woodforde's Wherry; guest beers Ⓗ
Quite hard to find, this country pub is 350 years old, named after two spinsters who lived here. It has been tastefully refurbished, with beams, wooden floorboards, a low ceiling in part and a log fire. The menu is interesting and varied, with a good choice of Sunday roasts, and the credit crunch lunch is popular. There is outdoor seating. The pub offers many specials (quiz nights, steak nights) and themed menus. Westons Old Rosie is on handpump. Child-friendly. ♨Q❀◑🍏P

Purleigh

Bell

The Street, CM3 6QJ
⏲ 11-3, 6-11; 12-3, 7-10.30 Sun ☎ (01621) 828348
Beer range varies Ⓗ
Situated next to the church, this friendly village pub with fine views over the low-lying surrounding area has a peaceful location. The building dates from the 14th century, with 16th-century modifications. Good pub food is served (phone in advance to book), made with locally-sourced produce where possible. A real fire and beams lend a cosy atmosphere, and a good-sized meeting room is available. ♨Q❀◑♣P⁵–

Rayleigh

Roebuck ✔

138 High Street, SS6 7BU (close to library)
⏲ 9am-midnight (1am Fri & Sat) ☎ (01268) 748430
Greene King Ruddles Best, Abbot; guest beers Ⓗ
A Wetherspoon house, the largest pub in Rayleigh High Street is located on the site of the Reverend James Pilkington's Baptist School and close to the shops. It stocks a good range of guest beers. Food is served all day until 10pm, and children are welcome, during the day, in a sectioned-off dining area. Outdoor drinking and smoking is permitted in a cordoned-off area at the front and side of the pub ❀◑♿⇌🚌🍏⁵–

Ridgewell

White Horse Inn

Mill Road, CO9 4SG (on A1017 between Halstead and Haverhill) TL736407
⏲ 12-3 (not Mon & Tue), 6-11; 12-10.30 Sun
☎ (01440) 785532 🌐 ridgewellwhitehorse.com
Beer range varies Ⓖ
This old established pub, dating from about 1860, has a great atmosphere and offers a wide choice of beers and real ciders, all dispensed by gravity from the cellar. A 'dark' winter beer festival is held in March, as well as a regular summer festival. There is a large dining room/restaurant serving excellent food. Accommodation is available for up to 25 people. ♨❀🛏◑♿♣🍏P⁵–

Rochford

Golden Lion

35 North Street, SS4 1AB (200m N of Town Square)
⏲ 11-midnight; 11-11 Sun ☎ (01702) 545487
🌐 goldenlionrochford.co.uk
Adnams Bitter; Crouch Vale Brewers Gold; Greene King Abbot; guest beers Ⓗ
Small, often busy, 16th-century traditional Essex weatherboarded free house complete with stained glass windows. It serves six ales, including three changing guests – one a dark beer – plus real cider. A large-screen TV shows major sporting events. Bar snacks are available. The decor includes hops above the bar and a fireplace with traditional log burner. A small but cosy beer garden at the back is suitable for smokers. Many times local CAMRA Pub of the Year. ♨❀◑⇌🚌(7,8,60)♣🍏⁵–

Horse & Groom

1 Southend Road, SS4 1HA
⏲ 11.30 (12 Sun)-11 ☎ (01702) 544015
Mighty Oak Maldon Gold; Sharp's Special; guest beers Ⓗ
Local CAMRA Pub of the Year recently, and currently Town Pub of the Year, it is only a few minutes' walk from the town centre or station. The four varying guest ales include a selection from Essex breweries as well as from further afield, and

real cider is also always available. Occasional beer festivals are held in the function room, which can be hired. Good quality and value-for-money food can be enjoyed in the separate restaurant or in the bar. ♛❀◐◑⇌⊟(7,8)●P⅋

Rowhedge

Olde Albion

High Street, CO5 7ES (3 miles S of Colchester)
✪ 12-3 (not Mon), 5-11; 12-11 Thu-Sat; 12-10.30 Sun
☎ (01206) 728972 ⊕ yeoldealbion.co.uk
Beer range varies Ⓗ/Ⓖ
Traditional free house with a strong community spirit, the Albion offers a wide range of ales from micro-breweries. Beers to come are featured above the bar. In summer, visitors can sit in front of the pub by the River Colne. In winter a woodburner makes you welcome. The function room upstairs can be hired out and provides space for regular beer festivals, including on St George's Day and during the village regatta in June. Small but perfect award-winning local. ♛❀⊟(66)♣⅋

Saffron Walden

Old English Gentleman

11 Gold Street, CB10 1EJ (E of B184/B1052 jct)
✪ 11-11 (2am Tue-Thu; 1am Fri & Sat) ☎ (01799) 523595
Adnams Bitter; Woodforde's Wherry; guest beers Ⓗ
This 18th-century town-centre pub has log fires and a welcoming atmosphere. It serves a selection of guest ales and an extensive menu of bar food and sandwiches that changes regularly. Traditional roasts and chef's specials are available on Sunday in the bar or the dining area, where a variety of works of art are displayed. Saffron Walden is busy on Tuesday and Saturday market days. The pub has a pleasant patio at the rear. ♛❀◐⅋

Railway

Station Road, CB11 3HQ (300m SE of war memorial)
✪ 12-3, 6-11 (midnight Thu-Sat); 12-11 Sun
☎ (01799) 522208
Young's Bitter; guest beers Ⓗ
Typical 19th-century town-centre railway tavern, now opened out. Railway memorabilia, including a model train trundling back and forth above the bar, add a nice touch. Six handpumps feature Elgood's and Mighty Oak guest beers. Beer festivals are held at Easter (24 beers) and Whitsun (12 beers). The pub also has Erdinger Weissbier on draught, as well as an extensive food menu available lunchtimes and evenings. There are occasional live bands, with folk and blue grass prevailing. ❀◐◑P⅋

Temeraire ✔

55 High Street, CB10 1AA
✪ 9am-midnight (1am Fri & Sat) ☎ (01799) 516975
Greene King Ruddles Best Bitter, Abbot; guest beers Ⓗ
Fine Georgian building which was once a working men's club. At least one local beer from either Mighty Oak or Nethergate is always available. In addition to the regular Wetherspoon beer festivals, the pub hosts occasional Meet the Brewer sessions and beer tastings. It was the winner of a regional Wetherspoon's food award, hosts a Monday quiz night, and always stocks draught ciders. Families are welcome, and there is a large garden and a covered smoking area. ❀◐◑♿⊟(5,301,312)●P⅋

Shenfield

Olde Green Dragon ✔

112 Shenfield Road, CM15 8EZ (on A1023 at jct with A129 Hutton Road)
✪ 11-11 (10.30 Mon; midnight Fri, Sat & summer); 12-10.30 Sun ☎ (01277) 212300
Adnams Bitter; Greene King IPA; guest beers Ⓗ
This is a 16th-century former coaching inn with an extensively wood-panelled bar. The pub is much-improved and traditional. In addition to the regular beers, two varying guest beers from the Punch range are normally available. No meals are served all day Monday or Sunday evening. There is a smokers' shelter outside with a patio and heater. Buses stop close by during the day, and the railway station is only a 10-minute walk. ❀◐⇌P⅋

Southminster

Station Arms

39 Station Road, CM0 7EW (near B1021)
✪ 12-2.30, 6 (5.30 Thu & Fri)-11; 2-11 Sat; 12-4, 7-10.30 Sun
☎ (01621) 772225 ⊕ thestationarms.co.uk
Dark Star Hophead; Mighty Oak Oscar Wilde; guest beers Ⓗ
This traditional Essex weatherboarded pub will make you want to stay longer – customers travelling by rail from nearby towns frequently do. Beer festivals are held in an adjoining out-building to the rear and a courtyard provides a pleasant space to enjoy the excellent and varied range of ales throughout the summer months. Regular live music nights and a weekly meat raffle are held. It has been Pub of the Year at CAMRA branch, county and regional level over the years.
♛Q❀⇌⊟(31X)♣●⅋

Stanford-le-Hope

Rising Sun

Church Hill, SS17 0EU (opp church and near A1014)
✪ 3-10.30 Mon; 12-11 Tue-Thu; 12-midnight Fri & Sat; 12-10.30 Sun ☎ (01375) 671097
Crouch Vale Brewers Gold; guest beers Ⓗ
Much-improved, single-bar traditional town pub in the shadows of the church. The four guest beers are mainly from independent breweries, including LocAle beers. Up to two ciders or perries are stocked. Freshly-prepared, locally-sourced food is available daily (not Mon and Tue) in a separate area at one end of the bar. Fortnightly cash quiz nights are held to raise money for a local charity, and there are beer festivals twice-yearly in summer and winter. ❀◐◑⇌⊟♣●P⅋

Stansted Mountfitchet

Dog & Duck

58 Lower Street, CM24 8LR
✪ 11-midnight; 12-10.30 Sun ☎ (01279) 812047
Greene King IPA, Abbot; guest beers Ⓗ
Making a welcome return to the Guide after a long absence, this fine weatherboarded pub is in the heart of the older part of the village, close to the railway station. Wednesday is Pie & Mash Night, and there is a conker competition every September. The pub retains a traditional public bar (with level access and a wide door) and a quiet lounge bar, and is dog-friendly. Outside is a large garden and a smaller decking area.
Q❀◐⊞♿⇌⊟♣P⅋

Rose & Crown

31 Bentfield Green, CM24 8HX (½ mile W of B1383)
TL507255
12-3, 6-midnight; 12-10 Sun ☎ (01279) 812107
Adnams Bitter; guest beers Ⓗ
Typical family-run Victorian pub near a duck pond on the edge of a small hamlet. This free house has been modernised to provide one large bar but retains the atmosphere of a village inn and is well used by locals. The front of the pub is brightened by floral displays. Food is traditional and good value, made from locally-sourced produce (no meals Sun eve). Guest beers are from local breweries. The smoking area is covered and heated. Children and dogs are welcome.
(7)P

Stapleford Tawney

Moletrap

Tawney Common, CM16 7PU (3 miles E of Epping)
TL500013
11.30-2.30, 6-11; 12-3.30, 7-10.30 Sun ☎ (01992) 522394
themoletrap.co.uk
Fuller's London Pride; guest beers Ⓗ
This superb old inn is a free house enjoying magnificent views over the surrounding countryside. Three guest beers are normally available, usually from small independent brewers. Good value traditional food is on offer (no food Sun and Mon eve). There is a covered and heated smoking area. QP

Stock

Hoop ✔

High Street, CM4 9BD (on B1007)
11-11 (midnight Fri & Sat); 12-10.30 Sun
☎ (01277) 841137 thehoop.co.uk
Adnams Bitter Ⓗ**; guest beers** Ⓗ/Ⓖ
A traditional, friendly drinkers' pub, the interior of this 15th-century timber-framed building retains plenty of character. Home-made food is served in the bar and in the upstairs restaurant. This award-winning hostelry has at least four guest beers on gravity dispense and a cider or perry is also usually available. The large garden is the setting for a renowned beer festival held over the spring bank holiday. During the summer months there is an outside bar and a barbecue. Q(100)

Stow Maries

Prince of Wales

Woodham Road, CM3 6SA (near B1012) TL830993
11-11 (midnight Fri & Sat); 12-11 Sun ☎ (01621) 828971
prince-stowmaries.co.uk
Beer range varies Ⓗ/Ⓖ
This 17th-century weatherboarded inn was previously a bakery, complete with working oven. It has three open-plan drinking areas, all with open fires. The beer range is widely varied, including bottled and draught Belgian ales, and Westons cider is served. Good food, served lunchtimes and evenings, includes seafood specialities. The pub's November fireworks display is locally renowned. En-suite accommodation is a recent addition.
QP

Thaxted

Star

Mill End, CM6 2LT
12-11 (midnight Fri & Sat) ☎ (01371) 830368
thestarinn-thaxted.co.uk
Adnams Bitter, Broadside, seasonal beers; Taylor Landlord Ⓗ
Popular with locals and visitors, the pub is now open plan with exposed beams, panelling and a large fireplace. Thaxted is an architectural gem, with a steep high street, timbered guildhall, windmill, almshouses and, towering above all, the huge parish church. Thaxted Morris Ring is an annual gathering of teams from all over the country on the weekend following the late spring bank holiday. Notable is the Abbots Bromley Horn Dance on the Saturday evening. There are regular poker nights. (5,313)P

Warley

Brave Nelson

138 Woodman Road, CM14 5AL (½ mile E of B186)
12-3, 5.30-11; 12-midnight Sat; 12-3.30, 7-10.30 Sun
☎ (01277) 211690
Greene King IPA; Nethergate Suffolk County Best Bitter; guest beer Ⓗ
Cosy local, featuring wood-panelled bars with understated nautical memorabilia, including pictures, drawings and plates. This is a rare, regular outlet in the area for Nethergate Suffolk County Best Bitter, while the guest beer is usually from either Brentwood or Cottage. The weekly Sunday evening quiz, which is usually well-attended, starts soon after 9pm. Darts, pool and crib are played, and widescreen TVs often show sport. Live music features twice a month. No food is served Sunday or Monday. There is a sheltered smoking area in the garden. P

Weeley

White Hart

Clacton Road, Weeley Heath, CO16 9ED (on B1441, 1 mile from Weeley station)
12-2.30, 4-11; 12-11 Fri-Sun ☎ (01255) 830384
Beer range varies Ⓗ
A good watering hole that is worth seeking out regularly, situated near Weeley train station and on the bus route from Clacton and Colchester. The friendly landlord is a real ale and local brewery supporter, with an active real ale club and beer festival, and there is no food to distract from enjoying a good pint. Up to four handpumps supply a wide range of beers. The pub is popular with locals, sports fans and CAMRA members alike.
P

Wendens Ambo

Bell

Royston Road, CB11 4JY (on B1039, 1 mile W of B1383/old A11 jct)
11.30-3, 6-11; 11.30-12.30am Fri & Sat; 12-11.30 Sun
☎ (01799) 540382
Adnams Bitter; Woodforde's Wherry; guest beers Ⓗ
Classic country pub at the centre of a picturesque village. A charity fundraising event is held in summer and there are small beer festivals throughout the year. Beers are straight from the cask. A chalkboard features beer tasting notes and

forthcoming guest beers. Traditional pub food is served lunchtimes, main meals in the evenings, and roast lunches on Sunday, including a vegetarian option. There is a large garden with a play area and a petanque pitch. A weekly quiz is held on Thursday. Dogs welcome.
⛫❀◑⇌(Audley End)▣P⚋

Westcliff-on-Sea

Cricketers

228 London Road, SS0 7JG (on A13)
⏲ 11.30-midnight (2am Fri & Sat); 12-midnight
☎ (01702) 343168
Greene King Abbot; guest beers Ⓗ
This large street-corner pub is on the edge of Southend. A Gray's pub, it serves up to four constantly changing guest ales, often from local micros. Ciders are kept in the back room and are dispensed on gravity. Beer festivals are held occasionally throughout the year. The music venue Club Riga adjoins the premises, so this popular pub can get busy on music nights. Good value meals are available lunchtimes and evenings.
❀◑⇌(Southend Victoria/Westcliff)▣●⚋

Lamb & Lion

270-274 Station Road, SS0 7SD (200m W of Westcliff station)
⏲ 2-11; 12-midnight Fri & Sat; 12-11 Sun ☎ (01702) 332380
Mighty Oak Maldon Gold, Burntwood Bitter; guest beers Ⓗ
A warm welcome is assured at this relaxed, friendly free house, with a roaring open fire on chilly evenings and traditional pub games including pool, darts and shove-ha'penny. The landlord enjoys supporting micro-breweries and often has Julian Church and Potbelly beers as well as real cider and perry. The excellent Bar Lambs music venue is downstairs. Westcliff station is opposite and First Bus 24 stops outside.
⛫❀⇌▣(24)♣●⚋▯

Widdington

Fleur de Lys

High Street, CB11 3SG TL538316
⏲ 12-3 (not Mon), 6-11; 12-midnight Fri & Sat; 12-11 Sun
☎ (01799) 543280 🌐 thefleurdelys.co.uk
Adnams Bitter; Greene King IPA; guest beer Ⓗ
Welcoming 400-year-old village local that is reputed to be haunted, with a large open fireplace and beams. A pitch penny 'hole' is located in the seat by the door. The games room has a full-sized pool table, fuzzball table and dartboard. This was the first pub to be saved from closure by the North West Essex branch of CAMRA after the branch's formation many years ago. Quality meals from fresh ingredients are offered, with ingredients sourced locally (no food Mon). The venue is close to the source of the River Cam and Priors Barn, an English Heritage site. ⛫Q❀◑♿▣(322)♣P

Wivenhoe

Horse & Groom ✔

55 The Cross, CO7 9QL (on B1028)
⏲ 10.30-3, 5.30-11 (midnight Fri); 12-4.30, 7-11 Sun
☎ (01206) 824928
Adnams Bitter, seasonal beers; guest beers Ⓗ
This pub on the outskirts of Wivenhoe has been run by the same landlord for 21 years, fostering a friendly atmosphere. It has two bars, one that is popular for darts. Adnams beers are on offer, with changing guests often including a mild. Good home-cooked food is served lunchtimes (Mon-Sat). At the rear is a garden with a covered and heated smoking area. Buses serve the pub and Wivenhoe station is a one-mile walk. ❀◖⊞▣(78)♣P⚋

Woodham Mortimer

Hurdlemakers Arms

Post Office Road, CM9 6ST (off A414)
⏲ 12-11 (10 Sun) ☎ (01245) 225169
🌐 hurdlemakersarms.co.uk
Greene King Abbot; Mighty Oak IPA; guest beers Ⓗ
Popular with diners, this is a 400-year-old Gray's country pub. The tenants are CAMRA members who like to promote local brewery beers, with regularly changing guest beers alongside real cider. The extensive menu is available daily; summer barbecues take place in the huge garden, which has a children's play area. Special events throughout the year include a beer festival on the last weekend in June. ⛫Q❀◑♿▣(D2)♣●P⚋

Writtle

Wheatsheaf

70 The Green, CM1 3DU (S of A1060)
⏲ 11-2.30 (3 Fri), 5.30-11; 11-11 Sat; 12-10.30 Sun
☎ (01245) 420695 🌐 wheatsheafph-writtle.co.uk
Adnams Bitter; Farmer's Ales Drop of Nelson's Blood; Greene King Abbot; Mighty Oak Oscar Wilde, Maldon Gold; Sharp's Doom Bar Ⓗ
Traditional village pub with a small public bar, an equally compact lounge and a covered patio for smokers by the road. Local CAMRA and East Anglia Pub of the Year in 2009, it serves a guest seventh beer from the wide Gray's list on gravity. The atmosphere is generally quiet, with Sky TV switched on only for occasional sporting events. A folk night is held on the third Friday of each month. Note the Gray's sign in the public bar.
Q⊞▣(45)♣P⚋

Choosing pubs

CAMRA members and branches choose the pubs listed in the Good Beer Guide. There is no payment for entry, and pubs are inspected on a regular basis by personal visits; publicans are not sent a questionnaire once a year, as is the case with some pub guides. CAMRA branches monitor all the pubs in their areas, and the choice of pubs for the guide is often the result of democratic vote at branch meetings. However, recommendations from readers are welcomed and will be passed on to the relevant branch: write to Good Beer Guide, CAMRA, 230 Hatfield Road, St Albans, Hertfordshire, AL1 4LW; or send an email to: **gbgeditor@camra.org.uk**

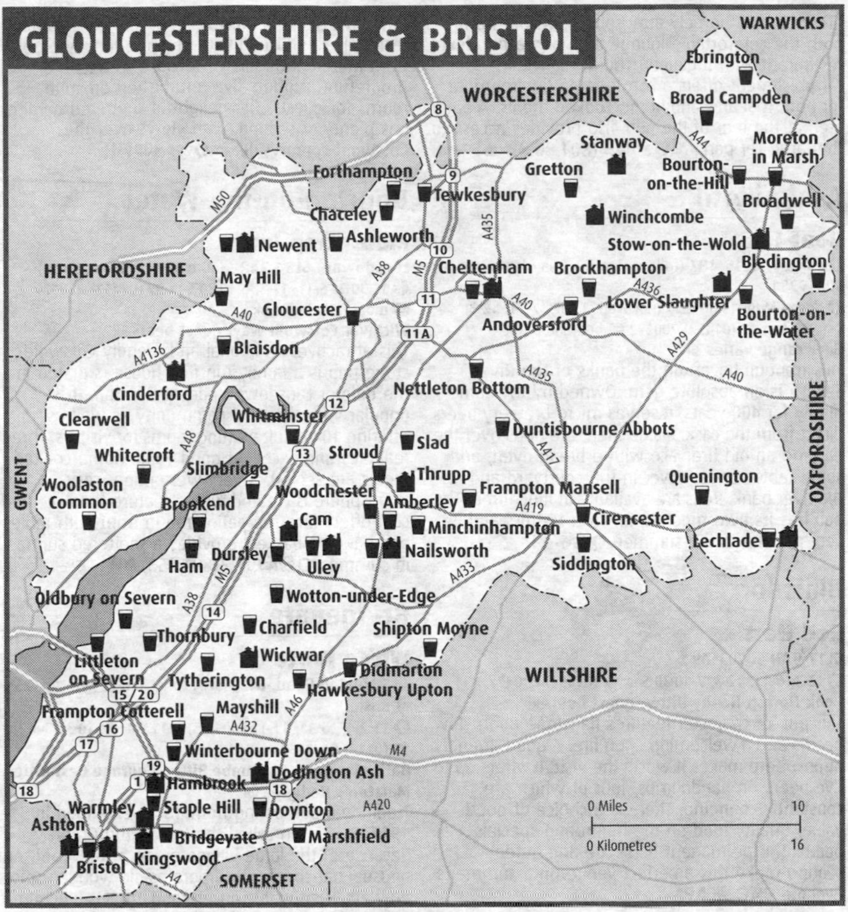

Amberley

Black Horse

GL5 5AL

12-11 (midnight Fri & Sat) ☎ (01453) 872556

blackhorseamberley.co.uk

RCH Old Slug Porter; Stroud Tom Long, Budding; Taylor Landlord; guest beers Ⓗ

Friendly, family-run pub on the edge of Minchinhampton Common, with stunning views across the Nailsworth Valley to Selsley Common. Good value food is served until 10pm daily. There are regular music and quiz nights and other themed evenings, including Pint of View, a discussion club. The terraced gardens command views of the River Severn and the Forest of Dean. Barbecues and occasional beer festivals are held in summer. Black Rat cider is served. Stroud CAMRA Pub of the Year 2009.

Andoversford

Royal Oak

Gloucester Road, GL54 4HR (on A436 in village centre) SP023195

11-3, 5-11; 12-10.30 Sun ☎ (01242) 820335

Sharp's Doom Bar; Stanway Stanney Bitter; guest beers Ⓗ

Popular, well-run local set in good walking country. The pub offers up to five quality real ales, including two from local Cotswold brewers. A large open log

INDEPENDENT BREWERIES

Arbor Bristol: Kingswood
Avon Bristol
Bath Ales Bristol: Warmley
Battledown Cheltenham
Bristol Beer Factory Bristol: Ashton
Cotswold Lower Slaughter
Cotswold Spring Dodington Ash
Donnington Stow-on-the-Wold
Festival Cheltenham
Freeminer Cinderford
Goff's Winchcombe
Great Western Bristol: Hambrook
Halfpenny Lechlade
Hetty Pegler Nailsworth (NEW)
Nailsworth Nailsworth
Prescott Cheltenham
Severn Vale Cam
Stanway Stanway
Stroud Thrupp
Uley Uley
Whittington's Newent
Wickwar Wickwar
Zerodegrees Bristol

fire creates a homely atmosphere, visible from both the comfortable lounge area and a two-level restaurant with a gallery. The attractive refurbishment offers a comfortable environment for both real ales and home-cooked meals. A patio area at the rear of the pub also provides access to the large car park. ⛫Q❀◐◑⊟(801,803)♣●P⁄–

Ashleworth

Boat Inn

The Quay, GL19 4HZ (follow sign for Quay from village) SO819251

✪ closed Mon; 11.30-2.30 (not Wed; 3 Sat), 7-11; 12-3, 7-10.30 Sun ☎ (01452) 700272 ⊕ boat-inn.co.uk

Beer range varies Ⓖ

This tranquil haven on the banks of the River Severn is an absolute gem. Owned by the same family for 400 years, it serves micro-brewery beers direct from the cask. Inside there are hops over the bar and an old fireplace with a bread oven, and some tables under cover in the courtyard and on the river bank. Rolls are available at lunchtime. The pub has its own mooring for river visitors and is very popular in the summer. Q❀♣●P

Blaisdon

Red Hart

GL17 0AH SO703169

✪ 12-3, 6-11; 12-3, 7-10.30 Sun ☎ (01452) 830477

Hook Norton Hooky Bitter; guest beers Ⓗ

This pub of character features flagstone floors, low beams and a welcoming open fire. A good, friendly atmosphere makes it worth the visit. It offers up to five beers on handpumps, four of which are constantly changing. There is a choice of good value, quality food on the menu and specials board. The permanent barbecue and outdoor seating make this a perfect venue on a summer's evening. ⛫Q❀◐◑P⁄–

Bledington

Kings Head ✔

The Green, OX7 6XQ (on village green) SP243228

✪ 11.30-3, 6-11; 12-10.30 Sun ☎ (01608) 658365

⊕ kingsheadinn.net

Hook Norton Hooky Bitter; guest beers Ⓗ

Local CAMRA Pub of the Year 2008, this delightful 16th-century honey-coloured stone inn overlooks the village green, with its brook and ducks. The original old beams, inglenook with kettle plus military brasses, open wood fire, flagstone floors and high-back settles and pews create a heart-warming atmosphere. Quality food is served in a separate dining area while 12 rooms offer charming accommodation. Guest ales are varied but they often come from Gloucestershire. ⛫Q♉❀⛺◐◑⊟⇌(Kingham)♣P⁄–

Bourton-on-the-Hill

Horse & Groom

GL56 9AQ

✪ 11-2.30 (3 Sat), 6-11; 12-3.30 Sun ☎ (01386) 700413

⊕ horseandgroom.info

Goff's Jouster; guest beers Ⓗ

Grade II-listed Georgian stone inn serving three local real ales. This is a family-run free house in private ownership since 2005, winning awards for excellent contemporary food served in an attractive dining area. The light, airy bar has been tastefully refurbished with an open fire. Two miles from Moreton in Marsh and close to Batsford Arboretum, it offers five refurbished en-suite rooms for guests. The delightful sheltered garden has plenty of seating, with views over the Cotswold countryside. ⛫Q❀⛺◐◑⊟P

Bourton-on-the-Water

Mousetrap Inn

Lansdowne, GL54 2AR (300m W of village centre)

✪ 11.30-3, 6-11; 12-3, 6-10.30 Sun ☎ (01451) 820579

⊕ mousetrap-inn.co.uk

Wickwar Cotswold Way; guest beers Ⓗ

This attractive, traditional and friendly Cotswold-stone pub is a family-run free house, situated in the quieter Lansdowne part of Bourton. It is popular with the local community as well as offering 10 en-suite letting rooms for visitors. Three real ales and excellent good value home-cooked meals are served. A very welcoming, cosy atmosphere is created with a feature fireplace and coal-effect fire. The patio area in front with tables and hanging baskets provides a sheltered suntrap in summer. Q❀⛺◐◑⊟(801,855)♣P

Bridgeyate

White Harte

111 London Road, BS30 5NA (on A420 jct wth A4175 E of Bristol)

✪ 11-2.45, 5-11; 11-11 Fri; 11-3, 6-11 Sat; 12-10.30 Sun ☎ (0117) 9673830

Bath Ales Gem; Butcombe Bitter; Courage Best Bitter; Marston's Pedigree Ⓗ

Traditional pub dating from 1860, extended in 1987. It is often called the Inn on the Green because of the large village green at the front. An unusual bar counter incorporates old wooden spice drawers. Reasonably priced food attracts lunchtime diners, and the pub also gets busy in the evening with people out for a drink. Pub games and sporting activities are likely conversation topics, and a quiz features on Monday evening. Black Rat cider is served. ⛫❀◐⊟(634,635)♣●P⁄–

Bristol: Central

Bank

8 John Street, BS1 2HR (take lane by arcade in All Saints Lane)

✪ 12-midnight (1am Thu-Sat) ☎ (0117) 930 4691

Beer range varies Ⓗ

Now well established as one of the better real ale pubs in Bristol, the Bank is right in the centre yet well hidden. A strong supporter of south-west micro-brewers, the three or four beers vary constantly, and the venue is not afraid to sell dark or very strong beers, always at keen prices; there are also guest ciders. Food is served 12-4pm daily, including popular Sunday roasts. Many live events take place in this compact one bar pub. Expect much quirky humour. ❀◐⇌(Temple Meads)⊟●⁄–

Barley Mow

39 Barton Road, The Dings, BS2 0LP (400m from rear exit of Temple Meads station over footbridge)

✪ 12-3 (not Mon), 5-11; 12-11 Fri & Sat; 12-10 Sun ☎ (0117) 930 4709 ⊕ myspace.com/barleymowbristol

Bristol Beer Factory Red, No. 7, Sunrise, seasonal beer; guest beer Ⓗ

A short walk from Temple Meads station brings you to this excellent pub, saved from closure by the Bristol Beer Factory in 2008. Located in the Dings renovation area, it is open plan with a pleasant courtyard area outside. Pictures of the area and local art feature strongly. There is occasional live music and a monthly quiz on Sunday night. Good food is served 12-2.30pm and 5.30-9pm. Seasonal ales include the award-winning Milk Stout, and a guest beer often appears.
⚔❀◐◑ ⇌(Temple Meads)🚌⚟

Bell ✔

Hillgrove Street, Stokes Croft, BS2 8JT (off Jamaica St)
⏲ 12-2 (not Sat), 5-midnight (1am Thu-Sat); 1-11.30 Sun
☎ (0117) 909 6612 🌐 bell-butcombe.com
Bath Ales Gem; Butcombe Bitter, Gold, seasonal beer Ⓗ
Pleasant, eclectic, two-roomed pub where DJs spin their discs from 10pm nightly in the back room. Friday evenings, in particular, attract drinkers on their way to nearby clubs. Local workers are regular customers for the lunchtime and early evening food. Sunday lunches are popular, too. A surprising feature is the pleasant rear garden with a patio, which is heated in colder weather. Local art on the wood-panelled walls adds a Bohemian feel. Plenty of buses serve Gloucester Road nearby. ❀◐◑🚌⚟

Bridge Inn

16 Passage Street, BS2 0JF
⏲ 12-11.30 (11 Sun) ☎ (0117) 929 0942
🌐 bridgeinnbristol.co.uk
Bath Ales SPA, Gem; guest beers Ⓗ
Tiny pub that changed hands early in 2009, close to the station and surrounding hotels, yet only a short walk from the city centre. Music industry memorabilia adorns the walls and a collection of vinyl records is available to play on a deck. Regular quizzes and other evening events are held. The pub is now much more adventurous in its choice of real ales, with two from Bath Ales usually available plus two from high-quality micro-breweries. Great to see it back in this Guide. ❀◐⇌(Temple Meads)🚌

Colston Yard ✔

Colston Street, BS1 5BD
⏲ 11 (12 Sun)-midnight ☎ (0117) 376 3232
🌐 colstonyard-butcombe.com
Butcombe Bitter, Gold, seasonal beers; Fuller's London Pride; guest beers Ⓗ
A tremendous renovation of the old Smiles brewery and tap site, reopened by Butcombe in late 2007. Unrecognisable internally and decorated to a high standard, it has a pleasant upmarket feel. In addition to the Butcombe range there are one or two guest ales, and a number of interesting foreign draught and bottled beers. An extensive bar and restaurant menu features local organic produce and fresh pizzas. Very handy for the Colston Hall and the Bristol Royal Infirmary. ◐◑🚌

Grain Barge

Mardyke Wharf, Hotwells Road, Hotwells, BS8 4RU (moored on opp bank to SS Great Britain)
⏲ closed Mon; 12-11 (11.30 Fri & Sat) ☎ (0117) 929 9347
🌐 grainbarge.co.uk
Bristol Beer Factory Red, No 7, Sunrise, seasonal beers Ⓗ
This moored boat, built in 1936 and recently a restaurant, was purchased by the Beer Factory in 2007 and converted into a floating pub offering good food. Great views of the SS Great Britain, the floating harbour and passing boats are available from the two top decks. Popular themed food nights are held some weekdays. The kitchen is open lunchtimes and evenings, and until 10pm Friday and Saturday. Thatchers cider is served. A downstairs bar and function room are available.
❀◐◑🚌●⚟

Green Man

21 Alfred Place, Kingsdown, BS2 8HD
⏲ 12-2.30 (Fri only), 5-11; 12-10.30 Sun ☎ (0117) 930 4824
🌐 thegreenmanbristol.org
Dawkins Green Barrel; guest beers Ⓗ
This small, dimly-lit Dawkins pub, formerly known as The Bell, aims to sell mainly organic or ethically produced food and drink. This extends to the real ales, which usually include three different guest beers, some on handpump and others via gravity. Home-cooked food from a small but interesting changing menu is served Wednesday to Saturday, and Sunday lunchtime. Note the limited lunchtime opening. Organic ciders also feature. Q◐◑🚌(20)●

Highbury Vaults

164 St Michaels Hill, Kingsdown, BS2 8DE (top of steep hill next to Bristol Royal Infirmary)
⏲ 12-midnight (11 Sun) ☎ (0117) 973 3203
Bath Ales Gem; Brains SA; Bristol Beer Factory Exhibition; St Austell Tribute; Young's Bitter; guest beers Ⓗ
In the same hands, and this Guide, for many years, this venue is popular with university students and hospital staff. Dating from the mid-19th century, its interior is dark and dingy, and features a small front snug bar, a main drinking area and a bar billiards table. Outside is a large heated patio and garden. Good quality, great value food is served lunchtimes and weekday evenings. The premises is owned by Young's but is allowed a lot of freedom with the beer range. Toilets are down steep stairs.
Q❀◐◑⇌(Clifton Down)🚌(8,9)♣⚟

Hillgrove Porter Stores

53 Hillgrove Street North, Kingsdown, BS2 8LT
⏲ 4-midnight (1am Fri); 2-1am Sat; 2-midnight Sun
☎ (0117) 924 9818 🌐 thehillgroveporterstores.com
Dawkins Brassknocker, Green Barrel, Bob Wall; guest beers Ⓗ
This was the first of the Dawkins Taverns, the brainchild of a local entrepreneur who also bought the Matthews brewery in 2009. An excellent community pub, it usually dispenses seven guest ales, including dark beers and rare styles, plus Westons cider. The interior is horseshoe-shaped, with a wonderfully comfy lounge area hidden behind the bar. Outside is a pleasant patio. Sunday night is quiz night. Frequent themed mini beer festivals are held in conjunction with the other Dawkins pubs. Q❀◐◑⇌(Montpelier)🚌♣●⚟

Hope & Anchor

38 Jacobs Well Road, BS8 1DR (between Anchor Rd and top of Park St)
⏲ 12-11 (10.30 Sun) ☎ (0117) 929 2987
Beer range varies Ⓗ
Popular and friendly city local offering up to six changing real ales, mostly from West Country micro-breweries. The pub has achieved a happy balance between those who come to eat the high quality food, served all day, and those who just want a pint. Subdued lighting, candles on the tables and hanging hop bines over the bar create atmosphere. On summer days the terraced garden

at the rear is very pleasant. Street parking is limited but buses pass nearby on Park Street or Anchor Road. ❀◐◑🚌⊱

Kings Head ★

60 Victoria Street, BS1 6DE

⏲ 11-11; 12-5, 7-11 Sat; 12-3, 7-11 Sun ☎ (0117) 927 7860

Butcombe Gold; Sharp's Cornish Coaster, Doom Bar; Wadworth 6X Ⓗ

Classic small pub, dating from pre-1660 and listed on CAMRA's National Inventory of Historic Pub Interiors. A narrow area around the bar leads to the tramcar snug at the rear. Pictures of old Bristol make fascinating viewing. An earlier landlady is reputed to haunt the pub. Popular food is served weekday lunchtimes only. A few minutes' walk from Temple Meads station on the way to town, the pub is also well served by buses. There are tables for outside drinking in summer.
Q❀◐⇌(Temple Meads)🚌♣

Knights Templar ✔

1 The Square, Temple Quay, BS1 6DG (adjacent to Temple Meads station rear car park)

⏲ 9am-midnight ☎ (0117) 930 8710

Greene King Ruddles Best Bitter, Abbot; Marston's Pedigree; guest beers Ⓗ

Pleasant Wetherspoon outlet housed at the base of a modern office complex. Outdoor seating in a paved area at the front is close to the floating harbour and river ferry service to the city centre and Hotwells. Eight real ales and three ciders are normally offered, plus the usual JDW fare. Silent sport is shown on the TVs.
Q❀◐◑♿⇌(Temple Meads)🚌(1,8,9)🍎

Old Fishmarket ✔

59-63 Baldwin Street, BS1 1QZ (200m from city centre)

⏲ 12-11.30 (midnight Fri & Sat); 12-10 Sun

☎ (0117) 921 1515

Butcombe Bitter; Fuller's Discovery, London Pride, ESB, seasonal beers Ⓗ

This spacious Fuller's pub, once a fish market, has become the main venue for those who enjoy a great pint with their TV sport – all main events are screened. It has a large front bar and a side indoor patio, as well as several discrete seating booths behind the bar for those wishing to avoid the sport. Thai and English meals are served at lunchtimes until 3pm, and evenings from 5pm (until 5pm only on Sun). ◐◑♿⇌(Temple Meads)🚌

Orchard Inn

12 Hanover Place, Spike Island, BS1 6XT (off Cumberland Rd near SS Great Britain)

⏲ 12-11; 9am-4, 7-11 Sat; 9am-10.30 Sun

☎ (0117) 926 2678

Bath Ales Gem; guest beers Ⓗ

The CAMRA National Cider Pub of the Year 2009 is a popular one-bar street-corner local, a 10-minute walk from the centre along the harbourside. The ferry service stops fairly close by. Up to three guest beers are served, usually including a dark beer in winter, and up to 24 different ciders at once. Good hearty food is served at lunchtimes, with snacks at most other times. Opening early at the weekend, the pub is known as the 'hangover cafe', serving breakfast from 9am and alcohol from 10am. Occasional live music is hosted. ❀◐🚌(500)♣🍎⊱

Seven Stars 🏆

1 Thomas Lane, Redcliffe, BS1 6JG (just off Victoria St)

⏲ 12-11 (10.30 Sun) ☎ (0117) 927 2845

Beer range varies Ⓗ

Small one-bar pub that has developed into one of Bristol's premier real ale venues since changing hands in 2009. It gives discounts to CAMRA members at all times and to everyone on Wednesdays. The venue has a pool table, rock-oriented jukebox and silent TVs set to sport channels, with outdoor seating in fine weather. Eight changing pumps include at least one dark beer and usually something strong. Live music takes place on Thursday evening and weekend afternoons. Local CAMRA Pub of the Year 2010.
❀⇌(Temple Meads)🚌♣

Bristol: East

Chelsea Inn

60-62 Chelsea Road, Easton, BS5 6AU

⏲ 1-midnight ☎ (0117) 902 9186 🌐 pickofthepubs.co.uk/thechelsea

Beer range varies Ⓗ

Street-corner community local with one large room and a collection of vintage sofas, armchairs and other furniture. Pictures from local artists are for sale or commission. Situated in a cosmopolitan area, it attracts a varied crowd, many relatively young. Free internet facilities and a small exchange library are available. Up to five beers are sold, some from the Marston's range, plus varied guest beers and two real ciders. Live music plays on Tuesday (jazz), Wednesday and Saturday.
❀⇌(Stapleton Rd)♣🍎⊱

Old Stillage

145-147 Church Road, Redfield, BS5 9LA (on A420)

⏲ 4-11 (12.30am Fri); 12-12.30am Sat; 1-10.30 Sun

☎ (0117) 939 4079

Arbor Ales Brigstow, Oyster Stout, Beech Blonde, seasonal beers; guest beers Ⓗ

Arbor's first pub acts as the brewery tap and testing ground for its many one-off brews. Low lighting and simple decor feature in this traditional town venue. A pool table, dartboard and jukebox are all available. There are plans to introduce food, to open longer, expand the beer range and open up the outdoor rear area. There is live music or a DJ at weekends, and Irish night on the last Thursday of the month. ⇌(Lawrence Hill)🚌♣

Bristol: North

Annexe

Seymour Road, Bishopston, BS7 9EQ (behind Sportsman pub)

⏲ 11.30-3, 5-11.30; 11.30-11.30 Sat; 12-11 Sun

☎ (0117) 9493931

Bath Ales Gem Bitter; Courage Best Bitter; Sharp's Doom Bar; Skinner's Cornish Knocker; Wye Valley HPA; guest beer Ⓗ

Community pub very close to the county cricket ground and not far from the Memorial Stadium. Inside is a converted skittle alley and a large conservatory/family room to one side. Several TVs show live sport, including one out on the partially covered patio outside. Good simple food, including quality pizzas, is served, and a pool table is available. Monday is quiz night in this pub, which continues to improve and impress.
Q⚘❀◐◑♿🚌♣⊱

Duke of York

2 Jubilee Road, St Werburghs, BS2 9RS (behind Mina Road Park close to M32 jct 3)
5-11 (midnight Thu & Fri); 4-midnight Sat; 3.30-11 Sun
☎ (0117) 941 3677
Beer range varies H
This well-hidden free house serves an eclectic clientele. Visit in daylight for the enchanted forest mural exterior, then at night experience the warm glow of the grotto-like interior. The decor comprises fairy lights, odd memorabilia, wooden floors, 1940s newspapers, a rare skittle alley and much more. There are two rooms and an extra bar upstairs. Three handpumps offer unusual beers, real ciders and a good range of bottled ales. Local CAMRA Pub of the Year 2008.
❀⊟≠(Montpelier)🚌(5,25)♣●⊱

Inn on the Green

2 Filton Road, Horfield, BS7 0PA (on A38 opp sports centre)
12-11 (midnight Fri & Sat) ☎ (0117) 952 1391
Butcombe Bitter; Cotleigh Tawny Owl; Draught Bass; guest beers H
A welcome return for this former local CAMRA Pub of the Year, offering an amazing 10 guest beers, ciders and perries. The interior is divided into three sections, catering for locals as well as rugby and football fans from the nearby Memorial Stadium. Note that the pub closes before some home football games. Good value pub food is served and a two-day beer festival is held on the first May bank holiday weekend. There is a charity quiz on Sunday night. Q❀◐◑♿🚌(75,76,77)♣●P⊱

Kellaway Arms

140 Kellaway Avenue, Horfield, BS6 7YQ (400m from A38)
12 (4 Mon-Thu winter)-11; 12-10.30 Sun
☎ (0117) 924 5368
Cheddar Ales Potholer; Sharp's Doom Bar; Shepherd Neame Spitfire; Skinner's Betty Stoggs; St Austell Tribute; guest beer H
Reputed to be geographically the highest pub in Bristol, this welcoming two-bar local near Horfield Common has come back strongly after a brief period of closure. There is a small and intimate bar, and a larger lounge geared towards diners. The large south-facing garden, complete with hen run, is a suntrap in summer. Wednesday is quiz night All beers are discounted on Monday and from 4-7pm Tuesday to Friday. The Memorial Stadium is a 15-minute walk. ❀◐◑⊟🚌(20)⊱

Miners Arms

136 Mina Road, St Werburghs, BS2 9YQ (400m from M32 jct 3)
4-11 (midnight Fri); 2-midnight Sat; 12-11 Sun
☎ (0117) 907 9874
Fuller's London Pride; St Austell Tribute; Sharp's Doom Bar; guest beers H
Located close to St Werburghs City Farm and Bristol Climbing Centre, this is an excellent three-roomed street-corner local, part of the local Dawkins chain. The split-level interior houses a hop-adorned bar where guest beers join the regulars. Another small quiet bar lies to the side, and a larger pool room to the rear. Dogs are welcome. The function room can be booked and houses an open mike night on Tuesday. Wednesday is cribbage night and Thursday is the quiz.
⛼❀⊟≠(Montpelier)🚌(5,25)♣

Bristol: South

Coronation

18 Dean Lane, Southville, BS3 1DD
3 (12 Sat)-11; 12-10.30 Sun ☎ (0117) 940 9044
Hop Back Crop Circle, Summer Lightning, seasonal beer; guest beers H
Hop Back's only Bristol pub, this busy street-corner local is a stone's throw from the River Avon, and a 10-minute walk from the centre. Up to five Hop Back beers feature, plus a guest – often from the associated Downton Brewery. The full range of Hop Back bottle-conditioned beers and a guest cider are also sold. Low-volume background music is played and a small TV is there for major sports events. Quiz night is Monday. Pizzas are served every evening 6-9pm. ◑≠(Bedminster)🚌(24)●

Windmill

14 Windmill Hill, Bedminster, BS3 4LU (next to Bedminster station)
11-11 (midnight Fri); 12-midnight Sat; 12-10.30 Sun
☎ (0117) 963 5440 🌐 thewindmillbristol.com
Bristol Beer Factory Red, No. 7, Sunrise H
With pastel colours and wooden flooring throughout, the pub is on two levels, with a family room on the lower area where children are welcome until 8pm. Three beers from the nearby Bristol Beer Factory are always on offer, plus real cider and foreign bottled beers. Good food is served all day. Board games are available, there is free Wi-Fi and an old 1970s jukebox. Outside is a small patio area to the front.
⛼❀◐◑≠(Bedminster)🚌●⊱

Bristol: West

Cambridge Arms

Coldharbour Road, Redland, BS6 7JS
12-11 (11.30 Fri & Sat) ☎ (0117) 973 9786
Butcombe Bitter; Fuller's Discovery, London Pride, ESB, seasonal beers H
Large, recently refurbished red-brick Fuller's pub, not far from the Downs, with wooden floors and pastel-coloured walls. It can get very busy with diners but drinkers are also welcome around the L-shaped room. There is a large south-facing garden at low level behind the pub. Fuller's seasonal beers and those from the former Gale's brewery are often available. Sunday roast is popular but no booking is allowed. Dogs are welcome.
⛼❀◐◑🚌P⊱

Lansdown

8 Clifton Road, Clifton, BS8 1AF
12 (4 Mon-Wed)-11; 12-10.30 Sun ☎ (0117) 973 4949
Bath Ales Barnstormer; Cheddar Ales Potholer; St Austell Tribute; guest beers H
Traditional pub that now specialises in a great real ale offering. Four of the five beers come from within 20 miles and the range always features an excellent mix of styles, including a dark beer and a golden ale. All beers are sold at similar upper-end prices irrespective of strength. There is an upstairs function room and live acoustic music events. Food is available evenings except Sunday and lunchtimes when open. The courtyard garden is heated and covered. ❀◐◑🚌(8,9)⊱

Merchants Arms

5 Merchants Road, Hotwells, BS8 4PZ
4 (12 Fri & Sat)-11; 12-10.30 Sun ☎ (0117) 9040037
Bath Ales SPA, Gem, Barnstormer, seasonal beer H

Traditional local located just before the Cumberland Basin, on all the main Bristol to North Somerset bus routes. It won a national CAMRA award for its refurbishment when Bath Ales first took it on. Conversation dominates in the two drinking areas, although live music is held occasionally and a quiz night on Thursday. The concealed TV is brought out now and again for football. Food is limited to bar snacks. Well-behaved dogs are welcome, and there is free Wi-Fi access. Q🚌

Portcullis

3 Wellington Terrace, Clifton, BS8 4LE (close to Clifton side of Suspension Bridge)

12-2 (Fri only), 4.30-11; 12-11 Sat; 12-10.30 Sun

☎ (0117) 908 5536

Dawkins Brassknocker, Green Barrel; guest beers Ⓗ

A pub since 1821 but rescued from closure by the Dawkins chain in early 2008, it has a downstairs bar and an quieter upstairs lounge that can be used for functions. All nine pumps are occupied by small micros, including at least six guest beers, with one pump dedicated to a changing beer from BrewDog. Ciders and foreign beers are also stocked. Frequent beer festivals and themed brewery weeks feature, plus a popular Thursday quiz, and there is good quality food. Dawkins beers are discounted to CAMRA members. Q◐◑🚌(8,9)🍎

Victoria

20 Chock Lane, Westbury on Trym, BS9 3EX (in small lane behind churchyard)

12-2.30, 6-11; 12-3, 7-10.30 Sun ☎ (0117) 950 0441

thevictoriapub.co.uk

Butcombe Bitter; Wadworth Henry's Original IPA, Horizon, 6X, seasonal beers Ⓗ

Once a courthouse, this quiet, relaxed and welcoming Wadworth-owned traditional pub has been in the same hands for many years. A raised garden to the rear is a suntrap in summer. Pictures of Westbury as a village adorn the walls. Popular home-cooked food is available daily, including pizzas. Entertainment includes quizzes, themed meals and live blues on Sunday evening. Various societies meet here. Bonus card offers are now available if you provide your email address.
Q❀◐◑🚌(1,20)⁵—

Vittoria

57 Whiteladies Road, Clifton, BS8 2LY

12-11 (midnight Fri & Sat); 12-10.30 Sun

☎ (0117) 3309414

Courage Best Bitter; Sharp's Doom Bar; Wells Bombardier; guest beers Ⓗ

Traditional single bar pub in an area surrounded by theme bars and restaurants. A real fire and jukebox add to the warm atmosphere. The licensee does his best to provide interesting guest beers within the terms of his lease. Pieminster pies are offered at very fair prices along with a snack menu. The outside covered seating to the front is useful in summer months. Several interesting malt whiskies can be sampled. Thursday is quiz night.
♨❀◐◑⇌(Clifton Down)🚌♣

Broad Campden

Bakers Arms ✔

GL55 6UR (signed from B4081) SP158378

11.30-2.30, 5.30-11; 11.30-11 Fri, Sat & summer; 12-10.30 Sun ☎ (01386) 840515

Donnington BB; Stanway Stanney Bitter; Wells Bombardier; guest beers Ⓗ

This genuine free house, where the owners are celebrating their 13th year, is characterised by Cotswold-stone walls, exposed beams, an inglenook fireplace and an attractive oak bar counter where the local Stanney Bitter is a popular choice. Home-cooked meals prepared by the landlady can be tried in the bar or in the dining room. A framed handwoven rug is a feature of this CAMRA County Pub of the Year 2005. A traditional Cotswold pub at its very best. ♨Q❀◐◑♣🍎P

Broadwell

Fox Inn

The Green, GL56 0UF (off A429 in village centre) SP202276

11-2.30, 6-11; 12-2.30, 7-10.30 Sun ☎ (01451) 870909

Donnington BB, SBA Ⓗ

This attractive stone-built pub overlooking the large village green was deservedly North Cotswold CAMRA Pub of the Year 2007. Donnington Beers are popular with visitors. The pub is a true local centre where good home-cooked food is enjoyed. Features include original flagstone flooring in the main bar area, jugs hanging from beams and the Aunt Sally game played in the garden. Behind the garden is a camping and caravan site. A special experience is assured at this attentive family-run pub. ♨Q❀◐◑⛺🚌♣P⁵—

Brockhampton

Craven Arms

Kingsbury Street, GL54 5XQ (off A436 in centre of village) SP035224

12-3, 6-11; 12-11 Sat; 12-6 Sun ☎ (01242) 820410

Butcombe Bitter; Otter Bitter; guest beers Ⓗ

A spacious 17th-century pub that is a proper free house, with carefully selected guest beers. Set in an attractive hillside village with outstanding views and walks, it has an open fire bar area and excellent dining separated by church-style stone windows. It was runner-up in the 2009 local CAMRA Pub of the Year. A beer festival is held annually in August in the sizeable garden. Handy for nearby Sudeley Castle, this is a well-managed gem, with very attentive family service.
♨Q❀⇄◐◑♿⛺♣P

Brookend

Lammastide Inn

GL13 9SF

12-3, 7-midnight; 6-midnight Fri; 12-midnight Sat; 12-11 Sun ☎ (01453) 811337

Draught Bass; Wye Valley Bitter; guest beers Ⓗ

Single-bar pub built in 1932. It has an imposing main bar with six beer engines. There is a raised seating area in the bay window, otherwise the pub, garden and toilets are accessible by wheelchair. The dining area overlooks the raised decking in the garden equipped with children's play equipment, and there are fine views towards the River Severn and Forest of Dean. The pub opens at 6.30pm Monday and Tuesday for takeaway fish and chips. Well-behaved dogs are welcome.
❀◐◑♿🚌♣P⁵—

Chaceley

Yew Tree Inn

Stock Lane, GL19 4EQ (½ mile from Chaceley village) SO856298

12-2.30 (3 Sat), 6-11.30 (midnight Fri & Sat); 12-3, 7-11 Sun ☎ (01452) 780333

Wye Valley Butty Bach; guest beers

Riverside pub set on the west bank of the Severn with visitor moorings. It has been altered and extended over 200 years and now has a spacious public bar, comfortable lounge and a skittle alley. The large restaurant serves good value food. Both the seating on the river bank in the summer and the real fire in the winter draw customers to this friendly pub. It holds a beer festival in the summer. P

Charfield

Pear Tree Inn

6 Wotton Road, GL12 8TP (1½ miles from jct 14 of M4)

12-12.30am (midnight Sun) ☎ (01454) 261663

peartreecharfield.webs.com

Butcombe Bitter; Otter Bitter; guest beer

A genuine free house, this traditional village pub is situated on the main Charfield road. It has a public bar and a comfortable lounge dining room where local artists display their work. A quiz evening is hosted on Wednesday and live music on Thursday. Dogs are welcome in the public bar. Customers vote for the guest ale every week. The pub specialises in locally reared Aberdeen Angus steaks. Q P

Cheltenham

Adam & Eve

8 Townsend Street, GL51 9HD (near Tesco superstore)

10-2 (not Thu), 4-11; 10-11 Sat; 12-2, 4-10.30 Sun

☎ (01242) 690030

Arkell's 2B, 3B, seasonal beers

Run by the same landlady for 32 years, this friendly and unpretentious terraced local is home to skittles, darts and quiz teams. It is a 15-minute walk from the town centre and, while parking is very limited, it is readily accessible by public transport: Stagecoach buses stop at the end of the street. There is a separate lounge, and the public bar is a focal point for the community. Charity events are often hosted. Q

Bath Tavern

68 Bath Road, GL53 7JT

11-11; 12-10.30 Sun ☎ (01242) 256122

Butcombe Bitter; Sharp's Cornish Coaster, Doom Bar

Located close to the town hall and nearby Cheltenham College with its cricket festival, there is always a warm welcome at this friendly and busy single-bar free house. Run for more than 100 years by the Cheshire family, it now has young owners. Local produce is freshly cooked on the premises and Sunday lunch is especially popular (booking is advisable). Music is played at a background level, but the volume may rise on weekend evenings.

Cheltenham Motor Club

Upper Park Street, GL52 6SA (access from A40 London Rd via Crown Passage)

7 (12 Sat)-midnight ☎ (01242) 522590 cheltmc.com

Donnington BB; guest beers

CAMRA members are welcome at this friendly club, just outside the town centre in the former Crown pub. Gloucestershire and SW Regional Club of the Year for the last five years, the club offers three different ales from breweries throughout the country, alongside Donnington BB and Thatchers cider. Parking is limited. Local league quiz, darts and pool teams are based here. Q (B) P

Jolly Brewmaster

39 Painswick Road, GL50 2EZ

12-11 (10.30 Sun) ☎ (01242) 772261

Beer range varies

Cheltenham CAMRA's Pub of the Year 2010. Seven handpumps feature a changing range of ales from local breweries and beyond, alongside Black Rat, Thatchers Heritage, Cheddar Valley and Westons Old Rosie ciders. Booking is advised for the excellent value Sunday lunch. Relaxed and friendly, this busy pub features original etched windows and open fires and appears in CAMRA's Good Cider Guide. The very attractive beer garden serves as an extra room in the summer and offers winter warmth for smokers. Q (10)

Kemble Brewery Inn

27 Fairview Street, GL52 2JF

11-11 (midnight Fri & Sat) ☎ (01242) 243446

Beer range varies

This small, popular back-street local is hard to find but well worth the effort. It can get very busy on race days or if nearby neighbours Cheltenham Town FC are at home. Six changing real ales from local breweries and others from further afield are usually available, alongside Westons Traditional Scrumpy. Booking is necessary for the excellent Sunday lunch (12-3pm) and a special is served 12-2.30pm daily. Smoking is permitted in the attractive walled drinking area at the rear.

Q

Royal Oak

43 The Burgage, Prestbury, GL52 3DL

11-11 (11-3, 5.30-11 Mon-Thu winter); 12-10.30 Sun

☎ (01242) 522344 royal-oak-prestbury.co.uk

Taylor Landlord; guest beers

This Cotswold stone-built local in Prestbury village with limited parking is the closest pub to Prestbury Park racecourse. The quiet public bar features oak beams, parquet flooring, equine prints and a log fire. Good quality food is served in the lounge bar, with daily specials (booking advised). Two changing guest beers (see website for details) feature alongside Thatchers cider. The Pavilion – a skittle alley and function room in the garden – hosts annual May beer and August cider festivals.

Q (A) P

Royal Union

37 Hatherley Street, GL50 2TT

12-11 (midnight Fri & Sat) ☎ (07957) 577450

Prescott Hill Climb; Sharp's Doom Bar; Skinner's Betty Stogs; Taylor Landlord

Three guest ales from near and far supplement the four regulars at this locals' pub, which has been brought into the 21st century. More than 20 single malts are also available, as well as a great range of good value wines. Traditional home-cooked food is served until 9pm (curries only on Friday) and buffets or banquets can be arranged. Both the lounge and skittle alley can be booked for functions. Smoking is permitted in the courtyard at the rear of the pub. Q (94)

Cirencester

Corinium Hotel

12 Gloucester Street, GL7 2DG (off A435 N of town centre)
✪ 11-11 (10.30 Sun) ☎ (01285) 659711
🌐 coriniumhotel.co.uk
Beer range varies Ⓗ
This agreeable two-star hotel has an almost discreet frontage that you enter through a narrow courtyard, which leads to the comfortable lounge area. A recently refurbished bar adjoins the wooden-floored restaurant. The varying thickness of the walls gives hints to its origin as an Elizabethan wool merchant's house. A pleasant rear garden is very popular in summer.
♨❀⇌◐◑♿P

Drillmans Arms

34 Gloucester Road, Stratton, GL7 2LJ (on old A417 N of jct with A435)
✪ 11-2.30, 5.30-midnight; 11-midnight Sat; 12-4.30, 7-11 Sun ☎ (01285) 653892
Sharp's Doom Bar; Three Castles Saxon Archer Ⓗ
A haven for skittles teams, this busy roadside local is a proper community pub. Its new decor marries well with the low-beamed ceilings and open fire to create a warm and welcoming atmosphere. The real ales are dispensed to the left of a slightly obtrusive fruit machine; the smaller public bar is adjacent to the large skittle alley/function room at the rear, which is dominated by a pool table and dartboard. Parking on match nights can be slightly awkward. ♨❀◐🚌♣P⚟

Clearwell

Lamb

High Street, GL16 8JU SO570081
✪ closed Mon-Wed; 6-11 Thu & Fri; 12-3, 6-11 Sat; 12-3, 7-10.30 Sun ☎ (01594) 835441
Wye Valley Bitter; guest beers Ⓖ
This local has two bars with open fires; two large settles flank the fire in the snug bar. The atmosphere is warm and welcoming and the locals are very friendly. The beer is served directly from casks in the cellar. This venue has been a long-time favourite with local CAMRA members. The three varying guest beers are usually sourced from local micros. ♨Q❀⊟♣🍎P

Didmarton

King's Arms

The Street, GL9 1DT (on A433)
✪ 11-11; 12-10.30 Sun ☎ (01454) 238245
🌐 kingsarmsdidmarton.co.uk
Exmoor Gold; Otter Ale; Taylor Landlord; Uley Bitter Ⓗ
Chatty locals and friendly bar staff can make this smartly attired village hostelry a hard place to leave. Its lively drinking area is adorned with copious amounts of reclaimed wood, which give a warmth to the stylish interior. This is all ably complemented by the smart furnishings of the popular restaurant. The low-key frontage only hints at the superb refurbishment contained inside this 17th-century coaching inn. The tidy, walled garden gets busy in summer and boasts a smart smokers' pavilion. ♨❀⇌◐◑🚌♣P⚟

Doynton

Cross House

High Street, BS30 5TF
✪ 11.30-3; 12-3, 6-11 Sat; 12-10.30 Sun ☎ (0117) 9372261
Bath Ales Gem; Courage Best Bitter; Draught Bass; Taylor Landlord; guest beer Ⓗ
Traditional country pub with a stone-walled exterior and a split-level interior. In a pleasant, small village not far from the A420 at Wick, it plays a pivotal role in village life. It is allegedly haunted by the ghost of Archie Carrow, who was landlord for 50 years. The garden is child-friendly and dogs are welcome. It represents a rare outlet for Timothy Taylor Landlord in these parts. The TV is used sparingly for live sport. ♨Q❀◐◑♣P

Duntisbourne Abbots

Five Mile House ☆

Old Gloucester Road, GL7 7JR (off A417 at services sign and S of petrol station)
✪ 12-3, 6 (7 Sun)-11 ☎ (01285) 821432
🌐 fivemilehouse.co.uk
Donnington BB; Taylor Landlord; Young's Bitter Ⓗ
After stooping to enter this welcoming pub, you can see why it features in the National Inventory of Historic Pub Interiors. The tap room's flagstones and large settle are complemented by the worn woodwork of the cosy bar, whose tables and benches have outlasted many generations. Two old living rooms and the cellar have been converted into dining rooms to cope with the demand for the classy menu. There is a well-appointed 'Palais Fumant' for the smokers. ♨Q❀◐◑♣P⚟

Dursley

Old Spot

Hill Road, GL11 4JQ (next to bus station)
✪ 11 (12 Sun)-11 ☎ (01453) 542870 🌐 oldspotinn.co.uk
Severn Vale Session; Uley Old Ric; guest beers Ⓗ
CAMRA National Pub of the Year 2007, this free house dates from 1776 and serves an extensive range of ales from independent brewers. It was named after the Gloucestershire Old Spot pig, and a porcine theme blends with the extensive brewery memorabilia. Low ceilings and log fires provide a cosy atmosphere. The pretty garden has a heated, covered area. Wholesome, freshly prepared dishes are available. This convivial local is on the Cotswold Way and holds regular beer festivals. There is a free car park opposite. ♨Q❀◐♿🚌♣🍎⚟

Ebrington

Ebrington Arms 🏆 ✔

GL55 6NH SP186399
✪ closed Mon; 12-3, 6-11; 12-11 Fri & Sat summer; 12-6 Sun
☎ (01386) 593223 🌐 theebringtonarms.co.uk
Stroud Organic Ale; Uley Bitter; guest beers Ⓗ
CAMRA North Cotswold Pub of the Year 2009, this is an outstanding 17th-century Cotswold-stone free house serving four selected beers, mainly from Gloucestershire. There is an attractive low-beamed bar with a cosy separate dining room, both with open fires. This family-run inn serves home-cooked meals from a varied menu using local ingredients. Situated two miles from Chipping Campden and popular with the local community, it has three en-suite letting rooms. In summer you can picnic in a beautiful walled garden. ♨Q❀⇌◐◑▲🍎P

Forthampton

Lower Lode Inn

GL19 4RE (follow sign to Forthampton from A438 Tewkesbury-Ledbury road) SO878317
12-midnight (2am Fri & Sat) ☎ (01684) 293224
lowerlodeinn.co.uk
Donnington BB; Sharp's Doom Bar; Wye Valley Golden Ale; guest beers Ⓗ
This brick-built pub has been licensed since 1590. Standing in three acres of lawned river frontage, it looks across the River Severn to Tewkesbury Abbey. It has its own moorings and a private slipway, and a ferry crosses the river to the Lower Lode picnic area outside Tewkesbury from April to September. The regular ales are complemented by two changing guests (three in summer). Lunchtime and evening meals are served, including Sunday lunch. En-suite accommodation is offered. Day fishing licences are available and the pub is a licensed touring park site. ♕Q♨❀⇔◐◑♿⛺♣P⌐

Frampton Cotterell

Rising Sun

43 Ryecroft Road, BS36 2HN
11.30-11.30 (midnight Fri & Sat); 12-11 Sun
☎ (01454) 772330
Butcombe Bitter; Draught Bass; Great Western Maiden Voyage, seasonal beers; Wadworth 6X; guest beer Ⓗ
Now the brewery tap for the Great Western Brewery, it's owned by the same family that has run this excellent free house for many years. At least two GWB beers are on and normally one guest beer. The three-roomed interior comprises the main bar, a small snug and a conservatory that acts as the restaurant during food hours. There is also a skittle alley/function room and a covered smoking area. It now has an enclosed child-safe beer garden and free Wi-Fi. Q❀◐◑🚌(581)♣P⌐

Frampton Mansell

Crown Inn

GL6 8JG (off A419 Cirencester to Stroud road opp Texaco garage)
12-11 (10.30 Sun) ☎ (01285) 760601
thecrowninn-cotswolds.co.uk
Butcombe Bitter; Stroud Organic Ale; Uley Laurie Lee's Bitter; guest beer Ⓗ
This pub dates back to at least 1633, when it was known to be a cider house with an adjoining village slaughterhouse. It was also one of the first premises to be recorded under the 1737 Licensing Act. A three-roomed local, each room has an open fire. There is a 12-bedroom hotel annexe, ample car parking and exquisite views over the Golden Valley. ♕Q❀⇔◐◑♿♣P⌐

Gloucester

Cross Keys Inn

Cross Keys Lane, GL1 2HQ
11-11 (midnight Fri & Sat); 7-11 Sun ☎ (01452) 523358
crosskeysinngloucester.co.uk
Beer range varies Ⓗ
Popular 18th-century free house off Southgate Street. The main bar's welcoming atmosphere encourages lively conversation among mature drinkers by day. From Wednesday to Sunday an evening entertainment programme offers live and recorded music, and there are 'smooth' Saturday afternoons. Home-prepared bistro-style food includes a changing daily special. One of the two ales is local. A smart sun terrace is ideal for relaxation in warm weather and serves the smokers. A small cocktail bar is available for private parties. Closed Sunday lunchtime. ❀◐◑⇌⌐

Fountain Inn

53 Westgate Street, GL1 2NW
11 (12 Sun)-11 ☎ (01452) 522562
fountain-inn-restaurant.co.uk
Greene King Abbot; Hook Norton Old Hooky; St Austell Tribute; Taylor Landlord Ⓗ
This 17th-century inn is on a site where ale was almost certainly served in 1216. A passage from Westgate Street leads into a courtyard ablaze with flowers in summer. The Cathedral bar has a panelled ceiling, carved stone fireplace and a real fire. The modernised orange room acts as a function room or bar overflow. A second function room is upstairs. All is deliberately traditional, including the food (no food Sun eve). The inn plays host to local morris dancers. ♕Q❀◐◑♿⇌♣⌐

Greyhound

Greyhound Gardens, Longlevens, GL2 0XH (near Elmbridge Court roundabout, jct A40/A417)
12-11 (midnight Fri & Sat) ☎ (01452) 506107
Banks's Mild, Bitter; guest beers Ⓗ
This attractive and welcoming community pub is close to the city's northern bypass. Bricks from Gloucester's demolished 18th-century infirmary were used in its construction in 1985, close to the site of a former greyhound stadium. A single bar serves three distinct seating areas, each with its own rich style of furniture and decor. Food is available until 9pm (8pm Sun). A small garden has a heated covered area for smokers. Two guest ales are from Marston's national list.
❀◐◑♿🚌(94)♣P⌐

Linden Tree ✔

73-75 Bristol Road, GL1 5SN (on A430 S of docks)
11.30-2.30, 6-11; 11.30-11.30 Sat; 12-11 Sun
☎ (01452) 527869
Wadworth Henry's Original IPA, Horizon, 6X, JCB, Bishop's Tipple; guest beers Ⓗ
Part of a Grade II-listed Georgian terrace, this is a very popular community pub. Its modest entrance masks an interior not untypical of a Cotswold pub. The open log fire, warm colour scheme and somewhat eccentric decorative features contribute to a homely atmosphere. A skittle alley opens up to provide extra space when required. Up to three guest beers are from family brewers. Substantial home-cooked meals are offered (no food Sat and Sun eves). Accommodation is reasonably priced.
♕Q❀⇔◐◑🚌(12)♣⌐

Pig Inn the City

121 Westgate Street, GL1 2PG
11-midnight (1.30am Fri & Sat) ☎ (01452) 421960
St George's Dragons Blood; Wickwar Long John Silver; guest beers Ⓗ
Behind the listed 19th-century facade is a family-run pub of real character(s). Lighthearted pig portraits capture the mood, which may extend to the entertainment on Tuesday, Friday and Sunday evenings. Up to four guest ales come from craft brewers nationwide, and there are ciders from Gwatkin, Broadoak and others. Excellent home-made food including roasts in three sizes (beware

the large) is available each lunchtime and on non-entertainment evenings. Local CAMRA City Pub of the Year 2009-2010. ❀◐◑⇌♣●⌐

Water Poet ✓

61-63 Eastgate Street, GL1 1PN
⏲ 9-midnight ☎ (01452) 783530
Greene King Abbot, Ruddles Best Bitter; guest beers [H]
Opened in 2007, this is a highly successful second venue for Wetherspoon in the city (the first was the Regal in Kings Square). An abundant use of wood, warm colour scheme, gilt-framed mirrors, potted palms and attractive lighting give an impression of quality. A large paved and bricked garden with mature trees and shrubs contains a spacious heated shelter for smokers. Up to four guest ales come from craft brewers, some local. The cider is from Westons. Food is served until 11pm. Q❀◐◑♿⇌●⌐

Gretton

Royal Oak

Gretton Road, GL54 5EP (at E end of village, 1½ miles from Winchcombe) SP014305
⏲ 12-3, 6-11; 12-4, 6-10.30 Sun ☎ (01242) 604999
Goff's Jouster; Stanway Stanney Bitter; guest beers [H]
A popular Cotswold pub where a warm welcome is assured from the family owners. Two regular beers are from Gloucestershire breweries, with varied guests. Excellent home-cooked food can be taken in the two bars and conservatory, with views across the vale. Bar areas have a mix of wood and flagstone floors, while the garden hosts an annual beer and music festival in July. There are walks nearby and the Gloucestershire Warwickshire Railway is a feature at the bottom of the garden. ⛫❀◐◑♣P⌐

Ham

Salutation 🏆

Ham Green, Berkeley, GL13 9QH (from Berkeley take road signed Jenner Museum) ST681984
⏲ 12-2.30 (not Mon), 5-11; 11-11 Sat; 12-10.30 Sun
☎ (01453) 810284
Cotswold Spring Old English Rose; Severn Vale Dursley Steam Bitter; guest beers [H]
Rural free house situated in the Severn Valley within walking distance of the Jenner Museum, Berkeley Castle and Deer Park. This friendly local sources its beers from nearby breweries and is popular with walkers and cyclists. The pub has two cosy bars, with a log fire and a skittle alley/function room. Food is served lunchtimes and early evening. There is a child-friendly garden at the front of the pub. CAMRA Gloucestershire Pub of the Year 2010. ⛫Q❀◐◑⊞♿♣P

Hawkesbury Upton

Beaufort Arms

High Street, GL9 1AU (off A46, 6 miles N of M4 jct 18)
⏲ 12-11 (10.30 Sun) ☎ (01454) 238217
🌐 beaufortarms.com
Wickwar BOB; guest beers [H]
This 17th-century Grade II-listed Cotswold stone free house is close to the historic Beaufort Monument. It has separate public and lounge bars, a dining room and skittle alley/function room. The pub contains a plethora of ancient brewery and local memorabilia. It serves four ales and Wickwar Screech cider. With an attractive garden, the pub is the hub of local community activities. A warm welcome is assured at this local CAMRA award winner. ⛫Q❀◐◑⊞♿▣♣●P

Lechlade

Crown Inn ✓

High Street, GL7 3AE (opp traffic lights at A417/A361 jct)
⏲ 12-midnight (11 Sun) ☎ (01367) 252198
🌐 crownlechlade.co.uk
Halfpenny Ha'penny Ale, Thames Tickler, Four Seasons, Old Lech, seasonal beer [H]
Cirencester CAMRA sub-Branch Pub of the Year 2010. This twin-roomed, wooden-floored brew-pub has flourished, with up to six of its ales available, to the delight of the regular clientele. Renowned for its parties and unusual choice of games, this enthusiastic pub makes for a memorable experience. Two fireplaces flank the front room, whose walls are adorned with an eclectic array of paraphernalia, while smokers can watch the brewing process from their covered patio at the rear. There are six letting bedrooms. ⛫❀⌂⛺▣♣⌐

Littleton on Severn

White Hart

BS35 1NR (signed from B4461 at Elberton)
⏲ 12-11 ☎ (01454) 412275
Bath Ales Gem; Young's Bitter, Special, seasonal beers [H]
Superlative Young's pub characterised by low ceilings, oak beams, flagstone floors and many nooks and crannies to hide in. Food is served throughout the pub. Outside features a sunny patio and a large front garden with views over the Severn estuary. The pub produces cider from its own orchard at the rear. Young's seasonal and occasional guest beers complement the regular beers. ⛫Q♋❀◐◑♣●P⌐

Marshfield

Catherine Wheel

High Street, SN14 8LR (off A420 between Chippenham and Bristol)
⏲ 12-11 ☎ (01225) 892220 🌐 thecatherinewheel.co.uk
Courage Best Bitter; guest beers [H]
Beautifully restored Georgian-fronted pub on the village high street with a pretty dining room. An extensive main bar leads down from the original wood-panelled area, via stone-walled rooms, to the patio area at the rear. A superb open fire warms in winter. There are up to two local guest ales available, and imaginative and well-presented food is served in the bar or garden (no meals Sun eve). Children are allowed and free Wi-Fi is available. ⛫Q❀⌂◐◑▣(635)P⌐

May Hill

Glasshouse

GL17 0NN (off A40 W of Huntley) SO710213
⏲ 11.30-3, 6.30-11; 12-3 Sun ☎ (01452) 830529
Butcombe Bitter; Fuller's London Pride [G]
A sympathetic refurbishment using reclaimed timber and bricks means this extended pub blends in with its surroundings. Flagstone floors, nooks

and crannies and an old cooking range make this a very popular venue. A fine food menu complements the two real ales. An interesting feature is the historic yew hedge in the small car park – it is shaped into a hollow with its own seat cut into it. The safe, enclosed garden is ideal for families. ⚲Q❀◑▶P

Mayshill

New Inn ✔

Badminton Road, BS36 2NT (on A432 between Coalpit Heath and Nibley)

❂ 11.45-2.30, 6-10.30 (11 Wed-Fri); 12-11 Sat; 12-10 Sun

☎ (01454) 773161

Beer range varies ⊞

This 17th-century inn is hugely popular for its food, so book ahead. Expect one beer from the nearby Cotswold Spring Brewery and three changing guests from far and wide, one of them likely to be dark. The main bar is warmed by a real fire in winter, and the rear area is more of a restaurant. Children are welcome until 8.45pm. The garden is pleasant in summer. Generous beer discounts are available to CAMRA members on Sunday and Monday evenings. Local CAMRA Pub of the Year 2009. ⚲Q❀◑▶🚌(X42,342)P⁄–

Minchinhampton

Weighbridge Inn

Longfords, GL6 9AL (on road from Nailsworth to Avening near Longford Mill)

❂ 12-11 (10.30 Sun) ☎ (01453) 832520 🌐 2in1pub.co.uk

Uley Old Spot; Wadworth 6X; guest beer ⊞

The Weighbridge Inn is on the original packhorse trail to Bristol, which is now a footpath and bridleway. The road at the front of the inn became a turnpike in 1822, and the weighbridge served the local mills. Today the pub is known for its 2-in-1 pies. Inside there are many exposed beams and open logs fires to provide winter warmth. The guest beer is usually from a local brewery. Children and dogs are welcome. ⚲Q❀◑▶⊟♿●P

Moreton in Marsh

Inn on the Marsh

Stow Road, GL56 0DW (on A429 at S end of town)

❂ 12-2.30, 7-11; 11-3, 6-11 (Thu-Sat & summer); 12-3, 7-11 Sun ☎ (01608) 650709

Banks's Mild; Marston's Burton Bitter, Pedigree; guest beer ⊞

A charming Marston's pub that usually has an interesting house guest ale, often from Ringwood. Next to a duckpond, this former bakery has woven hanging baskets on display. The bar area has a dedicated locals' section and a welcoming lounge area with open fire and comfortable seating. The large conservatory serves up food with a Dutch East Indies influence and is ideal for parties. If you're lucky, the enthusiastic landlord may even play his guitar. ⚲Q❀◑▶♿Ⅹ⇌🚌♣●P⁄–

Nailsworth

Village Inn

The Cross, Fountain Street, GL6 0HH (on A46 at N end of town)

❂ 11-11 (midnight Thu-Sat); 12-10.30 Sun

☎ (01453) 835715 🌐 villageinn-nailsworth.co.uk

Nailsworth Artist's Ale, Mayor's Bitter, Town Crier, Vicar's Stout, seasonal beers; guest beers ⊞

The Village Inn, which reopened in late 2006 as the Nailsworth Brewery brew-pub, is unrecognisable from the inn that closed in the mid 1990s – truly an ugly duckling reborn as a swan. An intricate warren of rooms and spaces has been created with care and flair, where salvaged furniture combines with new joinery. Stroud CAMRA sub-Branch Pub of the Year 2008. ⚲Q◑▶⊟🚌(40,46)●⁄–

Nettleton Bottom

Golden Heart

GL4 8LA (on A417)

❂ 11-3, 5.30-11; 11-11 Fri & Sat; 12-10.30 Sun

☎ (01242) 870261 🌐 thegoldenheart.co.uk

Brakspear Bitter; Festival Gold; guest beers ⊞

This 300-year-old Cotswold free house stands beside a tricky section of the Swindon to Gloucester road. Little has changed here in a century and the large log fire, bare stone walls, mixed furniture and assorted mementos ooze rustic charm. The best locally sourced produce contributes to the national award winning food and children are fully catered for. To the rear, a large stone-paved patio and lawn abut a cow pasture. There are two en-suite guest bedrooms. ⚲Q❀⛌◑▶P⁄–

Newent

George

Church Street, GL18 1PU (off B4215 and B4216 opp church)

❂ 11-11 (midnight Fri & Sat); 12-10.30 Sun

☎ (01531) 820203 🌐 georgehotel.uk.com

Butcombe Bitter; Cottage Golden Arrow; Freeminer Bitter; guest beers ⊞

This mid-17th century hotel has a quiet bar at the front with settles and window seats and a central serving area. A dartboard, fruit machines and TV screens are located in the rear bar. The former coach house is now the restaurant. A beer festival is held in September to coincide with Newent Onion Fair. Accommodation comprises en-suite bedrooms and a two-bedroom mews flat. Local attractions include the National Birds of Prey Centre. ⚲❀⛌◑▶♿🚌♣●P⁄–

Oldbury on Severn

Anchor Inn

Church Road, BS35 1QA

❂ 11.30-2.30, 6.30-11; 11.30-11 Sat; 12-10.30 Sun

☎ (01454) 413331

Butcombe Bitter; Draught Bass; Otter Bitter; guest beer ⊞

Converted riverside mill with two bars and a restaurant. People come from afar for the food, which is served in all areas when busy. The lounge has an L-shaped bar, wooden beams and an open fire. The more spartan public bar is popular with locals. One guest beer is added on Thursdays until it runs out. The large enclosed garden to the rear has a boules piste and access to the river footpath. Children are welcome in the restaurant. ⚲Q❀◑▶⊟♣P⁄–

Quenington

Keepers Arms

Church Road, GL7 5BL (from Fairford turn right at village green)
⊙ 12-3 Wed-Sun; 7-11 Mon-Sun ☎ (01285) 750349
⊕ thekeepersarms.co.uk
Butcombe Bitter; St Austell Tribute 🄷
This previously basic village local has been given a fresh breath of life under its young, enthusiastic landlord and slowly transformed into a modern pub. The new wood of the counter and floor make an attractive combination in the refurbished bar. The other two rooms are used for dining (except for quiz nights), where fish dishes predominate (no food Mon & Tue eve). Two fireplaces give a pleasant glow in winter. The tiny front garden is popular with cyclists, ramblers and smokers alike. ♨❀⇌◑◐♣P

Shipton Moyne

Cat & Custard Pot

The Street, GL8 8PN (on Tetbury road)
⊙ 11-3, 6-11.30; 11.30-3, 6-11 Sun ☎ (01666) 880249
Taylor Landlord; Wadworth Henry's Original IPA, 6X; Wickwar BOB 🄷
Blessed with a unique pub sign, this pretty village pub is mainly open plan, showing where rooms have been opened out to cope with the increasing popularity of its food. The busy main bar can appear to be the hub of the local dog-walking society at times, while the quieter snug behind it is popular with families. The memorabilia on the walls reflect the equestrian bent of the clientele, while the origins of the unusual pub name are also explained. ♨Q❀◑◐♣P

Siddington

Greyhound Inn

Ashton Road, GL7 6HR (S edge of village on main road)
⊙ 11-3, 6-midnight; 11.30-midnight Sat & Sun
☎ (01285) 653573 ⊕ thegreyhound-inn.co.uk
Wadworth Henry's Original IPA, 6X, JCB, The Bishops Tipple, seasonal beer 🄷
A large, multi-roomed hostelry boasting copious amounts of flagstones and beams throughout, complete with roaring fire and exposed stonework. This old village local's reputation for good food fills the large front dining room, with the renowned Sunday carvery a highlight. An L-shaped counter and a new entrance link it to the public bar. The modern function room, which leads off, is wood-panelled. There is a deceptively large garden, which gets busy in summer and on festival weekends, and a small smoking shelter by the entrance. ♨❀◑◐⊟♣P⌐

Slad

Woolpack

GL6 7QA (on B4070)
⊙ 12-3, 5-11.30; 12-10.30 Sun ☎ (01452) 813429
⊕ thewoolpackinn-slad.com
Uley Bitter, Old Spot, Pig's Ear; guest beers 🄷
Popular village inn dating from the 16th century, which affords superb views over the Slad Valley. It achieved fame through the late Laurie Lee, author of Cider With Rosie, who was a regular customer. The building has been thoughtfully restored and the bar extends to each of the four rooms, with wooden settles in the end room, where children are permitted. One of the guest beers is usually from the Stroud Brewery and real cider and perry are also available. Dogs and walkers are welcome. ♨Q❀◑◐⊟♣●P⌐

Slimbridge

Tudor Arms

Shepherds Patch, GL2 7BP (from A38 1 mile beyond Slimbridge village)
⊙ 11-11; 12-10.30 Sun ☎ (01453) 890306
⊕ thetudorarms.co.uk
Uley Pig's Ear; Wadworth 6X; guest beers 🄷
A family owned and operated free house near the Wildfowl and Wetlands Trust site. Two bars and five dining areas are constantly being improved and excellent home-cooked food is available all day. Children are welcome. High-class accommodation is offered in the modern lodge alongside and there is a caravan and camping park behind. Four guest ales come from Wickwar, Palmers and local micros, and there is a range of ciders and perry. Winner of local CAMRA Country Pub of the Year 2007-10. ❀⇌◑◐⊟♿⛺♣●P⌐

Staple Hill

Staple Hill Oak ✔

84-86 High Street, BS16 5HN
⊙ 9am-11 (midnight Thu; 1am Fri & Sat) ☎ (0117) 9568543
Greene King Ruddles Best Bitter, Abbot; Marston's Pedigree; guest beers 🄷
A busy Wetherspoon pub in a Bristol suburb that offers a total of eight beers. Once a post office, it is a split-level open plan affair with a small outdoor patio at the rear. It was voted Wetherspoon's regional community pub of the year 2008-2009. Local history is the theme of the decor, with reference to a local preacher, Robert Bateman, who was the band leader on the ill-fated Titanic. The usual JDW food offering is available. ❀◑◐♿⊟(7,49)⌐

Stroud

Crown & Sceptre

98 Horns Road, GL5 1EG
⊙ 3 (12 Sat)-11; 12-10.30 Sun ☎ (01453) 762588
Stroud Budding; Uley Bitter, Old Spot; guest beers 🄷
A lively free house where customers are encouraged to suggest guest beers – Blue Anchor Spingo Middle is a favourite. The front bar has a log fire in winter; the back bar has TV with Sky Sports. The terrace at the rear has panoramic views over Stroud and there is a large garden with a children's area. Very tasty snacks are available. Traditional games include bar billiards and shove ha'penny. Stroud CAMRA Pub of the Year 2010. ♨❀◑⇌♣P⌐

Prince Albert ✔

Rodborough, GL5 3SS
⊙ 4.30 (5 Sat)-11.30 (12.30am Fri & Sat); 12-10.30 Sun
☎ (01453) 755600 ⊕ theprincealbertstroud.co.uk
Fuller's London Pride; Otter Bitter; Stroud Budding; guest beers 🄷
This lively, cosmopolitan, stone-built pub near Rodborough Common manages to be simultaneously bohemian and homely. It has an imaginative colour scheme and an eclectic mix of furniture and fittings, including chandeliers. Art

exhibitions and themed nights are held, including quizzes, backgammon, crib and scrabble, folk music, stand-up comedy, live bands and even political hustings. Children and dogs are welcome. Bar meals are served Thursday-Saturday. Sunday lunch is sourced from Stroud's award-winning farmers' market. There is free internet access and Wi-Fi. ♨◑➤♣⊱

Queen Victoria
5 Gloucester Street, GL5 1QG
✪ 11-11 (late Fri & Sat); 12-10.30 Sun ☎ (01453) 762396
Beer range varies Ⓗ
This imposing building formerly housed the Gloucester Street forge and records show that it was owned by the Nailsworth Brewery in 1891. The large single bar offers a varying range of at least four beers from micro-breweries. The community pub fields quiz, darts and pool teams in local leagues. Across the courtyard, the spacious function room holds a beer festival at least once a year and provides live music on Thursday, Friday and Saturday evenings. ♨✿⑤⇒◨♣●⊱

Tewkesbury

Olde Black Bear
68 High Street, GL20 5BH
✪ 11 (12 Sun)-11 ☎ (01684) 292202
Beer range varies Ⓗ
Set on the east bank of the Avon, this is an extended riverside pub with visitor moorings. A central bar area serves separate rooms. It is reputed to be the oldest pub in the county, with parts of the building dating back to 1308. The garden overlooks the Avon and St John's Bridge. There are several interesting parts of the building; the lower restaurant area was once the stables and was used as a hospital during the Wars of the Roses. ♨Q⇆✿◑⑤⚞▲◨⊱

Royal Hop Pole ✓
94 Church Street, GL20 5RS (between the Abbey and Cross)
✪ 7 (8 Sat & Sun)-11 ☎ (01684) 274039
Greene King IPA, Abbot; Marston's Pedigree; guest beers Ⓗ
This well-known landmark is an amalgamation of historic buildings from the 15th and 18th centuries. It has been known as the Royal Hop Pole since a visit in September 1891 from Princess Mary of Teck (Queen Mary, Royal Consort of George V), and was mentioned in The Pickwick Papers. It was purchased by JD Wetherspoon to join its list of lodges. It reopened in 2008, following a £4 million refurbishment. ♨Q⇆✿◨◑⚞▲◨●P⊱

White Bear
Bredon Road, GL20 5BU (N of High St)
✪ 10-11; 12-10.30 Sun ☎ (01684) 296614
Draught Bass; guest beers Ⓗ
Family-run free house on the edge of the town centre, close to the river and marina. A multi-space bar, which was completely renovated following the floods of 2007, provides four handpumps with a range of guest beers plus local ciders. Darts, skittles and pool all feature here. A separate skittle alley can double as a function room. There is a small library, which includes children's books. Live music is performed most Sunday afternoons. Dogs welcome. ✿⚞▲◨♣●P⊱⊟

Thornbury

Anchor
Gloucester Road, Lower Morton, BS35 1JY
✪ 12-11 ☎ (01454) 281375
Draught Bass; guest beers Ⓗ
Licensed since 1695, this is the second oldest inn in Thornbury. Dogs are welcome in the public bar, which was the original pub, and also houses darts and dominoes teams. The more recent lounge includes the dining area, offering locally sourced home-cooked food. Daily specials and home made pies are popular. The garden includes a boules piste and children's play area. There are up to four guest beers, and it is the base for a newly formed CAMRA sub-Branch – new members welcome. ♨Q✿◑⚞♣P⊱

Tytherington

Swan Inn ✓
Duck Street, GL12 8QB (1 mile E of A38 between Falfield and Almondesbury)
✪ 12-2.30 (not Mon winter), 6-11; 12-10.30 (6 winter) Sun ☎ (01454) 412280 ⊕ swan-inn.com
Bath Ales Gem; Fuller's London Pride; guest beer Ⓗ
A 16th-century coaching inn situated in this quaint village, near to the A38 and junction 14 of the M5. Its friendly, welcoming atmosphere is enhanced by the low ceilings and two wood-burning inglenook fireplaces in the main bar. The pub has a reputation for food, which is freshly cooked and mainly sourced locally. The separate Village Bar has a dartboard and table games. There is a large function room, a spacious child-friendly garden with umbrellas and an extensive car park. ♨✿◑⚞⚞♣P⊱

Uley

Old Crown
The Green, GL11 5SN (at top end of village)
✪ 12-11 ☎ (01453) 860502
Uley Bitter, Pig's Ear; guest beers Ⓗ
An attractive 17th-century whitewashed coaching inn situated in the pretty village of Uley on the edge of the Cotswold Way. The pub has a pleasant walled garden and, besides being the village local, is also popular with passing walkers. The low-beamed single bar has a welcoming fire. Its beers are sourced mainly from micro-breweries. The pub offers four en-suite double bedrooms and food is served lunchtimes and evenings. There is a covered smoking area. ♨Q✿⚞◑♣P⊱

Whitecroft

Miners Arms
The Bay, GL15 4PE (on B4234 near railway crossing) SO619062
✪ 12-11 (10.30 Sun) ☎ (01594) 562483
⊕ minersarmswhitecroft.org
Banks's Mild; guest beer Ⓗ
A CAMRA winner of a beer and national cider award in 2005, this village pub offers a wide range of ales and a fine selection of good food. The skittle alley doubles as a blues music venue once a month. There is a sound structure for smokers in the back garden, from which you can hear the steam trains passing on the Dean Forest Railway. ♨✿⚞◑⚞⇒♣●P⊱

Whitminster

Old Forge Inn ✓

GL2 7NP (on A38, close to M5 jct 13)
✪ 12-11 (midnight Thu-Sat); 12-10.30 Sun
☎ (01452) 741306
Butcombe Bitter; Greene King IPA; guest beer Ⓗ
Most of this listed wood-framed building with mixed window styles dates from the 17th century. Oak beamed ceilings, carpeting and smart furniture create a homely atmosphere, enhanced by the landlady's personality, her aquariums, brasses and collection of over 500 commemorative spoons. Substantial meals are served lunchtimes and evenings (not Mon winter) and all day at weekends. A patio offers outdoor games and heated cover for smokers. There is bungalow accommodation for up to four. Q❀⇌◑▲⊟♣P⁵⁄

Winterbourne Down

Cross Hands

85 Down Road, BS36 1BZ
✪ 12-11 ☎ (01454) 850077
Courage Best Bitter; guest beers Ⓗ
Friendly 17th-century stone-built village free house with a spacious main bar, snug and an alcove used by local darts players. Old sewing machines feature as decoration, together with an interesting selection of old pump clips on a dummy beer engine near the entrance. The large rear garden includes a children's play area and a heated smoking shelter. A daytime bus service operates to nearby Hicks Common and the Frome Valley walkway is close. Three guest beers often include Taylor Landlord, and Thatchers and Taunton ciders are stocked. ♨❀♣●⁵⁄

Woodchester

Ram Inn

Station Road, GL5 5EQ (signed from A46)
✪ 11-11; 12-10.30 Sun ☎ (01453) 873329
Butcombe Bitter, Gold; Stroud Budding, Organic; Uley Old Spot; guest beers Ⓗ
The inn is more than 400 years old and stands in superb walking country near Woodchester Mansion. This is a dog-friendly village local which stocks an excellent range of ales, including those from the local Nailsworth or Stroud breweries. The food is highly recommended. There is good wheelchair access. The pub is a regular venue for the Stroud Morris Men.
♨Q❀◑◑⊟♿⊟(40,46)♣P⁵⁄

Woolaston Common

Rising Sun

GL15 6NU (1 mile off A48 at Woolaston) SO590009
✪ 12-2.30, 6.30-11.30; 12-3, 6.30-midnight Sat; 12-3, 7-11 Sun ☎ (01594) 529282
Butcombe Bitter; Wye Valley Bitter; guest beers Ⓗ
This 350-year-old stone-built pub has a cosy snug and main bar area. There are spectacular views over the Forest of Dean from the front of the pub. It is popular with walkers, as it lies on the circular pub walks of the forest. Good home-cooked food is available and, together with the well-kept real ales, makes it a pub worth finding. No food on Monday. ♨Q❀◑◑P

Wotton-under-Edge

Star Inn

21 Market Street, GL12 7AE (close to local museum and free car park at top of town)
✪ 12-11 (midnight Fri & Sat) ☎ (01453) 844651
Butcombe Bitter; Wickwar Coopers WPA; guest beer Ⓗ
Situated at the top of a historic town on the Cotswold Way, this comfortable 16th-century two-bar pub has an exposed Cotswold stone interior. It contains memorabilia of the White Star Line, famous for the ill-fated Titanic; John Cambridge, who started the company, was born in the pub in 1784. Major sporting events can be watched in the public bar or a quiet pint can be enjoyed in the lounge. It has a function room that is used for community events. Q☕❀◑⊟♿⊟●⁵⁄

Old Spot, Dursley (Photo: Roger Protz)

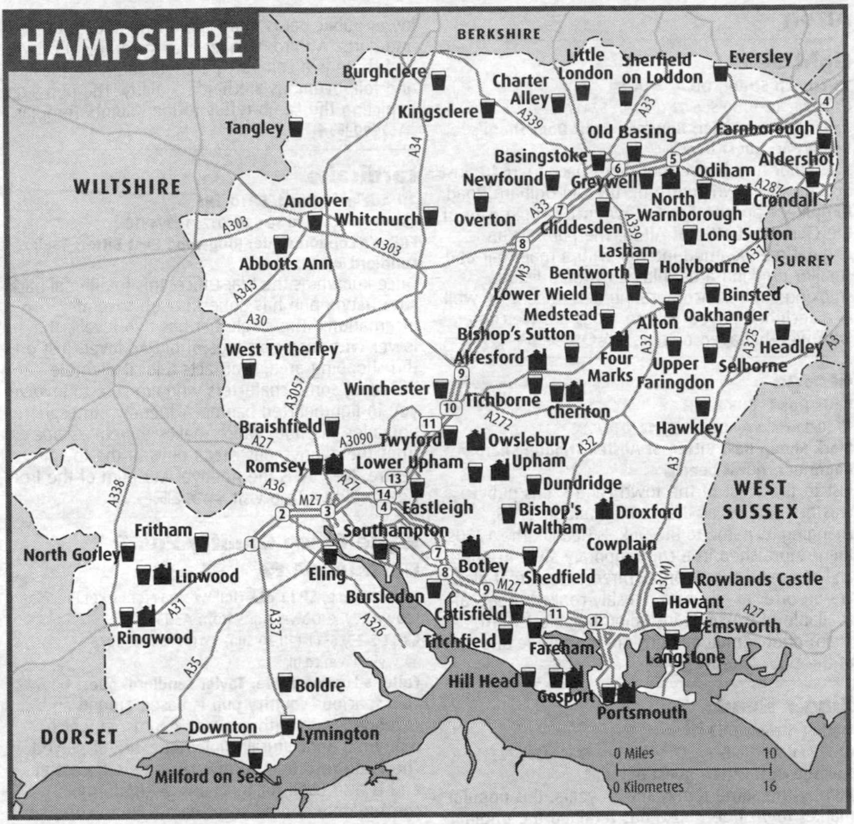

NOTE: Gale's Brewery has been bought and closed by Fuller's. The beers are now brewed in London at Fuller's Chiswick brewery. When a Guide entry serves only Gale's beer we list the beers as shown on pumpclips i.e. Gale's HSB, rather than Fuller's Gale's HSB. Please see Fuller's entry in the Independent Breweries section. Please note that Ringwood is now owned by Marston's – see New Nationals section.

Abbotts Ann

Eagle 🏆

Red Rice Road, SP11 7BG SU328435
⏲ 11.30-11; 12-10.30 Sun ☎ (01264) 710339
🌐 eagleabbottsann.co.uk
Skinner's Betty Stogs; guest beers Ⓗ
A superb village pub, two miles south-west of Andover, at the heart of the community. Similarly, real ale is at the heart of the pub – the regular Betty Stogs is supplemented by three changing southern and south-western guests, plus four ciders, on handpump. The public bar features a pool table and there is a skittle alley at the back of the pub. Note that food is not available Tuesday or Sunday evenings. ⛰Q❀◑◗⊟🚌(77,87)♣🍎P⚡

Aldershot

Garden Gate

Church Lane East, GU11 3BT
⏲ 5-midnight; 3-1am Fri; 12.30-1am Sat; 12-10 Sun
☎ (01252) 321051 🌐 gardengatepub.com

> What care I how time advances: I am drinking ale today. **Edgar Allan Poe**

Greene King IPA, Abbot, seasonal beer Ⓗ
Cosy and friendly local pub with one bar divided into two areas. Good value food is served and B&B offered in two en-suite rooms. A covered smoking area is provided with a sheltered garden to the side. Entertainment includes quiz night on Thursday, blue-grass music on the first Monday of the month, folk nights, and jazz on the last Sunday of the month. There is a piano and a dartboard, and a Sunday meal draw. ❀⛟◗≠🚌♣⚡

White Lion

20 Lower Farnham Road, GU12 4EA (200m from A331/A323 jct)
⏲ 1-11 (10.30 Mon; midnight Fri); 12-midnight Sat; 12-10.30 Sun ☎ (01252) 323832
Triple fff Alton's Pride, Pressed Rat & Warthog, Moondance, seasonal beers; guest beers Ⓗ
Genuine, small, two-bar locals' pub a mile east of the town. The publican's enthusiasm for scooters is evident in the various displays, while substantial bar stools complement the no-nonsense plain wooden tables and church pews. Open mike night is every other Thursday, quiz night is Monday and live music plays on some Saturdays. There are board games, and pizza snacks are available at all times. ⛰Q❀⊟🚌(3,20)♣⚡

Alton

Eight Bells

33 Church Street, GU34 2DA
⏲ 11-11; 12-10.30 Sun ☎ (01420) 82417
Ballard's Best Bitter; Bowman Swift One; Sharp's Doom Bar; guest beers Ⓗ
A popular free house that dates back to 1640, just outside the town centre on the Old Odiham Road turnpike. Opposite lies St Lawrence Church, site of the Civil War Battle of Alton. The pub has an original oak-beamed interior with a main bar and smaller drinking area, plus a restored listed smoking shelter incorporating a 17th-century well in a secluded paved garden. Dogs are welcome with well-behaved owners. ♨Q❀⇌🚌⚡

George

Butts Road, GU34 1LH
⏲ 10-11 (midnight Thu-Sat) ☎ (01420) 82331
Black Sheep Best Bitter; St Austell Tribute; Sharp's Doom Bar; guest beer Ⓗ
Just to the west of the town centre, this pub was first known as the Cumberland in 1745, changing its name to the Duke's Head in the 1750s, then refurbished in a contemporary style in 2008 and renamed the George. Three or four real ales are on offer at all times. Freshly cooked meals are available all sessions including breakfast from 10am-noon. Small gardens are at the side and rear of the pub. ♨❀◐♿🚌P⚡

King's Head

Market Street, GU34 1HA
⏲ 10 (11 Mon-Thu)-11; 12-10.30 Sun ☎ (01420) 82313
Courage Best Bitter; guest beers Ⓗ
Run by the same family for 26 years, this popular market town free house has retained the original two-bar layout. The ever-popular Courage Best is complemented by two guest beers, often from local breweries; recommendations from customers are welcome. Dominoes, darts and shove ha'penny are played and the pub regularly participates in local charity and sporting events. No food is served on Sunday. Well-behaved dogs are welcome. ❀◑⊟⇌🚌♣⚡

Railway Arms

26 Anstey Road, GU34 2RB
⏲ 12-11; 11-midnight Fri & Sat ☎ (01420) 82218
Triple fff Alton's Pride, Pressed Rat and Warthog, Moondance, Stairway, seasonal beers; guest beers Ⓗ
Friendly pub close to the Watercress Line and mainline station, owned by Triple fff Brewery, whose own beers are supplemented by ales from a host of micros. The extension at the rear has its own bar and is available for hire. The patio area, designed with a traditional railway theme, is ideal for barbecues and incorporates a covered, heated smoking area. There are tables outside the front of the pub, under a striking sculpture of a steam locomotive. Q❀⇌🚌♣⚡

Andover

Lamb Inn

21 Winchester Street, SP10 2EA (opp police station)
⏲ 12-2.30 (not Tue), 6-11 (midnight Thu; 1am Fri & Sat); 12-2.30, 7-11 Sun ☎ (01264) 323961
Wadworth Henry's IPA, 6X; guest beer Ⓗ
A traditional pub dating from the 1600s on the edge of the main shopping area. The small lounge retains a cosy and homely atmosphere, while the lower public bar is more sports oriented, with pool and darts. A third, smaller area separates the two, and there is a compact patio outside. Live music and folk evenings are held regularly. The pub sign depicting the Lamb refers to the Knights Templar. ♨Q❀⊟🚌♣

Lardicake

19 Adelaide Road, SP10 1HF
⏲ 11-11; 12-10.30 Sun ☎ (01264) 394810
Fuller's London Pride; Ringwood Best Bitter; Taylor Landlord Ⓗ
Once known as the War Office, this traditional back street-style pub has gone through several incarnations. The single bar has two levels, the lower with many pictures of old Andover. Just off the shopping area, it attracts a local clientele including some characters who are sure to involve you in lighthearted banter. A friendly atmosphere pervades the pub, which makes a great escape from the anonymous circuit pubs of the town centre. Nearby is the Andover Museum of the Iron Age, well worth a visit. ♨❀⊟🚌⚡

Wyke Down Country Pub & Restaurant ✔

Picket Piece, SP11 6LX (follow signs for Picket Piece and brown Wyke Down signs from A303)
⏲ 12-2.30, 6-11 (10.30 Sun) ☎ (01264) 352048
🌐 wykedown.co.uk
Fuller's London Pride; Taylor Landlord; guest beer Ⓗ
This spacious country pub is based around an extended barn with exposed beams, in which many old agricultural implements are displayed. The large restaurant draws customers from afar and is also used for functions. A comfortable conservatory and adjacent games room complete the facilities in the main building. Outside there is a campsite, children's play area, golf driving range and swimming pool. Various annual events take place in the grounds, from transport rallies to cycling activities. ♨🛏❀◐▲♣P⚡

Basingstoke

Basingstoke Sports & Social Club ✔

Mays Bounty, Fairfields Road, RG21 3DR
⏲ 12-3, 5-11; 12-11 Fri & Sat; 12-10.30 Sun
☎ (01256) 331646 🌐 basingstoke-sports-club.co.uk
Adnams Bitter; Fuller's London Pride; Gale's Seafarers Ale, HSB; guest beers Ⓗ
The club is home to cricket, rugby, football and hockey clubs as well as providing squash courts. County cricket week attracts large crowds in the

INDEPENDENT BREWERIES

Andwell North Warnborough
Botley Botley (NEW)
Bowman Droxford
Crondall Crondall
Flack Manor Romsey (NEW)
Flowerpots Cheriton
Havant Cowplain
Hensting Owslebury (NEW)
Irving Portsmouth
Itchen Valley Alresford
Oakleaf Gosport
Red Shoot Linwood
Ringwood (Marston's) Ringwood
Triple fff Four Marks
Upham Upham (NEW)

summer. There is a widescreen TV in the bar dedicated to sports events. A full programme of social activities is held throughout the year, and the clubhouse and grounds are available for hire. CAMRA members with a current membership card are welcome. Opening hours are flexible when sporting fixtures are held. Fuller's Discovery is also sold in summer. ❀◑◗🚌P

Maidenhead Inn ✔

17 Winchester Street, RG21 7ED (top of town)
9-midnight (1am Fri & Sat) ☎ (01256) 316030
Greene King Ruddles Best Bitter, Abbot; guest beers H
This attractive Wetherspoon pub is situated in the historic Top of Town area, with five pumps to dispense local and guest ales. Local beers from Andwell, Loddon and Triple fff breweries regularly feature. A large dining area leads to the compact bar, with further seating to the rear over two levels, complemented by an outdoor heated beer garden. Q❀◑◗♿⇌🚌⊬

Queens Arms ✔

Bunnian Place, RG21 7JE (150m E of railway station)
11-11 (10.30 Sun) ☎ (01256) 465488
Courage Best Bitter; Sharp's Cornish Coaster; guest beers H
A welcoming beacon of excellence, the 'Queens' attracts a wide-ranging clientele of all ages from all walks of life. The choice of guest beers is imaginative and the turnaround is such that a free text alert service, tailored to customers' tastes, is available. Good value home-cooked food is available Monday-Friday 12-2pm and 5-9.30pm, Saturday 12-3pm, Sunday 12-4pm (no food Mon eve). During warmer weather the shady courtyard garden is a popular attraction. Q❀◑◗⇌🚌♣⊬

Way Inn

Chapel Hill, RG21 5TB (opp Holy Ghost church)
12-11 (10.30 Sun) ☎ (01256) 321520
Caledonian Deuchars IPA; Greene King Abbot; Taylor Landlord; guest beers H
This extensively refurbished pub provides a comfortable environment for the 20+ age group. It has a spacious family room and dining area at the rear with access to the large car park, outside patio and south-facing sun-drenched garden. There are no TVs or bar games but there is an on-line jukebox. The menus offer a wide range of home-cooked traditional food, available 12-2.30pm and 6-9pm, with a good vegetarian range. Guest beers are sourced via SIBA. ⌂❀◑◗♿⇌🚌P⊬

Bentworth

Star Inn

GU34 5RB SU666401
12-3.30, 5-11.30; 12-11.30 Fri-Sun ☎ (01420) 561224
star-inn.com
Fuller's London Pride; Palmers Copper Ale; guest beers H
Dating back to 1841, this friendly free house has a bar warmed by open fires and an adjacent restaurant offering freshly cooked meals at all sessions. A social hub for the village community, its staff provide an active social calendar, including Tuesday curry evening, live music on Friday and a blues jam session on Sunday evening. Visitors, especially walkers, are always welcome. Guest beers are from within Hampshire, and local bottled cider is available. ⌂❀◑◗🚌(28)♣P⊬

Binsted

Cedars

The Street, GU34 4PB SU772411
11.30-3, 6 (4.30 Fri)-11:30, 11.30-11.30 Sat; 12-11 Sun
☎ (01420) 22112 thecedarspub.co.uk
Courage Best Bitter; guest beers H
Country pub with a quiet and cosy bar area where customers can enjoy pub games, with many teams in local leagues. There is an extensive garden that children will love. Occasional musical events are held as well as an annual beer festival. A warm welcome is extended to walkers, cyclists and campers at this convivial, friendly community pub. Caravans are also permitted. ⌂Q❀◑◗Å♣P⊬

Bishop's Sutton

Ship Inn ✔

Main Road, SO24 0AQ (on B3047)
12-2.30 (not Mon), 6-11; 12-3, 7-10.30 Sun
☎ (01962) 732863
Palmers Copper Ale; guest beers H
This comfortable, genuine family-run free house has a split-level bar and a log fire providing a cosy, relaxing atmosphere. There are separate areas for pub games, families and dining, plus a restaurant. The food is home-cooked, with many daily specials on the board. Popular with walkers from the nearby St Swithun's Way, this pub is the hub of the village. The regular bus between Winchester and Alton stops outside, and the Watercress Line steam railway is nearby. ⌂Q❀◑◗🚌(64)♣P⊬

Bishop's Waltham

Bunch of Grapes

St Peter's Street, SO32 1AD (follow signs to church)
12-1.45, 6-10.30; 12-1.45 (closed eve) Sun
☎ (01489) 892935
Courage Best Bitter; Goddards Ale of Wight; guest beer G
In an ancient lane between the church and the town, this small, idiosyncratic pub feels like a private house. It has been a regular in the Guide for many years, dispensing superb beer and nowadays the landlord's equally excellent locally produced wine. Outside is a tranquil town garden; inside the bar is right for conversation. Note that the pub may close even earlier if trade is quiet, and that prices are high (a price list is posted outside). Q❀🚌♣

Boldre

Red Lion

Rope Hill, SO41 8NE (on Rope Hill/Boldre Lane crossroads)
11-3, 5.30-11; 12-4, 6-10.30 (12-10.30 Jul & Aug) Sun
☎ (01590) 673177 theredlionboldre.co.uk
Marston's Pedigree; Ringwood Best Bitter, Fortyniner; guest beer H
This 'proper' New Forest pub dates back to the 15th century, and now incorporates original stables and old cottages. The interior feels cosy, with low beams, log fires and authentic decor. The converted stables are decorated with tack. The food on the traditional menu is all sourced locally and home-cooked, and often includes game and seafood. Home-made puddings are delicious. An infrequent bus service stops outside - not evenings. ⌂Q❀🛏◑◗🚌(112)P⊬

Braishfield

Newport Inn

Newport Lane, SO51 0PL (lane opp red phone box) SU373249
⏲ 12-2.30 (not Mon), 6-11 (7-10.30 Sun) ☎ (01794) 368225
Fuller's London Pride, seasonal beers; Gale's Seafarers Ale, HSB Ⓗ
Run by the same family for nearly 70 years, this two-bar pub, hidden away down a country lane, attracts a loyal clientele from miles around. Visitors would be forgiven for thinking they had strayed into an earlier age. There is often a folk session on Thursday evening, and on Saturday night the landlady leads a singalong around the piano. The simple bar menu offers sandwiches or ploughman's (choose ham or cheese) and their quality is legendary. ♨Q❀⊟♣P

Burghclere

Carpenters Arms

Harts Lane, RG20 9JY (opp Sandham Memorial Chapel)
⏲ 11-11; 12-10.30 Sun ☎ (01635) 278251
Arkell's 3B Ⓖ**, Kingsdown Ale** Ⓗ
A pleasant Arkell's pub on the edge of the village opposite the National Trust Sandham Memorial Chapel. A welcoming rest stop for weary walkers, it is open all day, serving a good selection of food every lunchtime and Tuesday-Saturday evenings. The well-kept beers are occasionally joined by a seasonal ale. Dogs are welcome. There is accommodation available in the converted house next door. Real cider is available in summer only. ♨Q❀🛏◑◐🍎P⚟

Bursledon

Vine Inn

High Street, Old Bursledon, SO31 8DJ SU485092
⏲ 12-3 (Fri only), 5.30-11; 12-4, 7.30-10.30 Sun
☎ (023) 8040 3836
Greene King IPA, Abbot Ⓖ
Well-kept village pub where little has changed over the years, one exception being putting the beer back onto gravity – the handpumps are now just for show. Pottery and copper vessels hang from the wood-beamed ceilings and there are local photographs from the early 1900s; Bursledon station has changed beyond recognition since then. The pub has a good community spirit, especially on Sunday afternoons. It is easier to find walking from the station (though hilly!) than by driving. Dog-friendly. ♨❀🛏⇌♣P⚟

Catisfield

Limes at Catisfield

34 Catisfield Lane, PO15 5NN (200m from Highlands Road bus route)
⏲ 12-2.30 (not Tue & Wed), 5-11; 12-3, 7-11 Sat (10.30 Sun)
☎ (01329) 842926
Gale's HSB; Hop Back Summer Lightning; Ringwood Best Bitter, Fortyniner, Old Thumper; Sharp's Doom Bar Ⓗ
A large free house that has seen previous lives as a farmhouse and country club, and is now an active community pub with many clubs and societies using its facilities. It has a long public bar with darts and a pool table, and a small, quiet lounge bar with access to a function room. A friendly assortment of regulars is present most evenings and the bar can become busy when the petanque club is playing at home. Seasonal beers may be available, including Ringwood XXXX Porter during the winter months. ❀⊟🚌(26,28)♣P⚟

Charter Alley

White Hart

White Hart Lane, RG26 5QA (1 mile W of A340) SU593577
⏲ 12-2.30 (3 Sat), 7-11; 12-3, 7-10.30 Sun
☎ (01256) 850048 🌐 whitehartcharteralley.com
Palmers Best Bitter; Triple fff Alton's Pride; guest beers Ⓗ
The oldest building in the village, this was the place where folk used to natter, hence 'chatter alley' (Charter Alley). Oak beams and log fires enhance the welcoming atmosphere of the pub. The bar now houses six pumps and the range of beers is forever changing. Quality food is served in a very pleasant restaurant converted from the skittle alley. There is a lovely terraced garden where water features enhance a peaceful drink. En-suite guest rooms available. ♨Q❀🛏◑◐⊟♣P▯

Cheriton

Flower Pots

SO24 0QQ (½ mile N of A272 between Winchester and Petersfield) SU581283
⏲ 12-2.30 (3 Sat), 6-11; 12-3, 7-10.30 Sun
☎ (01962) 771318 🌐 flowerpots-inn.co.uk
Flowerpots Perridge Pale, Bitter, Goodens Gold, seasonal beers Ⓖ
Four-square, warm, 1820s red-brick pub with two separate bars, popular with walkers and cyclists. A large rear marquee provides welcome overflow space on busy days. Two outbuildings house the pub's famous 10-barrel brewery and four comfortable B&B rooms. All the brewery's current beers (usually at least three) are served directly from casks. Good, home-cooked food is available daily (except Sun eve), with Wednesday evening featuring curries from a Punjabi chef. Westons Old Rosie cider is available. ♨Q❀🛏◑◐⊟🍎P⚟

Cliddesden

Jolly Farmer

Farleigh Road, RG25 2JL (on B3046)
⏲ 12-11 (10.30 Sun) ☎ (01256) 473073
Beer range varies Ⓗ
Busy, listed village pub close to Basingstoke offering a selection of beers from the Punch Taverns list. A cider such as Westons Old Rosie is usually available from the cellar. The quieter second bar may be used by families when not reserved for functions. At the rear, a large garden provides a secluded area for a peaceful drink, with a heated, covered area (with table football) for cooler evenings. The kitchen closes at 4pm on Sunday. ☺❀◐♣🍎P⚟

Downton

Royal Oak

Christchurch Road, SO41 0LA (on A337 between New Milton and Everton)
⏲ 11-11; 12-10.30 Sun ☎ (01590) 642297
Ringwood Best Bitter, Fortyniner; guest beer Ⓗ

Originally a 19th-century roadside inn, now much extended. A large car park and patio with gently sloping path leads to the main entrance. The tasteful restaurant area has tiling, a wood and carpeted floor and a large, central fireplace. Comfortable seating for drinkers is adjacent to the bar, which sells three ales, including a local guest, with full tasting notes. Traditional family values and home-cooked specialities cater for all visitors. The outside bar features occasional live music in summer, and barbecues are held.
⛰Q❀◑♿▲♣P⁵–

Dundridge

Hampshire Bowman

Dundridge Lane, Bishop's Waltham, SO32 1GD (1½ miles E of B3035) SU578184
⚙ 12-11 (10.30 Sun) ☎ (01489) 892940
🌐 hampshirebowman.com
Bowman Swift One, Wallops Wood, Quiver; Palmers 200; guest beers Ⓖ
Situated in an idyllic spot and catering for almost everyone, the old front bar retains its charm and leads to a larger extension, mainly used by diners enjoying the excellent food; families are welcome here until 9pm. Outside, the patio and large garden is a perfect place to pass summer days. In winter the pub has three real fires and in the summer real cider. Camping is available by prior arrangement, and there is disabled access by the rear patio. An annual sardine race is held in July.
⛰Q❀◑♿▲♣●P

Eastleigh

Wagon Works ✔

28 Southampton Road, SO50 9FJ (opp station)
⚙ 9-11 (midnight Fri & Sat) ☎ (023) 8062 2670
Greene King Ruddles Best Bitter, Abbot; Marston's Pedigree; guest beers Ⓗ
Pleasant, late-Victorian architecture with gables, curiously displaying differing 1887 and 1890 building dates. Originally the Home Tavern, the town's commercial hotel, it is now Eastleigh's first Wetherspoon pub, renamed to reflect the historic railway connections. On the small side for a typical Wetherspoon, it can get quite busy. Not obvious on entering, the beer pumps are in two banks of five. Guest ales frequently come from Hampshire breweries such as Itchen Valley and Oakleaf, and Westons real cider is sometimes available.
❀◑♿⇌🚌⁵–

Eling

King Rufus ✔

Eling Hill, SO40 9HE (400m S of tide mill) SU368121
⚙ 11-2.30, 6-11; 12-10.30 Sun ☎ (023) 8086 8899
Ringwood Best Bitter; guest beers Ⓗ
Single-bar Victorian pub with two separate drinking areas; interesting Victoriana adorns the walls and assorted bar games are available. It has a small, intimate dining room serving a varied range of food including vegetarian options and OAP Specials (no food Sun and Mon eves). There are usually three guest beers. The child-friendly garden has a petanque terrain. The pub is close to the UK's only working tide mill and convenient for the New Forest National Park. Dog-friendly.
⛰Q❀◑♿🚌(8,9,56)♣P⁵–

Emsworth

Coal Exchange ✔

21 South Street, PO10 7EG
⚙ 10.30-3, 5.30-11; 10.30-midnight Fri & Sat; 12-11 Sun
☎ (01243) 375866 🌐 thecoalexchange-emsworth.co.uk
Fuller's London Pride, seasonal beers; Gale's Seafarers Ale, HSB; guest beers Ⓗ
An unusual (for an ex-Gale's pub) green-tiled building set a short walk from Emsworth harbour. The single L-shaped bar is decorated with local photographs and charts. The pub began life as a pork butchery and ale house, and saw commerce as it became a place for locals to trade their produce with coal delivered by sea – hence the name. The award-winning lunchtime food is complemented by curry night on Tuesday and Thursday international evenings – an early arrival for these is recommended. ⛰❀◐⇌🚌(700)♣⁵–

Eversley

Golden Pot

Reading Road, RG27 0NB SU788617
⚙ 11.30-3, 6-11; 12-4 Sun ☎ (0118) 9732104
🌐 golden-pot.co.uk
Beer range varies Ⓗ
First-time Guide entrant, the interior has been broken up into numerous interconnected areas of various sizes, allowing people to form their own groups and creating a cosy atmosphere. The landlord recently bought the freehold from Greene King, and maintains three changing ales, frequently consulting his regulars as to choice, with at least one LocAle beer usually on. The pub has an excellent reputation for food. There are two outdoor areas – the Snug at the front and the Vineyard at the back. Q❀◑🚌(82)P

White Hart

Reading Road, RG27 0PJ SU774662
⚙ 12-11 (midnight Sat; 10.30 Sun) ☎ (0118) 9732817
Courage Best Bitter; Fuller's London Pride; guest beers Ⓗ
Dating from the 17th century, this is a traditional little country pub, with low oak-beamed ceilings and blazing log fires in winter. Guest beers are often from local breweries such as Andwell or Loddon. The simple furnishings are in keeping with the rural setting; the later extension at the back has a dartboard and TV, with an emphasis on rugby, as the pub is home to the internationally renowned White Hart Marauders seven-a-side team. Occasional live bands play on Saturday.
⛰Q◐◻♣P⁵–

Fareham

Crown ✔

40 West Street, PO16 0JW
⚙ 9am-midnight (1am Fri & Sat) ☎ (01329) 241750
Greene King Ruddles Best Bitter, Abbot; guest beers Ⓗ
A delightful, popular pub with character and an interesting history. From 1841 to 1911 this was the home of the Crown Brewery. After the closure of the brewery the pub remained as the Crown Inn, and Wetherspoon took over in 2009. Two regular ales are offered, with three changing guest beers from small local independents. Choice expands during occasional beer festivals. The pub opens for breakfast from 9am, with plans to open earlier for local business trade. Q❀◑♿⇌🚌🛈

Lord Arthur Lee ✔

100-108 West Street, PO16 0EP
⏲ 9-11 (midnight Fri & Sat) ☎ (01329) 280447
Greene King IPA, Abbot; Marston's Pedigree; guest beers Ⓗ
Popular with office workers and shoppers, this spacious Wetherspoon's pub is near the town centre, bus and train station. The walls are lined with photographs and historic details of the pub's namesake and other local figures. It has a separate family area often popular at lunchtimes. Three regular ales and up to five guest beers are offered, mainly selected from small independent breweries; occasional beer festivals offer increased choice. The usual range of food is available all day including breakfast. ❀◐◑♿⇌🚌⌐

Farnborough

Prince of Wales 🏆 ✔

184 Rectory Road, GU14 8AL
⏲ 11.30-2.30, 5.30-11; 11.30-11 Fri & Sat; 12-10.30 Sun
☎ (01252) 545578
Dark Star Hophead; Fuller's London Pride; Hop Back Summer Lightning; Ringwood Fortyniner; Young's Bitter; guest beers Ⓗ
The landlord celebrated 25 years at this hugely popular free house with his hostelry winning CAMRA Wessex Regional Pub of the Year. It is a traditional pub with a single bar surrounded by separate drinking areas, and a covered patio outside. Up to 10 beers are on handpump, with guests to be found in the snug. Ales from local breweries such as Ascot are often available. May is Mild Month and strong, warming ales are sold around Christmas. Good value lunches are served Monday to Saturday. ❀◐⇌(North)🚌(73)P⌐

Fritham

Royal Oak ✔

SO43 7HJ (1 mile S of B3078) SU232141
⏲ 11.30-2.30 (3 summer), 6-11; 11-11 Sat; 12-10.30 Sun
☎ (023) 8081 2606
Bowman Wallops Wood; Hop Back Summer Lightning; Ringwood Best Bitter, Fortyniner; guest beers Ⓖ
Thatched gem at the end of a New Forest track. The main bar leads to several interconnected areas featuring low beams and doors, colour-washed walls, log fires and wooden floors, all served via a hatchway. Guest ales are always from small local brewers; the house beer Royal Oak is Wallops Wood. Simple but excellent food includes local cheeses. The vast garden has plenty of picnic tables and hosts barbecues, hog roasts and occasional beer festivals. A perfect welcome awaits walkers, cyclists and equestrians (facilities provided); dogs abound. ♔Q❀◐▲

Gosport

Queen's Hotel

143 Queen's Road, PO12 1LG
⏲ 11.30-2.30 (Fri only), 5-11; 11.30-11 Sat; 12-3, 7-10.30 Sun
☎ (023) 9258 2645
Ringwood Fortyniner; Young's Bitter; guest beers Ⓗ
This award-winning back-street locals' pub has a nationwide reputation, with over 25 consecutive entries in this Guide. Three guest beers are normally available from Waverley. Fuller's ESB appears quite often in the winter months and real cider in summer. A regular beer festival takes place in October. Snacks are served Friday lunchtimes, and weekend opening times are often extended by up to half an hour. ♔❀🚌♣●⌐

Greywell

Fox & Goose

The Street, RG29 1BY (E end of village) SU 721518
⏲ 11-11; 12-10.30 Sun ☎ (01256) 702062
🌐 foxandgoosegreywell.co.uk
Courage Best Bitter Ⓗ
Sixteenth-century inn set in a picturesque village, a short distance from the Basingstoke Canal and King John's Castle from where he rode to Runnymede to seal the Magna Carta in 1215. An ideal stop-off for local walkers, there is a large field behind the pub used for various events. No food is served Sunday or Monday evening or Tuesday evening in winter. ♔Q❀◐◑P⌐

Havant

Old House At Home ✔

2 South Street, PO9 1DA
⏲ 11-11 (11.30 Fri & Sat); 12-10.30 Sun ☎ (023) 9248 3464
Fuller's Chiswick Bitter, London Pride, ESB; Gale's HSB Ⓗ
About 200 years after the date 1339 marked on the outside of the building, this pub started life as five cottages built from timber recovered from the Spanish Armada. Along with the neighbouring church it survived a fire in 1760 and was then converted into a bakery – the remains of the oven can be seen in the lounge. Later it became a comfortable two-bar pub. It is reputed to have shown the last dancing bear in England. ♔❀◐⊟⇌🚌♣⌐

Hawkley

Hawkley Inn

Pococks Lane, GU33 6NE SU747291
⏲ 12-3, 5.30-11; 12-11 Sat; 12-10.30 Sun ☎ (01730) 827205
🌐 hawkleyinn.co.uk
Beer range varies Ⓗ
Comfortable but basic three-room village pub with a veranda at the front. A genuine free house, depending on the time of year, it offers between five and nine beers on draught, mainly from small breweries. Locally-sourced fresh produce is used for the interesting menu. At least one cider is available from local producer Mr Whiteheads. Outside is a large secure garden. Local CAMRA Pub of the Year 2008. ♔Q❀⇄◐◑●

Headley

Holly Bush ✔

High Street, GU35 8PP
⏲ 11.30-11; 12-10.30 Sun ☎ (01428) 712211
Greene King Old Speckled Hen; St Austell Tribute; Sharp's Doom Bar; guest beers Ⓗ
The building dates from the early 19th century and is largely unchanged from the 1911 photograph displayed inside. There is plenty of comfortable seating and two working ornate tiled iron fireplaces. Behind and to the sides of the single bar are several pleasant dining areas, each with two or three tables. On the bar are six handpumps, three each for regular beers and changing guest ales. Food is available every lunchtime and Tuesday-Saturday evenings. ♔Q❀◐◑♿▲🚌(18)♣P⌐

Hill Head

Crofton

48 Crofton Lane, PO14 3QF
⌚ 11-11; 12-10.30 Sun ☎ (01329) 314222
🌐 thecroftonpub.co.uk
Sharp's Doom Bar; guest beers Ⓗ
This modern estate pub is situated in a housing area not far from the sea. Five guest beers are usually available, with beers from SIBA breweries in addition to those from the Punch Taverns portfolio. Oakleaf Hole Hearted appears regularly. The function room has a skittle alley where special events are held, including a beer festival in October. Home-cooked food is served all day at weekends, and real cider is available in summer.
♨Q❀◐◑⊟♿🚌(33,35)♣●P⚟

Holybourne

Queen's Head

20 London Road, GU34 4EG
⌚ 12-11 (11.30 Thu; 12.30am Fri & Sat); 12-10.30 Sun
☎ (01420) 86331
Greene King IPA; guest beers Ⓗ
This traditional and friendly pub highlights the best of Greene King, featuring a flexible and interesting guest beer list. The Queen's comprises two rooms plus a new extension and covered smoking area. Hearty food, served Thursday to Saturday, features local produce. Regular live music events take place throughout the year. The extensive garden features a children's play area. Alton Station is a 15-minute walk. Q❀◐◑⊟♿🚌(X65)♣P⚟

Kingsclere

Swan Hotel

Swan Street, RG20 5PP
⌚ 11-3, 5.30 (6 Sat)-11 (11.30 Fri & Sat); 12-3.30, 7-10.30 Sun ☎ (01635) 298314 🌐 swankingsclere.co.uk
Theakston XB; Young's Bitter; guest beer Ⓗ
Traditional inn frequented by an eclectic mix of customers, serving four beers including two frequently changing local guests. The 400-year-old pub is one of the county's oldest coaching inns, dating from 1449 and associated with the Bishop of Winchester for 300 years. The Grade II-listed building, close to the Watership Down beauty spot, retains original oak beams and fireplaces and offers nine en-suite bedrooms. Good food is served in both the dining room and the bar (no food Sun).
♨Q❀🛏◐◑🚌(32,32A)♣⚟

Langstone

Ship Inn ✔

Langstone Road, PO9 1RD
⌚ 11-11; 12-10.30 Sun ☎ (023) 9247 1719
Fuller's Discovery, London Pride; Gale's Seafarers Ale, HSB Ⓗ
An imposing building located next to the bridge to Hayling Island, this pub is an ideal spot to relax in after a walk along the coastal path or the track of the much-missed railway line from Havant. The remains of the railway swing bridge can still be seen but the site of the old train ferry berth is hard to locate. In addition to excellent beer, the meals are of very high quality, with seafood a prominent feature. ♨❀◐◑♿⛺🚌(30,31)P⚟

Lasham

Gliding Club

Lasham Airfield, GU34 5SS (signed from A339)
SU677438
⌚ 12-2, 5.30-11; 12-11 Sat, Sun & summer)
☎ (01256) 384900
Sharp's Doom Bar; guest beer Ⓗ
This club has a friendly, comfortable lounge bar and an excellent restaurant with a resident chef. Check in advance for availability of evening meals. It is open to the public at all times and children are welcome. An extensive patio area is a good place to enjoy your pint while watching the aircraft. The club holds a mini beer festival every Easter. Voted local CAMRA Club of the Year 2007-2009 and Wessex Regional Club of the Year 2009. ❀◐◑♿P⚟

Royal Oak ✔

GU34 5SJ (off A339 between Alton and Basingstoke)
SU676425
⌚ 12-11 (10.30 Sun) ☎ (01256) 381213 🌐 royaloak.uk.com
Gale's HSB; Ringwood Best Bitter; Triple fff Moondance; guest beers Ⓗ
Situated in the centre of a quiet village next to Lasham Airfield, well known for its gliding club, the pub is more than 200 years old and has two bars. Food is served lunchtimes and evenings (not Mon), all day on Sunday. A regular Monday quiz or bingo night is held and live music features occasionally. The pub is very popular with ramblers and cyclists. There is a large garden and children are welcome.
♨Q❀◐◑⊟🚌(28)♣P⚟

Linwood

Red Shoot ✔

Tom's Lane, BH24 3QT (4 miles NE of Ringwood, on unclassified road) SU187094
⌚ 11-11 ☎ (01425) 475792 🌐 redshoot.co.uk
Red Shoot New Forest Gold, Muddy Boot, Tom's Tipple; Wadworth Henry's IPA, 6X Ⓗ
This welcoming brew-pub for Red Shoot Brewery, along with its neighbouring campsite, provides a useful base for exploring the northern New Forest. Live music every Sunday and a quiz each Thursday provide entertainment for both locals and visitors. Two beer festivals in April and October and a cider festival in June add to the fun. Excellent food in generous portions is available every day, although food times are reduced on weekdays in winter. The pub welcomes children and dogs.
♨ᗢ❀◐◑♿⛺P⚟

Little London

Plough Inn

Silchester Road, RG26 5EP (1 mile off A340, S of Tadley)
⌚ 12-2.30 (3 Sat), 5.30 (6 Sat)-11; 12-3, 7-10.30 Sun
☎ (01256) 850628
Palmers Best Bitter; Ringwood Best Bitter Ⓗ**; guest beers** Ⓖ
Wonderful village pub where in winter you can enjoy a glass of beer in front of one of the log fires or play a game of bar billiards instead. Live music is on the second Tuesday of the month, quiz night the third Monday of the month. A good range of baguettes is available (not Sun eve). There is a secluded garden at the side of the pub. It is ideal for ramblers and cyclists visiting the Roman ruins at nearby Silchester or Pamber wood.
♨Qᗢ❀🚌(44)♣P⚟

Long Sutton

Four Horseshoes

RG29 1TA (off B3349, 1 mile E of village centre)
SU748471
12-2.30 (not Mon & Tue), 6.30-11; 12-2.30 (closed eve) Sun ☎ (01256) 862488 fourhorseshoes.com
Beer range varies H
This friendly local has a single bar divided by a fireplace. A small enclosed veranda offers fine views. Home-cooked meals are tasty and reasonably priced. Up to three beers may be available, usually one under 4% ABV. The second and fourth Tuesdays of the month are jazz nights, and the fourth Thursday is quiz night. Take-home real ale is only £1 a pint. There are just a few buses a day (not Sat) – check carefully. Accommodation is available and there is a grassed area for camping (enquire in advance). (201)P

Lower Upham

Woodman

Winchester Road, SO32 1HA (on B2177, by B3037 jct)
SU525194
12-2.30, 7.15 (6.15 Sat)-11; 12-2.30, 6.15-11 Sun
☎ (01489) 860270
Beer range varies H
A 17th-century pub, recently changed to a free house. The landlord has lived here for more than five decades. A cosy lounge and a friendly public bar serve two or three continuously changing real ales (usually one local), plus a choice of over 150 whiskies. Sandwiches and ploughman's are normally available at lunchtimes. Events include Sausage Saturday in March, a mini beer festival on the nearest Saturday to St George's Day, and live blues on the first Wednesday of each month.
(69)P

Lower Wield

Yew Tree

SO24 9RX SU 637308
closed Mon; 12-3, 6-11; 12-10.30 Sun ☎ (01256) 389224
the-yewtree.org.uk
Triple fff Alton's Pride; guest beer H
Out-of-the-way rural local set in picturesque rolling Hampshire countryside, with an old yew tree growing outside (hence the name), situated on a quiet country lane opposite the local cricket pitch. The house beer is Alton's Pride and the guest comes from a local brewery. The pub has a separate dining area and is a winner of a Good Food Award for 2010. The nearest bus stop is Medstead on route 28, Basingstoke-Alton, 1½ miles away. P

Lymington

Borough Arms

39 Avenue Road, SO41 9GP (off N end of New Street)
11 (4 Mon)-11 (midnight Fri & Sat); 12-10.30 Sun
☎ (01590) 672814
Ringwood Best Bitter, Fortyniner; guest beer H
Former post house, dating from 1855 and previously in the Jollifer family for three generations. Beers, both local and countrywide, are supplemented by bar snacks throughout opening times. A community pub, it has a mixed but friendly clientele. There is a lively bar that caters for pool and darts, with a jukebox and TV for live sport, and a carpeted lounge area available for quiet conversation. The pub is handy for the library, St Barbe Museum and High Street. Cider is Westons or Mr Whiteheads. (X2)P

Wheel Inn

Sway Road, Pennington, SO41 8LJ (Ramiley Road/Pitmore Lane jct, 2 miles W of Lymington)
10-midnight (1am Fri & Sat); 12-11 Sun
☎ (01590) 676122 thewheelinnpub.co.uk
Ringwood Best Bitter; guest beers H
Rare two-bar free house with a cosy lounge and large public bar, dog and family friendly with good value, imaginative home-prepared meals. Rolls and soup can be ordered from the bar. Two changing guest ales are sourced from local breweries for originality and differing styles. Breakfasts are served 10am-noon, Monday to Saturday. Acoustic night is Monday and small functions are catered for, supported by modern, multi-purpose entertainment equipment.
(X2)P

Medstead

Castle of Comfort

Castle Street, GU34 5LU SU654372
11.30-2.30 (3 Sat), 6-11; 12-3, 7-10.30 Sun
☎ (01420) 562112 castleofcomfort.co.uk
Black Sheep Best Bitter; Courage Best Bitter, Directors; Young's Bitter; guest beer H
Tucked behind the church, the Castle of Comfort is named after a ship whose timbers were used to build the original pub. This 17th-century village local has a public bar and small lounge that feels more like a family living room, with a wood-burning stove set in a large fireplace. Outside is a large garden and at the front a suntrap drinking area. Dogs are welcome and bar food is available at lunchtimes (not Mon). A perfect stopping-off place for ramblers. (28)P

Milford on Sea

Red Lion

32 High Street, SO41 0QD (on B3058, leave A337 at Everton)
11.30-2.30, 6-11; 12-3 (closed eve) Sun
☎ (01590) 642236 redlionpubmilfordonsea.co.uk
Fuller's London Pride; Ringwood Best Bitter; guest beers H
Imposing 18th-century inn with a notable feature fireplace. Run by Paul and June Lines for 12 years, it has featured in the Guide for 10 years. Friendly, comfortable and relaxing, the single bar area is split up and arranged on several levels, with carpeting throughout. One area is reserved for pool and darts, with an unobtrusive gaming machine. Good value quality food is served and occasional musical events are staged. The cider is Mr Whiteheads. Overnight accommodation is in three en-suite rooms. (X2)P

Newfound

Fox

Andover Road, RG23 7HH (B3400 W of Basingstoke at Oakley turning)
12-11.30 (10.30 Sun) ☎ (01256) 780493
Fuller's London Pride, seasonal beers; Gale's HSB H
A busy ex-Gale's Fuller's village pub. The public bar has an dining area to the side serving traditional

home-cooked food, and features a 40-metre deep well that used to supply the water for a cottage next door. There is a separate quiet private bar/snug and a function room that hosts regular Monday evening live jazz and blues. The garden and enclosed children's play area overlook fields and are a treat in fine weather. Food is served 12-2pm every day, 6.30-9pm Tuesday-Saturday. ⛼Q❀◑⊟♿⊟(76,78)P⁵—

North Gorley

Royal Oak

Ringwood Road, SP6 2PB (1½ miles S of Fordingbridge, ½m E of A338) SU161119

⏲ 11-11 (10.30 Sun) ☎ (01425) 652244

Sharp's Doom Bar; guest beers ⊞

A former hunting lodge, this attractive thatched-roof building became a pub in 1820. A spacious bar, including an annexe used as a family area or music venue, caters for summer visitors. Up to four guest beers are served in summer and two in winter, often from local breweries. There is no food Sunday or Monday evenings in winter, and it is advisable to phone first if arriving late. Friday night is live music night. The pub has hitching posts for your ponies. ⛼Q☋❀◑♿⊟(X3)P⁵—

Oakhanger

Red Lion

GU35 9JQ SU770360

⏲ 12-3, 6-11 (not Sun eve) ☎ (01420) 472232

Courage Best Bitter; Ringwood Fortyniner; guest beer ⊞

Dating from 1550 and part of the Oakhanger Estate until 1883, the pub was called The Rising Sun between 1700 and 1824. Acquired by Farnham United Brewery in 1927 and latterly Courage in 1951, the Red Lion is now an Enterprise Inn. A typical village pub catering for locals and visitors, there are views across the countryside from the front window seats. The restaurant boasts a two-level seating area, warmed by a log fire. Guest beers are from the SIBA list. ⛼Q❀◑⊟♣P⁵—

Odiham

Odiham & Greywell Cricket Club

King Street, RG29 1NF SU752500

⏲ 5 (2 Sat)-9; 12-10 summer; 1-7 (12-10 summer) Sun

☎ (01256) 703302 🌐 odihamandgreywell.play-cricket.com

Andwell seasonal beer; guest beer ⊞

The first recorded match at this club was in 1764, making it one of the oldest cricket clubs in the country. The club is set in countryside just south of the village, so you can enjoy a quiet beer while watching cricket in summer. A guest ale is available alongside one of the beers from Andwell brewery. Although a private members' club, CAMRA members are welcome on production of a membership card. ⛼❀♣P⁵—

Old Basing

Crown Inn

The Street, RG24 7BW (next to ruins of Basing House)

⏲ 11-3, 5-11; 11-11.30 Fri & Sat; 11.30-10.30 Sun

☎ (01256) 321424 🌐 thecrownoldbasing.co.uk

Fuller's London Pride; guest beers ⊞

A Grade II-listed building dating from the Civil War when Cromwell's Roundheads laid siege to Basing House, the inn is home to the Hawkins Regiment of the re-enactment society and a microlight club. There are two bars, one a cosy snug and the other with wheelchair access. Food is available every day and includes tapas. Two of the three guest beers are always from local micro-breweries, and a dark ale usually features. The pub uses oversized glasses, except branded ones. ⛼Q☋❀◑⊟♿⊟(12)P⁵—▯

Overton

Greyhound

46 Winchester Street, RG25 3HS (300m S of village centre)

⏲ 12-2 (not Mon), 5-11 (11.30 Fri & Sat); 12-3, 7-10.30 Sun

☎ (01256) 770241

Caledonian Deuchars IPA, seasonal beer; Greene King IPA, Abbot; Wadworth 6X ⊞

Recently refurbished and revitalised by the friendly couple who took over the pub in 2008, having been regulars themselves before that, the pub has a warm and inviting atmosphere. There is a games area with pool and darts and a lounge area to sit more quietly. The log fire inside the entrance is very welcoming. A typical traditional English village pub. ⛼Q❀⇌⊟(76,86)♣⁵—

Red Lion

37 High Street, RG25 3HQ (200m W of village centre on B3400)

⏲ 11.30-3, 6-11; 12-4 Sun ☎ (01256) 773363

🌐 redlion-overton.co.uk

Andwell King John; Flowerpots Bitter; Itchen Valley Winchester Ale; Ringwood Best Bitter ⊞

Just a short walk from the centre of the village, the Red Lion is gaining a good reputation for high quality food at reasonable prices. As well as the main menu, which includes a vegetarian dish, there are daily specials. Three tastefully decorated separate areas include a restaurant (bookings advisable) and a cosy snug, with the main bar sandwiched between the two. A good-sized garden with a covered wooden patio overlooks the car park. The staff are friendly and attentive. ⛼❀◑⇌⊟(76,86)P⁵—

Portsmouth

Artillery Arms

Hester Road, PO4 8HB

⏲ 12-3, 6-11.30; 11-12.30 Fri & Sat; 11-11.30 Sun

☎ (023) 9273 3611

Bowman Swift One; Fuller's ESB; guest beers ⊞

Traditional back-street free house selling a wide selection of up to six ales from many southern breweries. Located just minutes from Fratton Park football ground, it can get lively on match days. The pub has a large walled garden with equipment for children. It is famous for its good value Sunday lunches, and rolls are available on match days. The pub also supports darts and pool teams. Q❀⊟⊟(1c,6,15)♣P▯

Barley Mow ✔

39 Castle Road, Southsea, PO5 3DE

⏲ 12 (11 Sat)-midnight; 12-11 Sun ☎ (023) 9282 3492

Fuller's London Pride; Gale's HSB; guest beers ⊞

Good-sized Victorian street-corner pub with pool and darts in the public bar, and a wood-panelled lounge bar with plenty of seating. There are usually five guest ales on offer, one a dark beer. This lively

community pub hosts a wide range of events from theme nights to quizzes and music.
❀⊟♿⇌(Portsmouth & Southsea)⊟(1,23,40)♣●

Bridge Tavern ✔

54 East Street, Old Portsmouth, PO1 2JJ (follow Broad St round to East St and Camber Quay car park. Pub is at far end of car park)

11-11; 12-10.30 Sun ☎ (023) 9275 2992

Fuller's London Pride, ESB; Gale's Seafarers Ale, HSB; guest beer Ⓗ

Brightly coloured, this Fuller's pub is highly visible yet deceptively remote. On accessing it through the car park from Old Portsmouth you are rewarded with a large bar with timber and tiled floors. Popular for food, including Catch of the Day, it gets busy at mealtimes. Food is served all day Saturday, all afternoon Sunday. On fine days the outside seating is ideal for views over the boats in Camber Dock. There is a quieter restaurant area/function room upstairs. Q❀◑P

Duke of Devonshire

119 Albert Road, PO5 2SR

11-midnight (12.30am Fri & Sat); 12-11.45 Sun
☎ (023) 9282 3682

Fuller's London Pride; guest beers Ⓗ

A thoroughly traditional street-corner local in the popular Albert Road area of Southsea. The single bar has comfortable seating throughout and a real old-world feel. It is known to many as 'Mollie's' and has a thriving ladies' darts team. On warmer days, drinkers can enjoy the walled patio garden to the rear. You are certain of a warm welcome no matter what the weather. ❀⊟(17,18)♣⊱

Eastfield Hotel

124 Prince Albert Road, Southsea, PO4 9HT

11-11 (midnight Fri & Sat); 12-11 Sun ☎ (023) 9275 0102

Fuller's London Pride; Greene King Old Speckled Hen; guest beers Ⓗ

An imposing Edwardian pub in the back streets of Eastney, still displaying the tiled exterior and windows from its original construction in 1906 by AE Cogswell. The boisterous public bar shows sport and supports darts and pool teams, while the quieter lounge has original wood panelling. Two guest beers are sourced from many independent local breweries. The new bar manager is intending to continue regular Sunday night quizzes and summer barbecues, plus the popular local brewery guest slots. Q❀⊟⊟(1c,6,17)♣●

Fifth Hants Volunteer Arms ✔

74 Albert Road, Southsea, PO5 2SL

3-midnight (1am Fri); 12-1am Sat & Sun
☎ (023) 9282 7161

Fuller's London Pride; Gale's Seafarers Ale, HSB Ⓗ

A thriving two-bar street-corner local with something happening almost every evening. Last year was the landlord's 25th anniversary of running the pub. The lounge bar has comfortable seating and displays certificates commemorating the pub's many years in this Guide, while the lively public bar has probably the best jukebox in town. On Sunday evening there is often live music, and the pub has cricket and darts teams. ⊟⊟(17,18)♣

Florence Arms

18-20 Florence Road, Southsea, PO5 2NE

12-midnight (11 Sun) ☎ (023) 9287 5700

Adnams Bitter, Broadside; Shepherd Neame Spitfire; guest beers Ⓗ

One of Southsea's hidden gems, the Flo has a genuine public bar, a more select lounge, and a dining room serving excellent home-cooked food (no food weekends except Sun lunch). Live entertainment includes jazz, folk and poetry. Guest beers come from local independent breweries, each featuring for a month at a time. One of the main attractions is the excellent range of cider and perry, with at least 12 real ciders and perries on draught and 40-plus in bottles. Q◑◗⊟⊟(1,5,6)●

Hole in the Wall

36 Great Southsea Street, Southsea, PO5 3BY

4-11; 12-2, 4-midnight Fri; 4-midnight Sat
☎ (023) 9229 8085 🌐 theholeinthewallpub.co.uk

Oakleaf Hole Hearted; guest beers Ⓗ/Ⓖ

The Hole is one of the smallest pubs in Portsmouth, but for its size has one of the best beer ranges sourced from both local breweries and agencies. Hole Hearted, which was brewed for and named after the pub, is on sale by gravity from the back of the bar; cider and 'weapons grade' ginger beer are also available. There is no admittance after 11pm. Local CAMRA Pub of the Year 2007 and 2009.
◗⇌(Portsmouth & Southsea)⊟(1,23,40)●⊡

John Jacques ✔

78-82 Fratton Road, Fratton, PO1 5BZ

9-midnight (1am Fri & Sat) ☎ (023) 9277 9742

Greene King IPA, Abbot; Marston's Pedigree; Shepherd Neame Spitfire; guest beer Ⓗ

Situated in the former Portsmouth Co-operative (PIMCO) supermarket and named after a post-World War II chairman and driving force, this Wetherspoon's can be very busy, especially on match days. Standard Wetherspoon fare is available, in a plain building with no real architectural or decorative features. The outdoor smoking and drinking area is separated from the busy Fratton road by a low wall.
◑◗♿⇌(Fratton)⊟(3,13,14)⊱

Leopold Tavern 🏆 ✔

154 Albert Road, Southsea, PO4 0JT

11-11 (midnight Fri & Sat); 12-11 Sun ☎ (023) 9282 9748

Bowman Swift One; Hop Back Summer Lightning; Oakleaf Hole Hearted; guest beers Ⓗ

A traditional green-tiled exterior to this street-corner hostelry belies its modernised interior. The pub has however retained its two distinctive drinking areas; the one closest to Albert Road can become extremely lively on a weekend evening when the Albert Road crawls visit. The inner area is quieter but still busy. An outdoor heated beer garden does ease the pressure on space inside at busy times. The pub has a darts team, live football and Wi-Fi is available. Local CAMRA Pub of the Year 2010. ❀⇌(Fratton)⊟(17,18)♣⊱

Old Customs House

Gunwharf Quay, PO1 3TY

9-midnight (1.30am Sat); 9-11 Sun ☎ (023) 9283 2333

Fuller's London Pride, ESB, seasonal beers; Gale's Seafarers Ale, HSB Ⓗ

High-quality conversion from a pay office to a pub, this ex-naval building is enjoying a successful rebirth as a tasteful hostelry supplying both good food and excellent beer. The layout comprises several rooms spread over the ground and first floors, understated but attractively decorated. Well worth a visit for both natives of Portsmouth and visitors. ❀◑◗♿⇌(Harbour)⊟

Pembroke

20 Pembroke Road, Southsea, PO1 2NR

⏲ 10-midnight (11 Mon); 12-4, 7-11 Sun ☎ (023) 9282 3961

Draught Bass; Fuller's London Pride; Greene King Abbot Ⓗ

Purpose built as a street-corner hostelry in 1711, this now single room bar has a horseshoe-shaped interior and an L-shaped servery decorated with naval memorabilia. It is mentioned in the Captain Marryat novels under its original name of the Little Blue Line. It changed its name to the Pembroke in 1900. This pub is a rare haven for the discerning drinker, which explains its varied clientele, and it still serves probably the best pint of London Pride in Portsmouth. ♨♿🚌(6)

Phoenix

13 Duncan Road, Southsea, PO5 2QU

⏲ 10-midnight (1am Fri & Sat); 12-midnight Sun

☎ (023) 9278 1055

Beer range varies Ⓗ

A few minutes' walk from Albert Road, this hidden gem is well worth the detour. It still retains its two bars – the lounge features many signed photographs of people who have appeared at the nearby Kings Theatre over the years. A separate games room (which was part of the old Dock End Brewery) houses a pool table, and a small walled patio garden accommodates smokers. The pub often features live music at weekends.

❀⊟🚌(17,18)♣⚊

Rose In June ✔

102 Milton Road, PO3 6AR

⏲ 12-11.30 ☎ (023) 92824191

Fuller's London Pride; Gale's HSB; Oakleaf Hole Hearted; Otter Ale; Sharp's Doom Bar; guest beer Ⓗ

Imposing pub situated near to Kingston Prison and 20 minutes' walk from Fratton Park. It has two very different bars, a function room and a huge garden with play area, and hosts two annual beer festivals in February and June. A guest beer is served at a reduced price every weekend. There is a quiz on Tuesday and darts Tuesday-Friday and Sunday. The cider is Thatchers Cheddar Valley. If arriving by bus ask for the prison bus stop.

Q❀⊟♿🚌(1c,6,21)♣●⚊

Sir Loin Of Beef

152 Highland Road, PO4 9NH

⏲ 11-11.30 (midnight Fri & Sat); 12-11.30 Sun

☎ (023) 9282 0115

Hop Back Summer Lightning; guest beers Ⓗ

A large single-bar pub near to the old Royal Marines barracks. The pub has a nautical theme – time is called with a submarine klaxon. The extensive beer range, normally including eight guests, is mostly sourced from southern independent breweries, and every month one of them is featured in a special brewery evening. A good range of bottle-conditioned beers is also stocked. ⅄🚌(1,6,17)♣●

Taswell Arms ✔

42 Taswell Road, Southsea, PO5 2RG

⏲ 12-midnight (11 Sun) ☎ (023) 9285 1301

Hop Back Summer Lightning; Oakleaf Hole Hearted; Shepherd Neame Spitfire; guest beers Ⓗ

A lively locals' pub situated halfway between the seafront and Albert Road. Supporting both darts and pool teams, it also offers several more unusual pub games including table football. Outside is a pleasant secluded garden with a heated smoking area. Good value food is sold both lunchtimes and evenings (no food Sun eve); on Sunday roasts are available from midday-6pm. ❀◑♿🚌♣●⚊

White Swan ✔

26 Guildhall Walk, PO1 2DD

⏲ 9-11 (1am Fri & Sat) ☎ (023) 9289 1340

Greene King Ruddles Best Bitter, Abbot; Oakleaf Pompey Royal, Hole Hearted; guest beers Ⓗ

Situated near the Guildhall and Theatre Royal, the pub is popular with students and locals. This Grade II-listed, mock Tudor building was built in 1916, replacing the previous 17th-century pub of the same name. Restored by Wetherspoon in 2009, the venue has an impressive ornate exterior, and inside features a central floating bar and distinctive entrance vestibule with a clock. Notice the six handpumps in use. Regular ales from Oakleaf and Ringwood are available, plus guest ales and occasional beer festivals.

◑⇌(Portsmouth & Southsea)🚌

Winchester Arms

99 Winchester Road, Buckland, PO2 7PS

⏲ 3 (4 Mon)-11; 12-11 Sat & Sun ☎ (023) 9266 2443

🌐 thewinchpub.co.uk

Oakleaf Hole Hearted; Shepherd Neame Spitfire; guest beers Ⓗ

This is a friendly two-roomed community pub with two beers and one regularly changing guest. An open fire is set in the winter, there is a covered area in the garden for smokers, and games are available. There is a dartboard and the pub runs its own teams. A beer festival takes place on the spring bank holiday each year. On Sunday evening there is live music. The pub may stay open beyond 11pm on some Friday and Saturday evenings.

♨Q❀⊟♿♣●⚊

Wine Vaults

41-47 Albert Road, PO5 2SF

⏲ 12-11.30 (12.30am Fri & Sat) ☎ (023) 9286 4712

Fuller's Discovery, London Pride, ESB; Gale's HSB; guest beers Ⓗ

A large pub opposite the Kings Theatre, with several rooms over different floors, basic decor with wood-panelling, plus a couple of popular leather sofas. Vines, on the corner, is a quieter part of the pub laid out for dining. Previous visitors will be pleased to hear the toilets have been refurbished. There are several bars but, apart from Friday and Saturday when the pub door get very busy, only the main one is open.

♨❀◑🚌(17,18)⚊

Ringwood

Inn on the Furlong ✔

12 Meeting House Lane, BH24 1EY (opp market place car park and bus terminus)

⏲ 10-11 (midnight Fri & Sat); 11-11 Sun ☎ (01425) 475139

Jennings Cocker Hoop; Ringwood Best Bitter, Fortyniner, Old Thumper, seasonal beers; guest beers Ⓗ

Now a Marston's tied house, this cream-painted Victorian building escaped demolition in 1985 to become Ringwood Brewery's first pub. Centrally situated, it has a large flagstoned bar that serves several linked areas including a sunny conservatory and family area. Generally a quiet pub, it is a popular and lively meeting place for more mature customers. The full range of Ringwood-brewed beers is available, augmented with several other

Marston's group guests. Tuesday and Saturday are live music nights. No evening meals Saturday, Sunday or Tuesday. ⛰Q🛏❀◑◗♿⛺🚌♣⚊

Romsey

Abbey Hotel

11 Church Street, SO51 8BT

⏲ 11-3, 6-11; 12-3, 7-10.30 Sun ☎ (01794) 513360

🌐 abbeyhotelromsey.co.uk

Courage Best Bitter, Directors; Young's Bitter Ⓗ

Handsome, late 19th-century building facing the east end of Romsey Abbey, close to the tourist information centre and the medieval King John's House. The bar and adjoining dining area are decorated in Victorian style and are havens for those seeking respite from piped music and other modern-day auricular intrusions. Good, reasonably priced food adds to the attraction (no food Sun eve) and there is a tranquil garden beyond the car park. ⛰Q❀🛏◑◗≋🚌P⚊

Bishop Blaize

4 Winchester Road, SO51 8AA

⏲ 12-11 (midnight Fri & Sat; 10.30 Sun) ☎ (01794) 511777

Ringwood Best Bitter; guest beer Ⓗ

Named after the patron saint of wool combers, the Bishop Blaize is a modest drinkers' pub in a 300-year-old listed building warmed by a wood-burning stove. Expect a genuine welcome from the friendly staff. The long bar stretches from a quiet corner at one end to a large-screen TV and dartboard at the other. Sport is important: the pub has four darts teams and a crib team. The secluded garden includes a grand smoking shelter. Parking is behind the pub. ⛰❀≋🚌♣P⚊

Old House at Home

62 Love Lane, SO51 8DE

⏲ 11-11 (11.30 Fri & Sat); 12-10.30 Sun ☎ (01794) 513175

Fuller's Discovery, London Pride; Gale's Seafarers Ale, HSB; guest beer Ⓗ

Romsey's only thatched pub stands a stone's throw from the town centre and a world away from its environs. Well-kept ales, quality food, efficient service and a warm welcome may be enjoyed in the three distinct and comfortable internal areas, one usually dedicated to dining. Those wishing to take their pleasures alfresco will enjoy the handsome garden and patio; should it get too fresco, there are plenty of heaters. Food is available all day except Sunday evening. ⛰Q❀◑◗≋🚌P⚊

Rowlands Castle

Castle Inn ✔

1 Finchdean Road, PO9 6DA

⏲ 11 (12 Sun)-midnight ☎ (023) 9241 2494

Fuller's London Pride, seasonal beer; Gale's Seafarers Ale, HSB Ⓗ

Tucked away behind the railway bridge from the village green, this is a friendly village local. The island bar serves two small rooms – one is partly used as a restaurant serving excellent home-cooked food; the other is a basic public bar with an open fire where dogs, and their owners, are welcome. The pub has two garden areas – one dedicated to those who prefer a quiet drink outside. Although the pub shuts at midnight, last entry is usually 11pm. ⛰❀◑◗🀫♿≋♣P

Selborne

Selborne Arms ✔

High Street, GU34 3JR

⏲ 11-3, 6-11; 11-11 Sat summer; 12-11 Sun

☎ (01420) 511247 🌐 selbornearms.co.uk

Courage Best Bitter; Oakleaf Suthwyk Old Dick; Ringwood Fortyniner; guest beers Ⓗ

A traditional award-winning village pub with real fires and a friendly atmosphere, located at the foot of the zigzag path carved by famous naturalist Gilbert White. Extensive menus showcase local and home-made produce. Up to four guest beers come from local micro-breweries, and Mr Whiteheads ciders are always available. A play area in the huge garden is popular with children and parents, and houses heaters and a wood-burner keep you warm. ⛰Q❀◑◗🀫🚌(72,X72)♣●P⚊

Shedfield

Wheatsheaf Inn

Botley Road, SO32 2JG (on A334)

⏲ 12-11 (10.30 Sun) ☎ (01329) 833024

Flowerpots Bitter, Gooden's Gold, seasonal beer; guest beers Ⓖ

This ever-popular country pub has a selection of six locally-brewed real ales served directly from casks behind the bar. Thatchers Cheddar Valley cider is also available. The home-cooked food is excellent (evening meals available Tue and Wed only). Blues, jazz or folk music is played live most Saturday evenings. A beer festival is held on the late spring bank holiday weekend. The summer flowers in the garden are a delight. Parking is across a busy road. ⛰Q❀◑◗🀫🚌(69)♣●P⚊

Sherfield on Loddon

White Hart

Reading Road, RG27 0BT (just off A33)

⏲ 11-11 (midnight Fri & Sat); 12-11 Sun ☎ (01256) 882280

🌐 whitehartsherfield.co.uk

Young's Bitter, Special, seasonal beers Ⓗ

Traditional 17th-century coaching inn situated in the heart of the village, opposite the village green. The pub has a garden area to the rear and a heated smoking area to the front. Although it has had a makeover it retains many reminders of days gone by, including the mail rack above the fireplace, said to be one of only four remaining in England. The White Hart is a good base for walkers. ⛰Q❀◑◗♿🚌(14,15)P⚊

Southampton

Bitter Virtue Off Licence

70 Cambridge Road, SO14 6US

⏲ closed Mon; 10.30-8.30; 10.30-2 Sun ☎ (023) 8055 4881

🌐 bittervirtue.co.uk

Beer range varies Ⓖ

A real gem of the Portswood back streets, this award-winning beer shop specialises in American, British and Belgian bottled beers. German, Dutch, Czech and other countries' beers complete the range of some 400 different bottles. Bottled ciders and perries complement the many locally produced beers, earning it LocAle status. At least one draught real ale is available for takeaway, and draught cider is often stocked. Polypins from local breweries can be sourced to order. An extensive range of glasses, T-shirts and posters is also sold. 🚌

Guide Dog 🏆

38 Earl's Road, Bevois Valley, SO14 6SF (jct of Ancasta Rd, 100m W of Bevois Valley Rd, opp Aldi)

3 (12 Fri & Sat)-11; 12-10.30 Sun ☎ (023) 8022 5642

Flowerpots Goodens Gold; Fuller's ESB; guest beers H

Closed in 1981, it reopened in 1984 as the Guide Dog after the previous landlady had raised £14,000 for the charity. Eight handpumps serve a wide range of ales, mainly from small breweries. Beer can be served in four-pint carry-out containers and jugs. Within walking distance of St Mary's football stadium, it gets busy on match days. It hosts a variety of charity events, has a weekly meat draw on Friday, and an annual autumn beer festival. Local CAMRA Pub of the Year 2007-9.
≹(St Denys)♣–

Hop Inn

Woodmill Lane, SO18 2PH (corner of Oak Tree Rd)

11-11; 12.30-10.30 Sun ☎ (023) 8055 7723

Beer range varies H

By Riverside Park in Bitterne, the unassuming Hop Inn could easily be overlooked by passers-by. However, it is friendly and welcoming with attentive and knowledgeable staff, operating a 'try before you buy' policy on the excellent range of regularly changing ales. A pub quiz is held monthly on the first Sunday, with complementary cheese and biscuits for each team. In addition to the main bar there is a games room with pool and darts. City-centre buses pass by. ❀(3,8,U9)♣P–

Humble Plumb ✔

Commercial Street, Bitterne, SO18 6LY

11.30 (12 Mon)-2.30, 5-11; 11.30-11 Fri & Sat; 12-10.30 Sun ☎ (023) 8043 7577 wadworth.co.uk/southampton/humble_plumb

Jennings Sneck Lifter; Wadworth Henry's IPA, Strong in the Arm H**, 6X** G**, Bishops Tipple; guest beers** H

Friendly local in Bitterne with an excellent range of regularly changing ales, often including a guest from Wadworth's Red Shoot micro-brewery. It is a rare outlet for 6X, gravity-dispensed from wooden casks. All beers are offered on a 'try before you buy' basis. Good quality food is available lunchtimes and early evenings (no food Sun eve). Outside is a colourful garden and covered, heated patio for smokers. A meat draw is held on Sunday afternoon and a quiz night on Monday. Parking is behind the pub. ❀♿(18)P–

Junction Inn

21 Priory Road, St Denys, SO17 2JZ

12-11 (midnight Fri & Sat) ☎ (023) 8058 4486

thejunction-inn.co.uk

Greene King XX Mild, IPA, Abbot; guest beers H

Dawn and Martin manage this very friendly, welcoming local pub – a previous winner of Southampton's Best-Bar-None Community Pub of the Year award. The Junction is a Grade II-listed building, built circa 1860, with many original features. It serves excellent home-cooked food with vegetarian choices seven days a week. Friday quiz night, darts, crib, bar billiards, table football, karaoke and regular charity fundraising activities are hosted. Up to four guest ales are usually available. Dogs are welcome. Two minutes' walk from St Denys station. ❀≹(St Denys)♣–

Key & Anchor

90 Millbrook Road East, Freemantle, SO15 1JQ (corner of Cracknore Rd)

12-11 (midnight Fri & Sat; 10.30 Sun) ☎ (023) 8090 0747

Badger Tanglefoot; Ringwood Fortyniner; guest beers H

Popular 150-year-old local and corner pub at the heart of the community, friendly and most inviting, with a comfortable and lively atmosphere. There is regular entertainment: karaoke and disco every Saturday evening, quiz nights, darts evenings and live music. It has two original open log fireplaces and a superb old-fashioned Wizard jukebox filled with classics. Outside, the lovely south-facing garden hosts barbecues in summer. Dogs are welcome. Everything a real local pub should be, and more. ❀≹(Central/Millbrook)♣–

Park Inn ✔

37 Carlisle Road, Shirley, SO16 4FN (at jct of Shirley Park Rd)

11.30 (12 Sun)-midnight ☎ (023) 8078 7875

Wadworth Henry's IPA, 6X, Bishops Tipple, seasonal beers; guest beers H

A Wadworth pub since the late 1980s, it has six handpumps serving the Wadworth range plus seasonal and guest beers. A collection of brewery memorabilia mirrors graces the walls of the single bar, which has kept its two-bar feel. This friendly local has a meat draw on Sunday lunchtime and a Sunday evening quiz, and there is an annual beer festival. Outside is a paved and tabled garden with a covered area for smokers. Free Wi-Fi.
Q❀(8,10,18)♣–

Platform Tavern

Town Quay, SO14 2NY (rear entrance in Winkle St)

12-11 (midnight Thu-Sat) ☎ (023) 8033 7232

platformtavern.com

Fuller's London Pride; Gale's Seafarers Ale; guest beers H

Easily found, near Southampton Docks, almost opposite the Red Funnel ferry, the pub has a laid-back bar, decorated in muted earth colours adorned with Afro masks. Parts of the original town walls show in the structure. The adjoining fish restaurant is part of the pub. The Platform is a free house, focusing weekly on a different local brewery. Blues and jazz music feature strongly, including live performances. There is a wide pavement area outside for smokers and summer drinking. ❀♿–

South Western Arms

38-40 Adelaide Road, St Denys, SO17 2HW (adjoins St Denys station)

12-11 (midnight Fri & Sat) ☎ (023) 8032 4542

Bowman Swift One; guest beers H

Traditional pub, keeping 10 real ales and cider. There is always a good variety, with one popular local session beer and one strong Westons cider on permanently, one ale badged as house beer, up to six more local brews, and several from further afield. The walled beer garden, with heated smoking shelter, caters for 100 plus. Two beer festivals are held each year in May and November. The building has two levels – the quieter mezzanine with a pool table and table football. Dogs on leads are allowed. ❀≹(St Denys)♣P–

Waterloo Arms

101 Waterloo Road, Freemantle, SO15 3BS

12-11 ☎ (023) 8022 0022

Hop Back GFB, Crop Circle, Entire Stout, Summer Lightning, seasonal beers; guest beers H

A Hop Back pub since 1991 – the only one in Southampton. It has eight handpumps serving the

Hop Back range plus seasonal and guest beers. There is a single L-shaped bar, a rear conservatory and beyond that the garden for smokers and alfresco drinkers. Hot food is served 12-2pm and 5-8pm, Tuesday to Saturday, and Sunday roasts 12-2pm. Families are welcome in the conservatory until 8pm. Tuesday evening features a popular quiz. ⛵❀◐◑⇌(Millbrook)⊟(10,11,12)⁄–

Wellington Arms

56 Park Road, Freemantle, SO15 3DE
✪ 12-midnight ☎ (023) 8022 0356
Fuller's London Pride, ESB; Palmers Copper Ale; Ringwood Old Thumper; Wychwood Hobgoblin; guest beers Ⓗ
This back-street, mid-Victorian local is full of character and serves 11 ales – six regular beers and up to five guests. The Wellington is a two-bar, three-roomed pub with a small seating area outside at the rear. Iron Duke memorabilia lines the walls while the bar counters have many old pre-decimalisation coins set in them. There is live music on Tuesday and a popular quiz on Thursday. The building has the rare distinction of being the Redondan consulate. ❀⊞⇌(Millbrook/Central)⁄–

Tangley

Cricketers Arms

SP11 0SH (towards Lower Chute) SU327528
✪ 11-3 (not Mon & Tue), 6-11; 12-3, 7-10.30 Sun
☎ (01264) 730283 🌐 thecricketers.eu
Bowman Swift One, Wallops Wood Ⓖ
Situated in attractive countryside, this 16th-century drovers' inn sits below the Berkshire Downs. Dog-friendly, it has three resident black Labs. The two Bowman ales, served from stillage behind the bar, may be supplemented by a local guest in summer months. The front bar, with its huge inglenook fireplace, is used mainly for drinking, while traditional home-cooked food is served in the flagstoned dining area at the rear. Behind the pub is a large Scandinavian-style wooden chalet with 10 en-suite bedrooms. ♨Q❀🛏◐◑♿⊟(C6)P⁄–

Tichborne

Tichborne Arms

SO24 0NA SU571304
✪ 11.45-3, 6-11 (1am Fri); 12-4.30 Sun ☎ (01962) 733760
Palmers Copper Ale; guest beers Ⓖ
This welcoming village pub offers a range of guest ales, usually from local breweries such as Bowman. The high-quality, extensive menu changes daily and often includes local game. Darts and shove-ha'penny are popular and dogs are welcome in both bars. There is no piped music but a piano is available for spontaneous recitals. Mr Whiteheads cider is served in summer. A three-day beer festival is held every August. ♨Q❀◐◑⊞♣●P⁄–

Titchfield

Wheatsheaf

1 East Street, PO14 4AD (E end of East Street)
✪ 12-3, 6-11; 12-11 Fri & Sat; 12-10.30 Sun
☎ (01329) 842965
Flowerpots Bitter; guest beers Ⓗ
This friendly 17th-century free house is in a conservation area at the eastern end of the village. The interior is sympathetically decorated in a homely style and includes a main bar with real fire, cosy snug and family dining room. There is a beer garden and smoking area at the rear, with access to a private car park. Two varying guest beers are normally available. No food is served on Sunday night or Monday. ♨❀◐◑⊟P⁄–

Twyford

Bugle

Park Lane, SO21 1QT (jct of Park Lane and High St)
✪ 11.30-11; 12-10.30 Sun ☎ (01962) 714888
Bowman Swift One; Flowerpots Bitter; guest beer Ⓗ
For years the pub was the subject of bitter planner/developer battles in which, unusually and happily, the public interest prevailed. The Bugle reopened in 2008, modernised as a large, light and airy single bar, restoring the village's two-pub culture. One end has tables for dining, the other has deep, relaxing settees, but the central bar, with bar stools, still accommodates casual drinkers. A high-quality daily food menu is offered plus a popular Sunday roast lunch (no food Sun eve). The guest beer is usually another Bowman or Flowerpots brew. Wi-Fi hot spot.
♨Q❀◐◑⊟(69,49A)P⁄–

Phoenix ✔

High Street, SO21 1RF
✪ 11.30-2.30, 6-11; 11.30-11 Fri & Sat; 12-11 Sun
☎ (01962) 713322 🌐 thephoenixinn.co.uk
Greene King IPA; guest beers Ⓗ
Old coaching inn in the village centre, dating in parts from the 17th century. Once many-roomed, the pub is now one long, multi-level bar room, although to the rear there is a large skittle alley, with bar, which doubles as a family area. The pub is a rare rural outpost for mild. Food is a major feature, with a number of evening themes – Monday curry, Wednesday steak, Thursday fish and chips. Occasional live music sessions and quiz nights are hosted. ♨Q❀◐◑⊟(49A,69)♣P⁄–

Upper Farringdon

Rose & Crown

Crows Lane, GU34 3ED (signed off A32 at Farringdon crossroads) SU715351
✪ 12-3, 5.30-11; 12-11 Sat; 12-10.30 Sun ☎ (01420) 588231
🌐 roseandcrownfarringdon.co.uk
Hogs Back TEA; Triple fff Alton's Pride, Pressed Rat & Warthog, Moondance; guest beers Ⓗ
Built in 1810 by the Knight family of Chawton, the Rose & Crown is off the beaten track but worth seeking out. Enter this friendly pub to find a welcoming L-shaped bar with a seating area warmed by a log fire. Deeper inside is a dining area leading to a modern restaurant. An imaginative menu is supplemented by lunchtime bar snacks. Food is served lunchtimes and evenings, all day on Sunday. Families, walkers and dogs are always welcome and there is a spacious garden. A monthly jazz evening is held. ♨Q❀◐◑♣P⁄–

West Tytherley

Black Horse

North Lane, SP5 1NF SU275301
✪ 12-3 (not Mon & Tue winter), 6-11 (5.30-midnight Fri); 12-8 (later in summer) Sun ☎ (01794) 340308
🌐 theblackhorsewiltshire.co.uk
Bowman Wallops Wood; Hop Back GFB; guest beers Ⓗ

This delightful, welcoming 17th-century pub is the true hub of the village. It is home to football and skittles teams and a meeting place for other local groups including a monthly folk club. The pub comprises myriad rooms – the old stables has become a skittle alley. Guest beers come from breweries including Palmers and Stonehenge. Excellent food is served daily in the summer; in winter hours are reduced – phone to check.
♨Q❀◐▶⊟🚌(36)♣P⁵–

Whitchurch

Bell Inn

Bell Street, RG28 7DD
⏲ 10-11; 12-10.30 Sun ☎ (01256) 893120
Courage Best Bitter; Gale's Seafarers Ale, HSB; Goddards Special [H]
The half-timbered, family-run Bell is one of the town's oldest and most traditional pubs. Conversation and local gossip rule in the two bars, while a separate area off the lounge with exposed beams provides space for enjoying a quiet pint. There is a pool table in the public bar and a small library that raises funds for charity. Acoustic music events featuring local musicians are held on alternate Sunday afternoons. Outside is a pleasant patio. The public car park is opposite.
Q❀🛏◐⊟🚌(76,86)

White Hart Hotel ✔

The Square, RG28 7DN
⏲ 11-11; 12-10.30 Sun ☎ (01256) 892900
Arkell's 3B, Moonlight Ale, Kingsdown Ale [H]
Impressive, comfortable 15th-century coaching inn owned by Arkell's Brewery, with several separate areas. The popular public bar is lively at weekends, and occasional live music/discos are held. To the rear is a restaurant and quiet dining area. Breakfast is available from 8am, while lunch offers design-your-own-doorstop-sandwiches as well as full meals. Families are made very welcome. Local artists' work adorns the walls. Under its present ownership the pub has become a centre for community life. Q❀🛏◐▶⊟♿🚌(76,86)P⁵–

Winchester

Black Boy

1 Wharf Hill, SO23 9NQ (just off Chesil St, B3404)
⏲ 12-11 (midnight Fri & Sat, 10.30 Sun) ☎ (01962) 861754
🌐 theblackboypub.com
Flowerpots Bitter; Hop Back Summer Lightning; Ringwood Best Bitter; guest beers [H]
Centuries-old rambling building, comprising many interconnected rooms resembling a well-stocked folk museum, serviced from a central bar. One room is themed as a country kitchen complete with working Aga, another a butcher's, with papier-mâché joints, while other areas are tradesmen's workshops. Pub grub-style food is served from Tuesday evening to Sunday lunchtime (for full dining the pub owns the Black Rat restaurant opposite). Guest beers come from other local breweries, often including Bowman. A splendid 'medieval' smoking shelter graces the patio/garden. Good dogs are welcome. ♨Q❀◐▶⁵–

Fulflood

28 Cheriton Road, SO22 5EF (take Western Rd, off Stockbridge Rd)
⏲ 11-3, 5-11; 11-midnight Fri & Sat; 12-10.30 Sun
☎ (01962) 842996
Flowerpots Bitter; Greene King IPA; Itchen Valley Godfathers; Triple fff Moondance [H]
Original dark-green tiled facade and etched windows are evidence of this 19th-century pub's former Winchester Brewery ownership. Situated in a residential conservation area, a makeover has given the single bar a fresh look, with comfy sofas, newspapers and flowers. The loyal following of friendly locals, their banter, quizzes, occasional live music and special events all make for a good atmosphere. Bar billiards is also played. Outside, drinkers and smokers have small patios at both front and rear. Cider is from Westons.
❀◐▶⇌🚌♣🍎⁵–

Hyde Tavern

57 Hyde Street, SO23 7DY (on B3047)
⏲ 12.30-2 (not Mon-Wed), 5-11.30 (12.30am Fri); 12-12.30am Sat; 12-11 Sun ☎ (01962) 862592
Ballard's Midhurst Mild; Ringwood Best Bitter [H]**; guest beers** [H]/[G]
The exterior of this small, medieval, timber-framed building is dominated by an imposing double gable. The three-roomed interior is below street level – beware of low ceilings and undulating floors. A cellar bar is used for literature evenings, a sewing circle, folk music and other functions. Up to seven beers from small local breweries feature, many direct from the cask, and real cider is often available. There is no food, but customers may bring in takeaways (menus available and plates provided). Outside is a delightful, secluded garden.
♨Q❀⇌⁵–

Old Vine ✔

8 Great Minster Street, SO23 9HA (opp Winchester Cathedral green)
⏲ 11-11 (10.30 Sun) ☎ (01962) 854616
🌐 oldvinewinchester.com
Bowman Swift One; Ringwood Best Bitter; Taylor Landlord; guest beers [H]
Located in the heart of Winchester, with a vine growing over the front, this pub overlooks the Cathedral green. The cosy bar area features an oak-beamed ceiling, artwork from a local design house, leather sofas and an extensive selection of games. A heavy curtain divides the pub from the award-winning restaurant, where home-cooked food made from local produce is served. A no-smoking partially-covered terrace is at the rear. Accommodation is available, and well-behaved dogs are welcome. ♨❀🛏◐▶⇌🚌♣⁵–

Wykeham Arms ✔

75 Kingsgate Street, SO23 9PE (by entrances to Cathedral Close and college)
⏲ 11-11; 12-10.30 Sun ☎ (01962) 853834
Fuller's Chiswick Bitter, London Pride; Gale's Seafarers Ale, HSB [H]
Rambling, Georgian inn dating from 1755 with many interlinked rooms, immediately outside the city's ancient Kingsgate. An array of memorabilia, much of it Nelsonian, crams every available space. The Wykeham is frequently busy but always utterly civilised – a conversationalist's haven, away from 21st-century pressures. Advance booking is advised for meals at busy times. Beers may also include a Fuller's seasonal. More than 20 wines are available by the glass. Accommodation is highly rated. Dog-friendly. ♨Q🛏◐▶

HEREFORDSHIRE

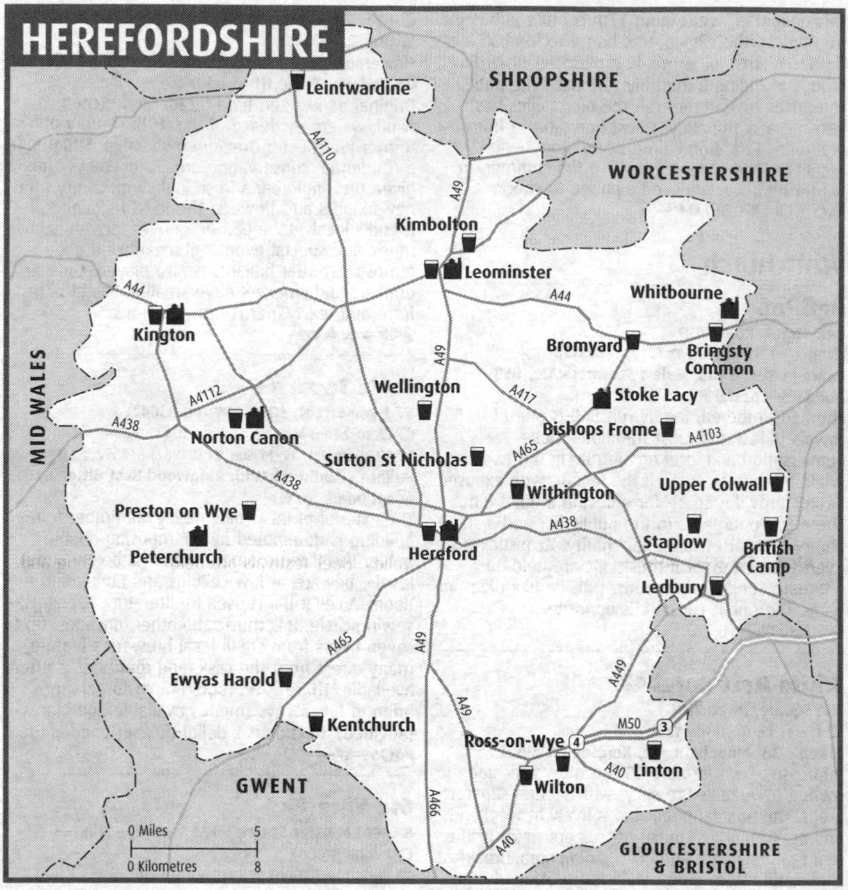

Bishops Frome

Green Dragon

WR6 5BP

☉ 5 (4 Fri; 12 Sat)-11.30; 12-4, 7-11 Sun ☎ (01885) 490607

Snowdonia Purple Moose; Taylor Golden Best; Theakston Best Bitter; Wye Valley Butty Bach; guest beer ⊞

The Green Dragon is everything a country pub should be. The rambling 17th-century inn has a maze of rooms with flagstone floors, low beams and real fires, and a paved yard outside. The inglenook in the main bar is particularly fine. Six handpumps dispense a range of local and regional beers, supplemented by real cider and perry in summer. Bar meals are served in the evenings (not Sun), with steaks a speciality. Two beer festivals are held every year. ⌂Q❀◐▶⊟♿♣●P⊱

Bringsty Common

Live & Let Live

WR6 5UW (off A44 – at cat & mouse sign follow right-hand track down to common) SO699547

☉ 5.30 (6.30 winter)-11; 12-11 Sat; 12-10.30 Sun

☎ (01886) 821462 ⊕ liveandletlive-bringsty.co.uk

Malvern Hills Black Pear; guest beers ⊞

A true survivor – this 17th century Grade II-listed ex cider house was subject to four planning applications for conversion into a private dwelling. Finally, after 11 years of closure, it reopened in 2007. Herefordshire's only thatched pub, it is accessed via a short track across the common. The owners have lovingly renovated the pub to a high standard – downstairs is much exposed timber, flagstone floors, settles and a fine fireplace; upstairs is the Thatch Restaurant, where diners can enjoy excellent locally-sourced food including Bringsty lamb. ⌂Q☕❀◐▶⊟(420)P

British Camp

Malvern Hills Hotel

Jubilee Drive, WR13 6DW (jct of A449 and B4232)

☉ 12-11 ☎ (01684) 540690 ⊕ malvernhillshotel.co.uk

Malvern Hills Black Pear; Wye Valley Bitter, HPA, Butty Bach; guest beer ⊞

Located high on the Malvern Hills, in the shadow of the Herefordshire Beacon, this comfortable venue has been popular with walkers and locals for

INDEPENDENT BREWERIES

Arrow Kington
Golden Valley Peterchurch
Hereford Hereford
Mayfields Leominster
Shoes Norton Canon
Willoughby Whitbourne
Wye Valley Stoke Lacy

generations. Drinkers come from near and far for the five local ales and enjoyable atmosphere in the wood-panelled main bar. A good range of bar meals is served and there are two stylish restaurants providing affordable quality dining. Refurbished accommodation and a conference room are also available. Dry dogs and children welcome – the latter until 4pm. ⚔Q❀⇔◑♿🚌(244)●P⚟

Bromyard

Rose & Lion

5 New Road, HR7 4AJ

✪ 11-11 (midnight Fri & Sat) ☎ (01885) 482381

Wye Valley Bitter, HPA, Butty Bach 🄷

The Rose & Lion was completely refurbished in contemporary style back in 2007, but retains the atmosphere of a traditional village inn moved into the town. The two small original rooms are complemented by a further bar to the rear plus disabled toilets. The 'Rosie' has always enjoyed a loyal local following and is never anything but friendly. A venue for live folk music on Sunday night, there is always a real buzz about the place. No food. ⚔Q❀⊟♿🚌♣P⚟

Ewyas Harold

Dog Inn ✔

HR2 0EX

✪ 10-midnight (1am Fri & Sat); 10-11 Sun ☎ (01981) 240598

Beer range varies 🄷

A welcoming stone-built village inn dating from the early 16th century, with a main bar plus games room and restaurant. Three ever-changing beers come from micro-breweries, mainly local. Home-prepared and locally sourced meals are served in the restaurant and also in the bar at lunchtime. Live music features from time to time, and a beer festival is held annually in the autumn. Two cricket teams and a football team have their social base here. ⚔Q❀⇔◑♿🚌(440)♣●⚟

Hereford

Barrels ✔

69 St Owen Street, HR1 2JQ

✪ 11-11.30 (midnight Fri & Sat) ☎ (01432) 274968

Wye Valley Bitter, HPA, Dorothy Goodbody's Golden Ale, Butty Bach; guest beers 🄷

This CAMRA multi-award winning pub enjoys a cult following. Once home to Wye Valley Brewery, and still the brewery's flagship outlet, it stocks most of the beer range plus Thatchers cider. Four distinct rooms cater for all age groups – a pool table occupies one bar, another has a pull-down TV screen for major sporting events, otherwise conversation rules. The cobbled and decked courtyard, and the stylish new bar in the old brewery, are home to an annual charity beer and music festival held over the August bank holiday weekend. ❀⊟≈🚌♣●⚟

Lichfield Vaults

11 Church Street, HR1 2LR

✪ 11-midnight (2am Fri & Sat) ☎ (01432) 266821

Adnams Broadside; Caledonian Deuchars IPA; Draught Bass; guest beers 🄷

A welcome return to the Guide for this 18th-century pub hidden away in a charming cobbled alley. Although opened out to a single bar, the panelled and bare-brick interior gives an intimate feel, while the secluded, decked garden extends some way beyond what is immediately visible. Speciality Greek Cypriot dishes feature on the lunchtime menu, while a traditional roast lunch is served on Sunday. One guest beer is always from a local brewery. Live blues plays on the last Sunday of the month. ⚔❀◐♿🚌⚟

Kentchurch

Bridge Inn

HR2 0BY (on B4347)

✪ 12-3 (not Mon & Tue), 5-11; 12-3, 7-10.30 Sun

☎ (01981) 240408

Golden Valley Hay Bluff; Otter Ale 🄷

Beautifully situated close to the Welsh border on the banks of the River Monnow, the building probably dates from the 14th century. It has a welcoming single front bar, plus a restaurant with excellent views. Outside are fine riverside gardens and a petanque piste for summer days. The freshly-prepared food ranges from bar snacks to full a la carte (not served Sun eve). Guest beers are from regional and local breweries, usually including Wye Valley. Beer festivals are held on the spring and August bank holidays. ⚔Q❀⇔◑♿P

Kimbolton

Stockton Cross

HR6 0HD (on A4112, W of village)

✪ 12-3, 7-11 (not Mon); 12-3 Sun ☎ (01568) 612509

Wye Valley HPA, Butty Bach 🄷

Prominently situated on the edge of the village, this single-bar black and white pub dates from the 16th century. The long, narrow bar with two cosy alcoves set either side of a large fireplace accommodates both drinkers and diners. The interesting menu, including a good vegetarian choice, is mainly sourced locally and freshly prepared. Regular events include an open mike night on the second Wednesday of the month and a curry and quiz night on the last Wednesday. ⚔☋❀◑P⚟

Kington

Olde Tavern 🏆 ☆

22 Victoria Road, HR5 3BX

✪ 6.30-midnight; 12 (4 winter)-midnight Fri, 12-midnight Sat & Sun ☎ (01544) 239033

Hobsons Mild; Ludlow Best; Wye Valley Butty Bach; guest beer 🄷

This diminutive Grade II-listed, two-room time warp is much improved by the removal of strip lights. An entrance lobby, still with its off-sales hatch, leads to a main bar with many original features, alcove seating and fascinating curios. The old smoke room to the right has a flagstone floor and bench seating, plus a serving hatch to the bar. Regulars take pride in pub-based and local activities, including the annual Kington Wheelbarrow Race. A warm welcome is assured from staff and locals alike. Q❀⊟🚌♣⚟

Oxford Arms Hotel

Duke Street, HR5 3DR

✪ 12-3, 6-midnight (closed Mon winter); 12-midnight Sat & Sun ☎ (01544) 231957 🌐 the-oxford-arms.co.uk

Beer range varies 🄷

Located on the edge of the town centre, this building was once the Earl of Oxford's hunting lodge and also a coaching inn – its 17th-century timber construction hides behind a Victorian frontage. The public bar is popular with locals, and attracts a younger clientele with pool, darts and quoits. The large dining lounge doubles as a function room, staging occasional live music. To the rear is a comfortably-furnished snug. Wholesome home-cooked food made with locally-sourced ingredients is served. Regularly-changing ales come from local breweries, usually including Spinning Dog. ♨Q❀⇌◐◑⊟⩓⊟P⚟

Ledbury

Prince of Wales ✓

Church Lane, HR8 1DL

✪ 11-11 (10.30 Sun) ☎ (01531) 632250 ⊕ powledbury.com

Hobsons Mild, Best Bitter; Sharp's Doom Bar; Wye Valley HPA, Butty Bach; guest beers Ⓗ

Set in a delightful cobbled alley leading to the church, this 16th-century timber-framed pub has two bars and a low-ceilinged alcove off to one side, where a folk jam session is held on Wednesday evening. Primarily a community pub, it is always bustling with locals and visitors. Two draught ciders from Westons are stocked, together with an excellent range of foreign beers, both draught and bottled. The unpretentious bar meals are excellent value and include very popular Sunday roasts. ♉❀◐⊟⇌⊟♣●⚟

Talbot Hotel

14 New Street, HR8 2DX

✪ 11-11 (midnight Fri & Sat) ☎ (01531) 632963

Wadworth Henry's IPA, 6X; Wye Valley Butty Bach; guest beer Ⓗ

This outstanding black and white half-timbered building dating back to the 1590s – with direct links to the Civil War – was restored and redecorated after surviving a fire in 2009. Various comfortably furnished seating areas with discreet corners surround a central bar which boasts a splendid fireplace. The restaurant, with its wood panelling, offers affordable fine cuisine using locally-sourced ingredients. Bar snacks are also available. The guest beer is from Wadworth's seasonal range or its Red Shoot subsidiary. ♨❀⇌◐◑⇌⊟♣⚟

Leintwardine

Sun Inn ★

Rosemary Lane, SY7 0LP (off A417)

✪ 12-3, 6-11; 11-11 Sat & Sun ☎ (01547) 540705

⊕ suninn-leintwardine.co.uk

Hobsons Mild, Best Bitter; guest beer Ⓖ

One of Britain's few remaining parlour pubs, the future of this Grade II-listed two-room marvel was cast into doubt when the landlady of 74 years died in 2009. CAMRA ran a 'Save the Sun' campaign, and it was ultimately bought by a locally-based consortium. The tiled public bar features simple furniture, a fireplace and gentle conversation. Beer is served straight from a stillage in the kitchen, together with Mahorall Farm cider. A beer festival is held each August bank holiday in the garden. No food. ♨Q♉❀⊟⩓●

Leominster

Bell Inn

39 Etnam Street, HR6 8AE

✪ 12-11.30 ☎ (01568) 612818

Malvern Hills Black Pear; Marston's Pedigree; Wye Valley Bitter, HPA; guest beer Ⓗ

A friendly pub with a single U-shaped island bar and light, modern decor, plus a pleasant garden to the rear. A premier venue for live music, the Bell features folk music every Tuesday and bands on Thursday evening. Reasonably priced, home-made food is served at lunchtime. Run by a young and cheery licensee who enjoys his beer. On-street parking is free and there is a large car park to the rear. ♨❀◐⇌⊟♣⚟

Grape Vaults

2-4 Broad Street, HR6 8BS

✪ 11-11 ☎ (01568) 611404

Hobsons Best Bitter; Ludlow Best; guest beers Ⓗ

Long ago this tiny pub was a hardcore cider house, but today it specialises in local ales. The main bar area has a fireplace, bench seating and much original woodwork, plus a pull-down TV screen used only for important matches. A small snug, tucked away to one side behind a part-glazed screen, is truly something to cherish. The pub has the smallest Gents' in the county. Traditional pub food is served at affordable prices (not Sun eve). Live music plays on Sunday afternoons. A beer festival is held in December. ♨Q◐◑⇌⊟

Linton

Alma Inn

HR9 7RY (off B4221, W of M50 jct 3) SO659255

✪ 12-3 (Sat only), 6-11; 12-3, 7-10.30 Sun

☎ (01989) 720355

Butcombe Bitter; Oakham JHB; Malvern Hills Black Pear; guest beer Ⓗ

The Alma is proud of its beer and continues to thrive, proving that village inns don't have to sell meals to survive. A CAMRA multi-award winner, it is a community pub run with real passion. The welcoming front bar – complete with a real fire – contrasts with a wood-panelled 'other' room and the rear pool room. There is always something happening here – major events include a well-established blues festival in June and an acoustic roots festival in late August – both include beer festivals and are held in the pub's extensive grounds. ♨Q♉❀⊟⩓♣●P⚟

Norton Canon

Three Horseshoes

HR4 7BH (On A480)

✪ 12-3 (Wed only), 6-11; 12-3, 7-10.30 Sun

☎ (01544) 318375

Shoes Light, Canon Bitter, Norton Ale, Peploe's Tipple, Farriers Beer Ⓗ

This red-brick roadside pub on the edge of the village is home to the Shoes Brewery. All the beers, brewed at the back of the pub, are available on handpump. A friendly atmosphere is assured, helped in winter by the glow of a huge log fire. Quoits is played, and there is a pool table in the large room beyond the bar. On the other side is a small lounge. The bus stop is half mile from the pub – alight at the 'Weobley Turn'.
♨Q♉❀⊟⊟(461,462)♣P⚟

Preston on Wye

Yew Tree

HR2 9JT SO385414
✪ 7-midnight (1am Fri & Sat); 12-3, 7-11 Sun
☎ (01981) 500359
Beer range varies Ⓖ
A delightfully old-fashioned, welcoming village local which also attracts canoeists and fishermen from the nearby River Wye. Simply furnished and warmed by a wood-burning stove in winter, the pub is home to boules, pool and quiz teams. The single beer, from a local or regional brewery, is served direct from the cask behind the small central bar, and draught Thatchers and Westons ciders are also stocked. Evening meals are available in summer if ordered in advance. Live music plays monthly on a Saturday. ♨Q❀▲♣●P⁵⁻

Ross-on-Wye

Mail Rooms ✔

Gloucester Road, HR9 5BS
✪ 9-midnight (1am Fri & Sat) ☎ (01989) 760920
Greene King Ruddles Best Bitter, Abbot; guest beers Ⓗ
Behind the fine red brick and stone facade of what was the town's main post office is a single modern bar with a vaulted ceiling, roof windows and a conservatory to the rear. At night the decor and subtle lighting combine to create an intimate atmosphere. Good value food is served all day, including a children's menu. The two regular beers are complemented by up to four guests from a diverse range of breweries, plus Westons Marcle Hill Cider. Q☋❀◐♿🚌●⁵⁻

Staplow

Oak Inn

HR8 1NP (on B4214)
✪ 12-3, 5.30-11; 12-3, 7-11 Sun ☎ (01531) 640954
🌐 oakinnstaplow.co.uk
Bathams Best Bitter; Sharp's Doom Bar; Wye Valley Bitter; guest beer Ⓗ
This stylishly-refurbished rural inn focuses primarily on food, and enjoys a county-wide reputation for first-class affordable dining, but drinkers are also very welcome. The front bar divides into two areas – one strictly for diners, featuring an open kitchen. At the rear is another room and a snug to one side. Book ahead for dining. New quality accommodation enjoys views across nearby orchards. ♨Q☋❀🛏◐♿🚌(417)●P⁵⁻

Sutton St Nicholas

Golden Cross

HR1 3AZ SO533455
✪ 12-3, 6-midnight (1am Fri); 12-1am Sat; 12-midnight Sun
☎ (01432) 880274 🌐 goldencrossinn.com
Beer range varies Ⓗ
Recently opened out and refurbished in contemporary style, the large main bar includes a games area with pool, darts and quoits. Striking a balance between village local and dining pub, there is a restaurant upstairs serving a good selection of traditional and modern cuisine, specialising in local steaks. Food and snacks are also served in the bar. Beers are predominantly from local breweries. Live music features on Friday evening. Q◑⊟♿🚌(426)♣P

Upper Colwall

Chase Inn

Chase Road, WR13 6DJ (off B4218, turn at upper hairpin bend signed British Camp) SO766431
✪ 11.30-3, 5-11; 11.30-11 Sat; 12-10.30 Sun
☎ (01684) 540276
Bathams Best Bitter; Hobsons Best Bitter; Sharp's Doom Bar; Wood Shropshire Lad; Wye Valley HPA; guest beers Ⓗ
Conversation rules at this two-bar, old-fashioned free house. Comprising a small lounge for informal dining and a narrow bar for drinkers, it is shoe-horned full of paraphernalia. The suntrap rear garden commands views across Herefordshire to the Welsh Hills. The pub is very much beer-first and always offers a guest ale from St George's Brewery. Cider and perry are from Westons. Booking is essential for Sunday roast.
Q☋❀◐⊟🚌(675)♣●P⁵⁻

Wellington

Wellington

HR4 8AT (½ mile W of A49)
✪ 12-3 (not Mon), 6-11; 12-3, 7-10.30 (not Winter eves)
☎ (01432) 830367 🌐 wellingtonpub.co.uk
Hobsons Best Bitter; Wye Valley HPA, Butty Bach; guest beer Ⓗ
A traditional village inn that also serves fine food. The public bar complements a separate barn-style restaurant. The award-winning food is a real speciality with an adventurous lunchtime and evening menu and Sunday roasts (no food Sun eve). The bar has interesting local photographs, board games and newspapers. Guest beers are mainly from micro-breweries, and Weston's Cider is served. A beer festival is held annually in July.
♨☋❀◐🚌(492)●P⁵⁻

Wilton

White Lion ✔

Wilton Lane, HR9 6AQ (just off B4260)
✪ 12-11 (10.30 Sun) ☎ (01989) 562785
🌐 whitelionross.co.uk
Wye Valley Bitter, HPA; guest beer Ⓗ
This pleasant riverside inn commands fine views from its patio and garden across the River Wye to Ross. The 16th-century building has a single, open main bar area, complete with original beams and stonework. Upstairs is the bistro-style Gaol Restaurant – originally part of a neighbouring prison house – where traditional English dishes made with locally-sourced produce are served. Draught cider from Broome Farm is stocked. Canoe hire is available. ♨❀🛏◐▲🚌(37,38)♣●P⁵⁻

Withington

Cross Keys

HR1 3NN (on A465 in Withington Marsh)
✪ 5 (12 Sat)-11; 12-4.30, 7-10.30 Sun ☎ (01432) 820616
Greene King Abbot; Wye Valley Butty Bach; guest beers Ⓗ
Conversation rules in this traditional local, run by the same landlord for more than 30 years. A long, narrow bar divides into two drinking areas, both with original beams and exposed stonework. A folk jam session is held on the last Thursday of the month. No food is available except on Saturday when filled rolls are served. ♨❀▲🚌(420)♣P

HERTFORDSHIRE

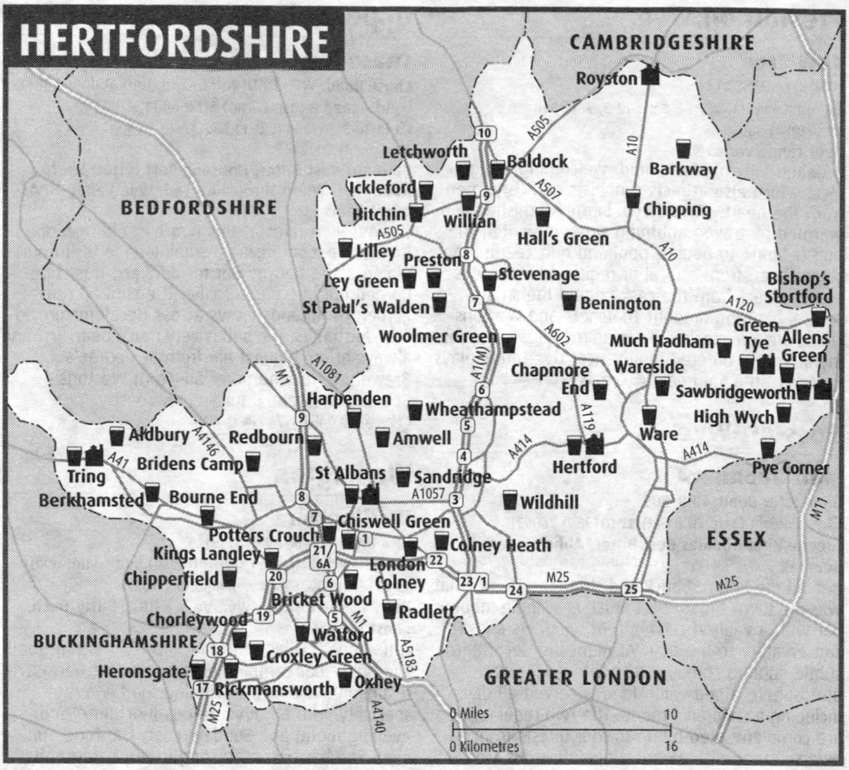

Aldbury

Valiant Trooper

Trooper Road, HP23 5RW (2 miles E of Tring)
☼ 12-11 (10.30 Sun) ☎ (01442) 851203
🌐 thevalianttrooper.co.uk
Brakspear Bitter; Fuller's London Pride; Tring Trooper; guest beers 🄷
A warm welcome awaits visitors, walkers and their dogs at this popular hostelry in an idyllic village in the Chilterns. The six ales are a mix of local and national brews, always including at least one Tring beer, as well as an occasional guest on gravity. The pub is olde worlde with a pleasant restaurant offering interesting menus featuring local produce. Outside, there's a courtyard for alfresco drinking and dining. ♨Q❀◐▶🚌(30,31,387)♣🍎P⅟

Allens Green

Queens Head 🏆

CM21 0LS TL455170
☼ 12-2.30 (not Mon & Tue), 5-11; 12-11 Sat; 12-10.30 Sun
☎ (01279) 723393 🌐 shirevillageinns.co.uk
Fuller's London Pride; Mighty Oak Maldon Gold 🄷**; guest beers** 🄷/🄶
Set in a small village, this building was once a large hostelry but was then closed down for many years. Two locals reopened the pub in 2002 in part of the building, the rest becoming a private house. Some of the beers are on handpump, but check the blackboard for guests served on gravity straight from the cellar. The third weekend of the month is 'Beer Lovers Weekend', with up to 10 beers on offer. Locals, walkers and cyclists all mix well. Good basic pub food is served. Q❀♿♣🍎P⅟

Amwell

Elephant & Castle ✔

Amwell Lane, AL4 8EA TL167131
☼ 12-2.30, 5.30-11; 12-11 Sat; 12-10.30 Sun
☎ (01582) 832175
Greene King IPA, H&H Bitter, Abbot 🄷
Welcoming and deservedly popular pub, dating from 1714, hidden away in a beautiful and peaceful setting. Two real fires warm the interior and there is a 200-feet deep well in the back bar. Lunches are served daily and evening meals Tuesday to Saturday. The pub hosts Amwell Day, a local charity fund-raising event, in June each year. With two large gardens (one for adults only), this is an excellent example of a successful country pub. ♨❀◐▶P⅟

Baldock

Victoria

Sun Street, SG7 6QA TL245340
☼ 12-11 ☎ (01462) 893153
St Austell Tribute; Caledonian Deuchars IPA 🄷
Formerly called The Sun, this pub was built in 1736 and acquired in 1925 by JW Green's Brewery of Luton. It stands in the centre of town on the Icknield Way Iron Age trading route. A friendly locals' pub, it has been under the same management for the past 30 years and is popular with horse-racing enthusiasts. ⇌🚌(700)♣P

Barkway

Tally Ho

London Road, SG8 8EX TL383350

11.30-11; 12-3 Sun ☎ (01763) 848389
tallyho-barkway.co.uk
Buntingford Highwayman IPA; Rebellion IPA Ⓗ
This friendly rural free house usually offers two real ales, sometimes three when there is the demand. Dark beers, mild and porter can often be found here. Bar snacks and home-made meals are available in the restaurant. The spirits menu offers 58 whiskies, 11 gins and nine rums. Look out for the large collection of cartoons, newspaper clippings and apocryphal stories. ⋒❀◐P

Benington

Lordship Arms
42 Whempstead Road, SG2 7BX TL307228
12-3, 6 (7 Sun)-11 ☎ (01438) 869665
lordshiparms.co.uk
Black Sheep Best Bitter; Crouch Vale Brewers Gold; Taylor Landlord Ⓗ
Single-room pub situated at the southern end of the village. A very tidy bar is decorated with telephone memorabilia – even some of the handpumps are modelled on telephones. Good quality sandwiches are available Monday to Saturday lunchtimes; Wednesday evening curries and Sunday roasts are popular. The well-tended garden sports superb summer floral displays and a classic car club meets here in summer. A repeat winner of local and county CAMRA Pub of the Year awards. ⋒Q❀◐🚌(384)P

Berkhamsted

Rising Sun
1 Canalside, George Street, HP4 2EG (on Grand Union Canal towpath next to Lock 55) SP997077
12-11 (midnight Thu-Sat) summer; 3-11 (midnight Thu) winter; 12-midnight Fri & Sat; 12-10.30 Sun
☎ (01442) 864913 theriser.co.uk
Tring Riser; guest beers Ⓗ
This welcoming two-room pub, with more space outside than in, has become an attraction for cider seekers as well as ale aficionados. Westons First Quality cider, perry and up to eight more ciders and perries are dispensed from the cellar. The pub holds three beer and cider festivals a year. Food is served in summer, home-made and locally sourced, with plenty of seating for diners on the patio and canal-side in warmer weather. Parking nearby is difficult; the bus stop on the High Street is a short walk. Branch and Regional Cider Pub of the Year 2010. ❀◐⇌🚌🍎⚡

Bishop's Stortford

Red Cow
58 Dunmow Road, CM23 5HL
4.30 (12 Sat)-1am; 12-midnight Sun ☎ (01279) 755784
Greene King IPA, Abbot; guest beer Ⓗ
Cosy neighbourhood pub in a mid 19th-century gabled building with leaded windows. The third handpump rotates between Buntingford Brewery beers. This is a pub for conversation – enter alone and you may soon be drawn into a chat with the landlord or friendly locals seated at the central bar. The bar serves several small drinking areas, and there is a pool room and a back garden to enjoy in the summer. ❀⇌🚌♣P

Bourne End

White Horse
London Road, HP1 2RH (½ mile from A41 jct) TL022063
11-11 (11.30 Fri & Sat); 12-10.30 Sun ☎ (01442) 863888
McMullen AK, Country Ⓗ
Large country-style roadside pub for all seasons and tastes. In winter there are cosy log fires; in summer the extensive patio and large lawned garden are the main attraction. The older front area of the interior is on several levels with traditonal exposed beams, with a large open-plan space near the bar. Bar snacks, main meals and a specials menu are available at all times, catering for a mixed clientele. Children are welcome, but no dogs. ⋒❀◐♿🚌(500)P⚡

Bricket Wood

Gate
Station Road, AL2 3PW TL136021
12-11 (10.30 Sun) ☎ (01923) 675801
Wells Bombardier; Young's Bitter Ⓗ
Friendly pub serving the local community, refurbished in 2006, with two bars and an extensive enclosed garden. The front bar has a tiled floor, large fireplace, rustic furniture and a dartboard. The side bar is carpeted and opens out on to the patio and large garden. All ages are very welcome. There is regular entertainment including a monthly quiz and occasional live music. The car park is large.
⋒Q❀◐⊟♿⇌🚌(320,655,656)♣P⚡

Bridens Camp

Crown & Sceptre 🏆
Red Lion Lane, HP2 6EY (from A4146 at Water End take Red Lion Lane for ½ mile) TL044111
12-3, 5.30-11; 12-11 Sat & Sun ☎ (01442) 234660
Greene King IPA, Abbot; St Austell Tribute; guest beers Ⓗ
This popular country inn with three interconnecting wood-beamed rooms around a U-shaped bar will make you nostalgic for the days when there were pubs like this all over England. It has a large patio and beer garden, and an outside bar for beer festivals and functions. Popular with walkers, the pub is home to a number of leisure activities, and there is a cricket pitch in an adjacent field. Local CAMRA Branch Pub of the Year 2010.
⋒Q❀◐🚌(X31)P⚡

Chapmore End

Woodman ✔
30 Chapmore End, SG12 0HF TL328164
12-2.30 (not Mon), 5.30-11; 12-11 Sat & Sun
☎ (01920) 463143 woodmanware.co.uk
Greene King IPA, Abbot Ⓖ

INDEPENDENT BREWERIES

Buntingford Royston
Green Tye Green Tye
McMullen Hertford
Old Cross Hertford
Red Squirrel Hertford
Sawbridgeworth Sawbridgeworth
Tring Tring
Verulam St Albans

Classic two-bar country pub in a quiet hamlet off the B158, popular with walkers. At this unspoilt gem the beer is served straight from cooled casks in the cellar behind the public bar. A local favourite is 'Mix' – half IPA and half Abbot. Home-made food is available Tuesday-Sunday (not Sun eve), including the Wednesday Supper Special featuring seasonal dishes. The large rear garden has a safe children's play area and petanque. Look out for beer and music festivals. ♨Q❀◑♣P⅃

Chipperfield

Royal Oak

1 The Street, WD4 9BH (at village crossroads)

⏲ 12-3, 6 (7 Sun)-11 ☎ (01923) 266537

Adnams Broadside; Fuller's London Pride; Young's Bitter; guest beer Ⓗ

A regular in the Guide for 30 years, this street-corner pub offers high quality ale and a warm welcome. The public and saloon areas are served by a central bar. A collection of foreign currency, matchbooks and historic car photographs lines the public bar, which has upholstered cask stools and copper-topped tables. The popular home-made lunches are served daily, evening meals by arrangement only. A function room to the rear is used by classic car groups. Dogs are welcome in the bar. ♨Q❀◐⊞⊟(R9,352)♣P⅃

Chipping

Countryman

Ermine Street, SG9 0PG TL356319

⏲ 12-11 Fri & Sat only; 12-10.30 Sun ☎ (01763) 272721

Beer range varies Ⓗ

Built in 1663 and a hostelry since 1760, the Countryman is a one-bar, split-level pub. The interior features some well executed carvings on the bar front, an impressive fireplace and a collection of obscure agricultural implements. Two real ales are usually available. The beer itself will vary, but tends to be brown and around 4-4.5% ABV. Note the restricted opening hours.
♨Q♉❀⊟(331)P⅃

Chiswell Green

Three Hammers ✔

210 Watford Road, AL2 3EA (on B4630 1 mile N of jct 21A M25) TL133045

⏲ 12-11 (midnight Fri & Sat) ☎ (01727) 846218

Courage Best Bitter; Fuller's London Pride; guest beers Ⓗ

Well-maintained 18th-century inn, originally a blacksmith's, with a contemporary interior and large garden, situated on the main Watford Road near the National Gardens of the Rose. Six real ales include five ever-changing guests, available in third of a pint taster glasses on request. The pub hosts regular beer festivals. Meals are served until 9pm every day. Quiz nights on Sunday and Tuesday offer a small cash prize. Buses stop directly outside and the pub is well placed for access to the M25 and M1. ♨Q❀◑♿⊟(320,321,724)♣P⅃

Chorleywood

Rose & Crown ✔

Common Road, WD3 5LW TQ026963

⏲ 11.30-2.30, 5.30-11; 11-11 Sat; 12-10 Sun

☎ (01923) 283841 🌐 roseandcrownchorleywood.co.uk

Fuller's London Pride; Young's Bitter Ⓗ

Small, one-bar pub dating back to the mid-19th century overlooking the western side of Chorleywood Common. The back bar was converted to a popular restaurant more than 15 years ago. The drinking area can get crowded, particularly as part of it may also be used for dining at busy times (no food Mon eve). Two guest beers are typically from fairly local breweries such as Buntingford, Rebellion or Vale.
♨❀◑⇚⊖⊟(336)♣P

Colney Heath

Crooked Billet

88 High Street, AL4 0NP TL202060

⏲ 11-2.30, 4.30-11; 11-11 Sat; 12-10.30 Sun

☎ (01727) 822128

Tring Side Pocket for a Toad Ⓗ

Popular and friendly cottage-style village pub dating back over 200 years. A genuine free house, it stocks three or four guest beers from national, regional and micro-breweries. A wide selection of good-value home-made food is served lunchtimes and Friday and Saturday evenings. Summer barbecues are held occasionally. This is a favourite stop-off for walkers on the many local footpaths. Families are welcome in the large garden where there is play equipment. Opens all day Saturday in summer. ♨❀◑⊞⊟(304)♣P⅃

Croxley Green

Sportsman 🏆

2 Scots Hill, WD3 3AD (at A412 jct with The Green) TQ069953

⏲ 12-11 (10.30 Sun) ☎ (01923) 443360

🌐 croxleygreen.com/sportsman

Red Squirrel Conservation Bitter; Taylor Landlord; Tring Side Pocket for a Toad Ⓗ

Comfortable, family-run pub with a warm welcome for all. Seven handpumps serve up to three guest beers and a real cider in addition to the regulars. The guests are often from LocAle brewers such as Buntingford, and craft brewers from further afield. Entertainment includes a popular quiz night on Wednesday, regular live music on Saturday evening, a monthly book club and twice-yearly beer festivals. The Sportsman is an excellent flagship for real ale.
♉◐♿⇚(Rickmansworth)⊖(Croxley)⊟♣P⅃

Green Tye

Prince of Wales

SG10 6JP TL443184

⏲ 12-3, 5.30-11 (1am Fri); 12-11 Sat; 11.15-10.30 Sun

☎ (01279) 842517 🌐 thepow.co.uk

Greene Tye Union Jack; Wadworth Henry's IPA; guest beers Ⓗ

Traditional village pub with the Green Tye Brewery situated in the car park. Green Tye beers are usually available, plus many guests from small independent breweries. Basic but decent pub food is served. The beer garden is covered by a tent twice a year to host the pub's beer festival.
♨❀◑♿♣●P⅃

Hall's Green

Rising Sun

SG4 7DR (approx 2 miles SE from Weston via Maiden St) TL275287

⌚ 11-2.30 (not Mon), 6-11; 11-11 Sat; 12-10.30 Sun
☎ (01462) 790487

McMullen AK, Cask Ale, Country Ⓗ

Traditional country pub in a small hamlet in the beautiful Hertfordshire countryside. A real fire in the winter and a large garden in the summer make it the ideal location for a pint of real ale all year round. The pub plays host to the local petanque league and classic car club. Good pub food is served in the conservatory and bar lunchtimes and evenings Monday to Saturday and all day Sunday. ᗑQ♿❀◑♿♣P⁵

Harpenden

Carpenters Arms

14 Cravells Road, AL5 1BD TL144133

⌚ 11-3, 5.30-11; 12-3, 7-10.30 Sun ☎ (01582) 460311

Adnams Bitter; Courage Best Bitter; Greene King Abbot; Harveys Sussex Best Bitter Ⓗ

Harpenden's smallest pub is cosy, comfortable and welcoming, with no fruit machines or loud music to distract the drinker. Five real ales are available including one guest. The pub is beautifully furnished and an open fire warms the bar in colder weather. Occasional themed food nights are held throughout the year (booking essential). In warm weather, barbecues are hosted on the secluded patio. ᗑ◐⇌🚌(321)P⁵

Cross Keys ✔

39 High Street, AL5 2SD (on Bowers Parade) TL133144

⌚ 11-midnight (1am Thu-Sat) ☎ (01582) 763989

🌐 cross-keys-harpenden.co.uk

Fuller's London Pride; Rebellion IPA; Taylor Landlord Ⓗ

This two-bar pub retains its traditional charm with a fine pewter bar top and flagstoned floors. The original oak-beamed ceiling has tankards from past and present customers hanging from it. In spring and summer you can enjoy your pint in the secluded, attractive rear garden, and in autumn or winter savour your pint in front of the saloon bar's real fire. Traditional home-cooked lunches are served Monday to Saturday lunchtimes. Last entry on Friday and Saturday is 11pm. ᗑQ❀◐⊟⇌🚌♣

Heronsgate

Land of Liberty, Peace & Plenty

Long Lane, WD3 5BS TQ023949

⌚ 12-11; 11-midnight Fri & Sat ☎ (01923) 282226

🌐 landoflibertypub.com

Red Squirrel Conservation Bitter; Tring Liberty Ale Ⓗ

Welcoming single-bar community pub popular with walkers, cyclists and real ale enthusiasts, named after a 19th-century Chartist community. It offers six or more beers, ciders, perries and single malts and has a policy of supporting smaller breweries. Liberty Ale is available elsewhere as Tring Brock Bitter. No children are allowed in the bar but outside is a large garden with a covered pavilion. Regular events include book and film clubs, beer tastings, quizzes and beer festivals. A CAMRA National Pub of the Year finalist in 2007. ᗑ❀◐⇌(Chorleywood)⊖(Chorleywood)🚌(R4)♣P⊟

Hertford

Old Barge ✔

2 The Folly, SG14 1QD (ask for Folly Island and you'll find the Old Barge) TL326128

⌚ 11-11 (midnight Fri & Sat); 12-11 Sun ☎ (01992) 581871

🌐 theoldbarge.co.uk

Red Squirrel Exmoor; Tring Colley's Dog; Woodforde's Wherry Ⓗ

The Old Barge is now a free house and hosts three beer festivals a year, one celebrating St George's Day. Enjoy great beer watching the passing narrowboats. On August bank holiday children under 12 can take part in the Crayfish Festival. The pub is proud of its home-cooked food, often featuring locally-sourced produce. A film night is hosted on the first Thursday of the month, jazz nights on the second and last Thursdays. Look out for the 'Folly at the Folly' Sunday festival in August. ᗑ◑⇌(East/North)🚌●P⁵

Old Cross Tavern

8 St Andrew Street, SG14 1JA TL323126

⌚ 12 (4 Mon)-11; 12-10.30 Sun ☎ (01992) 583133

Fuller's London Pride; Old Cross Tavern Laugh 'n' Titter; Taylor Landlord Ⓗ

Superb town free house offering a friendly welcome. Up to eight real ales, usually including a dark beer of some distinction, come from brewers large and small, including the pub's own micro-brewery. There is also a fine choice of Belgian bottle-conditioned beers. A popular beer festival is held over the spring bank holiday. There is no TV or music here, just good old-fashioned conversation. Filled rolls and pork pies are available well into the evening Monday to Saturday.
ᗑQ⇌(East/North)🚌♣

White Horse

33 Castle Street, SG14 1HH TL326124

⌚ 11-11 (midnight Fri & Sat); 12-10.30 Sun
☎ (01992) 501950

Fuller's Discovery, London Pride, ESB; Gale's Seafarers Ale Ⓗ

Charming old timber-framed building with two downstairs bars and additional rooms upstairs, one featuring bar billiards, another where children are welcome. Guest beers usually include either an Adnams or Butcombe bitter, and a beer festival is often held over one of the May bank holiday weekends. Home-made lunches are served daily. There are no gaming machines or TVs to disturb the pleasure of engaging conversation. Dog friendly – a 'must visit' for real ale lovers in Hertford.
ᗑQ♿◐⊟⇌(East/North)🚌♣

High Wych

Rising Sun

CM21 0HZ TL465142

⌚ 12-2.30, 5.30 (6 Sat)-11; 12-3, 7-10.30 Sun
☎ (01279) 724099

Courage Best Bitter; Mighty Oak Maldon Gold, Oscar Wilde; guest beers Ⓖ

A well-established roadside pub in the centre of the village, dedicated to serving excellent beers. Recently refurbished, this is now a smart, pleasant hostelry. Handpumps have never been installed here – the beers are always served on gravity. The Rising Sun has featured in all but one edition of the Guide and was local CAMRA Pub of the Year 2009. Q❀♿🚌(SW3,347)♣●⁵

Hitchin

Half Moon 🏆

57 Queen Street, SG4 9TZ TL186288

12-2.30, 6-midnight; 12-1am Fri & Sat; 12-11 Sun

☎ (01462) 452448

Adnams Bitter; Young's Special; guest beers Ⓗ

This split-level one bar pub dating back to 1748 was once owned by Hitchin brewer W&S Lucas. Two regular beers are supplemented by four guests, often from local micros. Two ciders and a perry are also available and plus a good choice of wines. Monthly quiz nights and curry nights are popular in this friendly community pub. Two beer festivals a year are held. Hertfordshire CAMRA Pub of the Year 2009 and Branch Pub of the Year 2010.

P

Nightingale 🏆

Nightingale Road, SG5 1RL TL192293

3-11 Mon; 2.30-11 Tue & Wed; 12-midnight Thu-Sat; 12-10.30 Sun ☎ (01462) 457448

Tring Brock Bitter, Colley's Dog; guest beers Ⓗ

This friendly Punch Taverns pub is around 150 years old and reputed to have three ghosts. It was formerly owned by Fordhams of Ashwell, whose name is set into the exterior stonework. The interior is open plan but retains the layout of the original rooms, with distinct seating areas. Five real ales and a cider are on handpump. Traditional entertainment includes darts, pool and board games. Sport is occasionally shown on the four TV screens. A barbecue is hosted every weekend, weather permitting. P

Ickleford

Cricketers

107 Arlesey Road, SG5 3TH TL184318

4-11; 12-midnight Sat (10.30 Sun) ☎ (07855) 2841285

thecricketersickleford.com

Courage Directors; Wells Eagle IPA; guest beers Ⓗ

Attractive traditional village pub situated at the North End of the village. Rejuvenated after recently becoming a free house and now a true part of the local community, the single bar has several seating areas, with some clustered around a real fire. Traditional pub games are available, with a quiz night every Thursday. Food on Monday and Tuesday evenings must be booked in advance.

(M2)

Kings Langley

Saracens Head

47 High Street, WD4 9HU

11-2.30, 5-11.30; 12.30-4, 7-10.30 Sun ☎ (01923) 400144

Adnams Bitter; Fuller's London Pride, ESB; Tring Ridgeway Ⓗ

Early 17th-century community-oriented pub proud of its status as a regular in the Guide and popular with a mixed clientele. The single room interior has a collection of Saracens' heads, old beer bottles, pottery jugs and bottles, and old telephones on display. The landlord often wins 'in bloom' prizes for his hanging baskets and window boxes. Lunchtime food is available every day. There are benches on the pavement for drinkers and smokers. No children are permitted under 14.

(500,501)P

Letchworth

Three Magnets ✔

18-20 Leys Avenue, SG6 3EW TL219326

7am-midnight Sun-Thu (1am Fri & Sat) ☎ (01462) 681093

Greene King Ruddles Best Bitter, Abbot; guest beers Ⓗ

The Wetherspoon chain aims to be all things to all people and this hostelry in a converted 1924 furniture/hardware shop (Brookers) succeeds very well. It is a family venue during the day (no alcohol served before 9am) and early evening, a regulars' pub later, a quiet meeting place except during international sports events, and a restaurant with competitively-priced food served all day. Many old photographs of early Letchworth adorn the walls.

Q

Ley Green

Plough

Plough Lane, SG4 8LA TL162243

12 (4 Mon & Tue)-11; 12-midnight Fri & Sat; 12-10.30 Sun

☎ (01438) 871394 kingswalden.blogspot.com

Greene King IPA, Abbot Ⓗ

Originally an ale house as far back as 1846, this is a warm and friendly traditional pub. Set in rolling farm country, it is a popular stop-off for walkers and cyclists exploring the area. The large patio enjoys idyllic views of the surrounding countryside – look out for the red kites. Visitors are welcome to join in the acoustic music session on a Tuesday evening. The snug bar is available for small functions. Hot and cold snacks, with real chips, are served Wednesday to Sunday lunchtimes.

Q(88)P

Lilley

Lilley Arms

41 West Street, LU2 8LN (N end of village off the green) TL117264

12-11 (10.30 Sun) ☎ (01462) 768371 lilley-arms.co.uk

Greene King IPA, Abbot Ⓗ

A 300-year-old former coaching inn set in the beautiful Hertfordshire countryside. It is a traditional country pub in an ideal location for horse riding, cycling or walking holidays. The Lilley Arms is included in one of the Chiltern Pub Walks. The restaurant is very popular so it is best to book, although on hotter days the garden has additional seating from where the chickens, ducks and other animals can be seen. (102)

London Colney

Bull

Barnet Road, AL2 1QU TL182037

12-11 (midnight Fri & Sat) ☎ (01727) 823160

thebullatlondoncolney.co.uk

Black Sheep Best Bitter; Greene King IPA; Young's Special; guest beers Ⓗ

Lovely old 17th-century timbered building by the River Colne with a cosy lounge and original fireplace. The large public bar features darts, pool and sport on TV. Outside there is a children's play area. Evening events include a quiz on Sunday, live music on Saturday and bingo on Thursday. Good value home-made meals are served Monday to Saturday lunchtimes, Wednesday is food night and curry evenings are held monthly.

(84,602,603)P

Much Hadham

Old Crown

Hadham Cross, SG10 6DF

12-3 (not Mon), 5.30-11; 12-11 Fri-Sun ☎ (01279) 842753

Greene King IPA; Woodforde's Wherry; guest beers H

Rejuvenated after a period of closure, this village community pub set deep in the Hertfordshire countryside is very much a part of local life. A free house, a beer from the local Green Tye Brewery is usually available. Good traditional food is served. This pub is proof that rural pubs can come back from closure and thrive. Q◐▶⊟(351)P

Oxhey

Villiers Arms

108 Villers Road, WD19 4AJ TQ121950

4-midnight ☎ (01923) 221556

Beer range varies H

Single-room family-run inn dating from the 19th century. It has recently become a free house and offers regularly changing guest ales, which can be enjoyed in front of the fire during the winter. The landlord is open to requests for new and different ales to add to the menu. The bar is decorated with a large range of interesting and idiosyncratic items including beer and drinks memorabilia, and boxing magazine and sheet music front covers. Dogs are welcome. ❀≠(Bushey)⊟♣

Potters Crouch

Holly Bush ✔

Bedmond Lane, AL2 3NN (off B4630 at jct of Potters Crouch Lane and Ragged Hall Lane) TL116052

12-2.30, 6-11; 12-2.30, 7-10.30 Sun ☎ (01727) 851792

thehollybushpub.co.uk

Fuller's Chiswick Bitter, London Pride, ESB H

An attractive early 17th-century pub in rural surroundings beautifully and tastefully furnished to a high standard and boasting large oak tables and period chairs. Spotless throughout, there are no jukeboxes, slot machines or TVs to disturb the drinker in any of the three drinking areas. The range of food is not extensive but is of high quality. The garden is lovely in summer and children are welcome here but no under-14s are permitted inside. The pub may be closed on Mondays – ring ahead. Q❀◐▶♿P⊱

Preston

Red Lion

The Green, SG4 7UD TL180247

12-2.30, 5.30-11; 12-3.30, 7-10.30 Sun ☎ (01462) 459585

Fuller's London Pride; Young's Bitter; guest beers H

This attractive Georgian free house on the village green is the first community-owned pub in Great Britain. It offers a constantly changing range of guest beers, many from micro-breweries. The landlord and landlady, Ray and Jo, continue to prepare fresh home-made food using locally sourced ingredients where possible (no food Tue and Sun eve). The pub is home to the village cricket teams and fundraises for charity. A regular CAMRA award winner. Q❀◐▶♿⊟(88)♣P⊱

Pye Corner

Plume of Feathers

Gilston, CM20 2RD TL449123

11 (12 Sun)-11 ☎ (01279) 424154

Adnams Broadside; Courage Best Bitter; guest beers H

Old coaching inn with a long L-shaped bar. At least one guest beer is available to supplement the regulars, often two on Friday and Saturday. The pub is very popular for its excellent food. Outside is a spacious courtyard patio and large grassed area, with plenty of tables for alfresco drinking and dining. There are rumours of a resident ghost. ❀◐▶

Radlett

Red Lion Hotel

78-80 Watling Street, WD7 7NP (on A5183) TQ163998

11-11.30 (midnight Fri & Sat); 12-10.30 Sun

☎ (01923) 855341 redlionradlett.co.uk

Young's Bitter, Special H

This Edwardian hotel dating from 1906 opposite the railway station was once a temperance house. It now has a spacious split level bar and a large restaurant. There are 14 guest rooms and a function room. A good menu of home-made meals is offered including daily specials. The patio at the front of the hotel overlooks Watling Street. ◐▶♿≠⊟(602,632)P⊱

Redbourn

Cricketers

East Common, AL3 7ND TL104119

12-11 (midnight Fri & Sat); 12-10.30 Sun

☎ (01582) 620612 thecricketersofredbourn.com

Greene King IPA; guest beers H

Attractive refurbished pub dating from 1725 overlooking the common and the historic cricket pitch established in the 18th century. A true free house, it serves up to four real ales. The pub has a large restaurant serving top class food freshly prepared using the finest ingredients. Local parking can be tricky. Q❀◐▶⊟(34,46,620)P⊱

Rickmansworth

Rose & Crown

Woodcock Hill, Harefield Road, WD3 1PP (jct of Harefield Road and Woodcock Hill, between Rickmansworth and Harefield) TQ060924

11-11 ☎ (01923) 897680 morethanjustapub.co.uk/theroseandcrown

Caledonian Deuchars IPA; Fuller's London Pride H

This countryside pub, part of which was originally a farmhouse, dates from the 1700s. It has a large garden with a marquee for functions, a small children's play area and a chicken run. Inside, winter visitors enjoy two real fires. The focus here is on providing good locally-sourced British food to complement well-chosen beers. A farmers' market is held on the second Saturday of the month with produce including meats, cheeses, ciders and beer carryouts. Dog owners and board gamers are made welcome. ❀◐▶♿≠⊖⊟(R21)♣P⊱

St Albans

Blacksmiths Arms ✔

56 St Peters Street, AL1 3HG TL150075

10-11 (midnight Fri & Sat); 12-11 Sun ☎ (01727) 868845

Taylor Landlord; Wells Bombardier; guest beers H

A great example of a town-centre hostelry, featuring two regular ales and six changing guests

including beers from local breweries. Recently redecorated, the pub has a friendly and lively feel, with regular beer festivals and live music every Friday and Saturday night. It opens at 10am for breakfast and serves food throughout the day.
❀◐♿⇌(City)🚌♣⚍

Boot

4 Market Place, AL3 5DG TL147072
⏲ 12-midnight (1am Fri & Sat); 12-11.30 Sun
☎ (01727) 857533
Black Sheep Best Bitter; Draught Bass; Taylor Landlord; guest beers Ⓗ
Dating back to the 1400s, the Boot has been restored and refurbished to create a typical market town pub, with low ceilings, exposed beams, a log fire and wood flooring. It is particularly busy on Wednesdays and Saturdays, bustling with market traders and shoppers. Live bands play on Sunday afternoon. Westons Old Rosie cider is available in summer. No food on Sunday or Monday.
🜂◐⇌(Abbey/City)🚌♣

Farmers Boy

134 London Road, AL1 1PQ TL152068
⏲ 12-11 (midnight Wed & Thu, 2am Fri & Sat)
☎ (01727) 860535 🌐 farmersboy.net
Fuller's London Pride; Taylor Landlord; Verulam Farmers Joy Ⓗ
One-room cottage-style hostelry just outside the city centre. A micro-brewery behind the pub supplies two of the real ales. The TVs are turned on only for major sporting events. Quiz night is Wednesday and live bands perform on Thursday evening. Closing time beyond 11pm depends on how busy the pub is and families may be admitted at the discretion of the management.
🜂◐⇌(City)♣⚍

Goat Inn ✔

37 Sopwell Lane, AL1 1RN (off Holywell Hill) TL147069
⏲ 12-3, 5-11 Mon; 12-11 (midnight Fri & Sat)
☎ (01727) 833934 🌐 goatinn.co.uk
St Austell Tribute; guest beers Ⓗ
Welcoming, traditional 15th-century pub, a short walk from the cathedral and situated on the old coaching route from London. Food is served in an award-winning restaurant at the rear of the pub. Families are welcome on Saturday and Sunday lunchtimes. Jazz/rock/funk jam sessions featuring local musicians are hosted on Wednesday evening, and a quiz on Sunday. The games room has bar billiards, darts, dominoes, shove-ha'penny and board games. Westons Old Rosie cider is available.
❀◐⇌(Abbey/City)🚌♣⚍

Mermaid ✔

98 Hatfield Road, AL1 3RL TL152074
⏲ 12-11 Mon, Tue & Thu; 12-midnight Wed, Fri & Sat; 12-10.30 Sun ☎ (01727) 837758 🌐 mermaidalehouse.com
Dark Star Hophead; guest beers Ⓗ
Small one-room pub, handy for both the railway station and the city centre. The guest beer range showcases a wide and ever-changing selection of real ale, always including a mild, porter or stout. LocAle brewers regularly feature, including the town's Verulam Brewery. A selection of foreign bottled beers and real cider is also stocked and beer festivals are held throughout the year. The pub is also home to chess and darts teams.
◐♿⇌(City)🚌♣P⚍

Six Bells 🏆

16-18 St Michaels Street, AL3 4SH TL137074
⏲ 12-11 (11.30 Fri & Sat); 12-10.30 Sun ☎ (01727) 856945
🌐 the-six-bells.com
Fuller's London Pride; Oakham JHB; Taylor Landlord; guest beers Ⓗ
This excellent, traditional 16th-century pub, now a true free house, is within walking distance of the city centre and cathedral, and close to Verulamium Park and Museum. The only licensed premises within the walls of Roman Verulamium, five beers are available, all in lined glasses. Food is served lunchtimes and evenings (not Sun eve). Occasional quiz nights and live music sessions feature at this popular, friendly pub. 🜂◐🚌(300,301)♣P⚍

White Hart Tap

4 Keyfield Terrace, AL1 1QJ TL150069
⏲ 12-11 ☎ (01727) 860974 🌐 whiteharttap.co.uk
Caledonian Deuchars IPA; Fuller's London Pride; guest beers Ⓗ
Welcoming single-bar back-street local featuring guest beers from the Punch Taverns range. Good value, home-made food is served every lunchtime and Tuesday to Friday evenings, with fish and chips on Friday and roasts on Sunday. Quiz night is Wednesday and occasional live music plays on Saturday night. There is a covered area for smokers outside. Barbecues are held in summer. A public car park is opposite the pub. 🜂❀◐⇌(Abbey)⚍

White Lion

91 Sopwell Lane, AL1 1RN (off Holywell Hill) TL149068
⏲ 12-11 ☎ (01727) 850540 🌐 thewhitelionph.co.uk
Black Sheep Best Bitter; Young's Special; guest beers Ⓗ
This friendly and quiet 16th-century two-bar pub is close to St Albans Abbey. Six beers are available from the Punch Taverns' list. Appetising home-made food is served daily including some intriguing dishes, and whenever possible the eggs are supplied by the landlord's own chickens. The large garden has a barbecue and boules pitch. A former local CAMRA Pub of the Year.
🜂Q❀◐⇌(Abbey/City)🚌(320,321,724)♣⚍

St Paul's Walden

Strathmore Arms

London Road, SG4 8BT TL193222
⏲ 6-11 Mon; 12-2, 5-11 Tue-Thu; 12-11 Fri & Sat; 12-10.30 Sun ☎ (01438) 871654
Buntingford Golden Plover; Fuller's London Pride Ⓗ
Situated on the Bowes-Lyon estate, this rural pub is divided into drinking, dining and games areas. A beer paradise, it offers a constantly changing range of beers and hosts regular beer festivals. A range of foreign bottled beers, particularly Belgian, is also available. Wild food nights are a highlight, with food made using local wild ingredients. A former winner of CAMRA Hertfordshire Pub of the Year and Branch Community Pub of the Year.
Q❀◐🚌(304)♣P

Sandridge

Green Man

31 High Street, AL4 9DD TL169104
⏲ 11-11 (midnight Fri & Sat); 12-11 Sun ☎ (01727) 854845
Black Sheep Best Bitter Ⓖ**; Greene King IPA** Ⓗ**, Abbot** Ⓖ

Located in the High Street, this pub is at the heart of Sandridge. The landlord is now in his 24th year of residence and has been nominated for a community award by a local newspaper for raising money through charity events. The family-run locals' pub extends a warm welcome to all discerning beer and cider drinkers, serving four real ales – three of them straight from the cask. Up to six real ciders from Westons are available.
⛰Q☕❀◐◑⊟🚌(304,620)♣P

Sawbridgeworth

Gate

81 London Road, CM21 9JJ
⌚ 11.30-2.30, 5.30-11; 11.30-11 Fri & Sat; 12-11 Sun
☎ (01279) 722313
Beer range varies Ⓗ/Ⓖ
This large pub with two bars in the centre of Sawbridgeworth attracts both beer and sports fans. The Sawbridgeworth Brewery is owned by the pub and located in the car park, and its beers are often among the changing range of countrywide ales. A famous collection of pump clips adorns the walls.
❀◐⇌🚌(333,510)♣🍎P⚟

Stevenage

Our Mutual Friend

Broadwater Crescent, SG2 8EH
⌚ 12-11 (11.30 Fri & Sat) ☎ (01438) 312282
Beer range varies Ⓗ
Real ale enthusiasts from far and wide come to sample the seven ever-changing cask beers available in this thriving community pub. Since being brought back from the cask ale graveyard in 2002 it has appeared in every edition of the Good Beer Guide. Real cider, perry and Belgian bottled beers complement the real ale. A beer festival brightens up January. Winner of many local CAMRA awards including Pub of the Year 2006-2008.
Q❀◐⊟🚌♣🍎P⚟⊡

Tring

King's Arms

King Street, HP23 6BE
⌚ 12-2.30, 7-11 (11.30 Fri); 11.30-3, 7-11 Sat; 12-4, 7-10.30 Sun ☎ (01442) 823318 🌐 kingsarmstring.co.uk
Wadworth 6X; guest beers Ⓗ
This 1830s back-street local is popular with all ages. The striking fuchsia pink building is a former local and regional CAMRA Pub of the Year. Run by the same family for 29 years, it offers a changing range of five ales and one real cider. Two real fires are welcoming in winter and outside is a secluded heated patio with canopies. Home-cooked food is based on an imaginative international menu. Children are welcome at all times.
⛰Q❀◐◑♿🚌(61,500,501)♣🍎⚟

Robin Hood ✔

1 Brook Street, HP23 5ED (jct B4635/B486)
⌚ 11.30-3, 5.30-11 (11.30 Fri); 12-4, 6-11.30 Sat; 12-4, 7-11 Sun ☎ (01442) 824912 🌐 therobinhoodtring.co.uk
Fuller's Chiswick Bitter, Discovery, London Pride, ESB; Gale's Seafarers Ale; guest beer Ⓗ
Olde worlde end of town hostelry with a split-level bar and warming stove creating a cosy feel. A busy pub with a mixed clientele, it has a popular patio courtyard designed to add extra drinking space. The enthusiastic landlords are dedicated to quality beer and food. One of Fuller's flagship outlets, six beers are on handpump, and fish is the speciality on the food menu. The Wednesday quiz is held in aid of a local charity. ⛰Q❀◐◑🚌(61,500)♣⚟

Ware

Crooked Billet

140 Musley Hill, SG12 7NL TL362150
⌚ 12-2.30 (Tue & Fri only), 5.30-11.30 (midnight Fri); 12-midnight Sat; 12-11.30 Sun ☎ (01920) 462516
Beer range varies Ⓗ
The 'Billet' celebrates over 10 years in the Guide, remaining one of the best local outlets for guest beers and, especially, dark ales – a mild, porter or stout is available throughout the year. Three ever-changing ales are on handpump, with a fourth often drawn direct from the cellar. The landlord is a supporter of Carlisle United and the bar is popular with football fans. It can become lively when matches are screened on TV and when Ware FC are playing. ⛰♿🚌(395)♣⚟

Worppell

35 Watton Road, SG12 0AD TL353147
⌚ 12-2.30, 5-11; 12-midnight Fri& Sat; 12-10 Sun
☎ (01920) 411666
Greene King IPA, Abbot Ⓗ
For more than 25 years George and Pat have run this pub, making them one of Hertfordshire's longest serving and much-loved landlords. Beers are always in exemplary condition – with no finer-kept Abbot for miles. A third ale is often also available – a seasonal Greene King offering or a genuine guest. A small, cosy, community pub, food is served weekday lunchtimes. Football on TV can be lively, with the customers often more entertaining than the match! ◐⇌♣

Wareside

Chequers

SG12 7QY (on B1004) TL394157
⌚ 12-3, 6-11; 12-4, 6-10.30 Sun ☎ (01920) 467010
Adnams Bitter; Taylor Landlord; guest beers Ⓗ
Traditional village free house, run by the same family for 14 years. Dating from the 15th century, it was originally a coaching inn and has three distinct bar areas plus a restaurant. There are no games machines or music, and swearing is banned. All food is home-made, with vegetarian options. Situated in beautiful unspoilt countryside, the pub is a popular stop-off for ramblers and cyclists. B&B accommodation is available.
⛰Q❀🛏◐◑♿🚌(M3,M4)P⚟

Watford

One Crown

156 High Street, WD17 2EN TQ112962
⌚ 12-11 (12.30am Fri & Sat); 12-9 Sun ☎ (01923) 222626
Tring Jack O'Legs, seasonal beer Ⓗ
This town-centre pub is the oldest in Watford, the building dating from the 16th century. The U-shaped bar divides into lounge and games areas, the latter with a pool table and dartboard. Outside, behind the pub, there is a patio with seating. The clientele is a mixture of locals and visitors to the town centre. The guest beers are often seasonal beers from Tring Brewery and change on a monthly basis. The pub frequently has karaoke and live music. ⛰❀◐◑⛺🚌

West Herts Sports Club

8 Park Avenue, WD18 7HP (S of A412, near town hall) TQ103964

4 (12 Fri & Sat)-11; 12-10.30 Sun (01923) 229239

westhertssports.co.uk

Fuller's London Pride; Young's Bitter

Clubhouse featuring a comfortable, modern bar, decorated with a sporting theme. Most major sporting events are screened here and pub games are played. Guest beers are mostly from small independents, served in oversized glasses. Rolls and pies are usually available. The function room, home of the CAMRA Watford Beer Festival for the past 15 years, is available for hire. The club is open to non-members up to three times a year – show a current CAMRA membership card or a copy of this Guide for entry.

Wheathampstead

Swan

56 High Street, AL4 8AR TL177139

11-11 (midnight Fri & Sat); 12-10.30 Sun

(01582) 833110 wheathampstead.net/swan/index.htm

Greene King IPA; St Austell Tribute; guest beers

Village inn dating from 1744, with exposed beams and three fireplaces including an inglenook. A thriving community village pub, it offers something for everyone – from live bands to Sunday roasts for all the family. The upper bar has Sky TV and a dartboard, lunch is served in the lower bar and there is a pool room to the rear. The landlord hosts an evening quiz on Wednesday. In early September there is a beer festival featuring a wide selection of real ales and several ciders.

Wildhill

Woodman

45 Wildhill Road, AL9 6EA (between A1000 and B158) TL264068

11.30-2.30, 5.30-11; 12-2.30, 7-10.30 Sun

(01707) 642618

Greene King IPA, Abbot; McMullen AK; guest beers

This small, friendly village pub extends a warm welcome to a varied clientele of all ages. Six beers are available including three guests, with at least one ale from a Herts brewery. Good pub grub is served at lunchtime but no chips (no food Sun). The large garden is ideal in summer. The pub holds an annual beer festival in June. An all-round superb boozer, the Woodman has won CAMRA South Herts Pub of the Year a record seven times.

Willian

Fox

Baldock Lane, SG6 2AE TL224306

12-11 (midnight Fri & Sat); 12-10.30 Sun

(01462) 480233 foxatwillian.co.uk

Adnams Bitter; Brancaster Best; Fuller's London Pride; Woodforde's Wherry

Built in 1860, this free house is in a pleasant village location next to to the main street. Extensively refurbished in 2004, the single room interior is now light and airy, with a restaurant to the rear. The ethos of the pub is to serve good beer, wine and food to a discerning clientele. The restaurant specialises in seafood, largely sourced on the Norfolk coast. Beers also come from Norfolk breweries including Brancaster and Woodforde's.

Woolmer Green

Chequers

16 London Road, SG3 6JP TL253185

12 (4 Mon)-11; 12-8.30 Sun (01438) 813216

benicksatthechequers.co.uk/

Adnams Bitter; Young's Bitter; guest beer

Large brick-built inn at the southern end of the village on the old Great North Road. Originally it had separate bars but the interior is now largely open plan, with a central fireplace sporting a real fire during the cooler months. Quality cask ale is very popular although the range is limited. The three cask beers on offer are well-liked, with the guest beer changing regularly. Home-cooked food made with fresh ingredients is served in the dining room or the more casual bar.

(300,301)

White Hart Tap, St Albans (Photo: Katie Hunt)

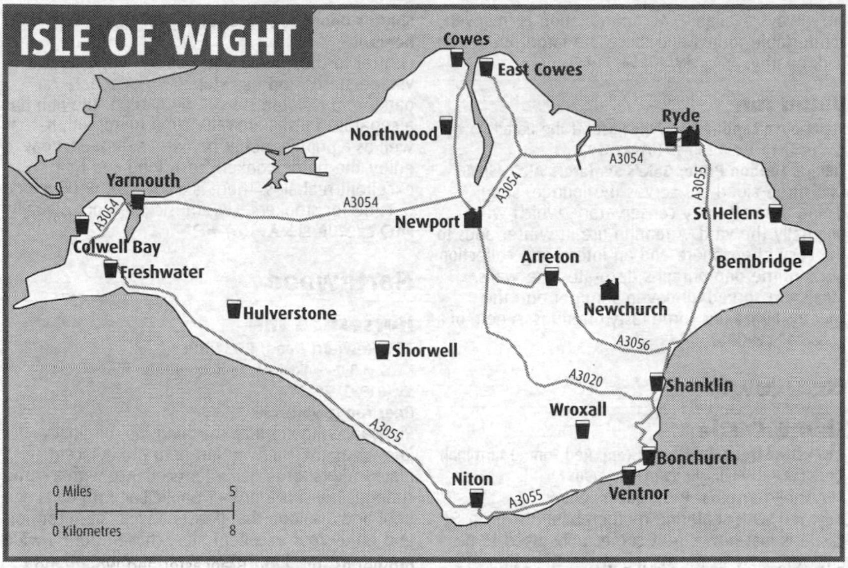

Arreton

White Lion ✔

Main Road, PO30 3AA

☼ 11-11; 12-10.30 Sun ☎ (01983) 528479

🌐 white-lion-arreton.com

Taylor Landlord; guest beers Ⓗ

A lovely old country pub a stone's throw from St George's 11th-century church with much character and charm. Black ceiling beams and interesting brassware complement the varied assortment of old signs and bric-a-brac. The pub has a fine reputation for food with an interesting specials board and popular curry night on Wednesday. One of the two guest beers is usually local. Families are welcome and there is a quiz fortnightly in the winter. ⌂Q♉❀◑♿▲🚌(8)♣P

Bembridge

Olde Village Inn

61 High Street, PO35 5SF

☼ 11-midnight; 12-11 Sun ☎ (01983) 872616

Greene King IPA, Abbot; Sharp's Doom Bar Ⓗ

Comfortable village local with a warm, friendly atmosphere. The one-bar interior is expansive but cosy. Older people are catered for Monday to Friday with lunchtime meals at reduced prices – food is served 12-3pm and 6-9pm. Live music plays on occasional Fridays and a popular quiz is held on the first Saturday in the month. There are two letting rooms, a patio area to the rear and a petanque terraine. ⌂❀⛌◑♿▲🚌(10,14)♣P⁄–

Bonchurch

Bonchurch Inn

The Shute, PO38 1NU (off Shanklin-Ventnor road)

☼ 11-3, 6.30-11; 12-3, 7-10.30 Sun ☎ (01983) 852611

🌐 bonchurch-inn.co.uk

Courage Best Bitter, Directors Ⓖ

Superbly preserved stone pub in a Dickensian courtyard, formerly the stables of the adjacent manor house. Little has changed since it gained its licence in the 1840s, making it one of the most unspoilt inns on the island. The pub featured in an episode of The Detectives, and displays mementos from many famous names who have popped in when visiting the Island. The fine food menu reflects an Italian influence and all dishes are cooked to order. Q♉❀⛌◑⊟▲🚌(3)♣P⁄–

Colwell Bay

Colwell Bay Inn

Colwell Road, PO40 9LZ (opp village green)

☼ 11-11; 12-10.30 Sun ☎ (01983) 756055

Fuller's London Pride; guest beers Ⓗ

This pub dates back more than 200 years. Originally called the Drum & Monkey, then the Nelson, for some years it was used as the coastguards' barracks. Well supported by locals and tourists, it has a huge car park and disabled access to the terrace and bar. The extensive beer garden has an adventure playground and toddler safe play area. Two guest ales are on offer, one from a local brewery. Food is served all day in summer. ⌂❀◑♿🚌(7,11)P⁄–

Cowes

Anchor Inn

1 High Street, PO31 7SA (opp Somerfields)

☼ 11-11 (midnight Fri & Sat); 12-10.30 Sun

☎ (01983) 292823 🌐 theanchorcowes.com

Fuller's London Pride; Goddards Fuggle-Dee-Dum; Ringwood Best Bitter; guest beers Ⓗ

Originally the Trumpeters back in 1704, this high-street pub is next to the marina and ferry. Hugely popular during the summer, it has a covered area outside with tables for smokers. An extensive food menu is available all day, with families welcome. Live music plays outside in summer and in the stable bar in winter. One Island ale and two guests

INDEPENDENT BREWERIES

Goddards Ryde
Island Newport (NEW)
Yates' Newchurch

are always available. Accommodation is in seven comfortable rooms and there is a large public car park nearby. ♛♞❀⊟◐◗⊡(1)♣⌐

Union Inn

Watchouse Lane, PO31 7QH (just off the Parade)
⊛ 11-11; 12-10.30 Sun ☎ (01983) 293163
Fuller's London Pride; Gale's Seafarers Ale, HSB ⊞
One three-sided bar serves the lounge, snug, dining area and airy conservatory, which was originally the yard. A roaring fire in winter adds to the cosy atmosphere and an interesting collection of maritime photographs decorates the walls. Meals are served all day in summer and the specials board has some tasty offerings. A gem of a pub. ♛♞❀◐◗⊡(1)⌐

East Cowes

Ship & Castle

21 Castle Street, PO32 6RB (opp Red Funnel terminal)
⊛ 12 (11 Sat)-midnight ☎ (01983) 290522
St Austell Dartmoor Best; guest beer ⊞
Adorned with seafaring memorabilia, the Ship & Castle is just how street corner pubs used to be, and very cosy in the winter when the wind whistles across the Red Funnel car park. Easy to find – turn left off the floating bridge or once around the block if arriving from Southampton. Despite the small bar there are always at least three beers on offer and Westons Old Rosie cider. Bustling on games nights, the pub runs four darts teams to keep the locals happy. ❀⊡(4,5)♣●⌐▯

Freshwater

Prince of Wales

Princes Road, PO40 9ED (just off shopping area)
⊛ 3-11; 11-11.30 Fri & Sat; 12-11 Sun ☎ (01983) 753535
Yates Undercliff Experience; guest beer ⊞
Fine, unspoilt gem of a town pub run by possibly the longest-serving landlord on the Isle of Wight. Situated just off the main Freshwater shopping centre, it has a large garden to relax in and pleasant public and lounge bars to sample the well-kept ales. It now offers five frequently-changing guest beers so there is always something new to try. A popular games area adds to the lively atmosphere. Q❀⊟▲⊡(11)♣P⌐▯

Hulverstone

Sun Inn

Main Road, PO30 4EH
⊛ 12-10.30; 11-11 summer ☎ (01983) 741124
⊕ sun-hulverstone.com
Beer range varies ⊞
This 600-year-old hostelry boasts uninterrupted views to the sea. It has a strong following for food with an extensive menu and daily specials served all day, plus a weekly curry night. There is a large restaurant and the pub caters for wedding parties in a stunning extension. Weekly music nights feature local musicians. Well-behaved children are welcome. The four ever-changing beers include at least one from the Island. ♛❀◐◗♿⊡(7)♣P

Niton

White Lion

High Street, PO38 2AT SZ507768
⊛ 11 (12 Sun)-11 ☎ (01983) 730293
Sharp's Doom Bar; Yates Undercliff Experience; guest beers ⊞
Central to the village, the pub sits opposite the village stores and bus stop, with adequate car parking, a children's area and garden. The pub has a separate formal area/function room with bar, as well as a popular public bar with extended areas to enjoy the home-cooked fresh food and four excellent real ales. There is a covered, decked area outside for smokers. Live music plays occasionally. ♛Q♞❀◐◗⊟♿▲⊡(6)♣P⌐

Northwood

Horseshoe Inn

353 Newport Road, PO31 8PL
⊛ 12-5.30, 7-midnight; 12-midnight Thu-Sun
☎ (01983) 292349
Beer range varies ⊞
Pleasant 17th-century coaching inn, originally known as the Halfway Inn until the adjacent blacksmith's forge gained precedence with a name change. There is a proper public bar with darts and pool and a saloon that boasts a well. Sit in comfort and enjoy four excellent ales, chosen from a wide range, with a dark beer often available. Always expect to see the latest big game on two massive TV screens. Well-behaved children are welcome. ♛Q♞❀⊟▲⊡(1)♣P⌐

Travellers Joy 🏆

85 Pallance Road, PO31 8LS (on A3020)
⊛ 11-2.30, 5-11; 11-midnight Fri & Sat; 12-3, 7-11 Sun
☎ (01983) 298024 ⊕ tjoy.co.uk
Shepherd Neame Spitfire; Yates Undercliff Experience; guest beers ⊞
Offering one of the best choices of cask ale on the Isle of Wight, this renovated and extended old country inn was the Island's first beer exhibition house. Six carefully chosen and interesting ales supplement the Undercliff and Spitfire, with Island beers always available – if you have mastered the 'Northwood nod' you may even get a special from the cellar. A good range of home-cooked food is available lunchtime and evening plus the occasional real cider. ♛♞❀◐◗▲⊡(1,30)♣●P⌐

Ryde

S Fowler & Co ✔

41-43 Union Street, PO33 2LF
⊛ 9-midnight (1am Fri & Sat) ☎ (01983) 812112
Courage Directors; Greene King Ruddles County, Abbot ⊞
This converted drapery store offers one of the most varied ranges of well-kept beers you will find anywhere. The pub's name was suggested by the local CAMRA branch – it was not just the name of the former drapery but also that of a founder member of CAMRA, whose life is commemorated in the pub. There is a selection of 12 ales, fewer at the quietest periods. Food served until 10pm. ♞◐◗⇛(Esplanade)⊡(4,9)

Simeon Arms

21 Simeon Street, PO33 1JG (opp Canoe Lake)
⊛ 11-11 (midnight Thu-Sat); 12-11.30 Sun
☎ (01983) 614954
Courage Directors; Goddards Special Bitter; guest beer ⊞
Thriving yet unlikely gem tucked away in a Ryde back street with a Tardis-like interior and annexed

function hall. The pub is immensely popular with the local community who come to participate in various leagues including darts, crib and pool, and petanque on the enormous floodlit terrain in summer. You can always expect to find a local ale, and food is available lunchtimes and weekend evenings. Live music plays on Saturday and Sunday night. The smoking area outside is heated and covered. ❀◑≋(Esplanade)🚌♣⁻

Solent Inn ✔

7 Monkton Street, PO33 1JW
11-11 (midnight Thu-Sat); 12-10.30 Sun
☎ (01983) 563546 🌐 solentinn.com
Banks's Bitter; guest beers Ⓗ
Excellent street-corner local with a warm, welcoming atmosphere. There is live music at least three times a week and a very friendly weekly quiz. An interesting range of ales includes four guests mainly from the Punch portfolio plus one local ale. Good home-cooked food is served at lunchtime and barbecues hosted in summer. Themed and karaoke nights are always popular. A local challenge is shove-ha'penny – Ryde is one of the few places that a local league can be found. ❀≋(Esplanade)🚌♣⁻

St Helens

Vine Inn

Upper Green Road, PO33 1UJ
11-11 (12.20am Fri & Sat); 11-11.30 Sun
☎ (01983) 872337 🌐 the-vine-inn.co.uk
Fuller's London Pride; guest beers Ⓗ
The front of the pub overlooks what is possibly the biggest village green in the kingdom, known locally as Goose Island. An eclectic selection of memorabilia reflecting local history, from railways to hunting to breweries to maritime, decorates the walls. From Easter to late summer there is an additional tented area outside. Three guest beers include one from an Island brewery, with two extra on the bar during the summer. It's close to a public car park. ❀◑♿▲🚌(10,14,16)♣⁻

Shanklin

Chine Inn

Chine Hill, PO37 6BW
11-4, 7-11; 12-10.30 Sun ☎ (01983) 865880
Sharp's Doom Bar; Taylor Landlord; guest beer Ⓗ
This inn is a classic. The pub, which has stood since 1621, must have some claim to being one of the oldest buildings with a licence on the Island. Completely refurbished, it has retained plenty of the original charm for which it was well known. Live music is hosted on Saturday night and Sunday afternoon. The Chine Inn ghosts – a girl in blue and an old man in the corner – have been seen by small children. The magnificent kitchens will be put to good use. Q❀◑🚌(3,16)⁻

King Harry's Bar

Glenbrook Hotel, 8 Church Road, PO37 6NU
11 (12 winter)-11; 12-11 Sun ☎ (01983) 863119
Fuller's ESB; guest beers Ⓗ
Charming 19th-century thatched property with two established Tudor bars, restaurants, decked gardens and the Chine walk, plus car parking front and rear. It offers five guest beers, chosen for their originality, and a real cider. The long-established Henry VIII kitchen specialises in steaks to die for. There are function facilities and entertainment in the summer months. Accommodation is available. Q❀◑♿▲🚌(3,16)♣P⁻

Shorwell

Crown Inn

Walkers Lane, PO30 3JZ SZ459830
10.30 (11.30 Sun)-11 ☎ (01983) 740293
🌐 crowninnshorwell.co.uk
Ringwood Fortyniner; Sharp's Doom Bar; guest beers Ⓗ
Expansive pub in the heart of the countryside with a central multi-sided bar and traditional bar areas offering a range of four beers and a good home-cooked pub menu. An area is set aside for dining and food is served all day. The pub has a trout stream running through the garden, ducks in abundance to keep the children amused, and plenty of car parking. The picturesque village of Shorwell features many thatched and traditional buildings. Q❀◑♿▲🚌(7)♣P

Ventnor

Volunteer

30 Victoria Street, PO38 1ES (50m from bus terminal)
11-11 (midnight Fri & Sat); 12-11 Sun ☎ (01983) 852537
🌐 volunteer-inn.co.uk
Courage Best Bitter; Greene King Abbot; guest beers Ⓗ
Built in 1866, the Volunteer is probably the smallest pub on the Isle of Wight. A past winner of local CAMRA Pub of the Year, between four and six guest beers are usually available including a local brew. No chips, no children, no fruit machines, no video games – just a pure adult drinking house and one of the few places where you can still play Rings and enjoy a traditional games night. Live music plays on Sunday afternoon. Q🚌(3,6)♣

Wroxall

Four Seasons

2 Clarence Road, PO38 3BY
11-12.30am ☎ (01983) 854701
🌐 the-fourseasons-inn.co.uk
Gale's HSB; Ringwood Best Bitter; guest beer Ⓗ
Formerly known as the Star, this pub was brought back to life after a fire when it could easily have been lost to housing. Now a successful village pub, it has an Island-wide reputation for good food, with all produce sourced locally and cooked fresh to order. Meals are served all day and under-10s eat free. There is a covered, heated smokers' area and a small car park. Q❀◑♿▲🚌(3)♣P⁻

Yarmouth

Kings Head

Quay Street, PO41 0PB (opp ferry terminal)
11-11; 12-10.30 Sun ☎ (01983) 760351
Beer range varies Ⓗ
Ancient 16th-century town pub with a big open fire and an interesting collection of old Island prints and local photographs. Stone floors, low ceilings and cosy corners in abundance help to create an intimate atmosphere. Home-cooked food includes fresh fish, with daily specials. Three changing ales are on offer, always including an Island beer. A handy place to wait for the Yarmouth-Lymington ferry. ❀◑🚌(7,11)⁻

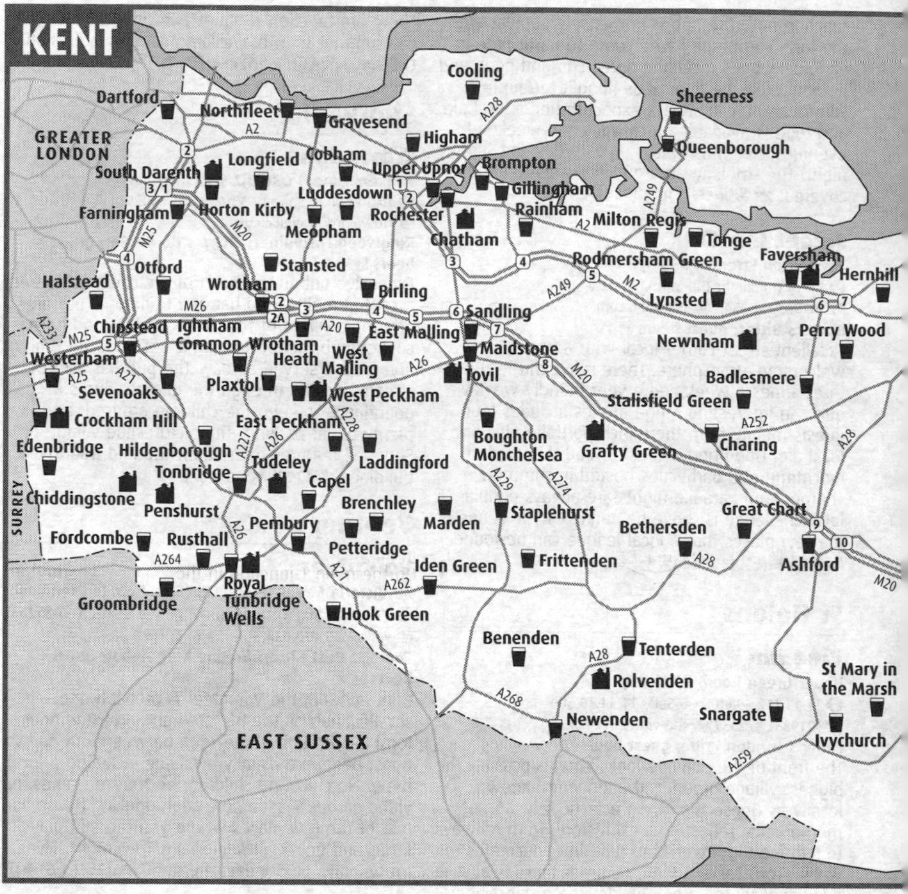

Ashford

County Hotel ✔

10 High Street, TN24 8TD

⏲ 9am-midnight (1am Fri & Sat) ☎ (01233) 646891

Greene King Ruddles Best Bitter, Abbot; guest beers Ⓗ

The building dates from circa 1710 when it was a doctor's home and medical practice. It became an inn around 1890 and was named the County Hotel in 1926. There are two bars in a split-level layout with three distinct seating areas. Wetherspoon's good value food is available from opening until late and children are permitted if dining. This pub is a welcome real ale oasis in the centre of Ashford, with four changing guest beers.

Q≿◑♿⇌🚌🍎P⊱

Pheasant

Trinity Road, TN25 4QH

⏲ 11-11 ☎ (01233) 647604 🌐 pheasantpub.co.uk

Marston's Pedigree; guest beers Ⓗ

Brand new, purpose-built pub near the Eureka Business Park with a quiet, relaxed atmosphere. Spice night is held on Thursday evening, with a choice of dishes and a drink included in the price, and a quiz is hosted on Sunday evening. Pub food is served daily until late. The bar is divided into three areas – a social drinking area, a quiet area, and a family dining area. ≿❀◑♿🚌(C,E)P

Badlesmere

Red Lion

Ashford Road, ME13 0NX TR009539

⏲ 12-11 (midnight Fri & Sat); 12-10.30 (9.30 winter) Sun ☎ (01233) 740320 🌐 redlionbadlesmere.co.uk

Shepherd Neame Master Brew Bitter; guest beers Ⓗ

Free house dating from 1546 with exposed timbers and low ceilings. Popular with walkers, it is dog and family friendly. Beer festivals are held on the Easter and August bank holidays with camping facilities available. Home-cooked food is served all hours except Friday, Sunday and Monday evenings. The pub gets busy on Friday evening when live music plays, and the large garden is popular in summer. Bus 666 from Ashford and Faversham runs hourly Monday to Friday and every two hours on Saturday, but not evenings or Sunday.

🔥❀◑⛺🚌(666)♣P⊱

Benenden

Bull

The Street, TN17 4DE

⏲ 12 (4 Mon)-midnight; 12-11 Sun ☎ (01580) 240054 🌐 thebullatbenenden.co.uk

Dark Star Hophead; Harveys Sussex Best Bitter; Larkins Traditional; guest beer Ⓗ

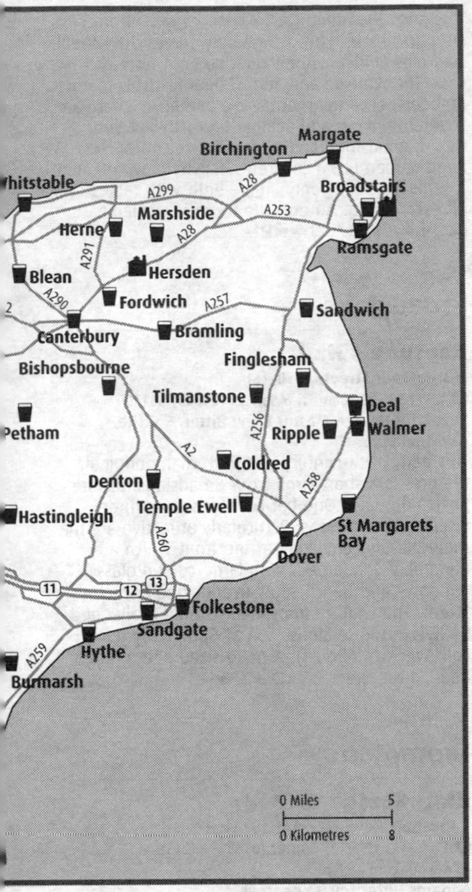

Award-winning free house next to a picturesque village green. The interior features multi-level wooden floors, exposed beams and an inglenook fireplace. There is a separate dining/function room, although meals are served throughout – excellent food includes a Sunday carvery (booking advisable), curry, fish 'n' chips and steak nights. An over-60s lunchtime menu is offered. A family summer fayre (with beer tent) is held in July and a beer festival in September. A monthly music club is hosted for local musicians plus occasional live music at weekends. ♨✿⇄◑♿🚌(297)♣P⁄

Bethersden

George Inn

The Street, TN26 3AG

⏲ 12-11.30 (10.30 Sun) ☎ (01233) 820235

Brakspear Bitter; Greene King Old Speckled Hen; Harveys Sussex Best Bitter; guest beer Ⓗ

Situated in the centre of the village, this former Style & Winch pub is now a free house offering a warm welcome to locals and visitors alike. Parts of the building are thought to date from the 16th century. Old pictures of the pub, village and inhabitants hang from the exposed beams and brickwork. Food is served every lunchtime and evening except Sunday evening. Beer festivals are held near to St George's Day and in the summer. ♨Q✿◑🚌(400)♣●P⁄

Birchington

Acorn Inn

6 Park Lane, CT7 0AW

⏲ 11-11; 12-10.30 Sun ☎ (01843) 841196

Fuller's London Pride; Shepherd Neame Master Brew Bitter; guest beers Ⓗ

A warm and friendly free house situated just off the main square with a beautiful flint wall leading to a restaurant. Excellent pub food is served as well as a more formal menu. The bar is well lit and has big mirrors behind it. Lots of exposed beams remains but the decor is 1970s. The pub caters for both local and passing trade, with a garden for the summer and a covered smoking area. ✿♿🚌(8)P⁄

Birling

Nevill Bull

1 Ryarsh Road, ME19 5JW

⏲ closed Mon; 11-3, 6.30-11; 12-3, 7-11 Sun

☎ (01732) 843193

Adnams Bitter; Shepherd Neame Master Brew Bitter; guest beer Ⓗ

On the main T-junction in the village, renamed in 1953 in memory of local man Michael Nevill, killed in WWII. The main bar, with brick walls and black, wooden beams decorated with brasses and copper items, is warmed by a real log fire. Blackboards list a popular food menu that is also available in the adjacent restaurant. Above the fire is an interesting display of bottled beers. Popular guest ales may stay for some time. ♨✿◑♿🚌(58)P

Bishopsbourne

Mermaid

The Street, CT4 5HX

⏲ 12-3.30, 6-11; 12-11 Sat; 12-3.30, 7-11 Sun

☎ (01227) 830581

Shepherd Neame Master Brew Bitter, Late Red Ⓗ

Built in 1865, this charming red-brick pub nestles in a pretty valley and is well worth the short detour from the A2. The two bars are a good place for a chat or a game of darts. Excellent home-cooked meals are served at lunchtimes (not Sun). There is live music monthly, and occasional quizzes and summer barbecues. A heated and covered area is provided for smokers. Walkers and dogs are welcome, but children are allowed only in the attractive enclosed garden. A ramp is available for wheelchair users. ♨Q✿◑♿♣⁄

INDEPENDENT BREWERIES

Goacher's Tovil
Hopdaemon Newnham
Larkins Chiddingstone
Millis South Darenth
Moodley's Penshurst (NEW)
Nelson Chatham
Old Dairy Rolvenden (NEW)
Ramsgate Broadstairs
Shepherd Neame Faversham
Swan West Peckham
Tonbridge Tudeley (NEW)
Tunbridge Wells Royal Tunbridge Wells (NEW)
Wantsum Hersden (NEW)
Westerham Crockham Hill
Whitstable Grafty Green

Blean

Hare & Hounds
4 Blean Hill, CT2 9EF (on A290)
☼ 12-11 (11.30 Fri & Sat); 12-10.30 Sun ☎ (01227) 471594
Ringwood Best Bitter; Taylor Landlord; guest beer Ⓗ
Attractive half-bricked building, formerly a Flint's inn. The pub has built up a considerable reputation for excellent, good value food, using local produce (no food Mon, or Sun after 5.30pm). The guest beer is often from a Kent brewery, usually Ramsgate or Wantsum. Sporting events can be viewed on an unobtrusive TV in the comfortable bar. Meals are served in the bar or separate restaurant, which can be booked for functions. Beer festivals are held at Whitsun and in early November.
ᗰQ❀◑➊🖟(4,6)P⅃—

Boughton Monchelsea

Cock Inn ✅
Heath Road, ME17 4JD
☼ 11-11; 12-10.30 Sun ☎ (01622) 743166
🌐 cockinnboughtonmonchelsea.com
St Austell Tribute; Young's Bitter; guest beer Ⓗ
Sixteenth-century picture postcard pub originally built to provide lodgings for Canterbury pilgrims. It has a huge inglenook fireplace with one of the best log fires around. Fine food and snacks are available in both the bar and restaurant. Ales are stored, piped and served at a constant 11°C, and a good selection of bottle-conditioned ales is stocked. The pub came top in Young's mystery customer ratings. Darts and board games are available and a quiz night held every third Sunday. Outside is an extensive summer dining patio. Child and dog friendly. ᗰQ❀◑≽🖟(59)♣P⅃—

Bramling

Haywain ⭐
Canterbury Road, CT3 1NB (on A257)
☼ 7-11 Mon; 12-3, 6-11 (midnight Fri & Sat); 12-4 Sun
☎ (01227) 720676 🌐 thehaywainpubbramling.co.uk
Fuller's London Pride; Wells Bombardier; guest beers Ⓗ
The welcoming main bar features hanging hop bines and assorted curios, while the small snug is mainly used for diners and meetings. Traditional games include darts and bat and trap, and there is a regular Monday night quiz. Guest beers usually come from small regional breweries, and two annual beer festivals are hosted in marquees in the attractive garden, on the Whitsun bank holiday and the last week in September. Excellent home-cooked food, using local produce, is served (not Mon). A regular bus service between Canterbury and Sandwich passes the door. The smoking shelter is heated and covered. ᗰQ❀◑🖟♣P⅃—

Brenchley

Halfway House ⭐ ✅
Horsmonden Road, TN12 7AX (½ mile SE of village)
TQ682413
☼ 12-11.30 (10.30 Sun) ☎ (01892) 722526
Goacher's Fine Light Ale; Skinner's Betty Stogs; Rother Valley Smild; Westerham 1965 Special; guest beers Ⓖ

This award-winning real ale Mecca goes from strength to strength. It routinely serves 10-12 real ales plus Chiddingstone cider straight from the cask. The Whitsun and August beer festivals feature 60 beers, entertainment and a barbecue. There are several drinking and seating areas to suit your mood, good food and a friendly welcome. The large garden has a children's activity play area and a separate adults only area – both with tables for alfresco dining. An en-suite room is available.
ᗰQ❀≽◑🖟(297)♣♦P⅃—

Broadstairs

Neptune's Hall
1-3 Harbour Street, CT10 1ET
☼ 12-11.30 (12.30am Fri & Sat) ☎ (01843) 861400
Shepherd Neame Master Brew Bitter, Spitfire, seasonal beers Ⓗ
This early 19th-century pub with many original features is a short stroll from Broadstairs' picture postcard beach. One bar counter serves three interconnected areas. Particularly attractive are the main bar and tiny snug at the front which are agreeably unadorned, with large curved glass windows and bench seats overlooking Harbour Street. The chatty atmosphere is only challenged by live music sessions (Sun at 5pm, daily during Folk Week in August). A good sized beer garden adds to the appeal. ᗰQ❀◑♣⅃—

Brompton

King George V ✅
1 Prospect Row, ME7 5AL TQ761687
☼ 11.45-11; 12-10.30 Sun ☎ (01634) 842418
🌐 kgvpub.com
Adnams Bitter; guest beers Ⓗ
Built in 1690 close to Chatham historic dockyard and Royal Engineers barracks, the pub is decorated with military memorabilia. Known locally as the 'KG Five', it has a single bar with three connected areas and a covered smoking area to the rear. Guest beers include a dark mild, alongside a wide selection of bottled Belgian beers, whiskies and Magic Bus cider. Food is served lunchtimes and evenings (not Sun eve or all day Mon), with pizzas available all day. On the route of the Saxon Shore Way long-distance footpath. Q≽◑🖟♦⅃—

Burmarsh

Shepherd & Crook ✅
Shear Way, TN29 0JJ (follow signs from A259 to E of Dymchurch) TR101320
☼ 11-4, 6.30-11 (not Tue); 11-11 Fri & Sat; 12-10.30 Sun
☎ (01303) 872336 🌐 shepherdandcrook.co.uk
Adnams Bitter; guest beers Ⓗ
Small and friendly country pub where dogs are welcome. The family-run free house has a bar and separate dining area. Guest ales are always available and change frequently. Traditional English food, all home-cooked using locally sourced ingredients where possible, is served every day except Tuesday, when there are bar snacks only. This pleasant, popular pub is situated on the Romney Marsh Cycle Route and thus makes a very welcome cyclists' stop. ᗰQ❧❀◑♣♦P

Canterbury

Bell & Crown

10-11 Palace Street, CT1 2DE (150m from cathedral)
12-12.30am (1.30am Fri & Sat) ☎ (01227) 784639
Hopdaemon Incubus; Ramsgate Gadds' No. 5, Gadds' No. 3; Whitstable East India Pale Ale Ⓗ
Grade II-listed characterful city pub with original signage, window etchings, Truman's lanterns and a fully-beamed interior. Outside seating on the pavement in front of the pub has excellent views of the Cathedral and the ancient King's School opposite. The pub stocks a range of continental bottled beers as well as local real ales. Palace Street is part of the King's Mile and contains many small shops and 17th-century buildings including the former King's School shop with its crooked door. ❀◐≠(West)

Eight Bells

34 London Road, CT2 8LN
3-11 (midnight Thu & Fri); 12-midnight Sat; 12-10.30 Sun ☎ (01227) 454794
Shepherd Neame Master Brew Bitter; Young's Bitter; guest beer Ⓗ
This small, traditional local dates from 1708 and was rebuilt in 1902. It has original embossed windows and is decorated with memorabilia. There is live music fortnightly on Friday, and a monthly quiz, usually on the last Wednesday. Five darts teams play every week and their trophies are on display. Roast lunches are served on Sunday, and a simple menu at other times. There is a heated, covered smoking area and an attractive, small walled garden. ❀◐●≠(West)▭(3,22)♣

King's Head

204 Wincheap, CT1 3RY (600m from ring road)
12-2.30, 4.45-midnight; 12-midnight Fri & Sat; 12-11.30 Sun ☎ (01227) 462885
Greene King IPA; Harveys Sussex Best Bitter; guest beer Ⓗ
Traditional and friendly Grade II-listed 15th-century local, 15 minutes walk from the city centre. Exposed beams, hanging hops and bric-a-brac add to its charm. Bar billiards and darts are played indoors, while bat and trap league matches are held in the garden in summer. There is a fortnightly Sunday quiz from September to April. Guest beers are normally sourced from micro-breweries. Three-star B&B is available, with parking for residents only. There is a heated and covered smoking shelter. ❀⊨◐●≠(East)▭(28,652)♣

New Inn

19 Havelock Street, CT1 1NP (off ring road near St Augustine's Abbey)
11-11 (11.30 Thu; midnight Fri); 11-3, 6-midnight Sat; 12-3, 6-11 Sun ☎ (01227) 464584
Greene King IPA; Harveys Sussex Best Bitter; St Austell Tribute; guest beers Ⓗ
This Victorian back-street terraced house is close to St Augustine's Abbey, the Cathedral and bus station. Guest beers are often from local breweries. The main bar has red walls, a jukebox, a wooden floor and old wooden bar. At the back is a long conservatory with two cosy alcoves, one of which is the 'library'. TV screens show sporting events. There are usually two beer festivals a year, on the Whitsun and August bank holiday weekends. Disabled access is through the garden and conservatory via Old Ruttington Lane. ❀◐●♿▭

Unicorn Inn

61 St Dunstan's Street, CT2 8BS
11.30-11 (midnight Fri & Sat) ☎ (01227) 463187
unicorninn.com
Caledonian Deuchars IPA; Shepherd Neame Master Brew Bitter; guest beers Ⓗ
This comfortable 1604 pub stands near the historic Westgate and boasts an attractive sun-trap garden. Bar billiards is played, and a quiz, set by regular customers, is held weekly on Sunday evening. The two guest beers often include a Kent micro-brewery ale. Imaginative food, available lunchtimes and evenings, ranges from pub favourites to exotic specials, and is excellent value, with two meals for £10 after 5pm (no food Sun eve). There is a covered and heated area for smoking. ⛼❀◐●≠(West)▭♣

Capel

Dovecote Inn

Alders Road, TN12 6SU (½ mile W of A228) TQ643441
5.30-10.30 Mon; 12-3, 5.30-11; 12-9.30 Sun ☎ (01892) 835966
Gale's HSB; Harveys Sussex Best Bitter; guest beers Ⓖ
Welcoming, traditional pub set in orchard country and popular with walkers. The cosy interior features exposed red brick, beams hung with hops and a real fire. Up to six ales are served direct from the cask from a cooled room through a mock barrel frontage, supplemented by Westons Old Rosie cider. Good food is available every day (not Sun and Mon eve). Drinks and food can be enjoyed on the sunny patio or large garden complete with children's climbing area. ⛼Q❀◐●♣●P

Charing

Bowl

Egg Hill Road, TN27 0HG (at jct of 5 Lanes) TQ950514
4 (12 summer)-11.30; 12-midnight Fri & Sat; 12-11 Sun ☎ (01233) 712256 bowlinn.co.uk
Fuller's London Pride; guest beers Ⓗ
A 16th-century free house located on top of the North Downs in an area of outstanding natural beauty, signposted from the A20 and A251. Guest beers come from Adnams, Harveys and Kentish micro-breweries, and a beer festival is held in mid-July. The large garden is popular in summer and camping is available (booking essential). Hearty snacks are served and there are regular themed food evenings. An impressive inglenook fire warms visitors in winter. Accommodation is in five rooms. ⛼Q❀⊨Ă♣P

Chipstead

Bricklayers Arms ✔

39 Chevening Road, TN13 2RZ
11.30-3.30, 5.30-11; 11.30-11 Fri & Sat; 11.30-10.30 Sun ☎ (01732) 743424 the-bricklayers-arms.co.uk
Harveys Sussex Best Bitter, seasonal beers Ⓗ
A warm and friendly village inn in a row of cottages with a lakeside view. The owners have much improved this pub and it now attracts locals and the many sailors who use the lake. A good range of food is served and regular steak and curry nights are held. Quiz night is Thursday. Live music is on offer occasionally. ⛼Q❀◐●♿▭(401)

Cobham

Darnley Arms
40 The Street, DA12 3BZ
⏲ 12-11 (10.30 Sun) ☎ (01474) 812218
Dark Star Hophead; Greene King IPA; guest beers Ⓗ
This cosy village local goes from strength to strength. The single bar has several distinct drinking areas. The decor features a wide range of local memorabilia including the coat of arms of the Darnley family who lived at nearby Cobham Hall. The extensive food menu features fish as a speciality. A quiz evening is hosted on the second Monday of each month. ♨Q❀🛏◑◗♿🚌(416)P

Coldred

Carpenter's Arms ★
The Green, CT15 5AJ
⏲ 6.30-11.30 ☎ (01304) 830190
Beer range varies Ⓗ/Ⓖ
Dating from the 18th century and largely unchanged for 50 years, this pub retains the character of a traditional village local. A short flight of stairs leads down to the main bar, which looks out on to the village green. To the left a smaller bar can be used if necessary. Two or three real ales are normally available, usually from local breweries Hopdaemon and Ramsgate. Note the display of silhouettes of regulars from days past. Darts, dominoes and skittles are played. Listed on CAMRA's National Inventory of Historic Pub Interiors. ♨Q🚌(88A)♣P⊱

Cooling

Horseshoe & Castle
Main Road, ME3 8DJ TQ759761
⏲ 11.30 (5.30 Mon)-11 (midnight Fri & Sat); 12-11.30 Sun
☎ (01634) 221691 🌐 horseshoeandcastle.co.uk
Shepherd Neame Master Brew Bitter; guest beer Ⓗ
Nestling in the quiet village of Cooling, this pub is near a ruined castle once owned by Sir John Oldcastle, on whom Shakespeare modelled his Falstaff character. The local graveyard was used in the film version of Great Expectations, where young Pip met the convict Magwich. Food is served in a separate dining area (no food Mon). Draught Addlestones cider is available. Accommodation is high quality. ♨Q❀🛏◑◗♿●P⊱

Crockham Hill

Royal Oak
Main Road, TN8 6RD (on B2026)
⏲ 12-3, 6-11 (midnight Fri); 12-11 Sun ☎ (01732) 866335
🌐 westerhambrewery.co.uk/OurPubs.htm
Westerham Finchcocks Original, SPA, British Bulldog, seasonal beers Ⓗ
This is the flagship pub for the local Westerham Brewery, serving the full range of its award-winning real ales, all well kept in a great local pub atmosphere. The Royal Oak is a small village inn with a great local community, a very warm welcome and home-cooked traditional pub food. Especially popular are the traditional roasts on Sunday, for which booking is advisable. Families, walking groups and societies are welcome.
♨Q❀◑◗P

Dartford

Malt Shovel
3 Darenth Road, DA1 1LP
⏲ 12-11 (midnight Fri) ☎ (01322) 224381
St Austell Tribute; Young's Bitter, Special, seasonal beers Ⓗ
Attractive country cottage-style pub just outside the town centre. The low-ceilinged tap room, which now features an original Dartford Brewery mirror, dates from 1673 and still exudes a rustic charm. The main bar has recently been extensively refurbished but retains the large wooden malt shovel on display. A large modern conservatory leads to the garden which overlooks the parish church. Good food is available lunchtimes (not Mon) and evenings (not Sun-Tue), with fish night on Friday. Quiz night is Monday.
♨❀◑◗⊟⇌🚌♣P⊱

Paper Moon ✔
55 High Street, DA1 1DS
⏲ 9-11 (midnight Fri & Sat) ☎ (01322) 281127
Courage Best Bitter; Greene King Ruddles Best Bitter, Abbot; Nelson Flying Moon; guest beers Ⓗ
Town-centre corner pub, formerly Lloyds Bank. The name reflects the town's historic connection with the papermaking industry and is decorated with memorabilia recalling Dartford past. The pub offers four regular beers including the exclusive Flying Moon and up to four rapidly changing guest ales. A LocAle pub, beers come from Kent and other south-east micro-breweries. The pub conducts regular brewery promotions and charity events and was Wetherspoon's 2008/09 Regional Community & Charity Pub of the Year. ♨◑◗♿⇌🚌●

Deal

Bohemian
47 Beach Street, CT14 6HY
⏲ 11-11 (midnight Sat); 9am-10 Sun ☎ (01304) 374843
🌐 bohemianbythesea.com
Beer range varies Ⓗ
In a prime position on Deal's seafront, this pub has a modern yet congenial interior. There are fine views of the pier and the Downs, as the sea in these parts is confusingly known, especially from the upstairs restaurant. Everyone's needs are catered for, with Kentish beers regularly available and cider from Westons. For the more adventurous there is a large range of draught and bottled beers from Belgium and further afield. Open for Sunday breakfast from 9am. Outside, there is a patio at the rear. ❀◑◗⇌🚌(13,14,15)●⊱

Dunkerley's
19 Beach Street, CT14 7AH
⏲ 8-11 ☎ (01304) 375016 🌐 dunkerleys.co.uk
St Austell Tribute Ⓗ
Formerly the Pier Hotel, this hostelry is situated in the heart of Deal, just a stone's throw from the beach and pier. Enjoy your pint in the warm and relaxing piano bar or on the alfresco terrace at the front watching the world go by. A full bar and restaurant menu is available with the emphasis on local seafood. Gentle live music plays during weekend lunchtimes and in the evening on Friday and Monday. ❀🛏◑◗♿⇌🚌(13,14,15)⊱

Prince Albert
187-189 Middle Street, CT14 6LW
⏲ 6 (12 Sun)-11 ☎ (01304) 375425
Beer range varies Ⓗ
On the corner of Middle Street and Alfred Square, this pub is a 15-minute walk north of the town centre and railway station, just 100 metres from the seafront. The unassuming Victorian exterior conceals a cheerful and welcoming local. The cosy bar serves an ever-changing range of three real ales from smaller, often local breweries. A small restaurant is open Wednesday to Saturday evenings with roast lunch on Sunday. The small garden is ideal in summer. B&B is available.
♨Q❀🛏◑≠🚌(15A)

Ship
141 Middle Street, CT14 6JZ
⏲ 11-11.30; 12-11 Sun ☎ (01304) 372222
Caledonian Deuchars IPA; Ramsgate Gadds' No. 7, Gadds' Seasider; guest beers Ⓗ
Situated about 10 minutes to the north of the town centre, you'll find this unspoilt house on historic, winding Middle Street, which runs parallel to the seafront. Beers are from Ramsgate and other small breweries. The cosy back bar overlooks a small garden. Conversation prevails, so if you are seeking fruit machines or a jukebox, look elsewhere. There are good displays of nautical memorabilia, though when the press gang visits these days it should only be a historical re-enactment! ♨Q❀≠🚌(15A)

Denton

Jackdaw
The Street, CT4 6QZ
⏲ 11-11 ☎ (01303) 844663 🌐 thejackdaw.info
Harvey's Sussex Best Bitter; Shepherd Neame Spitfire; guest beers Ⓗ
Called the Red Lion until 1964, the inn was renamed after the Jackdaw of Rheims, from the Ingoldsby Legends. The pub featured in the 1969 film The Battle of Britain, and RAF memorabilia abounds. Refurbished in early 2009, this is a popular watering hole for locals and visitors alike. Served by the regular Canterbury/Folkestone bus route, the welcoming ambience makes a stopover well worthwhile. Weather permitting, the rear gardens are well recommended. Not to be missed.
♨❀◑🚌(16)♣P

Dover

Blakes of Dover
52 Castle Street, CT16 1PJ
⏲ 12-11; closed Sun ☎ (01304) 202194
🌐 blakesofdover.com
Adnams Bitter Ⓗ**; guest beers** Ⓗ/Ⓖ
A town-centre cellar bar providing a quiet, restful haven. This is a great place to try a fine range of real ales and excellent food – from goat or mutton curry to superb home-smoked salmon. Real cider is available from Thatchers, Broomfield and many others. Peter and Kathryn are the archetypal host and hostess, providing good conversation to go with the food and beer. There is a restaurant upstairs and B&B facilities are offered. Three minutes' walk from Dover bus station.
Q❀🛏◐≠🚌●⁵⁻

Eight Bells ✔
19 Cannon Street, CT16 1BZ
⏲ 9-midnight (1am Fri & Sat) ☎ (01304) 205030
Courage Best Bitter; Greene King Ruddles Best Bitter, Abbot; Marston's Pedigree; Shepherd Neame Spitfire; guest beers Ⓗ
One of the relatively few pubs remaining in Dover's town centre, this Wetherspoon's is named after the bells of St Mary's Parish Church opposite. It was converted from a former cinema and has a two-level bar. Most of the 12 handpumps are normally in use, with the beer range usually including one or more Kent micro beers. A footpath by the side of the church and across a park leads to the nearby bus station which provides services to local towns and villages. ◑♿≠🚌●⁵⁻

Louis Armstrong
58 Maison Dieu Road, CT16 1RA
⏲ 2 (7 Sun)-1am ☎ (01304) 204759
Hopdaemon Skrimshander IPA; guest beers Ⓗ
Five minutes from Dover town centre, opposite Morrisons supermarket, this pub has been a home to live music for over 40 years. With an L-shaped bar and stage at the rear, it hosts live music Friday and Saturday and jazz on Sunday, and occasionally other days too. Up to four Kent real ales are available plus guests from elsewhere. Outside is a fine rear garden and a large car park opposite. On Wednesday you buy a meal and a pint for just £5.
❀◑🚌⁵⁻

East Malling

Rising Sun
125 Mill Street, ME19 6BX
⏲ 12-11 (10.30 Sun) ☎ (01732) 843284
Goacher's Fine Light Ale; guest beers Ⓗ
This long-time Guide entry offers the best value food and drink in the area. A free of tie, family-run pub, it hosts the local darts, football and cricket teams. All major football matches and other sports events are shown. The two guest beers come from far and wide. Look out for the collection of malt whiskies above the bar. Food is served Monday to Friday lunchtime only. A meat raffle is held every Sunday lunchtime. ❀◐≠🚌(58)♣⁵⁻

East Peckham

Bush, Blackbird & Thrush
194 Bush Road, Peckham Bush, TN12 5LW (1 mile NE of East Peckham, via Old Rd and Pond Rd) TQ664500
⏲ 11-3 (not Mon), 6-11; 12-3, 6-10.30 Sun
☎ (01622) 871349
Shepherd Neame Master Brew Bitter, Spitfire, seasonal beers Ⓖ
Attractive tile-hung 15th-century rural pub on a quiet lane outside the sprawling village. The bar and dining room areas are separated by a large well-used fireplace. Shepherd Neame beers are served on gravity from behind the bar. Good home-cooked food is available Tuesday to Sunday. A real community pub with strong local support, it is home to bat and trap, darts and cribbage teams.
♨Q❀◑♿♣P⁵⁻

Edenbridge

Old Eden

121 High Street, TN8 5AX
12-11 (midnight Fri & Sat) ☎ (01732) 862398
Harveys Sussex Best Bitter; Westerham British Bulldog; Whitstable Native Bitter; guest beers H
Situated just south of the historic bridge over the River Eden, a plaque is displayed by the bar showing the water level in the 1968 floods. This large, comfortable pub features plenty of beams, sofas and three log fires, as well as a secluded garden. Popular with diners (no food Sun and Mon evenings), it offers a range of beers from local brewer Westerham plus guests from Kent and Sussex breweries. The cider is Westons Old Rosie. (Edenbridge Town) (231,233) P

Farningham

Chequers

87 High Street, DA4 0DT (250m from A20 jct 3 M25)
12-11.30 (11 Sun) ☎ (01322) 865222
Fuller's London Pride, ESB; Taylor Landlord; guest beers H
Popular, cosy, one-bar corner local in an attractive riverside village. The unusual decor includes murals depicting local scenes, two large decorative candelabra and a life-size model waiter. Ten handpumps dispense three regular beers and up to seven guests. Food is served Monday to Saturday lunchtimes 12-3pm. Parking is difficult as the pub is situated in the village on a dangerous corner. (421,427)

Faversham

Bear Inn

3 Market Place, ME13 7AG
10.30-3, 5.30-11; 10.30-midnight Fri & Sat; 11.30-10.30 Sun ☎ (01795) 532668
Shepherd Neame Master Brew Bitter, Late Red, seasonal beers H
Opposite the historic Guildhall in Market Place, the Bear has three distinct bar areas off a long side corridor. All have wood panelling and their own separate character. The back bar has an unusual clock – instead of numbers it uses the pub's name spelled out around the dial. The landlord sources seasonal beers from Shepherd Neame's micro-brewery, and guests are sometimes featured. Wholesome home-cooked lunches are served every day. On Thursdays local folk musicians draw a crowd.

Elephant

31 The Mall, ME13 8JN
closed Mon; 3 (12 Sat)-11; 12-7 Sun ☎ (01795) 590157
Beer range varies H
Local CAMRA Pub of the Year 2010 for the fourth year running, offering five ever-changing beers including a mild. The licensee aims to present the best ale selection in town. Beers are sourced almost exclusively from micro-breweries, including several in Kent. The pub holds two beer festivals a year, in July and November/December. There is an open fire in winter and a well-tended walled garden for the summer, with rabbits and guinea pigs. There's lots of boxed games and bagatelle. (333,666)

Old Wine Vaults

75 Preston Street, ME13 8PA
11-11; 12-10.30 Sun ☎ (01795) 591817
theoldwinevaults.co.uk
Hopdaemon Incubus; guest beers H
Once the Old Albion Wine Vaults, it was then the Hole in the Wall before reverting to almost the original name. A deceptively large pub, it has ample seating and a nice garden. One ale comes from the local Hopdaemon Brewery plus two changing guests. Over 60s are offered a reduced price on a beer. All food is home cooked and freshly prepared using locally sourced meat, fruit and vegetables. There are daily specials and bar snacks (no food Sun eve).

Railway Hotel

Preston Street, ME13 8PE (opp railway station)
12-11 (10.30 Sun) ☎ (01795) 533173
railwayhotelfaversham.co.uk
Shepherd Neame Master Brew Bitter, seasonal beers H
This imposing Victorian street-corner hotel is located directly opposite the railway station's main entrance and has seven letting rooms. The ornate interior features a splendid bar back and many beautiful etched windows. The sound of conversation is not interrupted by music. There is a dartboard and bar billiards table. Tables are set outside during the summer. Breakfast for residents include the proprietors' own home-made preserves. Dogs are welcome. Q P

Shipwrights Arms

Ham Road, Hollowshore, ME13 7TU (1½ miles N of Faversham) TR017636
closed Mon winter; 11-3 (4 Sat), 6-10 (11 summer); 12-4, 6-10 (11 summer) Sun ☎ (01795) 590088
Goacher's Real Mild, Shipwrecked; Hopdaemon Incubus; Whitstable EIPA; guest beers G
A remote 300-year-old pub where Faversham and Oare creeks meet, about 45 minutes' walk from Faversham. The decor reflects the pub's nautical location. There are log fires for the winter months and a large garden for summer. The beers come from mostly Kentish micro-breweries, with the house beer, Shipwrecked, brewed by Goacher's. Food is served lunchtimes 12-2.30pm, evening meals 7-9pm in summer (not Sun), and Saturday only in winter. Q P

Finglesham

Crown

The Street, CT14 0NA
12-3, 6-11.30; 11-midnight Fri & Sat; 12-11.30 Sun (winter hours may vary) ☎ (01304) 612555
thecrownatfinglesham.co.uk
Beer range varies H
Situated in a quiet rural hamlet, this welcoming village pub and 16th-century restaurant specialises in beers from Kent and south-east brewers, with real cider from Biddenden's. The pub is proud of its award-winning, freshly prepared, home-cooked food, available lunchtimes and evenings, all day Sunday in summer. Themed food nights and quizzes are held throughout the year, and beer festivals in May and August. Bat and trap is played. Well-behaved dogs are welcome outside meal times. Caravan Club certified. Local CAMRA Pub of the Year 2007. (13,14) P

Folkestone

British Lion ✔

10 The Bayle, CT20 1SQ (close to the church off the pedestrian part of Sandgate Road)
✪ 12-4, 7-11 (10.30 Sun) ☎ (01303) 251478
Greene King IPA, Abbot; guest beers Ⓗ
Now the oldest pub in Folkestone, the building dates from 1460. Charles Dickens visited this former Hanbury, Mackeson and Whitbread house when writing Little Dorrit. The room he used is now the Dickens Room. Situated close to the town centre, adjacent to the church, a comfortable and relaxed atmosphere prevails. Two guest beers are always available, usually from the finest cask selection. Good pub food is served in generous portions. ♨Q☺◑♿🚌♣●⚟

Chambers

Radnor Chambers, Cheriton Place, CT20 2BB (off the Hythe end of Sandgate Road)
✪ 12-11 (1am Fri & Sat); 7-10.30 1st Sun of month only
☎ (01303) 223333 🌐 pubfolkestone.com
Adnams Bitter; Hopdaemon Skrimshander IPA; Ramsgate Faithful Dogbolter; Whitstable Kentish Reserve; guest beer Ⓗ
Surprisingly spacious cellar bar with a coffee shop upstairs under the same ownership, attracting a very varied clientele. Beer festivals are held over the Easter and August bank holiday weekends. Food includes Mexican and European choices plus daily specials. Guest ales are normally from local micro-breweries. Live music plays every Thursday and a quiz is hosted on the first Sunday of the month. Local CAMRA Pub of the Year 2008.
☺◑⇌(Central)🚌♣●

Guildhall ✔

42 The Bayle, CT20 1SQ (close to the church off the pedestrian part of Sandgate Road)
✪ 12-11 (midnight Fri & Sat); 12-10.30 Sun
☎ (01303) 251393
Greene King IPA; guest beers Ⓗ
Welcoming, traditional pub, close to the town centre, with a single bar. Large windows give the interior a light, airy feel. Good value food is served at lunchtimes. This is an ideal place to take a break from the hustle and bustle of the town centre and enjoy good ale. Three guest beers are on handpump. ❀◐♿🚌♣P⚟

Fordcombe

Chafford Arms ✔

Spring Hill, TN3 0SA
✪ 11 (12 Sun)-11 ☎ (01892) 740267 🌐 chaffordarms.co.uk
Harveys Sussex Best Bitter; Larkins Traditional Ale Ⓗ
Attractive Victorian tile-hung pub with an extensive garden affording fine views over the upper Medway valley. Close to the Wealdway long distance footpath and amid good walking country, walkers, dogs and children are welcome in the comfortable public bar, which was recently refurbished to a high standard, complete with log fire. Good quality food is available throughout the day and until 7pm on Sunday. Afternoon cream teas are served and a takeaway menu is available Monday to Saturday. ♨❀◑⊟Å🚌(231)♣P⚟

Fordwich

Fordwich Arms

King Street, CT2 0DB
✪ 11-midnight (1am Fri & Sat); 12-11 Sun
☎ (01227) 710444 🌐 fordwicharms.co.uk
Flowers Original; Shepherd Neame Master Brew Bitter; Wadworth 6X, Henry's IPA Ⓗ
Classic 1930s building listed in CAMRA's Kent Regional Inventory of Historic Pub Interiors. The large bar has a superb fireplace, a woodblock floor and a dining room with wood panelling. Excellent meals are served in both areas (not Sun eve). The garden and terrace overlook the River Stour, close to the Stour Valley Walk. The pub hosts regular themed evenings including a popular pudding night on the second Wednesday of the month, plus folk music at least every second and fourth Sunday night. The landlord can provide keys to the church and tiny town hall. ♨Q❀◑⇌(Sturry)🚌P⚟

Frittenden

Bell & Jorrocks ✔

Biddenden Road, TN17 2EJ TQ815412
✪ 12 (11 Sat & Sun)-11 ☎ (01580) 852415
🌐 thebellandjorrocks.co.uk
Adnams Bitter; Black Sheep Best Bitter; Harveys Sussex Best Bitter; guest beer Ⓗ
Fine community village pub incorporating a post office. The unusual name is a combination of two village pubs: the present pub – formerly the Bell – and John Jorrocks (named after a fictional fox-hunting Cockney created by RS Surtees in the 19th century), which closed in 1969. This old coaching inn has an L-shaped main bar and a small back room. Ask about the Heinkel propeller hanging over the fireplace. Beer festivals are held in April and September. No food on Wednesday.
♨❀◑Å♣●⚟

Gillingham

Frog & Toad ✔

38 Burnt Oak Terrace, ME7 1DR TQ774688
✪ 1 (4 Mon)-11; 12-10.30 Sun ☎ (01634) 852231
🌐 thefrogandtoad.com
Fuller's London Pride; guest beers Ⓗ
A typical back-street pub, three times previous winner of local CAMRA Pub of the Year, the Frog & Toad is 15 minutes' walk from Gillingham station. Frequently changing guest beers, Magic Bus cider and a selection of Belgian beers are available. A large patio garden area to the rear of the pub has bench tables and seats. There is an outside bar for beer festivals, held three times a year. Sandwiches are served throughout the week in addition to a traditional Sunday roast lunch. Q❀⇌🚌(176)●⚟

Hastings Arms

18 Lower Rainham Road, ME7 2YD (100m E of A289/B2004 jct) TQ793687
✪ 11-midnight (12.30am Fri & Sat) ☎ (01634) 851310
🌐 hastingsarms.co.uk
Shepherd Neame seasonal beers; Wells Bombardier; guest beers Ⓗ
Standing close to the west end of the Riverside Country Park, this area was historically governed by the Cinque Port of Hastings. Step inside to a horseshoe-shaped bar, one side leading to a large

function room and restaurant before opening to the enclosed garden. Three guest beers come mainly from the West Country, but LocAles can also be found. ❀◐♿🚌(176)♣P⊱

Upper Gillingham Conservative Club

541 Canterbury Street, ME7 5LF (160m from jct of Canterbury St and A2) TQ777670

⏲ 11-2.30, 7-11; 11-11 Sat; 12-10.30 Sun ☎ (01634) 851403

Shepherd Neame Master Brew Bitter; guest beers Ⓗ

A club since 1922, this former army store is handy for Gillingham football stadium. Show this Guide or your CAMRA membership card to gain entry. A finalist in the CAMRA National Club of the Year awards in 2001, the U-shaped bar stocks three real ales. There is a large-screen TV in the bar and a separate snooker room with two tables. Theme nights and live music are a feature of many Saturday evenings; raffles take place on Sunday. ♿🚌(116,327)♣

Will Adams

73 Saxton Street, ME7 5EG TQ770683

⏲ 12.30-4 (Sat only), 7-11; 12-3, 8-11 Sun

☎ (01634) 575902 🌐 thewilladams.co.uk

Hop Back Summer Lightning; guest beers Ⓗ

This friendly single bar local was local CAMRA Pub of the Year in 2008. The traditional back-street pub has a deserved reputation for well-kept beer. Three ales are usually on offer from breweries and micros across the country plus draught ciders and perry – Old Rosie is a regular. The pub is named after a local navigator adventurer, whose exploits are depicted on a mural. Opening times vary for Gillingham FC home games. Away fans are always welcome. ❀⇌🚌♣●⊱

Gravesend

Crown & Thistle

44 The Terrace, DA12 2BJ

⏲ 12-11 (10.30 Sun) ☎ (01474) 326049

Adnams Regatta; Dark Star Hophead; guest beers Ⓗ

Small Georgian terraced pub close to the river and town centre. The convivial atmosphere is free from music and games machines. Four frequently changing guest beers are on handpump. Chinese and Indian takeaways can be ordered and eaten on the premises. The pub is home to men's and women's rowing teams. Q❀⇌🚌(480,499)⊱

Jolly Drayman

1 Love Lane, Wellington Street, DA12 1JA

⏲ 12-11.30 (midnight Fri & Sat); 12-11 Sun

☎ (01474) 352355 🌐 jollydrayman.com

Dark Star Hophead; Everards Tiger; guest beers Ⓗ

Comfortable lounge-style pub and small hotel near the town centre with original low beams and wood panelling. It was once part of the Wellington Brewery – the power plant stood on the site and hence the pub is known locally as the 'Coke Oven'. The pub hosts dadlums (Kentish skittles) on alternate Sunday evenings and is home to darts, rowing and football teams. Occasional live music plays. The restaurant serves good food (booking advisable). Q❀🛏◐◑♿⇌🚌(490,499)♣P⊱

Rum Puncheon

87 West Street, DA11 0BL (on one way system, next to Tilbury Ferry)

⏲ 11-11 (9 Mon); 12-9 Sun ☎ (01474) 353434

Beer range varies Ⓗ

This pub reopened in 2008 after a lengthy closure for refurbishment. It is situated between new-build flats and next to the Tilbury Foot Ferry entrance. The beer range changes on a regular basis. The L-shaped bar has a log fire, wooden furniture and chandeliers. At the rear there is an outside drinking area and a first floor balcony with views of the River Thames. Food is served every lunchtime and Friday and Saturday evenings.
🔥Q❀◐◑♿⇌🚌(480,499)▯

Ship & Lobster

Mark Lane, Denton, DA12 2QB (end of Mark Lane)

⏲ 11-11; 12-4 Sun ☎ (01474) 324571

🌐 shipandlobster.co.uk

Beer range varies Ⓗ

Mentioned by Dickens as the Ship in Great Expectations, this welcoming historic pub can be found at the eastern end of the town, past the canal basin at the end of Mark Lane. It has a nautical theme and is used by walkers on the Saxon Shore Way and by locals fishing the River Thames. Book ahead for Sunday roasts as they are ever popular. ❀◐●P⊱

Great Chart

Hoodener's Horse

The Street, TN23 3AN

⏲ 11-11 (midnight Fri & Sat); 12-11 Sun ☎ (01233) 625583

St Austell Tribute; Sharp's Doom Bar; Young's Special; guest beers Ⓗ

This former Hooden Horse chain pub has been transformed to its former glory with basic furnishings, wooden floors and bar furniture. It offers a good selection of real ales and an interesting food menu which includes Mexican dishes and a range of pizzas. Outside, the unusual garden terraces mingle with the surrounding cottages. 🐄❀◐◑🚌(400)⊱

Groombridge

Crown Inn

TN3 9QH (A264 from Tunbridge Wells, then B2110)

⏲ 11-3, 6-11; 11-1.15am Sat; 11-11 (12-10.30 winter) Sun

☎ (01892) 864742 🌐 thecrowngroombridge.co.uk

Harveys Sussex Best Bitter; Larkins Traditional, seasonal beers Ⓗ

You step back in time when you visit this English Heritage-listed pub furnished with flagstones, wooden beams and an inglenook fireplace. Enjoy local beers sitting outside with a view of the old village and green. Home cooking features locally sourced food. Walkers, cyclists, children and dogs are welcome. The 291 bus stops nearby and the Spa Valley Railway is a five-minute walk, with a regular service from Tunbridge Wells in summer.
🔥Q❀◐◑⇌🚌(291)

Halstead

Rose & Crown

Otford Lane, TN14 7EA

⏲ 12-11 ☎ (01959) 533120

Larkins Traditional; Moorhouse's Black Cat; Whitstable East India Pale Ale; guest beers Ⓗ

Built in the 1860s, this two bar flint-faced free house offers a warm welcome to locals and visitors. It is host to a monthly Sunday quiz and a

number of darts teams. Three regularly changing guest ales from smaller breweries are served. Home-cooked food is on offer and the pub opens at 10am during the week for breakfast. Booking for Sunday lunch is advisable. Voted local CAMRA Pub of the Year in 2008 and 2009.
⚲Q⚲⚲⚲⚲⚲(R5,R10,402)♣P⚲

Hastingleigh

Bowl Inn

The Street, TN25 5HU TR 095449
⚲ closed Mon; 5 (12 Sat)-midnight; 12-10.30 Sun
☎ (01233) 750354 ⚲ thebowlonline.co.uk
Adnams Bitter; Harveys Sussex Best Bitter; Hopdaemon Incubus; guest beers Ⓗ
Lovingly restored village pub, this listed building retains many period features including a tap room (now used for playing pool), and is free from jukebox and games machines. Quiz night is Tuesday. The lovely garden has a tame European eagle owl and a cricket pitch to the rear where matches are played most Sundays in the summer. A beer festival is held on the August bank holiday. Excellent sandwiches and baguettes are available at the weekend. ⚲Q⚲⚲⚲♣⚲P⚲

Herne

Butcher's Arms

29A Herne Street, CT6 7HL (opp church)
⚲ closed Sun & Mon; 12-1.30, 6-9 (or later)
☎ (01227) 371000 ⚲ micropub.co.uk
Dark Star Hophead; Fuller's ESB; Harveys Sussex Best Bitter; guest beers Ⓖ
The smallest pub in Kent, and a real ale gem. Once a butcher's shop, it still has the original chopping tables, with hooks and other implements. There is seating for 12 customers and standing room for about 20 – the compact drinking area ensuring lively banter. An ever-changing variety of guest beers is offered, and customers can also buy beer to drink at home. The pub has won five CAMRA awards and was East Kent Pub of the Year in 2009. Broomfield cider is sold. Q⚲(4,6)

Smugglers Inn

1 School Lane, CT6 7AN (opp church)
⚲ 11-11 (1am Fri & Sat) ☎ (01227) 741395
Shepherd Neame Master Brew Bitter, seasonal beers Ⓗ
Welcoming village local with a smuggling history, situated just inland from Herne Bay. Parts of the pub date back 400 years, and it has been run by the same landlord for 16 years. The comfortable saloon bar has a low ceiling with birch thatching, hanging hops and wood panelling. The public bar has a pool table and dartboard. The garden has a bat and trap pitch and hanging flower baskets. Beers from Shepherd Neame's micro-brewery are occasionally available. Regular buses pass the door.
Q⚲⚲⚲⚲(4,6)♣⚲

Hernhill

Three Horseshoes

46 Staple Street, ME13 9UA TR060601
⚲ 12-3 (not Mon), 6-11; 12-11 Fri & Sat; 12-3, 7-10.30 Sun
☎ (01227) 750842 ⚲ 3shoes.co.uk
Shepherd Neame Master Brew Bitter Ⓖ**, Late Red, seasonal beers; guest beers** Ⓗ
Set in a hamlet amid orchards and hop gardens, less than a mile from Boughton Street, this hospitable and traditional pub has been run by the same husband and wife team for 11 years. The gravity-served Master Brew Bitter is rare in a Shepherd Neame house. The pub has a well deserved reputation for good home-cooked food (no meals Sun eve or Mon). Live music plays on alternate Saturday nights. A wheelie bin grand prix race is held in mid July. ⚲Q⚲⚲⚲(638)♣P

Higham

Stone Horse

Dillywood Lane, ME3 8EN (off B2000 Cliffe Road)
TQ732713
⚲ 12-11 (10.30 Sun) ☎ (01634) 722046
Courage Best Bitter; guest beers Ⓗ
Country pub with a large garden situated on the edge of Strood, surrounded by fields and handy for walkers. The unspoilt public bar sports a wood-burning range. Good value food is served and locals can participate in the cookery club. The pub is dog-friendly but no children are allowed in the bar. Up to three guest beers are usually available.
⚲Q⚲⚲⚲⚲♣P⚲

Hildenborough

Cock Horse

London Road, TN11 8NH (on B245 between Sevenoaks and Tonbridge)
⚲ 11-11.30; 12-11 Sun ☎ (01732) 833232
Shepherd Neame Master Brew Bitter, Spitfire Ⓗ
Family-run 16th-century coaching inn with a very comfortable bar and an inglenook fireplace to make you feel warm and welcome. Home-cooked food is available including Sunday lunches (booking recommended). An ideal location for walkers, outside this hospitable pub is a split-level decked area where you can sit and enjoy your food and drink. There is also a lawn area and ample parking space. ⚲Q⚲⚲⚲⚲⚲(402)P⚲

Hook Green

Elephant's Head ✔

Furnace Lane, TN3 8LJ
⚲ 12-3, 4.30-11; 12-11 Sat; 12-10.30 Sun ☎ (01892) 890279
Harveys Hadlow Bitter, Sussex Best Bitter, Armada Ale, seasonal beers Ⓗ
Striking Tudor building set back from the road by a small green and surrounded by lovely countryside for walking or cycling. Grade II-listed, built in 1489, it was formerly part of the famous Culpepper Estate and a pub since 1768. Owned by Harveys, it usually offers the full range of beers. A good selection of food is available including a children's menu, and there is plenty of space in the conservatory for dining. The garden has a children's play area.
⚲Q⚲⚲⚲⚲(256)♣P

Horton Kirby

Bull 🏆

3 Lombard Street, DA4 9DF

⌚ 12-11 (midnight Fri); 12-10.30 Sun ☎ (01322) 862274
🌐 thebullhk.info
Dark Star Hophead Ⓗ; guest beers Ⓗ/Ⓖ
Comfortable and friendly one-bar village pub with a large garden affording views across Darent Valley. One beer is on gravity stillage and seven are on handpump, often from Dark Star, Marble and other micro-breweries. Rotating cider and perry are also available on gravity. Good quality food is served at lunchtime and in the evening. Monday is quiz league, Tuesday curry night, first Thursday of the month is bingo quiz, and Saturday night is often a themed food evening. Local CAMRA Pub of the Year 2008/2009, and Regional Pub of the Year 2009.
♨Q❀◐◑♿⇌(Farningham Road)🚌(414)♣●⁵⁻🗑

Hythe

Three Mariners
37 Windmill Street, CT21 6BH
⌚ 12 (4 Mon)-11 (midnight Fri & Sat); 12-11 Sun
☎ (01303) 260406
Young's Bitter; guest beers Ⓗ
Traditional two bar local – the 'jewel in the crown' and a cask ale Mecca in a town with several other good outlets. Recently refurbished from a run-down Shepherd Neame establishment, it was runner-up local CAMRA Pub of the Year in 2010. The friendly and relaxed atmosphere makes this a worthwhile find for its ever-changing range of six guest ales, usually including two from local micro-brewers. Beer festivals are usually held on the spring and August bank holidays. ♨ఠ❀⊟♣●⁵⁻

Iden Green

Peacock
Goudhurst Road, TN17 2PB (1½ miles E of Goudhurst at A262/B2085 jct) TQ747374
⌚ 12-11 (6 Sun) ☎ (01580) 211233
Shepherd Neame Master Brew Bitter, Kent's Best, Bishop's Finger, seasonal beer Ⓗ
Picturesque country inn dating from the 17th century with a later sympathetic extension that has been recently refurbished. The original building houses a simply-furnished but comfortable bar with low beams and an inglenook fireplace, and a restaurant in an adjoining dining room. The newer bar in the extension opens out onto a large garden. Good quality food is served every lunchtime and Tuesday to Saturday evenings. One-off special beers from Shepherd Neame's in-house micro-brewery are regularly available.
♨Q❀◐◑♿🚌(297)♣P⁵⁻

Ightham Common

Old House ★
Redwell Lane, TN15 9EE (½ mile SW of Ightham village, between A25 & A227) TQ591598
⌚ 7-11 (9 Tue); 12-3, 7-11 Sat; 12-3, 7-10.30 Sun
Lodden Gravesend Shrimpers Bitter; Sharp's Cornish Coaster; guest beers Ⓖ
A rural gem from a bygone era, this Kentish red-brick and tile-hung cottage has no pub sign and is hidden away down a steep, narrow lane. Enter through a small lobby to find a dog-friendly public bar to the left with a Victorian wood-panelled bar counter and large inglenook fireplace. The parlour to the right features old-fashioned armchairs, a retired cash register and empty champagne bottles. The beers are served by gravity from a stillage in a back room. ♨Q⊟♣P

Ivychurch

Bell Inn 🏆
TN29 0AL (signed from the A2070 between Brenzett and Hamstreet) TR 028275
⌚ 12-11 (10.30 Sun) ☎ (01797) 344355
🌐 thebellinnromneymarsh.co.uk
Black Sheep Best Bitter; Sharp's Doom Bar; Wadworth Henry's Original IPA; guest beers Ⓗ
Picturesque 16th-century inn situated in the shadow of the village church. The large bar has a dining area to the left and a games room to the right. A good range of freshly prepared meals is available each evening and at weekends. The perfect place to relax and enjoy five well-kept real ales, this welcoming pub was voted local CAMRA Pub of the Year 2010. A large enclosed beer garden to the side is ideal for families.
♨ఠ❀◐◑⊟♿♣P⁵⁻

Laddingford

Chequers ✔
Lees Road, ME18 6BP (1 mile SW of Yalding) TQ 689481
⌚ 12-3, 5-11; 12-11 Sat; 12-10.30 Sun ☎ (01622) 871266
🌐 chequersladdingford.co.uk
Adnams Bitter; Fuller's London Pride; guest beers Ⓗ
Attractive oak-beamed 15th-century pub at the heart of village activities. A warm welcome is assured in the simply furnished, community-spirited bar, flanked by a split-level dining area. During the summer the frontage is adorned with colourful window boxes. There is a large garden with children's play equipment, which is busy during the beer festival held in April. Food theme nights include sausage Thursday and Charles' pie days on the first Tuesday and Wednesday of the month. Snacks only on Monday lunchtime. One double letting room is available.
♨Q❀🛏◐◑🚌(26)♣P⁵⁻

Longfield

Green Man ✔
Main Road, Longfield Hill, DA3 7AS (on B260)
⌚ 12-11 (midnight Fri & Sat); 12-10.30 Sun
☎ (01474) 702234
Harveys Sussex Best Bitter; Shepherd Neame Spitfire; guest beer Ⓗ
Dating back to the 17th century, this building was originally a farmhouse that brewed ale for the farm workers. Now a Vintage Inn pub and restaurant, it is situated on the B260 about a mile from Longfield town centre in the direction of Meopham. Three draught beers are usually available. The pub holds small beer festivals every three months with the focus on specific styles of beer. Good food is served daily. ♨Q❀◐◑♿P⁵⁻

Luddesdown

Cock Inn ✔
Henley Street, DA13 0XB (1 mile SE of Sole Street station) TQ664672

☼ 12-11 (10.30 Sun) ☎ (01474) 814208
⊕ cockluddesdowne.com
Adnams Bitter, Broadside; Goacher's Mild; Hogs Back Bitter; Shepherd Neame Master Brew Bitter; guest beers Ⓗ
In a pleasant rural setting, this superb, traditional English free house dating from 1713 has been under the same ownership since 1984. It has two bars and a conservatory, and plays host to many local clubs and societies. Outside is a specially designed under-cover heated smoking area complete with dartboard. Bar billiards can be played in the public bar while petanque is played in the garden. The landlord hosts a devious quiz every Tuesday. Local CAMRA Pub of the Year 2005-2007. ⚌Q❀◖➍➌P≛〒

Lynsted

Black Lion

Lynsted Lane, ME9 0RJ (close to church) TQ943609
☼ 11-3, 6-11; 12-3, 7-10.30 Sun ☎ (01795) 521229
Goacher's Mild, Light, Dark, seasonal beers Ⓗ
Friendly village pub sought out by drinkers as there are always three or four beers from Goacher's on offer. The main bar room has real fires in winter, and the other is home to a bar billiards table. Wooden floors throughout add to the character. Food is available daily. There is a large garden for alfresco drinking. The 345 bus runs every two hours or so from Sittingbourne via Teynham (not eves or Sun). There are three letting rooms separate from the pub. ⚌Q❀⊷◖☖🚋(345)➍P≛

Maidstone

Flower Pot ▼

96 Sandling Road, ME14 2RJ (off A229 N of town centre)
☼ 12 (11 Sat)-11; 12-10.30 Sun ☎ (01622) 757705
⊕ flowerpotpub.com
Goacher's Gold Star; Young's Bitter; guest beers Ⓗ
Filling a gap in Maidstone's pub portfolio, this genuine street-corner free house has much to offer real ale enthusiasts. The landlord is an evangelist for real ale and offers a diverse range of four guest ales to complement the two regular beers. The pub's top bar has panelling reputed to be from HMS Victory. Home-cooked pub food is available 12-6pm daily. Frequent live music and jam nights feature, as well as occasional beer festivals. A short walk from the railway station.
⚌Q❀◖≋(East)🚋(101,155)➍➍≛

Rifle Volunteers

28 Wyatt Street, ME14 1EU
☼ 11-3, 6 (7 Sat)-11; 12-3, 7-10.30 Sun ☎ (01622) 758891
Goacher's Real Mild, Fine Light, Crown Imperial Stout Ⓗ
Quiet street-corner single-bar pub owned by the local Goacher's Brewery. It retains most of its original features and has been a regular in this Guide for several years. The pub fields two quiz teams in the local league. Note the display of interesting old bottled beers and the unusual toy soldiers used to indicate a beer 'in the wood'. A good, old-fashioned pub free from music and fruit machines. Simple, good-value lunches are available during the week. Q❀◖≋(East)➍≛

Swan ✅

2 County Road, ME14 1UY (opp prison, near County Hall)
☼ 12-11 ☎ (01622) 751264 ⊕ theswaninnmaidstone.co.uk
Shepherd Neame Master Brew Bitter, Kent's Best, seasonal beers Ⓗ
Originally called The County Arms, this friendly locals' pub dates back to 1840 and is situated two minutes' walk from Maidstone East station and close to County Hall and Maidstone Prison. Shepherd Neame beers include seasonals and brews from the brewery's pilot micro-brewery, and the pub hosts regular mini festivals. The interior is adorned with swans in all shapes and sizes, and historic brewery and pub pictures. Occasional live music plays at weekends, plus folk nights and fun quiz nights on alternate Wednesdays.
⚌❀≋(East)➍≛

Wheatsheaf

301 Loose Road, ME15 9PY (S of Maidstone at A229/A274 jct)
☼ 4-11; 12-11.30 Fri & Sat; 12-10.30 Sun ☎ (01622) 752624
Courage Best Bitter; guest beers Ⓗ
The landlord of this busy out-of-town free house has been in residence now for 26 years. The pub, built in 1830, stands at a major road junction and is well served by buses. Regular beer festivals are held, usually four times a year. Saturday is quiz night, there is a golf society, and a TV at one end of the bar shows Sky Sports. Live music features occasionally, often on saints' days.
❀◖♿🚋(5,89)➍≛

Marden

Stile Bridge ✅

Staplehurst Road, TN12 9BH (S of Maidstone on A229 at foot of Linton Hill by jct with B2079)
☼ 5-10 Mon; 12-11 Tue-Sat; 12-6 Sun ☎ (01622) 831236
⊕ stile.co.uk
Shepherd Neame Master Brew Bitter; guest beers Ⓗ
The front bar of this large roadside pub is divided in two, with dining on the right and comfortable sofas on the left. A third area has a large-screen TV popular for big sporting events, and blackboards with tasting notes from local micro-breweries. At the rear is a large tithe barn restaurant/function room. Live music plays on Friday. Guest ales are usually from local micro-breweries, with a good selection of continental bottled beers and an adventurous choice of lagers. The cider is supplied by Biddenden and Double Vision. An extensive selection of quality food is available.
⚌Q❀◖🚋(5)➍P≛

Margate

Mechanical Elephant ✅

28-30 Marine Terrace, CT9 1XJ
☼ 9am-midnight (1am Fri & Sat) ☎ (01843) 234100
Greene King IPA; Marston's Pedigree; guest beers Ⓗ
Ideally located opposite Margate main sands with a summer balcony offering famous sunset views, a quiet daytime and evening pub during the week, it becomes a Lloyds No 1 bar on Friday and Saturday evenings. The name derives from a large roving mechanical elephant that used to give rides along the seafront in the 1920s. An ever-changing range of ales and regular beer festivals are offered in line with Wetherspoon's national promotions. Local beers are often available. ❧❀◖♿≋🚋(8)≛

Northern Belle
4 Mansion Street, CT9 1HE
☉ 11-11; 12-10.30 Sun ☎ (07810) 088347
Shepherd Neame Master Brew Bitter, Kent's Best, seasonal beers Ⓗ
Margate's oldest standing pub is situated down a tiny alleyway opposite the stone pier. In the year 1680 two fishermen's cottages were combined and a new pub Aurora Borealis was born. Its present name derives from a merchant ship that ran aground in 1857. Low ceilings and quirky little nooks make this a rather cosy pub. Mostly frequented by working men, the language can be somewhat colourful. ⊟⇌♣

Marshside

Gate Inn
Boyden Gate, CT3 4EB (off A28 at Upstreet)
☉ 11-2.30 (4 Sat), 6-11; 12-4, 7-10.30 Sun
☎ (01227) 860498
Shepherd Neame Master Brew Bitter, Spitfire, seasonal beers Ⓖ
Chris Smith is probably the longest-serving landlord in this Guide – the Gate has been continuously listed since 1977. A focal point for the community, the pub's events include mummers' plays, hoodeners and morris dancing. The bars have tiled floors, log fire and hanging hops, while the garden includes a stream, ducks and apple trees, which are protected by the annual wassailing ceremony. Excellent, good value food includes hotpots and black pudding sandwiches (not Mon eve or winter Tue). Shepherd Neame micro-brewery beers are occasionally available. ♨Q☺❀◐◑⛺♣P

Meopham

George Inn
Wrotham Road, DA13 0AH (on A227 near church)
☉ 11-11; 12-10.30 Sun ☎ (01474) 814198
Shepherd Neame Master Brew Bitter, Spitfire, Late Red, Bishops Finger, seasonal beers Ⓗ
The oldest public house in Meopham, this former coaching inn, dating in parts from the 15th century, has an attractive Kentish weatherboard exterior. Inside, there are two bars and a separate restaurant serving good food daily until 9.45pm (7.45pm Sun). To the rear is a large drinking and smoking area. The pub has a large car park and a floodlit petanque piste. A passageway under the road links the inn with the parish church. ♨Q❀◐◑♿⊟(306,308)♣P⚐

Milton Regis

Three Hats
High Street, ME10 2AR
☉ 11-11; 10-10 Sun ☎ (01795) 427645 ⊕ the3hats.com
Shepherd Neame Master Brew Bitter; guest beers Ⓗ
This popular, friendly local is situated in a historic village. The oldest pub in Milton Regis, it is a traditional single-roomed urban pub with two main areas. The front, known locally as the shallow end, has low beams and a small dining area providing good value lunch and evening bar meals (not Sat or Sun eve). The rear of the pub has a pool table and dartboard. Guest beers are from the Enterprise Inns list. ♨❀◐◑⇌(Sittingbourne)⊟♣⚐

Newenden

White Hart
Rye Road, TN18 5PN TQ834273
☉ 11-11; 12-10.30 Sun ☎ (01797) 252166
Harveys Sussex Best Bitter; Rother Valley Level Best; Sharp's Doom Bar; guest beers Ⓗ
This 500-year-old weatherboarded and old oak-beamed inn is reputedly haunted. It stands just within Kent's boundary with East Sussex. Regular customers score the two guest beers for quality and make suggestions for future ales. Good quality food is available and there is a large garden to sit out in the summer. The pub has six guest rooms and is a short walk from Northiam station on the Kent and East Sussex Railway. ♨Q☺❀⌂◐◑⇌⊟(340,341)♣P

Northfleet

Earl Grey
177 Vale Road, DA11 8BP (off Perry St)
☉ 12-11 (10.30 Sun) ☎ (01474) 365240
Shepherd Neame Master Brew Bitter, Spitfire, seasonal beers Ⓗ
Distinctive late 18th-century cottage-style building with a Kentish brick and flint exterior that is rarely seen in this area. The interior consists of an L-shaped bar, with a raised seating area at one end, and exudes a homely, convivial atmosphere. The Cygnet Leisure Centre in Perry Street is nearby. ❀⊟(498,499)♣P⚐

Otford

Crown ✔
10 High Street, TN14 5PQ (adjacent to village duck pond)
☉ 12-11 (11.30 Fri); 11-11.30 Sat; 11-11 Sun
☎ (01959) 522847 ⊕ crownpubandrestaurant.co.uk
Harveys Sussex Best Bitter; Westerham Otford Crown; guest beers Ⓗ
Attractive whitewashed cottage-style village pub dating from the 16th century. Two distinct bars include one that houses a suit of armour under a bygone stairwell, and banknotes and hotel keys adorn the beams. Excellent home-cooked meals are served every lunchtime and Wednesday to Saturday evenings. Booking for the Sunday roast is essential. Otford Crown (house beer) is a blend of Finchcocks and Freedom Ale. The hub of village community activities – beer festivals are held in April and October. ♨Q❀◐◑⇌⊟(431,432)♣●⚐

Pembury

Black Horse
12 High Street, TN2 4NY
☉ 11-11 (midnight Sat); 12-10.30 Sun ☎ (01892) 822141
⊕ blackhorsepembury.co.uk
Courage Best Bitter; Fuller's London Pride; Greene King Old Speckled Hen Ⓗ
Lovely, traditional Kentish local pub, well kept with hanging baskets and plant pots providing an array of colour out front, and a cosy, welcoming feel inside. Deceptively large, it has plenty of seating extending into the adjoining restaurant. The landlord's love of sport is reflected in the interesting display of trophies and memorabilia

comprising much of the decor. There is a large inglenook with log fire and central bar. The attractive garden has spacious, covered, heated areas for drinking, dining and smoking.
⚲Q❀◐♿⊟♣⊱

Perry Wood

Rose & Crown

ME13 9RY (1½ miles from Selling station, signed to Perry Wood) TR042552
⊙ 11.30-3, 6.30-11 (not Mon); 12-3, 7-10.30 Sun
☎ (01227) 752214 ⊕ roseandcrownperrywood.co.uk
Adnams Bitter; Harveys Sussex Best Bitter; guest beers Ⓗ
This historic free house was once a woodcutter's cottage and is in the middle of the wood, which is East Kent's highest point. Popular with walkers and cyclists, it is well regarded for its food and, of course, beer. The bar room has a large fireplace and is decorated with old wood-cutting tools and corn dollies. The large garden has a children's play area. Winner of Kent Environment Business of the Year 2009. No food is available Monday.
⚲Q❀◐♣P

Petham

Chequers

Stone Street, CT4 5PW (on B2068)
⊙ 12-3 (not Mon), 6-11; 12-4.30, 7-10.30 Sun
☎ (01227) 700734
Dark Star Hophead; Fuller's London Pride; Harveys Sussex Best Bitter; Hopdaemon Incubus; Wadworth Henry's IPA; Whitstable East India Pale Ale Ⓖ
On the Roman road from Canterbury to Hythe, the Chequers was built about 1830. The bar area has comfortable leather sofas, and there is a spacious dining area and restaurant at the back, with a tempting menu including a popular Sunday carvery (no food Sun and Mon eves). Darts and pool are played in the small side bar. The range of beers varies slightly but up to eight are available at busy times. All real ales are hand drawn from the cellar, and Biddenden Bushells cider is stocked. Petanque is played, and there is a covered smoking area.
⚲Q❀◐♿▲♣●P⊱

Petteridge

Hopbine

Petteridge Lane, TN12 7NE
⊙ 12-2.30, 6-11; 12-3, 7-10.30 Sun ☎ (01892) 722561
Badger K&B Sussex Bitter, First Gold, seasonal beer Ⓗ
The most easterly Hall & Woodhouse pub, so a rare outlet for its excellent range of beers in this part of the world, served in oversized lined glasses. The pub has an attractive and traditional Kentish white weatherboard and tile-hung exterior, while inside a cosy welcome awaits, with a log fire in winter. It recently received a CAMRA award for its 25th consecutive appearance in the Guide (23 with the current landlord). The landlady's home-cooked food is a draw and takeaways are available on request (no food Wed). ⚲Q❀◐⊟(296,297)P⊱⊡

Plaxtol

Golding Hop

Sheet Hill, Topps Hill, TN15 0PT (¾ mile N of village) TQ 600547
⊙ 11-3 (2.30 Mon), 6-11; 11-11 Sat; 12-3.30, 7-10.30 Sun
☎ (01732) 882150
Adnams Bitter; guest beers Ⓖ
Nestling in a secluded vale surrounded by orchards and woods, this timeless pub eschews modernity. Low beams and roaring fires add to the cosy atmosphere and a multitude of hanging baskets covers the whitewashed exterior. Beers are served direct from casks behind the bar and there are several real ciders on offer including the home-made house rough. Pub grub is served in hearty portions. Dogs and children are permitted in the garden where there is a large play area. The pub is a major contender in the local petanque league.
⚲Q❀◐⊟(222,404)♣●P

Queenborough

Old House At Home

1 High Street, ME11 5AA TQ907722
⊙ 12-11 (midnight summer; 1am Fri & Sat)
☎ (01795) 662463
Greene King IPA; guest beers Ⓗ
Waterfront pub next to the sea wall with views over the Medway estuary and a nautically themed rustic interior. It has two public bars and a saloon. Live music plays most Sundays and quiz night is Thursday. Ask at the bar for the DIY barbecue in the garden. Food is available until 9pm Monday to Saturday and 4pm Sunday. Bus 360/362 from Sheerness runs half-hourly Monday to Saturday, but not in the evening. ⚲❀◐⊟⇌⊟(360,362)P

Rainham

Angel

Station Road, ME8 7UH (N end of B2004) TQ825670
⊙ 12-11 (midnight Fri & Sat) ☎ (01634) 360219
⊕ theangelrainham.com
Adnams Bitter; guest beers Ⓗ
Less than 15 minutes' walk north from Rainham railway station, enter the Angel to be greeted by Buster the dog. An L-shaped bar serves Adnams Bitter plus two changing guest ales. Outside is a large walled garden with a smoking area set aside. Local CAMRA Pub of the Year 2004, 2005 and 2007.
⚲❀⇌⊟(131,327)♣P⊱

Mackland Arms

213 Station Road, ME8 7PS TQ820664
⊙ 10-midnight (1am Fri-Sat); 12-10.30 Sun
☎ (01634) 232178
Shepherd Neame Master Brew Bitter, seasonal beers Ⓗ
This small, unchanged pub in a part of old Rainham is only a few minutes' walk from the railway station. It offers a friendly welcome and good quality Shepherd Neame beers, including their seasonal range. Walk through the narrow bar to a paved garden and smoking area, which is a sun-trap in the summer. Well worth a visit.
❀⇌⊟(120,327)♣⊱

Ramsgate

Artillery Arms

36 Westcliff Road, CT11 9JS

12-11.30 (midnight Fri & Sat) (01843) 853282

Sharp's Doom Bar; guest beers H

The pub has a warm and welcoming atmosphere and focuses on its reputation as a traditional ale house. Stained glass windows depict battle scenes from the 19th century. The busy bar offers six handpumps featuring a constantly rotating choice of ales from local micros. Guest beers also come from other breweries across Britain to offer an eclectic mix of good quality ales. LocAle accredited. (9)

Churchill Tavern

19-22 The Paragon, CT11 9JX

11.30-11 (1am Fri & Sat); 12-11 Sun (01843) 587862 churchilltavern.co.uk

Fuller's London Pride; Ringwood Old Thumper; guest beers H

Built in 1816, this building has seen a number of changes through the centuries. Now known as 'the country pub in town', it offers pub and brasserie-style food. Oak beams and lowered ceilings feature heavily, giving the pub a warm and welcoming atmosphere. It offers superb views across Ramsgate Harbour and the English Channel. Live bands most weekends are very popular with locals and visitors alike. (34,88)

Montefiore Arms

1 Trinity Place, CT11 7HJ

12-2.30 (4.30 Sat), 7-11; closed Wed; 12-3, 7-10.30 Sun (01843) 593265 montefiorearms.co.uk

Ramsgate Gadds' No. 7; guest beers H

A quintessential English back-street pub offering a warm old-world feel in the front bar with pool and darts available, as well as a small snug for a more intimate evening. The pub is named after Sir Moses Montefiore, 1784-1885, a Jewish philanthropist, much-loved in Ramsgate. It was the first LocAle accredited pub in Kent and a firm supporter of CAMRA initiatives. This is not a food pub, but the friendly landlord will serve you reasonably priced ale in a convivial atmosphere.
Q (Dumpton Park) (9X,9)

Sir Stanley Gray

Pegwell Bay Hotel, 81 Pegwell Road, CT11 0NJ

11-11 (midnight Fri & Sat); 11.30-10.30 Sun (01843) 599590 pegwellbayhotel.co.uk

Greene King Abbot; Ramsgate Gadds' No. 5; guest beers H

Welcoming pub, part of the Thorley Tavern chain, situated in the village of Pegwell with scenic views over Pegwell Bay and across the Channel. Connected to the Pegwell Hotel via a tunnel, the atmosphere is old world and friendly, with low beams and a warm, intimate feeling. There is a separate games room with pool and darts, and a full pub-grub menu supplemented by home-cooked daily specials. The pub offers four real ales including regionals and independents, and is LocAle accredited. P

Ripple

Plough Inn

Church Lane, CT14 8JH TR348498

12-11 (01304) 360209 theploughripple.co.uk

Fuller's London Pride, ESB; Shepherd Neame Master Brew Bitter; guest beers H

This pub's tranquil rural setting feels like the middle of nowhere but in reality it is just outside Deal. A managed house, it is privately owned by Sutton Vale Caravan Park, about a mile away. Popular with walkers, the pub is easily accessible by field paths from Walmer. This is a renowned outlet for Fuller's ESB, a bit of a rarity in these parts. Don't be put off by six handpumps on the bar in such a quiet pub – somehow it works! Quiz night is Wednesday. Lunch is served Thursday and Sunday. P

Rochester

Britannia Bar Café

376 High Street, ME1 1DJ (⅓ mile E of railway station) TQ751678

10-11 (2am Fri & Sat); 12-11 Sun (01634) 815204 britannia-bar-cafe.co.uk

Goacher's Light; guest beers H

Situated between Rochester and Chatham railway stations, this bar can be busy at lunchtimes, attracting a mainly business clientele. The bar offers an extensive and popular daily menu, including breakfast and lunches Monday to Saturday. Evening meals are served Tuesday to Thursday at candle-lit tables, and there is a traditional Sunday lunchtime roast. A stylish bar leads out into a small walled garden that is a sun trap in summer. Occasional special events are hosted. No jukebox or fruit machine. Q

Good Intent

83 John Street, ME1 1YL TQ743678

12-midnight (11 Sun) (01634) 843118

Beer range varies G

Local CAMRA Pub of the Year in 2008, this back-street local for real ale enthusiasts is well worth searching out. An ever-changing selection of beers is available from a gravity-fed system. Various events are held in the garden throughout the year with additional ales available. The public bar features a large-screen TV for major sports events and a pool table. Live music gigs are hosted. Those wishing to enjoy their pint in a quieter atmosphere can retire to the back bar in comfort.
Q P

Man of Kent

6-8 John Street, ME1 1YN (200m off A2 from bottom of Star Hill) TQ744679

2-11; 12-midnight Fri & Sat; 12-11 Sun (07772) 214315 themanofkent.com

Goacher's Light; Hopdaemon Incubus; Whitstable East India Pale Ale; guest beers H

Local CAMRA Pub of the Year 2010, with ales from 14 Kent brewers served on eleven handpumps plus seven ciders and various Kent wines. Kentish produce is a feature of this LocAle pub. The lively and friendly venue also offers a large range of German and Belgian beers on tap and in bottles. Live music plays on several evenings during the week. The enclosed garden offers plenty of seating all year round.

Rodmersham Green

Fruiterers Arms

Bottles Lane, ME9 0PP TQ915613
11.30-2.30, 6-10 (11 Wed-Fri); 11.30-11 Sat; 12-6 Sun
(01795) 424198
Fuller's London Pride; Shepherd Neame Master Brew Bitter; Taylor Landlord H
A village local with two bars. The public bar has a log fire in winter, and dogs are welcome in here. The saloon bar has an emphasis on dining with a separate restaurant area. There is a garden for alfresco drinking in warmer months. A full a la carte menu is offered throughout the week, with bar snacks also available. No under 5s admitted on Sunday and no under 11s on weekdays. Bus 348 is infrequent and runs Monday to Friday only.
(348)P

Rusthall

Beacon

Tea Garden Lane, TN3 9JH (opp cricket pitch) TQ563392
11-11; 12-10 Sun (01892) 524252 the-beacon.co.uk
Harveys Sussex Best Bitter; Larkins Traditional; Taylor Landlord H
Set in 17 acres of grounds on a sandstone outcrop, the decking area has a 180 degree panoramic view of the Spa Valley below. The front bar is comfy with leather seating surrounded by a collection of old wirelesses. A member of Kentish Fayre, the varied food menu features locally-sourced produce, and food can be enjoyed in one of four dining rooms. The downstairs bar caters for functions and is licensed for weddings. Fishing is available in the grounds for a small fee.
Q(231,291)P

St Margaret's Bay

Coastguard

The Bay, CT15 6DY
10.30-11 (01304) 853176 thecoastguard.co.uk
Beer range varies H
The pub's superb location at the foot of the White Cliffs merits the descent of the cliff path, and even the climb afterwards. Lounge on the terrace and watch the shipping on the Strait of Dover while enjoying the view and good ale too. An ever-changing beer selection is always on offer, featuring smaller breweries from Kent and Scotland. Westons cider is served alongside a wide range of continental draught and bottled beers, and the pub has won several food awards.
P

St Mary in the Marsh

Star Inn

TN29 0BX (opp church) TR065279
12-11 (10.30 Sun) (01797) 362139
thestarinn-themarsh.co.uk
Adnams Bitter; Young's Bitter; guest beers H
Situated in the heart of Romney Marsh, this Grade II-listed building was built in 1476 and became an ale house in 1711. A cosy inn where a warm and friendly welcome always awaits you, this pretty village local offers real ale from four handpumps, home-cooked food and en-suite accommodation. Opposite is St Mary the Virgin Church where Edith Nesbit is buried. Noel Coward lodged in the adjacent cottages while writing his first play.
P

Sandgate

Ship Inn

65 Sandgate High Street, CT20 3AH (on A259)
11.30-11.30 (1am Fri & Sat); 12-11.30 Sun
(01303) 248525
Greene King IPA, St Edmunds, Abbot; Hop Back Summer Lightning; Hopdaemon Incubus; guest beer H
In spring 2010 the landlord and landlady celebrated 25 years at this two-bar community pub. A new dining area with sea views opened in 2010 and other facilities have been recently refurbished, but the range of nautical memorabilia remains. The front facing the High Street dates from 1798. Guest beers on gravity are available periodically and the August bank holiday beer festival specialises in summer ales. Biddenden medium and dry ciders are always available.

Sandling

Yew Tree

Grange Lane, ME14 3DB (take Boarley Lane by Running Horse pub) TQ757584
11-11 (midnight Fri & Sat); 12-10.30 Sun
(01622) 752882 yewtreesandling.co.uk
Shepherd Neame Master Brew Bitter, Spitfire, seasonal beers H
Relatively quiet pub down a narrow country lane close to the M2 motorway. The bar is divided into two distinct areas, one carpeted for dining, the other stone-floored for drinking. Several photographs of the pub dating from the 1890s to present times are displayed. The quiz machine and TV are normally muted. Fun quizzes are held on Tuesday evenings with various prizes, and half-time hot food is included in the entry fee. Good fresh food is cooked daily including ostrich steaks for the adventurous. QP

Sandwich

Fleur de Lis

6-8 Delf Street, CT13 9BZ
10-11 (midnight Fri); 10-10.30 Sun (01304) 611131
thefleur-sandwich.co.uk
Badger K&B Sussex Bitter; Greene King IPA; guest beer H
A popular and friendly old coaching office situated in the middle of this Cinque Port, catering for all types of customer. Each of the three areas that make up this pub has its own character, and there is a separate restaurant space with an unusual painted cupola ceiling. Good pub food is supported by a specials board. Live bands play every Friday, pictures painted by local artists are displayed for sale and dogs are welcome. No food on Sunday evening. (13,14,88)

Red Cow

12 Moat Sole, CT13 9AU
11-midnight (01304) 613243
theredcowpub.webs.com

St Austell Tribute; Taylor Landlord; guest beers Ⓗ
Located close to the town centre, this is one of the oldest inns in Sandwich. The pub is child and dog friendly and offers a welcoming atmosphere, enhanced by good food, fine beers and ciders from Thatchers and Westons, and two open fires. The large enclosed garden, with children's games, is a sun-trap in summer. A range of entertainment is provided including poker nights and two mini beer festivals. ♛❀◐♿⇌⊟♣●P⁻

Sevenoaks

Anchor

32 London Road, TN13 1AS
✪ 11-3, 6-11.30; 10-4, 6-midnight Fri; 10-4, 7-midnight Sat; 12-5, 7-11 Sun ☎ (01732) 454898
Harveys Sussex Best Bitter; Sharp's Doom Bar; guest beer Ⓗ
Friendly town-centre pub popular with all ages, the Anchor is a regular Guide entry and has the area's longest-serving licensee. A third handpump has recently been installed to provide a continually changing guest beer. Live blues music is performed on the first Wednesday of the month. Good food is available Monday to Friday lunchtimes, a smaller range at other times. Christmas lunches are recommended. When entering the pub observe the unusual circular lobby. ◐⊟♣⁻

Sheerness

Red Lion

61 High Street, Blue Town, ME12 1RW TQ911750
✪ 10-midnight (2am Thu-Sat); 12-midnight Sun
☎ (01795) 664354
Beer range varies Ⓗ
An oasis of choice in Sheppey – facing the former naval dockyard wall, this is the only real ale outlet remaining in the old Blue Town district of Sheerness, with its cobbled High Street. Three beers from regional and micro-breweries are served, with local customers having a say in the choice of beers. No meals, but there is a free buffet all day on Sunday. Outside are tables and a heated, covered smoking area. ♛❀⇌⊟♣⁻

Snargate

Red Lion ★

TN29 9UQ (on B2080, 1 mile W of Brenzett) TQ 990285
✪ 12-3, 7-10.30 ☎ (01797) 344648
Beer range varies Ⓖ
Beautiful, unspoilt, award-winning pub on the remote Welland Marsh. The interior is decorated with WWII and Women's Land Army posters, and features in CAMRA's National Inventory of Historic Pub Interiors. A haven for good conversation, it is also a friendly place to play one of the traditional games available. Several beer festivals are hosted annually; the main event is in June. Local CAMRA Pub of the Year 2009. ♛Q❀♣●P

Stalisfield Green

Plough Inn

ME13 0HY TQ955529
✪ closed Mon; 12-3, 6-11 (12.30am Fri); 12-midnight Sat; 12-8 (11 summer) Sun ☎ (01795) 890256
🌐 stalisfieldgreen.com
Beer range varies Ⓗ
Historic multi-roomed pub in an attractive setting on the North Downs. Beers mostly from micro-breweries are featured on a rotating basis, together with a local cider. The extensive menu features locally-sourced produce and has won many awards (no food Sun eve or Mon). The pub has a large family-friendly garden. Live music plays on some Fridays (phone for details). There is a beer festival over the August bank holiday weekend. The 660 bus from Faversham is infrequent. ♛❀◐▲⊟(660)♣P

Stansted

Black Horse

Tumblefield Road, TN15 7PR (1 mile N of A20 jct 2) TQ606620
✪ 11.30-11; 12-10.30 Sun ☎ (01732) 822355
Larkins Traditional; guest beers Ⓗ
Popular with ramblers and cyclists, this welcoming village local is free of any tie. Thai meals are available 6.30-9.30pm Tuesday to Saturday, bar meals lunchtimes and Sunday evening. The pub affords excellent views of the surrounding countryside from its garden at the rear which includes a children's play area. Irish folk music sessions are held on the second Sunday of each month. ♛Q☕❀⇔◐▲♣P⁻

Staplehurst

Bell

High Street, TN12 0AY
✪ 12-11 (10.30 Sun) ☎ (01580) 893366
🌐 bellinn-staplehurst.co.uk
Westerham Finchcocks Original; guest beers Ⓗ
A late-Victorian pub opposite the church, stylishly refurbished, revealing original panelling, tiling and wooden floors. The bar area has comfortable seating and a log fire with a fireback featuring a Charles I motif. A second room on a raised level provides additional seating and a dartboard. Snacks and meals using local produce are served daily in the bar or split-level restaurant. The large garden has a children's play area. Two guest beers are mainly from SIBA brewers. Biddenden Bushells cider is sold. ♛Q❀⇔◐⇌⊟(5)♣●P

Lord Raglan

Chart Hill Road, TN12 0DE (½ mile N of A229) TQ786472
✪ 12-3, 6.30-11.30; closed Sun ☎ (01622) 843747
Goacher's Light; Harveys Sussex Best Bitter; guest beer Ⓗ
A popular country free house with open log fires and a bar decorated with hops. Outside, the large orchard garden catches the evening sun. The guest beer changes frequently and local Double Vision cider is always available. Excellent meals and snacks are served and can be finished off with home-made ice cream. ♛Q❀◐⊟(5)●P

Temple Ewell

Fox

Hight Street, CT16 3DU
✪ 11.30-3.30, 6-11.30; 7-11.30 Sun ☎ (01304) 823598

Caledonian Deuchars IPA; Greene King Abbot; guest beers Ⓗ
The pub lies in the Dour river valley on the outskirts of Dover. Chalk downland rises behind the pub and a branch of the river flows through the garden. The single bar offers four real ales, and meals are served lunchtimes and evenings (not Sun eve) including a Sunday carvery. Traditional pub games include darts, skittles and dominoes. The pub runs weekly events including quiz evenings and curry and pie nights. A regular Guide entry and local CAMRA Pub of the Year 2005.
♨❀◑♿⇌(Kearsney)🚌(15,15A,68)♣P⅟

Tenterden

Vine Inn

76 High Street, TN30 6AU
⏲ 11-11 (midnight Fri & Sat); 11-10.30 Sun
☎ (01580) 762718
Shepherd Neame Master Brew Bitter, Spitfire, seasonal beers Ⓗ
Modernised Shepherd Neame flagship town-centre pub. Built in the 19th century, it was an old Obadiah Edwards' brewery pub until 1922 when Shepherd Neame bought it. There is almost nothing remaining of the old Vine. Facilities are very good, with all customers well catered for. The large open plan interior is divided into different areas, with a separate restaurant and pleasant patio and garden. Some of the slower-selling beers may have a cask breather on at quieter times.
♨❀◑♿⇌

White Lion Hotel

57 High Street, TN30 6BD
⏲ 10-11 (midnight Fri & Sat); 10-10.30 Sun
☎ (01580) 765077 🌐 marstonsinns.co.uk
Marston's Pedigree; Jennings Cumberland Ale; guest beers Ⓗ
A 16th-century coaching inn with an elegant frontage, pillared porch, bowed and dormer window, and the original coaching entrance. It was built facing the wide tree-lined street that includes many historic buildings and is convenient for the K&ES Railway. Inside there are aged ship timbered beams, inglenook fireplaces and much local memorabilia. The pub utilises the full range of beers from the Marston's list and encourages customers to ask for the beers they want on the bar. ⛵🛏◑🍴⇌(Town)🚌P

Tilmanstone

Plough & Harrow

Dover Road, CT14 0HX (signed off A256 between Dover & Sandwich)
⏲ 12-11; 12-10.30 Sun (hours vary in winter)
☎ (01304) 617582 🌐 ploughandharrowtilmanstone.co.uk
Shepherd Neame Master Brew Bitter, Spitfire, seasonal beers Ⓗ
The bar of this rural pub has a traditional feel to it, with wooden floors, sofas, a bar billiards table and an interesting collection of Kent coalfield memorabilia on the walls. Real ale includes limited-edition beers from Shepherd Neame's micro-brewery. Traditional home-cooked food is served in the conservatory restaurant overlooking the garden (no food Sun eve). The pub is popular with ramblers and walkers, families are welcome, as are dogs. ♨❀🛏◑🚌(87,88)♣P⅟

Tonbridge

Humphrey Bean ✔

94 High Street, TN9 1AP
⏲ 7am-midnight (1am Fri & Sat) ☎ (01732) 773850
Greene King Ruddles Best Bitter, Abbot; Marston's Pedigree; guest beers Ⓗ
This spacious Wetherspoon conversion of the former Crown post office building is named after the landlord of a pub which once occupied the site. The main part of the venue has a bright and airy feel, thanks to large roof windows. The spacious garden at the rear has views across the River Medway to Tonbridge Castle. Beers from local brewery Westerham are a regular feature on the beer list, alongside brews from King and Welton's.
Q❀◑⇌🚌♣P⅟

Tonge

Oast Golf Centre

Church Road, ME9 9AR TQ933643
⏲ 8.30am-10 ☎ (01795) 473527 🌐 oastgolf.co.uk
Adnams Bitter; Harveys Sussex Best Bitter; guest beer Ⓗ
An unusual outlet for the beer drinker, but non-golfers are very welcome in the comfortable bar. Either Adnams or Harveys Bitter is offered in winter, plus a differing second beer in summer. Facilities include a public par three golf course and floodlit driving range, with lessons available. There is also short mat bowls, pool and darts. Sandwiches and rolls are served. ❀♣P

Tunbridge Wells

Bull

79 Frant Road, TN2 5LH
⏲ 12-3, 5.30-11; 12-11 Sat; 12-10.30 Sun ☎ (01892) 536526
🌐 thebulltunbridgewells.co.uk
Shephard Neame Master Brew Bitter, Spitfire, seasonal beers Ⓗ
Warm and friendly locals' pub with an open fire in the winter and pleasant courtyard gardens for the summer. Excellent, home-made traditional food including Sunday roasts is served. Enjoy the use of a free pool table, dartboard and wireless internet. The Neville Cricket Ground is a 10-minute walk. Dogs are welcome. ♨❀◑♿🚌♣P⅟

Grove Tavern ✔

19 Berkley Road, TN1 1YR
⏲ 12-midnight ☎ (01892) 526549 🌐 grovetavern.co.uk
Harveys Sussex Best Bitter; Taylor Landlord; guest beer Ⓗ
Certainly the oldest pub in Tunbridge Wells, the Grove is also the friendliest. Visitors are made to feel very welcome and often stay for just another hour to enjoy the excellent ales, play pool or join in the friendly banter. The Grove is a locals' pub in the village area of the town and has an open fire during the colder months. Dogs are always welcome. Real ciders are available in the summer. Free wireless internet access. ♨❀♿⇌🚌♣🍎

Royal Oak

92 Prospect Road, TN2 4SY
⏲ 12-11.30 (10.30 Sun) ☎ (01892) 542546
🌐 theroyaloak.food.officelive.com

Dark Star seasonal beers; Harveys Sussex Best Bitter; Larkins Traditional Ⓗ
Very popular family pub with four real ale pumps dispensing excellent quality beers. A separate dining area serves home-made food, locally sourced whenever possible. Regular events include lunch with jazz on the last Sunday of the month and quiz night on the third Thursday of the month (book ahead for both). Real cider and perry are offered in the summer months. Dogs are welcome.
◐⇌⊟(285)P⊱

Sankeys

39 Mount Ephraim, TN4 8AA
⊙ 10.30-11 (midnight Fri & Sat); 12-midnight Sun
☎ (01892) 511422 ⊕ sankeys.co.uk
Sankeys Halfway to Paradise; Westerham Joey's Bite Ⓗ
Just a short walk from the town centre and station, if you fancy something different to drink this could be the right place. The pub has a good selection of continental and fruit beers in bottle and on draught along with two house beers from local breweries. The brassiere on the lower level is very busy, with fresh fish the speciality. This has proved so popular the owners have opened the town's only wet fish shop. ♔Q❀◐⇌⊟●⊱

Upper Upnor

King's Arms

2 High Street, ME2 4XG TQ757704
⊙ 11.30-11; 12-10.30 Sun ☎ (01634) 717490
Beer range varies Ⓗ
Set at the top of an enchanting cobbled High Street leading to the Castle and River Medway, this village local also houses a very popular restaurant offering traditional home-cooked pub grub alongside an a la carte menu. Five ales are well kept, always including a mild. Real cider and perry are also stocked. The large, picturesque garden gets very lively in the summer and is used to host regular beer festivals. Local CAMRA Pub of the Year 2009. Q❀◐◑⊟(197)●⊱

Tudor Rose

29/31 High Street, ME2 4XG TQ757704
⊙ 11 (12 Sun)-11 ☎ (01634) 715305
⊕ the-tudor-rose-upnor.co.uk
Shepherd Neame Canterbury Jack, Master Brew Bitter, Kent's Best, Spitfire, Bishops Finger, seasonal beers Ⓗ
This multi-roomed pub is situated at the bottom of the cobbled High Street next to Upnor Castle. Murals depicting historic scenes painted by a local artist adorn the walls. The garden is partly surrounded by the castle's 17th-century wall. Meals are served at all times except Monday evening. Winner of a Master of Beer award in 2008, this Shepherd Neame pub boasts a full range of its beers including seasonal offerings and those produced in the micro-brewery. ♔❀◐♣⊱

Walmer

Berry 🏆

23 Canada Road, CT14 7EQ
⊙ 11-2.30 Mon & Wed, 5.30-11.30; 11-11 Fri & Sat; 11.30-11 Sun ☎ (01304) 362411 ⊕ theberrywalmer.co.uk
Dark Star Hophead, American Pale Ale; Harveys Sussex Best Bitter; guest beers Ⓗ
The strength of this traditional community pub lies in the enthusiasm of the owner and staff for real ale and cider. As a result, Chris has won local CAMRA Pub of the Year in 2008, 2009 and 2010. The pub boasts a February beer festival, May cider festival and German-themed Oktoberfest. Ciders are from Thatchers and Westons. Social activities include euchre on Sunday, quiz nights, pool and darts. Dogs are welcome. The real McCoy for great beers in a warm, friendly atmosphere.
♔❀⊟(13,14,82)♣●⊱

West Malling

Bull

1 High Street, ME19 6QH (S from A20, on left after railway bridge)
⊙ 12-2.30, 5-11; 12-11 Fri & Sat; 12-10.30 Sun
☎ (01732) 842753
Young's Bitter; guest beers Ⓗ
This classic town-centre pub has been an inn since 1426. Divided into two rooms by a large brick fireplace that burns logs in winter, Kentish hops adorn both the oak beams and bar. There are WWII warplane paintings by a local artist on the walls. Lively at weekends, the quieter room to the left has a dartboard. The pub sells a wide range of beers and was judged runner-up local CAMRA Pub of the Year in 2009. ♔❀◐⇌⊟(72,151)♣⊱

West Peckham

Swan on the Green

The Green, ME18 5JW (1 mile W of B2016 at Mereworth) TQ644525
⊙ 11-3, 6-11 (8.30 Mon); 12-9 (5 winter) Sun
☎ (01622) 812271 ⊕ swan-on-the-green.co.uk
Swan Fuggles Pale, Trumpeter Best, Cygnet, Bewick, seasonal beers Ⓗ
This brew-pub occupies a peaceful rural location overlooking the village green and cricket pitch. The light and airy interior features exposed brickwork, hop-strewn beams and an open fire. The walls display amusing black and white photographs of village characters. Beers come from the micro-brewery behind the pub. Quality meals are available (not Sun and Mon eves). Situated on the Greensand Way, it is popular with walkers and there is plenty of outside seating. Know your Cobs from your Pens before visiting the toilet!
♔Q❀◐●P

Westerham

General Wolfe

High Street, TN16 1RQ (W end of town on A25)
⊙ 12-11 (12.30am Fri & Sat); 12-11 Sun ☎ (01959) 562104
Greene King IPA, Old Speckled Hen, Abbot Ⓗ
Traditional weatherboard pub named after a famous town resident (General Wolfe of Quebec). The garden forms part of the Old Black Eagle Brewery. The interior comprises a long room divided into a number of areas. The front area has a log fire in winter. The pub serves a varied food range (not Sun-Tue eves). A large range of malt whiskies is available. Quiz night is Wednesday with music nights held monthly.
♔Q❀◐⊟(401,409,410)♣P

Whitstable

Pearson's

Sea Wall, CT5 1BT (on seafront at end of High Street)
12-11 (midnight Fri & Sat) ☎ (01227) 272005
Harveys Sussex Best Bitter; Ramsgate Gadd's No. 7, Gadd's No. 5, Gadd's No. 3 Ⓗ
Pearson's Crab and Oyster House was built in 1577 and is just behind the sea wall. It has undergone many changes but retains the charm of an old-fashioned seaside inn and restaurant. There are two interlinking bar areas and an upstairs restaurant with stunning views over the Thames Estuary. It is a rare outlet for Gadd's beers in Whitstable. Outdoor drinking is on the pub forecourt or the sea wall itself. (4,6)

Ship Centurion ✔

111 High Street, CT5 1AY
11-11; 12-7 Sun ☎ (01227) 264740
Adnams Bitter; Elgood's Black Dog; guest beers Ⓗ
A mild is always served here, along with ever-changing guest beers, one from a local brewer. This centrally-located free house is festooned with colourful hanging baskets in summer. Fascinating photographs of old Whitstable hang in the comfortable bar, in which several TV screens display sporting events. There is live entertainment on Thursday evening (except Jan). Home-cooked bar food often features authentic German produce – the only food on Saturday is schnitzel. Kent CAMRA Pub of the Year 2007. (4,6)

Whitstable Labour Club

12 Belmont Road, CT5 1QP
12-11 (midnight Fri & Sat) ☎ (01227) 272023
Shepherd Neame Master Brew Bitter; guest beers Ⓗ
Formerly a pub (the Golden Lion), the cheerful bar has darts, a TV screen and quizzes. There is a function room at the back where pool and darts are played. Live music features every other Saturday evening, and every other Sunday afternoon from 3.30 to 6.30pm. The garden has a heated and covered smoking area, and a beer festival is held on the August bank holiday weekend. There are usually two constantly-changing guest beers from an interesting range of small breweries. Non-members can be signed in if they mention this Guide. (4,6)

Wrotham

Bull Hotel

Bull Lane, TN15 7RF
12-3, 6-11; 12-11 Sun ☎ (01732) 789800
thebullhotel.com
Dark Star Hophead; guest beers Ⓗ
Historic village-centre hotel dating from the 14th century. The large single bar features a modern interior with occasional echoes of the past. Jazz evenings are a highlight on the last Wednesday of the month. During the summer months there are occasional outdoor events in the courtyard. The restaurant features locally sourced food and holds a fish night on Friday. Q(306,308)P

Wrotham Heath

Moat

London Road, TN15 7RR (on A20 near M26 jct)
12-11 (10.30 Sun) ☎ (01732) 882263
Badger First Gold, Tanglefoot, seasonal beers Ⓗ
This rambling roadhouse has been extensively refurbished in recent years. Some of the original features have been retained in the bright and airy interior, including four log-burning fireplaces. Food is served daily until 9pm (7pm Sun). There is a quiz evening on Thursday from 9pm. The outside seating area has heated lamps and umbrellas. P

Churchill Tavern, Ramsgate (Photo: Chris Hunt)

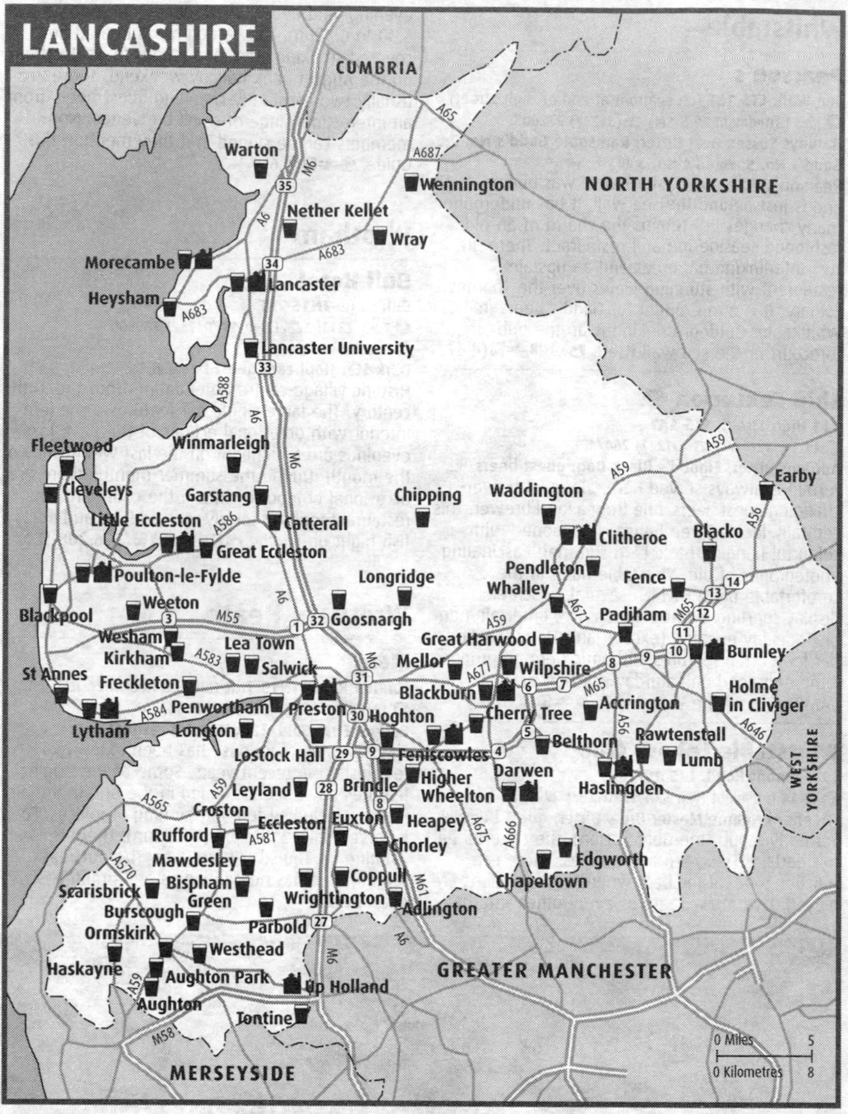

Accrington

Abbey

Bank Street, BB5 1HP

⏲ 12-midnight ☎ (01254) 237043

John Smith's Bitter; guest beers Ⓗ

Community pub on the edge of the town centre, with a small front room with a dartboard and a larger back room. The pub is popular with the locals and can be busy at times. There are up to seven guest beers alongside the regular John Smith's. The smoking area is covered and heated. ❀≠♣⅃

Peel Park

Turkey Street, BB5 6EW (200m from A679, adj to Peel Park school)

⏲ 12-11.30 ☎ (01254) 235830

Tetley Bitter; guest beers Ⓗ

A true free house opposite the site of the old Stanley football ground; eight beers are sold, mainly from micros. Two beer festivals a year are held, over the spring bank holiday and in November. The main bar is a large open front room which is divided into two sections. There is a separate little pool room, and a rear room used for a restaurant or meetings. ❀◐🚌(23,263)♣P⅃

Swan

117-119 Abbey Street, BB5 1EH

⏲ 11-11 (midnight Fri & Sat) ☎ (01254) 234050

Copper Dragon Golden Pippin; guest beers Ⓗ

Large open-plan pub located on the main road into town, the Swan is comfortably set back from the road. The patio area to the front has tables and chairs, ideal for warm afternoons and evenings. The main bus routes to the Rossendale Valley and Manchester pass the pub. At lunchtimes reasonably priced home-cooked food is served.
❀◐≠🚌(464,X41)♣P

Adlington

Spinners Arms

23 Church Street, PR7 4EX
⊙ 12-11 (midnight Fri & Sat) ☎ (01257) 483331
Bank Top Dark Mild; Moorhouse's Pride of Pendle; Taylor Landlord; guest beers ⊞
The pub is known as the 'Bottom' Spinners to differentiate it from the Spinners Arms in the village. Welcoming and friendly, a single bar serves three seating areas and there is a pleasant outdoor drinking area to the front. It has no pool table, TV or gaming machine, just an open log fire. The bar menu offers home-cooked food. Guest beers, which are often sourced from local breweries, always include a mild. A CAMRA Pub of the Season plaque is proudly displayed. ♨Q❀◐⇌⊟P⊬

Aughton

Derby Arms

Prescot Road, L39 6TA (at Bowker's Green on B5197, S of Ormskirk) SD407043
⊙ 11.30 (9am Sat)-midnight; 11.30-1am Fri & Sat; 12-midnight Sun ☎ (01695) 422237
Tetley Mild, Bitter; guest beers ⊞
This CAMRA-award-winning country pub is made special by the regulars, who help to create the atmosphere of a community local. Alongside the regular Tetley beers, the guest choice is extraordinary. The food is of excellent quality and value. Two real fires and a walled garden add to the character. Regular charity events go alongside other entertainments. Having benefited from a refurbishment, this pub is one worth seeking out. Breakfast is served on Saturday from 9am.
♨❀◐◑⊟♣P

Aughton Park

Dog & Gun ✔

233 Long Lane, L39 5BU (nr railway station) SD413064
⊙ 12-2 (not Mon-Wed), 4-midnight; 12-midnight Sat & Sun
☎ (01695) 423303
Banks's Original, Mild; Jennings Bitter; Marston's Pedigree; guest beers ⊞
An attractive community pub in a residential area regularly serving five real ales, including guests, from the Jennings and Marston's ranges. Despite alterations, the interior retains an intimacy, with two rooms, one with a real fire. The pub has darts teams, quiz teams, a golf society and cycle club, and is used by an archery club and football teams. There are outside drinking areas to the front and rear, and an award-winning floral display. Look for the pet parrot. ♨Q⚇❀◐◑♿⇌P⊬

Belthorn

Grey Mare Inn

Elton Road, BB1 2PG (on A6177 opp road to Edgworth) SD 731 240
⊙ 12-2, 6-11; 12-11 Fri & Sat; 12-10.30 Sun
☎ (01254) 53308
Thwaites Nutty Black, Original, Wainwright, Lancaster Bomber, seasonal beers ⊞
This is the highest pub on the old Grane road between Blackburn and Haslingden. Nestling under Oswaldtwistle Moor, the pub is popular with motorists and walkers alike, and is well-known for its good food (served until 9pm daily, 8pm Sun). The full range of Thwaites' beers is always available. The interior is divided into three areas including a conservatory; there is no TV or jukebox. Q❀♿P

Bispham Green

Eagle & Child

Maltkiln Lane, L40 3SG (off B5246)
⊙ 12-3, 5.30-11; 12-11 Sat; 12-10.30 Sun ☎ (01257) 462297
🌐 ainscoughs.co.uk/The-Eagle-Child/eagle-and-child-home
Beer range varies ⊞
Outstanding 16th-century local overlooking the village green, with antique furniture and stone-flagged floors. The pub is renowned for its food and features occasional themed menu evenings (booking advised). An annual beer festival is held on the first May bank holiday in a marquee on the lawn behind the pub. There is a jazz evening on the last Sunday of every month. It also has a guest cider range as well as a varying choice of ales. CAMRA Pub of The Season 2008. ♨Q❀◐◑♿●P

Blackburn

Postal Order ✔

15-19 Darwen Street, BB2 2BH (close to cathedral in town centre)
⊙ 9-midnight (1am Fri & Sat) ☎ (01254) 676400
Greene King IPA, Ruddles County; guest beers ⊞
This former post office has alleged ghostly goings-on upstairs. Offering the largest selection of real ales in town, this Wetherspoon's has a spacious main room with raised areas at both ends for dining. Food is served 9am-10pm. Beers are regularly from LocAle micros Hopstar and Three B's, as well as larger local breweries Moorhouse's and Thwaites; and there are up to two real ciders. Many locals meet here to wind down after work.
⚇◐◑♿⇌●

Blacko

Cross Gaits ✔

Beverley Road, BB9 6RF (off A682) SD867414
⊙ 5-11 Mon; 4.30-11 Tue; 4.30-midnight Wed & Thu; 12-3, 4.30-midnight Fri; 12-midnight Sat; 12-9 Sun
☎ (01282) 616312
Jennings Cumberland Ale; Marston's Burton Bitter; guest beers ⊞
A pleasant rural pub in good walking country, it has one large bar with two areas and a second small room available for families and/or darts. At least

INDEPENDENT BREWERIES

Arkwright's Preston (NEW)
Bowland Clitheroe
Bryson's Morecambe
Fallons Darwen
Fuzzy Duck Poulton-le-Fylde
Garthela Blackburn
Hart Little Eccleston
Hopstar Darwen
Lancaster Lancaster
Lytham Lytham
Mayflower Up Holland
Moonstone Burnley
Moorhouse's Burnley
Red Rose Great Harwood
Rossendale Haslingden
Three B's Feniscowles
Thwaites Blackburn

one roaring fire is lit during the winter, and a friendly clientele adds to the atmosphere. Bar snacks and full meals are served lunchtimes and evenings, and the garden is very popular in summer. 'Free ale tomorrow' is the motto above the door. ⛬Q♨❀◑◐Å🚌(P70,P71)♣P⁵—

Rising Sun ✔

330 Gisburn Road, BB9 6LS (on A682)
⌚ 12-2 (not Mon, Tue & winter), 5-11; 12-midnight Fri & Sat; 12-11 Sun ☎ (01282) 612173
Moorhouse's Black Cat, Premier Bitter, Pride of Pendle, Blond Witch; guest beers Ⓗ
This dog-friendly village local, still retaining a traditional tap room, is Moorhouse's only tied house within Pendle and featured on its TV commercial. Bar meals and snacks are served lunchtimes and evenings during the week and all day until 7pm at weekends. The Rising Sun is thought to be the last pub serving the old Pendleside delicacy of 'Stew and Hard'. Enjoy the view of Pendle Hill. ⛬Q❀◑◐⊟🚌(P70,P71)♣P

Blackpool

Churchills ✔

83-85 Topping Street, FY1 3AF (nr Winter Gardens)
⌚ 10-11 (midnight Fri & Sat); 11-11 Sun ☎ (01253) 622036
Batemans XXXB; Greene King Old Speckled Hen; Shepherd Neame Spitfire; Wells Bombardier Ⓗ
An example of that rare thing, a Blackpool town-centre pub with character, it has one room divided into various areas. The venue is lively, sometimes boisterous, and located a short stroll from the Winter Gardens. Singalongs, quizzes and live entertainment feature prominently. Spot the pub's earlier name at the front and the collection of old Guinness bottles. ❀⇌(North)⁵—

No 4 & Freemasons ✔

Layton Road, FY3 8ER (jct with Newton Drive)
⌚ 12-11 (midnight Tue; Fri-Sun) ☎ (01253) 302877
Thwaites Nutty Black, Original, Wainwright, Lancaster Bomber Ⓗ
This smart suburban pub fronts on to Newton Drive and is located a mile inland from the seafront, with bus stops directly outside. The main lounge has both dining and drinking areas with TV screens and pictures of Blackpool's heyday. The rear games room has pool and darts. Beers are served in top condition and meals are served lunchtimes and evenings Monday-Friday, all day Saturday and Sunday. ❀◑◐⊟♿🚌(2,15)♣P⁵—

Ramsden Arms

204 Talbot Road, FY1 3AZ
⌚ 10.30-midnight (1am Sat); 12-midnight Sun
☎ (01253) 623215
Beer range varies Ⓗ
After several years absence, the 'Rammy' is back! A new management team has brought back quality real ales as a central feature of this superb pub, located at the edge of the town centre by the North rail station. Four real ales are usually served, with London Pride a regular. An amazing array of beer tankards and sporting trophies adorns the walls, along with a couple of TV screens. The good value bar food is available until 6pm every day. ◑◐⊟⇌(North)🚌P⁵—

Saddle Inn ✔

286 Whitegate Drive, FY3 9PH (at Preston Old Road jct)
⌚ 12-11 (midnight Fri & Sat) ☎ (01253) 767827
Draught Bass; Thwaites Original; guest beers Ⓗ
Blackpool's oldest pub, established in 1770, the Saddle comprises a main bar and two side rooms, plus a large patio outside for drinking and dining during the summer. This excellent, friendly pub has six cask guest beers on offer. A good menu of food is served all day. ⛬❀◑◐♿🚌(2,4,61)♣P⁵—

Shovels

260 Common Edge Road, FY4 5DH (on B5261, ½ mile from A5230 jct)
⌚ 12-11 (midnight Thu-Sat) ☎ (01253) 762702
Lytham Shovels Best; guest beers Ⓗ
This large open-plan roadside pub was joint winner of local CAMRA Pub of the Year 2010. Six handpumps offer a wide range of beers from micros and brew-pubs, often changing on a daily basis. A quiz night is held every Thursday. The pub also holds an annual beer festival every October, which attracts people from all over the country. The food is popular, with many daily specials, served 12-9.30pm. ⛬❀◑◐♿🚌(14a,14)♣P⁵—

Brindle

Cavendish Arms ✔

Sandy Lane, PR6 8NG
⌚ 12-11 (midnight Fri-Sun) ☎ (01254) 852912
🌐 cavendisharms.co.uk
Banks's Bitter; guest beers Ⓗ
At the heart of this attractive village and opposite the 13th-century church, the Cavendish was sadly boarded up for most of 2008. Now under new management, the pub and village have been revitalised. With a small room on the left as you enter and the large main bar area with rooms off, the pub has been tastefully restored and expanded inside. Three guest beers are from the Marston's list. A beer festival is held in a marquee annually in June. ⛬Q❀◑◐⊟P

Burnley

Bridge Bier Huis

2 Bank Parade, BB11 1UH (behind shoppping centre)
⌚ closed Mon & Tue; 12-midnight (2am Fri & Sat); 12-11 Sun
☎ (01282) 411304 🌐 thebridgebierhuis.co.uk
Hydes Bitter; guest beers Ⓗ
This free house has a large open bar area and a small separate room to one side. A LocAle supporter, it offers up to five guest beers, usually from local micros. A good range of Belgian and other foreign bottled beer is on offer, plus five on tap. Real cider is also sold. The Bridge hosts a regular Wednesday night quiz and occasional live music at weekends. Check the website for event details. A frequent winner of CAMRA awards. ❀◑⇌(Central)🚌♣🍎

Gannow Wharf

168 Gannow Lane, BB12 6QH
⌚ 7 (5 Fri)-11; 3-11 Sat & Sun ☎ (07855) 315498
Beer range varies Ⓗ
Next to Leeds-Liverpool canal, on Gannow Bridge, this biker-friendly local offers a warm welcome to real ale enthusiasts. Six ales change weekly, most sourced from local breweries under the LocAle scheme. Try the gallon challenge if you dare! The venue has a cosy, covered heated smoking/drinking area. Facilities include live music, quizzes, karaoke, pool and satellite TV sports. ❀⇌(Rose Grove)🚌(4,65)⁵—

Ministry of Ale

9 Trafalgar Street, BB11 1TQ

❂ 5-11 Wed & Thu; 12.30 (11 Sat)-midnight Fri & Sat; 12-11 Sun ☎ (01282) 830909

Beer range varies ⊞

Home of the Moonstone Brewery, the 2½ barrel plant can be viewed in the front room. This small, friendly local places an emphasis on excellent beer and good conversation. Two Moonstone beers are sold alongside two rotating guests from micro-breweries. The Ministry holds regular alternative art exhibitions and a popular quiz takes place on Thursday night. The pub opens on Tuesday nights when Burnley FC are at home. Manchester Road railway station is a two-minute walk.
❀⇌(Manchester Road)⊟(X43,X44)⊱

Burscough

Hop Vine

Liverpool Road North, L40 4BY

❂ 10.30-midnight (12.30am Fri & Sat) ☎ (01704) 893799

🌐 thehopvine.co.uk

Moorhouse's Pendle Witches Brew; guest beers ⊞

The Hop Vine, previously known as the Royal Coaching House, has had a major refurbishment in 2009, and is now definitely an asset to the town of Burscough. It was built in 1874 as a coaching stop on the main road (now the A59) from Preston to Liverpool. The pub has its own house beer from Prospect Brewery, called Hop Vine Bitter, and is LocAle accredited. It is situated very close to Burscough Bridge station, and has two real fires.
♨❀◑◗⊟⇌⊟(2A,2B)P⊱

Catterall

Pickerings

Garstang Road, PR3 0HD (on B6430 S of Garstang)

❂ 11.30-midnight; 12-10.30 Sun ☎ (01995) 600999

🌐 pickerings-hotel.co.uk

Beer range varies ⊞

Though describing itself as a country house hotel – it has 12 en-suite rooms, including two four-poster suites – this elegant free house is informal in atmosphere and offers a warm welcome to non-residents. The building dates from the 18th century and is set in mature grounds. Up to five real ales are served, including beers from Bank Top, Black Sheep and George Wright (Pickerings Pride, 4%). Signs from the A6 still have the old name of Pickering Park. There is a heated area outside for smokers. ⛡❀⊟◑◗♿⊟(40,41,42)P⊱

Chapeltown

Chetham Arms

83 High Street, BL7 0EW (on B6391) SD734157

❂ 12-3, 5-11; 12-midnight Fri & Sat; 12-11 Sun

☎ (01204) 852279

Bank Top Flat Cap; Moorhouse's Pendle Witches Brew; guest beer ⊞

This 18th-century village inn is a meeting place for locals, visitors and walkers. It has been altered to provide rooms for dining, and has a part stone-flagged floor and real fire. The bar serves LocAle from Bank Top and Moorhouse's, with a through hatch to the hideaway room at the back. Opening times vary from winter to summer; it is best to call and check. Nearby are Turton Towers, originally a medieval pele tower, set in nine acres of woodland gardens, and Wayoh reservoir. ⛡◗♣P⊱

Cherry Tree

Station

391 Preston Old Road, BB2 5LW (at Cherry Tree railway station)

❂ 3-10; 12-1am Fri & Sat; 12-11.30 Sun ☎ (01254) 201643

Thwaites Nutty Black, Original, Wainwright, Lancaster Bomber, seasonal beers ⊞

Located next to the railway station, this may not be a quiet pub but it is a must-visit establishment for those seeking the full range of Thwaites beers. Patrons are a mixture of young and old, enjoying games of darts, dominoes and pool. Satellite sports are shown on three TVs and via a large projector screen. ❀♿⇌⊟(124, 152)♣P

Chipping

Tillotsons Arms

18 Talbot Street, PR3 2QE

❂ 12-3, 4.30-midnight; 12-midnight Fri-Sun

☎ (01995) 61568

Beer range varies ⊞

In a picturesque village in the Trough of Bowland, this two-roomed beamed pub built in 1836 has four to five real ales from local micros, always including at least one from Bowland and Moorhouse's, and often a Hawkshead beer. Child and dog friendly, it has two real fires and a beer garden to the rear. Locally sourced home-cooked food is available lunchtimes and evenings, and all day on Sunday. Live music plays on Saturday night. On the SIBA direct delivery scheme.
♨Q❀◑◗⛺⊟(4)♣⊱

Chorley

Malt 'n' Hops

50-52 Friday Street, PR6 0AH (behind railway station)

❂ 12-11 (10.30 Sun) ☎ (01257) 260967

🌐 caskaleschorley.com

Beartown Kodiak Gold; guest beers ⊞

Situated close to Chorley railway and bus stations, this pub has a long-standing reputation in the local area for fine cask ales. Originally converted from an old shop in 1989, it became a haven for local drinkers thanks to its selection of guest beers. Now owned by Beartown Brewery of Congleton, it still offers up to seven guests plus the permanent beer from Beartown. The pub is a short walk from the town centre and keeps traditional licensing hours.
❀⇌⊟●⊱

Potters Arms

42 Brooke Street, PR7 3BY (next to Morrisons)

❂ 3-11.30; 11-midnight Fri; 12-4, 7-midnight Sat; 12-5, 7-11 Sun ☎ (01257) 267954

Black Sheep Best Bitter; Three B's Doff Cocker; guest beers ⊞

Small, friendly free house named after the owners, situated at the bottom of Brooke Street alongside the railway bridge. The central bar serves two games areas, while two comfortable lounges are popular with locals and visitors alike. The pub displays a fine selection of photographs from the world of music, as well as vintage local scenes. Regular darts and dominoes nights are well attended and the chip butties go down a treat. The smoking area is covered. ♨⇌⊟(3,3A,10)♣P⊱

Prince of Wales ✔

9-11 Cowling Brow, PR6 0QE (off B6228)

❂ 12-11.30 (midnight Fri & Sat) ☎ (01257) 413239

Banks's Bitter; Jennings Cumberland Ale, seasonal beers; guest beers Ⓗ

Stone terraced pub in the south-eastern part of town, not far from the Leeds-Liverpool canal. An unspoilt interior comprises a traditional tap room, games room, large lounge and a comfortable snug with real fire. There is photographic evidence of the licensee's love of jazz, and collections of brewery artefacts and saucy seaside postcards are also on display. A large selection of malt whiskies is behind the bar and sandwiches are served on request. Note the no-swearing policy. ⛫❀⊟⊟(3,3A,10)♣⊱

Swan With Two Necks

Hollinshead Street, Chorley Bottoms, PR7 1EP (at foot of steps off Park Road behind St Lawrence church)

✪ 12-12.20am (1am Thu & Sun, 2.30am Fri & Sat)

☎ (01257) 266649 ⊕ swanchorley.co.uk

Beer range varies Ⓗ

Chorley's hidden gem, which prides itself on catering for all generations in enjoyable harmony. Five handpumps serve quality ales from LocAle breweries, with preference to Moorhouse's, Three B's, Bowland and Bank Top. Food served in the bar, and the picturesque Cygneture bistro, is of the highest standard, ranging from homely to exotic (booking recommended). High-quality entertainment is assured, with jazz, blue-grass, folk, pop, karaoke and disco. ⛫❀◐◑⇌⊟P⊱

White Bull

135 Market Street, PR7 2SG (S end of Market St near Big Lamp)

✪ 12-11 (midnight Fri); 11-midnight Sat ☎ (01257) 232745

Bank Top Dark Mild; Wells Bombardier; guest beers Ⓗ

This single bar pub is a beacon for real ale in an area where so many pubs around it are closing. The games room is partitioned to the right of the comfortable L-shaped lounge. The walls are adorned with memorabilia from the landlord's favourite football team, Preston North End. One of the guest beers is from the Bank Top range, the other from one of the regional brewers. Good value lunchtime meals are served Tuesday-Saturday. ❀◐⇌⊟♣⊱

Cleveleys

Victoria Hotel

183 Victoria Road West, FY5 3PZ (approx ½ mile from Cleveleys town centre, on B5412)

✪ 11-11; 12-11.30 Sun ☎ (01253) 853306

Samuel Smith OBB Ⓗ

A 1930s hostelry situated in a residential area close to the town centre, handy for the Blackpool-Fleetwood tramway and various bus routes. A very popular local with a spacious lounge and two real fires, it is well known in the area for its low-priced beer. There is a separate meeting room available. Quiz nights are held on Thursday and Sunday and Tuesday is games day. ⛫Q❀⊟♿⊖⊟(7,11,74)P

Clitheroe

Horseshoe Inn

1-5 Bawdlands, BB7 2LA (B6243, ½ mile W of town centre)

✪ 10 (12 Sun)-midnight ☎ (01200) 424391

Bowland Sawley Tempted; Caledonian Deuchars IPA; guest beers Ⓗ

Traditional local just outside Clitheroe town centre, run by two CAMRA members, with a central room and a pool room to one side. Guest beers are likely to be from micros such as Bowland or Three B's. A try-before-you-buy scheme is in operation. The pub is well-used by local sports teams, hence the trophies. Comfortable seating and stained glass add to the atmosphere. No hot food, but pies and sandwiches are available. East Lancs CAMRA Pub of the Season in 2009. ⛺⇌⊟(B10,B11)

New Inn 🏆

Parson Lane, BB7 2JN

✪ 11-11; 12-10.30 Sun ☎ (01200) 443653

Coach House Gunpowder Mild; guest beers Ⓗ

A real gem, nestling below the 12th-century castle near the town centre. A central bar connects four rooms, three with real fires, one with a TV – the only electronics other than the till. There are 10 handpumps operated by knowledgable and friendly staff. Beers come from Moorhouse's, Bowland or Shoes (Farriers), among others. The pub is a meeting place for local groups and has a real community feel; dogs are welcome. There is often live music on Friday and Saturday. ⛫Q❀⇌♣

Coppull

Red Herring

Mill Lane, PR7 5AN (off B5251 next to Coppull Mill)

✪ 3-11; 12-11.30 Fri & Sat; 12-11 Sun ☎ (01257) 470130

Moorhouse's Pride of Pendle; guest beers Ⓗ

This oasis of real ale is situated in the former offices of the next-door mill. It was converted to a pub some years ago and the bar area comprises a large single room plus an extension, with three micro-brewed beers usually available. TV sports fans are catered for, as are anglers who use the pond opposite. The pub hosts regular music nights and barbecues and has a large first-floor function room. Trainspotters will enjoy close proximity to the West Coast main line. ❀⊟(1,362)♣P⊱

Croston

Lord Nelson

Out Lane, PR26 9HJ

✪ 3.30-11 (midnight Tue-Thu); 12-midnight Fri & Sat; 12-11 Sun ☎ (01772) 600387 ⊕ lordnelsoncroston.co.uk

Copper Dragon Golden Pippin; Jennings Cumberland Ale; guest beers Ⓗ

This former Higsons pub was once a farmhouse facing on to the village green. It claims to be the oldest pub in Croston, with some parts dating from 1640. There is a cosy central bar area and two separate rooms. Good value food is served, and the pub continues to be a welcoming venue for drinkers to congregate. The two guests are sourced from micro-breweries and there is a changing guest cider. An annual beer festival is held in summer. ⛫❀◐◑⇌⊟(7,112)♣●P

Darwen

Black Horse

72 Redearth Road, BB3 2AF

✪ 12-11 ☎ (01254) 873040

Fallons seasonal beers; guest beers Ⓗ

A lively, friendly community local, this is the brewery outlet for Fallon's Exquisite Ales. Four or more beers and real cider from the cellar are usually available. There are meal deals on Sunday afternoon. Thursday music nights – jazz on the first Thursday of the month, otherwise groups/jam sessions – are popular with all comers. Other features are plasma TV sports, satellite jukebox, and a games room home to teams in local leagues. A paved, seated and tented smoking area to the rear is well used. ❀◐♿⇌♣●⊬

Park Inn

1 Cemetery Road, BB3 2LZ
⏲ 2-11; 12-midnight Fri & Sat; 12-11 Sun ☎ (01254) 774155
🌐 parkinndarwen.co.uk
Beer range varies Ⓗ
A prominent corner pub opposite Whitehall Park, with a tap room to the side with a quiet hidden corner, and a main open plan room. Three real fires create a warm, friendly and pleasant atmosphere. Fuller's ales, rare for this area, are served, alongside LocAle from a micro. Three plasma TVs offer sports events, or customers can play pool and darts. The pub is served by two main bus routes: Accrington-Darwen Cemetery and Clitheroe-Bolton. ♨⊟♣

Earby

White Lion

Riley Street, BB18 6NX
⏲ 12-11 (midnight Fri & Sat) ☎ (01282) 842377
Greene King IPA; Tetley Bitter; guest beer Ⓗ
Traditional village pub located on the village green; the building frontage dates from 1681. Inside are five rooms off a central bar: two dining rooms, a games room, a snug and main bar area. There is an open fire in the aptly name snug and, outside, a heated patio and beer garden. Pool, darts and dominoes are played. Popular with diners, food is served Monday-Friday 12-2pm, Thursday-Saturday 5-8pm, and Sunday 12-6pm. ♨Q❀◐♣P⊬

Eccleston

Original Farmers Arms

Towngate, PR7 5QS (on B5250)
⏲ 12-midnight (11.30 Sun) ☎ (01257) 451594
Beer range varies Ⓗ
This white-painted village pub has expanded over the years into the cottage next door, adding a substantial dining area. However, the original part of the pub is still used mainly for drinking. Up to six real ales are available, predominantly sourced from local micros – Bowland, Three B's and Southport breweries are favourites. Meals are available throughout the day seven days a week, and there is accommodation in four good value guest rooms. ❀⊭◐🚌(113,347)P⊬

Edgworth

White Horse

2-4 Bury Road, BL7 0AY SD742168
⏲ 12-3 (not Mon & Tue), 5-11 (midnight Thu & Fri); 12-midnight Sat; 12-11 Sun ☎ (01204) 852929
Bank Top Flat Cap; Greene King Ruddles Best Bitter; Marston's Pedigree; Taylor Landlord; guest beers Ⓗ
Large corner building situated prominently at the crossroads of the Bolton to Bury road. An impressively decorated interior offers tables set for exquisite cuisine and a good range of real ales. The bar has five handpumps, some with LocAle brews, and there is also a good selection of wine. The pub's name has heraldic origins dating back from 1714-1800 – white being the colour of peace and horse representing stead, or readiness for all events in the name of the King. An external wall plaque explains more. ♨❀◐♿P⊬

Euxton

Euxton Mills ✔

Wigan Road, PR7 6JD (at A49/A581 jct)
⏲ 11.30-10.30 (11 Wed & Thu; 11.30 Fri); 12-11.30 Sat; 12-10.30 Sun ☎ (01257) 264002
Jennings Bitter, Cumberland Ale; guest beers Ⓗ
A village inn that has won several Best Kept Pub awards, as well as the local CAMRA Pub of the Season. Outside, a large collection of hanging baskets and flowerpots are particularly attractive during the summer months. The pub is renowned for the quality of its food and serves up to three guest beers from the extensive Marston's range. Two beer festivals are held each year, with eight ales available at any one time. Quiz night is Wednesday. ❀◐⇌(Balshaw Lane)🚌(16,109)P⊬

Travellers Rest

Dawbers Lane, PR7 6EG (on A581)
⏲ 12-11 (10 Sun) ☎ (01257) 451184
🌐 thetravellersresteuxton.co.uk
Black Sheep Best Bitter; Young's Special; guest beers Ⓗ
Dating back to 1750 and made up of three former weavers' cottages, this pub is a wonderful example of the great British traditional country inn, with a lounge and separate games room. Winner of two Publican and one Morning Advertiser awards, the pub offers six real ales. The food is sourced as locally as possible and is classic British fare with a contemporary twist. ❀◐⊟♿🚌P

Fence

White Swan ✔

300 Wheatley Lane, BB12 9QA (off A6068) SD835381
⏲ 12-2.30 (not Mon), 5-11; 12-11.30 Fri & Sat; 12-10.30 Sun ☎ (01282) 611773 🌐 whiteswanatfence.co.uk
Taylor Golden Best, Best Bitter, Landlord Ⓗ
Known locally as t'Mucky Duck, this is one of only two Timothy Taylor tied houses in Lancashire. A fourth handpump regularly dispenses one of Taylor's other beers. Good, wholesome food is served lunchtimes and evenings, made with fresh local ingredients. A warm welcome awaits, especially in winter when two fires heat the small pub. Satellite TV sports is screened in the bar area. ♨Q◐🚌(65)P⊬

Feniscowles

Feildens Arms

673 Preston Old Road, BB2 5ER (at A674/A6062 jct)
⏲ 12-midnight (1.30am Fri & Sat; 10.30 Sun)
☎ (01254) 200988
Flowers IPA; Three B's Stoker's Slake; guest beers Ⓗ
Situated on a busy road junction, this stone-built pub is located three miles west of Blackburn. Feildens is a LocAle supporter and among the six handpumps you will always find one or two dispensing ales from local brewers. Customers can play darts, cards and dominoes or watch satellite TV sports. Buses stop just outside. ♨❀♿⇌(Pleasington)🚌(124,152)♣P⊬

Fleetwood

Steamer

1-2 Queens Terrace, FY7 6BT (opp market)
11-11 (midnight Fri & Sat); 12-11 Sun ☎ (01253) 771756
Wells Bombardier; guest beers Ⓗ
Opposite Fleetwood Market and convenient for bus and tram routes, the pub has an old blacksmith's workshop at the rear, dating from when the yard was used to stable horses. Snooker, pool, darts and dominoes are played, there are Wii nights, karaoke on Wednesday and Sunday, Fleetwood folk club meets on Thursday, and there is live entertainment on Friday and Saturday. The private function room can be booked. Children are welcome until 7pm. Local CAMRA Pub of the Season spring 2010.
❀◐♿⊖(Ferry Terminal)🚌(1,14,16)

Thomas Drummond ✔

London Street, FY7 6JY (between Lord St and Dock St)
9-11 (midnight Fri & Sat) ☎ (01253) 775020
Greene King Ruddles Best Bitter, Abbot; guest beers Ⓗ
A previous winner of a local CAMRA silver award and Pub of the Season, the pub is situated in a former church hall and furniture warehouse. It is named after a builder who helped construct Fleetwood. There are displays featuring the founders of Fleetwood, Sir Peter Hesketh Fleetwood and his architect, Decimus Burton. Food is served until 10pm daily. Marcle Hill and Old Rosie ciders are available. There is a covered and heated area for smokers.
❀◐♿⊖(London Street)🚌(1,14)

Freckleton

Coach & Horses ✔

Preston Old Road, PR4 1PD
11-midnight (1am Fri & Sat); 12-midnight Sun
☎ (01772) 632284
Boddingtons Bitter; guest beers Ⓗ
This community village local has retained its cosy atmosphere. It is home to Freckleton's award-winning brass band; a cabinet displays an impressive collection of trophies. A special place is reserved for mementos of the Eighth Air Force who served locally during WWII. The pub also has a golfing society. Meals are served 12-2pm Monday-Friday, 12-6pm Saturday. ❀◐♿🚌(2,7,68)♣P

Garstang

Wheatsheaf

Park Hill Road, PR3 1EL
10-midnight (1am Fri & Sat); 11.30-11.30 Sun
☎ (01995) 603398
Courage Directors; Hawkshead Pride of Garstang; guest beers Ⓗ
Built as a farmhouse in the late 18th century, this is now a Grade II-listed building and was greatly extended in 2002. A disco is held every Friday. The pub serves breakfast, lunch and supper and there is a covered outdoor smoking area. A welcoming pub that attracts a varied clientele from all age groups.
❀◐♿Ⅹ🚌(40,42)♣P

Goosnargh

Stag's Head ✔

990 Whittingham Lane, PR3 2AU
12-11 (10.30 Sun) ☎ (01772) 864071
thestagshead.co.uk
Theakston Best Bitter; guest beers Ⓗ
Large public house and restaurant close to the haunted Chingle Hall. Inside there are four seating areas served by a central bar, with a huge garden and a heated area for smokers. Up to four guest beers are from the Heineken UK's Cellarman's Reserve list. A mild or dark ale is usually available. Live music often plays and there is an annual beer festival. All food is from local producers and home-made pickles and chutneys are available to take away. ❀◐♿🚌(4)P

Great Eccleston

White Bull

The Square, PR3 0ZB (in village square)
11 (4.30 Tue)-11; 11-midnight Sat ☎ (01995) 670203
Black Sheep Best Bitter; Everards Tiger Best Bitter; St Austell Tribute; guest beers Ⓗ
Historic coaching inn in the heart of the village. A family-friendly, welcoming pub with flagged floors and an unspoilt atmosphere, it has a games room with pool, darts and the usual pub games. Three quieter rooms are for talking, drinking and eating. Locally sourced home-cooked food is good quality and excellent value. Interesting guest ales come from breweries on the SIBA list.
❀◐Ⅹ🚌(82,42)P

Great Harwood

Royal Hotel ✔

2 Station Road, BB6 7BE (jct of Princess St and Park Rd)
4-11; 12-midnight Fri & Sat; 12-10.30 Sun
☎ (01254) 883541
Beer range varies Ⓗ
Brewery tap for the Red Rose Brewery which is down in the cellar. Eight ales are on offer, including beers from the brewery and guests from near and far. There are always at least two dark ales as well as a good selection of bottled beers. The pub is well-served by public transport from Accrington, Blackburn and Manchester. A beer festival is held over the May bank holiday. ❀Ⅹ🚌(6,7)♣

Victoria ★ ✔

St John's Street, BB6 7EP
4 (3 Fri; 12 Sat)-midnight; 12-10.30 Sun
☎ (01254) 885210
Bowland Gold; Caledonian Deuchars IPA; guest beers Ⓗ
Built in 1905 by Alfred Nuttall and known locally as Butcher Brig, the pub features a wealth of original features. The lobby has floor-to-ceiling glazed tiling, and there is dark wood throughout the five rooms. On the horseshoe-shaped bar are eight handpumps dispensing beers sourced from small breweries throughout northern England and Scotland. There is an annual beer festival. The pub also sits on a cycleway. The smoking area is covered and heated. Q❀Ⅹ♣

Haskayne

Ship Inn 🏆

6 Rosemary Lane, L39 7JP (signed off A5147 between Maghull and Southport) SD364082
12-11 ☎ (01704) 840077
George Wright Ship Ahoy; guest beers Ⓗ

Eighteenth-century pub built specifically for the passing trade using the busy Leeds-Liverpool canal. The Ship has won a number of recent CAMRA Pub of the Year awards and supports LocAle. It has four real coal fires, and also caters for families with an outdoor playground, tables and beer garden. The house beer, Ship Ahoy, is brewed by George Wright, and the hard-to-find Southport Brewery beers also regularly feature. Good value food is served until 8pm.
♨Q☺✿◐◑⊟♿🚌(300,315)♣P⊱

Haslingden

Griffin Inn

84 Hud Rake, BB4 5AF (off A680 signed for Rossendale Ski Slope)
⏲ 12-midnight ☎ (01706) 214021
Pennine Floral Dance, Hameldon Bitter, Railway Sleeper, Rossendale Ale, Pitch Porter, Sunshine ⊞
With its own micro-brewery in the cellar, The Griffin is a staple for the community – a quiet pub but with lively local discussions. An open fire is very welcome in winter. As well as the Pennine range there are occasional guest beers and real cider. ♨Q☺♣P

Holden Arms

Grane Road, BB4 4PD (jct A6177 and B6235) SD775225
⏲ 12-midnight (2am Fri & Sat) ☎ (01706) 231461
🌐 holdenarms.co.uk
Jennings Cocker Hoop; guest beers ⊞
An award-winning pub with a large function room for meals, parties and receptions. You can always find a quiet corner in the main bar, and good food is available at all times. The landlord is passionate about ensuring a good atmosphere and is ever friendly. ◐◑♿🚌(11,244)P⊱

Heapey

Top Lock

Copthurst Lane, PR6 8LS (alongside canal at Johnson's Hillock)
⏲ 11.30-11; 12-10.30 Sun ☎ (01257) 263376
Beer range varies ⊞
Excellent canalside pub with an upstairs dining room. Up to nine real ales are served, mostly from micros, including a mild and either a porter or stout, together with a Timothy Taylor and a Coniston beer, and up to three real ciders. An annual beer festival is held in October with around 100 ales available in the pub and a marquee. There is a covered smoking area. Indian cuisine from Indian chefs is a speciality. Winner of local CAMRA Pub of the Year. Q✿◐◑♣P⊱▯

Heysham

Royal

7 Main Street, LA3 2RN (70m towards St Patrick's Chapel from Heysham Village bus terminus)
⏲ 12-11 (midnight Fri & Sat); 12-10.30 Sun
☎ (01524) 859298
York Guzzler; guest beers ⊞
A 15th-century inn in the heart of the village. As you enter, a tiny locals' bar is on the right and a restaurant is on the left; the main bar is accessed via a winding passage and opens on to a large landscaped garden. Six handpumps provide the beers, often including Lancaster Bomber and ales from York. York Guzzler is sold as Royal Ale 1504. Forthcoming guest beers are usually listed on the website. Outside is a covered and heated smoking area. Q☺✿◐◑⊟♿🚌(4,5)P⊱

Higher Wheelton

Golden Lion

369 Blackburn Road, PR6 8HP (on A674)
⏲ 12 (5 Mon)-12.30am; 12-1am Fri & Sat; 12-11 Sun
☎ (01254) 830855 🌐 goldenlionchorley.co.uk
Thwaites Nutty Black, Original, Wainwright, Lancaster Bomber, seasonal beers ⊞
Situated in the centre of the village, this stone-built single-bar pub has a comfortable bar/lounge with a partitioned-off games area. The walls are adorned with old photographs of the area, and TV sports fans are well catered for. Outside drinking areas are to the front and rear, and good value meals are served. ♨✿◐◑🚌(124)P⊱

Hoghton

Royal Oak

Blackburn Old Road, Riley Green, PR5 0SL (at A675/ A674 jct)
⏲ 11.30-11; 12-10.30 Sun ☎ (01254) 201445
Thwaites Nutty Black, Original, Wainwright, Lancaster Bomber, seasonal beers ⊞
Stone-built pub on the old road between Preston and Blackburn, near the Riley Green basin on the Leeds-Liverpool canal. The Royal Oak is popular with diners and drinkers. Rooms, including a dining room, and alcoves radiate from the central bar. Low-beamed ceilings and horse brasses give the pub a rustic feel. This Thwaites tied house is a regular award winner and acts as an outlet for its seasonal beers. Hoghton Towers is nearby, steeped in history and worth visiting. ♨Q✿◐◑🚌(152)P

Sirloin

Station Road, PR5 0DD (off A675 near level crossing)
⏲ 4-11.30; 12-midnight Sat; 12-10.30 Sun
☎ (01254) 852293 🌐 thymeout.net
Moorhouse's Jackie's Tea Thyme Tipple; guest beers ⊞
This 250-year-old, family-run country inn is near Hoghton Tower, where King James I knighted a loin of beef – his coat of arms hangs over one of the fireplaces. Sirloin steak is a speciality here and in the adjoining restaurant. Three handpumps dispense a choice of beers, often from micros. Jackie's Tea Thyme Tipple, named after the owner's dog, is brewed by Moorhouse's especially for the pub. Pub food is served Friday-Sunday lunchtime only, but the upstairs Thyme restaurant is open Tuesday-Sunday lunch and evening.
♨◐🚌(152)P⊱

Holme in Cliviger

Queen

412 Burnley Road, BB10 4SU (on A671 between Burnley and Todmorden)
⏲ 1-11 ☎ (01282) 436712
John Smith's Bitter; guest beers ⊞
Small friendly roadside local with two rooms both warmed by coal fires in winter. No music or machines means good conversation and beer are the norm here. Situated in the spectacular Cliviger Gorge, the pub displays a large collection of old photos of its people and scenery. Walkers are welcomed and are free to bring their own food.

The three guest beers are usually sourced from micro-breweries. There's a very small car park, but roadside parking no problem.
(589,592)

Kirkham

Black Horse

29 Preston Street, PR4 2YA (200m uphill from market square)
12-midnight (11 Sun) (01772) 671209
Greene King Ruddles County, Abbot; guest beers
First opened in the 13th century, this friendly two-roomed local on the main street attracts a wide range of customers. The smaller side room has a pool table and dartboard. There is a large-screen TV in the front room showing sports events. The beer range has increased of late: up to eight ales may be available at any one time. A beer festival is held over the Easter bank holiday. Outside there is a covered smoking area.
(Kirkham & Wesham)(2,6)P

Lancaster

Sun

63 Church Street, LA1 1ET
10-midnight (01524) 66006
thesunhotelandbar.co.uk
Lancaster Amber, Blonde, Black, Red; Thwaites Wainwright; guest beers
Quality is the name of the game here. The decor combines a mixture of exposed stonework, wood panelling and solid furniture, with ambient candlelight in the evenings. Some original features remain, including stone fireplaces and a well. The pub is the primary outlet for Lancaster Brewery in the city, as well as offering up to four guest beers. Wi-Fi internet access is available. Outside is a peaceful courtyard with a heated and covered smoking area.

Three Mariners

Bridge Lane, LA1 1EE (nr Parksafe car park entrance)
12-midnight (1am Fri & Sat) (01524) 388957
threemariners.co.uk
Black Sheep Best Bitter; guest beers
Commonly claimed to be the oldest pub in Lancaster, it had a comprehensive revamp in 2004. Built into the side of Castle Hill, the cellar is excavated at first-floor level. There is a narrow strip of cobbles at the front, occupied by tables for drinkers. The pub is now a popular watering hole with a thriving local clientele, and is involved with the maritime section of the Lancaster Music Festival in October. Home-cooked, reasonably priced food is available. Limited parking.

Water Witch

Tow Path, Aldcliffe Road, LA1 1SU (on canal towpath near Penny Street bridge)
11-midnight (11 Sun) (01524) 63828
thewaterwitch.co.uk
Lancaster Blonde; Thwaites Lancaster Bomber; York Guzzler; guest beers
The Water Witch was a passenger packet boat that once plied the Lancaster canal. The building, originally a canal company stable block, assumed its present name and use in 1978 – the first true canalside pub on this stretch of water. Wedged between the towpath and a retaining wall, it is long and narrow, with bare stone walls and floors. A mezzanine floor and the space underneath it are used mainly for dining. There are seats on the towpath. Quiz night is Thursday.

White Cross

Quarry Road, LA1 4XT (behind town hall, on canal towpath)
11.30-11 (12.30am Fri & Sat); 12-11 Sun (01524) 33999
Caledonian Deuchars IPA; guest beers
A modern renovation of an old canalside warehouse with an open-plan interior and a light, airy feel. French windows open on to extensive canalside seating, making this a popular location for summer afternoons and evenings. The 14 ales available, including Tirril's, concentrate on Lancastrian, Cumbrian and Pennine brewers, plus Old Rosie cider. Meals are available throughout the week, including a Sunday roast. There is a popular Tuesday night quiz, and a beer and pie festival each April. P

Yorkshire House

2 Parliament Street, LA1 1DB (opp Greyhound bridge)
7-midnight (1am Thu & Fri); 2-1am Sat; 2-11.30 Sun
(01524) 64679 yorkshirehouse.enta.net
Everards Tiger Best Bitter; Hawkshead Bitter; guest beers
A music pub, with a great jukebox and bands playing most evenings in the big room upstairs. The mix of ages, friendly service and intimate drinking spaces, including a cosy corner with a wood-burning stove, help to explain this pub's appeal. One handpump dispenses Westons Perry, Organic Cider, 1st Quality and Scrumpy on rotation. Table football is a further attraction. A popular quiz is held on the first Sunday of the month. The sheltered courtyard garden is recommended for summer drinking.

Lancaster University

Graduate College Bar

Barker House Village, LA2 0PF
7-11 (5-11.30 Fri & Sat term time) (01524) 592824
Beer range varies
The Graduate College can be found at Alexandra Park, south-west of the main campus, its bar attracting an age range higher than the average student watering hole. The choice of beer is good, with eight handpumps often offering Barngates, Hawkshead or Goose Eye. Gwynt-y-ddraig cider and a guest cider are also served. There is a beer fest in June and a cider fest in October. The bar is open to university members, staff, guests and visitors with a copy of this Guide. P

Lea Town

Smith's Arms

Lea Lane, PR4 0RP (rear of BNFL Salwick) SD 476311
12-midnight (01772) 760555
smithsarmspreston.co.uk
Thwaites Original, Wainwright, Lancaster Bomber, seasonal beers
Open-plan country pub situated near the Preston-Lancaster canal and on route 62 of the national cycle network, known as the Slip Inn from a time when farmers would slip in for a drink. The four handpumps see plenty of use in this Thwaites house, which regularly wins awards for its quality food, so it can get busy, especially on Sunday when

food is served all day. Home to darts and dominoes teams, it has a covered smoking area with a real log fire and leather sofas. ⚑Q❀◑♿🚌(77)♣P⚐

Leyland

Railway at Leyland

1 Preston Road, PR25 4NT
⏲ 12-11 (1am Fri & Sat) ☎ (01772) 458427
🌐 therailwayatleyland.co.uk
Black Sheep Best Bitter; guest beers Ⓗ
An outstanding example of a community local, the Railway has gone from strength to strength. Huge investment from Punch Taverns has transformed the interior and the new licensees have made this landmark Leyland pub a welcoming hostelry, with something for everyone. Four cask ales including three rotating guests make a fine accompaniment to the excellent food. There is occasional live music. An annual beer festival is held in summer (see website for details). ❀◑⇌🚌(111)P⚐

Little Eccleston

Cartford Inn

Cartford Lane, PR3 0YP (½ mile from A586)
⏲ 12-10 Mon & Sun; 12-11 Tue-Thu; 12-midnight Fri & Sat
☎ (01995) 670166 🌐 thecartfordinn.co.uk
Theakston Old Peculier; guest beers Ⓗ
The pub is a 300-year-old former farmhouse located on the banks of the River Wyre, by the toll bridge built on the site of a ford. Recently modernised and restyled inside and out by the current owner, future plans include better wheelchair access. The range of four local beers is complemented by excellent food, good enough to earn entries in the 2010 editions of the Good Food and Michelin Eating Out in Pubs guides. No lunchtime meals on Monday.
⚑ᘓ❀🛏◑⛺🚌(42,80)♣P

Longridge

Corporation Arms

Lower Road, PR3 2YJ (near B6243/B6245 jct)
⏲ 11-11; 12-10.30 Sun ☎ (01772) 782644
🌐 corporationarms.co.uk
Beer range varies Ⓗ
Eighteenth-century country inn close to the Longridge reservoirs and a handy base for local walks. A free house, it has a deserved reputation for excellent ale, food, service and accommodation. Four handpumps serve beers sourced from local breweries, with Moorhouse's, Bowland and Phoenix some of the favourites. There is an annual beer festival in June. Luxurious overnight rooms are popular, so booking is advised. Note the old horse trough outside, reputedly used by Oliver Cromwell on his way to the Battle of Preston. ⚑❀🛏◑♿🚌P⚐

Longton

Dolphin

Marsh Lane, PR4 5JY (take right fork 1 mile down Marsh Lane) SD459254
⏲ 12 (4 Mon & winter)-midnight; 10.30-midnight Sun
☎ (01772) 612032
Beer range varies Ⓗ
An isolated former farmhouse at the start of the Ribble Way, this local CAMRA award-winning marshland pub comprises a main bar, family room and conservatory, while a separate building houses a function room. The four or five ales on offer always include a mild and are sourced from micros near and far, plus at least one real cider. An annual beer festival is held in August. Outside there is a children's play area and a covered smoking space. ⚑ᘓ❀◑🖵●P⚐

Lostock Hall

Anchor ✔

43 Croston Road, PR5 5LA (300m from B5254)
⏲ 12-2 (summer only), 4.30-11.30; 4-midnight Fri winter; 11-midnight Sat; 12-midnight Sun ☎ (01772) 335637
Beer range varies Ⓗ
Located just a short distance from the Tardy Gate shopping area and alongside the railway line, this friendly community pub had been selling only keg beers for years, but has recently been revitalised and now offers five changing cask ales from the Cellarman's Reserve list. In May and September it holds a beer festival in marquees on a large grassy area adjacent to the pub. Lunchtime meals Sunday only. ❀◐⇌🚌♣P

Lumb

Hargreaves Arms

Burnley Road East, BB4 9PQ (on B6238 a couple of miles N of Waterfoot) SD837247
⏲ 12-midnight ☎ (01706) 215523
🌐 thehargreavesarms.co.uk
Theakston Old Peculier; guest beers Ⓗ
A traditional travellers' rest with original interior and roaring fire, this 17th-century country inn is situated in the beautiful Rossendale Valley. It has previously served as a counting house, drinking venue and funeral parlour, and reportedly has its own resident ghost – Mr Hargreaves. A wide selection of good pub food and ale is offered, including 'curry for a fiver' on Thursday evening. Nearby is the East Lancashire Steam Railway for a great day out. Q❀◑

Lytham

County Hotel ✔

Church Road, FY8 5LH
⏲ 12-11 (midnight Fri & Sat) ☎ (01253) 795128
Beer range varies Ⓗ
A comfortable hotel dating from the 1800s in the centre of town offering popular local ales. The large lounge is divided into two areas: sports viewing on plasma TV, and small quiet bays. At least two beers from the Lytham Brewery plus two to four changing guests are available. Good value, appetising food is served until 9pm, and on Thursday night a curry special is available 4-9pm followed by a quiz. Accommodation comprises 22 en-suite rooms. ❀🛏◑♿⇌🚌P

Ship & Royal ✔

91 Clifton Street, FY8 5EH
⏲ 11-11 (midnight Fri & Sat); 12-11 Sun ☎ (01253) 732867
Shepherd Neame Spitfire; guest beers Ⓗ
Named after a past business merger, this Grade II-listed mock-Tudor Victorian building is a prominent feature on the main street. The interior was refurbished in 2007 and retains many of the original fittings. It has an L-shaped bar and discrete areas on two levels with gas fires and a large-screen TV. Up to five guest beers are served, with

Lytham Brewery and more distant micros featuring regularly. Music nights are Friday and Saturday. Traditional British food is served daily.
❀◖◗♿⇌🚌(7,11,12)⚟

Taps 🏆 ✔

Henry Street, FY8 5LE
⏲ 11-11 (midnight Fri & Sat); 12-11 Sun ☎ (01253) 736226
🌐 thetaps.net
Titanic Taps Bitter; guest beers Ⓗ
This multi award-winning one-roomed pub was CAMRA Branch Pub of The Year 2010, with six varying guest beers including a cask mild. The pub supports the local lifeboat and rugby team, and much memorabilia is displayed. The landlord is the only person to win Branch Pub of the Year in two different pubs. The venue stocks a regularly changing real cider. ⌂Q❀◖♿⇌🚌(7,11,68)♣🍎⚟

Mawdesley

Black Bull ✔

Hall Lane, L40 2QY (off B5246)
⏲ 12-11 (7 Mon winter); 12-midnight Fri & Sat; 12-11 Sun
☎ (01704) 822202
Black Sheep Best Bitter; Jennings Cumberland Ale; Robinson's Unicorn; Taylor Landlord; guest beer Ⓗ
A pub since 1610, this low-ceilinged stone building boasts some magnificent oak beams. Older village residents know the pub as 'Ell 'Ob, a reference to a coal-fired cooking range. Certificates on display record the pub's success in Lancashire's Best Kept Village competition. It has also earned awards for its numerous hanging baskets. During summer months the well-kept beer garden is popular with both drinkers and diners. The guest beer is usually from a regional brewery. No evening meals on Monday. ⌂❀◖◗♿🚌(347)♣P

Robin Hood

Bluestone Lane, L40 2QY (off B5252)
⏲ 11.30-11; 12-10.30 Sun ☎ (01704) 822275
🌐 robinhoodinn.co.uk
Black Sheep Best Bitter; Jennings Cumberland Ale; Taylor Landlord; guest beers Ⓗ
Charming inn at the crossroads between the three old villages of Mawdesley, Croston and Eccleston. The 15th-century building was substantially altered in the 19th century. Run by the same family for over 40 years, it enjoys a reputation for good food. Wilsons restaurant upstairs is open Tuesday to Sunday evenings. Bar food is served all day at the weekend. It still finds room for those who have come for a drink only, offering three guest ales. 🐎❀◖◗🚌(347)P

Mellor

Traders Arms

Mellor Lane, BB2 7EW SD651309
⏲ 12-11 (midnight Fri & Sat); 12-11.30 Sun
☎ (01254) 812478 🌐 thetradersarms.co.uk
Thwaites Original, Wainwright, Lancaster Bomber Ⓗ
High on a hill top on the edge of Mellor, the Traders has views across to the Fylde coast. Dating from the 18th century, this low-beamed stone-built pub is a comfortable local with at least three Thwaites beers – a rarity for a Thwaites pub close to Blackburn – plus occasional seasonal beers. The food is exceptionally good value; try the smoked haddock stack or select from the extensive specials board. Quiz night is Wednesday. ❀◖◗P

Morecambe

Palatine

The Crescent, LA4 5BZ (overlooking prom opp clock tower)
⏲ 10.30-midnight (1am Fri & Sat; 11.30 Sun)
☎ (01524) 410503
Lancaster Amber, Blonde, Black, Red; Thwaites Nutty Black; guest beers Ⓗ
An Edwardian mid-terraced pub. The ground floor was completely transformed in late 2008 with much bare stone and woodwork. The bar room is quite small, with some intimate corners. An upstairs room is rather different. Cosy and carpeted, many of the fittings — leaded lights, shelving, fireplace — appear to be original. Enjoy the spectacular views across the Bay. ◖◗⇌🚌

Smugglers' Den ✔

56 Poulton Road, LA4 5HB
⏲ 12 (4 Oct, Nov, Jan & Feb)-midnight; 12-11.30 Sun
☎ (01524) 421684 🌐 thesmugglersden.com
Adnams Broadside; Brysons Union Flag; guest beers Ⓗ
The oldest pub in Morecambe, circa 1640, though remodelled, this is a welcoming hostelry, with six handpumps that have two lines for guest ales. Regular live folk music features throughout the year. An impressive open fire warms the bar during the colder months. There are ladies' and gents' darts teams, and a pub quiz team. Meals are available 5-8pm weekdays. Westons Traditional Scrumpy and a guest perry are served. There is a discount for CAMRA members. Games include shove-ha'penny. ⌂❀◗⇌🚌(5,430)♣🍎P⚟

York

87 Lancaster Road, LA4 5QH (where B5321 crosses railway)
⏲ 12-11 (midnight Fri & Sat) ☎ (01524) 425353
🌐 yorkhotelmorecambe.co.uk
Everards Beacon; Lancaster Blonde; guest beer Ⓗ
Large Victorian community pub on the edge of the town centre, with several rooms and some original plasterwork ceilings. It is the headquarters of Morecambe Royal British Legion, and St George's Day and Remembrance Day are celebrated. On Morecambe FC match days, away fans can relax with the locals in this football-friendly pub; check out the display of football scarves in the back room. A large function room (with catering if required) and a recently-opened patio complete the picture. ⌂❀🛏◖◗⇌🚌(2,2A)♣P⚟

Nether Kellet

Limeburner's Arms

32 Main Road, LA6 1EP
⏲ 7.30 (2 Sun)-midnight ☎ (01524) 732916
Beer range varies Ⓗ
Once – within living memory – most country pubs were like this: no food, no jukebox, plain and simply furnished. Minor improvements have not changed the character of the place. Unsurprisingly, most of the customers are locals; the landlord himself is a local farmer. The old photos in the bar are a rewarding study. ⌂Q❀🚌(49,55A)♣P⚟

Ormskirk

Disraelis

26 Church Street, L39 3AN (between clock tower and church)

⌚ 10 midnight (1am Tue, Fri & Sat) ☎ (01695) 570737
Marston's Pedigree, seasonal beers Ⓗ
Disraelis is in the market town of Ormskirk, situated close to the ancient parish church (well worth a visit). Prior to renovation it was a Burtonwood pub uniquely named the Snig's Foot. An extensive menu is competitively priced, much to the liking of students at Edge Hill University. The seasonal beers come from the Marston's portfolio, and encouragingly the phrase 'Always ask for cask' is written on the front of the till. ◑⇌🚌

Greyhound

100 Aughton Street, L39 3BS (250m S of clock tower)
⌚ 12-11.30 (10.30 Sun) ☎ (01695) 576701
Tetley Dark Mild, Bitter; guest beers Ⓗ
The Greyhound is a classic community pub, little changed over the years, with a diminutive public bar and a superb snug on the right as you enter. B&B is available and visitors are made welcome by a loyal customer base. A Walkers of Warrington Ales sign can be seen high up at the back of the public bar. Some of the handpumps are only visible in the larger back room.
Q❀♿⇌🚌(75,311,351)♣P

Queens Head

30 Moor Street, L39 2AQ (near bus station and clock tower)
⌚ 11-midnight (1am Fri); 10-1am Sat ☎ (01695) 574380
Tetley Mild, Bitter; guest beers Ⓗ
The Queen's Head is a Victorian town pub in the principal shopping street of the market town, close to both bus and train stations. The pub is one of the most adventurous in the area as regards its beer selection policy, with excellent ales drawn from a variety of sources, including some of the smaller breweries, as well as from Tetley. Food is available from 10am-6pm and children are welcome until 7pm. The pub can be very busy, especially on Thursday market days. ❀◑♿⇌🚌

Padiham

Free Gardeners

2 St Giles Street, BB12 8HL (behind parish church)
⌚ 5-midnight; 4-2am Fri; 2-2am Sat; 1-midnight Sun
☎ (01282) 772280
Beer range varies Ⓗ
Named after a Friendly Society, when a local branch was formed in 1827. The layout is welcoming, open plan, emphasising televised sport and live entertainment, particularly at weekends. However, there is an area offering a degree of privacy near the log-burning stove. Two handpumps dispense a rapidly changing selection of beers from across the country. The mirrors behind the bar were made from the old window panes and show the initials WA – referring to William Astley's Nelson Brewery – which closed in the 1920s. 🔥🚌(26,27,152)

Parbold

Wayfarer

1-3 Alder Lane, WN8 7NL (on A5209)
⌚ 12-3, 5-11 (1.30am Fri); 12-1.30am Sat; 12-11 Sun
☎ (01257) 464600 🌐 wayfarerparbold.co.uk
Tetley Bitter; guest beers Ⓗ
Conversion of a row of 18th-century cottages, with the focus very much on fine dining. In 2009 the Il Viandante Italian bistro was built onto the Wayfarer. There are now three menus to choose from: bar, restaurant and Italian. The bar has low-beamed ceilings with cosy little nooks and crannies, and is a popular stop in the summer and weekends, situated close to the Leeds-Liverpool canal and Parbold Hill with its panoramic views. Tetley Bitter and two guests are available.
❀◑♿⇌🚌P

Windmill

3 Mill Lane, WN8 7NW (off A5209 Wigan-Ormskirk Road)
⌚ 12-11 (midnight Fri & Sat) ☎ (01257) 462935
Tetley Bitter; guest beers Ⓗ
A former grain store to the adjacent windmill, parts of the building date back to 1794. Clean lines in the interior design and period furniture are in keeping with the building's history. There are two open fires, and a warm welcome is offered to drinkers, diners, bargees and walkers. The bar features mainly beers from the Prospect and George Wright breweries. There is a separate snug to the right of the doorway with delightful carved animals in the wooden panels. LocAle accredited. 🔥Q◑⇌P

Pendleton

Swan With Two Necks

Main Street, BB7 1PT (½ mile E of A59 turn-off)
⌚ 7-11 Mon; closed Tue; 12-2.30, 6-11 Wed-Sat; 12-10.30 Sun ☎ (01200) 423112 🌐 swanwithtwonecks.co.uk
Copper Dragon Golden Pippin; Phoenix Navvy; guest beers Ⓗ
Recently refurbished but losing none of its character, this is a friendly, comfortable village local run by two East Lancs CAMRA members. Popular with both locals and walkers from nearby Pendle Hill, it is warmed by two real fires. Alongside the regular beers, three other ales come from local micros such as Marble, Hopstar and Salamander. Real cider from Westons is also available. Food here is very good, but please check in advance for availability. Look out for the teapots and Rosie the white cat. 🔥Q❀◑●P

Penwortham

Fleece Inn ✔

39 Liverpool Road, PR1 9XD (200m from Penwortham Library)
⌚ 11-11; 12-11.30 Sun ☎ (01772) 745561
Tetley Bitter; Wells Bombardier; guest beers Ⓗ
An ex-sheriff's house with a heritage protection order on it, the interior has been extensively modernised and is now mostly open plan with wall dividers, but retains separate seating areas, including a quiet raised room. The guest beers, often from micros, change up to four times a week, with at least two usually on sale at any one time. The food from a varied menu is very popular and the pub can get busy at times. ❀◑♿🚌(2,3)

Poulton-le-Fylde

Grapevine (Café Bar)

19-21 Market Place, FY6 7AS
⌚ 6-11 (midnight Thu; 1am Fri & Sat) ☎ (01253) 896700
Thwaites Original, Wainwright; guest beers Ⓗ
The Grapevine café/wine bar is situated in the heart of historic Poulton-le-Fylde. Formerly an ironmongers' and hardware shop, it is thought to date back to 1754. Today the Grapevine serves as a

popular venue and meeting place for all ages. During the day it opens as an upmarket café with a selection of coffees, teas and home-cooked food available. By night it becomes a pleasant, informal wine bar with several quality cask ales on offer. Q⇌🚌

Old Town Hall

5 Church Street, FY6 7AP

11-11 (11.30 Fri & Sat); 12-11 Sun ☎ (01253) 892257

Beer range varies H

Used as council offices for much of the 20th century, it then became a pub formerly known as the Bay Horse. A first-floor bar is open weekend evenings and live bands often feature. Well-behaved families are welcome. The large TV screen is for football and racing fans. Guest beers are usually from Thwaites and Moorhouse's, and up to four real ales are served. There is a large municipal car park at the rear of the pub. ♿⛺⇌🚌(2,42,84)♣

Thatched House ✔

12 Ball Street, FY6 7BG

11-11 (midnight Fri & Sat); 12-11 Sun ☎ (01253) 891063

Bank Top Flat Cap; Lytham Amber; guest beers H

The present pub stands in the grounds of a Norman church, and was built on the site at the beginning of the 20th century. Various photos of sporting heroes of the past are displayed. Often loud with the chatter of customers, this local gets very busy at weekends. A true meeting and drinkers' pub, it is handy for bus and rail stations. Guest beers are from the SIBA list. ⛺⇌🚌(2,42,84)♣

Preston

Anderton Arms ✔

Longsands Lane, Fulwood, PR2 9PS (near Eastway and M6 jct 31A)

11.45-11 (midnight Thu-Sat) ☎ (01772) 700104

Thwaites Original; guest beers H

One of the Ember Inns chain, the Anderton Arms is a modern estate pub to the north of Preston, popular with residents and commuters alike. The interior is light and airy, with seating to a very high standard of comfort. Examples of modern art are on display. Up to six guest beers are usually available, often from small breweries. Third of a pint tasters are available. Good value food is served. No children under 14, please. Preston Orbit bus services stop outside. ❀♿🚌(88A,88C)P

Bitter Suite

53 Fylde Road, PR1 2XQ

12-3, 7 (6 Tue & Thu)-11; 12-3, 6-11.30 Wed; 12-3, 6-midnight Fri; 12-midnight Sat; 7-11 Sun ☎ (01772) 827007

bittersuitepreston.co.uk

Beer range varies H

Single-room bar set back from Fylde Road at the side of the unrelated Mad Ferret bar. A genuine free house, it serves six guest beers from micro-breweries that change almost hourly. There are at least four regular beer festivals each year, and simple home-cooked lunches are served Monday to Friday. Although opposite the Students Union and surrounded by university buildings, it is not primarily a student bar. ❀🚌(31,35,68)

Black Horse ★

166 Friargate, PR1 2EJ

10.30-11 (midnight Fri & Sat); 12-4.30 Sun

☎ (01772) 204855

Robinson's Old Stockport, Dizzy Blond, Unicorn, Double Hop, Old Tom, seasonal beers H

Classic Grade II-listed pub in the main shopping area close to the historic open market. With its tiled bar and walls and mosaic floor, it is an English Heritage/CAMRA award winner. The two front rooms bear photos of old Preston; the famous hall-of-mirrors seating area is to the rear, and memorabilia of a previous landlord is displayed. Up to seven Robinson's beers are regularly on sale. A new covered smoking area has been built upstairs through the modern non-real ale bar. ⇌

Grey Friar ✔

144 Friargate, PR1 2EJ (jct of Ringway)

9am-midnight (1am Fri & Sat) ☎ (01772) 558542

Greene King Ruddles Best Bitter, Abbot; Theakston Old Peculier; guest beers H

Modern open-plan Wetherspoon pub with raised areas to the side and rear in a fine real ale drinking part of the city, formerly a carpet store. Preston's students and citizens both young and old appreciate the range of ales and food at the best prices around, with up to seven guests ales on sale. The mix of students, workers and locals creates a bustling atmosphere and the bar can get extremely busy at weekends. The pub plays an active role in CAMRA recruiting. ♿⇌🚌

Market Tavern

33-35 Market Street, PR1 2ES

10.30-9 (11 Thu; midnight Fri & Sat); 12-6 Sun

☎ (01772) 254425

Beer range varies H

Small, popular city-centre local in pedestrianised area overlooking the historic Victorian outdoor market. Three handpumps serve a wide range of guest beers, usually from micros from all over the country. A suberb selection of imported bottled beers is also on offer, plus German weisse on draught. Outside seating is available in summer. With two intimate seating booths, conversation rules in this former local CAMRA Pub of the Year. No food is served, but you are welcome to bring your own. ❀⇌

Old Black Bull ✔

35 Friargate, PR1 2AT

10.30-11 (midnight Fri & Sat); 12-10.30 Sun

☎ (01772) 823397

Hydes Boddingtons Bitter, guests beers H

Mock-Tudor city-centre pub that is now completely free of tie for cask beers. A small front vault, a main bar with distinctive black and white floor tiles, two comfortable lounge areas and a pool table combine to make this a popular venue. There is also a patio to the rear. Live music is played on Saturday evenings and all TV sport is shown. Up to nine guest beers come from micros or small independents. Twice winner of local CAMRA Pub of the Year. ❀⇌🚌♣

Old Vic

78 Fishergate, PR1 2UH

11.30-11 (midnight Fri; 1am Sat); 12-midnight Sun

☎ (01772) 254690

Caledonian Deuchars IPA; Courage Directors; Theakston Best Bitter; guest beers H

Situated opposite the railway station and on bus routes into the city, the Old Vic can be rather busy at times. There are seven handpumps, with usually up to four guest beers, often two from Moorhouse's and one Three B's. Big screens show sports events and there is a large pool table. The pub also hosts a keen darts team. Meals are served 12-5pm (4pm Sun). A rear car park is available Sunday and evenings. ❀◐⇌▣♣P̶

Olde Dog & Partridge

41 Friargate, PR1 2AT

11-3, 6-11.30 (1am Sat); 12-5, 7-11.30 Sun

☎ (01772) 252217

Taylor Landlord; Tetley Dark Mild; Young's Special; guest beers Ⓗ

Down-to-earth city-centre pub that specialises in rock music. The student union Rock Society meets here. Five real ales often include one from the Museum Brewery. The landlord has been at the pub for over 30 years and there is a monthly live music night, a weekly quiz on Thursday and a rock DJ on Sunday evening. Excellent value pub lunches are served (not Sun) and a covered Smokey-O-Joes smoking area is provided at the rear.
❀◐⇌▣♣●P̶

Rawtenstall

White Lion

72 Burnley Road, BB4 8EW

4.30 (2 Fri; 12 Sat & Sun)-midnight ☎ (01706) 213117

Black Sheep Best Bitter; Copper Dragon Golden Pippin; Greene King Old Speckled Hen; Tetley Bitter; guest beers Ⓗ

A friendly pub with enthusiastic and loyal locals. Constant guest beers sourced from all around the country help add to the classic atmosphere. Home-made sandwiches are available from behind the bar as well as full meals at weekends. Situated on the main road from Manchester to Burnley, just out of Rawtenstall town centre. ▣(X43)♣P̶

Rufford

Hesketh Arms

81 Liverpool Road, L40 1SB (on A59 at jct with B5246) SD460155

12-11 (midnight Fri & Sat) ☎ (01704) 821002

Jennings Cumberland Ale; Moorhouse's Pride of Pendle; guest beers Ⓗ

The Hesketh Arms is a former Greenall's inn on the A59 Liverpool to Preston road in the small village of Rufford, close to the National Trust property of Rufford Old Hall. It was closed for major refurbishment for seven years, reopening in 2005. The pub was originally a forester's house from the Hesketh estate, built in the 17th century, with additions in the 19th and 20th centuries. The station is on the B5246, nearly opposite the pub.
❀◐♿⇌▣(2A,2B)P̶

St Annes

Fifteens ✔

42 St Annes Road West, FY8 1RF

11-11 (midnight Fri & Sat); 12-10.30 Sun

☎ (01253) 725852

Tetley Bitter; guest beers Ⓗ

Formerly Lloyds Bank, Fifteens has been refurbished in style and attracts a discerning clientele. Upstairs, a gallery displays local artists' work; in the main bar there is music, or enjoy the tranquillity of what must be the world's most luxurious bank vault. Martin and his team worked hard since their arrival in 2008, and within a year the pub was awarded CAMRA Pub of the Season, gaining Cask Marque accreditation along the way. Four ales are always on offer, including a local brew. ♿⇌▣♣P̶

Salwick

Windmill Tavern

Clifton Lane, PR4 0YE (off A583 via Clifton village)

closed Mon; 12-3, 5-11 Tue-Thu; 12-midnight Fri & Sat; 12-10.30 Sun ☎ (01772) 687203

Black Sheep Best Bitter; guest beers Ⓗ

Built around 1778, Clifton windmill is the Fylde's oldest and tallest windmill, constructed from stone. It has only been a pub since 1974 and the restaurant was still a working mill until quite recently. Up to five beers are on sale, with ales from York and local breweries featuring among the guests. You can drink and relax in comfort beneath the main tower of the mill, or dine in the ample restaurant area on excellent, locally-sourced food.
Q❀◐◑⇌▣(77,75)P̶

Scarisbrick

Heaton's Bridge Inn

2 Heaton's Bridge Road, L40 8JG (on B5242 between A570 and Burscough) SD404119

11-11.30 (12.30am Fri & Sat); 12-11.30 Sun

☎ (01704) 840549

Tetley Mild, Bitter; guest beers Ⓗ

Built in 1837, this is an attractive canalside pub with stained glass windows, separate snugs and historic wall portraits. Handy for walks or cycling along the Leeds-Liverpool canal, the pub welcomes dogs and has two real fires. It is a rare outlet for Tetleys mild in this area. Reasonably priced meals can be enjoyed, with a good menu selection; food is served 12-2.30pm and 5-8pm Monday-Saturday, and 12-8pm Sunday. Buses stop outside on the Southport-Wigan 375 route.
⛫❀◐◑♿▲▣(375)♣P̶

Tontine

Delph

Sefton Road, WN5 8JU (off B5206)

12-midnight (1am Fri & Sat; 11.30 Sun) ☎ (01695) 622239

Beer range varies Ⓗ

There is always a warm welcome and friendly atmosphere in this pub, which retains a separate vault with a pool table. Good value meals complement the real ales in a relaxed environment. Children are welcome although not in the vault area. Darts and dominoes are played in the local league and a quiz night is held on Wednesday. The beers are normally pale ones. Wigan CAMRA Pub of the Season Autumn 2006 and Autumn 2008, and LocAle accredited.
❀◐♿⇌(Orrell)♣P

Waddington

Waddington Arms

West View, BB7 3HU

11-11 (midnight Fri & Sat); 1-11 Sun ☎ (01200) 423262

waddingtonarms.co.uk

Moorhouse's Waddy Ale; Theakston Best Bitter; Thwaites Wainwright; guest beers Ⓗ

Situated in the heart of a multi-award-winning Best Kept Village, this stone-built pub usually serves four real ales, with the guest beer often from Tirril. This village inn is a convivial place to drink, eat and sleep, with an extensive menu and six en-suite rooms. There is a small beer garden at the rear and outdoor seating at the front overlooking the brook and the Coronation Gardens. ⛰Q✿⇄◐♿P⅃

Warton

George Washington

Main Street, LA5 9PJ
⚙ 12 (4 Mon)-11; 12-10.30 Sun ☎ (01524) 732865
Everards Beacon Bitter; Hawkshead Bitter; guest beers Ⓗ
Old inn at the heart of the village, with a number of distinct areas and a dining room, handily situated for Warton Crag, the old church and the Old Rectory. The pub's name is due to a distant family connection between this village and America's first president. Outside is a covered and heated area for smokers. ⛰✿⇄◐♿🚌(55)♣P⅃

Weeton

Eagle & Child ✔

Singleton Road, PR4 3NB (from Fleetwood, follow B5260 past Weeton army barracks)
⚙ 12-midnight ☎ (01253) 836230
🌐 theeagleandchild.co.uk
Caledonian Deuchars IPA; Theakston Best Bitter; guest beers Ⓗ
One of the most picturesque pubs in the area, with historical connections going back to Cromwellian times; some of the original features still remain. Although the beers have to be sourced from a limited list offered by the pub group, they are exceptionally well kept and presented. The food offered to customers has increased the pub's reputation and is reasonably priced. Meals are served 12-2.30pm and 5-8pm Monday-Friday, 12-8.30pm Saturday and Sunday.
⛰✿◐♿▲🚌(75,76)P⅃

Wennington

Bridge

Tatham, LA2 8NL (on B6480 S of Wennington)
⚙ 12-11 (10.30 Sun) ☎ (01524) 221326
Black Sheep Best Bitter; Everards Beacon Bitter; guest beers Ⓗ
Two linked buildings, one dating from 1642, the other from 1744, make up a small bar, cosy and low-beamed, and two dining rooms. The pub is set in an isolated spot south of Wennington, but attracts a surprisingly large number of local customers, as well as walkers in the summer months. It has not succumbed to the gastro market, but offers good, well-priced food. The pub features in a Turner painting. Quiz night is Friday. There is an associated caravan park and helipad.
⛰Q✿⇄◐▲≋🚌(80,81b)♣P⅃

Wesham

Lane Ends

Weeton Road, PR4 3DH
⚙ 12-midnight (11 Sun) ☎ (01772) 671216
🌐 laneends.co.uk
Thwaites Lancaster Bomber; guest beers Ⓗ
Situated on Weeton Road, this large community pub has four separate drinking areas. One has a pool table, the other areas have large-screen TVs. The enthusiastic landlord holds a beer festival once a year. Regular live music plays on Saturday evenings, and the pub is home to football, pool and darts teams. Buses pass close by.
Q✿⊟♿≋(Kirkham & Wesham)🚌(2,61)♣P⅃

Westhead

Prince Albert ✔

109 Wigan Road, L40 6HY (on A577 Skelmersdale road, 2 miles E of Ormskirk) SD441077
⚙ 12-11.30 (midnight Fri) ☎ (01695) 573656
Moorhouse's Pendle Witches Brew; Tetley Mild, Bitter; guest beers Ⓗ
Country pub with a warm atmosphere in the heart of the village. The Prince Albert has a small central bar that serves three snug rooms around it. The interior has been slightly modified but still retains charm, with real fires on cold days. The pub remains quiet because most mobile networks are out of range! Children are permitted during the afternoon. Excellent home-cooked lunches are served 12-3pm (12-4pm Sun). A supporter of LocAle. ⛰✿◖♿▲🚌(375,385)♣P⅃

Whalley

Swan Hotel

62 King Street, BB7 9SN
⚙ 12-11 (midnight Fri & Sat) ☎ (01254) 822195
Bowland Hen Harrier; Taylor Landlord; guest beer Ⓗ
Built in 1781, this haunted pub is situated, like all four Whalley pubs, in the heart of the historic village. It has a deceptively modern but comfortable interior and serves three local Bowland beers as well as Taylor Landlord. Weekends tend to be lively in the central bar and lounge, and Wednesday is quiz night. There is a popular market held on the last Sunday of each month on the car park at the rear of the pub.
✿⇄◗≋🚌(26,225,280)P

Wilpshire

Rising Sun

797 Whalley New Road, BB1 9BE (on A666)
⚙ 1.30 (12 Sat)-midnight; 12-11.30 Sun ☎ (01254) 247379
Theakston Best Bitter; guest beers Ⓗ
About a mile out of Blackburn you will find this traditional pub, a former Matthew Brown house; that lost brewery's name can be found on the pub's windows. Games of cards and dominoes are played in a separate bar room. The lounge has a real coal fire and piano for Saturday night entertainment. Smokers are protected from the elements by a covered and heated shelter.
⛰Q⊟≋(Ramsgreave & Wilpshire)🚌(225)♣⅃

Winmarleigh

Patten Arms

Park Lane, PR3 0JU (on B5272 3 miles N of Garstang)
⚙ 4 (12 Sat)-11; 12-10 Sun ☎ (01995) 791484
Black Sheep Best Bitter; Jennings Cumberland Ale; Tetley Bitter; guest beer Ⓗ
Genuine, isolated free house situated away from villages on a B-road, yet enjoying regular local custom. This early 19th-century Grade II-listed building has a single bar with a country pub feel, high-backed bench seats, cream-painted walls and open fires. There is a separate restaurant, and terraced seating overlooking a bowling green. No meals on Monday. ⛰✿◐▲♣P⅃

Wray

George & Dragon

Main Street, LA2 8QG (off B6480)

6-11 Mon; 12-2.30, 5-midnight; 12-11 Sat & Sun

☎ (01524) 221403

Everards Beacon Bitter; guest beers Ⓗ

A genuine village local that also has an excellent reputation for its food. Inside, there are two bar rooms of quite different sizes and a restaurant. Unusual pub games are available, as is Wi-Fi broadband. There is a Wednesday night quiz. The extensive beer garden has an aviary, as well as an unheated but covered smoking area. Wray hosts a popular scarecrow festival in May.

Q❀(80,81B)♣

Wrightington

White Lion

117 Mossy Lea Road, WN6 9RE (on B5290)

12-midnight (11 Mon & Wed; 10.30 Sun)

☎ (01257) 425977 thewhitelionlancs.co.uk

Jennings Cumberland Ale; guest beers Ⓗ

Extremely popular country pub, with a good mix of drinkers and diners. Four handpumps are in constant use, serving beers from the Marston's range. There is a weekly quiz on Tuesday and a poker league on Thursday. Themed evenings are held in the restaurant. The pub is family-friendly with a large outside garden area. It is reputed to be haunted by the ghost of an old lady who used to inhabit one of the cottages that now makes up the restaurant. ❀P

Greyhound, Ormskirk (Photo: Richard Brown)

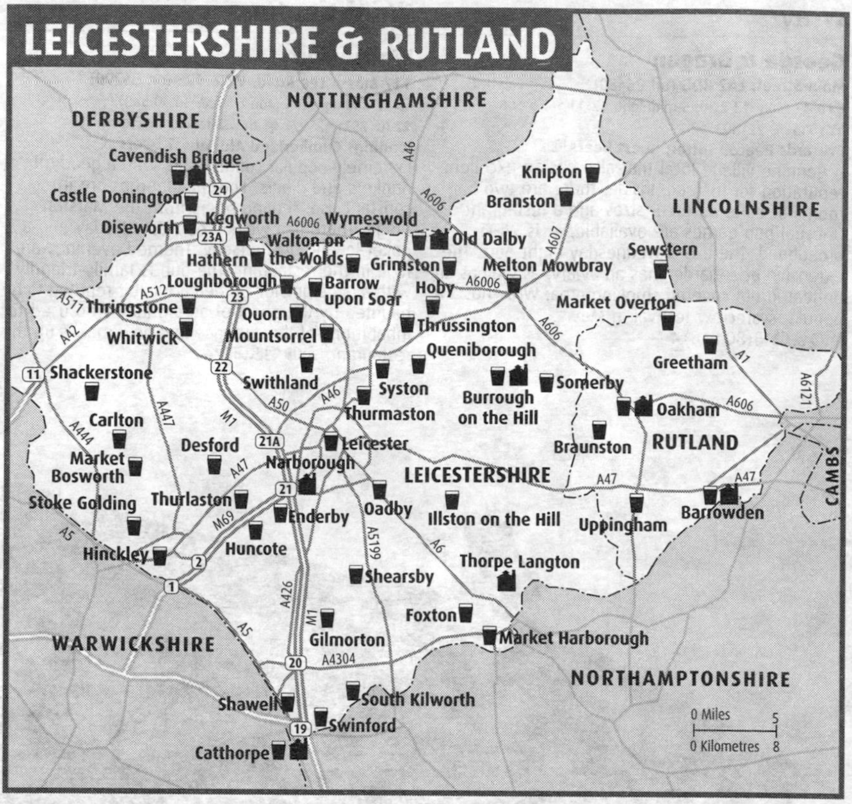

Barrow upon Soar

Soar Bridge Inn

29 Bridge Street, LE12 8PN

⏲ 12-11 (10.30 Sun) ☎ (01509) 412686

Castle Rock Elsie Mo; Everards Sunchaser, Tiger, Original; guest beer Ⓗ

Situated next to the bridge that gave it its name, this pub is popular with walkers, boaters and drinkers. The large single room interior divides into distinct areas, with a separate restaurant, function room and skittle alley. Outside there is a floodlit petanque court, beer terrace and garden. Well-behaved dogs and children are welcome. Home-made food is available Tuesday to Sunday. The first Monday of the month is Grand Union Folk Club night and a weekly quiz is held on Thursday. The annual beer festival is a highlight.
⌂❀◑⛺⇌🚌(K2,CB27)♣P⁄–

Barrowden

Exeter Arms

28 Main Street, Rutland, LE15 8EQ (1 mile S of A47)

⏲ 12-2.30 (not Mon), 6-11; 12-3.30, 6-11 Sat; 12-5 Sun ☎ (01572) 747247

Barrowden Beech, Hop Gear, Bevin, Blackadder Porter; Greene King IPA Ⓗ

Collyweston stone-built pub with a fantastic view overlooking the village green, duck pond and Welland Valley. It offers a warm welcome and serves highly regarded food. The patio drinking area outside is a wonderful place to spend a summer's day. Petanque is played in the summer, dominoes in the winter and darts all year round. Folk music and quiz nights alternate on Mondays. Barrowden Brewery is situated in a barn building behind the pub. ⌂Q❀⛟◑♿🚌(12)♣P⁄–

Branston

Wheel

Main Street, NG32 1RU

⏲ closed Mon; 11-11; 12-10.30 Sun ☎ (01476) 870376

🌐 thewheelinnbranston.co.uk

Batemans XB; guest beers Ⓗ

Like most of the buildings in the village, this attractive 18th-century pub is built using local stone. There is a small bar with some seating and a larger restaurant area that was originally two small rooms, now sympathetically renovated. The extensive food menu uses locally-sourced ingredients where possible, including produce from the nearby Belvoir Estate. ⌂Q❀◑♿●P⁄–

Braunston

Blue Ball

6 Cedar Street, Rutland, LE15 8QS

⏲ 11.30-3, 6-11; 11.30-11 Sat & Sun ☎ (01572) 722135

🌐 theblueballbraunston.co.uk

Jennings Cumberland Ale; Marston's Pedigree; guest beer Ⓗ

This pub is Rutland's oldest inn and the historic thatched building has been refurbished to a high standard but retains all its original features. The cosy bar has a roaring fire making it the ideal place to be on a cold evening. The rest of the pub is dedicated to serving good quality food on a daily basis. Up to three changing ales are available depending on the season. Walkers and dogs are welcome. ⌂Q✿◑🚌P⊬

Burrough on the Hill

Grant's Free House

Main Street, LE14 2JQ

✪ closed Mon; 12-2, 5-11; 12-midnight Sat; 12-11 Sun

☎ (01664) 452141 or 454801

Parish PSB, Farm Gold, Burrough Bitter Ⓗ**, Baz's Bonce Blower** Ⓖ

Formerly a 16th-century inn known as the Stag & Hounds, Grant's Free House is a completely refurbished two-room split-level pub, firmly established as the home of the Parish Brewery. A full range of Parish beers is always available from the adjacent brewhouse, which has an entry in the Guinness Book of Records for brewing Britain's strongest beer at 23% ABV. Guest beers from other local micros are also available. A 30-beer festival is to become a regular event over the late-May bank holiday weekend. Q✿◑🚌P⊬

Carlton

Gate Hangs Well

Barton Road, CV13 0DB (1 mile N of Market Bosworth) SK403043

✪ 6-11; 12-3, 6-midnight Fri & Sat; 7-10.30 Sun

☎ (01455) 291845

Draught Bass; Greene King Abbot; Marston's Burton Bitter, Pedigree Ⓗ

A Guide pub for eight consecutive years, this welcoming, traditional village inn has seating areas served by a central bar. Popular with walkers and cyclists, there is a pleasant garden and conservatory where children are welcome until mid-evening. Sandwiches and rolls are made to order. Darts is played and live music hosted on Wednesday and Saturday evenings. A smoking shelter is available. Convenient for Bosworth Battlefield, Bosworth Water Trust, Ashby Canal, the Leicestershire Round and The Battlefield Line at Shackerstone. ⌂Q✿♿🚌(153)♣P⊬

Castle Donington

Jolly Potters

36 Hillside, DE74 2NH

✪ 12 (11 Sat)-midnight; 12-10.30 Sun ☎ (01332) 811912

Draught Bass; Fuller's London Pride; Marston's Pedigree; Taylor Landlord Ⓗ

The landlord and locals are always happy to chat to visitors at this traditional, friendly pub, built at the turn of the 20th century. The open plan front room divides into bar and lounge areas – the basic stone-floored bar has traditional wooden pews and there is a back room with juke-box, TV and dartboard. A collection of framed beermats and cards decorates the walls, and cups, jugs and tankards hang from the ceiling. ⌂✿♣⊬

Catthorpe

Cherry Tree

Main Street, LE17 6DB

✪ 12-2.30 (Mon only), 5-11.30; 12-2.30, 5-12.30am Fri; 12-12.30am Sat; 12-10.30 Sun ☎ (01788) 860430

🌐 cherrytree-pub.co.uk

Adnams Bitter; guest beers Ⓗ

Welcoming and friendly, this genuine free house with a small decked garden to the rear is an ideal meeting place for those travelling by the notorious 'Catthorpe Junction' of M1/M6/A14. It has a bar plus a snug/dining area offering good food made using locally sourced ingredients, with an excellent cold table in summer. Guest beers come from local brewers including Dow Bridge, who have brewed in the village since 2002. The snug has an aviation and railway theme, including jet fighter ejection seats, and is the venue for the June beer festival. ⌂✿◑⛺♣P

Cavendish Bridge

Old Crown ✔

Shardlow, DE72 2HL (off A6)

✪ 11-11.30 (12.30am Fri & Sat); 11-11 Sun

☎ (01332) 792392 🌐 brilliantpubs.co.uk/oldcrownshardlow

Jennings Dark Mild, Cumberland Ale, Cocker Hoop; Marston's Pedigree, Old Empire; guest beers Ⓗ

Coaching inn dating from the 17th century with the original oak-beamed ceiling displaying an extensive collection of old jugs. The walls are covered with pub mirrors, brewery signs and railway memorabilia which even extend into the toilets. The cosy open-plan interior is divided into two areas with a large inglenook on the right. Good value food includes curry night on Wednesday. Local CAMRA Branch Pub of the Year 2009. ⌂✿🛏◑🚌P⊬

Desford

Blue Bell Inn

39 High Street, LE9 9JF

✪ 11-midnight (1am Fri & Sat); 12-midnight Sun

☎ (01455) 822901

Everards Beacon, Tiger, Original, seasonal beers; guest beers Ⓗ

Welcoming pub in the centre of the village with two rooms and a restaurant area with a central servery. A general knowledge quiz is held on Tuesday night. Food is available lunchtimes and evenings throughout the week including the traditional Sunday lunch. Dominoes and darts are played. Outside, the garden has a children's play area and there is a heated and covered space for smokers. Close to Mallory Park, B&B accommodation is provided. Q✿🛏◑⊟♿🚌(152,153)♣P⊬

Diseworth

Plough Inn

33 Hall Gate, DE74 2QJ

✪ 11.30-3, 5-11; 11.30-11 Fri & Sat; 12-10.30 Sun

☎ (01332) 810333 🌐 theploughdiseworth.co.uk

Draught Bass; Greene King Abbot; Marston's Pedigree; guest beers Ⓗ

INDEPENDENT BREWERIES

Barrowden Barrowden
Belvoir Old Dalby
Dow Bridge Catthorpe
Everards Narborough
Grainstore Oakham
Langton Thorpe Langton
Parish Burrough on the Hill
Shardlow Cavendish Bridge

Situated in a village that has many half timbered buildings, this is a cosy multi-roomed pub with parts dating back to the 13th century. Low beamed ceilings and exposed brickwork are just some of the original features discovered during renovation work in the 1990s. There is an interesting display of old photographs of the area. The restaurant serves tasty home-made food. Regular Skylink buses to Derby and Leicester via Loughborough pass by. Local CAMRA Village Pub of the Year 2009.
♨❀◑◐⊟●P⊱

Enderby

New Inn

51 High Street, LE19 4AG
✪ 12-2.30 (not Mon), 6-11; 12-3, 6 (5.30 Fri)-11.30 Thu-Sat; 12-3, 7-11 Sun ☎ (0116) 286 3126
Everards Beacon, Tiger, Original, seasonal beers; guest beers ⊞
Friendly thatched village local dating from 1549 tucked away at the top of the High Street. Everards' first tied house, the pub is well known locally for the quality of its beer and often frequented by Everards brewery staff. Three rooms are served by a central bar, with long alley skittles and a snooker room to the rear. Outside is a patio area and garden. Plentiful and imaginative lunches are served Tuesday to Saturday. ♨Q❀◑♿⊟♣P⊱

Foxton

Bridge 61 ✔

Bottom Lock, LE16 7RA
✪ 10-11 ☎ (0116) 279 2285 🌐 foxtonboats.co.uk
Adnams Bitter; Banks's Mild; guest beers ⊞
Canal-side pub situated at the bottom of the famous flight of 10 staircase locks at Foxton. The two-roomed interior has a small bar in the snug area and a larger conservatory with wide doors that open out onto the water in summer. The patio area is an ideal spot for watching the canal boats pass by. Meals are available all day. Nearby is a boatyard and canal shop with passenger trips and boats to hire; book in advance.
♨Q♉❀◑◐♿⊟●⊱

Foxton Locks Inn ✔

Bottom Lock, Gumley Road, LE16 7RA
✪ 11-11 (10.30 Sun) ☎ (0116) 279 1515
Caledonian Deuchars IPA; Greene King Old Speckled Hen; Theakston Black Bull, Old Peculier; guest beers ⊞
Refurbished canal-side inn situated at the foot of Foxton Locks, a major attraction on the Grand Union Canal. The canal director's office, once upstairs, has been recreated at the rear of the pub, complete with a collection of original share certificates on display. Outdoor seating runs down to the canal bank where boats may be moored. Families are welcome inside the pub and blankets are available for outdoor drinkers.
Q♉❀◑◐♿⊟♣P⊱

Gilmorton

Red Lion ✔

Main Street, LE17 5LT
✪ 12-2.30 (not Mon & Tue), 5-11; 12-10.30 Sun
☎ (01455) 203564 🌐 theredliongilmorton.co.uk
Banks's Mild; Marston's Pedigree; guest beers ⊞
This bistro village pub is popular with locals and people visiting to dine out, and can be busy at weekends. It is open plan, bright and spacious, with a friendly and modern feel. As well as the two regular beers, there are usually three guests from the Marston's list. Food is made with local produce where possible including eggs from the pub's chickens and herbs from the garden, and cooked on the premises. ♨❀◑◐♿P⊱

Greetham

Plough ✔

23 Main Street, Rutland, LE15 7NJ (1 mile off A1 towards Oakham on B668)
✪ 11-3, 5-11; 11-11 Thu-Sat; 12-10.30 Sun
☎ (01572) 813613 🌐 ploughgreetham.co.uk
Taylor Golden Best; guest beers ⊞
Well-run and much-loved village pub serving quality beers and excellent food. It is dog- and walker-friendly, with two camping sites and Rutland Water within easy reach by car or bicycle. Mild and draught cider are always available. Food includes a pie club on Sunday and bangers on Wednesday. Traditional pub games and pentanque are played. Runner up in the first Rutland CAMRA Pub of the Year award in 2009.
Q❀◑◐⊟♿⛺⊟(RF1,RF2)♣●P⊱

Grimston

Black Horse 🏆

Main Street, LE14 3BZ
✪ 12-3, 6-11; 12-6 Sun ☎ (01664) 812358
🌐 theblackhorsegrimston.com
Adnams Bitter; Marston's Pedigree; St Austell Tribute; guest beer ⊞
Overlooking the village green, this pub is very popular and busy both lunchtimes and evenings. It has a large open-plan bar on two levels where a wide range of good food is available. Real cider usually replaces one of the ales in summer. A petanque court hosts several local teams. A regular weekday daytime bus service from Melton Mowbray stops outside the pub.
♨Q❀◑◐⊟(23)♣●⊱

Hathern

Dew Drop ✔

49 Loughborough Road, LE12 5HY
✪ 12-3, 6-midnight; 12-3, 7-1am Fri-Sun ☎ (01509) 842438
Greene King XX Mild, H&H Bitter, Ruddles County; guest beers ⊞
Traditional two-roomed local with a large bar and comfortable small lounge with real fires. Don't miss a visit to the totally unspoilt toilets with their tiled walls and original features. A large range of malt whiskies is stocked and cobs are available at lunchtime. ♨Q❀⊟⊟♣P

Hinckley

Ashby Road Sports & Social Club

Hangmans Lane, LE10 3DA (on N edge of town off B4667 Ashby Road) SP429959
✪ 7 (5 Fri)-11; 12-11 Sat; 12-10.30 Sun ☎ (01455) 615159
Worthington's Bitter; guest beers ⊞
CAMRA members are welcome at this private sports and social club that offers a wide range of sporting activites and dancing. Its six acres of grounds have good facilities for team events.

Campers and camper vans are welcome. A large family bar area hosts traditional pub games, and there are two function rooms. Guest beers change each Thursday. Cold rolls are served. A smoking shelter is available outside. The club is on three bus routes and has a large car park and disabled access.
❀♿⛺🚌(48,81A,158)♣P⅃

New Plough Inn

Leicester Road, LE10 1LS (edge of town opp fire station)
SP431942
4.45-midnight; 12-midnight Fri-Sun ☎ (01455) 615057
Marston's Burton Bitter, Pedigree; guest beers ⊞
Traditional inn built in 1900 with original wood settles, comfortable lounges and a sports area. Local rugby memorabilia is much in evidence and the pub sponsors the Hinckley RFC Under-10s team. The venue is home to men's and women's darts, skittles and football teams. Money-raising events for charity are popular, with a quiz on the last Thursday of the month. An attractive and secure beer garden is located to the rear, with a covered area for smokers. A function room is available.
❀🚌(81,81A)♣P⅃

Hoby

Blue Bell

Main Street, LE14 3DT
12-11 ☎ (01664) 434247
Adnams Bitter; Everards Beacon, Tiger, Original; guest beer ⊞
This attractive thatched Everards' house has been tastefully and sympathetically refurbished following a serious fire a couple of years ago. The main building has two cosy rooms, with lunchtime and evening meals served in both. The pub also has a long skittle alley and function room. The garden to the rear enjoys excellent views across the Wreake Valley and provides a fine resting place for weary walkers using the well-marked footpath that follows the river. Q❀◑♿P

Huncote

Red Lion

Main Street, LE9 3AU
12-2.30 (not Mon & Sat), 5 (4 Sat)-11; 12-10.30 Sun
☎ (0116) 286 2233 🌐 red-lion.biz
Everards Beacon, Tiger; guest beers ⊞
Built in 1892, the Red Lion is a friendly local offering a warm welcome. With beamed ceilings throughout, it has a cosy lounge with a wooden fireplace and log fire. The bar has an adjoining dining area and a separate pool room. The sizeable garden has picnic tables and a children's play area. Good value home-cooked lunches are served and evening meals on Tuesday and Wednesday. Skittles can by played by prior arrangement.
♛❀◑🚌♣P⅃

Illston on the Hill

Fox & Goose

Main Street, LE7 9EG
12-2 (not Mon & Tue), 5.30 (7 Mon)-11; 12-3, 7-11 Sun
☎ (0116) 259 6430
Everards Beacon, Tiger, Original; guest beers ⊞
Cosy, unspoilt pub with a timeless feel, tucked away in the village and well worth seeking out. A fascinating collection of local mementos and hunting memorabilia is on display including original Mclaughlan cartoons. Popular annual events include conkers, an onion-growing championship and a fund-raising auction for local charities. ♛Q❀⊟♣

Kegworth

Red Lion 🏆

24 High Street, DE74 2DA
11.30-11; 12-10.30 Sun ☎ (01509) 672466
🌐 redlionkegworth.com
Adnams Bitter; Castle Rock Preservation; Greene King Abbot; Theakston Traditional Mild; guest beers ⊞
Georgian building standing on the 19th-century route of the A6, with four rooms served from one bar. There is bench seating and original features including coal fires. Eight cask ales and real cider are available plus a good selection of malt whiskies. Food is served every lunchtime and weekday evenings. Outside is a large car park and garden plus a petanque court and children's play area. En-suite accommodation is also available. Local CAMRA Branch Pub of the Year 2010.
♛Q❀🛏◑⊟🚌(65)♣●P⅃

Knipton

Manners Arms

Croxton Road, NG32 1RH
11-11; 12-10.30 Sun ☎ (01476) 879222
🌐 mannersarms.com
Belvoir Beaver Bitter; guest beers ⊞
Impressive Georgian hunting lodge beautifully renovated by the Duke and Duchess of Rutland. Served by one long bar, the lounge, with tall bookshelves and comfortable seating, and bar room are warmed by a huge open fireplace. Light bar dishes are available plus a wide range of interesting food made with local produce in the restaurant. A wonderful patio and garden area, overlooked by the conservatory, is ideal for lazing on a hot summer's day. ♛Q❀🛏◑♿P

Leicester

Ale Wagon

27 Rutland Street, LE1 1RE
11-11; 12-3, 7-10.30 Sun ☎ (0116) 2623330
🌐 alewagon.co.uk
Hoskins Hob, Best Mild, Brigadier, Bitter, EXS; guest beers ⊞
Run by the Hoskins family, this city-centre pub with 1930s interior, including an original oak staircase, has two rooms with tiled and parquet floors and a central bar. There is always a selection of Hoskins Brothers ales and guests available. The pub is popular with visiting rugby fans and real ale drinkers. It has a function room available with catering and is handy for the Curve Theatre.
♛⊟⇌🚌♣

Black Horse

65 Narrow Lane, Aylestone, LE2 8NA
12-2.30 (not Mon), 5-11; 12-midnight Fri & Sat; 12-11 Sun
☎ (0116) 2832811 🌐 philspub.co.uk
Everards Beacon, Sunchaser, Tiger, Original, seasonal beers; guest beers ⊞
Welcoming, traditional three-room Victorian pub with a distinctive bar servery in the Aylestone Village Conservation Area, three miles from the city centre. Home-cooked food is served lunchtimes Tuesday to Friday plus Friday evenings. Outside is a

large beer garden with children's play area. The skittle alley hosts a monthly comedy club and acoustic night, and is available for private parties. A popular quiz is held every Sunday. Regular beer festivals and community events are hosted. Dogs welcome. ♛Q❀◐◑⊟⊞♣●⁂

Criterion

44 Millstone Lane, LE1 5JN
✪ 12-11 ☎ (0116) 262 5418
Oakham Inferno, Bishops Farewell; guest beers ⊞
Two-roomed 1960s city-centre pub offering up to 10 guest ales from micros and regionals at weekends. Beer festivals are held regularly, with many beers on gravity from the cellar. More than 100 international bottled beers are stocked. Darts and dominoes are played in the bar. A pop quiz is hosted on Tuesday, general knowledge quiz on Wednesday and live music on Thursday and Saturday. Pub food is available Sunday and Monday; Italian-style pizzas Tuesday to Saturday. ❀◐◑♣●⁂

Globe

43 Silver Street, LE1 5EU
✪ 11-11 (midnight Fri & Sat); 12-10.30 Sun
☎ (0116) 262 9819
Everards Beacon, Sunchaser, Tiger, Original, seasonal beers; guest beers ⊞
More than 30 years ago this city-centre pub was hailed as Everards' first pub to return to a full real ale range after seven years as keg only. Major renovations in 2000 moved the bar to the centre of the pub. There is a snug and gas lighting throughout (electric too). An upstairs room is available for meetings. Leicester CAMRA first met here in 1974. Bar meals and snacks are served until 7pm. A warm welcome awaits from the landlord and staff. ◑⊟♿⇌⊞

Old Horse

98 London Road, LE2 1NE (on A6 opp Victoria Park)
✪ 11-11.30 (midnight Fri & Sat); 11-11 Sun
☎ (0116) 2548384 🌐 oldhorsepub.co.uk
Everards Beacon, Sunchaser, Tiger, Original, seasonal beers; guest beers ⊞
This 19th-century coaching inn was immortalised by Michael Green in The Art of Coarse Rugby. It is popular with all sections of the community including students and the local church choir. Women can leave their partners in the 'man creche' where they 'will look after him while you go shopping'! Lots of interesting bric-a-brac hangs from ceilings. The large garden features owls and a Tardis. CAMRA members receive a 15 per cent discount on beer. ❀◐◑♿⊞(31,31A)♣●P⁂

Pub 🏆

12 New Walk, LE1 6TF (opp council offices)
✪ 12-11 (midnight Fri & Sat); 12-6 Sun
🌐 thepubleicester.co.uk
Beowulf Dragon Smoke Stout; Oakham Inferno, Bishops Farewell; guest beers ⊞
Behind the small frontage lies a warm, welcoming interior with a modern bar offering a wide range of micro-brewery ales and continental draught and bottles. The pub is home to Leicester morris men and a favourite with rugby and football fans. LocAle breweries often feature among the 15 handpulls supporting up to 12 changing guests. Food is served lunchtimes Monday to Saturday and evenings Tuesday to Saturday. ◐◑♿⇌

Salmon

19 Butt Close Lane, LE1 4QA
✪ 12-8; closed Sun ☎ (0116) 2532301
Beer range varies ⊞
Corner back-street free house with a strong sports following, especially for rugby. There is a large open U-shaped bar offering a selection of varied beers, often from micro-breweries. Lunches are served 12-2.30pm. St Margaret's bus station is nearby. ❀◑⊞●⁂

Shakespeare's Head

Southgates, LE1 5SH
✪ 12-midnight (1am Fri & Sat); 12-11 Sun
☎ (0116) 262 4378
Oakwell Old Tom Mild, Barnsley Bitter ⊞
This two-roomed local was built alongside the underpass in the 1960s and has changed little since then, retaining all the charm of a typical town pub of its era. Two large glass doors lead to an off-sales area with a bar to the left and lounge to the right. Formerly a Shipstones pub, it now sells Oakwell beers at very reasonable prices. A selection of cobs is available on Friday and Saturday, and Sunday lunch is very popular. ◑♿⊞♣

Swan & Rushes

19 Infirmary Square, LE1 5WR
✪ 12-3, 5-11 (midnight Thu); 12-midnight Fri & Sat; 12-11.30 Sun ☎ (0116) 233 9167 🌐 swanandrushes.co.uk
Batemans XB; Oakham JHB, Bishops Farewell, seasonal beers; guest beers ⊞
Comfortable, triangular, two-roomed pub in the city centre with a relaxed atmosphere, filled with breweriana and framed photos on the wall. Up to nine real ales (no nationals) are available or you can choose from the bottled beer menu featuring more than 100 international classics. Several food-linked beer festivals are held each year plus cider and cheese events. Thursday is quiz night and live gigs take place on some Saturdays. Good value home-cooked food is served lunchtimes and Wednesday and Friday evenings. ❀◐◑⊟⊞♣●⁂▯

Tom Hoskins

131 Beaumanor Road, LE4 5QE
✪ 12-11; 11.30-midnight Fri & Sat ☎ (0116) 2669659
Black Sheep Best Bitter; Greene King IPA; Hook Norton Bitter; M&B Mild; guest beers ⊞
Hospitable, two-room, city-suburbs pub catering for the mature drinker. Between four and six ales are always available, including a mild, and if you are hungry there are freshly made cobs. Darts is played in the bar and the pub is very popular with local football and rugby teams. Regular Sunday evening quiz nights are held. ❀⊟♿♣P⁂

Western

70 Western Road, LE3 0GA
✪ 12-3, 5-11; 12-midnight Fri & Sat ☎ (0116) 2545287
Steamin' Billy Tipsy Fisherman, Bitter, Skydiver ⊞**; guest beers** ⊞/Ⓖ
Traditional two-roomed local in a residential location with a bar and lounge, popular with a good mixed clientele of all ages. Old pub signs decorate the walls. Food is served, with a carvery on Sunday. The pub gets busy on match days. ♛❀◑⊟⊞♣⁂

Loughborough

Moon & Bell ✔

6 Wards End, LE11 3HA

9-midnight ☎ (01509) 241504

Greene King Ruddles Best Bitter, Abbot; Marston's Pedigree H

Traditionally styled Wetherspoon venue set in the Grade II-listed Atherstone House, with a warm and welcoming atmosphere. It has a spacious beer garden to the rear, perfect for the summer months. An extensive food menu is available until 10pm every day. A fine selection of guest and house ales, always including a mild, is served to top Cask Marque quality, and frequent ale and cider festivals are hosted. Local CAMRA Mild Pub of the Year 2009 and Town Pub of the Year 2008. Q❀◑♿🚌●⚡

Paget Arms

41 Oxford Street, LE11 5DP

12-midnight ☎ (01509) 266216

Steamin' Billy Bitter, Skydiver; guest beers H/G

Located on a corner at the end of a row of terraced houses, this former Everards' pub has been refurbished and is now one of Steamin Billy's locals. It offers six real ales, with some served by gravity, direct from the cellar. Home-cooked food includes pizzas and doorstep sandwiches. There are two attractive rooms with ample seating, and a large, enclosed garden with a heated, covered area for smokers. Regular beer festivals are held. Old Rosie cider is available. ⌂❀◑⊟♿●⚡

Plough Inn

28 Thorpe Acre Road, LE11 4LF

12-11 (midnight Fri & Sat); 12-10.30 Sun

☎ (01509) 214101

Draught Bass; Jennings Cumberland Ale; Tetley Mild; guest beers H

Probably an early 19th-century building, part of the original Thorpe Acre village, now surrounded by modern houses. The unusual look of the pub is due to a change in road layout that has resulted in the back of the pub adjoining the road. To the 'front' there are gardens and a children's play area. The pub is split level with the bar and front entrance lower than the lounge, which is accessed via steps leading from the road. Live entertainment plays most weekends. ⌂❀⊟🚌(11,12)♣●P⚡

Swan in the Rushes

21 The Rushes, LE11 5BE

11-11 (midnight Fri & Sat); 12-11 Sun ☎ (01509) 217014

swanintherushes.co.uk

Adnams Bitter; Castle Rock Sheriff's Tipple, Harvest Pale, Elsie Mo; guest beers H

Traditional three-room Castle Rock pub comprising two quiet, comfortable rooms and the Charnwood Vaults, a lively bar with a jukebox and wooden bench seating. A constantly changing range of up to six guest beers always includes a mild. Real cider, perry, a limited range of continental bottled and draught beers and a good range of malt whiskies and country wines are also available. Upstairs is a skittle alley and function room that hosts comedy nights, live music and twice yearly beer festivals. ⌂Q☕❀🛏◑⊟♿⇌🚌♣●P⚡

Tap & Mallet

36 Nottingham Road, LE11 1EU

5 (11.30 Sat & Sun)-2am ☎ (01509) 210028

Abbeydale Moonshine; Marston's Burton Bitter; Oakham JHB; guest beers H

Genuine free house specialising in beers from micro-breweries not commonly found in the Loughborough area, plus seasonal brews from Abbeydale and Oakham. The interior has a large single room split into two distinct drinking areas – a public bar with pool table, darts and boxed games, and a quieter lounge area that can be partitioned off for functions. Outside there is a large, secluded lawned garden and patio area with children's play equipment and pets' corner. Thatchers cider is available. ⌂❀⇌🚌♣●⚡

Market Bosworth

Olde Red Lion Hotel

1 Park Street, CV13 0LL SK406031

11 (10 Wed & Sat)-11; 11-10.30 Sun ☎ (01455) 291713

redlionmarketbosworth.co.uk

Banks's Bitter; Jennings Sneck Lifter; Marston's Pedigree; guest beers H

The Olde Red Lion Hotel prides itself on providing a wide range of real ales, home-cooked food and en-suite B&B accommodation. More than 400 years old, it remains very traditional with a cosy atmosphere, original oak beams and an open fireplace. Excellent food is from local suppliers and home-cooked. The first Sunday of the month is quiz night. Smokers have a heated area outside. The pub opens early on Wednesday and Saturday market days. ⌂❀🛏◑♿🚌(153)♣P⚡

Market Harborough

Admiral Nelson

49 Nelson Street, LE16 9AX

12-2, 5-midnight; 12-midnight Fri & Sat; 12-11 Sun

☎ (07999) 655550

Wells Eagle IPA, Bombardier; guest beers H

Welcoming, friendly locals' pub, built in 1900, situated a short stroll from the centre of the historic market town. Just off the beaten track, this pub is the town's best kept secret, offering a lounge with TV (where they like their rugby) and bar with darts, pool, juke-box and another TV. Home-cooked food is served Monday-Saturday lunchtimes. A function room is available. Outside is a heated and covered smoking area with seating. Dogs are welcome. ❀◐⊟♣P⚡

Market Overton

Black Bull Inn

2 Teigh Road, Rutland, LE15 7PW (jct of Main Street and Teigh Road)

12-3, 6-11 (midnight Sat); 11.30-5, 7-11 Sun

☎ (01572) 767677 blackbullrutland.co.uk

Black Sheep Best Bitter; Theakston Black Bull Bitter; guest beers H

Situated close to the church, the Black Bull has been a traditional village pub for more than 200 years. It has a cosy, low-beamed bar and a separate dining area serving good quality food with delicious home-made desserts. B&B accommodation is available. It is ideally placed for visitors to nearby Rutland Water. Regular live music and monthly pudding club. ⌂❀🛏◑🚌(RF2)P⚡

Melton Mowbray

Anne of Cleves

12 Burton Street, LE13 1AE (just S of St Mary's Church)

11-11; 12-4, 7-10.30 Sun ☎ (01664) 481336

Everards Tiger, Original, seasonal beers; guest beers 🄷
One of Everards' most historic pubs and an icon for the town. Part of the property dates back to 1327 when it was home to monks. The house was gifted to Anne of Cleves by Henry VIII as part of her divorce settlement. It is now a popular and busy hostelry following a sympathetic conversion and restoration of the building, with stone-flagged floors, exposed timber roof beams and wall tapestries. The building is said to be haunted and psychic research evenings feature regularly. Up to three guest ales may be available.
⛰Q❀◑≠🚌P⌐

Kettleby Cross ✔
Wilton Road, LE13 0UJ (opp public library)
☉ 9-midnight ☎ (01664) 485310
Greene King IPA, Abbot; Marston's Pedigree 🄷
Standing close to the bridge over the nearby River Eye, and named after the cross that once directed travellers towards Ab Kettleby, this is Wetherspoon's flagship 'green' pub, with numerous energy-saving design features including a prominent wind turbine on the roof. There are 10 handpumps on the long bar, with five regular beers supplemented by up to five changing guests, often from local brewers Langton and Grainstore.
❀◑♿≠🚌⌐

Mountsorrel

Swan Inn
10 Loughborough Road, LE12 7AT
☉ 12-2.30, 5.30-11; 12-11 Sat; 12-3, 7-10.30 Sun
☎ (0116) 2302340 🌐 the-swan-inn.eu
Black Sheep Best Bitter; Greene King Ruddles County; Theakston XB, Old Peculier; guest beers 🄷
Traditional 17th-century, Grade II-listed coaching inn, under the present ownership since 1990. The split-level interior has open fires, stone floors and low ceilings, and includes a small dining area with a polished wood floor. Good quality, interesting food is cooked to order, with the menu changing weekly. Outside is a secluded riverside garden with moorings. Self-contained accommodation is available. ⛰❀🛏◑🚌P⌐

Oadby

Cow & Plough
Stoughton Farm Park, Gartree Road, LE2 2FB
☉ 12-3, 5-11; 12-11 summer ☎ (0116) 2720852
🌐 steamin-billy.co.uk
Fuller's London Pride; Steamin' Billy Scrum Down, Bitter, Skydiver; guest beers 🄷
Situated in a converted farm building with a conservatory, this pub is decked out with breweriana. It is home to Steamin' Billy beers, named after the owner's now departed Jack Russell who features on the logo and pump clips. All beers are brewed at Tower Brewery. A mild and Sheppy's cider are always available. A large restaurant has been added in the former Victorian dairy buildings.
Q👶❀◑⊟♿♣🍎P⌐

Wheel Inn
99 London Road, LE2 5DP
☉ 12-midnight; 12-10.30 Sun ☎ (0116) 271 2231
Draught Bass; Marston's Pedigree; guest beers 🄷
Sports-oriented community pub where there is always something going on. As well as darts, dominoes and skittles teams there are football, cricket, golf and fishing matches, casino nights, jazz evenings, train trips, cycle rides and anything else the landlord and customers can think of. Tasty home-cooked food and an extensive selection of wines and spirits add to the appeal. The Leicester bus stops outside. ❀☾⊟🚌(31)♣P⌐

Oakham

Grainstore 🏆
Station Approach, Rutland, LE15 6RE (next to Oakham station)
☉ 11-11 (midnight Fri & Sat); 12-11 Sun ☎ (01572) 770065
🌐 grainstorebrewery.com
Grainstore Rutland Panther, Cooking, Triple B, Ten Fifty, seasonal ales 🄷
Brewery tap showcasing the Grainstore's award-winning bitters and milds. The spacious open-plan bar has wooden seats and benches. The building is a converted Midland Railway grainstore, backing on to Oakham Station, with the two upper floors forming the brewery. Brewery tours are on offer but must be booked in advance. Take-out beers are stocked. The annual Rutland Beer Festival is held over the August bank holiday. Good honest pub food is served lunchtimes only. Occasional live music sessions are held. Q❀☾♿≠🚌♣P⌐

Wheatsheaf
2-4 Northgate, Rutland, LE15 6QS
☉ 11.30-3, 6-11; 12-3, 7-10.30 Sun ☎ (01572) 756797
🌐 rutnet.co.uk/Wheatsheaf
Adnams Bitter; Everards Beacon, Tiger; guest beers 🄷
An attractive thatched pub opposite the church, near the market place and medieval castle. It has a traditional cosy feel with an open fire and comfortable chairs. The building is listed and has some steps between levels which may cause difficulties for wheelchair users. A small, enclosed prize-winning garden has dining and smoking areas. Food is served at lunchtime. Two guest ales are usually available. ⛰Q👶❀☾⊟≠🚌⌐

White Lion Hotel
30 Melton Road, Rutland, LE15 6AY
☉ 12-3 (not Mon), 6-midnight; 12-3, 6-midnight Sun
☎ (01572) 724844
Fuller's London Pride; Taylor Landlord; Wells Bombardier; guest beers 🄷
Les and Maria are landlords from the old school, with Maria doing all the cooking and Les spruced up in a collar and tie doing the waiting. Traditional home-cooked meals come in one size only – large! The pub is directly opposite the thatched cottage that was home to Rutland's shortest man, Jeffrey Hudson. The building is on different levels and has a real fire. Dominoes and quiz teams compete weekly and the joanna sits gathering dust.
⛰Q🛏◑≠🚌♣P▯

Old Dalby

Crown Inn
Debdale Hill, LE14 3LF
☉ 5-11 Mon; 12-3, 6-11 Tue-Thu; 12-1am Fri & Sat; 12-10.30 Sun ☎ (01664) 823134
Belvoir Beaver; Castle Rock Harvest Pale; guest beer 🄷
Dating from 1590, this charming ivy-clad pub is situated in delightful gardens. It has a quirky selection of rooms, including the original brewing

room, now used as the bar, with stone floors and real ale casks on the back stillage. The extensive bar and restaurant menu uses local produce. The outdoor pentanque court is popular during the summer months. ♨Q✿◐⊟♣P⊱

Sample Cellar 🏆
Belvoir Brewery, Station Road, LE14 3NQ
⌚ 12-10 ☎ (01664) 823455
Belvoir Star Mild, Beaver Bitter, seasonal beers ⊞
The brick-fronted Sample Cellar on the outskirts of the village incorporates a bar, visitors' centre and function room. The comfortable, spacious interior, filled with brewing artefacts, has a traditional bar area and there is even room for long alley skittles and a bar billiard table. Two large internal windows provide views into the brewery. A full menu is served daily, with the focus on good wholesome food made with local produce. ✿◐♿♣P⊱

Queniborough

Britannia
47 Main Street, LE7 3DB
⌚ 12-2.30, 6-11; 12-11 Sun ☎ (0116) 260 5675
M&B Brew XI; Taylor Landlord; guest beers ⊞
Two-roomed, comfortable village local with a traditional bar and restaurant leading off the lounge. Both rooms have an open fire providing welcome warmth on cold winter evenings. Food is available seven days a week. Old pictures of the village are on the lounge wall. Guest beers come from the Punch list. ♨✿◐⊟🚌♣P⊱

Quorn

Manor House
Woodhouse Road, LE12 8AL
⌚ 12-11 (midnight Sat); 12-10 Sun ☎ (01509) 413416
🌐 themanorhouseatquorn.co.uk
Batemans XB; Draught Bass; guest beers ⊞
Built in 1899 by the Great Central Railway, the Manor House was designed to serve passengers arriving at Quorn and Woodhouse Station, which it still does today. It was refurbished in 2005 and now has an open-plan bar and award-winning restaurant with a separate function/meeting room available to hire. From the beer garden you can watch the preserved steam- and diesel-hauled trains pass by. The pub recently became a free house, with up to four guest beers available, usually from local breweries.
✿◐♿⛺⇌(Great Central Railway)🚌P⊱

Sewstern

Blue Dog
Main Street, NG33 5RQ
⌚ 11-11; 12-10.30 Sun ☎ (01476) 860097
Greene King IPA; guest beers ⊞
Friendly and welcoming pub west of the village, handy for walkers at the southern end of the Viking Way. The unusual name reflects the tradition of local farm workers on the Tollemache estate being paid partly in blue tokens. The 300-year-old building was once a war hospital and has a ghost – a drummer boy called Albert. Guest ales often come from local breweries and a beer festival is held in late May. A popular fish and chip menu is available on Wednesday evening.
♨Q🐴✿◐⛺🚌(55)♣P⊱

Shackerstone

Rising Sun
Church Road, CV13 6NN (3 miles E of Twycross, 3 miles SW of Ibstock) SK374066
⌚ 10.30-2.30, 6-midnight; 11.30-midnight Sun
☎ (01827) 880215 🌐 risingsunpub.com
Marston's Pedigree; Taylor Landlord; guest beers ⊞
A family-run free house since 1987 with a large, traditional wood-panelled bar area. The separate sports room has pool and Sky TV. Children are welcome in the conservatory and attractive beer garden. Two guest ales change regularly and Old Rosie real cider is sold. Meals are served daily in the bar and barn-conversion restaurant, with Sunday lunches always popular. The Battlefield Railway and Ashby Canal are nearby. Walkers are welcome. Regular charity fundraising walks support Guide Dogs for the Blind.
♨🐴✿◐⊟♿🚌(153)♣●P⊱

Shawell

White Swan
Main Street, LE17 6AG
⌚ closed Mon; 11 (5 winter)-11 Tue-Sat; 11-11 (12-7 winter) Sun ☎ (01788) 860357
Brakspear Bitter, Oxford Gold; guest beer ⊞
A cosy village inn with a friendly ambience in a quiet location. Built in 1865, this building has always been a public house. The main bar welcomes the visitor, with intimate seating areas and a real fire in winter. The original wood-beamed ceiling remains in the restaurant, where an extensive menu of pub classics is offered.
♨Q✿🛏◐♿P⊱▯

Shearsby

Chandlers Arms
Fenny Lane, LE17 6PL (close to A5199)
⌚ 12-3 (not Mon), 7 (6 Fri)-11; 12-4, 6-11 Sat; 12-4, 7-10.30 Sun ☎ (0116) 2478384 🌐 chandlersatshearsby.co.uk
Dow Bridge Acris; guest beers ⊞
Classic, quaint old country pub overlooking the village green. Popular with walkers, cyclists, diners and visitors from the city, it also has strong local support. It was the first pub in CAMRA's Leicester Branch to be accredited to the LocAle scheme. Micro-brewery beers are always on the bar, often locally sourced. Draught cider is available in summer. No food is served on Sunday evening or Monday. Leicester CAMRA County Pub of the Year 2010. ✿◐🚌♣●

Somerby

Stilton Cheese
Main Street, LE14 2PZ
⌚ 12-3, 6-11; 12-3, 7-10.30 Sun ☎ (01664) 454394
Grainstore Ten Fifty; Marston's Pedigree; Tetley Bitter; guest beers ⊞
Late 16th-century pub built in local ironstone, like most of the buildings in the village. The interior comprises two bars and a function room. Tall customers will note the wide range of pump clips on the low beams as they bang their heads on them. A popular and lively village pub, booking is advised for food. ♨Q🐴✿◐🚌(113)●P

South Kilworth

White Hart

Rugby Road, LE17 6DN
12-2.30 (not Wed), 5.30-11; 12-3, 6-11 Sat; 12-6, 7-11 Sun
☎ (01858) 575416
Banks's Bitter; Ringwood Bitter; guest beer Ⓗ
Former coaching inn on the Rugby to Market Harborough road with links back to Oliver Cromwell and the Battle of Naseby in 1645. The atmospheric L-shaped interior has low ceilings, open fires and a separate dining room. Good pub food is served, made with locally-sourced ingredients. The three beers include a guest from the Marston's portfolio. ♨❀◐◑🚌♣P⅟

Stoke Golding

White Swan

High Street, CV13 6HE SP397973
12-2.30 (not Mon) & 6.30- (11 Mon) midnight; 12-midnight Fri-Sun ☎ (01455) 212313
Adnams Bitter, Broadside; Everards Tiger, Original; guest beer Ⓗ
The Swan is situated close to the site where King Henry VII was crowned after the Battle of Bosworth. It was originally built over 200 years ago for the navvies employed on the construction of the nearby Ashby Canal. It remains a relatively unspoilt two-room village local. The pub is known for its money raising activities for village charities. The traditional British meals produced by the licensee are home-made where possible and are both good value and generously portioned.
♨Q❀◐◑🚌(86)♣P⅟

Swinford

Chequers ✔

High Street, LE17 6BL
7-11 Mon; 12-2.30, 6-11; 12-3, 7-11 Sun
☎ (01788) 860318 🌐 chequersswinford.co.uk
Adnams Bitter; guest beers Ⓗ
This open-plan, family-friendly village local was once separate cottages. The drinking area has a low ceiling, wood floor and wood-burning stove for winter nights. Traditional skittles is played in the bar and old pictures of village life adorn the walls. Outside, a large garden with children's play area provides enough space for the annual beer festival in July. The 16th-century Stanford Hall is nearby, with its caravan park, extensive gardens and museum. ♨❀◐◑▲🚌♣P⅟

Swithland

Griffin Inn

174 Main Street, LE12 8TJ
11-11 (10.30 Sun) ☎ (01509) 890535
🌐 griffininnswithland.co.uk
Everards Beacon, Tiger, Original; guest beers Ⓗ
Friendly and welcoming local with three comfortable rooms. Set in the heart of Charnwood Forest, there are many walking and cycling routes nearby. Swithland Reservoir, Bradgate Park and the preserved Great Central Railway are also close. Alongside the regular food menu, light snacks are available every afternoon including Melton Mowbray pork pies. Guest ales are chosen from Everards Old English Ale Club, with three regularly stocked in addition to the Everards regulars.
♨Q❀◐◑♿▲🚌♣P⅟

Syston

Queen Victoria

76 High Street, LE7 1GQ
12 (2 Mon & Tue)-11; 12-midnight Fri & Sat; 12-11 Sun
☎ (0116) 2605750
Everards Sunchaser, Beacon, Tiger; guest beers Ⓗ
This large bar has benefited from the addition of a very cosy snug, plus a separate restaurant to the side of the pub. The large patio and garden area are popular with families in summer. Guest beers come from the Everards Old English Ale Club, often including a Brunswick Brewery beer. There is plenty of street parking nearby. ❀◐◑🚌♣P⅟

Thringstone

George & Dragon

Ashby Rd, LE67 8UH
9am-3 (not Mon), 5.45-11; 10-11 Sat; 12-11.30 Sun
☎ (01530) 222282 🌐 georgeandragon.co.uk
Black Sheep Best Bitter; Greene King Abbot; guest beer Ⓗ
Separate dining and drinking areas allow this country pub to cater for families while remaining a community local. The pub serves quality beer, wine and food including good value breakfasts (eat in or take away), regular themed food nights and a Sunday lunchtime carvery. Occasional beer festivals are hosted. Live music plays on Saturday and quiz night is Sunday. ♨❀◐◑P

Thrussington

Blue Lion

5 Rearsby Road, LE7 4UD
12-2.30 (not Wed), 5.30-11; 12-3, 6-11 Sat; 12-3, 7-10.30 Sun ☎ (01664) 424266
Marston's Burton Bitter, Pedigree, seasonal beers; guest beers Ⓗ
Late 18th-century rural inn, once two cottages. Good value pub grub, using meat supplied by the local butcher, is served in the comfortable lounge. However, the bar is the heart of the pub, where locals meet for high-pressure darts and dominoes matches, kept under control by licensees Mandy and Bob. ♨Q❀◐◑▲🚌(128)♣P

Thurlaston

Elephant & Castle 🏆

26 Main Street, LE9 7TP SP502990
12-2.30 (not Mon or Tue), 6-11; 12-3, 7-10.30 Sun
☎ (01455) 888213
Everards Beacon, Tiger, Original; guest beers Ⓗ
The licensees of this CAMRA-award-winning village local offer the perfect combination of fine real ales, great food and friendly service. Also winner of the Midlands Great British Pub Best-Kept Cellar Award, its occasional themed mini beer festivals are highly popular. Excellent value home cooking includes speciality pies. Freshly caught Grimsby fish is served on Friday evening, and Sunday lunches and mid-week special offers are a treat. The garden and patios have seating areas. Walking and cycling routes pass by. A free Wi-Fi hotspot.
Q❀◐◑♿🚌(148)♣P⅟

Thurmaston

Harrow Inn

635 Melton Road, LE4 8EB

⏲ 11-11.30 (midnight Fri & Sat) ☎ (0116) 2602240
Belvoir Star Mild, Star Bitter; Taylor Landlord Ⓗ
A classic community local with local ales, live entertainment, live sports and traditional bar games. All are welcome to share the jovial and relaxed atmosphere. Good value food is served lunchtimes and evenings. The pub is the home of Glastonbudget Music Festival which features 130 bands from across Europe and nearly 200 real ales and ciders. It is also the home of the Tie Club which meets regularly and raises money for children with special needs. ❀◑♣P

Uppingham

Crown Hotel
19 High Street East, Rutland, LE15 9PY
⏲ 11-11; 12-10.30 Sun ☎ (01572) 822302
🌐 thecrownrutland.co.uk
Everards Tiger, Beacon, Original, seasonal beers; guest beers Ⓗ
A warm welcome is assured at this traditional market town pub which offers good quality, reasonably priced home-cooked food in the bar and restaurant. Dogs are permitted in the bar area. The licensee has been awarded Everards Gold Master of Beer status and hosts regular beer festivals in April and October. Live music plays monthly or more often. The pub is home to the local dominoes team. En-suite accommodation is available. ❀◑♿(RF1,12,747)♣P

Walton on the Wolds

Anchor Inn
2 Loughborough Road, LE12 8HT
⏲ 12-3 (not Mon), 7-11; 12-10.30 Sun ☎ (01509) 880018
Adnams Bitter; Black Sheep Best Bitter; Taylor Landlord; guest beer Ⓗ
Situated in the centre of a small village within easy reach of Leicester and Nottingham via the A46. The pub is a popular venue for walkers who stop for a well-earned home-cooked lunch in front of the log fire. There is a menu to suit all tastes plus an extensive specials board. Outside is an elevated seating area to the front and a garden and large car park to the rear. En-suite B&B accommodation is available. ❀◑P

Whitwick

Three Horseshoes ★
11 Leicester Road, LE67 5GN
⏲ 11-3, 6.30-11; 12-2, 7-10.30 Sun ☎ (01530) 83731
Draught Bass; Marston's Pedigree Ⓗ
Listed on CAMRA's National Inventory of Historic Pub Interiors, the nickname 'Polly's' is thought to come from a former landlady, Polly Burton. The pub was originally two separate buildings but now has two rooms. To the left is a long bar with quarry-tiled floor and open fires, wooden bench seating and pre-war fittings; to the right is a similarly furnished small snug. Q♣

Wymeswold

Three Crowns ✔
45 Far Street, LE12 6TZ
⏲ 12-11 ☎ (01509) 880153
Adnams Bitter; Marston's Pedigree; guest beers Ⓗ
Late-18th-century pub standing opposite the church. This friendly village local features a beamed ceiling in the bar and a split level snug/lounge. Guest beers are usually from local breweries including Castle Rock, Belvoir or Nottingham. Evening meals are available Thursday-Saturday. There is a regular daytime bus service. Q❀◑♿♣P

Olde Red Lion Hotel, Market Bosworth

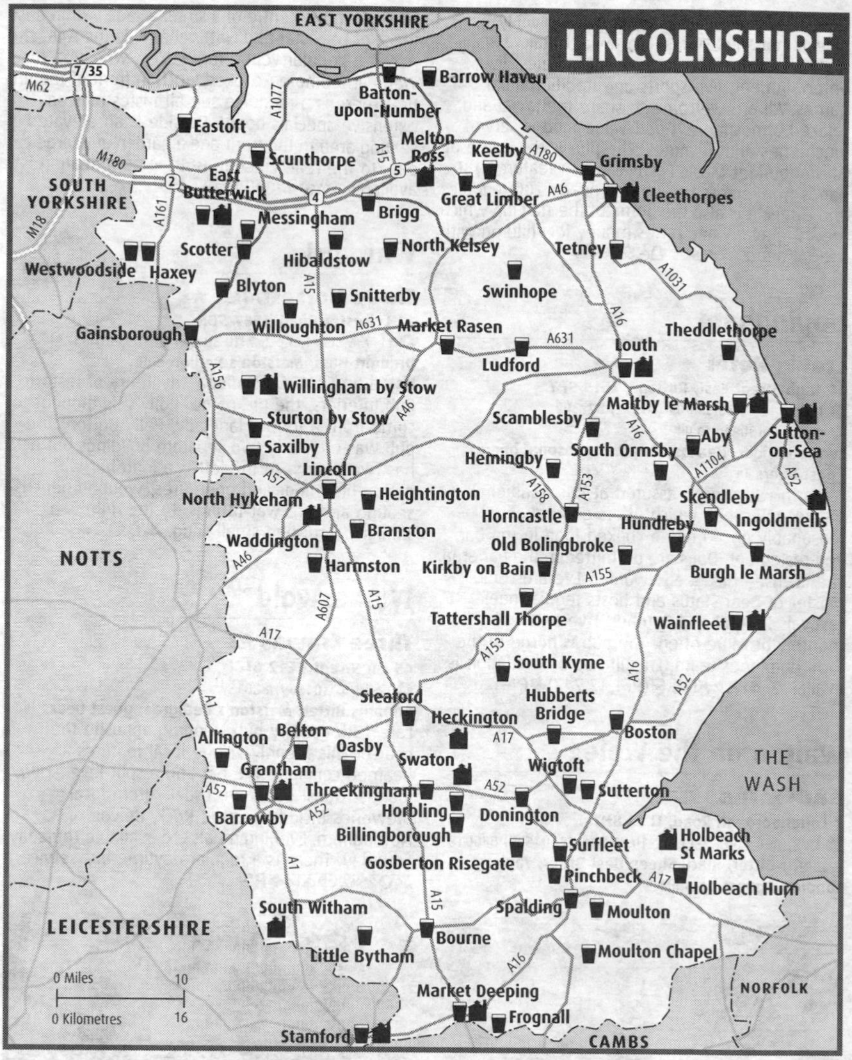

Aby

Railway Tavern

Main Road, LN13 0DR (off A16 via S Thoresby)

⌚ 12-midnight (closed Tue winter) ☎ (01507) 480676

Beer range varies Ⓗ

This cosy village pub is worth searching out for its varied beer list and excellent food. Plenty of railway memorabilia includes the original Aby platform sign, and even the lighting is railway-oriented. A real community pub with a warm welcome for all, it has an open fire and a Wednesday quiz night. Dogs are permitted and there are plenty of good walks close by. Food is usually available until 8.30pm. ⛫Q✿◑♿▲♣P⇌

Allington

Welby Arms ✔

The Green, NG32 2EA (1 mile from A1 Gonerby Moor jct or A52)

⌚ 12-2.30, 6-11; 12-10.30 Sun ☎ (01400) 281361

Draught Bass; Jennings Cumberland Ale; John Smith's Bitter; Taylor Landlord; guest beers Ⓗ

A welcoming and friendly traditional village pub. Six well-kept real ales accompany a splendid selection of bar snacks or full meals in the comfortable restaurant. Morris dancers visit during the summer, and the monthly quiz (held on the third Monday of the month) attracts entrants from afar. There are also three AA 3-star rooms and ample parking. ⛫Q✿⛿◑♿P

Barrow Haven

Haven Inn

Ferry Road, DN19 7EX (approx 1½ miles E of Barrow-upon-Humber) TA063230

⌚ 11.30-11 ☎ (01469) 530247 🌐 thehaveninn.co.uk

Black Sheep Best Bitter; Taylor Landlord; Tom Wood's Best Bitter Ⓗ

The Haven Inn was built in 1730 as a coaching inn for travellers using the nearby ferry, and has remained a place renowned for hospitality, good food and comfortable lodgings ever since. Full of character, the bars have traditional, beamed ceilings, and a warm welcome awaits the weary traveller by the open fire in the lounge. Themed food events such as pie night and stew/curry night make this a great pub for both good food and good beer. ⌂❀⇄◑◑⊟≑♣●P⁴–

Barrowby

White Swan 🏆 ✔

High Road, NG32 1BH

✪ 12-midnight (1am Fri-Sat) ☎ (01476) 562375

Adnams Bitter, Broadside, guests beers Ⓗ

Voted Grantham CAMRA Country Pub of the Year for the second year running. This cosy two-roomed traditional village local is situated close to the A1 and A52. The busy public bar plays host to darts and crib teams. There is also a pool table. The lounge is a quiet room with comfortable seating and an open fire. There is a regular quiz on the first Sunday of the month and occasional live music. ⌂Q❀◑⊟⊟(6)♣P⁴–

Barton-upon-Humber

Sloop Inn

81 Waterside Road, DN18 5BA (follow Humber Bridge viewing signs)

✪ 11-11; 12-10.30 Sun ☎ (01652) 637287

Tom Wood's Shepherd's Delight, Bomber County; guest beers Ⓗ

Welcoming pub with nautical-themed decoration and areas named after parts of a ship. The central bar serves a games section with a pool table and darts, plus a drinking/dining area and two further rooms. Real ales from the local Tom Wood Highwood Brewery are on offer plus rotating guests. A good range of home-cooked food, with many specials including the pub's own sausages, is popular with locals and walkers. The Far Ings Nature Reserve, Waterside Visitor Centre and Humber Bridge are nearby. Q❀◑◑♿▲≑⊟(250,350)♣P

Wheatsheaf

3 Holydyke, DN18 5PS

✪ 12-11.30 (12.30am Fri & Sat; 11 Sun) ☎ (01652) 633292

Batemans XB; Black Sheep Best Bitter; Theakston Best Bitter; Wells Bombardier; guest beers Ⓗ

Occupying a prominent position on the main road through Barton, this pub dates back to the 18th century, with a list of former licensees going back to 1791. It has an unspoilt, traditional atmosphere, with regulars enjoying classic bar games of dominoes and crib. The pub has a bar, snug and large drinking/dining area, plus a summer beer garden and private car park. A range of excellent food is served at lunchtimes and in the evenings. ⌂Q❀◑◑≑⊟(250,350)♣P⁴–

Belton

Crown

Church Lane, Churchtown, DN9 1PA (off A161, behind church)

✪ 1 (12 Sat & Sun)-11 ☎ (01427) 872834

Bradfield Farmers Blonde; Jennings Cumberland Ale, Cocker Hoop; Marston's Pedigree; guest beers Ⓗ

Difficult to find but well worth the effort, this hidden gem always offers six cask ales. A rotating ale from the nearby Glentworth Brewery and one other guest ale are on offer alongside the four regular beers. Quizzes, live music and traditional pub games are enjoyed at this friendly local, which has a games room at the rear. The Crown held its first beer festival in summer 2009, and more are planned in the future. ⌂Q❀⊟▲⊟(399)♣P⁴–▯

Billingborough

Fortescue Arms

27 High Street, NG34 0QB

✪ 12-3, 5.30-11; 12-midnight Sat & Sun ☎ (01529) 240228

Adnams Bitter; Everards Tiger; Greene King Abbot; guest beer Ⓗ

Fine Grade II-listed inn with an interesting multi-roomed interior and a rustic feel. The pub is also popular with diners, with a large patio to the rear providing a pleasant outdoor drinking area. The guest beer is sometimes from a local brewery. Nearby is the site of Sempringham Abbey and its monument to Gwenllian, daughter of the Prince of Wales, who was confined to the priory in the 12th century. Stone from the abbey was used to build part of the inn. ⌂Q❀◑◑⊟⊟P⁴–

Blyton

Black Horse

93 High Street, DN21 3JX

✪ closed Mon; 11.45-midnight ☎ (01427) 628277

Great Newsome Sleck Dust; guest beers Ⓗ

This is a 250-year-old establishment selling 'real ale, real food from a real pub'. It is a very well appointed and comfortable local but with a clean, fresh twist, serving good, home-made food made with fresh local meat, fish and vegetables prepared in a five-star-hygiene-rated kitchen. Guest beers often come from Lincolnshire's micro-breweries. Pool is played and darts and quiz nights are regular events. The pub has a real community feel while remaining very welcoming to visitors. ⌂Q❀◑◑⊟♿⊟♣●P⁴–

Boston

Coach & Horses

86 Main Ridge, PE21 6SY

✪ 4 (12 Sat & Sun)-midnight ☎ (01205) 362301

Batemans Dark Mild, XB, GHA Ⓗ

INDEPENDENT BREWERIES

- **8 Sail** Heckington (NEW)
- **Bacchus** Sutton-on-Sea (NEW)
- **Batemans** Wainfleet
- **Blue Bell** Holbeach St Marks
- **Blue Cow** South Witham
- **Brewsters** Grantham
- **DarkTribe** East Butterwick
- **Fulstow** Louth
- **Grafters** Willingham by Stow
- **Highwood/Tom Wood** Melton Ross
- **Hopshackle** Market Deeping
- **Leila Cottage** Ingoldmells
- **Malt B** Maltby le Marsh
- **Melbourn** Stamford
- **Newby Wyke** Grantham
- **Oldershaw** Grantham
- **Poachers** North Hykeham
- **Riverside** Wainfleet
- **Swaton** Swaton
- **Willy's** Cleethorpes

Well worth the short walk out of the town centre. The open-plan lounge includes tables with candles and soft lighting throughout. The pub hosts pool, darts, poker, football and quiz teams and is popular with football supporters. There is regular entertainment at weekends. 🔥❀♿♣⚟⊓

Cowbridge

Horncastle Road, PE22 7AX (on B1183, N of Boston)
⌚ 11 (7 Mon)-11 ☎ (01205) 362597
Greene King Old Speckled Hen; guest beers Ⓗ
Just out of town, this pub is popular with drinkers as well as diners. It divides into three main areas: the public bar is a no-nonsense drinking and darts environment with a large array of football scarves, the smaller lounge is cosy with an open fire, opening out into a restaurant that serves excellent freshly cooked food. The pub is frequented by members of Boston golf club, which is just across the road. 🔥Q♘❀◐◗⊟♿♣P⚟

Eagle

144 West Street, PE21 8RE (300m from railway station)
⌚ 11 (11.30 Thu)-11; 11-midnight Fri & Sat; 12-3, 6-10.30 Sun
☎ (01205) 361116
Banks's Bitter; Castle Rock Harvest Pale; guest beers Ⓗ
Part of the Castle Rock chain, the Eagle is known as the real ale pub of Boston. This two-roomed, friendly hostelry has an L-shaped bar with a large TV screen for big sports events. The small, cosy lounge has an open fire. The pub stocks a wide range of guest ales, usually including one or more Castle Rock beers, and at least one cider. A function room upstairs is home to Boston Folk Club on Monday. Thursday is quiz night – allegedly the hardest in town. 🔥❀⊟⇶🚌♣🍎⚟

Kings Arms

13 Horncastle Road, PE21 9BU
⌚ 5-11; 12-1am Sat & Sun ☎ (01205) 364296
Batemans Dark Mild, XB, Salem Porter, XXXB; Draught Bass; guest beer Ⓗ
This delightful, mid-18th-century, Grade II-listed, red brick and pantile pub was constructed to slake the thirsts of the navvies digging the Maud Foster drain. The internal layout has been altered over the years and now has a single bar and two snug dining rooms (for Sunday lunch only). The beers are on traditional stillage in the original and immaculate brick vaulted cellar. Across the drain from the pub is the tallest working windmill in the country. Visit them both! 🔥❀🛏◐♿⇶🚌♣P⚟

Bourne

Smith's

25 North Street, PE10 9AE
⌚ 10-11 (midnight Fri & Sat); 12-11 Sun ☎ (01778) 426819
🌐 smithsofbourne.co.uk
Fuller's London Pride; Ufford Ales White Hart; guest beers Ⓗ
Winner of a CAMRA/English Heritage award for an imaginative conversion of a three-storey family grocer's shop to produce a multi-roomed public house. It has a large, well-equipped patio, and a beer garden with a grassed area for children. It opens early for breakfast 8 (9 Sun)-11am. Evening meals are Monday-Thursday 6-9pm only. Wednesday is wine night, Thursday is real ale jug night, there is live music on Saturday evenings, and a quiz on alternate Sundays. The annual beer festival is in July. 🔥Q♘❀◐◗⊟♿🚌(101,102)⚟

Branston

Waggon & Horses

High Street, LN4 1NB
⌚ 12-2 (not Mon), 5-midnight; 12-1am Fri & Sat; 12-midnight Sun ☎ (01522) 791356 🌐 branstonwaggon.co.uk
Batemans XB; John Smith's Bitter; Taylor Landlord; guest beers Ⓗ
A welcoming community pub in the heart of the village. The public bar is home to darts and pool teams – spot the moose head if you can. The comfortable lounge hosts Monday quiz night, Tuesday jam night and live entertainment on Saturday. Regular fundraising events are held. Excellent home-cooked food is available until 8pm on weekdays and 6pm at weekends. The Waggon now offers B&B so getting home need not be an issue. Bikers are welcome. ❀🛏◐◗⊟🚌(2)♣P⚟

Brigg

Black Bull ✔

3 Wrawby Street, DN20 8JH
⌚ 11-3, 7-11.30 Mon; 11-11 ☎ (01652) 652153
John Smith's Bitter; guest beers Ⓗ
This popular, friendly pub in the middle of a small market town, run by the second generation of a local family, gets busy on market days (Thu and Sat). The guest beers change frequently. When available, Fulstow Sergeant's Bitter is a guest. Food is served 11.30-2pm Monday-Tuesday, 11.30-7pm Wednesday-Saturday and 12-2pm Sunday. Quiz night is Tuesday. Brigg can be reached by bus from Scunthorpe, Barton and Doncaster, and by train on Saturday on the Cleethorpes-Sheffield line.
❀◐⇶🚌(909)P⚟

White Hart

57 Bridge Street, DN20 8NS
⌚ 11-11 (11.30 Sat & Sun) ☎ (01652) 654887
Jennings Cumberland Ale; guest beers Ⓗ
The pub is one of the older Brigg buildings. Its beer garden runs alongside the old River Ancholme. It is traditionally decorated and has some old photos of Brigg. The lounge bar is at the front of the pub, with a pool table in the rear bar area. The regular beer is quite unusual for the area, and the guests are usually seasonal. Food is served lunchtime Monday to Sunday and early evening Monday to Friday. Quiz night is Thursday at 9pm.
🔥❀◐◗⇶🚌(909)P⚟

Burgh le Marsh

Red Lion

East End, PE24 5LW
⌚ 11-midnight; 12-11 Sun ☎ (01754) 810582
Batemans XB; guest beers Ⓗ
This low-ceilinged pub, located off the main road, offers constantly changing beers in addition to the regular session beer. The landlord is enthusiastic about his ales and for a small pub there is quite a high weekly turnover of casks. One of the rare pubs nowadays not to provide food, the Red Lion concentrates instead on beer quality.
🔥♘❀⊟⛺🚌♣P

Cleethorpes

No.1 Refreshment Room

1 Station Approach, DN35 8AX
⌚ 12-midnight (7 Mon) ☎ (01472) 691707

Everards Tiger; Hancock's HB; guest beer Ⓗ
Located in the original entrance to Cleethorpes station, this convivial local has a main lounge and a smaller bar, with an area off overlooking the platform, serviced from a central servery. An uncovered outside area fronting the street has benches and tables. Quiz night is on a Friday and there is a soul/motown music night on the first Friday of the month. Sunday lunch is served 12-4pm. ❀≹⁻

No.2 Refreshment Room 🏆
Station Approach, DN35 8AX (on station)
⏲ 7.30am-midnight ☎ (07905) 375587
Greene King H&H Olde Trip; Hancock's HB; M&B Mild; Worthington Bitter; guest beers Ⓗ
This small, single-roomed pub with its friendly atmosphere located on the railway station, just a few paces from the seafront promenade, is a favourite of both locals and visitors. Smokers may use the fenced, covered and heated area on the concourse. Thursday is quiz night and there is a free buffet provided on Sunday evenings. ❀≹⁻

Willy's Pub & Brewery
17 Highcliff Road, DN35 8RQ
⏲ 11-11 (2am Fri & Sat) ☎ (01472) 602145
Willy's Original Bitter; guest beers Ⓗ
A beach-view bar that is light and open, this pub also has a micro-brewery on site which may be viewed from inside the pub. A livelier crowd visits at weekends when music is played. There are generally four guest ales plus a guest cider, and a varied selection of bottled beers. The pub is a perennial Guide entrant. Meals are available every lunchtime plus Tuesday and Thursday evenings. There is a covered outdoor area. ❀◐≹🚌(9)🍎⁻

Donington

Black Bull ✔
Marketplace, PE11 4ST
⏲ 11 (12 Sun)-midnight ☎ (01775) 822228
🌐 blackbulldonington.co.uk
John Smith's Bitter; guest beers Ⓗ
Busy local just off the A52. Four handpumps feature a varying selection of guest beers from small brewers as well as larger regionals; Westons cider is on handpump. The comfortable bar has low, beamed ceilings, wooden settles and a cosy fire in winter. The restaurant offers a good choice of reasonably priced evening meals; lunches are served in the bar. Tables in the car park are used for outdoor drinking. Buses run from Boston and Spalding (not Sun). ♨❀◐🚌🍎P⁻

East Butterwick

Dog & Gun
High Street, DN17 3AJ (off A18 at Keadby Bridge E bank) SE837058
⏲ 5 (12 Sat & Sun)-11 ☎ (01724) 782324
DarkTribe Full Ahead, Captain Floyd; John Smith's Bitter Ⓗ
This traditional, small village centre pub dispenses excellent ales, usually two from a range of DarkTribe beers (brewed on site), plus John Smith's Bitter. A dartboard is available and a real fire in winter creates a warm, friendly atmosphere in the small but cosy bar. Families are welcome in the games room (under 18s must leave by 9pm). In summer customers can enjoy good beer and views of the Trent from the riverbank. Assisted wheelchair access is available on request.
♨❀⊟♿⛺🚌(12)♣P⁻

Eastoft

River Don Tavern
Sampson Street, DN17 4PQ (on A161 Goole-Gainsborough road)
⏲ 5-12.30am; closed Tue; 12-1am Sat; 12-12.30am Sun
☎ (01724) 798040
Beer range varies Ⓗ
Welcoming village local on the main road, traditionally styled with ceiling beams, rustic furnishings and black and white photos of village life. Open plan in design, a dividing wall separates the lively drinking area around the bar from a more sedate lounge often used for dining. The pub is renowned for good quality meals, including a Sunday carvery. It offers two rotating real ales (three in summer), generally from Yorkshire, Nottinghamshire and Lincolnshire micros. An annual beer festival is held in summer.
♨❀◐♿🚌(356)♣🍎P⁻

Frognall

Goat
155 Spalding Road, PE6 8SA
⏲ 11-3, 6-11; 12-10.30 Sun ☎ (01778) 347629
🌐 thegoatfrognall.com
Beer range varies Ⓖ
Friendly pub with a low-ceilinged bar, dining area and separate restaurant. Five varying cask ales, mostly from micros, include a low gravity beer and normally a strong dark ale, 6-10%, served direct from the cellar. A large range of single malt whiskies is also stocked. Good quality food is served – last orders for lunch are 2pm and evening meals 9pm. Food is served all day on Sunday. The large garden has a play area for children. A beer festival is held in July/August.
♨Q⛀❀◐♿⛺🚌(22,102)🍎P⊡

Gainsborough

Canute
Silver Street, DN21 2DP (50m S of Market Place)
⏲ 9am-midnight ☎ (01427) 678715
Wells Bombardier; guest beers Ⓗ
A typical lively town-centre pub with between three and five real ales always available. Wells Bombardier is a regular, while beers from the local Springhead and Grafters breweries often feature. TV screens, live music and quiz nights are a part of the pub's week. A wide variety of food is served all day. The pub can get very busy on Friday and Saturday nights and when football is on TV.
⛀❀◐♿P⁻

Eight Jolly Brewers
Ship Court, Silver Street, DN21 2DW
⏲ 11 (12 Sun)-midnight ☎ (07767) 638806
Beer range varies Ⓗ
In the Guide for 15 years, this real ale haven based in a Grade II-listed former carpenter's yard continues to offer eight varying beers. Many are sourced from northern micros, and Glentworth, Castle Rock and Rudgate breweries regularly feature. Leffe Blonde, real cider on draught and a wide selection of continental bottled beers are also available. Quality live music can be heard on

Thursday and Saturday nights. Sunday lunchtime conversations are lively, with customers bringing in food to share. Q❀♿♣P⊱

Elm Cottage

139 Church Street, DN21 2JU (100m W of Gainsborough Trinity football ground)

⌚ 12 (9am Tue)-2.30 (not Mon), 6-midnight; 12-midnight Fri-Sun ☎ (01427) 615474

Jennings Cumberland Ale; guest beers Ⓗ

This well-established pub features two bay windows with seating, and a separate dining area where good value, freshly-cooked food is available every lunchtime and Friday evening 6-8pm. Breakfast is served on Tuesday from 9am and the Sunday carvery is very popular. There are old pictures of the locality and a cabinet of trophies won by the sports teams based here. A charity quiz is held every other Tuesday, with live music on the last Saturday of the month. ❀◑◗🚌P⊱

R Bar

3 Lord Street, DN21 2DD (400m W of market square)

⌚ 10-midnight (1am Fri & Sat); 12-midnight Sun ☎ (01427) 611265

Grafters Moonlight; guest beers Ⓗ

Records show this building was The Old Boar's Head in 1821, although it may have been a pub before then. It was the Hickman Arms until about 1930 and then a Rechabite Hall until 2006. The current owner reopened the building as a pub in 2009. Ales from local, award-winning Grafters Brewery are always available. Beers sold under the name of Trentside Ales are brewed exclusively for R Bar and The Canute. A quiz is held every other Wednesday. ❀♣P⊱▯

Gosberton Risegate

Duke of York

105 Risegate Road, PE11 4EY

⌚ 12 (6.30 Mon)-11; 12-3.30, 7-10.30 Sun ☎ (01775) 840193

Batemans XB; Black Sheep Best Bitter; guest beers Ⓗ

A long-standing Guide entry, this friendly pub maintains its well-deserved reputation for value-for-money beers and food. As well as the regular beers, the guests generally come from independent brewers, and the landlord, a real ale stalwart, makes great efforts to ensure a varied and interesting range. A centre of local community life, the pub supports charities, sports teams and other social events. A large enclosed garden for children makes it popular for families in the summer. ♨❀◑◗⊟♿♣P⊱

Grantham

Chequers

25 Market Place, NG31 6LR (on narrow side street between High Street and Market Place known as Butchers Row)

⌚ 12-midnight (1am Fri & Sat) ☎ (01476) 570149

Beer range varies Ⓗ

This single-room Victorian pub has completely changed into a trendy public house. With individual drinking areas customised with luxury leather sofas and deep-cushioned chairs, it makes a welcome retreat, popular with all ages, a place to unwind during the day. As night-time descends an upmarket atmosphere takes over. LocAles feature on the handpumps. ♣

Grantham Railway Club

off Huntingtower Road, NG31 7AU

⌚ 11-3 Sat only, 7-11; 12-2, 7-10.30 Sun ☎ (01476) 564860

Beer range varies Ⓗ

A traditional working men's club, it was voted Grantham CAMRA's first-ever Club of the Year in 2010. With two changing beers on handpump, more than 100 different beers have been served in the last year. LocAles often feature, predominantly by Brewster's and Newby Wyke. The club plays host to a number of darts, dominoes and crib teams, and is the venue for Grantham CAMRA's August beer festival. Live entertainment plays every Saturday night. ❀♿⇌♣P

Lord Harrowby

65 Dudley Road, NG31 9AB

⌚ 4 (12 Sat & Sun)-11 ☎ (01476) 563515

Milestone Rich Ruby; Tom Wood's Best Bitter; guest beers Ⓗ

Traditional back-street local within walking distance of the town centre and well worth a visit. It retains separate bar and lounge areas, the latter featuring a large collection of aviation memorabilia, much of which reflects Lincolnshire's history as Bomber County. Live traditional jazz is a feature every third Friday of the month, and there is a weekly Sunday night quiz. ♨❀⊟♿♣⊱

Nobody Inn

9 North Street, NG31 6NU

⌚ 12-11 (10.30 Sun) ☎ (01476) 565288 🌐 nobodyinn.com

Greene King IPA; Newby Wyke Grantham Gold, Bear Island; guest beers Ⓗ

This is a traditional wooden-floored pub with a friendly and vibrant atmosphere. LocAles are supplied, mainly from Newby Wyke – Grantham Gold is brewed especially for this pub. Leave plenty of time to find the unusual entrance to the toilets. TV screens make this pub the place to be on big sports days. Regular Wii nights are held. Pool and table football are available, with live entertainment some weekends. ♿♣⊱

Stagger Inn

35 London Road, NG31 6EX

⌚ 11 (12 Sun)-midnight ☎ (01476) 565368

Beer range varies Ⓗ

A traditional family-run pub located just off the town centre on the corner of a major thoroughfare, offering a sports and games bar with three large TVs and a big screen. There is also a separate lounge bar. The pub hosts darts, pool, crib and dominoes. The beer garden has a TV and barbecue area. Wadworth 6X, Courage Directors and Wells Bombardier are rotated regularly. ❀⊟⇌♣⊱

Tollemache Inn ✔

17 St Peter's Hill, NG31 6PY

⌚ 9-midnight (1am Fri & Sat) ☎ (01476) 594696

Banks's Mild; Greene King Abbot; Newby Wyke Warrior Ⓗ

This well-established Wetherspoon pub, known locally as The Tolly, has deservedly won the local CAMRA Town Pub of the Year award for the last three years. It serves 10 real ales, with one dark beer always available. A committed supporter of LocAle breweries – Brewster's, Newby Wyke and Oldershaw's – it is easy to understand the pub's popularity with local real ale drinkers. Both the bus and railway stations are a short walk away. Q❀◑◗♿⇌🚌♣⊱

Great Limber

New Inn

2 High Street, DN37 8JL
11.30-3, 6-11; 11.30-11 Fri & Sat; 12-10.30 Sun
☎ (01469) 560257
Beer range varies Ⓗ
Under the care of skilled licensees, this Tom Wood pub makes a return to the Guide. On the Brocklesby Estate, the mausoleum is a short walk away. There are two changing beers from the Tom Wood guest list. A darts league is hosted in the bar and bingo is played on Thursday. Pub food is served in a separate dining room (no food Sun eve). Village hall facilities are available for caravan parties by arrangement. There is a covered area for smokers.
Q ≠(Ulceby) (X1)♣P

Grimsby

County Hotel

Brighowgate, DN32 0QU
12-11 (midnight Fri & Sat) ☎ (01472) 354422
Beer range varies Ⓗ
Formerly known as the Olde Musician, this one-room pub near the Salvation Army Hostel attracts a mixed clientele. The varied choice of cask ales on up to four handpumps comes from the Heineken guest list, with regular appearances of Fugelestou and Tom Wood. There is often a cider either on handpull or gravity. Live music features regularly Friday to Sunday. A lower alcove provides some relative quiet. Poker is played on Monday night.
≠(Town)

Rose & Crown

Louth Road, DN33 2HR (2 miles from town on A16)
11-11 (midnight Fri & Sat); 11.30-11 Sun
☎ (01472) 278517
Batemans XXXB; Caledonian Deuchars IPA; Taylor Landlord; Tetley Bitter; guest beers Ⓗ
This very popular and friendly pub, which is part of the Ember Inns chain, typically has an emphasis on good, reasonably priced food, but takes pride in its real ales. One large bar serves various seating areas. It is only a 10-minute ride on the Grimsby-Louth bus route from the town centre. A heated and seated patio is provided. (51)P

Swigs

21 Osborne Street, DN31 1EY
11-8 (5 Sun) ☎ (01472) 354773
Willy's Original; guest beers Ⓗ
Swigs is the second outlet for Willy's Cleethorpes brewery but also stocks three other changing guests. With a bare wood floor and an L-shaped servery at the far end, it is quieter than its sister pub and has an older-type feel. It has made a regular appearance in the Guide for a number of years. Close to Grimsby Town railway station and the town centre bus rank. ≠(Town)

Wheatsheaf ✔

47 Bargate, DN34 5AD
11.30-11 (midnight Thu-Sat) ☎ (01472) 246821
Taylor Landlord; Tetley Bitter; guest beers Ⓗ
This friendly, well-used Ember Inns chain pub typically supplies its clientele with good, affordable food, augmented by a fine selection of ales. Two bars serve a split-level layout with various seating areas. A heated patio is available for the use of smokers. It's on several bus routes from the town centre. ≠(Town) (8,9,13)P

Yarborough Hotel

29 Bethlehem Street, DN31 1JN
9am-midnight (1am Fri & Sat) ☎ (01472) 268283
Greene King Ruddles Best Bitter, Abbot; guest beers Ⓗ
Three times local CAMRA Pub of the Year, this spacious Wetherspoon pub uses the ground floor of an imposing Victorian former railway hotel, comprising two separate bar areas with a front and rear snug, plus a seated patio at the rear. It gets very busy, particularly at weekends, with good value meals served throughout the day until late evening. Up to eight guest beers are available. Located in the town centre adjacent to the railway station. Q ≠(Town)

Harmston

Thorold Arms

High Street, LN5 9SN
12-3 (not Mon & Tue), 6-11; 12-11 Sun ☎ (01522) 720358
thoroldarms.co.uk
Beer range varies Ⓗ
A true village community pub specialising in beers from micro-breweries, with four handpumps offering a varying range. The stone-built 17th-century building is fronted by a courtyard drinking area, while the small bar has a mixture of tables, settles and settees. Numerous regular events, feature nights and charity fundraisers are hosted. Excellent home-cooked meals are served in the bar or restaurant – ring to confirm food availability.
Q (1)♣P

Haxey

Loco

31-33 Church Street, DN9 2HY (from A161 follow B1396 into village)
4-midnight (1am Fri & Sat); 12-midnight Sun
☎ (01427) 752879 thelocohaxey.co.uk
John Smith's Bitter; guest beers Ⓗ
Converted from the village Co-op during the 1980s, this pub was originally decorated with railway memorabilia. Following extensive refurbishment, only a locomotive smoke box remains of the original design. The Loco is a fine example of diversity, offering four-star accommodation and a restaurant specialising in English and Indian cuisine. Lunches are available Sundays only. At least one guest beer is always on tap. The Loco takes part in the annual Haxey Hood contest each January. (291,292)

Heighington

Butcher & Beast

High Street, LN4 1JS
12-11 (10.30 Sun) ☎ (01522) 790386
butcherandbeast.co.uk
Batemans XB, GHA, XXXB, Victory; Greene King Abbot; guest beer Ⓗ
With welcoming staff, this old stone Batemans pub is in the centre of the village on a regular bus route. The pub features distinct areas showing old village photos, and has regular beer festivals, pub games, quizzes and meat raffles. Speciality bottled German and Belgian beers are available, plus a range of rare whiskies and gins. Meals are served using local produce, and there are weekly theme nights. Dogs are allowed in non-food areas.
Q (2)♣P

Hemingby

Coach & Horses

Church Lane, LN9 5QF (1 mile from A158)
⏲ 12-2 (not Mon & Tue; 3 Sat), 7 (6 Wed-Fri)-11; 12-3, 7-10.30 Sun ☎ (01507) 578280
Riverside Dixon's Major; guest beers Ⓗ
Recorded as Hemingebi in the Domesday Book, the village was on the route from Louth to Lincoln, and this former coaching inn stands prominently opposite the parish church. One of the few village facilities remaining, the free house hosts pool, darts, dominoes and quiz teams, and a golf society. Guest beers always include a mild, and award-winning, home-cooked meals are served. The beer garden and camping field overlook the rolling Lincolnshire wolds. ♨Q☋❀◐◑♿▲♣P🚬

Hibaldstow

Wheatsheaf

15 Station Road, DN20 9EB
⏲ 12-midnight ☎ (01652) 658386
Adnams Broadside; Black Sheep Best Bitter; guest beer Ⓗ
The central bar serves three large rooms. A public bar with wooden and slate floor has TV, pool table and games machine, and leads through to a large half-carpeted lounge with tables, sofas and a real fire. The third room is a smaller, more formal dining area with ramped access to the car park at the rear. All rooms are decorated in contemporary style. Meals can be eaten in any area. The semi-covered outdoor area at the rear has picnic tables. ♨Q☋❀🛏◐◑▤♿🚌P🚬

Holbeach Hurn

Rose & Crown

Low Road, PE12 8JN (off Marsh Road on N edge of village) TF395273
⏲ 10-midnight (1am Fri & Sat) ☎ (01406) 426085
🌐 roseancrown.co.uk
Elgood's Black Dog, Cambridge Bitter Ⓖ
The landlady and her team make sure that first-time visitors feel at home in this friendly and revitalised village local. The public bar can be lively with pool and games, but a quieter pint and good value food can be enjoyed in the lounge and adjoining dining room. The smoking lounge is a pleasant patio which leads to a large grassed area with facilities for camping and caravans. ♨❀◐◑▤♿▲♣P🚬

Horbling

Plough Inn

Spring Lane, NG34 0PF
⏲ closed Mon; 12-3, 5-11 (11.30 Thu); 12-midnight Fri & Sat; 12-11 Sun ☎ (01529) 240263 🌐 theploughinnhorbling.co.uk
Beer range varies Ⓗ
Low-beamed true community pub, built in 1832, in a quiet village, owned by the parish council. In addition to the lounge and bar, it has a snug that is surely one of the smallest and most intimate of its kind. Beers are usually from micro-breweries and change regularly. Home-cooked meals are available in the bar and restaurant. Steak and jazz feature on the first Wednesday of the month. Spring wells are a feature just a few yards down the lane. ♨❀◐◑▤♿🚌♣P🚬

Horncastle

Red Lion

Bull Ring, LN9 5HT
⏲ 11-11 (midnight Fri & Sat); 12-11 Sun ☎ (01507) 523338
Oakwell Barnsley Bitter Ⓗ
This typical market-town pub has a large bar/lounge with old bay windows overlooking the Bullring town centre. Above the bar a collection of 800 assorted keyrings hangs on display, while framed photographs of Lion Theatre productions from 1988 adorn the walls. The theatre is part of the pub premises, located at the rear, and run by the Horncastle Theatre Co – productions sometimes star the landlord. A snug and a dining room also feature. ☋❀◐▤♿🚌♣🚬

Hubberts Bridge

Wheatsheaf Inn

Station Road, PE20 3QR
⏲ 12-2.30 (not Mon), 5-11.30 ☎ (01205) 290347
🌐 thewheatsheafinn.org
Batemans XB; Wells Bombardier; guest beers Ⓗ
This pleasant rural free house has been a pub for well over 100 years and is now run by a family partnership. It stands on the banks of the South Forty Foot Navigation with moorings nearby. Eventually this waterway will link with the entire Midland canal system, with access currently available via the river Witham at Boston. The pub's first beer festival in 2009 was so successful that it has become an annual event. ♨Q❀◐◑▲⇌♣P🚬

Hundleby

Hundleby Inn

73 Main Road, PE23 5LZ
⏲ 12 (4 Mon & Tue)-11 (midnight Fri & Sat)
☎ (01790) 752577 🌐 thehundlebyinn.co.uk
Batemans XB; Black Sheep Best Bitter; guest beers Ⓗ
This welcoming and cosy free house features a wood-panelled bar/lounge decorated with pictures of aeroplanes and sport. Note the Black Sheep handpump. The dining room provides excellent, good value home-cooked food. A large outdoor space includes a children's play area, camping and caravanning, a patio and seating. The pub is located on the edge of the Wolds and has excellent walks. It is also in easy striking distance of the nearest town, Spilsby. ♨❀◐◑♿▲🚌♣P🚬

Keelby

Nag's Head

8 Manor Street, DN41 8EF
⏲ 12-midnight (10.30 Sun) ☎ (01469) 560660
John Smith's Bitter; Theakston Traditional Mild; guest beers Ⓗ
Situated opposite the village school, this two-roomed pub provides a warm welcome. It is one of very few regional pubs with a regular mild, and the two guest beers are sourced from smaller breweries. A small beer garden includes a children's play section and there is a covered, lit and heated smoking area. In addition to the Tuesday quiz, the pub hosts Wednesday bingo and live music most weekends. No food is available except the occasional barbecue on a summer weekend. ♨❀▤🚌(X1)♣P🚬

Kirkby on Bain

Ebrington Arms

Main Street, LN10 6YT
⏲ 12-3, 6-midnight; 12-11 Sun ☎ (01526) 354560
Black Sheep Best Bitter; Greene King Old Speckled Hen, Abbot; Taylor Landlord; Theakston Ebrington Arms Bitter Ⓗ
Attractive country pub dating from 1610 close to the River Bain, with a low-beamed ceiling in the bar/lounge that was used by aircrew during World War II; coins still slotted into the ceiling beams were intended to pay for beer when they returned from their missions. The popular restaurant offers good food made with local produce (booking advised). The garden has an awning to protect outside drinkers and there is a caravan campsite within a mile of the pub.
♨Q❀◑◐♿▲♣P⚡

Lincoln

Dog & Bone

10 John Street, LN2 5BH (off Monks Rd)
⏲ 12-3 (not Mon), 7-11 (midnight Fri & Sat); 12-11 Sun
☎ (01522) 522403 🌐 dogandbonelincoln.co.uk
Batemans XB, GHA, seasonal beers; guest beers Ⓗ
A welcoming, award-winning, community pub for all seasons, with cosy coal fires in the winter and a pleasant beer garden in summer. The pub is split into two seating areas, one lined with books as part of the pub's book exchange; this room also contains a variety of board games popular with the locals. Regular music events take place each month. 'Lite bites' lunchtime food is available Tuesday-Saturday. Seasonal beer festivals are hosted. ♨❀◑⇌🚌♣●⚡

Golden Eagle

21 High Street, LN5 8BD
⏲ 11 (12 Sun)-11 (11.30 Fri & Sat) ☎ (01522) 521058
🌐 goldeneagle.org.uk
Batemans XB; Castle Rock Harvest Pale, Preservation; guest beers Ⓗ
This traditional ale house has plenty of guest ales and a cider on offer. A Wednesday lunchtime music session is held monthly, quiz night is Friday, and there are regular crib and dominoes matches plus seasonal weekly fishing matches. The lounge features old Lincoln City football programmes; the pub is close to the Sincil Bank ground. Food is prepared using fresh local produce. There is a function room for hire and a large child-friendly garden at the rear.
♨Q❀◑⊟🚌♣●P⚡

Green Dragon

Magpie Square, Broadgate, LN2 5DH
⏲ 11-10.30 (11.30 Fri & Sat) ☎ (01522) 567155
🌐 greendragonpub.co.uk
Beer range varies Ⓗ/Ⓟ
Close to bus and rail stations, as well as the city centre, this 14th-century timber-framed pub offers a large choice of real ales. The Riverside bar has 12 handpumps serving varying Milestone ales, and micro-breweries from all over the country also feature. Good quality food is available 12-9pm, including Friday fish specials and a Sunday carvery. Up to five real ciders and perry are stocked. There is a riverside patio that caters for smokers.
❀◑◐⇌🚌●P⚡

Jolly Brewer

27 Broadgate, LN2 5AQ
⏲ 12-midnight (1am Fri & Sat); 12-11 Sun
☎ (01522) 528583 🌐 thejollybrewer.co.uk
Courage Directors; Young's Bitter; guest beers Ⓗ
This regular Guide entry welcomes a cosmopolitan clientele and plays host to regular live music, open mike and quiz nights. Local beers often feature on two of the six handpumps, plus Westons perry and a cider on gravity. The main bar area, which has a real fire, is supplemented by a corridor drinking area where the work of local artists is displayed. The ample outdoor drinking courtyard includes a covered area for smokers. ♨❀◑⇌🚌♣●P⚡

Magna Carta

1 Exchequer Gate, LN2 1PZ
⏲ 12-11 (midnight Fri & Sat); 12-10 Sun ☎ (01522) 538884
Marston's Pedigree; guest beers Ⓗ
Impressively situated at the top of Steep Hill, adjacent to the cathedral and with large windows overlooking the castle and square, this pub caters for tourists and locals alike. The interior is open plan but has drinking areas on many levels, plus a dining room on the top floor. Three or four guest beers are always from the extended Marston's range. Food is available 12-8pm (5pm Sun). ◑◐

Morning Star

11 Greetwell Gate, LN2 4AW
⏲ 11-midnight; 12-11 Sun ☎ (01522) 527079
Caledonian Deuchars IPA; Draught Bass; Greene King Ruddles Best Bitter, Abbot; Taylor Golden Best; Wells Bombardier Ⓗ
The walls within the main bar area of this busy traditional pub are adorned with WWI memorabilia celebrating Lincoln's association with the development of the first tank. The pub is situated uphill, close to the Cathedral, and reputed to have become an inn in the 18th century. While sampling the fine ales, visitors can sit back and play traditional pub games and enjoy the conversation that makes this pub so popular. Q❀◑🚌(2)♣P⚡

Ritz ✔

143-147 High Street, LN5 7PJ
⏲ 9am-midnight (1am Fri & Sat) ☎ (01522) 512103
Batemans XXXB; Greene King Ruddles Best Bitter, Abbot; guest beers Ⓗ
The neon lights of the Ritz have been a feature of the High Street since it opened as a cinema in 1937. It was the first picture house in the city to have Cinemascope installed, but the credits rolled for the final time in 1996. Two years later, it reopened as a pub, with Art Deco-style fittings recalling the building's heyday. Guest beers always include at least one from a local brewery. Westons Marcle Hill cider is a regular. ☕◑◐♿⇌●⚡

Strugglers 🏆

83 Westgate, LN1 3BG
⏲ 10.30-11 (midnight Tue & Wed, 1am Thu-Sat); 11-11 Sun
☎ (01522) 535023
Black Sheep Best Bitter; Draught Bass; Greene King Abbot; Rudgate Ruby Mild; Taylor Landlord; guest beers Ⓗ
This friendly old pub, under the north-west corner of Lincoln's Norman Castle, is in the city's historic cathedral quarter. Seven handpumps dispense at least two changing guest beers, often from the SIBA list. Affordable food is served in the cosy snug, with its real fire and photos of Lincoln past, and in the long public bar. A rear garden, of unexpected

size, includes a covered area for smokers. Close by are the Lawn Visitor Centre and Lincolnshire Life Museum. ♨Q❀☾⊟🚌(7,8)⚐

Tap & Spile ✔
21 Hungate, LN1 1ES
✪ 4-midnight; 12-1am Fri & Sat ☎ (01522) 534015
🌐 tapandspilelincoln.co.uk
Sharp's Doom Bar; Woodeforde's Wherry; Wychwood Hobgoblin; guest beers ⊞
An escape from the busy high street bars, this cosy pub has a friendly atmosphere welcoming young and old alike. Pictures of folk and blues artists are displayed around the walls, and there is a centre bar with eight handpumps often serving Oldershaw, Hambleton or Tom Woods beers. Friday nights feature live music and a jam session is hosted on early Sunday evenings. A music quiz is held on the second Wednesday of the month. Westons Old Rosie cider is available. ❀⇌♣●⚐

Victoria
6 Union Road, LN1 3BJ
✪ 11-midnight (1am Fri & Sat); 12-midnight Sun
☎ (01522) 541000 🌐 victoriapub.net
Batemans XB; Castle Rock Harvest Pale; Taylor Landlord; guest beers ⊞
A Guide entry for the last 26 years, the pub is now owned by Batemans. Situated beneath the castle wall, it has undergone some minor changes but has kept the old feel thanks to its long-term staff. The narrow bar hosts seven handpumps, with a further four in the small lounge area. A real cider is served direct from the cellar. Seasonal beer festivals are held in a marquee outside, where there is also a children's play area and outdoor seating. Q❀☾⊟🚌(7,8)●⚐

Little Bytham

Willoughby Arms ✔
Station Road, NG33 4RA
✪ 12-11 (10.30 Sun) ☎ (01780) 410276
🌐 willoughbyarms.co.uk
Batemans XB; Ufford White Hart; guest beers ⊞
Set in the heart of the Lincolnshire countryside, this 150-year-old former booking office and waiting room of a private railway serves four guest ales. There is always one dark beer available supplementing the Batemans XB and LocAle Ufford White Hart. Two beer festivals are held annually in May and October. Home-cooked food is served daily, and there is occasional live music.
♨❀⛿◐♿⛺●P⚐

Louth

Boars Head 🏆
12 Newmarket, LN11 9HH (next to cattle market)
✪ 5 (9.30am Thu, 4 Fri)-11; 12-11 Sat & Sun
☎ (01507) 603561
Batemans Dark Mild, XB; guest beers ⊞
A Batemans pub situated next to the cattle market, a short walk from the town centre, it has a good guest beer list. The interior includes two main rooms plus the old snug, which is now the games room. Warmed by real fires in the winter, it always provides a friendly welcome. Pub games include darts and dominoes. Thursday is cattle market day, which is why the pub opens earlier. Lunches are served Thursday-Sunday 12-2pm (no food Mon-Wed). ♨Q⛿◐⊟♣⚐

Cobbles Bar
2 New Street, LN11 9PU (pedestrian-only street off Cornmarket)
✪ 10-midnight (2am Fri & Sat); 12-10 Sun ☎ (07736) 275262
Black Sheep Best Bitter; guest beers ⊞
Cobbles Bar is a traditional pub-style bar based in the centre of town, with friendly staff at all times. This small but accommodating bar has multiple personalities, from bustling coffee shop serving light lunches to a busy pre-club with DJs and live music at the weekend. It has a good beer trade with carefully selected beers, lagers and two contrasting cask ales, as well as a huge selection of exotic spirits. Disabled access is right through the front doors. ☾♿🚌(10,51)

Newmarket Inn
133 Newmarket, LN11 9EG (jct of Church Street and Newmarket)
✪ 12-3 (not Mon & Tue), 5-midnight; 12-midnight Sat & Sun
☎ (01507) 605146
Adnams Bitter; Taylor Landlord; guest beer ⊞
This is a lively, family-run, pleasantly decorated two-roomed pub, formerly known as the Brown Cow, set in an urban location five minutes walk from town centre. A guest beer is always available. A popular free quiz is held every Sunday night, and the local folk club meets here on a Tuesday. The Hurdles bistro is always busy and booking is recommended; lunches are available, excluding Sunday when food is served 4-8pm. Q❀☾P

Ludford

White Hart Inn
Magna Mile, LN8 6AD
✪ 12-2 (not Mon-Thu), 6-11; 12-2.30, 6-11 Sat; 12-3.30, 7-10.30 Sun ☎ (01507) 313489
Beer range varies ⊞
This 18th-century coaching house was Louth and District CAMRA Pub of the Year 2009. A two-roomed rural village pub close to the Viking Way, it is very popular with hikers and ramblers. It offers four changing guest beers; the licensees pride themselves on serving real ale from micro-breweries. All food is home-made, using ingredients from local suppliers; meals are available lunchtimes and evenings. There is guest accommodation separate from the pub.
♨Q❀◐♣P

Maltby le Marsh

Crown Inn
Beesby Road, LN13 0JJ (jct of A157 and A1104)
✪ 12-11.30 (11 Sun) ☎ (01507) 450100
Batemans XB Bitter; Malt B Old Reliable, Smarty's Night Porter, PEA; guest beers ⊞
Up to six beers are on offer as well as ciders including Westons Old Rosie. A small micro-brewery has been installed mainly to supply the Crown, and its first beers have been well-received. The inn and its outdoor tables are in a good position for the nearby coastal strip with its many visitors, especially in summer. Bar skittles and shove ha'penny are played. Meals are availabe either in the bar or in the restaurant.
❀⛿◐⊟♿⛺🚌(10)♣●P⚐

Market Deeping

Vine ✔

19 Church Street, PE6 8AN

✪ 5 (12 Fri & Sat)-11; 12-10.30 Sun ☎ (01778) 344699

⊕ inn-the-vine.co.uk

Wells Eagle IPA, Bombardier; guest beer Ⓗ

Friendly pub built of local limestone and slate, once a Victorian prep school, now with a low-ceilinged front bar and a cosy back snug. Disabled access is at the rear along with a canopied courtyard, enclosed within the garden and children's play area. The venue hosts themed food nights and a quiz every second Sunday. Charity events include music fests and a summer panto. A thriving pub once again after a period of uncertainty about its future. ❀♿⊟(22,101,102)♣P⊱⊓

Market Rasen

Aston Arms

18 Market Place, LN8 3HL

✪ 11-11 (11.30 Fri & Sat); 12-11 Sun ☎ (01673) 842313

John Smith's Bitter; Wells Bombardier; guest beer Ⓗ

This large, popular pub holds a commanding position on the market square. A central bar serves three open-plan drinking areas. The guest ale changes frequently; the licensee favours beers from micro-breweries. The games area features pool, darts, shove ha'penny and a wide-screen TV. Good value food is served daily until 8pm, making it popular with families and walking groups (the Viking Way passes nearby). There is a covered and heated patio area outside with ramp access to the pub. ❀◑♿⇌⊟(3,23)♣P⊱

Red Lion

45 King Street, LN8 3BB (200m W of Market Square)

✪ 11.30-11 (11.30 Fri & Sat); 12-11 Sun ☎ (01673) 842424

Greene King Ruddles Best Bitter; Tom Wood's Best Bitter, Bomber County; guest beers Ⓗ

The pub was reopened in 2008 after restoration by local brewer Tom Wood. The mock-Tudor exterior has been retained, but inside the pub has been tastefully refurbished in an open-plan style, complemented with bygone relics, bar billiards and other bar game machines. Three drinking areas are served by one bar, with cask ale and cider from seven handpumps, Belgian beers and a large malt whisky range – and no keg lager. ♔Ω❀⊨⇌⊟(3,23)♣●P⊱

Messingham

Bird in the Barley

Northfield Road, DN17 3SQ (½ mile from Messingham on A159)

✪ closed Mon; 11.30-3, 5-11; 11.30-3.30, 5.30-10.30 Sun ☎ (01724) 764744

Jennings Snecklifter; Marston's Pedigree; guest beers Ⓗ

A country pub with a mix of traditional and modern design. The interior features oak beams, wooden flooring and a dining conservatory. A seated drinkers' area includes leather sofas and armchairs. There are two beer gardens; one includes a large canopy and heater. Good home-cooked food is made from locally-sourced ingredients. Two regular real ales from the Jennings/Marston's range are stocked, plus one or two guest beers. Cyclops tasting notes are displayed on the handpumps. ♔❀◑♿⊟(100,101,353)P⊱

Horn Inn

61 High Street, DN17 3NU

✪ 11-11 (midnight Sat) ☎ (01724) 762426

Black Sheep Best Bitter, Ale; guest beers Ⓗ

In the village centre on the A159, this venue is popular with locals and visitors, both for its regular and changing real ales and its excellent food. Meals are served lunchtimes and evenings except Wednesday and Saturday. Quiz night is Monday and local bands entertain on Wednesday and Saturday. There are several distinctive drinking areas plus a sheltered garden for use in the warmer months. ♔Q❀◑⊞♿⊟♣P⊱

Moulton

Swan ✔

13 High Street, PE12 6QB

✪ 11 (11.30 Sun)-2am ☎ (01406) 370349

Tetley Bitter; Wells Bombardier; guest beers Ⓗ

Family-run pub in the centre of an attractive village. Two changing guest ales are available, with the local Tydd Steam brewery often featuring, and two real ciders – Westons Traditional and a guest. The pub has an excellent reputation for food, with an interesting and varied menu, and credit crunch specials Monday-Wednesday. It is family and dog friendly, with a pleasant and popular garden. Enter before 11pm if you wish to take advantage of late evenings. ♔☕❀◑⊞⊟(505)●P⊱

Moulton Chapel

Wheatsheaf

4 Fengate, PE12 0XL

✪ 12-2.30 (not Mon), 5.30-11; 12-2, 6.30-11 Sat; 12-2, 7-10.30 Sun ☎ (01406) 380525

Beer range varies Ⓗ

The small quarry-tiled bar is at the heart of this village pub, with its splendid old black range that positively glows on winter evenings, and no noisy machines or TV to sully the atmosphere. The beer could be from far or near but is consistently good, as is the home-cooked food. Fish and chips night and other good value specials feature during the week. Two pleasant dining rooms showcase paintings by local artists. A games room is due to open soon. ♔Q❀◑Ⓐ⊟♣P

North Kelsey

Butcher's Arms

Middle Street, LN7 6EH

✪ 4-midnight (1.30am Fri); 12-1.30am Sat; 12-midnight Sun ☎ (01652) 678002

Tom Wood Best Bitter, Harvest Bitter; guest beer Ⓗ

Village local of open-plan design, retaining a traditional outlook. Simply but comfortably decorated in rustic style, the main bar features a welcoming real fire. Photographs of village life adorn the walls and a large hop bine overhangs the bar. Two beers from the Tom Wood range are featured, plus a rotating guest beer. A games area is used for darts, and table skittles is also played. The pub has an attractive beer garden for spring and summer drinking. ♔❀♿♣P⊱

Oasby

Houblon Arms

Village Street, NG32 3NB

closed Mon; 12-3, 6.30 (6 Sat)-11; 12-3, 6.30-10.30 Sun
☎ (01529) 455215 houblon-inn.co.uk
Everards Tiger; guest beers Ⓗ
Situated at the centre of the village, the pub is named after John Houblon, who was the first Governor of the Bank of England. Its flagstone floor, open real fire, large inglenook fireplace and cosy atmosphere make this a popular destination. LocAles are from Brewster's, Newby Wyke and Oldershaw. Excellent home-cooked food is served every day (no food Sun eve). B&B accommodation is provided in four cottages. ♨Q❀⇌◐♿♣●P⅟

Old Bolingbroke

Black Horse Inn

Moat Lane, PE23 4HH
closed Mon; 8.30-11 Tue; 12-3, 7-11 Wed-Sun
☎ (01790) 763388
Milestone Black Pearl; Young's Bitter; guest beers Ⓗ
Situated in a good walking area, this is a fine old country inn with its origins in the 17th century and extended in 1930. History is on the doorstep, with castle remains and the roses of Henry IV and the Duke of Lancaster dating from 1366. Guest beers are usually from micros and the pub stages regular beer festivals. Excellent food is served made with local organic produce. Ring to check food availability and book (no food Tue). Opening times may vary. ♨Q❀◐♿▲♣●P⅟

Pinchbeck

Bull Inn ✔

1 Knight Street, PE11 3RA (on B1356)
12-2.30, 5-11 (midnight Fri); 12-midnight Sat; 12-11 Sun
☎ (01775) 723022
John Smith's Bitter; guest beers Ⓗ
Welcoming, friendly village pub opposite the green, which still has the old stocks. The Bull has two comfortable bars: the public bar with a log fire, and the lounge, used mainly for dining. A carved bull's head features on the long bar front, with the bar rail representing its horns. The pub has a reputation for good food, from bar snacks to meals in the upstairs restaurant. Guest beers change regularly, often coming from local micros.
♨❀◐⊟♿⊞P⅟⊓

Saxilby

Anglers

65 High Street, LN1 2HA
11.30 (12 Sun)-11 ☎ (01522) 702200
Caledonian Deuchars IPA; Greene King IPA; guest beers Ⓗ
Although described as 'the local's local', this Victorian-built village pub welcomes all. The pub's name refers to trainloads of anglers from the Sheffield area who came to fish the nearby Foss Dyke – England's oldest canal. The place is home to many pub games teams and local societies, including the village history group – note the old photos in the lounge. Guest beers are from the Heineken guest list. Daytime buses from Lincoln to Gainsborough stop almost outside the door.
❀⊟⇌⊞(100,105)♣P⅟

Scamblesby

Green Man

Old Main Road, LN11 9XG
12-2.30 (not Mon), 5-midnight; 12-midnight Thu-Sun
☎ (01507) 343282
St Austell Tinners; Young's Bitter; guest beers Ⓗ
Welcoming village pub in picturesque Wolds countryside, popular with walkers and visitors to Cadwell Park race circuit just a mile away. Accommodation is available, together with traditional good value meals, served until 8.30pm. A spacious main bar and a quiet lounge are both patrolled by Harry the pub dog. Lots of motorcycle memorabilia is on display. The guest beer usually changes every month. ♨Q☋❀⇌◐♿▲P

Scotter

Sun & Anchor

54 High Street, DN21 3RX
12-midnight (1am Fri & Sat) ☎ (01724) 763444
Young's Bitter; guest beers Ⓗ
Village centre pub near to the A159, popular with locals both for the bar with traditional pub games and the large, comfortable lounge. There is a large outdoor seating area where visitors are free to use the pub barbecue. Several sports teams are based at the venue and a film club is held monthly. One regular beer and two guests, often from Lincolnshire breweries, are served.
♨❀⊟♿⊞(100,101,353)♣P⅟

Scunthorpe

Berkeley ★

Doncaster Road, DN15 7DS (½ mile from end of M181)
11.30-2.30, 5-11; 12-11 Fri & Sat; 12-10.30 Sun
☎ (01724) 842333
Samuel Smith Old Brewery Bitter Ⓗ
This large 1930s Art Deco Samuel Smith's hotel is 30 minutes' walk from the town centre and 10 minutes' walk from Glanford Park football ground. It comprises four rooms: a dining room, function room and lounge at the front, with a public bar at the rear. It also has seven guest rooms. Landscaped at the front, with a large car park, there is a beer garden at the back. Evening meals are available Monday to Saturday, with lunch on Sunday. The pub occasionally closes on match days (phone to check). ♨Q❀⇌◐⊟♿⊞(31A,32A,37)♣P⅟

Blue Bell ✔

1-7 Oswald Road, DN15 7PU (at town centre crossroads)
9am-midnight (1am Sat) ☎ (01724) 863921
Greene King Ruddles Best Bitter, Abbot; guest beers Ⓗ
Popular Wetherspoon town-centre pub 15 minutes' walk from the station, with an open-plan layout on two levels. The upper level is a carpeted family area, with guarded fire and tables for dining. The lower level has wooden flooring with a mix of high and low tables and chairs and sofas. The pub holds beer festivals and themed events such as Valentine's and Hallowe'en. Quiz night is Wednesday. Food is served daily until 10pm. A heated patio area at the rear has picnic tables and can be used by smokers. Q❀◐♿⇌⊞●⅟

Malt Shovel

219 Ashby High Street, Ashby, DN16 2JP (in Ashby Broadway shopping area)
10-11 (midnight Fri & Sat); 12-11 Sun ☎ (01724) 843318
Exmoor Gold; Tom Wood's Best Bitter; John Smith's Bitter; guest beers Ⓗ

Self-styled country pub in the town, always with eight real ales, bottled and draught foreign beers, and real ciders and perries served straight from the cellar. Beer festivals take place in spring and autumn. It gets busy lunch and teatimes for excellent value home-cooked food. Magazines, newspapers, a book swap and members-only snooker facilities are all available. Quizzes are on Tuesday and Thursday, and live music most Saturdays. It is handy for the shops, but do your shopping first, otherwise you just might not bother! ❀◑🚌●⊢

Skendleby

Blacksmiths Arms

Main Road, PE23 4QE

✪ 12-midnight (12-3, 5.30-midnight winter); 12-3, 7.30-midnight (not winter eve) Sun ☎ (01754) 890662

⊕ blacksmithspub.co.uk

Batemans XB; guest beers ⊞

Dating back to the 18th century, this country pub is set in an attractive Wolds village. Ducking beneath the low front door lintel, fortunately well-padded, into the quarry-tiled snug bar complete with period fireplace and settles, you discover a cosy and friendly atmosphere. The dining room at the rear has an enclosed well. The cellar is visible through a glass panel behind the bar. There are fine views of the Lincolnshire Wolds from the dining rooms. A cottage is available for overnight accommodation. ♛Q❀⇔◑⊟🚌♣P⊢

Sleaford

Packhorse Inn ✔

7 Northgate, NG34 7BH

✪ 9am-midnight ☎ (01529) 308730

Greene King Ruddles County, Abbot; Marston's Pedigree; guest beers ⊞

This 18th-century coaching inn on the London to Lincoln road has had several names during its lifetime, reverting to the original name when taken over by Wetherspoon a few years ago. Despite being remodelled as partly open plan, it retains an intimate atmosphere. As the Lion Hotel it hosted the opening dinner for the Sleaford Railway, an event that marked the start of the decline in the coaching trade. Q❀◑♿≥⊢

Snitterby

Royal Oak

High Street, DN21 4TP (½ mile off A15)

✪ 5 (12 Sat)-11; 12-10.30 Sun ☎ (01673) 818273

Fuller's Chiswick Bitter; Wold Top Bitter, Wold Gold; guest beers ⊞

Good old-fashioned community pub in a village setting, with a friendly welcome, going from strength to strength, now having up to eight real ales on at any one time. In 2009 75 different ales were offered, with a focus on CAMRA award winners. It has a traditional light and airy interior with wooden floors and real fires. Outside, a seating area overlooks the stream. High-quality food made from carefully sourced local produce is served Thursday to Sunday. ♛Q❀⇔◑▲●P⊢

South Kyme

Hume Arms

High Street, LN4 4AD

✪ 11.30-2.30 (not Mon), 6-11 (midnight Fri & Sat); 12-3, 6-midnight Sun ☎ (01526) 869143

Beer range varies ⊞

Situated in a quiet village, this country inn stands opposite the Kyme Eau where narrowboats often visit, especially for the May bank holiday gatherings. Three guest beers, often from micros, are available. The pub recently reverted to its previous name, and years before that was known as the Simon de Kyme. Tastefully refurbished in 2006, it offers excellent food menus. Two en-suite rooms are also available. A bus service stops near the pub twice per day. ♛Q❀⇔◑♿🚌P⊢

South Ormsby

Massingberd Arms

Brinkhill Road, LN11 8QS (1½ miles from A16)

✪ 12-2.30 (not Mon & Tue, 3 Sat), 6-11; 12-10.30 Sun ☎ (01507) 480492

Beer range varies ⊞

This pub, named after the local lord of the manor, is not on a main thoroughfare, but has a track to its door well-beaten by lovers of good food and beer. There are three changing real ales. The pub is a great stopping-off point for walkers and cyclists in a beautiful area of the country, on the edge of the Lincolnshire Wolds. Guide dogs only are admitted. ♛Q❀◑P

Spalding

Ivy Wall

18-19 New Road, PE11 1DQ

✪ 9-midnight (1am Fri & Sat) ☎ (01775) 719770

Greene King Ruddles Best Bitter, Abbot ⊞

This 2005 rebuilt Wetherspoon's pub stands on what was the north bank of the former Westlode river and takes its name from a site shown on a map from 1732. Changing guest ales are regularly sourced from local breweries. Westons Marcle Hill cider is served, and the usual range of all-day food and drink offers is available. CAMRA members receive a discount. A gallery of photographs and finds from the archaeology dig are displayed on the wall. ❀◑≥●⊢

Lincoln Arms

4 Bridge Street, PE11 1XA

✪ 11-3, 7-12.30am; 11-12.30am Fri & Sat; 11-4, 7-midnight Sun ☎ (01775) 710017

Marston's Mansfield Cask Ale; guest beers ⊞

Overlooking the River Welland, the pub has a relaxed atmosphere with the emphasis on conversation and pub games, with darts, cribbage and pool played. Some of the regular customers have been using this traditional town local for more than 25 years. Spalding Folk Club holds an informal jam session every second Thursday of the month, and karaoke is the entertainment on the second Saturday of the month. Guest ales come from the Marston's stable and change weekly. ≥♣⊢

Red Lion Hotel ✔

Market Place, PE11 1SU

✪ 10-midnight ☎ (01775) 722869

⊕ redlionhotel-spalding.co.uk

Draught Bass; Fuller's London Pride; Greene King Abbot; Marston's Pedigree ⊞

Refurbished 18th-century hotel situated in the centre of Spalding with a cosy and welcoming bar. A regular Guide entry due to its consistently well-kept ales, it is popular with locals and visitors. Meals and bar snacks are available all day, with an interesting Polish menu. There are tables and chairs outside for an alfresco pint in fine weather. Memorabilia over the fireplace marks the occasion when Jimi Hendrix stayed here in 1967 after playing a local gig. ❀🛏◑⇌

Stamford

Green Man
29 Scotgate, PE9 2YQ
☺ 11 (12 Sun)-midnight ☎ (01780) 753598
🌐 stamfordonline.co.uk/greenman
Caledonian Deuchars IPA; guest beers Ⓗ
Stone-built former coaching inn dating from 1796 featuring an L-shaped split-level bar. It offers seven beers, always including guests from micros, plus up to seven traditional ciders and perries, and a good range of European bottled beers. Two beer festivals each year are held on the secluded patio. Lunchtime food is served Monday, Friday and Saturday, with sandwiches available Tuesday to Thursday. It has a TV and jukebox, and pump clips and beer memorabilia adorn the walls.
♨❀🛏◐⇌🚌(201)♣●⅟–⊓

Jolly Brewer
1 Foundry Road, PE9 2PP
☺ 11-midnight; 12-11.30 Sun ☎ (01780) 755141
🌐 jollybrewer.com
Oakham JHB; Sharp's Doom Bar; guest beers Ⓗ
Stone-built pub, some 300 years old, with an L-shaped room around the bar and a small dining area. A good community hostelry, it is home to darts, crib, dominoes and pool teams. Push penny is also played – the world championships take place here. Locally sourced food is served every day, with Sunday lunches particularly popular. There is a good range of single malts.
♨❀◑⇌🚌♣●P

Mama Liz's 🏆
9A North Street, PE9 1EL
☺ 12-11.30; closed Tue; 12-2am Fri & Sat ☎ (01780) 765888
🌐 mamaliz.co.uk
Beer range varies Ⓗ
This welcome new entry to the Guide was built around 1901 as a Victorian wine and spirit warehouse. The New Orleans-style bar serves local beers through three handpumps, and American bottled beers are stocked. Upstairs, the Soul Food Shack serves Creole and Cajun food. Entertainment is provided in the downstairs Voodoo Lounge cellar bar, which is on a par with the famous Cavern. A split-level patio hosts a twice-yearly beer festival. Local Pub of the Year 2010 with a LocAle certificate.
❀◑♿🚌⅟–

Tobie Norris
12 St Paul's Street, PE9 2BE
☺ 12-11 (10.30 Sun) ☎ (01780) 753800 🌐 tobienorris.com
Adnams Bitter; Ufford Ales range; guest beers Ⓗ
Parts of this stone building date back to circa 1280, and in 1617 it was bought by Tobie Norris and used as a bell foundry. It was converted into a pub by Mick Thurlby, for which it won CAMRA Awards in 2008. It has seven rooms over two floors which have been restored to their former glory and is a must-visit gem. Five handpumps serve local and micro-breweries, with a good menu that includes pizzas with unusual toppings. ♨Q❀◑⇌♣⅟–

Sturton by Stow

Plough
2 Tillbridge Road, LN1 2BP
☺ 12-2 (not Mon & Tue), 5 (6.30 Mon; 6 Tue)-11 (1am Sat); 12-midnight Sun ☎ (01427) 788268
🌐 theplough-sturtonbystow.co.uk
Flowers Original; guest beers Ⓗ
A welcoming family-run pub, standing at the crossroads in the village centre. The Flowers beer is unusual for the area; three more handpumps dispense guest ales, often from the nearby Grafters brewery, Batemans, or other Lincolnshire brewers such as Oldershaw. Good value food is a feature, with fish and chips a speciality (not Sun and Mon eve). Westons Old Rosie cider is usually available. Buses between Lincoln and Gainsborough stop nearby during the daytime.
Q❀◑⊟🚌(100,105)♣●P⅟–

Surfleet

Riverside Inn
123 Station Road, PE11 4DG (on bank of River Glen)
☺ 12-2.30, 5.30-11; 12-midnight Fri-Sun ☎ (01775) 680675
Beer range varies Ⓗ
This pleasant riverside pub on the banks of the Glen is on the edge of an attractive village. It has an L-shaped bar/lounge with offshoot dining rooms and a conservatory that overlooks the river. Two guest beers, often from micros, change fairly regularly. Note the unusual marble table with supporting eagle near the entrance. Accommodation includes en-suite facilities. Riverside wildlife make this an attractive area for walks. ❀🛏◑♿♣P⅟–

Sutterton

Thatched Cottage ✔
Pools Lane, PE20 2EZ
☺ 11.30-11.30 ☎ (01205) 460870
🌐 thatchedcottagerestaurant.co.uk
Courage Directors; John Smith's Bitter; Theakston Best Bitter; guest beers Ⓗ
This picturesque thatched 17th-century listed building is a rarity in Fen Country, and was a private house until 1985. Although extended and modernised to the rear, the bar and separate dining room exhibit a wealth of ancient timbers and inglenook fireplaces. Tall people beware! Behind the pub is a country farm store, and meat is butchered and cured on the premises. A country park and arboretum extending to eight acres is being developed, with an area for outdoor games including petanque and quoits. Q❀◑⊟♿🚌P⅟–

Sutton-on-Sea

Bacchus Hotel
17 High Street, LN12 2EY (main A52 through town)
☺ 10-midnight (1am Fri & Sat) ☎ (01507) 441204
🌐 bacchushotel.co.uk
Courage Directors; Greene King Ruddles County; Wells Bombardier; guest beers Ⓗ
A long-established hotel in the centre of Sutton selling a varied range of beers, including several from local breweries and the hotel's new micro-brewery. Well-attended beer festivals are held over the late spring and autumn bank holiday weekends. The pub is used regularly by local clubs and societies and is also popular with tourists.

There is a large garden and patio area, and it is on the bus route between Skegness and Mablethorpe. ♨Q⛹❀⛺◑⊞♿Ă⊟(9)♣P⚟

Swinhope

Click'em Inn

LN8 6BS (2 miles N of Binbrook on B1203)
⌚ 5 (7 Mon)-11; 12-3, 5-11 Thu; 12-11.30 Fri & Sat; 12-10.30 Sun ☎ (01472) 398253
Batemans XXXB; Hook Norton Old Hooky; guest beers Ⓗ
Country pub set in the picturesque Lincolnshire Wolds, and a good stopping place for walkers and cyclists. The unusual name originates from the counting of sheep through a nearby clicking gate. Good home-cooked food is available in the bar and conservatory. A changing range of guest beers is offered alongside the house beer, Terry's Tipple (Hancock's HB). An outside covered but unheated area is available to smokers. Local CAMRA Branch Country Pub of the Year 2009. Q❀◑♣P⚟

Tattershall Thorpe

Blue Bell Inn

Thorpe Road, LN4 4PE
⌚ 12-3, 7-11 (10.30 Sun) ☎ (01526) 342206
Greene King IPA, H&H Bitter, Morland Original Bitter, Old Speckled Hen Ⓗ
A gem of a pub in a delightful location. You step back in time when you enter this lovely 13th-century inn, one of Lincolnshire's oldest pubs. It has a large open fire and beamed ceilings covered in signed photos from WW II RAF squadrons who used the pub, including the famous Dambusters. Food is served in the bar and dining room, and three ales are usually on offer. Outside is an attractive garden. ♨Q❀◑♿Ă♣P⚟

Tetney

Crown & Anchor

Tetney Lock Road, DN36 5UW
⌚ 12-11 ☎ (01472) 388291
Beer range varies Ⓗ
Positioned near the now defunct Louth Navigation canal, the pub's location attracts wildfowlers and anglers as well as walkers and cyclists. Dogs are welcome in the public bar, which has a cosy open fire. Good value home-cooked food is served in the restaurant every lunchtime (no food Mon) and early evening (not Sun and Mon out of season). Two changing real ales are offered. Outside, there is a children's playground at the rear and a covered smokers' area at the front. ♨Q❀◑⊞♣P⚟

Theddlethorpe

Kings Head Inn

Mill Road, LN12 1PB (signed from A1031)
⌚ 12-11 (closed Mon winter); 12-10.30 Sun (winter hours vary) ☎ (01507) 339798 🌐 kingsheadinn.com
Batemans XB Bitter; guest beers Ⓗ
Set on the edge of a picturesque village near the North Sea coast, this pub is the longest single-storey thatched public house in Britain, built in 1623. Entering it is like stepping back in time. Keep a lookout for two thrones in the restaurant. The bars are warmed by roaring open fires in the winter months. Note that the ceiling of the front bar is, to say the least, low. The restaurant has a good reputation and booking is recommended. There are picnic tables outside in the large garden. ♨Q❀◑⊞♿P

Threekingham

Three Kings Inn

Saltersway, NG34 0AU
⌚ closed Mon; 12-3, 6-11 (10.30 Sun) ☎ (01529) 240249
Draught Bass; Taylor Landlord; guest beers Ⓗ
A fine country inn retaining charm and character. Its comfortable lounge/bar with attractive and bright rural prints and its panelled dining room serving locally sourced food are deservedly popular with locals and visitors. Guest beers are usually from independent brewers. There is a pleasant terraced garden for the summer months, and a large function room is available. The pub name refers to the slaying of three Danish chieftains in 870 in a battle at nearby Stow; look for the effigies above the entrance. ♨❀◑ĂP⚟

Waddington

Three Horseshoes

High Street, LN5 9RF
⌚ 12 (3 Mon; 11 Sat)-midnight; 12-11 Sun ☎ (01522) 720448
John Smith's Bitter; guest beers Ⓗ
A varying range of ales, mainly from smaller brewers, can be found in this traditional inn tucked away in the heart of the village. Located close to the Viking Way footpath, and within easy access of local bus routes, a good time can be had by all in this hostelry that thrives on community spirit. The main bar is complemented by a smaller, quieter back room, both of which benefit from open fires during the winter months. ♨❀⊞⊟(1,13)♣P⚟

Wainfleet

Batemans Brewery Visitor Centre

Salem Bridge Brewery, Mill Lane, PE24 4JE
⌚ 11.30-3.30; evenings by appointment (winter hours may vary) ☎ (01754) 880317 🌐 batemans.co.uk
Batemans Dark Mild, XB, GHA, XXXB, seasonal beers Ⓗ
A pilgrimage for many, Batemans draws real ale fans from far and wide, so the bar in the iconic windmill is the ideal place to sample those Good Honest Ales. In addition to the core range, a seasonal beer is available. A good selection of Tastes of Lincolnshire food is also offered, and further entertainment is to be found in the Brewery Experience, brewery tours featuring the Theatre of Beers, traditional pub games and the relaxing beer garden. ♨❀◐⊞♿⇌⊟♣P⚟

Westwoodside

Carpenters Arms

Newbigg, DN9 2AT (on B1396 in centre of village)
⌚ 4 (2 Fri & Sat)-11; 12-10.30 Sun ☎ (01427) 752416
🌐 thecarps.co.uk
Caledonian Deuchars IPA; John Smith's Bitter; Wells Bombardier; guest beers Ⓗ
A popular village local, there has been a hostelry on this site since 1861. Distinct bar and lounge areas share a friendly ambience. Five real ales are available, with two usually sourced from micro-breweries. This venue is a major charity fundraiser and one of four participating pubs in the annual

Haxey Hood contest. There is a covered and heated smokers' area and the pub has ambitious plans for a restaurant. Buses are few and far between. Winner of local CAMRA Pub of the Season 2007. ❀⊟⊟(291,399)P⁼–

Wigtoft

Golden Fleece

Main Road, PE20 2NJ
✪ 12-3 (Fri & Sat only), 7-11.30; 12-3, 7-10.30 Sun
☎ (01205) 460021
Batemans Dark Mild, XB ⊞
The Golden Fleece is a remarkable survivor in an era of pub closures. Housed in the Blissbury charity building of 1818, it is still a 'wet only' local in a small Fenland village long bypassed by the A17. The original entrance porch leads to an open interior, formerly two or three separate rooms. The pool table is housed away from the main drinking area. Twin Gaskell and Chambers handpumps from 1900 grace the bar counter. ⛫⊟♣P

Willingham by Stow

Half Moon 🏆

23 High Street, DN21 5JZ (200m from B1241 jct)
✪ 12-2 (Wed-Fri only), 6-11; 12-11 Sat; 12-10.30 Sun
☎ (01427) 788340 🌐 graftersbrewery.com
Grafters Traditional, Over the Moon, Brewers Troop, Moonlight, Darker side of the Moon, Wobble Gob ⊞
Home to the award-wining Grafters Brewery, this popular village pub goes from strength to strength. It serves two permanent Grafters ales with five others on rotation. The renowned home-cooked fish and chip suppers are a must, served Thursday-Saturday evenings and Friday and Saturday lunchtimes. Sunday lunches are 12-3pm. The pub is home to the local football team and is involved in many local fundraising events. Moonlight was awarded champion beer of the Peterborough beer festival 2009. Grafters Greetings is a seasonal Christmas brew. ⛫Q◑⊟⊟(100)♣⁼–▯

Willoughton

Stirrup Inn

1 Templefield Road, DN21 5RZ
✪ 5 (12 Sat & Sun)-11 ☎ (01427) 668270
John Smith's Bitter; guest beers ⊞
Built from local Lincolnshire limestone, this hidden gem in an out-of-the-way location is well worth seeking out. The enthusiastic landlord keeps two varying guest ales to complement the regular beer. The pub attracts locals from the village as well as visitors from further afield, and offers a warm welcome to CAMRA members. Pub quizzes are always popular. ⛫Q❀♣P⁼–

Red Lion Hotel, Spalding

London Index

***Shown on Inner London map**

GREATER LONDON

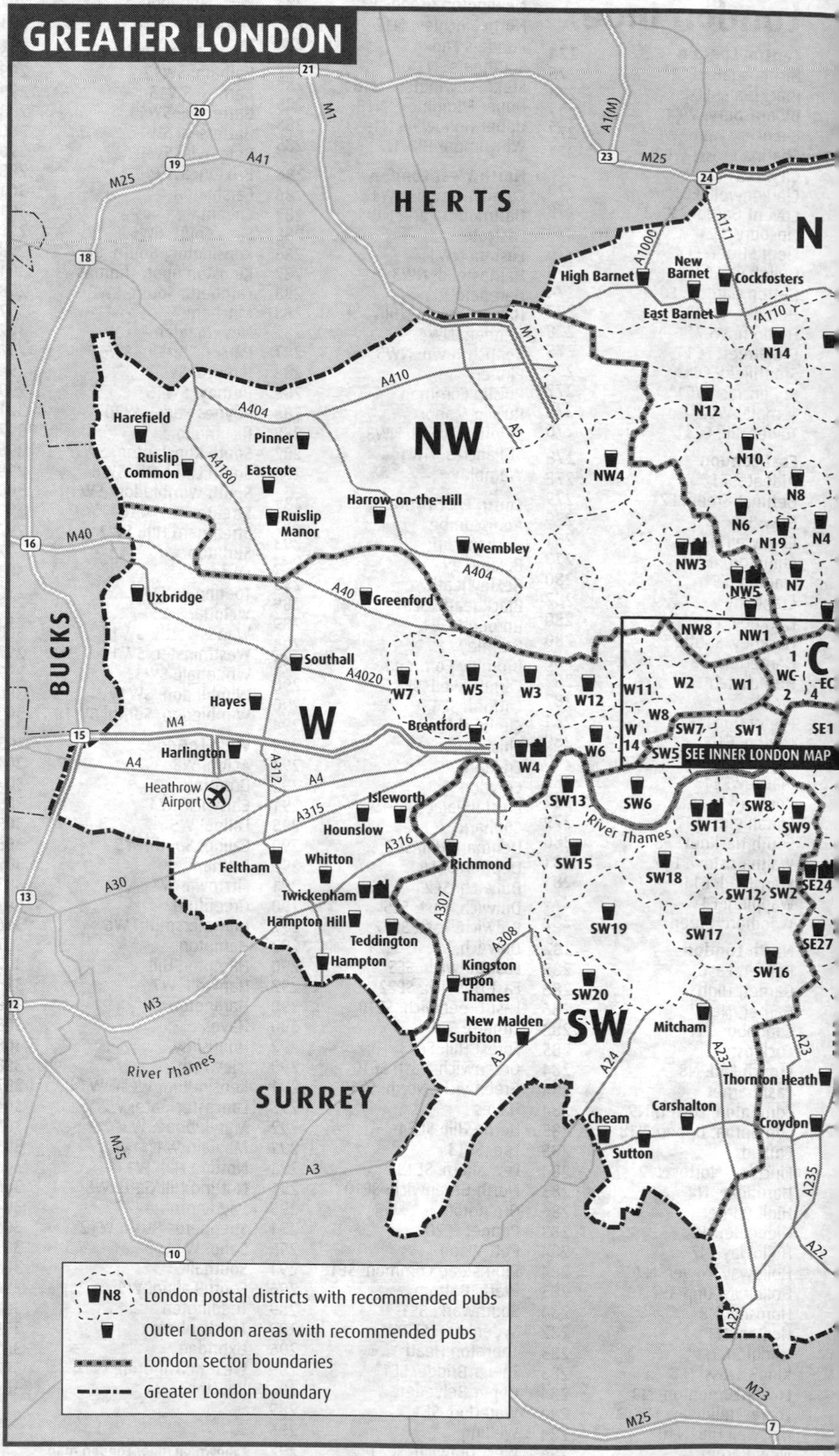

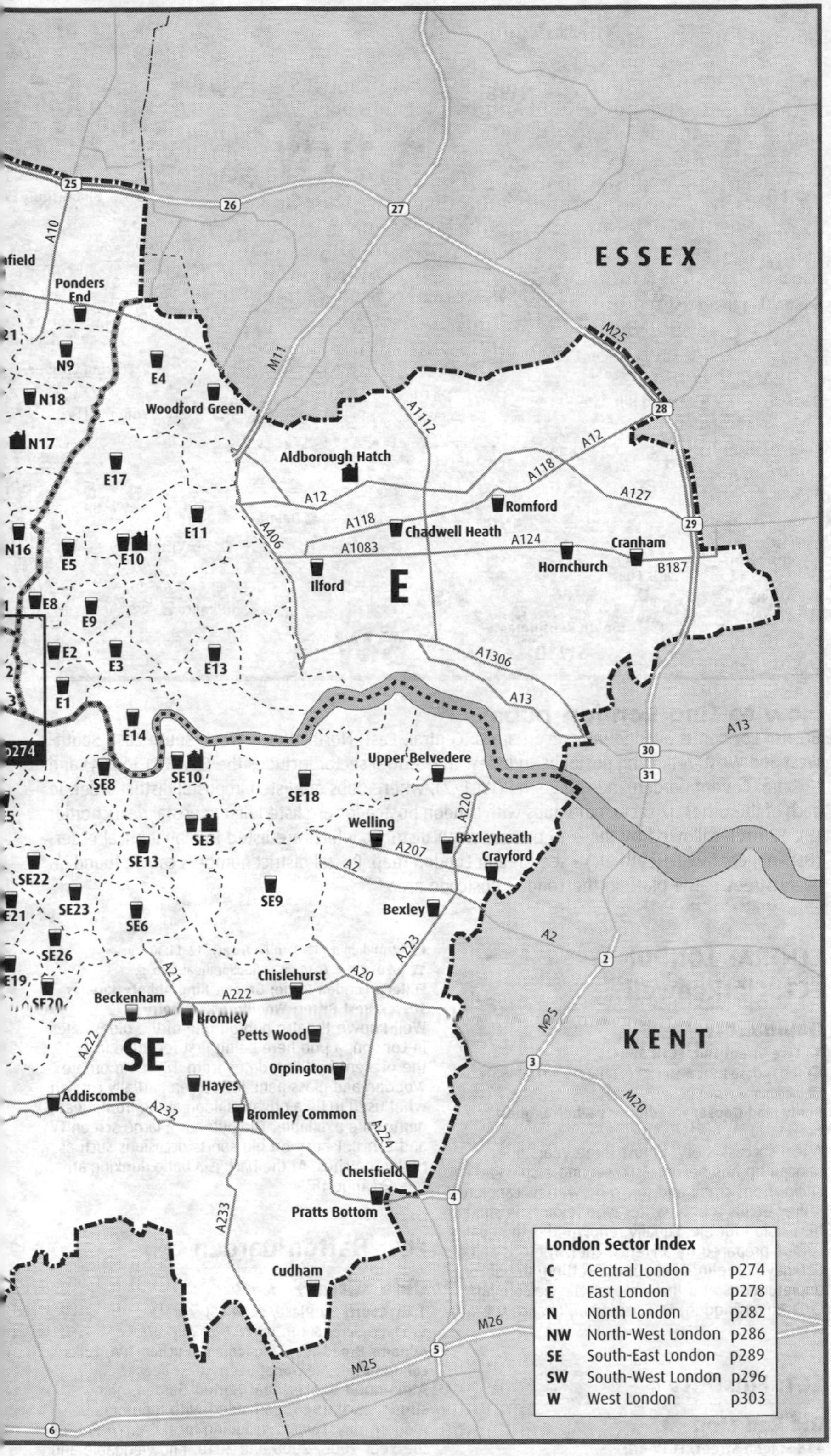
ESSEX
KENT
E
SE
Ponders End
N9
N18
N17
N16
E4
Woodford Green
E17
E11
E5
E10
E8
E9
E2
E3
E13
E1
E14
SE8
SE10
SE18
SE3
SE13
SE22
SE23
SE6
SE9
SE26
E19
SE20
E21
Aldborough Hatch
Romford
Chadwell Heath
Ilford
Hornchurch
Cranham
Upper Belvedere
Welling
Bexleyheath
Crayford
Bexley
Chislehurst
Beckenham
Bromley
Petts Wood
Orpington
Hayes
Addiscombe
Bromley Common
Chelsfield
Pratts Bottom
Cudham
p274
A10
M11
A1112
A12
A118
A127
A406
A1083
A124
B187
A1306
A13
A220
A207
A2
A223
A20
A21
A222
A232
A224
A233
M25
M26
M20
25
26
27
28
29
30
31
2
3
4
5
6
London Sector Index
C Central London p274
E East London p278
N North London p282
NW North-West London p286
SE South-East London p289
SW South-West London p296
W West London p303

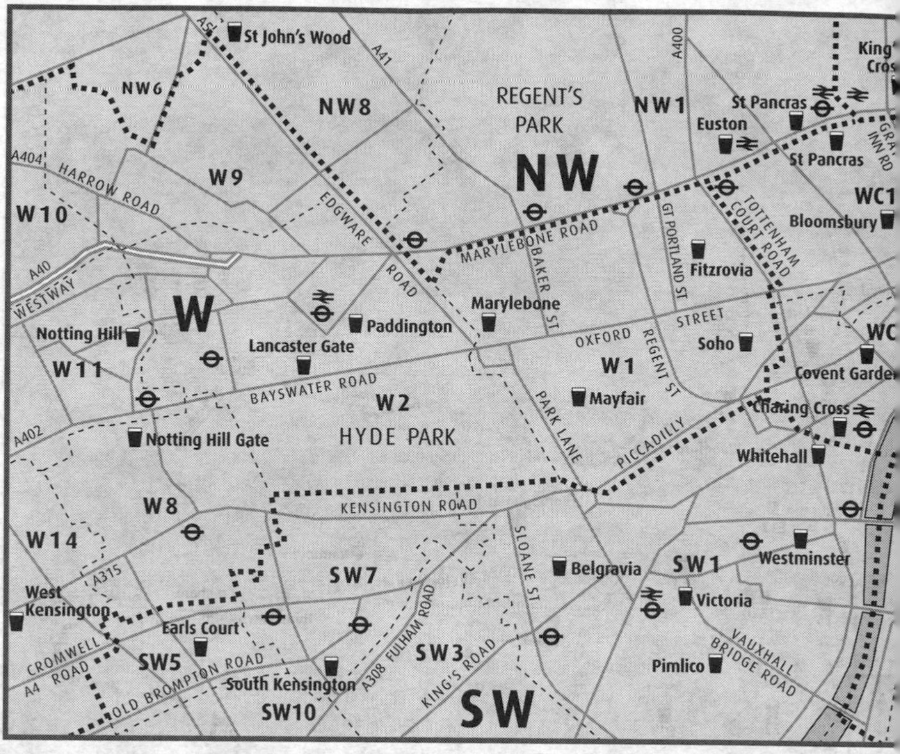

How to find London pubs

Greater London is divided into seven areas: Central, East, North, North-West, South-East, South-West and West, reflecting postal boundaries. The Central sector includes the City (EC1 to EC4) and Holborn, Covent Garden and The Strand (WC1/2), where pubs are listed in postal district order. In each of the other six sectors the pubs with London postcodes are listed first in postal district order (E1, E2 etc), followed by those in outer London districts, which are listed in alphabetical order (Barking, Chadwell Heath etc) – see Greater London map. Postal district numbers can be found on every street name plate in the London postcode area.

CENTRAL LONDON

EC1: Clerkenwell

Gunmakers

13 Eyre Street Hill, EC1R 5ET

⏲ 12-11; closed Sat & Sun ☎ (020) 7278 1022
🌐 thegunmakers.co.uk

Purity Mad Goose; Woodforde's Wherry; guest beers Ⓗ

A real success story: in just three years one handpump has become six, serving a splendid choice from small and micro-breweries. Landlord Jeffrey Bell is a beer writer who rejoices in sharing his passion for ale. Equally renowned is the quality cuisine prepared by a French chef. There is still a Cockney homeliness about the setting; the decor is unpretentious and the atmosphere welcoming.
Q◐ ⇌(Farringdon) ⊖(Farringdon/Chancery Lane) 🚌🍏🍺

EC1: Finsbury

Old Red Lion ✔

418 St John Street, EC1V 4NJ

⏲ 12-midnight (1.30am Fri & Sat); 12-11.30 Sun
☎ (020) 7837 7816 🌐 oldredliontheatre.co.uk

Fuller's London Pride; Greene King Abbot; Harveys Sussex Best Bitter; Woodforde's Wherry Ⓗ

Well-known theatre pub on one of the oldest sites in London, a pub here being first recorded in 1415; the present building dates from 1898. An ornate wooden and glass panelled screen partially cuts off what used to be a private saloon at the front. Board games are available. The pub has a large-screen TV and can get busy on big sports occasions such as rugby matches. At the back is a patio drinking area.
❀♿⊖(Angel)🚌⚟

EC1: Hatton Garden

Olde Mitre 🏆 ★ ✔

1 Ely Court, Ely Place, EC1N 6SJ

⏲ 11-11; closed Sat & Sun ☎ (020) 7405 4751

Adnams Broadside; Caledonian Deuchars IPA; Fuller's London Pride, seasonal beer; guest beer Ⓗ

A diamond boozer near Hatton Garden, going strong since 1546, garlanded with innumerable modern-day awards including local CAMRA Pub of the Year 2006, 2008 and 2010. Knowledgable and

welcoming hosts Kathy and Scotty keep six real ales impeccably. The only weekend opening is the one at the end of the Great British Beer Festival when devotional beer buffs nationwide make an annual pilgrimage. Toasties are a speciality among the popular bar snacks.
Q❀⊟⇌(Farringdon)⊖(Chancery Lane)⊟⚊

EC1: Old Street

Old Fountain

3 Baldwin Street, EC1V 9NU
11-11; closed Sat & Sun ☎ (020) 7253 2970
oldfountain.co.uk
Fuller's London Pride; guest beers Ⓗ
Delightful old free house that has been in the same family for nearly 50 years. It takes its name from one of the medicinal springs for which this part of the City is famous. Seven guest ales are available, often from Dark Star, Red Squirrel and Mighty Oak, with many new and unusual beers on the list. Traditional pub food is served 12-2.30pm and pizzas 5-9pm. ❀◑⊟⇌⊖⊟⚊

EC1: Smithfield

Fox & Anchor

115 Charterhouse Street, EC1M 6AA
8am (9.30am Sat & Sun)-10.30 ☎ (020) 7250 1300
foxandanchor.com
Sharp's Doom Bar; guest beer Ⓗ
Close to Smithfield Market, this pub has been rescued and refurbished back to its Victorian splendour as a smart gastro-pub with accommodation. A long, narrow bar, which can be difficult to navigate when busy, leads to small rooms mainly used by diners. Food is classic British with hearty portions. The house beer, Fox & Anchor Ale, is specially brewed by Nethergate, and seasonal ales are often available. Unusually, beer is served in pewter tankards.
⊟◑⇌(Farringdon)⊖(Barbican)⊟●

Hand & Shears ★

1 Middle Street, EC1A 7JA
11-11; closed Sat & Sun ☎ (020) 7600 0257
Adnams Bitter; Courage Best Bitter, Directors; Wadworth 6X Ⓗ
Hidden down a side street but one to seek out, this historic hostelry has, in different forms, served Smithfield since 1123. Its name reflects a medieval association with the Guild of Merchant Tailors and the cloth trading at Bartholomew Fair nearby. Appropriately, the excellence of its four ales and appetising bar snacks still appeals to members of the five guild livery halls that are within 100 metres. The upstairs room is attractive and frequently used. Q◑⊖(Barbican)⊟

EC2: Bishopsgate

Magpie ✔

12 New Street, EC2M 4TP
11-11; closed Sat & Sun ☎ (020) 7929 3889
Fuller's London Pride; Greene King IPA; Taylor Landlord; guest beer Ⓗ
Tucked away behind Bishopsgate police station, off the opposite side of Bishopsgate from Liverpool Street Station, this City gents' pub now sells up to six guest beers a week. The upstairs bar and restaurant specialises in pies and can also be hired for private functions. One of Mitchells & Butlers best Nicholsons houses and well worth seeking out. Q◑⊟♿⇌⊖(Liverpool St)⊟

EC2: Guildhall

Old Doctor Butler's Head

2 Masons Avenue, EC2V 5BT
11-11; closed Sat & Sun ☎ (020) 7606 3504
Shepherd Neame Master Brew Bitter, Spitfire, Bishops Finger, seasonal beer Ⓗ
Traditional City workers' hostelry originally established in 1610, its present building dating from after the Great Fire of London in 1666. A Shepherd Neame pub serving the full range including special brews from its micro-brewery, the single room comprises a raised rear seating area and a drinking area at the bar. Wood panelling and historic prints add to the atmosphere. On the first floor is a lunchtime restaurant, with a large function room above. ⇌⊖(Moorgate/Bank)⊟

Red Herring ✔

49 Gresham Street, EC2V 7EH
10-11; closed Sat & Sun ☎ (020) 7606 0399
Fuller's London Pride, ESB, seasonal beers Ⓗ
At the heart of the City of London, close to the Guildhall with its art gallery, library and the remains of the Roman ampitheatre, this pub is part of a 1990s office redevelopment. The ground floor bar is welcoming with high ceiling, large windows and light walls, and gets very busy at lunchtimes and early evenings. Food is available in the cellar brasserie which may be hired in the evenings, as can the whole pub at weekends. ◑⊖(St Pauls)⊟

EC3: City

Crosse Keys ✓

9 Gracechurch Street, EC3V 0DR

9am-11 (midnight Fri; 7 Sat); closed Sun

(020) 7623 4824

Greene King Ruddles County, Abbot; guest beers H

Wetherspoon pub housed in the former headquarters of the HSBC bank, complete with some oriental decor. Twenty four handpumps are available, all of them in use on Thursdays and Fridays. As well as the two regular Wetherspoon's beer festivals, the pub holds its own festivals, normally around the same time at weekends. Food is available all day until 10pm on weekdays. A large-screen TV shows terrestrial sporting events. (Cannon St/Liverpool St)(Monument/ Bank)

East India Arms

67 Fenchurch Street, EC3M 4BR

11.30-8.30; closed Sat & Sun (020) 7265 5121

Shepherd Neame Master Brew Bitter, Kent's Best, Spitfire, seasonal beers H

Small red-brick corner pub with limited inside seating, but full of standing customers and those leaning on stools at windows at lunchtimes and in the evening. Tables and chairs are available in a heated outside area. Prints on the walls show this pub has had different names, including the Station Tavern because of its proximity to Fenchurch Street, but it now celebrates the company that traded with and, for a time, ruled India. (Fenchurch St)(Aldgate/Tower Hill)

Ship

3 Hart Street, EC3R 7NB

11.30-11.30; closed Sat & Sun (020) 7481 1871

Butcombe Gold; Courage Best Bitter; Sharp's Doom Bar; guest beer H

This small pub packs a heavy punch. A friendly hostelry, there is plenty going on here, like the Cheesey Quiz every first Tuesday of the month – watch out for spot prize cheese (cheese straws or Babybel missiles being thrown). Customers select the guest ale from the Heineken Cellarman Reserve list. The pub supports charity Y2L (Yes to Life): sponsor a tie for £10. (Fenchurch St)(Tower Hill/Tower Gateway DLR)

EC3: Tower Hill

Crutched Friar ✓

39-41 Crutched Friars, EC3N 2AE

10-11; closed Sat & Sun (020) 7488 3243

Taylor Landlord; guest beers H

You walk into a large lobby where openings to the left and right have plenty of seating for drinking and dining, especially at lunchtimes. A couple of steps lead to the bar, lit by a skylight and serving three changing guests from the M&B lists. Beyond is another drinking area leading to a patio garden. (Fenchurch St)(Tower Hill/Tower Gateway DLR)

Peacock ✓

41 Minories, EC3N 1DT

12-midnight; closed Sat & Sun (020) 7488 3630

Black Sheep Ale; Butcombe Bitter; Harveys Sussex Best Bitter; guest beer H

On the corner of Ibex House, built in Art Deco style in about 1935. The name may reflect symbolism of the Peacock, supposedly wise because of its many 'eyes'. The house of minoresses or Clares, commemorated in the name of the street, was nearby. The single ground floor bar has a dartboard and board games available, but the main playing area for both darts and pool is upstairs. Show your CAMRA membership card for a discount on real ale. (Fenchurch St)(Aldgate/Tower Hill/Tower Gateway DLR)

EC4: Blackfriars

Black Friar ☆ ✓

174 Queen Victoria Street, EC4V 4EG

10-11 (11.30 Fri & Sat); 12-10 Sun (020) 7236 5474

Fuller's London Pride; Sharp's Doom Bar; Taylor Landlord; guest beer H

One of CAMRA's Real Heritage Pubs, this Art Nouveau Grade II*-listed M&B Nicholson's house is unique. The site was once a Dominican friary and hand-crafted sculptures, mosaics and metal reliefs display monkish scenes. Three regular beers and the guest beer are whatever the manager fancies from well-known independents to micro-breweries. Food is served all day.

Cockpit

7 St Andrews Hill, EC4V 5BY

11-11; closed Sat & Sun (020) 7248 7315

Adnams Bitter; Courage Best Bitter, Directors; Marston's Pedigree; guest beers H

Small pub on an old corner site, adapted from one of the Blackfriars Monastery's gateways and most recently rebuilt about 1865. Its shape recreates that of a cockpit and fighting cock prints adorn the walls. (It was renamed the Three Castles in 1849 when cockfighting was prohibited, reverting in 1970.) Enter by the corner door to a drinking area with a bar up a few stairs.

EC4: Fleet Street

Castle

26 Furnival Street, EC4A 1JS

11-11; closed Sat & Sun (020) 7405 5470

Nethergate Redcar Best Bitter; Young's Bitter; guest beers H

A tavern has stood on this site for around 700 years; the area was part of Lincoln's Inn in the 14th century. The current pub dates from 1901 and once had several rooms. The upstairs bar doubles as a restaurant, with food available downstairs as well. Six changing guest beers are on offer, often from small breweries and, interestingly, there are no keg beers on sale. Lunchtime food is available from 12-3pm. (Chancery Lane)

INDEPENDENT BREWERIES

Brew Wharf SE1
Brodie's E10: Leyton
Camden NW3: Hampstead/NW5: Camden
Florence SE24: Herne Hill
Fuller's W4: Chiswick
Ha'penny Aldborough Hatch
Kernel SE1 (NEW)
Meantime SE10: Greenwich
Redemption N17: Tottenham (NEW)
Sambrook's SW11: Battersea
Twickenham Twickenham
Zerodegrees SE3: Blackheath

WC1: Bloomsbury

Calthorpe Arms

252 Grays Inn Road, WC1X 8JR

⌚ 11-11.30 (midnight Fri & Sat); 12-10.30 Sun

☎ (020) 7278 4732

St Austell Tribute; Young's Bitter, Special, seasonal beers Ⓗ

Unusual double doors lead into this single-bar corner local. With no music and an unobstrusive TV in the corner, it is easy to strike up a conversation if you sit on a stool at the bar (sit at one of the tables along the sides for more privacy). The upstairs dining room is open for lunch (12-2.30pm) but can be booked at other times. Evening meals are served 6-9.30pm. Young's bottle-conditioned beers are stocked. There is pavement seating outside. ❀◐◑⇌(King's Cross)⊖(Russell Sq)🚌⛟

Jeremy Bentham

31 University Street, WC1E 6JL

⌚ 11.30-11, closed Sat & Sun ☎ (020) 7387 3033

Young's Bitter; guest beers Ⓗ

Despite appearing to be a one-bar corner pub, there are stairs leading up to the Ladies and a lounge providing welcome extra seating. Situated in the main University College London campus and attracting many academics from the university, it was renamed in 1982 to commemorate the 150th anniversary of the death of the recognised spiritual founder of UCL, in whose college vaults lies his mummified head. This Punch pub serves three regularly changing guests and a Westons cider. ❀◐⇌(Euston)⊖(Euston Sq/Warren St)🚌🍎⛟

Museum Tavern ✔

49 Great Russell Street, WC1B 3BA

⌚ 11.30-11.30 (midnight Fri & Sat); 11.30-10 Sun

☎ (020) 7242 8987

Sharp's Doom Bar; Taylor Landlord; Theakston Old Peculier; guest beers Ⓗ

Friendly and cosmopolitan Victorian bar with a long single room, thronging with locals and tourists. The sign shows Sir Hans Sloane, founder of the British Museum opposite. There has been a tavern on this site since the early 18th century. One of London's Real Heritage Pubs, many period features remain, including the bar back of 1889. A full menu and snacks are available until 10pm. Seven handpumps serve a rapidly changing selection of beers and usually Thatchers cider. Uncovered benches provide outside seating. ❀◐◑⊖(Tottenham Ct Rd)🚌🍎

WC1: Holborn

Penderel's Oak ✔

286-288 High Holborn, WC1V 7HJ

⌚ 8-11 (midnight Thu; 1am Fri); 9-1am Sat; 10-11 Sun

☎ (020) 7242 5669

Greene King Ruddles Best Bitter, Abbot; Marston's Pedigree; guest beers Ⓗ

This large, modern, L-shaped Wetherspoon's pub has a quiet ground floor room, with the full beer selection, and a downstairs bar screening sport with sound or music videos. Up to six regularly changing guest beers are available. French windows face out on to the street, where there are seats for the hardy and the smoker. A family area at the back of the main bar opens until 7pm, with last food orders at 6pm. Food is served until 10pm otherwise.

Q❀◐◑♿⊖(Chancery Lane/Holborn)🚌🍎⛟

WC1: St Pancras

Mabel's Tavern

9 Mabledon Place, WC1H 9AZ

⌚ 11-11 (midnight Thu-Sat); 12-10.30 Sun

☎ (020) 7387 7739

Shepherd Neame Master Brew Bitter, Kent's Best, Spitfire, Bishops Finger, seasonal beers Ⓗ

Named after Mabel Macinelly of Dublin and reportedly haunted by her, this busy pub is anything but eerie. Its closeness to Euston and St Pancras attracts tourists, locals and workers, giving a cross section of clientele, some attracted by the sport on the large TV screens at either end of the pub. A small snug is in an elevated area at one end of the bar. Food is served until 9.30pm (8.30pm Fri-Sun). ❀◐◑⇌⊖(King's Cross/St Pancras)🚌⛟

Skinners Arms

114 Judd Street, WC1H 9NT

⌚ 12-11; closed Sun ☎ (020) 7837 6521

Greene King IPA, Abbot, seasonal beer; guest beer Ⓗ

Taking its name from the City Livery Company, this popular pub has a long room in dark wood with an elevated section on the left as you enter. A smaller section at the rear has a more private feel with a real fire in colder months. Pavement seating is also available. Good value food is served 12-3pm and 5.30-9pm. Independently owned although Greene King products can predominate, it holds mini beer festivals from time to time.

♨❀◐◑⇌⊖(King's Cross/St Pancras)🚌⛟

WC2: Chancery Lane

Knights Templar ✔

95 Chancery Lane, WC2A 1DT

⌚ 9-11.30; 11-5 Sat; closed Sun ☎ (020) 7831 2660

Greene King Ruddles Best Bitter, Abbot; guest beers Ⓗ

The Knights Templar-owned land upon which Chancery Lane was built and this imposing, listed, Wetherspoon's conversion of a former banking hall appeared in the film of The Da Vinci Code. Stairs at the rear lead to interconnected mezzanine level rooms, one reserved until 8pm for families. The 12 handpumps generally dispense up to six guest beers and two draught ciders. The pub can be hired for weddings and private functions on Saturday evenings. TV screens show sport and the pub is Wi-Fi friendly. 🐎◐◑♿⊖🚌🍎

Seven Stars

53-54 Carey Street, WC2A 2JB

⌚ 11 (12 Sat)-11; 12-10.30 Sun ☎ (020) 7242 8521

Adnams Bitter, Broadside; Dark Star Hophead; guest beers Ⓗ

Small, historic, esoteric Enterprise pub, busy mainly with law courts trade. One of London's Real Heritage Pubs, it has a narrow central bar area and two rooms either side. Guest beers include seasonals from Dark Star and other micro-breweries. Film posters and caricatures with a legal theme adorn the walls and a spiral staircase leads to toilets identified by a bisected poster of film stars Audrey Hepburn and Spencer Tracy. The food menu is limited but adventurous. Q◐◑⊖🚌

WC2: Charing Cross

Ship & Shovell

2-3 Craven Passage, WC2N 5PH

⌚ 11-11; closed Sun ☎ (020) 7839 1311

Badger First Gold, Tanglefoot, seasonal beers ⊞
Listed Hall & Woodhouse gem located beneath Charing Cross main line station and uniquely divided into two halves on opposite sides of the passageway. Admiral Sir Cloudesley Shovell's portrait hangs in the main bar, which features bevelled mirrors, engraved glass, nautical pictures, wood panelling, a brass handrail and footrest, and TV for sports. The smaller bar opposite has a dartboard and Crows Nest upstairs room.
◑⇌⊖(Charing Cross/Embankment)🚲

WC2: Covent Garden

Cross Keys
31 Endell Street, WC2H 9EB
✪ 11-11; 12-10.30 Sun ☎ (020) 7836 5185
⊕ crosskeyscoventgarden.com
Brodie's English Best, IPA, Amarilla, seasonal beers ⊞
This unpretentious listed neighbourhood local in the heart of Covent Garden is an Enterprise pub leased by Brodie's. The exterior is covered in foliage. Inside, the walls are festooned with dozens of portraits and prints as well as a stuffed fish and memorabilia of the Fab Four from Liverpool collected over the years. Q❀◑⊖🚲♣

Freemasons Arms
81-82 Long Acre, WC2E 9NG
✪ 12-11 (11.30 Fri & Sat); 12-10.30 Sun ☎ (020) 7836 3115
Shepherd Neame Master Brew Bitter, Spitfire, Bishops Finger, seasonal beers ⊞
Situated near Covent Garden Piazza in the heart of theatreland, a pub has been on this site since 1704. This pub claims to be famous for everything, but one genuine claim to fame is that the Football Association was founded here in 1863. Decor is mock-Victorian, with raised seating towards the rear. ◑⊖🚲

Harp ♟ ✔
47 Chandos Place, WC2N 4HS
✪ 10-11.30 (11 Mon; midnight Fri & Sat); 12-10.30 Sun
☎ (020) 7836 0291 ⊕ harpcoventgarden.com
Dark Star Hophead; Harveys Sussex Best Bitter; Sambrook's Wandle; guest beers ⊞
This small, friendly, independent free house has become a haven for beer choice, generally including a mild or porter, Dark Star and London micro-brewery seasonals. Real ciders, perries and malt whiskies also feature strongly. The narrow bar is adorned with mirrors, theatrical memorabilia and portraits. There is no intrusive music or TV and a cosy upstairs room provides a refuge from the busy throng. To eat there are award-winning real sausages in baps. Local CAMRA Pub of the Year 2006, 2008 and 2010.
Q⇌(Charing Cross)⊖(Charing Cross/Leicester Sq)🚲♠

WC2: Holborn

Ship Tavern ✔
12 Gate Street, WC2A 3HP
✪ 11-11 (midnight Thu & Fri); 12-10 Sun ☎ (020) 7405 1992
⊕ theshiptavern.co.uk
Caledonian Deuchars IPA; Greene King Old Speckled Hen; Theakston Best Bitter; Wells Bombardier; guest beers ⊞
A pub has been on this site since 1549. This former Younger's house with six handpumps runs frequent regional beer festivals. Stripped oak flooring,

booths and maritime prints add to the atmosphere, which is far removed from the bustle of High Holborn. Look out for the pie night promotions. The upstairs restaurant can be booked for private functions. ◑⊖🚲

WC2: Temple

Devereux ✔
20 Devereux Court, WC2R 3JJ
✪ 11-11; closed Sat & Sun ☎ (020) 7583 4562
Fuller's London Pride; guest beers ⊞
This attractive, listed pub was built in 1844; part of the site used to be the Grecian Coffee House. The comfortable lounge has a wood-panelled bar with five handpumps dispensing beers from the Punch list. There are prints on the walls showing local places of interest and historical figures; judges' wigs reflect proximity to the Law Courts. Upstairs is a restaurant available to hire. ◑⊖🚲

Edgar Wallace
40 Essex Street, WC2R 3JF
✪ 11-11; closed Sat & Sun ☎ (020) 7353 3120
⊕ edgarwallacepub.com
Adnams Bitter; Nethergate Edgar's Pale Ale; guest beers ⊞
There has been a pub on this site since 1777. Now leased from Enterprise, this one has so far collected about 140 of the 170 or so books Edgar Wallace wrote. The comfortable downstairs room has a fine wooden bar with seven handpumps. Many of the prints and photos on the walls celebrate rugby and football. There is more seating available upstairs. Look out for beer festivals. Q◑⊖🚲

EAST LONDON
E1: Aldgate

Dispensary
19A Leman Street, E1 8EN
✪ 12-11; closed Sat & Sun ☎ (020) 7977 0486
⊕ thedispensarylondon.co.uk
Dark Star Hophead; Harveys Sussex Best Bitter; guest beers ⊞
The large and imposing cream frontage of this former hospital building leads you into a very smart interior where friendly and attentive staff offer fine wines and dining, but also a bar menu along with excellent, ever-changing ales. Meals are served lunchtimes and evenings daily, either in the main bar or upstairs in the gallery area. Unusually this is a dog-friendly pub, where Bibi, the landlady's cocker poodle, takes pride of place. Local CAMRA Pub of the Year 2009.
◑⊖(Aldgate East)🚲♣↳

Goodman's Field ✔
87/91 Mansell Street, E1 8AN
✪ 7.30am (10am Sat & Sun)-11 ☎ (020) 7680 2850
Greene King Ruddles Best Bitter, Abbot; guest beers ⊞
On the ground floor of an apartment block, this is a comfortable, contemporary and spacious Wetherspoon's pub where even the loos have won a national award. The very pleasant staff cater to a broad mix of office workers, locals and the many tourists who flock to the nearby attractions including the Tower of London, Tower Bridge, St Katharine Docks and the Royal Mint.
◑⇌(Fenchurch St)⊖(Tower Hill/Tower Gateway DLR)🚲

White Swan

21-23 Alie Street, E1 8DA

⏲ 11-11; closed Sat & Sun ☎ (020) 7702 0448

Shepherd Neame Master Brew Bitter, Spitfire, seasonal beer ⊞

This Grade II-listed building a short walk from the heart of the City offers a very warm welcome, hot home-made traditional food at lunchtimes and cold snacks. The half wood-panelled downstairs bar is furnished with large sofas and very cosy. Upstairs is a small room used for diners at lunchtimes and also for small groups holding meetings.
◖⇌(Fenchurch St)⊖(Aldgate/Aldgate East)🚌

E1: Spitalfields

Pride of Spitalfields

3 Heneage Street, E1 5LJ

⏲ 11-midnight (2am Fri & Sat) ☎ (020) 7247 8933

Crouch Vale Brewers Gold; Fuller's London Pride, ESB; Sharp's Doom Bar ⊞

Just off Brick Lane and close to the area's famous curry houses, the Pride has the only real ale in 'Bangla Town'. A genuine free house, the small bar is decorated with photos of the area in bygone days, especially of the Truman Brewery that was nearby. If a curry doesn't tickle your fancy, home-cooked food is served weekdays and roasts are available on Sunday. At busy times, drinkers spill out on to the benches on the pavement.
♛❀◖⇌(Liverpool St)⊖(Aldgate East)🚌⊱

E1: Wapping

Town of Ramsgate ✔

62 Wapping High Street, E1 2PN

⏲ 12-midnight (11 Sun) ☎ (020) 7481 8000

Fuller's London Pride; Sharp's Doom Bar; Young's Bitter ⊞

Welcoming riverside local, dog and children friendly, where historic surroundings contribute to the homely atmosphere. The fishermen of Ramsgate used to land their catch at nearby Wapping Old Stairs to avoid river taxes at Billingsgate. A long, narrow bar leads to a delightful patio overlooking the River Thames, which can be very popular in the summer. Home-cooked food is served until 9pm, Tuesday is steak night and Wednesday curry night.
⛴❀◖◗⊖🚌(100,D3)♣

E2: Bethnal Green

Camel

277 Globe Road, E2 0JD

⏲ 5-11 (midnight Sat); 12-10.30 Sun ☎ (020) 8983 9888

🌐 thecamele2.co.uk

Crouch Vale Brewers Gold; Harveys Sussex Best Bitter ⊞

A small street-corner pub, tucked away behind the Museum of Childhood. The exterior features beautiful brown and cream tiling from its days as a Taylor Walker house, while the interior has an intimate, candle-lit atmosphere. Food consists of pies, served London-style, with mash. The Harveys beer is sometimes replaced by a guest beer, with LocAle brewers supported. Occasional live music includes a local pianist and a banjo player. Hard to think we nearly lost the pub in 2000.
❀◖◗⇌(Bethnal Green/Cambridge Heath)⊖🚌●

Carpenters Arms

73 Cheshire Street, E2 6EG

⏲ 12 (4 Mon)-11.30 (12.30am Fri & Sat) ☎ (020) 7739 6342

🌐 carpentersarmsfreehouse.com

Adnams Bitter, seasonal beer; Taylor Landlord ⊞

A friendly street-corner free house handy for Brick Lane attractions, surviving where many have closed, with ongoing redevelopment changing the surrounding area. There is a cosy single bar, more seating away from the bar area, and a heated enclosed patio. Well worth a visit for the wide selection of bottled beers (UK and European) and ciders. Home-made food is served daily 1-10pm: see the blackboard for daily specials.
◖◗⇌(Liverpool St/Bethnal Green)⊖(Liverpool St)🚌⊱

E3: Bow

Eleanor Arms

460 Old Ford Road, E3 5JP

⏲ 12 (4 Mon)-11 (10.30 Sun) ☎ (020) 8980 6992

Shepherd Neame Kent's Best, seasonal beer; guest beers ⊞

You can be sure of a warm welcome at this wood-panelled family-run Shepherd Neame pub near Victoria Park, the Hertford Union Canal and the remains of the famous Roman Road Market. There are two separate, comfortable bars: the quiet front bar and a rear bar for games with pool table, dartboard and quiz machine as well as a large screen for rugby. The four beers served can include an offering from Shepherd Neame's micro-brewery. ❀⊟⊖(Bow Rd/Bow Church DLR)🚌(8)⊱

Palm Tree

127 Grove Road, E3 5RP (in Mile End Park, road access via Haverfield Rd)

⏲ 12-midnight (1.30am Fri & Sat); 12-late Sun

☎ (020) 8980 2918

Beer range varies ⊞

One of London's Real Heritage Pubs and run by the same family for over 30 years, this pleasantly old-fashioned two-bar pub now stands isolated with a large grassed outdoor drinking area very popular in summer. Generally 4-5% ABV offerings from smaller breweries, the two real ales change constantly. Sandwiches are available weekday lunchtimes. There is live jazz with floor singers on Sunday night, but note strictly no admittance after 10.45pm Friday-Sunday. Local CAMRA Pub of the Year 2007. ❀⊟♿⊖(Mile End)🚌●P⊱

E4: Chingford

Kings Ford ✔

250-252 Chingford Mount Road, E4 8JL

⏲ 9-midnight (1am Fri & Sat) ☎ (020) 8523 9365

Courage Directors; Greene King Ruddles Best Bitter, Abbot; guest beer ⊞

Spacious Wetherspoon pub at the heart of the Chingford community; pictures of Chingford history decorate the walls. Three of the six handpumps serve changing guest ales, including the LocAle beers from Brentwood. Occasional brewery beer festivals are held as well as the Wetherspoon's festivals. The pub is lively at weekends with a diverse customer base. The staff are friendly, efficient and willing to help. ❀◖◗♿🚌⊱

E5: Clapton

Anchor & Hope ✔

15 High Hill Ferry, E5 9HG (800m N of Lea Bridge Rd, along river path)
1 (12 Fri & Sat)-11; 12-10.30 Sun ☎ (020) 8806 1730
Fuller's London Pride, ESB; guest beer H
The easy way to find this pub is to walk northwards up the towpath from Lea Bridge Road. With its panoramic views of Walthamstow Marshes and the River Lea being cleaned up for the Olympics, this makes a special and welcome break for locals, walkers and cyclists on the Lea Valley route. A small one-bar, two-room pub, it offers a guest beer mostly from a micro-brewery. ❀≠(393)♣

Elderfield

57 Elderfield Road, E5 0LF
4 (1 Sat)-11 (midnight Thu-Sat); 1-11 Sun
☎ (020) 8986 1591
Adnams Broadside; Fuller's London Pride; Harveys Sussex Best Bitter; Taylor Landlord H
Friendly family pub, a real locals' local, offering beers from the Punch list in a quiet area of Hackney not normally known for selling real ales. Reverting back to its original name in 2008, it is one of London's Real Heritage Pubs, the panelling and concealed lighting well worth looking out for. Food can be ordered until one hour before closing.
❀≠(Homerton)(242,308)

E8: Hackney

Pembury Tavern

90 Amhurst Road, E8 1JH
12-11 ☎ (020) 8986 8597 individualpubs.co.uk/pembury
Milton Minotaur, Sparta, Nero; guest beers H
A massive 16 handpumps serving five house beers from Milton Brewery, rotating guests and a real cider make the Pembury a beer island in the hustle and bustle of Hackney. The large one-room free house offers bar billiards, pool and board games in peaceful surroundings without gaming machines or TV. At beer festivals held in March, July and November you will see all pumps offering beers, plus 10 extra. The original building dates from the mid-19th century.
Q♿≠(Hackney Central/Downs)♣

E8: South Hackney

Dove

24-28 Broadway Market, E8 4QJ
12-11 (midnight Fri & Sat) ☎ (020) 7275 7617
dovepubs.co.uk
Crouch Vale Brewers Gold; Taylor Landlord; guest beers H
One-bar, split level pub decorated in a European style. In 2009 it was the only British pub to be awarded the Orval Ambassadeur and it has possibly the best selection of Belgian beers in the country. Six handpumps offer two house beers and four changing guests. Tastings are held on a regular basis and are a must for any beer enthusiast. The food menu is superb and the mixed toilets are unique. Q♿≠(London Fields)(236,394)

E9: Homerton

Globe in Morning Lane

20 Morning Lane, E9 6NA
12-midnight (3am Thu & Fri); 11-3am Sat; 11-midnight Sun
☎ (020) 8985 6455
Shepherd Neame Spitfire; Young's Bitter H
A single-bar pub full of entertainment: live music is on offer, free to enjoy, six days a week. The walls are decorated with boxing photos and TVs advertise upcoming events and promotions. Two beers are served by friendly staff and traditional lunchtime pub food represents excellent value (no food Sun). Now the Hackney Empire is closed, this could easily be the best place in Hackney for live entertainment. ❀♿≠(Hackney Central)♣

E10: Leyton

Drum ✔

557-559 Lea Bridge Road, E10 7EQ
9am-midnight (1am Fri & Sat) ☎ (020) 8539 9845
Greene King Ruddles Best Bitter, Abbot; guest beers H
A very welcome return to this Guide for an early example of a Wetherspoon's pub, where manager David Kirby and his team now offer a choice of up to 10 different beers and ciders. They hold two Wetherspoon's festivals a year and also their own mini beer festivals and beer tastings, meet the brewer events and brewery trips. This split-level pub is a friendly place with a conservatory seating area and small patio garden.
❀≠(Leyton Midland Rd)

Leyton Orient Supporters Club

Matchroom Stadium, Oliver Road, E10 5NF
from 12.30 Sat match days; 5.30 week days, not during game. Closing time varies ☎ (020) 8988 8288
orientsupporters.org
Mighty Oak Oscar Wilde; guest beers H
A welcoming and popular social club with a vibrant match day real ale and cider culture, this was CAMRA National Club of the Year joint winner in 2008. Guest beers change rapidly, with LocAle breweries well supported. CAMRA members and those with a copy of this Guide are welcome. The club is open for special events, including 'Piglet' beer festivals normally in March and November, and also one-night brewery festivals: check website for details. The bar is manned by volunteers. ♿⊖

E11: Leytonstone

Birkbeck Tavern

45 Langthorne Road, E11 4HL
11-11 (midnight Fri & Sat); 12-11 Sun ☎ (020) 8539 2584
Beer range varies H
This basic and friendly Victorian corner pub in a back street behind Leyton Underground Station is split into two parts, one with a pool table and smaller bar and the other with the larger bar, screens to watch football (including the local team), three dartboards and more seating. Alongside house beer Rita's Special there are three ever-changing guests, many from micro-breweries and normally up to 4.5% ABV. Outside is a very pleasant garden. ❀♿⊖(Leyton)♣

North Star

24 Browning Road, E11 3AR
4 (12 Sat)-11; 12-10.30 Sun ☎ (07961) 226197
Caledonian Deuchars IPA; Wells Bombardier; guest beers H

Located in the Browning Road conservation area, which seems a million miles from the busy High Road nearby, this very friendly Victorian pub with four changing guest ales attracts a wide cross section of regulars. Original features include a hatch opening on one side of the bar. It also has a delightful beer garden. There is live music every third Sunday of the month, with charity nights three or four times a year. ❀⊟⊖⊟♣

E11: Wanstead

Nightingale ✔

51 Nightingale Lane, E11 2EY
11-midnight (1am Fri & Sat); 12-midnight Sun
☎ (020) 8530 4540
Courage Best Bitter; guest beers H
Tucked away in the back streets of Wanstead, this Enterprise establishment is a popular community pub with two main rooms round the bar plus an alcove and a separate room that can be used for meetings. The current leaseholder has been here for 22 years. Four guest beers change regularly and an excellent all round menu is available during the day. Tuesday is quiz night and Wednesday Irish music night. ⊖(Snaresbrook)⊟(W12)

E13: Plaistow

Black Lion ✔

59-61 High Street, E13 0AD
11-11; 12-10.30 Sun ☎ (020) 8472 2351
Courage Best Bitter; guest beers H
An early 16th-century coaching inn rebuilt about 280 years ago retaining some original features including low ceilings, oak beams and a cobbled courtyard. East Anglian breweries regularly appear on the guest list in this top quality free house in what is otherwise a real ale desert. Excellent home-cooked food is served lunchtimes and early evenings, excluding bank holidays. A function room is available for hire and there is a local boxing club alongside. ❀⊟⊖⊟P

E14: Isle of Dogs

Gun ✔

27 Coldharbour, E14 9NS
11-midnight (11 Sun) ☎ (020) 7515 5222
thegundocklands.com
Adnams Bitter; Greene King Abbot; Young's Bitter H
Historic Thames-side pub dating from 1710 and once tied to Hodgsons brewery of Bow. It survived a disastrous fire in 2001, reopening as a place that celebrates good beer and fine food. Besides the main dining area, there are three bars for drinkers to choose from and a riverside terrace overlooking the O2 arena. In summer the dining experience moves outside to a large terrace at the side of the pub. ❀⊟⊖(Blackwall DLR)⊟(D3,D7)

North Pole

74 Manilla Street, E14 8LG
11-3, 5-11; closed Sat & Sun ☎ (020) 7987 5443
Black Sheep Best Bitter; Fuller's London Pride; Taylor Landlord H
The pub is surrounded by new high rise offices. Walk from South Quay station along Marsh Wall for about 400 metres, turn down the steps on the left and the original glass fronted corner pub beckons you into a single horseshoe bar with wood-panelled walls. Although the interior is not original, it has not been modernised, and there is character and a warm welcome. The dartboard is used by the ladies team on a Monday. Food is available lunchtimes only. ⊖(South Quay DLR)⊟

E17: Walthamstow

Nags Head

9 Orford Road, E17 9LP
4 (2 Fri; 12 Sat)-11; 12-10.30 Sun ☎ (020) 8520 9709
thenagsheade17.com
Mighty Oak Oscar Wilde, Maldon Gold; Nethergate Augustinian; Taylor Landlord; guest beer H
Friendly one-bar pub in Walthamstow village. The Itinerant (3.8%) is specially brewed for the pub in honour of Tetley, the village cat, who is a regular visitor. There is a pleasant rear garden with a heated area for smokers and bench tables outside at the front. Occasional beer festivals are held and jazz oriented live music is performed on Sunday afternoon. There are no TVs and no food is served. Mild is always available – a rarity in London. ❀⇌⊖(Walthamstow Central)⊟(W12)

Olde Rose & Crown

53-55 Hoe Street, E17 4SA
10-11 (midnight Fri & Sat); 12-11 Sun ☎ (020) 8509 3880
yolderoseandcrowntheatrepub.co.uk
Beer range varies H
In under two years five friends have transformed this Enterprise inn into an exceptional local community pub, welcoming families, dogs and theatre-goers alike. It attracts many supporters to a wide range of events held in the pub itself or the two function rooms including an upstairs theatre. Mini cider festivals are held occasionally. The pub has an ever-changing range of beers normally from smaller breweries or micro-breweries. ♿⇌⊖(Walthamstow Central)⊟

Waltham Forest Corporation Sports & Social Club

Waltham Forest Town Hall, Forest Road, E17 4JF
12-11 (midnight Fri); closed Sat; 12-10.30 Sun
☎ (020) 8527 3944
Crouch Vale Essex Boys Bitter; guest beers H
This private members club, located behind the Town Hall, welcomes CAMRA members and visitors with a copy of the Guide. Two changing guest ales are available and beer festivals are held in April and November. Food is served lunchtimes and Friday evenings, with jerk dishes a speciality. There is a main bar and the smaller Hatters bar. Football is screened, especially Spurs matches. A charge of £1 on Friday covers live entertainment. ⊟⊟

Chadwell Heath

Eva Hart ✔

1128 High Road, RM6 4AH (on A118)
9am-midnight ☎ (020) 8597 1069
Courage Best Bitter, Directors; Greene King Ruddles Best Bitter, Abbot; Marston's Pedigree; guest beers H
This large, comfortable Wetherspoon's pub, previously the local police station, is named after a local singer and music teacher who was one of the longest-living survivors of the Titanic disaster: photographs and memorabilia are on display. Up to four guest ales are served on handpump, usually including at least one stout or porter. A real cider is available from Westons. Good value food is served until 10pm. Q❀♿⇌⊟P

Cranham

Thatched House ✓

St Mary's Lane, RM14 3LT (on B187)
12-11 (10.30 Sun) ☎ (01708) 641408
vintageinn.co.uk/thethatchedhouseupminster
Adnams Broadside; Fuller's London Pride; guest beer H
Considerably extended, popular, family M&B pub on edge of countryside, now rather dominated by its food trade; don't be put off by the 'please wait here to be seated' notice as you enter the bar area. The pub has one ever-changing guest beer. The fireplace that used to be at the back of the pub now marks the boundary between the bar and restaurant. There are tables and chairs on the open decking at the rear. ❀◐P

Hornchurch

JJ Moons ✓

Unit 3, 46-62 High Street, RM12 4UN (on A124)
9am-midnight (12.30am Fri & Sat); 9am-11.30 Sun
☎ (01708) 478410
Greene King Abbot; Marston's Pedigree; guest beers H
An impressive range of guest beers greets you at this busy Wetherspoon's pub near the end of the High Street. The usual collection of local historic photographs and information includes a feature on John Cornwall, the boy hero of the Battle of Jutland. Breakfast is served until midday and food up to 11pm. A family area is available until 6pm. At the back is a covered smoking area.
Q◐◑♿⇌(Emerson Pk)🚌⁻

Ilford

Prince of Wales

63 Green Lane, IG1 1XJ (on A1083)
12-11.30 ☎ (020) 8478 1326
Fuller's London Pride; Greene King IPA; Young's Bitter; guest beers H
This very pleasant local has a small, cosy saloon bar and a larger L-shaped public bar. Regular beers are supplemented by three guests. The public bar houses a dartboard and there is an outdoor pool table. Regular quiz nights are held. The rear garden is comfortable and well maintained, with a heated, covered smokers' area. There is ample parking. Meals are served 12-9pm. This S&N/Heineken establishment is a welcome addition to an area dominated by keg pubs. ❀◐◑⊡♿🚌(128,145)P⁻

Romford

Golden Lion ✓

2 High Street, RM1 1HR
11-midnight (1am Sat); 11-11 Sun ☎ (01708) 740081
Greene King IPA; guest beers H
Close to Romford Market, this Punch town-centre pub was a coaching inn on the route from London to Colchester. A Grade II-listed building, it dates back to the 15th century and still retains some of the original beams. The pub normally has five ales on handpump, with up to 10 during its beer festivals. Regular live music plays on Wednesday and Thursday evenings. There is a yard at the rear.
❀◑⇌🚌P

Woodford Green

Cricketers

299-301 High Road, IG8 9HQ (on A1099)
11-11 ☎ (020) 8504 2734
McMullen AK, Country Bitter, seasonal beers H
A comfortable local with a country feel, a dartboard in the public bar and plaques in the saloon for all 18 first-class cricket counties, together with photographs of local MP Sir Winston Churchill, whose statue stands on the green almost opposite. Good value food (including pensioners' specials) is served Monday to Saturday lunchtimes. There is patio seating at the front, a covered smoking area with picnic bench, and boules is played behind the pub. Q❀◐⊡♿🚌(179,W13)♣P⁻

Traveller's Friend 🏆

496-498 High Road, IG8 0PN (on slip road off A104)
12-11; 12-4, 7-11 Sun ☎ (020) 8504 2435
Adnams Broadside; Courage Best Bitter; Wells Bombardier; guest beer H
An absolute gem of a local and one of London's Real Heritage Pubs, this friendly, comfortable, Barracuda pub company establishment features oak-panelled walls and rare original snob screens. There are normally two guest beers. Small beer festivals are held in April and September. As far as is known, the pub has never sold keg bitter. There is a heated, covered patio/smoking area at the rear, and a very small car park. Local CAMRA Pub of the Year 2008 and 2010. Q❀♿🚌(20,179,W13)P⁻

NORTH LONDON

N1: Canonbury

Lord Clyde

340-342 Essex Road, N1 3PB
12-11 (midnight Sat); 12-10.30 Sun ☎ (020) 7288 9850
thelordclyde.com
Harveys Sussex Best Bitter; guest beer H
A welcoming locals' pub with original Charrington woodwork carefully blended to feel traditional yet comfy. The ethos of real ale and great service marries well with good fresh pub food at pub prices. It has a separate public bar, tranquil sunny decked area at the back for enjoying a Sunday roast, and seating in front to watch the world go by. Chill out with friends, join the popular quiz every other Monday or just relax with a quiet pint and your newspaper. ⚒❀◐◑⊡⇌(Essex Rd)🚌♣⁻

N1: Hoxton

Prince Arthur

49 Brunswick Place, N1 6EB
11.30-midnight (may close earlier); 12-6 Sat & Sun
☎ (020) 7253 3187
Shepherd Neame Canterbury Jack, Master Brew Bitter, Spitfire, seasonal beers H
This is a bow-windowed Victorian building which sticks out of a modern industrial area, down a turning off East Street. Serving mostly local residents, it is a small and friendly pub, with boxing (the landlord is former boxer Dixie Dean) and racing pictures. There is ample seating at the front and a prominent darts area with silverware on the mantelpiece down a couple of steps. Snacks are served at all times. In summer there is seating outside. ❀⇌⊖(Old St)🚌♣⁻

N1: Islington

Charles Lamb

16 Elia Street, N1 8DE
⏲ 12 (4 Mon & Tue)-11; 12-10.30 Sun ☎ (020) 7837 5040
🌐 thecharleslambpub.com
Butcombe Bitter; Dark Star Hophead; guest beer Ⓗ
The building dates from 1839 and was converted from three shops in the 1920s. A small, cosy free house in a residential area just south of the Regent's Canal, it serves distinctive food, chiefly in the rear room. The pub supports local artists, has a shove ha'penny board and boules is played in the street outside on Bastille Day. There are covered smokers' tables on the pavement. Cider is sold fresh in summer and mulled in winter.
❀◑⇌(Essex Rd)⊖(Angel)🚌♣●⌐

N1: King's Cross

King Charles I

55-57 Northdown Street, N1 9BL
⏲ 12-11 (1am Fri); 5-11 Sat; 5-10.30 Sun ☎ (020) 7837 7758
Beer range varies Ⓗ
Small, cosy, wood-panelled pub in a Georgian building, with a bar billiards machine and knick-knacks including African masks. A back-street single-room local serving workers and residents, it is just far enough from King's Cross to avoid tourists. One of the four handpumps features Brodie's beers; the rest have rotating guests. Snacks and board games are available, and poker tournaments are hosted. The outside seating is partly covered.
❀⇌⊖(King's Cross/St Pancras)🚌♣⌐

N1: Newington Green

Nobody Inn ✔

92 Mildmay Park, N1 4PR
⏲ 12-11 (midnight Thu-Sat) ☎ (020) 7249 6430
St Austell Tribute; Woodforde's Wherry; guest beer Ⓗ
Spacious pub facing Newington Green, attracting the 25+ crowd and featuring regular real ale festivals. The pub is divided into three areas, including one with a pool table and TV sports and another featuring a traditional telephone box. All areas have modern 'North London' decor and are furnished with a mix of scrubbed tables, chairs and sofas. The cider is Westons Traditional Scrumpy. Thai food is served lunchtimes 12-3.30pm and evenings 5-10pm (12.30-10pm Sun).
◑⇌(Canonbury)🚌●

N4: Harringay

Old Ale Emporium ✔

405 Green Lanes, N4 1EU
⏲ 11-midnight (1am Fri & Sat); 12-midnight
☎ (020) 8348 6200 🌐 oldaleemporium.co.uk
Fuller's London Pride; guest beers Ⓗ
This late 20th-century shop conversion offers a range of four ales. There is adequate seating with chairs and tables inside, and outside on the patio. With a late licence at weekends, three screens for sport, a jukebox, a dartboard and team, plus shelves of books, this pub has something for everyone. Friendly management and staff create a great ambience that makes this a true community pub. ❀♿⇌(Harringay Green Lanes)🚌♣⌐

Salisbury ★

1 Grand Parade, Green Lanes, N4 1JX
⏲ 5-midnight (1am Thu; 2am Fri); 12-2am Sat; 12-11.30 Sun
☎ (020) 8800 9617
Fuller's Discovery, London Pride, ESB; Gale's HSB; guest beer Ⓗ
One of CAMRA's Real Heritage Pubs, this Grade II*-listed 1899 building was the work of JC Hill, who also designed the Queens Hotel in nearby Crouch End. A wealth of high Victorian features is evident: stained glass windows, tiled walls, floor mosaics and the ever-popular skylights in the former saloon and billiards rooms. Fuller's beers are supplemented by occasional guests from micro-breweries. Excellent food, genuine Czech lagers, regular salsa, quiz and jazz nights can all be found here. ♛◑⇌(Harringay Green Lanes)🚌

N6: Highgate

Gatehouse ✔

1 North Road, N6 4BD
⏲ 9am-11.30 (midnight Fri & Sat); 9am-10.30 Sun
☎ (020) 8340 8054
Greene King Ruddles Best Bitter, Abbot; Marston's Pedigree; guest beers Ⓗ
This large, Tudor-style Wetherspoon's pub on a busy corner in Highgate village was once a toll house. The L-shaped bar with a profusion of booths leads to a dining area at the rear and ramped access to a fair-sized enclosed garden with heaters. The theatre upstairs generates plenty of business for pre- and post-performance drinks and meals. Disabled access is at the north door. The pub has recently launched its own Facebook site for regulars. Board games are available.
Q❀◑♿⊖🚌♣●⌐

Prince of Wales

53 Highgate High Street, N6 5JX
⏲ 12-11 (midnight Fri & Sat) ☎ (020) 8340 0445
Butcombe Bitter; guest beers Ⓗ
Squeezed between the bustle of Highgate High Street and the calm of Pond Square, this pub offers up to three guest beers and an interior relatively unchanged over the years. It can get busy, particularly on Tuesday quiz night, perhaps because the quiz is one of the most testing in the capital. Thai food is served Monday-Friday 12-3pm and 6-10pm, Saturday 12-10pm. Sunday roasts are available 12-9pm. At the back is an outdoor drinking/smoking area. Q❀◑⊖🚌♣⌐

Red Lion & Sun

25 North Road, N6 4BE
⏲ 12-11 (midnight Thu-Sat) ☎ (020) 8340 1780
🌐 theredlionandsun.com
Greene King IPA, Morland Original; Hook Norton Old Hooky; guest beer Ⓗ
Fronted by a large, open patio, this pub has been opened out into an L-shaped room, leading to a garden at the rear. Two bay windows at the front add character as do candles, subtle lighting, mixed tables, chairs and sofas, a log fire in winter and wood panelling. Dogs and children are welcome until 8pm, there is wireless Internet access and an imaginative menu is served until 10pm (9pm Sun). The guest beer changes every week.
♛❀◑♿⊖🚌⌐

N7: Holloway

Coronet ✔

338-346 Holloway Road, N7 6NJ
⏲ 9am-11 (11.30 Fri & Sat); 9am-10.30 Sun
☎ (020) 7609 5014
Greene King Ruddles Best Bitter, Abbot; Marston's Pedigree; guest beers Ⓗ
Impressive Wetherspoon's conversion of an old cinema, with large pictures of former screen stars adorning the walls. The main hall is dominated by an old projector mounted in the centre of a raised dais. Five or six guest ales can be depended upon here, one of very few real ale outlets in this area and popular with all age groups. Behind is a heated outdoor smoking area. Prices increase on Arsenal home match nights. Occasional single brewery mini-festivals are hosted.
Q❀◐◑♿⊖(Holloway Rd)🚌🍎⚟

N7: Lower Holloway

Duchess of Kent

441 Liverpool Road, N7 8PR
⏲ 12-11 (midnight Fri & Sat) ☎ (020) 7609 7104
Adnams Broadside; Sambrook's Wandle; guest beers Ⓗ
A smart corner pub with tables outside, divided into two main areas. The front has scrubbed tables and bare boards; the larger L-shaped rear part is carpeted, furnished with a mix of tables and comfy chairs, and principally set aside for dining. The regularly changing menu features dishes such as slow roast belly pork. Quiz night is Monday.
❀◐◑⇌⊖(Highbury & Islington)🚌⚟

N8: Crouch End

Harringay Arms

153 Crouch Hill, N8 9QH
⏲ 12-11.30 (midnight Fri & Sat) ☎ (020) 8340 4243
Adnams Broadside; Caledonian Deuchars IPA; Courage Best Bitter; Wells Bombardier Ⓗ
Easily Crouch End's most traditional real ale pub – small from the outside, cosy on the inside – and a regular Guide entry. One wall features historic local maps, another has old photos of Irish literary figures. There is televised sport, darts and chess on request, and a quiz night on Tuesday. Courage Best is the house beer, with two of the other three listed beers available on rotation. There is a small rear garden for smokers. ❀⇌(Crouch Hill)🚌♣⚟

N8: Hornsey

Three Compasses ✔

62 High Street, N8 7NX
⏲ 11-11 (midnight Fri & Sat); 12-11 Sun ☎ (020) 8340 2729
Caledonian Deuchars IPA; Fuller's London Pride; Taylor Landlord; guest beers Ⓗ
This Guide regular since 2006 has collected CAMRA National Community Pub of the Year and local Branch Pub of the Season awards along the way. The pub features three changing guest ales alongside the three regular brews. It also hosts two beer festivals a year. Food is served until 10pm (9.30pm Sun). There is a weekly Monday quiz as well as pool, darts and board games, and big screen sports coverage.
◐◑♿⇌(Hornsey)🚌(144,W3)♣⚟🥛

N9: Lower Edmonton

Beehive

24 Little Bury Street, N9 9JZ
⏲ 12-midnight (1am Fri & Sat); 12-11 Sun
☎ (020) 8360 4358
Draught Bass; Fuller's London Pride; Greene King IPA, Old Speckled Hen; guest beer Ⓗ
The lessee of this one-bar Punch house has improved it in all aspects, winning the local CAMRA Pub of the Year award in 2009. Home-cooked meals with vegetarian alternatives include a range of daily specials, with traditional London pie and mash available every day. Fish features on the menu Tuesday to Saturday; roast dinners are served on Sunday until 6pm. Outside is a heated, covered smoking area. No admittance after 11pm.
❀◐🚌(329,W8)♣P⚟

N10: Muswell Hill

John Baird

122 Fortis Green Road, N10 3HN
⏲ 11-11 (midnight Fri & Sat); 12-10.30 Sun
☎ (020) 8444 8830 🌐 johnbaird-muswellhill.co.uk
Black Sheep Best Bitter; Wells Bombardier; guest beers Ⓗ
A busy local built on a former bomb site, named after the television pioneer and popular with sports fans, shoppers and cinema-goers. The pub has wide-screen TV, a thriving Thai restaurant to the side and a secluded patio to the rear, which doubles as a heated smoking area in winter. Sunday roasts are served all day. Four varying guest beers are offered and occasional beer festivals hosted. Disabled access is via the mews and rear patio. 🔥❀◐◑♿🚌(102,234)♣🍎⚟

Maid of Muswell ✔

121 Alexandra Park Road, N10 2DP
⏲ 12-11 (11.30 Fri & Sat); 12-10.30 Sun ☎ (020) 8883 4971
🌐 themaidofmuswell.co.uk
Fuller's London Pride; Taylor Landlord; guest beers Ⓗ
This recently refurbished M&B pub, halfway between Muswell Hill and Bounds Green, is popular for lunchtime and evening family meals, including Sunday roasts. Lots of comfortable seating is available, and outside seating around the forecourt and in the rear garden, with a heated pergola for smokers. A large number of board games are provided, as well as a piano on Sunday afternoon and quiz on Tuesday evening. Note: lined half-pint glasses are used, but brim measure pints. ❀◐◑🚌(102,299)♣⚟

N12: North Finchley

Elephant Inn

283 Ballards Lane, N12 8NR
⏲ 11-11 (midnight Fri & Sat); 12-10.30 Sun
☎ (020) 8343 6110
Fuller's Discovery, London Pride, ESB; guest beer Ⓗ
Comfortable and spacious three-bar Fuller's pub with a large front patio. A Thai restaurant is open upstairs 6-10pm (12-10pm at weekends) and bar food is also available lunchtimes and evenings, all day Thursday to Sunday. Children may eat until 8pm in the bar, 10pm in the restaurant. Service is friendly with a landlady and staff keen to promote real ale. Theme, charity, quiz and poker nights are hosted, and occasional live music. WiFi available.
❀◐◑♿🚌♣⚟

N14: Southgate

New Crown ✔

80-84 Chase Side, N14 5PH

9-11.30 (12.30am Fri & Sat) ☎ (020) 8882 8758

Greene King Ruddles Best Bitter, Abbot; guest beers Ⓗ

This large Wetherspoon's pub is handily placed for shops, buses and Tube and can be busy at times, but service is generally efficient and there is plenty of seating. Four rapidly changing guest beers are normally available and pump clips from many past ales are on display above the bar. There are occasional brewery beer festivals in addition to the national ones where extra beers are on cooled gravity stillage. Sparklers may be used: if concerned, ask for removal.

N16: Stoke Newington

Daniel Defoe ✔

102 Stoke Newington Church Street, N16 0LA

12 (4 Mon-Fri Nov-Apr)-midnight ☎ (020) 7254 2906

thedanieldefoe.com

Courage Directors; St Austell Tribute; Wells Bombardier; guest beer Ⓗ

A friendly single-bar Victorian corner local with a reputation for convivial drinking and dining and a pleasant, well-furnished walled garden. The name acknowledges the area's subtantial literary heritage. The guest beer changes fortnightly, the list of malts is impressive and food is served from opening until 9.30pm. This Charles Wells pub often stays open beyond midnight. WiFi access is provided.

N18: Upper Edmonton

Gilpin's Bell ✔

50-54 Fore Street, N18 2SS

9am-11.30 (12.30am Fri & Sat) ☎ (020) 8884 2744

Greene King IPA, Abbot; guest beers Ⓗ

Brentwood and Itchen Valley beers are regular guests at this Wetherspoon's conversion, with the story of its unusual name framed on a wall. When there are home games at the nearby Spurs ground, entry is restricted to match ticket holders four hours prior to and after the match. The busy main bar has TV sports, but there are three separate quieter areas. The large rear patio has partial cover and heaters. Sparklers may be used: if concerned, ask for removal. (White Hart Lane)P

N19: Upper Holloway

North Nineteen ✔

194-196 Sussex Way, N19 4HZ

1-midnight; 12-1am Fri & Sat; 12-midnight Sun

☎ (020) 7281 2786 northnineteen.co.uk

Fuller's ESB; Skinner's Betty Stogs; guest beers Ⓗ

An unusual pub in these modern times, having two separate bars with entrances surrounded by two seating areas. The larger front bar has three real ales, a screen for sport and a raised area for singing, poetry etc. The smaller back bar has up to six real ales and 30 whiskies. Pint jugs are used in both bars and there is a discount for CAMRA members. The Sunday roast is recommended and there is a garden for summer barbecues.

(91,210)

N21: Winchmore Hill

Dog & Duck

74 Hoppers Road, N21 3LH

12-11 (10.30 Sun) ☎ (020) 8886 1987 dogandduck.info

Fuller's London Pride; Greene King IPA; Taylor Landlord; guest beer Ⓗ

This small, single bar back-street local has a loyal following and offers a warm welcome to visitors. Note the etched glass in the front doors indicating former saloon and public bars. The walls are adorned with old photographs and maps of the area, together with sports posters. Sporting events are shown on a large screen. The secluded garden has a covered and heated area for smokers. Try the complementary samosas and bhajis early on Friday evenings in winter. (W9)

Orange Tree

18 Highfield Road, N21 3HA

12-midnight (1am Fri & Sat); 12-11 Sun

☎ (020) 8360 4853

Greene King IPA, Old Speckled Hen; guest beer Ⓗ

A well maintained back-street local close to Green Lanes and the New River. The one main bar is divided into three distinct parts, one with a pool table and dartboard, another with large screen TVs for football and other sporting events, and a third quieter area. A wide selection of home-prepared food is available lunchtimes, plus Sunday roasts. The large family-friendly garden has a children's play area and barbecues in summer. There is no admittance after 11pm. (329)P

Cockfosters

Cock & Dragon ✔

14 Chalk Lane, EN4 9HU TQ277967

11-11 (11.30 Fri & Sat); 11-10.30 Sun ☎ (020) 8449 7160

cockanddragon-cockfosters.co.uk

Greene King IPA; guest beers Ⓗ

A pub with a history, set in the former royal hunting forest of Enfield Chase, now at the very end of the Piccadilly Line. The large main bar has several alcoves, creating a cosy atmoshere. A separate restaurant serves English meals lunchtimes and Thai food lunchtimes and evenings. The extensive rear garden has a large decked section. To the side is a covered, heated area.

(298)P

East Barnet

Prince of Wales ✔

2 Church Hill Road, EN4 8TB

11-11; 12-midnight Fri & Sat; 12-11 Sun

☎ (020) 8440 5392 theprinceofwalesbarnet.co.uk

Adnams Bitter; Fuller's London Pride; guest beer Ⓗ

A very large single bar with three distinct areas including a family area and sports bar. At the heart of East Barnet village, the pub provides a warm, relaxed and welcoming environment, much due to a long-standing landlady, and is known locally for its variety of guest beers and good pub food. Events include a Sunday night quiz, and poker on Tuesday. Disabled access is at the rear through the car park. (Oakleigh Pk)(184,307)P

Enfield

Moon Under Water ✔

115-117 Chase Side, EN2 6NN

✪ 9am-11 ☎ (020) 8366 9855
Courage Best Bitter; Greene King Ruddles Best Bitter, Abbot; Marston's Pedigree; guest beers Ⓗ
This spacious Wetherspoon's pub, a conversion from a dairy over 20 years ago, has two main seating areas around a U-shaped bar. It attracts a regular clientele. Breakfasts are served until noon, meals until 10pm (families welcome until 8.30pm). Various brands of real cider are served on gravity. Sparklers may be used: if concerned, ask for removal! ❀◐♿⇌(Gordon Hill)🚌(191,W9)●P⌐

Wonder

1 Batley Road, EN2 0JG (near jct of Chase Side and Lancaster Rd)
✪ 11-11 (midnight Fri & Sat); 12-11 Sun ☎ (020) 8363 0202
McMullen AK, Cask Ale, Country Bitter, seasonal beer Ⓗ
Timeless, traditional locals' pub that still retains two bars. A friendly atmosphere is enhanced on weekend evenings by a piano sing-along, often with a chap on spoons and the landlady on tea chest double bass or washboard. In winter there is a real fire that provides an additional homely feel. A football-free zone with no TV, there is however a dartboard in regular use. Local CAMRA Pub of the Year for three recent consecutive years.
♨Q❀⊟♿⇌(Gordon Hill)🚌(191,W8)P⌐

High Barnet

Lord Nelson

14 West End Lane, EN5 2SA
✪ 12-11 (midnight Fri & Sat); 12-10.30 Sun
☎ (020) 8449 7249 🌐 thelordnelsonph.co.uk
Wells Bombardier; Young's Bitter, Special, seasonal beer Ⓗ
A traditional one-bar back-street local just off Wood Street, with well-established tenants and a regular clientele where women will feel comfortable and dogs and cats are welcome. Look out for the interesting collection of cruet sets and nautical memorabilia. The popular home-cooked food (available until 8.30pm) is to die for and the pub has won many awards for its beer quality. There is also a good selection of bottled beers. Outside there are front and rear patios. ❀◐🚌♣⌐

Olde Mitre 🏆 ✔

58 High Street, EN5 5SJ
✪ 12-11 (1am Fri & Sat) ☎ (020) 8449 5701
Adnams Bitter; guest beers Ⓗ
There has been a pub on this site since 1553. The interior has extensive wood panels; the front area has wood flooring, basic seating and tables. The friendly licensee ensures there is a rapidly changing choice of up to four real ales, which outsell lager. The emphasis is on conversation although an adjacent function room has TV and is also available for private hire. Local CAMRA Pub of the Year 2010. Q❀◐♿⊖🚌♣●⌐

New Barnet

Builders Arms

3 Albert Road, EN4 9SH
✪ 12-11 ☎ (020) 8216 5678
Greene King IPA, Abbot; guest beer Ⓗ
Hidden away in a side street, this traditional two-bar pub can be difficult to find. The quiet saloon bar is tastfully decorated and free of piped music and gaming machines. The locals' tankards hang behind the bar and all you will hear is conversation. By contrast the lively public bar has a pool table, dartboard and Sky TV, and can get boisterous when football is being shown. Food is served 12-8pm on weekdays only.
Q❀◐⊟⇌🚌♣⌐

Ponders End

Picture Palace ✔

Howards Hall, Lincoln Road, EN3 4AQ (jct with Hertford Road)
✪ 9am-11 (midnight Fri & Sat) ☎ (020) 8344 9690
Brentwood guest beers; Courage Directors; Greene King Ruddles Best Bitter, Abbot; guest beers Ⓗ
Situated at a busy crossroads in an area otherwise deprived of real ale, this pub is a Wetherspoon's conversion of a 1920s cinema. Murals of silent movies adorn the walls of the main area which has two smaller adjoining areas. The addition of guests from Brentwood qualifies the pub for LocAle status. There is a patio beside the building. Sparklers may be used: if concerned, ask for removal.
❀◐♿⇌(Ponders End/Southbury)🚌●P⌐

NORTH-WEST LONDON

NW1: Camden Town

Prince Albert ✔

163 Royal College Street, NW1 0SG
✪ 12-11 (midnight Fri & Sat); 12-10.30 Sun
☎ (020) 7485 0270 🌐 princealbertcamden.com
Wells Bombardier; Young's Special; guest beer Ⓗ
A free house restored to excellent health by new owners drawing upon W&Y beers but also likely to feature something locally brewed. The ground floor horseshoe bar has lots of wood panelling, old Toby/Charrington branding on the leaded windows and a chunky wooden floor. The original tiling on the outside is stunning and at the front there's a pleasant garden. There is a separate restaurant on the first floor. Sunday is quiz night, from 8pm. Children and dogs welcome.
❀◐⇌(Camden Rd)⊖🚌(46,274)⌐

NW1: Euston

Bree Louise

69 Cobourg Street, NW1 2HH
✪ 11.30 (12 Sat & Sun)-11 or later if busy
☎ (020) 7681 4930 🌐 thebreelouise.com
Bateman's GHA; Redemption Pale Ale, Urban Dusk; Sambrook's Wandle, Junction Ⓗ**; guest beers** Ⓗ/Ⓖ
One-bar corner pub, usually busy with locals and Euston commuters, which was local CAMRA Pub of the Year in 2009/10. A cooled gravity stillage, complemented by handpumps, provides a large range of real ales plus up to eight Westons ciders. Regular beer festivals feature. CAMRA members get 50p off a pint and also a discount on the home-made pies (food is served 12-9pm daily). There is no music, just conversation, but occasional sport on TV (usually weekends). Outdoor seating is on the pavement. ❀◐⇌⊖(Euston/Euston Sq)🚌●⌐

Doric Arch

1 Eversholt Street, NW1 2DN
✪ 12-11 (10.30 Sun) ☎ (020) 7383 3359
Fuller's Discovery, London Pride, ESB; Gale's HSB; guest beers Ⓗ
Located east of the bus station and in front of the railway station, the pub's first-floor split-level

single bar is reached by two entrances. Fuller's continues to promote a range of up to four guest beers plus its own seasonals as well as Westons ciders. TV screens feature live sporting events. Food is served on weekdays all day until 9pm. There is an impressive display of railway artefacts from when it was the Head of Steam. ◑⇌⊖🚌🍎

NW1: St Pancras

Euston Flyer ✓

83-87 Euston Road, NW1 2RA

10-11 (midnight Tue & Wed; 1am Thu-Sat); 10-11.30 Sun
☎ (020) 7383 0856

Fuller's Discovery, London Pride, ESB, seasonal beers; Gale's HSB H

Across the road from the British Library, this is a popular spot for office workers, commuters, sports fans and travellers using St Pancras International. A large open-plan pub divided into different sections and levels, it can be boisterous in the evenings and during major football matches. Two large-screen TVs plus a smaller one are always on for sporting events, often showing different matches. Meals are served all day until 10pm. At times guest beers may also be available. ◑⇌⊖🚌

NW3: Hampstead

Duke of Hamilton

23-25 New End, NW3 1JD

12-11 (10.30 Sun) ☎ (020) 7794 0258

Fuller's London Pride, ESB; guest beers H

An inn for nearly 300 years, a Guide entry for more than 20, the Duke continues to promote real ale in an area badly served by pub closures in recent years. The regular beers at this free house come from Fuller's and the guests from Adnams and others. The pub also offers a real cider from Millwhites. Televised sport, particularly rugby, is regularly shown, and there is a generous outdoor drinking and smoking area at the front of the pub. ❀⇌(Hampstead Heath)⊖🚌(268,603)♣🍎⚡

Holly Bush ✓

22 Holly Mount, NW3 6SG

12-11 (10.30 Sun) ☎ (020) 7435 2892
hollybushhampstead.co.uk

Fuller's London Pride, ESB; Gale's HSB; Harveys Sussex Best Bitter H

An attractive multi-roomed Grade II-listed building in a charming location off Hampstead's beaten track, originally the stables of artist George Romney's house. A pub for 200 years, it retains many historic features, making it one of London's Real Heritage Pubs. British food is served in the pub and, at weekends, in the upstairs restaurant. Food service times are 12-3pm and 6-10pm (12-5pm and 6-10pm Sat, 12-5pm and 6-9 Sun). There is a small smoking area at the front.
Q❀◑⊖🚌(268,603)⚡

NW4: Hendon

Greyhound

52 Church End, NW4 4JT

12-midnight (1am Fri & Sat); 12-11 Sun
☎ (020) 8457 9730

Courage Best Bitter; Wells Bombardier; Young's Bitter, Special; guest beers H

Next to St Mary's church and a museum of local history, this popular three-bar Young's local in the centre of Old Hendon village has recently been redecorated yet keeps its old traditional charm. The site has been licensed since 1675, the pub rebuilt in 1896. There is free jazz once a month, two quizzes every week as well as a local book club. Wholesome home-prepared food is available lunchtimes and evenings, including pizzas from an authentic pizza oven. ◑🚌

NW5: Dartmouth Park

Lord Palmerston

33 Dartmouth Park Hill, NW5 1HU

12-11 (10.30 Sun) ☎ (020) 7485 1578

Adnams Broadside; Sharp's Doom Bar; guest beer H

Scrubbed wooden tables proclaim this a gastro-pub, with modern British food available from lunchtime through to 9.45pm (9.15pm Sun). A bright and airy conservatory on one side at the rear and a more formal restaurant on the other side are linked by a spacious bar. A function room upstairs is also available for hire, and there is ample pavement and rear garden seating. Quiz night is Wednesday, live music Sunday.
❀◑⊖(Tufnell Pk)🚌(4)♣⚡

NW5: Kentish Town

Junction Tavern

101 Fortess Road, NW5 1AG

12-11 (10.30 Sun) ☎ (020) 7485 9400
junctiontavern.co.uk

Sambrook's Wandle; guest beers H

Local CAMRA 2008 Pub of the Year and keen LocAle scheme promoter, with at least one of up to four guests locally sourced. Two large beer festivals and a number of mini-festivals are held during the year. The side door leads to a wood-panelled and mirrored bar, all part of the classic Victorian design. The restaurant serves gastro-style food. Behind the bar room is a beautiful conservatory and a flourishing garden with seating. Dogs are welcome. Q❀◑⇌⊖(Tufnell Pk)🚌(134)⚡

Oxford

256 Kentish Town Road, NW5 2AA

12-11.30 (midnight Fri & Sat) ☎ (020) 7485 3521

Beer range varies H

A friendly high street pub: although leaning towards the gastro-pub in decor, with a large dining area reached beyond an open kitchen, there is still a proper pub feel. Guest beers change frequently although Harveys Sussex is quite a regular. The function room upstairs currently offers poker on Monday, jazz on Tuesday, quiz night on Wednesday and comedy on Thursday. Outside is bench/table seating. ❀◑♿⇌⊖🚌⚡

Pineapple 🏆

51 Leverton Street, NW5 2NX

12-11 (10.30 Sun) ☎ (020) 7284 4631

Draught Bass; guest beers H

Saved from closure by local campaigning and under new management, this popular pub is local CAMRA Pub of the Year 2010 and one of London's Real Heritage Pubs. A range of guest beers includes ales from the newer London breweries. The front of the pub has a number of original features; beyond, alcoves and corridors lead to a spacious conservatory, where the pub's Thai food can be enjoyed. Q❀◑♿⇌⊖🚌⚡

NW8: St John's Wood

Clifton ✔

96 Clifton Hill, NW8 0JT

12-11 (10.30 Sun) ☎ (020) 7372 3427

cliftonstjohnswood.com

Ringwood Best; guest beers H

A hunting lodge 200 years ago, then a licensed bar, reputedly King Edward VII granted this pub hotel status so that he could visit Lily Langtry here, as royalty could not visit pubs! With three seasonal guests, it serves good food using choice ingredients to match the beer. There is a traditional drinking area around the island bar plus conservatory and restaurant areas. A hidden gem in a quiet backwater, a short walk from Kilburn High Road. (Kilburn High Rd) (Kilburn Pk)

Eastcote

Black Horse ✔

Black Horse Parade, Eastcote High Road, HA5 2EN

12-11 (midnight Fri & Sat); 12-10.30 Sun

☎ (020) 8866 9106

Fuller's London Pride; Young's Bitter; guest beers H

A comfortable local set back from the busy Eastcote High Road. Traditional pub games include pool, darts, cribbage, draughts and chess. Lunch is available every day except Sunday. Major sporting events are shown on widescreen TVs and there is live music on Friday evening and Sunday afternoon. The pub has a garden and decked patio at the front. The landlord planned to run his first beer festival during 2010. (282,H13)♣P

Case is Altered

Eastcote High Road, HA5 2EW

11-11 ☎ (020) 8866 0476 caseisalteredpinner.co.uk

Greene King IPA, Morland Original; Sharp's Doom Bar; guest beers H

This old English pub from the 17th century is one of London's Real Heritage Pubs. Set in the attractive village of Old Eastcote, next to the cricket pitch, at the front is a large beer garden. Inside, there is one bar with three seating areas. The barn to the back is a recent refurbishment and provides extra seating. There is a real fire in the main bar during the winter months. (282,H13)P

Harefield

Harefield

41 High Street, UB9 6BY

12-11 (10.30 Sun) ☎ (01895) 820003

Taylor Landlord; guest beers H

This Admiral pub has had several name changes before settling on the current one in 2007 after a complete refurbishment. It is well known for its good food made with fresh local produce and the quality and variety of its real ales. There is a full Sunday roast. A beer club on Wednesday offers discounted real ales. Outside there is a patio, but parking is limited. An annual beer festival is usually held in the autumn. (331,U9)P

Harrow-on-the-Hill

Castle ★ ✔

30 West Street, HA1 3EF

12-11 (midnight Fri & Sat) ☎ (020) 8422 3155

Fuller's Discovery, London Pride, ESB, seasonal beers; Gale's HSB H

Situated in the heart of historic Harrow on the Hill, this is a popular and friendly Fuller's house. Built in 1901 and Grade II-listed, it is one of CAMRA's Real Heritage Pubs. Food is served until 9pm every day; reservations are recommended for Sunday lunchtime. Three real coal fires help to keep the pub warm and cosy in the colder months and a secluded beer garden is popular during the summer. Q(258,H17)

Pinner

Queen's Head

31 High Street, HA5 5PJ

11-11 ☎ (020) 8868 4607 thequeensheadpinner.co.uk

Adnams Bitter; Greene King Abbot; Wells Bombardier; Young's Special; guest beers H

This historic pub in a conservation area is a Grade II-listed building dating back to 1540. Despite its suburban location, it has the appearance and feel of a traditional country inn, with its Tudor frontage, low ceiling and exposed beams. It is closely involved in local activities and celebrates St George's Day with a hog roast. There is no music or TV but a quiz is held on Monday. QP

Ruislip Common

Woodman ✔

Breakspear Road, HA4 7SE

11-midnight (1am Fri); 12-midnight Sun

☎ (01895) 635763

Draught Bass; Courage Best Bitter; guest beer H

A cheerful and welcoming two bar local in the northern area of Ruislip close to Ruislip Lido and woods, opposite Hillingdon Borough Football Club. The cosy lounge bar is traditional in atmosphere with no intrusive electronic machines, although the TV may be on for sports matches. Note the collection of bottled beers on display. There is also a good selection of single malt whiskies. The public bar is friendly and comfortable, with a dartboard. Q(331)♣P

Ruislip Manor

JJ Moons ✔

12 Victoria Road, HA4 0AA

9am-midnight (1am Fri & Sat) ☎ (01895) 622373

Courage Directors; Fuller's London Pride; Greene King Ruddles Best Bitter, Abbot; Marston's Pedigree; guest beers H

Large, busy Wetherspoon's opened in 1990 in a former Woolworths, and still with the same enthusiastic manager. Frequented mainly by locals, this pub gets very busy on Friday and Saturday evenings. There is a large raised area to the rear for diners. Accredited for LocAle in 2009, it now offers two guest ales from local breweries such as Rebellion, Twickenham and Tring in addition to London Pride. Two Westons ciders are also regularly available on handpump. (114,398,H13)

Wembley

JJ Moons ✔

397 High Road, HA9 6AA

9am-11.30 ☎ (020) 8903 4923

Greene King Ruddles Best Bitter, Abbot; Marston's Pedigree; guest beers H

Typical, medium-sized Wetherspoon's pub in a former shop premises. Three regular and two guest ales are always available, plus two ciders from polypins in the fridge. Situated in the culturally diverse London Borough of Brent, it has the feel of a community pub. However, its close proximity to Wembley Stadium and Arena makes it extremely busy and more expensive on match days.
Q❀◑♿⇌⊖(Wembley Central)🚌🍎⌐

SOUTH-EAST LONDON

SE1: Borough

Market Porter

9 Stoney Street, SE1 9AA
✪ 6-8.30am, 11-11; 12-11 Sat; 12-10.30 Sun
☎ (020) 7407 2495
Harveys Sussex Best Bitter; guest beers Ⓗ
This classic boozer (and past recipient of the Pub of the Year award from the local CAMRA branch) serves 10 real ales. The interior is largely open plan to cater for the large volume of market traders, shoppers and office workers, but a seating area is provided at the rear. The walls and ceiling display pump clips from the vast range of ales that have been served. Upstairs is a restaurant for lunch and available to hire for functions in the evening.
◐⇌⊖(London Bridge)🚌🍎

Rake

14 Winchester Walk, SE1 9AG
✪ 12 (10 Sat)-11; 12-10.30 Sun ☎ (020) 7407 0557
Beer range varies Ⓗ
Originally the Old Kings Head and later a greasy spoon cafe, the Utobeer off-licence from nearby Borough Market reopened the Rake as a pub in 2006. Two or sometimes three real ales from innovative breweries such as Otley, Dark Star and BrewDog are served, and an extensive range of bottled beers from the UK, USA, Belgium, Germany and elsewhere. One wall is signed by brewers from across the world whose comments include 'the best pub in London'. ❀◑♿⇌⊖(London Bridge)🚌

Royal Oak ✔

44 Tabard Street, SE1 4JU
✪ 11 (12 Sat)-11; 12-6 Sun ☎ (020) 7357 7173
Harveys XX Mild, Pale, Sussex Best Bitter, seasonal beers; guest beer Ⓗ
Traditional local, with two Victorian-style bars featuring decorative glass, carved woodwork and subdued corner lighting, creating a cosy atmosphere thankfully not marred by noisy music or fruit machines. A rarity in London, this pub is owned by Harveys, and many interesting photos of the brewery hang on the walls. Draught cider is available, excellent food is offered and there is a handy meeting room upstairs. The guest beer is from the Fuller's range.
Q◑⇌(London Bridge)⊖🚌🍎

Wheatsheaf

24 Southwark Street, SE1 1TY
✪ 11 (12 Sat)-11; 12-10 Sun ☎ (020) 7407 9934
Nethergate Redcar Best Bitter; Young's Bitter, Special; guest beers Ⓗ
This pub relocated round the corner from the Hop Cellars after the closure of the old Wheatsheaf in Stoney Street due to the Thameslink programme. Photos of the regulars from the old Wheatsheaf adorn the walls. Six changing guest beers are served, with dark beers and East Anglian ales featuring prominently. There are several alcoves, one with a darts area, the others with large tables. Live jazz plays on Sunday and occasional live music on Saturday. ◑⇌⊖(London Bridge)🚌

SE1: Southwark

Charles Dickens ✔

160 Union Street, SE1 0LH
✪ 11.30-11; 2-8 Sat; 12-6 Sun ☎ (020) 7401 3744
🌐 thecharlesdickens.co.uk
Adnams Bitter; guest beers Ⓗ
Popular one-bar, wooden floored free house with a large rear patio, promoting real ales from independent breweries. Charles Dickens lived in neighbouring Lant Street as a boy while his father was in Marshalsea Prison for debt. The lower walls are wood-panelled; upper walls carry framed illustrations from Dickens' stories. The house beer Charles Dickens Best is brewed by Nethergate and the four guests always include a mild. Above average, reasonably-priced meals are served lunchtimes and evenings. Quiz night is Wednesday.
Q❀◑⇌(Waterloo East)⊖(Southwark/Borough)
🚌⌐

SE1: Tower Bridge

Bridge House

218 Tower Bridge Road, SE1 2UP
✪ 12-11 (midnight Fri & Sat) ☎ (020) 7407 5818
Adnams Bitter, Explorer, Broadside; guest beer Ⓗ
This three-tier gastro-pub in a terrace of old shops immediately south of Tower Bridge has a modern edge with no traditional twists. With its brightly painted walls, it could put off the old-fashioned ale house lover, but you will always find the Adnams beers in top condition. The food is not bad either.
◑♿⇌(London Bridge)⊖(Tower Hill/London Bridge)🚌

SE1: Waterloo

Hole in the Wall

5 Mepham Street, SE1 8SQ
✪ 11-11 (10.30 Sun) ☎ (020) 7928 6196
Adnams Bitter; Hogs Back TEA; Marston's Pedigree; Sharp's Doom Bar; Young's Bitter Ⓗ
Appropriately named for its unusual location, this pub is in a railway arch just across from the main entrance to Waterloo Station. A two-bar free house, it is something of an institution, very popular with locals and commuters alike, having served an impressive range of real ales for longer than most people can remember. It gets busy most nights, and screens sporting events. Outside is a beer garden with patio heaters. ❀◑⊟⇌⊖🚌⌐

SE3: Blackheath

Princess of Wales ✔

1a Montpelier Row, SE3 0RL
✪ 12-11 (10.30 Sun) ☎ (020) 8852 5784
🌐 princessofwalespub.co.uk
Caledonian Deuchars IPA; Fuller's London Pride Ⓗ
Set a little way out of Blackheath village centre, this Georgian pub has a pleasant, spacious interior designed in an L-shape but with a cosy feel. From the central bar, patrons can order high quality beers plus a selection of good food. An inviting conservatory to the rear leads on to a garden. Additionally, during the summer, visitors can take

advantage of historic Blackheath Common's extensive natural beer garden in front of the pub. ✪❶&⟲⇌🍴P⟍

SE5: Camberwell

Bear

296a Camberwell New Road, SE5 0RP
✪ closed Mon; 4-11 (midnight Fri); 12-11 Sat; 12-10.30 Sun
☎ (020) 7274 7037 ⊕ thebear-freehouse.co.uk
Beer range varies Ⓗ
Popular with young professionals, this free house serves two or three changing guest ales often from Scottish and other micro-breweries, and several bottle-conditioned beers. The dark green decor combines traditional style and French bistro influences. Meals are British/French fusion dishes cooked by the head chef who is also the owner. Wednesday is pie and ale night. Quiz night is Tuesday. The upstairs room exhibits local artists and can be hired. ➳❶🍴🖥

Hermit's Cave

28 Camberwell Church Street, SE5 8QU
✪ 12-midnight (2am Fri & Sat) ☎ (020) 7703 3188
Brodie's Mild, IPA, Red; Loddon Gravesend Shrimpers Bitter Ⓗ
Close to a busy junction, yet you can escape from it all in this corner pub with eye-catching curved frontage. Watch the world go by through the etched glass Victorian windows that illuminate the grand marble fireplace beautifully. The bar has a homely atmosphere, bare floorboards, a variety of seating – banquette, small café tables and chairs, and bar stools. This is a family-run pub, with bar snacks, and is ideal for a break from shopping or an evening out. Q⇌(Denmark Hill)🚃●

SE5: Denmark Hill

Fox on the Hill ✪

149 Denmark Hill, SE5 8EH
✪ 9am-midnight (12.30am Fri & Sat) ☎ (020) 7738 4756
Greene King Ruddles Best Bitter, Abbot; Marston's Pedigree; guest beers Ⓗ
Large Wetherspoon's within its own grounds, unusually a conversion of a former pub. Unlike the company's more recent venues, its layout includes numerous cosy, small-screened booths. Children are permitted in two areas, one a small conservatory. Local notables and places of interest are displayed on the walls. Outside there is a spacious garden with a climbing frame. The pub holds its own mini fests. Q➳✪❶&⟲⇌🍴P⟍

SE5: East Dulwich

Hoopers

28 Ivanhoe Road, SE5 8DH
✪ 5.30-11 (11.30 Wed; midnight Thu-Sat); 12.30-11 Sun
☎ (020) 7733 4797 ⊕ hoopersbar.co.uk
Beer range varies Ⓗ
Formerly the Ivanhoe, this back-street local was renamed and revitalised by the current owner, turning it into an ale drinker's oasis. Ales change regularly and there is a large selection of bottled beers. Beer festivals are held frequently. There is plenty of space around the bar and a small room at the rear is ideal for meetings. Satellite TV shows regular sporting events. Quiz night is Thursday, there is live music every fortnight and comedy once a month. ⋈⟲❶⇌🚃(P13)●⟍

SE6: Catford

Catford Ram

9 Winslade Way, SE6 4JU
✪ 11-midnight (12.30am Fri & Sat); 11-11 Sun
☎ (020) 8690 6206
Young's Bitter, Special; guest beer Ⓗ
One of very few pubs left in Catford, this likeable Young's house has so far avoided the pub company's rampant 'restaurant-isation'. The spacious single room still has traditional decor and furniture, with plush carpets, wrought-iron drinking tables, subdued lighting and old photographs and prints on the walls. Despite the feel of an old Victorian pub, it occupies the ground floor of a 1970s building that is part of a modern shopping precinct. ❶&⇌(Catford/Catford Bridge)🚃

SE8: Deptford

Dog & Bell ✅

116 Prince Street, SE8 3JD
✪ 12-11.30 (11 Sun) ☎ (020) 8692 5664
Fuller's London Pride, ESB, seasonal beer Ⓗ
From the 1860s this pub was the Royal Marine, and its current name dates back to an earlier pub that existed here. A much loved, moderate sized Victorian free house, it has survived the now closed wharves and dockyard it was built to serve. It offers three guest ales and several Belgian bottled beers. The modern kitchen is reassuringly open to view from its walled yard behind the pub. Cuisine is uncomplicated and matches the traditional pub atmosphere. ⋈Q✪❶&⇌🚃(47,188,199)♣⟍

SE9: Eltham

Park Tavern

45 Passey Place, SE9 5DA
✪ 12-11 (midnight Fri & Sat); 12-10.30 Sun
☎ (020) 8850 8919
Fuller's London Pride; Harveys Sussex Best Bitter; St Austell Tribute; Taylor Landlord; guest beers Ⓗ
Attractive traditional Victorian Enterprise pub with tiled frontage and historic Truman and Burton signage. The beautifully and warmly refurbished interior has elegant drapes, bar lamps and chandeliers, an impressive wood bar and real log fire. Decorative plates and pictures line the walls. Vases of fresh flowers add to the relaxed atmosphere, with jazz and light classical background music, and an impressive selection of ales, whiskies and wines. A rear garden is available plus seating to the front and side. ⋈Q✪❶⇌🚃♣⟍

SE10: East Greenwich

Pelton Arms ✅

23-25 Pelton Road, Greenwich, SE10 9PQ
✪ 10-12.30am (1.30am Fri & Sat) ☎ (020) 8858 0572
⊕ peltonarmspub.com
Greene King IPA; Wells Bombardier; guest beers Ⓗ
Watch out! Due to ongoing filming for a TV series, this traditional corner pub also displays the name the Nags Head. Once inside though, there is no confusion about the quality of its up-to-five real ales. It has a warming decor and a real fire at the lounge end of its L-shaped drinking area. An unusual feature is the small shop on the Banning Street side where cups of tea and takeaway pub food can be bought from 7am onwards. ⋈✪❶&⇌(Maze Hill)🚃♣P⟍

SE10: North Greenwich

Pilot Inn ✔

68 River Way, West Parkside, SE10 0BE

✪ 11-11 ☎ (020) 8858 5910

Fuller's Discovery, London Pride, ESB, seasonal beer Ⓗ

Built in 1801 but left unscathed by the bulldozers that cleared the area for the Millennium Dome development, this good-sized pub and the short row of cottages next to it continue to be an architectural island. Its garden is tastefully landscaped and accommodates a good crowd, especially when giant Jenga or dominoes is being played during a summer barbecue. The pub has at least four Fuller's beers, with occasional ones from its wider stable. ❀⇄◑♿⊖🚌♣P⁻

SE13: Lee

Dacre Arms

11 Kingswood Place, SE13 5BU

✪ 12-11 (10.30 Sun) ☎ (020) 8852 6779

Black Sheep Best Bitter; Courage Best Bitter; Greene King IPA; Hogs Back TEA; Wells Bombardier Ⓗ

A fine example of that endangered species, the traditional back-street pub. Run by friendly people who have been here over a decade, all the right ingredients are here: comfortable banquette seating, brass jugs and other bric-a-brac on display and cosy wood panelling on the walls (possibly dating from the 1930s). Some small partitions add more intimacy. There is a garden at the rear for smokers. Seek this place out and remind yourself how wonderful pubs used to be!
Q❀♿≠(Blackheath)🚌⁻

SE13: Lewisham

Watch House ✔

198-204 High Street, Lewisham, SE13 6JP

✪ 9am-midnight (1am Fri & Sat) ☎ (020) 8318 3136

Greene King Ruddles Best Bitter, Old Speckled Hen, Abbot; guest beers Ⓗ

In busy Lewisham High Street, this Wetherspoon's pub provides a haven away from all the hustle and bustle. One of the smaller pubs in the chain, it offers a number of cosy areas to relax in, as well as tables situated by the large front windows. In good weather there is a small outside pavement terrace. Two small screens show selected live sporting events. Two draught ciders from Westons are on handpump. Q◑♿≠⊖(DLR)🚌🍎

SE18: Plumstead Common

Old Mill

1 Old Mill Road, SE18 1QG

✪ 11.30-11.30 (midnight Fri & Sat); 12-10.30 Sun
☎ (020) 8244 8592

Beer range varies Ⓗ

Popular, friendly local Enterprise pub built around a windmill that dates back to the 17th century. Beer has been served here since 1848 and today it offers six ever-changing ales. Baguettes are available all day Monday to Saturday. Live music plays on the first Sunday of the month. Many calendar dates are celebrated, including St George's Day and Halloween. The large garden has an aviary. No entry is allowed after 11pm on a Friday night. ❀◐≠(Plumstead)🚌(51,53,291)⁻

SE18: Woolwich

Prince Albert (Rose's)

49 Hare Street, SE18 6NE

✪ 11-11.30; 12-10.30 Sun ☎ (020) 8854 1538

Beer range varies Ⓗ

This free house, owned by local former brewery McDonnell's, has barely changed since the 1960s. It features six handpumps, with three changing guests from micro-breweries. Dockyard scenes by local artists adorn the walls and it hosts league darts and crib teams. Rose's, as it is known by all who love it, may look uninviting, but it is one of the friendliest pubs around – just ask the locals.
Q⇄≠(Woolwich Arsenal)⊖(Woolwich Arsenal DLR)🚌♣▯

SE19: Crystal Palace

Grape & Grain

2 Anerley Hill, SE19 2AA

✪ 11-11 (1am Fri & Sat); 12-10.30 Sun ☎ (020) 8778 8211
🌐 thegrapeandgrainse19.co.uk

Purity Pure Gold; guest beers Ⓗ

This CC Taverns pub has had many incarnations including Jack Beard's, the Sportsman and the Crystal Palace, but in its current format it is probably at its best. Rick the landlord excels, offering six guest ales concurrently, including such delights as Adnams Oyster Stout, and playing host to 'meet the brewer' events. An ideal place to meet friends for hearty food as well as good beer, this pub has monthly book club meetings and live music at weekends. ❀◑≠🚌🍎⁻▯

SE20: Penge

Moon & Stars ✔

164-166 High Street, SE20 7QS

✪ 9am-11 (10.30 Sun) ☎ (020) 8776 5680

Greene King Ruddles Best Bitter, Abbot; Ringwood Fortyniner; guest beers Ⓗ

This large Wetherspoon's pub in Penge High Street is worth a visit for its good selection of ales. With old-style booths and masses of wood panelling, it is a traditional boozer with bags of character. The hostelry also proves useful for a brief history lesson with the old photos on the walls. It is always a handy spot for a bite to eat too.
Q❀◑♿≠(Kent House)⊖(Beckenham Rd Tramlink)🚌🍎P⁻

SE21: Dulwich

Crown & Greyhound ✔

73 Dulwich Village, SE21 7BJ

✪ 11-11 (midnight Thu-Sat); 11-10.30 Sun
☎ (020) 8299 4976 🌐 thecrownandgreyhound.co.uk

Fuller's London Pride; Adnams Broadside; Harveys Sussex Best Bitter; guest beer Ⓗ

Built around 1900 and retaining many original features, this lovely M&B outlet is one of London's Real Heritage Pubs, with many separate areas, a large function room upstairs, split-level garden and conservatory. There is an over-18s bar with no music, but families are welcome in all other areas. The only pub in Dulwich Village, it boasts a friendly atmosphere, good bar service and excellent, reasonably priced food.
Q❀◑♿≠(North Dulwich)🚌(37,P4,P13)♣🍎⁻▯

SE21: West Dulwich

Alleyns Head ✔

Park Hall Road, SE21 8BW

11-11 (midnight Fri & Sat) ☎ (020) 8670 6540

Adnams Broadside; Fuller's London Pride; Greene King IPA; guest beers ⊞

Built in 1956 and part of the M&B Ember Inns chain, this pub is open plan, spacious and comfortable, with a restaurant area at one end that is kept as quiet as possible. Service is good, the food is excellent and includes three-course meals. There is an outside space with tables at the front of the pub. Children under 14 are not admitted and over 14s only if dining. ♨❀◐♿⇄🚌(3,P13)♣●P⊱−▯

SE22: East Dulwich

Herne Tavern

2 Forest Hill Road, SE22 0RR

12-11 (1am Sat) ☎ (020) 8299 9521 🌐 theherne.net

St Austell Tribute; Taylor Landlord; guest beers ⊞

The preservation of features from the inter-war refit earns this Punch pub a place among London's Real Heritage Pubs. Around 12 guest beers are on offer, varying from time to time. Rock and soul nights feature on Thursday, quiz nights on Sunday. A large garden, conservatory and children's play area are at the rear. ♨❀◐⊟🚌(63,363)

SE23: Forest Hill

Blythe Hill Tavern

319 Stanstead Road, SE23 1JB

11-midnight ☎ (020) 8690 5176

Adnams Broadside; Courage Best Bitter; Dark Star Hophead; Fuller's London Pride ⊞

Local CAMRA Pub of the Year 2008, this three-bar establishment is a shining example of how a pub should be, with its old-fashioned ambience, always warm and inviting. The staff are smart in shirt and tie, reminding patrons of the good old days. Old pictures and signs on the walls make for good conversation topics. One of London's Real Heritage Pubs.
Q❀⊟⇄(Catford/Catford Bridge)🚌(171,185)♣P⊱

Capitol ✔

11-21 London Road, SE23 3TW

9am-midnight (1am Fri & Sat) ☎ (020) 8291 8920

Greene King Ruddles Best Bitter, Abbot; Marston's Pedigree; guest beers ⊞

Circa 1929, formerly an ABC cinema, an impressive fascia opens to a cavernous interior that retains the original neo-classical mouldings throughout. The bar of this Wetherspoon's pub sits imposingly along the far wall, beneath what was the cinema screen, dispensing a wide selection of quality ales and ciders in a unique environment. If you are looking for a real piece of early cinema architectural history in south east London, this is an unmissable example. ❀◐♿⇄🚌⊱

Dartmouth Arms

7 Dartmouth Road, SE23 3HN

12-midnight (1am Fri & Sat); 12-11 Sun

☎ (020) 8488 3117 🌐 thedartmoutharms.com

Adnams Broadside; Fuller's London Pride; Taylor Landlord ⊞

Originally built by the Noakes brewing family to exploit trade from nearby Forest Hill station, this handsome 1866 pub has attractive stucco decorations around the windows. The interior was refurbished in 2005 but happily the three separate rooms remain. Decor is modern, with work by local artists displayed on the walls. The rear room (an 1899 extension) serves as a saloon bar during the day and a smart restaurant in the evening. There is a cosy courtyard behind. ❀◐⊟♿⇄🚌P⊱

SE24: Herne Hill

Florence ✔

131-133 Dulwich Road, SE24 0NG

11.30-midnight (1am Fri); 11-1am Sat; 11-midnight Sun

☎ (020) 7326 4987 🌐 florencehernehill.com

Adnams Explorer; Florence Bonobo, Weasel; guest beer ⊞

This attractive pub brews a few beers on the premises – at least two are always available from the bar. Exposed brickwork is interleaved with modern wall surroundings, with well-spaced tables and wood floors. The menu consists of pub classics in addition to roasts on Sundays. Smokers are provided for in the back garden and at tables at the front. There is table football and a retro-style games machine. Q☋❀◐⇄🚌⊱

Prince Regent

69 Dulwich Road, SE24 0NJ

12-11 (12.30am Thu-Sat); 12-10.30 Sun

☎ (020) 7274 1567 🌐 theprinceregent.co.uk

Black Sheep Best Bitter; guest beers ⊞

Substantial Victorian corner pub overlooking Brockwell Park and within a stone's throw of the Lido, with an ornate exterior boasting a life-size statue of the Prince Regent himself. Inside, some modern refurbishment and impressive full-height wood-and-glass screens create two separate rooms. The upstairs bar is available for hire. The menu consists of traditional food, with a gastro twist. The pub is family friendly and also welcomes dogs. Q❀◐⇄🚌(3,37,196)⊱

SE26: Sydenham

Dolphin

121 Sydenham Road, SE26 5HB

12-midnight (11 Mon); 12-10.30 Sun ☎ (020) 8778 8101

🌐 thedolphinsydenham.com

Adnams Broadside; Fuller's London Pride; Taylor Landlord ⊞

In 2007 the Dolphin's garden was given a horticultural makeover, transforming it into a great place to spend a balmy summer's evening. If you're lucky you may be treated to a local theatre group's latest Shakespeare production. Inside, the pub exudes a laid back atmosphere, perfect for reading the papers over a pint. ❀◐⇄🚌P⊱

SE27: West Norwood

Hope ✔

49 Norwood High Street, SE27 9JS

11-11.30 (midnight Fri & Sat); 12-11 Sun

☎ (020) 8670 2035 🌐 thehopepub.net

Young's Bitter, Special, seasonal beers ⊞

Built in the 1840s as part of the pub estate that would become Young & Co, this compact boozer is popular with a wide range of customers and, due to the proximity of West Norwood Cemetery, is often a venue for wakes. The terraced garden becomes a sun trap in summer, where you might find anything from live music to open air cinema and barbecue. Friday night entertainment includes weekly karaoke and folk singers once a month. A TV shows sporting events. ⛰❀⇌⊟⌐

Addiscombe

Claret Free House

5A Bingham Corner, Lower Addiscombe Road, CR0 7AA

⏲ 11.30-11 (11.30 Thu; 11.45 Fri); 12-11 Sun

☎ (020) 8656 7452

Palmers IPA; guest beers Ⓗ

This former wine bar now regularly features in this Guide: this is its 23rd consecutive appearance. The shop-style premises deceptively hides a friendly pub where conversation dominates, and is easily accessible by public transport. The regular Palmers beer is supplemented by a constantly changing range of guest ales on the other five handpumps, mostly from southern England and micro-breweries. Real cider is always available. Two TV screens cover sporting events. ♿⊖⊟

Cricketers

47 Shirley Road, CR0 7ER

⏲ 12-11 (10.30 Sun) ☎ (020) 8655 3507

Dark Star Hophead; Harveys Sussex Best Bitter; guest beers Ⓗ

Traditional community Enterprise pub with a mock-Tudor exterior. The interior has two almost separate areas, with real fires in winter. Guest beers often come from smaller breweries and micros. The keen landlord runs mini beer festivals periodically when the five beers on handpump are supplemented by ales on gravity. Outside there is a patio, a large garden and a covered area for smokers. Food is available until 7pm (not Sun). A large-screen TV shows sporting events.

⛰❀◐◑⊖(Addiscombe/Blackhorse Lane Tramlink) ⊟(130,367)♣●P⌐▯

Beckenham

Jolly Woodman

9 Chancery Lane, BR3 6NR

⏲ 12 (4 Mon)-11 (midnight Fri & Sat) ☎ (020) 8663 1031

Adnams Bitter; Harveys Sussex Best Bitter; Taylor Landlord; Young's Bitter Ⓗ; guest beers Ⓗ/Ⓖ

This charming little pub is tucked away from the main road and remains unchanged from yesteryear. Until some 20 years ago it had a beer licence only. A friendly local serving a discerning clientele, it has one bar with two areas: a small area at the front and a larger sitting area to the rear. Home-cooked lunches are available weekdays. There is outside seating at the front and side and in a rear patio area.

Q❀◐⇌(Beckenham Jct)⊖(Beckenham Jct Tramlink)⊟(227,367)♣⌐

Oakhill

90 Bromley Road, BR3 5NP

⏲ 10-11 (midnight Fri & Sat); 12-11 Sun ☎ (020) 8650 1279

Courage Best Bitter; St Austell Tribute; Westerham 1965 Ⓗ

This three-roomed pub consists of two modern bar areas and a separate, quiet lounge bar. Four Victorian fireplaces with gas fires bestow a cosy ambience during winter months. As well as a tasteful patio-style garden at the rear (allowing smoking under table umbrellas) there is further outdoor seating at the front. Stone-baked pizzas supplement standard meal options, Saturday brunch (from 10am) and Sunday roasts. Poker and quizzes can be enjoyed regularly on Monday and Tuesday nights respectively.

Q❀◐◑⇌(Beckenham Jct)⊖(Beckenham Jct Tramlink)⊟(227,367)P⌐

Bexley

Black Horse

63 Albert Road, DA5 1NT

⏲ 12-11.30 (midnight Fri) ☎ (01322) 523371

Courage Best Bitter; guest beers Ⓗ

Four bus routes stop within five minutes' walk of this friendly back-street local, which offers good value lunches on weekdays. The open-plan bar is split into two: to the left is an open space with a dartboard while to the right is a smaller, more intimate area and bar. The pub supports a local golf society. The publican continuously rotates six guest beers. ❀◐⇌⊟♣⌐

Railway Tavern

38 Bexley High Street, DA5 1AH

⏲ 11-11 (midnight Fri & Sat); 12-11 Sun ☎ (01322) 522779

Courage Best Bitter; guest beers Ⓗ

Traditional pub with live music on a Friday and Sunday and karaoke on Tuesday. Families are welcome as are dogs on a lead. There is a poker league on Thursday evening. The railway memorabilia are in keeping with the name and location of the pub. Continuously changing guest beers are drawn from a variety of smaller breweries and are often unusual for the area. Free Wi-Fi is available. ❀⇌⊟♣⌐

Bexleyheath

Furze Wren ✔

Broadway Square, 6 Market Place, DA6 7DY

⏲ 9-11 ☎ (020) 8298 2590

Courage Best Bitter; Greene King Ruddles Best Bitter, Abbot; Marston's Pedigree; Shepherd Neame Spitfire; guest beers Ⓗ

Located in the heart of Bexleyheath shopping centre, this modern pub is named after a once local bird, the Dartford Warbler. The large open-plan space and big windows afford great opportunities for people-watching. Unusually for a Wetherspoon's pub it is all on one level including the toilets – a pleasant environment to drink, eat and chat. ◐◑♿⊟●

Robin Hood & Little John

78 Lion Road, DA6 8PF

⏲ 11-3, 5.30 (7 Sat)-11; 12-4, 7-10.30 Sun

☎ (020) 8303 1128

Adnams Bitter, Broadside; Brakspear Bitter; Fuller's London Pride; Harveys Sussex Best Bitter; guest beers Ⓗ

This back-street pub dates from the 1830s and has eight real ales on offer. It has a reputation for its home-cooked food at lunchtime (not Sun), with themed specials and regular Italian pasta dishes, which can be eaten at tables made from old Singer sewing machines. London Regional CAMRA Pub of the Year winner three times and local Branch winner for the last decade. Over 21s only. Q❀◐

Bromley

Bitter End Off Licence
139 Masons Hill, BR2 9HW
✪ 12 (11 Sat)-9; 12-2, 7-9 Sun ☎ (020) 8466 6083
🌐 thebitterend.biz
Beer range varies Ⓖ
An off-licence selling a constantly changing range of gravity-dispensed real ale by the pint at significantly less than pub prices is a local treasure. Larger volumes, from minipins to firkins, of over 500 beers can be ordered and delivered, as can real cider. There is also an impressive range of bottled beers and ciders. The website reference to this offie being a 'beer festival in a shop' is an apt description. ≉(Bromley South)🚌🍎

Partridge ✔
194 High Street, BR1 1HE
✪ 12-11.30 (12.30am Fri & Sat); 12-11 Sun
☎ (020) 8464 7656
Fuller's Discovery, London Pride, ESB, seasonal beers; Gale's Seafarers Ale, HSB Ⓗ
Though the interior looks very much like most people's idea of the archetypal English pub, this building used to be a bank. Fuller's tasteful conversion retains the sumptuous Edwardian interior and is popular with shoppers, while the large-screen TVs attract sports fans. Although it is often rather busy, there are two quieter areas off the main bar. The splendid food and ales come with excellent service and clean tables.
❀◑♿≉(Bromley North)🚌

Red Lion
10 North Road, BR1 3LG
✪ 11 (12 Sun)-11.30 ☎ (020) 8460 2691
Greene King IPA, Abbot; Harveys Sussex Best Bitter; guest beers Ⓗ
A Red Lyon ale house was recorded on this site in 1731, long before the surrounding streets of quaint terraced housing appeared. Rebuilt in the early 1900s, this back-street local is one of a cluster to the north east of the town centre, all serving real ale. Normally a quiet pub with a living room atmosphere and well stocked library, try it for liveliness on a summer's evening when it hosts the Ravensbourne Morris Men.
♨Q❀◐≉(North)🚌(314)♣⌐

Bromley Common

Two Doves
37 Oakley Road, BR2 8HD
✪ 12-3, 5.30-11; 12-11.30 Fri & Sat; 12-10.30 Sun
☎ (020) 8462 1627
St Austell Tribute; Young's Bitter, Special; guest beer Ⓗ
Beautiful leaded windows and a warm welcome await in this immaculately kept pub with old plates, jugs and saucy postcards in the Gents. Home to the Ravensbourne Morris Men and a perfect stop off for walkers, it has a lovely large garden at the rear. Set in a semi-rural conservation area, you won't find any noisy big-screen TVs but you will get real conversation with locals and everything you'd hope for in a traditional pub.
♨Q❀◐🚌(320)⌐

Chelsfield

Five Bells 🏆
Church Road, BR6 7RE
✪ 11-11 (midnight Fri & Sat); 12-10.30 Sun
☎ (01689) 821044 🌐 thefivebells-chelsfieldvillage.co.uk
Courage Best Bitter; Harveys Sussex Best Bitter; Sharp's Doom Bar; guest beers Ⓗ
A warm welcome awaits you as you enter this gem of a pub, built around 1680 to celebrate the installation of five new bells in Chelsfield Church. Original beams, photographs and plates decorating the walls create a cosy atmosphere. An Enterprise pub with two bars and an increasingly popular restaurant, it hosts regular theme nights and entertainment. The large, pleasant garden welcomes walkers, families and dogs to this lovely, ancient village. The bus will drop you off right outside. Q❀◐◑🀱🚌(R3)♣P⌐

Chislehurst

Ramblers Rest ✔
Mill Place, BR7 5ND (off Old Hill)
✪ 11.30-11; 12-10.30 Sun ☎ (020) 8467 1734
Fuller's London Pride; Wells Bombardier; Courage Best Bitter; guest beers Ⓗ
Superb weatherboarded building in a scenic location on the edge of Chislehurst Common. This two-bar pub, laid out on two levels, is especially popular during the summer months with customers choosing to enjoy their beer on the grass outside by the pond. With the Chislehurst Caves nearby, it is always worth a visit. ♨Q❀≉🚌(162,269)

Crayford

Crayford Arms 🏆
37 Crayford High Street, DA1 4HH
✪ 2-11 Mon-Wed; 12-midnight Thu-Sat; 12-11 Sun
☎ (07907) 709710 🌐 thecrayfordarms.com
Shepherd Neame Master Brew Bitter, Kent's Best, Spitfire, Bishops Finger, seasonal beer Ⓗ
Following a sympathetic refurbishment, this pub boasts five handpumps and a traditional atmosphere with many original features. To the right is a cosy public bar and to the left a wood-panelled saloon bar from which an attractive oak staircase leads up to a function room. Occasional live music is performed. Despite being a Shepherd Neame tied house, the pub hosts at least one mini-festival a year. ❀🀱≉🚌(96,428,492)♣P⌐

Croydon

Dog & Bull
24 Surrey Street, CR0 1RG
✪ 11-11; 12-10.30 Sun ☎ (020) 8667 9718
🌐 dogandbull.com
Young's Bitter, Special, seasonal beers Ⓗ
In the heart of Croydon's historic street market, this Grade II-listed pub traces its history back to at least 1595. Rebuilt and leased to Young and Bainbridge in the 19th century, the pub currently has an island bar plus two rooms and a well-kept garden. Food is available every day until 9pm (6pm Sun). Poker night is Wednesday and there is a monthly comedy night. A function room is available for hire.
❀◐◑≉(E/W Croydon)⊖(Church St/George St Tramlink)🚌⌐

George ✔
17-21 George Street, CR0 1LA
✪ 9-midnight (1am Fri & Sat) ☎ (020) 8649 9077
Greene King IPA; Marston's Pedigree; guest beers Ⓗ

This Wetherspoon pub occupies former shop premises and dates from 1993. The town-centre location makes it convenient for business customers and shoppers, and it can be busy at any time. The long single room has a second bar at the rear and features a wider range of ales than is usually found in these pubs. Guest beers are often from micro-breweries. Two of the 15 handpumps usually offer draught cider. Beer festivals are held twice a year.
(E/W Croydon) (George St Tramlink)

Green Dragon ✓

58-60 High Street, CR0 1NA
10-midnight (1am Fri & Sat); 12-10.30 Sun
(020) 8667 0684 myspace.com/greendragonpub
Dark Star Hophead Ⓗ; Hogs Back TEA Ⓖ; Wells Bombardier; Westerham Freedom Ale Ⓗ; guest beers Ⓗ/Ⓖ
A Town & City pub on two floors in former bank premises at the south end of historic Surrey Street market. Ales are dispensed from six handpumps and two firkins on gravity. Wholesome food is served all day to customers of all ages. Entertainment upstairs includes acoustic music on Tuesday and Sunday afternoon jazz. There are board games, a pool table, occasional beer festivals and charity events, and the pub sponsors local arts and music.
(E/W Croydon) (George St Tramlink)

Half & Half

282 High Street, CR0 1NG
12 (3 Sat)-midnight; 3-11 Sun (020) 8726 0080
halfandhalf.uk.com
Dark Star Hophead; guest beer Ⓗ
Lounge bar on two floors with friendly and efficient service. Sofas, comfortable bar stools and soft background music create the atmosphere, well away from the central Croydon night life and handy for South Croydon restaurants for a pre-dinner drink. The rotating guest beer is from the Dark Star range, complemented by a small but interesting range of Belgian bottled beers and Czech beer on the tall fonts. Free Internet access is provided and the basement is available for private parties.
(George St Tramlink)

Royal Standard ✓

1 Sheldon Street, CR0 1SS
11-midnight (11 Sun) (020) 8688 9749
Fuller's Chiswick Bitter, London Pride, ESB, seasonal beers Ⓗ
This traditional street-corner local is a former CAMRA regional Pub of the Year. It is situated close to the bustle of central Croydon but provides a peaceful retreat with its sensitively restored interior of three distinct drinking areas. The fine beer quality reflects the landlord's assured cellarmanship. Beer festivals have been a popular innovation. There is a surprisingly quiet garden area opposite, almost beneath Croydon flyover.
Q (George St Tramlink)

Spreadeagle ✓

39-41 Katharine Street, CR0 1NX
11-11 (midnight Fri & Sat); 12-10.30 Sun
(020) 8781 1134
Fuller's Chiswick Bitter, Discovery, London Pride, ESB, seasonal beers; Gale's HSB Ⓗ
Well-appointed town centre pub in an old bank premises beside the old town hall. The interior has wood-panelled walls and displays local scenes. Two upstairs rooms are available and can be booked for functions. The full range of Fuller's ales is on offer plus a good range of bottled beers. Branded as a Fuller's Ale & Pie House, it serves food at reasonable prices. It can get busy after office hours, and has an outdoor canopied area for smokers.
(E/W Croydon) (George St Tramlink)

Cudham

Blacksmiths Arms

Cudham Lane South, TN14 7QB (opp New Barn Lane)
TQ446598
11-midnight (01959) 572678
theblacksmithsarms.co.uk
Adnams Bitter; Courage Best Bitter; Harveys Sussex Best Bitter; Hogs Back TEA Ⓗ
Quaint rural village pub, built in 1628 as a house and forge with the ale house business added in 1730. It is famous as the birthplace of Little Tich, the music hall entertainer with the large shoes, a pair of which is displayed in the bar. The pub has a large car park, heated smoking shed and spacious beer garden with barbecue area. Summer activities include bat and trap, with occasional visits from morris and clog dancing sides. Q (R5)P

Hayes

George ✓

29 Hayes Street, BR2 7LE
11.30-11 (020) 8462 1120
Courage Best Bitter; Harveys Sussex Best Bitter; guest beer Ⓗ
Only two miles from Bromley, Hayes still retains a village feel, with the George at its heart. Rebuilt in 1900 in the Arts and Crafts style, the pub is a locally listed building. Internally it has undergone many refurbishments, most recently in the modern decor of an M&B Ember Inn. This works very well and although the interior looks a million dollars, real ale prices are some of the lowest in Bromley. The food is also excellent value.
Q (119,146,353)P

Orpington

Cricketers

93 Chislehurst Road, BR6 0DQ
12-3, 5-midnight; 12-11 Sat; 12-10.30 Sun
(01689) 812648
Adnams Bitter, Broadside; guest beer Ⓗ
This well-hidden pub has been run by the same family for more than 30 years, and has a traditional feel to it. The back room is ideal for parties and meetings. It can get quite busy on a Thursday when the quiz is on and when sport is screened on TV.
Q (61)P

Petts Wood

Sovereign of the Seas ✓

109-111 Queensway, BR5 1DG
10-11 (11.30 Fri & Sat) (01689) 891606
Greene King Ruddles Best Bitter, Abbot; Shepherd Neame Spitfire; guest beers Ⓗ
Occupying what were originally three adjacent shops in a 1930s parade, this is another fine example of a noise-free, comfortable Wetherspoon's pub. The large lanterns and polished granite of the exterior give it a traditional

look. Although largely open-plan, the interior has five small booths offering some privacy. Well-researched wall displays provide interesting local history snippets, including the fact that the pub was named after a 1637 Royal Navy ship built by a local shipbuilding family. Q❀◐♿⇌🚌(208,R3)

Pratts Bottom

Bulls Head

Rushmore Hill, BR6 7NQ

11-11 (midnight Fri); 12-10.30 Sun ☎ (01689) 852553

thebullsheadpub.net

Courage Best Bitter; Fuller's London Pride; guest beers H

A genuine welcome awaits at this 17th-century coaching inn, boasting original features including the old hoist for lifting travellers' luggage, and the old stables. A haunt of Dick Turpin, it has roaring fires in winter and plenty in the way of theme nights and entertainment. Bat and trap and darts are played in the gaming room. A separate dining room serves great food. The large garden has a new children's play area and there is a popular annual beer festival. ♛❀◐🚌(402,R5)♣P⁵–

Thornton Heath

Victoria Cross

228 Bensham Lane, CR7 7EP

12-11 (midnight Sat) ☎ (020) 8684 3022

Courage Best Bitter; guest beer H

One of London's Real Heritage Pubs, this popular local was rebuilt in 'brewers' Tudor' style in 1937, comprising two bars with original wood panelling and prints of scenes of local historic interest. The public bar has a pool table and dartboard, and there are large TVs showing sport. The well kept garden holds barbecues in the summer. Meals are available in the evening, supplied by a local takeaway. ❀◑🚌(450)♣⁵–

Upper Belvedere

Prince of Wales

13a Woolwich Road, DA17 5EE

12-11 (midnight Fri & Sat) ☎ (01322) 433737

Courage Best Bitter; St Austell Tribute; guest beer H

A corner pub built around 1863 on what was once Lessness Heath and named after the future King Edward VII. Acquired by Beasleys of Plumstead in 1883 and consequently Courage, fortunately it was not ruined during its 60s makeovers. The horseshoe-shaped bar has lots of copper pots hanging from the ceiling. There is live music or karaoke most Saturday evenings. ❀◐🚌(99,401)⁵–

Welling

New Cross Turnpike ✔

55 Bellgrove Road, DA16 3PB

9am-midnight ☎ (020) 8304 1600

Courage Best Bitter; Greene King Ruddles Best Bitter, Abbot; Marston's Pedigree; Shepherd Neame Spitfire; guest beers H

Exemplary Wetherspoon's pub with an attractive layout on four levels including a gallery and two patios. Disabled access includes wheelchair lifts. Varied guest ales are dispensed by helpful staff. Special offers include steak night on Tuesday and curry night on Thursday. Q❀◐♿⇌🚌●⁵–

SOUTH-WEST LONDON

SW1: Belgravia

Antelope ✔

22-24 Eaton Terrace, SW1W 8EZ

12-11; closed Sun ☎ (020) 7824 8512

Fuller's Chiswick Bitter, Discovery, London Pride, ESB, seasonal beers H

Attractive 1827 mews pub with etched glass windows and a fine island bar. There is a comfortable rear section with a fire. Wood-panelled walls feature old photos of rugby and football scenes and one wall is dedicated to the pub's cricket team with photos and records. The upstairs and downstairs snug areas can be booked for parties and the main upstairs room, with bar, can be hired for functions. Q◐⊖(Sloane Sq)🚌

Horse & Groom

7 Groom Place, SW1X 7BA

11-11; closed Sat & Sun ☎ (020) 7235 6980

Shepherd Neame Master Brew Bitter, Kent Best, Spitfire, seasonal beers H

You may have to search a little to find this traditional mews pub but it is well worth seeking out. The main wood-panelled downstairs room has etched glass front windows. There is also an upstairs room that is mainly used for dining. Although closed on Saturday and Sunday, the pub is available for private hire.
◐⇌⊖(Hyde Pk Corner)🚌⁵–

Nag's Head

53 Kinnerton Street, SW1X 8ED

11-11; 12-10.30 Sun ☎ (020) 7235 1135

Adnams Bitter, Broadside, seasonal beer H

A small, unspoilt establishment with bars on two levels, the front one boasting the lowest bar counter in London, if not the country. Built circa 1833, it was first licensed as a beer house about seven years later and acquired by Benskins later that century. Actor Kevin Moran has been running it as a free house for many years. There are a considerable number of collectibles, including a 'What the Butler Saw' machine that still works.
♛Q❀◐⊖(Hyde Pk Corner/Knightsbridge)🚌

Star Tavern ✔

6 Belgrave Mews West, SW1X 8HT

11-11; 12-10.30 Sun ☎ (020) 7235 3019

Fuller's Chiswick Bitter, Discovery, London Pride, ESB, seasonal beers H

A Grade II-listed pub dating from 1848, the Star underwent a sensitive refurbishment in early 2008. No glass and chrome here – the ambience takes you back to when a pub looked like a pub. The landlord often organises a posse of regulars to take part in fundraising events to raise money for cancer research. Former local CAMRA Pub of the Year, the Star has featured in the Guide since its first edition.
Q◐♿⊖(Hyde Pk Corner/Knightsbridge)🚌

SW1: Pimlico

Cask Pub & Kitchen

6 Charlwood Street, SW1V 2EE

12 (4 Mon)-11; 12-10.30 Sun ☎ (020) 7630 7225

caskpubandkitchen.com

Dark Star Hophead; guest beers H

Leased from Greene King, this pub has been totally transformed by the current operator from a typical estate pub to a real ale haven. A good mix of local office workers and tourists from nearby hotels enjoy eight handpumps with Dark Star, Thornbridge and other guest beers. There is also an interesting range of German and Belgian bottled beers and keg foreign beers. No food on Monday. (Victoria) (Pimlico/Victoria)

Jugged Hare ✔
172 Vauxhall Bridge Road, SW1V 1DX
11-11 (11.30 Fri); 12-10.30 Sun ☎ (020) 7828 1543
Fuller's Chiswick Bitter, Discovery, London Pride, ESB, seasonal beers H
Situated in a former NatWest Bank dating from the 1800s, this Fuller's Ale & Pie House opened in 1996. It is named after the traditional English dish. The bar features fine brass chandeliers and attractive Art Deco lights. The back of the pub and the upstairs gallery can be booked for functions. (Victoria) (Pimlico/Victoria)

SW1: Victoria

Cask & Glass
39 Palace Street, SW1E 5HN
11-11; 12-9 Sat; closed Sun ☎ (020) 7834 7630
Shepherd Neame Master Brew Bitter, Kent's Best, Spitfire, Bishops Finger, seasonal beers H
First licensed in 1862 as the Duke of Cambridge, this attractive one-room pub between Buckingham Palace and Westminster Cathedral, adorned with flowers in summer, is a haven for tourists and local residents. The wood-panelled bar has pictures of local scenes and politicians, plus two gold-framed mirrors. Look out for the bullseye windows and the two paintings of the pub on the way to the toilets. A cosy place for a well-earned pint after visiting the sights.

Willow Walk ✔
25 Wilton Road, SW1V 1LW
9am-midnight (11.30 Sun) ☎ (020) 7828 2953
Greene King IPA, Ruddles Best Bitter, Abbot; Marston's Pedigree; guest beers H
This busy Wetherspoon's is opposite the side entrance to Victoria Station in Wilton Road, but there is also access via Vauxhall Bridge Road. The bar has 12 handpumps and supports LocAle, offering Twickenham Fine Ales among its selection. Prints on the walls give information on local history. The pub dates from 1999 and was previously a Woolworths.

SW1: Westminster

Buckingham Arms
62 Petty France, SW1H 9EU
11-11; 12-6 Sat; 12-10.30 Sun ☎ (020) 7222 3386
Caledonian Deuchars IPA; Wells Bombardier; Young's Bitter, Special, seasonal beers H
Originally a shop and later the Black Horse, this Young's pub acquired its present name in 1901. Recently refurbished, the pub has retained many heritage features. The facade is elegant with its small window panes and the notable heraldic shield next to the entrance. The front bar and window possess similar graceful curves and behind the bar is an impressive set of decorated mirrors. This real ale stalwart has featured in every edition of the Guide. Q (St James's Pk)

Sanctuary House Hotel ✔
33 Tothill Street, SW1H 9LA
11-11; 12-10.30 Sun ☎ (020) 7799 4044
sanctuaryhousehotel.com
Fuller's Chiswick Bitter, London Pride, ESB, seasonal beers H
A Fuller's Ale & Pie House plus 34-bedroom hotel in a building said to have formerly housed MI5. With plenty of wood panelling, bevelled mirrors, bright brass fittings at the bar, big tall windows, and generous, split-level hardwood or carpeted seating areas, it is comfortable and warm with a welcoming buzz, though the musak may be irritating. A curious medieval style 'Book of Hours' mural on the back wall is said to represent 'Sanctuary' at the nearby Westminster Abbey. (St James's Pk)

Speaker ✔
46 Great Peter Street, SW1P 2HA
12-11; closed Sat & Sun ☎ (020) 7222 1749
Shepherd Neame Spitfire; Young's Bitter; guest beers H
Located near the heart of Westminster, this Enterprise pub is popular with civil servants and MPs and, like most bars in the area, has its own division bell. There are caricatures of MPs and clay pipes throughout the wood-panelled interior. Regular themed beer festivals are held, utilising two handpumps. Q (St James's Pk)

St Stephen's Tavern
10 Bridge Street, SW1A 2JR
10-11.30 (midnight Fri); 10.30-10.30 Sun
☎ (020) 7925 2286
Badger First Gold, Tanglefoot, seasonal beers H
Built in 1875 and reopened in 2003 by Hall & Woodhouse after a period of restoration, this pub, located opposite the Houses of Parliament, is frequented by civil servants and tourists. Grade II-listed and one of London's Real Heritage Pubs, it gives an impression of discreet grandeur. Particularly of note are the high bar back, etched mirrors and splendid hanging brass lamps. The upstairs room has views to the main bar below and distinctive curved leather seating. Q

SW1: Whitehall

Lord Moon of the Mall ✔
16-18 Whitehall, SW1A 2DY
9am-11.30 (midnight Fri & Sat); 9am-11 Sun
☎ (020) 7839 7701
Greene King Ruddles Best Bitter, Abbot; Marston's Pedigree; guest beers H
Listed former bank dating from 1872 converted by Wetherspoon's in 1995 into a spacious, ornate, wood-panelled pub. A portrait of 'Lord Moon', aka Tim Martin, the pub chain's founder, is prominent; local history panels and prints otherwise cover the walls and pillars. Alongside six guest beers are two draught Westons ciders. Popular with civil servants and passing tourists, the pub welcomes accompanied children until 8pm in the dining area to the rear. Sport is screened on TV.
Q (Charing Cross) (Charing Cross/Westminster)

SW2: Streatham Hill

Crown & Sceptre ✔
2A Streatham Hill, SW2 4AH

9-midnight (1am Fri & Sat) (020) 8671 0843
Greene King Ruddles Best Bitter, Abbot; guest beers H
The first Wetherspoon's in south west London, this pub reverted to its original name soon after opening as JJ Moons. Standing on a busy junction of the south circular road, it retains its fine Truman's facade and tiling. The interior is divided into several distinct areas, with some unusual framed floral artwork on the walls. Guest beers usually include Sambrook's Wandle and Junction. Westons Marcle Hill, Organic Vintage and Old Rosie ciders are also available.

SW5: Earls Court

Courtfield

187 Earls Court Road, SW5 9AN
8am-12.30am; 9am-11.30 Sun (020) 7370 2626
Fuller's London Pride; guest beers H
Spacious Punch pub with a good atmosphere, right outside Earls Court Tube station. The staff really try to make your visit as pleasant as possible, with excellent service. Six ales are on handpump. Customers are invited to try the varied food menu throughout the day, and enjoy the quality guest ales.

SW6: Parsons Green

White Horse

1-3 Parsons Green, SW6 4UL
11-11.30 (midnight Thu-Sat); 11-11 Sun
(020) 7736 2115 whitehorsesw6.com
Adnams Broadside; Harveys Sussex Best Bitter; guest beers H
Large, light and airy M&B pub maintaining a long-standing international reputation for quality beer and food. There are six guest ales from regional and micro-breweries, a draught Severn cider/perry and unusual foreign beers. The former coach house at the rear is used as a restaurant or for stillage during four annual beer festivals. Upstairs a bar now opens in the evening and at weekends. The covered patio area in front accommodates outdoor drinkers and smokers all year, with barbecues in summer.

SW7: South Kensington

Anglesea Arms

15 Selwood Terrace, SW7 3QG
11-11; 12-10.30 Sun (020) 7373 7960
Adnams Bitter, Broadside; Fuller's London Pride; guest beers H
This listed Capital Pub Co establishment looks like a country pub with its hanging baskets and benches outside. Walk through the foliage and you discover a hidden gem. Numerous features from the past are apparent including an etched glass panel with the pub's name. A prominent wooden clock hangs above the bar. The front bar has a large brewery mirror and a diverse collection of paintings. A good range of cask ales is served.

SW8: South Lambeth

Priory Arms

83 Lansdowne Way, SW8 2PB
12-11 (10.30 Sun) (020) 7622 1884
Hop Back Summer Lightning; guest beers H
Welcoming free house, often and deservedly very busy. The listed frontage is a riot of colourful hanging baskets in summer. Guest beers come from a wide range of micro-breweries, with Hop Back and Downton beers often featured. Many German and other overseas bottled beers are also available. A regular, mixed clientele enjoy good beer, good food, free newspapers and big match sport. Ask about the upstairs function room.
(Wandsworth Rd) (Stockwell)

SW9: Brixton

Trinity Arms

45 Trinity Gardens, SW9 8DR
11-11 (midnight Fri); 12-midnight Sat; 12-11 Sun
(020) 7274 4544
Wells Bombardier; Young's Bitter, Special, seasonal beer H
Set in a quiet square off the bustle of Acre Lane and Brixton High Road, this is an oasis of calm and tranquillity where people come for a chat after work or to eat. Draught beer is a big seller as it is always good. Named after an ancient asylum nearby, the pub is very busy during Brixton Academy nights, often with performers. Families with children are welcome until 7.30pm and food is available until 10pm every day.

SW11: Battersea

Beehive

197 St John's Hill, SW11 1TH
11-11 (midnight Fri & Sat); 12-11 Sun (020) 7564 1897
Fuller's London Pride, ESB, seasonal beer H
A rare Fuller's tied house in south west London, the Beehive makes everyone welcome, including well behaved children, with its friendly landlord and staff. Major sporting events are shown on the flat screen TV at the rear of the pub. Good value lunches are served during the week. Background music is played from an old fashioned Wurlitzer jukebox. This is a great local, well worth the short walk from Clapham Junction. (Clapham Jct)

Draft House Westbridge

74-76 Battersea Bridge Road, SW11 3AG
12 (11 Sat)-11 (midnight Fri & Sat); 11-10.30 Sun
(020) 7228 6482 drafthouse.co.uk/westbridge
Adnams Bitter; Sambrook's Wandle, Junction H
Opposite the Royal College of Art at the south end of Battersea Bridge, this recently renamed pub draws a lively atmosphere from its student following. Brewery pump clips are always replaced with informative beer descriptions posted on each handpump. An eclectic collection of posters and arty album covers adorns the walls. The open plan kitchen next to the bar serves a tantalising menu of good, reasonably priced, home-cooked food, popular with regulars and students alike.

Eagle Ale House

104 Chatham Road, SW11 6HG
2 (12 Sat)-11; 12-10.30 Sun (020) 7228 2328
Sharp's Doom Bar; Westerham Best Bitter; guest beers H
A real ale haven with seven rapidly changing beers from Westerham and other micro-breweries, this is an unspoilt, dog-friendly local with a somewhat chaotic interior featuring leather sofas, old bottles and dusty books. A loyal clientele is welcoming to all. The large-screen TV shows major sporting

events. There is a heated marquee in the garden for special occasions and also used as a smoking area. Sunday is quiz night. ⚠❀♿🚌(319,G1)⚡

Falcon ☆ ✔

2 St John's Hill, SW11 1RU

⏲ 10-11 (midnight Thu-Sat); 10-10.30 Sun

☎ (020) 7228 2076

Adnams Broadside; Brakspear Bitter; Sharp's Doom Bar; St Austell Tribute; Taylor Landlord; guest beers Ⓗ

Close to Clapham Junction station and usually busy with passengers and local residents alike, the Falcon regularly serves up to 16 real ales drawn mainly from the M&B Nicholson's seasonal list, plus real cider in the summer. The enthusiastic manager also organises four beer festivals a year. A landmark in all senses, this late Victorian gem is a CAMRA Real Heritage Pub with an impressive island servery, partitions and etched and stained glass. ◐♿⇌(Clapham Jct)🚌🍎

SW12: Balham

Nightingale ✔

97 Nightingale Lane, SW12 8NX

⏲ 11 (12 Sun)-midnight ☎ (020) 8673 1637

Wells Bombardier; Young's Bitter, Special; guest beer Ⓗ

A Grade II-listed building, this friendly Young's house is a regular Guide entry and was runner up local CAMRA Pub of the Year 2009. It was also winner of the Publican's Community Pub of the Year 2009 and a Kennel Club Open for Dogs award, and organises an annual walk that raises money for charities. Food is served from 12-10pm daily and a tasting tray with third-of-a-pint glasses has been introduced.

⚠Q❀◐♿⇌(Wandsworth Common)
⊖(Clapham South)🚌(G1)⚡

SW13: Barnes

Red Lion ✔

2 Castelnau, SW13 9RU

⏲ 11-11; 12-10.30 Sun ☎ (020) 8748 2984

Fuller's Discovery, London Pride, ESB, seasonal beer Ⓗ

Large Victorian landmark pub, situated at the entrance to the Wetland Centre. It has been opened out in recent years, although the rear room still has a more exclusive feel, and leads to a decked patio area and the spacious garden. The landlord is twice winner of the Fuller's Cellarman of the Year award. Excellent food is always available from a varied, modern menu, and children are welcome during the day. ⚠❀◐♿🚌P⚡

SW15: Putney

Bricklayer's Arms

32 Waterman Street, SW15 1DD

⏲ 12-11 (10.30 Sun) ☎ (020) 8789 0222

🌐 bricklayers-arms.co.uk

Sambrook's Wandle; Taylor Dark Mild, Golden Best, Best Bitter, Landlord; guest beers Ⓗ

Local CAMRA Pub of the Year 2006 and 2008, and regional winner in 2007, this welcoming free house dating from 1826 reopened in 2005. The only pub in London with the full Timothy Taylor range, it also serves micro-brewery guest beers and Westons cider or perry. Decorated with Thames and Putney-related photos and cartoons, this community pub with its shove ha'penny, bar skittles, cricket team and regular beer festivals is very busy, particularly when Fulham FC are at home. ⚠❀⇌⊖(Putney Bridge)🚌♣🍎⚡

Green Man

Wildcroft Road, Putney Heath, SW15 3NG

⏲ 11-11 (midnight Fri & Sat); 12-10.30 Sun

☎ (020) 8788 8096

Wells Bombardier; Young's Bitter, Special; guest beer Ⓗ

On the edge of the heath opposite the bus terminus up Putney Hill, this charming, warm and welcoming Young's pub retains an intimate atmosphere. Ring the Bull is played in one of various rooms leading off the small bar. Outside are a sheltered front patio and a large, split level back garden ideal for families in summer. Quiz night is Tuesday; poker night Wednesday. Meals are served lunchtimes and evenings weekdays, all day Friday in summer, Saturday and Sunday.

⚠❀◐♿🚌♣⚡

SW16: Streatham

Earl Ferrers ✔

22 Ellora Road, SW16 6JF

⏲ 4 (12 Sat)-midnight; 12-11 Sun ☎ (020) 8835 8333

Sambrook's Wandle, Junction; guest beers Ⓗ

Imposing Victorian street-corner local seemingly named after the infamous fourth Earl who was hanged at Tyburn in 1760. Now a single roomed pub, it usually stocks four locally brewed beers supplied through Enterprise under the SIBA scheme and offers a full menu on weekday evenings and all day at weekends. A community noticeboard lists various activities including 'stitch and bitch' and a book club. Games are available for children.

⚠❀◑⇌(Streatham/Streatham Common)🚌⚡

SW17: Tooting

Antelope

76 Mitcham Road, SW17 9NG

⏲ 4 (12 Fri)-midnight; 12-1am Sat; 12-11 Sun

☎ (020) 8672 3888

Beer range varies Ⓗ

An old unspoilt Barclays pub restored in 2009 by Antic Ltd, this Tardis-like establishment has six handpumps offering a changing beer range, including customer suggestions. Of three distinct areas, the most striking is the huge back room, decorated with antelope skulls and a stuffed beetle collection, containing a pool table and giant screen for major sporting events. Excellent food is served on weekday evenings (not Mon) and all day Saturday and Sunday. A welcome new entry to the Guide. ⚠◑⊖(Tooting Broadway)🚌♣

JJ Moons ✔

56A Tooting High Street, SW17 0RN

⏲ 10-midnight ☎ (020) 8672 4726

Greene King Ruddles Best Bitter, Abbot; Marston's Pedigree; guest beers Ⓗ

Long, narrow Wetherspoon's pub opposite the Tube station and handy for the area and its many South Asian restaurants. The wood-panelled interior features photos of Edwardian Tooting. There are two large TV screens for sport, but the sound is usually turned down. This is a vibrant community pub; move to the rear for a quieter drink. Westons Marcle Hill and Organic Vintage cider are available. ◐⊖(Tooting Broadway)🚌🍎

Tooting Tram & Social

46-48 Mitcham Road, SW17 9NA

closed Mon; 5-midnight Tue-Thu, 4-2am Fri, 12-2am Sat; 12-midnight Sun (020) 8767 0278

Brakspear Bitter; Purity Pure Gold, Mad Goose, Ubu

Once a tramshed, this listed building became a pub in the late 1990s before it was acquired by the Antic pubco in 2007. The original interior tiling remains, now decorated with an eclectic mixture of framed pictures, mirrors and other paraphernalia. A balcony area is mainly open at weekends. Subdued lighting contributes to a relaxed ambience, enjoyed by a mostly young clientele. Two of the three Purity beers are usually available at any time. ⊖(Broadway)

SW18: Battersea

Roundhouse

2 Wandsworth Common Northside, SW18 2SS

12-11.30 (midnight Sat); 12-11 Sun (020) 7326 8580

theroundhousewandsworth.com

Sambrook's Wandle, Junction

A lively corner gastro-pub where the locally brewed real ales outsell the various keg lagers. Westons Organic cider is also available on handpump. There is no TV but the walls are adorned with some excellent Spanish B-film posters. Lunchtime food is served Friday to Sunday only, with evening meals available throughout the week. A dog-friendly pub, it provides water and free doggy treats. An outside seating area is heated on those chilly spring and autumn evenings. ≠(Clapham Jct)(77,219)♣

SW18: Wandsworth

Grapes

39 Fairfield Street, SW18 1DX

12-11 (midnight Fri & Sat); 12-10.30 Sun

(020) 8874 3414

Young's Bitter, Special

This traditional corner local has undergone a minor refurbishment recently but has not lost any of its charm. A heated patio is provided for smokers adjacent to a sun-trap garden which continues to be London's best-kept secret. Good value lunches are provided during the week. A regular finalist and former winner of the local CAMRA Pub of the Year competition, its outstanding beer quality remains the benchmark to which others are compared. ≠(Wandsworth Town)

Le Gothique

Royal Victoria Patriotic Building, John Archer Way, SW18 3SX (off Windmill Rd)

12-midnight; weekend hours vary (020) 8870 6567

legothique.co.uk

Beer range varies

Built in 1857 as an orphanage and used by intelligence services in WWII, the haunted, Gothic building now houses apartments and studios along with this well-established free house, French restaurant and wedding venue. Wall panels illustrate the building's history. Three real ales are on offer, usually one from Downton, Sambrook's and Shepherd Neame, although other small brewers may feature. Food is served 12-3pm and 6-10pm weekdays, times vary at weekends. Beer festivals are held in March and October (Halloween). (77,219)P

Spread Eagle

71 Wandsworth High Street, SW18 2PT

11-11 (midnight Fri & Sat); 12-11 Sun (020) 8877 9809

Young's Bitter, Special, seasonal beers

One of London's Real Heritage Pubs, this traditional drinkers' establishment sits at the heart of Wandsworth opposite the now sadly disused Young's Brewery. Behind the impressive counter of the saloon there is some fine glass and woodwork to admire, including a full-height partition behind which lies the plainer public bar. Although meals are only served weekdays 12-3pm, panini are available all day every day. ≠(Wandsworth Town)

SW19: South Wimbledon

Sultan

78 Norman Road, SW19 1BT

12-11 (midnight Fri & Sat) (020) 8544 9323

Hop Back GFB, Entire Stout, Summer Lightning; guest beer

Traditional, well-run street-corner local with a welcome for all seeking Hop Back beers in the brewery's only tied house in London. There are two bars – the smaller with a dartboard is usually only open in the evening. No food is available but occasional barbecues are held. Beer Club with reduced prices is Wednesday 6-9pm. A weekend beer festival is held in the autumn. The guest beer is usually a Hop Back seasonal or from the Downton Brewery. ⊖(Colliers Wood)(200)♣

Trafalgar

23 High Path, SW19 2JY

3 (12 Fri & Sat)-11; 12-11 Sun (020) 8542 5342

thetraf.com

Ascot Market Ale; Pilgrim Thru'ppenny Hop; guest beers

Local CAMRA Pub of the Year 2007 and 2009, and regional winner in 2008, this small back-street local just over two minutes' walk from the bus stop is a hidden gem. The two regular beers are specially brewed for the pub and four more beers change frequently. With jazz on Sunday afternoon, live music every week, food night on Thursday, an annual autumn beer festival, cricket and darts teams, this is a real community pub. ⊖(South Wimbledon)♣

SW19: Wimbledon

Hand in Hand

6 Crooked Billet, SW19 4RQ

11-11 (midnight Fri & Sat); 12-10.30 Sun

(020) 8946 5720

Courage Directors; Wells Bombardier; Young's Bitter, Special, seasonal beer; guest beers

This much-loved pub on the edge of Wimbledon Common was originally a bakehouse, and after becoming an ale house was acquired by Young's in 1974. It now has a number of distinct drinking areas around a central bar. During warm weather drinkers (with plastic glasses) spill out on to the grass triangle across the access road. There is regular live acoustic music, with quiz and poker nights each week. Q(200)♣

SW20: Raynes Park

Edward Rayne ✔

8-12 Coombe Lane, SW20 8ND

⏲ 9am-11.30 ☎ (020) 8971 0420

Greene King Ruddles Best Bitter, Abbot; Marston's Pedigree; guest beers Ⓗ

Opened in 2006 on the site of a supermarket, this large, single bar Wetherspoon's has become a firm favourite in the area, commemorating the 19th-century farmer whose lands became Raynes Park. Decorated in pastel shades, with wood panelling, half mirrored pillars and soft lighting, it shows TV news with subtitles but no sound, except for sports (not football). Westons Marcle Hill and Organic Vintage ciders and a perry are available. ◐≹🚌🍎⊨

Carshalton

Hope 🏆

48 West Street, SM5 2PR

⏲ 12-11 (10.30 Sun) ☎ (020) 8240 1255

🌐 hopecarshalton.co.uk

Dark Star Hophead; guest beers Ⓗ

A cosy little free house with a traditional atmosphere, the pub has a single bar and a large garden at the rear. There is a good rotating range of ales, with a mild and a real cider usually available. The staff and the regulars always make you feel welcome, and there is a lovely community feel. Regular real ale festivals are held throughout the year. Local CAMRA Pub of the Year 2009 and 2010. ♨Q❀♿≹🚌(127,157,S3)♣🍎P⊨

Railway Tavern ✔

47 North Street, SM5 2HG

⏲ 12-2.30, 5-11; 12-11 Sat & Sun ☎ (020) 8669 8016

Fuller's London Pride, ESB; Gale's Seafarers Ale Ⓗ

Built in Victorian times to serve the nearby station, this small corner local has featured many times in the Guide. A U-shaped bar has walls adorned with railway memorabilia and several beer quality certificates. The pub has outdoor floral displays and a small patio garden to the side and rear. Sporting events are screened on the TV. Lunches are served on weekdays only. ❀◐≹🚌(127,157,S3)⊨

Windsor Castle ✔

378 Carshalton Road, SM5 3PT

⏲ 11-11 (11.30 Fri & Sat); 12-10.30 Sun ☎ (020) 8669 1191

🌐 windsorcastlepub.com

Harveys Sussex Best Bitter; Shepherd Neame Kent's Best, seasonal beers; guest beers Ⓗ

Acquired by Shepherd Neame in 2009, this pub has been a CAMRA award winner many times. Food is available in the restaurant (not Sun and Mon eves). Quiz night is every Thursday. Local rock and blues bands play on Saturday, while Monday evening is jam night. A covered courtyard leads to the function room and garden. A wider selection of beers is provided at periodic beer festivals. ❀◐≹(Carshalton Beeches)🚌(154,407,S3)♣P⊨

Cheam

Claret Wine Bar

33 The Broadway, SM3 8BL

⏲ 11.30-11.30 (12.30am Fri & Sat); 12-11.30 Sun

☎ (020) 8715 9002

Shepherd Neame Master Brew Bitter, Spitfire; guest beers Ⓗ

A family-owned pub and wine bar in Cheam village, the Claret is run in tandem with its namesake in Addiscombe, which also features in the Guide. This shop conversion with a mock-Tudor interior is adorned with breweriana, and real ale is promoted. Quiz night is Monday, and Thursday is curry night. Local food is served including Sunday roasts, and parties are catered for. The TV screen shows sporting events, and free wireless access is available. ◐♿≹🚌⊨

Prince of Wales

28 Malden Road, SM3 8QF

⏲ 11-11 (midnight Fri & Sat); 12-10.30 Sun

☎ (020) 8641 8106

Pilgrim Progress; guest beers Ⓗ

This traditional pub in a pretty village location, convenient for the library, car park and buses, has an L-shaped bar, a rear garden and seating at the front. Dogs are welcome. There are at least two regularly changing guest beers and an extensive restaurant menu, available all day at weekends. The pub has a Sunday meat raffle, a golf society, a darts team and an annual charity cricket match. And after 75 years' regular custom you can qualify for free drinks! ♨Q❀◐♿≹🚌(151,213,X26)♣⊨

Railway

32 Station Way, SM3 8SQ

⏲ 12-11 (midnight Thu-Sat) ☎ (020) 8642 7416

🌐 therailwayonline.com

Courage Best Bitter, Directors; guest beers Ⓗ

Small 1810 pub, formerly an hotel, family owned since 2007 and located in a village setting near Cheam railway station. With a log fire in winter, it has a welcoming feel and friendly and helpful staff. The two guest beers change regularly and are often local. A quiz is held monthly on a Tuesday. There are also themed nights and events such as wild west, gangsters and Halloween. The pub is home to a local golf society. Sandwiches and rolls are served, and real coffee. ♨≹🚌(151,213,470)♣

Kingston upon Thames

Boaters Inn ✔

Lower Ham Road, KT2 5AU (off A307 via Woodside Rd)

TQ180699

⏲ 11-11; 12-10.30 Sun ☎ (020) 8541 4672

Beer range varies Ⓗ

Large, open-plan, modern pub on the bank of the River Thames, just outside the town centre in Canbury Gardens. Five beers are usually on draught, often from local breweries. Home-made traditional pub food is served alongside more adventurous daily specials. The spacious outside drinking area often overflows into the gardens on sunny summer days (plastic glasses must be used). Families and dogs are welcome. Live jazz plays on Sunday evening and blues on the last Saturday of the month. There is a small mooring for river craft, but please check. Q❀◐≹🚌(65)⊨

Druids Head ✔

3 Market Place, KT1 1JT

⏲ 11-11; 12-midnight Thu-Sat; 12-11 Sun

☎ (020) 8546 0723

Black Sheep Best Bitter; Greene King IPA, Ruddles County, Old Speckled Hen, Abbot, seasonal beer Ⓗ

Ex-coaching house split into two levels. The older part dates back to the 1600s and is Grade II-listed. Author Jerome K Jerome left an inscription on one of the windows. An upstairs room can be hired. There are smoking areas in the rear garden and on the first floor terrace. Meals are served every day 12-9pm and traditional roasts on Sunday. Occasional guest beers may feature. Busy with shoppers at weekends, children are not permitted. George the ghost makes the occasional appearance. ♨❀◐◑⇌🚌⸙

Willoughby Arms

47 Willoughby Road, KT2 6LN

🕓 10.30 (12 Sun)-midnight; 12-midnight Sun
☎ (020) 8546 4236 🌐 thewilloughbyarms.com

Fuller's London Pride; guest beers Ⓗ

Friendly Victorian back-street local, divided into a sports bar and a quieter lounge, with an upstairs function room for hire. Four guest beers always include at least one LocAle. Folk music is played on the last Friday of the month. Summer barbecues are provided in the garden, which has its own TV screen, a covered, heated smoking area and a pond with terrapins. Three beer festivals are held every year. Local CAMRA Pub of the Year 2009. Q❀⊟♿🚌(371,K5)♣⸙

Wych Elm ✔

93 Elm Road, KT2 6HT

🕓 11-3, 5-midnight; 11-midnight Sat; 12-11 Sun
☎ (020) 8546 3271

Fuller's Chiswick Bitter, London Pride, ESB, seasonal beer Ⓗ

Welcoming and friendly back-street local, with one of the longest standing landlords in the area. It has a smart saloon with a glass partition and a basic but tidy public bar. Local CAMRA Pub of the Year in 2005, it has also won many prizes for its garden and floral displays out front. Good quality home-cooked lunches are served daily (not Sun). Jazz sessions are held on the last Saturday of the month. Q❀◐⊟⇌🚌(K5)♣⸙

Mitcham

White Lion of Mortimer ✔

223 London Road, CR4 2JD

🕓 10-11 (midnight Fri & Sat) ☎ (020) 8646 7332

Greene King IPA, Abbot; guest beers Ⓗ

A Wetherspoon's pub in a pedestrianised area near the clock tower, the former Bucks Head has an L-shaped bar with 10 handpumps, including Westons Marcle Hill cider. Framed coats of arms decorate the walls. The management has some independence in choosing beers, and mini beer festivals are held monthly. Quiz night is every Wednesday with a charity quiz monthly. No music is allowed, games machines are silent and TV volume is raised only for major sports events. ❀◐◑♿⇌(Mitcham Eastfields)🚌⸙

New Malden

Woodies 🏆

Thetford Road, KT3 5DX TQ206673

🕓 11-11; 12-10.30 Sun ☎ (020) 8949 5824
🌐 woodiesfreehouse.co.uk

Adnams Broadside; Fuller's London Pride, ESB; Young's Bitter; guest beers Ⓗ

This competitively priced, dog and family friendly open-plan free house in a former sports pavilion is local CAMRA Pub of the Year 2010 (also 2006-2008). Show business and sporting artefacts cover the walls and ceiling. Three guest beers are sourced from mainly local small breweries, with forthcoming beers listed on the website. The large outdoor patio incorporates a heated and covered smoking area. Features include a Sunday carvery, fortnightly quiz night, summer weekend barbecues and annual beer festival in August. Thatchers Traditional Dry cider is sold.
♨❀◐♿🚌(265)♣🍎P⸙

Richmond

Roebuck ✔

130 Richmond Hill, TW10 6RN

🕓 12-11; 11-midnight Fri & Sat; 12-10.30 Sun
☎ (020) 8948 2329

Beer range varies Ⓗ

Overlooking the World Heritage view of Petersham Meadows and the Thames, this 200-year-old, reputedly haunted pub is close to Richmond Park Gate. Patrons are welcome on the terrace to enjoy the view cherished by their forebears and highwaymen for 500 years. A recent refurbishment has opened up a function room on the first floor. Four handpumps have regularly changing beers, and an updated food menu offers great choice (food is served till late). ♨❀◐◑🚌(371)

Shaftesbury Arms

121 Kew Road, TW9 2PN

🕓 12-11 (midnight Fri); 11-midnight Sat ☎ (020) 8255 2419
🌐 shaftesburyarms.com

Wells Bombardier; Young's Bitter, Special, London Gold, seasonal beer; guest beer Ⓗ

Friendly, comfortable Victorian pub, popular with the London Welsh RFC a short walk away. At the rear is a covered, heated patio garden. The two original bars were merged into one in 1988, with the addition of a restaurant area in 2001 serving Thai food all week. Acquired by Young & Bainbridge in 1860, this distinctive building was originally known as the Wheatsheaf, becoming the Shaftesbury Arms in 1878 and rebuilt in 1899. Wi-Fi and sports TV feature. ♨❀◐◑⇌⊖🚌⸙

White Cross

Riverside, Off Water Lane, TW9 1TH

🕓 11-11; 12-10.30 Sun ☎ (020) 8940 6844

Wells Bombardier; Young's Bitter, Special, seasonal beer; guest beer Ⓗ

This prominent Young's pub on Richmond's waterfront dates from 1835. A stained glass panel commemorates that this was once the site of a convent of the Observant Friars, whose insignia was a white cross. The entrance is reached by steps for good reason: the river often floods here. An island bar serves two side rooms (one a mezzanine); an unusual feature is a working fireplace beneath a window. The ground-level patio bar opens at busy times. Food is served all day. ♨Q❀◐◑⇌⊖🚌

Surbiton

Cap in Hand ✔

174 Hook Rise North, KT6 5DE (at A3/A243 jct)

🕓 10-midnight ☎ (020) 8397 3790

Greene King Ruddles Best Bitter, Abbot; guest beers Ⓗ

Originally the Southborough Arms, this spacious 1930s roadhouse is located on the Hook junction of the A3. A varied beer range often includes ales from Hogs Back, Itchen Valley, WJ King, Pilgrim,

ENGLAND

Twickenham and Triple fff, with a selection of Westons ciders also available. Local mini beer festivals complement Wetherspoon's national events. Food is served until 10pm. An airy conservatory is designated a family area until 9pm.

Coronation Hall

St Marks Hill, KT6 4LQ
9am-midnight ☎ (020) 8390 6164
Fuller's London Pride; Greene King Ruddles Best Bitter, Abbot; Shepherd Neame Spitfire; guest beers
One of the better Wetherspoon's conversions, this building has been a music hall, cinema, bingo hall and nudist health club. The decor is a mix of movie stars, film artefacts, the coronation of George V and the planets. The pub has LocAle accreditation and beers from local micros always feature among the regularly changing guests. Local beer festivals are also held occasionally featuring beers from a couple of local breweries. Westons Marcle Hill cider is served on handpump.

Lamb

73 Brighton Road, KT6 5NF (on A243)
12-11 (midnight Thu-Sat) ☎ (020) 8390 9229
homagedefromage.co.uk
Ringwood Best Bitter; Wychwood Hobgoblin; guest beer
Reopened in 2007, this small, cosy, family-run pub was built in 1850 and originally had a small brewery. Formerly divided into four separate bars, it retains the horseshoe-shaped bar from those times. The pub offers interesting guest ales, and a wide selection of British cheeses and terrines, pates and pies from the family farm in Dorset. There are regular events including music nights – the Lamb positions itself successfully as a community local.

Sutton

Robin Hood

52 West Street, SM1 1SH
11 (12 Sun)-11 ☎ (020) 8643 7584
robinhoodsutton.co.uk
Courage Directors; Young's Bitter, Special, seasonal beers
A warm welcome awaits you at this fine community pub located close to Sutton's main shopping street. The experienced bar staff have been here for years and the pub was a finalist in the 2009 British Pub Awards. Many groups meet here, including cribbage teams, and an informal borrowing library operates. The pub stocks the full range of Young's bottle-conditioned beers.
(Sutton/West Sutton)

WEST LONDON

W1: Fitzrovia

Hope

15 Tottenham Street, W1T 2AJ
11-11; 12-6 Sun ☎ (020) 7637 0896 thehopepub.com
Courage Directors; Fuller's London Pride; Greene King IPA; Sharp's Doom Bar; Taylor Landlord
Licensed since 1772, the present building, now an Enterprise pub, dates from 1867. The wood-floored bar has bench seating around the sides with additional stools. Six handpumps complement a varied food menu including a good range of sausages. Further seating is available in an upstairs lounge which can be hired for parties or functions. Two large TVs show sports. (Goodge Street)

W1: Marylebone

Carpenters Arms

12 Seymour Place, W1H 7NE
11-11; 12-10.30 Sun ☎ (020) 7723 1050
Adnams Broadside; Harveys Sussex Best Bitter; guest beers
Known locally as 'The Carp', the building was first licensed in 1776 and rebuilt by Meux Brewery in 1872. The U-shaped bar has a raised area with bench seating by the window. There are six handpumps in this Market Taverns pub, with a varied choice of beers. Three TV screens show most sporting events and it can get crowded. There is a dartboard at the back and an upstairs function room for hire. (Marble Arch)

W1: Mayfair

Coach & Horses

5 Bruton Street, W1J 6PT
11.30-11; 12-8 Sat; closed Sun ☎ (020) 7629 4123
Fuller's London Pride; Greene King IPA; Taylor Landlord; guest beers
An excellent refuge from the bustle of the nearby Bond Street shopping area. First licensed in 1738, this Punch pub was rebuilt in 1933 and has an imposing mock-Tudor exterior. Inside the atmosphere is traditional with wooden beams and panelling. Pictures on the walls feature caricatures of 19th-century politicians and clerics. Ale drinkers will be impressed by the collection of pump clips displayed above the bar. Four handpumps include regulars and a changing series of guest ales.
(Bond St/Green Pk/Oxford Circus)

Coach & Horses

5 Hill Street, W1J 5LD
12-11; closed Sat & Sun ☎ (020) 7355 1055
Shepherd Neame Kent's Best, Spitfire
This distinguished pub is the oldest surviving in Mayfair. Dating from 1744, it is also Grade II-listed. The splendid bar is outstanding with much polished wood, alcoves and mirrors. An unusual wooden canopy extends over the bar counter. Brass lanterns above contribute to the impression of grandeur. The real seating area features an attractive marble and wood fireplace. Pictures depict humorous drinking scenes from past times. The pub is popular with business people from the surrounding area. Q (Bond St/Green Pk)

W1: Soho

Crown

64 Brewer Street, W1F 9TP
10am-11 (11.30 Fri & Sat); 12-10.30 Sun
☎ (020) 7287 8420
Fuller's London Pride; Taylor Landlord; guest beers
Popular M&B Nicholson's pub in the heart of Soho on the site of the Hickford Rooms, which were London's main concert rooms in the 1740s and '50s. The front bar, with its banquettes, is a welcome retreat from the bustling street. Changing guest beers make for an interesting range of ales. The plush upstairs dining room has its own bar. Breakfast is served from 10am every day.
(Piccadilly Circus)

Dog & Duck ☆ ✓
18 Bateman Street, W1D 3AJ
11-11 (11.30 Fri & Sat); 12-10.30 Sun ☎ (020) 7494 0697
Fuller's London Pride; Taylor Landlord; guest beers [H]
In the bustling heart of Soho, this listed M&B Nicholson's pub built in 1897 is one of CAMRA's Real Heritage Pubs. Elaborate mosaic tiles depict dogs and ducks, and wonderful advertising mirrors adorn the walls. The upstairs Orwell Bar is a great place for looking out over the frenetic streets of West One. (Tottenham Ct Rd)

Old Coffee House
49 Beak Street, W1F 9SF
11-11; 12-10.30 Sun ☎ (020) 7437 2197
Brodie's English Ale, IPA, Special, seasonal beers [H]
The cosy back-street local atmosphere belies the pub's proximity to the chaos of Carnaby Street. While every available inch of wall and ceiling space is covered with vintage prints, paintings of naked ladies and brassware, the decor is intriguing but not oppressive. Food is available lunchtimes only (not Sun). An S&N/Heineken pub leased by Brodie's, prominently featuring five of its beers and rapidly becoming a London CAMRA favourite. (Oxford Circus/Piccadilly Circus)

Ship ✓
116 Wardour Street, W1F 0TT
11-11; closed Sun ☎ (020) 7437 8446
Fuller's Discovery, London Pride, ESB, seasonal beers [H]
A marvellous Fuller's pub. Charlotte and her staff have been here for a long time now and keep the beers in superb condition. Damaged during World War II, the pub was rebuilt with as many of the original 1895 fittings as possible: etched and leaded glasswork, decorative mirrors and an ornate wooden bar back. It has an extensive collection of indie music, reflecting the local music industry. (Tottenham Ct Rd)

W2: Lancaster Gate

Mitre
24 Craven Terrace, W2 3QH
11-11; 12-10.30 Sun ☎ (020) 7262 5240
mitrelancastergate.co.uk
Wells Bombardier; Young's Bitter, Special, seasonal beer [H]
Built in 1859 and Grade II-listed, with the interior mostly intact, this pub is one of London's Real Heritage Pubs with original etched glass, unusual rounded front doors at the corner entrance and four interconnecting rooms. An upstairs dining room can be hired for private parties and there is also a small outside space with seating. Children are welcome. Taken over by Young's in 2008, it attracts drinkers looking for well-kept beer and tourists looking mainly for good food. (Paddington)

W2: Paddington

Cleveland Arms
28 Chilworth Street, W2 6DT
11-11 (11.30 Fri & Sat); 12-10.30 Sun ☎ (020) 7706 1759
Greene King IPA; Taylor Landlord; guest beer [H]
A few minutes' walk from Paddington Station, this lovely Grade II-listed pub with its tiled ends is named after William Vane, first Duke of Cleveland, and was built by DM Austin in 1852. A friendly free house mainly serving local residents, its guest beer is often one seldom seen in London. The rear room with dartboard and pool table can be hired for functions. Quiz night is Tuesday; there is a free bar buffet Sunday lunchtime. Children and dogs are welcome.

Mad Bishop & Bear ✓
Upper Level, Paddington Station, W2 1HB
8-11 (11.30 Fri); 10-10.30 Sun ☎ (020) 7402 2441
Fuller's Chiswick Bitter, Discovery, London Pride, ESB, seasonal beers; guest beers [H]
Opened in 1999 in the shopping complex just behind the station concourse, the traditional interior features a long bar, mirrors, good prints and a rather grand chandelier, with screens for train information and two TVs for sports. The raised drinking space can be hired for events. It doesn't get too crowded even in the rush hour. The bar sometimes closes early and may also close, at police insistence, when football crowds are passing through the station.

Victoria ☆ ✓
10A Strathearn Place, W2 2HN
11-11; 12-10.30 Sun ☎ (020) 7724 1191
Fuller's Discovery, London Pride, ESB, seasonal beers [H]
There is plenty to admire in this listed mid-Victorian pub, one of CAMRA's Real Heritage Pubs, including ornately gilded mirrors above a crescent-shaped bar, painted tiles in wall niches and numerous portraits of Queen Victoria. The walls display cartoons, paperweights and a Silver Jubilee plate. A recessed area at the back is furnished with a leather bench seat. Upstairs, reached via a spiral staircase, there is a library and theatre bar available for public use. Tuesday is quiz night. Q (Lancaster Gate/Paddington)

W3: Acton

George & Dragon
183 High Street, W3 9DJ
12-11 (midnight Fri & Sat); 12-10.30 Sun
☎ (020) 8992 3712
Fuller's Chiswick Bitter, London Pride; Gale's HSB [H]
This 18th-century pub was wonderfully restored and improved in 2006 and is now a welcoming venue with three bars of real character. A traditional front bar, with a list of landlords dating back to 1759, leads into a heritage bar with exposed original features, and a stylish back room. At the heart of the historic Acton town centre, the pub is opposite the main High Street bus stop and a short walk from local stations. (Acton Central) (Acton Town)

Red Lion & Pineapple ✓
281 High Street, W3 9BP
9am-midnight ☎ (020) 8896 2248
Greene King Ruddles Best Bitter, Abbot [H]
A sizeable two-room Wetherspoon's with a large, circular bar in the main room. The large windows have etched and stained tops and the walls are decorated with photographs of old Acton. The smaller room is mainly for diners and families. Formerly owned by Fuller's, the site originally had two pubs until the neighbouring tram shed was built, hence the unusual name. Itchen Valley supplies additional beers including one named after the pub. Westons Marcle Hill cider is also on handpump. Q (Acton Town)

West London Trades Union Club

33-35 High Street, W3 6ND
✪ 7-midnight ☎ (020) 8992 4557
Beer range varies Ⓗ
This small and friendly club, run as a co-operative, combines excellent real ale with a busy cultural and social life. Two beers are normally served, at least one from the Nelson Brewery range, the other from a small independent brewery. The Acton Community Theatre is upstairs, and the club hosts regular special events including summer barbecues in the courtyard. The local CAMRA branch is an associate member: show a CAMRA membership card or this Guide for entry.
❀≠(Acton Central)🚌⚟

W4: Chiswick

Duke of Sussex

75 South Parade, Acton Green, W4 5LF
✪ 12-11 (midnight Fri & Sat); 12-10.30 Sun
☎ (020) 8742 8801
Beer range varies Ⓗ
A very friendly bar staff welcome you to this listed pub run by Realpubs Ltd, with three rotating guest ales. A large restaurant area serves a mix of English food and Iberian specials such as paella and salted cod. The current management has turned what was a failing pub into a local gem that can get very busy in the evenings. Family and dog friendly, it is both a local and a gastro-pub.
Q❀◐◑♿≠(South Acton)⊖(Chiswick Pk/Turnham Green)🚌(94,440)⚟

Fox & Hounds/Mawson Arms ✔

110 Chiswick Lane South, W4 2QA
✪ 10-8; closed Sat & Sun ☎ (020) 8994 2936
Fuller's Chiswick Bitter, London Pride, ESB, seasonal beers Ⓗ
On the corner of the Griffin Brewery and its de facto brewery tap, this listed pub is the start for the Fuller's brewery tour. The unusual double naming is an historical relic of the separate licences needed for beer, wine and spirits. Hot food is available at lunchtime, and the pub is well known for its home-made steak and ale pies. There is memorabilia of the brewery's history on the walls plus portraits of ancestors of the Fuller, Smith and Turner founders.
♨Q◐🚌(190)

George & Devonshire ✔

8 Burlington Lane, W4 2QE
✪ 12-11 ☎ (020) 8994 1859
🌐 thegeorgeanddevonshire.co.uk
Fuller's Chiswick Bitter, London Pride, ESB, seasonal beers Ⓗ
The alternative Fuller's brewery tap, a listed pub off the Hogarth roundabout with its flyover on the A4, parades its rich local history within the Old Chiswick area on a board on the front. Relatively insulated from the traffic noise, the pub serves a wide food menu including basic English main courses and desserts, plus curries and some unusual sandwiches, jackets and wraps. There are large-screen TVs for sports enthusiasts and live music one evening a week. ❀◐◑⊟🚌(190)♣P⚟

Old Pack Horse ✔

434 Chiswick High Road, W4 5TF
✪ 11-11 (midnight Fri & Sat); 12-10.30 Sun
☎ (020) 8994 2872
Fuller's Chiswick Bitter, Discovery, London Pride, ESB Ⓗ
A well-preserved Edwardian corner pub with a fine frontage often featured in photographs of the area, with a view across Turnham Green and its church. The pub interior retains ornate woodwork and glasswork including some stained glass panels; it is one of London's Real Heritage Pubs. Five drinking areas include a snug and a large Thai restaurant at the back. The walls are adorned with theatre memorabilia. Two TVs show sports events.
❀◐◑≠(Gunnersbury)⊖(Chiswick Pk/Gunnersbury)🚌⚟

W5: Ealing

Fox & Goose ✔

Hanger Lane, W5 1DP
✪ 12-11 (midnight Fri & Sat); 12-10.30 Sun
☎ (020) 8998 5864 🌐 foxandgoosehotel.com
Fuller's London Pride, ESB, seasonal beer Ⓗ
A large 1830s pub with period features, although since extended. A separate hotel has been built on the site, and the location is good for overnight stays when on trips to Wembley. A large central bar divides the main bar and restaurant area, with good service on both sides. A front patio and rear garden are available, with a heated smoking area. Food is well priced, and of good quality.
♨❀⇆◐◑♿⊖(Hanger Lane)🚌P⚟

Questors (Grapevine Bar) ✔

12 Mattock Lane, W5 5BQ
✪ 7-11; 12-2.30, 7-10.30 Sun ☎ (020) 8567 0011
🌐 questors.org.uk/grapevine
Fuller's London Pride; guest beers Ⓗ
This friendly theatre bar is set opposite Walpole Park just south of the town centre. It regularly serves guest beers, usually including one from a local brewery, and also runs CAMRA themed festivals twice a year. Books and board games are available, as are Belgian beers and obscure whiskies. The club is run by enthusiastic volunteers and is the current local CAMRA Club of the Year.
Q❀♿≠⊖(Ealing Broadway)🚌♣P⚟

Red Lion ✔

13 St Mary's Road, W5 5RA
✪ 11-11 (midnight Fri & Sat); 12-11 Sun ☎ (020) 8567-2541
Fuller's Chiswick Bitter, London Pride, ESB, seasonal beer; guest beer Ⓗ
A popular local, affectionately known as 'Stage 6', situated opposite Ealing Studios. Photographs of TV and film stars who have been associated with the studios are on display alongside other memorabilia of the films that gave them their reputation. The pub has gained its own reputation for home-made food in recent years and is unusual in the area for not having a TV or jukebox. The covered patio at the back hosts occasional beer festivals.
Q❀◐◑♿≠(Ealing Broadway)⊖(Ealing Broadway/S Ealing)🚌(65)⚟

Wheatsheaf ✔

41 Haven Lane, W5 2HZ
✪ 12-11 (10.30 Sun) ☎ (020) 8997 5240
🌐 wheatsheafealing.co.uk
Fuller's Chiswick Bitter, Discovery, London Pride, ESB, seasonal beer Ⓗ
A Fuller's pub tucked down a side street north of Ealing Broadway and the perfect place for a pleasant drink. The traditional interior has interesting features such as carved wood signs.

There is a small outside passageway for smoking, and the rear of the pub is a dining area. Quiz night is Monday. The pub promotes itself as Ealing's best kept secret, and that's probably not far wrong. ✿◐⇌⊖(Ealing Broadway)🚌⅃

W5: South Ealing

Ealing Park Tavern

222 South Ealing Road, W5 4RL

⏲ 11-11; 12-10.30 Sun ☎ (020) 8578 1879

Harveys Sussex Best Bitter; guest beers Ⓗ

One of London's Real Heritage Pubs, this large 19th-century pub was rescued through conversion into a gastro-pub, reverting back to its original name and retaining its original character. Five handpumps in a spacious front bar offer a changing variety of beers, often from micro-breweries thanks to the SIBA scheme. The restaurant serves excellent English and European dishes and bar snacks are also available. There is a large beer garden and old fashioned bar billiards has recently been introduced. ♛Q✿◐♿⊖🚌(65)♣●⅃

W6: Hammersmith

Andover Arms ✔

57 Aldensley Road, W6 0DL

⏲ 12-midnight ☎ (020) 8748 2155 🌐 andoverarms.co.uk

Fuller's Chiswick Bitter, London Pride, ESB, seasonal beers Ⓗ

Popular back-street local tucked away in the side streets of Hammersmith. A regular entry in this Guide, the pub holds regular quiz nights and occasional beer festivals. It underwent refurbishment recently and the improved kitchen offers a wide range of meals. There is a TV that is used occasionally for major sporting events. ♛◐⊖(Ravenscourt Pk)🚌

Dove ✔

19 Upper Mall, W6 9TA

⏲ 11-11; 12-10.30 Sun ☎ (020) 8748 9474

Fuller's Discovery, London Pride, ESB, seasonal beers Ⓗ

Traditional Fuller's pub, a listed building overlooking the Thames, with a quaint dark wood interior. One of London's Real Heritage Pubs, it also holds the Guinness world record for the smallest bar area. Classic food with a twist is served every day; meals can take up to 45 minutes to arrive at busy times, but are definitely worth the wait. Well-kept beer and a pleasant atmosphere make this one of the best pubs in the area. ♛Q✿◐⊖(Ravenscourt Pk)🚌♣⅃

W7: Hanwell

Fox 🏆

Green Lane, W7 2PJ

⏲ 11-11; 12-10.30 Sun ☎ (020) 8567 3912

🌐 thefoxpub.co.uk

Fuller's London Pride; Sharp's Doom Bar; Taylor Landlord; guest beers Ⓗ

Convivial back-street free house near Hanwell Locks, popular with walkers and canal users as well as locals. A traditional corner bar with plenty of seating, it offers a good range of beers and excellent food at reasonable prices. Booking is recommended for Sunday lunch. The pleasant garden has a games room. Local CAMRA Pub of the Year 2010. ♛✿◐🚌(195,E8)♣●⅃

W8: Notting Hill Gate

Churchill Arms ✔

119 Kensington Church Street, W8 7LN

⏲ 11-11 (midnight Thu-Sat); 12-10.30 Sun

☎ (020) 7727 4242

Fuller's Chiswick Bitter, Discovery, London Pride, ESB, seasonal beers Ⓗ

The winner of awards ranging from Boozers in Bloom to the Griffin Award for Fuller's Pub of the Year, this is also one of London's Real Heritage Pubs. As you enter, it looks as if there is an antique market hanging from the ceiling. There is even a signpost in the middle of the pub just in case you get lost. The Thai food is to be recommended as well as the beer. Q◐⊖🚌

Uxbridge Arms

13 Uxbridge Street, W8 7TQ

⏲ 12-11 (10.30 Sun) ☎ (020) 7727 7326

Fuller's London Pride; St Austell Tribute; Wells Bombardier Ⓗ

A popular back-street Enterprise local dating from 1836 as a beer house. Wood-panelled and carpeted throughout, the welcoming bar has a warm feel, with lots of photographs and plates as well as a lieutenant-colonel's dress tunic. The best seats are at the end of the bar by the Nicola Sunshine Fund charity collection bottle. Q✿⊖🚌⅃

W11: Notting Hill

Cock & Bottle

17 Needham Road, W11 2RP

⏲ 11-11; 12-10.30 Sun ☎ (020) 7229 1550

Fuller's London Pride; Hogs Back TEA; guest beers Ⓗ

Built in 1851 and formerly known as the Swan, this Enterprise pub is one of London's Real Heritage Pubs. Stained glass panels depict swans above the windows in the main bar. An impressively ornate bar back and Corinthian columns are prominent features. Sporting events are often shown on the TV in the main bar but the comfortable rear lounge provides a retreat. A notable portrait of the influential landlord is unmissable here. ♛Q✿◐⊖(Notting Hill Gate)🚌⅃

Duke of Wellington

179 Portobello Road, W11 2ED

⏲ 10.30 (9.30am Sat)-midnight; 11-10.30 Sun

☎ (020) 7727 6727

Wells Bombardier; Young's Bitter, Special, seasonal beers Ⓗ

Dating from 1854, this Young's pub is an interesting combination of traditional and modern. Partitions with etched glass give an indication of an earlier layout. The impressive island bar with its tall bar back is the most prominent feature and the front bar retains a traditional ambience. The comfortable raised area at the rear has an attractive marble fireplace. Located close to the famous Portobello antiques market, the pub attracts many visitors. ✿◐♿⊖(Ladbroke Grove/Notting Hill Gate) 🚌(23,52,452)⅃

W12: Shepherds Bush

Crown & Sceptre ✔

57 Melina Road, W12 9HY

⏲ 11-11 (midnight Fri & Sat); 12-10.30 Sun

☎ (020) 8746 0060

ENGLAND

Fuller's Chiswick Bitter, London Pride, ESB, seasonal beers Ⓗ
Large back-street local dating back to 1866, more recently converted from a two-bar establishment to an open-plan pub with a Thai kitchen. The walls show pictures from TV programmes Steptoe and Son and Minder, which were filmed on location in the Shepherds Bush area, and of Queens Park Rangers football legends. The heated garden is a beautiful place to sit back and enjoy great food and drink. Monday is the weekly quiz night. ⌂❀♿🚌⌐

W14: West Kensington

Albion ✔

121 Hammersmith Road, W14 0QL
✪ 12-midnight (10.30 Sun) ☎ (020) 7603 2826
Caledonian Deuchars IPA; Sharp's Doom Bar; guest beers Ⓗ
About halfway between Hammersmith Broadway and Olympia, this attractive S&N/Heineken corner pub dates from 1925 but there have been licensed premises here since 1864. The walls display posters for concerts by Queen, Johnny Cash, Elvis and Frank Zappa, and a photo of the Beatles near the fireplace. A good selection of food is available lunchtimes, and excellent, stone-baked pizzas in the evenings. Watch out for quiz nights and live music. The upstairs bar can be hired for functions. ◐⊖(Barons Court/Hammersmith)🚌⌐

Brentford

Brewery Tap

47 Catherine Wheel Road, TW8 8BD
✪ 12-midnight ☎ (020) 8560 5200
Fuller's Chiswick Bitter, Discovery, London Pride, seasonal beer; guest beer Ⓗ
Popular with locals and close to Kew Bridge Steam Museum, this Victorian pub is known for its music nights, except Monday (quiz night) and Wednesday. As well as the main bar, there is a games and TV room, and a back room that leads on to the covered and heated patio. The front terrace, overlooking steps down to the street, provides more outdoor drinking space during the summer. Meals are served until 7.30pm on weekdays, and Sunday lunchtime. ❀◐⇌🚌♣⌐

O'Brien's

11 London Road, TW8 8JB (near canal bridge at W end of High St)
✪ 11-11.30 (1am Fri & Sat); 12-11 Sun ☎ (020) 8560 0506
🌐 obrienspub.co.uk
Fuller's London Pride; guest beers Ⓗ
This compact and popular free house on the main road through Brentford features an ever-changing range of cask beers, frequently from the local Twickenham Brewery, as well as some Belgian specialities and at least one real cider or perry on handpump. Food is served 12-3pm and 6-9pm on weekdays, and 12-4pm Sunday lunchtime. Acoustic music sessions are held on Tuesday evening, a quiz night on Wednesday, and occasional music evenings at weekends. TV coverage of sporting events provides entertainment. ❀◐⇌🚌●⌐

Feltham

Moon on the Square ✔

30 The Centre, High Street, TW13 4AU
✪ 9am-midnight (10.30 Sun) ☎ (020) 8893 1293
Courage Best Bitter; Greene King Ruddles Best Bitter; Green King Abbot; guest beers Ⓗ
This real ale oasis continues to flourish in a changing Feltham. The interior is early Wetherspoon's: wood panels and glass partitioned booths, with pictures and local history panels. The welcome is warm and genuine. Eight real ales feature continuously varying guests including local brews, with a bar-top gravity cask usually on tap. Westons cider is available. The usual value-for-money food is served all day. Families with children are welcome until 7pm. Free Wi-Fi is available. ◐♿⇌🚌(117,235)●

Greenford

Black Horse ✔

425 Oldfield Lane, UB6 0AS
✪ 11.30-11 (midnight Fri & Sat); 12-11 Sun
☎ (020) 8578 1384
Fuller's London Pride, ESB Ⓗ
This friendly canalside pub, on the Grand Union, has a committed local following. Children are welcome and there is a strong community feel. Regular events are held in the evening during the week as well as occasional weekly themed events. The large garden at the back is very popular in the summer and there are moorings nearby that are regularly in use. The food is home-made with a changing specials board.
❀◐♿⇌⊖🚌(92,395)♣P⌐

Hampton

Railway Bell

Station Road, TW12 2AP
✪ 11-11; 12-10.30 Sun ☎ (020) 8979 1897
🌐 therailwaybell.ph
Courage Best Bitter; guest beers Ⓗ
'The Dip' is a small cottage-style pub with a large, comfortable front terrace down a driveway beside the bridge over the railway (Tudor Road) to the east of the station. Two separate bars are simply furnished and one is decorated with original photos of old Hampton. Four guest beers come from micro-breweries and small regional breweries all over the country. Crib night is every second week; quiz night the last Wednesday of the month.
⌂❀◐⇌🚌(111,216)♣⌐

Hampton Hill

Roebuck

72 Hampton Road, TW12 1JN
✪ 11-11 (11.30 Fri & Sat); 12-4, 7-10.30 Sun
☎ (020) 8255 8133
Sharp's Doom Bar, Special; Young's Bitter; guest beers Ⓗ
The bright red exterior of this Victorian street corner local does not prepare you for the amazing array of artefacts inside – even the tables are decorated with old newspapers, banknotes or coins. A wickerwork Harley-Davidson hangs from the ceiling. The award-winning garden has a heated smokers' gazebo and there is a separate garden room for hire, or just for cooler evenings. Two guest beers come mainly from south eastern micro-breweries. Local CAMRA Pub of the Year 2008. ⌂❀🛏◐⇌(Fulwell)🚌(285,R68,R70)♣⌐

Harlington

White Hart ✔

158 High Street, UB3 5DP
☉ 11-11 (11.30 Thu; midnight Fri & Sat); 12-11 Sun
☎ (020) 8759 9608
Fuller's London Pride, ESB, seasonal beer; guest beer Ⓗ
This large, Grade II-listed Fuller's pub, refurbished in 2009, stands proud at the north end of the village. The single bar allows access to an open-plan area for sport on large TV screens and through to a seated area favoured by diners. Local history is the theme of the wall displays enjoyed by locals and visitors from nearby Heathrow Airport. Food is home-cooked. ❀◑♿🚌(90,140,H98)P⚊

Hayes

Botwell Inn ✔

25-29 Coldharbour Lane, UB3 3EB
☉ 9am-midnight ☎ (020) 8848 3112
Courage Directors; Greene King Ruddles Best Bitter, Abbot; guest beers Ⓗ
A large Wetherspoon's shop conversion with several areas for dining and drinking, with large settees in one part. There is a paved region to the front and a patio at the rear with large market-type parasols with heaters. Wheelchair access is good. Several beer festivals are held annually. Westons Marcle Hill and Old Rosie cider are usually available, as is Farmer Henry's perry.
Q❀◑♿⇌(Hayes & Harlington)🚌🍎⚊

Hounslow

Moon Under Water ✔

84-86 Staines Road, TW3 3LF (W end of High St)
☉ 10 (12 Sun)-11 ☎ (020) 8572 7506
Courage Directors; Greene King Ruddles Best Bitter, Abbot; guest beers Ⓗ
Early Wetherspoon's shop conversion in original style and still displaying many local history panels and photos. Very popular, it has a diverse customer base. There are normally five guest ales, often locally sourced, but far more at festival times when all 12 handpumps offer different beers. Cider is from the Westons range. Children are welcome until 8.30pm; the rear is considered the family area, and off that is an outside patio.
Q❀◑♿⊖(Hounslow Central)🚌⚊

Isleworth

Red Lion 🏆 ✔

92-94 Linkfield Road, TW7 6QJ
☉ 12-11 (midnight Wed-Sat) ☎ (020) 8560 1457
🌐 red-lion.info
Greene King IPA; Twickenham Grandstand Bitter; Young's Bitter; guest beers Ⓗ
Spacious two-bar free house with a strong community focus and often something going on: a performance by its own theatre group, live music, Thursday quiz or darts and pool competitions. Up to six guest beers complement the regulars and three ciders/perries. Twice-yearly beer festivals feature champion beers and weekend festivals have regional themes. Lunches are offered daily (except Mon), evening meals Tuesday-Saturday. Local CAMRA Pub of the Year 2009. ❀◑⊟♿⇌🚌🍎⚊

Southall

Conservative & Unionist Club

Fairlawn, High Street, UB1 3HB
☉ 11.30-2.30, 7-11; 11.30-3, 6-11 Fri & Sat; 12-3, 7-10.30 Sun
☎ (020) 8574 0261
Rebellion IPA, seasonal beers; guest beers Ⓗ
Virtually the last real ale outlet in this historic market town, situated behind the former town hall. A selection of beers from the Rebellion range is to be found inside. Meals are served some lunchtimes, there are four snooker tables and various events are held most evenings. This is an ideal meeting place before enjoying a curry in one of the many local restaurants. Show this Guide or a CAMRA membership card for entry. ❀◐⇌🚌♣P⚊

Teddington

Adelaide

57 Park Road, TW11 0AU
☉ 12-11 (midnight Fri & Sat); 12-10.30 Sun
☎ (020) 8977 3616
Shepherd Neame Master Brew Bitter, Kent's Best, Spitfire, seasonal beer Ⓗ
Previously known as the Adelaide Inn and built around 1860, this popular and friendly community pub has a prominent central bar where you are invariably greeted by the landlord on arrival. At the rear is a secluded covered patio extending to a garden area. An extensive selection of good quality food is available lunchtimes and evenings during the week (not Mon) and 12-5pm Sunday. A folk club meets twice a month in the upstairs function room. ❀◑⇌🚌(481)⚊

Clock House

69 High Street, TW11 8HA
☉ 11-11.30 (midnight Fri & Sat); 11-11 Sun
☎ (020) 8977 3909 🌐 theclockhousepub.com
Fuller's London Pride; Taylor Landlord; Twickenham seasonal beer; guest beer Ⓗ
This light and airy former Isleworth Brewery pub underwent a major refurbishment in 2008 that included a new oak floor and a new name (it was the Kings Arms). It now caters for more upmarket customers. The bar separates a comfortable seating area from the main entrance, a side room and access to a large rear patio area. There is an attractive fireplace with seating. A selection of good quality food is available.
♨❀◑♿⇌🚌(281,285,R68)⚊

Lion

27 Wick Road, TW11 9DN
☉ 12-11.30 (11 Sun-Tue) ☎ (020) 8977 3199
🌐 thelionpub.co.uk
Fuller's London Pride; Sharp's Doom Bar; Twickenham seasonal beer; guest beer Ⓗ
Victorian single-bar corner pub, sympathetically modernised and extended, with a choice of good food until 9pm (Sun lunch until 5pm). Wednesday is quiz night and there is live music most Saturdays. The landlord has continued the tradition of holding an annual beer festival. There is a large patio and garden with a children's play area, pool table, sports TV and a function room. Regional CAMRA Pub of the Year 2006.
♨❀◑♿⇌(Hampton Wick)🚌(281,285)♣⚊

ENGLAND

Twickenham

Eel Pie

9-11 Church Street, TW1 3NJ
11-11 (midnight Thu-Sat); 12-10.30 Sun
(020) 8891 1717
Badger K&B Sussex Bitter, First Gold, Tanglefoot, seasonal beers H
Though originally a wine bar in this charming part of Twickenham, this has all the feel of a traditional pub, with a distinctly historic look and much rugby-orientated paraphernalia. There is a choice of drinking areas, including the bar itself, normally festooned with many regulars. All the food is home made, with lunches daily and superb Sunday roasts. One of Hall & Woodhouse's top performing pubs.

Prince Albert

30 Hampton Road, TW2 5QB
11-11 (midnight Fri & Sat) (020) 8894 3963
Fuller's Chiswick Bitter, Discovery, London Pride, ESB, seasonal beer H
Opened by the Star Brewery in 1840, the pub was later unofficially known as 'Wiffen's' as it was run by three generations of the same family whose name is still displayed behind the bar. Nowadays divided into three areas, it is popular for its convivial atmosphere and Thai restaurant. The attractive garden and patio are pleasant in summer. Live music is played on Saturday evening. Two annual beer festivals feature small brewers. The heated smoking patio has a sports screen.
Q (Strawberry Hill)

Prince Blucher

124 The Green, TW2 5AG
11-11 (midnight Fri & Sat); 12-11 Sun (020) 8894 1824
Fuller's Chiswick Bitter, Discovery, London Pride, ESB, seasonal beer H
Historic 1815 inn, the first to be built on the newly enclosed Twickenham Green and reputedly the only pub in the UK still paying homage to the Duke of Wellington's left flanker at Waterloo. Four separate bar areas suit most tastes. The enthusiastic landlord of 13 years' standing offers home-cooked food all day and in summer hosts hog roasts and barbecues in the ample, child-friendly garden. Food and real ale festivals also feature. Q (Strawberry Hill) P

Rifleman

7 Fourth Cross Road, TW2 5EL
12-11 (10.30 Sun) (020) 8898 8993
Courage Best Bitter; Young's Bitter; guest beers H
A gem of a late Victorian quiet street corner community pub retaining many original features and named allegedly for riflemen billeted nearby. Courage's golden cockerel remains perched atop the sign on the front terrace. Guest beers always include one or two from the Twickenham Brewery nearby. Locals gather for Monday quiz night and regular darts matches, greeted by Keeya, a friendly collie cross who is part of the establishment.
Q (Fulwell/Strawberry Hill)

Turk's Head

28 Winchester Road, St Margarets, TW1 1LF
12-11 (11.30 Thu; midnight Fri & Sat); 12-10.30 Sun
(020) 8892 1972
Fuller's Discovery, London Pride, ESB, seasonal beer H
Local corner pub built in 1902, offering fine beers, food and live music on Friday. Beatles fans used to flock here to see the pub's location for a scene from A Hard Day's Night. The Bearcat Comedy Club has been inviting top comedians to the function room every Saturday night for more than 20 years. Rugby fans form human pyramids on match days and try and stick their tickets on the high ceiling.
Q (St Margaret's) (H37)

Uxbridge

Good Yarn

132 High Street, UB8 1JX
9am-midnight (12.30am Fri & Sat) (01895) 239852
Fuller's London Pride; Greene King Ruddles Best Bitter; Marston's Pedigree; guest beers H
Formally the Pearson menswear shop (originally a tailor's founded in 1837 and supplying Queen Victoria), this Wetherspoon Lloyds No.1 bar has a slim frontage but extends back from the High Street some way, opening out into a larger room decorated with pictures of old Uxbridge. The bar covers a good third of the length of the pub. Guest beers from Rebellion and White Park feature alongside Westons Marcle Hill cider.

Load of Hay

33 Villier Street, UB8 2PU
11-11.45pm (01895) 234676
Sharp's Doom Bar; guest beers H
Originally the officers' mess of the Elthorne Light Militia, this became a pub in the 1870s. A genuine free house, it usually sells three guest beers, mostly from small and micro-breweries. The pub hosts darts matches, there is an open crib competition on Thursday and a quiz on Tuesday. Live music on Saturday includes folk and traditional and modern jazz. There are always at least two, and usually three, real ciders on the bar. Car parking is limited. (U3) P

Queens Head

54 Windsor Street, UB8 1AB
11-11 (10.30 Sun) (01895) 258750
Wadworth 6X; Young's Bitter; guest beers H
Grade II-listed pub in the old part of town. Rebuilt after an arson attack in 1986, it retains the feeling of an old English pub with its low ceilings and exposed brick. The bar is an irregular L-shape in the main part of the building and there is a small area to the rear that was formerly the no-smoking section and is a little quieter. It was named after Anne Boleyn, whose head appears outside.

Whitton

Admiral Nelson

123 Nelson Road, TW2 7BB
11-11 (midnight Fri & Sat); 11-10.30 Sun
(020) 8894 9998
Fuller's Chiswick Bitter, Discovery, London Pride, ESB, seasonal beers H
A former beer house, fully licensed in 1861 and rebuilt in the 1930s, this large landmark pub has a small patio area on the side and stands in a prominent position on the crossroads at the end of the High Street. Completely refurbished in 2008, it has both a Nelsonian and a rugby theme, being only 15 minutes from Twickenham Stadium and Twickenham Stoop, and is a haven for rugby fans on match days. Large TVs provide sports coverage.
(281,481,H22)

GREATER MANCHESTER

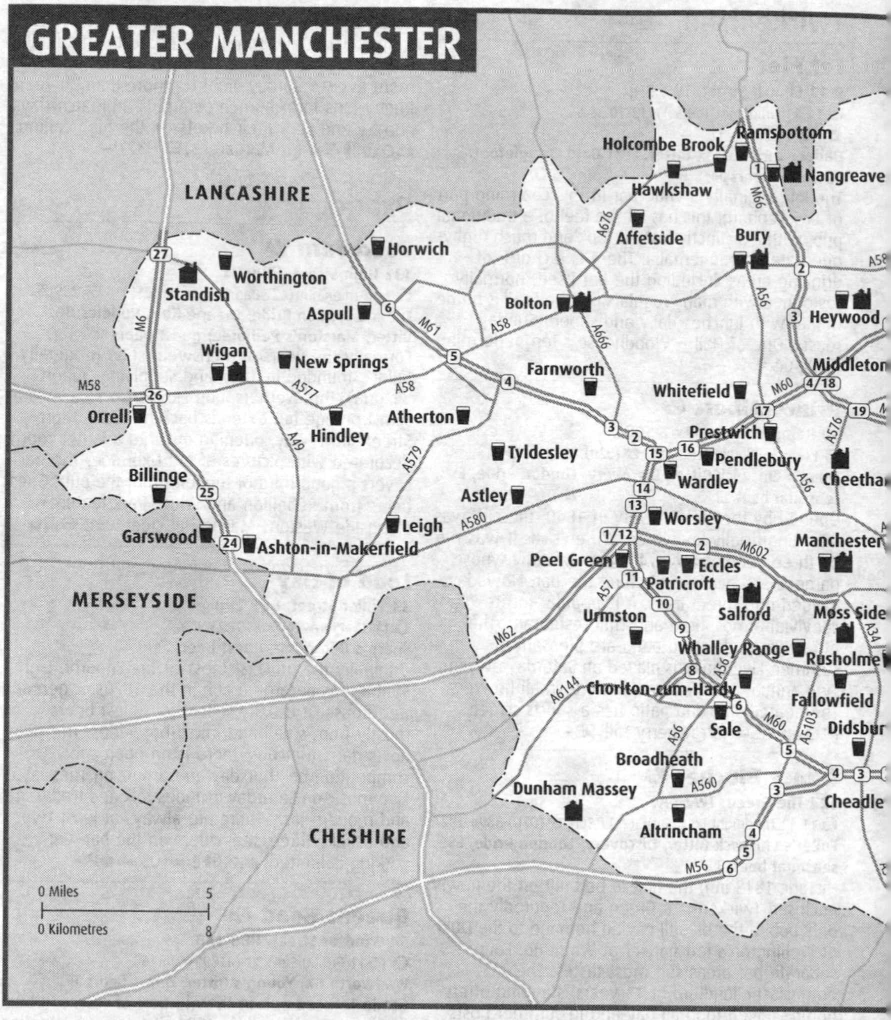

Affetside

Pack Horse ✓

52 Watling Street, BL8 3QW (approx 2 miles NW of Walshaw) SD755136

12-11 (1am Fri & Sat) ☎ (01204) 883802

packhorseaffetside.co.uk

Hydes Original Bitter, seasonal beers; guest beers Ⓗ

This country pub benefits from superb panoramic views thanks to its situation high up on a Roman road. The bar areas and cosy lounge with real fire are part of the original pub, dating from the 15th century. It has a function room and pool room, while the Hightop bar is used as a family room. Many a tale is told about the ghost of a local man whose skull is on view behind the bar. Good quality food is served all day. ⌂Q❀◗♿▲P⁵–

Altrincham

Old Market Tavern

Old Market Place, WA14 4DN (on A56) SJ 767880

12-11 (midnight Wed-Sat) ☎ (0161) 927 7062

oldmarkettavernaltrincham.co.uk

Caledonian Deuchars IPA; Phoenix Arizona; George Wright Drunken Duck, Northern Lights; guest beers Ⓗ

A welcoming pub where a wide range of events takes place – quiz night with free buffet on Wednesday, acoustic jam on Thursday, electric rock & blues Saturday and Sunday and live blues every second Friday. As well as the regular beers there are seven guests mainly sourced from micros, plus a draught cider. Good value meals are available until 6pm and children are welcome. The pub is dog-friendly and provides free Wi-Fi access. ⌂❀◗⇌⊖♣⁵–

Ashton-in-Makerfield

Sir Thomas Gerard ✓

2 Gerard Street, WN4 9AN (on A58)

9am-midnight (1am Fri & Sat) ☎ (01942) 713519

Greene King Ruddles County, Abbot; guest beers Ⓗ

Known locally as the Tom & Jerry, this Wetherspoon pub was once a supermarket. Interesting features include a tiled mural depicting aspects of Ashton-in-Makerfield's history. There are two raised areas away from the busy main floor and small booths to the rear which are good for a cosy drink. The pub

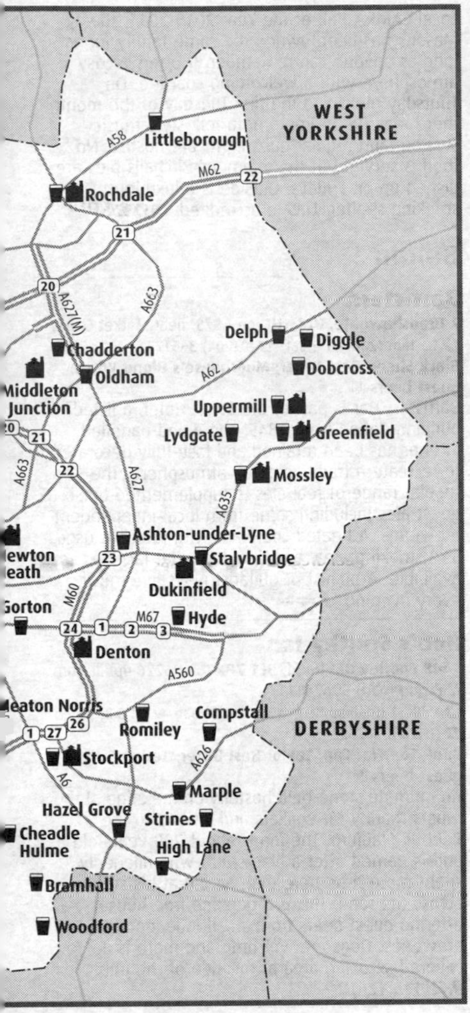

gets busy at weekends and on race days as it is within walking distance of Haydock Park racecourse. CAMRA LocAle accredited and winner of Winter Pub of the Season 2010.
❀◑♿🚌(320,600,601)P⚍

Ashton-under-Lyne

Dog & Pheasant

528 Oldham Road, OL7 9PQ
⌚ 12-11 (11.30 Fri & Sat); 12-10.30 Sun ☎ (0161) 330 4894
Banks's Mild; Marston's Burton Bitter, Pedigree; guest beers Ⓗ
This popular, friendly local near the Medlock Valley Country Park has been a regular Guide entry over the years and is nicknamed the Top Dog. It has a large bar serving three areas, plus another room at the front. The menu of good value food includes vegetarian options. On Tuesday and Thursday evenings a quiz is hosted. Up to three guest beers from the Marston's portfolio are available at all times. Home to a local hiking group known as the Bog Trotters. ♨❀◑🚌(409,419)P⚍

Junction Inn

Mossley Road, Hazelhurst, OL6 9BX (on A670 two miles north of town)
⌚ 12-3 (not Mon), 5-midnight; 12-midnight Sat & Sun
☎ (0161) 343 1611
Robinson's Hatters, Unicorn, seasonal beers Ⓗ
This small pub of great character remains little changed since the 19th century. Built of local stone, it is situated close to Ashton golf course and open country. The cosy, welcoming front rooms serve as a lounge; the recently-converted tap room is now a small restaurant. The famous home-made rag puddings, a Lancashire speciality, are available at lunchtimes alongside other pub food, served Tuesday to Friday. Traditional Sunday lunch is also popular. Q❀◑🚌(350)♣

Aspull

Gerrard Arms Hotel

615 Bolton Road, WN2 1PZ (on B5239)
⌚ 11.30 (4 Mon & Tue)-midnight ☎ (01942) 832346
Tetley Mild, Bitter; guest beers Ⓗ
One-room open-plan cosy pub with a light and airy interior, comfortable seating and a good atmosphere. Original Boddington and Smoke Room windows feature. There are six handpumps with Tetley Bitter and Mild as the regulars plus guests. Two TV screens show sport. Located on the edge of Borsdane Wood, a local nature reserve, it makes an ideal refreshment stop. Food is served lunchtimes and evenings, all day at the weekend, until 8pm.
❀◑P

Victoria

50 Haigh Road, WN2 1YA (on B5239)
⌚ 1-midnight ☎ (01942) 830869
Beer range varies Ⓗ
This traditional two-room local is Allgates Brewery's first pub. The smart yet intimate lounge displays photographs depicting the history of Aspull and Haigh. Two large-screen TVs cater for sports fans, although the one in the lounge is usually switched off. The pub is well located for Haigh Hall Country Park and is halfway between Bolton Wanderers and Wigan Athletic football grounds.

INDEPENDENT BREWERIES

AllGates Wigan
Bank Top Bolton
Bazens' Salford
Boggart Hole Clough Manchester: Newton Heath
Brewhouse Bolton (NEW)
Brightside Bury (NEW)
Dunham Massey Dunham Massey
Green Mill Rochdale
Greenfield Greenfield
Holt Cheetham
Hornbeam Denton
Hydes Moss Side
Lees Middleton Junction
Leyden Nangreaves
Marble Manchester
Millstone Mossley
Outstanding Bury
Phoenix Heywood
Pictish Rochdale
Prospect Standish
Robinson's Stockport
Saddleworth Uppermill
Shaws Dukinfield

Guest beers come from Allgates and other micro-breweries. There is a covered smoking area. LocAle accredited. ⊟🚌(575,715)♣P⁄–

Astley

Cart & Horses

221 Manchester Road, M29 7SD

⏲ 12-11 (1am Fri & Sat); 12-10.30 Sun ☎ (01942) 870751

Holt Mild, Bitter 🄷

Popular, friendly local with an open-plan lounge that was formerly two rooms and still retains a divided feel. There is also a busy tap room to the side of the bar, and a raised lounge area that leads to the walled garden and rear car park. The pub's frontage is worthy of a picture, with etched windows either side of the front door and a Holt's roof sign. Regular quiz nights are hosted. ❀◐⊟♣P⁄–

Ross's Arms

130 Higher Green Lane, Higher Green, M29 7JB

⏲ 12-11 (midnight Fri & Sat); 12-10.30 Sun

☎ (01942) 874405 🌐 rossarms.co.uk

Beer range varies 🄷

The Ross's is a family-run pub and restaurant in the village of Higher Green, situated next to the Astley Colliery Mining Museum and the Leigh Branch of the Bridgewater Canal at Bridge 58. Inside, the large open-plan pub offers various seating areas from a coffee lounge-style space to the standard table and chairs for dining, plus a big screen for popular sports events, regular food theme nights and occasional barbecues. At the rear of the pub is a garden with children's play park. ❀◐♿🚌P⁄–

Atherton

Old Isaacs

48 Market Street, M46 0DG

⏲ 12-11 (midnight Fri & Sat) ☎ (01942) 882885

Phoenix seasonal beers 🄷

Large, popular town-centre pub with two rooms at the front for dining or chatting. The main lounge has several comfortable seating areas. Very handy during the day for a rest from shopping for a drink and a snack, this is also a popular meeting place for various societies. Live music plays. More pumps on the bar are promised. Q◐

Pendle Witch 🍷 ✔

2-4 Warburton Place, M46 0EQ

⏲ 11 (12 Sun)-midnight ☎ (01942) 884537

Moorhouse's seasonal beers; guest beers 🄷

The Pendle is to be found hidden down Warburton Place (access from Market Street). The entrance, now part of a large conservatory, leads to an open-plan bar that serves the full range of Moorhouse's beers plus an occasional guest. The games room has a pool table and large-screen TV. Regular rock nights plus occasional beer festivals are held and there is a well-kept garden for summer. Current CAMRA Branch Pub of the Year. ❀◐♿♣⁄–

Billinge

Masons

99 Carr Mill Road, WN5 7TY (off A571)

⏲ 2-late; 12-late Sun ☎ (01744) 603572

🌐 masonsarmsbillinge.co.uk

Beer range varies 🄷

Local CAMRA Pub of the Year 2010-2011, the Masons has been owned the same family for as long as anyone can remember. It offers a cosy atmosphere with a welcoming coal fire. On Thursday night and the first Tuesday of the month there may be an impromptu folk-style music session, and regular quiz nights are hosted. No food is served but the infamous Birchalls pies are dished up on Fridays. Outside is a luxurious smoking shelter. LocAle accredited. ♨Q❀♿P⁄–

Bolton

Barristers

7 Bradshawgate, BL1 1HJ (on A575, near Market Cross)

⏲ 12-1am (2am Fri & Sat) ☎ (01204) 365174

Black Sheep Best Bitter; Moorhouse's Blond Witch; guest beers 🄷

Barristers Bar is part of the Swan Hotel, a listed building dating from 1845. The wood-panelled interior has been retained and tastefully decorated to recreate a traditional pub atmosphere. The regular range of real ales is supplemented by six guest ales including some from local independent breweries. A heated courtyard with tables is used as a smoking area, and disabled toilet facilities are available. A pianist or guitarist plays live music every evening. ❀⇌⁄–

Bob's Smithy Inn

1448 Chorley Old Road, BL1 7PX (on B6226 uphill from A58 ring road) SD674111

⏲ 4.30-11 (midnight Fri); 12-midnight Sat; 12-11 Sun

☎ (01204) 842622

Bank Top Flat Cap; Taylor Best Bitter; Tetley Bitter; guest beers 🄷

An intimate stone-built hostelry on the edge of the moors, handy for walkers and visitors to the Reebok Stadium. The inn is about 200 years old and is named after a blacksmith who allegedly spent more time here than he did at his smithy across the road. This is a genuine free house, offering guest beers from small independent breweries. Dogs are welcome and there is a covered smoking area at the side of the pub. ❀🚌(125,126)P⁄–

Flag Inn ✔

50 Hardmans Lane, Bromley Cross, BL7 9HL (off B6472 Darwen Road) SD717138

⏲ 12-11 (midnight Fri & Sat) ☎ (01204) 598267

Bank Top Flat Cap; Greene King IPA, Ruddles County, Old Speckled Hen; Moorhouse's Blond Witch; guest beers 🄷

Close to the Last Drop village, walkers are attracted to this pub in Bromley Cross for its proximity to good countryside. Ten handpumps include rotating Bank Top beers. The Saturday beer club must include a pint of traditional cider. Note the unusual viewing cellar. Locally-produced food, cooked on site, complements the already comprehensive menu. Live TV sport is shown on multi-screens. Sporadic and spontaneous piano sessions feature and a quiz is held on Sunday. People visit this pub from far and wide. ♨❀◐🚌(225,563)♣🍎⁄–

Hen & Chickens ✔

143 Deansgate, BL1 1EX (on B6204 opp post office)

⏲ 11.30 (7 Sun)-11 (later on request) ☎ (01204) 389836

Tetley Dark Mild, Bitter; guest beers 🄷

Cask beers are promoted enthusiastically – in addition to the Tetley ales, several regularly-changing guest beers are supplied from the Punch

Taverns portfolio. The pub is renowned for its excellent home-cooked lunchtime food and friendly atmosphere. Popular quiz nights are held during the week and there is a covered outdoor smoking area. The pub is available for private hire during the day on Sunday. There are steps at the door but staff are happy to assist. ◑⇌🚌⚐

House Without A Name ✔

75-77 Lea Gate, Harwood, BL2 3ET (on B6196, near A676 jct) SD737121
✪ 2-11.30 (midnight Fri); 12-midnight Sat; 12-11.30 Sun
☎ (01204) 306091
Holt Bitter; guest beers Ⓗ
Traditional village pub in Harwood dating from 1810 with a two-room layout. Memorabilia from the local Trafalgar Day group are on display and there are poignant pictures of the local area throughout. The pub is free of tie and supplements its regular Holt beer with an ever-changing selection of ales. The terrace is a sun trap in the early evening, with a covered area for smokers provided. Live entertainment is held every Sunday and a quiz on a Monday evening. ❀⊟🚌(507)♣⚐

Howcroft Inn

36 Pool Street, BL1 2JU
✪ 12-11 (midnight Fri & Sat) ☎ (01204) 366042
Greene King Old Speckled Hen; Taylor Landlord; guest beers Ⓗ
Traditional four-roomed pub, where a warm and friendly welcome is guaranteed. The atmosphere here is relaxed, with open fires in the winter months, a pub games room with TV and a function room where families are welcome. There is also an intimate snug and conservatory, overlooking the bowling green, leading to a large patio, incorporating a covered and heated smoking area. Guest ales invariably include one Bank Top brew. ♨♘❀◑🚌(501)♣P⚐

Kings Head 🏆

52 Junction Road, Deane, BL3 4NA (just off A676)
✪ 3.30 (12 Sat & Sun)-11 ☎ (01204) 62609
Bank Top Flat Cap; Wells Bombardier Ⓗ
Set back off the road in a lovely setting and close to Deane Parish Church, the oldest church in Bolton. The inn is a stone-built Grade II-listed building dating from the 17th century – it was named the Kings Head in 1824 and was primarily used as a travellers' overnight stop. It has three rooms, two with low timber-framed ceilings, the other with a cast-iron range. At the rear is a bowling green, children's play area and outdoor seating. Q❀🚌(540,715)P⚐

Masons Arms

156-158 Blackburn Road, Egerton, BL7 9SB (on A666) SD711144
✪ 4 (3 Fri)-11 (midnight Thu & Fri); 12-midnight Sat; 12-11 Sun ☎ (01204) 303517
Theakston Best Bitter; guest beers Ⓗ
This inviting pub with its brick and stone facade is situated in Egerton about three miles from Bolton and dates from the late Victorian era. Good-value beers including two constantly-changing guests are dispensed from four handpumps on an imposing bar. The hostelry is always packed for the Tuesday night quiz and live folk music on Wednesday evening. This is the place for those looking for a genuine friendly local. ❀🚌♣⚐

Spinning Mule ✔

Unit 2, Nelson Square, BL1 1JT
✪ 9-midnight (1am Fri & Sat) ☎ (01204) 533339
Green King Ruddles Best Bitter, Abbot; guest beers Ⓗ
Newly built in 1998, this town-centre pub, just off Bradshawgate, is an open-plan split-level building with a comfortable dining area in a modern Wetherspoon style. It is named after Samuel Crompton's Mule, a revolutionary invention in cotton spinning that made Bolton famous throughout the world. The original device may be seen in the town's museum and Crompton himself is immortalised by the statue in the square. The Mule supports Moorhouse's and other local breweries. Q◑◐♿⇌

Sweet Green Tavern

127 Crook Street, BL3 6DD (opp Sainsbury's, off A579)
✪ 11-11; 12-10.30 Sun ☎ (01204) 392258
Holt Bitter; Moorhouse's Pride of Pendle; guest beers Ⓗ
This busy, warm and friendly town-centre pub comprises four small rooms, served by a central bar. A genuine free house, the landlord offers up to 11 cask beers sourced from independent breweries. Used by many local clubs, groups and teams as a meeting place, there are traditional pub games as well as free use of a Nintendo Wii console. The beer garden incorporates a covered and heated smoking area. Free car parking (on street) after 6pm. ♨Q♘❀⇆♿⇌🚌♣P⚐

Volunteer

276 Radcliffe Road, Darcy Lever, BL3 1RS (1 mile from Bolton centre on B6209)
✪ 1-11; 12-midnight Sat & Sun ☎ (01204) 524271
Holt Bitter Ⓗ
Situated in Darcy Lever, a once-thriving village close to Leverhulme Park still with its own cricket ground. Originally a Victorian beer house, part of the old red sandstone frontage remains alongside a brick built extension. Inside this very popular local is one large room divided by a central bar, and there are areas for darts and pool games – the pub supports one pool and four darts teams. A quiz is held on Tuesday evening. ❀🚌(536)♣P⚐

Bramhall

Ladybrook Hotel ✔

Fir Road, SK7 2NP
✪ 11.30-11 (11.30 Fri & Sat) ☎ (0161) 440 0176
Boddingtons Bitter; Wells Bombardier; guest beers Ⓗ
Dating from the 1930s, this large, striking mock-Tudor house has a most welcoming interior, where wood dominates with panels, balustrades, columns and exposed beams. The large space is open plan but tastefully divided into separate drinking areas, all with plush upholstered seating. Beyond the bar in the back room is a large vault. Function room/conference facilities are available upstairs. Ideally situated for a visit to nearby historic Bramall Hall and its park. Food is served 12-9pm daily. ❀◑◐⊟♿🚌(378)♣P⚐

Broadheath

Railway ★

153 Manchester Road, WA14 5NT (on A56 adjacent to business park) SJ766892
✪ 11-11 (midnight Fri & Sat); 3-7 Sun ☎ (0161) 941 3383
Holt Mild, Bitter Ⓗ

This Victorian Grade II-listed pub features in CAMRA's National Inventory of Historic Pub Interiors. Once part of a row of cottages, it now stands alone on the edge of a business park. Inside, there are a tap room and bar parlour either side of a lobby that leads to the bar. To the right of the bar are two more rooms used for dining and games. The outside drinking area has an old-fashioned lamp-post and telephone kiosk. The car park does not belong to the pub and closes at 9pm.
♔Q☺❀⇄◐⊟⇌(Navigation Rd)⊖(Navigation Rd)⊟♣⁄–

Bury

Automatic

Derby Hall, Market Street, BL9 0BW (500m N from Interchange)
✪ 10am-midnight; 12-11 Sun ☎ (0161) 763 9399
🌐 themet.biz/automatic/
Outstanding Northern Light; guest beers Ⓗ
This welcoming independent café and restaurant shares the Derby Hall with the Bury Met theatres. It has extended into what was the tourist information office, creating the Malt Bar which, with the use of glass, gives a complete view of the beer cellar and its small electric hoist system. Serving excellent food, the bar does get busy at times and priority may be given to diners at lunchtime. Relaxed, safe and comfortable, this a popular choice for women and the discerning. Chess, dominoes and backgammon are played.
◐◑♿⇌(Bolton St ELR)⊖⊟♣⊓

Lamb Inn

533 Tottington Road, BL8 1UB (on B6123)
✪ 4.30-11 (midnight Fri); 1-midnight Sat; 1-10.30 Sun
☎ (0161) 764 2714
Beer range varies Ⓗ
Built in 1831, the Lamb is a very popular family-run pub. A stone fireplace with open fire and seating with plenty of scatter cushions help to create a traditional and comfortable ambience. The landlord is enthusiastic about his real ale and regularly features beers from George Wright, Phoenix, Salamander and Outstanding. A varied range of home-prepared pub fare is served early evenings and also at lunchtime at the weekend. The enclosed beer garden gets busy during the summer months. ♔❀◐◑⊟(468,469)P⁄–

Robert Peel ✔

5-10 Market Street, BL9 0BL (near the Robert Peel monument)
✪ 9-midnight (1am Fri & Sat) ☎ (0161) 764 7287
Greene King Abbot; Marston's Pedigree; guest beers Ⓗ
A larger Wetherspoon's pub opposite the parish church. Named after the former prime minister and founder of the police force who was born in Bury, it also has memorabilia of other well-known former Bury residents. Food is served daily 9am-10pm. Guest beers are usually sourced from local micros.
◐◑⇌(Bolton St)⊖

Trackside

East Lancashire Railway, Bolton Street Station, BL9 0EY (on East Lancashire Railway Platform 2)
✪ 12-11; 10-midnight Sat; 10-11 Sun ☎ (0161) 764 6461
Outstanding Piston Broke; guest beers Ⓗ
The Trackside is a small buffet bar boasting eight ever-changing real ales from all over the country. It also stocks a selection of continental beers from around Europe, cask cider and a fine choice of malt whiskies. The array of pump clips on the ceiling is a testament to the amount of different ales served in the past. The building is railway-themed with a café look to it. No food is available Monday or Tuesday.
❀◐⇌(Bolton St, East Lancs Railway)⊖⊟●P

Chadderton

Rifle Range Inn

372 Burnley Lane, OL1 2QP (200m from A663/A627M junction)
✪ 2 (12 Sat & Sun)-11 ☎ (0161) 678 6417
Lees Brewer's Dark, Bitter, seasonal beers Ⓗ
Originally a farmstead, first licensed around 1860, with a family-friendly atmosphere in its open-plan lounge and separate vault. Sports fans visiting nearby Boundary Park are welcome at all times (pie and peas available on match days), and sport is screened on TV. The pub runs football, darts and pool teams, plus a quiz night. It also hosts live entertainment on Saturday evening and barbecues on the heated patio in summer – a pub that caters for all the community. ❀⊟⊟(24,181)♣P⁄–

Rose of Lancaster ✔

7 Haigh Lane, OL1 2TQ (jct of A69 and B6195 by Rochdale Canal)
✪ 11.30-11 (midnight Fri & Sat); 12-11 Sun
☎ (0161) 624 3031
Lees Brewer's Dark, Bitter, seasonal beers Ⓗ
The Rose is one of Lees' busiest pubs with a high ale turnover. Situated by the Rochdale Canal and overlooking countryside, it is a popular watering hole and diner for walkers, canal boat enthusiasts and locals alike. The covered patio is busy during the summer months, and an open fire adds warmth in winter. A thriving vault, friendly management and an eclectic clientele always ensure a convivial visit to the Rose. Buses, trains and boats stop nearby.
♔❀◐◑⊟♿⇌(Mills Hill)⊟(59,64)♣P⁄–

Cheadle

Red Lion

83 Stockport Road, SK8 2AJ (on A560, jct Jackson St)
✪ 12-11 (10.30 Sun) ☎ (0161) 428 5507
Robinson's Hatters, Unicorn, Old Tom, seasonal beers Ⓗ
A large, solid-looking, half-rendered building on the fringe of the village. A mixed clientele of varying ages enjoys the well-appointed surroundings – plenty of dark wood, traditional fittings, fireplaces, toby jugs, old bottles, and snug corners to nestle in. Low ceilings add to the feeling of homeliness. Welcoming home-cooked food from a varied menu, including a salad bar, is served 12-8.30pm most days, with a carvery on Sunday. Much used by the community, weekly quiz and curry nights are always popular. Outside, there is a heated drinking and dining area.
♔Q☺❀◐◑♿⊟(310,371)♣P⁄–

Cheadle Hulme

Church

90 Ravenoak Road, SK8 7EG (jct A5149/B5095)
✪ 11-11 (midnight Thu-Sat); 12-11 Sun ☎ (0161) 485 1897
Robinson's Hatters, Unicorn, seasonal beers Ⓗ

ENGLAND

Once known as the Knapsack Inn, this friendly, family-run pub is the oldest in Cheadle Hulme – it has been in the hands of the Bromley family for 35 years. Its cottage-like appearance reflects a cosy interior with low ceilings, wood-panelling and brass plates. The busy restaurant serves excellent, freshly-prepared food lunchtimes and evenings (booking recommended). Darts is played in the snug, while the lounge boasts a real fire and quiet conversation. ♨Q❀◐◗⊟🚌(313,X57)♣P⁴—

Kings Hall ✔

11-13 Station Road, SK8 5AF (on A5149 near station)
⏲ 9-midnight (1am Fri & Sat) ☎ (0161) 482 0460
Greene King Ruddles Best Bitter, Abbot; guest beers Ⓗ
One of the earliest Wetherspoon pubs in Greater Manchester, opening in 1998. The pub was originally a dance hall and served latterly as a Chinese restaurant. It was extensively rebuilt a few years ago following a major fire, adding a large rear conservatory area that is popular with diners. A comfortable, modern pub, up to four guest ales are usually available including some from local micros. Value food is served daily until 11pm. Q❀◐◗♿⇌🚌(313,X57)P⁴—

Chorlton-cum-Hardy

Bar

531-533 Wilbraham Road, M21 0UE SJ 819939
⏲ 12-11.30 (midnight Thu; 12.30am Fri & Sat)
☎ (0161) 861 7576
Marble Manchester Bitter, Ginger Marble; guest beers Ⓗ
One of the first café bars to open in Chorlton in the early '90s, this is one of more than 20 real ale outlets on the Chorlton Challenge – the CAMRA branch's annual Chorlton survey. Three guest beers come from micro-breweries, not always local, and there is a range of continental beers both bottled and draught. Locally-sourced food is available daily until 8pm, with vegan and vegetarian options. A quiz night is held on Monday and children are welcome until 8pm. ❀◐◗🚌⁴—

Dulcimer

567 Wilbraham Road, M21 0AE SJ 817939
⏲ 4 (12 Sat)-12.30am (1.30am Fri & Sat); 12-12.30am Sun
☎ (0161) 860 0044 🌐 dulcimer.chorlton.co.uk
Beer range varies Ⓗ
This pub offers a good range of beer, with four ever-changing ales on handpump and a good selection of foreign bottles. There is a large music room upstairs that is used as a folk music venue and also to host regular beer and cider festivals. The pub attracts a varied age range and has very good home-made food, especially the cheese and paté selection. ❀◐◗♿⊖🚌●⁴—

Electrik

559 Wilbraham Road, M21 0AE SJ 817939
⏲ 3-midnight; 12-1am Fri & Sat; 12-midnight Sun
☎ (0161) 8813315
Thwaites Wainwright; guest beers Ⓗ
This new bar has a friendly, bohemian feel to it, from its home-made cakes to an excellent jukebox. It offers a very varied home-made food menu, served every day. On the beer front it concentrates on local breweries, with two ever-changing guests, and real cider is always available. Tuesday evening is quiz night and there is free Wi-Fi access. ❀◐◗♿🚌♣●⁴—

Marble Beer House

57 Manchester Road, M21 9PW (50m N of Chorlton Library) SJ816943
⏲ 12-11 (midnight Thu-Sat); 12-11.30 Sun
☎ (0161) 881 9206
Marble Pint, Manchester, JP Best, Ginger Marble, seasonal ales; guest beers Ⓗ
Marble Beer House has featured in this Guide since it first opened. Serving a selection of beers from the Soil Association registered Marble Brewery, the micro-brewery attached to the Marble Arch Inn, it also stocks a number of guest ales from local breweries plus a good choice of bottled beers from Marble and others. A welcoming atmosphere and interested staff create a relaxed place to meet mates or read the many books, with your dog by your side. Q❀🚌(47,84,86)♣●⁴—

Pi

99 Manchester Road, M21 9GA SJ816944
⏲ 11-11 (midnight Wed & Thu; 12.30am Fri); 12-12.30am Sat; 12-11 Sun ☎ (0161) 882 0000 🌐 pi-chorlton.co.uk
Bank Top Flat Cap; guest beers Ⓗ
Pi is a relaxed bar with a great mix of traditional and modern, but what makes it really stand out is the massive range of local and continental beers. Four real ales on handpump vary but are all sourced from local breweries, and there are over 80 bottles to choose from, most of which are excellent. Aiming to please everyone, there is even a hand-pulled cider. The various gourmet pies that complement the name come with mash, mushy peas and onion gravy. Q❀◐◗🚌(47,84,86)●⁴—

Compstall

Andrew Arms

George Street, SK6 5JD
⏲ 12-midnight ☎ (0161) 484 5392
Robinson's Hatters, Cumbria Way, Unicorn Ⓗ
Traditional detached stone-built pub in a quiet former mill village, constructed in the 1820s by George Andrew for his workers. It lies close to Etherow Country Park, with its wildlife and river valley walks. The pub features a comfortable lounge, a small, traditional games room and a separate dining room. A community local, popular with all ages, it is the centre for many social activities. The kitchen serves good, traditional food and holds themed nights such as Tuesday's Chippy night. ♨Q❀◐◗⊟🚌(383,384)♣P

Delph

Royal Oak (Th' Heights)

Broad Lane, Heights, OL3 5TX (via Tame Lane, off main Delph-Denshaw Road) SD982090
⏲ closed Mon; 7 (5 Thu & Fri)-11; 12-midnight Sun
☎ (01457) 874460
Black Sheep Best Bitter; guest beers Ⓗ
Isolated, 250-year-old stone-built pub on a packhorse route overlooking the Tame Valley. In a popular walking area, it benefits from outstanding views. The pub comprises a cosy bar and three rooms, each with an open fire. The refurbished side room boasts a hand-carved stone fireplace, while the comfortable snug has exposed beams and old photos of the inn. On Friday and Saturday evenings good home-cooked food is available. ♨Q❀◗P⊡

Didsbury

Fletcher Moss ✔

1 William Street, M20 6RQ (off Wilmslow Rd, A5145 via Albert Hill St)
⌚ 12-11 (midnight Fri & Sat); 12-10.30 Sun
☎ (0161) 438 0073
Hydes Mild, Original Bitter, Jekyll's Gold, seasonal ales; guest beers Ⓗ
Named in memory of Alderman Fletcher Moss who donated the nearby botanical gardens to the city. A thriving community local, down a side street near the village centre, it attracts people of all ages. Extended in the 1990s with a large conservatory at the rear, it retains a traditional feel in the front rooms, with separate areas and niches, and old photos of local places. A quiz or live acoustic music take place every Monday. There is always at least one guest beer available. **Q❀♿🚌(42,142)P⚡**

Royal Oak

729 Wilmslow Road, M20 6WF (on A5145, jct Albert Hill St)
⌚ 12-11 (10.30 Sun) ☎ (0161) 434 4788
Jennings Dark Mild; Marston's Burton Bitter, Pedigree, seasonal beers Ⓗ
Four-square Victorian house set on Didsbury's cosmopolitan main thoroughfare. The interior is somewhat open, but is essentially three areas around a central bar. The bar canopy boasts a collection of interesting spirit casks. Assured and welcoming service is the order of the day. Seldom quiet and often lively, it can become boisterous even, especially during televised football. If food is your thing, take comfort in the mammoth cheese lunches (served Mon-Fri). **❀◖🚌(42,142)⚡**

Diggle

Diggle Hotel

Station Houses, OL3 5JZ (½ mile off A670) SE007081
⌚ 12-3, 5-midnight (1am Fri); 12-1am Sat; 12-midnight Sun
☎ (01457) 872741 🌐 saddleworthlife.com/digglehotel
Black Sheep Best Bitter; Copper Dragon Golden Pippin; Taylor Landlord; Three B's Stoker's Slake; guest beers Ⓗ
Stone pub in a pleasant hamlet near the Standedge Canal Tunnel under the Pennines. Built as a merchant's house in 1789, it became an ale house and general store on the construction of the nearby railway tunnel in 1834. Affording fine views of the Saddleworth countryside, this makes a convenient base in a popular walking area. With a bar area and two rooms, the accent is on home-cooked food (served lunchtimes and evenings, all day Sat and Sun). Brass bands play on alternate summer Sundays. **Q❀🛏◖◗🚌(184)P**

Dobcross

Navigation Inn

21-23 Wool Road, OL3 5NS (on A670)
⌚ 12-2.30, 5-11 (midnight Fri); 12-11 Sat; 12-10.30 Sun
☎ (01457) 872418
Moorhouse's Pendle Witches Brew; Wells Bombardier; guest beers Ⓗ
Next to the Huddersfield Narrow Canal, this stone pub was built in 1806 to slake the thirst of navvies cutting the Standedge Tunnel. It comprises an open-plan bar and L-shaped interior. Live brass band concerts are staged on alternate Sundays in summer. The pub is the venue for the annual Beer Walk in spring and Rushcart Festival in August. Guest beers usually include an ale from Greenfield and a mild. Home-cooked food including weekday special offer meals are popular.
Q❀◖◗🚌(184,350)P⚡

Swan Inn (Top House)

The Square, OL3 5AA
⌚ 12-3, 5-11; 12-11.30 Sat; 12-10.30 Sun ☎ (04157) 873451
Brakspear Oxford Gold; Jennings Cumberland Ale, Cockerhoop; Marston's Pedigree; guest beers Ⓗ
Built in 1765 for the Wrigley family of chewing gum fame, part of the building was later used as a police court and cells. Overlooking the attractive village square, the pub has been well renovated, with flagged floor and three rooms, plus a fine function room that caters for 60 people. It gets very busy during the Whit Friday Brass Band Contest and the August Rushcart Festival. Home-cooked food features dishes from around the world (no food Sun eve). **⛫Q❀◖◗🚌(184,353)**

Eccles

Eccles Cross ✔

13 Regent Street, M30 0BP (opp tram terminus)
⌚ 9-midnight (1am Fri & Sat) ☎ (0161) 788 0414
Greene King IPA, Ruddles Best Bitter, Abbot; guest beers Ⓗ
The New Regent Picture House opened in 1920 and after various changes became this Wetherspoon's in 1999. It has retained the fine stone and brick frontage and inside the ceiling reflects the building's original use. Although open plan it is divided into four levels, creating distinct drinking areas. The three sunken snugs feature local historical information. The historic Eccles Cross, after which the pub is named, is just along the road in the town centre. **ᗢ❀◖◗♿⇌⊖🚌●⚡**

Lamb Hotel ★

33 Regent Street, M30 0BP (opp tram terminus)
⌚ 11.30-11.30 (midnight Sat); 12-11.30 Sun
☎ (07827) 850252
Holt Mild, Bitter, seasonal beers Ⓗ
Grade II-listed, red-brick and terracotta building dated 1906 —the interior comprises a vault, parlour, bar and lobby with adjoining lounge, plus a billiard room complete with full-size table in near-original condition. Period features include elaborate mahogany woodwork, glazed wall tiles, curved glazed hatches around the bar and mosaic flooring. A seasonal ale from the Holt's portfolio has now been added to the range and all are reasonably priced. **Q⊟⇌⊖🚌♣P⚡**

Royal Oak ★

34 Barton Lane, M30 0EN
⌚ 9.30am-11 (12.30am Sat) ☎ (07971) 835 029
Holt Mild, Bitter Ⓗ
This fine red-brick Edwardian pub was built in 1904. The mahogany central bar serves a large vault and a bar lobby, both very popular. The lobby leads to a pool room and a snug. There is a large back room where families are welcome and regular events are held. Darts is played in the vault on a traditional Manchester log end board. Hot pies and B&B are available at this well-run friendly pub.
⛫Qᗢ❀🛏⊟⇌⊖🚌♣⚡

ENGLAND

Fallowfield

Friendship ✔
353 Wilmslow Road, M14 6XS (B5093, jct Egerton Rd)
❂ 12-11 (midnight Fri & Sat) ☎ (0161) 224 5758
Hydes 1863, Original Bitter, Jekyll's Gold, seasonal beers; guest beers 🄷
Impressive, high-set Victorian mansion in the midst of this busy student area. That said, this is not purely the domain of the young, as it attracts a good mix of folk. A large horseshoe bar serves a variety of areas – some quiet, some raised. The rear extension completed a few of years ago has created the space for provision of interesting and popular Oriental food, including takeaways. TV screens abound, so it can get very busy on football days. ❀◑♿🚌(42,43)P⊱

Farnworth

Britannia
34 King Street, BL4 7AF (opp bus station, off A6053)
❂ 11-11 (midnight Fri & Sat); 12-11 Sun ☎ (01204) 571629
Beer range varies 🄷
Thriving local next to the market and bus station with a basic L-shaped vault and a slightly smaller lounge, both served by a central bar. The pub offers inexpensively priced guest beers from Moorhouses and Coach House. The good value home-cooked lunches are popular. Well-attended, mini-outdoor beer festivals are held on both the May bank holidays and in August. Behind the pub is a free car park. Children are welcome until 4.30pm.
❀◐⊟⇌♣⊱

Garswood

Railway Hotel ✔
4 Station Road, WN4 0SA
❂ 2-11 (11.30 Thu); 12-midnight Fri & Sat; 12-11 Sun
☎ (01942) 745187
Beer range varies 🄷
Corner pub opposite Garswood station with a large lounge overlooking the beer garden and children's play area, plus a separate TV lounge. The pub features three beers from the Punch range, served from a large bar in the centre of the pub. Outside is a covered, heated smoking terrace and ample car parking. Bar snacks are available every day until 10.30pm. The pub regularly holds charity events and is Wigan CAMRA Community Pub of the Year 2010. ❀◑⇌P⊱

Gorton

Vale Cottage
Kirk Street, M18 8UE (off Hyde Rd A57, east of jct with Chapman St)
❂ 12-3 (4 Sun), 5 (7 Sat & Sun)-11 ☎ (0161) 223 2477
Taylor Landlord; Theakston Black Bull; guest beers 🄷
Well-hidden in the Gore Brook conservation area, Vale Cottage has the feel of a country pub. Parts date from the 17th century, hence the low-beamed ceilings, multiple drinking areas and reputed ghost. A relaxed, friendly atmosphere, where conversation predominates, is disturbed only by the ever-popular, lively quizzes (Tuesday – general knowledge, Thursday – music). Indulge in an excellent home-cooked meal (available lunchtimes and early evening) in the garden to round off a visit. Don't miss this hidden gem.
Q❀◑⇌(Ryder Brow)🚌(201,203)P⊱

Greenfield

King William IV
134 Chew Valley Road, OL3 7DD
❂ 12-midnight ☎ (01457) 873933
Caledonian Deuchars IPA; Lees Bitter; Tetley Bitter; guest beers 🄷
Detached stone pub comprising a central bar area and two rooms, with a benched, cobbled forecourt for outdoor drinking and a backyard for smoking. Two changing guest beers are often local. Food is served Wednesday to Sunday until 7.30pm. The large car park makes this a handy base for local walks. The 'King Bill' is the centre of village life, participating in the annual Beer Walk and August Rushcart Festival, and hosting Greenfield's Whit Friday Brass Band Contest. Children and dogs are welcome. ❀◑⇌🚌(180,350)♣P⊱

Railway
11 Shaw Hall Bank Road, OL3 7JZ (opp station)
❂ 12-midnight (1am Thu-Sat) ☎ (01457) 872307
Caledonian Deuchars IPA; Elland Beyond the Pale; Millstone Tiger Rut; Theakston Old Peculier; Wells Bombardier; guest beer 🄷
Unspoilt pub where the central bar and games area draw a good mix of old and young. The tap room boasts a log fire and old photos of Saddleworth. In a picturesque area, the pub affords beautiful views across Chew Valley. The Railway is a popular venue for all styles of live music on Thursday, Friday (unplugged night – all players welcome) and Sunday. It is also a stop-off on the Transpennine Real Ale Trail that links eight pubs by rail. Westons and Thatchers cider are served on gravity.
♨❀🛏⊟⛺⇌🚌(180,184)♣🍎P

Hawkshaw

Red Lion
81 Ramsbottom Road, BL8 4JS (on A676 Burnley Road)
❂ 11-3, 6-11; 12-11 Sat; 12-10.30 Sun ☎ (01204) 856600
🌐 redlionhawkshaw.com
Lees Brewers Dark, Bitter, Coronation Street, seasonal beers 🄷
Attractive stone-built pub in a picturesque village. Inside is a single, large room that is popular with locals and visitors alike. The menu of freshly prepared dishes has made the inn popular with diners who can opt to eat in the pub or the restaurant. Meals are served all day at the weekend. The landlord is enthusiastic about his real ales and regularly features those from Phoenix, Acorn and Bank Top. Five en-suite bedrooms are available including one with a four poster bed. 🛏◑🚌P⊱

Hazel Grove

Grapes
196 London Road, SK7 4DQ (on A6, jct with Hatherlow Lane)
❂ 11.30-11 (midnight Fri & Sat); 12-10.30 Sun
☎ (0161) 483 4479
Robinson's Hatters, Unicorn 🄷
A very old building retaining its classic town pub layout – the central bar separates the large vault on the left from the three-roomed lounge on the right, which still has some original-looking wooden beams. The back room displays images of old Hazel Grove, and to the rear is a small beer garden. Mild is offered at two different temperatures according to taste. ❀⊟⇌🚌(192,199)♣P⊱

Heaton Norris

Nursery ★ ✔

258 Green Lane, SK4 2NA (off A6, jct with Heaton Road)
⏲ 11.30-11 (11.30 Fri; midnight Sat); 12-11.30 Sun
☎ (0161) 432 2044 🌐 hydesbrewery.co.uk
Hydes Mild, Owd Oak, Original Bitter, Jekyll's Gold, seasonal beers; guest beers Ⓗ
A former CAMRA National Pub of the Year and a Guide regular, the Nursery is a classic, unspoilt 1930s pub with its own bowling green, hidden away in a pleasant suburb. The multi-roomed interior includes a traditional vault with its own entrance and a spacious, wood-panelled lounge, used by diners at lunchtime. The home-cooked food draws customers from miles around (no food Mon, set lunches only Sun) – children are welcome if dining. There are two non-Hydes guest beers, usually one from Allgates. Q❀◐⊟🚌(22,364)♣P⚐

Heywood

Edwin Waugh ✔

10-12 Market Street, OL10 4LY
⏲ 9-1am; 10-midnight Sun ☎ (01706) 621480
Greene King Ruddles Best Bitter, Abbot; guest beers Ⓗ
Spacious single-floor Wetherspoon's with large windows at the front and to one side, and a small patio to the rear. The pub is named after the dialect poet Edwin Waugh, who died in 1890 and was described as the Burns of Lancashire. The pub is comfortably furnished with easy chairs, plus a few booths, and decorated with scenes of local history. The beer cellar is located on the first floor above the bar. Food is served until 10pm. Guest beers often come from local breweries.
Q❀◐◑♿🚌(471)⚐

High Lane

Royal Oak

Buxton Road, SK6 8AY
⏲ 12-3, 5-11; 12-10.30 Sun ☎ (01663) 762380
Marston's Burton Bitter; Jennings Cocker Hoop; guest beers Ⓗ
A well-appointed pub with a pleasing exterior. Although it has an open-plan layout, there are three distinct drinking areas, one used for games. Live entertainment is hosted most Fridays and an innovative food menu is served all sessions. The garden and outdoor play area make this a good summer and family pub. Guest beers are sourced from the Marston's range. Q❀◐◑♿🚌(199,394)P▯

Hindley

Edington Arms

186 Ladies Lane, WN2 2QJ (off A58)
⏲ 12-11.30 (12.30am Fri & Sat) ☎ (01942) 259229
Holt Mild, Bitter, seasonal beers Ⓗ
Also known as the Top Ale House, the Edington is a cosy, welcoming Holt's pub. The single bar is centrally situated in the front lounge. There is also a games room with a pool table that leads to the beer garden and smoking area at the rear. An upstairs function room is available by arrangement. Standing next to the Liverpool-Manchester rail line, it is ideally situated for any 'rail ale crawl' into Wigan or Manchester. LocAle accredited.
❀⇌♣P⚐

Hare & Hounds

31 Ladies Lane, WN2 2QA
⏲ 4 (2 Fri; 12 Sat & Sun)-midnight
Beer range varies Ⓗ
This small but traditional pub is located between Hindley railway station and the town centre. It has a large, cosy lounge and a bar/vault area. The lounge displays pictures of bygone Hindley and has a large-screen TV for sports. This is an All Gates pub serving its own beers plus guests. Darts is popular here and both men's and women's teams play in the local darts league. Quiz night is Thursday evening. LocAle accredited. 🔥⊟⇌

Holcombe Brook

Hare & Hounds ✔

400 Bolton Road West, BL0 9RY (on A676)
⏲ 12-11 (midnight Thu-Sat) ☎ (01706) 822107
🌐 hareandhoundsbury.com
Beer range varies Ⓗ
This large, rural community pub has a bright, friendly atmosphere where young, old and their dogs are all welcome. Ten cask ales on handpump include beers from across the country plus a range of continental lagers on tap. Two beer festivals are held annually in March and September (see website for details). There is space for small functions. The pub runs two pool teams and a quiz team, and offers free Wi-Fi.
🔥❀◐◑⊟♿🚌(472,474)♣P⚐

Horwich

Crown

1 Chorley New Road, BL6 7QJ (jct A673/B6226)
SD634118
⏲ 11-11 (midnight Fri & Sat); 12-11.30 Sun
☎ (01204) 693109
Holt Mild, Bitter, seasonal beers Ⓗ
A grand local landmark, handy for the Reebok Stadium, Rivington Pike and the West Pennine Moors. Lever Park across the road was a gift from Lord Leverhulme, the soap magnate and great benefactor to his home town. Darts and dominoes teams play on Tuesday and Thursday evenings and there is a vault and games room at the rear. Various artists provide entertainment on Sunday evening. Children are welcome at lunchtime when dining. ❀◐⊟♿🚌(125,575)♣P⚐

Original Bay Horse

206 Lee Lane, BL6 7JF (on B6226, 200m from A673)
⏲ 1-midnight; 12-12.30am Fri & Sat; 12-midnight Sun
☎ (01204) 696231
Bank Top Flat Cap; Coach House Gunpowder Mild; Lees Bitter; Moorhouse's Pride of Pendle; guest beers Ⓗ
Dating from 1777, this stone-built pub with small windows and low ceilings has been run by the same family for many years and is locally known as the 'Long Pull'. In the lounge, pool and darts are played and live sports coverage on TV is popular, while on the left a cosy, traditional vault has some interesting football memorabilia. A Moorhouse's beer is usually available. Nearby Lever Park is ideal for lovely woodland walks. ❀⊟🚌(125,575)♣🍎⚐

Hyde

Cheshire Ring

72 Manchester Road, SK14 2BJ

2 (1 Thu & Fri)-11; 12-11 Sat; 12-10.30 Sun
(07917) 055629
Beartown Kodiak Gold, Bearskinful, seasonal beers; guest beers H
A warm welcome is assured at this friendly pub, one of the oldest in Hyde and comprehensively overhauled by Beartown. Seven handpumps offer a range of Beartown ales and guests from micros in addition to ciders, perries and continental beers. A range of bottled beers is also stocked and occasional beer festivals offer additional drinking choice. Gentle background music plays and live bands perform. The opening hours vary with the season. (Central)

Cotton Bale

21-25 Market Place, Market Place, SK14 2LX
9am-midnight (1am Fri & Sat) (0161) 351 0380
Beer range varies H
A reminder of when cotton was king in Hyde, this popular, vibrant town-centre pub offers up to 12 handpumped real ales at Wetherspoon's value-for-money prices. A number of indoor drinking areas and another outside provide flexible space for drinking and dining, and TV screens are provided. Families are welcome and food is available all day. Hyde market and good public transport links are nearby. (Central)

Queens Inn

23 Clarendon Place, SK14 2ND
11-11 (0161) 368 2230
Holt Mild, Bitter, seasonal beers H
A town-centre community pub with a warm welcome. Home to several sports teams, the interior is divided into four distinct areas to cater for all needs, including a large function room that is a favourite for wedding receptions. Situated close to Hyde bus station and the market, the Queens is popular with shoppers during the day. A late licence is used for special events throughout the year. Rail travellers can use either Hyde Central or Newton for Hyde stations.
(Central/Newton for Hyde)

Sportsman

57 Mottram Road, SK14 2NN
11-11; 12-10.30 Sun (0161) 368 5000
Moorhouse's Black Cat; Pennine Floral Dance, Railway Sleeper, Pitch Porter, White Owl, Sunshine H
This Pennine Ales tied house offers the full range of Pennine beers plus three guests from micros. Bar snacks are served and there is a restaurant upstairs specialising in genuine home-cooked Cuban food and tapas. This former CAMRA Pub of the Region retains its character and has a full-size snooker table upstairs. The rear patio includes a covered and heated smoking area. Hyde Central and Newton for Hyde railway stations are within walking distance.
Q(Central/Newton for Hyde)P

Leigh

Boars Head

2 Market Place, WN7 1EG
11-11 (1am Thu-Sat) (01942) 673036
Beer range varies H
Opposite Leigh's parish church, the imposing red-brick exterior contains clues to the pub's history, from the Bedford Brewing Company to Walker's Warrington Ales, plus the odd Firkin memento inside. A real free house, there are four pumps, two dispensing Moorhouse's beers and two ever-changing guests. The large pool room houses a collection of Rugby League team photographs from various eras, and one of the lounges displays a collection of Lancashire colliery plates. Live music sessions are held most Saturdays, a quiz with hotpot on Sunday.

Bowling Green Inn

Manchester Road, WN7 2LD
11-midnight (1am Fri & Sat); 12-midnight Sun
(01942) 673964
Beer range varies H
Close to Butts Bridge Marina on the Bridgewater Canal (Leigh Branch), this large, popular roadside local attracts all ages. The main lounge contains many alcoves, making it an ideal meeting place for local societies. Two handpumps on the bar offer changing cask ales, and a separate lounge is used for dining and drinking. Pool, darts and doms are played in the well-supported tap room and there is a big screen for sports. Children are welcome until 9pm. P

Thomas Burke ✓

20A Leigh Road, WN7 1QR
9am-midnight (1am Fri & Sat) (01942) 685640
Beer range varies H
Gaining popularity in the town with all ages, this pub is named after a renowned tenor, known as the Lancashire Caruso, who was born in Leigh and sang in the building when it was the Hippodrome Theatre. The pub divides into three areas: the main long bar, a raised dining area and, in what was once the cinema foyer, lounge-style seating. Ten handpumps offer a changing range of beers from the Wetherspoon range.

Waggon & Horses ✓

68 Wigan Road, WN7 5AY
7 (4 Fri)-midnight; 12-1am Sat; 12-11 Sun
(01942) 673069
Hydes Mild, Original Bitter H
Friendly community pub that attracts all ages. The bar with side snug is a good spot for conversation. The main part of the lounge is hidden behind a large hearth that includes a big-screen TV for sporting events. A large games room with pool table, darts and dominoes is home to the pub's various teams. Regular theme nights are held throughout the year. Children are welcome until 8pm.

Littleborough

Moorcock

Halifax Road, OL15 0LD (on A58, 1 mile NE of Littleborough)
11.30-midnight (11.30 Sun) (01706) 378156
themoorcockinn.com
Taylor Landlord; guest beers H
Traditional country inn, originally a farmhouse built in 1681 and first licensed in 1840. Located at the foot of the Pennines with panoramic views of the surrounding countryside, the inn has a warm, friendly atmosphere, serving guest beers from Pictish and other local micro-breweries. Bar food is available at all times with a full à la carte menu served in the restaurant lunchtimes and evenings. Seven en-suite bedrooms make this an ideal base to explore the local area. The smoking area outside is covered. (528)P

White House

Halifax Road, OL15 0LG (on A58 towards Halifax)
⏲ 12-3, 6.30-midnight; 12.30-10.30 Sun ☎ (01706) 378456
Theakston Best Bitter; guest beers Ⓗ
The Pennine Way passes this 17th-century coaching house, situated 1300 feet above sea level. It is a landmark that benefits from panoramic views over the surrounding hills and as far away as Cheshire and Wales. A family-run inn extending a warm, friendly welcome, inside there are two bars, both with log fires. Three local guest ales, continental bottled beers and a good selection of wines complement the excellent menu and daily specials board. Meals are served all day Sunday.
⌂Q⚘◐◑▲🚌(528)P⚟

Lydgate

White Hart

51 Stockport Road, OL4 4JJ (on A6050 close to jct with A669)
⏲ 12-midnight (11 Sun) ☎ (01467) 872566
🌐 thewhitehart.co.uk
Lees Bitter; Taylor Golden Best, Best Bitter, Landlord; guest beers Ⓗ
A true free house in a classic weathered Yorkshire stone building dating from 1788, commanding impressive views over Greater Manchester and as far as the Welsh mountains on a clear day. The multi-room layout has log-burning stoves in two rooms. The guest beer is usually from a local micro such as Greenfield and a growing range of foreign bottled beer is also stocked. Quality food from an award-winning kitchen is served daily in the pub and separate restaurant.
⌂Q⚘⇄◐◑♿🚌(180,184)P

Manchester City Centre

Angel 🏆

6 Angel Street, M4 4BQ (off Rochdale Rd)
⏲ 12-11 (midnight Sat); closed Sun ☎ (0161) 833 4786
Bob's White Lion; guest beers Ⓗ
Formerly the famous Beer House, the revitalised Angel is just off Rochdale Road, north of the city centre. Under new management since 2009, it still has an upmarket restaurant upstairs, while downstairs there is space for drinkers, with bare floorboards and candlelit tables. Eight handpumps now grace the bar, two usually reserved for cider and perry. A wide range of beers is on offer from all over the country, mostly from small breweries. Regular live music plays.
⌂◐◑⇌(Victoria)⊖(Shudehill)🚌🍎P⚟

Bar Fringe

8 Swan Street, M4 5JN (next to Oldham Rd/Oldham St interchange)
⏲ 11-midnight (12.30am Fri & Sat); 12-midnight Sun
☎ (0161) 835 3815
Beer range varies Ⓗ
An interesting Belgian brown bar, popular with the discerning drinker, decorated with curios, including a motorcycle, plus weird and wacky knick-knacks. The bar features five handpumps dispensing guest ales and regulars from local breweries, including Bank Top, Phoenix, Allgates and Acorn. Real ciders and perries are available. Ten draught foreign beers are also on offer, with the accent on Belgian beers including Duvel Green, plus more than 50 bottles. Four mini festivals are held annually.
⚘◐⇌(Victoria)⊖(Shudehill)🚌🍎⚟

Bulls Head

84 London Road, M1 2PN (jct Fairfield Street)
⏲ 11.30-11; 12-10.30 Sun ☎ (0161) 236 1724
Banks's Mild; Jennings Cumberland Ale; Marston's Pedigree; guest beers Ⓗ
Dating from 1894 and dominating the corner opposite Piccadilly Station, this pub is ideal if you have an hour or so between trains. A single-roomed establishment, the large, open-plan interior has plenty of standing room. Around the periphery are tables and bench seating. The walls are adorned with the usual scatterings of old Manchester pictures. A good starting point for city centre nights out, the pub gets busy in the evening at weekends.
Q◐◑♿⇌(Piccadilly)⊖(Piccadilly)🚌(192,201)

Castle Hotel

66 Oldham Street, M4 1LE
⏲ 12-1am (2am Fri & Sat) ☎ (0161) 237 9485
🌐 thecastlehotel.info
Robinson's seasonal beers Ⓗ
Robinson's only Manchester city-centre pub, six beers from the Robinson's stable are available. This Grade II-listed building is undergoing a sympathetic renovation, returning the pub to its former glory – with no leaks! With its traditional tiled frontage and bar, the pub retains its old-fashioned feel and ambience. Food is provided, with good home-made soups and stews supplemented by an eclectic range of snacks. Live bands play and there is an indie/rock juke-box.
◐◑⇌(Victoria/Piccadilly)⊖(Market St)🚌⚟

City Arms ✔

46-48 Kennedy Street, M2 4BQ
⏲ 11-11 (midnight Fri); 12-midnight Sat; 12-8 Sun
☎ (0161) 236 4610
Tetley Bitter; guest beers Ⓗ
Busy little two-roomed hostelry found behind The Waterhouse pub which has appeared in the Guide for 16 consecutive years. It can be hectic at lunchtimes with office workers who come for the good food. Early doors can be busy, then it settles down and gives way to a quieter period with a local mood. There is no beer garden but in front of the pub is a small drinking area. Seven widely sourced guest beers are on offer along with the regular Tetley Bitter, making this a very popular city-centre pub. ◐⇌(Oxford Rd)⊖(St Peters Sq)🚌

Crown & Kettle

2 Oldham Road, Ancoats, M4 5FE (corner of Oldham St & Great Ancoats St)
⏲ 12-11 (midnight Fri & Sat); 12-10.30 Sun
☎ (0161) 236 2923 🌐 crownandkettle.com
Greenfield Crown & Kettle Ale; guest beers Ⓗ
This historic Grade II-listed pub reopened in 2005 after a closure of 16 years. Up to six handpumps dispense beers from an ever-changing list of local breweries including Dunham Massey and Howard Town, as well as breweries further afield. The main drinking hall has an adjoining modern snug and there is a separate vault with fully-restored ornate ceiling. Note the tiny smoking shelter in the backyard. ◐◑♿⇌(Victoria)⊖(Shudehill)🚌🍎⚟

Dutton

37 Park Street, Strangeways, M3 1EU (back of MEN Arena, corner of Dutton St)
⏲ 12-11 (10 Sun) ☎ (0161) 834 4508
Hydes Original Bitter Ⓗ

Back-street corner pub with a triangular snug bar and an eccentric shape to the rest of the interior. This popular local has a loyal following as well as attracting passing trade from the nearby MEN Arena, and it can get busy. Three rooms, including a large back room, festooned with antique oil lamps, are comfy and homely. The landlord will make a decision to stay open late if there is the demand. There is a smoking shelter at the rear.
⊟≠(Victoria)⊖(Victoria)🚌(89,135)♣⁻

Jolly Angler ✔

47 Ducie Street, M1 2JW
⏲ 12-3, 5.30-11; 12-11 Sat; 12-6, 8-10.30 Sun
☎ (0161) 236 5307
Hydes Original Bitter Ⓗ
Head down Ducie Street away from the bustle of Piccadilly Station and you will find a back-street pub of a type that is sadly becoming a rarity in most towns and cities. Run by the same family for more than 25 years, the 'Jolly' features live Irish music on Thursday night and hosts special events during Manchester's Irish Festival in March. Opening hours are restricted when nearby Manchester City FC play at home.
♛≠(Piccadilly)⊖(Piccadilly)🚌(1,2,3)♣

Knott 🏆

374 Deansgate, M3 4LY
⏲ 12-11.30 (midnight Thu; 12.30am Fri & Sat)
☎ (0161) 839 9229
Marble Manchester Bitter, Ginger Marble; guest beers Ⓗ
A well-established venue with a great mix of customers serving both local and national brewery beers. The excellent public transport links make this an ideal start/end point for a pub crawl. Food is served 12-8pm daily, with monthly themed epicurean nights a speciality. There is always a real cider available from a box, together with an extensive selection of foreign bottled beers.
❀◑♿≠(Deansgate)⊖(G-Mex)🚌🍎⁻

Marble Arch ☆

73 Rochdale Road, M4 4HY (on A664 200m from A665 jct)
⏲ 12-11 (midnight Fri & Sat); 12-10.30 Sun
☎ (0161) 832 5914 🌐 marblebeers.co.uk
Marble Pint, Manchester Bitter, JP Best Bitter, Lagonda IPA, Ginger Marble, seasonal beers Ⓗ
Classic tiled Victorian gem with a sloping floor down to the bar and an original decorated frieze around the tiled ceiling in the front room. Home of the award-winning Marble Brewery, this is a brew pub with up to 10 handpumps, though the accent is now more on food with a restaurant in a back room. Situated in the suburb of Collyhurst, this heritage pub retains links with the locality and is graced by local workers as well as the well-heeled from the city. Quality restaurant food is served until 9pm Monday to Saturday and 8pm on Sunday.
♛❀◑≠(Victoria)⊖(Shudehill)🚌🍎⁻

Micro Bar

Unit FC16, Manchester Arndale, 49 High Street, M4 3AH (in food market in shopping centre)
⏲ 12-6 (5 Sun) ☎ (0161) 277 9666
Boggart Hole Clough Rum Porter, seasonal beers; guest beers Ⓗ
Small compact bar – hence the name – situated within the Arndale Food Market. An ideal place to stop off during a day's shopping. This is the first brewery tap for the local Boggart brewery, who took over from Paradise Brewery in 2009 and completely refurbished the bar. Up to five handpumps offer two Boggart beers, two guests from an exotic and endless list, and real cider or perry. ◑♿≠(Victoria)⊖(Shudehill)🚌🍎P⊓

Odd Bar

30-32 Thomas Street, M4 1ER (off Shudehill)
⏲ 11-midnight (1am Thu; 1.30am Fri & Sat); 12-midnight Sun
☎ (0161) 833 0070 🌐 oddbar.co.uk
Beer range varies Ⓗ
Odd is an independent and self-proclaimed free-spirited bar in the heart of the trendy Northern Quarter. The beers are usually sourced from small breweries in the Manchester area. Despite only having one handpump, it manages to ring the changes on a regular basis. Often busy in the evenings, Odd is also a fine place to relax, with home-made food, free Wi-Fi, newspapers, a giant cinema screen downstairs and even an artist's gallery. A warm atmosphere pervades throughout this wonderfully eccentric bar.
❀◑≠(Victoria)⊖(Shudehill)🚌

Old Wellington Inn ✔

4 Cathedral Gates, M3 1SW (next to Cathedral)
⏲ 10-11 (midnight Fri & Sat); 10-10.30 Sun
☎ (0161) 839 5179
Jennings Cumberland Ale; guest beers Ⓗ
With part of the structure dating from the 16th century, this timber-framed inn moved to its present location as part of a redevelopment following the explosion of a terrorist bomb in 1996. Split over three levels, with up to four handpumps in use offering beers from national brands and local micro-breweries, this is a favourite stop on the Manchester tourist trail. There is an extensive food menu and large courtyard, which gets busy in good weather. Children are allowed inside until 8pm.
Q☺❀◑♿≠(Victoria)⊖(Victoria)🚌⁻

Paramount ✔

33-35 Oxford Street, M1 4BH
⏲ 9-midnight (1am Fri & Sat) ☎ (0161) 2331820
Greene King Abbot; Thwaites Wainwright; guest beers Ⓗ
Despite being very busy, this Wetherspoon's pub has a more relaxed ambience than some of the other somewhat frenetic city-centre pubs. However, what really gives it an edge is the zeal the managers and staff have for their cask beers, with many coming from local micros. The Paramount derives its name from its location in Manchester's old theatreland (note the old photos) and is very handy for modern day venues including the Palace Theatre, Bridgewater Hall and Manchester Central conference centre.
◑♿≠(Oxford Rd)⊖(St Peter's Sq)🚌(1,3)🍎⁻

Piccadilly ✔

71-75 London Road, Piccadilly, M1 2BS (on A6)
⏲ 8am-11 (midnight Fri; 1am Sat); 9am-11 Sun
☎ (0161) 236 3622
John Smith's Bitter; guest beers Ⓗ
Originally part of an old warehouse, the building was converted into a pub in the 1990s, with a split-level layout. After a shaky past, the pub is now thriving due to a keen licensee dedicated to real ale. The guest beers come from various micro and regional breweries. Food is served until 9.30pm. Wheelchair access and a disabled toilet are at street level.
◑♿≠(Piccadilly)⊖(Piccadilly Gardens)🚌

Sand Bar

120-122 Grosvenor Street, All Saints, M1 7HL (off Oxford Rd A34/B5117 jct)

12-midnight (1am Thu; 2am Fri); 4-2am Sat; 4-10.30 Sun

(0161) 273 1552 sandbaronline.net

Moorhouse's Black Cat; Phoenix All Saints; Taylor Landlord; guest beers H

Situated in the heart of the university area, the Sand Bar attracts custom from both students and lecturers alike, who come for the bohemian atmosphere and excellent range of UK and foreign beers, both draught and in bottle. Exhibitions of photographs and paintings usually line the walls, while DJs or live music often feature in the evening. Food is available until 6.30pm. The cider is a changing guest from a small maker.

(Oxford Rd)(42,43)

Smithfield Hotel & Bar

37 Swan Street, M4 5JZ (on A665 between Rochdale Rd and Oldham Rd)

12-midnight (0161) 839 4424

Robinson's Dark Mild; guest beers H

Handy for the Band On The Wall live music venue, as well as the Crowne Plaza Hotel, this pub is a long-standing bastion of real ale, with up to nine handpumps in use. The good-value Smithfield Bitter from Facers Brewery is always on offer, with the seven remaining beer engines mainly dedicated to micro-breweries near and far. Durham and Dunham Massey breweries are among the favourites. There are many beer festivals throughout the year. Recently refurbished both in and out to a high standard, accommodation is available. (Victoria)(Shudehill)

Waterhouse

67-71 Princess Street, M2 4EG

9am-midnight (1am Fri & Sat) (0161) 200 5380

Phoenix Wobbly Bob; Elland Waterhouse IPA; guest beers H

This multi-room Wetherspoon's is unlike any you may have visited before. It provides a fine range of cask ales plus well-presented food from the regular Wetherspoon's menu. A feature of this venue is the regular Meet the Brewer evenings, which are very popular. It also provides probably the best range of real ciders of all Manchester's Wetherspoon's.

(Oxford Road)(St Peter's Sq)

Marple

Hare & Hounds

Dooley Lane, Otterspool, SK6 7EJ

11.30-11; 12-10.30 Sun (0161) 427 0293

Hydes Bitter, Jekyll's Gold, seasonal beers H

An attractive pub by the River Goyt on the Marple-Romiley road. It is difficult to imagine that when this pub was first built it was at the end of a row of terraced cottages, demolished long ago when the road was realigned. The pub's Hydes beers now provide some welcome variety in the area. The interior is open plan with a separate dining area and conservatory plus an improved and pleasant outdoor space. The pub offers something for everyone including good value food. QP

Hatters Arms

81 Church Lane, SK6 7AW

12-midnight (0161) 427 1529 hattersmarple.co.uk

Robinson's Hatters, Unicorn, seasonal beers H

At the end of a row of stone-built hatters' cottages, this tiny pub was enlarged only a few years ago and retains an intimate atmosphere. There are three small rooms and an attractive panelled bar area. Numerous photographs on the walls reflect the pub's brass band connections. Much is done to attract regular custom, including games evenings and a quiz on Thursday. (Rose Hill)

Railway

223 Stockport Road, SK6 6EN

12-11 (11.30 Fri & Sat) (0161) 427 2146

Robinson's Hatters, Unicorn, seasonal beers H

This impressive pub first opened in 1878 alongside Rose Hill Station and many rail commuters still number among its customers. The pub has changed little externally, and is handy for walkers and cyclists on the nearby Middlewood Way. Two open-plan airy and relaxing rooms are complemented by an outside verandah and drinking area. A deservedly popular pub. (Rose Hill)P

Middleton

Old Boar's Head

111 Long Street, M24 6UE

12-11 (10.30 Sun) (0161) 643 3520

Lees Brewer's Dark, Bitter H

Striking half-timbered and stone-flagged pub dating back to at least 1632, handily situated on the main Middleton to Rochdale road. It attracts both locals and passing trade. The pub is divided into a number of cosy rooms and has a large sessions room at the side, which was a courtroom many years ago. The pub is home to a popular slimming club but nonetheless provides excellent value home-cooked meals. A rare outlet for the hard-to-find Brewer's Dark. (17)P

Mossley

Britannia Inn

217 Manchester Road, OL5 9AJ

3 (11 Sat)-11; 12-11 Sun (01457) 832799

Marston's Burton Bitter; guest beers H

Mossley's closest real ale outlet to the station. Thanks to SIBA, it now features beers from many local breweries among its constantly-changing range of five guests (Millstone's beers are among the favourites). The 'Brit' is semi open-plan inside with a secluded dining area, with meals served until 7.30pm, 5pm Sunday. A partially-covered front patio is available for smokers and drinkers. Sunday is poker night. (343,350)

Church Inn

82 Stockport Road, OL5 0RF

4-midnight; 2-1am Fri & Sat; 12-1am Sun

(07712) 07712 650607

Thwaites Original, Wainwright; guest beers H

Once the Hardman's Arms, the Church Inn takes its name from the nearby St John the Baptist church, which can be seen from the rear windows. The pub retains its tap room, which is becoming increasingly rare, and features splendid tile work just inside the front door. A traditional local, it is frequented by the Mossley morris men. There is a pavement patio for outdoor use. Dogs are welcome. (353)P

Dysarts Arms
Huddersfield Road, OL5 9BT (on B6175 ½ mile S of A635)
⏰ 12-midnight (1am Sat) ☎ (01457) 832103
Robinson's Unicorn, seasonal beers Ⓗ
Close to the pre-1974 Lancashire/Yorkshire border and backing on to open farmland, this pub was acquired by Robinson's in 1926, when it had another storey. The present steeply-pitched roof, with its deep eaves, dates from 1928 and transformed the pub's appearance. Inside, there is a comfortable bar area and cosy lounge. A partially covered patio to the side is available for drinkers and smokers. No food is served on Monday. The pub is home to walkers and cyclists' clubs.
🏔️🕏◗▲🖵(350)♣P⅃

Nangreaves

Lord Raglan
Mount Pleasant, BL9 6SP
⏰ 12-2.30, 6 (5 Fri)-11; 12-11 Sat; 12-10.30 Sun
☎ (0161) 764 6680
Leyden Rammy Rocket, Forever Bury, Crowning Glory, seasonal beers; guest beers Ⓗ
A country inn at the end of a cobbled lane with open views of the surrounding hills. The Leyden family has run this friendly pub for half a century and it is also the home of the Leyden Brewery – an impressive selection of its beers always features on the bar. Good food is served in the bar and a separate restaurant, prepared by the chef who is also the head brewer. The interior is decorated with antique glass, pottery and old photographs.
Q🕏◗🖵(477)P

New Springs

Crown Hotel
106 Wigan Road, WN2 1DP (on B5238 by canal bridge)
⏰ 7-midnight (1am Fri); 2-1am Sat; 2-11 Sun
Beer range varies Ⓗ
This is a community pub well worth a visit. A free house, it has three handpumps usually offering a selection of Prospect beers, and is LocAle accredited. Two real fires welcome visitors on winter evenings, and there is a pool table and dartboard. Outside is a beer garden and a smoking area. Cabaret entertainment takes place on Friday evening and karaoke on Saturday. Opening times may vary in winter. 🏔️🕏P⅃

Oldham

Ashton Arms ♈
28-30 Clegg Street, OL1 1PL (rear of Town Square shopping centre)
⏰ 11.30-11 (11.30 Fri & Sat); 11.30-10 Sun
☎ (0161) 630 9709
Beer range varies Ⓗ
Superb free house overlooking the old Town Hall, offering a warm welcome to all. The friendly and knowledgable staff serve a choice of seven ever-changing ales from both new and long-established breweries, specialising in local micro and seasonal beers. Traditional cider and continental bottles are also stocked and themed beer festivals are hosted. The food is highly recommended (meals served until 6pm Mon-Thu and 3pm Fri). Note the 200-year-old stone fireplace. Sunday is quiz night.
🏔️◗🖵♣♠⅃☐

Three Crowns ✓
1 Manchester Street, OL1 1LE (by bus station)
⏰ 11.30-8 (11 Fri & Sat); 12-4 Sun ☎ (0161) 628 6123
Beer range varies Ⓗ
This is a large town-centre pub with a smartly painted black-and-white exterior, situated centrally next to the bus station. It attracts a varied mix of customers of all ages. Seasonal ales from the Marston's stable are regularly available. The pub has three distinct drinking areas, one often used for small functions, and offers full disabled access and facilities. Quality food is served seven days a week.
◗🕭🖵♣⅃

Up Steps Inn ✓
17-23 High Street, OL1 3AJ (between town square and Tommyfield market)
⏰ 9am-midnight ☎ (0161) 627 5001
Greene King Ruddles Best Bitter, Abbot; guest beers Ⓗ
Traditional town-centre Wetherspoon's on the main shopping street near the bus station and market. There are usually two regular beers and six to eight rotating guests on offer, including several from local breweries under the LocAle scheme. The pub also hosts beer festivals featuring special beers and ciders. Food is available all day from 9am breakfast until 10pm. ◗🕭🖵♠

Orrell

Robin Hood
117 Sandy Lane, WN5 7AZ (near rail station)
⏰ 3-midnight; 12-1am Thu-Sat; 12-midnight Sun
☎ (01695) 627479
Beer range varies Ⓗ
Well worth seeking out, this small sandstone pub tucked away in a residential area has a reputation for serving good home-cooked food (Thu-Sun, lunchtime and evening; booking advisable). The lounge is used for dining at meal times. There is a separate bar area where sporting events are screened. Three handpumps provide semi-regular beers include Deuchars IPA, Old Speckled Hen and Taylor Landlord. Not surprisingly, the decor has a Robin Hood theme, with a large broadsword on display in the lounge. 🕏◗⇌♣P

Patricroft

Stanley Arms ★
895 Liverpool Road, M30 0QN (opp fire station on A57)
⏰ 12-midnight ☎ (0161) 788 8801
Holt Mild, Bitter Ⓗ
Dating from 1850 and originally known as the Red Lamp, this was Holt's last purchase in the area, in 1909, and is probably its smallest pub. The Stanley is the epitome of the unspoilt, street-corner local. Enter by a small door on the side street to find a tiny lobby with a serving hatch. The busy vault is at the front, with the best room just off the lobby. At the far end of the corridor is a third room with a mock cast-iron range. Holt's Mild, fast disappearing across the brewery's estate, is still highly popular here. Q🕏◗⇌(10,22,67)♣⅃

Peel Green

Grapes Hotel ★
439 Liverpool Road, M30 7HD (on A57 near M60 jct 11)
⏰ 11-11 (midnight Sat); 12-11 Sun ☎ (0161) 789 6971
Holt Mild, Bitter Ⓗ

Built by Holt's in 1906, this is a fine example of a large five-room Edwardian hostelry. Magnificent red brick outside, visitors enter via a bar lobby and bar parlour, with a large separate vault. A former billiards room to the rear is now a games room with a pool table (note the fine old fireplace). The pub is adorned with mosaic floors, tiled walls, etched glass, polished mahogany and an impressive staircase.
⚠⊟≠(Patricroft)⊟(10,67)♣P⁄–

Pendlebury

Lord Nelson

653 Bolton Road, M27 4EJ (A666/B5231 jct)
✪ 11-11 (11.30 Fri) ☎ (0161) 794 3648
Holt Mild, Bitter Ⓗ
Situated on Bolton Road near its junction with Station Road and Queensway, the Lord Nelson offers a friendly welcome. Built in 1969, it is a fine example of a classic 1970s community pub, with a lounge with a stage for live music, a vault with pool table and large-screen TV, and a small snug. There is a covered and heated outdoor area with a TV for smokers. ❀◑⊟≠(Swinton)⊟(8)♣P⁄–

Prestwich

Friendship

Scholes Lane, M25 0PD (on A6044 near Heaton Park)
✪ 12-11 (11.30 Fri & Sat); 12-11.30 Sun ☎ (0161) 773 2645
Holt Mild, Bitter, seasonal beers Ⓗ
An imposing red-brick building on the main Prestwich to Agecroft road. The pub comprises a dining area, neat snug bar and comfortable lounge. Both drinking areas are served by an impressive semi-island bar with wooden surrounds and hatches. Food is available all day until 8pm (9pm Fri and Sat). Outside, there is a large patio and seating area for smokers. The car park is small.
❀◑♿P⁄–

Ramsbottom

Major Hotel

158-160 Bolton Street, BL0 9JA
✪ 3.30-11 Mon; 12-midnight Tue-Sat; 12-11 Sun
☎ (01706) 826777
Harviestoun Bitter & Twisted; Sharp's Doom Bar; Taylor Landlord; guest beers Ⓗ
This traditional stone pub with a bar and lounge was originally three Lancashire terraced houses. The decor includes many historic photos of picturesque Ramsbottom and surroundings. The central bar offers four cask ales and a food menu listing old favourites as well as contemporary dishes (no eve meals Sat and Sun). There is a small beer garden with bench seating and a heated smoking area. A car park is available for those unlucky drivers. ❀◑⊟≠⊟♣P⁄–

Rochdale

Baum

33-37 Toad Lane, OL12 0NU (follow signs for Co-op Museum)
✪ 11.30-11 (midnight Fri & Sat); 11.30-10.30 Sun
☎ (01706) 352186 🌐 thebaum.co.uk
Beer range varies Ⓗ
A hidden gem within a conservation area, the Baum occupies part of the same building as the Pioneer Museum. A split-level inn with old world charm, the conservatory at the rear overlooks a large beer garden. Friendly staff serve ever-changing real ales, a large choice of worldwide bottled beers and five Belgians on draught. Fresh food and international tapas are served daily. Outside is a covered smoking area. CAMRA Branch Pub of the Year 2009 and Pub of Rochdale 2008.
Q❀◑≠⊟♣●P⁄–

Cask & Feather

1 Oldham Road, OL16 1UA
✪ 11-midnight (1am Fri & Sat); 12-midnight Sun
☎ (01706) 711476
Phoenix Navvy; guest beers Ⓗ
True free house a few minutes walk from the railway station with an open-plan interior including a long bar and pool area. Cask beers are keenly priced, with guests regularly sourced from local micros. Good value lunches are served until 2.30pm daily. Outside is a beer garden with covered smoking area. Pool and poker are played on Monday and Tuesday, there is a heavy rock disco on Friday and live music on Sunday.
❀◑≠⊟♣⁄–

Cemetery Hotel ★ ✔

470 Bury Road, OL11 5EU (on B62)
✪ 4-2am; 12-1am Thu-Sat; 12-10.30 Sun ☎ (01706) 645635
Beer range varies Ⓗ
Rochdale's original free house from the 1970s, this pub is listed in CAMRA's National Inventory of Historic Pub Interiors for its many original features. It has maintained its multi-roomed layout, which includes two lovely snugs. Upstairs is a large function room available for hire. There are usually four or five beers on offer from the Punch range and the food is good and well-priced. The pub can get very busy with Rochdale AFC fans on match days. Real cider is served during the summer months. ⚠Q❀◑⊟(469)♣P⁄–

Flying Horse Hotel

37 Packer Street, OL16 1NJ (next to town hall)
✪ 11-midnight (1am Fri & Sat); 12-midnight Sun
☎ (01706) 646412 🌐 theflyinghorsehotel.co.uk
Lees Bitter; Phoenix Arizona; Taylor Best Bitter, Landlord; guest beers Ⓗ
Impressive Edwardian free house with many original architectural features, owned by the same family for the past decade. Popular with local football teams, live sports events are shown on TV and live music plays most Saturdays. The menu features meat from the local butcher and pies made on the premises. A function room is available for hire and there is a heated smokers' area outside. The main bus station is three minutes' walk away. ⊟◑≠⊟♣⁄–

Healey Hotel

172 Shawclough Road, OL12 6LW
✪ 3-11.30; 12-midnight; 12-11.30 Sat & Sun
☎ (01706) 645453
Robinson's Hatters, Unicorn, Dizzy Blond, Old Tom Ⓗ
On the end of a row of terraced houses, this popular local retains many original features including a half-tiled bar area. Situated close to a local nature reserve, it has a beer garden to the side and a petanque piste to the rear. Four handpumps serve Robinson's beers. A quiz night is held on Tuesday. Buses stop outside the pub.
❀⊟(446,466)♣⁄–

Regal Moon ✔

The Butts, OL16 1HB (next to bus station)
☼ 9-midnight (1am Fri & Sat) ☎ (01706) 657434
Beer range varies Ⓗ
Impressive former cinema in the centre of town that retains many Art Deco features. A long bar serves several distinct drinking areas in an open plan interior. Eighteen handpumps dispense a wide variety of ales, with many local micro-breweries featured. The house beer is brewed by Elland. Spot the organist on his perch above the bar. Value meals are served including breakfast until noon. Real cider is from Westons. Q❀◑♿🚌●⚐

Romiley

Duke of York ✔

Stockport Road, SK6 3AN
☼ 11-midnight (1am Fri-Sat); 12-11.30 Sun
☎ (0161) 430 2806 🌐 dukeofyorkromiley.co.uk
Black Sheep Best Bitter; Caledonian Deuchars IPA; Fuller's London Pride; John Smith's Bitter; Wells Bombardier Ⓗ
Cosy, traditional village inn built in 1786 as the King's Head and renamed in Victorian times. The pub retains its character and historic feel, with open fires during the winter months adding to the warm welcome. Up to six handpulled real ales plus a real cider are on offer and food is available daily in the bar and first floor restaurant. A quiz is held on Monday evening, jazz on the first Wednesday of the month and a beer festival in September.
⛫Q❀◑⊟⇌🚌(383,384)●P⚐

Rusholme

Ford Madox Brown ✔

Unit 3 Wilmslow Park, Oxford Road, M13 9NG (opp Whitworth Park)
☼ 9-midnight ☎ (0161) 256 6660
Greene King Ruddles Best Bitter, Abbot; guest beers Ⓗ
This Wetherspoon's house, built under a student hall of residence, is named after the renowned Pre-Raphaelite Victorian painter who lived nearby in Victoria Park, whose work hangs in the City Art Gallery and town hall. Close to the university area and Whitworth Art Gallery, it is convenient for the famous Curry Mile. Deservedly the most popular pub in the area, it retains a warm atmosphere despite its size. Q❀◑♿🚌(42,43)⚐

Sale

Bulls Head

2 Cross Street, M33 7AE SJ785921
☼ 11-11; 12-1am Fri & Sat; 12-10.30 Sun ☎ (0161) 905 2859
Beer range varies Ⓗ
Situated in a prominent position in the centre of Sale, this Grade II-listed building was built in 1879. It has been recently refurbished by the current tenants and offers two cask ales selected from independent breweries. Downstairs is a large function room, with live entertainment held every Friday and Saturday evening. Food is available daily until 9pm (not Mon), with a carvery on Sunday.
⛫❀◑♿⊖🚌P⚐

J P Joule ✔

2a Northenden Road, M33 3BR SJ 790919
☼ 9-midnight (1am Fri & Sat) ☎ (0161) 962 9889
Greene King Ruddles Best Bitter, Abbot Ⓗ
Popular Wetherspoon's pub named after the physicist JP Joule, famous for heat experiments – exhibits of his work are on view in the pub. His gravestone can be seen in Brooklands Cemetery close by. The pub has two floors with an extensive bar on each one with at least eight handpumps. Real cider from Westons is available. Food is served daily from 9am until 10pm. Brewers and tasting evenings are held occasionally. ❀◑♿⊖🚌●P⚐

Volunteer Hotel

81 Cross Street, M33 7HH SJ 786924
☼ 12-midnight (11 Sun) ☎ (0161) 973 5503
Holts Mild, Bitter, seasonal beers Ⓗ
Dating back to the late-19th century, this once multi-roomed pub has been opened up into a large open-plan room served by a single bar. The interior is warm and welcoming, with friendly, helpful staff. Three darts teams are based here, and a quiz is hosted most Thursdays. There's an oak-panelled room upstairs available for meetings. ❀♿⊖🚌P⚐

Salford

Black Lion

65 Chapel Street, M3 5BZ
☼ 12-11 ☎ (0161) 836 4620
Beer range varies Ⓗ
Prominently sited on the corner of Blackfriars Street, this former keg-only pub reopened in 2009 under the same management as the nearby New Oxford. The pub has been impressively refurbished – the bar gantry is particularly fine. It now boasts eight handpumps serving beers free of tie, often featuring local brewers such as Hornbeam and Northern. The house beer comes from Phoenix, and an extensive selection of bottled Belgian beers is also stocked. Food is served daily except Sunday and Monday evenings. There is a large function room upstairs for hire. ◑⇌⊖(Victoria)🚌

Crescent

18-21 The Crescent, M5 4PF (opp Salford university)
☼ 12-midnight (1am Fri & Sat); 12-11 Sun
☎ (0161) 736 5600 🌐 thecrescentsalford.co.uk
Beer range varies Ⓗ
This Grade II-listed building dating from the 1860s has recently undergone exterior refurbishment and is now receiving attention to the interior. Popular with students and beer lovers, the pub caters for all tastes, with quiz, 'open mike' and curry nights (see the website for details). A dozen handpumps hosts beers from around the country, including ales from micro-breweries Mallinsons, Pictish and Phoenix. Ciders are from Thatchers, plus guests and perry. Regular beer festivals are hosted.
⛫❀◑⊟⇌⊖🚌♣●P⚐

King's Arms

11 Bloom Street, M3 6AN (off Chapel St)
☼ 12-11 (midnight Fri & Sat); 12-6 Sun ☎ (0161) 839 8726
Beer range varies Ⓗ
A fine pub on the Salford Real Ale Trail boasting an unusual oval-shaped lounge area, high ceilings and Grade II-listed features. A bohemian arts scene attracts an arty crowd that loves beer and music, alongside new regulars from the nearby posh flats. Up to six beers on handpump come from Bazens', Facers and Allgates among other breweries. Eclectic evenings include knitting night on Monday. The decorated and heated smoking shelter is of note. ❀◑⇌(Central)🚌P⚐

New Oxford ✔

11 Bexley Square, M3 6DB (by magistrates court)
✪ 12-midnight ☎ (0161) 832 7082 🌐 thenewoxford.co.uk
Beer range varies Ⓗ
In a historic square, this well-appointed two-room pub is dedicated to serving quality beer. Rescued from an unpromising past by a committed management team, it was crowned CAMRA Greater Manchester Pub of the Year in 2007. Up to 16 ales are on handpull, including guest beers and two house beers from Mallinsons and Moorhouse's, supplemented by a superlative range of Belgian beers, many rare for the UK, with several on draught. Regular popular beer festivals are held. Food serving times vary.
✿◑≠(Central)🚌●P⁻

Racecourse Hotel

Littleton Road, Lower Kersal, M7 3SE (next to River Irwell)
✪ 12-midnight (1am Fri & Sat); 12-11 Sun
☎ (0161) 792 1420
Oakwell Old Tom Mild, Barnsley Bitter Ⓗ
Large and imposing award-winning mock-Tudor building dating back to 1930, lovingly renovated to recall the glory days when it served the now long-gone Manchester Racecourse. Beautiful oak wood panelling and carvings feature throughout, complemented by many trophies and photographs of the old racecourse (now allotments). The pub has one large drinking hall and the largest bar you will ever see, a separate vault and two smaller lounges. Q♨✿⊟🚌(93,95)♣P⁻

Star Inn

2 Back Hope Street, Higher Broughton, M7 2FR (off Great Clowes St)
✪ 1.30 (4 Tue-Thu)-midnight; 1.30-1am Fri & Sat
☎ (0161) 792 4184 🌐 staronthecliff.co.uk
Beer range varies Ⓗ
Following its closure in 2009 by Robinson's Brewery, the Star was bought at auction by a determined group of locals and is now owned by a cooperative of 62-plus shareholders. The bar serves a house beer brewed by local small brewery Bazens', and a guest ale. This pub is hard to find for the first time, but is well-worth making the effort to seek out. There is a large-screen TV in the main room. Note: no admission after 11pm (10.30pm Sun). ✿⊟🚌(98)♣P⁻

Stalybridge

Old Hunter's Tavern

51-53 Acres Lane, SK15 2JR
✪ 12-midnight ☎ (0161) 303 9477
Beer range varies Ⓗ
This delightful hostelry has plenty of character and appeals to all ages. Note the splendid carpentry in the bar and the eye-catching brasswork throughout the pub including the brass poles holding circular shelves to accommodate standing drinkers' glasses. The licensees often organise extra-mural activities for their regulars. A local amateur radio club meets on the last Saturday of the month. No food is served at the weekend. ✿◑🚌♣P⁻

Stalybridge Labour Club ✔

Acres Lane, SK15 2JR
✪ 12-4.30, 7.30-11; 12-6, 7.30-10.30 Sun
☎ (0161) 338 4796
Taylor Landlord; Wells Bombardier; guest beers Ⓗ
This modern social club incorporates a lounge, TV room, function/concert room and a small meetings room. The comfortable and friendly atmosphere can be enjoyed while playing a variety of games including billiards and snooker. Guest beers are mainly sourced from local micros. A copy of this Guide or a CAMRA membership card will secure entry. ✿♿≠🚌P⁻

Stalybridge Station Refreshment Rooms (Buffet Bar) 🏆 ☆

Rassbottom Street, SK15 1RF (Platform 1)
✪ 9.30 (alcohol from 11)-11; 11 (alcohol from 12)-10.30 Sun
☎ (0161) 303 0007 🌐 buffetbar.freewebspace.com
Boddingtons Bitter; Flowers IPA; guest beers Ⓗ
Nobody minds delayed or missed trains at Stalybridge. This institution for educated drinkers serves an ever-changing range of up to nine cask beers, usually from micros, plus often rare brews. These can be enjoyed in convivial Victorian splendour by the roaring fire while enjoying simple traditionally cooked meals, or outside watching the world and the trains go by. The conservatory adds to the charm and character of this gem. Foreign bottled beers are available and a folk club plays on Saturday. 🔥Q✿◑◐⊟♿≠🚌●P⁻

Stockport

Arden Arms ★

23 Millgate, SK1 2LX (jct Corporation Street)
✪ 12-11 ☎ (0161) 480 2185 🌐 arden-arms.co.uk
Robinson's Hatters, Unicorn, Double Hop Ⓗ**, Old Tom** Ⓖ**, seasonal beers** Ⓗ
Grade II-listed and on CAMRA's National Inventory of Historic Pub Interiors, the Arden's distinctive curved, glazed bar, its hidden snug, chandeliers and grandfather clock conjure up a Victorian ambience. Gourmet lunches, quiz nights and wine tastings, however, add a contemporary touch. Conveniently close to Stockport's historic market, the place is abuzz at lunchtimes, but more intimate in the evenings. Formerly a mortuary, the cellars retain body niches in the walls. A beautiful courtyard shows off the old stables and outbuildings. Voted CAMRA Branch Pub of the Year in 2009, this is an unmissable gem.
🔥♨✿◑⊟🚌(300,384)♣P⁻

Armoury

31 Shaw Heath, SK3 8BD (on B5465, jct Greek St)
✪ 10.30-midnight (2am Fri & Sat); 11-midnight Sun
☎ (0161) 477 3711
Robinson's Hatters, Unicorn, Old Tom, seasonal beers Ⓗ
Busy local with a strong community involvement, with friendly and knowledgeable staff. Three rooms with original internal doors bear the old Bells Brewery logo in the glass panels, while the walls feature memorabilia relating to the Cheshire Regiment. Convenient for Edgeley Park football ground, bar food is often available when Stockport County or Sale Sharks are at home. Darts is a strong feature here, with two leagues often playing on the same night. Live folk music sessions are held in an upstairs room. CAMRA Branch Pub of the Year 2007 runner-up. Q✿⊟≠🚌(310,369)♣P⁻

Blossoms

2 Buxton Road, Heaviley, SK2 6NU (at A6/A5102 jct)
✪ 12-3, 5-11 (11.30 Fri); 12-11.30 Sat; 12-10.30 Sun
☎ (0161) 477 2397

Robinson's Hatters, Unicorn Ⓗ**, Old Tom** Ⓖ
Excellent, unspoilt local, with a vault, pool room and very cosy snug around the central bar, and a large function room upstairs. The snug has an elegant carved fireplace surround, stained glass panels and pictures of the town's past on the walls. A more basic room offers pinball and a TV, often used for screening football matches. Built as a coaching house in the 18th century, it is also reported to have been an exit place for an escape tunnel from nearby Bramall Hall.
Q❀◐⊟⇌(Davenport)🚌(192,199)♣P⅟—

Crown

154 Heaton Lane, SK4 1AR (jct of King Street West under viaduct)
⏲ 12-11 (10.30 Sun) ☎ (0161) 480 5850
🌐 thecrowninn.uk.com
Beer range varies Ⓗ
CAMRA National Pub of the Year 2009 runner-up, the Crown is a busy pub, especially in the evenings. It offers around 16 ever-changing beers – with helpful and knowledgable staff to advise those confused by the choice. Pictish and Copper Dragon are regulars and there is usually a mild, stout and cider. Four rooms radiate from the busy bar: two compact snugs, a large lounge, and a stand-up bar. Food is served lunchtimes Monday to Friday. Live music is a feature, with the rear yard often showcasing local bands at the weekend. A real gem. ⛼❀◐⊟⇌🚌(192)♣●⅟—

Magnet

51 Wellington Road North, SK4 1HJ (A6 jct Duke St)
⏲ 4-11; 12-11 Thu-Sun ☎ (0161) 429 6287
Beer range varies Ⓗ
Once a failing keg pub that then closed, this was rescued from certain destruction by a beer- and pub-loving family. Renovated with help from friends and local ale fans, it now boasts 14 handpumps for beer and a draught cider. A large foreign bottled range completes the now rosy picture. It has a bustling vault to the left, leading to a lower pool room, and a series of rooms separated by arched doorways on the right. Monday cheese night is popular. There are plans to establish an in-house brewery. Q❀⊟🚌(22,192)♣●P⅟—

Olde Vic

1 Chatham Street, SK3 9ED (jct of Shaw Heath)
⏲ Closed Mon; 3 (7 Sat) late (last entry 10.15); 7-10.30 Sun
☎ (0161) 480 2410 🌐 yeoldevic.com
Beer range varies Ⓗ
This quirky but extremely well-run free house was the first Stockport pub to offer changing guest beers, and continues to do the business to this day. Larger than life landlord Steve runs a tight ship (strictly no swearing) where conversation and banter are the order of the day. The ever-changing guest beers are sourced from micros near and far, and the guest cider often comes from a smaller maker. ⛼❀⇌🚌(310,369)●⅟—

Pineapple

159 Heaton Lane, SK4 1AQ (off A6, near viaduct)
⏲ 12-11 (10.30 Sun) ☎ (0161) 480 3221
Robinson's Hatters, Cumbria Way, Unicorn, seasonal beer Ⓗ
Old, low-set building with three rooms including a smart lounge and bar area where the walls are festooned with dozens of plates gathered on travels around the globe. At the rear is a spacious lower-level games room. A friendly welcome is offered to all, including regulars, shoppers and business people. Lunches are served daily except Sunday. One of the very few Robinson's houses in the town to offer Hartley's beer. ❀◐⇌🚌(192)♣⅟—

Railway

1 Avenue Street, SK1 2BZ (jct of Great Portwood St/ A560)
⏲ 12-11 (10.30 Sun) ☎ (0161) 429 6062
Pennine Floral Dance, Hameldon Bitter, Railway Sleeper, Porter, Sunshine, seasonal beers; guest beers Ⓗ
Bustling, street-corner house with 11 handpumps showcasing the full Pennine Brewery range, plus two guests. A changing mild and a real cider are also stocked, plus a wide selection of Belgian, German and other bottled beers. Home-made lunches are served Monday to Saturday. Look out for the model railway atop the bar canopy, and the amusing loco mural at the back. A bar billiards table is well used. Q❀◐🚌(325,330)♣●⅟—

Red Bull

14 Middle Hillgate, SK1 3AY
⏲ 12-11 (10.30 Sun) ☎ (0161) 480 1286
Robinson's Hatters, Unicorn, seasonal beers Ⓗ
Refurbished and enlarged three years ago, the pub retains a homely, rustic atmosphere. Situated 400 metres uphill from Robinson's – it is seen as a flagship house for the brewery. Numerous dining and drinking areas radiate from a large central bar area, with a wooden and tiled floor. Outside are a cobbled courtyard and small car park. Food is available lunchtimes and evenings, with Sunday lunch ever popular. Quiz night is Wednesday – with complementary curry. Live music plays on Saturday evening. ⛼Q❀⇋◐◑⇌🚌(313)P⅟—

Swan with Two Necks ★

36 Princes Street, SK1 1RY
⏲ 11-11; 12-6 Sun ☎ (0161) 480 2341
Robinson's Hatters, Dark Hatters, Unicorn Ⓗ**, Old Tom** Ⓖ**, seasonal beers** Ⓗ
Narrow-fronted with a mock-Tudor facade, the building was bought by Robinson's in 1924. Rejuventated of late by a young couple with ideas and vigour, it is impressively panelled in light oak throughout in familiar Robinson's style, with labelled doors to match. The front door leads to a vault, then the bustling bar-corridor, then a cosy snug with an attractive skylight, and at the rear a small lounge and diner. Outside is a compact, walled drinking area. Quality lunchtime meals are served daily. ❀◐⊟🚌(300,330)

Strines

Sportsman's Arms

105 Strines Road, SK6 7GE (on B6101)
⏲ 12-3, 5-11; 12-11 Sat & Sun ☎ (0161) 427 2888
🌐 the-sportsman-pub.co.uk
Beer range varies Ⓗ
Standing on the edge of the Goyt Valley with a great picture window giving views over the wooded countryside, a monumental fireplace accommodates log fires in winter and there is a small separate tap room. Five ever-changing guest beers, mainly from micros, are available and the landlord welcomes beer suggestions. Outside, a terrace and balcony are popular in summer and the pub is close to the Peak Forest Canal.
⛼Q❀◐◑⊟♿⛺⇌🚌(358)♣P⅟—

Tyldesley

Half Moon

115-117 Elliot Street, M29 8FL
⊙ 11-4, 7-midnight; 12-midnight Sat; 12-11 Sun
☎ (01942) 883481
Holt Bitter; guest beers Ⓗ
Well-kept town-centre two-room local popular with a clientele of all ages. The main lounge has various seating and standing areas, while the second lounge is comfortable and ideal for get-togethers. In summer the patio is a good place to take in the views of Winter Hill. ❀♣⌐

Mort Arms

235-237 Elliot Street, M29 8DG
⊙ 12-midnight (1am Fri & Sat); 12-11 Sun ☎ (01942) 883481
Holt Mild, Bitter Ⓗ
This 1930s pub has changed little over the years. From the facade to the interior it is recognisable as a Holt's hostelry. The entrance has two etched doors directing you into the tap room or lounge, with a central bar serving both rooms. The tap room is a bright contrast and just how a tap room should be. At the rear is a secluded patio area. ⊟♣

Uppermill

Cross Keys

Off Running Hill Gate, OL3 6LW (off A670, up Church Rd)
⊙ 12-11.30 (midnight Fri & Sat) ☎ (01457) 874626
Lees Brewer's Dark, Bitter, Coronation Street, seasonal beers Ⓗ
Overlooking Saddleworth Church, this attractive 18th-century stone building has exposed beams throughout. The public bar features a stone-flagged floor and Yorkshire range. The pub is the centre for many activities including mountain rescue and the Saddleworth Runners. It is especially busy during annual events such as the Rushcart Festival and the Road & Fell Race in August. A folk night is hosted on Wednesday. Home-cooked food features puddings, pies and real chips. Dogs are welcome. ⩕Q☪❀◐◑⊟♣P⌐

Urmston

Steamhouse

Station Approach, Station Road, M41 9SB SJ 766946
⊙ 12-11 (midnight Fri-Sun) ☎ (0161) 748 6487
⊕ thesteamhouse.co.uk
Beer range varies Ⓗ
Urmston station's old waiting room, this multi-roomed pub retains a number of the original features. The station itself is still operational, so getting to and from here is easy. The Sunday carvery (1-6pm) is very busy, to the point where advance booking is required. Cask ales change regularly and there is also an excellent choice of continental bottled beers. Live music is hosted on Thursday and Sunday, a quiz night on Monday and poker on Tuesday. ⩕Q❀◐◑♿⇌⊟♣●P⌐

Wardley

Morning Star

520 Manchester Road, M27 9QW (on A6 between Swinton and Walken)
⊙ 12-midnight (11 Sun) ☎ (0161) 794 4927
Holt Mild, Bitter, seasonal beers Ⓗ
Situated on the edge of Swinton, this is a good example of a community pub, with an active social club and darts and dominoes teams. As you enter, to the left is the vault, to the right is a small alcove lounge leading through to a large main lounge. Quiz night is Tuesday or Wednesday depending on football on TV. Musical entertainment is provided at weekends. The outdoor smoking area is covered and heated. ❀⊟⇌(Moorside)⊟(36,37)♣P⌐

Whalley Range

Hillary Step ✔

199 Upper Chorlton Road, M16 0BH SJ821950
⊙ 4-midnight (12.30am Fri); 12-1am Sat; 12-midnight Sun
☎ (0161) 881 1978
Beer range varies Ⓗ
Opened in 2004, the pub name refers to a plateau on Mount Everest. Thwaites provides the house beer, with four guests mostly from local micro-breweries. Draught and bottled continental beers are also served. No meals are available, although a large range of snacks is on offer. Events include live jazz on Sunday and quiz night the first Tuesday of the month. No TV or slot machines. Children are not permitted. Q❀⊟

Whitefield

Eagle & Child

Higher Lane, M45 7EY (on A665, 300m from A56)
⊙ 12-11 (midnight Fri & Sat)
Holt Mild, Bitter, seasonal beers Ⓗ
Detached, imposing double-fronted pub with a floodlit bowling green and patio at the rear. Set back from the road, the existing pub dates from 1936 although the site has been used since the 1800s. This large building has a spacious lounge and public bar, both served by a central bar. A smaller room is ideal for meetings or private parties. The bowling green at the rear is superbly maintained and well used by the pub's 11 teams. There is a covered patio for smokers.
❀⊟⊖(Besses o' th' Barn)⊟(98,135)♣P⌐

Wigan

Anvil ✔

Dorning Street, WN1 1ND (next to bus station)
⊙ 11-11; 12-10.30 Sun ☎ (01942) 239444
Beer range varies Ⓗ
Popular town-centre pub, a frequent winner of local CAMRA awards – note the array of certificates adorning the 'Wall of Fame'. Six handpumps offer beers from the nearby AllGates Brewery plus guests, and six draught continental ales and a range of bottled beers are also on offer. The pub can be busy on match days as it close to the JJB Stadium, home to Wigan Athletic and Wigan Warriors. Outside is a heated smoking terrace. LocAle accredited. ❀⇌(Wallgate/N.Western)⊟⌐

Berkeley ✔

27-29 Wallgate, WN1 1LD (opp Wallgate station)
⊙ 12-11 (midnight Fri & Sat); 12-10.30 Sun
☎ (01942) 242041 ⊕ berkeleybar.co.uk
Beer range varies Ⓗ
The Berkeley, a former coaching house, has a friendly, comfortable atmosphere, offering something for everyone. Regular sporting fixtures are shown on large-screen TVs in the open-plan bar. The pub's clever design means that the comfortable, split-level areas give the impression of distinct seating sections. Food is served daily

until 7pm. A first-floor function room is available for hire. There is a dress code on Saturday night. Three beers are on offer, at least one from the Prospect Brewery. LocAle accredited.
◑⇌(Wallgate/North Western)🚌

Boulevard

Wallgate, WN1 1LD (near Wallgate station)
⊙ 2-2am (2.30am Fri & Sat); 2-midnight Sun
☎ (01942) 497165
Beer range varies ⊞
This is a surprisingly spacious basement pub. From the bar you enter a large back room where regular entertainment is hosted including live music on Friday and Saturday. Open until very late, it is close to Wallgate and North Western train stations. Beers from Prospect and Allgates are usually among the range, and a cider can often be found on one of the handpumps. LocAle accredited.
⇌(Wallgate/North Western)🚌

Brocket Arms ✔

Mesnes Road, Swinley, WN1 2DD
⊙ 7am-midnight (1am Fri); 8am-1am Sat; 8am-midnight Sun
☎ (01942) 403500
Greene King Ruddles County, Abbot; Marston's Pedigree; guest beers ⊞
The Brocket Arms was built by brewer Peter Walker, and opened by Lord Brocket on 10 October 1957. Now a Wetherlodge, the open-plan interior is spacious, light and airy, with intimate booths and flexible seating to accommodate groups of all sizes. Two conference rooms are available for hire and a patio area to the front caters for smokers. Guest beers from local micro-breweries often feature. Regular comedy nights are hosted. LocAle accredited. ❀◑♿🚌P⊱

Crooke Hall Inn

Crooke Road, Standish Lower Ground, WN6 8LR (signed off B5375)
⊙ 12-midnight ☎ (01942) 247524
Beer range varies ⊞
Multi-roomed pub owned by Allgates Brewery featuring beers from the brewery and guests. Situated in an attractive village overlooking the Leeds-Liverpool canal to the rear and close by Crooke Marina, it attracts walkers and canal traffic all year round. Outside is a beer garden and children's play area overlooking the canal. Food is available until 8pm seven days a week, with children welcome until 9pm. There is a pool table and screens for sport. ❀◑⊟♣⊱

Moon Under Water ✔

5-7a Market Place, WN1 1PE
⊙ 9am-midnight (1am Fri & Sat) ☎ (01942) 323437
Greene King Ruddles Bitter, Abbot; Marston's Pedigree; guest beers ⊞
The former Halifax Building Society was converted into Wigan's first and largest Wetherspoon's, accessible from the Market Place and from the Wiend (Wigan's historic shopping street). Local beers are regularly available alongside the standard Wetherspoon offerings. Located in the town centre, the pub gets very busy at weekends and on match days for football and rugby.
Q◑♿⇌🚌●

Royal Oak

Standishgate, WN1 1XL (on A49 N of town centre)
⊙ 4-midnight; 12-1am Fri & Sat; 12-midnight Sun
☎ (01942) 323137 ⊕ royaloakwigan.co.uk
Beer range varies ⊞
The Royal Oak was built in the early 17th century and is now a listed building. It has always been a landmark pub on the town circuit due to its location on the A49 and close to Wigan centre. The multi-room interior is served by a long bar stocking foreign draught and bottled beers. The pub is the tap for Mayflower Brewery and hosts live music, beer and food festivals. It has a pleasant beer garden ideal for summer barbecues. LocAle accredited. ❀♿⊱

Woodford

Davenport Arms (Thief's Neck)

550 Chester Road, SK7 1PS (on A5102, jct Church Lane)
⊙ 11-11; 12-10.30 Sun ☎ (0161) 439 2435
Robinson's Hatters, Dark Hatters, Unicorn, Old Tom, seasonal beers ⊞
Unspoilt, red-brick farmhouse-style pub where the licence has been in the same family for more than 75 years. The cosy rooms are warmed by real fires, and children are welcome at lunchtimes in the right-hand snug. Excellent food is mostly home-made, with some adventurous specials. Outside, the spacious forecourt and attractive garden, set well away from the road, are popular in summer, when impressive floral displays are on show.
⩩Q⛄❀◑⊟🚌(X57)♣P⊱

Worsley

Bridgewater Hotel ✔

23 Barton Road, M28 2PD (on B5211 200m S of M60 jct 13)
⊙ 10-11 ☎ (0161) 794 6206
Boddington's Bitter; Wells Bombardier; guest beers ⊞
After many identity crises and mixed fortunes, this pub has now settled as a comfortable, family-friendly hostelry offering a good and varied selection of cask ales. A massive pub situated near the origins of the canal age, it is unchanged on the outside but much altered inside. The two-level interior is divided into eight distinct drinking and dining areas with carpeted upper floors and a mix of tiles and shiny boards around the bar. The emphasis is on food, with a specials board and a separate carvery. ⩩Q❀◑♿P⊱

Worthington

Crown Hotel 🏆 ✔

Platt Lane, WN1 2XF
⊙ 12-11 (10.30 Sun) ☎ (08000) 686678
⊕ thecrownatworthington.co.uk
Prospect Silver Tally; guest beers ⊞
Regional Pub of the Year and National Pub of the Year runner-up in 2009, this country inn offers 10 cask beers and is the tap for Prospect Brewery. High quality, home-cooked food is served in the bar and conservatory restaurant, while a decked sun terrace at the rear has patio heaters. Regular themed evenings and mini-beer festivals are hosted. There are 10 en-suite rooms. LocAle accredited. ❀🛏◑🚌P⊱

There can't be a good living where there is not good drinking. **Benjamin Franklin**

MERSEYSIDE

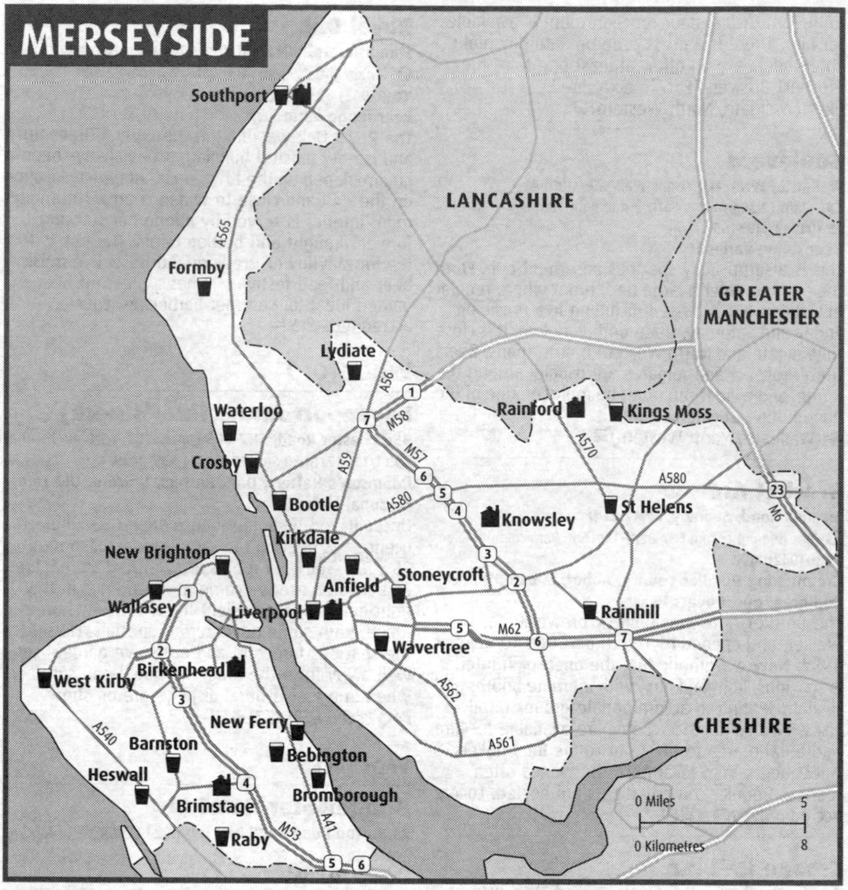

Barnston

Fox & Hounds ✓

107 Barnston Road, Wirral, CH61 1BW (on A551)

11-11; 12-10.30 Sun ☎ (0151) 648 7685

the-fox-hounds.co.uk

Brimstage Trappers Hat; Theakston Best Bitter, Old Peculier; guest beers Ⓗ

Village pub with bar, lounge and snug full of bric-a-brac, clocks, flying ducks, horse brasses, local photos and other memorabilia. The lounge, converted from tea rooms, is quiet with no music or games machines. The pub retains its original character including real fires in the bar and snug. The stone courtyard is a profusion of colour in the summer. Popular for its cask ales and real lunchtime food, it offers a fish dish of the day, daily specials and traditional Sunday roasts. CAMRA Wirral Pub of the Year 2008.
♨Q⛺❀◐⊟♿≠🚌♣P⁻

Bebington

Traveller's Rest

169 Mount Road, CH63 8PJ

12-11 (10.30 Sun) ☎ (0151) 608 2988

Black Sheep Best Bitter; Flowers IPA; Greene King Abbot; Taylor Landlord; Wells Bombardier; guest beers Ⓗ

Reputedly over 300 years old, this cosy pub is decorated throughout with brasses and bric-a-brac. A previous Wirral CAMRA Pub of the Year, all beers are served from a central bar, the guest ales often from local micro-breweries. At lunchtime the emphasis is on serving award-winning food (no food Sun), but in the evening this is very much a traditional pub. ♨Q◐♿🚌

Bromborough

Knockaloe Bar & Restaurant

28 Bridle Road, CH62 6AR

12-11 (midnight Fri & Sat) ☎ (0151) 328 5690

Brimstage Trappers Hat; Tetley Bitter; guest beer Ⓗ

Formerly the Associated Octel Social Club, the 'OC' is now a pub open to all. The club has undergone a tasteful refurbishment attracting a wide variety of

INDEPENDENT BREWERIES

Brimstage Brimstage
Cains Liverpool
Cambrinus Knowsley
George Wright Rainford
Liverpool One Liverpool (NEW)
Liverpool Organic Liverpool (NEW)
Peerless Birkenhead
Southport Southport
Wapping Liverpool

drinkers. There are extensive sports facilities, function and meeting rooms, plus a patio area. A well-attended quiz night is hosted. Local beers from Brimstage are popular – the brewery usually supplies the guest ale. Children are welcome until 9.30pm. Food is available throughout the day until 9pm (7pm Sun). ❀◐♿⇌🚌P

Formby

Freshfield Hotel ✔

1a Massams Lane, Freshfield, L37 7BD
☉ 12-11 (midnight Fri & Sat) ☎ (01704) 874871
Greene King IPA, Morland Original, Ruddles County, Abbot; Titanic Freshie Mild, Freshie Bitter Ⓗ
Less than five-minutes walk from the train station and 15 minutes from the famous red squirrel reserve and beach, this pub features stone and wooden floors along with a real fire and great character. It offers up to 12 beers plus a cider – six from the Greene King range and six guests mainly from micros. A function room at the rear hosts a comedy club and live music events. Food is served 12-9 daily. ⌂Q❀◐♿⇌🚌(162,165)♣●P⁼

Heswall

Dee View Inn

Dee View Road, CH60 0DH
☉ 12-midnight (11 Sun) ☎ (0151) 342 2320
Black Sheep Best Bitter; Caledonian Deuchars IPA; Taylor Landlord; Tetley Bitter; Wells Bombardier; guest beer Ⓗ
Homely, traditional local built in the late 1800s offering a warm welcome. Redecorated in 2008, it has retained its character and friendly atmosphere. It sits on a hairpin bend by the war memorial and famous mirror, with views over the Dee Estuary and close to the Wirral Way path. A popular and entertaining quiz night is held on Tuesday. Traditional home-cooked food is served and children are welcome if dining. ❀◐🚌♣P⁼

Johnny Pye

Pye Road, CH60 0DB (next to bus station)
☉ 11-11 (11.30 Thu; midnight Fri & Sat); 12-11 Sun
☎ (0151) 342 8215
Banks's Bitter; Marston's Burton Bitter; guest beers Ⓗ
Situated on the site of an old bus depot, this lively, modern pub is named after a local entrepreneur. Johnny Pye is associated with some other buildings nearby, and was responsible for starting the local bus service. A signed caricature of England's 1966 World Cup winning goalie, Gordon Banks, adorns the bar. The pub has wide-screen TVs, a strong football following and ladies and gents darts teams. Children are welcome on the patio area. ❀◐♿🚌♣P⁼

Kings Moss

Colliers Arms

Pimbo Road, WA11 8RD (follow signs to Houghwood Golf Club)
☉ 12-11 (10.30 Sun) ☎ (01744) 892894
🌐 theredcatcrank.co.uk/colliersarms.html
Black Sheep Best Bitter; guest beers Ⓗ
Situated in Kings Moss at the foot of Billinge Hill, with the austere sounding Hangman's Wood on the hill above. The pub is part of a row of miners' cottages next to the former site of the Hillside colliery. Unsurprisingly, there is mining memorabilia on display plus a selection of books to accompany a relaxing visit. A central bar serves four distinct areas. Outside, a small enclosed children's play area is accessed through premises to the rear. ⌂Q❀◐⊟🚌(152,356)P

Liverpool: Anfield

Strawberry Tavern

Breckfield Road South, L6 5DR (off Asda car park)
☉ 12-midnight (1am Fri & Sat) ☎ (0151) 261 9364
Oakwell Old Tom Mild, Barnsley Bitter Ⓗ
Situated at the corner of an Asda car park off Breck Road close to the old Ogden's tobacco factory, this large pub is the nearest real ale outlet for thirsty fans visiting Liverpool Football Club and very convenient for parking. Usefully, it may open early on match days with a lunchtime kick-off. The interior is divided to create a separate games area with a pool table and dartboard. ❀♿🚌(14)♣P

Liverpool: Bootle

Merton Inn ✔

42 Merton Road, L20 3BW
☉ 7am-1am (2am Thu-Sat) ☎ (0151) 934 7790
Greene King Ruddles Best Bitter, Abbot; guest beers Ⓗ
This spacious multi-level pub opened as a Wetherspoon's outlet in 2009. The walls are covered with panels illustrating and describing the local area and its history – several abstract paintings have been specially commissioned for the pub depicting the local landscape. Seating consists of a combination of bar stools, dining chairs, sofas and armchairs, catering for both diners and drinkers. The large single bar has up to 10 handpumps, often featuring ales from local and micro-breweries. ◐⇌(Oriel Road/New Strand)🚌

Wild Rose ✔

2a & 1b The Triad Centre, L20 3ET
☉ 7am-midnight (1am Fri & Sat) ☎ (0151) 922 0828
Greene King Ruddles Best Bitter, Abbot; guest beers Ⓗ
This Wetherspoon pub is situated at the base of the Triad tower block – a 240-foot structure that dominates the area. The open-plan layout is broken up by two large columns, with wheelchair access throughout. Recently refurbished, it features plenty of wood panelling, including the bar itself. Local photographs adorn the walls. Up to eight handpumps dispense an ever-changing selection of beers. ◐♿⊖🚌

Liverpool: City Centre

Augustus John

Peach Street, L3 5TX (off Brownlow Hill next to Blackwell's bookshop)
☉ 11-11 (11.30 Thu; midnight Fri); 12-midnight Sat; closed Sun ☎ (0151) 794 5507 🌐 liv.ac.uk/educatering/augustus_john.htm
Greene King Abbot; Tetley Bitter; guest beers Ⓗ
This '60s-style open-plan pub run by the University of Liverpool can be very busy, with an eclectic mix of students, lecturers and locals. Augustus John, the artist, was himself a lecturer at the University in 1901 and the pub was opened by his son. Up to three guest beers are available. Ask for real cider which is kept in a cooler. There is an annual beer festival. Sport is shown on a multitude of TV

screens and there is a juke-box. Closed over Christmas and New Year.
❀♿⇌(Lime St)⊖(Central)🚌(78,79)🍎⚐

Baltic Fleet

33 Wapping, L1 8DQ
⏲ 12-11 (11.30 Fri & Sat) ☎ (0151) 709 3116
🌐 wappingbeers.co.uk
Wapping Bitter, Baltic Gold, Summer, Stout, seasonal beers; guest beers Ⓗ
Conveniently located near the Albert Dock and Liverpool One, Liverpool's only brew-pub is based on a flat-iron shape resembling the bow of a ship. It is named after a 19th-century timber-importing fleet and the decor reflects this with displays of nautical memorabilia. Tunnels reaching out under the building add to the intrigue, but links to smuggling and press gangs are probably anecdotal. Good value hot and cold food is available, including daily lunches and evening meals Wednesday to Saturday. Q◐◑⊖(James St)🚌(500)🍎⊓

Belvedere ✔

8 Sugnall Street, L7 7EB (off Falkner Street)
⏲ 12-11 (midnight Fri & Sat); 12-10.30 Sun
☎ (0151) 709 0303
Beer range varies Ⓗ
A few years ago permission was granted to convert this 1830s listed building into a house, but fortunately it has now reopened as a pub. Many of the original fixtures and fittings feature in the two small rooms, including some interesting glasswork. Although it is close to the city centre, it is very much a community pub – proximity to the Philharmonic Hall has made it a popular watering hole for members of the orchestra. The missing back bar has recently been rediscovered.
♨Q❀◐◑⊟🚌

Cracke

13 Rice Street, L1 9BB (off Hope St near Philharmonic Hall)
⏲ 12-11.30 (12.30am Fri & Sat); 12-11 Sun
☎ (0151) 709 4171
Cains Bitter; Thwaites Original; Wem Cherry Bomb; guest beers Ⓗ
The door to the bar – the original part of the pub – is once again marked Houlding's, the brewery from Everton that was taken over by Ind Coope in 1938. Now part of an independent group of three local pubs, all the real ales are directly delivered. Outside, there is a small seating area for drinkers. It is reported that John Lennon was a regular here when he was studying at art school.
❀◐⊟⇌(Lime St)⊖(Central)🚌(86)🍎

Dispensary 🏆

87 Renshaw Street, L1 2SP
⏲ 12-11 (midnight Fri & Sat) ☎ (0151) 709 2180
Cains IPA, Bitter, FA, seasonal beers; guest beers Ⓗ
The Dispensary has a welcoming atmosphere and great beer quality. Bought by Robert Cain in 1998, it gained the CAMRA/English Heritage Refurbishment award and was Merseyside Pub of the Year in 1999. It serves Cains ales together with a varied selection of four or five guests. Dark lovers will usually find a stout or porter on offer. Beer festivals are a recent addition, with 10 handpulls devoted to guest beers. A Pub of Excellence award in 2009 recognises the sustained beer quality.
♿⇌(Lime St)⊖(Central)🚌🍎

Doctor Duncan's

St John's House, St John's Lane, L1 1HF (opp St George's Gardens)
⏲ 10-11 (midnight Fri & Sat); 10-10.30 Sun
☎ (0151) 709 5100
Cains IPA, Bitter, FA, seasonal beers; guest beers Ⓗ
This flagship Cains pub is named after Doctor Duncan, a campaigner against poor living conditions in Liverpool during the Victorian era. Medical history memorabilia features throughout, including, near the entrance, a pharmacy cabinet displaying various old-fashioned preparations and surgical instruments. The pub serves the full range of Cains beers and up to two guests. It has four distinct rooms including a magnificent tiled room with mosaic floor and fireplace. There is also a covered beer garden.
♨❀◐♿⇌(Lime St)⊖(Lime St)🚌⚐

Everyman Bistro ✔

5-9 Hope Street, L1 9BH (beneath Everyman Theatre)
⏲ 12-midnight (2am Fri & Sat); closed Sun
☎ (0151) 708 9545 🌐 everyman.co.uk
Cains Bitter; Caledonian Deuchars IPA; guest beers Ⓗ
The Everyman Bistro is as much a Liverpool institution as the adjoining theatre. Much thought is given to the award-winning home-produced food, and equally the ale range which concentrates on Yorkshire and north west beers, with regulars from York, Derwent, George Wright, Liverpool Organic and Brimstage. The bar can be busy in the early evening before a performance, attracting an eclectic mix of students, professors, media types and locals. Q◐◑⇌(Lime St)⊖(Central)🚌🍎

Fly in the Loaf ✔

13 Hardman Street, L1 9AS
⏲ 11-11 (midnight Fri & Sat) ☎ (0151) 708 0817
Okells Bitter, seasonal beers; guest beers Ⓗ
The second Manx Cat inn to be opened on the mainland by the Isle of Man brewer Okells. The previous Kirkland's bakery – slogan: 'no flies in the loaf' – was refurbished in 2004. There are usually up to seven guests from micro-breweries alongside the Okells range, and a good selection of foreign bottled beers. It's very popular on weekends and evenings, and when Sky Sports screens sports fixtures. There is an upstairs function room with handpumps. A new food menu has recently been introduced. ◐◑♿⇌(Lime St)⊖(Central)🚌

Globe

17 Cases Street, L1 1HW (opp Liverpool Central Station)
⏲ 11 (10 Sat)-11; 12-10.30 Sun ☎ (0151) 707 0067
Black Sheep Best Bitter; Cains Bitter; Caledonian Deuchars IPA; guest beers Ⓗ
Small traditional two-roomed local in the city centre, handy for the main shopping area and railway stations. A lively pub, it is popular with both regulars and visitors to the area. Drinkers need to be aware of an unusual sloping floor which leads you through to the quiet back room, where the inaugural meeting of the Merseyside branch of CAMRA, held here in 1974, is commemorated with a brass plaque. ⇌(Lime St)⊖(Central)🚌

Hole in Ye Wall

4 Hackins Hey, L2 2AW
⏲ 11-11; 12-10.30 Sun ☎ (0151) 227 3809
George Wright Drunken Duck, Longboat; Tetley Bitter; guest beers Ⓗ
Allegedly Liverpool's oldest public house, dating back to the start of the city's maritime heyday in

1726. The cellar is not downstairs but on the first floor because the pub was constructed over an ancient Quaker burial site that it was thought irreverent to disturb. More recently, in 1977, the Hole became the last pub in Liverpool to allow entry to women. The pub boasts oak-panelled walls and various pictures of old Liverpool scenes. ⊖(Moorfields)

James Monro

69 Tithebarn Street, L2 2EN

12-11 (1am Fri & Sat); 12-9 Sun ☎ (0151) 236 9700

themonro.com

Beer range varies H

Once a Burtonwood house known as the Brunswick, and under the same ownership as its namesake in Duke Street, the James Monro styles itself as a gastro-pub, with candles on the tables. It serves a range of real ales to accompany British and international cuisine, featuring local produce. This is an ideal location for those who wish to enjoy good beer with fine food. Guest beers come from all over the country – you are welcome to try before you buy. ⊖(Moorfields)

Lady of Mann

19 Dale Street, L2 2EZ

11.30-11; 12-10.30 Sun ☎ (0151) 236 5556

Okells Bitter; guest beers H

Formerly the Courtyard Restaurant, the Lady adjoins Thomas Rigby's and they share a large outside drinking area. The pub, named after the eponymous Manx ferry, and owned, like Rigby's, by Okells, is essentially open plan with a single bar located in a separate drinking area approached from the Courtyard via a flight of steps. There is occasional live music and snacks are served at all times. The large rear room can be booked for events. ⇌⊖(Moorfields)

Lion Tavern ☆

67 Moorfields, L2 2BP

11-11; 12-10.30 Sun ☎ (0151) 236 1734

Caledonian Deuchars IPA; Lees Bitter; Young's Bitter; guest beers H

The Grade II-listed Lion is named after the locomotive that worked the Liverpool to Manchester railway. In 1915, the original building was amalgamated with the adjoining licensed premises, creating the existing layout. The interior features exquisite tile work, etched and stained glass, carefully restored wood panelling and an ornate glass dome in one of the two lounges. The pub attracts a mixed clientele, including office staff and journalists. Bar food is available, with hand-made pork pies particularly recommended. ⇌(Lime St)⊖(Moorfields)

Peter Kavanagh's ★

2-6 Egerton Street, L8 7LY (off Catharine St)

12-midnight (1am Fri & Sat) ☎ (0151) 709 3443

Greene King Abbot; guest beers H

Situated in an area once occupied by rich merchants, this splendid back-street local is a gem and features in CAMRA's National Inventory of Historic Pub Interiors. It boasts stained glass windows with wooden shutters, and two snugs with wooden benches – note the carved arm rests, allegedly caricatures of the politically incorrect Peter Kavanagh. There are also murals by Eric Robinson, which are thought to have been commissioned to cover a debt. Up to four rotating guest beers are offered. Q(86)

Philharmonic ★ ✔

36 Hope Street, L1 9BX

10-midnight ☎ (0151) 707 2837

Caledonian Deuchars IPA; Jennings Cumberland Ale; guest beers H

Featuring in CAMRA's National Inventory of Historic Pub Interiors, this magnificent Grade II-listed building was described by historic pub expert Geoff Brandwood as the finest of its kind. Opposite the Philharmonic Hall, the interior is divided into several discrete and highly ornate drinking areas, notably the splendidly refurbished Grand Lounge. There is an upstairs restaurant where food is served until 10pm. While ladies are invited to visit the amazingly ornate gentlemen's toilet, it is polite to check before doing so.
Q♿⇌(Lime St)⊖(Central)(86)

Pilgrim

34 Pilgrim Street, L1 9HB

10-11 ☎ (0151) 709 2302 thepilgrimpub.co.uk

Beer range varies H

This friendly, long-roomed cellar bar, with booth style seating, is popular with students. The juke-box plays a wide selection of albums from reggae to rock, and Beatles murals adorn the walls. A wrought-iron spiral staircase leads up to the function room. Entry is via a covered courtyard where tables and benches provide an outside drinking area. Up to four handpumps serve a selection of regional and national beers.
⇌(Lime Street)⊖(Central)

Richard John Blackler ✔

1-2 Charlotte Row, L1 1HU

7am-midnight (1am Fri & Sat) ☎ (0151) 709 4802

Greene King Ruddles Best Bitter, Abbot; guest beers H

This recently-refurbished Wetherspoon pub is the ground floor of the former Blackler's department store. Close to Lime Street station, the Queen Square bus station and St John's precinct shopping mall, it is always busy – a good place to take a break before, during or after shopping in the city centre. Two bookshelves to the rear provide copious reading material to enjoy while relaxing over a pint. ♿⇌(Lime St)⊖(Central)

Richmond Hotel

32 Williamson Street, L1 1EB (in pedestrian precinct, off Williamson Square)

10-11; 11-midnight Fri-Sun ☎ (0151) 709 2614

Draught Bass; Southport Golden Sands; Taylor Landlord; guest beers H

Lively family-run corner house in the pedestrianised shopping area of the city centre. It offers up to three guest ales from local breweries and is a rare outlet for Southport Brewery beers. Formerly a Bass house, the original Bass mirror remains. More than 50 malt whiskies are usually available, and satellite TV shows sports fixtures. The pub sign, simply saying 'Richmond Pub', depicts WWII veteran Paddy Golden, a much-missed regular and one of the first to land on the Normandy beaches.
♿⇌(Lime St)⊖(Central)

Roscoe Head

24 Roscoe Street, L1 2SX

11.30-11 (midnight Fri & Sat); 12-11 Sun

☎ (0151) 709 4365

Jennings Bitter; Marston's Burton Bitter; Tetley Mild, Bitter; guest beers H

Welcoming side-street local where conversation is king. One of the few pubs to appear in every edition of the Guide, this traditional hostelry has been run by the same family for more than 20 years. The interior retains the original small rooms and snugs, with a sensitive redecoration. Guest beers may come from micros. Quiz night is Tuesday and cribbage night Wednesday. Children are welcome until 6pm.
⛰Q♂◐🛏≋(Central)⊖(Lime St)🚌(86)♣

Ship & Mitre

133 Dale Street, L2 2JH (by Birkenhead tunnel entrance)
✪ 11-11 (midnight Thu-Sat) ☎ (0151) 236 0859
🌐 theshipandmitre.com
Beer range varies Ⓗ
The Ship, as it is known locally, has an impressive Art Deco exterior retaining some original features in the upstairs room. Inside is equally impressive, with a bar boasting 13 handpulls dispensing real ale at all times, and a similar number of fonts for foreign brews, plus a large selection of German and Belgian bottled beers. Quality fresh food is also available. Nearby are some of Liverpool's more famous landmarks, including St George's Hall.
Q◐◑♿≋(Lime St)⊖(Moorfields)🚌♣🍎P

Swan Inn

86 Wood Street, L1 4DQ
✪ 12-11 (2am Thu-Sat); 12-10.30 Sun ☎ (0151) 709 5281
🌐 myspace.com/swaninn
Hydes Original; Phoenix Wobbly Bob; guest beers Ⓗ
With its distinctive blue-tiled facade and stained glass windows, the Swan has changed little over the years. A rockers' pub, it is famous for its rock juke-box. Seating is a combination of wooden pews and traditional bar stools, and the walls are adorned with an eclectic mix of posters, swan-themed paintings and drawings. Eight handpumps serve a selection of beers from both national and micro-brewers, and Westons Old Rosie Scrumpy.
♿≋(Lime St)⊖(Central)🚌🍎

Thomas Rigby's

23-25 Dale Street, L2 2EZ
✪ 11.30-11 (10.30 Sun) ☎ (0151) 236 3269
Okells Bitter, Dr Okells IPA, seasonal beers; guest beers Ⓗ
This multi-roomed Grade II-listed building, bearing the name of wine and spirit dealer Thomas Rigby, now supplies an extensive world beer range on draught and in bottles, with at least four regularly-changing guest ales. Good-value food is served daily until early evening, including specials, with one room offering a friendly and efficient table service. The outdoor courtyard is shared with the Lady of Mann. ❀◐◑🛏≋⊖(Moorfields)

Vernon Arms

69 Dale Street, L2 2HJ
✪ 11.45-11.30 (12.30am Fri & Sat); 12-11 Sun
☎ (0151) 236 6132 🌐 vernonarms.co.uk
Boggart Rum Porter; Brains The Rev James; guest beers Ⓗ
A welcome return to the Guide for a pub that has the friendly feel of a street-corner local despite its city-centre location, with patrons from all walks of life, from students to office workers. The Vernon reopened in 2009 after being closed down and badly neglected for around four and a half years. Thanks to the present licensee it is once again thriving and an essential port of call on the Dale Street area pub circuit. ◐◑⊖(Moorfields)

White Star

2-4 Rainford Gardens, L2 6PT
✪ 11.30-11; 12-10.30 Sun ☎ (0151) 231 6861
🌐 thewhitestar.co.uk
Caledonian Deuchars IPA; Draught Bass Ⓗ
A rare traditional Victorian two-roomed public house located among the glitzy and often noisy establishments of the historic Mathew Street area. The White Star is packed with fascinating local memorabilia and pictures of White Star liners as well as an abundance of boxing photography. Live football matches are screened. The pub is twinned with bars in the Czech Republic and Norway. A range of beers from the Bowland brewery are regularly available.
◐🛏≋(Lime St)⊖(Central/Moorfields)⛳

Liverpool: Crosby

Stamps Bar

4 Crown Buildings, Crosby, L23 5SR (centre of Crosby village, just off A565)
✪ 12-11 (midnight Fri & Sat) ☎ (0151) 286 2662
🌐 stampsbar.co.uk
Beer range varies Ⓗ
This cosy two-floor bar is situated in what was once the local post office, hence the name. The tasteful conversion features wooden floors and plain brick walls covered with paintings and prints. Six handpumps serve an ever-changing selection of beers from local and micro-breweries, and good food is available. A renowned live music venue, there is live entertainment most evenings. The pub provides free Wi-Fi internet access and newspapers. ◐◑♿≋(Blundellsands & Crosby)🚌🍎P

Liverpool: Kirkdale

Thomas Frost ✔

177-187 Walton Road, Kirkdale, L4 4AJ
✪ 7-11.30 ☎ (0151) 207 8210
Beer range varies Ⓗ
The open-plan layout of this former drapery store gives a light and airy feel to the pleasant venue. This branch generally has a greater number of beers on offer than many other Wetherspoon outlets. Note that at busy times the well-trained regulars will form a queue at the bar – you should join it! The pub has a family area, but children are not allowed on match days due to the proximity of Goodison Park and Anfield grounds.
♂◐◑♿🚌(20)⛳

Liverpool: Stoneycroft

Navigator ✔

694 Queens Drive, L13 5UH
✪ 7-11.30 ☎ (0151) 220 2713
George Wright Dream; guest beers Ⓗ
This branch of Wetherspoon's, named after St Brendan – the patron saint of navigators who is reputed to have discovered America – occupies a former showroom. A welcome oasis on the edge of a busy shopping area, it has an open-plan layout punctuated with alcoves along one side. A raised area is set aside for families, with children welcome until 9pm if dining. George Wright beers appear regularly and the pub participates enthusiastically in Wetherpoon's national beer festivals. ♂❀◐◑♿🚌(10,61,81)⛳

ENGLAND

Liverpool: Waterloo

Stamps Too
99 South Road, L22 0LR (opp Waterloo Station)
12-11 (midnight Fri & Sat); 12-11.30 Sun
(0151) 280 0035
Beer range varies; H
This friendly, continental-style bar became the local CAMRA branch's first LocAle pub in 2009. Up to six handpumps serve national, regional and local beers including ales from Liverpool Organic and Southport breweries. With café-style seating at the front, this one-room bar is a popular live music and comedy venue. Lively banter can often be heard at the bar. The walls are adorned with pump clips from beers that have come and gone.
❀◑♿⇌🚌(53)⚽

Volunteer Canteen ★
45 East Street, L22 8QR
12-11 (10.30 Sun) (0151) 928 4676
Black Sheep Best Bitter; Caledonian Deuchars IPA; Tetley Bitter; guest beers H
The 'Volly' is a fine example of a traditional community local in a residential side street. The building dates from 1827 and has been a public house since 1871. It is a good place to go for a pint in a warm convivial atmosphere with no irritating intrusions from juke-box or large-screen TV. Table service is available in the wood-panelled lounge. Note the old Higson's Brewery mirror, etched windows and other Higson's external decorations.
Q❀⊟⇌🚌(53)

Liverpool: Wavertree

Edinburgh
4 Sandown Lane, L15 8HY
12-midnight (0151) 733 3533
Cains Bitter, FA, seasonal beers; guest beers H
This pub was part of the original Cains tied estate that is now owned by the new company. It was awarded Best Community Pub 2008 by the local CAMRA branch, in recognition of its popularity with locals and its support of charities. Irish music can be heard on Monday nights and there is a quiz on Tuesday. Televised sports are shown. Recently, the guest beer range has expanded to include ales from local micros. ❀🚌♣⚽

Willowbank ✓
329 Smithdown Road, L15 3JA
12-11 (11.30 Wed & Thu; midnight Fri & Sat)
(0151) 733 5782
Greene King Abbot; guest beers H
This Spirit group pub is still signed as a Festival Ale House. It offers up to six guest beers from a variety of breweries and beer festivals are held regularly. The lounge area is used by diners during the day but in the evening it is given over to drinkers, many from the large local student population. Quiz night is Wednesday. Sport is shown on a number of screens including one in the drinking area outside. Food is served lunchtimes and early evenings.
☕❀◑⊟♿🚌(86)♣●P⚽

Lydiate

Scotch Piper ★
Southport Road, L31 4HD (on A5147)
12-midnight (0151) 526 0503 scotchpiper.co.uk
Black Sheep Best Bitter; guest beers H
Centuries-old Grade II-listed thatched inn set back from the road overlooking farmland. The name can be traced back to 1745 when a highland piper, injured in the 1745 Jacobite rebellion, took refuge at the inn. This quiet, cosy pub has a small bar area ideal for reading the papers by a roaring fire in winter. Two cask beers are always available. There is a disabled outdoor toilet but the pub itself is not wheelchair accessible. ♨Q❀🚌(300)♣P

New Brighton

Clarence
89 Albion Street, CH45 9JQ
11.30-11.30 (midnight Fri & Sat) (0151) 639 3860
clarencehotelnewbrighton.co.uk
Weetwood Eastgate Ale; Young's Bitter; guest beer H
A worthwhile 10-minute uphill walk from the centre of New Brighton, this former Whitbread pub has a split-level lounge with a dining/function room, patio and garden. The pub is the last survivor of the original New Brighton real ale festival and celebrates this event every July and October. Local micro-brewers are well supported and there is usually a guest beer. Food is served Wednesday-Sunday lunchtimes and evenings, and home-made pies are available throughout the week. A quiz is hosted on Tuesday and live music on Thursday and Saturday. ☕❀◑⊟♿⇌♣⚽

Magazine Hotel
7 Magazine Brow, CH45 1HP (above Egremont Promenade)
11-11 (midnight Fri & Sat) (0151) 639 3381
Draught Bass; Taylor Landlord; guest beers H
This multi-roomed low-beamed pub of great character, dating from 1759, makes a welcome return to the Guide. Situated above Egremont Promenade, the pub affords fine views of the River Mersey. Three separate rooms lead off the main central bar area. Renowned for many years for its Draught Bass, it also offers three guest ales, always including a local beer from Brimstage, Liverpool Organic or Peerless. Good value lunchtime bar meals are served. Local CAMRA Pub of the Season spring 2010. ♨Q☕❀◐♣⚽

Queen's Royal
Marine Promenade, Wirral, CH45 2JT
10.30-11 (10.30 Sun) (0151) 691 0101
thequeensroyal.com
Brimstage Trappers Hat; guest beers H
An airy, modern bar in an imposing Victorian building overlooking Marine Promenade, Marine Lake and Fort Perch Rock. A strong supporter of local ales and a popular CAMRA meeting venue, it only stocks local beers, with ales from Brimstage and Weetwood among the favourites. The drinking area outside affords superb views over Liverpool Bay. Good value, hearty meals are served in the bar; the adjoining restaurant offers excellent quality food including a popular Sunday carvery.
❀◑⊟♿⇌🚌⚽

Stanley's Cask
212 Rake Lane, Wirral, CH45 1JP
11-11 (midnight Sat) (0151) 691 1093
John Smith's Bitter; guest beers H
This ever-popular local returned to the Guide in 2010 after an absence of 14 years, and continues to thrive, due in no small part to the landlady who has a track record of serving good beer. Up to four guest beers are served, mainly from national and

regional breweries. A traditional, single-roomed community local, it hosts various sports teams, quiz nights and entertainment. ❀🚌(410)♣⅟–

Telegraph Inn ✓

25-27 Mount Pleasant Road, Wirral, CH45 5EW

11.30-11; 12-10.30 Sun ☎ (0151) 639 1508

Wells Bombardier; guest beers 🄷

This traditional, friendly multi-roomed local is believed to be New Brighton's oldest as well as highest pub. It has a conservatory extension where good value home-cooked food is served daily. The handpumps are in the main bar area, with four varying guest ales on offer from a mixture of national and micro-breweries. Two very popular annual beer festivals are hosted in the rear garden. Live folk music plays regularly here. Wirral CAMRA Pub of the Year 2009. ❀⌚🚌(410)♣P⅟–

New Ferry

Freddie's Club

36 Stanley Road, CH62 5AS

5 (12 Sat)-11; 12-11 Sun

Brimstage Trappers Hat 🄷

Popular social club converted from a former Conservative Club into a single-storey lounge bar with snooker room, with two full-size tables. Situated in a residential street, a short walk from New Ferry centre, Freddie's is a former Wirral CAMRA Club of the Year. A LocAle outlet, the two handpumps often both serve local beer. Freddie's fun quiz is hosted every Friday, as well as regular live entertainment. Guests are welcome – for entry show a CAMRA membership card or a copy of this Guide. ⇌(Bebington)🚌(41,401)P⅟–

John Masefield ✓

70-72, New Chester Road, CH62 5AD

7am-11 (11.30 Fri & Sat) ☎ (0151) 644 4250

Greene King Ruddles Best Bitter, Abbot 🄷

In 2007, JD Wetherspoon converted a large shop into this comfortable open-plan pub, in the centre of New Ferry. Controversy surrounded the opening, after locals suggested that the pub sign's portrait of the former Poet Laureate John Masefield looked more like Adolf Hitler – judge for yourself. Four handpumps serve regular and guest beers. The pub features the usual JDW meal deals and a quiz is held every Wednesday.
❀⌚⇌(Bebington)🚌(41,401)●⅟–

Raby

Wheatsheaf Inn 🏆

Raby Mere Road, CH63 4JH SJ311798

11.30-11 ☎ (0151) 336 3416

Brimstage Trappers Hat; Greene King Old Speckled Hen; Taylor Landlord; Tetley Bitter; Thwaites Original, Wainwright 🄷

Ancient thatched building celebrating its 400th anniversary since being rebuilt after a fire in 1611. Wirral's oldest pub, known locally as the Thatch, it has been an inn for more than 350 years, and in 2010 was Wirral CAMRA Pub of the Year. It is reputed to be haunted by 'Charlotte', who died here. The walls are decorated with old photographs of Raby. The bar with eight handpumps serves two rooms and a dining room in a converted cowshed. The two guest beers are usually from local breweries. No evening meals Sunday and Monday. ⛫Q❀⌚♿🚌(85)P⅟–

Rainhill

Commercial Hotel ✓

12 Station Road, L35 0LL (20m from Rainhill station)

11.30-11; 12-10.30 Sun ☎ (0151) 4308473

Tetley Mild, Bitter; Weetwood Best Bitter; guest beers 🄷

Once owned by the long defunct Joseph Jones Brewery, whose livery can still be seen, the original bar has been preserved. It is situated adjacent to Rainhill railway station, home of the Railway Trials of 1829 won by Stephenson's Rocket – the event is depicted pictorially in the pub along with scenes of old Prescot and Rainhill. The pub is always busy, and screens sports channels on large TVs positioned throughout. A worthy stop-off point on the journey from Liverpool to Manchester. Quiz night is Tuesday. ⌚♣P⅟–

Ship Inn 🏆 ✓

804 Warrington Road, L35 6PE (on A57, 400m W of jct 7 M62)

12-11 (10.30 Sun) ☎ (0151) 4264165

George Wright Ship to Shore; guest beers 🄷

Situated in a semi-rural location, the pub oozes atmosphere with candles on the tables and open fires in the winter months. One bar has big screens showing sport, another is quieter, and there is a separate restaurant. Outside, there are decked areas front and rear with lighting and jumbrellas. Children are welcome until 8pm. Breakfast is available daily 7am-9am, and main meals from noon until late. Coach parties are welcome by prior arrangement. Free Wi-Fi. ⛫❀⌚♿🚌P⅟–

St Helens

Eccleston Social Club

Holme Road, off Knowsley Road, WA10 4QB (next to St Helens Rugby League Club)

7-11.30; 12-midnight Sat; 12-10.30 Sun ☎ (01744) 27986

Beer range varies 🄷

Originally known as the Triplex Club, one of Pilkington Brothers works' social clubs, the venue is now owned by Ruskin Leisure and boasts a games room with snooker, darts and dominoes, large-screen TV for sports, a spacious, comfortable, newly-refurbished lounge, and a function room for up to 200 people with stage, in-house sound system and large dance floor. CAMRA members are welcome on production of a membership card.
⌚♿🚌P⅟–

Glass House ✓

5 Market Street, WA10 1NE

9am-midnight (1am Fri & Sat) ☎ (01744) 762310

Beer range varies 🄷

This former discount store, named to reflect the town's historic link with glassmaking, is situated a short distance from the award-winning World of Glass Visitor Centre, and the main shopping centre in Church Street. Bargain prices ensure the pub is always busy, and meal times are best avoided as there are rarely enough staff to cope with demand. Large-screen TVs dominate the upper bar. Disabled access is via the rear patio area, and the toilets are situated upstairs. Children are allowed in the lower bar only if dining. ❀⌚♿🚌●⅟–

Phoenix Hotel

34 Canal Street, WA10 3LL

12-11 (1am Fri & Sat); 12-midnight Sun ☎ (01744) 751890

Beer range varies 🄷

Built in 1903, the pub retains many original features, including its name in mosaic tiles on an outer wall. A community local, it was one of the original CAMRA Pubs of the Year in the 1980s. A smallish bar is home to pool, darts and dominoes, and a large lounge is comfortable. Sky Sports is shown on numerous TVs, with a large screen in the lounge. Music dominates, with jam night on Tuesday, karaoke on Friday night, and live Irish bands on Saturday. A yard at the back has been converted into a heated smoking area. ❀⊟♿⁻

Turks Head

49-51 Morley Street, WA10 2DQ
✪ 2-11.30 (12.30am Fri); 12-12.30am Sat; 12-11.30 Sun
☎ (01744) 751289
Beer range varies Ⓗ
A short distance from town, this popular pub was a previous CAMRA national Pub of the Year runner-up, and is currently St Helens Pub of the Year. Half-timbered, with etched glass windows, it was built in the 1870s by Ellis Warde Brewery, and features a distinctive turret inset with the brewery logo. It offers a constantly-changing beer range, with 12 handpulls in use over the weekend, six at other times. Draught and bottled continental beers are stocked. Thursday is curry and jazz night, and on Tuesday night there is a free quiz. Darts and dominoes are played. ♨❀◑⊟🚌♣▯

Southport

Baron's Bar (Scarisbrick Hotel) ✔

239 Lord Street, PR8 1NZ (on A565, opp Eastbank St)
✪ 11-11 (midnight Fri; 1am Sat); 12-11 Sun
☎ (01704) 543000 🌐 baronsbar.com
Moorhouse's Pride of Pendle; Tetley Bitter; guest beers Ⓗ
The Barons is the flagship real ale Mecca of Southport, based within the privately-owned Scarisbrick Hotel, a premier hotel in the town. A CAMRA LocAle supporter, it hosts the SIBA northern beer judging contest. Home to two quiz league teams, it also stages regular live music and fun competitions – such as a Welsh quiz on St David's Day, with beers from Wales on tap. The bar holds an annual May Day beer festival. Flag & Turret is the house beer. Q⊟♿⇌🚌♣⁻

Bold Arms ✔

59-61 Botanic Road, Churchtown, PR9 7NE
✪ 11.30-11 (midnight Fri); 12-11 Sun ☎ (01704) 228192
Tetley Dark Mild, Bitter; guest beers Ⓗ
Built in the 17th century before Southport existed, the Bold was originally named the Griffin, changing its name in 1759. The pub is one of the two oldest in modern Southport, and still has the old stables intact at the rear. The room that was the ale house three centuries ago is now the public bar. The lounge was converted from two old cottages and keeps the original fireplaces. Good pub food is served including the traditional Sunday lunch. ♨Q❀◑⊟♿🚌(49,49A)♣P⁻

Cheshire Lines

81 King Street, PR8 1LQ
✪ 11.30-midnight (1am Thu-Sat) ☎ (01704) 532178
Tetley Dark Mild, Bitter Ⓗ
The Cheshire Lines is a little Tudor-style gem. It features regularly in the Guide despite only serving Tetley Bitter and Dark Mild, proving that these are fine beers when kept really well. The pub has an attractive exterior with flower baskets, original windows and seating out front. Inside, there is a little snug to the left and a bar to the right where domino games are played. The back room is sometimes dedicated to food, also of excellent quality. Buses stop in Lord Street. ♨Q❀◑⊟⇌🚌♣⁻

Beer is proof that God loves us and wants us to be happy. **Benjamin Franklin**

Guest House 🏆 ✔

16 Union Street, PR9 0QE
✪ 11.30-11 (11.30 Fri & Sat); 12-10.30 Sun
☎ (01704) 537660
Adnams Bitter; Caledonian Deuchars IPA; Greene King Ruddles Best Bitter; Jennings Cumberland Ale; Theakston Traditional Mild, Best Bitter; guest beers Ⓗ
This attractive half-timbered Edwardian pub has been altered very little over the years, retaining three separate drinking areas. As well as the regular beers there are up to five changing guests, often including an ale from Southport Brewery (the pub supports LocAle). Quiz night is Thursday and acoustic folk nights are held on the first and third Monday evenings of the month. There is outdoor seating to the front and a pleasant courtyard to the rear. Buses stop in Lord Street. Q❀◑⊟⇌🚌⁻

Lakeside Inn

Marine Lake, The Promenade, PR9 0EA
✪ 11-11 ☎ (01704) 530173
Fuller's London Pride; Tetley Bitter Ⓗ
Perched on the Promenade overlooking the Marine Lake, this one-roomed inn displays a Guinness Book of Records certificate verifying that it was the smallest pub in Britain. Large windows provide a panoramic view across the lake. The interior has a nautical theme, outside there is a balcony and two further drinking areas, making the venue popular with families and holidaymakers in summer. The comfortable pub also has its own band of regulars. Buses stop in Lord Street. Q❀⇌🚌⁻

Mason's Arms

44 Anchor Street, PR9 0UT (behind main post office)
✪ 11-1am ☎ (01704) 534123
Robinson's Unicorn, seasonal beers Ⓗ
This small town-centre back-street pub two minutes' walk from the railway station is popular with locals and shoppers. Two cosy wood panelled rooms contain golfing memorabilia, the smaller room warmed by a real fire in winter. It is the only outlet in Southport for Robinson's beers. Acoustic folk nights are held on the first and third Wednesday evenings of the month, and a pub piano is available. You can enjoy the hidden roof garden in summer. Buses stop in Lord Street. ♨❀⇌🚌⁻

Sir Henry Segrave ✔

93-97 Lord Street, PR8 1RH (on A565)
✪ 7-midnight (1am Fri & Sat) ☎ (01704) 530217
Greene King Ruddles Best Bitter, Abbot; Moorhouse's Pendle Witches Brew; Phoenix Wobbly Bob; guest beers Ⓗ
The Sir Henry Segrave, named after the motor racing hero, has a typical Wetherspoon's interior, with spacious rooms used for both dining and drinking. (Take a moment before entering to look at the most attractive 19th-century exterior.) Beers on offer are invariably in excellent condition and

drawn from a large range of breweries, including locals such as George Wright. Food is reasonably priced and of good quality, served 7am-9pm.
Q⚘❀◑♿⛺⇌(Southport)🚌🍎⚊

Willow Grove ✔
387 Lord Street, PR9 0AG (on A565)
✪ 7-midnight (1am Fri; 2am Sat) ☎ (01704) 517830
Greene King Ruddles Best Bitter, Abbot; guest beers Ⓗ
Situated on the renowned Lord Street close to the war memorial, this is a typical Lloyds No 1 Bar. The modern L-shaped interior has a brightly-lit long bar displaying a great range of bottled beers. There are flat-screen TVs and comfortable couches around a 'living flame' fire. Popular with young people in the evening, the dance area is vibrant until the small hours. An upstairs bar is quieter, but real ale is not available there. Food is served 7am-9pm.
◑♿⇌🚌🍎⚊

Windmill
12-14 Seabank Road, PR9 0EL (off Lord St)
✪ 11.30-11 (midnight Thu-Sat); 12-10.30 Sun
☎ (01704) 547319
Moorhouse's Black Cat; Theakston Best Bitter; guest beers Ⓗ
Excellent community pub with a large front garden and an ornate heated shelter. Opposite is a Pugin-designed Catholic church. Inside there are alcoves to enjoy the beers – this is Southport's only outlet for Moorhouse's famed Black Cat. Quality food is served at reasonable prices (no food Wed). The pub is home to league-winning ladies and gents darts teams, a Wednesday quiz, and live Irish music on Thursday. The landlord claims to be the town's longest-serving publican. Buses stop in Lord Street.
❀◑♿⇌🚌♣⚊

Wallasey

Cheshire Cheese ✔
2 Wallasey Village, CH44 2DH
✪ 12-11 (midnight Fri & Sat) ☎ (0151) 638 3641
🌐 thecheesewallasey.com
Theakston Best Bitter; guest beers Ⓗ
Friendly local, Wallasey's oldest licensed premises, with a separate bar, snug and lounge. Outside is a walled beer garden where regular beer festivals are held. The handpumps are located in the lounge, with four guest beers on offer including a local ale, often from Liverpool Organic Brewery. Excellent home-cooked food is served until early evening (no food Thu). Quiz nights are Monday and Wednesday, and the pub hosts a golf society and football, darts and bowls teams. Q❀◑◧⇌🚌♣⚊

West Kirby

White Lion
51 Grange Road, CH48 4EE
✪ 12-11 (10.30 Sun) ☎ (0151) 625 9037
Black Sheep Best Bitter; Courage Directors; guest beers Ⓗ
Traditional local freehouse in a 200-year-old sandstone building close to West Kirby centre and the Wirral Way. The pub enjoys fine views of the Welsh hills and coastline, and Marine Lake, Promenade and the beach are all within easy walking distance. This is a warm, welcoming retreat, especially in the colder months with a real fire by the bar – perfect after that Wirral Way ramble! An ever-changing range of guest beers is on offer and food is served lunchtimes (not Sun). Quiz night is Monday. Outside is a large beer garden. Sorry, no children or dogs.
♨Q❀◐⇌🚌(22,437)⚊

Baltic Fleet, Liverpool (Photo: Dennis Jones)

Edinburgh Pub Walks

NEW FOR 2010

Bob Steel

A practical, pocket-sized travellers' guide to the pubs in and around Scotland's capital city. Featuring 25 town, park and costal walks, **Edinburgh Pub Walks** enables you to explore the many faces of the city, while never straying too far from a decent pint. Featuring walks in the heart of Edinburgh, as well as routes through its historic suburbs and nearby towns along the Firth of Forth, all accessible by public transport, why not stray off the Royal Mile and explore the history, architecture and landscape of the city.

£9.99 ISBN 978-1-85249-274-8 CAMRA members' price £7.99 160 pages

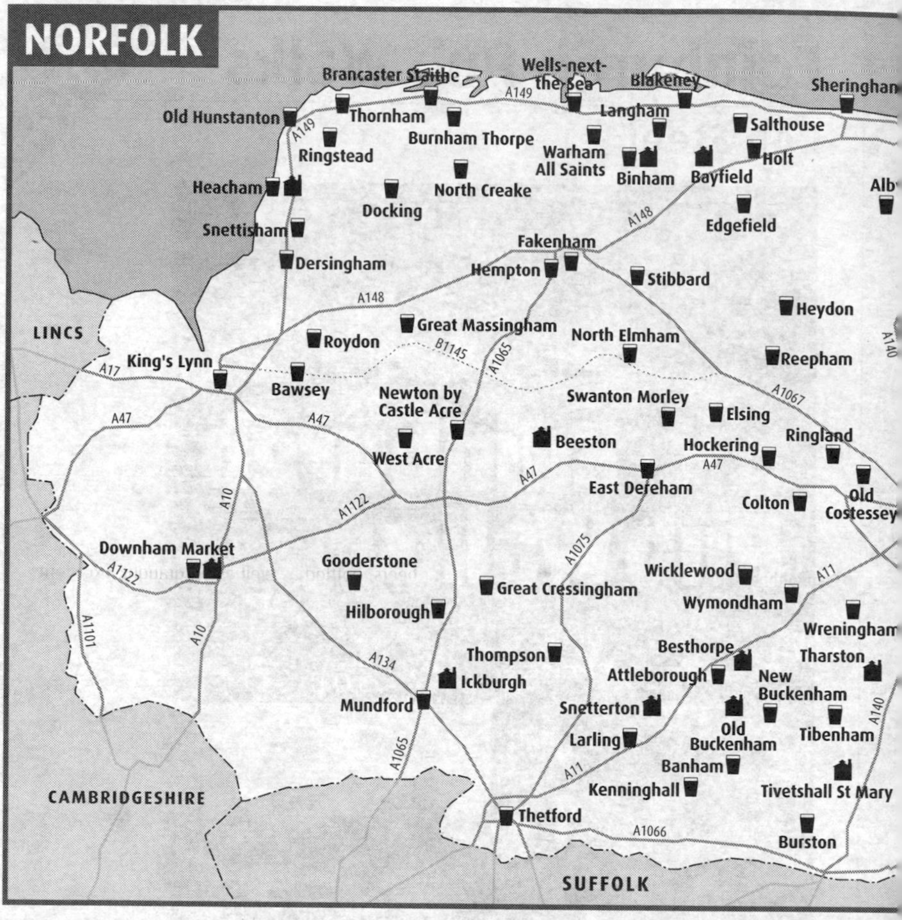

Alby

Horse Shoes

Cromer Road, NR11 7QE (on A140 halfway between Cromer and Aylsham) TG208324

12-2.30 (not Wed), 6.30-11; 9-10.30 Sun & Mon winter

(01263) 761378 albyhorseshoes.co.uk

Woodforde's Wherry; guest beers H

A 19th-century inn on the main Norwich-Cromer road that offers four real ales: Woodforde's Wherry and three guests, usually from local brewers such as Humpty Dumpty and Tipples. There are two bars – one with an unusually low counter – a wood-burning stove, and a separate restaurant. The traditional games of Ring the Bull and Twister are located in the ceiling. Pictures of old cars adorn the walls, the landlord being a classic car enthusiast. Folk music nights are held monthly. Locally sourced home-cooked food is available most lunchtimes and evenings. (X5,44,50)

Attleborough

London Tavern

Church Street, NR17 2AH

11-11 (1.30am Fri); 10-1.30am Sat; 10-11 Sun

(01953) 457415

Wolf Werewolf; guest beers H

Family-friendly pub in the town centre, opposite the main bus stops and 10 minutes' walk from the railway station. The range of three guest beers comes from all over the UK. Occasionally a fourth may be served on gravity. The pub has a dining room and serves breakfast and lunch every day. Evening meals are by arrangement. Outside is a covered smoking area and the garden. An annual beer festival takes place in September.

Banham

Barrel

The Appleyard, Kenninghall Road, NR16 2HB (opp Banham Zoo) TM056875

4 (2 Wed & Thu summer)-11; 2-midnight Fri & Sat; 12-midnight Sun (01953) 888593 banhambarrel.co.uk

Adnams Bitter H**; Wolf Coyote; guest beer** G

Formerly a cattle shed, the Barrel is home to Jonty's Cider. The large single room features an eclectic range of furniture and a wood-burning stove. The guest beer is chosen from a range of local micro-breweries. The pub is children and dog friendly and renowned for its live music; details of acts and artists can be found on its website. Camping and caravan facilities are available opposite at Banham Zoo. The rum cask cider is not to be missed.

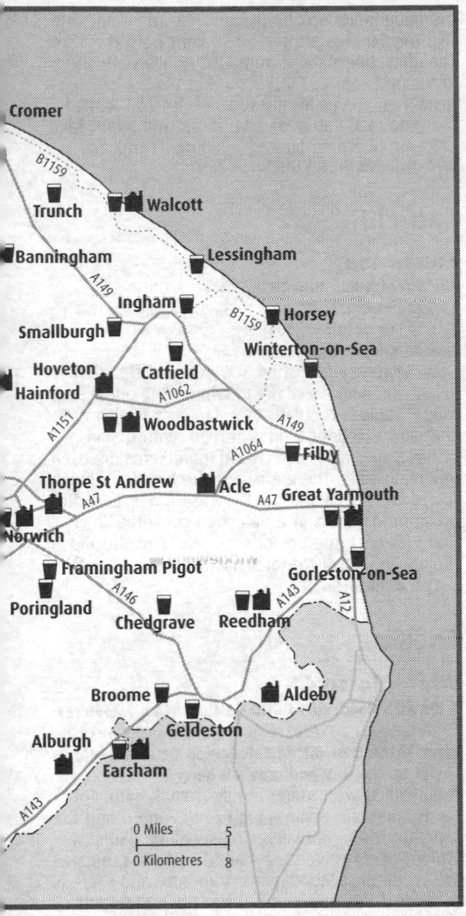

Banningham

Crown Inn

Church Road, NR11 7DY (adjacent to village green, just off B1145 or E of A140) TG217294
⌚ 12-2.30, 6.30-11; 12-10.30 Sun ☎ (01263) 733534
🌐 banninghamcrown.co.uk
Adnams Broadside; Greene King IPA, Abbot; guest beer H
Traditional, friendly local in the heart of the village, opposite the parish church and village green. Interior features include old beams and a large working fireplace, in a building that has housed an inn since the 17th century. The rear door leads out on to a patio with a covered smoking shelter and large garden with a barbecue. Quality food, often made with locally sourced produce, is available lunchtimes and evenings. Monthly quiz nights and other special events are held throughout the year (see website). ⛫❀◑P⚐

Bawsey

Sandboy

Gayton Road, PE32 1EP
⌚ 11-11 ☎ (01553) 630527 🌐 thesandboy.com
Beer range varies H
This village pub is situated near the local sandpits, hence the name, and used to be next to the railway bridge. The pub has a function room, beer garden and parking at the front and rear of the building. Three real ales are on offer, with beers from local breweries always among the range. There is a varied menu including Thai food. Camping and caravan facilities are also available. Q≋❀◑⊟♿⛺🚌(48)P⚐

Binham

Chequers Inn

Front Street, NR21 0AL (3km S of Stiffkey) TF983396
⌚ 11.30-2.30, 6-11 (11.30 Fri); 11.30-11.30 Sat; 12-11 (12-2.30, 7-11 winter) Sun ☎ (01328) 830297
🌐 binhamchequers.co.uk
Front Street Binham Cheer, Callums Ale, Unity; guest beers H
Chequers is a short walk from the historic and picturesque English Heritage Binham Priory. You enter past a series of outdoor tables into a single-room bar that has welcoming roaring fires in winter. The pub hosts its own micro-brewery, Front Street, with a range of 17 real ales, four of which are always available, as well as guest beers. There is also an extensive range of Belgian and German beers, bottled as well as on draught. Excellent meals are served. ⛫Q❀◑♿🚌(46)P⚐

Blakeney

Kings Arms

Westgate Street, NR25 7NQ (nr Blakeney harbour) TG026440
⌚ 11-11; 12-10.30 Sun ☎ (01263) 740341
Adnams Bitter G**; Greene King Old Speckled Hen; Marston's Pedigree; guest beers,** H
Situated close to the harbour of one of Norfolk's most picturesque coastal villages, this old building was originally three fishermen's cottages, with an interior comprising a series of interconnecting rooms. Note the plaque halfway up the wall denoting the 1953 flood level. Real ales here are

INDEPENDENT BREWERIES

Bees Walcott
Beeston Beeston
Blackfriars Great Yarmouth
Buffy's Tivetshall St Mary
Chalk Hill Norwich
Elmtree Snetterton
Fat Cat Norwich
Fox Heacham
Front Street Binham
Grain Alburgh
Humpty Dumpty Reedham
Iceni Ickburgh
Norfolk Cottage Norwich
Norfolk Square Great Yarmouth
Ole Slewfoot Hainford
Opa Hay's Aldeby
Spectrum Tharston
Tipples Acle
Uncle Stuarts Hoveton
Wagtail Old Buckenham
Waveney Earsham
Why Not Thorpe St Andrew
Winter's Norwich
Wissey Valley Downham Market
Wolf Besthorpe
Woodforde's Woodbastwick
Yetman's Bayfield

dispensed by handpump and gravity. There is a patio and large garden to the side of the pub. Children and dogs are welcome and food is served all day. En-suite accommodation is available. ⌂Q❀⇌◐▲⊟(36)P

Brancaster Staithe

White Horse

Main Road, PE31 8BY
⊙ 11-11; 12-10.30 Sun ☎ (01485) 210262
⊕ whitehorsebrancaster.co.uk
Adnams Bitter; Fuller's London Pride; Woodforde's Wherry [H]
A large, modern pub which sits on the edge of the salt marshes on the beautiful north Norfolk coast. The village is a wonderful place to explore and is home to many seafood stalls. Now an outlet for Brancaster Brewery, the pub bridges the gap between local and tourist pub, catering well for both types of pubgoer. Three beers are always available, and the menu features fresh seafood. ⌂Q❀⇌◐♿⊟♣P⊬

Broome

Artichoke

162 Yarmouth Road, NR35 2NZ (just off A143) TM352915
⊙ closed Mon; 12-11 (midnight Fri & Sat) ☎ (01986) 893325
⊕ theartichokeatbroome.co.uk
Adnams Bitter, Broadside [H]**; Elgood's Black Dog** [G]**; guest beers** [H]/[G]
Situated just off the A143, this early 19th-century inn was the home of the long-defunct Crowfoot Brewery. Flagstones, wooden floors and a large fireplace with a real fire give a rural ambience to this welcoming, friendly pub. Home-cooked food is available in the dining area and conservatory. A range of up to eight beers is offered, with an emphasis on local breweries, with some served by gravity from a tap room. The pub also boasts a range of around 70 malt whiskies. Norfolk CAMRA Pub of the Year 2009. ⌂Q❀◐▲⊟(580,588)P⊬

Burnham Thorpe

Lord Nelson

Walsingham Road, PE31 8HN (off B1355)
⊙ closed Mon winter; 11-11 (12-3, 6-11 winter); 11-11 (12-3, 6.30-10.30 winter) Sun ☎ (01328) 738241
⊕ nelsonslocal.co.uk
Greene King Abbot; Woodforde's Wherry [G]
Situated in the village of Nelson's birth, this pub was the first to be named in his honour. In 1793 it was used by the Norfolk hero to throw a farewell party, paid for by his wife. The dispense is all gravity from a traditional tap room, the beer served in a bar that contains the original settles. The modern world is catered for by live bands on Thursdays. There is a Nelson memorabilia shop. No evening meals on Sunday. ⌂Q❀◐♣P⊬

Burston

Crown Inn

Crown Green, IP22 5TW (2 miles W of A140) TM138834
⊙ 12-11 (10.30 Sun) ☎ (01379) 741257
⊕ burstoncrown.com
Adnams Bitter; Greene King Abbot [G]**; guest beer** [H]
Welcoming 16th-century Grade II-listed pub with exposed beams, deep sofas and a blazing fire in the huge inglenook fireplace in the main bar. The two regular ales are served straight from the cask. The guest beers come from East Anglian breweries including Elmtree, Blackfriars and Wolf. A small restaurant serves locally-sourced, freshly-cooked food (no food Sun eve). Live music and a quiz take place on alternate Sunday evenings. Families welcome. ⌂❀◐♿⊟P⊬

Catfield

Crown Inn

The Street, NR29 5AA TG387218
⊙ closed Mon; 12-2.30, 7-11; 12-3, 7-midnight Sat; 12-3, 7-10.30 Sun ☎ (01692) 580128
Greene King IPA; guest beers [H]
Cosy, tastefully furnished 300-year-old traditional village inn with a real fire in winter. The guest beer range changes regularly. The landlord is also the chef and excellent food is served, with Italian dishes a speciality; fresh, local ingredients are used where possible. There is a separate function/dining room and a secluded garden in summer. En-suite accommodation is in a detached converted hall that was once the doctor's surgery. Close to the Broads and north Norfolk coast. ⌂Q❀⇌◐⊟(54)P

Chedgrave

White Horse ✔

5 Norwich Road, NR14 6ND (just off A146) TM360993
⊙ 12-11 ☎ (01508) 520250 ⊕ whitehorsechedgrave.co.uk
Black Sheep Best Bitter; Caledonian Deuchars IPA; Taylor Landlord; Woodforde's Wherry [H]
A genuinely welcoming family-friendly pub. The bar is open plan, with a log fire in winter, and the separate restaurant serves roasts all day Sunday. Various beer festivals are staged each year, quizzes are on the first Monday every month, and there is occasional live music plus other themed events. The pub is wheelchair-friendly and there are excellent baby changing facilities. Pub games including backgammon and chess are played and in summer the bowls green is busy. Outside, there is a covered smoking area with tables. ⌂❀◐♿⊟(X2)♣P⊬

Colton

Ugly Bug Inn

High House Farm Lane, NR9 5DG (2 miles S of A47. Turn off on roundabout on Honingham Road) TG104908
⊙ 12-2.30 (not Tue), 5-10.30 (11 Fri & Sat); 12-3 Sun ☎ (01603) 880794 ⊕ uglybuginn.co.uk
Humpty Dumpty Cheltenham Flyer; guest beers [H]
Large rural pub with extensive gardens, eight en-suite bedrooms and a fine dining room. The large single bar is divided into smaller cosy sections, creating a pleasant environment for drinkers. Regular ales are sourced from the local Humpty Dumpty and Beeston micro-breweries, and in addition there is usually a national guest beer. The pub is closed Tuesday lunchtime, but plans to open on Sunday evening in the near future. Live jazz takes place monthly. ❀⇌◐♿P

Cromer

Red Lion

Brook Street, NR27 9HD (in back street close to church)

⏲ 10-11 (10.30 Sun) ☎ (01263) 514964
🌐 yeolderedlionhotel.co.uk
Adnams Bitter; Woodforde's Wherry; guest beers H
A Victorian pub situated at the top of the cliff, with commanding views of the promenade and sea. The interior comprises two bars; one a traditional Edwardian bar with mahogany panels, the other with flint and brick walls adorned with photos of Cromer's maritime past. There is also the Galleons Restaurant offering an extensive menu.
🛏◑♿⛺⇌🚌♣P

Dersingham

Coach & Horses

77 Manor Road, PE31 6LN
⏲ 12-midnight (11 Sun) ☎ (01485) 540391
🌐 norfolkinns.co.uk/coachhorse/index.htm
Woodforde's Wherry H
Busy 19th-century carrstone pub close to Sandringham House. Entertainment includes quiz nights, bingo, poker games and live music on Friday nights and some Sundays. It is a popular pub for food, enjoyed by locals as well as tourists. There is a large beer garden including a children's play area, music stand, old red phone box and heated smoking shelter. Three en-suite rooms are available to let. A beer festival takes place in September, with around 20 real ales and some cider. ⛰Q❀🛏◑⊟⛺🚌(41A)P⚟

Docking

Railway Inn

Station Road, PE31 8LY
⏲ 12-11 ☎ (01485) 518620
Buffy's Bitter; guest beers H
Lovely cosy pub situated at one end of the village near the old railway house and adjacent to the disused railway line. A railway theme is continued inside including railway pictures and a high level working model train. The main bar boasts three handpumps, two dispensing different guest beers. Another bar has lounge settees and a small dining area. The main restaurant is a large conservatory built on the side, serving locally produced food. ⛰👶❀◑⊟♿♣P⚟

Downham Market

Crown Hotel

12 Bridge Street, PE38 9DH
⏲ 9.30am (11 Sun)-11 ☎ (01366) 382322
Adnams Bitter; Greene King IPA, Abbot; Woodforde's Wherry; guest beers H
Popular with locals and visitors alike, this 17th-century coaching inn can be found at the heart of the old town. The bar has a beamed ceiling, a large fireplace and five handpumps with four regular beers and one guest. There is a restaurant and a separate function room that caters for parties and weddings. The smoking area is located under the coaching arch and bench seats are situated along the yard. ⛰Q👶❀🛏◑⇌🚌P⚟

Railway Arms

Downham Market Railway Station, PE38 9EN
⏲ 10-10.30 (5.30 Mon-Wed); closed Sun ☎ (01366) 386636
Beer range varies H
This small, welcoming pub is an ideal place to wait for a train at Downham Market. The entrance is off the platform and two to three real ales are offered. A member of the LocAle scheme, one of the beers is generally from Elgood's, sometimes from another local brewery. Cider drinkers are also catered for with one real cider, normally from Crones. Light bar snacks, made from locally sourced products, are available. ⛰⇌♣🍎

Earsham

Queens Head

Station Road, NR35 2TS (turn left off A143 signed Earsham) TM321891
⏲ 12-3, 5-11; 12-11 Sat; 12-10.30 Sun ☎ (01986) 892623
Waveney East Coast Mild, Lightweight; guest beers H
A 17th-century pub with a large front garden overlooking the village green. The main bar features flagstone floors, wooden beams, an old fireplace and a ceiling decorated with pumpclips of guest ales that have previously featured here. Home to the Waveney Brewing Co, two Waveney beers are usually on offer plus two guests from other brewers. Food is served at lunchtime (not Mon and Tue). Successful darts, pool and football clubs are based here. The smoking area is unheated. ⛰Q👶❀◐🚌(580)♣P⚟

East Dereham

George Hotel

Swaffham Road, NR19 2AZ (near war memorial)
⏲ 10-11 (midnight Fri & Sat); 12-11 Sun ☎ (01362) 696801
🌐 lottiesrestaurant.co.uk
Adnams Bitter, Broadside; Beeston Worth the Wait; Fuller's London Pride; Woodforde's Wherry H
An 18th-century coaching inn situated just to the north end of the market place of this busy mid-Norfolk market town. The well-designed bar is open to non-residents, with alcoves, wood-panelling, leather chairs and pictures of local historic interest. There is a fine air-conditioned conservatory with disabled access, a heated outdoor patio lined with bamboo for drinkers, and a separate smokers' corner. It has a secure car park and is handily situated for the Mid-Norfolk Railway. Q👶❀🛏◑♿⇌🚌(X1)P⚟

Edgefield

Pigs

Norwich Road, NR24 2RL (off B1149) TG090313
⏲ 11-3, 6-11; 12-10 Sun ☎ (01263) 587634
🌐 thepigs.org.uk
Adnams Bitter, Broadside; Greene King Abbot; Wolf Old Spot; Woodforde's Wherry; guest beers G
Multi award-winning pub with its own local news sheet – The Pig Issue – and famed for its barter system where fresh produce can be exchanged for beer. Enter through the foyer displaying fresh local produce for sale. Beer is served by gravity from barrels behind the bar. There is a room to the left, a restaurant area to the right and outdoor seating areas to the front and rear. The pub can become very busy during peak times. Accommodation is now also available. ❀🛏◑♿🚌♣P⚟

Elsing

Mermaid Inn

Church Street, NR20 3EA (opp church) TG053165
⏲ 12-3.30, 7-11 (midnight Fri & Sat); 12-3, 6.30-11 Sun
☎ (01362) 637640

Adnams Broadside; Wolf Golden Jackal; Woodforde's Wherry; guest beers Ⓖ
This 17th-century pub is located opposite a large 14th-century parish church in a small village in the charming upper Wensum Valley. The interior has a large bar with a new log-burning fire at one end and a pool table at the other. There is also a dining area. Cask ales sold here are mainly from local brewers and are dispensed by gravity from small casks. Home-made traditional English food is available, with steak and kidney and jam roly-poly the local specialities. Quiz night features occasionally. ♨❀◗♿▲🚌♣P⁻

Fakenham

Bull

Bridge Street, NR21 9AG TF856264
✪ 10 (12 Sun)-midnight ☎ (01328) 853410
🌐 thefakenhambull.co.uk
Woodforde's Wherry Ⓗ
Walk through an outdoor seating area to enter this single-room pub with its superbly finished wooden floor, alcoves and comfortable leather settees. Three guest ales are always available from all over the country, including the Isle of Man, totalling around 300 different ales each year, as well as the regular Woodforde's Wherry and a real cider. The Bull is one of only two premises locally to be awarded five stars for its food standards by the local council. Steak night is Wednesday.
♨❀🛏◗♿🚌♣⁻

Filby

Kings Head

Main Road, NR29 3HY (on main A1064 just E of village) TG483133
✪ 12 (6 Mon)-11; 12-midnight Fri & Sat; 12-10.30 Sun
☎ (01493) 730992
Taylor Landlord Ⓗ
This traditional dog-friendly village local in an east Norfolk village is a true free house, with beers sourced from several local breweries. The lounge/dining room has a log-burning fireplace surrounded by comfortable Chesterfields. Traditional quality seasonal food is served. The pub is home to a number of sports teams. Two beer festivals are held annually in June and November offering 20 or more real ales and five ciders.
♨❀◗◗▣▲🚌♣♣P⁻

Framingham Pigot

Gull

Loddon Road, NR14 7PL (on A146) TG285038
✪ 12-3, 5.30-11 ☎ (01508) 492039
Greene King Abbot; Woodforde's Wherry; guest beer Ⓖ
On the main road from Norwich to Beccles, this pub is divided into four distinct areas, with three for dining and one for drinking, plus a pool room. All beers are served on gravity, with the guest beer coming from either Brandon or Woodforde's. The pub is noted for its food, which is served at all sessions. The menu is an interesting mix of English and continental food. The X2 bus stops nearby. Families are welcome. ♨❀◗♿🚌(X2)P

Geldeston

Locks Inn

Locks Lane, NR34 0HW (through village centre, turn left into Station Rd, after 300m turn left onto track across marshes) TM390908
✪ 12-midnight Fri, Sat & summer; 5-midnight (closed Mon & Tue) winter; 12-midnight (7 winter) Sun ☎ (01508) 518414
🌐 geldeston.locks.co.uk
Green Jack Canary Pale Ale, Orange Wheat Beer, Trawler Boys Best Bitter, Gone Fishing, seasonal beers; guest beers Ⓗ
Stunningly situated on the banks of the River Waveney and accessed by a long, meandering track between dykes and marshes. Extensive gardens lead to overnight moorings. The small main bar, with low ceiling beams and clay pamment floor, retains an authentic, welcoming feel, with the candlelit lighting adding to the atmosphere, and modern extensions allowing the pub to maintain an active live music scene. Owned by Green Jack Brewery, its range of beers is supplemented by guests and a selection of real ciders and perries. ♨Q⛴❀◗♣♣P

Gooderstone

Swan Inn

The Street, PE33 9BP (opp church)
✪ 3 (12 Fri-Sun)-midnight ☎ (01366) 328365
Adnams Bitter; guest beers Ⓗ
After a short closure, the Swan has reopened and is once again an important part of the local community. There is one main bar, with guest beers from small independent breweries, and a garden room containing a pool table and dartboard overlooking the large enclosed garden. Traditional Sunday roasts are served as well as regular themed food nights, and there is occasional live music. During October the regulars produce cider from apples grown in the garden and donated by villagers. ♨❀♣P⁻

Gorleston-on-Sea

Mariners Compass

21 Middleton Road, NR31 7AJ
✪ 11-1.30am (2.30am Thu-Sat); 12-12.30am Sun
☎ (01493) 659494
Beer range varies Ⓗ
On the town route to Lowestoft, this large two-bar pub was opened in the 1930s and fitted out in 'brewers' Tudor' style. It was saved from demolition in 2008 and since then has become one of the major real ale venues for the area. It retains many of its original fittings inside. The pub has two defined drinking areas, the real ale bar occupying the old saloon area. Beers are always changing and invariably interesting. Good value bar snacks are always available. ♨❀◗▣♿♣P⁻▯

New Entertainer

80 Pier Plain, NR31 6PG (off Englands Lane)
✪ 12-11 ☎ (01493) 441643
Greene King IPA; guest beers Ⓗ
Traditional street-corner local with an interesting design and layout including a triangular-shaped corner. There is always an interesting choice of beers on offer, with many ales coming from local brewers. This dedicated free house is only a short walk from the seafront, and is well worth seeking out, though the signposting is not always obvious. Some Belgian beers are also available. Q🚌♣⁻

Great Cressingham

Windmill Inn

Water End, IP25 6NN (off A1065 S of Swaffham) TF846019

⌚ 9-11 ☎ (01760) 756232 🌐 oldewindmillinn.co.uk

Adnams Bitter, Broadside; Greene King IPA ⊞; guest beers ⊞/Ⓖ

A multi-roomed pub which is full of character and provides a different atmosphere in each of its drinking areas, ranging from 'olde worlde' with open fires and real beams to a modern extension. A good selection of real ales includes the house beer Windy Miller by Hancock's, while guest beers are rotated weekly. Thirty different malt whiskies are also stocked. The pub features live music and a talent night. Good home-cooked food is available. A worthwhile detour from the Peddars Way walk. ♨Q🛏❀🛏◐◑⊟♿▲♣P⊱

Great Massingham

Dabbling Duck

11 Abbey Road, PE32 2HN

⌚ 12-11 (10.30 Sun) ☎ (01485) 520827

🌐 thedabblingduck.co.uk

Adnams Broadside; Beeston Worth the Wait; Greene King IPA; Woodforde's Wherry; guest beers ⊞

Large pub located in a beautiful village with a number of duck ponds. There is a bar for drinkers and several areas for dining, including a separate restaurant. A log fire warms in winter and during the summer the large beer garden is popular. Despite its popularity for food, this remains a village local with events such as quizzes, poker nights, live music and even film screenings. There are a number of B&B rooms available. ♨❀🛏◐◑⊟♿🚌(48)♣P⊱

Great Yarmouth

Mariners Tavern 🏆

69 Howard Street South, NR30 1LN (between harbour and Market Place)

⌚ 11-11 (midnight Fri-Sat); 12-11 Sun ☎ (01493) 332299

Greene King IPA; guest beers ⊞

A former Lacons pub with a pleasant red brick and flint exterior. This family-run friendly community local comprises a main bar and a smaller cider bar, with a large range of real ciders available. It hosts a number of themed beer festivals during the year including one held to coincide with the Yarmouth maritime weekend in September. Most of the seven guest ales come from local micros, and there is a selection of foreign beers available. Voted Norwich and Norfolk CAMRA Branch Pub of the Year 2010. ♨🛏❀⊟▲⇌🚌(X1)♣●

Oliver Twist

62-63 North Market Road, NR30 2DX (to NE of Market Gates complex)

⌚ 12-11 (1am Sat) ☎ (07768) 120714

Blackfriars Twos, Old Habit ⊞

This is a well-established street-corner pub with a thriving local trade. Beers from Blackfriars Brewery are always available and the full range is constantly rotated. Live music features rock 'n' roll and skiffle, reflecting the landlord's passion, as does a display cabinet full of model scooters and cars, and the original jukebox (with 2000 singles to choose from). Midday food and very local cider are also available. ❀◐⊟♿⇌🚌(X1)♣●⊱

St Johns Head

58 North Quay, NR30 1JB

⌚ 12-midnight ☎ (01493) 843443

Elgood's Cambridge Bitter; guest beers ⊞

This former Lacons Brewery pub is reputed to be built on land confiscated from monks of the Carmelite Order. Now a free house, it has a traditional flintstone facade and oval windows at the front. A single bar houses a large TV screen for live sports, which are very popular here. There is a pool table in one area. Four real ales include three changing guests. The smoking shelter is minimalist but heated. ❀♿▲⇌(Vauxhall)🚌(X1)♣●⊱

Heacham

Fox & Hounds

22 Station Road, PE31 7EX

⌚ 12-11 (10.30 Sun) ☎ (01485) 570345

Adnams Broadside; guest beers ⊞

Popular with locals and visitors, this is the home of the Fox Brewery and was CAMRA's West Norfolk Branch Pub of the Year 2008. It offers six beers, four from Fox, one guest and a house beer. Bottled beer is also available, including the brewery's own, plus a range of foreign beers. The restaurant offers beer recommendations to match the cuisine. There is live music on Tuesday and a quiz on Thursday. Beer festivals are hosted throughout the year. Very posh loos. ❀◐◑♿🚌(40,41)♣P⊱

Hempton

Bell

The Green, NR21 7LG (turn by the Fakenham Garden Centre off the A1065) TF913293

⌚ 11-2.30 (not Tue), 5-midnight; 11-midnight Sat; 11-4, 7-midnight Sun ☎ (01328) 864579 🌐 hemptonbell.co.uk

John Smith's Bitter; Woodforde's Wherry; guest beer ⊞

A rare example of a rural pub that does not serve food, the Bell is friendly, very traditional, and retains a two-bar layout little altered since the early 1970s. It has been at the centre of the village community for around 400 years. The guest beer always changes and comes from a micro or independent brewery. Trad jazz sessions take place on the second and fourth Thursdays of each month. ⊟⊱

Heydon

Earle Arms

The Green, NR11 6AD (W of B1149, opp village green) TG113273

⌚ closed Mon; 12-3, 6-11; 12-10.30 Sun ☎ (01263) 587376

🌐 earlearms.vpweb.co.uk/default.html

Adnams Bitter; Black Sheep Bitter; Woodforde's Wherry ⊞

Delightful old coaching inn set opposite the picture postcard village green. The village is privately owned, quiet and quintessentially English, and has often been used as a film location. The bar is mainly candle-lit, with a welcoming, relaxing atmosphere and a log fire in winter; it also has an interesting collection of horse racing memorabilia. The food is locally sourced, cooked to order and of the highest quality. The restaurant is separate, so booking is advisable. Superb pub, not to be missed. ♨Q❀◐◑P

Hilborough

Swan

Brandon Road, IP26 5BW (on A1065)
11-midnight ☎ (01760) 756380 hilboroughswan.co.uk
Greene King IPA; guest beers H
On the A1065 between Mundford and Swaffham, featuring a cosy new settle in the bar, the Swan offers an extensive menu with a good Sunday carvery. Greene King IPA sits alongside two guest ales, usually Beeston beers and Wadworth's Henry's IPA. If you are passing on your way to the coast, this pub is an ideal stop-off for a pint or a meal. With B&B accommodation, it's also a good base for exploring Breckland. Q P

Hockering

Victoria

The Street, NR20 3HL (just off A47) TF863355
12-3, 6-11; 12-6 Sun ☎ (01603) 880507
Beer range varies H
Just off the A47 and opposite the X1 bus stop, this friendly pub offers a warm welcome and a real fire. The bar has two changing guest beers from all over the UK. The walls are adorned with old photos of the village, framed beer mats and Arsenal memorabilia. The garden is a lovely spot to enjoy a pint on a summer's evening. Bar snacks are available at lunchtime. An annual beer festival is held in the summer. (X1) P

Holt

Kings Head

19 High Street, NR25 6BN (along Holt High Street) TG078388
11 (12 Sun)-11 ☎ (01263) 712543
kingsheadholt.org.uk
Adnams Bitter, Broadside; Blackfriars Whyte Angel; Wolf Straw Dog; Woodforde's Wherry H
This 19th-century inn situated in the middle of Holt on the High Street offers five real ales, including Woodforde's Wherry, plus real cider. Guest ales are usually from local brewers. The interior has two bars with open fires. Food is available lunchtimes and evenings, with meat sourced from a local butcher. Outside there is a large beer garden. B&B accommodation is available.

Horsey

Nelson Head

The Street, NR29 4AD (300m N of B1159 coast road) TG460228
11-11; 12-10.30 Sun ☎ (01493) 393378
nelsonheadhorsey.co.uk
Woodforde's Wherry, Nelson's Revenge H
Rural pub close to the coast, Horsey Mere Nature Reserve, the Broads and a famous mill. It is quiet, with a timeless atmosphere enhanced by a log fire in winter. The bar has a large collection of marshman's implements. A good selection of home-cooked meals made with locally sourced produce is available lunchtime and evenings. Families are welcome, and there is a large garden area for children. This venue is popular with artists, walkers, boaters and locals alike. Well worth seeking out. Q P

Ingham

Swan Inn

Swan Corner, Sea Palling Road, NR12 9AB (1 mile NE of Stalham on B1151) TG390260
12-3, 6-11 (10.30 Sun) ☎ (01692) 581099
Woodforde's Wherry; guest beers H
Rural 14th-century thatched and flint-built pub situated close to the church. The interesting split-level beamed interior has a wealth of warm brick and traditional flint. The drinkers' area is small, with most of the pub devoted to diners. Beers are selected from the full Woodforde's range. Freshly prepared meals are made with local produce. High quality en-suite rooms in a separate block are available all year round, with short break rates to include dinner and B&B. Q P

Kenninghall

Red Lion ☆

East Church Street, NR16 2EP (opp church) TM042859
12-3, 5.30-11 (midnight Fri & Sat); 12-10 Sun
☎ (01953) 887849 redlionkenninghall.co.uk
Greene King IPA H**, Abbot** G**; Woodforde's Wherry; guest beers** H
Four-hundred-year-old pub comprising a bar with a real fire, a pine-panelled snug and a separate restaurant. Abbot is from a cask behind the bar and Elmtree Bitter is one of the regular guests. Good quality, home-cooked food with interesting vegetarian options is served every day. Four rooms are available for B&B. There are regular theme nights. Directions for a short local walk can be obtained from the bar. P

White Horse

Market Place, NR16 2AH TM038862
11.30-3, 5-11; 11.30-11 Sat; 12-11 Sun ☎ (01953) 888857
Adnams Bitter; Greene King IPA; guest beer H
The pub is situated at the centre of the village, with a main bar that features a large inglenook fireplace and plenty of beams. It also has a family/games room, function room and restaurant. The guest beer is chosen from a variety of local micro-breweries, including Wolf, Buffys and Humpty Dumpty. Food is served every day lunchtimes and evenings. The pub also offers accommodation with five letting rooms. P

King's Lynn

Globe Hotel ✔

Tuesday Market Place, King Street, PE30 1EZ
9 (8 Fri-Sun)-midnight ☎ (01553) 668000
Greene King Ruddles Best Bitter, Abbot; Marston's Pedigree; guest beers H
On the corner of the larger of the town's two market places, this Wetherspoon Lloyds No1 Bar is a sympathetic conversion of a former coaching inn. In stark contrast to its sister pub the Lattice House, several screens show a variety of music videos and live sport. The Globe can get very busy evenings and weekends. Food is served all day until 10pm. The heated outdoor drinking area goes down towards the river. Wetherspoon Lodge accommodation includes rooms adapted for disabled guests.

Lattice House ✔

Chapel Street, PE30 1EG
9-11 (1am Fri & Sat) ☎ (01553) 769585

Greene King Ruddles Best Bitter, Abbot; guest beers H
Just off the Tuesday Market Place in the town centre, this was one of the pioneering pubs of the real ale renaissance in the early 1980s. It is a truly beautiful building, with many small drinking areas inside, and a much quieter Wetherspoon's than the Globe, although still busy on weekends. It offers the usual Wetherspoon food options until 10pm. Good to see one of the original icons of the CAMRA movement return. ▲Q⊱❀❀《◗

Stuart House Hotel
35 Goodwins Road, PE30 5QX
🕑 6-11; 7-10.30 Sun ☎ (01553) 772169
🌐 stuart-house-hotel.co.uk
Beer range varies H
The bar of an independent hotel situated down a gravel drive off Goodwins Road, near to the football ground and the Walks park. There is a roaring fire in the winter and a beer garden for summer use. Food is served in the evening in the bar and restaurant, and regular events include live music and themed meals. Each year a beer festival coincides with the King's Lynn festival in late July. Two or three beers are always available, mostly from East Anglian breweries. ▲Q❀⇔《◗♣P

Langham

Bluebell ✓
22-24 Holt Road, NR25 7BX (take B1156 S from Blakeney, then turn right into village) TG012411
🕑 11-3 (4 Sat), 7-11; 11-11 Fri; 12-4, 7-11 Sun
☎ (01328) 830502
Greene King IPA H; **Woodforde's Wherry** G; **guest beer** H
Situated two miles inland from the Norfolk coast road at Blakeney, this village local is small from the outside but visitors, including families and dogs, can be sure of a big welcome inside. The main bar area is at the front, with a split-level dining room to the side. To the rear is a games room, leading to the large rear garden. Home-cooked food, using locally sourced products where possible, is available every day lunchtime and evening (no food Wed). ▲❀《◗ᗢ♣P⇐

Larling

Angel Inn ♆
NR16 2QU (off A11 between Thetford and Norwich, signed by B1111 East Harling) TL983890
🕑 10-midnight; 11-11 Sun ☎ (01953) 717963
🌐 larlingangel.moonfruit.com
Adnams Bitter; guest beers H
A brilliant all-around pub run by the same family for over 80 years, recognised as West Norfolk CAMRA Branch Pub of the Year for 2010. Five real ales are always on handpump, including a mild. There is superb food, over 100 whiskies, and both the lounge and bar have open fires. The bar is frequented by friendly locals, passers-by and campers who enjoy the Angel's caravan park. A summer beer festival features more than 70 ales and the pub also hosts a whisky week. ▲Q❀⇔《◗ᗢᗺ▲✦(Harling Road)P⇐

Lessingham

Star Inn
School Road, NR12 0DN (300m off B1159 coast road) TG388283
🕑 12-3 (not Mon), 6-11; 12-11 Sat & Sun ☎ (01692) 580510
🌐 thestarlessingham.co.uk
Adnams Bitter; Buffy's Bitter; Greene King IPA; guest beer H
This excellent village local situated not far from the Norfolk coast has an easy-going feel. It is convenient for those visiting nearby East Ruston Old Vicarage Garden. The Star is now under new ownership and goes from strength to strength, offering well-kept beers to regulars from near and far. The large beer garden is the perfect place to relax in summer. The cider is Westons Old Rosie. Dogs are welcome in the bar, and meals are available lunchtimes and evenings except Monday. ▲Q❀⇔《◗▲➾(34,36)♣❀P

Mundford

Crown Hotel
Crown Road, IP26 5HQ
🕑 11-midnight ☎ (01842) 878233 🌐 the-crown-hotel.co.uk
Courage Directors; Marston's Pedigree; guest beer H
The Crown dates back to 1652 and is a lovely old building. There are two bars to choose from and a quiet, beautifully-appointed restaurant upstairs. The food is all excellent and locally sourced. Two roaring fires in the winter welcome you in for a pint or a dram of whisky; there are more than 70 to choose from. A high standard of accommodation is offered to visitors to the Breckland area, but the pub remains very much a village local. ▲Q❀⇔《◗ᗺ⇐

New Buckenham

King's Head
Market Place, NR16 2AN (opp village green) TM088905
🕑 12-3, 7-11 (1am Fri; 12.30 Sat; 10.30 Sun)
☎ (01953) 860487
Adnams Bitter; guest beer H
This friendly free house is opposite the village green in the centre of this orthogonal medieval grid-pattern village. The rear drinking area is furnished with pine tables and wooden chairs, and has a woodburner in the large inglenook fireplace. Traditional home-cooked food is available at all sessions and Sunday lunch is especially popular with pubgoers. Quiz night is every second Thursday. The guest beer comes mainly from a local brewery. ▲Q《◗⇐

Newton by Castle Acre

George & Dragon
Swaffham Road, PE32 2BX (on main road between Fakenham and Swaffham)
🕑 12-2.30, 6-11; 12-3 Sun ☎ (01760) 755046
Beer range varies H
Situated by a busy road, the large car park and entrance are at the rear. On arrival you pass a cosy meeting room into the main bar, where the interior is split into three rooms featuring wooden beams, a restaurant and a welcoming open fire. The pub supports LocAle and two local beers are available at all times. A varying food menu is offered and entertainment includes regular music nights and quiz nights. ▲Q⊱❀《◗ᗺᗺP

North Creake

Jolly Farmers

1 Burnham Road, NR21 9JW
closed Mon and Tue; 11-2.30, 7-11; 12-3, 7-10.30 Sun
(01328) 738185 jollyfarmers-northcreake.co.uk
Woodforde's Wherry, Admiral's Reserve; guest beers G
This traditional, cosy pub has small rooms with pine furniture, beams and tiled floors which are enhanced by a roaring log fire in the winter. The beer is on gravity and the menu features local produce, including game in winter and seafood in summer. There is classical music in the background at lunchtime and jazz in the evening.
P

North Elmham

Railway Hotel

Station Road, NR20 5HH TF995202
11-11 (01362) 668300
Beer range varies H/G
This rural gem, situated close to an ancient Anglo-Saxon cathedral, is a fine example of a community local. There is an adjacent function room with a first-floor balcony that hosts many local events, plus a patio at the rear of the pub. Most of the beers on sale here are from local breweries such as Beeston, Humpty Dumpty and Wolf. Home-cooked meals using mainly locally-sourced ingredients are available at lunchtimes and in the evenings. The pub now offers accommodation. P

Norwich

Alexandra Tavern

16 Stafford Street, NR2 3BB
10.30-11 (midnight Fri & Sat); 12-11 Sun
(01603) 627772 alexandratavern.co.uk
Chalk Hill Tap, CHB, Gold; guest beers H
This is a friendly 19th-century street-corner local, serving a mixed age group. Three Chalk Hill beers and two or three guests, usually from micro-breweries, are available. The interior is decorated with mementos of the landlord's past as a submariner and transatlantic rower. Home-cooked food is available, from filled rolls to the pub's speciality Mexican dishes. There is a pool table and dartboard, and other pub games are available.
Q (19,20)

Beehive

30 Leopold Road, NR4 7PJ (just off Newmarket Road)
12 (5 Mon)-11; 12-midnight Fri & Sat; 12-11 Sun
(01603) 451628 beehivepubnorwich.co.uk
Fuller's London Pride; Wolf Golden Jackal, Ale; guest beers H
A pleasant community local situated between the Unthank and Newmarket roads, the pub is home to three darts teams, one pool and one korfball. It hosts an annual beer festival in the first week of July. Charity barbecues are frequently held in the garden during the summer months. Free Wi-Fi and pub games round out the entertainment. A selection of Belgian bottled beers is available. Pub grub is served at lunchtime.

Duke of Wellington

91-93 Waterloo Road, NR3 1EG
12-11.30 (10.30 Sun) (01603) 441182
dukeofwellingtonnorwich.co.uk
Elgood's Black Dog; Fuller's London Pride; Oakham JHB, Bishop's Farewell; Wolf Golden Jackal, Straw Dog; guest beers H/G
A pub with bags of character. The current landlord has been here for nearly 10 years and has certainly put his own stamp on the place, from the redesigned back patio area which holds the pub's annual beer festival in late August to the choice of ales, many served from a small tap room behind the bar. There is no food available but customers may bring in their own. Tuesday is folk night.
(9A,16)P

Fat Cat

49 West End Street, NR2 4NA (just off Dereham Road)
12-11 (midnight Fri & Sat) (01603) 624364
fatcatpub.co.uk
Adnams Bitter H**; Fat Cat Bitter, Honey Cat, Wild Cat** H/G**; Fuller's London Pride; Woodforde's Wherry** H
A real ale lover's paradise, with over 25 guest ales plus regulars from Adnams, Crouch Vale, Elgood's, Fuller's, Green Jack, Oakham and Woodforde's, as well as its own Fat Cat range. Twelve draught continental beers and over 50 bottled beers from around the world are also available. There is a small back room that plays host to the committee meetings of the local CAMRA branch. Food is limited to good value rolls and pies. Simply outstanding – a Mecca for visitors to Norwich.
(16,19,20)

Gate House

391 Dereham Road, NR5 8QJ
12-11 (midnight Fri & Sat) (01603) 620340
Grain Oak G**; Greene King IPA, Abbot; Woodforde's Wherry** H
This quiet local can be found two miles west of Norwich city centre. There is always a warm welcome in winter thanks to a log fire in the larger of the two oak-panelled bars. In the summer the garden area overlooking the Wensum is a delight. There is live music on Friday and Saturday and the pub is proud of its crib, ladies' darts and three pool teams. Prices are among the most attractive in the area, making this lovely pub excellent value.
Q (19,20)P

Ketts Tavern

29 Ketts Hill, NR1 4EX
12-midnight (11 Sun) (01603) 449654
Wolf Golden Jackal; Woodforde's Wherry; guest beers H
At the bottom of Ketts Hill and not far from the yacht station, this pub serves up to six guest ales, many from Norfolk. It also hosts many beer festivals with a geographical theme throughout the year. There is a conservatory, which is children-friendly, and a smoking area at the rear. Many sports teams call this pub home, and quizzes are held once a fortnight. The local Indian takeaway provides an ordering service for customers in the evening. (19,20)P

King's Arms

22 Hall Road, NR1 3HQ
11-11 (11.30 Fri & Sat); 12-10.30 Sun (01603) 766361
kingsarmsnorwich.co.uk
Adnams Bitter; Batemans XB, XXXB; Beeston Worth the Wait; Hop Back Summer Lightning; guest beers H
Situated just to the south of the city centre, this warm, welcoming gem of a pub is well worth a visit. Most of the Batemans range of beers is available, complemented by a large number of

guests. Famed for allowing customers to bring in their own grub (plates and condiments provided), food is served at lunchtimes, as well as amazing value Sunday roasts. The pub has regular quiz nights and hosts a well-attended festival of beer in November. Batemans Customer Service Pub of the Year. ❀◐♿♣●⚡

King's Head

42 Magdalen Street, NR3 1JE
✪ 12-midnight (11 Sun) ☎ (01603) 620468
🌐 kingsheadnorwich.co.uk
Winter's Kings Head Bitter; Woodforde's Nelson's Revenge; guest beers Ⓗ
This warm, welcoming, fantastic pub is well stocked with a rotating range of reasonably priced real ales mostly from Norfolk and East Anglia. It has won local CAMRA Pub of the Year twice in recent years, and carries an excellent range of continental bottled beers. No keg beers of any sort are sold here. One of just a few pubs in the area with its own bar billiards table, it even hosts a league. A small selection of sandwiches and locally-sourced pies is available. Q🚌♣●⚡▯

Murderers/Gardeners Arms

2-8 Timberhill, NR1 3LB (close to Norwich Castle)
✪ 10-11.30 (1.30am Fri & Sat); 12-10.30 Sun
☎ (01603) 621447
Adnams Bitter; Woodforde's Wherry Ⓗ
This popular city-centre free house is located in Norwich's main shopping area and close to the Castle, with the somewhat odd double name of The Gardeners Arms and The Murderers. The interior contains a number of drinking areas on split levels. In 1991 the pub took over the adjacent property, naming it The Murderers Café Bar, to provide an extra room which can be booked for private functions. The range of nine real ales includes a house beer. ❀◐♿🚌

Ribs of Beef ✔

24 Wensum Street, NR3 1HY
✪ 11-12.30am (1am Fri & Sat); 12-12.30am Sun
☎ (01603) 619517 🌐 ribsofbeef.co.uk
Adnams Bitter; Courage Best Bitter; Elgood's Black Dog; Woodforde's Wherry Ⓗ
A popular city-centre local, on the banks of River Wensum, next to Fye Bridge and close to the cathedral. The Ribs is famous for its range of cask ales, local cider and traditional English food, much of which is sourced locally. There is a nearby jetty where in the summer visiting boats can moor to enjoy the pub's facilities. Sports enthusiasts can enjoy live sports on the large screens in the bar. A riverside room is available for hire.
◐◑⇌🚌(21,22)●

Take 5

17 Tombland, NR3 1HF TG233088
✪ 11-11 ☎ (01603) 763099
Woodforde's Wherry, Norfolk Nog Ⓗ
This Grade II-listed building, parts of which date from the 17th century, is at the north end of Norwich's historic Tombland. It opened under its present name in 2004. It has a continental café bar feel to it, especially at lunchtime, providing home-cooked food. A range of around four real ales is available, including Woodforde's and guests, often from local brewers. There is also a selection of bottled beers plus real cider. A large function room is upstairs. ◐◑⇌🚌(21,22)●

Trafford Arms ✔

61 Grove Road, NR1 3RL
✪ 11-11 (11.30 Fri & Sat); 12-10.30 Sun ☎ (01603) 628466
Adnams Bitter; Woodforde's Wherry; guest beers Ⓗ
Welcoming, well-run community local close to the city centre. The row of handpumps that greets you shows the extensive choice and quality of the beers on offer. There is always at least one dark mild available. The pub is open plan, with a pool table and a large TV screen on one side. Delicious food is served lunchtimes and early evenings. The Valentine's beer festival is a highlight not to be missed. A previous Norfolk Pub of the Year winner.
❀◐◑🚌(9,17)♣●P⚡

Vine

7 Dove Street, NR2 1DE (close to market near Guildhall)
✪ 11-11; 12-9 Sun ☎ (01603) 627362 🌐 vinethai.co.uk
Oakham JHB; Wolf Coyote Bitter Ⓗ
Located just off the Market Place, this former Adnams house is Norwich's smallest pub. Dating from 1842 but closed down in 2006, it reopened in late 2008 as a combination of a traditional English pub and a Thai restaurant. The restaurant, offering excellent quality Thai cuisine, is upstairs, although some customers prefer to eat downstairs in the bar area. In summer tables and chairs are set out in the pedestrianised street outside where customers can while away their time watching shoppers go by.
Q◐◑⇌🚌♣⚡

White Lion

73 Oak Street, NR3 3AQ (just off the inner link road, near Barn Road roundabout)
✪ 12-2.30, 5-11; 12-11 Fri & Sat; 12-10.30 Sun
☎ (01603) 632333 🌐 individualpubs.co.uk/whitelion
Milton Dionysus, Minotaur, Pegasus, Sparta; guest beers Ⓗ
A three-roomed pub, now owned by Milton Brewery, serving a range of its own beers plus guests from across East Anglia. Food is served lunchtimes and early evenings. A good malt whisky selection is stocked. There are many pub games and weekly quiz nights. An outside smoking area adjoins the main building. Historic details of the surrounding area, and the many pubs that existed close by, have been researched by the pub landlord and put on view. Q❀◐◑🚌♣⚡

Wig & Pen

6 St Martins Palace Plain, NR3 1RN (near Cathedral)
✪ 11.30-11 (midnight Fri & Sat); 11.30-6 Sun
☎ (01603) 625891 🌐 thewigandpen.com
Adnams Bitter; Caledonian Deuchars IPA; Fuller's London Pride; guest beers Ⓗ
Renowned, friendly, 17th-century free house with a spacious outside patio. A range of at least six local and national guest beers is available and a number of themed beer festivals are held throughout the year. The owner is proud of his Cask Marque accreditation and offers a 'try before you buy' policy. The small back room can be used for meetings. Major sporting events are shown on a large-screen TV. A comprehensive lunchtime and evening menu is served. ♨❀◐◑⇌🚌⚡

Old Costessey

Bush

58 The Street, NR8 5DD TG174119
✪ 11 (12 Sun)-11 ☎ (01603) 747227

Fuller's London Pride; Theakston Traditional Mild; Woodforde's Wherry H
Village pub dating back to the 19th century and once frequented by the artist Alfred Munnings. Inside, the pub has been modernised yet retains a beamed ceiling. The interior is divided into two bars, one with a dartboard, the other with a large open fire. Outside there is a large beer garden leading down to the river. Regular beers are from Woodforde's and Fuller's, with one guest beer. ♣P

Old Hunstanton

Ancient Mariner

Golf Course Road, PE36 6JJ
11 (12 Sun)-11 (01485) 534411
theancientmariner.co.uk
Adnams Bitter, Broadside; guest beers H
A popular pub with beer gardens with views of the sea and beaches. The inn has been created from old barns and stables and adjoins the Le Strange Arms Hotel. There is also a children's room and restaurant. Four real ales are available. The lawns, including a children's play area, stretch down to the dunes and beach. Old Hunstanton is the only village on the east coast to face west, and offers superb views of spectacular sunsets over the sea. Q(36)P

Poringland

Royal Oak

44 The Street, NR14 7JT (on B1332) TG267023
12-3, 5-11; 12-midnight Fri & Sat; 12-11 Sun
(01508) 493734
Fuller's London Pride; Woodforde's Wherry H
Voted CAMRA Norfolk Pub of the Year in 2007, this is unashamedly a beer-oriented pub, offering a large range of beers from brewers across the UK, together with ales from a number of the best local breweries. There are always eight to 10 ales on at any time. The interior is warmly and invitingly laid out, with numerous nooks and small seating areas for drinkers. No food is available, but an excellent fish and chip shop adjoins the pub for those in need of more solid fare. Q(587,588)♣P

Reedham

Lord Nelson

38 Riverside, NR13 3TE TG418016
12-midnight; closed Mon Nov-Mar (01493) 701548
lordnelsonpub.com
Green Jack Lurcher Stout; Greene King IPA; Humpty Dumpty Little Sharpie; guest beers H
This welcoming village free house is situated on the banks of the River Yare, with an outdoor seating area offering fine views of the river and marshes. Free moorings just outside the pub are available to boaters. The beer range always includes ales from local brewers such as nearby Humpty Dumpty, and increases in summer. The menu contains locally-sourced food including vegetarian options. Regular folk sessions and periodic live music enliven an already vibrant pub. Q♣P

Ship

19 Riverside, NR13 3TQ (on banks of River Yare by railway swing bridge) TG422016
11-11; 12-10.30 Sun (01493) 700287
Adnams Bitter, Broadside; Woodforde's Wherry; guest beers H
The pub is beautifully located on the Yare underneath the famous railway swing bridge. At the front there is a large riverside garden that includes a children's play area and a smoking shelter. There is a main bar with a separate public bar complete with pool table and two dining areas where families are welcome. The rear dining room is full of historic paraphernalia with accordions and brass instruments, bedwarmers and chamber pots. Good food is a part of the pub's trade. P

Reepham

King's Arms

Market Place, NR10 4JJ (in market square) TG099231
11.30-3, 5.30-11; 12-3, 7-10.30 Sun (01603) 870345
Adnams Bitter, Broadside; Elgood's Cambridge Bitter; Greene King Abbot; Woodforde's Wherry; guest beer H
An old 17th-century former coaching inn situated in the market square of this picturesque mid-Norfolk village. There are several drinking and dining areas on split levels. Charm and character have been retained, with many original beams, brickwork and open fires. An original glass-topped well can be viewed in the conservatory. The comprehensive menu includes food sourced from nearby butchers and bakers. Regular live jazz bands play in the rear forecourt on Sunday afternoons. Dogs are welcome. Cars can be parked on the market square. Q♣P

Ringland

Swan Inn

The Street, NR8 6AB TG140138
11-11 (1am Fri & Sat); 12-11 Sun (01603) 868214
tasteofoz.com/swaninn
Adnams Bitter; Woodforde's Wherry, Nelson's Revenge H
Situated close to the banks of the River Wensum, this 400-year-old pub combines a traditional local with an Australian-themed restaurant, The Taste of Oz, offering Australian and Asian cuisine. English-style traditional bar snacks can be purchased in the Riverview restaurant within the pub area. Although the beer menu in the restaurant concentrates mainly on Australian beers, a choice of at least two real ales, usually from local brewers, is available in the pub. Disabled access is via the restaurant. P

Ringstead

Gin Trap Inn

6 High Street, PE36 5JU
11.30-11 summer; 11-2.30 (2 Sun), 6-11 winter
(01485) 525264 gintrapinn.co.uk
Adnams Bitter; Woodforde's Wherry; guest beers H
Attractive village inn with whitewashed walls and a pantile roof, set in the centre of the village. The large single bar has a beamed ceiling, log burner and walls adorned with old artefacts. Up to five ales are available and excellent home-cooked food is served in various rooms as well as the restaurant. Also available are three en-suite double rooms. A popular quiz night is held every Sunday. Dogs are welcome. P

Roydon

Union Jack
30 Station Road, PE32 1AW
⏲ 12 (4 Tue-Thu)-midnight ☎ (01485) 601347
Beer range varies ⊞
A village drinkers' pub that relies solely on its beer trade, a rare find in this area. It offers up to four guest beers, mostly around 4.2% ABV, with a mild often featuring. Ales are chosen in consultation with the regulars and occasional beer festivals are held. The pub supports many sports activities and a good quantity of trophies is on display. Live music is performed some weekends. Dogs are welcome in the bar. Voted local CAMRA Pub of the Year 2009. ⛫❀🚌(48)♣

Salthouse

Dun Cow ✔
Coast Road, NR25 7XA (on A149) TG073439
⏲ 11 (12 Sun)-11 ☎ (01263) 740467
🌐 theduncow-salthouse.co.uk
Adnams Bitter; Greene King Abbot; Taylor Landlord; Woodorde's Wherry ⊞
Busy inn situated on the north Norfolk coast road overlooking Salthouse Marshes, a popular location for bird watchers. The main bar has a double-pitched roof and the wooden trough that forms the central gutter is visible in the ceiling. An extensive food menu offering many local dishes is available all day. Adnams Bitter is only available from Easter to September. Walkers, children and dogs are welcome. ⛫❀⇄◖◗♿🚌(36)P⁄

Sheringham

Crown ✔
East Cliff, NR26 8BQ (on promenade)
⏲ 10 (12 Sun)-11 ☎ (01263) 823213
🌐 crownsheringham.co.uk
Adnams Broadside; Fuller's London Pride; Greene King IPA, Abbot; Woodforde's Wherry ⊞
This venue is situated on the promenade next to Sheringham lifeboat museum and offers commanding views of Sheringham beach and the North Sea. The interior comprises three wood-panelled lounges and a central bar. One bar contains a pool table and there is a dartboard in another room. A range of five real ales is usually available. ❀◖◗♿⛺≠🚌♣P⁄

Two Lifeboats Hotel
2 High Street, NR26 8JR (far end of High St)
⏲ 11-11; 12-12.30 Sun ☎ (01263) 822401
🌐 twolifeboats.co.uk
Adnams Bitter, Broadside; Greene King IPA ⊞
A friendly locals' pub situated at the end of the High Street. Both the pub's bars are named after famous old Sheringham lifeboats, hence the name. There is the Duncan Bar, frequented predominantly by locals, and the Augusta Bar, a lounge offering great views of Sheringham beach. Patio doors lead out to a beer terrace facing the sea. En-suite accommodation is available. This pub can become busy with tourists during the summer season. Q❀⇄◖◗⊟♿⛺≠🚌♣

Windham Arms
15-17 Wyndham Street, NR26 8BA (just off High St)
⏲ 12-11 (11.30 Fri-Sun) ☎ (01263) 822609
🌐 thewindhamarms.co.uk
Greene King Abbot; Wolf Straw Dog; Woodforde's Wherry, Norfolk Nog ⊞
This cosy two-bar local with its Dutch-style gables is situated on a narrow back street just behind the High Street. There is a main bar plus restaurant and a separate function room. Outside is a small drinking area with views of the North Sea. Four regular real ales are served plus guests in summer. Greek food is the pub speciality, available lunchtimes and evenings. Robert Sunman, the pub's first landlord, built Sheringham's first lifeboat, The Augusta, and the pub is still frequented by lifeboat men. Q♨❀◖◗⊟⛺≠🚌●P⁄

Smallburgh

Crown
North Walsham Road, NR12 9AD (on A149 NE of Wroxham) TG330245
⏲ 12-3 (not Mon), 5.30 (7 Sat)-11; 12-3 Sun
☎ (01692) 536314
Adnams Bitter; Greene King IPA; Woodforde's Wherry; guest beers ⊞
Friendly former coaching inn in the village with a thatched roof and original timbers lending character to the interior. Five ales with two guests give plenty of choice, while seasonal local produce is used in the home-cooked food. Meals may be enjoyed in the dining room, the bar or, in summer, the peaceful tree-fringed garden. The log fire provides a cosy winter atmosphere. Outside is a covered, heated smoking area. Close to the Broads and the north Norfolk coast, a warm welcome awaits at this popular gem. ⛫Q❀⇄◖◗🚌♣P⁄

Snettisham

Rose & Crown
Old Church Road, PE31 7LX
⏲ 11-11; 12-10.30 Sun ☎ (01485) 541382
🌐 roseandcrownsnettisham.co.uk
Adnams Bitter, Broadside; Woodforde's Wherry; guest beers ⊞
Village inn dating back to the 14th century with a modern hotel facility at the rear with 16 rooms. The front bars are small and unspoilt with old fireplaces, tiled floors, exposed beams and low ceilings. A larger back bar is reached through a narrow passage. Home-cooked meals are prepared using local produce. Dogs are welcome. Very busy during the summer months.
⛫Q♨❀⇄◖◗⊟🚌(40,41)P⁄

Stibbard

Ordnance Arms
Guist Bottom, NR20 5PF (on A1067) TF987267
⏲ 12-3 (Sat only), 5.30-midnight; 12-10.30 Sun
☎ (01328) 829471 🌐 ordnancearms.co.uk
Greene King IPA; Woodforde's Nelson's Revenge; guest beer ⊞
Situated on the Norwich to Fakenham road, this is a traditional, welcoming establishment and one of the few remaining estate-owned public houses in the county. The bar area has three small rooms: a cosy main bar with comfortable seating and a real fire, a second bar with stone flooring and simple wooden furniture, and a third room with a pool table. To the back is a popular Thai restaurant offering excellent food five nights a week (closed Sun and Mon). ⛫Q◗🚌(X29)P⁄

Swanton Morley

Angel

66 Greengate, NR20 4LX (on B1147 towards S edge of village) TG012162
✪ 12-11; 12-10 (6 winter) Sun ☎ (01362) 637407
🌐 theangelpub.co.uk
Hop Back Summer Lightning; Mighty Oak Oscar Wilde; Woodforde's Wherry; guest beers Ⓗ
Parts of this old inn date back to 1610, and it boasts a connection with Abraham Lincoln's family. The present owners are keen CAMRA members. The interior comprises a spacious main bar with real fire, and dried hops adorning the beams, a dining room serving food lunchtimes and evenings, and a small games room with pool, darts, shove ha'penny and skittles. Five beers are usually available. The garden includes a bowling green. Two beer festivals are held annually at Easter and in November. **♨Q❀◐▣(4)♣P**

Thetford

Albion

93-95 Castle Street, IP24 2DN (opp Castle Hill)
✪ 12-11 (11.30 Thu); 12-12.30am Fri; 11-12.30am Sat
☎ (01842) 752796
Greene King IPA, Abbot Ⓗ
Small, friendly local set in a row of flint cottages, run by the same family for over 40 years. It overlooks Castle Park with its highest Norman motte in England. There is a quiet, conversational main bar and a lower room with a pool table. Quiz nights are the first and third Sundays at 8pm. Live music features frequently on Saturday night. No food is available but you can order takeaways from local restaurants for delivery to the pub.
Q❀⇌♣⌐

Black Horse

64 Magdalen Street, IP24 2BP
✪ 12-11; 11-1am Fri; 11-midnight Sat ☎ (01842) 762717
Greene King IPA; guest beers Ⓗ
Lovable local run by a mother and son duo, a true free house with four real ales and a penchant for small local breweries. Great pub food with added flair is prepared by a Swiss chef. This is a well-supported local that hosts three dart leagues and one cribbage league. There is a separate dining room and three distinct drinking areas served by a wraparound bar. A large garden offers drinkers another option when the weather co-operates.
Q❀◐⇌♣P⌐

Thompson

Chequers

Griston Road, IP24 1PX (signed to left in village if travelling from Watton)
✪ 11-3, 6.30-11; 12-3, 7-10.30 Sun ☎ (01953) 483360
🌐 thompsonchequers.co.uk
Beer range varies Ⓗ
A beautiful thatched 16th-century inn in the middle of Breckland on the ancient Peddars Way, the Chequers has two to three guest ales normally from Greene King, Adnams and Elgood's. The approach to the bar is obstructed by a low beam so if you are more than 16th-century-sized keep your head down! Food is served seven days a week, and booking is advisable for Sundays. The pub is food-focused without much nattering space, but in summer it is very pleasant to sit outside.
♨❀⛿◐♣P

Thornham

Lifeboat ✔

Ship Lane, PE36 6LT (signed off A149 coast road)
✪ 11-11 (10.30 Sun) ☎ (01485) 512236 🌐 lifeboatinn.co.uk
Adnams Bitter; Greene King IPA, Abbot; Woodforde's Wherry; guest beers Ⓗ
Busy pub on the edge of the salt marsh with a wide range of places to drink, from the dark and cosy bar lit by oil lamps, to the light and airy conservatory with a huge grapevine. There is extensive seating in the garden and an exciting play area for children. A hotel and restaurant are attached. Whether sheltering from a northerly gale in January or in from a day on the beach, this is a very comforting place for a pint. **♨Q⛴❀⛿◐♿⛺▣♣P**

Tibenham

Greyhound

The Street, NR16 1PZ TM136895
✪ 6.30 (6 Fri)-midnight; 12-midnight Sat & Sun
☎ (01379) 677676
Adnams Bitter, Broadside; Fuller's London Pride; guest beer Ⓗ
A two-bar pub in what is supposedly Norfolk's remotest village. The public bar features a jukebox and games machines. The saloon is quiet and comfortable, displaying memorabilia from film actor James Stewart's service at the nearby airfield in World War II. The pub also boasts a function room, dining room and a games room in a separate barn. Bar snacks are available at all sessions, and there are facilities for camping. Guest beers are normally from local breweries. **♨⛴❀◑⊟⛺♣P⌐**

Trunch

Crown

Front Street, NR28 0AH (opp church) TG287348
✪ 12-3 (not Mon), 5.30-11 (11.30 Fri); 12-3.30, 5.30-11.30 Sat; 12-4.30, 7-10.30 Sun ☎ (01263) 722341
🌐 trunchcrown.co.uk
Batemans XB, GHA, XXXB; Greene King IPA; guest beers Ⓗ
Set in the middle of this charming north Norfolk village with fine old flint cottages, the Crown is Batemans only pub in the area, and offers an excellent choice of beers, with frequently changing guests. XXXB is sometimes replaced by a Batemans seasonal beer. The website has details of beer festivals and forthcoming events such as the monthly quiz night. Dogs are welcome in the bar. Trunch is not far from the north Norfolk coast.
♨Q❀◐♿▣(5,34)P

Walcott

Lighthouse Inn ✔

Coast Road, NR12 0PE (on B1159) TG359319
✪ 11-11 ☎ (01692) 650371 🌐 lighthouseinn.co.uk
Beer range varies Ⓗ
This large, family-friendly pub is located on the coast road between Cromer and Great Yarmouth. It has been owned and run by the same landlord for over 20 years. A rotating range of four real ales is available in summer, but fewer in winter. There is a separate function/family room and a large beer garden with a family marquee during the summer season. Hot, quality home-made food is available daily from 11-10.30pm, including a children's menu. **♨⛴❀◐⛺♣P**

Warham All Saints

Three Horseshoes

Bridge Street, NR23 1NL (2 miles SE of Wells) TF948417
✪ 12-2.30, 6-11 (10.30 Sun) ☎ (01328) 710547
Greene King IPA; Woodforde's Wherry; guest beers Ⓗ/Ⓖ
This old rural gem has been serving beers for nearly 300 years and has stone floors, scrubbed pine furniture and gas lighting. Its three connected rooms are filled with a jumble of antiques and pictures, including the traditional game of Norfolk Twister in the first bar. The pub is renowned for good plain cooking, featuring soups, pies and puddings. It can be busy with diners at lunchtime and early evening in the summer, but is often quieter at other times. ♨Q❀⇌◑◐♿Ⓐ♣●P

Wells-next-the-Sea

Albatros

The Quay, NR23 1AT (moored on quayside)
✪ 12-11 ☎ (07979) 087228 🌐 albatros.eu.com
Woodforde's Wherry, Nelson's Revenge; guest beer Ⓖ
The Albatros is a North Sea clipper sailing ship built in 1899 and the last commercial sailing boat of this type in the UK. It has been located centrally in Wells harbour since 2001. The bar, situated in the hold of the ship, is adorned with much nautical memorabilia including many shipping maps. Dutch pancakes, savoury or sweet, are a speciality here. Live bands perform regularly. Being a 19th-century vessel it is not disabled friendly. ⇌◑◐🚌(36)

West Acre

Stag

Low Road, PE32 1TR
✪ closed Mon; 12-3, 6.30-11; 12-11 Fri; 6.30-11 Sat
☎ (01760) 755395 🌐 westacrestag.co.uk
Beer range varies Ⓗ
The pub can be found at the east end of picturesque West Acre, a village renowned for its historic ruins. Local CAMRA Pub of the Year 2005 and a member of LocAle, it has maintained a high standard, with three varying ales. There is a very popular restaurant with a wide choice of food. Annual beer festivals and battle re-enactments take place. The large car park has a water trough for horses and is also popular with walkers and cyclists. ♨Q❀◑◐🚂♿Ⓐ🚌(A48)♣P

Wicklewood

Cherry Tree

116 High Street, NR18 9QA TG075022
✪ 5-11; 3-1am Fri; 12-1am Sat; 12-midnight Sun
☎ (01953) 606962
Buffy's Bitter, Polly's Folly, Norwegian Blue Ⓗ/Ⓖ**; guest beers** Ⓗ
One of Buffy's two tied houses, the L-shaped bar boasts an unusual naturally curved top made from planks of solid oak. The pub hosts a number of evening entertainments including a monthly quiz night, bingo, jam session and folk night, and every Sunday lunchtime a Chase the Ace game. Home-cooked food is available evenings and all day Friday, Saturday and Sunday. Guest beers are normally from the Buffy's range, although beers from other breweries are sometimes available as guests. ❀◐P

Winterton-on-Sea

Fisherman's Return

The Lane, NR29 4BN (off B1159) TG495194
✪ 11-2.30, 5-11; 11-11 Sat; 12-10.30 Sun ☎ (01493) 393305
🌐 fishermans-return.com
Woodforde's Wherry, Norfolk Nog; guest beers Ⓗ
Situated in an attractive coastal village, close to the beach, the Broads and the resort of Great Yarmouth, this traditional brick and flint 17th-century pub has an interesting collection of memorabilia inside. The beers are complemented by Westons Old Rosie cider. Meals are home-prepared using local produce when available and may be enjoyed in the bar or dining room. Log fires feature in winter. A separate function/family room can cater for all occasions, and three en-suite bedrooms are available all year.
♨☋❀⇌◑◐🚂♿🚌♣●P⚋

Woodbastwick

Fur & Feather Inn

Slad Lane, NR13 6HQ (just off B1140) TG328151
✪ 10 (11 Sun)-11.30 ☎ (01603) 720003
🌐 thefurandfeatherinn.co.uk
Woodforde's Mardlers, Wherry, Sundew, Nelson's Revenge, Norfolk Nog, Admiral's Reserve, Headcracker Ⓖ
This independently-run large country pub was opened in the early 1990s as a conversion from three cottages. It serves as the brewery tap for Woodforde's Brewery, which is next door. A visit to the brewery can be pre-booked and combined with your visit. There have been recent extensions sympathetically incorporating a function and dining room. It is a fairly food-oriented pub offering an extensive menu. There is a large garden where regular events are held. Q☋❀◑◐♿P⚋

Wreningham

Bird in Hand

Church Road, NR16 1BJ (7 miles from Norwich on B1113) TM166988
✪ 11-3, 5.30-11.30; 12-3.30, 7-11 Sun ☎ (01508) 489438
🌐 birdinhandwreningham.com
Adnams Bitter; Draught Bass; Woodforde's Wherry; guest beers Ⓗ
Very much a food-oriented pub, with two restaurants, one very stylishly decorated and furnished in a Victorian style. Bar meals are available in the spacious tie-beam-roofed main bar, which is decorated with agricultural implements and breweriana. Of special note is the massive Bass mirror. Food is available at all sessions and families are welcome. The two guest beers come from East Anglian breweries.
❀◑◐♿P⚋

Wymondham

Cross Keys

Market Place, NR18 0AX (at top end of Market Place)
✪ 11-2.30, 5-11 winter; 11-3, 5-11 (Fri & Sat 11-11) summer; 12-6.30 winter; 12-10.30 summer Sun ☎ (01953) 602152
Adnams Bitter; Fuller's London Pride; Wolf Straw Dog Ⓗ
Timbered Grade II-listed 16th-century town-centre pub conveniently situated at the top end of the market place, adjacent to Market Cross and bus stops. Most of the present exterior is Victorian apart

from the old timbers. The interior has recently been sympathetically refurbished to a high standard. A large range of around nine real ales is usually available, including beers from Wolf and Timothy Taylor. Real cider is served in summer. Food is available lunchtimes and evenings.
(14,14B,15)

Feathers Inn

13 Town Green, NR18 0PN (just off bottom end of Market Place)

11-2.30, 7-11; 6-midnight Fri; 7-11.30 Sat; 12-2.30, 7-10.30 Sun ☎ (01953) 605675

Adnams Bitter; Fuller's London Pride; Greene King Abbot; guest beers

Only a short walk from Wymondham Abbey and close to the market place, the Feathers is an excellent local pub that dates from the early 18th century. It has a cosy bar with alcoves and the walls are adorned with farming and other memorabilia, including an old bike. The real ale range includes two guest beers plus a house beer, Feathers Tickler, brewed by Elgood's. A folk music night is held in the upstairs function room on the last Sunday of the month.
(14,14B,15)

Green Dragon

6 Church Street, NR18 0PH (just off Market Place nr Wymondham Abbey)

12-3, 5-11 (midnight Thu & Fri); 12-midnight Sat; 12-10.30 Sun ☎ (01953) 607907

Beer range varies

This magnificent old half-timbered inn dates from the late 15th century, and is located between the Market Place and Wymondham Abbey. In 1615 a great fire struck Wymondham and this building was one of the few to survive; you can see the scorch marks on the external timbers. The interior has two bars and a snug which retain many of their original beamed timbers. The rotating beer range of four real ales usually includes Nethergate Umbel Magna and beers from Green Jack, Wolf and Woodforde's.
(14,14B,15)

Bull, Fakenham (Photo: Warren Wordsworth)

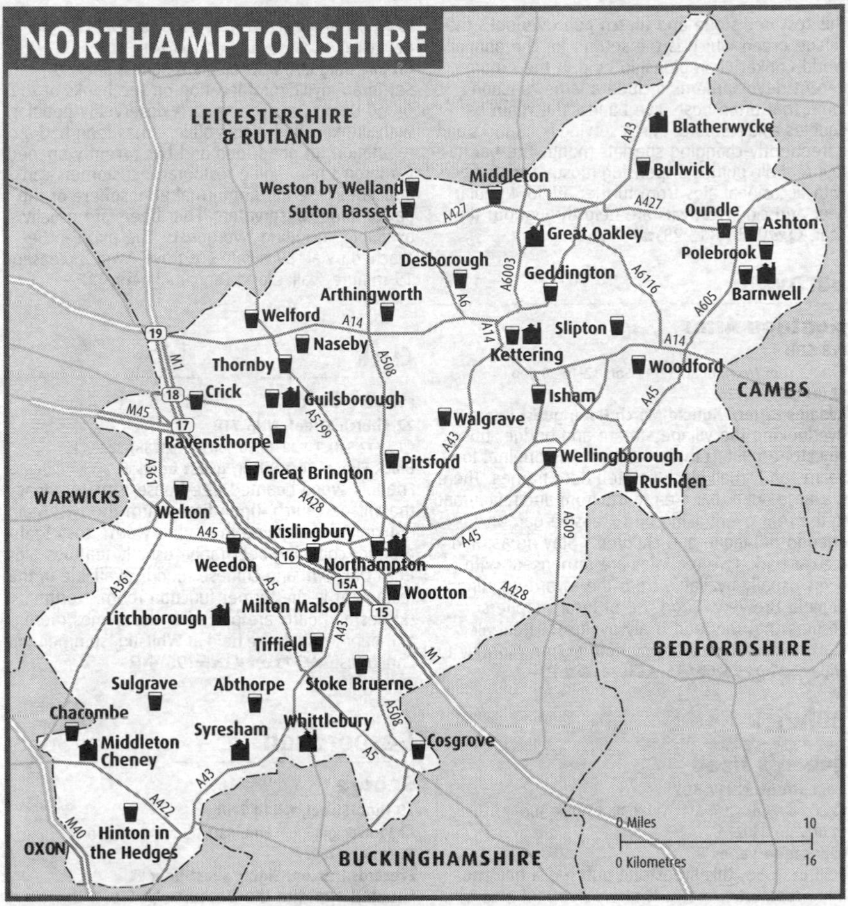

Abthorpe

New Inn

Silver Street, NN12 8QR SP648465

12-2.30 (not Mon & Tue), 6-11 (11.30 Sat); 12-4, 7-10.30 Sun ☎ (01327) 857306

Hook Norton Hooky Bitter, Gold, Old Hooky Ⓗ

This quintessentially English pub is hard to find, tucked away down a back street, though it is definitely worth the search. Traditional pub food is served in all bars, much of it locally sourced, including meat from the couple's own farm. Dating back to the early 19th century, the pub is built from local stone and features an inglenook fireplace. It offers ales from Hook Norton including the pub's house bitter, Abthorpe Ale, as well as occasional guests. No food served Sunday to Tuesday evenings. ♨❀◑♣P⚐—

Arthingworth

Bull's Head

Kelmarsh Road, LE16 8JZ (off A508)

12-3, 6-11; 12-10.30 Sun ☎ (01858) 525637

thebullsheadonline.co.uk

Thwaites Original, Lancaster Bomber; guest beers Ⓗ

A rural village pub in rolling countryside originally built as a 19th-century farmhouse. The pub has an opened-up bar room with several drinking areas and a restaurant to the front. Stables and barns to the rear have been converted into B&B accommodation. An annual August bank holiday beer festival is held on the suntrap patio. Popular with ramblers and cyclists, this is an ideal place to start or finish a walk in the local area. Home-cooked food is served using fresh produce. ♨Q❀⇌◑♿⛺♣●P⚐—

Ashton

Chequered Skipper

The Green, PE8 5LD

11.30-3, 6-midnight; 11.30-midnight Sat; 12-11.30 Sun ☎ (01832) 273494 chequeredskipper.co.uk

Brewster's Hophead; guest beers Ⓗ

INDEPENDENT BREWERIES

Cherwell Valley Middleton Cheney
Dare Whittlebury
Digfield Barnwell
Frog Island Northampton
Great Oakley Great Oakley
Hoggleys Litchborough
Julian Church Kettering
Nobby's Guilsborough
Potbelly Kettering
Rockingham Blatherwycke
Silverstone Syresham

This restored stone and thatch pub overlooks the village green which is the setting for the annual World Conker Championship held in the autumn. Recent developments include a large function room that often hosts live bands. The main bar doubles as a restaurant area serving bar snacks and a frequently-changing specials menu. The bar has four real ale pumps dispensing mostly LocAle beers with occasional ales from further afield. Regular beer and cider festivals are held throughout the year. Q❀◑♿🚌(15,25)●P⁻

Barnwell

Montagu Arms
PE8 5PH
✪ 12-3 (not Mon), 6-11; 12-11 Sat; 12-10.30 Sun
☎ (01832) 273726
Adnams Bitter; Digfield March Hare; guest beers Ⓗ
Overlooking the village stream and bridge, this limestone-built 16th-century inn has original low beams and small black painted door frames. There is a large public bar area to the front and restaurant to the rear overlooking an extensive garden offering petanque and children's play areas, and the car park. Five real ales are dispensed, with beers usually available from the award-winning Digfield Brewery. Good use of local suppliers ensures that the food is always fresh. Real ale drinkers can enjoy a happy hour 6-7pm Monday to Friday. ♨Q❀◑♿▲🚌(24)♣●P⁻

Bulwick

Queen's Head
Main Street, NN17 3DY
✪ closed Mon; 12-3, 6-11; 12-4.30, 7-10.30 Sun
☎ (01780) 450272
Beer range varies Ⓗ
Built in 1653, this limestone pub has a bar and three restaurant areas. It offers five real ales from small breweries around the country, usually including two local beers and a dark mild, porter or stout. The food is locally sourced with game coming from nearby country estates. The pub has won many awards for its well-kept beer and was Northamptonshire Dining Pub of the Year 2009. ♨Q❀◑♣P⁻

Chacombe

George & Dragon ✔
1 Silver Street, OX17 2JR (between A361 and B4525 near Banbury)
✪ 12-11 (midnight Fri & Sat); 12-10 Sun ☎ (01295) 711500
🌐 georgeanddragon.org
Everards Beacon, Tiger; guest beers Ⓗ
A village centre pub with bare stone walls and stone flooring creating a lovely country pub atmosphere. There are two rooms for drinkers and two for diners, including three very impressive fireplaces. Quiet background music plays. Outside is a pretty sun terrace. This Everards pub has two regular beers and one changing guest – another may be added if there is the demand. The 500 bus from Banbury-Brackley stops outside the pub. ♨Q❀◑♿🚌(500)♣P⁻

Cosgrove

Navigation
Thrupp Wharf, Station Road, MK19 7BE (off A508)
✪ 12-3, 5.30-11 (11.30 Fri); 12-11.30 Sat; 12-10.30 Sun
☎ (01908) 543156 🌐 navigationinn.net
Greene King IPA, H&H Olde Trip; guest beers Ⓗ
Set in an idyllic rural location on the banks of the Grand Union Canal, the pub is deservedly popular with drinkers and diners alike. It has long had a reputation for good food and has recently opened Cameron's fine dining restaurant. Customers can also eat in the more informal atmosphere of the bar or large conservatory. Four beers are usually available, including two guests. The pub can be reached by an 89 bus to Cosgrove, with a pleasant 15-minute walk along the canal. ♨❀◑P⁻

Crick

Royal Oak
22 Church Street, NN6 7TP
✪ 3 (12 Sat)-11; 12-10.30 Sun ☎ (01788) 822340
Black Sheep Best Bitter; guest beers Ⓗ
Friendly wood-beamed free house, situated near the village church. Open fires warm the two main drinking areas, giving the pub a warm, cosy feel. An ever-changing beer range usually features ales from Oakham, and Chinese food is available in the restaurant in the former function room. Northants skittles and darts are played in the games room and beer festivals are held at Whitsun, summer and Christmas. ♨Q❀◑▲🚌(96)♣P⁻

Desborough

George
79 High Street, NN14 2NB
✪ 11-midnight (1am Fri & Sat); 12-midnight Sun
☎ (01536) 760271
Everards Beacon, Tiger; guest beer Ⓗ
Situated opposite the Desborough Cross, this coaching inn built from local ironstone dates from the 17th century. The interior has been modernised with two main drinking areas and a separate lounge. Home to football, cricket, darts and pool teams, this community-oriented pub is popular with sports fans and has large TV screens. In summer the part-covered suntrap yard comes into its own. Guest ales are from the Everards list. Bar meals are served at lunchtime. ♨❀🛏◑♿🚌(19)♣P⁻

Geddington

Star Inn
2 Bridge Street, NN14 1AZ (follow signs for Eleanor Cross)
✪ 12-3, 6-11.30 (midnight Fri & Sat); 12-11.30 Sun
☎ (01536) 742386
Greene King IPA; guest beers Ⓗ
Dating from 1817, the pub stands opposite the Eleanor Cross. There are four rooms – a bar, lounge, raised dining area and a separate dining room serving home-cooked food made with local produce. The landlord is a keen supporter of the LocAle scheme – the beer range includes at least two local ales alongside interesting beers from further afield. Real cider is also available. The pub holds a quiz night every second Tuesday of the month and a beer festival in September. ♨❀◑♿🚌(8)♣●P⁻

Great Brington

Althorp Coaching Inn (Fox & Hounds)

Main Street, NN7 4JA

11-11 (11.45 Fri & Sat); 12-10.30 Sun ☎ (01604) 770651

althorp-coaching-inn.co.uk

Fuller's London Pride; Greene King IPA, Abbot; guest beers H

An ale house since 1765, this is a lovely traditional stone and thatch country pub with low ceilings, oak beams, flagstone floors and a large inglenook fireplace. The exterior is also a delight with a flower-filled garden, a garden room with fireplace, stables and an enclosed courtyard with seating. Close to Althorp House, home of the Spencer family and Princess Diana, whose burial place is nearby. The pub can be very busy at times but is well-worth seeking out. ⌂Q❀◐▶♣P⚟

Guilsborough

Ward Arms

High Street, NN6 8PY

12-2.30 (not Mon), 5.30-11; 12-11 Fri-Sun

☎ (01604) 740265

Nobby's Best, Guilsborough Gold; guest beers H

This 17th-century pub is situated in the heart of the village. Built from local ironstone with white rendering and a thatched roof, the old stables have been converted into Nobby's Brewery and visitor centre. A selection of Nobby's beers plus guest beers from the SIBA direct delivery scheme are on handpump. Traditional home-cooked, locally-sourced food is served. Live music plays on the last Saturday of the month. ⌂Q❀◐▶♣●P⚟

Hinton in the Hedges

Crewe Arms

Sparrow Corner, NN13 5NF (off A43/A422)

6-11 (midnight Thu-Sat); 12-11 Sun ☎ (01280) 705801

thecrewearms.com

Hook Norton Hooky Bitter; guest beers H

This gem is tucked away in a village that can be hard to find. Following a two-year closure, the pub was bought by two local villagers in 2004 who refurbished and redecorated it throughout. The interior is divided into four comfortable areas, retaining a traditional bar. Dining is popular, accompanied by local micro-brewery guest beers. A folk evening is held on the last Sunday of the month, and a quiz night on the first Monday. ⌂Q❀▶♿P⚟

Isham

Lilacs ✔

39 Church Street, NN14 1HD (off A509 at church)

12-3, 5.30-midnight; 12-1am Fri & Sat; 12-midnight Sun

☎ (01536) 723948

Greene King IPA, St Edmunds, Abbot; guest beers H

Named after a breed of rabbit, this hard-to-find village pub is at the heart of the community – popular with locals, diners and drinkers enjoying a well-kept pint. The pub has a lounge and a cosy snug at the front, complemented by a large games room towards the rear with two pool tables, darts and Northants skittles. Quiz and live music nights are held regularly. The guest beers are from the Greene King range. ⌂Q❀◐🚌(X4)♣P⚟

Kettering

Alexandra Arms

39 Victoria Street, NN16 0BU (400m from bus station)

2-11; 12-midnight Fri & Sat; 12-11 Sun ☎ (01536) 522730

Beer range varies H

Several times local CAMRA Pub of the Year, this two-room back-street local boasts 14 handpumps serving an interesting range of beers from new and unusual micros, with more than 5,000 different beers from more than 600 breweries over the last six years. Julian Church Brewery is now brewing in the cellar on the former Nobby's plant, with at least one beer from both breweries available at all times. The front bar is covered with pump clips. Northants skittles is played in the larger back room. Under 14s are not permitted. Well-worth the 10-minute walk from the railway station. Q❀🛏⚙≠🚌♣⚟

Beeswing

226 Rockingham Road, NN16 9AL (on A6003)

11-11 (midnight Fri & Sat); 12-11 Sun ☎ (01536) 481790

Everards Beacon, Tiger, Sunchaser, Original, seasonal beers H

A large estate pub with two rooms. The spacious front bar is divided into three areas: a lounge with large leather sofas and TV for football, a bar area and a dining area. The back room, the Vault, is usually quiet – no beer is served in this room. Not far from Kettering Town Poppies football ground, well-behaved away fans are made welcome. Sunday lunches, served 12-3pm, are a speciality (booking recommended). ❀◐♿🚌(B,X4)♣P⚟

Piper ✔

Windmill Avenue, NN15 6PS

11-3, 5-11; 11-4, 6-11 Sat; 12-10.30 Sun

☎ (01536) 513870

Hook Norton Hooky Bitter; Potbelly Best; guest beers H

Popular 1950s two-roomed pub and Potbelly Brewery tap, run by an enthusiastic CAMRA member who offers five changing beers from the Enterprise Inns direct delivery scheme. There is a quiet lounge serving home-cooked food until 10pm, complemented by a more lively bar/games room. Sunday is quiz night. Two beer festivals are held each year. Ideal for visitors to Wicksteed Park, Britain's first theme park. Q❀◐▶⚙♿🚌(B,X4)♣●P⚟

Kislingbury

Sun Inn

6 Mill Road, NN7 4BB

11.30-2, 5-11; 12-2.30, 6-11 Sat; 11.30-3.30, 7-11.30 Sun

☎ (01604) 833571

Tetley Bitter; guest beers H

Tucked away in the village, this thatched building has four cosy areas inside, with low beams and church pew seating. Complementing this olde-worlde feel are toby jugs and pub memorabilia adorning the walls. For the competitive pubgoer, Northants skittles and darts can be played as well as other traditional table games. Eight handpumps offer well-known guest ales and a couple of local Northants beers, including one from the Hoggleys Brewery. Good food is recommended. For smokers, a purpose-built under-cover heated area is to the front. ❀▶🚌♣●P⚟

Middleton

Red Lion

7 The Hill, LE16 8YX (off A427)
12-3, 6-midnight; 12-1am Sat; 12-11.30 Sun
(01536) 771268
Great Oakley Welland Valley Mild, Wot's Occuring; guest beer H

A large village pub with an extended bar, games room, lounge and restaurant, with a large garden that comes into its own during the Welland Valley Beer Festival in June. The landlord is a keen supporter of CAMRA's LocAle scheme and the guest beer is usually from a county brewery. Reasonably-priced food is sourced locally. Awarded CAMRA Pub of the Season in 2009, it always stocks a real cider from the local Rockingham Forest Cider which is pressed near the pub.

Milton Malsor

Compass

61 Green Street, NN7 3AT (between A43 & A508)
5-11 (midnight Fri); 12-midnight Sat; 12-11 Sun
(01604) 858365
Beer range varies H

Based in the heart of the village just outside Northampton, the Compass is a drinkers' pub and no food is served. It offers two changing beers, usually local, with Hoggleys Brewery a favourite. The long L-shaped interior has Northants skittles at one end and darts at the other. Two beer festivals are held each year in the outbuildings and live music features occasionally. Well-behaved children are welcome until 8pm.

Naseby

Royal Oak

Church Street, NN6 6DA (on B4036)
4.30 (3 Sat)-midnight; 12-7 Sun (07985) 408240
royaloaknaseby.co.uk
Beer range varies H

A well-supported former CAMRA Pub of the Season dating from the 1930s. The L-shaped single room is divided into three areas with a real fire in the wall between the main bar and games room. Recently a new kitchen has been added, enabling the pub to serve traditional basket meals. The lounge walls are adorned with farming implements, plates and other knick-knacks. Northants skittles, pool and darts are played. Adjoining barns host popular beer festivals in April and October. Recently Oakham Ales of Excellence accredited, five rotating guest beers are always available including a local beer.

Northampton

Bantam

7 Abington Square, NN1 4AE (on A4500)
12-midnight (4am Fri & Sat) (01604) 632534
Caledonian Deuchars IPA; Fuller's London Pride; St Austell Tribute; guest beers H

A new entry to the Guide, this pub is just off the town centre and has now gone back to its original name. The bar is in the centre of a large U-shaped room with tables, chairs and an area where food is cooked, and another area for live music. Three regular beers and several guests are available. Beer festivals are held with live music and comedy.

Bold Dragoon

48 High Street, Weston Favell, NN3 3JW
11.30-11.30; 12-3, 6-11.30 Sat; 12-10.30 Sun
(01604) 401221
Fuller's London Pride; Greene King IPA, Abbot; guest beers H

This 1930s pub is situated in a village now absorbed by the expansion of Northampton. There are at least three ever-changing guest beers available, with local breweries often represented. The lively bar has a pool table, darts and a sports TV. The lounge is quieter and the restaurant in the rear conservatory is a peaceful haven. Good quality food and bar snacks feature on the menu.

Eastgate

98-100 Abington Street, NN1 2BP (E end of pedestrianised zone)
9-midnight (1am Fri & Sat) (01604) 633535
Greene King Ruddles Best Bitter, Abbot; guest beers H

A former Lloyds No 1 Bar refurbished to become a Wetherspoon in 2009, offering two regular ales and two frequently-changing guest beers. The number of pints of real ale sold each week is displayed, with 1,000+ at the time of the survey. Westons' bag-in-a-box cider is stocked. The quiet two-level pub attracts a varied daytime clientele; Friday and Saturday nights are much busier with a younger crowd. TVs are mostly mute except for major sporting events. Two beer festivals are held a year.

Malt Shovel Tavern

121 Bridge Street, NN1 1DF (opp Carlsberg brewery)
11.30-3, 5-11; 12-3, 7-10.30 Sun (01604) 234212
Frog Island Natterjack; Fuller's London Pride; Great Oakley Wot's Occuring, Harpers; Tetley Bitter; guest beers H

Just off the town centre, this is a popular, award-winning pub. The tap for the Great Oakley Brewery, its beers always feature among the 14 handpumps. A real cider and Belgian draught and bottled beers are also available. The walls and ceilings are adorned with breweriana. At least two beer festivals are held each year, usually over bank holidays. Blues bands play on Wednesday nights. The pub has a strong rugby following and stays open all day at weekends when live games are screened. Well-worth visiting.

Queen Adelaide

50 Manor Road, Kingsthorpe, NN2 6QJ (2 miles from town centre off A5199)
11.30-11; 12-10.30 Sun (01604) 714524
queenadelaide.com
Adnams Bitter, Broadside; Copper Dragon Golden Pippin; guest beers H

This friendly pub retains a village inn feel although Kingsthorpe has been slowly swallowed up by the town's expansion. The interior is divided into three rooms, with a lounge, public bar and games room where Northants skittles is played. It serves up to four guest ales, often from local micro-breweries, and good home-made food is available most times. Rugby matches are shown on a large TV in the bar. A beer festival is held in the first week of September on the patio in the back garden.

Racehorse

15 Abington Square, NN1 4AE (on A4500)
⌚ 12-midnight (1am Sat) ☎ (01604) 631997
Beer range varies ⊞
A friendly pub with a relaxed atmosphere attracting a mixed clientele. A central bar divides the single room in two, with plenty of wood panelling and bench seating. A varied range of up to seven ales focuses on local micro-breweries, and at least one cider is available along with draught and bottled continental beers. Live bands play in the back bar. ❀🚌🍎⚡

Road to Morocco

Bridgewater Drive, Abington Vale, NN3 3AG (off A4500, near Abington Park)
⌚ 12-11 (midnight Fri & Sat); 12-10.30 Sun
☎ (01604) 632899
Greene King IPA, Abbot; Theakston Old Peculier; guest beers ⊞
A popular and welcoming two-roomed estate pub run by a landlord who enthusiastically promotes real ale, offering up to four guest beers as well as the regulars. Numerous themed events are held. Pool and darts are played in the lively public bar, Tuesday night is quiz night and poker is played on Thursday in the quieter lounge. All live sports are shown on screens in both bars. Wi-Fi internet access is available. ❀🍺♿🚌(5B)♣P⚡

Victoria Inn

2 Poole Street, NN1 3EX
⌚ closed Mon; 4-midnight (1am Fri); 12-1am Sat; 12-midnight Sun ☎ (01604) 633660
Vale Best, Gravitas; guest beers ⊞
Close to the racecourse, this difficult-to-find pub is well-worth seeking out. The Vic is owned by Vale Brewery but features many guest beers on its eight handpumps. Vale Gravitas is usually available on gravity. The single-roomed pub is always busy, with curry and cask nights, quiz nights and live music. There is a small decked area outside to the rear. Local CAMRA Pub of the Season 2009.
❀◐♣⚡

Oundle

Ship

18 West Street, PE8 4EF
⌚ 11-11.30 (midnight Fri & Sat), 12-11 Sun
☎ (01832) 273918 🌐 theshipinn-oundle.co.uk
Brewster's Hophead; Digfield March Hare; Elgood's Black Dog; guest beers ⊞
This old Grade II-listed coaching inn is on the main street, to the west of the town centre. The pub has many rooms and two separate bars, with black wooden beams and white-painted walls adding to the old world charm. The pub is reputedly haunted by a previous landlord who threw himself from an upstairs window. There are recent stone-built annexes and a little cottage on the site providing accommodation. 🔥Q🛏❀🛏◐🍺♿⛺🚌(X4)♣P⚡

Pitsford

Griffin Inn

25 High Street, NN6 9AD (between A43 & A508)
⌚ 6 (5 Fri)-11; 12-2.30, 7-11 Sun ☎ (01604) 880346
🌐 griffinpitsford.co.uk
Greene King Abbot; Potbelly Best; guest beers ⊞
A warm welcome is assured at this friendly 17th-century ironstone family owned and run free house. Locals gather in the small cosy bar room or around the small bar area in the larger comfortable lounge. The Griffin has kept most of its original character and is festooned with fascinating artefacts. The separate restaurant serves a high quality, reasonably priced short menu. Potbelly beers are among the regular guests.
Q❀◐🍺♿🚌(X7,62)P⚡

Polebrook

Kings Arms ✔

Kings Arms Lane, PE8 5LW
⌚ 12-3, 6-11 (midnight Fri); 12-11.30 Sat; 12-11 Sun
☎ (01832) 272363 🌐 thekingsarms-polebrook.co.uk
Adnams Bitter; Digfield Barnwell Bitter; guest beers ⊞
Located at the heart of the small village of Polebrook, this traditional thatched stone pub has a three-sided bar and three dining areas including the conservatory. The four handpumps are fitted with unusual wooden handles, dispensing a choice of beers from the nearby Digfield Brewery among others. The main rooms have a great deal of character with stone walls, inglenook fireplaces and wooden beams. There is an extensive food menu including specials and tapas. A good-sized enclosed garden is ideal for children to play.
🔥Q❀◐◐🍺⛺🚌(15,25)♣P⚡

Ravensthorpe

Chequers

Chequers Lane, NN6 8ER (between A428 and A5199)
⌚ 12-3, 6-11; 12-11 Sat; 12-3, 7-10.30 Sun
☎ (01604) 770379
Fuller's London Pride; Greene King IPA; Jennings Bitter; guest beers ⊞
Popular with locals, walkers and fishermen alike, you can be sure of a warm welcome from the lively, affable hosts of 20 years at this friendly pub. The brick-built Grade II-listed free house has an outdoor children's adventure play area and a separate building for Northants skittles. There is a collection of jugs on the beams, and bank notes on the half-panelled walls. The pub and restaurant area serve an extensive menu of good-value food.
🛏❀◐◐🚌(96)♣P⚡

Rushden

Rushden Historical Transport Society

Station Approach, NN10 0AW (on ring road)
⌚ 7.30 (12 Sat)-11; 12-3, 7.30-10.30 Sun ☎ (01933) 318988
🌐 rhts.co.uk
Fuller's London Pride; Oakham Bishops Farewell; guest beers ⊞
National winner of CAMRA Club of the Year 2010 and East Midlands regional winner in 2009, the station bar offers up to seven ales including a dark beer at weekends. The platform lounge bar is gas lit and enamel advertisements adorn the walls. Visitors are charged £1 per person or couple. Open weekends are held during the summer with steam and diesel hauled train rides. In May a traction engine and vintage vehicles cavalcade is held. A hidden gem – not to be missed. 🔥Q❀♿♣⚡🥛

Slipton

Samuel Pepys

Slipton Lane, NN14 3AR (off A6116)
⏲ 12-3, 6-11; 12-11 Sat & Sun ☎ (01832) 731739
🌐 samuel-pepys.com
Digfield Fools Nook; Greene King IPA; Oakham JHB Ⓗ**; guest beers** Ⓗ/Ⓖ
A popular ironstone pub dating from the 16th century encompassing several drinking and dining areas. To the front is a traditional low-beamed bar with brick flooring and leather chairs, to the side is the main lounge bar. There are further intimate drinking areas to the rear, and a restaurant in the conservatory. The guest beer on handpump is either from Digfield or Potbelly, with two further guests on gravity, often from other local micro-breweries. ♨Q❀◐◑⊟🚌(16)P⊬

Stoke Bruerne

Boat Inn

Bridge Road, NN12 7SB (opp canal museum)
⏲ 11-11; 12-10.30 Sun ☎ (01604) 862428 🌐 boatinn.co.uk
Banks's Bitter; Frog Island Best Bitter; Jennings Cumberland Ale; Marston's Burton Bitter, Pedigree, Old Empire Ⓗ
Situated on the banks of the Grand Union Canal, the Boat Inn has been run by the same family since 1877. The delightful tap bar's interconnecting rooms have canal views, open fires and window seats. A large, modern timber and stone barn-style extension upstairs houses a lounge, restaurant and cocktail bar. There is a small shop on site selling basic groceries, refreshments and souvenirs. Northants skittles is played adjacent to the front bar. ♨Q❀◐◑⊟♿🚌(86)♣P⊬

Sulgrave

Star Inn ✔

Manor Road, OX17 2SA (follow brown signs for Sulgrave Manor)
⏲ 12-11 summer; 12-3, 6-11 (closed Mon) winter; 12-11 (4 winter) Sun ☎ (01295) 760389 🌐 thestarinnsulgrave.com
Hook Norton Hooky Bitter, Old Hooky, seasonal beers Ⓗ
In a lovely village, this attractive 300-year-old ivy-clad stone pub is situated almost opposite Sulgrave Manor, the ancestral home of the George Washington family. The smart bar area retains its traditional look and feel with a stone-flagged floor, beamed ceiling, wooden settles and inglenook fireplace. The larger rear room is motor sport themed, and there is a small hospitality room on the other side of the bar. Accommodation is provided in four comfortable rooms.
♨Q❀🛏◐◑🚌(409,508)P

Sutton Bassett

Queen's Head

Main Street, LE16 8HP (on B664)
⏲ 12-3, 5-11; 12-10.30 Sun ☎ (01858) 463530
Adnams Bitter; Greene King IPA, Old Speckled Hen; Oakham JHB; Phipps Red Star; guest beers Ⓗ
A welcome return to the Guide for this 18th-century two-room pub with low-beamed ceilings and adorned with pictures. In the cosy bar to the rear is an open fire and a piano covered in silverware won by the pub's darts teams. Guest beers come from local micro-breweries. Locally-sourced home-cooked food is served, with Sunday roasts especially popular (booking recommended). A terrace to the rear offers fine views of the Welland Valley, with the pub taking part in the Welland Valley Beer Festival in June.
♨Q❀🛏◐◑♣P⊬

Thornby

Red Lion

Welford Road, NN6 8SJ (on A5199)
⏲ 12-2.30 (not Mon; 3 Thu & Fri), 5-11; 12-11.30 Sat; 12-10.30 Sun ☎ (01604) 740238
Wadworth Henry's IPA; guest beers Ⓗ
Situated on the old A50, this traditional village pub dates back more than 400 years. The simple bar has three drinking areas featuring wooden beams, and a wood-burning open fire in the lounge. To the rear is a compact restaurant. A motley collection of beer tankards, steins and paintings is displayed throughout. Five guest beers are available, usually from larger breweries and often from Dow Bridge on the county border. During the summer, classic car meetings are held along with pig roasts.
♨❀◐◑♿🚌P⊬

Tiffield

George Inn ✔

21 High Street, NN12 8AD (off A43)
⏲ 12-3 (not Tue), 6-midnight; 12-3, 5.30-1am Fri; 12-1am Sat; 12-7 Sun ☎ (01327) 350587 🌐 thegeorgeattiffield.co.uk
Vale Best Bitter; guest beers Ⓗ
A popular and welcoming village pub near Towcester dating from the 16th century with Victorian and more recent additions. It has three rooms – a cosy bar, games room featuring Northants skittles and a back room with an eclectic range of furniture and artwork. Two ever-changing guest beers and a Thatchers cider are on offer, with current and forthcoming beers detailed on the website. A quiz is held twice a month on Saturday and other events including beer festivals are hosted. ♨🐾❀◐◑♣🍎P⊬

Walgrave

Royal Oak

Zion Hill, NN6 9PN (2 miles N of A43)
⏲ 11.30-2.30, 5.30 (5 Fri & Sat)-11; 12-10.30 Sun
☎ (01604) 781248
Adnams Bitter; Greene King Abbot; guest beers Ⓗ
A classic Northamptonshire stone-built village pub. The front entrance leads to a central bar area flanked by two dining areas. The traditional interior features beams with hanging jugs and a stone inglenook fireplace. To the rear is a small lounge bar leading to a function room, and an outdoor room has Northants skittles. The garden has robust children's play equipment. There are three changing guest beers, with local breweries often featuring. ♨❀◐◑🚌(39)♣P

Weedon

Globe Hotel

High Street, NN7 4QD (jct A5/A45)
⏲ 10-11 ☎ (01327) 340336 🌐 globehotelweedon.co.uk
Hook Norton Hooky Bitter; guest beers Ⓗ
The Globe Hotel is a 19th-century posting house that was originally patronised by cavalry officers from the training centre in Weedon. Now a white-

painted privately owned hotel, the bar has a friendly and cosy pub atmosphere. Frequently changing guest beers come from local micro-breweries. There is also a separate room with a pool table, and a restaurant with a bar.
(D1,D2)P

Welford

Wharf Inn

NN6 6JQ (on A5199 N of village)
12-11 ☎ (01858) 575075
Marston's Burton Bitter, Pedigree; guest beers
Situated on the Leicestershire border, this brick-built inn lies at the end of the Welford Arm of the Grand Union Canal and is popular with narrow boat travellers, locals and tourists alike. There are several pleasant walks close by, including the Jurassic Way. Inside, the main bar and dining area are separated by a large open fire. A smaller bar is on a lower level to the front. Beer festivals and themed events are held regularly. Three to six guest beers are on offer, often from established micro-breweries. Wireless internet access is available. Q P

Wellingborough

Coach & Horses

17 Oxford Street, NN8 4HY
12-11 ☎ (01933) 441848
Beer range varies
Town-centre local fully committed to quality real ales. Up to 10 are available, with Adnams and local micro-breweries featuring regularly. Good, traditional home-cooked food is served lunchtimes and evenings. Lots of breweriana can be found in the front bar area which has a real fire. The large garden has a heated smoking shelter. Free Wi-Fi is available. CAMRA East Midlands regional Pub of the Year runner-up in 2009.

Golden Lion

19 Sheep Street, NN8 1BL (off A45 London Rd)
12-11 ☎ (01933) 227130
Beer range varies
This former Squires Lodge, close to the town centre, dates back to 1540. Converted into a public house in 1800, it retains many of the original features. Inside are two distinct areas, one boasting a high vaulted ceiling, minstrel gallery, oak panelling, wooden flooring and a huge framed mirror over an open stone fireplace; the other with red quarry brick flooring and a black-beamed ceiling. Up to four guest beers are available.

Locomotive

111 Finedon Road, NN8 4AL (on A510)
11 (12 Sun)-11 ☎ (01933) 276600
Hop Back Summer Lightning; Oakham JHB; Phipps IPA; Wychwood Hobgoblin; guest beers
A popular locals' pub on the outskirts of the town, not far from the railway station. A railway theme runs throughout, with a display of classic '00' gauge locomotives behind the bar and a railway running above the servery. With three rooms, the front bar has a relaxed atmosphere with armchairs and a piano, while the other rooms are more traditional. Themed beer festivals are held and there is always an unusual beer among the range of seven ever-changing ales, including many from local micro-breweries. (45)♣P

Welton

White Horse

High Street, NN11 2JP (off A361 betwen Rugby and Daventry)
12-3, 5-11; 12-midnight Sat & Sun ☎ (01327) 702820
Batemans XB; Black Sheep Best Bitter; Oakham Bishops Farewell; Purity Gold; guest beer
Charming 17th-century country pub heated with wood burners. There are two bars – a split-level public bar where skittles and darts are played, and a traditional beamed lounge leading to the restaurant. A large canopied patio overlooks the garden. Restaurant and bar food are available, and children and dogs are welcome. Traditional cider is served. Live bands play in the garden during the summer. Local CAMRA Country Pub of the Year 2008. Q♣P

Weston by Welland

Wheel & Compass

Valley Road, LE16 8HZ (off B664)
12-3, 5-11; 12-11 Fri & Sat; 12-10.30 Sun
☎ (01858) 565864 thewheelandcompass.co.uk
Banks's Bitter; Greene King Abbot; Marston's Burton Bitter, Pedigree; guest beers
The pub stands on the edge of the village opposite a farmyard and surrounded by fields. Inside it has two drinking areas and a large dining room serving good quality food at reasonable prices. A large family-friendly garden contains swings and slides – a big attraction in the summer. Guest beers come from all over the country. QP

Woodford

Duke's Arms

83 High Street, NN14 4HE (off A14/A510)
12-11 ☎ (01832) 732224
Greene King IPA, Abbot, H&H Olde Trip; guest beer
This popular village pub overlooking the village green was once called the Lord's Arms, named after the Duke of Wellington, who was a frequent visitor to Woodford. A games-oriented hostelry, it features Northants skittles, darts and pool. Home-cooked food is served daily (no food Sun eve). A beer festival is held on the Whit Sunday bank holiday weekend. (16)♣P

Wootton

Wootton Working Men's Club

High Street, NN4 6LW (off A508 near jct 15 M1)
12-2 (not Wed & Thu), 7-11; 12-3, 7-11.30 Fri & Sat; 11.30-10.30 Sun ☎ (01604) 761863
Great Oakley Wagtail; guest beers
This ironstone building was previously a pub and is now a multi-award-winning club. It was rescued from closure by the regulars and now supports local sports groups. There are many areas in which to enjoy a pint, including the bar, cosy lounge, function room and games room with Northants skittles. Up to five guest beers are available. Show this Guide or a CAMRA membership card for admittance. Local CAMRA Club of the Year 2008.
Q♣P

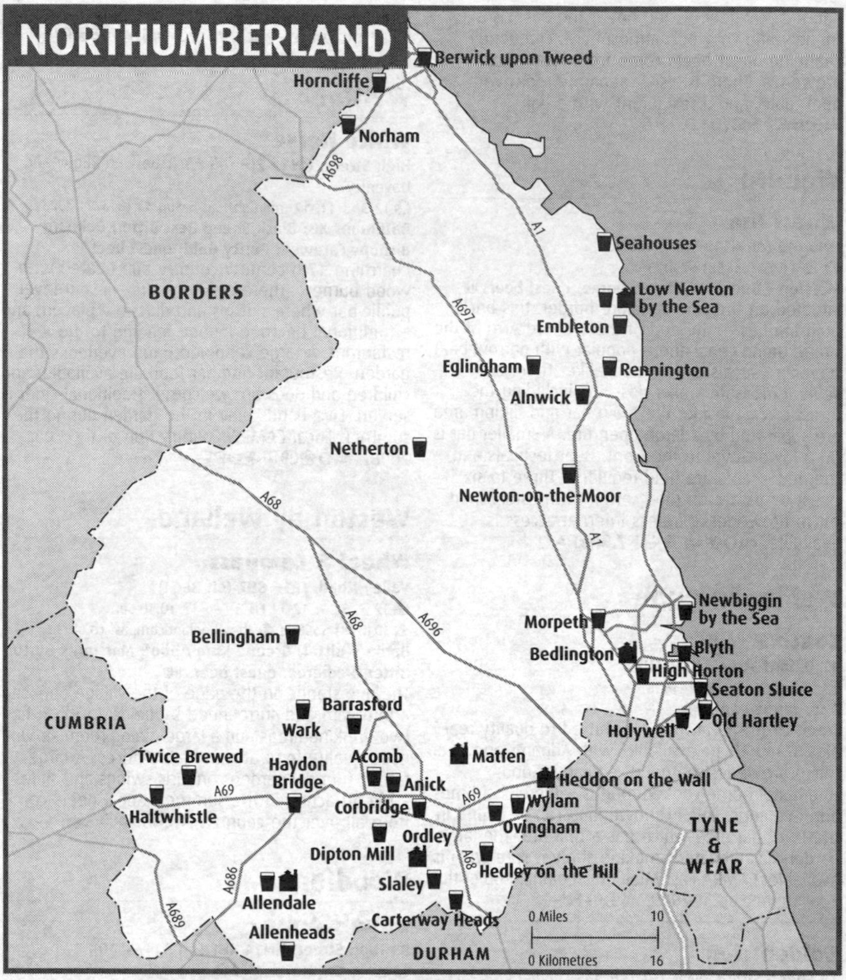

Acomb

Miners Arms

Main Street, NE46 4PW

5 (12 Sat & Sun)-midnight ☎ (01434) 603909

theminersacomb.com

Mordue Five Bridge Bitter; Yates Bitter; guest beers Ⓗ

Superb, traditional 1746 inn. Family-run, the staff empathise with real ale drinkers. Ale is served in oversize glasses. The pub hosts regular music and folk nights. The bar, divided by a central staircase, has a genuine, cosy feel. The miners have long gone but this pub is a superb legacy that lives on in a popular hamlet. (880,882)

Allendale

Allendale Inn

Market Place, NE47 9BY

12-midnight ☎ (01434) 683246

Beer range varies Ⓗ

A new landlord has made a big impact at this pleasant hostelry nestling in the corner of Market Square. The pub is well-supported, popular with visitors and locals, and runs darts, dominoes and pool teams. The nearby Allen Banks and superb countryside attract large numbers of ramblers who gladly quench their thirst here. Food is served lunchtimes and early evenings. Handy for the PlusBus via Hexham rail station. (688)

Kings Head

Market Place, NE47 9BD (opp Co-Op)

12-midnight ☎ (01434) 683681

Banks's Mild; Jennings Cumberland Ale Ⓗ

A welcoming, upmarket inn situated in the town square. The refurbished bar retains original features including an open log fire, and serves traditional pub food all day. The pub is popular with ramblers, cyclists and day trippers taking advantage of nearby countryside walks. Rail and bus links to Allendale are good, and this small market town is well-worth a visit. Handy for the PlusBus via Hexham rail station. (688)

Allenheads

Allenheads Inn

NE47 9HJ

12-4, 7-11; 12-11 Sat; 12-10.30 Sun ☎ (01434) 685200

Black Sheep Best Bitter; Greene King Abbot; Harviestoun Bitter & Twisted; Mordue Five Bridge Bitter; guest beers H
Superb rural pub, very popular with local ramblers and tourists. Good bar meals are available at a decent price. Originally the home of Sir Thomas Wentworth, this 18th-century multi-room building has a public bar with log fire, games room and dining room. The premises are filled with memorabilia and knick-knacks from a bygone age.
(688)♣P

Alnwick

John Bull Inn

12 Howick Street, NE66 1UY
12-3 (Sat only), 7-11; 12-3, 7-10.30 Sun
☎ (01665) 602055 john-bull-inn.co.uk
Beer range varies H
Current CAMRA North Northumberland Pub of the Year winner, this 180-year-old inn thrives on its reputation as a 'back-street boozer'. The passionate landlord offers four cask-conditioned ales at varying ABVs, real cider, the widest range of bottled Belgian beers in the county and 120 different single malt whiskies. The pub runs a darts team in the local league and continues to uphold the north-east tradition of an annual leek show.
Q♣

Anick

Rat Inn

NE46 4LN (signed from Hexham A69 roundabout)
12-3, 6-11; 12-11 Sat & Sun ☎ (01434) 602814
theratinn.com
Draught Bass; Caledonian Deuchars IPA; guest beers H
Superb 1750 country inn with spectacular views across the Tyne Valley. The interior has a welcoming and friendly feel to it, with an open log fire and chamber pots hanging from the ceiling. The pub is renowned in the area for excellent food prepared with locally-sourced ingredients, and features in the prestigious Michelin Red Guide. If you don't want to drive, the Rat is well worth the short taxi ride from Hexham rail station.
QP

Barrasford

Barrasford Arms

NE48 4AA
12-2 (not Mon), 6.30-9; 12-3 Sun ☎ (01434) 681237
barrasfordarms.co.uk
Beer range varies H
Top chef Tony Binks took over this 1870s pub situated at the heart of Barrasford village in the North Tyne Valley in 2006. It regularly hosts quoits tournaments, hunt meets, darts finals and vegetable competitions, and the friendly bar is the focus for hand-pulled real ales and general banter. Voted Destination Restaurant of the Year, it has two public dining rooms and a small private dining room accommodating visitors from all over the north, drawn by the landlord's formidable reputation in the kitchen. Q♣

Bellingham

Riverdale Hall Country House Hotel

NE48 2JT (5 mins walk W of Bellingham on road to Kielder)
11-11 (10.30 Sun) ☎ (01434) 220254
riverdalehallhotel.co.uk
Beer range varies H
Originally built as a Victorian mansion for a leading railway developer in 1866, the present owners, the Cocker family, purchased the hotel from Lord Stafford in the late 1970s. The superb patio enjoys excellent views of the rear garden with its full-size cricket pitch. Games are played in the summer, creating a traditional tranquil English setting for a leisurely pint on a Sunday afternoon.
Q(880)P

Berwick upon Tweed

Barrels Ale House

59-61 Bridge Street, TD15 1ES (in old part of town)
11.30 (3 winter)-midnight; 11.30-1am (midnight winter) Fri & Sat; 12-midnight Sun ☎ (01289) 308013
thebarrels.co.uk
Shepherd Neame Spitfire; Stewart Pentland IPA; guest beers H
There is an original, 'old curiosity shop' ambience to this pub – note the dentist's chair at the side of the bar. Serving excellent real ale, it is a regular winner of CAMRA Pub of the Year awards. Located in the old part of Berwick next to the original road bridge over the Tweed, the downstairs bar is used by DJs and bands at weekends. A unique rear open drinking area is surrounded by very high walls.

Pilot

31 Low Greens, TD15 1LX
12 (11 Sat)-midnight ☎ (01289) 304214
Caledonian Deuchars IPA; guest beers H
Well patronised by locals and sought out by train trippers who have heard about this gem. The stone-built end of terrace pub dates from the 19th century and is one of the North East England's Real Heritage Pubs. It retains the original small room layout and boasts several nautical artefacts over 100 years old. The pub runs darts and quoits teams and hosts music nights. The bar staff are warm and friendly. ♣

Blyth

Olivers

60 Bridge Street, NE24 2AP
12 (2 Tue & Sat)-11; 12-10.30 Sun ☎ (01670) 540356
Allendale Golden Plover; Greene King Old Speckled Hen; guest beers H
This warm and friendly one-roomed hostelry was converted from a newsagent's shop and is a welcome real ale outlet within a beer desert. It is located close to the regenerated quayside of a port better known for the FA Cup exploits of its famous

INDEPENDENT BREWERIES

Allendale Allendale
Hexhamshire Ordley
High House Farm Matfen
Northumberland Bedlington
Ship Inn Low Newton by the Sea
Wylam Heddon on the Wall

Spartans Football Club. Three real ales are available, one usually locally sourced. Bus 308 passes the door and the bus station for services to Blyth is a five-minutes walk. (308)♣

Carterway Heads

Manor House Inn

DH8 9LX (on A68 S of Corbridge)
12-11 (11.30 Sun) (01207) 255268
themanorhouseinn.com
Beer range varies
Excellent country inn run by a licensee keen on supporting local micros. The multi-room interior with three open fires has a comfortable and welcoming feel. Situated just off the A68, it is very popular with tourists. Home-cooked food is served, made with local produce. Accommodation is in four ensuite rooms. ♣P

Corbridge

Angel Inn

Main Street, NE45 5LA
11-11 (midnight Fri & Sat); 12-10.30 Sun
(01434) 632119 angelofcorbridge.co.uk
Black Sheep Best Bitter; Durham Magus; Hadrian & Border Tyneside Blonde; Taylor Landlord; guest beers
Superb former 1726 coaching inn located on the main road with good transport links. Family-friendly, it has a reputation for good food, and attracts tourists, ramblers and locals. The interior includes a contemporary bar and attractive lounge area with comfortable sofas and leather armchairs, and outside there is a pleasant area with seating. A wonderful selection of malt whiskies is on offer. The town has strong links with the Romans and Hadrian's Wall is nearby.
Q(602,604)P

Dyvel's Inn

Station Road, NE45 5AY (30m from railway station)
12-11 (01434) 633633 dyvelsinn.co.uk
Caledonian Deuchars IPA; guest beers
Family-friendly country inn easily accessible by train along the beautiful Tyne Valley, 20 minutes from Newcastle. Cosy in winter and open and sunny in summer, it has a public bar and a separate dining area, although food is served throughout. An ideal base for visiting this historic Tyne Valley town, the pub has beautiful town and country walks on the doorstep. It has its own secluded garden, a private car park and three rooms for overnight stays. (602,685)P

Dipton Mill

Dipton Mill Inn

Dipton Mill Road, NE46 1YA
12-2.30, 6-11; 12-3 Sun (01434) 606577
diptonmill.co.uk
Hexhamshire Devil's Elbow, Shire Bitter, Devil's Water, Whapweasel, Old Humbug
The tap for Hexhamshire brewery, this small inn is run by a keen landlord who brews his own excellent beers. To complement the ales there is great home-cooked food. A cosy atmosphere and warm welcome make this pub well-worth seeking out. The large garden has a stream running through it and there is plenty of countryside to explore.
QP

Eglingham

Tankerville Arms

15 The Village, NE66 2TX
12-11 (12.30am Fri & Sat); 12-10.30 Sun
(01665) 578444
Black Sheep Best Bitter; Hadrian & Border Tyneside Blonde; guest beers
Well-appointed, traditional country pub dating from 1851. The bar is decorated with several framed pictures that enhance the surroundings, complemented by an excellent open-beamed restaurant. Popular with tourists and ramblers, the pub welcomes dogs and families, and hosts meetings for local golf and cricket clubs. Accommodation is in en-suite rooms. Well-worth a visit. QP

Embleton

Greys Inn

Stanley Terrace, NE66 3XJ
12-11 (10.30 Sun) (01665) 576983
Black Sheep Best Bitter; guest beers
Pleasant, traditional pub in a lovely seaside hamlet, with three open fires adding welcome warmth in the winter. A framed 1904 grocery list hangs on the wall. This is an excellent venue to catch a bite to eat washed down with a locally-sourced real ale – hopefully sitting outside on the superb patio. A short walk takes you to a wonderful beach. Opening hours may vary in winter.
(501,518)♣

Haltwhistle

Black Bull

Market Square, NE49 0BL (down a cobbled lane)
12-11 (midnight Fri & Sat); 12-10.30 Sun
(01434) 320463
Caledonian Deuchars IPA; Greene King IPA; guest beers
Warm, friendly two-room pub close to Hadrian's Wall, popular with locals and ramblers. Situated just off Market Place down a cobbled lane, it has a traditional ambience with an open fire, low-beamed timber ceiling and horse brasses. There are six handpumps for real ales. Regular themed nights are hosted. Ring to check winter hours.
Q(685)

Haydon Bridge

Railway

Church Street, NE47 6JG
11-midnight; 12-10.30 Sun (01434) 684254
Black Sheep Best Bitter; Caledonian Deuchars IPA
Homely, traditional one-room pub with friendly customers and staff, offering good home-cooked food at reasonable prices. Folk and R&B evenings are hosted on the second and fourth Monday of the month, and the pub is home to two cricket teams, darts and dominoes teams. Situated near the railway station, an hourly bus service stops round the corner. The pub is handy for Hadrian's Wall, Vindolanda and Chesters Roman forts, and close to popular rambling areas. (685)♣

Hedley on the Hill

Feathers

NE43 7SW

⏲ 12 (6 Mon)-11 ☎ (01661) 843607 🌐 thefeathers.net
Hadrian & Border Gladiator; Mordue Workie Ticket; guest beers Ⓗ
Much-acclaimed country pub set in a pleasant hamlet with superb views of three counties. The young and welcoming staff serve high-quality home-cooked food to complement the real ales. A beer festival is held every Easter including an uphill barrel race on Easter Monday. The pub has a genuine, comfy feel with exposed stone walls and beams. An award winner for quality food, booking is recommended for Sunday lunch. ♨Q☕◑◗P

High Horton

Three Horse Shoes

Hathery Lane, NE24 4HF (off A189 N of Cramlington, follow A192) N7276793
⏲ 11-11 (midnight Fri & Sat); 12-11 Sun ☎ (01670) 822410
🌐 3horseshoes.co.uk
Greene King Abbot; guest beers Ⓗ
Extended former coaching inn, privately owned, at the highest point in the Blyth Valley, with views of the Northumberland coast. The pub is open-plan with distinct bar and dining areas plus a conservatory. Dedicated to real ale, it holds regular beer festivals, with real cider and perry also available. Guest ales are sourced from all over the country including local micro-breweries. If you get the chance, take a look at the impressive modern cellar. An extensive range of meals and snacks is served lunchtimes and evenings, all day Friday to Sunday. Q❀◑◗P⚟

Holywell

Olde Fat Ox Inn

NE25 0LJ
⏲ 12-11 ☎ (0191) 237 0964
Caledonian Deuchars IPA; guest beers Ⓗ
Family-friendly, well-appointed former coaching inn, popular with cyclists and walkers. Regular themed nights are hosted. There is comfortable leather seating and a selection of books if you fancy a quiet read with your pint. No meals are available but snacks, tea and coffee are served – try the hot beef sandwich. More than 30 whiskies are stocked. The award-winning beer garden with a heated outdoor smoking area leads down to a local beauty spot, Holywell Dene. Dogs are welcome. ❀P

Horncliffe

Fishers Arms

Main Street, TD15 2XW
⏲ 12-3 (2 Sun), 6-10.30 ☎ (01289) 386866
Northumberland Fog on the Tyne; guest beer Ⓗ
Traditional pub at the heart of community life, offering a once a month buskers' session, food-themed nights, quiz nights, OAP lunch every Thursday, and the 'Hooky Mats' club on Wednesday lunchtime. Part of a terrace in the village centre, the pub has separate dining and drinking areas. Reasonably priced home-cooked food is very popular. The Tweed Cycle Way is nearby. B&B accommodation is in en-suite rooms. 🛏◑◗🚌(67)♣

Low Newton by the Sea

Ship Inn

Newton Square, NE66 3EL
⏲ 11-11; 12-10.30 Sun ☎ (01665) 576262
🌐 shipinnnewton.co.uk
Ship Inn Sandcastles at Dawn, Sea Coal, Sea Wheat, Ship Hop, Dolly Daydream Ⓗ
Nestling in the corner of a three-sides-of-a-square arrangement of former fishermen's cottages and graced by a small village green, this pub's location is unique. Virtually on the beach, fine sea views can be enjoyed on the short walk from the car park. A very popular hostelry, it does get busy – opening times may vary in the winter so phone first. An excellent food menu features fresh locally-sourced ingredients. The pub brews its own beer on the premises. ♨Q❀◑◗⊟⚟

Morpeth

Old Red Bull ✔

Dark Lane, NE61 1ST
⏲ 12-11 (midnight Fri & Sat); 12-10.30 Sun
☎ (01670) 513306
Beer range varies Ⓗ
The walls of this building proudly display the level of the floods in Morpeth at the latter end of 2008 – the pub has since been renovated and has a modern yet comfortable feel. Inside, there is a main bar area and a smaller second room with a pool table and dartboard. Three real ales are available, with guest beers sourced both locally and from further afield. ♨⇌⚟

Tap & Spile

23 Manchester Street, NE61 1BH
⏲ 12-2.30, 4.30-11; 12-11 Fri & Sat; 12-10.30 Sun
☎ (01670) 513894
Everards Tiger; guest beers Ⓗ
Cosy, popular local, welcoming to all and handy for the nearby bus station. It has a busy narrow bar to the front and quieter lounge to the rear. A good choice of ales is available, often including local brews from Northumbrian breweries. Westons Old Rosie cider is stocked as well as a selection of fruit wines from Lindisfarne Winery. Winner of local CAMRA awards. Q⊟⇌🚌♣●⚟

Netherton

Star Inn ★

NE65 7HD
⏲ 7.30-10.30 (closed Mon, Thu and Sun) ☎ (01669) 630238
Camerons Strongarm Ⓖ
The only pub in Northumberland to appear in every issue of the Guide. Stepping into this gem is like entering the private living room of a large house – beer is served on gravity from the cellar at a hatch in the panelled entrance hall. The bar area is basic with bench seating. The walls display the many awards won by the pub. Children are not allowed in the bar. Please ring to check opening hours. Q❀P

Newbiggin by the Sea

Queens Head (Porters) ✔

7 High Street, NE64 6AT
⏲ 9.45am to midnight ☎ (01670) 817293
Marston's Burton Bitter; guest beers Ⓗ

One of the North East England's Real Heritage Pubs, it's original Edwardian layout has been retained with a public bar area, lounge displaying many photographs of bygone Newbiggin, and a snug to the rear. Outstanding features include the curved bar counter, bench seating, fireplace, etched windows and mosaic floors. The landlord sells competitively priced real ales and displays an ever-growing collection of guest beer pump clips. All Newbiggin buses pass the door.

Newton-on-the-Moor

Cook & Barker Inn

NE65 9JY (exit off A1, 5 miles S of Alnwick)
11 (12 Sun)-11 ☎ (01665) 575234
cookandbarkerinn.co.uk
Black Sheep Best Bitter; guest beers H
A real traditional Northumbrian country inn with outstanding views of the Northumberland coast and the Cheviot Hills. Situated close to the A1, the pub is an old dwelling that has been tastefully updated but retains part of the original blacksmith's forge next door. The pub is split into several rooms, all featuring exposed beams and stone walls. Real ales are both locally and nationally sourced, and excellent food is available. P

Norham

Mason's Arms

17 West Street, TD15 2LB
12-3, 7-11; 12-10.30 Sun ☎ (01289) 382326
tweed-sports.co.uk
Belhaven 80/-; Caledonian Deuchars IPA; guest beer H
The Mason's Arms is a classic pub situated in the historic village of Norham, near the River Tweed, which marks the border between England and Scotland. There is a traditional bar with excellent, locally-sourced, handpulled draught beers, a dining room and well-appointed en-suite family accommodation. The pub is renowned in the area for high quality home-cooked meals made with locally grown produce in season.
(67)

Old Hartley

Delaval Arms

NE26 4RL (jct of A193/B1325 S of Seaton Sluice)
12-11 (10.30 Sun) ☎ (0191) 237 0489
Caledonian Deuchars IPA; guest beers H
Multi-roomed Grade II-listed building dating from 1748, with a listed WWI water storage tower behind the beer garden. Good quality, affordable meals complement the beer, with guest ales coming from both local and national breweries. To the left as you enter there is a room served through a hatch from the bar and to the right a room where children are welcome. Q P

> Not all chemicals are bad. Without chemicals such as hydrogen and oxygen, for example, there would be no way to make water, a vital ingredient in beer.
> **Dave Barry**

Ovingham

Bridge End Inn

West Road, NE42 6BN
4 (12 Sat)-11; 12-3.30, 7-10.30 Sun ☎ (01661) 832219
bridgeendcc.org
Jennings Cumberland Ale; Taylor Landlord; Tetley Bitter; Wylam Gold Tankard; guest beer H
Traditional family-run 'wet led' pub with a friendly customer base, run by the same licensee for the past 35 years. The pub's back door opens onto the village green where a goose fair is held annually on the third Saturday in June, supported by the whole village. There is access to the pub from Prudhoe over the bridge by a pedestrian walkway. Monthly music nights are held featuring blues, rock, '60s and more.
Q (Prudhoe) (684,686,687) P

Rennington

Horse Shoes Inn

6 Rennington Village, NE66 3RS
closed Mon; 12-3, 7-11 ☎ (01665) 577665
Hadrian & Border Farne Island, Tyneside Blonde H
Traditional family-run village pub dating from 1851. The bar is warm and friendly with dry hops hanging over the serving area, and a large restaurant serving good food made with locally-sourced produce. Outside at the front is a pleasant beer garden. The pub hosts a scarecrow competition every August bank holiday Saturday.

Seahouses

Olde Ship Inn

7-9 Main Street, NE68 7RD
11 (12 Sun)-11 ☎ (01665) 720200 seahouses.co.uk
Black Sheep Best Bitter; Courage Directors; Greene King Old Speckled Hen, Ruddles County; Hadrian & Border Farne Island; Theakston Best Bitter H
One of the North East England's Real Heritage Pubs, this 1745 farmhouse was converted to the licensed trade in 1812 and has been in the same family since 1910. Three quality bars are adorned with a veritable treasure trove of 19th and 20th century maritime memorabilia. The pub offers a wholesome menu of fish, fresh crab meals and snacks (no chips!). Seahouses harbour is nearby and handy for boat trips to the famous Farne Islands. Q P

Seaton Sluice

Melton Constable

Beresford Road, NE26 4QL
12-11 (10.30 Sun) ☎ (0191) 237 7741
Theakston Best Bitter; Wells Bombardier; guest beers H
Large roadside inn a few minutes walk from the beach, overlooking a small harbour cut out of the rock by the famous Delavals and still in use today. The pub is named after the southern seat of Lord Hastings, also a member of the Delaval family. A popular quiz is held on Wednesday evening. The ruins of Starlight Castle can be seen from the conservatory. (308)P

Slaley

Travellers Rest ✔

NE46 1TT (on B6306 1 mile N of village)
✪ 12-11 (10.30 Sun) ☎ (01434) 673231
🌐 travellersrestslaley.com
Black Sheep Best Bitter; Caledonian Deuchars IPA; Mordue Travellers Ale; guest beers H
Former farmhouse dating from the 16th century and licensed for more than 150 years. The pub has an excellent reputation for good food and accommodation. The bar has a large open fire, flagstone floors and comfortable furniture. Children are welcome and there is a safe play area outside. Q➢❀⇌⦶◑♣P⁴—

Twice Brewed

Twice Brewed Inn

Bardon Mill, NE47 7AN (on B6318)
✪ 11 (12 winter)-11.30; 12-10.30 Sun ☎ (01434) 344534
🌐 twicebrewedinn.co.uk
Yates Twice Brewed Bitter; guest beers H
Superb, remote inn, close to Hadrian's Wall, well patronised by tourists and ramblers. It offers five ales including guests sourced from all over the UK, plus a range of bottled beers named 'beers of the world'. The interior includes a drinks-only lounge and an IT suite with internet connection. It has 14 bedrooms, six en-suite. The inn serves as a rural transport interchange and has full disabled access. ♔Q➢❀⇌⦶◑⊟♿⊞P

Wark

Battlesteads Hotel

NE48 3LS
✪ 11-11; 12-10.30 Sun ☎ (01434) 230209
🌐 battlesteads.com
Black Sheep Best Bitter; Durham Magus; Wylam Gold Tankard; guest beers H
Well-appointed former 1747 farmhouse with a superb rear walled garden and large conservatory. The pub supports local micros but also offers guest ales from further afield. Ingredients for the excellent food menu come from local farms and traders. Motorists may wish to try organic soft drinks such as Fentimans Dandelion & Burdock. Hadrian's Wall is nearby and excellent accommodation includes ground floor rooms with disabled access. Handy for the PlusBus via Hexham Rail Station. Note that the pub usually closes in February for sprucing up. ♔➢❀⇌⦶◑⊟♿P⁴—

Wylam

Black Bull

Main Street, NE41 8AB
✪ 4 (12 Fri-Sun)-11 ☎ (01661) 853112
🌐 blackbull-wylam.co.uk
Wylam Gold Tankard; guest beers H
Cheerful pub on the main street in Wylam with a friendly landlord and staff, very popular with the locals. Regular themed nights are hosted, many to raise funds for charities. Local home-cooked specialities feature in the newly-redecorated restaurant area. Nearby is Wylam Waggonway, a popular walk that passes George Stephenson's cottage. Winner of a Morning Advertiser Best Pub Award. ⇌◑⥂♣⁴—

Boathouse Inn 🏆

Station Road, NE41 8HR
✪ 11-11 (midnight Sat); 12-10.30 Sun ☎ (01661) 853 431
Beer range varies H
Superb, well-managed, two-roomed real ale emporium with 15 handpulls, three dedicated to cider. Beers are sourced locally and nationwide, and every bank holiday there is a themed beer festival. Meals are served lunchtimes and evenings during the week, with Sunday lunches particularly popular. This is a favourite stopping off point for 'Whistle Stop' travellers as you can fall off the railway platform straight into the pub. Winner of several CAMRA awards, including North East Regional Pub of the Year 2009. ♔Q➢❀⦶◑⥂●P

Battlesteads Hotel, Wark

NOTTINGHAMSHIRE

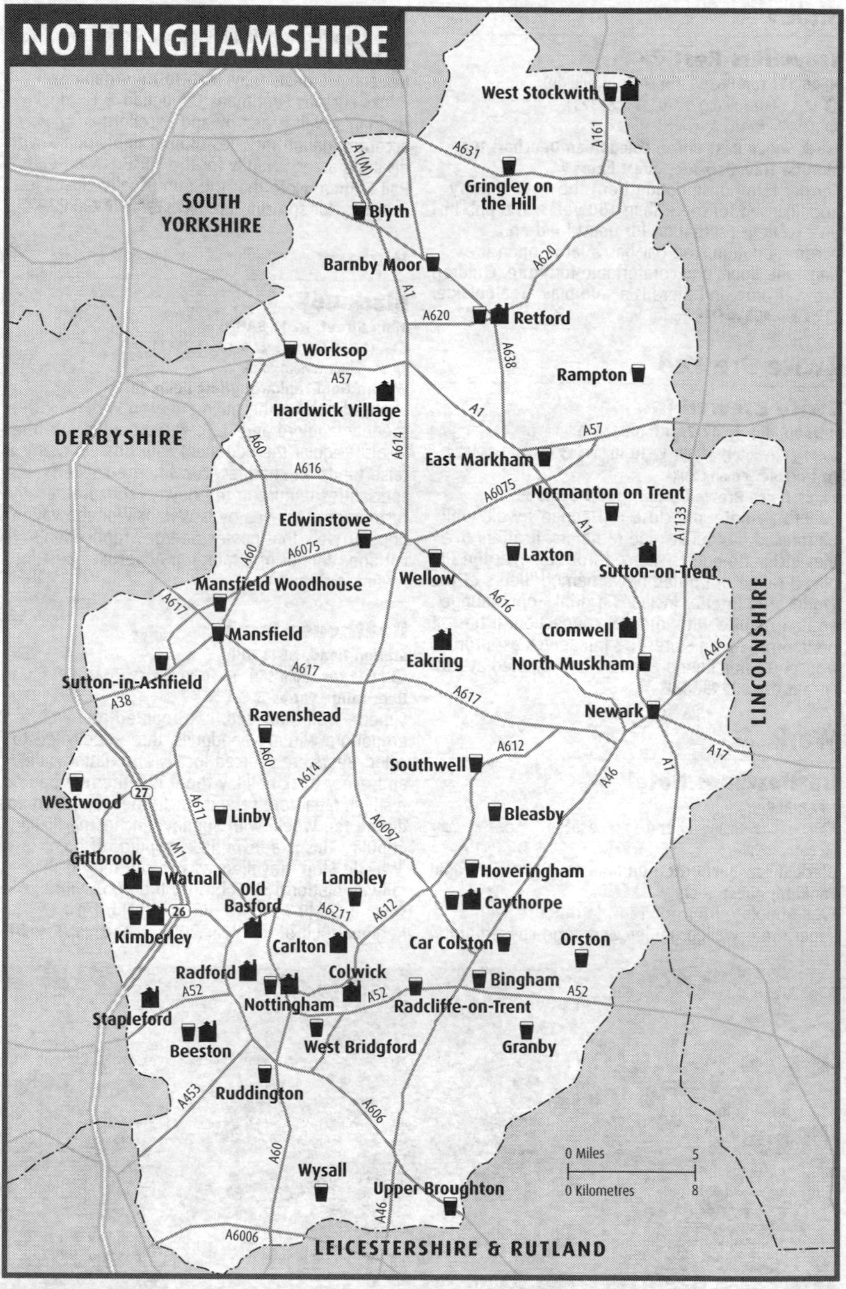

Barnby Moor

White Horse

Great North Road, DN22 8QS (on A638)

11-3, 6-11; 11-11 Sat; 12-11 Sun ☎ (01777) 707721

Beer range varies Ⓗ

This attractive village pub situated at the side of the A638 has a large lounge bar with separate dining area and a smaller public bar area, which now houses a large-screen TV for sport. The beer range varies depending on the time of the year, most ales originating from local micro-breweries. The walls in the lounge bar are covered with paintings, some connected to the local Grove & Rufford Hunt that has its kennels across the road.
⌂Q❀◑⊟P⁵–

Beeston

Crown 🏆

Church Street, NG9 1FY

11 (12 Sun)-11 ☎ (0115) 925 4738

Leatherbritches CAD, Bounder; Everards Tiger; Fuller's London Pride; guest beers Ⓗ

This former Hardys & Hansons house has been transformed into a cask-drinking emporium by Everards with a genuine warm welcome. A multi-roomed pub with low-beam ceilings, it has a 'confessional' snug that was once used as a hideaway for the vicar next door after a service. The four regular beers and many guests are complemented by four cask ciders and perries from breweries both local and national, with an emphasis on micros. Basic snacks and rolls are provided. Q❀◘♿⇌🚌●P⁄—

Malt Shovel ✔

1 Union Street, NG9 2LU

11-11 (11.30 Fri & Sat); 12-11 Sun ☎ (0115) 922 2320

Nottingham Rock Mild, Rock Bitter; guest beers Ⓗ

Just off the pedestrianised High Road, this one-room pub offers a friendly welcome. A modern interior makes thoughtful use of furnishings and decor to provide a sense of separate drinking areas. Bright colours and comfortable leather sofas create a light, airy ambience with a cosy atmosphere. There is a good value food menu (no meals Sun eve), a quiz night on Wednesday and live music on Friday. Guest beers are from micro and regional brewers. ♨❀◑♿🚌♣●P⁄—

Victoria Hotel

85 Dovecote Lane, NG9 1JG (off A6005 by station)

10.30 (12 Sun)-11 ☎ (0115) 925 4049

victoriabeeston.co.uk

Castle Rock Harvest Pale; Everards Tiger; guest beers Ⓗ

Buzzing Victorian architectural gem – note the fine windows. This former Nottingham CAMRA Pub of the Year is popular with drinkers and diners alike. The multi-roomed layout includes a dining area, public bar and covered heated outside drinking space, fully no-smoking. Fourteen beers are served including a local ale, mild, stout and two real ciders. High quality freshly-cooked food, including a wide choice of vegetarian dishes, is available all day. Regular beer and music festivals are held throughout the year. ♨Q❀◑◘♿⇌🚌(13,14)●P

Bingham

Horse & Plough 🏆 ✔

25 Long Acre, NG13 8AF

11-11 (11.30 Fri & Sat); 12-11 Sun ☎ (01949) 839313

horseandploughbingham.com

Caledonian Deuchars IPA; Wells Bombardier; guest beers Ⓗ

Situated in the heart of a busy market town, this warm, friendly, one-room free house was a former Methodist chapel and has a cottage-style interior and flagstone floor. Six cask ales are always available including four guests, with a 'try before you buy' policy, and a cider from Westons. The first floor à la carte restaurant offers a varied seasonal menu. A fresh bar menu is served weekday lunchtimes and evenings. Local CAMRA Pub of the Year 2007 and 2010. ◑♿⇌🚌●

Bleasby

Waggon & Horses

Gipsy Lane, NG14 7GE

12-2 (not Mon & Tue), 5-11; 12-midnight Sat; 12-11 Sun ☎ (01636) 830283

Blue Monkey Original, Evolution; Nottingham Rock Mild; guest beers Ⓗ

Reversing the trend of village pub closures, the Waggon has been reborn. Now a free house, it offers six real ales including two from the award-winning Blue Monkey Brewery and a mild. This is a true village pub overlooking the church and green with no gimmicks or electronic gizmos, just conversation and banter. Well-worth finding in a lovely Trent Valley village close to Southwell Minster and races. ♨Q❀◑◘⇌♣●P⁄—

Blyth

Red Hart

Bawtry Road, S81 8HG

12-midnight (11.30 Sun) ☎ (01909) 591221

Beer range varies Ⓗ

An attractive village pub situated in the centre of Blyth – a previous winner of best-kept village. It has separate lounge and bar areas with a reasonably-sized dining room. The walls in the lounge are decorated with photos and paintings of various locations around the village. Guest ales change regularly, with beers from micro-breweries usually available. Restaurant quality food at pub prices is served daily. The pub now hosts an annual beer festival on the May bank holiday. ♨Q❀◑◘🚌P⁄—

White Swan

High Street, S81 8EQ

12-3, 6-11 ☎ (01909) 591222

Beer range varies Ⓗ

This village pub situated off the green has a single bar serving one long room with a large open fire. Good home-cooked food is served lunchtimes and evenings. A quiet pub with no juke-box or pool table, there are a small number of tables outside at the front overlooking the green. Two real ales are available. A regular bus service from Worksop stops near the pub. ♨Q❀◑🚌

Car Colston

Royal Oak ✔

The Green, NG13 8JE

11.30-3 (not Mon), 5.30-midnight; 11.30-midnight Fri & Sat; 12-10.30 Sun ☎ (01949) 20247

Jennings Cumberland Ale; Marston's Burton Bitter, Mansfield Cask Bitter; guest beer Ⓗ

Impressive country inn situated on one of England's largest village greens. The two-room

INDEPENDENT BREWERIES

Alcazar Nottingham: Old Basford
Blue Monkey Giltbrook
Castle Rock Nottingham
Caythorpe Caythorpe
Copthorne Sutton-on-Trent (NEW)
Flipside Colwick (NEW)
Full Mash Stapleford
Grafton Retford
Holland Kimberley
Idle West Stockwith
Magpie Nottingham
Mallard Carlton
Maypole Eakring
Milestone Cromwell
Nottingham Nottingham: Radford
Prior's Well Hardwick Village (NEW)
Reality Nottingham: Beeston (NEW)
Springhead Sutton-on-Trent

interior includes a lounge and restaurant on one side and bar with comfortable seating on the other. Note the bar's vaulted brickwork ceiling – a legacy from the building's previous life as a hosiery factory. Good quality, traditional food is served lunchtimes and evenings. There is a skittle alley to the rear. Local CAMRA Pub of the Year 2009 – the landlord maintains his 100 per cent record of entries in the Guide. ⛫Q❀◐◑⊟♿⛺♣P⌐

Caythorpe

Black Horse

29 Main Street, NG14 7ED

⏲ closed Mon; 12-2.30, 6-11; 12-5, 8-11 Sun

☎ (0115) 966 3520

Caythorpe Dover Beck, One Swallow; Greene King Abbot; guest beers Ⓗ

Classic unspoilt 18th-century country inn run by the same family for 37 years and reputedly a former haunt of Dick Turpin. Little has changed over the years – there is a comfortable lounge, a tiny snug bar with hatch servery, inglenook, bench seats, beams and wood panelling. A dining room is available for dinner parties (but no children allowed). Bar food is very popular, mostly cooked to order using fresh ingredients – booking essential. The home of Caythorpe Brewery, guest beers are often from other local micros.
⛫Q❀◐◑⊟🚌(103)♣P

East Markham

Queen's Hotel

High Street, NG22 0RE

⏲ 12-11 (10.30 Sun) ☎ (01777) 870288

Adnams Bitter; Everards Beacon, Tiger; guest beers Ⓗ

Situated on the village main street, this cosy public house has a friendly atmosphere enhanced by an open fire in winter. A single bar serves the lounge, pool room and dining area. Food, ranging from hot and cold snacks to full home-cooked meals, is available Tuesday-Sunday. There is a large garden area at the rear of the premises where you can enjoy a drink on a warm summer's day. A previous winner of local CAMRA branch awards.
⛫Q❀◐◑🚌♣P⌐

Edwinstowe

Forest Lodge Hotel ✔

2 Church Street, NG21 9QA (on A6075 Mansfield-Ollerton road)

⏲ 11.30-3, 5.30 (5 Fri)-11; 12-3, 6-10.30 Sun

☎ (01623) 824443 🌐 forestlodgehotel.co.uk

Courage Directors; Kelham Island Pale Rider; Wells Bombardier; guest beer Ⓗ

Situated in the heart of Sherwood Forest country, this family-run free house offers a fine choice of five real ales together with a first class menu. There is a large function area for private parties. A coaching inn dating back to the 17th century, it has been restored and refurbished to a high standard. Accommodation is in 13 en-suite rooms. A golf course and riding stables are only a five-minute drive away. ⛫Q🚸❀🛏◐◑♿🚌(10,14,16)P⌐

Granby

Marquis of Granby

Dragon Street, NG13 9PN

⏲ 4-11 (midnight Fri); 12-midnight Sat; 12-11 Sun

☎ (01949) 859517

Brewster's Hophead, Marquis; guest beers Ⓗ

Believed to be the original Marquis of Granby, dating back to 1760 or earlier, this small, two-roomed pub is now the brewery tap for Brewster's Brewery. York stone floors complement the yew bar tops and wood-beamed rooms, period wallpaper features throughout and the lounge has a welcoming open fire in winter months. Guest beers complement the Brewster's range and come from micros, usually including a mild, stout or porter. Fish and chips night is Friday. Local CAMRA Pub of the Year 2008. ⛫❀⊟♿♣P

Gringley on the Hill

Blue Bell

High Street, DN10 4RF

⏲ 7 (12 Sat)-11; 12-3, 7-11 Sun ☎ (01777) 817406

Beer range varies Ⓗ

The Blue Bell is a traditional country pub, around 300 years old. A single entrance door off the High Street leads to two large rooms served by one bar, with a warming open fire for winter days. Three real ales are available. The local morris men can often be seen dancing outside the pub on bank holidays. Food is served Sunday lunchtime and in the evenings. ⛫Q❀◑

Hoveringham

Reindeer Inn

Main Street, NG14 7JR SK699469

⏲ 12-2 (not Mon & Tue), 5-11.30; 12-11.30 Sat & Sun

☎ (0115) 966 3629 🌐 thereindeerinn.com

Blue Monkey Original; Castle Rock Harvest Pale; Caythorpe Stout Fellow; guest beers Ⓗ

Genuine free house in a pleasant country village with traditional beams and a log fire for cold winter nights. A central servery divides the bar and restaurant areas of the pub. Good home-cooked food includes vegetarian and vegan choices. The outside drinking area overlooks a cricket pitch. Dog-friendly. ⛫Q❀◐◑♣P⌐

Kimberley

Nelson & Railway

12 Station Road, NG16 2NR

⏲ 11-midnight; 12-11 Sun ☎ (0115) 938 2177

🌐 nelsonandrailway.co.uk

Greene King H&H Bitter; guest beers Ⓗ

Run by the same family for more than 40 years, this popular pub lies in the shadow of the defunct Kimberley Brewery buildings. Beers are usually from the Greene King portfolio but guests also appear. A refurbishment featuring several shades of wood adds to the character of this friendly local. Renowned for its quality food and accommodation, it has 11 rooms available. There are attractive gardens at the front and rear.
❀🛏◐◑⊟♿🚌(1)♣P⌐

Stag Inn ✔

67 Nottingham Road, NG16 2NB

⏲ 5 (1.30 Sat)-11; 12-10.30 Sun ☎ (0115) 938 3151

Adnams Bitter; Black Sheep Best Bitter; Marston's Pedigree; Taylor Landlord; guest beer Ⓗ

Situated on the main road into the town, this historic two-room pub is adjacent to Kimberley Town FC's ground, which is named after the pub.

Low wooden beams are adorned with old photographs of Shipstones, the former brewery that once owned the pub. Traditional pub games such as table skittles and dominoes are played, but at most times conversation reigns. The spacious rear garden includes a children's play area and ample seating. An annual beer festival is hosted on the late May bank holiday weekend, raising money for charity. Q❀♿🚌(1)♣P⅃

Lambley

Woodlark

Church Street, NG4 4QB

⏲ 12-3 (4 Mon & Sat), 5.30-midnight, 12-midnight Fri; 12-5.30, 7-11 Sun ☎ (0115) 931 2535

Castle Rock Harvest Pale; Copper Dragon Best Bitter; Courage Directors; Taylor Landlord Ⓗ

Tucked away on the edge of the village, this delightful red-brick local is mercifully free of electronic machines. The bare brick and beamed bar is welcoming and dog-friendly while the comfortable lounge has a justifiable reputation for home cooking (booking recommended, even at lunchtime). A popular downstairs steak bar is open on Friday and Saturday evenings from 7-9pm. ♨Q❀◑◐🀫🚌(7,61)♣P⅃

Laxton

Dovecote Inn ✔

Cross Hill, NG22 0SX

⏲ 12-11 ☎ (01777) 871 586 🌐 dovecoteinnlaxton.co.uk

Beer range varies Ⓗ

This traditional inn is situated in the centre of Laxton, a village known for having the last remaining working open field farming system in the country. The pub boasts three cosy wining and dining rooms, a locals' drinking room and a welcoming foyer. Three real ales are available and the pub holds an annual beer festival. Food is served daily lunchtimes and evenings, 12.30-6.30pm on Sunday. The large beer garden has access to Laxton's Visitor Centre. ♨❀🛏◑◐🀫P⅃

Linby

Horse & Groom

Main Street, NG15 8AE

⏲ 12-11 (10.30 Sun) ☎ (0115) 963 2219

Greene King IPA, Old Speckled Hen, Abbot; Theakston Traditional Mild; Wells Bombardier; guest beers Ⓗ

Charming and unspoilt Grade II-listed village pub dating back to 1800. The multi-roomed establishment has an inglenook in the public bar, a snug and roaring open fires. The Green Room welcomes families. Fine food is available at lunchtime from an extensive and varied menu, evening dining is on Friday and Saturday only. There is a conservatory and the extensive garden has a children's play area. ♨Q👶❀◑◐🀫🚌(141)♣P⅃

Mansfield

Bold Forester ✔

Botany Avenue, NG18 5NF

⏲ 11-11 (midnight Fri-Sat); 12-11.30 Sun ☎ (01623) 623970

Greene King IPA, Old Speckled Hen, Ruddles County, Abbot; guest beers Ⓗ

Run by the same landlord for the past 11 years, this Hungry Horse pub and restaurant offers 12 real ales. The spacious interior has an open-plan layout with several raised areas for dining and drinking, and large-screen TVs for live sports coverage. Two beer festivals are held annually. Local CAMRA Pub of the Season and Pub of the Year winner 2005-2007. ❀◑◐♿⇌🚌P⅃

Court House

Market Place, NG18 1HX (next to town hall)

⏲ 9am-11 (midnight Fri & Sat) ☎ (01623) 412720

Greene King Ruddles Best Bitter, Abbot; guest beers Ⓗ

This friendly community pub in the town centre gets busy, especially at weekends. It offers a comprehensive range of at least five beers from local micro-breweries including Milestone, Springhead, Derventio and Amber Ales, plus three guest ciders. Food is served all day until 10pm, offering typical excellent value and quality associated with Wetherspoon's. Families are welcome. Local CAMRA Branch Pub of the Season. Q◑◐♿⇌🚌🍎⅃

Nell Gwyn

117 Sutton Road, NG18 5EX (on A38 out of town at jct of Sheepbridge Lane and Skegby Road)

⏲ 2 (12 Fri-Sun)-midnight ☎ (01623) 659850

Beer range varies Ⓗ

One of the first dwellings on Sutton Road, originally a farmhouse, the building became a gentlemen's club in 1927 and now claims to be Mansfield's best-kept secret – a pub not a club. A fine community hostelry with a loyalty card scheme, it holds regular charity fundraising events in comfortable surroundings. Darts and dominoes teams meet on Monday and Wednesday, and it has a football team. Two constantly-changing real ales, often from local micro-breweries, are served from a central bar. ♨Q❀🚌♣⅃

Railway Inn

9 Station Street, NG18 1EF

⏲ 11-11 (8 Tue); 12-6 Sun ☎ (01623) 623086

Beer range varies Ⓗ

A true independent real ale gem in an area of themed pubs and keg outlets, with a strong community focus. It offers three constantly-changing, mainly light-coloured beers, often sourced from local micro-breweries within the LocAle radius, plus a good selection of bottled beers. Excellent value home cooked food is available every lunchtime and Tuesday to Thursday evenings 5-8pm. There is a small walled garden and heated smoking area in the courtyard. Dogs are welcome. Q👶❀◑◐🀫⇌🚌⅃

Redgate

189 Westfield Lane, NG19 6EH

⏲ 4 (12 Fri-Sun)-11 ☎ (01623) 624406

Beer range varies Ⓗ

Saved from threat of change of use to an Indian restaurant, the landlord has transformed the pub into a thriving community-focused venue with a welcoming and friendly atmosphere. It features a comfortable lounge and large public bar, with regular entertainment and events planned. Three constantly-changing beers come from local and national micro-breweries, with Brampton Brewery's Redgate Rocket a regular guest. There is a skittle alley and traditional pub games with men's and women's teams. Dogs are welcome. ❀🀫🚌(6,23B)♣P⅃

Rufford Arms

335 Chesterfield Road South, NG19 7ES (at main traffic lights with A6075)
11-11 (midnight Fri & Sat); 11-10.30 Sun
(01623) 623286 marstontavens.co.uk
Beer range varies H
Large food-oriented open-plan pub with plenty of seating, dispensing two real ales from the Marston's stable. A daily carvery is offered lunchtimes and evenings during the week and all day Friday to Sunday. There is a table for pool and a prize quiz on Sunday night. A large function area is available for private parties. Local buses run past the door up until 11pm.
Q (Mansfield Woodhouse) (23,53)P

Sir John Cockle

Sutton Road, NG18 5EU
11-11 (midnight Fri & Sat) (01623) 623459
sirjohncocklepub.co.uk
Marston's Mansfield Cask Ale, seasonal beers H
Traditional community pub offering three real ales from Marston's. Good value pub food is available every day plus a specials board. Live entertainment is hosted fortnightly on a Friday and a quiz is held on Sunday and Wednesday evenings. Sky Sports and ESPN feature on large-screen TVs. The pub has an outdoor drinking area, plus a heated and covered space for smokers. The football ground is a five-minute walk. P

Widow Frost

41 Leeming Street, NG18 1NB
9am-midnight (1am Fri & Sat) (01623) 666790
Greene King Ruddles Best Bitter, Abbot; guest beers H
Spacious pub not far from the town centre, it gets very busy, especially at weekends, but it is still possible to find a quiet corner. The full range of excellent value-for-money Wetherspoon's meals is available until 10pm, with a separate family dining area. There are usually five beers on offer plus two real ciders, served by friendly staff from a large bar. Local CAMRA Pub of the Season. Q

Mansfield Woodhouse

Greyhound

82 High Street, NG19 8BD
12-11 (midnight Fri & Sat); 12-10.30 Sun
(01623) 464403
Adnams Broadside; Caledonian Deuchars IPA; Theakston Traditional Mild; guest beers H
Classic stone-built two-roomed pub dating from around the 1700s with a public bar with a pool table and a comfortable lounge. A regular entry in the Guide for the past 17 years, the Greyhound offers a fine choice of up to six ales, always including a mild. Two mini beer festivals are staged each year. No food is served. Traditional pub games include darts and dominoes.
Q (1,10)P

Newark

Castle & Falcon

10 London Road, NG24 1TW
12-3 (not Mon-Thu), 7-11.30 (01636) 703513
John Smith's Bitter; guest beers H
A popular, busy and well-run pub with a varied clientele, offering interesting guest beers, often from small breweries, it has a small front bar, a larger rear bar, plus another distinct drinking area. A function room is across the courtyard. In the shadow of the former James Hole Brewery, it is near to the town centre and bus station. No food is served. Home to a number of pub teams. Local CAMRA Pub of the Year 2008. (Castle)

Vine

117 Barnbygate, NG24 1QZ
12-2 (Sun only), 4-11
Springhead Liberty, Roaring Meg; guest beers H
A five-minute walk from the town centre, this Victorian street-corner local is owned by Springhead Brewery. The large L-shaped, no-frills bar with pool table and gaming machines contrasts with a more luxurious lounge with a dartboard. Landlord Paul, an enthusiastic CAMRA supporter, offers two guest beers from micro-breweries from all over the country. Very much a drinkers' pub.
(Northgate)

Normanton on Trent

Crown

South Street, NG23 6RQ (exit A1 at B1164, follow signs to Normanton) SK792688
12-11 (01636) 821973 milestonebrewery.co.uk
Milestone Dark and Stormy, Lions Pride, Rich Ruby; guest beer H
The brewery tap for Milestone Brewery, this sympathetically refurbished pub was once the village shop and post office, and is still very much at the heart of the community. The attractive interior is open-plan but has secluded places for dining in peace. Although very much a village pub, it has a good menu and an excellent Sunday roast. The chef uses local meat and vegetables to match the locally-produced beers. A safe play area is provided to the rear. (39)P

North Muskham

Muskham Ferry

Ferry Lane, NG23 6HB
12-midnight (01636) 704943
Greene King Morland Original; guest beers H
Formerly known as the Newcastle Arms (named after the Dukes of Newcastle who owned much of the parish), the pub became the Muskham Ferry in 1976, with reference to a period in the 1930s when the landlord would ferry school children to and from school. The traditional riverside pub stocks beer from the Greene King portfolio as well as local ales, and serves no-nonsense staple pub food. A terraced beer garden overlooks moorings for visiting boats. (37,39)P

Nottingham: Central

Canalhouse

48-52 Canal Street, NG1 7EH
12-11 (midnight Thu; 1am Fri & Sat); 12-10.30 Sun
(0115) 955 5060
Castle Rock Harvest Pale; guest beers H
This listed three-storey Castle Rock pub has a canal inlet on the inside, traversed by wooden walkways. It used to house a canal museum before it was converted into an open-plan pub that retains a certain quiet cosiness. One floor doubles as a function room that has hosted multiple beer festivals including SIBA champions. The canal-side decked patio is very popular in summer, half-

covered and heated for overcast evenings. Food, available daily, is varied in choice.
Q❀◐♿⇌⊖(Station St)🚌🚭

Dragon

67 Long Row, NG1 6JE
⏲ 12-11 (midnight Thu & Fri; 1am Sat); 11-11 Sun
☎ (0115) 941 7080 🌐 the-dragon.co.uk
Adnams Bitter; Castle Rock Harvest Pale Ⓗ
Small, unspoilt pub with a long, split-level and fairly narrow interior and laid-back ambience. Seating is a combination of bar stools and comfy benches, perfect for whiling away a happy hour or two. There is a delightful enclosed beer garden at the back. An extensive menu of fresh home-cooked food is available until 9pm weekdays and 5pm weekends. ❀◐⊖(Market Sq)🚌🚭

Hand & Heart

65 Derby Road, NG1 5BA
⏲ 4-11 Mon; 12-midnight; 12-10.30 Sun ☎ (0115) 958 2456
Blue Monkey Sanctuary; Full Mash Hand & Heart; guest beers Ⓗ
A short walk from the city centre, this relaxing pub is carved deep into Nottingham's sandstone caves. The front bar is decorated with restored Victorian wood, and mood lighting and background gypsy jazz music add further to the mellow atmosphere. There is an art gallery on the upper floor and live jazz plays on Tuesday and Thursday. An excellent choice of food attracts regular visitors – the home-made cakes are a speciality. Q◐🚌

Kean's Head

46 St Mary's Gate, NG1 1QA (opp St Mary's Church)
⏲ 11.30-11 (12.30am Fri & Sat); 12-10.30 Sun
☎ (0115) 947 4052 🌐 castlerockbrewery.co.uk
Castle Rock Harvest Pale, Preservation, Screech Owl; guest beers Ⓗ
Cosy one-room pub opposite the imposing St Mary's Church in the historic Lace Market district – the building was once a lace factory. Named in honour of the 19th-century actor Edmund Kean, it is busy at weekends and attracts a diverse and varied clientele. Owned by the Castle Rock group, it offers inventive, freshly-prepared food from an ever-changing menu. Three guest beers are usually available, including an ale from Castle Rock's Natural Selection series. ◐♿⇌⊖(Lace Market)🚌

King William IV

6 Eyre Street, Sneinton, NG2 4PB
⏲ 12 (11 Fri & Sat)-11; 12-10.30 Sun ☎ (0115) 958 9864
Oakham JHB, Bishops Farewell; guest beers Ⓗ
Nicknamed the King Billy, this cosy Victorian gem nestling on the edge of town is just a stone's throw from the Trent FM Arena. A family-run free house that oozes charm and character, it is a haven for real ale drinkers, with a choice of seven micro-brewery ales from near and far, as well as a cider. Occasional live music and unusual televised sports feature. A fine selection of rolls is available. This is one not to miss on a visit to Nottingham. ❀🚌🍏🚭

Lincolnshire Poacher

161-163 Mansfield Road, NG1 3FR (on A60 N of city centre)
⏲ 11-11 (midnight Thu & Fri); 10-midnight Sat; 12-11 Sun
☎ (0115) 941 1584
Batemans XB; Castle Rock Harvest Pale, Screech Owl; Everards Tiger; guest beers Ⓗ
Atmospheric two-roomer with a conservatory and enclosed patio to the rear. Eleven handpumps offer an ever-changing range of ales, mainly from micro-breweries, always including a local ale, mild, stout or porter and cider. Continental bottled beers and 80 whiskies provide even more choice. Popular home-cooked food uses locally-sourced, fresh ingredients. Live music plays on Sunday night and brewery evenings and micro-brewery trips are offered. Proudly twinned with the In de Wildeman bar in Amsterdam, the pub is a winner of many local CAMRA awards. Q❀◐♿🚌♣🍏🚭

Newshouse

123 Canal Street, NG1 7HB
⏲ 12-11 (midnight Fri & Sat) ☎ (0115) 950 2419
Castle Rock Harvest Pale; guest beers Ⓗ
Comfortable, friendly, two-roomed Castle Rock local. Note the brewery names etched into wall tiles in the public bar where sport is shown, sometimes on a large screen. Memorabilia from BBC Radio Nottingham and the local Evening Post adorn the walls. Darts, bar billiards and table skittles are played. A fun quiz night is held on Thursday. Up to eight cask beers from micro and regional brewers always include a mild, stout or porter and a cider. Local CAMRA 2010 Pub of the Year winner. ❀◐🀫⇌⊖(Station St)🚌♣🍏🚭

Olde Trip to Jerusalem ★ ✔

1 Brewhouse Yard, NG1 6AD (below castle)
⏲ 12-11; 11-midnight Fri & Sat; 11-11 Sun
☎ (0115) 947 3171 🌐 triptojerusalem.com
Greene King IPA, H&H Olde Trip, Old Speckled Hen, Abbot; Nottingham Rock Mild, EPA; guest beers Ⓗ
This world-famous pub is reputed to date from 1189. It has a number of rooms, some cut out of the castle rock. Upstairs, the rock lounge is home to the Cursed Galleon and a museum room houses a tapestry depicting Nottingham's history – both rooms can be reserved for functions. A covered courtyard and a seated pavement drinking area, next to Brewhouse Yard, with waitress service, are available Easter to August. Cellar tours by appointment. Children are welcome until 7pm.
🔥Q❀◐🀫⇌⊖(Station St/Market Sq)🚌♣🚭

Salutation Inn

Hounds Gate, Maid Marian Way, NG1 7AA
⏲ 12-midnight (2am Fri & Sat) ☎ (0115) 988 1948
🌐 salutationpub.com
Beer range varies Ⓗ
Steeped in history, this lively 17th-century inn with oak beams and stone floor is a favourite venue with young and old. Regular live rock music plays upstairs while downstairs there are quiet snugs for drinking and conversation. The pub sells a range of ciders and perries and promotes local beers. A Halloween beer festival is an annual highlight. Good food is based on local produce and cooked on the premises. The labyrinth of caves under the pub is reputed to be haunted.
🔥❀◐⊖(Market Square)🚌🍏🚭

VAT & Fiddle

12-14 Queen's Bridge Road, NG2 1NB
⏲ 11-11 (midnight Fri & Sat); 12-11 Sun ☎ (0115) 985 0611
Castle Rock Harvest Pale, Hemlock, Preservation, Elsie Mo, Screech Owl; guest beers Ⓗ
The Castle Rock brewery tap is a minute's walk from the railway station, and welcomes both regulars and visitors. With 12 handpumps, their full range is offered, including the monthly 'Wildlife Trust' beers. Guests include a mild, and a real cider. The Art Deco frontage boasts an attractive floral

display, which can be admired from the outside seating area. Although primarily a drinkers' pub, freshly-made cobs are available.
Q❀♿⇌(Nottingham)⊖(Station Street)🚌(Railway Station)♣●⌐

Nottingham: East

Bread & Bitter

153 Woodthorpe Drive, Mapperley, NG3 5JL
⏲ 10-11 (midnight Thu-Sat); 11-11 Sun ☎ (0115) 960 7541
Castle Rock Black Gold, Harvest Pale, Preservation; Everards Tiger; Fuller's London Pride; guest beers Ⓗ
Castle Rock pub built in 2007 on the premises of the old Judge's bakery on Mapperley Top. The original baker's oven fronts are still embedded in an inside wall, giving the place a warm and welcoming feel. The pub started a revival of real ale outlets in Mapperley. Food is all home-cooked and varies frequently – look for the specials board. Up to 12 beers, always including a local ale and a mild, are available along with an extensive foreign bottled beer list. Q❀◐◑♿🚌(25,44,45)●⌐

Nottingham: North

Gladstone ✔

45 Loscoe Road, Carrington, NG5 2AW (off A60)
⏲ 5-11 (11.30 Thu); 3-11.30 Fri; 12-11.30 Sat; 12-11 Sun
☎ (0115) 912 9994
Castle Rock Harvest Pale; Courage Directors; Fuller's London Pride; Nottingham EPA; Taylor Landlord; guest beer Ⓗ
Two-roomed back-street local located in the middle of a Victorian terrace. Memorabilia is on display in the narrow public bar, and the TV shows sporting events. A similarly shaped lounge is pleasantly decorated with old bottles, brass ornaments and classic pictures. A shelf of books is available for customers to peruse. The Carrington Folk Club has been meeting in the upstairs function room on a Wednesday night for the last 25 years.
❀⊟🚌♣⌐

Horse & Groom ✔

462 Radford Road, Basford, NG7 7EA
⏲ 12-11; 11-11.30 Fri & Sat ☎ (0115) 970 3777
🌐 horseandgroombasford.com
Caledonian Deuchars IPA; Fuller's London Pride; guest beers Ⓗ
This popular corner pub is situated a few yards away from the defunct Shipstones Brewery. The main entrance is via steps to the front door, but there is disabled access towards the rear on request. Although small, the pub has several distinct areas on two levels, including a function room, each with its own character. The bar accommodates nine handpumps serving mainly micro-brewery beers, including a mild, and at least one local guest. There is a quiz on Monday night.
♨Q◐♿⊖(Shipstone St)🚌(80/81)

Hotel Deux

Clumber Avenue, Sherwood Rise, NG5 1AP
⏲ 5-11 (11.30 Thu-Sat) ☎ (0115) 985 6724
🌐 theguitarbar.co.uk
Blue Monkey seasonal beer; Everards Tiger; Oakham Bishops Farewell; Whim seasonal beer Ⓗ
Formerly a hotel, it no longer provides accommodation or food. A friendly main bar is comfortably furnished and overlooks the front garden space and car park. The range of four beers may vary from those listed. Off the main bar is the Guitar Bar, featuring live entertainment at weekends from local, national and sometimes international artists (see website for details). A separate function room is much used by the local community. Board games are available.
❀🚌(NCT Yellow Route)P

Lion Inn ✔

44 Mosley Street, New Basford, NG7 7FQ
⏲ 12-11 (midnight Thu-Sat); 12-10.30 Sun
☎ (0115) 970 3506 🌐 thelionatbasford.co.uk
Castle Rock Harvest Pale; Draught Bass; guest beers Ⓗ
This suburban pub overlooks the former Shipstones Brewery and is adjacent to the Shipstone Street tram stop. The central bar serves up to 11 beers, mostly from micro-breweries. A real cider is available on gravity. Meals are served lunchtimes and evenings. The large beer garden and patio area are a pleasant setting for lazy summer afternoons. Live bands play on Friday, Saturday and Sunday evenings, with live jazz on Sunday lunchtime. Tuesday is folk night and Thursday is 'open mike' night. ♨❀◐◑♿⊖(Shipstone St)●P⌐

Nottingham: South

Globe

152 London Road, NG2 3BQ
⏲ 11.30-11.30 (12.30am Fri); 11-12.30am Sat; 12-10.30 Sun
☎ (0115) 986 6881 🌐 theglobenottingham.com
Nottingham Legend, EPA; guest beers Ⓗ
Light, airy, popular pub near Nottingham's cricket, football and rugby grounds, named after an old cinema on an adjacent site. Cold snacks are served on match days only, lunches on Sunday. Sport features regularly on several screens. Six handpumps serve ales mainly from micro-breweries, with Nottingham beers usually available. Ask about the CAMRA discount. An upstairs function room holds up to 100 people with catering facilities. Quiz night is Thursday and vinyl night Sunday. 🚌P⌐

Nottingham: West

Johnson Arms ✔

59 Abbey Street, Dunkirk, NG7 2NZ
⏲ 12-midnight (1am Fri & Sat) ☎ (0115) 978 6355
🌐 johnsonarms.co.uk
Adnams Bitter; guest beers Ⓗ
This former Shipstone's house still proudly displays the defunct brewery's name in its etched windows to complement the green-brick-tiled frontage. Once three rooms, the open-plan split-level bar is popular with undergraduates, locals and nearby QMC hospital staff. Quarterly beer festivals are not to be missed, along with the annual Johnsonbury Music Festival, held in the magnificent beer garden. Outside is a petanque court. Traditional home-cooked food – try the house burgers – is available along with a real cider and a LocAle.
❀◑🚌(13,14)♣●⌐

Plough ✔

17 St Peters Street, Radford, NG7 3EN
⏲ 12-midnight ☎ (0115) 970 2615
Nottingham Rock Mild, Rock Bitter, Legend, EPA; guest beers Ⓗ
This pleasant two-bar local is the brewery tap for Nottingham Brewery (situated behind the pub). One bar is quiet, with Sky TV in the other. There is a

covered smoking area and long alley skittles in the yard at the back. A quiz is held on Thursday with a free bowl of chilli on offer. CAMRA members receive a discount of 15p a pint, Monday to Thursday, 12-7pm. Traditional cider and the occasional guest can also be found on the bar. ⩕Q❀◐⊟⊟(2,28,30)♣●P⊱

Orston

Durham Ox ✓

Church Street, NG13 9NS

⊙ 12-3, 6-11; 11.30-11 Sat; 12-3, 7-10.30 Sun

☎ (01949) 850059

Fuller's London Pride; Greene King IPA; Marston's Mansfield Cask Ale; Wells Bombardier Ⓗ

A delightful pub for locals and visitors alike, situated opposite the village church. Outside, there are hitching rails for horses and ferrets. The large but cosy bar area features many equine pictures and prints, reflecting the landlady's interest in the local area. Bar meals are served. Regular well-attended charity fund-raising events are held at the pub all year round. An attractive garden and outdoor drinking space are popular in summer. Q⊂❀◐◑♿P⊱

Radcliffe-on-Trent

Horse Chestnut ✓

49 Main Road, NG12 2BE

⊙ 12-11 (11.30 Fri); 11-11.30 Sat ☎ (0115) 933 1994

⊕ horsechestnutradcliffe.com

Batemans XB; Castle Rock Harvest Pale; Fuller's London Pride; guest beers Ⓗ

Previously known as the Cliffe Inn, this LocAle-accredited pub was totally refurbished in 2006 with a smart 1920s-style decor. Seven reasonably priced real ales are served including ever-changing guests. Very much a smart local pub that sells food, rather than a restaurant that sells beer, but it does offer quality dishes made with local ingredients. Sunday is quiz night, on Monday there is a themed food night, and Tuesday to Thursday are steak nights. ❀◐◑♿⇌⊟●P⊱

Rampton

Eyre Arms

Main Street, DN22 0HR

⊙ 12-11 ☎ (01777) 248771 ⊕ eyre-arms.co.uk

Beer range varies Ⓗ

Recently refurbished pub situated in the centre of the village. The front bar area has a pool table, real fire and comfortable seating. A rear room acts as a dining area where lunchtime and evening meals are served. One bar serves all areas, with three changing real ales available. Outside is a large beer garden for sunny days. ⩕Q❀◐◑P⊱

Ravenshead

Hutt ✓

Nottingham Road, NG15 9HJ (A60 Nottingham-Mansfield road)

⊙ 11-11 (11.30 Fri & Sat); 11.30-10.30 Sun

☎ (01623) 792325

Castle Rock Harvest Pale; Courage Directors; Theakston Old Peculier; Wells Bombardier Ⓗ

The Hutt has all the character of a traditional British pub – an excellent venue for good food and a choice of up to five real ales. Built on the site of the first building in Ravenshead, opposite Newstead Abbey gates, the original building was recorded as one of the Royal Huts put up by King John in 1400. Owned by the Byron family from 1540, it used to be known as the Royal Hutt. There has been a coaching inn on this site since the 17th century. ⩕Q❀◐◑♿⊟(141)P⊱

Little John Inn

177 Main Road, NG15 9GS (on B6020 between Larch Farm and Blidworth)

⊙ 11.30-11.30 ☎ (01623) 792670

Jennings Cocker Hoop; Marston's Burton Bitter, Pedigree; Wychwood Hobgoblin; guest beers Ⓗ

A road house and local for the modern development of Ravenshead, the Little John is still proudly signed a Mansfield Ales pub. It regularly offers six real ales from the Marston's range. Good home-cooked food, with vegetarian options, is available all day. Games include darts, dominoes, and skittles played in the adjoining alley. Outside there is a covered smoking area and a large grassed playground. ⩕❀◐◑⊟(141)♣P⊱

Retford

Rum Runner

Wharf Road, DN22 6EN (by fire station)

⊙ 12-11 ☎ (01777) 860788

Batemans XB, XXB; guest beers Ⓗ

Formerly home to the now-closed Broadstone Brewery. The interior includes a long room warmed by a real fire and a second room with its own serving hatch through to the bar, which can be used for meetings. A quiz night is held on Wednesday and frequent music nights are hosted. Mini beer festivals are a regular feature. Outside is a large enclosed beer garden. ⩕Q❀◐◑⊟♣P⊱

Turks Head

Grove Street, DN22 6LE

⊙ 11-4, 7-11; 11-11 Sat; 12-11 Sun ☎ (01777) 702742

Beer range varies Ⓗ

Situated close to the main Market Square, entry to this pub is via two large oak doors, which both lead into an open-plan area served by an L-shaped bar. The room features plenty of oak panelling and has a large warming open fire. At the far end is a pool table. Four real ales are served. ⩕⊟♣

Ruddington

White Horse

60 Church Street, NG11 6HD

⊙ 12-11 (11.30 Thu-Sat); 12-10.30 Sun ☎ (0115) 984 4550

⊕ whitehorseruddington.co.uk

Black Sheep Best Bitter; Wells Bombardier; guest beers Ⓗ

Lads', dads' and grandads' two-roomed local with a pool table and darts in the bar. Up to three guest beers include a LocAle from Nottingham Brewery. CAMRA members receive a discount on pints and halves. The pub is a host of the annual village beer festival around the first weekend in June, held in its spacious, attractive courtyard complete with sunny aspects and barbecue. Quiz night is Thursday. Situated on the south side of the village, with regular bus services to Nottingham and a large, secure car park. ❀◐⊟⊟(10)♣P⊱

Southwell

Bramley Apple

51 Church Street, NG25 0HQ

⏲ 12 (5 Mon)-midnight (1am Fri & Sat); 12-11 Sun

☎ (01636) 813675

Springhead Liberty, Charlie's Angel; guest beers Ⓗ

The first (or last) pub on the famed 'sunset strip' run, this Springhead Brewery-owned hostelry offers an excellent beer selection from eight handpumps with a choice of ales from all over the country. Located just yards from the original Bramley Apple tree, this single room pub has a U-shaped interior. It offers something for everyone, with lunchtime specials, a Sunday carvery and curry night every Thursday. Q❀◐🚌(90,100)♣🍎⊱

Hearty Goodfellow 🏆

81 Church Street, NG25 0HQ

⏲ 12-3 (not Mon), 5-midnight; 12-1am Fri & Sat; 12-midnight Sun ☎ (01636) 812365

Everards Tiger; guest beers Ⓗ

Local CAMRA Pub of the Year 2010, this venue has been rejuvenated by the present tenants. The outside appearance belies an interior with a feeling of genuine age. An Everards house, it offers five guest beers, including a LocAle, as well as real perry and cider, plus a range of continental beers. The pub serves wholesome, home-made food made with locally-sourced produce at lunchtime. Outside is a large garden suitable for families and a car park. ❀◐🚌(90,100)♣P⊱

Old Coach House ✔

69 Easthorpe, NG25 0HY

⏲ 5 (12 Sun)-midnight; 4-1am Fri; 12-1am Sat

☎ (01636) 813289

Wells Bombardier; guest beers Ⓗ

Superb LocAle inn at the edge of the village serving six different ales mainly from micros. The pub has cosy areas with real fires and traditional pub games, and a beer garden for a welcome change in the summer. Live jazz plays on the first Sunday of the month, live folk music on a Monday and 'open mike' every Wednesday. Dogs are welcome. ♨♞❀🚌(101)♣🍎⊱

Sutton-in-Ashfield

Snipe ✔

Alfreton Road, NG17 1JE (jct of A38 and B6023) SK478575

⏲ 11-11 (midnight Fri & Sat) ☎ (01623) 443604

Greene King H&H Olde Trip, Old Speckled Hen, Abbot, seasonal beers Ⓗ

A large, open-plan pub situated on the A38. Half the interior is devoted to family dining – an extensive menu that caters for all needs is served all day. There is also ample space for drinkers, as well as a covered outdoor seating area. The pub is served well by public transport, with buses stopping outside. ❀◐◑♿🚌(9.1,9.2)P⊱

Upper Broughton

Golden Fleece

Main Street, LE14 3BG

⏲ 12-11 (10.30 Sun) ☎ (01664) 822262

Belvoir Beaver; guest beers Ⓗ

Large, attractive pub situated just off the main A606 Nottingham to Melton road. A dining pub, the spacious interior has a small area for drinkers and a larger restaurant space and conservatory. The wide and varied menu receives very good reports locally. A guest ale often comes from a micro-brewery and occasional beer festivals are hosted. ♨♞❀◐◑♿🚌(19)♣P⊱

Watnall

Queens Head

40 Main Road, NG16 1HT

⏲ 12-11.30 ☎ (0115) 938 6774

Adnams Broadside; Everards Tiger, Original; Greene King Old Speckled Hen; Wells Bombardier; guest beers Ⓗ

A 17th-century rural gem with a lounge/dining space, a small snug hidden behind the bar and an unusual locals' area with a grandfather clock. The extensive garden has children's play equipment and a recently installed marquee, making the pub popular all year. The internal fittings around the bar are original, and old photos adorn the walls adding to the pub's ambience. Home-cooked English food is served lunchtimes and weekday evenings. The pub is reputedly haunted. ♨Q❀◐◑⊟▲🚌(331)P⊱

Wellow

Olde Red Lion

Eakring Road, NG22 0EG (opp maypole)

⏲ 12-11 ☎ (01623) 861000

Beer range varies Ⓗ

This 400-year-old village pub is situated opposite the village green with its maypole and participates in a large event on May Day. The traditional wood-beamed interior includes a restaurant, lounge and bar areas with photographs and maps depicting the history of the village. Three real ales are available including a house beer from the local Maypole Brewery. Situated close to both Sherwood Forest and Clumber Park. Q❀◐◑⊟P⊓

West Bridgford

Southbank

1 Bridgford House, Trent Bridge, NG2 5GJ

⏲ 11-midnight (11 Tue; 2am Fri); 10-2am Sat; 10-midnight Sat ☎ (0115) 945 5541 🌐 southbankbar.co.uk

Beer range varies Ⓗ

Large, lively bar near Trent Bridge, handy for the cricket and football grounds. It has comfortable seating and a patio overlooking the Trent. Part of a small local pub group, it always offers a beer from Mallard and Nottingham. A varied and interesting selection of food is available, including breakfast on Saturday from 10am. Live music plays on most nights. Multiple TVs show sport, with two large screens for major games. ◐◑♿🚌⊱

Stratford Haven

2 Stratford Road, NG2 6BA

⏲ 10.30-11 (midnight Thu-Sat); 12-11 Sun

☎ (0115) 982 5981

Batemans XB, XXXB; Castle Rock Harvest Pale, Sheriff's Tipple; Everards Tiger; Hop Back Summer Lightning; guest beers Ⓗ

Busy, gimmick-free Castle Rock pub, tucked down a side street, handy for Trent Bridge cricket ground and the centre of West Bridgford. A former pet shop, it was named as a result of a local newspaper competition. The large beer range includes a rotating mild, and a good food menu includes vegetarian options. Live music plays at monthly brewery nights. Q❀◐◑♿🚌⊱

West Stockwith

White Hart

Main Street, DN10 4ET
✪ 12-11 ☎ (01427) 890176
Beer range varies Ⓗ
Small country pub with a little garden overlooking the River Trent, Chesterfield Canal and West Stockwith Marina. One bar serves the through bar, lounge and dining area. The Idle Brewery is situated in outbuildings at the side of the pub. The range of five real ales usually includes three from Idle. The area is especially busy during the summer, due to the river traffic. **Q◑◐♿⅄🚌♣P**

Westwood

Corner Pin 🏆

75 Palmerston Street, NG16 5HY (off B6016.)
✪ 1-11 (midnight Fri); 12-midnight Sat & Sun
☎ (07908) 531901
Beer range varies Ⓗ
Corner pub with a lounge and separate public bar, both with open fires. A genuine free house, six handpumps dispense beers from local micros – and a real cider. The landlady regularly brews special beers for the pub at Amber Ales. The interior includes a pool room, function room and indoor skittles alley – table skittles can be played in the bar. Dogs are welcome. An annual St George's beer festival is held. **⛰❀⊟♿⅄🚌(1,90)♣●⊢**

Worksop

Mallard

Station Approach, S81 7AG (on railway platform)
✪ 5 (2 Fri)-11 (midnight Sat); 12-11 Sun ☎ (01909) 530757
Beer range varies Ⓗ
Formerly the Worksop station buffet, the Mallard is situated within the railway station buildings, with access from the car park. The pub offers a warm welcome as well as three real ales including a porter, a selection of foreign bottled beers and country fruit wines. A further room is available downstairs for special occasions such as the three beer festivals the pub holds each year. **Q⅄⇌🚌P**

Shireoaks Inn

Westgate, S80 1LT
✪ 11.30-4, 6-11; 11.30-11 Sat; 12-10.30 Sun
☎ (01909) 472118
Beer range varies Ⓗ
Warm, friendly pub converted from cottages. The public bar houses a pool table and large-screen TV, and the comfortable lounge bar has a newly extended separate dining area. Tasty home-cooked food represents good value for money. The two handpulls dispense regularly changing guest ales. A small outside area with tables is available in the summer. **Q❀◑⊟⅄⇌🚌♣⊢**

Station Hotel

Carlton Road, S81 7AG (opp railway station)
✪ 11-11 (10.30 Sun) ☎ (01909) 474108
Acorn Barnsley Bitter; guest beers Ⓗ
Formerly the Regency, the Station Hotel has now reverted to its original name, situated opposite Worksop railway station, on the edge of the town centre. Four real ales are available, always including Barnsley Bitter. One bar serves a large bar area with a separate dining room, and a further small room suitable for meetings. Food is available lunchtimes and evenings. **❀◑◐⅄⇌🚌P**

Wysall

Plough Inn

Main Street, Keyworth Road, NG12 5QQ (jct of Widmerpool Rd and Main St)
✪ 12-midnight ☎ (01509) 880339 🌐 ploughatwysall.co.uk
Draught Bass; Fuller's London Pride; Greene King Abbot; Taylor Landlord; guest beers Ⓗ
This traditional village free house, run by the same family for more than 10 years, occupies an elevated position overlooking the main road. Originally built as three cottages, it retains the old beamed ceilings. Period features transport you back to the Victorian era, with separate alcoves and comfortable seating creating a welcoming atmosphere. A popular choice for rural dining at lunchtimes, guest beers are sourced from local micros. Quiz night is Tuesday. **⛰Q❀◑🚌(51)♣P⊢**

LocAle

A growing number of entries in the guide refer to pubs supporting the LocAle system. This was devised by CAMRA members in Nottingham and is now in widespread use in England, Wales, Scotland and Northern Ireland. The aim is to encourage publicans to stock at least one cask beer that comes from a local brewery – the distance between pub and brewery varies but is now generally accepted to be not more than 30 miles. The scheme also encourages publicans to use the Direct Delivery Scheme run by SIBA, the Society of Independent Brewers. SIBA members deliver direct to pubs in their localities rather than going through the central warehouses of pub-owning companies.

The overall aim of LocAle is to cut down on 'beer miles'. Research by CAMRA shows that food and drink transport accounts for 25 per cent of all HGV vehicle miles in Britain. Taking into account the miles that ingredients have travelled on top of distribution journeys, an imported lager produced by a multi-national brewery could have notched up more than 24,000 'beer miles' by the time it reaches a pub.

£10 spent on locally-supplied goods generates £25 for local economies. Keeping trade local helps enterprises, creates more economic activity and jobs, and makes other services more viable. The scheme also generates consumer support for local breweries. Pubs that support the LocAle scheme receive a special window sticker. For more information, see the CAMRA website: **www.camra.org.uk**.

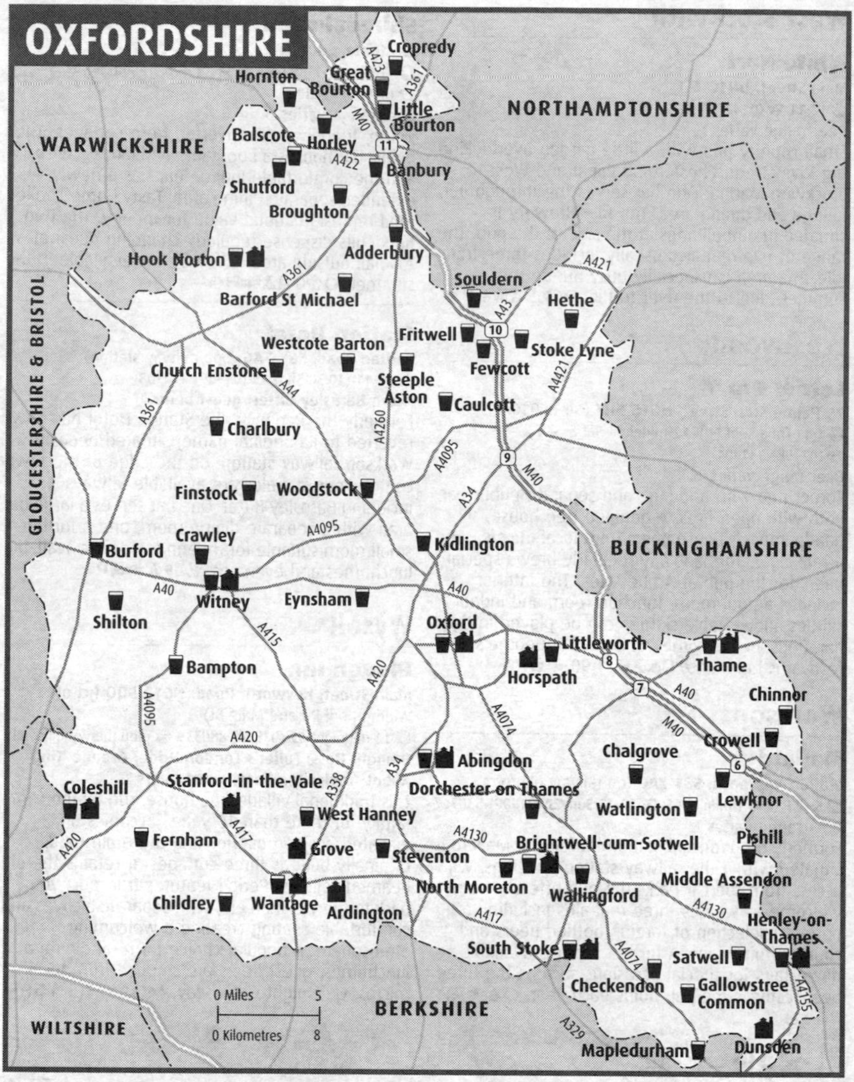

Abingdon

Brewery Tap ✓

40-42 Ock Street, OX14 5BZ

11-11.30 (1am Fri & Sat); 12-11 Sun ☎ (01235) 521655

thebrewerytap.net

Greene King H&H Bitter, Morland Original; guest beers Ⓗ

Morland created a tap for its brewery in 1993, in an award-winning conversion of three Grade II-listed town houses. The brewery closed and its site was redeveloped in 2000, following a takeover by Greene King, but the pub, run by two generations of the same family since it first opened, has thrived. Although the bar stays open until 1am on Friday and Saturday nights, last admission is midnight. ❀⇌◗♣⅟

Crown & Thistle (Stocks Bar)

Bridge Street, OX14 3HS

11-11 (1am Fri & Sat); 12-10.30 Sun ☎ (01235) 522566

crownandthistle.com

Brakspear Bitter; guest beers Ⓗ

The Stocks Bar is a free house within the 17th-century Crown and Thistle Hotel. Popular with tourists and locals alike, the publican is a keen supporter of local ale and sources his guest beers mainly from local breweries including Hook Norton and White Horse. The bar has many original features including a cobbled courtyard, galleried bar, authentic cannon and working stocks. A varied pub menu is offered – CAMRA members receive a 25 per cent discount. Live music plays at the weekends. Occasional beer festivals are held and real cider is sold. ❀⇌◑◗♿🚌(X3)♣🍎P⅟

Adderbury

Bell Inn ✓

High Street, OX17 3LS

12-2.30, 6-11 (midnight Fri & Sat); 12-3, 7-11 Sun

☎ (01295) 810338 the-bell.com

Hook Norton Hooky Dark, Hooky Bitter, Hooky Gold, seasonal beers; guest beers Ⓗ

In the heart of a beautiful village, this Tardis-like 18th-century ale-house retains its character with old beams, panelling and an inglenook fireplace. Discounts are available to CAMRA members who join the cask ale drinkers club. Freshly-cooked quality food is served and the pub hosts darts, dominoes, bar billiards, Aunt Sally and regular quiz nights. Folk nights are the first and third Mondays of the month. Well-behaved dogs, children, walkers and morris dancers are welcome. A Beautiful Beer award-winning pub, and CAMRA Branch Pub of the Year 2008.
♛☕❀⇄◑⊟⊟(59)♣⇀

Balscote

Butchers Arms

Shutford Road, OX15 6JQ (off A422)

✪ 12.30-2.30, 5-11 ☎ (01295) 730750 ⊕ balscote.com/butchersarms

Hook Norton Hooky Dark, Hooky Biitter; guest beer Ⓖ

A Hook Norton pub since 1878, this traditional village inn was once an abbatoir and still has the ice house in the garden. A cosy pub with an open fire, it serves Hooky ales straight from the cask, including monthly and guest ales. Come and try the traditional home-made pub grub, including weekly themed curry and steak nights. The family-friendly garden has Aunt Sally and children's activities. Walkers, muddy boots and dogs on a lead are always welcome here. ♛❀◑♣●P

Bampton

Morris Clown

High Street, OX18 2JW

✪ 5 (1 Sat)-11; 12-10.30 Sun ☎ (01993) 850217

Brakspear Bitter; West Berkshire Good Old Boy; guest beers Ⓗ

The 600-year-old morris dancing tradition thrives in this village and in this inn. A true free house, run by two generations of the same family for years, the pub is a regular in the Guide. Guest ales are usually sourced directly from smaller breweries. The interior is decorated with murals featuring past customers, and the pub is heated by a huge log fire. Bar billiards and Aunt Sally are played. Perry is available in the summer months.
♛❀⊟(18)♣●P⇀

Banbury

Bell Inn ✔

12 Middleton Road, OX16 4QJ

✪ 12.30-3 (not Mon & Tue), 7-11; 12-midnight Fri & Sat; 12-5.30, 8-11 Sun ☎ (01295) 253169

Hobsons Bitter; guest beers Ⓗ

This friendly and thriving community pub is close to the railway station and a regular entry in the Guide. There is a comfortable lounge with a blazing fire in winter and a traditional bar with a pool table. At least two guest ales are usually served and beer festivals are sometimes held. The pub hosts traditional sports such as darts and Aunt Sally. Outside is an attractive patio area. The pub was CAMRA North Oxon Pub of the Year in 2007.
♛❀◑⊟≠⊟♣P⇀

Barford St Michael

George Inn

Lower Street, OX15 0RH (off B4031)

✪ 7 (6 Fri)-11; 12-3, 7-11 Sat; 12-4 Sun ☎ (01869) 338226

Beer range varies Ⓗ

Nestling in the centre of this delightful village, the George is a thatched free house dating from 1672. Landlord Martin and his labrador Dillon offer a warm welcome and a choice of up to four changing real ales, plus a real cider and perry. Although no food is served, Martin is happy to cater for wedding receptions or functions, and picnics and barbecues are welcomed in the large beer garden. The pub hosts an annual summer beer festival.
Q❀⊟⛺♣●P⇀

Brightwell-cum-Sotwell

Red Lion

Brightwell Street, OX10 0RT

✪ 11-3, 6-11.30; 12-3, 7-10.30 Sun ☎ (01491) 837373 ⊕ redlion.biz

Appleford Power Station; Loddon Hoppit; guest beers Ⓗ

This is a fine 16th-century village pub, very popular with both locals and visitors – a warm welcome is assured. It offers excellent ales from local breweries such as Loddon, Appleford and West Berkshire, and from further afield. Quality, locally sourced food is served including beef and lamb from Little Wittenham and vegetarian choices. Pub and community events are well-supported, including pudding nights, pub quizzes, music festivals and parent and baby coffee mornings. Firmly established as one of south Oxfordshire's outstanding pubs – well-worth seeking out.
♛Q❀◑⊟(131)P⇀

Broughton

Saye & Sele Arms ✔

Main Road, OX15 5ED (3 miles W of Banbury on B4035)

✪ 11.30-2.30 (3 Sat), 7-11; 12-5 Sun ☎ (01295) 263348 ⊕ sayeandselearms.co.uk

Adnams Bitter; guest beers Ⓗ

Welcoming 17th-century free house at the edge of Broughton Castle grounds. Four real ales are always available in the flagstoned bar, with guest beers often available from local breweries. There is something for everyone on the menu – including the landlord's excellent 'proper' pies and wonderful desserts. In summer, the beautifully landscaped garden is perfect for alfresco dining. Don't drive past. Q❀◑♿⊟(480)♣P⇀

INDEPENDENT BREWERIES

Adkin Wantage
Appleford Brightwell-cum-Sotwell
Best Mates Ardington
Brakspear (Marston's) Witney
Hook Norton Hook Norton
Loddon Dunsden
Loose Cannon Abingdon (NEW)
Lovibonds Henley-on-Thames
Old Bog Oxford
Old Forge Coleshill (NEW)
Pitstop Grove
Ridgeway South Stoke
Shotover Horspath (NEW)
Thame Thame (NEW)
White Horse Stanford-in-the-Vale
Wychwood (Marston's) Witney

Burford

Royal Oak

26 Witney Street, OX18 4SN (off A361)
⏲ 11-2.30 (not Tue), 6.30-11; 11-11 Sat; 11-3, 7-10.30 Sun
☎ (01993) 823278
Wadworth Henry's IPA, 6X; guest beer Ⓗ
Tucked away down a side street in a tourist town, this is a genuine local with a long-serving landlord and landlady and a traditional pub atmosphere. The flagstoned front bar leads to a long carpeted side bar with a bar billiards table at the end. The walls of both bars are covered in interesting pictures and memorabilia. An ancient clock chimes melodiously and around 1,000 tankards hang from the ceiling. Excellent home-made food features local produce. Walkers are welcome – boot scraper provided.
⛫Q❀⇌◑▶⛺⊟♣●P⁵⁻

Caulcott

Horse & Groom 🏆

Lower Heyford Road, OX25 4ND (on B4030 between Middleton Stoney and Lower Heyford)
⏲ 12-3, 6-11; 12-3, 7-10.30 Sun ☎ (01869) 343257
🌐 horseandgroomcaulcott.co.uk
Hook Norton Hooky Bitter; guest beers Ⓗ
A small pub with a big welcome. The French landlord/chef offers excellent food and the Bastille Day celebration and beer festival is not to be missed. A genuine free house, the three guest ales could come from any part of the country – local micros and Cornish breweries feature strongly. Real cider is sold in summer. Booking is advised for meals, especially Sunday lunch. The garden is popular in summer. No dogs or under sevens permitted inside. Car parking is available nearby. A gem. ⛫Q❀◑▶♿●

Chalgrove

Red Lion

115 High Street, OX44 7SS SU635970
⏲ 11.30-3, 6-11 (later at weekends); 12-11.30 Sun
☎ (01865) 890625 🌐 redlionchalgrove.co.uk
Adnams Bitter; Fuller's London Pride; Taylor Landlord; guest beers Ⓗ
Picturesque 16th-century local in a village with three good pubs. Owned by the parish church, the interior is divided into several distinct areas, with an open fire and plenty of exposed beams. The husband and wife licensees are very welcoming. Both are trained chefs and good food is a speciality. Gardens at the front and rear have seating for drinkers. Car parking is available opposite.
⛫❀◑▶♿⊟(101,122)♣⁵⁻

Charlbury

Rose & Crown ✔

Market Street, OX7 3PL
⏲ 12-11 (midnight Wed & Thu; 1am Fri) 11-1am Sat
☎ (01608) 810103 🌐 myspace.com/theroseandcrownpub
Ramsbury Bitter; guest beers Ⓗ
Traditional town-centre free house, 24 years in this Guide, with a simply-furnished split-level bar and a large lounge with patio courtyard. On the Oxfordshire Way, walkers are welcome to bring their own food. A pub for the discerning drinker who enjoys an excellent pint, with seven real ales it offers one of the best selections in the area and strongly supports micro-breweries. Fortnightly music nights feature some of the best touring artists around. Four times local CAMRA Pub of the Year. ⛫❀⛺⇄⊟(X9,69,53)♣●⁵⁻

Checkendon

Black Horse

Burncote Lane, RG8 0TE SU666841
⏲ 12-2, 7-11 (10.30 Sun) ☎ (01491) 680418
Hook Norton Hooky Bitter; West Berkshire Old Father Thames, Good Old Boy Ⓖ
Run by generations of the same family for over 100 years, parts of the pub date from the early 18th century. This free house is difficult to find but well-worth seeking out – it is situated up an unmarked lane on the left of the Checkendon/Stoke Row road which appears to go nowhere. A selection of filled baguettes is available at lunchtime but there is no hot food. ⛫Q❀⛺⊟(142,145)P

Childrey

Hatchet Inn

Main Street, OX12 9UF (on B4001)
⏲ 12-2.30 (not Mon & Tue; 3 Sat), 7-11; 12-3.30, 7-10.30 Sun
☎ (01235) 751213
Greene King Morland Original; guest beers Ⓗ
One-room, split-level pub with a small, quiet area off to one side, offering a warm welcome to all. At the centre of a small village community, it is close to the historic Uffington White Horse. Thriving and well-supported quiz and Aunt Sally teams represent the pub in local leagues. Well-behaved dogs are welcome. A regular entry in the Guide, the pub is a previous winner of the local CAMRA Pub of the Year. ❀▶♿⛺⊟(38,67)♣P⁵⁻

Chinnor

Red Lion ✔

3 High Street, OX39 4DL (on B4009)
⏲ 12-2, 5-11; 12-11 Sat; 12-10.30 Sun ☎ (01844) 353468
🌐 redlionchinnor.co.uk
Greene King IPA; Skinner's Cornish Knocker; guest beers Ⓗ
Situated near the centre of the village, this 300-year-old local was originally three cottages. It is near a local steam railway station and also close to the fine Chiltern countryside. Guest ales usually change twice weekly and quiz nights are held monthly. Outside, there is decking with lighting and heating for drinkers. Families and well-behaved dogs are welcome. No meals Sunday evening. ⛫Q❀◑▶⊞⊟(40)♣P⁵⁻

Church Enstone

Crown

Mill Lane, OX7 4NN (off A44, on B4030)
⏲ 12-3, 6-11; 12-4 Sun ☎ (01608) 677262
Hook Norton Hooky Bitter; guest beers Ⓗ
This picturesque 17th-century stone free house, overlooking the quiet village green, is a real gem. Comfortable inside, there is an inglenook and old village photographs on the walls. Conversation flourishes without intrusive background music or games machines. The restaurant features award-winning menus including fresh fish, seafood, game (in season) and local produce. The pub is popular with both locals and walkers keen to explore the beautiful surrounding countryside.
⛫Q❀◑▶⊟(20)P

Coleshill

Radnor Arms

32 Coleshill, SN6 7PR (on B4019)
⏲ 12-11 (10.30 Sun) ☎ (01793) 861575
🌐 radnorarmscoleshill.co.uk
Beer range varies Ⓗ/Ⓖ
Set in a beautiful National Trust village, the 18th-century building was the former smithy to the Coleshill estate. Old blacksmith's tools are displayed in the split-level two-room interior, one of which has its own snug. This pub is the brewery tap for the on-site Old Forge brewery and also the main outlet for Halfpenny beers in Oxfordshire, and their products can be enjoyed along with the traditional home-cooked pub fare. Walkers (boots off), children and well-behaved dogs are welcome. ♨Q❀◐◑♿🚌(64)♣P⚡

Crawley

Lamb Inn ✔

Steep Hill, OX29 9TW (off B4022 Charlbury/Witney Road)
⏲ 11-3, 6-11 (not Sun) ☎ (01993) 703753
🌐 thelambcrawley.com
Brakspear Bitter; guest beer Ⓗ
This 18th-century traditional pub offers a warm welcome from friendly staff. The low-beamed main bar has tasteful wooden furniture and a log fire, together with well-kept Brakspear and Wychwood beer. The chef/landlord is passionate about food, which is freshly prepared, home-cooked and locally sourced. There are two restaurants: the first is small and cosy (formerly the village shop), the second – approached through a small snug – is large and airy, an ideal venue for private parties and meetings. Large patio and garden. ♨Q❀◐◑P⚡

Cropredy

Red Lion ✔

8 Red Lion Street, OX17 1PB (opp church) SP469467
⏲ 12-2.30 (3.30 Sat), 6 (5.30 Tue & Fri)-11 (midnight Fri & Sat); 12-10.30 Sun ☎ (01295) 750224
🌐 redlioncropredy.co.uk
Hook Norton Hooky Bitter; guest beers Ⓗ
This four-room part-thatched pub is at the hub of a historic village. Four handpumps dispense ales from the Punch Taverns list. There is a restaurant area as well as a family room where both locals and canal users dine on changing daily specials or à la carte. Log fires, one in an inglenook, blaze in winter and there is a garden area for summer use. The pub hosts a range of evening entertainment including quiz night on Thursday and fish and chips on Friday. ♨Q❀◐◑♿P⚡

Crowell

Shepherd's Crook

The Green, OX39 4RR (off B4009 between Chinnor and M40 jct 6) SU 744997
⏲ 11.30-3, 5-11; 11-11 Sat; 12-10.30 Sun ☎ (01844) 351431
🌐 theshepherdscrook.co.uk
Enville Ale; Holden's Black Country Bitter; Vale seasonal beers; guest beers Ⓗ
In the foothills of the Chilterns, this comfortable inn is renowned for the quality and choice of its ales. The landlord is a real ale fanatic, and the pub is a mecca for horse racing and cricket enthusiasts. The pub is well known for its food quality – fish is a speciality. Steaks and steak and kidney for the pies come from local butchers. A beer festival is held every August bank holiday weekend. Well-behaved dogs are welcome. ♨Q❀◐◑🚌(40)P

Dorchester on Thames

Fleur de Lys

9 High Street, OX10 7HH (off A4074 from Shillingford to Berinsfield) SU578942
⏲ 12-3 (not Mon), 5-midnight; 12-midnight Sat & Sun
☎ (01865) 340502 🌐 fleurdelys-dorchester.co.uk
Brakspear Bitter; Hook Norton Hooky Bitter; guest beer Ⓗ
The Fleur is situated in the historic village of Dorchester opposite the Abbey and nearby Thames walks. Once a coaching inn, parts of the pub date from the 16th century. A free house, it offers a friendly welcome, with three handpumps and an excellent affordable bar and à la carte menus, a roaring fire in winter and newspapers on the bar. There is a large enclosed rear garden where Aunt Sally is played in the summer. A dog- and family-friendly pub. ♨❀🛏◐◑🚌♣●P⚡

Eynsham

Queens Head

17 Queens Street, OX29 4LH
⏲ 12-2.30 (3 Sat & Sun), 6-11 ☎ (01865) 881229
🌐 thequeenshead.net
White Horse Village Idiot; Sharp's Doom Bar; guest beer Ⓗ
This 18th-century inn is tucked away in the back streets of Eynsham. Popular with locals and visitors alike, it has two bars – one with a wood-burning stove, decorated with railway memorabilia, the other more spacious with a seating area, TV and pool table. Outside is a spacious garden. The landlord, with 25 years at the helm, has long been a keen supporter of small breweries and offers a wide range of guest beers.
♨Q❀◐◑🀫♿⛺🚌(S1)♣⚡

Fernham

Woodman Inn

SN7 7NX (on B4508)
⏲ 11-11; 12-10.30 Sun ☎ (01367) 820643
🌐 thewoodmaninn.net
Taylor Landlord; guest beers Ⓖ
First licensed in 1652, this delightful and spacious inn caters for all. Most of the building's internal walls were removed years ago but many original features remain including the huge roaring fire. There are close links with horse racing. Although renowned locally for its food, there is always a warm welcome for drinkers who come to sample the four ever-changing cask ales all stored behind the bar and dispensed by gravity. Thatchers cider is available in the summer.
♨Q❀◐◑♿🚌(65,67)●P⚡

Fewcott

White Lion

Fritwell Road, OX27 7NZ (1 mile from jct 10 M40)
⏲ 7 (5.30 Fri; 12 Sat)-11; 12-6.30 Sun ☎ (01869) 346639
Beer range varies Ⓗ
A true free house and hub of the community, offering a constantly-changing choice of four ales

mainly from micros near and far. Stout and porter often feature. This popular village pub is ideal for enjoying conversation and watching sport on TV, though it can get busy on darts nights. One en-suite room has recently been added. The large garden is popular in summer but is closed for the winter. ⋒❀⇌♿♣P

Finstock

Plough Inn

The Bottom, OX7 3BY (off B4022)
✪ closed Mon; 12-2.30, 6-11; 12-11 Sat; 12-6 Sun
☎ (01993) 868333 ⊕ theplough-inn.co.uk
Adnams Broadside; Butts Organic Jester; guest beer Ⓗ
Thatched free house dating from the mid-18th century with a simply furnished flagstoned public bar. Attractive features include old local photos, a piano and a library. The low-beamed dining room offers excellent food from a small but interesting menu. There is also a snug with comfortable settees around an inglenook fireplace. Walkers (with boots off), well-behaved children over five and dogs on leads are welcome. The well-kept garden is a pleasant place to relax in summer. North Oxon CAMRA Cider Pub of the Year 2006. ⋒Q❀◐◑⊟🚌(X9,69,53)♣●P

Fritwell

Kings Head

92 East Street, OX27 7QF (2 miles W of M40 jct 10 at S end of village)
✪ 11 (3 Mon)-11; 11-midnight Fri & Sat; 12-10.30 Sun
☎ (01869) 346738 ⊕ thekingsheadfritwell.co.uk
Fuller's London Pride; Taylor Golden Best; guest beer Ⓗ
Stone-built north Oxfordshire pub with a single-room bar and separate dining room, warmed by a welcoming fire on colder days. A regularly-changing guest ale usually comes from a national brewery. Food is served daily, with Jamaican and Spanish dishes featuring, and fish and chips on Friday. The Kings Head is home to many sports teams as the trophies testify, including Aunt Sally, fishing and pool. Disabled access is through the back door from the car park. ⋒❀◐◑♿♣P⁵–

Gallowstree Common

Reformation

Horsepond Road, RG4 9BP (between Cane End and Rotherfield Peppard) SU690801
✪ 12-3; 5.30-11(12 Fri and Sat); 12-8 ☎ (0118) 972 3126
⊕ the-reformation.co.uk
Brakspear Bitter, seasonal beers Ⓗ
This award-winning country pub is a great example of a community hostelry, hosting many village events. It is divided into three distinct areas, and boasts a large garden with separate children's play area, complete with pirate ship. Families and well-behaved dogs are welcome, and good-quality food is available at every session, all home-made, using local produce wherever possible. However, one bar area is always kept free for those who just want to enjoy a pint. A recent finalist for a national community pub of the year, look out for the log-splitting contest, ploughing day and the ever-popular summer evening tractor runs.
⋒Q❀◐◑⊟♣P⁵–

Great Bourton

Bell Inn

Manor Road, OX17 1QP (off A426) SP455455
✪ 12-2.30 (not Tue; 3 Sat), 6-11 (midnight Fri & Sat); 12-3, 7-11 Sun ☎ (01295) 750504
Hook Norton Hooky Dark, Hooky Bitter, Hooky Gold Ⓗ
The genial hosts, Frank and Freya, have transformed this establishment. Centrally located in a delightful village, it sits opposite the unusual detached bell tower of the church with its associated lychgate. At least three Hooky beers are usually on offer, and there is a popular restaurant area for diners. Numerous themed evenings are hosted throughout the year. A true community pub, it runs darts and dominoes teams. An annual beer festival is held in March/April. Dogs are welcome. ⋒Q❀◐◑⊟♣●P

Henley-on-Thames

Bird in Hand 🏆

61 Greys Road, RG9 1SB SU760824
✪ 11.30-2, 5-11; 11.30-11 Sat; 12-10.30 Sun
☎ (01491) 575775 ⊕ henleybirdinhand.co.uk
Brakspear Bitter; Fuller's London Pride; Hook Norton Hooky Dark; guest beers Ⓗ
This pub was local CAMRA Pub of the Year in 2006 and 2008. Henley's only genuine free house, the combination of town-centre location and friendly atmosphere makes it popular with locals and visitors alike. A one-bar pub, it has a large, secure garden with an aviary, pond and friendly dogs. Two guest beers usually come from micro-breweries. Good value lunches are available Monday to Friday. Beer festivals are usually held in May and September. ❀◐▲⇌🚌♣⁵–

Hethe

Whitmore Arms

Main Street, OX27 8ES (in village, off A421) SP593295
✪ 12-2.30 (not Mon-Fri), 7-11; closed Tue; 12-2.30, 7-10.30 Sun ☎ (01869) 277654
Brakspear Bitter; Hook Norton Hooky Bitter; St Austell Tribute Ⓗ
This 18th-century stone-built village pub is set in a locality that offers plenty of easy walking in Flora Thompson's Lark Rise country. The open bar area with its large inglenook fireplace at one end warms the cockles in winter and there is a pleasant garden for summer use. Aunt Sally and dominoes teams flourish – there is also a separate outside room with two pool tables. Good value food is served 7-9.30pm and weekend lunchtimes. Children and dogs are welcome. ⋒Q❀◐◑♿♣P⁵–

Hook Norton

Pear Tree ✔

Scotland End, OX15 5NU (off A361, follow signs to brewery)
✪ 11.30-11.30 (1.30am Fri & Sat) ☎ (01608) 737482
Hook Norton Hooky Dark, Hooky Bitter, Hooky Gold, Old Hooky; guest beers Ⓗ
This much-loved village local is the brewery tap for Hook Norton, situated close to the Victorian tower brewery and visitor centre. The full range of Hooky beers is served. With three guest rooms it provides the ideal base for a brewery tour and to explore the Cotswolds. The large beer garden is family friendly. Open all day, every day, with a cosy log

fire in winter. Live music is hosted three times a month and there is free Wi-Fi.
(488)P

Horley

Red Lion

OX15 6BQ (centre of village) SP418438
closed Mon; 6-11; 12-6 Sun ☎ (01295) 730427
Hook Norton Hooky Bitter; Taylor Landlord
At the heart of the local community, this popular locals' pub offers a friendly welcome to visitors. Little changed over the years, it is a traditional beer-only pub. Poker, darts and dominoes are played during the week, and sport is screened on TV. Aunt Sally is played during the summer. The pub also hosts occasional beer and music festivals. ♣

Hornton

Dun Cow

West End, OX15 6DA (signed from village green) SP392449
6 (12 Sat)-11; 12-10.30 Sun ☎ (01295) 670524
drunkenmonk.co.uk
Hook Norton Hooky Bitter; Wells Bombardier; guest beers
Thatched, low-beamed and flagstone-floored Grade II-listed pub, located in a quiet and attractive village. There is good walking locally and ramblers and dogs are welcome. The family runs the Vitis Wines and Drunken Monk outlets and stocks historical ales, meads and fruit and country wines alongside real ciders. Beer festivals are held in February and July. Freshly-cooked food is available in the evening and weekday lunchtime by arrangement. A previous local CAMRA Cider and Perry Pub of the Year. ♣P

Kidlington

King's Arms

4 The Moors, OX5 2AJ (close to jct of High St and Church Rd)
11-3, 5.30-11.30; 11-midnight Fri & Sat; 12-11.30 Sun
☎ (01865) 373004
Greene King IPA; Wells Bombardier; guest beers
Traditional community pub with two small front rooms in possibly England's largest village. Guest beers are a major attraction and can be any style from any brewery, with dark beers often making an appearance. The heated, covered patio is used to play Aunt Sally and also for a twice-yearly beer festival. Darts is popular. Good value, traditional lunches are served Monday to Saturday. The outside seating area includes a heated smoking shelter. (2A)♣P

Lewknor

Leathern Bottle

1 High Street, OX49 5TW SU716976
11-2.30 (3.30 Sat), 6-11; 12-3.30 7-10.30 Sun
☎ (01844) 351482 theleathernbottle.co.uk
Brakspear Bitter, seasonal beers; Marston's Pedigree
Situated close to junction 6 of the M40 yet in the centre of the village of Lewknor, this classic 450-year-old pub has featured in all but one edition of the Guide. It has a reputation for great, home-cooked pub food featuring locally-sourced meats and daily specials. There is now an outdoor facility for playing boules. The Oxford Tube bus breaks its journey from Oxford to London near here.
Q(124,M1,W1)P

Little Bourton

Plough

Southam Road, OX17 1RH (beside A423)
12-2.30, 6.30-11; 12-3, 7-10.30 Sun ☎ (01295) 750222
Hook Norton Hooky Bitter; Purity Ubu
This welcoming, family-run roadside free house dispenses two beers on handpump. The large bar opens out into a large, well-lit dining area popular for lunches and evening meals, particularly on Wednesday curry night and Friday fish and chips night – eat in or take away. Sunday lunches are also popular. Functions are catered for by booking in advance. Dominoes is played. The pub is a focal point for both the nearby holiday caravan park and the local community. Q♣P

Littleworth

Cricketer's Arms

38 Littleworth, OX33 1TR
12-3, 6-11; 12-3, 7-10.30 Sun ☎ (01865) 872738
cricketers-arms.co.uk
Hook Norton Hooky Bitter, seasonal beer; Shotover Prospect; guest beer
A friendly, family-run free house, 'The little pub with a big welcome' was the first in Oxford to gain LocAle accreditation. Four cask ales are available – one from the nearby Shotover Brewery, two from Hook Norton and a local guest – plus a huge range of local bottled ales. Great value home-made food is served every day, with roasts on Sunday. Popular with walkers, and dogs and children are welcome. Live music is hosted on the first Friday of the month, and beer festivals in February and September. Q(U1,280)♣P

Mapledurham

Pack Saddle

Chazey Heath, RG4 7UD (on A4074) SU696772
11-3, 6-11; 11-midnight Fri & Sat; 12-midnight Sun
☎ (0118) 946 3000 thepacksaddleinn.co.uk
Wadworth Henry's IPA, Horizon, 6X, Bishops Tipple, seasonal beers; guest beer
This is a genuine pub with traditional features – large fireplace, wood beams and panelling, and horticultural memorabilia. It is located between two golf courses on the Mapledurham estate just a mile or so from the main house. The bar area is divided into two, the lower bar primarily for drinkers. Food is served at all sessions and is freshly made, of high quality and excellent value, with the emphasis on locally-sourced, traditional fare. There is a large enclosed garden with a children's play area. Q(X39,X40)♣P

Middle Assendon

Rainbow

RG9 6AU (on B480) SU738858
12-3, 6-11 (not Mon eve winter); 12-3, 7-10.30 Sun
☎ (01491) 574879
Brakspear Bitter, seasonal beers
Small and easily missed pub hidden away in the Stonor Valley. Ideally situated for Chiltern walks, it is a popular stop for local horse-drawn carriage

tours. There is always a warm and friendly welcome. The bar is divided into two – the lounge serving home-cooked fresh food, including locally-sourced game. This is a lively local pub, very much the hub of the village. Q❀◐◑⊟♣P

North Moreton

Bear at Home

High Street, OX11 9AT (S off A4130) SU561894
✪ 12-3, 6-11; 12-11 Sat; 12-3, 6-11 (12-11 summer) Sun
☎ (01235) 811311 🌐 bear-at-home.co.uk
Taylor Landlord; West Berkshire Bear Beer; guest beers Ⓗ
This friendly village local dates back to the 15th century, when it was a coaching inn. The main bar features sofas, an open fire and plenty of tables for diners to enjoy the excellent pub food. The varying range of mostly local ales includes Bear Beer, brewed exclusively for the pub by West Berkshire. The Bear adjoins the village cricket ground and cricket matches are played on most weekends throughout the summer. A four-day Beer and Cricket Festival is held at the end of July.
⛰❀◐◑🚌(31,95)♣P

Oxford

Bear Inn

6 Alfred Street, OX1 4EH
✪ 11-11 (midnight Sat); 11-10.30 Sun ☎ (01865) 728164
Beer range varies Ⓗ
This cosy pub claims to be the oldest pub in Oxford. Hidden away from the busy High Street, down Bear Lane, it is frequented by students, locals and tourists alike. The interior comprises two small wood-beamed rooms with low ceilings, decorated by a colourful collection of ties. The small bar serves a collection of four Fuller's ales, plus two guests. Quiz night is Tuesday. ⛰Q❀◐◑⇄🚌⊱

Far from the Madding Crowd 🏆 ✔

10-12 Friars Entry, OX1 2BY (alley off Magdalen St)
✪ 11.30-11 (midnight Thu-Sat); 12-10 Sun
☎ (01865) 240900 🌐 maddingcrowd.co.uk
Brakspear Bitter; guest beers Ⓗ
A free house in the centre of Oxford, the pub opened in 2002 as a conversion of shop units. There are six handpumps and real cider is always available. Four beer festivals are held yearly, and Sunday night is quiz and curry night. Food is served daily from mid-day until 8pm. Live music features occasionally and local morris dancers perform. Convenient for theatres, cinemas, shops and taxis. Local CAMRA Pub of the Year 2009. ◐◑♿⇄🚌●

Harcourt Arms

Cranham Terrace, Jericho, OX2 6DG (off Walton St)
✪ 12-2, 5.30-11 (midnight Fri & Sat); 12-2, 7-11 Sun
☎ (01865) 310630
Fuller's Chiswick, Discovery, London Pride, ESB; guest beers Ⓗ
Situated just outside the city centre in Jericho, which remains a good area for pubs, this typical 1930s brick hostelry has an atmospheric interior with subdued lighting and background jazz. The walls are decorated with modern art prints and an impressive selection of international bank notes. Toasted sandwiches are available, as is Fuller's 1845 bottle-conditioned ale. While away the time playing games including Scrabble, or read the New Scientist or Private Eye magazines. ⛰❀🚌(17)♣

King's Arms

40 Holywell Street, OX1 3SP
✪ 10.30 (12 Sun)-midnight ☎ (01865) 242369
🌐 kingsarmsoxford.co.uk
Caledonian Deuchars IPA; St Austell Tribute; Young's Bitter, Special, seasonal beers; guest beers Ⓗ
This 17th-century Oxford institution is set among the university buildings and owned by Wadham College, with student accommodation above the drinking floors. The multi-roomed, wood-panelled pub serves locals, tourists and academics alike. Up to seven beers are on offer, with food served until 9pm. The King's Arms can be very busy, but the service is ever-efficient. ⛰Q👶◐◑⇄🚌

Lamb & Flag

12 St Giles, OX1 3JS
✪ 12-11 (10.30 Sun) ☎ (01865) 515787
Palmers IPA; Shepherd Neame Spitfire; Skinner's Betty Stoggs; Theakston Old Peculier; guest beers Ⓗ
At the heart of the university and run by St John's College as a free house, this Grade II-listed building has been an ale house since around 1695. The spacious, multi-roomed pub was saved from conversion into student accommodation by a vigorous campaign by the local CAMRA branch some years ago. Guest beers often come from the West Country, and Lamb & Flag Gold is brewed by Palmers of Bridport as a house beer. Q◐⇄🚌

Mason's Arms ✔

2 Quarry School Place, Headington Quarry, OX3 8LH
✪ 5 (11 Sat)-11; 12-4, 7-10.30 Sun ☎ (01865) 764579
🌐 masonsquarry.co.uk
Brains The Rev James; Harviestoun Bitter & Twisted; West Berkshire Good Old Boy; guest beers Ⓗ
Family-run community pub full of character – a meeting place for local darts and Aunt Sally teams. Guest ales change weekly and a popular annual beer festival is held in September. A selection of bottled Belgian beers is also stocked and cider is on handpump. Beers from the pub's own micro-brewery, the Old Bog, are often available at weekends and sell out fast – contact the pub to check availability. A heated decking area is popular all year round and there is a room available for private functions. ❀♣●P⊱

Rose & Crown

14 North Parade Avenue, OX2 6LX (½ mile N of city centre, off Banbury Road)
✪ 10-midnight (1am Fri & Sat – may vary); 12-11 Sun
☎ (01865) 510551 🌐 rose-n-crown.com
Adnams Bitter; Hook Norton Old Hooky; guest beers Ⓗ
Popular Victorian local in vibrant north Oxford. Andrew, the landlord of some 25 years, is noted for greeting every customer when at home. The pub has recently become a genuine free house. There still exists a friendly and warm atmosphere for locals, students, and academics, with excellent beer and lively conversations. A covered heated courtyard makes for an old colonial club feeling. No mobile phones, dogs, or children permitted. The pub is 50 metres from the bus stop.
Q❀◐◑🚌(2,2A,7,7A)⊱

Royal Blenheim

13 St Ebbe's Street, OX1 1PT
✪ 11-11 ☎ (01865) 242355
White Horse Village Idiot, Wayland Smithy; guest beers Ⓗ

This street-corner, city-centre pub is owned by Everards, but is leased to White Horse Brewery. There are 10 handpumps, with a good range of White Horse beers and one from Everards always on offer, plus guests from all over the country. The interior feels light and airy with plenty of natural wood in evidence. Live sport is regularly shown on the large TV screen, with rugby and American football regularly pulling in the crowds. ◑♿⇌🚌

Turf Tavern ✔

4 Bath Place, OX1 3SU (in alley off Holywell St, next to Bath Hotel)

11-11; 12-10.30 Sun ☎ (01865) 243235

theturftavern.co.uk

Greene King IPA, Old Speckled Hen, Abbot; guest beers 🄷

Traditional 16th-century pub with two bars, popular with students and always busy during university term times. Outside there are three flagstoned courtyards, one retaining parts of the original city wall standing three storeys high, all with heating and umbrellas for drinkers and smokers. Up to 11 real ales are available plus Westons Old Rosie cider. Two beer festivals are held each year in spring and autumn. Winner of Publican Perfect Pub Award in 2007. ♨❀◑⇌🚌●⚊

White Horse ✔

52 Broad Street, OX1 3BB

11-midnight ☎ (01865) 204801

whitehorseoxford.co.uk

St Austell Tribute; Sharp's Doom Bar; Shotover Prospect; White Horse Wayland Smithy; Wychwood Hobgoblin; guest beer 🄷

Claiming to be the smallest pub in Oxford and sandwiched between the two entrances to Blackwell's famous bookshop, this classic Grade II-listed 16th-century city-centre inn has a long and narrow bar and a small snug at the rear. Up to six cask ales are dispensed. Popular with students and tourists, the pub featured regularly in Inspector Morse and more recently Lewis. Both Winston Churchill and Bill Clinton are reputed to have frequented the pub in their Oxford days. Q◑⇌🚌

Pishill

Crown Inn

RG9 6HH (on B480) SU718902

11.30-2.30, 6-11; 12-3, 7-10.30 Sun ☎ (01491) 638364

thecrowninnpishill.co.uk

Brakspear Bitter; guest beers 🄷

This 15th-century coaching inn may have origins dating back as far as the 11th century. The renovated 400-year-old barn complements the brick and flint main pub and holds functions and music nights. With warming log fires in winter, and a picturesque beer garden in summer, the pub is always welcoming. Brakspear ales feature, with one or two regularly changing guest beers, although this is a free house. ♨Q❀🛏◑🄿P

Satwell

Lamb ✔

Satwell, Rotherfield Greys, RG9 4QZ (50m E of B481 Reading-Nettlebed road, signed to Shepherds Green) SU706833

12-3, 6-11; 12-11 Fri; 10-midnight Sat; 12-10.30 Sun ☎ (01491) 628482 thelambpub.net

Black Sheep Best Bitter; Loddon Leaping Lamb; guest beer 🄷

Quintessential 16th-century country pub rescued from the ruins of the Antony Worrall Thompson restaurant empire by local entrepreneur and beer lover Chris Smith. The cosy interior, home to George the ghost, is quirkily split into two areas, one dedicated to diners, with seating at a premium in the main bar. Outside, the ample garden, set amid pine trees, features an enormous barbecue and chickens roaming free. The pub has its own beer, Leaping Lamb, from local brewery Loddon. ♨❀◑♿🚌(M1)P

Shilton

Rose & Crown

OX18 4AB (off B4020 SE of Burford)

12-3, 6-11; 12-11 Fri & Sat; 12-10 Sun ☎ (01993) 842280

Young's Bitter; guest beer 🄷

This authentic 17th-century Cotswold stone pub has two rooms – the welcoming front bar warmed by a log fire in winter and the rear room with a wood-burning stove for dining. The pub is the focus of the local community, with food sourced locally and cooked by the chef/landlord. The rotating guest beer often comes from a local brewer. Well-behaved dogs are welcome in the front bar. There is a large, attractive garden for summer drinking. ♨Q❀◑♣●P⚊

Shutford

George & Dragon ✔

Church Lane, OX15 6PG (3 miles off A422 next to church)

closed Mon; 12-2.30, 5.30-11; 12-10.30 Sun

☎ (01295) 780320 thegeorgeanddragon.com

Hook Norton Hooky Bitter; guest beers 🄷

This traditional 13th-century listed building in the heart of the village nestles into the hill beside the church. Four real ales are available in the lively bar with its inglenook fireplace and tiled flooring. Hooky Bitter is always on handpump as well as three guest ales which regularly come from local breweries. Good food is also available. The pub hosts traditional games including darts and Aunt Sally. For the adventurous there is a yard of ale hanging above the bar. ♨Q❀◑🄿♣🄳

Souldern

Fox Inn ✔

Fox Lane, OX27 7JW (off B4100)

12-3, 5-11; 12-11 Sat; 12-4, 6-11 Sun ☎ (01869) 345284

thefoxatsouldern.co.uk

Hook Norton Hooky Bitter; guest beers 🄷

A free house situated at the centre of the village – a cul-de-sac off the B4100. Two guest ales come from local breweries or national micros, with Yorkshire brewers proving popular, especially Copper Dragon. A beer festival is held on the fourth weekend of July, when northern micros feature strongly. The large garden is busy in good weather where Aunt Sally is played. The car park is small, but there is on-road parking nearby. Accommodation is available in four en-suite rooms. ♨❀🛏◑♣P

South Stoke

Perch & Pike

The Street, RG8 0JS (off B4009)
✪ 11.30-3, 5.30-11; 11.30-11 Sat; 12-10.30 Sun
☎ (01491) 872415 🌐 perchandpike.co.uk
Brakspear Bitter, Oxford Gold Ⓗ
Traditional 17th-century brick and flint pub at the hub of the village. An adjoining barn has been converted into a restaurant and four en-suite bedrooms. The menu is varied and at lunchtime focuses on homely real pub food. A la carte is available in the evening, with a traditional roast on Sunday. The original part of the pub has three separate areas with low beams, a real fire, comfortable seating and daily newspapers. The pub is situated by the Ridgeway path. It now has its own darts team and dogs are welcome.
♨Q❀⇌◐◑♿🚌(134,135)♣P⊬

Steeple Aston

White Lion

Southside, OX25 4RR
✪ 12-midnight ☎ (01869) 340307
Taylor Golden Best, Landlord Ⓗ
Family-run single-room community pub dating from the 19th century. There is always something happening here, with chess by the fire, satellite TV, pool, occasional live music and free Wi-Fi Internet access. Guest beers can come from local micros or national brewers. Fresh food is served all day every day and a heated shelter is provided for smokers in the garden. The Oxford to Banbury bus stops outside and the pub is a mile or so from the canal and Heyford station over the river.
♨❀◐◑🚌(X59)♣⊬

Steventon

North Star ★

2 Stocks Lane, OX13 6SE (end of the Causeway off High St)
✪ 5 (3 Fri)-11; 12-11.30 Sat; 12-11 Sun ☎ (01235) 831677
Butts Traditional; Greene King Morland Original; West Berkshire Good Old Boy; guest beers Ⓗ
National Heritage pub situated next to the Causeway, a listed ancient monument. This wonderful unspoilt village pub has been run by the same family for 160 years. It is popular with locals and visitors and hosts a monthly tractor club as well as many village clubs. Inside it has two rooms, one with a snug space with three settles around an open fireplace. There is no bar counter – beers are served through a stable door or hatch. An ideal stop-off for walkers and their dogs.
♨Q❀▲🚌(32C,X2)♣P⊬

Stoke Lyne

Peyton Arms

Main Street, OX27 8SD (¾ mile off B4100) SP567284
✪ closed Mon; 12-2, 5-11; 12-11 Sat; 12-7 Sun
☎ (01869) 345285
Hook Norton Hooky Bitter, Old Hooky Ⓖ
This classic gem, just two miles from junction 10 of the M40, is a national treasure. Once inside, travellers from far and wide are transported far from the madding crowd. Genial and welcoming hosts provide much of the pub's character, as well as the charming, cosy bar room with its memorabilia-adorned walls. Beers are dispensed on gravity, conversation abounds and no one is allowed to go hungry, with freshly prepared rolls available on request. ♨Q❀⊬

Thame

Cross Keys

1 Park Street, OX9 3HP
✪ 12-2, 5-11; 12-11 Sat; 12-10.30 Sun ☎ (01844) 218202
Vale Best Bitter; guest beers Ⓗ
Closed for nine months, the Cross Keys reopened again in 2009. Six handpumps feature guest beers from micro-breweries, usually including a mild. No food is available although there is no objection to bringing in a takeaway from one of the local fish & chip shops. Lots of games are available and a piano for those who are musical. The pub is also home to Thame Brewery. Brews are created about twice a week and don't hang around very long.
♨❀🚌(280)♣🍎⊬

Wallingford

Coachmakers Arms

37 St Marys Street, OX10 0EU SU606891
✪ 12-3, 5-11; 12-11 Fri-Sun ☎ (01491) 832231
🌐 thecoachmakersarmswallingford.co.uk
Brakspear Bitter Ⓗ
Situated close to the centre of a historic market town, this lively and friendly drinkers' pub offers a warm welcome to all. Known locally as The Cat, the interior is divided into two rooms – the Ramping Cat Bar and a second room where music sessions and themed nights are held. Good value food is served at lunchtimes and the pub is renowned for its excellent Sunday lunches. It is popular for darts and has its own cycling club that meets each Thursday in summer. As well as excellent public transport, Wallingford can be reached by heritage train or riverboat on some weekends.
❀⇌◐⊟♿▲⇌🚌(X39,40)♣⊬

Wantage

Royal Oak Inn 🏆

Newbury Street, OX12 8DF (S of Market Square)
✪ 5.30-11; 12-2.30, 7-11 Sat; 12-2, 7-10.30 Sun
☎ (01235) 763129 🌐 royaloakwantage.co.uk
Wadworth 6X Ⓗ/Ⓖ**; West Berkshire Maggs Mild, Dr Hexter's Wedding Ale, Dr Hexter's Healer; guest beers** Ⓖ
This multi-award-winning street-corner pub is a mecca for the discerning drinker and is a meeting place for many local clubs. Photographs of ships bearing the pub's name adorn the walls. The lounge bar features wrought-iron trelliswork covered in more than 300 pumps clips. This is the primary outlet for Pitstop and West Berkshire ales in the area – two beers carry the landlord's name. An extensive changing range of ciders and perrys is also on offer. Local, county, regional and national finalist CAMRA Pub of the Year. ⊟🚌♣🍎

Watlington

Carriers Arms

Hill Road, OX49 5AD (off B4009) SU692944
✪ 10-midnight (11 Sun) ☎ (01491) 613470
Adnams Bitter; Brains The Rev James; Sharp's Doom Bar Ⓗ
This thriving local free house has four darts teams and Aunt Sally in the summer. There is a quiz on

Thursday evening and a curry night every Saturday. The pub offers a late breakfast and serves food lunchtimes and Thursday to Saturday evenings. From the large garden there is a good view of the White Mark, a chalk triangle on Watlington Hill. It should also be possible to catch sight of the once rare red kite. For walkers the Ridgeway long distance footpath passes close by. ⩓❀◑⅄⊟♣P

West Hanney

Plough ✔

Church Street, OX12 0LN

✪ 12-3, 6-11; 12-7 Sun ☎ (01235) 868674

🌐 ploughwesthanney.co.uk

Brakspear Bitter Ⓗ**; Taylor Landlord; guest beers** Ⓗ/Ⓟ

Welcoming, atmospheric, 16th-century thatched free house. The Grade II-listed building has a cosy, beamed and alcoved split-level bar with an open fire and separate dining room serving locally renowned, traditional British food. A large garden plays host to Aunt Sally and outdoor skittles in summer. Two beer festivals are held annually. The late May bank holiday festival features Oxfordshire ales. The August festival is a real village and family occasion – a weekend of live music and a variety of entertainments for everyone. ⩓Q☕❀◑⊟♣P⚍

Westcote Barton

Fox Inn

27 Enstone Road, OX7 7BL (on B4030 Enstone-Bicester road)

✪ 12-3, 5-11 (midnight Fri & Sat); 12-11 Sun

☎ (01869) 340338 🌐 thefoxinnmiddlebarton.co.uk

Hook Norton Hooky Bitter; Ringwood Fortyniner; guest beer Ⓗ

Seventeenth-century stone-built roadside pub with up to three guest ales from bigger micros and the SIBA list; Skinner's, Sharp's and Wickwar feature regularly. The innovative landlords run a fortnightly crop swap, monthly bike nights, quizzes, and a music and beer festival over the August bank holiday. Good quality food is available lunchtimes and evenings (not Sun eve or Mon) – the South African landlord makes his own biltong. The pub hosts darts and Aunt Sally teams. ⩓❀◑♣P

Witney

Eagle Tavern

22 Corn Street, OX28 6BL

✪ 11-3, 5-midnight (2am Fri); 11-2am Sat; 12-midnight Sun

☎ (01993) 849564

Hook Norton Hooky Bitter, Hooky Gold, Old Hooky, seasonal beers Ⓗ

Expect to find excellent beer and friendly staff and locals here. Wood panelling, a real fire, exposed stone walls and a rich colour palette create a welcoming atmosphere. The landlord has been running pubs on Corn Street for 20 years and is proud of his award-winning cellar, which can be viewed from a window in the pub. The Hook Norton seasonal beer changes on a monthly basis. A juke-box plays eclectic but unobtrusive music. ⩓◐⊟(S1)♣⚍

New Inn ✔

111 Corn Street, OX28 6AU

✪ 5-midnight; 12-1am Sat; 12-midnight Sun

☎ (01993) 703807

Black Sheep Best Bitter; Brakspear Bitter; Jennings Cumberland Ale; Wychwood Hobgoblin; guest beers Ⓗ

Slightly away from the town centre, the New Inn is a relaxing place to enjoy a quiet pint during the week. With six well-kept real ales, there is something for everyone. Friday and Saturday nights are busy, as are televised rugby match nights, when the atmosphere is lively. The pub itself dates back to 1805, though the cellar is older. A separate building at the rear is used for occasional beer festivals. Live music plays on some Fridays. ⩓⊟(S1)♣⚍

Woodstock

Black Prince

2 Manor Road, OX20 1XJ (on A44 just N of town centre)

✪ 12-11 ☎ (01993) 811530

Vale Best Bitter; guest beer Ⓗ

Situated opposite Blenheim Park, this 16th-century pub has a delightful riverside garden. Inside, features include ancient fireplaces, stone walls, beams and a suit of armour. Three real ales are available. Fresh home-cooked food is served at reasonable prices ranges from a good selection of sandwiches to full meals plus daily specials. A side room is available for meetings. The venue is famous for Mock Mayor celebrations in August and Duck Race Day in June. There is occasional live music in the evening. Walkers, families and dogs are welcome. ⩓Q❀◐◑P⚍

Beers suitable for vegetarians and vegans

A number of cask and bottle-fermented beers in the Good Beer Guide are listed as suitable for vegetarians and vegans. The main ingredients used in cask beer production are malted grain, hops, yeast and water, and these present no problems for drinkers who wish to avoid animal products. But most brewers of cask beer use isinglass as a clearing agent: isinglass is derived from the bladders of certain fish, including the sturgeon. Isinglass is added to a cask when it leaves the brewery and attracts yeast cells and protein, which fall to the bottom of the container. Other clearing agents – notably Irish moss, derived from seaweed – can be used in place of isinglass and the Guide feels that brewers should take a serious look at replacing isinglass with plant-derived finings, especially as the sturgeon is an endangered species.

Vegans avoid dairy products: lactose, a bi-product of cheese making, is used in milk stout, of which Mackeson is the best-known example.

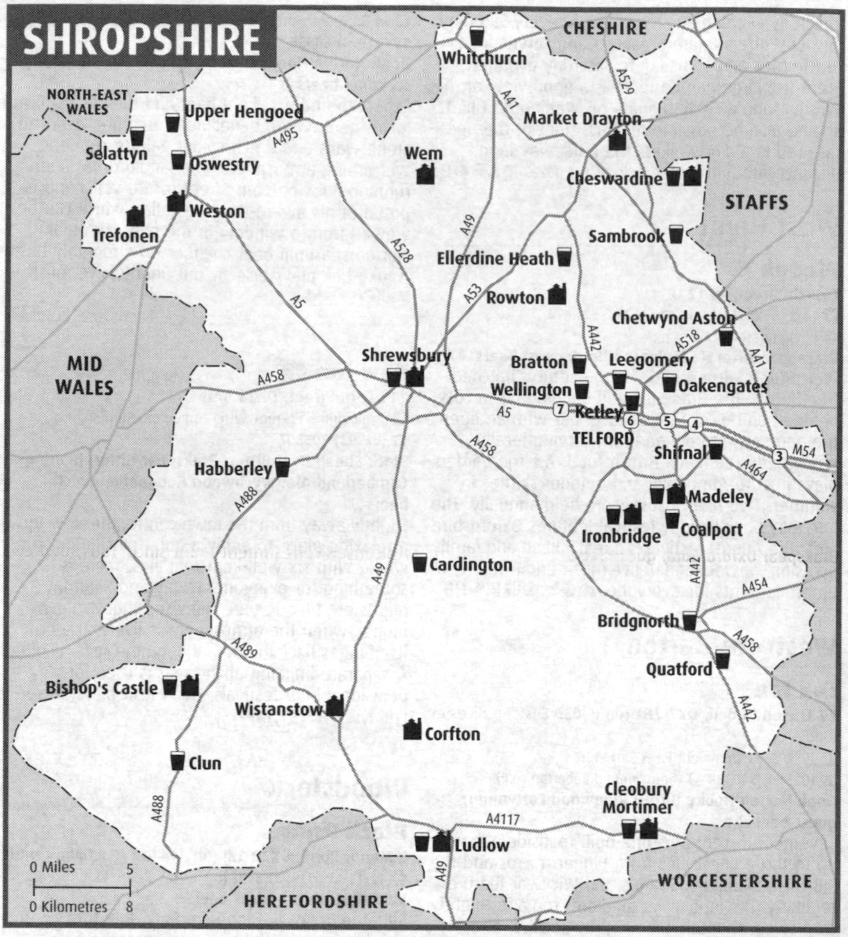

Bishop's Castle

Six Bells

Church Street, SY9 5AA

12-2.30 (not Mon), 5-11; 12-11 Sat; 12-3.30, 7-10.30 Sun

☎ (01588) 638930 sixbellsbrewery.co.uk

Six Bells Big Nevs, Goldings, 1859, Cloud Nine; guest beers Ⓗ

This is the Six Bells brewery tap – the adjoining Six Bells Brewery was re-established on the site of the original one, which closed in the early 1900s. You can be sure of a friendly greeting in the wooden beamed bar where four real ales are on handpump, plus monthly specials and Montgomery Cider in summer. Excellent fresh food is served in the dining/lounge bar (no food Sun eve or Mon). A local beer festival in July offers around 20 ales and real ciders plus live music in the courtyard.

Three Tuns

Salop Street, SY9 5BW

12-11 (10.30 Sun) ☎ (01588) 638797

thethreetunsinn.co.uk

Three Tuns 1642, XXX, Clerics Cure; guest beer Ⓗ

One of the truly historic pubs in the country, this is one of the Famous Four that were still brewing in the early 1970s. Together with the adjoining, but separately owned, Three Tuns Brewery, it has been on this site since 1640. Now extended into four rooms, on one side is the dining lounge, on the other the front bar leading to the central characterful snug and the extended timber and glass dining room. Music sessions, including jazz, are hosted in the top room on a regular basis. Dogs welcome. Q (443,745)

Bratton

Gate Inn

TF5 0BX (on B5063 just N of Shawbirch)

12 (5 Mon)-11; 12-11.30 Fri & Sat; 12-10.30 Sun

☎ (01952) 244207 lets-group.co.uk/thegate

Rowton Bitter; Three Tuns XXX; guest beers Ⓗ

Dating from 1779, this pub is noted locally for its food and real ale. Situated less than a mile from Shawbirch on the B5063, it is also at the northern extent of the Silkin Way. Sympathetically refurbished, the interior mixes a modern decor with original features including the oak floor, quarry tiles and exposed ceiling beams. Nigel and Yvonne serve freshly-cooked local English food. At the rear is a large fenced garden and children's play area. Two beer festivals are held each year in May and December. Q P

Bridgnorth

Bell & Talbot
2 Salop Street, High Town, WV16 4QU
5-11.30 (midnight Fri & Sat); 5.30-11 Sun
☎ (01746) 763233 odleyinns.co.uk
Bathams Best Bitter; Hobsons Town Crier; guest beers ⊞
This old coaching inn is a beer drinkers' and musicians' local, with live music on a Friday and Sunday. The larger bar has a memorable ceiling display of records and musical instruments. Outside a foliage-adorned conservatory leads to the umbrella-covered smoking area. Bridgnorth's first LocAle pub, guest beers are always local and are selected from Shropshire or Black Country breweries. Cider is occasionally served in the summer. CAMRA members receive a discount.
⩓⊭⇌⊟♣⌐

George
Hollybush Road, WV16 4AX (opp Severn Valley Railway entrance)
11 (12 Sun)-midnight ☎ (01746) 768868
Brakspear Oxford Gold; guest beers ⊞
A family-owned inn, recently renovated to a very high standard with four star accommodation. It has a comfortable, small snug bar and a large lounge bar featuring exposed beams and real fires where occasional live music plays at weekends. Locally-sourced food is served in the lounge and in a separate dining area. There is a large patio and a small covered space for smoking. The guest ales will usually include one LocAle beer.
⩓Q✿⊭◑♿⇌⊟⌐

Golden Lion ✔
83 High Street, High Town, WV16 4DS
11.30-2.30, 5-11; 11-11 Fri & Sat; 12-10.30 Sun
☎ (01746) 762016 goldenlionbridgnorth.co.uk
Greene King IPA; Hobsons Town Crier; Wye Valley HPA; guest beers ⊞
Originally a 17th-century coaching inn, this traditional town-centre hostelry has retained separate public and lounge bars, and continues to offer accommodation. The history of the inn is displayed in two pleasant lounge bars. The public bar is the venue for dominoes, darts and quiz teams. A fine collection of pump clips adorn the beams throughout. Home-cooked food is served at lunchtime. At the rear there is a covered smoking area, and an outdoor patio near the car park.
Q✿⊭◐⊟⇌⊟♣P⌐

Hare & Hounds
8 Bernards Hill, Low Town, WV15 5AX (200m up hill from A442 by the Fox)
5-midnight; 12-1am Sat; 12-midnight Sun
☎ (01746) 768819 hareandhounds.biz/index.php
Hobsons Mild, Town Crier; guest beers ⊞
This family-run traditional pub has wonderful views of the Severn Valley Railway and Bridgnorth from its raised beer garden. Inside you will find three distinct drinking areas, two with real fires. All guests are made most welcome – regulars, visitors, families, walkers and well-behaved dogs alike. Ideal for quiet conversation mid-week, the pub comes alive on Saturday with a varied entertainment programme. There is a daily happy hour 5-7pm and keenly-priced cocktails at all times. ⩓✿⊟⛺⊟♣●⌐

Kings Head
3 Whitburn Street, High Town, WV16 4QN
11-11 (midnight Fri & Sat); 12-10.30 Sun
☎ (01746) 762141 kingsheadbridgnorth.co.uk
Bridgnorth Apley Ale, Best; Hobsons Best Bitter, Town Crier; guest beers ⊞
Grade II-listed, 16th-century coaching inn, sympathetically renovated featuring timber beams, flagstone floor, leaded windows and roaring log fires in winter. Local beers are always available and there is a constantly-changing selection of guest ales. Lunch and evening menus offer plenty of variety, with char-grills featuring local produce a speciality. The Stable Bar to the rear has seven handpulls and an impressive display of wine bins. The courtyard has a pleasant seated area.
⩓Q✿◑♿⇌⊟⌐☐

Railwaymans Arms
Hollybush Road, WV16 5DT (follow signs for SVR)
11.30-4, 6-11; 11.30-11 Fri; 11-11 Sat; 12-10.30 Sun
☎ (01746) 764361
Bathams Best Bitter; Hobsons Best Bitter; guest beers ⊞
A licensed refreshment room since 1861, owned by SVR, this is an exceptionally busy drinking spot, attracting beer drinkers and steam buffs from around the country. The platform drinking area is perfect for soaking up the atmosphere of the steam era, with plenty of fine railway memorabilia on display. A free house, the three guest beers tend to be from smaller, often local, brewers plus one changing Belgian beer. A large selection of local and European bottled beers is also available. Sandwiches and pies are occasionally on offer. A CAMRA beer festival is hosted in the car park every September. ⩓Q✿⇌⊟●P⌐☐

White Lion
3 West Castle Street, WV16 4AB
10.30-11 (midnight Fri & Sat); 10.30-10.30 Sun
☎ (01746) 763962 whitelionbridgnorth.co.uk
Banks's Bitter; Ludlow Gold; St Austell Tribute; Titanic Mild; guest beers ⊞
This 18th-century inn with two bars offers a warm welcome to regulars and visitors. Murals by a local artist adorn the lounge and outside walls. Good pub lunches are prepared from locally-sourced produce, and seven handpulls offer a selection of LocAles, national beers and Thatchers traditional cider. Outside is a terrace, lawned garden and children's play area. A regular venue for a story-telling group, folk club and quiz teams, folk & blues

INDEPENDENT BREWERIES

Corvedale Corfton
Dolphin Shrewsbury
Hobsons Cleobury Mortimer
Ironbridge Ironbridge
Joules Market Drayton (NEW)
Lion's Tail Cheswardine
Ludlow Ludlow
Offa's Dyke Trefonen
Rowton Rowton
Salopian Shrewsbury
Shires Madeley
Shropshire Wem
Six Bells Bishop's Castle
Stonehouse Weston
Three Tuns Bishop's Castle
Wood Wistanstow

music and beer festivals are held in summer and winter. CAMRA members receive a discount. ♨Q⚘❀⌂◑♿⇌⊟♣●⁄

Cardington

Royal Oak

SY6 7JZ

✪ closed Mon; 12-2.30, 6.30-midnight; 12-2.30, 7-1am Fri & Sat; 12-3.30, 7-midnight Sun ☎ (01694) 771266

🌐 at-the-oak.com

Draught Bass; Hobsons Best Bitter; guest beers Ⓗ

Ancient 15th-century free house in a conservation village, reputedly the oldest continuously licensed inn in Shropshire. It retains the character of a country pub – the low-beamed bar has a roaring fire in winter in a vast inglenook fireplace. The dining room has exposed old beams and studwork. Guest beers are predominantly from local breweries. The menu includes Fidget Pie made to a Shropshire recipe that has been handed down from landlord to landlord. Dog-friendly during non-dining times – phone for details. ♨Q❀◑▲♣P⁄

Cheswardine

Red Lion

High Street, TF9 2RS

✪ 6 (5 Thu & Fri; 12 Sat)-11; 12-3, 7-10.30 Sun

☎ (01630) 661234

Lion's Tail Blooming Blonde, Lionbru, Chesbrewnette; Marston's Burton Bitter Ⓗ

Dating from the 1750s, the pub is set in the heart of rural Shropshire a couple of miles from the A529. Home to the Lion's Tail Brewery, the interior includes a large bar with a small snug and a room suitable for meetings. A huge range of single malt whiskies is stocked. A community pub where locals, visitors and well-behaved dogs are welcome, it is within walking distance of bridges 52 and 53 of the Shropshire Union Canal. Well worth seeking out, especially by boat. ♨Q❀⊟♿P⁄

Chetwynd Aston

Fox

Pave Lane, TF10 9LQ (½ mile W of A41)

✪ 12-11 (10.30 Sun) ☎ (01952) 815940

🌐 fox-newport.co.uk

Brunning & Price Original Bitter; Salopian Oracle; Wood Shropshire Lad; guest beers Ⓗ

Originally called the Fox & Duck, the pub is open plan, providing extensive dining and drinking areas. There is a large open fire in the main bar area for the winter months and an extensive garden for the summer. The pub hosts mini beer festivals and food weeks and offers a varied range of excellent food, made with locally-sourced ingredients wherever possible. The clientele is a mixture of locals and travellers from further afield, including visitors to the Lilleshall National Sports Centre nearby. ♨Q❀◑♿♣P⁄

Wheatsheaf

TF10 9LF (½ mile from A41)

✪ 4.30 (12 Sat)-midnight; 12-10 Sun ☎ (01952) 811447

🌐 wheatsheafinn.co.uk

Banks's Mild; Marston's Burton Bitter, Pedigree; guest beer Ⓗ

This very popular locals' pub with traditional quarry-tiled floors and an open fire makes a second appearance in the Guide. In addition to the usual bar games the pub hosts pickled onion, damson and sloe gin competitions. It is also a meeting place for local cyclists. Although it is situated in a rural area it attracts many visitors from outside the village. ♨Q❀⊟♣●P⁄Ȗ

Cleobury Mortimer

Kings Arms

6 Church Street, DY14 8BS

✪ 10-11 (midnight Thu-Sat); 10-10.30 Sun

☎ (01299) 271954 🌐 kingsarms-cleobury.co.uk

Hobsons Mild, Twisted Spire, Best Bitter, Town Crier; guest beer Ⓗ

This 15th-century inn with wooden floors and beamed ceilings is set in the centre of a market town – the gateway to the Shropshire Hills. The tap for Hobsons Brewery, it is overlooked by St Mary's Church, famous for its twisted spire – hence the name of Hobsons' blond beer. Breakfast and morning coffee are available as well as a lunch menu of locally-sourced produce with daily changing specials. There is free Wi-Fi access and a covered, heated terrace for smokers. ♨❀⌂◑♿⊟♣⁄

Clun

White Horse Inn ✔

The Square, SY7 8JA

✪ 11 (12 Sun)-midnight ☎ (01588) 640305

🌐 whi-clun.co.uk

Hobsons Mild, Best Bitter; Salopian Shropshire Gold; Three Tuns XXX, 1642; Wye Valley Butty Bach; guest beers Ⓗ

Comfortable, 16th-century coaching inn and post house in the old market square at the centre of a wonderfully timeless town, described by A E Housman as 'one of the quietest places under the sun', and now with its own 'nano' brewery. A friendly local, it has an L-shaped bar with low beams and adjoining dining room serving excellent, reasonably priced food. Westons cider, perry and an interesting range of foreign bottled beers are stocked. Jam nights are held once a month. Outside is a secluded garden. Dogs are welcome. A previous local CAMRA Pub of the Year. ♨Q⚘❀⌂◑▲⊟♣●⁄Ȗ

Ellerdine Heath

Royal Oak

TF6 6RL (2 miles off A442 towards A53) SJ604225

✪ 12-midnight (10.30 Sun) ☎ (01939) 250300

Hobsons Best Bitter; Salopian Shropshire Gold; Wye Valley HPA; guest beer Ⓗ

Still known as 'the Tiddly' because of its former size, although an extension and disabled access have seen the pub grow in recent years. The small central bar and roaring fire haven't changed one bit, nor has the quality of the keenly priced local beers. Friendly staff and locals, from farmhands to landed gentry, all mix with town folk and visitors to give a truly cosmopolitan feel to this popular rural pub. Various local ciders are regularly rotated. No food is available on Wednesday. Camping is in the pub's grounds. ♨Q❀◑♿▲♣●P⁄

Habberley

Mytton Arms

SY5 0TP (S of Pontesbury off A488) SH398035

⏲ 4 (12 Fri-Sun)-11 ☎ (01743) 792490

Hobsons Best Bitter; Three Tuns XXX; guest beers Ⓗ

This quintessential country pub has survived despite recent closures and is now at the heart of the small village. Off the entrance lobby are a separate lounge and open-plan U-shaped bar divided into various nooks and crannies. The venue is home to several pub teams. Outside, there are seats to the front and a paved area with a pagoda. A rare example of a country pub thriving on mainly wet sales, but sandwiches are available at lunchtime. Guest beers come from local and national breweries and tend to be around the 4.0% ABV mark. ♔Q❀⊟♣P⁵⁄

Ludlow

Charlton Arms

Ludford Bridge, SY8 1PJ (S approach 350m from town centre by medieval Ludford Bridge)

⏲ 11-midnight (1am Fri & Sat) ☎ (01584) 872813

🌐 thecharltonarms.co.uk

Hobsons Mild, Twisted Spire, Best Bitter; Ludlow Gold; Wye Valley Butty Bach; guest beers Ⓗ

Now extensively refurbished, this fine building, to the south of the town, looks over the River Teme across the historic Ludford Bridge and up toward Ludlow's last remaining fortified gate and the town centre. It has an attractive bar with a spacious lounge off which is a separate dinning room with a terrace. The impressive function suite and roof bar all give fine views across the river toward the town. Dogs are allowed in the bar.

♔Q❀⇌◐⊟♿⛺P⁵⁄▯

Church Inn

The Buttercross, SY8 1AW

⏲ 11-11 (11.30 Fri & Sat); 12-11 Sun ☎ (01584) 872174

🌐 thechurchinn.com

Hobsons Mild, Town Crier; Ludlow Boiling Well, Gold; Weetwood Eastgate Ale; Wye Valley Bitter; guest beers Ⓗ

Situated in the centre of Ludlow, close to the castle and market square, the Church is the only free house within the town walls and now has a residential ale conner to ensure the quality of the beer. The landlord, a former mayor of Ludlow, is a great advocate of real ale and also owns the Charlton Arms at Ludford Bridge. Guests ales are usually from national micro-breweries. The upstairs bar affords a wonderful view of the South Shropshire Hills and the church. Dogs are welcome.

♔Q☋⇌◐⇌🚌▯

Nelson Inn

Rocks Green, SY8 2DS (on A4117 Kidderminster road from Ludlow bypass)

⏲ 5-11; 1-midnight Fri; 12-11 Sat & Sun ☎ (01584) 872908

🌐 nelsoninn-ludlow.co.uk

Sharp's Doom Bar; guest beers Ⓗ

On the outskirts of Ludlow, the Nelson dates back some 300 years and is a fine example of a traditional beer house. The bar has a pool table, darts, quoits and a juke-box featuring '70s and '80s music. The lounge is decked out with musical instruments and spontaneous music events sometimes occur. The pub holds beer festivals at Easter and late summer. Real cider and, from time to time, perry are sold.The tasty real chips on the menu are highly recommended. Evening meals are occasionally available on Friday to order only. Dogs are welcome.

♔Q❀⇌◐⊟♿⛺🚌(192,292)♣●P⁵⁄▯

Oswestry

Oak Inn

47 Church Street, SY11 2SZ

⏲ 12-11 ☎ (01691) 659254

Draught Bass; Stonehouse Station Bitter, Cambrian Gold; guest beer Ⓗ

An early 18th-century listed building, formerly the coach house of the large hotel next door, close to the town centre opposite the parish church. To the front is a small public bar/games room and behind is a much larger comfortable lounge with two screens for sports events. The lounge is accessed via the public bar or alternatively via a passage that runs down the side of the bar, which also serves as a covered smoking area. There is an outdoor drinking area at the rear of the pub. Q❀⊟♿🚌♣⁵⁄

Quatford

Danery

WV15 6QJ

⏲ 12-3 (4 Sat), 6-midnight; 12-7 Sun ☎ (01746) 762255

Hobsons Town Crier; Wye Valley Butty Bach; guest beers Ⓗ

A family-run freehold food pub, dating back well before 1840, nestling in a hollow just off the A442 in the village of Quatford. A fine selection of mainly LocAles is expertly cared for by Andy. Chef and owner Roz shows off her culinary skills with an ever-changing specials board and a traditional Sunday lunch offering four types of roast. A Wednesday roast and theme nights, such as Bangers & Mash on Monday, are also well attended. The large beer garden is popular in summer. ♔Q❀◐♿⛺🚌P⁵⁄

Sambrook

Three Horseshoes

TF10 8AP (½ mile E of A41)

⏲ 12-2 (not Mon), 5 (4 summer)-11; 11-10.30 (11 summer) Sun ☎ (01952) 551133

Banks's Mild; St Austell Tribute; Salopian Shropshire Gold; guest beers Ⓗ

Five consecutive years in the Guide are well earned for this true country pub that attracts customers from near and far. The only music is traditional and live, performed by local groups. Darts and dominoes are played in the quarry-tiled bar which has a wood burner for winter months. In fine weather there is an attractive beer garden to enjoy. This excellent establishment also provides good home-cooked local food (no food Mon lunch or Sun eve). ♔Q❀◐⊟♿♣●P⁵⁄

Selattyn

Cross Keys ★

Glyn Road, SY10 7DH (on B4579 Oswestry to Glyn Ceiriog road)

⏲ closed Mon & Tue; 7 (6 Fri)-11; 12-5, 7-11 Sun ☎ (01691) 650247

Stonehouse Station Bitter; guest beers Ⓗ

Situated next to the church in a small village close to the Welsh border and Offa's Dyke, this building, dating from the 17th century, has been a pub since

1840. Listed in CAMRA's National Inventory of Historic Pub Interiors, it includes a cosy, small, quarry-tiled bar, two further rooms and a function room. Above the fireplace in the bar is a large topical cartoon redrawn each December. The pub opens at lunchtimes Monday to Saturday only by prior arrangement. Two guest beers are usually available. Accommodation is in a self-catering cottage attached to the pub. ♨Q❀⇌⊟⅄♣P

Shifnal

White Hart ✔

4 High Street, TF11 8BH

⊙ 12-11 ☎ (01952) 461161

Holden's Black Country Mild; Salopian Shropshire Gold; guest beers ⊞

This Grade II-listed half-timbered free house received the first Cask Marque accreditation in Shropshire, and continues to provide superb beers and a warm welcome. Good wholesome pub grub is offered at lunchtime (no food Sun). The pub, with its beamed traditional bars, feels warm and cosy, with the evening trade focusing on good conversation and fine ales. Regular quiz, darts and dominoes matches are held during the winter. Groups and coaches are welcome but please telephone in advance. Q❀◐⊟≷⊟♣P⊱

Shrewsbury

Abbey Hotel ✔

83 Monkmoor Road, SY2 5AZ (15 mins walk from Shrewsbury Railway Station via Castle footbridge)

⊙ 11.30-11 (midnight Fri & Sat); 12-11 Sun

☎ (01743) 236788

Fuller's London Pride; Holden's Black Country Mild; M&B Brew XI; guest beers ⊞

This large imposing pub on a suburban road offers a range of up to nine different cask ales. Gary the landlord runs what must be Ember Inns flagship real ale house – this is the only outlet within the pub group to offer a permanent cask mild. Quiz nights are held twice a week. Children under 14 years of age not permitted. ♨Q❀◐◑♿⊟P⊱

Admiral Benbow

24 Swan Hill, SY1 1NF (just off main square)

⊙ 5 (12 Sat)-11; 7-10.30 Sun ☎ (01743) 244423

Ironbridge Gold; Ludlow Gold; Six Bells Cloud Nine; Shropshire Stout; Wye Valley HPA; guest beer ⊞

This spacious free house specialises in a variety of Shropshire and Herefordshire ales and ciders. A good range of Belgian beers is also available. The house beer, Benbow IPA, is brewed by Six Bells Brewery in Bishop's Castle. Ciders are Gwatkin's Foxwhelp and Yarlington Mill, and the perry is Gwatkin's Golden Valley. Outside seating and a smoking area are available at the rear. Children are not permitted and under 30s are served at the management's discretion. ♨Q❀⊟≷♣●⊱

Bull in the Barne

52-54 The Mount, SY3 8PW

⊙ 4-11; 2-12.30am Fri; 12-midnight Sat & Sun

☎ (01743) 344798

Salopian Shropshire Gold, Oracle, Golden Thread; guest beers ⊞

The brewery tap for the local Salopian Brewery, the pub is set in a Georgian terrace on the outskirts of town. The original Bull in the Barne pub, which was situated not far from here, is said to have conducted 'unusual weddings'. The large single-room interior is divided into bar and lounge areas and is home to darts, dominoes and pool teams. Satellite TV shows major sporting events. The outside terrace affords views over the old West Midlands Showground and the River Severn. Hot pies and sausage rolls are sometimes available. ⛀❀♿⊟♣⊱

Coach & Horses ✔

Swan Hill, SY1 1NF

⊙ 11.30-midnight (12.30am Fri & Sat); 12-11.30 Sun

☎ (01743) 365661 🌐 odleyinns.co.uk

Salopian Shropshire Gold; Wye Valley HPA; guest beers ⊞

Set in a quiet street off the main shopping area, the Coach & Horses provides a quiet haven. In summer it has magnificent floral displays. Victorian in style, the pub has a wood-panelled bar, a small side snug area and a large lounge where meals are served lunchtimes and evenings. Cheddar Valley cider is sold. Live music, electro-acoustic in the main, plays most Sunday evenings in the lounge/restaurant. Q◐◑⊟♿≷⊟●⊱

Loggerheads ★ ✔

1 Church Street, SY1 1UG (off St Mary's Street)

⊙ 11-11; 12-3, 7-11 Sun ☎ (01743) 344226

Banks's Bitter; Brakspear Oxford Gold; Draught Bass; Jennings Snecklifter; guest beers ⊞

This classic 18th-century Grade II-listed town-centre pub features in CAMRA's National Inventory of Historic Pub Interiors. The pub has a small bar, servery and three further rooms. The bar to the left has scrubbed tables, a shove ha'penny board and up until 1975 was reserved for 'gents only'. Folk music plays on Thursday evening. Good-value lunchtime food is available until 2.30pm (no food Sun). Q◐⊟≷⊟♣

Montgomery's Tower ✔

Lower Claremont Bank, SY1 1RT

⊙ 9am-midnight (2am Fri & Sat; 1am Sun)

☎ (01743) 239080

Greene King Ruddles Best Bitter, Abbot; Salopian Shropshire Gold; Wood Shropshire Lad; guest beers ⊞

Located close to the Quarry Park and handy for Theatre Severn, this Lloyds No 1 conversion from a former nightclub offers a choice of two bars. To the left is a large open area rich in natural light. In contrast, the bar to the right with its subdued lighting provides quieter surroundings, except on Friday and Saturday when a DJ plays. Many prints are displayed illustrating local history and famous Salopians. Food is available 8am to 10pm. Marcle cider is usually available. ◐◑♿≷●⊱

Nags Head

Wyle Cop, SY1 1XB (on RH side of Wyle Cop)

⊙ 11.30-midnight (1am Fri & Sat); 12-midnight Sun

☎ (01743) 362455

Caledonian Deuchars IPA; Courage Best Bitter, Directors; Hobsons Best Bitter; Taylor Landlord; Wychwood Hobgoblin; guest beer ⊞

Situated on the historic Wyle Cop, the main features of this timber-framed building are best appreciated externally, in particular the upper storey jettying and to the rear the timber remnants of a 14th-century hall house including a screened passage that provided protection from draughts (and now provides shelter for smokers). The traditional interior has remained unaltered for many years. The pub can be very busy at times, attracting a mixed clientele. It has a reputation for being haunted and features on the Shrewsbury Ghost Trail. ❀⊟⇆⊟♣⊱

Prince of Wales

Bynner Street, Belle Vue, SY3 7NZ
⊙ 5-11.30; 12-midnight Fri-Sun ☎ (01743) 343301
⊕ princeofwaleshotel.co.uk
Greene King IPA; St Austell Tribute; Salopian Golden Thread; Theakston Traditional Mild; guest beers Ⓗ
Welcoming two-roomed community pub with a large decked suntrap garden and heated smoking shelter with bowling green. The green is overlooked by an 18th-century maltings. Darts, dominoes and bowls teams abound. Two beer festivals are held – a winter ales fest in February and another in May. Popular themed nights are hosted. Shrewsbury Town FC memorabilia adorn the building inside and out, with some of the seating from the old Gay Meadow ground skirting the bowling green. Good value food is available Friday-Sunday lunchtimes. ♔♨❀⊂⊟♿⊟♣P⊱⊓

Salopian Bar

Smithfield Road, SY1 1PW (200m from bus station)
⊙ 12-11 (midnight Wed, Fri & Sat) ☎ (01743) 351505
⊕ thesalopianbar.co.uk
Dark Star Hophead; Oakham Bishops Farewell; Stonehouse Station Bitter; guest beers Ⓗ
This pub has a modern, comfortable atmosphere with tasteful, subtle decor. The dedicated management continually strives to increase the beer, cider and perry range to satisfy public demand – real cider and perry come from Westons and Thatchers. An ever-increasing range of Belgian, American and British bottled beer is also available. Major sports events are shown on a large-screen TV. Local artists' paintings on display are for sale. Winner of local CAMRA Pub of the Year and Shropshire CAMRA Pub of the Year 2008 and 2009. ♿⇆⊟♣●⊱

Three Fishes 🍷

Fish Street, SY1 1UR
⊙ 11.30-3, 5-11; 11.30-11.30 Fri & Sat; 12-4, 7-10.30 Sun
☎ (01743) 344793 ⊕ realaleshrewsbury.com
Bath Gem; Taylor Landlord; guest beers Ⓗ
This 15th-century building stands in the shadow of two churches, St Alkmund's and St Julian's, within a maze of streets and passageways in the medieval quarter of the town. The pub offers a range of up to six local and national beers, with some dark ales featuring regularly although not guaranteed. Real cider and perry are also stocked. Freshly prepared food is available at lunchtime and early evening Monday to Saturday, Sunday lunches are served during winter months only. Local CAMRA Pub of the Year 2010. Q⊂◗⇆⊟♣●

Wheatsheaf

50 High Street, SY1 1ST
⊙ 11-midnight; 12-11 Sun ☎ (01743) 272702
Banks's Bitter; Brakspear Oxford Gold; Jennings Sneckllifter, Cumberland Ale; Ringwood Old Thumper; guest beers Ⓗ
Comfortable town-centre street-corner pub with views to St Julian's Church. It has three distinct bar areas for regulars, visitors and shoppers, decorated with many pictures of old Shrewsbury. Food is served at lunchtime made with locally-sourced produce (no food Sun). Beer festivals are held in March and October. Live electro-acoustic music plays on Thursday and Sunday evenings. In fine weather seating is available out on the pavement. A good range of Belgian bottled beers is stocked. ⊂⇆⊟♣⊱

Woodman Inn

Coton Hill, SY1 2DZ (750m from train station on Ellesmere Rd A528)
⊙ 4 (2 Sat)-11; 12-11 Sun ☎ (01743) 351007
Salopian Shropshire Gold; Wye Valley Butty Bach; guest beers Ⓗ
Brick and timber black-and-white corner-pub originally built in the 1800s but destroyed by fire in 1923 and rebuilt in 1925. The pub is reputedly haunted by an ex-landlady who died when the pub burned down. It has a wonderful oak-panelled lounge with two real log fires and traditional settles. The separate bar has the original stone-tiled flooring, wooden seating, log fire and listed leaded windows. The courtyard seating area doubles as a heated smoking area. Real cider is usually available. ♔Q♨❀⊟♿⇆⊟♣●⊱⊓

Telford: Coalport

Shakespeare Inn

High Street, TF8 7HT
⊙ 5-11; 12-midnight Sat & Sun ☎ (01952) 580675
⊕ shakespeare-inn.co.uk
Enville Ale; Everards Tiger; guest beers Ⓗ
Warm, welcoming family-run pub with wonderful views of the Severn Gorge and River, ideally situated for the Coalport China and Tar Tunnel museums. Nearby is a youth hostel and the Silkin Way leading to the Blists Hill Museum. A good selection of guest ales is on offer – mostly LocAles and regular favourites Hobsons Twisted Spire and Three Tuns XXX. The tempting menu of excellent home-cooked dishes is always popular, so book ahead (eve meals served Mon-Sat only). The large beer garden has children's play equipment. Q❀⇄⊂◗♿⊟♣P⊱

Telford: Ironbridge

Golden Ball

Newbridge Road, TF8 7BA (off B4373 Madeley Road Hill)
⊙ 12-11 (10.30 Sun) ☎ (01952) 432179
⊕ goldenballinn.com
Everards Tiger; guest beers Ⓗ
Hidden away off the Telford to Ironbridge road, this historic inn is well worth seeking out. The interior is divided into three areas set around a central bar plus a separate dining space. Good food is served along with an ever-changing selection of guest beers. An added bonus is the range of foreign bottled beers that is stocked. Friendly and welcoming, the pub is handy for local museums around the Ironbridge Gorge. ♔Q❀⇄⊂◗⊟♣P

Robin Hood Inn

33 Waterloo Street, TF8 7HQ
⊙ 10-midnight ☎ (01952) 433100
Holden's Black Country Bitter, Golden Glow; Salopian Golden Thread; Sarah Hughes Dark Ruby; guest beers Ⓗ
This 18th-century pub overlooks the River Severn opposite the Jackfield Bridge. It has two warm and cosy bars with oak beams, wooden floors and open fires. The main bar has two smaller rooms leading off it, decorated with murals depicting local landscapes. Food is served daily with a carvery on

Sunday. Live folk music plays fortnightly and a disco is held once a month. Outside is a small garden and large car park. ⩔Q❀⇌◑♿⊟♣●P⊓

Telford: Ketley

Compasses

72 Beveley Road, TF2 6SD (just off Holyhead Rd at Ketley)

⊙ 12-11 (10.30 Sun) ☎ (01952) 617997 ⊕ jenkos.co.uk

Hobsons Best Bitter; Salopian Hop Twister; guest beer Ⓗ

Located on the original line of Watling Street, now bypassed, this pub is well worth seeking out. Two regular bitters plus one guest are always available. This is a venue of two halves – at the front is a traditional local inn with regular lively trade, at the rear in a spectacular contemporary log cabin is Jenko's Mongolian Barbeque restaurant. Traditional roasts are served on Sunday lunchtime. Cask ale can be ordered to accompany your meal. ❀◗♿⇌(Oakengates)⊟(44)♣P⊬

Telford: Leegomery

Malt Shovel

Hadley Park Road, TF1 6QG (off A442 near Leegomery roundabout)

⊙ 12-2.30, 5-11; 12-11 Fri & Sat; 12-10.30 Sun

☎ (01952) 242963

Banks's Mild; Marston's Burton Bitter, Pedigree; guest beer Ⓗ

Popular two-roomed local on the northern edge of Telford near the Silkin Way and Apley Woods. A long-standing entry in the Guide, the landlord has added the prestigious Telford & Wrekin hygiene award to the pub's portfolio. The lounge features tankards and mugs hanging from the ceiling beams. Guest beers come from the Marston's list. A highly popular charity quiz is held once a month. Check out the sausage and onion sandwiches. Highly recommended. ⩔Q◖⊟⊟(25)♣P

Telford: Madeley

All Nations 🏆

20 Coalport Road, TF7 5DP (off Legges Way opp Blists Hill Museum)

⊙ 12-midnight ☎ (01952) 585747

Shires Coalport Dodger Mild, Dabley Ale, Dabley Gold; guest beer Ⓗ

A local institution more than a pub, the brewing kettle out back is home to the Shires Brewery – sample its beers in this popular historic inn. Close to the Blists Hill Victorian Museum, it opens its friendly doors to all (hence the name). No frills here, just well-priced quality ales, good banter and a real fire. The best-selling snack is a 'black puddding & cheese toasty'. Outside you will find various drinking areas and the toilets. Westons cider or perry is always available. Branch Pub of the Year 2010. ⩔Q❀⇌♣●P⊬

> Wer Kein Bier hat,
> Hat nichts zu trinken.
> **Martin Luther**
>
> When you have no beer,
> You have nothing to drink.
>
> Luther (1483-1546), was an Augustinian friar who rebelled against the excesses of the Papacy and sparked the Protestant reformation. When he was put on trial for heresy at the Diet of Worms in 1521, he was refreshed with supplies of beer from Einbeck in Lower Saxony. Einbeck gave its name to the strong German beer style known as Bock.

Telford: Oakengates

Crown Inn ✔

Market Street, TF2 6EA

⊙ 12-11 (11-11 Sat) ☎ (01952) 610888

⊕ crown.oakengates.net

Hobsons Best Bitter; guest beers Ⓗ

This multi-award-winning pub has 14 handpulls offering ever-changing beers – some 11,000 guest ales have now passed through the pumps – including mild, stout or porter, plus cider and perry. A town pub with a friendly atmosphere, it has three distinct drinking areas and a rear courtyard. An acoustic club is hosted on Wednesday, quality live music on Thursday, and good conversation every day, with a cosmopolitan clientele. Beer festivals with up to 60 ales are held on the first weekends in May and October.
Q❀⊟♿⇌⊟♣●P⊬

Station Hotel

42 Market Street, TF2 6DU

⊙ 10-11; 10.30-3.30, 7-11 Sun ☎ (01952) 612949

Holden's Black Country Mild; Salopian Shropshire Gold; guest beers Ⓗ

Dating from 1861, this multi-roomed pub has a main bar plus two further comfortable seating areas. The bar room has a GWR theme with a painted railway mural across the bar front. Up to eight handpumps dispense an imaginative range of beers alongside the regular ales. Additionally, there is always a hand-pulled cider and continental beers and fruit wines. Food is confined to 'monster baps' and a regular curry night on Wednesday.
⩔Q⊟⇌⊟♣●⊬

Telford: Wellington

Cock Hotel

148 Hollyhead Road, TF1 2DL

⊙ 4 (12 Thu)-11.30; 12-midnight Fri & Sat; 12-4, 7-11 Sun

☎ (01952) 244954 ⊕ cockhotel.co.uk

Hobsons Mild, Best Bitter; guest beers Ⓗ

CAMRA West Midlands and local branch Pub of the Year in 2009, this 18th-century coaching inn continues to add attractions for the serious drinker. The lively main bar, known as the Old Wrekin Tap, is hop festooned with eight handpulls serving constantly-changing beers, always including a mild and a stout or porter. Those seeking peace can drink in the wood-panelled dining room. The front bar has recently been converted into the Belgian-inspired Brasserie de Haan, with 40 quality beers from across Europe on offer. Outside, there is a drinking and smoking area in the stable yard.
⩔Q❀⇌⊟⇌⊟♣●P⊬

Wrekin Inn

26 Wrekin Road, TF1 1RH
⏲ 4-11; 2-midnight Fri; 12-midnight Sat; 12-10.30 Sun
☎ (01952) 244865
Oakham White Dwarf; Titanic Steerage; guest beers Ⓗ
Now firmly established on the real ale scene, this pub has something for everyone. There are several distinct areas within an open-plan layout, plus a decked outdoor seating area. Six ales are on handpull alongside a cider dispensed by gravity. Beer and cider festivals are held four times a year. Simple snacks are usually available. Sunday afternoon entertainment is popular and there is an 'open mike' night on Tuesday. Regular quiz nights also feature. ❀♿⇌🚌♣●P⅟

Upper Hengoed

Last Inn

SY10 7EU (off B4579 at Weston Rhyn sign)
⏲ 5-midnight (1am Fri & Sat); 12-11.30 Sun
☎ (01691) 659747 🌐 thelastinn.net
Banks's Mild; Oakham Bishops Farewell; guest beers Ⓗ
Large pub at a rural crossroads with an inn sign exhibiting a lengthy Latin tag. This former cobbler's workshop has a games room beyond the public bar as well as a dining room. The extensive function room at the rear has been recently refurbished and hosts folk music and other entertainment. There are always six cask ales on offer from regional and micro-breweries. A separate restaurant offers evening meals Tuesday to Saturday and Sunday lunchtimes. Q❀◐◑🚌♣P⅟

Whitchurch

Old Town Hall Vaults

SY13 1QU (behind Barclays Bank off High Street)
⏲ 10-2.30, 6-11; 12-2.30, 7-11 Sun ☎ (01948) 662251
Brains The Rev James; Hancock's HB; M&B Mild; guest beers Ⓗ
Locally known as 'The Backstreets', Whitchurch's only established real ale pub has seven handpulls on the bar, four serving rotating local and national guest ales. An open log fire helps to create a cosy atmosphere in the winter. Locally-sourced home-cooked food is served. The pub has successful quiz and dominoes teams competing in local leagues. There is a rear courtyard at the back. The pub was the birthplace of composer Sir Edward German.
♨Q❀◐◑♿⇌♣●⅟

Whitchurch Cricket Club

SY13 3JG (via Greenfoot Lane off Tilstock Road)
⏲ 6-11 Wed-Fri summer; 7-11 Thu-Sat winter; 10-11.30 Sat; 7-11.30 Sun ☎ (01948) 663923
🌐 whitchurchcc.play-cricket.com
Thwaites Nutty Black; Woodlands Midnight Stout; guest beers Ⓗ
This CAMRA local Club of the Year 2009 and 2010 is home to four senior cricket teams, two junior teams and two quiz teams. The bar has nine handpulls, one serving real cider, and holds two beer festivals each year. The venue is sometimes closed for private parties so please check the website or telephone before travelling. A CAMRA membership card or copy of this Guide will admit you to this family-friendly club.
❀♿▲⇌🚌(511)♣●P⅟🗑

Wheatsheaf, Shrewsbury (Photo: Dave Kirkby)

SOMERSET

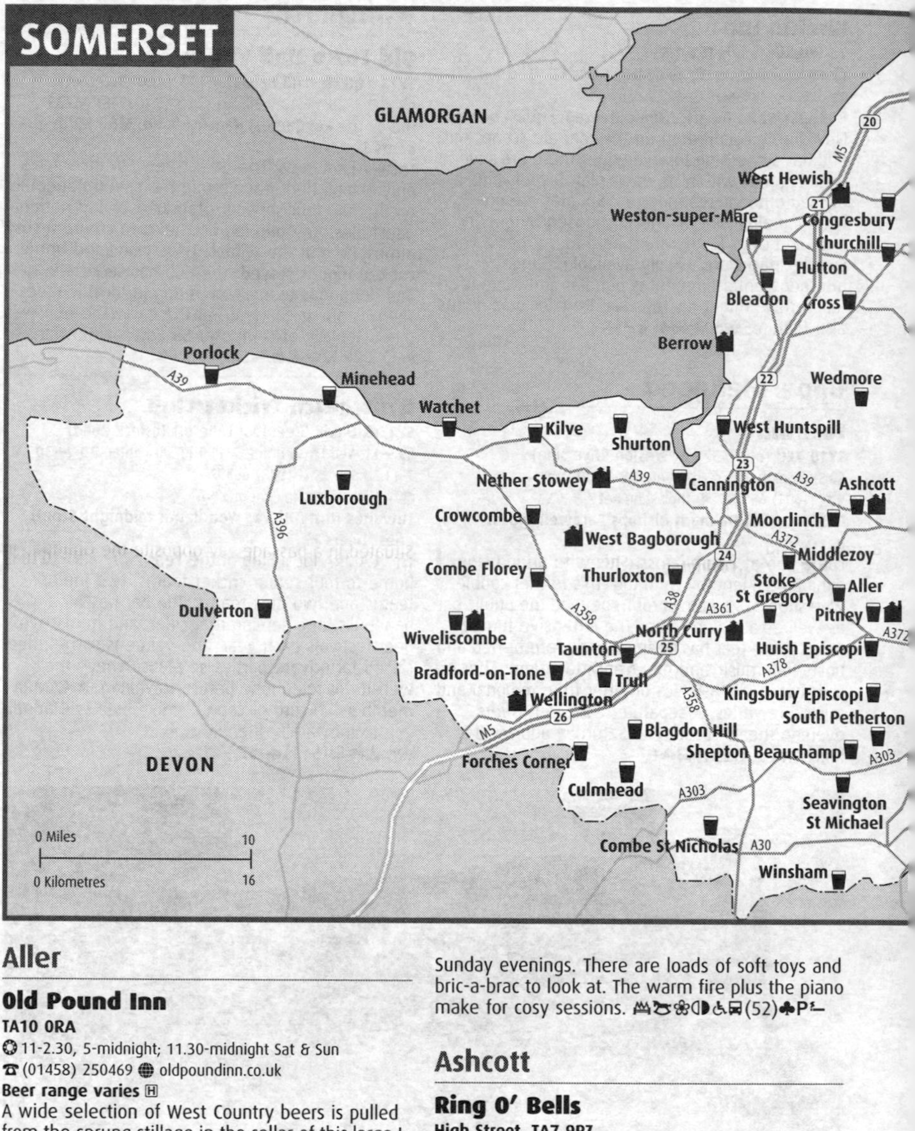

Aller

Old Pound Inn

TA10 0RA

⌚ 11-2.30, 5-midnight; 11.30-midnight Sat & Sun

☎ (01458) 250469 🌐 oldpoundinn.co.uk

Beer range varies Ⓗ

A wide selection of West Country beers is pulled from the sprung stillage in the cellar of this large L-shaped 16th-century inn. It has eight letting rooms, a skittle alley and a restaurant spur from the main bar, lounge/family area and kitchen. Those visiting the restaurant to sample the excellent food will be able to enjoy the amazing murals of domestic and wild animals. Dogs are always welcome in the bar area. ♨❀⊭◑♿🚌(16)♣P⁻

Ash

Bell Inn

3 Main Street, TA12 6NS

⌚ 12-midnight ☎ (01935) 822727 🌐 thebellinnash.co.uk

Fuller's London Pride; Wickwar BOB; guest beers Ⓗ

This fine local village inn is what a pub should be – good beers from local breweries dispensed from four handpumps by well-trained staff. Quality food is usually on offer at reasonable prices and the Sunday lunchtime carvery is exceptional. Live music is well supported, as is a quiz night most Sunday evenings. There are loads of soft toys and bric-a-brac to look at. The warm fire plus the piano make for cosy sessions. ♨❀◑♿🚌(52)♣P⁻

Ashcott

Ring O' Bells

High Street, TA7 9PZ

⌚ 12-2.30, 7-11 (10.30 Sun) ☎ (01458) 210232

🌐 ringobells.com

Beer range varies Ⓗ

Delightful family-run pub where you are sure of a warm welcome. The skittle alley doubles as a large function room with modern facilities. There is disabled access through the function room but the upper bar areas have steps between. Old fireplaces and beams exude tradition but are tempered by soft carpeting. The pub is near the church and signposted off the A39. There is always a great selection of ales, mostly from the West Country, and Wilkins cider. Q❀◑♿🚌(29,375)♣●P⁻

Babcary

Red Lion

TA11 7ED (off A37 N of Podimore jct with A303)

⌚ 12-3, 6-midnight; 12-midnight Sun ☎ (01458) 223230

🌐 redlionbabcary.co.uk

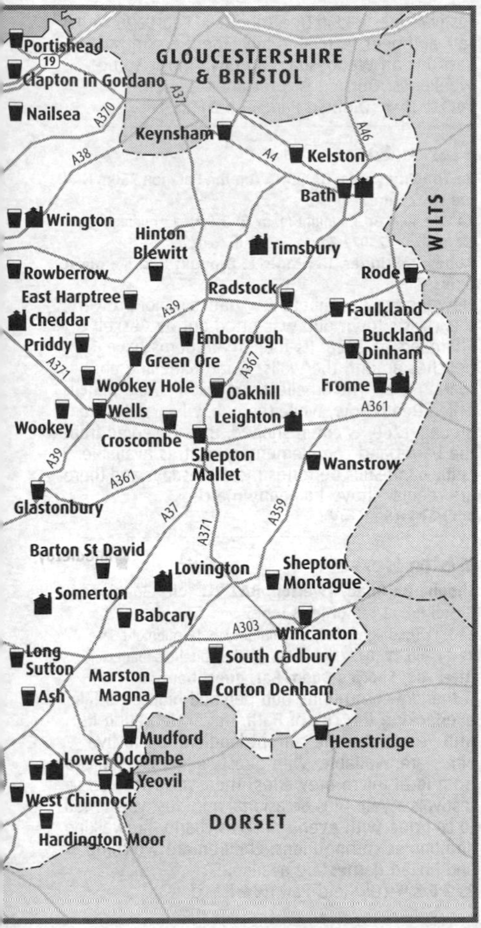

Otter Bright; Teignworthy Reel Ale; guest beers Ⓗ
Thatched pub in the heart of the village. A large restaurant offers everything from fine dining to classic pub food, using local produce wherever possible. Bread is baked daily on the premises. Bar snacks are also available. The pub is at the heart of the local community and supports its own cricket team. Table skittles is very popular in the bar. There is an attractive garden in which to sit in the sun and enjoy the surroundings. ♨❀◐◑⊟♿●P

Barton St David

Barton Inn

Main Street, TA11 6BZ ST540321
⏲ 12-2.30, 4.30-11 (midnight Sat & Sun) ☎ (01458) 850451
Beer range varies Ⓖ
Park the muddy dog next to the fire to dry before sampling some of the local ales racked behind the counter, or real cider if you prefer. This is a proper country pub full of both character and characters, where eccentricity appears to be the norm.
The single bar manages to retain the appearance of the original two rooms and maintain a cosy feeling. While this pub is somewhat off the beaten track, those making the effort to find it will be rewarded. ♨❀◐◑♿🚌(667)♣●P⚲

Bath

Bell

103 Walcot Street, BA1 5BW
⏲ 11.30-11; 12-10.30 Sun ☎ (01225) 460426
🌐 walcotstreet.com
Abbey Bellringer; Bath Ales Gem; Hop Back Summer Lightning; Otter Bitter; RCH Pitchfork; Stonehenge Danish Dynamite; guest beers Ⓗ
The Bell features bands performing on Monday and Wednesday evenings and Sunday lunchtimes. There is a long main bar and a number of seating areas. The wall space inside is taken up with posters for gigs and other events in the Walcot area. A computer is available for free internet access with Wi-Fi facilities. At the back of the pub is a garden with plenty of covered seating, behind which is the love lounge and launderettette (sic). ❀⇌(Spa)🚌♣⚲

Coeur de Lion

17 Northumberland Passage, BA1 5AR
⏲ 11-11 (1am Fri & Sat); 12-10.30 Sun ☎ (01225) 463568
🌐 coeur-de-lion.co.uk
Abbey Ales Bellringer; guest beers Ⓗ
Situated in a passageway opposite the Guildhall in the centre of Bath, this pub claims to be the smallest in the city. Containing just four tables in a single small bar, this may well be true. However, seating capacity is increased in summer by tables outside. Food is served 12-6pm every day in the newly added dining room upstairs. The stained glass window at the front of the pub is a good example of its kind. ◐⇌(Spa)🚌

Garrick's Head

8 St John's Place, Saw Close, BA1 1ET (next to Theatre Royal)
⏲ 12-11.30 (midnight Sat; 10.30 Sun) ☎ (01225) 318368
🌐 garricksheadpub.com
Beer range varies Ⓗ
Bath's theatre pub for over 200 years, the Garrick's Head is reputedly the most haunted pub in the city. Up to six beers, mostly from local micro-breweries, include some rarities. At least two Somerset ciders are often complemented by a local perry. Traditional food sourced from local ingredients is served lunchtimes and evenings. Tables in the pedestrianised area outside are an ideal place to watch the world go by. ❀◐◑⇌(Spa)🚌●⚲

King William

36 Thomas Street, London Road, BA1 5NN (on A4 London Road around ½ mile NE of city centre)
⏲ 12-3 (not Mon), 5-11 (midnight Fri); 12-midnight Sat; 12-11 Sun ☎ (01225) 428096 🌐 kingwilliampub.com
Beer range varies Ⓗ
This tiny, two-bar Victorian pub has kept the look and feel of a bustling street-corner local, while garnering awards for the quality of its home-cooked, locally sourced food. The varying range of local beers generally includes one from Palmers and three from local micro-breweries. Local cider is also available. A monthly book club meets in the restaurant upstairs and the quiz on the first Monday of each month is gaining in popularity. ◐◑🚌●

New Inn

23-24 Monmouth Place, Upper Bristol Road, BA1 2AY
⏲ 12-2.20, 5-11; 12-11 Sat; 12-3, 7-11 Sun
☎ (01225) 332643
Wadworth Henry's Original IPA, Horizon, 6X, seasonal beer; guest beer Ⓗ

This traditional local, which opened as a beer house in 1837, has separate snug and public bars, real fires, home-cooked food and one of the longest serving landlords in the city. Only 150 metres south-west of Queen's Square, yet very much a locals' pub, this hidden gem is well worth seeking out. Look for the traditional Ring the Bull game in the main bar – not as easy as it looks.
♨◑◗⊟⇌(Spa)⊟♣●

Old Green Tree ★

12 Green Street, BA1 2JZ
✪ 11-11; 12-10.30 Sun ☎ (01225) 448259
Blindmans Green Tree Bitter; RCH Pitchfork; guest beers Ⓗ
Classic, unspoilt pub in a 300-year-old building. An atmosphere of quiet cosiness pervades the three oak-panelled rooms. The panelling dates from the 1920s. The lounge bar at the front is decorated with pictures of World War II aircraft. The pub can get very crowded, but space can sometimes be found in the comfortable back bar. The beer range, which always includes a porter, usually Wickwar Station Porter, is complemented by an occasional cider or perry and a choice of malt whiskies. Q◑⇌(Spa)⊟

Pulteney Arms ✔

37 Daniel Street, BA2 6ND
✪ 12-3 (not Mon & Tue), 5-11; 12-midnight Fri & Sat; 12-10.30 Sun ☎ (01225) 463923 🌐 thepulteneyarms.co.uk
Fuller's London Pride; Taylor Landlord; Young's Bitter; guest beers Ⓗ
The building dates from 1759 and is known to have been a pub as early as 1792. Gas light fittings are a feature of the interior, with five lights above the bar. The decor shows an emphasis on sport, particularly rugby. The pub sponsors a number of sports teams, including a hockey team and Bath Ladies Rugby. The food menu is extensive and deservedly popular. The cat symbol on the pub sign refers to the Pulteney coat of arms.
Q♉❀◑◗⊟⇌(Spa)⊟♣

Raven

6-7 Queen Street, BA1 1HE
✪ 11.30-11 (midnight Fri & Sat); 12-10.30 Sun
☎ (01225) 425045 🌐 theravenofbath.co.uk
Blindmans Raven, Raven Gold, Start Raven; guest beers Ⓗ
Local CAMRA Pub of the Year 2006, this busy city-centre free house occupies an 18th-century building. Six real ales are available, three brewed exclusively for the Raven by Blindmans, and three varying guests, featuring many rarities. The same beer range is available on both the ground floor and in the quieter first-floor bar. Mini beer festivals are held throughout the year. Famous for its selection of sausages and Pieminister pies, the Raven is one of the few pubs in Bath to serve food Sunday evenings. ◑◗⇌(Spa)●

Royal Oak (Twerton)

Lower Bristol Road, Twerton, BA2 3BW (1 mile W of city centre on A36, 200m from Oldfield Park station)
✪ 12-11 (midnight Fri & Sat; 10.30 Sun) ☎ (01225) 481409
🌐 theroyaloak-bath.co.uk
Beer range varies Ⓗ
Local CAMRA Pub of the Year 2007, 2008 and 2009, with a range of up to 10 beers from micro-breweries near and far, including ale from the pub's own brewery – Art Brew. Local ciders and bottled Belgian beers are also available. Beer festivals are held in December and February, with a folk and beer festival in July. There are music sessions on Wednesdays and live music some weekends. Outside is a secluded garden.
♨Q❀◑◗⇌(Oldfield Park)⊟♣●P

Star ★ ✔

23 The Vineyards, BA1 5NA (on the Paragon 750m N of the city centre)
✪ 12-2.30, 5.30-midnight (1am Fri & Sat); 12-midnight Sun
☎ (01225) 425072 🌐 star-inn-bath.co.uk
Abbey Bellringer, Heritage Ⓗ**; Draught Bass** Ⓖ**; guest beers** Ⓗ
Now the tap for Abbey Ales, Bath's major brewery, this classic town pub was fitted out by Gaskell & Chambers in 1928. Its four small rooms have benches around the walls, wood panelling and roaring fires. The smallest has just a single bench, called Death Row, while the pub, which dates from around 1760, is coffin-shaped. Bass is served from the barrel and complementary snuff is available. Celtic band Sulis performs most Tuesdays and there are regular shove-ha'penny matches.
♨Q⊟⇌(Spa)⊟♣

White Horse

Shophouse Road, Twerton, BA2 1EF (off A36 Lower Bristol Rd, at top of Jews Lane)
✪ 3-11 (midnight Thu); 2-midnight Fri; 12-midnight Sat; 12-11 Sun ☎ (01225) 340668 🌐 thewhitehorsebath.com
Otter Ale; Sharp's Doom Bar; guest beers Ⓗ
A friendly community pub perched high on a hill overlooking the city of Bath, now celebrating its fifth year under the current landlord. Up to five beers are available, with guests generally sourced from local micro-breweries. There are two beer festivals a year plus occasional mini-festivals timed to coincide with events such as charity firewalking and boules competitions. Children are welcome and boxed games are available.
♉❀◗♿⇌(Oldfield Park)⊟♣P⊱⊓

Blagdon Hill

Lamb & Flag

TA3 7SL (4 miles S of Taunton)
✪ 11-11 (midnight Fri); 12-10.30 (4 winter) Sun
☎ (01823) 421736 🌐 lambandflag.co.uk
Otter Bitter; guest beers Ⓗ

INDEPENDENT BREWERIES

Abbey Ales Bath
Berrow Berrow
Blindmans Leighton
Butcombe Wrington
Cheddar Ales Cheddar
Cotleigh Wiveliscombe
Cottage Lovington
Dawkins Timsbury
Exmoor Wiveliscombe
Glastonbury Somerton
Isle of Avalon Ashcott (NEW)
Milk Street Frome
Moor Pitney
North Curry North Curry
Odcombe Lower Odcombe
Quantock Wellington
RCH West Hewish
Stowey Nether Stowey
Taunton West Bagbrough
Yeovil Yeovil

Privately owned free house with frequently changing real ales. Located on the northern slopes of the Blackdown Hills, this 16th-century pub is popular with locals and visitors. The main bar has the original flagstone floor and candlelit dining area. Good food is locally sourced and home-made. A skittle alley and function room are situated beyond the bar. The large garden has panoramic views from the Brendon to the Mendip hills. ⛫♉❀◑♣P⁄–

Bleadon

Queens Arms ✔

Celtic Way, BS24 0NF (off A370)
✪ 11.30-11; 12-10.30 Sun ☎ (01934) 812080
Butcombe Bitter, Gold, seasonal beers; guest beer Ⓗ
Seventeenth-century stone-built pub, situated in the centre of the village. Three rooms converge on the bar; the largest is the main dining area. Food sales are strong, but not at the expense of ale drinkers – the pub is owned by the local Butcombe Brewery. Thatchers cider is also sold. Two real fires and exposed beams add to the atmosphere. There is also a garden/patio with a sales hatch and families are welcome. Morris men perform on May Day Monday. ⛫Q❀◑🚌(83)●P⁄–

Bradford-on-Tone

White Horse Inn

Regent Street, TA4 1HF (off A38 between Taunton and Wellington)
✪ 12-11 ☎ (01823) 461239
Exmoor Ale; Sharp's Doom Bar; guest beers Ⓗ
Very much a community pub at the centre of the village, with a shop run by villagers in the outbuildings. Guest beers are sourced from south-west breweries. Excellent home-cooked food is served (booking advised) and speciality evenings are planned. Real fires warm both bars in winter, while the beautiful large garden hosts barbecues in summer. The skittle alley doubles as a function room. Customers are welcome to try out the piano. Buses stop a 15-minute walk away. ⛫❀◑♿🚌(22,92)P⁄–

Buckland Dinham

Bell

High Street, BA11 2QT (on A362 Frome-Radstock road, around 3 miles from Frome centre) ST752512
✪ 12-3 (not Mon & Tue), 6-midnight; 12-2.30, 7-11.30 Sun
☎ (01373) 462956 🌐 bellatbuckland.co.uk
Butcombe Bitter; Wychwood Hobgoblin; guest beers Ⓗ
This warm and cosy local pub is involved in community activities. It holds film nights, has produced a village recipe book and uses local beers in its dishes. It also offers a facility to order and pay for beer online. A three-day summer beer festival is run with live music in August, and a cider festival in October. The pub is convenient for on-site campers. Boules is played. ⛫♉❀◑⊟♿⛺🚌♣●P⁄–

Cannington

Rose & Crown

30 High Street, TA5 2HF (off A39)
✪ 12-11 (10.30 Sun) ☎ (01278) 653190
Brains The Rev James; Greene King IPA, Abbot; guest beers Ⓗ
An atmospheric, friendly 17th-century pub with a loyal local following. Original beams are covered with interesting objects donated by locals and there is a collection of clocks. The single bar has a pool table, table skittles and a collection of games hand-made by locals. The Outside Inn is a covered, comfortable smoking area in a large award-winning garden. ⛫❀🚌(14)♣P⁄–

Churchill

Crown Inn

The Batch, Skinners Lane, BS25 5PP (off A38, ¼ mile S of A368 jct)
✪ 11.30-11 (midnight Fri & Sat); 12-10.30 Sun
☎ (01934) 852995
Bath Ales Gem; Butcombe Bitter; Cotleigh Batch; Palmers IPA; RCH Hewish, PG Steam; guest beers Ⓖ
This long-time Guide regular and winner of many CAMRA awards has been in the same hands for 24 years. It is tucked away down a small lane yet close to the village centre. Several small rooms with stone-flagged floors are warmed by two log fires and offer an assortment of seating. Excellent food is provided lunchtimes only using local ingredients. Up to nine beers are served from the cask, usually from local breweries. There is outside drinking to the front and rear. ⛫Q❀◐⛺🚌(121)P⁄–

Clapton in Gordano

Black Horse

Clevedon Lane, BS20 7RH (2 miles from M5 jct 19) ST473739
✪ 11-11; 12-10.30 Sun ☎ (01275) 842105 🌐 thekicker.co.uk
Bath Ales Gem Ⓗ**; Butcombe Bitter** Ⓖ**; Courage Best Bitter; Wadworth 6X** Ⓗ**; guest beer** Ⓖ
Excellent 14th-century pub hidden away down a small lane. The snug was once the village lock-up. A large fireplace with a display of old rifles dominates the main bar. Beers are served from a small serving hatch. The games room doubles as a family room, and there is a children's play area in the pleasant garden. The Gordano Valley cycle route is nearby. Dogs are welcome. Thatchers Dry and Moles Black Rat cider are sold. Bar meals are served 12-2pm Monday to Saturday. ⛫Q♉❀◐⛺♣●P⁄–

Combe Florey

Farmers Arms

TA4 3HZ (on A358 between Bishops Lydeard and Williton)
✪ 12-11 (10.30 Sun) ☎ (01823) 432267
🌐 farmersarmsatcombeflorey.co.uk
Cotleigh Tawny Owl; Exmoor Ale, Gold; St Austell HSD; guest beers Ⓗ
This family-owned and run 16th-century thatched inn is set in picturesque countryside close to the West Somerset Railway. Comprising a bar area with inglenook fireplace and a restaurant, it is justly famous for the quality of its local ales, which are popular with regulars and tourists alike. It has a lovely beer garden in which to soak up the summer sun. The pub has featured in the Sunday Times list of Top 10 Pubs. ⛫Q❀◑🚌(28)P⁄–

Combe St Nicholas

Green Dragon

TA20 3NG

✪ 12-2.30 (not Mon), 6-midnight; 12-midnight Sat; 12-4, 7-11 Sun ☎ (01460) 63311

Otter Bitter; guest beer Ⓗ

A large green dragon carved by the landlord greets visitors to this friendly free house, which has origins in the 17th century. Wood carvings adorn both bars. The guest beer usually comes from a West Country brewery. A varied menu of good value, home-cooked food is served Tuesday to Sunday. Local ingredients are used where possible and there is a popular Pie and a Pint night on Wednesday. Live music plays once a fortnight on Friday. Q◐⊟▲🚌(99)♣P⁵—

Congresbury

Old Inn

18 St Pauls Causeway, BS49 5DH

✪ 11.30-11.30 (12.30am Fri & Sat); 12-11.30 Sun ☎ (01934) 832270

Wells Bombardier; Young's Bitter, Special; guest beer Ⓗ

Popular 16th-century village local, owned by Young's and tucked away in the heart of the village. It has a wonderful inglenook fireplace that burns chunky logs during the winter. There are low ceilings throughout and a main bar area plus two smaller rooms, one with a TV for sport and the other for families. The main bar has leather straps hanging from the ceiling to steady yourself after one too many! No food is served. Dogs and children are welcome. The cider is Thatchers. ♨Q☎❀🚌(X1,353)●⁵—

Plough

High Street, BS49 5JA (off A370 at B3133 jct)

✪ 11.30-2.30, 4.30-11; 11.30-midnight Fri; 12-3, 7-11 Sun ☎ (01934) 877402 🌐 the-plough-inn.net

Butcombe Bitter; St Austell Tribute; guest beers Ⓗ

Characterful village pub with flagstone floors and many original features, decorated with interesting local artefacts. Three or four guest beers are served from a row of old barrel heads behind the bar powered by a flo-jet system, sourced mainly from local breweries. Thatchers cider is also stocked. Food is served daily 12-2pm and 7-9pm except Sunday evening which is quiz night. The pub has real fires, no TV, and children and dogs are welcome. Mendip Morris Men meet here. ♨Q❀◑🚌(X1,353)♣●P⁵—

Corton Denham

Queen's Arms

DT9 4LR (3 miles from A303)

✪ 11-3, 6-11; 11-11 Sat; 12-10.30 Sun ☎ (01963) 220317 🌐 thequeensarms.com

Moor Queen's Revival; guest beers Ⓗ

Very popular village pub about three miles from the A303. Nestling beneath the beautiful hills of south Somerset, the pub has a wood and flagstone floor and a fire at both ends of the large bar. Fine food and locally made pork pies are available. There is also a separate dining room. Dogs and muddy boots are welcome and passing walkers call in most days, summer and winter. The pub supports LocAle and serves Burrowhill and Thatchers cider. ♨Q❀⇌◑●P

Croscombe

George Inn

Long Street, BA5 3QH (on A371 between Wells and Shepton Mallet) ST589443

✪ 12-3.30, 6-11 ☎ (01749) 342306 🌐 thegeorgeinn.co.uk

Blindmans King George the Thirst; Butcombe Bitter; Cheddar Gorgeous George; guest beers Ⓗ

This 17th-century inn, refurbished by the landlord, serves at least two guest ales and hosts two beer festivals a year, at Whitsun and late October. There is a large main bar, a snug with a fireplace, a family room and a separate dining room. The food is home-cooked using locally-sourced ingredients. At the rear is a skittle alley and a garden with a covered terrace. The guests are from West Country independents. (Gorgeous George is a 3.8% ABV late-hopped semi-regular guest.) ♨Q❀⇌◑♿🚌♣●P⁵—

Cross

New Inn ✔

Old Coach Road, BS26 2EE (on A38/A361 jct)

✪ 12-11 ☎ (01934) 732455

Otter Ale; guest beers Ⓗ

Roadside inn on the A38, close to the historic medieval town of Axbridge. Popular for its extensive food menu and twice-yearly beer festivals, it usually has three guest beers which can often be adventurous and unusual for the area. There is a separate dining area and a pool room on the first floor. A large hillside garden with children's play facilities offers a fine view of the Mendip Hills and Somerset Levels. Families are welcome – dogs too. There is a small car park opposite. ❀◑🚌(126)♣P

Crowcombe

Carew Arms

TA4 4AD (off A358)

✪ 11-11.30 (1am Sat); 12-4, 7-11.30 Sun ☎ (01984) 618631 🌐 thecarewarms.co.uk

Exmoor Ale; Otter Bright; Yeovil Ruby; guest beers Ⓗ

Village inn situated in a picture-postcard village at the bottom of the Quantock Hills, the ancient flagstoned public bar includes benches and an inglenook, and is popular with locals and their dogs. A larger lounge/restaurant overlooks a spacious patio garden and the Brendon Hills. Real cider is served and a music and beer festival is held in August. Food is sourced locally where possible, and the ales are mostly from the West Country. ♨Q☎❀⇌◑⊟♿🚌(18,28)●P

Culmhead

Holman Clavel

TA3 7EA (¼ mile off B3170)

✪ 12-11; 12-3, 7-11 (summer only) Sun ☎ (01823) 421432

Butcombe Bitter, Gold; guest beers Ⓗ

The only pub in England with this name – a clavel is a beam across the fireplace made from holm oak. Fresh fish and game when in season feature on the food menu, which has choices to suit all tastes and budgets. Guest beers come from both micro-breweries and regional brewers. The pub is allegedly haunted by the ghost of a defrocked monk – but a warm welcome is assured. Tricky Cider is served. ♨Q❀◑▲♣●P⁵—

Dulverton

Bridge Inn ✔

20 Bridge Street, TA22 9HJ
⏲ 12-3, 6-11 (not Mon winter), 12-11 Fri-Sun
☎ (01398) 324130 🌐 thebridgeinndulverton.com
Exmoor Ale; Otter Ale; guest beers Ⓗ
Situated close to the River Barle, this warm, welcoming pub dating from 1845 has a cosy single-room bar featuring a wood-burning stove and Exmoor memorabilia. Good food is available lunchtimes and evenings. The pub hosts a beer festival in July at the time of the local fete. Situated at the southern gateway to Exmoor, good walking and country pursuits are nearby. The Bridge holds a Green Tourism Award in recognition of the environmentally-friendly way it is run.
♨❀◑🚌(25B,398)♣P⁵⁄

East Harptree

Castle of Comfort

BS40 6DD (on B3134 just N of jct with B3135)
⏲ 12-3, 6-11; 12-11 Sun ☎ (01761) 221321
🌐 castleofcomfort.com
Butcombe Bitter; Sharp's Doom Bar; guest beers Ⓗ
Splendid sprawling inn on the Mendip Hills, within reach of both Cheddar Gorge and Wookey Hole caves. The name is said to derive from the time when the pub housed condemned criminals on their last night. A hostelry since 1684, it is popular for its locally sourced and generously portioned food. Two guest beers feature regularly from the south-west and sometimes further afield. The child-friendly garden is busy in summer. Dogs are allowed in the lower bar. Moles Black Rat is the cider. ♨Q❀◑♣●P⁵⁄

Emborough

Old Down Inn

BA3 4SA ST628513
⏲ 12-2, 6.30-11.30 ☎ (01761) 232398
Butcombe Bitter; Draught Bass; guest beers Ⓖ
A free house first licensed in 1640, this establishment was once an important coaching inn. The spirit of the past lives on in the wood-panelled main bar, where beer is served straight from the cask. Guests from local breweries are generally available. Bar snacks are excellent value, likewise the main meals. The building has recently been refurbished throughout. This friendly and popular hostelry is a classic example of a traditional Somerset inn. Q❀🛏◑⊟▲🚌●P⁵⁄

Faulkland

Tucker's Grave ★

BA3 5XF (on A366 1 mile E of village) ST751551
⏲ 11.30-3, 6-11; 12-3, 7-10.30 Sun ☎ (01373) 834230
Butcombe Bitter; Draught Bass Ⓖ
This pub was built in the mid-17th century and has changed very little since then. It was named after Tucker, who hanged himself and was buried at the crossroads outside. Beers and Thatchers cider are served from an alcove rather than a bar. Shove-ha'penny is played and there is a skittle alley. Camping is available in the grounds. A warm welcome is guaranteed in this traditional pub, which featured in a song by the 1970s punk band The Stranglers. ♨Q❀▲♣●P⁵⁄

Forches Corner

Merry Harriers

EX15 3TR (3 miles SE of Wellington) ST182171
⏲ closed Mon; 12-3, 6.30-11; 12-3 Sun ☎ (01823) 421270
🌐 merryharriers.co.uk
Beer range varies Ⓗ
Friendly, family-owned free house on an attractive ridge of the Blackdown Hills bordering Somerset and Devon. The bar effectively separates the dining area from the lounge. Three changing beers are offered from local micro-breweries, with Cotleigh and Otter featuring regularly as well as Bollhayes and Thatchers ciders. Despite a somewhat remote location, the pub has a thriving local trade attracted by its reputation for excellent quality food. The large, pleasant garden is ideal for families in summer. ♨Q⛺❀◑♿♣●P⁵⁄

Frome

Griffin Inn 🏆

Milk Street, BA11 3DB
⏲ 5-11; 4-1am Fri & Sat; 1-7 Sun ☎ (01373) 467766
🌐 milkstreetbrewery.co.uk
Milk Street Nick's, Zig Zag, Beer Ⓗ
Situated in the older part of Frome, known as Trinity or Chinatown, it is owned by Milk Street Brewery, with the small brewhouse at the back. It produces a wide range of ales, served alongside guests and seasonal beers. The single bar retains original features including open fires, etched windows and wooden floors. Live music plays regularly. A small garden opens all year. Barbecue and Thai food nights are held. A stained glass griffin is behind the bar. The cider is Thatchers. Local CAMRA Pub of the Year 2010.
♨❀⇌🚌♣●P⁵⁄

Lamb

1 Christchuch Street East, BA11 1QA
⏲ 12-3, 5-11; 12-midnight Fri & Sat; 12-10.30 Sun
☎ (01373) 472042 🌐 thelambinnfrome.co.uk
Blindmans Buff, Lamb Gold, Lamb Ale, Mine Beer, Icarus; guest beers Ⓗ
Reopened by Blindmans Brewery after a long closure, this pub, once the brewery tap for the now defunct Lamb Brewery, has been refurbished to a very high standard, including the hotel accommodation and restaurant. The pub, which is very near the town centre, is light and spacious throughout, with a slate floor and local artwork on the walls. Guest beers come from local breweries, cider from Thatchers. 🛏◑♿⇌🚌●P⁵⁄

Glastonbury

Riflemans Arms ✔

4 Chilkwell Street, BA6 8DB
⏲ 12-11 (midnight Fri & Sat); 12-10.30 Sun
☎ (01458) 831023
Butcombe Bitter; Skinner's Cornish Knocker; guest beers Ⓗ
With a well-worn 16th-century facade and great views from the rear entrance, this tavern spans centuries and generations. The wide, low front doorway leads to a traditional bar where a more mature clientele gathers; pass through a portholed archway to the modern building where younger drinkers congregate. Real log fires warm both bars. There is also a pool room and function room for occasional live music. Wilkins Cider is served.
♨Q❀◑🚌●P⁵⁄

Green Ore

Ploughboy Inn

BA5 3ET (on A39/B3135 crossroads)
⊙ closed Mon; 11-2.30, 6.30-11; 12-2.30, 7-11 Sat; 12-3, 7-10.30 Sun ☎ (01761) 241375 ⊕ ploughboyinn.com
Butcombe Bitter; Otter Ale; guest beers Ⓗ
In the same safe hands for well over 20 years, this substantial stone free house to the north of Wells occupies a corner plot by the traffic lights in the hamlet of Green Ore. The 376 Wells to Bristol bus runs nearby and there is a large car park and pleasant beer garden to the rear. A single good-sized L-shaped bar provides reasonably priced, excellent food and the local butcher's huge, meaty sausages are recommended. Up to two guest beers are kept. ♨Q❀◑🚌(376)P

Hardington Moor

Royal Oak

Moor Lane, BA22 9NW (turn left off A30 at Yeovil Court Hotel)
⊙ 11.30-3.30 (not Mon), 6.30-11; 11.30-5, 6.30-10.30 Sun
☎ (01935) 862354
Beer range varies Ⓗ
'Sonny's', as it is locally known after a previous landlord, is a superb community pub in the centre of Hardington. The small dining room has scrubbed wooden tables to support a fine menu, which accompanies the cider from a local farm and the West Country beers. Dogs are welcome but are expected to make way for the occasional christening or wake. The pool table is in a room apart and skittles is very popular. Beer festivals are held in May and October. ♨❀◑♿♣●P⊬

Henstridge

Bird in Hand

2 Ash Walk, BA8 0RA (100m S of A30/A357 jct)
⊙ 11-2.30, 5.30-11; 11-11 Sat; 12-3, 7.30-10.30 Sun
☎ (01963) 362255
Beer range varies Ⓗ
This cosy village pub, with thick stone walls and low ceilings, is a real find. The bar is attractively set in a beamed room with a fire at both ends. Although main meals are not available, the bar snacks are superb and real value for money. To the rear is a skittle alley/games room. Three real ales are usually available as well as Taunton Cider. Well worth a short diversion off the nearby A30.
♨Q❀◑♿🚌♣●P

Hinton Blewitt

Ring O' Bells ✔

Upper Road, BS39 5AN ST594569
⊙ 12-3, 5-11 (midnight Fri); 12-midnight Sat; 12-11 Sun
☎ (01761) 452239
Butcombe Bitter, seasonal beer; Fuller's London Pride Ⓗ
This Butcombe pub dates from the 19th century. Enter via a small yard with a pleasant garden to the side; you are soon in the warmth of the bar where many cricketing mementos feature – the pub runs its own team. The food is popular and children and dogs are welcome. The guest or seasonal beer is usually available Thursday to Sunday but up to five beers are offered in the summer months. Thatchers Cheddar Valley Cider features. ♨Q❀◑♣●⊬

Huish Episcopi

Rose & Crown (Eli's) ☆

Wincanton Road, TA10 9QT (on A372)
⊙ 11.30-2.30, 5.30-11; 11.30-11 Fri & Sat; 12-10.30 Sun
☎ (01458) 250494
Teignworthy Reel Ale; guest beers Ⓗ
This traditional thatched inn, known locally as Eli's, has been in the same family for generations. The character and unusual features remain unchanged, giving visitors the feeling they have stepped back in time. There are several cosy rooms, with drinks served in the counterless, flagstoned tap room. Good wholesome food is available at lunchtime and in the early evening (no food Mon and Sun eves). Burrow Hill cider is stocked. The 54 bus stops a 20-minute walk away. ☺❀◑♿🚌(54)♣●P⊬

Hutton

Old Inn

Main Road, BS24 9QQ
⊙ 11.30 (12 Sun)-11 ☎ (01934) 812336
Butcombe Bitter; Fuller's London Pride; RCH Hewish IPA Ⓗ
The year 2009 saw a hugely welcome return to the trade for John and Carol Hayes, former owners of the Guide regular Coopers at Highbridge, and they have set about transforming this venue. Now a thriving local, it offers a varied range of guest ales, often from nearby brewers including RCH, and several more handpumps are planned. John has revealed his previously hidden cooking skills and the pub is gaining a great food reputation. The Sunday carvery is highly recommended. Dogs welcome. ♨☺❀◑♿🚌♣P⊬

Kelston

Old Crown ✔

Bath Road, BA1 9AQ (3 miles from Bath on A431)
⊙ 11.30-11; 12-10.30 Sun ☎ (01225) 423032
Butcombe Bitter, Gold, seasonal beer; Draught Bass; Fuller's London Pride Ⓗ
This attractive multi-roomed 18th-century coaching inn is owned by Butcombe Brewery. The old beer engine in the bar, flagstone floors, open fires and settles all help to create a friendly atmosphere. No restaurant food is served Sunday or Monday evenings, but from 6pm on Monday the landlord and regular customers contribute tapas dishes. In summer barbecues and live musical events are occasionally held in the large, attractive garden. Tuesday is quiz night. ♨Q❀🛏◑🚌(319,332)P

Keynsham

Lockkeeper

Keynsham Road, BS31 2DB (on A4175)
⊙ 11-midnight; 12-11 Sun ☎ (0117) 9862383
⊕ lockkeeperbristol.com
Young's Bitter, Special, seasonal beers; guest beer Ⓗ
Multi-roomed Young's pub by Keynsham lock on the River Avon. The original 17th-century cottage once brewed its own beer and was named the White Hart until quite recently. Now noted for its food, it divides into two parts, with the older bar facing the canal while the large conservatory and heated veranda overlook the river, petanque pitches and the popular garden. Young's seasonal ales and a guest from the likes of Bath Ales or St Austell always feature. ❀◑♿⇌🚌(318)♣P⊬

Old Bank
20 High Street, BS31 1DG
✪ 10am-11 (midnight Fri & Sat); 12-9 Sun
☎ (0117) 904 6356
Sharps Doom Bar; guest beers Ⓗ
Located at one end of the High Street, this is a basic and welcoming pub with a single bar decorated with pictures of bygone Keynsham. Quiz night is Monday. The two or three guest beers are often unusual and interesting and there is a small selection of foreign beers. Full English breakfast served 9.30am-2.45pm Monday-Saturday (no food Sun). A rear car park is accessed via a narrow entrance at the side of the pub. ❀≋⊟♣P⊱

Ship ✔
93 Temple Street, BS31 1ER
✪ 12-3, 6-11; 12-11 Fri-Sun ☎ (0117) 9869841
Marston's Burton Bitter, Pedigree; Ringwood Best Bitter; guest beers Ⓗ
Grade II-listed 17th-century coaching inn, apparently in the Domesday Book, and one of the oldest buildings in Keynsham, retaining some original features, with a number of different areas for dining and drinking. The garden at the rear overlooks the park and the River Chew beyond. No food is available Sunday or Monday evenings. The car park is very small, but local buses pass close by. The three or four guest beers tend to come mainly from other Marston's group breweries.
❀◑⊟≋⊟(318,339,349)♣P⊱

Kilve

Hood Arms
TA5 1EA (on A39)
✪ 11-11 ☎ (01278) 741210 🌐 thehoodarms.com
Otter Head; guest beers Ⓗ
This 17th-century former coaching inn in the centre of the village is set beside the main road. It has oak beams, an open fireplace, a comfortable bar and a separate restaurant. There is also a landscaped walled garden where boules is played in summer. A bar billiards knockout takes place every Sunday night. Well-behaved dogs are welcome. Special events for charities are held regularly. Hecks cider is served. There are 12 en-suite guest rooms and a lodge available for rent.
♨❀⇌◑♿⅄⊟(14)♣●P⊱

Kingsbury Episcopi

Wyndham Arms ✔
TA12 6AT
✪ 12-11 (midnight Sun) ☎ (01935) 823239
🌐 wyndhamarms.com
Butcombe Bitter; guest beers Ⓗ
This marvellous old pub, around 400 years old, offers a warm welcome to visitors as well as regulars. Beers are mostly local and Burrow Hill cider is usually available. The dining room has a log fire, as does the bar. Outside there is a smoking area with patio heaters and a well-used pool table. There is also a skittle alley/function room, and upstairs is another function room often featuring live music. ♨Q❀◑⊟(633)♣●P⊱

Long Sutton

Devonshire Arms
TA10 9LP
✪ 12-3, 6-11 (10.30 Sun) ☎ (01458) 241271
🌐 thedevonshirearms.com
Beer range varies Ⓗ
Grade II-listed former hunting lodge facing an idyllic village green. A combined bar and restaurant area in a pleasing contemporary style includes comfy chairs around the log fire. Real ales always include a beer from Moor Brewing Company served by gravity. A blackboard gives tasting notes for beers on handpump. Burrow Hill cider is served, and the extensive menu details local suppliers. Alfresco areas include a courtyard, a large walled garden and a terrace overlooking the green. Nine modern en-suite bedrooms are available.
♨❀⇌◑⅄●P⊱

Lower Odcombe

Masons Arms
41 Lower Odcombe, BA22 8TX (off Yeovil to Montacute road)
✪ 12-2.30, 6-midnight ☎ (01935) 862591
🌐 masonsarmsodcombe.co.uk
Odcombe No 1, Spring; guest beers Ⓗ
This welcoming thatched free house in the main street of a chocolate box village has a small brewery at the back of the pub supplying it exclusively with regular and seasonal beers. Good locally sourced food is on offer and bookings are advised as demand is high. Try the very popular monthly curry night. Children and dogs are welcome. At the rear is a caravan site with hook-ups, showers and laundry room. Local events are held on the pub field. ❀⇌◑⅄⊟(81)●P⊱

Luxborough

Royal Oak Inn
TA23 0SH (about 2½ miles from B3224 between Wheddon Cross and Raleghs Cross)
✪ 12-2.30, 6-11; 12-11 Sat & Sun ☎ (01984) 640319
🌐 theroyaloakinnluxborough.co.uk
Cotleigh Tawny; Exmoor Ale; St Austell Tribute; guest beers Ⓗ
Ancient village pub known locally as the Blazing Stump, with an original stone-flagged public bar, serving hatches, large inglenook fireplace and a further bar/children's room to the rear. Alongside is a hotel and dining complex. The pub is popular in season with shooting parties and walkers as well as locals. Folk music and quiz evenings are held. Up to three real ciders are usually available. In an Exmoor valley, it is an ideal base for walking.
♨Q☋❀⇌◑⊟♣●P⊱

Marston Magna

Red Lion
Rimpton Road, BA22 8DH (200m from A359)
✪ closed Mon & Tue; 12-3.30, 6 (7 Sun)-11.30
☎ (01935) 851723
Sharp's Doom Bar; Yeovil Summerset; guest beers Ⓗ
Homely and friendly, this former Eldridge Pope house (note the plaque by the front door) is now free of tie. It is just outside the village centre but signposted from the main road. The single bar has wooden chairs and tables, and paintings on the walls. The licensee enthusiastically supports the LocAle scheme – the guest beer is often from Yeovil Ales. Good value food includes daily specials. The monthly quiz night is popular. Opening hours may vary in winter. ❀◑♿⊟(1)P⊱

Middlezoy

George Inn

42 Main Street, TA7 0NN (off A372, 1 mile NW of Othery)
☼ 12-3 (not Mon), 7-midnight (11.30 Sun)
☎ (01823) 698215 🌐 thegeorgeinnmiddlezoy.co.uk
Butcombe Bitter; guest beers Ⓗ
Dating from the 17th century, little has changed over the years, with exposed beams, a huge fireplace and stone-flagged floor. From the middle bar you should beware of the step up lest you are heckled good naturedly by the locals or the booming South African voice of the landlord. The pub is dog-friendly but children should be well-behaved. There is always a selection of two or three guest ales, real cider and hearty home-cooked food. At Easter there is the bonus of a beer festival, now approaching its 20th year.
♨☕❀◑◐⊟🚌(16)♣●P⚡

Minehead

Old Ship Aground

Quay Street, TA24 5UL (beside Minehead harbour)
☼ 11 (12 Sun)-11 ☎ (01643) 702087
Courage Best Bitter; Greene King Ruddles County; St Austell Dartmoor Best, Tribute Ⓗ
Well-established 1906 pub set in the picturesque part of Minehead between the harbour and lifeboat station, with fantastic views of the Bristol Channel. This dog-friendly pub offers good quality food and has a recently refurbished function room for hire. Its 12 en-suite rooms all have good views. The West Somerset Railway and town centre are just a short walk, and Exmoor is a 20-minute drive. Fishing trips are available from the harbour.
♨☕❀🛏◑◐♿⇌🚌(15,28)♣P⚡

Moorlinch

Ring O' Bells

Pit Hill Lane, TA7 9BT (between A39 and A361 near Street) ST 400365
☼ 5-8 Mon; 12-2, 5-11 Tue-Fri; 12-11 Sat & Sun
☎ (01458) 210358 🌐 ringobellsmoorlinch.co.uk
Butcombe Gold; Greene King IPA; St Austell Dartmoor Best; guest beers Ⓗ
This traditional village inn offers at least two West Country beers plus Greene King IPA, all served by handpump. Locally sourced home-cooked food is available in the public bar, big lounge bar or the separate dining room. Darts, skittles and pool are played and there is a jukebox. Families are welcome and dogs too. Although a little off the beaten track, this pub is well worth seeking out.
♨Q❀◑◐⊟♿🚌(19)♣P⚡

Mudford

Half Moon

Main Street, BA21 5TF (on A359 between Yeovil and Sparkford)
☼ 12-11 (10.30 Sun) ☎ (01935) 850289
🌐 thehalfmooninn.co.uk
Beer range varies Ⓖ
Welcoming 17th-century village free house restored to its original condition. The single bar is divided into small areas which makes for a convivial atmosphere. Each area is festooned with an eclectic selection of memorabilia. Beers, usually from Arbor or Quantock, are served from a stillage behind the bar. Good food and snacks, available all day, feature strongly, but drinkers are also welcome here. Accommodation is available both in the pub and a converted former skittle alley. Westons cider is served. ❀🛏◑◐♿🚌(1)●P⚡

Nailsea

Blue Flame

West End, BS48 4DE (1 mile off A370 at Chelvey) ST449691
☼ 12-3, 6-11; 12-10.30 Sun ☎ (01275) 856910
Butcombe Bitter; Fuller's London Pride Ⓖ**; guest beer** Ⓗ
Lovely rustic 19th-century free house comprising two rooms, one with a bar and a snug, and coal fires in winter. The toilets are outside. Live music features on the first and third Tuesdays of the month. The large rear garden is ideal for families in summer. Camping is available but phone first. Food is limited to filled rolls. The guest beer may be unavailable and the opening hours a little erratic. All beers are on gravity from the cask. The cider is Thatchers. ♨Q❀⛺♣●P

Oakhill

Oakhill Inn

Fosse Road, BA3 5HU (on A367 between Radstock and Shepton Mallet) ST 635472
☼ 12-3, 5-11 (midnight Fri); 12-midnight Sat & Sun
☎ (01749) 840442 🌐 theoakhillinn.com
Beer range varies Ⓗ
Formerly very much a village local, this has been completely refurbished as a family-friendly gastro-pub with a strong emphasis on organic and locally sourced food. Regular quiz nights and live music sessions are held. The ambience is more French bistro than country pub, but up to four changing guest ales are available along with a range of ciders. There is no food Sunday evening and the car park is 20 metres up the road. ♨❀🛏◑◐🚌●P

Pitney

Halfway House

Pitney Hill, TA10 9AB (on B3153)
☼ 11.30-3, 5.30-11; 12-3.30, 7-11 Sun ☎ (01458) 252513
🌐 thehalfwayhouse.co.uk
Butcombe Bitter; Hop Back Summer Lightning; Otter Bright; Teignworthy Reel Ale; guest beers Ⓖ
Thriving traditional village pub serving a variety of local ales on gravity alongside a range of international bottled beers, with superb home-cooked food based on local produce (ploughman's only Sun lunch, no food Sun eve). No music or fruit machines disturb the buzz of conversation in this multiple award winning pub. CAMRA National Pub of the Year 1996, Telegraph Pub of the Year 2007, and local CAMRA Pub of the Year 2008. Local ciders, including Wilkins and Hecks, are served. A real gem, not to be missed. ♨Q❀◑◐🚌(54)●P⚡

Porlock

Ship Inn ✔

High Street, TA24 8QD
☼ 11-midnight ☎ (01643) 862507 🌐 shipinnporlock.co.uk
Exmoor Ale; Otter Bitter; St Austell Tribute, Proper Job; guest beers Ⓗ
Known locally as the Top Ship, this 13th-century inn was recorded in RD Blackmore's Lorna Doone. The

bar appears not to have changed much since then, with flagstoned floors, inglenook fireplaces and a good selection of real ales and Cheddar Valley cider. Located at the bottom of the notorious Porlock Hill, this gem offers good home-cooked food, a three-tiered patio garden, skittle alley and four en-suite bedrooms. The dog-friendly hostelry also welcomes well-behaved children.
⛬Q⛄❀⇌◑⊟♿⛺⊟(39,300)♣●P⅟–

Portishead

Windmill Inn

58 Nore Road, BS20 6JZ (next to municipal golf course above coastal path)
✪ 11-11; 12-10.30 Sun ☎ (01275) 843677
Butcombe Gold; Courage Best Bitter; Draught Bass; RCH Pitchfork; guest beers 🄷
Large split-level free house with a spacious patio to the rear, with a recent extension enjoying panoramic views. Above the coastal path on the edge of town, the Severn estuary and both Severn bridges can be seen on clear days. A varied menu is served all day and is enormously popular. One large area is set aside for families. The two guest ales are often locally sourced and there is an Easter beer festival. Thatchers cider is stocked.
Q⛄❀◑♿⊟(359)●P⅟–

Priddy

Hunters Lodge

BA5 3AR (isolated crossroads 1 mile from A39) ST549500
✪ 11.30-2.30, 6.30-11; 12-2, 7-11 Sun ☎ (01749) 672275
Blindmans Mine Beer; Butcombe Bitter; Cheddar Potholer 🄶**; guest beers** 🄷
Timeless, classic roadside inn near Priddy, the highest village in Somerset, popular with cavers and walkers. The landlord has been in charge for well over 40 years. Three rooms include one with a flagged floor; the beer casks are behind the bar. Simple home-cooked food is excellent and exceptional value. A folk musicians' drop-in session is held on Tuesday evening in the back room. Wilkins cider is served. The garden is pleasant and secluded. Mobile phones are not welcome.
⛬Q⛄❀◑⊟♣●P

Queen Victoria Inn ✔

Pelting Drove, BA5 3BA (on minor road to Wookey Hole, S of village centre)
✪ 12-3, 6-11; 12-11.30 Sat; 12-11 Sun ☎ (01749) 676385
Butcombe Bitter, Gold; guest beer 🄷
Creeper-clad inn, a pub since 1851 with four rooms that feature low ceilings, flagged floors and three log fires. This is a wonderfully warm and relaxing haven on cold winter nights, and is popular during the Priddy Folk Festival in July and the annual fair in August. Reasonably priced, home-cooked food is a speciality. Children and dogs are allowed and there is a play area by the car park. Cheddar Valley cider is sold. Beers are now via handpump, not gravity as before. ⛬Q❀◑⛺♣●P⅟–

Radstock

Fromeway

Frome Road, BA3 3LG (¾ mile from Radstock centre on A362 Frome Road)
✪ closed Mon; 12-3; 6 (7 Sun)-11 ☎ (01761) 432116
🌐 fromeway.co.uk
Butcombe Bitter; Wadworth 6X; guest beer 🄷
This friendly free house has been in the same family for five generations, and the present landlord has been in charge for over 30 years. The pub is combined with a butcher's shop, which supplies all the meat for the excellent bar and restaurant meals. Well-used by locals, the Fromeway has a warm and relaxing atmosphere. A single bar serves a number of adjoining areas. Guest beers are sourced from local and national breweries. Q⛄❀⇌◑♿⊟P⅟–

Rode

Bell Inn

13 Frome Road, BA11 6PW (on A361 between Beckington and Southwick opp church) ST808535
✪ 11-11; 12-10.30 Sun ☎ (01373) 839356
🌐 flatcappers.co.uk
Three Castles Barbury Castle, Vale Ale, Knight's Porter; guest beers 🄷
Large former coaching house, acquired by local chain Flatcappers and refurbished in 2009. There are four bar areas, with original flagstones and reclaimed wooden floorboards, including a snug. Victorian lampshades are a feature. The venue caters for diners, grazers and drinkers, and the menu offers a rich variety of proper pub grub. Beers are sourced from local micros, with the two stronger regulars badged as Flatcappers. A large car park is to the rear. The bus shelter is right next to the pub. ⛬Q❀◑⊟♿⊟P⅟–

Rowberrow

Swan Inn ✔

Rowberrow Lane, BS25 1QL (signed off A38)
✪ 11.30-3, 6-11; 11.30-11 Fri & Sat; 12-10.30 Sun
☎ (01934) 852371
Butcombe Bitter, Gold, seasonal beer; guest beer 🄷
Believed to date from around the late 17th century, this Butcombe Brewery-owned country pub enjoys an attractive setting, nestling beneath the Dolebury Iron Age hill fort. A convenient stop for walkers on the Mendip Hills, the emphasis is on home-cooked food with unusual specials, but customers who just want a drink are very welcome. There is a collection of artefacts around the walls and a grandfather clock. Thatchers cider is available. The large, attractive beer garden and car park are opposite. ⛬Q❀◑●P⅟–

Seavington St Michael

Volunteer ✔

New Road, TA19 0QE (on former A303, 2 miles E of Ilminster)
✪ 12-2.30, 6.30-11; 12-3, 7-11 Sun ☎ (01460) 240126
🌐 thevolly.co.uk
Beer range varies 🄷
Five ales are available in this comfortable village pub, which is to be found on the old A303 between South Petherton and Ilminster. Mini-pin take-outs are available for all draught beers. Pie night on Wednesday has become a popular speciality, so booking is suggested. Situated in the heart of the countryside, walkers and their dogs are welcome – dogs are permitted in both bar areas.
⛬Q❀⇌◑⊟♿⊟(91)♣P⅟–

Shepton Beauchamp

Duke of York

North Street, TA19 0LW
12 (6 Mon)-11 ☎ (01460) 240314
thedukeshepton.co.uk
Otter Bright; Teignworthy Reel Ale; guest beers H
This friendly village pub hosts several local darts and skittles teams. On pleasant days, the tables on the raised pavement outside enable patrons to enjoy a voyeuristic view of rural Somerset life: the butcher's, post office, school, church and village hall all panoramically displayed. Dogs and walking boots are welcomed. The pool room is separate from the bar area. Recently built accommodation is popular with visitors. No food Sunday evening or Monday. (633)♣P

Shepton Mallet

Swan Inn

27 Town Street, BA4 5BE (N of town centre) ST618437
11-midnight ☎ (01749) 344995 swanatshepton.co.uk
Matthews Bob Wall; guest beers H
Formerly called The Stumbles Inn until it was renamed in 2008, this pub is situated in a terrace of small shops. Inside, the front area is arranged mainly for diners (no meals Mon afternoon or Sun, Mon and Tue eves), with chairs and tables extending out onto the pavement. The bar area at the rear offers darts and shove-ha'penny. Live music features once or twice a month. Guest ales are chosen from local small brewers. ♣P

Shepton Montague

Montague Arms

BA9 8JW (signed off A359 and A371) ST675315
closed Mon; 12-3, 6-11; 12-3 Sun ☎ (01749) 813213
Bath Ales Gem; Greene King Abbot; Wadworth IPA; guest beers G
An attractive pub in a sparsely populated village between Wincanton, Castle Cary and Bruton, well-known in the region for its outstanding cuisine, complemented by its real ales, often in pins in an anteroom behind the bar. Thatchers cider is usually available. The single bar is cosy and welcoming, with diners catered for in a restaurant at the rear of the building. From here there is access to a wide terrace and garden that enjoy spectacular views towards the famous folly, Alfred's Tower.
QP

Shurton

Shurton Inn

TA5 1QE (3 miles N of A39 near Nether Stowey)
12-3 (not Mon & Tue), 6-11; 12-3.30, 7-10.30 Sun
☎ (01278) 732695
Sharp's Doom Bar, Special; guest beers H
This 17th-century coaching inn is situated in a rural hamlet. Excellent freshly prepared local produce is served in a friendly atmosphere, with fresh fish the speciality. Four real ales are available along with an extensive wine list. There are restaurant and conservatory dining rooms, a beautiful beer garden and four en-suite guest rooms. Children and well-behaved dogs are made welcome. There is a smoking shelter and skittle alley, and beer festivals are held. QP

South Cadbury

Camelot

Chapel Road, BA22 7EX (just off A303 between Sparkford and Wincanton)
11-midnight (closed 3-5 winter); 11.30-11 Sun
☎ (01963) 440448 thecamelotpub.com
Beer range varies H
Easily located in the village, this deceptively large pub with flagstoned bar features a glass display case with information on the history of Cadbury Castle and artefacts found there. The ancient hill fort is a short walk away. Flagstones continue to the dining area, with a log burner at both ends. Beers from local breweries such as Yeovil Ales are always available, and usually a local cider from the next village as well. A blackboard tempts you with a Next Available list. All food is home-cooked.
Q♣P

South Petherton

Brewers Arms

18 St James Street, TA13 5BW (½ mile off A303)
11.30-2.30, 6-11; 11.30-midnight Fri & Sat; 12-11 Sun
☎ (01460) 241887
Otter Bitter; guest beers H
Local CAMRA Pub of the Year 2009, the pub has served 1500 ales in 15 years and attentive staff ensure that your glass will not be empty for long. It organises trips to the races and cricket, hosts two beer festivals a year, and supports myriad village functions and themed evenings. Dogs on leads and children are welcome. There is a good adjoining restaurant in the old bakehouse. Within a couple of minutes of the A303, this is a pub not to be missed.
(81,91)♣

Stoke St Gregory

Royal Oak

TA3 6EH (opp church)
closed Mon; 12-3, 7-11 (1am Fri); 12-1am Sat; 12-3, 7-midnight Sun ☎ (01823) 490602
theroyaloaktaunton.co.uk
St Austell Tribute; guest beers H
A warm, friendly pub in the centre of the village. It has become a real part of the community, with several skittles teams plus darts and pool. A family concern since 2005, in the course of a visit you will probably meet most of its members. The pub is ideally positioned for taking a break when walking the Somerset Levels or the long distance Parrett Trail. (51)♣P

Taunton

Castle Green Inn

Castle Green, TA1 4AE (by Castle Hotel)
9am-11 (10.30 Sun) ☎ (01823) 257688
Beer range varies H
Open-plan town-centre pub with a country pub atmosphere. There is a central bar area with a bricked floor and seating/dining areas on either side. Good value food is served both lunchtimes and evenings. Beers normally include offerings from Somerset breweries such as Cotleigh, Exmoor, Moor and Taunton, as well as other West Country breweries, and there is usually at least one beer on offer at an advantageous price. Occasional live music plays. Situated close to Taunton bus station.

Racehorse ✔

East Reach, TA1 3HT
⏲ 12-4, 6-11 (midnight Thu); 12-12.30am Fri & Sat; 12-11 Sun ☎ (01823) 327513
St Austell Dartmoor Best Bitter, Tribute, Proper Job Ⓗ
Friendly, popular pub just off the town centre at the top of East Reach. Multi-roomed, with front and rear bars, a small lounge with comfortable armchairs and two other indoor drinking areas as well as a large walled beer garden, this traditional town hostelry is the place to go for good conversation and a great atmosphere. On display are various pieces of memorabilia such as old tin signs and musical instruments. No food is served. ❀⊟⊟♣⁴⁄–

Wyvern Club

Mountfields Road, TA1 3BJ
⏲ 7-11; 12-3, 7-10.30 Sun ☎ (01823) 284591
🌐 wyvernclub.co.uk
Exmoor Ale; guest beers Ⓗ
Large, busy sports and social club, home to cricket, rugby and squash teams. It offers a variety of West Country beers, with guest ales changing frequently – beers from three different breweries are usually on offer, at club prices. Meals are available each evening until 9pm, plus Sunday lunchtime. The club premises are available for daytime meetings and evening functions. Show this Guide or your CAMRA membership card to be signed in as a guest. A real ale festival is held in October. Children are welcome. ♉❀◐♿⊟(1A,99)♣P

Thurloxton

Maypole Inn

TA2 8RF (just off A38 between Taunton and North Petherton)
⏲ 12-3, 6-11 (7-10.30 Sun) ☎ (01823) 412286
🌐 maypole-inn.co.uk
Beer range varies Ⓖ
Originally a cider house dating back to 1880, local Rich's cider is still served, together with two local beers direct from the cask. A large, cosy village hostelry, it is split into various areas, mainly for dining but with ample space for those who just want a drink. It is a family-friendly pub with an extensive menu emphasising local produce and a children's menu designed by the landlord's children. The large garden includes a children's play area. There is a skittle alley and large function room. ♨❀◐⊟(15,21)♣●P⁴⁄–

Trull

Winchester Arms

Church Road, TA3 7LG (turn E off main road by village shop, just past school and church) ST 217221
⏲ 12-3, 6.30-11 ☎ (01823) 284723 🌐 winchattrull.co.uk
Draught Bass; Sharp's Doom Bar; St Austell Tribute; guest beers Ⓗ
This well-appointed pub is run by a brother and sister and has tasteful furnishings. There is a long dining area and an L-shaped section with comfortable seating and some bar stools. An impressive coal-effect fireplace separates the two areas. There is an excelllent choice of menu, with lunchtime specials and theme nights every Wednesday. The chefs use local produce and all meals are home-made. B&B is very reasonable and there is a large car park at the rear.
Q❀⇚◐♿⊟(97)♣P⁴⁄–

Wanstrow

Pub

Station Road, BA4 4SZ (on A359 halfway between Nunney Catch services and Bruton) ST711416
⏲ 6.30-11 Mon; 12-2.30 (3 Fri & Sat), 6-11; 12-3, 7-10.30 Sun
☎ (01749) 850455
Draught Bass; Hop Back GFB; guest beers Ⓗ
An absolute gem, this friendly village local has a lounge bar with open fire and flagstone floors that leads to a small restaurant. The pub serves two regular and two guest beers, sourced from almost anywhere, along with Thatchers Traditional and Cheddar Valley ciders. Games include skittles, bar billiards and ring the bull. A small but imaginative menu is offered and all food is home cooked.
♨Q❀◐⊟♣●P

Watchet

Esplanade Club ✔

The Esplanade, TA23 0AJ (opp marina)
⏲ 12-3 (Sun), 7-midnight ☎ (01984) 634518
Cotleigh Tawny Owl; St Austell Tribute; guest beers Ⓗ
The club has splendid views over the marina and Bristol Channel. Decked out with old photographs and memorabilia, it was built in the 1860s as a sail-making factory, but has been a club since the 1930s. There is live entertainment every weekend, with folk and open mike nights in the week. A short walk from the West Somerset Railway, visitors showing this Guide or a CAMRA membership card are very welcome and will be signed in by staff. Also home to the boat owners' club. ♿▲⇌⊟(14,18,28)♣

Star Inn 🏆 ✔

Mill Lane, TA23 0BZ
⏲ 12-3.30, 6.30-midnight; 12-4, 7-midnight Sun
☎ (01984) 631367
Butcombe Bitter; guest beers Ⓗ
The Star has four (five in summer) different beers from both local and regional breweries. There is a cosy main bar with small side rooms and a large, pleasant garden. Mouth-watering food, including seafood, locally sourced where possible, is served. There are quiz teams, skittle teams and the infamous Sunday Bad Boys Club. Close to the marina, West Somerset Railway and bus routes, it is handy for walks on the Quantock Hills and for sea fishing. Dogs are welcome.
♨❀◐♿▲⇌⊟(14,18,28)♣●⁴⁄–

Wedmore

New Inn

Combe Batch, BS28 4DU
⏲ 12-2.30, 5-midnight; 12-2am Fri (1am Sat); 12-10.30 Sun
☎ (01934) 712099
Butcombe Bitter; guest beers Ⓗ
Traditional pre-1800s village inn and the current venue for the Turnip Prize. Other annual competitions include conkers, spoof, penny chuffin' and apple bobbin'. There are three main areas: public, lounge and dining, beer gardens front and rear, and a skittle alley/function room. A chalkboard lists forthcoming guest ales from mainly local breweries. Local award-winning Wilkins cider is also served. Traditional pub food is available lunchtimes and evenings (no food Sun eve). Q❀◐▲⊟(668,670)♣●P⁴⁄–

Wells

City Arms ✔

69 High Street, BA5 2AG ST547456
☼ 10-11; 9am-midnight Fri & Sat; 10-10.30 Sun
☎ (01749) 673916 ⊕ thecityarmsatwells.com
Butcombe Bitter; Cheddar Gorge Best, Pot Holer; Glastonbury Hedgemonkey, Golden Chalice; Greene King IPA Ⓗ
In 1810 the City of Wells Jail closed and later became the City Arms. The main bar retains the small barred windows and low-vaulted ceilings of its former existence. The building encloses a courtyard on three sides, with outdoor seating. The upstairs restaurant serves tapas and snacks and all food is made to order using fresh local produce. Up to seven beers are available, sourced mainly from nearby micros, and real cider including Ashton Press. ⚲❀◑⊒♣●╚

West Chinnock

Muddled Man

Lower Street, TA18 7PT
☼ 11-2.30 (not Mon winter), 7-midnight; 11-midnight Fri & Sat; 12-10.30 Sun ☎ (01935) 881235
Beer range varies Ⓗ
Well-worth seeking out, this family-owned and run free house has three handpumps serving a range of West Country ales. Superb, reasonably priced home-cooked food is available – Sunday lunch must be booked. Numerous visitors have been converted to real ale here, many becoming regulars at this fine LocAle-supporting pub. Burrow Hill cider is available. Dogs are permitted and the skittle alley can be hired for meetings or functions. Charities are well supported. ⚲❀◑&♣●

West Huntspill

Crossways Inn

TA9 3RA (on A38)
☼ 11-11 (2am Thu-Sat); 12-10.30 Sun ☎ (01278) 783756
Butcombe Bitter; Fuller's London Pride; guest beers Ⓗ
This 17th-century hostelry has recently been refurbished by the new landlord. The skittle alley/games area is now accessed off the bar area and has a large-screen TV. A changing selection of guest beers is available alongside Rich's cider. There is a new food menu complemented by specials on the blackboard and themed menus for events such as Burns Night or Shrove Tuesday. Please note that accommodation is no longer available. ⚲Q❀◑&⊒(15,21,21A)♣●P╚

Weston-super-Mare

Criterion

45 Upper Church Road, BS23 2DY (100m from sea front)
☼ 12-11 (10.30 Sun) ☎ (01934) 622673
Courage Best Bitter; RCH Hewish IPA; guest beers Ⓗ
Genuine free house and traditional community pub, just off the sea front in the Knightstone area. Possibly one of the oldest pubs in town, it has interesting local photos on the walls. Pub games feature strongly, with darts, bar billiards and table skittles, plus a quiz on Tuesday. Dogs are welcome. Two guest beers are offered, with local breweries well-supported, and Thatchers cider is sold. The Raglan is almost opposite, making for a handy two-pub crawl. ⚲⊒(1)♣●

Off the Rails

Station Approach, BS23 1XY (on railway station concourse)
☼ 7am-11.30; 9am-11 Sun ☎ (01934) 415109
RCH PG Steam; guest beers Ⓗ
This genuine free house, conveniently situated at the railway station, is also the station buffet. Two guest beers usually come from West Country micro-breweries, with occasional beer and cider guests from further afield. The landlord is happy to receive suggestions from his regulars for which beers to stock. Two-pint carry-out containers are a handy feature for train travellers. Three TVs show sporting events, often silently. Quiz night is Tuesday and there is a free jukebox. Dogs are welcome. ⇌⊒(112,126)●

Raglan

42-44 Upper Church Road, BS23 2DX (100m from sea front via Greenfield Place)
☼ 4 (12 Sat & Sun)-midnight ☎ (01934) 429942
⊕ myspace.com/theraglanarms
Beer range varies Ⓗ
Two-roomed corner house in the older part of town. A log fire is at the centre of the lounge bar where all four handpumps are located. This bar, with a piano, is also where live music takes place regularly. Every Friday is open folk night – bring an instrument and join in. The public bar has a pool table, Sky Sports and real cider – real ale is served here too, so don't be scared off by the lack of pumps. O'Hanlons, Cotleigh and Exmoor beers often feature. A monthly quiz is held on a Thursday. ⚲⊟⊒♣●

Wincanton

Nog Inn

South Street, BA9 9DL (50m from Market Sq opp Nat West Bank)
☼ 10.30-11 (midnight Fri & Sat); 12-11 Sun
☎ (01963) 32998 ⊕ thenoginn.com
Otter Bitter; Sharp's Doom Bar; guest beers Ⓗ
Tucked away a short distance from the town's market square, this attractive listed pub is not to be missed. A striking Georgian facade fronts a long, narrow building with parts dating back to the 16th century. A secluded sunny garden with covered seating can be found at the far end of the property. The guest ales are often seasonal and an extensive range of continental draught beers is always available. A beer festival and live music events are hosted regularly, and a charity quiz night is held on the last Thursday of the month.
⚲Q❀◑&⊒♣●P╚

Unicorn Inn

Bayford, BA9 9NL (1 mile E of Wincanton on old A303)
☼ closed Mon; 12-11.30 (6 Sun) ☎ (01963) 34941
Butts Jester; Sharp's Doom Bar; guest beers Ⓗ
This former 17th-century coaching inn has a comfortable bar with a woodburner and a deep well concealed beneath a large flagstone. The pub is reputed to be haunted by the ghost of a young boy who was run over by a horse-drawn coach. This inn is a favourite of Terry Pratchett (Discworld) fans, and also Wincanton race-goers. The guest ales are often from local micros. The landlord is enthusiastic about real ale and regularly holds beer and cider festivals. ⚲⇌◑⊒♣●P

Winsham

Bell Inn

11 Church Street, TA20 4HU
☉ 12-2.30 (not Mon; 3 Sat & Sun), 7-11 ☎ (01460) 30677
⊕ thebellwinsham.co.uk
Branscombe Branoc; guest beers Ⓗ
Popular village-centre pub with a large open-plan bar and a function room where darts and skittles are played. Up to three guest ales, mostly from the West Country, are usually available. Many village activities are hosted on the patio. Good value food is offered 12-1.30pm and 7-8.45pm. Children are made welcome. Q⚯❀◑⊟♿⊟(99)♣P⚍

Wiveliscombe

Bear Inn

10 North Street, TA4 2JY
☉ 11-11 Mon-Wed & Fri; 11-midnight Thu & Sat; 12-11 Sun
☎ (01984) 623537
Cotleigh Harrier; Otter Amber; Sharp's Doom Bar; guest beers Ⓗ
Lively community pub in the centre of a traditional brewing town, with two rooms sharing a single bar. There is a children's play area and a garden at the rear, as well as a skittle alley. This is an ideal base for exploring Exmoor and the Brendon Hills. Both Cotleigh and Exmoor breweries are just a short walk away. ♨❀⊏◑⊟(25,25B)♣P⚍

Wookey

Burcott Inn

Wookey Road, BA5 1NJ (on B3139, 2 miles W of Wells)
☉ 11-2.30 (3 Sat), 6-11; 12-3, 7-10.30 Sun
☎ (01749) 673874 ⊕ burcottinn.co.uk
Beer range varies Ⓗ
Cosy country pub featuring a copper-clad, L-shaped bar counter always serving two or more ales, mostly from independent West Country brewers. This stone-built roadside inn is characterised by low beams, pine tables and flagstone flooring. The front bar is warmed by a cheery log-burning stove in winter, leading to a long room where darts, cribbage and shove-ha'penny are played. Freshly prepared food is served throughout the pub (no food Sun or Mon eves, or Mon lunchtime in winter). ♨Q⚯❀⊏◑⛺⊟(670)♣P

Wookey Hole

Wookey Hole Inn

High Street, BA5 1BP (opp Wookey Hole caves)
☉ 12-11 (6 Sun) ☎ (01749) 676677 ⊕ wookeyholeinn.com
Beer range varies Ⓗ
Charismatic, picturesque gastro-pub with a unique contemporary style, situated opposite the major tourist attraction of the famous caves. Two to four changing guest beers from small, often unusual brewers are served, plus Wilkins cider and a wide choice of draught continental beers and lagers. Top-quality food is available at restaurant prices, ideal for special occasions (book ahead at weekends). The huge sculpted rear garden is superb in summer. A lurid pink function room and five highly individual bedrooms complete the picture. ❀⊏◑⛺⊟●P⚍

Wrington

Golden Lion

Broad Street, BS40 5LA
☉ 2.30-11.30; 12-midnight Fri & Sat; 12-11.30 Sun
☎ (01934) 862205 ⊕ goldenlionwrington.co.uk
Butcombe Bitter; guest beers Ⓗ
Family-run village-centre free house, which prides itself on offering a warm welcome. It runs its own football team, golfing society and shooting syndicates, and is popular with the local community. No food is served, but great attention is paid to offering quality beer. Three guest ales are usually sourced from West Country brewers and the landlord will consider customers' suggestions. Events include a beer festival on the late May bank holiday weekend, a summer hog roast and live music on Saturday nights. ♨❀⊟(121)♣⚍

Yeovil

Great Western

47 Camborne Grove, BA21 5DG (signed off Lyde Road, NE of town centre)
☉ 12-2 (not Mon), 5-midnight; 12-midnight Fri-Sun
☎ (01935) 431051 ⊕ greatwestern-pub.co.uk
Butcombe Bitter; Wadworth 6X, seasonal beers Ⓗ
Friendly, comfortable local in a residential area. The single bar features a collection of railway memorabilia, much of it relating to the Great Western Railway, who built the nearby station. There is a pool table and skittle alley, and an upstairs function room is available for hire. Certificates on the wall testify to the cellar skills of the landlady. Good-value food includes an excellent Sunday lunch (no food Mon and Tue lunchtime or Mon eves).
❀◑⇌(Yeovil Pen Mill)⊟(57,58)♣⚍

Quicksilver Mail ✔

168 Hendford Hill, BA20 2RG (at jct of A30 and A37 W of town centre)
☉ 10.30-midnight (1am Sat); 12-11 Sun ☎ (01935) 424721
⊕ quicksilvermail.com
Adnams Broadside; Butcombe Bitter; St Austell Tribute Ⓗ
Friendly, comfortable pub in an imposing position at the roundabout that bears its name. It is the only pub with this name, commemorating a high-speed mail coach. Some interesting old photographs of the inn are displayed in the single bar, which has a lower section for diners. Note also the sporting memorabilia and an earlier pub sign. Good value food is served, including a popular Sunday lunch. Well-behaved children and dogs are welcome. The large function room features regular live music.
❀⊏◑♿⊟(4,99)♣P⚍

Join CAMRA

The Campaign for Real Ale has been fighting for over 35 years to save Britain's proud heritage of cask-conditioned ales, independent breweries, and pubs that offer a good choice of beer. You can help that fight by joining the campaign: use the form at the back of the guide or see **www.camra.org.uk**

STAFFORDSHIRE

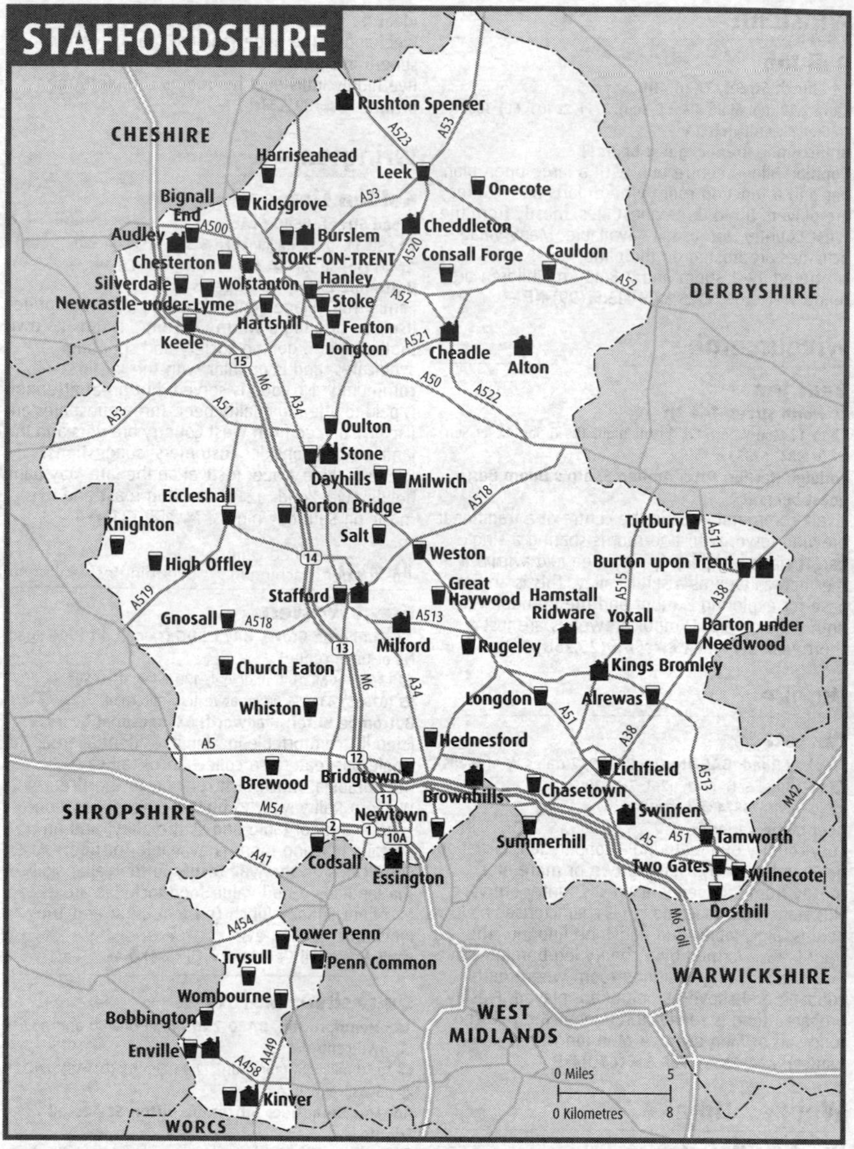

Alrewas

George & Dragon

120 Main Street, DE13 7AE SK171150
⏲ 11 (12 Sun)-11 ☎ (01283) 791476
Marston's Burton Bitter, Pedigree; guest beer Ⓗ
Three-storey, welcoming village local, dating back to the early 1700s. The comfortable main bar area is split into three distinct sections, and there is a separate lounge/dining room to one side. The guest beer is usually from the Marston's list. Meals are not served Sunday evening. Reasonably priced accommodation comprises one family room and two doubles. The Trent & Mersey canal runs along the edge of the village, about 300m distant. National Memorial Arboretum is one mile to the east. ⛺❀⇌◑♿▲🚌(7,12)♣P⊱

Barton under Needwood

Royal Oak ✔

74 The Green, DE13 8JD (½ mile from B5016 via Wales Lane) SK182180
⏲ 12-midnight (1am Fri & Sat); 12-11 Sun ☎ (01283) 713852
Marston's Pedigree; guest beers Ⓗ/Ⓖ
Bustling, community local situated on the southern edge of the village, home to many traditional pub games and an over-40s football team. While parts of the building date back to the 16th century, the pub has only existed since the mid-1800s. Public bar and lounge customers are served from a central sunken bar, set below the level of the rest of the ground floor. Beers are available on handpump or on gravity, direct from the cask, on request. ⛺Q🍺❀⊟🚌(7,12)♣P⊱

Shoulder of Mutton ✔

16 Main Street, DE13 8AA (on B5016) SK189186
⏲ 12-midnight (1am Fri & Sat) ☎ (01283) 712568
🌐 shoulderofmutton.com
Draught Bass; Marston's Pedigree; guest beer Ⓗ
This 17th-century former coaching inn, with some 19th-century additions, is located at the centre of this historic village, opposite the church. The front entrances, illuminated by two rather smart Bass lanterns, lead directly into the simple public bar and comfortable lounge, the latter featuring a low-beamed ceiling, wood panelling and inglenook, plus a dining area to one side. There is a delightful landscaped garden to the rear, adjoining the car park. Live music features occasionally (see website for details). 🏰❀⇌◐▢🚌(7,12)♣P⁻

Waterfront ✔

Barton Marina, DE13 8DZ (off B5016, ½m E of village) SK197181
⏲ 11-11 (12.30am Fri & Sat) ☎ (01283) 711500
🌐 bartonmarina.co.uk
Blythe Marina Bitter; Marston's Pedigree; St Austell Tribute; guest beers Ⓗ
Large, imposing pub, opened in 2007, within a retail complex and leisure park adjacent to the Barton Marina, which is linked to the nearby Trent & Mersey canal. The main open-plan room features a low ceiling with wooden beams, and has lounge and dining areas amid wood partitioning. There is a separate restaurant, the Quarterdeck. An outdoor terrace overlooks the marina, where short-stay moorings are available. A function room, the Crow's Nest, is located upstairs. No meals after 8pm Sunday. 🏰❀◐♿🚌(7,12)P⁻

Bignall End

Bignall End Cricket Club

Boon Hill, ST7 8LA (off B5500)
⏲ 7 (12 Sat & Sun)-midnight ☎ (01782) 720514
Beer range varies Ⓗ
Welcoming village cricket club in a semi-rural location, not far from the main road, with splendid rural views over Cheshire from the clubhouse. Established for over 100 years, the club hosts two popular beer festivals in summer and winter, and many other events in the upstairs function room. A public bar and also a snooker room are downstairs, and a wide range of cask beers is supplied by an independent wholesaler. CAMRA members are welcome as guests. 🚌(34)P⁻

Swan

Chapel Street, ST7 8QD (200m off B5500)
⏲ 12-11 (10.30 Sun) ☎ (01782) 720622
Draught Bass; Oakham Inferno; guest beers Ⓗ
The Swan is a multi-award-winning, traditional, two-roomed pub serving up to eight real ales and four traditional ciders. Staffordshire County Pub of the Year 2008 and 2009, it has a traditional bar and a quieter, comfortable lounge, both warmed by real fires. A regular beer festival is held over the August bank holiday weekend. The pub is easily reached by frequent bus services from Newcastle and Hanley. 🏰❀▢🚌(34)♣●⁻

Bobbington

Red Lion

Six Ashes Road, DY7 5DU
⏲ 12-3, 5-11; 12-11 Sat; 12-10.30 Sun ☎ (01384) 221237
🌐 redlioninn.co.uk
Enville Ale; Theakston Old Peculier; Wye Valley HPA Ⓗ
First recorded as an ale house in 1820, this pub has been family-run for more than 20 years. The bar leads to a room housing traditional and modern games. The restaurant provides good quality food, which is also served in the bar. An expansive garden with a children's play area provides a pleasant place to enjoy a beer on a summer's afternoon. Seventeen modern en-suite rooms, including two suites, provide excellent accommodation (CAMRA members receive a discount, ring for details). Q♉❀⇌◐▢♿▲♣P⁻

Brewood

Swan Hotel 🏆

15 Market Place, ST19 9BS
⏲ 11.45-midnight ☎ (01902) 850330
🌐 swanbrewood.co.uk
Caledonian Deuchars IPA; Courage Directors; Theakston Black Bull Bitter; guest beers Ⓗ
Located in the centre of the picturesque village and with low-beamed ceilings and seasonal log fires, this former coaching inn is five minutes' walk from the Shropshire Union canal. Cosy snugs displaying pictures of old Brewood flank the bar, while there is a skittle alley upstairs. The two guest beers are usually from local micro-breweries and, with new host named Robbie Burns, there is a wide selection of single malt whiskies. Hourly buses from Wolverhampton and evening buses from Stafford serve the pub. 🏰Q❀♿🚌(3,76)♣P

Bridgtown

Stumble Inn

264 Walsall Road, WS11 0JL (200m from A34/A5/M6 toll jct)
⏲ 12-3, 6 (5 Fri)-11; 7-midnight Sat; 12-10.30 Sun
☎ (01543) 502077
Beer range varies Ⓗ
Arguably the area's most consistent real ale choice, with four varied guest ales, the pub was runner-up in the local CAMRA Pub of the Year awards in 2008 and 2009. A small meeting/function room plus pool/darts area add to the split-level main room. Music is integral here: discos on Fridays, jam

INDEPENDENT BREWERIES

Beowulf Brownhills
Black Hole Burton upon Trent
Blythe Hamstall Ridware
Burton Bridge Burton upon Trent
Burton Old Cottage Burton upon Trent
Enville Enville
Kinver Kinver
Leek Cheddleton
Lymestone Stone
Marston's Burton upon Trent
Morton Essington
Peakstones Rock Alton
Quartz Kings Bromley/Swinfen
Shugborough Milford
Slater's Stafford
Titanic Burslem
Toft Cheadle (NEW)
Tower Burton upon Trent
Town House Audley
Wincle Rushton Spencer

sessions on the second and last Tuesdays every month, live bands on Saturday evenings. It organises a beer festival in September, and there is free Wi-Fi broadband.
❀◐♿≹(Cannock)🚌(1,351)♣P⊱

Burton upon Trent

Alfred

51 Derby Street, DE14 2LD (on A5121) SK243236
⌚ 11-2, 4.30-11; 11-midnight Fri & Sat; 11-5 Sun
☎ (01283) 562178 🌐 bbb-thealfred.co.uk
Burton Bridge Golden Delicious, Bridge Bitter, Burton Porter, Stairway to Heaven, Bramble Stout, Festival Ale; guest beer Ⓗ
This double-fronted terrace pub, now part of the Burton Bridge estate, was once the Trumans Brewery tap. A central bar counter serves two rooms, each featuring wood partitions topped with leaded stained glass. An area in the left-hand room is generally set aside for dining. There is also a small snug/family room to the rear. The pub is known locally for its range of English fruit wines, Monday poker nights, and Wednesday quiz nights. No meals Tuesday, Wednesday evening or Sunday.
❀◐◑▭≹🚌♣P⊱

Burton Bridge Inn 🏆

24 Bridge Street, DE14 1SY (on A511, at town end of Trent Bridge) SK254233
⌚ 11.30-2.30, 5-11; 11.30-11.30 Fri & Sat; 12-3, 7-11 Sun
☎ (01283) 536596 🌐 burtonbridgebrewery.co.uk
Burton Bridge Golden Delicious, Sovereign Gold, Bridge Bitter, Burton Porter, Festival Ale; guest beer Ⓗ
This 17th-century pub is the flagship of the Burton Bridge Brewery estate and fronts the brewery itself. Refurbished in 2000, it has two rooms served from a central bar: a smaller front room, with wooden pews and displaying brewery memorabilia, and a back room featuring oak beams and panels. The beer range is supplemented by a selection of malt whiskies and fruit wines. A small dining/function room and a skittle alley are upstairs and available for hire. No lunches Sunday. ♨Q❀◐🚌♣⊱

Coopers Tavern ☆

43 Cross Street, DE14 1EG (off Station Street) SK245231
⌚ 12-2.30 (not Mon & Tue), 5-11; 12-midnight Fri & Sat; 12-11 Sun ☎ (01283) 532551
Castle Rock Harvest Pale Ⓗ**; Draught Bass** Ⓖ**; guest beers** Ⓗ/Ⓖ
A classic, unspoilt 19th-century ale house that was once the Bass Brewery tap and bottle store, now a free house. The inner tap room has barrel tables and bench seats. The beer is served from a small counter next to the cask stillage, using a mixture of gravity and handpumps. Up to four draught ciders and perries, plus fruit wines, are also available. The more comfortable lounge leads to a third small room. Meals are available Sunday lunchtime only.
♨Q❀◐▭≹🚌●⊱

Devonshire Arms

86 Station Street, DE14 1BT SK245232
⌚ 11.30-2.30 (not Mon), 5.30-11.30; 11.30-midnight Fri & Sat; 12-3, 7-11 Sun ☎ (01283) 562392
Burton Bridge Golden Delicious, Bridge Bitter, Burton Porter, Stairway to Heaven; guest beer Ⓗ
Popular old pub, dating from the 19th-century and Grade II-listed; one of five Burton Bridge Brewery hostelries in the town. It comprises a public bar at the front and a larger, more comfortable, split-level lounge to the rear. Note the 1853 map of Burton, old photographs, and the unusual arched wooden ceilings. An enclosed rear patio features flower borders and hanging baskets. A number of continental bottled beers and English fruit wines are also stocked. No lunches Sunday.
♨Q❀◐▭≹🚌♣P⊱

Lord Burton ✔

154 High Street, DE14 1JE SK248231
⌚ 9-midnight (1am Fri & Sat) ☎ (01283) 517587
Greene King Ruddles Best Bitter, Abbot; Marston's Pedigree; guest beers Ⓗ
Named after Michael Bass, the brewer and first Lord Burton, this busy Wetherspoon's pub was formerly a Woolworths store and is close to the town centre. Old photographs of Burton adorn the walls of the large single room, with the rear section designated a family area. An attractive, enclosed mixed grass and paved beer garden to the rear overlooks the Memorial Gardens, with the River Trent beyond. Guest beers are often from local micro-breweries. Real cider is Westons Marcle Hill. Q❀◐◑♿🚌●⊱

Old Cottage Tavern

36 Byrkley Street, DE14 2EG (off Derby Street A5121, behind town hall) SK240236
⌚ 12-11 ☎ (01283) 511615
Old Cottage Oak Ale, Stout, Halcyon Daze; guest beers Ⓗ
This welcoming local is now a privately leased free house, but still operates as the Old Cottage Brewery tap, although no longer owned by the brewery. The main public bar at the front and the wood-panelled lounge to the rear are served from a central bar. There is also a cosy snug to one side of the public bar, a small restaurant beyond the lounge, and a games/function room (with skittle alley) upstairs. No meals Monday, or Sunday evening. ♨❀🛏◐◑▭≹🚌♣⊱

Cauldon

Yew Tree Inn

ST10 3EJ (1 mile S of A523 at Waterhouses)
⌚ 11-2.30 (3 Sat), 6-midnight; 12-3, 7-midnight Sun
☎ (01538) 308348
Burton Bridge Bitter; Draught Bass; Rudgate Ruby Mild Ⓗ
Enjoy a great pint while studying the many antiques in this famous moorlands pub, which lies close to the Manifold Valley and Alton Towers. There is plenty of old world charm to soak up inside, and the collection of antiques must surely be unique. The pub has been in the same family for nearly 50 years, and bar snacks such as pork pies are always available. This truly is a pub with a difference and one not to be missed.
♨Q❀♿⛺🚌♣●P⊱

Chasetown

Uxbridge Arms

2 Church Street, WS7 3QL
⌚ 12-midnight ☎ (01543) 677852
Draught Bass; guest beers Ⓗ
Up to four guest ales and two real ciders greet weary travellers in this busy corner pub and Guide regular. A wide range of country wines and malt whiskies is also available. Sport is popular here,

with bowls, darts and football teams. The bar features bar billiards as well as sport on a large screen. Good food is available in the lounge and upstairs restaurant (no food Sun eve). Dogs are welcome in the bar. ❀◖◗⊟🚌♣🍎P

Chesterton

Black Horse

Sutton Street, ST5 7JH

⌚ 12-3 (4 Sun), 7-11 (10.30 Sun) ☎ (01782) 561313

Coach House Ollers Duck; Greene King Old Speckled Hen, Abbot; guest beers Ⓗ

The Black Horse is a community pub with a beer garden for the summer and hot mulled wine for the winter. You can be sure of a warm welcome from the friendly landlord and staff waiting to serve you from a magnificent wooden bar, well-stocked with ale, cider, whisky and more. The walls are lined with books, and assorted games can be played in a separate public bar with a jukebox. A place to bring your granny to.
❀◖⊟🚌(34,34A)♣🍎⁻

Church Eaton

Royal Oak

High Street, ST20 0AJ

⌚ 5 (12 Sat)-midnight; 12-10.30 Sun ☎ (01785) 823078

Banks's Mild, Bitter; Marston's Pedigree; guest beer Ⓗ

The only pub in the village, a few years ago it was threatened with closure, but was saved by a small consortium of local people and is now the hub of the community. It has a modern interior split into four interconnecting rooms – a bar, restaurant, TV room and a room with a pool table. Children are welcome until 7pm, or later if dining in the restaurant. The varied guest beers are mostly sourced from local micro-breweries.
⛟❀◖◗♿🚌(482)♣P⁻

Codsall

Codsall Station

Chapel Lane, WV8 2EJ

⌚ 11.30-2.30, 5-11; 11.30-11.30 Fri & Sat; 12-10.30 Sun

☎ (01902) 847061

Holden's Mild, Bitter, Golden Glow, Special; guest beers Ⓗ

This award-winning pub was once the waiting room and stationmaster's house in this Grade II-listed building. It has a bar, lounge, snug and conservatory, and displays world wide railway memorabilia. A raised outdoor terrace allows you to sit in peace and watch the trains, including the occasional steam locomotive. There are free acoustic music sessions every other Sunday. Sunday lunch must be booked and there is no food on Sunday evening. A popular beer festival is held the weekend after the August bank holiday.
♨Q❀◖◗♿⇌🚌(535,880)P⁻

Consall Forge

Black Lion ✔

ST9 0AJ (from A522 turn to Consall into Nature Reserve; on U-bend go straight on; ignore No Through Road to Trains sign; bottom of hill turn left along track)

⌚ 12-midnight ☎ (01782) 550294 🌐 blacklionpub.co.uk

Peakstones Rock Black Hole; guest beers Ⓗ

A truly beautiful pub located in the heart of the Churnet Valley; watch steam trains go by while enjoying the excellent range of beers and ciders. Inside, there is a single bar with a quarry-tiled floor, plus plenty of room to sit and enjoy the home-cooked food. A beer festival is held in conjunction with the Churnet Valley Railway at the start of February. An excellent pub to bring the family to that rewards the effort of getting there.
♨Q⛟❀◖◗▲⇌(Churnet Valley)♣🍎P⁻

Dayhills

Red Lion

Uttoxeter Road, ST15 8RU (3 miles E of Stone on the B5027)

⌚ 5 (4 Fri)-11; 2-midnight Sat; 12-10.30 Sun

☎ (01889) 505474

Draught Bass; Worthington's Bitter; guest beer Ⓗ

This welcoming country pub is known locally as the Romping Cat. Unspoilt and full of character, it has been in the same family, along with the adjoining farm, since 1920. The main room has a timeless feel with its quarry-tile floor, meat hooks in the ceiling and inglenook fireplace. The atmosphere is undisturbed by music, gaming machines or TV.
♨Q♣P⁻

Dosthill

Fox Inn ✔

105 High Street, B77 1LQ

⌚ 4 (6 Mon)-11; 2-1am Fri; 12-1am Sat; 12-11 Sun

☎ (01827) 280847

Greene King Abbot; Marston's Pedigree; Wychwood Hobgoblin; guest beer Ⓗ

Welcoming local to the south of Tamworth, around three miles from the town centre. This three-roomed pub has a traditional bar and very comfortable lounge. The separate Fox's Lounge is quiet and may be used for meetings by local groups and societies. The changing guest beer can be from anywhere in the country. Quiz night is popular on Sunday, Wednesday is poker night. The pub is close to the West Midlands Water Ski Centre and Kingsbury Water Park. Q❀◖◗⊟♿🚌♣P⁻

Eccleshall

Bell Inn

16 High Street, ST21 6BZ

⌚ 11am-11.30 (1am Fri & Sat); 12-11.30 Sun

☎ (01785) 850378

Black Sheep Best Bitter; Holden's Golden Glow; Marston's Pedigree; guest beers Ⓗ

A busy pub in the centre of a small market town. A former coaching inn with a multi-room layout, it was recently rescued from closure and sympathetically refurbished, including an extensive rear beer garden. It has an increasing number of handpulls, including a guest from Titanic, and a selection of South African wines. The pub also hosts beer festivals throughout the year. There is a regular Thursday night quiz, together with live music events. ♨⛟❀◖◗♿🚌(350,432)♣P⁻

George Hotel

Castle Street, ST21 6DF (at Eccleshall's main crossroads)

⌚ 11-midnight (1am Fri & Sat); 12-midnight Sun

☎ (01785) 850300 🌐 thegeorgeeccleshall.com

Slater's Bitter, Original, Top Totty, Premium, Supreme; guest beers Ⓗ

Slater's brewery has moved to Stafford, but the six handpulls serving nearly the full range of Slater's award-winning ales are still the main attraction at the George, with Thatchers cider available and the pub having a LocAle accreditation. Originally a 17th-century coaching inn, the George has thrived under the Slater family's ownership. It now boasts an attractive bar and lounge area, with food available all day everyday. There are evenings of live music on a monthly basis.
♨Q🐴🛏◑◐🚌(350,432)P🚭

Star Inn ✔

Copmere End, ST21 6EW (leave Eccleshall on B5026, turn left at sign for Copmere End. Pub is on the crossroads) SJ803294
🕘 6-11 Mon winter only; 12-3, 6-11; 12-11 Sat summer; 12-6 (11 summer) Sun ☎ (01785) 850279
🌐 thestarinn-eccleshall.co.uk
Draught Bass; Wells Bombardier; guest beers 🄷
A thriving 100-year-old pub situated in the heart of the beautiful Staffordshire countryside adjacent to the Cop Mere lake and central to numerous walks. The next-door post office has been closed for a number of years but a Victorian postbox remains. An excellent selection of bar meals and an a la carte menu are offered lunchtimes and evenings – the pub was recently awarded third place in the Taste of Staffordshire good food awards.
♨Q🐴❀◑◐⊟♿▲♣P🚭

Enville

Cat

Bridgnorth Road, DY7 5HA (on A458)
🕘 closed Mon; 12-2.30 (3 Sat), 6.30-11; 12-6 Sun
☎ (01384) 872209 🌐 thecatinn.talktalk.net
Enville Ale; guest beers 🄷
Parts of this traditional pub date back to the 16th century. It has three oak-beamed rooms, two with real fires, and a family/function room. Hanging baskets adorn the beer garden and courtyard during summer months. Up to five guest ales are served, including beers from Enville and other local breweries. Home-made dishes and daily specials, using local produce whenever possible, are served. A separate menu is offered in the restaurant.
♨Q🐴❀◑◐♿P

Gnosall

Royal Oak

Newport Road, ST20 0BL (on A518)
🕘 12-midnight; 12-3 Sun ☎ (01785) 822362
Ansells Mild; Greene King IPA, Abbot; guest beer 🄷
Popular village local, once a coaching inn although the exact age of the building is not clear. The pub hosts a music night every other Tuesday evening and upstairs is a function room with a skittle alley for hire. There is a large beer garden with swings and a climbing frame. Outside is a large heated smoking area. No food on Monday, Tuesday and Sunday evenings. Dogs are welcome.
♨🐴❀◑◐⊟🚌(481)♣P🚭

Great Haywood

Clifford Arms ✔

Main Road, ST18 0SR (off A51 4 miles NW of Rugeley, 200m from canal junction)
🕘 12-11.30 (midnight Fri & Sat); 12-11 Sun
☎ (01889) 881321
Adnams Broadside; Draught Bass; Greene King Old Speckled Hen; guest beers 🄷
Village-centre inn with a large bar providing plenty of seating, and a restaurant adorned with past photos of the pub. A busy local, home to cribbage, dominoes and quiz teams, it also has a tug of war team. Popular with walkers, cyclists, boaters and visitors to the nearby Shugborough Estate (National Trust), the Staffordshire Way and bridge 73 of the Trent & Mersey Canal are 200 metres along Trent Lane. The pub is dog-friendly.
♨❀◑◐⊟♿▲🚌♣P🚭

Harriseahead

Royal Oak

High Steeet, ST7 4JT
🕘 7-11; 5-midnight Fri & Sat; 12-4, 7-10.30 Sun
☎ (01782) 513262 🌐 royaloak-harriseahead.com
Courage Directors; Fuller's London Pride; Samuel Smith OBB; guest beers 🄷
Popular two-roomed village pub, totally free of tie. Three guest beers are available from a wide selection of micro-breweries, plus a good range of bottled Belgian beer, with one on draught. There is a small room upstairs for meetings, which plays host to a beer festival in early December. There are pork pies and barms to fill the stomachs of hungry walkers. Well-behaved dogs are always welcome. Mow Cop Folly is a mile away. ♨Q❀⊟🚌♣P🚭

Hednesford

Cross Keys Hotel

42 Hill Street, WS12 2DN
🕘 12-midnight ☎ (01543) 877285
Greene King Old Speckled Hen; Skinner's Betty Stogs; guest beers 🄷
An 18th-century former coaching inn serving several different real ales, including five that always change. The licensee, who has been here since 1997, used to play for and later managed Hednesford Town football club, which at one time had its ground behind the pub. Voted CAMRA Staffs area Pub of the Year 2008 and runner-up 2009, it also has Cannock Chase, an area of outstanding natural beauty, in close proximity. Sky and ESPN sports are available to view on TV.
❀🛏⊟♿🚌(33,60)♣P📺

High Offley

Anchor Inn ☆

Peggs Lane, Old Lea, ST20 0NB (by bridge 42 of the Shropshire Union canal) SJ775256
🕘 12-3, 7-11 Easter-Oct; winter hours vary
☎ (01785) 284569
Wadworth 6X 🄷
A Victorian canalside inn that has changed little, run by generations of the same family since 1870. A rare example of an unspoilt country pub, it has two small bars where cask ale and Westons cider are often served from jugs. Although hard to reach by road, it is well worth finding. Freshly made sandwiches are always available. There is a large award-winning garden. Winner of the Best Public House 2008 by the Caravan Club of Great Britain. Check winter opening times beforehand.
♨Q❀⊟▲♣🍎P

Keele

Keele Postgraduate Association (KPA)

Horwood Hall, University Campus, ST5 5BG
⏲ 11 (Sat 2)-2am; 3-midnight Sun ☎ (01782) 734228
🌐 keele.ac.uk/kpa
Beer range varies Ⓗ
The KPA was founded in 1967 as the Keele Research Association, but changed its name and moved to its present site in 1994. It comprises a one-room bar and a function room upstairs, and has a quiet reading area with with newspapers. Three real ales, often from local breweries, are always on offer, covering a wide range of beer styles. CAMRA members are welcome as guests. There is a bus stop close by. ❀◑♿🚌(25)⚡

Kidsgrove

Blue Bell

Hardingswood, ST7 1EG (off A50 near Tesco)
⏲ closed Mon; 1-4 (Sat only), 7.30-11 Sat; 12-10.30 Sun
☎ (01782) 774052 🌐 bluebellkidsgrove.co.uk
Beer range varies Ⓗ
Genuine free house that benefits from the absence of TV, games machines and other intrusions to make a conversational atmosphere that draws everyone in. Informal and spontaneous live music plays on Sunday evening and the pub attracts customers from a wide area, together with visitors from the Trent & Mersey and Macclesfield canals, which meet a few metres away. Six handpumps deliver a wide range of beers from independent and micro-brewers. Foreign beers, plus real cider, are always available. Q❀⇌🚌🍏P

Kinver

Kinver Constitutional Club

119 High Street, DY7 6HL
⏲ 5-11; 4-midnight Fri; 11.30-midnight Sat; 12-10.30 Sun
☎ (01384) 872044
Draught Bass; Enville Ale; Hobsons Best Bitter, Town Crier; Wye Valley HPA; guest beers Ⓗ
A converted hotel with three main areas: a smart restaurant, large snooker room, and bar dispensing up to 18 real ales. The club enjoys an enviable sporting reputation and hosts regular quiz and music nights. Meals are served Sunday lunchtime and Thursday to Saturday evenings (booking advised). CAMRA members are welcome but must be signed in; groups should book ahead. The bus from Stourbridge stops nearby. Local CAMRA Branch Club of the Year every year since 2007. ❀◑♿🚌(227,228)♣🍏P⚡

Knighton

Haberdasher's Arms

ST20 0QH (between Adbaston and Knighton) SJ753275
⏲ 12.30 (7 Wed & Thu)-midnight; 12.30-1am Fri & Sat; 12-midnight Sun ☎ (01785) 280650
Banks's Mild, Bitter; guest beer Ⓗ
Traditional country inn, built around 1840, offering a warm, friendly welcome. This former local CAMRA Pub of the Year has four compact rooms, all served from a small central bar. It hosts a range of events such as the annual Potato Club Show, and occasional music festivals. It is also available for private hire. It is well worth the drive through leafy country lanes to get here. ♨Q🚼❀⊟♿⛺♣P⚡

Leek

Wilkes Head

15 St Edward Street, ST13 5DS
⏲ 12 (3 Mon)-midnight; 12-11 Sun ☎ (07976) 592787
Whim Arbor Light, Hartington Bitter, IPA, Flower Power; guest beers Ⓗ
The Wilkes Head is the second oldest pub in Leek and is a must visit in this lovely market town. A popular venue for music, the licensee is a skilled musician. Acoustic night is every Monday; three music festivals are held in the large outside area, plus many another gig. All this plus a great jukebox. The pub is also the tap for the Whim Brewery, with quality ales and cider available on the bar. ♨Q❀🚌♣🍏⚡

Lichfield

Bowling Green ✔

Friary Road, WS13 6QJ
⏲ 11.30-11 (midnight Fri & Sat) ☎ (01543) 257344
🌐 emberinns.co.uk/thebowlinggreenlichfield
Beer range varies Ⓗ
A large Tudor-fronted inn located on a large traffic island, which is also home to an independent bowling club. The interior is divided into several distinct areas, with a large central bar offering up to four different guest ales. Regulars can request forthcoming beers from the comprehensive Ember Inns list. An excellent selection of food is served daily until 9pm. Quiz nights are Tuesday and Sunday. ♨❀◑⇌(City)🚌⚡

Duke of Wellington 🏆

Birmingham Road, WS14 9BJ
⏲ 4 (12 Fri-Sun)-11 ☎ (01543) 263261
Fuller's London Pride; Marston's Pedigree; guest beers Ⓗ
A warm welcome awaits at this traditional pub, well worth the 15-minute walk from the city centre. The interior is essentially open plan, with three distinct drinking areas. The excellent, quality ales on handpump include up to five guests, with many examples from micros. During the summer months the large back garden is very popular. Dogs are welcome if accompanied by well-behaved owners. Check out the noticeboard for the speciality food evenings. ♨❀◐🚌♣P⚡

Duke of York

23-25 Greenhill, WS13 6DY
⏲ 11-11 (midnight Fri & Sat); 12-11 Sun ☎ (01543) 300386
Draught Bass; guest beers Ⓗ
A recently refurbished 17th-century Grade II-listed building, which features ales from the owning Joule's Brewery, plus guests. The pub offers a warm welcome but no music, TV or fruit machines. The oak-timbered bar features an open logburner. The lounge has oak panelling and leather seating, also with a logburner. There is an outside patio area with a bowling green and car park to the rear. A strict 18-plus admittance policy is enforced. ♨Q❀◐⊟⇌🚌♣🍏P⚡

George & Dragon ✔

28 Beacon Street, WS13 7AJ
⏲ 11-midnight (1am Fri & Sat); 12-11.30 Sun
☎ (01543) 254854
Banks's Mild, Bitter; Marston's Pedigree; guest beers Ⓗ
A deservedly popular local close to the cathedral, with a public bar and an exceptionally cosy lounge.

Up to four guest ales are from the Marston's portfolio. To the rear of the pub is a very large garden that hosted an artillery barrage during the siege of Lichfield in 1643. For the active, darts and dominoes along with board games are played, and a charity quiz is held on a Tuesday night. The pub is dog-friendly. ❀⊟Ʌ≠(City)⊟♣P⊱

Horse & Jockey

8-10 Sandford Street, WS13 6QA
✪ 12-11 (midnight Fri & Sat; 10.30 Sun) ☎ (01543) 410033
Draught Bass; Holden's Golden Glow; Marston's Pedigree; guest beers Ⓗ
After a dismal spell as a Rock Café, this welcoming city-centre pub has been restored to its original name and original role as a friendly haven for real-ale enthusiasts. Up to eight ales are available, often from local breweries. There is an over-21s entry policy and alcopops are banned. Locally-produced bar snacks are served. Friday and Saturday nights are particularly lively with a good cross-section of customers, while there is live entertainment on offer once a month. ⋒❀◐≠P⊱

Longdon

Swan with Two Necks

40 Brook End, WS15 4PN (250m off A51)
✪ 12-3, 6-11 (midnight Sat); 12-11 Sun ☎ (01543) 490251
Marston's Pedigree; guest beers Ⓗ
A meeting place for locals from the village and surrounding countryside, this fine pub has been in the Guide for more than 30 years. Up to three guest beers are served, mainly from local micro-breweries, with Bathams Best Bitter a Friday regular. Meals are of a very high quality, and the restaurant area is open on Friday and Saturday evenings. Takeaway fish and chips are available. With three open coal fires, this is a cosy pub for the winter. ⋒Q❀◐◑♿P⊱

Lower Penn

Greyhound

Market Lane, WV4 4UN (at Market Lane/Greyhound Lane jct)
✪ 12-3.30, 5.30-11; 12-11 Fri-Sun ☎ (01902) 620666
🌐 thegreyhoundlowerpenn.co.uk
Enville Ale; guest beers Ⓗ
Dating from 1830, this village local has recently been refurbished. It is around three miles from Wolverhampton city centre, and is popular with walkers and cyclists using the South Staffordshire Railway walk. Canal moorings are available at nearby Dimmingsdale. The bar area features memorabilia of Wolves teams and players from the past 100 years. The Greyhound's own beer, Hare of the Dog (Wye Valley), and other local ales are regularly available, including Slater's Top Totty and Kinver Edge. ⋒❀◐◑♿P⊱

Milwich

Green Man

ST18 0EG (on B5027)
✪ 12-2.30 Thu & Fri, 5-11; 12-11 Sat; 12-10.30 Sun
☎ (01889) 505310 🌐 greenmanmilwich.com
Adnams Bitter; Draught Bass; guest beers Ⓗ
A pub since 1775, this free house offers guest beers from regional and micro-breweries nationwide – see the website for forthcoming guests. The current licensee is in his 20th year at the pub and a list of his predecessors dating back to 1792 is displayed. A popular pub with walkers and cyclists, it has a restaurant section within the bar (lunches served Thu-Sun, eve meals Wed-Sat). Westons or Thatchers cider is stocked. Local CAMRA Pub of the Year 2007. ⋒Q☕❀◐◑♿♣●P⊱

Newcastle-under-Lyme

Boat & Horses ✔

2 Stubbs Gate, ST5 1LU (opp Morrisons supermarket, 500m from bus station)
✪ 3-11; 2-midnight Fri; 12-midnight Sat; 12-10.30 Sun
☎ (01782) 662789 🌐 boatandhorses.com
Draught Bass; Greene King Abbot; guest beer Ⓗ
This traditional pub with an open-plan design has lost none of its cosy charm. A friendly, no-frills venue with a warm welcome for regulars and strangers alike, here you can enjoy good beer and, if you like, wholesome food provided by on-site caterers. It is a popular location for viewing sports fixtures, with numerous screens for easy viewing, and for listening to the nostalgic jukebox. The pub is easy to spot as it is painted bright blue. ◐◑⊟⊱

Castle Mona ✔

4 Victoria Street, ST5 1NT
✪ 4 (12 Sat)-midnight; 12-11.30 Sun ☎ (01782) 257764
Marston's Pedigree; Wells Bombardier; Wychwood Hobgoblin; guest beers Ⓗ
Small traditional terraced pub, with a central bar dividing the bar and a comfortable, pleasantly decorated lounge. A pool table can be found at the back of the bar area and there is a separate area for darts players to enjoy a game. To the rear is a large beer garden with a heated area and plenty of seating. Live sports events are shown. Three regular ales as well as up to two guest ales are available. ❀⊟⊟♣⊱

Old Brown Jug ✔

Bridge Street, ST5 2RY
✪ 5-midnight (1am Wed); 12-1am Fri-Sun
☎ (01782) 711393 🌐 oldbrownjug.com
Marston's Pedigree; guest beers Ⓗ
This large, one-roomed Marston's pub at the edge of town is popular with both locals and students, and renowned for its beer and cider as well as for its varied music. A popular jazz venue, it also hosts a salsa night and a rock and blues evening; check the website as the opening hours can vary. There is a large beer garden to the rear. Winner of local CAMRA Cider Pub of the Year; well-worth a visit. ❀⊟♣●P⊱

Newtown

Ivy House 🏆

62 Stafford Road, WS6 6AZ (on A34)
✪ 12-11.30 (11 Sun) ☎ (01922) 476607
🌐 ivyhousepub.co.uk
Banks's Mild, Bitter; Marston's Pedigree; guest beers Ⓗ
This local CAMRA Pub of the Year 2005-2007 was first listed as an ale house in 1824. This traditional pub comprises three rooms plus a purpose-built restaurant. The beer garden retains a country feel, backing onto open farm land. A visit is highly recommended and a warm welcome assured. Q❀◐◑♿⊟(1,2,351)P⊱

Norton Bridge

Railway Inn

Station Road, ST15 0NT

⏲ 4.30-11; 12-10.30 Sun ☎ (01785) 760289

Thwaites Original, Lancaster Bomber; guest beer Ⓗ

Saved from closure, this local is now a thriving community village pub which plays host to a variety of traditional pub games and an annual rally of BSA motorcycles. A good range of home-cooked meals is served in the bar (Mon-Sat eves). Not to be missed, with the food to be savoured with a traditional pint and atmosphere. ♨Q♘❀◗⊟♿⛺🚌(490)♣P⚋

Onecote

Jervis Arms

ST13 7RU (on B5053 N of A53 Leek-Ashbourne road)

⏲ 12-midnight summer; 12-3, 7 (6 Sat)-midnight winter; 12-midnight Sun ☎ (01538) 304206

Titanic Iceberg; Tower Bitter; Wadworth 6X; guest beers Ⓗ

Seventeenth-century free house in a small village in an idyllic location at the southern edge of the Peak District National Park and close to Alton Towers. It is very family-friendly, with a family room, playground and a garden running down to the river Hamps. Quality home-cooked food is always available. Guest beers concentrate on independents and micro-breweries. A beer festival is held in May, with cask ales and ciders sourced by the landlord; a cider festival is held in September. ♘❀◐◗⛺P⚋

Oulton

Brushmakers Arms ✔

8 Kibblestone Road, ST15 8UW (500m W of A520, 1 mile NE of Stone)

⏲ 12-3, 6-midnight; 12-1am Fri & Sat; 12-midnight Sun ☎ (01785) 812062

Thwaites Original, Lancaster Bomber; guest beer Ⓗ

Named after a local cottage industry, the Brush is a pub where time stands still. It has a traditional quarry-tiled bar and a small ornate lounge. Pictures and postcards adorn the walls reflecting a bygone era. The small rear patio garden doubles as a smoking area and is a real suntrap. With no games machines or jukebox, conversation flows in this excellent village local. Well-behaved dogs are welcome. The guest ale may come from a local micro. ♨Q❀⊟♿🚌(250)♣P⚋

Penn Common

Barley Mow

Pennwood Lane, WV4 5JN (follow signs to Penn Golf Club from A449) SO901949

⏲ 12-3, 6-11; 12-11 Sat & Sun ☎ (01902) 333510

Caledonian Deuchars IPA; Greene King Abbot; Taylor Landlord; guest beers Ⓗ

On the edge of Penn Common and sharing an access driveway with Penn Golf Club, this venue takes a bit of finding but is well worth the effort. Built around 1630, it has low-beamed ceilings and steps down into the main drinking and dining area. The small single bar has a display of beer mats, foreign bank notes and a selection of five quality real ales. The licensee is also the local butcher, so take the opportunity to sample the fare. Q❀◐◗P

Rugeley

Plaza ✔

Horsefair, WS15 2EJ

⏲ 9am-11.30 (12.30am Fri & Sat) ☎ (01889) 586831

Greene King Ruddles Best Bitter, Abbot; guest beers Ⓗ

This multi-level, characterful Wetherspoon's was converted from a cinema in 1988 and has been the heartbeat of the town ever since. Step inside and you will see that a lot of the old 1930s cinema still remains. Guest beers are mostly local, including an ever-present offering from nearby Blythe Brewery. There are regular Meet the Brewer evenings. Try the balcony or large beer garden for outdoor drinking. Arriva 825 Stafford-Lichfield bus goes by the pub. Q❀◐◗♿≋🚌●P⚋

Salt

Holly Bush Inn

ST18 0BX (turn left off A518 opp Weston Hall) SJ959277

⏲ 12-11 (midnight Fri & Sat) ☎ (01889) 508234

🌐 hollybushinn.co.uk

Adnams Bitter; Marston's Pedigree; guest beer Ⓗ

The Holly Bush claims to have origins as far back as 1190 and is believed to be the second English inn to be granted a licence. The oldest part of the building retains a thatched roof. With extensions and alterations over the centuries there are now three distinct areas: a bar towards the middle, a dining room, and a snug which is mainly used by diners. Food is available until 9.30pm (9pm Sun). Many awards have been won for the superb quality yet reasonably priced meals. ♨Q❀◐◗♿⛺P⚋

Silverdale

Bush

High Street, ST5 6JZ

⏲ 12-11 (midnight Fri & Sat; 10.30 Sun) ☎ (01782) 713096

Wells Bombardier; guest beers Ⓗ

Situated at the top of a former mining village, the Bush has three rooms and a large, enclosed garden. Six beers are available on handpump; the guest beers can come from both local and regional brewers. The pub has its own darts, dominoes, pool and football teams, and there is entertainment on Friday night. Good value food is available 12-2pm lunchtimes and 5-8pm weekday evenings, and all day at weekends. Easily reached by bus from Newcastle town centre. ♨♘❀◐◗⊟♿🚌♣P⚋

Stafford

Greyhound

12 County Road, ST16 2PU (off A34, opp jail)

⏲ 4 (2 Fri)-11; 12-11 Sat & Sun ☎ (01785) 222432

Wells Bombardier; guest beers Ⓗ

A short walk from the town centre, opposite Stafford's jail, this site has housed a pub since the 1830s. The pub was threatened with closure a few years ago, and the car park had to make way for a block of flats. However, the Greyhound has lost none of its vitality and energy. Eight hand-pulled ales are usually on offer, mostly from local micro-breweries and regional brewers. Cold snacks are available. Local CAMRA Pub of the Year in 2009. ♨⊟≋🚌♣⚋

Joxer Bradys

4 St Martin's Place, ST16 2LA (in the corner of Market Square)
⏲ 11.30-11 (midnight Thu-Sat) ☎ (01785) 228183
Jennings Cumberland Ale; Marston's Pedigree; Wychwood Hobgoblin; guest beer ⊞
This friendly multi-roomed pub in the corner of Stafford's market square was once an Irish-themed pub but has now fully recovered! At least four real ales are usually available, as well as a traditional cider (Thatchers Heritage). The pub was formerly known as The Chains, and is reputed to have an underground tunnel leading to the dungeons of the once-nearby Crown Court. Regular live music and comedy nights feature; phone for details.
◐♿⇌🚌♣🍎

Lamb Inn ✔

Broad Eye, ST16 2QB (opp Sainsbury's on Chell Road)
⏲ 12-11 (midnight Fri & Sat; 10.30 Sun) ☎ (01785) 603902
Fuller's London Pride; Wells Bombardier; guest beer ⊞
A traditional street-corner local situated in the town centre and within easy reach of the railway station, making it a prime stop-off for those looking for a quality pint. The nearby lorry park and bus stops also generate walk-in trade. With a warm, friendly and welcoming atmosphere, the pub has great charm and community spirit. The car park is small but there are numerous local authority parking spaces close by. ❀♿⇌🚌(1,3,9)♣P⊱

Picture House ✔

Bridge Street, ST16 2HL
⏲ 7am-midnight (1am Fri & Sat) ☎ (01785) 222941
Greene King Ruddles Best Bitter, Abbot; Marston's Pedigree; guest beers ⊞
A tasteful Wetherspoon conversion of a 1914 cinema in this county town, first opened as a pub in 1997. Many original features have been retained – the entrance foyer, projection booth, and a profusion of posters from the golden age of cinema. The pub is often busy in the evenings, with a mixed clientele of all ages. LocAle accredited in 2009, a good selection of real ales is offered.
☕❀◐♿⇌🚌♣🍎⊱

Spittal Brook ✔

106 Lichfield Road, ST17 4LP (1 mile SE of centre off A34)
⏲ 12-3, 5-11; 12-11 Fri & Sat; 12-10.30 Sun
☎ (01785) 245268
Black Sheep Best Bitter; Everards Tiger; Fuller's London Pride; Marston's Pedigree; St Austell Tribute; guest beer ⊞
A thriving traditional two-roomed ale house supporting a variety of pub games, sporting clubs and societies, including water polo, netball and golf. Entertainment includes a folk night on Tuesday and a quiz on Wednesday. Dogs travelling with their owners are welcome overnight. Local CAMRA Branch Pub of the Year 2008.
♨Q❀🛏◐⊟♿🚌(1,3,6)♣P⊱

Stoke-on-Trent: Burslem

Bulls Head

St John's Square, ST6 3AJ
⏲ 3-11 (11.30 Wed & Thu); 12-11.30 Fri & Sat; 12-11 Sun
☎ (01782) 834153 🌐 titanicbrewery.co.uk/bulls
Everards Tiger; Titanic Steerage, Anchor, Iceberg, White Star; guest beers ⊞
The Bulls Head is situated in the middle of Burslem and is now the flagship of an expanding fleet of taps for the renowned Titanic Brewery. Five of Titanic's award-winning range can be found on the bar, along with four guest ales. With its coal fire, old-style jukebox and bar billiards, this great pub has a retro feel to it. Themed beer-related events are often held and it is proud of Port Vale Football Club. ♨⊟🚌♣🍎⊱

Leopard

Market Place, ST6 3AA
⏲ 11-11 (midnight Fri & Sat); 12-10.30 Sun
☎ (01782) 819644
Beer range varies ⊞
A three-roomed pub with a separate dining room and large function room at the rear, this multi-award winning local is steeped in history. The former Georgian hotel was once known as the Savoy of the Midlands, with a long history of famous residents, and the first meeting to discuss the building of the Trent & Mersey canal was held here. A very popular pub with the locals, and very welcoming to away football supporters. Truly a must-visit pub. Q❀◐🚌🍎⊱

Post Office Vaults

3 Market Place, ST6 3AA
⏲ 10-10.45 (12.45am Fri & Sat); 10-10.30 Sun
☎ (01782) 811027
Greene King Abbot; Oakham Inferno, Bishops Farewell; Thornbridge Jaipur; guest beers ⊞
This is a small, one-roomed pub in the centre of Burslem, popular with the local football club and community. Guest beers can hail from a wide variety of micro-breweries. Real cider is also available from the cellar. Sport and live music feature on the array of TV screens. There is a heated smoking area to the rear with its own TV. Post Office memorabilia adorn the walls, including a factory clocking-in machine. The pub is dog-friendly. ❀🚌(20,21,98)🍎⊱

Stoke-on-Trent: Fenton

Malt 'n' Hops

295 King Street, ST4 3EJ
⏲ 12-4, 7-11; 12-midnight Fri & Sat; 12-10.30 Sun
☎ (01782) 313406
Greene King Abbot; guest beers ⊞
This family-run pub is one of the few traditional free houses remaining in the area. The venue is split into two levels, creating an impression of separate bar and lounge spaces. The house beers are brewed by Tower, and there is a changing range of guest ales. A good selection of bottled Belgian beers is also stocked, as well as some on draught. The pub has been a regular among CAMRA's top Potteries pubs for many years.
⇌(Longton)🚌⊱

Stoke-on-Trent: Hanley

Coachmakers Arms 🏆 ★

Lichfield Street, ST1 3EA (off A5008 Potteries Way ring road)
⏲ 12-11 (midnight Fri & Sat); 12-10.30 Sun
☎ (01782) 262158 🌐 thecoachmakers.co.uk/
Draught Bass; guest beers ⊞
A warm atmosphere and friendly character welcome you to the Coachmakers Arms, situated near Hanley bus station. This pub, voted CAMRA

Potteries Branch Pub of the Year 2009, provides six different guest beers including a mild and stout, along with hand-pulled cider. The pub is popular with local drinkers as well as many fans from outside Stoke-on-Trent. Possible renovation to the area has put this pub in jeopardy, so don't miss the opportunity to visit this gem. Q

Unicorn

Piccadilly, ST1 1EG

12-1am (midnight Sun) (01782) 281809

Fuller's London Pride; guest beers H

Located in the centre of Hanley's cultural quarter, it is indeed a cultural experience stepping inside this little oasis of a pub, with toby jugs and brass paraphernalia hanging from the oak beams. Popular with visitors to the Regent Theatre opposite, you can order your interval drinks before the start of the show. The current winner of the Fuller's National Award for the quality of its London Pride, the pub also stocks two varying guest beers. One to cherish.

Stoke-on-Trent: Hartshill

Greyhound

67 George Street, ST5 1JT

12-11.30 (midnight Wed & Thu; 12.30am Fri & Sat) (01782) 635814 titanicbrewery.co.uk/greyhound.html

Everards Tiger; Titanic Steerage, Iceberg, White Star; guest beers H

Situated on the edge of Newcastle town centre, this roadside pub is a joint venture between Titanic and Everards. There are nine handpumps on the bar, dispensing a range of Titanic, Everards and guest beers. Hot and cold snacks are served at lunchtimes, with local oatcakes a speciality; a monthly sausage and mash evening is also organised. The pub has an L-shaped, open-plan layout, with a separate room to the right-hand side. Traditional pub games are available on request. Q

Stoke-on-Trent: Longton

Congress

Sutherland Road, ST3 1HJ (opp police station)

12-11 (midnight Fri & Sat); 12-4, 7-11 Sun (01782) 763667

Holden's Mild; Hydes Original; Townhouse Gladstone Strong Ale; Wadworth 6X H**; guest beers** H/G

Spacious, two-roomed pub just off the main road through Longton town centre, comprising a large bar area and meeting room. The landlord has transformed this pub into one of the best real ale establishments in the Potteries; it won second place in the 2009 local CAMRA Pub of the Year competition. A beer festival is held every May, when the regular range is supplemented by two more ales. A proper traditional pub – a pleasure to drink in.

Stoke-on-Trent: Stoke

Wheatsheaf

84-92 Church Street, ST4 1BU

7am-midnight (1am Fri & Sat) (01782) 747462

Greene King Ruddles Best Bitter, Abbot; Marston's Pedigree; guest beers H

This town-centre Wetherspoon's outlet is now becoming a fixture in the Guide, and justifiably so, with a good selection of well-kept beers sourced from across the country. The staff always take that extra step to ensure customer satisfaction. Meet the Brewer and brewery-themed beer festivals are becoming fixtures and the pub supports local brewers, with ales from Lymestone and Slater's often to be found on the bar. A most convivial addition to the JDW chain. Q

White Star

63 Kingsway, ST4 1JB (off Church Street, close to King's Hall)

11-11 (midnight Fri & Sat); 12-11 Sun (01782) 848732 titanicbrewery.co.uk/thewhitestar.html

Everards Tiger; Titanic Steerage, Anchor, Iceberg, White Star; guest beers H

This open-plan, town-centre pub is a joint venture between Everards and Titanic breweries. Ten handpumps dispense a range of Titanic, Everards and guest beers. Home-cooked food and snacks are available until 2.30pm every day. There are pub and board games available to play, plus a book exchange scheme. There is also a separate upstairs function room, with a bar for hire. Entertainment includes live music, and the pub is friendly to dogs. (23,25,26)

Stone

Pheasant Inn

Old Road, ST15 8HS SJ901346

12 (3 Mon)-11; 12-midnight Fri & Sat (01785) 814603

Banks's Mild; Marston's Pedigree; Wye Valley HPA; guest beer H

A friendly local town pub that is close to the railway station and the canal, and within easy walking distance of the town centre. It has a quarry-tiled floor, horse brasses on the walls, and a wide range of traditional pub games including darts, cribbage and dominoes. The pub also has its own fishing group.

Poste of Stone

1 Granville Square, ST15 8AB (top of High Street)

9am-midnight (1am Fri & Sat) (01785) 827920

Greene King Ruddles Best Bitter, Abbot; guest beers H

Large, open-plan Wetherspoon pub, formerly a post office. Breakfast and beer are served from 9am daily. Children are welcome in the restaurant until 9pm. With Tuesday grills and Thursday curries complementing a good range of food at all times at competitive prices, it is understandably popular. Lymestone, Titanic, Thornbridge and Slater's ales often feature, alongside occasional Meet the Brewer sessions. The Trent & Mersey canal is a short walk and the bus stops outside. There is a disabled lift to restaurant level. (101,350,490)

Royal Exchange

Radford Street, ST15 8DA (on corner of Northesk St and Radford St)

12-11 (midnight Fri & Sat) (01785) 812685

Everards Tiger; Titanic Steerage H**, Iceberg** H/G**, White Star; guest beers** H

Refurbished in 2008, this Everards and Titanic establishment has four distinct drinking areas. A welcome addition to the town's real ale scene, up to six guest ales, many from micros, and a real cider, complement ales from the Titanic and Everards ranges. Acoustic music features occasionally on a Tuesday night. Basic lunchtime food, locally sourced, is good value. There is also a good selection of single malts. Well-behaved dogs are welcome, and children are allowed until 9pm. ⚜Q🍴◐⇌🚌(101,250)♣🍏⊱

Swan Inn 🍷
18 Stafford Street, ST15 8QW (on A520)
☉ 11-midnight (1am Thu-Sat); 12-11 Sun ☎ (01785) 815570
Coach House John Joule Old Priory; guest beers 🄷
Grade II-listed and renovated in 1999, this thriving free house is one of Stone's premier real ale venues, with over 450 breweries so far represented. A changing range of guest ales from Lymestone, Slater's, Thornbridge, Abbeydale, Townhouse, Sharp's, Blythe and Dark Star are on offer. Tuesday is quiz night, there are four nights of live music, and a free Sunday buffet. The annual beer festival is in the second week of July. Real cider is available. Over-18s only.
⚜❀♿⇌🚌(101)🍏⊱

Summerhill

Boat
Walsall Road, WS14 0BU
☉ 12-3, 6-11; 12-11 Sun ☎ (01543) 361692
🌐 oddfellowsintheboat.com
Beer range varies 🄷
This is a free house for real ale and a heaven for lovers of gourmet food. Relax in the reception area and peruse the extensive chalkboard menu while watching the cooking. There is no processed or pre-cooked food and all ingredients are delivered daily. Excellent chefs prepare delectable dishes that can be accompanied by the ever-surprising range of beers sourced locally and nationally. There is a spacious enclosed garden area next to the large car park. ⚜Q❀◐◑♿P⊱

Tamworth

Globe Inn
Lower Gungate, B79 7AT
☉ 11-11; 12-3, 7-10.30 Sun ☎ (01827) 60455
🌐 theglobetamworth.com
Draught Bass; Holden's Mild; Worthington's Bitter; guest beer 🄷
Comfortable town-centre hotel bar, attracting a clientele of all ages. The three public areas include a raised dining area where inexpensive Sunday lunches are very popular. The changing guest beer sometimes comes from a local micro-brewery. Popular karaoke nights are held on Sunday and Thursday; beware if you want a quiet drink! The pub can get very busy when live sporting events are shown on the two large-screen TVs. A separate function room is available for hire. 🛏◐◑⇌♣

Sir Robert Peel
13-15 Lower Gungate, B79 7BA
☉ 2-11 (midnight Fri); 12-midnight Sat; 12-11.30 Sun
☎ (01827) 300910
Beer range varies 🄷
Although only a pub since the 1970s, this is one of the oldest buildings in the town. Up to four guest beers and a regular real cider, usually Westons, are always available. Guest beers vary, with most from micro-breweries throughout the country. There are also regular appearances of ales from local brewers. Weekends can be very busy; Monday and Wednesday are ideal for a quiet pint. Local CAMRA Pub of the Year 2007 and 2009. ⇌🍏

White Lion
1 Aldergate, B79 7DJ
☉ closed Mon; 12-11 (midnight Fri-Sun) ☎ (01827) 64630
🌐 whiteliontamworth.co.uk
Banks's Bitter; Greene King Abbot; guest beer 🄷
Three real ales are regularly available at this street-corner pub. The guest beer is sometimes sourced from Blythe or Church End. Good home-cooked food is served (no food Sun eve and Mon). Sport is popular here, with live matches often shown on the big screen. The pub has two pool tables, and plays host to both a pool and football team.
❀◐◑🀫♿⇌♣⊱

Trysull

Bell 🍷
Bell Lane, WV5 7JB SO852940
☉ 11.30-3, 5-11.30; 11.30-midnight Fri & Sat; 11.30-11.30 Sun ☎ (01902) 892871
Bathams Best Bitter; Holden's Bitter, Golden Glow, Special; guest beers 🄷
A fine 18th-century building next to the village church, comprising a smallish but cosy bar, pleasant lounge and a large restaurant/dining room. Food is served 12-2pm and 6-9pm; 12-4pm Sun. As well as the Holden's range, Bathams Best Bitter is a regular, together with a guest often sourced from a micro-brewery. A patio area is to the front of the pub. Popular with walkers – the Staffordshire & Worcestershire canal is a 15-minute walk away. Q🍴❀◐◑🀫♿P

Tutbury

Cross Keys
39 Burton Street, DE13 9NR (E side of village) SK215287
☉ closed Mon eve; 10-3, 5.30 (6 Sat)-11; 12-3, 7-10.30 Sun
☎ (01283) 813677
Tetley Draught Burton Ale; guest beer 🄷
Popular privately-owned late 19th-century free house, overlooking the Dove Valley and with a view of Tutbury Castle along Burton Street. The two split-level rooms, public bar and lounge have a homely feel and are served from a similarly split-level bar. There is a separate large function room to the rear. This is one of the few pubs in the area to have remained loyal to Draught Burton Ale since its launch by Ind Coope in Burton in 1976. No lunches Sunday. Q❀◐🀫♿🚌(1,V1)P

Two Gates

Bull's Head
446 Watling Street, B77 1HW (on A51 and B5404 crossroads)
☉ 11-3, 5-11; 12-midnight Fri & Sat; 12-11 Sun
☎ (01827) 287820
Marston's Pedigree; guest beer 🄷
Popular locals' pub situated on the old Roman road of Watling Street. Just a few minutes walk from Wilnecote railway station, it is also served by regular bus services from Tamworth. The two-roomed pub has a split-level lounge leading to the patio and outside smoking area, and a small friendly bar with large-screen TV. It is home to many games and sports clubs, including the long-standing Golf Society. The guest beer comes from the Marston's portfolio.
Q❀◐◑🀫⇌(Wilnecote)🚌(116,767)♣P⊱

Weston

Saracens Head

Stafford Road, ST18 0HT (on A518) SJ971270
✪ 12-3 (not Mon), 5-11; 12-11 Sat; 12-10.30 Sun
☎ (01889) 270286
Greene King IPA; Marston's Pedigree; guest beer Ⓗ
Very friendly family pub situated in a delightful village, it caters for visitors en route to Alton Towers, narrowboats on the nearby Trent & Mersey canal, and the local community. The name of the pub commemorates the grant of a Saracens head crest to local landowner Lord Ferrers during the third crusade. Diners can enjoy views over open countryside in the conservatory. Drinkers can make themselves at home in the public bar, or more comfortable in the lounge.
⛫Q☕❀◑◗⊟♿▲⊟♣P⁄–

Whiston

Swan Inn

ST19 5QH (in Penkridge turn off A449 at George & Fox pub) SJ895144
✪ 12-3 (not Mon), 5-11; 12-11 Sun ☎ (01785) 716200
Holden's Mild, Bitter; Slater's Top Totty; guest beers Ⓗ
Although remotely situated, high quality, well-kept ales and superb food make this a thriving pub. Built in 1593, burnt down and rebuilt in 1711, the oldest part today is the small bar housing an inglenook fireplace. The lounge features an intriguing central double-sided log fire. Six acres of grounds include a children's obstacle course, aviary and rabbits. Food is served 12-2pm and 6-9pm, 12-8.30pm Sunday, and varying seasonal specialities and vegetarian meals are available. ⛫Q☕❀◑◗⊟♿▲⊟♣●P⁄–

Wilnecote

Globe Inn

91 Watling Street, B77 5BA (on B5404 opp Wilnecote Church)
✪ 1-3.30, 7-11 (11.30 Fri & Sat); 12-3, 7-11 Sun
☎ (01827) 280885
Marston's Pedigree Ⓗ
A real community pub, where a warm welcome is guaranteed. A regular Guide entry, the pub is renowned for the quality of its Pedigree. Like a good Pilsener, it takes the landlord around seven minutes to pull – but is well worth the wait. Situated near the M42 junction, the pub is a 15-minute walk from Wilnecote railway station. A regular bus service from Tamworth passes close by. Good natured banter is assured from a long-standing and popular landlord. Q❀⊟(9)♣⁄–

Wolstanton

New Smithy Inn

21 Church Lane, ST5 0EH
✪ 12-11 (10.30 Sun) ☎ (01782) 740467
Greene King Morland Bitter; Hop Back Summer Lightning; Marston's Pedigree; guest beers Ⓗ
This building dates back to the late 1700s and was made a Grade II-listed building when it was threatened with demolition a few years ago; it is now owned by the Hop Back Brewery. There are three regular beers, two guests and two ciders on at any one time. The interior is open-plan, but with the feel of a separate bar and lounge area, as well as a bar where sports can be watched. There is a patio for smokers. ❀⊟♣●P⁄–

Wombourne

New Inn

1 Station Road, WV5 9EY (Station Rd/Ounsdale Rd jct)
✪ 12-11 (11.30 Thu); 12-midnight Fri & Sat
☎ (01902) 892037
Banks's Mild, Bitter Ⓟ**; guest beers** Ⓗ
Large open-plan pub with a strong emphasis on good quality food at reasonable prices. There are separate areas for food (mainly in the lounge) and for drinkers (at the other end of the pub). Both areas are served from a central horseshoe-shaped bar. Banks's beers are on offer plus three changing guests from the Marston's range. There is a large garden at the rear and a patio at the front, which get especially busy in summer. Regular karaoke and quiz nights are hosted. ☕❀◗♿⊟P⁄–

Yoxall

Golden Cup

Main Street, DE13 8NQ (on A515) SK142191
✪ 12-3, 5-midnight; 12-1am Fri & Sat; 12-midnight Sun
☎ (01543) 472295 ⊕ goldencupyoxall.co.uk
Marston's Pedigree; guest beer Ⓗ
Impressive family-run 300-year-old inn at the centre of the village, opposite St Peter's church, bedecked with attractive floral displays for much of the year. The pub features a smart L-shaped lounge with beamed ceiling, primarily catering for diners, and a plainer public bar with Sky Sports TV. Colourful murals with a classical theme enhance both the ladies' and men's toilets. The award-winning pub gardens stretch down to the River Swarbourn and include a camping area (caravans and motor-homes only).
⛫Q❀⇌◑◗⊟♿▲⊟(7)♣P⁄–

Gone for a Burton

Burton upon Trent is almost wholly give up to the manufacture of beer. The place is nothing more than a huge brewery or nest of breweries. Then there is Bass – his extensive beer-mills covering a hundred acres of land, and using two or three hundred quarters of malt every day, requiring the barley grown on sixty thousand acres of good English land, besides the hops grown on two thousand acres – yearly rolls into the groggeries of London and other great towns in England something like a million barrels of beer.

John B Gough, 1880

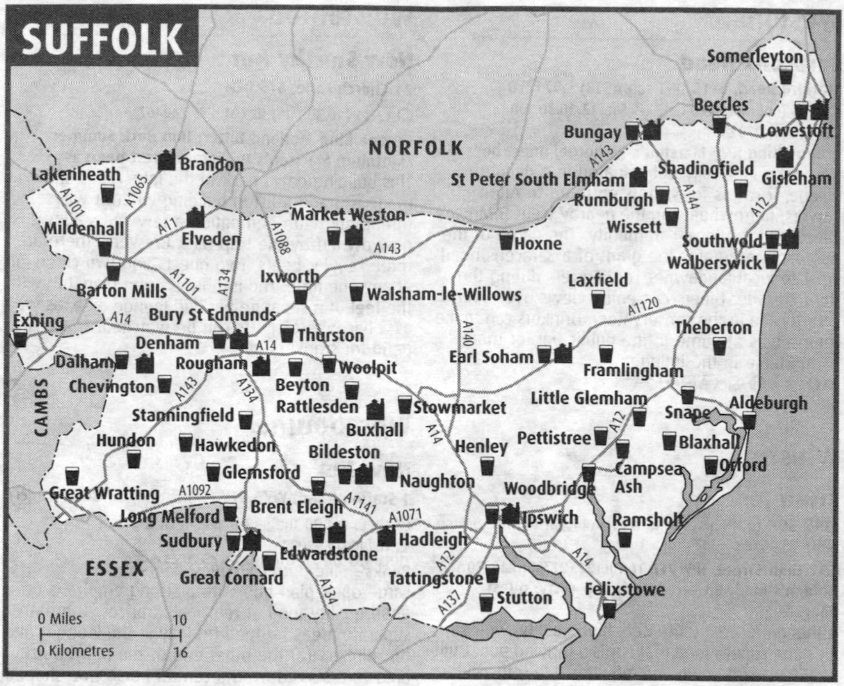

Aldeburgh

Mill Inn

Market Cross Place, IP15 5BJ (opp Moot Hall)

11.30 (11 Sat)-11; 12-10.30 Sun (01728) 452563

themillinnaldeburgh.com

Adnams Bitter, Broadside, seasonal beers

Friendly and comfortable pub close to the town centre and sea front. Two bars are divided by an impressive gas fire. To the rear is a small restaurant area serving good food made from locally-sourced ingredients including fresh fish from the nearby fishermen's huts, lunchtimes and evenings. Themed food nights are popular including Chinese, medieval, Indian, Spanish and more.

White Hart

222 High Street, IP15 5AJ

11-11; 12-10.30 Sun (01728) 453205

Adnams Bitter, Broadside, seasonal beers; guest beers

This traditional drinkers' pub is adjacent to the town's renowned fish and chip shop. It is a popular meeting place for locals and visitors alike in a popular coastal town. The lively single room, decorated with nautical pictures, was formerly a public reading room.

Barton Mills

Olde Bull Inn

The Street, IP28 6AA

11-11 (01638) 711001 bullinn-bartonmills.com

Adnams Bitter, Broadside; Greene King IPA; guest beer

The Olde Bull Inn at Barton Mills is a welcoming, family-owned and managed pub with a log fire in winter and a fantastic courtyard for the summer. It offers a choice of four ales, with guests from local micro-breweries such as Brandon and Humpty Dumpty. Alongside the great beer you can enjoy delicious home-made food served in the bar and the award-winning restaurant.

Beccles

Caxton Club

Gaol Lane, NR34 9SJ

12-1.30, 7-11 (not Wed); closed Tue; 12-2, 6.30-11 Fri; 12-11 Sat; 12-10.30 Sun (01502) 712828

Theakston Black Bull; guest beers

This spacious club is situated close to the town centre. A large central bar area offers up to four real ales, often from micro-brewers. On one side is a TV and darts room, leading to a snooker room. On the other is a large function room. Outside, the garden has a children's play area and hosts

INDEPENDENT BREWERIES

Adnams Southwold
Bartrams Rougham
Brandon Brandon
Cliff Quay Ipswich
Cox & Holbrook Buxhall
Earl Soham Earl Soham
Elveden Elveden
Green Dragon Bungay
Green Jack Lowestoft
Greene King Bury St Edmunds
Hellhound Hadleigh (NEW)
Kings Head Bildeston
Mauldons Sudbury
Mill Green Edwardstone
Old Cannon Bury St Edmunds
Old Chimneys Market Weston
Red Rat Denham
St Jude's Ipswich
St Peter's St Peter South Elmham
Trinity Gisleham (NEW)

barbecues in summer. Show this Guide or a CAMRA membership card to be signed in as a guest. ♘❀♿⇌🚌♣🚬

Beyton

Bear Inn

Tostock Road, IP30 9AG

🕓 12-2, 5-11; 12-4, 7-10.30 Sun ☎ (01359) 270249

Brandon Rusty Bucket; Earl Soham Victoria; Greene King IPA; Woodforde's Wherry ⊞

Rebuilt in 1900 after the original thatched Bear burned down in a July thunderstorm – you can read a full account of this event in the bar. The pub has been run by the same family since 1922. The current landlord has updated the building without spoiling a traditional inn, with two bars and a separate dining room (for residents only at present). There is easy access from the A14 as the building was originally on the main Ipswich to Cambridge road. ♨Q❀🛏⊟▲🚌♣P🚬

Bildeston

Kings Head

132 High Street, IP7 7ED (on B1115 Stowmarket to Hadleigh road)

🕓 closed Mon & Tue; 6-midnight Wed & Thu; 4 (12 summer)-midnight Fri; 12-midnight Sat; 12-10.30 Sun ☎ (01449) 741434 🌐 bildestonkingshead.co.uk

Earl Soham Victoria; Kings Head Landlady, Brettvale Ale; Mill Green Bulls Cross ⊞

The home of the Kings Head Brewery since 1996, this large former coaching inn dating from around 1530 has a single bar and retains exposed carved timbers and an inglenook fireplace. A friendly drinking house atmosphere has evolved, with food available at the weekend only. There is a fully enclosed rear garden with covered patio area, lawns and play equipment. The May bank holiday beer festival is well established. ♨❀◑🍎

Blaxhall

Ship

School Road, IP12 2DY

🕓 12-3, 6-midnight ☎ (01728) 688316

🌐 blaxhallshipinn.co.uk

Adnams Bitter; Taylor Landlord; Woodforde's Wherry; guest beers ⊞

Traditional 16th-century pub on the edge of Suffolk Sandlings with a long reputation for singing in the bar. It has re-established a very good reputation for food, served lunchtimes and evenings. The menu offers a wide choice of options made with locally-sourced ingredients and cooked on the premises. Occasional folk music plays and there are live bands on Friday night. Eight chalets provide B&B accommodation for those with more time to explore the local area. Q♘❀🛏◑▲🚌♣P

Brent Eleigh

Cock Inn ☆

Lavenham Road, CO10 9PB

🕓 12-4, 6-11; 12-11 Fri & Sat; 12-10.30 Sun

☎ (01787) 247371

Adnams Bitter; Greene King Abbot; guest beer ⊞

Shock horror, the Brent Eleigh Cock is now serving food! This gem, listed on CAMRA's National Inventory of Historic Pub Interiors, remains unspoilt. In winter both bars are snug and warm; in summer with the doors open, the bar is at one with its surroundings. The Bitch & Stitch knitting club meets here every Wednesday evening. Walkers and cyclists exploring the Brett Valley and Lavenham will be pleased to hear that Deborah is a great cook and that food, available at all times, is not intrusive. ♨Q❀🛏◑⊟♣🍎P

Bungay

Green Dragon

29 Broad Street, NR35 1EE

🕓 11-3, 5-11; 11-midnight Fri; 12-midnight Sat; 12-3, 7-11 Sun ☎ (01986) 892681

Green Dragon Chaucer Ale, Gold, Bridge Street, seasonal beers ⊞

Bungay's only brew-pub – the home of the Green Dragon Brewery – is a regular entry in the Guide. Ales are brewed in outbuildings next to the car park at the rear of the property and brewery tours are available by appointment. This lively town pub has a separate public bar and a spacious lounge with a small side garden. Bottle-conditioned and seasonal beers are often available. During the summer months more flexible opening hours depend on demand. ♨♘❀⊟▲🚌P

Bury St Edmunds

Dove 🏆

68 Hospital Road, IP33 3JU

🕓 5-11; 12-3, 6-11 Sat; 12-3, 6-10.30 Sun ☎ (01284) 702787

🌐 thedovepub.co.uk

Crouch Vale Brewers Gold; Woodforde's Wherry, seasonal beers; guest beers ⊞

A traditional ale house dating back to 1837, situated just outside the town centre. There are six handpumps with some additional beers served direct from the cellar. The main bar is rustic with scrubbed floorboards, and there is a separate parlour area. No music, TV or gaming machines. The landlord and staff are knowledgable about the beers they sell and offer a warm and friendly welcome. A high percentage of the ales are from East Anglian breweries. Q❀♣P🚬

Old Cannon Brewery

86 Cannon Street, IP33 1JR

🕓 12-3, 5-11; 12-11 Sat & Sun ☎ (01284) 768769

🌐 oldcannonbrewery.co.uk

Adnams Bitter; Old Cannon Best Bitter, Black Pig, Gunner's Daughter; guest beers ⊞

Formerly the St Edmunds Head, this brew-pub is on the site of the original Cannon Brewery. It is regarded as the best place in town for real ale, offering its own beers and a good range of guest and foreign beers. Excellent food focusing on local produce is served most days (not Sun eve or Mon lunch) and comfortable accommodation is available. ♨Q❀🛏◑♿⇌🚌P🚬▯

Rose & Crown ✔

48 Whiting Street, IP33 1NP

🕓 11.30-11 (11.30 Thu & Fri); 11.30-3, 7-11.30 Sat; 7.30-11 Sun ☎ (01284) 755934

Greene King XX Mild, IPA, Abbot; guest beers ⊞

Listed red-brick street-corner pub with two bars and a rare off-sales counter, run by the same family for more than 30 years. Good value lunches are available Monday to Saturday in this homely hostelry. The pub is in sight of Greene King's Westgate Brewery. Q❀◖⊟♣🚬

Campsea Ash

Dog & Duck

Station Road, IP13 0PT
🕒 11-2.30 (closed Wed), 7-11; 12-2.30, 7-10.30 Sun
☎ (01728) 748439
Adnams Bitter; Woodforde's Wherry 🄶
Large, welcoming single bar, divided into two drinking areas by a fireplace, with a separate restaurant. There are high ceilings and lots of interesting pictures throughout. The handpumps are for display only. Traditional, home-cooked, locally-sourced food, with seasonal game and vegetarian options, is served lunchtimes and evenings. Wi-Fi is available in the bar. Popular with cyclists and ramblers, the pub is located close to Wickham Market station and offers accommodation for those wishing to stay a bit longer.
♛⛟❀⇆◑⇌(Wickham Market)♣P

Chevington

Greyhound

2 Chedburgh Road, IP29 5QS
🕒 12-3, 7-11; 7-10.30 Sun ☎ (01284) 850765
Adnams Bitter, Broadside; guest beer 🄷
The Greyhound is in its 22nd year serving excellent authentic Indian cuisine. It also offers an extensive menu for the non curry lover, with home-cooked lunches, evening meals and a Sunday roast, as well as an Indian takeaway. Barbecues and buffets are available by arrangement. Regular guest ales range from old favourites to the more unusual. The traditional bar has a log-burning fireplace. Outside is a garden with swings, slide and climbing frame.
♛Q⛟❀◑⊟♣P⚟

Dalham

Affleck Arms

Brookside, CB8 8TG
🕒 12-2.30 (not Mon), 5-11; 12-11 Sun ☎ (01638) 500306
Adnams Bitter; Greene King IPA 🄷
Situated in the thatched village of Dalham, dating back to the 16th century, this friendly pub offers a cosy restaurant and a sleepy bar with original beams and a prominent inglenook fireplace. It offers two cask ales from local micro-breweries and hosts annual beer fests every June. The home-cooked food is exceptional and very well priced, catering for families and walking parties. Outside is a rear patio and a garden for diners and drinkers overlooking the river. ♛Q❀⇆◑♿⊟♣P⚟

Earl Soham

Victoria

The Street, IP13 7RL (on A1120)
🕒 11.30-3, 6-11; 12-3, 7-11 Sun ☎ (01728) 685758
Earl Soham Victoria, Albert, Brandeston Gold, seasonal beers 🄷
Popular and very traditional Victorian pub with two small bars, with a relaxed, friendly ambience that has changed little over the years. It offers an interesting, ever-changing food menu lunchtimes and evenings alongside locally-brewed beers – the brewery is 150m from the pub. The pub can be busy during weekends and especially on summer days when even a seat in the garden may be difficult to find. A rare gem and a must for visitors to the area who appreciate good pubs – it still has an outside loo, too! ♛Q❀◑⊟P

Edwardstone

White Horse

Mill Green, CO10 5PX TL951426
🕒 12-3 (not winter), 5-11; 12-midnight Fri-Sun
☎ (01787) 211211 🌐 edwardstonewhitehorse.co.uk
Adnams Bitter 🄷**; Crouch Vale Gold** 🄶**; Mill Green Mawkin Mild, Loveleys Fair; guest beer** 🄷
Well off the beaten track, this lovely rural free house has been recently extended and refurbished. An ideal holiday base, it has two self-catering chalets and a windmill supplies power to the pub, chalets and a new green eco-brewery. Delicious home-made food uses locally-sourced and seasonal organic ingredients when available. Beer festivals are held and the pub has a late licence when trade demands. Regular live music plays. Castlings Heath Cottage Ciders are stocked.
♛Q❀⇆◑⛺●P⍌

Exning

White Horse

Church Street, CB8 7EH
🕒 12-11 ☎ (01638) 577323
Wells Bombardier; Woodforde's Wherry 🄷
The Exning White Horse has been run by the same family since 1923 and is mentioned in the Domesday Book. It is a real village pub with a thriving restaurant and public bar. An excellent menu of home-cooked food specialises in seafood, steaks and classic British dishes (booking advisable). Happy hour is 5.30-6.30pm, extended to 7.30pm on Friday. ❀♿⊟♣P⚟

Felixstowe

Half Moon

303 Walton High Street, Walton, IP11 9QL
🕒 12-2.30 (not Mon), 5-11; 12-11 Sat; 12-3, 7-10.30 Sun
☎ (01394) 216009 🌐 felixstowe-halfmoon.co.uk
Adnams Bitter, Broadside, seasonal beers; guest beers 🄷
Traditional two-bar pub away from the drama and bustle found in other parts of this popular seaside town. It has a large, comfortable lounge bar and a small, basic public bar that retains an air of a bygone era with darts, crib and a welcoming fire on winter days. The spacious garden has a new secluded decking area for warmer days. No food is available except pickled eggs. Occasional live music and regular quiz nights are held.
♛Q⛟❀⊟⊟♣P

Framlingham

Station

Station Road, IP13 9EE (on B1116)
🕒 11-2.30, 5-11; 12-2.30, 7-10.30 Sun ☎ (01728) 723455
🌐 thestationhotel.net
Earl Soham Gannet Mild, Victoria, Albert, seasonal beers 🄷
Characterful venue with a wealth of attractions. This former station buffet, built in 1859 – the branch line closed in 1963 – is usually busy with patrons soaking up the atmosphere. The food menu is displayed on chalkboards and beers are dispensed from a set of Edwardian German silver handpumps. A small snug bar leads to an enclosed patio area. A beer festival is held on the last weekend of July. Q⛟❀◑⊟♣P

Glemsford

Angel ✔
Egremont Street, CO10 7SA
⏲ 5-midnight; 12-1am Fri & Sat; 12-midnight Sun
☎ (01787) 281671
Greene King IPA, Abbot [H]
One of the oldest buildings in the village, dating back to the 15th century in parts, the Angel breathes history inside and out. The well maintained exterior is worth more than a second glance before making your way into the cosy two-bar interior. Very much a community hostelry, this is a popular meeting place for local and not so local musicians, with regular open mike nights and tuition available for novices. A friendly welcome is assured – and what a pleasure to sit in a pub with no food smells. A refreshing experience. ♨❀♣⅟

Great Cornard

Five Bells
63 Bures Road, CO10 0HU
⏲ 11-midnight (1am Sat); 11-11.30 Sun ☎ (01787) 379016
🌐 5bells.co.uk
Greene King XX Mild, IPA, Abbot [H]
Friendly community ale house next to Great Cornard church (home of the five bells). The pub fields several teams playing traditional games plus some more unusual ones such as petanque and uckers. The landlord has invested in a large adventure playground that is big enough for adults and was used in the 2008 Pub Olympics. Home-cooked English food now includes the monthly Sunday morning breakfast club fry-up, which is likely to drift into Sunday lunch by all accounts. ♨Q❀◐◑⊟♿⊟♣P⅟

Great Wratting

Red Lion
School Road, CB9 7HA (on B1061 2 miles N of Haverhill)
⏲ 11-2.30, 5-11; 11-1am Fri & Sat; 12-3, 7-10.30 Sun
☎ (01440) 783237
Adnams Bitter, Broadside, seasonal beers; guest beers [H]
Good beer, food and conversation are the mainstays of this traditional village local. Ideal for families in the summer months, it has a huge back garden with plenty to keep children occupied. Take a look at the collection of copper and brass while sampling the Adnams beers or occasional guest. Good food is served in the bar and restaurant. Look out for the whale's jawbone that you pass through as you enter the front door. ♨❀◐◑P⅟

Hawkedon

Queen's Head
Rede Road, IP29 4NN
⏲ 4 (12 Fri-Sun)-11 ☎ (01284) 789218
🌐 hawkedonqueen.co.uk
Adnams Bitter; Woodforde's Wherry; guest beers [H]/[G]
The Queens Head is a 15th-century free house with an unspoilt interior and an enormous open fire in the bar. Voted local CAMRA Pub of the Year for 2007, it holds an excellent beer festival in July. As well as good beers it also serves traditional cider and perry. The food is home cooked and of excellent quality. A warm and friendly welcome is assured at this village pub. ♨Q❀◐◑⛺♣●P⅟

Henley

Cross Keys 🏆 ✔
Main Road, IP6 0QP
⏲ 11-11 (midnight Thu-Sat); 12-10.30 Sun
☎ (01449) 760229 🌐 henleycrosskeys.co.uk
Cliff Quay Bitter; Mauldons Black Adder; Woodforde's Wherry; guest beers [G]
Situated in Suffolk countryside, this building has three bars, two with real fires, plus a large, attractive garden. It is open all day every day, offering traditional food including a popular roast lunch on Sunday and a selection of up to six local ales served directly from the cask. Pub games include pool and darts. Quiz nights, karaoke, folk nights, live music and seasonal beer festivals are hosted. ♨❀◐◑⊟♿⊟♣●P⅟

Hoxne

Swan ✔
Low Street, IP21 5AS
⏲ 12-3, 6-11; 12-10.30 Sun ☎ (01379) 668275
🌐 hoxneswan.co.uk
Adnams Bitter, Broadside [G]**; Woodforde's Wherry; guest beers** [H]
Timber-framed Grade II country pub with plenty of history. Originally built for the Bishop of Norwich (c1480), it was used as a brothel for many years after. Good food made with fresh, seasonal, locally-sourced ingredients is served alongside a selection of real ales on gravity dispense or handpump. It has three main rooms including a front bar with a large fireplace and high beamed ceiling. The spacious garden backs onto the river. A beer festival is held in summer. ♨❀◐◑⊟P⅟

Hundon

Plough Inn
Brockly Green, CO10 8DT (follow brown signs from Hundon village)
⏲ 12-3, 6-11; 12-7 Sun ☎ (01440) 786789
🌐 theploughhundon.co.uk
Beer range varies [H]/[G]
Set high above Hundon with wonderful views, this is a traditional inn with great character. Serving two cask ales in winter and up to four in summer, you are assured of a good range of exceptional beers. The menu provides a choice of delicious home cooked food – eat in the bar or more formal restaurant, or the large garden in summer. Beer festivals are held in April and September with mainly East Anglian ales. ♨❀⊟◐◑♿⊟P⅟

Ipswich

Arboretum
43 High Street, IP1 3QL
⏲ 11 (12 Sun)-11 ☎ (01473) 222177 🌐 the-arboretum.net
Beer range varies [H]
Single-bar pub with a new restaurant and function room upstairs, specialising in good, locally-sourced, freshly-prepared food available lunchtimes and evenings. Food is mainly traditional English with some European influences and modern twists. Beers from local small brewers including Humpty Dumpty and St Peter's are complemented by a selection of local bottled beers. Imported German bottled beers and traditional cider from Thatchers or Cheddar Valley are also stocked. There is a patio garden to the rear. ❀◐◑⇌⊟●⅟

Brewery Tap
Cliff Quay, IP3 0AZ
⏲ 11-3, 6-11; 11-11 Sat; 11-10.30 Sun ☎ (01473) 225501
🌐 thebrewerytap.org
Cliff Quay Bitter, Tolly Roger, seasonal beers Ⓗ
Chef and landlord Mike took over this pub set in the historic brewer's house adjacent to the former Victorian Tolly Cobold brewery in 2009 and has introduced an extensive food menu based on quality, home-produced fare. Themed food nights, home-made pickled eggs, tapas and various bar snacks are prepared in a new kitchen. The bar remains unchanged with wooden floors, fine decor and stunning views of the River Orwell through a massive bay window. Live acoustic music plays fortnightly on Friday evening. A function room is available. ♨Q☺❀◐◑♿🚌(1,6)♣P⍉

Dove Street Inn
St Helens Street, IP4 2LA
⏲ 12-midnight; 12-10.30 Sun ☎ (01473) 211270
🌐 dovestreetinn.co.uk
Adnams Broadside; Crouch Vale Brewers Gold; Hop Back Summer Lightning Ⓗ**; Woodforde's Wherry** Ⓖ**; guest beers** Ⓗ/Ⓖ
This vibrant cask ale house serves more than 20 real ales in oversized glasses, including milds, traditional ciders plus an array of draught continental beers. Three popular beer festivals are held annually with more than 60 cask ales available. Good home-cooked food and bar snacks are on offer at all times. Well-behaved dogs and children are welcome during the day. East Anglian CAMRA Pub of the Year in 2006/07 and former nationwide runner-up. Note that last entry is 10.45pm. Q☺❀◐◑⊟♿🚌♣●⍉⊓

Fat Cat
288 Spring Road, IP4 5NL
⏲ 12-11 (midnight Fri & Sat) ☎ (01473) 726524
🌐 fatcatipswich.co.uk
Crouch Vale Brewers Gold; Fuller's London Pride; Woodforde's Wherry; guest beers Ⓖ
As popular as ever, with up to 14 gravity beers dispensed from a tap room behind the bar. This intimate drinking pub is a joy to visit, with no background music or games machines. Original enamel signs, posters and other artefacts are scattered around the walls. There is a garden and patio for summer evenings. Snacks are available and plates provided for customers to order in takeaways (not Fri or Sat eve). Children and dogs are not permitted. Q❀⇌(Derby Rd)🚌(2,75)♣⍉

Greyhound
9 Henley Road, IP1 3SE
⏲ 11-2.30, 5-11; 11-11 Sat; 12-10.30 Sun ☎ (01473) 252862
Adnams Bitter, Explorer, Broadside, seasonal beers; guest beers Ⓗ
Popular pub just a short walk from the town centre, close to Christchurch Park and the town museum. It has a cosy, small public bar at the front and a larger drinking and dining area to the rear. An outside drinking space is also popular in the summer months. Fresh home-made food from a blackboard menu is served daily. The present landlord has been in the Guide for 12 consecutive years since taking over this pub. ❀◐◑⊟♿⇌🚌♣P⍉

Mannings
8 Cornhill, IP1 1DD (next to town hall)
⏲ 11-8 (11 Thu-Sat); 12-5 Sun ☎ (01473) 254170
Adnams Bitter, Broadside; Fuller's London Pride; Greene King Old Speckled Hen Ⓗ
A gem of a pub providing an oasis of calm in the town centre, especially on Friday and Saturday evenings. The ales are of excellent quality and outdoor tables and chairs in the summer provide an ideal place to sit and watch the world go by. There is also a small enclosed patio at the back. A popular provisions market is held on the Cornhill four days a week. Q❀◐♿⇌🚌⍉

Robert Ransome ✔
Trafalgar House, Tower Street, IP1 3BE
⏲ 9am-midnight (2am Fri & Sat); 11-11 Sun
☎ (01473) 341920
Beer range varies Ⓗ
This large two-storey pub next to the bus station is a Lloyds No 1 Wetherspoon's hostelry. It opened in 2009 to replace a Yates nightclub that was formerly in the building. Two bar serveries offer a wide range of up to seven beers alongside the usual value fare from this popular national pub chain. Occasional live music plays into the late evening at the weekends. ◐◑♿⇌🚌●

Woolpack ✔
1 Tuddenham Road, IP4 2SH
⏲ 11.30-3, 4.30-11; 11-11 Fri, Sat & summer; 11-10.30 Sun
☎ (01473) 253059
Adnams Bitter, Broadside; Black Sheep Best Bitter; St Austell Tribute; Woodforde's Wherry; Young's Bitter Ⓗ
Attractive community local with three bars – a tiny snug, public bar and lounge/diner with a welcoming fire in the winter months. An ever-popular paved garden area to the front includes wooden benches and umbrellas. The extensive menu of home-cooked food is served lunchtimes and evenings (not Sun or Mon eve), with fresh fish and seafood dishes plus more traditional fare. Located close to Christchurch Park, with its famous Tudor mansion. ♨Q☺❀◐◑⊟♣P

Ixworth

Greyhound
High Street, IP31 2HJ
⏲ 11-3, 6-11; 12-3, 7-11 Sun ☎ (01359) 230887
Greene King XX Mild, IPA, Ruddles Best Bitter, Abbot; guest beers Ⓗ
Situated on the town's pretty High Street, this traditional inn has three bars including a lovely central snug. The heart of the building dates back to Tudor times. The pub is a rare outlet for XX Mild. Good value lunches and early evening meals are served in the restaurant. A beer festival is held in November. Dominoes, crib, darts and pool are played in leagues and for charities. ❀◐◑⊟🚌♣P⍉

Lakenheath

Brewer's Tap
54 High Street, IP27 9DS
⏲ 12-midnight; 12-4.30, 7-midnight Sun ☎ (01842) 862328
Beer range varies Ⓗ
A true free house, this village pub is full of character. Bigger than it looks from the outside, there is also a patio area at the back. Three or four handpumps offer local and national beers, and traditional Sunday lunches are popular. Crib, darts and poker are played. A public car park is nearby. Q❀◐🚌♣⍉

Laxfield

King's Head (Low House) ★

Gorams Mill Lane, IP13 8DW (behind churchyard)
12-3, 6-midnight; 11-midnight Fri & Sat summer; 12-4, 7-11 Sun ☎ (01986) 798395 laxfieldkingshead.co.uk
Adnams Bitter, Broadside, seasonal beers G; guest beer H
Known locally as the Low House, this gem dates from the 16th century and has changed little over the years, with a warren of rooms, low ceilings and high-back settles. Beer is served straight from casks in the tap room – there is no bar counter. Home-cooked food is served in a separate dining room. Outside, there is a large seating area and garden to the rear where croquet is played on the lawn. En-suite accommodation is available. The Guildhall and local museum are nearby. Beer festivals are held in May and September. Q P

Little Glemham

Lion Inn

on A12, IP13 0BA
closed Mon; 12-2.30, 6-11; 12-3, 7-10.30 Sun
☎ (01728) 746505 lioninnlittleglemham.co.uk
Adnams Bitter; Woodforde's Wherry; guest beer H
Friendly pub on the main A12 – an ideal stopping off point for visitors to the Suffolk heritage coast. Food is traditional, home cooked and locally sourced, with vegetarian options, a special menu for children and various meal deals. Themed food evenings are always popular, especially 'starters & puddings' and curry nights. Monthly bingo sessions and quiz nights are hosted. Car park and garden are to the rear. Q P

Long Melford

Crown

Hall Street, CO10 1JL
11.30-11; 12-10.30 Sun ☎ (01787) 377666
thecrownhotelmelford.co.uk
Adnams Bitter; Greene King IPA; Nethergate seasonal beers; Taylor Landlord H
In the antiques centre of Long Melford, the Crown is a family-run free house dating back to the 17th century. The last reading of the Riot Act in West Suffolk took place here in 1885. The bar area is set round a central servery, with a choice of seating for diners and drinkers inside or on the patio. Excellent food ranges from traditional favourites to modern cuisine. The 12 en-suite guest rooms vary in style. P

Lowestoft

Mariner's Rest

60-62 Rotterdam Road, NR32 2HA
11-midnight (2am Fri & Sat); 12-11.30 Sun
☎ (01502) 538813
Beer range varies H/G
This pub, formerly known as the Lacon Arms, is now part of the Mariners pub chain and close to the nearby cemetery, hence the name. The comfortable open-plan interior has been refurbished but retains the darts alley. Metal artwork and cast-iron light covers adorn the walls. The garden to the rear has a covered and heated area. Up to six beers are on offer, either hand-pulled or gravity fed from the tap room, plus a cider.

Norman Warrior

Fir Lane, NR32 2RB
11-midnight (12.30am Fri & Sat); 12-10.30 Sun
☎ (01502) 561982 thenormanwarrior.co.uk
Greene King IPA; Marston's Pedigree; guest beers H
Situated between Lowestoft town centre and Oulton Broad, this is a popular community pub. It has a public bar with a pool table and dartboard, and a comfortable lounge leading to a spacious restaurant serving home-cooked food daily, ranging from full meals to bar snacks. Outside there is a large garden and terrace. A beer and cider festival is held over the August bank holiday weekend with live music. Guest beers are usually supplied by local brewers and traditional cider is available. (Oulton Broad North) P

Oak Tavern

Crown Street West, NR32 1SQ
10.30-11; 12-10.30 Sun ☎ (01502) 537246
Adnams Bitter; Greene King Abbot; guest beers H
On the northern side of town, this lively drinkers' pub has an open-plan bar divided into two areas – one festooned with Belgian memorabilia, the other for pool and darts, with a large-screen TV for sporting events. Four real ales are always available, often including dark beers in winter. The bar is renowned for its extensive range of Belgian draught and bottled beers. P

Triangle Tavern

29 St Peters Street, NR32 1QA
11-11 (midnight Thu; 1am Fri & Sat); 12-10.30 Sun
☎ (01502) 582711 thetriangletavern.co.uk
Green Jack Canary, Orange Wheat, Trawler Boys, Mahseer IPA, seasonal beers; guest beers H
This popular town-centre tavern, the brewery tap for Green Jack, is situated close to the Triangle Market Place. It has two contrasting bars – the cosy front bar adorned with many awards for fine ales, and the back bar with pool table, TV and brewery memorabilia, where the younger generation congregates. The full range of Green Jack beers is usually available plus guest ales and cider. Regular beer festivals are held. Local CAMRA Pub of the Year 2009.

Market Weston

Mill Inn

Bury Road, IP22 2PD (on B1111)
12-3 (not Mon), 5-11; 12-3, 7-11 Sun ☎ (01359) 221018
Adnams Bitter; Greene King IPA; Old Chimneys Military Mild, Great Raft; guest beer H
This striking white brick-and-flint faced inn stands at a crossroads and is the closest outlet to the Old Chimneys Brewery, located on the other side of the village. It has been run by the same landlady for more than 12 years. An excellent choice of beers is complemented by a good menu of home-cooked meals (no food Mon eve). Q P

Mildenhall

Queens Arms

42 Queensway, IP28 7JY
12-2.30, 5-11.30; 12-11.30 Fri-Sun ☎ (01638) 713657
Woodforde's Wherry; guest beers H
Comfortable and homely pub, used as a community centre by locals. Extremely popular with real ale drinkers since being taken over by Admiral Taverns, four handpumps are in constant

use. The landlord is very keen on real ale and holds an annual beer festival on the August bank holiday to coincide with a cycle rally in the town. A range of alternating Belgian beers is stocked and real cider is occasionally available. Q❀♣P⅂

Naughton

Wheelhouse

Whatfield Road, IP7 7BS (450m off B1078 close to airbase)

✪ 5-11 (9 Mon; 8 Tue); 6-11 Sat; 12-10.30 Sun

☎ (01449) 740496

Beer range varies Ⓗ

Splendid two-bar rural pub, well worth seeking out. Set in a thatched, timber framed building, the low ceiling in the main bar remains a hazard, despite the tiled floor being much lower than it once was. The more spacious public bar is brighter and leads to a games room with pool table and darts. Outside there is a pleasant garden. An interesting selection of beers is always available. Opening times vary to suit demand. ♨Q❀♿🚌♣P

Orford

Jolly Sailor

Quay Street, IP12 2NU ☎ (01394) 450243

🌐 thejollysailor.net

Adnams Bitter, Broadside, seasonal beers Ⓗ

Formerly six cottages, this late 16th-century building was built mainly from old ship timbers. It is situated close to the modern quay – the historic original quay silted up and is now used as a huge car park. The pub has been extensively but sympathetically refurbished, and the main bar remains largely unaltered. A snug and three other rooms are used as restaurants offering fresh fish dishes and a wide range of local produce. Shove ha'penny, dominoes and boules can be played. A highlight is the traditional sea shanty singing once a month. ♨Q❀🛏◑♿⛺🚌P⅂

Pettistree

Greyhound

The Street, IP13 0HP

✪ 11-2.30 (not Mon), 6-11; 12-3, 7-10.30 Sun

☎ (01728) 746451 🌐 pettistreepub.co.uk

Woodforde's Wherry; guest beers Ⓗ

This historic inn dating from 1349 adjacent to the church has been extensively refurbished but retains several interesting features. Good food and beer are available in two comfortable bars, one used mainly for dining. Various themed food nights and barbecues are held. The garden is very popular on summer evenings and can host car rallies and other events. Folk music plays on the second Monday evening of the month. Note the traditional outdoor toilets. ♨☕❀◑♿🚌P

Ramsholt

Ramsholt Arms

Dock Road, IP12 3AB (signed off B1083)

✪ 11.30-11.20; 11.30-10.30 Sun ☎ (01394) 411229

Adnams Bitter; Greene King H&H Olde Trip, Abbot Ⓗ

Popular riverside pub, especially during the summer and at weekends. It offers excellent views of the River Deben and is an ideal stopping off point for local walkers. Increasingly, the owners are sourcing the ingredients for their excellent food menu and draught beers from local producers. Meals, including various fish and vegetarian options, are served lunchtimes and evenings. Outside, the tranquil garden provides an excellent spot for a relaxed few moments away from the noise of the modern world. The pub is both child and dog friendly. ♨Q☕❀◑🚍♣P

Rattlesden

Five Bells

High Street, IP30 0RA

✪ 12-12.30am (11.30 Sun) ☎ (01449) 737373

Beer range varies Ⓗ

Set beside the church on the high road through the picturesque village, this is a good old Suffolk drinking house – few of its kind still survive. Three well chosen ales on the bar are usually sourced direct from the breweries. The cosy single room has a games room on a lower level. Occasional live music plays. ♨Q❀●

Rumburgh

Buck

Mill Road, IP19 0NS

✪ 11.45-3, 6.30-11; 12-3, 7-10.30 Sun ☎ (01986) 785257

Adnams Bitter, seasonal beers; guest beers Ⓗ

Full of character and charm, this splendid pub was originally a guest house for a medieval priory. It has a long narrow front bar with a games room extension. The back rooms are used as dining areas where you can enjoy good food made with local ingredients. The original bar is timber framed with a flagstone floor. Outside there is a small enclosed garden. Quiz nights and sporting events are held regularly. ❀◑🚍⛺🚌♣P

Shadingfield

Fox

London Road, NR34 8DD (on A145)

✪ 12-3, 6-11.30; 12-5 Sun ☎ (01502) 575100

🌐 shadingfieldfox.co.uk

Adnams Bitter; guest beers Ⓗ

Situated in a tiny village on edge of Sotterley Park, the Fox straddles the boundary of two parishes – Shadingfield and Willingham St Mary. This 16th-century inn has undergone refurbishment but the original arched doors and carved fox heads on beams have been retained. The interior comprises a bar, lounge/dining area and conservatory. Outside, a patio and small garden are popular in summer months. Beer festivals are held twice yearly. Good food made with locally-sourced produce is prepared on the premises (booking advisable). ♨Q☕❀◑P⅂

Snape

Golden Key

Priory Lane, IP17 1SA

✪ 12-3.30, 6 (7 Sun)-11 ☎ (01728) 688510

🌐 snape-golden-key.co.uk

Adnams Bitter, Broadside, seasonal beer Ⓗ

Popular with ramblers in summer, this pub is just off the main road and offers a refuge from the modern world. The drinking area has a tiled floor, large open fireplace, low-backed settle and a tiny 'grotto' for the locals. Elsewhere, the spacious building is mainly used for dining, with two restaurant areas, one more secluded with a low-beamed ceiling. Locally-sourced, well-cooked food is prepared on the premises. There is a large car park to the rear. ♨☋❀◑P⚑

Somerleyton

Duke's Head

Slugs Lane, NR32 5QX
⏲ 11-11; 12-10.30 Sun ☎ (01502) 730281
🌐 somerleyton.co.uk/dukeshead
Adnams Bitter; Woodforde's Wherry; guest beers Ⓗ
Situated in a picturesque village, the Duke's Head overlooks marshes near the River Waveney and attracts river users, railway travellers and ramblers visiting the Angles Way. The interior includes a public bar, lounge and restaurant. Guest beers are often from local micros. Barbecues, an outside bar and musical events take place in the large garden. A converted barn in the grounds is used by local musicians once a month. ♨❀◑⊟▲⇌▣P

Southwold

Lord Nelson ✔

42 East Street, IP18 6EJ
⏲ 10.30-11; 12-10.30 Sun ☎ (01502) 722079
Adnams Bitter, Explorer, Broadside, seasonal beers Ⓗ
This pub is popular with locals and holidaymakers alike, situated next to the Sailors' Reading Room and just a stone's throw from the sea. It offers three drinking areas – the main bar has a flagstone floor and open fire in winter, and there is a side room where children and dogs are welcome. Outside is a partly covered and heated patio area. As to be expected, much naval memorabilia adorns the walls throughout. ♨☋❀◑▲▣⚑

Stanningfield

Red House

Bury Road, IP29 4RR
⏲ 12-3 (not Wed), 5-11.30; 12-11.30 Sat & Sun
☎ (01284) 828330 🌐 theredhouse.zoomshare.com
Greene King XX Mild, IPA; guest beers Ⓗ
Built in 1866 in Victorian red brick, the building was originally a cobbler's workshop, but licensed in 1900 and now a free house. It was named after the red tunics of the Suffolk Regiment. Neat and clean inside and out, this single-bar local has a relaxed and comfortable atmosphere. Live music plays monthly and pub games and sports are well supported. Food is served daily, lunchtimes and evenings (not Sun eve). The pub is soon to offer accommodation. ♨❀⊨◑♿▣♣P⚑

Stowmarket

King's Arms

Station Road, IP14 1RQ
⏲ 11-11 ☎ (07570) 097739
Fuller's London Pride; Taylor Landlord; Woodforde's Wherry Ⓗ**; guest beers** Ⓗ/Ⓖ
Closed for 51 years, this excellent and much-needed addition to the town finally reopened in 2009. A back to basics pub, it is deceptive in size and gets very busy in the evenings. Always friendly and welcoming, it is an ideal stop off if travelling by train, and just a short walk from the town centre. Dogs are welcome during non-busy periods. The popular Museum of East Anglian Life is nearby, which holds its own beer festival in early July. ☋❀◑♿⇌▣(87B,88)♣P⚑

Royal William

53 Union Street, IP14 1HP (off Stowupland St)
⏲ 11-11; 12-10.30 Sun ☎ (01449) 674553
Beer range varies Ⓖ
Tucked away down a side street and just a short walk from the station and town centre, this is a gem of a pub. An end of terrace back-street boozer, it is well supported by locals and visitors alike. Regular team games are played and sports shown on TV. Ales are served from a small cellar behind the bar by gravity dispense. ❀⇌▣♣⚑

Stutton

Gardeners Arms

Manningtree Road, IP9 2TG
⏲ 12-3, 6-11; 12-10 Sun ☎ (01473) 328868
Adnams Bitter; guest beers Ⓗ
A traditional village roadside inn with a small pretty restaurant and a larger main bar leading to an ornamental garden. Ideal as a base for walkers exploring the River Stour area, it offers excellent food and ale. Children and dogs are welcome. The pub displays a large collection of knick-knacks to keep visitors interested. Enjoy the atmosphere on the popular jazz night held on the second Tuesday of the month. ♨Q☋❀◑♿▲▣P⚑

Sudbury

Brewery Tap

21 East Street, CO10 2TP (200m from Market Place)
⏲ 11-11 (midnight Fri & Sat); 12-10.30 Sun
☎ (01787) 370876 🌐 blackaddertap.co.uk
Mauldons Mole Trap, Silver Adder, Suffolk Pride Ⓗ
Mauldons Brewery's first pub, after many years of searching. Formerly the Black Horse, this street corner local has been transformed. Up to six Mauldons beers are available here, four or more on gravity dispense, as well as guest beers. Soups and snacks are served and takeaway meals can be ordered in. Live music plays including jazz on the first Sunday of the month. Q❀⇌▣♣⚑▽

Tattingstone

White Horse

White Horse Hill, IP9 2NU
⏲ 12-3, 6-11; 12-11 Fri & Sat; 12-10.30 Sun
☎ (01473) 328060 🌐 whitehorsetattingstone.co.uk
Crouch Vale Brewers Gold; Woodforde's Wherry; guest beers Ⓗ
Located just north of Alton Water Reservoir, this 17th-century Grade II-listed inn remains relatively untouched. The heavily-beamed main bar with log-burning stove hosts folk nights and other events. Excellent home-cooked food available lunchtimes and evenings (not Sun eve) includes gluten-free options. Curry night on the last Thursday of the month is always popular. Beers include a changing mild. Dog and biker friendly, there is a caravan and camp site at the rear. ♨Q☋❀◑▲▣♣P

Theberton

Lion

Main Road, IP16 4RU
⏲ 12-3, 6-11; 12-3, 7-10.30 Sun ☎ (01728) 830185
🌐 thebertonlion.com
Adnams Bitter; Woodforde's Wherry; guest beers Ⓗ

Friendly pub with a comfortable large main bar area divided into two seating areas by a central fireplace. Another seating area mainly used for dining has been recently refurbished. Food is served lunchtimes and evenings. Outside there is a beer garden and two log cabins available to let. The pub hosts a weekly quiz night and live music once a month. Crib, dominoes and shove ha'penny are played.

Thurston

Fox & Hounds ✔

Barton Road, IP31 3QT

12-2.30, 5-11; 12-midnight Fri & Sat; 12-10.30 Sun

(01359) 232228 web thurstonfoxandhounds.co.uk

Adnams Bitter; Greene King IPA; guest beers [H]

Dating from 1800, this listed building is now a regular entry in the Guide. A busy village local, it offers a good selection of ever-changing real ales on handpump, served by the ever-cheerful landlord and staff. Good home-cooked food is available. The public bar has a pool table, darts and Sky TV while the lounge is quieter and more comfortable. Local CAMRA Pub of Year 2007, 2008 & 2009.

Walberswick

Anchor

Main Street, IP18 6UA

11-4, 6-11; 11-11 Sat; 12-11 Sun (01502) 722112

web anchoratwalberswick.com

Adnams Bitter, Broadside, seasonal beers [H]

Situated in a picturesque coastal village, the Anchor has a main bar, a cosy snug and a spacious restaurant committed to serving seasonal local produce. Various events are catered for including beer festivals and seminars in a converted barn that has its own cinema screen. Family, walker and dog friendly, the pub is accessible from Southwold via footbridge or ferry. Accommodation is available in the main building or chalets in a large garden.

Walsham-le-Willows

Blue Boar

The Street, IP31 3AA (next to church)

12-2.30, 5-midnight; 12-1am Fri & Sat; 12-11.30 Sun

(01359) 258533

Adnams Bitter [H]; Woodforde's Wherry; guest beers [H]/[G]

An ale house most of time since 1420, this true free house offers a fine selection of beers on handpump and gravity and is a supporter of local breweries. Regular themed food nights and live music evenings are hosted. A May bank holiday beer festival is held in a marquee in the garden.

Wissett

Plough

The Street, IP19 0JE

10.30-12.30am; 11.30-11.30 Sun (01986) 872201

Adnams Bitter; guest beers [H]

Popular local at the heart of village life supporting charities and fundraising events. Inside there is a central bar area with wooden flooring and original beams, and a cosy snug known as the 'potting shed'. The pub's owners have also opened a village shop in a converted outbuilding. A well-supported annual beer and cider festival is held in July with live music and barbecue. Camping is available in the large garden.

Woodbridge

Cherry Tree Inn

73 Cumberland Street, IP12 4AG

7.30am-11; 9am-11 Sat & Sun (01394) 384627

web thecherrytreepub.co.uk

Adnams Bitter, Explorer, Broadside, seasonal beers; Taylor Mild; guest beers [H]

Spacious open-plan bar with a large central counter that helps to create several distinct seating areas. The long-standing landlord has a very good reputation for keeping quality real ale. Eight beers are usually on offer and two beer festivals are held. Traditional food is served all day. Family games are available to play. Accommodation is offered in a converted barn beside the pretty garden and car park. Child, wheelchair and dog friendly.

Old Mariner ✔

26 New Street, IP12 1DX

11-3.30, 5 (6 Sat)-11; 12-10.30 Sun (01394) 382679

Adnams Bitter; Fuller's London Pride; Shepherd Neame Spitfire; Young's Bitter [H]

Cosy intimate two-bar pub with a small restaurant area to the rear. The decor is simple and traditional throughout, with quarry-tiled floors and scrubbed wooden tables. The large TV is well used on rugby days, when the locals gather in the lively front bar. Food is popular, with casseroles, stews and roasts all freshly prepared on the premises (booking recommended for Sun lunch). There is a smoking area and garden outside.

Sekforde Tap

76 Seckford Street, IP12 4LZ

12-2, 5.30-11; 12-2.30, 6-11 Sat; 12-2.30, 7-10.30 Sun

(01394) 384446 web thesekfordetap.com

Earl Soham Victoria; Greene King IPA; guest beers [H]

Cosy and well-furnished multi-roomed pub away from the busy town centre, offering an interesting and changing selection of up to nine beers. The front bar is accessed via a few steps up from the roadside patio. The back bar leads to a series of secluded rooms including a restaurant, and also to a hidden garden. Food options include tapas and Sunday roast, and takeaways by arrangement. A good place to get to know the locals, especially at the weekend.

Woolpit

Bull

The Street, IP30 9SA

11-3, 6-11 (midnight Fri); 12-4, 6-midnight Sat; 12-4, 7-10.30 Sun (01359) 240393 web bullinnwoolpit.co.uk

Adnams Bitter; guest beers [H]

Large family-run inn on the old Ipswich to Cambridge road through the village. Visitors can choose between the community-minded front bar, hosting various charity events throughout the year, games room, comfortable conservatory and a spacious restaurant to the rear. Wholesome, home-cooked food is served (not Sun). A garden with children's play area leads off the car park beside the pub.

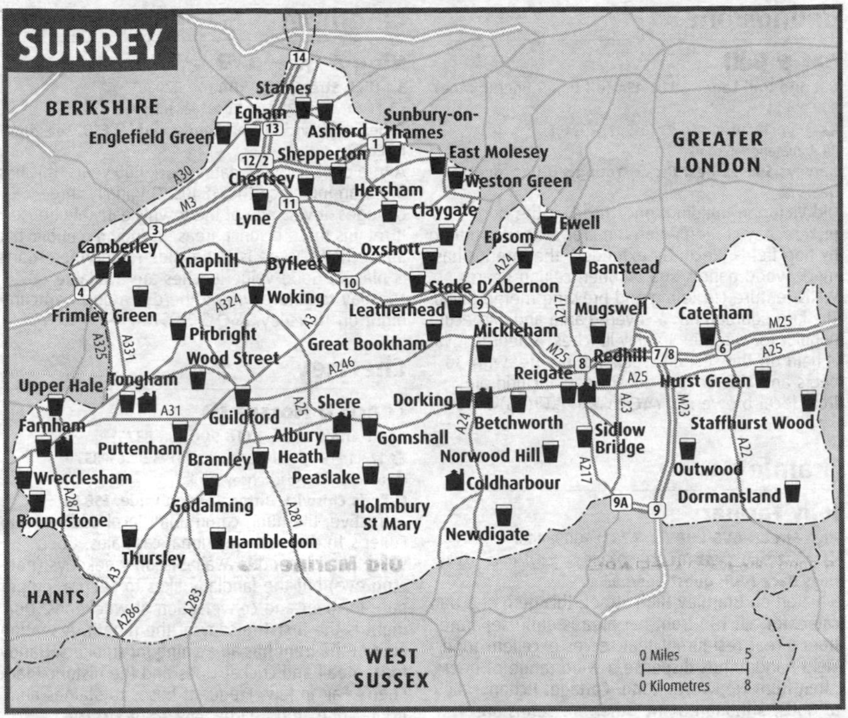

Albury Heath

William IV

Little London, GU5 9DG TQ066467
11-3, 5.30-11; 12-3, 7-10.30 Sun ☎ (01483) 202685
williamivalbury.com
Flowers IPA; Hogs Back TEA; Surrey Hills Ranmore Ale, Shere Drop Ⓗ
A magnificent wood-burning fire warms the cosy main bar of this secluded and unspoilt 16th-century country pub with flagstone floor and wood beams. Meals served in the restaurant include Gloucestershire Old Spot pork from the pigs kept in the field behind the pub (no food Sun eve). Westons Bounds real cider is sold on the fifth handpump. In summer the tables in the front garden are well used. ♨Q✿◑▶♣P⊢

Ashford

Kings Fairway ✔

91 Fordbridge Road, TW15 2SS (on B377)
11.30-11 (midnight Fri & Sat) ☎ (01784) 423575
Adnams Broadside; Fuller's London Pride; Young's Bitter; guest beers Ⓗ
This comfortable Ember Inns pub offers relaxed seating partitioned into a number of areas on two levels. The friendly staff keep six beers including three constantly-changing guests from around the UK. Food is served daily until 9pm, with grill night Tuesday and curry night Thursday. Quiz nights are Wednesday and Sunday. Real ale, world lager and wine festivals feature throughout the year.
✿◑♿🚌(290)P⊢

Banstead

Woolpack ✔

186 High Street, SM7 2NZ (on B2217)
11-11; 12-10.30 Sun ☎ (01737) 354560
thewoolpackbanstead.co.uk
Shepherd Neame Master Brew Bitter, Spitfire, seasonal beer; guest beers Ⓗ
Well-run pub offering excellent beer and food. Although now owned by Shepherd Neame, two ever changing guest beers are sold, often from local breweries. The single room interior is divided up into smaller areas. Home-made food is served all day, with all ingredients sourced locally, always featuring a number of specials. A beer festival is held over the August bank holiday. Live jazz on the first Tuesday afternoon of the month. ✿◑▶♿🚌P⊢

Betchworth

Red Lion

Old Road, RH3 7DS (off A25) TQ214504
11-11.30 (midnight Fri & Sat); 11-11 Sun
☎ (01737) 843336 redlionbetchworth.co.uk
Fuller's London Pride; guest beers Ⓗ
Backing on to a local cricket club ground, this pub dates back to the early 18th century, with parts of the main building built around 1730. The wisteria at the rear is said to be 230 years old. Excellent home-cooked meals are served in the large bar and six en-suite rooms are available for bed and breakfast. The guest beers often come from Adnams or Sharp's. ♨Q✿🛏◑▶🚌(32)P

Boundstone

Bat & Ball

Bat and Ball Lane, GU10 4SA (off Upper Bourne Lane) SU833444
✪ 11-11; 12-10.30 Sun ☎ (01252) 792108
🌐 thebatandball.co.uk
Harveys Sussex Best Bitter; Young's Bitter; guest beers ⊞
Old Victorian building, once used as the hop pickers' pay station when the area was surrounded by hop fields. Recently extended, the interior has mock wood panels and wooden ceiling beams. Walls feature cricketing and brewing memorabilia. The large garden has a covered area and barbecue, popular for summer Sunday lunches. A beer festival is held on the second weekend in June, with 30 beers and ciders. Four guest beers include ales from local breweries. ♨Q❀◑◐♿🚌(16)♣●P⊬

Bramley

Jolly Farmer

High Street, GU5 0HB (on A281) TQ008448
✪ 11 (12 Sun)-11 ☎ (01483) 893355 🌐 jollyfarmer.co.uk
Hogs Back HBB; guest beers ⊞
Situated on Bramley High Street, this gem of a pub caters for all. The front bar area is quite separate from a rear restaurant that serves excellent food. Eight handpumps dispense a wide range of beers, often from Hepworth, King, Cottage, Itchen Valley or Goffs, although many other breweries are represented. A large fish tank sits in the bar area among much rural and brewery related memorabilia adorning the walls. Quiz night is Sunday. Q❀🛏◑◐🚌(53,63)♣P⊬

Byfleet

Plough ✔

104 High Road, KT14 7QT (off A245) TQ064611
✪ 11 (12 Sat)-3, 5-11; 12-10.30 Sun ☎ (01932) 354895
Fuller's London Pride; guest beers ⊞
Long-term Guide entry with eight ever-changing guests, many from local micros – none of which lasts very long as the numerous pump clips behind the bar testify. The L-shaped bar has two roaring fires, exposed brickwork, solid furniture and a variety of agricultural artefacts. The emphasis here is on conversation – mobile phones are banned. Children are allowed in the conservatory. Don't ignore the garden. No lunches Saturday and alternate Sundays. ♨Q❀◑🚌P

Camberley

Claude du Vall ✔

77-81 High Street, GU15 3RB SU875606
✪ 9-midnight ☎ (01276) 672910
Greene King Ruddles Best Bitter, Abbot; guest beers ⊞
Originally high street shops, this 2002 Wetherspoon's has a long bar and modern decor. 'The Claude' has become a popular meeting place for a wide variety of people – helped by its location within 100 metres of the station and bus stops. It offers the usual competitively-priced range of food and drinks, including five real ales, one usually a LocAle. TV screens play with the sound off. Quiz night is Monday. ❀◑◐♿⇌🚌●⊬

Caterham

King & Queen ✔

34 High Street, CR3 5UA (on B2030)
✪ 11-11; 12-10.30 Sun ☎ (01883) 345438
Fuller's Chiswick Bitter, London Pride, ESB, seasonal beers ⊞
A true drinkers' pub, dating back 400 years, this has been an inn since the 1840s. Originally three cottages, it was one of the town's early ale houses. It retains three distinct areas, including a public bar at the front. There is also a side room where darts is played. Good value lunches are available Tuesday to Saturday, and there is a quiz and curry night on Thursday. ♨Q❀◑⊟🚌♣P⊬

Chertsey

Coach & Horses ✔

14 St Ann's Road, KT16 9DG (on B375)
✪ 12-11; 12-3, 7-10.30 Sun ☎ (01932) 563085
🌐 coachandhorseschertsey.co.uk
Fuller's Chiswick Bitter, London Pride, ESB ⊞
Attractive, tile-hung community local dedicated to Fuller's three main traditional cask ales. Good-value English food is available on weekdays (not Mon eve) but the landlady likes to keep a 'proper pub' for beer and conversation at weekends. Quiz night is the first Thursday of the month. A seating area at the front has an awning for smokers. Handy for football and cricket clubs and the historic Black Cherry Fair in July. Frequent buses to Staines and Addlestone stop nearby. ♨❀🛏◑◐🚌♣P⊬

Claygate

Swan

2 Hare Lane, KT10 9BS TQ147640
✪ 12-11 (11.30 Fri & Sat) ☎ (01372) 462582
Fuller's London Pride; guest beers ⊞
A former Isleworth Brewery pub, rebuilt in 1905, this is an open plan, light and airy free house. The old cricket green opposite is used as an overspill drinking area, especially during the August bank holiday beer festival. Up to three guest ales come from local and nationwide breweries. English and Thai food is available, and a takeaway service is offered. At the side is a fenced garden, and tables overlook the green. Accommodation is in six en-suite rooms. ♨❀🛏◑◐♿⇌🚌(K3)P⊬

Dorking

Cricketers ✔

81 South Street, RH4 2JU (on A25 one-way system westbound)
✪ 12-11 (midnight Thu & Sat; 1am Fri) ☎ (01306) 889938
Fuller's Chiswick Bitter, London Pride, ESB; guest beer ⊞
Family-run pub with a Georgian walled patio garden that has a large umbrella heated for smokers when it is cold. Hot and cold sandwiches

INDEPENDENT BREWERIES

Ascot Camberley
Dorking Dorking
Farnham Farnham
Hogs Back Tongham
Leith Hill Coldharbour
Pilgrim Reigate
Surrey Hills Shere

and a choice of main meals are available weekday lunchtimes. Children are welcome until early evening. As well as the regular beers there is often a fourth which may be a Fuller's seasonal beer or a guest, usually from an independent brewery. Beer festivals are held three times a year and monthly music nights are hosted. ✿◐♣⊱

Dormansland

Old House at Home

63 West Street, RH7 6QP TQ402422

✪ 11.30-3.30, 6-midnight; 12-4, 7-midnight Sun

☎ (01342) 832117

Shepherd Neame Master Brew Bitter Ⓗ, Kent's Best Ⓖ, Spitfire Ⓗ, seasonal beers Ⓖ

Traditional and friendly Victorian village pub on the western side of the village. Although hidden away, it is signposted from surrounding roads. There is a separate dining area and a public bar with a dartboard off the main bar. The pub is renowned for its excellent home-cooked food served in the bar and restaurant (not Sun eve). There is a patio for outdoor drinking. A quiet pub with occasional live music. ⋒Q✿◑⊟⊟(409)P⊱

Plough

44 Plough Road, RH7 6PS (just off B2028) TQ406427

✪ 12-11 (midnight Fri & Sat; closed 3-5 Mon)

☎ (01342) 832933 ⊕ ploughdormansland.com

Fuller's London Pride; Harveys Sussex Best Bitter Ⓗ; guest beers Ⓗ/Ⓖ

Traditional 18th-century pub with wood beams and an inglenook log fire. One side is run as a genuine Thai restaurant but traditional pub fare is also available at lunchtime. The large garden is popular and barbecues are held as well as the occasional beer festival. Conveniently situated near to Lingfield racecourse. There is a covered smoking area. ⋒Q✿◑⊟(236,409)P⊱

East Molesey

Europa

171 Walton Road, KT8 0DX (on B369)

✪ 11-11 (midnight Fri & Sat); 12-11 Sun ☎ (020) 8979 5183

Caledonian Deuchars IPA; Courage Best Bitter; Fuller's London Pride; Greene King Abbot; Harveys Sussex Best Bitter; Young's Bitter Ⓗ

Friendly local pub retaining three bars – public, cabin and saloon – as well as a children's play area and large garden. The public bar has a TV, dartboard and pool table, while the saloon has a comfortable feel with its stained glass signs and skylights. The cabin bar features photographic memories of Hurst Park racecourse, which closed in 1962. Sunday is jazz night, and a quiz is hosted once a week. ✿◐⊟♿⊟(411,514)♣P⊱

Egham

Compasses

158 Thorpe Lea Road, Pooley Green, TW20 8HA (on B376)

✪ 12 (3 Mon)-11; 12-10.30 Sun ☎ (01784) 454354

⊕ compassespub.com

Rebellion IPA; guest beers Ⓗ

Thanks to a keen licensee, this 102-year-old free house has gradually been returned to its former glory with a restored log fire and the introduction of micro-brewed ales. It was built in 1909 by Hodgson's Kingston Brewery – a fact that is still celebrated with a wonderful pediment above the entrance featuring the old brewery logo. Inside, it has three rooms including a rear sports bar for darts, pool and TV sports events. Heated umbrellas outside for smokers. ⋒✿◐♿⊟(71,441)♣P⊱

United Services Club

111 Spring Rise, TW20 9PE

✪ 12-11 (midnight Fri & Sat) ☎ (01784) 435120

⊕ eusc.co.uk

Rebellion IPA; guest beers Ⓗ

Friendly LocAle-accredited club that proudly promotes real ale. The five handpumps offer an ever-changing range of unusual ales, often including stouts and milds, from independent and micro-breweries. Real cider, usually Mr Whiteheads, is from a separate stillage. The social calendar includes music nights, snooker and darts leagues plus seasonal beer festivals. Sunday roasts are gut-busters. There is satellite TV and free Wi-Fi. Show a copy of this Guide or CAMRA membership card for entry. ✿◐♿⇌⊟♣●P⊱

Englefield Green

Happy Man

12 Harvest Road, TW20 0QS (off A30)

✪ 12-11.30 (midnight Fri & Sat); 12-10.30 Sun

☎ (01784) 433265

Hop Back Summer Lightning; guest beers Ⓗ

Originally two Victorian cottages, the building was converted to a pub to serve the workers building Royal Holloway College, and is now a popular student haunt. The internal layout has barely changed since, with separate rooms either side of the bar and a back room for darts. Shut the box is played. Four handpumps dispense a changing range of guest ales from micro-breweries. Beers on gravity from the cellar are sometimes also on offer, and up to three real ciders. The rear smokers' refuge is heated. ✿◑⊟⊟♣●

Epsom

Assembly Rooms ✔

147-153 High Street, KT19 8EH (on A24 northbound)

✪ 9-midnight (1am Fri & Sat) ☎ (01372) 737290

Greene King Ruddles Best Bitter, Abbot; guest beers Ⓗ

The building dates from the late 17th-century when Epsom was a leading health spa. It was previously a draper's shop, then a building society, and converted to a pub by Wetherspoon in 2002. As well as supporting JDW's national beer festivals, the pub often showcases local micro breweries. The pub is handy for the market. Children are welcome until 8pm. Q☋◑♿⇌⊟●

Jolly Coopers

84 Wheelers Lane, KT18 7SD TQ197605

✪ 12-11 (midnight Fri & Sat); 12-10.30 Sun

☎ (01372) 723722 ⊕ jollycoopersepsom.co.uk

Beer range varies Ⓗ

This traditional pub is more than 200 years old, situated in the middle of a residential area, just over half a mile west of the town centre. It has a quiet lounge bar and a sports bar where pool and darts are played. There is also a snug area. Dogs are welcome. There are three changing beers in the range, often from local micros. ⋒Q✿◐⊟⊟(E9)P⊱

Ewell

Wheatsheaf

34 Kingston Road, KT17 2AA (off A240)
⌚ 11-11; 12-10.30 Sun ☎ (020) 8393 2879
Wells Bombardier; Young's Bitter; guest beer Ⓗ
This cosy local, built in 1858, stands across the road from the Hogsmill River. Original leaded Isleworth Brewery windows can be seen behind the bar. The adjoining Longhurst Lounge is accessed through an arch and from the lounge there is a connection to the nearby undertakers. Photographs of old Ewell decorate the walls. Live music plays on Saturday evenings. Food is served 11-2pm weekdays. ❀◐≷(West)🚌♣⌐

Farnham

Hop Blossom ✔

50 Long Garden Walk, GU9 7HX (off Castle St) SU839469
⌚ 12-3, 5-11; 12-midnight Fri & Sat; 12-10.30 Sun
☎ (01252) 710770
Fuller's Chiswick Bitter, Discovery, London Pride, ESB, seasonal beers; guest beer Ⓗ
Friendly pub in the town centre tucked down a quiet back street. The interior comprises an L-shaped bar and three drinking areas – the cosy main bar with a fire in winter (chestnuts and crumpets provided), a good-sized room for meetings at the back and a conservatory in between. The walls are decorated with an eclectic collection of mementos and artefacts. All Fuller's beers make an appearance at some time during the year. ♨Q♉◐≷🚌

Lamb

43 Abbey Street, GU9 7RJ (off A287) SU842466
⌚ 11-2.30, 5-11; 11-11 Sat; 12-10.30 Sun ☎ (01252) 714133
Shepherd Neame Kent's Best Ⓗ**, Spitfire** Ⓖ**, seasonal beers** Ⓗ/Ⓖ
Long-term Guide entry just off the town centre on the way to the railway station. The single L-shaped bar is normally quiet and relaxed, but gets noisier on match days when games are screened on TVs, and on Fridays when live music is hosted. To the rear is a covered area for smokers and access to an elevated garden via a metal staircase. Food is excellent (not available Tue eve or all day Sun). ♨Q◐≷🚌⌐

Shepherd & Flock ✔

22 Moor Park Lane, GU9 9JB (centre of roundabout at A325/A31 jct E of town) SU854474
⌚ 12-11 (10.30 Sun) ☎ (01252) 716675
🌐 shepherdandflock.co.uk
Hogs Back TEA; Theakston Old Peculier; Triple fff Alton's Pride; guest beers Ⓗ
The 'great little pub on the great big roundabout' is hard to miss at the east end of town. An array of handpumps dispenses a varying selection of beers, and a cider from Thatchers or Westons is added in summer. Excellent home-cooked food is served in a separate dining area (no food Sun eve). The front garden is an interesting place to contemplate the frenetic activity of modern motoring, whereas the back garden offers peace and quiet with a heated area for smokers. ♨❀◐🚌(14,X65)P⌐

Frimley Green

Rose & Thistle ✔

1 Sturt Road, GU16 6HT (on B3411) SU888566
⌚ 12-midnight (1am Fri & Sat) ☎ (01252) 834942
🌐 theroseandthistlefrimleygreen.co.uk
Beer range varies Ⓗ
Taken over by new management with a genuine interest in cask ale a couple of years ago, this pub made its first entry into the Guide in 2010, and continues to offer outstanding ales. It has recently also gained Cask Marque accreditation. The pub offers three or four changing beers, and draught Westons cider. A good range of food is available, served in the conservatory, the bar and the beer garden. ❀◐♿🚌♣🍎P⌐

Godalming

Jack Phillips ✔

48-56 High Street, GU7 1DY SU971438
⌚ 9-11 (midnight Thu; 1am Fri & Sat) ☎ (01483) 521750
Greene King Ruddles Best Bitter, Abbot; Hogs Back TEA; guest beers Ⓗ
A long, narrow pub, stretching back from the High Street, featuring a modern decor with a hint of Art Deco. A lower area beyond the bar is favoured by families, with children welcome until 9.30pm. Guest beers are chosen from the Wetherspoon list and from many local breweries. Q♉❀◐♿≷🚌🍎

Star

17 Church Street, GU7 1EL SU968438
⌚ 11-11 (midnight Thu; 1am Fri & Sat); 12-10.30 Sun
☎ (01483) 417717 🌐 thestargodalming.co.uk
Greene King St Edmunds, H&H Olde Trip Ⓗ**; guest beers** Ⓗ/Ⓖ
Friendly pub in a 17th-century, oak-beamed building, attracting drinkers of all ages. Up to eight ales are offered – beers from the Greene King range sit alongside genuine guests – as well as real ciders. Themed beer festivals at Easter and Halloween focus on ales from one area of the country. Regular live music nights are hosted, and there's a quiz on Sunday. Evening meals are served Thursday to Saturday only. ❀◐≷🚌♣🍎⌐

Gomshall

Compasses

50 Station Road, GU5 9LA (on A25)
⌚ 11-11; 12-10.30 Sun ☎ (01483) 202506
🌐 thecompassesinn.co.uk
Surrey Hills Ranmore Ale, Shere Drop, seasonal beers Ⓗ
Standing in the centre of the village and next to the River Tillingbourne, this pub has a large bar leading through to a larger dining room (no meals Sunday eve). The traditional bar features exposed wooden beams and pillars, and is adorned with a display of old-fashioned farming implements. There are two en-suite rooms for bed and breakfast. Live music plays every Friday and a music festival is held in August (see website for details). ❀🛏◐≷🚌P⌐

Great Bookham

Anchor ✔

161 Lower Road, KT23 4AH (off A246 via Eastwick Road)
⌚ 11-11; 12-10.30 Sun ☎ (01372) 452429
Courage Best Bitter, Directors; Fuller's London Pride; Harveys Sussex Best Bitter; Surrey Hills Shere Drop Ⓗ
This Grade II-listed inn dates from the 15th century. Low beamed ceilings, wooden floors, exposed brickwork and an inglenook with a real fire burning

in winter give the pub a traditional feel. Live music features occasionally and a quiz is hosted on Tuesday. The pub is also home to a golf society. Lunchtime meals are available Monday to Saturday. The pub is LocAle accredited, serving Surrey Hills beer. ⚐Q❀◐🚌(479)♣P⚟

Royal Oak 🏆

16 High Street, KT23 4AG (off A246) TQ144552
⏲ 11-11; 12-10.30 Sun ☎ (01372) 452533
Caledonian Deuchars IPA; Courage Best Bitter; guest beers Ⓗ
Welcoming village pub dating from 1450, with a separate public bar with dartboard and TV. The parlour features original beams, a flagstone floor and an inglenook fireplace, and hosts folk singers every Saturday. Guest beers are selected from the Heineken list and local breweries. Three beer festivals are held during the year. Sunday is poker night, and a quiz is held on Monday. Carvery meals are served all day in the dining room (no food Sun eve). Local CAMRA Pub of the Year 2009 and 2010. ⚐Q❀◐◑⊟♿🚌(479)♣P⚟

Guildford

Bench

Surrey Sports Park, University of Surrey, Richard Meyjes Road, GU2 7AD (off A3 near hospital) SU975498
⏲ 11-11 (7 Sat); 12-10.30 Sun ☎ (01483) 689111
Beer range varies Ⓗ
This university sports bar has recently moved within the new Surrey Sports Park, but the same team still offers an excellent range of up to six ever-changing ales. Enter via the reception and head to the first floor of the complex where you will find a large modern bar and an outside decked area, where you can watch various sports. Changing Hogs Back and Andwell beers are always on offer and other local breweries are well supported. Food is available at all times. ❀◐◑♿🚌P

Keystone

3 Portsmouth Road, GU2 4BL (on A3100) SU993493
⏲ 12-11 (midnight Fri & Sat); 12-5 Sun ☎ (01483) 575089
🌐 thekeystone.co.uk
Black Sheep Best Bitter; Wadworth 6X; guest beers Ⓗ
A modern and comfortable over-21s town-centre pub with sofas, wooden floors and large tables for groups. It hosts many events during the year including barbecues, morris dancing and hog roasts (check the website for details). Excellent freshly-made food is served with themed evenings always popular (no food Fri-Sun eve). The rear patio is heated and lit, with giant umbrellas for smokers. Live music plays weekly. ❀◐◑⇌🚌⚟

Rowbarge ✔

7 Riverside, GU1 1LW (off A320 via Stoughton Rd) SU997511
⏲ 12-midnight (11 Sun) ☎ (01483) 573358
Andwell King John; Ascot On The Rails, Posh Pooch Ⓗ**; guest beer** Ⓖ
Following years of neglect, this pub was revived late in 2008 by a new landlord. Unofficially the brewery tap for Ascot Ales, guest beers come from local micros. Situated on the River Wey, the pub is a pleasant stroll from the town centre along the towpath. Overnight moorings are available to customers. A beer festival is held on the late May bank holiday. Frequent live music includes regular Friday and Saturday night bands. Food is served until 7pm, 5pm on Sunday. ❀◐◑⊟🚌♣P⚟

Hambledon

Merry Harriers

Hambledon Road, GU8 4DR SU968392
⏲ 11.30-3 (not Mon), 5.15-10.30 (11 Thu & Sat; midnight Fri); 11-8 Sun ☎ (01428) 682883 🌐 merryharriers.com
Hop Back Crop Circle; Surrey Hills Shere Drop; Triple fff Alton's Pride; guest beers Ⓗ
Sixteenth century pub off the beaten track and recently updated but retaining three separate bar areas, a large open fire, panelled walls and a wooden floor. Five beers are available with two guests from local breweries. Good, traditional food is made with locally-sourced ingredients. The pub hosts many events including quizzes, live music and films. Winter opening hours may vary. Opposite the pub is its large car park, campsite and the Surrey Hill Llama Centre. ⚐❀◐◑⛺♣P⚟

Hersham

Royal George

130 Hersham Road, KT12 5QJ (off A244)
⏲ 11-11 (midnight Fri & Sat); 12-11 Sun ☎ (01932) 220910
Young's Bitter, Special Ⓗ
Built in 1964, the Royal George is a popular local two bar pub and a regular entry in the Guide. It is named after a ship of the line dating back to the Napoleonic wars, and there is a plan of one of the ships displayed on the wall. Excellent Thai food is served in the evenings, traditional English pub food at lunchtime. There is a garden at the rear with a covered awning for smokers. Local CAMRA Pub of the Year 2007. ⚐❀◐◑⊟♿🚌(218)♣P⚟

Holmbury St Mary

King's Head

Pitland Street, RH5 6NP (off B2126) TQ112442
⏲ 12 (4 Mon)-11; 12-10.30 Sun ☎ (01306) 730282
Dark Star Hophead; King Horsham Best Bitter; Pilgrim Surrey; Surrey Hills Shere Drop Ⓗ
This wonderful unspoilt pub proudly serves locally sourced beers and food. It's popular with ramblers and mountain bikers exploring the lovely Surrey Hills countryside. Excellent food is served in the restaurant including daily specials and a changing fish menu in the evening (no food Sun eve or Mon). The wooden-floored bar has a bar billiards table, real fire and interesting old shooting photos on the walls. Beer festivals are held on the spring and August bank holidays. ⚐Q❀◐◑🚌(21)♣P

Hurst Green

Diamond

Holland Road, Holland, RH8 9BQ TQ407503
⏲ 12-11; 12-10.30 Sun ☎ (01883) 716040
Fuller's London Pride; Harveys Sussex Best Bitter; Young's Bitter; guest beer Ⓗ
Now making a third consecutive appearance in the Guide, this dog-friendly community pub on the southern edge of Hurst Green has gained many new customers due to its reputation for fine ale and good value dining (no food Sun eve). The interior has several different drinking areas, with a large collection of clocks on display throughout. Note Morag who keeps a watchful eye on the bar from above the fireplace. CAMRA members receive a discount on real ales. ⚐❀◐◑🚌(410)♣P⚟

Knaphill

Garibaldi ✔

134 High Street, GU21 2QH SU960585
✪ 12-11 (midnight Fri & Sat); 12-10.30 Sun
☎ (01483) 473374 🌐 thegaribaldi-knaphill.co.uk
Greene King IPA; guest beers Ⓗ
Cosy two-room pub with one bar, situated on the crossroads with Chobham Road on the west side of Knaphill. One or two guest beers are on offer alongside the IPA, and occasional real cider. Food is available every day until 9.30pm, and children are welcome. There is a family area at the back of pub. Curry night is Tuesday from 6pm. Sunday is quiz night. Sports are screened on TV. Outside there is a covered patio and garden. ❀◑P⁄

Leatherhead

Edmund Tylney ✔

30-34 High Street, KT22 8AW
✪ 9-midnight (1am Fri & Sat) ☎ (01372) 362715
Greene King Ruddles Best Bitter, Abbot; guest beers Ⓗ
This small Wetherspoon pub is named after a Leatherhead resident who was Master of Revels to Queen Elizabeth I and censor of Shakespeare's plays. The Elizabethan theme is evident in the artwork around the upper gallery. The one room bar has a more secluded raised area to the right. LocAle accredited, expect to find guest beers from Dorking, Hogs Back, Pilgrim and other local breweries. Westons ciders are served from a fridge. Food is available until 10pm. Q◑♿⇌🚌●

Lyne

Royal Marine

Lyne Lane, KT16 0AN (off B386) TQ012663
✪ 12-2.30, 5.30-11; 12-2.30, 6.30-11.30 Sat; 12-3 Sun
☎ (01932) 873900 🌐 royalmarinelyne.co.uk
Sharp's Doom Bar; guest beers Ⓗ
The pub started life as two cottages over 160 years ago and has much Marines paraphernalia on display. It offers three guest beers, often from micro-breweries. The food is home cooked and of generous proportions. A bookcase displays Dickens and Enid Blyton classics. Outside, the peaceful garden backs on to the village green, where cricket matches can be enjoyed during the summer. Note that the pub closes some winter Saturday evenings – ring first to check. ⛫Q❀◑🚌(P3)♣P⁄

Mickleham

King William IV

Byttom Hill, RH5 6EL (off A24 southbound) TQ174538
✪ 11-3, 6.30-11; 12-4.30 Sun ☎ (01372) 372590
🌐 king-williamiv.com
Hogs Back TEA; Surrey Hills Shere Drop; Triple fff Alton's Pride; guest beer Ⓗ
Friendly rural 18th-century free house clinging to a hillside overlooking the Mole Valley. It has two separate rooms, both with real fires. An extensive home-cooked menu offers traditional pub food plus more exotic dishes and vegetarian options. The patio and terraced garden are extremly popular on sunny days, and barbecues are hosted. Opening hours are extended in summer months. Steep steps make access for the infirm difficult. The shared car park is on the A24. ⛫Q❀◑🚌(465)⁄

Mugswell

Well House Inn ✔

Chipstead Lane, CR5 3SQ (off A217) TQ259552
✪ 12-11.30 (10.30 Sun) ☎ (01737) 830640
🌐 wellhouseinn.co.uk
Adnams Bitter; Fuller's London Pride; Surrey Hills Shere Drop; guest beers Ⓗ
Grade II-listed, 16th-century pub with two drinking areas, a conservatory and a restaurant serving generous portions of good food made with local ingredients (not Sun or Mon eve). The main bar displays an excellent collection of pewter and ceramic tankards. The Domesday Book mentions the well outside – known as Mags Well, hence the area name – its water level is still monitored by the Environment Agency. Harry the monk's ghost is a pub regular. ⛫Q❀◑⊟●P⁄

Newdigate

Surrey Oaks 🏆

Parkgate Road, RH5 5DZ (on road to Leigh from Newdigate) TQ205436
✪ 11.30-2.30 (3 Sat), 5.30 (6 Sat)-11; 12-10.30 (8 Nov-Feb) Sun ☎ (01306) 631200 🌐 surreyoaks.co.uk
Harveys Sussex Best Bitter; Surrey Hills Ranmore Ale; guest beers Ⓗ
A strong supporter of micro-breweries from near and far, the Soaks has been a deserving winner of local CAMRA Pub of the Year for the last eight years. There are several drinking areas, including the 16th-century bar featuring low beams, flagstones and an inglenook. Good home-made food is served in the restaurant and bar (not Sun or Mon eve). Outside is a lovely garden with two boules pitches. Beer festivals are held on the late spring and August bank holidays. Third-of-a-pint glasses are available. ⛫Q❀◑♣●P

Norwood Hill

Fox Revived

RH6 0ET TQ240435
✪ 11-11.30 (10 Sun) ☎ (01293) 862312
🌐 thefoxrevived.co.uk
Dark Star Hophead; guest beers Ⓗ
Within easy reach of Gatwick Airport, this is a smart country inn offering good food and beer. Meals are all home made and of a very high standard, served lunchtimes and evenings, all day at the weekend. However this is still very much a pub, with LocAle beers to the fore. The interior mixes modern and traditional features, and there is a conservatory plus a large garden. ❀◑P

Outwood

Bell

Outwood Lane, RH1 5PN TQ328457
✪ 12-11 (10.30 Sun) ☎ (01342) 842989
Fuller's London Pride, ESB, seasonal beers Ⓗ
Dating from 1635, the Bell was previously a coaching stop. The quarter-ton bell from which the pub takes its name is by the front door. The emphasis here is on food, especially fresh fish, with a separate restaurant area, but drinkers and dogs are welcome in the comfortable bar with its large inglenook. Outside is an umbrella with heaters for smokers. If the pub is busy it may stay open slightly later, or occasionally may shut earlier on a Sunday if quiet. ⛫❀◑P⁄

ENGLAND

Oxshott

Bear

Leatherhead Road, KT22 0JE (on A244)
⏲ 12-11 (10.30 Sun) ☎ (01372) 842747
🌐 thebearoxshott.co.uk
Young's Bitter, Special, seasonal beers 🄷
This refurbished Young's pub dates from before 1816. The central bar is surrounded by several distinct areas and there is a restaurant to the rear. Two spare handpumps may feature either Wells beers or Young's seasonals. There is a decked area at the front, part covered and heated for smokers, and a garden at the rear with a barbecue. Tea and coffee are served from 10am and food is served lunchtimes and evenings, all day on Sunday. Tuesday is quiz night. 🜂❀◐♿🚌(408)P⊬

Peaslake

Hurtwood Inn

Walking Bottom, GU5 9RR TQ086446
⏲ 12-11 (midnight Fri; 10.30 Sun) ☎ (01306) 730851
🌐 hurtwoodinnhotel.com
Hogs Back TEA; Surrey Hills Shere Drop; guest beers 🄷
The bar at this three star hotel is open to both locals and residents. It has a bright contemporary design with a new inglenook fireplace. A wide range of bar snacks is served to complement the real ales from micro-breweries, mostly qualifying as LocAle beers. Peaslake is in the heart of Surrey Hills walking country, at the centre of the 3,000-acre Hurtwood, making it a popular lunch stop for ramblers. 🜂❀🛏◐🚌(25)P

Pirbright

Cricketers Inn ✔

The Green, GU24 0JT (off A324) SU947559
⏲ 12-2.30, 6-11; 12-11 Sat; 12-10.30 Sun ☎ (01483) 473198
Fuller's London Pride; Surrey Hills Shere Drop; guest beer 🄷
Set overlooking the large triangular village green with pond and cricket pitch, the Cricketers attracts both locals and those enjoying the countryside between Woking and Guildford. A narrow area in front of the bar is set with small tables, while a more open area to the side has sofas and high tables for larger groups. No food is served on Sunday evening. 🜂❀◐🚌(28,91)P

Puttenham

Good Intent

The Street, GU3 1AR (off B3000) SU931478
⏲ 12-3, 6-11; 12-11.30 Sat; 12-10.30 Sun ☎ (01483) 810387
🌐 thegoodintentpub.co.uk
Harveys Sussex Best Bitter; Ringwood Best Bitter; Taylor Landlord; guest beers 🄷
Welcoming 16th-century former coaching inn situated on the North Downs and Pilgrims Way and National Cycle Route 22. Popular with walkers and cyclists, families and dogs are welcome. The last field still growing hops in Surrey is situated in the village – the hops are used in Harveys Best. Guest beers from local breweries regularly feature and an annual beer festival is held over the late May bank holiday weekend. No food Sunday and Monday evenings. 🜂Q❀◐⛺♣●P⊬

Redhill

Garland ✔

5 Brighton Road, RH1 6PP (on A23)
⏲ 11.30-11.30 (12.30 Fri; midnight Sat); 12-11.30 Sun
☎ (01737) 760377
Harveys Sussex XX Mild, Hadlow Bitter, Sussex Best Bitter, Armada Ale, seasonal beers 🄷
This classic Victorian street-corner local is one of the older buildings in Redhill. Although just off the town centre, it has the atmosphere of a country pub, and is home to a number of darts and quiz teams. Eight handpumps supply the full range of Harveys beers, including all seasonal and one-off brews. A side room is available for private use and well-behaved children are welcome until 7.30pm. Lunchtime meals during the week offer good value. ❀◐⇌🚌♣P⊬

Home Cottage

3 Redstone Hill, RH1 4AW (on A25)
⏲ 11-11.30; 12-10.30 Sun ☎ (01737) 762771
St Austell Tribute; Young's Bitter, Special, seasonal beers 🄷
Just off the town centre, this large mid 19th-century community pub has three distinct drinking areas. The front bar has a relaxing atmosphere warmed by a real fire and displays an interesting old bank of five handpumps. Children are welcome in the back conservatory. A separate room is the venue for comedy on the last Friday of the month. Good food is available lunchtimes and evenings (until 8pm Sun). Live music plays every other Saturday. 🜂☕❀◐⇌🚌♣P⊬

Reigate

Yew Tree

99 Reigate Hill, RH2 9PJ (on A217)
⏲ 12-11 (10 Sun) ☎ (01737) 244944
Beer range varies 🄷
A pub site for 300 years, the current building dates back to 1938 and has a mock-Tudor exterior and wood-panelled walls. Good-quality locally-sourced food is available all day from a changing menu. The single bar serves two distinct areas – one mainly for drinkers and one for diners – separated by a large chimney breast with a real fire. Two guest beers vary, one is often from a micro-brewery. 🜂❀◐🚌(420,460)P

Shepperton

Barley Mow 🏆

67 Watersplash Road, TW17 0EE (off B376)
⏲ 12-11 (10.30 Sun) ☎ (01932) 225326
Hogs Back TEA; Hop Back Summer Lightning; guest beers 🄷
Perennial Guide entry and extremely welcoming dog-friendly local. Five handpumps often offer unusual micro-brewery beers complemented by real cider from Mr Whiteheads. Bar billiards is played. A popular music venue, it hosts jazz on Wednesday evening (the only time food is served), and rock and blues on Friday and Saturday evenings. A traditional pub quiz is held on Thursday night. Local CAMRA Pub of the Year 2007, 2009 and 2010. ❀🚌♣●P⊬

Sidlow Bridge

Three Horseshoes

Ironsbottom, RH2 8PT (off A217) TQ252461
⚙ 12-11 (7 Sun) ☎ (01293) 862315 🌐 sidlow.com
Fuller's London Pride, ESB; Harveys Sussex Best Bitter; Young's Bitter; guest beers 🄷
The Shoes is a very fine old-fashioned country pub, with parts of the building dating back 300 years. It was once home to a forge, hence the name. Up to four guest beers are available, including local ales, and a beer festival is held on the first May bank holiday. Very good food, with daily specials, is available lunchtimes and evenings, with barbecues held in the large garden. Q❀◐⊟(324)♣P

Staffhurst Wood

Royal Oak ✔

Caterfield Lane, RH8 0RR TQ407485
⚙ 11-11 (closed 3-5 Mon & Tue winter); 12-10.30 Sun
☎ (01883) 722207
Adnams Bitter; Harveys Sussex Best Bitter; Larkins Traditional; Westerham Staffhurst Ale 🄷**; guest beers** 🄷/🄶
This hidden away rural free house is run by an enthusiastic landlord, with guest beers usually coming from local micro-brewers. A range of interesting bottled beers is also stocked, plus real ciders and perry. Excellent quality meals made from locally-sourced ingredients are available in the bar and restaurant (not Sun eve). The pub enjoys superb views across the countryside. CAMRA members receive a discount on real ales and bar meals. A dog-friendly pub. ♨Q❀◐●P⅟

Staines

Bells

124 Church Street, TW18 4YA (off B376)
⚙ 12-3, 5-11; 12-midnight Fri & Sat; 12-11 Sun
☎ (01784) 454240 🌐 thebellspub.co.uk
Wells Bombardier; Young's Bitter, Special, seasonal beers 🄷
Traditional 18th-century English pub in a quiet location opposite St Mary's Church and close to the Thames but within easy walking distance of the town centre. This community pub with friendly bar staff serves impressive beers and food, with fish dishes a speciality. The pleasant rear patio garden has a large heated smoker's canopy and is especially popular in summer, attracting local workers and shoppers. Q❀◐♿⊟⅟

George ✔

2-8 High Street, TW18 4EE (on A308)
⚙ 9-midnight (1am Fri & Sat) ☎ (01784) 462181
Courage Directors; Greene King Abbot; Marston's Pedigree; guest beers 🄷
Ever popular large two-storey Wetherspoon pub built in the 1990s. The large downstairs bar with its mixture of tables and intimate booths is always busy but a quieter bar can be reached via a spiral staircase. Up to six guest ales, often from local breweries such as Twickenham and Loddon, are dispensed from one bank of handpumps, with the national brands and up to two real ciders from Westons on the rear bank. ◐♿⇌⊟●⅟

Swan Hotel ✔

The Hythe, TW18 3JB (off A308/A320 roundabout)
⚙ 12-11.30 (midnight Fri & Sat) ☎ (01784) 452494
Fuller's Discovery, London Pride, ESB, seasonal beers 🄷
This 18th-century flagship Fuller's hotel is on a site that has been home to a 'Swan' since at least the 15th century. It is well-named with the long riverside terrace overlooking a stretch of the Thames where numerous swans congregate. The hotel has has had a number of refurbishments and enlargements over the years. It has its own moorings and in centuries past bargemen would tie up here to exchange part of their wages in tokens for food and drink. ♨❀⊨◐♿⊟⅟

Stoke D'Abernon

Old Plough ✔

2 Station Road, KT11 3BN (off A245)
⚙ 11-11; 12-10.30 Sun ☎ (01932) 862364
🌐 theoldplough.net
Courage Best Bitter; guest beers 🄷
Large pub offering four ever-changing guest beers, with a strong emphasis on local and seasonal ales. There are several distinct areas inside and a spacious garden to the rear. An extensive food menu is available lunchtimes and evenings (not Sun eve). Regular quiz and poker nights are held and there are occasional beer tastings. Families and dogs on leads are welcome. The pub is popular with commuters. ♨❀◐♿⇌⊟(408)♣P⅟

Sunbury-on-Thames

Grey Horse

63 Staines Road East, TW16 5AA (on A308)
⚙ 11-11; 12-10.30 Sun ☎ (01932) 782981
Fuller's London Pride; Twickenham Original; guest beer 🄷
This friendly, comfortably furnished little community pub started life as a beer house in the 1840s. Situated between Sunbury Station and Kempton Park racecourse, it has a surprisingly rural feel. The regularly-changing guest beer is often from Twickenham Ales. Live sports are shown on TV. The large beer garden has a covered heated smoking area. There are rumours of resident ghosts, including a woman who burned to death. No evening meals Friday-Sunday. ♨❀◐⇌⊟⅟

Thursley

Three Horseshoes

Dye House Road, GU8 6QD (off A3) SU904397
⚙ 12-3, 5.30-11; 12-11 Sat; 12-10.30 Sun ☎ (01252) 703268
🌐 3hs.co.uk
Hogs Back TEA; Surrey Hills Shere Drop; guest beers 🄷
Saved from closure and bought out by local supporters in 2004, the pub is now a thriving concern. The friendly and welcoming traditional inn boasts roaring log fires and a two-acre garden popular with families. The excellent guest ale range includes beers from local breweries, and quality home-cooked food is served. The Devil's Punch Bowl and Thursley Nature Reserve are within walking distance. ♨Q❀◐♿●P⅟

Tongham

Hogs Back Brewery Shop

Manor Farm Business Centre, The Street, GU10 1DE (off A31) SU886485
⚙ 9-6 (8.30 Wed-Fri); 10-4.30 Sun ☎ (01252) 784495
🌐 hogsback.co.uk/breweryshop.htm

Hogs Back HBB, TEA, Hop Garden Gold, seasonal beers [G]
Situated in a barn partially overlooking the brewery, the shop sells the full range of Hogs Back draught beers. It also stocks a large selection of bottled beers from Britain and all over the world and a good choice of country wines, plus some excellent Hogs Back souvenir merchandise. Cider from Westons or Mr Whiteheads is also available. Show your CAMRA membership card to receive a 5% discount on all shop products. 🚌🍎P

White Hart ✓

76 The Street, GU10 1DH (off A31) SU886489
🕘 12-11 (midnight Fri & Sat); 12-10.30 Sun
☎ (01252) 782419 🌐 whiteharttongham.co.uk
Beer range varies [H]
Set in the centre of the village, the pub offers a warm welcome to drinkers, with at least four real ales and one cider on offer – check the blackboard before ordering in case there are more beers in the bar next door. Meals are served lunchtimes and evenings (not Sun eve), and snacks at most other times. Two beer festivals are hosted in March and September. Children are welcome until 9pm, and dogs on leads. Live bands play and there is a quiz every other Tuesday. ♨❀◐🍽🚌(3,20)♣🍎P⊱

Upper Hale

Alfred Free House

9 Bishops Road, GU9 0JA (off A3016) SU837490
🕘 hours vary ☎ (01252) 820385
Beer range varies [H]
This establishment was known as the King Alfred in previous editions of the Guide. A new name and a new look bring it back into the Guide once more. It's a classic pub serving traditional food and ales. Phone ahead for opening times as they vary depending on the landlord's inclination.
♨❀◐🚌⊱

Weston Green

Marney's Village Inn

Alma Road, KT10 8JN (off A309)
🕘 11-11; 12-10.30 Sun ☎ (020) 8398 4444
Courage Best Bitter; Fuller's London Pride; Twickenham Original [H]
This 10th century hunting lodge became a public house in the mid-1800s and was originally called the Alma Arms. The current name comes from the family that owned a wood yard next door. The pub is tucked away from the main road near a pond and church. It has a small, cosy, traditional bar with a wood floor, low ceiling and just two tables. A raised area, used mostly for dining, leads out to the garden. ❀◖⇌(Esher)🚌(515)P

Woking

Herbert George Wells 🏆

51-57 Chertsey Road, GU21 5AJ TQ008589
🕘 9-midnight (1am Fri & Sat); 9-12 Sun ☎ (01483) 722818
Courage Best Bitter, Directors; Greene King Abbot; Hogs Back TEA; guest beers [H]
Long-established Wetherspoon outlet serving an ever-changing range of guest beers. There is something for everyone here – office workers and shoppers during the day and a wide range of drinkers young and old in the evening. Named after HG Wells who lived locally and wrote War of the Worlds, artefacts on display include a magnificent invisible man bandaged in tin. Close to both bus and rail stations, this a comfortable alternative to a waiting room. Local CAMRA Pub of the Year 2010. Q❀◐♿⇌🚌🍎⊱

Sovereigns ✓

Guildford Road, GU22 7QQ (on A320) TQ004584
🕘 12-11 (midnight Fri & Sat) ☎ (01483) 751426
Adnams Broadside; Caledonian Deuchars IPA; Ringwood Best Bitter, Fortyniner; guest beers [H]
A large and welcoming Ember Inns pub on the south west side of the town with a commitment to real ale evident from the eight handpumps on the bar. The beer choices are made from a national list, and real cider is often available in the summer months. Food is served daily until 9pm. A quiz is held every Monday and Wednesday. There is a quiet area for relaxed drinking and outside is a sheltered and heated seating area. A former local CAMRA Pub of the Year. ♨Q❀◐♿⇌🚌P⊱

Woking Railway & Athletic Club

Goldsworth Road, GU21 6JT TQ003585
🕘 10.30-11; 12-10.30 Sun ☎ (01483) 598499
Beer range varies [H]
Friendly and resourceful working men's club with more than 200 beers sold during the year, including ales from micro-breweries such as Andwell and Bowman. A meeting place for organisations such as the Gurkhas, Royal Naval Association, trade unions and Woking Beer Festival, the club is generally quiet and relaxed, although it can be noisy when sports fixtures are screened on TV. Children are welcome and there is disabled access at the side. For entry show a CAMRA membership card or copy of this Guide. Local CAMRA Club of the Year 2010. ♿⇌🚌♣⊱

Wood Street

Royal Oak

89 Oak Hill, GU3 3DA SU958510
🕘 11-3, 5-11; 12-3.30 Sun ☎ (01483) 235137
Courage Best Bitter; Surrey Hills Shere Drop; guest beers [H]
An excellent and genuine free house with a range of guest beers that always includes some surprises, including an ever-changing mild. Many well-deserved CAMRA awards are displayed beside the bar – look for the pump clips above the bar for the beers coming next. Lunches are highly recommended (not served Sun), with plenty of vegetables but no chips. Children will enjoy the large garden. Q❀◖🚌(17)♣🍎P

Wrecclesham

Sandrock

Sandrock Hill Road, GU10 4NS (off B3384) SU830444
🕘 12-11 (10.30 Sun) ☎ (01252) 715865 🌐 thesandrock.com
Beer range varies [H]
Set in leafy suburbia but only a stone's throw from the forest and commons south of Farnham, the Sandrock is proudly a community pub. Firmly beer led, local breweries are always well represented among its eight real ales. The furniture in the bars helps create a contemporary feel. Children are allowed in the side bar which leads to the garden. The food is winning local and national awards and themed nights are proving popular (no food Sun eve). ♨Q❀◐🚌(16)P

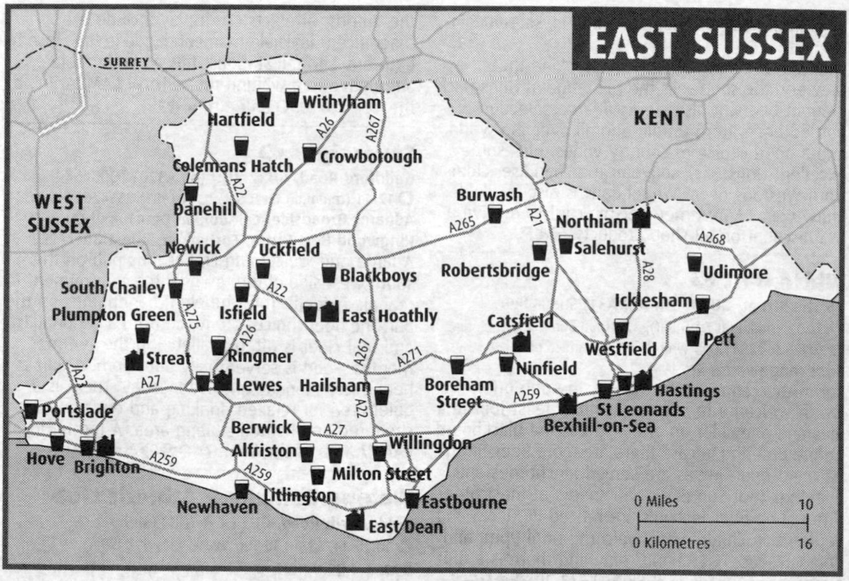

SUSSEX (EAST)

Alfriston

Olde Smugglers Inne

Waterloo Square, BN26 5UE (by market cross)
✪ 11-11; 12-10.30 Sun ☎ (01323) 870241
⊕ yeoldesmugglersinne.co.uk
Harveys Sussex Best Bitter; Skinner's Betty Stogs Bitter; Taylor Landlord; guest beers Ⓗ
Set in the heart of the village, this cosy venue with plenty of character dates from 1358. It has a large garden, including hard-paved and grass areas with picnic tables, reached via several interconnecting rooms from the main bar area. A good range of food is offered. Evening entertainment from live music to toad in the hole competitions is hosted.
♨Q☕❀⇄◑◗🚌(126)

Berwick

Cricketers' Arms ✔

Berwick Village, BN26 6SP (S of A27)
✪ 11-3, 6-11; 11-11 Sat & summer; 12-10.30 Sun
☎ (01323) 870469 ⊕ cricketersberwick.co.uk
Harveys Sussex Best Bitter, Armada Ale, seasonal beers Ⓖ
This popular traditional 18th-century pub specialises in serving Harveys ales straight from the cask. Good quality home-cooked food using local produce is served all day at weekends and all week during the summer. You will find welcoming surroundings with cricket memorabilia adorning the walls, and real fires to keep you warm in the winter. Outside, large front and rear gardens with plenty of seating can be enjoyed in the summer. Toad in the hole is played here. ♨Q❀◑◗♣P

Blackboys

Blackboys Inn ✔

Lewes Road, TN22 5LG (on B2192 S of village)
✪ 11-11; 12-9 Sun ☎ (01825) 890283
⊕ theblackboysinn.co.uk
Harveys Hadlow Bitter, Sussex Best Bitter, seasonal beers Ⓗ
This 14th-century village pub has two bars serving Harveys ales and two restaurants tastefully decorated with old prints, hop bines and interesting artefacts. Outside there is a large terraced area overlooking the pond, with a covered smoking area and gardens, plus a 'secret' garden set aside for adults. Food is served lunchtimes and evenings, all day on Sunday. New this year are a children's play area, Wi-Fi, accommodation with breakfast, and a function room available for hire.
♨Q❀⇄◑◗⊡P⌐

Boreham Street

Bull's Head ✔

BN27 4SG (on main road in village)
✪ 12-3, 6-11; 12-11 Fri & Sat; 12-10.30 (6 winter) Sun
☎ (01323) 831981 ⊕ bullsheadborehamstreet.co.uk
Harveys Hadlow Bitter, Sussex Best Bitter, seasonal beers Ⓗ
Harvey's first-ever tied house makes a welcome return to the Guide; after a short closure it is now thriving under new management. A traditional village pub, wood dominates the interior, which comprises a main bar area plus two smaller rooms. A selection of Harveys seasonal beers is served, but Old Ale is available throughout the winter, Olympia in the summer. Food is sourced locally wherever possible (no meals Sun or Mon eves).
♨Q❀◑◗Ā🚌(98)♣P⌐

Brighton

Basketmakers Arms ✔

12 Gloucester Road, BN1 4AD
✪ 11-11 (midnight Fri & Sat); 12-11 Sun ☎ (01273) 689006
⊕ thebasketmakersarms.co.uk
Fuller's Discovery, London Pride, ESB, seasonal beers; Gale's HSB; guest beers Ⓗ
Located in the North Laine area of the city, this busy tied house stocks a wide range of Fuller's beers along with the occasional guest ale. It is also noted for its decent and inexpensive pub food (no

meals Sat and Sun eves) and large choice of malt whiskies. An odd feature is the dozens of metal tins attached to the walls, sometimes containing bizarre notes from other pubgoers – feel free to leave your own message. ◑≹🚌⊱

Constant Service ✔

96 Islingword Road, BN2 9SJ

✪ 3-midnight; 12-1am Sat; 12-11 Sun ☎ (01273) 607058

Harveys Sussex Best Bitter, Armada Ale, seasonal beers Ⓗ

Formerly a pumping station for the Constant Service Water Company, this is a traditional street-corner local in the Hanover area of the city. This friendly one-bar Harveys house has a varied clientele, and among the decorations on the walls is a display of pressure gauges from the building's previous incarnation. Outside is a walled garden with a smoking shelter. Either Old Ale (winter) or Olympia (summer) is always available. Meals are served every day, with pie and mash a speciality, 6-9pm Monday-Friday, 12-8pm Saturday and Sunday roasts 12-6pm. ❀◑🚌(23,37)⊱

Evening Star 🏆

55-56 Surrey Street, BN1 3PB (400m S of station)

✪ 12-11; 11.30-midnight Fri & Sat ☎ (01273) 328931

🌐 eveningstarbrighton.co.uk

Dark Star Hophead, seasonal beers; guest beers Ⓗ

The original home of the Dark Star brewery, this pub serves four Dark Star beers and three guest beers from micro-breweries, along with a wide selection of bottle-conditioned and imported beers. Draught cider or perry is also available. The walls are festooned with certificates for awards gained by the pub and brewery, together with old beer bottles. Regular beer festivals and occasional live music events are held, which make this pub even more popular and busy, especially at weekends. ❀≹🚌🍎⊱

Greys

105 Southover Street, BN2 9UA (500m E of A270 opp The Level)

✪ 4-11 (11.30 Thu; 12.30am Fri); 12-12.30am Sat; 12-11 Sun ☎ (01273) 680734 🌐 greyspub.com

Harveys Sussex Best Bitter; Taylor Landlord Ⓗ

Inviting, ever popular, Victorian corner pub in the Hanover area, with a relaxed atmosphere that makes it very popular with locals. As well as a packed events calendar, including various themed quizzes, there is live music and several beer festivals (see website for details). Restaurant-quality food from a well-priced menu is served Tuesday-Thursday and Saturday evenings, with a three-course roast lunch available on Sunday. A varying list of around 14 Belgian bottled beers is stocked. Dogs are welcome. ❀◑🚌(37,37B)⊱

Hand in Hand

33 Upper St James's Street, BN2 1JN

✪ 12-midnight (11.30 Sun) ☎ (08721) 077077

Kemptown Bitter, China; guest beers Ⓗ

Claimed to be the smallest brew-pub in the UK, this tiny street-corner establishment is situated in the Kemp Town area of the city. It is the home of the Kemptown Brewery, a tower brewery incorporated within the building at the rear of the premises. The pub also serves a selection of four guest beers, mainly sourced from local breweries, and Gwynt y Ddraig cider is available in summer. Locally sourced pies are available at the bar. Occasional live music plays on Sunday night. 🚌(37,47)

Lion & Lobster

24 Sillwood Street, BN1 2PS (jct of Bedford Square and Bedford Place)

✪ 11-11 (2am Fri & Sat); 12-midnight Sun ☎ (01273) 327299

Dark Star Festival, Hophead; Greene King Abbot; Harveys Sussex Best Bitter; guest beers Ⓗ

Behind the stunningly restored Bandstand on Brighton seafront is Bedford Square, and just above is this impressive back-street pub. Spacious inside with an upstairs restaurant and two-level terrace, closing times are generously late, including food to 10pm and takeaway pizzas until last orders. Real cider is stocked in summer only. An eclectic mix of pictures and framed mirrors adorns the walls. With a wide range of customers, the pub blends a modern feel with a traditional atmosphere. The subdued lighting includes candles. ♛❀◑🚌⊱

Lord Nelson Inn ✔

36 Trafalgar Street, BN1 4ED

✪ 12-11 (11.30 Fri & Sat; 10.30 Sun) ☎ (01273) 695872

🌐 thelordnelsoninn.co.uk

Harveys XX Mild, Hadlow Bitter, Sussex Best Bitter, Armada Ale, seasonal beers Ⓗ

A Guide and Ale Trail regular that is deservedly popular with locals as well as visitors to the city. It is conveniently located for the station and many bus routes. The entire range of Harveys regular and seasonal beers is stocked. There is a folk club on the first Monday of the month and Tuesday is quiz night. Evening food is by arrangement with a nearby Italian restaurant (not Sun). The conservatory can be booked for meetings. Thatchers cider is available on handpump. ◑≹🚌🍎⊱

Prestonville Arms ✔

64 Hamilton Road, BN1 5DN (between Preston Circus and Seven Dials)

✪ 5-11; 12-midnight Fri & Sat; 12-11 Sun ☎ (01273) 701007

🌐 theprestonvillearms.co.uk

Fuller's London Pride, seasonal beers; Gale's HSB; guest beers Ⓗ

A Fuller's tied house, the pub has wood-panelled walls covered with historic pictures of Brighton. There is plenty of seating indoors and a patio garden outside. Special nights include a Tuesday music quiz, Wednesday curry night and Sunday general knowledge quiz. This easy-going pub with its horseshoe-shaped bar is situated on a hilly corner. Good pub food is served along with up to five real ales. ❀◑≹⊱

Pump House ✔

46 Market Street, BN1 1HH

✪ 10-11 (midnight Fri & Sat) ☎ (01273) 827421

Harveys Sussex Best Bitter; Shepherd Neame Spitfire; guest beers Ⓗ

INDEPENDENT BREWERIES

1648 East Hoathly
Beachy Head East Dean
Fallen Angel East Hoathly
FILO Hastings
Full Moon Catsfield
Harveys Lewes
Kemptown Brighton
Rectory Streat
Rother Valley Northiam
White Bexhill-on-Sea

Set in the historic Laines area of the city and close to the seafront, this bow-windowed and wood-panelled free house offers a warm welcome. Tasting notes are displayed on each of the five handpumps, and third-of-a-pint taster trays of these beers are also available. The interior is divided into three rooms, with a heated patio area and an upstairs family-friendly restaurant. Children are welcome in the pub until 8pm. Breakfast is available during the morning. ❀◐◑🚌🍏⚋

Sir Charles Napier

50 Southover Street, BN2 9UE
⏲ 4-11.30; 3-12.30am Fri; 12-12.30am Sat; 12-11 Sun
☎ (01273) 601413
Fuller's London Pride, seasonal beers; Gale's Seafarer, HSB; guest beers Ⓗ
This unspoilt Victorian street-corner community venue in Brighton's lively Hanover quarter is the favourite of a broad spectrum of customers. Many of the original 19th-century features remain intact. Food is served until late evening; lunchtime meals are available at the weekend. The small, attractive, walled beer garden is popular in summer. The pub is the headquarters of the Brighton Morris Men and it stages one of the city's most popular and longest running quizzes every Sunday.
⩩Q❀◐◑🚌(37,81)♣⚋

Station

1 Hampstead Road, Preston Park, BN1 5NG (opp Preston Park station)
⏲ 11-11 (midnight Thu-Sat); 12-11 Sun ☎ (01273) 501318
Harveys Sussex Best Bitter; guest beers Ⓗ
On an elevated corner above the station, the pub has a mixed clientele of sports fans and beer-loving locals. Sometimes a lively match will be on the screens, or there will be a quiz, or it could just be a quiet night. The bar is curved like the pub and raised up; the staff tower above you! Two varying guest beers and Westons vintage cider are offered. Pizzas are the chief bar food plus snacks such as sweets and chocolate bars. Two cats and a dog live here. ⩩❀◐◑⇌(Preston Park)🚌🍏⚋

West Quay ✔

Old Jacksons Wharf, Brighton Marina Village, BN2 5UT (first floor level near roundabout)
⏲ 9am-midnight (1am Sat & Sun) ☎ (01273) 645780
Courage Directors; Greene King Ruddles Best Bitter, Abbot; guest beers Ⓗ
Best approached from the steps near the main roundabout at Brighton marina, this venue offers harbourside views from its four bars spread over two floors. Each level has a balcony with seating, which also serves as a smoking area. Local micro-breweries are favoured, and each month a brewery is featured, with at least one of its beers on offer. The spacious panelled interior gives the comfortable bar areas a traditional air, unlike some Wetherspoon pubs. Q❀◐◑♿🚌(7,21)🍏⚋

Burwash

Rose & Crown ✔

Ham Lane, TN19 7ER (signed from High Street)
⏲ 11-3, 5-11; 11-11 Sat & Sun ☎ (01435) 882600
🌐 roseandcrown-burwash.co.uk
Harveys Sussex Best Bitter, seasonal ales Ⓗ
Built in the 1480s, this attractive, quiet village local, with an exposed well by the main entrance, offers a good range of up to four Harveys beers. The single bar has low beams and an inglenook fireplace. The separate restaurant offers a good choice of English and continental dishes made with locally-sourced produce, with fish the speciality. This large, welcoming pub is easily missed, situated in a lane off the High Street. There are four guest rooms. ⩩Q❀🛏◐◑🍴🚌P⚋

Colemans Hatch

Hatch Inn

TN7 4EJ (400m S of B2110)
⏲ 11.30-2.30, 5.30-11; 12-10.30 Sun ☎ (01342) 822363
🌐 hatchinn.co.uk
Harveys Sussex Best Bitter, Old Ale; Larkins Traditional; guest beers Ⓗ
Originally three 15th-century cottages, this building has been an inn for the last 200 years. An attractive low-beamed building, it is extremely popular with visitors to the nearby Ashdown Forest and has two large gardens for summer dining. The daily changing menus of locally-sourced food are well known and have earned several accolades. There is also an extensive wine list. Close by is (Winnie the) Pooh Bridge and the llama farm. The pub has featured in many TV adverts.
⩩❀◐◑♿🚌(261,291)P

Crowborough

Cooper's Arms

Coopers Lane, TN6 1SN
⏲ 12-2.30 (not Mon), 6-11; 12-11 Sat; 12-10.30 Sun
☎ (01892) 654796
Dark Star Hophead, Best Bitter; guest beers Ⓗ
The property comprises a main bar, a small bar with a TV, and a separate dining room, all simply furnished. Food is served lunchtimes and Wednesday to Saturday evenings. The pub is a free house and offers a changing range of beers, many from Sussex breweries. Petanque, darts and toad in the hole can be played. Beer festivals are held at Easter and on the August bank holiday, using the 12 available handpumps, and themed weekends also feature occasionally. Q❀◐◑🚌♣P

Wheatsheaf ✔

Mount Pleasant, Jarvis Brook, TN6 2NF
⏲ 12-11 (10.30 Sun) ☎ (01892) 663756
🌐 wheatsheafcrowborough.co.uk
Harveys XX Mild, Hadlow Bitter, Sussex Best Bitter, seasonal beers Ⓗ
Dating from 1750, this Harvey's tied house has three separate drinking areas located around a square bar. It serves a varying selection of the regular beers and most seasonals, supplemented by beer festivals at the end of May and October. Lunches are served daily except Sunday, and evening meals Tuesday to Thursday only. Crib, dumps and petanque can be played and live music is performed on alternate Saturdays. The charity jar benefits by £1 each time a mobile phone rings.
⩩❀🛏◐◑⇌🚌♣P⚋

Danehill

Coach & Horses

School Lane, RH17 7JF (off A275) TQ412286
⏲ 12-3, 6-11; 12-11 Sat & Sun ☎ (01825) 740369
🌐 coachandhorsesinn.co.uk
Dark Star Best Bitter; Harveys Sussex Best Bitter; guest beer Ⓗ

A traditional country pub built in 1847 and retaining many original features. The former adjoining stables have been converted to a restaurant serving locally-sourced food. There are separate public and saloon bars with real fires and simple farmhouse-type furniture. Outside is a large garden to the front and a rear patio with extensive farmland views. Although on a minor rural road there is a convenient bus stop outside.
 filfQ❀◑▶🖳🖳(270)♣🐾P🕿⏤🖫

East Hoathly

King's Head
1 High Street, BN8 6DR
✪ 11-11 (midnight Fri & Sat); 12-11 Sun ☎ (01825) 840238
🌐 1648brewing.co.uk
1648 Brew Master, Signature, seasonal beers; Harveys Sussex Best Bitter; guest beers 🅷
This traditional 17th-century hostelry mainly serves beers from the 1648 Brewery next door. As well as the main bar, there is a function room and a family area. An extensive range of home-cooked food is available. Outside, there is a walled beer garden to the rear, but in the summer months picnic tables at the front are an ideal place to watch the world go by. filfQ🌜❀◑▶🖳(54)🐾P🕿

Eastbourne

Dewdrop Inn
37-39 South Street, BN21 4UP (E of town hall)
✪ 12-midnight (1.30am Fri & Sat) ☎ (01323) 723313
Greene King IPA, H&H Olde Trip; guest beers 🅷
Situated in the 'Little Chelsea' area, this small, friendly inn is close to the Saffrons sports grounds, home to football, hockey and cricket clubs. The pub is popular with drinkers of all ages, but draws a mainly younger crowd in the evenings. The drinking area is horseshoe-shaped and divided in two, and there is a pleasant garden to the rear. Food is served until 6pm. fil❀◑🖧≠🖳🖳

Eagle
57 South Street, BN21 4UT
✪ 11-11 (1am Fri & Sat) ☎ (01323) 417799
Beer range varies 🅷
Originally a Kemptown Brewery pub with some of the original emblems preserved, it has a large single bar area with a wooden floor. There is a pool table and a number of TV screens that show various sports events. Five regularly changing ales are served from local breweries, with 1648 beers prominent, plus a real cider. A wide variety of pies is available. Well-behaved children and dogs are welcome. There is a roof terrace for warmer days. fil❀◑🖧≠🖳🖫⏤

Hurst Arms 🍷 ✓
76 Willingdon Road, BN21 1TW (on A2270)
✪ 11-11; 12-10.30 Sun ☎ (01323) 721762
Harveys XX Mild, Hadlow Bitter, Sussex Best Bitter, Armada Ale, seasonal beers 🅷
This welcoming Victorian local has two widely differing bars: an inviting, cosy lounge, and a lively public bar with two wide-screen TVs, a jukebox, dartboard, bar billiards and pool table. There is a small rear garden and a larger front patio. The full range of Harveys regular and seasonal beers is served in excellent condition. Two beer festivals are held each year in May and September. CAMRA Pub of the Year 2010. ❀🖳🖧♣🖫⏤

Ship
33-35 Meads Street, BN20 7RH
✪ 10-11 (midnight Fri; 10.30 Sun) ☎ (01323) 733815
Beachy Head Original; Harveys Sussex Best Bitter; Shepherd Neame Kent's Best; guest beer 🅷
Located in the centre of Meads village, convenient for the start of the South Downs Way and the seafront, the large bar has separate drinking areas with comfortable seating and TV, and a restaurant area serving good-quality food. There is a conservatory leading to a spacious garden with a decked area and food bar for summer use. This is one of the few pubs in the area offering Beachy Head Brewery beers. Q❀◑▶🖳(3)

Terminus Hotel ✓
153 Terminus Road, BN21 3NU
✪ 9am-1am ☎ (01323) 733964
Harveys XX Mild, Hadlow Bitter, Sussex Best Bitter, Armada Ale, seasonal beers 🅷
Popular town-centre pub offering the full range of Harveys beers. The spacious single bar features a large skylight, and front windows overlook a pleasant outside drinking area with seating in the shopping precinct. There is a restaurant area to the rear and a conservatory to the side. Good value pub food is available 12-5pm. Varying entertainment takes place each evening and there is a large function room upstairs. ❀◑🖧≠🖳🐾🖫⏤

Victoria Hotel ✓
27 Latimer Road, BN22 7BU (behind TAVR Centre, off A259)
✪ 11-11 (midnight Fri & Sat); 12-10.30 Sun
☎ (01323) 722673 🌐 victoriaeastbourne.co.uk
Harveys XX Mild, Sussex Best Bitter, Armada Ale, seasonal beers 🅷
Traditional, friendly, family-run local close to the seafront and Redoubt fortress. It has a large open bar area and a smaller back bar with sports TV, pool, darts, bar billiards and toad in the hole. There is a small secluded garden at the rear. The pub holds beer festivals at Easter and in November. Food is served lunchtimes and evenings Thursday to Saturday, and 12.30-4pm Sunday, with the emphasis on value and home cooking.
❀🖾◑▶🖳♣🖫⏤

Hailsham

King's Head ✓
146 South Road, BN27 3NJ
✪ 5-11; 12.30-3, 4.30-11 Fri; 12-3, 6-11 Sat; 12-3, 7-10.30 Sun ☎ (01323) 440447
Harveys Sussex Best Bitter, seasonal beers 🅷
A community pub and popular local, the building dates from 1700 and has been a tied Harvey's house since 1841. It has three separate drinking areas including a quiet snug, featuring exposed beams and open fireplaces. Outside there is a large rear garden with a sheltered smoking area. Activities supported by the enthusiastic staff and friendly locals include darts, pool, dominoes, crib, toad in the hole and a knitting club.
filfQ❀🖳🖳♣P🖫⏤

Hartfield

Anchor
Church Street, TN7 4AG
✪ 11-11; 12-10.30 Sun ☎ (01892) 770424

Harveys Sussex Best Bitter; Larkins Traditional; guest beers Ⓗ
Of the two pubs in the village, this is where the locals drink. Dating from the 14th century, it has two bars and a separate restaurant available for functions. The bars are heated by wood-burning stoves in winter. Locals enjoy the all-day opening, where friendly bar staff add to the relaxed atmosphere. The pub is situated close to Ashdown Forest and is not far from Pooh Bridge. The two guest beers usually come from local breweries. ♛Q❀⇌◑▲🚌♣P⊢

Hastings

Dolphin ✔
11-12 Rock-a-Nore Road, TN34 3DW
⏲ 11-11 (midnight Sat) ☎ (01424) 431197
Courage Directors; Dark Star Hophead; Harveys Sussex Best Bitter; guest beers Ⓗ
Overlooking the unique Hastings fishermen's huts, this old town pub is at the heart of the fishing community. The U-shaped bar is decorated with fishing memorabilia and is very busy at weekends and holidays. Food is served, with a fish platter the speciality; evening meals are available Monday to Friday only. Live music and quiz nights take place during the week. ♛Q❀◑🚌⊢▢

First In Last Out
14-15 High Street, TN34 3EY (in old town, near Stables Theatre)
⏲ 12-11 (midnight Fri); 11-midnight Sat ☎ (01424) 425079
🌐 thefilo.co.uk
FILO Mike's Mild, Crofters, Ginger Tom, Cardinal, Gold; guest beers Ⓗ
Home of the FILO Brewery since 1985, the building dates from the 1500s and has been dispensing beer since at least 1896. The popular old town pub has a large bar warmed by a central open fire. Four beers are usually available, sometimes including guests. Fresh home-cooked food is served Monday to Saturday lunchtimes, and tapas on Monday evening. Beer festivals are held in the covered garden at the rear on most bank holiday weekends, with real cider also available. ♛Q❀◑🚌♣▢

Stag Inn
14 All Saints Street, TN34 3BJ
⏲ 12-midnight (11 Sun) ☎ (01424) 425734
Shepherd Neame Kent's Best, Spifire, Bishops Finger, seasonal beers Ⓗ
Possibly the oldest surviving pub in Hastings, in its present form it dates from 1547 and has many interesting and quirky features (mummified cats on display!). It is on Shepherd Neame's list of pubs that take beers from its new pilot micro-brewery and these are often available to complement the regular ales. Guest beers are also occasionally stocked. Food is usually on offer (check first in winter months). Monday is quiz night, Tuesday folk night, Wednesday bluegrass and Thursday singers. ♛Q❀◑🚌♣⊢

White Rock Hotel
1-10 White Rock, TN34 1JU
⏲ 10 (12 Sun)-11 ☎ (01424) 422240
🌐 thewhiterockhotel.com
Beer range varies Ⓗ
Located next door to the White Rock Theatre, opposite the pier, this hotel has a stylish, refurbished, contemporary bar with ample seating and a spacious outside terrace that overlooks the seafront. A good range of freshly prepared food is available throughout the day; the four beers on offer are always from independent Sussex breweries. Many guest rooms in the hotel have sea views. Q❀⇌◑⇄🚌●

Hove

Downsman
189 Hangleton Way, BN3 8ES (N of Hangleton)
⏲ 11.30-4, 6-11; 12-4.30, 7-11 Sun ☎ (01273) 711301
Harveys Sussex Best Bitter; guest beers Ⓗ
A traditional family run pub in the Hangleton district of North Hove, adjacent to the start of the old Dyke Railway Trail. The Saloon Bar has a log-burning stove and is decorated with rural prints. There is a separate dining area and Sunday roasts are very popular; meals are available every lunchtime and Monday to Friday evenings. Smokers are catered for in a heated and lit shelter. Two guest beers are usually available alongside the regular Harveys Best. ♛❀◑⊡🚌(5)P⊢

Neptune Inn
10 Victoria Terrace, Kingsway, BN3 2WB (on Coast Road E of King Alfred leisure complex)
⏲ 12-1am (2am Fri & Sat); 12-midnight Sun
☎ (01273) 736390 🌐 theneptunelivemusicbar.co.uk
Greene King Abbot; Harveys Sussex Best Bitter; guest beers Ⓗ
A traditional local free house on the Brighton to Shoreham seafront road and close to Hove's shopping area. There is a strong live music theme with gigs on Friday and Sunday evenings – mostly blues and rock. The narrow single bar interior has wood-panelled walls and a small raised stage. The walls are decorated with pictures of musicians and posters for forthcoming events. There are up to five real ales available plus a selection of bottled beers and spirits. 🚌(700)

Icklesham

Queen's Head
Parsonage Lane, TN36 4BL (signed off A259, opp village hall)
⏲ 11-11; 12-10.30 Sun ☎ (01424) 814552
🌐 queenshead.com
Greene King IPA; Harveys Sussex Best Bitter; guest beers Ⓗ
A Guide regular, and local CAMRA Pub of the Year in 2009. Five beers are served – up to eight at weekends – in strengths and styles to suit all, and locally produced cider. All this, plus an interesting, affordable menu, means the pub can get busy. There is an autumn mini beer festival and live music most Sundays. The interior has five areas, three log fires in winter, and an eclectic mix of decorations and memorabilia. A spacious garden offers great views towards Rye. ♛❀◑🚌(100)♣●P⊢▢

Robin Hood
Main Road, TN36 4BD
⏲ 11.30-3, 7-11; 11.30-11 Fri & Sat; 12-5, 7-10.30 Sun
☎ (01424) 814277
Greene King IPA; guest beers Ⓗ
A family-run roadside pub dating from 1607 with parts rebuilt in 1812 following fire damage. Up to five beers are available, often from local breweries. There are two bars, one with a pool table and open

fire, the other leading to a dining area where excellent home cooked food is served (no food Tue eve). The garden has a children's play area. In July the pub hosts the very popular Icklesham village beer festival. ⛫❀◑◐⊟♿🚌(100)♣P⁻

Isfield

Laughing Fish ✔

Station Road, TN22 5XB (off A26 between Lewes and Uckfield) TQ 452172
✪ 11.30-11 ☎ (01825) 750349 🌐 laughingfishonline.co.uk
Greene King IPA, H&H Olde Trip, seasonal beers; guest beers Ⓗ
Built in the 1860s as the Station Hotel, the pub was renamed in the 1960s by local request. The railway line was closed in 1969 but the preserved Lavender Line now uses the station. Tenants since 2001, Andy and Linda have made many improvements including disabled access, a heated outdoor smoking area and a large children's play area. Annual events include the Easter beer race and the village fete. The pub hosts successful bar billiards and toad in the hole teams.
⛫❀◑◐⊟♿⛺🚌(29,29B)♣P⁻

Lewes

Brewers Arms

91 High Street, BN7 1XN (near Lewes Castle)
✪ 10-11; 12-10.30 Sun ☎ (01273) 475524
🌐 brewersarmslewes.co.uk
Harveys Sussex Best Bitter; guest beers Ⓗ
A two-bar free house situated in the historic High Street close to Lewes Castle. The spacious public bar at the rear has a pool table, toad in the hole and a wide-screen TV showing sport. The front bar decorations include an architect's drawing of the pub from long ago; although more sedate than the public bar, it can get busy on Thursday evenings when cribbage rules. Outside, seek out the Page and Overton ceramic plaques and the Shirley Brewery windows. Q❀◑⊟⇌🚌(28,29)♣●⁻

Elephant & Castle

White Hill, BN7 2DJ (off Fisher Street, near police station)
✪ 11.30-11 (midnight Fri & Sat); 12-11 Sun
☎ (01273) 473797 🌐 elephantandcastlelewes.co.uk
Harveys Sussex Best Bitter; Taylor Landlord; guest beers Ⓗ
Situated behind the Castle Mound and originally built as a hotel in 1838 for the long defunct East Grinstead & Southdown Brewery of Lewes, this Enterprise Inn offers changing guest beers and Westons Old Rosie cider on handpump. The 'Elly' is the hub of the local community. One of Lewes's famous Bonfire societies meets here, as well as the folk club. The locally-sourced home-made Ellyburgers are the house speciality. Sky Sports and free Wi-Fi are available. ⛫❀◑◐🚌(127)♣●⁻

Gardener's Arms

46 Cliffe High Street, BN7 2AN
✪ 11-11; 12-10.30 Sun ☎ (01273) 474808
Harveys Sussex Best Bitter; guest beers Ⓗ
Compact, two-bar, genuine free house decorated with pictures of bygone days. Harveys Best is a regular and the guest beers come from small independent breweries; a real cider is always available on handpump. The pub is home to cricket, stoolball and toad in the hole teams. Many community groups are also supported including the Cliffe Bonfire Society. Locally-sourced pies, sausage rolls and pasties are on offer. A former landlord's football allegiances can be viewed in the Gents.
⇌🚌(28,29)♣●

John Harvey Tavern ✔

Bear Yard, Cliffe High Street, BN7 2AN (opp Harveys Brewery)
✪ 11-11; 12-10.30 Sun ☎ (01273) 479880
🌐 johnharveytavern.co.uk
Harveys Hadlow Bitter, Sussex Best Bitter, Armada Ale, seasonal beers Ⓗ
This two-room venue is located opposite the entrance to Harveys and may be described as the brewery tap. The busy main bar has a slate-flagged floor and wood-panelled walls decorated with horse brasses on the columns and beams, together with unusual seats on either side of the fireplace converted from old fermenting vessels. There is a quieter side room and an upstairs meeting room. A good selection of food and wines is available 12-2.30pm and 6-9.30pm Monday to Saturday, 12-4.30pm on Sunday. ⛫Q☋◑◐⇌🚌(28,29)⁻

Lewes Arms ✔

1 Mount Place, BN7 1YH
✪ 11-11 (midnight Fri & Sat); 12-11 Sun ☎ (01273) 473152
🌐 thelewesarms.co.uk
Fuller's London Pride, ESB; Gale's Seafarers Ale, HSB; Harveys Sussex Best Bitter; guest beers Ⓗ
This quirky, historic venue is split into three rooms and is popular with the locals. There are five regular beers including Harveys Best plus one guest ale. The pub is the home of the world pea-throwing championships, dwyle flunking and other unusual events. In 2009 it started hosting a regular August bank holiday festival – a three-day event of music, poetry and a toad in the hole competition. It also puts on its own pantomime, and the upstairs function/meeting room hosts writing and bonfire groups. ⛫Q☋❀◑◐⊟⇌🚌(28,29)♣⁻

Snowdrop Inn

119 South Street, BN7 2BU
✪ 12-midnight (11 Sun) ☎ (01273) 471018
🌐 thesnowdropinn.com
Dark Star Hophead, seasonal beers; Harveys Sussex Best Bitter, seasonal beers; guest beers Ⓗ
A recently revived free house, the Snowdrop now sports an interior decorated with wood panelling and the 'roses and castles' traditional painted motifs of narrowboats. Describing itself as 'dog and family friendly', it features a wide variety of live music nearly every evening, and meals are served 12-9pm. The pub is named after the 1836 avalanche that buried several local houses and led to the deaths of eight people. ❀◑◐🚌(28,29)♣⁻

Litlington

Plough & Harrow

The Street, BN26 5RE
✪ 11 (12 Sun)-11 ☎ (01323) 870632
🌐 ploughandharrowlitlington.co.uk
Dark Star Hophead; Harveys Sussex Best Bitter, seasonal beer; guest beer Ⓗ
With the oldest parts dating from the 16th century, this pretty village free house has a flint-knapped and tile-hung exterior. The interior has a variety of comfortable seating, including cut-down beer casks. As well as the main bar area there is a separate dining area and an unusual snug with an

inglenook fireplace. To the rear is a garden with seating. Food is served with an emphasis on home-cooked local produce and home-made desserts.
⛼❀◐◑♣P

Milton Street

Sussex Ox

BN26 5RL (signed off A27) TV 533040
⊙ 11.30-3, 6-11; 12-3, 6-10.30 (12-5 winter) Sun
☎ (01323) 870840 🌐 thesussexox.co.uk
Harveys Sussex Best Bitter; guest beers Ⓗ
Located in a small hamlet at the end of a country lane, the pub has a large garden with pleasant country views. The bar area is small compared with a good-sized seating area and separate restaurant. This pub was originally a Ballard house, but now serves a good selection of well-kept beers from Dark Star and other Sussex brewers. Excellent home-cooked food is available. ⛼Q❀◐◑P

Newhaven

Jolly Boatman

133-135 Lewes Road, BN9 9SJ (N of town centre)
⊙ 11-11 (midnight Sat); 11-10.30 Sun ☎ (01273) 510030
Harveys Sussex Best Bitter; guest beers Ⓗ
A friendly street-corner local with a single bar on two levels. Four handpumps offer Harveys Best plus three changing guest beers, focusing on local and independent brewers. Pump five offers Westons Scrumpy all year round. In winter the pub has a welcoming real log fire. Quiz nights are held twice-monthly, with jazz on Thursday. Crib and darts are played, and Sky Sports is screened. Bar snacks, sweets and chocolates are always available. Dog-friendly.
⛼⇌(Newhaven Town)🚌(123)♣🍎⊱

Newick

Royal Oak

1 Church Road, BN8 4JU
⊙ 11-11; 12-10.30 Sun ☎ (01825) 722506
Fuller's London Pride; Harveys Sussex Best Bitter; guest beers Ⓗ
This weatherboarded local is situated in a quiet side road off the village green. The front patio area provides seating for diners and drinkers. The low, beamed interior is divided into a main bar with attached dining area, and a public bar with pub games and a pool table. Points of interest in the pub are a large log-burning fire, a hanging jug collection, and a section of wall cut out to expose the ancient wattle and daub construction.
⛼❀◐◑🀫🚌(31,121)♣P⊱

Ninfield

Blacksmith's Inn

The Green, TN33 9JL (on A269)
⊙ 12-11 (10.30 Sun) ☎ (01424) 892462
Harveys Sussex Best Bitter; guest beers Ⓗ
You can be sure of a warm welcome from the knowledgable landlord at this genuine local, with up to four different guest beers. There is plenty of brewery memorabilia on the walls, a friendly atmosphere, and dogs are most welcome. Excellent locally-sourced food is served. There is a separate restaurant which is quieter than the main bar. ❀◐◑♿⛺🚌(98)♣P⊱

Pett

Two Sawyers

TN35 4HB
⊙ 12-11 (10.30 Sun) ☎ (01424) 812255
🌐 twosawyers.co.uk
Harveys Sussex Best Bitter; guest beers Ⓗ
This excellent village pub is extremely welcoming and regularly serves three real ales and a real cider. Featuring mostly local beers and providing an excellent menu, it is popular with villagers, walkers and campers. It comprises two main bars with real fires, a separate restaurant and a number of dining areas. The bars are decorated with an interesting array of saws. There are three B&B rooms available, a large beer garden and a petanque piste. ⛼Q❀🛏◐◑🀫♿⛺🚌(347)♣🍎P⊱

Plumpton Green

Plough Inn ✔

South Road, BN7 3DF (N of village)
⊙ 12-11 (10.30 Sun) ☎ (01273) 890311
Harveys Sussex Best Bitter, seasonal beers; guest beers Ⓗ
A memorial to Polish Spitfire crews operating from the nearby wartime airfield at Chailey stands in the car park of this family-run Harvey's pub. Both bars are warmed by open fires in winter, and bar billiards and darts can be played. Quality meals from an extensive menu are available in the restaurant area or in the large beer garden during the summer. Children and dogs are welcome. The 166 bus stops right outside the pub.
⛼❀◐◑🀫♿🚌(166)♣P⊱

Portslade

Stanley Arms

47 Wolseley Road, BN41 1SS (100m S of Old Shoreham Road, on corner of Wolseley Road and Stanley Road)
⊙ 3 (4 Mon)-11; 12-11 Sat; 12-10.30 Sun ☎ (01273) 430234
🌐 thestanley.com
Beer range varies Ⓗ
This family-run free house has seven handpumps serving a range of real ales, alongside a wide choice of bottled beers, real cider and perry. Seven dwarves in football strips peer down from above the bar, from where the stained glass proclaims 'Welcome to the Stanley Arms'. The pub screens sport in one bar, and has its own football team. Hot and cold snacks are available. Three beer festivals are held annually, together with monthly cellar tours. Local CAMRA Pub of the Year 2009.
⛼❀🀫⇌(Fishersgate)🚌(2,46)♣🍎⊱🍺

Ringmer

Cock Inn ✔

Uckfield Road, BN8 5RX (1 mile from village on slip road off A26)
⊙ 11-3, 6-11.30; 11-11 Sun ☎ (01273) 812040
🌐 cockpub.co.uk
Fuller's London Pride; Harveys Sussex Best Bitter, seasonal beers; guest beers Ⓗ
A traditional family-run pub with an extensive menu of exceptional quality dishes catering for all tastes, including vegetarian, vegan and gluten-free. Guest beers rotate with the seasons and include Harveys Old, Adnams Broadside and Dark Star Hophead. Harveys bottled beers feature all year round, including Kiss, Bonfire Boy and

Christmas Ale. The bar has a huge inglenook fireplace, exposed beams and a flagstone floor. There is a large separate dining area, beer garden and car park. ♨Q❀◐◑⊟⛺🚌(29,29A)P⚟

Robertsbridge

George Inn

High Street, TN32 5AW

⏲ 11-11; 12-9 Sun ☎ (01580) 880315

🌐 thegeorgerobertsbridge.co.uk

Harveys Sussex Best Bitter; guest beers Ⓗ

Three handpumps offer a varying choice of ales, including local Rother Valley beers, in this friendly 18th-century coaching inn. The small bar is next to an impressive inglenook fireplace at the head of a long dining area. Food is home-cooked, and ingredients are supplied from within a 30-mile radius. There is live music on the last Sunday of the month. Hotel accommodation comprises four en-suite boutique rooms. ♨Q❀🛏◐◑♿⇌🚌🍎P⚟

St Leonards

Horse & Groom

4 Mercatoria, TN38 0EB

⏲ 11-11; 12-10.30 Sun ☎ (01424) 420612

🌐 horseandgroomstleonards.co.uk

Adnams Broadside; Greene King IPA; Harveys Sussex Best Bitter; guest beers Ⓗ

This free house is found at the heart of old St Leonards. The outside gives no clue to the unusual horseshoe-shaped bar, with a separate, narrow, quieter room at the rear. Food is not served in the pub, but there is an adjoining restaurant open Tuesday to Saturday evenings and Sunday lunchtime. The pub is a short walk from the seafront and Warrior Square.
♨Q❀♿⇌(Warrior Square)♣⚟

Salehurst

Halt

Church Lane, TN32 5PH (by church)

⏲ closed Mon; 12-3, 6-11 Tue & Wed; 12-11 Thu-Sun

☎ (01580) 880620 🌐 salehursthalt.co.uk

Harveys Sussex Best Bitter; guest beers Ⓗ

Originally a railway stop on a hop-picking line, this free house was saved from redevelopment by the two local families who now own it. The traditional bar features an open fire, low beams, oak floors, wooden furniture and a comfortable snug, while the rear patio and garden look over the picturesque Rother Valley. Good food is served including locally-reared meat and there is a purpose-built pizza oven. Live music plays every second Sunday from 4pm. ♨Q❀◐♣🍎⚟

South Chailey

Horns Lodge

South Street, BN8 4BD (on A275)

⏲ closed Tue; 11.30-2.30, 5.30-11; 11.30-11 Sat; 12-10.30 Sun ☎ (01273) 400422 🌐 hornslodge.com

Harveys Sussex Best Bitter; guest beers Ⓗ

This roadside pub was originally one of the London to Brighton Postal Service coaching inns. The main bar room, warmed by log fires in winter, has a games area at the end of the bar where bar billiards and darts are played. There is a separate restaurant area serving traditional home-cooked food. For summer there is a large garden with a patio. An annual beer festival is held on the second weekend in September. The 121 bus from Lewes stops outside. B&B accommodation is available.
♨❀🛏◐◑🚌(121)♣🍎P⚟

Uckfield

Alma ✔

65 Framfield Road, TN22 5AJ (on B2102)

⏲ 11-11 (midnight Fri & Sat); 12-10.30 Sun

☎ (01825) 762232

Harveys XX Mild, Hadlow Bitter, Sussex Best Bitter, seasonal beers; guest beers Ⓗ

Situated close to Uckfield town centre, railway station and buses, this is a large, friendly two-bar community local. All Harveys seasonal beers are stocked, including Olympia in summer and Old Ale in winter. Traditional pub games such as crib, darts, dominoes and shove-ha'penny are played in the public bar. Food is available 12-2pm and 6-9pm Monday-Saturday, with a Sunday afternoon carvery. Opening hours may vary in winter. There is a separate beer garden and smoking area at the rear of the car park. Q❀◐◑⊟♿⇌🚌(318)♣P⚟

Udimore

King's Head

Rye Road, TN31 6BG (on B2089, W of village)

⏲ 11-3.30 (not Mon), 6-11; 11-4.30 Sun ☎ (01424) 882349

Harveys Sussex Best Bitter; guest beers Ⓗ

The King's Head celebrated 15 consecutive years in this Guide in 2010. Built in 1535 and extended in the 17th century, the traditional village ale house has a long bar featuring exposed beams and open fires. The pub serves one or two guest ales, often from Harveys, plus excellent home-cooked food at all sessions. Situated in an area of outstanding natural beauty, there are many scenic walks nearby, while pleasant views over the surrounding countryside unfold from the garden.
♨Q🚸❀◐◑⊟🚌♣🍎P

Westfield

Old Courthouse

Main Road, TN35 4QE TQ812154

⏲ 12-11 (10.30 Sun) ☎ (01424) 751603

🌐 oldcourthousepub.com

Harveys Sussex Best Bitter; guest beers Ⓗ

Located on the 1066 Country Walk, this popular community-focused village pub welcomes ramblers and locals alike. Hot food is served 12-9pm daily, with roasts on Sunday lunchtime. The main bar has an open fire and low ceiling; the smoking shelter is heated. Bar billiards and darts can be played. The first Friday of each month is curry night. A mini beer festival is held on the August bank holiday weekend. The pub was CAMRA Branch Pub of the Year 2007 and remains as excellent as ever.
♨Q❀◐◑⊟♿🚌(340,341)♣P⚟

Willingdon

Red Lion

99 Wish Hill, BN20 9HQ (S end of village)

⏲ 11-3, 5-11; 11-11 Fri & Sat; 11-10.30 Sun

☎ (01323) 502062 🌐 redlion-willingdon.co.uk

Badger First Gold, Tanglefoot, seasonal beers Ⓗ

Situated at the foot of the South Downs, this friendly village community pub is popular with locals and walkers. The function room, located at the rear, leads to a well-used split-level garden with good, solid wooden furniture. Excellent home-cooked food, using many locally-sourced ingredients, is available lunchtimes and evenings Monday to Thursday, all day Friday and Saturday until 9pm, and all day Sunday until 5.30pm. A popular annual beer festival is held over the August bank holiday weekend. ⩩❀◐◑⊟P⸗

Withyham

Dorset Arms ✔

TN7 4BD (on B2110)
⊛ 11.30-3, 6-11; 12-10.30 Sun ☎ (01892) 770278
⊕ dorset-arms.co.uk
Harveys Hadlow Bitter, Sussex Best Bitter, seasonal beers Ⓗ
Set back from the B2110, this attractive 16th-century Harvey's pub is a regular entry in the Guide. Close to Ashdown Forest, it is an ideal stopping off point for those on a Wealden tour. The large dining area is separate from the bar, which has bare floorboards and a welcoming open fire in winter. A varied choice of meals is available and booking is advisable. Dogs are welcome.
⩩☋❀◐◑⊟(291)P⸗

SUSSEX (WEST)

Amberley

Sportsman 🏆

Rackham Road, Cross Gates, BN18 9NR (½ mile E of village off B2139) TQ039135
⊛ 11 (12 Sun)-11 ☎ (01798) 831787
Dark Star Hophead; Harveys Sussex Best Bitter; guest beers Ⓗ
This small, picturesque village in the Arun Valley happily supports two fine pubs, together with other amenities that have long since disappeared elsewhere. Here, a warm welcome awaits drinkers, diners, cyclists and walkers alike. Fine local beers and an enticing menu with daily specials featuring locally-sourced produce can be savoured in three separate areas. There is also a conservatory and outside decking overlooking the Wild Brooks. Popular with bird watchers. Local CAMRA Pub of the Year 2010. ⩩Q❀⇌◐◑⊞⊟(73)♣P

Angmering

Spotted Cow

1 High Street, BN16 4AN (off B2265, half mile E of village)
⊛ 11-3, 5.30-11; 11-11.30 Fri & Sat; 12-10.30 Sun
☎ (01903) 783919 ⊕ spottedcowangmering.co.uk
Fuller's London Pride; Greene King Old Speckled Hen; Harveys Sussex Best Bitter; Ringwood Best Bitter; Taylor Landlord; guest beer Ⓗ
Old smuggling inn with a rotating range of at least five real ales. The pub boasts a spinning jenny on the ceiling, morris dancing on the Summer Solstice and a hugely popular charity conker tournament on the second Sunday in October. There is a busy seated restaurant with bar snacks and a small, separate drinkers' bar where dogs are welcome. Boules can be played in the pretty garden, which has a children's play area. The pub can get busy in summer. ⩩Q☋❀◐◑⊞▲⊟(9)♣P⸗

Barns Green

Queens Head ✔

Chapel Road, RH13 0PS TQ123271
⊛ 11.30-2.30, 6-11; 11.30-11 Fri & Sat; 12-10.30 Sun
☎ (01403) 730436 ⊕ thequeensheadbarnsgreen.co.uk
Fuller's London Pride; King Horsham Best Bitter Ⓗ**; guest beers** Ⓗ/Ⓖ
Warm and cosy village venue with low ceilings and a large open fireplace. During the warmer weather two casks dispense ale direct; these are owned by the landlord and filled by local breweries. There are also four handpumps. The menu features locally-sourced food; the landlord also owns a farm and a country market (where you can buy real ale in a bottle). TV, Wi-Fi access and a bar billiards table are all available. LocAle accredited.
⩩Q❀◐◑♿▲⊟♣P⸗

Bepton

Country Inn

Severals Road, GU29 0LR (1 mile SW of Midhurst, down Bepton Rd) SU870206
⊛ 11.30-3, 5-11; 11.30-midnight Fri & Sat; 12-10.30 Sun
☎ (01730) 813466 ⊕ thecountryinn.co.uk
Ballard's Midhurst Mild; Young's Bitter; guest beers Ⓗ
Cosy rural local in a quiet spot, an easy walk down the lane from Midhurst and the bus stop from Chichester. The single bar has a drinking area and dartboard, plus tables by the log fire that burns in winter, where food is served (book for Sun lunch; no food Sun eve). Outside at the front there are tables, while the large enclosed garden to the side has children's play equipment. The two guest beers usually include at least one from a micro-brewery.
⩩Q❀◐◑⊟(60)♣P⸗

Burgess Hill

Watermill Inn

1 Leylands Road, RH15 0QF
⊛ 11-midnight (1am Fri); 10-1am Sat; 12-midnight Sun
☎ (01444) 235517
Fuller's London Pride, ESB; Goddards Ale of Wight; Harveys Sussex Best Bitter Ⓗ
This regular on the local CAMRA Ale Trail is a single bar community local situated in the World's End area of Burgess Hill. The walled garden is ideal for families in summer and has an adjacent covered smoking area. There is live music on the first Friday of every month and Sky Sports on TV.
⩩❀⇌(Wivelsfield)⊟(40,40X)♣P⸗

Byworth

Black Horse

GU28 0HL (just off A283, 1 mile SE of Petworth)
⊛ 11 (12 Sun)-11 ☎ (01798) 342424
⊕ theblackhorsebyworth.com
Dark Star Hophead; Flowerpots Bitter; Fuller's London Pride; guest beers Ⓗ
Hospitable old village pub full of character, with a rustic front bar and large fire. There are many areas for diners, some secluded. An iron staircase leads to games and function rooms. The steeply terraced garden is one of the finest in Sussex. Food is all prepared on the premises using locally-sourced ingredients. The pub is LocAle accredited and guest beers are local. The hourly bus from Worthing and Midhurst stops nearby. ⩩Q❀◐◑⊞⊟(1)♣P

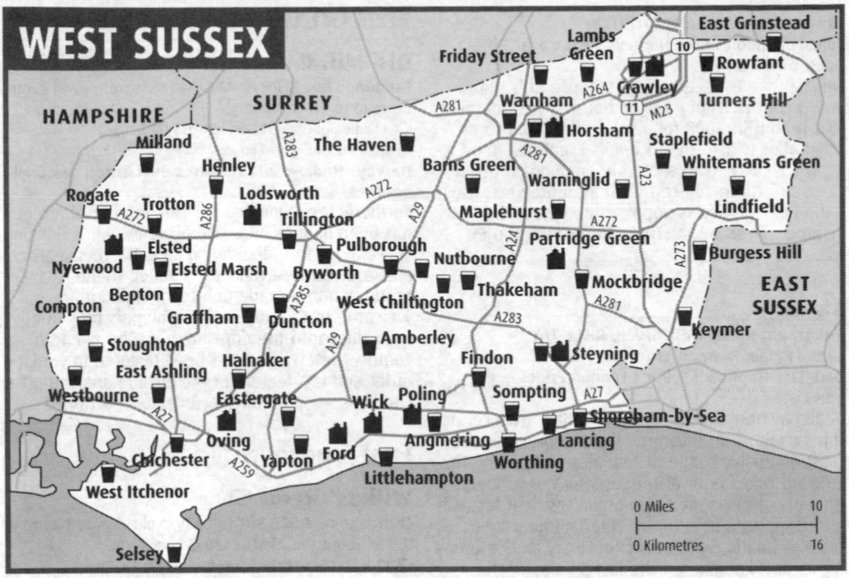

Chichester

Bell Inn

3 Broyle Road, PO19 6AT (on A286 just N of Northgate)
⏲ 11.30-2.30, 5-midnight; 12-3, 7-midnight Sun
☎ (01243) 783388 🌐 thebellinnchichester.com
Beer range varies Ⓗ
Cosy, comfortable city local especially popular with theatregoers, where the ambience is enhanced by exposed brickwork, wooden panelling and beams. The beer range usually comprises two from the Enterprise range and one from a local micro, and an extensive blackboard menu is offered (no food Sun eve). The rear suntrap garden has a covered smoking area heated by a coal stove. The bar gets busy after 10pm when the Festival Theatre empties out. Q❀◐◑⇌🚌(60)♣P⌐

Eastgate Inn ✔

4 The Hornet, PO19 7JG (500m E of Market Cross)
⏲ 12 (11 Wed)-11; 12-midnight Fri; 10-1am Sat
☎ (01243) 774877 🌐 theeastgatepub.org.uk
Fuller's London Pride; Gale's Seafarers Ale, HSB; guest beer Ⓗ
An attractive open-plan bar with a wood-burning stove and an area for diners. Good value traditional pub meals are home-cooked and served daily, with organic roasts offered on Sunday. There is a heated patio garden to the rear, which is the venue for a beer festival in July. The pub attracts locals, holidaymakers and shoppers from the nearby market with its warm welcome and traditional pub games, such as darts, cribbage, pool and backgammon. ♨❀◐⇌🚌(55,700)♣⌐

Four Chesnuts

234 Oving Road, PO19 7EJ (900m E of Market Cross)
⏲ 12-11 (midnight Fri & Sat); 12-10.30 Sun
☎ (01243) 779974 🌐 the4chesnuts.co.uk
Ballard's Mild; Langham Hip Hop; Taylor Landlord; guest beers Ⓗ
Traditional town hostelry and local CAMRA Pub of the Year 2007, the Chesnuts has been converted to a single bar but with distinct drinking areas. The skittle alley doubles as a dining room at busy times and occasionally as a venue for beer festivals. The menu of hearty meals includes a 'pie of the moment' (no food Sun eve). There is a Saturday music night, local folk club on Tuesday, plus a quiz night on Wednesday. Sports are shown on TV. ♨◐◑⇌🚌(51,700)♣P

Compton

Coach & Horses

The Square, PO18 9HA (on B2146, in village centre)
⏲ 12-3, 6-11; 12-4, 6-10.30 Sun ☎ (023) 9263 1228
Dark Star Hophead, Original; Harveys Sussex Best Bitter; guest beers Ⓗ
Sixteenth-century pub in a remote but charming village, close to lovely local walks. The front bar is warm and welcoming, with two open fires and internal window shutters. The rear bar is for dining; this is the oldest part of the pub and features exposed beams and another open fire (no food Sun and Mon). Up to five beers from independent breweries are usually available. There is a bar billiards table, and seats outside in the village square. ♨Q❀◐◑⛺🚌(54)♣▯

Crawley

Frogshole Farm ✔

Maidenbower Drive, Maidenbower Village, RH10 7QF

INDEPENDENT BREWERIES

Adur Steyning
Anchor Springs Wick (NEW)
Arundel Ford
Ballard's Nyewood
Dark Star Partridge Green
Gribble Oving
Hammerpot Poling
Hepworth Horsham
King Horsham
Kissingate Crawley (NEW)
Langham Lodsworth
Welton's Horsham

✪ 11-11; 12-10.30 Sun ☎ (01293) 885081
Fuller's London Pride; Harveys Sussex Best Bitter; guest beers Ⓗ
Originally a 16th-century farmhouse, this pub, which is now within a large housing development, was rebuilt in 2008 following a fire. Built to an open plan with restored original features, food is served all day, with a carvery on Sunday. Guest beers are often sourced from local brewers. The large beer garden is popular throughout the summer. ♨❀◑♿⇌(Three Bridges)🚌(100)P

Swan
1 Horsham Road, West Green, RH11 7AY
✪ 12-11 (1am Fri & Sat) ☎ (01293) 527447
Dark Star Hophead; Fuller's London Pride; guest beers Ⓗ
Within a short walking distance of the town centre, this excellent local community pub provides the most extensive range of real ales in Crawley. The landlord takes note of requests for guest beers from his regulars, and also organises beer festivals in the spring and autumn. Entertainment takes place regularly, with music on Friday and Saturday nights and karaoke on the last Sunday of the month. This very popular local also supports a number of charities. ♨❀⊟♿⇌🚌(23,34)♣●⊬

Duncton

Cricketers
High Street, GU28 0LB (on A285)
✪ 11 (12 Sun)-11 ☎ (01798) 342473
🌐 thecricketersduncton.co.uk
King Horsham Best Bitter; Skinner's Betty Stogs; guest beers Ⓗ
Renovated to a high standard, this hospitable 16th-century coaching inn has strong links with cricket, with much memorabilia evident including many prints. There is a room for diners at a higher level and local ingredients are used for the enjoyable food – try the field mushroom stack! The pub supports the LocAle scheme, and Arundel Gold is the extra beer in summer. The splendid garden is lined with trees. The Compass bus stops when pre-booked on (01903) 264776.
♨Q❀◑♿🚌(99)●P⊬

East Ashling

Horse & Groom 🏆
PO18 9AX (on B2178 in village)
✪ 12-3, 6-11; 12-6 Sun ☎ (01243) 575339
🌐 thehorseandgroomchichester.co.uk
Dark Star Hophead; Harveys Sussex Best Bitter; Hop Back Summer Lightning; Young's Bitter; guest beer Ⓗ
This welcoming 17th-century inn features flagstones, settles, half-panelled walls and a fine old cooking range in the bar. It has been improved, but remains unspoilt, attracting drinkers and diners equally. The beers benefit from a deep cellar under the handpumps and are sold at consistently good-value prices. The restaurant offers a diverse, high-quality menu of home-made dishes, all sourced locally (no food Sun eve). Dog-friendly accommodation is en-suite, some in a converted 17th-century oak-beamed flint barn. Local CAMRA Pub of the Year 2010.
♨Q❀🛏◑♿⛺⇌(Bosham)🚌(54)♣P⊬

East Grinstead

Old Mill ✔
Dunnings Road, RH19 4AT (half mile from town centre on road to West Hoathly)
✪ 11-midnight; 12-11 Sun ☎ (01342) 326341
🌐 theolddunningsmill.co.uk
Harveys Hadlow Bitter, Sussex Best Bitter, seasonal beers Ⓗ
Formerly the Dunnings Mill, the interior of the pub has been divided into several areas, with a drinking space away from the dining area. Harveys seasonal ales are usually available. A varied menu features home-made pub food. Children are welcome in the pub and dog owners may bring their dogs into the drinking area. The old 16th-century water wheel has been restored to working order and is a feature of the outside drinking area. Food is served all day. ♨❀◑♿⛺⇌🚌(84)P⊬

Eastergate

Wilkes' Head ✔
Church Lane, PO20 3UT (off A29 in old village, 300m S of B2233 roundabout) SU 943053
✪ 12-3, 5-11; 12-11 Fri-Sun ☎ (01243) 543380
Adnams Bitter; Hop Back Summer Lightning; Sharp's Doom Bar; guest beers Ⓗ
Named after 18th-century Radical John Wilkes, this listed, red-brick pub dates from 1803. There is a cosy lounge to the left of the central bar and a larger public bar with inglenook and low beams to the right. Up to two guest beers come from Punch's Finest Cask range. A restaurant has been added in a modern extension and there is a large garden with tables for outdoor drinking, plus a comfortable, heated smokers' shelter. Beer festivals are staged at Easter and in late September.
♨Q❀◑⊟⇌(Barnham)🚌(66,66A)♣P⊬

Elsted

Three Horseshoes
GU29 0JY (E end of village) SU 819196
✪ 11-2.30, 6-11; 12-3, 7-10.30 Sun ☎ (01730) 825746
Ballard's Best Bitter; Bowman Wallops Wood; Flowerpots Bitter; Young's Bitter; guest beer Ⓖ
Low-beamed cosy rural pub with small rooms. The furthest room is for dining only, while another room with a blazing log fire in winter is also used for diners. There is a large, pleasant garden with superb views over the Downs. This is an old, comfortable and homely pub that you will be reluctant to leave. In summer there are five beers, three in winter, all served by gravity dispense from a stillage alongside the bar. ♨Q❀◑🚌(91)P

Elsted Marsh

Elsted Inn
Elsted Road, GU29 0JT (2 miles S of A272 between Midhurst & Petersfield) SU 834206
✪ 5-10 Mon; 12-2.30, 5-10.30 Tue-Thu; 12-3, 5-midnight Fri; 11-11 Sat; 11-10 Sun ☎ (01730) 813662
🌐 theelstedinn.co.uk
Otter Bitter; St Austell Tribute; guest beer Ⓗ
Elsted, or 'Halesteed' in the Domesday Record, means 'the place where elder grows'. Today this Victorian pub, built originally to cater for a station on the Petersfield-Midhurst branch railway, is surrounded by the glorious countryside of the South Downs. In addition to the bar and restaurant

it has four en-suite rooms in a detached coach house alongside, at one time the home of Ballard's Brewery, whose Best Bitter or Nyewood Gold continue to be available on handpump. No food Monday, or Sunday evening.
⩋Q❀⛟◐◑🚌(91,92)P⸗

Findon

Snooty Fox

High Street, BN14 0TA (between A24 and village centre)
⏲ 12-2.30, 6-11; 12-10.30 Sun ☎ (01903) 872733
🌐 findonmanor.com
Fuller's London Pride; Harveys Sussex Best Bitter; Taylor Landlord; guest beers ⊞
Part of the historic 16th-century Findon Manor Hotel, with outstanding service assured. The bar has a peaceful, cosy atmosphere with lots of wooden beams overhead. Excellent restaurant-quality food is available at pub prices. Guest beers are sourced locally. The large garden is delightful in summer. There is a half-hourly bus service from Worthing. ⩋Q❀⛟◐◑♿🚌(1)P⸗

Friday Street

Royal Oak 🏆

RH12 4QA (on Rusper to Capel road, signed down side road) TQ183367
⏲ 12-3, 5-11 (9 Mon); 12-11 Sat; 12-9 Sun
☎ (01293) 871393
Surrey Hills Ranmore Ale; guest beers ⊞
An isolated but welcoming low-beamed free house featuring seven real ales, which vary from local micro-brewery beers to several from a long-established relationship with brewers from Devon. There is a strong emphasis on the community and the locals, with annual events including a pantomime horse race, snail race and weed show. Food is home-cooked using produce from nearby farms. CAMRA Surrey/Sussex Pub of the Year in 2008 and 2009, and National Pub of the Year runner-up in 2009 and 2010. ⩋Q🚼❀◐◑♣🍎P⸗▢

Graffham

White Horse

Heyshott Road, GU28 0NT (200m W of village centre) SU 925176
⏲ 11-3, 6-12; 11-midnight Sat; 12-midnight Sun
☎ (01798) 867331 🌐 thewhitehorsegraffham.co.uk
Dark Star Hophead; Hogs Back TEA; Skinner's Betty Stogs; guest beers ⊞
A new entry to the Guide, this traditional village pub comprises a bar with large open fireplace and an area for the three darts teams. Behind the pub is a conservatory restaurant, where booking is recommended at weekends (no food Sun eve or winter Mon). Up to two guest beers may include ales from local micros. There is a beer garden with fine views of the South Downs and a trampoline for children. A new B&B block will be ready for 2011.
⩋Q❀⛟◐◑⛺🚌(99)♣P⸗

Halnaker

Anglesey Arms

Stane Street, PO18 0NQ (on A285)
⏲ 11-3, 5.30-11.30; 11-11 Sat; 12-10.30 Sun
☎ (01243) 773474 🌐 angleseyarms.co.uk
Black Sheep Best Bitter; Hepworth Prospect Organic; Langham Hip Hop; Young's Bitter; guest beer ⊞
Family-run, listed Georgian venue featuring a wood and flagstone floored public bar with a log fire, plus a comfortable restaurant renowned for good food made with local produce (reservation essential). Three of the regular ales plus one hoppy SIBA guest are usually available, along with several Belgian beers. Hepworth Prospect Organic is badged Goodwood Organic as the pub belongs to the Estate. Cribbage and cricket are played by pub teams. There is a two-acre rear garden with a petanque court, and dogs are welcome in the bar.
⩋Q❀◐◑♿⛺🚌(55,99)♣P

Henley

Duke of Cumberland Arms

Henley Village, GU27 3HQ (off A286, 3 miles N of Midhurst) SU 894258
⏲ 11-11; 12-10.30 Sun ☎ (01428) 652280
🌐 dukeofcumberland.com
Beer range varies Ⓖ
Stunning 15th-century inn nestling against the hillside and set in three and a half acres of gardens with extensive views. Often threatened with redevelopment, the pub was rescued in 2007 by a group of locals. The single rustic bar, with scrubbed-top tables and benches plus a log fire at both ends, is soon to be augmented by extra space in an extension at the back. Three or four beers, usually including Langham, are dispensed from a gravity stillage behind the bar. Local CAMRA Pub of the Year 2009. No evening meals Sunday or Monday. ⩋Q❀◐◑🚌(70)♣P⸗

Horsham

Beer Essentials

30A East Street, RH12 1HL
⏲ 10-6 (7 Fri & Sat); closed Sun & Mon ☎ (01403) 218890
🌐 thebeeressentials.co.uk
Beer range varies Ⓖ
Specialist beer shop, with a variety of ales drawn straight from the cask. An extensive range of bottled beers from around the UK plus some foreign beers are always in stock. JB Medium Cider is available along with a range of bottled ciders and lagers. Draught products can be taken away in minipins, polypins or two-pint containers. The proprietor runs a popular autumn beer festival in a local hall. 🚌🍎

Malt Shovel

15 Springfield Road, RH12 2PG
⏲ 11-11 (midnight Fri & Sat) ☎ (01403) 254543
🌐 maltshovel.com
Brakspear Bitter; Fuller's London Pride; Harveys Sussex Best Bitter; guest beers Ⓖ
This lively town-centre hostelry regularly has up to eight beers served directly from the cask, and real cider and perry are available. Friendly locals and staff grace the bar and at weekends the emphasis is on rugby in season and live bands in the evenings. Quiz night is every Sunday. There is a real fire during the winter months. The pub hosts an annual CAMRA Mild Day event and was runner up local CAMRA Pub of the Year in 2009.
⩋❀♿⇌🚌♣🍎P⸗

Keymer

Greyhound Inn

Keymer Road, BN6 8QT (on B2116 between Hassocks and Ditchling opp church)
⊙ 11-midnight (11-3, 6-midnight Mon-Wed winter); 12-11 Sun ☎ (01273) 842645 ⊕ greyhoundkeymer.com
Adnams Bitter; Gale's HSB; Harveys Sussex Best Bitter; guest beers Ⓗ
Situated in the older part of the village, the inn dates back approximately 450 years and retains many original features. The comfortable beamed main bar has a dining room attached, and the smaller public bar has darts and bar billiards. The landlord and chef, Hassan, prides himself on his excellent food from an extensive menu. There is a rear garden with a covered barn for smokers, and an dining area for summer. Families and dogs are welcome. ⌂Q✿◑◗⊟🚌(33,41)♣P⅃

Lambs Green

Lamb Inn

RH12 4RG (2 miles N of A264) TQ 220368
⊙ 11.30-3, 5.30-11; 11.30-11 Fri & Sat; 12-10.30 Sun
☎ (01293) 871336 ⊕ thelambinn.org
Beer range varies Ⓗ
Until autumn 2007 this was WJ King's only tied house. Now a free house, it offers rotating guest ales normally from Sussex brewers and an annual autumn beer festival. This is a delightful country pub where visitors are surrounded by oak beams and cosy nooks, and a real log fire adds to the timeless atmosphere in winter. Home-cooked food is served lunchtimes and evenings, all day at the weekend, and a large conservatory provides an extension to the dining area. Biddenden cider is stocked. ⌂✿◑◗🚌●P

Lancing

Crabtree Inn

140 Crabtree Lane, BN15 9NQ
⊙ 12-11 (11.30 Thu); 12-12.30am Fri & Sat
☎ (01903) 755514
Beer range varies Ⓗ
An unexpected oasis towards North Lancing, this is a traditional Kemp Town house with a large public bar, with pool, darts and table football. The Spitfire lounge provides a quiet area to enjoy the range of guest beers. The pub offers live music monthly and the bar is available for private functions. There is a spacious child and dog-friendly garden and a heated, covered smoking area. The Crabtree supports the LocAle scheme. There is a carvery Sunday lunchtimes. ✿◑◗⊟♿⇌🚌(7)♣P⅃

Lindfield

Stand Up Inn

47 High Street, RH16 2HN
⊙ 11.30-11.30 (midnight Fri & Sat); 12-11.30 Sun
☎ (01444) 482995 ⊕ standupinn.co.uk
Dark Star Hophead, Best, seasonal beers; guest beers Ⓗ
This popular Dark Star house is situated in the high street of this pleasant village. Real log fires create a warm and comfortable atmosphere in winter. A courtyard at the rear provides a covered area for smokers and contains the old outbuildings of the long defunct Durrant's Brewery. Two beer festivals are held annually plus one cider/perry event. Draught real cider and perry are a regular feature of this pub, together with a good selection of bottled continental beers. ⌂Q✿◑🚌(30,270)♣●⅃

Littlehampton

Crown

29 High Street, BN17 5EG
⊙ 9am-midnight (1am Thu-Sat) ☎ (01903) 719842
⊕ thecrownlittlehampton.co.uk
Beer range varies Ⓗ
Recently refurbished by new owners, this large town-centre pub attracts a cosmopolitan clientele and always has a lot going on. The Crown is a Greene King free tenancy, and features up to 25 very competitively priced beers each month from six pumps. It is also the brewery tap for the nearby Anchor Springs Brewery, which started production in spring 2010. Westons Old Rosie cider is available on draught. ⌂☕✿◑◗⇌🚌(9,700)♣●⅃

Maplehurst

White Horse

Park Lane, RH13 6LL TQ190245
⊙ 12-2.30, 6-11 (11.30 most Fri); 12-3, 7-11 Sun
☎ (01403) 891208
Dark Star Best Bitter; Harveys Sussex Best Bitter; Welton's Pride 'n' Joy; guest beers Ⓗ
Now in its 24th year in the Guide, this delightful country pub with its roomy interior oozes character, with an imposing timber bar and different drinking areas including a large conservatory opening onto an attractive garden. While food is available, the emphasis is very firmly on conversation washed down with the numerous ales on offer, including guest beers often sourced from small independents. Real cider is also stocked. The landlord is a classic car enthusiast; examples are frequently parked outside.
⌂Q✿◑◗⊟🚌(108)♣●P

Milland

Black Fox Inn

Portsmouth Road, GU30 7JJ (1½ miles S of Liphook on B2070) SU 829291
⊙ 12-2, 6-11; 12-4 Sun ☎ (01428) 723218
⊕ theblackfoxinn.co.uk
Gale's HSB; Triple fff Alton's Pride; guest beers Ⓗ
Situated on the B2070 and the West Sussex Border Path, this remote and comfortable free house has an air of spaciousness about its L-shaped bar, high ceilings and brick arches. Food from the extensive menu can be enjoyed in the restaurant, overlooking the patio and an enclosed garden with a play house for children. There is also a skittle alley for hire and four B&B rooms. The guest beers will often come from local micros.
Q✿🛏◑◗⇌(Liphook)P

Mockbridge

Bull Inn

London Road, BN5 9AD (on A281)
⊙ 11.30-3, 6-11; 12-10.30 Sun ☎ (01273) 492232
⊕ thebullinnhenfield.co.uk
Fuller's London Pride; Harveys Sussex Best Bitter; King seasonal beers Ⓗ
The Bull is a traditional roadside country pub with an unusual tile-fronted bar, real log fires in winter, and a large garden at the rear with a children's

play area for the summer. A separate restaurant serves Italian-accented quality food, including daily specials, lunchtimes and evenings, all day until 9pm Sunday. A vast range of pizzas is a speciality and takeaways are available. The skittle alley also serves as a function room available for hire (see website for details). ♨Q❀◐◑♿🚌(17)P⁻

Nutbourne

Rising Sun

The Street, RH20 2HE (off A283, E of Pulborough)
⊛ 11-3, 6-11; 12-3, 7-10.30 Sun ☎ (01798) 812191
🌐 therisingsunnutbourne.co.uk
Beer range varies Ⓗ
Well off the beaten track, this is a venerable stone building dating back to the 16th century, fronted by an ivy-clad Victorian facade. A genuine free house, it has been owned by one family for 30 years, with a total absence of corporate makeover that afflicts so many rural pubs. Four interesting beers are usually available. The main bar has a roaring log fire and summer visitors enjoy the large rustic garden featuring resident poultry and a listed outside privy. ♨Q☕❀◐◑⊟⁻

Pulborough

White Hart

Stopham Road, Stopham Bridge, RH20 1DS (off A283 1 mile W of Pulborough, near bridge over River Arun)
⊛ 11.30-11 (10.30 Sun) ☎ (01798) 873321
🌐 whitehartstophambridge.co.uk
Arundel Gold; Hammerpot Woodcote; King Horsham Best Bitter Ⓗ
Situated next to the 14th-century Stopham Bridge, this was once a coaching inn. The central bar serves four rooms split over two levels, with a log fire in one of the lower rooms. There are cosy alcoves and oak-beamed ceilings throughout. A quiz is held every Thursday evening and live music on the last Friday of the month. Food is served all day at weekends. The outdoor drinking area offers views across the valley. There is an hourly bus service from Worthing. ♨Q❀◐◑🚌P⁻

Rogate

White Horse Inn ✔

East Street, GU31 5EA (on A272)
⊛ 11-midnight (1am Fri & Sat); 12-midnight Sun
☎ (01730) 821333
Harveys Hadlow Bitter, Sussex Best Bitter, Armada Ale, seasonal beers Ⓗ
Dating from the 16th century, this old coaching inn has oak beams, flagstone floors and a huge log fire. At this Harvey's tied house you can expect up to five of its draught beers, including Mild or Old (depending on season) plus seasonal brews. Half the pub is used for dining – a large range of meals includes steaks and vegetarian choices, plus specials on the blackboard (no food Sun eve). The car park overlooks the village sports field behind the pub. ♨Q❀◐◑🚌(91,92)♣P⁻

Rowfant

Rowfant House

Wallage Lane, RH10 4NG (follow Wallage Lane towards jct with B2028. Entrance is about halfway along on left) TQ 325373
⊛ 11.30-11; 12-10.30 Sun ☎ (01342) 714823
🌐 rowfanthouse.co.uk
Harveys Sussex Best Bitter; King Horsham Best Bitter; guest beers Ⓗ
This handsome 16th-century manor house is owned by the Latvian Lutheran Church. A country club set in 22 acres of parkland, the bar is open for all to enjoy. It has seen many famous visitors in past years including Tennyson and Dickens. There are several rooms available for functions. The bar manager is justly proud of his beer quality and local brews are available. ♨☕❀🛏◐◑♿🚌P⁻

Selsey

Seal Hotel ✔

6 Hillfield Road, PO20 0JX (on B2145)
⊛ 10.30-12.30am; 12-11 Sun ☎ (01243) 602461
🌐 the-seal.com
Dark Star Hophead; Greene King IPA; Oakleaf Hole Hearted; Young's Bitter; guest beers Ⓗ
Family-run for 39 years, this spacious free house is popular with locals and visitors alike. Quality home-cooked food and locally-caught fish await in the restaurant (booking advised), and guest beers are mostly from local micros. Acoustic live music often features on Sunday. A patio caters for smokers, with umbrellas and seating. Upstairs 12 en-suite B&B rooms are a recent addition, returning the pub to its former hotel status. There is camping nearby at West Sands Caravan Park. Local CAMRA Pub of the Year 2008.
Q❀🛏◐◑♿⛺🚌(51)♣⁻

Shoreham-by-Sea

Buckingham Arms

35 Brunswick Road, BN43 5WA (opp railway station)
⊛ 11-11; 12-10.30 Sun ☎ (01273) 453660
Greene King Abbot; Harveys Sussex Best Bitter; Hop Back Summer Lightning; Sharp's Doom Bar; Taylor Landlord; guest beers Ⓗ
As you enter you will be met by an array of 11 handpumps dispensing six regular and five guest beers. Harveys XX Mild has recently joined the regulars and is deservedly popular. In July Tom Paine Porter always makes an appearance, with sales consistently better than in most Harvey's tied houses. Keith, the landlord, is justifiably proud of this achievement. Beer festivals are held in February and August. Lunchtime food is available Monday to Saturday. ❀◐⇌🚌(2,9)🍎⁻

Duke of Wellington

368 Brighton Road, BN43 6RE (on A259)
⊛ 12-11 (midnight Fri & Sat); 12-10.30 Sun
☎ (01273) 389818
Dark Star Hophead, seasonal beers; guest beers Ⓗ
Situated just east of the town centre, this Dark Star pub is easily recognised by the large wellington boot pub sign. The building facade still has some of the original Kemp Town Brewery motifs. The spacious rear garden has a barbecue area. The pub is renowned for live music at the weekend, for which an entry fee may be charged. A summer beer festival is held annually. Real cider, normally Thatchers, is served. ❀⇌🚌(2,700)♣🍎⁻

Red Lion

Old Shoreham Road, BN43 5TE
⊛ 12-11 (10.30 Sun) ☎ (01273) 453171
🌐 theredlionshoreham.co.uk

Beer range varies Ⓗ
Historic former coaching inn situated in the old part of town close to the early-Norman church and River Adur. The pub comprises a low-ceilinged, oak-beamed bar with a separate drinking area and a restaurant. Five handpumps serve a wide choice of beers, mainly from Sussex micros. An outdoor seating area offers views of the airport and Lancing College, while the secluded garden has an air of tranquillity. The Adur Beer Festival is held here every Easter. ♨Q❀◐🚌(2A)♣P⁻

Sompting

Gardener's Arms

West Street, BN15 0AR (on S side of West Street)
⏲ 11-11 (midnight Fri); 12-midnight Sat; 12-11 Sun
☎ (01903) 233666
Draught Bass; Harveys Sussex Best Bitter; Sharp's Doom Bar; guest beers Ⓗ
This fine hostelry stands in what was originally Sompting's main street. Reopened last year after an unobtrusive extension to the eastern elevation, it has been sympathetically redecorated by the hands-on landlord. The landlady prepares the home-cooked food herself (no food Mon). Four handpumps are in operation, with plans for a fifth one. There is an outside patio area. A half-hourly bus service runs from Worthing and Lancing. ♨❀◐⊟♿🚌(7)P⁻

Staplefield

Jolly Tanners ✔

Handcross Road, RH17 6EF
⏲ 11-3, 5.30 (5 Fri winter)-11; 11-11 Fri summer & Sat; 11-10.30 Sun ☎ (01444) 400335
Fuller's London Pride; Harveys Sussex Best Bitter; guest beers Ⓗ
On the north corner of the cricket green, this welcoming pub combines all the best elements of a village inn. The spacious bar is divided into two distinct areas and a log fire adds to the cosy feel. The large range of guest beers always includes a mild, and real cider is also served. A good range of tasty food is available at all sessions and popular; however, this is still very much a locals' pub. Beer festivals are held during May and November. ♨Q❀◐🚌(271)♣🍏P

Steyning

Chequer Inn ✔

41 High Street, BN44 3RE
⏲ 10-11 (midnight Fri & Sat) ☎ (01903) 814437
🌐 chequerinnsteyning.co.uk
Gale's HSB; Harveys Sussex Best Bitter; Taylor Landlord; guest beers Ⓗ
Fifteenth-century coaching inn which retains many original architectural features. There are several drinking areas including a covered courtyard garden and cosy saloon bar with an open log fire in winter, and a 100-year-old, three-quarter-size snooker table. Guest ales always include one from Dark Star. Home-cooked, traditional and speciality food makes use of locally-sourced ingredients, with breakfasts ever popular. There is an hourly 2A bus service from Brighton and Shoreham, with Compass bus services from other Sussex towns. ♨Q❀⇌◐⊟🚌(2A,100)♣P⁻

Stoughton

Hare & Hounds

PO18 9JQ (off B2146) SU802115
⏲ 11-3, 6-11; 11-11 Fri & Sat; 12-10.30 Sun
☎ (023) 9263 1433 🌐 hareandhoundspub.co.uk
Ballard's Best Bitter; Harveys Sussex Best Bitter; Taylor Landlord; guest beer Ⓗ
An ideal base for walking, this is a traditional country pub in a beautiful downland valley. A large dining room serves fresh local produce, while the public bar is the locals' choice. There are three open fires in all which, along with stone-flagged floors, beams and simple furniture, create a wonderful atmosphere. Outside is a paved drinking area at the front and a garden at the back. The bus stops on the B2146, a mile away. Cider is Westons. ♨Q❀◐⊟🚌(54)♣🍏P

Thakeham

White Lion Inn

The Street, RH20 3EP (just off B2139)
⏲ 11-11; 12-10.30 Sun ☎ (01798) 813141
Caledonian Deuchars IPA; Fuller's London Pride; Harveys Sussex Best Bitter; guest beers Ⓗ
A genuine free house situated in an idyllic village setting, this part 17th-century ale house offers a warm and friendly ambience. It has a central bar with three different drinking areas and a separate dining room. The food is excellent, with the dining room fireplace used to smoke local ham, cheese and sausages. Thankfully, the White Lion has remained virtually unchanged over its 371-year history. Long may this continue! Dog friendly. ♨Q❀◐⊟♿🚌(74)♣P⁻

The Haven

Blue Ship ★ ✔

RH14 9BS TQ084305
⏲ 11-3, 6-11; 12-4, 7-8.30 Sun ☎ (01403) 822709
Badger K&B Sussex Best, First Gold Ⓖ
The Blue Ship is 15th/16th century, welcoming and snug, with very friendly staff and customers. It has four rooms, featuring log fires and a coal burning stove. There are red-brick, wooden and carpeted floors, and various old wooden tables, settles, wood-beamed ceilings and leaded-glass windows, with a display cabinet for bar billiards trophies. Beer is on stillage and pub food is excellent. The local clay shoot meets here. On the CAMRA National Inventory of Historic Pub Interiors. ♨Q❀◐♿♣P⁻

Tillington

Horseguards Inn

Upperton Road, GU28 9AF
⏲ 12-11 (11.30 Fri & Sat) ☎ (01798) 342332
🌐 thehorseguardsinn.co.uk
Harveys Sussex Best Bitter; Langham Hip Hop; Skinner's Betty Stogs Ⓗ
Originally three cottages, this old pub sits high up from the road opposite the charming All Hallows church and its unusual tower. Its name refers to a regiment that was stabled in Petworth Park during the Napoleonic Wars. The main bar has an open fire, while there are three other rooms at different levels, one with a cosy stove. Outside is a small front terrace plus a larger rear garden. Top quality food is served. ♨❀⇌◐♿🚌(1)♣

Trotton

Keepers Arms

Love Hill, Terwick Lane, GU31 5ER (on A272, 3 miles W of Midhurst) SU839222

⊙ 12-3, 6-11 (7-10.30 Sun) ☎ (01730) 813724

🌐 keepersarms.co.uk

Dark Star Hophead; Otter Bitter; Ringwood Fortyniner; guest beer 🄷

Set high above the road and the River Rother near Trotton Bridge, this 17th-century inn boasts low ceilings, bare wood floors and a comfortable sofa by an open log fire. A smart dining area features an adventurous menu, but the bar remains welcoming to drinkers. The elevated patio around two sides of the pub is popular in fine weather. Real cider is usually available in the summer. There is level access from the car park. ♨❀◑♿🚌(92)♣●P⸗

Turners Hill

Red Lion ✔

Lion Lane, RH10 4NU (off North St, B2028)

⊙ 11 (12 Sun)-11 ☎ (01342) 715416

Harveys XX Mild, Sussex Best Bitter, seasonal beers 🄷

Still very much the village local, a friendly welcome is assured at this split-level pub with an inglenook fireplace. Mild ale is now available as a result of customer demand. Twice-monthly quiz nights are held in aid of local charities. Occasional live music is played in the garden during summer months. Wi-Fi Internet access is available. Children and dogs are welcome. North Sussex CAMRA held its first meeting here in 1974. ♨Q❀◑🚌(82)♣P⸗

Warnham

Sussex Oak ✔

2 Church Street, RH12 3QW

⊙ 11-11 (10.30 Sun) ☎ (01403) 265028

🌐 thesussexoak.co.uk

Adnams Bitter; Fuller's London Pride; Taylor Landlord; Young's Bitter; guest beers 🄷

Parts of this pub, situated in the centre of the village, date back to the 16th century. The large L-shaped bar area is broken up by pillars and partitions, and a room opposite the bar has a stone floor and large inglenook fireplace. There is a separate restaurant and, outside, a large garden. A wide selection of food is available including daily specials and roast lunches on Sunday. The outside smoking area is heated. Families and dogs are welcome. ♨❀◑🚌(93)♣●P⸗

Warninglid

Half Moon

The Street, RH17 5TR (on B2115 crossroads)

⊙ 11.30-2.30, 5.30-11; 11-11 Sat; 12-10.30 Sun

☎ (01444) 461227 🌐 thehalfmoonwarninglid.co.uk

Harveys Sussex Best Bitter; Greene King Old Speckled Hen; guest beers 🄷

Large village pub dating back in parts to the 16th century. The entrance leads straight into the bar, with oak beams, wooden floors, an open fire and a long wooden table. To the right are smaller rooms with three more fires and a conservatory restaurant with a covered and illuminated well flush with the floor. Locally sourced ingredients are used in the excellent food. LocAle accredited and dog friendly. ♨Q❀◑🚌♣P⸗

West Chiltington

Five Bells

Smock Alley, RH20 2QX (1 mile SE of village centre) TQ091170

⊙ 12-3, 6-11 (7-10.30 Sun) ☎ (01798) 812143

🌐 fivebellsinn.co.uk

Arundel Sussex Mild; Harveys Sussex Best Bitter; Palmers Copper Ale; guest beers 🄷

The genial hosts have been welcoming drinkers, diners, walkers and dog lovers to their CAMRA award-winning pub, easily accessed by daily buses, for nearly three decades. Formerly King & Barnes tenants, Bill and Joan bought the freehold and added en-suite accommodation and a conservatory restaurant. The menu features locally-sourced produce, usually including a hearty home-made steak and kidney pie and proper fish and chips (takeaway available). No food Sunday or Monday evenings. A rare outlet for mild.
♨Q❀🛏◑🚌(1,74)♣●P

West Itchenor

Ship Inn

The Street, PO20 7AH (on main street, 100m from waterfront)

⊙ 11-11; 12-10.30 Sun ☎ (01243) 512284 🌐 theshipinn.biz

Arundel Castle; Ballard's Best Bitter; King Horsham Best Bitter; guest beer 🄷

Attractive 1930s-built pub in the main street of the village leading down to the picturesque harbour. Many original features remain, including parquet floors and wood-and-brick fireplaces. Homely wood-panelled bars decorated with yachting memorabilia add to the pub's character, and the wide front patio is a suntrap in summer. Two rooms are dedicated to dining, offering a wide range of traditional meals, often including locally-landed fish. Up to four ales are normally available from local breweries, with competitively-priced session beers. ♨Q❀🛏◑⊟🚌(52,53)♣P⸗

Westbourne

Cricketers

Commonside, PO10 8TA (N from The Square, turn E at Lashley's Garage) SU 758082

⊙ 5-11.30; 12-midnight Thu-Sun ☎ (01243) 372647

Fuller's London Pride; Gale's HSB; guest beers 🄷

This 300-year-old local is the only true free house in a village of good pubs. Situated on the northern outskirts, it is hard to find but well worth the effort. Conversation abounds in the single L-shaped, half-panelled bar. There is a suntrap garden to the side, with a covered and heated smoking area. Up to three guest beers come from mainly Hampshire and Sussex micros, often from Suthwyk Brewery (brewed by Oakleaf), as well as Timothy Taylor Landlord. ♨Q❀⇌(Emsworth)🚌(11,36)♣P⸗

Stag's Head

The Square, PO10 8UE (on B2147, in village centre)

⊙ 12-11 (10.30 Sun) ☎ (01243) 372393

Oakleaf Hole Hearted; Ringwood Best Bitter; guest beers 🄷

A very welcome new entrant to the Guide, this early 19th-century pub was built on the site of the village market and subsequently extended into a neighbouring shop. The newer area is mainly used for dining (no food Sun eve or Mon), leaving the remainder of the L-shaped bar with its real fire for drinkers. There is an outside bar in the yard that

comes into its own during beer festivals, when the usual diet of local micros is supplemented by beers from far and wide.
♨Q❀◖◗♿≠(Emsworth)🚌(11,36)♣⌐

Whitemans Green

Ship Inn

RH17 5BY (N of Cuckfield at B2115/B2036 jct)
⏲ 12-2 (not Wed), 5.30-11; 12-11 Sat; 12-4 Sun
☎ (01444) 413219
Harveys Sussex Best Bitter; guest beers Ⓖ
Located at the north end of Cuckfield, this is a family-run pub. The handpumps are for decorative purposes only – the beers are served by gravity from a cooled back room. The bar features a double-sided fireplace decorated with pottery steins, and has a dining area at one end. A pool table and dartboard are in a separate games room. Food is served lunchtimes (not Wed) and evenings (not Sun), with a changing range of specials in addition to the regular menu. B&B available.
♨Q❀🛏◖◗🚌(271,272)P⌐

Worthing

Cricketers

66 Broadwater Street West, Broadwater, BN14 9DE (on A24 opp Broadwater Green)
⏲ 11-3, 6-11 Mon & Tue; 11-11 Wed & Thu; 11-11.30 Fri & Sat; 12-10.30 Sun ☎ (01903) 233369
Fuller's London Pride; Harveys Sussex Best Bitter; Hop Back Summer Lightning; Ringwood Fortyniner; Shepherd Neame Bishops Finger; guest beers Ⓗ
Overlooking Broadwater Green, this friendly pub has been serving locals for more than 160 years. The spacious single bar retains a cosy feel, with distinct areas for a restaurant and games. There are real fires in winter. The keen landlord hosts three annual beer festivals. A fenced-off area where children can play safely allows adults to enjoy the large rear garden. Accompanied children are welcomed in the lower bar up to 9pm. Evening meals served Friday-Sunday. ♨❀◖◗🚌⌐

George & Dragon ✔

1 High Street, Tarring, BN14 7NN (S end of Tarring High Street)
⏲ 11-11 (midnight Fri & Sat); 12-10.30 Sun
☎ (01903) 202497 🌐 ganddtarring.co.uk
Courage Directors; Greene King Abbot; Harveys Sussex Best Bitter; Hop Back Summer Lightning; Young's Bitter; guest beers Ⓗ
This traditional 17th-century village pub enjoys strong local support. Low-beamed ceilings and a warm decor create a cosy atmosphere with universal appeal. There are distinct drinking areas including a suntrap patio and garden space. Locally sourced, home-cooked food is available lunchtimes and some evenings. There is a meat raffle on Sunday lunchtime, jazz on the first Tuesday of the month, and live music twice a month at weekends. Home to a darts team and golf society, charity fundraising events are also held.
❀◖≠(West Worthing)🚌(6,6A)♣P⌐

Richard Cobden ✔

2 Cobden Road, BN11 4BD
⏲ 11-11 (11.30 Fri & Sat); 12-4, 7-10.30 Sun
☎ (01903) 236856 🌐 therichardcobden.co.uk
Harveys Sussex Best Bitter; Hop Back Summer Lightning; guest beers Ⓗ
An archetypal street-corner pub that continues to welcome a wide cross-section of the local community. The cosy L-shaped bar offers conversation, darts, cards, a popular Sunday lunchtime meat raffle, jazz (Thu eve) and occasional live music on other nights. Outside is a pleasant courtyard garden. This is the spiritual home of a local morris side who perform a traditional mummers' play on New Year's Day featuring the pub's Father Christmas, with folk singing later. Daily buses stop nearby. ❀◖♿≠♣⌐

Selden Arms

41 Lyndhurst Road, BN11 2DB (nr Worthing Hospital)
⏲ 11-11 (11.30 Fri); 12-11.30 Sat; 12-10.30 Sun
Dark Star Hophead; Ringwood Fortyniner; guest beers Ⓗ
A regular for many years in this Guide and a must for real ale fans. A chalkboard lists 1,200 different ales served in the last 12 years, another tempts with 'What's on Soon'. Six handpumps dispense the varied range, with one dark ale always available. Bottled Belgian beers and over 30 malt whiskies are stocked. A beer festival is held in January, Wi-Fi is available and dogs are welcome. Some TV sport is shown quietly and there is occasional acoustic live music. ◖≠🚌(9,106)

Swan Inn

79 High Street, BN11 1DN
⏲ 11-11 (midnight Fri & Sat); 12-11 Sun ☎ (01903) 232923
Greene King Abbot; Harveys Sussex Best Bitter; Hop Back Summer Lightning; guest beers Ⓗ
Just five minutes' walk from Worthing town centre, this traditional 19th-century Sussex pub has flint walls, beams, brasses and agricultural implements a-plenty. Two fireplaces and stained glass windows from the days of the Kemp Town Brewery lend an historic feel. Cheerful staff and consistently well-kept ales ensure that this is a popular haven for shoppers and locals. Evening attactions include bar billiards, quizzes and musical entertainment Friday to Sunday. There are extensive lunchtime menus with generous portions, and a freshly cooked Sunday roast. Runner up local CAMRA Pub of the Year. ♨❀◖≠🚌(9,106)♣⌐

Yapton

Maypole Inn

Maypole Lane, BN18 0DP (off B2132 1km N of village; pedestrian access across railway from Lake Lane) SU978042
⏲ 11.30-11 (midnight Fri & Sat); 12-11 Sun
☎ (01243) 551417 🌐 themaypoleinn.co.uk
Dark Star Hophead; Greene King XX Mild; Skinner's Betty Stogs; guest beers Ⓗ
This small flint-built inn is hidden away from the village centre, down a narrow lane ending in a pedestrian crossing over the railway. The cosy lounge boasts two open fires and an imposing row of eight handpumps, dispensing a variety of up to four guest beers. The public bar has a jukebox, darts, pool and a TV for sports events. A skittle alley/function room with bar billiards table can be booked. There is a covered veranda for smokers. The cider is Thatchers Gold.
♨Q❀◖⊟⛺≠(Barnham)🚌(66,66A,700)♣⬟P⌐

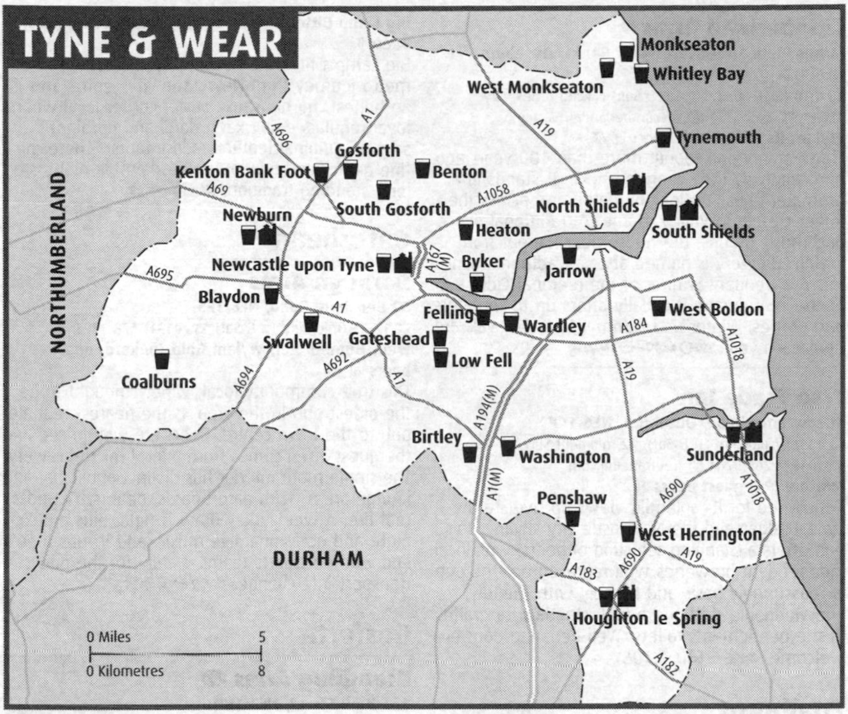

Benton

Benton Ale House

Front Street, NE7 7XE

⊙ 11-11 (11.30 Wed; midnight Fri & Sat); 12-11 Sun
☎ (0191) 266 1512 ⊕ bentonalehouse.com

Banks's Bitter; Jennings Cumberland Ale; Marston's Pedigree; guest beers ⊞

Traditional pub with a horseshoe bar and large bay windows giving a light and airy feel. There is plenty of good quality seating throughout. Be sure to check the monthly beer menu on the bar. Reasonably-priced good-quality food is available – Sunday lunchtime booking is essential. The pub is family-friendly. ☺◑♿⊖(Four Lane Ends)P⁄–

Birtley

Barley Mow Inn ✔

Durham Road, Barley Mow, DH3 2AG (jct of Durham Road and Vigo Lane)

⊙ 11.30-midnight (12.30am Fri & Sat); 10-midnight Sun
☎ (0191) 410 4504 ⊕ thebarleymowinn.co.uk

Rudgate Viking; guest beers ⊞

On the border with County Durham, this 1930s roadhouse has a split-level lounge, dining area and dog-friendly public bar. With one regular beer and seven guests, often from northern England, it has the widest range of real ales for some distance and is a CAMRA LocAle member. A real cider is also stocked. The pub hosts a weekly quiz, dominoes and darts (the landlord is a keen player). There is also frequent live music and an annual music and beer festival is held in February.
❀◑⊟♿⊟♣●P⁄–

Blaydon

Black Bull ✔

Bridge Street, NE21 4JJ

⊙ 2-11; 12-midnight Fri & Sat; 12-11 Sun ☎ (0191) 414 2846

Black Sheep Best Bitter; Caledonian Deuchars IPA; guest beers ⊞

Traditional two-roomed pub with old-fashioned values: 'No pool table, no juke-box, no bandit' boasts the proud landlord. There has been a pub on this site since the 1800s and the pub displays many framed photographs of old Blaydon. Two folk nights are held weekly, plus a buskers' night, quiz night and live bands once a month. There are barbecues in the superb rear beer garden during the summer months, which enjoys excellent views of the River Tyne and Tyne Valley. Dog-friendly.
♨∩⊟⇌⊟(10,602)♣P

Byker

Cluny

36 Lime Street, Ouseburn, NE1 2PQ

⊙ 11.30-11 (midnight Thu; 1am Fri & Sat); 12-10.30 Sun
☎ (0191) 230 4474 ⊕ theheadofsteam.com

Beer range varies ⊞

Large, former industrial building converted into a pub, art gallery and live music venue. The pub runs frequent themed beer festivals and always has a good selection of British and foreign draught and bottled products on offer. The art gallery displays work of all kinds ranging from final degree shows to local independent established artists. Live music sessions are held most evenings featuring a wide range of British, European and American musicians.
❀◑♿⊖●

Cumberland Arms ★

James Place Street (off Byker Bank), Ouseburn, NE6 1LD

☼ 4.30 (3.30 Fri; 12.30 Sat & Sun)-closing times vary
☎ (0191) 265 6151 ⊕ thecumberlandarms.co.uk

Wylam Rapper; guest beers ⊞/ⓖ

Three-storey pub rebuilt more than 100 years ago and relatively little changed since. It stands in a prominent position looking down and across the lower Ouseburn Valley. Home to traditional dance and music groups, the house beer Rapper from Wylam Brewery is named after a traditional dance form. A frequent winner of the regional Cider Pub of the Year award, it usually offers up to six ciders and perries. Winter and summer beer festivals are held each year. ▲Q☞⏌⊖♣♨P

Free Trade Inn

St Lawrence Road, Ouseburn, NE6 1AP

☼ 11-11 (midnight Fri & Sat); 12-midnight Sun
☎ (0191) 265 5764 ⊕ freetradeinn.com

Mordue IPA; guest beers ⊞

Renowned for its splendid views up river to the Tyne Bridges and the Newcastle city skyline, this pub offers a changing selection of beers, with local independent breweries well represented. The pub is reassuringly basic and homely with friendly, knowledgable staff and a high standard of graffiti in the gentlemen's toilets. Well-behaved dogs are welcome. ▲❀⊖⏛(Q2,106)

Coalburns

Fox & Hounds (Coalies)

NE40 4JN

☼ 4-11; 1-midnight Sat; 2 (11 summer)-11 Sun
☎ (0191) 413 2549

Black Sheep Best Bitter; Caledonian Deuchars IPA; guest beers ⊞

Welcoming, traditional pub with friendly management and bar staff on the outskirts of Greenside. Dating from 1795, the walls and ceilings are decorated with memorabilia from the local industries of centuries ago. The traditional open fire has a granny's oven, giving the pub a homely feel. Although flooded last year, the pub was reopened within a day with help from the local villagers in order to hold their annual leek show. It also holds regular themed cookery nights, a folk club on Sunday, quiz night on Wednesday and live music on Saturday. ▲Q◑♣P

Felling

Old Fox

10-14 Carlisle Street, NE10 0HQ

☼ 3 (1 Fri-Sun)-11 ☎ (07941) 393075

Castle Rock Harvest Pale; Fuller's London Pride; guest beers ⊞

Pleasant real ale pub a short walk from Felling Metro. The open fire gives the bar a homely feel. A live band plays on the first Saturday of the month. Monday night is local buskers' night, and darts and quiz nights are hosted. The present landlord has returned after several years away and is busy restoring the pub to its former glory. ▲❀☞⊖♣♨└

Wheatsheaf

26 Carlisle Road, NE10 0HQ

☼ 5 (12 Fri & Sat)-11; 12-10.30 Sun ☎ (0191) 420 0659

Big Lamp Bitter, Prince Bishop, Sunny Daze; guest beers ⊞

Big Lamp's first tied house is well-worth the short metro journey from Newcastle city centre. This is an honest, no-nonsense street-corner local where loyal regulars enjoy keen darts and dominoes schools. Original features add interest – note the fine gantry and windows. Tuesday folk night is a long-standing tradition. ▲◑⊖⏛♣♨

Gateshead

Borough Arms

82 Bensham Road, NE8 1PS

☼ 12-11 (midnight Fri & Sat) ☎ (0191) 478 1323

Wells Bombardier; Wylam Gold Tankard; guest beers ⊞

This true community local, widely thought to be the oldest pub in the area, is the nearest real ale pub to the town centre. Beers are well-priced and the guest often comes from a local micro-brewery. The single room interior has distinct public bar and lounge areas, with bare boards, beams, TV and a real fire. A weekly key draw is held, plus a poker night and occasional live music, and it runs men's and women's darts teams. Handy for the public transport interchange. ▲❀⊖⏛♣P

Gosforth

Brandling Arms ✓

176 High Street, NE3 1HD

☼ 11-11 (midnight Fri & Sat); 12-10.30 Sun
☎ (0191) 285 4023 ⊕ thebrandlingarmsgosforth.co.uk

Caledonian Deuchars IPA; Mordue Workie Ticket; guest beers ⊞

Set back in the middle of Gosforth High Street, this is a large pub with an emphasis on food. The original name is thought to come from the Brandlings, a family of merchants and land owners. Tastefully refurbished, there are distinct areas for dining while remaining drinker-friendly. Two rotating guests are served alongside the regular beers. Quiz night is Wednesday. ❀◑♿⊖(Regent Centre)♨

Job Bulman ✓

St Nicholas Avenue, NE3 1AA

☼ 9-11 ☎ (0191) 223 6230

Greene King IPA, Abbot; Marston's Pedigree; guest beers ⊞

Impressive Wetherspoon conversion of the old Post Office building just off busy Gosforth High Street. Catering equally for diners and drinkers, the unusual horseshoe-shaped interior houses a large bar area in the centre, with more discrete dining areas to each side. Outside is a courtyard with an area for smokers. Three regular beers are complemented by a constantly rotating guest list, with up to eight ales on at any one time. At least two guests are from local micro-breweries. ⏃◑⊖(Regent Centre)♨└

INDEPENDENT BREWERIES
Big Lamp Newburn
Bull Lane Sunderland
Darwin Sunderland
Double Maxim Houghton le Spring
Hadrian & Border Newcastle upon Tyne
Jarrow South Shields
Mordue North Shields

Heaton

Chillingham

Chillingham Road, NE6 5XN
☼ 11-11 (midnight Fri & Sat); 12-10.30 Sun
☎ (0191) 265 5915
Black Sheep Best Bitter; Jarrow Bitter; Mordue Workie Ticket; guest beers Ⓗ
A large two-roomed pub in contrasting styles, appealing to the widest possible customer base. The traditional public bar has dark wood panelling and a historic mirror recalling the past glories of nearby Wallsend, while the lounge has a contemporary feel with excellent artwork depicting the sights of Newcastle, plus flat-screen TVs showing sports. An upstairs function room holds live music and comedy nights. Look out for bottled beer, whisky and the wine of the month.
◐Ⓔ⊖(Chillingham Road)⊒(62,63)●

Houghton le Spring

Burn Inn

Hetton Road, DH5 8JN
☼ 12-11 (11.30 Fri; midnight Sat) ☎ (0191) 584 2130
⊕ burninnpub.co.uk
Banks's Mild; Marston's Pedigree; guest beers Ⓗ
Family-friendly inn located centrally to both Hetton le Hole and Houghton le Spring. A Marston's pub, it offers a varied selection of quality guest ales. Food is available at very competitive prices with themed menus for special occasions such as Mother's Day, Valentine's Day, and so on. There is a separate room with a pool table. ◐⊒(M1,20,35)♣P

Copt Hill

Seaham Road, DH5 8LU (on B1404)
☼ 11-midnight; 11.30-11.30 Sun ☎ (0191) 584 4485
Maxim Ward's Bitter, Samson; guest beer Ⓗ
Commanding views over Houghton and close to the famous local landmark, this former Vaux pub shares many connections with the local Maxim brewery and acts as its unofficial tap. Two of its beers are always available, complemented by three guest ales, often locally sourced. Excellent food is available all day from an extensive menu – booking for the recently refurbished restaurant is advisable as it can get very busy at evenings and weekends. Live music plays every Sunday night. ◐Ⅎ⊒(20)P

Three Horseshoes

Pit House Lane, Leamside, DH4 6QQ (½ mile N of A690 at West Rainton)
☼ 11 (12 Sun)-11 ☎ (0191) 584 2394
⊕ threehorseshoesleamside.co.uk
Taylor Landlord; guest beers Ⓗ
Four years ago this pub underwent extensive alterations and building work – the result is well-worth a visit. The landlord is a past winner of CAMRA branch and regional Pub of the Year competitions with previous pubs. The traditional bar has a large open fire, to the rear is a smart modern restaurant, and outside a spacious garden area. Fresh food is served in both rooms, with a varied menu in the restaurant (booking advisable). The pub is home to local cycle and clay pigeon clubs. Traditional cider comes from Westons.
♨❀◐Ⅎ&●P

Jarrow

Robin Hood

Primrose Hill, NE32 5UB (on Roman Road below A194)
☼ 12-11 (11.30 Fri & Sat) ☎ (0191) 428 5454
⊕ jarrowbrewery.co.uk
Jarrow Bitter, Rivet Catcher, Joblings Swinging Gibbet, McConnells Irish Stout; guest beers Ⓗ
A winner of CAMRA local and regional Pub of the Year awards, the Robin Hood is not to be missed. The interior comprises two bars, a conservatory and restaurant. Outside are covered and heated drinking and smoking areas, plus a purpose-built music and function room (look for the ghostly manservant in the royal box!). Four Jarrow ales are on offer plus a guest. Beer festivals are held twice a year. Live music plays Friday-Sunday and on the first Tuesday of the month. A quiz is hosted on Sunday, and poker night on Thursday.
☽❀◐Ⅎ&⊖(Fellgate)⊒(88,89)♣●P¹⌐

Kenton Bank Foot

Twin Farms

22 Main Road, NE13 8AB
☼ 11.30-11 (10.30 Sun) ☎ (0191) 286 1263
Black Sheep Best Bitter; Taylor Landlord; guest beers Ⓗ
Large stone-built former farmhouse standing in its own grounds, it has various comfortable areas inside and out to sit and enjoy the extensive selection of beers on offer. The management runs various events for regulars including brewery visits and Meet the Brewer sessions. Good classic British food is served – the pub aims to reduce food miles and uses locally-sourced ingredients from named suppliers. ♨Q☽❀◐&⊖⊒(X77,X78)●P

Low Fell

Aletaster

706 Durham Road, NE9 6JA
☼ 12-11 (midnight Fri); 11-midnight Sat ☎ (0191) 487 0770
Durham White Amarillo; Everards Tiger; Jennings Cumberland Ale; Taylor Landlord; Theakston Best Bitter, Old Peculier Ⓗ
With 11 handpulls, this suburban ale house offers the greatest number of real ales (and a real cider) for miles around. It is a member of CAMRA's LocAle scheme and guest beers come from regional brewers anywhere in the country. The pub has been a regular in the Guide under the same landlord for nearly 20 years. It has an L-shaped public bar with bare boards and TVs plus a cosy lounge. It hosts a weekly quiz, occasional live music, and beer festivals from time to time. Ⓔ⊒♣●P

Monkseaton

Black Horse

68 Front Street, NE25 8DP
☼ 11-midnight; 12-11.30 Sun ☎ (0191) 253 6931
Caledonian Deuchars IPA; Durham Magus; Jarrow Rivet Catcher; guest beers Ⓗ
Active town pub with darts, dominoes, football, cricket and even a whist team. The bar area is decked out in signed Newcastle United and Whitley Bay FC shirts. Young actors practise in a room upstairs and perform a live show on the second Saturday of the month. Occasional free barbecues are held on Sunday in the summer months. The

cheerful landlord typifies the atmosphere in this happy pub. A disabled ramp is provided for easy access. Q☕◑⊞♿⊖♣⟵

Newburn

Keelman
Grange Road, NE15 8NL
⏲ 11-11; 12-10.30 Sun ☎ (0191) 267 0772
Big Lamp Sunny Daze, Bitter, Summerhill Stout, Prince Bishop; guest beers Ⓗ
This tastefully converted Grade II-listed former pumping station is now home to the Big Lamp Brewery and Keelman brewery tap. A conservatory has been added to accommodate a growing band of diners and drinkers who come to sample the full range of Big Lamp beers. Quality accommodation is provided in the adjacent Keelman's Lodge and Salmon Cottage. Attractively situated by Tyne Riverside Country Park, the Coast to Coast cycleway and Hadrian's Wall National Trail. ❀🛏◑🚌(22)P

Newcastle upon Tyne

Bacchus
4248 High Bridge, NE1 6BX
⏲ 11.30-11 (midnight Fri & Sat); 7-10.30 Sun
☎ (0191) 261 1008
Jarrow Rivet Catcher; guest beers Ⓗ
Current CAMRA Tyneside Pub of the Year, this smart, comfortable city-centre pub offers a wide range of rapidly-changing guest beers. Regular 'brewery weekends' are held when all eight handpumps are given over to beers from a single brewery and food is matched to individual beers. Photographs and posters showing the industries in which this region used to lead the world cover the walls. Ciders are served direct from the cellar – check the list on the bar for what is available.
◑♿⇌(Central)⊖(Monument)🍎

Bodega
125 Westgate Road, NE1 6BX
⏲ 11-11 (midnight Fri & Sat); 12-10.30 Sun
☎ (0191) 221 1552
Big Lamp Prince Bishop; Durham Magus; guest beers Ⓗ
Two fine stained-glass domes are the architectural highlight of the pub, which stands next to the Tyne Theatre and attracts football and music fans. The interior offers a number of standing and seating areas, with separate booths for more intimate drinking. A number of old brewery mirrors adorns the walls. TVs show sporting events and the pub can be busy on match days.
◑⇌(Central)⊖(Central)🍎

Bridge Hotel
Castle Garth, NE1 1RQ
⏲ 11.30-11 (midnight Fri & Sat); 12-10.30 Sun
☎ (0191) 232 6400
Black Sheep Best Bitter; Caledonian Deuchars IPA; guest beers Ⓗ
Situated next to the High Level Bridge, built by Stephenson, and facing the keep of the 'new' castle, which gives the city its name. The rear windows and the patio have views of the city walls, River Tyne and Gateshead Quays. The main bar area, adorned with many stained-glass windows, is divided into a number of seating areas, with a raised section at the rear used for dining at lunchtime. Among the live music events held in the upstairs function room is what is claimed to be the oldest folk club in the country.
❀◑⇌(Central)⊖(Central)🍎

Centurion
Central Station, Neville Street, NE1 5DG
⏲ 10-11 (10 Fri & Sat) ☎ (0191) 261 6611
🌐 centurion-newcastle.co.uk/bar.asp
Black Sheep Best Bitter; Caledonian Deuchars IPA; guest beers Ⓗ
This beautiful bar was built in 1893 as a sumptuous waiting lounge for first class passengers – a major feature being the exquisite tiling. It was closed during the 1960s when the British Transport Police used it as cells. Since its restoration the grandeur of the John Dobson-designed interior has been enjoyed by thousands of customers, both locals and visitors to Newcastle. This is the starting point for Whistle Stops real ale outings.
☕◑⊞♿⇌(Central)⊖(Central)🚌🍎

Crown Posada ★
33 Side, NE1 3JE
⏲ 12 (11 Thu)-11; 11-midnight Fri; 12-midnight Sat; 7-10.30 Sun ☎ (0191) 232 1269
Hadrian Gladiator; Jarrow Bitter; Mordue Workie Ticket; guest beers Ⓗ
An architecturally fine pub, listed in CAMRA's National Inventory of Historic Pub Interiors. Behind the narrow street frontage with its two impressive stained-glass windows lies a small snug, bar counter and a longer seating area. There is an interesting coffered ceiling, local photographs and cartoons of long-gone customers and staff on the walls. Local small brewers are enthusiastically supported. The pub has been sympathetically refurbished over the years by the owners and is an oasis of calm and peace near the busy Quayside drinking, dining and clubbing circuit.
Q⇌(Central)⊖(Central)🚌(Q1,Q2)⟵

Duke of Wellington ✔
High Bridge, NE1 1EN
⏲ 11-11; 12-10.30 Sun ☎ (0191) 261 8852
Caledonian Deuchars IPA; Taylor Landlord; guest beers Ⓗ
Recently acquired by an enthusiastic real ale supporter, the Duke has retained its independent identity with a mixed clientele drawn by the selection of beers from near and far. The pub is near the infamous Bigg Market area, but just far enough away to ensure that it is off the young revellers' circuit. Home-made lunchtime and afternoon food is simple and good value. Very busy on match days. ◑⇌(Central)⊖(Monument)🍎

New Bridge
2 Argyle Street, NE1 6PF
⏲ 11-11 (11.30 Thu); 12-10.30 Sun ☎ (0191) 232 1020
Beer range varies Ⓗ
Just east of Newcastle city centre, well-served by buses and the Metro, this pub offers an ever-changing choice of ales from independent brewers. It is very much a locals' pub, but all are made welcome. Situated next to a business park and facing a new large extension to Northumbria University, it attracts a mixed lunchtime and early-evening crowd enjoying the beer and home-made food. ◑⊖(Manors)

Newcastle Arms
57 St Andrew's Street, NE1 5SE (20m from Chinese Arch at Gallowgate end of Stowell St)

11-11; 12-10.30 Sun ☎ (0191) 260 2490
newcastlearms.co.uk
Caledonian Deuchars IPA; guest beers ⊞
Popular single-roomed pub near St James' Park and Chinatown, the 'Top Arms' is a multiple winner of local CAMRA Pub of the Year competitions. The staff are committed to giving the customer what they want – an impressive range of beer is sourced from far and wide, including a seasonal house beer from Big Lamp Brewery. Beer festivals are held regularly, when a portable bar brings the number of beers available to 13.
Q⊟♿⇌(Central)⊖(Monument/St James)●

North Shields

Magnesia Bank
1 Camden Street, NE30 1NH
12-11 (midnight Fri & Sat) ☎ (0191) 257 4831
magnesiabank.com
Durham Magus; guest beers ⊞
The 'Maggie Bank' was once a bank, then a social club before conversion into a pub. The hostelry is now a popular music venue, with free live music every Wednesday, Friday and Saturday, and a buskers' night on Monday. As well as the pub, there is Café Black Door, open Wednesday to Saturday evenings, which offers an extensive food menu. A former CAMRA Pub of the Year, this is now a much-improved boozer. ◗⊖

Oddfellows
7 Albion Road, NE30 2RJ
11 (12 Sun)-11 ☎ (0191) 257 4288
oddfellowspub.co.uk
Greene King Abbot; Jarrow Bitter; guest beer ⊞
The walls of this small, friendly, single-room lounge bar are covered with historic maps and photographs of pre-war North Shields. Run along traditional lines, this is a wet-led pub with only a small range of lunchtime bar meals on offer. The venue has strong sporting links with past boxing champions and current national darts players. Home to football and darts teams, the pub fundraises for charity and a beer festival is held annually in May. Bottle-conditioned beers are also available. ❀♿⊖🚌(306)●⌐

Prince of Wales
2 Liddell Street, NE30 1HE
12 (3 Mon & Tue)-11; 12-10.30 Sun ☎ (0191) 296 2816
Samuel Smith OBB ⊞
Records for this pub date back to 1627 but the current building, faced with green-glazed brick, dates from 1927. The premises lay empty for some years before restoration in traditional style by Samuel Smith, reopening in 1992. A rare outlet for Sam Smiths this far north, it is well-worth a visit. Close to the Fish Quay where the fish and chips are renowned, there is a replica wooden doll outside which gives the pub its 'Old Wooden Dolly' nickname. ♨Q❀⊟⊖🚌(333)

Penshaw

Monument
Old Penshaw Village, DH4 7ER (off A183 signed Old Penshaw)
11 (12 Sun)-11 ☎ (0191) 584 1027
Beer range varies ⊞
Situated at the foot of Penshaw Monument, a local landmark and folly, this is a popular locals' pub. The small bar is dominated by a roaring real fire in winter and there is a separate games room. The walls are decorated with old pictures tracing the history of the village. Food is limited to simple snacks and toasties. Handy for Herrington Country Park. ♨❀⊟♿🚌(78,78A)●

South Gosforth

Victory
43 Killingworth Road, NE3 1SY
12-11 (midnight Fri & Sat); 12-10.30 Sun
☎ (0191) 285 1254
Caledonian Deuchars IPA; Courage Directors; Mordue IPA; Taylor Landlord; Theakston Best Bitter; Wells Bombardier ⊞
Established on this site since 1861, the pub takes its name from Nelson's flagship and once served the local mining community. Essentially a single room, the bar has different levels and areas with wood ceilings, traditional decor and two fireplaces. A range of malt whiskies complements the quality beers. Busy at weekends with tables outside during the summer, there is a covered and heated area for smokers. ◖♿⊖P⌐

South Shields

Maltings
Claypath Lane, NE3 4PG (off Westoe Road)
12-11.30 (10.30 Sun) ☎ (0191) 427 7147
jarrowbrewery.co.uk
Jarrow Rivetcatcher, Joblings Swinging Gibbet; guest beer ⊞
Large former dairy with a modern micro-brewery on the ground floor. An impressive staircase leads to a large wood-panelled room dominated by a imposing central bar with a number of raised seating areas. At least two Jarrow beers are always available, complemented by four ever-changing guest ales and a varied range of imported European draught and bottled beers. Food is available daily with Thai food a speciality on the extensive menu. Q❀◖◗♿⊖🚌●⌐

Old Ship
147 Sunderland Road, Harton Village, NE34 8DG
11-11.30 (midnight Fri & Sat) ☎ (0191) 456 2196
Beer range varies ⊞
The Old Ship is reputed to be the oldest public house in South Shields, established around 1803. It was originally a coaching inn on the road between Westoe and Sunderland – an old mounting stone once used by horsemen to make it easier to get into the saddle remains outside the front entrance. This friendly establishment has a combined bar/lounge area and a function room upstairs. There are two handpumps providing an ever-changing range of beers. Q❀🚌P

Stag's Head ☆
45 Fowler Street, NE33 1NS
11-11 (midnight Fri & Sat); 12-midnight Sun
☎ (0191) 427 2911
Draught Bass; Greene King Abbot; guest beer ⊞
Traditional single-room town-centre pub dominated by an attractive alcove back bar. Listed on CAMRA's National Inventory of Historic Pub Interiors, this pub has retained many other original design features including colourful entrance tilework and a wide acid-etched bay window at the front. Three beers are usually available, always

including Bass. This popular local can get busy at times. An extra room is available upstairs complete with its own small bar – also available to hire for private functions. ⊖♣

Steamboat 🏆 ✔

Coronation Street, Mill Dam, NE33 1EQ

🕒 12-11 (10.30 Sun) ☎ (0191) 454 0134

Beer range varies 🄷

A former Vaux pub close to the North Shields ferry and Custom House Theatre, the Steamboat has been awarded CAMRA local Pub of the Year for the past two years. It has a large bar with a raised seating area and a small lounge. Eight handpumps offer an impressive range of beers from independent and micro-brewers all over the country. The pub hosts regular beer festivals and Meet the Brewer nights. ⊞⊖🚌●

Sunderland

Chesters

Chester Road, SR4 7DR

🕒 11-11; 12-10.30 Sun ☎ (0191) 565 9952

Beer range varies 🄷

This popular pub just outside the city centre was recently refurbished and has a very smart yet comfortable interior with a large main bar and a more intimate area at the back. There is always at least one ale on offer from Maxim Brewery as well as guest ales from other brewers. Outside is ample car parking and a large beer garden. A function room with private bar is also available. ❀◑♿⊖(University)🚌P╘

Clarendon

143 High Street, SR1 2BL

🕒 12-midnight (11 Sun) ☎ (0191) 510 3200

🌐 bull-lane-brewing.co.uk

Bull Lane Ryhope Tug 🄷

Classic old-fashioned brew-pub licensed since 1753 with all the character you would hope for in a local inn. The single-room bar has a large window overlooking the River Wear. It hosts a buskers' night on Wednesday and live music on Sunday afternoon. Up to six Bull Lane beers are available. A little out of the way but definitely worth a visit. ♿🚌(5,5A)

Fitzgerald's

10-12 Green Terrace, SR1 3PZ

🕒 11-11 (midnight Fri & Sat); 12-10.30 Sun

☎ (0191) 567 0852 🌐 sjf.co.uk

Black Sheep Best Bitter; Taylor Landlord 🄷

Part of the Sir John Fitzgerald chain, this is a mecca for real ale lovers with 11 handpumps dispensing beers mainly sourced from local breweries. Students from Brewlab supply beers they have brewed on their training courses. The pub is on two levels – the smaller Chart Room downstairs is quieter than the main bar. Quiz nights are Tuesday and Thursday. A former CAMRA North East Pub of the Year winner. ❀◑⇌⊖(University)🚌●╘

Harbour View

Benedict Road, Roker, SR6 0NL

🕒 10.30-11.30 (7 Fri; 12.30am Sat) ☎ (0191) 567 1402

Caledonian Deuchars IPA; Taylor Landlord; guest beers 🄷

Modern pub overlooking Roker Marina and a short walk from Roker Beach. The ground-floor bar features exposed brickwork and has a horseshoe-shaped bar with six handpumps offering four guest beers sourced from local breweries. A Sunday carvery is served in the first floor Benedict's Bar, with fine views over the marina. Bar food is available on Saturdays. Quiz nights are Monday and Wednesday. The pub can get very busy when Sunderland are playing at home. ◑♿⊖(Stadium of Light)🚌(E1)

King's Arms

Beach Street, Deptford, SR4 6BU

🕒 12-11 (midnight Fri & Sat); 12-10.30 Sun

☎ (0191) 567 9804

Taylor Landlord; guest beers 🄷

CAMRA Branch and Regional Pub of the Year for three years from 2006 to 2008, the King's Arms is an old-fashioned pub with an unspoilt interior. Nine handpumps offer an ever-changing range of beers from micro-breweries from the north east and across the country as well as a cider. It has large-screen TVs for sport and can get very busy when Sunderland are at home. Live music plays in the marquee during the summer. ♨❀⊖(Millfield)🚌(10,11)●╘▯

Rosedene ✔

Queen Alexandra Road, SR2 9BT

🕒 11-11; 12-10.30 Sun ☎ (0191) 528 4313

🌐 therosedene.co.uk

Greene King IPA, Old Speckled Hen, Abbot, seasonal beers 🄷

Now part of the Greene King chain, the building was originally a Georgian mansion built in 1830, pulled down in 1876 and rebuilt in its current location brick by brick. It was converted to a pub by Vaux in 1964. The venue now has a reputation for quality food, with a separate restaurant, bar area, function room and outside smoking area with TV. The function room is licensed for weddings. ❀◑♿🚌(10)P╘

Saltgrass ✔

Hanover Place, Deptford, SR4 6BY

🕒 12-11 ☎ (0191) 565 7229

Caledonian Deuchars IPA; guest beers 🄷

Situated at the bottom of a hill adjacent to a once-bustling shipyard, this welcoming two-roomed pub oozes character. It has several open fires, polished wooden floors and beamed ceilings, and is decorated with wonderful old photographs and nautical artefacts depicting the industrial heritage of the area. The pub gets its name from the tough saltgrass that used to dominate the area before the shipyards. ♨Q❀◑⊞⊖(Millfield)🚌(11)

Smugglers

3 Marine Walk, Roker, SR6 0PL

🕒 2 (12 Sat & Sun)-midnight ☎ (0191) 514 3844

🌐 the-smugglers.com/

Beer range varies 🄷

Family-owned and family-friendly, the Smugglers is yards from Roker Beach and near the Marina. It has a large single-room interior and hosts live music five nights a week. Three handpumps offer two local guest ales and a real cider. The pub gets very busy during the International Air Show in July. ❀●

TJ Doyles

Hanover Place, Deptford, SR4 6BY

🕒 11.30-2 (not Mon), 4-11; 11-late Fri & Sat; 11.30-11 Sun

☎ (0191) 510 1554 🌐 tjdoyles.com

Bull Lane Neck Oil; guest beers 🄷

This former Vaux pub is now a stylish Irish bar providing a range of beers from local micro-breweries – ales from Bull Lane and Maxim are regularly available as well as guest beers from further afield. The bar is large with very comfortable Chesterfield leather sofas for relaxed drinking. Live music plays at weekends and free ukulele lessons are given on Wednesday evenings. ⊖(Millfield)(11)

Wolsey

40 Millum Terrace, Roker, SR6 0ES

11-11 (midnight Fri & Sat) ☎ (0191) 567 2798

Theakston Best Bitter; guest beers H

This friendly pub overlooks Roker Marina and is only a short walk from the beach. The large open-plan lounge has two handpumps dispensing the regular beer and a guest. Live music plays every Saturday evening and a popular free quiz takes place on Thursday night. Good reasonably-priced food is available every day. Specials such as curry night on Wednesday and steak night on Thursday are very popular. Q(E1)P

Swalwell

Sun Inn

Market Lane, NE16 3AL

11 (12 Sun)-11

Jennings Cocker Hoop; guest beers H

Situated in the modern village of Swallwell just a stone's throw from the Metro Centre shopping complex, this pub has been in existence for more than 100 years. The central bar divides the interior into two rooms with an additional room open for buskers' night on Saturday. The enthusiastic landlord has increased the handpulls from one to four and also has real cider on draught. Bar food and snacks are available and free on Sunday. ⇌(Metro Centre)♣

Tynemouth

Cumberland Arms ✔

17 Front Street, NE30 4DX

12-11 (10.30 Sun) ☎ (0191) 257 1820

cumberlandarms.co.uk

Courage Directors; Jennings Cumberland Ale; Tetley Bitter; guest beers H

A friendly welcome awaits you at this cosy split-level pub with two bars featuring attractive stained-glass windows and historic maritime artefacts. Each bar dispenses three regular ales and up to three nationally-sourced guests. Quiet background music plays and there are large-screen TVs for live football matches. Families are welcome in a dining area at the rear of the pub, where good value meals are served. ⊖(306)♣

Turks Head ✔

41 Front Street, NE30 4DZ

11-11 (midnight Fri & Sat) ☎ (0191) 257 6547

Caledonian Deuchars IPA; Courage Directors; Mordue Five Bridge Bitter; Wells Bombardier H

Popular main-street pub with a white-tiled exterior and stained-glass windows. Inside, it has two linked rooms with wooden floors and a wide range of seating. The front bar tends to be more lively with the rear room much quieter, welcoming families up to 7pm. TVs throughout screen live sport. Food is available all day. Look for the infamous stuffed dog. ⊖(306)♣

Tynemouth Lodge Hotel

Tynemouth Road, NE30 4AA

11-11; 12-10.30 ☎ (0191) 257 7565

tynemouthlodgehotel.co.uk

Belhaven 80/-; Caledonian Deuchars IPA; Draught Bass; guest beer H

This attractive externally tiled free house was built in 1799 and has featured in every issue of the Guide since 1983 – the local CAMRA branch presented the licensee with a certificate for this achievement in 2009. The comfortable U-shaped lounge, with a bar on one side and hatch on the other, is noted in the area for its Scottish ales and for selling reputedly the highest volume of Draught Bass on Tyneside. The pub is near the Coast to Coast cycle route. Q⊖P

Wardley

Green

White Mare Pool, NE10 8YB (at Leam Lane B1288/A184 jct)

11-11 (10.30 Sun) ☎ (0191) 495 0171

Beer range varies H

This bar and brasserie, part of the highly respected Sir John Fitzgerald group, has eight handpulls dispensing four real ales sourced from throughout the British Isles. Furnished throughout to a very high standard, the lounge is in the style of a hunting lodge while the public bar has a large-screen TV and many black-and-white motor racing photographs. A weekly quiz is hosted. The excellent restaurant makes good use of locally-sourced produce. P

Washington

Courtyard

Arts Centre, Biddick Lane, Fatfield, NE38 8AB

11-11 (midnight Fri & Sat); 12-11 Sun ☎ (0191) 417 0445

Taylor Landlord; guest beers H

This small, open plan bar/café with outside seating in the courtyard is an adjunct to the Washington Arts Centre, and offers a friendly welcome to customers. There are eight handpumped beers, sourced locally and from around the country. Old Rosie real cider is also available. Beer festivals are held at Easter and late August. The café is renowned for its fish and chips. Home of the famous Davy Lamp Folk Club. Q(M1,M3)♣P

William de Wessyngton ✔

2-3 Victoria Terrace, Concord, NE37 2SY (opp bus station)

9-11.30 ☎ (0191) 418 0100

Greene King Ruddles Best Bitter; Marston's Pedigree; guest beers H

This large open-plan Wetherspoon conversion was formerly an ice cream parlour and billiard hall. It is the only real ale outlet in Concord and offers the typical JDW features of value-for-money beer and food. The regular ales are complemented by up to

> Good ale is the true and proper drink of Englishmen. He is not deserving of the name of Englishman who speaketh against ale, that is good ale.
> **George Borrow**, Lavengro

four guests, often from north-east micros including Maxim. Occasional beer festivals are held.
Q

West Boldon

Black Horse

Rectory Bank, NE36 0QQ (off A184)
11-11; 12-10.30 Sun ☎ (0191) 536 1814
Black Sheep Best Bitter; guest beer
The Black Horse is a typical village pub but with unusual decor and design – the interior is filled with eclectic bric-a-brac and photographs. It has one small bar and can get very busy due to the popular restaurant serving high quality food. Two beers are usually available. There is live music on Sunday evenings. (9,30)

West Herrington

Stables

McLaren Way, DH4 4ND (off B1286)
12-11 (midnight Fri & Sat) ☎ (0191) 584 9226
Black Sheep Best Bitter; Taylor Landlord; guest beers
From the outside this looks like a private dwelling as there is no pub sign. However, walk through the small beer garden and you will find a long, narrow pub with a stone floor, low ceiling and subdued lighting. The introduction of quality food, including the local speciality - panaculty - means this pub is always busy. A warm welcome is guaranteed at this hidden gem. Q (35)P

West Monkseaton

Beacon Hotel

Earsdon Road, NE25 9PT
11.30-11 (midnight Fri & Sat); 11-11.30 Sun
☎ (0191) 253 6911
Caledonian Deuchars IPA; guest beers
Superb modern pub serving excellent food at reasonable prices. The cellar has been updated to ensure ales are dispensed at the correct temperature. Guest beers change monthly. Look for the 'rack of ale' – a wooden rack that serves any three ales the customer chooses in third of a pint glasses. Food themed nights include the Tuesday grill and Thursday curry. Quiz nights are Sunday and Wednesday. Children over 14 are welcome with an accompanying adult. P

Whitley Bay

Briar Dene

71 The Links, NE26 1UE
11-11; 12-10.30 Sun ☎ (0191) 252 0926
Black Sheep Ale; guest beers
This Fitzgerald's pub has a large, attractive lounge with sea views to the Links and St Mary's Lighthouse, and a more compact rear bar with wide-screen TV, pool and darts. The pub is well-known for its food, with local fish and chips a speciality. Guest beers change regularly. Children are welcome in a family area in the lounge. There is seating outside at the front of the pub.
P

Rockcliffe Arms

Algernon Place, NE26 2DT
11-11 (11.15 Fri & Sat); 12-11 Sun ☎ (0191) 253 1299
Beer range varies
Outstanding back-street Fitzgerald's pub, a few minutes walk from the Metro station. This one-room establishment has distinct bar and lounge areas with a snug in between. Four constantly-changing guest ales are available, with beer details on notices above the dividing arch. Regular darts and dominoes matches are held in the snug.

Free Trade Inn, Byker (Photo: Richard Brown)

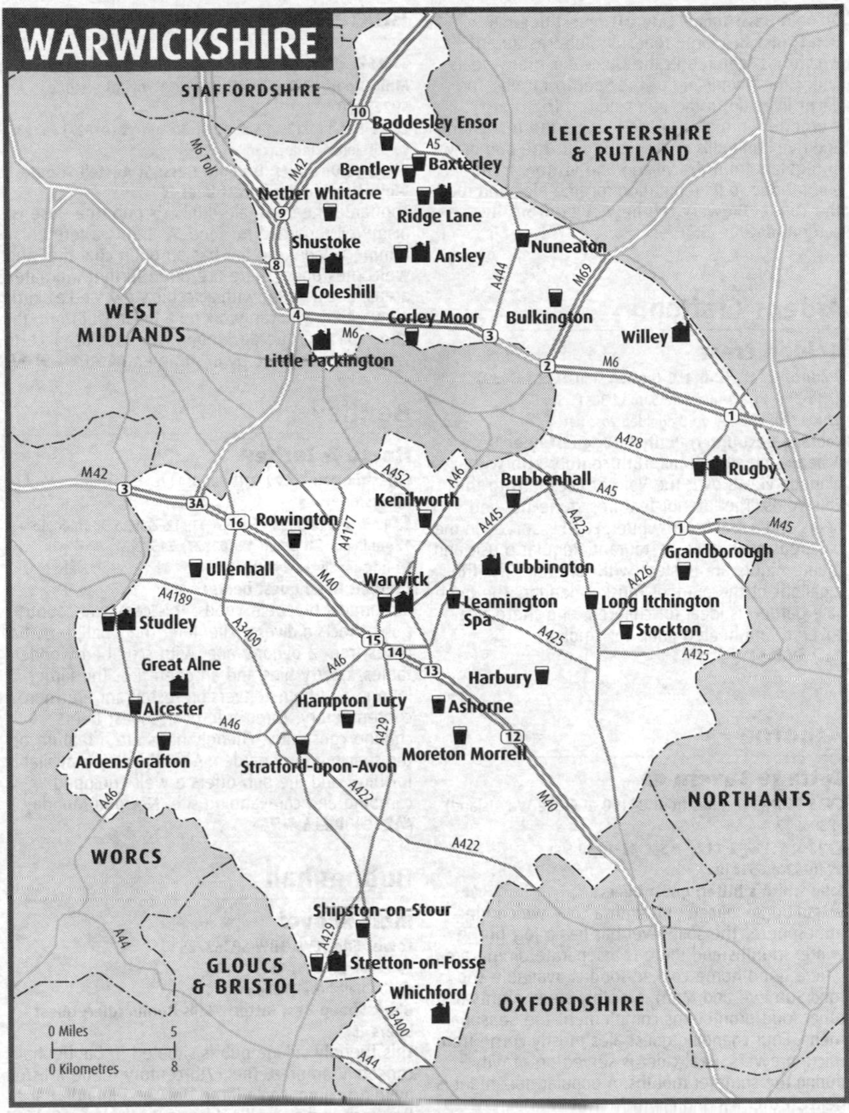

Alcester

Holly Bush

37 Henley Street, B49 5QX (behind church and town hall)

☼ 12-11 ☎ (01789) 762482 theholllybushpub.com

Black Sheep Best Bitter; Purity Pure Gold, Mad Goose; Sharp's Doom Bar; Uley Bitter; guest beers Ⓗ

This traditional 17th-century local in an historic market town is a frequent CAMRA Branch Pub of the Year. Restoration has preserved its five rooms and many original features. There is also a function room and a pretty walled garden at the rear. Five regular ales and up to three guests are available and beer festivals are held in June and October. It has both traditional English and à la carte menus (not Sun eve). Regular folk sessions are held monthly and spontaneous music may strike up at any time. White Hart morris men practise here on Monday evenings. (26,246,247)♣

Three Tuns

34 High Street, B49 5AB (next to post office)

☼ 12-2, 5-11; 12-11 Sat & Sun ☎ (01789) 762626

Hobsons Best Bitter; guest beers Ⓗ

This local CAMRA award-winning pub is a must visit; no music, no pool and no food – how a real pub should be. Inside there is a single room with low beams, stone-flagged floor and an exposed area of wattle and daub. Up to eight ales from micros and independents provide a permanent yet ever-changing mini beer festival. The pub stays open on weekday afternoons if custom warrants it, or by prior arrangement. Q(26,246,247)♣

Ansley

Lord Nelson Inn

Birmingham Road, CV10 9PQ

☼ 12-11 (10.30 Sun) ☎ (024) 7639 2305

thelordnelsoninnansley.co.uk

Draught Bass; Tunnel Late OTT; guest beers ⊞
Don't miss this large roadside pub/restaurant which has featured in the Guide for many years under the ownership of the Sperrin family. The decor lives up to the pub's name. There are themed food nights in the lounge and restaurant, and five handpulls in the public bar. The pub draws in regulars from the village and visitors from near and far due to its reputation for fine ales and food. The Tunnel Brewery can be viewed from the garden. ♛❀◐◑⊟⊞P⚟

Ardens Grafton

Golden Cross

Wixford Road, B50 4LG (brown signs from B439)
⚙ 11-3, 6-11, 11-midnight Sat; 11.30-11 Sun
☎ (01789) 772420 ⊕ thegoldencross.net
Courage Best Bitter; Purity UBU; guest beer ⊞
A beautiful, stone-built 18th-century pub with glorious views over the Vale of Evesham to the Cotswolds. The interior features stone-flagged floors and a real fire in winter. Food is served in the bar areas or separate restaurant. Regular music and theme nights are hosted, with 'Graftonbury' the highlight of the outdoor music calendar. The large safe garden is ideal for children, and there is a covered and heated patio for smokers.
♛Q❀◐◑♿P⚟

Ashorne

Cottage Tavern ✔

CV35 9DR (1½ miles from B4100 at Fosse Way Island) SP304577
⚙ 12-3; 5-11; 12-11 Fri & Sat; 12-10.30 Sun
☎ (01926) 651410
John Smith's Bitter; guest beers ⊞
A traditional village pub with a cosy welcoming atmosphere. The split-level bar has a log fire in winter months and there is a separate dining area where good home-cooked food is available (no food Sun eve and Mon). Monthly steak nights and other food promotions complement the seasonal menu. Four changing guest ales mostly come from micro-brewers. Real cider is served on gravity during the summer months. A popular quiz night is held on the last Sunday of the month.
♛Q♉❀◐◑♣🍎⚟

Baddesley Ensor

Red Lion

The Common, CV9 2BT (from Grendon roundabout on A5 go S up Boot Hill)
⚙ 7 (4 Fri)-11; 12-3, 7-11 Sat; 12-3, 7-10.30 Sun
☎ (01827) 718186
Everards Tiger; Greene King IPA; Marston's Pedigree; guest beers ⊞
Now the only pub in the village, this is a popular community local where ale is king and food does not feature. Enjoy instead the open fire and the buzz of conversation in a cosily decorated, music-free environment. Two or three guest ales are featured, and the landlord willingly removes the sparkler. Off-street parking is available opposite the pub. Note the restricted opening hours.
♛Q⊞(765)♣🍎

Baxterley

Rose Inn ✔

Main Road, CV9 2LE (off B4116, W of Atherstone) SP277970
⚙ 12-3, 7-11 ; 12-11 Sat; 12-10.30 Sun ☎ (01827) 713939
⊕ roseinnbaxterley.com
Courage Directors; Draught Bass; St Austell Tribute; Wells Bombardier; guest beer ⊞
Though at heart an ale drinker's pub, the Rose is also well-regarded for food. As befits a former mining village, the bar has an open coal fire, and welcomes dogs. There are three further intimate areas, a restaurant with a scenic view, and a skittle alley where you can work up a thirst. Out front, the large, picturesque duck pond is a popular place to watch the world go by in summer. ♛❀◐◑⊟⊞♣P

Bentley

Horse & Jockey

Coleshill Road, CV9 2HL (on B4116, 2½ miles SW of Atherstone)
⚙ 12-3 (not Mon), 6 (7 Mon)-11; 12-2.30, 5.30-midnight Fri; 12-midnight Sat & Sun ☎ (01827) 715236
⊕ horseandjockeybentley.co.uk
Draught Bass; guest beers ⊞
Set amidst bluebell woods, this convivial country pub attracts a diverse clientele. The small, busy bar dates from a bygone age, with scrubbed wooden tables, quarry tiles and an open fire. The larger lounge and barn-conversion restaurant are more contemporary. Three free-of-tie guest beers change constantly. Friendly hens are a feature of the spacious beer garden. A skittle alley is available for hire, and the pub offers a well-equipped camping and caravanning site. No food Monday.
♛♉❀◐◑⊟▲♣P⚟

Bubbenhall

Malt Shovel

Lower End, CV8 3BW SP362725
⚙ 12-11 ☎ (024) 7630 1141
⊕ themaltshovelbubbenhall.co.uk
Black Sheep Best Bitter; Wells Bombardier; guest beers ⊞
This friendly village pub is situated in Bubbenhall conservation area. The 17th-century Grade II-listed building comprises a large L-shaped lounge bar at the front and a small public bar to the rear. Behind the spacious car park lies a large walled garden and adjacent bowling green (woods available from the bar in summer). Traditional home-cooked food is available, with daily specials. One or more of the guest beers is usually local. Convenient for Ryton Pools Country Park. Q❀◐◑⊟▲⊞♣P⚟

INDEPENDENT BREWERIES

Alexandra Ales/Atomic Rugby
Church End Ridge Lane
Discovery Little Packington
Griffin Inn Shustoke
North Cotswold Stretton-on-Fosse
Patriot Whichford (NEW)
Purity Great Alne
Slaughterhouse Warwick
Tunnel Ansley
Warwickshire Cubbington
Weatheroak Studley
Willey Willey (NEW)

Bulkington

Olde Chequers Inn

Chequers Street, CV12 9NH

⏲ 12-11.30 (10.30 Sun) ☎ (024) 7631 2182
🌐 homepage.ntlworld.com/timothy.clews

Draught Bass; M&B Brew XI; guest beer Ⓗ

The oldest pub in the village, this renowned hostelry has a well-appointed bar divided into two areas with an open fire, a small snug and two games rooms at the rear. The regulars support the pub teams in local darts and dominoes leagues. The picturesque exterior is adorned with hanging baskets, with a seating area where you can watch the local Anker morris men when they entertain the village. There is a heated, covered smoking area. ♨❀♿⊟(56,75)♣P⚟

Weavers Arms

12 Long Street, Ryton, CV12 9JZ (off Wolvey Road B4109)

⏲ 1 (12 Sun)-midnight ☎ (024) 7631 4415

Draught Bass; guest beers Ⓗ

Classic two-room family-run free house for more than 20 years and a regular in the Guide. The stone-floored traditional bar with a log fire is home to darts and dominoes teams who play in local leagues. To one end is a small wood-panelled games room with a bar billiards table. Two guest beers come from local micro and independent breweries. Outside is a covered and heated area for smokers. ♨❀⊡⊟(56,75)♣⚟

Coleshill

Green Man ✔

68 High Street, B46 3AH

⏲ 11-11; 12-10.30 Sun ☎ (01675) 463376

Draught Bass; M&B Brew XI; guest beers Ⓗ

Prominent three-storey pub on the main town crossroads. The sprawling interior features a boisterous bar and servery area, a comfy lounge to the rear, and a quiet side room. Internal beams and pillars show the age of the building. The decor is pleasantly dated, with a display of '80s beermats that may appeal to nostalgia fans. No juke-box or food (although there are filled rolls at lunchtime). The two guest beers are from the Punch Finest Cask range. ⊡⊟♣P

Corley Moor

Bull & Butcher

Common Lane, CV7 8AQ SP279850

⏲ 10-midnight (1am Fri & Sat; 11 Sun) ☎ (01676) 540241

Draught Bass; Greene King Abbot; M&B Brew XI; guest beer Ⓗ

Attractive village pub adorned with a wonderful display of hanging baskets most of the year. There is a large, busy restaurant at the rear, which does not detract from the traditional atmosphere of the public bar and cosy snug. The large garden has plenty of children's play equipment, including a bouncy castle. Food is served throughout the day until 9.30pm – home-made pies are highly recommended. One guest beer is available.
♨Q❀◑⊡♿⛺P⚟

Grandborough

Shoulder of Mutton

Sawbridge Road, CV23 8DN (off A45)

⏲ 12-3 (not Mon), 6-11; 12-3, 7-10.30 Sun
☎ (01788) 810306 🌐 shoulderofmuttongrandborough.co.uk

Black Sheep Best Bitter; Greene King Abbot; guest beer Ⓗ

This friendly and welcoming village pub with beamed ceilings and open fires has recently won Rugby CAMRA summer Pub of the Year. Excellent food is served with vegetarian options (booking is advisable). The garden has a large pond full of large fish. The pub hosts two-stroke and classic motorcycle days on the last Sunday of the month plus a Thursday quiz and Sunday poker evenings. Cyclists and walkers welcome.
♨Q♂❀◑⊡♿⊟♣P⚟

Hampton Lucy

Boars Head 🏆

Church Street, CV35 8BE

⏲ 11-11 (closed 3-5 Mon-Thu Nov-Mar); 12-10 Sun
☎ (01789) 840533 🌐 theboarsheadhamptonlucy4food.co.uk

Beer range varies Ⓗ

Shakespeare CAMRA Pub of the Year 2009, this friendly, comfortable village pub dates back to the 17th century. Situated on a Sustrans route and close to the river Avon, it is popular with cyclists, walkers and visitors to nearby Charlecote Park, as well as with the local Young Farmers. A walled rear garden hosts Sunday afternoon barbecues in summer, with 'steak on a stone' also available. Six beers are served from a constantly changing range, always including at least one ale from a small local brewery. ♨❀◑P⚟

Harbury

Old New Inn

Farm Sreet, CV33 9LS

⏲ 3 (11 Fri & Sat)-12.30am; 11-12.30am Sun
☎ (01926) 614023

Beer range varies Ⓗ

A large village pub supporting two teams each for pool, dominoes and men's and women's darts. The pub is built of local Jurassic White Lias limestone and was once several rooms. The former lounge has been refurbished and integrated with the larger bar, TV and games area. The rear garden is a mass of colour in summer. The landlord sponsors a village football and rugby team. Ever-changing Church End and Hook Norton beers feature, with three available at weekends.
♨Q♂❀⊡♿⛺⊟(64)♣P⚟

Kenilworth

Clarendon Arms

44 Castle Hill, CV8 1NB

⏲ 11.30-3, 5.30-11.30 (12.30am Fri); 11.30-12.30am Sat; 12-11.30 Sun ☎ (01926) 852017 🌐 clarendonarmspub.co.uk

Beer range varies Ⓗ

Multi-roomed pub opposite Kenilworth Castle offering a choice of four beers, regularly from Purity, Slaughterhouse and Church End breweries in Warwickshire, and also from nearby Sadler's and Hook Norton breweries. An extensive range of food is available daily. A log-burning stove provides warmth in winter and outside there is a paved rear patio for smokers. An upstairs room is available for functions. The TV is turned on for Six Nations and World Cup sport only. The pub opens all day in December. ♨❀◑⊟(540)⚟

Old Bakery

12 High Street, CV8 1LZ (near A429/A452 jct)
5.30 (5 Fri & Sat)-11; 5-10.30 Sun ☎ (01926) 864111
theoldbakeryhotel.co.uk
Wye Valley Bitter; guest beers ⊞
Attractively restored former bakery in a 400-year-old building in the old town, with two rooms plus a small outside patio. The single bar hosts three frequently-changing guest beers – often Cornish as well as more local offerings. Fish and chip suppers are proving popular, available Monday 5.30-7.30pm only. Disabled access is via the rear car park. Located near Abbey Fields and a 10-minute walk from the castle. Q❀♿(12)P

Virgins & Castle

7 High Street, CV8 1LY (A429/A452 jct)
11-11 (10.30 Sun) ☎ (01926) 853737
Everards Beacon Bitter, Sunchaser, Tiger, Original; guest beer ⊞
The oldest pub in Kenilworth, dating from 1563, with a multi-room interior including a central L-shaped bar and lots of separate drinking areas. Oak-panelled walls, assorted furniture and many pictures add to the character of the pub. English and Filipino food is available. There is limited parking at the front, but a public car park is close by. Well-served by buses from Coventry, Leamington Spa and Warwick University, it's the only Everards pub in Kenilworth. Q❀(12)

Wyandotte Inn

Park Road, CV8 2GF (jct of Park Rd and Stoneleigh Rd)
11.30-11.30 (10.30 Sun) ☎ (01926) 854897
thewyandotteinn.com
Jennings Cocker Hoop; Marston's Burton Bitter, Pedigree; guest beers ⊞
Named after a tribe of native American Indians – the landlord and his son are honorary chiefs of the tribe. A pleasant community corner pub on the north side of the town, it is renowned for good beer, music and atmosphere. Large screens show sport. The pub hosts a disco and live bands – details can be found on the website. The two guest beers are usually from the Marston's stable and Thatchers cider is also available. ❀♿(16,X17)P

Leamington Spa

Green Man

Lower Tachbrook Street, CV31 2BQ
4 (12 Fri-Sun)-12.30am ☎ (01926) 316298
Wells Bombardier; guest beer ⊞
You can be sure of a warm welcome from the friendly landlady at this late Victorian pub, situated on the corner of a South Leamington back street, a 15-minute walk from the train station. It has a spacious open plan interior with one large bar. The guest beer changes on a weekly basis. The pub has a popular pool table and hosts a weekly quiz among many other community activities.
❀♿

Talbot Inn

34 Rushmore Street, CV31 1JA
12-11 (midnight Fri & Sat) ☎ (01926) 428883
Wye Valley HPA, Butty Bach; guest beers ⊞
Genuine local free house in the south of the town, well-worth seeking out for its ever-changing range of ales sourced from micro-breweries across the country. It is also a rare local outlet for real cider. Just a few minutes' walk from the Grand Union canal, it is popular with walkers and boaters, especially in the summer months. Local CAMRA Pub of the Year for 2009. Q❀

Long Itchington

Green Man ✔

Church Road, CV47 9PW
5 (12 Sat & Sun)-midnight ☎ (01926) 812208
greenmanlongitchington.co.uk
Black Sheep Best Bitter; Fuller's London Pride; Tetley Bitter; guest beer ⊞
The building dates in parts from 1700 with a traditional interior comprising a series of linked drinking areas and a function room. A popular community pub, it is home to several games teams and hosts regular folk music on a Tuesday night. The landlord plays a full part in the village's May Day weekend beer festival. A fish and chips van arrives on a Friday evening and punters can use the pub benches, garden or bring them inside.
Q❀(64)P

Harvester Inn

6 Church Road, CV47 9PG (off A423 at village pond, then first left)
12-2.30, 6-11; 12-3, 7-10.30 Sun ☎ (01926) 812698
theharvesterinn.co.uk
Hook Norton Hooky Bitter; guest beers ⊞
A Guide regular, the Harvester has been run by the hands-on Mills family since 1984. The bar and restaurant are comfortable and unpretentious, serving reliably good fare. Budvar and Budvar Dark plus three real ales are usually available – see the website for what's currently on offer. The pub is exceptionally busy during the village May Day weekend beer festival. The Harvester is the world's most northerly commissary for Gruntfuttocks speciality pickles. Q(64)P

Two Boats Inn ✔

Southam Road, CV47 9QZ
12-11 ☎ (01926) 812640 2boats.co.uk
Adnams Broadside; Greene King Abbot; Wells Eagle IPA; guest beer ⊞
This large canalside inn on the Grand Union Canal was originally three cottages built around 1743. Inside, it has a separate bar and comfortable lounge offering food ranging from snacks to full meals. Access to the pub is via a flight of steps at the side or direct from the towpath. A beer festival is held each May Day weekend and an extra guest beer is added in summer. ❀(64)P

Moreton Morrell

Black Horse

CV35 9AR
11.30-3, 7-11; 12-3, 7-10.30 Sun ☎ (01926) 651231
Hook Norton Hooky Bitter; guest beer ⊞
A rural pub in the heart of the village, where beer and banter come first. Nothing seems to have changed here since the 1960s, including the music on the juke-box. Wooden settles are arranged around the walls of the cosy, compact bar. A popular destination for walkers, the pub is also a handy stop-off for travellers on the Fosse Way and M40. The landlord takes great pride in the quality of his ales – the guest beer is usually fairly high gravity and from a small independent brewery.
♿(77)

Nether Whitacre

Gate Inn

Gate Lane, B46 2DS

12-11 (10.30 Sun) ☎ (01675) 481292 thegateinn.com

Banks's Mild; Jennings Cumberland Ale; Marston's Pedigree; Ringwood Fortyniner Ⓗ

Popular community hub with a variety of rooms, ales and food, all topped off with a warm welcome. Diners tend to favour the conservatory and large lounge while drinkers gravitate to the quarry-tiled bar. Interesting old photos of the locality decorate the walls. The pool table is in a room off the bar. Outside is a large, child-friendly garden. Do not miss the yearly beer festival. ❀◐⊟▲♣P

Nuneaton

Crown 🏆

10 Bond Street, CV11 4BX

12-11 (midnight Fri & Sat) ☎ (024) 7637 3343

thecrownnuneaton.com

Oakham JHB; Wychwood Hobgoblin; guest beers Ⓗ

Eight ales and two ciders or perries are on offer at this popular town-centre split-level bar. The walls feature an interesting collection of photographs ranging from George Eliot to John Lennon. Live bands play on Saturday night and a there is a quiz on Sunday. There is an outside drinking area and a function room available for hire. Foreign beers are available on draught and in bottles, and beer festivals are held in June and December. ♔❀≹⊟●P⁵⁻

Hearty Goodfellow

285 Arbury Road, Stockingford, CV10 7NQ

11-11; 12-10.30 Sun ☎ (024) 7638 8152

Marston's Burton Bitter; guest beers Ⓗ

Lively large one-roomed community local where sport rules the day – your favourite sport can be viewed on numerous TVs. Pool and darts are popular and the Ford Sports football club is based here. Numerous trophies, pennants and shirts adorn the walls. The regular Burton Bitter is complemented by three guest beers from the Marston's group. ❀⊟♣⁵⁻

Rose Inn

Coton Road, CV11 5TW (opp Our Lady of the Angels Catholic Church)

11-11.30 (11 Sun) ☎ (07957) 376787

Marston's Burton Bitter, Pedigree; guest beer Ⓗ

The Rose was the venue for CAMRA's first AGM – an account of this occasion hangs on the wall alongside a brass plaque. Landlord Tony is passionate about his ales and also his clock collection on display around the L-shaped lounge. The bar at the front has a pool table and dartboard. There is a covered and heated area for smokers. The pub is handy when visiting Nuneaton Museum across the road in Riversley Park. ❀⊟♿⊟♣P⁵⁻

Ridge Lane

Church End Brewery Tap

109 Ridge Lane, CV10 0RD (2 miles SW of Atherstone) SP295947

closed Mon-Wed; 6 (12 Fri & Sat)-11; 12-10.30 Sun

☎ (01827) 713080 churchendbrewery.co.uk

Beer range varies Ⓗ/Ⓖ

Ever-popular brewery tap, usually offering eight beers from the adjoining brewery, visible through a large glass panel. You can try a 'coffin' of one-third of a pint tasters. Keg beers are banned here, but there is a good range of Belgian bottled beers plus at least one real cider. A mild is always available. While dogs are welcome inside, children and smokers are relegated to the extensive rural beer garden. No food is served, but customers can bring in their own. Q❀♿▲♣●P⊟

Rowington

Rowington Club

Rowington Green, CV35 7BX (just E of B4439) SP1998070150

2 (12 Sat & Sun)-11 ☎ (01564) 782087 rowington.org/Rowington/rowington_club.html

Flowers IPA; Wye Valley HPA; guest beers Ⓗ

Overlooking the village cricket ground, this community club is in an idyllic location. Two frequently changing guest ales and a guest cider are offered alongside the house beers. Visitors are guaranteed a warm welcome – with day membership for a nominal fee and free to CAMRA members. Two snooker tables are available. Live music, bingo and other social and family-friendly events are held, including barbecues in summer. A popular beer, cider and music festival is hosted over the August bank holiday.

Q❀♿≹(Lapworth)♣●P⁵⁻

Rugby

Alexandra Arms

72 James Street, CV21 2SL (next to John Barford multi-storey car park)

11.30-11 (11.30 Fri & Sat); 12-11 Sun ☎ (01788) 578660

alexandraarms.co.uk

Alexandra Petit Blonde; Fuller's London Pride; Greene King Abbot; guest beers Ⓗ

Friendly pub with a comfortable L-shaped lounge where lively debate flourishes among an eclectic group of locals. A back bar/games room features a fabulous rock juke-box along with pool, skittles and table football. The large comfortable garden serves as a venue for summer beer festivals, complete with live jazz. At the rear of the pub is a micro-brewery which is home to the Alexandra Ales and Atomic ranges. The pub is a seven-times winner of CAMRA Rugby Pub of the Year.

Q❀◐⊟♿≹(Rugby)♣⁵⁻

Lawrence Sheriff ✔

28-29 High Street, CV21 3BW

9am-midnight (1am Thu; 2am Fri & Sat)

☎ (01788) 517640

Greene King Ruddles Best Bitter, Abbot; Shepherd Neame Spitfire; guest beers Ⓗ

Rugby's reputation for real ale and pub diversity is ever-increasing and this pub is an outstanding addition to the scene. A classic Lloyds No 1 bar, it offers a choice of value real ales. Situated a stone's throw from Rugby School, it is named after the Elizabethan gentleman and grocer to Elizabeth I who founded the school. ☕◐♿≹⊟⁵⁻

Merchants Inn ✔

5-6 Little Church Street, CV21 3AW (behind Marks & Spencer)

12-midnight (1am Fri & Sat; 11 Sun) ☎ (01788) 571119

merchantsinn.co.uk

B&T Shefford Bitter; Batemans XB; Purity Mad Goose; Oakham Bishop's Farewell; guest beers Ⓗ

This 'must visit' pub boasts 10 regularly-changing real ales plus two ciders on gravity dispense and a large range of Belgian beers. It has one of the country's largest collections of breweriana and a warm, cosy atmosphere, with comfortable sofas, flagstone floors and an open fire. Home-cooked food is served every lunchtime. Live rugby features on big screens at the weekend. Beer festivals are held in April and October, plus an annual Belgian night in February. A former Warwickshire CAMRA Pub of the Year. ⌂◖♿🚌♣🍎⚡

Raglan Arms 🏆

50 Dunchurch Road, CV22 6AD (opp Rugby School)
⏲ 4-midnight; 3-1am Fri; 12-1am Sat; 12-midnight Sun
☎ (01788) 544441 🌐 raglanarmsinn.co.uk
Ansells Mild; Fuller's London Pride, ESB; Greene King Abbot; Raglan Original Bitter; guest beers Ⓗ
Rescued from closure and reopened three years ago, this three-room town pub has had a tasteful refurbishment. In 2008 it was awarded Rugby CAMRA Pub of the Year and Warwickshire Pub of the Year in 2009. The interior has a comfy feel and a friendly atmosphere. Up to 12 real ales are kept in the pub's two cellars, sourced from across the country. Regular poker nights and live music are hosted and major sporting events screened on TV. A cosy snug bar with a real fire is available to hire. Snacks are available all day. ❀◖◗🍴🚌♣P⚡

Squirrel Inn

33 Church Street, CV21 3PU
⏲ 12 (4 Sun)-11 ☎ (01788) 544154
Dow Bridge Ratae'd; Marston's Pedigree; guest beers Ⓗ
This high quality true town local is hard to miss with its bright pink 'wedge of cheese' exterior. A supporter of LocAle, it usually offers a Dow Bridge beer as well as varied guests including a mild. A large range of indoor games is played including scrabble, chess and table skittles, and live music hosted on Wednesday (yes, bands do fit in!). Visitors are welcome to join in the ever-changing discussions at the bar. ⌂Q⇌🚌♣🍎

Three Horse Shoes Hotel ✔

22-23 Sheep Street, CV21 3BX (in pedestrian precinct)
⏲ 11-midnight; 12-11 Sun ☎ (01788) 544585
Greene King IPA, Abbot; guest beer Ⓗ
This 17th-century town-centre hotel has been restored to reveal original oak beams and an open fireplace. The bar provides a haven away from Rugby centre – an ideal place to dine, drink or simply relax in comfortable leather sofas and armchairs. The restaurant is popular with residents, visitors and locals alike. ⌂Q❀🛏◖◗🍴♿⇌🚌⚡

> Here old John Randal lies,
> Who counting from this tale,
> Lived three score years and ten,
> Such vertue was in ale.
> Ale was his meat,
> Ale his drink;
> Ale did his heart revive,
> And if he could have drunk his ale,
> He still had been alive.
> **Epitaph of 1699**, formerly at Great Wolford, Warwickshire

Victoria Inn

1 Lower Hillmorton Road, CV21 3ST
⏲ 4 (12 Thu)-midnight; 12-1am Fri & Sat; 12-midnight Sun
☎ (01788) 544374 🌐 downthevic.com
Atomic Strike, Fission, Meltdown, Half Life, Bomb; guest beers Ⓗ
Victorian hostelry with ornate windows and a comfortable snug and lounge. Brewery tap for the Atomic Brewery, six guests from other breweries are also available as well as a selection of bottled Belgian beers. Regular beer, curry and chilli festivals are hosted. A quiz is held and the pub is home to three football teams, plus cricket, pool and darts teams. Sky Sports and ESPN are screened. Dogs are welcome. Q❀🍴⇌⊖🚌♣🍎⚡

Shipston-on-Stour

Horseshoe Inn

6 Church Street, CV36 4AP (A3400 S of church)
⏲ 11-11.30 (midnight Thu; 1am Fri & Sat); 12-11 Sun
☎ (01608) 662190 🌐 horseshoeshipston.com
Sharp's Doom Bar; guest beers Ⓗ
Refurbished since the floods of 2007 and with a new landlord, this half-timbered pub has a carpeted open-plan bar and a separate restaurant. Sharp's Doom Bar is always available and three further handpumps offer changing beers from breweries including Copper Dragon and Purity. Delicious food is available lunchtimes and evenings. A heated, covered garden area is good for smokers and Aunt Sally is played in summer. A favourite real cider is Hogan's Warwickshire Wobbler. Q❀◖◗♿🚌(23,50,50A)♣🍎P⚡

Shustoke

Griffin Inn 🏆

Church Road, B46 2LB (on B4116)
⏲ 12-2.30, 7-11; 12-3, 7-10.30 Sun ☎ (01675) 481205
Banks's Mild; Hook Norton Old Hooky; Marston's Pedigree; RCH Pitchfork; Theakston Old Peculier; guest beers Ⓗ
Thriving family-run Guide regular with its own brewery next door. A Griffin Inn Brewery beer is usually available as well as the regulars and four guests. The music and TV-free interior features low beams and inglenooks with solid fuel stoves, while outside there is patio seating and a large grassy play area. Children are welcome in the conservatory. Food is served Monday to Saturday lunchtimes – local eggs and cheeses are on sale at the bar. ⌂Q🚼❀◖⛺P⚡

Stockton

Crown

8 High Street, CV47 8JZ SP436638
⏲ 11-midnight (1am Fri & Sat) ☎ (01926) 812255
Ansells Bitter; guest beers Ⓗ
Popular recently refurbished village local serving two changing guest beers from local and national breweries. The public bar is divided into two areas with seating around a real fire on one side and a dartboard on the other. There is a restaurant to the other side of the servery. Outside, the barn hosts a folk night on the last Tuesday of the month. The petanque team visits French and German teams on an annual exchange. The collection of Guinness memorabilia and whiskies is a reminder of the landlord's Irish roots. ⌂❀◖◗🍴♿🚌(63,64)♣P⚡

Stratford-upon-Avon

Bear at the Swan's Nest Hotel

Swan's Nest Lane, CV37 7LT (S end of Clopton Bridge)
✪ 12-11 ☎ (01789) 265540 🌐 thebearfreehouse.co.uk
Everards Tiger; Hook Norton Old Hooky; guest beers Ⓗ
A traditional English pub with a waterside location, five minutes' walk from the town centre. It serves seven real ales focusing on local and regional brewers such as Wye Valley, Hook Norton, Hobsons and Warwickshire, with seasonal beers available. The Bear is decked out with wood panelling and has a pewter bar. Excellent, home-made bar meals are served in a warm, friendly, welcoming atmosphere. Board games and newspapers are available. ⇆◑◐🚌(23)♣

Stretton-on-Fosse

Plough Inn

GL56 9QX
✪ 11.30-2.30, 6-11; 11.30-3, 6-11 (closed eve Oct-Apr) Sun
☎ (01608) 661053
Ansells Mild; Hook Norton Hooky Bitter; guest beers Ⓗ
Delightful 17th-century stone built village inn with oak beams and flagstoned bar. The large inglenook fireplace is used on winter Sundays to slow-roast a joint of meat – Sunday lunch is a speciality, served 12-3pm. Delicious food is home cooked by the owner, French chef Jean-Pierre. Traditional pub games and quiz nights are hosted. Four real ales and a cider are available. Local CAMRA Pub of the Year 2008, and Morning Advertiser Best Freehouse, East and West Midlands 2010. ♨Q❀◑◐♣●P⁻

Studley

Little Lark

108 Alcester Road, B80 7NP (Tom's Town Lane jct with A435) SP075632
✪ 12-3, 6-11; 12-midnight Fri & Sat; 12-10.30 Sun
☎ (01527) 853105
Adnams Bitter; Ansells Mild; Taylor Landlord; guest beers Ⓗ
A former Mad O'Rourke pub, this popular village local serves a great selection of traditional fruit wines and single malt whiskies as well as real ale. The pub is divided into four sections surrounding a central bar, with a patio smoking area towards the back. The Lark used to publish its own newspaper and the walls are decorated with framed front pages. Food is served lunchtimes and evenings – the Desperate Dan Cow Pie is a speciality. The pub also runs an annual cheese festival.
♨Q❀◑◐♿🚌(67,246,247)⁻

Ullenhall

Winged Spur 🏆 ✔

Main Road, B95 5PA SP122674
✪ 8.30am-2.30am ☎ (01564) 792005
Fuller's London Pride; Greene King Abbot; guest beers Ⓗ
An unassuming village pub, with nooks and crannies creating different drinking areas. The name derives from a past local landowner Robert Knight whose family crest was the spur – the medieval symbol of knighthood. Up to four guest beers and occasional traditional ciders are stocked. Good food, including breakfasts, takeaways and vegetarian dishes, is offered, with fish a speciality – the menu changes daily. Regular quiz nights are hosted and a real fire is welcoming on cold nights. There is a heated area outside for smokers.
♨Q❀◑◐♿♣●P⁻□

Warwick

Cape of Good Hope

66 Lower Cape, CV34 5DP (off Cape Road)
✪ 12-11 (midnight Fri & Sat); 12-10.30 Sun
☎ (01926) 498138 🌐 capeofgoodhope.co.uk
Church End Two Llocks; Greene King IPA, Abbot; Tetley Bitter Ⓗ**; Weatheroak Keystone Hops** Ⓖ**; guest beer** Ⓗ
This canalside pub offers a very friendly welcome to visitors and locals. The walls of the traditional front bar are adorned with local history pictures. Rugby match tickets and pump clips from previous guest beers line the wall behind the bar. The larger lounge provides ample seating to enjoy the good-value home-cooked food or tackle the famous 'Cape Fear' mixed grill. The guest beer is usually from Cottage, Purity or Slaughterhouse breweries.
Q❀◑◐⊞▲⇌🚌(G1)♣P

Old Fourpenny Shop 🏆

27/29 Crompton Street, CV34 6HJ (between A429 and A4189)
✪ 12-11 ☎ (01926) 491360 🌐 fourpennyshophotel.co.uk
RCH Pitchfork; guest beers Ⓗ
The plain white facade of this hotel fronts an attractive open-plan, split-level interior that stretches far back from the roadside, with a restaurant at the rear. The comfortable bar is well-known locally for its ever-changing range of five guest beers, with beer notes on a large blackboard. Unusually, it takes a similar approach with its wines. Ideal for a quiet drink, the pub is also handy for Warwick racecourse, where you can park your caravan. Q⇆◑▲🚌(16,18,68)P

The soul of beer

Brewers call barley malt the 'soul of beer'. While a great deal of attention has been rightly paid to hops in recent years, the role of malt in brewing must not be ignored. Malt contains starch that is converted to a special form of sugar known as maltose during the brewing process. It is maltose that is attacked by yeast during fermentation and turned into alcohol and carbon dioxide. Other grains can be used in brewing, notably wheat. But barley malt is the preferred grain as it gives a delightful biscuity / cracker / Ovaltine note to beer. Unlike wheat, barley has a husk that works as a natural filter during the first stage of brewing, known as the mash. Cereals such as rice and corn / maize are widely used by global producers of mass-market lagers, but craft brewers avoid them.

WEST MIDLANDS

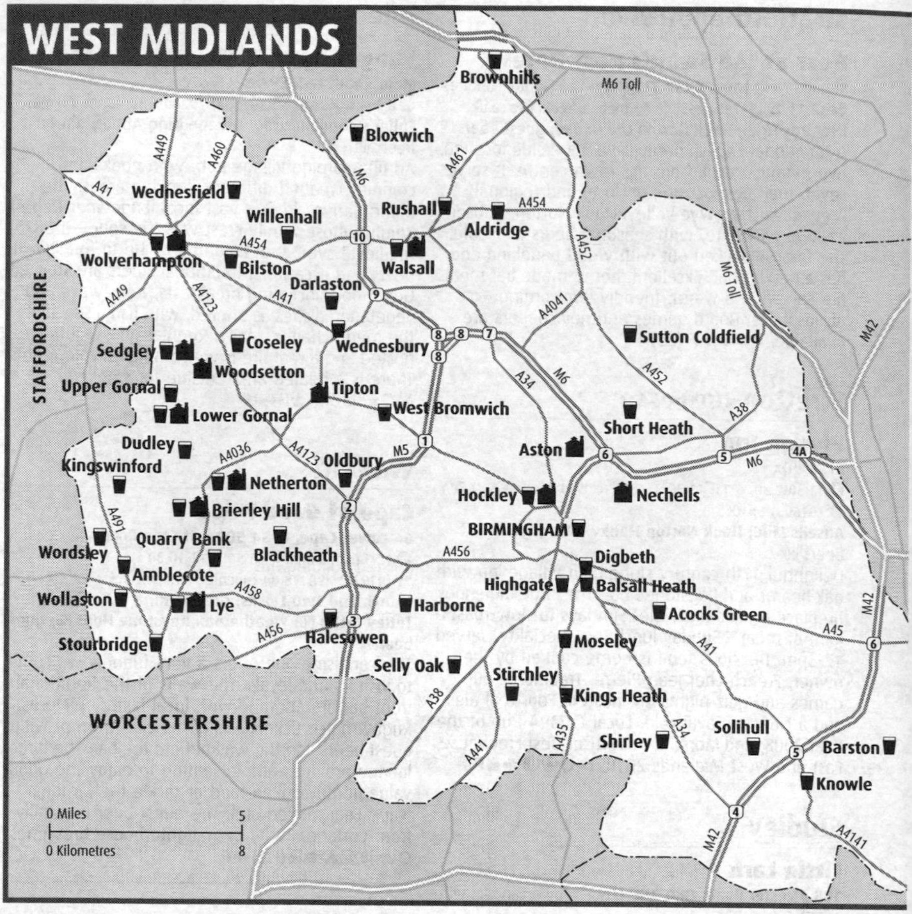

Aldridge

Lazy Hill Tavern

196 Walsall Wood Road, WS9 8HB

12-2.30 Sat, 6-11; 12-2.30, 7-10.30 Sun

☎ (01922) 452040

Caledonian Deuchars IPA; Courage Best Bitter; Greene King Abbot; Marston's Pedigree; Theakston Traditional Mild; guest beer H

Spacious, welcoming, family-run free house with the same licensee for more than 30 years. Originally a farmhouse, it became a country club, then finally a pub in 1986. Four separate rooms are all similarly and comfortably furnished, with original beams exposed in the middle two. The large function room is used mid-week by local sports organisations and can be booked for weddings and other functions. ⌂Q⊟(7,56)P

Amblecote

Maverick ✔

Brettell Lane, DY8 4BA (on jct of A491 and A461)

12-midnight (1am Wed, Fri & Sat); 12-11 Sun

☎ (01384) 824099

Jennings Cumberland Ale; guest beers H

Local Branch Pub of the Year for 2009, the Maverick is a large street-corner pub. A Wild West room doubles as a venue for folk, blues, roots, blue-grass and other music. There is also a Mexican-themed room. A corridor leads to a covered smoking area to the rear with a small garden. There are always four beers on tap, usually with two from micros. Several screens show Sky Sports when no live music is playing. ❀⊟(256,257)♣⁻

Robin Hood ✔

196 Collis Street, DY8 4EQ (on A4102 off Brettell Lane A461)

12-3 (not Mon & Tue), 5-11; 12-1am Fri; 12-midnight Sat; 12-11 Sun ☎ (01384) 821120

Bathams Best Bitter; Enville Ale, Ginger; guest beers H

In the Glass Quarter and close to the canal network, this family owned and run free house prides itself on the range and quality of its award-winning ale. The restaurant opens seven days a week, and features good home-made food that has earned the pub plaudits. En-suite accommodation is available including a family room, and guests are served a hearty breakfast.
⌂❀⊨◑⊟(246)♣P⁻⊡

Starving Rascal ✔

1 Brettell Lane, DY8 4BN

4 (12 Sat & Sun)-11 ☎ (07843) 670163

Beer range varies H

This unusually named new entry to the Guide is run by an enthusiastic young landlord. A warm and

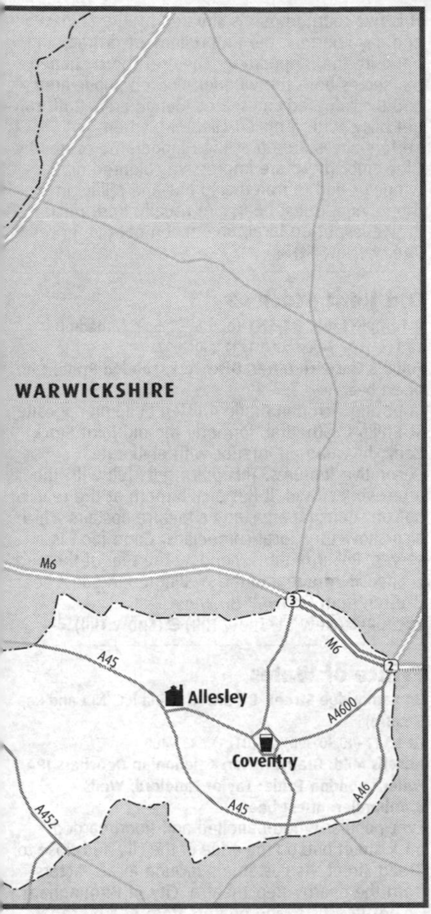

friendly atmosphere is to be found among an array of ornaments, beer bottles and pictures on the wall. The pub consists of three linked rooms around a central bar. Three real ales are available, often paler beers from local breweries. A large range of single malt whiskies is also on offer. ♨🚌(246)♣P

Swan

10 Brettell Lane, DY8 4BN (on A461, ⅓ mile after A491)
⏲ 12-2.30 (not Tue-Thu), 7-11; 12-11 Sat; 12-3, 7-11 Sun
☎ (01384) 76932
Beer range varies Ⓗ
A free house that boasts a comfortable lounge, a separate public bar and a delightful garden. There is a TV in the bar for watching sporting events. This friendly neighbourhood pub supports several local charities including the Air Ambulance. Drinkers can choose from the three varied real ales on offer. There is also an interesting selection of whiskies and a heated smoking area. ❀🍺🚌(246)♣⅃

Barston

Bull's Head ✔

Barston Lane, B92 0JU (in village, on main road)
SP2073378090
⏲ 11-2.30, 5-11; 11-11 Fri & Sat; 12-10.30 Sun
☎ (01675) 442830 🌐 thebullsheadbarston.co.uk
Adnams Bitter; Hook Norton Hooky Bitter; guest beers Ⓗ
Winner of the local CAMRA Pub of the Year award in 2009, as well as three times in previous years, this tranquil, unspoilt pub is a former coaching inn. Two comfortable bars, featuring real fires in winter, and a 20-cover restaurant, afford plenty of room and ambience. There is a regular menu plus ever-changing specials, featuring seasonal home-cooked food. Beers include regularly changing guests. With a beer garden flanked by fields, the pub is popular with locals, cyclists, ramblers and others. ♨Q❀◑♣P⅃

Bilston

Olde White Rose

20 Lichfield Street, WV14 0AG
⏲ 11-11 (11.30 Wed & Thu); 10-11.30 Fri & Sat
☎ (01902) 498339
Beer range varies Ⓗ
The pub features 12 changing real ales sourced from far and wide, plus Westons cider on gravity. The ale is complemented by a standard menu and specials board, with food available 12-9pm. This Grade II-listed building has been extended into the former printers at the rear to provide en-suite accommodation. Quiz nights take place every Tuesday and Wednesday evening and acoustic music often plays on Sunday evening. The downstairs bierkeller is available for private functions and has its own bar.
❀🛏◑♿⊖(Central)🚌🍎

Trumpet

58 High Street, WV14 0EP
⏲ 12-4, 7.30-11.30 ☎ (01902) 493723 🌐 trumpetjazz.org.uk
Holden's Black Country Mild, Black Country Bitter, Golden Glow, Special; guest beer Ⓗ
Busy and welcoming, this compact one-room local serves Holden's award-winning ales at reasonable prices. Plenty of musical memorabilia is on display, including posters from Basie to Bird and musical instruments on the walls and ceiling. There is live jazz and blues seven nights a week plus Sunday lunchtime. A collection plate is passed around for the bands. Outside at the back is a drinking and smoking area. The bus and metro stations are a five-minute walk away. ❀⊖(Central)🚌⅃

Birmingham: Acocks Green

Westley Hotel

80 Westley Road, B27 7UJ
⏲ 11-11; 12-10.30 Sun 🌐 westley-hotel.co.uk
Wye Valley HPA; guest beer Ⓗ
Smart hotel with a comfortable lounge and dining area at the far side of the bar, where meals can be ordered from the restaurant's extensive menu. Sport is shown on a large-screen TV. There is also a spacious function room. A covered but unheated smoking area leads onto a patio and large rear car park. The Wye Valley beer may at times be Butty Bach, supplemented by a different guest.
Q🛏◑⇌🚌(11)P⅃

Birmingham: Balsall Heath

Old Moseley Arms

53 Tindal Street, B12 9QU
⏲ 12-11 (10.30 Sun) ☎ (0121) 440 1954

Black Sheep Best Bitter; Enville Ale; Wye Valley HPA; guest beers Ⓗ
The landlord now owns the freehold at this fine back-street pub, and improvements are obvious. Home-made curry nights are Tuesday and Thursday, and quiz night is Tuesday. Chaos Acoustic Club performs on Sunday evening. Sporting events are shown on a big screen in one of the two bars and in the heated and covered smoking area. Above the fireplace is a history of the pub including a list of landlords since 1838. Regular beer festivals are held. Guest beers can include locals.
❀⊟🚌(50)⚲

Birmingham: City Centre

Bull

1 Price Street, B4 6JU (off St Chads Queensway)
⏲ 12-11; closed Sun ☎ (0121) 333 6757
🌐 thebull-pricestreet.com
Adnams Broadside; Marston's Pedigree; guest beer Ⓗ
One of Birmingham's oldest pubs, this popular and friendly back-street local is in the Gun Quarter, close to Aston University and the Childrens' Hospital. Two main rooms are served by a central bar, with a quiet room at the rear. Traditional food is available until 9.30pm (children welcome). There is a vast collection of jugs and plates, along with photos, on the shelves and walls around the pub bar. The windows have etched Ansells insignia. The guest beer is often from a micro.
Q❀⇄◐◑♿⇌(Snow Hill)⊖(Snow Hill)🚌⚲

Metro Bar & Grill

94 Cornwall Street, B3 2DF
⏲ 10-11 (closed Sun) 🌐 metrobarandgrill.co.uk
Enville White; guest beer Ⓗ
Simple yet chic open-plan wine bar behind Colmore Row and close to many offices. It can be busy in the evenings with an eclectic clientele. There is a large wooden bar on one side and a U-shaped seating area on the other. The bar extends through to a large mirrored wall, and then on to a main dining area serving restaurant-style food. One or two ales are always from a local brewery.
Q◐◑♿⇌(Snow Hill/New St)🚌

Old Contemptibles ✔

176 Edmund Street, B3 2HB (100m from Snow Hill station)
⏲ 10 (12 Sat)-11; 12-5 Sun ☎ (0121) 200 3831
Marston's Pedigree; St Austell Tribute; Taylor Landlord; guest beers Ⓗ
Recently refurbished to a high standard, the pub is very busy lunchtimes and early evenings. It has a long wood-panelled bar and a comfortable separate snug at the rear used for dining. The tasteful decor features mementos commemorating World War I military campaigns of the British Expeditionary Force, after whom the pub is named. Excellent food is served until 10pm. Guest ales are from a seasonally changing portfolio. Tasting racks are available to sample the beers. Toilets are upstairs.
Q◐◑♿⇌(Snow Hill/New St)⊖(Snow Hill)🚌

Old Fox ✔

54 Hurst Street, B5 4TD (opp Hippodrome Theatre)
⏲ 11-midnight (2.30am Fri & Sat); 11-11 Sun
☎ (0121) 622 5080
Greene King Old Speckled Hen; St Austell Tribute; Tetley Bitter; guest beers Ⓗ
This two-roomed pub is situated by the Chinese and gay quarters, the entertainment district, and opposite the Hippodrome Theatre. The U-shaped bar serves both the wooden-floored public area and the carpeted and seated lounge area. Both can get busy, with a mixed clientele, when performances are on at the Hippodrome or nearby Glee Club. There are impressive coloured glass windows and mirrored columns and pillars in the lounge. Guest beers are usually from micro-breweries, often local, and at competitive prices.
◐◑♿⇌(New St)🚌

Old Joint Stock ✔

4 Temple Row, B2 5NY (opp St Philip's cathedral)
⏲ 11-11; 12-5 Sun ☎ (0121) 200 1892
Fuller's Chiswick Bitter, Discovery, London Pride, ESB; guest beers Ⓗ
Imposing Victorian Grade II-listed building opposite St Philip's cathedral, formerly the old Joint Stock Bank, boasting an interior with elaborate decorative features. This place gets full with the after-work crowd. It has a club room at the rear, a balcony drinking area, and a theatre upstairs which also showcases local comedians. Good food is served. Poker night is Monday. The rear of the pub is opposite the rear of the Wellington. A guest beer is often from Beowulf Brewery.
♨❀◐◑⇌(New St/Snow Hill)⊖(Snow Hill)🚌⚲

Prince of Wales

84 Cambridge Street, B1 2NP (behind ICC/NIA and Rep Theatre)
⏲ 12-11 (10.30 Sun) ☎ (0121) 643 9460
Ansells Mild; Brains Bitter; Caledonian Deuchars IPA; Fuller's London Pride; Taylor Landlord; Wells Bombardier; guest beers Ⓗ
Ever-popular wood-panelled and floorboarded back-street pub on the edge of the city and close to Broad Street, its customers include locals, actors from the nearby Rep Theatre, City of Birmingham Orchestra artists, and boaters from nearby canal boats. Home-cooked food is served until 7pm. It can get busy when major events are held at the nearby International Convention Centre, National Indoor Arena and Theatre. The handpumps mainly dispense national brands, but a guest beer changes regularly. Live music plays most Sunday afternoons. ◐♿⇌(New St)⊖(Snow Hill)🚌

Pub du Vin

25 Church Street, B3 2NR
⏲ 12-11; closed Sun 🌐 hotelduvin.com/pub-du-vin
ABC Heartlands; Kinver Light Railway; Purity Mad Goose Ⓗ

INDEPENDENT BREWERIES

ABC Birmingham: Aston
Backyard Walsall
Bank's & Hanson's (Marston's) Wolverhampton
Batham Brierley Hill
Birmingham Nechells
Black Country Lower Gornal
Broughs Netherton
Holden's Woodsetton
Olde Swan Netherton
Rainbow Allesley
Sadler's Lye
Sarah Hughes Sedgley
Toll End Tipton
Two Towers Birmingham: Hockley (NEW)

Cellar bar beneath the Hotel du Vin, with relaxed seating to all sides creating a peaceful atmosphere for office types, though all are welcome. It also has the Snuggles Room for cosier drinking and relaxing. There is a large-screen TV in one corner. Beers from local micros are served in old-style pewter tankards. 'Pie and a pint' is available, as well as a range of baps and home-made pies that changes daily.
⇄◑♿⇌(Snow Hill/New St)⊖(Snow Hill)🚌(Colmore Row)

Sack of Potatoes ✔
10 Gosta Green, B4 7ER
⏲ 11.30-11 (midnight Thu & Fri; 1am Sat); 12-midnight Sun
Harviestoun Bitter & Twisted; Shepherd Neame Spitfire; Taylor Landlord Ⓗ
A comfortable wooden-floored street-corner pub that is popular with students from the adjacent Aston University and office workers alike. It has a U-shaped bar with several distinct seating areas around it, and outside seating available for warmer days. The walls are decorated with photos of old Birmingham scenes. The food is good value and the beer prices low for the area. TV screens feature in most areas for sports coverage but the volume is normally off.
❀◑⇌(Snow Hill)⊖(Snow Hill)🚌(14,66)🍎🚬

Wellington 🏆
37 Bennetts Hill, B2 5SN
⏲ 10-midnight ☎ (0121) 200 3115
🌐 thewellingtonrealale.co.uk
Black Country BFG, Fireside, Pig on the Wall; Purity Mad Goose; Wye Valley HPA; guest beers Ⓗ
Birmingham CAMRA Pub of the Year for three of the past four years, its 15 active handpumps plus three changing ciders make every day a mini-festival here. Equidistant from Snow Hill and New Street stations, its location is also convenient for buses. Bring your own food or order in from nearby as cutlery is provided. Regular cheese and quiz evenings are held as well as quarterly beer festivals from January. The pub can get busy evenings and weekends.
Q⇌(New St/Snow Hill)⊖(Snow Hill)🚌🍎🚬

Birmingham: Digbeth

Anchor ★
308 Bradford Street, B5 6ET
⏲ 11 (12 Sun)-11 ☎ (0121) 622 4516
🌐 anchorinndigbeth.co.uk
Hobsons Mild; Tetley Bitter; guest beers Ⓗ
Always a contender for CAMRA Birmingham Branch Pub of the Year, the Anchor is a must-visit for the ale enthusiast. The pub, in the heart of Birmingham's Irish Quarter, has been in the care of the Keane family for 37 years and brings a local pub feel to a city-centre location. The beer range is always changing, with house favourites from Church End making regular appearances. Live sporting events are shown on large screens. Regular themed beer festival weekends are held.
Q❀◑⊟♿⇌(New St/Moor St)🚌(2,5,6)🍎🚬

Spotted Dog
104 Warwick Street, B12 0NH
⏲ 7-11; 4-midnight Fri; 12-midnight Sat; 7-12.30am Sun
☎ (0121) 772 3822
Ansells Mild; guest beers Ⓗ
Family-owned old-fashioned Irish boozer frequented by an eccentric mix of oddballs, artists, mountaineers with vertigo and anarchists. The same landlord has been at the helm since 1985 and is permanantly at odds with various authorities, and a leading figure in the campaign to keep live music in this part of the city. The pub has Birmingham's most spectacular smoking shelter in the beautiful, spacious beer garden. Sport is shown on large screens, especially rugby, and the venue is home to the Digbeth Olympics.
❀⊟♿🚌(2,12,31)🚬

White Swan ★ ✔
276 Bradford Street, B12 0QY
⏲ 12-11 (1am Fri & Sat) ☎ (0121) 622 2586
Banks's Mild; Jennings Cocker Hoop, Cumberland Ale; guest beer Ⓗ
This unspoilt Victorian red-bricked pub has had the same wonderful landlady since 1969, a fact acknowledged by the local branch with the presentation of a special award certificate. A long, narrow bar opens onto an impressive ornately-tiled hallway leading to a small lounge and smoking area at the rear. Both bars have large-screen TVs showing sporting events. A popular pub with locals and visitors alike, it is close to Digbeth coach station. Guest beers are from the Marston's/Jennings portfolio.
⊟♿⇌(New St/Moor St)🚌(2,12,31)

Birmingham: Harborne

Harborne Club
219 Albany Road, B17 9JX
⏲ 5.30-midnight; 12.30-3.30 Sat & Sun
🌐 theharborneclub.co.uk
Holden's Black Country Bitter; guest beer Ⓗ
There is always an exceptionally warm welcome at this rather anonymous private members' club with a distinct living-room atmosphere. The ales are well-kept, and it is worth noting that they rarely exceed 4% ABV. Guest beers tend to be mainly local to the area such as Wye Valley, Purity, Beowulf or Sadlers. Show a CAMRA membership card or a copy of this Guide for entry. A smoking facility is planned. Q🚌(21,22,29)

Plough ✔
21 High Street, B17 9NT
⏲ 11-11 (midnight Thu & Fri); 10-midnight Sat; 10-10.30 Sun
🌐 theploughharborne.co.uk
Purity Mad Goose; Wye Valley Dully Dach, guest beer Ⓗ
This refurbished pub with an enthusiastic manager and helpful staff has now been brought up to date. The lively, busy atmosphere appeals to both young and old. Events include film screenings on Sunday, live music on Thursday and a quiz on Tuesday. Two-for-one burgers are a speciality. There is a pleasant rear garden. Two regular beers are served plus one changing guest, usually local. Traditional sweets and nuts are dispensed in paper bags.
❀◑🚌(22,23,103)🚬

White Horse ✔
2 York Street, B17 0HG
⏲ 11-11 (11.30 Tue-Thu; midnight Fri & Sat)
🌐 whitehorseharborne.com
Greene King Abbot; Purity Pure Gold; guest beers Ⓗ
This former Festival Ale House just off the main High Street is having a new lease of life. A basic wooden-floored main bar area with seating and tables leads off from the carpeted snug to a rear area that shows live sport events and, often, music

acts including jam sessions on Sunday as well as quiz nights. The beer range includes varying Purity and Greene King beers, with guests tending to come from regionals and small local micros. Cider also varies. Q◑◗🚌(21,23,29)●

Birmingham: Highgate

Lamp

157 Barford Street, B5 6AH (500m from Pershore Road)
⏲ 12-11 ☎ (0121) 622 2599
Church End Gravediggers Mild; Everards Tiger; Stanway Stanney Bitter; guest beers Ⓗ
Popular back-street single-bar pub close to the Hurst Street entertainment area attracting beer enthusiasts from far and wide. Small tables and bar stools together with a long seated area look in toward the bar. The Lily Langtree room at the rear is spacious and caters for meetings and live acts. Guest beers are never above 4.3% ABV and often include a locally-brewed mild, and are sourced from smaller breweries. The pub often has a late licence. ♿⇌(New St)🚌(35,45,47)

Birmingham: Hockley

Black Eagle

16 Factory Road, B18 5JU (in Jewellery Quarter)
⏲ 11-3, 5.30-11; 11-11 Fri; 12-3, 7-11 Sat; 12-3 Sun
☎ (0121) 523 4008 🌐 blackeaglepub.co.uk
Ansells Mild; Bathams Best Bitter; Marston's Pedigree; Taylor Landlord; guest beers Ⓗ
This back-street four-times CAMRA Branch Pub of the Year retains many original features, including Minton tiles. It has two rooms at the front, with a larger rear room for relaxed seating. The restaurant at the rear offers excellent food, from sandwiches and light meals to more substantial dishes. An annual beer festival in July is held in the garden, which has a patio and grassed area and a covered smoking section to the front. Also in the CAMRA Good Food Guide.
Q❀◑◗⊟♿⊖(Soho Benson Road)🚌(11,101)⚟

Lord Clifden

34 Great Hampton Street, B18 6AA
⏲ 10-midnight ☎ (0121) 523 7515 🌐 thelordclifden.co.uk
Bathams Best Bitter; Wye Valley HPA; guest beers Ⓗ
Birmingham CAMRA Branch Pub of the Year silver award winner for the past two years, this establishment continues to impress. A quieter and smaller wooden-floored room at the front and a part-wooden-floored, part-carpeted larger room behind lead to an even larger suntrap garden area. There is artwork by Banksy on the walls. A DJ features on Monday and Friday; quiz night is Tuesday. Guest beers are from Urban Arts Brewery based next door. Good quality food is served.
❀◑◗⊟♿⇌(Jewellery Quarter)⊖(Jewellery Quarter)🚌♣⚟

Red Lion

94/95 Warstone Lane, B18 4NG
⏲ 10am-midnight ☎ (0121) 233 9144
🌐 theredlionbirmingham.com
Purity Mad Goose; Wye Valley Butty Bach; guest beers Ⓗ
Everything a good pub should be, this smart, clean, true free house shows that its owners really care about food and ale. Located 100m down from the Jewellery Quarter clock, the front bar has an unobtrusive TV for sport while the rear lounge doubles as a restaurant for the excellent menu that complements four real ales. A well-appointed first floor function room for hire also hosts various pub events. The rear patio has a smoking area with shelter.
❀◑◗⊟♿⇌(Jewellery Quarter)⊖(Jewellery Quarter)🚌(8,101)♣⚟

Birmingham: Kings Heath

Kings Heath Cricket Club ✔

Charlton House, 247 Alcester Road South, B14 6DT
⏲ 12-midnight ☎ (0121) 444 1913
Fuller's London Pride; Wye Valley Butty Bach, HPA; guest beers Ⓗ
This well-run, friendly and welcoming sports club has two rooms, with the smaller lounge area for more relaxed drinking and the larger room more populated with drinkers watching sporting events on two large screens, and also housing two full size snooker tables. Beer festivals are held in April and November as well as other social events, including live music in the large function room. CAMRA members are welcome on production of a membership card (maximum 10 visits per year).
Q❀◑◗♿🚌(50)♣P⚟

Birmingham: Moseley

Fighting Cocks ✔

St Marys Row, B13 8HW
⏲ 12-11 (10.30 Sun) ☎ (0121) 449 0811
🌐 thefightingcocksmoseley.co.uk
Purity Pure Ubu; Young's Bitter; guest beers Ⓗ
Great destination pub located in the heart of Moseley. The bar at the front has wooden-floored areas to the front and sides, with more relaxed seating at the rear. Four ales are on at any one time, with the range constantly changing. The pub also offers a good food menu available daily until 10pm. This is an extremely popular pub, with Fridays and Saturdays particularly busy. The music is generally unintrusive but there are DJs on at the weekend. ❀◑◗♿🚌(1,50)●⚟

Prince of Wales ✔

118 Alcester Road, B13 8EE
⏲ 12-11.30 (1am Fri & Sat); 12-11 Sun ☎ (0121) 449 4198
Greene King Abbot; St Austell Tribute; Wells Bombardier; guest beers Ⓗ
Busy three-roomed community pub now selling nine beers from the Punch list. The bar leads to a tiled passage with two quieter rooms, and then out to the extensive garden. There is a covered and heated smoking area, plus a large marquee which hosts productions of the Prince of Wales Players. Most nights there is some entertainment and every Saturday is hog roast night. Occasional beer festivals are held. Q⚭❀◑◗⊟♿🚌(50)♣⚟

Birmingham: Selly Oak

Country Girl ✔

1 Raddlebarn Road, B29 6HJ
⏲ 11.30-11 (midnight Fri & Sat) ☎ (0121) 472 7639
Greene King Old Speckled Hen; M&B Brew XI; guest beers Ⓗ
Large but welcoming open-plan Ember Inn, with seating around high and low tables and settees. Smoking areas are at the front and in the large garden with heated and covered spaces. Tuesday is grill night, Thursday curry night, Monday and

Wednesday are quiz nights. Guest beers are from the Waverley portfolio, including micros and locals, and change on a monthly basis, often chosen by customers. Third-of-a-pint tasting racks are available. The manager celebrated 10 years in charge in 2010. ♔Q❀◐♿⇌P⅟

Birmingham: Stirchley

British Oak ★

1364 Pershore Road, B30 2XS (on main A441 close to Bournville station)

⏲ 11-11 (1am Fri & Sat); 12-11 Sun ☎ (0121) 458 1758

Black Sheep Best Bitter; M&B Mild; guest beers Ⓗ

This splendid example of a roadside 1920s-style ale house has a fine interior and features in CAMRA's National Inventory of Historic Pub Interiors. The front bar can be very boisterous at times, with a large-screen TV for sports, while the rear rooms are more peaceful. Notice the fine wood panelling and superb fireplace in the rear bar. There is a large smoking area and a garden for alfresco dining in the summer months. Guest beers come from a seasonal portfolio.
♔☋❀◐◑⊟♿⇌(Bournville)⊟(45,47)♣P⅟

Blackheath

Britannia ✔

124 Halesowen Street, B65 0ES

⏲ 9-midnight (1am Fri & Sat) ☎ (0121) 559 0010

Greene King Ruddles Best Bitter, Abbot; guest beers Ⓗ

In the centre of Blackheath with a wide customer mix, this pub is open plan but with a homely feel. Food is served until 10pm daily, and an adventurous range of up to seven guest beers is available. In the summer a rear garden area makes for a pleasant, secluded location. The pub is reasonably close to Rowley Regis railway station, and buses from Birmingham, West Bromwich and Dudley stop nearby.
☋❀◐◑♿⇌(Rowley Regis)⊟(128,129,140)♣P⅟

Malt Shovel

61 High Street, B65 0EH

⏲ 11-11 (2am Fri); 10-2am Sat; 12-11 Sun

☎ (0121) 561 2321

Enville Ale, Ginger Beer; Holden's Golden Glow; guest beer Ⓗ

Just a few minutes' stroll from Blackheath centre, where many buses stop, you will find a welcome in this friendly pub. There is a pronounced sports theme in the L-shaped, one-roomed house, with four screens showing many live events. There is a distinct community feel and a good customer mix. The guest beer varies. A marquee is erected several times a year in the garden to host various events such as live music and children's entertainment.
☋❀♿⇌(Rowley Regis)⊟(258,404)♣⅟

Bloxwich

Turf Tavern ★

13 Wolverhampton Road, WS3 2EZ (opp Bloxwich Park)

⏲ 12-3, 7-11; 12-2.30, 7-10.30 Sun ☎ (01922) 407745

Oakham JHB; Olde Swan Bumble Hole Bitter; Otter Otter Bright; RCH Pitchfork; guest beer Ⓗ

Grade II-listed building, known locally as Tinky's, which has been in the same family for more than 130 years. The three rooms are dominated by the bar with its splendid tiled floor. The building is steeped in nostalgia and is a haven for quiet conversation, which adds to its traditional charm. Outside is a charming courtyard that serves as a pleasant spot for the summer drinker. Not to be missed. ♔Q☋❀⊟♿⇌⊟(301,908)⅟

Brierley Hill

Vine (Bull & Bladder)

10 Delph Road, DY5 2TN

⏲ 12-11 (10.30 Sun) ☎ (01384) 78293

Bathams Mild Ale, Best Bitter, XXX (winter) Ⓗ

Classic, unspoilt brewery tap with an ornately decorated facade. Step inside and you enter an elongated pub with a labyrinthine feel. The rooms have contrasting characters. The front bar is small and staunchly traditional while the larger rear bar, with its own servery and leather seating, houses the dartboard at the far end. On the other side of the central passageway is a homely lounge partly converted from former brewery offices. Good value Black Country lunches are served weekdays.
♔Q☋❀◐⊟⊟(X96)♣P⅟

Brownhills

Royal Oak ✔

68 Chester Road, WS8 6DU (on A452 approx 500m from Anchor Bridge)

⏲ 12-11 (midnight Thu & Fri); 11-midnight Sat; 11-11 Sun

☎ (01543) 452089 🌐 theroyaloakpub.co.uk

Greene King Abbot; St Austell Tribute; Taylor Landlord; Tetley Bitter; Titanic Anchor Bitter; guest beers Ⓗ

Known locally as the Middle Oak, this beautifully decorated Art Deco-style pub is set back from the main road. The traditional bar plays host to darts and dominoes teams and there is poker on Sunday night, while the very comfortable lounge provides a more relaxed atmosphere. The pub also boasts its own skittle alley, a separate dining room, and a patio drinking area that leads down to a large garden at the rear. Q☋❀◐◑⊟♿⊟(10)♣⅟

Coseley

New Inn

35 Ward Street, WV14 9LQ (backs on to A4123)

⏲ 4-11; 12-11.30 Sat; 12-10.30 Sun ☎ (07927) 459470

🌐 thenewinncoseley.co.uk

Holden's Black Country Mild, Black Country Bitter; guest beers Ⓗ

Warm and cosy one roomed local, best approached from the Birmingham New Road (126 bus route). The bar in the older 19th-century part of the building is divided by a modern bar counter that is the hub of the establishment. The lounge is housed in a late 20th-century extension. An extensive food menu offered Tuesday-Friday evenings uses meat from an award-winning local butcher. Family parties and events can be catered for. There is a covered, heated outside patio area.
♔Q☋◑♿⇌⊟(126)♣P⅟

Coventry

Burnt Post ✔

Kenpas Highway, CV3 6AW (jct of A45 and Wainbody Avenue North)

⏲ 12-11 (midnight Thu-Sun) ☎ (024) 7669 2671

Beer range varies Ⓗ

Former Bass local, recently refurbished. One of several Ember Inns pubs, it has an open-plan bar and lounge shared by drinkers and diners. An extensive food menu accompanies five changing cask beers, with comprehensive beer tasting notes printed monthly. Tasting trays comprising three third-of-a-pint measures are available for those wishing to sample a range of beers.
♨✿◐◑♿🚌(15,801)P⚟

City Arms ✔

1 Earlsdon Street, CV5 6EP (on roundabout at centre of Earlsdon)
⚙ 7am-midnight (1am Fri & Sat) ☎ (024) 7671 8170
Greene King Ruddles Best Bitter, Abbot; guest beers Ⓗ
Wetherspoon's pub in the centre of Earlsdon, popular with both locals and students. Guest beers regularly come from Purity and other Warwickshire breweries. Westons Marcle Hill cider is kept on gravity in the chilled cabinet. The bar is often busy weekend evenings and on Thursday curry night, but more relaxed at other times. Buses from the city centre and the university stop outside. There is a paved patio area together with outside seating for smokers. Food is served all day until 10pm.
✿◐◑♿🚌(12,19)🍎P⚟

Craven Arms

58 Craven Street, Chapelfields, CV5 8DW (1 mile W of city centre, off Allesley Old Road)
⚙ 12-11.30; 12-12.30am Fri; 11-12.30am Sat; 12-11 Sun
☎ (024) 7671 5308
Flowers Original; Holden's Golden Glow; Oakham JHB; Sarah Hughes Dark Ruby; guest beer Ⓗ
An unpretentious street-corner local adjoined by terraced houses, the Craven Arms is in a conservation area with several other interesting pubs nearby. The single-roomed local consists of a long bar area with seating and tables, and has a raised area to the left for pool and games. There is a paved area outside with a heated covered area for smokers. Live music is performed on Sunday evening. The pub is a regular outlet for Sarah Hughes Dark Ruby. ♨✿🚌(10,32)♣⚟

Gatehouse Tavern

46 Hill Street, CV1 4AN (near jct 8 of ring road)
⚙ 11-3, 5-11; 11-11 Thu-Sat; 12-10.30 Sun
☎ (024) 7663 0140 🌐 gatehousetavern.com
Beer range varies Ⓗ
Pub converted by the landlord from the gatehouse of the former Leigh Mill, with one of the few gardens in the city centre. An eclectic clientele keeps the hostelry busy. Stained glass windows depicting the Six Nations give clues to the sporting nature of the place, where rugby, speedway, cricket, golf and the ubiquitous football feature on a large screen. It can therefore get quite noisy when big games are shown. Food is served in large portions at reasonable prices. ✿◐◑🚌(10,32)🍎⚟

Greyhound Inn 🏆

Sutton Stop, Hawkesbury Junction, CV6 6DF (off Grange Rd at jct of Coventry & Oxford canal)
⚙ 11-11; 12-10.30 Sun ☎ (024) 7636 3046
🌐 thegreyhoundinn.com
Marston's Pedigree; Theakston Traditional Mild; guest beers Ⓗ
Winner of the 2005-2009 Godiva Award for best pub in Warwickshire, this canalside inn dates from 1830 and has many original features. An extensive menu of freshly cooked food is available and regular beer festivals are held on St George's Day weekend and in mid-July. The terrace and rear garden have their own outside bar in the summer, with an additional four cask ales served on gravity. Within 25 minutes' pleasant canalside walk of the Ricoh Arena. ♨Q✿◐◑🚌♣P⚟

Hare & Hounds

Watery Lane, Keresley End, CV7 8JA (jct of Bennetts Road and Watery Lane) SP318837
⚙ 11-11.30 (12.30am Fri); 9am-12.30am Sat; 9am-11.30 Sun
☎ (024) 7633 2716 🌐 hareandhounds.co.uk
Draught Bass; Hook Norton Old Hooky; M&B Brew XI; guest beer Ⓗ
Located on the northern fringes of the city, this pub is popular with country walkers and locals alike. A large, comfortable L-shaped bar area includes real fires. Good value bar meals are available, with a more diverse food choice served in the restaurant. The garden has outside seating and a children's play area. The pub features live music most Saturdays and there is a large function room available for hire. ♨Q✿◐◑⊟♿🚌(36)♣P⚟

Nursery Tavern

38-39 Lord Street, Chapelfields, CV5 8DA (1 mile W of city centre, off Allesley Old Road)
⚙ 12-11.30; 11-midnight Fri & Sat; 12-11 Sun
☎ (024) 7667 4530
Courage Best Bitter; Fuller's London Pride; John Smith's Bitter; Taylor Golden Best; guest beer Ⓗ
This family-run community pub is a long-standing entry in the Guide. It has two front rooms served by a central bar. The third room at the rear generally hosts live music, with free entry on the second Wednesday of every month. This room is also used for other social events and doubles as a restaurant on Sunday lunchtime. Beer festivals are held in the rear garden every June and December. Dogs (with well-behaved owners) are welcome.
Q♉✿◐🚌(10,32,33)♣🍎⚟

Old Windmill

22-23 Spon Street, CV1 3BA
⚙ 11 (12 Wed & Thu)-11; 11-1am Fri-Sun ☎ (024) 7625 2183
Greene King Old Speckled Hen; Sharp's Doom Bar; Taylor Landlord; Theakston Old Peculier; Wychwood Hobgoblin; guest beer Ⓗ
Popular half-timbered pub in the medieval Spon Street, known locally as Ma Brown's, and probably the oldest pub in Coventry. It has lots of small rooms, one of which is the old brewhouse where the old mash tun and copper can be seen. A 10 per cent discount is offered to CAMRA members on all beers. The pub can get very busy at weekends with people getting a decent pint before hitting the nearby clubs. Meals are served 11-5pm Wednesday-Sunday. ♨◐🚌🍎

Rose & Woodbine

40 North Street, Stoke Heath, CV2 3FW
⚙ 12-11 (11.30 Fri & Sat); 12-5, 7-11.30 Sun
☎ (024) 7645 1480
Draught Bass; guest beers Ⓗ
Keenly priced food (lunchtimes only) and ales make this village pub in a back-street urban setting easy on the pocket. The pub is home to three dominoes, three darts, and two pool teams, and offers up to four guest ales. Children are welcome until 7pm. There is a covered and heated area for smokers. ✿◐⊟♿🚌(10,36)♣⚟

Royal Oak
22 Earlsdon Street, CV5 6EJ (100m from Earlsdon roundabout)
⏲ 5-11 (midnight Fri & Sat); 12-11 Sun ☎ (024) 7667 4140
Draught Bass; Hook Norton Hooky Bitter; Tetley Bitter; guest beer 🄷
Earlsdon's only remaining traditional pub, with a charismatic landlord and attentive bar staff. This venue was refurbished after flooding in 2006 but the opportunity for change was resisted, much to the delight of locals. The pub is music-free and attracts a diverse clientele where convivial banter dominates. A U-shaped slate-topped bar serves two drinking areas where table service is also available. The patio leading to the rear bar has magnificent hanging baskets and provides a pleasant outdoor drinking area. ⩩Q❀🚌(12,19)⚊

Town Wall Tavern ✔
Bond Street, CV1 4AH (behind Belgrade Theatre)
⏲ 12 (11.30 Sat)-midnight; 12-7 Sun ☎ (024) 7622 0963
Adnams Bitter, Broadside; Caledonian Deuchars IPA; Draught Bass; Fuller's London Pride; M&B Brew XI; guest beer 🄷
A welcoming and popular city-centre pub located behind the Belgrade Theatre. It has three rooms including a delightful snug called The Donkey Box. Freshly cooked lunchtime and early-evening meals are available (no food Sun). A good range of regular beers and guests comes from breweries such as St Austell and Black Sheep.
⩩Q◐◑⊟♿🚌(10,32)🍎⚊

Whitefriars Olde Ale House
114-115 Gosford Street, CV1 5DL
⏲ 12-midnight (1am Fri & Sat); 12-11 Sun
☎ (024) 7625 1655 🌐 whitefriarscov.com
Sharp's Doom Bar; guest beer 🄷
The original building dates back to the 14th and 17th centuries and many features are still discernible today. Five changing guest beers are served – a discount is available on selected beers on Monday evening. Beer festivals are held on many public holidays in the summer in the semi-covered garden at the back; winter beer festivals are also held inside. Quiz night is Tuesday, open mike Wednesday, karaoke Sunday and live music features occasionally on Friday or Saturday.
⩩Q❀◐♿🚌(27,32)♣⚊

Darlaston

Prince of Wales
74 Walsall Road, WS10 9JJ
⏲ 3-11 Mon, Wed & Thu; 12-11 Tue, Fri & Sat; 12-10.30 Sun
☎ (0121) 526 6244
Holden's Black Country Bitter, Golden Glow; guest beer 🄷
The snug lounge has old maps and photos of the town's football teams on display. The long narrow bar has drinks and cigarette mirrors, and darts is played at the far end. At the rear is a large garden with a play area, benches and conservatory. In the early 1900s the pub hosted the Butcroft Judge and Jury Club. There are occasional trips out on local ale trails. Fresh rolls are available daily, with lunches served on Tuesday, Friday and Sunday.
🐴❀◐⊟🚌(333,334)♣⚊

Spring Head Tavern
83 Walsall Road, WS10 9JU
⏲ 12-midnight ☎ (0121) 526 6636
Black Country BFG, Pig on the Wall, Fireside; guest beer 🄷
The small front bar has advertisements of sports equipment from yesteryear on display. The large lounge has soft bench seats with old world prints on the walls; a big screen shows sports events at one end. The yard at the rear has benches and a sheltered area, plus a covered area for smokers. Darts is played, with karaoke every fortnight. There is a free-and-easy guitar session every Sunday lunchtime. Various cobs are available daily.
❀⊟🚌(333,334)♣P⚊

Dudley

Court House
30 New Street, DY1 1LP (short walk from bus station towards police station)
⏲ 12-11 (10.30 Sun) ☎ (01384) 240062
🌐 blackcountryrealales.co.uk
Black Country BFG, Pig on the Wall, Fireside; guest beers 🄷
Acquired by Black Country Traditional Inns, this pub opened mid-2009 as a specialist real ale venue. The regular beers come from the company's own brewery, accompanied by a wide selection of guests, usually including a dark beer. Cider drinkers are well catered for with a choice of Thatchers Traditional and Heritage regularly available, as well as guests. The small snug and the upstairs function room complement the facilities. Meals available 12-7pm. Q◐♿🚌🍎

Full Moon ✔
58-60 High Street, DY1 1PS
⏲ 9am-11.30 (midnight Fri & Sat) ☎ (01384) 212294
Greene King Ruddles Best Bitter, Abbot 🄷**; guest beers** 🄷/🄿
The Full Moon is a large, centrally-located Wetherspoon pub with a friendly, comfortable atmosphere, offering good value food and drink. It opened in 1996 and was originally a town-centre department store and then a pizza restaurant. Historic local photographs and facts adorn the walls. It is not far from the main Dudley bus station where buses from all over the region terminate. Food is served 9am-10pm. 🐴◐♿🚌♣🍎

Lamp Tavern
116 High Street, DY1 1QT
⏲ 12-11 (10.30 Sun) ☎ (01384) 254129 🌐 bathams.co.uk
Bathams Mild Ale, Best Bitter, XXX (winter) 🄷
Classic Bathams pub with a large front bar with traditional games and a cosy back room with a more relaxed feel. The old Queens Cross brewery has been converted into a large function room used for staging music nights and is available for hire. An outside area for drinking overlooks the southern area of the Black Country to the Clent Hills beyond. B&B accommodation is in the adjacent Lamp Cottage (with a discount for CAMRA members – ring for details).
Q🐴❀🛏⊟♿🚌(242A,243)♣P⚊

Halesowen

Coombs Wood Sports & Social Club
Lodgefield Road, B62 8AA (just off A4099 Coombs Road, 1 mile from town centre)
⏲ 6.30 (12.30 Sat)-11; 12-10.30 Sun ☎ (0121) 561 1932
🌐 coombswood.co.uk
Beer range varies 🄷

Originally set up for employees of the local steel works that is now long gone, happily the club continues to thrive. Located adjacent to a cricket pitch, various sports teams including cricket, bowls and darts operate from the club. The less energetic can enjoy Sky Sports and ESPN TV. Up to six real ales, including a mild, are usually available. Bar snacks are available at weekends. Show a current CAMRA membership card or a copy of this Guide to gain admission. ❀🚌(242)♣⚟

Hawne Tavern

76 Attwood Street, B63 3UG (opp Tesco Express)

⏲ 4.30 (12 Sat)-11; 12-10.30 Sun ☎ (0121) 602 2601

Bank Top Dark Mild; Banks's Bitter; Bathams Best Bitter; Bob's White Lion; guest beers Ⓗ

This busy former CAMRA Pub of the Year is now in its 11th consecutive year in the Guide and is a wonderful example of a community free house, offering four regular and up to six guest beers. You can drink in the small lounge or the livelier open bar area with pool, darts area and TV for sports results. Sun worshippers and smokers enjoy the enclosed rear garden. Bar snacks are served evenings and Saturday. Children allowed until 9pm. Q❀🚌(9)♣P⊓

Waggon & Horses

21 Stourbridge Road, B63 3TU (on A458, ½ mile from bus station)

⏲ 12-11.30 (12.30am Fri & Sat) ☎ (0121) 550 4989

Bank Top Dark Mild; Bathams Best Bitter; Bob's White Lion; Holden's Golden Glow; Nottingham EPA; Oakham White Dwarf; guest beers Ⓗ

A pub with a national reputation but with a real community feel, the regular beers sit alongside eight guest ales, two real ciders, a perry and up to five Belgian beers on draught. There are three rooms, a traditional bar with a sloping floor, and quieter rooms at both ends. CAMRA awards include County and Branch Pub of the Year. Owner Bob has been here over 22 years, most of them in the Guide. Cobs and snacks are available until 6.30pm. Q🚌(9)♣●

Kingswinford

Bridge

110 Moss Grove, DY6 9HH (on A491)

⏲ 12-11.30 (11.45 Fri & Sat); 12-11 Sun ☎ (01384) 352356

Banks's Mild, Bitter; guest beers Ⓗ

In addition to a healthy local trade, this pub is most welcoming to visitors. The bar, popular for pub games and sports TV, extends across the front of the building. There is a cosy lounge behind. Outside is an enclosed garden with children's play equipment. One or two guest beers come from the Marston's list. There is occasional live entertainment at weekends. Hot pies and pasties are available, plus sandwiches made to order. Q❀♿🚌(256,257)♣P⚟⊓

Knowle

Vaults

St John's Close, B93 0JU (off High Street A4141) SP181768

⏲ 12-2.30, 5-11; 12-11.30 Fri & Sat; 12-11 Sun

☎ (01564) 773656

Highgate Vaults Bitter; Tetley Bitter; Wadworth 6X; guest beers Ⓗ

This popular drinkers' pub has frequently been local CAMRA Branch Pub of the Year, most recently in 2008. The range of guest beers always varies, including ales from small breweries and old favourites. Real cider from the Westons range is also available. Major sporting events can be viewed on ESPN Sports TV, and the pub also has Wi-Fi. Regular beer festivals take place, and there is an annual pickled onion competition. Light meals are served lunchtimes Monday to Saturday. (🚌(S2,S3)●⚟

Lower Gornal

Black Bear

86 Deepdale Lane, DY3 2AE

⏲ 5 (4 Fri)-11; 12-11 Sat; 12-10.30 Sun ☎ (01384) 253333

Kinver Black Bear IPA; guest beers Ⓗ

Charming, traditional pub built on the hillside, with impressive views over the edge of the Black Country and beyond. Originally an 18th-century stone farmhouse, it has acquired a slight gradient over the years, requiring a supporting buttress. The interior comprises a split-level lounge with several distinct cosy corners. Guest beers are usually from smaller micro-breweries. It's a 10-minute uphill walk from Gornal Wood bus station. ⛰❀🚌(257,297)♣

Fountain

8 Temple Street, DY3 2PE (on B4157 5 mins from Gornal Wood bus station)

⏲ 12-11 (10.30 Sun) ☎ (01384) 242777

Greene King Abbot; Hobsons Town Crier; Hook Norton Old Hooky; RCH Pitchfork; guest beers Ⓗ

Frequent finalist and twice winner of Dudley CAMRA Pub of the Year, this excellent free house serves nine real ales accompanied by draught and bottled Belgian beers, real cider and 12 fruit wines. The busy, vibrant bar is complemented by an elevated dining area serving excellent food 12-2.30pm and 6-9pm Monday-Friday, 12-9pm Saturday and Sunday lunches until 5pm. During the summer months the rear garden is a suntrap and a pleasant area to while away an hour or two. ❀◑♿🚌(541)♣●

Lye

Shovel

81 Pedmore Road, DY9 7DZ (on A4036, just S of Lye Cross)

⏲ 5.30 (2.30 Sat)-midnight; 12-midnight Sun

☎ (01384) 423998

Enville Ale; Greene King Old Speckled Hen, Abbot; Holden's Golden Glow; guest beers Ⓗ

Good old-fashioned traditional pub, serving 13 real ales. It's home of the Rale Ale Wall – 800 pump pulls from the last 24 years. The building has ornate gates featuring two malt shovels intertwined with grape vines. There is a central bar serving three separate seating areas, and two TVs ensure most sporting events are covered. There is also a dartboard and general knowledge machine. Outside there is a partly-covered patio and a heated smoking area. ❀◑♿⇌🚌(9,276,297)♣⚟

Netherton

Olde Swan (Ma Pardoe's) ☆

89 Halesowen Road, DY2 9PY (on A459 Dudley-Old Hill road)

⏲ 11-11; 12-4, 7-11 Sun ☎ (01384) 253075
Olde Swan Original, Dark Swan, Entire, Bumble Hole; guest beer Ⓗ
One of the last four remaining English home-brew pubs from 1974, deservedly on CAMRA's National Inventory of Historic Pub Interiors, and home to the Olde Swan Brewery, resurrected in 2000. The front bar is an unspoilt treasure, and there is a cosy rear snug. Food is available in the lounge Monday-Friday lunchtimes and Monday evening. The upstairs restaurant is highly regarded for its a la carte menu (open Tue-Sat); Sunday lunches are also served, with booking essential.
♨Q❀◐◑⊟♿🚌(242A,243,283)P

Oldbury

Jolly Collier
43 Junction Street, B69 3HD (off A457)
⏲ 12-3, 5-11; 12-11 Fri & Sat; 12-10.30 Sun
☎ (07817) 286827
Beer range varies Ⓗ
At the end of a side street, this friendly locals' pub is popular with a mixed clientele. It offers traditional pub games and comprehensive TV coverage of live sporting events. There is a heated, covered smoking patio and a large, elevated, decked area overlooking the garden. The beers, which change regularly, are nearly always LocAles. Three beer festivals are organised each year, one usually coinciding with Cask Ale Week. Sandwiches are available at the bar.
🚼❀⇌(Sandwell & Dudley)🚌(87,120)♣⚊

Waggon & Horses ★ ✔
17A Church Street, B69 3AD
⏲ 12-11 (midnight Fri & Sat); 12-10.30 (7 Nov-Apr) Sun
☎ (0121) 552 5467
Enville White; guest beers Ⓗ
In Oldbury town centre opposite Sandwell council buildings, this pub is popular with office workers and shoppers. Up to five guest beers are available, often one from owners SA Brains. A long-standing entry in CAMRA's National Inventory of Historic Pub Interiors, the pub has some wonderfully noteworthy architectural features such as the panelled ceiling, ornately tiled walls and etched windows. A tasty selection of freshly cooked, good value food is served, with a vegetarian option always available.
♨Q🚼◐◑⊟♿⇌(Sandwell & Dudley)🚌(87,120)

Quarry Bank

Church Tavern
36 High Street, DY5 2AA
⏲ 12-11 (10.30 Sun) ☎ (01384) 560249
Beer range varies Ⓗ
This friendly community-centred pub is a Brains house but the landlord has the freedom to select a changing range of four guest beers. It has a traditional L-shaped bar and a separate lounge with a real fire. Children are welcome in the lounge. The pub gets very busy at weekends when live music alternates with a disco. Frequent buses pass by en route to Merry Hill shopping centre. There is a small car park to the rear.
♨🚼⊟🚌(123,222)♣P

Rushall

Manor Arms ★
Park Road, off Daw End Lane, WS4 1LG (off B4154 at Canal Bridge)
⏲ 12-midnight (11 Sun) ☎ (01922) 642333
Banks's Mild, Bitter; Jennings Cocker Hoop; Ringwood Old Thumper; guest beers Ⓗ
This pub is thought to have been built around 1105 and to have held a licence to serve ale since 1248. Exposed wood beams remain, and there is an open fire in both bars. The beer pulls come straight out of the wall; the pub is known locally as 'the pub with no bar'. Its large beer garden is near the canal and a local country park. Good food is served on Saturday and Sunday from April through to September. Dog-friendly. ♨Q🚼❀◐🚌(997)P⚊

Sedgley

Beacon Hotel 🏆 ★
129 Bilston Street, DY3 1JE (A463)
⏲ 12-2.30, 5.30-11; 12-3, 6-11 Sat; 12-3, 7-10.30 Sun
☎ (01902) 883380
Sarah Hughes Pale Amber, Surprise, Dark Ruby; guest beers Ⓗ
This beautifully-restored Victorian tap house and tower brewery is the home of Sarah Hughes ales. The heart of this popular pub is the small island servery with hatches serving the central corridor, a small, cosy snug, and the large main room. It also has a benched tap room and a family room leading to a garden. Cobs are available. Local CAMRA Pub of the Year 2008, 2009 and 2010. The strong barley wine Snowflake is on sale during the Christmas period. Q🚼❀🚌(545)P⚊

Bulls Head
27 Bilston Street, DY3 1JA (A463)
⏲ 9am-11 ☎ (01902) 661676
Holden's Black Country Mild Ⓗ**, Black Country Bitter** Ⓗ/Ⓟ**, Golden Glow; guest beer** Ⓗ
This is a double-fronted, street-corner, listed building close to the centre of Sedgley village. The locals like their sports TV but this is confined to the bar area across the front of the pub. Go up the steps into the lounge area for a quieter drink. There is a yard at the back with smoking shelters. Breakfasts and lunches are served; check availability of evening meals – a takeaway option may be available. Bitter is served on both electric and handpump. ♨🚼❀◐◑🚌(541,558)♣⚊▭

Mount Pleasant (Stump)
144 High Street, DY3 1RH (A459)
⏲ 6.30 (7 Mon & Tue)-11; 12-3, 7-10.30 Sun
☎ (07950) 195652
RCH Stumpys; guest beers Ⓗ
Known locally as the Stump, this popular free house serves an interesting selection of up to eight beers. It possesses a Tardis-like interior and a mock-Tudor frontage. The front bar has a convivial, warm atmosphere while the lounge has an intimate feel, with two rooms on different levels. Food is limited to ham or cheese cobs. Stumpys Ale is brewed by RCH. Dog-friendly, it is on the 558 Dudley/Wolverhampton bus route, or a five-minute walk from Sedgley centre.
♨Q❀⊟🚌(558)♣P⚊

Shirley

Bernie's Real Ale Off-Licence

266 Cranmore Boulevard, B90 4PX (off A34, opposite TRW research site) SP1287077635

⏲ 11.30-2, 4.30-10; 11.30-9.30 Sat; 6-9 Sun

☎ (0121) 744 2827

Taylor Landlord; guest beers Ⓗ

This off-licence has definitely deserved 28 consecutive years in this Guide. It sells the largest number of micro-brewery beers available anywhere in this area. Many are from northern England, but unusual beers could come from anywhere in the UK. Three or four guest beers are constantly changing and there is usually a pale, hoppy beer on sale. Samples are offered and containers are always available to take home. Over 100 bottled beers complement the cask ales. 🚌(5,6,76)●

Woodman's Rest ✓

Union Road, B90 3DB (between Stratford Rd and Marshall Lake Rd) SP1270078490

⏲ 11.30-11 (11.30 Thu); 11.30-midnight Fri & Sat

☎ (0121) 745 3904

Greene King IPA, Abbot; guest beers Ⓗ

Refurbished in 2000, this venue is now an Ember Inn aimed at the older market. A single central bar serves the vast but comfortable space around it. Popular with the locals, it can get very busy, so if you want to sit down get there early. Four guest beers come from the Ember Inns monthly list; one is usually Black Sheep Bitter, or the local Purity UBU. Children over 14 are allowed only if dining. ⛫Q❀◐♿🚌(6,76)P⁻

Short Heath

Duke of Cambridge

82 Coltham Road, WV12 5QD

⏲ 12-11 ☎ (01922) 712038

Black Country BFG, Pig on the Wall, Fireside; guest beers Ⓗ

Originally converted from 17th-century farm cottages around 200 years ago, the pub has been given a new lease of life after an 18-month closure. The public bar is heated by a solid fuel burner, while the lounge, with an aquarium built into the dividing wall, features original beams in the front half. The large family room has a pool table and a quiz machine, and a garden is planned for 2010. ⛫♘⊟🚌(341,342)♣⁻

Solihull

Assembly Rooms ✓

21 Poplar Road, B91 3AD (100m from John Lewis, 150m from White Swan) SP1517579645

⏲ 8.30am-1.00am Mon-Wed; 8am-2am Thu-Sat; 9am-1am Sun ☎ (0121) 711 6990

Greene King Ruddles Best Bitter, Abbot; guest beers Ⓗ

Formerly Solihull's Council House, this imposing Lloyds No 1 bar offers a choice of up to six guest beers and two regular ales. Sky Sports is screened upstairs, reached via a spiral staircase. Downstairs is quieter, with background music, except on Thursday-Saturday nights when there is a DJ from 9pm onwards. The usual Wetherspoon's menu is available, with special offers and a children's option. Beers from local breweries are often represented, with Meet the Brewer nights from time to time. ◐♿⇌🚌⁻

White Swan ✓

32-34 Station Road, B91 3SB (by main bus stops opp Touchwood shopping centre) SP1500579615

⏲ 7am-midnight (1am Fri & Sat) ☎ (0121) 7115180

Greene King Ruddles Best Bitter, Abbot; guest beers Ⓗ

This was the first Wetherspoon pub in Solihull, opening in 2004 from a converted shop, with a mix of open seating and cosy alcoves. It now runs beer festivals and occasional events such as Meet the Brewer. The five most prominent handpumps offer changing guest beers. Centrally located by Touchwood, it is a popular place from breakfast to midnight; although there is no music, the conversation does get quite animated, so it is not a quiet pub. ◐♿⇌🚌⁻

Stourbridge

Plough & Harrow 🏆

107 Worcester Street, DY8 1AX (on A451 at jct of B4186 Heath Lane)

⏲ 12-11 (11.30 Fri & Sat); 12-10.30 Sun ☎ (01384) 397218

Hobsons Best Bitter; Taylor Landlord; Wye Valley HPA; guest beer Ⓗ

A cheerful welcome awaits at this local, where the main priority is well-kept real ale and cider. The servery is a U-shaped bar, and good conversation is not interrupted by TV or loud music. Three real fires create a cheerful atmosphere inside, where dogs on leads are welcome. Outside there is a garden with covered smoking areas. The nearby park has public car parking, but beware of park closing times. Current CAMRA Branch Pub of the Year. ⛫Q❀⇌🚌♣●⁻

Royal Exchange

75 Enville Street, DY8 1XW

⏲ 1 (12 Sat)-11; 12-10.30 Sun ☎ (01384) 396726

Bathams Mild Ale, Best Bitter, XXX (winter) Ⓗ

This perennial Guide entry is in a row of terraced houses. A narrow passageway contains an entrance to a bustling public bar and leads to a paved patio/heated smoking area. A comfortable lounge is at the rear of the building, with a function room upstairs. There is no hot food, but cobs are available, with pork pies at weekends. A December visit might land you the elusive XXX on draught. There is a public car park opposite. Q❀⊟⇌🚌♣P⁻

Sutton Coldfield

Bishop Vesey 🏆 ✓

63 Boldmere Road, B73 5UY

⏲ 9-11 (midnight Fri & Sat) ☎ (0121) 355 5077

Courage Directors; Greene King Abbot; Marston's Pedigree; guest beers Ⓗ

Named after the town's Tudor benefactor, this busy and popular Wetherspoon's provides a convenient and welcoming meeting place. It has an open-plan layout with upstairs seating, and a patio area for smokers. Children are allowed in the family area if dining until 9pm. Themed evenings and regular beer festivals feature. Three regular beers are complemented by up to six guests, some from local micros. ❀◐♿⇌(Wylde Green)🚌⁻

Butlers Arms

444 Lichfield Road, B74 4BL

⏲ 12-11 (midnight Fri & Sat; 10.30 Sun) ☎ (0121) 308 0765

🌐 butlersarms.co.uk

Caledonian Deuchars IPA; Greene King Abbot; guest beers Ⓗ
Shaken into an eclectic mix of styles, the interior features leather sofas, Shaker chairs, modern lamps and mirrors dotted around the tall bar. The fabulous food includes a chalkboard full of fish specials and a menu with meat and vegetarian alternatives, all with great prices. This is a family-run pub with a comfortable feel. There is a spacious car park, railway station at Butlers Lane, and buses nearby at Mere Green.
❀◑♿⇌(Butlers Lane)🚌P⊬

Crown ✔
66 Walsall Road, Four Oaks, B74 4RA
✪ 11.30-11 (midnight Thu-Sat) ☎ (0121) 323 2715
🌐 emberinns.co.uk/thecrownsuttoncoldfield
M&B Brew XI; guest beers Ⓗ
A magnificent pub with a large car park fronted by flower borders and shrubs, and heated patio areas. The interior is spacious but with a warm, friendly and welcoming atmosphere. An Ember Inn, it offers four guest beers and great food for all tastes served by attentive staff. Grill night is Tuesday and curry night Thursday. A strong community spirit is cemented by local events, including beer and wine tasting and charity fundraisers.
♨❀◑♿⇌(Butlers Lane)🚌(366)♣P⊬

Upper Gornal

Britannia (Sally's) ☆
109 Kent Street, DY3 1UX (on A459)
✪ 12-11 (10.30 Sun) ☎ (01902) 883253
Bathams Mild Ale, Best Bitter, XXX (winter) Ⓗ
The Britannia owes its CAMRA National Inventory of Historic Pub Interiors listing to the tap room at the rear, with its wall-mounted handpumps. Service is from the main front bar, a very comfortable place to be, with both rooms warmed by a roaring open fire. There is also a family/games room with a TV occasionally in use. Behind the pub is the former brewhouse, a delightful backyard, smoking shelter and garden. A good selection of bar snacks is available. ♨Q☕❀⊟♿🚌(558)♣⊬

Jolly Crispin
25 Clarence Street, DY3 1UL (A459)
✪ 4 (12 Fri & Sat)-11; 12-10.30 Sun ☎ (01902) 672220
🌐 thejollycrispin.co.uk
Titanic Crispy Nail; guest beers Ⓗ
Sat atop a major watershed where the Black Country ridge meets the sky, the back of the pub drains into the Trent, the front into the Severn. This 18th-century building stands out as a major star in the firmament that is the Gornals. The locals and their dogs are friendly, the fires glow and the beer – a regular Titanic – and eight guest pulls with a real cider or perry is bostin'. A twice-yearly cider festival is held. ♨❀⊟🚌(558)♣●P⊬

Walsall

Black Country Arms 🏆
High Street, WS1 1QW (in market, opp Asda)
✪ 12-11.30 (1am Fri & Sat; midnight Sun) ☎ (01922) 640588
Black Country BFG, Pig on the Wall, Fireside; guest beers Ⓗ
Imposing three-level pub, originally the Green Dragon Inn, dating back to at least the 18th century. It was refurbished in 1976, incorporating a former music shop next door, and renamed in 2008. The impressive mahogany bar boasts 16 handpulls serving up to 12 micro-brewery guest beers from all over the UK. A quiz is held every Tuesday and live jazz is played on the first Monday of each month. Local CAMRA Pub of the Year 2009.
Q❀◐⇌🚌●P⊬

Butts Tavern
44 Butts Street, Butts, WS4 2BJ (200m from Arboretum Lichfield St entrance)
✪ 12-11 (midnight Fri & Sat) ☎ (01922) 629332
🌐 buttstavern.co.uk
Beer range varies Ⓗ
Friendly community local with a large main bar with a stage at one end, and a smaller room with a pool table and dartboard. Six handpulls serve two permanent and up to four changing guest beers. Quiz night is Tuesday, there is entertainment most Fridays and Saturdays, and the last Sunday of the month is acoustic night. Sky Sports and ESPN are screened. There is an external smoking area. Crusty cobs on sale at £1 each are excellent value.
☕♿⇌🚌(10,22,977)♣⊬

King Arthur
59 Liskeard Road, WS5 3EY (off A34 next to Gillity shopping centre)
✪ 12-11 (midnight Sat) ☎ (01922) 631400
🌐 thekingarthurpub.co.uk
Greene King Ruddles Best Bitter, Old Speckled Hen, Abbot; Taylor Golden Best; Wye Valley HPA; guest beers Ⓗ
An urban gem located in Park Hall estate, which is hard to find but definitely worth the effort. A two-roomed community pub, it has a bar area with a big screen and five TVs boasting comprehensive sports viewing. The front lounge is popular with diners and is famous for its steaks (booking required for four people or more). There is a heated smoking area outside next to the large car park, and front and rear beer gardens.
❀◑⊟♿🚌(74)P⊬

Lyndon House Hotel
9-10 Upper Rushall Street, WS1 2HA (between market and St Matthew's Church)
✪ 11.30-11 (2am Fri & Sat); 12-11 Sun ☎ (01922) 612511
🌐 lyndonhousehotel.co.uk
Caledonian Deuchars IPA; Greene King Abbot; Theakston Traditional Mild, Best Bitter; guest beers Ⓗ
Situated in the heart of the town, this pub is part of a complex with a hotel and Italian restaurant. The bar (formerly the Royal Exchange) was converted about 15 years ago. It features old brick and many old timbers to warm and cosy effect. The luxurious hotel was formerly a Salvation Army hostel. Popular with business people, a mixed clientele is drawn from all over the town to give a slice of Walsall life. ♨Q❀🛏◑⊟⇌🚌(51,77)P⊬

Walsall Cricket Club
Gorway Road, WS1 3BE (off A34, by university campus)
✪ 8-10.30; 7.30-midnight Fri; 12-midnight Sat; 12-10 (8 winter) Sun ☎ (01922) 622094 🌐 walsallcricketclub.com
Wye Valley HPA; guest beers Ⓗ
Established in 1830, the club has occupied this site since 1907. The comfortable single-roomed lounge displays cricket memorabilia, with two large screens for sporting events. The bar is manned by members. On match days the cricket can be viewed through panoramic windows; in good weather the lounge is opened onto the patio. On summer evenings this is a rural retreat in the heart

of town. Beer festivals are held. Entry to the club for non-members is by CAMRA membership card.
❀♿🚌(51)♣P

White Lion ✔

150 Sandwell Street, WS1 3EQ (at jct of Sandwell Sreet and Little London)
🕐 12-11 (midnight Thu-Sat) ☎ (01922) 628542
Adnams Bitter; Greene King IPA, Abbot; Taylor Landlord; guest beer Ⓗ
Imposing late-Victorian back-street local. The classic sloping bar, with its deep and shallow ends, is the best in town. There is a plush, comfortable lounge for the drinker who wants to languish. This venue is a great community melting pot. A monthly jazz night and quiz night are hosted. Outside is a little walled garden.
🔥❀🍺🚌(404)♣⊱

Wednesbury

Bellwether ✔

3-4 Walsall Street, WS10 9BZ
🕐 9am-midnight (1am Fri & Sat) ☎ (0121) 502 6404
Beer range varies Ⓗ
Lively town-centre Wetherspoon's outlet in the heart of Wednesbury with a friendly atmosphere and a diverse clientele. It offers a selection of 10 ales, with a minimum of eight available at any one time. Situated near to the bus station, it is popular with shoppers. Food is served from 9am until 10pm every day. At the rear is a pleasant garden convenient for smokers, and ideal in the summer.
🔥❀◐♿⊖🚌⊱

Old Blue Ball

19 Hall End, WS10 9ED (just off B4200 Whitley Street)
🕐 12-3, 5-11; 12-11 Fri; 12-4.30, 7-11 Sat; 12-3.30, 7-11 Sun
☎ (0121) 5560197
Everards Original; Taylor Landlord; guest beers Ⓗ
Friendly back-street local with a small bar on the right with a sliding door, a family room on the left with a dartboard, and a quiet snug across the corridor with a serving hatch. On Friday and Saturday chips and hot pork and stuffing sandwiches are served. The pub has crib and darts teams, and hosts the local historians' society. There is a large garden with seating and a children's play area. Dogs are welcome on a leash.
Q⛵❀🍺⊖(Great Western St)🚌(311A,313)♣⊱

Olde Leathern Bottel ✔

40 Vicarage Road, WS10 9DW (just off A461)
🕐 12-2.30 (not Mon), 6-11; 12-2, 6-11.30 Fri; 11-11.30 Sat; 12-4, 7-11 Sun ☎ (0121) 505 0230
Beer range varies Ⓗ
Traditional pub set in cottages dating from 1510, with four rooms including a snug which is also used as a function room. Old photographs adorn the walls. There are two guest ales which vary in strength; Jennings ales feature regularly. The home-cooked food proves popular, and vegetarian dishes are available. Children are welcome. The pub hosts a quiz on Sunday, and a dominoes team and other organisations meet here. Dogs are permitted in the bar.
🔥❀◐◑🍺⊖(Great Western St)🚌(311)♣⊱

Rosehill Tavern

80 Church Hill, WS10 9DJ (nr top of Church Hill off A461)
🕐 12-11 (12.30am Fri & Sat) ☎ (0121) 5308128
Banks's Mild; guest beers Ⓗ
This modern pub attracts a diverse clientele. The bar is adorned with sports memorabilia and various TV screens showing sporting events. There is also a family room and a function room upstairs. The pub has four handpumps, with three changing guest ales. Outside there is a spacious garden with a covered smoking area including a wall-mounted TV. Many teams are based here, including football, crib and dominoes. Cobs are available daily.
🔥⛵❀🍺♿⊖(Great Western St)🚌(311A,313)♣P⊱

Wednesfield

Pyle Cock ✔

Rookery Street, WV11 1UN (on old Wolverhampton Rd)
🕐 10.30 (11 Thu)-11; 10.30-11.30 Fri & Sat; 12-11 Sun
☎ (01902) 732125
Banks's Mild, Bitter Ⓟ**; guest beers** Ⓗ
A friendly welcome awaits regulars and visitors to this traditional pub dating back to 1860. It features a bar with wooden settle backs, a small smoke room, and a more modern lounge at the rear reached by a corridor. The pub supports LocAle and offers three guest beers from the Marston's list, to complement Banks's mild and bitter. On a main bus route, it is easy to reach by public transport. Local CAMRA Pub of the Year 2008.
❀🍺🚌(559)♣P⊱

Royal Tiger ✔

41-43 High Street, WV11 1ST
🕐 9am-midnight (1am Fri & Sat) ☎ (01902) 307816
Banks's Mild; Greene King Ruddles Best Bitter, Abbot; guest beers Ⓗ
The Royal Tiger opened in 2000, and took its name from a pub nearby which closed some years previously. It is basically a large one-room pub with a patio at the back, overlooking the canal, with a heated smoking area. This venue is popular with the locals for food and drink. LocAle accredited, it also serves two real ciders. ❀◐◑♿🚌(525,559)●⊱

Vine ★

35 Lichfield Road, WV11 1TN
🕐 12-11 ☎ (01902) 733529
Black Country BFG, Pig On The Wall, Fireside; guest beers Ⓗ
A rare intact example of a simple inter-war working-class pub built in 1938. On CAMRA's National Inventory of Historic Pub Interiors and Grade II-listed, it retains its bar, lounge and snug. Guest beers from local micro-breweries are often available, alongside beers from all over the country. Good value home-cooked food is served lunchtime and evening (booking recommended for Sunday lunch). No food Sunday evening or all day Monday. A covered shelter is provided outside for smokers. Local CAMRA Pub of the Year 2009.
🔥Q❀◐◑🍺🚌(525,559)♣P⊱

West Bromwich

Greets Green Sports & Social Club

101 Whitehall Road, B70 0HG (on B4166)
🕐 11.30-11 (midnight Fri & Sat; 10.30 Sun)
☎ (0121) 5571388
Beer range varies Ⓗ
Popular local community club set back from the main road in the Greets Green area. There are two large comfortable rooms, one available for functions. Free and Easy is on Thursday and Sunday,

with live entertainment on Saturday night. Children are welcome at all times. The cider is Thatchers. The Club Café serving traditional fittle is open 7am-2pm Monday-Saturday. Darts, dominoes, crib and Sky Sports regularly feature.
(401,402A)P

Horse & Jockey ✔

49 Stoney Lane, B71 4EZ (100m from Sandwell Hospital)
12-11 (midnight Fri & Sat) ☎ (0121) 525 3655
thehorseandjockey.org
Banks's Mild, Bitter; Marston's Old Empire; Jennings Cocker Hoop; guest beers H
Atmospheric two-roomed pub with a conservatory and enclosed patio area to the rear. This is a true drinkers' pub, an institution for the real ale fraternity. Tied to Marston's, it has access to micro-breweries including Jennings, Ringwood, Wychwood and Brakspear, to name a few. Entertainment includes live music on Sunday evening. Popular home-cooked food is served daily. (404,405)

Old Hop Pole

474 High Street, B70 9LD
12-1am ☎ (07946) 579957
Hop Back Summer Lightning; Wye Valley HPA; guest beer H
Traditional bustling pub that always guarantees a warm welcome, located a brisk walk from the centre of West Bromwich. It has a spacious, open-plan design and its walls are packed with West Bromwich Albion football memorabilia. The pub gets very busy on Saturday evenings and on match days. Saturday nights often feature a disco-karaoke. Children are welcome until 9pm.
(Dartmouth St)(74,79)

Royal Oak ✔

14 Newton Street, B71 3RQ (down side road off Hollyhedge Rd)
4-11; 12-midnight Fri & Sat; 12-11 Sun ☎ (0121) 532 5692
Sharp's Doom Bar; Taylor Landlord; Wye Valley HPA; guest beer H
Traditional back-street pub with two small rooms and a friendly atmosphere. One bar is adorned with WBA pictures, while the lounge features entertainment once a month on a Sunday. The pub hosts reunions for the Territorial Army, and a cheese club on a Tuesday night. Cards and dominoes are also played here. There is a terrace in the rear yard for smokers, and two benches out front to bask on in the summer.

Wheatsheaf

379 High Street, B70 9QW
12-11 (1am Fri); 11-1am Sat; 11-11 Sun
☎ (0121) 553 4221
Holden's Black Country Mild H**, Black Country Bitter** H/P**, Golden Glow, Special; guest beers** H
Every high street should have at least one pub like this classic town boozer. Early-Victorian in style, it has a lively, basic front bar and a plush, more genteel lounge at the rear. It is much-beloved of office workers during the week, footie fans at weekends and horse racing enthusiasts all week long. A quiz night takes place on the first Wednesday of each month, with live music every fortnight. Good value food is served weekday lunchtimes.
Q(Guns Village)(74,79)

Willenhall

Falcon

77 Gomer Street West, WV13 2NR (off B4464, behind flats)
12-11 (10.30 Sun) ☎ (01902) 633378
Olde Swan Dark Swan, Bumble Hole Bitter; RCH Pitchfork; Salopian Oracle; guest beers H
Local CAMRA Pub of the Year 2005-7 and joint winner in 2009, the Falcon remains the flagship real ale venue in Willenhall. Boasting seven keenly priced beers, the pub has been run by the same family for over 25 years and has established a strong following. Built in 1936, it has two rooms – a lively bar and a quieter lounge – and is home to popular crib and darts teams. There is an outside drinking area. Handy for Willenhall Lock Museum.
Q(525,529)

Wollaston

Foresters Arms

Bridgnorth Road, DY8 3PL (on A458 towards Bridgnorth)
12-2.30 (not Mon), 6-midnight; 12-3, 7-11 Sun
☎ (01384) 394476
Ansells Mild; Marston's Pedigree; Wye Valley HPA; guest beer H
Located on the ridge – ideal for ramblers – this friendly local is on the outskirts of Wollaston on the edge of the countryside. It has an L-shaped interior where diners can sample good-value quality food. Quizzes are usually held on the first and third Sundays of the month and a poker night on Monday. The annual Wollaston Fun Run starts from outside the pub and is followed by a barbecue in the beer garden. There is a heated and covered smoking area. (X96,227,228)P

Unicorn

145 Bridgnorth Road, DY8 3NX (on A458 towards Bridgnorth)
12-11; 12-3, 7-11 Sun ☎ (01384) 394823
Bathams Mild Ale, Best Bitter, XXX (winter) H
This former brewhouse was purchased by Bathams in the early 1990s following the death of the last member of the Billingham family. Since joining the estate it has become widely recognised as serving one of the best pints. The original brewhouse remains at the side but sadly will never brew again. The pub itself is still a two-bar drinking house, popular with all ages. It serves generous cobs and pork pies at lunchtime. There is free Wi-Fi.
Q(227,228,X96)P

Wolverhampton

Chindit ✔

113 Merridale Road, WV3 9SE
4 (12 Sat & Sun)-11 ☎ (01902) 425582 thechindit.co.uk
Enville Ale; Hop Back Summer Lightning; Wye Valley HPA; guest beers H
Street-corner local, built in the 1950s originally as an off-licence. The history of the Chindit regiment is displayed in the lounge. The bar contains a pool table and a large TV and is decorated with music memorabilia. Quiz night is Wednesday and live music features on Friday evening (see the website for upcoming bands). Guest beers are usually from local micro-breweries. A covered shelter is provided at the back of the pub for smokers.
(513,543)P

ENGLAND

Combermere Arms

90 Chapel Ash, WV3 0TY (on A41 Tettenhall Road)
11-3, 5.30-11; 12-midnight Fri & Sat; 12-10.30 Sun
☎ (01902) 421880
Banks's Mild, Bitter; guest beers ⊞
Award-winning, family-friendly local close by Banks's Brewery, comprising an intimate bar plus two rooms off a central corridor with servery, leading to an outside courtyard with awning and heaters where live music features on Saturday night. There is a large beer garden to the rear with seating, and an outside Gents famously built around a tree. Home-cooked food is served 12-2pm weekdays. Popular with home supporters on Wolves match days. P

Dog & Gun

1 Wrottesley Road, Tettenhall, WV6 8SB (off A41 Wergs Road)
12-11 (midnight Thu-Sat) ☎ (01902) 747943
Banks's Bitter; Wells Bombardier; guest beers ⊞
This comfortable, welcoming pub has individual seating areas around a large U-shaped bar. It attracts a wide age range, including a local writers' group and a rambling club who meet here regularly. Food quality and a varying range of beers, often including a dark, ensure a busy, friendly atmosphere. There is a patio for outside drinking and a covered, heated area for smokers. Children must be over 14 and dining with an adult. (501,891)P

Great Western

Sun Street, WV10 0DJ (via subway from high-level station and city centre)
11-11 (10.30 Sun) ☎ (01902) 351090
Bathams Best Bitter; Holden's Black Country Mild, Bitter, Golden Glow, Special; guest beers ⊞
This Grade II-listed 150-year-old pub was extended twice in the 1990s. Near the old low-level station, the former CAMRA National Pub of the Year has four distinct drinking areas served by a central bar. There are three real fires, wonderfully warming on a cold winter's day. The interior features both railway and Wolves memorabilia and is always busy when Wolves are at home.
(St George's)P

> Over the mahogany, jar followed jorum, gargle, tincture and medium, tailor, scoop, snifter and ball of malt, in a breathless pint-to-pint. Discreet barman, Mr Sugrue thought, turning outside the door and walking in the direction of Stephen's Green. Never give anything away – part of the training. Is Mr so-and-so there, I'll go and see, strict instructions never to say yes in case it might be the wife. Curious now the way the tinge of wickedness hung around the pub, a relic of course of Victorianism, nothing to worry about as long as a man kept himself in hand.
> **Jack White**,
> The Devil You Know

Hog's Head

186 Stafford Street, WV1 1NA
10-midnight (1am Fri & Sat); 12-midnight Sun
☎ (01902) 717955
Wells Bombardier; guest beers ⊞
This popular city-centre pub, built in 1894 as the Vine, closed in 1984 before reopening as the Hogshead in 1998. Locally listed for its superb terracotta exterior, the pub's single-room interior is divided into many areas, featuring pool tables and TVs showing major sporting events and music videos. In the LocAle scheme for its commitment to local micro-breweries, beers often come from Enville and Wood. CAMRA members receive a discount. (St George's)

Horse & Jockey

64 Robert Wynd, Woodcross, WV14 9SB
12-11 (11.30 Fri & Sat) ☎ (01902) 662268
Banks's Mild; Draught Bass; Greene King Abbot; St Austell Tribute; guest beers ⊞
Very popular community pub. In the bar there are pictures of horses from the Grand National and other races. Through to the lounge there is an old Black Country canal map. Quiz nights raise money for local charities. Good-value food is served every day (no food Sun eve and Mon lunchtime). A large beer garden is at the rear and families are welcome until 8.30pm. LocAle accredited.
(581)P

Moon Under Water

53-55 Lichfield Street, WV1 1EQ (opp Grand Theatre)
9am-midnight (1am Fri & Sat) ☎ (01902) 422447
Banks's Mild; Greene King Ruddles Best Bitter; Holden's Golden Glow; Marston's Pedigree; guest beers ⊞
This busy city-centre Wetherspoon's is in its 15th year and serves a wide range of guest ales typical of the chain, and also hosts regular micro-brewery beer festivals. Food is available from opening until 10pm. In demand for pre-theatre drinks, it gets very busy at peak times. A popular meeting place for younger drinkers at weekends, it is also a handy stop-off for commuters on their way home due to the close proximity of the bus and railway stations.
(St George's)

Newhampton

19 Riches Street, Whitmore Reans, WV6 0DW
11-11 (midnight Fri & Sat); 12-11 Sun ☎ (01902) 746747
Caledonian Deuchars IPA; Courage Directors; Enville Ale; Fuller's London Pride; Taylor Landlord; Wye Valley HPA; guest beers ⊞
Locals from all walks of life are catered for here, with three main bars supplemented by a bowls pavilion bar, function room and an award-winning garden around the bowling green. The pub's street-corner location disguises an extensive range of drinking areas, with eight handpumps offering seven real ales and a real cider. Hot food from the pot is almost always available. CAMRA members receive a discount on beer.

Posada

48 Lichfield Street, WV1 1DG (opp art gallery)
12-11 (midnight Fri & Sat); closed Sun
Adnams Broadside; Brains SA; Caledonian Deuchars IPA; Shepherd Neame Spitfire; guest beers ⊞
City-centre pub with original features; much of the tile work remains as well as the fireplace and bar. It enjoys a mixed and friendly clientele, and is an excellent spot for a quiet afternoon drink, though

more lively on a weekend evening. The location is ideal for a drink before a visit to the theatre or local concert venues. A cobbled courtyard to the rear is popular for outside drinking in the summer months. CAMRA members receive a discount on cask beer. ❀≋⊖(St George's)🚌⚟

Summer House

290 Newhampton Road West, Whitmore Reans, WV6 0RS

⏲ 12-11 (midnight Fri & Sat) ☎ (01902) 745213

Adnams Bitter; Fuller's London Pride; guest beers Ⓗ

Recently refurbished, this friendly community pub's bar features a roaring real fire in winter and football memorabilia. The central servery links a cosy, comfortable lounge and a dining area where a chalkboard advertises the chef's renowned traditional home cooking and pies. Sky Sports is available. There is a crown bowling green and pavilion used by the Summer House Bowls Club, a large garden for barbecues and outside drinking, and a covered, heated area for smokers.
⛼❀◑⊟♿🚌♣⚟

Wordsley

New Inn

117 High Street, DY8 5QR (A491)

⏲ 12-11 (10.30 Sun) ☎ (01384) 295614

Bathams Mild, Best Bitter, XXX (winter) Ⓗ

On the main Wolverhampton to Stourbridge road, the building has an imposing three-storey Victorian facade. An L-shaped bar serves a single room with a small annexe at one end, and a patio area outside. Car parking is at the rear. Children are not allowed inside but there is a play area in the garden for the summer. Bar snacks are available. The pub largely caters for the surrounding community and has the feel of a proper local. Occasional live music plays.
♘❀♿🚌(256,257)♣●P⚟

Queens Head

129 High Street, DY8 5QS (A491)

⏲ 4-11.30; 12-12.30am Sat; 12-10.30 Sun

☎ (07904) 390950

Enville Ale, Ginger, Old Porter; Olde Swan Bumble Hole; Sarah Hughes Surprise, Dark Ruby; guest beers Ⓗ

Comfortable roadside watering hole on the main Stourbridge to Kingswinford Road. Its layout echoes its multi-roomed past, though most of the walls have gone. The decor is cosy Victorian/Edwardian in style. Renowned locally for its generous Sunday carvery, food is restricted to cobs at other times. One guest ale and an Enville seasonal offering complement the regular range.
♘❀🚌(256,257)♣P⚟

Bull's Head, Barston

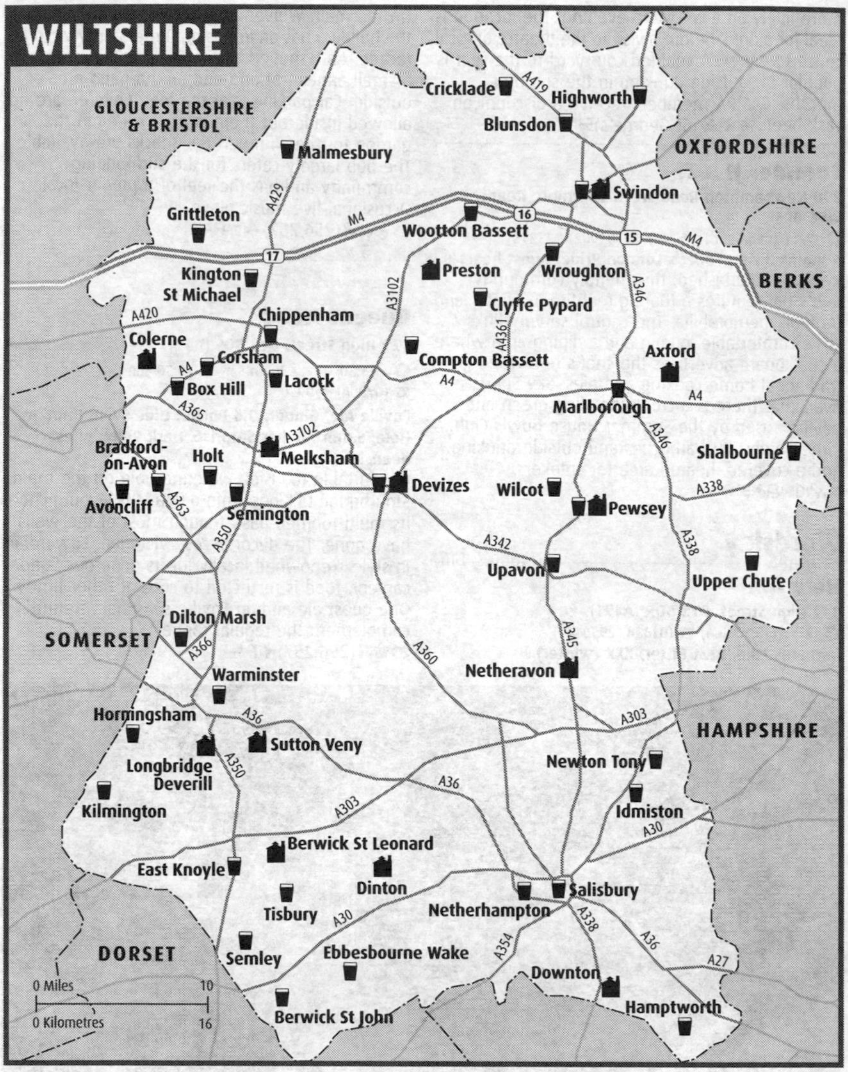

Avoncliff

Cross Guns

BA15 2HB ST804599

10-midnight (1am Sat) ☎ (01225) 862335

crossguns.net

Box Steam Cog, Golden Bolt, Tunnel Vision, seasonal beers; guest beers H

Sixteenth-century canalside inn with sloping terraces down to the River Avon, popular with walkers and cyclists. Features include an inglenook fireplace, priest's hole, garden bar, weekend barbecues and a resident ghost. Children and dogs are welcome. Four beers from Box Steam are complemented by two guests sourced from far and wide, always with a dark and a blond in the mix. Up to nine real ciders are also available. Just 100 metres from Avoncliff station, there are car parks nearby. Accommodation includes en-suite B&B and self-contained apartments. ♨Q❀⇌◑♿⇌♣●

Berwick St John

Talbot

The Cross, SP7 0HA (S of A30, 5 miles E of Shaftesbury)

12-2.30, 6-11; 12-4 Sun ☎ (01747) 828222

Draught Bass; Ringwood Best Bitter; Wadworth 6X; guest beers H

Set in a small, rural, peaceful village, the Talbot opened as a beer house circa 1832 despite vehement opposition from the local parson's wife. The building is predominantly stone-built with a long, low bar with beams and an inglenook fireplace. As well as offering three regular beers, the landlord is keen to promote local micro-breweries with a choice of guest ales. The more inquisitive visitor may find the cosy dining room behind the inglenook. The pub is very popular with walkers from the local downs and cyclists on the 160-mile Wiltshire Cycleway.
♨Q❀◑♿⊟(29)♣P⁄-

Blunsdon

Blunsdon Arms

Thamesdown Drive, SN25 2NA
11-11 (midnight Thu-Sat) ☎ (01793) 729801
emberinns.co.uk/theblunsdonarmsswindon
Beer range varies Ⓗ
One of Swindon's newest pubs, the Blunsdon Arms opened in 2006. This large open-plan Ember Inns pub has plenty of comfortable seating, with columns and partial walls to break up the interior. A range of 18 beers is served on six handpumps throughout the month. The three-brew tasting rack allows you to choose three beers in third-of-a-pint measures for the price of a pint. Wednesday and Sunday are quiz nights. (24)P

Box Hill

Quarrymans Arms

SN13 8HN (S of A4 between Corsham and Box) ST834693
11-3, 6-11.30; 11-midnight Fri & Sat; 11-11.30 Sun
☎ (01225) 743569 quarrymans-arms.co.uk
Butcombe Bitter; Moles Best Bitter; Wadworth 6X; guest beer Ⓗ
This pub is tucked away off the main routes, but is well-worth seeking out. A 300-year-old miner's pub offering a friendly welcome, it is renowned for high quality food and ales. These can be enjoyed in the bar, restaurant or garden, which has a heated area for smokers. Quiz night is every second Wednesday, and occasional county-themed beer festivals are held. Black Rat cider is occasionally on offer. Accommodation is available in four rooms. Q (231)P

Bradford-on-Avon

Castle Inn

10 Mount Pleasant, BA15 1SJ ST827612
9-11; 10-10.30 Sun ☎ (01225) 865657
flatcappers.co.uk
Three Castles Barbury Castle, Vale Ale, Knight's Porter; guest beers Ⓗ
Acquired by pubco Flatcappers in 2006 and transformed by wholesale refurbishment, this quiet, cosy, relaxing pub caters for a wide clientele. The interior comprises a large bar with flagstone floor, lime-washed walls, open fireplace and magnificent reclaimed mahogany bar, and three smaller rooms with elm floorboards, exposed walls and worn club chairs. Food is served throughout the premises. The garden with a flagstone terrace has commanding views towards Salisbury Plain. The Three Castles beers are badged as Flatcapper, served alongside three guest beers sourced from local micros. Q P

Rising Sun

231 Winsley Road, BA15 1QS
12 (4 Tue)-11; 12-10.30 Sun ☎ (01225) 862354
therisingsunatbradfordonavon.co.uk
Courage Best Bitter; guest beers Ⓗ
Popular local at the top of a hill with two bars: a small, quiet lounge and a more spacious, livelier saloon with TV screens. Out back is a walled beer garden with patio. The pub is home to darts, quiz, crib, pool and football teams, and hosts regular live music including a Rhythm & Brews beer festival over the August bank holiday. Guest beers usually come from local breweries and the cider is Cheddar Valley. The pub's ancient spaniel is still there, ready to welcome you.

Chippenham

Gladstone Arms

34 Gladstone Road, SN15 3BW
11-3, 5.30-11; 11-midnight Fri & Sat; 12-11 Sun
☎ (01249) 660535 thegladstonearms.co.uk
Butcombe Bitter; St Austell Tribute; Taylor Landlord Ⓗ
Friendly and welcoming town-centre pub near the bus station catering for a broad age range of customers. Lively at weekends, the lounge is mainly used for bistro-style dining but there is a comfortable separate public bar. A TV shows news, with the volume only turned up for major sporting events. The town coat of arms appears in the stone front. The large garden adjoins an innovative eco-friendly house, designed and occupied by a local architect. P

Old Road Tavern

Old Road, SN15 1JA (200m from railway station, over bridge from station front)
11-11.30 (12.30am Fri & Sat); 12-11.30 Sun
☎ (01249) 652094
Fuller's London Pride; Hop Back Summer Lightning; Otter Bitter; guest beers Ⓗ
A basic, unpretentious local, featuring a traditional bar, lounge, separate pool room and large enclosed garden. Live French music plays every second Sunday evening and folk music every first and third Sunday evening. Live local bands are also often to be found playing here at the weekend. The 'Credit Crunch Munch' lunch menu serves traditional satisfying pub grub and is good value for money. Main sporting events are screened although this is not a sports-oriented pub.

Clyffe Pypard

Goddard Arms

Wood Street, SN4 7PY SU074769
12-2.30, 7-11; 12-11 Sat; 12-10.30 Sun ☎ (01793) 731386
Beer range varies Ⓗ
This friendly community pub is a true free house, with three regularly changing beers, mainly from local micro-breweries. Westons cider is also served. The pub has a large beer garden with a covered area and houses a YHA hostel, open all year round. The White Horse Trail passes nearby, making this village pub a welcome pit stop for weary cyclists, walkers and dogs. There is food available every day. Open all day on bank holidays.
Q (70)P

INDEPENDENT BREWERIES

Arkell's Swindon
Box Steam Colerne
Braydon Preston
Downton Downton
Hidden Dinton
Hop Back Downton
Keystone Berwick St Leonard
Moles Melksham
Plain Ales Sutton Veny
Ramsbury Axford
Stonehenge Netheravon
Three Castles Pewsey
Wadworth Devizes
Wessex Longbridge Deverill
World's End Pewsey (NEW)

Compton Bassett

White Horse Inn

SN11 8RG (2 miles off A4 Calne to Marlborough road)
⌚ 12-3, 6-11; 12-4 Sun ☎ (01249) 813118
Bath Ales Gem; Ramsbury Gold; Wadworth Henry's IPA, 6X Ⓗ
A real gem with very friendly hosts and staff. This traditional country inn is situated on the edge of the Marlborough Downs in an area of outstanding beauty, ideal for walkers. All food is prepared on the premises with fresh fish from Brixham and locally-sourced meat and vegetables. It has a large beer garden, function room and holds a monthly quiz night. Black Rat cider is available on draught. Accommodation is available in eight en-suite rooms and Avebury and Stonehenge are close by. ♔Q❀⌂◑♿🚌♣●P⁴⁻

Corsham

Hare & Hounds ✔

48 Pickwick, SN13 0HY
⌚ 11-11 ☎ (01249) 701106
Bath Ales Gem; Caledonian Deuchars IPA; Gale's HSB; guest beers Ⓗ
A large, busy 17th-century coaching inn on the A4. Five ales are usually available including two ever-changing guest beers from local breweries. The occasional beer festival and a Tuesday evening quiz are held. A variety of good food is always on the menu. The pub has three drinking areas – the large lounge can be reserved for private functions. Dogs are welcome. Outside seating is available in the new garden, which includes cider apple trees and a covered, heated smoking area.
♔Q❀◑🚌(231,233)P⁴⁻

Two Pigs

38 Pickwick, SN13 0HY
⌚ 7-11; 12-2.30, 7-10.30 Sun ☎ (01249) 712515
🌐 the2pigs.info
Stonehenge Pigswill; guest beers Ⓗ
This classic free house is a gem of a pub. Several times local CAMRA Pub of the Year, it has featured in the Guide continuously for 21 years. With flagstone floors and wood-panelled walls, the pub dates back to the 18th century. Four ales are usually available – Hop Back Summer Lightning alternates with Stonehenge Danish Dynamite and there are two additional guest beers. Live music plays on Monday evenings, usually local blues bands. The covered outdoor drinking area is known as The Sty. ❀♿🚌(231,233)

Cricklade

Red Lion

74 High Street, SN6 6DD
⌚ 12-11 (10.30 Sun) ☎ (01793) 750776
Moles Best; Ramsbury Gold; Sharp's Doom Bar; Wadworth 6X; guest beers Ⓗ
Friendly ale house dating in parts back to the 16th century. It offers a range of up to nine real ales from smaller local breweries and some from a bit further afield, giving drinkers a chance to sample a wide variety of beers. Food is served in what used to be the back bar and is now the restaurant (no food Mon). There is a large garden at the back. Local CAMRA Pub of the Year 2007 and a past winner of CAMRA South West Regional Pub of the Year. ♔Q❀⌂◑🚌(51)♣P

Devizes

British Lion ✔

9 Estcourt Street, SN10 1LQ (on A361 London road)
⌚ 11-11 (midnight Fri & Sat); 12-11 Sun ☎ (01380) 720665
Beer range varies Ⓗ
A proper free house in every sense of the word, run by a long-standing and committed landlord. With a welcoming atmosphere, wooden floors and settles, it attracts a mixed group of regulars, from builders to teachers. Four handpumps dispense changing, well-kept beers from south-western breweries as far afield as Sharp's, Skinner's and St Austell, as well as favourites from Abbey, Bath Ales, Palmers, Stonehenge and Hop Back. Juke-box, pool, darts and friendly banter rule throughout. A must when visiting Devizes. ❀🚌(49)♣●P⁴⁻

Hare & Hounds ✔

Hare & Hounds Street, SN10 1LZ
⌚ 11-2.30 (3 Sat), 7-11; 12-3, 7-10.30 Sun
☎ (01380) 723231
Wadworth Henry's IPA, 6X, seasonal beers Ⓗ
Very much a place to enjoy a quiet drink, the pub is well-worth the short walk to get here from the town centre. Carpeted, cosy and friendly, with a welcoming landlord, it has one long bar and serves arguably the best-kept Wadworth's beer in town. The locals tend to occupy the bar stools, leaving the tables for casual visitors. A weekly quiz night is held and pub games feature strongly. Some food is served and well-behaved children are made as welcome as their parents. ♔Q❀◑🚌(49)♣P⁴⁻

Lamb

20 St John's Street, SN10 1BT
⌚ 11-midnight (1am Fri & Sat); 12-midnight Sun
☎ (01380) 725426
Wadworth Henry's IPA, 6X, seasonal beers Ⓗ
Small, back-street pub, full of character, with a varied clientele. It has a single U-shaped bar area with lots of old beams and cosy wooden seating. The compact courtyard is a suntrap in summer. The walls are adorned with photographs of the locals and old pub signs. Live music is hosted in the function room upstairs, a side room features a rifle range and there is a separate room for the pool table. Pull up a chair and soak up the warmth from the open log fire. ♔❀🚌(49)♣P⁴⁻

Silk Mercer ✔

38 St John's Street, SN10 1BL
⌚ 9am-midnight (1am Fri & Sat) ☎ (01380) 736760
Beer range varies Ⓗ
The Mercer opened in 2008, occupying a Grade II-listed 18th-century building which has been attractively renovated with comfortable seating and pristine toilets. The long wooden bar always has at least five beers available from a wide range from major and regional breweries, and one of these is always well under £2 per pint. Food is served throughout the day. The managers have been particularly supportive of the local CAMRA branch and arrange beer tasting evenings.
❀◑♿🚌(49)⁴⁻

Dilton Marsh

Prince of Wales

94 High Street, BA13 4DZ ST843497
⌚ 12-2.30 (not Mon & Tue), 7-11 (midnight Thu & Fri); 12-3, 7-midnight Sat & Sun ☎ (01373) 865487
Draught Bass; Ringwood Best Bitter; guest beers Ⓗ

Friendly village local with a single bar serving two drinking areas plus a pool table area and skittle alley. One of the guest beers comes from Sharp's brewery (usually Own or Special) and the other is a session beer that could come from anywhere. The pub participates in local skittles, crib and pool leagues and there is a weekly Sunday evening quiz. Moles (not necessarily the beer) are something of a feature at the pub. Can you spot the error on the pub sign? Q❀◑♿⇌⊟♣P⊱

East Knoyle

Fox & Hounds

The Green, SP3 6BN (signed from B3089 close to jct A303) ST871313

⊛ 11.30-3, 5.30-11 ☎ (01747) 830573

⊕ foxandhounds-eastknoyle.co.uk

Beer range varies Ⓗ

Attractive old thatched black-and-white pub situated high on a hillside with extensive panoramic rural views. Comfortable and cosy inside, the warm welcome is enhanced in winter by a blazing log fire in a huge inglenook fireplace. Three ales are always available encompassing a wide range of ABVs and varying continuously, with local beers given prominence. The real cider is Thatchers Cheddar Valley. Food is served at all sessions. An adjacent skittle alley doubles as a function room. ♨Q❀◑♣●P

Ebbesbourne Wake

Horseshoe Inn

The Cross, SP5 5JF (just off A30) ST993239

⊛ 12-3 (not Mon), 6.30-11; 12-4 Sun ☎ (01722) 780474

Bowman Swift One; Otter Bitter; Palmers Copper Ale; guest beer Ⓖ

Unspoilt 18th-century pub in a remote rural setting at the foot of an old ox drove. This friendly pub has two small bars which display an impressive collection of old farm implements, tools and lamps, a restaurant, conservatory and a pleasant garden. Good local food is served Tuesday-Sunday and the five beers are served direct from casks stillaged behind the bar. The original serving hatch just inside the front door is still in use. Cider is often available. Q❀⇆◑⊟⊟(29)●P

Grittleton

Neeld Arms

The Street, SN14 6AP

⊛ 12-3, 5.30-11; 12.30-4, 7-11 Sun ☎ (01249) 782470

⊕ neeldarms.co.uk

Wadworth Henry's IPA, 6X; guest beers Ⓗ

Cosy, comfortable 17th-century inn set in a beautiful and unspoilt south Cotswold village with old prints and photographs adorning the walls and a welcoming log fire in winter. A good selection of home-made food is offered and an ever-changing choice of guest beers means there is always something different to try. Popular with locals and visitors, the pub is central to the community. Tourist attractions including Castle Combe, Malmesbury and Bath are close by. ♨Q☋❀⇆◑♿⊟(35)P⊱

Hamptworth

Cuckoo Inn

Hamptworth Road, SP5 2DU (follow signs from A36 for Hamptworth Golf Club) SU244197

⊛ 11.30-2.30, 5.30-11; 11.30-11 Sat; 12-10.30 Sun

☎ (01794) 390302

Bowman Elderado; Hop Back GFB, Summer Lightning; Ringwood Best Bitter; guest beers Ⓖ

Beautiful thatched pub within the New Forest National Park. Inside are four small rooms, three served from the same bar. Ales are dispensed direct from casks racked in the ground floor cellar. GFB and Elderado are listed as Old School and Cuckoorado. At least two guest ales, and up to six in summer, are available alongside Frams scrumpy cider. The large garden has a quiet adults-only space. An annual beer festival is held in late summer. Lunches are available Tuesday to Sunday. CAMRA Branch Pub of the Year 2009. ♨Q❀♣●P⊱

Highworth

Rose & Crown ✔

19 The Green, SN6 7DB (off A361) SU200922

⊛ 12-3, 5-11 (1am Thu); 12-2am Fri & Sat; 12-1am Sun

☎ (01793) 766287

Courage Best Bitter; Wadworth 6X; Wells Bombardier; guest beers Ⓗ

Built around 1768, this is one of the oldest pubs in Highworth. Good food is genuinely home-cooked on the premises, with custom menus available for larger parties (lunch Thu-Sun, evening meals Wed-Sat). Live music plays every Friday, and occasionally on Sunday lunchtime. The landlord is a lover of whisky as well as real ale and hosts a tasting evening on the last Sunday of the month showcasing his stock of 70 malts. ♨❀◑♿⊟(7,64,74)♣P⊱

Holt

Tollgate Inn

Ham Green, BA14 6PX (on B3105 between Bradford-on-Avon and Melksham) ST858616

⊛ closed Mon; 11-2.30, 5.30-11; 11.30-2.30 Sun

☎ (01225) 782326 ⊕ tollgateholt.co.uk

Beer range varies Ⓗ

This old village pub is a real gem with an upmarket atmosphere featuring a wood-burning stove, oak floors and comfy sofas to relax in. The range of four or five beers, which changes daily, is very imaginative, with a good selection of local beers alongside many from smaller breweries further afield. The food in both the upstairs restaurant and the bar is excellent. The garden at the rear overlooks a pretty valley. ♨❀⇆◑⊟(237)●P⊱

Horningsham

Bath Arms

Longleat Estate, BA12 7LY ST810416

⊛ 11-11 ☎ (01985) 844308 ⊕ batharms.co.uk

Wessex Horningsham Pride; guest beer Ⓗ

This 17th-century stone building on the edge of Longleat Estate was first a public house with rooms in 1732. Known then as the New Inn, it became the Marquess of Bath Arms in 1850. It now offers two bars, a restaurant and accommodation. The house beer is Horningsham Pride, brewed locally, and one guest is always available, usually sourced from a local micro. The idyllic village of Horningsham has the oldest free congregational chapel in England, known as The Old Meeting House, built in 1556 and still in use. ♨☕❀⇌◑⊟♿⛺⊟♣●P⁄

Idmiston

Earl of Normanton

Tidworth Road, SP4 0AG (on A338) SU195382
✪ 12-2.30, 6-11; 12-3, 7.45-10.30 Sun ☎ (01980) 610251
⊕ earlofnormanton.co.uk
Flowerpots Bitter; Hop Back Summer Lightning; guest beers ⊞
Popular roadside pub with a loyal village clientele and a welcoming atmosphere enhanced by the two real fires in winter months. Formerly the Plough Inn, the pub was renamed to commemorate previous ownership by the Normanton estate. LocAle accredited, it offers two guest ales mostly from local breweries. Good value home-cooked food is available (not Sun eve). There is a small, pleasant garden on the steep hill behind the pub and a heated, covered smoking area. B&B is available. A former Salisbury CAMRA Pub of the Year. ♨Q❀⇌◑♿⊟(63,64)P⁄

Kilmington

Red Lion Inn 🍷 ✔

BA12 6RP (on B3092 to Frome)
✪ 11-2.30, 6.30-11; 12-3, 7-10.30 Sun ☎ (01985) 844263
Butcombe Bitter; Butts Jester; guest beers ⊞
This 16th-century building, located close to Stourhead House and Gardens, originally stabled the extra horses needed to climb the steep hill on the adjacent coach road. The single bar is mainly stone-flagged with two real fires. Excellent, value-for-money food is served at lunchtimes only. The landlord has been in residence for 32 years. Walkers and dogs are welcome. The large garden has a superb smoking facility. Real cider is always available. ♨Q❀◐♣●P⁄

Kington St Michael

Jolly Huntsman 🍷

80 Kington St Michael, SN14 6JB (signed from A350, between Chippenham and M4 jct 17)
✪ 11.30-2.30, 6-11 (midnight Fri & Sat); 12-3, 7-10.30 Sun
☎ (01249) 750305 ⊕ kingtonstmichael.com
Moles Tap Bitter; Wadworth 6X; guest beers ⊞
Situated on the high street, at the heart of the village, you can be sure of a friendly welcome at this free house, with an open log fire in winter. A varying range of real ales and ciders is always on offer. The excellent food menu features regularly changing chef's specials as well as themed evenings. Quiz night is the first Monday of the month and other entertainment includes live jazz and blues. Accommodation is all en-suite with free Wi-Fi. ♨Q☕⇌◑♿⛺⊟(99)♣●P⁄

Lacock

Bell Inn

The Wharf, Bowden Hill, SN15 2PJ
✪ 11.30-2.30, 5-11; 11.30-11 Sat; 12-10.30 Sun
☎ (01249) 730308
Bath Ales Gem; Palmers Best Bitter; guest beers ⊞
Family-run, well-established free house on the edge of the beautiful National Trust village of Lacock. Local CAMRA Pub of the Year for five consecutive years, it has an excellent reputation for its food and constantly-changing stock of real ales. An annual winter beer festival is held in late January/early February. Originally canal cottages, the pub lies beside the National Cycle Route, with excellent cycle tracks and walks between Chippenham and Melksham. Q❀◑♿♣●P⁄

Rising Sun

32 Bowden Hill, SN15 2PP (1 mile E of Lacock)
ST9377680
✪ 12-3, 6-11; 12-midnight Sat; 12-11 Sun ☎ (01249) 730363
Moles Best Bitter, Elmo's Fire, Molecatcher, seasonal beers ⊞
Stone-built 17th-century pub with flagstone floors and traditional settles. The spacious conservatory and large terraced garden provide stunning views over the Avon Valley. All the beers come from the Moles Brewery, which is less than six miles away. Beer festivals are run occasionally as well as themed events. A wide choice of home-cooked food is available including daily specials. A welcoming and convivial pub with live music on Wednesday evenings. Q❀◑♣●P⁄

Malmesbury

Smoking Dog ✔

62 High Street, SN16 9AT (lower end of High Street)
✪ 12-11 (midnight Fri & Sat); 12-10.30 Sun
☎ (01666) 825823
Brains Rev James; Butcombe Bitter; guest beers ⊞
People of all ages, locals and visitors, frequent this popular picturesque pub. The only Brains pub in Wiltshire, it is full of character, with Cotswold stone walls, wooden floors and a fire. It is popular for reading newspapers or after taking the dog for a walk. There is a restaurant and a good-sized enclosed garden for warmer weather. The pub is famous for its annual Beer and Sausage Festival held on the last bank holiday weekend in May. ♨❀◑⊟⁄

Whole Hog

8 Market Cross, SN16 9AS
✪ 11-11.30; 12-10.30 Sun ☎ (01666) 825845
Wadworth 6X; Wickwar Coopers; Young's Bitter; guest beers ⊞
Located between the 15th-century Market Cross and Abbey, the building has at various times served as a cottage hospital, gas showroom and café/restaurant before becoming a licensed premises. With a warm, friendly atmosphere, the pub attracts locals and visitors alike, serving up to five real ales including two guests often from local breweries. Meals can be eaten in an area adjacent to the bar (no food Sun eve). Traditional cider is from Westons. Q◑⊟●

Marlborough

Sun Inn

90 High Street, SN8 1HF
✪ 8.30am-11.30 (midnight Fri & Sat) ☎ (01672) 515011
⊕ thesunmarlborough.co.uk
Ringwood Fortyniner; Shepherd Neame Spitfire; Wadworth 6X; guest beer ⊞
Originally a 15th-century coaching inn, this pub has bags of character and a choice of three bars to tempt the visitor. The public bar retains its Tudor wood panelling and has a roaring log fire in the winter. For the summer there is a small terraced

garden at the back. Good food and recently refurbished B&B accommodation make this a popular overnight stay. A jazz night is held every other Thursday and live music plays on Friday and Saturday night. (70,95)

Netherhampton

Victoria & Albert

SP2 8PU (opp church) SU108298

11-3.30, 5.30-11; 12-3, 7-10.30 Sun ☎ (01722) 743174

Beer range varies H

A classic thatched country pub built in 1540 with a large garden and heated patio. Inside is a real log fire and low beams which add to the atmosphere on a cold night. The three or four ever-changing real ales are from small independent brewers. The menu ranges from snacks to restaurant meals, with all food prepared in the pub. Camping is available at the nearby racecourse. Salisbury CAMRA Pub of the Year 2005 and 2007. Dogs are welcome.

Q P

Newton Tony

Malet Arms

SP4 0HP (opp village green) SU215403

11-3, 6-11; 12-3, 7-10.30 Sun ☎ (01980) 629279

Beer range varies H

Traditional village pub named after a local family who are well represented in the village churchyard. Inside, the main bar features a large fireplace and a window reputed to come from an old galleon. There is a separate restaurant serving a daily-changing menu based on local produce. LocAle accredited, the pub offers four beers including at least one from Ramsbury Brewery, and other local brewers feature regularly. The cider is Westons Old Rosie. Q (63,64)P

Pewsey

Crown Inn

60 Wilcot Road, SN9 5EL

12-midnight (1am Sat & Sun) ☎ (01672) 562653

Wadworth 6X; guest beers H

The Crown Inn started to brew its own beers in 2009 and now always offers one of its own brews, a Three Castles ale and three more guests, mainly local. Ciders and perries are also available. The traditional village local has a small bar where pool and darts are played and a lounge with an attractive stone and brick fireplace in the centre. Live music plays regularly. Food is available lunchtimes and evenings Wednesday to Sunday. (5,95)

Salisbury

Anchor & Hope

59 Winchester Street, SP1 1HL

10 (11 Sun)-11 ☎ (01722) 501660

Beer range varies H

This is a friendly, traditional pub, close to the town centre. The landlord is a keen diver and the pub hosts the Hidden Depths Dive Club. It is also home to pool, darts and cribbage teams. Three draught beers, varying seasonally, are served on handpump. Six varieties of pizza are available throughout opening hours. There is a courtyard garden with a covered, heated area for smokers.

Deacons

118 Fisherton Street, SP2 7QT

5 (4 Fri; 12 Sat)-11; 12-10 Sun ☎ (01722) 504723

Hop Back GFB, Summer Lightning; Sharp's Doom Bar H

A warm welcome is guaranteed at this good old-fashioned local pub, whether you are one of the loyal band of regulars or a visitor to the city. Convenient for the city centre and railway station, it has a small front bar with woodblock flooring and a larger back room with table football and TV for sport. The walls and ceilings are adorned with some unusual artefacts. Last entry is around 10.40pm. The pub is LocAle accredited.

Kings Head Inn ✔

Bridge Street, SP1 2ND

7am-midnight (1am Thu & Fri); 8am-1am Sat; 8am-midnight Sun ☎ (01722) 342050

Greene King IPA, Abbot; Marston's Pedigree; guest beer H

This Wetherspoon Lloyds No 1 is arranged over two floors of what was formerly the County Hotel. There has been a pub on the site since 1470 when it was known as Bones Place – it became the Kings Head around 1520 and the County Hotel in the 1880s. Three ever-changing guests include one from a local brewery when possible, and there is a large selection of bottled beers and ciders. The food is Wetherspoon's standard fare and beer festivals are held twice a year.

Rai d'Or

69 Brown Street, SP1 2AS

5-11; closed Sun ☎ (01722) 327137 raidor.co.uk

Beer range varies H

Dating from about 1292, this is the oldest pub in Salisbury, with an inglenook, murals by Glastonbury artists and a fascinating history. Excellent, reasonably-priced Thai food is served until 10.30pm, with an early-evening discount before 6.30pm (booking essential). The pub offers two ales, usually from local micro-breweries, and there is always space at the bar for drinkers who just want to enjoy the warm welcome and CAMRA ale discount. Salisbury CAMRA Pub of the Year 2008 and LocAle accredited.

Royal George ✔

17 Bedwin Street, SP1 3UT (close to Salisbury Arts Centre)

12-midnight; 12-3, 7-10.30 Sun ☎ (01722) 327782

Hop Back GFB; Ringwood Best Bitter; Sharp's Doom Bar H

This Grade II-listed 15th-century inn is named after the sister ship of HMS Victory and features a wood beam said to be from that ship. The low-beamed bar is decorated with pictures of ships and sea battles. A city pub with the feel of a country local, it is well known for its involvement in crib, darts and pool leagues. Outside is a large secluded garden. LocAle accredited. P

Village Freehouse

33 Wilton Road, SP2 7EF (on A36 near St Paul's roundabout)

12-midnight ☎ (01722) 329707

Downton Quadhop; Hop Back Taiphoon; guest beers H

A friendly LocAle accredited pub that serves three changing guest beers, focusing on local micro-breweries and beers unusual for the area, with requests welcome. It is the only regular outlet in the city for dark beers, with a dark ale, mild, porter or stout always available. Cricket, rugby and football are screened on a small TV. There is no food but plates can be provided if you want to bring in a takeaway. Close to the station, it is popular with travellers waiting for a train. A former Salisbury CAMRA Pub of the Year. ≠⊟

Winchester Gate 🏆

113-117 Rampart Road, SP1 1JA

✪ 12 (2 Mon & Tue)-11 ☎ (01722) 322834

Hop Back Crop Circle; guest beers Ⓗ

This welcoming free house is a former coaching inn on the site of the city's east tollgate. LocAle accredited, the pub offers beers from near and far. One of the four handpumps often has a real cider and beer festivals are held twice a year. There is live music every weekend in the second bar. The large stepped garden features a petanque terrain. Food is served 12.30-5.30pm Friday and Saturday, Sunday roast 1-5.30pm. Salisbury CAMRA Pub of the Year 2010. ❀●P⅟

Wyndham Arms

27 Estcourt Road, SP1 3AS

✪ 4.30 (12 Fri & Sat)-midnight; 12-11.30 Sun
☎ (01722) 331026

Downton seasonal beers; Hop Back GFB, Crop Circle, Summer Lightning, seasonal beers Ⓗ

This is the original home of the Hop Back Brewery although brewing has long since moved to nearby Downton. LocAle accredited, it offers six real ales, usually five from Hop Back and one from Downton. There is also a selection of bottled ales including Entire Stout. A carved head of Bacchus greets you as you enter the pub. A genuine local, it caters for all, with a small bar and two further rooms, one where children are welcome. Salisbury CAMRA Pub of the Year 2006. ⊟(57)♣

Semington

Somerset Arms

High Street, BA14 6JR

✪ 10-11 ☎ (01380) 870067

⊕ somersetarmssemington.co.uk

Bath Ales Gem; Box Steam Golden Bolt; guest beers Ⓗ

This handsome old village inn was recently bought by a local family who have turned it into a smart, upmarket and very welcoming pub, specialising in locally-brewed real ales. As well as the two regular beers, it always has at least two guests available, plus a local real cider. The food is highly regarded. Close to the Kennet and Avon canal, it is popular with boaters. ⛫❀⇄◑♿▲⊟(234)♣●P⅟

Semley

Benett Arms

SP7 9AS (off A350, 4 miles N of Shaftesbury) ST891270

✪ 12-3, 5-11 ☎ (01747) 830221 ⊕ thebenettarms.co.uk

Beer range varies Ⓗ

A former Gibbs Mew country pub sitting by the village green and pond in a quiet village, it has a single small bar with separate dining areas. The beer choice varies but regularly includes an ale from the nearest brewery, Keystone, as well as Ringwood Best Bitter. Excellent home-cooked food is available at all sessions. A warm welcome is extended to all, including families and dogs, in an area popular with walkers. ⛫❀⇄◑♿♣P⅟

Shalbourne

Plough

Kingston Road, SN8 3QF

✪ closed Mon; 12-3, 6-11; 7-11 Sun ☎ (01672) 870295

⊕ ploughshalbourne.co.uk

Butcombe Bitter; Wadworth Henry's IPA; guest beer Ⓗ

This friendly village pub has been a Wadworth house since 2007 (Butcombe Bitter survived the change). The interior, with wood beams and low ceilings, includes a bar and restaurant that can cater for large parties. The menu is wide-ranging and interesting. Quiz nights, live music and community events are enjoyed by the locals. The pub is frequented by ramblers. There is also a gliding club nearby. ⛫❀◑⊟⊟(20,22)P⅟

Swindon

Glue Pot

5 Emlyn Square, SN1 5BP

✪ 12 (4 Mon)-11; 11.30-11 Fri & Sat; 11-10.30 Sun
☎ (01793) 325993

Hop Back Odyssey, Crop Circle, Summer Lightning, seasonal beer; White Horse Oxfordshire Bitter; guest beers Ⓗ

A friendly pub with strong links to the local CAMRA branch, situated in the heart of the Great Western Railway workers' village. A range of six Hop Back beers and two guests is offered, with four real ciders alongside. Good pub grub is served at lunchtime including doorstep sandwiches and ham and chips. The pub is usually quiet but gets busy on weekend evenings. Major sporting events are screened but the TV is not obtrusive or loud. ❀◐≠⊟(8,54)

Roaring Donkey ✔

6 Albert Street, SN1 3HJ

✪ 5-midnight (1am Fri & Sat); 5-11.30 Sun
☎ (01793) 529916 ⊕ roaringdonkey.com

Wadworth 6X; guest beers Ⓗ

Although called the Rising Sun for more than a century, this traditional back-street local was always known as the Roaring Donkey and formally adopted the name in 1999. As you enter the pub there is a small wood-panelled bar on the right and a larger lounge to the left which hosts an acoustic night on the first Wednesday of the month and live music on Sunday. It also has a free juke-box. ⛫Q⊟⊟♣

Savoy ✔

38-40 Regent Street, SN1 1JL

✪ 9-midnight (1am Fri & Sat) ☎ (01793) 533970

Greene King Ruddles Best Bitter, Abbot; guest beers Ⓗ

Formerly an Art Deco cinema, situated just outside the busiest area of the town centre, this is now a popular Wetherspoon pub. Deceptively large, irregularly shaped and on several levels, it has plenty of niches, including a slightly quieter book-lined area. Local ales often feature, with Three Castles a favourite brewery, and there are regular beer festivals offering 10 or more real ales. Westons Marcle Hill cider is served. ❀◑♿≠⊟●

Sir Daniel Arms ✔

Fleet Street, SN1 1RQ

✪ 9am-midnight (2am Thu-Sat); 9am-1am Sun
☎ (01793) 509270

Greene King Ruddles Best Bitter, Abbot; Marston's Pedigree; guest beer [H]
Located in the heart of the town centre, this Wetherspoon Lloyds No 1 pub has two floors to choose from. The ground floor has a dance area used on weekend evenings, when it can get quite busy. Upstairs is more relaxed with an open gas fire and balconies. Background music plays and there are several TV screens. Occasional themed nights are held throughout the year. ❀◑♿⇌🚌🍎🚬

Steam Railway

14 Newport Street, SN1 3DX
⏲ 12-11 (1am Fri & Sat); 12-10.30 Sun ☎ (01793) 538048
🌐 thesteamrailway.co.uk
Fuller's London Pride; Wadworth 6X; Wells Bombardier; guest beers [H]
Originally a coaching inn, this large pub now has a split personality. To the right is a small wood-panelled bar serving up to eight real ales, five of them guest beers. The larger part of the pub is given over to live sports coverage and music. The pub is home to the Real Ale Tasting Society (RATS) and hosts its own beer festival in May. Good-value food is available every day. 🔥❀◑♿🚌(11)♣🚬

Wheatsheaf ✔

32 Newport Street, SN1 3DP
⏲ 5-11; 4-midnight Fri & Sat; 12-10.30 Sun
☎ (01793) 523188
Wadworth Henry's IPA, Horizon, 6X; guest beers [H]
Popular and friendly two-bar Old Town pub dating back to the 1820s. The front bar is small and quiet with a traditional feel, ideal for those looking for a more peaceful pint. The larger, livelier back bar incorporates what was originally the courtyard and has a pool table. Wednesday is real ale night with reduced prices on beers. Cider and perry are available throughout the summer.
🔥Q❀⊟🚌♣🍎🚬

Tisbury

Boot Inn

High Street, SP3 6PS
⏲ 12-2.30, 7 (5 Fri)-11; 12-4 Sun ☎ (01747) 870363
Beer range varies [G]
Fine village pub built of Chilmark stone, licensed since 1768, with a relaxed, friendly atmosphere appealing to locals and visitors alike. Run by the same landlord since 1976, it became a free house in 2009. LocAle accredited, it offers three or four ales sourced from local breweries as well as from further afield. Excellent food is served (pizza only on Tuesday) and there is a spacious garden. A former local CAMRA Pub of the Year.
🔥❀◑⇌🚌(25,26)♣P🚬

Upavon

Ship

10 High Street, SN9 6EA
⏲ 11-12.30am (1am Thu-Sat); 11.30-12.30am Sun
☎ (01980) 630313 🌐 upavonpc.co.uk/ship.htm
Beer range varies [H]
The Ship Inn is a free house dating from the 15th century. It has been completely refurbished, combining traditional wooden beams with a light, open appearance. The decorations, including a huge model of the Cutty Sark in the dining room, have a nautical or local theme. A large covered area is available for smokers in the beer garden. Beers from Stonehenge and Three Castles regularly feature alongside a range of guests. Westons and Cheddar Valley ciders are served. Limited parking outside. Dogs welcome. 🔥❀◑♿🚌(5,6)♣🍎P🚬

Upper Chute

Cross Keys Inn ✔

SP11 9ER (signed from Upper Chute village) SU 295538
⏲ 12-2.30, 6-11 (midnight Sat) ☎ (01264) 730295
🌐 upperchute.com
Fuller's Seafarers, London Pride; guest beers [H]
Situated at the top of a hill with magnificent views, the pub was built in 1705 and became a pub in 1715. In 2006 it was saved from conversion to housing. An old drovers' pub, it still welcomes walkers, cyclists and riders. LocAle accredited, two guest beers usually include one from Hop Back and often a dark beer. An extensive menu of freshly-prepared meals is available (not Sun eve). Families and dogs are welcome and accommodation includes stabling for horses. 🔥❀🛏◑♣P🚬

Warminster

Fox & Hounds

6 Deverill Road, BA12 9QP ST870445
⏲ 11-11 ☎ (01985) 216711
Wessex Foxy's Best [A]**, Warminster Warrior; guest beer** [H]
Friendly two-bar local just off the town centre. One of the bars is a cosy snug, the other has a pool table and TV at the back. A new large skittle alley and function room with its own bar opened in 2009. Three real ciders from Rich's and Thatchers are a mainstay of the pub. A regular outlet for the Wessex Brewery, the guest beer is usually sourced from another local micro. Closing time may be later than 11pm. 🔥Q❀⊟♿⇌🚌(24,264,265)♣🍎P🚬

Mason's Arms

34 East Street, BA12 9BN ST876449
⏲ 11-midnight ☎ (01985) 212792 🌐 masonsarmspub.com
Plain Ales Innmasons; guest beers [G]
This 400-year-old building was refurbished in 2009, creating a family-friendly traditional pub specialising in gravity-served cask beers, real cider and wholesome food. The interior comprises two bars and a back room, with a function room behind the main building. Four beers are usually available – three from Plain Ales, Wessex and Yeovil and another from a micro-brewery within a 40 mile radius. A regular outlet for the nearby Plain Ales Brewery, Innmasons is the house beer.
Q❀◑⊟⇌🚌(24,264,265)♣🍎P🚬

Organ Inn ✔

49 High Street, BA12 9AQ ST872451
⏲ 4 (12 Sat)-midnight; 4-11 Sun ☎ (01985) 211777
🌐 theorganinn.co.uk
Beer range varies [H]
The Organ was converted from a fish and fruit shop in 2006. The building dates from around 1770 and was a public house up until 1913. The landlords have created a welcoming pub with a traditional feel. There are three rooms including a snug, games room and skittles alley. Five ciders are served from a separate bar. The beer range includes three ever-changing guests usually sourced from local micros. The brewer of house beer Organ Bitter is a closely-guarded secret.
🔥Q❀⊟♿⛺⇌🚌(24,264,265)♣🍎🚬

Wilcot

Golden Swan ✔

SN9 5NN

⏲ 12-3 (not Mon), 6-midnight ☎ (01672) 562289

🌐 thegoldenswan.co.uk

Wadworth Henry's IPA, 6X, guest beer Ⓗ

Friendly mid-19th-century village pub with a steep thatched roof, popular with locals, people coming for Sunday lunch and campers. There is a barn for private functions and a large camping field behind. It has a small public bar with an open fire and a lounge where home-cooked food is served. The last Thursday of the month is folk night. The pub also has its own darts, cricket and cribbage teams. Set in the Vale of Pewsey, the Kennet & Avon Canal and a Sustrans cycle route are nearby.

⛰❀◐◑⊟♿⛺🚌(L2)♣P

Wootton Bassett

Five Bells ✔

Wood Street, SN4 7BD

⏲ 12-3, 5-11.30; 12-midnight Fri & Sat; 7-11 Sun

☎ (01793) 849422

Black Sheep Best Bitter; Fuller's London Pride; guest beers Ⓗ

Busy and cosy thatched local with a beamed ceiling. It opened before 1841 and absorbed the adjoining cottage in 1921. The bar sports five handpumps for two regular and three guest beers. Another pump serves real cider. The large blackboard displays an interesting selection of lunchtime meals. A themed food evening is held every Wednesday night 6-8.30pm. Robert Burns and St George are honoured with suppers. The pub is home to crib and darts teams.

⛰❀◐◑⊟🚌(54,55)♣🍎P⚟

Wroughton

Carters Rest 🏆 ✔

High Street, SN4 9JU

⏲ 5-midnight (1am Fri); 12-1am Sat; 12-11 Sun

☎ (01793) 812288

Cotswold Spring Old English Rose; Plain Ales Innocence; Sharp's Doom Bar; guest beers Ⓗ

Decorated with photographs of bygone Wroughton, this large two-bar traditional pub offers a genuinely warm welcome. Three regular and nine frequently-changing guest ales are on offer from numerous breweries. A beer festival is held in December and social events such as Meet the Brewer evenings, poker and weekly quiz nights are hosted throughout the year. The pub welcomes children until early evening and well-behaved pets. A good honest pub, well-worth a visit.

❀⊟🚌(54,71)♣P⚟

Tollgate Inn, Holt

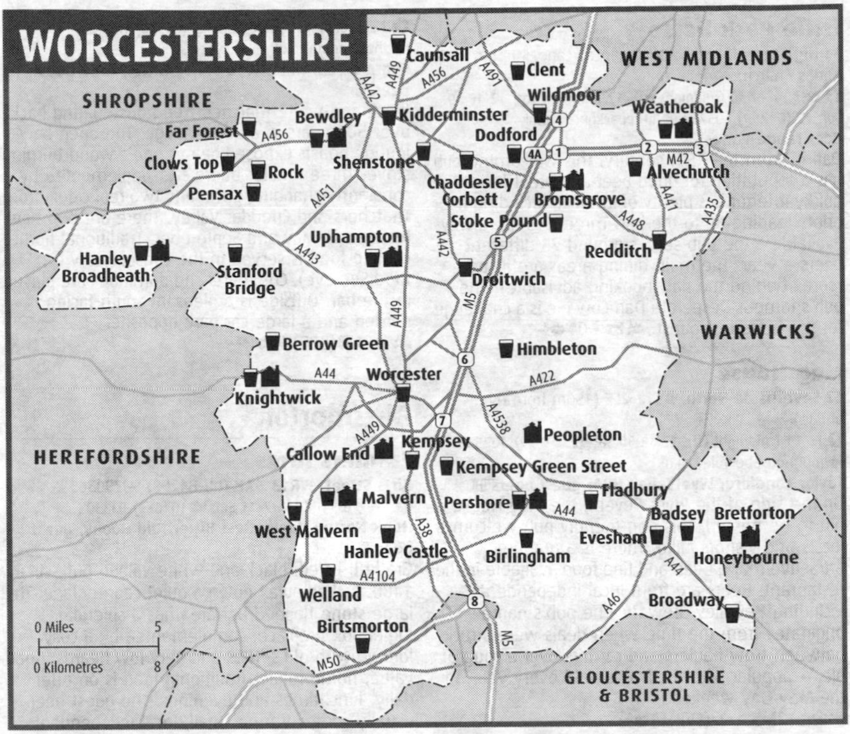

Alvechurch

Weighbridge 🏆

Scarfield Wharf, Scarfield Hill, B48 7SQ SP022721

12-3 (4 Sat summer), 7-11; 12-3, 7-10.30 Sun

☎ (0121) 445 5111 the-weighbridge.co.uk

Kinver Bargee's Bitter; Weatheroak Ale; guest beers Ⓗ

Cosy authentic canalside pub with two lounges and a public bar – a popular retreat for walkers, boaters and morris dancers. Good value home-cooked food is served lunchtimes and evenings (no food Tue and Wed). There is seating outside close to the canal and a heated marquee for functions. Two changing guest beers are stocked as well as real cider or perry on handpump. Two beer festivals are held annually – one in the summer and one in the autumn - featuring ales from local breweries and live entertainment. ⛬Q⚘❀◐⊟≢⊟♣●P⁵–

Badsey

Round of Gras

47 Bretforton Road, WR11 7XQ (B4035/B4085 jct)

11-11 ☎ (01386) 830206 roundofgras.co.uk

Flowers IPA; Uley Pig's Ear; guest beer Ⓗ

Uniquely named and decorated with ornaments, photographs and old farming implements celebrating the Vale of Evesham's world-famous asparagus crop, which features prominently on the menu from March to July. The open-plan roadside inn has a separate restaurant area, games area with pool table, comfortable bar and seating, and an attractive beer garden. Food is served all day every day with a reasonably-priced carvery 12-2pm Tuesday to Thursday. Real ciders include Westons Old Rosie and a cider or perry from Thatchers. ⚘❀◐♿⊟(247,554)♣●P⁵–

Berrow Green

Admiral Rodney

WR6 6PL SO748583

12-3 (not Mon), 5-11; 11-11 Sat & Sun ☎ (01886) 821375

admiral-rodney.co.uk

Wye Valley Bitter, HPA; guest beers Ⓗ

This light, airy country pub is not to be missed. It has three main bar areas where bar food is available, and a restaurant serving locally produced food and excellent fish and chips (booking advised Fri & Sat eves). Guest ales are often from local micro-breweries, along with real cider and perry. The accommodation is popular with walkers – the Worcestershire Way passes the front door. The pet-friendly pub features a skittle alley, floodlit garden, covered and heated patio, disabled toilet and baby-changing facilities. Folk music plays on the third Wednesday of the month. ⛬⇌◐Ẳ●P

Bewdley

Black Boy ✔

50 Wyre Hill, DY12 2UE (follow Sandy Bank from B4194 at Welch Gate)

12-3, 6-11; 12-11 Fri-Sun ☎ (01299) 403523

Banks's Mild, Bitter; Marston's Pedigree; guest beer Ⓗ

This long-standing Guide entry is worth the heart-thumping climb up a steep hill away from the town centre. The building dates back several hundred years and has an open fire and wooden beams. Two main rooms are served from a single bar. A small separate room may be used by families at the landlord's discretion. There are many awards for cellarmanship on display. Guest beers come from Banks's list. ⛬Q⚘❀⊟♿≢(SVR)⊟♣●⁵–

Little Pack Horse

31 High Street, DY12 2DH (near Lax Lane, 500m from St Annes Church)

12-3, 6-11.30 (midnight Fri); 12-midnight Sat; 12-10.30 Sun ☎ (01299) 403762 littlepackhorse.co.uk

Beer range varies H

Dating from the 15th century, this welcoming pub has a reputation for good beer and great food. The quirky interior has plenty of interest, including hoof prints leading up to the bar. Three ales are always available – the pub serves around 75 different beers a year. The main dining areas are in two rooms behind the bar (booking advisable). The pub's famous Desperate Dan Cow Pie is a challenge for the hungriest guest.

Mug House

12 Severnside North, DY12 2EE (150m from river bridge)

12-11 (midnight Fri); 12-11.30 Sat ☎ (01299) 402543
mughousebewdley.co.uk

Taylor Landlord; Wye Valley HPA; guest beers H

On the side of the River Severn, the Mug House is not to be missed. This dog-friendly pub welcomes locals and visitors alike. There is a real fire, attractive rear garden and fine food available in the restaurant. Beers are from local independents including Bewdley Brewery. The pub's name originates from the time when deals were struck between trow haulers and carriers over a mug of ale. A popular beer festival is held every year on the May Day weekend.
(SVR)

Waggon & Horses

91 Kidderminster Road, DY12 1DG (on Bewdley to Kidderminster road, Wribbenhall side of river)

12-3, 5-11; 12-midnight Fri & Sat; 12-11 Sun
☎ (01299) 403170

Banks's Mild, Bitter; Bathams Best Bitter; guest beer H

Popular locals' pub with a single bar serving three distinct areas. The small, wooden-floored snug has settles, tables and a dartboard; a larger room has a large roll-down screen for major sporting events, bench seating and TV. An old kitchen range in the dining area adds to the cottagey feel. Food is available lunchtimes and evenings, with a carvery on Sunday (booking advised). A terraced garden is to the side. Guest ales come from local independents. (SVR) ♣ P

Woodcolliers Arms

76 Welch Gate, DY12 2AU

12-3 (not Mon Easter-Nov), 5-midnight; 12-midnight Sat & Sun ☎ (01299) 400589 woodcolliers.co.uk

Beer range varies H

An old-style, dog-friendly pub with open fires and beams, offering a constantly changing range of guest beers, many from local independents, as well as a bottled beer menu. The Cordon Bleu chef offers a speciality Russian menu as well as traditional food – a microwave is never used. Bikes and fishing tackle can be stored for visitors and a special service is available for Severn Way walkers – ring for details. Quiz night is Tuesday.
Q (SVR) ♣

Birlingham

Swan

Church Street, WR10 3AQ

12-3, 6.30-11 (10.30 Sun) ☎ (01386) 750485
theswaninn.co.uk

Sharp's Doom Bar; Wye Valley Bitter, HPA; guest beer H

Black-and-white thatched free house dating back over 500 years in a quiet village. The open bar/lounge boasts exposed beams and a wood-burning stove. Three regular beers are supplemented by a constantly-changing guest and two real ciders from Thatchers and Cheddar Valley. There are two beer festivals in May and September. Traditional home-cooked food is served in the conservatory (no food Sun eve). Crib, darts and dominoes are played in the bar. Outside is a pleasant south-facing garden and a large car park opposite.
(382) ♣ P

Birtsmorton

Farmers Arms

Birts Street, WR13 6AP (off B4208) SO790363

11-4, 6-11; 12-4, 7-11 Sun ☎ (01684) 833308

Hook Norton Hooky Best Bitter, Old Hooky; guest beer H

Grade II-listed, black-and-white village pub, circa 1480, tucked away down a quiet country lane. The large stone-flagged bar area has a splendid inglenook fireplace, complemented by a cosy lounge with old settles and very low beams. Good value, home-made, traditional food is on offer daily, lunchtimes and evenings. The guest beer usually comes from a small, local independent brewer. The spacious safe garden with swings enjoys fine views of the Malvern Hills.
Q ♣ P

Bretforton

Fleece Inn ★

The Cross, WR11 7JE

11-3, 6-11 (closed 3-6 Mon-Thu Sept-May); 11-11 Sun
☎ (01386) 831173 thefleeceinn.co.uk

Hook Norton Hooky Bitter; Uley Pig's Ear; guest beers H

Famous old National-Trust-owned village pub sympathetically restored following a fire in 2005 and voted CAMRA's 2006 Worcestershire County Pub of the Year. It is home to a world-renowned collection of 17th-century pewter. Up to five ciders are available including one produced at the Fleece itself using apples from various National Trust premises. The pub has its own orchard garden where visitors may drink in fine weather. Buckle Street Brewery in nearby Honeybourne was started in 2008 by the landlord and a fellow morris dancer.
Q (554) ♣

INDEPENDENT BREWERIES

Bewdley Bewdley
Birds Bromsgrove
Brandy Cask Pershore
Buckle Street Honeybourne
Cannon Royall Uphampton
Joseph Herbert Smith Hanley Broadheath
Malvern Hills Malvern
St George's Callow End
Teme Valley Knightwick
Weatheroak Hill Weatheroak
Wyre Piddle Peopleton

Broadway

Crown & Trumpet ✔

Church Street, WR12 7AE (on road to Snowshill)
✪ 11-11 (closed 2.30-5 Mon-Thu winter) ☎ (01386) 853202
Marston's Pedigree; guest beers ⊞
Unpretentious 17th-century Cotswold stone inn, popular with locals and tourists. Oak beams, log fires and plenty of Flowers Brewery memorabilia create a warm ambience. The pub offers an unusual range of games, jazz and blues on Thursday and live music on Saturday evening. Locally sourced, home-cooked food is served daily. Seasonal beers from Stanway and Stroud breweries are available throughout the year, as well as up to three additional guests and real cider. A mini-beer fest runs in December. ⩕❀⇄◑♿⊟(559)♣P⅟

Bromsgrove

Golden Cross Hotel ✔

20 High Street, B61 8HH
✪ 7am-midnight (1am Fri & Sat) ☎ (01527) 870005
Greene King Ruddles Best Bitter, Abbot; Marston's Pedigree; guest beers ⊞
Rebuilt in 1932 on the site of one of Bromsgrove's oldest coaching inns, the Golden Cross Hotel was opened by Wetherspoon in 1994. Interesting facts about the town's local history are displayed on panels around the walls. Local micro-brewery ales are usually stocked, with up to 12 different cask ales on offer, and monthly beer events are held. Good value food, including special deals, is served daily 7am-11pm. There is pay and display parking to the rear. CAMRA members are offered a discount on real ales. ❀◑♿⇶⊟●P⅟

Caunsall

Anchor Inn

DY11 5YL (off the A449 Kiddie-Wolverhampton road)
✪ 11-4, 7-11; 11-3, 7-10.30 Sun ☎ (01562) 850254
⊕ theanchorinncaunsall.co.uk/
Enville Ale; Hobsons Best Bitter, Town Crier; Wye Valley HPA; guest beer ⊞
A gem of a pub, this popular, friendly, traditional local has been run by the same family for 80 years. Little changed over the years, the original 1920s tables and chairs remain in the two main rooms served by a long bar. Renowned for its filling cobs served with salad, the pub offers four real ales and a cider. A lovely atmosphere and location, kind and friendly staff, and a good-humoured atmosphere attract an impressive mix of customers. Easily reached from the nearby canal. Q☋❀♿♣●P⅟

Chaddesley Corbett

Swan

The Village, DY10 4SD SO892737
✪ 11-3, 6-11; 11-11 Fri & Sat; 12-10.30 Sun
☎ (01562) 777302
Bathams Mild Ale, Best Bitter, XXX (winter) ⊞
Lovely village pub dating from 1606 with a large lounge, snug and comfy public bar. The restaurant serves evening meals Thursday to Saturday. Lunch is available daily; however, there is no hot food on Monday. Jazz nights are held in the lounge every Thursday. Dogs are welcome in the public bar and garden. The pub is well-used by walkers. Outside is a large garden and play area. The cider is Westons Old Rosie. ⩕Q☋❀◑⊟♿⊟♣●P⅟

Talbot

The Village, DY10 4SA SO892736
✪ 11-3, 5-11; 11-11 Sat summer; 12-3, 6-11 Sun
☎ (01562) 777388 ⊕ talbotinn.net
Banks's Mild, Bitter; guest beers ⊞
This half-timbered historic pub occupies a site that has been an inn since 1600. Inside there is a public bar with pool table, two cosy wood-panelled lounges with hidden alcoves and an upstairs restaurant. Food is served daily, lunchtimes and evenings. Outside there is a large rear veranda shaded by a grape vine, car park and garden with children's play area. Guest beers are from the Marston's portfolio. ⩕Q☋❀◑⊟♿⊟♣P⅟

Clent

French Hen

Bromsgrove Road, DY9 9PY SO918798
✪ 12-midnight (11 Sun) ☎ (01562) 883040
Greene King Old Speckled Hen; Wye Valley HPA; guest beer ⊞
Large pub formerly owned by the O'Rourke Company and typically rather eccentric – a French theme runs throughout. Rear and side rooms are set out for dining but there is a bar and lounge at the front for drinkers as well as an extensive patio and garden outside. Jazz nights are held on Tuesday and Thursday. The National Trust Clent Hills are nearby. ☋❀⇄◑⊟▲⊟P⅟

Clows Top

Colliers Arms

Tenbury Road, DY14 9HA (on main A456 Kidderminster-Tenbury road)
✪ 11-3, 6-11; 11-11 Sat; 11-6 Sun ☎ (01299) 832242
⊕ colliersarms.com
Beer range varies ⊞
A family owned and run free house set in Worcestershire countryside with fine views from the restaurant and garden. Open fires are welcoming in winter and friendly staff give good service and advice on beers and food. A lounge area offers comfortable seating and a pool table. Beers come from local independents and excellent quality, home-cooked food is made with seasonal, locally sourced ingredients – the pub features in Michelin and AA food guides. There are regular live music events and quiz nights as well as celebratory specials. ⩕❀◑♿⊟P⊽

Dodford

Dodford Inn

Whinfield Road, B61 9BG SO939729
✪ 12 (5 Mon)-11 ☎ (01527) 575815 ⊕ thedodfordinn.com
Beer range varies ⊞
Set in eight acres of rolling countryside, this pub is known as 'the pub in the field'. This real ale haven attracts walkers, ramblers, bikers and horse riders. It offers up to four ales from local brewers and from micro-breweries further afield, and hosts regular beer festivals. Up to three local real ciders are also stocked. Home-cooked meals and themed food events add to the attraction. Occasional music evenings are held. Families with children and dogs are all welcome. ⩕☋❀◑♿▲●P⅟

Droitwich

Hop Pole

40 Friar Street, WR9 8ED (near town centre) SO898634
12-11 (10.30 Sun) ☎ (01905) 770155 thehoppole.com
Malvern Hills Black Pear; Wye Valley HPA, Butty Bach; guest beers Ⓗ
Just a short walk from the town centre, this 18th-century pub provides a relaxing haven for drinkers and shoppers alike. There is a raised alcove for those who enjoy quiet conversation as well as bar-side seating for the locals. Adjoining the bar is a separate pool room and outside is a heated patio for smokers. Guest beers are mostly from Wye Valley and Malvern Hills breweries. Good-value home-cooked food is served 12-2pm.
ቖ❀☾⇌▭♣⌐

Evesham

Old Red Horse

17 Vine Street, WR11 4RE
10 (12 Sun)-11 ☎ (01386) 442784
Draught Bass; M&B Brew XI; guest beer Ⓗ
This popular and friendly two-bar local is in Evesham's historic centre, attracting young and old alike. The attractive black-and-white building features an award-winning floral display. The public bar has a TV and dartboard, and there is a lounge bar with an area set aside for dining. Note the gargoyles and grotesques decorating the bar and rear courtyard. Traditional home-cooked food is served lunchtimes and evenings. An excellent value, weekly steak night is popular, and a quiz is held on the last Tuesday of the month.
♨❀⛟☾◑⊟⇌▭●⌐

Far Forest

Plough Inn ✔

Cleobury Road, DY14 9TE (½ mile from A456/ B4117 jct)
12-11.30; 11-11 Sat ☎ (01299) 266237
nostalgiainns.co.uk
Wye Valley HPA; guest beers Ⓗ
Food is the main focus at this friendly, family-run free house with open fires and rustic decor. The main bar serves a number of drinking and dining areas – the front bar/lounge has an open fire with bench seating. The beer range varies, with ales coming from local breweries. For diners there is a renowned carvery and extensive menu offering local produce. Food is served all day (booking advisable at busy times). Children are welcome in the dining areas. ♨ቖ❀☾◑⊟♿⚠▭♣●P⌐

Fladbury

Anchor Inn

Anchor Lane, WR10 2PY (off A44, on village green)
11.30-11.30 ☎ (01386) 860391 anchorfladbury.co.uk
Fuller's London Pride; Hobsons Best Bitter; Sharp's Doom Bar Ⓗ
A traditional country pub with a welcoming landlord set on the village green at the heart of the picturesque village of Fladbury. The beamed interior has two open fires creating a cosy feel. There is a pool room and darts as well as card games for those in search of entertainment. Food is limited to award-winning pork pies and filled rolls. Real cider is available on gravity dispense on the bar. ♨❀♿▭(551)♣●P

Hanley Broadheath

Fox Inn

B4204, WR15 8QS
5-midnight; 12-12.30am Fri & Sat; 12-11 Sun
☎ (01886) 853189
Bathams Best Bitter; JHS Amy's Rose, Foxy Lady; guest beer Ⓗ
Black-and-white timbered, 16th-century, rural free house. Three local real ales are on offer including at least two from the pub's own JHS brewery, plus occasional real cider in summer. The friendly, family-owned pub has a welcoming wood-burning stove lit throughout the winter. Annual lawnmower racing is held in the adjoining field in August. Meals are served on Friday, Saturday evening and Sunday lunchtime, but lunches may be ordered ahead on other days and sandwiches are available in the daytime. The pub has a games room and garden with a play area.
♨Qቖ❀☾◑⊟▭(309)♣P⌐

Hanley Castle

Three Kings ☆

Church End, WR8 0BL (signed off B4211) SO838420
12-3, 7-11 (10.30 Sun) ☎ (01684) 592686
Butcombe Bitter; Hobsons Best Bitter; guest beers Ⓗ
Former CAMRA National Pub of the Year and on CAMRA's National Inventory of Historic Pub Interiors, this unspoilt 15th-century country pub on the village green near the church has been run by the same family since 1911 and will be celebrating the centenary this year. The three-room beamed interior has a small snug with large inglenook, serving hatch and settle wall, a family room and a lounge with another inglenook. Three interesting guest ales are on offer, often from local breweries. A popular beer festival is held in November.
♨Qቖ❀☾▭(363)●P

Himbleton

Galton Arms

Harrow Lane, WR9 7LQ
12-2 (closed Mon), 4.30-11; 11-11 Sun ☎ (01905) 391672
Banks's Bitter; Bathams Best Bitter; Wye Valley Galton Arms Pale Ale; guest beers Ⓗ
Popular village local with a welcoming atmosphere. The main bar area has original beams and an open log fire, and there is a separate dining room. Guest beers often come from unusual breweries, including Berrow Brewery in Somerset, who supply Recession Bitter at a reasonable price. Special food nights are held regularly, offering good value meals (no food is available Sun or Mon eve). ♨Qቖ❀☾◑♿P⌐

Kempsey

Walter de Cantelupe ✔

34 Main Road, WR5 3NA (next to post office) SO852489
closed Mon; 12-2, 6-11; 12-3, 7-10.30 Sun
☎ (01905) 820572 walterdecantelupe.co.uk
Cannon Royall Kings Shilling; Taylor Landlord; guest beers Ⓗ
A Guide regular, named after a 13th-century bishop of Worcester. The cosy drinking area features a large settle from the 1700s and an imposing inglenook fireplace. The pub is renowned for serving high-quality food made with local ingredients where possible. Regular events are

held throughout the year including a paella party in the attractive walled garden in July. During the summer the pub may stay open all day. ⛫Q❀⇄◑⊟(32)P⁻

Kempsey Green Street

Huntsman Inn

Green Street, WR5 3QB SO868490
⏲ 12-3.30 (Sat only), 5-11; 12-3.30, 7-10.30 Sun
☎ (01905) 820336
Bathams Best Bitter; Greene King IPA, Morland Original 🄷
This cosy and friendly multi-roomed local with exposed beams and a real fire was originally a farmhouse 300 years ago. A separate restaurant serves reasonably priced home-cooked food. There is also a skittle alley with its own bar, an attractive garden and a large car park. Dogs are welcome in the bar and lounge. ⛫♨❀◑⊞♣P

Kidderminster

King & Castle

SVR Station, Comberton Hill, DY10 1QX (next to mainline station)
⏲ 11-11; 12-10.30 Sun ☎ (01562) 747505
Bathams Best Bitter; Hobsons Mild; Wyre Piddle Royal Piddle; guest beers 🄷
Atmospheric recreation of a GWR refreshment room, attracting both locals and visitors to the Severn Valley Railway. A cosy interior offers ample seating and a roaring log fire in winter months. Six handpumps dispense the regular beers plus three frequently-changing guests, which may be from local breweries such as Kinver and Bewdley or from breweries as far flung as Cornwall and Scotland. The Royal Piddle is brewed especially for the pub. Good value lunchtime meals are served daily in the adjacent Refreshment Room. ⛫Q◐♿⇌⊟P

Olde Seven Stars

13-14 Coventry Street, DY10 2BG
⏲ 11 (12 Sun)-11 ☎ (01562) 755777
🌐 yeoldesevenstars.co.uk
Beer range varies 🄷
This popular town-centre pub is the oldest in Kidderminster, with wood panelling throughout, wooden floors and an inglenook fireplace. Five well-kept constantly changing guest beers often come from local independents. The large garden has a covered, heated smoking area and resident hens. No food is served but customers are welcome to order in takeaways, and plates, cutlery and condiments can be supplied. Live music plays on some Friday evenings and dogs are welcome. A pub not to be missed. ❀⊞♿⇌⊟♣●⁻▯

Knightwick

Talbot

WR6 5PH (on B4197, 400m from A44 jct)
⏲ 11-midnight; 12-10.30 Sun ☎ (01886) 821235
🌐 the-talbot.co.uk
Hobsons Best Bitter; Teme Valley This, That, T'Other 🄷
A pub at the heart of the community. The kitchen sources all its ingredients locally, including wild food from the fields and hedgerows and vegetables and salads grown in its own gardens. Delicious seasonal dishes are available in the bar all day and in the separate restaurant. The Teme Valley Brewery is located behind the pub and grows its own hops for brewing – three or four of its beers are on offer at the bar. There is a farmers' market on the second Sunday of the month, and the Green Hop Beer Festival in early October is very popular. ⛫Q❀⇄◑⊞♿⊟(420)♣●P

Malvern

Great Malvern Hotel ✔

Graham Road, WR14 2HN
⏲ 10-11; 11-10.30 Sun ☎ (01684) 563411
🌐 great-malvern-hotel.co.uk
Draught Bass; Malvern Hills Black Pear; guest beers 🄷
This popular hotel public bar just a short walk from the Malvern Theatres complex is an ideal venue for pre- and post-performance refreshment. At least one beer comes from a local brewery. Meals are served in the bar and adjoining brasserie. There is also a lounge with comfortable sofas. Tuesday is 'open mike' night and there are free newspapers and Wi-Fi access. Parking on-site is limited but nearby public parking is plentiful. The railway station is a short walk down the hill and most local buses stop close by. Q♨⇄◑⇌⊟P▯

Morgan ✔

52 Clarence Road, WR14 3EQ
⏲ 12-3.30, 5-11.30; 12-3, 6.30-11 Sun ☎ (01684) 578575
🌐 wyevalleybrewery.co.uk/pubs/the-morgan-great-malvern.html
Wye Valley Bitter, Butty Bach, HPA; guest beers 🄷
The first Wye Valley Brewery tenanted pub outside Herefordshire, named after the Morgan car, which is made nearby. This previously unloved side-street pub is now a real-ale magnet. The open-plan interior is divided into a games area with bar billiards and darts, a drinking area and a seating area with comfy settees. Outside, the front yard has been much improved with landscaping, a fish pond and 'Them Organ' gates to provide an attractive seating area. The pub runs occasional trips to visit the brewery.
Q♨❀◐♿⇌(Great Malvern)♣⁻

Nags Head ✔

21 Bank Street, WR14 2JG
⏲ 11-11.15 (11.30 Fri & Sat); 12-11 Sun ☎ (01684) 574373
Banks's Bitter; Bathams Best Bitter; St Georges Friar Tuck, Charger, Dragons Blood; Sharp's Doom Bar; guest beers 🄷
Eight regular beers and up to nine guests provide the biggest choice for miles around, including St George's ales brewed in the owner's brewery. The pub gets very busy in the evening and at the weekend, and the restaurant, which serves good quality food, is also popular. There is a no-swearing rule which is strictly enforced. Newspapers are provided. There is ample covered space outside for smokers and a pleasant garden to the rear. Dog-friendly. ⛫❀◑⇌⊟(44,44A)●⁻

Star

59 Cowleigh Road, WR14 1QE
⏲ closed Mon; 4.30-11 (midnight Fri & Sat); 12-10.30 Sun
☎ (01684) 891918
Beer range varies 🄷
An unusual fusion of Chinese and English, the Star has a separate restaurant serving high quality Chinese food (booking essential Fri and Sat), and a light and airy bar room with a fabulously ornate bar for drinkers. The outside patio has a sheltered area for smokers. A take-away service is offered from what was once the snug, with comfortable leather

benches to relax and enjoy a beer while waiting for your food. Wye Valley HPA is a regular guest ale. ❀◐◑🍴⇌(Malvern Link)🚌(44,44A,675)P⚟

Wyche Inn

Wyche Road, WR14 4EQ (Upper Wyche) SO76964376
⏲ 12 (11 Sat)-11; 11-10.30 Sun ☎ (01684) 575396
🌐 thewycheinn.co.uk
Hobsons Best Bitter; Malvern Hills Black Pear; guest beers Ⓗ
Set on the side of the Malvern Hills adjacent to the Wyche Cutting, this free house has panoramic views towards the Cotswolds and is ideally situated for hill walkers. It offers two bars, traditional games, a dining area and a patio. Tony and Stephanie serve an ever-changing ale list, tempting enough to convert even die-hard lager drinkers – check the website for upcoming beers. Good home-cooked food and themed food nights are offered. ❀🛏◐◑🍴🚌(363,675)♣

Pensax

Bell 🏆

WR6 6AE (on B4202, Clows Top to Great Witley)
⏲ 12-2.30 (not Mon), 5-11; 12-10.30 Sun ☎ (01299) 896677
Hobsons Best Bitter; guest beers Ⓗ
A consistent Guide regular and CAMRA Pub of the Year winner, this pub is not to be missed. The friendly hostelry serves at least five superbly kept, constantly changing ales, plus local cider and perry. The wooden floors, hanging hops, open fires and pew seating give a true country feel. Dog-friendly, it has a separate dining room with superb views and a snug where families are welcome. The food menu features local seasonal ingredients. A beer festival is held at the end of June.
🔥Q🐾❀◐◑🍴♿⛺🍎P🍷

Pershore

Brandy Cask

25 Bridge Street, WR10 1AJ
⏲ 11.30-2.30, 7-10.30 (11.30 Thu); 11.30-3, 7-11.30 Fri & Sat; 12-3, 7-11 Sun ☎ (01386) 552602
Brandy Cask Whistling Joe, Brandysnapper, John Bakers Original; guest beers Ⓗ
Superb brew-pub offering three regular house ales as well as seasonal brews and a wide range of often unusual guest beers. Real cider is also usually available. Food is good and reasonably priced (not served Tue in winter). The beautifully kept rear garden runs down to the River Avon where mooring for boats is available. A 'must visit' when in Pershore. 🔥Q❀◐◑🚌(382,550,551)🍎

Redditch

Gate Hangs Well ✔

98 Evesham Road, B97 5ES (on main Evesham to Redditch road) SP037659
⏲ 11-2.30, 6-11; 11-2.30, 5.30-11.30 Fri; 6-11.30 (closed lunch) Sat; 12-3, 7-11 Sun ☎ (01527) 401293
🌐 gatehangswell.com
Greene King Abbot; Hobsons Best Bitter; Hook Norton Hooky Bitter; St Austell Tribute; Wadworth 6X; guest beer Ⓗ
Friendly and cosy local with up to six beers usually available and future guests advertised in advance. The single-room interior has a dartboard at one end and is home to sports and games teams. A quiz is held on Sunday and Monday nights from 9pm.
Good value bar snacks are served at lunchtime Monday to Friday. There is no loud music and the small TVs are only turned on for sporting events. The pub does not have facilities for children. A free public car park is located at the top of nearby Birchfield Road. 🔥Q❀◐♿🚌(70)♣⚟

Rising Sun ✔

4 Alcester Street, B98 8AE (opp Town Hall)
⏲ 7am-midnight (1am Fri & Sat); 10-midnight Sun
☎ (01527) 62452
Greene King IPA, Ruddles County, Abbot; guest beers Ⓗ
A popular meeting place for evening drinkers, this Wetherspoon's pub has a large L- shaped interior with several booths and plush settees. A figure on horseback is the room's centrepiece. Historic information about the town's needle and hook industry adorns the walls. Outside seating includes shelter from the elements. At least one local beer is always available and real cider is served from the box. Food is available until 10pm. ◐◑♿⇌🚌🍎⚟

Woodland Cottage

102 Mount Pleasant, Southcrest, B97 4JH SP038668
⏲ 12 (5 Tue)-midnight ☎ (01527) 402299
Greene King Abbot; Taylor Landlord; guest beers Ⓗ
Friendly locals' pub with an open-plan single room interior, including a separate bar area. Sport is shown on TV and darts is played. The pictures on the walls are painted by a well-known local artist. Local bands play live most Saturday evenings and also occasionally on other nights of the week. Guest beers are usually sourced from local independent brewers. The balcony has a sheltered smoking area overlooking the garden.
🔥❀⇌🚌P⚟

Rock

Rock Cross Inn

Rock Cross, DY14 9SD (follow signs from A456)
⏲ 5 (4 Fri)-midnight; 12-midnight Sat; 12-11 Sun
☎ (01299) 832533 🌐 therockcrossinn.co.uk
Bewdley Worcestershire Way; Hobsons Best Bitter; guest beer Ⓗ
A popular, genuine pub at the heart of the community set on the village crossroads. The beamed interior has log fires and a central bar. Traditional pub games are played, with a pool table and dartboard in an area off the bar where there is a TV and music. The lounge is quieter and includes a raised dining area where good food is served. Walkers, dogs and children are all welcome in the bar. 🔥❀◑🍴♿🚌(297)♣P⚟

Shenstone

Plough

Shenstone Village, DY10 4DL (off A450/A448) SO865735
⏲ 12-3, 6 (7 Sun)-11 ☎ (01562) 777340
Bathams Mild Ale, Best Bitter, XXX (winter) Ⓗ
A pub since 1840, this Bathams house is just off the A450 and well-worth seeking out. It was once frequented by members of Led Zeppelin (scenes from The Song Remains The Same were filmed locally). Bar snacks and delicious locally-made pork pies are available. Children are allowed in the enclosed courtyard. Harvington Hall, a 16th-century Elizabethan moated manor house with priest holes, is nearby. 🔥Q🐾❀🍴♿♣P⚟

Stanford Bridge

Bridge Hotel

WR6 6RU (off B4203) SO715658
✪ 12-midnight (1am Wed-Sat) ☎ (01886) 812771
🌐 stanfordbridgepub.co.uk
Hobsons Twisted Spire; Wye Valley HPA; guest beers Ⓗ
A former hotel in a pleasant riverside location, this community pub is popular with local residents and has a lively, friendly atmosphere. Three real ales from local breweries are always stocked alongside Thatchers Heritage cider and Westons perry in summer. Traditional pub games including pool and darts are played in the separate games room. Food is served Friday to Sunday lunchtimes and Tuesday to Saturday evenings. The summer beer festival features live bands and lawnmower racing. Note the fascinating door closers.
Q❀◐♿🚌(758)♣●P

Stoke Pound

Queen's Head ✔

Sugarbrook Lane, B60 3AU SO962679
✪ 12-3, 5-11; 12-11 Fri-Sun ☎ (01527) 877777
🌐 queens-head-inn.co.uk
Wye Valley HPA; guest beers Ⓗ
A warm welcome awaits at this cosy canalside country pub with an award-winning restaurant. The interior has a modern feel with a friendly and relaxed atmosphere. Two guest beers are available, often from the local Weatheroak Brewery. In summer the patio and garden are the perfect place to drink and dine alfresco while watching the boats drift by. Dogs are welcome in the garden. Local CAMRA Pub of the Season Summer 2009. ❀◐♿P

Uphampton

Fruiterer's Arms

Uphampton Lane, WR9 0JW (off A449 at Reindeer Pub) SO838648
✪ 12.30-3.30, 7-11.30 (midnight Fri); 12-midnight Sat; 12-11.30 Sun ☎ (01905) 620305
Cannon Royall Fruiterer's Mild, Kings Shilling, Arrowhead Bitter, IPA; guest beer Ⓗ
The Fruiterer's Arms is in a lovely rural location not too far down a lane off the A449 Worcester to Kidderminster road, served by a regular bus during the day. Beers are provided by Cannon Royall Brewery at the rear of the pub, which is a separate business – seasonal ales are also available. The reasonably priced ales are served in both the bar and the cosy oak-beamed lounge decorated with working horse memorabilia and pictures. Filled rolls are available Friday to Sunday and children under 14 are welcome up to 9pm. Q🚌♣P

Weatheroak

Coach & Horses

Weatheroak Hill, B48 7EA (Alvechurch to Wythall road) SP057741
✪ 11.30-11; 12-10.30 Sun ☎ (01564) 823386
Hobsons Mild, Best Bitter; Holden's Special; Weatheroak Hill Icknield Pale Ale, Bitter; Wood Shropshire Lad; guest beers Ⓗ
This attractive rural pub on the corner of Icknield Street and Weatheroak Hill is the Home of the Weatheroak Hill Brewery. It has a quarry-tiled public bar with a real fire, a split level lounge/bar and a modern restaurant with disabled access and toilets. Outside is a large family-friendly garden and patio. Beer festivals, barbecues and morris dancing are frequent attractions. The pub is a winner of numerous local CAMRA awards. Children under 14 are not allowed in the bars.
Q❀◐♿●P

Welland

Pheasant Inn

Drake Street, WR13 6LP (jct of A4104 & B4208) SO796400
✪ 12-2.30 (not Mon), 5-11 (midnight Fri); 12-midnight Sat; 12-11 Sun ☎ (01684) 310400 🌐 thepheasantwelland.co.uk
Banks's Bitter; guest beers Ⓗ
Relax on comfortable leather couches by the fire enjoying local guest ales in the welcoming main bar. The restaurant serves locally-sourced, home-cooked food (no eve meals Sun and Mon). There is also a large function room with bar and dance floor available to hire and live music plays occasionally. The extensive garden with fine views of the Malvern Hills has a miniature assault course for children. Occasional ferret racing evenings raise money for charity. The pub also offers B&B, camping/caravan facilities, barbecues and a large car park. Q❀◐♿▲🚌(362,363)♣P

West Malvern

Brewers Arms 🏆

Lower Dingle, WR14 4BQ (down track by pub sign on B4232) SO76404565
✪ 12-3, 6-midnight; 12-midnight Fri-Sun ☎ (01684) 568147
🌐 brewersarmswithaview.co.uk
Malvern Hills Black Pear; Marston's Burton Bitter; Wye Valley HPA; guest beers Ⓗ
A comfy traditional pub, the Brewer's Arms serves as both the centre of the village community and an ideal refreshment stop for visitors to the Malvern Hills. Up to eight real ales are available and a beer festival is held in October. Home-cooked food is served lunchtimes and evenings. The cosy bar can get busy at times, but extra dining space is available in the function room or the garden with its award-winning view to the Black Mountains.
Q❀◐🚌(675)

Wildmoor

Wildmoor Oak

Top Road, B61 0RB SO953757
✪ 12-3 (not Mon), 5-11; 12-11.30 Fri & Sat; 12-10.30 Sun ☎ (0121) 453 2696 🌐 wildmooroak.com
Wells Bombardier; guest beers Ⓗ
This rural country inn by a stream is both a local pub and a destination restaurant. Serving traditional British food, international cusine and Caribbean specialities, it has a growing reputation for fine food. Diverse themed nights ranging from comedy to quizzes, Chinese buffet to cheese and wine, attract a varied clientele. The real ale range is always interesting, with two guests. One or two local ciders are also featured.
❀◐♿🚌♣●P

Worcester

Bell

35 St Johns, WR2 5AG (W side of the Severn off A44)

10 (11 Sun)-11.30 ☎ (01905) 424570
Fuller's London Pride; M&B Brew XI; guest beers Ⓗ
This community local has the main bar on one side of a corridor running through the centre of the pub, with two small family rooms on the other side. At the rear is a skittles alley and a second bar only used at busy times, also available for functions. The guest beer range usually includes one from Fuller's and two frequently from local independent brewers. Occasional live music plays at the weekend. ♣

Bridges

Hindlip Lane, WR3 8SB
closed Mon; 12-3, 6-11.30; 12-3 (closed eve) Sun
☎ (01905) 757117 bridgesworcester.co.uk
Malvern Hills Black Pear; Wye Valley Bitter; guest beers Ⓗ
Situated in Hindlip Lane off the B4550 Blackpole Road, this is a lively, vibrant carvery, bar and entertainment venue with live variety acts. There are quieter moments on Sunday lunchtimes or early doors. The landlord is fanatical about the quality of his ales, sourced from mainly local breweries. Coach parties are welcome as are guide dogs with owners. Outside is a large heated gazebo and seating area. ♿P

Dragon Inn

51 The Tything, WR1 1JT (on A449, 300m N of Foregate St Station)
12-3 (not Mon & Tue), 4.30-11 (11.30 Fri); 12-11 Sat; 1-4.30, 7-10.30 Sun ☎ (01905) 25845 thedragoninn.com
Beer range varies Ⓗ
This real-ale-centric pub features six ever-changing beers from smaller independent brewers, including at least one from the co-owned Little Ale Cart Brewery in Sheffield. Bottle-conditioned Belgian beers are also offered. The walls feature mementos of life in the pub, but note the list of banned conversation topics! A partially covered rear patio is pleasant for outdoor drinking in warmer weather. Good value lunchtime meals are offered on Friday and Saturday only. Well-behaved dogs are welcome. ⇌(Foregate St)

Firefly

54 Lowesmoor, WR1 2SE
5-midnight; 3-1am Fri; 1-1am Sat; 3-11 Sun
☎ (01905) 616996
Cannon Royall Arrowhead; Hobsons Twisted Spire; guest beers Ⓗ
Offering period comfort in a regenerated part of the industrial city, the old vinegar works manager's Georgian residence is now a delightful venue with soft furnishings and subtle lighting, warmed by a cosy fire. Downstairs is a candlelit snug with bench sofas. The upstairs bar opens at weekends and occasionally during the week for live music. There is a sun terrace overlooking the city as well as a paved beer garden. ⇌

Plough

23 Fish Street, WR1 2HN (next to fire station)
12-11 (midnight Fri & Sat) ☎ (01905) 21381
Hobsons Best Bitter; Malvern Hills Black Pear; guest beers Ⓗ
This friendly Grade II-listed pub offers four ever-changing guest ales from breweries in Worcestershire and surrounding counties, and draught cider and perry from local producers. A short flight of stairs leads to a bar flanked by two rooms, each with a fire and many original features. A small outside patio area provides views towards the Cathedral. Good food is served (Fri & Sat lunch), with roast dinners on Sunday. Dog-friendly. ⇌(Foregate St)♣

Postal Order ✔

18 Foregate Street, WR1 1DN
9am-midnight (1am Fri & Sat) ☎ (01905) 22373
Greene King Ruddles Best, Abbot; Marston's Pedigree; guest beers Ⓗ
A classic Wetherspoon pub created from the old Worcester telephone exchange. The Postal Order has one of the largest real ale sales in Wetherspoon's West Midlands region, offering up to six guest beers from the quarterly list plus beers from local micros. Local brewers' beers are showcased regularly. Traditional cider is also available. Good-value food is served daily until 10pm. Foregate Street railway station is close by. Q♿⇌(Foregate Street)(32,144,303)

The beauty of hops

When Sean Franklin, who runs Roosters Brewery in Yorkshire, described hops as the 'grapes of brewing' he opened a debate that has led to a much greater appreciation of the role of the small green plant in brewing.

There are many varieties of hops: global brewers use 'high alpha' varieties (high in alpha acids) purely for bitterness. Craft brewers prefer to use varieties that deliver aroma and flavour as well as bitterness. The two most widely used English hops are Fuggles and Goldings, often blended together in the same beer, the Fuggle primarily for bitterness but with earthy and smoky notes, the Golding for its superb resiny, spicy and peppery character. Bramling Cross delivers rich, fruity (blackcurrant) notes, Challenger has a citrus/lime edge while the workhorse of the hop fraternity, Target, offers citrus and pepper. First Gold is the most successful of the newer 'hedgerow' varieties that grow to only half the height of conventional hops and are therefore easier to pick. It offers piny and apricot notes. American varieties used in Britain include Willamette (an offshoot of the Fuggle) and Cascade, both of which give rich citrus/grapefruit aromas and flavours. The Styrian Golding (actually a type of Fuggle) from Slovenia is widely used as an aroma hop in Britain for its luscious floral and citrus character.

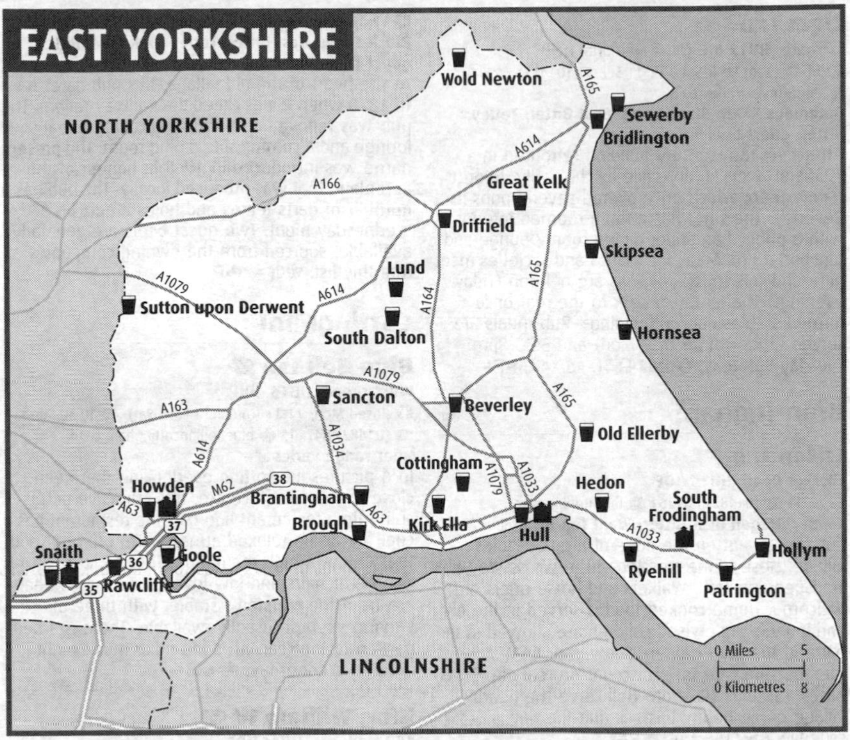

YORKSHIRE (EAST)

Beverley

Dog & Duck

33 Ladygate, HU17 8BH

11-4, 7-midnight; 11-midnight Fri & Sat; 11.30-3, 7-11 Sun
☎ (01482) 862419

Black Sheep Best Bitter; Copper Dragon Best Bitter; John Smith's Bitter; guest beers Ⓗ

Just off the main Saturday Market, next to the historic Picture Playhouse building, the Dog & Duck was built in the 1930s and has been run by the same family for over 35 years. It comprises three areas: a bar with a period brick fireplace and bentwood seating, a front lounge, and a rear snug. The good value, home-cooked lunches are popular. Guest accommodation is in six purpose-built, self-contained rooms to the rear. Local CAMRA Town Pub of the Year 2008. ♨🛏◖🚌♣

Green Dragon ✔

51 Saturday Market, HU17 8AA

11-11 (midnight Thu-Sat); 12-11 Sun ☎ (01482) 889801

Beer range varies Ⓗ

This historic Tudor-fronted inn was renamed the Green Dragon in 1765. Up to seven beers from breweries throughout the UK are featured. Beer festivals are held at Easter and Halloween and regular Meet the Brewer evenings take place. The pub was extensively refurbished and extended 12 years ago; most internal fittings of note were lost, although some wood panelling remains. Meals are served daily until 10pm; Tuesday and Wednesday are quiz nights. Weekends are busy. CAMRA East Yorkshire Town Pub of the Year 2009. ❀◖♿🚌🍎⊱

Molescroft Inn

75 Molescroft Road, HU17 7EG

11.30-11 (midnight Fri & Sat); 12-11 Sun
☎ (01482) 862968

Jennings Bitter, Sneck Lifter, seasonal beers Ⓗ

Much-enlarged village local dating back to the 18th century. The building was comprehensively altered in the 1980s, with the loss of some small rooms to create a large L-shaped lounge/dining room with separate bar area around a central servery. There is a dining area adjacent to the pub's large car park. Meals are served lunchtime and evenings, and all day Sunday until 8pm. ❀◖🚌(121)♣P⊱

Moulders Arms

32 Wilbert Lane, New Walkergate, HU17 0AG

3-11; 12-midnight Fri & Sat; 12-11 Sun ☎ (01482) 867033

John Smith's Bitter; Taylor Golden Best, Landlord Ⓗ

Built around 1870, this street-corner local was named after the nearby Crosskills iron foundry. The Moulders was extended into the adjoining house in 1996 and comprises three drinking areas: a public bar with pool table and darts, a central entrance area with wooden floor, and a comfortable lounge area. A solid wooden bar servery connects these areas. The walls display old photographs of Beverley and the pub. It opens from 12 noon on race days. A guest beer is available occasionally. ❀⇌🚌♣⊱

INDEPENDENT BREWERIES

Bird Brain Howden (NEW)
Great Newsome South Frodingham
Old Mill Snaith
Whalebone Hull

Tiger Inn

Lairgate, HU17 8JG (near Memorial Hall)
11-11 (1am Fri & Sat); 12-11 Sun ☎ (01482) 869040
tiger-inn-beverley.co.uk
Batemans XXXB; Black Sheep Best Bitter; Tetley Bitter; guest beer Ⓗ
Attractive 18th-century building refronted in a 1930s brewers' Tudor style by the sadly defunct Darley & Co, which once owned several pubs in Beverley. The Tiger has a multi-roomed interior with a public bar, snug, dining room/lounge and function room. Many local clubs and societies meet here and folk music sessions are held on Friday evenings. The large car park to the rear once formed stables and outbuildings. Pub meals are served at lunchtime (not Mon) and 5.30-8pm Tuesday-Saturday. Q (X46,X47)P

Brantingham

Triton Inn

Ellerker Road, HU15 1QE
12-11 ☎ (01482) 667261 thetritoninn.com
Copper Dragon Best Bitter; Wold Top Bitter Ⓗ
Pub/restaurant on the edge of a quiet Wolds village, close to the crossing of the Wolds Way and Transpennine Trail. Walkers and horse riders are welcome. Home-cooked food is served in the bar and lounge. Supervised children are allowed in the bar and the beer garden. Show your CAMRA membership card for a discount on real ale. EYMS buses 155 and 156 from Hull serve the nearby village on an hourly basis during the day.
(155,156)P

Bridlington

Marine Bar

North Marine Drive, YO15 2LS (1 mile NE of centre)
11-11 (11.30 Sat) ☎ (01262) 675347
John Smith's Bitter; Taylor Landlord; Wold Top Bitter; guest beer Ⓗ
Large, triangular-shaped, open-plan bar, part of the Expanse Hotel, situated on the seafront to the north east of the town. The bar attracts a good mix of regulars throughout the year and is welcoming to the influx of summer visitors. A good menu of home-cooked food, including vegetarian, is available daily. There is ample car parking on the promenade at the front.

Prior John ✔

34-36 The Promenade, YO15 2QD (near bus station)
9am-midnight ☎ (01262) 674256
Greene King Ruddles Best Bitter, Abbot; guest beers Ⓗ
Large, busy Wetherspoon's pub in the town centre and close to the bus station. Modern in appearance, the interior is basically one large half-moon shaped room. To the right of the serving area is a first-floor gallery, reached by a sweeping metal staircase. The downstairs room is a clever mix of metal and wood, with a segmented ceiling supported by steel pillars. The decor is plain and bright, using mainly pastel colours. Five guest beers are usually available, including a dark beer.
Q

Brough

Buccaneer

47 Station Road, HU15 1DZ (near railway station)
12-11 (midnight Thu-Sat) ☎ (01482) 667435
Black Sheep Best Bitter; Tetley Dark Mild, Bitter; guest beers Ⓗ
At the heart of the old village, this pub dates back to 1870 when it was called the Railway Tavern. The pub was renovated in 2000 to provide a rear lounge and a comfortable dining room. The present name was introduced in 1968 in honour of the aeroplane that was produced locally. The pub has a number of darts teams and holds a quiz on a Wednesday night. Two guest beers are generally available, sourced from the owning company's monthly list. P

Cottingham

Blue Bell Inn ✔

West Green, HU16 4BH
closed Mon; 11-11 (midnight Fri & Sat); 12-10.30 Sun
☎ (01482) 847113 bluebellinncottingham.co.uk
Beer range varies Ⓗ
In a picturesque setting overlooking the green close to the village centre, this attractive pub is split into a restaurant and bar. The restaurant has a coal fire and a relaxed atmosphere, offering food that enjoys a high reputation. The modern bar has deep armchairs and low-level piped music. Beers are from the Marston's stable, with three of varying strength usually available. There is a beer garden to the rear. An open mike music night is held on Wednesday.

King William IV ✔

152 Hallgate, HU16 4DF
11-11 (11.30 Fri & Sat); 12-11 Sun ☎ (01482) 875996
Jennings Cumberland Ale; Marston's Pedigree, seasonal beers Ⓗ
Village-centre pub with a traditional bar and lounge, both free of music. At the rear a former brewery has been converted into a function room offering live music, sport on large-screen TV and special events. The pub also hosts weekly quiz nights and an annual music festival. The rear beer garden and side courtyard have covered smoking areas. Excellent value meals are served in large and small portions. CAMRA East Yorkshire Village Pub of the Year runner-up. Q

Driffield

Bell Hotel ✔

46 Market Place, YO25 6AN
9.30am-11; 12-10.30 Sun ☎ (01377) 256661
Beer range varies Ⓗ
This inn has a feeling of elegance, featuring a long, wood-panelled bar and red leather seating, substantial fireplaces, antiques and prints. Two or three real ales are available, usually from Hambleton or Highwood breweries. Over 300 malt whiskies are stocked. A covered courtyard functions as a bistro, and there is a splendid lunchtime carvery buffet Monday to Saturday; Sunday lunch must be booked. Children are welcome until 7.30pm. Q(121)P

Mariners Arms

47 Eastgate South, YO25 6LR (near old cattle market)
3 (12 Sat & Sun)-midnight ☎ (01377) 253708
Banks's Bitter; Jennings Bitter, seasonal beers Ⓗ
This street-corner local is well worth seeking out as an alternative to the John Smith's outlets that dominate the capital of the Wolds. Formerly part of

the Hull Brewery estate, its four small rooms have now become two: a basic bar and a more comfortable lounge. Live sport is shown and the pub fields various sports teams. The long-standing licensees enjoy a loyal following among locals and offer a friendly welcome to all visitors.
❀⊟⇌🚌(121)♣P⊱

Tiger Inn ✓

65 Market Place, YO25 6AW

⊙ 10.30-midnight; 11.30-10.30 Sun ☎ (01377) 257490

🌐 thetigeratdriffield.co.uk

John Smith's Bitter; guest beers Ⓗ

This 18th-century coaching inn was tastefully refurbished a few years ago but has retained most of the original tap room at the front. To the rear is a beer garden with a large decked area and children's play area. The pub is one of the venues for the town's annual folk festival. CAMRA East Yorkshire Town Pub of the Year 2009 runner-up.
⛫Q❀♿⇌🚌(121)♣P⊱

Goole

Macintosh Arms

13 Aire Street, DN14 5QW (from Boothferry Rd roundabout, take North St then right onto Aire St)

⊙ 10.30-midnight (1am Tue & Thu; 2am Fri & Sat)

☎ (01405) 763850

Marston's Burton Bitter; Tetley Mild, Bitter; guest beers Ⓗ

This Grade II-listed building, originally a magistrates' court, is a gem. Left alone by town planners, it retains a traditional feel, with three rooms set around a central bar, and panelled walls featuring pictures of old Goole. A glass ceiling in the pool room allows a glimpse of the original plaster ceiling. A motorcycle club meets here, and live music plays on the last Friday of the month, with karaoke on Sunday night. The smokers' area outside is covered and heated. ⛫❀♿⇌🚌♣🍎⊱

Great Kelk

Chestnut Horse

Main Street, YO25 8HN

⊙ closed Mon & Tue; 6 (5.30 Fri & Sat)-11; 12-10.30 Sun

☎ (01262) 488263

Wold Top Bitter; guest beers Ⓗ

Built in 1793, this delightful Grade II-listed rural community pub is situated between the Wolds and Holderness. It has a cosy bar with a real fire and a comfortable games room that doubles as a daytime family room. Darts, dominoes and chess are played. Two guest beers are available alongside draught Peroni beer; Belgian bottled beers are served in authentic glasses. The restaurant offers fine home-cooked English and Italian meals until 8.45pm daily (7.30pm Sun).
⛫Q❀◐◑♿♣P⊱

Hedon

Haven Arms

Havenside, Sheriff Highway, HU12 8HH (½ mile S of A1033 crossroads)

⊙ 12-11 (midnight Fri & Sat; 10.30 Sun) ☎ (01482) 897695

Black Sheep Best Bitter; Taylor Landlord; Tetley Bitter; guest beers Ⓗ

This pub is situated in the historic Haven area of town, once the largest port on the Humber. The bar is divided into different areas, and the concert and cabaret room serves as the focal point for the activities of a number of community clubs and teams. Reasonably priced pub food, freshly prepared from local ingredients, is served all day. Two guest beers are available, one usually from a local micro-brewery. One real cider increases to two or three from April to September.
❀◐◑♿⛺🚌(75,76,77)♣🍎P⊱

Hollym

Plough Inn

Northside Road, HU19 2RS

⊙ 12 (5 Mon; 2 Tue-Thu winter)-midnight; 12-midnight (11 winter) Sun ☎ (01964) 612049 🌐 theploughinnhollym.co.uk

Tetley Bitter; guest beers Ⓗ

This family-run, 200-year-old free house of wattle and daub construction has undergone considerable refurbishment. Primarily a locals' pub, it is a haven for discerning holidaymakers in summer. Part of the pub dates from the 16th century, while photographs in the bar depict its role as a WWII ARP station. The room on the right doubles as a dining room, and booking is essential on a Sunday. Accommodation comprises three en-suite letting rooms ⛫❀🛏◐◑⛺🚌(75,76,77)♣P⊱🍺

Hornsea

Rose & Crown

33 Market Place, HU18 1AN

⊙ 11 (12 Sun)-midnight ☎ (01964) 535756

Banks's Mild, seasonal beers Ⓗ

Attractive Tudor coaching inn, rebuilt in 1932 following a fire, and run by real ale enthusiasts. Popular with tourists and walkers, it is ideally situated for the nearby Hornsea Mere and other local attractions. The pub is home to a number of pool and darts teams in the separate games room, and holds Wii and quiz nights. Up to three beers are available – all from the Marston's portfolio. Dog-friendly. ⛫❀◐⊟♿🚌(240,246)♣P⊱

Howden

Barnes Wallis

Station Road, DN14 7LF (adjoins railway station)

⊙ 5 (12 Sat)-11; 12-10.30 Sun ☎ (01430) 430639

🌐 barneswallisinn.com

John Smith's Bitter; Taylor Landlord; guest beers Ⓗ

The country pub you don't have to drive to! Located alongside Howden railway station, Kieron and Kirsty have run this pub for seven years now, and have a well-established formula. There are two permanent Yorkshire beers with two varying guests, one usually dark. One large room abounds with Barnes Wallis and Dambusters memorabilia, and there is a large beer garden. Local produce is used for meals, which are cooked in a country style. Sunday hours on bank holidays.
⛫Q❀◐◑♿⇌P⊱

Hull

George Hotel

Land of Green Ginger, HU1 2EA

⊙ 12-11.30 (midnight Fri & Sat) ☎ (01482) 226373

Fuller's London Pride; Hop Back Summer Lightning; St Austell Tribute; guest beer Ⓗ

Situated in the old town, this traditional pub has beamed ceilings, wood-panelled walls and pictures of old Hull on the walls, with faux gas lamps providing subdued lighting. The bar offers darts and dominoes, TV and piped music. Meals are served 12-3pm Tuesday-Thursday and 12-6pm Friday-Sunday. An upstairs function room is available. The pub is reputed to have England's smallest window, dating back to coaching days and excise searches. A main bus route is close by.

Hop & Vine

24 Albion Street, HU1 3TG (near Hull New Theatre)
11-11; closed Sun & Mon (07500) 543199
hopandvinehull.co.uk
Beer range varies
Atmospheric basement bar with rare bentwood seating. This free house serves three changing guest ales from independents, plus rare farmhouse ciders and a perry. An interesting menu of freshly made snacks and hot drinks is available until 9pm. CAMRA Hull & East Yorkshire Cider Pub of the Year 2009 and Yorkshire Regional Cider Pub of the Year 2009 runner-up. Closed between Christmas and New Year.

Nelly's Bar

48 High Street, HU1 1QE
12-11 (01482) 225212
Beer range varies
Replacing the original Lion & Key public house, this building has had various uses before once again becoming a traditional pub. Dark wood is the prevailing theme here, with an impressive imitation bar back. There is a small separate room on the first floor that offers extra seating. Ten handpumps offer six real ales, usually including beers from local breweries Great Newsome and Wold Top, and four real ciders. This is a sister pub to the nearby award-winning Walters.

Three John Scotts

Lowgate, HU1 1XW
9am-midnight (1am Fri & Sat) (01482) 381910
Greene King Ruddles Best Bitter, Abbot; guest beers
Originally an Edwardian post office in the old town, this open-plan Wetherspoon's features modern decor and works of art. It is named after three past incumbents of the church opposite. The clientele is mixed at lunchtime, with circuit drinkers appearing at weekends. Up to five guest beers are available, plus Westons cider and perry. Food is served until 10pm, with a steak club on Tuesday and a curry club on Thursday. A finalist in CAMRA's Hull Pub of the Year 2009 competition.

Walters

21 Scale Lane, HU1 1LF
12-11 (01482) 224004 waltersbar.co.uk
Beer range varies
The pub's name recalls an 1820s barber shop on the same premises. Although Walters is modern café bar in style, it is a haven in an area of the old town that is overpopulated by fashion bars. Sixteen handpumps offer 10 real ales, usually including beers from local breweries Great Newsome and Wold Top, and six ciders. Belgian and German draught and bottled beers are also available. An over-21s door policy operates. CAMRA Hull Pub of the Year 2009.

Wellington Inn

55 Russell Street, HU2 9AB
4-11; 12-midnight Fri & Sat; 12-11 Sun (01482) 329486
thewellington-hull.co.uk
Tetley Bitter; guest beers
This hidden free house gem just off Freetown Way is a former Hull Brewery pub dating from 1861. It serves up to six guest beers and features a walk-in cooler stocking over 100 European bottled beers; note the glass-fronted display in the back bar. Farmhouse ciders and perry can also be found, plus specialist European beers on draught and Lindisfarne fruit wines. No food is served, but you can bring your own sandwiches. A finalist in CAMRA's Hull Pub of the Year 2009 competition.

Whalebone

165 Wincolmlee, HU2 0PA (500m N of North Bridge on W side of river)
11-midnight (01482) 226648
Copper Dragon Best Bitter; Taylor Landlord; Whalebone Diana Mild, Neckoil Bitter, seasonal beers; guest beer
Built in 1796, the pub is situated in a former industrial area – look for the illuminated M&R Ales sign. The comfortable saloon bar is adorned with photos of bygone Hull pubs, CAMRA awards, and the city's sporting heritage. The adjacent Whalebone Brewery opened in 2003. Two real ciders and a real perry, together with European draught and bottled beers, are also stocked. Hot snacks are available. A CAMRA Hull & East Yorkshire Cider Pub of the Year 2009 finalist.

Kirk Ella

Beech Tree

Southella Way, HU10 7LY
11.30 (12 Sun)-11 (01482) 654350
Black Sheep Best Bitter; Caledonian Deuchars IPA; Taylor Landlord; Tetley Bitter; guest beers
Open-plan pub on the western outskirts of Hull, owned by a pub company that is committed to cask ale. A rack of three third-of-a-pints can be ordered, and 'try before you buy' is encouraged. Food is available 12-9pm every day. Tuesday is grill night and Thursday is curry night – both are served from 5pm. Monday and Wednesday are quiz nights. Children under 14 are not allowed on the premises. EYMS buses 154 and 180 pass nearby until early evening. (154,180)P

Lund

Wellington Inn

19 The Green, YO25 9TE
12-3 (not Mon), 6.30-11 (11.30 Fri & Sat); 12-11 Sun
(01377) 217294 thewellingtoninn.co.uk
Black Sheep Best Bitter; John Smith's Bitter; Taylor Landlord; guest beers
Enjoying a prime location on the green in this award-winning Wold village, most of the pub's trade comes from the local farming community. Renovated by the present licensee, it features stone-flagged floors, beamed ceilings and three real fires. The multi-roomed interior includes a games room and candle-lit restaurant serving evening meals Tuesday-Saturday. Good food can also be enjoyed at lunchtime from the bar menu and specials board. A CAMRA East Yorkshire Village Pub of the Year finalist.

Old Ellerby

Blue Bell
Crabtree Lane, HU11 5AJ
✪ 12-4 (Sat only), 7-11.30 (midnight Fri & Sat); 12-5, 8-11.30 Sun ☎ (01964) 562364
Greene King Old Speckled Hen; Tetley Bitter; guest beers H
This 16th-century inn has an L-shaped bar and a single room divided into distinct areas, including a snug to the right and a rear pool area where children are welcome until 8.30pm. The pub has a strong community feel, hosting several darts and dominoes teams. Three guest beers in winter increase to four in summer. Outside is a fish pond and bowling green. Popular with walkers (wipe your shoes please). ♨Q❀♿▲♣P⚌

Patrington

Holderness Inn
9 High Street, HU12 0RE
✪ 12-11 ☎ (01964) 630335
Tetley Bitter; guest beers H
The original entrance porch and two rooms to the left have now become one large L-shaped room. To the right, a door takes you into the comfortable front lounge, which retains some of its original features, and extends into a more basic room behind it. There are three guest beers available, with Black Sheep Best Bitter, Copper Dragon Golden Pippin, Fuller's London Pride and Taylor Landlord making regular appearances. Food is served from noon until 8pm every day.
♨Q❀◑⚅♿▲⛟(75,76,77)♣P⚌

Station Hotel ✪
Station Road, HU12 0NE
✪ 12-11 (midnight Sat) ☎ (01964) 630262
Tetley Bitter; guest beers H
A family-owned free house on the western edge of the village, this hotel used to service passengers on the Hull-Withernsea railway, which closed in the 1960s. The Anglo-German owners have completely refurbished the old building in a welcoming modern-rustic style, and have added a snug. The hotel is renowned locally for the quality of its food, as well as one or two guest beers sourced from far and wide. ❀◑♿▲⛟(75,76,77)P⚌

Rawcliffe

Jemmy Hirst at the Rose & Crown ▼
26 Riverside, DN14 8RN (from village green turn N on Chapel Lane)
✪ 6 (12 Sun)-11; 5-midnight Fri & Sat ☎ (01405) 831038
⊕ jemmyhirst.freeservers.com
Taylor Landlord; guest beers H
Much loved by visitors across the region, you can be sure of a warm welcome from the owners, locals and Bruno the dog. Four changing guest ales and Westons cider suit every taste. A rustic interior with a real fire and book-lined walls provides a welcome retreat, with lazy summer days on the patio or riverbank. A real gem, six times winner of local CAMRA Pub of the Year including 2010, and Yorkshire runner-up in 2007.
♨Q❀♿⛟(88,400)♥P⚌

Ryehill

Crooked Billet ✪
Pitt Lane, HU12 9NN (400m off A1033 E of Thorngumbald)
✪ 5-midnight; 12-1am Sat & Sun ☎ (01964) 622303
Banks's Bitter; Jennings Cumberland Ale, seasonal beers H
At the heart of the community, this 16th-century coaching inn has stone floors, upholstered bench seats and a rear dining area. A warm welcome is guaranteed in the colder months, with a real fire next to the entrance door. Four handpumps offer two regular beers and at least one other Jennings or Marston's beer, plus an occasional guest. High quality home-cooked food is served on Friday evening, Saturday lunchtime and evening, and Sunday lunchtime. ♨❀◑⛟(76)♣P⚌

Sancton

Star
King Street, YO43 4QP
✪ 12-3, 6-11 ☎ (01430) 827269 ⊕ thestaratsancton.co.uk
Beer range varies H
First licensed in 1710, the Star is now a roadside village pub and restaurant. Bar meals, served lunchtimes and evenings, include vegetarian food. Meals are sourced from local produce, and apple juice and real cider are made by a local farmer. Booking is recommended for the restaurant. The guest beers are sourced from local breweries and oversized lined glasses are available on request. Building work is soon to be completed on a public bar and facilities for disabled customers. ♨❀◑♥P⚌

Sewerby

Ship Inn ✪
Cliff Road, YO15 1EW
✪ 11-11 ☎ (01262) 672374 ⊕ shipinnsewerby.co.uk
Banks's Bitter; seasonal beers H
Village-centre pub serving both locals and those holidaying to the north of Bridlington. One bar is wood-panelled with a beamed ceiling, and food comprises main meals and snacks. The pub is family-friendly, welcoming children and dogs, and the beer garden has a children's play area. Nearby attractions include a model village, Sewerby Hall and cliff-top walks. The pub sponsors the local cricket club that plays only 100 metres away.
♨⛱❀◑⚅♿▲⛟(103,110)♣P⚌

Skipsea

Board Inn
Back Street, YO25 8SU
✪ 6 (7 winter)-11; 12-midnight Sat; 12-11 Sun ☎ (01262) 468342
Wychwood Hobgoblin, seasonal beers H
Traditional village local dating from the 17th century, with distinct public and lounge bars as well as a recently extended restaurant. The public bar, with its sporting focus (especially Rugby League), is home to two darts teams, two pool teams and a dominoes team. The comfortable lounge features the landlady's water jug collection. Home-cooked food is served daily from 6pm, and in summer many holidaymakers come for the Sunday lunch (booking advisable). Dogs are welcome. ♨Q❀◑♿▲♣P⚌

Snaith

Brewer's Arms

10 Pontefract Road, DN14 9JS (on A645)
⏲ 11.30-11.30 ☎ (01405) 862404
Old Mill Bitter, Blonde Bombshell, Bullion, seasonal beers Ⓗ
This impressive former town house is the flagship pub and brewery tap for the Old Mill estate. Converted in 1986, it is of split-level design, with four distinct drinking-dining areas, and includes a well, complete with fake but realistic skeleton at the bottom. Seeing is believing! Four Old Mill ales are on offer, plus a real cider. Excellent, freshly cooked food is available daily from noon until 8.45pm. The licensee trained under Gordon Ramsay at Claridges. ❀⇔◑◗≈♣●P⅟

South Dalton

Pipe & Glass

West End, HU17 7PN (follow signs from B1248)
⏲ closed Mon; 12-3, 6.30-11; 12-11 Sat; 12-10.30 Sun
☎ (01430) 810246 🌐 pipeandglass.co.uk
Black Sheep Best Bitter; guest beers Ⓗ
This delightful hostelry stands at the site of the original gatehouse to Dalton Hall. It features exposed beams and custom-made furniture. Local produce is used as much as possible in high quality meals including children's specials. The restaurant has recently gained a prestigious Michelin Star for its food. Three guest beers come from Yorkshire micros. The pub is open on bank holidays, but closes for a week in January. Two double rooms are available to let. Walker-friendly. ♨❀⇔◑◗⊟●P

Sutton upon Derwent

St Vincent Arms

Main Street, YO41 4BN (on B1228 S of Elvington)
⏲ 11.30-3, 6-11; 12-3, 6.30-11 Sun ☎ (01904) 608349
🌐 stvincentarms.co.uk
Fuller's London Pride, ESB; Old Mill Bitter; Taylor Golden Best, Landlord; Wells Bombardier; York Yorkshire Terrier; guest beer Ⓗ
This pretty white-painted pub on a bend in the road through the village has been family owned and run for many years. The L-shaped bar to the right is popular with locals; note the large old Fuller Smith & Turner mirror. Another small bar with a serving hatch to the left leads to the dining rooms. The excellent restaurant menu includes many fish dishes. Q❀◑◗⊟P

Wold Newton

Anvil Arms

Bridlington Road, YO25 3YL
⏲ 12-midnight ☎ (01262) 470279
Black Sheep Best Bitter; Theakston Best Bitter; guest beer Ⓗ
Reputedly haunted, this Grade II-listed building stands opposite the pond in a picturesque village on the edge of the Wolds. Sympathetically restored, it comprises a bar, games room with pool table, and a restaurant that opens Friday and Saturday evenings and Thursday and Sunday lunchtimes (booking essential). Snacks are sometimes on offer – ask at the bar. The pub fields darts and dominoes teams. The guest beer is likely to come from Great Newsome, Hambleton, Daleside or Rudgate. ♨Q☋❀◑◗⊟♿⛺♣P⅟

YORKSHIRE (NORTH)

Acomb

Sun Inn

35 The Green, YO26 5LL SE571513
⏲ 11-midnight ☎ (01904) 798500 🌐 thesuninnacomb.com
Flowers IPA; guest beers Ⓗ
A welcome source of beer variety in the Acomb area of York, this attractive, traditional pub overlooks Acomb village green, opposite the bus stop for links east to York city centre. It has a lunchtime menu, a very comfortable lounge, a quiet side bar and a public bar with dartboard and TVs for sporting events, and tables outside at the front and a rear courtyard. Live music features, with open-mike and jam sessions. A friendly community pub. ❀◑⊟♿🚌(1,4)♣P⅟

Aldbrough St John

Stanwick Inn

High Green, DL11 7SZ (1 mile from B6275)
⏲ 12-3, 5.30 (6.30 Sat)-11; 12-10.30 Sun ☎ (01325) 374258
🌐 thestanwickinn.co.uk
Jarrow Rivet Catcher; Black Sheep Best Bitter; guest beers Ⓗ
In a picturesque North Yorkshire village on England's second-largest village green, this welcoming 19th-century inn overlooks the meandering beck. It has two bars: one for drinkers and one for the two excellent restaurants, serving food seven days a week, sourced locally. The pub has three guest beers coming from local micros including the village's Mithril Ales, and was CAMRA Branch Pub of the Season. There is a quiz every second Wednesday of the month. You can stay at the pub and explore the Yorkshire Dales and Teesdale. ♨Q❀⇔◑◗⊟🚌(29)♣P⅟🗑

Appletreewick

Craven Arms Inn

BD23 6DA
⏲ 11.30-3, 6-11 Mon & Tue; 11.30-11 Wed & Thu; 11.30-midnight Fri & Sat; 11.30-10.30 Sun ☎ (01756) 720270
🌐 craven-cruckbarn.co.uk
Dark Horse Hetton Pale Ale; guest beers Ⓗ
Built originally in 1548 as a farm, many historic features have been restored to this building including oak beams, stone-flagged floors, gas lighting and open fires. To the rear is a cruck barn, the first one built for 400 years in the Dales. The menu ranges from a la carte to bar meals, and the public bar boasts a rare Ring the Bull pub game and dartboard. The house beer, Cruck Barn Bitter, is from Moorhouse's. ♨Q☋❀◑◗⊟⛺🚌(74)♣P

Askrigg

Kings Arms

Main Street, DL8 3HQ
⏲ 11.30-3, 5.30-11.30; 11-midnight Sat; 12-10.30 Sun
☎ (01969) 650817
Black Sheep Best Bitter; Theakston Best Bitter; Yorkshire Dales Kings Arms Ale; guest beers Ⓗ
At the heart of a pretty Dales village, this imposing building of character was originally a 1760s racing stables, only becoming an inn a century later. A variety of rooms includes the stone-flagged bar with its open fire, which was originally the tack room, and a games room to the rear featuring a

barrel-vaulted ceiling. Close to the market cross, it achieved TV stardom as the Drovers Arms in the BBC series All Creatures Great and Small about vet James Herriot. ♛Q❀⇄◑⊟♿⊟(157)♣⚐

White Rose Hotel

Main Street, DL8 3HG
⚙ 11.30-midnight (1am Fri & Sat) ☎ (01969) 650515
🌐 thewhiterosehotelaskrigg.co.uk
Black Sheep Best Bitter; John Smith's Bitter; Theakston Best Bitter; Yorkshire Dales Askrigg Ale Ⓗ
At the heart of Wensleydale, Askrigg featured in the James Herriot TV series and was also home to Dales historian Marie Hartley. Originally a Victorian town house, the White Rose was sympathetically refurbished in 2006 and is now a family-run country house hotel. Its spacious 19th-century rooms include a lounge bar, restaurant and residents' lounge/pool room, while a conservatory overlooks the sheltered rear garden. Twelve en-suite bedrooms provide good-value accommodation. ♨❀⇄◑♿⊟(157)♣P⚐

Aysgarth

George & Dragon

DL8 3AD (on main A684 Wensleydale road)
⚙ 11.30 (12 Sun)-2am ☎ (01969) 663358
🌐 georgeanddragonaysgarth.co.uk
Black Sheep Best Bitter; John Smith's Bitter; Yorkshire Dales George & Dragon; guest beers Ⓗ
This 17th-century former coaching inn provides a fine base for exploring Wensleydale, including the spectacular Aysgarth Falls. The cosy bar with its decor of dark wood is ideal for relaxing with a local beer after a walk. The restaurant offers good food with friendly service, while for a fine day the patio has flowers and glorious views. Dogs are welcome in the bar and in some letting rooms. Three beers from the nearby Yorkshire Dales brewery are usually available. ♛Q♨❀⇄◑⛺⊟(156)♣P⚐

Barkston Ash

Boot & Shoe ✔

Main Street, LS24 9PR (100m off A162 in village)
⚙ closed Mon; 12-2 (not Tue & Wed), 5-11 (midnight Fri & Sat); 12-11 Sun ☎ (01937) 557374 🌐 bootandshoe.info
Black Sheep Best Bittter; Tetley Bitter; guest beer Ⓗ
A friendly welcome awaits you in this traditional two-roomed village free house which dates back to the start of the 18th century. Full of character, it boasts three roaring fires. Three cask ales are always available. Food is traditional and good value, including Sunday lunch. There is a decked beer garden. The annual beer festival is run each July. ♛❀◑♿⊟♣P

Beck Hole

Birch Hall Inn 🏆 ★

YO22 5LE (1 mile N of Goathland)
⚙ 11-11 summer; 11-3, 7.30-11 (closed Mon eve & Tue) winter ☎ (01947) 896245 🌐 beckhole.info
North Yorkshire Beckwatter; Black Sheep Best Bitter; guest beers Ⓗ
Unspoilt gem resting in a hamlet of nine cottages. A CAMRA multi-award winner, including Pub of the Year 2010, it comprises two bars sandwiching a sweet shop. The house ale, Beckwatter, is organically brewed by North Yorkshire, while guests are sourced locally. A painting of the Murk Esk by Algernon Newton, RA, has been hanging outside the pub since 1944 – donated as a thank you during his seven-year residency. Sandwiches, pies and beer cake are available. Take a look at the informative website. ♛Q❀⇄◑⊟♣●P

Bilbrough

Three Hares

Main Street, YO23 3PH (off A64) SE530465
⚙ 12 (4.30 Mon)-11; 12-midnight Thu-Sat
☎ (01937) 832128
Copper Dragon Golden Pippin; Taylor Landlord; guest beers Ⓗ
This pretty whitewashed village pub is a former blacksmith's with a 200-year history. Excellent beers and food are served in an elegant, modern atmosphere, with a mix of dining and bar areas to suit the needs of all customers. A large garden terrace is set aside for dining and drinking in the summer. Darts and dominoes are played on Monday evening and live music features occasionally. ❀◑♿♣P⚐

Bishop Monkton

Lamb & Flag

Boroughbridge Road, HG3 3QN (off A61)
⚙ closed Mon & Tue; 12-2, 5.30-11; 12-3, 7-10.30 Sun
☎ (01765) 677322 🌐 lambandflagbarn.co.uk
Tetley Bitter; guest beer Ⓗ
Warm and cosy inside, this immaculately kept traditional village pub supports local charities and fundraising events. Two comfortable rooms adorned with knick-knacks and brasses are served from one central bar, but each has its own open coal/log fire. Good home-cooked food is offered and AA 4-star accommodation is available. A garden and large car park are at the rear, with tables at the front ♛Q❀⇄◑⛺⊟(56)♣P

INDEPENDENT BREWERIES

Black Sheep Masham
Brown Cow Barlow
Captain Cook Stokesley
Copper Dragon Skipton
Cropton Cropton
Daleside Harrogate
Dark Horse Hetton
East Coast Filey
Great Heck Great Heck
Hambleton Melmerby
Litton Litton
Marston Moor Tockwith
Mithril Aldbrough St John (NEW)
Moorview Nesfield
Naylor's Cross Hills
North Yorkshire Pinchinthorpe
Redscar Redcar
Richmond Richmond
Rooster's/Outlaw Knaresborough
Rudgate Tockwith
Samuel Smith Tadcaster
Stokesley (Wainstones) Stokesley (NEW)
Storyteller Terrington
Theakston Masham
Three Peaks Settle
Wensleydale Bellerby
Wold Top Wold Newton
York York
Yorkshire Dales Askrigg

NORTH YORKSHIRE

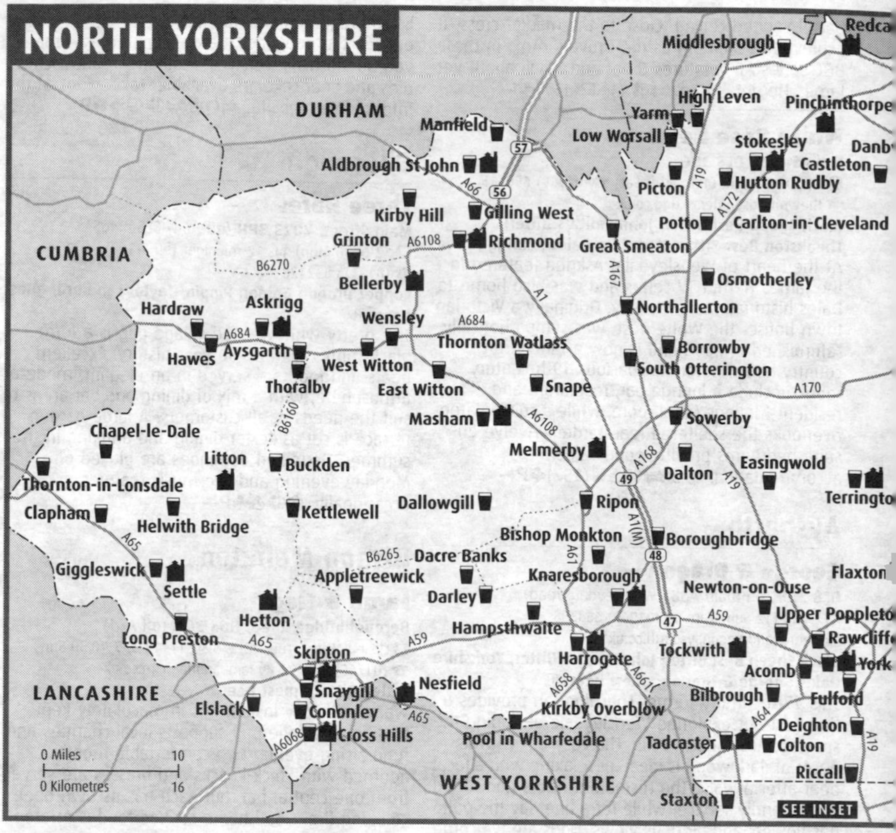

Boroughbridge

Black Bull Inn

6 St James Square, YO51 9AR

⊙ 11-midnight; 12-11 Sun ☎ (01423) 322413

John Smith's Bitter; Taylor Best Bitter; guest beer Ⓗ

Situated in the main square, this 13th-century Grade II-listed inn is popular with locals and visitors. There are several discrete dining and drinking areas as well as a separate restaurant that boasts an international menu. A traditional snug has wall settles, a larger distinctive bar serves good value beers, and there is a wide choice of bar meals. This classic pub, complete with friendly locals, is well worth a visit. Free town parking nearby. ⌂Q⇌◑⊟▲⊟♣P

Borrowby

Wheatsheaf

Main Street, YO7 4QP (1 mile from A19 in village centre)

⊙ 5.30 (2 Sat)-11; 12-4, 7-10.30 Sun ☎ (01845) 537274

⊕ borrowbypub.co.uk

Daleside Bitter; guest beers Ⓗ

This attractive 17th-century free house is near the North York moors. A huge stone fireplace dominates the low-beamed public bar, with another drinking area to the rear and a small dining room across the passage. Home-cooked food is served Wednesday-Saturday evenings and Sunday lunchtimes, when roast dinners are popular. However, this is predominantly a thriving and friendly locals' pub. ⌂Q♨❀◑⊟▲♣P⚊

Buckden

Buck Inn

BD23 5JA

⊙ 11-11 (10.30 Sun) ☎ (01756) 760228

⊕ thebuckinnbuckden.co.uk

Black Sheep Best Bitter; Taylor Landlord Ⓗ

Situated on the Dales Way National Trail, this Georgian coaching inn sits snugly below Buckden Pike among the stunning scenery of Upper Wharfedale. The main room is split between a stone-flagged bar area and comfortable lounge. The Courtyard Restaurant is open evenings for home-cooked food made from local ingredients. Outside is a seating area with fantastic views. The house beer is Buckden Pike from Yorkshire Dales. Accommodation is in 14 en-suite rooms. ⌂❀⇌◑⊟(72,74)P

Burn

Wheatsheaf

Main Road, YO8 8LJ (on A19 3 miles S of Selby) SE594286

⊙ 12-11 ☎ (01757) 270614 ⊕ wheatsheafburn.co.uk

John Smith's Bitter; Taylor Best Bitter; guest beers Ⓗ

A renowned roadside free house stocking four reasonably priced guest beers, often from local breweries including Brown Cow and Great Heck. A narrow entrance leads to the bar and spacious lounge with its huge open fire. A collection of bottled beers, artefacts from bygone days and memorabilia of 578 Squadron stationed at Burn in

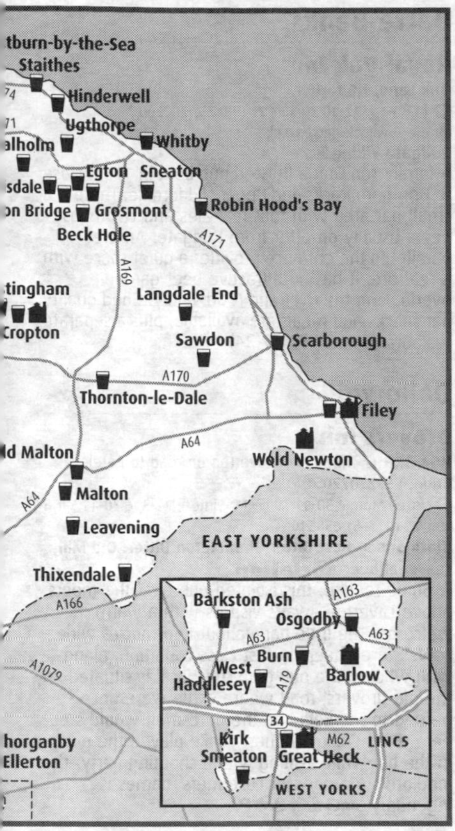

World War II adorn the walls. Food is served every lunchtime and Thursday to Saturday evenings. Frequent beer festivals and a monthly jazz night are held. ⛫Q❀◐◑🚌♣P⚟

Carlton-in-Cleveland

Blackwell Ox Inn

Main Street, TS9 7DJ (400m off A172)

⏲ 11.30-11 ☎ (01642) 712287 🌐 theblackwellox.co.uk

Black Sheep Best Bitter; Worthington's Bitter; guest beers 🄷

Located in a beautiful area on the edge of the National Park, this impressive, multi-roomed village inn is renowned for its good value cuisine. Winter Monday evening Thai buffets, washed down with a pint or two, can easily become habit forming. Look out also for early-evening year-round specials. But you don't have to eat! Drinkers are also made most welcome. Four handpumps, including two guests, provide an eclectic range of varying beer styles. The garden has an extensive children's play area. ⛫Q❀⛟◐Å🚌(80,89)P

Castleton

Eskdale Inn

Station Road, YO21 2EU (next to railway station)

⏲ 12-midnight (11 Sun) ☎ (01287) 660333

🌐 eskdaleinn.co.uk

Black Sheep Best Bitter; Tetley Bitter; guest beers 🄷

Situated between the railway station and the Esk, a friendly welcome is assured at this former station hotel. The casks of ale sit in a cool cellar directly beneath the handpumps and well away from the warming fire. Guest ales are often chosen by the locals themselves. Good value meals are supplemented by a specials board and an extensive children's menu. The pub supports two darts and one pool team. A disabled toilet is provided. Two letting bedrooms are available. ⛫Q❀⛟◐◑♿⇌🚌♣P⚟⊓

Chapel-le-Dale

Hill Inn

LA6 3AR (on B6255) SD374477

⏲ closed Mon; 12-11 ☎ (01524) 241256 🌐 oldhillinn.co.uk

Black Sheep Best Bitter; Dent Aviator; Theakston Best Bitter 🄷

The inn dates from 1615 and is beloved of generations of hikers and potholers. Well-worn paths run from here to both Whernside (Yorkshire's highest peak) and Ingleborough (its best known). Lots of exposed wood and some stonework feature in the bar. Run by a family of chefs, the pub is popular with diners – puddings are a speciality, and there is a sugar sculpture exhibition in an adjoining room (booking advisable for meals). ⛫Q❀⛟◐◑ÅP⚟⊓

Clapham

New Inn

LA2 8HH

⏲ 11-midnight ☎ (01524) 251203 🌐 newinn-clapham.co.uk

Black Sheep Best Bitter; Copper Dragon Best Bitter, Golden Pippin; guest beers 🄷

Situated in a major tourist village, this spacious 18th-century coaching inn features two lounge bars. One includes oak panelling, the other has walls with photos and cartoons depicting caving and is home to pub games. Children are welcome in the restaurant. The railway station is a mile away. ⛫❀⛟◐◑♿⇌🚌(581)♣P

Old Manor House

Church Avenue, LA2 8EQ

⏲ 12-6 (7 Fri & Sat) ☎ (01524) 251144

🌐 claphambunk.com/

Beer range varies 🄷

The old manor house, dating back to circa 1620, houses a bunkhouse, craft emporium and a bar called the Reading Room. A huge fireplace (dated 1701) holds a wood-burning stove, the floor is flagged, and art for sale hangs on the walls. Snacks such as soup, paninis and baked potatoes are available. Giant Jenga is played. Do not overlook the bottled beers and ciders. The draught cider is Westons Scrumpy. The station is a mile away. ⛫Q❀⛟Å⇌🚌(581)●

Colton

Old Sun Inn ✔

Main Street, LS24 8EP (left into village, along Colton Lane, 1 mile S of Bilbrough Services on A64) SE542448

⏲ 12-2.30 (not Mon), 6-11; 12-11 Sun ☎ (01904) 744261

🌐 yeoldsuninn.co.uk

Black Sheep Best Bitter; Taylor Landlord; guest beers 🄷

Seventeenth-century country village pub with an award-winning restaurant and deli. Cosy and friendly with a real fire, it has low-beamed ceilings and traditional decor. Great food is served

lunchtimes and evenings daily (Sun to 7pm, no food Mon lunch). In a pleasant rural setting, there is a formal patio garden at the front and a large informal picnic area behind the car park. Special events are staged including cooking demonstrations (details available on the website). B&B is available at nearby Walnut Lodge.
⌂Q❀⇌◑♿P⊟

Cononley

New Inn

Main Street, BD20 8NR

✪ 12-2.30, 5.30-midnight; 12-1am Fri & Sat; 12-10.30 Sun ☎ (01535) 636302 ⊕ newinncononley.co.uk

Taylor Dark Mild, Golden Best, Best Bitter, Landlord, Ram Tam Ⓗ

Mullioned windows, low ceilings, wooden beams and Yorkshire hospitality abound in this whitewashed village pub. A Timothy Taylor tied house, it stocks the full range of beers. The main room serves as both a drinking and dining area, with a small room available for quiet dining. The Knowle Spring room upstairs is available for functions. The railway station is a five-minute walk. Note: If catching a train south allow time to get over the level-crossing barrier.
⌂❀◑⛺⇌⊟(78A)♣

Cropton

New Inn

Woolcroft, YO18 8HH (5 miles off the A170 Pickering-Kirkbymoorside road) SE755888

✪ 11-11; 11.30-10.30 Sun ☎ (01751) 417330

⊕ newinncropton.co.uk

Cropton seasonal beers; guest beers Ⓗ

Set on the edge of North Yorkshire Moors National Park, this is a perfect base for walking and cycling. It is the brewery tap for Cropton Brewery, with a fantastic beer range, good food and accommodation. A beer festival is held every November, plus a music festival in summer. The New Inn sets the standard for how a rural pub should be run. For those not wanting to drive, the Moors bus service runs regularly from both Pickering and Kirkbymoorside.
Q⛴❀⇌◑⛺⊟♣P⊟

Cross Hills

Old White Bear

6 Keighley Road, BD20 7RN (on A6068, close to jct with A629)

✪ 11.30-11; 12-10.30 Sun ☎ (01535) 632115

Naylor's Pinnacle Pale Ale, Bitter, Blonde, seasonal beers Ⓗ

Four-room village pub with timbers said to have come from a ship of the same name. Built in 1735, it has had a chequered history as a hotel, brothel, council meeting room and dance hall before becoming a pub. The top room, with stone-flagged floor, is used mainly for dining; there are three other rooms, two with open fires. The back room has darts and ring the bull. Quiz night is Thursday. It's a regular outlet for Naylor's Brewery, and local CAMRA Pub of the Year 2009.
⌂❀◑⊟(66,66A)♣P⚟

Dacre Banks

Royal Oak Inn

Oak Lane, HG3 4EN

✪ 11.30-11; 12-10.30 Sun ☎ (01423) 780200

⊕ the-royaloak-dacre.co.uk

Rudgate Viking Ⓗ

A family-run Grade II-listed pub built in 1752, close to Brimham Rocks and Upper Nidderdale. There is a small bar area with four real ales and two house beers usually on offer from Rudgate. An area parallel to the entrance provides a quiet space with a real fire. It has an attractive beer garden overlooking the river and Nidd Valley. Good quality bar snacks and meals are available, plus a separate restaurant. ⌂❀⇌◑⊟(24)♣P

Dallowgill

Drovers Inn

HG4 3RH (2 miles W of Laverton on road to Pateley Bridge) SE210720

✪ closed Mon; 6.30-11.30 (7-11 winter); 12-3, 6.30-11 Sat & Sun ☎ (01765) 658510

Black Sheep Best Bitter; Hambleton Bitter; Old Mill seasonal beer Ⓗ

A Guide regular, this isolated pub near the moors above Laverton awaits visitors with a warm welcome. The little bar – about two metres wide – serves three beers in first-class condition, along with wholesome pub grub. This local is situated on the old drovers' road where cattle were once herded to markets and the herdsmen would stop here. Bing Crosby (honest) once played the piano in the bar while visiting with a shooting party. The landlord's memory for customers' names is legendary. ⌂Q❀◑⛺♣P⚟

Dalton

Jolly Farmer

Brookside, YO7 3HY (off A19 or A168)

✪ 7-11 Mon-Wed; 12-3, 6 (7 Sun)-11 ☎ (01845) 577359

Tetley Bitter; Theakston Traditional Mild Ⓗ

Popular with locals, this family-run pub dating from the mid-1800s is at the heart of the village. Its six handpumps feature beer from local micros chosen by the regulars, as well as a real cider and perry. Freshly prepared home-made dishes using local produce are served from the kitchen (booking advisable for Sunday lunch). Three en-suite rooms provide an ideal base for exploring the Dales and North Yorkshire moors. ⌂Q❀⇌◑♿⛺♣●P⚟

Danby

Duke of Wellington

2 West Lane, YO21 2LY (200m N of railway station)

✪ 12-3 (not Mon), 7-11; 12-11 Fri & Sat; 12-3, 7-10.30 Sun ☎ (01287) 660351 ⊕ dukeofwellingtondanby.co.uk

Copper Dragon Scotts 1816; Daleside Bitter; guest beers Ⓗ

This 18th-century inn, and 2009 local CAMRA Pub of the Season award winner, is set in idyllic National Park countryside, close to the Moors Visitor Centre. It was used as a recruiting post during the Napoleonic Wars, and a cast-iron plaque of the first Duke of Wellington, unearthed during restoration work, hangs above the fireplace. All the ales always come from local breweries, while the menu offers traditional British meals using locally-sourced meat, fish and game. ⌂Q❀⇌◑⇌⊟♣

ENGLAND

Darley

Wellington Inn

HG3 2QQ (on B6451 to W of village)
⏲ 11.30-11; 12-10.30 Sun ☎ (01423) 780362
🌐 wellington-inn.co.uk
Black Sheep Best Bitter; Copper Dragon Golden Pippin; Taylor Landlord; Tetley Bitter Ⓗ
Spacious stone roadside inn much extended in the 1980s. The beer garden gives excellent views over Nidderdale, an area of outstanding natural beauty. The original bar operates as a tap room. The extension has an impressive inglenook fireplace and is used more as a dining area. There is a separate restaurant and the pub makes an ideal starting point for exploring the dales.
⛰❀🛏◑⊟🚌♣P

Deighton

White Swan ✔

YO19 6HA (on A19 between York and Selby) SE628441
⏲ 12-2.30, 5.30-11; 12-11 Sat; 12-10.30 Sun
☎ (01904) 728287 🌐 whiteswandeighton.co.uk
Banks's Bitter; Jennings Bitter; Marston's Pedigree; guest beer Ⓗ
An oasis on a busy highway, this quite large pub has a front bar opening up from the entrance, a separate dining area off to one side, and a lounge/dining room to the other side. Although now partly open plan, much of the original layout is unchanged. The comprehensive menu of good quality, good value food is the main draw, supplemented by a daily specials board and children's dishes. Q❀◑🚌(415)P

Easingwold

George ✔

Market Place, YO61 3AD
⏲ 11-11 ☎ (01347) 821698 🌐 the-george-hotel.co.uk
Black Sheep Best Bitter; Moorhouse's Pride of Pendle; guest beers Ⓗ
An 18th-century coaching inn occupying a prime site in the cobbled market square of this pretty Georgian town, it has retained much of its original character, with open fires, a wealth of beams and horse brasses. A friendly, family-run inn, the George enjoys a good reputation as both a pub and a restaurant, with dining available in the restaurant or Courtyard Bar. It has the widest choice of beers in town. ⛰Q🛏◑♿P

East Witton

Cover Bridge Inn

DL8 4SQ (½ mile N of village on A6108) SE144871
⏲ 11-midnight; 12-11.30 Sun ☎ (01969) 623250
🌐 thecoverbridgeinn.co.uk
Black Sheep Best Bitter; John Smith's Bitter; Taylor Landlord; Theakston Best Bitter, Old Peculier; guest beers Ⓗ
Outstanding country inn situated where the rivers Cover and Ure meet. A CAMRA multi-award winner, it serves up to eight cask ales on a regular basis. Once you have fathomed out the door latch, you enter the ancient public bar with its splendid hearth and open fire. A tiny lounge leads to a very attractive riverside garden with a play area. The pub has an enviable reputation for food, with lunchtime and evening meals served daily.
⛰Q🛝❀🛏◑⊟🚌(159)♣P⊱🥛

Egton

Wheatsheaf Inn

High Street, YO21 1TZ
⏲ closed Mon; 11.30-2.30, 5.30-11; 11.30-11 Sat & Sun
☎ (01947) 895271 🌐 wheatsheafegton.com
Black Sheep Best Bitter; Taylor Landlord; guest beer Ⓗ
This Grade I-listed 19th-century pub, now in its 11th year in the Guide, is under the stewardship of a licensee who has had 24 years of continuous Guide recognition, and was a local CAMRA award winner in 2009. Church pews, collectables from auctions and a roaring range add to the character. The upmarket menu features local meats, fish and game. The grassy area to the front, and boules to the rear, are ideal for summer. Six bedrooms and a holiday cottage are available.
⛰❀🛏◑⊟♿⇌🚌(99)♣P⊱

Egton Bridge

Horseshoe Hotel

YO21 1XE (down hill from Egton station)
⏲ 11.30-3, 6.30-11; 11.30-11 Sat; 12-11 Sun
☎ (01947) 895245
Black Sheep Best Bitter; John Smith's Bitter; guest beers Ⓗ
Secluded gem in a hollow accessed from the station or across the stepping stones of the Esk. Old-fashioned settles and a large fire adorn the bar. Five handpumps provide a wide beer selection, with guests usually from Copper Dragon and Durham. A beer festival is held on Yorkshire Day, 1 August. A raised grassy area makes outdoor drinking a pleasure. The regular menu and specials are locally sourced and good value. It's a former local CAMRA Pub of the Year winner.
⛰Q🛝❀🛏◑♿⇌🚌(99)P⊱

Ellerton

Boot & Shoe

Main Street, YO42 4PB (just off B1228 road to Howden)
⏲ 5.30-late; 12-late Sat & Sun ☎ (01757) 288346
Dark Horse Old Boot; Leeds Best; Old Mill Bitter Ⓗ
This welcoming country village inn dates from the 17th century and features low-beamed ceilings. There is a cosy bar area with exposed brick and an open fire, plus two separate dining rooms. Three real ales are on offer, including Old Boot brewed by the Dark Horse brewery. Food is served Friday and Saturday evenings and Sunday lunchtime. ⛰Q♣

Elslack

Tempest Arms

BD23 3AY (off A56 Skipton-Colne road)
⏲ 11-11; 12-10.30 Sun ☎ (01282) 842450
🌐 tempestarms.co.uk
Dark Horse Hetton Pale Ale; Taylor Landlord; Theakston Best Bitter; Thwaites Wainwrights Ⓗ
In a pleasant rural setting in a hamlet of stone-built houses, this large country inn offers a wide choice of excellent food, served in the comfortable bar or separate restaurant area. The decor reflects the historic association with the local Tempest family. During the winter months there is a welcoming log fire that greets you as you enter. Conference facilities, a function room and accommodation are all available. The house beer, Elslack Ale, is brewed by Moorhouse's. ⛰❀🛏◑♿🚌(215)P

Filey

Bonhommes Bar

Royal Crescent Court, The Crescent, YO14 9JH

✪ 11 (12 winter)-midnight; 11-1am Fri & Sat; 12-midnight Sun ☎ (01723) 514054

East Coast Bonhomme Richard; guest beers Ⓗ

Situated just off the fine Victorian Royal Crescent Hotel complex, the bar's name celebrates John Paul Jones, father of the American Navy. His ship, the Bonhomme Richard, was involved in a battle off nearby Flamborough Head during the War of Independence. Six handpumps serve one East Coast beer plus five rotating guests. A fun quiz is held on Saturday, and the main quiz on Sunday. Voted local CAMRA Rural Pub of the Year 2008 and 2009. ⇌🚌🍎

Flaxton

Blacksmith's Arms

YO60 7RJ (1 mile from A64, opp York Lane jct) SE678 624

✪ closed Mon; 12-2 Thu & Fri; 6-11 Tue-Sat; 12-3, 6-10.30 Sun ☎ (01904) 468210 🌐 blacksmithsarmsflaxton.co.uk

Copper Dragon Best Bitter; Taylor Landlord; Theakston Best Bitter; York seasonal beers; guest beer Ⓗ

Built in the 1700s as a coaching inn and now over 250 years old, the Blacksmiths Arms has retained plenty of charm and character. Family owned and run, this village pub has an L-shaped main bar with a dining room and snug off to one side, and a welcoming real fire for the winter months. Four regular ales are served, all Yorkshire brewed, with an occasional guest on the fifth pump. The snug houses a Yorkshire board for darts matches. Good food is served evenings and Sunday lunch. ⛫🛏◑♣P

Fulford

Saddle Inn

Main Street, YO10 4PJ (on A19 2 miles S of York city centre)

✪ 11.30-4, 6.30-midnight; 11.30-midnight Fri & Sat; 11.30-11 Sun ☎ (01904) 633317

Banks's Bitter; guest beers Ⓗ

A prominent 153-year-old pub on a main road into York, with a comfortable L-shaped lounge and an adjacent dining area where children are welcome. The good-value food accompanies the best selection of beers in this part of the city. Sports TV, darts and pool are also a draw. An unusual petanque terrain features in the attractive rear garden, with open sessions for visitors to join in. Accommodation is available. No food Monday lunchtime. ❀🛏◑🚌(7,415)♣P⌐

Giggleswick

Hart's Head Hotel

Belle Hill, BD24 0BA (on B6480 ½ mile N of Settle)

✪ 12-2.30 (not Tue & Thu), 5.30-11; 12-11 Fri & Sat; 12-10.30 Sun ☎ (01729) 822086 🌐 hartsheadinn.co.uk

Copper Dragon Golden Pippin; Tetley Bitter; guest beers Ⓗ

A warm welcome is assured at this open-plan 18th-century coaching inn. There is a bar area for pub games and sport on TV, while the comfy lounge area has sofa seating. Freshly prepared meals from a varied menu are served in the adjacent dining room. Snooker can be played on a full-sized table in the recently refurbished cellar. Four varying guest beers are available, often from Dent, Barngates, Black Sheep or Bowland breweries. ⛫❀🛏◑♿🚌(580,581)♣P⌐

Gilling West

White Swan Inn

51 High Street, DL10 5JG (2 miles W of Scotch Corner, off A66)

✪ 12-11 (10.30 Sun) ☎ (01748) 821123

Black Sheep Best Bitter; John Smith's Bitter; guest beers Ⓗ

Friendly 17th-century country inn with an open-plan bar with a real fire and a dining room offering an extensive menu. This free house sources guest beers from local and national micro-breweries. The bar's beams are covered in bank notes, old and new. The beer garden has tables, chairs, sunshades and features an unusual collection of objects to be spotted. Live acoustic music plays on alternate Wednesdays. Occasional themed food nights are hosted. Be careful if you sit in the Grumpy Seat. ⛫Q❀◑⛺🚌(29)♣⌐

Glaisdale

Arncliffe Arms

1 Arncliffe Terrace, YO21 2QL (at bottom of village next to station)

✪ 12-2.30, 5-11 (not Fri); 12-11 Sat & Sun ☎ (01947) 897555 🌐 arncliffearms.co.uk

Copper Dragon Golden Pippin; guest beers Ⓗ

In a scenic location close to the River Esk and Beggars Bridge, the pub is popular with both locals and holidaymakers. Two guest beers are sourced from local micro-breweries, while restaurant meals and substantial bar food use local produce wherever possible. A happy hour features mid-week. Children are welcome until 9pm. An excellent pub website gives details of a number of circular walks, together with details of the Esk Valley and NYMR train services. Accommodation is in four bedrooms. Dog-friendly. ⛫Q❀🛏◑⇌🚌(99)♣P

Great Heck

Bay Horse Inn

Main Street, DN14 0BQ (follow signs to village from A19) SE 594210

✪ closed Mon; 5-11 (11.30 Thu-Sat); 12-10.30 Sun ☎ (01977) 661125 🌐 thebayhorseinn.org

Old Mill Bitter, seasonal beers Ⓗ

Originally three cottages, this is a charming old inn, complete with original beams displaying horse brasses and various artefacts. The pub currently keeps up to three real ales and provides hearty home-cooked meals at various times of the day and evening. A quiz is hosted on Thursday evening. There is a car park and the pub is situated on a bus route. All in all, a very warm welcome awaits you. ⛫Q❀◑🚌(476)P⌐

Great Smeaton

Black Bull

DL6 2EH (on A167)

✪ 5-late (midnight Sat & Sun) ☎ (01609) 881219

Daleside Blonde; John Smith's Bitter Ⓗ

Popular 17th-century coaching inn situated at the end of a row of roadside cottages on the Darlington to Northallerton road. Inside it has a linked bar, lounge and games room, with low-beamed ceilings. Underneath the games room were once cells that detained the legendary highwayman Dick Turpin on the way to his execution in York. Accommodation is available in four rooms. Handy for exploring the North Yorkshire Moors and Yorkshire Dales, with the Croft Circuit nearby. Dogs are welcome. ⛬♨❀⇌◐♿Å⊟(72)♣P⅟

Grinton

Bridge Inn

DL11 6HH (on B6270, 1 mile E of Reeth) SE 046984
⏲ 12-midnight (1am Fri & Sat); 12-11 Sun
☎ (01748) 884224 🌐 bridgeinn-grinton.co.uk
Jennings Bitter, Cumberland Ale; guest beer ⊞
On the banks of the River Swale below Fremington Edge, this former coaching inn has been sensitively renovated to retain its character. Inside there is a lounge with wooden panelling and beams, a restaurant to the left and a games room to the right. Food prepared from local seasonal produce is served daily. Families and pets are welcome but mobile phones are not, and their use incurs a fine. Thursday is musicians' night.
⛬Q♨❀⇌◐⊟Å⊟(30)♣P⅟

Grosmont

Crossing Club

Co-operative Building, Front Street, YO22 5QE (opp NYMR car park)
⏲ 8-11 (closed Mon winter) ☎ (01947) 895040
Beer range varies ⊞
Opposite the NYMR and Esk Valley railway stations, this railway-themed club was converted from the Co-operative store's upstairs delivery bay. Five busy handpumps, one usually from Wold Top, have served more than 700 different beers during the club's 10-year existence. CAMRA members are made most welcome. Access is through the ground level door (ring the bell). A summer beer festival is held and beer is also supplied for the Esk Valley Music Train that runs on Friday evenings during the summer. Q⇌⊟(99)♣

Hampsthwaite

Joiners Arms

High Street, HG3 2EU (off A59)
⏲ 12-2, 5-11; 12-11 Sat & Sun ☎ (01423) 771673
Rudgate Viking; Tetley Bitter ⊞
On entering this popular village local visitors are presented with the traditional choice of tap room or lounge, but behind the bar these are linked by an unusual snug with a stone floor and vaulted ceiling, which was once the cellar. The lounge features an inglenook fireplace and leads to an attractive dining room adorned with a collection of rare gravy boats. Here food is served Wednesday to Saturday evenings, although bar meals are available every lunchtime. Q◐⊟⊟(24)P

Hardraw

Green Dragon

DL8 3LZ 868913
⏲ 10-1am (2am Fri & Sat) ☎ (01969) 667392
🌐 greendragonhardraw.com
Taylor Landlord; Theakston Best Bitter, Old Peculier; guest beers ⊞
Rambling old Dales pub of great character at the entrance to England's highest single drop waterfall Hardraw Force, a noted beauty spot (£2 admission, pay at the bar). With a strong commitment to traditional beer and music, the pub host several folk festivals and a brass band contest each year. The main bar is divided into three rooms featuring stone flagged floors, low beams and two impressive ranges, with guest beers in summer. Meals are served all day, every day. Opening times may vary in winter. ⛬❀⇌◐⊟ÅP

Harrogate

Blues Bar

4 Montpelier Parade, HG1 2JJ (by Betty's Tea Room)
⏲ 10 (12 Sun)-1am ☎ (01423) 566881 🌐 bluesbar.org.uk
Beer range varies ⊞
Small single-room bar in the town centre overlooking the lovely Montpelier gardens. Noted for live music seven days a week, with two sessions on a Sunday, it is very popular with music lovers and can get very busy. Modelled on an Amsterdam café bar, it has been going for more than 20 years. Food is served lunchtimes (except Sun) and upstairs there is an Egyptian restaurant open from Tuesday to Saturday. ◐⇌⊟

Coach & Horses

16 West Park, HG1 1BJ (opp The Stray)
⏲ 11-11; 12-10.30 Sun ☎ (01423) 568371
🌐 thecoachandhorses.net
Copper Dragon Golden Pippin; Daleside Bitter; Taylor Landlord; Tetley Bitter; guest beers ⊞
A central bar is surrounded by snugs and alcoves, creating a cosy atmosphere. Excellent meals are served at lunchtime and there are frequent themed food evenings. Many of these, together with a Sunday-night quiz, raise money for a local children's hospice. Five real ales are usually sourced from local breweries, including one from Rooster's always available. A few tables and chairs are placed outside for smokers. Window boxes provide year-round colour, with a quite spectacular display in summer. Q◐⇌⊟(36)

Empress

10 Church Square, HG1 4SP (nr roundabout at jct of Wetherby and Knaresborough roads)
⏲ 11.30 (12 Sun)-11.30 ☎ (01423) 567629
Daleside Blonde; John Smith's Bitter; Tetley Bitter; guest beer ⊞
Situated in the oldest part of Harrogate, this increasingly popular pub has a central entrance lobby separating the pool table/TV area from the large, comfortable lounge. Guest beers usually include another from the Daleside list or one from Bowland brewery. Good value food is served every lunchtime and some evenings, including Sunday. The large upstairs room, overlooking the famous Stray, can be hired for functions such as parties and meetings. ◐⇌⊟♣

Hales Bar ✔

1-3 Crescent Road, HG1 2RS
⏲ 12-midnight (1am Thu-Sat; 11.30 Sun) ☎ (01423) 725570
🌐 halesbar.co.uk
Copper Dragon Golden Pippin; Daleside Special Bitter; Draught Bass; Taylor Golden Best, Landlord ⊞
Harrogate's oldest pub, on CAMRA's Regional Inventory of Historic Pub Interiors, and used in the filming of Chariots of Fire. The lounge has a Victorian-style interior with gas lighting over the

bar, stuffed birds and old brewery prints and mirrors. There are six handpumps, one serving a changing range of guest beers. Karaoke features on a Thursday night and occasional party nights are hosted – see the website for details. The pub prides itself on its floral displays in season. Food is available lunchtimes and evenings. ◑◐⊟♿⇌⊟⚐

Montpellier

14 Montpellier Parade, HG1 2TG (near Betty's Tea Room)

⏲ 11-11 ☎ (01423) 818247

Black Sheep Best Bitter; Daleside Old Leg Over; Taylor Landlord Ⓗ

Readily accessible from both bus and train stations, this single-room pub offers three locally brewed real ales. The pub is situated in the Montpellier Quarter and framed prints with French commentary help preserve this connection. Photographs of an older Harrogate also adorn the walls. The clientele is a mix of all age groups. Tables are placed outside in summer and the pub looks out on to beautiful gardens. A number of antique and art shops are nearby. ❀◑⇌⊟(36)⚐

Old Bell Tavern ✔

6 Royal Parade, HG1 2SZ (500m W of A61)

⏲ 12-11 (10.30 Sun) ☎ (01423) 507930

Black Sheep Best Bitter; Theakston Best Bitter; guest beers Ⓗ

Originally the site of the Blue Bell Inn, which closed in 1815 and was later demolished, the Old Bell opened in 1999. In 2001 it expanded into the former Farrah's toffee shop – plenty of Farrah memorabilia is still on show. Eight real ales are always available; many are local and the guest ales always include a Rooster's, Timothy Taylor and a mild, plus a good range of bottled beers. Excellent quality bar food is served every day and a separate upstairs restaurant opens evenings (not Sun).
Q◑◐⇌⊟

Tap & Spile

Tower Street, HG1 1HS (100m E of A61)

⏲ 11.30-11; 12-10.30 Sun ☎ (01423) 526785

Rooster's Yankee; Theakston Old Peculier; guest beers Ⓗ

A central bar links the three drinking areas in this quality ale house. Visitors are spoilt for choice with a range of guest beers, many sourced from local micros. The venue is well established and popular with all age groups. A quiz is held on Monday evening, folk music on Tuesday and rock music on Thursday. Darts is played on alternate Tuesdays and Wednesdays. Some outdoor seating is provided.
❀⇌⊟(36)♣●⚐

Winter Gardens ✔

4 Royal Baths, HG1 2RR

⏲ 9am-midnight (1am Fri & Sat) ☎ (01423) 877010

Greene King Ruddles Best Bitter, Abbot; Marston's Pedigree Ⓗ

Tasteful conversion of the main hall of the Victorian Royal Baths complex, retaining many original features, with Harrogate Turkish Baths next door. The sweeping stone staircase carries you down to the vast bar area. At least five guest ales are always available at reasonable prices, plus a comprehensive range of bottled beers. Regular mini beer festivals are hosted. Good food is served all day. Children are welcome until 9pm on weekdays. There is a separate function room and courtyard drinking area. ♉❀◑◐♿⇌⊟●⚐

Hawes

Fountain Hotel

Market Place, DL8 3RD

⏲ 11.30-midnight ☎ (01969) 667206

🌐 fountainhawes.co.uk

Black Sheep Best Bitter, Ale, Riggwelter; John Smith's Bitter; guest beer Ⓗ

The capital of Upper Wensleydale, Hawes is home to the famous Creamery, Ropeworks and Countryside Museum, as well as being on the Pennine Way and a centre for many other walks and events. Under the same management for 22 years, the Fountain has an opened-out front bar serving bar meals, and a large dining room to the rear. Tuesday market days are especially busy. On a fine day try people-watching with a pint on the pavement-side patio.
♨♉❀⇌◑◐⛺⊟(156,157)♣P⚐

Helwith Bridge

Helwith Bridge ✔

BD24 0EH (turn off B6479 at Helwith Bridge and cross river) SD810695

⏲ 2.30 (12 Fri-Sun)-11 ☎ (01729) 860220

🌐 helwithbridge.com

Caledonian 80; John Smith's Bitter; Three Peaks Brewery Pen-y-Ghent Bitter; Wells Bombardier; guest beers Ⓗ

Despite its relative isolation in the tiny hamlet of Helwith Bridge, this is a welcoming, thriving, no-frills local, run with warmth and a sense of humour. The three separate rooms are stone flagged and adorned with railway artefacts, paintings and photos. Pie and peas are served all day every day, with full meals available Thursday to Sunday evenings, Saturday and Sunday lunch. The three guest beers are usually sourced from the Heineken list. ♨❀◑◐♿⛺⊟(B1)♣P⚐

High Leven

Fox Covert

Low Lane, TS15 9JW (on A1044, 1½ miles E of Yarm)

⏲ 11.30-11 (midnight Fri & Sat); 12-11 Sun

☎ (01642) 760033 🌐 thefoxcovert.com

Caledonian Deuchars IPA; Theakston Old Peculier Ⓗ

A previous local CAMRA Pub of the Season award winner, this popular, long-established and uniquely-named inn has been in the same family for more than 25 years. Originally a farmhouse, it is built in the traditional longhouse style, with whitewashed walls and a pantiled roof. Inside it is warm and cosy, with two open fires and two drinking areas offering superbly kept beers. The pub is noted for its food, served all day every day. Conference facilities are available.
♨❀◑◐♿⊟(507)P

Hinderwell

Brown Cow

55 High Street, TS13 5ET (on A174)

⏲ 11 (12 Sun)-1am ☎ (01947) 840694

Beer range varies Ⓗ

Between the moors and the coast, this family-run pub has a strong local following as well as attracting holiday visitors. Two busy handpumps serve weaker beers mid-week and stronger beers at weekends. The pub supports darts teams, charity nights, dominoes and whist drives, and has a separate pool room. Smokers are well accommodated. Children and dogs are also welcome. There are snacks in addition to lunchtime and evening meals. Accommodation is in three bedrooms. A previous local CAMRA Pub of the Season award winner. ♨☕❀⇄◑⊟♿⊟(5)♣P⊱

Hutton Rudby

King's Head

36 North Side, TS15 0DA (W end of village)
⌚ 12-11.30 (12.30am Fri & Sat) ☎ (01642) 700342
Camerons Strongarm; Jennings Cocker Hoop, Cumberland Ale; guest beer Ⓗ
Set in a beautiful village, this previous local CAMRA Pub of the Season award winner is a traditional community pub comprising a main bar and a snug where children are welcome. Four handpumps include a guest from the Marston's range. Happy hour on Friday has become a 20-year-old tradition for some. Friendly locals, real fires, a popular quiz night on Tuesday and monthly jazz/blues nights add to the experience. Outside is a smokers' paradise, complete with TV. ♨☕❀◑⊟(82)⊱

Kettlewell

Kings Head

The Green, BD23 5RD (top of village near church)
⌚ 11-midnight (12.30am Fri & Sat); 12-midnight Sun
☎ (01756) 760242 🌐 kingsheadkettlewell.co.uk
Black Sheep Best Bitter; Tetley Bitter; Yorkshire Dales Butter Tubs Ⓗ
Situated in a village mentioned in the Domesday Book, this 17th-century hostelry boasts an impressive inglenook fireplace and flagstone floors. The simple single-bar interior welcomes visitors to the Yorkshire Dales as well as providing a haven for locals. Food is locally sourced and accommodation is available. The pub welcomes walkers and dogs. A regular outlet for the local Yorkshire Dales brewery.
♨❀⇄◑Å⊟(72,72R,874)♣P

Kirby Hill

Shoulder of Mutton

DL11 7JH (2½ miles from A66, 4 miles NW of Richmond)
⌚ 12-3 (Sat only), 6-11.30; 12-3, 6-11 Sun
☎ (01748) 822772 🌐 shoulderofmutton.net
Daleside Bitter; guest beers Ⓗ
Ivy-fronted country inn in a beautiful hillside setting overlooking Lower Teesdale and the ruins of Ravensworth Castle. The pub has an opened-out front bar that links the lounge with a cosy restaurant to the rear. Three guest beers are chosen by the pub's regulars. Situated on the edge of the Yorkshire Dales, this is a popular venue for walkers. There are five en-suite guest bedrooms available. Highly-recommended, excellent food is available Wednesday to Sunday, although the bar area remains for drinkers. ♨Q❀⇄◑⊟♣P⊱

Kirk Smeaton

Shoulder of Mutton

Main Street, WF8 3JY
⌚ 5 (11.30 Sun)-midnight; 12-1am Fri & Sat
☎ (01977) 620348
Black Sheep Best Bitter; guest beer Ⓗ
Traditional village inn comprising a large lounge with open fires and a cosy, dark-panelled snug. The superb beers are sourced directly from independent breweries – the guest is usually from Dark Horse. Outside there is ample parking and a spacious beer garden complete with a covered and heated shelter for smokers. This attractive pub is popular with the local community and walkers from the nearby Went Valley and Brockadale Nature Reserve. Quiz night is Tuesday.
♨❀⊟(409)P⊱

Kirkby Overblow

Shoulder of Mutton ✔

Main Street, HG3 1HD
⌚ 11.30-3, 6-11; 12-11.30 Sun ☎ (01423) 871205
🌐 shoulderatkirkbyoverblow.com
Black Sheep Best Bitter; Taylor Landlord; Tetley Bitter; guest beers Ⓗ
This long-established village hostelry has gained an enviable reputation for good food. The L-shaped bar covers two servery areas, with welcoming real fires greeting visitors. The chef/proprietor is a real ale enthusiast and has won awards for the quality of his beer. Occasional guest beers are served in special glasses. A converted outbuilding houses a village store. ♨Q❀◑♿P

Knaresborough

Blind Jack's

18a Market Place, HG5 8AL
⌚ 4 (5.30 Mon; 3 Fri)-11; 12-11 Sat; 12-10.30 Sun
☎ (01423) 869148 🌐 blindjacks.co.uk
Black Sheep Best Bitter; Harviestoun Bitter & Twisted; Taylor Landlord; guest beers Ⓗ
Cosy multi-roomed pub with bare brick walls, wooden floorboards and dark wood panelling. A vibrant, award-winning ale house, it provides a focal point for both locals and the many visitors who appreciate the excellent selection of beers, warm ambience and lively banter. The changing guest beers usually include a mild. Cheese and pâté platters complement the beers. Of particular interest is the trompe-l'oeil painting to the exterior which features the pub's namesake Blind Jack Metcalfe. Q⇌⊟(100,101,102)🍺

Mitre Hotel ✔

4 Station Road, HG5 9AA (opp railway station)
⌚ 12-11 (midnight Fri & Sat) ☎ (01423) 868948
🌐 themitreinn.co.uk
Black Sheep Ale; Copper Dragon Golden Pippin; Thwaites Wainwright; guest beers Ⓗ
This venue comprises a split-level lounge, side function room, brasserie/restaurant and an outside drinking area. Five guest ales featured include a dark beer, rotating beers from the Rooster's/Outlaw label, Timothy Taylor and mainly local beers. Look out for the speciality bottled beer menu; some foreign beers are also available on draught. There is live acoustic music on Sunday evenings. Dogs are welcome.
Q☕❀⇄◑♿⇌⊟(1A,1B,1C)

Langdale End

Moorcock Inn

YO13 0BN SE938912
⌚ closed Mon; 11-2, 6.30-11 (Thu-Sat only winter); 12-3, 6.30-10.30 Sun ☎ (01723) 882268
Beer range varies Ⓗ/Ⓖ

Sympathetically restored some years ago, the pub is situated in the picturesque hamlet of Langdale End, near the end of the Dalby Forest Drive. The beers are usually from York, Wold Top and Slater's breweries, and served through a hatch to both bars. Open daily (except Mon) after Easter but winter hours vary, so ring to check. There is a grassy area for outdoor drinking and/or smoking. Bar meals prepared from local produce include a popular steak pie. ♨Q❀◑▲♣P⁄

Lastingham

Blacksmith's Arms

Front Street, YO62 6TL (4 miles N of A170 between Helmsley and Pickering) SE728904
⊙ 12 (Tue 5)-11 ☎ (01751) 417247
⊕ blacksmithslastingham.co.uk
Theakston Best Bitter; guest beers ⊞
Twice winner of York CAMRA Country Pub of the Season, this pretty stone inn is in a conservation village opposite St Mary's Church, famous for its 11th-century crypt. The cosy bar has a York range lit in winter. A snug and two dining rooms complete the interior. Excellent food including local game is served lunchtimes and evenings (no food Tue lunch winter) alongside interesting guest beers. Well worth seeking out, this remote pub also has a secluded rear beer garden. ♨Q❀⊨◑

Lealholm

Board Inn

Village Green, YO21 2AJ (by River Esk)
⊙ 9am-midnight (2am Fri & Sat) ☎ (01947) 897279
Black Sheep Best Bitter; Camerons Strongarm; guest beers ⊞
This family-run, picturesque 17th-century free house has four handpumps, three real ciders and a huge selection of whiskies. The menu, which reflects the seasons, is virtually all sourced within 500 metres of the pub. Breakfasts are served from 9am, while the restaurant stays open all day. And how many licensees air-cure their hams, keep 45 laying hens, a herd of prime beef, and also have local fishing rights? A beer festival is held at Easter on the riverside patio. There are five letting bedrooms. ♨Q☕❀⊨◑⊟♿▲⇌⊡(99)♣●P⁄

Leavening

Jolly Farmer

Main Street, YO17 9SA SE785631
⊙ 7 (6 Fri)-midnight; 12-midnight Sat & Sun
☎ (01653) 658276
Black Sheep Best Bitter; Taylor Landlord; Tetley Bitter; guest beers ⊞
This 17th-century pub is on the edge of the Yorkshire Wolds between York and Malton. The multi-room interior has been extended but still retains a cosiness in two small bars, a family room and dining rooms. Former York CAMRA Pub of the Year, varied guest beers from independent breweries and two beer festivals per year make this an essential visit. The extensive menu includes locally-caught game dishes in season.
♨☕❀◑♿♣P⁄⊓

Long Preston

Maypole Inn 🍷 ✔

Main Street, BD23 4PH
⊙ 11 (12 Sun)-11 ☎ (01729) 840219 ⊕ maypole.co.uk
Moorhouse's Premier Bitter; Taylor Landlord; guest beers ⊞
Situated on the village green complete with maypole, this friendly, welcoming pub has been in the same capable hands for 26 years. Dogs are welcome in the tap room, which has carved Victorian bench seating. Good quality home-cooked food is available all day in the separate dining room or in either bar. Two guest beers are usually available, often from Bowland, Moorhouse's or other local breweries. Two Westons ciders are served. Local CAMRA Branch Pub of the Year 2010.
♨Q❀⊨◑⊟▲⇌⊡(580)♣●P⁄

Low Worsall

Ship

TS15 9PH (on B1264)
⊙ 12-11 (10.30 Sun) ☎ (01642) 780314
Greene King Old Speckled Hen; guest beers ⊞
The Ship sits beside the old Richmond to Yarm turnpike and near a disused quay that marks the centuries-old limit of navigation for boats on the River Tees. Guest beers are usually premium bitters, while the pub is known for the quality of its good value food, served all day every day. Smaller portions are available for those unable to tackle the impressively large helpings. The pub is child friendly, with a small play area in the garden.
Q❀◑♿P⁄

Malton

Crown Hotel (Suddaby's)

12 Wheelgate, YO17 7HP
⊙ 11-11 (11.30 Fri & Sat); 12-11 Sun ☎ (01653) 692038
⊕ suddabys.co.uk
Black Sheep Best Bitter; John Smith's Bitter; Suddaby's Double Chance, seasonal beers; guest beers ⊞
This Grade II-listed market town pub has been in the same family for 139 years. Double Chance is brewed by Leeds Brewery, other Suddaby's beers by Brown Cow. Beer festivals are held at Easter, summer and Christmas. The on-site shop stocks over 200 different beers, specialising in Belgian and German brews, British micro-breweries, wine and breweriana. A covered smoking patio is at the rear. Accommodation includes two en-suite family rooms – a small discount is available for CAMRA members. ♨Q❀⊨▲⇌⊡♣P⁄

Manfield

Crown Inn

Vicars Lane, DL2 2RF (500m from B6275)
⊙ 5 (12 Sat)-11.30; 12-11 Sun ☎ (01325) 374243
⊕ crowninn.villagebrewer.co.uk
Village White Boar; guest beers ⊞
Yorkshire CAMRA Pub of the Year 2005 and a regular local award winner, this attractive 18th-century inn sits in a quiet village. It has two bars, a games room, a large beer garden and a trellised heated smoking area. A mix of locals and visitors creates a friendly atmosphere. Seven guest beers come from micro-breweries countrywide, along with up to two ciders or perries. Three beer festivals and a cider festival are held, and there is a monthly quiz on a Tuesday night. Dog friendly.
♨Q❀◑⊡(29)♣●P⁄⊓

Masham

Black Sheep Brewery Visitors Centre ✔

Wellgarth, HG4 4EN (follow the brown tourist signs)
⏲ 10.30-4.30 (11 Thu-Sat) ☎ (01765) 680101
🌐 blacksheepbrewery.com
Black Sheep Best Bitter, Ale, Riggwelter H
This popular tourist attraction is housed in the spacious former maltings. As well as offering the opportunity to sample the brewery's products at the 'baaar', there is a high quality café/bistro serving snacks and full meals, with an emphasis on local ingredients. A 'sheepy' shop stocks the bottled product and Black Sheep souvenirs. Visitors can book a 'shepherded' tour of the brewery. A small garden overlooks scenic lower Wensleydale and the River Ure. Q❀◑♿🚌P

White Bear ✔

12 Crosshills, HG4 4EN (follow brown tourist signs on A6108)
⏲ 12-11 (10.30 Sun) ☎ (01765) 689319
🌐 thewhitebearhotel.co.uk
Theakston Best Bitter, Black Bull Bitter, XB, Old Peculier; guest beers H
A recently extended and refurbished brewery tap – the extension making extra room for diners as well as adding 14 bedrooms and conference facilities. The pub has not lost any of its charm as an award-winning hostelry and is a great favourite with the locals, as well as directors and staff from the Theakston Brewery. The full range of the brewery's products is usually available. Outside is a pleasant drinking and dining area. ♨❀◑♿🚌♣P

Middlesbrough

Star

14 Southfield Road, TS1 3BX
⏲ 11-11 (1am Fri & Sat); 12-11 Sun ☎ (01642) 245307
Beer range varies H
A large and very popular pub situated opposite the university campus, recently sympathetically modernised. With a licensee dedicated to promoting a wide variety of real ales, four beers are usually available, together with Westons Old Rosie cider. A contemporary, relaxed atmosphere prevails, with sofas and easy chairs adding to the ambience. The pub attracts a wide-ranging clientele and gets extremely busy at weekends. Good value pub food is on offer. The smoking area is heated and covered. ❀◑♿⇌🚌

Newton-on-Ouse

Blacksmith's Arms

Cherry Tree Avenue, YO30 2BN
⏲ 5.30 (12 Sat)-11; 12-3, 5.30-11 Fri; 12-9.30 Sun
☎ (01347) 848249
Jennings Bitter; Ringwood Best Bitter H
A former CAMRA Pub of the Season, this comfortable L-shaped pub has a dining area at one end, bar in the middle and raised area with pool table and retractable TV screen at the other. Note the interesting old photographs of the village and old boards advertising various beers including Cameron's. Four beers from the Marston's range are usually available. It has a covered and heated smoking area. The splendid Beningborough Hall is nearby. ♨❀◑♣P

Northallerton

Standard

24 High Street, DL7 8EE (on A167, 400m N of town centre opp Sainsbury's)
⏲ 12-2.30, 5-11.30; 12-11.30 Fri-Sun ☎ (01609) 772719
🌐 thestandard-pub.co.uk
Caledonian Deuchars IPA; Hambleton Stallion; Taylor Landlord; guest beer H
Want to see a real Jet Provost aircraft close up? The Standard's beer garden is the place, with an example restored for display. Located just north of the town centre, the pub is named after the famous nearby Battle of the Standard of 1138, an English victory over the Scots. A real community local, it offers good value, hearty food daily (no food Sun-Tue eves) in the opened-out, stone-flagged bar, and is home to the Stallions – the local Rugby League club. Spring bank holiday sees an annual beer festival. Q❀◑🚌♣

Station Hotel

2 Boroughbridge Road, Romanby, DL7 8AN (outside railway station)
⏲ 12-2 (3 Sat), 5-11; 12-3, 8-11 Sun ☎ (01609) 772053
Caledonian Deuchars IPA; John Smith's Bitter; Tetley Bitter; guest beer H
An imposing Edwardian building prominently located near the railway station. Previously known as the Railway Hotel, as can be seen from the impressive etched windows, other period features include a lovely tiled entrance hall, while the bar has been sympathetically renovated. Ten rooms are available for accommodation and food is served Monday-Thursday evenings. Sunday lunch is very popular. ♨Q❀◑⇌🚌♣P

Tithe Bar & Brasserie ✔

2 Friarage Street, DL6 1DP (just off High Street near hospital)
⏲ 12-11 (midnight Fri & Sat) ☎ (01609) 778482
Beer range varies H
Just off the town's busy High Street, this CAMRA award-winning bar is part of the small Market Town Taverns chain, renowned for its strong commitment to cask beer. The six handpumps usually feature ales from Black Sheep, Timothy Taylor and Durham breweries, plus guests from smaller brewers, supplemented by an array of foreign beers. The downstairs bar has the feel of a continental beer café, offering good value meals, and there is a brasserie upstairs, open Tuesday-Saturday evenings. Q◑♿⇌🚌♣

Old Malton

Royal Oak

47 Town Street, YO17 7HB (400m off A64 Malton bypass)
⏲ closed Mon; 5-midnight; 12-1am Fri & Sat; 12-midnight Sun
☎ (01653) 699334
Tetley Bitter; York Guzzler; guest beers H
Popular hostelry set in a picturesque village close to the Eden Camp military museum. At the front of the pub is a cosy snug, to the rear is a larger room leading to an extensive beer garden with a large covered smoking area. Guest beers are usually from York or Moorhouse's. Traditional meals featuring locally-sourced produce are served weekend lunchtimes, Friday and Saturday night – Thursday is pie night. The bus stops outside. Finalist CAMRA Branch Pub of the Year 2009.
♨Q❀◑▲⇌🚌♣P

Osgodby

Wadkin Arms ✓

Cliffe Road, YO8 5HU (just off A63 in village) SE641335
☼ 12-11 (midnight Fri & Sat) ☎ (01757) 702391
⊕ wadkinarms.co.uk
John Smith's Bitter; Rudgate Ruby Mild; guest
beers ⊞
Cosy old pub in the centre of the village, featuring
real fires and wholesome food served at limited
times – teatimes can be very busy. Guest beers
regularly come from nearby breweries such as
Great Heck and Brown Cow. The pub has a good
local atmosphere and is frequented by both
Osgodby residents and nearby villagers alike.
🏚🛏🌮♣P🍴

Osmotherley

Golden Lion

6 West End, DL6 3AA (in village centre, 1 mile E of A19)
☼ 12-2.30 (not Mon & Tue), 6-11; 12-midnight Sat; 12-10.30
Sun ☎ (01609) 883526 ⊕ goldenlionosmotherley.co.uk
Taylor Best Bitter, Landlord; guest beers ⊞
On the edge of the National Park in a popular
walking area, whitewashed stone walls with
mirrors, candlelit tables at night and a magnificent
fireplace distinguish this bar. There is a restaurant
upstairs and tables on the pavement outside.
Popular with diners, the emphasis here is on food,
but drinkers are welcome at the bar and there is a
strong local trade. Guest ales include one from a
local Yorkshire brewery. A beer festival is hosted in
November. 🏚Q🌮🛏◑▲🚌(80,89)🍴

Picton

Station

TS15 0AE (at level crossing on Kirklevington-Picton rd)
☼ 11-2.30 (Sat only), 6-11; 11-11.30 Sun ☎ (01642) 700067
Black Sheep Best Bitter; Taylor Landlord ⊞
Situated beside the Middlesbrough to York railway,
this remote pub is well worth the journey, though
sadly not by train, as the adjacent station was
closed in the 1960s. The one-roomed bar is
warmed by an open fire, where railway
memorabilia adorns the walls. The two ales are
served alongside an impressive and varied food
menu, using local produce where possible, with
portion sizes renowned for their generosity.
🏚Q🌮◑P

Pool in Wharfedale

Hunters Inn

Harrogate Road, LS21 2PS (on A658 between Otley and
Harrogate)
☼ 11-11; 12-10.30 Sun ☎ (0113) 2841090
Tetley Bitter; Theakston Best Bitter; guest beers ⊞
When you enter this welcoming roadside pub,
don't forget to check out the impressive range of
up to nine cask ales shown on the board on the
right. A separate board gives tasting notes. The
large single-room interior incorporates a raised
area with a warming real fire during the colder
months. Well-behaved children are allowed in the
pub until 9pm accompanied by an adult.
🏚🌮🚌♣P🍴

Potto

Dog & Gun ✓

2 Cooper Lane, DL6 3HQ
☼ 12-3, 5.30-midnight; 12-midnight Sat; 12-11.30 Sun
☎ (01642) 700232 ⊕ thedogandgunpotto.com
Black Sheep Best Bitter; guest beers ⊞
This recently refurbished country ale house is under
the stewardship of an enthusiastic licensee who
only provides the very best in food, drink, service
and accommodation. Friendly staff ensure a laid-
back ambience prevails in this contemporary
setting comprising a comfortable main bar, classy
restaurant, private dining areas, five luxury
bedrooms and conference facilities. Outside, open
terraces are ideal for summer drinking. Sunday
lunches are served until 6pm. CAMRA members
receive a discount across the range of real ales.
🏚🌮🛏◑&P

Rawcliffe

Lysander Arms

Manor Lane, YO30 5TZ (Manor Lane is opp Park & Ride
site on A19 N of York) SE582550
☼ 11-11 (12.30am Sat) ☎ (01904) 640845
⊕ lysanderarms.co.uk
Caledonian Deuchars IPA; Copper Dragon Golden
Pippin; York Guzzler; guest beers ⊞
A little gem hidden away at the end of a new
housing estate, this building replaces the original
caravan site clubhouse. The pub still has a 10-pitch
caravan site and is popular with Dutch and German
visitors. Well-kept LocAle is served alongside basic
pub grub in the bar area. There is also a dedicated
restaurant area. The lounge is big enough to have
two sports showing on large-screen TVs and to
leave a quiet space. Free Wi-Fi is available.
🛏🌮◑&▲♣P🍴

Riccall

Greyhound Inn ✓

Main Street, YO19 6TE (on A19 10 miles S of York)
SE620380
☼ 12 (3 Mon-Wed Nov-Feb)-midnight; 12-11.30 Sun
☎ (01757) 249101 ⊕ thegreyhoundriccall.co.uk
Copper Dragon Golden Pippin; Tetley Mild, Bitter;
guest beers ⊞
Situated in a quiet village between Selby and York,
this pub offers a friendly welcome and an
enthusiastic guest beer policy. Home-made food
produced by the landlord is available weekdays
except Monday (Sat and Sun lunchtime only).
Home to keen darts and dominoes teams, it is also
popular with cyclists and walkers using the York-
Selby cycle path (note the old Cyclist's Touring Club
emblem on the front). There is a large garden to
the rear for summer meals and drinks.
🏚Q🌮🛏◑🚌(415)♣P🍴

Richmond

Ralph Fitz Randal ✓

6 Queens Road, DL10 4AE (edge of town centre on main
Scotch Corner rd)
☼ 9am-midnight (1am Fri & Sat) ☎ (01748) 828080
Greene King Ruddles Best Bitter, Abbot; guest
beers ⊞
Wetherspoon hostelry in a converted post office on
three levels, with an informal seating area just
inside the main entrance, a main bar area a few

steps down and a large family dining area to the rear. The interior is simple and modern with the minimum of fuss, sometimes reverberating to the sound of loud conversation; flat-screen TVs offer solace for sports fans although the volume is usually quite low. Themed monthly beer festivals feature up to eight guest beers focusing on a local brewery or a particular beer style. ❀◑♿🚌🍎⁄–

Ripon

One-Eyed Rat 🏆 ✔

51 Allhallowgate, HG4 1LQ (near bus station)
⏲ 5 (12 Fri & Sat)-11; 12-10.30 Sun ☎ (01765) 607704
🌐 oneeyedrat.com
Black Sheep Best Bitter; guest beers Ⓗ

Situated in a terrace of 200-year-old houses, the small frontage gives no clue to the award-winning beer garden situated at the rear. This independent family-run pub is everything a good cask ale house should be, with a warm and welcoming atmosphere complete with coal fire plus one regular and six changing guest beers. There is always a pump dedicated to a stout/mild or porter and another for a stronger beer at around 5% ABV. ♨Q❀🚌♣🍎⁄–

Royal Oak ✔

36 Kirkgate, HG4 1PB (just off Market Square)
⏲ 11-11 (midnight Fri & Sat); 12-10.30 Sun
☎ (01765) 602284 🌐 royaloakripon.co.uk
Timothy Taylor Golden Best, Best Bitter, Landlord, Ram Tam Ⓗ

This old coaching inn adjacent to the cathedral and Market Square retains its original facade but has an airy feel to its interior. While stocking the full range of Taylor's beers there is also a strong emphasis on locally-sourced food. Nearby attractions are Fountains Abbey and Ripon Racecourse. At the Obelisk in Market Square every night at 9pm the Ripon Hornblower sets the night watch – which has happened for 1,000 years. The pub has six en-suite bedrooms. ♨❀🛏◑🚌⁄–

Robin Hood's Bay

Victoria Hotel

Station Road, YO22 4RL (at top of cliff)
⏲ 12-11 Fri-Sun & summer; 12-2, 6-11 winter
☎ (01947) 880205 🌐 thevictoriahotelrobinhoodsbay.co.uk
Camerons Bitter, Strongarm; Daleside Old Leg Over; guest beers Ⓗ

A warm welcome awaits you at this family-run 19th-century hotel, set in a superb location on the edge of the cliffs, overlooking the bay of this picturesque seaside resort. The busy and friendly bar, popular with regulars and visitors, serves six beers including three guests. A good value, highly regarded menu, including daily specials, is served lunchtimes and evenings. There are stunning views from the restaurant and gardens. A separate family room is available and there are 11 letting bedrooms. ♨Q👶❀🛏◑🚌(56,93)P▯

Saltburn-by-the-Sea

Saltburn Cricket, Bowls & Tennis Club

Marske Mill Lane, TS12 1HJ (next to leisure centre)
⏲ 8-midnight (1am Fri & Sat); 2-midnight Sat match days; 11.30-3, 8-midnight Sun ☎ (01287) 622761
Beer range varies Ⓗ

This private sports club, which is well-supported by the local community, fields cricket, tennis and bowls teams, and also acts as the watering hole for the local diving club. A spacious lounge can be divided for different functions and social events. The balcony, ideal for those lazy sunny afternoons, overlooks the cricket field. Two varying beers are served. Casual visitors are made most welcome without having to join the club.
❀♿⇌🚌(X4,48)♣P⁄–

Sawdon

Anvil Inn

Main Street, YO13 9DY (2 miles off A170)
⏲ closed Mon; 12-2.30, 6.30-11; 12-3, 7-10.30 Sun
☎ (01723) 859896 🌐 theanvilinnsawdon.co.uk
Copper Dragon Best Bitter; guest beers Ⓗ

A heart of the village pub, on the edge of the North York Moors National Park, Dalby Forest and close to the coast, in excellent walking, cycling and mountain biking country. Formerly the village blacksmith's, it still retains the forge and of course the anvil. A cosy bar, with a separate lounge and dining area, serves two guest beers from local independents, and food of the highest standard (booking recommended; no food Sun eve). There are two well-appointed letting cottages.
♨❀◑♣P

Scarborough

Angel

46 North Street, YO11 1DF
⏲ 11-midnight ☎ (01723) 365504
Copper Dragon Golden Pippin; John Smith's Bitter; Tetley Bitter; Wells Bombardier Ⓗ

Friendly town-centre local close to the main shopping area, with a single-room horseshoe bar displaying an excellent collection of saucy seaside postcards. An interest in sport and games is reflected in the impressive array of trophies won by various pub teams and the large-screen TVs for viewing sporting events. Occasional guest beers are added in summer. Note the Tardis-like quality of the surprisingly spacious and well-appointed patio garden at the rear. ❀⇌🚌♣⁄–

Cellars

35-37 Valley Road, YO11 2LX
⏲ 4-11; 12-midnight Sat & Sun; 12-10.30 Sun
☎ (01723) 367158 🌐 scarborough-brialene.co.uk
Black Sheep Riggwelter; guest beers Ⓗ

Family-run pub converted from the cellars of a Victorian house. The bar keeps six beers – ales come from Black Sheep and Durham plus guests mainly from Yorkshire micros. Excellent, good value, home-cooked food made with locally sourced produce is served lunchtimes and evenings. Live music night is Saturday, with an open mike night on Wednesday. Tuesday is quiz night and Sky Sports. Beer festivals are an occasional feature. The patio gardens are popular for alfresco drinking. Children and dogs are welcome. 👶❀🛏◑⛺⇌🚌♣P⁄–

Leeds Arms

26 St Mary's Road, YO11 1QW
⏲ 11-11; 11.30-3, 7-11 Wed; 11-midnight Fri & Sat; 12-11 Sun ☎ (01723) 361699
Draught Bass; Taylor Landlord; guest beers Ⓗ

Small, thriving one-roomed pub situated in the Old Town area of Scarborough behind the harbour. Fishing and yachting pictures and memorabilia adorn the walls. An eclectic mix of locals gives rise to lively conversation. Up to four guest beers are served, especially in the summer season. There is always a magnificent display of hanging baskets outside. The pub is dog but not sprog friendly! Q

North Riding Hotel

161-163 North Marine Road, YO12 7HU

12-midnight (1am Fri & Sat) ☎ (01723) 370004

northridinghotel.co.uk

Taylor Landlord; York Guzzler; guest beers H

Friendly community pub situated on the North Bay, just down from the cricket ground and opposite the bowls centre. Local CAMRA Town Pub of the Year in 2009, it has served well over 1,000 guest beers. Two or more guests come from micro-breweries – Elland, Thornbridge and Yorkshire Dales feature regularly. Monthly brewery weekends are also held. The pub has a public bar, a quiet, refurbished lounge and an upstairs dining room serving home-cooked food. Quiz night is Thursday.

Q

Old Scalby Mills

Scalby Mills Road, YO12 6RP

11 (12 winter)-11 ☎ (01723) 500449

Copper Dragon Black Gold; Wold Top Premium; guest beers H

Popular seafront local, the building was originally a watermill but has seen many uses over the years – old photographs and prints chart its history. Admire the superb views of the North Bay from the sheltered patio or lounge. The Cleveland Way reaches the seafront here and there is a Sealife Centre nearby. Children are welcome in the lounge. Premium beer from the local Wold Top Brewery is only available here; guest beers invariably include a stout, porter or mild. Q (3A)

Scholars

Somerset Terrace, YO11 2PW

4.30 (12 Sat & Sun)-midnight ☎ (01723) 360084

Copper Dragon Golden Pippin; Hambleton Nightmare; Theakston Black Bull; guest beers H

A warm, friendly atmosphere prevails in this town centre pub located at the rear of the main shopping centre. It has a large front bar and a games room. Three handpumps serve rotating beers, mainly from Yorkshire Dales, York and Ossett breweries. Numerous screens show major sporting events. Twenty eight pints are the prize at the Thursday quiz, and more free beer can be won rolling dice on Monday, Tuesday, Wednesday and Sunday nights.

United Sports Bar

94-100 St Thomas Street, YO11 1DU (entrance opp Atlas Taxis off St Thomas Street)

4-midnight; 12-1am Fri & Sat; 12-midnight Sun

☎ (01723) 503350

John Smith's Bitter; guest beers H

A former social club now open to all, offering a warm welcome to locals and tourists alike. This comfortable bar is to be found situated on the first floor via a door opposite Atlas Taxis. The bar plays host to a number of indoor sports teams as well as a Sunday football team. Most major sports events are shown on TV. Live music plays on some Saturdays.

Valley

51 Valley Road, YO11 2LX

12-midnight (1am Thu-Sat) ☎ (01723) 372593

valleybar.co.uk

Theakston Best Bitter; guest beers H

CAMRA National Cider Pub of the Year 2007 and local CAMRA Town Pub of the Year 2005 and 2007. This family-run, multi-roomed pub has a popular cellar bar. Seven handpumps feature beers mainly from micro-breweries, plus up to eight real ciders and perries. One hundred different bottled Belgian beers are also stocked. Excellent, reasonably priced sandwiches are available all day. Want to stay in an award-winning pub? Accommodation is available at a discount to CAMRA members. Free Wi-Fi throughout.

Skipton

Devonshire

22 Newmarket Street, BD23 2HR

9-midnight (1am Fri & Sat) ☎ (01756) 692590

Greene King Ruddles Best Bitter, Abbot; guest beers H

Sympathetic Wetherspoon conversion of the Grade II-listed former town house of the Duke of Devonshire, dating from 1702. Four rooms of varying character give a choice of drinking environments, retaining some original features. The walls are decorated with old photographs of the building and its surroundings, and the impressive Queen Anne-style facade overlooks a large off-street patio drinking area. Busy Friday and Saturday nights.

Narrow Boat

38 Victoria Street, BD23 1JE (alleyway off Coach St near canal bridge)

12-11 ☎ (01756) 797922 markettowntaverns.co.uk

Black Sheep Best Bitter; Copper Dragon Best Bitter, Golden Pippin; Taylor Landlord; guest beers H

Market Town Taverns' pioneer free house is traditionally furnished with church pews and decorated with canal-themed murals. No piped music, jukebox or gaming machines disturb the conversation. Guest ales, always including a dark beer, are mainly from northern independents and there is a good selection of continental bottled and draught beers. A folk club is hosted on Monday evening and a quiz night on Wednesday. Children under 14 are admitted if dining with adults. Dogs with well-behaved owners are welcome.

Q

Red Lion Hotel

High Street, BD23 1DT

11-11 (midnight Fri & Sat) ☎ (01756) 790718

Greene King IPA, Old Speckled Hen, Abbot; guest beers H

Built in 1205, this is probably Skipton's oldest pub. Recently improved, it now serves up to eight real ales from the Greene King range and others. It can get busy at weekends and when major sporting events are shown on the large-screen TVs; the tasteful smoking area at the back has a TV so there is no need to miss the action. The main bar features a large original fireplace and there is a small, quieter room set back from the hubbub of the bar.

ENGLAND

Snape

Castle Arms

DL8 2TB (off B6268 Bedale-Masham road)
⏲ 12-3, 6-midnight (1am Thu-Sat) ☎ (01677) 470270
🌐 castlearmsinn.com
Banks's Bitter; Jennings Bitter; Marston's Pedigree; guest beer ⊞
This pretty village is handy for Thorpe Perrow Arboretum, a mile away. Catherine Parr, the wife who outlasted Henry VIII by far, once lived at Snape Castle, a short walk from the pub. The cosy stone-flagged bar has an impressive open fire and locally renowned food, served here and in the restaurant (no food Sun eve winter). Nine letting rooms and a small caravan park to the rear add to a thriving local trade. ♨Q❀⇌◑◐⊟Ä♣P

Snaygill

Copper Dragon Bistro

Snaygill Industrial Estate, Keighley Road, BD23 2QR (just off A6131, at Snaygill Ind Est)
⏲ 11.30-3 (9 Fri & Sat); 12-4 Sun ☎ (01756) 704560
🌐 copperdragon.uk.com
Copper Dragon Black Gold, Best Bitter, Golden Pippin, Scotts 1816, Challenger IPA ⊞
Large modern bar-bistro decorated with black and white photos of the equally large and modern adjacent brewery. The emphasis is on informal dining using locally-sourced ingredients, but drinkers are welcome. The bistro opens for breakfast 9.30-11.30am Monday-Saturday. The full range of Copper Dragon ales is available. The brewery shop, visitor centre, private function room and conference suite are on the same premises. Brewery tours can be pre-booked, noon Monday-Saturday. ◑◐🚌(66,66A)P

Sneaton

Wilson Arms

Beacon Way, YO22 5HS (400m off B1416)
⏲ closed Mon winter; 12-2 (Sat only), 6.30-11; 12-4.30, 6.30-11 (not winter) Sun ☎ (01947) 602552
🌐 thewilsonarms.co.uk
Black Sheep Best Bitter; John Smith's Bitter; guest beers ⊞
Historic Grade II-listed 18th-century pub in a quiet village a couple of miles from Whitby and close to the Monks' Pathway, Sneaton Beacon and Beacon Farm, famous for its ice cream. A warm welcome is guaranteed in this single bar with beamed ceilings and roaring fires. Three handpulled beers, including a guest from Timothy Taylor, and a fine selection of whiskies, complement the excellent, traditional home-cooked meals. There is a pool room and seven letting bedrooms. Quiz night is Tuesday. ♨Q❀⇌◑◐♣P⊱

South Otterington

Otterington Shorthorn

DL7 9HP (on A167)
⏲ 12-2 (not Mon & Tue), 5-11.30 (12.30am Fri); 12-12.30am Sat; 12-11 Sun ☎ (01609) 773816
Black Sheep Best Bitter; John Smith's Bitter; Taylor Landlord; guest beer ⊞
Named after a local prize bull of bygone years, this thriving and comfortable village local is at the heart of the community. Monthly music nights feature folk and other genres, while themed food nights are also a regular attraction. Meals are served in the bar or the small restaurant (no food Mon). The guest beer varies and there is a beer festival on the spring bank holiday. ♨❀⇌◑◐Ä🚌(153)P⊱

Sowerby

Crown & Anchor

138 Front Street, YO7 1JN (in village ½ mile from Thirsk town centre)
⏲ 12-midnight (1am Thu-Sat) ☎ (01845) 522448
🌐 crownandanchorsowerby.co.uk
John Smith's Bitter; guest beers ⊞
Just what a local should be, at the heart of this village on the edge of Thirsk, offering at least three guest ales, a range of continental beers and, in summer, real cider. Good no-nonsense food ranges from bar snacks to specials and Sunday lunches (booking advised). There are three distinct drinking areas, and a beer garden with a covered outdoor smoking area adjoins the large car park to the rear. Occasional live music plays and an annual beer festival is held in September.
Q❀◑◐♿Ä🚌(146,148,149)♣P⊱

Staithes

Captain Cook Inn

60 Staithes Lane, TS13 5AD (off A174, by village car park)
⏲ 11-midnight ☎ (01947) 840200 🌐 captaincookinn.co.uk
Bank Top Bitter; guest beers ⊞
CAMRA multi-award winning pub near the Staithes railway viaduct and Boulby Cliffs, the highest in England. Six handpumps provide an eclectic mix of beer styles, including milds, porters and stouts. The house bitter, Bank Top, is brewed by Tower. The range extends to 12 handpumps during the pub's four annual beer and pork pie/sausage festivals, held to celebrate St George's Day, Lifeboat Week, Halloween/Guy Fawkes and Winter Warmers week. Four letting bedrooms and a holiday cottage are available. ♨Q❀⇌◑◐🚌(5)♣P

Staxton

Hare & Hounds

Main Street, YO12 4TA
⏲ 12-11.30 ☎ (01944) 710243
Black Sheep Ale; Stones Bitter; Theakston Old Peculier; guest beers ⊞
Imposing former coaching inn on the A64 – an excellent stopping-off point when travelling to the East Coast. The bar and lounge/dining area feature low beams and real fires. Guest beers are usually sourced from the Enterprise/SIBA scheme and often come from Wold Top and Copper Dragon breweries on six handpumps. Home-cooked meals are available all day every day, with seafood sourced from Flamborough a speciality in summer. There are large grassed drinking areas at the front and rear of the pub. ♨Q❀◑◐Ä🚌P⊱

Stokesley

Spread Eagle

39 High Street, TS9 5BL
⏲ 11-1am; 12-12.30am Sun ☎ (01642) 710278
Camerons Strongarm; Marston's Pedigree; guest beers ⊞
A fine welcome is assured at this small, unspoilt market town pub. Friendly regulars drink at one

end and an open fire welcomes diners at the other. Excellent, good value home-cooked food, complete with details of where the ingredients have been sourced, is served all day. Two interesting and stronger guest beers are always available. Children are welcome. A rear garden leads down to the tranquil River Leven, where over-fed ducks amuse children and adults alike. Tuesday is live music night. ⛰Q❀◐◑⛺🚌(29,81)⚐

White Swan ✔

1 West End, TS9 5BL (at W end of town)
⏲ 11.30 (12 Sun)-11 ☎ (01642) 710263
🌐 thewhiteswanstokesley.co.uk
Captain Cook Sunset, Slipway, Black Porter; Consett Ale Works White Hot, Red Dust; guest beers ⊞
A recent local CAMRA Pub of the Year, this traditional one-room 18th-century local is the brewery tap for both the prize-winning Captain Cook Brewery and Consett Ale Works. The bar has seven handpumps, with two guest ales always available. Well-supported by the local community, the pub holds a quiz on Wednesday, and monthly music nights. Beer festivals feature at Easter and in October. Ploughman's lunches are served Wednesday-Saturday. Children are not allowed in the pub. ⛰Q❀◐🚌(29,81)

Tadcaster

Angel & White Horse

23 Bridge Street, LS24 9AW
⏲ 11 (12 Sat)-11; 12-10.30 Sun ☎ (01937) 835470
Samuel Smith OBB ⊞
This old limestone coaching inn is a warm and welcoming town-centre hostelry and the brewery tap for Samuel Smith's, one of the oldest breweries in England. The interior is wood-panelled, with a huge log fire in the winter. A rear door leads to a courtyard with the brewery behind and, in front, the stables for the grey dray Shire horses that are still used to deliver beer to local pubs. The bitter is pulled from a wooden cask. ⛰Q❀◐🚌⚐

Terrington

Bay Horse Inn

Main Street, YO60 6PP SE668706
⏲ closed Mon; 12-3, 5.30-11; 12-7.30 Sun
☎ (01653) 648416
Beer range varies ⊞
Welcoming village free house in the Howardian Hills, run by a real ale enthusiast. Home to the Storyteller Brewery, at least three of its beers are available, including seasonal specials. Guest beers from other micro-breweries are sometimes also stocked. The pub features distinct areas for drinkers and diners and serves excellent food using local produce Wednesday to Sunday. It is ideally situated for refreshment when visiting local tourist attractions including Castle Howard and the Yorkshire Lavender Centre. Children and dogs are welcome. ⛰Q❀◐◑♿♣P

Thixendale

Cross Keys

YO17 9TG SE845611
⏲ 12-3 (not Mon), 6-11; 12-3, 7-10.30 Sun
☎ (01377) 288272
Jennings Bitter; Tetley Bitter; guest beer ⊞
Evidence of activity in Thixendale has existed for 10,000 years. This single-room hostelry appears on a map dated 1851. At the focus of 16 dry valleys, the pub is popular with walkers, including those on the Wolds Way. Guest beer comes from independent breweries and is usually not more than 4% ABV. Children are welcome in the beer garden. Good value, traditional food is served. Accommodation is in the adjoining converted stable. A remote pub well worth seeking out. ⛰Q❀🛏◐◑♣

Thoralby

George ✔

DL8 3SU (1 mile off A684 near Aysgarth, or just off B6160 Bishopsdale rd)
⏲ 12-3, 6.30-11 (1am Fri & Sat; 10.30 Sun)
☎ (01969) 663256 🌐 thegeorge.tv
Black Sheep Best Bitter; guest beer ⊞
Hidden away in a tiny, picturesque village in Bishopdale, a quiet branch of Wensleydale in the heart of the National Park, this one-room pub built in 1732 is divided into two main areas, with a cobbled area outside at the front for summer drinking. Guest beers include one from Copper Dragon and other local ales. An irregular bus service passes through the village. Opening hours may vary. ⛰Q❀🛏◐◑⛺🚌(156)♣P

Thorganby

Ferryboat Inn 🏆

Ferry Lane, YO19 6DD (1 mile NE of village, signed from main road) SE697427
⏲ closed Mon; 7-11; 12-midnight Sat; 12-4, 7-11 Sun
☎ (01904) 448224
Beer range varies ⊞
This warm and welcoming local CAMRA award-winning pub is in a beautiful rural setting with a large beer garden running down to the River Derwent. It is popular with birdwatchers, ramblers and cyclists, while the river attracts fishermen and boaters. Run by the same family for more than 60 years, the landlady makes beautiful home-made sandwiches and the landlord gives meticulous attention to his guest beers. Dogs are welcome in the garden. ⛰Q☕❀♿⛺🚌♣P⚐🥛

Thornton Watlass

Buck Inn ✔

The Village Green, HG4 4AH (off B6268 between Bedale and Masham)
⏲ 11-11 ☎ (01677) 422461 🌐 thebuckinn.net
Black Sheep Best Bitter; Theakston Best Bitter, Black Bull Bitter; guest beers ⊞
Overlooking the village green, this traditional country inn features a cosy bar room with real fire, a lounge/function room and separate dining area. Regular beers are from Black Sheep and Theakston breweries just down the road in Masham, with two rotating guests usually from northern micros. The pub hosts regular jazz sessions. Food is sourced locally and served lunchtimes and evenings. Outside is an attractive tree-lined beer garden. ⛰Q❀🛏◐◑🀄P

Thornton-in-Lonsdale

Marton Arms ✔

LA6 3BP (¼ mile from A65/A687 jct)

⏲ 10-11; 12-10.30 Sun ☎ (01524) 241281
🌐 martonarms.co.uk
Black Sheep Best Bitter; Moorhouse's Black Cat; Sharp's Doom Bar; Taylor Golden Best; Theakston Best Bitter; guest beers Ⓗ
In a hamlet with a parish church, old stocks and little else, the pub relies almost entirely on tourists drawn by the 16 handpumps, although there are other interesting beverages including a stunning range of malt whiskies. Behind the 1679 datestone and old oak door, a flagged passage leads to a modern bar. Ten minutes' walk from the start of the Waterfalls Walk, buses 80 and 80A run along the main road. The cider is Westons Old Rosie.
⛫❀⇆◑◗♿⛺🍏P⊱

Thornton-le-Dale

Hall Inn

Chestnut Avenue, YO18 7RR (250m from village centre towards Scarborough)
⏲ 11 (12 winter)-11; 12-11.30 Sat; 11-11 Sun
☎ (01751) 475046 🌐 thehallpub.co.uk
Black Sheep Best Bitter; Copper Dragon Golden Pippin; Tetley Bitter Ⓗ
This venue has the traditional feel of an English pub housed inside a building steeped in history, yet with a contemporary atmosphere. Food includes inexpensive seasonal pub-grub delights and an a la carte menu using local produce. There is a separate dining area and meals are served all day every day until 9.30pm. The warm welcome extends to visitors and locals alike and everyone is made to feel at home. The pub uses part of the ground floor, the rest being a residential home for the elderly.
⛫❀◑◗🚌(128,840)P

Ugthorpe

Black Bull Inn

Postgate Way, YO21 2BQ (1 km E of A171)
⏲ 12-2 (not Mon), 6-midnight (11 Sun) ☎ (01947) 840286
Theakston Old Peculier; guest beer Ⓗ
This comfortable, family-run, Grade II-listed country inn, with photographs of yesteryear adorning the walls, comprises a main bar, snug, restaurant and games room. The guest beer changes weekly. Portions of home-cooked food are such that going hungry is not an option, and diners travel from far and wide for the impressive Sunday lunches (booking advisable). The venue has a pool table, three darts teams and a quoits team. A holiday cottage is available. ⛫Q❀⇆◑◗⊟♿⛺🚌(93)♣P⊱

Upper Poppleton

Lord Collingwood

The Green, YO26 6DP (on village green)
⏲ 12-3, 5-midnight; 12-midnight Fri-Sun ☎ (01904) 794388
Beer range varies Ⓗ
This fine pub is set in a lovely 17th-century Grade II-listed building. Up to seven ales from the Marston's list are on offer, including seasonals. You will find friendly, welcoming staff and good honest pub lunches and dinners (no food Mon). The comfortable single-room interior features a timbered ceiling, real fires and a 19th-century carved oak bar. A fairy-lit beer garden, patio and children's play area are to the rear. Popular with locals, particularly for evening meals, it is accessible from York by bus or rail.
⛫❀◑◗⇌🚌(10)♣P

Wensley

Three Horseshoes

DL8 4HJ (on A684)
⏲ 11-3 (not Mon), 5.30-11; 12-10.30 Sun ☎ (01969) 622327
🌐 3horseshoeswensley.com
Black Sheep Best Bitter; John Smith's Bitter; Taylor Landlord; guest beers Ⓗ
A classic whitewashed country pub in the picturesque village of Wensley on the A684, with superb views across the dale from the beer garden to the rear. The cosy bar and adjoining dining room both have low beams and real fires. Major rebuilding work has created inside toilets with disabled access and a new cellar. Excellent, reasonably priced lunchtime and evening meals are served daily.
⛫Q⛾❀◑◗⊟♿🚌(156,157)♣P⊱

West Haddlesey

George & Dragon

Main Street, YO8 8QA (1 mile W of A19, 5 miles S of Selby) SE565266
⏲ 5-midnight (1am Fri); 2-1am Sat; 12-10.30 Sun
☎ (01757) 228198
Brown Cow White Dragon; guest beers Ⓗ
Privately owned free house with an enthusiasm for local micro-brewery beers – the house beer is from Brown Cow. It has low-ceilinged cosy bars, with a separate area for restaurant users (no eve meals Sun). The wide-screen TV stands over a well, proof that there has always been liquid refreshment here! There are weekly quiz and jazz music nights. Beer festivals are held frequently with a regular event close to St George's Day, 23 April.
⛫Q❀◑◗♿🚌♣P⊱

West Witton

Fox & Hounds

Main Street, DL8 4LP (on A684)
⏲ 12-4, 6-midnight; 12-midnight Sat & Sun
☎ (01969) 623650 🌐 foxwitton.com
Black Sheep Best Bitter; John Smith's Bitter; Yorkshire Dales seasonal beers; guest beer Ⓗ
Parts of this Grade II-listed, family-run, CAMRA award-winning free house date from the 1400s, when it was a rest house for the Jervaulx Abbey monks. Today, a central fireplace separates the friendly bar from a games room, while an inglenook fireplace, complete with beehive oven, gives the small dining room character. To the rear there is a pleasant patio and garden with quoits pitch. One of the two guest beers is usually from the Yorkshire Dales Brewery. Good value meals are served all week, with a roast on Sunday.
⛫❀◑◗🚌(156)♣P⊱

Whitby

Black Horse ✔

91 Church Street, YO22 4BH (E side of bridge on approach to Abbey steps)
⏲ 11-11; 12-10.30 Sun ☎ (01947) 602906
🌐 the-black-horse.com
Adnams Bitter; Black Dog Rhatas; Taylor Landlord; guest beers Ⓗ
Dating from the 1600s, this previous local CAMRA award winner offers a warm welcome. The frontage, with its frosted glass windows, together with one of Europe's oldest public serving bars,

was built in the 1880s and remains largely unchanged. Beer is dispensed from five handpumps alongside hot meals available during the winter months. Snuff, tapas, olives, Yorkshire cheeses and hot drinks are on offer all year round. The cider is Westons Traditional Scrumpy. Accommodation is in four bedrooms and an apartment. Q🛏◑◐⊞♿⛺≋🚌(93)♣●

Endeavour

66 Church Street, YO22 4AS (on E side of river, 50m S of swing bridge)
✪ 12-1am (11.30 Sun) ☎ (01947) 603557
John Smith's Bitter; guest beers Ⓗ
Named in celebration of James Cook's three-year voyage to the South Seas, this cosy one-room town pub has an open fire which adds to the warm welcome. As well as the John Smith's, five busy handpumps serve approximately 140 different guest ales annually, sourced from throughout the country. A tremendous atmosphere prevails, enhanced during folk week and Gothic weekends, while regular folk/Irish music sessions are held on Friday/Saturday evenings, and Sunday afternoons. Two bedrooms are available. ♨🛏⛺≋🚌(93)

First In Last Out

1 York Terrace, Fishburn Park, YO21 1PT (300m S of railway station)
✪ 12-midnight (11.30 Sun) ☎ (01947) 602149
🌐 firstinlastoutpub.co.uk
Camerons Strongarm; Tetley Bitter Ⓗ
One of only three pubs with this name in the country, documents dating from 1868 show that this street-corner gem of a local was once a fruit and vegetable shop. It is popular with locals and with those holidaying visitors who have discovered it. Tuesday is folk night, while on Friday live bands play. The pub supports darts and dominoes teams. There is no food, but one of Whitby's finest fish and chip shops, the Railway Chippy, is directly opposite. ❀⊞⛺≋🚌(93)♣P⚟▯

Station Inn ✔

New Quay Road, YO21 1DH (opp bus station)
✪ 10-midnight (11.30 Sun) ☎ (01947) 603937
Black Dog Whitby Abbey Ale; Copper Dragon Challenger IPA; Taylor Golden Best; guest beers Ⓗ
Next to the harbour and marina, a warm welcome awaits you at this popular multi-roomed pub where you can have your own beer festival. Enthusiastic licensees ensure that the eight real ales always represent a superb range of varying beer styles, while Westons cider and a dozen fruit wines mean there is something for everyone. Now the discerning traveller's waiting room, it is situated opposite the bus station and the NYMR/Esk Valley railway terminus. Live entertainment plays on Wednesday, Friday and Saturday. ≋🚌(93)●

Yarm

Black Bull ✔

42 High Street, TS15 9BH (by town hall)
✪ 10-midnight (1am Fri & Sat) ☎ (01642) 791251
Black Sheep Best Bitter; Draught Bass; guest beers Ⓗ
With the best beer garden in the area, this popular 17th-century much-extended hostelry has been well known as the favourite haunt of Teesside's 30-somethings, and older, for decades. It is busy most evenings but manic at weekends, when the clientele queue to gain entry. Two bars are inside, and there is a third outside on the large heated patio. Good value pub food is served all day. A plaque commemorates Bob Tillson, who decided to climb up the pub's chimney – from the inside! ♨❀◑◐♿🚌(7)⚟

York

Blue Bell ★

53 Fossgate, YO1 9TF
✪ 11-11; 12-10.30 Sun ☎ (01904) 654904
Black Sheep Best Bitter; Copper Dragon Golden Pippin; Rudgate Ruby Mild; Taylor Landlord; guest beers Ⓗ
Small glazed and brick-clad building dating from 1798 with an unchanged cosy Edwardian interior as listed in CAMRA's National Inventory of Historic Pub Interiors. Wood-panelled throughout, it has two small rooms and a serving hatch to the corridor. A three-times winner of local CAMRA Pub of the Year, the venue is also well known for fundraising activities. Guest beers are usually from small Yorkshire breweries. Good value sandwiches are served at lunchtimes. Groups are discouraged due to the lack of space. Q◑⊞🚌♣

Brigantes Bar & Brasserie ✔

114 Micklegate, YO1 6JX (100m from Micklegate Bar)
✪ 12-11 ☎ (01904) 675355 🌐 markettowntaverns.co.uk
Beer range varies Ⓗ
This real ale haven just inside the city walls was the birthplace of Joseph Aloysius Hansom, inventor of the hansom cab. Part of the acclaimed Market Town Taverns chain, its range of guest beers is constantly rotating, with Yorkshire beers a regular feature. A fine selection of continental beers as well as a draught cider can also be found. The excellent menu features daily specials and a pie of the day. Q◑◐♿≋🚌●

Golden Ball ★

2 Cromwell Road, YO1 6DU
✪ 5-11 (11.30 Thu); 4.30-11.30 Fri; 12-11.30 Sat; 12-11 Sun
☎ (01904) 652211 🌐 goldenball-york.co.uk
Caledonian Deuchars IPA; Everards Tiger; Greene King Ruddles County; John Smith's Bitter; Wells Bombardier; guest beer Ⓗ
Situated in the residential Bishophill district, this is a fine, welcoming Victorian street-corner local. It has an impressive glazed brick exterior and was extensively refurbished by John Smith's in 1929. A worthy inclusion in CAMRA's National Inventory of Historic Pub Interiors, it has four very different rooms – a main bar with TV, back room with bar billiards and TV, comfortable lounge and snug. It also has a large south-facing beer garden. Q❀♿≋♣⚟

Maltings

Tanners Moat, YO1 6HU (below Lendal Bridge)
✪ 11-11; 12-10.30 Sun ☎ (01904) 655387 🌐 maltings.co.uk
Black Sheep Best Bitter; York Brewery Guzzler; guest beers Ⓗ
An institution on York's real ale scene, this pub serves seven ales and several ciders plus a good range of bottled beers. Guest ales, often including stouts or porters, come from all over the country, and are usually different from those found in other York pubs. You will find quirky decor, with friendly licensees and staff. Home-cooked and filling food is available every lunchtime. Very handy for the railway station, so often the first or last call for visitors by train. ♨◑≋🚌●

Minster Inn
24 Marygate, YO30 7BH
⏲ 2-11; 11-midnight Fri & Sat; 12-10.30 Sun
☎ (01904) 624499 🌐 pangalactictrading.com
Jennings Sneckliftер; Marston's Burton Bitter; guest beers Ⓗ
A fine, traditional inn overlooking the Bar walls, with a warm welcome from staff and regulars alike. This multi-roomed pub makes an ideal place to escape the bustling city. Beers are from the Marston's range and always include a wide selection of regulars and seasonals. Traditional pub games are available to while away an afternoon or evening. This gem is one that you will certainly want to return to time and time again.
♔Q☕❀⊟≹⊟♣⚡

Rook & Gaskill
12 Lawrence Street, YO10 3WP (near Walmgate Bar)
⏲ 12-11 (midnight Thu-Sat) ☎ (01904) 674067
🌐 castlerockbrewery.co.uk
Castle Rock Black Gold, Harvest Pale, Screech Owl; guest beers Ⓗ
Northern outpost of the Castle Rock Brewery estate. The widest beer range in York is dispensed from 12 handpumps featuring three or four Castle Rock ales plus a wide variety of guests, always including a mild, stout or porter. A further two handpumps are used for traditional ciders. The pub has weekly live music and quiz nights, with beer festivals several times a year. ◗⊟🍎⚡

Swan Inn ★
16 Bishopgate Street, YO23 1JH
⏲ 4-11 (11.30 Thu; midnight Fri); 12-midnight Sat; 12-10.30 Sun ☎ (01904) 634968
Copper Dragon Golden Pippin; Taylor Landlord; Tetley Bitter; guest beers Ⓗ
This Tetley Heritage Inn and local CAMRA Pub of the Year 2009 features a West Riding layout. Three regular and three rapidly changing guest beers, plus two real ciders, are served from a central bar to the drinking lobby, lounge and public bar. One of only three York pubs included in CAMRA's National Inventory of Historic Pub Interiors, it has a comfortable paved and walled garden to the rear with a large covered and heated smoking area.
♔❀⊟♿≹⊟♣🍎⚡

Tap & Spile
29 Monkgate, YO31 7PB (200m outside city walls at Monkbar)
⏲ 12 (3 Mon)-11; 12-midnight Thu-Sat; 12-10.30 Sun
☎ (01904) 656158 🌐 tapandspileyork.co.uk
Rooster's Yankee; guest beers Ⓗ
Imposing Flemish-style house dating from 1897, formerly known as the Black Horse. It was renamed in 1988 when it became one of the first Tap & Spiles in the chain. The spacious interior has a raised bar area at one end and a separate library-style lounge with an imposing fireplace at the other. Five guest ales come mainly from the SIBA scheme. Regular music nights are held and the annual pork pie festival is a highlight. ❀◐⊟P⚡

Waggon & Horses
19 Lawrence Street, YO10 3BP
⏲ 4 (12 Fri-Sun)-midnight ☎ (01904) 637478
🌐 waggonandhorsesyork.co.uk
Batemans Dark Mild, XB Bitter, seasonal beers; guest beers Ⓗ
Some of York's finest establishments are just outside the city walls, this being an excellent example. Batemans' most northerly pub regularly provides four house beers and four guests such as locally brewed Rooster's, York or Rudgate ales. York Autumn 2009 Pub of the Season, it has an award-winning publican, six comfortable B&B rooms with secure parking, four bars (one with satellite TV) and good food – you may never leave.
♔☕❀⊨◗⊟♿⊟♣🍎⚡

Yorkshire Terrier
10 Stonegate, YO1 8AS
⏲ 11-11 (midnight Fri & Sat); 12-11 Sun ☎ (01904) 676722
🌐 york-brewery.co.uk/yorkshire_terrier.html
York Guzzler, Constantine, Yorkshire Terrier, Centurion's Ghost; guest beers Ⓗ
This York Brewery pub is one of the city's best-known secrets. Hidden away behind the brewery shop, it offers a safe haven from the busy tourist street. Beers from York Brewery feature alongside a varying range of guest ales. Tasting trays are available for the indecisive. The attractive lunchtime menu includes home-made soup as well as steak and ale pies. Thursday is quiz night and there is often live music on Sunday. Q☕◐♿≹⊟

YORKSHIRE (SOUTH)

Aston

Roland Arms
117 Mansfield Road, S26 2BR (corner of A618 Mansfield Road and Lodge Lane, 1½ miles from M1 jct 31)
⏲ 12-11 (Fri & Sat 11.30) ☎ (0114) 287 6199
Taylor Landlord; guest beers Ⓗ
A welcome return to real ale for a past branch favourite, turned around by the tenant who did the same with the Chequers. Despite a recent internal refurbishment, it retains a two-room layout served by a central bar. The comfortable lounge is complemented by a traditional tap room. Copper Dragon beers often feature among the guests. Quality, back to basics food is served including home-made curries, real chips and Sunday roasts. Winner of the local CAMRA Branch Pub of the Season award autumn 2009. Handy for visiting Rother Valley Country Park.
❀◐◗⊟♿⊟(21,27,29)♣P⚡

Barnsley

Conservative Club
36 Pitt Street, S70 1AW (200m out of town centre)
⏲ 11.30-3.30 (Fri & Sat only), 6.30-midnight; closed Sun
☎ (01226) 282571
Phoenix Wobbly Bob; guest beer Ⓗ
This club is a recent Barnsley CAMRA Pub of the Season award winner. The two real ales on offer have become very popular with members; the changing guest beer is usually a local/session beer. There is very comfortable seating only feet away from the bar, which runs down the right-hand side of the room. Snooker tables are for members and are situated to the back of the room. Show a CAMRA membership card or copy of this Guide to be welcomed in. ≹♣

Dove Inn
102 Doncaster Road, S70 1TP (edge of town following signs for Doncaster)
⏲ 2-11; 1-midnight Fri; 12-midnight Sat; 1-11 Sun
☎ (01226) 288351
Old Mill Bitter, seasonal beers Ⓗ

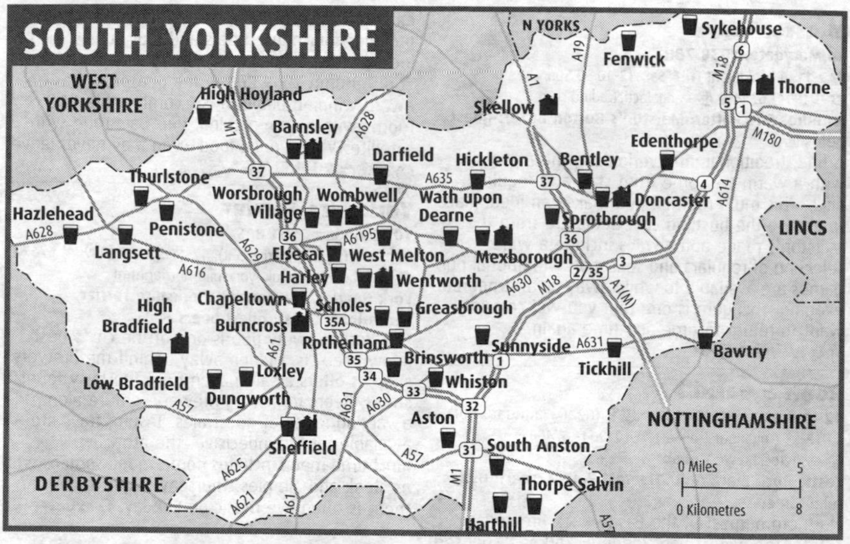

The Dove was rescued from John Smith's brewery ownership by Old Mill Brewery, creating a warm, bright, welcoming house, with plenty of outside space in the rear paved beer garden and veranda which overlooks Oakwell Stadium. The pub is at its busiest on match days when both home and away fans meet up here. The corner bar serves a public bar to the left and games/TV area to the right. The smaller back room leads to a smokers' balcony and beer garden. ❀⇌🚌(6,219,222)♣⊬

Shaw Lane Sports Club (Barnsley RUFC)

Shaw Lane, S70 6HZ (200m up the lane from Holgate School on edge of town)

⏲ 11-11 (11.30 Sat & Sun) ☎ (01226) 203509

Acorn Barnsley Bitter; guest beers 🄷

Many times CAMRA Club of The Year award winner, this venue is always a hive of activity, home to sports such as rugby, cricket and bowling. It has two plush rooms – the lounge overlooks the cricket pitch and TVs show live sporting events. Outside there is plenty of room to sit and watch the match, or just the world go by. The three real ales are usually sourced from local breweries, and good value food is always available. Caravans are allowed on site, but not tents. ❀◐♿▲♣P⊬

Silkstone Inn ✔

64 Market Street, S70 1SN (160m from Peel Square up Market St)

⏲ 9am-midnight (1am Fri & Sat) ☎ (01226) 320860

Greene King Ruddles Best Bitter, Abbot; guest beers 🄷

Situated in the heart of the town centre, this is the 700th outlet for JD Wetherspoon. The interior has a coal theme (the Silkstone Seam stretched under Barnsley), even down to the black pendants in the lights and the subdued nature of the lighting. A central, modern fireplace creates a warming effect in contrast to the long black bar, where two permanent beers and up to four guest ales plus a real cider satisfy the client mix. Popular with families and older couples, it is a recent CAMRA Pub of the Season winner. Q❀◐♿⇌🍏⊬

Bawtry

Ship ✔

Gainsborough Road, DN10 6HT (on A631 near traffic lights)

⏲ 12-11 (10.30 Sun) ☎ (01302) 710275

🌐 theship-bawtry.com

Beer range varies 🄷

Probably the most improved pub in Doncaster CAMRA's branch area. Once a run-down roadside pub, the Ship has been extensively refurbished inside and out. Four cask ales are available, with the Marston's and Jennings ranges always represented. It was Doncaster CAMRA's Pub of the Season for autumn 2008 and has been Cask Marque accredited since 2008. The Ship is also renowned for its high quality meals at reasonable prices. Quizzes and theme nights are popular. ❀◐⊟♿▲🚌♣P⊬

Turnpike

28-30 High Street, DN10 6JE (on A638)

⏲ 11-11; 12-10.30 Sun ☎ (01302) 711960

Greene King Ruddles Best Bitter; John Smith's Bitter; Thorne Pale Ale; guest beers 🄷

Opened in 1986 and still with the original licensee, the Turnpike celebrates 23 years in this Guide. Situated opposite the old market place, it is arranged over three levels, and features glass and

INDEPENDENT BREWERIES

Abbeydale Sheffield
Acorn Wombwell
Bradfield High Bradfield
Brew Company Sheffield
Concertina Mexborough
Crown Sheffield
Glentworth Skellow
Kelham Island Sheffield
Little Ale Cart Sheffield
Oakwell Barnsley
Sheffield Sheffield
Thorne Thorne
Toad Doncaster (NEW)
Wentworth Wentworth
White Rose Burncross

wood panelling together with flagstone floors. The decor includes a county cricket tie collection and photographs of the former RAF Finningley, now Robin Hood Airport. The venue has been voted local CAMRA Pub of the Season on four occasions. A good selection of lunchtime food is served.
❀◑🚌(25)⊁

Bentley

Three Horseshoes

St Mary's Bridge, Town End, DN5 9AG (on the roundabout where the A638 meets the new bridge on route N from Doncaster)
✪ 4-11; 3.30-midnight Fri & Sat; 12-11 Sun
☎ (07878) 757474
Tetley Bitter; guest beers ⊞
Traditional, friendly, multi-roomed free house situated between Bentley and Doncaster on the banks of the River Don and just five minutes' walk from Doncaster town centre. A newly created beer garden overlooks the river. Karaoke evenings are held on alternate Saturdays, and the local morris men meet at the pub on Wednesday. Pool is competitive on Tuesday and Thursday, darts and dominoes on Monday. A private room is available at no charge. Note the unchanged pub frontage with leaded glass.
⛬Q❀⊟♿⇌(Doncaster)🚌♣P⊁

Brinsworth

Phoenix Sports & Social Club ✔

Pavilion Lane, S60 5PA (off A631 Bawtry Road, 1½ miles from M1 jct 33 look for sign)
✪ 10.30-11; 12-10.30 Sun ☎ (01709) 363788
Stones Bitter; Wentworth seasonal beers; Worthington's Bitter; guest beers ⊞
Members of the public are very welcome at the Phoenix. A regular outlet for local Wentworth beers, the comfortable refurbished lounge now offers five cask ales, all expertly kept by the enthusiastic stewards. The club boasts a family room, TV room, snooker room and large function room. Lunchtime and evening meals are available. It has won numerous local branch and Yorkshire regional CAMRA awards. A wide variety of outdoor and indoor sports is played. Dances and quiz nights are held. ⛄❀◑◗♿🚌(32,33)♣P⊁

Chapeltown

Commercial

107 Station Road, S35 2XF
✪ 12-3, 5.30-11; 12-11 Fri & Sat; 12-10.30 Sun
☎ (0114) 2469066
Wentworth Imperial, WPA, Bumble Beer; guest beers ⊞
Built in 1890 and a former Stroutts pub, it is a regular outlet for Wentworth beers as well as five guest ales including a stout or porter. A rotating cider is generally available. An island bar serves the lounge, public/games bar and the snug. Successful beer festivals are held during the last weekends of May and November. Outdoor drinking facilities are to the side and rear. Children are welcome. Hot roast pork sandwiches are available from 10pm on Saturday. No meals Sunday evenings.
⛬Q❀◑◗⊟♿⇌🚌(265)♣●P⊁

Darfield

Cross Keys

Church Street, S73 9JX (jct of School St and Church St next to village church)
✪ 12-3 (4 Sat & Sun), 7-midnight (11 Sun)
☎ (01226) 752130
John Smith's Bitter; Tetley Bitter ⊞
The Cross Keys is situated in the heart of the village of Darfield close to the village church and Maurice Dobson Museum. The pub is known for its good value food and impressive floral displays during spring and summer. The interior comprises two rooms: a plush lounge and a traditional tap room. Quiz night is Tuesday. The pub is an ideal stop for local walkers, with the River Dearne and Old Moor Wetlands both within a short walking distance.
❀◑♿🚌(218,219,X19)♣P

Doncaster

Corner Pin ✔

145 St Sepulchre Gate West, DN1 3AH (on W side of dual carriageway)
✪ 12-midnight ☎ (01302) 340670
Beer range varies ⊞
A traditional street-corner pub situated just a short walk from the town centre and the Travel Interchange. Recently reprieved from demolition, the Corner Pin celebrated by earning the Cask Marque and a local CAMRA Pub of the Season award. The pub comprises a smart lounge and a public bar, with an outside drinking area to the rear. Up to three guest beers are on offer, often sourced from local micro-breweries. Reasonably priced Sunday lunches are available.
❀◑⇌🚌♣⊁▯

Gatehouse

Priory Walk, DN1 1TS (pedestrian walkway between High St and Printing Office St)
✪ 9am-midnight (1am Fri & Sat) ☎ (01302) 554540
Greene King Ruddles Best Bitter; Marston's Pedigree; guest beers ⊞
More of a bar than a traditional pub, this recently built Wetherspoon's branch on the site of a gatehouse to a medieval priory is an oasis in the middle of a desert of non-real ale outlets in the town. Beer drinkers are encouraged to vote for their favourite ale to appear on the bar. Guest beers from South Yorkshire breweries are featured, as well as those from further afield. ❀◑◗♿⇌🚌⊁

Plough ★

8 West Laith Gate, DN1 1SF (close to Frenchgate shopping centre)
✪ 11-11; 11-3, 7-11 Sun ☎ (01302) 738310
Acorn Barnsley Bitter; guest beers ⊞
Close to the Frenchgate Centre, the (Little) Plough, as the locals know it, is a haven for those wishing to escape the town centre hustle and bustle. The unchanged interior dates back to 1934, and features in CAMRA's National Inventory of historic pub interiors. There is a basic public bar at the front and a comfortable lounge at the rear. Note the unusual pictures of old agricultural scenes in the lounge. Winner of several CAMRA awards, this pub is well worth a visit. Q⊟⇌🚌♣⊁

Red Lion ✔

37-38 Market Place, DN1 1NH (S corner of Market Place, near fish market)
✪ 9am-11 (midnight Fri & Sat) ☎ (01302) 732120

Greene King Ruddles Best Bitter, Abbot; guest beers Ⓗ
Large, historic pub enjoying a renaissance as a Wetherspoon's. A strong commitment to real ale, and micro-breweries in particular, has earned two consecutive local CAMRA Pub of the Year awards. A lively front drinking area contrasts with a quieter haven towards the rear. Although much altered over the years, it was here in 1778 that discussions took place to organise the St Leger Stakes classic horse race – an association commemorated by a wall display listing post-war winners of the race.
Q◑♿⇌🚌🍏⚍

Salutation Hotel ✔

14 South Parade, DN1 2DR (close to traffic lights on main route S from town centre)
✪ 12-11 (11.30 Tue & Thu; 1am Fri & Sat) ☎ (01302) 340705
Tetley Bitter; guest beers Ⓗ
Originally a coaching inn on the Great North Road and now a popular pub on the edge of Doncaster town centre. 'The Sal' has cosy drinking areas downstairs, a large function room upstairs and a patio area out back. The bar features seven handpumps with a constantly changing range of beers and a cider. Quiz night is on Tuesday, and Meet the Brewer evenings take place during the winter months. Local CAMRA Branch Pub of the Season 2008-9. ❀◑🚌🍏⚍

Tut 'n' Shive

6 West Laith Gate, DN1 1SF (next to Frenchgate shopping centre)
✪ 11-11 (1am Fri & Sat); 12-midnight Sun ☎ (01302) 360300
Black Sheep Best Bitter; Greene King IPA, Abbot; guest beers Ⓗ
Up to six real ales in excellent condition are available at this busy town-centre pub with its stone floor, boarded ceilings and walls decorated with pump clips from past guest ales. A large screen shows major sporting events. Quiz night is Sunday and classic rock is on the jukebox. Shopping and the Transport Interchange are very close. A relaxed but lively atmosphere ensures all are welcome. This pub has won several local CAMRA awards in recent times. ◑⇌🚌⚍

Dungworth

Royal Hotel

Main Road, S6 6HF (next to church) SK280898
✪ 6 (12 Sat)-11; 12-4, 7-11 Sun ☎ (0114) 285 1213
🌐 royalhotel-dungworth.co.uk
Crown Royal Bitter Ⓗ
A small 19th-century rural pub north-west of Sheffield, with panoramic views over the Loxley Valley. Children, walkers and well-behaved pets are welcome. One bar serves two drinking areas. Early evening meals are available on weekdays, lunch and evening meals on Saturday, and lunch on Sunday. Try the home-made pies. A highlight on Sunday from mid-November is the popular lunchtime carol singing. Three en-suite rooms are available in the adjoining lodge. Open on bank holiday Mondays for lunch.
⛰Q❀🛏◑▲🚌(61,62)♣P

Edenthorpe

Eden Arms ✔

Edenfield Road, DN3 2QR (off A18 next to Tesco)
✪ 12-11 (midnight Thu-Sat) ☎ (01302) 888682
Taylor Landlord; Tetley Bitter; guest beer Ⓗ
Modern, food-based pub with a choice of seating areas, warmed by gas-effect and real fires. Music is zoned so there is at least one quiet area. Outside is a heated patio. The pub has a large car park and good disabled access. No children under 14 are allowed. An occasional cask ale weeks take place, with up to six real ales. Monday and Wednesday are quiz nights, and a variety of games is available. There is a frequent local bus service.
⛰Q❀◑♿🚌(87,88)♣P⚍

Elsecar

Market Hotel 🏆

2-4 Wentworth Road, S74 8EP
✪ 12-11; 11-1am Sat ☎ (01226) 742240
Wentworth WPA; guest beers Ⓗ
Multi-room pub with a popular drinking corridor. The varied beers are from micro-breweries and there is always a LocAle; beers are charged at the same price regardless of strength. To the rear is a beer garden with a barbecue in summer. Above the front window look for the 'Horse and gig for hire' sign. The Market is popular for meetings of various clubs, societies and walking groups, and stands next door to the Elsecar Heritage Centre, near plenty of scenic countryside.
Q❀⇌🚌(66,67,227)P⚍

Milton Arms

Armroyd Lane, S74 8ES
✪ 12-3, 7 (6 Fri)-midnight; closed Wed; 12-5, 7-midnight Sun
☎ (01226) 742278
Black Sheep Best Bitter; Stones Bitter; guest beers Ⓗ
Welcoming three-roomed pub with a conservatory overlooking an award-winning garden. You will find open fires, real ales and good food. Meals are served Thursday to Sunday; the landlord is an accomplished chef and offers variety and quality. Guest beers change regularly. The venue is close to Elsecar Heritage Centre, and is the start and finish line for the Milton Six race that takes place in June, attracting athletes from all around Yorkshire. Meals are served lunchtimes and evenings Thursday to Saturday, 12-4pm Sunday.
⛰❀◑⇌🚌(66,67,227)P⚍🍺

Fenwick

Baxter Arms

Fenwick Lane, DN6 0HA
✪ 5.30 (11.30 Sat & Sun)-midnight ☎ (01302) 702671
Theakston Best Bitter; guest beer Ⓗ
This pub is a treasure – a little off the beaten track but well-worth seeking out. Formerly a farmhouse until 1973, it has a lounge with an open fire and a smaller bar with a snooker table and another open fire. Bar meals are available and cooked to order. Theakston Best Bitter is a regular, plus one guest ale. Outside is a large, sheltered garden with a small play area. On Wednesday evening there is a quiz. ⛰❀◑♿▲🚌(89)♣P⚍

Greasbrough

Prince of Wales

9 Potters Hill, S61 4NU
✪ 11-4, 7-11; 12-3, 7-10.30 Sun ☎ (01709) 551358
Beer range varies Ⓗ
The Prince celebrates its 16th consecutive entry in the Guide. This popular street-corner local has a

well-decorated lounge and tap room. The friendly landlord recently celebrated his 30th year of tenancy and continues to provide cask beers from a variety of breweries. The guest beer can change up to three times a day, ensuring its quality. In summer outside tables and chairs allow customers to watch the world go by. Winner of many local CAMRA Branch awards. Q❀⊟⊟(43A,227)♣

Harley

Horseshoe Inn

9 Harley Road, S62 7UD (off A6135 on B6090)

4 (1 Sat)-11; 12-10.30 Sun ☎ (01226) 742204

John Smith's Bitter; Wentworth WPA, seasonal beers; guest beers H

This street-corner pub is situated close to the local Wentworth Brewery and stocks at least one Wentworth beer. The hostelry hosts regular events and is home to a pool team. Guest beers change regularly to ensure their quality, with ales often coming from local breweries. A carvery is held on Sunday 12-3pm; book to avoid disappointment. The venue hosts regular events and is the hub of the local community. Handy for walking around the Wentworth estate. ❀◐⊟(44)♣

Harthill

Beehive Inn

16 Union Street, S26 7YH (opp church)

12-3 (not Mon), 6-11; 11-11 Sat & Sun ☎ (01909) 770205

Kelham Island Easy Rider; Taylor Landlord; Tetley Bitter H

A welcoming village inn close to Rother Valley Country Park and on the Five Churches Walk. It provides space for drinkers and diners and is home to a number of local clubs. The rear room houses a full-sized snooker table. There is a function room upstairs with stairlift access, which is available to hire. The pub is home to a thriving Friday folk club and the Harthill Morris Men. Family-run, with good home-cooked food available. Q❀◐⊟♿⊟(25)♣P

Hazlehead

Dog & Partridge

Bord Hill, S36 4HH (1¼ miles westbound on A628 Flouch roundabout) SE179011

12-midnight ☎ (01226) 763173

dogandpartridgeinn.co.uk

Acorn Barnsley Bitter; guest beers H

Set in the Dark Peak District high on the Woodhead Pass, this is the jewel in Barnsley's pub crown, always serving at least one locally-brewed beer (LocAle). The warm open fire provides a welcome shelter from the often wild weather outside. Enlarged over the years, the Dog & Partridge has grown to include modern accommodation and all-day quality food, and has always supported CAMRA's aims. It is an attraction to the regular passing trade – both walkers and motorists. ⌂❀◐P

Hickleton

Hickleton Village Hall

Castle Hill Lane, DN5 7BG (just off A635)

closed Mon; 8 (7 Fri & Sat)-12.30am; 5-midnight Sun

☎ (01709) 306371

Beer range varies H

Tucked away in a quiet conservation village, this stone-built private members club (the building is owned by Lord Halifax) was transformed into a real ale haven in 2007, and won a local CAMRA award. Beers from local South Yorkshire breweries are usually available, and food is served from Wednesday to Saturday (eves only) and on Sunday lunchtime. If you enjoy great ale in a friendly, relaxed atmosphere you will love it here. CAMRA members welcome. ⌂◐⊟(X19,219)♣

High Hoyland

Cherry Tree

Bank End Lane, S75 4BE

12-3, 5.30-midnight; 12-midnight Fri-Sun

☎ (01226) 382541

Black Sheep Best Bitter; Greene King Old Speckled Hen; John Smith's Bitter; guest beers H

Located near to Cannon Hall Country Park in a picturesque location, the Cherry Tree has far-reaching views over Barnsley and the countryside. It is popular with locals and visitors alike. Good value, quality food is offered (booking advised). There is a long central bar with dining areas to both sides. Outside, there is plenty of seating to enjoy the views. Walkers are welcome. The bus service to the pub is 10am-5pm (not Sun). ❀◐♿⊟(95)P

Langsett

Waggon & Horses

Manchester Road, S36 4GY (on A616)

closed Mon; 12-3, 6.30-11; 12-3 Sun ☎ (01226) 763147

langsettinn.com

Bradfield Farmers Bitter; Taylor Landlord H

This Grade II-listed rural pub alongside Langsett Barn Visitors' Centre and woods gives wonderful access to the Dark Peak District. It has been in the hands of the same family for 37 years and has a legendary reputation for home-made food; the pie is a speciality. Locally sourced produce is prominent on the plate and LocAle prominent on the bar. ⌂Q❀◐⊟(20A)♣P

Low Bradfield

Plough Inn ✔

New Road, S6 6HW SK263916

12-3.30, 6 (7 Tue)-midnight; 12-midnight Wed-Sun

☎ (0114) 285 1280

Bradfield Farmers Blonde, Plough; guest beers H

Nestled in the heart of the Loxley Valley, this former farm, built in the early 18th-century, celebrated 200 years as a pub during 2009. A true free house, it provides guest beers – one from Sheffield, the others usually sourced from Yorkshire or the north-east. Good home-cooked food is available at lunchtimes all week, evenings Wednesday to Saturday and all day Sunday, made from locally-sourced produce, with the pies a speciality. A music evening is held on the first Tuesday of every month.
⌂❀◐⊟♿⊟(61,62)♣P

Loxley

Nag's Head

Stacey Bank, S6 6SJ SK906289

6-11.30 Mon; 12-3, 5.30-11.30 Tue & Wed; 12-11.30 Thu & Sun; 12-midnight Fri & Sat ☎ (0114) 285 1202

Bradfield Farmers Blonde, Yorkshire Farmer, seasonal beers Ⓗ
A two-roomed country pub on the main road out of Loxley, birthplace of Robin Hood, towards High Bradfield. Was this the merry men's local? Probably not, but today they would find Bradfield beers, as this is the brewery's recently acquired tap, with up to five from the range, including seasonal beers and specials. Good home-cooked food is available lunchtimes, evenings (not Sun and Mon), and all day Saturday. A three-quarter-size snooker table fills the room to the left of the entrance.
🏚❀◑◗🖫🖬(61,62)♣P🖴

Mexborough

Concertina Band Club
9A Dolcliffe Road, S64 9AZ (off Bank Street, half-way up the hill)
❂ 12 (2 Wed)-4, 8.45-11; 12-5, 7-11 Fri; 12-4, 7-11 Sat; 12-3, 8.45-10.30 Sun ☎ (01709) 580841
Concertina Club Bitter, Bengal Tiger; John Smith's Bitter Ⓗ
This now-unique club brewery is a regular in this Guide. The Tina, as it is known locally, was originally home to a band for many years. Photographs from previous decades, plus many well-deserved CAMRA awards, are on display. The club has a bar area above the cellar brewery, a small TV and pool room, and a large lounge-concert room. CAMRA members are very welcome; just show this Guide or your membership card to gain entry. ❀🖫≠🖬(220,221,222)♣🖴🖵

George & Dragon
Church Street, S64 0HE (not far from roundabout and flyover, off Doncaster Road)
❂ 12-midnight ☎ (01709) 584375
Beer range varies Ⓗ
Popular with locals, this very welcoming pub has a double-sided bar with six handpumps serving three distinct drinking areas, and a conservatory restaurant/function room. Reasonably priced home-cooked food is available Thursday-Sunday lunchtimes and Thursday-Saturday evenings. The landlord here has been the recipient of various local CAMRA awards while licensee of two other south Yorkshire establishments. In olden times, horses that worked on the nearby shipping canal were stabled at the back of the pub.
❀◑&▲≠🖬(220,221,222)♣♠P🖴

Penistone

Wentworth Arms
Sheffield Road, S36 6HG (off train station approach)
❂ 12.30-11 (1am Fri & Sat) ☎ (01226) 762494
Banks's Bitter; guest beers Ⓗ
Handy for both Trans-Pennine walking trail and train station. The Wentworth's long-serving landlord has always lovingly cared for his three handpulled beers from the Marston's range. This is a proper no-frills boozer, with a handy fish and chip shop beside it. There is an airy feel to the large lounge, with its open fire and an old-fashioned jukebox. The cosy public bar is where the locals banter, and the TV in the corner gives a homely feel. A back room has pool and darts.
🏚🛏❀🖫▲≠🖬(24,29)P🖴

Rotherham

Bluecoat ♈ ✔
The Crofts, S60 2JD (behind town hall)
❂ 7am-midnight (1am Fri & Sat) ☎ (01709) 580841
Greene King Ruddles Best Bitter, Abbot; Marston's Pedigree; guest beers Ⓗ
Originally a school, opened in 1776, it became a pub called Ffeoffes in 1981 and then a Wetherspoon's in 2001. Tucked behind the town hall, it is well worth seeking out. It offers a wide selection of beers from national and local breweries, and frequently holds Meet the Brewer nights. Westons Old Rosie or Organic Cider are on handpull; other ciders may be offered. Winner of local CAMRA Branch Pub of the Year 2006-2008 and 2010. ❀◑&≠🖬♿P🖴

Scholes

Bay Horse
Scholes Lane, S61 2RQ (off A629, 1 mile from M1 jct 35. Turn at side of Sportsman pub)
❂ 5 (12 Sat & Sun)-11 ☎ (0114) 246 8085
Kelham Island Pale Rider; Taylor Landlord; guest beers Ⓗ
Traditional village pub by the cricket ground, on the Rotherham Round Walk and the Trans-Pennine Trail. It serves home-cooked food including Dan's Cow Pie (you get a certificate if you finish everything on the plate), curries and Sunday lunches. Pork pie competitions are held and hog roasts feature up to four times a year. Entertainment is provided by a choir on Thursday and two quizzes. Local CAMRA Pub of the Year 2009. 🏚Q❀◑&🖬(44)P🖴

Sheffield: Central

Bath Hotel ★
66 Victoria Street, S3 7QL
❂ 12-11; 7-10.30 Sun ☎ (0114) 249 5151
Abbeydale Moonshine; Acorn Barnsley Bitter; Tetley Bitter; guest beers Ⓗ
A careful restoration of the 1930s interior gave this two-roomed pub a conservation award and a place on CAMRA's National Inventory of Historic Pub Interiors. The bar lies between the tiled lounge, a small corridor drinking area and the cosy well-upholstered snug. There are usually three guest beers from local breweries and micros from further afield, plus a good choice of malt whiskies and continental beers. Live jazz/blues plays most Sundays, Irish music on Monday and a blues session on the first Wednesday of the month.
Q◑⊖(West St/Sheffield University)🖬🖵

Devonshire Cat ✔
49 Wellington Street, S1 4HG
❂ 11.30-11 (midnight Fri & Sat); 12-10.30 Sun
☎ (0114) 279 6700 🌐 devonshirecat.co.uk
Abbeydale Moonshine, Absolution; Theakston Old Peculier; Thornbridge Jaipur; guest beers Ⓗ
With 12 handpumps adorning the bar (the house beer is brewed by the local Brew Company brewery) and over 100 beers from around the world, the Dev Cat is a great place for the discerning drinker. The menu features light snacks through to hearty meals. Throughout the day the clientele is a mix of beer enthusiasts, students and anyone else in search of an excellent range of the best beers. An essential calling point if you are on a short visit to the city. ◑&⊖(West St)🖬

Fat Cat

23 Alma Street, S3 8SA

⏲ 12-11 (midnight Fri & Sat) ☎ (0114) 249 4801

Kelham Island Best Bitter, Pale Rider; Taylor Landlord; guest beers Ⓗ

Opened in 1981 and still ferociously independent, this is the pub that started the real ale revolution in the area. Beers from around the country are served alongside those from the adjacent Kelham Island brewery. Vegetarian and gluten-free dishes feature heavily on the menu (evening food to 8pm, not Sun). The walls are covered with the many awards presented to the pub and brewery. Beer festivals are held every August and at various other times. Monday is curry and quiz night.

Q❀◐♿⊖(Shalesmoor)🚌⁴–

Harlequin

108 Nursery Street, S3 8GG

⏲ 11.30-11 ☎ (0114) 275 8195 🌐 theharlequinpub.co.uk

Brew Company Abyss, Blonde; guest beers Ⓗ

Now operated by the Brew Company, the Harlequin (formerly the Manchester) takes its name from another former Wards pub around the corner, now demolished. The large open-plan interior features a central bar, with seating on two levels. As well as local brews, the nine handpumps serve beers from far and wide, with an emphasis on micro-breweries, and there are regular highly regarded beer festivals. Wednesday is quiz night and there is live music Tuesday, Thursday and Saturday nights.

Q❀◐⊖(Castle Square)🚌(47,48,53)♣🍎⁴–

Kelham Island Tavern 🏆 ✔

62 Russell Street, S3 8RW

⏲ 12-11 (midnight Fri-Sun) ☎ (0114) 272 2482

🌐 kelhamislandtavern.co.uk

Acorn Barnsley Bitter; Bradfield Farmers Blonde; Pictish Brewers Gold; Thwaites Nutty Black; guest beers Ⓗ

Selected as CAMRA's National Pub of the Year for 2009 and 2010 - the first pub to achieve the award in successive years - this small gem was rescued from dereliction in 2002. An impressive 12 handpumps dispense a range of beers always including a mild, a stout and a porter, so you are sure to find something to suit your palate. In the warmer months you can relax in the pub's multi award-winning beer garden. Regular folk music features on Sunday and quiz night is Monday; no meals Sunday. Q❀◐♿⊖(Shalesmoor)🚌🍎⁴–▢

Museum ✔

25 Orchard Square, S1 2FB

⏲ 11-11 (midnight Fri & Sat; 10.30 Sun) ☎ (0114) 275 5016

Abbeydale Brimstone; Greene King IPA, Old Speckled Hen, Abbot, seasonal beer; guest beers Ⓗ

Located at the heart of the Orchard Square shopping precinct, this is a traditional pub in the city centre, with many regulars among a clientele that also includes shoppers and office workers. Inside there are contrasting seating areas on three levels. The guest beers are regularly rotated and usually from local breweries, with an emphasis on Abbeydale and Kelham Island. Food is served throughout the day to 10pm (6pm Sun).

◐♿⇌⊖(Cathedral/City Hall)🚌

Old House

113-117 Devonshire Street, S3 7SB

⏲ 12-1am (2am Fri & Sat) ☎ (0114) 272 0569

🌐 theoldhousesheffield.com

Abbeydale Moonshine; Kelham Island Pale Rider; guest beers Ⓗ

A fairly recent addition to the trendy strip of bars that form Division Street/Devonshire Street, the Old House provides a homely atmosphere. There are seating areas either side of the entrance corridor leading into the main bar area, which is decorated with classic album covers and old photos, while the shelves are stacked with retro rammel (junk). Food ranging from snacks to hearty mains is home-cooked and available throughout the day. Guest beers are mostly local.

♛◐⊖(West St)🚌

Red Deer

18 Pitt Street, S1 4DD

⏲ 12-11 ☎ (0114) 2722890 🌐 red-deer-sheffield.co.uk

Black Sheep Best Bitter; Caledonian Deuchars IPA; Taylor Landlord; Tetley Bitter; guest beers Ⓗ

A genuine, traditional local in the heart of the city, the small frontage of the original three-roomed pub hides an open-plan interior extended to the rear with a gallery seating area. As well as the impressive range of cask ales, including up to four guest beers from local breweries, there is also a selection of continental bottled beers. Lunches are served until 3pm weekdays and 6pm Saturday and Sunday. Evening meals Tuesday and Wednesday only, 5-8pm. Q❀◐⊖(West St)🚌🍎⁴–

Rutland Arms

86 Brown Street, S1 2BS

⏲ 12-11 (midnight Fri & Sat) ☎ (0114) 272 9003

Jennings Cumberland Ale; Sheffield Crucible Best, Blanco Blonde; guest beers Ⓗ

Occupying a corner spot in the Cultural Industries Quarter and near Sheffield's main station, this reopened as a free house in 2009. The comfortable interior provides ample seating either side of the central entrance, and the walls are decorated with changing displays of work from local artists, as well as photos of old Sheffield pubs. Most of the guest beers are sourced from local breweries, and both beer and cider festivals are held annually. Food is served throughout the day to 8pm.

❀◐⇌⊖🚌🍎⁴–

Sheffield: East

Carlton

563 Attercliffe Road, S9 3RA

⏲ 11-9 (11 Thu-Sat) ☎ (0114) 244 3287

Beer range varies Ⓗ

Built in 1862, this former Gilmour's house lies behind a deceptively small frontage, but offers the most impressive range of real ales in the area. The main room around the bar is comfortably furnished in traditional style. To the rear is a newly extended games room and a recently created garden. A strict no-swearing policy enhances the friendly atmosphere. Beers are mainly from local breweries, often Clark's and Wentworth, with some from further afield.

❀⊖(Woodbourn Rd)🚌(52,69)♣⁴–

Sheffield: North

Gardeners Rest

105 Neepsend Lane, S3 8AT

⏲ 3-11; 12-midnight Fri & Sat; 12-11 Sun ☎ (0114) 272 4978

🌐 gardenersrest.com

Sheffield Crucible Best, Five Rivers, seasonal beers; guest beers Ⓗ
The tap of the Sheffield Brewery reopened in late 2009 after refurbishment following severe flooding in 2007. The clean, bright interior has retained the cosy lounge. The main bar features art exhibitions, live music Friday and Saturday, and the restored bar billiards table. To the rear is a conservatory leading to the beer garden overlooking the River Don. There are usually four Sheffield beers, together with up to six guests from other local and regional breweries. The popular quiz night is on Sunday. Q❀♿⊖(Infirmary Rd)🚌(53)♣🍏⚐⊓

Hillsborough Hotel

54-58 Langsett Road, S6 2UB
✪ 12-11 (midnight Fri & Sat) ☎ (0114) 232 2100
🌐 hillsborough-hotel.com
Crown Middlewood Mild, HPA, Traditional Bitter, Stannington Stout, seasonal beers; guest beers Ⓗ
Family-run hotel serving home-cooked food. Ever-changing guest ales are supplemented by beers from the house brewery in the cellar, which brews under the Crown name, with at least four of its beers always available. Brewery tours can be booked. The conservatory and raised terrace at the rear feature panoramic views along the upper Don Valley. Attractions include seasonal beer festivals, regular themed events, folk music on Sunday and a popular quiz night on Tuesday.
Q❀🛏◐♿⊖(Langsett Primrose View)🚌♣⚐

New Barrack Tavern

601 Penistone Road, S6 2GA
✪ 11-11 (midnight Fri & Sat); 12-11 Sun ☎ (0114) 234 9148
Acorn Barnsley Bitter; Bradfield Farmers Bitter; Castle Rock Harvest Pale, Screech Owl; guest beers Ⓗ
An essential stop-off for football fans visiting nearby Hillsborough, this pub offers 11 handpumps and pre-match sustenance. The home-cooked food is available late night Friday and Saturday, with a carvery on Sunday. The front bar has darts, the main room features live music Friday and Saturday, there is a comedy club on the first Sunday of the month, plus folk on Monday. A wide choice of continental beers, single malts and a real cider are served. Outside is an award-winning heated, covered patio garden.
🔥Q❀◐⊖(Bamforth St)🚌(53,77,78)♣🍏⚐

Rawson Spring ✔

Langsett Road, Hillsborough, S6 2LN
✪ 7am-11.30 (midnight Fri & Sat) ☎ (0114) 285 6200
Greene King Ruddles Best Bitter, Abbot; guest beers Ⓗ
Large Wetherspoon pub in the former Hillsborough swimming baths, popular on match days and featuring past Wednesday team photos, along with other historic prints. The pub takes its name from the local spring that supplied fresh water to the nearby barracks. The eponymous house beer is provided by Bradfield, and six other handpumps supply a range of guest ales. Food is available every day until 10pm. Family-friendly throughout, it has a beer garden and covered, heated patio area. ❀◐♿⊖(Hillsborough)🚌🍏⚐

Wellington

1 Henry Street, S3 7EQ
✪ 12-11; 12-3.30, 7-10.30 Sun ☎ (0114) 249 2295
Millstone Baby Git; guest beers Ⓗ
This popular street-corner pub, also known as the Bottom Wellie, champions a varying range of beers from small independent brewers, with 10 handpumps always offering a stout or porter and a real cider, plus a range of continental bottled beers. The house brewery, which adjoins the secluded garden at the rear, recommenced brewing late in 2009. It now produces a wide range of brews, usually pale and hoppy, under the Little Ale Cart name, normally with three on sale.
🔥Q❀⊖(Shalesmoor)🚌🍏⚐⊓

Sheffield: South

Archer Road Beer Stop

57 Archer Road, S8 0JT
✪ 11 (10.30 Sat)-10; 5-10 Sun ☎ (0114) 255 1356
Beer range varies Ⓗ
Small, well-established corner shop off-licence stocking an extensive range of bottle-conditioned ales, Belgian beers and other world favourites. Up to four real ales are also available dispensed by handpump, largely from independent micro-breweries, usually from within the LocAle area. A certificate from the local CAMRA branch for its outstanding contribution to real ale is proudly displayed. 🚌(97,98)

Sheaf View

25 Gleadless Road, Heeley, S2 3AA
✪ 11.30-11.30 ☎ (0114) 249 6455
Bradfield Farmers Blonde; Kelham Island Easy Rider; guest beers Ⓗ
Formerly derelict pub reopened in 2000 after considerable renovation as a genuine free house. At least six rotating guest ales supplement the regular beers. These are sourced from across the UK and are supplemented by an extensive range of draught and bottled continental beers. The source of the cider varies. The choice, superb quality and great value make the Sheaf a drinkers' paradise. The pub is particularly busy at weekends, Wednesday quiz night and after Sheffield United home games. Q❀♿🚌(20,20A,53)♣🍏P⚐

White Lion

615 London Road, Heeley, S2 4HT
✪ 2-11; 3-11.30 Fri; 12-11.30 Sat; 12-11 Sun
☎ (0114) 255 1500
Kelham Island Easy Rider; Taylor Landlord; Tetley Bitter; guest beers Ⓗ
Superb multi-roomed pub situated in the busy Heeley Bottom area. Many parts are Grade II-listed. Small rooms lead off the original tiled corridor. The larger room at the rear is a venue for the local bands that play most Thursdays. The two guest ales are chosen from the Punch list and often include LocAles. Westons Old Rosie cider is sometimes available. First-time visitors should note the original Gilmour's windows with the unusual spelling of Windsor. ❀🚌(20,20A,53)♣⚐

Sheffield: West

Ball Inn ✔

171-173 Crookes, S10 1UD
✪ 11-11.30 (12.30am Fri & Sat); 12-11.30 Sun
☎ (0114) 266 1211
Greene King IPA, Ruddles County, Old Speckled Hen, Abbot; guest beers Ⓗ
Situated at the heart of Crookes, this is a traditional pub dating back to around 1901, replacing an earlier inn which started life as a farmhouse. The old-fashioned wooden decor incorporates the oak

panelling of the former tap room. The Ball has become a very popular cask ale house thanks to the policy of rotating guest beers mainly from local brewers. A good selection is usually available, ranging from pale to dark, to complement the core range from Greene King. ❀♿🚌(52)♣⚡

Champs Sports Bar

315 Ecclesall Road, S11 8NX

⏲ 10-midnight (1am Fri & Sat) ☎ (0114) 266 6333

🌐 champssportsbar.co.uk

Kelham Island Champs Special, Pale Rider; Thornbridge Wild Swan, Lord Marples, Jaipur IPA; guest beers Ⓗ

At the heart of the Ecclesall Road drinking circuit, the pub comprises a large open-plan bar area and a raised restaurant space. A refurbishment in 2009 saw the introduction of 10 additional handpumps, which dispense up to four beers each from Kelham Island and Thornbridge, in addition to guests from local and regional breweries. Meals are served throughout the day, starting with breakfast at 10am, and last orders in the restaurant are 9.30pm (10pm Sat and Sun). ❀◐♿🚌

Cobden View

40 Cobden View Road, Crookes, S10 1HQ

⏲ 1-midnight (1am Fri); 12-1am Sat; 12-midnight Sun

☎ (0114) 266 1273

Black Sheep Best Bitter; Bradfield Farmers Blonde; Caledonian Deuchars IPA; Greene King Old Speckled Hen; Wychwood Hobgoblin Ⓗ

Off the main Crookes thoroughfare, this busy community pub caters for a varied clientele, ranging from students to retired folk. The original room layout is still apparent, with the bar serving a snug at the front, a games area with pool table to the rear, and a lounge to the right of the front entrance. A quiz is held on Sunday evening and there is live music most Thursdays and Saturdays. The well-kept rear garden hosts summer barbecues. ❀♿🚌♣●⚡

Fox & Duck

227 Fulwood Road, Broomhill, S10 3BA

⏲ 11-11.30 (12.30am Fri & Sat); 12-11.30 Sun

☎ (0114) 263 1888

Abbeydale Moonshine; John Smith's Bitter; guest beers Ⓗ

Although run by the Sheffield University Students Union, this busy pub at the heart of the Broomhill shopping area is popular with locals as well as students. Originally a two-roomed venue, it was converted to its present open-plan format in the 1980s and extended recently into an adjacent shop. Fresh sandwiches are available but drinkers may also bring in their own food from the numerous nearby takeaways up to 7pm. The guest beers are sourced from local and regional breweries. ❀♿🚌(51,52)●⚡

Ranmoor Inn ✔

330 Fulwood Road, S10 3GD

⏲ 11.30-11; 12-10.30 Sun ☎ (0114) 230 1325

Abbeydale Moonshine; Bradfield Farmers Bitter, Farmers Blonde; Taylor Landlord; guest beers Ⓗ

This renovated Victorian local with original etched windows lies in the shadow of Ranmoor Church. Now open plan, the seating areas reflect the old room layout. A friendly, old-fashioned pub, it has a diverse clientele that includes choirs and football and rugby teams. The piano by the bar is often played by regulars. Outside, the small front garden is supplemented by the former stableyard, which has been opened as a partly-covered and heated drinking area. Lunches are available Tuesday to Saturday. Q❀◐🚌(4,120)♣⚡

Rising Sun

471 Fulwood Road, S10 3QA

⏲ 12-11 ☎ (0114) 230 3855 🌐 risingsunsheffield.co.uk

Abbeydale Daily Bread, Brimstone, Moonshine, Absolution, seasonal beers; guest beers Ⓗ

Operated by local brewer Abbeydale, this is a large suburban roadhouse in the leafy western side of the city. The two rooms are comfortably furnished, with a main bar and raised area to the rear. A range of Abbeydale beers is always available, with up to six guests, mainly from micros, dispensed from the impressive bank of handpumps. Entertainment includes live music on Monday and quizzes on Sunday and Wednesday. An annual beer festival, Sunfest, is held in July.

Q❀◐♿🚌(40,120)♣P⚡

University Arms

197 Brook Hill, S3 7HG

⏲ 12-11; closed Sun ☎ (0114) 222 8969

Thornbridge Wild Swan; guest beers Ⓗ

Owned by the University of Sheffield, this venue became a pub in 2007. There is a bar with a small alcove seating area adjoining, and a main lounge area. A conservatory at the rear leads to the extensive beer garden. Up to five guest beers always include one from Thornbridge, with the others mostly sourced locally. There is no food on Saturday evening. Entertainment includes a quiz on Tuesday night and regular live jazz and blues at weekends. A LocAle pub.

Q❀◐⊖(Sheffield University)🚌(51,52)♣⚡

Walkley Cottage

46 Bole Hill Road, S6 5DD

⏲ 11-11.30 (12.30am Fri & Sat) ☎ (0114) 234 4968

Kelham Island Easy Rider; Taylor Landlord; Tetley Bitter; Wells Bombardier; guest beers Ⓗ

This spacious roadhouse-style suburban local is open plan, with an L-shaped lounge providing separate seating areas. A fine display of photographs shows some of Sheffield's interesting buildings. Built for Gilmours between the wars on a large site, the extensive garden affords panoramic views over the Rivelin Valley. A lively pub, it holds a popular quiz on Thursday. In addition to the four regular cask ales, there are two rotating guest beers from local and regional brewers. No evening meals Sunday. ❀◐♿🚌(52,94,95)♣P⚡

South Anston

Loyal Trooper ✔

34 Sheffield Road, S25 5DT (off A57, 3 miles off M1 jct 31 heading for Worksop)

⏲ 12-11 (midnight Fri & Sat) ☎ (01909) 562203

Adnams Bitter; Taylor Landlord; Tetley Bitter; guest beers Ⓗ

Friendly village local selling a range of real ales and good wholesome food. Guest beers often come from local breweries. Parts of the building date back to 1690; the interior comprises a public bar, snug, lounge and a function room upstairs used by many local groups including a thriving folk club. On the Five Churches Walk and handy for Anston Stones and the nearby Butterfly Farm.

Q❀◐⊞🚌(19,29)P⚡

Sprotbrough

Boat Inn ✔

Nursery Lane, DN5 7NB (down hill from village; walk along canalside)

11.30-11 (10.30 Sun) ☎ (01302) 858500

Beer range varies Ⓗ

Popular riverside pub dating back to the 17th century, situated near the Trans-Pennine Trail, frequented by walkers, diners and the local community. After suffering damage from flooding, the pub has been restored, taking care to maintain its original style. Good food from an extensive menu is served throughout the day, and background music is unobtrusive. Outside is a large courtyard drinking area and ample parking. CAMRA Doncaster Pub of the Season, summer 2007.

Sunnyside

Woodman

Woodlaithes Road, Woodlaithes Village, S66 3ZL (off A631, 1½ miles from M18 jct 2)

12-11 (midnight Fri & Sat) ☎ (01709) 533854

Marston's Pedigree; guest beers Ⓗ

A new pub situated on the Woodlaithes village estate, opened around three years ago by Marston's, with guest beers sourced from its portfolio. It offers an extensive menu of locally-sourced food, with popular curry nights and quiz nights held regularly. Winner of local CAMRA Branch Pub of the Season award for summer 2008. (3,3A)P

Sykehouse

Old George

Broad Lane, DN14 9AU

12-midnight ☎ (01405) 785635

Tetley Bitter; guest beers Ⓗ

A 200-hundred-year old building in this linear village, the Old George is worth seeking out, with an open fire in winter and a warm welcome from staff. A free house, Tetley Bitter is the regular choice complemented by various guest ales, usually two in summer. Excellent meals are served in the restaurant and throughout the pub, including OAP specials and a Sunday carvery. Outside is a patio area where barbecues are held in summer, and a large playground including a swimming pool. (89)♣P

Thorne

Windmill Inn

19 Queen Street, DN8 5AA (mid-way between Thorne North station and centre of town)

2-11 (midnight Fri); 12-midnight Sat & Sun ☎ (01405) 812866

Black Sheep Best Bitter; John Smith's Bitter; guest beers Ⓗ

Near the former Darley Brewery tower, this well-kept pub is one of a growing number in Thorne serving beer from the local Thorne Brewery. Popular with the local community, sports fans enjoy the pool table and TVs showing most major sporting events. The pub appeals to young and old alike, and can be lively during the evening. Smokers are catered for in the outdoor heated area. P

Thorpe Salvin

Parish Oven

Worksop Road, S80 3JU

12-2.30 (not Mon), 5.30-11 (11.30 Fri); 12-midnight Sat; 12-10.30 Sun ☎ (01909) 770685

Black Sheep Best Bitter; guest beers Ⓗ

Built on the site of a former communal bakery, this award-winning pub is a popular venue for Sunday lunch and evening meals, offering a variety of home-cooked dishes (booking advisable). There is a large play area outside, and well-behaved dogs are welcome in the bar area. Situated on the Five Churches and Round Rotherham walks, it is also close to the Chesterfield Canal and the ruins of medieval Thorpe Salvin Hall. There is often a guest beer from Hambleton Brewery. P

Thurlstone

Huntsman

136 Manchester Road, S36 9QW (on the A628)

6 (5 Sat)-11; 12-10.30 Sun ☎ (01226) 764892

thehuntsmanthurlstone.co.uk

Black Sheep Best Bitter; Taylor Landlord; Tetley Bitter; guest beers Ⓗ

The positioning of this village local on the main East-West Pennine route (the A628 towards Woodhead) provides an interesting mixture of regular and passing trade customers. Genuine and friendly meeting, drinking and talking are this pub's lifeblood. Throw in old-fashioned pub games, LocAle and a warm welcome for dogs – it just should not be passed by. Q(20,20A)♣

Tickhill

Scarbrough Arms

Sunderland Street, DN11 9QJ (on A631 between motorway bridge and the Buttercross)

12-11 (10.30 Sun) ☎ (01302) 742977

Courage Directors; Greene King Abbot; John Smith's Bitter; guest beers Ⓗ

Celebrating 20 years in this Guide, this three-roomed stone pub has won several local CAMRA awards, including Pub of the Year in 2003. Originally a farmhouse, the building dates back to the 16th century, although structural changes have taken place. The snug is a delight, with its barrel-shaped tables and real fire, while bar billiards can be played in the bar. An outbuilding doubles as covered smoking area and beer festival extension in May and September. Accommodation is available. (22)♣P

Wath upon Dearne

Church House ✔

Montgomery Square, S63 7RZ

9am-midnight (1am Fri & Sat) ☎ (01709) 879518

Greene King Ruddles Best Bitter; Marston's Pedigree; guest beers Ⓗ

Wetherspoon's pub with an impressive frontage set in a pedestrian square in the town centre, with excellent access to local bus services. The building was originally used by the nearby church before becoming a pub. Handy for exploring the RSPB Old Moor Wetlands Centre and for Manvers, it serves a wide variety of beers from both national and local brewers, including the nearby Acorn and Wentworth breweries. Westons ciders are on handpull. (220,229)P

Wentworth

George & Dragon

85 Main Street, S62 7TN

⌚ 10-11 (10.30 Sun) ☎ (01709) 742440

Taylor Landlord; Wentworth WPA, seasonal beers; guest beers Ⓗ

In a picturesque village, just 500 metres from Rotherham's only brewery, the pub offers up to four ales from the brewery along with beers from local and national brewers. This local is set back from the road, with car park and patio, and a grassed area at the rear with a children's adventure playground and a craft shop. Home-cooked food is very popular. The pub is handy for historic Wentworth Woodhouse. The cider from Addlestones is not considered real by CAMRA due to use of apple concentrate.
Q(44,227)P

West Melton

Plough Inn ✔

144 Melton High Street, S63 6RG

⌚ 12-12.30am (2am Fri & Sat) ☎ (01709) 872995

John Smith's Bitter; guest beer Ⓗ

Popular pub standing back from the road, the front bar serves as both a lounge and tap area. There is a separate function room, family room and sizeable outside area. The real ales are well kept and food is served every lunchtime (except Mon), Tuesday to Friday evenings, and all afternoon on Sunday. Poker matches are played here. Handy for the RSPB Old Moor Wetlands Centre and Manvers. Local CAMRA Branch Pub of the Season winter 2008.
(220,229)♣P

Whiston

Chequers Inn

Pleasley Road, S60 4HB (on A618, 1½ miles from M1 jct 33)

⌚ 12 (4 Mon & Tue)-11; 12-11.30 Fri & Sat

☎ (01709) 829168

Tetley Bitter; guest beers Ⓗ

Next to a 13th-century thatched barn, this friendly local replaced an old coaching inn when the road was widened in 1933. One side of the bar acts as a tap room, with a split level lounge to the right. The large garden features a barbecue area. Situated in the heart of Whiston, the pub is a regular local CAMRA award winner. The food is home-cooked by chefs. Features include quiz nights, discos, occasional live music and scooter club meets. Close to Whiston Meadows. **(21,25,29)♣P**

Golden Ball ✔

7 Turner Lane, S60 4HY (off A618, 1½ miles from M1 jct 33)

⌚ 11-11.30; 11.30-12.30am Fri & Sat; 11.30-11.30 Sun

☎ (01709) 726911

Taylor Landlord; Tetley Bitter; guest beers Ⓗ

Small cottage-style pub in the old part of Whiston, with parts of the building dating back more than 500 years. Recently refurbished, the interior has several small enclaves and a comfortable snug to the rear. There are large gardens at the back and a patio area in front. The car park is across the road. Popular with both drinkers and diners, tasting racks with three third-of-a-pint glasses are available. The nearby parish church and stocks are worth visiting. Handy for Ulley Country Park. **QP**

Hind ✔

285 East Bawtry Road, S60 4ET (on A631 link road between M1 and M18)

⌚ 12-11 (midnight Thu-Sat) ☎ (01709) 704351

Taylor Landlord; Tetley Bitter; guest beers Ⓗ

This large pub was built for the Mappins Brewery of Rotherham in 1936. Originally known as King Edward VIII, it was renamed when the king abdicated. Since refurbishment the interior has been opened out, creating good disabled access. There are extensive gardens and a patio to the rear, and a snooker table upstairs (membership required to play). Daytime and evening food is popular. Third-of-a-pint tasting racks are available.
Q(10,19B)P

Wombwell

Anglers Rest

66 Park Street, S73 0HS (on Park St 5 mins walk from town centre)

⌚ 5 (7 Wed winter)-midnight; 12-1am Sat; 12-midnight Sun

☎ (01226) 751031

Black Sheep Best Bitter; guest beer Ⓗ

This small roadside pub is a little gem and well worth a visit. The landlady is a big cider fan and a guest draught cider is always available. The guest ale is often sourced from the nearby Acorn Brewery. The venue comprises three small rooms and offers a selection of traditional pub games. It hosts various events and prides itself on being a traditional community local. B&B is available.
Q(222,226)♣P

Horseshoe ✔

30 High Street, S73 0AA (on main shopping street)

⌚ 7am-midnight (1am Fri & Sat) ☎ (01226) 273820

Greene King Ruddles Best Bitter, Abbot; guest beers Ⓗ

Splendid, spacious, red-brick pub built in the 1930s to replace an earlier terraced pub of the same name on the same site. It has been expertly converted in typical Wetherspoon style, with a large open space divided into convenient, comfortable areas, each with a different feel. Children are welcome. **(222,227,229)P**

Worsbrough Village

Edmunds Arms

25 Worsbrough Road, S70 5LW (off A61 onto Worsbrough Rd)

⌚ 11.45-3 (4 Sat), 6-11; 12-4, 7-10.30 Sun

☎ (01226) 206865

Samuel Smith OBB Ⓗ

Attractive stone-built pub opposite the historic church. A range of bar meals is served daily in the tap room and lounge, while full meals can be enjoyed in the restaurant 12-2pm (not Wed) and 6-8pm Tuesday, Thursday and Friday. There is a popular outside seating area at the front of the pub and a garden to the rear. The regular Tuesday night quiz is well attended. **Q(67,265)♣P**

YORKSHIRE (WEST)

Ackworth

Angel

Wakefield Road, WF7 7AB (on A638 ½ mile W of A628/A638 roundabout)

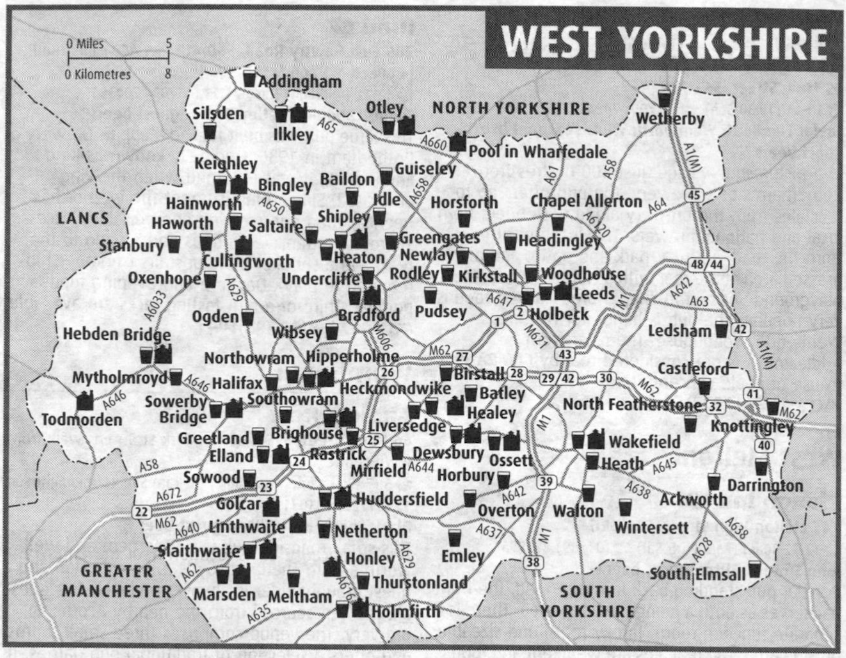

☉ 12-3, 5-11 (11.30 Fri & Sat); 12-11 Sun ☎ (01977) 611276
Black Sheep Best Bitter; guest beer Ⓗ
One of eight real ale pubs and clubs in the village, the Angel has a thoughtful and well-designed open-plan layout centred around a large arched wooden bar. High quality home-made bar meals using local produce are served Monday-Saturday lunchtimes and evenings, plus a Sunday carvery 12-4pm. There is a very popular quiz on Wednesday evening. The adjacent Dando Way provides a good start and finish point for walking/cycling in the nearby Country Park and surrounding area. ⛼❀◗◪♿🚌(35,245)P⚟⊡

Addingham

Swan Inn ✔
106 Main Street, LS29 0NS
☉ 12-2 (not Mon & Tue), 5.30-11; 12-midnight Sat; 12-10.30 Sun ☎ (01943) 831999 🌐 swan-addingham.co.uk
Tetley Bitter; guest beers Ⓗ
This friendly village local retains a four-room layout arranged around a central bar. The main area is stone-flagged, and there is a separate tap room and snug, all warmed by real fires in winter. Live bands perform on Saturday evening and Monday is folk night. Good food is served Wednesday to Friday and at weekend lunchtimes. The three guest beers are sourced via the SIBA scheme. Well-behaved dogs are welcome.
⛼◗🚌(X84,762,765)♣P

Baildon

Junction
1 Baildon Road, BD17 6AB (on Otley road)
☉ 12-midnight (1am Fri & Sat) ☎ (01274) 582009
Dark Star Hophead; Fuller's ESB; Tetley Bitter; guest beers Ⓗ
A friendly community local, this CAMRA multi-award-winning pub has three rooms: a main bar, lounge, and games room with a pool table, dartboard and pinball machine. Beers change constantly, including ales from local micros, and one pump is dedicated to ales from the nearby Saltaire Brewery. Home-cooked food is served on weekday lunchtimes. Most Sunday evenings a music jam session is hosted, and sporting events are shown on TV. There is an annual beer festival in July. ❀◖≠(Shipley)🚌(656,658,653)♣●⚟

Batley

Cellar Bar
51 Station Road, WF17 5SU (opp Batley rail station)
☉ 4-11; 12-midnight Fri & Sat; 12-11 Sun ☎ (01924) 423419
🌐 downthecellar.com
Black Sheep Best Bitter; Copper Dragon Golden Pippin; guest beers Ⓗ
Atmospheric, welcoming single-room bar in the basement of a Grade II-listed building in an historic area occasionally used as a film set. Comfortable seating includes two Chesterfield settees, while candles on the tables add to the ambience. A pool table is located on a raised section at the rear. The pub hosts two annual beer festivals. Quiz night is Thursday, and live music plays on most Saturday evenings. ≠♣●⚟

Bingley

Brown Cow ✔
Ireland Bridge, BD16 2QX
☉ 12-3, 5-11 (midnight Fri); 12-midnight Sat; 12-10.30 Sun
☎ (01274) 564345
Taylor Dark Mild, Golden Best, Best Bitter, Landlord, Ram Tam Ⓗ
Riverside destination pub next to a 13th-century bridge. Both drinkers and diners are welcome in this comfortable wood-panelled hostelry. Not all tables are laid for food, and low-level settees and armchairs as well as bar stools are provided. An

upstairs function room, for 45, plays host to a variety of local groups. A small range of Belgian bottled beers is stocked. Book ahead for meals, particularly at weekends. ♨❀◑♿⇌🚌P⚡

Harvester

Chapel Lane, BD16 1AW

9-11 ☎ (07779) 694308

Beer range varies Ⓗ

New life has been given to this previously closed pub, rescued by the relaxation of its beer tie and the addition of four handpumps, making seven in all. The publican is a cask ale enthusiast and obtains his ales from UK regional breweries, and local micros who deliver direct. The competitively priced, frequently changing beers reward return visits to this basic back-street hostelry. Janet's Jungle Juice cider is a staple. Handy for the railway station. ❀◑⇌🚌🍎⚡

Myrtle Grove ✔

141 Main Street, BD16 1AJ

9am-midnight ☎ (01274) 568637

Greene King Ruddles Best Bitter, Abbot; guest beers Ⓗ

Popular town-centre Wetherspoon pub, now in its 11th year. A conversion of an old cinema, the high ceiling, 20th-century artworks, curved fittings and pillars lend an Art Nouveau atmosphere to the large single room. Cosy alcoves with comfy high-backed settles occupy the back wall. Five guest beers are always available, with local breweries well represented, especially Saltaire, Naylor's, Elland, Ossett, Moorhouse's and Daleside. The bus stop and train station are close by. Q◑♿⇌🚌

Birstall

Black Bull

5 Kirkgate, WF17 9PB (off A652/A643)

12-11 (10.30 Sun) ☎ (01274) 873039

blackbullbirstall.co.uk

Sharp's Doom Bar; John Smith's Bitter; guest beer Ⓗ

Dating in parts from the 17th century, this inn has a vital place in local history, playing a part in celebrations, auctions, local elections and even acting as the local magistrates' court – the last trial was held in 1839. The courtroom function room retains the magistrates' box and prisoner's dock. The snug is popular for small meetings, while the remainder is divided into several cosy areas. The independent guest beer changes rapidly. Lunches are 12-1.45pm, evening meals 6-8.30pm Wednesday-Saturday. ☕❀◑♿🚌(220,283)P⚡

Bradford

Castle Hotel

20 Grattan Road, BD1 2LU

12 (1 Sun)-midnight ☎ (07967) 144474

Jennings Cumberland Ale; guest beers Ⓗ

An established real ale pub in the city centre within easy reach of the transport network. This former Webster's house now stocks a changing range of beers, usually including an ale from the local Old Spot Brewery. A real cider is also often available. The 19th-century building features a semi-circular wrap-around bar, forming two almost separate areas, with a dartboard and TV at one end. Ring the pub for live music details.
♿⇌(Forster Square/Interchange)🚌🍎

City Vaults

33 Hustlergate, BD1 1NS

10.30-11 (midnight Fri & Sat) ☎ (01274) 739697

Black Sheep Best Bitter; Copper Dragon Golden Pippin; Salamander Mud Puppy, Golden Salamander; Tetley Bitter Ⓗ

Bustling city-centre pub in former bank premises opposite Bradford's famous wool exchange. There are now five ales on handpump. Home-cooked food is served 12-7pm week days and until 6pm on Saturday. The pub retains a traditional feel, with lovely stained glass and a wrought-iron spiral staircase to the upper drinking area. There is live music every alternate Saturday, jazz every Sunday evening and a popular quiz on Wednesday.
❀◑♿⇌(Forster Square/Interchange)🚌⚡

Corn Dolly

110 Bolton Road, BD1 4DE

11.30-11; 12-10.30 Sun ☎ (01274) 720219

Black Sheep Best Bitter; Draught Bass; Everards Tiger; Moorhouse's Pride of Pendle; guest beers Ⓗ

Opened in 1834, this was formerly called the Wharfe because of its location near the end of the Bradford canal. This award-winning local is a short walk from the city centre. Four changing guest beers are sold alongside the regulars. Good value food is served weekday lunchtimes. The open-plan layout incorporates a separate games area. A large collection of pump clips adorns the walls.
♨❀◐♿⇌(Forster Square/Interchange)
🚌(612,640,641)♣P⚡

INDEPENDENT BREWERIES

Anglo Dutch Dewsbury
Atlas Mill Brighouse
Barearts Todmorden
Bob's Healey
Brass Monkey Sowerby Bridge
Bridestones Hebden Bridge
Bridgehouse Keighley (NEW)
Briscoe's Otley
Clark's Wakefield
Eastwood Elland
Elland Elland
Empire Slaithwaite
Fernandes Wakefield
Five Towns Wakefield
Fox Beer Leeds
Golcar Golcar
Goose Eye Keighley
Halifax Steam Hipperholme
Ilkley Ilkley
Leeds Leeds
Linfit Linthwaite
Little Valley Hebden Bridge
Mallinsons Huddersfield
Nook Holmfirth
Old Bear Keighley
Old Spot Cullingworth
Ossett Ossett
Ridgeside Leeds (NEW)
Riverhead Marsden
Rodham's Otley
Salamander Bradford
Saltaire Shipley
Summer Wine Honley
Tigertops Wakefield
Timothy Taylor Keighley
WharfeBank Pool in Wharfedale (NEW)

Fighting Cock

21-23 Preston Street, BD7 1JE
⌚ 11.30-11; 12-10.30 Sun ☎ (01274) 726907
Bob's White Lion; Copper Dragon Golden Pippin; Greene King Abbot; Taylor Best Bitter, Landlord; Theakston Old Peculier; guest beers 🄷
Popular, unassuming pub, just a short walk or bus ride from the city centre. Twelve real ales are usually available, including at least one dark beer. Additionally, this regular local CAMRA award-winner serves ciders, foreign bottled beers and fruit wines. It attracts a wide variety of customers from loyal locals to well-travelled real ale enthusiasts. Lunches are served Monday to Saturday. ⛰◐♿🚌●

Haigy's

31 Lumb Lane, Manningham, BD8 7QU
⌚ 5 (12 Sat)-2am; 2-11 Sun ☎ (01274) 731644
Tetley Dark Mild, Bitter; guest beers 🄷
Friendly locals' pub, a former winner of Bradford CAMRA Pub of the Year, situated on the edge of the city centre. It offers up to four guest ales, mainly from local micros. The comfortable lounge sports a fine collection of porcelain teapots and an extensive range of pictures. It has a heated, covered smoking area and large TV screen, and is popular with Bradford City fans on match days. Pool players excel on the unusual revolving hexagonal table.
❀⇌(Forster Square/Interchange)🚌(620,621) ♣P⚟

New Beehive Inn ★

171 Westgate, BD1 3AA
⌚ 12-11 (3am Fri-Sun) ☎ (01274) 721784
Beer range varies 🄷
Gas-lit pub on the fringe of the city centre. Built in 1901, this imposing building deserves its place on CAMRA's National Inventory of Historic Pub Interiors for its multi-roomed interior. Note its external features too. Beers are almost exclusively from micros, with local ales prominent. Three-star en-suite accommodation is available. A separate cellar bar offers an eclectic selection of music. Folk and jazz can also be experienced in the pub itself on occasions. See the splendid paintings in the back bar. No food Sunday.
⛰❀⛟◐◑⊟⇌(Forster Square)🚌(617,618)♣P⚟

Shoulder of Mutton

28 Kirkgate, BD1 1QL
⌚ 12-11 ☎ (01274) 726038
Samuel Smith OBB 🄷
This small, multi-roomed city-centre pub, a former coaching inn, dates from the early 1800s. it has a large suntrap garden to the rear. The interior has been refurbished without ruining its traditional atmosphere, and pictures, photographs and drawings of old Bradford abound. The pub is the main base for the Airedale quiz league.
❀⇌(Forster Square/Interchange)⚟

Sir Titus Salt ✔

Unit B, Windsor Baths, Morley Street, BD7 1AQ (behind Alhambra Theatre)
⌚ 9am-midnight (1am Fri & Sat) ☎ (01274) 732853
Greene King Ruddles Best Bitter, Abbot; guest beers 🄷
Splendid Wetherspoon conversion of the original swimming baths, now named after a local industrialist and philanthropist. An upstairs seating area overlooks the main bar, where framed pictures depict the educational heritage of the city. The pub draws a cosmopolitan clientele including students, theatregoers, clubbers and diners from nearby Indian restaurants. The location is handy for the National Media Museum. A Bradford CAMRA Pub of the Season.
Q⛟◐◑♿⇌(Forster Square/Interchange)🚌●

Brighouse

Old Ship Inn 🏆

34 Bethel Street, HD6 1JN
⌚ 12-11 (midnight Fri & Sat; 10.30 Sun) ☎ (01484) 719543
🌐 theoldshipinnbrighouse.co.uk
Black Sheep Best Bitter; Copper Dragon Golden Pippin; guest beers 🄷
Friendly pub in the town centre with a growing reputation for real ale. The bar area has a stone-flagged floor and wood-panelled walls. Three constantly changing beers plus a rotating ale from Brass Monkey Brewery complement the regular beers. Good home-cooked food is served at lunchtime, using ingredients sourced from local suppliers. Winner of local CAMRA Pub of the Year 2010 and Pub of the Season summer 2008. It holds an annual beer festival (FestivALE) in early March.
Q❀◐⇌(Brighouse)🚌⚟

Red Rooster

123 Elland Road, Brookfoot, HD6 2QR (on A6025)
⌚ 3 (12 Fri & Sat)-11; 12-10.30 Sun ☎ (01484) 713737
Abbeydale Moonshine; Harviestoun Bitter & Twisted; Marble Pint; Moorhouse's Blond Witch; Taylor Landlord; guest beers 🄷
This small stone pub lies on the inside of a sharp bend approximately half a mile out of town. Its former four-roomed layout is still apparent, with a stone-flagged floor throughout. A charity week is held in mid-August and a beer festival in September. Part of the decking area to the front is covered to provide a smoking shelter. Live music features on the afternoon of the last Sunday of the month. Guest ales always include a dark beer.
❀🚌(571,E8)♣⚟

Richard Oastler ✔

Bethell Street, HD6 1JN SE145227
⌚ 9am-11 (1am Fri & Sat) ☎ (01484) 401756
Greene King Ruddles Best Bitter, Abbot; guest beers 🄷
A Grade II-listed former Methodist chapel converted to a very successful Wetherspoon pub. Inside, a magnificent but inaccessible upper floor with original chapel pews and impressive ceiling is retained. Eight guest beers are served, including one from Elland Brewery. Other local micro-breweries feature regularly, and there is always at least one dark beer. Winner of local CAMRA 2009 winter Pub of the Season. Food is served until 10pm. ❀◐◑♿⇌🚌⚟

Castleford

Glass Blower ✔

15 Bank Street, WF10 1JD (just off town centre)
⌚ 9am-midnight (1am Fri & Sat) ☎ (01977) 520390
Greene King Ruddles Best Bitter, Abbot; guest beers 🄷
Former post office converted by Wetherspoon. It was initially to be called the Glass House, referring to the town's history of glass bottle manufacture, but local people objected because of the link with

prison. Pictures of the work of locally-born sculptor Henry Moore adorn the walls. Up to eight guest beers are available. The pub is a popular venue for families and rugby supporters when Castleford Tigers are at home. Excellent value food is served all day and children are welcome. Q❀◐♿⇌🚌⊬

Shoulder of Mutton

18 Methley Road, WF10 1LX (on A6032)
⏲ 12-3, 7-midnight; 12-4, 7-1am Sat & Sun
☎ (01977) 736039
Tetley Dark Mild, Bitter; guest beers Ⓗ
This free house started life as a farmhouse in 1632 and is packed with breweriana. The landlord, "Tetley" Dave Parker, an ex-Tetley drayman, is a fount of knowledge on pubkeeping, a great supporter of micro-brewers and proud of the many awards he has received for his cellarmanship. Expect lively conversation and a warm welcome from landlord and locals. Ring the bull, nine men's morris and wooden puzzles are played, and the George Formby Society meets here on the last Wednesday of each month.
⛫Q❀◑♿⇌🚌(153,189)♣P⊬

Darrington

Spread Eagle

Estcourt Road, WF8 3AP (½ mile W of A1 on main road through village and 4 miles E of Pontefract)
⏲ 12-3, 5-11 (midnight Fri; 11 Sat); 12-10.30 Sun
☎ (01977) 699698
Black Sheep Best Bitter; guest beers Ⓗ
A welcoming, friendly community pub in the heart of the village. Popular with a wide cross-section of the community, it is well-frequented in the evenings. Good quality food is served either in the bar or in a small restaurant-style area. A quiz is held on Monday and Wednesday evening and there is a pleasant function room for hire. Children are allowed in the pub until 9pm. No food Sunday evening and all day Monday. There is a patio.
Q❀◐♿🚌(408,409)P⊬

Dewsbury

Huntsman

Chidswell Lane, Shaw Cross, WF12 7SW (400m from A653/B6128 jct)
⏲ 12-3 (not Mon), 7 (5 Thu-Sat)-11 ☎ (01924) 275700
Taylor Landlord; guest beers Ⓗ
Situated in a semi-rural area and enjoying fine views across open fields to the north, the pub has been tastefully converted from farmworkers' cottages and has a large lounge leading to two further rooms. The smaller room has a Yorkshire range and is decorated with militaria and horse brasses, offering a friendly atmosphere to all. Lunches are served Tuesday-Saturday and evening meals 5-7.30pm Thursday and Friday. The house beer, Chidswell Bitter, is brewed by Highwood.
⛫❀◐⛺🚌(117,205)P

Leggers Inn

Calder Valley Marina, Mill Street East, WF12 9BD (off B6409; follow brown signs to Canal Basin)
⏲ 10.30-11 (midnight Fri & Sat) ☎ (01924) 502846
Everards Tiger; guest beers Ⓗ
Once the hayloft of a stable block by the canal basin, this pub has featured in the Guide for the 12 years it has been open. Low beams and quirky items on display make it very atmospheric. Six handpumps feature ales from Leeds and Rooster's, with one pump for cider. Outside, a large decking and seating area is excellent for summer. Light meals are served all day until 9pm, and there is a function room. Bus and rail stations are nearby.
⛫❀◐♣●P⊬

Shepherds Boy ✔

157 Huddersfield Road, WF13 2RP (on A644 ½ mile from town centre)
⏲ 3-11; 12-midnight Fri & Sat; 12-11 Sun ☎ (01924) 454116
Ossett Pale Gold; guest beers Ⓗ
Outside the town centre, this is an excellent pub reconstruction with many original features retained or reinstated. Four comfortable drinking areas are provided and a trademark brick arch separates the front room from the rear. The nine handpumps dispense a well-balanced range of beers from the Ossett group and various small breweries, plus one from Fuller's, and a real cider and perry. Tuesday is quiz night. Well-supported beer festivals are hosted twice annually, supplemented by popular seasonal ale trails. ❀◐♿🚌♣●P⊬

West Riding Licensed Refreshment Rooms ✔

Railway Station, Wellington Road, WF13 1HF (platform 2 Dewsbury Station)
⏲ 12-11 Mon; 11-11 Tue, Wed & Sun; 11-midnight Thu & Fri; 10-midnight Sat ☎ (01924) 459193 🌐 imissedthetrain.com
Black Sheep Best Bitter; Taylor Dark Mild, Landlord; guest beers Ⓗ
Multi-award-winning pub in a Grade II-listed Victorian building. A Transpennine Real Ale Trail mainstay, the pub serves a well-kept range of rotating beers from local independents – one of the eight handpumps is reserved for the local Anglo-Dutch Brewery. The pub is justly famed for good value, quality food. Beer festivals are held twice annually, and there is occasional live music. A large, decked, partially-covered patio serves as a beer garden. Evening meals are available Tuesday-Thursday only. ⛫❀◐♿⇌🚌⊬

Elland

Barge & Barrel

10-20 Park Road, HX5 9HP (on A6025 N of Elland Bridge)
⏲ 12-midnight ☎ (01422) 373623
Abbeydale Moonshine; Elland Bargee; Phoenix Wobbly Bob; guest beers Ⓗ
A large roadside pub built to serve the former Elland station. Its three-sided bar serves the comfortable lounge, with a bottle collection and views over the canal and river to Elland town. Opposite, an area warmed by a fire is partly divided from the bar by a partition of modern stained glass. Quiz night is Wednesday and curries feature on Sunday. The nine guest beers are mainly from micro-breweries. The smoking shelter is heated. ⛫❀◐🚌(537,538,E8)♣P⊬

Emley

White Horse ✔

Chapel Lane, HD8 9SP (on main road through village)
⏲ 4-11; 3-11.30 Fri-Sun ☎ (01924) 840937
Fuller's London Pride; Ossett Pale Gold, Emley Cross, Excelsior; guest beers Ⓗ
An Ossett Brewery pub with a large stone-flagged main bar with a cast-iron range. The regular Ossett

beers are complemented by a further four guests. A small flight of steps leads up to another room with a stove, which is used as a family room. The separate restaurant is open for à la carte meals 5-9pm Wednesday-Sunday, and traditional Sunday lunches are served. A quiz is held every Tuesday evening. ⋔Ⴆ❀◗⊟(232)♣P⁄

Greengates

Albion Inn ✔

25 New Line, BD10 9AS (on main Keighley-Leeds road)
⚙ 12-11 (midnight Fri & Sat) ☎ (01274) 613211
Acorn Barnsley Bitter; Tetley Bitter; guest beers Ⓗ
This busy roadside local has an L-shaped lounge and a separate tap room where pub games are played. A thriving social club is in existence, and strangers are made most welcome. Traditional values are kept in this friendly neighbourhood pub. Moonshine cider and Broadoak perry are usually available. ⊟(760)♣●P

Greetland

Greetland Community & Sporting Association

Rochdale Road, HX4 8JG (on B6113)
⚙ 5-11; 4-midnight Fri & Sat; 12-11 Sun ☎ (01422) 370140
Beer range varies Ⓗ
Award-winning sports and social club set back from the road at the top of Greetland village. The club is a past winner of both the CAMRA Yorkshire and National Club of the Year awards. It has a wooden decked area outside, which in summer affords excellent views over Halifax. A very warm welcome is offered to all visitors. Beers from Timothy Taylor feature. ❀⊟(557,559)P⁄

Guiseley

Coopers ✔

4-6 Otley Road, LS20 8AH (opp Morrisons on A65)
⚙ 12-11 ☎ (01943) 878835
Black Sheep Best Bitter; Taylor Landlord; guest beers Ⓗ
One of the Market Town Taverns chain, this light, airy, modern bar/diner serves eight ales, generally from Yorkshire micros and independents. It also stocks a large selection of continental bottled beers. A diverse range of meals is available until 9pm in a separate dining area. The large upstairs function room has regular jazz and musical events and also serves as a dining room.
Q❀◖◗♿⇌⊟(33,33A,97)⁄

Guiseley Factory Workers Club

6 Town Street, LS20 9DT (off A65, near St Oswald's Church)
⚙ 1-4 (5 Mon), 7-11; 1-midnight Fri; 11.30-midnight Sat; 11-midnight Sun ☎ (01943) 874793
Tetley Bitter; guest beers Ⓗ
Small, friendly working men's club, a meeting place for community groups, local clubs and societies. The traditional three-roomed layout includes a lounge, snooker room and concert room hosting Saturday night turns. Quiz night is Sunday; sports are shown on a large-screen TV or in the lounge. There is a large garden at the rear. A beer festival is held in April. Show your CAMRA membership card or a copy of this Guide for entry. National CAMRA Club of the Year 2008.
❀⇌⊟(33A,97,737)♣P⁄

Hainworth

Guide

Keighley Road, BD21 5QP (Keighley Rd/Rycroft Rd jct) SE065387
⚙ 4-11.30; 12-12.20am Sat; 12-11 Sun ☎ (07807) 998537
Beer range varies Ⓗ
Bradford CAMRA's most isolated pub, but well-worth searching out. At least two real ales are on offer, one from the local Old Spot Brewery and the other from Naylor's Brewery. This friendly two-roomed pub features a log fire and pictures of motorbikes and landscapes. Dog walkers, hikers, bikers, campers and caravanners are all made welcome. There is no bus service on Sunday. A Bradford Pub of the Season. ⋔Q❀▲⊟(915)♣P⁄

Halifax

Big Six

10 Horsfall Street, Saville Park, HX1 3HG (off A646, Skircoat Moor road at King Cross)
⚙ 5-11; 3.30-11.30 Fri; 12-11.30 Sat; 12-11 Sun
☎ (01422) 350169
Adnams Bitter; guest beers Ⓗ
Busy, friendly mid-terrace pub close to the Free School Lane recreation ground. A through-corridor divides two lounges from the bar and games room. Brewery memorabilia plus relics of the former Big Six mineral water company which operated from the premises a century ago are displayed throughout the pub. A varying range of guest beers from regional and micro-breweries is served. There is a small beer garden to the rear of the pub. Dogs are welcome. ⋔Q❀⊟♣

Sportsman Inn

Bradford Old Road, Swalesmoor, HX3 6UG (off A647, 1 mile N of centre)
⚙ 12-2.30 (not Mon), 6-11 (midnight Fri); 12-midnight Sat; 12-11 Sun ☎ (01422) 367000
Taylor Landlord; Tetley Bitter; guest beer Ⓗ
Situated on the hillside, the inn has stunning views towards Halifax and Queensbury. There are two bars, one serving as a family room, plus a separate restaurant area. Four guest beers are served, usually from local breweries. The Sportsman is adjacent to a dry ski slope and a children's adventure playground, and has its own play area.
⋔QႦ❀◖◗♿⊟(576)♣P⁄

Three Pigeons ★ ✔

1 Sun Fold, South Parade, HX1 2LX
⚙ 3 (12 Fri-Sun)-11.30 ☎ (01422) 347001
Ossett Pale Gold, 3 Pigs, Excelsior; guest beers Ⓗ
A comfortable Art Deco town house lying conveniently between the railway station and the Shay football and Rugby League ground. The present owner, Ossett Brewery, has sensitively restored the interior, which features an impressive central octagonal drinking lobby from which three of its four rooms radiate. Generally, five guest ales are on offer, including one from the Ossett group and a dark beer. A small selection of Belgian beers and a real cider is also stocked. ⋔❀⇌⊟●⁄

William IV

247 King Cross Road, HX1 3JL
⚙ 11-11; 11.30-10.30 Sun ☎ (01422) 354889
Tetley Bitter Ⓗ
Popular pub situated in the main shopping street at King Cross. Buses from the town centre stop at the door. The lounge has a standing area and

comfortable seating. There is a small public bar to the rear, and an extension into a former shop provides further seating at a raised level. Lunches are served Monday to Saturday. Sporting fixtures feature on TV screens in both bars. Benches are provided at the rear for smokers and outdoor drinkers. ❀◐⊟⊞♣

Haworth

Fleece Inn ✔

67 Main Street, BD22 8DA

⏲ 12 (10 Sat)-11 (11.30 Fri & Sat); 10-10.30 Sun
☎ (01535) 642172 ⊕ fleece-inn.co.uk

Taylor Dark Mild, Golden Best, Best Bitter, Landlord, Ram Tam Ⓗ

A three-storey former coaching inn situated halfway up the historic steep cobbled Haworth main street. The Haworth brass band can be heard outside on some evenings rehearsing in their band room above the pub. Offering good beer, food and accommodation, it is popular with locals as well as visitors. The beer garden is three storeys up from the bar. A large range of foreign bottled beers is available. ♨❀⇔◐♿⅄⇌(KWVR)⊞(664,665)♣

Heath

King's Arms ☆

Heath Common, WF1 5SL (off A655 Wakefield-Normanton road)

⏲ 12-3, 5-11 (all day summer); 12-11 Fri; 12-midnight Sat; 12-11 Sun ☎ (01924) 377527 ⊕ kingsarmswakefield.co.uk

Clark's Classic Blonde; Taylor Landlord; Tetley Bitter Ⓗ

Built in early 1700 and converted into a pub in 1841, the King's Arms is one of a small number of pubs owned by Clark's Brewery. It has three oak-panelled rooms lit by gaslight, with original open fires lit during the colder months. To the rear is a conservatory overlooking two large beer gardens where children and dogs are welcome. There is wheelchair access to the pub and toilets. A quiz is held every Tuesday from 9.30pm.
♨Q⇋❀◐♿⊞(188)♣P⊱

Heaton

Kings Arms

10 Highgate, BD9 4BB (off A650 Keighley Rd, opp St Bede's School)

⏲ 12-midnight ☎ (01274) 543165 ⊕ kingsarmsheaton.co.uk

Copper Dragon Black Gold, Golden Pippin; guest beers Ⓗ

Traditional Victorian pub situated at the heart of the urban village of Heaton. There is a large single room downstairs, an upstairs games room and a choice of front or rear outdoor areas. This is a true community pub, popular with local residents who enjoy quizzes and games nights, plus live music at weekends. The landlord is a keen CAMRA supporter and sources beers from local independents such as Empire, Goose Eye and Elland. ❀⊞(629,680)⊱

Hebden Bridge

New Delight Inn ✔

Jack Bridge, Colden, HX7 7HT SD 962282

⏲ 12-2.30, 5-11; 12-11 Sat; 12-10 Sun ☎ (01422) 846178

Bridestones Bottleneck Bride; Young's Bitter; guest beers Ⓗ

A cosy rural pub in the delightful Colden Valley, well-placed for the Pennine Way and Calderdale Way footpaths, as well as the Pennine Bridleway. Cyclists and dog walkers are always welcome. To one side of the bar is a comfortable lounge, on the other a stone-flagged room favoured by locals and hikers. This hostelry is family-run, as is the nearby Bridestones Brewery. Guest beers usually include two from Bridestones. Camping is available in the grounds. ♨❀◐⊟⅄⊞(E)P

Heckmondwike

New Charnwood 🏆

4 Westgate, WF16 0EH (on A638 near green)

⏲ 11-11; 12-10.30 Sun ☎ (01924) 406512
⊕ thenewcharnwood.co.uk

Taylor Landlord; guest beers Ⓗ

An inviting front garden leads to an attractive bay-windowed former Oddfellows Hall, now described as a pub and dining room. Guest beers are mostly from local breweries and usually include a dark mild or old ale, all also available in the 80-seat function room. CAMRA members get a 10 per cent discount on real ales. Monday to Saturday lunch and evening menus provide high quality contemporary cuisine. A Sunday menu, served until 7pm, offers a choice of four roasts. Good bus links.
❀◐♿⊞P⊱

Hipperholme

Cock o' the North

The Conclave, South Edge Works, Brighouse Road, HX3 8EF (on A644)

⏲ 5 (4 Fri)-11; 12-11 Sat & Sun ☎ (07974) 544980

Halifax Steam Cock o' the North, Jamaican Ginger, Uncle Jon; guest beers Ⓗ

The sectional building shared with the brewery, situated next to the imposing red-brick Vulcan works, belies a well-fitted-out single-roomed bar with polished floors and fittings, inspired by 1930s Art Deco ocean liners. The atmosphere is relaxed, with a friendly, varied clientele. The bar is a showcase for the extensive range of Halifax Steam beers, with at least 10 ales on offer, together with occasional guests, increasing to 25 during frequent beer festivals, all served cold through a cooler.
Q❀⊞(548,549)P

Travellers Inn ✔

53 Tanhouse Hill, HX3 8HN (on A58, back of camping centre)

⏲ 12-midnight (11 Mon; 11.30 Tue & Wed)
☎ (01422) 202494

Fuller's London Pride; Ossett Pale Gold, Excelsior; guest beers Ⓗ

Opposite the former railway station, this traditional 18th-century, stone-built local has taken in adjoining cottages to create a series of distinct spaces. The floor is stone-flagged in the lower area, with plain floorboards in the upper part. Children and dogs are welcome until 7pm when quiet. There is a small south-facing roadside seating area. A covered yard with heating is provided for smokers. Guest beers include two from Ossett, a Riverhead or Fernandes ale, and a dark beer.
♨❀⊞(255,548,549)♣⊱

Holmfirth

Rose & Crown (Nook)

7 Victoria Square, HD9 2DN (down alley off Hollowgate)

⏲ 11.30 (12 Sun)-midnight ☎ (01484) 682373
🌐 thenookholmfirth.co.uk
Nook Yorks, Best, Blond, Red; guest beers Ⓗ
Eighteeenth-century records mention an inn and brewhouse on this site. The Nook is a deceptively spacious, multi-roomed pub with a traditional fireplace. It is the brewery tap for the Nook Brewhouse, serving LocAle beers, and has featured over 30 times in the Guide. Home-cooked food is available from 2pm each day. The Nook is renowned for its live music and open mike night every third Wednesday of the month. Beer festivals are held throughout the year. ♨❀◑◐♿🚌♣●⚟

Horbury

Boons ✔

6 Queen Street, WF4 6LP (off High Street)
⏲ 11-3, 5-11; 11-11 Fri & Sat; 12-10.30 Sun
☎ (01924) 277267
Clark's Classic Blonde; John Smith's Bitter; Taylor Landlord; guest beers Ⓗ
Centrally situated just off the High Street, this Clark's Brewery tied house caters for all age groups and is a real community pub. Four rotating guest beers are always available alongside beers from the Clark's range. At the back of the pub is a large outdoor drinking area which is that for the annual summer beer festival. ♨❀🚌(126,127,231)♣

Huddersfield

Cherry Tree ✔

16-18 John William Street, HD1 1BA
⏲ 9am-midnight (1am Fri & Sat) ☎ (01484) 448190
Greene King Ruddles Best Bitter; guest beers Ⓗ
This town-centre pub, on the ground floor of a 1960s office block, may not be the most elegant building in the Wetherspoon's chain, but what it lacks in outward aesthetics it makes up for inside. It has one large room, with a raised family dining area at the rear and a small downstairs seating space. There are many guest beers on sale and also a real cider. Management and staff are happy to advise before you buy. Q◑◐♿⇌🚌●

Grove

2 Spring Grove Street, HD1 4BP
⏲ 12-11 (midnight Thu-Sat) ☎ (01484) 430113
🌐 groveinn.co.uk
Empire Grove Grog; Fuller's London Pride; Taylor Golden Best, Landlord; Thornbridge Jaipur IPA; guest beers Ⓗ
Extensive is the only word to describe the beer choice at the Grove. There are five permanent beers, four pumps dedicated to beers from Thornbridge, Marble, Durham and BrewDog breweries, with a further nine guest beers, many rare for the region. Mild, stout and strong ale are usually available. This is complemented by the 200-plus bottled beers and nine foreign draughts. Enjoy your beers in airy, traditional surroundings and decide which is more bizarre – the bar snacks or the artwork. Q❀⊟⇌🚌⊤

King's Head

St George's Square, HD1 1JF (in station buildings, on left when exiting station)
⏲ 11.30-11; 12-10.30 Sun ☎ (01484) 511058
🌐 the-kings-head-huddersfield.co.uk
Taylor Golden Best, Landlord; guest beers Ⓗ
Formerly the Station Tavern, this pub displays a quirky and distinctive individuality, and owes its success to sound management and loyal, friendly staff. The main room has a splendid mosaic-tiled floor, and hosts live bands Sunday afternoon, piano singalongs Tuesday evening and monthly folk and blues sessions. Two smaller rooms provide extra seating. A choice of 10 beers is available, plus a range of sandwiches. The pub notably appeared on TV on Oz and James Drink to Britain. ♨♿⇌🚌⚟

Rat & Ratchet 🏆 ✔

40 Chapel Hill, HD1 3EB (on A616 below ring road)
⏲ 3-midnight; 12-12.30am Fri & Sat; 12-11 Sun
☎ (01484) 542400
Fuller's London Pride; Ossett Pale Gold, Silver King, Excelsior; guest beers Ⓗ
A perennial entry in the Guide, this pub was Branch Pub of the Year 2008, regional Cider Pub of the Year 2008 and Branch Mild Pub of the Year 2009. Thirteen handpumps feature Riverhead, Fernandes and guest beers including mild and porter, and numerous ciders. It has a jukebox, pin table and two real fires. Pub games are available and a quiz is held on Wednesday. Beer festivals are held in May (milds only) and September. There is an outdoor drinking terrace. ♨❀⇌🚌♣●P⚟

Sportsman ✔

1 St John's Road, HD1 5AY
⏲ 12-11; 11-midnight Fri & Sat ☎ (07866) 901162
🌐 undertheviaduct.com
Black Sheep Ale; Taylor Landlord; guest beers Ⓗ
A 1930s corner pub given a new lease of life with the reintroduction of real ale. Decorated in a contemporary style complementing the Art Deco features, it retains its Hammond's Brewery etched windows and corner vestibule door. It has a spacious lounge with two side rooms featuring brewery advertising. There are eight handpumps serving LocAle beers, including a mild. Home-cooked food is available 12-3pm Sunday-Thursday, 6-8pm Monday-Thursday, and 11-4pm Friday-Saturday. There is occasional live music. On the Real Ale Rail Trail. ♨❀◑◐⇌🚌⚟

Star Inn

7 Albert Street, Folly Hall, HD1 3PJ (off A616)
⏲ closed Mon; 5 (12 Sat)-11; 12-10.30 Sun
☎ (01484) 545443 🌐 thestarinn.info
Pictish Brewers Gold; Taylor Best Bitter, Landlord; guest beers Ⓗ
The deserved winner of many CAMRA awards, this welcoming pub is visited by people from all over the country. There is an emphasis on a variety of guest ales, all individually sourced and researched, including milds, stouts and porters. There is a fire during winter months, no jukebox, pool table, or games machines – just a great atmosphere. The pub holds three excellent beer festivals a year in its marquee – known nationally as some of the best in the country. ♨Q❀♿🚌⚟

White Cross Inn

2 Bradley Road, Bradley, HD2 1XD (on A62, 3 miles from town centre)
⏲ 11.45-11; 12-10.30 Sun ☎ (01484) 425728
Copper Dragon Golden Pippin; John Smith's Bitter; guest beers Ⓗ
This award-winning, local community pub is no stranger to this Guide. Situated on the busy Leeds/Bradley Road junction, the White Cross extends a warm welcome to all. The lunchtime food menu

offers good, value-for-money, home-cooked fare, and is popular with local business workers. A large lounge extends each side of the central bar area, where up to three guest beers are available. A former CAMRA Huddersfield Pub of the Year, it holds an annual February beer festival. ❀◑♿🚌(202,203)♣P⅐

Idle

Symposium Ale & Wine Bar ✔

7 Albion Road, BD10 9PY

⏲ 12-2 (not Mon & Tue), 5.30-11; 12-11 Fri & Sat; 12-10.30 Sun ☎ (01274) 616587

Beer range varies Ⓗ

A member of the Market Town Taverns group, this popular bar/restaurant offers rolling beer festivals showcasing a range of beers from brewery after brewery, primarily from the north of England. Excellent meals are available from an inventive menu. A wide selection of foreign beers is available in bottle and draught, and the wine list is extensive. The rear snug leads to an elevated terrace, popular in summer. A warm and quiet pub in an old suburban village that is remarkably easy to find. Q❀◑▶🚌(610,611,612)⅐

Ilkley

Bar T'at ✔

7 Cuncliffe Road, LS29 9DZ

⏲ 12-11 ☎ (01943) 608888

Black Sheep Best Bitter; Copper Dragon Golden Pippin; Ilkley Mary Jane; Taylor Landlord; guest beers Ⓗ

Popular side-street pub from the Market Town Taverns group, renowned for the quality of its beer and food. Guest ales usually include a mild or porter, plus brews from Yorkshire micros. A wide choice of good foreign beers is available in bottles and on draught, including Belgian fruit beers. Home-cooked food is on the menu every day. This three-storey building has a music-free bar area. It stands next to the main town centre car park. Q❀◑▶⇌🚌⅐

Riverside Hotel

Riverside Gardens, Bridge Lane, LS29 9EU

⏲ 10-11 (10.30 Sun) ☎ (01943) 607338

🌐 ilkley-riversidehotel.co.uk

Copper Dragon Best Bitter; Samuel Smith OBB; Tetley Bitter Ⓗ

Family-run hotel with 13 rooms, set by the River Wharfe in a popular park. The adjacent fish and chips shop and ice cream servery, also run by the hotel, are popular in summer. Meals are served until early evening and the bar runs a happy hour on weekdays, 4-8pm. The open fire is a welcome sight in cold weather. The start of the Dalesway is at the old Pack Horse Bridge close to the hotel. ⚘❀🛏◑▶⇌🚌P⅐

Keighley

Boltmakers Arms ✔

117 East Parade, BD21 5HX

⏲ 11-midnight (11 Mon); 12-11 Sun ☎ (01535) 661936

Taylor Dark Mild, Golden Best, Best Bitter, Landlord, Ram Tam; guest beer Ⓗ

Classic Keighley town-centre pub – the de facto Taylor's brewery tap. It has a tiny split-level layout, but this just serves to add to the character of the place. The licensees take pride in the pub and it is always very welcoming. Brewery, whisky and music memorabilia adorn the walls. The guest beer and hand-pulled cider are from various sources at the licensee's whim, and there is a fine selection of single malts. Quiz night is every Tuesday and occasional live music plays. ⚘❀⇌🚌♣●⅐

Brown Cow ✔

5 Cross Leeds Street, BD21 2LQ (bottom of West Lane, corner of Oakworth Rd)

⏲ 4-11; 12-10.30 Sun 🌐 browncowkeighley.co.uk

Taylor Dark Mild, Golden Best, Best Bitter, Landlord, Ram Tam; guest beers Ⓗ

This popular, friendly local is comfortably furnished. It features local breweriana including the original sign from Bradford's Trough Brewery. The licensees are keen local historians and the landlord is the official town mace bearer and steward. A Timothy Taylor tied house, it has two regularly changing guest beers, usually from local micros, often Brown Cow. Bad language is banned. ⚘❀🚌♣P

Cricketers Arms

Coney Lane, BD21 5JE

⏲ 11.30-midnight; 12-11.30 Sun ☎ (01535) 669912

🌐 cricketersarmskeighley.co.uk

Moorhouse's Premier Bitter; guest beers Ⓗ

Back-street pub revitalised by frequent live music sessions featuring bands from near and far. The ground-floor bar is now complemented by a downstairs bar, open Friday and Saturday evenings. Note the interesting montage of photographs taken of regulars at the top of the stairwell. The venue serves five guest ales from regional and micro-breweries nationwide, and a range of foreign bottled beers. Occasional beer festivals are held. ❀⇌🚌⅐

Livery Rooms ✔

89-97 North Street, BD21 3AA

⏲ 9am-midnight (1am Fri & Sat) ☎ (01535) 682950

Greene King Ruddles Best Bitter, Abbot; guest beers Ⓗ

This typical large open-plan Wetherspoon's in the town centre has previously been stables, a temperance hall, a bingo hall and various shops. The history of the building is displayed, using different art forms, on the walls throughout the pub. The guest beer policy strongly supports beers from local micros. The pub is very handily positioned for the bus station, and can get busy at weekends. ⚘❀◑▶♿⇌🚌●⅐

Knottingley

Steampacket

2 Bendles, Racca Green, WF11 8AT (200m off the A645 next to the Aire & Calder Canal)

⏲ 12 (11 Sun)-11 ☎ (01977) 671862

Beer range varies Ⓗ

On the banks of the Aire & Calder Navigation, this historic pub is still known locally as the Commercial, its name until 1986, due to its association with the former adjacent dockyard. A massive anchor in the porch remains. In 1893 the first screw steamer, the Message, was launched from here. This venue is the only real ale outlet in town. A decked area overlooks the tow path and moorings, with a secure children's play area at the rear. ⚘❀🖵🚌(145,148,149)P

Ledsham

Chequers Inn

Claypit Lane, LS25 5LP

11-11; closed Sun ☎ (01977) 683135

Brown Cow Bitter, seasonal beers; John Smith's Bitter; Taylor Landlord; Theakston Best Bitter H

A cosy old English country pub with a well-regarded restaurant and enigmatic garden in the picturesque village of Ledsham, across the road from All Saints – possibly Yorkshire's oldest church. It has two main rooms either side of the bar, plus two smaller rooms complete with oak beams, wood fires, jugs, brasses, sporting memorabilia, old photographs and beer mats from previous guest beers. An extensive range of meals and sandwiches is served at all times – outside in the summer.

Leeds: Chapel Allerton

Further North

194 Harrogate Road, LS7 4NZ

5.30-11 (midnight Thu & Fri); 4-midnight Sat; 4-11 Sun

☎ (0113) 237 0962 furthernorth.co.uk

Beer range varies H

The sister bar to North in the city centre, this former car spares shop was converted to a one-room bar three years ago. It describes itself as a small, beautiful retreat away from the bustle of the centre of Chapel Allerton. The bijou bar is well stocked with a good selection of world bottled beers in addition to two often varying draught ales from Rooster's, Marble, Elland and Ossett.

Regent

15-17 Regent Street,, off Harrogate Road, LS7 4PE

11-11 (midnight Fri & Sat); 12-10.30 Sun

☎ (0113) 293 9395

Tetley Mild; guest beers H

Stone-built two-roomed pub dating from 1827. Recently refurbished but still retaining a traditional feel, it is popular with locals and visitors alike. Five beers are offered, including the rare Tetley Mild. The introduction of guest beers from near and far has been a great success. Quiz nights on Monday, Tuesday and Thursday have general knowledge, music and movie themes. Sky and ESPN screen sports events. Look for the TV in the beer garden. Food is available until 8pm. P

Three Hulats

13 Harrogate Road, Chapel Allerton, LS7 3NB

9am-midnight (1am Fri & Sat) ☎ (0113) 262 0524

Greene King Ruddles Best Bitter, Abbot; guest beers H

An L-shaped bar, three drinking areas, eight changing and two regular ales give The Hulats the widest beer choice in Chapel Allerton. Formerly The Mexborough, this pub is a popular meeting place for groups and organisations by day and night. Food is served all day and families are welcome until 9pm. The landlord holds themed beer festivals throughout the year; don't miss the Moorhouse's Halloween event. Trips to local breweries are occasionally arranged. Q P

Leeds: City

Mr Foley's Cask Ale House

159 The Headrow, LS1 5RG (opp town hall)

11?11 (midnight Fri & Sat) ☎ (0113) 242 9674

Beer range varies H

Occupying the ground floor of the impressive Pearl Assurance building, this multi-layered pub offers something for everyone, even the most discerning drinker. A fine array of handpumps – which always dispense a beer from York and Elland breweries – adorns the bar, which is backed by fridges full of bottles of world beers. Sporty TV is popular here, but it is possible to find a quieter corner. There is a Tuesday quiz, and acoustic music on the first Sunday of the month.

North

24 New Briggate, LS1 6NU

12-2am (1am Mon & Tue); 12-midnight Sun

☎ (0113) 242 4540 northbar.com

Outlaw Wild Mule; guest beers H

Superficially, North is just like many bars in Leeds; it has an unassuming exterior which is easy to miss, and a compact interior which is sparsely decorated. But dig deeper and one of the great treasures of Leeds is discovered. You will find three changing guest beers, always a dark beer and usually a local ale, a wall of beer names, 100 plus global bottles, at least two beer festivals a year and some of the best pies in the north.

Palace

Kirkgate, LS2 7DJ

11-11.30 (midnight Fri & Sat); 12-11 Sun

☎ (0113) 244 5882

Draught Bass; Tetley Bitter; guest beers H

The Palace is situated adjacent to the old East Bar Stone, which once marked the City boundary and allowed those within the Bar special privileges. This spacious two-tiered pub still has traces of its former three-roomed layout, as well as the stone flags in the lower tier. Myriad guest ales are available, including a mild or stout, along with Westons Old Rosie for the cider lovers.

Reliance

76-78 North Street, LS2 7PN (near the inner ring road and Leeds College of Building)

12-11 (midnight Fri & Sat); 11-10.30 Sun

☎ (0113) 295 6060 the-reliance.co.uk

Acorn Reliance Bitter; guest beer H

Don't be fooled by the shabby-looking exterior, the interior is a wonder to behold, offering views of the surrounding area through the massive windows of this Victorian building. The food offerings are above that of standard pub grub, including the signature Erdinger battered fish finger sandwiches. Local artists' work adorns the walls, changing every six weeks. Alfresco drinking is available on the pavement outside. A weekly quiz is held every Sunday. The pub features a dedicated cider/perry handpump.

Scarbrough Hotel

Bishopgate Street, LS1 5DY

11-midnight; 10-10.30 Sun ☎ (0113) 243 4590

Black Sheep Best Bitter; Fuller's London Pride; Taylor Landlord; Tetley Bitter H

A busy city-centre pub, now part of the JJ Nicholson brand. Pies are the featured food offering, available all day, along with the usual pub fare. The national ale brands are supplemented by a selection of guests, usually from Yorkshire micros. Two real ciders are kept on gravity dispense. Both beer and cider festivals feature. Reputed to offer the best Tetley Bitter in the city centre. (1)

Templar
2 Templar Street, LS2 7NU
11-11; 12-10.30 Sun ☎ (0113) 245 9751
Tetley Mild, Bitter; guest beers Ⓗ
One of the few pubs remaining in Leeds with the cream and green glazed Burmantofts tiles on the exterior of the building, and examples of the Bowing Courtier logo in the leaded upper window panes from the days of being a Melbourne's pub. The interior is divided into two areas, with a corridor separating them. At one end of the bar there are some drinking booths and at the other an area with an attractive red-tiled fireplace.

Town Hall Tavern ✔
17 Westgate, LS1 2RA
11.30-11; closed Sun ☎ (0113) 244 0765
townhalltavernleeds.co.uk
Taylor Golden Best, Best Bitter, Landlord, Ram Tam, seasonal beers Ⓗ
Neatly tucked between taller office buildings, this three-storey brick building is decorated in the recognisable livery of owners Timothy Taylor. Tasteful decoration with lots of pictures gives it a traditional feel, with the light-wood panelling adding a fresh, modern look. Pies and jackets are served to the suits at lunchtime, whereas the evening crowd makes the pub a city-centre local. The friendly, efficient staff effortlessly make the transition between the two, ensuring everyone is made welcome.

Victoria Family & Commercial
28 Great George Street, LS1 3DL (behind town hall)
10-11 (midnight Thu-Sat); 12-6 Sun ☎ (0113) 245 1386
Acorn Barnsley Bitter; Taylor Landlord; Tetley Dark Mild, Bitter Ⓗ
Despite being five storeys high, this pub is hidden away behind the town hall. The need to accommodate travelling judges has long since passed, but the Vic F&C still provides sustenance to those visiting the area. Divided into three rooms, the pub has an air of grandeur about it. Few pubs can boast such a long ornate bar or numerous styles of glass decoration, let alone working snob screens. Up to five guest beers are on offer.

Whitelocks First City Luncheon Bar ★ ✔
Turks Head Yard, off Briggate, LS1 6HB
11-11 (midnight Fri & Sat); 12-6 Sun ☎ (0113) 245 3950
whitelocks.co.uk
Caledonian Deuchars IPA; Theakston Best Bitter, Old Peculier; guest beers Ⓗ
Situated on one of the city's main shopping streets, this long, narrow, classic Leeds yard pub was said to be 'the very heart of Leeds' by Sir John Betjeman. Licensed since 1715, although the building has been around a lot longer, the present delightfully atmospheric Victorian interior dates from 1895. The fine ceramic bar counter and brewery mirrors are of particular note. Five changing guest beers are offered. The restaurant is famous for its hearty fare, plus bar snacks. The newer bar, Ma Gamps, further up the yard, is open at weekends. Q

Leeds: Headingley

Arcadia Ale & Wine Bar 🏆 ✔
34 Arndale Centre, Otley Road, LS6 2UE (corner of Alma Road)
12-11 ☎ (0113) 274 5599
Black Sheep Best Bitter; Taylor Landlord; guest beers Ⓗ
Arcadia has recently been cleverly extended into the adjoining unit and now includes a disabled toilet. The bar has ground-floor rooms plus an upstairs mezzanine level. Eight beers are offered, including ales from Copper Dragon, Elland and Leeds breweries, plus guests from around the region. Draught and bottled foreign beers plus a range of wines also feature. Food is served Thursday to Sunday. Children are not allowed, but dogs are welcome. Waiter service is sometimes offered on busy nights. Q

Leeds: Holbeck

Cross Keys
Water Lane, LS11 5WD
12-11 (midnight Fri & Sat; 10.30 Sun) ☎ (0113) 243 3711
the-crosskeys.com
Beer range varies Ⓗ
Exposed beams, stone flags, tiles and bare brickwork abound in this pub, which is under the same ownership as the city-centre North Bar and Reliance. Up to four guest beers are served, with one handpump for a stout or porter. There is also a range of bottled beers from Germany, Belgium and the US. Downstairs, two rooms wrap around a central bar area, each with its own wood-burning stove. Upstairs is another bar and function room. Sunday meals are served 12-5pm.

Grove Inn
Back Row, LS11 5PL
12-11 (midnight Fri & Sat) ☎ (0113) 243 9254
Daleside Blonde; Moorhouse's Black Cat, Pride of Pendle; guest beers Ⓗ
Just outside the city centre, next to the tallest building in Yorkshire, the Grove is an oasis of history in a rising sea of modernity. A rare surviving example of a traditional West Riding corridor pub, first mentioned in a survey of Leeds in 1850, its four rooms include a concert room and a tap room. Guest beers are all sourced through SIBA and concentrate on West Yorkshire micros. Dogs are welcome, provided resident Donut approves.
Q (1,2,3)

Midnight Bell
101 Water Lane, LS11 5QN (near Globe Rd jct)
11.30-11 (midnight Fri & Sat); 12-11 Sun
☎ (0113) 244 5044 midnightbell.co.uk
Leeds Pale, Best, Midnight Bell; guest beers Ⓗ
Part of the heritage Round Foundry area, a pioneering early industrial revolution works, in Holbeck Urban Village. The premises were excellently converted from rundown buildings in 2008 by Leeds Brewery. The pub is on two levels, with quality modern decor and a sunny rear terrace adjoining Wonderwood – a novel micro-park. All Leeds beers including a seasonal special are offered, plus two guests. An a la carte menu is available 6-9pm, plus bar meals 12-3, 6-9pm.
Q

Leeds: Horsforth

Old Kings Arms
The Green, LS18 5JB (opp The Green)
9am-11 (11.30 Wed & Thu; midnight Fri & Sat); 11-midnight Sun ☎ (0113) 281 9709

Copper Dragon Golden Pippin; Tetley Bitter; guest beers H
This former Tetley Festival Ale House is situated opposite The Green, at the bottom of Town Street. One of the guest ales is from Saltaire Brewery, and Westons Old Rosie cider is served on handpump. The pub hosts occasional live music, and there is lively karaoke on Sunday evening. Good value food is served at lunchtime. Many unusual photographs and pictures adorn the walls of this bare-boarded pub, which is popular for live TV sport.
❀◑♿🚌(50,50A)●P⌐

Town Street Tavern ✔
16-18 Town Street, LS18 4RJ
✪ 12-11 (10.30 Sun) ☎ (0113) 281 9996
Black Sheep Best Bitter; Copper Dragon Golden Pippin; Leeds Pale; Taylor Best Bitter; guest beers H
Conveniently situated on several bus routes in the centre of Horsforth's Town Street, this modern bar has eight handpumps featuring guest ales mainly from northern micro-breweries. Draught and bottled continental beers are also available. The upstairs brasserie serves evening meals from 6pm, while a bar menu is available during the day. Accompanied children are allowed in the bar until 6pm. There is a small outdoor drinking area which doubles as a smoking area. Q❀◑♿🚌(50,50A)⌐

Leeds: Kirkstall

West End House ✔
26 Abbey Road, LS5 3HS
✪ 11.30-11; 12-midnight Thu-Sat; 12-11 Sun
☎ (0113) 228 9108
Copper Dragon Golden Pippin; Taylor Landlord; guest beers H
This traditional, welcoming pub close to Kirkstall Abbey has a central bar surrounded by comfortable seating and a dining area serving high quality food. The TV in one corner does not intrude on the main area, which provides a convivial atmosphere for visitors and locals alike. Popular quiz nights are Tuesday and Thursday. The regular beers rotate on four handpumps, with guests from regional breweries such as Salamander and Jennings, together with an additional pump for Old Rosie cider. ❀◑♿⇌(Headingley)🚌(33,33A,757)●⌐

Leeds: Newlay

Abbey
99 Pollard Lane, LS13 1EQ (vehicle access from B6157 only) SE239367
✪ 12-11 (10.30 Sun) ☎ (0113) 258 1248
🌐 theabbey-inn.co.uk
Leeds Pale; guest beers H
Grade II-listed building with low ceilings, situated between the River Aire and the Leeds-Liverpool canal, with moorings nearby. The pub takes its name from the 12th-century Kirkstall Abbey just over a mile away, and is popular with walkers exploring the valley. Guest beers are mainly from local breweries, with some from further afield. There are jam sessions on Tuesday, live music on Saturday and a quiz night on Sunday. An annual beer festival is held. ❀◑🚌♣P⌐

Leeds: Rodley

Owl
1 Rodley Lane, LS13 1LB (on corner of Bagley Lane)
✪ 12-11 (midnight Fri & Sat) ☎ (0113) 256 5242
🌐 theowlatrodley.co.uk
John Smith's Bitter; Taylor Landlord; guest beers H
The large lounge has a conservatory leading to the beer garden, which has a children's play area. Dogs are welcome in the tap room, where pool and darts are played. Guest ales include beers from Copper Dragon and Leeds breweries. Food is served until 7.30pm Monday to Saturday, with a carvery on Sunday until 5pm. A beer festival is held over the August bank holiday weekend. Live music is on Friday and Saturday, with a quiz on Thursday.
♨❀◑◐♿🚌(8,9,16A)♣P⌐

Rodley Barge
182-184 Town Street, LS13 1HP
✪ 12-3, 5-11; 12-11 Fri-Sun ☎ (0113) 257 4606
🌐 therodleybarge.wetpaint.com
Clarks Rodley Barge Bitter; Tetley Bitter; guest beers H
This comfortable stone-built pub next to the Leeds-Liverpool canal serves up to five real ales, with guest ales mostly from local micro-breweries. There are two rooms served by a central bar; children are welcome in the back bar. Various quizzes are hosted throughout the week, and a beer festival is held over the August bank holiday weekend. The Barge Anglers angling team meet at the pub once a month. Food is served 12-2pm, Monday to Friday. ♔♨❀◑◐♿🚌(8,9,16A)♣⌐

Leeds: Woodhouse

Chemic ✔
9 Johnston Street, LS6 2NG
✪ 12-midnight (1am Fri & Sat); 12-11.30 Sun
☎ (0113) 245 7670 🌐 myspace.com/chemictavern
Black Sheep Best Bitter; Leeds Pale, Best, Midnight Bell; Taylor Landlord H
This local CAMRA award-winning pub is the perfect blend of locals, students and ex-students, a true community pub. There are two clean and tidy rooms that are served from a central wood-panelled bar. The front room is a cosy, almost country-pub-like lounge, oddly shaped and simply decorated. The rear room is a traditional bare-boarded bar, not quite as plush but still comfortable. Several events are held throughout the week, including a comedy writers' club.
❀◐🚌(51,55,62)♣●P

Liversedge

Black Bull ✔
37 Halifax Road, WF15 6JR (on A649, near A62)
✪ 12-midnight (1am Fri & Sat) ☎ (01924) 403779
Fuller's London Pride; Ossett Pale Gold, Black Bull Bitter, Silver King, Excelsior; guest beers H
Ossett Brewery's first pub is a fine example of a sociable community hostelry where conversation with strangers comes easy. Although opened out slightly, each of the five rooms has its own unique style. The new stained glass and woodwork in one has led some regulars to call it the chapel. Most of the nine handpumps dispense Ossett, Fernandes or Riverhead beers, including a mild or dark ale. Other drinks are all selected for quality. Last admission is 30-60 minutes before closing time.
♔♨❀🚌(254)♣P⌐

Marsden

Riverhead Brewery Tap ✓

Argyle Street, HD7 6BR (overlooking River Colne)
⏲ 12-midnight (1am Fri); 11-1am Sat ☎ (01484) 841270
Ossett Pale Gold, Silver King; Riverhead Sparth Mild, Butterley Bitter, March Haigh; guest beers Ⓗ
Formerly a Co-op, now part of Ossett Brewery's estate, this pub is at the centre of village life. It offers a relaxed atmosphere and pleasant surroundings. Great pictures of Marsden adorn the walls. Fantastic food is served in the restaurant and there is a riverside terrace for alfresco drinking. The micro-brewery is visible from the bar – LocAle does not get any more local than this. Up to 10 beers are available: usually six from Riverhead, two from Ossett, London Pride and a guest. Dogs are welcome. Q❀♿⇌🚌(185)

Meltham

Wills O' Nats ✓

Blackmoorfoot Road, HD9 5PS SE 009124
⏲ 11.45-3, 5-midnight; 11.45-midnight Sat & Sun
☎ (01484) 850078
Black Sheep Best Bitter; Taylor Landlord; Tetley Bitter; guest beers Ⓗ
In 1890, William, son of Nathaniel, became landlord of the Spotted Cow. Soon it became known as the Wills, and eventually the name was changed to Wills O' Nats. Today it is renowned for its locally sourced, home-cooked food and Cask Marque beers. Live music events are held on the last Saturday of each month in the summer. In Summer Wine country, close to the Peak District, the views are stunning. A welcome stop for families, walkers and their dogs.
♨❀◐◑♿🚌(388)P⚟

Mirfield

Navigation Tavern

6 Station Road, WF14 8NL (between rail station and canal)
⏲ 11.30-11 (midnight Fri & Sat); 12-10.30 Sun
☎ (01924) 492476
John Smith's Bitter; Theakston Best Bitter, Black Bull Bitter, XB, Old Peculier; guest beers Ⓗ
Popular canalside free house serving Theakston, John Smith's and up to five guest ales. The pub is a registered ambassador for Theakston beers at competitive prices. Situated between Mirfield railway station and the Calder and Hebble Navigation, adjacent to a boatyard and marina, it features on the Transpennine Real Ale Trail. It has very active sports and pool teams, with a quiz night Thursday and karaoke on Sunday night. The landlord is a beer enthusiast and hosts occasional beer festivals. ❀⛴⇌🚌♣P⚟

Old Colonial Club

Dunbottle Lane, WF14 9JJ (off A644 up Church Lane, 1 mile NNE of station)
⏲ 5-midnight; 4-1am Fri; 1-1am Sat; 12-11 Sun
☎ (01924) 496920 🌐 theoldcolonial.co.uk
Copper Dragon Best Bitter; guest beers Ⓗ
Formerly a working men's club, this is now run by an enthusiastic real ale supporter. The five guest beers are from a wide range of brewers and often include one-off or commemorative brews. The excellent value Sunday lunch is very popular. There is a Royal British Legion memorial in the garden, and the National Pie-eating Championship is held here. The spacious conservatory is popular for meetings and functions. Evening meals are available Thursday 6-8pm, Friday 5.30-8pm, and Saturday 5.30-7.30pm. ⛄❀◑♿🚌(202,205)P⚟

Mytholmroyd

Shoulder of Mutton

86 New Road, HX7 5DZ (on B6138, near station)
⏲ 11.30-3, 7-11; 11.30-11 Sat; 12-10.30 Sun
☎ (01422) 883168
Black Sheep Best Bitter; Copper Dragon Best Bitter, Golden Pippin; Taylor Landlord; guest beers Ⓗ
Village inn with a strong community feel and a warm welcome for walkers and other visitors. Excellent value, quality home-cooked food is available lunchtimes and evenings (not Mon and Tue). Guest beers are from the Enterprise list. Major sporting events are shown on large-screen TV, but there is normally a quiet corner to be found. The bar displays memorabilia relating to the Cragg Vale Coiners, a gang of 18th-century forgers. A smoking shelter is located at the rear. ❀◐◑⇌🚌♣P⚟

Netherton

Beaumont Arms

396 Meltham Road, HD4 7EL (on B6108)
⏲ 12-2, 4-11 (10 Mon); 12-11 Fri & Sun; 2.30-11 Sat
☎ (01484) 661984
Tetley Bitter; guest beers Ⓗ
A convivial pub, popular with locals and visitors alike, and a regular meeting place for local clubs and organisations. A large-screen TV shows sports events, and prize quizzes are held every Wednesday and Sunday night. Food is served lunchtimes Monday-Friday and Monday evening (5-8pm) only. The first Monday evening of the month is a well-attended curry night. Although popular for its real ales, the pub also carries a good range of wines by the glass or bottle.
❀◐◑🚌(321,324,323)⚟

North Featherstone

Bradley Arms

96 Willow Lane, WF7 6BG (on B6421)
⏲ 3 (12 Sat & Sun)-midnight ☎ (07833) 762360
Black Sheep Best Bitter; John Smith's Bitter; guest beers Ⓗ
Lovely old ex-farm building with several rooms and levels. This inn has a rich history and was a key location in the infamous Featherstone Massacre of 1893, when soldiers fired on striking miners, killing two. Cunninghame Graham, co-founder of the Scottish Labour Party and workers' rights champion, spoke here at the time of the massacre. Candle-lit evenings in the lounge are a feature, with Sky Sports available in the bar. Much Featherstone Rovers memorabilia is on display.
♨Q❀◐◑🖵🚌(147,157,177)♣P⚟

Northowram

Yew Tree

20 Northowram Green, HX3 7JE
⏲ 2-midnight (1am Fri); 11.30-1am Sat; 12-midnight Sun
☎ (01422) 202316
Beer range varies Ⓗ
A village-centre local with an L-shaped lounge with pictures and plates displayed. The bar also serves the pool room, which has a display of trophies. A

snooker club and a ladies' walking club are among the diverse groups that meet here. The pub's name comes from a yew tree that was reputed to grow in a former adjacent cemetery.
♔✿⊟(508,681,682)♣P⅟

Ogden

Causeway Foot

13 Causeway Foot, Keighley Road, HX2 8XX (on A629)
✪ 12-2.30 (not Mon & Tue), 5.30 (6 Tue)-11; 12-11 Sat & Sun
☎ (01422) 240273 🌐 thecausewayfootinn.co.uk
Black Sheep Best Bitter; Taylor Landlord; guest beers ⊞
A biker, dog and walker-friendly main road inn near Ogden Water. The comfortable lounge has an adjoining area with settees and a large fireplace. A small dining room lies beyond. Guest beers are from regional and micro-breweries and always include one from Goose Eye. Camping is available on land to the rear of the pub. Bus services are restricted to daytime. ♔♉✿◑⛺⊟(502,504)P

Ossett

Brewer's Pride

Low Mill Road, WF5 8ND (at bottom of Healey Road, 1½ miles from town centre)
✪ 12-11 (10.30 Sun) ☎ (01924) 273865
🌐 brewers-pride.co.uk
Bob's Brewing Co White Lion; Rudgate Ruby Mild; guest beers ⊞
A genuine free house on the outskirts of Ossett, five minutes' walk from the Calder & Hebble canal. Two resident beers are offered plus seven varying guest ales from a wide range of micro-breweries. An excellent menu and evening specials are available (Mon-Sat 12-2pm; Tue-Thu 6-9pm). Monday is quiz night with a hot supper, and there is live music on the first Sunday of each month. Dogs are welcome and well-behaved children until 7pm. There is an August bank holiday beer festival.
♔Q✿◑⊟(102)⅟

Tap ✔

2 The Green, WF5 8JS (from town centre turn left onto Queen St, which becomes The Green)
✪ 3 (12 Thu & Sun)-1am; 12-2am Fri & Sat
☎ (01924) 272215
Ossett Pale Gold, Silver King, Excelsior; guest beers ⊞
Formerly the Mason's Arms, the pub was bought by Ossett Brewery and is now its brewery tap. Alongside the three regular Ossett beers there is usually a special/seasonal beer from Ossett, plus five guest ales. A real wood fire and stone-flagged floors give an old fashioned feel. ♔Q✿⊟(117)P⅟

Otley

Junction

44 Bondgate, LS21 1AD (corner of Bondgate and Charles Street)
✪ 11-11 (midnight Fri & Sat); 12-10.30 Sun
☎ (01943) 463233
Leeds Pale; Taylor Best Bitter, Landlord; Theakston Best Bitter, Old Peculier; guest beers ⊞
This popular street-corner ale house boasts 11 handpumps, with four guest ales from around the country supplementing the seven regular beers. It also serves real cider, and has a collection of over 50 malt whiskies and eight gins. Inside, irregular wooden beams and a tiled floor are complemented by pictures of old Otley, and various unusual artefacts, including some interesting metal beer advertisements and mirrors. There is live music on Tuesday, and a DJ on Sunday. ♔✿⊟♣●⅟

Manor House

Walkergate, LS21 1HB (between library and maypole)
✪ 12-midnight (1am Fri & Sat) ☎ (01943) 463807
Thwaites Nutty Black, Original, Lancaster Bomber, Wainwright's, seasonal beers ⊞
This friendly pub located between the library and the maypole is a rare outlet for Thwaites ales in the Leeds area. The pub is carpeted throughout, with an open-plan layout and a real fire. Thursday is music night, with the house DJ and live acts alternating weekly. The outdoor drinking area to the rear features trestle tables and a heated smoking shelter. Various local clubs meet here, including the darts and dominoes teams on Mondays. ♔✿♿⊟♣⅟

Overton

Reindeer 🏆

204 Old Road, WF4 4RL (turn left off A642 in Middlestown, continue for 1 mile, pub on right)
✪ 12 (4 Mon)-midnight; 12-11 Sun ☎ (01924) 848374
John Smith's Bitter; guest beers ⊞
A traditional free house and Wakefield CAMRA Pub of the Year 2009. Guest beers are mainly from local breweries and there is also real cider on handpull. Home-cooked food, including real chips, is served in the separate restaurant or conservatory which leads to the beer garden overlooking the National Coal Mining Museum. A free quiz and supper are hosted on Wednesday night. The games room has a pool table, dartboard, dominoes and games machines. Outside is a covered smoking area.
♔Q♉✿◑⊟(128,232)♣●P⅟

Oxenhope

Waggon & Horses Inn

Dyke Nook, Hebden Bridge Road, BD22 9QE
✪ 12-11 ☎ (01535) 643302
🌐 waggonandhorsesoxenhope.co.uk
Beer range varies ⊞
West Yorkshire's highest free house affords magnificent views across the Worth Valley. Surrounded by rugged moors, the location can be bliss on a sunny day and foul when the weather gets angry. Nonetheless, the pub offers fine sanctuary, with a warm welcome, roaring fires in winter, an ever-changing range of up to five cask ales mainly from micro-breweries, and fine home-cooked food. ♔✿⛟◑⊟(500)P

Pudsey

Fleece

100 Fartown, LS28 8LU
✪ 12-11 (10.30 Sun) ☎ (0113) 236 2748
Taylor Landlord; Tetley Bitter ⊞
On the edge of Pudsey and set back from the road, this stone-built pub is a comfortable two-roomed local. To the left is a small tap room known as the Snug where you can catch up on the latest sporting action. The larger lounge is divided into two; the front has parquet flooring and the rear is carpeted. The carefully chosen guest beer often comes from one of the many quality local breweries.
✿⊡⊟(40,40A,205)P

Rastrick

Globe

66 Rastrick Common, HD6 3EL
⊙ 12 (4 Mon)-midnight ☎ (01484) 713169
Greene King IPA; Tetley Bitter; guest beers Ⓗ
About 300 years old, known as the Red Lion in the 18th century and said to be haunted by a former landlady, the Globe was orginally a terrace of cottages. Nowadays, this popular locals' pub has a very pleasant conservatory extension for diners. The decor celebrates Shakespeare and the Globe Theatre – look for the timeline of Shakespeare's life near the pool table. Pool teams play in a Monday night league. The guest beers are from the Punch list. ❀◐⇌(Brighouse)🚌(547,570)♣P⁻

Saltaire

Fanny's Ale & Cider House 🏆

63 Saltaire Road, BD18 3JN (on A657 opp fire station)
⊙ 12 (5 Mon)-11; 12-midnight Fri & Sat ☎ (01274) 591419
🌐 fannysalehouse.com
Taylor Golden Best, Landlord; Theakston Old Peculier; guest beers Ⓗ
Near the historic Salts Mill complex and the world heritage site of Saltaire Village, this cosy pub was originally a beer shop. It is now a fully licensed free house stocking an excellent range of beers and also serving a number of draught ciders. A recent extension increased the seating capacity downstairs and added disabled access, while an upstairs room has comfortable seating. The gas-lit lounge is adorned with breweriana; real fires add nicely to the warm welcome. Bradford CAMRA Pub of the Year 2009. ♨♿⇌(662)♣●

Victoria

192 Saltaire Road, BD18 3JF (5 minutes' walk from railway station)
⊙ 11.30-11.30 (12.30am Fri & Sat) ☎ (01274) 595090
Copper Dragon Golden Pippin; Greene King Abbot; Tetley Bitter; guest beers Ⓗ
Traditional community pub, close to Saltaire Village world heritage site, with a friendly atmosphere where children and dogs are welcome. There is a lounge with real fires and a separate public bar with a pool table and pinball machine. A quiz is held on Wednesday night and live music plays each Saturday, with an acoustic jam session on Thursday. See the Facebook group 'The Vic, Saltaire' for information. Three regular ales and two guests are served, including beers from local breweries. ♨❀◫⇌🚌(662,677)♣P⁻

Shipley

Sir Norman Rae ✔

Victoria House, Market Square, BD18 3QB (50m from clock tower)
⊙ 9am-midnight (1am Fri & Sat) ☎ (01274) 535290
Greene King IPA, Ruddles Best Bitter, Abbot; guest beers Ⓗ
Centrally located in the town, adjacent to the bus station and five minutes from the train station, this former department store originally opened as a Lloyds No 1 bar, but is now a standard Wetherspoon outlet. The large open-plan layout provides comfortable surroundings in which to enjoy the wide ranging beer and food menu. Many ales come from local micros. The pub hosts regular Meet the Brewer events and is a Bradford CAMRA Pub of the Season winner. ◑◐♿⇌🚌●

Silsden

Kings Arms ✔

Bolton Road, BD20 0JY
⊙ 12-midnight ☎ (01535) 653216
Theakston Best Bitter; guest beers Ⓗ
A vibrant pub featuring regular folk sessions, quizzes and live music. Originally three cottages, the pub is now divided into three rooms, one containing a coal fire. Pub games include darts, dominoes, cards and cribbage. Two regularly changing guest beers are from the Punch Finest Cask list. A real cider or perry is also available. Dogs and well-behaved children are welcome. ♨❀🚌(70,712,762)♣●P⁻

Slaithwaite

Commercial

1 Carr Lane, HD7 5AN (off A62)
⊙ 12-midnight ☎ (01484) 846258
Empire Commerciale, Moonraker Mild; guest beers Ⓗ
Genuine free house, owned by the licensees of the nearby Swan. It reopened in 2009 and, following a radical overhaul, is now a far cry from the sorry state it was in previously. The venue displays modern and traditional features, including a useful meeting room – available free of charge. Nine handpumps dispense a bitter and a mild from the nearby Empire Brewery, plus six guests and a traditional cider. Sandwiches and snacks are served Thursday-Saturday. Ramblers and their dogs are welcomed. Q❀⇌🚌♣●⁻

Swan

Carr Lane, HD7 5BQ (off A62, turn right at village centre, under viaduct)
⊙ 4-midnight (1am Fri); 12-1am Sat; 12-midnight Sun
☎ (01484) 843225
Taylor Golden Best; guest beers Ⓗ
Friendly roadside pub overlooked by a railway viaduct, a short stroll from its partner pub The Commercial, run by the same licensees. The Swan is very community focused, with local causes readily supported. Two excellent beer festivals are staged in May and October. The pub's rotating beer range usually includes one from the Empire brewery, plus two more, all at the same price. A light food menu is served at weekends. The pub features on the Transpennine Real Ale Trail ❀◫⇌🚌♣P⁻

South Elmsall

Barnsley Oak

Mill Lane, WF9 2DT (on B6474, off A638 Doncaster-Wakefield road)
⊙ 12 (11.30 Sun)-11.30 ☎ (01977) 643427
John Smith's Bitter; guest beers Ⓗ
This former mining area is fortunate to be served by such a fine community pub. Demand for cask ale continues to grow and this venue often features a guest ale brewed in Yorkshire. Excellent value food is served all day until 7.45pm (4.30pm Sun); in addition, there are occasional themed food evenings. Children are welcome and meals can be served in the conservatory, which affords panoramic views. Quiz nights are Tuesday and Sunday.
❀◑◐◫⇌(South Elmsall/Moorthorpe)🚌(46,496) P⁻

Southowram

Shoulder of Mutton ✔

14 Cain Lane, HX3 9SB
⏲ 12-midnight (11 Sun) ☎ (07707) 358697
Beer range varies Ⓗ
This busy village local has won awards including Best Community Pub in Yorkshire and the north-east, and a Pubs in Bloom award for its floral display enhancing the roadside frontage. The building is thought to be over 300 years old. The interior has an L-shaped lounge and a busy pool room. Blonde and gold beers are favourites for the two guest beers. 🚌(571,572)♣⅃

Sowerby Bridge

Firehouse

1 Town Hall Street, HX6 2QD
⏲ 4-11.30; 12-11.30 Fri-Sun ☎ (01422) 832586
🌐 firehouserestaurant.co.uk
Taylor Golden Best, Landlord; guest beers Ⓗ
Situated in Sowerby Bridge centre, this modern bar and restaurant is not your typical real ale venue. This prominent building dating from 1874 has been stylishly converted from offices. The guest beers always include an ale from a local brewery plus one from a regional outlet. A family-run concern, this bar and restaurant has a growing reputation, not just for its ales but also for food. In particular the open pizza oven produces authentic-style Italian pizzas. ◑♿⇌🚌⅃

Jubilee Refreshment Rooms

Station Road, HX6 3AB (at railway station)
⏲ 12-11 (10.30 Sun) ☎ (01422) 648285
🌐 jubileerefreshmentrooms.co.uk
Beer range varies Ⓗ
Set in a lovingly restored compact railway station building dating from 1876, the café bar serves predominantly local beers on up to six handpumps, plus a choice of bottled ciders and European lagers. Photographs, railway memorabilia and breweriana are on display. The bar makes an ideal stop on a Calder Valley Rail Ale trip, while walking (on a Calderdale Way link path), cycling (near national routes 66 and 68) or canal cruising (Rochdale canal basin is 400 metres away). ♨Q❀◑♿⇌P

Puzzle Hall

21 Hollins Mill Lane, HX6 2RF (400m from A58)
⏲ 3-11.30 (12.30am Fri & Sat) ☎ (01422) 835547
🌐 thepuzzlehall.com
Taylor Golden Best, Landlord; guest beers Ⓗ
Nestling between the canal and river and dating from the 1700s, this former brew-pub is dominated by the tower of the old brewery. It offers six beers, one from Goose Eye and one from Saltaire, plus two rotating guests. Well known as a music venue, live bands play on Thursday and Saturday and jazz on Tuesday. Chess is on Monday, poker on Wednesday and poetry on the first Monday of the month. ♨❀⇌🚌⅃

Shepherd's Rest ✔

125 Bolton Brow, HX6 2BD (on A58 towards Halifax)
⏲ 3-11.30; 12-11.30 Fri-Sun ☎ (01422) 831937
Ossett Pale Gold, Shepherd's Rest, Excelsior; guest beers Ⓗ
Acquired in 2003 by Ossett Brewery, this is a good example of a local pub. The open-plan interior helps to provide a welcoming atmosphere, with quiet corners if you wish. Built in 1877, the pub has a stone-flagged floor. Quiz night is Monday and a beer festival is held in July each year. Local CAMRA pub of the year in 2008. ♨Q❀⇌🚌♣⅃

White Horse

Burnley Road, Friendly, HX6 2UG
⏲ 12-11 (10.30 Sun) ☎ (01422) 831173
Tetley Bitter; guest beer Ⓗ
White painted pub set back from the busy A646 Burnley Road, on the main bus route from Halifax to Todmorden and next to a bus stop. The welcoming local has a tap room and a large lounge partitioned in two. A strong community following includes members of the Friendly football club, Friendly brass band and dominoes club. There is a smoking area to the rear and an outside seating area to the front. ❀🚌(590,591,592)♣P⅃

Sowood

Dog & Partridge

Forest Hill Road, HX4 9LB SE075182
⏲ 12-5 (Sun only), 7-11 ☎ (01422) 374249
Black Sheep Best Bitter; Taylor Landlord; guest beer Ⓗ
An unchanged rural pub, run by the same family since 1956. Visitors can soon find themselves in conversation with the locals. There is no TV, music or gaming machines, just the ticking of a seven-day mill clocking-in clock. Other textile mill memorabilia are displayed, including a textile yard quadrant. An impressive collection of Corgi buses features in the side lounge, which doubles as the family room. Beware of the witch seemingly hovering over the bar on her broomstick. Q☕❀♿▲🚌(537,538)♣P

Stanbury

Friendly

54 Main Street, BD22 0HB (on Colne Road between Haworth and Colne)
⏲ 12-11 (10.30 Sun) ☎ (01535) 645528
Goose Eye Bronte Bitter; Young's Bitter; guest beer Ⓗ
A pleasant village in scenic Bronte country which is quite easily accessible by car, bus or footpath. Stanbury is only two miles from Haworth but a million miles from its tourist hustle and bustle. The pub offers comfortable sanctuary to both locals and visitors alike. It is quite small, with a main drinking area split in two by a central bar, along with a separate TV area. ❀♿▲🚌(664,M3,M4)♣P

Thurstonland

Rose & Crown ✔

The Village, HD4 6XU (off A616)
⏲ 12-midnight ☎ (01484) 660790
🌐 therosethurstonland.co.uk
Bradfield Farmers Blonde; Brass Monkey Son of Silverback, Bitter; Greene King IPA; Tetley Bitter Ⓗ
This welcoming rural inn serves as the brewery tap for the Brass Monkey Brewery, with always at least four of its beers on handpull, with other well-kept guests available too. It is a lively, true local pub at the centre of village life, with themed food nights, regular live music, and quizzes every Wednesday and Sunday – it even carries a small stock of household essentials. Food is served 12-3pm and 5.30-9.30pm Monday-Saturday, 12-6pm on Sunday. Three en-suite rooms are available. ♨🛏◑♿🚌(341,911)P

ENGLAND

Undercliffe

Milners Arms

126 Undercliffe Road, BD2 3BN (300m from Eccleshill library)

4 (12 Sat & Sun)-11 ☎ (01274) 639398

Beer range varies H

This friendly two-roomed traditional community pub is a short bus ride from Bradford city centre. The small bar serves both tap room and lounge. Wednesday quiz night is popular, with a regular and loyal clientele. Three handpumps offer a varied range of beers from both national and local breweries. Up to seven different ales are served each week. There is a pleasant beer garden at the side of the pub and ample on-street parking. (670)♣

Wakefield

Alverthorpe WMC

111 Flanshaw Lane, WF2 9JG (between Dewsbury and Batley roads, 2 miles from city centre)

11.30-4, 6.30-11.30; 11.30-11.30 Fri & Sat; 12-3.30, 7-11 Sun ☎ (01924) 374179

Tetley Mild, Bitter; guest beers H

Multi-roomed CIU-affiliated club with a cosy interior featuring unusual stained glass and an extensive collection of pot horses. It stocks a wide selection of guest beers, mostly from local micros, and holds an annual beer festival in November. There is live entertainment on Saturday and Sunday, while snooker and darts are among the traditional games. A large-screen TV is provided for armchair sports enthusiasts. Outside is a floodlit bowling green. Joint third in CAMRA Yorkshire Club of the Year 2009/10. (114)♣P

Black Rock

19 Cross Square, WF1 1PQ (at top of Westgate, near Bull Ring)

11-11 (midnight Sat); 12-10.30 Sun ☎ (01924) 375550

Tetley Bitter; guest beers H

An arched, tiled facade leads into an L-shaped compact city-centre local. The Rock has been a bastion of comfort to the ale drinkers of Wakefield for eons. It is an enclave from the surrounding bars and discos of the yoof zone. A warm welcome and comfy interior with many photographs of old Wakefield add to the proper pub feel. A three-minute walk from the bus station.
(Westgate/Kirkgate)

Fernandes Brewery Tap & Bier Keller ✔

5 Avison Yard, Kirkgate, WF1 1UA

Pub: 4-11 (midnight Thu); 11-1am Fri & Sat; 12-midnight Sun. Bier Keller: 6.30-midnight Thu; 4-midnight Fri & Sat; 12-10.30 Sun ☎ (01924) 386348

Fuller's London Pride; guest beers H

This outlet is owned by Ossett Brewery and the beer range includes Ossett and Fernandes beers. The pub has 10 handpulls, one dedicated to a mild, stout or porter. The Bier Keller has 12 premier foreign beers on draught plus Ossett Silver King and a cider on handpump. There is live music on Sunday afternoon, with free stew on Sunday evening. Pie and peas are served on Tuesday evening, for which there is a small charge. Pets are welcome. Q(Westgate/Kirkgate)

> Bread is the staff of life, but beer is life itself.
> **Traditional**

Harry's Bar

107B Westgate, WF1 1EL

5-11.30 (midnight Fri & Sat); 12-11.30 Sun
☎ (01924) 373773

Bob's Brewing Co White Lion, Chardonnayle; Leeds Pale; Ossett Silver King; guest beer H

Winner of Wakefield CAMRA Branch Pub of the Year for 2007, this small, one-roomed pub has an exposed brick and wood interior complemented by a sun deck and a shady yard. Hidden away down an alley off Westgate, it is secluded from the fizz and music yoof zone of the city centre. Harry's is a thriving community local with many new friends to meet. Live music features on Monday and Wednesday. There is a pay-and-display car park adjacent. (Westgate/Kirkgate)

Hop ✔

19 Bank Street, WF1 1EH (left off Westgate, opp Opera House)

4-midnight; 3 (12 Sat)-2am Fri & Sat; 12-11 Sun
☎ (01924) 367111

Ossett Pale Gold, Silver King, Excelsior; guest beers H

This converted Victorian building has been transformed into a multi-faceted venue for drinking, socialising, music appreciation and conversation. It retains the bare brick walls, fireplaces and other original features. The draught beers are complemented by an extensive wine list and a selection of bottled Belgian beers. There is acoustic music on Monday and live music on Friday and Saturday. Tuesday is quiz night and the first Monday of each month features a live Comedy Store. Rooms are available for hire.
Q(Westgate/Kirkgate)

O'Donoghues

60 George Street, WF1 1DL

5-11; 12-midnight Fri & Sat; 12-11 Sun ☎ (07877) 520013

East Coast SSB; Theakston XB; guest beers H

After a period of decline, this pub once again has a good following among real ale fans in the city, with two CAMRA Pub of the Season awards under its belt. It holds a Thursday quiz and an annual beer festival. Comfy sofas, secluded corners and a real fire complement the warm welcome.
(Westgate/Kirkgate)(443,444)

Wakefield Labour Club (The Red Shed)

18 Vicarage Street, WF1 1QX

12-4 (Fri only), 7-11; 11-4, 7-11 Sat; 7-11 Sun
☎ (01924) 215626 theredshed.org.uk

Beer range varies H

The Red Shed is an old army hut which has survived the redevelopment of the area. Home to many trade union, community and charity groups, quiz night is Wednesday and live music plays on the second and last Saturdays of the month. There are three rooms; two can be hired for functions. An extensive collection of union plates and badges is displayed over the bar, together with numerous CAMRA awards adorning the walls. The beers are usually from northern and Midland micros.
Q(Westgate/Kirkgate)♣P

Walton

New Inn

144 Shay Lane, WF2 6LA SE 382157
⏲ 12-midnight ☎ (01924) 255447 🌐 newinnwalton.co.uk
Black Sheep Best Bitter; Leeds Pale; Taylor Landlord; guest beers Ⓗ
Traditional 18th-century vernacular stone building with a flagstone roof, it has several areas, including a restaurant that offers exceptionally good food (no food Mon). It is a community-focused pub attracting people from all walks of life. There is live folk music each Wednesday (details can be found on the pub website). It hosts an annual summer beer festival, and is an ideal start or finish to rural walks along the route of the former Barnsley canal. No disabled access to toilets.
❀◑♿🚌(194,195,196)P⊱

Wetherby

Muse Ale & Wine Bar ✔

16 Bank Street, LS22 6NQ
⏲ 11-11; 12-10.30 Sun ☎ (01937) 580201
Black Sheep Best Bitter; Copper Dragon Golden Pippin Ⓗ
Located in a quiet area just off Wetherby's main shopping district, this Market Town Taverns bar/ brasserie has a light, bright and cosy feel. It serves quality home-cooked meals lunchtime and evening, and offers a recently increased range of cask ales. Copper Dragon and Black Sheep beers are the regulars, with four rotating guests mainly from northern micros. A large range of quality continental bottled and draught beers is also available. Q❀◑♿🚌P⊱

Wibsey

Dog & Gun

St Enoch's Road, BD6 3BU
⏲ 2-11; 12-midnight Fri & Sat; 12-11 Sun ☎ (01274) 677727
Tetley Bitter; Theakston Best Bitter; guest beers Ⓗ
Warm and welcoming traditional local on the outskirts of Bradford with three distinct areas. The bar serves the smart front lounge, which has a small games room at the side. A further lounge at the rear often shows live sport. Two guest beers are always available from the Cellarman's Reserve list. Monday is poker night and a weekly quiz is held on Wednesday. The pub may open earlier Monday-Thursday during the summer.
❀🚌(570,571,640)♣P

Wintersett

Angler's Retreat

Ferry Top Lane, WF4 2EB (between Crofton and Ryhill) SE 382157
⏲ closed Tue; 12-3, 7-11; 12-11 Sat; 12-3.30, 7-10.30 Sun
☎ (01924) 862370
Acorn Barnsley Bitter; John Smith's Bitter; Samuel Smith OBB; guest beer Ⓗ
This rural ale house is an increasingly rare example of an old-fashioned, no frills community pub. There is a loyal local clientele with many old pitmen and many old tales to be told. Close to the Angler's Country Park, it is also frequented by birdwatchers, walkers and bikers. There are benches and a garden for fine weather drinking, with a large car park opposite. ♔Q❀⊟🚌(194,195,196)♣P⊱

Yorkshire Terrier, York, North Yorkshire (Photo: Melissa Reed & Allan Conner)

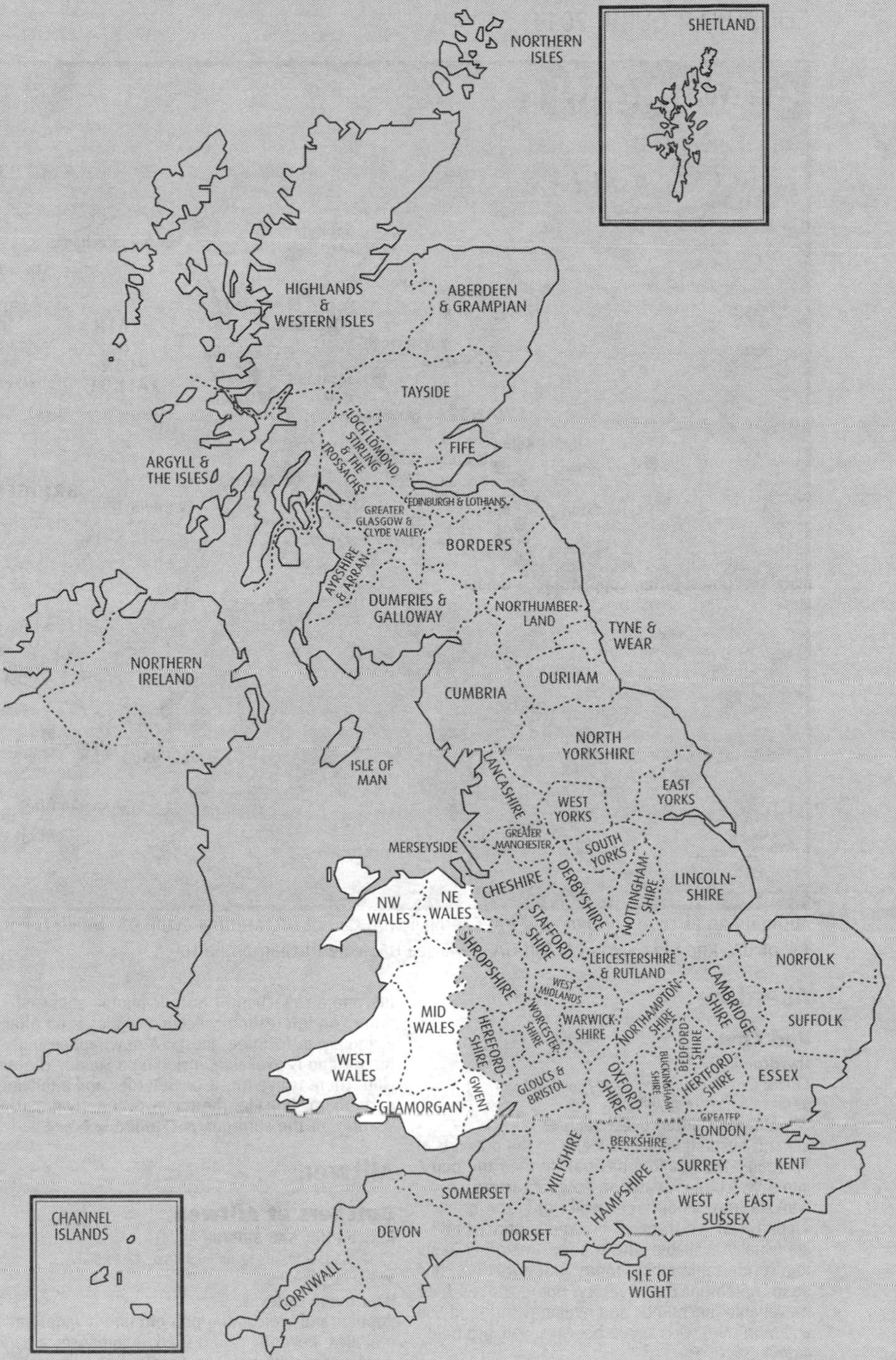
SHETLAND
NORTHERN ISLES
HIGHLANDS & WESTERN ISLES
ABERDEEN & GRAMPIAN
TAYSIDE
LOCH LOMOND, STIRLING & THE TROSSACHS
FIFE
ARGYLL & THE ISLES
EDINBURGH & LOTHIANS
GREATER GLASGOW & CLYDE VALLEY
BORDERS
AYRSHIRE & ARRAN
DUMFRIES & GALLOWAY
NORTHUMBERLAND
TYNE & WEAR
NORTHERN IRELAND
DURHAM
CUMBRIA
NORTH YORKSHIRE
ISLE OF MAN
LANCASHIRE
WEST YORKS
EAST YORKS
GREATER MANCHESTER
SOUTH YORKS
MERSEYSIDE
CHESHIRE
DERBYSHIRE
NOTTINGHAMSHIRE
LINCOLNSHIRE
NW WALES
NE WALES
STAFFORDSHIRE
SHROPSHIRE
LEICESTERSHIRE & RUTLAND
NORFOLK
WEST MIDLANDS
CAMBRIDGESHIRE
MID WALES
HEREFORDSHIRE
WORCESTERSHIRE
WARWICKSHIRE
NORTHAMPTONSHIRE
SUFFOLK
BEDFORDSHIRE
BUCKINGHAMSHIRE
WEST WALES
GWENT
GLOUCS & BRISTOL
OXFORDSHIRE
HERTFORDSHIRE
ESSEX
GLAMORGAN
GREATER LONDON
WILTSHIRE
BERKSHIRE
SURREY
KENT
SOMERSET
HAMPSHIRE
WEST SUSSEX
EAST SUSSEX
CHANNEL ISLANDS
DEVON
DORSET
CORNWALL
ISLE OF WIGHT

Wales

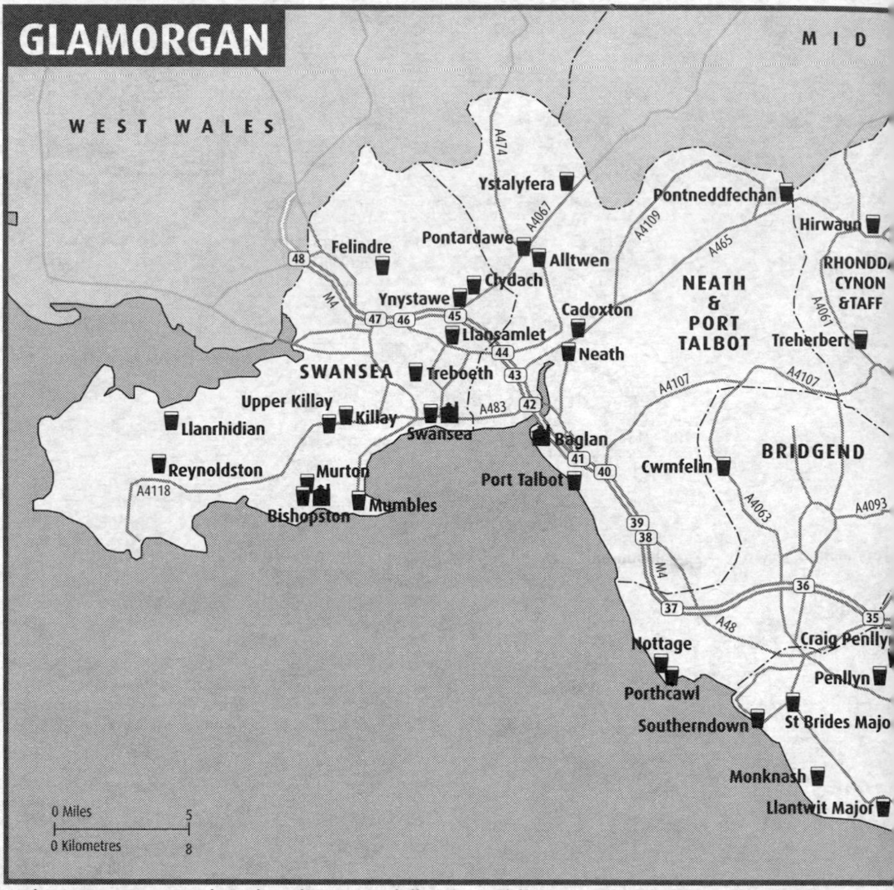

Authority areas covered: Bridgend UA, Caerphilly UA, Cardiff UA, Merthyr Tydfil UA, Neath & Port Talbot UA, Rhondda, Cynon & Taff UA, Swansea UA, Vale of Glamorgan UA

Aberdare

Red Cow

Llwydcoed, CF44 0YE

12-2 (not Mon), 6-midnight; 12-midnight Sun

(01685) 873924 theredcowpub.co.uk

Worthington's Bitter; guest beers H

Vibrant, bustling village hostelry on the outskirts of Aberdare. The landlord has transformed the pub into a welcoming watering-hole, attracting drinkers from all different walks of life. A great supporter of Welsh micro-breweries, three beers are usually available. The spacious main bar leads to a comfortable dining room with a real fire, and on to a pleasant conservatory. Home-cooked food is available lunchtimes and evenings (no food Sun and Mon eve). Occasional beer festivals are held. (6)P

Aberthin

Hare & Hounds

Aberthin Road, CF71 7LG (on A4222)

12 (4 Mon)-midnight (01446) 774892

Marston's Pedigree H**, Old Empire** G**; Ringwood Bitter** H

A friendly, welcoming and comfortable old village pub. The pleasant bar has wooden settles, an open fire and a collection of historic photographs and prints. An interesting collection of ales is on offer including up to three guests. A new, appetising food menu is available, including a Sunday cheese club. There is live music on Saturday and a thriving darts team. Outside, there is a beer garden and seating for the summer. Q

Alltwen

Butchers at Alltwen

Alltwen Hill, SA8 3BP (off A474)

12-3.30, 6-11.30; 12-midnight Sat; 12-11 Sun

(01792) 863100

Beer range varies H

Popular and welcoming pub offering a variety of real ales. Recently refurbished, it comprises a bar/dining area with an open fireplace and separate restaurant. There is also a veranda with excellent views. The pub has a good reputation for freshly cooked food, with steak nights on Monday and Tuesday. Live music plays on Sunday evenings. Q(122)P

Barry

Barry West End Club

54 St Nicholas Road, CF62 6QY

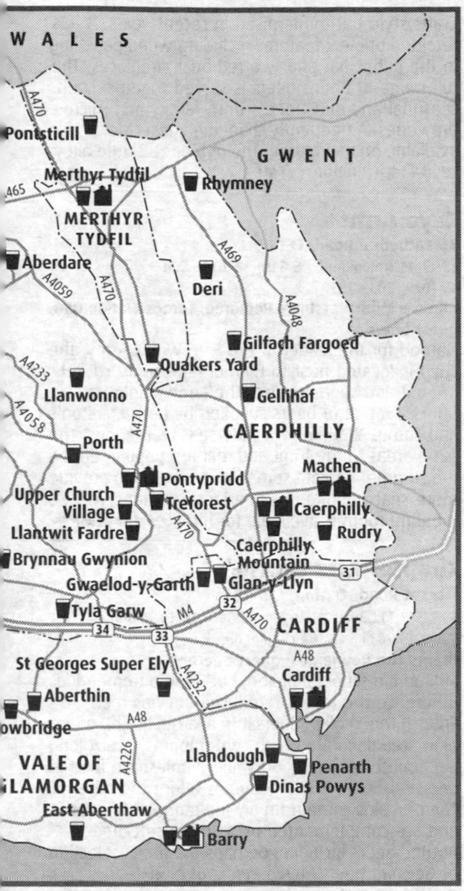

⏲ 2 (11.30 Sat)-11.30; 12-10.30 Sun ☎ (01446) 735739
Brains Dark, Bitter; guest beer Ⓗ
Set on a hill overlooking Barry Old Harbour, this friendly establishment has been voted Local CAMRA Club of the Year for the past three years. It has the feel and lively atmosphere of a real local, with a regular quiz night and snooker, crib, darts and skittles all played. CAMRA members are most welcome and an annual beer festival is held in the autumn. ❀⊟♿⇌⊡♣⊱

Castle Hotel
44 Jewel Street, CF63 3NQ (900m from rail station)
⏲ 12-11.30 (midnight Fri & Sat); 12-11 Sun
☎ (01446) 408916
Brains Bitter, SA; guest beers Ⓗ
Friendly Victorian former hotel close to the historic docks area. A past local CAMRA Branch Pub of the Year and regional runner-up in 2008, with regularly changing guest ales, the public bar features regular live music and has a large-screen TV for sports. The quieter lounge bar has many original features and serves food five nights a week plus Sunday lunch. There is a skittle alley, snooker room and darts, and a local folk club meets upstairs. ❀⊟⇌(Docks)⊡

Sir Samuel Romilly
4-6 Romilly Buildings, Market Street, CF62 7AU
⏲ 9-midnight (1am Fri & Sat) ☎ (01446) 724900
Greene King Ruddles Best Bitter, Abbot; guest beers Ⓗ
Originally a market hall built in the late 19th-century recently converted into a Wetherspoon's pub. Previously the building was used as a cinema and bingo hall. This is more of a community establishment and patrons are encouraged to bring their own cards and board games, with local events well-supported. Local breweries such as Bullmastiff, Rhymney and Vale of Glamorgan are a feature along with breweries from further afield, and real cider. A great Wetherspoon's pub. Q❀◐♿⇌⊡●⊱

Bishopston

Joiners Arms
50 Bishopston Road, SA3 3EJ
⏲ 11.30 (2 Mon)-11; 12-10.30 Sun ☎ (01792) 232658
Courage Best Bitter; Marston's Pedigree; Swansea Bishopswood, Three Cliffs Gold, Original Wood; guest beers Ⓗ
Situated in the heart of the village, this 1860s pub is popular with locals and is busy in both bars. Home of the Swansea Brewing Company, beer festivals and music events are held occasionally, adding to the excellent ale range. Good value-for-money food is served and social events are organised. The pub has won several local CAMRA awards. There is a small car park – if full, try 100 metres down the hill. ♨Q❀◐⊟⊡(14,114)P⊱

Brynnau Gwynion

Mountain Hare
Brynna Road, Pencoed, CF35 6PG (off A473 between Pencoed and Llanharan on B4280)
⏲ 5-11.30; 2-midnight Fri & Sat; 12-11 Sun
☎ (01656) 860458 🌐 mountainhare.co.uk
Bullmastiff Welsh Gold; Evan Evans BB; guest beers Ⓗ
Full of character, this family-owned village pub is situated where the Vale of Glamorgan meets the former mining valleys. It has a large, comfortable lounge, and a traditional public bar where at least one guest ale is available at all times. A second guest is added on Friday, which rarely sees out the weekend. The pub has a pool room and runs a Sunday night quiz. Outside is a garden patio area for warmer days. An annual Ales of Wales beer festival is hosted here. Q❀⊟♿⊡♣P

Cadoxton

Crown & Sceptre
Main Road, SA10 8AP
⏲ 11-11; 12-10.30 Sun ☎ (01639) 642145
🌐 crownandsceptreinn.co.uk
Greene King Old Speckled Hen; Tomos Watkin OSB Ⓗ

INDEPENDENT BREWERIES

Artisan Cardiff
Brains Cardiff
Bullmastiff Cardiff
Carter's Machen
Celt Experience Caerphilly
Neath Baglan (NEW)
Newmans Caerphilly
Otley Pontypridd
Rhymney Merthyr Tydfil
Swansea Bishopston
Tomos Watkin Swansea
Vale of Glamorgan Barry
Zerodegrees Cardiff

Popular hostelry built in 1835 as the tap for the old Vale of Neath Brewery. The locals' bar and lounge have a central servery offering a wide range of hand-pulled cask ales. The pub has an excellent reputation for freshly cooked food, with fresh fish, home-made pies and a specials board providing an excellent choice of meals served in the bar, as well as an à la carte menu in the restaurant in the old stables. A large car park is opposite the pub.
❀◖◗⊟♿🚌(154,158)P🚬

Caerphilly

Masons Arms

Mill Road, CF83 3FE (on B4263, N of town centre.)
⏲ 12-11.30 (midnight Fri & Sat) ☎ (029) 2088 3353
Brains Bitter; guest beers ⊞
A friendly welcome is assured at this roadside local just 10 minutes' walk from Caerphilly Castle and the town centre. The Masons offers two very different drinking areas – a traditional sports bar and a spacious, quiet lounge. Good value meals are served, usually in the lounge that backs onto the local park. Cask beers, including two guests, can be found in the lounge, and a blackboard in the bar lets drinkers know what is on tap. The front bar features a juke-box, pool and darts, plus TV sport. The nearest station is Aber, a 15-minute walk.
Q❀◖◗⊟🚌♣P🚬

Caerphilly Mountain

Black Cock Inn ✔

Waunwaelod Way, CF83 1BD (off Watford Road A469)
⏲ 10.30 (12 Sun)-midnight ☎ (029) 2088 0534
🌐 theblackcockinn.co.uk
Hancock's HB; Theakston Old Peculier; guest beers ⊞
This rural pub and restaurant nestles in the hilltop forest close to Castle Heights Golf Club. Access is easiest from Caerphilly Mountain, but also through narrow lanes from Pantmawr and Tongwynlais. Two guest beers are stocked, usually from small brewers, and traditional cider is now a permanent feature. Food and drink have a Welsh focus. The bar is popular with ramblers and is dog-friendly. The first 'Cocktoberfest' beer festival was held in 2009, and is set to become an annual event. The outdoor smoking area is heated and lit. ♨❀◖◗⊟♿🍎P🚬

Cardiff

Albany

105 Donald Street, CF24 4TL
⏲ 12-11 (11.30 Sat); 12-10.30 Sun ☎ (029) 2031 1075
Brains Dark, Bitter, SA, seasonal beers; guest beers ⊞
This friendly neighbourhood pub attracts a mixed clientele of students and locals, and offers a popular range of guest beers. The main area is very lively and has a large-screen TV used by customers to play Wii games, while the lounge is quieter. The pub has live music on Saturday in addition to its twice-weekly poker league and weekly quiz. It has a covered and heated smoking area, skittle alley and large beer garden. Q❀◖⊟🚌🚬

Birchgrove ✔

Caerphilly Road, CF14 4AE
⏲ 12-11 (11.30 Thu-Sun) ☎ (029) 2031 1319
Brains Dark, Bitter, SA, The Rev James, SA Gold; guest beer ⊞
Busy suburban community pub in a prominent position at a major crossroads. Built in Arts and Crafts style but modernised in recent years, it has retained original features including wood panelling in the public bar and two red brick fireplaces. The full range of Brains beers is served together with seasonal and guest beers from family and micro-breweries. A frequently changing guest cider is also available on handpump. The pub has a skittle alley.
❀◖◗⊟≋(Birchgrove)🍎🚬

Cayo Arms

36 Cathedral Road, CF11 9LL
⏲ 12-11 (midnight Fri & Sat); 12-10.30 Sun
☎ (029) 2039 1910
Banks's Mild; Marston's Pedigree; Tomos Watkin OSB; guest beers ⊞
Named for the leader of the Free Wales Army, the Cayo is located near to Glamorgan county cricket ground and sports centre. The large single bar offers a range of beers supplied by both Marston's and Tomos Watkin from their seasonal ranges. The patio areas to the front and rear are popular during the summer and are sometimes covered to provide more space during peak periods in winter. A meeting room is available for hire. ❀🛏◖◗▲🚌P🚬

Chapter Arts Centre

Market Road, Canton, CF5 1QE
⏲ 12-11 (12.30am Fri; midnight Sat); 12-10.30 Sun
☎ (029) 2031 3431 🌐 chapter.org
Brains The Rev James; guest beers ⊞
Still an old school building, but what a tremendous difference the recent refurbishment has made. Enter through glass doors into a large, bright, open-plan area decorated with contemporary art. A long bar counter serves good-value wholesome food at one end, while six handpumps adorn the other. The real ales come from a wide range of breweries and are complemented by a strong selection of bottled beers including perhaps the finest selection of German beers anywhere. ❀◖◗♿🚌P🚬

Cottage ✔

25 St Mary Street, CF10 1AA
⏲ 11-11 (midnight Sat) ☎ (029) 2033 7195
Brains Dark, Bitter, SA, The Rev James, SA Gold ⊞
The slender but handsome black frontage of the Cottage conceals the true size of this long and narrow pub. Refurbishment a few years ago has created a tidy and well-presented pub that nonetheless feels thoroughly traditional and is certainly a welcome retreat from the busy nightlife nearby. The full range of Brains beers is proudly presented and fresh food is prepared in the kitchen, which is on full view at the rear.
◖◗♿≋(Central)🚌

Discovery

Celyn Avenue, CF23 6EH
⏲ 11-11 (midnight Fri & Sat); 12-10.30 Sun
☎ (029) 2075 5015
Adnams Broadside; Greene King Abbot; Hancock's HB; Sharp's Doom Bar; guest beers ⊞
Large, modern pub in a residential area close to Roath Park Lake where there are few other pubs. The Discovery is divided into a public bar, quieter lounge and a function room, which is used as a sports bar from Monday to Friday. The landlord is particularly proud of the unique collection of original photos from Captain Scott's ill-fated expedition to the Antarctic.
♨Q❀◖◗⊟♿≋(Heath High Level/Low Level)
🚌P🚬

Fox & Hounds ✔

Old Church Road, CF14 1AD

11 (12 Sun)-11 ☎ (029) 2069 3377

Brains Dark, Bitter, SA, The Rev James, SA Gold; guest beers Ⓗ

A friendly community pub not to be missed if you are in the Whitchurch area. The wood-panelled interior houses one long bar and has large screens showing sporting events and a quiet area for dining and drinking. The pleasant garden is popular in summer and has a canopy and heaters for cooler days. Festivals are organised during the year.
❀◐♿⇌(Whitchuch)🚌P⁻

Goat Major ✔

33 High Street, CF10 1PU

12-midnight (11 Sun) ☎ (029) 2033 7161

Brains Dark, Bitter, SA, SA Gold Ⓗ

Popular city-centre Brains pub with a traditional appearance and friendly bar staff, attracting a brisk trade from both locals and visitors. It is named for the mascot of the Royal Welsh Regiment, a fact that is proudly illustrated in the many photographs that adorn the interior. Traditional Welsh food is served into the early evening. ◐♿⇌(Central)🚌

Heathcock ✔

58 Bridge Street, Llandaff, CF5 2EN

12-11 Mon, Tue, Thu & Sun; 12-11.30 Wed, Fri & Sat
☎ (029) 2057 5005

Black Sheep Best Bitter; St Austell Tribute; Sharp's Doom Bar; guest beers Ⓗ

Busy two-bar community pub, popular with locals and visitors to the historic area of Llandaff. The pub has built a reputation for draught beer, and guest ales are sourced from south Wales micro-breweries including Otley, Rhymney and Celt Experience. At the rear is an attractive garden with a covered area, and a skittle alley. There is live music on Wednesday night. The menu includes a choice of curries. ❀◐🚌⁻

Mochyn Du

Sophia Close, CF11 9HW

12-11 (midnight Fri & Sat); 12-10.30 Sun
☎ (029) 2037 1599

Vale of Glamorgan Cwrw'r Mochyn Du; guest beers Ⓗ

Located near Glamorgan county cricket ground, this popular free house is as well known for its Welsh pride as it is for its real ale. Originally a Victorian park-keeper's lodge, the 'Black Pig' is now a busy retreat for sports fans, local residents and nearby office workers. Four real ales are on offer, mostly from Welsh micro-breweries. A refurbished conservatory area provides a smart and comfortable place to enjoy the menu of freshly cooked Welsh food. ❀◐Å🚌P⁻

Old Arcade ✔

14 Church Street, CF10 1BG

11.30-11 (12.45am Fri & Sat); 12-11 Sun
☎ (029) 2021 7999

Brains Dark, Bitter, SA, SA Gold; guest beers Ⓗ

Tidy but basically furnished traditional boozer with two distinct bars, renowned throughout Cardiff. It attracts a loyal local following as well as those seeking a break from shopping. Outside at the rear is a newly-constructed covered smoking area with a gate leading to Cardiff market. Guest beers are invariably from Brains' seasonal range.
◐⇌(Central)⁻

Pen & Wig 🏆 ✔

1 Park Grove, CF10 3BJ

9-midnight; 10-1am Fri & Sat; 10-11.30 Sun
☎ (029) 20371217

Brains Bitter; Hancock's HB; guest beers Ⓗ

Lively pub with traditional furnishings tucked away just out of town and well-worth seeking out. Often busy after work, it attracts a mix of customers, including legal professionals by day and students by night. The pub has a variety of seating including settles, chairs and stools, and has board games for customers. The selection of guest ales changes weekly, which ensures they are available at most times. The beer garden is popular in summer. Branch Pub of the Year 2010.
❀◐♿⇌(Queen St)🚌⁻

Yard ✔

42-43 St Mary Street, CF10 1AD

10-11 (midnight Thu; 2am Fri & Sat) ☎ (029) 2022 7577
yardbarkitchen.co.uk

Brains Dark, Bitter, SA, The Rev James, SA Gold Ⓗ

Large two-storey pub in the heart of the main entertainment district of the city centre. Converted partly from The Albert, the former brewery tap for Brains Brewery, and partly from the former brewery, the use of metal staircases and copper and brass pipework gives an industrial feel in keeping with its heritage. The paved outdoor drinking area overlooks the restaurants and bars of the Old Brewery Quarter. A full range of Brains beers is served, including seasonal beers.
❀◐⇌(Central)🚌⁻

Clydach

New Inn

The Lone, SA6 5SU (on road to Craig-Cefn-Parc)

11-3 (not Mon & Tue), 6-11; 12-10.30 Fri-Sun
☎ (01792) 842839 newinnclydach.co.uk

Beer range varies Ⓗ

Friendly family-run country pub with a public bar and log-burning fire in winter, games room and lounge. Outside is a children's play area, beer garden and car park. Good food is served in the bar and lounge. The pub is next to the Cwm Clydach RSPB nature reserve where you can walk along the river and look for kingfishers and red kites, so it is a handy place to stop off after a walk.
🔥Q❀◐♿🚌(121)♣P

Cowbridge

Vale of Glamorgan Inn 🏆

53 High Street, CF71 7AE

11.30-11 (midnight Fri & Sat); 12-10.30 Sun
☎ (01446) 772252

Celt Experience Bronze; Hancock's HB; Shepherd Neame Bishops Finger; Wye Valley HPA; guest beers Ⓗ

Friendly pub in the centre of town. This one-room bar has a comfortable carpeted lounge area and a bar area with wooden floors and a warming fire. There is no background music or games machines. Excellent home-cooked lunches are on offer (no food Sun). The outbuildings were once the home of the Vale of Glamorgan Brewery (no connection with the current business of that name) which was taken over by Hancock's in 1913. A beer festival is hosted in autumn. 🔥Q❀◐🚌(X1,X2)●⁻

Craig Penllyn

Barley Mow

CF71 7RT (off A48)

⏲ 12-11 ☎ (01446) 772558 ⊕ barleymow.net

Worthington's Bitter; guest beers Ⓗ

This old inn is popular with locals and visitors and is well-worth the effort of finding. The selection of guest beers along with the log fire make the bar cosy and welcoming on chilly days. Quality meals are served in the bar and dining room (12-3 and 6-9, 12-4 Sunday). There is a small beer garden and a patio at the front with a large car park across the road. The house beer is from a South Wales brewery. ♕Q❀◐◑⊟🚌(V2)P⊬

Cwmfelin

Cross Inn

Maesteg Road, CF34 9LB (on A4063)

⏲ 11.45-midnight (1am Fri & Sat); 11-midnight Sun

☎ (01656) 732476

Brains Bitter; Wye Valley Butty Bach; guest beers Ⓗ

A real locals' pub, where you are sure to get a friendly welcome, in an area where a decent pint is hard to find. This multi-roomed hostelry is situated on the main Bridgend to Maesteg road, with excellent local public transport. Children are welcome until 7pm, well-behaved dogs are permitted too (please ask first). The back room displays some interesting photographs. The pub has plans for its own small brewery.
Q❀⊟♿⇌(Garth)🚌⊬

Deri

Old Club ✔

93 Bailey Street, CF81 9HX

⏲ 5 (12 Sat & Sun)-midnight ☎ (01443) 830278

⊕ theoldclub.netfirms.com

Beer range varies Ⓗ

The Old Club is an oasis in a beer desert. Two guest beers are always available, rising to three at weekends. The vast collection of pump clips records the eclectic beer range, with ales mainly from small independent brewers supported by some of the more interesting regionals. An hourly bus service links Deri with Bargoed railway station, though the path along the former Darran & Deri Branch offers a leisurely alternative to the undulating road. Slightly further is Cwm Darran country park and hilltops popular with paragliders. Ă🚌(1,4)♣

Dinas Powys

Star ✔

Station Road, CF64 4DE

⏲ 11.30-11 (midnight Fri & Sat); 12-10.30 Sun

☎ (029) 2051 4245

Brains Dark, Bitter, SA, SA Gold; guest beers Ⓗ

Comfortable Brains house in the village centre, full of character, welcoming and cheerful. This spacious, open-plan pub has cosy seating and dining areas where good home-cooked food is available. There is a large car park and patio to the rear with disabled access to the pub by wheelchair lift. ❀◐◑♿⇌🚌P

East Aberthaw

Blue Anchor

CF62 3DD (on B4265)

⏲ 11-11; 12-10.30 Sun ☎ (01446) 750329

⊕ blueanchoraberthaw.com

Brains Bitter; Theakston Old Peculier; Wadworth 6X; Wye Valley HPA; guest beer Ⓗ

Fourteenth-century family-run pub with an adjoining restaurant, rebuilt and restored after a serious fire. Beneath the thatched roof of this historic inn lies a multi-room, flagstone-floored pub with thick stone walls that defeat most mobile phones. The guest beer is often from a local brewery. The car park is across the road and regular buses pass by. ♕Q◐◑⊟🚌●P⊬

Felindre

Shepherds Inn

18 Heol Myddfai, SA5 7ND

⏲ 12-3 (not Mon & Tue), 6-11.30; 12-11.30 Fri-Sun

☎ (01792) 794715 ⊕ shepherdsinn.co.uk

Felinfoel Double Dragon; guest beers Ⓗ

Well-kept community pub incorporating the village stores and post office. It has a single bar and separate restaurant offering reasonably priced meals, with regular specials on chalk boards. A free house, guest ales are sourced from Welsh breweries. The pub hosts occasional quiz and music evenings. The large patio has country views and overlooks the play area, with a covered, heated area for smokers. En-suite accommodation is ideal for keen walkers exploring the nearby country park and beyond. ❀⛟◐◑P⊬

Gellihaf

Coal Hole

Bryn Road, NP12 2QE (on A4049 S of Fleur-de-Lys)

⏲ 12-3, 6.30-11; 11-11 Fri & Sat; 12-10.30 Sun

☎ (01443) 830280

Greene King Old Speckled Hen, Abbot; guest beer Ⓗ

Close to the main road but easy to miss, this friendly one-bar pub was converted from farm buildings during the 19th century. One guest beer is sometimes stocked. Excellent food is available daily, served in both the bar and restaurant, with traditional Sunday lunches a highlight. The pub enjoys commanding views of the iconic Hengoed Viaduct spanning the Rhymney Valley. ❀◐◑P⊬

Gilfach Fargoed

Capel Hotel

Park Place, CF81 8LW

⏲ 12-11 (11.30 Fri & Sat); 12-10.30 Sun ☎ (01443) 830272

John Smith's Bitter; guest beers Ⓗ

This impressive Edwardian hotel retains much of its original character, and is known for its warm welcome. Guest beers and ciders are from smaller, often local, producers, and are listed on notice boards. Look for gravity cider and perry, served from a cold cabinet. An annual beer festival is held in May. Many visitors arrive by rail, alighting at the 'halt' at the bottom of the hill. Take care to select a journey that stops here. Q❀⛟⇌🚌(50)♣●⊬

Glan-y-Llyn

Fagins Ale & Chop House

9 Cardiff Road, CF15 7QD

11-midnight (1am Fri); 12-1am Sat; 12-11 Sun
☎ (029) 2081 1800 faginsalehouse.co.uk
Otley O1, OF Ⓗ; guest beers Ⓖ
A superb free house to rival anything in nearby Cardiff. Set in a typical Valleys terrace, the flagstone floor and welcoming log burner greet you on chilly days. Guest beers are gravity dispensed, with up to three available. Otley OF is exclusively brewed for Fagins. Two handpumped ciders are Gwynt y Ddraig Happy Daze and Farmhouse. Excellent value meals are served (no food Sun or Mon eves). Outside, there are tables by the roadside. Just off the M4, the pub is well-served by buses from Cardiff. Voted CAMRA Mid-Glamorgan Pub of the Year in 2008.
(26,132)

Gwaelod-y-Garth

Gwaelod-y-Garth Inn
Main Road, CF15 9HH
11-11 (1am Fri & Sat); 11-10.30 Sun ☎ (029) 2081 0408
gwaelodinn.co.uk
Wye Valley Bitter; guest beers Ⓗ
This friendly and atmospheric community pub stocks four or five changing real ales, many sourced from local breweries. It is renowned locally for its good food served in the upstairs restaurant. Real fires will keep you warm in the winter months and, in the summer, you can enjoy superb views over the surrounding valley from the beer garden. Dog- and child-friendly.
Q (26B) P

Hirwaun

Glancynon Inn
Swansea Road, CF44 9PH
11-11 ☎ (01685) 811043 glancynoninn.co.uk
Greene King Abbot; guest beers Ⓗ
This large country pub with oak beams and a friendly atmosphere is the main real ale outlet for the area. A little off the beaten track, it is nevertheless easy to find. The pub features a pleasant lounge and public bar leading to a well-kept beer garden. Guest beers are usually from Welsh breweries and the popular restaurant uses local organic produce whenever possible. Lunches are served daily, evening meals Monday to Saturday. Demand is high at weekends and booking is advisable. (9)P

Killay

Black Boy
444 Gower Road, SA2 7AL
11-11 (midnight Fri & Sat); 12-11 Sun ☎ (01792) 299469
Brains Bitter, SA, The Rev James Ⓗ
Large, comfortable, friendly pub popular with locals, situated on the main road to Gower. It is divided into several distinct areas – a bar with TV (mainly for sport including Sky and ESPN), the main dining area and a darts space. Food is available all day until 9pm. Recently refurbished, the decor is traditional. Monday is quiz night.
(20,21)P

Village Inn
5-6 Swan Court, Gower Road, SA2 7BA
10.30-11.30; 12-11 Sun ☎ (01792) 203311
Fuller's London Pride; Taylor Landlord; guest beer Ⓗ
Split-level L-shaped bar tucked away in the shopping precinct of a suburban Swansea village. The single room has several nooks and crannies, some with displays of plates and sporting memorabilia. Quiz nights are Sunday and Tuesday. Food is served lunchtimes and occasionally on special themed evenings. There is free public parking within 50 metres. (20,21)P

Llandough

Merrie Harrier ✔
117 Penlan Road, CF64 2NY
12-11; 11.30-11.30 Fri; 11-11.30 Sat ☎ (029) 2030 3994
Brains Bitter, SA; guest beers Ⓗ
One of the Cardiff area's best known landmarks, this large and traditionally styled road house lies on a busy road junction between Cardiff, Penarth and Dinas Powys. It has a spacious, comfortable lounge bar where there is live coverage of major sporting events. An extensive menu of freshly cooked food is available all day. A friendly and relaxing stop at any time. (Cogan)(X45,95)P

Llanrhidian

Dolphin Inn
SA3 1EH (just off B4295, N Gower Road)
1 (6 Mon)-11 summer; 6 (1 Fri-Sun)-11 winter; 1-11 Sun
☎ (01792) 391069 thedolphininngower.co.uk
Brains The Rev James; Fuller's London Pride Ⓗ
Dating from the 18th century and overlooking Llanrhidian Marsh and the Burry Inlet, the pub reopened in 2007 after 12 years' closure. There are panoramic views from the pleasant beer garden, which adjoins St Illtyd's Church. Refurbished in traditional style, it has a long single room and stone-faced bar. Local artwork and photography are on display. Light snacks including a classic local lava bread and cockles dish are available. Look for the yellow dolphin stickers to show you the way here. (116)P

Greyhound Inn
Old Walls, SA3 1HA
11 (12 Sun)-11 ☎ (01792) 391027
thegreyhoundinnoldwalls.co.uk
Draught Bass; Fuller's London Pride; Hancock's HB; guest beers Ⓗ
Welcoming to locals and visitors alike, this large and popular inn usually has up to five real ales available. Families are well-catered for and there are separate dining and function rooms, as well as a pleasant garden with fine views. The pub has a reputation for good food, served in all bars until 9pm Monday to Saturday (Sunday lunchtime only). There is plenty of parking and caravans are allowed. Q (116,119)P

Llansamlet

Plough & Harrow
57 Church Road, SA7 9RL
12-11 ☎ (01792) 772263
ploughandharrowllansamlet.co.uk
Beer range varies Ⓗ
Semi-rural Marston's pub with a large bar and comfortable seating. Good-quality meals are served at lunchtime in the bar and upstairs dining/function room. Curry is available on Wednesday evening. Outside is a covered, heated patio area for smokers. Popular with the community, a charity

quiz is hosted every Wednesday by the vicar from the church next door. Good disabled access and facilities are provided. ᗑ❀◑♿P⁵–

Llantwit Fardre

Bush Inn

Main Road, CF38 2EP

⏲ 11-11; 12-10.30 Sun ☎ (01443) 203958

Tomos Watkin OSB; guest beers Ⓗ

Lively, comfortable village local with a separate games area for pool and darts. Something is going on most nights here, including darts on Sunday and quizzes on Tuesday and Wednesday. 'Open mike' night is Thursday, and a band plays on Saturday, when the pub can be very busy and may stay open later. The guest ales can come from anywhere, but generally smaller breweries, and often Welsh, and there is sometimes a run of a particular brewer's beers for a few weeks. Forthcoming ales and bands are listed outside. ❀🚌(100,400)♣P⁵–

Crown Inn

Main Road, CF38 2HL

⏲ 12 (4 Tue)-midnight; 12-3, 7-midnight Sun

☎ (01443) 218277

Hancock's HB; guest beers Ⓗ

Bright one-room pub with a comfortable lounge area. Chalkboards outside tell customers which beers and activities are on offer. One or two guest ales may be from smaller Welsh breweries, but are often beers unusual to the area. Outdoor beer and cider festivals are becoming a regular feature. Bar food is prepared with Welsh-Italian flair and includes Sunday lunches and special event dinners. Live music on Friday or Saturday is usually country, blues or folk. ❀◑◐🚌(100,400)P⁵–

Llantwit Major

Kings Head

East Street, CF61 1XY

⏲ 11.30-11; 12-10.30 Sun ☎ (01446) 792697

Brains Dark, Bitter, SA; guest beers Ⓗ

Well-established local with a reputation for quality ale and excellent lunchtime meals. The large and popular bar has pool, darts, dominoes and a large-screen TV for sport. The quieter lounge is comfortably furnished and retains the character cherished by locals for many years. The pub is a rare outlet in Vale of Glamorgan for Brains Dark, available in the front bar.
ᗑQ❀◑🍴▲⇌🚌♣P⁵–

Old Swan Inn

Church Street, CF61 1SB

⏲ 12-11 (10.30 Sun) ☎ (01446) 792230

Beer range varies Ⓗ

The oldest pub in a historic town, this excellent hostelry has won numerous awards for its fine ales and excellent food. Two real ales are on offer during the week, four at weekends, with an emphasis on south Wales breweries alongside regular supplies from Cottage in Somerset. The lively back bar has pool and a juke-box while the traditional front lounge is quieter and attracts diners and drinkers. The smoking area is heated.
ᗑ❀◑◐🍴▲⇌🚌♣🍎⁵–

Llanwonno

Brynffynon Hotel

CF37 3PH ST030955

⏲ 12-11 (10.30 Sun) ☎ (01443) 790272

🌐 brynffynonhotel.com

Draught Bass; guest beers Ⓗ

This isolated country pub nestles in the forest between the Cynon and Rhondda-Fach valleys. Situated in a tiny hamlet – just the pub and St Gwynno's Church – the pub welcomes locals and visitors alike. It serves a range of up to five ales alongside a varied choice of food, and occasional beer festivals are held. Often surprisingly busy for such a remote pub, booking is a must for meals, especially Sunday lunch (no food Sun eve). Camping is available at the nearby Daerwynno Outdoor Centre. ᗑ❀🛏◑◐▲♣P

Machen

White Hart

Nant-y-Ceisiad, CF83 8QQ 203892

⏲ 12-2.30 (not Wed), 6-11.30; 7-11 Sun ☎ (01633) 441005

Beer range varies Ⓗ

An unlikely mix of old and new, the interior of this inn features fittings from the liner Empress of France. Although close to the main road, the original reason for the pub was to serve the old Rumney Tramroad which now forms part of National Cycle Route 4. An independent free house, it stocks up to three guest beers, mainly from smaller breweries. Brews from the resident brewery Carters make the occasional appearance.
❀🛏◑◐🚌(50)♣P

Merthyr Tydfil

Rose & Crown

20 Morgan Street, The Quarr, CF47 8TP (off A4102 Brecon Rd S of Cyfarthfa Park)

⏲ 4 (1 Mon)-midnight: 1-12.30am Fri; 12-midnight Sat; 11.30-midnight Sun ☎ (01695) 723743

Greene King Abbot; guest beers Ⓗ

This comfortable, back-street local is just a whisker from Brecon Road, easiest approached on foot via Mount Street. It is well-worth finding for the warm welcome. A good range of beers, usually from Welsh micros, is kept by an enthusiastic landlord. The interior is divided into separate areas, each with its own character. Historic maps and photographs proudly illustrate how industry shaped Merthyr Tydfil. Thursday is curry night. 🚌(26)♣⁵–

Monknash

Plough & Harrow

CF71 7QQ (off B4265 between Wick and Marcross)

⏲ 12-11 (10.30 Sun) ☎ (01656) 890209

🌐 theploughmonknash.com

Draught Bass Ⓗ/Ⓖ**; Otley 01; Worthington's Bitter; Wye Valley HPA** Ⓗ

Renowned throughout Wales, this historic pub serves up the finest of foods to complement an excellent ale range. Customers in the lounge should note that the beer and cider range is displayed in the bar. The large garden is perfect in summer, especially for the annual July beer festival. Proudly supporting Welsh brewers and cider makers, the pub offers a home delivery service. CAMRA Branch Cider Pub of the Year 2008 and 2009. ᗑ❀◑◐🍴🚌♣🍎P⁵–

Mumbles

Newton Inn

New Well Lane, Newton, SA3 4SR (1 mile N of Mumbles on Newton Road)
✪ 12-11 (10.30 Sun) ☎ (01792) 363226
Draught Bass; Worthington's Bitter; guest beers Ⓗ
Popular refurbished village local that retains bar and lounge areas in a semi-open-plan layout. The pub offers excellent meals lunchtimes and evenings Tuesday to Saturday (no food Sun eve). The bar has a large-screen TV which is used for sporting events. The landlord regularly changes the guest beers. A quiz is held on Wednesday. ❀◐◑⊟⊱

Park Inn

23 Park Street, SA3 4AD
✪ 4 (12 Fri-Sun)-11 ☎ (01792) 366738
Cambrian Bitter; Felinfoel Stout; guest beers Ⓗ
A regular Swansea CAMRA Pub of the Year, with five handpumps dispensing an ever-changing range of beers, with particular emphasis on independent breweries from Wales and the west of England. The convivial atmosphere in this small establishment attracts discerning drinkers of all ages, though the games room is particularly popular with younger people. Alongside a fine display of pump clips are pictures of old Mumbles and its pioneering railway. ♨Q🚌(2,3)♣⊱

Murton

Plough & Harrow

88 Oldway, SA3 3DJ
✪ 11-11; 12-10.30 Sun ☎ (01792) 234459
Brains Best Bitter, SA; guest beers Ⓗ
One of Gower's oldest pubs, the Plough & Harrow has been enlarged and renovated in recent times, but retains its character and popularity. The pub combines a busy food trade with the traditions of a local. The bar area has TV and pool, and there is a quieter space for conversation or a meal. Tuesday is quiz night. Heaters are used to warm the large, covered and decked outdoor area, which unusually also has a pool table. Q❀◐◑⊟🚌(14,114)♣P⊱

Neath

Borough Arms

2 New Henry Street, SA11 1PH (off A474 Briton Ferry Road)
✪ 4 (12 Sat)-11; 12-3 Sun ☎ (01639) 644902
Beer range varies Ⓗ
Welcoming, traditional pub with a loyal local following. The new landlady continues to uphold the pub's reputation for quality ale. A central bar serves two distinct areas with a constantly changing range of up to four beers, many from outside the region. The pub has strong rugby connections and can be particularly busy on days when the Ospreys or Neath are playing. Voted CAMRA Regional Pub of the Year 2008 and Branch winner for three consecutive years. Q❀♿⇌🚌♣⊱

David Protheroe ✔

7 Windsor Road, SA11 1LS
✪ 9-midnight (1am Fri & Sat) ☎ (01639) 622130
Beer range varies Ⓗ
This popular Wetherspoon is situated opposite the railway station and bus stop so is easily accessible. A former police station, it is named after Neath's first policeman, posted here in 1836. It has an open plan interior with a family area at the rear. A wide range of food is available and steak and curry nights are always popular. Drinks prices are reduced on Monday. Guest ales are usually available. ⛟❀◐◑♿⇌🚌●⊱

Highlander

2 Lewis Road, SA11 1EQ
✪ 12-midnight (10.30 Sun) ☎ (01639) 633586
Beer range varies Ⓗ
Large one-room public house with a central bar and elevated dining area serving reasonably priced meals. Two or more changing guest ales are supplied from independent breweries. There is a TV but conversation is the norm. Upstairs is a restaurant and function room. ◐◑⇌🚌

Nottage

Farmers Arms

Lougher Row, CF36 3TA
✪ 11-midnight; 11.30-11 Sun ☎ (01656) 784595
🌐 farmersarms.co.uk
Brains SA; Draught Bass; Greene King Abbot; Hancock's HB Ⓗ
Nottage is now effectively part of Porthcawl, but retains a village atmosphere of its own. This traditional stone-built pub overlooks the village green, with benches for outside drinking. Inside, the comfortable lounge has a long bar down one side and a large-screen TV for sport. Live entertainment draws a crowd, with music on Tuesday, Friday and the weekend. There is a separate restaurant at the back. ♨❀◐◑♿🚌P⊱

Rose & Crown Hotel

Heol y Capel, CF36 3ST
✪ 12-11, 12-1am Fri & Sat ☎ (01656) 784850
Brains Bitter, SA, The Rev James Ⓗ
Traditional pub with a friendly feel in a small, picturesque village. Three bars including the cosy real ale bar offer up to two guest beers. Very popular with local residents, children are welcome. The restaurant provides a good selection of food throughout the week. For overnight guests, four doubles and four twin rooms are available. Q❀🛏◐◑⊟♿🚌●P⊱

Penarth

Bears Head

37-39 Windsor Road, CF64 1JD
✪ 9am-11.30pm ☎ (029) 2070 6424
Bullmastiff Son of a Bitch; Greene King Ruddles Best Bitter, Abbot; guest beers Ⓗ
A very varied clientele is found in this town-centre pub. With a typical Wetherspoon layout, South Wales breweries feature strongly, and the venue is a regular outlet for Bullmastiff, where the brewers often gather to ensure their beer quality. Bears Head is an English translation of Penarth. Q⛟❀◐◑⇌🚌●⊱

Windsor

93 Windsor Road, CF64 1JF (on A4160 N of town centre)
✪ 9-midnight; 9-11.30 Sun ☎ (029) 2070 2871
Brains Bitter, SA Gold; Greene King Abbot; Taylor Landlord; guest beers Ⓗ
Lively, traditional hostelry offering a beer exhibition every day, with up to seven real ales. The pub hosts a jazz club on Wednesday and a poker school on many evenings, and is also home

to other clubs and social groups including morris dancers. A separate function room/restaurant is available. A good range of food is served all day. ◑◗⇌(Dingle Rd)🚌(92,93,94)⊱

Penllyn

Red Fox

CF71 7RQ (off A48) SS973763
⊙ 12-midnight; 12-11 Sun ☎ (01446) 772352
Hancock's HB; Tomos Watkin OSB; guest beers [H]
Popular with the residents of this scattered community as well as visitors enjoying nearby walks, the pub offers quality food and drink in a friendly atmosphere. The main room, with its flagstone floor and nooks and crannies, has a large log fire, while a separate room is used as a dining area. Exposed stone walls are decorated with pictures, mostly relating to the red fox and its pursuit. An attractive patio to the front and a rear garden are pleasant for outdoor drinking. Quiz night is the last Thursday of the month.
♨Q❀◑◗⊟🚌(V3)P⊱

Pontardawe

Pink Geranium ✔

31-33 Herbert Street, SA8 4EB
⊙ 10-midnight (1am Sat & Sun) ☎ (01792) 862255
Beer range varies [H]
Busy town-centre pub, handy for the Arts Centre. The L-shaped main bar is to the right of the entrance. There is a lounge and a music room with a stage where live bands play on Friday and Saturday nights. This leads to a large covered patio, popular with smokers and alfresco drinkers in the summer. Up to three ales are available, usually including a Welsh guest – Brains Rev James and Celt Bronze are among the favourites.
❀⊟🚌(120,125)⊱

Pontardawe Inn ✔

123 Herbert Street, SA8 4ED
⊙ 12-midnight (11.30 Sun) ☎ (01792) 830791
🌐 pontardaweinn.co.uk
Banks's Mild; Marston's Pedigree; guest beers [H]
Up to four beers are available at this 16th-century former coaching inn known locally as the Gwachel, situated next to the River Tawe bridge and Route 43 of the National Cycle Network. The new landlord has a minimalist approach to the decor in the bar, music room and snug. Music club is Wednesday and live bands play on Saturday evening. Beer festivals are held during National Cask Week and the Pontardawe festival week.
❀◑◗⊟♿🚌(120,122,132)♣P⊱

Pontneddfechan

Angel Inn

Pontneathvaughan Road, SA11 5NR (just off A465)
⊙ 11.30-11.30 summer; 11.30-4, 6.30-11.30 winter; 12-11.30 Sun ☎ (01639) 722013
Courage Best Bitter; Rhymney Bitter [H]
The Angel is situated opposite the National Park Waterfalls Centre and convenient for the famous waterfall walks. It is mainly food-oriented and has a deservedly high reputation for the quality and range of its dishes. One main central bar serves a large dining area on one side and a locals' and walkers' bar on the other. The tables in front of the pub are popular in summer. Q❀◑◗♿P⊱

Pontsticill

Red Cow ✔

CF48 2UN (follow signs for Brecon Mountain Railway)
⊙ 11-midnight ☎ (01685) 384828
Wye Valley Bitter; guest beers [H]
Set within the Brecon Beacons National Park, this traditional establishment has flagstone floors and an enthusiastic landlord. A popular locals' pub, it is also popular with walkers and visitors to the nearby Dolygaer Outdoor Education Centre. The Brecon Mountain Railway is a modest but steep walk away. ♨❀◑🚌(24)♣P⊱

Pontypridd

Bunch of Grapes

Ynysangharad Road, CF37 4DA (off A4054)
⊙ 12-midnight; 11-1am Fri & Sat; 11-midnight Sun
☎ (01443) 402934 🌐 bunchofgrapes.org.uk
Otley 01 [H]**; guest beers** [H]/[G]
Just a few minutes' walk from the town centre stands this multi-award-winning flagship for Otley Brewing Company. The eclectic range of beers on offer includes guests from near and far – often other Welsh craft breweries – and an interesting range of continental beers. Real cider and perry are available on gravity. The pub also has a much-esteemed restaurant, where the emphasis is on quality, locally-sourced foods and friendly service (booking advisable). Allow time to experience the fabulous atmosphere here – this is a hostelry you will not want to leave. ♨❀◑◗♣♣P⊱

Llanover Arms

Bridge Street, CF37 4PE (opp N entrace to Ynysangharad Park)
⊙ 12-midnight (11 Sun) ☎ (01443) 403215
Brains Bitter; Felinfoel Double Dragon; guest beer [H]
This free house stands opposite the Memorial Park and is just a short stroll from Pontypridd's historic Old Bridge and Museum. The pub's three rooms and passageway each have their own distinct atmosphere and attract a loyal clientele. Walls are festooned with a variety of artefacts including old mirrors, equine paintings, maps and clocks. But for many, the major attraction here is the constantly changing guest beer. There is outside drinking on the patio. Q❀⊟⇌🚌♣P

Port Talbot

Lord Caradoc ✔

69-73 Station Road, SA13 1NW
⊙ 9-midnight (1am Fri & Sat) ☎ (01639) 896007
Brains SA; Rhymney Dark; Green King Abbot; guest beers [H]
Wetherspoon pub situated in the centre of town a short distance from the railway station. The bar has an L-shaped layout with a raised drinking area. Children are welcome in the family area towards the rear of the pub and the patio area outside. The usual value-for-money fare is served, with steak and curry nights always popular. ❀◑◗♿⇌🚌

Porth

Rheola

Rheola Road, CF39 0LF
⊙ 2-midnight; 1-1am Fri; 12-1am Sat; 12-midnight Sun
☎ (01443) 682633
Brains The Rev James; Draught Bass; guest beer [H]

This comfortable and friendly detached free house with a lively bar and cosy lounge was winner of the Rhondda Cynon Taf Community Pub Award for 2009. Situated at the point where the Rhondda Fach and Fawr divide, the pub is overshadowed by a recent bridge carrying a bypass. One guest beer appears at weekends to supplement the regulars. A beer festival accompanies Porth Carnival in July. The outdoor smoking area is sheltered. Access is easy by bus or train. Note that last admission is strictly 10.30pm. ❀⊟⇌⊟♣P⚡

Porthcawl

Lorelei Hotel

36-38 Esplanade Avenue, CF36 3YU

✪ 5-11; 11-11 Fri & Sat; 12-10.30 Sun ☎ (01656) 788342

Draught Bass Ⓖ; Rhymney Export Ⓗ; guest beers Ⓗ/Ⓖ

This inconspicuous hotel in a terraced street is a real-ale oasis. The number of pump clips on display reflects the bar's commitment to a wide range of interesting guest ales, further enhanced by beer festivals at Grand National weekend and Halloween. Czech Budvar is served on draught along with other European beers, and real cider is available in summer. ♔Q♉❀⊟◑⊟♣●⚡

Quakers Yard

Glantaff Inn

Cardiff Road, CF46 5AH

✪ 11-midnight ☎ (01443) 410822

Rhymney Bevan's Bitter; guest beers Ⓗ

Comfortable Valleys pub with a riverside setting featuring a large collection of water jugs, boxing memorabilia and old photographs of local interest. Guest beers are frequently from local Welsh micro-breweries, bringing in the locals as well as walkers and cyclists on the Taff Trail from Cardiff to Brecon. The village's name comes from an old Quaker burial ground. A good range of home-cooked food is offered (no meals Sun eve). ◑⊟(7,78)

Reynoldston

King Arthur Hotel

Higher Green, SA3 1AD (on village green)

✪ 10-11 ☎ (01792) 390775 ⊕ kingarthurhotel.co.uk

Draught Bass, Felinfoel Double Dragon; Tomos Watkin OSB; guest beers Ⓗ

Set in the heart of Gower's beautiful countryside, this splendid hotel is deservedly popular with locals, walkers and tourists. During the summer the large outside area offers idyllic surroundings for drinking and dining. In winter the atmosphere in the bar is enhanced by a fire. An excellent menu featuring local produce is served in the restaurant, family room and bar, available until 9pm (9.30pm Fri and Sat). ♔♉❀⊟◑⊟⊟(115,118)♣P⚡

Rhymney

Farmers Arms

Old Brewery Lane, NP22 5EZ

✪ 12-11; 12-3.30, 7-11 Sun ☎ (01685) 840257

Fuller's London Pride; Everards Tiger Ⓗ

Large traditional pub close to the original Andrew Buchan Rhymney Brewery, recalled in photographs and displays of breweriana. Three rooms, full of individual character, surround a central serving area. The bar is particularly traditional with a flagstone floor and real fire. An easy walk from Rhymney terminus station, the Farmers is the most northerly Guide entry in the Valley. Thursday quiz nights are often busy. A large function room is available to hire. No evening food Sunday and Monday. ♔Q❀◑⇌♣P

Rudry

Maenllwyd Inn ✔

CF83 3EB

✪ 12-11 (10.30 Sun); 12-10.30 ☎ (029) 2088 2372

Adnams Broadside; Butcombe Bitter; Fuller's London Pride; Greene King Old Speckled Hen Ⓗ

Popular and often very busy Chef & Brewer dining pub in a tranquil setting near Rudry Common, just over the mountain from north-east Cardiff. Spectacular views can be enjoyed from the large beer garden. The Maenllwyd has won many awards for its food and drink, all proudly displayed near the bar. Beers may occasionally change. ♔Q❀◑⊟P

St Brides Major

Farmers Arms

Wick Road, Pitcot, CF32 0SE

✪ 12-3, 6-11; 12-10.30 Sun ☎ (01656) 880224

Brains The Rev James; Greene King Abbot; Hancock's HB; Wadworth 6X; Wychwood Hobgoblin Ⓗ

Known as 'the pub by the pond', this spacious, attractive roadside hostelry opposite the pond on the edge of the village enjoys a good reputation for both food and beer. The lounge bar is comfortably furnished and has china jugs hanging from the wood beams; there is also a separate restaurant. Live entertainment is hosted at the weekend. ♔Q❀◑⊟♿⊟P

St Georges Super Ely

Greendown Inn

Drope Road, CF5 6EP

✪ 12-2 (not Mon & Tue), 6-11; 12-11 Sat & Sun ☎ (01446) 760310 ⊕ greendownhotel.co.uk

Beer range varies Ⓗ

Dating back to the 15th century, this pub nestles in beautiful surroundings on the edge of a small village just outside the city of Cardiff. The single handpump dispenses a varying rotation of often local Welsh beers, and real cider and perry are also available. Look for the darts score ready reckoner – no need for mental arithmetic here. The pub may close early when trade is quiet. Q❀⊟◑⊟⛺⊟♣●P

Southerndown

Three Golden Cups

Southerndown Road, CF32 0RW

✪ 11-midnight ☎ (01656) 880432 ⊕ tuskasurf.co.uk/threegoldencups

Courage Best Bitter; Sharp's Doom Bar; guest beer Ⓗ

This 16th-century pub overlooks Dunraven bay and its spectacular heritage coast. Dogs are welcome and the pub is very popular with hikers where crackling fireplaces and oak beams add to a restful scene after the walk. The nearby sand-bar is popular with surfers and the local beach has been used to film scenes for Dr Who. Live music is a regular and popular draw for the pub. There is a large car park. ❀◑⊟(45)♣P⚡

WALES

Swansea

Brunswick Arms

3 Duke Street, SA1 4HS
11.30-11; 12-10.30 sun ☎ (01792) 465676
brunswickswansea.co.uk
Courage Best Bitter; Greene King Old Speckled Hen, Abbot Ale H; guest beer G
This well-run side-street pub has the air of a country inn in the city. Wooden beams and comfortable seating create a traditional, relaxing atmosphere. The walls are adorned with an interesting, ever-changing display of artwork, with pictures for sale. Food is available until 8pm during the week, 3pm at the weekend. A quiz is held on Monday evening and live music plays on Sunday, Tuesday and Thursday. The frequently changing guest beer is gravity dispensed, often from a local micro-brewery.

Potters Wheel

85 The Kingsway, SA1 5JE
9-midnight (1am Fri & Sat) ☎ (01792) 465113
Brains SA; Greene King Ruddles Best Bitter, Abbot; Marston's Pedigree; guest beers H
City-centre Wetherspoon outlet named after the old pottery industry. The long sprawling bar area has various seating layouts and attracts customers of all ages and backgrounds. The pub's display of a range of beers from local micros and an interesting selection of guest ales has boosted its sale of real ales. It also offers two draught ciders.
(High St)

Queens Hotel

Gloucester Place, SA1 1TY
11-11; 12-10.30 Sun ☎ (01792) 521531
Brains Buckley's Best Bitter; Theakston Best Bitter, Old Peculier; guest beers H
This vibrant free house, local CAMRA Pub of the Year 2008, is located near the Dylan Thomas Arts Centre, City Museum, National Waterfront Museum (featuring science and industry) and marina. The walls display photographs depicting Swansea's rich maritime heritage. The pub enjoys strong local support and the home-cooked lunches are popular. Evening entertainment includes a Sunday quiz and live music on Saturday. This is a rare local outlet for Theakston Old Peculier as well as a seasonal guest beer from a local micro-brewery.

Vivian Arms

Gower Road, Sketty, SA2 9BZ (Sketty Cross, jct of A4118 and A4216)
12-11 (midnight Fri & Sat) ☎ (01792) 516194
sabrain.com/vivianarms
Brains Bitter, SA, The Rev James; guest beers H
Situated on the main crossroads in Sketty, this spacious pub attracts a wide range of customers young and old. It has a mixture of seating areas including comfortable sofas, and plenty of TV screens throughout the pub show live sport. Two frequently changing guest beers are available alongside the Brains standards. The pub has a small meeting room and is suitable for family dining. Meals are served until 9pm Monday to Saturday and 6pm on Sunday. (20,21)

Westbourne

1 Brynymor Road, SA1 4JQ (on Bryn Y Mor Rd)
11-11 (11.30 Tues & Wed; midnight Thu; 12.30am Fri & Sat)
☎ (01792) 476637 westbourneswansea.com
Greene King Abbot; guest beers H
Located on the western fringe of the city centre, this street-corner single-bar pub has been recently refurbished. Renowned in the area, it has become the place to go for young and old alike. It hosts a quiz on Tuesday evening and has large plasma screens offering comprehensive multi-channel sports. Four ales are always available. Food is served 11-6pm (4pm Sun). (2,3)

Wig

134-136 St Helen's Road, SA1 4BL
11-11 (midnight Fri & Sat); 12-11.30 Sun
☎ (01792) 466519 thewigswansea.co.uk
Beer range varies H
A short walk from the city centre, the Wig is approached by a number of steps, with disabled access to the right. The L-shaped interior includes a bright, comfortable open-plan area to the front and a smaller games area with darts and pool to the rear. Outside seating is popular in summer, with a covered smoking area. Five handpumps serve a rotating range of beers, often from Adnams, Cottage and Rhymney breweries. High quality food is available until 8pm (6pm Sun). (2,3)

Treboeth

King's Head

Llangyfelach Road, SA5 9EL
12-11 (midnight Fri & Sat) ☎ (01792) 773727
Draught Bass; guest beer H
Pleasant roadside pub with patio tables at the front. Inside, the two-tier lounge, decorated in mock-Tudor style, has an upper area which can be used separately. One of the walls features an interesting royal family tree, another has a large chalkboard listing reasonably priced bar meals. Quiz nights are Sunday and Tuesday. A function room/restaurant with its own bar is available for private hire. (36,36A)P

Treforest

Otley Arms

Forest Road, CF37 1SY (on Treforest gyratory system)
11-12.30am (1.30am Fri & Sat); 12-12.30am
☎ (01443) 402033
Otley 01, OG; guest beers H
This much-extended end-of-terrace hostelry has a number of drinking areas, always in demand by the mixed clientele of locals and Glamorgan University students – as is the range of beers, which may include others from Otley Brewery. A beer festival is held each October. There is a large following for sport on multiple TV screens. A good local rail service makes the pub easily accessible from Cardiff and many valley towns. The outdoor smoking area is heated and covered.
(100,244)

Rickard Arms

61 Park Street, CF37 1SN (100m N of railway station)
10-midnight (1am Fri & Sat); 11-11 Sun ☎ (01443) 402305
Otley 01 H
Very much a part of the Treforest community, attracting locals and students alike, activities range from quizzes to dance lessons. A comfortable single-bar conversion of an old muti-roomed local, four distinct drinking areas remain downstairs, including the old cellar. Upstairs is the dining room and outside is the beer garden. The 01 may be replaced by another Otley beer.

Treherbert

Baglan Hotel

30 Baglan Street, CF42 5AW
✪ 11-11 ☎ (01443) 776111
Brains The Rev James; guest beers Ⓗ
This welcome oasis for real ale has been in the same family for more than 60 years. Photographs of well-known visitors adorn the walls. Its location at the head of the Rhondda Valley makes the hotel a good base for the more active visitor, particularly followers of outdoor pursuits such as hill walking and mountain biking. Guest beers frequently come from local Welsh breweries. Breakfast is available from 7.30am. No food is served on Sunday evening. ❀⇌◐◑⊟≈(Ynyswen)⊞(120,130)♣

Tyla Garw

Boar's Head

Coedcae Lane, CF72 9EZ (600m from A473 over level crossing) ST029815
✪ 12 (4 Mon)-11 ☎ (01443) 225400
Beer range varies Ⓗ
Visitors to this multi-award-winning pub are rewarded by a superb beer range. Now sporting eight handpumps, the choice is diverse and focuses on tasty beers from far and near. The pub's interior retains separate rooms, each with a cosy and welcoming character of its own. Talk at the bar often revolves around the beers of the day. The restaurant is extremely popular, especially for Sunday lunch (bookings a must), Tuesday steak night and Wednesday curry night. A direct path here from Pontyclun station cuts through a small industrial area. ♨Q❀◐◑⊟≈(Pontyclun)P⁵–

Upper Church Village

Farmers Arms

St Illyd Road, CF38 1EB
✪ 3-11 Mon-Wed; 12-midnight Thu-Sat; 12-10.30 Sun
☎ (01443) 205766
Black Sheep Best Bitter; Brains The Rev James Ⓗ
Popular, one-roomed village local with a friendly welcome for all. Tuesday's quiz draws in the crowds and Thursday's live music – usually singers – is also enjoyable. However, beer and conversation are the main attractions unless there is a major rugby match showing on the TV. Outside is a sizeable two-level beer garden. Curry night is Wednesday. No food Monday evening.
❀◐◑⊞(11,1000)P

Upper Killay

Railway Inn

553 Gower Road, SA2 7DS (down hill from Killay Square)
✪ 12-11 (10.30 Sun) ☎ (01792) 203946
Swansea Deep Slade Dark, Bishopswood, Three Cliffs Gold, Original Wood; guest beers Ⓗ
Built in 1864, this friendly pub is a popular local offering a warm welcome to visitors. Various social events are held mainly in the summer. The old railway route that runs alongside this former station house is now a footpath and cycle way forming part of the Swansea Bay and South Wales cycle network. Good value food is served at lunchtime. No children are permitted inside. A former local and regional CAMRA Pub of the Year. ♨❀◐⊟⊞(20,21)♣P⁵–

Ynystawe

Millers Arms

634 Clydach Road, SA6 5AX (on B4603, ½ mile N of M4 jct 45)
✪ 11-3, 6-11; 12-3, 7-10.30 Sun ☎ (01792) 842614
Greene King Abbot; Rhymney Hobby Horse; guest beers Ⓗ
Cosy roadside pub with a relaxed atmosphere. Check out the amusing teapot collection and historic local photographs. There is even a picture of the landlord with Welsh icon Tom Jones. Three ales are available, with a focus on Welsh breweries. The pub is always popular for food. Home-cooked, reasonably priced meals are served either in the bar, separate restaurant or outside in the garden, which has a heated, covered area for smokers. ❀◐◑♿♣P⁵–

Ystalyfera

Wern Fawr

47 Wern Road, SA9 2LX
✪ 7 (6.30 Fri & Sat)-11; 12-11 Sun ☎ (01639) 843625
Bryncelyn Holly Hop, Buddy Marvellous, Oh Boy, seasonal beers Ⓗ
Old-fashioned pub full of charm, character and characters. All the cask beers are from the Bryncelyn Brewery, formerly housed in the cellar. The Buddy Holly-themed beers range from the dark Buddy Marvellous at 4% ABV to the light, hoppy and refreshing Oh Boy at 4.5% ABV. The bar houses an amazing collection of memorabilia and a large wood and coal stove for cold winter evenings.
♨Q❀⊟⊞(120,125)♣●

Fishing for beer

Ah! My beloved brother of the rod, do you know the taste of beer – of bitter beer – cooled in the flowing river? Take your bottle of beer, sink it deep, deep in the shady water, where the cooling springs and fishes are. Then, the day being very hot and bright, and the sun blazing on your devoted head, consider it a matter of duty to have to fish that long, wide stream. An hour or so of good hammering will bring you to the end of it, and then – let me ask you avec impressement – how about that beer? Is it cool? Is it refreshing? Does it gurgle, gurgle and 'go down glug' as they say in Devonshire? Is it heavenly? Is it Paradise and all the Peris to boot? Ah! If you have never tasted beer under these or similar circumstance, you have, believe me, never tasted it at all.
Francis Francis, By Lake and River, 16th century

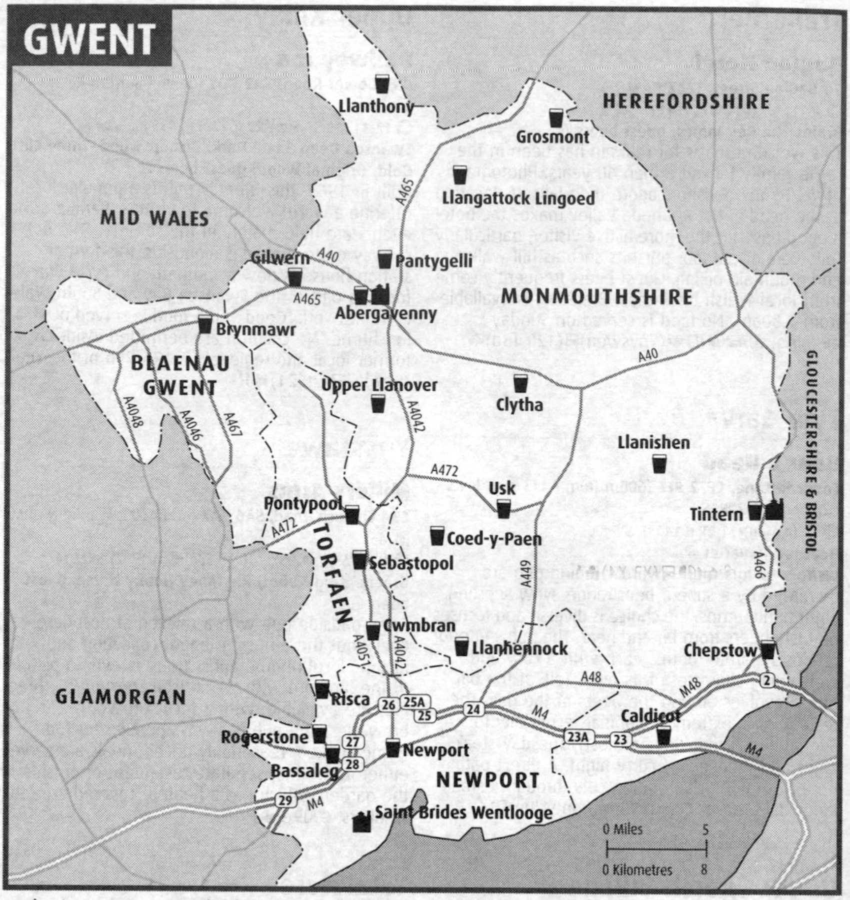

Authority areas covered: Blaenau Gwent UA, Monmouthshire UA, Newport UA, Torfaen UA

Abergavenny

Angel Hotel

15 Cross Street, NP7 5EN

10-3, 6-11 (11.30 Fri & Sat); 11-3, 6-10.30 Sun

☎ (01873) 857121 angelhotelabergavenny.com

Draught Bass; Wye Valley HPA; guest beer Ⓗ

This historic Georgian former coaching inn has served as a high quality hotel for decades. The half wood-panelled Foxhunter Bar is popular with drinkers and diners, with comfy sofa seating. A smaller, cosy lounge offers a tranquil alternative. Outside there is an area for alfresco dining. The restaurant has an excellent reputation and the hotel figures prominently during the hugely popular Abergavenny annual food and drink festival in September. ⛰Q❀⇔◐◑⇌🚌(X3,X4)P⅃

Coach & Horses

41 Cross Street, NP7 5ER

11-11 (midnight Fri & Sat); 12-3, 7-10.30 Sun

☎ (01873) 859411

Brains SA; Greene King IPA; Wadworth 6X Ⓗ

Near the bus station, this listed building was once part of the Gunter Mansion which unsuccessfully hid the last Catholic priest to be burnt at the stake in Britain. Now making a welcome return to the Guide, the Coach & Horses has a spacious open-plan bar with wood beams and a large fireplace reflecting its Tudor origins, plus a separate pool room. A quiet rear garden belies the town-centre location. Wadworth, the best-seller for years, is rare in this area. ❀⇌🚌(X3,X4)♣

Grofield

Baker Street, NP7 5BB (opp cinema on Lewis Lane)

5-midnight Mon; 11-11.30 ☎ (01873) 858939

Rhymney Bitter; guest beers Ⓗ

This smart side-street pub has benefited from a tasteful, modern refurbishment, with comfortable seating areas on both sides of the bar. The lounge bar decor with contemporary artwork distinguishes it from other pubs in town. Good quality lunches are available daily. The philosophy of offering local ales alongside more well-known brands seems to be reaping rewards. ❀◐🚌(X4,X43)⅃

Hen & Chickens ✔

Flannel Street, NP7 5EG

10.30-midnight; 12-11 Sun ☎ (01873) 853575

sabrain.com/henandchickens

INDEPENDENT BREWERIES

Kingstone Tintern
Tudor Abergavenny
Warcop Saint Brides Wentlooge

Brains Bitter, The Rev James; Draught Bass; guest beer Ⓗ
A welcome return to the Guide for this friendly town institution. It is very popular with the Tuesday market crowd and has its own eclectic mix of regulars. The original bar has been extended into the next door premises and there is a full calendar of events including jazz on Sunday, monthly karaoke, and spring and autumn mini-beer festivals. Home-cooked food is available throughout the day on market days. ❀◑◗▣(X3,X4)

Kings Head Hotel

60 Cross Street, NP7 5EU
⏲ 10.30-11 (10 Tue & Fri); 11-4, 7-11 Sun ☎ (01873) 853575
Wells Bombardier; guest beer Ⓗ
Behind the old etched windows of the bar you will find an open-plan room broadly divided into two sections, each with a fireplace. By day this is a popular haunt for market folk and shoppers, while later music comes to the fore, particularly at weekends. There is a large screen for big sporting occasions. A function room and good quality accommodation can be found upstairs. The affiliated Venue 59 offers tasty lunches and an à la carte menu. ❀⇄◑◗▣(X3,X4)♣⊢

Bassaleg

Tredegar Arms ✔

4 Caerphilly Road, NP10 8LE (1 mile N of M4 J28)
⏲ 12-11 (midnight Fri & Sat); 12-10.30 Sun
☎ (01633) 894237
Greene King IPA, St Edmunds, Ruddles County Ⓗ**, Abbot** Ⓖ**; guest beer** Ⓗ
Attractive pub dominating a busy roundabout in a residential area west of Newport. Known locally as the 'bottom TA', it offers a selection of ales from the Greene King stable, with one or more on gravity dispense. Refreshingly, a guest ale occasionally appears from a small independent brewery. The larger of two bars has space for dining, and the family area leads to a large garden and play area, which are very popular in fine weather. ❀◑◗▣(37,50)P⊢

Brynmawr

Hobby Horse Inn

30 Greenland Road, NP23 4DT (off Alma St)
⏲ 12-3, 7-midnight; 11.30-midnight Sat & Sun
☎ (01495) 310996 🌐 hobbyhorse.cjb.net
Beer range varies Ⓗ
Near the town centre but unashamedly serving its local community, this is a vibrant and popular pub offering a variety of real ales from a wide range of breweries. The interior is largely open-plan, but at its heart is the comfortable inner sanctum around the bar where everyone is drawn into conversation. Here the ceiling is covered with sports jerseys and representative pump clips illustrating the wide variety of beers that have been sold over the years. Great value prices for drinks and food. ❀⇄◑◗▣♣⊢

Caldicot

Castle

64 Church Road, NP26 4HN (opp St Mary's Church)
⏲ 12-11 (midnight Fri & Sat) ☎ (01291) 420509
Beer range varies Ⓗ
Set in attractive surroundings with a backdrop of trees, in the distance lies the 12th-century Caldicot Castle and Country Park. The low-beamed interior has a central servery with a room broadly divided between dining on one side and a cosy bar with a large fireplace on the other. An extensive menu of good food is always popular. The garden has a play area for young folk. ⛫❀◑◗⛺▣(X11/14,74)P⊢

Chepstow

Bell Hanger

9-10 St Mary Street, NP16 5EW
⏲ 9am-midnight ☎ (01291) 637360
Butcombe Blond, Brunel IPA; Greene King Ruddles Best, Abbot; Marston's Pedigree; guest beers Ⓗ
Once the premises of a skilled ironmonger, bell-hanger and nailer, this imaginative and comfortable conversion of two former shops now rings with the custom of the broad local community. Its roomy split-level interior appeals to regulars of all ages, from mums-and-toddlers groups to senior citizens. Families feel particularly welcome. Ale is the priority and festivals focus on regional breweries. At least seven ales are available, some from Wales. Opened in 2008, this Wetherspoon newcomer can be busy at peak times. ❀◑◗♿⇌▣(X11/14,74)⊢

Chepstow Athletic Club

Mathern Road, NP16 5JJ (off Bulwark Road)
⏲ 7-11 (11.30 Fri); 12-midnight (11.30 winter) Sat; 12-11 (12-3.30, 7-11 winter) Sun ☎ (01291) 622126
Brains SA; Flowers IPA; Rhymney Bitter; guest beers Ⓗ
This thriving and comfortable local club provides a hub for footballers, archers, cricketers, tennis and bowls players while pleasing the many regulars and visitors who just enjoy a fine pint. A popular community venue where CAMRA members are always welcome, the club hosts gatherings of many local organisations. Six value-for-money ales set the pace – three are guests, often from local breweries. Real ale is also available in the upstairs function room. ❀⇌▣(X11/14,74)♣P⊢

Coach & Horses

Welsh Street, NP16 5LN
⏲ 12-11 (10.30 Sun) ☎ (01291) 622626
🌐 coachandhorsesinn.co.uk
Brains Dark, SA, The Rev James; guest beers Ⓗ
Once a coaching inn, this popular pub warmly welcomes travellers and regulars. Ales from independent breweries, including four beers from Brains (three in summer when the Dark gives way to a cider, often from Westons), are complemented by two guest ales – expect to see six different guests from all parts of the UK each week, including distinctive light-coloured brews which are always popular here. A summer beer and cider festival coincides with the town's folk festival to keep everyone smiling. ❀⇄◑⇌▣●⊢

Clytha

Clytha Arms

NP7 9BW (on B4598 Old Road between Raglan & Abergavenny) SO366088
⏲ 12-3 (not Mon), 6-11; 12-11 Sat; 12-10.30 Sun
☎ (01873) 840206 🌐 clytha-arms.com
Beer range varies Ⓗ

Winner of many accolades for its beers, food and accommodation, this family-run free house is a south Wales institution. A wide range of ever-changing ales, always including beers from Welsh independents, is supplemented by various draught ciders and perry. The annual festival of Welsh cider and a summer festival of Welsh beers and cheeses are among many highlights of the year, held in the extensive grounds, which have wide views towards the Black Mountains. ♨Q❀⛟◐◑⊟♣●P

Coed-y-Paen

Carpenters Arms

NP4 0TH SO334986

⊛ 12-3 (not Mon), 6-11; 12-11 Sat; 12-5 Sun

☎ (01291) 672621 ⊕ thecarpenterscoedypaen.co.uk

Beer range varies Ⓗ

This 200-year-old hostelry is an ideal place to unwind after a strenuous walk or perhaps after watching the sailing and windsurfing on Llandegveth reservoir just half a mile away. The building is currently being extended to add a new dining room and function room. The pub's owner is also the chef and he is very proud of his food, made with locally-sourced ingredients where possible. Two beers are sold, one usually from Cottage, Rhymney or Wye Valley. ♨Q❀◐◑ÅP⚟

Cwmbran

Queen Inn

Upper Cwmbran Road, NP44 5AX

⊛ 12-midnight (11 Sun) ☎ (01633) 484252

Beer range varies Ⓗ

Located on the outskirts of Cwmbran, the pub is in a countryside setting, situated beside a mountain stream with wildfowl swimming in it. The interior has three areas – choose from the lounge, bar or dining room. Over the fireplace is a large framed photograph of the pub during the big freeze of 1963. A choice of three beers usually includes one from Wye Valley or Cottage breweries.
♨❀◐◑⊟⊞(1,25)P⚟

Gilwern

Corn Exchange

Crickhowell Road, NP7 0DG (on A4077 NW of village)

⊛ 12 (5 Mon & winter)-11.30 ☎ (01873) 832404

Brains The Rev James; Wye Valley Bitter; guest beer Ⓗ

Attractive pub situated at the gateway to the Brecon Beacons National Park in a pretty village surrounded by mountain scenery. Popular with local villagers, it offers a warm and friendly greeting to all and attracts visitors from the narrowboats on the nearby Monmouthshire & Brecon Canal as well as walkers. Good food is served in the restaurant. The guest beer is an occasional treat. Accommodation is available in a self-catering cottage. ♨Q❀⛟◐◑⊟⊞(X4)♣P⚟

Grosmont

Angel Inn

Main Street, NP7 8EP (off A465 at either Llanfihangel Crucorney or Llangua)

⊛ 12-2.30 (not Mon), 6-11; 12-11 Sat; 12-3, 7-11 Sun

☎ (01981) 240646 ⊕ grosmont.org/group/the-angel-inn

Beer range varies Ⓗ

Raise a glass to a success story as this pub was acquired by local residents to save it from closure. A short stroll from Grosmont Castle on the Three Castles Walk, if you're lucky you may catch music at weekends when the pub may close later. The regular beers are from Tomos Watkin and Wye Valley, plus a guest. There are cider and beer festivals in the summer. While good food is available, this is first and foremost a pub for drinking. ♨❀◐◑Å♣P

Llangattock Lingoed

Hunter's Moon

NP7 8RR (right from the unclassified Llanfihangel Crucorney to Grosmont road, or left off the B4521 at Llanvetherine) SO363201

⊛ 12-3 (not Mon-Fri Oct-March), 6.30-midnight; 12-3, 6.30-11 Sun ☎ (01873) 821499 ⊕ hunters-moon-inn.co.uk

Wye Valley HPA Ⓗ**; guest beers** Ⓖ

This small pub, set in a tiny hamlet, has ancient origins. Two well-maintained outside areas, one featuring a waterfall and pool, the other decked and looking out towards the medieval church, are beautiful. Guest beers from local Welsh breweries, often Otley and Newmans, are served direct from casks at the back of the bar to complement the regular handpumped beer and cider. The pub also offers good food and accommodation. Check out the pub cat's blog on the website. ♨❀⛟◐◑●P⚟

Llanhennock

Wheatsheaf

NP18 1LT ST353927

⊛ 11-11; 12-3, 7-10.30 Sun ☎ (01633) 420468

⊕ thewheatsheafllanhennock.co.uk

Fuller's London Pride; guest beers Ⓗ

A pub since the 19th century, this traditional, unspoilt two-bar village inn was formed from two much older cottages that were knocked together. The snug and public bar are both crammed with bric-a-brac, memorabilia and old photographs. With a blazing fire in winter and a pleasant garden, it is an ideal place to visit in all seasons. The owner tries to serve as many locally-brewed beers as possible. Boules has a very strong following.
♨❀◐⊟♣P

Llanishen

Carpenters Arms

NP16 6QH (on B4293 between Monmouth and Devauden) SO478032

⊛ closed Mon; 12-3 (not Tue & Wed), 5.30 (6 Tue)-11; 12-3, 7-10.30 Sun ☎ (01600) 860812

Wadworth 6X; guest beers Ⓗ

Impressive on the outside and very comfortable inside, this 400-year-old inn is a fine example of a country pub. Open-plan, with the bar and dining area partitioned from the pool table and dartboard, it also has a side room for busy occasions or small parties. The curries have a very high local reputation and the landlady prides herself on her fish dishes. The landlord likes to source guest beers from local breweries, particularly Kingstone. Self-catering flats are available. Q⛟◐◑⊞(65)♣P

Llanthony

Llanthony Priory Hotel

NP7 7NN (7 miles on unclassified road from Llanvihangel Crucorney) SO288278

⏲ 11-3 (not Mon or winter), 6-11; 11-11 Sat Jul & Aug; 11-10.30 (4 winter) Sun ☎ (01873) 890487
Felinfoel Best Bitter, Double Dragon; guest beers ⊞
Unsurpassed for location, this cellar bar, once part of the abbot's house, has possibly the best beer garden in the country. The stunning 11th-century ruins are situated in the heart of the Black Mountains where the views are magnificent and tranquillity welcomed. Accommodation is in ancient rooms reached via a spiral staircase in the old abbey tower. Check for opening times and note that severe weather can restrict access.
Q❀⇆◑▲♣P⚡

Newport

Godfrey Morgan ✔
Chepstow Road, Maindee, NP19 8EG
⏲ 9am-midnight (1am Fri & Sat) ☎ (01633) 221928
Brains SA, The Rev James; Greene King Ruddles Best, Abbot; guest beers ⊞
Well-appointed cinema conversion in the busy Maindee area which has a good number of pubs and restaurants. The pub is named after Godfrey Morgan who took part in and survived the Charge of the Light Brigade. The main entrance, formerly the cinema foyer, has a high ceiling and is light and airy. The often-busy spacious main bar has some interesting artwork and pictures of famous stars with local connections. Note the car park is pay and display, refundable with your order at the bar.
Q❀◑♿🚌♣P

John Wallace Linton ✔
10-12 The Cambrian Centre, Cambrian Road, NP20 1GA
⏲ 9-midnight (1am Fri & Sat) ☎ (01633) 251752
Brains SA; Greene King Ruddles Best, Abbot; Rhymney Export; guest beers ⊞
Newport's first Wetherspoon pub, named after WWII hero 'Tubby' Linton VC, showcases an excellent selection of micro-brewery beers as well as the core range. Its location near the railway station, shops and local nightlife makes it a popular venue for drinkers and diners. The interior is spacious with a variety of seating, some handily placed to view the news channel on TV. Attractive modern artwork shares wall space with pictures of Newport's past history and local personalities.
Q❀◑♿⇌🚌♣⚡

Olde Murenger House
53 High Street, NP20 1GA
⏲ 11-11; 12-3, 7-10.30 Sun ☎ (01633) 263977
🌐 murenger.com
Samuel Smith OBB ⊞
The ancient timbers of this Tudor house continue to resound to chat and laughter as they have for centuries. The interior has a cosy, dark decor with low beams, and offers a choice of seating areas, some with high-back settles. Here you can drink in the atmosphere as well as the beer and look at pictures depicting former sporting heroes or old town scenes. This well-managed pub remains hugely popular, having seen off some glitzy neighbours. Q◐⇌🚌

Red Lion
47 Charles Street, NP20 1JH (on jct with Stow Hill)
⏲ 12-midnight (1am Fri & Sat); 12-11.30 Sun
☎ (01633) 264398
Beer range varies ⊞
Traditional locals' pub just off the beaten track but handy for central amenities. It has a strong sporting theme with Rugby Union featuring prominently, particularly Newport RFC, and a large screen showing major rugby and football matches. Shove-ha'penny, a sport long associated with Newport, is played, with the pub competing in a local league. The two rotating guest beers are favourites sourced from regional and family brewers on the Punch list. The log fire is a welcoming sight in cold weather.
♨❀⇌🚌♣

St Julian Inn ✔
Caerleon Road, NP18 1QA
⏲ 11.30-11.30 (midnight Thu-Sat); 12-11 Sun
☎ (01633) 243548 🌐 stjulian.co.uk
John Smith's Bitter; Wells Bombardier; Young's Bitter; guest beer ⊞
Obliging staff ensure a warm welcome at this popular pub. It offers a choice of drinking areas arranged around a central bar, and outside a suntrap terrace gives scenic views over the River Usk and surrounding countryside towards historic Caerleon. Local breweries such as Celt, Newman and Rhymney are frequent visitors to augment the staple favourites. The Celtic Manor Resort, host to the 2010 Ryder Cup, is nearby.
❀◑🚌(28,29,60)♣P⚡

Pantygelli

Crown 🏆
Old Hereford Road, NP7 7HR SO302178
⏲ 12-2.30 (3 Sat, not Mon), 6-11; 12-3, 6-10.30 Sun
☎ (01873) 853314 🌐 thecrownatpantygelli.com
Draught Bass; Rhymney Best Bitter; Wye Valley HPA; guest beers ⊞
Busy and popular family-run free house with a reputation for serving quality food and actively promoting real ales. The guest beer comes from a Welsh independent brewery, supplemented by a second on high days and holidays, complementing the well-balanced portfolio of regular ales. Original artwork and fresh flowers add cheer. Outside, the patio, with extensive views towards Skirrid Mountain, is popular on warm days. ♨❀◐◑♣P

Pontypool

John Capel Hanbury ✔
130-131 Osborne Road, NP4 6LT
⏲ 9am-11 (midnight Thu; 1am Fri & Sat) ☎ (01495) 767080
Greene King Ruddles Best, Abbot; guest beers ⊞
This popular Wetherspoon pub is a real-ale beacon in a town with very little choice. Interesting guest ales tend to appear and soon disappear. The spacious interior has a central fireplace as its focal point and a clutter of varied furniture, while a pictorial history of Pontypool is dotted around the walls. The pub gets packed on Friday and Saturday evenings and is a handy watering hole for rugby supporters. John Capel Hanbury was Lord Lieutenant of the County. ❀◑♿🚌(24,X24)♣⚡

Risca

Commercial 🏆 ✔
Commercial Street, Pontymister, NP11 6BA (on B4501 jct with Brookland Rd)
⏲ 11 (12 Sun)-11.30 ☎ (01633) 612608
Beer range varies ⊞

WALES

Gwent CAMRA's Town Pub of the Year 2010 is a vibrant community hub with a comfortable interior comprising a lounge/dining room and a public bar with games. A number of TVs show horse racing and other sports. Outside, the large patio with a retractable awning is very popular – look out for the striking cask ale mural. Five real ales are sourced from far and wide, usually including a local beer, while tasty food is available from a varied menu. ❀◑♿🚌(X15,151)♣●⚟

Rogerstone

Tredegar Arms

157 Cefn Road, NP10 9AS

⏲ 12-3, 5.30-11; 12-11 Fri-Sat; 12-10.30 Sun

☎ (01633) 664999

Courage Best Bitter; Draught Bass; guest beer Ⓗ

Nicknamed the 'top TA', this roadside pub has been a regular Guide entry for years. The attractive interior is full of character, with a cosy public bar, lounge with a large fireplace and dining room. The food is popular and the menu, which changes lunchtimes and evenings, offers a tempting choice of dishes including daily specials (no food Sun eve). The guest ale is often from a local brewery. ❀◑🚂🚌(56)♣P⚟

Sebastopol

Open Hearth

Wern Road, NP4 5DR

⏲ 11.30-midnight; 12-11.30 Sun ☎ (01495) 763752

Wye Valley HPA; guest beers Ⓗ

Popular canalside pub well supported by the local community. This traditional low-beamed venue has several rooms in which to drink or dine. Tasty food is served from an appetising menu, available daily except Monday. Outside is an extensive garden and family play area, and the canal towpath is a popular place to drink in fine weather. ❀◑🚂🚌(23,X24)♣P⚟

Sebastopol Social Club

Wern Road, NP4 5DU (jct with Austin Road)

⏲ 12-11.30 (12.30am Fri & Sat); 12-11 Sun

☎ (01495) 763808

Beer range varies Ⓗ

Award-winning club offering six or more competitively priced ales sourced from micro-breweries UK-wide. The enthusiastic bar team stages a popular beer and cider festival in the summer. The main room hosts bingo, league darts and live weekend entertainment. Wide-screen TVs in the bar and lounge show major sporting events. Live jazz is hosted in the upstairs function room on Friday. Skittles and pool are played in the games room. Non-members are welcome subject to normal visitor rules. ❀🚌(23,X24)♣P⚟

> Up the street, in the Sailors Arms, Sinbad Sailors, grandson of Mary Ann Sailors, drew a pint in the sunlit bar. The ship's clock in the bar says half past eleven. Half past eleven is opening time. The hands of the clock have stayed still at half past eleven for fifty years. It is always opening time in the Sailors Arms.
>
> **Dylan Thomas**, Under Milk Wood

Tintern

Cherry Tree Inn

Forge Road, NP16 5TH (off A466 at Royal George Hotel)

⏲ 12-11 (winter hours vary); 12-10.30 Sun

☎ (01291) 689292 🌐 thecherry.co.uk

Hancock's HB; guest beers Ⓗ

Follow the Angiddy brook up from Tintern and you will soon find the welcoming Cherry Tree Inn with its vintage Hancock's sign. Hancock's Brewery is long gone but its HB flows on – the one permanent ale in a frequently changing range of guests from independents from across the UK, including local breweries. Cask and bottled cider are popular too (often Bulmers, sometimes Thatchers). The Cherry's excellent home-cooked food and its idyllic location make this pub a welcome re-entry to the Guide and well-worth discovering. 🔥Q❀🛏◑🚌(69)●P⚟

Moon & Sixpence

NP16 6SG

⏲ 12-midnight ☎ (01291) 689284

Wye Valley Bitter, Butty Bach; guest beer Ⓗ

The pub was named after the novel The Moon and Sixpence by Somerset Maugham in the 1940s. Two Wye Valley ales are always available here plus a guest, often from the nearby Kingstone brewery. Sunny days allow you to embrace the splendour of the Wye Valley itself on a split-level terrace overlooking the river. Within, a complexity of small rooms and a natural indoor spring add to the pub's distinctive interior. Good value food is available daily. Visitors and locals alike invariably return. 🔥❀◑⛺🚌(69)P

Upper Llanover

Goose & Cuckoo

NP7 9ER SO292073

⏲ closed Mon; 11.30-3, 7-11; 11.30-11 Fri & Sat; 12-10.30 Sun ☎ (01873) 880277 🌐 gooseandcuckoo.co.uk

Beer range varies Ⓗ

If there was a list of 100 pubs to visit before you die, this would surely feature. Situated at the end of a narrow, twisting lane two miles uphill from the main road, the pub has remained unchanged for many years. It features beers from independent Welsh brewers. Offering breathtaking views, it is a haunt of walkers and mountain bikers. Twice winner of Gwent CAMRA Country Pub of the Year, it hosts two annual beer and music festivals. 🔥Q❀🛏◑♣P

Usk

Kings Head Hotel

18 Old Market Street, NP15 1AL

⏲ 11-11; 12-10.30 Sun ☎ (01291) 672963

Fuller's London Pride; Taylor Landlord Ⓗ

A short corridor leads into a cosy bar on two levels with low-beamed ceilings and a mixture of furniture. With much hunting and fishing memorabilia scattered about along with a good selection of books, it has plenty of old-world charm. A good selection of appetising food is available both in the bar and the adjoining Lionel Sweet dining room. A mixture of en-suite and budget accommodation makes this a useful base for exploration of the surrounding area. 🔥🛏◑🚌(60,63)P

Nags Head Inn

Twyn Square, NP15 1BH

⚙ 11-2.30, 5-11; 12-2.30, 5-10.30 Sun ☎ (01291) 672820

Brains The Rev James; guest beers Ⓗ

A fascinating old multi-roomed pub, dating from 1641, it has been in the same family for over 40 years. Situated in the main town square, the long-time Guide entry is well known for a good range of locally-sourced produce. Note the unusual brass taps on the front panel of the bar, a fine collection of plaques from old businesses, and numerous old photos and adverts adorning the walls. The Tack Room has a racing theme. Q☡◑♿🚌(60,63)

Royal Hotel

26 New Market Street, NP15 1AT

⚙ 12-3, 7-11 (not Mon); 12-10.30 Sun ☎ (01291) 672931

Draught Bass; guest beers Ⓗ

A cosy two-roomed pub, famous for its steaks, and popular with locals and visitors alike. The entrance brings you immediately to the bar, with a dining area to the left and a charming public bar to the right with a high-backed settle. Excellent food is cooked to order, and may take a little while to prepare, but is worth the wait. The pub has a devoted following, with some customers coming from the other side of the River Severn.
⛼❀◑⊟🚌(60,63)P⁻

Usk Conservative Club

The Grange, 16 Maryport Street, NP15 1AB

⚙ 12-3, 7-11; 12-3, 7-10.30 Sun ☎ (01291) 672634

St Austell Tribute; guest beers Ⓗ

Well-appointed private members' club set in its own grounds. As you enter, you are greeted with the welcome sight of three handpulls mounted on an elegant bar at the centre of a comfortably furnished lounge, with a games area on one side and a dining room on the other. A large function room is to the rear. An air of old-fashioned gentility pervades this friendly club. Non-members are welcome but club entry rules may be applied.
Q❀◑🚌(60,63)♣P⁻

Red Lion, Newport (Photo: Dave Kirkby)

WALES

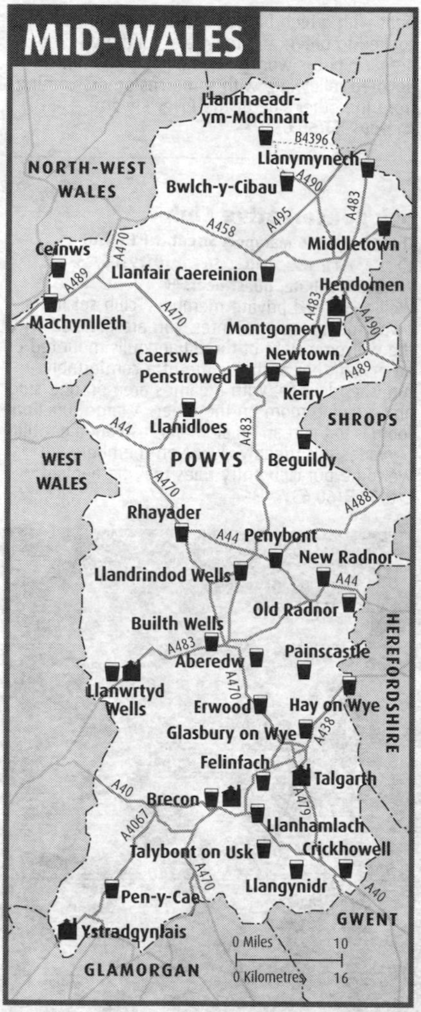

Authority area covered: Powys UA

Aberedw

Seven Stars

LD2 3UW (off B4567)

12-3, 6.30 (6 Fri & Sat)-11; 12-3.30, 6.30-10.30 Sun

☎ (01982) 560494 7-stars.co.uk

Beer range varies Ⓗ

Cosy pub with exposed beams, open stonework and flagstone floors. Legend has it that Llywelyn ap Gruffudd, the last true Prince of Wales, had his horse shod with reversed shoes here by a local smith to enable him to escape his pursuers. Tragically the ruse was unsuccessful and Llywelyn was killed at nearby Cilmeri. The smithy is now part of the inn. The pub opens around 9am most mornings for tea and coffee.

⩩Q❀⇆◑◑⊟♿⩓♣P⊱

Beguildy

Radnorshire Arms ✓

LD7 1YE (on B4355)

closed Mon; 7-midnight (1am Fri & Sat); 12-3, 7-midnight Sun ☎ (01547) 510354

Fuller's London Pride; Wye Valley Beguildy Bitter; guest beers Ⓗ

Picturesque 16th-century roadside inn very close to the English border, which would have been used by drovers. It has a cosy bar with an inglenook and an equally small, appealing dining area. The guest beers are sourced from a range of breweries including Breconshire, Hobson's, Six Bells and Wye Valley. No meals are served on Sunday evening. The outdoor smoking area is heated.

Q❀◑◑⊟♣P⊱

Brecon

Boar's Head

Ship Street, LD3 9AL (by bridge over River Usk)

11-midnight (2am Fri & Sat); 12-1am Sun

☎ (01874) 622856

Breconshire Welsh Pale Ale, Golden Valley, Cribyn, Ramblers Ruin, seasonal beers Ⓗ

The Breconshire Brewery tap is a popular and lively town-centre pub with two distinct bars – the wood-panelled front bar houses the majority of the handpumps and tends to be a little quieter than the larger back bar, which has a pool table and gets very busy on match days when rugby internationals are shown on TV. Live music evenings and quiz nights are held throughout the year, and the pub is a favourite spot during the jazz festival. The riverside patio garden enjoys superb views over the river and up to the Brecon Beacons.

⩩❀◑◑⊟♿⊟♣●P⊱

Olde Cognac

High Street, LD3 7AP

11-11 (11.30 Sat) ☎ (01874) 622725

Draught Bass; Hancock's HB; guest beer Ⓗ

Situated in the heart of Brecon, the Cognac is a small, quiet pub, well-used and well-loved. The public and snug bars both boast parquet floors and a wide selection of photographs, sketches and rugby memorabilia on the walls. Food is basic pub fare, served at lunchtime. The ever-changing guest ale may be local or from further afield.

Q◑⊟♿⩓⊟(X43)

Builth Wells

Greyhound Hotel

3 Garth Road, LD2 3AR

12-midnight (noon-1am Fri & Sat) ☎ (01982) 553255

thegreyhoundhotel.co.uk

Greene King Abbot; guest beers Ⓗ

Pleasant modern hotel with open-plan bars, a restaurant and a large function room. Excellent food, including a Sunday carvery, is served, with the menu featuring local produce. A glass panel above the door harks back to when there was a brewery at the hotel. A beer festival is held every year. ❀⇆◑◑♿⊟♣P⊱

INDEPENDENT BREWERIES

Breconshire Brecon
Bryncelyn Ystradgynlais
Heart of Wales Llanwrtyd Wells
Monty's Hendomen
Rotters Talgarth (NEW)
Waen Penstrowed

Bwlch-y-Cibau

Stumble Inn

SY22 5LL

⏲ 11-11 summer; 6-11 Mon & Tue, closed Wed, 11-11 Thu-Sat winter; 12-3 Sun ☎ (01691) 648860

Beer range varies Ⓗ

This roadside pub, once called the Cross Keys, has a public bar and a cosy lounge with a well-appointed restaurant seating up to 50 people. The varied food menu makes this a popular venue and two changing guest beers are available. The bar features a large twin-bladed propeller with a plaque bearing the name EW Alcock, which came from the Air Force Club in Manchester. ♛❀◑⊟⊟♣P

Caersws

Red Lion

Main Street, SY17 5EL (on B4569)

⏲ 3-11 (midnight Fri, Sat & summer) ☎ (01686) 688023

Beer range varies Ⓗ

Friendly wood-beamed village pub comprising two bars attracting a varied clientele of all ages. Early evenings can be busy as many villagers call in on the way home from work. The four changing ales usually include two locally-produced beers. A summer beer festival is held outside in the large car park and there are outside drinking areas to the front and rear. ♛❀⇌◑⊟⇶⊟(X75,X85)♣P

Ceinws

Tafarn Dwynant

SY20 9HA (off A487 3 miles N of Machynlleth) SH760060

⏲ closed Mon; 5.30 (12 Sat)-11; 12-7 Sun ☎ (01654) 761660

🌐 tafarndwynant.co.uk

Purple Moose Snowdonia Ale; guest beer Ⓗ

Situated in a quiet village, this friendly community free house is three miles from the nearest town and railhead of Machynlleth and a mile from the Centre of Alternative Technology. Both bars have solid-fuel/log-burning stoves. The landlord's own artwork is on display and for sale. Home-prepared food uses locally and ethically sourced ingredients. Occasional mini-beer festivals are held, with real cider also available. Buses stop on the main road, just across the river from the village. ♛◑⅄⊟(X32)⊱

Crickhowell

Bridge End Inn

Bridge Street, NP8 1AR (by River Usk bridge, off A40 on A4077 to Gilwern)

⏲ 11-11; 12-10.30 Sun ☎ (01873) 810338

🌐 thebridgeendinn.com

Brains The Rev James; Fuller's London Pride; Greene King Old Speckled Hen; Rhymney Best Bitter Ⓗ

Cosy and friendly 16th-century coaching inn in a superb location by the River Usk. Local and guest beers are of consistently high quality, and good value locally-sourced food is served in the restaurant. The beer garden by the river is a wonderful spot for catching the sun on long summer evenings. Accommodation is available in an adjoining cottage. ♛Q♉❀⇌◑⅄⊟P

Erwood

Erwood Inn

LD2 3EZ (in village centre)

⏲ 2-midnight; 12-midnight Thu-Sun ☎ (01982) 560218

🌐 erwoodinn.com

George Wright Wandering Minstrel Ⓗ

Welcoming community pub in the village centre, undergoing a sympathetic modernisation. The servery is a simple bar, next to a large iron stove lurking in a huge fireplace. There is a smart seating area to one side, with access to the riverside terrace garden. At the other end of the building, there is a large games room, complete with pool table, darts, quoits and a big screen for the main sporting events. ♛❀⇌◑♿⊟♣P⊱

Felinfach

Griffin

LD3 0UB (just off A470 3 miles NE of Brecon)

⏲ 12-11.30 ☎ (01874) 620111 🌐 eatdrinksleep.ltd.uk

Breconshire Cribyn; Otley 01; Wye Valley Bitter, Butty Bach Ⓗ

The pub's ethos – the simple things in life done well – says it all. A welcoming country pub, restaurant and hotel, the emphasis here is on good beer and excellent food. The multi-roomed layout allows for discrete areas for drinking and dining. The huge fireplace between the bar and the main dining area dominates during the winter, while a full-sized Aga lurks in a side room, providing warmth throughout the building. The large garden, very popular in summer, affords superb views of the Brecon Beacons and Black Mountains. ♛Q❀⇌◑♿⊟P⊱

Glasbury on Wye

Harp Inn

HR3 5NR (on Hay Road)

⏲ 6-10.30 Mon; 12-3, 6-11 Tue-Thu; 12-midnight Fri; 12-3, 6-midnight Sat; 12-3, 7-11 Sun ☎ (01497) 847373

🌐 theharpinn.co.uk

Wye Valley Dorothy Goodbody's Golden Ale; guest beers Ⓗ

Traditional country inn dating from around 1720 with low ceilings, wood beams and a large horseshoe-shaped servery. It offers a range of cask ales from local brewers and guests from further afield. A welcoming community pub, quoits, darts and poker are played on a regular basis and a quiz is hosted on Thursday. The rear garden area and veranda boast river views. ♛Q❀⇌◑⅄⊟♣P⊱

Hay on Wye

Kilverts ✔

The Bull Ring, HR3 5AG

⏲ 11-11 (midnight Fri & Sat) ☎ (01497) 821042

🌐 kilverts.co.uk

Breconshire Kilverts Gold; Marston's Pedigree; Wye Valley Butty Bach; guest beers Ⓗ

Nestling at the foothills of the Brecon Beacons in the famous book and festival town, this 12-bedroomed inn boasts five handpumps alongside an extensive range of wines, ciders and malt whiskies. Locally sourced, home-made food is served in the bar, restaurant and large beer garden, which hosts beer festivals and live jazz. Tuesday is the ever-popular 'open mike' night. ♛❀⇌◑⊟♿●⊱

Kerry

Kerry Lamb
SY16 4NP (on A489)
✪ 5-11 (midnight Thu); 4-midnight Fri; 12-midnight Sat; 12-11 Sun ☎ (01686) 670226 🌐 thekerrylamb.co.uk
Hobson's Best Bitter; guest beers Ⓗ
This popular village pub has two bars: the front bar with comfortable sofas is mainly used for dining, whilst the large wooden-floored rear bar has a wood-burning stove creating a homely feel. There is also a games room with a pool table. The inn attracts a varied clientele of all ages. The pub's name refers to a breed of sheep named after the village. No food is served on Monday evening. ⩠❀◑♣P⌐

Llandrindod Wells

Conservative Club
South Crescent, LD1 5DH
✪ 11-2, 5.30-11; 11-11.30 Fri & Sat; 11.30-10.30 Sun
☎ (01597) 822126
Hancock's HB; Fuller's London Pride; guest beers Ⓗ
A quiet, comfortable haven overlooking the Temple Gardens, the 'Con' has a large lounge, TV room, games bar, snooker and pool tables, and a small front patio. Lunches are available Thursday to Saturday. Live entertainment is hosted occasionally in the evening. CAMRA members are welcome but non-members must be signed in. Q❀◐♿⇌🚌♣⌐

Llanfair Caereinion

Goat Hotel
High Street, SY21 0QS (off A458)
✪ 11-11 (midnight Fri & Sat) ☎ (01938) 810428
Beer range varies Ⓗ
This excellent inn has a welcoming atmosphere and attracts both locals and tourists. The plush lounge, dominated by a large inglenook with an open fire, has comfortable leather armchairs and sofas, complemented by a dining room serving home-cooked food and a games room at the rear. The choice of three real ales always includes one from the Wood Brewery. ⩠❀⛌◐◑♣P

Llangynidr

Red Lion
Duffryn Road, NP8 1NT (off B4558)
✪ 11-11; 12-10.30 Sun ☎ (01874) 730223
Beer range varies Ⓗ
Popular village local, off the beaten track, which offers a warm welcome to walkers, boaters, families and dogs. The beer range changes regularly and good value home-cooked food is served in the bar. A separate games area, outside seating and children's play area make this a pub for all. ⩠Ƨ❀⛌◐◑⊟♣P

Llanhamlach

Old Ford Inn
LD3 7YB (on A40 3 miles E of Brecon)
✪ 12-11 ☎ (01874) 665220
Beer range varies Ⓗ
This 12th-century coaching inn has been much extended but retains its original character. The central bar features some unusual copper work and a collection of nip bottles. A larger room beyond the bar, used mainly by diners, has panoramic views of the Brecon Beacons. The excellent food includes regional dishes. Beers are usually sourced from local breweries. ⩠QƧ❀⛌◐◑⊟♿🚌P

Llanidloes

Angel Hotel
High Street, SY18 6BY (off A470)
✪ 11.30-2.30 (not Wed), 5-1am; 12-3, 7-midnight Sun
☎ (01686) 412381
Everards Tiger; Greene King Abbot; guest beer Ⓗ
Friendly edge-of-town pub with two comfortable bars. The larger of the two rooms has a large stone fireplace with old photographs on the wall. The smaller room has an interesting bar inlaid with old pennies. There is a restaurant at the rear that can seat 40 people (booking recommended). The pub was built in 1748 and Chartists held meetings here between 1838 and 1839. ⩠❀◐◑🚌(X75,525)♣

Crown & Anchor Inn ★
41 Long Bridge Street, SY18 6EF (off A470)
✪ 11-11; 12-10.30 Sun ☎ (01686) 412398
Brains The Rev James; Worthington's Bitter Ⓗ
Wonderful, unspoilt town-centre gem with a relaxed and friendly atmosphere, featuring in CAMRA's National Inventory of Historic Pub Interiors. The landlady has been in charge since 1965 and throughout that time the pub has remained unchanged, retaining its public bar, lounge, snug and two further rooms, one with a pool table and games machine. ⊟🚌(X75,525)♣

Red Lion Hotel
Long Bridge Street, SY18 6EE (off A470)
✪ 11-midnight (1am Fri & Sat) ☎ (01686) 412270
Taylor Landlord; guest beers Ⓗ
Wood-beamed town-centre hotel with a plush lounge and red leather sofas. The public bar is divided into two areas – the front area has an interesting wood-panelled fireplace, the rear space has a pool table and games machines. Up to four real ales are usually available. There is a patio outside at the rear for warmer weather.
⩠❀⛌◐◑⊟🚌(X75,525)♣

Stag Inn ✔
15 Great Oak Street, SY18 6BU (off A470)
✪ 11.30-3, 5-11; 12-midnight Sat; 1-11 Sun
☎ (01686) 412700 🌐 staginnllanidloes.co.uk/index.htm
Shepherd Neame Bishops Finger; guests beers Ⓗ
Dog-friendly town-centre pub offering three real ales. The long premises is divided into two – the front has wall seating and a wood-burning stove, the rear area through an archway has wood beams, a couple of sofas and barrels for tables. Live music is hosted at the weekend, with a folk and roots session on Sunday afternoon. Outside, there is space for alfresco drinking. ⩠❀◐◑♣●

Llanrhaeadr-ym-Mochnant

Plough Inn ✔
SY10 0JR (on B4580)
✪ 12-midnight (1.30am Fri; 2.30am Sat) ☎ (01691) 780654
Beer range varies Ⓗ
This true community local was converted from a private house. The multi-roomed interior retains the timber beams and tiled floors, and the front bar features a large open fireplace. A games area at the rear has a pool table and table football, and there is a separate restaurant. The range of beers

often includes Brains Rev James and Black Sheep Best Bitter. Wales' highest waterfall, Pistyll Rhaeadr, is close to the village.

Llanwrtyd Wells

Neuadd Arms Hotel

The Square, LD5 4RB

11-midnight (2am Fri & Sat); 11-11 Sun

(01591) 610236 neuaddarmshotel.co.uk

Heart of Wales Aur Cymru, Bitter, Welsh Black, Noble Eden, Innstable, seasonal beers; guest beer H

This large Victorian hotel serves as the tap for the Heart of Wales Brewery. The Bells Bar features a large fireplace and an eclectic mix of furniture. The bells formerly used to summon servants remain on one wall, along with the winners' boards from some of the town's more unusual competitions, such as bog-snorkelling or man v. horse. The lounge bar is a little more formal, with deep carpets, sofas and paintings on the walls. The hotel takes part in the town's annual events including a beer festival in November and food festivals. Local Cider Pub of the Year.

Stonecroft Inn

Dolecoed Road, LD5 4RA

5-midnight; 12-1am Fri-Sun (01591) 610332

stonecroft.co.uk

Brains The Rev James; guest beers H

This warm and friendly community pub acts as a hub for the town's many and varied festivities – bog-snorkelling, beer and food festivals, real ale rambles and much more. The hostelry has three main areas for drinking, dining and games, plus a large riverside garden with an aviary. Excellent food complements the fine range of beers. Lodge accommodation is popular with walkers and mountain bikers.

Llanymynech

Bradford Arms

North road, SY22 6EJ (on A483)

11.30-3, 6-11 (01691) 830582

bradfordarmshotel.com

Black Sheep Best Bitter; guest beers H

Small but popular hotel near Offa's Dyke with a varied clientele. The cosy bar has a real fire and the walls are adorned with pump clips and RAF photographs. Three beers are available with guest ales from local breweries. A real cider is planned for the summer months and third of a pint glasses are available for sampling. This AA four-star hotel has a restaurant to the rear and five guest rooms.

Machynlleth

White Horse

42 Maengwyn Street, SY20 8DT

12-3 (Wed-Fri only), 7 (6 Fri)-11.30; 12-11.30 Sat & Sun

Beer range varies H

Friendly locals' pub standing on the main street of this bustling market town, once the capital of Wales – just across the street is the site of Owain Glyndwr's Parliament House of 1404. Both bars have open log fires in winter, and the beer garden at the rear affords access for disabled customers. Two real ales are usually on offer, drawn from a wide range of family and micro-brewers. Bar meals available at certain times.

Middletown

Breidden Hotel

SY21 8EL (on A458)

12-2.30, 5-11; 12-midnight Sat; 11-midnight

(01938) 570880

Beer range varies H

This village local has a large wood-beamed L-shaped bar with comfortable seating, a pool table and games machines. At one end of the bar is a small, cosy restaurant area, and the pub has a good reputation for eastern cuisine. The hotel takes its name from Breidden Hill, topped by the 18th-century Admiral Rodney's Pillar, which dominates the neighbourhood. There is a large outside drinking area that is partly covered.

(X75)

Montgomery

Crown Inn

Castle Street, SY15 6PW

11-11 (midnight Sun) (01686) 668533

Beer range varies H

This pub attracts a mixed clientele from the local area with a wood-burning stove and wall seating at the front and a long public bar with a pool table and games machines at the rear. The walls are covered with local photographs. There is also a small lounge bar with a comfortable sofa and sports trophies. Three beers are on offer, at least one from a local brewery. (81)

New Radnor

Radnor Arms

Broad Street, LD8 2SP

12-2.30, 5-11; 12-midnight Sat; 12-11 Sun

(01544) 350232

Beer range varies H

Set in the Welsh Marches close to the English border, this cosy pub is an ideal base for an away-from-it-all break. The area offers excellent walking, trekking and cycling – Offa's Dyke is nearby and Hereford 25 miles away by car or bus. Food, served every day, includes a take-away service and a popular Sunday carvery (booking advisable). Guest beers are mainly from smaller breweries including Cottage, Six Bells and Wye Valley. Real cider and perry are available.

Newtown

Elephant & Castle

Broad Stree, SY16 2BQ (off A483)

11-11 (01686) 626271 elephantandcastlehotel.co.uk

Six Bells Big Nev's; guest beers H

Open-plan town-centre hotel next to the River Severn with a number of drinking areas off the main bar. Old photographs and prints adorn the walls. A number of TV sets show sporting events. Three local beers are on offer, usually from Monty's or Six Bells breweries. To the rear is a separate function building. Outside, there is bench seating by the river wall.

Railway Tavern

Old Kerry Road, SY16 1BH (off A483)

12-2.30, 6-midnight Mon, Wed & Thu; 11-1am Tue, Fri & Sat; 12-11 Sun (01686) 626156

Draught Bass; Worthington's Bitter; guest beer H

Traditional pub on the edge of the town centre and handy for the railway station. The pub owes its welcoming atmosphere and devoted following to the long-serving landlord and landlady who have been in charge for more than 25 years. The pub has a successful darts team and match nights can get busy. Guest beers come from a wide range of independent breweries. ❀⇌🚌(X75)♣

Old Radnor

Harp Inn

LD8 2RH

⏲ closed Mon; 12-3 (Sat & Sun only), 6-11

☎ (01544) 350655 🌐 harpinnradnor.co.uk

Beer range varies Ⓗ

This early 15th-century Welsh longhouse commands a fine view over the Radnor Valley. The interior is a tasteful mix of old and new – slate-flagged floors, beamed ceilings, an open fireplace, settles, a modern restaurant and en-suite accommodation. The beers are sourced mainly from micro-breweries both local (Hobson's, Three Tuns, Wye Valley) and far-flung (Bath, Leadmill, Millstone). There is also a good range of malt whiskies. ♨Q❀🛏◑⊟♿♣●P

Painscastle

Roast Ox

LD2 3JL ☎ (01497) 851398 🌐 roastoxinn.co.uk

Hook Norton Hooky Bitter Ⓗ

Village-centre pub that specialises in both cask ales and real ciders, with up to five ciders on offer at most times. Renovated and refurbished following a disastrous fire some years ago, the 500-year-old inn is steeped in history. With stone-flagged floors, a wooden bar and ale and cider casks on view behind the bar, it has the feel of an old and much-loved premises. In the corner behind the bar there is a well – an unusual feature for any pub. ♨❀◑●P⁄–

Pen-y-Cae

Ancient Briton 🏆

Brecon Road, SA9 1YY (on A4067 between Ystradgynlais and Dan-yr-Ogof caves)

⏲ 12-midnight ☎ (01639) 730273 🌐 ancientbriton.co.uk

Wye Valley Butty Bach; guest beers Ⓗ

Excellent country inn within the Fforest Fawr Geopark in the Brecon Beacons National Park, close to Dan-Yr-Ogof Caves and Henrhyd Waterfalls, frequented by walkers, cavers and cyclists. Up to six ales and one real cider are always on handpump, and an annual beer festival is held every September. The restaurant serves à la carte and bar meals. There is a large beer garden at the rear and en-suite accommodation. Local CAMRA Pub of the Year on three occasions including 2010. ♨Q❀🛏◑♿⛺🚌(X63)♣●P⁄–⊟

Penybont

Severn Arms 🏆

LD1 5UA

⏲ 11.30-3, 6-midnight (1am Fri & Sat); 12-3, 7-11 Sun

☎ (01597) 851224 🌐 severn-arms.co.uk

Beer range varies Ⓗ

This 18th-century coaching inn was built to serve the Hereford to Aberystwyth route (today's A44). The spacious bar with its large open fireplace leads to gardens overlooking the River Ithon – six miles of free fishing is available to residents. There is also a quiet, secluded restaurant and a games room. Guest beers are sourced from a wide range of breweries and a fine selection of malt whiskies is on offer. Champion Pub of South and Mid-Wales 2009. ♨Q❀🛏◑⊟⛺🚌♣P⁄–

Rhayader

Crown Inn

North Street, LD6 5BT

⏲ 11 (6 Mon Jan & Feb)-11 (midnight Fri & Sat); 12-10.30 Sun

☎ (01597) 811099 🌐 thecrownrhayader.co.uk

Brains Dark, Bitter, The Rev James, seasonal beers Ⓗ

This 16th-century beamed pub has an open-plan bar with many photographs of local residents and scenes, nearly all with written descriptions – look for the item referring to the eccentric Major Stanscombe, a former owner. This is a rare outlet locally for real mild, and the current Brains seasonal or one-off beer is usually available. The outdoor smoking area is covered. Q❀🛏◑⊟⛺🚌♣⁄–

Talybont on Usk

Star Inn 🏆

LD3 7YX (on B4558 between Brecon and Crickhowell) SO114226

⏲ 11-3, 5-11; 12-11 Sun ☎ (01874) 676635

🌐 starinntalybont.co.uk

Beer range varies Ⓗ

Large and lively pub alongside the Brecon and Monmouth canal. The spacious garden is extremely popular in summer. The beer range is mostly from local breweries, with some better-known ales added from time to time. Locally-produced cider is also available. Live music evenings are held regularly, and quiz nights are popular. The excellent food makes good use of local produce. A successful beer festival looks set to become a regular event. Brecknock Pub of the Year 2009 and 2010. ♨❀🛏◑⊟♿⛺🚌(X43)♣●

Learned drinker

He was a learned man, of immense reading, but is much blamed for his unfaithfull quotations. His manner of studie was thus, he wore a long quilt cap, which came two or rather three inches at least over his eies, which served him as an umbrella to defend his eies from the light. About every three houres his man was to bring him a roll and a pot of ale to refocillate (refresh) his wasted spirits so he studied, and dranke, and munched some bread and this maintained him till night, and then he made a good supper.
An Oxford man, William Prynne (1600-69), as described by **John Aubrey** in Brief Lives, ed. John Buchanan-Brown, 2000

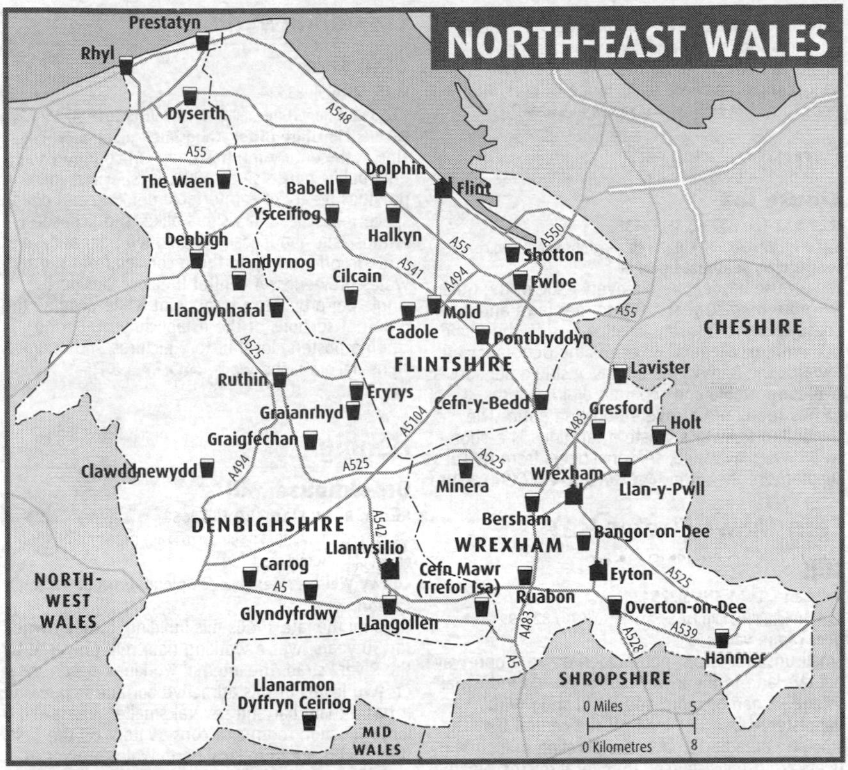

Authority areas covered: Denbighshire UA, Flintshire UA, Wrexham UA

Babell

Black Lion

CH8 8PZ (village signed from B5121) SJ155735
⌚ closed Mon & Tue; 6-11 Wed-Fri; 12-midnight Sat; 12-11 Sun ☎ (01352) 720239
Beer range varies H
Just 10 minutes' drive from the main A55, this rural pub has a reputation for locally-sourced food, freshly made and served until 9pm. The interior comprises two small bars and a separate overspill room. Celtic music evenings are held on the last Wednesday of the month and the local British Legion branch meets here bi-monthly. This former coaching inn offers something for everyone, including a house beer Black Lion Bitter from the local brewery Facer's. ⛫Q❀◑⊟⛺♣P⁄–

Bangor-on-Dee

Buck House Hotel

LL13 0BU (just off A525 Wrexham-Whitchurch road, opp church)
⌚ 11.30-midnight (1am Fri & Sat) ☎ (01978) 780336
🌐 buckhousehotel.co.uk
Plassey Border Mild; Tetley Bitter; guest beers H
Traditional twin-roomed pub with a warm, friendly, family atmosphere, accommodation and good pub food. The main bar has a pool table, jukebox, darts and sports for entertainment. The lounge is quieter with an amazing collection of teapots. Interesting features include a red telephone box and an old well in the lobby. The pub is a rare outlet for Plassey Border Mild and is also noted for its selection of tasty cakes. ⛫Q☕❀⛟◑♿♣P⁄–

Bersham

Black Lion ✔

LL14 4HN (off B5099 near Bersham Heritage Centre)
⌚ 12-12.30am (1am Fri-Sun) ☎ (01978) 365588
Hydes Original Bitter, seasonal beers H
Known locally as the Hole in the Wall, this very friendly pub with a long-serving landlord overlooks the delightful Clwyedog River and is adjacent to the Clwyedog Industrial Trail. It is popular with locals, walkers and visitors to the nearby Heritage Centre. The wood-panelled bar serves two rooms, both with real fires in winter, and a games room. Basic hot bar food is available all day. There is a play area in the garden. ⛫❀⊟♿🚌♣P⁄–

Cadole

Colomendy Arms

Village Road, CH7 5LL (off A494 Mold-Ruthin road)
⌚ 7 (6 Thu; 4 Fri; 2 Sat)-11; 2-10.30 Sun ☎ (01352) 810217
Beer range varies H
Delightful, traditional village local on the edge of Loggerheads Country Park. This frequent local CAMRA Pub of the Year winner is popular with

INDEPENDENT BREWERIES

Abbey Grange (Llangollen) Llantysilio (NEW)
Facer's Flint
Gertie Sweet Eyton (NEW)
Jolly Brewer Wrexham
McGivern Wrexham
Plassey Eyton
Sandstone Wrexham

families, walkers, cavers and runners. Friendly conversation is the main entertainment. The cosy single bar has a roaring fire in winter. Five handpumps provide a wide range of ales, many from local breweries. ⛫Q☺❀⊟♿🚌♣P

Carrog

Grouse Inn

LL21 9AT (on B5437) SJ113435
⏲ 11-11 ☎ (01490) 430272 🌐 thegrouseinncarrog.co.uk
Lees Bitter, seasonal beers Ⓗ
The Grouse has featured in every issue of the Guide for more than 20 years. This former farm and brew house is set in a lovely location beside the River Dee with excellent views across the Dee Valley and towards the Berwyn Mountains. A single bar serves two comfortable and separate dining rooms, a games room and a covered outside patio. The Llangollen Railway's western terminus is a short walk. When available, seasonal beers from JW Lees supplement the Bitter. ⛫Q❀◐▲⇌🚌(X94)♣P⊱

Cefn Mawr (Trefor Isa)

Mill

Mill Lane, LL14 3NL SJ275424
⏲ 12-midnight (1am Fri & Sat) ☎ (01978) 821799
Beer range varies Ⓗ
Small unspoilt locals' pub hidden down a one-way narrow lane in the lower part of an old industrial village. A games room and small snug with upholstered benches lead off the central bar. The smoking area backs on to the gurgling mill stream. Beers are usually sourced from local micros. Nearby are the famous Pontcysyllte Aqueduct on the Llangollen Canal and Cefn Druids FC. Parking can be difficult but buses pass nearby. ❀⊟🚌(2,5)♣⊱

Cefn-y-Bedd

Ffrwd

Ffrwd Road, LL12 9TS (1 mile along B5102 from A541)
⏲ 5.30-11.30; 1 (6.30 winter)-11.30 Sat; 12-9 Sun
☎ (01978) 757951
Beer range varies Ⓗ
The Ffrwd sits in an attractive wooded valley alongside the River Ceigidog. It was built on top of a former pub which was buried when the bridge replaced the original ford across the river. The pub has separate dining and bar areas served by a central bar. The two guest beers are often unusual brews for this area and real cider is also available. Generous portions of excellent food are served in the evenings and at weekends. ⛫❀◐♿⇌●P⊱

Cilcain

White Horse

The Square, CH7 5NN (signed from A451 Mold to Denbigh Road) SJ177651
⏲ 12-3, 6.30-11; 12-11 Sat; 12-10.30 Sun ☎ (01352) 740142
Banks's Bitter; guest beers Ⓗ
Picturesque whitewashed pub in an attractive village beside the foothills of Moel Famau, part of the Clwydian range. It has a split-level lounge and a separate public bar with a quarry-tiled floor, where walkers and dogs are welcome. Four log fires keep the pub warm in winter. The guest beer is often from the Marston's portfolio. Meals are served lunchtimes and evenings throughout the week. ⛫Q◐⊟♣P

Clawddnewydd

Glan Llyn

LL15 2NA SJ083524
⏲ 5 (12 summer)-midnight; 12-11 Sun ☎ (01824) 750754
Facer's Flintshire Bitter, Landslide; guest beer Ⓗ
This 16th-century inn has been Clawddnewydd's only public house since 1906. Its spacious interior provides plenty of comfortable drinking and dining space for locals and visitors alike. The licensee is enthusiastic about cask-conditioned beer and takes pride in offering up to three choices from north Wales breweries. A central fireplace beside the single bar provides a focal point while dividing the different sections of the establishment. Period cinema posters, local history pictures and enamel signs decorate the walls. ⛫Q❀◗▲♣P⊱

Denbigh

Brookhouse Mill

Ruthin Road, LL16 4RD SJ072658
⏲ 12-3, 6-11.30; 12-11 Sun ☎ (01745) 813377
🌐 brookhousemill.co.uk
Conwy Welsh Pride; Facer's Splendid; Great Orme Cambria Ⓗ
Up until the late 1960s this building, family-owned for 30 years, was a working flour mill powered by the River Ystrad. The internal workings are on show on two levels of this attractive bar and restaurant. It has a main bar and several smaller areas, and a large function room and conservatory on the first floor. Beers are from local north Wales breweries. A complimentary minibus operates to local areas within an eight-mile radius on Friday and Saturday. ❀◐♿🚌(51,53,150)P⊱

Railway

2 Ruthin Road, LL16 3EL SJ059664
⏲ 12-midnight (1am Fri & Sat) ☎ (01745) 812376
Purple Moose Glaslyn; guest beers Ⓗ
Denbigh railway station is long gone but the pub's name retains a link with the past. This basic local has five separate areas – a public bar and rooms for pool, dominoes and darts. The beers are usually from north Wales breweries. The pub is half a mile from the town and historic Denbigh Castle, built by Edward I. Bus route 51 from Rhyl to Ruthin stops nearby. ▲🚌(51,76,150)♣P⊱

Dolphin

Glan yr Afon Inn

CH8 8HE SJ195739
⏲ 12-11 (11.30 Fri & Sat); 12-10.30 Sun ☎ (01352) 710052
🌐 glanyrafoninn.co.uk
Beer range varies Ⓗ
With views of the Dee Estuary, this 16th-century inn, set off the A55 in a quiet location, is family, walker and dog friendly, and offers good quality accommodation. The multi-area pub serves food and drink all day in the bar or more secluded restaurant. The regular beer is Glan 450, brewed for the pub by Facer's of Flint to celebrate its 450 year anniversary. Local history displays and information about the nearby network of caves provide interest. ⛫Q❀🛏◐⊟🚌(126)♣P⊱

Dyserth

New Inn

Waterfall Road, LL18 6ET (on B5119 close to Dyserth Waterfall) SJ055794

12-11 ☎ (01745) 570482 thenewinndyserth.co.uk

Banks's Mild, Bitter; Marston's Burton Bitter, Pedigree; guest beer H

Close to the foot of Dyserth Waterfall tourist attraction, this old pub – now greatly modernised and extended – focuses on food. Nevertheless, five real ales are a good reason to call in for a drink at this TV-free zone. Pictures of days gone by attest to the age of this pub and village. There is a pleasant outdoor drinking area.
❀(35,36)P

Erydrys

Sun Inn

Village Road, CH7 4BX

3.30-11; 1-10.30 Sun ☎ (01824) 780402

Theakston Best Bitter; guest beers H

Built of local stone, the pub is situated in the centre of the village in an attractive area on the Flintshire and Denbighshire border, attracting both locals and walkers. The cosy interior, with low beamed ceilings, has an open fire in winter and – bizarrely – a gravestone in the floor. One or two guest ales, frequently from local brewers, are available. Good quality home-produced food including locally-sourced meat is cooked to order (no food Mon and Sun eve). P

Ewloe

Boars Head ✔

Holywell Road, CH5 3BS (jct of B5125/B5127, just off A55 expressway)

12-2.30 (not Mon), 5.30-11; 12-11 Sat & Sun ☎ (01244) 531065

Black Sheep Best Bitter; Draught Bass H

Cosy, traditional pub built in 1704. Brasses and an inglenook fireplace dominate the small, half-timbered front bar, with a real fire blazing on cold evenings. More seats are provided in the mezzanine lounge and the beer garden/smoking area. Food is served in the dining room at the rear of the pub (not Sat lunch or Sun/Mon eve). Quiz night is Thursday. There are no buses in the evening. Q❀P

Glyndyfrdwy

Sun

LL21 9HG SJ150426

6-11 ☎ (01490) 430517

Facer's Flintshire Bitter; guest beers H

Situated a fairly short climb from Glyndyfrdwy station on the Llangollen Railway, this free house is set back from the A5 in a picturesque Dee Valley setting between LLangollen and Corwen. The accommodation comprises three spacious drinking areas, a games room and a terraced garden leading down from the rear car park. The beer range often includes a mild and guests from other local breweries. In summer, the pub sometimes opens on weekend lunchtimes. Q❀(X94)♣P

Graianrhyd

Rose & Crown

Llanarmon Road, CH7 4QW SJ218560

4 (12 Fri & Sat)-11; 12-10.30 Sun ☎ (01824) 780727

theroseandcrownpub.co.uk

Flowers IPA; guest beers H

Friendly, welcoming, traditional pub, winner of many CAMRA awards. Popular with both locals and walkers, it is split into two rooms served by a single bar – one with an open fire, the other with a wood burner. Two ever-changing guest beers are sourced from local breweries and real cider is occasionally on offer. The cheery landlord is justifiably proud of his excellent pub food and fine ales. Snacks are served at lunchtime, no evening meals on Monday.
QP

Graigfechan

Three Pigeons

LL15 2EU (on B5429 about 3 miles from Ruthin) SJ145545

12-3, 5.30-11; 12-11 Sat; 12-10.30 Sun ☎ (01824) 703178

threepigeonsinn.co.uk

Hancock's HB; guest beers H/G

Within this fine old pub is a lounge decorated with shipping artefacts – including a large model of Bismarck on the mantlepiece – and a public bar area. The restaurant offers much locally-sourced produce (closed Sun eve). All beers can be served by handpump or straight from the cask – see the website or the in-house Pigeon Post newsletters for the latest guest ales. The licensees support CAMRA and hold a beer festival for St David's Day as well as participating in July's Route 76 inter-pub festival. Q❀(76)♣P

Gresford

Griffin

Church Green, LL12 8RG

4-11 ☎ (01978) 852231

Adnams Bitter; guest beers H

Welcoming community hostelry adjacent to the 15th-century All Saints Church – its bells are one of the Seven Wonders of Wales. The pub is a picturesque white building just off the road in an attractive part of the village. Pictures of the Gresford mining disaster adorn the walls, offering some historical perspective. There is a lawned area to the side of the building with seating. Children are welcome in some areas of the pub until 8pm.
Q❀(1)♣P

Pant-yr-Ochain

Old Wrexham Road, LL12 8TY (off A5156, E from A483, follow signs to The Flash) SJ347534

12-11 (10.30 Sun) ☎ (01978) 853525

pantyrochain-gresford.co.uk

Brunning & Price Original; Flowers IPA; guest beers H

Converted manor house set in award-winning landscaped gardens, overlooking a small lake to the rear. Inside, a central bar serves two main areas, but a walk around will reveal numerous other rooms plus nooks and crannies for more intimate seating. You could sit by the splendid 16th-century inglenook fireplace in the winter or relax in the modern garden room in summer. Half a dozen real ales are offered, plus real cider in the summer. Good food is very popular.
Q❀P

WALES

Halkyn

Blue Bell Inn

Rhosesmor Road, CH8 8DL (on B5123) SO209703
⏲ 5-11 (midnight Fri); 12-midnight Sat; 12-11 Sun
☎ (01352) 780309 🌐 bluebell.uk.eu.org
Facer's Blue Bell Bitter, Dark Blue Porter; guest beers Ⓗ
Situated on Halkyn Mountain, with spectacular views across both the Dee Estuary and local countryside, this pub is a focal point for the local community. Activities include a walking club, Welsh lessons, Sunday afternoon sessions for jazz enthusiasts and games nights. Recently, the pub has won several local and regional CAMRA awards. Two ciders and a perry are usually available alongside the two house beers brewed locally by Facer's. Keep up to date with the pub's informative website and beer and cider blog.
⛫Q❀◐▲🚌(126)♣●P⊱

Hanmer

Hanmer Arms Hotel

SY13 3DE
⏲ 11-11 ☎ (01948) 830532 🌐 hanmerarms.co.uk
Adnams Bitter; Stonehouse Station Bitter; Taylor Landlord Ⓗ
Situated on the borders of Shropshire, Wrexham and Cheshire, this picturesque hotel is only five miles from Whitchurch and 10 miles from Wrexham. A traditional inn with a warm ambience, it offers fresh produce, friendly service and a warm welcome. A full a la carte menu and light snacks are available lunchtimes and evenings, plus a Sunday carvery, alongside a good choice of quality ales. Accommodation is in 13 rooms, all furnished to a high standard. ⛫Q❀🛏◐⊟♿🚌●P⊱

Holt

Peal O' Bells

12 Church Street, LL13 9JP (400m S of Holt-Farndon bridge)
⏲ closed Mon; 4 (12 Sat)-11 (11.30 Thu; 12.30am Fri); 12-10.30 Sun ☎ (01829) 270411 🌐 pealobells.co.uk
Beer range varies Ⓗ
Family-friendly village pub situated next to St Chad's Church on the road down to the River Dee. The bar serves two front rooms and a back room with a dartboard and pool table. The large fully-enclosed garden with a small play area has excellent views of the Dee Valley and Peckforton Hills. Real perry is available on handpump and guest ales come from the SIBA list.
⛫❀♿🚌(C56)●P⊱

Lavister

Nag's Head

Old Chester Road, LL12 0DN (on B5445, Old Chester-Wrexham road)
⏲ 5.30-midnight; 12-2am Fri & Sat; 12-midnight Sun
☎ (01244) 570486
Boddingtons Bitter; Everards Tiger; Flowers IPA; Purple Moose Snowdonia Ale; guest beers Ⓗ
Large roadside pub with a single bar, spacious central area with tables and several alcoves, plus a separate area for pool and darts. The pub has connections with the origins of CAMRA. The lively clientele is a mix of locals and visitors. Food is available Friday to Sunday. Guest beers usually include at least one from a local micro. Outside is a covered, heated smoking area, beer garden and children's play area. ⛫❀◑⊟♿🚌♣P⊱

Llan-y-Pwll

Gredington Arms ✔

Holt Road, LL13 9SD (on A534)
⏲ 12-2.30, 5-11; 12-11 Sat & Sun ☎ (01978) 661728
🌐 gredingtonarms.co.uk
Hydes Original Bitter, seasonal beers; guest beers Ⓗ
Modernised bar and bistro on the outskirts of Wrexham with a relaxing atmosphere and a reputation for good-quality locally-produced food. The owner is proud of his cask ale and also offers an extensive wine list. The Hyde-Out bar is in a separate room above the stables and is a good place to watch sport on TV – it can also be hired for functions. Look out for a beer festival over the August bank holiday weekend. No evening or Sunday buses. ❀◐⊟🚌(C56)P⊱

Llanarmon Dyffryn Ceiriog

Hand Hotel

LL20 7LD (at end of B4500 from Chirk) SJ157328
⏲ 11-11 (12.30am Fri & Sat); 12-11 Sun ☎ (01691) 600666
🌐 thehandhotel.co.uk
Beer range varies Ⓗ
Superbly situated hotel at the head of the Ceiriog Valley surrounded by the Berwyn Mountains. Once you've settled into the cosy and atmospheric bar with its black beams and inglenook fireplace, it's hard to leave. There is always a cask beer on offer from an independent such as Weetwood, and two at busier times. Food and accommodation are both of a very high standard. This is a popular base for walkers and cyclists, and well-behaved dogs are welcome. ⛫Q🐕❀🛏◐⊟♿🚌♣P⊱

Llandyrnog

Golden Lion ✔

LL16 4HG (on B5429, opp village stores) SJ108650
⏲ 4-11 (midnight Thu); 3-1am Fri; 2-1am Sat; 2-11 Sun
☎ (01824) 790373
Facer's DHB; Tetley Bitter Ⓗ
In the village centre, this locals' pub has a central bar serving two drinking areas – the lounge with pictures of old Llandyrnog, and the public bar with games and TV for sports fans. The local football team frequents the pub after a game on match days. This is a drinking pub – if you want to eat, the nearby sister inn, The White Horse (see below), is recommended. The pub participates in the July Bus Route 76 beer festival. ⛫❀◐⊟▲🚌(76)♣●⊱

White Horse (Ceffyl Gwyn) ✔

LL16 4HG
⏲ 12-3, 6-11.30; closed Mon & Tue ☎ (01824) 790582
Facer's Flintshire Bitter; guest beer Ⓗ
Situated next to the village church building, this pub has a good reputation for food. Two real ales are available, at least one from a local brewery, usually Facer's of Flint. One hundred metres away, Llandyrnog's other pub The Golden Lion (see above) shares the same licensee. The Denbigh to Ruthin 76 bus stops nearby and the pub participates in the Route 76 beer festival in July.
⛫❀◐▲🚌(76)●P⊱

Llangollen

Corn Mill

Dee Lane, LL20 8PN SJ214421
⏲ 12-11 (10.30 Sun) ☎ (01978) 869555
🌐 brunningandprice.co.uk/cornmill
Beer range varies ⊞
Step inside the Corn Mill and you enter a superbly converted flour mill complete with water wheel, abundant wooden beams, stone and pine flooring and stone walls. Explore the numerous open-plan rooms split over three levels or venture outside onto the extensive decking overlooking the racing River Dee and the restored steam railway station. And of course sample the four guest beers from local micro-breweries and the high-quality food from a varied and lengthy menu. Q❀◐♿🚌🍎

Sun Inn

49 Regent Street, LL20 8HN (§ mile E of town centre)
⏲ 12-1am (2am Fri & Sat) ☎ (01978) 860079
Salopian Shropshire Gold; Thwaites Original; guest beers ⊞
Often lively pub, particularly at weekends. The large single room interior has a slate floor, three real fireplaces and a games area. A small snug leads to a covered seating area outside for smokers and drinkers. Six real ales, including four changing guests plus continental beers, are available, plus over 50 single malt whiskies and 10 varieties of rum. Live music plays on Wednesday to Saturday nights featuring jazz, folk, blues or rock bands.
♨❀◐♿🚌♦♣⛳

Llangynhafal

Golden Lion Inn

LL16 4LN (at village crossroads) SJ131634
⏲ closed Mon; 6-11 Tue-Thu; 4-midnight Fri; 12-midnight Sat; 12-11 Sun ☎ (01824) 790451 🌐 thegoldenlioninn.com
Bathams Best Bitter; Coach House Gunpowder Mild; Holt Bitter; guest beer ⊞
Positioned at a pleasant rural crossroads, this pub has been successful in recent CAMRA Branch and Regional Pub of the Year activities – the licensees play an enthusiastic part in the now annual inter-pub beer festival along the local 76 bus route each July. Beer and cider is served in lined glasses and a selection of bottled beers is often stocked. With good food, music evenings, quiz nights, rural walks, whisky-tasting events and B&B accommodation, the pub offers something for everyone. ♨Q❀🛏◐🚂⛺🚌(76)♣🍎P⊡

Minera

Tyn-y-Capel

Church Road, LL11 3DA (off B5426) SJ268519
⏲ closed Mon & Tue; 11-11 (midnight Sat); 12-11 Sun
☎ (01978) 757502 🌐 tyn-y-capel.co.uk
Beer range varies ⊞
Tyn-y-Capel or Chapel House, situated opposite the village church, was first listed as an ale house in 1764. The attractive whitewashed exterior with sturdy stone-flanked windows belies a modern multi-level interior comprising lounge/dining areas and function rooms. Outside, stunning views of Esclusham Mountain can be enjoyed from the decked gardens, now extending down to the valley stream. Up to six guest ales are available, often from local micros. Quality food is served until 9pm (8pm Sun). ♨♉❀◐♿P⛳

Mold

Glasfryn

Raikes Lane, CH7 6LR (off A5119) SJ240649
⏲ 11.30-11; 12-10.30 Sun ☎ (01352) 750500
🌐 glasfryn-mold.co.uk
Facer's Flintshire Bitter; Flowers Original; Purple Moose Snowdonia Ale; Thwaites Original; guest beer ⊞
The Glasfryn is situated in its own grounds, near Theatr Clwyd, with views of the town and surrounding hills. Originally a residence for circuit judges attending the court opposite, it was converted to its present use by Brunning & Price in 1999. The spacious interior is popular with diners but real ale fans also come here for the wide range of guest beers on offer. Ales from local breweries are served regularly. ♨❀◐♿🚌(28,X44)P⛳

Gold Cape ✔

8 Wrexham Road, CH7 1ES (near Market Square)
⏲ 9am-midnight ☎ (01352) 705920
Greene King Ruddles Best Bitter, Abbot; guest beers ⊞
This former store has been converted in typical Wetherspoon style. The staff take the trouble to promote cask ales and the venue offers the best choice of beer (and usually three real ciders) in the market town centre. The pub is named after a Bronze Age relic found in a field within walking distance, and the walls display illustrations reflecting the town's historic past. Q♉◐🚌🍎⛳

Overton-on-Dee

White Horse

21 High Street, LL13 0DT
⏲ closed Mon; 12-3, 5.30-midnight (11 Tue); 12-midnight Sat; 12-11 Sun ☎ (01978) 710111
🌐 thewhitehorseoverton.co.uk
Beer range varies ⊞
This attractive red brick and mock Tudor building is situated in the heart of the village and is part of the small but impressive Joules Brewery estate. A CAMRA pub design award winner, inside it features frosted and latticed windows, pristine wooden partitioning and restored fireplaces. A former pantry, coal shed and wash house to the rear have been converted into dining spaces, each decorated with Joules breweriana. ♨Q❀◐🚌(146)

Pontblyddyn

Druid Inn ✔

Wrexham Road, CH7 4HG (on A541)
⏲ 11.30-2.30, 5-11; 11.30-11 Sat & Sun ☎ (01352) 770292
🌐 druidinn.co.uk
Beer range varies ⊞
The Druid Inn is a traditional stone-built village pub with a restaurant serving modern British food. Wooden beams, open fires and original features give the pub a cosy feel, matched by the warmth of the welcome. The large single room interior has several alcoves, and outside is an attractive beer garden. Draught beer is always sourced from local micros and the pub's own bottle beer, Druid's Ale, is produced locally. ♨Q♉❀◐🚌P⛳

Prestatyn

Halcyon Quest

17 Gronant Road, LL19 9DT

✪ 3 (12 Fri)-11; 12-midnight Sat; 12-11 Sun
☎ (01745) 852442 🌐 halcyonquest-hotel.com
Facer's Flintshire Bitter; guest beers ⊞
Situated within 50 metres of Offa's Dyke, this hotel bar has two drinking areas served by a single bar. The interior features sporting memorabilia including an upside-down boat hanging from the ceiling. Comedy prints and historic illustrations also add interest. A friendly atmosphere, welcoming staff and sunny beer garden complemented by the best selection of cask beers in town make this a bar not to be missed. ✿▲⇌P⅟

Rhyl

Queen's Arms

118-120 Vale Road, LL18 2PD (on A525)
✪ 11-midnight (1am Fri-Sun) ☎ (01745) 345311
Brains The Rev James; guest beer ⊞
Now fully refurbished, this popular two-roomed locals' pub has reverted from The Galley back to its original name. The front room with a small seating area and bar leads to the games area with TV, pool table and dartboard. Alongside is a tastefully decorated lounge with leather seating, coffee tables and TV. Local north Wales breweries often supply the guest beers. ⛴⊟♿▲⇌🚌(35,36,51)⅟

Sussex ✔

26 Sussex Street, LL18 1SG
✪ 9am-midnight (1am Sat); 9am-10.30 Sun
☎ (01745) 362910
Greene King Abbot; Marston's Pedigree; guest beers ⊞
Medium-sized Wetherspoon outlet situated in a pedestrianised part of the town centre with an open-plan design covering three areas. Originally a Welsh Wesleyan Chapel, then The Old Comrades Club, it was converted to The Sussex in 1992. Interesting displays of Rhyl's cultural and social past decorate the walls, together with modern art. Guest beers often come from local north Wales breweries. Q⛴◐◑♿⇌🚌●

Swan ✔

13 Russell Road, LL18 3BS
✪ 11-11 (11.30 Fri & Sat); 12-10.30 Sun ☎ (01745) 336694
Thwaites Nutty Black, Original, Lancaster Bomber ⊞
One of Rhyl's oldest pubs, this popular local is situated just off the town centre. The interior comprises a lounge and public bar with a pool table, dartboard and large TVs showing major sporting events. Historic photos of Rhyl are displayed on the lounge walls, and colourful ornaments decorate shelves and windowsills. It is thought that, in 1951, The Swan was one of the first public houses in Britain to hold a TV licence. ✿◐⊟⇌🚌♣⅟

Ruabon

Bridge End Inn 🏆

5 Bridge Street, LL14 6DA (on B5605)
✪ 5 (4 Fri)-11; 12-11 Sat & Sun ☎ (01978) 810881
🌐 mcgivernales.co.uk
Beer range varies ⊞
Former coaching inn near the station now owned by the McGivern Brewery, with brewing soon to be transferred to the pub premises. This welcoming three-roomed local has a whitewashed exterior and a cosy public bar reputed to be 300 years old, with a beamed ceiling and walls adorned with old Wrexham breweriana. Families are welcome in the lounge and there is a rear pool room. Drinkers come from afar for the five changing guest ales including a stout and often a McGivern ale, plus a real cider. ♔Q⛴✿⊟⇌🚌♣●P⅟⊓

Ruthin

Farmers Arms

Mwrog Street, LL15 1LB
✪ 5-11; 12-midnight Fri-Sun ☎ (01824) 707290
Conwy Castle Bitter ⊞
A short walk from the town centre, close to Ruthin Gaol, this free house has a spacious interior with separate drinking areas served by a central bar. There is also a well-appointed games room, restaurant and comfortable snug with a real fire and an old brewery mirror. Home to several sports teams, the pub is the main sponsor for Ruthin RUFC. Good value B&B en-suite accommodation is available. ♔✿🛏◑🚌♣P⅟

Shotton

Castle Inn

Brookside, Brook Road, CH5 1HL (off B5129) SJ302688
✪ 12-11 (midnight Fri & Sat) ☎ (01244) 813317
Jennings Cumberland Ale; guest beer ⊞
Friendly local pub tucked away at the end of a narrow lane. The interior is open plan with a central bar serving both the TV viewing area and lounge/dining area. The pub can be lively at weekend evenings, especially on Friday karaoke nights. Guest beers come from the Marston's list. Sensibly priced meals are served, including a popular carvery on Sunday. ✿◐◑⊟♿⇌🚌P⅟

The Waen

Farmers Arms

LL17 0DY (S of A55 jct 28, signed for Trefnant) SJ061730
✪ closed Mon; 5.30-11; 12-2, 5.30-11 Sun
☎ (01745) 582190 🌐 the-farmers-arms.co.uk
Facer's Farmer's Ale, Cwrw y Waen ⊞
Formerly known as The Waen Tavern, this is now the meeting place for several local societies including Rhyl Motoring Club. The pub dates back to the 1700s in parts and pictures and artefacts on the walls reflect its historic rural pedigree. Private parties can be catered for and a monthly jazz night is hosted – see the website for details. Both beers are house ales brewed by local brewer Dave Facer. Q✿◐◑⊟♿▲P⅟

Ysceifiog

Fox ★

Village Road, CH8 8NJ SJ153714
✪ 6-11; closed Wed; 12 (4 winter)-11 Sat & Sun
☎ (01352) 720241
Beer range varies ⊞
Often described as a gem, the Fox is the only pub in north east Wales that features on CAMRA's National Inventory of Historic Pub Interiors. The front bar with its sliding door and wooden seat alongside the counter is of particular interest. Two ever-changing guest beers are available but, sadly, not at the prices listed on the old Chester Northgate Brewery list displayed in the corridor! ♔Q✿◑⊟

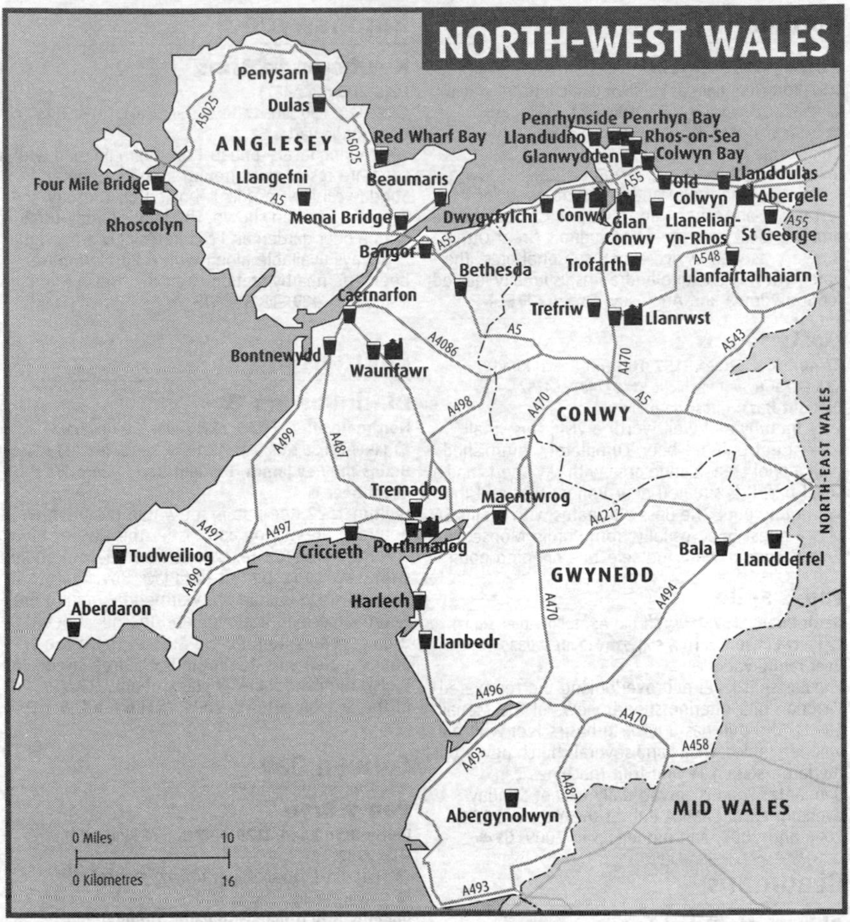

Authority areas covered: Anglesey UA, Conwy UA, Gwynedd UA

Aberdaron

Ship Hotel

LL53 8BE

11-11 ☎ (01758) 760204 theshiphotelaberdaron.co.uk

Beer range varies

The Ship is situated in the centre of the village at the tip of the Lleyn Peninsula. You can be sure of a friendly welcome in the two bars, one with a games area. Excellent food made with locally-sourced fresh ingredients is highly recommended. Two handpumps in summer and one in winter dispense local Welsh beer. The village has a bus service but check times first.

Abergynolwyn

Railway Inn

LL36 9YN (on B4405)

12-midnight (11 Sun) ☎ (01654) 782279

Beer range varies

Friendly community local in the centre of the village not far from the Talyllyn Railway. You can still see the remains of the old incline that brought goods traffic down from the railway to the village. Excellent food is served and, following a recent refit, the range of beers is set to increase. The pub has stunning views of the nearby hills and there is wonderful walking nearby.

Bala

Olde Bulls Head

78 High Street, LL23 7AD (on A494) SH927361

12-11 (1am Fri; 2am Sat) ☎ (01678) 520438

Greene King Abbot; Purple Moose Glaslyn

Reputedly haunted, this black-and-white coaching inn is the oldest in Bala, dating back to at least 1692. Inside, it has a spacious L-shaped lounge with a large stone fireplace and pictures of old Bala on the walls. There is also a smaller bar and games room. The heated smoking area has a dartboard. A wall panel tells of the whisky distillery that was situated nearby. The Wrexham to Barmouth bus stops outside. (X94)

INDEPENDENT BREWERIES

Conwy Conwy
Great Orme Glan Conwy
Nant Llanrwst
North Wales Abergele
Purple Moose Porthmadog
Snowdonia Waunfawr

Bangor

Abbeyfield Hotel

LL57 3UR (turn right at Penrhyn Castle into Tal-y-Bont)
⏲ 12-3, 6.30-midnight; 12-midnight Sat & Sun
☎ (01248) 352219 🌐 abbeyfieldhotel.co.uk
Great Orme Orme, Merlyn Ⓗ
Initially a 17th-century farmhouse, this is now a popular country hotel and inn, renowned for its restaurant and fine cuisine. The pub is a free house offering local beer from Llandudno's Great Orme Brewery as well as occasional seasonal ales. The hotel, with 11 en-suite bedrooms, is ideally located for Snowdonia and Anglesey. 🛏❀⇄◐🚌♣P

Mostyn Arms

27 Ambrose Street, LL57 1BH (off Beach Road)
⏲ 3 (1 Sat & Sun)-midnight ☎ (01248) 364752
Draught Bass; guest beer Ⓗ
Very friendly and well-worth a visit, this small back-street pub has been completely refurbished with a pool area, lounge area with Sky Sports and a small bar. It is situated near Bangor Pier and the swimming pool. The Bass alternates with Brains SA plus a guest beer, usually from Purple Moose. No food is served. Note the selective opening hours.

Tap & Spile

Garth Road, LL57 2SW (off old A5, follow pier signs)
⏲ 12-11 (11.30 Tue, Fri & Sat) ☎ (01248) 370835
Beer range varies Ⓗ
Popular split-level pub overlooking the renovated Victorian pier offering superb views of the Menai Straits. The pub has a back-to-basics feel with old wooden tables, chairs and several church pews, but the large-screen TV and fruit machines can dominate. Food is served daily except Sunday evening. Local CAMRA Pub of the Year in 2004, 2006 and 2007, and runner-up in 2009. ◐♣

Beaumaris

Olde Bulls Head Inn

Castle Street, LL58 8AA
⏲ 11-11; 12-10.30 Sun ☎ (01248) 810329
🌐 bullsheadinn.co.uk
Draught Bass; Hancock's HB; guest beer Ⓗ
Grade II-listed building that was the original posting house of the borough. In 1645 General Mytton, a parliamentarian, commandeered the inn while his forces laid siege to the nearby castle. The Royalists surrendered on 25 June 1646. Dr Johnson and Charles Dickens were famous guests and each bedroom is named after a Dickens character. The beamed bar has a large open fire. Parking is limited. ♨Q⇄◐🚌P

Bethesda

Douglas Arms Hotel ★

London Road, LL57 3AY
⏲ 6-11; 3.30-midnight Sat; 1-3, 7-11 Sun ☎ (01248) 600219
Marston's Burton Bitter, Pedigree; guest beer Ⓗ
Built in 1820, this was an important coaching inn on the historic Telford post route from London to Holyhead. The Grade II-listed building features in CAMRA's National Inventory of Historic Pub Interiors. The four-room interior has not changed since the 1930s and includes a snug, lounges and a large tap room with a full size snooker table. Bethesda, originally a town built on slate quarries, is convenient for buses to the Ogwen Valley and the surrounding mountains. Q⊟⛺🚌♣

Bontnewydd

Newborough Arms

LL55 2UG (on A487)
⏲ 12-11 (11.30 Sat); 12-10.30 Sun ☎ (01286) 673126
Beer range varies Ⓗ
Welcoming locals' pub just off the main road with a separate restaurant offering a good menu and Sunday carvery. A quiz is hosted on Tuesday and live sport is often shown. The pub is family-friendly with a beer garden and children's play area. A mild is always available along with a Purple Moose beer. The nearby station is on the Welsh Highland Railway. ❀◐⊟♿⛺⇌🚌P

Caernarfon

Black Boy Inn ✔

Northgate Street, LL55 1RW (near the marina)
⏲ 11-11 (11.30 Fri & Sat); 12-10.30 Sun ☎ (01286) 673604
Brains the Rev James; Draught Bass; Hancock's HB; guest beer Ⓗ
Built in 1522, the pub is set within the town walls between the marina and castle. This historic town, a world heritage site, is well-worth a visit, ending with a welcome pint at the Black Boy. The public bar and small lounge are warmed by roaring fires. Good value food is served and the guest beer usually comes from Purple Moose. There is a drinking area outside on the traffic-free street. The Welsh Highland Railway starts nearby. CAMRA Pub of the Season autumn 2009. ♨❀⇄◐⊟⛺⇌P

Colwyn Bay

Pen-y-Bryn

Pen-y-Bryn Road, LL29 6DD (top of King's Rd) SH842782
⏲ 11.30-11; 12-10.30 Sun ☎ (01492) 533360
🌐 penybryn-colwynbay.co.uk
Phoenix B&P Original; Thwaites Original; guest beers Ⓗ
Open-plan pub popular with all ages, with large bookcases, old furniture and real fires in the winter months. The walls are decorated with old photographs and memorabilia from the local area. Panoramic views of Colwyn Bay and the Great Orme can be admired from the terrace and garden. Excellent imaginative bar food is served – the menu is updated daily on the website. There are four guest beers mainly from local and independent breweries. A former local CAMRA Branch Pub of the Year and Food Pub of the Year 2010. ♨Q❀◐♿🚌♣P🍺

Picture House ✔

24-26 Princes Drive, LL29 8LA SH849791
⏲ 9-midnight (1am Fri & Sat) ☎ (01492) 535286
Courage Directors; Greene King Ruddles Best Bitter, Abbot; Marston's Pedigree; guest beers Ⓗ
Wetherspoon pub in the former Princess Cinema, now a Grade II-listed building. Theatre memorabilia adorn the walls of the three-level building, which also has an upper balcony. There are eight handpumps featuring at least one beer from a local brewery such as Conwy. Local beer festivals, in addition to Wetherspoon's national events, are held throughout the year. This popular pub is enjoyed by a wide range of locals and holidaymakers. Quiz night is Monday.
Q◐♿⇌🚌(12,14,15)🍎

Conwy

Old White House

Bangor Road, LL32 8DP (½ W of Conwy on old A55) SH770780
⏲ 4-11; 12-midnight Thu-Sun ☎ (01492) 573133
🌐 oldwhitehouseconwy.com
Thwaites Original Ⓗ
This 17th-century building was once a coach house stable for a now-demolished hotel. The long central bar, featuring a large log-burning stove and a high-beamed roof space, serves the open-plan front lounge and a small rear dining area. There is usually a quiz on Friday night and live entertainment on Saturday night. Food is available Thursday to Sunday evening, all day every day in summer. Guest beers are added occasionally.
♨❀◑▲⇌🚌(5,X5)♣P⊬

Criccieth

Castle Inn

LL52 0RW
⏲ 12-11 ☎ (01766) 523515
Beer range varies Ⓗ
Traditional three-roomed pub just off the A497 Porthmadog to Pwllheli road, catering for locals and tourists alike. Three handpumps dispense an ever-changing range of beers from regional and small breweries, as well as cider in summer. Well-served by public transport, the Cambrian Coast railway station is less than 100 metres away. There is a small outdoor area for enjoying a pint on a warm summer evening. ♨❀◑⊟▲⇌🚌♣●

Dulas

Pilot Boat Inn

LL70 9EX (on A5025)
⏲ 11 (12 Sun)-11 ☎ (01248) 410205
Robinson's Unicorn Ⓗ
Friendly rural family pub with a play area and converted double decker bus to keep children amused. Originally a cottage-type building, now much extended, the lounge features an unusual bar created from half a boat. The pub is much used by walkers – the coastal path passes through the car park. It is worth visiting Mynydd Bodafan for its spectacular views and Traeth Lligwy for the sands. Meals are served all day. Q❀◑▲🚌♣P⊬

Dwygyfylchi

Gladstone ✔

Ysgubor Wen Road, LL34 6PS (off jct 16 A55) SH730772
⏲ 12-11 (midnight Fri & Sat) ☎ (01492) 623231
🌐 thegladstone.co.uk
Beer range varies Ⓗ
Renowned for its magnificent sea views, this pub has been refurbished by the current owners but retains many original features including the alcoves and traditional decor with wood panelling and old photographs. A central bar serves both dining and drinking areas. Comfortable sofas surround a wood-burning stove and a galleried balcony with tables and booths overlooks the bar. Beers are served in the correct glasses. The restaurant offers imaginative food sourced locally. Function rooms and luxury accommodation are also on offer. ♨❀⇄◑♿▲🚌P⊬

Four Mile Bridge

Anchorage Hotel

LL65 2EZ (on B4545, just past bridge to Holy Island)
⏲ 11 (12 Sun)-11 ☎ (01407) 740168
Draught Bass; Taylor Landlord; Theakston XB; guest beer Ⓗ
This family-run hotel is situated on Holy Island close to Trearddur Bay. It has a large, comfortable lounge bar and a dining area serving a wide selection of meals. The hotel is near some fine, sandy beaches and coastal walks. Its proximity to the A55 makes it a useful stopping-off point for Holyhead Port. Q❀⇄◑▲🚌P⊬

Glanwydden

Queen's Head

LL31 9JP SH817804
⏲ 11.30-3, 6-10.30; 11.30-10.30 Sat; 11.30-10.30 Sun
☎ (01492) 546570 🌐 queensheadglanwydden.co.uk
Adnams Bitter; Great Orme Orme; guest beer Ⓗ
This former wheelwright's cottage in the centre of the village welcomes locals and holidaymakers alike. Run by the same owner for more than 20 years, the olde-worlde pub has a traditional front bar with a cosy atmosphere and a rear bar with a dining area. Excellent quality locally-sourced food includes fish and chips in Great Orme beer batter and steak and ale pie with Great Orme ale. There is a heated seating area outside. Guest beers come from breweries such as Weetwood and Coach House. ♨Q❀⇄◑⊟▲🚌P⊬

Harlech

Branwen Hotel

Ffordd Newydd, LL46 2UB (on A462 below Harlech Castle) SH583312
⏲ 11-11 ☎ (01766) 780477 🌐 branwenhotel.co.uk
Beer range varies Ⓗ
Warm and welcoming family-run hotel and bar overlooked by Harlech Castle. The hotel is named after a princess whose tales are found in a collection of Welsh myths known as Y Mabinogion. The popular and stylish bar offers a wide range of cask ales as well as foreign beers. A large selection of wines and malt whiskies is also stocked. Ask for your favourite malt – they're sure to have it. CAMRA Pub of the Season spring 2009.
❀⇄◑♿▲⇌🚌♣P⊬

Llanbedr

Ty Mawr Hotel

LL45 2HH
⏲ 11-11 ☎ (01341) 241440
Worthington's Bitter; guest beers Ⓗ
Small country hotel set in its own grounds. The modern lounge bar has a slate-flagged floor and cosy wood-burning stove. Unusual flying memorabilia reflect connections with the local airfield. French windows open out on a veranda and landscaped terrace with seating. A beer festival is held in a marquee on the lawn each year. Popular with locals and walkers, dogs and children are welcome. Meals are served all day.
♨❀⇄◑♿▲⇌P

Llandderfel

Bryntirion Inn 🏆

LL23 7RA (on B4401 3 miles E of Bala) SJ986364
⏲ 11 (12 Sun)-11 ☎ (01678) 530205 🌐 bryntirioninn.co.uk
Purple Moose Madog's; guest beer Ⓗ
Fine old coaching inn dating from 1695 in a rural setting offering a choice of rooms, including a spacious restaurant available for private functions. Outside is a pleasant courtyard and a large car park. Good-value accommodation is available. Dogs are welcome in the pub and guest rooms. The X94 Wrexham to Barmouth bus stops outside. Visitors to the area will be rewarded with a warm welcome and excellent fare. ♨Q☕❀🛏◐⊟🚌(X94)♣P⊱

Llanddulas

Valentine

Mill Street, LL22 8ES SH908781
⏲ 4-11; 3-midnight Fri; 12-midnight Sat & Sun
☎ (01492) 518189
Ringwood Fortyniner; guest beers Ⓗ
Local CAMRA's Most Improved Pub 2008, this traditional village inn dates from the 18th-century. It has a well-furnished, comfortable lounge with an open fire in winter, and a separate public bar with a TV. Two beer festivals are held annually – Ales in Wales on the spring bank holiday and Celtic Ales on the August bank holiday. Brewery memorabilia and many old framed photographs relating to the Valentine decorate the walls. Quiz night is Thursday. Dogs are welcome.
♨Q❀⊟⛺🚌(12,13)♣⊱

Llandudno

King's Head ✔

Old Road, LL30 2NB (next to Great Orme Tramway) SH778827
⏲ 12-midnight (11 Sun) ☎ (01492) 877993
Greene King IPA, Abbot; guest beers Ⓗ
The 300-year-old King's Head is the oldest inn in Llandudno. It has a traditional split level bar dominated by a large open fire and a grill restaurant at the rear serving good quality food. The pub makes an ideal stop after walking on the Great Orme or riding on Britain's only cable-hauled tramway. The suntrap patio with its award-winning flower display is a great place to watch the trams pass by. Wednesday is quiz night.
♨☕❀◐⛺⊖🚌P⊱

Llanelian-yn-Rhos

White Lion

LL29 8YA (off B583) SH863764
⏲ closed Mon; 11.30-3, 6-midnight; 12-4, 6-11 Sun
☎ (01492) 515807 🌐 whitelioninn.co.uk
Marston's Burton Bitter, Pedigree; guest beer Ⓗ
In the Guide for 19 years, this 16th-century inn situated in the hills above Old Colwyn, next to St Elian's Church, greets you with a warm welcome. Gracing the entrance are two stone white lions, leading into the bar area with its slate-flagged flooring and large comfortable chairs around the log fires. Decorative stained glass is mounted above the bar in the tiny snug. A spacious restaurant serves delicious home-cooked food, with a wide menu choice. ♨Q☕❀◐⊟⛺♣P⊱

Llanfairtalhaiarn

Swan Inn

Swan Square, LL22 8RY SH928702
⏲ 12-3 (not Wed), 6-11; 12-3, 6-midnight Fri & Sat; 12-11.30 Sun ☎ (01745) 720233
Black Sheep Best Bitter; Marston's Burton Bitter; guest beers Ⓗ
Located in a peaceful village, this is a good example of an unspoilt traditional village inn, thought to date from the 16th century, exuding warmth and hospitality. It has a front dining room/bar, a separate lounge bar with an open fire, a family room with a pool table, dartboard and juke-box, and a beer garden where children are welcome until 9.30pm. There is seating outside at the front in the square. Occasional entertainment is hosted on Saturday evening. ♨☕❀◐♿🚌♣⊱

Llangefni

Railway Inn

48-50 High Street, LL77 7NA
⏲ 4 (3 Thu & Fri)-11; 12-midnight Sat; 12-11 Sun
☎ (01248) 722166
Lees Bitter Ⓗ
Classic friendly small-town pub with a warm welcome, next to the old railway station, displaying photographs of the railway and old Llangefni. The main bar is hewn out of the stone wall. Near the centre of this county town, the pub is also close to Oriel Mon (museum) where you can find out about the history of Anglesey, see Tunnicliffe's bird books and pictures and view Sir Kyffin Williams' paintings. 🚌♣⊱

Llanrwst

Pen-y-Bryn

Ancaster Square, LL26 0LH SH798617
⏲ 4.30-11; 12-midnight Sun ☎ (01492) 640678
Beer range varies Ⓗ
Traditional stone-built pub much favoured by locals with a hospitable landlord and friendly regulars offering a warm welcome. A long bar serves a large, comfortable open-plan lounge area with an original inglenook fireplace. This is a great community pub with a games room at the rear for pool and darts. Traditional pub games are featured and there is a TV for sporting events. Tuesday is poker night. Beers are mainly from the local Nant Brewery, with Mwnci Nell always a favourite.
❀⊟⛺⇌🚌♣⊱

Maentwrog

Grapes Hotel

LL41 4HN (on A496 near A487 jct)
⏲ 12-late ☎ (01766) 590365 🌐 grapes-hotel.co.uk
Evans Evans Cwrw, Best, Warrior, seasonal beers Ⓗ
A former coaching inn, this hotel dates back to the 17th century and overlooks the Vale of Ffestiniog. The interior comprises a lounge, public bar, veranda and large dining room. All the beers are from the local Evan Evans Brewery in Llandeilo, including the full seasonal range. Good value food is popular, especially the ribs. The railway station nearby is on the Ffestiniog line.
♨Q❀🛏◐⊟♿⛺⇌(yes)🚌(yes)♣P⊱

Menai Bridge

Tafarn y Bont (Bridge Inn)

Telford Road, LL59 5DT

⏲ 11-midnight; 12-10.30 Sun ☎ (01248) 716888

Banks's Bitter; Marston's Pedigree; guest beers Ⓗ

Mid-19th-century former shop and tea rooms, close to the famous bridge, now a brasserie-style pub with an excellent restaurant. A beamed interior, log fires and numerous hideaway rooms give the pub an old-fashioned feel. Snowdonia is a short drive away and the Anglesey Coastal Path is very close. CAMRA Pub of the Season winter 2009. ♔☕❀◐⚠🚌⊱

Victoria Hotel

Telford Bridge, LL59 5DR (between bridge and town centre)

⏲ 11-11; 12-10.30 Sun ☎ (01248) 712309

Draught Bass; guest beers Ⓗ

Situated 300 metres from the Menai Suspension Bridge, this 19-room hotel overlooks the Straits and affords delightful views from the garden and patio. It is licensed for weddings and has a spacious function room with widescreen HD TV for sports. Live music is a regular added attraction. There is easy access to Snowdonia and the hotel is near the Anglesey Coastal Path. ☕❀🛏◐⊡♿🚌P⊱

Old Colwyn

Red Lion

385 Abergele Road, LL29 9PL (on main Colwyn Bay to Abergele road) SH868783

⏲ 5-11; 4-midnight Fri; 12-midnight Sat; 12-11 Sun

☎ (01492) 515042

Brains Dark; Marston's Burton Bitter; guest beers Ⓗ

This ever-popular local serves up to five guest beers from independent and local brewers. The free house has won many CAMRA awards and is a former Branch Pub of the Year and Mild Pub of the Year. The cosy L-shaped room is warmed by a real coal fire and features antique brewery mirrors and other memorabilia. The traditional public bar has a pool table, darts and TV. To the rear is a covered and heated smoking area. Westons cider is stocked. ♔Q❀⊡🚌♣●⊱

Sun Inn

383 Abergele Road, LL29 9PL (on main Colwyn Bay to Abergele road) SH868783

⏲ 12-11 (midnight Fri & Sat); 12-11.30 Sun

☎ (01492) 517007

Courage Directors; Marston's Burton Bitter; Theakston Traditional Mild; guest beers Ⓗ

The only original pub building in Old Colwyn, dating from 1844. A typical beer-drinker's local, the central bar serves a cosy lounge area with a welcoming real coal fire. CAMRA literature is displayed prominently on top of the piano. The bar also serves a side room with TV and juke-box. There is a large games/meeting room at the back with a dartboard and pool table. Outside is a heated and covered smoking area. Westons Old Rosie cider is available. ♔Q❀⊡🚌♣●⊱

Penrhyn Bay

Penrhyn Old Hall

LL30 3EE SH816815

⏲ 12-3, 5.30-11; 12-3, 7-10.30 Sun ☎ (01492) 549888

Draught Bass; guest beer Ⓗ

Medieval hall dating from the 12th century which has been in the Marsh family since 1963. The main Tudor lounge dates back to 1420 and features a wood-panelled bar and a large fireplace concealing a priest hole. Good value meals are served daily in the restaurant at the rear – Sunday lunches are a speciality. The hall is available for hire for functions and has a skittle alley. The Penrhyn Bay Players stage occasional pub theatre here. ❀◐⚠🚌♣P⊱

Penrhynside

Penrhyn Arms 🏆

Pendre Road, LL30 3BY (off B5115) SH814816

⏲ 5.30 (4.30 Thu; 4 Fri)-midnight; 12-1am Sat; 12-11 Sun

☎ (07780) 678927 🌐 penrhynarms.com

Banks's Bitter; Marston's Pedigree; guest beers Ⓗ

Multi-award-winning pub including CAMRA Regional and Welsh Cider Pub of the Year, National Cider Pub of the Year runner-up and Branch Pub of the Year 2010. This welcoming local is a real gem, with real ciders and perries plus up to four guest beers including local ales, Belgian beers and a winter ale on gravity at Christmas. The spacious L-shaped bar has pool, darts and a widescreen TV. Framed pictures of notable drinkers and brewery memorabilia adorn the walls. Thursday is cheese night. ♔❀🛏⚠🚌♣●⊱

Penysarn

Bedol

LL69 9YR

⏲ 12 (2 winter Mon-Fri)-11; 12-11 Sat; 12-11 (2-10.30 winter) Sun ☎ (01407) 832590

Robinson's Hartleys XB, seasonal beers Ⓗ

The Bedol (Horseshoe) was built in 1985 to serve a small village, but the regulars now come from a much wider area. This Robinson's tied house hosts regular live entertainment. Food is available all day except mid-week lunchtime in winter. Anglesey's beautiful beaches and the coastal path are nearby. Q❀◐⚠🚌♣P⊱

Porthmadog

Spooner's Bar

Harbour Station, LL49 9NF

⏲ 10-11; 12-10.30 Sun ☎ (01766) 516032 🌐 festrail.co.uk

Beer range varies Ⓗ

An all year round mini-beer festival – Spooner's has built its reputation on an ever-changing range from small breweries, including the local Purple Moose. Situated in the terminus of the world famous Ffestiniog Railway, steam trains are outside the door most of the year. Food is served every lunchtime, but out of season only Thursday to Saturday in the evening. Local CAMRA Pub of the Year 2005 and 2007. Q☕❀◐♿⇌🚌P

Station Inn

LL49 9HT (on mainline station platform)

⏲ 11-11 (midnight Thu-Sat); 12-11 Sun ☎ (01766) 512629

Brains The Rev James; Purple Moose Snowdonia; guest beer Ⓗ

Situated on the Cambrian Coast railway platform, this pub is popular with locals and visitors alike. It has a large lounge and smaller public bar and can get very busy at the weekend and on nights when live football is shown on TV. A range of pies and sandwiches is available all day. ❀⊡♿⚠⇌🚌♣P

WALES

Red Wharf Bay

Ship Inn ✔

LL75 8RJ (off A5025 between Pentraeth and Benllech)
11-11 (10.30 Sun) ☎ (01248) 852568
shipinnredwharfbay.co.uk
Adnams Bitter; Brains SA; guest beers 🄷
Red Wharf Bay was once a busy port exporting coal and fertilisers in the 18th and 19th centuries. Previously known as the Quay, the Ship enjoys an excellent reputation for its bar and restaurant, with meals served lunchtimes and evenings. It gets busy with locals and visitors in the summer. The garden has panoramic views across the bay to south-east Anglesey. The resort town of Benllech is two miles away and the coastal path passes the front door. Beer can be expensive. CAMRA Pub of the Season summer 2009. Q P

Rhos-on-Sea

Colwyn Bay Cricket Club ✔

Penrhyn Avenue, LL28 4LR
11.30-2, 4.30-11 (midnight Fri); 11.30-midnight Sat; 12-3, 7-11 (12-11 summer) Sun ☎ (01492) 544103
colwynbaycricketclub.co.uk
Tetley Dark Mild, Bitter, guests beers 🄷
A frequent local CAMRA Club of the Year winner, including 2010, this comfortably furnished club features wide-screen TVs showing sporting events, usually cricket. The games room has two full size snooker tables. Several function rooms are for hire. Good value snacks are available. Glamorgan County Cricket Club play at least of one of their home matches here. An annual beer festival is held over the spring bank holiday weekend. P

Toad

West Promenade, LL28 4BU SH847795
11-11.30 (10.30 Sun) ☎ (01492) 532726
Jennings Cumberland Ale; guest beers 🄷
Attractively furnished traditional inn on the Colwyn Bay promenade with stunning sea views from the pub and front beer garden. Winner of Local CAMRA Pub Food of the Year in 2009, it serves modern British cuisine freshly prepared with quality local produce, and excellent value Sunday lunches. The downstairs pool room is enjoyed by people of all ages. Professional, friendly and approachable staff offer a warm welcome to locals and visitors. ♣P

Rhoscolyn

White Eagle

LL65 2NJ (off B4545 signed Traeth Beach) SH271755
12-3, 6-11; 12-11 Sat; 12-10.30 Sun ☎ (01407) 860267
white-eagle.co.uk
Marston's Burton Bitter, Pedigree; Weetwood Eastgate Ale; guest beers 🄷
Saved from closure by new owners, this pub has been renovated and rebuilt with an airy, brasserie-style atmosphere. It has a fine patio enjoying superb views over Caernarfon Bay and the Lleyn Peninsula to Bardsey Island. The nearby beach offers safe swimming with a warden on duty in the summer months. The pub is also close to the coastal footpath. Excellent food is available lunchtimes and evenings, all day during the school holidays. Q P

St George

Kinmel Arms

LL22 9BP SH974758
closed Sun & Mon; 12-3, 6-11 (11.30 Fri & Sat)
☎ (01745) 832207 thekinmelarms.co.uk
Facer's Flintshire Bitter; guest beers 🄷
Local CAMRA Branch Pub of the Year 2009, this former 17th-century coaching inn is set on the hillside overlooking the sea. An L-shaped bar serves a large combined dining and drinking area with a real log fire in one corner and a spacious conservatory at the rear. Two guest beers come from independent breweries, plus a cider and a selection of Belgian beers. The pub has a reputation for good food. Luxury accommodation is available in four comfortable suites.
Q P

Trefriw

Old Ship (Yr Hen Long)

LL27 0JH (on B5106) SH781632
12-3, 6-11; 12-11 Sat; 12-10.30 Sun ☎ (01492) 640013
the-old-ship.co.uk
Banks's Bitter; guest beers 🄷
Dating from the 16th century, this former customs house is now a busy village local. A small central bar serves a cosy L-shaped lounge with an open fire, brass ornaments and pictures of historic and nautical interest. The dining room features an inglenook and serves excellent home-cooked food. This genuine free house offers a good range of guest beers from independent and local breweries such as Conwy, Great Orme and Nant. There is a popular Sunday quiz night. P

Tremadog

Golden Fleece

Market Square, LL49 9RB (on A487)
11.30-3, 6-11; 12.30-3, 6-10.30 Sun ☎ (01766) 512421
goldenfleeceinn.com
Draught Bass; Purple Moose Glaslyn Ale; guest beer 🄷
Situated in the old market square, this former coaching inn is now a friendly local. The pub has a lounge bar, snug and a covered area outside with decking and bench seats. Bar meals are good value and there is a bistro upstairs (booking advisable). Guest beers come from small breweries. Live acoustic music plays on Tuesday night.
Q

Trofarth

Holland Arms

Llanrwst Road, LL22 8BG SH840708
12-3, 7 (6 Fri & Sat)-11; closed Wed & Thu; 12-10.30 Sun
☎ (01492) 650777 thehollandarms.co.uk
Beer range varies 🄷
Family-run pub with a warm welcome for locals and visitors alike. The 18th-century coaching house is set in a country landscape within sight of Snowdonia. Recently tastefully refurbished in keeping with its origins, it has a pleasantly furnished bar, lounge and restaurant areas. Excellent good value meals are available lunchtimes and evenings. A big supporter of LocAle, it features beers from Conwy, Great Orme and Purple Moose. Well-worth seeking out – although this is the only pub in the area not accessible by public transport. Q ♣P

Tudweiliog

Lion Hotel

LL53 8ND (on B4417)

11-11 (12-2, 6-11 winter); 11.30-11 Sat; 11-10.30 (12-3 winter) Sun ☎ (01758) 770244

Beer range varies Ⓗ

Village pub on the glorious, quiet north coast of the Lleyn Peninsula. The cliffs and beaches are a mile away by footpath, a little further by road. The origins of this free house go back over 300 years. Up to three beers are served depending on the season, with Purple Moose a firm favourite. The pub is accessible by No 8 bus from Pwllheli during the day only. Closed Monday lunchtimes in winter. **Q**

Waunfawr

Snowdonia Park

Beddgelert Road, LL55 4AQ

11-11 (10.30 Sun) ☎ (01286) 650409

snowdonia-park.co.uk

Marston's Mansfield Dark Mild, Burton Bitter, Pedigree; guest beers Ⓗ

Home of the Snowdonia Brewery, this is a popular pub for walkers, climbers and families, with children's play areas inside and outside. Meals are served all day. The pub adjoins Waunfawr station on the Welsh Highland Railway – stop off here before continuing on one of the most scenic sections of narrow gauge railway in Britain (you can watch the trains while enjoying your drink in the beer garden). There is a large campsite by the pub on the riverside. **Q** **P**

Queen's Head, Glanwydden

WALES

WEST WALES

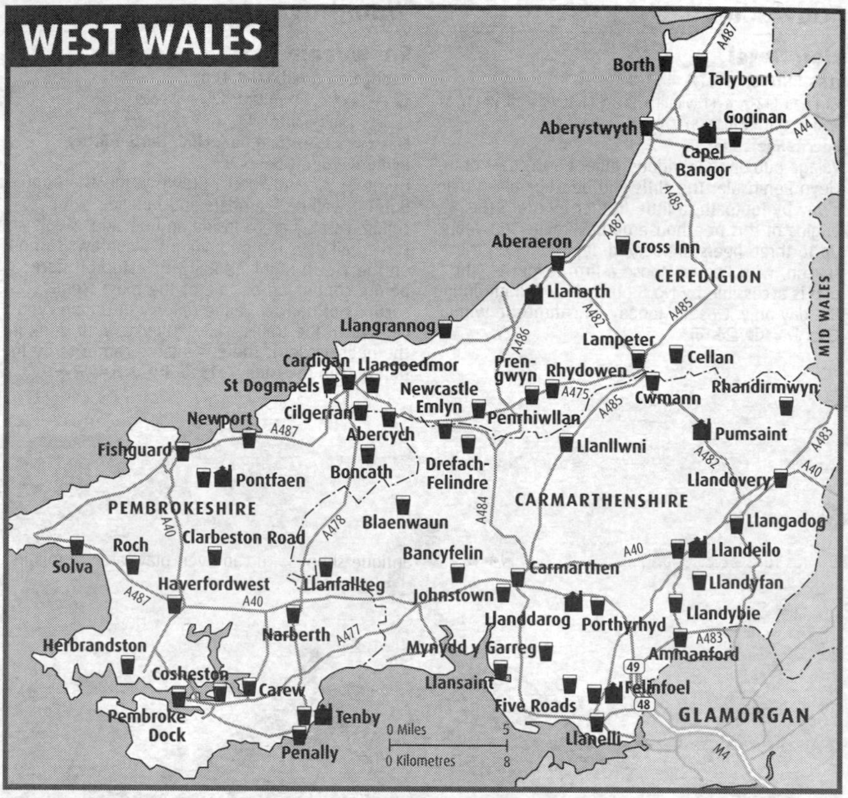

Authority areas covered: Carmarthenshire UA, Ceredigion UA, Pembrokeshire UA

Aberaeron

Harbourmaster

2 Quay Parade, SA46 0BT (off A487, overlooking harbour)

☼ 10-midnight ☎ (01545) 570755 ⊕ harbour-master.com

Evan Evans BB; Purple Moose Glaslyn; guest beer ⊞

Light, comfortable and expertly renovated bar and restaurant overlooking Aberaeron harbour. Welsh culture is celebrated, staff are bilingual, and paintings by Welsh artists adorn the walls. Award-winning food is locally sourced. A guest beer, available Easter to October, comes from a Welsh brewery and there are plans for a house beer from Purple Moose. While the bar is usually free of electronic entertainment, an exception is made for rugby internationals on TV. In the summer, pints can be enjoyed outside overlooking the water. Q⇌◑♿⛺🚌(X40,X50,550)P

Monachty ✔

Market Street, SA46 0AS (off A487)

☼ 12-11 (11.30 Fri & Sat); 12-10.30 Sun ☎ (01545) 570389

⊕ monachtyaberaeron.com

Brains Bitter, The Rev James ⊞

Situated next to the inner harbour, this Brains tied house has a comfortable front bar with wood-burning stove. Further drinking areas lead through to the restaurant, while the spacious beer garden at the rear offers stunning views of the harbour – an excellent place to relax on a summer's day. ♨❀⇌◑♿⛺🚌(X40,X50,550)⚑

Abercych

Nags Head

SA37 0HJ (on B4332 between Cenarth and Eglwyswrw)

☼ 11-3 (not Mon), 6-11; 12-10.30 Sun ☎ (01239) 841200

Beer range varies ⊞

This well-restored old smithy boasts a beamed bar and riverside garden. The bar area is furnished with collections of old medical instruments, railway memorabilia, and timepieces showing the time in various parts of the world. Space is also found for an extensive display of beer bottles. House beer Old Emrys is brewed for the pub. ♨⛄❀◑♿P⚑

Aberystwyth

Nags Head

23 Bridge Street, SY23 1PZ

☼ 12 (11 Sat)-midnight (1am Thu-Sat); 12-11.30 Sun

☎ (01970) 624725

Banks's Mild, Bitter ⊞

INDEPENDENT BREWERIES

Coles Llanddarog
Evan Evans Llandeilo
Felinfoel Felinfoel
Gwaun Valley Pontfaen
Gwynant Capel Bangor
Jacobi Pumsaint
Penlon Cottage Llanarth
Preseli Tenby

This good old-fashioned drinkers' pub serves a loyal clientele of townsfolk along with students, especially on Wednesday evening when there is free pool after 7pm. The main bar, with part-quarry-tiled floor, has pool and TV, and there is a quieter lounge up a step to the right. At the rear, a corridor lined with photographs of bygone darts teams leads to a large games room and outdoor drinking area where smokers are accommodated. Handled glasses are available. ❀⊟⅄⇌⊟♣⌐

Ship & Castle 🏆

1 High Street, SY23 1JG

☉ 2-midnight (1am Fri & Sat) ☎ (07773) 778785

⊕ shipandcastle.co.uk

Wye Valley HPA; guest beers Ⓗ

The best just got better. A total refit has given this flagship real-ale pub improved facilities while retaining its original character. A Mecca for townsfolk, students and visitors of all ages, five draught beers are usually available, mainly from micros, alongside Westons Old Rosie and Perry. Bottled offerings include Gwynt y Ddraig cider and a small European range including Duvel. Beer festivals are held in spring and autumn, and CAMRA runs occasional quiz nights. ⅄⇌⊟♣●

Ammanford

Ammanford Hotel

Wernolau House, 31 Pontamman Road, SA18 2HX

☉ 5.30 (1 Sat)-11; 12-10.30 Sun ☎ (01269) 592598

Beer range varies Ⓗ

Originally a colliery manager's house, this pleasant hotel stands on the outskirts of the town, set in five acres of landscaped grounds and woodland. It is renowned not only for the choice and quality of its beer but also for the warm welcome. Log fires burn in winter and there is a large function room catering for weddings and private events.
♔Q❀⇔◐⅄⊟P

Bancyfelin

Fox & Hounds

SA33 5ND (just off A40)

☉ 11-midnight summer; 11-3, 5.30-midnight winter

☎ (01267) 211341 ⊕ foxandhounds-bancyfelin.co.uk

Beer range varies Ⓗ

Situated in the heart of the village, this is a pub with a real Welsh welcome. Lunches and evening meals are served in the lounge/dining area and there is a separate locals' bar with a pool table, juke-box and games machines for those who prefer a more traditional bar atmosphere.
Q♉❀◐⊟♿⊟♣P

Blaenwaun

Lamb Inn

SA34 0JD SN236271

☉ 4.30-midnight ☎ (01994) 448839

Beer range varies Ⓗ

Friendly and comfortable pub with a welcoming landlord and a good selection of well-kept real ales. Three beers and a cider are available during the winter months, four or more beers and two ciders during the summer. Guest beers change frequently. The pub has an old-world look with drop beams and an open fire and wonderful panoramic views. Entertainment includes TV, pool, darts and occasional quiz nights. ♔❀◐♿⅄●⌐

Boncath

Boncath Inn

SA37 0JN (on B4332 between Cenarth and Eglwyswrw)

☉ 11-11; 12-8.30 Sun ☎ (01239) 841241

Worthington's Bitter; guest beers Ⓗ

Pembrokeshire CAMRA Pub of the Year 2006 and 2007, this pub dates back to the 18th century and is the centre of village life. The interior is divided into several seating areas creating an intimate atmosphere, and the walls display items of local historic interest. The home-cooked meals are recommended. A beer festival is held each August bank holiday weekend. ♔❀◐♿⅄⊟♣P⌐

Borth

Friendship Inn

High Street, SY24 5JA

☉ 12.30-3, 7-late ☎ (01970) 871213

⊕ friendshipinn.fsnet.co.uk

Beer range varies Ⓗ

Renowned for real ale, real people, and real music and singing, the Friendship has a traditional cosy front bar, family room, beer garden and upstairs antique shop – you can even play table tennis in the back room. The guest beer frequently comes from a Welsh micro such as Evan Evans. Snacks and ploughman's lunches are available in summer. Dogs and children are welcome. No background music, but there is a TV in the bar. It may open all day in summer. ♔Q♉❀⅄⇌⊟(510,512)♣P⌐

Cardigan

Grosvenor

Bridge Street, SA43 1HY

☉ 11-11; 12-10.30 Sun ☎ (01239) 613792

Greene King Abbot; Worthington's Bitter; guest beer Ⓗ

Situated at the southern entrance to Cardigan next to Cardigan Castle and the River Teifi, this large pub provides the best choice of ales in town, including a selection of bottled beers. Recently refurbished, the large open-plan bar/lounge provides various areas to relax, eat and drink. There is an extra room upstairs for dining or for functions. Good value food is served. ❀◐⊟♣⌐

Carew

Carew Inn

SA70 8SL (off A477 before Pembroke Dock)

☉ 11-11 (11.30 Sun) ☎ (01646) 651267 ⊕ carewinn.co.uk

Brains The Rev James; Evan Evans Cwrw Ⓗ

Situated close to Carew's historic Celtic Cross, castle and tidal mill, the pub makes an ideal stop-off with its village location and many local attractions. A pine-boarded bar features photographs of the local area from the past. Outside there is a marquee and a large grassed garden with a children's play area.
♔❀◐⅄P⌐

Carmarthen

Queen's Hotel

Queen Street, SA31 1JR

☉ 11-11 ☎ (01267) 231800

Beer range varies Ⓗ

Town-centre pub near Carmarthenshire county hall with a bar, lounge and small function room. The public bar is used by locals and has TV for sporting

WALES

events. Local beers are usually on sale. The patio nestles beneath the castle walls and is a suntrap during the summer months. Upstairs rooms are available for conferences and meetings and the local CAMRA branch meets here. ❀⇌🚌⊱

Yr Hen Dderwen ✓
47-48 King Street, SA31 1BH
✪ 9-midnight (11 Sun) ☎ (01267) 242050
Greene King Ruddles Best Bitter, Abbot 🄷
This Wetherspoon pub opened in 2000. It is named after the Carmarthen legend of Merlin and the Old Oak – the story is told in pictures and plaques on the walls. The interior is divided into two distinct spaces – the bar and drinking area at the front and a dining area to the rear. A good selection of real ales is offered. Food is served all day including good value meal deals. ◑⇌🚌●⊱

Cellan

Fishers Arms
SA48 8HU (on B4343)
✪ 12 (4.30 winter)-11 ☎ (01570) 422895
Tetley Bitter; guest beer 🄷
Situated close to the River Teifi, one of Wales' premier trout and salmon rivers, the pub dates from 1580 and was first licensed in 1891. The main bar has a logburner and flagstone floor. The guest beer changes weekly and is usually from a Welsh micro-brewery, though the house beer is from Tetley. The pub is served by buses from Lampeter and Aberystwyth. ⛺Q❀◑▲🚌(585)♣P

Cilgerran

Pendre Inn
High Street, SA43 2SL
✪ 12-11 (10.30 Sun) ☎ (01239) 614223
Shepherd Neame Spitfire; guest beers 🄷
Welcoming, traditional, unspoilt 14th-century pub standing at the heart of a large village whose attractions include a castle, wildlife centre and the Teifi Gorge. The public bar leads to a lounge area and separate restaurant. Up to two guest beers change regularly and real cider often makes an appearance. Though bar snacks are generally available, evening meals are served Wednesday to Saturday only. Sunday lunch is popular (booking advisable). ⛺❀◑🚌♣●P

Clarbeston Road

Cross Inn ✓
SA63 4UL SN019211
✪ 12-midnight (1am Fri & Sat) ☎ (01437) 731506
Courage Directors; Worthington's Bitter; guest beer 🄷
Multi-roomed village inn with stone and wood floors and original oak beams in abundance, comprising a spacious bar area, two small snugs and a restaurant. There is a large TV for sports, pool table and juke-box in the main bar. Good home-cooked food is on offer at reasonable cost, served in the restaurant. A beer festival is held in the summer. Outside there are spacious drinking areas. A pub well-worth seeking out. ⛺❀◑♿🚌♣P⊱

Cosheston

Brewery Inn
SA72 4UD
✪ closed Mon; 12-3, 6-11; 12-4, 7-11 Sun ☎ (01646) 686678
Courage Best Bitter; guest beers 🄷
Set between Cosheston Pill and the Carew Estuary just north-east of Pembroke, this light and airy stone-built inn boasts a traditional slate floor and bar, roof beams and comfortable seating with old tables. Paintings and drawings by local artists adorn the walls. The outdoor smoking area is heated in winter. Q☕❀◑♿P⊱

Cross Inn

Rhos Yr Hafod Inn
SY23 5NB (at B4337/B4577 crossroads)
✪ 5-11 (open Mon Jul, Aug & bank hols only); 12-3, 6-11 Sun
☎ (01974) 272644 🌐 rhos-yr-hafod-inn.co.uk
Young's Bitter; guest beer 🄷
This quiet, friendly pub in a small village offers a regularly changing guest beer alongside Young's Bitter. Linked drinking areas cluster around a central bar, with some attractive paintings and photographs of local scenes and wildlife in the back room. There's an outside drinking area at the front and a sizeable garden at the rear. Excellent food is home-made and good value, with most ingredients sourced locally (meals served Sun lunch and Mon-Sat eves). ⛺☕❀◑▲♣P⊱

Cwmann

Cwmann Tavern
SA48 8DR (jct of A482/A485)
✪ closed Mon; 4 (12 Sun)-midnight ☎ (01570) 423861
Beer range varies 🄷
Built in 1720 on a drovers' route, a short walk from Lampeter, the pub is popular with locals and students. Three drinking areas around the central bar feature wooden beams, posts and floors. Beers are from small breweries and Westons Old Rosie cider is always stocked, backed up with a good range of bottled beers. ⛺❀◑🚌(X40)♣●P⊱

Tafarn Jem
SA48 8HF (on A482 4 miles SE of Cwmann) SN615438
✪ 12-11 (10.30 Sun); closed Wed end Oct-Easter
☎ (01558) 650633
Breconshire Brecon County, Ramblers Ruin 🄷
Welcoming 19th-century pub, originally an old drovers' ale house, with stunning views over the valley from outside. Although the interior is open-plan there are two distinct areas – the bar and the lounge/restaurant. Food is served daily except Tuesday and Wednesday until 9.30pm. The menu changes every six weeks. There is excellent access for wheelchair users off the car park. ❀◑♿P

Drefach-Felindre

Tafarn John y Gwas
SA44 5XG
✪ 12-11 ☎ (01559) 370469 🌐 johnygwas.co.uk
Beer range varies 🄷
This traditional village inn was built in the early 1800s. A locals' pub, there is always a friendly welcome for tourists and their pets. Two real ales are on offer in winter, three in summer. Reasonably priced home-cooked food is available until 9pm every day, with a roast on Sunday. The beer garden has a covered area for smokers. Pool and darts are played, and a quiz night is held on the last Sunday of the month. Loca CAMRA Pub of the Year 2008. ⛺❀◑⊟▲🚌(460)♣P⊱

Felinfoel

Harry Watkins

2 Millfield Road, SA14 8HY (on A476)
⏲ closed Mon; 12-11 ☎ (01554) 776644
Beer range varies 🄷
Renamed after a local rugby hero of yesteryear who features on the pub walls, the pub was originally called the Bear. The open-plan, split-level, family-friendly pub has defined dining areas and a function room. There are covered and open drinking areas outside. Although there is no car park, there is usually ample room on the road. National cycle and walking paths to the Swiss Valley and beyond are nearby. 🐴❀◐◑🚌🚲

Fishguard

Pendre Inn

High Street, SA65 9AT (on A487 300m SW of market square)
⏲ 11 (4 Mon)-midnight; 12-11.30 Sun ☎ (01348) 874128
Worthington's Bitter; guest beers 🄷
This friendly, traditional pub on the outskirts of town has a good local following, with a growing reputation for its beer. Two guest beers change regularly and may come from anywhere in the UK. Pool and darts are played in the big back bar. No food is served except packet snacks.
♨❀🍺🚌(412,413)P🚲

Royal Oak Inn

Market Square, SA65 9HA
⏲ 11-11; 12-10.30 Sun ☎ (01348) 872514
Beer range varies 🄷
This charming, friendly, comfortable pub has connections with the last invasion of mainland Britain, by a French force at nearby Carregwastad Point in 1797, and displays some fascinating memorabilia from the period. Full of character, it has a bustling public bar and pleasant beer garden. Home-cooked meals are served at affordable prices from a varied menu. Two changing Brains beers are available alongside one or more guests. A beer and folk festival takes place over the spring bank holiday weekend, with 18 real ales on offer.
❀◑♿⛺🚌(412,413)♣🚲

Five Roads

Waun Wyllt Inn

Horeb Road, SA15 5AQ (off B4329)
⏲ 11-11 ☎ (01269) 860209 🌐 waunwyllt.com
Greene King Abbot; guest beers 🄷
Situated just off National Cycle Trail 47 (the Celtic trail), the Waun Wyllt is set in the heart of the Carmarthenshire countryside. It was built in the 18th century and although refurbished retains many original features. The inn is now the flagship of the Great Old Inns group. It offers a warm welcome, fine food and good ale, including a range of bottled real beers. ♨Q❀🛏◐◑♿⛺P

Goginan

Druid Inn

High Street, SY23 3NT (on A44 6 miles E of Aberystwyth)
⏲ 12-midnight (1am Fri & Sat) ☎ (01970) 880650
🌐 goginan.com/druid
Wye Valley Bitter, Butty Bach; guest beer 🄷
This thriving community local continues to draw crowds for its quality ales and excellent home-cooked food, including curries and regular specials. Live bands are hosted from time to time and there are occasional beer festivals featuring Welsh micros. The guest beer is typically from a micro in Wales or the Marches, often a Wye Valley monthly special. Local CAMRA Pub of the Year 2008 and 2009. 🐴❀◐◑🚌(525)♣P🚲

Haverfordwest

Bristol Trader ✔

Quay Street, SA61 1BE
⏲ 11-11 (1am Sat); 12-10.30 Sun ☎ (01437) 762122
Worthington's Bitter; guest beers 🄷
Dating back to Haverfordwest's days as a port, this pub retains some character despite recent modernisation. A quiet venue in the daytime, popular for dining, food is served in a large dining area or at outside tables overlooking the river. It gets lively in the evening. Two guest ales are served – beers can be dispensed without tight sparkler on request. ◐♿🚌P

Mariners Hotel

Mariners Square, SA61 2DU
⏲ 12-3, 5.30-11 ☎ (01437) 763353 🌐 hotelmariners.co.uk
Beer range varies 🄷
Family-run hotel in the centre of town with a cosy bar and exposed wood beams, it is known locally for good home-made food, from bar snacks to main meals in the restaurant. The exterior states 'established in 1625' but this claim was a whim of a previous proprietor in the 1920s. Two guest beers are available, often from far afield. The pub is a popular meeting place for many local societies and organisations. Q❀🛏◐◑🚌

Pembroke Yeoman

11 Hill Street, SA61 1QQ
⏲ 11-11 ☎ (01437) 762500
Draught Bass; Flowers IPA; guest beers 🄷
In this local pub conversation is king, though there is a well-stocked juke-box should it flag. Two guest ales come from small breweries and change often. Food is served in generous portions. Known as the Upper Three Crowns until the 1960s, the pub's name was changed to reflect the presence nearby of the local yeomanry headquarters. ♨Q◐◑🚌♣

Herbrandston

Taberna Inn

SA73 3TD (3 miles W of Milford Haven)
⏲ 12-11 ☎ (01646) 693498
Hop Back Summer Lightning; guest beers 🄷
Built in 1963 in a village dominated by a large oil refinery, this pub has a pleasant atmosphere and welcoming locals. Two guest beers are served alongside Westons and Moles Black Rat cider, and the pub issues its own listing of all the guest beers sold throughout the year. ♨Q❀🛏◐◑🍺♿🚌🍎P🚲

Johnstown

Friends Arms

Old St Clears Road, SA31 3HH
⏲ 12-11 (midnight Fri); 11-midnight Sat; 11-11 Sun
☎ (01267) 234073
Banks's Bitter; guest beers 🄷

Excellent local hostelry with a cosy and friendly atmosphere and a warm welcome, enhanced by two open fires. The pub is situated within half a mile of Carmarthen town centre and on a regular bus route. Popular with sports fans, it has Sky Sports and ESPN on two screens, plus pool and darts. A quiz is held on the the first and third Tuesday of the month and bingo on the second and fourth Tuesday. Happy hour is 5-6pm Monday to Friday. Dogs welcome. ♨Q❀🚌⚟

Lampeter

Kings Head

14 Bridge Street, SA48 7HG

⏲ 1 (5 Mon)-late; 12-2am Fri-Sun ☎ (01570) 421498

Jennings Cumberland Ale; Marston's Old Empire; guest beer Ⓗ

This town-centre pub has two bars and a large function room, with a good mix of customers – locals, students and tourists – in this university town, which is home to the oldest established rugby club in Wales. Good food is served all day, with dishes such as rabbit stew on the menu. Although the pub is tied to Marston's, the guest ale changes frequently and may come from Ringwood, Jennings and others. ♨❀◐◗▲🚌♣P⚟

Llandeilo

Sal

New Road, SA19 6DF

⏲ 12-midnight (11 Sun) ☎ (01558) 823325 🌐 thesal.co.uk

Greene King Abbot; guest beers Ⓗ

Vibrant and welcoming pub, just off the centre of the town, with a central bar area serving an open plan bar. Live music plays on a monthly basis – ring first to check bands and dates. Major sporting events are screened. At the rear of the pub are an extensively renovated restaurant area and a covered area outside. ♨❀♿🚌⚟

White Horse

Rhosmaen Street, SA19 6EN

⏲ 11-11; 12-10.30 Sun ☎ (01558) 822424

Evan Evans Cwrw, seasonal beers; guest beers Ⓗ

Grade II-listed coaching inn dating from the 16th century. The brewery tap for the Evan Evans range of Welsh beers, this multi-roomed pub is popular with all ages. There is a small outdoor drinking area to the front and a large council car park to the rear with access to the pub down a short flight of steps. The covered area for smokers has its own TV to watch the sport. ❀🚌♣⚟

Llandovery

Kings Head Inn

1 Market Square, SA20 0AB (in centre of town)

⏲ 10am-11pm ☎ (01550) 720393

🌐 kingsheadcoachinginn.co.uk

Evan Evans Cwrw Ⓗ

Former coaching inn dating from the 1700s in a historic town on the edge of the Brecon Beacons. Newly refurbished yet still traditional, it is a popular base for many organisations including the Rotary Club and cattle breeders. Good food ranges from bar meals to à la carte. Guest beers usually include local Welsh ales. Across the courtyard is the Red Lion, a CAMRA National Inventory pub whose limited opening hours depend on whether the local rugby team is playing. Q⇌♿▲≹🚌P

Llandybie

Ivy Bush

Church Road, SA18 3HZ (100m from church)

⏲ 12-midnight (11 Mon); 11-midnight Sat & Sun

☎ (01269) 850272

Taylor Landlord; guest beer Ⓗ

The oldest pub in the village, this friendly local dates back nearly 300 years. The single bar has two comfortable seating areas. Pub games and quizzes are run weekly and a large-screen TV shows sport. The guest beer changes regularly. The pub is close to the railway station on the Heart of Wales line. ❀≹🚌(103,X13)♣●P⚟

Llandyfan

Square & Compass

SA18 2UD (between Ammanford and Trap)

⏲ 12 (1 Sat)-11 summer; 5-11 winter; 12-6 Sun

☎ (01269) 850402

Beer range varies Ⓗ

This 18th-century building was originally the village blacksmith's. It was converted into a pub in the 1960s. Nestling on the western edge of the Brecon Beacons National Park, it offers magnificent local views and plenty of walking opportunities. A traditional family pub, it has a wonderful rustic charm and a warm, friendly welcome. Usually two, occasionally three guest beers are kept, at least one from a local brewery. Opening hours vary in winter – ring first to check. Q◗♿▲P⚟

Llanelli

Lemon Tree

2 Prospect Place, SA15 3PT

⏲ 12-11 (10.30 Sun) ☎ (01554) 775121

Evan Evans Best Bitter; guest beer Ⓗ

Situated on a side road on the roundabout entering the town from Felinfoel, this is a no-frills bar with a true local atmosphere. There is a major sports theme to this pub, with many mementos adorning the walls. A pool room is next to the main bar. The outdoor area has a covered space to allow smokers to stay dry. There are also tables outside which are popular on a summer's day. ❀♣⚟

Llanfallteg

Plash

SA34 0HN (off A40 at Llanddewi Velfrey)

⏲ 5-11; 12-midnight Wed-Sun ☎ (01437) 563472

Brains Bitter; Wye Valley Butty Bach; guest beer Ⓗ

Terrace-style cottage pub with a garden. An inn for more than 180 years, it has had four different names in that time. The pub is the centre of village life, with welcoming locals who will talk to anyone who wishes to join in. The attractive bar was rescued from a local outfitters shop. Traditional home-made dishes are served in the small restaurant. The guest beer is usually from a small, independent brewery. A disabled entrance is to the rear. ♨Q❀⇌◐◗♿♣P

Llangadog

Red Lion

Church Street, SA19 9AA

⏲ 12-midnight ☎ (01550) 777357

🌐 redlioncoachinginn.co.uk

Evan Evans Cwrw; guest beers Ⓗ

Refurbishment of this Grade II-listed 16th-century coaching inn has taken it back to its origins. It was reputed to be a safe house for Royalist soldiers during the Civil War. Family-friendly, it is full of character and atmosphere. Its excellent, fresh, locally-sourced food attracts locals and tourists alike. Guest beers include Welsh ales as well as those from across the border. Car parking is through the arch. ⛼❀⇌◑♿⛺⇌⊟P

Telegraph Inn

Station Road, SA19 9LS

4 (12 Sat)-midnight; 12-11 Sun ☎ (01550) 777727

Beer range varies H

On the edge of the village, the inn is next to the railway station on the spectacular Heart of Wales line. Built around 1830, the welcoming pub has a basic bar area and comfortable lounge. Food including takeaways is available Wednesday to Saturday. Curry night is Wednesday. Self-catering accommodation sleeps five. Large car park to the side of the building. ⛼❀◗⛺⇌⊟(280)P⁻

Llangoedmor

Penllwyndu

SA43 2LY (on B4570, 4 miles E of Cardigan) SN241458

3.30 (12 Sat)-11; 12-10.30 Sun ☎ (01239) 682533

Brains Buckleys Best Bitter; guest beers H

Old-fashioned ale house standing at an isolated crossroads where Cardigan's evil-doers were once hanged – the pub sign is worthy of close inspection. The cheerful and welcoming public bar has a slate floor and inglenook with wood-burning stove. Snacks are usually available and there is a separate dining area where good value home-cooked meals are served. The guest beer is often from Cottage Brewery. ⛼❀◗♣P⁻

Llangrannog

Pentre Arms

SA44 6SP (at seaward end of B4321/B4334)

12-midnight ☎ (01239) 654345 pentrearms.co.uk

Evan Evans Cwrw; St Austell Tribute H

Right on the shore in arguably Ceredigion's finest seaside village, this traditional pub offers stunning sea views. Built of local stone, it has a comfortable bar with a separate games room. Its welcoming atmosphere makes it popular with both locals and tourists. Eight letting bedrooms are available. ⛴⇌◑⛺♣

Ship (Y Llong)

SA44 6SL (at seaward end of B4321/B4334)

11-11 (1am Fri & Sat) ☎ (01239) 654510

Tomos Watkin Cwrw Braf; guest beers H

Slightly set back from the seafront, the larger of Llangrannog's two pubs is enthusiastically run with a focus on locally sourced produce and Welsh beers. One guest beer is kept in winter, two in summer, usually from Purple Moose. A stylish refurbishment featuring bare stone and wood has created a bright, modern interior – look for the 'ship-shape' bar. The pub is popular with locals and tourists alike. ⛼⛴❀◑⛺P

Llanllwni

Belle Vue Inn

SA40 9SQ (on A485 2 miles N of B4336 jct)

12-2.30 (Sat only), 5-10.30 (11 Fri & Sat); closed Tue; 12-2.30, 6-10.30 Sun ☎ (01570) 480495

bellevueinn.co.uk

Beer range varies H

Set on the main road in a long and straggling village, this former 17th-century farmhouse and smithy was converted to an inn in the 1800s. Both licensees are classically trained chefs and have gained a reputation for excellence, with the emphasis on local produce – the special themed evenings are very popular. With two rotating guest ales plus bottled beers, this friendly family-run free house is a magnet for locals and visitors alike – an oasis in a desert of blandness. Q❀◑⊟(X40)P⁻

LLansaint

King's Arms

13 Maes yr Eglwys, SA17 5JE

12-2.30, 6-11; closed Tue; 12-2.30, 6.30-10.30 Sun ☎ (01267) 267487

Brains Buckley's Best Bitter; guest beer H

This friendly village local, a former Carmarthenshire CAMRA Pub of the Year, has been a pub for more than 200 years. Situated near an 11th-century church, it is reputedly built from stone recovered from the lost village of St Ishmaels. Music and poetry nights are held on the third Friday of the month. Good value home-cooked food is served. Carmarthen Bay Holiday Park is a few miles away. ⛼Q❀⇌◑⛺⊟♣P

Mynydd y Garreg

Prince of Wales 🏆

SA17 4RP

5-11; closed Sun ☎ (01554) 890522

Bullmastiff Brindle, Son of a Bitch; guest beers H

This little gem of a pub, Carmarthenshire CAMRA Pub of the Year 2010, is well-worth seeking out for both its beer range and its ambience. As well as the two regular Bullmastiff beers there are up to four rotating guest ales, usually from smaller breweries. A real cider is also often available. The cosy single-room bar is packed with a treasure trove of miscellaneous items. ⛼Q❀●P

Narberth

Angel Inn

43 High Street, SA67 7AS

11-3, 5.30-11; 7-10.30 Sun ☎ (01834) 860215

Brains The Rev James; guest beer H

Cosy, modernised pub in the town centre with a separate, small public bar and larger lounge/dining area. It offers two guest beers and very popular food. With a warm and friendly welcome, it can be busy at times. Outside is a good-sized beer garden for the summer months. Q◑⊟⛺⊟⁻

Newcastle Emlyn

Pelican Inn

Sycamore Street, SA38 9AP

2.30 (12 Fri & Sat)-11.30 ☎ (01239) 710606

Draught Bass; guest beer H

If you want to enjoy a decent pint while you watch the rugby, this friendly local in the heart of town is the place to be. It has an inviting open fire and there are plenty of cosy nooks for a quiet chat. The bar has Sky TV, a dartboard and pool table. ⛼❀⊟(460)♣⁻

Newport

Castle Hotel

Bridge Street, SA42 0TB

✪ 11-11; 12-10.30 Sun ☎ (01239) 820472

Greene King Old Speckled Hen; Theakston Best Bitter, XB; guest beer Ⓗ

This friendly, popular local in a small town full of character has an attractive bar with some impressive wood panelling. Food is served at lunchtimes and in the evening in the extensive dining area. An off-street car park is situated behind the hotel. A wealth of prehistoric remains adds interest to the many local walks. ♨♞❀⇚◐◑▲⊟(412)P⚟

Golden Lion

East Street, SA42 0SY (on A487)

✪ 12-midnight (11 Sun) ☎ (01239) 820321

Brains The Rev James; Draught Bass; guest beers Ⓗ

Another of Newport's sociable locals, this one is reputed to have its own resident ghost. A number of internal walls have been removed to form a spacious open-plan bar area, with distinct sections helping to retain a cosy atmosphere. Car parking space is available on the opposite side of the road. ♨Q◐◑▲⊟(412)P⚟

Pembroke Dock

Flying Boat Inn

6 Queen Street, SA72 6JL

✪ 10-12.30am; 12-10.30 Sun ☎ (01646) 682810

Beer range varies Ⓗ

Featuring exposed stone and black beams, the bar of this relaxed and friendly pub displays memorabilia from the heyday of flying boats stationed locally. Sky Sports is shown on the large screen, a beer festival is held annually, and the local folk club meets every Friday evening. Irish Ferries sails twice daily from Pembroke Dock to Rosslare. ♨Q♞❀⇚⊡♿⇌⊟♣⚟

Station Inn

Hawkestone Road, SA72 6JL (in station building)

✪ 7-11 Mon; 11-3, 6-midnight (12.30am Fri & Sat); 12-3, 7-10.30 Sun ☎ (01646) 621255

Beer range varies Ⓗ

Housed in the town's railway station where trains still depart for Carmarthen and Swansea, this town-centre pub is close to both the Irish Ferries terminal and popular Pembrokeshire Coast Path. Meals are excellent value (no lunches Mon, evening meals Wed-Sat only). Three real ales are generally on sale, with Young's Bitter a frequent visitor and a new beer coming on every Tuesday. The June beer festival offers around 20 beers. Live music is performed on Saturday evenings. ♨Q❀⇚◐◑⊡♿⇌⊟P⚟

Penally

Cross Inn

SA70 7PU

✪ 12-11 (12.30am Fri & Sat); 12-midnight Sun ☎ (01834) 844665

Hancock's HB; guest beers Ⓗ

Situated in a picturesque village, the pub has a wood and brick bar leading to the restaurant. Local pictures and shields of regiments stationed in a nearby barracks adorn the walls. The sporting prowess of the locals is evident from the cups and shields on the trophy shelf. A signed photo and a set of darts used by Phil 'The Power' Taylor is framed in an alcove. Food is available at some times of the year – ring to check first. ❀▲⇌⊟⚟

Penrhiwllan

Daffodil

SA44 5NG (on A475 in village)

✪ 11.30-midnight ☎ (01559) 370343

Beer range varies Ⓗ

Formerly the Penrhiwllan Inn, the Daffodil is a family-run pub and restaurant dating from 1750, in a country village 20 minutes from Newquay on the Ceredigion coast. It has been modernised in an elegant style to provide separate, intimate dining areas and cosy drinking areas catering for all, and has excellent disabled facilities. Two handpumps, three in the summer, dispense beers mostly from nationals, with guest beers from Welsh breweries. Occasional live music nights. ♨Q♞❀◐◑♿♣P⚟

Pontfaen

Dyffryn Arms ★

SA65 9SG (off B4313)

✪ opening hours vary ☎ (01348) 881305

Draught Bass; Tetley Burton Ale Ⓖ

This much-loved pub, run by a landlady in her 80s, resembles a 1920s front room where time has stood still. The beer is still served by the jug through a sliding serving hatch. Conversation is the main form of entertainment, and the pub's relaxed atmosphere is captivating. Set in the beautiful Gwaun Valley between the Preseli Hills and Fishguard, the pub is at the heart of almost all local community activity. ♨Q❀▲♣

Porthyrhyd

Mansel Arms

Banc y Mansel, SA32 8BS (on B4310)

✪ 5-11; 3-midnight Sat; 12-6 Sun ☎ (01267) 275305

Beer range varies Ⓗ

Friendly 18th-century former coaching inn with wood fires in each room. The original limestone flags have been broken up and used in the fireplace. Low beams have been added to create atmosphere, and numerous jugs hang from them in the bar. Pool and darts are played in a room to the rear which was originally used for slaughtering pigs. Food is served Friday and Saturday evenings and Sunday lunch. ♨Q◐◑▲⊟♣●

Pren-gwyn

Gwarcefel Arms

SA44 4LU

✪ 12-midnight (1am Fri & Sat); closed Wed; 12-11 Sun ☎ (01559) 362720 🌐 gwarcefelarms.co.uk

Beer range varies Ⓗ

Country pub situated at the junction of five roads. The main bar has an open fire with cosy seating and a games area for pool and darts. A separate bar serves the restaurant, which caters for functions and parties as well as lunch and evening meals – the specials menu changes frequently. Guest ales are usually from large and small Welsh brewers including some of the newer ones. ♨❀◐◑▲⊟P⚟

Rhandirmwyn

Royal Oak

SA20 0NY

✪ 12-3 (2 winter), 6-11; 12-2, 7-10.30 Sun

☎ (01550) 760201 🌐 theroyaloakinn.co.uk

Beer range varies Ⓗ

Remote, stone-flagged inn with excellent views of the Tywi Valley and close to an RSPB bird sanctuary. Originally built as a hunting lodge for the local landowner, it is now a focal point for community activities and popular with fans of outdoor pursuits. A fine range of bottled beers and whiskies is stocked, and the good wholesome food is recommended. There are panoramic views from the beer garden situated to the side of the pub. Voted Carmarthenshire CAMRA Pub of the Year four times. ♔Q❀⛿◑▲♣P

Rhydowen

Alltyrodyn Arms

SA44 4QB (at A475/B4459 crossroads)

✪ closed Mon; 3 (12 Sat)-midnight; 12-8 Sun

☎ (01545) 590319

Beer range varies Ⓗ

This 400-year-old family-run country pub has an excellent reputation for both food and real ales (no keg beer sold), with an extended range stocked for its August bank holiday beer festival. The pub has recently undergone refurbishment to return the bar and restaurant areas back to one room. A games room with pool and darts complements the main bar. Good home-made food is served. The beer garden and covered decking area have lovely valley views. Families and dogs are always welcome. ♔❀◑🚌(551)♣P⌐

Roch

Victoria Inn

SA62 6AW (on A487)

✪ 12-2.30am (10.30 Sun) ☎ (01437) 710426

🌐 victoriainnroch.co.uk

Beer range varies Ⓗ

A little gem with views across St Brides Bay, this locals' pub offers a warm welcome to all. The inn was established in 1851 although some parts of the building date back to the 18th century. It has retained much of its old-world charm with beamed ceilings and low doorways. The menu features home-made Welsh dishes made with local produce where possible. Curry and a pint night is Friday. For those in a hurry there is a beer carry-out service. Occasional live music.
♔Q♨❀⛿◑⊟♿🚌(411)♣P

St Dogmaels

Teifi Netpool Inn

SA43 3ET

✪ 10-11.30 (12.30am Fri & Sat) ☎ (01239) 612680

Beer range varies Ⓗ

A tastefully modernised pub overlooking the Teifi River. The bar and ceiling feature many wooden beams. Old photographs of the village adorn the walls and a large number of beer jugs and steins hang from the ceiling. In front of the pub is a large village green and play area leading to the river. There is additional parking in the free council car park nearby. ♔Q❀◑♿▲🚌●P⌐

Solva

Cambrian Inn

SA62 6UU (on A487 by bridge)

✪ 11-11 ☎ (01437) 721210

Tomos Watkin OSB; guest beers Ⓗ

Situated in a popular coastal village, renowned as one of the most delightful places in Pembrokeshire, this sympathetically restored local pub has a reputation for good beer and food. The bar area is decorated with local crafts, creating a cosy atmosphere enjoyed by village residents and visitors alike. Q◑🚌(411)P⌐

Harbour Inn ✔

SA62 6UU (on A487 next to harbour)

✪ 11-11 ☎ (01437) 720013

Brains Dark, SA; guest beers Ⓗ

This delightful seaside inn, next to the harbour where emigrants once left for North America, remains the same from year to year. A community pub with a traditional atmosphere, it serves as a base for many village activities and is popular with locals who come to enjoy a quiet, relaxing pint. The nearby camping facilities cater for both caravans and tents. ♔Q❀⛿◑♿🚌(411)P⌐

Ship 🏆

15 Main Street, SA62 6UU (on A487)

✪ 12 (4 Mon-Thu winter)-11.30 (midnight Fri, Sat & summer Sun) ☎ (01437) 721247

Banks's Bitter; Jennings Cocker Hoop; Marston's Pedigree; guest beer Ⓗ

Families are made particularly welcome at this traditional pub. The Sunday roast is popular; authentic Indian curries are served in the evening with a free delivery service subject to a minimum order value. An outdoor smoking area is covered and heated, and ample parking is available nearby at the harbour. Pembrokeshire CAMRA Pub of the Year 2010. ♔❀⛿◑♿▲🚌(411)⌐

Talybont

White Lion (Llew Gwyn) ✔

SY24 5ER (7 miles N of Aberystwyth on A487)

✪ 12-late ☎ (01970) 832245

Banks's Mild, Bitter; guest beer Ⓗ

Popular with locals and holidaymakers alike, this friendly community pub faces the village green. Welcoming staff offer quality beer and good-value food – Thursday curry night and generous Sunday lunches are weekly highlights. The guest beer comes from the Marston's group. Pleasant accommodation is offered in rooms overlooking the green or large back garden.
♔♨❀⛿◑🚌(28,X32)♣P⌐

Tenby

Crown Inn

Lower Frog Street, SA70 7HU

✪ 12-11 (11.30 Sun) ☎ (01834) 842796

🌐 thecrowninn-tenby.co.uk

Brains The Rev James; guest beers Ⓗ

Close to the town's famous beaches and within the old town wall, the pub is convenient for Tenby's many attractions and is on the coastal footpath. Up to four guest beers are available. A poker night is held each week and numerous charity events are hosted throughout the year. Good value-for-money food includes a Sunday carvery. ❀◑♿▲⇌●⌐

Good Bottled Beer Guide

Jeff Evans

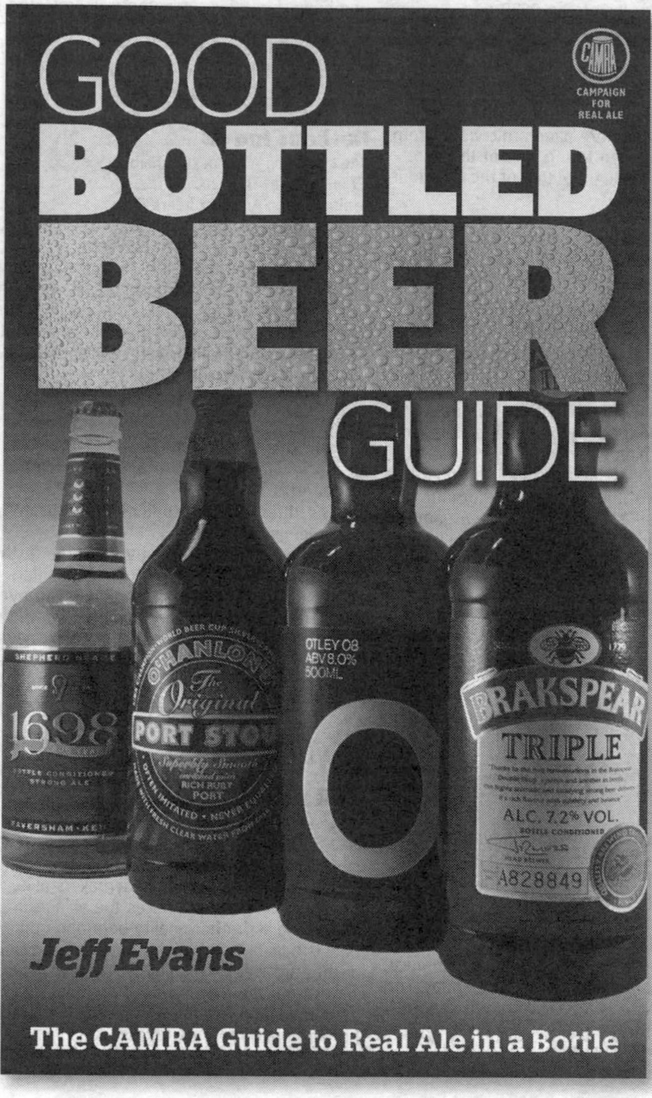

A pocket-sized guide for discerning drinkers looking to buy bottled real ales and enjoy a fresh glass of their favourite beers at home. The 7th edition of the **Good Bottled Beer Guide** is completely revised, updated and redesigned to showcase the very best bottled British real ales now being produced, and detail where they can be bought. Everything you need to know about bottled beers; tasting notes, ingredients, brewery details, and a glossary to help the reader understand more about them.

£12.99 ISBN 978-1-85249-262-5 CAMRA members' price £10.99 384 pages

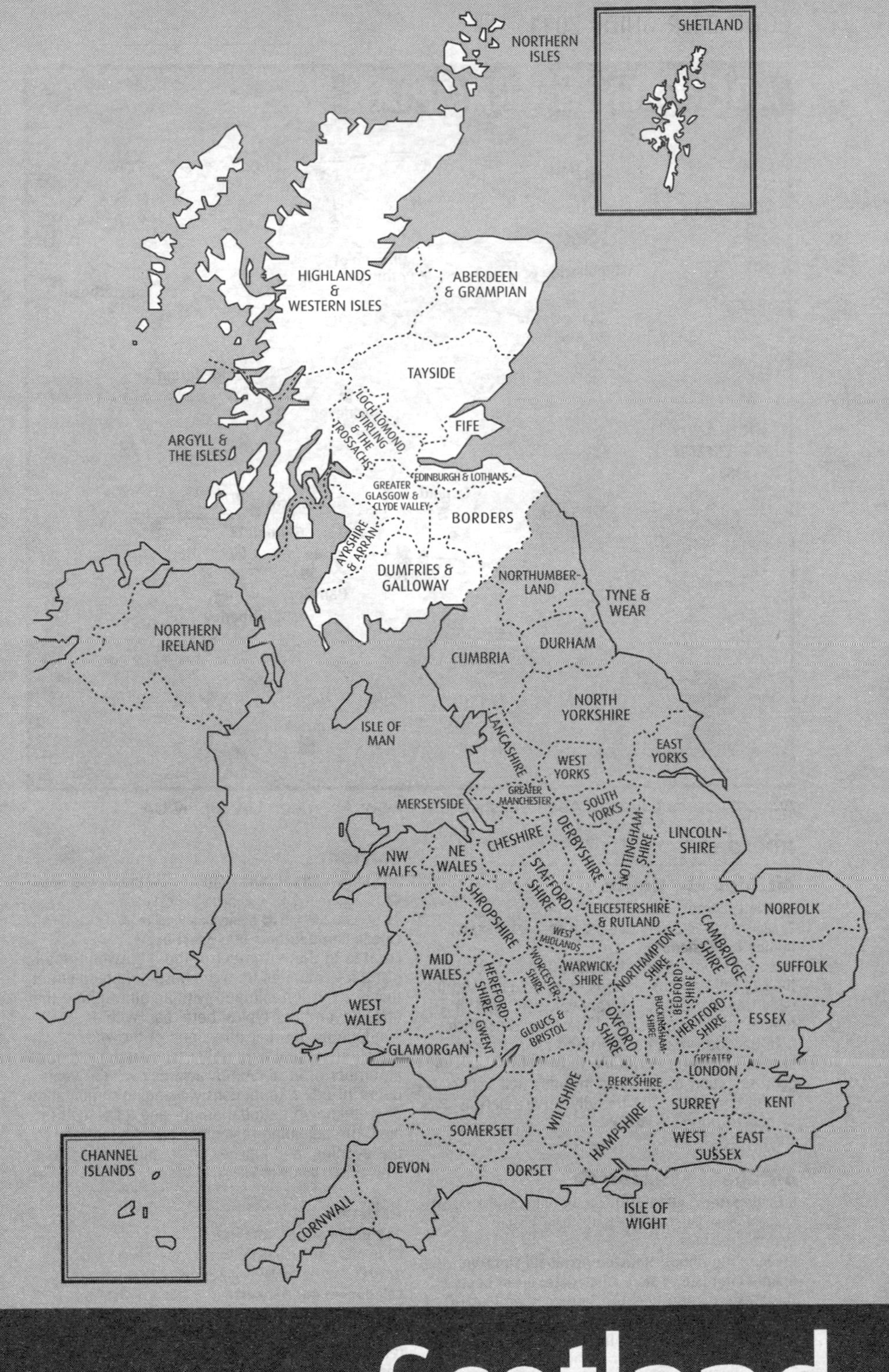

NORTHERN ISLES
SHETLAND
HIGHLANDS & WESTERN ISLES
ABERDEEN & GRAMPIAN
TAYSIDE
LOCH LOMOND, STIRLING & THE TROSSACHS
FIFE
ARGYLL & THE ISLES
EDINBURGH & LOTHIANS
GREATER GLASGOW & CLYDE VALLEY
BORDERS
AYRSHIRE & ARRAN
DUMFRIES & GALLOWAY
NORTHUMBERLAND
TYNE & WEAR
NORTHERN IRELAND
DURHAM
CUMBRIA
NORTH YORKSHIRE
ISLE OF MAN
LANCASHIRE
EAST YORKS
WEST YORKS
GREATER MANCHESTER
MERSEYSIDE
SOUTH YORKS
CHESHIRE
DERBYSHIRE
NOTTINGHAMSHIRE
LINCOLNSHIRE
NW WALES
NE WALES
STAFFORDSHIRE
SHROPSHIRE
LEICESTERSHIRE & RUTLAND
NORFOLK
WEST MIDLANDS
CAMBRIDGESHIRE
MID WALES
HEREFORDSHIRE
WORCESTERSHIRE
WARWICKSHIRE
NORTHAMPTONSHIRE
SUFFOLK
BEDFORDSHIRE
BUCKINGHAMSHIRE
WEST WALES
GWENT
GLOUCS & BRISTOL
OXFORDSHIRE
HERTFORDSHIRE
ESSEX
GLAMORGAN
GREATER LONDON
BERKSHIRE
WILTSHIRE
SURREY
KENT
SOMERSET
HAMPSHIRE
WEST SUSSEX
EAST SUSSEX
CHANNEL ISLANDS
DEVON
DORSET
ISLE OF WIGHT
CORNWALL

Scotland

ABERDEEN & GRAMPIAN

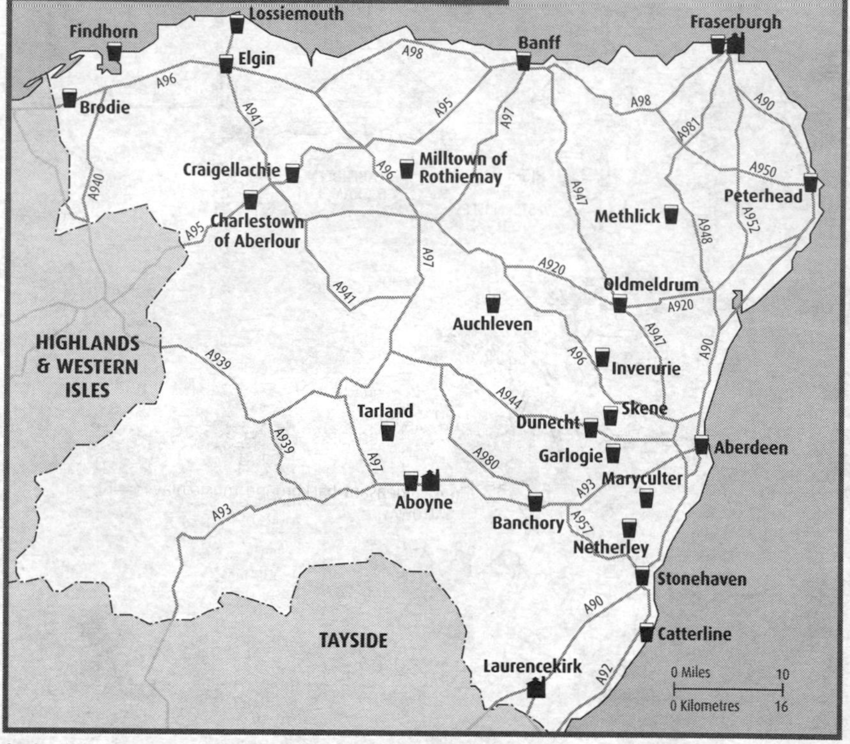

Authority areas covered: Aberdeenshire UA, City of Aberdeen UA, Moray UA

Aberdeen

Aitchies Ale House

10 Trinity Street, AB11 5LY
8am-10 (11 Fri & Sat); closed Sun (01224) 581459
Orkney Dark Island H
This small corner bar is the closest real ale outlet to the city rail and bus stations, with hours to suit the early traveller. Although renovated in 1994, it retains the flavour of an old-fashioned Scottish pub. Bar food may be described as traditional Scottish pub grub, including roast beef stovies. A good selection of whiskies includes Bell's special edition decanters. The friendly service here is second to none.

Archibald Simpson ✔

5 Castle Street, AB11 5BQ (corner Union St & King St)
10am-midnight (1am Fri & Sat); 10am-11 Sun
(01224) 621365
Greene King Abbot; Houston Archibald Simpson, Granite City; Isle of Skye Castlegate; guest beers H
This Wetherspoon was the former Aberdeen HQ of the Clydesdale Bank, designed by Archibald Simpson, the architect behind many of the splendid granite buildings in central Aberdeen. The main room is in the high-ceilinged central hall and retains many original architectural features. There are also seating areas to the side of the hall. A long bar features 12 handpumps offering an ever-changing variety of beers. The pub was CAMRA local pub of the year in 2009. Free Wi-Fi.

Carriages

101 Crown Street, AB11 6HH (below Brentwood Hotel)
11-2.30 (not Sat), 4.30-midnight; 6-11 Sun
(01224) 595440 brentwood-hotel.co.uk
Caledonian Deuchars IPA; guest beers H
Located in the basement of the Brentwood Hotel just a few minutes from the bustle of Union Street, this is a comfortable pub with an atmosphere that goes beyond the typical hotel bar. With 10 handpumps, the bar offers one of the widest selections of real ale in Aberdeen, and has earned a number of local CAMRA awards over the years. Beers include a continuously changing combination of well-known national brands and local Scottish ales. The adjoining restaurant offers good food in the evening, and lunches are available in the bar. Free Wi-Fi.

Grill ★

213 Union Street, AB11 6BA
10-midnight (1am Fri & Sat); 12.30-midnight Sun
(01224) 573530 thegrillaberdeen.co.uk
Caledonian 80; Harviestoun Bitter & Twisted; Shepherd Neame Spitfire; guest beers H
With an exquisite interior redesigned in 1926 and remaining largely unchanged since, this is the only CAMRA National Inventory of Historic Pub Interiors

INDEPENDENT BREWERIES

BrewDog Fraserburgh
Burnside Laurencekirk (NEW)
Deeside Aboyne

pub in the Aberdeen area. For men only until 1975, ladies toilets were eventually provided in 1998. Situated across from the Music Hall, musicians often visit during concert breaks. Guest beers may include Landlord or something from Isle of Skye. An extensive collection of malt whiskies is offered. Bar snacks are available. UK Whisky Bar of the Year 2009. ♿⇌🚌

Ma Camerons ✔

6-8 Little Belmont Street, AB10 1JG (just off Union St beside St Nicholas churchyard)

11-midnight (1am Fri & Sat); 12.30-midnight Sun

☎ (01224) 644487

Greene King IPA; Inveralmond Lia Fail; guest beers H

Known simply as Ma's, this is one of the oldest pubs in Aberdeen. It has a listed, unspoilt snug bar with serving hatch, and a modern, expansive lounge where meals are served until 9pm every day. Children are permitted, if dining, until 8pm. There are three handpumps in each bar offering the regular beers plus a guest, usually from the Greene King/Belhaven range. A quiz is held on Monday, live music one Friday a month, and sport is screened on the TV in the lounge. The snug may close early if quiet. Free Wi-Fi. ❀◐♿⇌🚌

Moorings

2 Trinity Quay, AB11 5AA (opp quayside at bottom of Market St)

12-midnight (1am Fri & Sat); 12.30-midnight Sun

☎ (01224) 587602

Beer range varies H

Hard rock meets real ale in this unique, laid-back dockside haven, CAMRA's City Pub of the Year 2008 and 2010. The pub has a friendly welcome for all, with relatively low prices for the city centre. Five handpumps dispense an ever-changing selection of ales, usually from Scottish micro-breweries, and Thatchers cider. Note the unusual 'elastic band' method of quality control. Frequent live rock bands play, and there may be a charge on Saturday nights. The juke-box tends to be in constant use, but be prepared to be surprised – Highland sword dancers were spotted recently. ⇌♣

Old Blackfriars

52 Castle Street, AB11 5BB

11-midnight (1am Fri & Sat); 11-11 Sun

☎ (01224) 581922 🌐 old-blackfriars.co.uk

Caledonian Deuchars IPA; Greene King Old Speckled Hen; Inveralmond Ossian Ale; guest beers H

Located on the Castlegate in the historic centre of the city, this was local CAMRA Pub of the Year in 2007. It is owned by Belhaven pubs, the Scottish arm of Greene King. On two levels, with bars on both levels, it offers up to six guest beers, with a bias towards Scottish micro-breweries. Unobtrusive background music plays, but there is no TV. The pub has a reputation for good pub food served daily until 9.30pm. Quiz night is the first Tuesday of the month. Occasional themed beer festivals are hosted. Free Wi-Fi. ◐♿⇌🚌

Prince of Wales

7 St Nicholas Lane, AB10 1HF (opp Marks & Spencer)

10-midnight (1am Fri & Sat); 11-midnight Sun

☎ (01224) 640597

Caledonian 80; Inveralmond Prince of Wales; Theakston Old Peculier; guest beers H

A past winner of CAMRA City Pub of the Year and listed in Scotland's True Heritage Pubs, this is one of the oldest bars in Aberdeen, with possibly the longest bar counter in the city. It has a friendly atmosphere and a traditional feel. The usual Greene King/Belhaven suspects are supplemented by a varied selection of Scottish and English ales and a house beer. Folk music plays on Sunday evening and a quiz is held every Monday at 9pm. Good value food is served daily till 8pm (5pm Sat & Sun). Q◐⇌🚌

Under The Hammer

11 North Silver Street, AB10 1RJ (3 mins from Union St, off Golden Square)

5 (4 Fri)-midnight (1am Thu & Fri); 2-1am Sat; 5-11 Sun

☎ (01224) 640253

Caledonian Deuchars IPA; Inveralmond Ossian Ale; guest beer H

Atmospheric, comfortable and inviting basement pub, next door to an auction house – hence the name. Paintings by local artists displayed on the walls are for sale if they take your fancy. Convenient for the Music Hall and His Majesty's Theatre, the large noticeboard has posters advertising forthcoming events in town. Guest beers tend to contrast in style from the two regulars, with local Deeside beers frequent guests. Pleasant background music plays. ⇌🚌

Aboyne

Boat Inn

Charleston Road, AB34 5EL (N bank of River Dee next to Aboyne Bridge)

11-11 (midnight Fri & Sat) ☎ (01339) 886137

🌐 theboatinnaboyne.co.uk

Inveralmond Ossian Ale; guest beers H

Popular riverside inn with a food-oriented lounge bar and a public bar to the rear. Good food is made with locally-sourced produce. Junior diners (and adults!) may request to see the model train, complete with sound effects, traverse the entire pub at picture-rail height upon completion of their meal. Two guest beers are usually from Scottish micros. Self-catering accommodation is available with full disabled facilities in one room. Q❀◐♿P

Auchleven

Hunter's Moon

3 The Belts, AB52 6QB

closed Mon; 5-11; 4-1am Fri; 12-12.30am Sat; 11-11 Sun

☎ (01464) 820380

Beer range varies H

A friendly welcome is assured at this village local, refurbished a couple of years ago, with green wood panelling all around. An interesting, seasonal menu of freshly-cooked, locally-sourced food is available in both the restaurant and spacious bar. Children are permitted until 8pm. Pool and darts are played and a quiz night is held on the first Tuesday of the month. Ever-changing beers often come from Inveralmond and Deeside, with ales from the Cellarman's Reserve list selected by the regulars. The Archaeolink Prehistory Park at Oyne is a short drive. Breakfast and papers from 10am Sunday. ❀◐♿♣P

Banchory

Douglas Arms Hotel

22 High Street, AB31 5SR

✪ 11-midnight (1am Fri & Sat); 11-11 Sun
☎ (01330) 822547 ⊕ douglasarms.co.uk
Beer range varies Ⓗ
Built in the 1840s and one of the oldest buildings in Banchory, this small hotel offers up to three ales, mainly from Scottish micros. The bar, pool area and snug room all feature plasma TV systems where different sports are screened. The public bar, included in Scotland's True Heritage Pubs, is a classic Scottish long bar with etched windows and vintage mirrors. The lounge area is mainly used for bar suppers. There is a separate function room. Outside is a large, south-facing decked area, ideal for summer afternoons and evenings.
♨Q♉❀⇌◑◗♿▲🚌(201,202)♣P

Ravenswood Club (Royal British Legion)

25 Ramsay Road, AB31 5TS (N of main A93)
✪ 11-11 (midnight Fri & Sat) ☎ (01330) 822347
⊕ banchorylegion.com
Beer range varies Ⓗ
Large British Legion club that welcomes CAMRA members as guests. A comfortable lounge adjoins the pool and TV room and there is a spacious function room. Darts and snooker are popular and played most evenings. The two handpumps offer excellent value and the beer choice is constantly changing, with ales consistently the best quality in the village. An elevated terrace has fine views of the Deeside hills. Show a copy of this Guide for entry. ❀⇌◑♿▲♣P

Banff

Ship Inn

8 Deveronside, AB45 1HP (at the mouth of the Deveron, close to the harbour)
✪ 12-midnight (1am Fri & Sat); 12.30-midnight Sun
☎ (01261) 812620 ⊕ theshipbanff.co.uk
Greene King Old Speckled Hen Ⓗ
The interior of this historic nautical-themed inn featured in the film Local Hero. It has a wood-panelled bar and lounge with sea views through the small windows. A blocked carriage arch hints at the earlier history of the building. Banff Marina, Duff House Gallery (National Gallery of Scotland) and the Macduff Aquarium are close by, as are several golf courses. The pub has a fine view across the mouth of the Deveron to Macduff. Bar snacks are served all day. Wi-Fi is available. ♨◗▲🚌(305)

Brodie

Old Mill Inn

IV36 2TD (on main A96 between Forres and Nairn)
✪ 11.30-11 (10.30 Sun) ☎ (01309) 641605
⊕ oldmillinnbrodie.com
Beer range varies Ⓗ
Beautifully refurbished old flour mill with rustic decor and a conservatory overlooking a suntrap garden. Well-chosen Scottish and English ales are served. The pub is famed for its imaginative menu of home-cooked food, including cream teas and traditional Scottish high teas. The inn is next to a caravan and campsite, Brodie Castle and a large tourist shopping venue are close by.
♨Q♉❀⇌◑◗♿▲🚌(10,305)P⁻

Catterline

Creel Inn

AB39 2UL (on coast off A92, 5 miles S of Stonehaven) NO868782
✪ 12-3, 6-midnight (1am Fri & Sat); 12-midnight Sun
☎ (01569) 750254 ⊕ thecreelinn.co.uk
Beer range varies Ⓗ
This small pub, in a scenic clifftop location, has been successfully extended to incorporate a restaurant in an adjacent row of fishermen's cottages. The pub is primarily a food operation but the bar area remains dedicated to drinking and serves as a popular village local. Up to four beers, usually from Scottish micros, and over 100 bottled beers from around the world, are on offer. Crawton Bird Sanctuary is two miles north, while Todhead Lighthouse and Kinneff Old Church lie two miles south. ♨Q❀◑◗♣P

Charleston of Aberlour

Mash Tun

8 Broomfield Square, AB38 9QP (follow sign for Speyside Way visitor centre)
✪ 12-12.30am (1am Fri & Sat); 12.30-12.30am Sun
☎ (01340) 881771 ⊕ mashtun-aberlour.com
Beer range varies Ⓗ
Built in 1896 as the Station Bar, this unusual, round-ended building has an airy interior featuring extensive use of timber. A pledge in the title deeds allowed a name change if the railway closed but it must revert to the Station Bar if a train ever pulls up again outside. The Speyside Way now runs past the door and patrons may drink their ale and enjoy the view on the former station platform. Up to two guest ales come from Cairngorm, Atlas, Houston or Deeside breweries. Note the display case at end of the bar containing Glenfarclas Family Casks from 1952 to 1994 – bring your credit card! Q❀⇌◑◗🚌

Craigellachie

Highlander Inn

10 Victoria Street, AB38 9SR (on A95)
✪ 12-11 (12.30am Fri & Sat) ☎ (01340) 881446
⊕ whiskyinn.com
Cairngorm Trade Winds; guest beers Ⓗ
Picturesque whisky and cask-ale bar on Speyside's Whisky Trail, close to the Speyside Way, offering a fine selection of malts and good value tasting sessions with occasional special promotions. CRAC (Craigellachie Real Ale Club) meets monthly and its members, whose etched glass tankards hang above the bar, help to choose the pub's guest ales with the support of the owners and staff. The area is good for fishing and walking. Opens at 11am for coffee. Q❀⇌◑◗🚌(336)♣P⁻

Dunecht

Jaffs

AB32 7AW (on the corner of the A944/B977)
✪ 12-11.30 (1am Fri); 11-midnight Sat ☎ (01330) 860808
⊕ jaffsbarandrestaurant.co.uk
Taylor Landlord; guest beer Ⓗ
A friendly country pub and restaurant at the heart of the village. This traditional pub has been run by the same team for four years and is gaining a reputation for good beer and fine food. The pub is popular with the locals and extends a friendly welcome to all visitors. Quiz night is the last

Sunday of the month. The guest beer is usually from Inveralmond Brewery, often Ossian Ale.
✿◑🚌(X15,215)P⚍

Elgin

Muckle Cross ✔

34 High Street, IV30 1BU
⏲ 11-midnight (1am Fri & Sat); 12.30-midnight Sun
☎ (01343) 559030
Greene King Abbot; guest beers Ⓗ
Typical small Wetherspoon converted from what was once a bicycle repair shop, then a Halfords branch. The pleasant long room has ample seating, a family area and a long bar. It can get very busy, particularly at weekends. Five handpumps offer a wide range of beers from national and micro-breweries, including Scottish (particularly Isle of Skye, who brew the house beer). The pub also stocks a wide range of malt whiskies from more than 20 local distilleries. Opens at 7am for coffee and breakfast. Q✿◑♿⇌🚌●

Sunninghill Hotel

Hay Street, IV30 1NH
⏲ 12-2.30, 5-11 (12.30am Fri & Sat) ☎ (01343) 547799
🌐 sunninghillhotel.com
Beer range varies Ⓗ
Friendly family-run hotel set in its own grounds in a quiet residential area, very close to the town centre and the railway station. The comfortable lounge includes a dining area and there are additional tables in the conservatory, making it a popular venue for families. Three handpumps serve a variety of beers, often from Scottish micros, and a large selection of whiskies is also on offer. Outside, there is seating on the patio and an attractive garden. ✿🛏◑♿⇌🚌P

Findhorn

Crown & Anchor Inn

44 Findhorn, IV36 3YF
⏲ 12-11 (12.30am Fri & Sat) ☎ (01309) 690243
🌐 crownandanchorinn.co.uk
Caledonian Deuchars IPA; Taylor Landlord Ⓗ
A spacious seaside inn, set in a charming village by the beautiful Moray Firth. The bar has solid, rustic decor, and there are two separate dining areas where home cooked, locally sourced food is served. Outside are many picnic tables and a fine 'Smokooterie' for smoking in comfort. The pub is popular with locals and summer visitors, who come for sailing, camping or strolling along the sands.
♨Q👶✿🛏◑♿⛺🚌(336)♣P⚍

Kimberley Inn

94 Findhorn, IV36 3YG
⏲ 12-midnight ☎ (01309) 690492 🌐 kimberleyinn.com
Beer range varies Ⓗ
This pub, under new management, styles itself Moray's seafood pub. Situated right on the shore of Findhorn Bay, it has superb views from the tables on the patio outside. The bar is wood-panelled with snugs at either end. Two handpumps dispense a wide variety of beers, mainly from Scottish micros. The menu of home-cooked food features local fish and even local ice-cream. Findhorn is a breezy village with views over the sands to the Moray Firth, framed by distant hills.
♨Q👶✿◑♿⛺🚌(336)♣P⚍

Fraserburgh

Elizabethan Lounge

36 Union Grove, AB43 9PH (jct Union Grove and Dennyduff Rd)
⏲ 9.30am (12 Sun)-1am ☎ (01346) 515148
Beer range varies Ⓗ
This friendly neighbourhood pub is located about half a mile from Fraserburgh town centre. The post-war building has three bars, all offering a warm welcome to regulars and visitors. Two handpumps serve a selection of beers, mainly from Scottish micro-breweries, including the local brewery, BrewDog. Pub games include darts, dominoes, pool and snooker. 👶🖵♿🚌(267,268,269)P⚍

Garlogie

Garlogie Inn

AB32 6RX (on B9119)
⏲ 11-2.30, 5-10.30 (11.30 Fri & Sat); 12.30-9 Sun
☎ (01224) 743212 🌐 garlogieinn.co.uk
Beer range varies Ⓗ
This traditional village pub run by the same family for 24 years was originally known as the Port & Ale House, and has been providing refreshments for travellers along the road from the early 1800s. The original bar and shop now form the lounge bar area, while the house next door has been converted into a restaurant (booking advised). The pub is renowned for its excellent food but drinkers are also very welcome. A single ale is from Inveralmond Brewery. ✿◑♿🚌(210)P⚍

Inverurie

Edwards

2 West High Street, AB51 3SA
⏲ 10am-1am (2am Fri & Sat) ☎ (01467) 629788
🌐 edwardsinverurie.co.uk
Caledonian Deuchars IPA; guest beers Ⓗ
Stylish café bar converted from an old hotel several years ago. The decor is light and modern with a hint of Art Deco about it. There is a series of comfortable snugs to relax in while enjoying a snack and browsing the newspapers. Up to two guest beers may be available. The upstairs function room doubles as a disco at weekends. It's extremely close to the railway station, and buses stop nearby. ✿◑♿⇌🚌(10,307,737)⚍

Lossiemouth

Skerry Brae Hotel

Stotfield Road, IV31 6QS
⏲ 11-11 (12.30am Fri & Sat); 12-11 Sun ☎ (01343) 812040
🌐 skerrybrae.co.uk
Beer range varies Ⓗ
Modern lounge bar in an old hotel building with stunning views over the Moray Firth and the golf course. Very much a food-based premises, the venue is popular with families, especially from the nearby RAF base, and the bar wall is adorned with a collection of squadron insignia. Three beers are available, mostly from Scottish micro-breweries.
✿🛏◑🚌(329)P

Maryculter

Old Mill Inn

South Deeside Road, AB12 5FX (jct B979/B9077)
⏲ 11 (12 Sun)-11 ☎ (01224) 733212 🌐 oldmillinn.co.uk

Caledonian Deuchars IPA; Taylor Landlord; guest beer Ⓗ
Small, privately-owned hotel, dating from 1797, in a rural location close to the River Dee, five miles west of Aberdeen city centre. Real ale is served in the comfortable lounge bar, furnished with sofas and decorated with fishing memorabilia, as well as in the adjacent restaurant. The large function room is popular for weddings. The children's attraction Storybook Glen and the Blairs Museum of Scotland's Catholic Heritage are close by. Fishing may be arranged on the river. ❀⇌◐⊟ÅP

Methlick

Ythanview Hotel

Main Street, AB41 7DT
⏲ 11-2.30, 5-11 (1am Fri); 11-12.30am Sat; 11-11 Sun
☎ (01651) 806235 🌐 ythanviewhotel.co.uk
Beer range varies Ⓗ
Traditional inn in the village centre, home to the MCC (Methlick Cricket Club) and numerous other local clubs. The small public bar at the rear is heavily sports-themed. Bands play on some Saturdays and quiz nights are also hosted. A log fire warms the large lounge/restaurant. The pub is renowned for Jay's special curry with whole chillis – a challenge worth taking! Beers mainly come from Scottish micros and from the Waverley guest list. Haddo House, Tolquhon Castle and Pitmedden Garden are close by. ♨❀⇌◐⊟🚌♣

Milltown of Rothiemay

Forbes Arms Hotel

AB54 7LT
⏲ 12-2.30 (not Mon & Tue), 5-11 ☎ (01466) 711248
🌐 forbesarms.co.uk
Beer range varies Ⓗ
Small family-run hotel in a pleasant country location near the River Deveron. It has public and lounge bars and a separate dining area. Fishing and shooting activities are nearby. The local folk club hosts a live session on the second Thursday of the month. Two beers are usually available, sourced from Scottish micros and from Welsh breweries, including Brains. Accommodation is in six en-suite rooms. ❀⇌◐⊟♿P

Netherley

Lairhillock Inn

AB39 3QS (¼ mile E of B979, signed from B979 and A90)
⏲ 11-11 (midnight Fri & Sat) ☎ (01569) 730001
🌐 lairhillock.co.uk
Caledonian Deuchars IPA; Taylor Landlord; guest beer Ⓗ
The 'INN' sign on the roof of this rambling building in attractive open countryside makes it easy to spot from the road. It has a traditional, wood-panelled bar warmed by a large log fire in winter, and a lounge with a large conservatory area, popular for dining. A separate restaurant, the Crynoch, is available for finer dining. The guest beer is usually from Cairngorm Brewery. Convenient for the attractions of Stonehaven and Royal Deeside. ♨Q⚑❀◐⊟♿♣P

Oldmeldrum

Redgarth Hotel

Kirk Brae, AB51 0DJ (off A947 towards golf course, signed on A947)
⏲ 11-3, 5-11 (11.45 Fri & Sat); 12-3, 5-11 Sun
☎ (01651) 872353 🌐 redgarth.com
Beer range varies Ⓗ/Ⓖ
Winner of many local CAMRA awards, this renowned hotel has imposing views over the eastern Grampian mountains. A successful blend of popular family restaurant and marvellous real ale pub, it is appreciated by a dedicated core of regulars who come from miles around to sample the imaginatively chosen beers. During occasional Brewers in Residence evenings, three handpumped ales may be supplemented by many more on gravity. ⚑❀⇌◐Å🚌(305,325)♣⚊

Peterhead

Cross Keys ✔

23-27 Chapel Street, AB42 1TH
⏲ 7am-11pm (midnight Fri & Sat) ☎ (01779) 483500
Caledonian Deuchars IPA; Greene King Abbot; Isle of Skye Cross Keys; guest beers Ⓗ
This welcome Wetherspoon's outlet in a beer desert was opened in 2008. The name derives from a chapel dedicated to St Peter, which previously stood on the site. It has a single long room with the bar towards the front and a large seating area to the rear. A sheltered and heated area outside caters for hardy souls and smokers. There are at least two guest ales, typically one Scottish and one English. Opens 7am for coffee and breakfast; children are welcome until 8pm if dining.
❀◐♿🚌🍎⚊

Skene

Red Star

Kirktown of Skene, AB32 6XE
⏲ 12-2.30 Wed & Thu (summer only), 5-11; 12-2.30, 5-1am Fri; 11-12.30am Sat; 12.30-11 Sun ☎ (01224) 743264
Beer range varies Ⓗ
This friendly community pub is situated in the centre of a small village at the edge of the Aberdeen commuter belt. Opened in 1948, the pub has a restaurant/lounge and a public bar, well-patronised by local residents. One handpump serves a beer from Deeside Brewery.
❀◐⊟🚌(215)P⚊

Stonehaven

Marine Hotel 🏆

9-10 Shorehead, AB39 2JY (on harbour front)
⏲ 11-midnight (1am Fri & Sat); 11-midnight (11 winter) Sun
☎ (01569) 762155 🌐 marinehotelstonehaven.co.uk
Inveralmond Dunnottar Ale; Taylor Landlord; guest beers Ⓗ
This small harbourside hotel features simple wood panelling in the bar and a rustic lounge with an open fireplace. Upstairs, the restaurant has been recently refurbished and has its own handpumps. Outside seating is available. The bar offers an unusual selection of Belgian beers on draught and a large choice of bottled beers from around the world. Historic Dunnottar Castle is one mile south. Scottish CAMRA Pub Of The Year 2008 and local Branch Pub of the Year 2009 and 2010.
♨❀⇌◐Å🚌(107,117)⚊▯

Ship Inn

5 Shorehead, AB39 2JY (on harbour front)
11-midnight (1am Fri & Sat); 12-midnight Sun
(01569) 762617 shipinnstonehaven.com
Beer range varies H
Traditional harbour-front bar with an outdoor seating area overlooking the water protected by a low wall. Inside, a mirror from the defunct Devanha Brewery is a prominent feature. Two beers are offered, one usually from the Inveralmond Brewery, and an extensive range of malt whiskies is stocked. A modern restaurant, with panoramic harbour views, is adjacent to the bar, with food available all day at the weekend.
(107,117)

Tarland

Aberdeen Arms

The Square, AB34 4TX
12-midnight (1am Fri & Sat); 12.30-11 Sun
(01339) 881225
Inveralmond Minstrel Ale; guest beer H
Three-hundred-year-old listed building situated on the town square. On cold days there is a roaring coal fire in the public/lounge bar and pool is played in an adjacent side room. Excellent home-made food is served. Regular music evenings take place in the bar on Tuesday, often featuring star fiddler and village resident Paul Anderson. The guest ale supplementing the Minstrel house beer is usually also from Inveralmond Brewery.
(210)P

Douglas Arms Hotel, Banchory

ARGYLL & THE ISLES

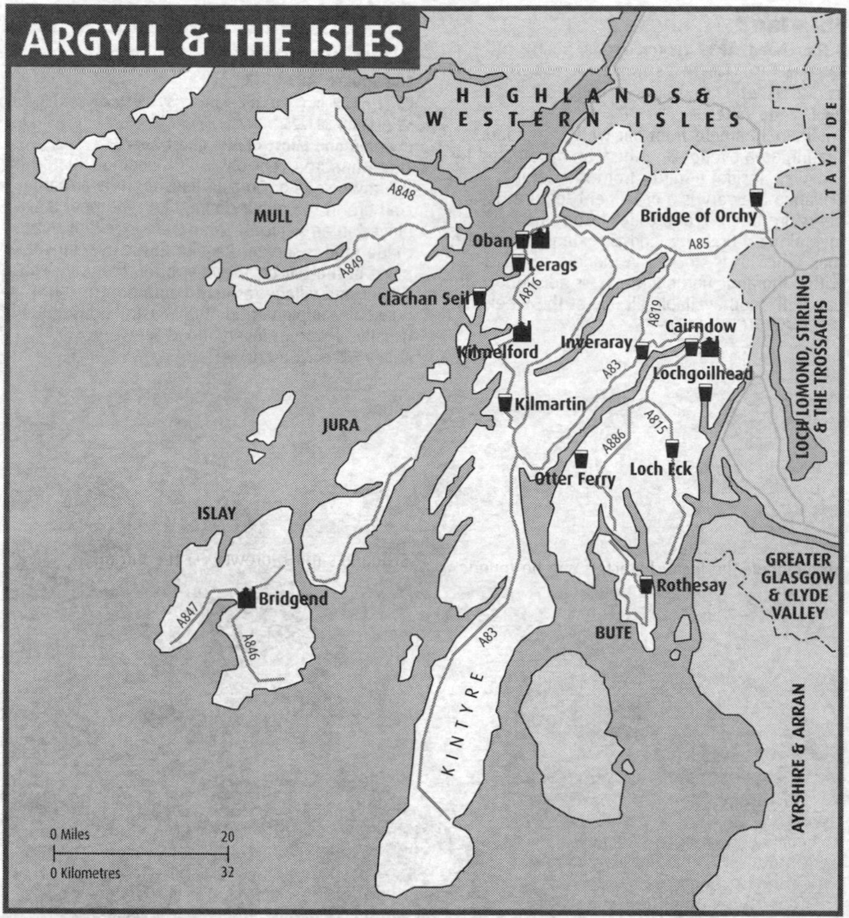

Authority area covered: Argyll & Bute UA

Bridge of Orchy

Bridge of Orchy Hotel ✓

PA36 4AD (on A82 at N end of Glen Orchy between Tyndrum & Glencoe) NN296396
11-11 (11.45 Fri & Sat); 12.30-11 Sun ☎ (01838) 400208
bridgeoforchy.co.uk
Caledonian Deuchars IPA; guest beers H
A stopping-off point en-route to Glencoe and the Western Highlands, this hotel has a recently refurbished café-style bar, which opens to the restaurant with views of the glen. The river and mountains around are well-worth exploring. The three handpumps dispense mainly Scottish ales, and good quality food and coffee are served. The West Highland Way, Citylink buses and West Coast Railway pass close to the hotel. The hotel also offers excellent on-site bunkhouse accommodation popular with walkers, climbers, skiers and trekkers. May close temporarily in winter.
(914) P

Cairndow

Stagecoach Inn

PA26 8BN (near head of Loch Fyne just off A83) NN181109
11-11 (1am Fri & Sat); 12-11 Sun ☎ (01499) 600 286
cairndowinn.com
Fyne Avalanche; guest beers H
Tucked away on the original main road, now a quiet backwater, look for the signs on the A83 to find this charming old coaching inn. This is the de facto tap room for nearby Fyne Ales and not to be missed if you are in the area. The hotel has a cosy bar, several further rooms and a pool table. Food is available at all times and there are great views over the loch and surrounding mountains.
(926,976) P

Clachan Seil

Tigh an Truish

PA34 4QZ (on B844 5 miles W of A816 jct, by Clachan Bridge) NM785197
11-11 (11-2.30, 5-10 winter) ☎ (01852) 300242
tighantruish.co.uk
Beer range varies H

INDEPENDENT BREWERIES

Fyne Cairndow
Islay Bridgend
Oban Kilmelford (NEW)
Oban Bay Oban

Glasgow CAMRA Argyll Pub of the Year 2009, this friendly locals' pub is an essential stop for anyone travelling in the area, reached by crossing the Atlantic (Clachan Sound) over the famous bridge. In the main bar room the rustic L-shaped counter serves two changing beers, normally from Fyne Ales. There is a smaller lounge and separate restaurant/dining room. Clachan Bridge can be viewed from the bay windows and also from the garden, which is a treat in summer.
⛰❀⇄◑♿🚌(418)P

Inveraray

George Hotel

Main Street East, PA32 8TT
⏲ 11-midnight (12.30am Fri & Sat); 12-midnight Sun
☎ (01499) 302111 🌐 thegeorgehotel.co.uk
Beer range varies Ⓗ
The George lies in the centre of a historic conservation town. It was founded 150 years ago in buildings completed 90 years earlier and is still family run. At the heart of the building is a restaurant area leading to a cocktail bar at the rear, with stone floors and walls, and roaring fires throughout. The local characters can be found watching TV in the vibrant public bar to one side. Beers come from Houston and Fyne Ales.
⛰Q⇄❀⇄◑⊟♿⛺🚌(926,976)P⊱

Kilmartin

Kilmartin Hotel

PA31 8RQ (on A816 10 miles N of Lochgilphead) NR835989
⏲ 11 (5 winter)-11 (1am Fri & Sat); 12-11 Sun
☎ (01546) 510250 🌐 kilmartin-hotel.com
Caledonian Deuchars IPA, 80; guest beers Ⓗ
A visit to scenic Kilmartin Glen is a must for anyone interested in stone carvings, standing stones, burial cairns and other prehistoric relics, dating back 5000 years. After a day exploring, this 19th-century family-run hotel is the perfect retreat. Offering up to three Scottish ales and a wide range of excellent home-made meals, it is so cosy and welcoming that you might be tempted to stay the night.
Q❀⇄◑🚌(423)P⊱

Lerags

Barn

Cologin, PA34 4SE (down minor road off A816) NM853260
⏲ 12-1am summer (closed Mon-Thu; 5-11 Fri; 12-11 Sat winter); 12-11 Sun ☎ (01631) 571313 🌐 myspace.com/barnbar
Fyne Highlander; guest beer Ⓗ
The Barn is part of a holiday complex of chalets and lodges situated in isolated hills just south of Oban. Once a cattle shed, the slate slats are still in place and help to maintain a cosy atmosphere. Despite the remote location, scenic hills and coastlines make it popular with visitors and locals, and it is a centre for outdoor activities. Out of season it is wise to check opening times. The guest beer is often from Fyne Ales. Q❀◑♿⛺P⊱

Loch Eck

Coylet Inn

PA23 8SG (on A815 near S end of Loch Eck) NS143885
⏲ closed Mon (& Tue winter); 11-midnight; 12-10.30 Sun
☎ (01369) 840426 🌐 coyletinn.co.uk
Fyne Highlander; guest beers Ⓗ
This hotel nestles in an idyllic setting near the southern end of Loch Eck. The views of loch and mountains will have you reaching for your camera. The cosy bar room has a large log fire and a wooden corner-counter with two handpumps. Good bar food includes local game and seafood, with a more formal restaurant upstairs. Excellent, seasonal, locally-sourced food and grand views make the restaurant popular so booking is recommended. ⛰❀⇄◑🚌(484)P⊱

Whistlefield Inn

PA23 8SG NS144933
⏲ 12.30-11 (midnight Fri & Sat) ☎ (01369) 860440
🌐 whistlefield.com
Beer range varies Ⓗ
This small but popular inn is situated up a hill close to the junction of the Ardentinny road off the A815. The views of Lock Eck below are truly striking. The cellar dates originally from the 15th-century but most rooms are more modern. Three handpumps supply beers sourced mainly from south-west Scotland's micro-breweries. The inn offers hotel rooms upstairs and there is also good value bunkhouse accommodation. ⛰⇄❀⇄◑🚌P

Lochgoilhead

Shore House Inn

PA24 8AD (at head of Loch Goil) NN198015
⏲ closed Tue; 12 (5 winter)-11; 12-11 Sun
☎ (01301) 703340 🌐 theshorehouse.net
Fyne Highlander; guest beers Ⓗ
Built in the 1850s, this former parish manse is set amid spectacular scenery at the head of Loch Goil. It is also within the Argyll Forest and Loch Lomond and the Trossachs National Parks, making it an ideal base for outdoor pursuits. The comfortable bar has two handpumps serving Fyne Ales. Views of the loch and mountains from the waterside lawn and large restaurant are impressive. The varied food menu includes authentic pizzas cooked in a wood-fired oven. Q❀⇄◑♿🚌(484)♣P⊱

Oban

Lorne Bar

Stevenson Street, PA34 5NA
⏲ 12-1am (2am Fri & Sat); 12.30-2am Sun
☎ (01631) 570 020
Caledonian Deuchars IPA; guest beer Ⓗ
It is worth exploring the smaller streets of the 'Gateway to the Isles' to find this welcoming local. The family-friendly traditional pub has an impressive island bar with twisted brass pillars. The food is popular with locals and there is an extended choice of real ale in summer. Outside is a sheltered garden area – a rarity in the town. Oban can be reached on a day trip from Glasgow and is an ideal base for taking ferries to the islands.
❀◑⇌🚌⊱

Tartan Tavern

3 Albany Terrace, George Street, PA34 5NY
⏲ 11 (12.30 Sun)-1am ☎ (01631) 562118
Beer range varies Ⓗ
Compact locals' bar with comfortable tartan upholstered seating and neat tables. Unusually, the walls are covered with padded tartan and brown

cushions. A grand display of whisky miniatures surrounds the top of the bar room. A small corner-counter dispenses two ever-changing guest ales. Low spot and wall lighting adds to the cosy feel. Quiet background music plays or sport is screened. Worth seeking out in a narrow street.

Otter Ferry

Oystercatcher

PA21 2DH (on B8000 on E coast of Loch Fyne) NR930845
11 (12 Sun)-11 ☎ (01700) 821229
theoystercatcher.co.uk
Fyne Highlander; guest beer
Large, friendly pub, serving local Fyne Ales and guests such as Taylor Landlord, located on the scenic eastern side of Loch Fyne. Accessible by car, bicycle or boat, the pub has its own pontoon and seven moorings. A spacious lawn borders the sea loch beach, popular for swimming and boating. Giant Jenga and chess are available in the bar, plus interesting books. Quality, locally-sourced food is served in the large bar and separate restaurant. Telephone to check opening hours in winter. P

Rothesay: Isle of Bute

Black Bull Inn

3 West Princess Street, PA20 9AF (on promenade)
11 -11 (midnight Fri & Sat); 12.30-11 Sun
☎ (01700) 502366
Caledonian Deuchars IPA
Leave the mainland from the Edwardian splendour of Wemyss Bay station, disembark in Rothesay and visit the superb Victorian toilets before enjoying a beer in this pub with two bars. Outside, join a tour to Mount Stuart House and gardens, returning to the pub, conveniently situated near the ferry terminal, for good food and a final pint before departing for the mainland – a perfect day out.

George Hotel, Inveraray

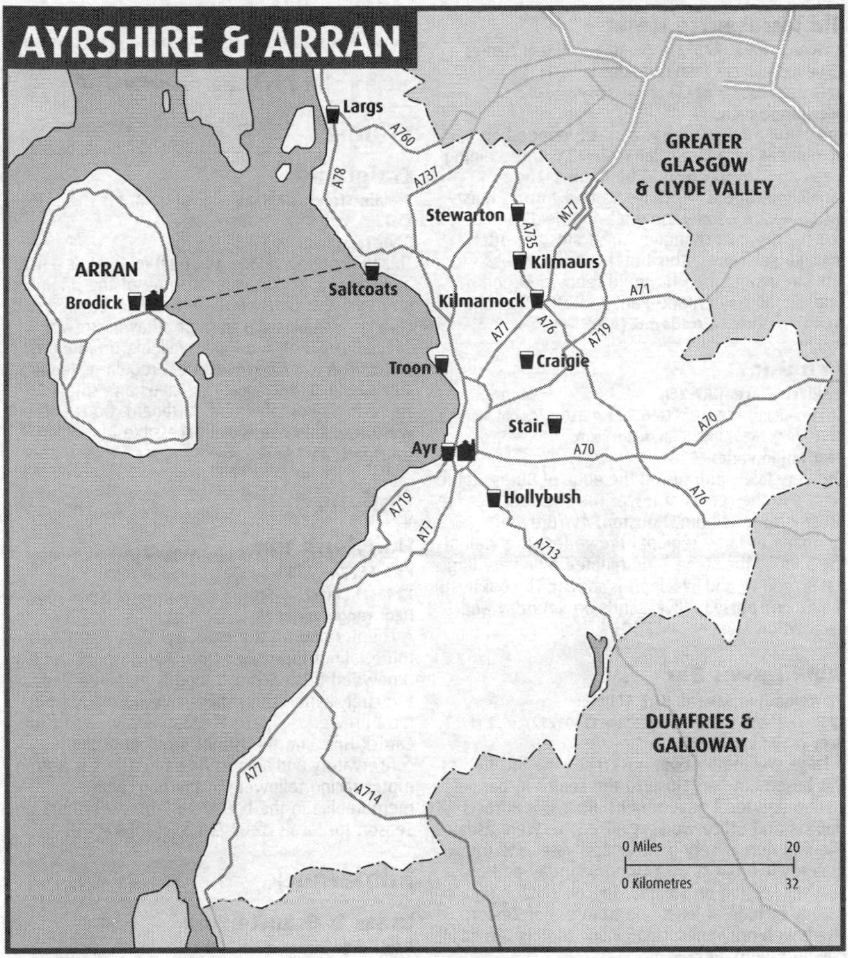

Authority areas covered: East Ayrshire UA, North Ayrshire UA, South Ayrshire UA

Ayr

Chestnuts Hotel

52 Racecourse Road, KA7 2UZ (A719, 1 Mile S of centre)

11-midnight (12.30am Sat); 12-midnight Sun

(01292) 264393 chestnutshotel.com

Beer range varies H

This hotel was once a centre for the town's Jewish community. It has a warm, comfortable lounge bar with a wood-panelled ceiling and an unusual collection of water jugs. The two real ales change constantly, sourced from both local and national breweries. Meals are of a very high standard and served in the bar or restaurant. The venue is handy for the seafront and golf courses.

(A9)P

Geordie's Byre

103 Main Street, KA8 8BU (N of centre, over river towards Prestwick)

11-11 (midnight Thu-Sat); 12.30-11 Sun

(01292) 264925

Beer range varies A

This CAMRA award-winning gem of a pub serves up to four guest ales sourced from far and near. The owners have reigned supreme for more than 30 years. Both the public bar and the lounge feature a wealth of memorabilia. A wide range of malt whiskies and rums is also available – ask for the list. CAMRA Branch Pub of the Year 2009.

(Newton-on-Ayr)

Glen Park Hotel

5 Racecourse Road, KA7 2DG

10-12.30am; 12-midnight Sun (01292) 263891

glenparkhotel.com

Ayr Leezie Lundie, Jolly Beggars, Towzie Tyke H

This hotel is in an 1860s B-Listed Victorian residence at the corner of Miller and Racecourse roads, midway between the seafront and the station. The lounge bar has an open fire within a magnificent mahogany surround, and there is an excellent restaurant. The hotel is now home to Ayr Brewing Company and offers three beers from the micro-brewery. The outdoor seating area at the front has sunset views in the summer months.

(A9)P

INDEPENDENT BREWERIES

Arran Brodick
Ayr Ayr (NEW)

Old Racecourse Hotel

2 Victoria Park, KA7 2TR (A719 1 mile S of centre)
11-midnight (12.30am Fri & Sat); 12.30-11 Sun
☎ (01292) 262873 oldracecoursehotel.co.uk
Beer range varies H
This family-run hotel has a small lounge bar dominated by a large flat-screen TV, three dining areas and seven en-suite bedrooms. The racecourse in the name refers to a former horse-racing venue nearby, now playing fields and a golf course. The two changing guest ales are often unusual selections. This hotel is an ideal base to visit the nearby beach, world-renowned golf courses, Burns Heritage Park and other delights of south Ayrshire. (A9)P

Twa Dugs

4 Killoch Place, KA7 2EA
11-midnight (12.30am Fri & Sat); 12.30-midnight Sun
☎ (01292) 288971 thetwadugs.co.uk
Beer range varies H
This very lively pub sits on the edge of Burns Statue Square in the centre of town. The two real ales are usually from Kelburn, Houston, Ayr Brewing Company or large regional breweries. The wall at the back of the stage is dominated by a very large flat-screen TV and live sport is shown. The bar hosts a quiz on Thursday, live bands on Saturday and karaoke on Sunday.

Wellingtons Bar

17 Wellington Square, KA7 1EZ
11-12.30am; 12.30-midnight Sun ☎ (01292) 262794
Beer range varies H
A large Wellington boot advertises the location of this basement bar. Close to the seafront, bus station and local government offices, it attracts tourists and office workers alike. The Wednesday evening quiz is very popular and weekend music features live bands or a DJ on Saturday and an acoustic session on Sunday. The two changing ales usually include at least one from either Kelburn or Strathaven breweries. Good value food is served all day until 9pm.

West Kirk ✔

58A Sandgate, KA7 1BX
10-12.30am; 10-midnight Sun ☎ (01292) 880416
Caledonian Deuchars IPA; guest beers H
This Wetherspoon's conversion of a former church retains many of the original features – access to the toilets is via the pulpit. Up to six changing guest ales are offered and local micros are usually well-represented. Meals are available all day, with breakfast from 9am. The pub is centrally located and close to the bus station. The front drinking area has a shelter for smokers.

Brodick: Isle of Arran

Ormidale Hotel

Knowe Road, KA27 8BY (off A841 at W end of village)
12-2.30 (summer only), 4.30-midnight; 12-midnight Sat & Sun ☎ (01770) 302293 ormidale-hotel.co.uk
Arran Ale, Blonde; guest beers A
This large red sandstone hotel is set in seven acres of grounds, including a large wooded area. The bar serves its ales through traditional tall founts. Beer prices are rather expensive considering the proximity of Arran Brewery. The public bar has tables in the shape of Arran and the large conservatory hosts discos and live music during the summer. There is an attractive beer garden with views across Brodick Bay. Accommodation is only available in summer, when guest beers will occasionally be available. P

Craigie

Craigie Inn

5 Main Street, KA1 5LY (signed off B730)
12-2, 5-11 ☎ (01563) 860286
Beer range varies H
This welcoming village inn, built in 1604, is a listed building and still maintains some of the original features. The function room has a lovely beamed ceiling. Real ales are from Strathaven Brewery. Special offers on food are available on Monday evening. A folk club meets here regularly, featuring jam sessions with local musicians and singers. There is a pool table and dartboard. Dogs are welcome. This pub is not accessible by public transport. QP

Hollybush

Hollybush Inn

KA6 6EY (on A713 Ayr-Dalmellington road)
11-11 (1am Fri & Sat); 12.30-midnight ☎ (01292) 560580
Beer range varies H
A country pub on the main Ayr-Galloway tourist route, about four miles from Ayr Hospital. Locally renowned fresh Scottish food is prepared daily by the chef owner. Guest beers are normally from local breweries. There are stunning views of the Carrick Hills and the Isle of Arran from the conservatory and an outside patio. There is a strong motor racing following in the pub, with memorabilia in the bar and a fantasy Formula One Season for locals. (52)P

Kilmarnock

Brass & Granite

53 Grange Street, KA1 2DD
11-midnight (12.30am Thu-Sat); 12.30-midnight Sun
☎ (01563) 523431
Beer range varies H
Open-plan town-centre pub in a quiet street behind the main post office, popular with all ages. Guest beers tend to be from Scotland or Cumbria, and Belgian fruit beers are available on draught as well as a variety of bottled ales. Food is served all day. Several large TVs screen mostly sporting events. A pub quiz is held on Sunday, Monday and Wednesday. Many bus routes pass close by, and bus and railway stations are within walking distance.

Wheatsheaf Inn ✔

70 Portland Street, KA1 1JG
10-11 (midnight Thu; 1am Fri & Sat); 10-midnight Sun
☎ (01563) 572483
Caledonian Deuchars IPA; Greene King Abbot; guest beers H
Large town-centre Lloyds No 1 bar a short walk from the bus and rail stations. It is divided into various seating areas, with booths, sofas and a raised dining space. No music plays Sunday to Wednesday, but a DJ entertains on Friday and Saturday – however the pub is large enough to find a quiet space if desired. The food menu is standard Wetherspoon fare. Real cider is stocked from the usual JDW range.

Kilmaurs

Weston Tavern

27 Main Street, KA3 2RQ
11-midnight (1am Fri & Sat); 12.30-midnight Sun
(01563) 538805 westontavern.co.uk
Beer range varies Ⓗ
Housed in the former manse of reformist minister David Smeaton, a contemporary of Robert Burns, this is a classic country pub and restaurant. It sits beside the former jailhouse and tollbooth. The public bar features a tiled floor, stone walls and a wood-burning fire, and hosts live music on the last Saturday of the month. The popular restaurant is to the rear. (1,337)

Largs

Charlie Smith's

14 Gallowgate Street, KA30 8LX (on A78, opp pier)
10-midnight (1am Fri & Sat); 12.30-midnight Sun
(01475) 672250
Beer range varies Ⓗ
Situated on the seafront opposite the pier and Cumbrae ferry terminal, and close to the railway station, this is a child-free pub serving good value food all day. The ever-changing beer is sometimes local but often from one of the larger regional brewers. Handy for the Waverley paddle steamer in summer. (585,901)

MacAulays

85-87 Main Street, KA30 8AJ (opp railway station)
11-midnight (1am Fri & Sat); 12.30-midnight Sun
(01475) 687359
Beer range varies Ⓗ
Busy but friendly one-room pub situated on the main street of this popular Clyde Coast town. Opposite the railway station, it is also on main bus routes and close to the ferry to Cumbrae. One real ale from the Belhaven guest list tends to be 4% ABV or below. There is also a good range of malt whiskies. A simple menu of good honest home-cooked food is available all day. The pub hosts karaoke evenings. (585,901)♣

Saltcoats

Salt Cot ✔

7 Hamilton Street, KA21 5DS
10-11 (midnight Thu; 1am Fri & Sat); 12.30-11 Sun
(01294) 465924
Greene King Abbot; guest beers Ⓗ
A good Wetherspoon's conversion of a former cinema. The pub gets its name from the original cottages at the salt pans. It has an area where children are permitted and there is a family menu. One guest beer usually comes from Strathaven Ales. Although there are TVs in the bar area the sound is only turned on a few times a year for rugby internationals. Licensed from 10am, it opens at 9am for breakfast. Q

Stair

Stair Inn

KA5 5HW (on B730 7 miles E of Ayr)
12-11 (1am Fri & Sat); 12.30-11 Sun (01292) 591650
stairinn.co.uk
Beer range varies Ⓗ
This family-run hotel, on the banks of the River Ayr, is not accessible by public transport but is well-worth seeking out. The comfortable bar and restaurant feature bespoke hand-made furniture and the bedrooms are furnished in a similar style. A single real ale is available, often from Houston Brewery. The food menu relies heavily on local produce – fish from the inn's own smokehouse is a speciality. Booking for meals at weekends is strongly recommended. QP

Stewarton

Millhouse Hotel

6-8 Dean Street, KA3 5EQ
11-midnight (1am Fri & Sat); 12-midnight Sun
(01560) 482255
Beer range varies Ⓗ
Enthusiastic owners have brought real ale back to the 'Bonnet Toun' after a long absence. Beer is available in the bar and on request in the restaurant/function suite. One of the two ales is usually from Kelburn, Houston or Strathaven breweries, with guests from just about anywhere. The bar is dog-friendly and the side courtyard is a suntrap in summer. The pub is a meeting place for the Bonnet Guild that organises the town's annual festival. (1)P

Troon

Bruce's Well

91 Portland Street, KA10 6QN
12 (11 Sat)-12.30am; 12-midnight Sun (01292) 311429
Caledonian Deuchars IPA; guest beers Ⓗ
Friendly, spacious and comfortable lounge bar close to Troon town centre. The bar benefits from a temperature-controlled cellar situated next door. Major sporting events are shown on a number of flat-screen TVs and the pub gets extremely busy during big matches. Occasional live music nights are hosted. Guest beers are often from Cairngorm Brewery. (14,10/110)

Cheeky Charlie's

47 Templehill, KA10 6BQ
10-12.30 (midnight Sun) (01292) 311038
Beer range varies Ⓗ
An entertainment-led pub with karaoke, quiz nights and poker evenings as well as darts and dominoes. The juke-box and pool table are free to play in the early part of the week. The beer is often Belhaven 80/-, a Stewart Brewing beer or a seasonal beer from the Belhaven list. The pub is at its busiest late on weekend evenings, and sports events are shown on TV. Over-60s receive a discount on all drinks. (15,10/110)♣

Harbour Bar

169 Templehill, KA10 6BH (opp P&O ferry terminal)
11 (10 Sat & Sun)-12.30am (01292) 312668
Fuller's London Pride; guest beers Ⓗ
Overlooking Troon's North Bay, a central bar serves the lounge and public bars. Both are nautically themed and decorated with pictures and artefacts from the now-closed Ailsa Shipyard. The public bar has a pool table and a well-stocked juke-box, the lounge bar has a dartboard. Two real ales (three in summer) are offered, with guests mostly from local breweries and reasonably priced for the area. A good range of malt whiskies and rums is also available. Popular meals are served throughout the day. (15,10/110)♣P

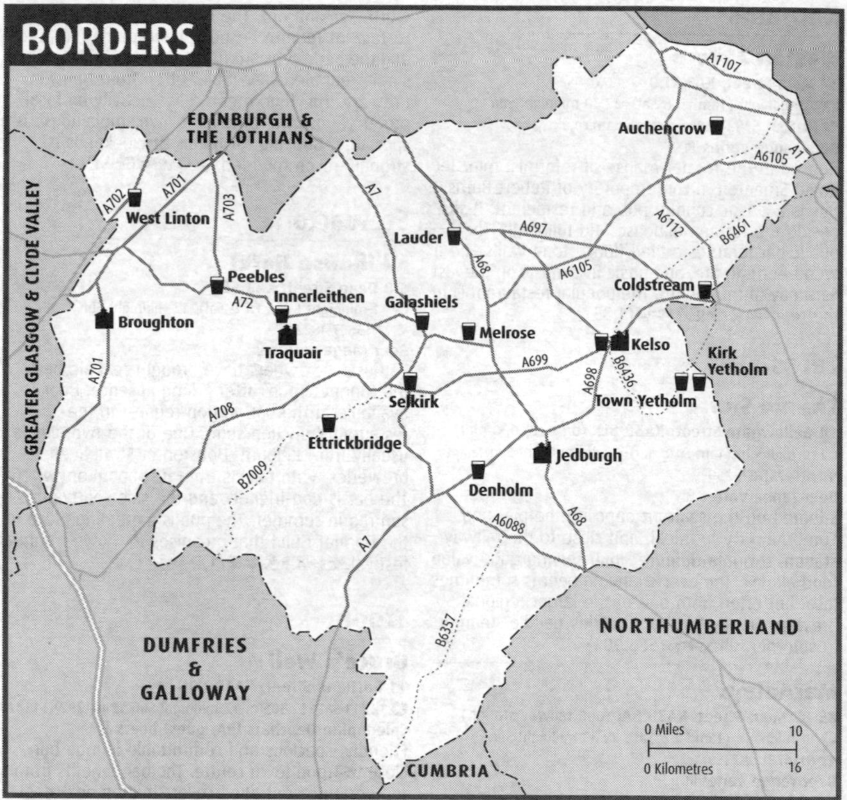

Authority area covered: Scottish Borders UA

Auchencrow

Craw Inn 🏆

TD14 5LS (signed from A1)

⏲ 12-2.30, 6-11 (midnight Fri); 12-midnight Sat; 12.30-11 Sun ☎ (01890) 761253 🌐 thecrawinn.co.uk

Beer range varies Ⓗ

This friendly 17th-century village inn is really the hub of the community. The traditional single bar features beams festooned with pump clips, a wood-burning stove, numerous tables and ample seating. Excellent home-cooked food is served every day in both the bar and the well-appointed restaurant. Summer drinking and dining can be enjoyed on decking outside. Children are welcome. A beer festival is held in November.
⌂Q✿⇌◑♿⊟♣P

Coldstream

Besom

75-77 High Street, TD12 4AE

⏲ 11-midnight (1am Fri & Sat); 12.30-midnight Sun ☎ (01890) 882391

Caledonian Deuchars IPA; guest beer Ⓗ

The first and last pub in Scotland, this little three-roomed gem has remained relatively unchanged since it was built in the 1890s and revamped circa 1910. The cosy bar retains its original counter and gantry, while the diverse range of memorabilia, bookshelves and comfortable seating creates the feel of a living room rather than a pub. Leading through from the lounge is a room dedicated entirely to the memory of the Coldstream Guards. Children are welcome in the lounge, dogs permitted in the bar. ⌂Q✿◑⊟⊟♣⊢

Denholm

Auld Cross Keys Hotel

Main Street, TD9 8NU

⏲ 12 (12.30 Sun)-11 (midnight Thu, 1am Fri & Sat) ☎ (01450) 870305 🌐 crosskeysdenholm.co.uk

Beer range varies Ⓗ

Overlooking the green, this small hotel retains the character of a village inn. The plain and functional public bar may be favoured by drinkers; however, there is also a more comfortable lounge bar. The beer is from Hadrian & Border or Northumberland breweries. Folk music sessions and concerts are regular events. Meals are served 1-7pm on Sunday. Children are welcome until 9pm, and dogs are permitted in the bar. ⌂Q✿⇌◑⊟⊟(20)♣P

Fox & Hounds Inn

Main Street, TD9 8NU

⏲ 11.30-3, 5-midnight Mon & Tue; 11.30-midnight (1am Fri & Sat); 12.30-midnight Sun ☎ (01450) 870247

Wylam Gold Tankard; guest beer Ⓗ

INDEPENDENT BREWERIES

Broughton Broughton
Scottish Borders Jedburgh (NEW)
Tempest Kelso (NEW)
Traquair Traquair

Village local, built in 1728, overlooking the village green. The small bar is half wood-panelled and a real fire adds a cosy warmth in winter. Pictures and memorabilia decorate the walls. The rear lounge has a coffee-house feel and there is a dining room upstairs open in the evening. In summer the courtyard offers sheltered outdoor drinking and has a smoking area. Children are welcome until 8pm. Free Wi-Fi. Dogs permitted. ⏣❀✉◗ ⏚❑(20)♣⌐

Ettrickbridge

Cross Keys Inn
TD7 5JN
✪ closed Mon-Wed winter; 12 (12.30 Sun)-2.30, 6.30-10.30 (11 Thu-Sat) ☎ (01750) 52224 ⏣ cross-keys-inn.co.uk
Beer range varies Ⓗ
Situated in the historic Ettrick valley, this inn dates from the 17th century. The cosy and welcoming bar and dining room are decorated with old photographs, water jugs and the odd stuffed animal. The emphasis here is on food and tables are set for dining, however there are stools at the bar and a smaller room available for drinkers. The real ales are often from smaller Scottish breweries such as Broughton and Inveralmond. Children are welcome. ⏣Q❀✉◗よ♣◗P

Galashiels

Salmon Inn
54 Bank Street, TD1 1EP
✪ 11-11 (midnight Thu; 1am Fri & Sat); 12.30-midnight Sun ☎ (01896) 752577
Caledonian Deuchars IPA; guest beers Ⓗ
Comfortable, friendly, centrally-situated pub, which can be very lively when sports events are screened on TV. The L-shaped room is decorated with historic photographs of the Galashiels area. Guest beers are often from smaller Scottish and English breweries. Good home-cooked meals are popular (no food Sun or Tue and Sat eves). Children are welcome at lunchtime only. Dogs permitted. ❀◗よ⏚❑♣⌐

Innerleithen

St Ronan's Hotel
High Street, EH44 6HF
✪ 11-midnight (12.45am Fri & Sat); 12-midnight Sun ☎ (01896) 831487 ⏣ stronanshotel.co.uk
Beer range varies Ⓗ
This village hotel takes its name from a local saint. The functional public bar is long and thin with a brick and wooden fireplace. There are two alcoves – one with seating, the other with a dartboard and a photograph of the village. There is also a pool room. Meals are served daily until 8pm (times and menu vary in winter). Children and dogs are welcome. The pub offers a pick-up service for Southern Upland Way walkers. Wi-Fi access is available. ⏣❀✉◗ ▲❑(62)♣P⌐

Traquair Arms Hotel
Traquair Road, EH44 6PD (B709, off A72)
✪ 11-11 (midnight Fri & Sat); 12-11.30 Sun ☎ (01896) 830229 ⏣ traquairarmshotel.co.uk
Caledonian Deuchars IPA; Taylor Landlord; Traquair Bear Ale Ⓗ
Elegant 18th-century hotel in the scenic Tweed Valley. The comfortable lounge bar features a welcoming real fire in winter and a relaxing tropical fish tank. An Italian bistro area and

separate restaurant provide plenty of room for diners. Food is served all day at weekends. This is one of the few outlets for draught ales from Traquair House. Children are welcome and dogs permitted. ⏣❀✉◗よ▲❑(62)P

Kelso

Cobbles Inn
7 Bowmont Street, TD5 7JH (off NE side of town square)
✪ 11-3, 5-10 (1am Fri); 11-midnight Sat; 12-3, 5-10 Sun ☎ (01573) 223548 ⏣ thecobblesinn.co.uk
Tempest Emanation Pale Ale, Elemental Porter, Into the Light Blonde Ⓗ
An award-winning gastro-pub offering an eclectic mix of British classics, Pacific Rim and modern European cuisine using the finest locally-sourced and seasonal ingredients. To the right of the main dining area is a lounge bar where beers from the inn's own micro-brewery are featured. Though the focus is on food, drinkers are always welcome here. Private functions are catered for upstairs. Free Wi-Fi access. ⏣❀◗よ❑

Kirk Yetholm

Border Hotel 🏆
The Green, TD5 8PQ
✪ 11-midnight (1am Fri & Sat); 12-11 winter; 12-midnight Sun ☎ (01573) 420237 ⏣ theborderhotel.com
Beer range varies Ⓗ
This 260-year-old coaching inn is a mecca for walkers, situated at the beginning of the Pennine Way and on the ancient St Cuthbert's Way. The walls of the wood-beamed bar are adorned with photographs of local gypsies and friezes showing country pursuits. The hotel is noted for its hearty food served in the bar and conservatory. Dogs and children are welcome. Voted local CAMRA Pub of the Year 2010. Free Wi-Fi access. ⏣❀✉◗ ▲❑♣P

Lauder

Black Bull Hotel
Market Place, TD2 6SR
✪ 11-11 (midnight Fri & Sat); 12-11 ☎ (01578) 722208 ⏣ blackbull-lauder.com
Caledonian Deuchars IPA; Taylor Landlord; guest beer Ⓗ
Overlooking the small square, this well-appointed coaching inn enjoys a reputation for good food. Meals are served all day on Saturday and Sunday. The small wood-panelled bar, adorned with artefacts and retaining much of the character of yester-year, leads through to various dining areas. Dogs and children are welcome. Free Wi-Fi access. Q❀✉◗よ▲❑(29)♣P

Melrose

Burt's Hotel
Market Square, TD6 9PL
✪ 11 (12 Sun)-2, 5 (6 Sun)-11 ☎ (01896) 82225 ⏣ burtshotel.co.uk
Caledonian Deuchars IPA; guest beer Ⓗ
An elegant, family-run hotel in the main square, with colourful window boxes in summer. In the lounge bar the decor reflects the country sporting interests of many of the clientele. Here the focus is unashamedly on food, so those going in solely for a drink may find space at a premium. But the food is very good, so treat yourself. Weather permitting,

the beer garden is an option but only at lunchtime. Children and dogs are welcome. Free Wi-Fi access. ⛼Q❀⇌◐♿⚠🚌♣P

George & Abbotsford Hotel

High Street, TD6 9PD

11-11 (midnight Fri & Sat); 12-11 Sun ☎ (01896) 822308

georgeandabbotsford.co.uk

Beer range varies Ⓗ

Spacious hotel overlooking the main street. The comfortable bar and lounges offer real ales from both sides of the border. There is also a small shop selling an interesting selection of bottled beers. Look out for the hotel's beer festivals. Meals are served all day until 8.30pm. Children are welcome. ❀⇌🚌♣P

Peebles

Bridge Inn

Portbrae, EH45 8AW

11-midnight (1am Thu-Sat); 12-midnight Sun

☎ (01721) 720589

Caledonian Deuchars IPA; Stewart Pentland IPA; Taylor Landlord Ⓗ**; guest beer** Ⓖ

Cheerful single room town-centre local, also known as the 'Trust'. The mosaic entrance floor is evidence that this was once the Tweedside Inn. The bright, comfortable bar is decorated with jugs, bottles, memorabilia of outdoor pursuits and photographs of old Peebles. An outdoor heated patio area overlooks the river. The Gents is superb, with well maintained original Twyford Adamant urinals. It's a child-free zone, but dogs are welcome. Free Wi-Fi access. ❀⚠🚌(62)♣⊱

Cross Keys Hotel

Northgate, EH45 8RS

11-midnight (1am Fri & Sat); 12-11 Sun

☎ (01721) 724222 crosskeyspeebles.co.uk

Stewart Pentland IPA; guest beers Ⓗ

Old coaching inn dating from 1654, just off the High Street, with a spacious L-shaped lounge bar. The imposing bar and gantry were reclaimed from a demolished Edinburgh pub. Although generally relaxed, the pub can be lively during weekend evenings. Dogs are welcome. There are rumours of a resident ghost. ⛼❀⇌◐♿⚠♣P

Selkirk

Town Arms

1 Market Place, TD7 4BT

11 (12.30 Sun)-midnight (1am Fri & Sat) ☎ (01750) 20185

Beer range varies Ⓗ

A typical working men's pub, situated just off the market square within the historic centre of Selkirk. The interior is very traditional, with a massive island bar dominating the small main room and wood-panelled walls adorned with numerous brewery mirrors. Two rooms, one with a dartboard, lead off the bar and there is a further room upstairs with modern bar fittings. Note the rare metal Drybrough's fly screens in the front windows. Dogs are welcome. ⛼🚌(X95,72)♣

Town Yetholm

Plough Hotel

High Street, TD5 8RF

11-midnight (1am Fri & Sat) ☎ (01573) 420215

ploughhotelyetholm.co.uk

Black Sheep Ale; guest beer Ⓗ

A friendly village inn dating from 1710 set in rural surroundings near the end of the Pennine Way. A large wood-burning stove sitting beneath two stags heads dominates the bar where the locals mingle happily with visitors. A separate functional games room has a pool table and video machine. Hearty home-cooked meals are served in the bar and the attractive little dining room. Children are welcome until 8pm. ⛼❀⇌◐◧♿⚠🚌♣P

West Linton

Gordon Arms Hotel

Dolphinton Road, EH46 7DR (on A702)

11-11 (midnight Tue; 1am Fri & Sat); 12-11 Sun

☎ (01968) 660208 thegordon.co.uk

Caledonian Deuchars IPA; guest beer Ⓗ

Situated in a picturesque village, the pub has a large L-shaped, airy bar with stone walls and cornicing more reminiscent of an Edinburgh tenement pub than a village local. There is a roaring log fire in winter and comfortable sofas to relax in. Meals are available lunchtimes and evenings during the week and all day Saturday and Sunday in the bar, restaurant or dining area outside. Children and dogs are welcome. ⛼❀⇌◐◧⚠🚌(100,101)♣P⊱

What is real ale?

Real ale is also known as cask-conditioned beer or simply cask beer. In the brewery, the beer is neither filtered nor pasteurised. It still contains sufficient yeast and sugar for it to continue to ferment and mature in the cask. Once it has reached the pub cellar, it has to be laid down for maturation to continue, and for yeast and protein to settle at the bottom of the cask. Some real ale also has extra hops added as the cask is filled, a process known as 'dry hopping' for increased flavour and aroma. Cask beer is best served at a cellar temperature of 11-12 degrees C, although some stronger ales can benefit from being served a little warmer. Each cask has two holes, in one of which a tap is inserted and is connected to tubes or 'lines' that enable the beer to be drawn to the bar. The other hole, on top of the cask, enables some carbon dioxide produced during secondary fermentation to escape. It is vital that some gas, which gives the beer its natural sparkle or condition, is kept within the cask: the escape of gas is controlled by inserting porous wooden pegs called spiles into the spile hole. Real ale is a living product and must be consumed within three or four days of a cask being tapped as oxidation develops.

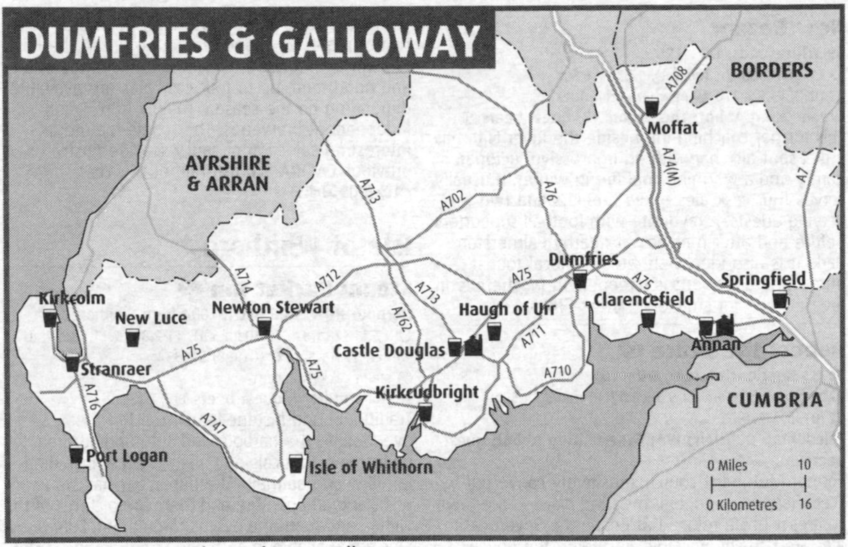

Authority area covered: Dumfries & Galloway UA

Annan

Bluebell Inn

10 High Street, DG12 6AG

11-11 (midnight Thu-Sat); 12.30-11 Sun

(01461) 202385

Caledonian Deuchars IPA; Greene King IPA; guest beers

A focus for cask ale enthusiasts in the Annan area for many years, this pub has won CAMRA's regional Pub of the Year title on several occasions. A former coaching inn, it is a busy, friendly hostelry offering three or four ales from throughout the UK. The outside courtyard at the rear provides a pleasant seated area in summer. The pub retains traditional features from its time within the Gretna & District State Management Scheme, notably the wood-lined interior.

Castle Douglas

Sulwath Brewery Tap Room

The Brewery, 209 King Street, DG7 1DT

10-5; closed Sun (01556) 504525

sulwathbrewers.co.uk

Beer range varies

Sulwath Brewery is the principal brewery in Dumfries & Galloway. Its ales have won a number of awards at various beer festivals north and south of the border. It has seven regular brews, with other seasonal ales featuring from time to time. The Tap Room is popular with real ale lovers around Castle Douglas. It offers four beers from the Sulwath range, with guest ales from other parts of the country on occasions. Q

Clarencefield

Farmers Inn

Main Street, DG1 4NF (on B724)

11-2.30, 6-11.30 (12.30am Fri); 12-12.30am Sat; 12.30-11.30 sun (01387) 870675 farmersinn.co.uk

Beer range varies

A small village pub with a good atmosphere and service. The building includes a post office and has a small bar and lounge with a warming stove and a separate games room. It serves a good mix of freshly prepared food and up to three ales from breweries nationwide. The pub is well-placed for a range of activities and nearby attractions include the eighth-century Ruthwell Cross and the world's first Savings Bank. P

Dumfries

Cavens Arms

20 Buccleuch Street, DG1 2AH

11-11 (midnight Thu-Sat); 12.30-11 Sun

(01387) 252896

Beer range varies

A busy town-centre pub with three house ales and four guest beers drawn from breweries from north and south of the border. Great value meals are served until 9pm daily except Monday. Occasional themed nights are hosted. Dumfries & Stewartry CAMRA Pub of the Year 2006-2009 and runner-up Scotland and Northern Ireland Pub of the Year in 2009.

Globe Inn

56 High Street, DG1 2JA (opp Loreburn Centre)

11-11 (midnight Thu-Sat); 12.30-midnight Sun

(01387) 252335

Caledonian Deuchars IPA; Sulwath Criffel

Steeped in tradition, this is the oldest pub in Dumfries (established 1610), and has been awarded a Pubs in Time plaque by CAMRA for its historic importance. Robert Burns was a frequent visitor to the Globe, his favourite 'howff'. A town-centre pub, situated just off the High Street, it has a large public bar with adjoining small snug bar and two small dining rooms. Lunch is served every day including Sunday and private dinners can be arranged. Live traditional music is often hosted on Sunday. Q

INDEPENDENT BREWERIES

Madcap Annan (NEW)
Sulwath Castle Douglas

New Bazaar

39 Whitesands, DG1 2RS

⏲ 11-11 (midnight Thu-Sat); 12.30-11 Sun

☎ (01387) 268776 🌐 newbazaardumfries.co.uk

Greene King Abbot; Theakston XB; guest beers Ⓗ

This former coaching inn beside the River Nith has a pleasant airy bar with an impressive Victorian gantry and a warming coal fire in winter. It usually serves four cask ales – two regulars and two varying guests. A favourite with football supporters before and after matches at nearby Palmerston Park, it is also ideally situated for local tourist attractions. Sky Sports is screened on TV. There is an area outside for smokers. ♨❀⇌🚌♣⚐

Robert the Bruce ✔

81-83 Buccleuch Street, DG1 1DJ

⏲ 11-midnight (1am Fri & Sat); 12.30-midnight Sun

☎ (01387) 270320

Caledonian Deuchars IPA; Greene King Abbot; guest beers Ⓗ

Former Methodist church sensitively converted by Wetherspoon. A popular meeting place in the town centre, it has a relaxed atmosphere. Seven cask ales are usually available, including the house beer, Robert the Bruce, brewed by Strathaven Brewery. Real ale festivals are a regular feature, with up to 40 ales on offer. The food menu is varied with a range of good value meals served all day every day. There is a pleasant seating area outside. ♿❀◑♿⇌🚌⚐

Tam o' Shanter

114-117 Queensberry Street, DG1 1BH

⏲ 11-midnight (11 Mon & Tue); 12.30-7.30 Sun

☎ (01387) 254055

Beer range varies Ⓗ

Well-positioned just off the high street, this 17th-century coaching inn, established in 1630, has featured highly in the Dumfries real ale scene for many years. A small, traditional pub with a main bar and a couple of small quiet rooms behind, it is comfortable, with a warming gas fire in the bar. It features a rotating range of three ales, two always from the Borders-based Broughton Brewery. Food is served from the Italian restaurant upstairs. Dog-friendly. Q⇌🚌♣

Waverley Bar

19 St Mary's Street, DG1 1LX (100m from railway station)

⏲ 11 (12.30 Sun)-11 ☎ (01387) 247878

Sulwath Waverley Steamer; guest beer Ⓗ

This Victorian free house, a traditional family-run pub close to Dumfries railway station, is a recent addition to the Dumfries real ale scene. The busy hostelry has a large traditional bar and a small quiet room at the back. It features satellite sports TV, weekly pub games and quiz nights. One or two cask ales are offered. The house beer is the 4.1% Waverley Steamer. Food is served all day, every day. A dog-friendly pub with a large covered smoking area outside. ❀◑⇌🚌⚐

Haugh of Urr

Laurie Arms Hotel

11-13 Main Street, DG7 3YA (on B794, 1 Mile S of A75)

⏲ 12 (12.30 Sun)-3, 5.30-midnight ☎ (01556) 660246

Beer range varies Ⓗ

Welcoming family-run pub and restaurant on the main street in a charming, quiet location. It has a genuine village pub atmosphere, helped on cold winter nights by the warming log fire in the bar. Popular with locals and visitors for its range of ales and good food, up to four cask ales are available depending on the season, mainly from small independent breweries. The toilets feature an interesting selection of saucy seaside postcards. A previous CAMRA Scottish Pub of the Year. ♨Q❀◑🚌♣P

Isle of Whithorn

Steam Packet Inn ✔

Harbour Row, DG8 8LL (B7004 from Whithorn)

⏲ 11-11 (1am Fri; 12.30am Sat); 11-2.30, 6-11 Mon-Thu winter; 12-11 Sun ☎ (01988) 500334

🌐 steampacketinn.com

Taylor Landlord; guest beers Ⓗ

Traditional and historic family-run hotel overlooking the harbour and surrounding area, welcoming to locals and visitors alike, including families and animals. The public bar has stone walls and an open fire and there are pictures of the village and maritime events throughout. Four guest ales are available in both bars, from a wide variety of breweries. The extensive food menu features local produce – the Sunday hot buffet is a speciality. Local CAMRA Branch Pub of the Year 2008. ♨Q♿❀🛏◑⊟♿🚌(415)♣

Kirkcolm

Blue Peter Hotel

23 Main Street, DG9 0NL (A718 5 miles N of Stranraer)

⏲ 6 (4 Fri)-11.30; 12-midnight Sat; 12.30-11.30 Sun

☎ (01776) 853221 🌐 thebluepeterhotel.co.uk

Beer range varies Ⓗ

A small independent hotel with two bars packed with memorabilia, and outside a decked patio for viewing the abundant wildlife – including red squirrels. Four handpumps dispense a constantly changing range of ales. Home-cooked food is available at weekends, using fresh and local produce. Popular with walkers, bird and wildlife watchers and real ale enthusiasts, good value B&B is available with discounts for CAMRA members. CAMRA Scotland & Northern Ireland Pub of the Year 2007. ♨Q❀🛏◑⊟⛺🚌(408)♣⚐

Kirkcudbright

Masonic Arms

19 Castle Street, DG6 4JA

⏲ 11 (12.30 Sun)-midnight ☎ (01557) 330517

Beer range varies Ⓗ

A sociable bar, welcoming to locals and visitors, and a firm favourite with real ale enthusiasts over many years. The tables and bar fronts are made from old malt whisky casks from Islay's Bowmore Distillery. It has a smaller back bar and a garden with a smoking area. One ale is always available, two during the summer months. A selection of over 30 bottled beers from all over the world is also stocked, plus a choice of 100 malt whiskies. ♨Q⛺🚌♣

Selkirk Arms

High Street, DG6 4JQ

⏲ 11-11 (midnight Fri & Sat); 12.30-11 Sun

☎ (01557) 330402 🌐 selkirkarmshotel.co.uk

Beer range varies Ⓗ

This traditional hotel has been upgraded recently and has an excellent reputation for meals and accommodation. Two cask ales are available in the lounge and public bars. Outside is a large garden area with tables for the summer months. Kirkcudbright is notable for its artistic heritage and houses a number of interesting galleries and museums. Robert Burns is reputed to have written his famous Selkirk Grace while visiting the hotel, hence the name of the house ale, The Grace, from local brewers Sulwath. Q❀⇄◑⊟♿🚌P⁄–

Moffat

Buccleuch Arms Hotel

High Street, DG10 9ET
⏲ 11-11 (midnight Thu & Fri; 1am Sat); 12-11 Sun
☎ (01683) 220003 🌐 buccleucharmshotel.com
Beer range varies Ⓗ
Dating from 1760, this Georgian coaching inn has recently introduced real ale in the Coachman Bar. One beer is from the Broughton Brewery, situated just up the road in the Borders, the other is an English guest ale. The hotel is renowned for excellent food and service, offering lunchtime and evening meals with options for all tastes. It has a eight-foot screen for sports and shows live fixtures. ♨❀⇄◑♿⛺🚌P⁄–

New Luce

Kenmuir Arms Hotel

31 Main Street, DG8 0AJ (8 miles N of Glenluce along old military road)
⏲ 11-midnight ☎ (01581) 600218
🌐 kenmuirarmsnewluce.com
Beer range varies Ⓗ
Situated in a beautiful village on the banks of the River Luce, this picturesque hotel has well-kept gardens by the river. The public bar serves one real ale all year round and two in summer, sourced from all over the UK. Home-cooked, freshly prepared food is served at lunchtimes and in the evenings. This is a popular stopping point for walkers on the Southern Upland Way and the pub offers a luggage transfer service. Q❀⇄◑⛺♣P⁄–

Newton Stewart

Creebridge House Hotel

Minigaff, DG8 6NP (on old main road, E of river)
⏲ 12-2.30, 6-11.30 (midnight Sat) ☎ (01671) 402121
🌐 creebridge.co.uk
Houston Creebridge Gold; guest beers Ⓗ
This traditional country house hotel is set in three acres of garden and woodland next to the River Cree and close to the town centre. The bar area offers a friendly and pleasant atmosphere, with a real wood fire. It offers two real ales including a house brew by Houston and a regularly changing guest. There are 18 bedrooms and a separate restaurant and brasserie serving fresh local produce. The hotel is in an ideal location for fishermen and walkers.
♨🐄❀⇄◑♿🚌(X75,430)♣P⁄–

Port Logan

Port Logan Inn

Laigh Street, DG9 9NG (15 mins S of Stranraer, off A716)
⏲ 12-midnight ☎ (01776) 860272 🌐 portloganinn.co.uk
Beer range varies Ⓗ
This pleasant seaside inn appeared in the TV series 2000 Acres of Sky. It has a large, cosy bar, a restaurant used mainly in summer and a beer garden overlooking the beach. The menu offers a good range of dishes made with high quality, locally-sourced ingredients. One real ale is available in winter (often Greene King Abbot) and two in the summer, including ales from Scottish breweries. ♨🐄❀⇄◑♿🚌(407)P

Springfield

Queens Head

Main Street, DG16 5EH
⏲ 5 (12 Sat)-11 (midnight Thu & Fri); 12.30-11 Sun
☎ (01461) 337173
Caledonian Deuchars IPA Ⓗ
This single-room village pub, although slightly off the beaten track, is actually little more than a stone's throw from Gretna, wedding capital of the country. It is very close to the A74(M) and about a mile from Gretna Green railway station. Just one real ale is served in this friendly, unpretentious local. Note there is no lunchtime opening on weekdays. ❀🚌♣P

Stranraer

Grapes

4-6 Bridge Street, DG9 7HY
⏲ 11-11.30 (midnight Fri & Sat); 12.30-11.30 Sun
☎ (01776) 703386
Beer range varies Ⓗ
A Stranraer institution, this traditional 1940s-style town-centre bar has a warm and welcoming atmosphere and a historic interior. One real ale from the Belhaven guest list is available in the bar as well as a wide selection of malt whiskies, rums and vodkas. There is a separate snug and an upstairs lounge where weekend entertainment is hosted. The rear courtyard is well-equipped with tables and umbrellas. Occasional beer festivals are held. ❀⊟⇌🚌♣⁄–

SCOTLAND

Choosing pubs

CAMRA members and branches choose the pubs listed in the Good Beer Guide. There is no payment for entry, and pubs are inspected on a regular basis by personal visits; publicans are not sent a questionnaire once a year, as is the case with some pub guides. CAMRA branches monitor all the pubs in their areas, and the choice of pubs for the guide is often the result of democratic vote at branch meetings. However, recommendations from readers are welcomed and will be passed on to the relevant branch: write to Good Beer Guide, CAMRA, 230 Hatfield Road, St Albans, Hertfordshire, AL1 4LW; or send an email to: **gbgeditor@camra.org.uk**

EDINBURGH & THE LOTHIANS

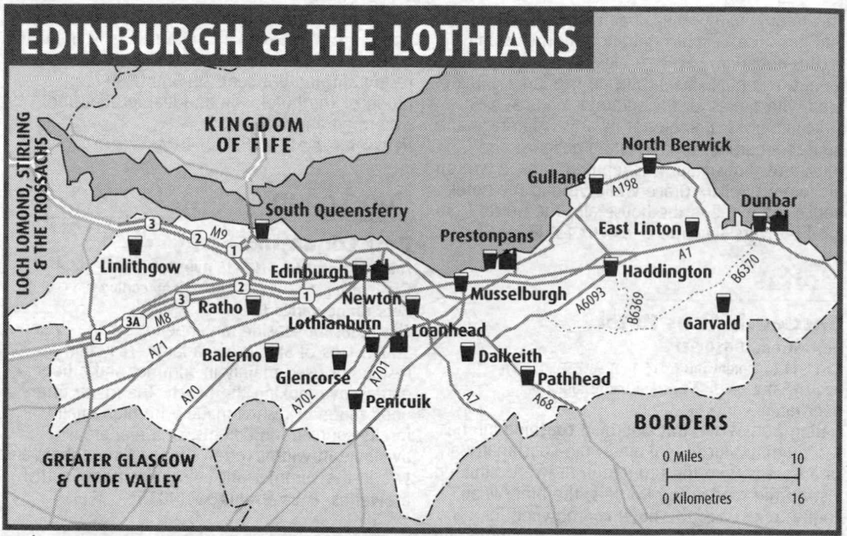

Authority areas covered: City of Edinburgh UA, East Lothian UA, Midlothian UA, West Lothian UA

Balerno

Grey Horse

20 Main Street, EH14 7EH (off A70, in pedestrian area)
10 (12.30 Sun)-1am ☎ (0131) 449 2888
Caledonian Deuchars IPA; Greene King Old Speckled Hen; guest beer Ⓗ
Traditional 200-year-old stone-built village-centre pub. The public bar retains some original features, with wood panelling and a fine Bernard's mirror. The pleasant lounge has green banquette seating. The café next door is part of the pub, so you can have an ale with your meal. Children are permitted in the lounge until 9pm. Dogs are welcomed with water and biscuits. Free Wi-Fi access.
Q(44)♣

Dalkeith

Blacksmith's Forge ✔

Newmills Road, EH22 1DU
9am-11 (midnight Fri & Sat); 10-11 Sun
☎ (0131) 561 5100
Greene King Ruddles Best Bitter, Abbot; guest beer Ⓗ
Wetherspoon's establishment with a mixture of different seating areas. It has a reasonably quiet atmosphere despite two small TVs and a gaming machine. Dimmed lighting helps to produce a soothing ambience, although the pub does tend to get busy at weekends. Meals are served all day. An outdoor drinking area can be used until 10pm. Children are welcome, but not dogs. Free Wi-Fi access available. (3,86)P

Dunbar

Volunteer Arms

17 Victoria Street, EH42 1HP
12-11 (midnight Thu; 1am Fri & Sat); 12.30-midnight Sun
☎ (01368) 862278
Beer range varies Ⓗ
Close to Dunbar harbour, this is a friendly, traditional locals' pub. The cosy panelled bar is decorated with lots of fishing- and lifeboat-oriented memorabilia. It offers two real ales, usually from smaller breweries. Local real cider is occasionally available. Upstairs is a restaurant serving an excellent, good value menu with an emphasis on seafood. In summer, meals are served all day until 9.30pm. Children are welcome until 8pm and dogs after 9pm. ♣

East Linton

Crown

25-27 Bridge Street, EH40 3AG
11 (4 Mon-Thu winter)-11 (1am Fri & Sat); 11-midnight Sun
☎ (01620) 860335 thecrowneastlinton.co.uk
Adnams Broadside; Caledonian Deuchars IPA; guest beers Ⓗ
Small 18th-century stone-built hotel in the centre of a historic conservation village. The functional, cosy bar has a real log fire, lots of wood panelling and original Dudgeon windows. To the rear is a large lounge/restaurant that serves pub meals and takeaways all day in summer (no food Sun-Wed eve winter). Children are permitted in the lounge and a small family room. Dogs are also welcome. A charge is made for Wi-Fi access.

Edinburgh

Abbotsford Bar & Restaurant ★

3 Rose Street, EH2 2PR (centre)
11-11 (midnight Fri & Sat); 12.30-11 Sun
☎ (0131) 225 5276 theabbotsford.com
Beer range varies Ⓐ
A traditional Scottish bar listed in CAMRA's National Inventory of Historic Pub Interiors. The magnificent island bar and gantry in dark mahogany have been a fixture since 1902. The ornate plasterwork and corniced ceiling, highlighted by concealed lighting, are also outstanding. Beers usually come from

INDEPENDENT BREWERIES

Belhaven (Greene King) Dunbar
Caledonian Edinburgh
Prestonpans Prestonpans
Stewart Loanhead

Scottish micro-breweries. Children are welcome in the restaurant upstairs. No evening meals in the bar Friday and Saturday. Q❀◐◑≹(Waverley)🚌

Athletic Arms (Diggers)

1-3 Angle Park Terrace, EH11 2JX (1 mile SW of centre)
⏲ 11 (12.30 Sun)-1am ☎ (0131) 337 3822
Caledonian Deuchars IPA; Stewart 80/- Ⓐ; guest beers Ⓗ
Situated between two graveyards, the name 'Diggers' became synonymous with this Edinburgh pub legend, which opened in 1897. Banquette seating lines the walls, and a compass drawing in the floor aids the geographically challenged. A smaller back room has a dartboard and further seating. Quieter now than in its heyday, though packed when Hearts are at home, it continues to extend a warm welcome to local characters and visitors alike. Dogs are welcome.
≹(Haymarket)🚌♣

Auld Hoose

23/25 St Leonards Street, EH8 9QN
⏲ 12 (12.30 Sun)-12.45am ☎ (0131) 668 2934
🌐 theauldhoose.co.uk
Caledonian Deuchars IPA; Wychwood Hobgoblin; guest beer Ⓗ
Traditional pub dating back to the 1860s with large central U-shaped bar featuring lots of pictures of old Edinburgh. Located in the student quarter, this is a friendly pub with a wide clientele. Enter the quiz on Tuesday evening or try the metal, punk or goth on the juke-box. Good pub food is served all day including vegetarian and vegan options, with a 10 per cent discount for students. The guest beer is usually from a Scottish micro. Dogs are welcome on a lead, and there is free Wi-Fi access. 🚌(2)♣

Blue Blazer

2 Spittal Street, EH3 9DX (SW side of centre)
⏲ 11 (12.30 Sun)-1am ☎ (0131) 229 5030
Cairngorm Trade Winds Ⓐ; Orkney Dark Island Ⓗ; Stewart Pentland IPA Ⓐ, 80/-; guest beers Ⓗ
Nestling in the shadows of Edinburgh castle, the wooden floors, high ceilings and old brewery window panels give this two-roomed pub a traditional feel, complemented by candles on the bar when the sun goes down. The pub specialises in beers from Scottish micros. Named after a local school uniform, there is a blue blazer inlaid on the floor. The pub stays open later during the festival in August. Dogs are welcome. Keep up to date on the pub's Facebook page, I Love The Blue Blazer.
≹(Haymarket)🚌♣

Bow Bar

80 West Bow, EH1 2HH (Old Town, off Grassmarket)
⏲ 12-11.30; 12.30-11 Sun ☎ (0131) 226 7667
Caledonian Deuchars IPA; Stewart 80/-; Taylor Landlord; guest beers Ⓐ
A late 20th-century pastiche of a classic Scottish one-roomed ale house, dedicated to traditional Scottish air pressure dispense and perpendicular drinking. The five guest beers can be from anywhere in the UK. The walls are festooned with original brewery mirrors and the superb gantry does justice to an award-winning selection of single malt whiskies. A map of the original 33 Scottish counties hangs above the fireplace. Bar snacks are available at lunchtime (not Sun). Dogs welcome. Q≹(Waverley)🚌

Café Royal ☆ ✔

19 West Register Street, EH2 2AA (centre, off E end of Princes St)
⏲ 11-11 (midnight Thu; 1am Fri & Sat); 12.30-11 Sun
☎ (0131) 556 1884 🌐 caferoyal.org.uk
Caledonian Deuchars IPA; guest beers Ⓗ
One of the finest Victorian pub interiors in Scotland, listed in CAMRA's National Inventory of Historic Pub Interiors. It is dominated by an impressive oval island bar with ornate brass light fittings, and magnificent ceramic tiled murals of innovators made by Doulton from pictures by John Eyre. The superb sporting windows of the Oyster Bar were made by the same firm that supplied the windows for the House of Lords. Guest beers are usually from Harviestoun, Inveralmond and Kelburn. Meals are served all day. Children are welcome in the restaurant. ≹(Waverley)🚌

Cask & Barrel

115 Broughton Street, EH1 3RZ (E edge of New Town)
⏲ 11-12.30am (1am Thu-Sat); 12.30-12.30am Sun
☎ (0131) 556 3132 🌐 caskandbarrel.co.uk
Caledonian Deuchars IPA, 80; Draught Bass; Hadrian & Border Broughton St Domestic Ale; Harviestoun Bitter & Twisted; Young's Special; guest beers Ⓗ
Spacious and busy ale house drawing a varied clientele of all ages, ranging from business people to football fans. The interior features an imposing horseshoe bar, bare floorboards, a splendid cornice and a collection of brewery mirrors. Old barrels act as tables. The guest beers, often from smaller Scottish breweries, come in a range of strengths and styles. Sparklers can be removed on request.
❀◐♿≹(Waverley)🚌

Cloisters Bar

26 Brougham Street, EH3 9JH (SW edge of centre)
⏲ 12-midnight (1am Fri & Sat); 12.30-midnight Sun
☎ (0131) 221 9997
Cairngorm Trade Winds; Stewart Pentland IPA, Holy Grale; Taylor Landlord; guest beers Ⓗ
A former parsonage, this bare-boarded ale house with large bench seats is popular with a broad cross-section of drinkers. A fine selection of brewery mirrors adorns the walls and a wide range of single malt whiskies does justice to the outstanding gantry. A spiral staircase makes visiting the loo an adventure. Freshly cooked bar meals are served daily (no food Mon and Fri-Sun eves). Dogs are welcome. Joint winner of CAMRA Edinburgh Pub of the Year 2010. Q◐◑🚌♣🍎

Dagda Bar

93-95 Buccleuch Street, EH8 9NG (¾ mile S of centre)
⏲ 12 (1 Sun)-1am ☎ (0131) 667 9773 🌐 dagda.co.uk
Beer range varies Ⓗ
Convivial, cosy bar in the university area attracting a wide-ranging clientele. The single room has banquette seating on three sides and the bar counter on the other. The stone-flagged floor is a little uneven in places. Three real ales are available, usually from smaller breweries, and the staff are happy to let you try before you buy. Fresh ground coffee and quality tea are also available. Dogs welcome. 🚌♣

Foot of the Walk ✔

183 Constitution Street, Leith, EH6 7AA (1 mile S of centre)
⏲ 9-11 (midnight Thu-Sat); 12.30-11 Sun ☎ (0131) 553 0120
Caledonian Deuchars IPA, 80; Greene King Abbot; guest beers Ⓗ

SCOTLAND

This Wetherspoon's pub attracts a large cultural cross-section of Leith's citizens. Reasonably priced food is served in a spacious room with low ceilings, divided into discrete dining areas by the trademark dias in one corner and waist-high wood panels with brass railings. Situated on a corner, it has two main entrances, and a third in Constitution Street allowing disabled access. Food is served all day and children are welcome until 8pm. Free Wi-Fi access.

Guildford Arms

1 West Register Street, EH2 2AA (off east end of Princes St)

11-11 (midnight Fri & Sat); 12.30-11 Sun

(0131) 556 4312 guildfordarms.com

Caledonian Deuchars IPA; Fyne Avalanche; Harviestoun Bitter & Twisted; Orkney Dark Island; guest beers H

This large city-centre pub was built in the golden age of Victorian pub design. The high ceiling, cornices and friezes are spectacular, as are the window arches and screens. An unusual gallery above the main bar, where the restaurant is located, is also noteworthy. There is plenty of standing room around the canopied bar, plus seating areas to the rear. Ten handpumps dispense a diverse beer range, including ales from various Scottish micros. (Waverley)

Halfway House

24 Fleshmarket Close, EH1 1BX (up steps opp station's Market St entrance)

11-midnight (1am Fri & Sat); 12.30-midnight Sun

(0131) 225 7101 halfwayhouse-edinburgh.com

Beer range varies H

Cosy, characterful bar hidden half-way down an old town 'close'. Railway memorabilia and current timetables adorn the interior of this small, often busy, bar. Four interesting beers from smaller Scottish breweries are usually on offer. Good quality, reasonably priced food is served all day. At busy times of the year the pub may stay open until 1am. Children over five and small dogs are welcome. (Waverley)

Kay's Bar

39 Jamaica Street, EH3 6HF (New Town, off India St)

11-midnight (1am Fri & Sat); 12.30-11 Sun

(0131) 225 1858

Caledonian Deuchars IPA; Theakston Best Bitter; guest beers H

This small, cosy and convivial pub is a popular haunt for lawyers in the early evening and offers an impressive range of beers. One wall is decorated with whisky barrels, and there is a good whisky selection behind the bar. Traditional Scottish fare is served at lunchtime. The building was once used as a wine merchant's and the remains of the pipes can still be seen around the light rose. Dogs are welcome after 2.30pm.

Q

Leslies Bar ★

45 Ratcliffe Terrace, EH9 1SU

11-11 (11.30 Thu; 12.30am Fri & Sat); 12.30-11.30 Sun

(0131) 667 7205 lesliesbar.com

Caledonian Deuchars IPA; Stewart 80/-; Taylor Landlord; guest beers H

Outstanding Victorian pub, listed in CAMRA's National Inventory of Historic Pub Interiors, retaining the original fine ceiling, cornice, leaded glass work and half-wood panelling. The island bar has a spectacular snob screen that divides the pub. Small 'ticket window' hatches allow customers to order drinks. A plaque near the fireplace gives further details of this busy, orderly pub. Two guest beers are usually from smaller breweries. Bar snacks are served. Live jazz plays on Monday evening. Dogs welcome. (42)

Oxford Bar ★

8 Young Street, EH2 4JB (New Town, off Charlotte Sq)

11-midnight (1am Thu-Sat); 12.30-11 Sun

(0131) 539 7119 oxfordbar.com

Caledonian Deuchars IPA; guest beers H

Small, basic, vibrant New Town drinking shop unchanged since the late-19th century. It is renowned as one of the favourite pubs of Inspector Rebus and his creator Ian Rankin, and a haunt of many other famous and infamous characters over the years – you never know who you might bump into. Guest beers are usually from Scottish micro-breweries. A real taste of New Town past, it features in CAMRA's National Inventory of Historic Pub Interiors. Bar snacks are available. Dogs welcome.

Regent

2 Montrose Terrace, EH7 5DL (¾ mile E of centre)

11 (12.30 Sun)-1am (0131) 661 8198

theregentbar.co.uk

Caledonian Deuchars IPA; guest beers H

Large, tenement bar with two rooms, one music-free, popular with gay and lesbian real ale drinkers. The comfortable seating includes banquettes, leather sofas and armchairs. It offers an interesting range of three guest beers. Bar snacks and meals are served all day. A novel slant on pub games is the pommel horse by the toilets. Children are permitted until 8pm. There is free Wi-Fi access. Voted local CAMRA branch Pub of the Year 2010.

Sandy Bell's

25 Forrest Road, EH1 2QH (½ mile S of centre)

11.30-1am; 12.30-11 Sun (0131) 225 2751

Caledonian Deuchars IPA, 80; Courage Directors; Inveralmond Ossian H

Very much a piece of Edinburgh folklore, the pub has been part of the traditional music scene for many years. An arch, the gantry bar counter and wall panelling are all in dark wood, in marked contrast to the atmosphere, which is far from gloomy. Folk music is played every night and on Saturday and Sunday afternoons. Bring along an instrument and join in! Dogs welcome.

(Waverley)

St Vincent Bar

11 St Vincent Street, EH3 6SW (New Town)

11 (12.30 Sun)-1am (0131) 225 7447

Caledonian Deuchars IPA; guest beers H

This unpretentious but comfortable basement pub with beautiful stained glass windows attracts a fairly mixed clientele due to its location in the New Town, just a little way from the popular and upmarket area of Stockbridge. The bar has a fine gantry incorporating a clock. Brass cribbage boards are built into some of the tables, and there is a pool table. Third of a pint glasses are available in a custom made wooden carrier. Meals are served all day, dogs are welcome and there is free Wi-Fi access. (25,42)

Stable Bar

Mortonhall Park, 30 Frogston Road East, EH16 6TJ
11-11 (midnight summer); 12.30-11 Sun
☎ (0131) 664 0773 mortonhall.co.uk
Caledonian Deuchars IPA; Stewart Copper Cascade, 80/- H
A real country pub on the edge of the city. Numerous paths are ideal for exploring the surrounding woods. The comfortable bar is dominated by a large stone fireplace that boasts a roaring log fire in the winter. Food is served all day until 9pm (10pm summer). With real ales coming from breweries less than three miles away, this is a true local ale pub. Watch out if in the Little Miss Muffet seat. Children and dogs are welcome. Wi-Fi access available. (11,18)P

Starbank Inn

64 Laverockbank Road, EH5 3BZ (1½ miles N of centre)
11-11 (midnight Thu-Sat); 12.30-11 Sun
☎ (0131) 552 4141 starbankinn.co.uk
Belhaven 80/-; Caledonian Deuchars IPA; Taylor Landlord; guest beers H
Bright, airy, bare-boarded ale house, with a U-shaped layout extending into a conservatory dining area. The walls sport several rare brewery mirrors. Up to five guest ales, often from Scottish independent breweries, are usually available. Meals are served all day at the weekend. Children are welcome until 9pm and dogs permitted if on a lead. Jazz plays on the second Sunday of the month. Enjoy the superb views across the Firth to Fife. Free Wi-Fi access. Q(7,16)

Stockbridge Tap

2-4 Raeburn Place, Stockbridge, EH4 1HN
12-midnight (1am Fri & Sat); 12.30-midnight Sun
☎ (0131) 343 3000
Cairngorm Trade Winds; Caledonian Deuchars IPA; Stewart 80/-; guest beers H
Very much a specialist real ale house, the pub stocks unusual and interesting beers from all over the UK and holds occasional beer festivals. The L-shaped room, with a bright bar area, boasts mirrors from lost breweries, including Murray's and Campbell's. The seating is a mixture of comfortable chairs and church pew-style benches, with ample room for vertical drinking. The food menu is excellent, available all day Friday to Sunday. Dogs welcome.

Tass

1 Jeffrey Street, EH1 1SR
11-midnight (1am Fri & Sat); 12.30-midnight Sun
☎ (0131) 556 6338
Caledonian Deuchars IPA; guest beers H
Wooden-floored bar with a small dining room serving a mixture of real ales, malt whiskies and fine wines to a clientele that includes locals, tourists and musicians. Live traditional music sessions are hosted in the evening (not Tue and Sun). Beer can be served in a third of a pint glass on request. Located at the lower end of the world-famous Royal Mile High Street, John Knox's house is nearby. Meals and bar snacks are served all day. Children over five are welcome if dining. (Waverley)

Teuchters Landing

1c Dock Place, Leith, EH6 6LU
11 (12.30 Sun)-1am ☎ (0131) 554 7427 aroomin.co.uk
BrewDog Trashy Blonde; Caledonian Deuchars IPA; Inveralmond Ossian; Taylor Landlord H
Formerly the Waterfront Wine Bar, this comfortable venue, with a half-wood-panelled, half-stone interior, displays interesting Scottish place names around the walls. To the rear is a larger restaurant and bistro, with a conservatory extension that opens out onto a pontoon floating on the Water of Leith. Meals are served all day and children are welcome until 10pm. Q(16,22)

Thomson's ✔

182/184 Morrison Street, EH3 8EB (W edge of centre)
12-11.30 (midnight Thu & Sat; 1am Fri); 4-11.30 Sun
☎ (0131) 228 5700
Caledonian Deuchars IPA; guest beers A
This award-winning pub is dedicated to the style of Glasgow architect Alexander 'Greek' Thomson and the traditional Scottish air pressure dispense system. The superb hand-made gantry is inlaid with scenes from Greek mythology and the walls feature a range of mirrors, adverts and elaborate point of sale material from long-forgotten Scottish breweries. Beers from Hop Back and Dark Star are regulars as well as a wide range of Scottish ales. No food is served on Sunday and pies only on Saturday. Dogs welcome. Q(Haymarket)

Winston's ✔

20 Kirk Loan, Corstorphine, EH12 7HD (3 miles W of centre, off St John's Rd)
11-11.30 (midnight Thu-Sat); 12.30 11 Sun
☎ (0131) 539 7077
Caledonian Deuchars IPA; guest beers H
This comfortable lounge bar is situated in Corstorphine, just over a mile from Murrayfield Stadium and not far from the zoo. The small, modern building houses a warm and friendly community pub used by old and young alike, with children welcome until 3pm. The decor is golf and rugby themed. Lunchtime meals include wonderful home-made pies (not available Sun). Dogs are welcome.

Garvald

Garvald Inn

EH41 4LN
closed Mon; 12-3, 5-11 (midnight Fri & Sat); 12.30-11 (5 winter) Sun ☎ (01620) 830311
Beer range varies H
Family-run 18th-century pub in a pretty village by the Lammermuir Hills. The bar is cosy and welcoming, with half-panelled walls, a crimson colour scheme and a large wood-burning stove. The single real ale is frequently from Stewart Brewing. The inn is popular for food, served in both the bar and tiny dining room – the dinner menu is particularly impressive. Occasional live music is hosted. Children and dogs welcome. QP

Glencorse

Flotterstone Inn

Milton Bridge, EH26 0PP
11.30 (12.30 Sun)-11 ☎ (01968) 673717
flotterstoneinn.com
Stewart Pentland IPA; guest beers H
Large, rectangular lounge bar with church-pew seating and numerous toby jugs and plates around the walls. A modern timber-clad extension overlooks the enclosed garden. Good food is served all day in two dining rooms, which have bare stone walls and wood ceilings. This is a handy

place to recover from a day on the Pentland Hills, and it can be busy at weekends. Dogs are permitted in the bar if on a lead. Children welcome. ✿♿🚌(100)♣P

Gullane

Old Clubhouse

East Links Road, EH31 2AF (W end of village, off A198)
11-11 (midnight Thu-Sat); 12.30-11 Sun
☎ (01620) 842008 oldclubhouse.com
Caledonian Deuchars IPA; Taylor Landlord; guest beers P
There's a colonial feel to this pub, which looks out over the golf links to the Lammermuir Hills. The half-panelled walls are adorned with historic memorabilia and stuffed animals. Caricature statuettes of the Marx Brothers and Laurel and Hardy look down from the gantry. Food features highly and is served all day – the extensive menu includes seafood, pasta, barbecue, curries, salads and burgers. Children are welcome until 8pm. This is Gullane's only real ale outlet. Dogs are also welcome. ✿🚌(X5,124)●

Haddington

Victoria Inn

9 Court Street, EH41 3JD
11-11 (midnight Fri & Sat); 12.30-11 Sun
☎ (01620) 823332 theavenuerestaurant.co.uk
Beer range varies H
Renowned for its colourful window baskets in summer, this stylish inn is in the town centre. The focus is on quality food; however, drinkers are made most welcome in the cosy bar with its horseshoe counter. Beers are mainly from the Belhaven/Greene King lists. Upstairs is the Avenue restaurant and five comfortable bedrooms. Children are welcome until 9pm. Free Wi-Fi access. Q✿◑♿🚌

Linlithgow

Four Marys ✔

65-67 High Street, EH49 7ED
11-midnight (1am Fri & Sat); 12.30-midnight Sun
☎ (01506) 842171 thefourmarys.co.uk
Belhaven 80/-, St Andrews Ale; Caledonian Deuchars IPA; guest beers H
A stone's throw from Linlithgow Palace, birthplace of Mary Queen of Scots, the building dates back to around 1500. The pub is named after the Queen's four ladies-in-waiting. Initially a dwelling house, the building has had several changes of use over the years – at one time it was a chemist's run by the Waldie family whose most famous member, David, established the anaesthetic properties of chloroform in 1847. Beer festivals are held in May and October when 12 more handpumps are added. ✿◑⇌🚌

Platform 3 ✔

1A High Street, EH49 7AB (next to railway station)
10.30-midnight (1am Fri & Sat); 12.30-midnight Sun
☎ (01506) 847405 platform3.co.uk
Caledonian Deuchars IPA; guest beers H
Small, friendly hostelry on the railway station approach, originally the public bar of the hotel next door. It was purchased and renovated in 1998 as a pub in its own right, and is now very much involved with the local community. Look out for the train running above the bar. A rotating guest ale from Cairngorm, Harviestoun or Stewart breweries is usually found on the second handpump. Occasional live music is staged. Dogs are welcome with biscuits 'on tap'. ⇌🚌♣

Lothianburn

Steading ✔

118-120 Biggar Road, EH10 7DU
11-midnight (earlier if quiet); 12.30-midnight Sun
☎ (0131) 445 1128
Caledonian Deuchars IPA; Taylor Landlord; guest beer H
Originally a row of farm cottages, the pub has a split bar, with areas of comfortable chairs and settees ideal for relaxing with a drink, and higher tables for eating. The restaurant includes a conservatory extension and food is served all day. The outside drinking area has excellent views of the Pentland Hills and the pub is ideally placed for a relaxing pint after walking in the hills. Children and dogs are welcome.
✿🚌(4,15/15A)P

Musselburgh

Levenhall Arms

10 Ravensheugh Road, EH21 7PP
12-11 (midnight Thu; 1am Fri & Sat); 12.30-midnight Sun
☎ (0131) 665 3220
Stewart Pentland IPA P**; guest beers** H
This three-roomed hostelry dates from 1830 and is popular with locals and racegoers. The lively, cheerfully decorated public bar is half timber-panelled, leading to a smaller area with a dartboard and pictures of old local industries. The quieter lounge area, with vinyl banquettes, is used for dining, with food served all day until 8pm. Children are permitted in the lounge until 8.30pm. Opening times/menu may vary in winter. Dogs are welcome in the bar. Q✿▲⇌(Wallyford)🚌♣P

Volunteer Arms (Staggs) 🏆

81 North High Street, EH21 6JE (behind Brunton Hall)
12-11 (12.30 Thu; midnight Fri); 11-midnight Sat; 1-11 Sun
☎ (0131) 665 9654 staggsbar.com
Caledonian Deuchars IPA; guest beers H
Superb pub run by the same family since 1858. The bar and snug are traditional with a wooden floor, wood panelling and mirrors from defunct local breweries. Old casks top the superb gantry. The snug has a nascent history collection featuring local breweries. The more modern lounge opens at the weekend. Three guest beers, often pale and hoppy, change regularly. Dogs are welcome in the bar, but don't bring the kids. CAMRA Lothian Pub of the Year 2010. ✿🚌♣

Newton

Duddingston Arms

13-15 Main Street, EH52 6QE (½ mile west of South Queensferry on the A904 Boness/Linlithgow road)
12-3, 4.30-11; 12-midnight Fri & Sat; 12.30-11 Sun
☎ (0131) 331 1948 duddingstonarms.com
Beer range varies H
This award-winning pub has been a family-owned business since 1832 and attracts a mixed clientele including locals, fishermen, ramblers, cyclists, dog-walkers and business people. Three handpumps serve a variety of real ales, with Belhaven, Kelburn,

Stewart and Tryst rotating regularly. The pub also acts as an art gallery for local artists, with pictures available for sale. ⛪❀◗♿🚌(474)

North Berwick

Nether Abbey Hotel

20 Dirleton Avenue, EH39 4BQ

11-11 (midnight Thu; 1am Fri & Sat) ☎ (01620) 892802 netherabbey.co.uk

Caledonian Deuchars IPA; Taylor Landlord Ⓐ; guest beers Ⓟ

Busy, family-run hotel in a stone-built villa with an open-plan, single-room interior and a bright, contemporary feel. On two levels, the lower area is a bar and the upper a restaurant. The marble-topped bar counter boasts a row of modern chrome founts – the middle ones, with horizontally moving levers, dispense the real ales. Food is served all day at the weekend. Children are welcome until 9pm. Dogs are also welcome. Free Wi-Fi access. ❀🛏◗♿⛺🚆🚌(X5,124)♣P⊱

Pathhead

Stair Arms Hotel

EH37 5TX (on A68, N of village)

11-11 (1am Fri & Sat); 12-11 Sun ☎ (01875) 320277 stairarmshotel.com

Stewart Edinburgh Gold Ⓗ

Originally a farm steading, in 1841 the building was converted into a coaching inn – a reminder of the hotel's past stands outside. Now extended, the elegant roadside venue has comfortable lounge areas, bar, dining room, wood beams and an impressive fireplace. Hidden to the rear are TV and function rooms. The restaurant menu features fine Scottish food. Children are welcome and dogs are allowed in the bar. ⛪Q❀🛏◗♿⛺🚌(51,52)♣P⊱

Penicuik

Navaar

23 Bog Road, EH26 9BY

12-1am (midnight Sun) ☎ (01968) 672693

Stewart Pentland IPA Ⓗ

A lively pub with a strong community spirit, situated in an old private house, from circa 1870. The large bar is open-plan with a real fire and TV screens. The restaurant, with an extensive à la carte menu, serves meals all day. Snacks are available in the bar. A large patio and decked area is popular in summer. Dogs are welcome. ⛪❀🛏◗🚌♣P⊱

Prestonpans

Prestoungrange Gothenburg ☆

227 High Street, EH32 9BE

closed Mon; 12-3, 5-11; 12-midnight Fri & Sat; 12.30-11 Sun ☎ (01875) 819922 thegoth.co.uk

Fowler's Gothenburg Porter, Prestonpans 80/- Ⓟ

This superb Gothenburg pub features in CAMRA's National Inventory of Historic Pub Interiors. The magnificent painted ceiling in the bar has to be seen to be appreciated. Fowler's micro-brewery can be viewed from the bar area. There is also a bistro and upstairs is a lounge and function room with superb views over the Forth. The walls throughout are covered in murals and paintings depicting past local life. Meals are served all day Friday to Sunday. Children welcome. ⛪◗🖧♿⛺🚌(26,129)P

Ratho

Bridge Inn

27 Baird Road, EH28 8RA (by Union Canal, Bridge 15)

11.30-11 (midnight Fri & Sat); 12.30-11 Sun ☎ (0131) 333 1320 bridgeinn.com

Beer range varies Ⓗ

The older part of this canalside inn, originally a farmhouse dating from around 1750 and predating the canal, is used as a restaurant. The lounge bar and dining area are in a modern extension with views over the canal. The inn was a focal point during the long campaign to restore the Union Canal, part of the Millennium Link project. The focus here is on food and meals are served all day. Children are allowed until 8pm. Free Wi-Fi access is available. ❀◗♿🚌(48)♣P⊱

South Queensferry

Orocco Pier

17 High Street, EH30 9PP

9.30am-1am ☎ (0131) 331 1298 oroccopier.co.uk

Caledonian Deuchars IPA, 80 Ⓟ

Smart and hospitable hotel in the old part of town. The Antico bar, with its modern and relaxing decor, welcomes diners and drinkers alike – the panoramic windows give a splendid view of the bridges and the Firth of Forth. Meals and bar snacks are served all day. The hotel's contemporary restaurant offers a good choice of seasonal dishes, with seafood prominent on the menu. Families are welcome until 7pm. Wi-Fi access available. ❀🛏♿🚆(Dalmeny)🚌(43)⊱

Johnnie Dowie was the sleekest and kindest of landlords. Nothing could equal the benignity of his smile when he brought in a bottle of 'the ale' to a company of well-known and friendly customers. It was a perfect treat to see his formality in drawing the cork, his precision in filling the glasses, his regularity in drinking the healths of all present in the first glass (which he always did, and at every successive bottle), and then his douce civility in withdrawing. Johnnie lived till within the last few years (he died in 1817), and, with laudable attachment to the old costume, always wore a cocked hat, and buckles at the knees and shoes, as well as a cane with a cross top, somewhat like an implement called by Scottish gardeners 'a dibble'. **William Hone, The Year Book, 1839**

Dowie's Tavern in Edinburgh was famously frequented by Robert Burns. Other habitues included Henry Raeburn, Adam Smith and the ballad collector, David Herd. The ale served was invariably Younger's, whose reputation the inn helped to make. After Dowie's death it became Burns Tavern but was demolished in 1831.

GREATER GLASGOW & CLYDE VALLEY

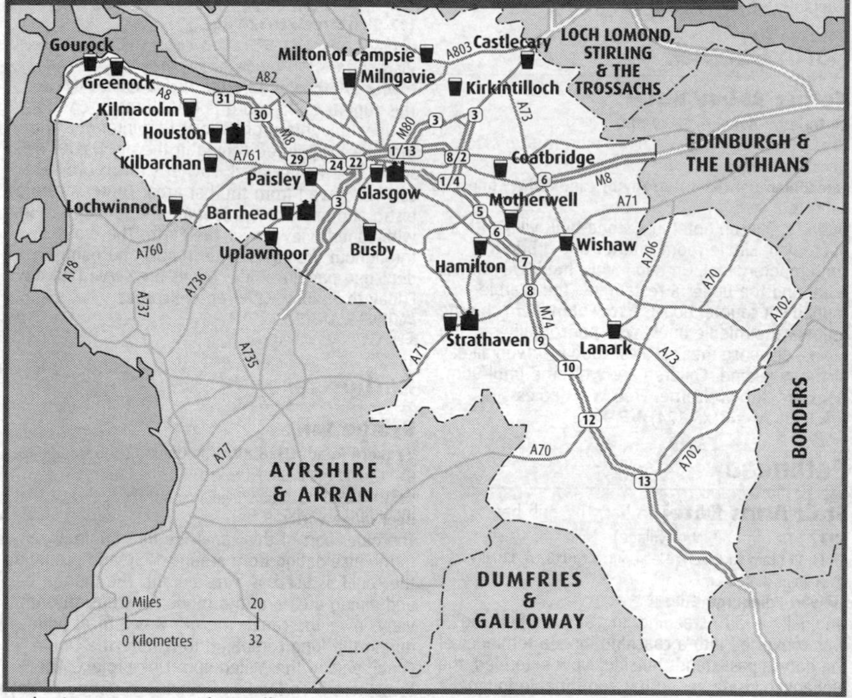

Authority areas covered: Argyll & Bute UA, Ayrshire UAs, City of Glasgow UA, Dunbartonshire UAs, Inverclyde UA, Lanarkshire UAs, Renfrewshire UAs

Barrhead

Cross Stobs Inn

4 Grahamston Road, G78 1NS (on B7712)

11-11 (midnight Thu & Sat; 1am Fri); 12.30-11 Sun

(0141) 881 1581

Kelburn Misty Law; guest beers H

Eighteenth-century coaching inn on the road to Paisley. The public bar has a real coal fire and retains much of its original charm with antique furniture and service bells. The lounge is spacious and leads out to an enclosed rear garden. There is also an outside drinking area at the front of the pub. The bar leads to a pool room and a function suite that can be hired privately. The guest beer is always from the nearby Kelburn brewery.

Waterside Inn

Glasgow Road, The Hurlet, G53 7TH (A736 near Hurlet)

11-11 (midnight Fri & Sat); 12.30-11 Sun

(0141) 881 2822

Kelburn Red Smiddy; guest beer H

Comfortable and friendly bar and restaurant near Levern Water. Food is the main focus here but there is a cosy area with a real log fire for those just wanting to enjoy a relaxing drink. The decor includes old local photographs on the walls. Themed nights are held fairly regularly, often musical, such as an Abba tribute night. The guest beer varies but is always from the local Kelburn Brewery. P

Busby

White Cart

61 East Kilbride Road, G76 8HX (on A726 near station)

11 (12.30 Sun)-11 (0141) 644 2711

Beer range varies H

A friendly welcome awaits you at this large Chef & Brewer pub. The emphasis here is on food service but there are two handpumps dispensing a changing choice of beers, one always from the Kelburn Brewery. A patio area at front is popular in summer and there is an area for families inside. P

Castlecary

Castlecary House Hotel

Castlecary Road, G68 0HD (just off A80 near M80 jct 4)

11-11 (11.30 Thu-Sat); 12.30-11 Sun (01324) 240 233

castlecaryhotel.com

Beer range varies H

Tucked away behind the busy Glasgow to Stirling highway lies a small village, home to this large hotel, which has long provided real ales. Two or three handpumps deliver an ever-changing range of beers from micro-breweries, especially local Williams Brothers, Harviestoun and Tryst, who brew their house beer, Bottleneck. The bars are inter-connected centrally so real ales can be enjoyed anywhere, though you might not see the pumps. The main Poachers lounge is large, with several separate alcoves.

Q (X37,X39)P

Coatbridge

Vulcan
181 Main Street, ML5 3HH (jct with Dunbeth Rd)
11-1am; 12.30-midnight Sun ☎ (01236) 437 972
Caledonian Deuchars IPA; Greene King Abbot; guest beers Ⓗ
Named after an old local iron works as a reminder of the area's industrial heritage, this Wetherspoon pub lies close to Coatbridge's town and shopping centre. It must be one of the chain's smallest Scottish pubs and has the feel of a traditional local. The bar offers three ever-changing guest beers from Scotland and south of the border, as well as two regular ales. ◑♿⇌(Sunnyside)🚌(262)●

Glasgow

1901 Bar & Bistro
1534 Pollokshaws Road, G43 1RF (jct with Haggs Rd)
11-11 (midnight Fri & Sat); 12.30-11 Sun
☎ (0141) 632 0161
Caledonian Deuchars IPA; guest beers Ⓗ
The large L-shaped room of this corner tenement pub is sub-divided by a partition, providing a cosy area adjacent to the main bar. The pub has a reputation for good food and meals may be taken here or in the more formal Mediterranean Bistro. The curved counter offers up to two changing guests along with the regular beer. With a bus stop outside, this is a convenient place to end a day visiting nearby Pollok Park, with its Burrell Collection.
◑♿⇌(Pollokshaws West/Shawlands)🚌⁻

Babbity Bowster
16-18 Blackfriars Street, Merchant City, G1 1PE
(between High St and Walls St/Albion St)
11 (12.30 Sun)-midnight ☎ (0141) 552 5055
Caledonian Deuchars IPA; Kelburn Misty Law; guest beers Ⓐ
For 25 years this pub's unique and friendly atmosphere has pulled in regulars from the local and business communities. Good food is served on polished wood tables overlooked by pictures of local scenes. Folk music events are advertised on posters and an improvised folk session takes place around the peat fire on Saturday afternoon. Three beers are dispensed by – now rare – air pressure, from traditional tall founts. Summer barbecues are held in the beer garden.
Q❀◑⇌(High Street/Argyle St/Queen St)
⊖(Buchanan St)🚌P⁻

Blackfriars
36 Bell Street, Merchant City, G1 1LG (corner of Albion St)
11 (12.30 Sun)-midnight ☎ (0141) 552 5924
blackfriarsglasgow.com
Beer range varies Ⓗ
Welcoming, popular and lively pub in the heart of the Merchant City with low lighting and candles on the table creating an intimate atmosphere. The walls and pillars are decorated with posters advertising local events. The bar downstairs hosts a Comedy Club at weekends, while upstairs bands play on Tuesday and Sunday nights. The five ales are mostly from Scottish brewers, particularly Kelburn, plus others from all over Britain. A range of bottled beers comes from the USA and Europe.
❀◑♿⇌(High St/Argyll St/Queen St)
⊖(Buchanan St)🚌(18,62)●⁻

Bon Accord
153 North Street, G3 7DA
11-midnight; 12.30-11 Sun ☎ (0141) 248 4427
bonaccordweb.co.uk
Caledonian Deuchars IPA; Harviestoun Bitter & Twisted; Marston's Pedigree; guest beers Ⓗ
The name says it all. This treasured Glasgow real ale legend is the pub that originally introduced ale to the city. A counter runs along the front half of the multi-level room, with up to ten real ales and one traditional cider from various sources available, plus a range of foreign bottled beers, whiskies and liqueurs. Good home-made food is served until 8pm. Live music plays at the weekend, and a quiz is hosted on Wednesday night.
❀◑♿⇌(Charing Cross/Anderston)●⁻

Clockwork Beer Co ✔
1153-1155 Cathcart Road, Mount Florida, G42 9HB
11-11 (midnight Thu-Sat); 12.30-11 Sun
☎ (0141) 649 0184 clockworkbeercompany.co.uk
Caledonian Deuchars IPA; guest beers Ⓐ
Opened 13 years ago, the brewery of this large brew-pub can be viewed from the spacious bar room. The interior is divided into various areas including a cosy corner and a raised dining space, plus an upstairs mezzanine room. Five guest ales accompany a range of the Clockwork Beer Co's own beers – the strongest are cask conditioned and the others are in tanks with a unique system retaining the CO2 from secondary fermentation. A good range of foreign bottled beers is also available.
❀◑♿⇌(Mount Florida/Cathcart)🚌P⁻

Esquire House ✔
1487 Great Western Road, Anniesland, G12 0AU
11-11 (midnight Thu-Sat); 12.30-11 Sun
☎ (0141) 341 1130
Caledonian Deuchars IPA; Greene King Abbot; guest beers Ⓗ
The smallest, and perhaps friendliest, of Glasgow's Wetherspoon pubs. Although located in the far west of the city, it is readily accessible from the city centre – just 10 minutes by train from either Central or Queen Street stations. It is blessed with extremely knowledgeable and amiable staff.
❀◑♿⇌(Anniesland)🚌(20,66,118)●P⁻

Horseshoe Bar ★ ✔
17-21 Drury Street, G2 5AE
10 (2.30 Sun)-midnight ☎ (0141) 229 5711
horseshoebar.co.uk
Caledonian Deuchars IPA, 80 Ⓗ**; Shepherd Neame Spitfire; guest beer** Ⓐ
The only remaining example in Glasgow of the large drinking establishments that flourished in Victorian times that is still largely unchanged. The front of the island bar is dominated by a black horse atop the gantry and the motif is continued on mirrors and stained glass panels. The long counter was originally horseshoe shaped; the rear section was added later. The pub gets busy so you will need to go early to appreciate the mosaic floor.
◑⇌(Central/Queen St)⊖(St Enoch/Buchanan St)
🚌

INDEPENDENT BREWERIES

Clockwork Glasgow
Houston Houston
Kelburn Barrhead
Strathaven Strathaven

SCOTLAND

Mulberry St

778 Pollokshaws Road, G41 2AE

11-11 (midnight Fri & Sat), 12.30-11 Sun

(0141) 424 0858 mulberrystbarbistro.com

Harviestoun Bitter & Twisted; guest beers H

This South Side bar/bistro serves three real ales. The clientele is mainly local, drawn by the Yorkshire and Scottish ales and good food ranging from Scots specialities to Thai curries. Imported bottled beers are also on offer. Background music is played at a level that enables conversation and the screen showing sports is kept silent. Large windows look to the street and catch the sun, as does the drinking and dining area outside. Good bus and rail links to the city centre.

(Queen's Park/Pollokshields West)

Samuel Dow

69 Nithsdale Road, G41 2PZ

11-11 (midnight Fri & Sat); 12.30-11 Sun

(0141) 423 0107

Beer range varies H

This friendly one-roomed bar is affectionately known as Sammy Dows. The old Ind Coope mirrors and decor help to create an ambience reminiscent of the '60s. A large real ale menu board behind the bar shows the commitment to the real ales, served on three pumps, usually Scottish and often from the Glasgow area, particularly Houston. Here, dominoes is played in preference to watching sport on screen. A large rear function room hosts rock bands Thursday to Saturday nights.

(Pollokshields West/Queen's Pk)

Sir John Moore

260-292 Argyle Street, G2 8QW

8 (12.30 Sun)-midnight (0141) 222 1780

Caledonian Deuchars IPA; Greene King Abbot; guest beers H

Originally a row of shops, this is now a Wetherspoon venue, with seating at the front giving views of busy Argyle Street. The long bar room has raised family areas at both ends providing quieter retreats from the three large screens that show sport, mostly football. These open out in summer to blend with seating on the pavement, covered by an awning. Six ales are on handpump. Close to Central Station and popular with commuters and city workers.

(Central) (St Enoch)

Sir John Stirling Maxwell

Unit 14B, 140 Kilmarnock Road, Shawlands, G41 3NN

11-11 (midnight Fri & Sat); 12.30-11 Sun

(0141) 636 9024

Caledonian Deuchars IPA; Greene King Abbot; guest beers H

This old Safeway supermarket is the only Wetherspoon on Glasgow's South Side and is named after the former owner of Pollok Estate, now Pollok Park, home to the famous Burrell Collection. Two regular beers and up to four guests are on offer, sometimes including Strathaven Brewery's Red Ale badged with the pub name. A raised TV-free area at the rear is popular with families. Locals frequent the main bar, which can get busy at weekends.

(Pollokshaws East)

Society Room

151 West George Street, G2 2JJ

9 (12.30 Sun)-midnight (0141) 229 7560

Caledonian Deuchars IPA; Greene King Abbot; guest beers H

The friendly staff at this increasingly popular, spacious Lloyds No 1 Bar serve a wide clientele – families out for a meal, 'silver suppers' enjoying the beers by day, and younger pre-clubbers attracted by the evening music, which can be loud at busy weekends, with a DJ from 8pm Friday and Saturday. Six handpumps dispense a range of ales. There are family dining areas at the rear, and window seats for those wishing to read.

(Queen St/Central) (Bucanan St)

State Bar

148 Holland Street, G2 4NG

11 (12.30 Sun)-midnight (0141) 332 2159

Caledonian Deuchars IPA, 80; Houston Killellan; Stewart Edinburgh No.3 Premium Scotch Ale; guest beers H

The impressive reproduction wood and brass island bar and gantry of this city pub look convincingly Victorian. A rear alcove hosts a blues band on Tuesday night, and comedy on Saturday and occasional concerts feature downstairs. The front of the bar is well-lit by large windows, while the back has cosy soft lighting. Partitions offer privacy in some areas. Three guest beers and four regulars accompany the good value lunches. Near to the Kings Theatre.

(Charing Cross) (Cowcaddens)

Station Bar

55 Port Dundas Road, G4 0HF

11-midnight; 12.30-11.45 Sun (0141) 332 3117

Caledonian Deuchars IPA; Greene King Abbot; guest beers H

Corner city bar frequented by nearby workers and locals. Art Deco glass panels behind the bar pay homage to fire, police and ambulance services based locally, and a steam engine image is a reminder of the now defunct station. The bar displays a large McEwans Brewery mirror and there are two large-screen TVs showing sport. There are quieter areas to the side of the main bar. Good lunches are popular, served 11am to 4pm. Near to the Royal Concert Hall and Pavilion Theatre.

(Queen St) (Buchanan St)

Tennents

191 Byres Road, G12 8TN

11-11 (midnight Thu-Sat); 12.30-11 Sun

(0141) 339 7203

Broughton Old Jock; Caledonian Deuchars IPA; Fuller's London Pride; Harviestoun Bitter & Twisted; Orkney Dark Island; Taylor Landlord; guest beers H

Traditional Victorian corner pub with friendly staff in the centre of Glasgow's busy West End. The sizeable room is sub-divided by partitions and alcoves, and the three-sided square bar and gantry offers 12 handpumps dispensing nine regular and three guest beers. The proximity to the university makes the pub popular with students and staff as well as locals and city workers, with good value meals served until 10pm. Very busy when big games are shown on the TVs.

(Hillhead/Kelvinhall) (44)

Three Judges

141 Dumbarton Road, G11 6PR

11-11 (midnight Thu-Sat); 12.30-11 Sun

(0141) 337 3055

Beer range varies A

Traditional Glasgow locals' corner bar, where striking up a conversation with regulars is easy. The staff are friendly and efficient, serving an ever-changing selection of beers from mostly small breweries on nine pumps plus one changing real cider. A corner TV shows sports with the sound off. A raised corner at the front overlooks busy Partick Cross and stages live jazz music on Sunday afternoon. To the rear is a quieter area. Current CAMRA Scottish Cider Pub of the Year.
(Partick) (Kelvinhall) (9,16,62)

Gourock

Spinnaker Hotel

121 Albert Road, PA19 1BU
11-midnight (12.30am Thu; 1am Fri & Sat); 12.30-midnight Sun ☎ (01475) 633107 spinnakerhotel.co.uk
Belhaven 80/-; guest beers H
Family-run hotel situated in a listed sandstone Victorian building on the coast road heading west out of Gourock. Three ever-changing guest ales supplement the regular beer. All food is home-made, with an accent on local produce. A highlight for any first-time visitor to this pub is the view from the large bay windows and front patio looking out across the Firth of Clyde to Dunoon and the beginning of the Highlands. Q

Greenock

James Watt

80-92 Cathcart Road, PA15 1DD
11-11 (midnight Thu; 1am Fri & Sat); 12.30-midnight Sun
☎ (01475) 722640
Caledonian Deuchars IPA; Greene King Abbot; guest beers H
Easy to find near the Central train station, this is a roomy, town-centre Wetherspoon with typical JDW trimmings. It has good wheelchair access and a separate area for families. Food is popular and served all day. Guest beers come from local breweries as well as further afield. Outside is a heated patio. (Central)

Hamilton

George Bar

18 Campbell Street, ML3 6AS (off Cadzow St)
11-11.45 (1am Fri); 12.30-11.45 Sun ☎ (01698) 424225
thegeorgebar.com
Beer range varies H
A favourite of the local CAMRA branch, this single-bar room is quite small, but there is plenty of standing room, and several tables for diners to enjoy tasty home-cooked lunches. In warmer weather there are more tables and chairs outside at the front in a pedestrianised area. The three handpumps deliver a varying range of beers from Scottish and English micro-breweries. A welcoming community pub and regular CAMRA Lanarkshire Pub of the Year winner, the awards are proudly displayed on the wall. (Central)

Houston

Fox & Hounds

South Street, PA6 7EN
11-midnight (12.30am Fri & Sat); 12.30-midnight Sun
☎ (01505) 612448 houston-brewing.co.uk
Houston Killellan, Peter's Well, Texas, Warlock Stout, seasonal beers; guest beers H
Established in 1779, this coaching inn is home to the Houston Brewing Company. The Fox & Vixen lounge, serving the full range of Houston beers, has a viewing window to the brewery. The Stables bar serves three Houston beers and has multiple TV screens for all sporting occasions. The Huntsman bar and an à la carte restaurant are upstairs. Themed beer festivals are held every May and August. P

Kilbarchan

Glen Leven Inn

25 New Street, PA10 2LN
12.15-11 (midnight Thu; 1am Fri & Sat); 12.30-11 Sun
☎ (01505) 702481
Beer range varies H
Situated in a conservation village, this friendly pub offers a warm welcome to locals and visitors alike. Live music plays on Saturday evening and Sunday afternoon. Sunday is a quiet night and a ladies quiz is held on the first Tuesday evening of the month. Two guest beers are usually available.
(35)

Trust Inn

8 Low Barholm, PA10 2ET
11.45-11.30; 11-1am Fri & Sat; 12.30-11.30 Sun
☎ (01505) 702401
Caledonian Deuchars IPA; guest beer H
At this large and spacious single-roomed pub enthusiastic staff check with the regulars to see which ale they would like to see as the guest – Houston Brewery beers are always popular. Regular entertainment includes the Tuesday night quiz and live bands on Friday evening. Children are permitted until 8pm. Close to the National Trust for Scotland's Weaver's Cottage. (36)

Kilmacolm

Pullman Tavern

Eithinstone Court, Lochwinnoch Road, PA13 4LG
11-11 (midnight Wed; 1am Fri & Sat); 12.30-11 Sun
☎ (01505) 874501
Beer range varies H
The only pub in the village, this Mitchells & Butlers hostelry is a converted railway station on the Sustrans cycle path from Paisley to Gourock. The outside seating area is popular with families, walkers and cyclists during the summer. Although the beer range varies, Timothy Taylor Landlord is a regular choice. P

Kirkintilloch

Kirky Puffer

1-11 Townhead, G66 1NG (next to canal)
11 (12.30 Sun)-midnight ☎ (0141) 7754140
Caledonian Deuchars IPA; Greene King Abbot; Strathaven Kirky Puffer Red; guest beers H
Originally a police station and now a Wetherspoon venue, the large and diverse interior is divided into different areas including what used to be the cells. The adjacent Forth & Clyde Canal is the main focus for tourists and can be viewed from the side rooms. There are historic pictures of boats – the pub name refers to the old puffer steamboats. Cyclists and walkers travel the towpath and also the nearby Roman Antonine Way. Easy to reach from Glasgow via bus. Q (84,85,88)

SCOTLAND

Lanark

Clydesdale Inn ✔

15 Bloomgate, ML11 9ET
✪ 11-midnight (1am Fri, 11.45 Sat); 12.30-midnight Sun
☎ (01555) 678 740
Caledonian Deuchars IPA; Greene King Abbot; guest beers Ⓗ
Wetherspoon pub in the centre of an historic county town, catering for the whole community including drinkers, diners and especially families. It has several small areas with a good ambience, and the bar boasts a varied range of ales from all over the UK. Only an hour from Glasgow, this is a friendly hostelry you will find hard to leave. New Lanark village nearby is worth a look.
♞◐◑♿≹🚌🍎

Lochwinnoch

Brown Bull

33 Main Street, PA12 4AH
✪ 12-11 (midnight Fri; 11.45 Sat); 12.30-11 Sun
☎ (01505) 843250
Caledonian Deuchars IPA; guest beers Ⓗ
More than 200 years old, this friendly family-run village free house, popular with visitors and locals alike, was local CAMRA Branch Pub of the Year in 2007. The restaurant upstairs makes full use of local produce. Quiz night is Tuesday and live music features every second Sunday. ♨◐◑♿⚊

Milngavie

Talbot Arms

30 Main Street, G62 6BU
✪ 11-midnight; 12.30-11 Sun ☎ (0141) 955 0981
Caledonian Deuchars IPA, 80; guest beers Ⓗ
This traditional bar, with modern furniture, attracts mainly locals but is also handy for walkers on the West Highland Way. Entertainment includes regular live bands, an 'open mike' night and a quiz at the weekend. Three screens show big football matches and other sporting events. Lunchtime food is popular. Customers playing traditional board and card games during the week get free snacks, and local clubs are encouraged to meet here. Staff welcome guest ale suggestions from their regular ale drinkers. ◐◑♿≹🚌(8,10)♣

Milton of Campsie

Kincaid House Hotel

Birdston Road, G66 8BZ (signed on B757, just S of village) NS650760
✪ 12-11.30 (1am Fri & Sat); 12.30-midnight Sun
☎ (0141) 776 2226 🌐 kincaidhouse.com
Beer range varies Ⓗ
Country house hotel, at the end of a long wooded driveway. The bar room, which lies behind the main building, is wood-panelled, with horse brasses and an old Alloa Brewery mirror, and has a pool table. The bar has two handpumps for real ale. There is a fire in the lounge/dining area and next to the conservatory restaurant is a child-safe garden. Food is served all day, attracting locals, tourists and walkers on the nearby Campsie Hills.
♨❀🛏◐◑♿🚌(88)P⚊

Motherwell

Brandon Works ✔

54-60 Merry Street, ML1 1JJ
✪ 11-midnight (1am Fri & Sat); 12.30-midnight Sun
☎ (01698) 210280
Caledonian Deuchars IPA; Greene King Abbot; guest beers Ⓗ
This Wetherspoon outlet, conveniently sited in a shopping centre, is named after a former ironworks that once occupied the site behind the pub, now a public car park. The large single room is on several levels and divided into drinking and dining areas. Motherwell was Britain's largest town without real beer before this pub opened – unsurprisingly it was warmly welcomed by local ale fans. The long bar dispenses up to three guest beers to accompany the regulars. Q◐◑♿⛺≹🚌🍎

Paisley

Bull Inn ★ ✔

7 New Street, PA1 1XU
✪ 11-11 (1am Fri & Sat); 12.30-11 Sun ☎ (0141) 849 0472
🌐 bullinnpaisley.co.uk
Caledonian Deuchars IPA; guest beers Ⓗ
Established in 1901, this National Inventory of Historic Pub Interiors-listed pub is the oldest in Paisley. It retains many original features including stained glass windows, bar gantry and three small snugs. Guest ales are primarly Scottish, from local breweries and further afield. Football fixtures are shown on a huge screen and on match days the pub can be full to bursting, especially when Scotland or St Mirren are playing at home.
◐≹(Gilmour St)🚌

Harvies Bar

86 Glasgow Road, PA1 3NU
✪ 11-midnight (1am Fri & Sat); 12.30-midnight Sun
☎ (0141) 889 0911
Caledonian 80; Kelburn Goldihops Ⓗ
Popular local, situated on the main road to Glasgow, with a well-preserved interior. Inside there is a large open-plan bar room with plenty of comfortable seating. Three plasma screens show sports and music videos with the volume turned down low. The pub hosts a popular quiz night on Sunday. The recent introduction of ale from the nearby Kelburn Brewery has been well-received.
◐◑♿≹(Hawkhead)

Last Post ✔

2 County Square, PA1 1BN
✪ 11-midnight (1am Fri & Sat); 12.30-midnight Sun
☎ (0141) 849 6911
Caledonian Deuchars IPA; Greene King Old Speckled Hen, Abbot; guest beers Ⓗ
Large Wetherspoon hostelry in a building that used to be the town's main post office. It has an open-plan design, plenty of seating downstairs and more on the upstairs balcony. The standard Wetherspoon food menu is available. Situated next to the entrance to Gilmour Street railway station, the pub is handy for a pint between trains.
Q◐◑♿≹(Gilmour St)

Sandpiper ✔

Glasgow Airport, Abbotsinch, PA3 2SW
✪ 5am-midnight ☎ (0141) 848 4877
Caledonian Deuchars IPA; Greene King Abbot; guest beers Ⓗ

A relatively recent addition to the Airport's retail outlets, this pub has six handpumps offering the Wetherspoon standards as well as a good selection of guest beers from around the country. The pub is named after the bird that visits nearby Paisley Moss Local Nature Reserve. Easy to reach by bus. (66,500,747)

Wee Howff

53 High Street, PA1 2AN

11-midnight (1am Fri & Sat); 12.30-midnight Sun
(0141) 889 2095

Caledonian 80; guest beers

An oasis in an area of cheap drinking establishments, this pub has appeared in the last 21 editions of the Guide. The Howf is a small, traditional pub with a loyal regular clientele and features an 'open mike' night on the first Monday of the month, along with a pub quiz every Thursday. The juke-box caters for the most eclectic of tastes. Guest ales come from all four corners of Britain. (Gilmour St)

Strathaven

Weavers

1-3 Green Street, ML10 6LT

11 (4 Tue-Thu)-midnight (1am Sat); 7-1am Sun
(07749) 332 914

Beer range varies

Current Glasgow CAMRA Lanarkshire Pub of the Year, this independently run pub takes its name from the town's traditional industry. The decor is light and modern – the walls filled with photographs of Hollywood stars. One handpump is dedicated to LocAle from the Strathaven Brewery, while the other three deliver an ever-changing range of beers from Scottish and English micros. There is also a selection of malt whiskies and bottled imported beers. (13)

Uplawmoor

Uplawmoor Hotel

66 Neilston Road, G78 4AF (off A736)

11-11 (midnight Sat); 12.30-11 Sun (01505) 850565
uplawmoor.co.uk

Houston Killellan; Kelburn Misty Law; guest beer

Situated in a tranquil village setting just over 10 miles from Glasgow, the building dates back to the 18th century. It was originally a coaching inn used by travellers and customs officers chasing smugglers en-route between Glasgow and the south-west coast of Scotland. Today the hotel continues to offer travellers the opportunity to relax and explore. The interior is rustic and cosy, with a separate pool room. Bar meals are served until 9.30pm and the guest beer is from Houston. QP

Wishaw

Wishaw Malt

62-66 Kirk Road, ML2 7BL

11-11 (midnight Thu; 1am Fri & Sat); 12.30-midnight Sun
(01698) 358806

Caledonian Deuchars IPA; Greene King Abbot; guest beers

This Wetherspoon pub opened over 10 years ago and has done wonders for real ale in an area with few alternatives. Popular with locals, it also attracts drinkers from out of town. The large room is on different levels, each with its own character to cater for regular drinkers and diners, as well as families, and the outside patio area is pleasant in summer. Two guest ales may come from local breweries or further afield, so there is always something interesting to try.
(240,267)

SCOTLAND

Bon Accord, Glasgow

HIGHLANDS & WESTERN ISLES

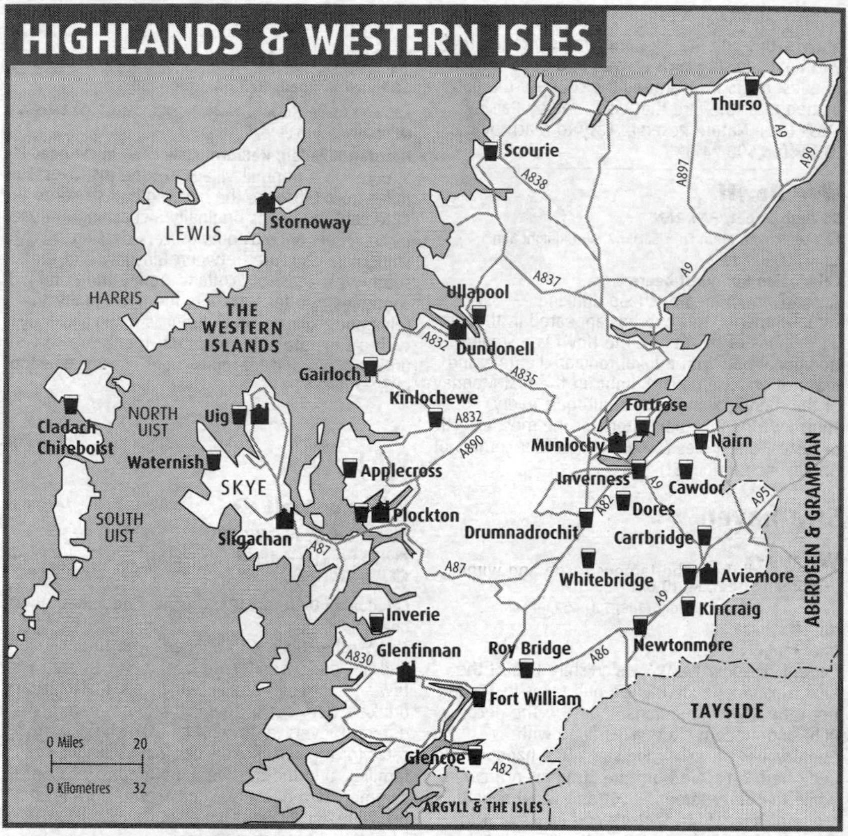

Authority areas covered: Highland UA, Western Isles UA

Applecross

Applecross Inn

Shore Street, IV54 8LR (on unclassified road off A896)
NG710444
11-11.30 (midnight Fri); 12.30-11.30 Sun
(01520) 744262 applecross.uk.com/inn
Beer range varies
Owned by the same family since 1989, the inn is spectacularly situated on the shore of the Applecross Peninsula enjoying views of the Isles of Skye and Raasay. It is reached by a single track road over the highest vehicular ascent in Britain, or by a longer scenic route. Two Isle of Skye beers are served alongside a large malt whisky selection. Accommodation is available and local seafood is a speciality. The area is ideal for climbing, walking and wildlife watching.

Aviemore

Cairngorm Hotel

Grampian Road, PH22 1PE (opp train station)
11-midnight (1am Fri & Sat); 11.30-midnight Sun
(01479) 810233 cairngorm.com
Cairngorm Stag, Gold
The lounge bar of this privately owned hotel, though large, has a cosy feel, enhanced by two bay windows, distressed wooden furniture and a large coal effect fire. Though the trade is mainly holidaymakers, the bar is very popular with locals, with a large-screen TV showing sport. There is a Scottish theme throughout the hotel with tartan wall coverings and Scottish entertainment on many afternoons and evenings.

Dalfaber Golf & Country Club

Dalfaber Drive, Dalfaber, PH22 1ST
11 (12.30 Sun)-midnight (01479) 811244
Cairngorm Trade Winds; guest beer
Dalfaber Lounge Bar serves Trade Winds and a guest ale from the local Cairngorm Brewery. With live entertainment most evenings and a Sunday night pub quiz, the bar has a lively, friendly and informal atmosphere where families are welcome. It has two full-size snooker tables and there is a leisure club attached with swimming pool and sports hall hosting tournaments for local teams. All major sports are screened on TV.

Old Bridge Inn

Dalfaber Road, PH22 1PU NH894117
11-midnight (1am Fri & Sat); 12.30-midnight Sun
(01479) 811137 oldbridgeinn.co.uk
Caledonian Deuchars IPA; guest beers
Busy pub, popular with outdoor enthusiasts, serving good quality food. Originally a cottage and now greatly enlarged, it lies on the road to the Strathspey Steam Railway, overlooking the River Spey. The two guest handpumps usually dispense a beer from the local Cairngorm Brewery plus another from a Scottish micro. Live music plays weekly. Children are welcome and there is a bunkhouse attached.

Carrbridge

Cairn Hotel
PH23 3AS (on B9153)
11-midnight (1am Fri & Sat); 12.30-11 Sun
☎ (01479) 841212 cairnhotel.co.uk
Beer range varies H
In the centre of a pleasant village, just off the A9 and close to the Landmark Heritage Park, the busy, cosy bar is part of the hotel. It is popular with locals and visitors, particularly walkers and cyclists. Two handpumps dispense mainly Scottish ales, usually from Cairngorm, Black Isle, Isle of Skye, Caledonian, Orkney and Atlas. Bar meals, soup and toasties are available all day. ♣P

Cawdor

Cawdor Tavern ✔
The Lane, IV12 5XP
11-11 (midnight Fri & Sat); 11-3, 5-11 (midnight Fri) Oct-Apr; 12.30-11 Sun ☎ (01667) 404777
cawdortavern.com
Beers range varies H
At the heart of this conservation village, the pub is a short walk from the famous castle and within easy reach of Fort George and Culloden battlefield. A pub full of character, it has a spacious lounge bar and cosy public bar, both wood panelled with log fires, and a large restaurant. The public bar features a splendid antique mahogany bar and a ceiling covered in old maps. Up to four handpumps offer ales from Atlas and Orkney, breweries belonging to the family that owns the pub. ♣P

Cladach Chirebost: North Uist

Westford Inn
HS6 5EP (5km NW of A867/865 jct) NF781655
12 (5 Oct-Mar)-11; 12.30-midnight Sun ☎ (01876) 580653
westfordinn.co.uk
Beer range varies H
A Georgian listed building, set in a remote area of the Outer Hebrides on the edge of the Atlantic. Popular with local fishermen, walkers, shooting parties and tourists, this friendly pub has a traditional atmosphere where a quick drink can turn into a ceilidh. Home-cooked pub food is available late into the evening and there are real peat-fuelled fires from the pub's own peat cutting. Dogs are welcome. Note that winter times depend on custom. Beers are from the Isle of Skye Brewery. Q♣P

Dores

Dores Inn
IV2 6TR (on B862 from Inverness at jct with B852)
11-11 (midnight Fri & Sat); 12-11 Sun ☎ (01463) 751203
thedoresinn.co.uk
Beer range varies H
Situated on the south side of Loch Ness just eight miles from Inverness, this inn enjoys spectacular views. The cosy wood-finished bar serves up to four ales, nearly always from Scottish independent breweries such as Highland, Orkney and Atlas, with the occasional English ale featured. The welcoming, extended dining room serves very good food made with locally-sourced ingredients and can get busy at times. Home baking is available and the inn opens at 10am for coffee.
Q(302,303)P

Drumnadrochit

Benleva Hotel
Kilmore Road, IV63 6UH (signed, 800m from A82)
12-midnight (1am Fri); 12.30-11 Sun ☎ (01456) 450080
benleva.co.uk
Beer range varies H/G
Popular, friendly village inn near Loch Ness, catering for locals and visitors. A 400-year-old former manse, the sweet chestnut outside was once a hanging tree. Four handpumps dispense mainly Highlands and Islands beers, usually one from Isle of Skye. Westons cider is on handpump. Good evening meals, lunches and Sunday roasts are available all year. The pub hosts the Loch Ness Beer Festival in September, occasional quiz nights and traditional music. Dogs are welcome. A former local CAMRA Pub of the Year.
Q♣P

Fort William

Ben Nevis Inn
Claggan, Achintee, PH33 6TE (at start of Ben Nevis footpath) NN125729
12-11 (closed Mon-Wed Nov-Mar); 12.30-11 Sun
☎ (01397) 701227 ben-nevis-inn.co.uk
Beer range varies H
Located at the start of the Ben Nevis path in Glen Nevis, this traditional, stone-built barn inn is famous for its friendly, informal atmosphere. The bar, with long beer-hall style tables, is an ideal setting for regular live music. Food is served all day and local produce features in the mix of traditional favourites and international dishes. Three real ales are offered from local breweries. There is a bunkhouse downstairs. QP

Cobbs at Nevisport
Aird's Crossing, High Street, PH33 6EU
11-11 (1am Fri & Sat); 12.30-11 Sun ☎ (01397) 704790
cobbs.info
Beer range varies H
A warming open fire welcomes winter visitors to this large but cosy bar, located beneath the Nevisport shop. At the West Highland Way finish and Great Glen Way start, close to Glen Nevis and convenient for Aonach Mor, this is a favourite meeting place for outdoor enthusiasts. Mostly Scottish beers are served, often from local Highlands and Islands breweries. Food is served in the bar or upstairs restaurant where children are welcome. Five minutes' walk from the railway station.

Grog & Gruel ✔
66 High Street, PH33 6AE
12 (4 Mon-Fri winter)-11.30; 12-12.30am Fri & Sat; 12 (5 winter)-11.30 Sun ☎ (01397) 705078 grogandgruel.co.uk
Beer range varies H

INDEPENDENT BREWERIES

An Teallach Dundonell
Black Isle Munlochy
Cairngorm Aviemore
Cuillin Sligachan
Glenfinnan Glenfinnan
Hebridean Stornoway
Isle of Skye Uig
Plockton Plockton

SCOTLAND

In the shadow of Britain's highest mountain, this bare-floored traditional ale house keeps up to six beers in summer, fewer in winter. Owned by the same family as the Clachaig Inn in Glencoe, it holds regular live music and beer festivals. The beers are predominantly Scottish, often from the local Glenfinnan Brewery, and the bar is busy with locals, outdoor enthusiasts and tourists. Home-cooked food is available in the upstairs dining room and light meals and snacks in the bar.
❀◑▲⇌🚌⚍

Fortrose

Anderson

Union Street, IV10 8TD
🕒 4-11.30; 12.30-11.30 Sun ☎ (01381) 620236
🌐 theanderson.co.uk
Beer range varies Ⓗ
Homely bar in a quiet seaside village, part of a nine-bedroom hotel. The owners are an international beer writer and self-confessed 'beer geek' and his wife, a New Orleans-trained chef. Serving ales and ciders from independent breweries, this eclectic beer drinkers' mecca also offers more than 200 malts and 100 Belgian beers, earning it several prestigious UK awards and the Belgian Ambassadeur d'Orval 2010. In the winter there is a barley wine festival. The food is reasonably priced, high-quality international cuisine. CAMRA members are offered a discount on accommodation. ♨☋❀⇌◑⊟▲🚌(26)♣●P⚍

Gairloch

Old Inn

Flowerdale, IV21 2BD (opp harbour) NG811751
🕒 11-1am (11.45 Sat); 12-11.15 Sun ☎ (0800) 542 5444
🌐 theoldinn.net
An Teallach Ale; Greene King Abbot; Isle of Skye Red Cuillin; guest beers Ⓗ
Traditional Highland coaching inn situated in a delightful riverside setting at the foot of the picturesque Flowerdale Glen. Close to Loch Maree, Inverewe Gardens and the Beinn Eighe Nature Reserve, this is an ideal base for exploring the delights of Wester Ross. The finest quality local produce, including West Coast seafood and Highland game dishes, takes pride of place on the menu. Six real ales are on handpump (three in winter), including brews from Isle of Skye and An Teallach breweries. ♨☋❀⇌◑⊟▲♣●P

Glencoe

Clachaig Inn

PH49 4HX (on slip road ½ mile off A83) NN128567
🕒 11-11 (midnight Fri; 11.30 Sat); 12.30-11 Sun
☎ (01855) 811 252 🌐 clachaig.com
Beer range varies Ⓗ
Situated at the base of the mountains in the centre of Glencoe, this pub attracts mainly walkers and climbers, but the hotel rooms and lounge bar are also very welcoming to the less active. The large stone-floored, stove-warmed Boots Bar offers mainly Scottish beers. Local musicians play most weekends and the pub hosts occasional mountaineering lectures. Beer festivals are held regularly. A youth hostel and two campsites are within staggering distance (bring a torch and midge repellent). ♨Q☋❀⇌◑⊟♿▲🚌(916)●P

Inverie

Old Forge

PH41 4PL (100m from ferry terminal)
🕒 11 (4 Tue & Thu; 12 Sat winter)-midnight; 11 (12 winter)-midnight Sun ☎ (01678) 462267
🌐 theoldforge.co.uk
Beer range varies Ⓗ
The most remote pub in mainland Britain can be reached only by ferry from Mallaig or a 15-mile hilly walk. In a spectacular setting on the shore of Loch Nevis, it provides an ideal location for walking the rough bounds of Knoydart. Moorings welcome waterborne visitors. Two handpumps usually include a beer from Isle of Skye or Glenfinnan breweries. Excellent food is served all day featuring locally-caught seafood specials. ♨Q❀◑▲⚍

Inverness

Blackfriars ✔

93-95 Academy Street, IV1 1LU
🕒 11-midnight (1am Fri, 12.30am Sat); 12.30-11 Sun
☎ (01463) 233881 🌐 blackfriarshighlandpub.co.uk
Caledonian Deuchars IPA; guest beers Ⓗ
This popular traditional pub is well worth the short walk from the centre of town. It has a spacious single room interior with a large standing area by the bar and ample seating in comfortable alcoves. The five handpumps are split between English and Scottish ales, with Scottish beers often from Inveralmond and Highland. A further two handpumps dispense real cider. Good-value meals feature home-cooked Scottish fare with daily specials. A welcoming, music-oriented pub, it hosts ceilidh, folk, country and a singing landlord, with local bands performing at weekends. ◑♿⇌🚌●

Castle Tavern 🏆

1 View Place, IV2 4SA (top of Castle Street) NH666449
🕒 11-1am (12.30am Sat); 12.30-midnight Sun
☎ (01463) 718178 🌐 castletavern.net
Beer range varies Ⓗ
Minutes from the city centre, this 19th-century listed building faces Inverness Castle and overlooks the River Ness. A favourite haunt for discerning visitors and locals, there is always a warm welcome and a lively buzz in the bar. Six handpumps dispense an Isle of Skye Brewery house beer plus changing guests mostly from Scottish independents. Good-value bar meals are served all day, and there is a restaurant on the first floor. A Victorian-style canopy covers the large beer patio. CAMRA Highlands & Western Isles Pub of the Year 2010. ❀◑▲⇌🚌⚍

Clachnaharry Inn

17-19 High Street, Clachnaharry, IV3 8RB (on A862 Beauly Road) NH648466
🕒 11-11 (1am Thu-Fri; 12.30am Sat); 12-11.45 Sun
☎ (01463) 239806 🌐 clachnaharryinn.co.uk
Adnams Broadside; guest beers Ⓗ
Popular with locals and visitors, this friendly 17th-century coaching inn offers high-quality food made with locally-sourced ingredients lunchtimes and evenings. Families are made welcome. Five handpumps dispense mainly Scottish guest beers, often from Inveralmond and Cairngorm breweries. The large patio area affords fine views over the Caledonian Canal sea lock and Beauly Firth toward the distant Ben Wyvis. The beer garden was once the platform of the old village station on the north railway line. ♨Q❀◑⊟▲🚌(18A)P

Kings Highway ✓

72-74 Church Street, IV1 1EN

11-11 (midnight Thu & Sat; 1am Fri); 12.30-11 Sun

☎ (01463) 251830

Caledonian Deuchars IPA; Greene King Abbot; guest beers Ⓗ

This former hotel is now a Wetherspoon pub with a 27-room lodge attached. The vast single roomed bar is broken up by several pillars and plenty of comfortable seating in alcoves. Up to 10 handpumps serve the regular ales and a good mix of guests, usually including beers from Houston and Cairngorm. Real cider is also available. Food is standard Wetherspoon's, with breakfasts served from 7am. Customers are the typical eclectic mix and the pub gets busy at weekends.

Snowgoose ✓

Stoneyfield, IV2 7PA (on A96)

12-11 (10.30 Sun-Thu Jan-Mar) ☎ (01463) 701921

Caledonian Deuchars IPA; guest beers Ⓗ

This traditional inn supports a popular bar trade with an area reserved for drinkers. Situated next to a Holiday Inn and a Travelodge, most of the custom comes from the local area. A converted 1788 coach house, the single large L-shaped room has alcoves and log fires to give it a more cosy and intimate feel. A wide variety of food is offered all day at reasonable prices. The two guest handpumps feature ever-changing ales from the Mitchells & Butlers Vintage Inn list. Q(1,10)P

Kincraig

Suie Hotel

PH21 1NA

5-11 (1am Fri & Sat) ☎ (01540) 651344 suiehotel.com

Cairngorm Trade Winds; guest beer Ⓗ

Cosy wooden extension to a seven-bedroomed Victorian character hotel, run by the second owner in 105 years. The wooden floored bar features a large stove and open fire and has an alcove with a pool table and jukebox. Situated between the Cairngorms and Monadhliath mountain ranges and close to the River Spey and Loch Insh, the bar is popular with locals, hillwalkers, skiers and cyclists. Traditional Scottish music features occasionally. A second handpump usually dispenses another Cairngorm brew. Very good food is served.

P

Kinlochewe

Kinlochewe Hotel

IV22 2PA NH028619

11-11 ☎ (01445) 760253 kinlochewehotel.co.uk

Isle of Skye Red Cuillin, Beinn Eighe Ⓗ

The ambience in this recently refurbished bar is friendly and welcoming, and a wood-burning stove provides extra warmth on chilly evenings. Home-cooked food uses the very best of seasonal high-quality local produce, including seafood, game and beef, all freshly cooked with an emphasis on simplicity and flavour. Set in the heart of the magnificent Torridon Mountains at the foot of Beinn Eighe, this is an ideal base for exploring the wild scenery of the North Western Highlands. Isle of Skye Brewery beers are served.

QP

Nairn

Braeval Hotel ✓

Crescent Road, IV12 4NB

12-midnight (12.30am Thu-Sat); 12.30-midnight Sun

☎ (01667) 452341 braevalhotel.co.uk

Beer range varies Ⓗ

Part of the Braeval Hotel, close to Nairn beach, the Bandstand Bar has five handpumps serving Scottish ales, mainly from Skye and Orkney, and a varying selection of English ales. Another handpump serves real cider. The family-run hotel is renowned for its Scottish and seafood menu served in the impressive restaurant offering spectacular sea views overlooking the Moray Firth. The bar hosts a beer festival every March featuring up to 50 ales. CAMRA Highlands & Western Isles Pub of the Year 2009. (10,11,305)P

Newtonmore

Glen Hotel ✓

Main Street, PH20 1DD

11 (12.30 Sun)-midnight ☎ (01540) 673203

theglenhotel.co.uk

Beer range varies Ⓗ

Small, welcoming, family-run hotel in Monarch of the Glen country in the Cairngorms National Park. It has a good local trade and is also popular with outdoor enthusiasts and tourists. Regular quiz and games nights are held. There is a large bar with separate games and dining rooms. Up to four handpumps usually dispense an English ale and Scottish beers, usually from Cairngorm, plus a Westons cider or perry. An extensive menu includes a good selection of vegetarian dishes.

P

Plockton

Plockton Hotel ✓

41 Harbour Street, IV52 8TN NG803335

11-midnight; 12.30-11 Sun ☎ (01599) 544274

plocktonhotel.co.uk

Beer range varies Ⓗ

Sheltered by mountains and fanned by the warm air of the Gulf Stream, the hotel, overshadowed by palm trees, is set in a sweep of whitewashed Highland cottages at the edge of Loch Carron and boasts breathtaking views across the bay. Seafood is the speciality on an excellent menu that also features locally-reared beef and Highland venison. The village has much to offer and is a regular haunt for outdoor enthusiasts. Brews from the local Plockton Brewery are regularly on handpump.

QP

Plockton Inn ✓

Innes Street, IV52 8TW NG803333

11-1am (12.30am Sat); 11-11 Sun ☎ (01599) 544222

plocktoninn.co.uk

Beer range varies Ⓗ

This popular village inn, set in the heart of the beautiful village of Plockton, has been owned and run by a local family for many years. Locally-caught fish and shellfish take pride of place on the menu and the seafood platter includes fish smoked on the premises. Every Tuesday and Thursday there are live music sessions in the public bar and all are welcome to join in. A regularly changing selection of real ales includes locally-brewed Plockton Brewery ales. QP

SCOTLAND

Roy Bridge

Stronlossit Inn

PH31 4AG

⏲ 11-11.45 (1am Thu-Sat); 12.30-11.45 Sun

☎ (01397) 712253 🌐 stronlossit.co.uk

Beer range varies Ⓗ

Traditional family-run Scottish inn, surrounded by landscaped gardens. Situated at the foot of the Nevis mountain range, the inn is an ideal base for outdoor activities or touring in the Highlands. Bar meals featuring local seasonal produce are available all day. The three handpumps dispense a selection of Scottish beers, often from Highland and Islands breweries, and an occasional cider. Opening times may vary in December and January. ♨❀🛏◑♿▲⇌🚌●P

Scourie

Scourie Hotel

IV27 4SX (on A894 between Laxford Bridge and Kylesku)

⏲ 11-2.30, 5-11 summer; 5-9.30 (10.30 Fri); 12-2.30, 5-11 Sat winter; 12-2.30, 6-10.30 Sun ☎ (01971) 502396

🌐 scourie-hotel.co.uk

Beer range varies Ⓗ

This historic coaching inn on the site of an old fortified house is a popular retreat for fishermen. Overlooking Scourie Bay, it is also handy for the bird reserve of Handa Island and the peaks of Ben Stack, Arkle and Foinavon. In addition to the bar menu, the dining room serves high-quality meals featuring local seafood. Four handpumps dispense mainly Scottish beers, usually from Cairngorm in winter, and one or two Westons ciders. Q❀🛏◑⊟▲♣●P⊬

Thurso

Central Hotel

3 Traill Street, KW14 8EJ

⏲ 11-11.45 (1am Fri & Sat); 12.30-11.45 Sun

☎ (01847) 893129

Beer range varies Ⓗ

Lively town-centre hotel bar, two miles from the Orkney Ferry Terminal at Scrabster, on the Pentland Firth. The downstairs bar has four handpumps, with two or three ales available all year round. Beers are mainly from the Highland Brewing Company, but a wide selection of other breweries also features. Live sport is regularly shown on the big screen. Children are not permitted in the bar, but are most welcome in the popular upstairs play area. ♉🛏◑⊟♿▲⇌🚌♣⊬▯

Uig: Isle of Skye

Bakur Bar

The Pier, IV51 9XX

⏲ 11.30-11 (midnight Thu; 1am Fri; 12.30am Sat); 12.30-11.30 Sun ☎ (01470) 542212

Beer range varies Ⓗ

This traditional West Coast bar is conveniently located on the pier at Uig adjacent to the Western Isles ferry terminal and a stone's throw from the Isle of Skye Brewery, who supply all the pub's ales. During the summer months up to four beers are available, with a more limited range in the quieter winter season. The Bakur also has a pool table and is popular with the locals. ❀◑♿▲🚌P⊬

Ullapool

Argyll Hotel

18 Argyll Street, IV26 2UB

⏲ 11-1am (midnight Sat); 12.30-11.30 Sun

☎ (01854) 612422 🌐 theargyllullapool.com

Beer range varies Ⓗ

This busy, small hotel offers breakfast, lunch and dinner all made with locally-sourced produce wherever possible. The beer range includes a changing English guest plus another from An Teallach. Live music sessions feature on Monday, and regular live bands on Tuesday and Saturday. Weekly quiz and poker nights keep the lounge bar busy. A pool table is available through the back and a dartboard in the public bar. Dogs are welcome. Hours vary out of season. ♨❀🛏◑⊟♿▲♣●P⊬

Morefield Motel

North Road, IV26 2TQ (off A835) NH125947

⏲ 12 (12.30 Sun)-11 ☎ (01854) 612161

🌐 morefieldmotel.co.uk

Beer range varies Ⓗ

Locally-caught seafood is the speciality on the menu at this friendly and welcoming hostelry. Three ales are predominantly from local Highland breweries. Landlord Tony organises the annual Ullapool Beer Festival, held at the Morefield in October. Comfortable accommodation makes this an excellent base for discovering the surrounding area. The Western Isles ferry terminal is a short distance away. Q❀🛏◑♿▲♣P⊬

Waternish: Isle of Skye

Stein Inn ✔

Waternish, IV55 8GA (N of Dunvegan, on B886) NG263564

⏲ 11-midnight (1am Fri; 12.30am Sat); 12-11 (midnight Fri & Sat) winter; 11.30 (12.30 winter)-11 Sun ☎ (01470) 592362

🌐 steininn.co.uk

Isle of Skye Red Cuillin; guest beers Ⓗ

Family-run 18th-century inn, nestling in a row of cottages on the shores of Loch Bay. An open central fireplace warms the cosy low-beamed bar. Home-cooked local produce, including fresh seafood, is served in the bar and restaurant from a menu that changes daily in accordance with the season's availability. Both bar and large shoreside garden afford stunning views over the sea loch to Rubha Maol. Facilities for seafarers include council moorings, showers, food supplies (by arrangement) and a message relay service. ♨Q♉❀🛏◑⊟♿♣P⊬

Whitebridge

Whitebridge Hotel

IV2 6UN

⏲ 11-11 Apr-Oct; 11-2.30, 5-11 Nov-Mar; 12.30-11 Sun

☎ (01456) 486226 🌐 whitebridgehotel.co.uk

Beer range varies Ⓗ

Built in 1899, this hotel is situated on an original Military Road through the foothills of the Monadhliath mountains. There is a classic Wade Bridge nearby and the famous Falls of Foyers are close. It has fishing rights on two local lochs. The attractive pitch pine panelled bar has an alcove with a pool table. One or two local Highland beers are served and most of the traditional pub food is home cooked. The hotel has a green tourism policy. ♨Q❀🛏◑⊟♿🚌♣P

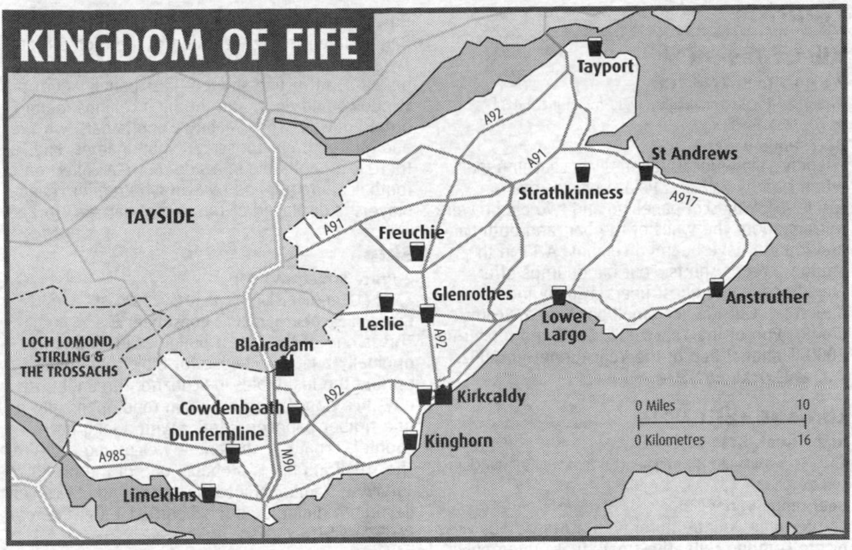

Authority area covered: Fife UA

Anstruther

Dreel Tavern

16 High Street, KY10 3DL

11 (12.30 Sun)-midnight; 12.30-midnight

(01334) 310727

Caledonian Deuchars IPA; guest beers H

A former Fife CAMRA Pub of the Year, situated in an old fishing village with links to James IV, the Dreel is an old stone building with traditional crow-step gables and a pantile roof. The public and lounge bars are separated by an open fire. Wood panelling and stone walls with an ornamental stove at one end of the bar all add to a cosy atmosphere. The games room has a pool table and the conservatory to the rear provides a pleasant dining area. Q (X26,95)

Ship Tavern

49 Shore Street, KY10 3AQ (next to Scottish Fisheries Museum)

11-midnight (1am Fri & Sat); 12.30-midnight Sun

(01333) 310347

Beer range varies H

This old, traditional pub on the harbour front is a popular meeting place for fishermen, locals and visitors to the museum next door. The main bar has a flagstone floor and a picture window overlooking the harbour, which provides berths for around 100 boats. Above the mirror behind the bar, covering two walls, is a mural of the harbour. A back room has a pool table. Ales from micro-breweries often feature. (X26)

Cowdenbeath

Woodside Hotel

109 Broad Street, KY4 8JR

11 (12.30 Sun)-midnight (01383) 510475

Beer range varies H

Large single-roomed bar with two handpumps serving ales from local micro-breweries in lined glasses. At one side of the room there is a pool table and dartboard, and around the room there are four plasma screens showing sport. A warm, friendly atmosphere prevails, with poker played on Thursday night and live entertainment at the weekend. A separate lounge is available for small functions. There is a covered, outdoor decked area with seating at the rear, which is a lovely suntrap in summer. (X54,19,30) P

Dunfermline

Commercial Inn

13 Douglas Street, KY12 7EB

11-11 (midnight Fri & Sat); 12.30-11 Sun

(01383) 733876

Caledonian Deuchars IPA, 80; Courage Directors; Theakston Old Peculier; guest beers H

Well-known ale house in a building dating back to the 1820s. A cosy town-centre pub, it is situated opposite the main post office off the High Street. This is a pub for conversation, with quiet background music. Good-quality food and friendly service attract an eclectic clientele. Seven ales are always available plus one cider. An extensive food menu includes regular specials at lunchtime. Evening meals are served Monday-Wednesday and Saturday. Fife CAMRA Pub of the Year 2005, 2006 and 2008.

East Port

7 East Port, KY12 7JG

11.30-11 (midnight Fri & Sat); 12.30-11 Sun

(01383) 736678 eastportbar.co.uk

Caledonian Deuchars IPA H

Busy town-centre pub with very friendly staff. The interior features wood panelling and a wood bar and gantry, alcove seating and comfortable sofas at the rear. An old Maclay mirror decorates the stairs leading to the beer garden. Two plasma screens show sport, and soft background music usually plays. Value-for-money bar food is served at lunchtime. The pub received a Best Bar None award in 2008 and 2009 from Fife Constabulary.

SCOTLAND

Freuchie

Albert Tavern

2 High Street, KY15 7EX

5 (12 Fri & Sat)-midnight; 12.30-midnight Sun

(07765) 169342

Beer range varies

Friendly village local, reputedly a coaching inn when nearby Falkland Palace was a royal residence. Wainscot panelling and two old brewery mirrors adorn the walls of the bar, and both bar and lounge have beamed ceilings. A TV in the lounge screens sports. Four handpumps offer weekly-changing guest beers, usually including a dark mild. Outside is a small patio area. Scottish CAMRA Pub of the Year 2002, 2009 and runner-up 2008. National Pub of the Year runner-up 2002.

Q (X54,64)P

Lomond Hills Hotel

High Street, KY15 7EY

11-2, 5-midnight; 11-midnight Fri & Sat; 12.30-midnight Sun (01337) 857329

Beer range varies

Comfortable country hotel with a marvellous view of the Lomond Hills. The small, welcoming public bar sports a carved bar top and wood panelling on the walls. A plasma screen shows sports. Two beers are always available. Meals are served in the family lounge and a separate dining room. Outside there is a smoking area and beer garden. The hotel has a leisure area with heated pool and sauna available to guests.

(X54, 64)P

Glenrothes

Golden Acorn

1 North Street, KY7 5NA (next to bus station)

11 (12.30 Sun)-midnight (01592) 751175

Greene King Abbot

Large Wetherspoon venue with its own accommodation. In the bar, scenes of the local area in days gone by decorate various pillars. Real ale on four handpumps and an occasional cider are on offer, as well as the usual Wetherspoon beer festivals and special deals. The local Fyfe Brewing Company sometimes also holds a beer festival. Families are welcome if dining until 6pm. Breakfast is served before 11am. Plasma screens show sport and there is a smoking area and seating outside.

P

Kinghorn

Auld Hoose

6-8 Nethergate, KY3 9SY

12 (11 Sat; 12.30 Sun)-midnight (01592) 891074

Fuller's London Pride; guest beers

Busy village local situated on a steep side street leading off the east end of Kinghorn main street, handy for the station, Kinghorn beach and the Fife Coastal Path. Popular with locals and visitors, the main bar has a TV and pool table to keep sports fans happy and features dominoes competitions at the weekend. The lounge is quieter and more comfortable, with a relaxed atmosphere.

(6,7)

Crown Tavern

55-57 High Street, KY3 9UW

11 (12.30 Sun)-11.45 (01592) 890340

Beer range varies

Bustling two-roomed local, also called The Middle Bar, situated to the west end of the High Street. Two ever-changing ales are dispensed by cheery bar staff. Attractive stained glass panels adorn the windows and door, and the high ceilings feature ornate plaster work. Mainly a sports bar, two TVs and a large projector screen show games, and there is a pool table in a side room. A collection of footballs autographed by Scottish Premier League players is displayed at the end of bar. (6,7)

Ship

2 Bruce Street, KY3 9TJ

12 (12.30 Sun)-midnight (01592) 890655

Caledonian Deuchars IPA; guest beer

This is one of the oldest buildings in Kinghorn, originally built as a house for Bible John, who printed the first bibles in Scotland. The unobtrusive entrance door facing the main road opens into a fine timber-panelled interior with a long bar counter, ornate gantry and a welcoming coal fire. The small jug bar is probably one of the finest surviving traditional interiors in Fife. An attractively decorated dining area has been added at the rear.

(6,7)

Kirkcaldy

Harbour Bar

471-475 High Street, KY1 1JL

11-3, 5-midnight; 11-midnight Thu-Sat; 12.30-midnight Sun (01592) 264270 fyfebrewery.co.uk

Beer range varies

Situated on the ground floor of a tenement building, this unspoilt local with a brewery on the premises has been described by regulars as a 'village local in the middle of town'. It has a light and airy lounge with ornate cornices. Six handpumps sell up to 20 different beers each week from micros all over Britain, including its own Fyfe Brewery ales. CAMRA Fife Pub of the Year on numerous occasions and Scottish Pub of the Year runner-up in 2000. Q

Robert Nairn

2-6 Kirk Wynd, KY1 1EH

11 (12.30 Sun)-midnight (01592) 205049

Caledonian Deuchars IPA; Greene King Abbot

A Lloyds No 1 with a split-level lounge and a separate family area. The walls feature pictures of old Kirkcaldy. Six handpumps sell a variety of beers including local ales from Fyfe Brewery – check the noticeboard to see the ales that are on and what to look forward to. There is also a good selection of bottled ciders. Frequent beer festivals are held throughout the year. Meals are served until 10pm.

Leslie

Burns Tavern

184 High Street, KY6 3DB

12 (11 Fri & Sat)-midnight; 12.30-midnight Sun

(01592) 741345

Taylor Landlord; guest beers

Typical Scottish two-room main-street local in a town once famous for paper making. The public bar

INDEPENDENT BREWERIES

Fyfe Kirkaldy
Loch Leven Blairadam

is on two levels, the lower lively and friendly with an open fire, the upper with a large-screen TV, pool table and football memorabilia on the walls. The lounge bar is quieter and more spacious. Competitions and quizzes are held weekly with karaoke on Saturday. Leslie folk club meets and plays here on a Sunday. Two beers are usually available. A real gem. (X1,201)P

Limekilns

Ship Inn

Halkett's Hall, KY11 3HJ (on promenade)
11-11 (midnight Fri & Sat); 12.30-11 Sun
(01383) 872247
Beer range varies
Traditional white coastal building on the waterfront with seating outside providing superb views of the River Forth to watch the ships go by. There is always a friendly welcome here, with fresh flowers, cosy alcoves and a maritime theme throughout. Three guest ales on handpump are complemented by the occasional real cider. Meals are served lunchtimes and evenings, with fish and seafood the speciality. Bar snacks are available outside meal service times. Q(73,76)P

Lower Largo

Railway Inn

1 Station Wynd, KY8 6BU
11 (12.30 Sun)-midnight (01333) 320239
Beer range varies
Small two-room pub with a cosy real fire close to the picturesque harbour. The bar has a railway theme and displays photographs of the last trains to pass on the viaduct overhead before the Beeching measures of the 1960s. TV screens in each room show sports. The four handpumps serve various beers from all over Britain. Bar snacks are available. Q

St Andrews

Central Bar

77-79 Market Street, KY16 9NU
11-11.45 (1am Fri & Sat); 12.30-11.45 Sun
(01334) 478296
Courage Directors; Fuller's London Pride; Inveralmond Lia Fail; Theakston Old Peculier
A good mix of students, locals, business folk and tourists make this an interesting, bustling hostelry. It has a Victorian-style island bar, large windows and ornate mirrors creating a late 19th-century feel. The only pub in town that serves food until 10pm, pavement tables are available, weather permitting. The bar manager is dedicated to his ales and the staff are very friendly.

Criterion

99 South Street, KY16 9QW
11-midnight (1am Fri & Sat); 12.30-midnight Sun
(01334) 474543
Caledonian Deuchars IPA; guest beers
This lovely pub has a big picture window and oak-panelled walls adorned with photographs of St Andrews in days gone by. The hostelry is famous for its home-made pies including steak and ale, chicken and ham, and lamb and rosemary, available until 5pm. Background music plays and a plasma screen shows sport. Monday is open music night and a quiz is hosted during the week.

Whey Pat Tavern

2 Argyle Street, KY16 9EX
11-11.30 (11.45 Fri & Sat); 12.30-11.30 Sun
(01334) 477740
Greene King IPA; guest beers
Town-centre pub on a busy road junction just outside the old town walls. There has been a hostelry on this site for several centuries. The front bar is L-shaped with a dartboard and TV, and there is an airy lounge and meeting room to the rear. Four beers are served on handpump. A mixed clientele of all ages frequents this usually busy venue.

SCOTLAND

Strathkinness

Tavern

4 High Road, KY16 9RS (just off A91)
5 (12 Fri & Sat)-midnight; 12.30-midnight Sun
(01334) 850085
Beer range varies
Public bar with seating and a comfortable lounge at one end, with two handpulls offering a choice of changing guest ales. There is a separate room with a pool table, and brain-teaser games to test your sobriety. Lunches and evening meals are served in the bar or you can dine in the restaurant. There is a beer garden at the rear. The front of the pub affords lovely views over the river estuary – a good location for plane spotting.
Q(64,96)P

Tayport

Bellrock Tavern

4-6 Dalgleish Street, DD6 9BB (opp harbour)
11-midnight (1am Thu-Sat); 12.30-midnight Sun
(01382) 552388
Beer range varies
Small, friendly town local, opposite the picturesque harbour with wonderful views across the Tay to Dundee and Broughty Ferry. The pub is on three levels, each with a mainly nautical theme, including old charts, photographs of ships and aircraft, old Dundee and the Tay ferries. Good-value home cooking is served at lunchtimes Monday to Saturday, evening meals Friday and Saturday, and high tea on Sunday. One ale is always available, supplemented by a second during busy times. Close to the Fife Coastal Path.
Q(96)P

LOCH LOMOND, STIRLING & THE TROSSACHS

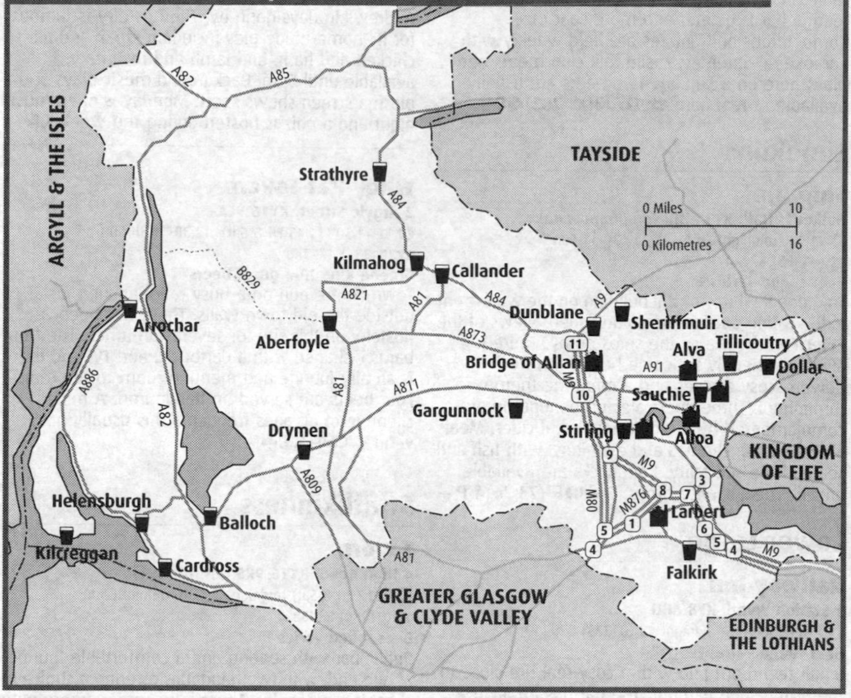

Authority areas covered: Argyll & Bute UA (part), Clackmannanshire UA, Falkirk UA, Stirling UA, West Dumbartonshire UA

Aberfoyle

Forth Inn Hotel

Main Street, FK8 3UQ

11-midnight (1am Fri & Sat) ☎ (01877) 382372

forthinn.com

Beer range varies

This 100-year-old, family-run inn is a magnet for tourists and locals. The bar and lounge are wood panelled and have a very cosy atmosphere, complemented by courteous and friendly staff. Entertainment is laid on most weekends and the pub hosts a beer festival at least once a year. The restaurant uses local produce and accommodation is available. ♨Q❀⇌◑◐♿⛺♣P⁵⁻

Arrochar

Village Inn ✓

Shore Road, G83 7AX (on A814) NN293034

11-midnight (1am Fri & Sat); 12-midnight Sun

☎ (01301) 702279 villageinnarrochar.co.uk

Beer range varies

A regular in the Guide, this atmospheric inn is well worth seeking out. Up to four beers, generally Scottish and especially from local Fyne Ales, can be enjoyed with a good meal from the extensive menu. The inn provides some grand views of the Arrochar Alps and Loch Long, particularly from the attractive garden. ♨Q❀⇌◑♿⛺(926,976)P⁵⁻

Balloch

Balloch House ✓

Balloch Road, G83 8LQ

12-11 (10.30 Sun) ☎ (01389) 752579

vintageinn.co.uk/theballochhouselochlomond

Caledonian Deuchars IPA; guest beers

Set on the banks of the River Leven, with tremendous views of Loch Lomond, it would be hard to find a better location so close to Glasgow. Balloch is a great place from which to explore the National Park, take a boat trip, or walk. After your exertions, you can relax in the cosy bar and sample beers from the ever-changing Vintage Inns range. Good food is available in the bar and restaurant. Children are welcome. ♨Q❀⇌◑♿⛺⇶P⁵⁻

Callander

Waverley Hotel ✓

88-92 Main Street, FK17 8BD

11-midnight (1am Fri & Sat) ☎ (01877) 330245

thewaverley.co.uk

Beer range varies

This popular pub is known for the quality of its ales. Beer festivals are held in September and at Christmas. The hotel is situated on the Perthshire whisky trail with the Trossachs National Park, Stirling and Loch Lomond within easy reach. Children are allowed in the bar until 10pm, dogs on a lead welcome. Q❀⇌◑♿⛺⁵⁻

Cardross

Coach House Inn

Main Road, G82 5JX NS347775
12-midnight (1am Thu-Sat) ☎ (01389) 841358
coachhouseinn-cardross.com
Caledonian Deuchars IPA; guest beers Ⓗ
A welcoming inn set in a quiet village, with separate bars including an area for playing pool and a sizeable dining room serving a varied menu. It's a good place to start or finish a ramble along the Clyde. At weekends there is a guest beer, sourced from a wide range of breweries. (216)P

Dollar

King's Seat ✔

19-23 Bridge Street, FK14 7DE
12-midnight (1am Fri & Sat); 12.30-midnight Sun
☎ (01259) 742515 kingsseat.com
Caledonian Deuchars IPA; Harviestoun Bitter & Twisted; guest beers Ⓗ
This old coaching inn with low ceilings and a cosy, comfortable feel is located in the main street of this historic and attractive village on the southern edge of the Ochil Hills. The pub is well placed for rambling, golf and fishing. Up to five ales are on handpump with the guests usually including a Harviestoun seasonal beer. The restaurant offers high quality meals. Q (23,65,70)

Drymen

Clachan Inn

2 Main Street, G63 0BG
11-midnight (1am Fri & Sat); 12.30-midnight Sun
☎ (01360) 660824 clachaninndrymen.co.uk
Beer range varies Ⓗ
Situated on Drymen's village green, this family-run inn is Scotland's oldest registered licensed premises, dating from 1774. It is popular with walkers on the West Highland Way as well as tourists and locals. The guest ale is from a Scottish brewery on the Belhaven list, such as Houston or Inveralmond. A wood-burning stove warms the traditional bar. The food is very popular, so it is best to book ahead.

Dunblane

Dunblane Hotel ✔

10 Stirling Road, FK15 9EP
11-midnight (1am Fri & Sat) ☎ (01786) 822178
Greene King IPA; Taylor Landlord; guest beers Ⓗ
Situated opposite the railway station, the bar is decorated with brewery mirrors and the comfortable lounge features pictures with an angling theme. Four cask ales are available, two usually from local brewers. An excellent view of the River Allan can be enjoyed from the rear window, which overlooks the patio. A popular pub quiz is held every other Thursday. B&B is available. Last orders for food is 8pm. P

Tappit Hen 🏆

Kirk Street, FK15 0AL
11-midnight (1am Fri & Sat); 12.30-midnight Sun
☎ (01786) 825226
Caledonian Deuchars IPA; Greene King IPA; guest beers Ⓗ
Forth Valley CAMRA Pub of the Year 2010, the Tappit Hen offers an ever-changing range of five real ales from local breweries and from further afield. Visitors are assured of a friendly welcome from the very knowledgable staff, and beer festivals held in May and October are popular with locals and visitors alike. Entertainment includes a folk night on Tuesday every week. Dunblane's famous cathedral is opposite.

Falkirk

Behind the Wall

14 Melville Street, FK1 1HZ
5-9 (11 summer); 5-1am Fri & Sat; 12.30-midnight Sun
☎ (01324) 633338 behindthewall.co.uk
Caledonian Deuchars IPA, 80; guest beers Ⓗ
This spacious venue for drinking, dining and entertainment, was created from a former bra factory. Very popular for watching live sports events, with lots of seating and several large screens in a large room which doubles as a live music venue for local bands. Eglesbrech is the ale and whisky bar upstairs, divided into two rooms with timber furnishings and a large wood-burning stove, offering a choice of cask beers.

Carron Works ✔

Bank Street, FK1 1NB
9.30-11 (midnight Thu; 1am Fri & Sat); 12.30-11 Sun
☎ (01324) 673020
Beer range varies Ⓗ
Situated in a recently converted cinema, this is an excellent Wetherspoon venue, with friendly and helpful staff dispensing the chain's regular and constantly changing guest beers. Centrally situated, with a spacious interior, and handy for the railway and bus stations, it is very popular with locals and CAMRA members. It has frequent festivals and is keen to promote real ale. The standard Wetherspoon menu is available all day.

Wheatsheaf Inn

16 Baxters Wynd, FK1 1PF
11-midnight (1am Fri & Sat); 12.30-midnight Sun
☎ (01324) 638282
Caledonian Deuchars IPA; guest beers Ⓗ
A firm favourite with locals and real ale enthusiasts alike, this public house dates from the late 18th century and retains much of its original character. The wood panelled bar is furnished in traditional style with plenty of interesting features from the past. Guest beers come from micro-breweries in Scotland and England, with two on offer mid-week and three at the weekend – this is definitely one to visit. (Grahamston/Falkirk High)

Gargunnock

Gargunnock Inn

Main Street, FK8 3BW
5 (12 Sat)-11 (1am Fri & Sat); 12-11 Sun
☎ (01786) 860333 gargunnockinn.co.uk

INDEPENDENT BREWERIES

Devon Sauchie
Harviestoun Alva
Tinpot Bridge of Allan (NEW)
Traditional Scottish Ales Stirling
Tryst Larbert
Williams Alloa

SCOTLAND

Beer range varies Ⓗ
Managed by a keen CAMRA member, the original building was an 18th-century staging inn, since extended to provide a restaurant and a function room. Serving both passing tourists and the village community, the pub sponsors the local football and cricket teams and holds charity events. The bar offers a rotating range of local and regional ales. Regular entertainment is hosted and a beer festival is held in a marquee in the car park on the second Sunday in August. ❀◑♿🚌(12)♣P

Helensburgh

Commodore Hotel ✔

112-117 West Clyde Street, G84 8ES
⏲ 11-11; 12.30-10.30 Sun ☎ (01436) 679 924
🌐 vintageinn.co.uk/thecommodorehelensburgh
Caledonian Deuchars IPA; guest beer Ⓗ
Overlooking the Gare Loch, this bar is ideal for submarine spotting. The hotel's large garden is a joy on a warm summer day. Inside, the spacious bar provides plenty of room to relax and enjoy the national brand beers on rotation. The restaurant has a varied menu to tempt you after working up an appetite walking along the seafront. Well worth a trip from Glasgow. ♨❀🛏◑♿⇌🚌(216)P

Kilcreggan

Kilcreggan Hotel 🏆

Argyll Road, G84 0JP NS238805
⏲ 11.30-midnight (1am Fri & Sat); 12.30-midnight Sun
☎ (01436) 842 243 🌐 kilcregganhotel.com
Beer range varies Ⓗ
It is a short ferry trip from Gourock, then a modest walk from the quaint pier, to this Victorian village mansion and Dunbartonshire CAMRA Pub of the Year 2009. The lounge bar, decorated with nautical ephemera, provides stunning Clyde views. Up to four ales are usually supplied by local micros, alongside beers from all over Britain. If you stay later than the last ferry, you can return to Glasgow via Helensburgh. ❀🛏◑🚌(316)P⚋

Kilmahog

Lade Inn

FK17 8HD (A84/A821 jct, 1 mile W of Callander)
⏲ 12-11 (1am Fri & Sat); 12.30-11 Sun ☎ (01877) 330152
🌐 theladeinn.com
Trossachs Waylade, Ladeback, Ladeout Ⓗ
On the edge of the Trossachs National Park, this pub is popular with locals and tourists alike. The three ales are unique to the Lade. All food is locally sourced and served in either the bar, restaurant or beer garden. Entertainment is laid on most weekends. The Scottish Real Ale shop, adjacent to the pub, offers the largest selection of bottled ales in Scotland. ♨Q❀◑♿⛺🚌P

Sauchie

Mansfield Arms ✔

7 Main Street, FK10 3JR
⏲ 11-11.30 (12.30am Fri & Sat); 12.30-11.30 Sun
☎ (01259) 722020 🌐 devonales.com
Devon Original, Thick Black, Pride Ⓟ
This pub and micro-brewery, brewing the three Devon ales, is the oldest operating brewery in the county. Family owned and run, and situated within an ex-mining community, the pub is very popular with the locals, and families come to enjoy good value meals served in the lounge. The pub is on the Stirling via Alloa circular bus route.
◑♿⇌(Alloa)🚌(60,62,63)P▯

Sheriffmuir

Sheriffmuir Inn

FK15 0LN NN 827022
⏲ 12 (5 Mon)-10; closed Tue; 12.30-10 Sun
☎ (01786) 823285 🌐 sheriffmuirinn.co.uk
Beer range varies Ⓗ
This late 18th-century drovers' inn, set in glorious countryside close to the 1715 battlefield site, features flagstone floors and an open fire in the restaurant. Food is sourced locally. Two handpumps serve regularly changing beers. The inn has two rooms for accommodation, and it's popular with locals, hillwalkers and tourists. The garden has a children's play area. ♨Q❀🛏◑♿P⚋

Stirling

Portcullis Hotel

Castle Wynd, FK8 1EG
⏲ 11.30-midnight ☎ (01786) 472290
🌐 theportcullishotel.com
Beer range varies Ⓗ
Situated close to Stirling Castle in the ancient heart of Stirling, the Portcullis has been sensitively converted, retaining interior stone walls and a real fire. The bar, which attracts a mix of tourists, regulars and diners, is renowned for its food, and diners are advised to reserve a table. There are usually two real ales from Scottish brewers. Outside is a pretty garden. ♨Q❀🛏◑⇌P⚋

Strathyre

Inn & Bistro

Main Street, FK18 8NA (on A84)
⏲ 12 (12.30 Sun)-11 ☎ (01877) 384224
🌐 innatstrathyre.com
Beer range varies Ⓗ
Cosy village pub serving excellent meals in the bar and bistro, all made using local produce. Dogs and children are welcome in the bar at all times. The beer terrace enjoys panoramic views to Ben Sheann and beyond. Hill-walking, fishing, golf and watersports are all close at hand. Stirling, Callander and the Trossachs are within easy travelling distance. Entertainment is regularly laid on.
♨Q❀🛏◑♿⛺🚌♣P⚋

Tillicoultry

Woolpack Inn

1 Glassford Square, FK13 6AU
⏲ 11-midnight (1am Fri & Sat); 12.30-midnight Sun
☎ (01259) 750332
Black Sheep Best Bitter; Greene King Old Speckled Hen; guest beer Ⓗ
Originally a coaching inn, the pub retains low ceilings and a comfortable feel. Recently refurbished, it now offers daytime meals. The hostelry is popular with the local rugby club and more mature locals – you will always find someone with a tale to tell propping up the bar. Situated on the southern foothills of the Ochil Hills, the pub is a popular stop-off for walkers. There is also golfing and fishing nearby, and Stirling is 12 miles away on a regular bus route. Q◑⛺🚌(23,62,63)▯

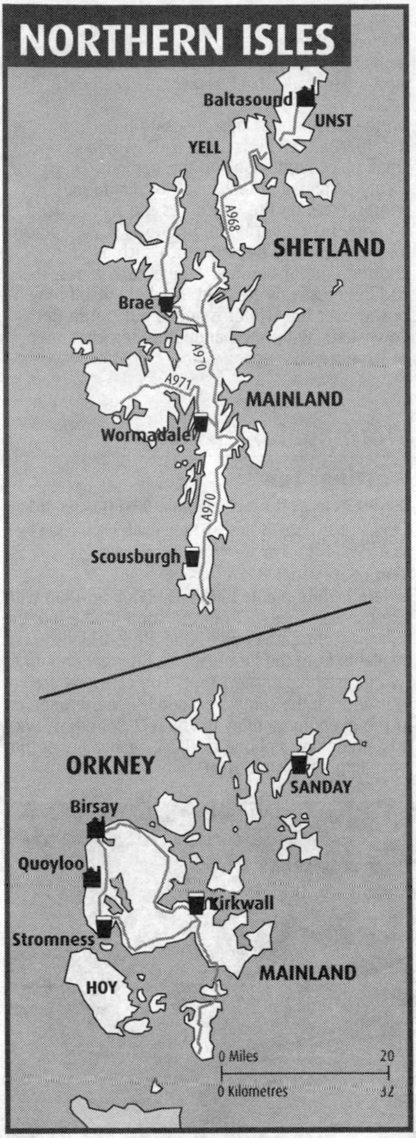

Authority area covered: Highland UA

Brae: Shetland

Busta House Hotel

ZE2 9QN HU345669

11 (12 Sun)-11 ☎ (01806) 522506 bustahouse.com

Beer range varies

Rambling mansion house on many levels, dating from 1588, with numerous later additions. It is now a friendly country house hotel, set in extensive grounds running down to the shore of sheltered Busta Voe. The beamed main bar area is lined with drawings of ships. A single ale is available, usually from local brewery Valhalla, and an extensive range of malt whiskies is stocked in the lounge bar. The hotel is situated near the centre of the Shetland mainland and Mavis Grind, where the Atlantic and the North Sea are separated only by the width of the road. Q P

Kirkwall: Orkney

Bothy Bar (Albert Hotel)

Mounthoolie Lane, KW15 1HW

11-midnight (1am Thu-Sat); 12-midnight Sun

☎ (01856) 876000 alberthotel.co.uk

Highland Scapa Special; Orkney Red MacGregor, Dark Island, seasonal beers

Risen from the ashes of a fire around four years ago, the bar has been rebuilt using much of the original timber and is now on just one level. As a result, it is more spacious than before and as popular as ever. Ideally located in the centre of town, it is busy after work and a lively part of the night scene at weekends. Meals are served daily. Beware of premium prices when buying half pints. Handy for shops, buses and ferries to the outer isles.

Helgi's Bar

14 Harbour Street, KW15 1LE

11-midnight (1am Thu-Sat); 12.30-midnight Sun

☎ (01856) 879273

Highland Scapa Special

Converted from a former shipping office, this small, smart bar has the look of a modern café. Take your drinks to the cosy upstairs room overlooking the harbour while filling in time before island-hopping on the many ferries to the outlying parts.

Shore

6 Shore Street, KW15 1LG

11.30-11 (midnight Fri); 10-midnight Sat; 10-11 Sun

☎ (01856) 872200

Highland Scapa Special

Smart, modern bar in a refurbished hotel overlooking the harbour. An ideal base for island-hopping using the many ferries available to Westray, Sanday and most of the other Orkney Islands. A darts player's haven, it has a dartboard at both ends of the bar room.

Sanday: Orkney

Kettletoft Hotel

KW17 2BJ (a few miles N of ferry terminal)

12 (12.30 Sun)-midnight ☎ (01857) 600217

kettletofthotel.co.uk

Beer range varies

Small, family-run hotel by the sea close to the local shops and with direct access to one of the most beautiful beaches on the island, Backaskaill Bay. Watch the seals and wildlife from the comfort of the well stocked bar. Good food is served using local produce wherever possible with a wide selection of home-made puddings. Meals are available throughout the day, and a fish and chip takeaway is available on Wednesday and Saturday evenings. The beer is from the Highland Brewery.

Scousburgh: Shetland

Spiggie Hotel

Dunrossness, ZE2 9JE (signed from A970 off B9122) HU379174

INDEPENDENT BREWERIES

Highland Birsay
Orkney/Atlas Quoyloo
Valhalla Baltasound

SCOTLAND

⏲ 12-2, 5-11 (midnight Fri); closed Mon & Tue winter; 12-midnight Sat; 12.30-11 Sun ☎ (01950) 460409
🌐 thespiggiehotel.co.uk
Beer range varies Ⓗ
Small family-run hotel built as the original terminus of the Northern Isles ferries. It has a small stone-floored bar and adjacent restaurant on an elevated site, with views of St Ninians Isle and the Loch of Spiggie. Birdwatching and trout fishing on the loch can be arranged. There is seating outside for warmer days. One ale is usually available from the local Valhalla Brewery and up to two guests in summer. Phone to check opening hours in winter. **Q❀🛏◐◑P**

Stromness: Orkney

Ferry Inn

John Street, KW16 3AA (100m from ferry terminal)
⏲ 9-midnight (1am Thu-Sat); 9.30-midnight Sun
☎ (01856) 850280 🌐 ferryinn.com
Highland Scapa Special, seasonal beers; Orkney Red MacGregor, Dark Island, seasonal beers; guest beer Ⓗ
A former temperance hotel, this inn is a welcome sight after the ferry crossing from Scrabster. The hostelry is popular with locals and visitors alike, particularly the divers who come to Orkney to explore the wrecks of Scapa Flow. Local folk musicians meet here regularly. Music features throughout the year and the pub hosts annual blues and folk festivals in conjunction with the Stromness Hotel. **❀🛏◐◑⛺🚌**

Stromness Hotel

15 Victoria Street, KW16 3AA (opp pier head)
⏲ 12-2, 5-midnight (1am Fri & Sat) ☎ (01856) 850298
🌐 stromnesshotel.com
Highland Scapa Special, seasonal beers; Orkney Red MacGregor, Dark Island, seasonal beers; guest beers Ⓗ
On the first floor of this imposing hotel is a large bar, the Hamnavoe Lounge, with windows and a small balcony overlooking the harbour. There are comfy settees and tables set for dining, and in winter a roaring fire welcomes the visitor. Used as an army HQ during WWII, the hotel is well placed for visiting world heritage sites such as Scara Brae and the Ring of Brodgar. Annual jazz, blues, folk and beer festivals are held. The hotel itself may be closed over the winter months, but Flattie Bar downstairs, with one handpump, remains open. **♨❀🛏◐◑⛺🚌P**

Wormadale: Shetland

Westings Inn

ZE2 9LJ (8 miles N of Lerwick on A 971) HU 403 465
⏲ 12.30-2.30, 5.30 (6.30 Sun)-10.30 (midnight if busy)
☎ (01595) 840242 🌐 westings.shetland.co.uk
Beer range varies Ⓗ
Isolated white-painted inn in a hilltop position with extensive sea views from the comfortable lounge and adjacent games area. One ale is usually available from the local Valhalla Brewery and up to two guests in summer. Tents and caravans are welcome on the campsite. Food is generally served in the evening Monday to Friday 7-8pm; however, it is advisable to phone to check availability before travelling. **Q❀🛏◑♿⛺♣P**

Ferry Inn, Stromness, Orkney (Photo: George Howie)

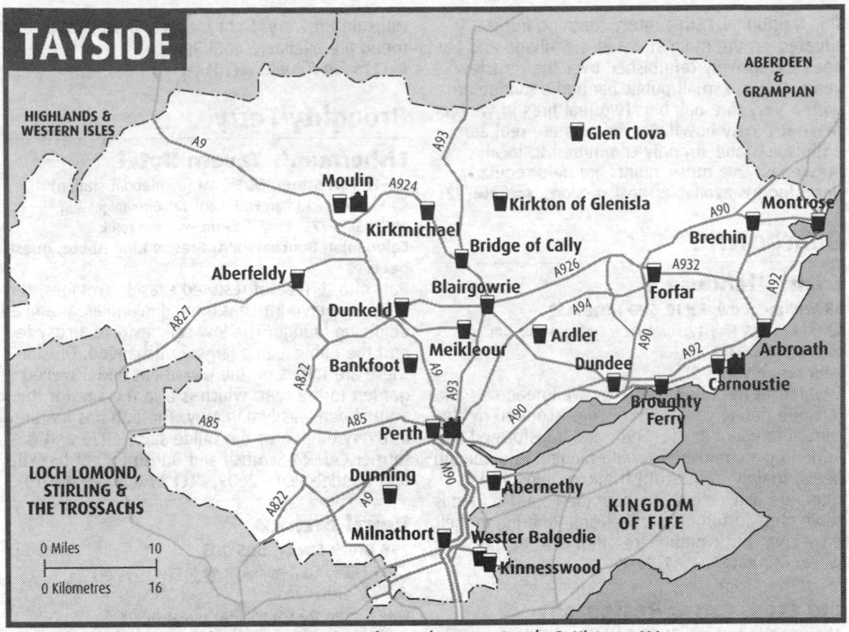

Authority areas covered: Angus UA, City of Dundee UA, Perth & Kinross UA

Aberfeldy

Black Watch Inn

Bank Street, PH15 2BB

⏲ 11-11 (11.45 Thu; 12.30 Fri & Sat); 12.30-11.30 Sun

☎ (01887) 820699 🌐 theblackwatchinn.co.uk

Beer range varies Ⓗ

A traditional community pub with a warm welcome, the family-run 'Blackie' is situated on a crossroads at the western end of the village. Two ales come from mainly Scottish breweries. Black Watch tartan adorns the furniture, with paintings of famous battles on the walls and the badge and motto – nemo me impune lacessit (no one touches me with impunity) – engraved on the glass entrance. Good food available. ❀◑⊟♿⊟(23)♣⊱

Abernethy

Crees Inn

Main Street, PH2 9LA

⏲ 11-2, 5-11; 11-11 Sat & Sun ☎ (01738) 850714

🌐 creesinn.co.uk

Beer range varies Ⓗ

A free house in a quiet village this pub is in the shadow of the imposing Abernethy Tower, one of only two Pictish watch towers in Scotland. Once a farmhouse, its timber panels and beams now display an impressive collection of pump clips reflecting the diverse beer range. Up to six ales are available, often from English breweries. A good varied selection of meals is available made with fresh local produce. Q❀⊟◑♿⊟(36)P

Arbroath

Corn Exchange ✔

Market Place, DD11 1HR

⏲ 11-midnight (1am Fri & Sat); 12.30-midnight Sun

☎ (01241) 432430

Greene King Abbot; guest beers Ⓗ

Situated in the heart of Arbroath, this Wetherspoon conversion of a former corn exchange dating from 1854 is run by an enthusiastic manager and friendly team. A recent winner of Angus CAMRA Pub of the Year, the pub offers constantly changing guest beers and holds popular beer festivals in spring and autumn, with up to 30 beers available. Although open plan there are several booths in which to hide away. ◑♿⇌⊟(39)●

Ardler

Tavern

Main Street, PH12 8SR

⏲ 6-11; 5-midnight Fri; 11-12.30am Sat; 12.30-midnight Sun

☎ (01828) 640340

Beer range varies Ⓗ

This friendly pub is a community asset – the only meeting place in the village. It was refurbished a few years back, and has a finely-crafted elm bar. A large open fire adds warmth in winter, with cosy sofas to settle into. Beers from Inveralmond, Sinclair and Angus breweries are regularly served, and soups and light snacks are available. Pool and darts are played. Outside is a nice little drinking area. A nearby disused railway line forms part of a rural path network. ♨Q❀♿♣P⊱

Bankfoot

Bankfoot Inn

Main Street, PH1 4AB (just off A9) NO067354

⏲ 5.30-11 (11.45 Thu; 12.30am Fri); 12-12.30am Sat; 12.30-11.30 Sun ☎ (01738) 787243 🌐 bankfootinn.co.uk

Inveralmond Ossian, Lia Fail; guest beer Ⓗ

INDEPENDENT BREWERIES

Angus Carnoustie (NEW)
Inveralmond Perth
Moulin Moulin

SCOTLAND

This traditional 18th-century coaching inn is situated on the main street in the village and has been extensively refurbished over the past few years. It has a small public bar and a lounge area with a very fine oak bar. Two real fires in winter make it a cosy howff. The owners are real ale enthusiasts and strongly committed to local breweries. Live music nights are held regularly. Good food is available most sessions. ⇌◐🚌(22)

Blairgowrie

Ericht Alehouse 🏆

13 Wellmeadow, PH10 6ND NO180452

⌚ 1-11 (11.45 Thu; 12.30am Fri & Sat); 1-11.30 Sun

☎ (01250) 872469

Beer range varies Ⓗ

Situated in the town centre by Wellmeadow Park, this pub dating back to 1802 was acquired by the current landlord in the 1990s and transformed into a friendly ale house. Six wide-ranging and varying beers, mainly from Scottish micros, plus a real cider, are available throughout the year. No food is served but customers are welcome to bring in their own. Live music nights are often held at the weekend. ♨Q♿🚌(57,59)

Old Cross Inn & Restaurant

Alyth Road, Rattray, PH10 7DY NO191457

⌚ 12-2.30, 5-11; 12-11 Sun ☎ (01250) 875502

🌐 theoldcrossinn.co.uk

Beer range varies Ⓗ

The Old Cross, originally named the Rattray Hotel, is part of a Victorian building standing in an elevated position at the eastern end of the village. This free house has two handpumps on the bar dispensing ales from Scottish micros, with bar meals and a la carte available. There is a pleasant beer garden with timber decking to the rear, where barbecues are occasionally held in summer. ❀◐⊟🚌(57)

Brechin

Caledonian Hotel

43-47 South Esk Street, DD9 6DZ

⌚ 5-11 (midnight Fri); 11.30-1am Sat; 12.30-11 Sun

☎ (01356) 624345

Beer range varies Ⓗ

Taking its name from the privately-run Caledonian Railway whose terminus is opposite, the pub has a large bar and dining area with a warm and inviting ambience. Houston and Inveralmond provide the regular ales, and one of the guests is often from a Hampshire brewery. A wide range of British and Belgian bottled beers is also available. Live folk music plays on the last Friday of the month. Lunch is available weekends only. ♨Q❀⇌◗🚌(30)♣

Bridge of Cally

Bridge of Cally Hotel

PH10 7JJ (6 miles N of Blairgowrie on A93) NO140513

⌚ 11-11 (12.30am Fri & Sat); 12-11 Sun ☎ (01250) 886232

🌐 bridgeofcallyhotel.com

Beer range varies Ⓗ

Situated where Strathardle meets Glen Shee, this hotel is ideally situated for access to a wide range of outdoor pursuits including downhill skiing during the winter. The 63-mile Cateran Trail, Scotland's newest long-distance walk, starts and finishes at nearby Blairgowrie and passes the door. Two ever-changing ales are available, often from the Houston Brewery. Light meals and a full a la carte menu are available until 9pm. ♨Q☋❀⇌◐⊟♿🚌(71)♣P

Broughty Ferry

Fisherman's Tavern Hotel

10-16 Fort Street, DD5 2AD (by lifeboat station)

⌚ 11-midnight (1am Fri & Sat); 12.30-midnight Sun

☎ (01382) 775941 🌐 fishermanstavern.co.uk

Caledonian Deuchars IPA; Greene King Abbot; guest beers Ⓗ

Part of a terrace of restored seaside cottages, this long-time favourite has three drinking areas and an adjoining lounge. The low ceilings give a cosy feel and the public bar is largely unchanged. Outside there are tables on the pavement and a walled garden to the rear, which is also the site for the annual beer festival in May. The pub has featured in every edition of the Guide since 1975 and is a former CAMRA Scottish and British Pub of the Year and Dundee POTY 2009. ♨Q❀⇌◐⊟♿≋🚌(9X)

Royal Arch ✔

258 Brook Street, DD5 2DS

⌚ 11 (12.30 Sun)-midnight ☎ (01382) 779741

🌐 royal-arch.co.uk

Caledonian Deuchars IPA; guest beers Ⓗ

A strikingly decorated, welcoming street-corner local in the heart of the town. The ale is in the public bar, a mecca for sports fans with three TVs showing different events. The ornate bar counter and gantry were rescued from a demolished Dundee pub. The walls are covered with sporting photos and cartoons of customers past and present. There is an area outside for drinkers and smokers on the pavement. Meals are served in the comfortable lounge. ❀◐⊟≋🚌(9X)

Carnoustie

Station Hotel

23 Station Road, DD7 6AR (next to railway station)

⌚ 12-2.30, 4-midnight (1am Fri); 11-1am Sat; 12.30-midnight Sun ☎ (01241) 852447

🌐 stationhotel.uk.com

Beer range varies Ⓗ

Formerly the Panmure Arms, the Station has been in the same family since 1977 and is now part of the town's history. The owner is a cask ale enthusiast and offers a constantly changing guest beer in both the public and lounge bars. Excellent food is available, with fresh fish collected daily from Arbroath a speciality. The steak pie is also recommended. The Carnoustie golf course is a five-minute walk. ☋⇌◐⊟♿≋🚌(39A,73/73A)♣P

Dundee

Bank Bar

7-9 Union Street, DD1 4BN

⌚ 11am-11.45pm; 12.30-11.45 Sun ☎ (01382) 205037

Beer range varies Ⓗ

One of the first bank-to-pub conversions in the city, this smallish venue has a cosy feel, with a wood floor and fittings, and discrete seating areas separated by wood and glass panels. The Bank has impressed on the real ale front for some years now, with three beers usually available, frequently from Scottish micros, attracting real beer drinkers on a regular basis. Food is served all day, prepared by the boss. ◐≋🚌

Phoenix

103 Nethergate, DD1 4DH
⏲ 11 (12.30 Sun)-midnight ☎ (01382) 200014
Caledonian Deuchars IPA; Taylor Landlord; guest beers Ⓗ
A popular pub with a striking interior – the ceiling and pillars are original, the bar and gantry reputedly came from a demolished Welsh pub. Unusual metal adverts, brewery mirrors (including a rare Ballingall's of Dundee), bric-a-brac, a 12-pointer stag's head and secluded seating alcoves all contribute to a place of great character. Five fonts of special design have been installed by the owner, who will discuss them with customers at the drop of a hat. Several draught foreign beers are also available. ◑⇌🚌

Town

85 Commercial Street, DD1 2AB
⏲ 11-9 (11 Wed & Thu; midnight Fri & Sat); 12.30-midnight Sun ☎ (01382) 201042 🌐 thetownbars.co.uk
Beer range varies Ⓗ
This former insurance building was restored to its original magnificence in 2009, featuring fine wood-panelled walls, mosaic floors, wonderful plasterwork and a glass-domed ceiling. The large establishment has many secluded sections, and a more modern area upstairs. There are six handpulls offering a good variety of beers, especially local ales. Food is served all day, with breakfast from 9am, and lunchtimes are very busy. Live music sessions are held in the evening. ◑⇌🚌

Dunkeld

Royal Dunkeld Hotel

Atholl Street, PH8 0AR NO026428
⏲ 11-11 (12.15am Fri & Sat); 12-11 Sun ☎ (01350) 727322
🌐 royaldunkeld.co.uk
Cairngorm Trade Winds; Stewart Pentland IPA; guest beer Ⓗ
Formerly a coaching inn, the Royal Dunkeld is a comfortable hotel with a restaurant, lounge and public bar. The bar provides a warm welcome with an open fire and three handpulls dispensing the ale. There is a pool room with dartboard next to it. Outside, the large beer garden is a real suntrap in summer. Do not miss the nearby Hermitage woodland containing some of Britain's tallest trees as well as the Black Linn waterfall and Ossian's Folly. ♨❀🛏◑🍴🚌P⚊

Dunning

Kirkstyle Inn & Restaurant ✔

Kirkstyle Square, PH2 0RR
⏲ 11-2.30 (not Mon winter), 5-11 (midnight Fri); 11-midnight Sat; 12.30-11 Sun ☎ (01764) 684248
🌐 kirkstyle-dunning.co.uk
Beer range varies Ⓗ
Traditional village inn dating from 1760 overshadowed by the impressive Norman steeple of St Serf's Church, which contains the ancient Dupplin Cross and other Pictish relics. Up to three ales in the small public bar often come from Harviestoun, Cairngorm and Greene King. A small snug area is next to the bar and there is a separate restaurant and pool room. Around a mile west of Dunning village stands a 20ft high stone cross, a memorial to Maggie Wall who in 1657 was burned here as a witch. ♨Q❀◑🍴🚌(17)

Forfar

Plough Inn

48 Market Street, DD8 3EW
⏲ 11-midnight (1am Fri & Sat); 12.30-midnight Sun
☎ (01307) 469288 🌐 bebo.com/ThePloo
Inveralmond Ossian, Thrappledouser; guest beers Ⓗ
Handily placed for Forfar FC's ground, 'The Ploo' serves up to three beers, with an emphasis on Scottish micros. Frequent live music and occasional beer festivals are a feature of this traditional pub. Good food including high teas are served daily. It's an ideal pub to end the day after exploring the Angus glens. Your visit to Forfar will not be complete without sampling a Forfar Bridie – available from bakers nearby. ☕◑🚌(20)♣

Glen Clova

Glen Clova Hotel

DD8 4QS (on B955 15 miles N of Kirriemuir) NO327731
⏲ 11-11 (1am Fri & Sat); 12-11 Sun ☎ (01575) 550350
🌐 clova.com
Beer range varies Ⓗ
Situated near the head of one of Scotland's most beautiful glens, the hotel's bar has been recently renovated, retaining a large log-fired stove and plenty of character. Popular with walkers after a day on the hills, the bar has two handpumps usually supplying ale from Scottish breweries including Stewart and Houston. Local food served in both bar and restaurant includes venison. The hotel has a range of accommodation from bunkhouse to en-suite rooms to a self-catering luxury lodge. ♨Q❀🛏◑🍴♿♣P⚊

Kinnesswood

Lomond Country Hotel

Main Street, KY13 9HN
⏲ 11-11 (midnight Fri & Sat) ☎ (01592) 840253
🌐 lomondcountryinn.co.uk
Beer range varies Ⓗ
This country inn sits in the listed village of Kinnesswood on the A911 east of Milnathort, at the foot of Bishop Hill. The large bar and separate restaurant with a central open fire enjoy stunning views over Loch Leven. Meals are served until 9pm. Inveralmond beers are regulars, and the gantry displays an extensive whisky range. A number of scenic trails are accessible such as the Tetley Trail, a three-mile circular walk, and the Loch Leven Heritage Trail. ♨Q☕❀🛏◑♿🚌(31,201,202)P

Kirkmichael

Strathardle Inn

PH10 7NS (on A924) NO082599
⏲ 12-2, 6-11 (11.30 Fri & Sat) ☎ (01250) 881224
🌐 strathardleinn.co.uk
Beer range varies Ⓗ
The Strathardle is a former coaching inn dating back to the late 1700s, retaining the original barn and stables. It has an attractive woodland garden as well as a 700-metre beat of the River Ardle offering salmon and trout fishing, and is popular with walkers and skiers in the winter. The owners are real ale enthusiasts and offer up to three ales depending on the season, often from Scottish micros. There is also a strong commitment to locally-sourced food – the venison is highly recommended. ♨Q☕❀🛏◑♿P

Kirkton of Glenisla

Glenisla Hotel

PH11 8PH (on B951 10 miles N of Alyth) NO215605
✪ 12-2, 5-11; 12-1am Sat; closed Mon; 12-11 Sun
☎ (01575) 582223 ⊕ glenisla-hotel.com
Beer range varies ⊞
A welcoming hostelry in a magnificent Angus glen, this 17th-century former coaching inn has been refurbished to a high standard but retains a traditional feel. Beer from local breweries is served from two handpumps in the cosy, oak-beamed bar, which features an open log fire. Good-value traditional food is available and the menus are often enhanced by a southern African dish or two. ♛Q❀⇌◑♿♣P⊬

Meikleour

Meikleour Hotel

PH2 6EB
✪ 11-3, 6-11 (midnight Fri); 11-midnight Sat; 12-11 Sun
☎ (01250) 883206 ⊕ meikleour-inn.co.uk
Beer range varies ⊞
Warm and welcoming country inn with an excellent reputation for quality meals. Built in 1820 as a coach and posting house, it was then used as a fishing and shooting lodge for guests of the Meikleour Estate. It has a stone-flagged bar, comfortable lounge and pleasant beer garden. The house beer, Lure of Meikleour, is brewed by Inveralmond, and guest ales come from Scottish micros. Nearby is the Beech Hedge (100ft high, a third of a mile long) the tallest hedge in the world. ♛Q❀⇌◑⊟♿⊟(58)P

Milnathort

Village Inn

36 Westerloan, KY13 9YH
✪ 2-11; 11-11.30 Fri & Sat; 12.30-1am Sun
☎ (01577) 863293
Inveralmond Thrappledouser; guest beer ⊞
Located in the heart of the village and family-owned since 1985, this is a friendly local with a relaxing atmosphere. The semi-open-plan interior has a comfortable lounge area with low ceilings, exposed joists and stone walls at one end and a bar area with log fire at the other. The games room at the rear has a pool table. Unobtrusive background music plays. Nearby places of interest include the island castle of Loch Leven where Mary Queen of Scots was imprisoned and the RSPB site at Vane Farm. ♛❀♿⊟(56/56B)♣

Montrose

Picture House

12 Hume Street, DD10 8JB
✪ 11-midnight (1am Fri & Sat); 12.30-midnight Sun
☎ (01674) 676991
Beer range varies ⊞
Former cinema converted by Belhaven in 2009, conveniently situated between the railway station and High Street. Stylishly furnished, it attracts sports fans, with plasma TVs on the walls and a big screen for live fixtures. However it is usually possible to find a quiet corner to sample one or two real ales on offer from the Greene King list. Families are welcome and there is an emphasis on food with table service from 11am to 9pm each day. ◑⛺⇌⊟(39)

Moulin

Moulin Inn

11-13 Kirkmichael Road, PH16 5EH
✪ 11-11 (11.45 Fri & Sat); 12-11 Sun ☎ (01796) 472196
⊕ moulininn.co.uk
Moulin Light, Braveheart, Ale of Atholl, Old Remedial ⊞
A delightful haven of authentic Scottish highland hospitality, this inn was founded in 1695. Set in the village square close to the holiday town of Pitlochry, the cosy hostelry is divided into small alcoves warmed by two log fires. Its four ales are produced in its own brewery in the former coach house and stable behind the hotel. A good choice of home-prepared local fare is served all day. A very popular destination for tourists and hillwalkers descending from Ben Vrackie. ♛Q☋❀⇌◑♣P

Perth

Capital Asset ✔

26 Tay Street, PH1 5LQ
✪ 11-11 (11.30 Thu; 12.30am Fri & Sat); 12.30-11 Sun
☎ (01738) 580457
Caledonian Deuchars IPA; Greene King Abbot; guest beers ⊞
The name of this Wetherspoon pub reflects the building's original purpose as a savings bank and Perth's status as medieval capital of Scotland. The bank's large safe has been retained, along with high ceilings and ornate cornices. Pictures of old Perth adorn the walls. A large open-plan lounge overlooking the River Tay is popular with shoppers and convenient for audiences at the nearby theatre and concert hall. Five ales from throughout the UK are available, with local Inveralmond beers featuring regularly. ☋◑♿⇌⊟(7)⊬

Cherrybank Inn

210 Glasgow Road, PH2 0NA
✪ 11-11 (11.45 Sat & Sun) ☎ (01738) 624349
⊕ cherrybankinn.co.uk
Inveralmond Independence, Ossian; guest beers ⊞
The Cherrybank has been a popular venue for passing travellers and locals since 1761. Originally a drovers' inn where horse-drawn carriages stopped for a break, the pub now enjoys an excellent reputation for bar lunches, evening meals and accommodation. There are five handpumps, split between the bar and larger lounge. Ales come from the local Inveralmond Brewery and other Scottish micros. A range of more than 100 malt whiskies is also available. Q⇌◑⊟⊟(7)P⊬

Wester Balgedie

Balgedie Toll Tavern

KY13 9HE
✪ 11-11 (11.30 Thu; 12.30am Fri & Sat); 12.30-11.30 Sun
☎ (01592) 840212
Harviestoun Bitter & Twisted; guest beer ⊞
Welcoming and comfortable rural tavern dating from 1534 where travellers had to break their journey to pay tolls. Now much extended, the oldest part of the building (the toll house) is at the southern end. It has three seating areas plus a small bar with low ceilings, oak beams, horse brasses, wooden settles and works of art by a local painter. A good selection of meals and bar snacks is available. ❀◑⊟(201,205)P⊬

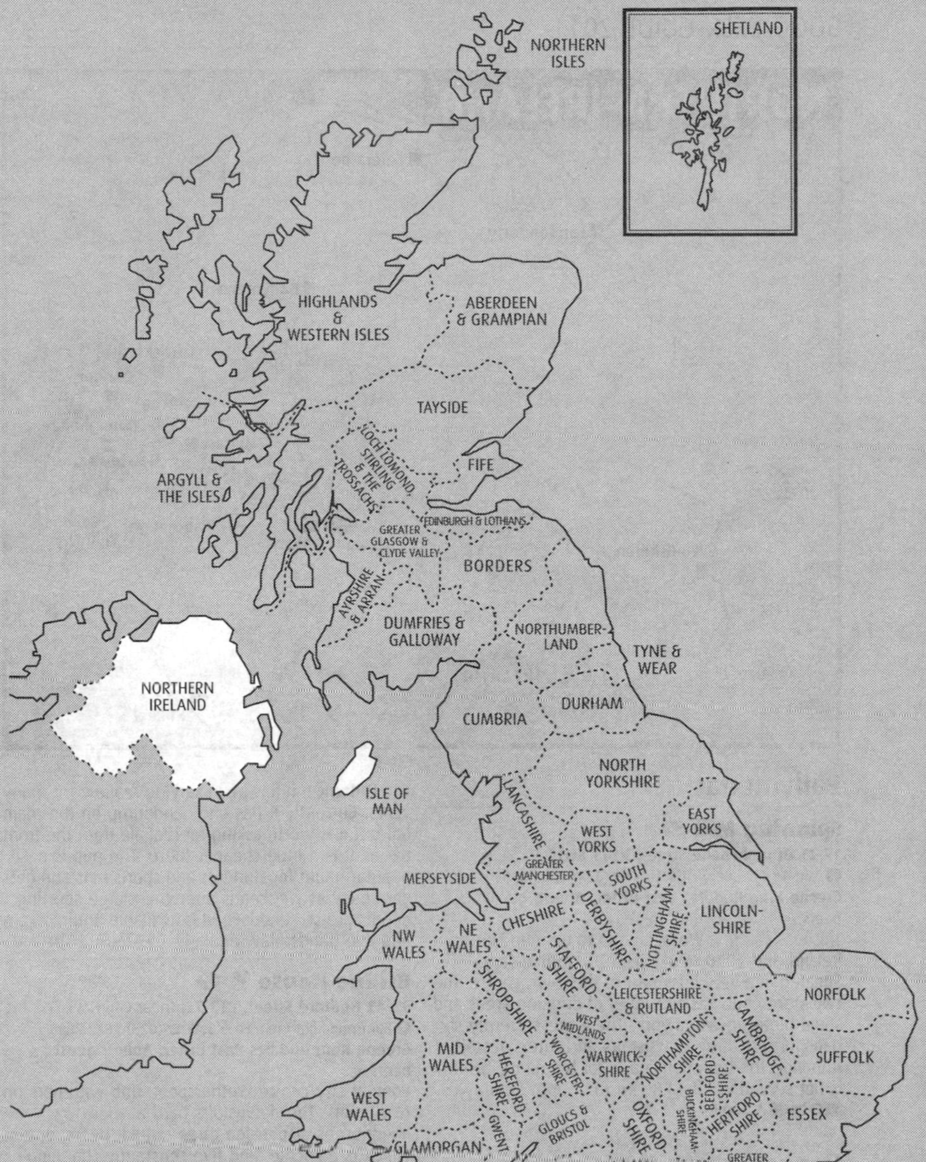

Northern Ireland Channel Islands Isle of Man

NORTHERN IRELAND

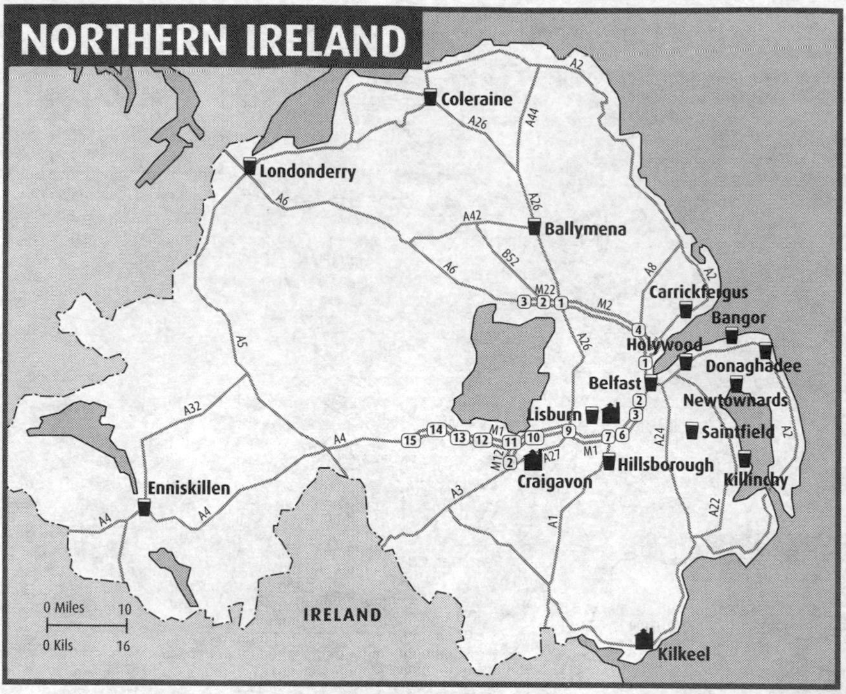

Ballymena

Spinning Mill ✔

17-21 Broughshane Street, BT43 6EB

9am-11 (12.30am Fri & Sat) ☎ (028) 2563 8985

Greene King Ruddles Best Bitter, Abbot; guest beers H

This was the first Wetherspoon to open in Northern Ireland and 2010 marks its 10th anniversary. Situated in a very busy part of the town centre, the two-storey pub has a number of drinking areas and some pleasing woodwork. There are currently six handpumps, three downstairs and three upstairs. Although the bar opens early for breakfast, alcohol is not served untill 11.30am (12.30pm Sunday).

Bangor

Esplanade

12 Ballyhome Esplanade, BT20 5LZ

11.30-11; 12.30-10 Sun ☎ (028) 9127 0954

Whitewater Belfast Ale; guest beers H

Comfortable seaside pub in the suburbs of Bangor, with commanding views over Ballyholme Bay from the lounges. Three handpumps offer local Whitewater ales and guests in the public bar, and staff will serve these in other parts of this former hotel. Four screens show sport and the pub has a golfing society. The pub stays open up until 1am on Friday and Saturday if there is the demand. (302A)

Belfast

Botanic Inn

23-27 Malone Road, BT9 6RU

11.30-1am; 12-midnight Sun ☎ (028) 9050 9740

Whitewater Belfast Ale H

The Botanic Inn has been serving real ale for many years. Currently it has one handpump on the main bar but it is worth asking for real ale from the front bar as it is a little cheaper there. The pub is a popular haunt for students and sports fans and gets very busy at weekends and when large sporting events are screened. Food is available until 7.45pm and live bands play regularly. (8B)

Bridge House 🏆 ✔

37-43 Bedford Street, BT2 7EJ (near City Hall)

8am-midnight (1am Fri & Sat) ☎ (028) 9072 7890

Greene King Ruddles Best Bitter, Abbot; guest beers H

Popular city-centre Wetherspoon pub with bars on two levels. The downstairs bar has eight handpumps dispensing three regular beers, one of which is a LocAle, and five constantly changing guest beers, all served by friendly, knowledgable staff. The pub is the region's highest selling real ale outlet and two festivals each year feature beers not usually available. Breakfast is served daily from 8am, alcohol from 11.30am (12.30pm Sun). (Gt Victoria St)

Crown ★ ✔

46 Great Victoria Street, BT2 7BA (opp Europa Hotel and Great Victoria St station)

11.30-midnight; 12.30-11 Sun ☎ (028) 90243187

crownbar.com

Whitewater Belfast Ale, Crown Glory; guest beer H

If you need one reason to visit Belfast, this is it. Featuring on CAMRA's National Inventory of Historic Pub Interiors, the Crown is easily the most

INDEPENDENT BREWERIES

Clanconnel Craigavon
Hilden Lisburn
Whitewater Kilkeel

ornate bar in Belfast. It has just about every feature a Victorian bar requires, from gas lighting to comfortable snugs, and attracts a mixture of tourists and city-centre drinkers. Three ales are provided by the Whitewater Brewery and good food is available downstairs and in the dining room upstairs. ◑♿≹(Gt Victoria St)🚌

John Hewitt

51 Donegal Street, BT1 2FH (100m from St Anne's Cathedral)
⏲ 11.30 (12 Sat)-1am; 7pm-midnight Sun
☎ (028) 9023 3768 🌐 thejohnhewitt.com
Hilden Ale; guest beer Ⓗ
The John Hewitt offers something different for the discerning drinker. Unlike most other bars, it is not owned by an individual or a commercial company – it is an arm of the Unemployed Resource Centre, and the profits are used to finance the organisation's work among the unemployed and others. The guest beer is usually from the Hilden Brewery. Well worth the short walk from the city centre. Q◐♿🚌

King's Head

829 Lisburn Road, BT9 7GY (opp Kings Hall at Balmoral)
⏲ 12-1am (midnight Sun & Mon) ☎ (028) 9050 9950
Whitewater Belfast Ale; guest beer Ⓗ
One of the first venues to sell real ale in Belfast, the King's Head has undergone a transformation in recent years. There is now a public bar, gastro eaterie and comfortable lounge downstairs, and upstairs is a 120-seat restaurant. The real ale is in the public bar, with two handpumps serving Whitewater ales. Regular live acts perform in the bar and the attached Live Lounge. Convenient for buses and Balmoral railway stop.
Q❀◑🀫♿≹(Balmoral)P⚐

Kitchen Bar

1 Victoria Square, BT1 4QB (adjacent to Victoria Shopping Centre, Victoria St side)
⏲ 11.30-11.30 (midnight Mon; 1am Fri & Sat); 12-6 Sun
☎ (028) 9024 5368 🌐 thekitchenbar.com
Whitewater Belfast Ale; guest beer Ⓗ
Modern one-room bar, built at the same time as the Victoria Shopping Centre, just a five-minute walk from the city centre. It is often very busy – packed with shoppers, sports and music fans. There are two real ale handpumps mainly dispensing beers from the Whitewater Brewery. Food is a major draw here, with the famous Kitchen Bar Special Paddy Pizza always a highlight. The bar is becoming something of a music venue, with live acts playing four times a week. ❀◑♿🚌⚐

McHugh's

29-31 Queens Square, BT1 3FG (near Albert Clock)
⏲ 12-1am (midnight Sun) ☎ (028) 9050 9999
🌐 mchughsbar.com
Whitewater Belfast Ale; guest beer Ⓗ
The old McHugh's has been sympathetically renovated and extended into the adjacent premises, which once housed Belfast's most celebrated house of ill repute. The ground floor now comprises a series of cosy interlinked drinking spaces, and a restaurant meanders at first floor level. The new arrangements are mellowing nicely, allowing the bar to retain its heritage status while remaining a community pub with a devoted regular clientele with interests in ice hockey, beer and rugby. ◑🀫♿≹(Central)🚌⚐

Molly's Yard

1 College Green Mews, Botanic Avenue, BT7 1LN
⏲ 12-9 (9.30 Fri & Sat); closed Sun ☎ (028) 9032 2600
🌐 mollysyard.co.uk
College Green Molly's Chocolate Stout, Headless Dog Ⓗ
This is a licensed restaurant, the only one in Belfast selling real ale. A quiet and relaxed haven in the often busy university area, it has a small bistro-style eaterie downstairs with a larger dining area upstairs. There are two handpumps dispensing College Green ales, brewed at Hilden. Good food is served, some of it accompanied by Molly's Chocolate Stout Wheaten Bread, which is made on the premises. Q❀◑♿≹(Botanic)🚌(7A)⚐

Ryan's

116-118 Lisburn Road, BT9 6AH
⏲ 11.30-1am; 12-midnight Sun ☎ (028) 9050 9850
Whitewater Belfast Ale Ⓗ
Ryans, a fairly recent convert to real ale, is situated near the City Hospital, about a mile from the city centre. The handpump is on the downstairs bar hidden among a number of charity boxes. The bar is mainly frequented by a mixture of students, locals, sports fans and hospital workers. Other attractions are the twice-weekly quizzes, live music and the bistro-style restaurant upstairs.
◑♿🚌⚐

Carrickfergus

Central Bar ✔

13-15 High Street, BT38 7AN (opp Carrickfergus Castle)
⏲ 9am-11 (1am Fri & Sat) ☎ (028) 9335 7840
Greene King Ruddles Best Bitter, Abbot; guest beers Ⓗ
Two storey centre-of-town hostelry providing a lively ground floor public bar and a family-friendly first floor bar/restaurant in standard Wetherspoon style. Guest ales are frequently from Scottish micros. The pub opens early for breakfast and alcoholic refreshments are served from 11.30am (12.30pm Sun). There are excellent views over Belfast Lough and the adjacent 12th-century Carrickfergus Castle from the multi-windowed first floor room. ♘◑🀫♿≹🚌(563)●

Coleraine

Old Courthouse ✔

Castlerock Road, BT51 3HP
⏲ 9am-11 (1am Fri & Sat) ☎ (028) 7032 5820
Greene King Ruddles Best Bitter, Abbot; guest beers Ⓗ
This remarkable Wetherspoon conversion retains the look of the old courthouse it once was, with pillars and black-and-white tiled flooring. Five handpumps dispense a changing range of beers. As well as the in the main bar area, food can be enjoyed in the balcony area upstairs or at outside tables. Although open from 9am, alcohol is not available until 11.30am (12.30pm Sun).
♔♘❀◑♿⚐

Donaghadee

Moat Inn

102 Moat Street, BT21 0ED
⏲ 11.30-11.30; 12.30-11 Sun ☎ (028) 9188 3297
🌐 moatinn.co.uk
Beer range varies Ⓗ

Two handpumps supply ales from the local Whitewater Brewery at this traditional pub with a compact public bar and a larger lounge. Upstairs is Henry's Bistro Restaurant, and a private room is available to hire for wedding receptions or private parties. Situated 300 metres from the harbour, there is off street parking and a garden area. ❀◑⊟♿⊡P⚟

Enniskillen

Linen Hall ✔

11-13 Townhall Street, BT74 7BD
✪ 9am-11 (1am Fri & Sat) ☎ (028) 6634 0910
Greene King Ruddles Best Bitter, Abbot; guest beers Ⓗ
An oasis of real ale that stands out among the busy nightlife of Enniskillen's Townhall Street. The Linen Hall was a pub even before it was converted into a modern Wetherspoon's. The interior is long and narrow, with a choice of areas to eat and drink in, and five handpumps on the centrally-located bar. The venue is very popular with locals and tourists alike, and well seeking out if you are visiting the Fermanagh Lakelands. ⏰❀◑♿🍏⚟

Hillsborough

Hillside

21 Main Street, BT26 6AE
✪ 12-11.30 (1am Fri & Sat); 12-11 Sun ☎ (028) 9268 9233
🌐 hillsidehillsborough.co.uk
Whitewater Belfast Ale, Copperhead Ale; guest beer Ⓗ
The Hillside is in the historic village of Hillsborough some 12 miles from Belfast, and well worth a visit. An early convert to real ale, it now has three handpumps serving a selection of beers. The pub has two drinking areas – the front bar and a main bar area. There is a bistro at the back and an a la carte restaurant upstairs. Outside is a heated beer garden where the annual beer festival is held. ♨Q❀◑⊟♿⊡(38,238)⚟

Plough Inn

The Square, BT26 6AG
✪ 11.30-11 (12.30am Fri & Sat); 12-11 Sun
☎ (028) 9268 2985
Hilden Ale Ⓗ
A former winner of local CAMRA Pub of the Year, the Plough has re-introduced real ale after a number of years as a keg-only bar. The interior is multi-levelled and comfortable, decorated with lots of wood and equine memorabilia. In addition there is an upstairs restaurant and the more modern Bar Retro next door. A very welcome return to the Guide. ♨❀◑♿⊡(38, 238)⚟

Holywood

Dirty Duck Ale House

3 Kinnegar Road, BT18 9JN (300m from railway station)
✪ 11.30-11.30 (1am Thu-Sat); 12.30-midnight Sun
☎ (028) 9059 6666 🌐 thedirtyduckalehouse.co.uk
Beer range varies Ⓗ
This well-situated pub, on the shore of Belfast Lough, has superb views of the shipping and the County Antrim coast from both bar and upstairs restaurant. A previous winner of local CAMRA Pub of the Year, four handpumps dispense beers from Hilden, Inveralmond and Highwood (Tom Wood) breweries, along with guest ales. Tuesday is quiz night and live music plays on Thursday to Sunday nights. The pub has a golfing society. ♨❀◑♿⇌⚟

> Beer: a high and mighty liquor.
> **Julius Caesar**

Killinchy

Daft Eddy's

Sketrick Island, BT23 6QH (2 miles N of Killinchey at Whiterock Bay)
✪ 11.30-11.30 (1am Fri); 12-10.30 Sun ☎ (028) 9754 1615
Beer range varies Ⓗ
Eddy's is in a beautiful location nestling off Sketrick Island, about two miles from the town of Killinchy. Excellent fresh food is highly recommended and the real ale comes from Whitewater Brewery. Other attractions include the nearby ruins of Sketrick Castle. There is no public transport to get you here but this bar is well worth seeking out. Q❀◑⊟♿P⚟

Lisburn

Tap Room

Hilden Brewery, Hilden, BT27 4TY (5 minutes' walk from Hilden railway halt)
✪ closed Mon; 12-2.30, 5.30-9; 12.30-3 Sun
☎ (028) 9266 3863 🌐 hildenbrewery.co.uk
Hilden Molly Malone; guest beer Ⓗ
Situated in the Scullions' Georgian mansion, the Tap Room is a licensed restaurant attached to the Hilden Brewery, not far from the A1 Belfast to Lisburn road and Hilden train halt. The restaurant is a long, narrow, wooden-floored building with a bar in the centre and a real fire. Good food, some of it cooked with real ale, is available. The venue hosts music events, brewery tours and an annual beer festival. ♨Q❀◑♿⇌(Hilden)⊡(325H)P⚟

Tuesday Bell ✔

4 Lisburn Square, BT28 1TS
✪ 9am-11.30 (1am Fri & Sat); 9am-11 Sun
☎ (028) 9262 7390
Greene King Ruddles Best Bitter, Abbot; guest beers Ⓗ
This two-floored pub is the centrepiece of the Lisburn Square shopping centre. Both bars have three handpumps and usually serve the same ales. The upper floor has three screens tuned to Sky Sports News and occasional rugby and football matches. Both floors can be very busy at lunchtimes and weekends. Although open from 9am, alcohol is not served until 11.30am (12.30pm Sun). Children are welcome upstairs. ◑♿⇌⊡🍏⚟

Londonderry

Diamond ✔

23-24 The Diamond, BT48 6HP (centre of walled city)
✪ 9am-11 (midnight Wed & Thu; 1am Fri & Sat); 9am-midnight Sun ☎ (028) 7127 2880
Greene King Ruddles Best Bitter, Abbot; guest beers Ⓗ
This is one area where the Maiden City fares better than Belfast – it has two Wetherspoon pubs. The Diamond, a department store conversion, is a large building with two floors. Up to 10 handpumps are available to dispense real ale, which is handy at beer festival time. From its elevated position, the

bar has a pleasant view over the city. Despite opening early, alcohol can only be served from 11.30am (12.30pm Sun).

Ice Wharf

Strand Road, BT48 7AB

9am-midnight (1am Thu-Sat) ☎ (028) 7127 6610

Greene King Ruddles Best Bitter, Abbot; guest beers Ⓗ

This Lloyds No 1 Bar was the second Wetherspoon to open in the city – 2002 saw the ground floor of the former Strand Hotel transformed into a large, bright, one-roomed pub. Situated on one of the main thoroughfares in the city, it can get very busy. It is a short walk from Guildhall Square and the chain's other pub, the Diamond. In common with other Wetherspoons, alcohol is served from 11.30am (12.30pm Sun).

Newtownards

Spirit Merchant

54-56 Regent Street, BT23 4LP (next to bus station)

9am-11 (1am Thu-Sat) ☎ (028) 9182 4270

Greene King Ruddles Best Bitter, Abbot; Marston's Pedigree; guest beers Ⓗ

Wetherspoon bar conversion with the feel of a friendly local, close to the town centre. It has an open-plan smoking area at the front and a heated side courtyard. Knowledgable staff dispense three regular and two guest beers from five handpumps, and two annual festivals are hosted, often featuring ales not usually available locally. Three screens show sports. Breakfast is served daily from 9am, beer from 11.30am (12.30pm Sun).
(5,7,9)P

Saintfield

White Horse

49 Main Street, BT24 7AB

11.30-11.30; 12-10.30 Sun ☎ (028) 9751 1143

Whitewater Copperhead Ale, Crown & Glory, Belfast Ale; guest beers Ⓗ

This many times winner of Northern Ireland CAMRA Pub of the Year is in Saintfield village 10 miles from Belfast. It is the Whitewater Brewery tap and features four of its ales and occasional guests. Ale and food can be enjoyed at the bar, in the lounge/restaurant area, upstairs above the bar and in a room downstairs. The pub has a lively community feel, especially during the spring beer festival.
(15,215)

NORTHERN IRELAND

Bridge House, Belfast (Photo: James Taylor)

CHANNEL ISLANDS

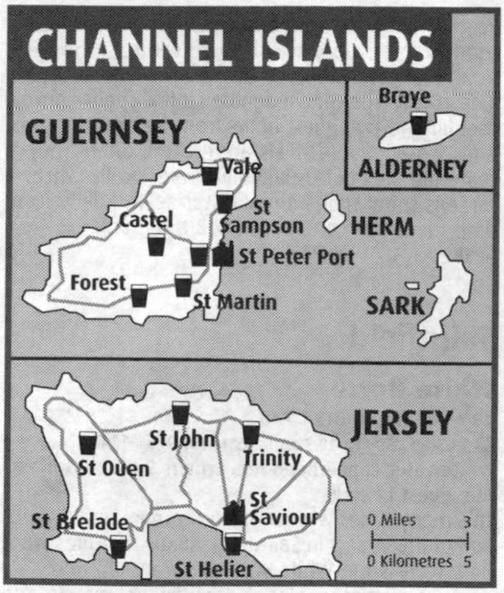

ALDERNEY

Braye

Coxswain Bar

Braye Street, GY9 3XT

9-11 (01481) 822421

Randalls Patois; guest beer

The small Coxswain Bar and Boathouse Bistro together form The Moorings, a venue that is popular with locals as well as visitors. The bar's welcoming landlords are enthusiastic about quality real ale. Another attraction is the lovely location just 100 metres from the harbour. Good value food is served from April to October.

GUERNSEY

Castel

Fleur du Jardin

Kings Mills, GY5 7JT

10.30-11.45 (01481) 257996 fleurdujardin.com

Beer range varies

A building of unique charm with two bars – one traditional, small and cosy, attached to the restaurant, the other recently renovated in a more contemporary style to create a comfortable, relaxing area to enjoy a beer. A door from this area leads to a large covered patio and out to the garden. Menus in both the bar and restaurant feature fresh local produce. Q P

Rockmount Hotel

Cobo, GY5 7HB

10.30-midnight (12.45am Fri & Sat) (01481) 256757

Randalls Patois

A pub for all seasons with a choice of bars – a public to the rear, and a newly-refurbished front bar by the road. A warming fire in winter makes it a cosy retreat from the gales. A good range of tasty food is served and the pub is just across the road from a sandy beach. The perfect place to relax and enjoy one of Guernsey's legendary sunsets P

Forest

Deerhound

Le Bourg, GY8 0AN

11-11 (01481) 238585

Beer range varies

Modern bar on the main road to the airport. The emphasis is on food here, and a good choice of tasty meals is served (booking advised at the weekend). There is a large, sunny, decked patio perfect for summer dining, and benches dotted about on the grass. Car parking spaces fill up quickly at busy times. P

St Martin

Captain's Hotel

La Fosse, GY4 6EF

11-11 (midnight Fri & Sat); 12-4 Sun (01481) 238990

Fuller's London Pride; guest beers

In a secluded location down a country lane, this is a popular locals' pub with a lively, friendly atmosphere. There is a small, raised area in front of the bar furnished with a sofa to make a 'comfy zone'. Meals can be eaten in the bar or the newly refurbished bistro area at the rear, and you can even take away a pizza. A meat draw is held on Friday. There is a car park to the rear which can fill up quickly. P

St Peter Port

Cock & Bull

Lower Hauteville, GY1 1LL

11-2.30, 4-12.45am; 11-12.45am Fri & Sat; 4-11 Sun (01481) 722660

Beer range varies

Popular pub, just up the hill from the town church, with five handpumps providing a changing range of beers. Live music takes place through the week, with salsa, baroque or jazz on Monday, open mike night on Tuesday, jazz on Wednesday and Irish on Thursday. Seating is on three levels. The pub only opens on Sunday when there is rugby on. CAMRA Branch Pub of the Year 2008.

Cornerstone Café

La Tour Beauregard, GY1 1LQ

10 (8am Thu & Fri)-midnight; 12-6 Sun (01481) 713832

cornerstoneguernsey.co.uk

Randalls Patois; guest beers

Situated across the road from the States Archives, the café has a small bar area to the front with bar stools, and further seating to the rear. Regular quiz evenings are held. The menu offers a wide range of good quality hot and cold meals, plus a daily specials board (no food Sun). There is a large screen for sporting events. Check the website for current beers on handpump.

Drunken Duck

La Charroterie, GY1 1EL (opp Charles Frossard House)

11 (12 Sun)-12.45am (01481) 726170

Badger Sussex Bitter, seasonal beers

A welcome return to the Guide for this public house. Since its last appearance it has had a name change and a refurbishment, which made it look more like a coffee shop than a pub. With a new owner (the landlady of the nearby Randy Paddle), the pub has returned to its distinctive name and original welcoming interior. The real fire will also

INDEPENDENT BREWERIES

Jersey St Saviour: Jersey

Randalls St Peter Port: Guernsey

be back for the winter months. There are also plans to install a third handpump as real ale is proving popular. Light lunches are served. ⛼🚭

Ship & Crown

North Esplanade, GY1 2NB (opp Crown Pier car park)
⏲ 10-12.45am; 12-10 Sun ☎ (01481) 721368
Beer range varies Ⓗ
Now a free house, the pub has a nautical theme. Situated across the road from Victoria Pier, this busy pub attracts a varied clientele of all ages. Real cider – Westons 1st Quality – is available on handpump. Excellent bar meals are served in generous portions throughout the day, with a daily changing range of specials. The Crows Nest above the pub serves meals lunchtimes and evenings but has no handpump, only bottles. ◐◑🍎

St Sampson

Pony Inn

Les Capelles, GY2 4GX
⏲ 11-10.30 ☎ (01481) 244374
Badger Tanglefoot Ⓗ
The pub was heavily modernised some years ago and the emphasis now is on good quality food. The handpump is on the bar in the dining area. To the side there is a public bar with its own separate entrance and although there is no handpump here the bar staff will happily bring you a pint from the main bar. Large car park to the front. ❀◐◑🂠P

Vale

Houmet Tavern

Rousse, GY6 8AR (between Vale Church and Rousse Tower)
⏲ 10-12.45am; 10-6 Sun ☎ (01481) 242214
Beer range varies Ⓗ
The pub has a public bar to the rear, popular with locals, with pub games and a TV to watch sporting events. To the front, there is a large lounge with an attached conservatory, giving fabulous views of the bay and local fishing boats. Bar meals are served in the lounge lunchtimes and evenings (not Sun eve). The pub may shut around 11.45pm. ◐◑🂠🚌P🚭

JERSEY

St Brelade

Old Court House

Le Boulevard, St Aubin's Harbour, JE3 8AB
⏲ 11-11 ☎ (01534) 746433
Draught Bass; Wells Bombardier Ⓗ**; guest beer** Ⓗ/Ⓖ
Situated on the bulwarks of St Aubin's harbour, The Old Court House featured prominently in the TV series Bergerac, under the pseudonym of The Royal Barge. The venue is primarily a restaurant and hotel, but the granite bar and conservatory are popular for drinking. A real ale from Skinner's is usually available on gravity. There is a regular bus service from St Helier town centre, and it is a short walk from here over the hill to the Smugglers at Ouaisne. Q❀◐◑🚌(15)🚭

Old Smugglers Inn

Le Mont du Ouaisne, JE3 8AW
⏲ 11-11 (winter opening hours vary) ☎ (01534) 741510
🌐 oldsmugglersinn.com
Draught Bass Ⓗ**; Greene King Abbot** Ⓖ**; Wells Bombardier; guest beers** Ⓗ
Perched on the edge of Ouaisne Bay, the Smugglers has been the jewel in the crown of the Jersey real ale scene for many years. Set on several levels within granite-built fishermen's cottages dating back hundreds of years. Up to four real ales are usually available including one from Skinner's, and mini beer festivals are regularly held. The pub is well known for its good food and fresh daily specials. CAMRA Pub of the Year 2007. ⛼Q◐◑

St Helier

Lamplighter 🏆 ✔

9 Mulcaster Street, JE2 3NJ
⏲ 11-11 ☎ (01534) 723119
Ringwood Best Bitter, Fortyniner Ⓗ**, Old Thumper** Ⓖ**; Wells Eagle IPA, Bombardier** Ⓗ**; guest beers** Ⓖ
A traditional pub with a modern feel. The gas lamps that gave the pub its name remain, as does the original antique pewter bar top. An excellent range of up to eight real ales and sometimes a real cider are available including one from Skinner's – four are served direct from the cask. Local CAMRA Pub of the Year 2009. ◐🚌(5)🍎

St John

L'Auberge du Nord

La Route du Nord, JE3 4AJ
⏲ 11-11 ☎ (01534) 861697
Ringwood Best Bitter Ⓗ
A 10-minute walk towards the north coast from St John village, this 16th-century farm house was converted to a pub in the 1950s. The restaurant was refurbished in 2009 and joins The Boat House, Tree House and Beach House in this popular chain serving locally-sourced produce. A guest ale often replaces the Ringwood on the bar. Parking and outside seating make the pub a useful meeting place for the north coast. ⛼Q❀◐◑🚌(5)P🚭

St Ouen

Moulin de Lecq

Le Mont de la Greve de Lecq, JE3 2DT
⏲ 11-11 (winter opening hours vary) ☎ (01534) 482818
🌐 moulindelecq.com
Greene King Old Speckled Hen Ⓗ**, Abbot** Ⓖ**, seasonal beers; Wells Bombardier; guest beers** Ⓗ
Another free house on the island offering a range of real ales, the Moulin is a converted 12th-century watermill situated in the valley above the beach at Greve de Lecq. The waterwheel is still in place and the turning mechanism can be seen behind the bar. A restaurant adjoins the mill. There is a children's play area and a barbecue area used extensively in the summer. ⛼Q❀◐◑🚌(9)🍎P🚭

Trinity

Trinity Arms

La Rue Es Picots, JE3 5JX
⏲ 11-11 ☎ (01534) 864691
Jersey Liberation Ⓗ**, Best** Ⓐ
Sporting the parish's ancient symbol of the Trinity, this 1976-built pub is modern by Jersey country pub standards but has plenty of character. Owned by the Jersey Brewery, the pub is central to and popular in village community life. It has a public bar and restaurant where food is served lunchtimes and evenings. Outside is seating, a children's play area and car parking. ❀◐◑♿🚌(4)♣P🚭

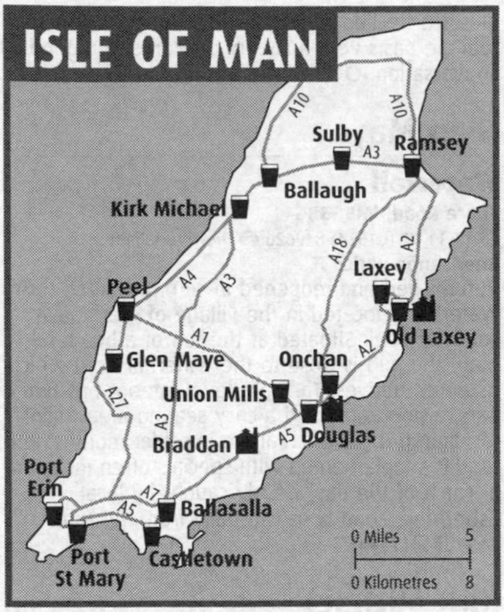

Ballasalla

Whitestone ✔

Station Road, IM9 2DD
✪ 12-11 (midnight Fri & Sat) ☎ (01624) 822334
Beer range varies Ⓗ
Large multi-roomed pub in the centre of the village with a small, separate public bar with pool and TV, which can be lively at weekends. The main area of the pub is divided into three with a dining space and two lounge areas with comfortable seating. There is an emphasis on food here, but plenty of seating for non-diners. A guest beer is usually available, frequently Bass by popular request from the regulars. No food is served on Sunday evening. Q❀◑⊟🚌(1,2)♣P⊬

Ballaugh

Raven

The Main Road, IM7 5EG
✪ 12-11 (midnight Fri & Sat) ☎ (01624) 896128
Okells Bitter, Ravens Claw; guest beers Ⓗ
Situated on the TT course close to the famous Ballaugh Bridge, the Raven provides an excellent vantage point during the races. This old coaching inn dating back to 1740 is a family-friendly locals' pub, popular for food, with Thai cuisine a speciality. The house brew is Ravens Claw, brewed by Okells. There is a large TV in the main bar, but no sport, and drawings of TT stars adorn the walls. The separate games room has a jukebox for those wanting some sounds with their game of pool or darts. Q❀◑🚌(5,6)♣P⊬

Castletown

Castle Arms (Glue Pot) ✔

The Quay, IM9 1LD
✪ 12-11 (midnight Fri); 10-midnight Sat ☎ (01624) 824673
Draught Bass; Okells Bitter; guest beers Ⓗ
The pub is popularly known as the Glue Pot due to the difficulty some of its clientele seem to have in extricating themselves. This attractive, historic inn nestles on the picturesque quayside in the shadow of Castle Rushen, and is also handy for Castletown's other heritage attractions. The Castle Arms has the distinction of being the only pub to appear on a bank note (Manx £). Inside, two cosy, nautically-themed rooms are served from one through-bar featuring up to four seasonal/guest beers.
❀◐⇌(IMR)🚌(1,2)♣⊬

Sidings

Victoria Road, IM9 1EF (next to railway station)
✪ 11.30-11 (midnight Fri & Sat) ☎ (01624) 823282
Bushy's Mild, Bitter, Castletown Bitter; guest beers Ⓗ
The Sidings is next to the steam railway station in the island's ancient capital. The clientele is a mix of seasonal visitors exploring the island and a base of loyal regulars. The three reasonably-priced local cask ales are always popular and up to seven ever-changing guests are also offered. The pub hosts a July beer festival with up to 60 real ales and ciders available over the week-long event, which grows in popularity each year. 🜂❀◐⇌(IMR)🚌(1,2)♣P⊬

Douglas

Albert Hotel ✔

3 Chapel Row, IM1 2BJ (next to bus station)
✪ 10-11 (11.45 Fri & Sat); 12-11 Sun ☎ (01624) 673632
Bushy's seasonal beers; Okells Mild, Bitter; guest beers Ⓗ
The Albert is next to the bus station and is also the nearest real ale pub to the sea terminal. This busy, unspoilt local has a traditionally laid out central bar with dark wood panelling. Sport on TV is a regular feature, but rarely loud enough to spoil a conversation. The three resident beers include Okells Mild, Okells Bitter and a seasonal Bushy's. Holts beers also make a regular appearance. Q⊟⇌(IMR)🚌♣⊬

Cat With No Tail ✔

Hailwood Court, Hailwood Avenue, Governors Hill, IM2 7EA
✪ 12-11 (midnight Fri & Sat) ☎ (01624) 616364
Okells Bitter; guest beers Ⓗ
The 'Cat' is a large, modern community pub serving the Governors Hill housing estate, two miles from central Douglas, with a good local bus service. There are two bar areas – the public bar on the right has pool and darts, and a large screen TV for sport; to the left, the lounge bar caters for food, served lunchtimes and evenings (not Sun). There is a large conservatory and popular outside seating area with extensive views over the central rural part of the island. ⚇❀◑⊟🚌(25A,28)P⊬

Manor Hotel

School Road, Willaston, IM2 6PQ
✪ 12-11 (midnight Fri & Sat) ☎ (01624) 676957
Okells Bitter; guest beers Ⓗ
A community pub on the Willaston Estate, close to the TT Grandstand and Isle of Man College. This large multiple roomed pub has separate darts and pool rooms. There is a spacious lounge area with dark wood panelling. The public bar has large TV screens and a sporting emphasis. An upstairs meeting room is used by many local societies and clubs. Q⊟🚌(22)♣P⊬

INDEPENDENT BREWERIES

Bushy's Braddan
Okells Douglas
Old Laxey Old Laxey

Prospect Hotel

Prospect Hill, IM1 1ET

⏲ 12-11 (midnight Fri); 6-midnight Sat; closed Sun

☎ (01624) 616773

Okells Bitter; guest beers Ⓗ

Busy, comfortable pub located in the business area of Douglas, and very popular with office workers. The large single room has plenty of seating and separate areas for a quiet chat, and plenty of elbow room at the long bar. In winter this is a warm and cosy place to meet friends. Wednesday is quiz night and there is surf and turf on Thursday. Guest beers change constantly, from brewers including Black Sheep, Brakspear and Theakston.
◖⇌(IMR)🚌⁄–

Queens Hotel

Queens Promenade, IM2 4NL (on seafront)

⏲ 12-midnight (1am Fri & Sat) ☎ (01624) 674438

Okells Bitter; guest beers Ⓗ

Large, busy, seaside pub, popular with locals and holidaymakers. The lounge has a Victorian feel, with original wood panelling and old pictures, and is usually quiet except for live entertainment on Friday and Saturday nights. The public bar has a large TV screen and an area set aside for games. The excellent heated area outside under awnings is now enclosed by a plastic hedge. In summer, drinkers can watch the horse trams passing by and look out on to Douglas Bay to see the ferries coming and going. Q❀◖◗⊟♿🚌(24,26)♣⁄–

Rovers Return

11 Church Street, IM1 2AG (behind town hall)

⏲ 12-11 (midnight Fri & Sat) ☎ (01624) 676459

Bushy's Mild, Bitter, seasonal beers; guest beers Ⓗ

Popular pub close to the town centre, busy at weekends. Six handpumps offer three regular beers and three frequently-changing guests. A recent addition is wireless broadband. The lively main bar has an MP3 jukebox and a real fire in winter. There are five more rooms for enjoying a quiet, more intimate drink, including one that features a large collection of Blackburn Rovers FC memorabilia. Outside is a heated seating area for smokers. ⩕❀◖⇌(IMR)🚌♣🍎⁄–

Terminus Tavern ✔

Strathallan Crescent, IM2 4NR

⏲ 12-11 (midnight Thu-Sat) ☎ (01624) 624312

Okells Bitter; guest beers Ⓗ

Refurbished a couple of years ago, the Terminus offers one or two guest beers alongside Okells Bitter. The large front bar is comfortable, with alcoves around the large front windows. Very popular for dining, the pub can get busy during food hours. There is also a back bar/games room. The large seating area outside is next to the starting point for the seasonal horse trams and Manx Electric Railway, with views across Douglas Bay. ⛴❀◖◗⊟♿⇌(MER)🚌(25,26,27)♣P⁄–

Woodbourne Hotel

Alexander Drive, IM2 3QF

⏲ 5 (12 Fri-Sun)-midnight ☎ (01624) 676754

Okells Mild, Bitter, seasonal beers; guest beers Ⓗ

Large Victorian brick-built tied pub, within walking distance of the town centre. The three bar pub used to have a bar for gentlemen only, and this room is now used to showcase real ale on six handpumps, with beers mainly from Okells. In recent years the pub has been used to promote Okells' new beers and seasonal launches. Guest ales are stocked alongside. The Woody is a friendly real ale oasis with a cheery welcome and good conversation. Q❀⊟🚌♣⁄–

Glen Maye

Waterfall

Shore Road, IM5 3BG

⏲ 12-11 ☎ (01624) 840626 🌐 thewaterfall.im

Beer range varies Ⓗ

Refurbished and reopened in summer 2009, the Waterfall is located in the village of Glen Maye, south of Peel. Situated at the top of a beautiful glen, the pub is close to the waterfall from which its name derives. The split-level interior has two bars, a pool table and a cosy seating area mainly for dining. There is a real fire in colder months. Pub food is supplemented with specials often including a 'catch of the day' freshly caught by local fishermen. Food is served daily from 12-9pm. ⩕❀◖◗🚌(7)♣P⁄–

Kirk Michael

Mitre ✔

IM6 1AJ (just N of the A3/A4 jct, Douglas Road Corner)

⏲ 12-2 (not Mon), 5-11; 12-2, 5-midnight Fri; 12-midnight Sat ☎ (01624) 801244

Okells Bitter; guest beers Ⓗ

You can expect a warm welcome, good beer and home-cooked food at this traditional village pub. Two rooms provide a choice of atmosphere and there is an additional room for pool and darts. Large gardens at the front and rear are popular in the summer months and an open fire is lit in winter. The pub is a good vantage point for the TT and hosts an excellent weekly quiz night. ⩕Q❀◖◗⊟⛺🚌♣P⁄–

Laxey

Queen's Hotel

New Road, IM4 7BP

⏲ 12-11 (midnight Fri & Sat) ☎ (01624) 861195

Bushy's Bitter; guest beers Ⓗ

This popular village pub is closely situated to the famous Laxey Wheel, the world's largest working waterwheel, and the Victorian Snaefell Mountain Railway train, which departs to the island's highest point. The walls of the pub are a shrine to the famous TT races, covered with photographs and memorabilia, as well as featuring photos of the locality. There are comfortable benches for seating, a snug porch area and an outside space. A relaxed, friendly pub for chilling out. ⩕🛏⇌(MER)🚌(3,13)♣P⁄–

Old Laxey

Shore Hotel

IM4 7DA

⏲ 12-midnight ☎ (01624) 861509

Old Laxey Bosun Bitter Ⓗ

The island's sole brew-pub, with the landlord acting as assistant brewer. A welcoming community hostelry, its convivial atmosphere makes it a pleasant destination all year round. As the name suggests, the pub is located close to the beach and has a subtle nautical theme. Themed music weekends are a highlight. More than 120 whiskies are stocked – ask for a card so you can tick them off as you go. ⩕❀◖◗⛺♣P⁄–

Onchan

Creg-Ny-Baa

Creg-Ny-Baa, Mountain Road, IM4 5BP (on A18 mountain road Douglas to Ramsey) SC393818
✪ 12-11 (9 Sun) ☎ (01624) 676948 🌐 creg-ny-baa.com
Beer range varies ⊞
The Creg is a homely country pub with superb views, especially at sunset. It has a separate restaurant with lunch and evening menus including daily specials. Renowned as one of the most spectacular landmarks on the TT mountain course, it offers a superb vantage point for watching the races, with a marquee and grandstand seating on site. Creg-ny-baa is Manx Gaelic for 'rock of the cow'. ❀◑♿P⊱

Peel

Creek Inn ✔

Station Place, IM5 1AT (by harbour)
✪ 10am-midnight ☎ (01624) 842216
Okells Bitter; guest beers ⊞
Located on the quayside adjacent to the House of Manannan museum, the Creek Inn dates back to around 1852. This two-roomed pub serves food all day, with four guest beers plus seasonal ales on a regular basis. Beer festivals are held throughout the year. The rear bar is a popular live music venue. There is ample seating outside with magnificent views over the revamped marina and castle. Local CAMRA Pub of the Year runner-up in 2009.
❀◑▲(5,6)♣⊱

White House Hotel 🏆 ✔

Tynwald Road, IM5 1LA (150m from bus station)
✪ 11-midnight ☎ (01624) 842252
Bushy's Mild, Bitter; Moorhouses Pride of Pendle; Okells Bitter; Taylor Landlord; guest beers ⊞
Although a fishing village, Peel is the island's only true city. This popular free house near the bus station has a three-room interior served by a central bar. The cosy Captain's Cabin snug has its own real fire and seafaring artefacts. Live music from local artists is hosted on Friday and Saturday. The pub has been run by the same family for many years. IoM CAMRA Pub of the Year 2009.
Q❀▲(5,6)♣P

Port Erin

Bay Hotel

Shore Road, IM9 6HL
✪ 12-midnight (1am Fri & Sat) ☎ (01624) 832084
Bushy's Bitter, Ruby Mild, Castletown Bitter, Old Bushy Tail, seasonal beers; guest beers ⊞
Bushy's flagship pub is located on the seashore where beach concerts are held during the summer. A good selection of Bushy's brews is available, and the pub is also well known for good food. The interior is effectively divided into four rooms – to the left the public bars where live music plays on many Fridays; to the right the quieter dining areas, which have Wi-Fi facilities. The pub is very much a destination for bikers in June during TT week and real ale fans all year round.
◑♿⇌(IMR)♣⊱

Falcon's Nest Hotel

Station Road, IM9 6AF
✪ 10.30-midnight (1am Fri & Sat); 10.30-11 Sun
☎ (01624) 834077 🌐 isleofman.com/business/f/falconsnest/
Bushy's Bitter; Okells Bitter, seasonal beers; guest beers ⊞
The Falcon's Nest Hotel on the south-west coast, overlooking the beautiful crescent-shaped bay, is a free house with two bars. The residents' lounge bar, also open to the public, is in the true tradition of the public house, where visitors can enjoy an ever-changing range of guests and local beers relaxing in front of an open fire. The Victorian-style Gladstone restaurant offers an extensive a la carte menu and an ever-popular Sunday lunch carvery.
Q◑⇌(IMR)♣

Port St Mary

Albert Hotel

Athol Street, IM9 5DS (next to bus terminal)
✪ 11-midnight; 12-1am Fri & Sat; 12-midnight Sun
☎ (01624) 832118
Bushy's Bitter, Old Bushy Tail; Okells Bitter; guest beers ⊞
Traditional pub in a quaint harbour setting. Previously called 'The Temperance Hotel' and 'The Ship', a nautical theme is retained in the internal decoration and a handsome sailing ship pub sign. Three rooms include a spacious public bar/games room and a cosy lounge with a real fire and an impressive collection of original local watercolour landscapes. Regular beers come for the island's two main breweries plus seasonal ales. Beware the low doorway to the Gents. ❀◑♣P⊱

Shore Hotel

Shore Road, Gansey, IM9 5LZ (on main Castletown-Port St Mary road)
✪ 12-midnight (1am Fri & Sat) ☎ (01624) 832269
Bushy's Bushy Tail; Okells Bitter; guest beers ⊞
This friendly free house occupies a prominent beachside position on Carrick Bay – an idyllic location in summer but somewhat exposed to winter gales, as can be seen in some spectacular old photographs displayed in the main bar. Regular beers hail from both the island's main breweries plus seasonal or guest ales. The separate dining room displays many fine photographs taken by the landlady's father-in-law featuring both local and more far-flung scenes. B&B accommodation is offered with four en-suite bedrooms.
❀◑(2,2A)♣P⊱

Ramsey

Swan

Parliament Square, IM8 1AH
✪ 12-11 (midnight Fri & Sat) ☎ (01624) 814236
Okells Mild, Bitter ⊞
This busy, friendly pub is well situated on the famous TT course, close to the bus station, railway station, quayside and town-centre shopping area. Food is served lunchtimes and evenings. The larger of the two bars has a dartboard, pool table and plasma TV screens. There are heated drinking areas outside. Guest ales are served on important Manx occasions like the Manx Grand Prix and also at Christmas. ❀◑♿⇌(MER)(3,5)♣⊱

Trafalgar Hotel ✔

West Quay, IM8 1DW (on quayside)
✪ 11-11 (12.15am Fri & Sat); 11.30-11 Sun
☎ (01624) 814601
Cains IPA; Moorhouses Black Cat; Okells Bitter; guest beers ⊞

ISLANDS

Established in 1870, this cosy, friendly and popular pub is a traditional quayside free house, overlooking the Sulby River, a short walk from the shopping area and TT course. A good selection of seasonal, guest and local ales is always available – beers are listed on a chalkboard for convenience.
QÅ⇌(MER)⊟(3,5,6)♣⊱

Sulby

Ginger Hall

Ballamanagh Road, IM7 2HB
✪ 11-midnight ☎ (01624) 897231
Beer range varies Ⓗ
The Ginger Hall is instantly recognisable by its colour. Inside the welcoming one-room bar area there is a real fire in the colder months and a impressive beer engine dominating the bar, dispensing Moorhouse's, Okells and Jennings ales. A recent addition to the decor are the unusual window decorations of black and white photographs of the TT. As well as a popular restaurant, the Ginger Hall offers reasonably priced accommodation, with some rooms en-suite.
⛼⇄◐♿P

Sulby Glen Hotel ✔

Main Road, IM7 2HR
✪ 12-midnight (1am Fri & Sat); 12-11 Sun
☎ (01624) 897240 ⊕ sulbyglen.net
Bushy's Bitter; Okells Bitter; guest beers Ⓗ
Situated beside the TT course, you can be sure of a friendly welcome at this large pub. It has two lounges served by a communal bar, with old photographs adorning the walls. Wonderful home-cooked food is available from two menus – one for the bar and one for the separate dining room. Regular mini beer and food festivals are hosted. Look out for the motorcycle beer engine (non-real ale). En-suite accommodation is available. The pub is blessed with its own bus stops on the Peel to Ramsey route. Cask Marque accredited.
⛼Q☕❀⇄◐⊟♿Å⊟♣P⊱

Union Mills

Railway Inn

Main Road, IM4 4NE (on main A1 Douglas-Peel road)
✪ 12-midnight (1am Fri & Sat) ☎ (01624) 853006
Okells Mild, Bitter, seasonal beers; guest beers Ⓗ
This popular village inn has been in the same family for five generations and dates back to 1841. Located on the TT course, the elevated beer garden is a favourite spot for viewing the famous races. Inside, there are three separate rooms including the characterful lounge which takes you back to the Victorian era. The beer range includes a choice of three guest ales plus a seasonal. Local CAMRA Pub of the Year 2000 and 2007.
⛼Q❀Å⊟(5,5A,6)♣P⊱

Creek Inn, Peel (Photo: Tom Stainer)

The Breweries

How to use the Breweries section

Breweries are listed in alphabetical order. The independents (regional, smaller craft brewers and brew-pubs) are listed first, followed by the nationals and the globals. Within each brewery entry, beers are listed in increasing order of strength. Beers that are available for less than three months are described as 'occasional' or 'seasonal' brews. If a brewery also produces bottle-conditioned beers, this will be mentioned in the main description: these are beers that have not been pasteurised and contain live yeast, allowing them to continue to ferment and mature in the bottle as a draught real ale does in its cask.

Symbols

A brew-pub: a pub that brews beer on the premises.

♦ CAMRA tasting notes, supplied by a trained CAMRA tasting panel. Beer descriptions that do not carry this symbol are based on more limited tastings or have been obtained from other sources.

Tasting notes are not provided for brew-pub beers that are available in fewer than five outlets, nor for other breweries' beers that are available for less than three months of the year.

A CAMRA Beer of the Year in 2009.

One of the 2010 CAMRA Beers of the Year: a finalist in the Champion Beer of Britain competition held during the Great British Beer Festival in London in August 2010, or the Champion Winter Beer of Britain competition held earlier in the year.

The brewery's beers can be acceptably served through a 'tight sparkler' attached to the nozzle of the beer pump, designed to give a thick collar of foam on the beer.

The brewery's beers should NOT be served through a tight sparkler. CAMRA is opposed to the growing tendency to serve southern-brewed beers with the aid of sparklers, which aerate the beer and tend to drive hop aroma and flavour into the head, altering the balance of the beer achieved in the brewery. When neither symbol is used it means the brewery in question has not stated a preference.

Abbreviations

OG stands for Original Gravity, the measure taken before fermentation of the level of 'fermentable material' (malt sugars and added sugars) in the brew. It is only a rough indication of strength and is no longer used for duty purposes.

ABV stands for Alcohol by Volume, which is a more reliable measure of the percentage of alcohol in finished beer. Many breweries now only disclose ABVs but the Guide lists OGs where available. Often the OG and the ABV of a beer are identical, i.e. 1035 and 3.5 per cent. If the ABV is higher than the OG, i.e. OG 1035, ABV 3.8, this indicates that the beer has been 'well attenuated' with most of the malt sugars turned into alcohol. If the ABV is lower than the OG, this means residual sugars have been left in the beer for fullness of body and flavour: this is rare but can apply to some Milds or strong old ales, barley wines and winter beers.

NOTE: The Breweries section was correct at the time of going to press and every effort has been made to ensure that all cask-conditioned beers are included.

The independents

SIBA indicates a member of the Society of Independent Brewers; IFBB indicates a member of the Independent Family Brewers of Britain; EAB indicates a member of the East Anglian Brewers Co-operative. See feature on page 839.

1648 SIBA

1648 Brewing Co Ltd, Old Stables Brewery, Mill Lane, East Hoathly, East Sussex, BN8 6QB
☎ **(01825) 840830**
✉ **brewmaster@1648brewing.co.uk**
🌐 **1648brewing.co.uk**
Tours by arrangement

⊗ The 1648 brewery, set up in the old stable block at the King's Head pub in 2003, derives its name from the year of the deposition of King Charles I. One pub is owned and more than 40 outlets are supplied. Seasonal beers: see website. Bottle-conditioned beers are also available.

Brew Master (OG 1040, ABV 3.9%)
A chestnut/brown-coloured bitter with a long aftertaste.

Triple Champion (OG 1041, ABV 4%)
A chestnut-coloured traditional English ale, deeply flavoured and full-bodied.

Signature (OG 1043, ABV 4.4%)
Very pale, light, crisply refreshing ale with a bitter aftertaste.

8 Sail (NEW)

8 Sail Brewery, Heckington Windmill, Hale Road, Heckington, Lincolnshire, NG34 9JW
☎ **07866 183479** ✉ **a.pygott@btinternet.com**

8 Sail Brewery was established in 2010 and operates on a six-barrel brew plant. The brewery nestles in the shadow of Heckington Windmill, Britain's only eight sailed windmill, from where the brewery takes its name. Bottle-conditioned beers are planned.

Ale (ABV 3.8%)

Abbey Ales SIBA

Abbey Ales Ltd, Abbey Brewery, Camden Row, Bath, Somerset, BA1 5LB
☎ **(01225) 444437** ✉ **enquiries@abbeyales.co.uk**
🌐 **abbeyales.co.uk**
Tours by arrangement

⊗ Abbey Ales was the first brewery in Bath for nearly 50 years. It supplies more than 80 regular accounts within a 20-mile radius of Bath, while selected wholesalers deliver beer nationally. It has four tied houses one of which, the Star Inn in Bath, is listed on CAMRA's National Inventory of Historic Pub Interiors. Seasonal beers: see website.

Bellringer (OG 1042, ABV 4.2%) ◆
A notably hoppy ale, light to medium-bodied, clean-tasting, refreshingly dry, with a balancing sweetness. Citrus, pale malt aroma and dry, bitter finish.

Abbeydale SIBA

Abbeydale Brewery Ltd, Unit 8, Aizlewood Road, Sheffield, South Yorkshire, S8 0YX
☎ **(0114) 281 2712**
✉ **info@abbeydalebrewery.co.uk** 🌐 **beerworks.co.uk**

⊗ Since starting in 1996, Abbeydale Brewery has grown steadily; it now produces upwards of 70 barrels a week, and the gradual expansion programme is set to continue. The regular range is complemented by ever-changing seasonals, each available for two months – see website. It also produces beers under the 'Beer Works' name.

Matins (OG 1034.9, ABV 3.6%)
Pale and full flavoured; a hoppy session beer.

Daily Bread (OG 1037, ABV 3.8%)

Brimstone (OG 1039, ABV 3.9%)
A russet-coloured bitter beer with a distinctive hop aroma.

Moonshine (OG 1041.2, ABV 4.3%)
A beautifully balanced pale ale with a full hop aroma. Pleasant grapefruit traces may be detected.

Absolution (OG 1050, ABV 5.3%)
A fruity pale ale, deceptively drinkable for its strength. Sweetish but not cloying.

Black Mass (OG 1065, ABV 6.7%)
A strong black stout with complex roast flavours and a lasting bitter finish.

Last Rites (OG 1097, ABV 11%)
A pale, strong barley wine.

Abbey Grange (NEW)

Abbey Grange Brewing Ltd, Llangollen Brewery, Abbey Grange Hotel, Llantysilio, Llangollen, LL20 8DD
☎ **(01978) 860753**
✉ **steven.evans10@btconnect.com**

The brewery began in 2010 on a 2.5-barrel plant.

Bitter (ABV 3.4%)

Llangollen Bitter (ABV 5.1%)

ABC SIBA

ABC Brewery Ltd, Unit 21, Birch Road, Witton, Aston, Birmingham, West Midlands, B6 7DD
☎ **(0121) 328 2655** ✉ **paul@abcbrewery.co.uk**
🌐 **abcbrewery.co.uk**
Tours by arrangement

⊗ ABC started brewing in 2008 and is situated near Villa Park football ground. It distributes to more than 60 outlets in the West Midlands. Bottle-conditioned beers are available.

Aston Mild (ABV 3.6%)

Hoppy Gold (ABV 3.8%)

Celtic Pride (ABV 4%)

Heartlands Bitter (ABV 4.2%)

Dizzy Blonde (ABV 4.4%)

Sporting Gold (ABV 4.4%)

Rotunda Red (ABV 4.8%)

Aston Distressway (ABV 6%)

THE BREWERIES

Acorn SIBA

Acorn Brewery of Barnsley Ltd, Unit 3, Aldham Industrial Estate, Mitchell Road, Wombwell, Barnsley, South Yorkshire, S73 8HA
☎ (01226) 270734 ✉ sales@acorn-brewery.co.uk
⊕ acorn-brewery.co.uk
Shop Mon-Fri 9am-5pm
Tours by arrangement

☺Acorn Brewery was set up in 2003 with a 10-barrel ex-Firkin plant. Expansion to a 20-barrel plant was completed when the brewery moved to larger premises. All beers are produced using the original Barnsley Bitter yeast strain, dating back to the 1850s. The brewery currently has a 100-barrel a week capacity. Seasonal beers: see website. Bottle-conditioned beers are also available.

Barnsley Bitter (OG 1038, ABV 3.8%) ◆
A bitter full of complex aromas and tastes including malt, fruit, hops and chocolate. Creamy texture with a bitter finish.

Blonde (OG 1040.5, ABV 4%)
A balanced pale ale with a crisp, clean finish.

Barnsley Gold (OG 1041.5, ABV 4.3%) ◆
Fruit in the aroma and taste. There is also a hoppy flavour throughout. A well-hopped, clean, dry finish.

Old Moor Porter (OG 1045, ABV 4.4%) ◆
A rich aroma of malt and hops with chocolate, liquorice and cherry flavours. A smooth porter.

Sovereign (OG 1044, ABV 4.4%) ◆
Plenty of fruit in both the aroma and taste in this well-balanced bitter.

IPA (OG 1047, ABV 5%) ◆
Full of hoppy and fruit aromas. A hoppy dry and fresh citrus fruit and bitter flavour leads to a crisp citrus, hoppy finish.

**Gorlovka Imperial Stout
(OG 1058, ABV 6%)** 🗂 🍷 ◆
A rich malt and hoppy aroma with liquorice. Fruit, hop and liquorice also carry through the duration of this full-bodied stout. Malty finish.

Adkin

Adkin Brewery, correspondence only: c/o 52 Adkin Way, Wantage, Oxfordshire, OX12 9HW
☎ 07709 086149 ✉ adkinbrewery@googlemail.com
⊕ adkinbrewery.co.uk
Tours by arrangement (limited to 4 persons)

⊠ Adkin was established on a 0.5-barrel plant in 2007 after producing charity beers in 2005 and 2006 at the Oxford Beer Festival. Six brews are rotated and are produced when required (prior orders only). No beer is kept at the correspondence address. Bottle-conditioned beers are available.

Adnams SIBA

Adnams plc, Sole Bay Brewery, East Green, Southwold, Suffolk, IP18 6JW
☎ (01502) 727200 ✉ info@adnams.co.uk
⊕ adnams.co.uk
Shop 10am-6pm daily
Tours by arrangement – see website

⊠ The company was founded by George and Ernest Adnams in 1872, who were joined by the Loftus family in 1902; a member of each family is still a director of the company. New fermenting vessels have been installed to cope with demand while a new eco-friendly distribution centre was opened in neighbouring Reydon. Real ale is available in all 70 pubs and there is national distribution. All beers are now from a new energy efficient 300-barrel brewery, built within the confines of the present site. Seasonal beers: see website. Bottle-conditioned beers are also available.

Bitter (OG 1037, ABV 3.7%) ◆
Hoppy aroma with hints of malt and fruit. Well-balanced malt and hop flavour with fruit overtones, giving way to a lingering bitter and surprisingly sweet aftertaste.

Explorer (OG 1042, ABV 4.3%) 🗂 ◆
Brewed with American hops, hence the name. Citrus fruit in the mouth, with a long, sweet aftertaste.

Broadside (OG 1049, ABV 4.7%) ◆
Strong, hoppy and fruity flavours with a long, sweet aftertaste.

Adur SIBA

Adur Brewery Ltd, Brick Barn, Charlton Court, Mouse Lane, Steyning, West Sussex, BN44 3DG
☎ (01273) 467527

Office: Adur Business Centre, Little High Street, Shoreham-by-Sea, West Sussex, BN43 5EG
✉ info@adurbrewery.com ⊕ adurbrewery.com

⊠ Adur Brewery was launched in 2008 on a 5.5-barrel plant, marking the return of brewing to the Adur Valley after an interval of nearly 100 years. A large part of the output is sold as bottle-conditioned beer and plans are underway for online sales.

Ropetackle Golden Ale (OG 1036, ABV 3.4%)
A light, golden ale with an initial sweetness and delicate aroma balanced by a dry finish.

Hop Token: Amarillo (OG 1040, ABV 4%)
An amber bitter with notes of peach and grapefruit in both aroma and taste, a good bitterness and a long, dry finish.

Velocity (OG 1044, ABV 4.4%)
Traditional best bitter with a hoppy aroma and a hint of marmalade in the taste.

Black William (OG 1055, ABV 5%)
A rich, black stout with dark chocolate aromas and roasted flavours.

Robbie's Red (OG 1050, ABV 5.2%)
A strong red-brown ale with an aroma of malt and hops. Slight initial sweetness leads into complex flavours including smoky orange peel and a satisfying bitterness which persists into the long finish.

Merry Andrew (OG 1062, ABV 6.2%)
Dark, strong ale with complex aroma and a rounded, fruity flavour. The initial sweetness is balanced by a dry finish.

**St Cuthman's Red Wheelbarrow
(OG 1082, ABV 10.5%)**
A Belgian Abbey-style Triple. The complex flavour has hints of caramel, fruit and spice with a long, warming aftertaste.

Alcazar SIBA

⬒ **Sherwood Forest Brewing Co Ltd, Alcazar Brewery, Church Street, Old Basford, Nottingham, NG6 0GA**

☎ (0115) 978 2282

Office: Turnstone Taverns, c/o The Railway Tavern, 188 Station Road, Langley Mill, Nottinghamshire, NG16 4AE ☎ (01773) 510863
✉ alcazarbrewery@tiscali.co.uk
⊕ alcazarbrewery.co.uk
Tours by arrangement

⊠ Alcazar was established in 1999 and is located behind its brewery tap, the Fox & Crown. The brewery is full mash with a 10-barrel brew length. Production is mainly for the Fox & Crown and other freehouses within the Turnstone Taverns estate. Seasonal beers: see website.

Sheriffs Gold (OG 1036, ABV 3.6%) ◆
Slightly sweet yellow session bitter made with First Gold and Goldings hops.

Alcazar Ale (OG 1040, ABV 4%) ◆
Flagship golden ale, full of citrus hops with a dry, bitter aftertaste.

New Dawn (OG 1045, ABV 4.5%) ◆
Full-bodied golden ale, brewed with Cascade hops.

Foxtale Ale (OG 1050, ABV 4.9%) ◆
A strong malty and bitter brown ale. Named 'Brush Bitter' in the brewery tap.

Vixen's Vice (OG 1052, ABV 5.2%) ◆
A premium strength hoppy pale ale.

Windjammer IPA (OG 1060, ABV 6%) ◆
Hoppy and bitter IPA brewed with five American hop varieties.

Bombay Castle IPA (OG 1065, ABV 6.5%) ◆
Strong IPA brewed with English hops.

Alehouse

See Verulam

Ales of Scilly SIBA

Ales of Scilly Brewery, 2b Porthmellon Industrial Estate, St Mary's, Isles of Scilly, Cornwall, TR21 0JY
☎ (01720) 423233 ✉ mark@alesofscilly.co.uk
Tours by arrangement

Opened in 2001 as a two barrel plant and expanded in 2004 to five barrels, Ales of Scilly is the most south-westerly brewery in Britain. Nine local pubs are supplied, with regular exports to mainland pubs and beer festivals. The brewery moved to new premises in 2007. Seasonal beers: Three Sheets (ABV 4.1%, summer), Firebrand (ABV 4.2%, Mar-Oct). Bottle-conditioned beer is also available.

Scuppered (ABV 4.6%) ◆
Rich tawny ale with sweet malt, honeycomb and fruity bitter taste and a hoppy aroma. Long bitter finish mellowed by sweetness.

Alexandra Ales

⬚ Alexandra Ales, 72-73 James Street, Rugby, Warwickshire, CV21 2SL
☎ (01788) 578660

The brewery is located behind the Alexandra Arms. The landlord of the pub produces one beer for use in the pub. Atomic Ales (qv) also brew on site.

Petite Blonde (ABV 3.9%)

Allendale

Allendale Brew Co Ltd, Allen Mills, Allendale, Hexham, Northumberland, NE47 9EQ
☎ (01434) 618686 ✉ tom@allendalebrewery.com
⊕ allendalebrewery.com
Shop Mon-Sat 9am-5pm
Tours by arrangement

Allendale was set up in 2006 and is run by father and son team, Jim and Tom Hick. Their locally themed ales are on sale in nearby free houses and also in Newcastle, Durham and surrounding areas. The brewery tap is the Crown in Catton, which was saved in 2008 after nine years of closure. Seasonal beers: Black Grouse Bitter (ABV 4%, Aug-Jan), Curlew's Return (ABV 4.2%, Feb-Jul).

Best Bitter (OG 1037, ABV 3.8%) ◆
Amber bitter with spicy aromas and a long, bitter finish.

Golden Plover (OG 1039, ABV 4%) ◆
Light, refreshing, easy-drinking blonde beer with a clean finish.

Adder Lager (ABV 5%)
A traditionally cold-fermented Pilsner-style lager.

Wolf (OG 1053, ABV 5.5%) ◆
Full-bodied red ale with bitterness in the taste giving way to a fruity finish.

AllGates SIBA

AllGates Brewery Ltd, The Old Brewery, Brewery Yard, off Wallgate, Wigan, WN1 1JU
☎ (01942) 234976
✉ information@allgatesbrewery.com
⊕ allgatesbrewery.com
Tours by arrangement (max. of 36)

⊕AllGates commenced brewing in 2006 in a Grade II-listed building at the rear of Wigan Main Post Office. The building is an old tower brewery that has been lovingly restored, but with a modern five-barrel plant. With the brewery now at full capacity, expansion plans are under consideration. Beers are distributed through its own estate of six pubs, regionally and through wholesalers. Seasonal beers and monthly specials: see website. Bottle-conditioned beer is also available.

California (OG 1037, ABV 3.8%) ◆
A clean-drinking, pale gold coloured ale with a strong floral aroma. Full-bodied despite its strength and dryness.

Mild at Heart (OG 1037, ABV 3.8%) ◆
Dark brown beer with a malty, fruity aroma. Creamy and malty in taste, with blackberry fruits and a satisfying aftertaste.

Napoleon's Retreat (OG 1038, ABV 3.9%)
A deep golden/copper-coloured traditional session bitter.

Twitter & Bisted (OG 1038, ABV 3.9%)
A seriously hoppy, straw-coloured ale.

Caskablanca (OG 1040, ABV 4.1%)
A generously hopped golden ale with a fruity, slightly floral aroma.

Reverend Ray (OG 1046, ABV 4.6%)
A traditional style best bitter with a peppery hop, ripe vine fruit and biscuity malt flavour.

Yankee Pale Ale (OG 1048, ABV 5%)

An American-style pale ale, light in colour and dry to enhance the crispness and full aroma of the hops.

All Nations

See Shires

Allsaints (NEW)

Allsaints Brewery, c/o Coastal Brewery, Unit 10B, Cardrew Industrial Estate, Redruth, Cornwall, TR15 1SS
☎ 07831 388829

Formerly known as Doghouse Brewery, which closed in 2007, Allsaints recommenced production in 2008 using spare capacity at Keltek Brewery. In 2009 the brewery began using spare capacity at Coastal Brewery in Redruth. See Coastal for beer list.

Alnwick

See Hadrian & Border

Amber

Amber Ales Ltd, Unit A, Asher Lane Business Park, Pentrich, Ripley, Derbyshire, DE5 3SW
☎ (01773) 512864 ✉ info@amberales.co.uk
⊕ amberales.co.uk
Shop Thu-Fri 2-6pm; Sat 10am-1pm
Tours by arrangement

⊗ Amber Ales began production in 2006 on a five-barrel plant from the Firkin brewpub chain. Part-time at first, it switched to full time ahead of plan due to strong local interest. Amber produces five core beers plus a seasonal ale. Its brewery tap, the Talbot Taphouse in Ripley, opened in late 2009. Around 100 outlets are supplied direct. Bottle-conditioned beers are available and are suitable for vegetarians and vegans.

Chocolate Orange Stout (OG 1040, ABV 4%) 🗐 🍾

Original Stout (OG 1040, ABV 4%)

Barnes Wallis (OG 1036, ABV 4.1%)

Samuel Slater (OG 1038, ABV 4.2%)

Imperial IPA (OG 1060, ABV 6.5%)

Anchor Springs (NEW)

Anchor Springs Brewery Co Ltd, Lineside Way, Wick, West Sussex, BN17 7EH
☎ (01903) 719842/715111
✉ debbie@jenkinslittlehampton.co.uk

Kevin Jenkins, owner of the Crown in Littlehampton, established Anchor Springs Brewery in 2010 using the five-barrel plant previously used at the Dark Star Brewery. The beer is mostly sold in the Crown.

Best (ABV 3.7%)

IPA (ABV 4.7%)

Andwell SIBA

Andwell Brewing Co LLP, Lodge Farm, North Warnborough, Hampshire, RG29 1HA
☎ (01256) 704412 ✉ beer@andwells.com
⊕ andwells.com

Brewing commenced in 2008 on a 10-barrel plant. Beer is distributed within a 30-mile radius of the brewery and to the Isle of Wight. More than 150 outlets are supplied.

Resolute Bitter (OG 1036, ABV 3.8%) ◆
A pleasant, well-balanced session bitter. Little aroma, with an initially malty flavour with some bitterness and a sweetish finish.

Gold Muddler (OG 1038, ABV 3.9%) ◆
A light golden ale with a hoppy, citrus aroma. These characteristics are carried into the flavour with a solid bitterness and a short, dry finish.

King John (OG 1042, ABV 4.2%) ◆
Malty best bitter, low in hops with a short initial bitterness and some dryness in the finish.

Ruddy Darter (OG 1047, ABV 4.2%)

Anglo Dutch SIBA

Anglo Dutch Brewery, Unit 12, Saville Bridge Mill, Mill Street East, Dewsbury, West Yorkshire, WF12 9AF
☎ (01924) 457772 ✉ angdutchbrew@yahoo.co.uk
⊕ anglodutchbrewery.com
Tours by arrangement

Paul Klos (Dutch) set up the brewery with Mike Field (Anglo) in a former dye mill near Dewsbury Minster in 2000. The brew length was doubled in 2007. Some beers contain wheat, Spike and Tabatha use lager malt. Seasonal beers: Devil's Knell (ABV 4.8%, Jan), Wild Flower (ABV 4.2%, Sep).

Apistus (OG 1040, ABV 4%)
A pale honey beer.

Dusk Till Dawn (OG 1040, ABV 4%)
Session version of Tabatha.

Kletswater (OG 1039, ABV 4%)
Pale-coloured beer with a hoppy nose and a good hop and citrus fruit flavour.

Spike's on 't' Way (OG 1041.6, ABV 4.2%) ◆
Pale bitter with citrus/orange flavour and dry, fruity finish.

Spikus (OG 1041.6, ABV 4.2%)
Made with organic lager malt and New Zealand hops.

Ghost on the Rim (OG 1043, ABV 4.5%)
Pale, dry and fruity.

Tabatha the Knackered (OG 1054, ABV 6%) ◆
Golden Belgian-style Tripel with a strong fruity, hoppy and bitter character. Powerful and warming, slightly thinnish, with a bitter, dry finish.

Angus (NEW)

Angus Ales, 14b Panmure Industrial Estate, Carnoustie, DD7 7NP
☎ 07708 011649 ✉ info@angus-ales.co.uk
⊕ angus-ales.co.uk
Tours by arrangement

⊗ Angus Ales was established in 2009 and is the brainchild of Alan Lawson and Graeme Duguid, both CAMRA members. The ales follow a golfing theme, the brewery being situated in the famous golfing town of Carnoustie.

Gowfers' Gold (ABV 3.8%)

A pale, refreshing golden ale.

Mashie Niblick (ABV 4.2%)
A full-flavoured malty ale.

Ann Street

See Jersey

An Teallach

An Teallach Ale Co Ltd, Camusnagaul, Dundonnell, Garve, Ross-shire, IV23 2QT
☎ (01854) 633306 ✉ ataleco1@yahoo.co.uk
Tours by arrangement

An Teallach was formed in 2001 by husband and wife team David and Wilma Orr on Wilma's family croft on the shores of Little Loch Broom, Wester Ross. The business has grown steadily each year. 60 pubs are supplied. All beers are also available bottled.

Beinn Dearg Ale (OG 1038, ABV 3.8%) ◆
A well-balanced malty, sweetish beer with a long, malty aftertaste.

Ale (OG 1042, ABV 4.2%) ◆
A classic pint in the Scottish 80/- tradition. Plenty of malt in the nicely-balanced bittersweet taste.

Crofters Pale Ale (OG 1042, ABV 4.2%) ◆
A good quaffing, lightly-flavoured golden ale. Hops in the taste and with a slight astringency in the finish.

Suilven (OG 1043, ABV 4.3%) ◆
A refreshing golden ale with a creamy sweetish taste and a pleasant sulphurous nose.

Brew House Special (OG 1044, ABV 4.4%) ◆
A golden ale with a nutty, malty taste and some hoppy bitterness balancing the pleasant sulphur background.

Kildonan (OG 1044, ABV 4.4%) ◆
Plenty of fruit and a good smack of bitterness in this golden ale.

Appleford SIBA

Appleford Brewery Co Ltd, Unit 14, Highlands Farm, High Road, Brightwell-cum-Sotwell, Wallingford, Oxfordshire, OX10 0QX
☎ (01235) 848055
✉ sales@applefordbrewery.co.uk
⊕ applefordbrewery.co.uk

Appleford Brewery opened in 2006 when two farm units were converted to house an eight-barrel plant. Deliveries are made to a number of local outlets as well as nationally, via the brewery or wholesalers. Bottle-conditioned beers are available.

River Crossing (ABV 3.8%)
A dark, hoppy session beer

Brightwell Gold (ABV 4%)

Power Station (ABV 4.2%)
A copper-coloured, slightly malty bitter.

Arbor

Arbor Ales Ltd, Unit 10a, Bridge Road Industrial Estate, Bridge Road, Kingswood, Bristol, BS15 4TA
☎ (0117) 957 0899 ✉ beer@arborales.co.uk
⊕ arborales.co.uk

Arbor Ales opened in 2007 in the back of the Old Tavern pub. In 2008 it moved to Kingswood and expanded to a 5.5-barrel plant. Further expansion took place in 2009. Arbor Ales also bought their first pub, the Old Stillage, in 2009. A wide range of beers are brewed with particular pride taken in the darker ales due to the brewer's involvement with the Bristol & District Rare Ales Group (www.badrag.co.uk). Seasonal beers are available: see website. Around 160 outlets are supplied direct.

Bushcraft (OG 1039, ABV 3.9%)

Single Hop (OG 1037, ABV 4%)

Hunny Beer (OG 1041, ABV 4.2%)

Brigstow (OG 1042, ABV 4.3%)

Oyster Stout (OG 1046.5, ABV 4.6%)

Beech Blonde (OG 1046, ABV 4.9%)

Archers

See Evan Evans

Arkell's IFBB SIBA

Arkell's Brewery Ltd, Kingsdown, Swindon, Wiltshire, SN2 7RU
☎ (01793) 823026 ✉ arkells@arkells.com
⊕ arkells.com
Brewery merchandise can be purchased at reception
Tours by arrangement

Arkells Brewery was established in 1843 and is still run by the family. The brewery owns 105 pubs in Berkshire, Gloucestershire, Oxfordshire and Wiltshire. Seasonal beers: Summer Ale (ABV 4%), JRA (ABV 3.6%), Noel Ale (ABV 5%), Bees Organic Beer (ABV 4.5%).

2B (OG 1032, ABV 3.2%) ◆
Light brown in colour, malty but with a smack of hops and an astringent aftertaste. It has good body for its strength.

3B (OG 1040, ABV 4%) ◆
A medium brown beer with a strong, sweetish malt/caramel flavour. The hops come through strongly in the aftertaste, which is lingering and dry.

Moonlight Ale (OG 1046, ABV 4.5%)

Kingsdown Ale (OG 1051, ABV 5%) ◆
A rich, deep russet-coloured beer, a stronger version of 3B. The malty/fruity aroma continues in the taste, which has a hint of pears. Hops come through in the aftertaste.

Arkwright's (NEW)

Arkwright's Brewery, c/o The Real Ale Shop, 47 Lovat Road, Preston, Lancashire, PR1 6DQ
☎ (01772) 201591 ✉ info@realaleshop.net
⊕ realaleshop.net

Arkwright's began brewing at the rear of the Real Ale Shop in 2010 using a 2.5-barrel plant.

Trouble at Mill (ABV 4%)

Run of the Mill (ABV 4.1%)

Arran SIBA

Arran Brew Ltd t/a Arran Brewery, Cladach, Brodick, Isle of Arran, North Ayrshire, KA27 8DE
☎ (01770) 302353 ✉ info@arranbrewery.co.uk
🌐 arranbrewery.com
Shop Mon-Sat 10am-5pm; Sun 12.30-5pm (reduced hours in winter)
Tours by arrangement

⊗ The brewery opened in 2000 using a 20-barrel plant. Production is up to 100 barrels a week with additional bottling capability. 50 outlets are supplied. Bottle-conditioned beer is available occasionally. Seasonal beers: Sunset (ABV 4.4%, Feb-Oct), Fireside (ABV 4.7%, Dec-Feb).

Ale (OG 1038, ABV 3.8%) ◆
An amber ale where the predominance of the hop produces a bitter beer with a subtle balancing sweetness of malt and an occasional hint of roast.

Dark (OG 1042, ABV 4.3%) ◆
A well-balanced malty beer with plenty of roast and hop in the taste and a dry, bitter finish.

Red Squirrel (OG 1038, ABV 4.5%)

Clyde Puffer (OG 1045, ABV 4.9%)

Blonde (OG 1048, ABV 5%) ◆
A hoppy beer with substantial fruit balance. The taste is balanced and the finish increasingly bitter. An aromatic strong bitter that drinks below its weight.

Arrow

Arrow Brewery, c/o Wine Vaults, 37 High Street, Kington, Herefordshire, HR5 3BJ
☎ (01544) 230685 ✉ deanewright@yahoo.co.uk

Former Bridge Street brewer Deane Wright has built his five-barrel brewery at the rear of the Wine Vaults and re-started brewing in 2005.

Bitter (OG 1042, ABV 4%)

Art Brew

Art Brew, The Art Brew Barn, Northend Farm, off Venn Lane, North Chideock, Dorset, DT6 6JY
☎ 07881 783626 ✉ artbrewdorset@googlemail.com
🌐 artbrew.co.uk

⊗ Brewing started in 2008 on a five-barrel plant with its own water source near the Jurassic Coast. The Royal Oak in Bath is also owned, which serves as the brewery tap. Around 60 outlets are supplied, mostly in Dorset, Devon and Somerset. Seasonal beers: see website.

Art Nouveau (OG 1039, ABV 3.9%)
Golden and hoppy.

iBeer (OG 1039, ABV 4%)
Speciality vanilla beer.

Renaissance (OG 1044, ABV 4.5%)
A mid-brown bitter.

Tempest Stout (OG 1046, ABV 4.6%)

Monkey IPA (OG 1058, ABV 6.4%)
Massively hopped proper IPA.

Spanked Monkey IPA (OG 1058, ABV 6.4%)
As above but with root ginger and chilli added to the cask.

Artisan

Artisan Brewing Co Ltd, 183a Kings Road, Cardiff, Glamorgan, CF11 9DF
☎ 07505 401939 ✉ info@artisanbeer.co.uk
🌐 artisanbeer.co.uk
Tours by arrangement (small groups only)

⊗ Artisan was established in 2008. All beers are unfiltered, without additives or preservatives and suitable for vegans. Bottle-conditioned beers are available.

Bavarian Style Wheat Beer (ABV 4.6%)

Chocolate Wheat (ABV 4.9%)

ALT Beer (ABV 5%)

Bohemian Style Pils (ABV 5%)

Helles Style Lager (ABV 5%)

Kolsch (ABV 5.1%)

The 'Real' IPA (ABV 5.6%)

Baltic Porter (Espresso) (ABV 6%)
Infused with coffee beans.

Arundel SIBA

Arundel Brewery Ltd, Unit C7, Ford Airfield Industrial Estate, Ford, Arundel, West Sussex, BN18 0HY
☎ (01903) 733111
✉ arundelbrewery@dsl.pipex.com
🌐 arundelbrewery.co.uk
Off-sales available Mon-Fri 9am-4pm at brewery

⊗ Founded in 1992, Arundel Brewery is the historic town's first brewery in more than 70 years. A range of occasional brands is available in selected months. Seasonal beers: see website.

Sussex Mild (OG 1037, ABV 3.7%) ◆
A dark mild. Strong chocolate and roast aromas, which lead to a bitter taste. The aftertaste is not powerful but the initial flavours remain in the dry and clean finish.

Castle (OG 1038, ABV 3.8%) ◆
A pale tawny beer with fruit and malt noticeable in the aroma. The flavour has a good balance of malt, fruit and hops, with a dry, hoppy finish.

Sussex Gold (OG 1042, ABV 4.2%) ◆
A golden-coloured best bitter with a strong floral hop aroma. The ale is clean-tasting and bitter for its strength, with a tangy citrus flavour. The initial hop and fruit die to a dry and bitter finish.

ASB (OG 1045, ABV 4.5%)
A special bitter with a complex roast malt flavour leading to a fruity, hoppy, bittersweet finish.

Stronghold (OG 1047, ABV 4.7%) ◆
A smooth, full-flavoured premium bitter. A good balance of malt, fruit and hops comes through in this rich, chestnut-coloured beer.

Trident (OG 1050, ABV 5%)
A strong golden ale.

Ascot

Ascot Ales Ltd, Unit 5, Compton Place, Surrey Avenue, Camberley, Surrey, GU15 3DX
☎ (01276) 686696 ✉ info@ascot-ales.co.uk
🌐 ascot-ales.co.uk
Tours by arrangement

⊗ Ascot Ales began production in 2007 on a four-barrel plant. Current owners Chris & Suzanne Gill took over the brewery in late 2007. Since adding a third fermenter the extra capacity has given scope for more seasonal/one off brews in addition to their five regular ales. Seasonal beers: see website. Bottle-conditioned beers are also available and are suitable for vegetarians and vegans.

Alley Cat Ale (OG 1038, ABV 3.8%) ◆
A pale brown session bitter with citrus hop present throughout, but balanced by malt. Dry with a lasting bitter finish.

On the Rails (OG 1039, ABV 3.8%) ◆
Dark, fruity and roasty mild with a faint hop character throughout, bittersweet in the taste and aftertaste. Notably dry finish.

Posh Pooch (OG 1042, ABV 4.2%) ◆
A hoppy best bitter with balancing biscuity malt sweetness. The citrus fruitiness lasts throughout. Clean hoppy aftertaste.

Alligator Ale (OG 1047, ABV 4.6%) ◆
American hops provide grapefruit notes in this golden ale. The biscuit in the aroma fades as hop and bitterness dominate the taste, but a residual sweetness remains even in the sharp, dry finish.

Anastasia's Exile Stout (OG 1049, ABV 5%) ▯ ◆
Burnt coffee aromas lead to a roast malt flavour in this black beer. Notably fruity throughout. The presence of some hop feeds into the bittersweet aftertaste.

Ashover

▤ Ashover Brewery, 1 Butts Road, Ashover, Chesterfield, Derbyshire, S45 0EW
☎ 07803 708526
✉ ashoverbrewery@googlemail.com
⊕ ashoverbrewery.com
Tours by arrangement

⊠ Ashover Brewery first brewed in early 2007 on a 3.5-barrel plant in the garage of the cottage next to the Old Poet's Corner pub. The brewery caters mainly for this and its sister pub, the Poet & Castle in Codnor, but other local free houses and festivals are also supplied. Seasonal beer: Winter Warmer (ABV 7%).

Light Rale (OG 1038, ABV 3.7%) ◆
Light in colour and taste, with initial sweet and malt flavours, leading to a bitter finish and aftertaste.

Poets Tipple (OG 1041, ABV 4%) ▯ ◆
Complex, tawny-coloured beer that drinks above its strength. Predominantly malty in flavour, with increasing bitterness towards the end.

Hydro (OG 1043, ABV 4.3%) ◆
Easy to drink golden beer with a predominantly hoppy aroma. Hop and fruit flavours and an initial sweetness lead to a dry, clean finish and aftertaste.

Rainbows End (OG 1045, ABV 4.5%) ◆
Slightly smooth, bitter golden beer with an initial sweetness. Grapefruit and lemon hop flavours come through strongly as the beer gets increasingly dry towards the finish, ending with a bitter, dry aftertaste.

Coffin Lane Stout (OG 1050, ABV 5%) ◆
Excellent example of the style, with a chocolate and coffee flavour, balanced by a little sweetness. Finish is long and quite dry.

Butts Pale Ale (OG 1055, ABV 5.5%) ◆

Pale and strong yet easy to drink golden bitter. Combination of bitter and sweet flavours mingle with an alcoholic kick, leading to a warming yet bitter finish and aftertaste.

Aston Manor

Aston Manor Brewery Co Ltd, 173 Thimble Mill Lane, Aston, Birmingham, West Midlands, B7 5HS
☎ (0121) 328 4336 ✉ sales@astonmanor.co.uk
⊕ astonmanor.co.uk

Aston Manor is the former owner of the Highgate Brewery in Walsall (qv). Its own plant concentrates on cider. Beer is bottled at Highgate but is not bottle-conditioned.

Atlantic

Atlantic Brewery, Treisaac Farm, Treisaac, Newquay, Cornwall, TR8 4DX
☎ (0870) 042 1714 ✉ stuart@atlanticbrewery.com
⊕ atlanticbrewery.com

Atlantic started brewing in 2005. All beers are organic, Soil Association certified and suitable for vegetarians and vegans. It concentrates on bottle-conditioned beers: Gold (ABV 4.6%, summer), Blue (ABV 4.8%), Red (ABV 5%), Fistral (ABV 5.2%).

Atlas

See Orkney

Atlas Mill

▤ Atlas Mill Brewery Ltd, The Tipp Inn, Atlas Mill Road, Brighouse, West Yorkshire, HD6 1ES
☎ (01484) 720440
✉ enquiries@atlasmillbrewery.com
⊕ atlasmillbrewery.com
Tours by arrangement

⊛Atlas Mill opened in early 2007 on the first floor of a converted mill. The brewery tap, the Tipp Inn, is situated on the ground floor of the mill and was opened in September 2007.

Dark Mild (ABV 3.6%) ◆
Grainy dark red mild. It has a roast and sulphurous aroma followed by a well-balanced, light, hoppy, fruity and malty taste.

Gold (ABV 3.6%) ◆
Lightly-flavoured and refreshing thirst-quencher with a subtle fruity palate and a delicate aftertaste.

Bitter (ABV 3.8%) ◆
Pale brown grainy session bitter. A sulphurous aroma leads to a fruity taste with light hop levels.

Basset Brown Ale (ABV 4.4%) ◆

Gwinness (ABV 4.4%) ◆
Creamy dark brown stout with a chocolate roast aroma. Complex, rich, fruity roast flavours develop in the mouth. It has a long, bittersweet aftertaste.

Hercules (ABV 4.5%) ◆
A distinctly sulphurous best bitter in both taste and aroma. Grainy and pale brown in colour, it has a malty, bitter aftertaste.

Irish Gold (ABV 4.8%) ◆
Grainy golden ale with a floral, hoppy aroma. Fruity on the tongue with a strong, bitter aftertaste.

IPA (ABV 5%) ◆

Amber-coloured strong beer with a creamy smoothness. It has a fruity rich flavour with a hoppy character. Bitterness develops in the aftertaste.

Atomic

Atomic Brewery, c/o Sounds Expensive, 12 Regent Street, Rugby, Warwickshire, CV21 2QF
☎ (01788) 542170 ✉ sales@atomicbrewery.com
atomicbrewery.com
Tours by arrangement

Atomic Brewery started production in 2006 and is run by CAMRA members Keith Abbis and Nick Pugh. One pub is owned, the Victoria Inn in Rugby, which acts as the brewery tap and features beers swapped with other micro-breweries. Atomic uses the Alexandra Ales brew plant behind the Alexandra Arms in Rugby.

Strike (OG 1039, ABV 3.7%)

Fission (OG 1040, ABV 3.9%)

Fusion (OG 1042, ABV 4.1%)

Reactor (OG 1047, ABV 4.5%)

Half-Life (OG 1051, ABV 5%)

Bomb (OG 1054, ABV 5.2%)

Avon

Avon Brewing Co Ltd, Unit 4, Russell Town Avenue Industrial Centre, Russell Town Avenue, Bristol, BS5 9LT
☎ (0117) 955 3353 ✉ beer@avonbrewing.co.uk
avonbrewing.co.uk

Avon began brewing in 2008 on an eight-barrel plant. Around 12 outlets are supplied direct.

Re-Session (OG 1040, ABV 3.8%)
An amber bitter berwed with organic malt and hops.

Gurt Lush (OG 1046, ABV 4.5%)
A rich golden ale brewed with organic malt and hops.

GPS (ABV 5.3%)

AVS

See Loddon

Ayr SIBA (NEW)

Ayr Brewing Co Ltd, 5 Racecourse Road, Ayr, KA7 2DG
☎ (01292) 263891
✉ anthony.valenti@btinternet.com
Tours by arrangement

Ayr began brewing in 2009 on a five-barrel plant and is located in the Glen Park Hotel. As well as the hotel around 25 other outlets are supplied in central and southern Scotland and the north of England.

Leezie Lundie (OG 1037.5, ABV 3.8%)

Jolly Beggars (OG 1041, ABV 4.2%)

Rabbies Porter (OG 1042.5, ABV 4.3%)

Towzie Tyke (OG 1044.5, ABV 4.6%)

B&T SIBA EAB

B&T Brewery Ltd, The Brewery, Shefford, Bedfordshire, SG17 5DZ
☎ (01462) 815080 ✉ brewery@banksandtaylor.com
banksandtaylor.com
Tours by arrangement

Banks & Taylor – now just B&T – was founded in 1982. It produces an extensive range of beers, including monthly special brews together with occasional beers: see website for details. Five tied houses, all operated with guest beers as well as B&T beers.

Two Brewers (OG 1036, ABV 3.6%)
Bronze-coloured bitter with citrus hop aroma and taste and a dry finish.

Shefford Bitter (OG 1038, ABV 3.8%)
A pale brown beer with a light hop aroma and a hoppy taste leading to a bitter finish.

Shefford Dark Mild (OG 1038, ABV 3.8%)
A dark beer with a well-balanced taste. Sweetish, roast malt aftertaste.

Golden Fox (OG 1041, ABV 4.1%)
A golden, hoppy ale, dry tasting with a fruity aroma and citrus finish.

Black Dragon Mild (OG 1043, ABV 4.3%)
Black in colour with a toffee and roast malt flavour and a smoky finish.

Dunstable Giant (OG 1044, ABV 4.4%)
Dark tawny bitter with a subtle blend of malt and hops.

Dragonslayer (OG 1045, ABV 4.5%)
A golden beer with a malt and hop flavour and a bitter finish. More malty and less hoppy than is usual for a beer of this style.

Edwin Taylor's Extra Stout (OG 1045, ABV 4.5%)
A complex black beer with a bitter coffee and roast malt flavour and a dry bitter finish.

Fruit Bat (OG 1045, ABV 4.5%)
A warming straw-coloured beer with a generous taste of raspberries and a bitter finish.

Shefford Pale Ale (SPA) (OG 1045, ABV 4.5%)
A well-balanced beer with hop, fruit and malt flavours. Dry, bitter aftertaste.

SOD (OG 1050, ABV 5%)
SOS with caramel added for colour, often sold under house names.

SOS (OG 1050, ABV 5%)
A rich mixture of fruit, hops and malt is present in the taste and aftertaste of this beer. Predominantly hoppy aroma.

Bacchus (NEW)

Bacchus Brewing Co, Bacchus Hotel, 17 High Street, Sutton-on-Sea, Lincolnshire, LN12 2EY
☎ (01507) 441204 ✉ info@bacchushotel.co.uk
bacchushotel.co.uk
Tours by arrangement

Bacchus began brewing in 2010 on a one-barrel plant mainly to supply their own bar.

Best Bitter (OG 1043, ABV 4.3%)

Backyard SIBA

Backyard Brewhouse, Unit 8a, Gatehouse Trading Estate, Lichfield Road, Brownhills, Walsall, West Midlands, WS8 6JZ
☎ 07591 923370
✉ enquiries@thebackyardbrewhouse.com
🌐 thebackyardbrewhouse.com
Tours by arrangement

Backyard began brewing in 2008 on a five-barrel plant. Three core beers are produced plus seasonal and monthly specials – see website for further details. Around 40 outlets are supplied direct.

The Hoard (ABV 3.9%)

D&B Porter (ABV 4.3%)

Nipin (ABV 4.6%)
Straw-coloured with a fruity hop aroma. Sweet start then a dry hoppy finish.

Badger

See Hall & Woodhouse

Ballard's SIBA

Ballard's Brewery Ltd, Unit 3, The Old Sawmill, Nyewood, Rogate, Petersfield, Hampshire, GU31 5HA
☎ (01730) 821301/821362
✉ info@ballardsbrewery.org.uk
🌐 ballardsbrewery.org.uk
Shop Mon-Fri 8am-4pm
Tours by arrangement

Launched in 1980 by Mike and Carola Brown at Cumbers Farm, Trotton, Ballard's has been trading at Nyewood since 1988 and now supplies around 60 free trade outlets. Seasonal beers: see website. Bottle-conditioned beers are also available.

Midhurst Mild (OG 1034, ABV 3.5%)
Traditional dark mild, well-balanced, refreshing, with a biscuity flavour.

Golden Bine (OG 1038, ABV 3.8%)
Amber, clean-tasting bitter. A roast malt aroma leads to a fruity, slightly sweet taste and a dry finish.

Best Bitter (OG 1042, ABV 4.2%)
A copper-coloured beer with a malty aroma. A good balance of fruit and malt in the flavour gives way to a dry, hoppy aftertaste.

Wild (ABV 4.7%)
A blend of Mild and Wassail.

Nyewood Gold (OG 1050, ABV 5%)
Robust golden brown strong bitter, hoppy and fruity throughout, with a balanced finish.

Wassail (OG 1060, ABV 6%)
A strong, full-bodied, tawny-red, fruity beer with a predominance of malt throughout, but also an underlying hoppiness.

Bank Top SIBA

Bank Top Brewery Ltd, The Pavilion, Ashworth Lane, Bolton, Lancashire, BL1 8RA
☎ (01204) 595800 ✉ dave@banktopbrewery.com
🌐 banktopbrewery.com
Tours by arrangement

Bank Top was established in 1995 by John Feeney. Since 2002 the brewery has occupied a Grade II listed pavilion. In 2007 the brewing capacity was doubled with the installation of a new 10-barrel plant and in 2008 David Sweeney became the sole proprietor. Bottle-conditioned beers are available.

Barley to Beer (OG 1036, ABV 3.6%)
A pale bitter with a citrus lemon and herbal finish.

Sweeney's (OG 1038, ABV 3.8%)
An amber bitter with a bold, crisp flavour and a delicate, slightly spicy aroma.

Bad to the Bone (OG 1040, ABV 4%)
A tan-coloured beer with floral qualities and delicate citrus notes.

Dark Mild (OG 1040, ABV 4%)
Dark brown beer with a malt and roast aroma. Smooth mouthfeel, with malt, roast malt and hops prominent throughout.

Flat Cap (OG 1040, ABV 4%)
Amber ale with a modest fruit aroma leading to a beer with citrus fruit, malt and hops. Good finish of fruit, malt and bitterness.

Gold Digger (OG 1040, ABV 4%)
Golden coloured, with a citrus aroma, grapefruit and a touch of spiciness on the palate; a fresh, hoppy citrus finish.

Pavilion Ale (OG 1045, ABV 4.5%)
A yellow beer with a citrus and hop aroma. Big fruity flavour with a peppery hoppiness; dry, bitter yet fruity finish.

Blonde (ABV 5%)
An extremely pale ale made with New Zealand hops resulting in a pleasant woody flavour and distinct berry aroma.

Port O Call (OG 1050, ABV 5%)
Dark brown beer with a malty, fruity aroma. Malt, roast and dark fruits in the bittersweet taste and finish.

Banks's

See Marston's in New Nationals section

Barearts

Barearts Ltd t/a Barearts Brewery, Studio Bar & Gallery: 108-110 Rochdale Road, Todmorden, West Yorkshire, OL14 7LP
☎ (01706) 839305 ✉ info@barearts.com
🌐 barearts.com
Shop Wed-Fri 4-9.45pm, Sat 12-9.45pm, Sun 12-8.45pm

A four-barrel craft brewery that began production in 2005 and is named after an art gallery dedicated to nude artwork. Beer is only available from the beer shop and studio bar or by mail order. All beers are bottle-conditioned, even those sold to drink on the premises.

Barge & Barrel

See Eastwood

Barlow SIBA (NEW)

Barlow Brewery Ltd, Units 5 & 6, Shippen Rural Business Centre, Church Farm, Barlow, Derbyshire, S18 7TR

THE BREWERIES

☎ (0114) 289 1767
✉ enquiries@barlowbrewery.co.uk
🌐 barlowbrewery.co.uk

Barlow began brewing in 2010 and is located in renovated farm buildings in a village on the edge of the Peak District.

Heath Robinson (OG 1039, ABV 3.8%)
A dark bitter with a malty background and a balanced, bitter finish.

Carnival Ale (OG 1042, ABV 4%)
A light, golden pale ale with a citrus finish.

Black (OG 1051, ABV 5%)
A dark ale with strong roast and malty flavours and a well-balanced, bitter finish.

Barngates SIBA

Barngates Brewery Ltd, Barngates, Ambleside, Cumbria, LA22 0NG
☎ (015394) 36575 ✉ info@barngatesbrewery.co.uk
🌐 barngatesbrewery.co.uk
Tours by arrangement

Barngates Brewery started brewing in 1997 and initially provided only the Drunken Duck Inn. The brewery became a limited company in 1999 upon expansion to a five-barrel plant. Further expansion in 2008 included a brand new, purpose-built 10-barrel plant. Around 150 outlets are supplied direct throughout Cumbria, Lancashire, Yorkshire and Northumberland. Occasional beer: 1077 10th Anniversary Ale (ABV 3.9%).

Cat Nap (OG 1037, ABV 3.6%)

Mothbag (OG 1037, ABV 3.6%)

Cracker Ale (OG 1038, ABV 3.9%) ◆
A flavoursome malty bitter, fruity but not sweet. Dry in taste rather than finish.

Pride of Westmorland (OG 1042, ABV 4.1%) ◆
A well-crafted pale brown beer with bitterness dominant throughout.

Westmorland Gold (OG 1043, ABV 4.2%) ◆
A golden ale with a good balance of malt and hops, perhaps not as intense as previously.

Tag Lag (OG 1044, ABV 4.4%) ◆
A pale amber beer, smooth and sweetly malty to begin but a lasting, bitter finish.

Red Bull Terrier (OG 1048, ABV 4.8%)
A deep red tone and a complex hop nose are complemented by tangy fruit and malt flavours with a spicy aftertaste.

Chester's Strong & Ugly (OG 1052, ABV 5.2%) ◆
Complex and well-balanced, a richly satisfying dark beer with plenty of roast and hop bitterness.

Barrowden SIBA

Barrowden Brewing Co, c/o Exeter Arms, 28 Main Street, Barrowden, Rutland, LE15 8EQ
☎ (01572) 747247
✉ enquiries@exeterarmsrutland.co.uk
🌐 exeterarmsrutland.co.uk

The brewery was established by Peter Blencowe in 1998. Martin Allsopp bought the pub and brewery in 2005, which is situated in a barn at the back of the Exeter Arms.

Beech (OG 1038, ABV 3.8%)

Own Gear (ABV 4%)

Hop Gear (OG 1044, ABV 4.4%)

Bevin (OG 1045, ABV 4.5%)

Black Five (ABV 5%)

Bartrams SIBA EAB

Bartrams Brewery, Rougham Estate, Ipswich Road (A14), Rougham, Suffolk, IP30 9LZ
☎ (01449) 737655 ☎ 07768 062581
✉ marc@bartramsbrewery.co.uk
🌐 bartramsbrewery.co.uk
Shop Tue & Sat 12-6pm
Tours by arrangement

The brewery was set up in 1999. In 2005 the plant was moved to a building on Rougham Airfield, the site of Bartram's Brewery between 1894 and 1902 run by Captain Bill Bartram. His image graces the pump clips. Beers are available in a selection of local pubs and there is a large amount of trade through local farmers' markets. Marld, Beltane Braces and all porters and stouts are suitable for vegetarians and vegans, as are all bottled beers. Seasonal beers: see website.

Marld (ABV 3.4%)
A traditional mild. Spicy hops and malt with a hint of chocolate, slightly smoky with a light, roasted finish.

Rougham Ready (ABV 3.6%)
A light, crisp bitter, surprisingly full bodied for its strength.

Trial and Error (ABV 3.6%)
A full malty bitter, fruity with a lot of character.

Premier (ABV 3.7%)
A traditional quaffing ale, full-flavoured but light, dry and hoppy.

Little Green Man (ABV 3.8%)
A golden bitter with the peppery and delicate citrus tones of subtle coriander. Dry and bitter.

Red Queen (ABV 3.9%)
Typical IPA style, chocolate malt in the foreground while the resiny hop flavour lingers.

Cats Whiskers (ABV 4%)
A straw-coloured beer with ginger and lemons added; a unique flavour experience.

Grozet (ABV 4%)
Using Little Green Man as the base beer, gooseberries are added to give an appealing extra dimension.

Bees Knees (ABV 4.2%)
An amber beer with a floral aroma; honey softness on the palate leads to a crisp, bitter finish.

Catherine Bartram's IPA (ABV 4.3%)
A full-bodied malty IPA style; tangy hops lead the malt throughout and dominate the dry, hoppy aftertaste.

Mother McCleary's Milk Stout (ABV 4.3%)

Jester Quick One (ABV 4.4%)
A sweet reddish bitter using fruity American Ahtanum hops.

Beltane Braces (ABV 4.5%)
Smooth and dark.

Coal Porter (ABV 4.5%)
Plenty of body in this ruby beer, supported by ample hops.

Stingo (ABV 4.5%)

A sweetish, fruity bitter with a hoppy nose. Light honey softens the bitter finish.

Beer Elsie Bub (ABV 4.8%)
Originally brewed for a Pagan wedding, this strong honey ale is now brewed all year round.

Captain Bill Bartram's Best Bitter (ABV 4.8%)
Modified from a 100-year old recipe, using full malt and traditional Kentish hops.

Captain's Stout (ABV 4.8%)
Biscuity dark malt leads to a lightly smoked aroma, plenty of roasted malt character, coffee notes and a whiff of smoke.

Cherry Stout (ABV 4.8%)
Sensuous hints of chocolate lead to a subtle suggestion of cherries.

Damson Stout (ABV 4.8%)
A robust, full-bodied stout with the chocolate and smoky aroma giving way to a lingering finish.

Trafalgar Squared (ABV 4.8%)
Brewed using malt grown a few miles from Nelson's birthplace and Goldings hops.

Suffolk 'n' Strong (ABV 5%)
A light, smooth and dangerously potable strong bitter, well-balanced malt and hops with an easy finish.

Comrade Bill Bartram's Egalitarian Anti-Imperialist Soviet Stout (ABV 6.9%)
A Russian stout by any other name, a luscious easy-drinking example of the style.

Barum SIBA

Barum Brewery Ltd, c/o Reform Inn, Pilton, Barnstaple, Devon, EX31 1PD
☎ (01271) 329994 ✉ info@barumbrewery.co.uk
barumbrewery.co.uk
Tours by arrangement

Barum was formed in 1996 by Tim Webster and is housed in a conversion attached to the Reform Inn which acts as the brewery tap and main outlet. Distribution is exclusively within Devon. Seasonal beers: Mild (ABV 4.2%, spring), Barnstablasta (ABV 6.6%, winter), Agincourt (ABV 4.5%, St Crispins Day).

Basil's Best (OG 1040, ABV 4%)

Gold (OG 1040, ABV 4%)

Original (OG 1044, ABV 4.4%)

Breakfast (OG 1048, ABV 5%)

Baskerville (NEW)

The Baskerville Brewery Co Ltd, Lower Yelland Farm, Yelland, Devon, EX31 3EN
☎ (01271) 860355
✉ baskervillesbrewery@yahoo.com
Brewing began in 2010 using a five-barrel plant. Seasonal beer: Surf Sup (ABV 4.2%, summer).

Golden Hound (ABV 4.2%)

Fremington IPA (ABV 4.5%)

Black Hound (ABV 5%)

Batemans IFBB SIBA

George Bateman & Son Ltd, Salem Bridge Brewery, Mill Lane, Wainfleet, Lincolnshire, PE24 4JE
☎ (01754) 880317 ✉ enquiries@bateman.co.uk
bateman.co.uk
Visitor Centre & Shop 11.30am-3.30pm daily
Tours Nov-1st Apr 1pm, Apr-end Oct 12.30 & 2pm (no booking necessary); Evening tours by arrangement

Bateman's Brewery is one of the few remaining independent family-owned brewers. Established in 1874 it has been brewing award-winning beers for four generations of the family. All but one of the 68 tied houses serve cask-conditioned beer. See website for seasonal and speciality beers.

Dark Mild (OG 1030, ABV 3%)
Gentle roast fruity airs preface this red-brown, caramel-infused brew. Malt and a stewed plummy sweetness initially give depth. Caramel dominates the short simple finish.

XB Bitter (OG 1037, ABV 3.7%)
A well-rounded, smooth malty beer with a blackcurrant fruity background. Hops flourish initially before giving way to a bittersweet dryness that enhances the mellow malty ending.

GHA Pale Ale (OG 1042, ABV 4.2%)

Salem Porter (OG 1048, ABV 4.7%)
A black and complex mix of chocolate, liquorice and cough elixir.

XXXB (OG 1048, ABV 4.8%)
A brilliant blend of malt, hops and fruit on the nose with a bitter bite over the top of a faintly banana maltiness that stays the course. A russet-tan brown classic.

Bath Ales SIBA

Bath Ales Ltd, Units 3-7, Caxton Business Park, Crown Way, Warmley, Bristol, BS30 8XJ
☎ (0117) 947 4797 ✉ hare@bathales.co.uk
bathales.com
Shop Mon-Fri 9am-5pm; Sat 9am-12pm
Tours by arrangement

Bath Ales started brewing in 1995 and moved in 1999 to new premises with a 15-barrel plant. The company now has a purpose-built site on the edge of east Bristol, and can brew 300 barrels a week. Around 350 outlets are supplied direct. Ten pubs are owned, all serving cask ale. Seasonal beers: Festivity (ABV 5%), Rare Hare (ABV 5.2%). Most beers are available for purchase from the website or shop.

SPA (OG 1037, ABV 3.7%)
Gold/yellow colour, this is a light-bodied dry, bitter beer with a citrus hop aroma. Long malty, dry and bitter finish with some fruit.

Gem Bitter (OG 1042, ABV 4.1%)
This well-balanced, medium-bodied bitter is malty (pale and crystal with caramel), fruity and hoppy throughout. Amber-coloured, it is dry and bitter at the end.

Golden Hare (OG 1046, ABV 4.4%)
A full-flavoured, crisp, light ale.

Barnstormer (OG 1047, ABV 4.5%)
Malt, hops and fruit aroma with a faint hint of roast, with toffee sweetness. Dark brown, well balanced and smooth with a malty, bitter, dry finish.

THE BREWERIES

Batham IFBB

Daniel Batham & Son Ltd, Delph Brewery, Delph Road, Brierley Hill, West Midlands, DY5 2TN
☎ (01384) 77229 ✉ info@bathams.com
🌐 bathams.com

A classic Black Country small brewery established in 1877. Tim and Matthew Batham represent the fifth generation to run the company. The Vine, one of the Black Country's most famous pubs, is also the site of the brewery. The company has 11 tied houses and supplies around 30 other outlets. Batham's Bitter is delivered in 54-gallon hogsheads to meet demand. Seasonal beer: XXX (ABV 6.3%, Dec).

Mild Ale (OG 1036.5, ABV 3.5%)
A fruity, dark brown mild with malty sweetness and a roast malt finish.

Best Bitter (OG 1043.5, ABV 4.3%)
A pale yellow, fruity, sweetish bitter, with a dry, hoppy finish. A good, light, refreshing beer.

Battledown

Battledown Brewery llp, Keynsham Works, Keynsham Street, Cheltenham, Gloucestershire, GL52 6EJ
☎ (01242) 693409 ☎ 07734 834104
✉ roland@battledownbrewery.com
🌐 battledownbrewery.com
Shop open Wed/Thu/Sat am
Tours by arrangement

Established in 2005 by Roland and Stephanie Elliott-Berry, and joined in 2006 by Ben Jennison-Phillips (ex-Whittingtons), Battledown operates an eight-barrel plant from an old engineering works and supplies more than 150 outlets. Visitors are always welcome. There is an online shop for mail order purposes. Seasonal beer: Porter (ABV 4.5%, Oct-Mar).

Standard (ABV 3.6%)
A golden pale ale with a refreshing aroma and sharp but smooth taste, leaving a dry, hoppy aftertaste which lingers on the palate.

Sunbeam (OG 1039, ABV 4%)
A California Common (aka American Steam Beer) golden ale.

Natural Selection (ABV 4.2%)
A deep golden beer, the malts evident but giving way to the triple hop addition giving a spicy and slightly citrus finish.

Premium (ABV 4.6%)
A rich amber ale. A malty aroma and taste with a deep satisfying, full-bodied fruit and malt texture leaving a well-rounded mellow aftertaste.

Special (ABV 5.2%)
A well-balanced and crisp pale ale.

Four Kings (OG 1066, ABV 7.2%)
A strong ale with a heady aroma.

Battlefield

See Tunnel

Bays SIBA

Bays Brewery Ltd, Aspen Way, Paignton, Devon, TQ4 7QR
☎ (01803) 555004 ✉ info@baysbrewery.co.uk
🌐 baysbrewery.co.uk
Shop Mon-Fri 8am-5pm
Tours by arrangement

Bays Brewery opened in early 2007 in an old steel fabrication unit in Paignton on a 20-barrel plant. Around 400 outlets are supplied direct. Seasonal beers: Spooky (ABV 4.5%, Halloween), Jingle (ABV 4%, Xmas). Bottle-conditioned beers are also available.

Best (OG 1037, ABV 3.7%)

Topsail (ABV 4%)

Gold (OG 1042, ABV 4.3%)

Breaker (OG 1046, ABV 4.7%)

Devon Dumpling (OG 1048, ABV 5.1%)

Bazens' SIBA

Bazens' Brewery, Rees Bazen Brewing Co Ltd, Unit 6, Knoll Street Industrial Park, Knoll Street, Salford, Greater Manchester, M7 2BL
☎ (0161) 708 0247 ✉ bazensbrewery@mac.com
🌐 bazensbrewery.co.uk
Tours by arrangement for CAMRA groups

Run by husband and wife Richard and Jude Bazen, Bazens' Brewery was established in 2002 and moved to its present location a year later. Around 50 pubs are supplied direct.

Black Pig Mild (OG 1037, ABV 3.6%)
A dark brown beer with malt and fruit aromas. Roast, chocolate and fruit flavours, with an underlying bitterness, lead to a dry, malty and slightly smoky aftertaste.

Pacific Bitter (OG 1039, ABV 3.8%)
Gold-coloured bitter with a fruity nose. Hops and citrus fruit dominate the taste and there is a bitter, hoppy finish.

Flatbac (OG 1042, ABV 4.2%)
Well-balanced, distinctive and refreshing blonde beer. A full hop character has pronounced citrus/floral notes.

Zebra Best Bitter (OG 1043, ABV 4.3%)
A complex premium bitter, loaded with full malt flavour and crisp fruity hop character.

Blue Bullet (OG 1045, ABV 4.5%)
Yellow in colour, this golden ale has a fruity aroma. Hops, fruit and bitterness are in the taste and linger in the finish.

Knoll Street Porter (OG 1055, ABV 5.2%)
Dark brown beer with a chocolaty and malt aroma. Roast and chocolate malt, hops and fruit to taste, with a satisfying complex finish.

Beachy Head

Beachy Head Brewing Co Ltd, Seven Sisters Sheep Centre, Birling Manor Farm, Gilberts Drive, East Dean, East Sussex, BN20 0AA
☎ (01323) 423906 ✉ charlie@beachyhead.org.uk
🌐 beachyhead.org.uk
Tours by arrangement

The 2.5-barrel brew plant was installed at the rear of the Seven Sisters Sheep Centre in late 2006. Beachy Head Brewery produces both cask and bottle-conditioned ales, supplied regularly to around 15 outlets, three of which are local pubs. The full range of ales (including seasonals) can be sampled at the Tiger Inn in East Dean village, which is the brewery tap.

Parson Darbys Hole (ABV 4%)

Beachy Original (ABV 4.5%)

Legless Rambler (ABV 5%)

Beartown SIBA

Beartown Brewery Ltd, Bromley House, Spindle Street, Congleton, Cheshire, CW12 1QN
☎ (01260) 299964
✉ headbrewer@beartownbrewery.co.uk
⊕ beartownbrewery.co.uk
Tours by arrangement

Congleton's links with brewing can be traced back to 1272. Two of its most senior officers at the time were Ale Taster and Bear Warden, hence the name of the brewery. Both the brewery's Navigation in Stockport and the Beartown Tap have been named CAMRA regional pubs of the year. There are plans to extend the tied estate to 15 outlets over the next two years. Beartown supplies 250 outlets and owns five pubs. A new 25-barrel plant has been installed.

Bear Ass (OG 1040, ABV 4%) ◆
Dark ruby-red, malty bitter with good hop nose and fruity flavour with dry, bitter, astringent aftertaste.

Ginger Bear (OG 1040, ABV 4%)
The flavours from the malt and hops blend with the added bite from the root ginger to produce a quenching finish.

Kodiak Gold (OG 1040, ABV 4%) ⬚ ◆
Hops and fruit dominate the taste of this crisp yellow bitter and these follow through to the dryish aftertaste. Biscuity malt also comes through on the aroma and taste.

Bearskinful (OG 1043, ABV 4.2%) ◆
Biscuity malt dominates the flavour of this amber best bitter. There are hops and a hint of sulphur on the aroma. A balance of malt and bitterness follow through to the aftertaste.

Bearly Literate (OG 1045, ABV 4.5%)

Polar Eclipse (OG 1048, ABV 4.8%) ◆
Classic black, dry and bitter stout, with roast flavours to the fore. Good hop on the nose follow through the taste into a long dry finish.

Black Bear (OG 1050, ABV 5%) ⬚ ◆
Advertised as a strong mild, this beer is rather bitter for the style. Bitter and malt flavours are balanced and there is also a good roast character along with a hint of liquorice. Aftertaste is short and reasonably dry.

Bruins Ruin (OG 1050, ABV 5%)

Beckstones SIBA

Beckstones Brewery, Upper Beckstones Mill, The Green, Millom, Cumbria, LA18 5HL
☎ (01229) 775294
✉ david@beckstonesbrewery.com
⊕ beckstonesbrewery.co.uk

⊠ Beckstones started brewing in 2003 on the site of an 18th-century mill with its own water supply. It's a five-barrel, one-man operation and the plant is always working to capacity. The beer names often have a connection to the long-closed Millom Iron Works or local characters.

Barley Juice (ABV 3.4%)

Beer O'Clock (ABV 3.5%)
A golden, hoppy beer.

Leat (OG 1038, ABV 3.6%) ◆
A refreshing golden bitter with tangy fruit and a rising hop finish.

Black Gun Dog Freddy Mild (OG 1040, ABV 3.8%) ⬚ ◆
A full-bodied, beautifully balanced ruby dark mild, replete with fruit and roast malt.

Iron Town (OG 1040, ABV 3.8%) ◆
Creamy sweet brown ale full of well-balanced fruit and hop.

Border Steeans (OG 1042, ABV 4.1%)
Scottish Borders style, bittersweet with berry fruit undertones.

Rev Rob (OG 1046, ABV 4.6%) ⬚
A strong, golden, hoppy bitter.

Hematite (OG 1058, ABV 5.5%) ◆
A luscious strong dark mild, mellow but punchy and full of dark fruit.

Beer Engine SIBA

⧉ Tuttles Unique Co Ltd t/a The Beer Engine, Newton St Cyres, Devon, EX5 5AX
☎ (01392) 851282 ✉ info@thebeerengine.co.uk
⊕ thebeerengine.co.uk
Tours by arrangement

⊠ Beer Engine was developed in 1983 and is the oldest continuously-working micro-brewery in Devon, still employing the original brewer, Ian Sharp. The brewery is visible behind glass downstairs in the pub. Four outlets are supplied as well as all local beer festivals. Seasonal beer: Whistlemas (ABV around 7%, Dec-Jan).

Rail Ale (OG 1037, ABV 3.8%) ◆
A straw-coloured beer with a fruity aroma and a sweet, fruity finish.

0-4-0 Shunter (OG 1040, ABV 4%)
An amber-coloured beer with a hoppy, sweet aftertaste.

Silver Bullet (OG 1040, ABV 4%)
A light, medium-strength summer beer with a bitter aftertaste.

Piston Bitter (OG 1043, ABV 4.3%) ◆
A mid-brown, sweet-tasting beer with a pleasant, bittersweet aftertaste.

Sleeper Heavy (OG 1052, ADV 5.4%) ◆
A red-coloured beer with a fruity, sweet taste and a bitter finish.

Beer Works

See Abbeydale

Bees (NEW)

Bees Brewery, Plot 2, Coast Road, Walcott, Norwich, NR12 0LS
☎ 07971 577526 ✉ bees-brewery@hotmail.co.uk

Bees first brewed in 2008 and was initially based at Queniborough near Leicester. It relocated to Norfolk towards the end of 2009 and the five-barrel plant is now located in a static caravan overlooking the sea. Brewer Alec Brackenbury operates the brewery on a part-time basis and mainly supplies pubs within a 10-mile radius of Walcott.

Amber (ABV 3.8%)

Navigator (ABV 4.5%)

Stripey Jack (ABV 4.6%)

Wobble (ABV 5%)

Honey (ABV 5.2%)

Beeston

Beeston Brewery Ltd, Fransham Road Farm, Beeston, Norfolk, PE32 2LZ
☎ (01328) 700844 ☎ 07768 742763
✉ mark_riches@tesco.net 🌐 beestonbrewery.co.uk
Tours by arrangement

⊗ The brewery was established in 2006 in an old farm building using a five-barrel plant. Brewing water comes from a dedicated borehole and raw ingredients are sourced locally whenever possible. All beers are available bottle conditioned and in 5 litre mini casks.

The Squirrels Nuts (ABV 3.5%)

Afternoon Delight (OG 1036, ABV 3.7%)
An easy-drinking blonde ale.

Worth the Wait (OG 1041, ABV 4.2%) ◆
Well-balanced and complex with a soft hoppy nose. An initial burst of passion fruit mingles with malt and hops in a delightful first taste. A long-lasting finish develops a bittersweet dryness.

Stirling (ABV 4.5%)
Rich malty red bitter with toffee notes.

The Dry Road (ABV 4.8%)

On the Huh (OG 1048, ABV 5%) ◆
Deceptively smooth bitter with a fruity raisin aroma. A bittersweet maltiness jousts with caramel and roast. A dry hoppiness gives depth to a strong finale.

Norfolk Black (OG 1060, ABV 6%)
A warming, full-bodied strong stout.

Belhaven

See Greene King in New Nationals section

Belvoir SIBA

Belvoir Brewery Ltd, Crown Park, Station Road, Old Dalby, Leicestershire, LE14 3NQ
☎ (01664) 823455 ✉ colin@belvoirbrewery.co.uk
🌐 belvoirbrewery.co.uk
Tours by arrangement

⊗ Belvoir (pronounced 'beaver') Brewery was set up in 1995 by former Shipstone's brewer Colin Brown. Long-term expansion has seen the introduction of a 20-barrel plant that can produce 50 barrels a week. There is also a visitor centre incorporating brewery memorabilia, a bar, restaurant and shop (open seven days a week). Around 150 outlets are supplied direct. Seasonal beers: Whippling Golden Bitter (ABV 3.6%, spring/summer), Peacock's Glory (ABV 4.7%, spring/summer). Bottle-conditioned beers are also available.

Star Mild (OG 1034, ABV 3.4%) ◆
Reddish/black in colour, this full-bodied and well-balanced mild is both malty and hoppy with hints of fruitiness leading to a long, bittersweet finish.

Star Bitter (OG 1039, ABV 3.9%) ◆
Reminiscent of the long-extinct Shipstone's Bitter, this mid-brown bitter lives up to its name as it is bitter in taste but not unpleasantly so.

Gordon Bennett (OG 1041, ABV 4.1%)
Light chestnut beer with a biscuity character and a pleasant hop finish.

Beaver Bitter (OG 1043, ABV 4.3%) ◆
A light brown bitter that starts malty in both aroma and taste, but soon develops a hoppy bitterness. Appreciably fruity.

Melton Mowbray Oatmeal Stout (OG 1044, ABV 4.3%)
A full-bodied creamy dark stout.

Old Dalby (OG 1050, ABV 5.1%)
A rich, smooth ruby red strong ale with pleasant hop character.

Beowulf SIBA

Beowulf Brewing Co, Chasewater Country Park, Pool Road, Brownhills, Staffordshire, WS8 7NL
☎ (01543) 454067 ✉ beowulfbrewing@yahoo.co.uk
🌐 beowulfbrewery.co.uk
Tours by arrangement

Beowulf Brewing Company beers appear as guest ales predominantly in the central region but also across the country. The brewery's dark beers have a particular reputation for excellence. Seasonal beers: see website. Bottle-conditioned beer is also available.

Beorma (OG 1038, ABV 3.9%) ◆
A pale session ale with a malty hint of fruit giving way to a lingering bitterness.

Noble Bitter (OG 1039, ABV 4%) ◆
Golden with a sweet malty aroma. Malty start becomes very hoppy then bitter, but not an over-long finish.

Wiglaf (OG 1043, ABV 4.3%) ◆
Powerful fruity aroma from this golden ale with subtle hop and fruit tastes. Bitterness develops as a surprise from the sweet start.

Chasewater Bitter (OG 1043, ABV 4.4%) ◆
Golden bitter, hoppy throughout with citrus and hints of malt. Long mouth-watering, bitter finish.

Dark Raven (OG 1048, ABV 4.5%) ◆
So dark with apple and bonfire in the aroma, so sweet and smooth like liquid toffee apples with a sudden bitter finish.

Swordsman (OG 1045, ABV 4.5%) ◆
Pale gold, light fruity aroma, tangy hoppy flavour. Faintly hoppy finish.

Dragon Smoke Stout (OG 1048, ABV 4.7%) ◆
Black with a light brown creamy head. Tobacco, chocolate, liquorice and mixed fruity hints on the aroma. Bitterness fights through the sweet and roast flavours and eventually dominates. Hints of a good port emerge.

Finn's Hall Porter (OG 1049, ABV 4.7%) ◆
Complex tasting porter with strong hints of coffee and a sweet roasty nose. Maltiness comes out strongly on the palate, with a vinous aftertaste.

Heroes Bitter (OG 1046, ABV 4.7%) ◆

Gold colour, malt aroma, hoppy taste but sweetish finish.

Mercian Shine (OG 1048, ABV 5%)
Amber to pale gold with a good bitter and hoppy start. Plenty of caramel and hops with background malt leading to a good bitter finish with caramel and hops lingering in the aftertaste.

Berrow SIBA

Berrow Brewery, Coast Road, Berrow, Burnham-on-Sea, Somerset, TA8 2QU
☎ (01278) 751345
Tours by arrangement

The brewery opened in 1982 and production is now around five barrels a week. All the beers have won prizes at beer festivals. 15-20 outlets are supplied. Seasonal beers: Carnivale (ABV 4.7%, Oct-Nov), Christmas Ale (ABV 4.7%, Nov-Dec).

Best Bitter/4Bs (OG 1038, ABV 3.9%)
A pleasant, pale brown session beer, with a fruity aroma, a malty, fruity flavour and bitterness in the palate and finish.

Berrow Porter (OG 1046, ABV 4.6%)
A ruby-coloured porter with a pronounced hop character.

Topsy Turvy (OG 1055, ABV 5.9%)
A gold-coloured beer with an aroma of malt and hops. Well-balanced malt and hops taste is followed by a hoppy, bitter finish with some fruit notes.

Best Mates

Best Mates Brewery Ltd, Sheep House Farm, Ardington, Wantage, Oxfordshire, OX12 8QB
☎ (01235) 835684
✉ bestmatesbrewery@btconnect.com
bestmatesbrewery.co.uk
Tours by arrangement

Best Mates Brewery was established in 2007 on a five-barrel plant and uses locally sourced water. Seasonal beer: Midsummer Madness (ABV 3.9%). Bottle-conditioned beers are available.

Scutchaman's Knob (OG 1036, ABV 3.6%)

Vicar's Daughter (OG 1037, ABV 3.7%)

Ardington Ale (ABV 4.2%)

Alfie's (OG 1044, ABV 4.4%)

Satan's Sister (OG 1045, ABV 4.5%)

Bewdley SIBA

Bewdley Brewery Ltd, Unit 7, Bewdley Craft Centre, Lax Lane, Bewdley, Worcestershire, DY12 2DZ
☎ (01299) 405148
✉ bewdleybrewery@hotmail.co.uk
bewdleybrewery.co.uk
Tours by arrangement

Bewdley began brewing in 2008 on a six-barrel plant in an old school. Brewing experience days are offered, please ring for details. Beers are brewed with a railway theme for the nearby Severn Valley Railway. Seasonal beers: see website. Bottle-conditioned beers are available.

Junior School Bitter (ABV 3.4%)
A light summer pale ale.

Worcestershire Way (ABV 3.6%)
A light beer with citrus notes.

Old School Bitter (ABV 3.8%)
Session bitter with a hoppy finish.

Senior School Bitter (ABV 4.1%)
A premium bitter, amber-coloured with malty taste and hoppy finish.

Big Lamp

Big Lamp Brewers, Grange Road, Newburn, Newcastle upon Tyne, Tyne & Wear, NE15 8NL
☎ (0191) 267 1689
✉ admin@biglampbrewers.co.uk
biglampbrewers.co.uk
Tours by arrangement

Big Lamp started in 1982 and relocated in 1997 to a 55-barrel plant in a former water pumping station. It is the oldest micro-brewery in the north-east of England. Around 35 outlets are supplied and two pubs are owned. Seasonal/occasional beers: Old Genie (ABV 7.4%), Blackout (ABV 11%), Embers (ABV 5.5%, Nov-Apr).

Sunny Daze (OG 1036, ABV 3.6%)
Golden, hoppy session bitter with a clean taste and finish.

Bitter (OG 1039, ABV 3.9%)
A clean-tasting bitter, full of hops and malt. A hint of fruit with a good, hoppy finish.

One Hop (OG 1040, ABV 4%)
Dark amber beer with a smooth finish and a hint of hazelnut.

Summerhill Stout (OG 1044, ABV 4.4%)
A rich, tasty stout, dark in colour with a lasting rich roast character. Malty mouthfeel with a lingering finish.

Prince Bishop Ale (OG 1048, ABV 4.8%)
A refreshing, easy-drinking bitter. Golden in colour, full of fruit and hops. Strong bitterness with a spicy, dry finish.

Premium (OG 1052, ABV 5.2%)
Hoppy ale with a good bitter finish.

Keelman Brown (OG 1057, ABV 5.7%)
A full-bodied ale with a hint of toffee.

Bird Brain (NEW)

Bird Brain Brewery Ltd, 30 Hailgate, Howden, East Yorkshire, DN14 7SL
☎ (01430) 432166 ☎ 07790 615915
✉ birdbrainbrewery@tiscali.co.uk

Bird Brain began brewing in 2009 using a two-barrel brew plant that operates twice a month. No regular beers are brewed at present.

Birds SIBA (NEW)

Birds Brewery, Ladybird Barn, Old Burcot Lane, Bromsgrove, Worcestershire, B60 1PH
☎ (01527) 889870
✉ brewmaster@birdsbrewery.co.uk
birdsbrewery.co.uk
Tours by arrangement

Birds began brewing in 2009 and is situated on Ashborough Farm. The brewer is Ian Hughes, a well-known local landlord as well as brewer at the

THE BREWERIES

Red Cross Brewery in Bromsgrove between 1995 and 1999. Bottle-conditioned beers are planned.

Ashborough Pale (ABV 4%)
A light golden session beer with a crisp, dry citrus taste and hoppy aroma.

Ashborough Gold (ABV 4.5%)
An amber gold ale with an initial slightly sweet malty taste which gives way to a smooth, hoppy finish.

Birmingham SIBA

Birmingham Brewery Ltd, Unit 45, Mount Street Business Centre, Nechells, Birmingham, West Midlands, B7 5RD
☎ (0121) 328 2120
✉ sales@birminghambrewery.co.uk
🌐 birminghambrewery.co.uk

The brewery was opened in 2008 by novice brewers Mark Norridge and Tim Watson. A six-barrel brew plant is operated and around 20 outlets are supplied direct.

Dark Mild (BDM) (OG 1038, ABV 3.8%)
Dark-brown, traditional Midlands mild with balanced sweet and roast malt flavours.

Pale Ale (OG 1041, ABV 4.1%)
A traditional, lightly-hopped English pale ale with a dry aftertaste.

Bitter End

Bitter End Brewery, Unit 11, Derwent Mills, Cockermouth, Cumbria, CA13 0HT
☎ (01900) 823300
✉ sales@bitterendbrewingco.com
Tours by arrangement

The brewery was established by Mike Askey in 1995, behind glass at the back of the Bitter End pub, and transferred to new premises in 2009. Output from the brewery is steadily increasing with expansion into the free trade. Three regular beers are brewed along with seasonals and a range of traditional English beer styles. One-off and festival beers are also produced.

Lakeland Bitter (ABV 3.8%)
An easy-drinking fruity bitter with a notably sweet follow through.

Lakeland Pale Ale (ABV 4%)

Lakeland Best Gold (ABV 4.3%)

Blackawton SIBA

Blackawton Brewery, Unit 7, Peninsula Park, Moorlands Trading Estate, Saltash, Cornwall, PL12 6LX
☎ (01752) 848777 ☎ 07971 871546
✉ enquiries@blacawtonbrewery.co.uk
🌐 blackawtonbrewery.com

Blackawton was once Devon's oldest operating brewery, but relocated to Cornwall in 2000 and ownership changed in 2004 and again in 2010. Around 30 outlets are supplied. Seasonal beers: see website. Bottle-conditioned beers are also available.

Original Bitter (OG 1037, ABV 3.8%)
A copper-coloured bitter; an ideal session beer with a fresh floral hop aroma.

West Country Gold (OG 1039, ABV 4.1%)
A light, golden, fresh-tasting summer beer with sweet malt flavours and delicate vanilla and fruit hints from Styrian Goldings hops.

44 Special (OG 1044, ABV 4.5%)
A premium, full-strength bitter that is rich and sweet with the aroma of ripe hops and fruit.

Moorland Ale (OG 1046, ABV 4.6%)
A dark amber-coloured premium bitter with a hoppy, bitter finish.

Exhibition Ale (OG 1047, ABV 4.7%)

Headstrong (OG 1048, ABV 5.2%)
A deceptively smooth beer with a bitter malt taste.

Blackbeck

Blackbeck Brewery, Blackbeck Inn, Egremont, Cumbria, CA22 2NY
☎ (01946) 841661
✉ drink@blackbeckbrewery.co.uk
🌐 blackbeckbrewery.co.uk

Blackbeck Brewery is owned and run by Kenny O'Hara. It was established in 2009 using a five-barrel, purpose-built system.

Belle (ABV 3.8%)

Trial Run (ABV 3.8%)
A fresh and fruity yellow beer with a lasting hoppy finish.

Black Country

Black Country Ales, Rear of Old Bulls Head, 1 Redhall Road, Lower Gornal, Dudley, West Midlands, DY3 2NU
☎ (01384) 480156
Office & Beer Deliveries: Unit 4, Tansey Green Road, Pensnett, Dudley, West Midlands, DY5 4TL
✉ info@blackcountryales.co.uk
🌐 blackcountryinns.co.uk
Tours by arrangement

Brewing started on the site around 1834. In 1900, oak vessels were installed that have now been refurbished and brought back into production. The brewery was closed down in 1934 but reopened in 2004, with many original features still remaining. Seasonal beers: English Summer (ABV 4.1%), English Winter (ABV 5.5%).

Bradley's Finest Golden (OG 1041, ABV 4.2%)
A straw-coloured quaffing beer with a bold citrus hop aroma, fruity balanced sweetness and a lingering, refreshing aftertaste.

Pig on the Wall (OG 1042, ABV 4.3%)
A refreshing chestnut brown beer with a complex flavour of light hops giving way to a bittersweet blend of roasted malt. Suggestions of chocolate and coffee undertones.

Fireside (OG 1047, ABV 5%)
A well-rounded premium bitter, amber in colour, clean in taste leading to a pleasant, dry finish.

Black Dog

Black Dog Brewery, Foulsyke Farm, Fylingdales, Whitby, North Yorkshire, YO22 4QL
☎ 0845 301 2337

Black Dog started brewing in 1997 in the centre of Whitby, but closed in 2000. In 2006 Tony Bryars purchased the original Black Dog recipes, and re-established the brewery. The beers are contract brewed by Hambleton Ales (qv) in Melmerby, North Yorkshire.

Blackfriars

Blackfriars Brewery Ltd, The Courtyard, Main Cross Road, Great Yarmouth, Norfolk, NR30 3NZ
☎ (01493) 850578 ✉ pints@blackfriars-brewery.co.uk 🌐 blackfriars-brewery.co.uk
Shop: Mon-Fri 9am-4.30pm
Tours by arrangement

⊗ The brewery was established in 2004 using a purpose-built five-barrel plant and was extended in 2007. In 2008 the brewery relocated and now has a shop, visitor centre and fully-licensed bar. More than 50 outlets are supplied. All beers (with the exception of specials) are available in bottle-conditioned form. Special beers: Holy Smoke (ABV 6.7%), Audit Ale (ABV 8%). Seasonal beers: see website.

Mild (ABV 3.4%) ◆
Sweet and malty in true Norfolk fashion. Red-hued with a gentle roast malt aroma. Stewed prunes and caramel lurk in the background as the finish lingers long and sweet.

Yarmouth Twos (ABV 3.6%)
A mix of Yarmouth Bitter and Mild.

Yarmouth Bitter (OG 1036, ABV 3.8%) ◆
A malt-dominated brew. Pale brown and smooth drinking with a distinctly malty nose. A bittersweet fruitiness in the taste turns to an increasing bitterness to rival the malt character.

Mitre Gold (OG 1044, ABV 4%)

Springtide (ABV 4.2%)
A traditional, well-hopped bitter.

Whyte Angel (ABV 4.5%) ◆
Fragrant hoppy aroma leads to a strong bitter first taste. Golden hued with honey notes softening the dryness of the bitter hops. Gentle malt background throughout.

Maritime (ABV 5%) ◆
Copper-coloured, rich, heavy and malty brew. Vinous, fruitcake characteristics supplement the richness of taste. A muted hoppy bitterness can be detected in the long finish.

Old Habit (OG 1052, ABV 5.6%) ◆
Old-fashioned mix of roast, malt and plummy fruitiness. Smooth and aromatic with coffee notes and a heavy mouthfeel. Finish softens to a malty character.

Black Hole SIBA

Black Hole Brewery Ltd, Unit 63, Ground Floor, Imex Business Park, Shobnall Road, Burton upon Trent, Staffordshire, DE14 2AU
☎ (01283) 534060 ✉ beer@blackholebrewery.co.uk
🌐 blackholebrewery.co.uk
Tours by arrangement

⊗ The brewery was established in 2007 on a purpose-built 10-barrel plant in the former Ind Coope bottling stores. There are plans to increase the fermenting capacity to allow the production of a brew per day. Occasional beers are produced to mark special anniversaries and occasions. Around 300 outlets are supplied. Seasonal beers: Starry Night (ABV 4.4%, Xmas/New Year), Titan (ABV 4.4%, Mar/Apr), Hubble Bubble (ABV 5.5%, Oct/Nov).

Bitter (OG 1040, ABV 3.8%) ◆
Gentle malt and hop aroma from this amber beer. After a grassy start the bitterness develops into a satisfying hop bite. There is a dry finish with some fruitiness and malt.

Cosmic (OG 1044, ABV 4.2%)

Red Dwarf (OG 1046, ABV 4.5%)

Supernova (OG 1048, ABV 4.8%)

No Escape (OG 1053, ABV 5.2%)

Milky Way (OG 1059, ABV 6%)

Black Isle SIBA

Black Isle Brewery Ltd, Old Allengrange, Munlochy, Ross-shire, IV8 8NZ
☎ (01463) 811871
✉ greatbeers@blackislebrewery.com
🌐 blackislebrewery.com
Shop: Mon-Sat 10am-6pm; Sun 11am-6pm (Apr-Sep)
Tours offered between 10am-5pm

⊛ Black Isle Brewery was set up in 1998 in the heart of the Scottish Highlands. The five-barrel plant was upgraded to a 30-barrel plant in 2010. All beers are organic, suitable for vegetarians and vegans and have Soil Association certification. Bottled (including bottle-conditioned) beers are available by mail order to anywhere in mainland Britain. Seasonal beer: see website.

Yellowhammer (OG 1038, ABV 3.9%) ◆
A refreshing, hoppy golden ale with light hop and passion fruit throughout. A short bitter finish with a light yeasty background.

Red Kite (OG 1042, ABV 4.2%) ◆
Tawny ale with light malt on the nose and some fruit on the palate. Slight sweetness in the taste and a short bitter finish.

Porter (OG 1046, ABV 4.6%) ◆
A hint of liquorice and burnt chocolate on the nose and a creamy mix of malt and fruit in the taste.

Blonde (OG 1046, ABV 5%)

Black Sheep SIBA

Black Sheep Brewery plc, Wellgarth, Masham, Ripon, North Yorkshire, HG4 4EN
☎ (01765) 689227 🌐 blacksheepbrewery.co.uk
Shop and Bistrol 10am-5pm daily
Tours by arrangement

⊛ Black Sheep was established 1992 by Paul Theakston, a member of Masham's famous brewing family, in the former Wellgarth Maltings. The company has enjoyed continued growth and now supplies a free trade of around 700 outlets, but owns no pubs. The brewery specialises in cask ales (70% of production) and bottled ales.

Best Bitter (OG 1038, ABV 3.8%) ◆
A hoppy and fruity beer with strong bitter overtones, leading to a long, dry, bitter finish.

Golden Sheep (OG 1039, ABV 3.9%)
A balanced blonde beer with a dry and refreshing bitterness. Light golden in colour with fresh citrusy fruit flavours and a clean, crisp finish.

Ale (OG 1044, ABV 4.4%)

THE BREWERIES

A premium bitter with robust fruit, malt and hops.

Riggwelter (OG 1059, ABV 5.9%)
A fruity bitter, with complex underlying tastes and hints of liquorice and pear drops leading to a long, dry, bitter finish.

Blackwater

Blackwater Brewery, Brewers Wholesale, Unit 2b Gainsborough Trading Estate, Rufford Road, Stourbridge, West Midlands, DY9 7ND
☎ (01384) 374050
✉ enquiries@thebrewerswholesale.co.uk
🌐 thebrewerswholesale.co.uk

Beers are contract brewed by Salopian Brewery (qv).

Blakemere

See Northern

Blencowe

See Barrowden

Blindmans SIBA

Blindmans Brewery Ltd, Talbot Farm, Leighton, Frome, Somerset, BA11 4PN
☎ (01749) 880038 ✉ info@blindmansbrewery.co.uk
🌐 blindmansbrewery.co.uk
Tours by arrangement

Blindmans Brewery was established in 2002 in a converted milking parlour. In 2004 the brewery was bought by Paul Edney and Lloyd Chamberlain. The brewery has its own exclusive water spring. The brewery opened its first pub in 2008, the Lamb Inn in Frome, serving several exclusively brewed ales and is in the process of renovating a second pub, the Bear in Bradford on Avon. Seasonal beers: Siberia (ABV 4.7%), Bah Humbug! (ABV 4.5%).

Buff (ABV 3.6%)
Amber-coloured, smooth session beer.

Golden Spring (ABV 4%)
Fresh and aromatic straw-coloured beer, brewed using selected lager malt.

Eclipse (ABV 4.2%)
A porter full of chocolate flavours and subtle bitterness

Mine Beer (ABV 4.2%)
Full-bodied, copper-coloured, blended malt ale.

Icarus (ABV 4.5%)
Fruity, rich, mid-dark ruby ale.

Blue Anchor SIBA

Blue Anchor Inn Brewery, 50 Coinagehall Street, Helston, Cornwall, TR13 8EL
☎ (01326) 565765
✉ theblueanchor@btconnect.com 🌐 spingoales.com
Tours by arrangement

Dating back to the 15th century, this is the oldest brewery in Cornwall and was originally a monks' hospice. After the dissolution of the monasteries it became a tavern brewing its own uniquely flavoured beer called Spingo at the rear of the premises. Brewing has continued to this day and people travel from all over the world to sample the delights of this wonderful inn, untouched by time. Five outlets are supplied. Seasonal beers: Spingo Bragget (ABV 6.1%, Apr-Oct), Spingo Easter Special (ABV 7.6%), Spingo Christmas Special (ABV 7.6%). All draught beers are available in bottle-conditioned form. Bragget is a recreation of a medieval beer style.

Spingo Jubilee/IPA (OG 1045, ABV 4.6%)

Spingo Middle (OG 1050, ABV 5.1%)
A copper-red beer with a fruity aroma, a hint of vanilla and a peppery note from the hops. The palate is nutty, with a fruit cake note. The complex bittersweet finish is fruity and dry.

Spingo Special (OG 1066, ABV 6.7%)
Darker than Middle with a pronounced earthy character on the nose balanced by rich fruit. Fruit and peppery hops dominate the mouth, followed by a long finish with malt, fruit and hops.

Blue Bell

Blue Bell Brewery, Sycamore House, Lapwater Lane, Holbeach St Marks, Lincolnshire, PE12 8EX
☎ (01406) 701000 ☎ 07813 819746
✉ beer@bluebellbrewery.co.uk
🌐 bluebellbrewery.co.uk
Tours by arrangement

The Blue Bell Brewery was founded in 1998 in a former potato shed located behind the Blue Bell pub, Whaplode St Catherine. The brewery operates as a separate business from the Blue Bell pub but the pub does act as the brewery tap. Around 30 outlets are supplied.

Frightened Pheasant (OG 1037, ABV 3.7%)

Old Honesty (OG 1040, ABV 4.1%)

Old Resurgence (ABV 4.3%)

Old Gold (OG 1045, ABV 4.5%)

Old Fashioned (OG 1045, ABV 4.8%)

Old Comfort (OG 1050, ABV 5%)

For Blue Bell Inn, Whaplode St Catherine:

Ingle Dingle (OG 1054, ABV 5.1%)

Blue Cow

Blue Cow Inn & Brewery, High Street, South Witham, Lincolnshire, NG33 5QB
☎ (01572) 768432 ✉ enquiries@bluecowinn.co.uk
🌐 bluecowinn.co.uk
Tours by arrangement

Owned by Simon Crathorn since 2005, Blue Cow is a traditional 13th-century pub with a brewery. The beer is only available in the pub.

Best Bitter (OG 1038, ABV 3.8%)

Blue Monkey

Blue Monkey Brewing Ltd, 10 Pentrich Road, Giltbrook Industrial Park, Giltbrook, Nottinghamshire, NG16 2UZ
☎ 0800 028 0329 / 07500 555595
✉ john@bluemonkeybrewery.com
🌐 bluemonkeybrewery.com

Blue Monkey was established in 2008 by John Hickling. Five core beers are produced with numerous one-off and seasonal specialities. 250 outlets are supplied direct.

Original (OG 1039, ABV 3.6%)
Full-bodied pale brown session bitter. Slightly sweet but predominantly malty.

BG Sips (OG 1041, ABV 4%)
Pale golden hoppy beer, brewed mainly with Brewers Gold hops. Very fruity and bitter.

99 Red Baboons (OG 1042, ABV 4.2%)
Red in colour with a malty fruitiness. Not overly hoppy.

Evolution (OG 1043, ABV 4.3%)
Amber-coloured ale with a floral hop aroma. Bitter and hoppy with a dry aftertaste.

Guerrilla (ABV 4.9%)
A creamy stout, full of roast malt flavour and a slightly sweet finish.

Ape Ale (OG 1052, ABV 5.4%)

Blythe SIBA

Blythe Brewery, Blythe Farm House, Lichfield Road, Hamstall Ridware, Rugeley, Staffordshire, WS15 3QQ
☎ 07773 747724 ✉ info@blythebrewery.plus.com
blythebrewery.co.uk
Tours by arrangement

Robert Greenway started brewing in 2003 using a 2.5-barrel plant in a converted barn on a farm. As well as specials, seasonal beers are produced on a quarterly basis. Fifteen outlets are supplied. Seasonal beer: Old Horny (ABV 4.6%, Sep-Nov). All cask beers are also available bottle conditioned.

Bitter (OG 1040, ABV 4%)
Amber with a full hoppy aroma and sweet touch. Immediate full hoppy taste that develops into an intense hoppy, lingering finish.

Ridware Pale (OG 1042, ABV 4.3%)
Bright and golden with a bitter floral hop aroma and citrus taste. Good and hop-sharp, bitter and refreshing. Long, lingering bite with ripples of citrus across the tongue.

Chase Bitter (OG 1044, ABV 4.4%)
Slight smoky aroma and traditional colour. Sweetish with malt, fruit and developing hops. Good mouthfeel and hoppiness to finish.

Staffie (OG 1044, ABV 4.4%)
Hoppy and grassy aroma with hints of sweetness from this amber beer. A touch of malt at the start is soon overwhelmed by hops. A full hoppy, mouth-watering finish

Palmer's Poison (OG 1045, ABV 4.5%)
Refreshing darkish beer. Tawny but light headed. Coffee truffle aroma, pleasingly sweet to start but with a good hop mouthfeel.

Johnson's (OG 1056, ABV 5.2%)
Black with a thick head. Refreshingly hoppy and full bodied with lingering bitterness of chocolate, dates, coal smoke and liquorice.

BMG Brewing

BMG Brewing Ltd, c/o Tower Brewery, Old Water Tower, Walsitch Maltings, Glensyl Way, Burton upon Trent, Staffordshire, DE14 1LX
☎ (01283) 561330

Beers are contract brews by Tower Brewery (qv) for Beer My Guest distributors.

Bob's

Bob's Brewing Co Ltd, Healey Brewery, Low Mill Road, Healey, West Yorkshire, WF5 8ND
☎ 07789 693597

The brewery was founded in 2002 by Bob Hunter, a former partner in Ossett Brewery, in outbuildings behind the Red Lion pub. During 2009 brewing relocated to a new eight-barrel plant. The beers appear regularly in around 25 freehouses across West Yorkshire and in the West Midlands via wholesalers.

White Lion (OG 1043, ABV 4.3%)
Pale, flowery, lager-style beer using American Cascade hops.

Yakima Pale Ale (OG 1045.5, ABV 4.6%)
A hoppy and bitter yellow beer that uses hops from the Yakima Valley in Washington State, U.S.

Chardonnayle (OG 1051.5, ABV 5.1%)
Complex, stylish strong pale ale with hints of lemongrass and fruits, with Willamette hops for aroma.

Boggart Hole Clough

Boggart Hole Clough Brewing Co, Building 7, Wilsons Park, Monsall Road, Newton Heath, Manchester, M40 8WN
☎ (0161) 277 9666 ✉ boggartoffice@btconnect.com
boggart-brewery.co.uk

The brewery was set up by Mark Dade in 2001 next to Boggart Hole Clough Park in former engineering works. In 2009 the brewery moved to the former Wilson's Brewery site. The site also houses Boggart Beer/Cider Distribution, launched in 2003 delivering to more than 250 outlets throughout the country. A large number of monthly specials are produced as are bottle-conditioned beers from the regular beer list. In 2009 the brewery opened its first outlet, the Micro Bar, in the food hall of Manchester's Arndale Centre.

Ruby Tuesday (ABV 3.8%)
A reddish, hoppy session ale.

Ray of Sunshine (ABV 3.9%)
A very pale, light and hoppy session ale.

Cascade (ABV 4%)
A bitter, hoppy session ale.

Boggart's Brew (OG 1043, ABV 4.3%)
A quaffable ruby-red beer.

Rum Porter (ABV 4.6%)
A classic porter with a smooth roast finish, enhanced by a sweet spicy hop taste, complemented with a hint of dark rum.

Sun Dial (OG 1047, ABV 4.7%)
A pale beer with a refreshing, fruity hop taste and aroma.

Waterloo Sunset (ABV 5%)
Traditional porter with an oak roast flavour.

Bollington SIBA

Bollington Brewing Co Ltd, Adlington Road, Bollington, Cheshire, SK10 5JT
☎ (01625) 575380 ✉ lee@bollingtonbrewing.co.uk
bollingtonbrewing.co.uk
Tours by arrangement

THE BREWERIES

Lee Wainwright bought the Vale Inn, a closed freehouse in Bollington in 2005. His love of real ale became the focus of the pub and he started brewing in 2008. The brewery is situated just 50 metres from the pub. Around 40 outlets are supplied direct. All cask ales are also available bottle conditioned.

Bollington Nights (OG 1038, ABV 3.9%)

Happy Valley (OG 1040, ABV 4%)

White Nancy (OG 1041, ABV 4.1%)

Best (OG 1042, ABV 4.2%)

Dinner Ale (OG 1043, ABV 4.3%)

Oat Mill Stout (OG 1048, ABV 5%)

Borough Arms

Borough Arms, 33 Earle Street, Crewe, Cheshire, CW1 2BG
☎ (01270) 254999
info@borougharmscrewe.co.uk
borougharmscrewe.co.uk
Tours by arrangement

A two-barrel brewery opened in 2005 to supply the pub. The beers are available at the pub and local beer festivals. Regular seasonal ales are brewed.

Blonde Temptation (ABV 3.8%)
A light session ale.

Extra Pale Ale (ABV 4.1%)

Borough Gold (ABV 4.2%)
A hoppy, golden ale.

Pilsner (ABV 4.6%)
A Pilsner-style ale brewed with Czech hops and yeast.

Botley (NEW)

Botley Brewery, The Old Cooperage, The Square, High Street, Botley, Hampshire, SO30 2EA
☎ (01794) 518918 (Sales) ☎ 07830 369573 (Brewery) botleybrewery@hotmail.co.uk

Botley Brewery began production in 2010 using a five-barrel brewery.

Mill (ABV 3.8%)

Botta's Best (ABV 4.2%)

Gringo's Gold (ABV 4.5%)

Old Cooperage (ABV 5%)

Bottle Brook

Bottle Brook Brewery, Church Street, Kilburn, Belper, Derbyshire, DE56 0LU
☎ (01332) 880051 ☎ 07971 189915

Bottle Brook was established in 2005 using a 2.5-barrel plant on a tower gravity system. The traditional brewery specialises in using rare and unusual hop varieties and at one point there was no range of permanent beers – most are now repeated occasionally. New fermenters were added in 2008 to boost output. Over 30 outlets are supplied.

Two Tuns Pale Ale (OG 1037, ABV 3.6%)

Columbus (OG 1040, ABV 4%)

Pot of Gold (OG 1042, ABV 4.1%)

Full Moon (OG 1045, ABV 4.6%)

Roadrunner (OG 1047, ABV 4.8%)

Midnight Mash (OG 1050, ABV 5.1%)

Louisiana Smoked Porter (OG 1055, ABV 5.6%)

Slum Dog (OG 1060, ABV 5.9%)

Bowland SIBA

Bowland Beer Co Ltd, Bashall Town, Clitheroe, Lancashire, BB7 3LQ
☎ (01200) 443592 ☎ 07952 639465
richardbakerbb@btconnect.com
bowlandbrewery.com
Shop Mon-Sun 10.30am-5pm
Tours by arrangement

Bowland started brewing in 2003 and has steadily expanded capacity to 50 barrels per week, supplying more than 100 outlets in the north west. Five litre mini-casks are sold through the on-site shop and visitor centre. A new range of quirky bottled beers was launched in 2008. At least one new cask ale is brewed each month. Seasonal beers include Patriot, Sorceress, Headless Peg and Sleigh Belle.

Hunters Moon (OG 1039, ABV 3.7%)
A dark mild with chocolate and coffee flavours.

Sawley Tempted (OG 1038, ABV 3.7%)
A copper-coloured fruity session bitter with toffee in the mouth and a spicy finish.

Bowland Gold (OG 1039, ABV 3.8%)
A hoppy golden bitter with intense grapefruit flavours.

Chipping Steamer (OG 1040, ABV 3.9%)
A mid-gold bitter with hints of orange and a slightly floral finish.

Hen Harrier (OG 1040, ABV 4%)
A pale gold bitter with soft citrus, peach and apricot flavours throughout.

Oak (OG 1041, ABV 4%)
A light chestnut coloured bitter with generous maltiness balanced by lime marmalade hop flavours.

Dragon (OG 1043, ABV 4.2%)
A golden bitter with rounded fruit in the mouth and a refreshing finish.

Black Dragon Porter (OG 1046, ABV 4.5%)
A deep, dark porter with chocolate and dark fruit flavours.

Bowman

Bowman Ales Ltd, Wallops Wood, Sheardley Lane, Droxford, Hampshire, SO32 3QY
☎ (01489) 878110 info@bowman-ales.com
bowman-ales.com
Tours by arrangement

Brewing started in 2006 on a 20-barrel brew plant in converted farm buildings. The brewery supplies more than 100 outlets. In addition to the standard beers a range of celebratory and seasonal brews are produced. Seasonal beer: Nutz (ABV 5%, winter). Bottle-conditioned beers are also available.

Elderado (OG 1035, ABV 3.5%)
Straw-coloured beer containing elderflower. A citrus aroma with a fruity, bitter taste. Good

hoppiness and a background sweetness. A dry, bitter finish.

Swift One (OG 1038, ABV 3.8%) ◆
A glorious golden ale characterised by strong hoppiness throughout. Aroma of grapefruit leads to a pleasing bitterness and a background sweetness. A long, dry finish.

Wallops Wood (OG 1040, ABV 4%) ◆
Well-balanced bitter, with no particular flavour dominating this well crafted beer. Malt flavours throughout are balanced by toffee notes in the flavour and a slightly dry finish.

Quiver Bitter (OG 1045, ABV 4.5%) ▣ ◆
A golden best bitter with a strong hoppy aroma leading through a bittersweet taste to a refreshing, hoppy finish.

Box Steam

Box Steam Brewery, Oaks Farm, Rode Hill, Colerne, Wiltshire, SN14 8AR
☎ (01225) 858383 ✉ info@boxsteambrewery.com
⊕ boxsteambrewery.com
Tours by arrangement

⊗ The brewery was founded in 2004 and boasts a Fulton steam-fired copper, hence the name. Under present ownership since 2006, the brewery has undergone a series of expansion work to increase production capacity. Two pubs are owned and more than 100 outlets are supplied. Seasonal beers: Xmas Dark Box (ABV 5%), Xmas Blonde Box (ABV 5.2%), Derail Ale (ABV 5.2%), Broad Gauge Bitter (ABV 4.5%).

Golden Bolt (OG 1037.5, ABV 3.8%)
A light, straw-coloured bitter with a hoppy aftertaste.

Cog (OG 1040, ABV 4%)
A traditional best bitter, dark amber in colour, with a light, fragrant nose and hoppy character.

Tunnel Vision (OG 1040.5, ABV 4.2%)
A well-rounded traditional bitter. Clean-tasting with a slight bitterness on the palate.

Funnel Blower (OG 1045, ABV 4.5%)
Dark brown in colour with a subtle vanilla aroma. The vanilla sweetness contrasts with the slight bitterness from the roasted barley and chocolate malts.

Dark & Handsome (OG 1047.5, ABV 5%)
Brewed in the style of a traditional old ale, this is a smooth, creamy beer with hints of lemon and subtle blackcurrant and liquorice undertones with a sweet start and finish.

Piston Broke (OG 1047.5, ABV 5%)
A subtle, single-hopped, golden-coloured beer with a hoppy aroma and a dry finish.

Bradfield

Bradfield Brewery, Watt House Farm, High Bradfield, Sheffield, South Yorkshire, S6 6LG
☎ (0114) 285 1118 ✉ info@bradfieldbrewery.com
⊕ bradfieldbrewery.co.uk
Shop Mon-Sat 10am-4pm

⊕ Bradfield Brewery is a family-run business, based on a working farm in the Peak District. Only the finest ingredients are used, along with pure Milstone Grit spring water from a borehole. More than 200 outlets are supplied. In 2009 the brewery

bought its first brewery tap – the Nags Head, Loxley. Seasonal beer: see website. Bottle-conditioned beers are also available along with five-litre mini kegs.

Farmers Bitter (OG 1039, ABV 3.9%)
A traditional copper-coloured malt ale with a floral aroma.

Farmers Blonde (OG 1041, ABV 4%)
Pale, blonde beer with citrus and summer fruits aromas.

Farmers Brown Cow (OG 1042.5, ABV 4.2%)
Deep chestnut-coloured ale with a smooth, creamy head. A citrus taste gives way to a long, dry finish.

Farmers Stout (OG 1045, ABV 4.5%)
A dark stout with roasted malts and flaked oats and a subtle, bitter hop character.

Farmers Pale Ale (OG 1049, ABV 5%)
A full-bodied pale ale with a powerful floral bouquet leaving a predominantly dry aftertaste.

Farmers Sixer (OG 1056, ABV 6%)
A strong, lager-type ale with a fruity, pleasant finish.

Brains IFBB

S A Brain & Co Ltd, Cardiff Brewery, PO Box 53, Crawshay Street, Cardiff, CF10 1SP
☎ (029) 2040 2060 ✉ brains@sabrain.com
⊕ sabrain.com

⊕ Brains began trading at the Old Brewery in Cardiff in 1882 when Samuel Arthur Brain and his uncle Joseph Benjamin Brain purchased a site founded in 1713. The company has remained in family ownership ever since. The full range of Brains ales is now produced at the company's Cardiff Brewery (formerly Hancock's), bought from Bass in 1999. The company owns more than 270 pubs, spread throughout Wales, the West Country and the Midlands. Brains is the official sponsor of the Wales Rugby Union team, the Football Association of Wales and Glamorgan County Cricket Club. Seasonal beers: see website.

Dark (OG 1035.5, ABV 3.5%) ▯ ▣ ◆
A tasty, classic dark brown mild, a mix of malt, roast, caramel with a background of hops. Bittersweet, mellow and with a lasting finish of malt and roast.

Bitter (OG 1036, ABV 3.7%) ◆
Amber coloured with a gentle aroma of malt and hops. Malt, hops and bitterness combine in an easy-drinking beer with a bitter finish.

SA (OG 1042, ABV 4.2%) ◆
A mellow, full-bodied beer. Gentle malt and hop aroma leads to a malty, hop and fruit mix with a balancing bitterness.

Rev James (OG 1045.5, ABV 4.5%) ◆
A faint malt and fruit aroma with malt and fruit flavours in the taste, initially bittersweet. Bitterness balances the flavour and makes this an easy-drinking beer.

SA Gold (OG 1047, ABV 4.7%) ▯ ◆
A golden beer with a hoppy aroma. Well balanced with a zesty hop, malt, fruit and balancing bitterness; a similar satisfying finish.

Brakspear

See Marston's in New Nationals section

Brampton SIBA

Brampton Brewery Ltd, Unit 5, Chatsworth Business Park, Chatsworth Road, Chesterfield, S40 2AR
☎ (01246) 221680 ✉ info@bramptonbrewery.co.uk
bramptonbrewery.co.uk
Shop via website
Tours by arrangement

The old Brampton Brewery existed in the town for more than 100 years before being taken over in 1955. After a lapse of 52 years the Brampton name was re-registered for a new brewery a stone's throw away from the original. The first commercial brew took place in 2007 on the eight-barrel plant. Around 35 outlets are supplied. Seasonal beer: Jerusalem (ABV 4.6%, St George's Day), Golden Bud Speciale (ABV 5.8%), 1302 (ABV 4%, summer).

Golden Bud (OG 1037, ABV 3.8%)
Crisp and refreshing golden bitter with a pleasant balance of citrus, sweetness and bitter flavours. Light and easy to drink.

Best (OG 1041, ABV 4.2%)
Classic, drinkable bitter with a predominantly malty taste, balanced by caramel sweetness and a developing bitterness in the aftertaste.

Impy Dark (OG 1047, ABV 4.3%)
Strong roasted coffee aroma and a rich flavour of vine fruit and chocolate combine to make this a tasty mild ale.

Mild (OG 1054, ABV 4.9%)

Wasp Nest (OG 1049, ABV 5%)
Strong and complex with malt and hop flavours and a caramel sweetness.

Brancaster EAB

Brancaster Brewery, c/o Jolly Sailors, Brancaster Staithe, Norfolk, PE31 8BJ
☎ (01485) 210314 ✉ info@brancasterbrewery.co.uk
brancasterbrewery.co.uk

Brancaster opened in 2003 with a five-barrel plant squeezed into a converted ocean-going steel container adjacent to its own pub/restaurant. The brewery closed in 2008 but has been resurrected by the current licensee, James Nye. In 2009 the plant was moved to the site of the Iceni Brewery where the head brewer brews the beers to the Brancaster recipes (see Iceni listing for regular beers). Seasonal beers: Oystercatcher (ABV 4.2%, summer), The Wreck SS Vina (ABV 4.9%, winter).

Brandon

Brandon Brewery, 76 High Street, Brandon, Suffolk, IP27 0AU
☎ (01842) 878496 ☎ 07876 234689
✉ enquiries@brandonbrewery.co.uk
brandonbrewery.co.uk
Shop Mon-Sat 9am-5pm (please ring before visiting)
Tours by arrangement

Brandon started brewing in 2005 in the old dairy of a 15th-century cottage. Visitors are welcome and encouraged to sample from the beer shop. 60 outlets are supplied. The entire range of beer is also available bottle conditioned.

Breckland Gold (OG 1037, ABV 3.8%)
A combination of Goldings and Fuggles hops give a delicate, smooth, slightly spicy taste and a dry, lingering, malty finish.

Bitter (OG 1040, ABV 4%)
Malt aroma with a hint of fruitiness. Dry palate.

Saxon Gold (ABV 4%)
A pale, golden beer with a subtle aroma of hops. The taste is a clean, crisp mix of spice and bitter fruits with a dry, hoppy finish.

Molly's Secret (ABV 4.1%)
A pale ale based on an old recipe.

Norfolk Poacher (ABV 4.1%)
Light aromas and flavours, with a gentle lemony hop taste. Soft fruit gives way to a bittersweet finish.

Royal Ginger (ABV 4.1%)
A refreshing summer ale with a distinctive mix of malt and hoppy spice, balanced with a gentle ginger flavour and finish.

Gun Flint (OG 1041, ABV 4.2%)
Roasted malts are used to produce a malty, chocolate flavour. This combines well with spicy, citrus hops to give a dry, bittersweet, roasted malt finish.

Wee Drop of Mischief (ABV 4.2%)
An amber-coloured premium bitter. Gentle malt flavours give way to a delightful hop character and a dry, increasingly bitter aftertaste.

Rusty Bucket (OG 1043, ABV 4.4%)
Malty and hoppy flavour with overtones of chestnut stuffing. Some fruitiness in finish.

Slippery Jack (OG 1044, ABV 4.5%)
A dark brown stout. Complex but well-balanced flavours of roasted grain and hop bitterness. Dry with a lingering, pleasantly bitter finish.

Nappertandy (OG 1047, ABV 4.8%)
A reddish amber beer, full-bodied with a malty aroma. Crisp and spicy with an underlying citrus flavour and a dry, malty, bitter fruit finish.

Grumpy Bastard (OG 1048, ABV 5%)

Brandy Cask SIBA

Brandy Cask Pub & Brewery, 25 Bridge Street, Pershore, Worcestershire, WR10 1AJ
☎ (01386) 552602
Tours by arrangement

Brewing started in 1995 in a refurbished bottle store in the garden of the pub. Brewery and pub now operate under one umbrella, with brewing carried out by the owner/landlord.

Whistling Joe (ABV 3.6%)
A sweet, fruity, copper-coloured beer that has plenty of contrast in the aroma. A malty balance lingers but the aftertaste is not dry.

Brandy Snapper (ABV 4%)
Golden brew with low alpha hops. Plenty of fruit and hop aroma leads to a rich taste in the mouth and a lingering aftertaste.

Ale Mary (ABV 4.8%)
A rich malt and fruit aroma leads to an equally complex taste with no one flavour dominating. A dry finish.

John Baker's Original (ABV 4.8%)
A superb blend of flavours with roasted malt to the fore. The rich hoppy aroma is complemented by a complex aftertaste.

Branscombe Vale SIBA

Branscombe Vale Brewery Ltd, Branscombe, Devon, EX12 3DP
☎ (01297) 680511
✉ branscombebrewery@yahoo.co.uk

The brewery was set up in 1992 by former dairy workers Paul Dimond and Graham Luxton in cowsheds owned by the National Trust. Paul and Graham converted the sheds and dug their own well. The NT built an extension for the brewery to ensure future growth. In 2008 a new 25-barrel plant was added to the brewhouse. Around 80 outlets are supplied. Seasonal beers: Anniversary Ale (ABV 4.6%, Feb-Mar), Hells Belles (ABV 4.8%), Yo Ho Ho (ABV 6%, Xmas). Bottle-conditioned beer is also available.

Branoc (OG 1038, ABV 3.8%)
Pale brown brew with a malt and fruit aroma and a hint of caramel. Malt and bitter taste with a dry, hoppy finish.

Draymans Best Bitter (OG 1042, ABV 4.2%)
A mid-brown beer with hop and caramel notes and a lingering finish.

BVB Best Bitter (OG 1045, ABV 4.6%)
Reddy/brown-coloured beer with a fruity aroma and taste, and bitter/astringent finish.

Summa That (OG 1049, ABV 5%)
Light golden beer with a clean and refreshing taste and a long hoppy finish.

Brass Monkey

Brass Monkey Brewery Co Ltd, Unit 25, Asquith Bottom Mill, Sowerby Bridge, West Yorkshire, HX6 3BS
☎ (01422) 316040
✉ richard@thebrassmonkeybrewery.co.uk
🌐 thebrassmonkeybrewery.co.uk
Tours by arrangement

Brass Monkey was established in 2008 on a seven-barrel brew plant. Capacity was doubled in 2009 with the addition of two fermenters. Around 150 outlets are supplied. Seasonal beer: Very Mild Monkey (ABV 3.6%).

Son of Silverback (ABV 3.6%)
Straw-coloured grainy bitter with a light hoppiness in the aroma. Fruity and hoppy in the mouth with bitterness developing in the aftertaste.

Bitter (ABV 3.8%)
Pale brown grainy bitter with a pronounced hoppy aroma and flavour. It has a long-lasting, satisfying bitter finish.

Golden Monkey (ABV 4.1%)
Smooth, tawny-coloured best bitter. It has a full hoppy flavour and a citrus spicy aroma finishing with a bitter finish.

Mandrill (ABV 4.2%)
This grainy golden ale has a floral hoppy nose. Hops fill the mouth balanced by tangy fruit. The finish is deep and long.

Silverback (ABV 5%)
Grainy yellow pale ale. A hoppy aroma is followed by a mellow fruity flavour. There is a lingering bitter aftertaste.

Braydon SIBA

Braydon Ales Ltd, The Brewhouse, Preston West Farm, Preston, Chippenham, Wiltshire, SN15 4DX
☎ (01249) 892900 ✉ info@braydonales.co.uk
🌐 braydonales.co.uk
Tours by arrangement

Braydon began brewing in 2009 on a five-barrel plant. Seasonal beers are planned.

Gibbles (OG 1040, ABV 3.8%)

Yertiz (OG 1042, ABV 4.1%)

Potwalloper (OG 1043, ABV 4.4%)

Breconshire SIBA

Breconshire Brewery Ltd, Ffrwdgrech Industrial Estate, Brecon, Powys, LD3 8LA
☎ (01874) 623731
✉ sales@breconshirebrewery.com
🌐 breconshirebrewery.com
Shop Mon-Fri 8.30am-4.30pm
Tours by arrangement

Breconshire Brewery was founded in 2002 as part of C H Marlow, a wholesaler and distributor of ales, beers, wines and spirits in the south Wales area for more than 30 years. The 10-barrel plant uses British malts blended with a range of British whole hops. The beers are distributed throughout Wales and the west of England to around 200 outlets. Seasonal beers: see website. Bottle-conditioned beers are also available. Beers are bottled on site.

Brecon County Ale (OG 1037, ABV 3.7%)
A traditional amber-coloured bitter. A clean hoppy flavour, background malt and fruit, with a good thirst-quenching bitterness.

Welsh Pale Ale (OG 1037, ABV 3.7%)
Pale golden, mildy hopped session ale. Brewed to an old Welsh style of pale ale.

Golden Valley (OG 1042, ABV 4.2%)
Golden in colour with a welcoming aroma of hops, malt and fruit. A balanced mix of these flavours and moderate, building bitterness lead to a satisfying, rounded finish.

Cribyn (OG 1045, ABV 4.5%)
A pale, straw-coloured aromatic best bitter. Brewed with Northdown, Challenger and Bramling Cross hops.

Red Dragon (OG 1047, ABV 4.7%)
A red-hued premium ale brewed with a complex grist and a blend of hops for extra bite.

Ramblers Ruin (OG 1050, ABV 5%)
Dark amber, full-bodied with rich biscuity malt and fruit flavours; background hops and bitterness round off the beer.

Brentwood SIBA

Brentwood Brewing Co Ltd, Frieze Hall Farm, Coxtie Green Road, South Weald, Essex, CM14 5RE
☎ (01277) 375577 ✉ brentwoodbrewing@aol.com
🌐 brentwoodbrewing.co.uk
Tours by arrangement

THE BREWERIES

⊗ Since its launch in 2006 Brentwood has steadily increased its capacity and distribution. A major expansion and relocation in 2007/08 means an 18-barrel plant is now being used. It supplies more than 50 local outlets as well as beer festivals and selected tied houses through its own distribution and the SIBA Direct Distribution Scheme. Seasonal/occasional beers: see website. Bottle-conditioned beers are also available.

IPA (ABV 3.7%)
A lightly hopped, pale session beer.

Marvellous Maple Mild (OG 1038, ABV 3.7%)
Dark brown mild with a hint of maple syrup.

Spooky Moon (OG 1040, ABV 3.8%) ◆
Well-balanced session bitter. The sweet marmalade aroma hints at the citrus bitterness to be found in the finish.

Best (OG 1042, ABV 4.2%)
A traditional, light-coloured best bitter with a well-rounded flavour and aroma.

Gold (OG 1043, ABV 4.3%)
A heavily hopped golden beer with a fruity taste and bitter finish.

Hope & Glory (OG 1046, ABV 4.5%)
A dark, full-bodied bitter.

Lumberjack (OG 1052, ABV 5.2%)
A strong bitter with a rounded, hoppy finish.

Brew Company

Brew Company Ltd, Unit C, G4 Business Centre, Carlisle Street East, Sheffield, South Yorkshire, S4 7QN
☎ (0114) 270 9991 ✉ thebrewcompany@gmail.com
thebrewcompany.co.uk
Tours by arrangement

⊗ Brewer Pete Roberts set up this eight-barrel plant in part of a former factory in Sheffield's industrial east end in 2008. Seasonal beers include St Petrus Stout (ABV 5%), Bock (ABV 5%) and Spring Bock (ABV 3.8%). A monthly special is also brewed exclusively for the nearby Harlequin pub.

Slaker Pale Ale (ABV 3.8%)
Pale, crisp and fruity.

Elixir Bitter (ABV 4%)
Amber-coloured traditional English bitter with a dry roasted flavour.

Abyss Best Bitter (ABV 4.2%)
Dark walnut in colour and full of malty bitter flavours.

Hop Ripper IPA (ABV 4.3%)
A pale IPA, bitter and hoppy.

Eclipse Porter (ABV 4.7%)
A traditional, heavy-bodied, dark, malty porter with a thick mouthfeel, a dry palate and a delicate toasted coffee grain finish.

Frontier IPA (ABV 4.7%)
Straw-coloured, crisp and dry with a bitter aftertaste.

For Devonshire Cat, Sheffield:

Devonshire Cat Brewers Gold (ABV 3.8%)

BrewDog

BrewDog Ltd, Unit 1, Kessock Workshops, Kessock Road, Fraserburgh, AB43 8UE
☎ (01346) 519009 ✉ info@brewdog.com
brewdog.com
Tours by arrangement

BrewDog was established in 2007 by James Watt and Martin Dickie. Most of the production goes into bottles but a limited amount of cask ale is available.

Trashy Blonde (OG 1042, ABV 4.1%)

77 Lager (OG 1046, ABV 4.9%)

Punk IPA (OG 1052, ABV 6%)

Dogma (OG 1072, ABV 7.8%)

Rip Tide (OG 1074, ABV 8%)

Hardcore IPA (OG 1085, ABV 9%)

Paradox (OG 1092, ABV 10%)

Brewhouse (NEW)

Brewhouse Brewery / Welcome Taverns Ltd, The Brewhouse, 987 Blackburn Road, Bolton, BL7 7LG
☎ (01204) 301372 ✉ jjones@welcometaverns.co.uk
Tours by arrangement

The Brewhouse (formerly the Cheetham Arms) began brewing in late 2009 on a four-barrel plant, visible to customers behind a large glazed panel. Beer is only available in the pub at present but there are plans for expansion.

Lancashire Boiler (ABV 3.8%)
A traditional, pale bitter.

Eagley Brook (ABV 4.2%)
A dark ale.

Dunscar Bridge (ABV 4.3%)
An amber ale.

Winter Hill (ABV 4.7%)
A best bitter with a strong chocolate/caramel taste.

Brewster's SIBA

Brewster's Brewing Co Ltd, Unit 5, Burnside, Turnpike Close, Grantham, Lincolnshire, NG31 7XU
☎ (01476) 566000 ✉ sara@brewsters.co.uk
brewsters.co.uk
Tours by arrangement

⊗ Brewster is the old English term for a female brewer and Sara Barton is a modern example. Brewster's Brewery was set up in the heart of the Vale of Belvoir in 1998 and moved in 2006 to its current premises. Beer is supplied to around 250 outlets throughout central England and further afield via wholesalers. Seasonal beers: see website.

Hophead (OG 1036, ABV 3.6%) ◆
This amber beer has a floral/hoppy character; hops predominate throughout before finally yielding to grapefruit in a slightly astringent finish.

Marquis (OG 1038, ABV 3.8%) ◆
A well-balanced and refreshing session bitter with maltiness and a dry, hoppy finish.

Daffys Elixir (OG 1042, ABV 4.2%)
A pale golden best bitter, well-balanced with a big hop finish.

Hop A Doodle Doo (OG 1043, ABV 4.3%)
A copper-coloured ale with a rich, full-bodied feel and fruity hop character.

Decadence (ABV 4.4%)
Well-balanced, full-flavoured golden ale with pronounced hop notes.

Rutterkin (OG 1046, ABV 4.6%)
A premium bitter with a golden appearance. A zesty hop flavour from American Mount Hood hops combines with a touch of malt sweetness to give a rich, full-bodied beer.

Wicked Women Range (OG 1048, ABV 4.8%)
(Varies seasonally)

Porter (ABV 5%)
Rich and roasty.

Belly Dancer (OG 1050, ABV 5.2%)
Well-balanced, ruby-red ale with a full-bodied taste from crystal and roast malts, with a subtle hop finish from Bramling Cross and Fuggles.

Brew Wharf

Brew Wharf Co Ltd, Brew Wharf Yard, Stoney Street, London, SE1 9AD
(020) 7378 6601 brewer-brewwharf@vinopolis.co.uk brewwharf.com

Brew Wharf opened in 2005 and has a bar plus a restaurant where dishes are matched with beer. Two changing special beers are brewed each month.

Bridestones

Bridestones Brewing, Smithy Farm, Long Causeway, Blackshaw Head, Hebden Bridge, West Yorkshire, HX7 7JB
(01422) 847104 bridestones@hotmail.co.uk
bridestonesbrewery.co.uk

Bridestones started brewing in 2006 and supplies over 60 outlets. Its brewery tap is the New Delight Inn, Blackshaw. Seasonal and bottle-conditioned beers are available.

Sandstone (ABV 3.9%)
A pale session ale with a smooth, clean taste.

Pennine Gold (ABV 4.3%)
Good hop aroma and flavour; fruity, refreshing and easy to drink best bitter.

Dark Mild (ABV 4.5%)
Dark brown strong mild with a complex nose of caramel and roasted malt. Good balance of sweetness and bitterness on the palate. Upfront bitterness in the finish.

American Pale Ale (ABV 5%)
A strong but easy-drinking pale ale.

Bridgehouse (NEW)

Bridgehouse Brewery Ltd, Unit 2, Pitt Street, Keighley, West Yorkshire, BD21 4PE
07970 038667 bridgehousebrewery.co.uk

Bridgehouse began brewing in 2010 using a 10-barrel plant.

Diken Gold (ABV 3.6%)

Best Bitter (ABV 3.8%)

Buffers Bitter (ABV 4%)

Barnstormer (ABV 4.4%)

Headshunt Stout (ABV 5%)

Bridgetown

Bridgetown Brewery, Albert Inn, Bridgetown Close, Totnes, Devon, TQ9 5AD
(01803) 863214

Bridgetown started brewing in 2008 on a 2.5-barrel plant. Seasonal beers are available.

AA (The Real Emergency Service) (OG 1036, ABV 3.8%)

Bridgestone Spring Ale (OG 1040, ABV 4.2%)

Realaleativity (OG 1046, ABV 4.8%)

Bridgnorth

Bridgnorth Brewing Co Ltd, The Old Brewhouse, Kings Head Courtyard, Whitburn Street, Bridgnorth, Shropshire, WV16 4QN
(01746) 762889 info@bridgnorthbrewing.com
bridgnorthbrewing.com
Tours by arrangement

Brewing started in 2007 with the original four-barrel plant expanding to 16 barrels by 2008. The King's Head Stable Bar opened next door as the brewery tap, serving real ale and fine wines. It supplies to more than 30 outlets in Shropshire and through SIBA. Brewing is temporarily suspended. Beers are currently brewed by Holdens under licence.

Brightside (NEW)

Brightside Brewing Co, c/o 1 New George Street, Bury, Lancashire, BL8 1NW
07870 207442 carley_friedrich@msn.com
brightsidebrewing.co.uk

Brightside is a family business established in 2010. Beer list not available at present.

Brimstage

Brimstage Brewing Co Ltd, Home Farm, Brimstage, Wirral, CH63 6HY
(0151) 342 1181 07870 968323
info@brimstagebrewery.com
brimstagebrewery.com
Tours by arrangement (max of 20 people)

Brewing started in 2006 on a 10-barrel plant in a redundant farm dairy in the heart of the Wirral countryside. This is Wirral's first brewery since the closure of the Birkenhead Brewery in the late 1960s. Around 60 outlets are supplied. Seasonal beers: Sandpiper Light Ale (ABV 3.4%, spring/summer), Frosty Ferret Winter Warmer (ABV 5%, winter).

Trappers Hat Bitter (ABV 3.8%)
Gold-coloured with a complex bouquet. It provides a mouthful of fruit zest, with hints of orange and grapefruit. A refreshingly hoppy session brew.

Rhode Island Red Bitter (ABV 4%)
Red, smooth and well-balanced malty beer with a good dry aftertaste. Some fruitiness in the taste.

Scarecrow Bitter (ABV 4.2%)
Orange marmalade in colour, this well-balanced session brew has a distinct citrus fruit bouquet.

Oyster Catcher Stout (ABV 4.4%)
A smooth, easy-drinking stout with rich chocolate aromas leading to a mellow roasted coffee flavour and lingering bitter finish.

THE BREWERIES

Briscoe's

Briscoe's Brewery, 16 Ash Grove, Otley, West
Yorkshire, LS21 3EL
☎ (01943) 466515 ✉ briscoe.brewery@virgin.net

The brewery was launched in 1998 by
microbiologist/chemist Dr Paul Briscoe in the cellar
of his house with a one-barrel brew length.
Following a spell brewing on a larger scale at the
back of a local pub, Dr Briscoe is currently
producing two occasional brews on his original
plant.

Chevin Chaser (OG 1043, ABV 4.3%)
A refreshing, pale-coloured, all-malt bitter with a
distinct hop finish.

Three Peaks Ale (OG 1045, ABV 4.5%)
A strong, pale premium bitter brewed with only
pale malt and traditional hops.

Bristol Beer Factory

Bristol Brewing Co Ltd, t/a Bristol Beer Factory, Unit
A, The Old Brewery, Durnford Street, Ashton, Bristol,
BS3 2AW
☎ (0117) 902 6317
✉ enquiries@bristolbeerfactory.co.uk
⊕ bristolbeerfactory.co.uk
Tours by arrangement

The Beer Factory is a 10-barrel micro-brewery in a
part of the former Ashton Gate Brewing Co, which
closed in 1933. 50 outlets are supplied.

Red (OG 1038, ABV 3.8%)
Dark ale with slight roast barley taste, fruity aroma
and ruby red tint.

No. 7 (OG 1042, ABV 4.2%) ◆
Mid-brown, old-fashioned style, malty best bitter.
Good body and mouthfeel, some apple-type fruit
flavours, with a drying bitter and astringent finish.

Sunrise (OG 1044.5, ABV 4.4%) ◆
Light, gold-coloured best bitter, with a strong
hoppy finish.

Milk Stout (OG 1059, ABV 4.5%) ⊓ ◆
Dark creamy stout, reviving an old Bristol tradition.
Black colour with a creamy mouthfeel.

Exhibition (OG 1051, ABV 5.2%)
A classic, strong, dark ale. Crystal and chocolate
malts give a full rich, estery flavour.

Brodie's SIBA

Brodie's Brewery, 816a High Road, Leyton, London,
E10 6AE
☎ 07828 498733 ✉ james@brodiesbeers.com
⊕ brodiesbeers.com
Tours by arrangement

⊠ Siblings James and Lizzie began commercial
brewing in 2008 on a five-barrel plant at the back
of the William IV pub in East London. Beers are
available at the William IV and their small chain of
family-owned pubs as well as other local outlets.
All cask ales are available bottle conditioned.
Seasonal ales and festival specials are also brewed
regularly – see website for more information.

Mild (OG 1038, ABV 3.6%) ◆
Roast notes on the nose of this well-balanced black
fruity mild. Some bitter character from the dark
malt on the palate, which lingers into a dry finish.

English Best (OG 1040, ABV 3.9%) ◆

Hops dominate the smell and taste in this brown
beer. The hoppy bitterness lingers but is balanced
by some malty sweetness and a pleasant dryness.

IPA (OG 1040, ABV 4%) ◆
A light drinking beer with a citrus flavour and finish
that is balanced by a little dry bitterness. Aroma
has traces of fruit and malt.

Sunshine (OG 1040, ABV 4%) ◆
A golden beer with lots of citrus character thanks to
the American hops that lingers into the bitter
aftertaste.

Red (OG 1042, ABV 4.3%) ◆
A fruity, light-drinking red beer with some biscuity
malt flavour and a sweetish berry fruit aftertaste.

Brothers

See Freedom

Broughs

Broughs Ltd, Olde Swan Brewery, 89 Halesowen
Road, Netherton, West Midlands, DY2 9PY
☎ 07814 158292 ✉ broughsltd@yahoo.co.uk

Broughs is currently using spare capacity at the
Olde Swan Brewery in Netherton and is a small
family-run company. Beer is brewed by Andrew
Brough, former head brewer at Sarah Hughes in
Sedgley. Bottle-conditioned beer is available.
Around 40 outlets are supplied direct.

Bitter (OG 1043, ABV 4.3%)

Pale Ale (OG 1048, ABV 4.8%)

Superior (OG 1058, ABV 5.8%)

Broughton SIBA

Broughton Ales Ltd, Broughton, Biggar, Peeblesshire, ML12 6HQ
☎ (01899) 830345 ✉ beer@broughtonales.co.uk
⊕ broughtonales.co.uk
Shop Mon-Fri 8am-5pm
Tours by arrangement

☺Founded in 1979 in Scottish Border country,
Broughton Ales has been brewing cask beers for
more than 25 years but more than 60% of
production goes into bottle for sale in Britain and
export markets. Seasonal beers: see website. All
bottled beers are suitable for vegetarians and
vegans.

Coulsons EPA (OG 1034, ABV 3.5%)
A light, yellow-coloured ale with a mellow
lingering flavour and tangy aftertaste.

The Reiver (OG 1038, ABV 3.8%)
A light-coloured session ale with a predominantly
hoppy flavour and aroma on a background of fruity
malt. The aftertaste is crisp and clean.

Bramling Cross (OG 1041, ABV 4.2%)
A golden ale with a blend of malt and hop flavours
followed by a hoppy aftertaste.

Clipper IPA (OG 1042, ABV 4.2%)
A light-coloured, crisp, hoppy beer with a clean
aftertaste.

Merlin's Ale (OG 1042, ABV 4.2%) ◆
A well-hopped, fruity flavour is balanced by malt in
the taste. The finish is bittersweet, light but dry.

Exciseman's 80/- (OG 1045, ABV 4.6%)

A traditional 80/- cask ale. A dark, malty brew. Full drinking with a good hop aftertaste.

Old Jock (OG 1070, ABV 6.7%)
Strong, sweetish and fruity in the finish.

Brown Cow

Brown Cow Brewery, Brown Cow Road, Barlow, Selby, North Yorkshire, YO8 8EH
☎ (01757) 618947
✉ susansimpson@browncowbrewery.co.uk
🌐 browncowbrewery.co.uk

Established in 1997 by Susan Simpson and joined by husband Keith in 2004, the brewery has steadily expanded, the five-barrel plant now brewing at its capacity of 15 barrels per week. The cask range has been consolidated to four regulars and in addition a range of seasonal and one-off beers is crafted. Beers are supplied throughout Yorkshire and to outlets in southern counties. Bottle-conditioned beer is also available.

Sessions (OG 1033, ABV 3.6%)

White Dragon (OG 1039, ABV 4%)
A pale, aromatic beer with a good level of bitterness, citrus undertones and a clean finish.

Captain Oates Mild (OG 1044, ABV 4.5%)
A dark mild with complex mix of malts and oats. Well-balanced with undertones of coffee and chocolate.

Suddaby's After Dark Coffee Porter (OG 1052, ABV 5%)
A deep, full-flavoured porter with subtle hints of coffee; long and full on the finish.

Brunswick SIBA

Brunswick Brewery Ltd, 1 Railway Terrace, Derby, Derbyshire, DE1 2RU
☎ (01332) 290677 🌐 brunswickinn.co.uk
Tours by arrangement

The Brunswick is a purpose-built tower brewery that started brewing in 1991. A viewing area allows pub users to watch production. Bought by Everards in 2002, it is now a tenancy supplying beers to local outlets and the Everard's estate. Seasonal beer: Rambo (ABV 8%, winter).

White Feather (OG 1038, ABV 3.6%)
Very pale citrus/floral session beer. Full-bodied with a grassy finish.

Triple Hop (OG 1038, ABV 4%)
A pale gold colour and citrus hop bouquet promise sweetness but the hops deliver a firm, dry, lasting bitterness.

Second Brew (OG 1042, ABV 4.2%)
This tawny best bitter, also known as The Usual, presents an aroma of sulphur and hops that continue throughout, accompanied by a striking bitterness and astringency.

Porter (OG 1045, ABV 4.3%)
Typical English porter – dark black chocolate and caramel with deep bitter undertones.

Station Approach (OG 1048, ABV 4.7%)
Straw-coloured bitter with lingering hints of citrus, with a hoppy aftertaste.

Old Accidental (OG 1050, ABV 5%)
A well-balanced, malty beer leading to a bitter finish with warming aftertaste. A light, vinous floral hop has underlying malt notes.

Father Mike's Dark Rich Ruby (OG 1055, ABV 5.8%)
A smooth, near black mild with a hint of red. Well-balanced and filled with sweet roast flavours that conceal its strength.

Black Sabbath (OG 1058, ABV 6%)
A genuine mild with a voluptuous feast of coffee, chocolate and caramel flavours. High alcohol balanced with fine body.

Bryncelyn

Bryncelyn Brewery, Unit 303, Ystradgynlais Workshops, Trawsffordd Road, Ystradgynlais, SA9 1BS
☎ (01639) 841900
✉ bryncelynbrewery@hotmail.co.uk
🌐 bryncelynbrewery.org.uk

A one-quarter barrel brewery was opened in 1999 by William Hopton (owner) and Robert Scott (brewer) and capacity was increased to a three-quarter barrel plant in the same year. The brewery relocated to its present premises in 2008 with a six-barrel plant acquired from the old Webb's Brewery of Ebbw Vale. As the beer names imply, the owner is fond of Buddy Holly: Feb 59 (seasonal) commemorates the singer's death. Seasonal beers: see website.

Everyday Ale (OG 1038, ABV 3.8%)

Holly Hop (ABV 3.9%)
Pale amber with a hoppy aroma. A refreshing hoppy, fruity flavour with balancing bitterness; a similar lasting finish. A beer full of flavour for its gravity.

Buddy Marvellous (OG 1040, ABV 4%)
Dark brown with an inviting aroma of malt, roast and fruit. A gentle bitterness mixes roast with malt, hops and fruit, giving a complex, satisfying and lasting finish.

Buddy's Delight (OG 1042, ABV 4.2%)

Cwrw Celyn (OG 1044, ABV 4.4%)

CHH (OG 1045, ABV 4.5%)
A pale brown beer with hints of red malt and an inviting hop aroma, with fruit and bitterness adding to the flavour. The finish is clean and hoppy-bitter.

Oh Boy (OG 1045, ABV 4.5%)
An inviting aroma of hops, fruit and malt, and a golden colour. The tasty mix of hops, fruit, bitterness and background malt ends with a long, hoppy, bitter aftertaste. Full-bodied and drinkable.

Buddy Confusing (OG 1050, ABV 5%)

Rave On (OG 1050, ABV 5%)

Brysons

Brysons Brewery, Newgate Brewery, White Lund Industrial Estate, Morecambe, Lancashire, LA3 3PT
☎ (01524) 39481 ✉ petermcross@msn.co.uk
🌐 brysonsbrewery.co.uk

Established in 2000 by George Palmer, the four-barrel plant is due to be expanded in the near future. More than 200 outlets are supplied.

Westmorland Bitter (OG 1036, ABV 3.6%)

THE BREWERIES

Lifesaver Bitter (OG 1039, ABV 3.8%)
A golden bitter brewed for charity (RNLI).

Union Flag (OG 1040, ABV 3.9%)

Bring Me Sunshine (OG 1040, ABV 4%)

Hurricane Bitter (OG 1040.5, ABV 4.1%)

John McGuinness Bitter (OG 1042, ABV 4.2%)

Patrick's Porter (OG 1050.5, ABV 5%)

Buckle Street

Buckle Street Brewery Ltd, 2 Shires Industrial Estate, Buckle Street, Honeybourne, Evesham, Worcestershire, WR11 7QF
☎ **(01386) 831173 (Fleece Inn)**
✉ **info@bucklestreetbrewery.co.uk**
🌐 **bucklestreetbrewery.co.uk**
Tours by arrangement

Buckle Street was set up in 2008 by Andy Davies and Nigel Smith from the Fleece Inn, Bretforton. It is named after the adjacent Roman road. It currently only supplies the Fleece but there are plans for expansion. Bottle-conditioned beer is available.

No. 1 Bitter (OG 1034, ABV 3.8%)
Pale, golden and smooth on the mouth. Grassy with slight lemon on the nose and a complex hoppy finish.

Pandora's Box (OG 1040, ABV 4.3%)
Copper-coloured with orange on the nose. Well-balanced with a dry hoppiness and caramel undertone.

Porter (OG 1043, ABV 4.6%)
Dark with rich liquorice and intense chocolate malt, smoky overtones and a creamy head.

Buffy's SIBA EAB

Buffy's Brewery Ltd, Rectory Road, Tivetshall St Mary, Norfolk, NR15 2DD
☎ **(01379) 676523** ✉ **buffysbrewery@gmail.com**
🌐 **buffys.co.uk**

Buffy's was established in 1993. The brewing capacity is 45 barrels, but a move to bigger premises is in hand with plans for a bottling plant. The brewery owns two pubs, the Cherry Tree at Wicklewood and the White Hart at Foulden. Barley for all brewing is grown in Norfolk. Around 150 outlets are supplied. Seasonal beers: Sleigher (ABV 4.1%, Dec-Jan), Hollybeery (ABV 5.5% Dec-Jan). Bottle-conditioned beers are also available.

Norwich Terrier (OG 1036, ABV 3.6%)
A fragrant peachy aroma introduces this refreshing, gold-coloured bitter. Strong bitter notes dominate throughout as hops mingle with grapefruit to produce a long, increasingly dry finish.

Bitter (OG 1039, ABV 3.9%)
The strong malty aroma contrasts totally with the dry bitterness of the taste. A pale brown beer with an increasingly hoppy finish that grows and grows.

Mild (OG 1042, ABV 4.2%)
A complex brew, deep red with a smooth but grainy feel. Caramel and blackcurrant bolster the heavy malt influence that is the main characteristic of this understated, deceptively strong mild.

Polly's Folly (OG 1043, ABV 4.3%)
Complex and well-balanced with a definitive malty spine. An elderberry sweetness complements the malty character throughout as a bittersweet dryness defines the long finale.

Hopleaf (OG 1044.5, ABV 4.5%)
Pale brown beer with a gentle hop nose. Strawberries mingle with the hops and malt, remaining as the malt gently subsides to leave a bittersweet, dry finish.

Mucky Duck (OG 1044, ABV 4.5%)
Roasted malt with sweet fruitiness giving depth without becoming dominant. Chewy mouthfeel and lingering finish.

Norwegian Blue (OG 1049, ABV 4.9%)
A gentle hoppy nose belies the rich warming character of the taste explosion. A complex, ever-changing mix of malt, hops, bitterness and fruit. A long, lingering, bittersweet ending.

Buffy's Ale (OG 1055, ABV 5.5%)

Festival 9X (OG 1089, ABV 9%)

Bull Lane

Bull Lane Brewing Co, Clarendon Hotel, 143 High Street East, Sunderland, Tyne & Wear, SR1 2BL
☎ **(0191) 510 3200**
✉ **bullanebrewingco@hotmail.co.uk**
🌐 **bull-lane-brewing.co.uk**
Tours by arrangement

Sunderland's first brew-pub started production in 2005 in the cellar of the Clarendon pub. The beers are supplied direct to pubs within a 30-mile radius of Sunderland and are regularly available in Sir John Fitzgerald's pubs.

Nowtsa Matta BB (OG 1037, ABV 3.7%)

Ryhope Tug (OG 1039, ABV 3.9%)

Terry's All Gold (OG 1042, ABV 4.3%)

Mutt's Nutts (OG 1044, ABV 4.4%)

Jack's Flag (OG 1045, ABV 4.5%)

Jason's Jinja Ale (OG 1045, ABV 4.5%)

Nowtsa Matta XB (OG 1045, ABV 4.5%)

Sauce of the Niall (OG 1045, ABV 4.5%)

Double Barrel (OG 1052, ABV 5.5%)

For TJ Doyles, Sunderland:

Neck Oil (ABV 4.3%)

Bullmastiff SIBA

Bullmastiff Brewery, 14 Bessemer Close, Leckwith, Cardiff, CF11 8DL
☎ **(029) 2066 5292**

An award-winning small craft brewery run by brothers Bob and Paul Jenkins since 1987. The name stems from their love of the bullmastiff breed. They have no ambitions for expansion or owning any pubs, preferring to concentrate on quality control. 30 outlets are supplied. Seasonal beers: Summer Moult (ABV 4.3%), Mogadog (ABV 10%, winter).

Welsh Gold (OG 1039, ABV 3.8%)
A hoppy and fruity aroma leads into the same juicy blend of flavours. Bittersweet initially, an easy-drinking and refreshing beer.

Jack the Lad (OG 1041, ABV 4.1%)

Thoroughbred (OG 1046, ABV 4.5%)

A good hop aroma leads to a hoppy flavour with accompanying fruit, malt and balancing bitterness. There is a quenching hoppy bitterness in the finish.

Welsh Black (OG 1050, ABV 4.8%)

Welsh Red (OG 1048, ABV 4.8%)

Brindle (OG 1050, ABV 5.1%)
A full-bodied, flavoursome pale beer. Good hop aroma with a mix of malt, hops, fruit and bitterness in the taste. A lasting and satisfying finish.

Son of a Bitch (OG 1062, ABV 6%)
A complex, warming amber ale with a tasty blend of hops, malt and fruit flavours, with increasing bitterness.

Buntingford SIBA

Buntingford Brewery Co Ltd, Greys Brewhouse, Therfield Road, Royston, Hertfordshire, SG8 9NW
☎ (01763) 250749 ☎ 07879 698541
contact@buntingford-brewery.co.uk
buntingford-brewery.co.uk
Tours by arrangement

Brewing commenced on the current site in 2005 and has expanded to a capacity of around 50 barrels per week. Further expansion is planned. Two regular beers are brewed year round alongside seasonal/occasional brews and various themed specials. The beers are brewed using water from an on-site well and all liquid waste is treated in a reed bed. The brewery is located on a conservation farm and there is a wide variety of bird life visible from the doors of the brewhouse, often including rare and endangered species.

Highwayman (ABV 3.6%)

Twitchell (ABV 3.8%)

Burnside (NEW)

Metcalfes Burnside Brewery, Laurencekirk Business Park, Laurencekirk, AB30 1EY
☎ (01561) 377316 info@brewmet.com
brewmet.com

Burnside began brewing in 2010 using a 2.5-barrel plant. Beer festivals and local outlets are supplied. Seasonal beers are planned.

3 Bullz (ABV 3.8%)

Wild Rhino (ABV 4.5%)

M-Pire (ABV 5.2%)

Burton Bridge SIBA

Burton Bridge Brewery Ltd, 24 Bridge Street, Burton upon Trent, Staffordshire, DE14 1SY
☎ (01283) 510573
bbb@burtonbridgebrewery.fsnet.co.uk
burtonbridgebrewery.co.uk
Shop at Bridge Inn 11.30am-2.15pm, 5-11pm
Tours by arrangement (Wed evenings)

A brewery established in 1982 by Bruce Wilkinson and Geoff Mumford. The brewery owns five pubs in the town, including its CAMRA award-winning brewery tap. More than 300 outlets are supplied direct. An ever-changing range of seasonal/monthly beers is available. Bottle-conditioned beers are also available.

Golden Delicious (OG 1037, ABV 3.8%)
A Burton classic with sulphurous aroma and well-balanced hops and fruit. An apple fruitiness, sharp and refreshing start leads to a lingering mouth-watering bitter finish with a hint of astringency. Light, crisp and refreshing.

Sovereign Gold (OG 1040, ABV 4%)
Minimal aroma but a grassy hop start with malt overtones. Hoppy taste and good dry finish.

XL Bitter (OG 1039, ABV 4%)
Another Burton classic with sulphurous aroma. Golden with fruit and hops and characteristic lingering aftertaste.

Bridge Bitter (OG 1041, ABV 4.2%)
Gentle aroma of malt and fruit. Good balanced start finishing with a robust hop mouthfeel.

Burton Porter (OG 1044, ABV 4.5%)
Chocolate aromas and smooth taste of smoky roasted grain and coffee.

Stairway to Heaven (OG 1049, ABV 5%)
Golden bitter. A perfectly balanced beer. The malty and hoppy start leads to a hoppy body with some astringency.

Top Dog Stout (OG 1049, ABV 5%)
Black and rich with a roast and malty start. Fruity and abundant hops give a fruity, bitter finish with a mouth-watering edge. Also available as Bramble Stout.

Festival Ale (OG 1054, ABV 5.5%)
Caramel aroma with plenty of hop taste balanced by malty sweetness.

Thomas Sykes (OG 1095, ABV 10%)
Kid in a sweetshop aroma. Rich fruity spirited tastes – warming and dangerously drinkable.

Burton Old Cottage

Burton Old Cottage Beer Co Ltd, Unit 10, Eccleshall Business Park, Hawkins Lane, Burton upon Trent, Staffordshire, DE14 1PT
☎ 07909 931250 jwsaville@tiscali.co.uk
oldcottagebeer.co.uk
Tours by arrangement

Old Cottage was originally installed in the old Heritage Brewery, once Everard's production plant in Burton. When the site was taken over, the brewery moved to a modern industrial unit. The brewery was sold in 2005 and 2006 saw heavy investment in new production and storage facilities by the new owners. Around 10 outlets are supplied. Seasonal beers: Snow Joke (ABV 5.2%, winter), Prancers Pride (ABV 4.7%, winter).

Pail Ale (OG 1040, ABV 3.8%)
A well-balanced, light-coloured ale with a full measure of maltiness and hop aroma.

Oak Ale (OG 1044, ABV 4%)
Tawny, full-bodied bitter. A sweet start gives way to a slight roast taste with some caramel. A dry, hoppy finish.

Chestnut (ABV 4.2%)
A dark session ale with a touch of bitterness and a pleasant, full aftertaste.

Cottage IPA (OG 1047, ABV 4.4%)
An intense, complex brew with elegant hop flavours.

Redwood (OG 1046, ABV 4.6%)
A unique flavour of fruit and hops with a slightly malty background and aftertaste.

THE BREWERIES

Cloughy's Clout (OG 1047, ABV 4.7%)
A chestnut-coloured ale with light malty undertones and a touch of bitterness.

Stout (OG 1047, ABV 4.7%) ◆
Dense black but not heavy. Sweet with lots of caramel, hints of liquorice and a roast and bitter finish.

Pastiche (OG 1050, ABV 5.2%)
A smooth, balanced ale with a complex taste and aroma.

Halcyon Daze (OG 1050, ABV 5.3%) ◆
Tawny and creamy with touches of hop, fruit and malt aroma. Fruity taste and finish.

Burtonwood

Thomas Hardy Burtonwood Ltd, Bold Lane, Burtonwood, Warrington, Cheshire, WA5 4TH
☎ (01925) 220022 ⊕ thomashardybrewery.co.uk

Burtonwood is now Thomas Hardy's only brewery, run by Peter Ward as a contract operation. All cask beer production has stopped with the demise of Webster's Green Label and Yorkshire Bitter.

Bushy's SIBA

Mount Murray Brewing Co Ltd, Mount Murray Brewery, Mount Murray, Braddan, Isle of Man, IM4 1JE
☎ (01624) 661244 ✉ info@bushys.com
⊕ bushys.com
Tours by arrangement

☺Set up in 1986 as a brew-pub, Bushy's moved to its present site in 1990 when demand outgrew capacity. It owns four tied houses and the beers are also supplied to 25 other outlets. Bushy's goes one step further than the Manx Pure Beer Law, which permits only malt, hops, sugar and yeast, preferring the German Reinheitsgebot (Pure Beer Law) that excludes sugar. Seasonal beers are numerous and include Oyster Stout (ABV 4.2%) – see website.

Castletown Bitter (OG 1035, ABV 3.5%)
A light, golden beer full of floral and citrus hints. A refreshing session beer.

Ruby (1874) Mild (OG 1035, ABV 3.5%)
An authentic malt brewed mild with a fine aroma of crystal malt and Fuggles.

Bitter (OG 1038, ABV 3.8%) ◆
An aroma full of pale malt and hops introduces a beautifully hoppy, bitter beer. Despite the predominant hop character, malt is also evident. Fresh and clean-tasting.

Shuttleworth Snap (OG 1040, ABV 4%)
A light-bodied beer, IPA in style with light citrus hints and well-rounded mouthfeel. Floral in aroma and light on the palate.

Manx Pride (OG 1042, ABV 4.2%)
Dry-hopped, reddish beer with a very distinctive citrus/floral aroma and a full palate.

Old Bushy Tail (OG 1045, ABV 4.5%)
A reddish-brown beer with a pronounced hop and malt aroma, the malt tending towards treacle. Slightly sweet and malty on the palate with distinct orangy tones. The full finish is malty and hoppy with a hint of toffee.

Piston Brew (OG 1045, ABV 4.5%)

A ruby-coloured ale, slightly sweet with subtle hop flavours coming through from the late addition of Challenger and Fuggles hops. Malty with hints of toffee.

Weiss Beer (OG 1040, ABV 4.5%)
A light, refreshing, cloudy wheat beer.

Butcombe SIBA

Butcombe Brewery Ltd, Cox's Green, Wrington, Bristol, BS40 5PA
☎ (01934) 863963 ✉ info@butcombe.com
⊕ butcombe.com
Shop Mon-Fri 9am-5pm; Sat 9am-12pm
Tours by arrangement

⊗ Established in 1978 by Simon Whitmore and sold to Guy Newell and friends in 2003, Butcombe moved to a new purpose-built brewery in 2005. It supplies about 500 outlets and similar numbers via wholesalers and pub companies. Butcombe has an estate of 16 freehouses. Seasonal beers: Blond (ABV 4.3%, Jun-Aug), Christmas Steps (ABV 4.2%, Dec).

Bitter (OG 1039, ABV 4%) ⬚ ◆
Amber-coloured, malty and notably bitter beer, with subtle citrus notes. Hoppy, malty, citrus and a slight sulphur aroma, and a long, dry, bitter finish.

Gold (OG 1045.5, ABV 4.4%) ◆
Aroma of pale malt, citrus hops and fruit. Medium bodied, well-balanced, with good pale malt, hops and bitterness. It is fruity, slightly sweet, with an abiding dryness.

Brunel IPA (OG 1049, ABV 5%)
Clean-tasting, dry and hoppy authentic recipe IPA. Pale in colour and full-bodied with a bittersweet finish.

Butts SIBA

Butts Brewery Ltd, Northfield Farm, Wantage Road, Great Shefford, Hungerford, Berkshire, RG17 7BY
☎ (01488) 648133 ✉ sales@buttsbrewery.com
⊕ buttsbrewery.com

⊗ The brewery was set up in a converted Dutch barn in 1994. In 2002, the brewery took the decision to become dedicated to organic production: all the beers brewed use organic malted barley and organic hops when suitable varieties are available. All beers are certified by the Soil Association. Around 60 outlets are supplied. Seasonal and occasional beers: Mudskipper (ABV 4.5%, summer), Bit o'Posh (ABV 4.2%, autumn), Blackguard Porter (ABV 4.5%), Golden Brown (ABV 5%), Le Butts (ABV 5%), Coper (ABV 6%). Bottle-conditioned beers are also available.

Jester (OG 1036, ABV 3.5%) ◆
A pale brown session bitter with a hoppy aroma and a hint of fruit. The taste balances malt, hops, fruit and bitterness with a hoppy aftertaste.

Traditional (OG 1040, ABV 4%) ◆
A pale brown bitter that is quite soft on the tongue with hoppy citrus flavours accompanying a gentle bittersweetness. A long, dry aftertaste is dominated by fruity hops.

Barbus Barbus (OG 1046, ABV 4.6%) ◆
Golden ale with a fruity hoppy aroma and a hint of malt. Hops dominate taste and aftertaste, accompanied by fruitiness and bitterness, with a hint of balancing sweetness.

Buxton

Buxton Brewery, Units 7D & E, Staden Business Park, Staden Lane, Buxton, Derbyshire, SK17 9RZ
☎ (01298) 24420 ☎ 07754 015743
✉ geoff@buxtonrealale.co.uk ⊕ buxtonrealale.co.uk

▧ Buxton Brewery was set up in 2009 and has recently acquired the Wild Walker Brewery. All beers are brewed using natural spring water from the Buxton Spring Water Company. Bottle-conditioned beers are available.

SPA (Special Pale Ale) (OG 1042, ABV 4.1%)
Light and refreshing, delicately hopped ale with a clean taste, a creamy mouthfeel and nutty notes.

Blonde (OG 1045, ABV 4.6%)
A classic blonde – clear, crisp and malty, mashed with a blend of barley and wheat for a zesty, fruity character.

Kinder Sunset (OG 1050, ABV 5%)
A ruby red bitter with a complex taste profile and malty richness, tempered by a bitter, citrus finish.

Under Wild Walker Brewery name:

Last Orders (ABV 3.8%)

Old Big 'ead (OG 1042, ABV 4.1%)

Great Escape (OG 1050, ABV 5%)

Robert Cain SIBA

Robert Cain Brewery, Stanhope Street, Liverpool, Merseyside, L8 5XJ
☎ (0151) 709 8734 ✉ info@cains.co.uk
⊕ cains.co.uk
Shop 12-10pm daily
Tours by arrangement

☺The Dusanj brothers, Ajmail and Sudarghara, bought the brewery in 2002, but after investing heavily and following a reverse takeover of the Honeycombe leased pubs estate, Cains Beer Co went into administration in 2008. The brewing operation was then sold back to the Dusanj family. Nine pubs are owned all serving cask beer and around 300 outlets are supplied. Seasonal beers including Dark Mild, see website.

IPA (OG 1036, ABV 3.5%)
A light, full-flavoured session beer with a subtle hop aroma.

Finest Bitter (OG 1041, ABV 4%) ◆
Blackcurrant fruit and malt dominate the aroma. A sweetish malty bitter with hints of roast and caramel. Hops come through in the dry, bitter aftertaste.

Fine Raisin Beer (ABV 5%)

Formidable Ale/FA (OG 1049, ABV 5%) ◆
A bitter and hoppy beer with a good dry aftertaste. Sharp, clean and dry.

Cairngorm SIBA

Cairngorm Brewery Co Ltd, Unit 12, Dalfaber Industrial Estate, Aviemore, Highlands, PH22 1ST
☎ (01479) 812222 ✉ info@cairngormbrewery.com
⊕ cairngormbrewery.com
Shop Mon-Sat 10am-5pm (online shop also available)
Tours: Mon-Fri 10.30am & 2.30pm by arrangement

☺The brewery produces seven regular cask beers along with a rolling programme of seasonal ales

throughout the year. Expansion has taken the weekly capacity to 140 barrels. The free trade is supplied as far as the central belt with national delivery via wholesalers. Seasonal beers: See website.

Stag (OG 1040, ABV 4.1%) ◆
A fine best bitter with plenty of roast and hop bitterness throughout. This tawny brew also has plenty of malt in the lingering bitter aftertaste.

Trade Winds (OG 1043, ABV 4.3%) ◆
A spectacular multi-award winning beer. A massive citrus fruit, hop and elderflower nose leads to hints of grapefruit and apricot in the mouth. The exceptional bitter sweetness in the taste lasts through the long, lingering aftertaste.

Black Gold (OG 1044, ABV 4.4%) ⏷ ◆
With a hint of smoked sausage, roast malt dominates throughout, but the liquorice and blackcurrant in the taste and nose give it a background sweetness. Very long, dry bitter finish.

Nessies Monster Mash (OG 1044, ABV 4.4%) ⏷ ◆
A good traditional English-type bitter with plenty of bitterness and strong malt flavour and a Tia Maria background. Lingering bitterness in the aftertaste with diminishing sweetness.

Cairngorm Gold (OG 1044, ABV 4.5%) ◆
Fruit and hops to the fore, with a hint of caramel in this sweetish brew.

Sheepshaggers Gold (OG 1044, ABV 4.5%) ◆
A golden amber brew with faint aromas and tastes of grapefruit and passion fruit. Some light bitterness in the otherwise sweet aftertaste.

Wildcat (OG 1049.5, ABV 5.1%) ◆
A full-bodied strong bitter. Malt predominates but there is an underlying hop character through to the well-balanced aftertaste.

Caledonian

See Heineken in Global Giants section

Callow Top

See Haywood Bad Ram

Calvors

Calvors Brewery Ltd, Home Farm, Coddenham, Ipswich, Suffolk, IP6 9UN
☎ (01449) 711055 ✉ info@calvors.co.uk
⊕ calvors.co.uk

No real ale. Calvors Brewery was established in 2008 and brews three real lagers, Calvors Suffolk Lager (ABV 3.8%), Calvors Premium (ABV 5%) and Calvors Dark (ABV 4.7%), which are available bottled and on draught.

Cambridge Moonshine

Cambridge Moonshine Brewery, Hill Farm, Shelford Road, Fulbourn, Cambridgeshire, CB21 5EQ
☎ (01223) 514366 ☎ 07906 066794
✉ mark@moonshinebrewery.co.uk

Established in 2004, the brewery has recently moved to larger premises incorporating a five-barrel plant. Locally produced ingredients are used including water from the brewery's own well. It mainly concentrates on supplying CAMRA beer

festivals, with two outlets supplied direct. Bottle-conditioned beers are available.

Sparkling Moon (ABV 3.6%)
A light blond lager beer with a delicate hop aroma and a crisp, clean taste with hints of vanilla.

Harvest Moon Mild (OG 1040, ABV 3.9%)
Smooth fruit notes combine with coffee and chocolate flavours, lightly hopped. A well-balanced beer, slightly sweet with plenty of character.

Barton Bitter (ABV 4%)
Pale brown with red and amber highlights, balanced malt and hops and a fruity backdrop on both nose and palate. A bittersweet flavour dries as fruit and sweetness diminish.

Thunder Moon (ABV 4.1%)
A light-bodied golden ale with a citrus fruit bouquet and taste that contines through to a pleasantly refreshing, clean and dry finish.

CB1 (ABV 4.2%)
Amber-coloured traditional best bitter with a good blend of malt and hops with a rounded, hoppy finish.

Red Watch (ABV 4.2%)
A red-coloured beer brewed with fresh blueberries. A thirst-quenching, refreshing, fruity summer ale.

Pigs Ear Porter (ABV 4.5%)
Five types of malts, four varieties of hops plus black honey from the Cambridge Beekeepers Association are blended together to create a unique and rounded flavour.

Minion of the Moon (ABV 4.6%)
A premium, light-coloured, full-flavoured fruity beer. Rich malt, fruit and hops dominate the taste, the fullness of flavour is sustained throughout leading to an uplifting and satisfying bittersweet finish.

Black Hole Stout (ABV 5%)
Full-bodied stout with a complex malt and caramel profile, dry-roasted bitter flavour that is rich, smooth and long lasting.

Budding Moon (ABV 5.1%)
A smooth, refreshing golden wheat beer. With a citrus hop bouquet and a rich, malty fruit flavour. The addition of locally produced honey gives a moderately bittersweet finish.

Chocolate Orange Stout (ABV 6.7%)
Full-bodied, rounded soft stout. Loaded with chocolate and coffee flavours with a good hop balance that has a hint of orange on the nose.

Cambrinus SIBA

Cambrinus Craft Brewery, Home Farm, Knowsley Park, Knowsley, Merseyside, L34 4AQ
☎ (0151) 546 2226 ✉ john@cambrinus.myzen.co.uk

Established in 1997, Cambrinus is housed in part of a former farm building on a private estate. It produces around 250 hectolitres a year on a five-barrel plant. Some 45 outlets are supplied on a regular basis in and around Lancashire, Cheshire and Cumbria. Seasonal beers: Bootstrap (ABV 4.5%, spring), Fruit Wheat Beer (summer), St Georges Ale (ABV 4.5%, Apr), Clogdance (ABV 3.6%, May), Solstice (ABV 3.8%, Jun), Honeywheat (ABV 3.7%, Jul), Dark Harvest (ABV 4%, autumn), Hearts of Oak (ABV 5%, Oct), Parkin (ABV 3.8%, Nov), Lamp Oil (ABV 4.5%, winter), Celebrance (ABV 5.5%, Xmas).

Herald (OG 1036, ABV 3.7%)
Light summer drinking bitter, pale and refreshing.

Yardstick (OG 1040, ABV 4%)
Mild, malty and lightly hopped.

Deliverance (OG 1040, ABV 4.2%)
Pale premium bitter.

Endurance (OG 1045, ABV 4.3%)
IPA-style, smooth and hoppy, fermented in oak.

Camden

Camden Town Brewery, 55-58 Wilkin Street Mews, Camden Town, London, NW5 3NN
☎ (020) 7485 1671
Second Brewery: The Horseshoe, 28 Heath Street, Hampstead, London, NW3 6TE ☎ (020) 7431 7206
✉ brewingbeer@camdentownbrewery.com
camdentownbrewery.com
Tours by arrangement

Formerly known as McLaughlin Brewhouse. The original micro-brewery was built in 2006 in honour of the landlord's late grandfather, who owned Mac's Brewery in Rockhampton, Australia. In 2007 the name changed to Camden Town Brewery and in 2010 a 20-hectolitre brewery was established in Camden. The original plant at the Horseshoe is now used for small batch sizes and single runs.

Wheat Beer (ABV 4.5%)

Hells Lager (ABV 4.8%)

Black Barrel Ale (ABV 5%)

Pale Ale (ABV 5%)

Camerons

Camerons Brewery Ltd, Lion Brewery, Stranton, Hartlepool, Co Durham, TS24 7QS
☎ (01429) 852000
✉ martindutoy@cameronsbrewery.com
cameronsbrewery.com
Shop Mon-Sat 12-4pm
Tours by arrangement

Founded in 1865, Camerons was bought in 2002 by Castle Eden brewery, which moved production to Hartlepool. In 2003 a 10-barrel micro-brewery, the Lions Den, opened to produce and bottle small brews of guest ales and to undertake contract brewing and bottling. 75 pubs are owned, with five selling real ale. Seasonal beers have been dropped in favour of monthly guest beer production.

Best Bitter (OG 1036, ABV 3.6%)
A light bitter, but well-balanced, with hops and malt.

Strongarm (OG 1041, ABV 4%)
A well-rounded, ruby-red ale with a distinctive, tight creamy head; initially fruity, but with a good balance of malt, hops and moderate bitterness.

Trophy Special (ABV 4%)
An amber ale, slightly sweet and malty, fruity and hoppy from the addition of Styrian Golding hops in the cask.

Cannon Royall SIBA

Cannon Royall Brewery Ltd, Fruiterer's Arms, Uphampton Lane, Uphampton, Worcestershire, WR9 0JW

☎ (01905) 621161 ✉ info@cannonroyall.co.uk
🌐 cannonroyall.co.uk
Tours by arrangement (CAMRA only)

Cannon Royall's first brew was in 1993 in a converted cider house behind the Fruiterer's Arms. It has increased capacity from five barrels to more than 16 a week. The brewery supplies a number of outlets in Worcestershire and the West Midlands. Seasonal beers are regularly produced. Bottle-conditioned beers are also available.

Fruiterer's Mild (OG 1037, ABV 3.7%)
This black-hued brew has rich malty aromas that lead to a fruity mix of bitter hops and sweetness, and a short balanced aftertaste.

King's Shilling (OG 1038, ABV 3.8%)
A golden bitter that packs a citrus hoppy punch throughout.

Arrowhead Bitter (OG 1039, ABV 3.9%)
A powerful punch of hops attacks the nose before the feast of bitterness. The memory of this golden brew fades too soon.

IPA (OG 1048, ABV 4.6%)
An aromatic hop aroma precedes a clean, citrus bitterness in this pale coloured beer.

Captain Cook SIBA

Captain Cook Brewery Ltd, White Swan, 1 West End, Stokesley, North Yorkshire, TS9 5BL
☎ (01642) 710263
✉ jeff.hind@thewynyardrooms.com
🌐 captaincookbrewery.co.uk
Tours by arrangement

The Captain Cook Brewery is located within the 18th-century White Swan pub. The brewery celebrated its 10th anniversary in 2009. With a four-barrel plant, it is brewing up to 12 barrels a week in order to supply other local outlets. Seasonal beer: Easter Island (ABV 4.1%, spring).

Sunset (OG 1040, ABV 4.1%)
An extremely smooth light ale with a good balance of malt and hops.

Slipway (OG 1042, ABV 4.2%)
A light-coloured hoppy ale with bitterness coming through from Challenger hops. A full-flavoured ale with a smooth malt aftertaste.

Endeavour (OG 1043, ABV 4.3%)
Mid brown ale with a bitter finish.

Black Porter (OG 1044, ABV 4.4%)
Chocolate notes and dominant roast flavours lead to a dry, bitter finish.

Carter's

Carter's Brewery, White Hart Inn, White Hart Lane, Machen, CF83 8QQ
☎ (01633) 441005

Carter's started in 2002 on a 1.5-barrel plant and only brews for special occasions and local beer festivals. There are plans to step up production and brew more regularly in the future.

Castle Rock SIBA

Tynemill Ltd t/a Castle Rock Brewery, Queensbridge Road, Nottingham, Nottinghamshire, NG2 1NB
☎ (0115) 985 1615
✉ admin@castlerockbrewery.co.uk
🌐 castlerockbrewery.co.uk
Shop: In brewery tap (Vat & Fiddle, Nottingham) 11 (12 Sun)-11am
Tours by arrangement (groups of 10 or more Sat & Sun 11am)

Castle Rock was established in 1998 producing 30 barrels weekly. Since then capacity has steadily increased with the largest expansion taking place in 2010 when additional brewing equipment was installed in the neighbouring building giving a total capacity of 300 barrels a week. Beers are distributed through its own estate of 22 pubs and further afield through wholesalers. A different beer is brewed monthly to support the Nottinghamshire Wildlife Trust. Seasonal beers: see website. Bottle-conditioned beers are also available.

Black Gold (OG 1037, ABV 3.8%)
A dark ruby mild. Full-bodied and fairly bitter.

Harvest Pale (OG 1037, ABV 3.8%)
Pale yellow beer, full of hop aroma and flavour. Refreshing with a mellowing aftertaste.

Hemlock Bitter (OG 1040, ABV 4%)
A bitter malty brown ale with slight caramel characteristics without being overly sweet.

Preservation Fine Ale (OG 1043, ABV 4.4%)
A traditional copper-coloured English best bitter with malt predominant. Fairly bitter with a residual sweetness.

Elsie Mo (OG 1045, ABV 4.7%)
A strong golden ale with floral hops evident in the aroma. Citrus hops are mellowed by a slight sweetness.

Screech Owl (OG 1052, ABV 5.5%)
A classic golden IPA with an intensely hoppy aroma and bitter taste with a little balancing sweetness.

Castle SIBA

Castle Brewery, Unit 9a-7, Restormel Industrial Estate, Liddicoat Road, Lostwithiel, Cornwall, PL22 0HG
☎ (01726) 871133 ☎ 07800 635831
✉ castlebrewery@aol.com

Castle started brewing in early 2008 on a two-barrel plant. Only bottle-conditioned ales are produced; Cornish Best Bitter (ABV 4.2%), Moat Mild (ABV 4.4%), Battle Stout (ABV 4.6%), Once A Knight (ABV 5%), Bodmin Beast (ABV 6.2%), Lostwithiale (ABV 7%), Hung, Drawn & Slaughtered (ABV 10%).

Castor (NEW)

Castor Ales, 30 Peterborough Road, Castor, Peterborough, Cambridgeshire, PE5 7AX
☎ (01733) 380337 ✉ duncan@castorales.co.uk
🌐 castorales.co.uk
Tours by arrangement

This three-barrel brewery, established in 2009, is located in a specially converted outhouse in the garden of the founder brewer Duncan Vessey. The first two beers were launched at the Peterborough beer festival. The Prince of Wales Feathers in Castor features the beers on gravity dispense as a permanent feature.

Roman Gold (OG 1037, ABV 3.7%)

THE BREWERIES

Golden-coloured session bitter.

Castor Oil (OG 1041, ABV 4.1%)
Golden and hoppy with a citrus aftertaste.

Serene Nene (OG 1045, ABV 4.5%)
Traditional copper-coloured bitter.

Castor & Pollux (OG 1048, ABV 4.8%)
Winter ale infused with seasonal spices and a strong clove finish.

Caythorpe SIBA

Caythorpe Brewery Ltd, c/o Black Horse, 29 Main Street, Caythorpe, Nottinghamshire, NG14 7ED
☎ (0115) 966 4933 ☎ 07913 434922
✉ caythorpebrewery@btinternet.com
Tours by arrangement

Caythorpe was set up using a 2.5-barrel brewery in a building at the rear of the Black Horse pub in 1997. Ownership changed in 2005 but the brewery continues to produce its small range of beers that have a big reputation in the local area. Seasonal beers: Winter Light (ABV 3.6%, autumn/winter), One Swallow (ABV 3.6%, spring/summer).

Bitter (OG 1034.7, ABV 3.7%)

Dover Beck (OG 1037, ABV 4%) ◆
Pale brown well-balanced session bitter. Initial malt is offset by a slight hoppy bitterness.

Stout Fellow (OG 1038.6, ABV 4.2%) ◆
A dark creamy stout with strong roast flavours.

Celt Experience

Celt Experience Ltd, Unit 2E, Pontygwindy Industrial Estate, Pontygwindy Road, Caerphilly, CF83 3HU
☎ (02920) 867707 ☎ 0870 803 3876
✉ celt@theceltexperience.co.uk
🌐 theceltexperience.co.uk
Shop Mon-Fri 10am-4.30pm
Tours by arrangement

⊗ Celt Experience first brewed in late 2007. A sister brewery to Newmans (qv), they share the 40-barrel plant. A bottling plant was installed in 2009 and an on-site off-licence is operated. 200 outlets are supplied direct. A small brewery (Y Bragdy Fach) is also situated at its tied house, the Wheatsheaf in Llantrisant.

Celt Golden (OG 1045, ABV 4.2%)

Celt Native Storm (OG 1044, ABV 4.4%)

Celt Bronze (OG 1046, ABV 4.5%)

Chalk Hill

Chalk Hill Brewery, Rosary Road, Norwich, Norfolk, NR1 4DA
☎ (01603) 477078 ✉ chalkhillinns@ntlworld.com
Tours by arrangement
Chalk Hill began production in 1993 on a 15-barrel plant. It supplies local pubs and festivals.

Tap Bitter (OG 1036, ABV 3.6%) ◆
Easy-drinking, well-balanced bitter with a light, malty character in both aroma and taste. Initially hops provide contrast but fade rapidly in a quick, clean finish.

CHB (OG 1042, ABV 4.2%) ◆
Malt comes to the fore as a fruity cooking apple beginning melds into the hoppy bittersweet background. A gentle malt aroma and sticky mouthfeel. Long finish.

Gold (ABV 4.3%) ◆
A gentle but well-defined hoppiness is the signature of this well-balanced amber-coloured brew. Elderflower on the nose continues throughout and provides depth and contrast. Short, dry finish.

Dreadnought (OG 1049, ABV 4.9%) ◆
A rich, resinous aroma fittingly introduces a heavily malt-influenced brew. Raisin and plum vie with each other to match the sweet malty backbone. Malt remains in an otherwise abrupt ending.

Flintknapper's Mild (OG 1052, ABV 5%) ◆
Red hued with a creamy mouthfeel. Malt emerges from a well-balanced mix of flavours including roast, sweetness and dates. Eventually only a malty sweetness remains.

Old Tackle (OG 1056, ABV 5.6%) ◆
A strong banana aroma overshadows a somewhat understated malty body. Banana notes swirl in the background to give depth and sweetness. A smooth, undemanding brew.

Cheddar Ales

Cheddar Ales Ltd, Winchester Farm, Draycott Road, Cheddar, Somerset, BS27 3RP
☎ (01934) 744193 ✉ brewery@cheddarales.co.uk
🌐 cheddarales.co.uk
Shop Mon-Fri 8am-4pm; Sat-Sun by appointment
Tours by arrangement

⊗ Cheddar Ales is a 20-barrel brewery set up in 2006 with a capacity of 17,000 pints per week. It is a local brewery serving a local market and has received many awards during its short history. Around 80 outlets are supplied regularly. Bottle-conditioned beers are available.

Mild Cheddar (OG 1036.5, ABV 3.6%)
A dark brown ale with a rounded blend of rich malt flavours, balanced with a light hop bitterness.

Bitter Bully (OG 1038.5, ABV 3.8%)
A straw-coloured session beer with a big hop aroma and a dry citrus finish.

Gorge Best Bitter (OG 1040, ABV 4%)
A best bitter with warm malt flavours and a clean, bitter finish.

Potholer (OG 1043.5, ABV 4.3%) ◆
Amber malty ale with a biscuity aroma and citrus in the mouth. Bitter fruit finish.

Festive Totty (OG 1044.5, ABV 4.5%)
Dark porter enriched with ruby port to give a smoother, slightly sweeter taste with hints of chocolate and fruit in the finish.

Totty Pot (OG 1044.5, ABV 4.5%)
A rich, dark porter with hints of roasted coffee and a creamy malt finish.

Goat's Leap (OG 1054.5, ABV 5.5%)
A contemporary IPA that stays close to the style's traditional roots. Full-bodied, strong and with a striking bitter finish. Brimming with hop character.

Cherwell Valley

Cherwell Valley Brewery Ltd, Bellfield House, 6 Queen Street, Middleton Cheney, Oxfordshire, OX17 2NP

☎ 07841 902427 ✉ tythinggraham@aol.com
🌐 cherwellvalleybrewery.com

⊗ Cherwell Valley started brewing in 2008 using a 2.5-barrel plant in Brackley before moving to its present address in 2010. Seasonal beers: Larkrise (ABV 4%, summer), Old Noll (ABV 4.8%, winter). Bottle-conditioned beers are also available.

Kineton Flight (ABV 3.8%)

Cropredy Bridge 1644 (ABV 4.2%)

Chiltern SIBA

Chiltern Brewery, Nash Lee Road, Terrick, Aylesbury, Buckinghamshire, HP17 0TQ
☎ **(01296) 613647** ✉ **info@chilternbrewery.co.uk**
🌐 **chilternbrewery.co.uk**
Shop Mon-Sat 9am-5pm
Tours every Sat (Jan-Nov) or mid-week by arrangement. Booking essential (see website)

Founded in 1980, the brewery is one of the first dozen micro-breweries to have been established in the country and is the oldest independent brewery in the Chilterns. This second generation family brewery produces a broad range of award-winning beers with English ingredients. The brewery tap is the Farmers' Bar at the King's Head in Aylesbury. Seasonal beers: see website. Bottle-conditioned beers are also available.

Chiltern Ale (OG 1037, ABV 3.7%) ◆
An amber, refreshing beer with a slight fruit aroma, leading to a good malt/bitter balance in the mouth. The aftertaste is bitter and dry.

Beechwood Bitter (OG 1043, ABV 4.3%) ◆
This pale brown beer has a balanced butterscotch/toffee aroma, with a slight hop note. The taste balances bitterness and sweetness, leading to a long bitter finish.

Chough SIBA

Chough Brewery, Unit 1, Higher Bochym, Cury Cross Lanes, Helston, Cornwall, TR12 7AZ
☎ **(01326) 241555**
Tours by arrangement

⊗ Established in 2000 by Andy Hamer and formerly known as Organic Brewery, its mini tower system was exclusively organic. The brewery now produce six regular beers in either standard or organic styles, hence the name change. The beers can be found locally in more than 20 outlets and further afield through wholesalers. They are still produced using the brewery's own source of natural mineral water. Bottle-conditioned beers are available.

Halzephron Gold (OG 1033, ABV 3.6%)

Kynance Blonde (OG 1039, ABV 4.2%)

Serpentine (OG 1042, ABV 4.5%)
A big malty nose, a bittersweet palate and a finish balanced by rich malt and tangy hops.

Black Rock (OG 1043, ABV 4.7%) ◆
Hop and apple aroma masked by complex roast overtones.

Wolf Rock (OG 1046, ABV 5%)

Julian Church

Julian Church Brewing Company, c/o Alexandra Arms, 39 Victoria Street, Kettering, Northamptonshire, NN16 0BU
☎ **07794 289559** ✉ **julianchurch@ymail.com**
🌐 **julianchurchbrewing.co.uk**
Tours by arrangement

Julian Church started brewing in early 2009 on Nobby's Brewery's old five-barrel plant when Nobby expanded and moved to Guilsborough. The brewery is based beneath the renowned Alexandra Arms in Kettering. Parson's Nose is rebadged as Father Nip for the Alexandra Arms. Seasonal and one-off beers are produced.

Parson's Nose (OG 1037, ABV 3.9%)
Mahogany-coloured with a nutty taste and a warm, spicy finish.

Martyr (OG 1040, ABV 4.1%)
An amber-coloured beer with a caramel flavour and a light, bitter finish.

Midnight Mass (OG 1040, ABV 4.2%)
A dark, rich, malty stout.

Wonky Spire (OG 1045, ABV 4.7%)
A fruity light ale.

5000 (OG 1048, ABV 5%)
A copper-coloured bitter.

Headstoned (OG 1056, ABV 5.8%)
A strong, dark, full-bodied old-style ale.

Church End SIBA

Church End Brewery Ltd, Ridge Lane, Nuneaton, Warwickshire, CV10 0RD
☎ **(01827) 713080**
✉ **stewart@churchendbrewery.co.uk**
🌐 **churchendbrewery.co.uk**
Shop during tap opening hours
Tours by arrangement

⊗ Stewart Elliot started brewing in 1994 in an old coffin shop in Shustoke. He moved to the present site and upgraded to a 10-barrel plant in 2001 with further expansion to a 20-barrel plant in 2008. The brewery tap opened in 2002. A portfolio of around 60 non-regular beers is produced as well as many one-off specials, including fruit, herb and spice beers. 500 outlets are supplied. Seasonal beers: Without-a-Bix (ABV 4.2%), Pews Porter (ABV 4.5%), Old Pal (ABV 5.5%), Arthurs Wit (ABV 6%), Rest-in-Peace (ABV 7%). Bottle-conditioned beers are also available.

Poachers Pocket (ABV 3.5%)

Pheasant Plucker (ABV 3.7%)

Cuthberts (ABV 3.8%) ◆
A refreshing, hoppy beer, with hints of malt, fruit and caramel taste. Lingering bitter aftertaste.

Goat's Milk (ABV 3.8%)

Gravediggers Ale (ABV 3.8%) 🍺 ◆
A premium mild. Black and red in colour, with a complex mix of chocolate and roast flavours, it is almost a light porter.

Hop Gun (ABV 4.1%)

What the Fox's Hat (ABV 4.2%) ◆
A beer with a malty aroma, and a hoppy and malty taste with some caramel flavour.

Pooh Beer (ABV 4.3%)

Brewed with honey.

Vicar's Ruin (ABV 4.4%) ◆
A straw-coloured best bitter with an initially hoppy, bitter flavour, softening to a delicate malt finish.

Stout Coffin (ABV 4.6%)

Fallen Angel (ABV 5%)

For Cape of Good Hope, Warwick:

Two Llocks (ABV 4%)

City of Cambridge EAB

City of Cambridge Brewery Co Ltd, Ely Road, Chittering, Cambridge, CB5 9PH
☎ (01223) 864864 ✉ sales@cambridge-brewery.co.uk ⊕ cambridge-brewery.co.uk

⊗ City of Cambridge opened in 1997 and moved to its present site in 2002. The brewery site is in the process of being redeveloped, with the intention of keeping the brewery on the site. At present all brewing is being done under contract by Elgoods Brewery (qv). In addition to prizes for its cask beers, the brewery holds a conservation award for the introduction of native reed beds at its site to treat brewery water. Seasonal beers: Mich'aelmas (ABV 4.5%, Xmas), Holly Heaven (ABV 4.8%, Xmas).

City of Stirling

See Traditional Scottish Ales

Clanconnel

Clanconnel Brewing Co Ltd, PO Box 316, Craigavon, Co Down, BT65 9AZ
☎ 07711 626770 ✉ info@clanconnelbrewing.com ⊕ clanconnelbrewing.com

Clanconnel started producing bottled beer in late 2008: Weaver's Gold (ABV 4.5%).

Clark's SIBA

HB Clark & Co (Successors) Ltd, Westgate Brewery, Wakefield, West Yorkshire, WF2 9SW
☎ (01924) 373328 Ext 211 ✉ rickp@hbclark.co.uk ⊕ hbclark.co.uk
Tours by arrangement

☺Founded in 1906, Clark's recently celebrated its centenary. It ceased brewing during the 1960s/70s but resumed cask ale production in 1982 and now delivers to around 220 outlets. Four pubs are owned, all serving cask ale. Seasonal beers: see website.

Classic Blonde (OG 1039, ABV 3.9%)
A light-coloured ale with a citrus and hoppy flavour, a distinctive grapefruit aroma and a dry finish.

No Angel (OG 1040, ABV 4%)
A bitter with a dry hop finish, well-balanced and full of flavour. Pale brown in colour with hints of fruit and hops.

Westgate Gold (OG 1042, ABV 4.2%)
A light-coloured, fruity beer with a full body and rich aroma.

Rams Revenge (OG 1046, ABV 4.6%) ◆

A rich, ruby-coloured premium ale, well-balanced with malt and hops, with a deep fruity taste and a dry hoppy aftertaste, with a pleasant hoppy aroma.

Clearwater SIBA

Clearwater Brewery Ltd, 2 Devon Units, Hatchmoor Industrial Estate, Torrington, Devon, EX38 7HP
☎ (01805) 625242
✉ sales@clearwaterbrewery.co.uk

Clearwater took over the closed St Giles in the Wood brewery in 1999. The brewery was sold in 2009 to businessman Barry Raynes, who installed a new brewer named Barrie Marden. The brewery was re-launched in 2010 with four beers being brewed. Around 30 outlets are supplied direct, which is expected to increase. Bottle-conditioned beers are available.

Real Smiler (ABV 3.7%)

Devon Dympsy (ABV 4%) ◆
Mid-brown, full-bodied best bitter with a burnt, rich malt aroma and taste, leading to a bitter, well-rounded finish.

Proper Ansome (ABV 4.2%)

Devon Darter (ABV 4.5%)

Cliff Quay SIBA

▤ **Cliff Quay Brewery, Cliff Road, Ipswich, Suffolk, IP3 0BS**
☎ (01728) 684097
✉ cliffquaybrewery@btconnect.com
⊕ cliffquay.co.uk
Tours by arrangement

Cliff Quay was established in 2008 by former Wychwood brewer Jeremy Moss and John Bjornson on part of the historic Tolly Cobbold riverside site. Regular seasonal beers are brewed every two months: see website.

Bitter (OG 1035, ABV 3.4%) ◆
Pleasantly drinkable, well-balanced malty sweet bitter with a hint of caramel, followed by a sweet/malty aftertaste. A good flavour for such a low gravity beer.

Black Jack Porter (OG 1042, ABV 4.2%) ◆
Unusual dark porter with a strong aniseed aroma and rich liquorice and aniseed flavours, reminiscent of old-fashioned sweets. The aftertaste is long and increasingly sweet.

Tolly Roger (OG 1043, ABV 4.2%) ◆
Well-balanced, highly drinkable, mid-gold summer beer with a bittersweet hoppiness, some biscuity flavours and hints of summer fruit.

Tumblehome (OG 1047, ABV 4.7%)

Clockwork

▤ **The Clockwork Beer Co, Maclay Inns PLC, 1153-5 Cathcart Road, Glasgow, G42 9HB**
☎ (0141) 649 0184 ✉ clockwork@maclay.co.uk
⊕ maclay.com
Tours by arrangement

⊗ The brewpub, the oldest in Glasgow, was established in 1997. The beers are kept in cellar tanks where fermentation gases from the conditioning vessel blanket the beers on tap (but not under pressure). A wide range of ales, lagers and specials are produced. Most beers are naturally gassed while the Original Lager and Seriously Ginger are pressurised. Having taken ownership of the Maclay's cookbook when Maclay Inns took over two years ago, some old recipes including Wallace IPA (ABV 4.5%), Oat Malt Stout (ABV 4.4%), Honey Weizen (ABV 4.6%) and Maclay's 90/- (ABV 6%) have been brewed with more to come.

Amber IPA (ABV 3.8%)

Red Alt (ABV 4.4%)

Gosch (ABV 4.8%)

Original Lager (ABV 4.8%)

Hazy Daze Seriously Ginger (ABV 5%)

Oregon IPA (ABV 5.5%)

Strong Ale (ABV 6%)

Thunder & Lightning (ABV 6%)

Coach House SIBA

Coach House Brewing Co Ltd, Wharf Street, Warrington, Cheshire, WA1 2DQ
☎ (01925) 232800 ✉ neil@coach-house-brewing.co.uk 🌐 coach-house-brewing.co.uk
Tours by arrangement for CAMRA groups only

Coach House was founded in 1991 and in 1995 increased its brewing capacity to cope with growing demand. The brewery also brews a large number of one-off and special beers. Seasonal beers: see website.

Coachman's Best Bitter (OG 1037, ABV 3.7%) ◆
A well-hopped, malty bitter, moderately fruity with a hint of sweetness and a peppery nose.

Gunpowder Mild (OG 1037, ABV 3.8%) ◆
Biscuity dark mild with a blackcurrant sweetness. Bitterness and fruit dominate with some hints of caramel and a slightly stronger roast flavour.

Honeypot Bitter (OG 1037, ABV 3.8%)

Farrier's Best Bitter (OG 1038, ABV 3.9%)

Dick Turpin (OG 1042, ABV 4.2%) ◆
Malty, hoppy pale brown beer with some initial sweetish flavours leading to a short, bitter aftertaste. Sold under other names as a pub house beer.

Flintlock Pale Ale (OG 1044, ABV 4.4%)

Innkeeper's Special Reserve (OG 1045, ABV 4.5%) ◆
A darkish, full-flavoured bitter. Quite fruity, with a strong, bitter aftertaste.

Postlethwaite (OG 1045, ABV 4.6%) ◆
Thin bitter with a short, dry aftertaste. Biscuity malt dominates.

Gingernut Premium (OG 1050, ABV 5%)

Posthorn Premium (OG 1050, ABV 5%) ◆
Dry golden bitter with a blackcurrant fruitiness and good hop flavours leading to a strong, dry finish. Well-balanced but slightly thin for its gravity.

For John Joule of Stone:

Old Knotty (ABV 3.6%)

Old Priory (ABV 4.4%)

Victory (ABV 5.2%)

Coastal SIBA

Coastal Brewery, Unit 10B, Cardrew Industrial Estate, Redruth, Cornwall, TR15 1SS
☎ 07875 405407 ✉ coastalbrewery@tiscali.co.uk
🌐 coastalbrewery.co.uk

Coastal was set up in late 2006 on a five-barrel plant by Alan Hinde, former brewer and owner of the Borough Arms in Crewe, Cheshire. It moved to larger premises in 2009. Around 150 outlets are supplied. Seasonal beers and two monthly specials are produced as well as bottle-conditioned beers.

Reflection (OG 1036, ABV 3.6%)

Hop Monster (OG 1038, ABV 3.7%)

Handliner (OG 1040, ABV 4%)

Merry Maidens Mild (OG 1040, ABV 4%)

Angelina (OG 1042, ABV 4.1%)

Golden Hinde (OG 1044, ABV 4.3%)

Gaddle Gold (OG 1047, ABV 4.7%)

Seafarer (OG 1051, ABV 5%)

Golden Sands (OG 1058, ABV 5.8%)

St Pirans Porter (ABV 6%)

Erosion (OG 1080, ABV 8%) ◆
After an aroma promising roast caramel this powerful, warming dark old ale bursts with molasses and roast malt. Liquorice adds to the finish.

Kernow Imperial Stout (OG 1090, ABV 9%)

For Allsaints Brewery:

St Piran Cornish Best Bitter (ABV 4%)

St Arnold (ABV 4.6%)

Coles

Coles Family Brewery, White Hart Thatched Inn & Brewery, Llanddarog, Carmarthen, SA32 8NT
☎ (01267) 275395 ✉ marcusrcoles@aol.com
🌐 thebestpubinwales.co.uk

The brewery is based at the ancient White Hart Inn, built in 1371. Centuries ago beer was brewed on site, but brewing only started again in 1999 on a nine-gallon plant. A one-barrel plant was fitted in 2000. Coles produces many unique ales throughout the year, style depends on the season.

Roasted Barley Stout (ABV 4%)

Golden Ale (ABV 4.2%)

Llanddarog (ABV 4.2%)

Swn y Dail (ABV 4.2%)

White Stag (ABV 4.2%)

Cwrw Blasus (ABV 4.4%)

College Green

College Green Brewery, 1 College Green Mews, Botanic Avenue, Belfast, BT7 1LW
☎ (02892) 660800/(02890) 322600
✉ irishbeers@hildenbrewery.co.uk
🌐 hildenbrewery.co.uk

College Green was set up in 2005 by Owen Scullion as a sister brewery to Hilden Brewery. All beers are brewed at the Hilden Brewery.

THE BREWERIES

Colonsay

Colonsay Brewery, The Brewery, Isle of Colonsay, PA61 7YT
☎ (01951) 200190 ✉ info@colonsaybrewery.co.uk
colonsaybrewery.co.uk

Colonsay began brewing in 2007 on a five-barrel plant. Beer is mainly bottled or brewery conditioned for the local trade: Lager (ABV 4.4%), 80/- Ale (ABV 4.2%), IPA (ABV 3.9%).

Compass (NEW)

Compass Brewery, Office: 6 Compass Close, Oxford, OX4 3SX
☎ 07988 928724 ✉ info@compassbrewery.com
compassbrewery.com

Compass is currently brewing using Cotswold Brewing Company's facilities. Head Brewer Mattias Sjoberg previously worked for Scottish & Newcastle at the Reading brewery. It brews experimental, innovative recipes and beer is available filtered in bottles, cask-conditioned in five-litre mini casks and occasionally in local pubs and at beer festivals. As well as brewing its own beer, Compass contract brew small batches for the public in its Bespoke Beer Program. Please see Cotswold for beer list.

Concertina SIBA

Concertina Brewery, 9a Dolcliffe Road, Mexborough, South Yorkshire, S64 9AZ
☎ (01709) 580841
Tours by arrangement

The brewery started in 1992 in the cellar of a club once famous as the home of a long-gone concertina band. The plant produces up to eight barrels a week for the club and other occasional outlets. Other beers are brewed on a seasonal basis, including Room at the Inn at Xmas.

Club Bitter (ABV 3.9%)
A fruity session bitter with a good bitter flavour.

Old Dark Attic (OG 1038, ABV 3.9%)
A dark brown beer with a fairly sweet, fruity taste.

One Eyed Jack (OG 1039, ABV 4%)
Fairly pale in colour with plenty of hop bitterness. Brewed with the same malt and hop combination as Bengal Tiger, but more of a session beer. Also badged as Mexborough Bitter.

Bengal Tiger (OG 1043, ABV 4.6%)
Light amber ale with an aromatic hoppy nose followed by a combination of fruit and bitterness.

Dictators (OG 1044, ABV 4.7%)

Ariel Square Four (OG 1046, ABV 5.2%)

Concrete Cow

Concrete Cow Brewery, 59 Alston Drive, Bradwell Abbey, Milton Keynes, Buckinghamshire, MK13 9HB
☎ (01908) 316794
✉ dan@concretecowbrewery.co.uk
concretecowbrewery.co.uk

Concrete Cow opened in 2007 on a 5.5-barrel plant. The beers are named after aspects of local history and all are available bottle conditioned as well as in casks. The brewery supplies pubs, farmers markets, local shops and restaurants. Seasonal beers: Black Monk (ABV 3.6%, May), Cowzat! (ABV 3.9%, summer), Midsummer Ale (ABV 3.8%), Winter Ale (ABV 5%).

Pail Ale (OG 1036, ABV 3.7%)

Iron Bridge Brew (ABV 3.9%)

Fenny Popper (OG 1039, ABV 4%)

Cock 'n' Bull Story (OG 1041, ABV 4.1%)

Watling Gold (OG 1044, ABV 4.5%)

Old Bloomer (OG 1045, ABV 4.7%)

Coniston SIBA

Coniston Brewing Co Ltd, Coppermines Road, Coniston, Cumbria, LA21 8HL
☎ (01539) 441133 ✉ beer@conistonbrewery.com
conistonbrewery.com
Shop (in Black Bull Inn) 11am-11pm
Tours by arrangement

A 10-barrel brewery set up in 1995 behind the Black Bull inn, Coniston. It now brews 40 barrels a week and supplies 70 local outlets while the beers are distributed nationally by wholesalers. One pub is owned. Some bottle-conditioned Coniston beers are brewed using Hepworth's Horsham plant: Bluebird (ABV 4.2%), Bluebird XB (ABV 4.4%), Oldman Ale (ABV 4.8%). Others are bottled on site.

Oliver's Light Ale (OG 1035, ABV 3.4%)
A fruity, hoppy, straw-coloured bitter with plenty of flavour for its strength.

Bluebird Bitter (OG 1036, ABV 3.6%)
A yellow-gold, predominantly hoppy and fruity beer, well-balanced with some sweetness and a rising bitter finish.

Bluebird Premium XB (OG 1040.5, ABV 4.2%)
Well-balanced, hoppy and fruity golden bitter. Bittersweet in the mouth with dryness building.

Old Man Ale (OG 1040.5, ABV 4.2%)
Delicious fruity, winey beer with a complex, well-balanced richness.

Special Oatmeal Stout (OG 1044, ABV 4.5%)
A well-balanced, easy-drinking stout, fruity with a balanced ratio of malt to hop bitterness. A good starting point for novice stout drinkers.

Blacksmiths Ale (OG 1047.5, ABV 5%)
A well-balanced strong bitter with hints of Xmas pudding.

Consett Ale Works

Consett Ale Works Ltd, Grey Horse Inn, 115 Sherburn Terrace, Consett, Co Durham, DH8 6NE
☎ (01207) 591540 ✉ jeffhind@aol.com
thegreyhorse.co.uk
Tours by arrangement

The brewery opened in 2006 in the stables of a former coaching inn, the Grey Horse, Consett's oldest pub. It expanded in 2007 to cope with demand. More than 100 outlets are supplied direct.

Steel Town Bitter (ABV 3.8%)

White Hot (ABV 4%)

Cast Iron (ABV 4.1%)

Consett Stout (ABV 4.3%)

Last Tap (ABV 4.3%)

Red Dust (ABV 4.5%)

Conwy

Conwy Brewery Ltd, Unit 3, Morfa Conwy Enterprise Park, Parc Caer Selon, Conwy, LL32 8FA
☎ (01492) 585287
✉ enquiries@conwybrewery.co.uk
🌐 conwybrewery.co.uk
Shop Mon-Fri 9am-5pm (please ring if making special trip)
Tours by arrangement

☺Conwy started brewing in 2003 and was the first brewery in Conwy for at least 100 years. Around 50 outlets are supplied. Seasonal beers: see website. Bottle-conditioned beers are also available including Welsh Honey Bitter (ABV 4.5%, brewed for Marks & Spencer). The brewery is currently developing a new range of beers named 'Heritage Ales', which will be available both cask and bottle conditioned.

Castle Bitter/Cwrw Castell (OG 1037, ABV 3.7%)

Welsh Pride/Balchder Cymru (OG 1040, ABV 4%)
A clean-tasting, malty bitter. Fruit in aroma and taste with a crisp, grainy mouthfeel and a lingering hoppy bitter aftertaste.

Celebration Ale (OG 1041, ABV 4.2%) ◆
Sweetish best bitter with a fruity nose and palate, and a good hoppy finish.

Honey Fayre/Cwrw Mel (OG 1044, ABV 4.5%) ◆
Amber best bitter with hints of honey sweetness in the taste balanced by an increasingly hoppy, bitter finish. Slightly watery mouthfeel for a beer of this strength.

For Cobdens Hotel, Capel Curig:

Cobdens Hotel Bitter/Cwrw Gwesty Cobdens (OG 1042, ABV 4.1%)

Copper Dragon SIBA

Copper Dragon Brewery Ltd, Snaygill Industrial Estate, Keighley Road, Skipton, North Yorkshire, BD23 2QR
☎ (01756) 702130 ✉ post@copperdragon.uk.com
🌐 copperdragon.uk.com
Bistro/Bar/Shop: Ring for opening hours as times vary for each
Tours by arrangement

☺Copper Dragon began brewing in 2003. Commissioned during October 2000, the purpose built 'double 60' brewhouse is the centrepiece of an impressive and technologically advanced operation. The site also boasts a visitor centre, shop, conference facilities and a bar/bistro. Beer distribution is widespread across northern England.

Black Gold (OG 1036, ABV 3.7%) ◆
This dark ale has a roast character throughout with coffee flavours and a tangy fruit note in the background. The finish is bitter and malty.

Best Bitter (OG 1036, ABV 3.8%) ◆
A traditional Yorkshire bitter with a gentle, hoppy, fruity aroma. A hoppy bitterness in the taste is balanced by nutty malt and hints of fruit and followed by a bitter, hoppy finish.

Golden Pippin (OG 1037, ABV 3.9%) ◆
This golden ale has an intense citrus aroma and flavour, characteristic of American Cascade hops. The dry, bitter astringency increases in the aftertaste.

Scotts 1816 (OG 1041, ABV 4.1%) ◆

A well-balanced, full-bodied, copper-coloured premium bitter with a tropical fruit character. Bitterness continues in the finish and leaves a dry, hoppy fruitiness.

Challenger IPA (OG 1042, ABV 4.4%) ◆
Amber-coloured, this is a best bitter in the traditional style. Initial maltiness gives way to fruit, hops and a growing bitter, dry finish.

Copthorne (NEW)

🏠 Copthorne Brewery, Nags Head, Old Great North Road, Sutton-on-Trent, Nottinghamshire, NG23 6QJ
☎ 07523 340989

Former Milestones brewer Dean Penney started production in 2010 in converted outbuildings at the Nags Head. The 3.5-barrel plant was previously installed at the former Cathedral Brewery in Lincoln.

Classic (ABV 3.6%)
A light, hoppy session ale.

Gold (ABV 4%)
A hoppy golden ale with a bitter finish.

Corvedale SIBA

🏠 Corvedale Brewery, Sun Inn, Corfton, Craven Arms, Shropshire, SY7 9DF
☎ (01584) 861239 ✉ normanspride@aol.com
🌐 corvedalebrewery.co.uk
Tours by arrangement

☺Brewing started in 1999 in a building behind the pub. Landlord Norman Pearce is also the brewer and he uses only British malt and hops, with water from a local borehole. One pub is owned and 100 outlets are supplied. Seasonal beers: Green Hop (ABV 4.5%, autumn), Teresa's Pride (ABV 4.8%, Jan). All beers are on sale in the pub in bottle-conditioned form and are suitable for vegetarians and vegans.

Molly Morgan (OG 1041, ABV 4%)

Katie's Pride (OG 1040, ABV 4.3%)

Norman's Pride (OG 1043, ABV 4.3%)
A golden amber beer with a refreshing, slightly hoppy taste and a bitter finish.

Farmer Ray Ale (OG 1045, ABV 4.5%)
A clear, ruby bitter with a smooth malty taste. Customers are invited to guess the hop!

St George's Stout (ABV 4.5%)

Dark and Delicious (OG 1045, ABV 4.6%)
A dark ruby beer with hops on the aroma and palate, and a sweet aftertaste.

Cotleigh SIBA

Cotleigh Brewery Ltd, Ford Road, Wiveliscombe, Somerset, TA4 2RE
☎ (01984) 624086 ✉ sales@cotleighbrewery.com
🌐 cotleighbrewery.co.uk
Shop Mon-Fri 9am-4pm
Tours by arrangement for select CAMRA groups

⊠ Situated in the historic brewing town of Wiveliscombe, Cotleigh has become one of the most successful independent breweries in the West Country. The brewery, which started trading in 1979, is housed in specially converted premises with a modern plant capable of producing 165 barrels a week. 300 pubs and 250 retail outlets are supplied; the beers are also widely available through select wholesalers. Cotleigh's charitable partner is The Hawk and Owl Trust. Seasonal beers: See website. Bottle-conditioned beers are also available.

Harrier (OG 1035, ABV 3.5%)
A golden beer with a delicate floral and fruity aroma and a refreshing, sweet and lightly hopped finish.

Tawny Owl (OG 1038, ABV 3.8%) ◆
Well-balanced, tawny-coloured bitter with plenty of malt and fruitiness on the nose, and malt to the fore in the taste, followed by hop fruit, developing to a satisfying bitter finish.

25 (OG 1040, ABV 4%)
A golden beer with a fresh aroma and fruit filled finish.

Golden Seahawk Premium Beer (OG 1042, ABV 4.2%) ◆
A gold, well-hopped premium bitter with a flowery hop aroma and fruity hop flavour, clean mouthfeel, leading to a dry, hoppy finish.

Barn Owl Premium Ale (OG 1045, ABV 4.5%) ◆
A pale to mid-brown beer with a good balance of malt and hops on the nose; a smooth, full-bodied taste where hops dominate, but balanced by malt, following through to the finish.

Buzzard Dark Ale (OG 1048, ABV 4.8%)
A traditional dark ale, deep copper red in colour. The chocolate malt gives a dry, nutty flavour with hints of amarone biscuit. The finish in the mouth is dry with a smoky but smooth finish.

Cotswold

Cotswold Brewing Co Ltd, College Farm, Lower Slaughter, Gloucestershire, GL54 2HN
☎ 07760 889100 ✉ info@cotswoldlager.com
⏺ cotswoldlager.com
Tours by arrangement

Cotswold Brewing Co is an independent producer of lager and speciality beers. The brewery was established in 2005 in rented accommodation on part of a working farm in Foscot, Oxfordshire. It moved to its current location in 2010. More than 60 outlets are supplied. Seasonal beers: Autumn Ale (ABV 4.3%), Winter Lager (ABV 5.3%). Bottle-conditioned beer is also available.

Three Point Eight Lager (OG 1035, ABV 3.8%)

Wheat Beer (OG 1040, ABV 4.2%)

Premium Lager (OG 1044, ABV 5%)

For Compass Brewery:

Baltic Night Stout (ABV 4.8%)

Isis Pale Ale (ABV 4.9%)

The King's Shipment (ABV 6%)

Cotswold Spring

Cotswold Spring Brewery Ltd, Dodington Ash, Chipping Sodbury, Gloucestershire, BS37 6RX
☎ (01454) 323088 ✉ info@cotswoldbrewery.com
⏺ cotswoldbrewery.com
Shop Mon-Fri 9am-5pm; Sat 10am-1pm
Tours by arrangement

⊙Cotswold Spring opened in 2005 with a 10-barrel refurbished plant that produces beers brewed using only the finest malted barley, subtle blends of hops and natural Cotswold spring water. All the beers are fermented in traditional vessels using specialist strains of yeast. They contain no artificial preservatives, flavourings or colourings. Seasonal beers: see website. Bottle-conditioned beers are also available.

Old English Rose (OG 1040, ABV 4%) ◆
Beautifully balanced quaffing ale with delicate floral aroma and hints of tropical fruit. Bittersweet finish.

Gloucestershire's Glory (OG 1041, ABV 4.1%)
A golden beer with a distinctive citrus hop nose, mouth-filling malt and fruit and a deep, dry finish. Brewed to celebrate the 1000th anniversary of Gloucestershire becoming a county.

Codrington Codger (OG 1042, ABV 4.2%) ◆
Mid-brown best bitter with the emphasis on malt. Nutty character.

Codrington Royal (OG 1045, ABV 4.5%) ◆
Ruby in colour with dark, sweet malt. Fruity with a hint of dandelion and burdock.

Cottage SIBA

Cottage Brewing Co Ltd, The Old Cheese Dairy, Hornblotton Road, Lovington, Somerset, BA7 7PS
☎ (01963) 240551
Tours by arrangement

⊠ The brewery was established in 1993 in West Lydford and moved to larger premises in 1996, doubling brewing capacity at the same time. In 2001, Cottage installed a 30-barrel plant. 1,500 outlets are supplied. The names of beers mostly follow a railway theme. Seasonal beers: Goldrush (ABV 5%), Santa's Steaming Ale (ABV 5.5%).

Southern Bitter (OG 1039, ABV 3.7%) ◆
Gold-coloured beer with malt and fruity hops on the nose. Malt and hops in the mouth with a long fruity, bitter finish.

Broadgauge Bitter (OG 1040, ABV 3.9%)
A light tawny-coloured session bitter with a floral aroma and a balanced bitter finish.

Champflower Ale (OG 1041, ABV 4.2%) ◆
Amber beer with a fruity hop aroma, full hop taste and powerful bitter finish.

Somerset & Dorset Ale (OG 1044, ABV 4.4%)
A well-hopped, malty brew, with a deep red colour.

Golden Arrow (OG 1043, ABV 4.5%) ◆
A hoppy golden bitter with a powerful floral bouquet, a fruity, full-bodied taste and a lingering dry, bitter finish.

Goldrush (OG 1051, ABV 5%)
A deep golden strong ale brewed with Cascade hops.

Norman's Conquest (OG 1066, ABV 7%) ◆
A dark strong ale, with plenty of fruit in the aroma and taste; rounded vinous, hoppy finish.

Country Life SIBA

Country Life Brewery, The Big Sheep, Abbotsham, Bideford, Devon, EX39 5AP

☎ (01237) 420808 ☎ 07971 267790
✉ simon@countrylifebrewery.co.uk
⊕ countrylifebrewery.co.uk
Shop 12-4pm daily
Tours by arrangement

⊠ The brewery is based at the Big Sheep tourist attraction that welcomes more than 100,000 visitors in the summer. The brewery offers a beer show and free samples in the shop during the peak season (Apr-Oct). A 15.5-barrel plant was installed in 2005, making Country Life the biggest brewery in north Devon. Bottling is now carried out on site. Around 100 outlets are supplied. All cask ales are also available in bottle-conditioned form plus Devonshire Ten-der (ABV 10%). Seasonal beer: Black Boar (ABV 5%, winter). All beers are also available in the brewery's managed pub, Laceys in Bridge St Bideford.

Old Appledore (OG 1037, ABV 3.7%)

Lacey's Ale (OG 1042, ABV 4.2%)

Pot Wallop (OG 1044, ABV 4.4%)

Golden Pig (OG 1046, ABV 4.7%)

Country Bumpkin (OG 1058, ABV 6%) 🍴

Cox & Holbrook EAB

Cox & Holbrook, Manor Farm, Brettenham Road, Buxhall, Suffolk, IP14 3DY
☎ (01449) 736323
Tours by arrangement

⊠ First opened in 1997, the brewery concentrates on producing a range of bitters, four of which are available at any one time, along with more specialised medium strength beers and milds. There is also a strong emphasis on the preservation and resurrection of rare and traditional styles. Bottle-conditioned versions of draught beers are available at varying times of the year.

Crown Dark Mild (OG 1037, ABV 3.6%) ◆
Thin tasting at first but plenty of malt, caramel and roast flavours burst through to give a thoroughly satisfying beer.

Shelley Dark (OG 1036, ABV 3.6%)
Full-flavoured and satisfying.

Beyton Bitter (OG 1038, ABV 3.8%)
A traditional bitter, pale tawny in colour, malty with Fuggles and Goldings hops.

Old Mill Bitter (OG 1038, ABV 3.8%)
Pale, hoppy and thirst quenching.

Rattlesden Best Bitter (OG 1043, ABV 4%)
A full-bodied and malty best bitter.

Albion Pale Ale (OG 1042, ABV 4.2%)
Refreshingly clean, hoppy ale.

Goodcock's Winner (OG 1050, ABV 5%)
An amber ale, rather malty yet not too heavy, with a sharp hop finish.

Ironoak Single Stout (OG 1051, ABV 5%)
Full-bodied with strong roast grain flavours and plenty of hop bitterness plus a distinct hint of oak.

Remus (OG 1051, ABV 5%)
An amber ale, soft on the palate with full hop flavours but subdued bitterness.

Stormwatch (OG 1052, ABV 5%)
An unusual premium pale ale with a full, slightly fruity flavour.

Stowmarket Porter (OG 1056, ABV 5%) ◆
Strong caramel flavour and lingering caramel aftertaste, balanced by full malt and roast flavours. The overall impression is of a very sweet beer.

Uncle Stan Single Brown Stout (OG 1053, ABV 5%)
Unusual soft malt and fruit flavours in a full and satisfying bit of history.

East Anglian Pale Ale (OG 1059, ABV 6%)
Well-matured, pale beer with a strong Goldings hops character.

Prentice Strong Dark Ale (OG 1083, ABV 8%)
A strong porter.

Croglin (NEW)

Croglin Brewery, Croglin Castle Hotel, South Road, Kirkby Stephen, Cumbria, CA17 4SY
☎ (01768) 371389
✉ anthony@croglinbrewery.co.uk
⊕ croglinbrewery.co.uk
Tours by arrangement

☺The brewery started in 2010 and is situated in the cellar of the Croglin Castle Hotel. There are plans to increase the range of beers.

Loki Original (OG 1037, ABV 3.7%)
An amber ale with initial sweetness overlaid with bitterness leading to a dry finish.

Trickster (OG 1041, ABV 4.2%)
A golden ale with a hint of bitterness.

Crondall

Crondall Brewing Co Ltd, Lower Old Park Farm, Dora's Green Lane, Dora's Green, nr Crondall, Hampshire, GU10 5DX
☎ (01252) 319000
✉ crondallbrewery@btinternet.com
⊕ crondallbrewery.co.uk
Shop Fri 3-7pm; Sat 10am-4.30pm

Crondall was established in 2005 using a 10-barrel plant in a converted granary barn. The company sells to the general public and to local free houses in the area, and supplies around 75 outlets. Seasonal beers include Easter Gold, Mr T's Wedding Ale, Ghoulies, Rocket Fuel, Crondall's Stocking Filler.

Best (ABV 4%) ◆
A pleasant and uncomplicated bitter. A modest hoppy bouquet and initially bitter palate lead to a satisfying dry, bitter aftertaste.

Sober as a Judge (ABV 4%) ◆
A complex brown bitter with a noticeably malty aroma. Toffee characteristics combine with a sharp flavour, which leads to a balanced finish but remains noticeably biscuity throughout.

Mitchell's Dream (ABV 4.5%) ◆
Sweet bitter with a pronounced malty nose. Maltiness remains present throughout with roast and caramel flavours building into a rich rounded aftertaste

Cropton SIBA

New Inn & Cropton Brewery, Cropton, Nr Pickering, North Yorkshire, YO18 8HH
☎ (01751) 417330 ✉ office@croptonbrewery.com
⊕ croptonbrewery.com
Tours by arrangement

THE BREWERIES

⊛Cropton was established in the cellars of the New Inn in 1984 on a five-barrel plant. This was extended in 1988, but by 1994 it had outgrown the cellar and a purpose-built brewery was installed behind the pub. A brand new state of the art brewery was opened in 2006. All the beers are available bottle conditioned and are suitable for vegetarians and vegans. Seasonal beer: Rudolph's Revenge (ABV 4.6%, winter).

Endeavour Ale (OG 1038, ABV 3.6%)
A light session ale, made with best quality hops, providing a refreshing drink with a delicate fruity aftertaste.

Two Pints (OG 1040, ABV 4%) ◆
A good, full-bodied bitter. Malt flavours initially dominate, with a touch of caramel, but the balancing hoppiness and residual sweetness come through.

Honey Gold (OG 1042, ABV 4.2%) ◆
A medium-bodied beer, ideal for summer drinking. Honey is apparent in both aroma and taste but does not overwhelm. Clean finish with a hint of hops.

Scoresby Stout (OG 1042, ABV 4.2%)
A traditional stout; rich, dark and aromatic.

Balmy Mild (OG 1044, ABV 4.4%)
Gives a mouthful of chocolate, complementing a light hoppiness.

Yorkshire Moors Bitter (OG 1046, ABV 4.6%)
A fine ruby beer brewed with Fuggles and Progress hops. A hoppy beer with a fruity aftertaste.

Blackout (OG 1051, ABV 5%)
A smooth, rich porter from an original 1930s recipe.

Monkmans Slaughter (OG 1060, ABV 6%) ◆
Rich tasting and warming; fruit and malt in the aroma and taste, with dark chocolate, caramel and autumn fruit notes. Subtle bitterness continues into the aftertaste.

Old Goat (OG 1080, ABV 8%)
A pale bitter with a strong malty flavour, finely balanced with English hops to give a hint of citrus and a surprisingly smooth finish for such a strong beer.

Crouch Vale SIBA

Crouch Vale Brewery Ltd, 23 Haltwhistle Road, South Woodham Ferrers, Essex, CM3 5ZA
☎ (01245) 322744 ✉ info@crouchvale.co.uk
⊕ crouchvale.co.uk
Shop Mon-Fri 8.30am-5pm
Tours by arrangement

⊠ Founded in 1981 by two CAMRA enthusiasts, Crouch Vale is now well established as a major craft brewer in Essex, having moved to larger premises in 2006. The company is also a major wholesaler of cask ale from other independent breweries, which it supplies to more than 100 outlets as well as beer festivals throughout the region. One tied house, the Queen's Head in Chelmsford, is owned. Seasonal beers: one beer available each month, details on website.

Essex Boys Bitter (OG 1035, ABV 3.5%) ◆
Light-bodied bitter with a malty, biscuity taste and an astringent finish.

Blackwater Mild (OG 1037, ABV 3.7%) ◆
A dark bitter rather than a true mild. Roasty and very bitter towards the end.

Brewers Gold (OG 1040, ABV 4%) ◆
Pale golden ale with a striking citrus nose. Sweet fruit and bitter hops are well matched throughout.

Crouch Best (OG 1040, ABV 4%) ◆
Dry, fruity session bitter with biscuity malt taste and pronounced bitterness in the finish.

Amarillo (OG 1050, ABV 5%)
A strong golden ale with a spicy aroma, juicy malt mouthfeel and an extremely long and bitter hop finish.

Crown

▤ **Crown Brewery, Hillsborough Hotel, 54-58 Langsett Road, Sheffield, South Yorkshire, S6 2UB**
☎ (0114) 232 2100 ✉ crown-brewery@btconnect.com ⊕ crownbrewery.co.uk
Tours by arrangement

⊠ The brewery was set up in 2001 with a four-barrel plant in the cellar of the hotel. It was sold to Edale Brewery in 2004 and has been owned by the Walker family since 2006. Around 25 outlets are supplied direct. Seasonal beer: Wheetie-Bits (ABV 4.4%), Middlewood Mild (ABV 3.8%), Primrose Pale Ale (ABV 4.2%). Bottle-conditioned beers are also available.

Middlewood Mild (OG 1039, ABV 3.8%) ◆
A dark traditional mild with flavours of chocolate and liquorice, and toffee in the aftertaste.

Hillsborough Pale Ale/HPA (OG 1038, ABV 3.9%) ◆
A straw-coloured bitter with a citrus nose, flowery head and petal undertones.

Traditional Bitter (OG 1039, ABV 4%) ◆
A traditional style, amber-coloured malty bitter.

Primrose Pale Ale (OG 1042, ABV 4.2%) ◆
Fairly bitter yellow ale with medium hoppiness and hints of grapefruit in the aftertaste.

Loxley Gold (OG 1043, ABV 4.5%) ◆
Golden coloured premium pale ale, hoppy with a clean, dry finish.

Stannington Stout (OG 1050, ABV 5%) ◆
Jet black, rich tasting, bitter yet smooth.

Samuel Berry's IPA (OG 1049, ABV 5.1%) ◆
Fairly dark IPA style fruity bitter, with some sweetness in the aftertaste.

Cuillin

▤ **Cuillin Brewery Ltd, Sligachan Hotel, Sligachan, Carbost, Isle of Skye, IV47 8SW**
☎ (01478) 650204 ☎ 07795 250808
✉ steve@cuillinbrewery.co.uk
⊕ cuillinbrewery.co.uk
Tours by arrangement

⊛The five-barrel brewery opened in 2004 and is situated in central Skye, close to the famous Cuillin mountain. The water provides a distinctive colour and taste to the ales. Specials are brewed throughout the year. The brewery is closed in winter. Seasonal beer: Eagle Ale (ABV 3.8%, Easter-Aug), Skye Amber (ABV 4.5%).

Skye Ale (ABV 4.1%)

Black Face (ABV 4.3%)
A good balance of blackcurrant fruit and malts highlight this dark ruby red strong mild. Liquorice and roast also evident in the creamy mouthfeel.

Glamaig (ABV 4.5%)

Pinnacle (OG 1047, ABV 4.7%) ◆
The hoppy and fruity nose leads to more hop and plenty of pale malt flavour in this very drinkable golden amber bitter.

Cumberland

Cumberland Breweries Ltd, The Green, Great Corby, Carlisle, Cumbria, CA4 8LR
☎ (01228) 560899
✉ enquiries@cumberlandbreweries.co.uk
⊕ cumberlandbreweries.co.uk
Tours by arrangement

Cumberland was established in 2009.

Corby Ale (ABV 3.8%)

Cumbrian Legendary SIBA

Cumbrian Legendary Ales Ltd, Old Hall Brewery, Esthwaite Water, Hawkshead, Cumbria, LA22 0QF
☎ (01539) 436436
✉ info@cumbrianlegendaryales.com
⊕ cumbrianlegendaryales.com
Tours by arrangement

The Old Hall Brewery was established in 2006 in a renovated barn on the shores of Esthwaite Water. It was taken over in early 2009 by Loweswater Brewery with Hayley Barton as head brewer. 50 outlets are supplied. The success of Loweswater Gold has meant the brewery is thriving and extra fermenting and conditioning tanks have been installed. All brewing and commercial activities for Loweswater Brewery have transferred to this site.

Loweswater Pale Ale (OG 1035, ABV 3.6%) ◆
A refreshing, straw-coloured ale with plenty of pithy fruitiness and a dry finish.

Melbreak Bitter (OG 1035.5, ABV 3.7%)

Dickie Doodle (OG 1040, ABV 3.9%)
A golden bitter with distinctive flavour and aroma of American Cascade hops.

Langdale (OG 1037.5, ABV 4%)

Grasmoor Dark Ale (OG 1041, ABV 4.3%)

Loweswater Gold (OG 1041, ABV 4.3%)

For Loweswater Brewery:

Gold (ABV 4.3%)

Daleside

Daleside Brewery Ltd, Camwal Road, Starbeck, Harrogate, North Yorkshire, HG1 4PT
☎ (01423) 880022
✉ enquiries@dalesidebrewery.com
⊕ dalesidebrewery.com
Shop Mon-Fri 9am-4pm (Off sales only)

Opened in 1991 in Harrogate with a 20-barrel plant, beer is now supplied to around 200 local outlets, via wholesalers nationally and through SIBA's DDS. Seasonal beers: see website.

Bitter (OG 1039, ABV 3.7%) ◆
Pale brown in colour, this well-balanced, hoppy beer is complemented by fruity bitterness and a hint of sweetness, leading to a long, bitter finish.

Blonde (OG 1040, ABV 3.9%) ◆
A pale golden beer with a predominantly hoppy aroma and taste, leading to a refreshing hoppy, bitter but short finish.

Old Leg Over (OG 1043, ABV 4.1%)
Well-balanced mid brown refreshing beer that leads to an equally well-balanced fruity bitter aftertaste.

Old Lubrication (ABV 4.1%)

Special Bitter (OG 1043, ABV 4.1%)
A mid-amber beer with a malty nose and a hint of fruitiness. Hops and malt carry over to leave a clean, hoppy aftertaste.

Bobek Export (ABV 5%)

Monkey Wrench (ABV 5.3%)

Morocco Ale (ABV 5.5%)

Dare

Dare Brewery Ltd, Stable Store, Home Farm Business Park, Whittlebury, Northamptonshire, NN12 8XS
☎ 07812 366369 ✉ john.evans@nomadbeers.com

Dare Brewery opened in 2007 using a 5.5-barrel plant in a refurbished barn at the Falcon Inn in Godreaman. In 2010 the brewery was sold and moved to its current address in Northamptonshire.

Whittlebury SPA (ABV 3.7%)

Whittlebury Best Bitter (ABV 4.1%)

Green Dragon (ABV 4.4%)

Falcon Flyer (ABV 5.2%)

Old Daredevil (ABV 7.9%)

Dark Horse

Dark Horse Brewery, Coonlands Laithe, Hetton, Nr. Skipton, North Yorkshire, BD23 6LY
☎ (01756) 730555

Formerly the Wharfedale Brewery, Dark Horse opened in late 2008 with new owners. The brewery is based in an old hay barn within the Yorkshire Dales National Park. 15 outlets are supplied direct. Bottle-conditioned beer is also available.

Best Bitter (OG 1038, ABV 3.8%) ◆
This mid-brown bitter has dark malts and fruit on the nose, which continue into the taste. Bitterness increases in the finish, with a spicy hint. Background roast throughout.

Hetton Pale Ale (OG 1041, ABV 4.2%) ◆
A well-balanced and full-bodied golden pale ale with bitterness on the palate overlaying a malty base and a strong fruit character.

Dark Star SIBA

Dark Star Brewing Co Ltd, 22 Star Road Industrial Estate, Partridge Green, Horsham, West Sussex, RH13 8RA
☎ (01403) 713085 ✉ info@darkstarbrewing.co.uk
⊕ darkstarbrewing.co.uk
Shop Mon-Fri 9am-5pm; Sat 9am-1pm
Tours by arrangement

Dark Star started as a hobby in the cellar of the Evening Star in Brighton, moved to a 15-barrel brewery near Haywards Heath in 2001 and in 2010 moved to its current premises using a 45-barrel plant. The range of beers is divided between

THE BREWERIES

permanent, seasonal and monthly specials. More than 150 outlets are supplied. Seasonal beers: See website. Bottle-conditioned beer is also available.

Hophead (OG 1040, ABV 3.8%) 🍺 ◆
A golden-coloured bitter with a fruity/hoppy aroma and a citrus/bitter taste and aftertaste. Flavours remain strong to the end.

Best Bitter (OG 1041, ABV 4%)
A malt flavour with a hint of smokiness is complemented by East Kent Goldings hops.

Espresso (OG 1043, ABV 4.2%) 🍺 🍺
A black beer brewed with freshly ground coffee.

American Pale Ale (OG 1047, ABV 4.7%) 🍺
Brewed with American hops and yeast.

Festival (OG 1050, ABV 5%)
A chestnut, bronze-coloured bitter with a smooth mouthfeel and fruit aroma.

Original (OG 1052, ABV 5%) 🍺 ◆
Dark, full-bodied ale with a roast malt aroma and a dry, bitter, stout-like finish.

DarkTribe

🍺 **DarkTribe Brewery, Dog & Gun, High Street, East Butterwick, Lincolnshire, DN17 3AJ**
☎ (01724) 782324 ✉ dixie@darktribe.co.uk
🌐 darktribe.co.uk
Tours by arrangement

☺A small brewery was built during the summer of 1996 in a workshop at the bottom of his garden by Dave 'Dixie' Dean. In 2005 Dixie bought the Dog & Gun pub and moved the 2.5-barrel brewing equipment there. The beers generally follow a marine theme, recalling Dixie's days as an engineer in the Merchant Navy and his enthusiasm for sailing. Local outlets are supplied. Seasonal beers: Dixie's Midnight Runner (ABV 6.5%, Dec-Jan), Dark Destroyer (ABV 9.7%, Aug onwards), Daft Bat (ABV 4.9%, Halloween), Starburst (ABV 5.1%, Bonfire Night), Ruddy Christmas (ABV 4.3%, Dec).

Dixie's Mild (ABV 3.6%)

Honey Mild (ABV 3.6%)

Admiral Sidney Smith (ABV 3.8%)

Full Ahead (ABV 3.8%) ◆
A malty smoothness is backed by a slightly fruity hop that gives a good bitterness to this amber-brown bitter.

Captain Floyd (ABV 3.9%)

Albacore (ABV 4%)

Red Duster (ABV 4%)

Red Rock (ABV 4.2%)

Sternwheeler (ABV 4.2%)

Intelligent Whale (ABV 4.3%)

RAMP (Richard's Amazing Magical Potion) (ABV 4.3%)

Bucket Hitch (ABV 4.4%)

Dixie's Bollards (ABV 4.5%)

Dr Griffin's Mermaid (ABV 4.5%)

Old Gaffer (ABV 4.5%)

Galleon (ABV 4.7%) ◆

A tasty, golden, smooth, full-bodied ale with fruity hops and consistent malt. The thirst-quenching bitterness lingers into a well-balanced finish.

Twin Screw (ABV 5.1%) ◆
A fruity, rose-hip tasting beer, red in colour. Good malt presence with a dry, hoppy bitterness coming through in the finish.

Dartmoor SIBA

Dartmoor Brewery Ltd, The Brewery, Station Road, Princetown, Dartmoor, Devon, PL20 6QX
☎ (01822) 890789 ✉ ale@dartmoorbrewery.co.uk
🌐 dartmoorbrewery.co.uk

⊠ Established in 1994, it is the highest brewery in England at 1,400 feet above sea level. It moved into a new purpose-built building in 2005 with equipment manufactured in Germany. In early 2010 the capacity was increased to 300 barrels per week by the addition of two 60-barrel fermenters. The brewery changed name from Princetown to Dartmoor in May 2008 with no change to the structure or ownership of the company. Bottle-conditioned ales are available. It is the first brewery to market its own brand of crisps, Jail Ale Crisps. Bottle-conditioned beers are available.

Dartmoor IPA (OG 1039.5, ABV 4%) ◆
There is a flowery hop aroma and taste with a bitter aftertaste to this full-bodied, amber-coloured beer.

Legend (OG 1043.5, ABV 4.4%)

Jail Ale (OG 1047.5, ABV 4.8%) ◆
Hops and fruit predominate in the flavour of this mid-brown beer, which has a slightly sweet aftertaste.

Dartmouth

🍺 **Dartmouth Brewery, Dartmouth Inn, 63 East Street, Newton Abbot, Devon, TQ12 2JP**
☎ 07969 860184
Tours by arrangement

Dartmouth Brewery was established in 2007 and only supplies the Dartmouth Inn. Brewing is currently suspended.

Big 5 (OG 1050, ABV 5%)

Darwin SIBA

Darwin Brewery Ltd, 63 Back Tatham Street, Sunderland, Tyne & Wear, SR1 2QE
☎ (0191) 514 4746 ✉ info@darwinbrewery.com
🌐 darwinbrewery.com
Tours by arrangement (based at Brewlab)

☺The Darwin Brewery first brewed in 1994 and expanded with the construction of its Wearside brewery in central Sunderland in 2002 after a move from the Hodges brewhouse in Crook, Co Durham. Darwin specialises in recreations of past beers and also produces trial beers from the Brewlab training and research unit at the University of Sunderland, and experiments in the production of novel and overseas styles for occasional production. Output from the brewery grew significantly in 2005. The brewery also produces the beers of the closed High Force Brewery in Teesdale. A changing portfolio of unique brews (developed by Brewlab) is available in limited edition bottles.

Sunderland Best (OG 1041, ABV 3.9%)
A light and smooth-tasting session bitter, full of hop character and moderate bitterness. Amber malt provides a smooth body and creamy character.

Evolution Ale (OG 1041, ABV 4%)
A dark amber, full-bodied bitter with a malty flavour and a clean, bitter aftertaste.

Ghost Ale (OG 1041, ABV 4.1%)

Richmond Ale (OG 1047, ABV 4.5%)

Rolling Hitch (OG 1055, ABV 5.2%)

Killer Bee (OG 1065, ABV 6%)
A strong but light ale matured with honey.

Extinction Ale (OG 1084, ABV 8.3%)

For High Force Hotel:

Forest XB (OG 1044, ABV 4.2%)

Cauldron Snout (OG 1056, ABV 5.6%)

Dawkins SIBA

Dawkins Ales, The Now Thus Brewery, Unit 7, Timsbury Workshop Estate, Hayeswood Road, Timsbury, Bath, BA2 0HQ
☎ (01761) 472242 ✉ glen@dawkins-taverns.co.uk
🌐 dawkins-ales.co.uk
Tours by arrangement

⊗ The established Dawkins Taverns group of independent Bristol pubs bought the former Matthews Brewery in late 2009. The regular Matthews recipes continue unchanged under the Dawkins banner. Five pubs are owned and around 80 outlets are supplied direct. Green Barrel Organic is certified by the Soil Association. Seasonal beers: see website.

35 Organic (OG 1034, ABV 3.5%)
A pale gold, light and quenching brew with plenty of flavour for its strength.

Brassknocker (OG 1037, ABV 3.8%) ◆
A pale gold beer with a full, hoppy, citrus flavour and a satisfying dry finish.

Double Dawkins (OG 1039, ABV 4%)
Amber-coloured, malty and well-rounded best bitter that is not too hoppy.

Green Barrel Organic (OG 1039, ABV 4%)
Am amber, classically well balanced best bitter with a distinctively refreshing, clean bitter finish.

Bob Wall (OG 1041, ABV 4.2%) ◆
Fruity best bitter; roasty hint with intense forest fruit and rich malt flavour continuing to a good balanced finish.

Deeside

Hillside Brewery Ltd t/a Deeside Brewery, c/o Deeside Activity Park, Dess, Aboyne, Aberdeenshire, AB34 5BD
☎ (01339) 883777 ☎ 07966 033451
✉ rob@deesidebrewery.com
🌐 deesidebrewery.co.uk
Tours by arrangement

⊗ Originally established as Home Brewery (Hillside Brewery) in 2005. The brewery relocated to the Deeside Activity Park in 2008 with a new 10-barrel plant. 50 outlets are supplied direct. Seasonal beers: see website. Bottle-conditioned beers are also available.

Brude (OG 1036, ABV 3.8%)

Macbeth (OG 1038, ABV 4.1%)

Nechtan (OG 1037, ABV 4.1%)

Talorcan (OG 1051, ABV 4.5%)

Dent SIBA

Dent Brewery Ltd, Hollins, Cowgill, Dent, Cumbria, LA10 5TQ
☎ (015396) 25326 ✉ paul@dentbrewery.co.uk
🌐 dentbrewery.co.uk
Merchandise available from George & Dragon, Dent
Tours by arrangement

⊗ Dent was set up in 1990 in a converted barn next to a former farmhouse in the Yorkshire Dales National Park. In 2005 the brewery was completely refurbished and capacity expanded. One pub is owned. Over 150 outlets are supplied direct.

Ale (OG 1036, ABV 3.7%)
A copper-coloured refreshing light session ale with hints of grapefruit in the nose accompanying hops and malt in the taste leading to a light bitter aftertaste.

Golden Fleece (OG 1035, ABV 3.7%)
A thirst-quenching light and hoppy ale with a balance of sweetness to the taste.

Porter (OG 1042, ABV 3.8%)
A dark traditional porter with delicate tones of five different malts, a rich, smooth head and lingering, light bitter aftertaste.

Aviator (OG 1039, ABV 4%) ◆
This medium-bodied amber ale is characterised by strong citrus and hoppy flavours that develop into a long bitter finish.

Rambrau (OG 1042, ABV 4.5%) 🗍
A cask-conditioned lager.

Ramsbottom Strong Ale (OG 1042, ABV 4.5%) ◆
This complex, mid-brown beer has a warming, dry, bitter finish to follow its unusual combination of roast, bitter, fruity and sweet flavours.

Kamikaze (OG 1047, ABV 5%) ◆
Hops and fruit dominate this full-bodied, golden, strong bitter, with a dry bitterness growing in the aftertaste.

T'owd Tup (OG 1056, ABV 6%) ◆
A rich, full-flavoured, strong stout with a coffee aroma. The dominant roast character is balanced by a warming sweetness and a raisiny, fruitcake taste that linger on into the finish.

Derby SIBA

Derby Brewing Co Ltd, Masons Place Business Park, Nottingham Road, Derby, Derbyshire, DE21 6AQ
☎ (01332) 242888 ☎ 07887 556788
✉ sales@derbybrewing.co.uk 🌐 derbybrewing.co.uk
Tours by arrangement

⊗ A purpose-built brewery, established 2004, in the varnish workshop of the old Masons Paintworks by owner/brewer Trevor Harris, former brewer at the Brunswick Inn, Derby. The business has grown massively over the years and two pubs are now owned – the Brewery Tap, Derby's Royal Standard and the Greyhound. More than 180 outlets are supplied. Seasonal beer: White Christmas (ABV 5.5%), Christmas Porter (ABV 5%). Two new beers are brewed each month.

Hop Till You Drop (OG 1039, ABV 3.9%)

Triple Hop (OG 1041, ABV 4.1%)

Business As Usual (OG 1044, ABV 4.4%)

Dashingly Dark (OG 1045, ABV 4.5%)

Double Mash (OG 1046, ABV 4.6%)

Penny's Porter (OG 1046, ABV 4.6%)

Old Intentional (OG 1050, ABV 5%)

Quintessential (OG 1058, ABV 5.8%)

Derventio SIBA

Derventio Brewery Ltd, The Brewhouse, Trusley Brook Farm, Trusley, Derbyshire, DE6 5JP
(01283) 733111
enquiries@derventiobrewery.co.uk
derventiobrewery.co.uk
Tours by arrangement

Derventio Brewery was established in 2005 and first brewed in early 2006. A shop and management training centre opened in 2008, followed by a brewery tap, which is available for hire. The brewery is involved in sponsorship of local cricket teams as well as numerous outside events. Derventio is also one of the founder members of the Derbyshire Brewers' Collective. Seasonal beers: Barbarian (ABV 5.5%), Winter Solstice (ABV 5%), Summer Solstice (ABV 4%), Chariot (ABV 4.3%), Anubis (ABV 4.4%, Mar-Jun).

Roman Pale Ale/RPA (ABV 3.6%)

Aquilifer (ABV 3.8%)

Maia Mild (ABV 4%)

Cupid (ABV 4.1%)

Emperor's Whim (ABV 4.2%)

Centurion (ABV 4.3%)

Arminius (ABV 5%)

Venus (OG 1048, ABV 5%)

Caesar (ABV 6%)

Versuvius (ABV 6.5%)

Derwent Rose

See Consett Ale Works

Derwent

Derwent Brewery, Units 2a-2c, Station Road Industrial Estate, Silloth, Cumbria, CA7 4AG
(01697) 331522 sales@derwentbrewery.co.uk
derwentbrewery.co.uk

Derwent was set up in 1996 in Cockermouth and moved to Silloth in 1998. It is involved with the Silloth Beer Festival every September and has supplied Carlisle State Bitter to the House of Commons, a beer that recreates one produced by the former state-owned Carlisle Brewery. Around 200 outlets are supplied in the north of England. Seasonal beers: see website.

Carlisle State Bitter (OG 1036, ABV 3.7%)
Amber bitter with a fruity mouthfeel and slightly astringent bitterness that fades in the finish.

W&M Mild (OG 1036, ABV 3.7%)

Parsons Pledge (OG 1039, ABV 4%)
Amber ale with a biscuity tang and a slightly fruity finish.

Blonde (OG 1039, ABV 4.2%)

Mutineer (OG 1043, ABV 4.4%)

W&M Pale Ale (OG 1042, ABV 4.4%)
A sweet, fruity, hoppy beer with a bitter finish.

Devil's Dyke

Devil's Dyke Brewery, Dyke's End, 8 Fair Green, Reach, Cambridgeshire, CB25 0JD
(01638) 743816
Tours by arrangement

Devil's Dyke came on stream in 2007 using a plant bought from the Red Rose Brewery. It is situated in outbuildings to the rear of the Dyke's End pub, the freehold of which was bought by the village in the late 1990s to save it from being turned back into a private house. Several outlets are supplied in the area. Seasonal beer: IPA (ABV 5.5%).

Bitter (OG 1036.7, ABV 3.8%)

No. 7 Pale Ale (OG 1039.8, ABV 4.1%)

Victorian (OG 1044, ABV 4.7%)

Strong Mild (OG 1049, ABV 5%)

London Porter (ABV 5.2%)

Devon

Devon Ales Ltd, Mansfield Arms, 7 Main Street, Sauchie, Clackmannanshire, FK10 3JR
(01259) 722020 info@devonales.com
devonales.com
Tours by arrangement

Established in 1992 to produce high quality cask ales for the Mansfield Arms, Sauchie, Devon is the oldest operating brewery in the county. A second pub, The Inn at Muckhart, was purchased in 1994.

Original (OG 1038, ABV 3.8%)

Thick Black (OG 1042, ABV 4.2%)

Pride (OG 1046, ABV 4.8%)

Devon Earth

Devon Earth Brewery, Office: 7 Fernham Terrace, Torquay Road, Paignton, Devon, TQ3 2AQ
07927 397871 info@devonearthbrewery.co.uk
devonearthbrewery.co.uk

Devon Earth was launched in 2008 on a 2.5-barrel plant located on the edge of Dartmoor (Buckfastleigh) and is run on a part-time basis. It supplies beer festivals and pubs, mainly in the Torbay area. As well as three regular ales, seasonal specials are also produced.

Devon Earth (ABV 4.2%)

Grounded (ABV 4.7%)

Lost in the Woods (ABV 5.2%)

Digfield

Digfield Ales, North Lodge Farm, Barnwell, Peterborough, Cambridgeshire, PE8 5RJ
☎ (01832) 293248 ✉ brewery@digfield-ales.co.uk
digfield-ales.co.uk

With equipment from the Cannon Brewery, Digfield Ales started brewing in 2005 as part of a farm diversification scheme. Digfield operates on a seven-barrel plant run by three partners. It supplies the local Barnwell pub, the Montagu Arms, as well as 30 other outlets. Seasonal beer: March Hare (ABV 4.4%, spring).

Fools Nook (OG 1037, ABV 3.8%)
The floral aroma, dominated by lavender and honey, belies the hoppy bitterness that comes through in the taste of this golden ale. A fruity balance lasts.

Barnwell Bitter (OG 1039, ABV 4%)
A fruity, sulphurous aroma introduces a beer in which sharp bitterness is balanced by dry, biscuity malt.

Shacklebush (OG 1044, ABV 4.5%)
Dry tawny bitter with a roasty, astringent finish.

I.P.A. (OG 1046, ABV 4.7%)
A strong flavoured pale ale with a hoppy aroma and a dry, lingering finish.

Mad Monk (OG 1047, ABV 4.8%)
Fruity beer with bitter, earthy hops in evidence.

Discovery

Discovery Ales, Brook Farm, Packington Lane, Little Packington, Warwickshire, CV7 7HN
☎ (01675) 463809

Correspondence: 52 Doris Road, Coleshill, Birmingham, 39, B46 1EJ
✉ simonamanda@btinternet.com

Discovery Ales began brewing on a part-time basis in 2007 on a 2.5-barrel plant.

Pioneer (OG 1039.6, ABV 4.2%)

Darwin's Delight (OG 1041.1, ABV 4.4%)

Lightening Frank (ABV 4.5%)
Light brown in colour with a gently sharp bitterness and clean finish.

Colombus (OG 1043.4, ABV 4.7%)
A copper-coloured, well-balanced beer with a pleasant mouthfeel and smooth bitterness.

Newton's Cream (OG 1044.2, ABV 4.8%)
A pale ale made using only pale malt and hopped with First Gold. An uncomplicated, satisfying ale.

Dynamite (OG 1045.8, ABV 5%)
A copper-coloured beer with a pleasant aroma that drinks below its gravity.

Doghouse

See Allsaints

Dolphin

Dolphin Brewery Ltd, The Dolphin, 48 St Michael's Street, Shrewsbury, Shropshire, SY1 2EZ
☎ (01743) 350419 ✉ mark@dolphin-shrewsbury.co.uk dolphin-shrewsbury.co.uk

Dolphin was launched in 2000 and upgraded to a 4.5-barrel plant in 2001. In 2006 both the pub and brewery were taken over by present owner Mark Oseland. After pub alterations the brewery was re-opened with a new range of beers.

Dizzy Lizzy (OG 1042, ABV 4.2%)

Ollie Dog (OG 1042, ABV 4.2%)

Donnington SIBA IFBB

Donnington Brewery, Upper Swell, Stow-on-the-Wold, Gloucestershire, GL54 1EP
☎ (01451) 830603 ✉ info@donningtonales.com
donningtonales.com
Shop Mon-Fri 8am-3pm

Thomas Arkell bought a 13th-century watermill in 1827 and began brewing on the site in 1865; the waterwheel is still in use. Thomas' decendant Claude owned and ran the brewery until his death in 2007, supplying 20 outlets direct. It has now passed to Claude's cousin, James Arkell, also of Arkells Brewery, Swindon (qv). Bottle-conditioned beer is available.

BB (OG 1035, ABV 3.6%)
A pleasant amber bitter with a slight hop aroma, a good balance of malt and hops in the mouth and a bitter aftertaste.

SBA (OG 1045, ABV 4.4%)
Malt dominates over bitterness in the subtle flavour of this premium bitter, which has a hint of fruit and a dry malty finish.

Dorking SIBA

Brewery at Dorking Ltd, Engine Shed, Dorking West Station Yard, Station Road, Dorking, Surrey, RH4 1HF
☎ (01306) 877988 ✉ info@dorkingbrewery.com
dorkingbrewery.com
Tours by arrangement

Dorking started brewing in July 2008 and supplies an increasing number of local pubs and clubs. Seasonal beers are available.

DB Dry Hop Gold (ABV 3.8%)
A hoppy bitterness dominates this golden coloured ale but balancing malt is also present. New Zealand hops result in a green hop character. Dry bitter finish.

DB Number One (ABV 4.2%)
Hoppy best bitter with underlying orange fruit notes. Some balancing malt sweetness in the taste leads to a dry bitter finish.

Red India Ale (ABV 5%)

DB Winter Ruby (ABV 5.2%)
Fruity dark old ale with roast malt evident throughout. Raisin and banana notes. Slightly sweet but with a dryness coming through.

Northdowns Bel (ABV 5.5%)

Dorset SIBA

Dorset Brewing Co Ltd, Hope Square, Weymouth, Dorset, DT4 8TR
☎ (01305) 777515 ✉ info@dbcales.com
dbcales.com
Shop at Brewers Quay 10am-5.30pm daily
Tours by arrangement via Timewalk at Brewers Quay or private tours via DBC direct

⊗ The Dorset Brewing Company, formerly the Quay Brewery, is the most recent in a long succession of breweries in Hope Square. Brewing first started there in 1256 but in more recent times it was famous as the home of the Devenish and Groves breweries. Brewing stopped in 1986 but restarted in 1996, when Giles Smeath set up Quay in part of the old brewery buildings. His beers are available in local pubs and selected outlets throughout the South-west. In 2008 Dorset took over the running of Dorchester's brewpub, Tom Brown's (Goldfinch Brewery). Seasonal beers: see website.

Weymouth Harbour Master (OG 1036, ABV 3.6%) ◆
Light, easy-drinking session beer. Well-balanced, with a long, bittersweet, citrus finish.

Weymouth Best Bitter (OG 1038, ABV 4%) ◆
Complex bitter ale with strong malt and fruit flavours despite its light gravity.

Chesil (OG 1038, ABV 4.1%)

Jurassic (OG 1040, ABV 4.2%) ◆
Clean-tasting, easy-drinking bitter. Well balanced with lingering bitterness after moderate sweetness.

Ammonite (OG 1043, ABV 4.5%)

Durdle Door (OG 1046, ABV 5%) ◆
A tawny hue and fruity aroma with a hint of pear drops and good malty undertone, joined by hops and a little roast malt in the taste. Lingering bittersweet finish.

For Goldfinch Brewery (qv):

Stormbroker (ABV 4%)

Tom Brown's (ABV 4%)

Flashman's Clout (ABV 4.5%)

Midnight Sun (ABV 4.5%)

Dorset Piddle

Dorset Piddle Brewery Ltd, Unit 7, Enterprise Park, Piddlehinton, Dorchester, Dorset, DT2 7UA
☎ (01305) 849336 🌐 dorsetpiddlebrewery.co.uk

Dorset Piddle began brewing in late 2007 on an eight-barrel plant. Monthly seasonals are available as are bottle-conditioned beers.

Jimmy Riddle (ABV 3.7%) ◆
Pale brown session beer with a good depth of malty flavours for its strength.

Piddle (ABV 4.1%) ◆
An enjoyable, well-balanced bitter with a lingering bitter finish.

Cocky Hop (ABV 4.7%)

Yogi Beer (ABV 4.9%)

Silent Slasher (ABV 5.1%)

Double Maxim

Double Maxim Beer Co Ltd, Maxim Brewery, 1 Gadwall Road, Rainton Bridge South, Houghton le Spring, County Durham, DH4 5NL
☎ (0191) 584 8844 ✉ admin@dmbc.org.uk
🌐 maximbrewery.co.uk
Tours by arrangement

⊗ Initially the former Vaux beer, Double Maxim, was contract brewed by Robinsons for this company but in summer 2007 it opened its own 20-barrel plant on the site of the old Canongate Brewery. 100 outlets are supplied direct and four pubs are owned, three serving cask ales.

Maxim Sladek (OG 1038, ABV 3.8%)
A deep golden beer that has a classic hop aroma with a touch of citrus, a full-bodied taste with residual malt flavour and subtle hop bitterness that leaves a lingering, balanced aftertaste.

Samson (OG 1040, ABV 4%)
A distinctive, well-balanced beer with a lingering, smooth flavour.

Ward's Best Bitter (OG 1040, ABV 4%)
A subtle aroma with hop overtones complements the taste of this malty, full-flavoured traditional Yorkshire Bitter.

Double Maxim (OG 1048, ABV 4.7%)
A brown ale with a well-balanced, smooth flavour leaving a pleasant, slightly sweet aftertaste.

Maximus (OG 1062, ABV 6%)
A strong premium ale, dark ruby in colour, with a sweet liquorice taste. Warming and easy to drink.

Dow Bridge

Dow Bridge Brewery, 2-3 Rugby Road, Catthorpe, Leicestershire, LE17 6DA
☎ (01788) 869121
✉ dowbridge.brewery@virgin.net
🌐 dowbridgebrewery.co.uk
Tours by arrangement

⊗ Dow Bridge commenced brewing in 2001 and takes its name from a local bridge where Watling Street spans the River Avon. The brewery adheres to using English whole hops and malt with no adjuncts or additives. The brewery expanded in 2006 but is looking to relocate as extra capacity is needed. Over 50 outlets are supplied direct. Seasonal beers: Summer Light (ABV 3.6%), Festivas (ABV 4.6%), Praetorian Porter (ABV 5%). Bottle-conditioned beers are also available.

Bonum Mild (OG 1035, ABV 3.5%) ◆
Complex dark brown, full-flavoured mild, with strong malt and roast flavours to the fore and continuing into the aftertaste, leading to a long, satisfying finish.

Acris (OG 1037, ABV 3.8%)

Legion (OG 1038, ABV 3.9%)

Centurion (OG 1039, ABV 4%)

Ratae'd (OG 1042, ABV 4.3%) ◆
Tawny-coloured, bitter beer in which bitter and hop flavours dominate, to the detriment of balance, leading to a long, bitter and astringent aftertaste.

Dow Bridge Dark (DBD) (OG 1043, ABV 4.4%)

Fosse Ale (OG 1046, ABV 4.8%)

For Morgan Ales:

Chedhams Ale (OG 1039, ABV 3.8%)

Downton SIBA

Downton Brewery Co Ltd, Unit 11, Batten Road, Downton Industrial Estate, Downton, Wiltshire, SP5 3HU
☎ (01725) 513313
✉ martins@downtonbrewery.com
🌐 downtonbrewery.com

⊗ Downton was set up in 2003 with equipment leased from the Hop Back Brewery (qv). The brewery has a 20-barrel brew length and three fermenting vessels producing 1,500 barrels a year. Seasonal and ever-changing monthly specials are available in addition to five regular beers. Around 80 outlets are supplied direct. Seasonal beers: see website. Bottle-conditioned beers are also available.

New Forest Ale (OG 1037, ABV 3.8%)

Quadhop (OG 1038, ABV 3.9%)

Elderquad (OG 1039, ABV 4%)

Honey Blonde (OG 1041, ABV 4.3%)

Dark Delight (OG 1053, ABV 5.5%)

Draycott EAB (NEW)

Draycott Brewery, Low Farm, 30 Mill Road, Buckden, Cambridgeshire, PE19 5SS
☎ (01480) 812404 ☎ 07740 374710
✉ sales@draycottbrewery.co.uk
draycottbrewery.co.uk

Jon and Jane Draycott set up Draycott Brewery in 2009 and produce bottle-conditioned ales including Buckden Bronze Bitter (ABV 4.1%). The beers are delivered by hand to local outlets and to a shop catering for holiday makers at Dunster Beach in Somerset where the owners have a holiday chalet.

Driftwood

Driftwood Brewery, Driftwood Spars Hotel, Trevaunance Cove, St Agnes, Cornwall, TR5 0RT
☎ (01872) 552428 ✉ driftwoodspars@hotmail.com
driftwoodspars.com
Shop 10am-5pm daily (Apr-Oct); Sat & Sun 10am-5pm (Oct-Mar)
Tours by arrangement

⊗ Brewing commenced in 2000 in the famous 17th-century pub, Driftwood Spars. The brewery, a custom built five-barrel plant, is located across from the pub. The range has expanded to seven regular beers and an alcoholic ginger beer called Furnace. The full range of beers is available in the adjacent brewery shop along with other local ales and produce. The cask ales are currently only available at the Driftwood Spars but expansion during 2010 will enable regular supply to other outlets. Bottle-conditioned beers are available.

Bawden Rocks (OG 1037, ABV 3.8%)
A hoppy and clean flavoured bitter named after the rocks located just beyond Trevaunance Cove.

Blackheads Mild (OG 1037, ABV 3.8%)
Traditional mild with smoky malt flavours and peppery aftertaste.

Blue Hills Bitter (OG 1039, ABV 4%)
A light session bitter with a big hop flavour.

Badlands Bitter (OG 1047, ABV 4.8%)
A strong, malty bitter.

Bolster's Blood Porter (OG 1049, ABV 5%)
A rich, dark, chocolaty, malty porter with a slight bitter finish.

Lou's Brew (OG 1049, ABV 5%)
Light and hoppy with citrus and grassy aromas.

Alfie's Revenge (OG 1060, ABV 6.5%)

Dunham Massey

Dunham Massey Brewing Co, 100 Oldfield Lane, Dunham Massey, WA14 4PE
☎ (0161) 929 0663
✉ info@dunhammasseybrewing.co.uk
dunhammasseybrewing.co.uk
Shop Mon-Fri 10am-5pm; Sat-Sun 11am-4pm

Dunham Massey commenced brewing in late 2007, brewing traditional North-western ales using only English ingredients and no added sugars. The beer range is also available bottle conditioned, which is suitable for vegetarians and vegans. Around 30 outlets are supplied direct. Seasonal beers are available.

Little Bollington Bitter (OG 1036.5, ABV 3.7%)

Chocolate Cherry Mild (OG 1040.5, ABV 3.8%)

Dark Mild (OG 1040.5, ABV 3.8%)

Light Mild (OG 1040.5, ABV 3.8%)

Big Tree Bitter (OG 1040.5, ABV 3.9%)

Milk Stout (OG 1051, ABV 4%)

Ruby Sunset (OG 1043, ABV 4.1%)

Stamford Bitter (OG 1044, ABV 4.2%)

Stout (OG 1046, ABV 4.2%)

Duerr's Blossom Honey Beer (OG 1043.5, ABV 4.3%)

Deer Beer (OG 1047, ABV 4.5%)

Cheshire IPA (OG 1047, ABV 4.7%)

Porter (OG 1056, ABV 5.2%)

Durham SIBA

Durham Brewery Ltd, Unit 5a, Bowburn North Industrial Estate, Bowburn, Co Durham, DH6 5PF
☎ (0191) 377 1991 ✉ steve@durham-brewery.co.uk
durham-brewery.co.uk
Shop Mon-Fri 8am-4pm; Sat 10am-12.00pm
Tours by arrangement

Established in 1994, Durham now has a portfolio of around 20 beers. These are not all available as regular beers – please see website for full list. Bottles and five litre mini-casks can be purchased via the online shop and an own label/special message service is available. 70-80 outlets are supplied direct. Seasonal beers are brewed. Bottle-conditioned beers are also available and suitable for vegans.

Magus (ABV 3.8%) ◆
Pale malt gives this brew its straw colour but the hops define its character, with a fruity aroma, a clean bitter mouthfeel, and a lingering dry, citrus-like finish.

Earl Soham SIBA

Earl Soham Brewery, The Street, Earl Soham, Woodbridge, Suffolk, IP13 7RT
☎ (01728) 684097 ✉ info@earlsohambrewery.co.uk
earlsohambrewery.co.uk
Shop is village store next to brewery
Tours by arrangement

⊗ Earl Soham was set up behind the Victoria pub in 1984 and continued there until 2001 when the brewery moved 200 metres down the road. The Victoria and the Station in Framlingham both sell the beers on a regular basis, as does the Brewery

THE BREWERIES

Tap in Ipswich. When there is spare stock, beer is supplied to local free houses and as many beer festivals as possible. 30 outlets are supplied and three pubs are owned. Seasonal beer: Jolabrugg (ABV 5%, Dec). Most of the beers are bottle conditioned for the shop next door and other selected outlets.

Gannet Mild (OG 1034, ABV 3.3%)
A beautifully balanced mild, sweet and fruity flavour with a lingering, coffee aftertaste.

Victoria Bitter (OG 1037, ABV 3.6%)
A light, fruity, amber session beer with a clean taste and a long, lingering hoppy aftertaste.

Sir Roger's Porter (OG 1042, ABV 4.2%)
Smooth and easy drinking porter with an initial roasty flavour which is soon replaced by a sweet, lingering aftertaste.

Albert Ale (OG 1045, ABV 4.4%)
Hops dominate every aspect of this beer, but especially the finish. A fruity, astringent beer.

Brandeston Gold (OG 1045, ABV 4.5%)
Easy-drinking, light-coloured seasonal ale. Well-balanced fruity bitterness with a creamy mouthfeel and a long, sweet finish.

East Coast

East Coast Brewing Co, 3 Clay House Yard, Rear of Mitford Street, Filey, North Yorkshire, YO14 9DX
☎ (01723) 514865
✉ eastcoastbrewing@hotmail.co.uk
eastcoastbrewingcompany.co.uk
Tours by arrangement

The brewery is housed in a converted stable and coach house. Six regular beers are produced plus at least one special per month. 20 outlets are supplied direct.

Bonhomme Richard (ABV 3.6%)

Mary Rose (ABV 3.8%)

Commodore (ABV 4.1%)

John Paul Jones (ABV 4.3%)

Alfred Moodies Mild (ABV 6%)

Empress of India (ABV 6%)

Eastwood

Eastwood the Brewer, Barge & Barrel, 10-12 Park Road, Elland, West Yorkshire, HX5 9HP
☎ 07949 148476 ✉ taggartkeith@yahoo.co.uk
Tours by arrangement

The brewery was founded by John Eastwood at the Barge & Barrel pub. 50-70 outlets are supplied direct. Seasonal beers are produced.

Stirling (ABV 3.8%)
An amber-coloured session beer with a pleasant, long-lasting, fruity finish.

Best Bitter (ABV 4%)
Creamy, yellow, hoppy bitter with hints of citrus fruits. Pleasantly strong bitter aftertaste.

Gold Award (ABV 4.4%)
Complex copper-coloured beer with malt, roast and caramel flavours. It has a hoppy and bitter aftertaste.

Black Prince (ABV 5%)
A distinctive strong black porter with a blend of pale and chocolate malts and roasted barley.

Eccleshall

See Slater's

Edinburgh

See Greene King in New Nationals section

Elgood's IFBB SIBA

Elgood & Sons Ltd, North Brink Brewery, Wisbech, Cambridgeshire, PE13 1LN
☎ (01945) 583160 ✉ info@elgoods-brewery.co.uk
elgoods-brewery.co..uk
Shop Tue-Thu 11.30am-4.30pm (May-Sep)
Tours by arrangement

The North Brink Brewery was established in 1795 and was one of the first classic Georgian breweries to be built outside London. In 1878 it came under the control of the Elgood family and is still run today as one of the few remaining independent family breweries, with the fifth generation of the family now helping to run the company. The beers go to 42 Elgood's pubs within a 50-mile radius of Wisbech and free trade outlets throughout East Anglia, while wholesalers distribute nationally. Elgood's has a visitor centre, offering a tour of the brewery and the gardens. Seasonal beers: see website.

Black Dog (OG 1036.8, ABV 3.6%)
Roast malt and underlying caramel characterise the aroma of this dark brown/red mild. Roast and malt are supported by hints of fruit on a bittersweet palate ending with roast bitterness.

Cambridge Bitter (OG 1037.8, ABV 3.8%)
A session bitter with a robust dry finish. Malty notes on aroma and palate are complemented by subtle hops.

Golden Newt (OG 1041.5, ABV 4.1%)
Golden ale with floral hops and sulphur aroma. Floral hops and a fruity presence on a bittersweet background lead to a short, muted hoppy and fruity finish.

Pageant Ale (OG 1043.8, ABV 4.3%)
A premium ale with an aroma of hops and malt giving a well-balanced bittersweet flavour and a satisfying finish.

Greyhound Strong Bitter (OG 1052.8, ABV 5.2%)
A tawny/brown beer with a malty aroma. Malt and raisin fruit on the palate balanced by pleasing dryness. Dry finish with faint malt and hops.

For City of Cambridge Brewery:

Boathouse Bitter (ABV 3.7%)
Copper-brown and full-bodied session bitter, starting with impressive citrus and floral hop; grassy fruit notes are present with finally a gentle bitterness.

Hobson's Choice (ABV 4.1%)
This golden ale has a predominantly spicy hop aroma. Bittersweet on the palate with plenty of hops leading through to a dry, hoppy finish.

Atom Splitter (ABV 4.5%)

Robust copper-coloured strong bitter with a hop aroma and taste, and a distinct sulphury edge.

Parkers Porter (ABV 5%) ◆
Impressive reddish brew with a defined roast character throughout, and a short, fruity, bittersweet palate.

Elland SIBA

Elland Brewery Ltd, Units 3-5, Heathfield Industrial Estate, Heathfield Street, Elland, West Yorkshire, HX5 9AE
☎ (01422) 377677 ✉ eands@btconnect.com
⊕ ellandbrewery.co.uk
Tours by arrangement

☺The brewery was originally formed as Eastwood & Sanders in 2002 by the amalgamation of the Barge & Barrel Brewery and West Yorkshire Brewery. The company was renamed Elland in 2006 to reinforce its links with the town. The brewery has a capacity to brew 50 barrels a week and offers more than 12 seasonal specials every month as well as a monthly Head Brewer's Reserve range of beers. More than 150 outlets are supplied. 1872 Porter was crowned overall champion at the National Winter Ales Festival 2010.

Bargee (OG 1038, ABV 3.8%) ◆
Amber, creamy session bitter. Fruity, hoppy aroma and taste complemented by a bitter edge in the finish.

Best Bitter (OG 1041, ABV 4%) ◆
Creamy, yellow, hoppy ale with hints of citrus fruits. Pleasantly strong bitter aftertaste.

Beyond the Pale (OG 1042, ABV 4.2%) ⬚ ◆
Gold-coloured, robust, creamy beer with ripe aromas of hops and fruit. Bitterness predominates in the mouth and leads to a dry, fruity and hoppy aftertaste.

Eden (OG 1042, ABV 4.2%) ◆
A yellow, fruity, hoppy, creamy bitter. Citrus fruit with assertively bitter taste to finish.

Nettlethrasher (OG 1044, ABV 4.4%) ◆
Grainy amber-coloured beer. A rounded nose with some fragrant hops notes followed by a mellow nutty and fruity taste and a dry finish.

1872 Porter (OG 1065, ABV 6.5%) ⬚ ▮ ◆
Creamy, full-flavoured porter. Rich liquorice flavours with a hint of chocolate from roast malt. A soft but satisfying aftertaste of bittersweet roast and malt.

Elmtree

Elmtree Beers, Snetterton Brewery, Unit 10, Oakwood Industrial Estate, Harling Road, Snetterton, Norfolk, NR16 2JU
☎ (01953) 887065 ✉ sales@elmtreebeers.co.uk
⊕ elmtreebeers.co.uk
Shop Mon-Wed, Fri-Sat 11am-4pm

⊠ Elmtree was established in 2007 using a five-barrel plant and moved in 2008 to new premises. 80 outlets are supplied direct. Bottle-conditioned beers are available and are suitable for vegetarians and vegans.

Burston's Cuckoo (OG 1038, ABV 3.8%)

Bitter (OG 1041, ABV 4.2%)

Dark Horse (OG 1048, ABV 5%) ◆

A roast, slightly salty aroma and matching initial taste introduce this coal black stout. The roast notes are aided by a fruity, prune-like background. Increasingly malty finish.

Golden Pale Ale (OG 1048, ABV 5%)

Nightlight Mild (OG 1057, ABV 5.7%) ◆
A heavy mix of liquorice, roast and malt infuses aroma and taste. The heavy character is lightened by a sweet, spicy, slowly-developing aftertaste.

Elveden EAB

Elveden Ales, The Courtyard, Elveden Estate, Elveden, Thetford, Norfolk, IP24 3TA
☎ (01842) 878922

Elveden is a five-barrel brewery based on the estate of Lord Iveagh, a member of the ennobled branch of the Guinness family. The brewery is run by Frances Moore, daughter of Brendan Moore at Iceni Brewery (qv) and produces three ales: Elveden Stout (ABV 5%) and Elveden Ale (ABV 5.2%), which are mainly bottled in stoneware bottles. The third is Charter Ale (ABV 10%) to mark the celebrations for the award of a Royal Charter for Harwich in 1604. The beer is available in cask and bottle-conditioned versions. The phone number listed is shared with Iceni. The majority of sales take place through the farm shop, adjacent to the brewery. During 2007 the brewery building was restored as part of the development of the outbuilding of the Elveden estate as a tourist attraction. The visitor centre re-opened in summer 2008, giving regular tours – please phone for details.

Empire

Empire Brewing, The Old Boiler House, Unit 33, Upper Mills, Slaithwaite, Huddersfield, West Yorkshire, HD7 5HA
☎ (01484) 847343 ☎ 07966 592276
⊕ empirebrewing.com
Tours by arrangement

☺Empire Brewing was set up 2006 in a mill on the bank of the scenic Huddersfield Narrow Canal, close to the centre of Slaithwaite. The five-barrel plant produces 20 barrels a week. Beers are supplied to local free houses and through independent specialist beer agencies and wholesalers. Seasonal beers are available, as are bottle conditioned ales.

Golden Warrior (OG 1039.5, ABV 3.8%)
Pale bitter, quite fruity with a sherbet aftertaste, moderate bitterness.

Strikes Back (OG 1041, ABV 4%)
Pale golden bitter with a hoppy aroma and good hop and malt balance with a citrus flavour, very light on the palate. Good session beer.

Valour (OG 1042.5, ABV 4.2%)

Imperium (OG 1050, ABV 5.1%)

Enville SIBA

Enville Ales Ltd, Enville Brewery, Coxgreen, Hollies Lane, Enville, Stourbridge, West Midlands, DY7 5LG
☎ (01384) 873728 ✉ info@envilleales.com
⊕ envilleales.com
Tours by arrangement for small groups only

Enville Brewery is sited on a picturesque Victorian, Grade II-listed farm complex. Using natural spring

water, traditional steam brewing and a reed and willow effluent plant. Enville Ale is infused with honey and is from a 19th century recipe for beekeeper's ale passed down from the former proprietor's great-great aunt. Seasonal beers: see website.

LPA (Light Pale Ale) (ABV 4%)
Traditional session bitter; dry and golden with a mellow, hoppy flavour.

Nailmaker Mild (OG 1041, ABV 4%)
A well-defined hop aroma and underlying sweetness give way to a dry finish.

Simply Simpkiss (ABV 4%)

Cherry Blonde (ABV 4.2%)

Saaz (OG 1042, ABV 4.2%) ◆
Golden lager-style beer. Lager bite but with more taste and lasting bitterness. The malty aroma is late arriving but the bitter finish, balanced by fruit and hops, compensates.

White (OG 1041, ABV 4.2%) ◆
Yellow with a malt, hops and fruit aroma. Hoppy but sweet finish.

Ale (OG 1044, ABV 4.5%) ◆
Sweet malty aroma and taste, honey becomes apparent before bitterness finally dominates.

Porter (OG 1044, ABV 4.5%) ◆
Black with a creamy head and sulphurous aroma. Sweet and fruity start with touches of spice. Good balance between sweet and bitter, but hops dominate the finish.

Ginger Beer (OG 1045, ABV 4.6%) ◆
Golden bright with gently gingered tangs. A drinkable beer with no acute flavours but a satisfying aftertaste of sweet hoppiness.

Epping

See Pitfield

Evan Evans

Evan Evans Brewery, The New Brewery, 1 Rhosmaen Street, Llandeilo, Carmarthenshire, SA19 6LU
☎ (01558) 824455 ✉ info@evan-evans.com
⊕ evan-evans.com
Shop Mon-Fri 10am-4pm
Tours by arrangement

Evan Evans opened in 2004 with a brand new Canadian brewing plant. Additional fermenting capacity was added in 2009, taking brewing capacity to 8,000 barrels per annum. Eight pubs are owned. It is Wales' first Soil Association organic-approved brewery. A large range of seasonal ales is available. In 2009 the brewery bought Archers Brewery of Swindon's brands and now brew some of Archers' regular and seasonal ales.

BB/Best Bitter (OG 1038, ABV 3.8%)
An easy-drinking best bitter. Malty with a clean hop palate.

Cwrw (OG 1043, ABV 4.2%) ⊟ ▮

Warrior (OG 1046, ABV 4.6%)

Under Archers Brewery name:

Village (ABV 3.6%)

Best Bitter (ABV 4%)

Golden (ABV 4.7%)

Everards IFBB SIBA

Everards Brewery Ltd, Castle Acres, Narborough, Leicestershire, LE19 1BY
☎ (0116) 201 4100 ✉ mail@everards.co.uk
⊕ everards.co.uk
Shop Mon-Fri 10am-5pm; Sat 10am-2pm
Tours by arrangement for parties of 8-12

Established by William Everard in 1849, Everards brewery remains an independent family-owned brewery. Four core ales are brewed as well as a range of seasonal beers – see website for more details. Everards owns a pub estate of more than 160 tenanted houses throughout the Midlands.

Beacon Bitter (OG 1036, ABV 3.8%) ◆
Light, refreshing, well-balanced pale amber bitter in the Burton style.

Sunchaser Blonde (OG 1038, ABV 4%) ◆
A golden brew with a sweet, lightly-hopped character. Some citrus notes to the fore in a quick finish that becomes increasingly bitter.

Tiger Best Bitter (OG 1041, ABV 4.2%) ◆
A mid-brown, well-balanced best bitter crafted for broad appeal, benefiting from a long, bittersweet finish.

Original (OG 1050, ABV 5.2%) ◆
Full-bodied, mid-brown strong bitter with a pleasant rich, grainy mouthfeel. Well-balanced flavours, with malt slightly to the fore, merging into a long, satisfying finish.

Brewed under contract for Coors:

Stones Cask Bitter (OG 1040, ABV 4.1%)

Exeter

Exeter Brewery Ltd, 5-6 Lions Rest, Station Road, Exminster, Exeter, Devon, EX6 8DZ
☎ (01392) 823013 ✉ sales@exeterbrewery.co.uk
⊕ exeterbrewery.co.uk

The Exeter Brewery, formerly named the Topsham & Exminster, remains on the same site amid the beautiful Exminster marshes, where it has brewed since 2003. The brewery has been completely refurbished and re-equipped, providing much greater production capacity and enabling a greater range of ales.

Lighterman (ABV 3.6%)

Avocet (ABV 3.9%)
An organic beer.

Ferryman (ABV 4.2%)

County Best (ABV 4.6%)

Darkness (ABV 5.1%)

Exe Valley SIBA

Exe Valley Brewery, Silverton, Exeter, Devon, EX5 4HF
☎ (01392) 860406 ✉ info@exevalleybrewery.co.uk
⊕ exevalleybrewery.co.uk
Tours for groups by arrangement (charge made)

⊠ Exe Valley was established as Barron's Brewery in 1984. The brewery is located in a converted barn overlooking the Exe Valley and Dartmoor hills. Locally sourced malt and English hops are used, along with the brewery's own spring water. Around 100 outlets are supplied within a 45-mile radius of the brewery. Beers are also available nationally via wholesalers. Seasonal beers: see website. Bottle-conditioned beer is also available.

Bitter (OG 1036, ABV 3.7%) ◆
Mid-brown bitter, pleasantly fruity with underlying malt through the aroma, taste and finish.

Barron's Hopsit (OG 1040, ABV 4.1%) ◆
Straw-coloured beer with strong hop aroma, hop and fruit flavour and a bitter hop finish.

Dob's Best Bitter (OG 1040, ABV 4.1%) ◆
Light brown bitter. Malt and fruit predominate in the aroma and taste with a dry, bitter, fruity finish.

Devon Glory (OG 1046, ABV 4.7%)
Mid-brown, fruity-tasting pint with a sweet, fruity finish.

Mr Sheppard's Crook (OG 1046, ABV 4.7%) ◆
Smooth, full-bodied, mid-brown beer with a malty-fruit nose and a sweetish palate leading to a bitter, dry finish.

Exeter Old Bitter (OG 1046, ABV 4.8%) ◆
Mid-brown old ale with a rich fruity taste and slightly earthy aroma and bitter finish.

Exmoor SIBA

Exmoor Ales Ltd, Golden Hill Brewery, Wiveliscombe, Somerset, TA4 2NY
☎ (01984) 623798 ✉ info@exmoorales.co.uk
⊕ exmoorales.co.uk
Tours by arrangement

⊗ Somerset's largest brewery was founded in 1980 in the old Hancock's brewery, which closed in 1959. Around 250 outlets in the South-west are supplied and others nationwide via wholesalers and pub chains. Seasonal beers: see website.

Ale (OG 1039, ABV 3.8%) ◆
A pale to mid-brown, medium-bodied session bitter. A mixture of malt and hops in the aroma and taste lead to a hoppy, bitter aftertaste.

Antler (ABV 4%)

Fox (OG 1043, ABV 4.2%)
A mid-brown beer; the slight maltiness on the tongue is followed by a burst of hops with a lingering bittersweet aftertaste.

Gold (OG 1045, ABV 4.5%) ◆
A yellow/golden best bitter with a good balance of malt and fruity hop on the nose and the palate. The sweetness follows through an ultimately more bitter finish.

Stag (OG 1050, ABV 5.2%) ◆
A pale brown beer, with a malty taste and aroma, and a bitter finish.

Beast (OG 1066, ABV 6.6%)
A dark beer brewed with chocolate and crystal malts.

Facer's SIBA

Facer's Flintshire Brewery, A8-9, Ashmount Enterprise Park, Aber Road, Flint, North Wales, CH6 5QT
☎ 07713 566370 ✉ dave@facers.co.uk
⊕ facers.co.uk
Tours by arrangement for CAMRA groups only

Bragdy Sir y Fflint Facer's (Facer's Flintshire Brewery) is the only brewery in Flintshire, having moved west from Salford in 2006. Ex-Boddington's head brewer Dave Facer ran the brewery single-handed from its launch in 2003 until 2007, when the first employee was recruited. The brewery was expanded to twice the floor space in early 2008. Around 70 outlets are supplied.

Clwyd Gold (OG 1034, ABV 3.5%) ◆
Clean tasting session bitter, mid-brown in colour with a full mouthfeel. The malty flavours are accompanied by increasing hoppiness in the bitter finish.

Flintshire Bitter (OG 1036, ABV 3.7%) ▮ ◆
Well-balanced session bitter with a full mouthfeel. Some fruitiness in aroma and taste with increasing hoppy bitterness in the dry finish.

North Star Porter (ABV 4%) ◆
Dark, smooth, porter-style beer with good roast notes and hints of coffee and chocolate. Some initial sweetness and caramel flavours followed by a hoppy bitter aftertaste.

Sunny Bitter (OG 1040, ABV 4.2%) ◆
An amber beer with a dry taste. The hop aroma continues into the taste where some faint fruit notes are also present. Lasting dry finish.

DHB (Dave's Hoppy Beer) (OG 1041, ABV 4.3%) ◆
A dry-hopped version of Splendid Ale with some sweet flavours also coming through in the mainly hoppy, bitter taste.

This Splendid Ale (OG 1041, ABV 4.3%) ◆
Refreshing tangy best bitter, yellow in colour with a sharp hoppy, bitter taste. Good citrus fruit undertones with hints of grapefruit throughout.

Landslide (OG 1047, ABV 4.9%) ◆
Full-flavoured, complex premium bitter with tangy orange marmalade fruitiness in aroma and taste. Long-lasting hoppy flavours throughout.

Fach

See Celt Experience

Fallen Angel

Fallen Angel Brewery, 14 Carriers Way, East Hoathly, East Sussex, BN8 6AG
☎ (01825) 841307
✉ sales@fallenangelbrewery.com
⊕ fallenangelbrewery.com
Tours by arrangement

The brewery was launched in 2004 and has been expanded from a one-barrel to a four-barrel plant. In 2009 the brewery moved from Battle to its present address. Bottle-conditioned beers are produced for outlets around Kent, Sussex, Surrey and Hampshire. Bottle-conditioned beers: Fire in the Hole Chili Beer (ABV 3.9%), St Patrick's Irish Stout (ABV 3.9%), Englishman's Nut Brown Ale (ABV 3.7%), College Cluster (ABV 4.2%), Cowgirl Gold (ABV 4.2%), Gamekeeper's Bitter (ABV 4.2%), Kama Sumatra (ABV 4.2%), Gardeners Delight (ABV 4.3%), Angry Ox Bitter (ABV 5.3%), Lemon Weissbier (ABV 5.4%), Black Death (ABV 5.5%), Naughty Nun (ABV 5.6%), Howlin' Red (ABV 6.5%), Black Cat (ABV 7.1%). Seasonal beers are also available.

Fallons

Fallons Exquisite Ales, Unit 15, Darwen Enterprise Centre, Railway Road, Darwen, Lancashire, BB3 3EH
☎ 07905 246810 ✉ info@fallonsales.com
⊕ fallonsales.com

⊚Fallons is a small family brewery established in 2008 with a 10-barrel plant in a unit on railway sidings. It now also has a small test brew plant in the Black Horse, the brewery tap. Beers are supplied to local pubs and festivals. Test and experimental beers appear under the name Graffiti Brewery.

TJ Fallon (OG 1035.9, ABV 3.7%)

Angel Tears (OG 1036.8, ABV 3.8%)

Lancastrian Gold (OG 1038.8, ABV 4%)

Red Merkin (OG 1038.8, ABV 4%)

Tattooers Arms (OG 1039.7, ABV 4.1%)

Jax Best (OG 1047.7, ABV 4.2%)

Original Dark Night (OG 1041.7, ABV 4.3%)

Dark Prince (OG 1047.1, ABV 4.8%)

Hex Original (OG 1048.8, ABV 5%)

Falstaff

▤ Falstaff Brewery, 24 Society Place, Normanton, Derby, DE23 6UH
☎ (01332) 342902 ✉ info@falstaffbrewery.co.uk
⊕ falstaffbrewery.co.uk
Tours by arrangement

⊠ Attached to the Falstaff freehouse, the brewery dates from 1999 but was refurbished and re-opened in 2003 under new management and has since doubled capacity to 15 barrels. Since 2005 Falstaff has also brewed themed monthly specials for the Babington Arms in Derby. More than 30 outlets are supplied.

3 Faze (OG 1040, ABV 3.8%)
Light gold in colour with a malt and honey nose. Smooth malt flavours lead to a clean, balanced malt and hop finish.

Fist Full of Hops (OG 1044, ABV 4.5%)
An amber ale with lots of hop.

Phoenix (OG 1047, ABV 4.7%) ◆
A smooth, tawny ale with fruit and hop, joined by plenty of malt in the mouth. A subtle sweetness produces a drinkable ale.

Smiling Assassin (OG 1050, ABV 5.2%)
A copper-coloured beer with sweet malt flavours.

Famous Railway Tavern

▤ Famous Railway Tavern Brewing Co, 58 Station Road, Brightlingsea, Essex, CO7 0DT
✉ famousrailway@yahoo.co.uk
Tours by arrangement

The brewery started life as a kitchen-sink affair in 1998 but Crouch Vale Brewery assisted the development and increased production. The brewery expanded in 2006 and it is now able to brew up to 135 gallons of beer a week for the pub, other local pubs and beer festivals. Seasonal beers are also available. Many of the beers are suitable for vegetarians and vegans.

Crab & Winkle Mild (ABV 4%) ◆
Thin-bodied mild with a pear drop aroma and a rather roasty taste. The aftertaste is slightly ash-like with suggestions of bitter chocolate.

Bladderwrack Stout (ABV 5%) ◆

Full-bodied stout with an intense roast grain character that is initially underpinned by subtle sweetness, which subsides to leave a drier finish.

Farmer's Ales EAB

Farmer's Ales, Stable Brewery, Silver Street, Maldon, Essex, CM9 4QE
☎ (01621) 851000 ✉ info@maldonbrewing.co.uk
⊕ maldonbrewing.co.uk
Shop open for beer sales at the brewery
Tours by arrangement for small parties only

Situated in a restored stable block behind the historic Blue Boar Hotel, this eight-barrel brewery started in 2002 and continues to enjoy success in local pubs and beer festivals. The beers are available at the Blue Boar, selected Gray & Sons houses as well as in a number of local pubs. Other outlets are supplied through Crouch Vale Brewery. All cask beers are available in bottle-conditioned form. Seasonal beers: see website.

Farmer's IPA (ABV 3.6%)

**Drop of Nelson's Blood
(OG 1038, ABV 3.8%)** ⬚ ◆
Red-brown session bitter. Initially quite sweet and fruity, with a pleasing bite to the aftertaste.

Hotel Porter (OG 1041, ABV 4.1%) ◆
Roast grain dominates this oatmeal stout, but an unusual fresh hop character is evident.

Pucks Folly (OG 1042, ABV 4.2%) ⬚ ◆
Pale golden ale with spicy notes and sweet fruit. Biscuity malt in the taste fades and the finish is dominated by bitterness.

Captain Ann (OG 1045, ABV 4.5%)
A deep ruby traditional malty best bitter.

Golden Boar (OG 1050, ABV 5%) ◆
Powerful, deep-golden ale. The hop character is initially full and citrus, but becomes more spicy in the aftertaste.

Dark Horse (ABV 6.6%)

Farnham

▤ Farnham Brewery, Claverton Marketing Ltd, t/a the Ball & Wicket Public House, 104 Upper Hale Road, Farnham, Surrey, GU9 0PB
☎ (01252) 735278 ✉ ballwick@ntlworld.com

⊠ The Farnham Brewery opened in 2006 and supplies the Ball & Wicket pub as well as around 10 other local outlets. Seasonal beers: Honeymoon (ABV 6.5%, Feb), Elderflower Spring Ale (ABV 6.3%, Apr-May), Rockin' Robin (ABV 6.5%, Aug-Sep).

Bishop Sumner (OG 1040, ABV 3.8%)

William Cobbett (ABV 4.3%)

Mike Hawthorn (OG 1055, ABV 5.3%)

Far North

Far North Brewery, c/o 1 Keoltag Drive, Reay, KW14 7SD
☎ (01847) 811118 ✉ info@farnorthbrewery.co.uk
⊕ farnorthbrewery.co.uk

Originally at the Melvich Hotel, Far North is now a part-time operation based at the brewer's home. Two bottled beers are contract brewed in Scotland; Real Mackay (ABV 4.5%) and Caithness Gold (ABV 4%).

Fat Cat

Fat Cat Brewing Co, The Cidershed, 98-100 Lawson Road, Norwich, Norfolk, NR3 4LF
☎ (01603) 788508 / 624364 ☎ 07795 633368
✉ pints@fatcatpub.co.uk 🌐 fatcatbrewery.co.uk
Tours by arrangement

Fat Cat Brewery was founded by the owner of the Fat Cat free house in Norwich. Brewing started in 2005 at the Fat Cat's sister pub, the Cidershed, under the supervision of former Woodforde's owner Ray Ashworth. Seasonal beers: Meow Mild (ABV 4.3%), Top Cat (ABV 4.8%), Fat Cat Porter (ABV 4.9%). Bottle-conditioned beers and occasional one-off brews are also available.

Bitter (OG 1038, ABV 3.8%) ◆
Abundantly hoppy with a dry bitter finish. Some citrus notes bulk out the hoppy aroma and continue through to the initial taste. Little complexity in the slightly astringent finish.

Honey Cat (OG 1043, ABV 4.3%) ◆
A malty/hoppy brew with a taste of honey. A pleasant, low key mix of malt and hops bound together with a sweetish honey background. Gold coloured with a grainy mouthfeel.

Stout Cat (OG 1046, ABV 4.6%)
A deep red/brown beer with a sweet, rich flavour of roast malt and molasses, well-balanced with a pronounced hop flavour and aroma.

Wild Cat (OG 1050, ABV 5%)
A classic, brown-coloured strong bitter with a markedly bitter finish. Full-bodied but easy-drinking.

Marmalade Cat (OG 1055, ABV 5.5%) ◆
A complex beer with a growing malt influence over a dry hoppy beginning. Sweet fruity notes in the nose continue into the taste. A heavy grainy feel for such a complex, well-balanced brew.

Felinfoel SIBA

Felinfoel Brewery Co Ltd, Farmers Row, Felinfoel, Llanelli, Carmarthenshire, SA14 8LB
☎ (01554) 773357 ✉ info@felinfoel-brewery.com
🌐 felinfoel-brewery.com
Shop 9am-4pm
Tours by arrangement

Founded in the 1830s, the company is still family-owned and is now the oldest brewery in Wales. The present buildings are Grade II* listed and were built in the 1870s. It supplies cask ale to half its 84 houses, though some use top pressure dispense, and to approximately 350 free trade outlets.

Best Bitter (OG 1038, ABV 3.8%) ◆
A well-balanced beer, with a low aroma. Bittersweet initially with an increasing moderate bitterness.

Cambrian Best Bitter (OG 1039, ABV 3.9%)
A full-hopped and refreshing session beer.

Stout (OG 1041, ABV 4.1%)
A Welsh stout created with a subtle blend of chocolate malt giving a predominantly roast barley flavour and a rich, creamy head.

Double Dragon (OG 1042, ABV 4.2%) ◆
This pale brown beer has a malty, fruity aroma. The taste is also malt and fruit with a background hop presence throughout. A malty and fruity finish.

Celtic Pride (OG 1045, ABV 4.5%)
A light, golden premium ale with a bright, clean flavour and citrus overtones.

Felstar EAB

Felstar Brewery, Felsted Vineyards, Crix Green, Felsted, Essex, CM6 3JT
☎ (01245) 361504 ☎ 07973 315503
✉ sales@felstarbrewery.co.uk
🌐 felstarbrewery.co.uk
Shop 10am-dusk daily
Tours by arrangement

⊗ The Felstar Brewery opened in 2001 with a five-barrel plant based in the old bonded warehouse of the Felsted Vineyard. A small number of outlets are supplied. Seasonal beers: Rayne Forest (ABV 4%), Chick Chat (ABV 4.1%), Dark Wheat (ABV 5.4%), Xmas Ale (ABV 6%). Bottle-conditioned beers are also available.

Felstar (ABV 3.4%)

Crix Forest (ABV 4%)

Shalford (ABV 4%)

Good Knight (ABV 5%)

Hoppy Hen (ABV 5%)

Peckin' Order (ABV 5%)

Dancin' Hen (ABV 6%)

Fernandes SIBA

Fernandes Brewery, 5 Avison Yard, Kirkgate, Wakefield, West Yorkshire, WF1 1UA
☎ (01924) 291709
Tours by arrangement

The brewery opened in 1997 and is housed in a 19th-century malthouse. Ossett Brewing Company purchased the brewery and tap in 2007 but independent brewing continues. The former home-brew shop has been turned into a Bavarian style 'Bier Keller' and sells continental beers as well as real ale. The tap sells Fernandes and Ossett beer as well as guest ales. Fernandes beers are more widely available through Ossett's supply chain. Many occasional beers are produced.

Malt Shovel Mild (OG 1038, ABV 3.8%)
A dark, full-bodied, malty mild with roast malt and chocolate flavours, leading to a lingering, dry, malty finish.

Triple O (OG 1041, ABV 3.9%)
A light, refreshing, hoppy session beer with a lingering fruity finish.

Ale to the Tsar (OG 1042, ABV 4.1%)
A pale, smooth, well-balanced beer with some sweetness leading to a nutty, malty and satisfying aftertaste.

Centennial (OG 1043, ABV 4.1%)
Light-coloured extremely hoppy beer with a long, lingering aftertaste.

Great Northern (OG 1050, ABV 5.1%)
Pale, citrussy and extremely hoppy.

Double Six (OG 1062, ABV 6%)
A powerful, dark and rich strong beer with an array of malt, roast malt and chocolate flavours and a strong, lasting malty finish, with some hoppiness.

Festival

Festival Brewery Ltd, Unit 17, Malmesbury Road, Kingsditch Trading Estate, Cheltenham, Gloucestershire, GL51 9PL
☎ (01242) 521444 ✉ info@festivalbrewery.co.uk
🌐 festivalbrewery.co.uk
Tours by arrangement

Festival was established in 2007 on a 10-barrel plant. 220 outlets are supplied direct.

Amber (OG 1036.8, ABV 3.8%)
An amber-coloured session beer with a refreshing balance of hops and malt.

Emerald (OG 1038.8, ABV 4%)
Fresh and zesty with crisp floral flavours, a background of sweet malt and a hoppy grapefruit bitter finish.

Pride (OG 1039.7, ABV 4.1%)
A classic English best bitter giving a hint of berry with a fruity, herbal aroma.

Gold (OG 1042.6, ABV 4.4%)
Refreshing golden ale with sweet floral aroma and a dry finish.

Ruby (OG 1045.5, ABV 4.7%)
A strong bitter, ruby-coloured with a rich and warming character.

FILO SIBA

FILO Brewing Co Ltd, First In Last Out, 14-15 High Street, Hastings, East Sussex, TN34 3EY
☎ (01424) 425079

Office: Torfield Cottage, 8 Old London Road, Hastings, East Sussex, TN34 3HA ✉ office@thefilo.co.uk
🌐 thefilo.co.uk
Tours by arrangement

The FILO Brewery was established in 1985, with the current owners taking over in 1988. There is a possibilty of the brewery moving to a barn at Torfield Cottage. Two outlets are supplied direct.

Mike's Mild (ABV 3.4%)

Crofters (ABV 3.8%)

Ginger Tom (ABV 4.5%)

Cardinal (ABV 4.6%)

Gold (ABV 4.8%)

Texas Tea (ABV 5%)

Five Towns

Five Towns Brewery, 651 Leeds Road, Outwood, Wakefield, West Yorkshire, WF1 2LU
☎ (01924) 781887
✉ malcolmbastow@googlemail.com

Five Towns began production on a 2.5-barrel plant in 2008 and mostly supplies outlets in Yorkshire. Seasonal beers: Indian Summer Ale (ABV 3.8%, Sep), Jimmy Riddle (ABV 3.7%, Oct), Davy Jones' Locker (ABV 3.9%, Nov), Christmas Ale (ABV 4%, Dec). Bottle-conditioned beers are also available.

Outwood Bound (OG 1040, ABV 4.2%)
A chestnut beer with a toffee nose and strong, dry, bitter finish.

Callum's Best (OG 1041, ABV 4.6%)
A dark-coloured bitter with a full flavour and bitter finish.

Ponte Carlo Stout (OG 1048.7, ABV 4.6%)

Niamh's Nemesis (OG 1053, ABV 5.7%)

Flack Manor (NEW)

Flack Manor Brewery Ltd, 8 Romsey Industrial Estate, Greatbridge Road, Romsey, Hampshire, SO51 0HR
☎ (01794) 518520 ✉ info@flackmanor.co.uk
🌐 flackmanor.co.uk

Flack Manor began brewing in 2010 using a 20-barrel plant.

Flack's Double Drop (ABV 3.7%)

Flipside (NEW)

Flipside Brewery, The Brewhouse, East Link Trade Estate, Private Road No. 2, Colwick, Nottinghamshire, NG4 2JR
☎ (0115) 987 7500 ☎ 07970 025863
✉ andrew.dunkin@flipsidebrewery.co.uk
🌐 flipsidebrewery.co.uk

Flipside began brewing in 2010 on a six-barrel brewery.

Sterling Pale (ABV 3.9%)

Flipping Best (ABV 4.6%)

Florence

The Florence Brewpub, Capital Pub Co PLC, 131-133 Dulwich Road, Herne Hill, London, SE24 0NG
☎ (020) 7326 4987
✉ enquiries@florencehernehill.com
🌐 florencehernehill.com

The Florence has been brewing since opening in 2007. Beer is supplied to four outlets, the Florence itself, the Clarence in Balham and the Merchant of Battersea and the Victoria Inn in Peckham.

Bonobo (ABV 4.5%)
A well-balanced brown beer with a strong citrus hop character, some butterscotch and a dry aftertaste.

Weasel (ABV 4.5%)
Citrus hops dominate this light-drinking, straw-coloured beer, including in the finish, which is dry and bitter.

Beaver (ABV 4.8%)

Flowerpots

Flowerpots Brewery, Cheriton, Alresford, Hampshire, SO24 0QQ
☎ (01962) 771534 🌐 flowerpots-inn.co.uk

Flowerpots began production in 2006. Iain McIntosh and Julie Jones are the brewers alongside the brewery owner, Paul Tickner. Many local outlets are supplied direct. Seasonal beers: see website.

Perridge Pale (OG 1035, ABV 3.6%)
Very pale, easy-drinking session beer with high hops and bitterness throughout. Some citrus notes; extremely tasty for its strength.

Bitter (OG 1038, ABV 3.8%)
Dry, earthy hop flavours balanced by malt and toffee. Good bitterness with a hoppy aroma and a sharp finish. A refreshing, easy-going bitter.

Goodens Gold (OG 1046, ABV 4.8%)

A yellow-coloured, full-bodied strong bitter. A complex beer, bursting with hops and fruit in the aroma and taste, leading to a long, dry finish.

Forge

Forge Brewery, Ford Hill Forge, Hartland, Devon, EX39 6EE
☎ (01237) 440015 ✉ dave@forgebrewery.co.uk
forgebrewery.co.uk
Tours by arrangement

Forge is situated in a coastal village near Bideford in North Devon and began brewing in 2008 on a five-barrel plant. 35 outlets are supplied direct.

Hartland Blonde (OG 1040, ABV 4%)
A light, hoppy beer with citrus notes.

Maid in Devon (OG 1040, ABV 4%)
Copper-coloured ale with a hoppy finish.

Forged Porter (OG 1042, ABV 4.2%)
A dark, smooth porter.

Litehouse (OG 1042, ABV 4.3%)
Light with a citrus bite.

IPA (OG 1044, ABV 4.5%)
A light, hoppy beer with grapefruit and citrus notes.

Dreckly (OG 1046, ABV 4.8%)
A warm, ruby-coloured strong premium ale fortified with gorse and heather, rich in malt with a spicy aroma and a malty aftertaste.

Forgotten Corner

Forgotten Corner Brewery, The Stables, Maker Barracks, Maker Heights, Cornwall, PL10 1LA
☎ (01752) 829363

Postal Address: 64 West Street, Millbrook, Torpoint, Cornwall, PL10 1AE ✉ gibsonb45@yahoo.com
Tours by arrangement

The brewery began production in 2008 and several local outlets are supplied.

J.P. (OG 1038, ABV 3.7%)
Crisp, clean and refreshing pale beer.

Solstice Salute (ABV 4%)

Trust Ale (OG 1040, ABV 4%)
A session bitter, full of malty flavours.

Hunters Porter (OG 1054, ABV 5.5%)
Full-bodied, rich, chocolaty molasses flavour with bitterness to follow.

Dragon IPA (ABV 6%)

Four Alls

Four Alls Brewery, Ovington, North Yorkshire, DL11 7BP
☎ (01833) 627302 ✉ john.stroud@virgin.net
thefouralls-teesdale.co.uk
Tours by arrangement

The one-barrel brewery was launched in 2003 by John Stroud, one of the founders of Ales of Kent, using that name. In 2004 it became Four Alls, named after the pub where it is based, the only outlet except for two beers supplied twice yearly to Darlington beer festivals. Phone first to check if beer is available.

Iggy Pop (OG 1036, ABV 3.6%)
A honey-coloured beer made from pale, crystal and wheat malts and hopped with First Gold and Goldings.

30 Shillings (OG 1039, ABV 3.8%)
A dark session ale made from pale, crystal and chocolate malts with First Gold and Fuggles hops.

Swift (OG 1038, ABV 3.8%)
A dark mild made with pale, crystal and chocolate malts. Hopped with Fuggles and Goldings to give a smooth, pleasant character.

Red Admiral (OG 1041, ABV 3.9%)
A deep red beer that uses pale and crystal malts and is hopped with Fuggles. A malty beer with flowery notes.

Smugglers Glory (OG 1041, ABV 4%)

Tallyman IPA (OG 1041, ABV 4%)
A citrus bitter foretaste gives way to a biscuity and malty aftertaste with further citrus notes.

Fowler's

See Prestonpans

Fox EAB

Fox Brewery, 22 Station Road, Heacham, Norfolk, PE31 7EX
☎ (01485) 570345 ✉ info@foxbrewery.co.uk
foxbrewery.co.uk
Tours by arrangement

Based in an old cottage adjacent to the Fox & Hounds pub, Fox brewery was established in 2002 and now supplies around 50 outlets as well as the pub. All the Branthill beers are brewed from barley grown on Branthill Farm and malted at Crisp's in Great Ryburgh. A hop garden next to the brewery, trialled during 2009, is to be enlarged. All cask beers are also available bottle conditioned.
Seasonal beers: Nina's Mild (ABV 3.9%), Flaming Bullet (ABV 4.2%), Fresh as a Daisy (ABV 4.2%), Fox's Willie (ABV 4.4%), Cerberus Stout (ABV 4.5%), Santa's Nuts (ABV 4.8%), Heacham Kriek (ABV 5.1%), Punt Gun (ABV 5.9%), 60 Minute IPA (ABV 6.1%).

Branthill Best (OG 1037, ABV 3.9%)

Heacham Gold (OG 1037, ABV 3.9%)
A gentle beer with light citrus airs. A low but increasing bitterness is the major flavour as some initial sweet hoppiness quickly declines.

Red Knocker (OG 1037, ABV 3.9%)
Copper coloured and malty.

IJB (OG 1040, ABV 4%)
A well-balanced malty brew with a hoppy, bitter background. The long finish holds up well, as a sultana-like fruitiness develops. Mid-brown with a slightly thin mouthfeel.

Branthill Norfolk Nectar (OG 1043, ABV 4.3%)
Slightly sweet. Brewed only with Maris Otter pale malt.

Warrior (OG 1043, ABV 4.4%)

Grizzly Beer (OG 1048, ABV 4.8%)
Honey wheat beer brewed from an American recipe.

Cascade (OG 1051, ABV 5%)
A very light beer with a hoppy flavour.

Bullet (OG 1050, ABV 5.1%)

THE BREWERIES

Pale golden yellow beer with resinous hop aroma and tropical fruit flavours.

Nelson's Blood (OG 1049, ABV 5.1%)
A liquor of beers. Red, full-bodied; made with Nelson's Blood Rum.

IPA (OG 1051, ABV 5.2%)
Based on a 19th-century recipe. Easy drinking for its strength.

Fox Beer SIBA

Fox Beer Co Ltd, Fox & Newt, 7-9 Burley Street, Leeds, West Yorkshire, LS3 1LD
☎ (0113) 245 4505 ✉ foxandnewt@googlemail.com
Tours by arrangement

⊛The brewery was re-commissioned by the ex-Tetley's head brewer, Ian Smith, in 2008. The brewery started as a Whitbread malt extract pub in the 1980s, with the mash tun added in the 1990s. 15 outlets are supplied direct.

Clarendon Dark Mild (OG 1036, ABV 3.6%) ◆
Almost black in colour with a red tinge. Faint aroma but rich flavour of sweet malt and roast with a balancing bitterness, moving to a long malt and roast finish.

Fox Blond (OG 1040, ABV 4.1%)

Mr Tod (OG 1043, ABV 4.3%)

Red Kite (OG 1046, ABV 4.6%)

Fox IPA (OG 1047, ABV 4.7%)

Nightshade (OG 1049, ABV 4.9%)

Foxfield

Foxfield Brewery, Prince of Wales, Foxfield, Broughton in Furness, Cumbria, LA20 6BX
☎ (01229) 716238 ⊕ princeofwalesfoxfield.co.uk
Tours by arrangement

⊛Foxfield is a three-barrel plant in old stables attached to the Prince of Wales inn. A few other outlets are supplied. Tigertops in Wakefield is also owned. The beer range constantly changes so the beers listed here may not necessarily be available. There are many occasional and seasonal beers. Dark Mild is suitable for vegetarians and vegans.

Sands (OG 1038, ABV 3.4%)
A pale, light, aromatic quaffing ale.

Fleur-de-Lys (OG 1038, ABV 3.6%)

Dark Mild (OG 1040, ABV 3.7%)

Brief Encounter (OG 1040, ABV 3.8%)
A fruity beer with a long, bitter finish.

Freedom

Freedom Brewery Ltd, Bagots Park, Abbots Bromley, Staffordshire, WS15 3ER
☎ (01283) 840721
✉ freedom@freedombrewery.com
⊕ freedomlager.com
Shop Mon-Fri 9am-4pm
Tours by arrangement

No real ale. Brothers Brewery was established in 2005 by acquiring Freedom Brewery, and specialises in lagers produced to the German Reinheitsgebot purity law. In 2008 it reverted to the name Freedom Brewery Ltd. It currently produces three beers, Freedom Organic Lager (ABV 4.8%), Freedom Pilsener (ABV 5%) and Freedom Organic Dark Lager (ABV 4.7%). All are suitable for vegetarians and vegans.

Freeminer SIBA

Freeminer Ltd, Whimsey Road, Steam Mills, Cinderford, Gloucestershire, GL14 3JA
☎ (01594) 827989 ✉ sales@freeminer.co.uk

⊗Founded by Don Burgess in 1992, Freeminer – previously Freeminer Brewery – has grown to be one of the vanguard of the quality bottled beers revival. It has two major national listings and bottled Fairtrade beers are being developed. These are sometimes released on draught. The brewery changed hands in 2006 but Don Burgess remains in post. Bottle-conditioned beers are available (brewed for Co-op). Co-op beers are now brewed with barley grown on Co-op farms and malted at Warminster. Fairtrade and organic beers are also produced, with limited edition cask versions available for Fairtrade fortnight.

Bitter (OG 1038, ABV 4%) ◆
A light, hoppy session bitter with an intense hop aroma and a dry, hoppy finish.

Strip & At It (OG 1035, ABV 4%)

Slaughter Porter (OG 1047, ABV 4.8%)

Speculation (OG 1047, ABV 4.8%) ◆
An aromatic, chestnut-brown, full-bodied beer with a smooth, well-balanced mix of malt and hops, and a predominately hoppy aftertaste.

Frodsham

Frodsham Brewery, Lady Heyes Craft Centre, Kingsley Road, Frodsham, Cheshire, WA6 6SU
☎ (01928) 787917
✉ enquire@frodshambrewery.co.uk
⊕ frodshambrewery.co.uk
Shop 10am-4pm daily
Tours by arrangement

⊗ Frodsham has been brewing since 2005 (initially as Stationhouse Brewery in Ellesmere Port). A 5-barrel electric and propane powered unit is used to produce the core range as well as seasonal and celebration brews. 115 outlets are supplied direct. Seasonal/occasional beers: see website. Bottle-conditioned beers are also available.

1'st Lite (OG 1037, ABV 3.8%) ◆
Light, hoppy bitter with clean lemon/grapefruit hop flavours and the trademark Station House bitterness and dry aftertaste. Clean and refreshing.

Maiden's Cross (ABV 3.8%)
A traditional bitter.

Devil's Garden (ABV 3.9%)
An amber bronze traditional beer with biscuit flavour and raisin aftertaste.

Mynza Mild (ABV 3.9%)
A mahogany mild with fruity aftertaste.

Splash (ABV 3.9%)
A blonde, refreshing summer beer. Crisp and citrus with hoppy flavours.

Froda's Ale (ABV 4.2%)
A traditional tawny bitter with a hoppy taste and hints of liquorice.

Buzzin' (OG 1042, ABV 4.3%) ◆
Golden fruity bitter dominated by a honey sweetness. Good hop flavours in initial taste and a long, lasting dry finish.

Iron Man (ABV 4.6%)
An amber, hop-rich beer with fruity aftertones.

800 (ABV 4.7%)
A golden bitter. Floral with late wine flavours.

Nightmail (ABV 4.7%)
A dry, jet black stout. Sharp with a mellow aftertaste.

Aonach (ABV 4.9%)
A typical Scottish style 80/- beer. Dark amber in colour.

Blush (ABV 5%)
A pink fruit beer with raspberry and blackcurrant flavours.

Lammastide (ABV 5%)
An English wheat beer with distinct elderflower aromas.

Wintafest (ABV 5.5%)
A dark, malty beer with citrus fruit, raisin and spice flavours and rich, hoppy aromas.

Frog Island SIBA

Frog Island Brewery, The Maltings, Westbridge, St James Road, Northampton, Northamptonshire, NN5 5HS
☎ (01604) 587772 ✉ beer@frogislandbrewery.co.uk
⊕ frogislandbrewery.co.uk
Tours by arrangement to licensed trade only

⊠ Started in 1994 by home-brewer Bruce Littler and business partner Graham Cherry in a malt house built by the long-defunct Thomas Manning brewery, Frog Island expanded by doubling its brew length to 10 barrels in 1998. It specialises in beers with personalised bottle labels, available by mail order. Some 40 free trade outlets are supplied, with the beer occasionally available through other micro-brewers. Bottle-conditioned beers are available.

Best Bitter (OG 1040, ABV 3.8%) ◆
Blackcurrant and gooseberry enhance the full malty aroma with pineapple and papaya joining on the tongue. Bitterness develops in the fairly long Target/Fuggles finish.

Shoemaker (OG 1043, ABV 4.2%) ◆
An orangey aroma of fruity Cascade hops is balanced by malt. Citrus and hoppy bitterness last into a long, dry finish. Amber colour.

That Old Chestnut (ABV 4.4%)

Natterjack (OG 1048, ABV 4.8%) ◆
Deceptively robust, golden and smooth. Fruit and hop aromas fight for dominance before the grainy astringency and floral palate give way to a long, dry aftertaste.

Fire Bellied Toad (OG 1050, ABV 5%) ◆
Amber-gold brew with an extraordinary long bitter/fruity finish. Huge malt and Phoenix hop flavours have a hint of apples.

Croak & Stagger (OG 1056, ABV 5.6%) ◆
The initial honey/fruit aroma is quickly overpowered by roast malt then bitter chocolate and pale malt sweetness on the tongue. Gentle, bittersweet finish.

Front Street

▤ Front Street Brewery, 45 Front Street, Binham, Fakenham, Norfolk, NR21 0AL
☎ (01328) 830297
✉ steve@frontstreetbrewery.co.uk
⊕ frontstreetbrewery.co.uk
Tours by arrangement

The brewery is based at the Chequers Inn and is probably Britain's smallest five-barrel plant. Brewing started in 2005 and three regular beers are produced as well as seasonal and occasional brews. Both cask and bottled beers are delivered to the free trade and retail outlets throughout East Anglia. Seasonal beers: China Gold (ABV 5%, winter), The Tsar (ABV 8.5%, winter), Old Sid (ABV 10.2%, Oct-Mar). Bottle-conditioned beers are also available.

Binham Cheer (OG 1039, ABV 3.9%)

Callums Ale (OG 1043, ABV 4.3%)

Unity Strong (OG 1051, ABV 5%)

Fugelestou

See Fulstow

Fuller's IFBB SIBA

Fuller, Smith & Turner plc, Griffin Brewery, Chiswick Lane South, London, W4 2QB
☎ (020) 8996 2000 ✉ fullers@fullers.co.uk
⊕ fullers.co.uk
Shop Mon-Fri 10am-8pm; Sat 10am-6pm
Tours by arrangement

⊠ Fuller, Smith & Turner's Griffin Brewery has stood on the same site in Chiswick for more than 350 years. The partnership from which the company now takes its name was formed in 1845 and members of the founding families are still involved in running the company today. Three different Fuller's beers have won the Champion Beer of Britain title, Chiswick Bitter, London Pride and ESB. At the end of 2005 Fuller's announced an agreed acquisition of Hampshire brewer George Gale. The company now operates 366 pubs and hotels. Fuller's stopped brewing at the Gale's Horndean site in 2006 and all of the brands, including some seasonals, are now brewed at Chiswick. Seasonal beers: see website. Bottle-conditioned beers are also available.

Chiswick Bitter (OG 1034.5, ABV 3.5%) 🍶 ◆
Hops are complemented by a little citrus and a malty toffee in the nose and palate of this pale brown bitter. Finish is slightly bitter with light, dry character.

Discovery (OG 1039.5, ABV 3.9%) ◆
A golden ale with citrus fruit and a little malty sweetness. Trace of hops in the flavour and aftertaste with some bitterness. Low aroma due to being served cold.

London Pride (OG 1040.5, ABV 4.1%) ◆
A balanced smooth pale brown best bitter with a malt character that lingers pleasantly with a citrus fruitiness and some bitterness. Aroma can have some creamy caramel notes when mature.

ESB (OG 1054, ABV 5.5%) ◆
This complex, rich strong bitter has orange marmalade on the nose and palate, starting fruity

and then developing into a long, bitter, dry finish complemented by sweet malt.

Under the Gale's brand name:

Seafarers Ale (OG 1036.8, ABV 3.6%)
This is a soft, smooth-drinking pale brown bitter with hops in the flavour, fading in the aftertaste with a touch of sweetness and a little peach and citrus.

HSB (OG 1050, ABV 4.8%)
A good, consistent interpretation of the flagship Gale's beer. A rich, complex traditional bitter; sweet and full-bodied with dark fruit aromas and hints of caramel, leading to a bittersweet finish.

Full Mash

Full Mash Brewery, 17 Lower Park Street, Stapleford, Nottinghamshire, NG9 8EW
☎ (0115) 949 9262 ✉ fullmashbrewery@yahoo.com
fullmash.net

Full Mash started brewing in 2003 with a quarter-barrel plant. The brewery has now expanded to four barrels and, with the addition of extra fermenters, 16 barrels a week are now produced. Trade is expanding with five regular beers supplied to 45 outlets.

Ouija (OG 1043, ABV 3.7%)
A dark mild with intense roast flavour despite its low strength.

ESP (OG 1039, ABV 3.8%)
Sweet and hoppy yellow beer with a little bitterness.

Seance (OG 1041, ABV 4%)
Predominantly hoppy golden beer, with a refreshing bitter finish.

Spiritualist (OG 1044, ABV 4.3%)
A reddish-brown traditional malty best bitter with delicate hop flavours.

Apparition (OG 1046, ABV 4.5%)
A pale hoppy bitter brewed with Brewers Gold hops.

Full Moon

Full Moon Brewery Ltd, Sharpes Farm, Henley Down, Catsfield, Battle, East Sussex, TN33 9BN
☎ 07832 220745 fullmoonbrewery.com

Full Moon was established in 2008 by James Pryke and Professor Philip Parsons.

Hopdance (OG 1039, ABV 3.9%)
A hoppy, refreshing bitter.

Darkerside (OG 1045, ABV 4.4%)
A rich porter.

Fulstow

Fulstow Brewery, 13 Thames Street, Louth, Lincolnshire, LN11 7AD
☎ (01507) 608202 ✉ fulstow.brewery@virgin.net
fulstowbrewery.co.uk
Tours by arrangement

Fulstow operates on a 2.5-barrel plant and started brewing in 2004 in a garage at the home of the head brewer in Fulstow. The brewery moved to Louth in 2006 and was the first brewery to be established there for more than 100 years. 'Fugelstou Ales' are distributed throughout Britain and one-off brews are produced on a regular basis.

Fulstow Common (OG 1038, ABV 3.8%)
A copper-coloured, medium-bodied beer with a strong hop character and malt discernable in the taste.

Marsh Mild (OG 1039, ABV 3.8%)
Traditional mild with a malty aroma. Chocolate malt on the palate with toffee and caramel overtones.

Village Life (OG 1040, ABV 4%)
Ruby red ale with great depth of malt and hop balance.

Northway IPA (OG 1042, ABV 4.2%)
A clean, crisp ale with a citrus aroma; very hoppy with a dry finish.

Imperial Stout (OG 1044.5, ABV 4.4%)
A full-flavoured stout with rich liquorice flavours with fruit and raisins. A satisfying, bitter aftertaste.

Pride of Fulstow (OG 1045, ABV 4.5%)
Copper-coloured bitter with a ripe malt taste in the mouth and a good hop balance. A dry finish with blackcurrant fruit notes.

Funfair

Funfair Brewing Co, Office: 34 Spinney Road, Ilkeston, Derbyshire, DE7 4GL
☎ 07971 540186
✉ sales@funfairbrewingcompany.co.uk
funfairbrewingcompany.co.uk

Funfair was launched in 2004 at the Wheel Inn in Holbrook. The brewery relocated to Ilkeston and in 2006 relocated again to its present site. A bottling plant was installed in 2007. The Chequers Inn in Elston was purchased in 2010, which serves as a brewery tap. There are plans to relocate the brewing plant to the pub and expand capacity to 20 barrels. Over 50 outlets are supplied. Seasonal beers: see website. Bottle-conditioned beers are also available.

Gallopers (OG 1038, ABV 3.8%)

Teacups (ABV 4%)

Waltzer (OG 1045, ABV 4.5%)

Dive Bomber (OG 1047, ABV 4.7%)

Dodgem (OG 1047, ABV 4.7%)

Cakewalk (OG 1060, ABV 6%)

Fuzzy Duck

Fuzzy Duck Brewery, 18 Wood Street, Poulton Industrial Estate, Poulton-le-Fylde, Lancashire, FY6 8JY
☎ 07904 343729 ✉ ben@fuzzyduckbrewery.co.uk
fuzzyduckbrewery.co.uk
Tours by arrangement

Fuzzy Duck was started on a half-barrel plant at the owner's home in 2006. It relocated to an industrial unit and expanded capacity to eight barrels. There are plans to introduce a bottle-conditioned range of beers. 30 outlets are supplied.

Thumb Ducker (OG 1040, ABV 3.9%)

Feathers (OG 1040, ABV 4%)

Stout (OG 1042, ABV 4%)

Cunning Stunt (OG 1044, ABV 4.3%)

Fyfe SIBA

▌Fyfe Brewing Co, 469 High Street, Kirkaldy, Fife, KY1 2SN
☎ (01592) 646211 ✉ fyfebrew@tiscali.co.uk
⊕ fyfebrewery.co.uk
Tours by arrangement

☺Fyfe was established in an old sailmakers behind the Harbour Bar in 1995 on a 2.5-barrel plant. Most of the output is taken by the pub, the remainder being sold direct to around 30 local outlets, including a house beer for JD Wetherspoon in Glenrothes. Seasonal beer: Cauld Turkey (ABV 6%, winter but can be brewed on request all year round).

Auld Alliance (OG 1040, ABV 4%) ◆
A bitter beer with a lingering, dry, hoppy finish. Malt and hop, with fruit, are present throughout, fading in the finish.

Lemon Twist (OG 1042, ABV 4.2%)

Lime-ited Edition (OG 1042, ABV 4.2%)

Lion Slayer (OG 1042, ABV 4.2%)
Amber-coloured ale with malt and fruit on the nose. Fruit predominates on the palate. A slightly dry finish.

Northern Brewer (OG 1042, ABV 4.2%)

Weiss Squad (OG 1045, ABV 4.5%)
Hoppy, bitter wheat beer with bags of citrus in the taste and finish.

Fyfe Fyre (OG 1048, ABV 4.8%)
Pale golden best bitter, full-bodied and balanced with malt, hops and fruit. Hoppy bitterness grows in an increasingly dry aftertaste.

Fyne SIBA

Fyne Ales Ltd, Achadunan, Cairndow, Argyll, PA26 8BJ
☎ (01499) 600120 ✉ jamie@fyneales.com
⊕ fyneales.com
Shop Mon-Sat 10am-4pm; Sun seasonal
Tours by arrangement

☺Fyne Ales has been brewing since 2001. The 10-barrel plant was installed in a redundant milking parlour on a farm in Argyll, set in a beautiful highland glen at the head of Loch Fyne. Around 430 outlets are supplied. The range of beers is supplemented by ale brewed for special events. Seasonal beers: Cairn Dhu (ABV 3.3%), Innishail (ABV 3.6%), Crannog (ABV 4.1%), Holly Daze (ABV 5%).

Piper's Gold (OG 1037.5, ABV 3.8%) ◆
Fresh, golden session ale. Well bittered but balanced with fruit and malt. Long, dry, bitter finish.

Maverick (OG 1040.5, ABV 4.2%) ◆
Full-bodied, roasty, tawny best bitter. It is balanced, fruity and well hopped.

Hurricane Jack (ABV 4.4%)

Vital Spark (OG 1042.5, ABV 4.4%)
A rich, dark beer that shows glints of red. The taste is clean and slightly sharp with a hint of blackcurrant.

Avalanche (OG 1043.5, ABV 4.5%) ◆
This true golden ale starts with stunning citrus hops on the nose. Well-balanced with good body and fruit balancing a refreshing hoppy taste, it finishes with a long bittersweet aftertaste.

Highlander (OG 1045.5, ABV 4.8%) ◆
Full-bodied, bittersweet ale with a good dry hop finish. In the style of a Heavy although the malt is less pronounced and the sweetness ebbs away to leave a bitter, hoppy finish.

Gale's

See Fuller's

Gargoyles

See Isca

Garthela

Garthela Brewhouse, Garthela, Beardwood Brow, Blackburn, Lancashire, BB2 7AT
☎ 07515 648630 ✉ garthelabrewhouse@gmail.com
⊕ garthelabrewhouse.co.uk
Tours by arrangement

☺Garthela Brewhouse began production in late 2008 on a 2.5-barrel plant. Further beers are planned. All beers are also available bottle conditioned.

Barm Cake Bitter (OG 1038, ABV 3.8%)
Golden-coloured with a malty nose and a clean bitterness through to the finish.

Oven Bottom Blonde (OG 1040, ABV 4%)
A classic blonde with a fresh taste of citrus throughout.

Eccles Cake Ale (OG 1041, ABV 4.2%)
Rich in colour with a hint of ruby. A touch of roast with a clean-tasting, delicate hoppiness throughout.

Pint O' Parkin (OG 1043, ABV 4.3%)
A malty dark ale with a subtle hint of blackcurrant.

Black Pudding Porter (OG 1045, ABV 4.5%)
Dark with a velvety sweetness and creaminess.

Geltsdale

Geltsdale Brewery Ltd, Unit 6, Old Brewery Yard, Craw Hall, Brampton, Cumbria, CA8 1TR
☎ (016977) 41541 ✉ geltsdale@mac.com
⊕ geltsdalebrewery.com
Tours by arrangement (max. 15 persons)

☺Geltsdale Brewery was established in 2006 by Fiona Deal and operates from a small unit in Brampton's Old Brewery, dating back to 1785. The beers are named after local landmarks within Geltsdale. Around 70 outlets are supplied direct.

Black Dub (OG 1036, ABV 3.6%)

King's Forest (OG 1038, ABV 3.8%)

Cold Fell (ABV 3.9%)

Bewcastle Brown Ale (ABV 4%)

Brampton Bitter (ABV 4%)

Tarnmonath (OG 1040, ABV 4%)

Hell Beck (OG 1042, ABV 4.2%)

Lager (ABV 4.5%)

George Wright

See under Wright

Gertie Sweet (NEW)

Gertie Sweet Brewing Co, c/o Plassey Brewery, Eyton, nr Wrexham, LL13 0SP
☎ (01939) 235022 ☎ 07769 155874
✉ gertie.sweet@googlemail.com

Following the closure of Hanby Ales, Jack Hanby felt that after 35 years of brewing he was not yet old enough to put down his bungriser! He began brewing from the Plassey Brewery in late 2009. Three regular ales are currently available.

New World Pale (OG 1039, ABV 3.9%)

Traditional (OG 1043, ABV 4.3%)

Winter Belle (OG 1048, ABV 4.8%)

Gidley's SIBA

Gidley's Brewery, 5 Gidleys Meadow, Christow, Exeter, Devon, EX6 7QB
☎ (01647) 252120 ✉ beer@gidleysbrewery.co.uk
🌐 gidleysbrewery.co.uk

⊗ Gidley's started brewing in 2009 using a five-barrel plant after taking over and rebranding the former Scattor Rock Brewery. The unofficial brewery tap is the Teign House Inn in Christow. Around 50 outlets are supplied direct.

Valley (OG 1041, ABV 4%)

Spinney (OG 1040, ABV 4.1%)
A dark, ruby red malty ale.

Meadow (OG 1043, ABV 4.5%)
A golden, hoppy ale.

Glastonbury SIBA

Glastonbury Ales, Unit 11, Wessex Park, Somerton Business Park, Somerton, Somerset, TA11 6SB
☎ (01458) 272244 ✉ pnash@glastonbury.com
🌐 glastonburyales.com
Shop Mon-Fri 10am-4pm; Sat 10am-12.30pm
Tours by arrangement

⊗ Glastonbury Ales was established in 2002 on a five-barrel plant. In 2006 the brewery changed ownership and has recently grown to a 20-barrel outfit. A shop opened in late 2009. Seasonal beers: see website.

Mystery Tor (OG 1040, ABV 3.8%) ◆
A golden bitter with plenty of floral hop and fruit on the nose and palate, the sweetness giving way to a bitter hop finish. Full-bodied for a session bitter.

Lady of the Lake (OG 1042, ABV 4.2%) ◆
A full-bodied amber best bitter with plenty of hops to the fore balanced by a fruity malt flavour and a subtle hint of vanilla, leading to a clean, bitter hop aftertaste.

Hedge Monkey (OG 1048, ABV 4.6%)
A well-rounded deep amber bitter. Malty, rich and very hoppy.

Golden Chalice (OG 1048, ABV 4.8%)
Light and golden best bitter with a robust malt character.

Glenfinnan

Glenfinnan Brewery Co Ltd, Sruth A Mhuilinn, Glenfinnan, PH37 4LT
☎ (01397) 704309 ☎ 07999 261010
✉ info@glenfinnanbrewery.co.uk
🌐 glenfinnanbrewery.co.uk

◎ Glenfinnan opened in 2007 and operates on a four-barrel plant. It produces around 600 litres per week during the tourist season. Further expansion is planned. Seasonal beer: Dark Ale (ABV 5.2%, winter).

Gold Ale (OG 1040, ABV 3.8%)

Standard Ale (OG 1044, ABV 4.2%)

Glentworth SIBA

Glentworth Brewery, Glentworth House, Crossfield Lane, Skellow, Doncaster, South Yorkshire, DN6 8PL
☎ (01302) 725555

◎ The brewery was founded in 1996 and is housed in former dairy buildings. The five-barrel plant supplies more than 80 pubs. Production is concentrated on mainly light-coloured, hoppy ales. Seasonal beers (brewed to order): Oasis (ABV 4.1%), Happy Hooker (ABV 4.3%), North Star (ABV 4.3%), Perle (ABV 4.4%), Dizzy Blonde (ABV 4.5%), Whispers (ABV 4.5%).

Lightyear (OG 1037, ABV 3.9%)

Globe

Globe Brewpub, 144 High Street West, Glossop, Derbyshire, SK13 8HJ
☎ (01457) 852417 🌐 globemusic.org

⊗ Globe was established in 2006 on a 2.5-barrel plant in an old stable behind the Globe pub. The beers are mainly for the pub but special one-off brews are produced for beer festivals.

Amber (ABV 3.8%)

Comet (ABV 4.3%)

Eclipse (ABV 4.3%)

Sirius (ABV 5.2%)

Goacher's

P & DJ Goacher, Unit 8, Tovil Green Business Park, Burial Ground Lane, Tovil, Maidstone, Kent, ME15 6TA
☎ (01622) 682112 🌐 goachers.com
Tours by arrangement

⊗ A traditional brewery that uses only malt and Kentish hops for all its beers. Phil and Debbie Goacher have concentrated on brewing good wholesome beers without gimmicks. Two tied houses and around 30 free trade outlets in the mid-Kent area are supplied. Special is brewed for sale under house names. Seasonal beers: Silver Star (ABV 4.3%), Old 1066 Ale (ABV 6.7%).

Real Mild Ale (OG 1033, ABV 3.4%) ◆
A moderately bitter mild with a base of chocolate malt and hints of roast barley and coffee.

Fine Light Ale (OG 1036, ABV 3.7%) ◆
A pale, golden brown bitter with a strong, floral, hoppy aroma and aftertaste. A hoppy and moderately malty session beer.

Special/House Ale (OG 1037, ABV 3.8%)

Best Dark Ale (OG 1040, ABV 4.1%) ◆
A bitter beer, balanced by a moderate maltiness, with a complex aftertaste.

Crown Imperial Stout (OG 1044, ABV 4.5%) ◆
A good, well-balanced roasty stout, dark and bitter with just a hint of caramel and a lingering creamy head.

Gold Star Ale (OG 1050, ABV 5.1%) ◆
A strong pale ale brewed from 100% Maris Otter malt and East Kent Goldings hops.

Goddards SIBA

Goddards Brewery Ltd, Barnsley Farm, Bullen Road, Ryde, Isle of Wight, PO33 1QF
☎ (01983) 611011 ✉ office@goddardsbrewery.com
⊕ goddardsbrewery.com

⊠ Goddards was established in 1993 on a farmstead on the Isle of Wight. Originally occupying an 18th-century barn, expansion has meant that a new brewery was built in 2008. 300 outlets are supplied. Seasonal beers: see website.

Ale of Wight (OG 1037, ABV 3.7%)
An aromatic, fresh and zesty pale beer.

Special Bitter (OG 1039, ABV 4%) ◆
Well-balanced session beer that maintains its flavour and bite with compelling drinkability.

Fuggle-Dee-Dum (OG 1047, ABV 4.8%) ◆
Brown-coloured strong ale with plenty of malt and hops.

Goff's SIBA

Goff's Brewery Ltd, 9 Isbourne Way, Winchcombe, Cheltenham, Gloucestershire, GL54 5NS
☎ (01242) 603383 ✉ brewery@goffsbrewery.com
⊕ goffsbrewery.com

⊠ Goff's is a family concern that has been brewing cask-conditioned ales since 1994. The ales are available regionally in more than 200 outlets and nationally through wholesalers. The addition of the seasonal Ales of the Round Table provides a range of 12 beers of which four or five are always available: see website for details.

Jouster (OG 1040, ABV 4%) ◆
A drinkable, tawny-coloured ale, with a light hoppiness in the aroma. It has a good balance of malt and bitterness in the mouth, underscored by fruitiness, with a clean, hoppy aftertaste.

Tournament (OG 1038, ABV 4%) ◆
Dark golden in colour, with a pleasant hop aroma. A clean, light and refreshing session bitter with a pleasant hop aftertaste.

White Knight (OG 1046, ABV 4.7%) ◆
A well-hopped bitter with a light colour and full-bodied taste. Bitterness predominates in the mouth and leads to a dry, hoppy aftertaste.

Golcar SIBA

Golcar Brewery, 60a Swallow Lane, Golcar, Huddersfield, West Yorkshire, HD7 4NB
☎ (01484) 644241 ☎ 07970 267555
✉ golcarbrewrey@btconnect.com
Tours by arrangement

⊕ Golcar started brewing in 2001 and production has increased from 2.5 barrels to five barrels a week. The brewery owns one pub, the Rose & Crown at Golcar, and supplies other outlets in the local area.

Dark Mild (OG 1034, ABV 3.4%) ▣ ◆

Dark mild with a light roasted malt and liquorice taste. Smooth and satisfying.

Bitter (OG 1039, ABV 3.9%) ◆
Amber bitter with a hoppy, citrus taste, with fruity overtones and a bitter finish.

Pennine Gold (OG 1038, ABV 4%)
A hoppy and fruity session beer.

Weavers Delight (OG 1045, ABV 4.8%)
Malty best bitter with fruity overtones.

Guthlac's Porter (OG 1047, ABV 5%)
A robust all grain and malty working man's porter.

Golden Valley

Golden Valley Ales, Old Forge Industrial Estate, Peterchurch, Herefordshire, HR2 0SD
☎ (01981) 252998 ☎ 05603 123209 / 07733 891314 ✉ beer@goldenvalleyales.co.uk
Tours by arrangement

☺ Golden Valley was set up in 2009 at the Bull Ring Pub, Kingstone with equipment from the Dunn Plowman Brewery. After a year of rapid growth the brewery moved to an industrial unit in 2010 with a 35-barrel capacity and delivers direct to over 50 outlets. Seasonal beer: Hop, Stock & Barrel (ABV 4.6%, winter). Bottle-conditioned beers are planned.

Hay Bluff (ABV 3.7%)

.410 (OG 1039, ABV 4.1%)

Brewers Choice (ABV 4.5%)

Kenyons Original Oatmeal Stout (ABV 4.7%)

Goldfinch

⬛ Goldfinch Brewery, 47 High Street East, Dorchester, Dorset, DT1 1HU
☎ (01305) 264020 ✉ info@goldfinchbrewery.com
⊕ goldfinchbrewery.com
Shop 11am-11pm daily
Tours by arrangement

⊠ Goldfinch has been brewing since 1987 and is situated behind the Tom Brown public house. In 2008 the brewery and pub were purchased by Dorset Brewing Co (qv). Eight outlets are supplied. Seasonal beer: Midnight Blinder (ABV 5%, Nov-Feb). All beers are currently brewed in Weymouth by Dorset Brewing Co (qv).

Goodall's SIBA (NEW)

⬛ Goodall's Brewery, The Lodge, 88 Crewe Road, Alsager, Staffordshire, ST7 2JA
☎ (01270) 873669
✉ goodalls.brewery@hotmail.co.uk
Tours by arrangement

⊠ Goodall's began brewing in 2010 at the Lodge in Alsager using a 2.5-barrel plant.

Datum (OG 1039, ABV 4%)

Snoweater (OG 1049, ABV 4.9%)

Goose Eye SIBA

Goose Eye Brewery Ltd, Ingrow Bridge, South Street, Keighley, West Yorkshire, BD21 5AX
☎ (01535) 605807
✉ gooseeyebrewery@btconnect.com
⊕ goose-eye-brewery.co.uk

⊚Goose Eye is a family-run brewery supplying 60-70 regular outlets, mainly in Yorkshire and Lancashire. The beers are available through national wholesalers and pub chains. It produces monthly occasional and seasonal beers with entertaining names.

Barm Pot Bitter (OG 1038, ABV 3.8%) ◆
The bitter hop and citrus flavours that dominate this amber session bitter are balanced by a malty base. The finish is increasingly dry and bitter.

Bronte Bitter (OG 1040, ABV 4%) ◆
A brown, malty best bitter. Bitterness increases to give a lingering, dry finish.

No-Eye Deer (OG 1040, ABV 4%) ◆
A faint fruity and malty aroma. Strong hoppy flavours and an intense, bitter finish characterise this pale brown bitter.

Chinook Blonde (OG 1042, ABV 4.2%) ◆
An increasingly tart, bitter finish follows an assertive grapefruit hoppiness in both the aroma and taste of this satisfying blonde brew.

Golden Goose (OG 1045, ABV 4.5%)
A straw-coloured beer light on the palate with a smooth and refreshing hoppy finish.

Over and Stout (OG 1052, ABV 5.2%) ◆
A full-bodied stout with a complex palate in which roast and caramel flavours mingle with malt, dark fruit and liquorice. Look also for tart fruit on the nose and a growing bitter finish.

Pommies Revenge (OG 1052, ABV 5.2%)
An extra strong, single malt bitter.

Graffiti

See Fallons

Grafters

▤ Grafters Brewery, Half Moon, 23 High Street, Willingham by Stow, Lincolnshire, DN21 5JZ
☎ (01427) 788340 ✉ phil@graftersbrewery.com
⊕ graftersbrewery.com
Tours by arrangement

⊚Brewing started on a 2.5-barrel plant in 2007 in a converted garage adjacent to the owner's freehouse, the Half Moon. Seasonal beer: Grafters Greeting (ABV 4.4%, Dec).

Moonlight (OG 1038, ABV 3.6%)

Traditional Bitter (ABV 3.8%)

Over the Moon (ABV 4%)

Brewers Troop (ABV 4.2%)

Darker Side of the Moon (OG 1045, ABV 4.2%)

Golden (OG 1046, ABV 4.3%)

Wobble Gob (OG 1048, ABV 4.6%)

Grafton

▤ Grafton Brewing & Pub Co, Packet Inn, Bescoby Street, Retford, Nottinghamshire, DN22 6LJ
☎ (01909) 476121 ☎ 07837 962688

Head Office: 8 Oak Close, Worksop, Nottinghamshire, S80 1GH ✉ allbeers@oakclose.orangehome.co.uk
Shop open during licensing hours
Tours by arrangement

⊚The brewery became operational in early 2007 and is housed in a converted stable block at the Packet Inn. The recipes for the re-named beers were purchased from Broadstone Brewery when that closed in 2006. Around 200 outlets are supplied. Seasonal beers: Snowmans Folly (ABV 4.2%, Oct-Mar), Winters Dream (ABV 4.5%, Oct-Mar), Summer Bliss (ABV 4.5%), Yule Fuel (ABV 4%), Fairground Attraction (ABV 4.2%), Encore (ABV 4.5%).

Two Water Grog (OG 1040, ABV 4%)

Lady Julia (OG 1042, ABV 4.3%)

Lady Catherine (OG 1044, ABV 4.5%)

Royal Blonde (ABV 4.5%)

Blondie (OG 1046, ABV 4.8%)

Lady Mary (OG 1050, ABV 5%)

Grain EAB SIBA

Grain Brewery, South Farm, Tunbeck Road, Alburgh, Harleston, Norfolk, IP20 0BS
☎ (01986) 788884 ✉ info@grainbrewery.co.uk
⊕ grainbrewery.co.uk
Shop Mon-Sat 10am-4pm
Tours by arrangement

⊗ Grain Brewery was launched in 2006 by Geoff Wright and Phil Halls. The five-barrel brewery is located in a converted dairy on a farm in the Waveney Valley. 80 outlets are supplied. Seasonal beers: see website. Bottle-conditioned beers are also available.

Oak (OG 1038, ABV 3.8%) ◆
A superbly balanced mix of malt and hops with bitter overtones. A lingering hint of molasses develops in the long, uplifting finish. Tawny hued with gentle malt airs.

Best Bitter (OG 1042, ABV 4.2%)

Harvest Moon (OG 1045, ABV 4.5%) ◆
An aroma of coffee vanilla introduces this complex but well-balanced amber hued brew. Malt and hops vie with a bitter citrus fruitiness for dominance. Mandarins make a late appearance.

Blackwood Stout (OG 1050, ABV 5%)

Porter (OG 1052, ABV 5.2%) ◆
A creamy, vanilla-enhanced brew. Well-rounded maltiness flows through both bouquet and taste and gives depth to the creamy, coffee-like roast character. A big, warming finish.

India Pale Ale (OG 1062, ABV 6.5%)

Grainstore SIBA

Davis'es Brewing Co Ltd (Grainstore), Grainstore Brewery, Station Approach, Oakham, Rutland, LE15 6RE
☎ (01572) 770065 ✉ grainstorebry@aol.com
⊕ grainstorebrewery.com
Tours by arrangement

Grainstore, the smallest county's largest brewery, has been in production since 1995. The brewery's curious name comes from the fact that it was founded by Tony Davis and Mike Davies. After 30 years in the industry Tony decided to set up his own business after finding a derelict Victorian railway grainstore building. 80 outlets are supplied. Seasonal beers: Springtime (ABV 4.5%, Mar-May), Gold (ABV 4.5%, May-Sep), Tupping Ale (ABV 4.5%,

Sep-Oct), Three Kings (ABV 4.5%, Nov-Dec). Bottle-conditioned beer is also available.

Rutland Panther (OG 1034, ABV 3.4%) ◆
This superb reddish-black mild punches above its weight with malt and roast flavours combining to deliver a brew that can match the average stout for intensity of flavour.

Cooking (OG 1036, ABV 3.6%) ◆
Tawny-coloured beer with malt and hops on the nose and a pleasant grainy mouthfeel. Hops and fruit flavours combine to give a bitterness that continues into a long finish.

Triple B (OG 1042, ABV 4.2%) ◆
Initially hops dominate over malt in both the aroma and taste, but fruit is there, too. All three linger in varying degrees in the sweetish aftertaste of this brown brew.

Ten Fifty (OG 1050, ABV 5%) ◆
Full-bodied, mid-brown strong bitter with a hint of malt on the nose. Malt, hops and fruitiness coalesce in a well-balanced taste; bittersweet finish.

Rutland Beast (OG 1053, ABV 5.3%)
A strong beer, dark brown in colour. Well-balanced flavours blend together to produce a full-bodied drink.

Nip (OG 1073, ABV 7.3%)
A true barley wine. A good balance of sweetness and bitterness meld together so that neither predominates over the other. Smooth and warming.

For Phipps Northampton Brewery Co:

Red Star (OG 1038, ABV 3.8%)

IPA (OG 1042, ABV 4.2%)

Great Gable

Great Gable Brewing Co Ltd, Unit 2G, Bridge End Industrial Estate, Egremont, Cumbria, CA22 2RD
☎ **(01946) 823846** ✉ **thegreatgable@btconnect.com**
🌐 **greatgablebrewing.com**
Tours by arrangement

Great Gable began brewing in 2002 using a five-barrel plant at the Wasdale Head Inn in Gosforth. It moved to its current location in 2010. Seasonal and bottle-conditioned beers are available.

Great Gable (OG 1035, ABV 3.7%) ◆
Refreshing, hoppy, fruity bitter with a pleasant, bitter aftertaste.

Burnmoor Pale Ale (OG 1040, ABV 4.2%) ◆
A dry, hoppy bitter, refreshing and clean-tasting. Straw-coloured with a fruity taste and grapefruit overtones. Long, bitter finish.

Wasd'ale (OG 1042, ABV 4.4%)
Ruby-coloured best bitter

Yewbarrow (OG 1054, ABV 5.5%) ◆
Strong, mild dark ale with robust roast flavours, rich and malty. Satisfying with hints of spice and fruit. Smooth chocolate and coffee aromas.

Great Heck

Great Heck Brewing Co Ltd, Harwinn House, Main Street, Great Heck, North Yorkshire, DN14 0BQ
☎ **(01977) 661430** ☎ **07723 381002**
✉ **denzil@greatheckbrewery.co.uk**
🌐 **greatheckbrewery.co.uk**

Great Heck began production in 2008 on a four-barrel plant in a converted slaughterhouse. Capacity was increased to 12 barrels per week in 2009. Over 100 outlets are supplied.

Dave (OG 1039, ABV 3.8%)

White Rabbit (OG 1038, ABV 3.8%)

Yorkshire Navigator (OG 1038, ABV 3.9%)

Yorkshire Pale Ale (OG 1043, ABV 4.3%)
A premium pale ale with a complex malt character and zesty finish.

Slaughterhouse Porter (OG 1046, ABV 4.5%)
Very black, full-bodied porter with a smooth malt character.

Staggering Genius (OG 1049, ABV 5%)
A pale Yorkshire wheat beer.

Super-Dave (OG 1050, ABV 5%)

Great Newsome

Great Newsome Brewery Ltd, Great Newsome Farm, South Frodingham, Winestead, East Yorkshire, HU12 0NR
☎ **(01964) 612201** ☎ **07808 367386**
✉ **enquiries@greatnewsomebrewery.co.uk**
🌐 **greatnewsomebrewery.co.uk**

Nestled in the Holderness countryside, Great Newsome began production in 2007 on a 10-barrel plant, brewing in renovated farm buildings. Beer is distributed throughout Yorkshire as well as North Lincolnshire. Seasonal beers: see website.

Sleck Dust (OG 1037, ABV 3.8%)
Straw-coloured, refreshingly bitter session beer with floral aroma and subtle dry finish.

Pricky Back Otchan (OG 1042, ABV 4.2%)
Hoppy golden bitter with fresh citrus aroma.

Frothingham Best (OG 1042, ABV 4.3%)
Dark amber best bitter with subtle dry finish.

Holderness Dark (OG 1042, ABV 4.3%)
Dark, strong mild. Malty notes with a hint of sweetness.

Jem's Stout (OG 1044, ABV 4.3%)
Dark, smooth beer with smoky, roasted malt flavours and aroma.

Great Oakley SIBA

Great Oakley Brewery, Bridge Farm, 11 Brooke Road, Great Oakley, Northamptonshire, NN18 8HG
☎ **(01536) 744888** ✉ **tailshaker@tiscali.co.uk**
🌐 **greatoakleybrewery.co.uk**
Tours by arrangement

The brewery started production in 2005 and is housed in converted stables on a former working farm. It is run by husband and wife team Phil and Hazel Greenway. More than 50 outlets are supplied, including the Malt Shovel Tavern in Northampton, which is the brewery tap. Seasonal beers: see website. Bottle-conditioned beers are also available.

Welland Valley Mild (OG 1037, ABV 3.6%)
A dark, traditional mild. Full of flavour.

Wagtail (OG 1040, ABV 3.9%)
Light coloured with a unique bitterness derived from New Zealand hops.

Wot's Occurring (OG 1040, ABV 3.9%)

THE BREWERIES

A mid-golden session bitter with a subtle hop finish.

Marching In (OG 1041, ABV 4.1%)
A golden, clean-tasting beer.

Harpers (OG 1045, ABV 4.3%)
Traditional mid-brown bitter with a malty taste and slight hints of chocolate and citrus in the finish.

Gobble (OG 1046, ABV 4.5%) 🍺
Straw-coloured with a pleasant hop aftertaste.

Delapre Dark (OG 1047, ABV 4.6%)
A dark, full-bodied ale made from five different malts.

Abbey Stout (ABV 5%)
A dark, rich stout.

Tailshaker (OG 1051, ABV 5%)
A complex golden ale with a great depth of flavour.

Great Orme

Great Orme Brewery Ltd, Nant y Cywarch, Glan Conwy, Conwy, LL28 5PP
☎ (01492) 580548 ✉ info@greatormebrewery.co.uk
⊕ greatormebrewery.co.uk

😊Great Orme is a five-barrel micro-brewery situated on a hillside in the Conwy Valley between Llandudno and Betws-y-Coed, with views of the Conwy Estuary and the Great Orme. Established in 2005, it is housed in a number of converted farm buildings. Around 50 outlets are supplied.

Cambria (ABV 3.8%)
A modern IPA with a full hop flavour and dry finish.

Welsh Black (OG 1042, ABV 4%) ◆
Smooth-tasting dark beer with roast coffee notes in aroma and taste. Sweetish in flavour and having some characteristics of a mild ale with hoppiness also present in the aftertaste.

Orme (OG 1043, ABV 4.2%) ◆
Malty best bitter with a dry finish. Faint hop and fruit notes in aroma and taste, but malt dominates throughout.

Celtica (OG 1045, ABV 4.5%) ◆
Yellow in colour with a zesty taste full of citrus fruit flavours. Some initial sweetness followed by peppery hops and a bitter finish.

Merlyn (OG 1051, ABV 5%)
A strong ale with balanced hop bitterness and sweet malt.

Great Western

Great Western Brewing Co Ltd, Stream Bakery, Bristol Road, Hambrook, Bristol, BS16 1RF
☎ (0117) 957 2842
✉ contact@greatwesternbrewingcompany.co.uk
⊕ greatwesternbrewingcompany.co.uk
Shop Mon/Wed/Thu 10am-5pm; Fri 10am-5pm; Sat 10am-3pm
Tours by arrangement

⊗ Great Western is a 12-barrel brewery set up in 2008 by Kevin Stone in a former bakery. The property has been renovated resulting in a bespoke showpiece brewery retaining many of the buildings original features. 150 outlets are supplied and one pub is owned.

Maiden Voyage (OG 1040, ABV 4%)

Bees Knees (OG 1041, ABV 4.2%)

Classic Gold (OG 1044, ABV 4.6%)

Old Higby (OG 1045, ABV 4.8%)

Ruby Porter (OG 1048, ABV 5.2%)

Green Dragon

⊟ **Green Dragon Brewery, Green Dragon, 29 Broad Street, Bungay, Suffolk, NR35 1EF**
☎ (01986) 892681
Tours by arrangement

⊗ The Green Dragon pub was purchased from Brent Walker in 1991 and the buildings at the rear converted to a brewery. In 1994 the plant was expanded and moved into a converted barn across the car park. The doubling of capacity allowed the production of a larger range of ales, including seasonal and occasional brews. The beers are available at the pub and beer festivals. Seasonal beer: Wynnter Warmer (ABV 6.5%).

Chaucer Ale (OG 1037, ABV 3.7%)

Gold (OG 1045, ABV 4.4%)

Bridge Street Bitter (OG 1046, ABV 4.5%)

Strong Mild (ABV 5.4%)

Greene King

See under New Nationals section

Greenfield SIBA

Greenfield Real Ale Brewery, Unit 8 Waterside Mills, Greenfield, Saddleworth, Greater Manchester, OL3 7NH
☎ (01457) 879789 ✉ office@greenfieldrealale.co.uk
⊕ greenfieldrealale.co.uk
Shop 9am-5pm daily
Tours by arrangement

😊Greenfield was launched in 2002 by Peter Percival, former brewer at Saddleworth. Tony Harratt joined Peter in 2005 as a partner. The brewery space was doubled in 2008 to provide extra storage and bottling facilities. 100-120 outlets are supplied. Seasonal beers: see website. Bottle-conditioned ales are also available.

Black Five (OG 1040, ABV 4%) ◆
A dark brown beer in which malt, roast, toffee, fruit and chocolate can all be found in aroma and taste. Smooth, malty aftertaste.

Monkey Business (OG 1041, ABV 4%) ◆
Yellow in colour with a fruit and hop aroma. Hops and grapefruit in the mouth, with a dry, astringent finish.

Delph Donkey (OG 1041, ABV 4.1%)

Dobcross Bitter (OG 1041, ABV 4.2%)

Summer Ice (OG 1041, ABV 4.2%)

Green Jack SIBA

Green Jack Brewing Co Ltd, Argyle Place, Love Road, Lowestoft, Suffolk, NR32 2NZ
☎ (01502) 562863 ✉ info@green-jack.co.uk
⊕ green-jack.com
Tours by arrangement

Green Jack started brewing in 2003 and in 2009 moved to a 35-barrel brew house built in an old Lowestoft smoke house. 150 outlets are supplied and two pubs are owned. Seasonal beers: see website. Bottle-conditioned beers are also available. Beers are also brewed for Hektors Brewery Ltd.

Canary Pale Ale (OG 1038, ABV 3.8%) ◆
Slight lemon aroma. Hoppy, fruit bitterness continues through to a gentle bittersweet finish.

Orange Wheat Beer (OG 1041, ABV 4.2%) ◆
Well-balanced, lightly hopped but full-bodied beer with a distinctive orange aroma and flavour.

Trawlerboys Best Bitter (OG 1045, ABV 4.6%)

Lurcher Stout (OG 1046, ABV 4.8%) ◆
Rich, roasty dark ale with mature blackcurrant in the aroma and fruity, hoppy bitterness in the taste quickly giving way to a long, sweetish aftertaste.

Mahseer IPA (OG 1048, ABV 5%)

Gone Fishing ESB (OG 1052, ABV 5.5%)

Ripper Tripel (OG 1074, ABV 8.5%)

Baltic Trade Export Stout (OG 1092, ABV 10.5%)

Green Mill

Green Mill Brewery, Queensway Snooker Club, Green Mill, Well I' Th' Lane, Rochdale, OL11 2LS
☎ 07967 656887 ✉ greenmillbrewery@msn.com
🌐 greenmillbrewery.co.uk

Green Mill started brewing in 2007 on a 2.5-barrel plant. A number of seasonal and occasional ales are brewed. Around 30 outlets are supplied either directly or through wholesalers.

Gold (ABV 3.6%)

Bitter T'ale (ABV 4%)

Chief (ABV 4.2%)

Northern Lights (ABV 4.5%)

Big Chief (ABV 5.5%)

Greenodd (NEW)

Greenodd Brewery, Ship Inn, Main Street, Greenodd, Cumbria, LA12 7QZ
☎ 07782 655294

Greenodd was established in 2010 in a building behind the Ship Inn using a two-barrel plant.

Best Bitter (ABV 4.1%)

GPA (Greenodd Pale Ale) (ABV 4.4%)

Green Room (NEW)

Green Room Ales Ltd, c/o St Stephen Road, Sticker, St Austell, Cornwall, PL26 7HA
☎ 07843 010950 ✉ letstalk@greenroomales.co.uk
🌐 greenroomales.co.uk

Stephen Burton started brewing in 2009 on a 2.5-barrel plant at the listed address. Due to increased demand he started using spare capacity at Keltek Brewery (qv), along with its bottling facilities. Production was relocated from early 2010, with the original plant subsequently moved to Keltek to increase flexibility. Cask beers are produced but much of the output is bottled, although at present only some of the special brews are bottle-conditioned.

Icon (ABV 4%)

IPA (ABV 4%)

Kudos (ABV 5%)

Rogue (ABV 7.6%)

Green Tye EAB

Green Tye Brewery, Green Tye, Much Hadham, Hertfordshire, SG10 6JP
☎ (01279) 841041 ✉ info@gtbrewery.co.uk
🌐 gtbrewery.co.uk
Tours by arrangement for small groups

⊗ Established in 1999 near Much Hadham, on the edge of the Ash Valley. The local free trade and neighbouring counties are supplied, and further afield via beer agencies and swaps with other micro-breweries. Cask beers are also available bottle conditioned. Seasonal beers: Snowdrop (ABV 3.9%, winter/spring), Mad Morris (ABV 4.2%, summer), Green Tiger (ABV 4.2%, summer), Autumn Rose (ABV 4.2%), Conkerer (ABV 4.7%, autumn), Coal Porter (ABV 4.5%, winter).

Union Jack (OG 1036, ABV 3.6%)
A copper-coloured bitter, fruity with a citrus taste and a hoppy, citrus aroma, with a balanced, bitter finish.

Hertfordshire Hedgehog (OG 1042, ABV 4%)
Traditional, chestnut-coloured bitter with a deep, hoppy nose. Starts soft and full with malt fruit flavours and bitterness, developing through to a full bitter finish.

East Anglian Gold (OG 1042, ABV 4.2%)

Gribble

▤ Gribble Brewery Ltd, Gribble Inn, Oving, West Sussex, PO20 2BP
☎ (01243) 786893 ✉ info@gribbleinn.co.uk
🌐 gribbleinn.co.uk

⊗ The Gribble Brewery was established in 1980. Until 2005 it was run as a managed house operation by Hall & Woodhouse (qv) but is now an independent micro-brewery owned by the publicans of the inn on the same site. Around 20 outlets are supplied direct. Seasonal beer: Wobbler (ABV 7.2%, Xmas).

Pukka Mild (ABV 3.5%)

CHI P A (ABV 3.8%)

Sussex Quadhopper (ABV 4%)
A full-flavoured beer with lots of hops.

Ale (ABV 4.1%)

Fuzzy Duck (ABV 4.3%)

Mocha Mole (ABV 4.5%)
A dark old ale with chocolate and coffee flavours.

Reg's Tipple (ABV 5%)
Reg's Tipple was named after a customer from the early days of the brewery. It has a smooth nutty flavour with a pleasant afterbite.

Plucking Pheasant (ABV 5.2%)

Pig's Ear (ABV 5.8%)

Griffin

▤ Griffin Brewery, Church Road, Shustoke, Warwickshire, B46 2LB
☎ (01675) 481205
Tours by arrangement

Brewing started in 2008 in the old coffin shop premises adjacent to the pub (formerly occupied by Church End Brewery). The brewery is a venture between Griffin licensee Mick Pugh and his son Oliver. At present the brewery only supplies the Griffin Inn and beer festivals.

Slurcher (OG 1041, ABV 4%)

'Ere It Is (OG 1045, ABV 4.5%)

Black Magic Woman (OG 1047, ABV 4.7%)

Pricklee 'olly (OG 1066, ABV 6.3%)

Gwaun Valley

Gwaun Valley Brewery, Kilkiffeth Farm, Pontfaen, Fishguard, SA65 9TP
☎ (01348) 881304

Gwaun Valley began brewing in 2009 on a four-barrel plant. They are open for sampling and visitors during business hours.

Bitter (ABV 4%)

Dark (ABV 4%)

Light (ABV 4%)

Gwynant

Bragdy Gwynant, Tynllidiart Arms, Capel Bangor, Aberystwyth, Ceredigion, SY23 3LR
☎ (01970) 880248 tynllidiartarms.com
Tours by arrangement

Brewing started in 2004 in a 4' 6" x 4' former men's toilet at the front of the pub, with a brew length of nine gallons. Beer is only sold in the pub. The brewery has now been recognised as the smallest commercial brewery in the world by the Guinness Book of Records. Brewing recommenced in late 2009 after a period of suspension.

Cwrw Gwynant (ABV 4.5%)

Hadrian & Border SIBA

Alnwick Ales Ltd t/a Hadrian & Border Brewery, Unit 11, Hawick Crescent Industrial Estate, Newcastle upon Tyne, Tyne & Wear, NE6 1AS
☎ (0191) 276 5302 hadrianborder@yahoo.co.uk
hadrian-border-brewery.co.uk
Tours by arrangement

Hadrian & Border is based at the former Four Rivers 20-barrel site in Newcastle but is relocating to Newburn in the near future as a larger plant is required. The company's brands are available from Glasgow to Yorkshire, and nationally via wholesalers. The beers are popular on Tyneside; the Sir John Fitzgerald Group stocks them regularly. Around 100 outlets are supplied.

Gladiator (OG 1036, ABV 3.8%)
Tawny-coloured bitter with plenty of malt in the aroma and palate leading to a strong, bitter finish.

Tyneside Blonde (OG 1037, ABV 3.9%)
Refreshing blonde ale with zesty notes and a clean, fruity finish.

Farne Island Pale Ale (OG 1038, ABV 4%)
A copper-coloured bitter with a refreshing malt/hop balance.

Flotsam (OG 1038, ABV 4%)
Bronze coloured with a citrus bitterness and a distinctive floral aroma.

Legion Ale (OG 1040, ABV 4.2%)
Well-balanced, amber-coloured beer, full bodied with good malt flavours. Well hopped with a long bitter finish.

Newcastle Pioneer (ABV 4.2%)
Light amber ale, well hopped with only Pioneer hops to give a light spicy/fruity finish.

Secret Kingdom (OG 1042, ABV 4.3%)
Dark, rich and full-bodied, slightly roasted with a malty palate ending with a pleasant bitterness.

Reiver's IPA (OG 1042, ABV 4.4%)
Golden bitter with a clean citrus palate and aroma with subtle malt flavours breaking through at the end.

Centurion Best Bitter (OG 1043, ABV 4.5%)
Smooth, clean-tasting bitter with a distinct hop palate leading to a good, bitter finish.

Ouseburn Porter (ABV 5.2%)
A traditional, robust and satisfying porter made with the finest ingredients.

Halfpenny

Halfpenny Brewery, Crown Inn, High Street, Lechlade, Gloucestershire, GL7 3AE
☎ (01367) 252198 halfpennybrewery.co.uk
Tours by arrangement

Halfpenny was established in late 2008 on a four-barrel plant. Two more fermentation vessels are planned to keep up with demand as are more beers. Bottle-conditioned beers are available.

Ha'penny Ale (OG 1039, ABV 4%)

Thames Tickler (OG 1040, ABV 4%)

Anniversary Ale (OG 1042, ABV 4.2%)

Four Seasons' Ale (OG 1042, ABV 4.3%)

Cockle Warmer (OG 1045, ABV 4.5%)

Old Lech (OG 1045, ABV 4.5%)

Halifax Steam

Halifax Steam Brewing Co Ltd, The Conclave, Southedge Works, Brighouse Road, Hipperholme, West Yorkshire, HX3 8EF
☎ 07974 544980 david@halifax-steam.co.uk
halifax-steam.co.uk

Halifax Steam was established in 2001 on a five-barrel plant and only supplies its brewery tap, the Cock o' the North, which is adjacent to the brewery. Approximately 150 different rotating beers are produced, three of which are permanent. The brewery also produces the only rice beers in the country. 10-12 Halifax Steam beers are available at any one time, plus occasional guests on a fair trade basis.

Emerald (ABV 3.8%)

Crock O' Tears (ABV 4%)

Jamaican Ginger (ABV 4%)
Refreshing yellow, grainy speciality beer. The ginger dominates but is not too fiery. It finishes sweet with the ginger receding on the palate.

Lily Fogg (ABV 4%)

Uncle John (ABV 4.3%)
Roast predominates in this creamy, dark brown stout. The finish is smooth with no harsh edges.

Child Catcher (ABV 4.8%)

Cock o' the North (ABV 5%) ◆
Amber-coloured, grainy strong bitter. Predominantly malty nose and taste, with a dry and astringent finish.

Hall & Woodhouse (Badger) IFBB

Hall & Woodhouse Ltd, Blandford St Mary, Blandford Forum, Dorset, DT11 9LS
☎ (01258) 452141 ✉ info@hall-woodhouse.co.uk
hall-woodhouse.co.uk
Shop Mon-Sat 9am-6pm; Sun 11am-3pm (Easter-Oct)
Tours by arrangement (call to book)

Founded by Charles Hall in 1777, Hall & Woodhouse is an independent family brewer, today run by the fifth generation of the Woodhouse family. The Badger logo was adopted in 1875. The company moved from Ansty to its present site in 1900 and a new brewery is planned on part of the current site by the end of 2011. Cask beer is sold in all 240 pubs. Seasonal beers: see website.

K&B Sussex Bitter (OG 1036, ABV 3.5%) ◆
Traditional, lightly-hopped, easy-drinking session bitter with hints of malt and caramel and the traditional Badger fruit flavour predominating in the lingering bitter aftertaste.

First Gold (OG 1041, ABV 4%) ◆
Good example of a best bitter with good, but not overpowering, hop aromas and flavours and a bittersweet aftertaste.

Tanglefoot (OG 1047, ABV 4.9%) ◆
Relatively sweet-tasting and deceptive, given its strength. Pale malt provides caramel overtones and bittersweet finish.

Hambleton SIBA

Nick Stafford's Hambleton Ales, Melmerby Green Road, Melmerby, North Yorkshire, HG4 5NB
☎ (01765) 640108 ✉ sales@hambletonales.co.uk
hambletonales.co.uk
Shop Mon-Fri 7.30am-5pm
Tours by arrangement

Hambleton Ales was established in 1991 on the banks of the River Swale in the heart of the Vale of York. Expansion over the years has resulted in relocation to larger premises on several occasions, the last being in 2007. Brewing capacity has increased to 100 barrels a week and a bottling line caters for micros and larger brewers, handling more than 20 brands. More than 100 outlets are supplied throughout Yorkshire and the North-east. Four core brands are produced along with an additional special brew every month. The company also brew beers under contract for the Village Brewer and Black Dog Brewery.

Bitter (ABV 3.8%)
A golden bitter with a good balance of malty and refreshing citrus notes leading to a mellow, tangy finish.

Stallion (OG 1041, ABV 4.2%) ◆
A premium bitter, moderately hoppy throughout and richly balanced in malt and fruit, developing a sound and robust bitterness, with earthy hops drying the aftertaste.

Stud (OG 1042.5, ABV 4.3%) ◆
A strongly bitter beer, with rich hop and fruit. It ends dry and spicy.

Nightmare (OG 1050, ABV 5%) ◆
This impressively flavoured beer satisfies all parts of the palate. Strong roast malts dominate, but hoppiness rears out of this complex blend.

For Black Dog Brewery, Whitby:

Whitby Abbey Ale (ABV 3.8%)
A light-coloured, hoppy bitter.

Schooner (ABV 4.2%)

Rhatas (ABV 4.6%)
A dark, rich bitter. Creamy and smooth to the palate.

For Village Brewer:

White Boar (OG 1037.5, ABV 3.8%) ◆
A light, flowery and fruity ale; crisp, clean and refreshing, with a dry-hopped, powerful but not aggressive bitter finish.

Old Raby (OG 1045, ABV 4.8%) ◆
A full-bodied, smooth, rich-tasting dark ale. A complex balance of malt, fruit character and creamy caramel sweetness offsets the bitterness.

Hammerpot

Hammerpot Brewery Ltd, Unit 30, The Vinery, Arundel Road, Poling, West Sussex, BN18 9PY
☎ (01903) 883338 ✉ sales@hammerpot-brewery.co.uk hammerpot-brewery.co.uk

Hammerpot started brewing in 2005 and the brew plant has been upgraded to a five-barrel brew-length. The brewery supplies a wide area between Southamptom and Eastbourne and north to the M25. All cask beers are available in bottle-conditioned form. Seasonal beers: Martlet (ABV 3.5%, Apr-Sep), Bottle Wreck Porter (ABV 4.7%, Oct-Mar), Shepherd's Warmer (ABV 5.5%), Vinery Mild (ABV 3.4%, May & Sep), HPA (ABV 4.1%, Jun-Aug).

Meteor (OG 1038, ABV 3.8%)

White Wing (OG 1039, ABV 4%)

Red Hunter (OG 1046, ABV 4.3%)

Woodcote (OG 1047, ABV 4.5%)

Madgwick Gold (OG 1050, ABV 5%)

Hanby

See Shropshire

Ha'penny

Ha'penny Brewing Co Ltd, Cuckoo Hall Brewery, Unit 8, Aldborough Hall Farm, Aldborough Hatch, Ilford, Essex, IG2 7TD
☎ (020) 8599 1338 ☎ 07961 161869
✉ info@hapenny-brewing.co.uk
hapenny-brewing.co.uk
Tours by arrangement

Ha'penny was established in 2009 by two CAMRA members in a disused stable block, with a former life as a pub and beer house for the Aldborough Hall Estate workers.

Sixteen-String Jack IPA (ABV 3.8%) ◆
A fruity pale brown bitter with hops and malt throughout. The bitterness builds on drinking and

lingers in the dry aftertaste, which has a hint of toffee.

London Particular Ruby Ale (ABV 4%)

Spring-Heeled Jack Porter (ABV 4%)

London Stone Bitter (ABV 4.5%)

Gog Magog Golden Ale (ABV 5%)
A dark gold beer with a little sulphur on the nose with floral parma violets and vanilla. Flavour is sweet and fruity. Finish is short and dry.

Mrs Lovett's Most Efficacious Stout Porter (ABV 5%)
A light-drinking, black, dry stout with a chocolate aroma. Roast notes and molasses in the flavour with a lingering sweetness balanced by the dryness.

Hardknott

Hardknott Brewery, Devonshire Road Industrial Estate, Millom, Cumbria, CA22 2RD
☎ (01229) 779309 ✉ dave@hardknottale.co.uk
hardknottale.co.uk
Tours by arrangement

Hardknott Brewery opened in 2005 using a two-barrel plant at the Woolpack Inn in Boot. The brewery relocated to Millom and expanded in 2010. Many occasional beers are brewed and seasonal and bottle-conditioned beers are also available.

Light Cascade (ABV 3.4%)
A well-hopped light ale. The hoppy bitter taste diminishes into an intense bitter finish.

Continuum (ABV 4%)

For Woolpack Inn, Boot:

Woolpacker (ABV 3.9%)

Hardys & Hansons

See Greene King in New Nationals section

Hart

Hart Brewery Ltd, Cartford Lane, Little Eccleston, Lancashire, PR3 0YP
☎ (01995) 671686
✉ johnsmith@hartbreweryltd.co.uk
hartbreweryltd.co.uk
Tours by arrangement

The brewery opened 1995 behind the Cartford Hotel on rural Lancashire's Fylde Plain. Hart supplies a number of local outlets and arranges exchanges with other micro-breweries. Monthly specials are also available.

Cartford Gold (ABV 3.6%)

Dishy Debbie (OG 1040, ABV 4%)

Ice Maiden (OG 1040, ABV 4%)
Hoppy, crisp, straw-coloured bitter with floral notes and a dry finish.

Squirrels Hoard (OG 1040, ABV 4%)

Nemesis (OG 1041, ABV 4.1%)

Cait-Lin Gold (OG 1042, ABV 4.2%)

Hart of Stebbing EAB

Hart of Stebbing Brewery, White Hart, High Street, Stebbing, Essex, CM6 3SQ
☎ (01371) 856383
✉ nick@hartofstebbingbrewery.co.uk
hartofstebbingbrewery.co.uk
Tours by arrangement

The brewery was established in 2007 by Bob Dovey and Nick Eldred, who is also the owner of the White Hart pub where the brewery is based. At present only the White Hart and local beer festivals are supplied. Bottle-conditioned beer is available.

Hart IPA (OG 1035, ABV 3.5%)

Hart Beat (OG 1041, ABV 4.1%)

Hart Prospector (OG 1042, ABV 4.5%)

Black Hart (OG 1045, ABV 5%)

Harveys IFBB

Harvey & Son (Lewes) Ltd, Bridge Wharf Brewery, 6 Cliffe High Street, Lewes, East Sussex, BN7 2AH
☎ (01273) 480209 ✉ maj@harveys.org.uk
harveys.org.uk
Shop Mon-Sat 9.30am-4.45pm
Tours by arrangement (currently two year waiting list)

Established in 1790, this independent family brewery operates from the banks of the River Ouse in Lewes. A major development in 1985 doubled the brewhouse capacity and subsequent additional fermenting capacity has seen production rise to more than 45,000 barrels a year. Harveys supplies real ale to all its 48 pubs and 450 free trade outlets in Sussex and Kent. Seasonal beers: see website. Bottle-conditioned beer is also available.

Sussex XX Mild Ale (OG 1030, ABV 3%)
A dark copper-brown colour. Roast malt dominates the aroma and palate leading to a sweet, caramel finish.

Hadlow Bitter (OG 1033, ABV 3.5%)
Formerly Sussex Pale Ale

Sussex Best Bitter (OG 1040, ABV 4%)
Full-bodied brown bitter. A hoppy aroma leads to a good malt and hop balance, and a dry aftertaste.

Armada Ale (OG 1045, ABV 4.5%)
Hoppy amber best bitter. Well-balanced fruit and hops dominate throughout with a fruity palate.

Harviestoun SIBA

Harviestoun Brewery Ltd, Alva Industrial Estate, Alva, Clackmannanshire, FK12 5DQ
☎ (01259) 769100 ✉ info@harviestoun.com
harviestoun.com
Tours by arrangement

Harviestoun started in a barn in the village of Dollar in 1985 with a five-barrel brew plant, but now operate on a state-of-the-art 60-barrel brewery in Alva. The brewery supplies local outlets direct and nationwide via wholesalers. It was bought by Caledonian Brewing Co in 2006 but is now independent following the takeover of Caledonian by Scottish & Newcastle in 2008. Further expansion is planned. Seasonal beers: see website.

Bitter & Twisted (OG 1036, ABV 3.8%)

Refreshingly hoppy beer with fruit throughout. A bittersweet taste with a long bitter finish. A golden session beer.

Ptarmigan (OG 1045, ABV 4.5%)
A well-balanced, bittersweet beer in which hops and malt dominate. The blend of malt, hops and fruit produces a clean, hoppy aftertaste.

Schiehallion (OG 1048, ABV 4.8%)
A Scottish cask lager, brewed using a lager yeast and Hersbrucker hops. A hoppy aroma, with fruit and malt, leads to a malty, bitter taste with floral hoppiness and a bitter finish.

Harwich Town EAB

Harwich Town Brewing Co, Station Approach, Harwich, Essex, CO12 3NA
☎ (01255) 551155 ✉ info@harwichtown.co.uk
harwichtown.co.uk
Shop – see website
Tours by arrangement

Brewing started in 2007 on a five-barrel plant next to Harwich Town railway station. The brewer is a CAMRA member and former customs officer. Beers are named after local landmarks, characters or events. 50 outlets are supplied. Seasonal beer: Hoppy Poppy (ABV 3.6%, Oct/Nov). An annual festival special is brewed for Harwich & Dovercourt Bay Winter Ale Festival in December. Bottle-conditioned beers are also available.

Ha'Penny Mild (ABV 3.6%)

Leading Lights (ABV 3.8%)

Misleading Lights (ABV 4%)

Bathside Battery Bitter (OG 1042, ABV 4.2%)

Redoubt Stout (ABV 4.2%)

Parkeston Porter (ABV 4.5%)

Lighthouse Bitter (ABV 4.8%)

Phoenix APA (OG 1052, ABV 5.1%)

Imperial Redoubt Stout (OG 1084, ABV 8%)

Havant SIBA

Havant Brewery, c/o 29 Gladys Avenue, Cowplain, Waterlooville, Hampshire, PO8 8HT
☎ (02392) 252118
✉ mike@thehavantbrewery.co.uk
thehavantbrewery.co.uk

Havant began brewing in 2009 on a one-barrel plant with two fermenters. Expansion is planned with production increasing to 16 barrels per week. Seasonal beers: Havant Dropped (ABV 3.8%, Sep-Nov), Havant Unwrapped (ABV 5.2%, Xmas).

Started (ABV 4%)

Stopped Dancing (ABV 4.4%)

Finished (ABV 5%)

Hawkshead SIBA

Hawkshead Brewery Ltd, Mill Yard, Staveley, Cumbria, LA8 9LR
☎ (01539) 822644
✉ info@hawksheadbrewery.co.uk
hawksheadbrewery.co.uk
Shop Mon-Tue 12-5pm; Wed-Sun 12-6pm

Hawkshead brewery complex is a showcase for real ale. The brewery expanded in 2006, having outgrown its original site (opened in 2002) in a barn at Hawkshead. Further expansion in 2010 means the complex now contains two bars – the Beer Hall (a function room) and the Brewery Tap (a pub), which are built around two 11,000-litre fermenting vessels. The beer cellar is visible behind glass and the brewing process can be watched from both bars. It also includes a beer shop and visitor centre. More than 150 outlets are supplied direct. Bottle-conditioned beers are available. Pure Brewed Organic Stout is suitable for vegans.

Windermere Pale (OG 1036, ABV 3.5%)
Crisp and fruity yellow beer with hints of melon and grapefruit and a strong bitter aftertaste.

Bitter (OG 1037, ABV 3.7%)
Well-balanced, thirst-quenching beer with fruit and hops aroma, leading to a lasting bitter finish.

Red (OG 1042, ABV 4.2%)
An impressive colour for this richly flavoured beer; lots of fruitiness and good hop flavour with a lingering aftertaste.

Lakeland Gold (OG 1043, ABV 4.4%)
Fresh, well-balanced fruity, hoppy beer with a clean bitter aftertaste.

Pure Brewed Organic Stout (OG 1044, ABV 4.5%)
A dry oatmeal stout brewed without any treatments or brewing aids.

Lakeland Lager (OG 1045, ABV 4.8%)
A cask-conditioned lager.

Brodie's Prime (OG 1048, ABV 4.9%)
Complex, dark brown beer with plenty of malt, fruit and roast taste. Satisfying full body with clean finish.

Haywood Bad Ram

Haywood Bad Ram Brewery, Callow Top Holiday Park, Sandybrook, Ashbourne, Derbyshire, DE6 2AQ
☎ 07974 948427 ✉ acphaywood@aol.com
callowtop.co.uk
Shop 9am-5pm (seasonal)
Tours by arrangement

The brewery was based in a converted barn but a new 2,500 sq ft brewery and bottling plant became operational in 2010. One pub is owned (on site) and several other outlets are supplied. The brewery is not operational during the winter. Bottle-conditioned beers are available.

Dr Samuel Johnson (ABV 4.5%)

Bad Ram (ABV 5%)

Lone Soldier (ABV 5%)

Woggle Dance (ABV 5%)

Callow Top IPA (ABV 5.2%)

Headless

Headless Brewing Co Ltd, The Flowerpot, 19-25 King Street, Derby, DE1 3DZ
☎ (01332) 204955
Tours by arrangement

Headless is situated at the rear of the Flowerpot pub in Derby and was established in 2007 on a 10-barrel plant. Seasonal beers: Ebenezer (ABV 6%, Xmas), Zymosis (ABV 7.5%, Over and Out Stout (ABV 4.5%).

THE BREWERIES

King Street Ale (KSA) (OG 1038, ABV 3.8%)

First Bloom (OG 1040, ABV 4.3%)

Five Gates (OG 1046, ABV 5%)

Heart of Wales

▤ Neuadd Arms Brewing Co t/a Heart of Wales Brewery, Stables Yard, Zion Street, Llanwrtyd Wells, Powys, LD5 4RD
☎ (01591) 610236
✉ Lindsay@heartofwalesbrewery.co.uk
⊕ heartofwalesbrewery.co.uk
Shop 10am-6pm daily
Tours by arrangement

⊠ The brewery was set up with a six-barrel plant in 2006 in old stables at the rear of the Neuadd Arms Hotel. Selected ales are conditioned in oak barrels prior to being casked. Beers are brewed using water from the brewery's own borehole. Seasonal brews celebrate local events such as the World Bogsnorkelling Championships. Seasonal and bottle-conditioned beers are available. All bottle-conditioned beers are suitable for vegetarians and vegans. Cambrian Heart (which is Noble Edean ale rebadged) is sponsored by the Prince of Wales Cambrian Mountain Initiative which helps to sustain local farms and farmers.

Irfon Valley Bitter (ABV 3.6%)

Aur Cymru (ABV 3.8%)

Bitter (ABV 4.1%)

Welsh Black (ABV 4.4%)

Noble Eden Ale/Cambrian Heart Ale (ABV 4.6%)

Inn-stable (ABV 6.8%)

Hebridean SIBA

Hebridean Brewing Co, 18a Bells Road, Stornoway, Isle of Lewis, HS1 2RA
☎ (01851) 700123 ✉ info@hebridean-brewery.co.uk ⊕ hebridean-brewery.co.uk
Shop open in summer months only
Tours by arrangement

☺The company was set up in 2001 on a steam powered plant with a 14-barrel brew length. A shop is attached to the brewery. Seasonal beers are produced for Mods, Gaelic festivals that are the Scottish equivalent of the Welsh Eisteddfod. These include Pagan Dark Winter Ale (ABV 4.8%, Mar-May).

Celtic Black Ale (OG 1036, ABV 3.9%)
A dark ale full of flavour, balancing an aromatic hop combined with a subtle bite and a pleasantly smooth caramel aftertaste.

Clansman Ale (OG 1036, ABV 3.9%)
A light Hebridean beer, brewed with Scottish malts and lightly hopped to give a subtle bittering.

Seaforth Ale (ABV 4.2%) ◆
A light, quaffable beer with a delicate nose. A complex mixture of biscuity malt and fruit in the taste leads to a lasting, bittersweet finish.

Islander Strong Premium Ale (OG 1044, ABV 4.8%) ◆
A malty, fruity strong bitter drinking dangerously below its ABV.

Berserker Export Pale Ale (OG 1068, ABV 7.5%) ◆

This malty, fruity winter warmer is packed full of flavour, with toffee apple and caramel notes right through to the long, satisfying aftertaste.

Hektors

Hektors Brewery Ltd, The Office, Henham Park, Southwold, Suffolk, NR34 8AN
☎ 07900 553426 ✉ hektor@henhampark.com
⊕ hektorsbrewery.com

⊠ Beers are currently brewed under contract by other breweries, including Green Jack and Oakham. However, there are plans to install a brewery in a converted barn at Henham Park in the future. Hektor's beers are provided to Henham Park's 65,000 annual visitors in addition to five other outlets and local events.

Pure (OG 1038, ABV 3.8%)

House (OG 1042, ABV 4.2%)

Scarecrow (OG 1050, ABV 5%)

Hellhound (NEW)

Hellhound Brewing Ltd, 6 Seager Court, Crockatt Road, Hadleigh, Suffolk, IP7 6RL
☎ 07850 076202 ✉ jack@hellhoundbrewery.co.uk
⊕ hellhoundbrewery.co.uk

Hellhound began brewing in 2010 using a six-barrel plant. No beer list was available at the time of going to press.

Hensting SIBA (NEW)

Hensting Brewery Ltd, Hill View Farm, Hensting Lane, Owslebury, Hampshire, SO21 1LE
✉ rebecca@henstingbrewery.org.uk
⊕ henstingbrewery.org.uk

⊠ Hensting Brewery was established in 2010 using a 0.5-barrel plant on the owner's farm. The beer is made with Maris Otter barley grown on the farm. The farm grows 50 acres of Maris Otter and are the first LEAF Marque farm producing real ale in the UK.

Winchester Mild (OG 1048, ABV 3.8%)

Winchester Gallon (OG 1048, ABV 4.4%)

Winchester Porter (OG 1060, ABV 4.6%)

Winchester Pale (OG 1058, ABV 4.8%)

Winchester IPA (OG 1090, ABV 8%)

Hepworth SIBA

Hepworth & Co (Brewers) Ltd, The Beer Station, Railway Yard, Horsham, West Sussex, RH12 2NW
☎ (01403) 269696 ✉ mail@hepworthbrewery.co.uk
⊕ hepworthbrewery.co.uk
Sales 9am-6pm daily
Tours by arrangement

⊠ Hepworth's was established in 2001, initially bottling beer only. In 2003 draught beer brewing was started with Sussex malt and hops. In 2004 an organic lager was introduced in bottle and on draught. 274 outlets are supplied. Seasonal beers: Summer Ale (ABV 3.4%), Harvest Ale (ABV 4.5%, autumn), Old Ale (ABV 4.8%, winter), Christmas Ale (ABV 7.5%), Dark Horse (ABV 3.8%, spring).

Traditional Sussex Bitter (OG 1035, ABV 3.6%) ◆

A fine, clean-tasting amber session beer. A bitter beer with a pleasant fruity and hoppy aroma that leads to a crisp, tangy taste. A long, dry finish.

Pullman First Class Ale (OG 1041, ABV 4.2%) ◆
A sweet, nutty maltiness and fruitiness are balanced by hops and bitterness in this easy-drinking, pale brown best bitter. A subtle bitter aftertaste.

Prospect Organic (ABV 4.5%)
A well-balanced and traditional brew.

Classic Old Ale (OG 1046, ABV 4.8%)
A traditional winter brew, rich with a variety of roasted malts balanced with sweetness and the bitterness of Admiral hops.

Iron Horse (OG 1048, ABV 4.8%) ◆
There's a fruity, toffee aroma to this light brown, full-bodied bitter. A citrus flavour balanced by caramel and malt leads to a clean, dry finish.

Blonde (ABV 5%)
Organic lager. Suitable for vegans.

Hereford SIBA

Hereford Brewery, 88 St Owen Street, Hereford, HR1 2QD
☎ **(01432) 342125** ✉ **jfkenyon@aol.com**
Tours by arrangement

The brewery was built in a room of the Victory in 2000 by Jim Kenyon, following the purchase of the pub. Initially only serving the pub, it has steadily grown from a four-barrel to a 10-barrel plant. In 2010 the brewery changed it's name from Spinning Dog to Hereford Brewery. Around 300 other outlets are supplied. Bottle-conditioned beer is available. Seasonal/special beers: Mutleys Springer (ABV 4.4%), Christmas Cheer (ABV 4.3%), Original Oatmeal Stout (ABV 4.4%), Gamekeepers Bitter (ABV 4.2%).

Original Bitter (ABV 3.7%)
Light in colour with a distinctive fruitiness from start to finish.

Herefordshire Owd Bull (ABV 3.9%)
A good session beer with an abundance of hops and bitterness. Dry, with citrus aftertaste.

Cathedral Bitter (OG 1040, ABV 4%)
A crisp amber beer made with local hops, producing a well-rounded malt/hop bitterness throughout and a pleasing, lingering aftertaste.

Herefordshire Light Ale (ABV 4%)
Brewed along the lines of the award-winning Mutleys Pitstop. Light and refreshing.

Mutleys Dark (OG 1040, ABV 4%)
A dark, malty mild with a hint of bitterness and a touch of roast caramel. A smooth drinkable ale.

Best Bitter (ABV 4.2%)

Celtic Gold (OG 1045, ABV 4.5%)
A bright gold best bitter, full of fruit and blackcurrant flavours.

Mutleys Revenge (OG 1048, ABV 4.8%)
A strong, smooth, hoppy beer, amber in colour. Full-bodied with a dry, citrus aftertaste.

Mutts Nuts (OG 1050, ABV 5%)
A dark, strong ale, full bodied with a hint of a chocolate aftertaste.

Hereward

Hereward Brewery, 50 Fleetwood, Ely, Cambridgeshire, CB6 1BH
☎ **(01353) 666441**
✉ **michael.czarnobaj@ntlworld.com**

A small home-based brewery launched in 2003 on a 10-gallon kit. The brewery supplies mainly beer festivals and also brews festival specials (brewed to order). Real cider is sometimes produced. Seasonal beer: Uncle Joe's Winter Ale (ABV 5%).

Michael's Mild (ABV 3.4%)

Bitter (ABV 3.8%)

St Ethelreda's Golden Bitter (ABV 4%)

Porta Porter (ABV 4.2%)

Oatmeal Stout (ABV 4.5%)

Hesket Newmarket SIBA

Hesket Newmarket Brewery Ltd, Old Crown Barn, Back Green, Hesket Newmarket, Cumbria, CA7 8JG
☎ **(01697) 478066** ✉ **admin@hesketbrewery.co.uk**
🌐 **hesketbrewery.co.uk**
Shop Mon-Fri 8.30am-5pm; Sat 10am-2pm (summer)
Tours by arrangement

The brewery was established in 1988 and was bought by a co-operative of villagers in 1999, anxious to preserve a community resource. Most of the original recipes have been retained, all named after local fells except for Doris's 90th Birthday Ale. An 11-barrel plant was installed in 2005 followed by a small-scale bottling plant in 2006. Around 50 regular outlets are supplied. Bottle-conditioned beers are available.

Great Cockup Porter (OG 1035, ABV 3%)
A refreshing, dark and chocolatey porter with a dry finish.

Blencathra Bitter (OG 1035, ABV 3.3%) ◆
A malty, tawny ale, mild and mellow for a bitter, with a dominant caramel flavour.

Haystacks Refreshing Ale (OG 1037, ABV 3.7%) ◆
Light, easy-drinking, thirst-quenching blond beer; very pleasant for its strength.

Skiddaw Special Bitter (OG 1037, ABV 3.7%)
An amber session beer, malty throughout, well-balanced with a dryish finish.

Helvellyn Gold (OG 1039, ABV 4%)
A smooth, golden bitter. light in colour but full-flavoured.

High Pike Dark Amber Bitter (OG 1042, ABV 4.2%)

Doris's 90th Birthday Ale (OG 1045, ABV 4.3%)

Scafell Blonde (OG 1043, ABV 4.3%)
Pale with bags of hop flavour, not too bitter. A good introduction to real ale for lager drinkers.

Catbells Pale Ale (OG 1050, ABV 5%) ◆
Golden ale with a nice balance of fruity sweetness and bitterness, almost syrupy but with an unexpectedly dry finish.

Old Carrock Strong Ale (OG 1060, ABV 6%) ◆
Reddy brown strong ale, vine-fruity in flavour with slightly astringent finish.

Hetty Pegler (NEW)

 Hetty Pegler Brewery, Village Inn, Bath Road, Nailsworth, Gloucestershire, GL6 0HH
☎ (01453) 835715 ⊕ villageinn-nailsworth.co.uk

Hetty Pegler Brewery began in 2010 and is based at the same location as the Nailsworth Brewery but operates on a separate 2.5-barrel plant upstairs. Seasonal beers are available and bottle-conditioned beers are planned.

Indian Summer (ABV 3.8%)

Hetty (ABV 4%)

Satisfaction (ABV 4.2%)

Admirals Ale (ABV 4.5%)

Hexhamshire SIBA

Hexhamshire Brewery, Leafields, Ordley, Hexham, Northumberland, NE46 1SX
☎ (01434) 606577 ✉ ghb@hexhamshire.co.uk
⊕ hexhamshire.co.uk

Hexhamshire was founded in 1992 and is operated by one of the founding partners and his family. 40 outlets are supplied direct. A relocation to the Dipton Mill Inn is planned.

Devil's Elbow (OG 1036, ABV 3.6%) ◆
Amber brew full of hops and fruit, leading to a bitter finish.

Shire Bitter (OG 1037, ABV 3.8%) ◆
A good balance of hops with fruity overtones, this amber beer makes an easy-drinking session bitter.

Devil's Water (OG 1041, ABV 4.1%) ◆
Copper-coloured best bitter, well-balanced with a slightly fruity, hoppy finish.

Whapweasel (OG 1048, ABV 4.8%) ◆
An interesting smooth, hoppy beer with a fruity flavour. Amber in colour, the bitter finish brings out the fruit and hops.

Old Humbug (OG 1055, ABV 5.5%)

Hidden SIBA

Hidden Brewery Ltd, Unit 1, Oakley Industrial Estate, Wylye Road, Dinton, Salisbury, Wiltshire, SP3 5EU
☎ (01722) 716440 ✉ sales@thehiddenbrewery.com
Tours by arrangement

The Hidden Brewery, founded in 2003, focusses on bottling, with particular emphasis on the export market. The brewery is named after its location, hidden away in the Wiltshire countryside. Seasonal beers: Hidden Spring (ABV 4.5%), Hidden Fantasy (ABV 4.6%).

Pint (OG 1039, ABV 3.8%)
A clean-tasting, tangy bitter with good hop content, and a citrus fruit and malt balance. Dry finish, mid-brown in colour; light hop aroma.

Old Sarum (OG 1042, ABV 4.1%)
A well-balanced bitter with a complex combination of malts and hops. The aroma is floral and spicy, full-flavoured with a dry bitterness.

Potential (OG 1042, ABV 4.2%)
A traditional bitter with a balanced malty flavour. Clean tasting with slight citrus tones.

Quest (OG 1042, ABV 4.2%)
An amber-coloured bitter with a malt background, fruity aroma and a dry finish.

Pleasure (OG 1049, ABV 4.9%)
A deep golden coloured, strong, dry, traditional IPA with a hoppy finish.

Highgate

Highgate & Davenports Brewery Ltd, Sandymount Road, Walsall, West Midlands, WS1 3AP
⊕ highgatedavenports.co.uk

☺The brewery closed in June 2010. There's a campaign underway to save it but brewing has ceased at present.

High House Farm SIBA

High House Farm Brewery, Matfen, Newcastle upon Tyne, Tyne & Wear, NE20 0RG
☎ (01661) 886192/886769 (Sales line)
✉ info@highhousefarmbrewery.co.uk
⊕ highhousefarmbrewery.co.uk
Shop Sun-Tue 10.30am-5pm, Thu-Sat 10.30am-9pm, closed Wed
Tours by arrangement

⊗ The brewery was founded in 2003 on a working farm with visitor centre, brewery shop and exhibition and function room. Over 350 outlets are supplied. Seasonal beers: see website.

Auld Hemp (OG 1038, ABV 3.8%) ⬚ ◆
Tawny coloured ale with hop, malt and fruit flavours and a good bitter finish.

Nel's Best (OG 1041, ABV 4.2%) ◆
Golden hoppy ale full of flavour with a clean, bitter finish.

Matfen Magic (OG 1046.5, ABV 4.8%) ◆
Well-hopped brown ale with a fruity aroma. Malt and chocolate overtones with a rich, bitter finish.

Highland

Highland Brewing Co Ltd, Swannay Brewery, Swannay by Evie, Birsay, Orkney, KW17 2NP
☎ (01856) 721700
✉ info@highlandbrewingcompany.co.uk
⊕ highlandbrewingcompany.co.uk
Tours by arrangement

☺Brewing began in 2006 and bigger plant was installed a year later. A visitor centre, café and 20-barrel plant are planned. Around 100 outlets are supplied. Seasonal beers: Light Munro (ABV 3%, Apr-May), Christmas Light (ABV 3.8%), Orkney Porter (ABV 9%, Nov-Mar).

Orkney Best (OG 1038, ABV 3.6%) ◆
A refreshing, light-bodied, low gravity golden beer bursting with hop, peach and sweet malt flavours. The long, hoppy finish leaves a dry bitterness.

Dark Munro (OG 1040, ABV 4%) ⬚ ⬚ ◆
The nose presents an intense roast hit which is followed by summer fruits in the mouth. The strong roast malt continues into the aftertaste.

Scapa Special (OG 1042, ABV 4.2%) ◆
A good copy of a typical Lancashire bitter, full of bitterness and background hops, leaving your mouth tingling in the lingering aftertaste.

Sneaky Wee Orkney Stout (OG 1044, ABV 4.2%)

St Magnus Ale (OG 1045, ABV 4.5%) ◆
A complex, tawny bitter with a stunning balance of malt and hop and some soft roast. Full-bodied.

Orkney IPA (OG 1048, ABV 4.8%)
A traditional bitter, with light hop and fruit flavour throughout.

Strong Northerly (OG 1055, ABV 5.5%)

Orkney Blast (OG 1058, ABV 6%)
Plenty of alcohol in this warming strong bitter/barley wine. A mushroom and woody aroma blossoms into a well-balanced smack of malt and hop in the taste.

Old Norway (OG 1082, ABV 9%)

Highlands & Islands

See Orkney

Highwood SIBA

Highwood Brewery Ltd, Melton High Wood Farm, Melton High Wood, Melton Ross, Lincolnshire, DN38 6AA

Office: Grimsby West, Birchin Way, Grimsby, Lincolnshire, DN31 2SG ☎ (01472) 255500
tomwood@tom-wood.com tom-wood.com

Highwood, best known under the Tom Wood brand name, started brewing in a converted Victorian granary on the family farm in 1995. The brew-length was increased from 10 barrels to 30 in 2001, using a plant from the Ash Vine brewery. In 2002, Highwood bought Conway's Licensed Trade Wholesalers. It now distributes most regional and national cask ales throughout Lincolnshire and Nottinghamshire. More than 300 outlets are supplied. Seasonal beers: see website.

Best Bitter (OG 1034, ABV 3.5%)
A good citrus, passion fruit hop dominates the nose and taste, with background malt. A lingering hoppy and bitter finish.

Dark Mild (OG 1034, ABV 3.5%)

Hop and Glory (ABV 3.6%)
Hoppy golden bitter made using English-grown Cascade hops.

Shepherd's Delight (OG 1040, ABV 4%)
Malt is the dominant taste in this amber brew, although the fruity hop bitterness complements it all the way.

Harvest Bitter (OG 1042, ABV 4.3%)
A well-balanced amber beer where the hops and bitterness just about outdo the malt.

Old Timber (OG 1043, ABV 4.5%)
Hoppy on the nose, but featuring well-balanced malt and hops. A slight, lingering roast/coffee flavour develops, but this is generally a bitter, darkish brown beer.

Bomber County (OG 1046, ABV 4.8%)
An earthy malt aroma but with a complex underlying mix of coffee, hops, caramel and apple fruit. The beer starts bitter and intensifies to the end.

Hilden

Hilden Brewing Co, Hilden House, Hilden, Lisburn, Co Antrim, BT27 4TY
☎ (02892) 660800
irishbeers@hildenbrewery.co.uk
hildenbrewery.co.uk

Shop Tue-Sun 12-2.30pm (3pm Sun) – Taproom Restaurant
Tours by arrangement (Tue-Sat 11.30am & 6.30pm)

Hilden was established in 1981 and is Ireland's oldest independent brewery. Now well into the second generation of the family-owned business, the beers are widely distributed across the UK. Around 15 outlets are supplied direct and two restaurants are owned. More beers are planned: see website.

Ale (OG 1038, ABV 4%)
An amber-coloured beer with an aroma of malt, hops and fruit. The balanced taste is slightly slanted towards hops, and hops are also prominent in the full, malty finish.

Silver (OG 1042, ABV 4.2%)
A pale ale, light and refreshing on the palate but with a satisfying mellow hop character derived from a judicious blend of aromatic Saaz hops.

Molly Malone (OG 1045, ABV 4.6%)
Dark ruby-red porter with complex flavours of hop bitterness and chocolate malt.

Scullion's Irish (OG 1045, ABV 4.6%)
A bright amber ale, initially smooth with a slight taste of honey that is balanced by a long, dry aftertaste that lingers on the palate.

Halt (OG 1058, ABV 6.1%)
A premium traditional Irish red ale with a malty, mild hop flavour. This special reserve derives its name from the local train stop, which was used to service the local linen mill.

For College Green Brewery:

Molly's Chocolate Stout (OG 1042, ABV 4.2%)
A dark chocolate-coloured beer with a full-bodied character.

Headless Dog (OG 1042, ABV 4.3%)
A well-hopped bright amber ale.

Hill Island

Michael Griffin t/a Hill Island Brewery, Unit 7, Fowlers Yard, Back Silver Street, Durham, DH1 3RA
☎ 07740 932584 mike@hillisland.freeserve.co.uk
myspace.com/hillisland

Hill Island is a literal translation of Dunholme from which Durham is derived. The brewery began trading in 2002 and stands by the banks of the Wear in the heart of Durham City. Many of the beers produced have names reflecting local history and heritage. Brews can also be made exclusively for individual pubs. Around 40 outlets are supplied. The brewery is open to visitors one weekend most months for a mini beer festival, during which six different house ales are served. Bottled ales and draught beer can be bought most Saturdays from the brewery's stall in Durham open market. Seasonal beers: Priory Summer Ale (ABV 3.5%), Miner's Gala Bitter (ABV 3.7%), Festive Ale (ABV 4.2%), St Oswald's Xmas Ale (ABV 4.5%).

Peninsula Pint (OG 1036.5, ABV 3.7%)
Blonde and hoppy with a zesty aroma.

Bitter (OG 1038, ABV 3.9%)
Red-gold in colour with pronounced caramel notes, balanced with grassy hop aromas.

Dun Cow Bitter (OG 1041, ABV 4.2%)
Golden ale with hints of caramel and citrus hop flavours.

THE BREWERIES

Cathedral Ale (OG 1042, ABV 4.3%)
Ruby red with hints of roast malts and crisp
bitterness.

Griffin's Irish Stout (OG 1045, ABV 4.5%)
Black and bitter. Traditional Irish-style stout.

Hillside

See Deeside

Hobden's

See Wessex

Hobsons SIBA

**Hobsons Brewery & Co Ltd, Newhouse Farm, Tenbury
Road, Cleobury Mortimer, Worcestershire, DY14 8RD**
☎ (01299) 270837 ✉ beer@hobsons-brewery.co.uk
⊕ hobsons-brewery.co.uk
Tours by arrangement

☺ Established in 1993 in a former sawmill,
Hobsons relocated to a farm site with more space
in 1995. A second brewery, bottling plant and a
warehouse have been added along with significant
expansion to the first brewery. It now uses
environmentally sustainable technologies where
possible. Beers are supplied within a radius of 50
miles. Hobsons also brews and bottles for the local
tourist attraction, the Severn Valley Railway (Manor
Ale, ABV 4.2%). Seasonal beer: Old Henry (ABV
5.2%, Sep-Apr). Bottle-conditioned beers are also
available.

Mild (OG 1034, ABV 3.2%) ◆
A classic mild. Complex layers of taste come from
roasted malts that predominate and give lots of
flavour.

Twisted Spire (OG 1036, ABV 3.6%)
A blond beer with a sweet, floral aroma. The initial
sweetness gives way to a burst of hop flavour
which lingers through to a crisp, dry finish.

Best Bitter (OG 1038.5, ABV 3.8%) ◆
A pale brown to amber, medium-bodied beer with
strong hop character throughout. It is consequently
bitter, but with malt discernible in the taste.

Town Crier (OG 1044, ABV 4.5%) 🍺
An elegant straw-coloured bitter. The hint of
sweetness is complemented by subtle hop
flavours, leading to a dry finish.

Postman's Knock (OG 1047, ABV 4.8%)
A rich ruby porter. The combination of subtle
flavour notes gives an initial rich sweetness leading
to a velvety chocolate finish.

Hoggleys SIBA

**Hoggleys Brewery, Unit 12, Litchborough Industrial
Estate, Northampton Road, Litchborough,
Northamptonshire, NN12 8JB**
☎ (01604) 831762 ☎ 07717 078402
✉ enquiries@hoggleys.co.uk ⊕ hoggleys.co.uk
Tours by arrangement

⊗ Hoggleys was established in 2003 as a part-
time brewery. It expanded to an eight-barrel plant
in 2006, became full-time and moved to larger
premises. Around 35 outlets are supplied. Solstice
Stout and Mill Lane Mild are suitable for

vegetarians and vegans as are all bottle-
conditioned beers.

Kislingbury Bitter (OG 1040, ABV 4%)

Mill Lane Mild (OG 1040, ABV 4%)
Brewed from mild, black and crystal malts and
hopped with Challenger and Fuggles.

Northamptonshire Bitter (OG 1040, ABV 4%)
A straw-coloured bitter brewed with pale malt
only. The hops are Fuggles and Northdown, and
the beer is late hopped with Fuggles for aroma.

Reservoir Hogs (OG 1042, ABV 4.3%)
Mid golden, hoppy and refreshing.

Pump Fiction (OG 1045, ABV 4.5%)
Light copper, complex but easy drinking.

Solstice Stout (OG 1050, ABV 5%)

Hogs Back SIBA

**Hogs Back Brewery Ltd, Manor Farm, The Street,
Tongham, Surrey, GU10 1DE**
☎ (01252) 783000 ✉ info@hogsback.co.uk
⊕ hogsback.co.uk
Shop – see website
Tours by arrangement

⊗ This traditionally-styled brewery, established in
1992, boasts an extensive range of award-winning
ales, brewed using the finest malted barley and
whole English hops. The shop sells all the
brewery's beers and related merchandise plus over
400 beers and ciders from around the world. See
website for more info. Around 400 outlets are
supplied direct. Seasonal beers: see website. Six
bottle-conditioned beers are produced for home
and export.

HBB/Hogs Back Bitter (OG 1039, ABV 3.7%) ◆
An aromatic session beer. Biscuity aroma with
some hops and lemon notes. Well-balanced, plenty
of hoppy impact in the mouth with a long-lasting
dry hoppy bitter aftertaste.

**TEA/Traditional English Ale
(OG 1044, ABV 4.2%)** ◆
A tawny-coloured best bitter with both malt and
hops present in the nose. These carry through into
a well-rounded flavour with malt slightly dominant
and more fruity sweetness than bitterness.

Hop Garden Gold (OG 1048, ABV 4.6%) ◆
Pale golden best bitter. Full-bodied and well-
balanced with an aroma of malt, hops and fruit.
Hoppy bitterness grows in an increasingly dry
aftertaste with a hint of sweetness.

**A Over T/Aromas Over Tongham
(OG 1094, ABV 9%)** 🗂 ◆
A full-bodied, tawny-coloured barley wine. The
malty aroma with hints of vanilla lead to a well-
balanced taste where the hops cut through the
underlying sweetness and dominate in the finish.

Hogswood SIBA (NEW)

**Hogswood Brewing Co, Higher Goshen, Mithian, St
Agnes, Cornwall, TR5 0QE**
☎ (01872) 554224 ✉ vaughan@hogswood.com
⊕ hogswood.com

⊗ Hogswood was established in 2009. Five outlets
are supplied direct. Seasonal beer: Yo Crimbo (ABV
4.8%).

Stoked (ABV 3.6%)

North Shore IPA (ABV 3.8%)

Goshen Ale (ABV 4%)

Broken Piston (ABV 4.2%)

Holden's IFBB

Holden's Brewery Ltd, George Street, Woodsetton, Dudley, West Midlands, DY1 4LW
☎ (01902) 880051 ✉ holdens.brewery@virgin.net
holdensbrewery.co.uk
Shop Mon-Fri 9am-5pm
Tours by arrangement

A family brewery going back four generations, Holden's began life as a brew-pub in the 1920s. The company continues to grow with 19 tied pubs and supplies around 70 other outlets.

Black Country Mild (OG 1037, ABV 3.7%)
A good, red/brown mild; a refreshing, light blend of roast malt, hops and fruit, dominated by malt throughout.

Black Country Bitter (OG 1039, ABV 3.9%)
A medium-bodied, golden ale; a light, well-balanced bitter with a subtle, dry, hoppy finish.

XB (OG 1042, ABV 4.1%)
A sweeter, slightly fuller version of the Bitter. Sold in a number of outlets under different names.

Golden Glow (OG 1045, ABV 4.4%)
A pale golden beer with a subtle hop aroma plus gentle sweetness and a light hoppiness.

Special (OG 1052, ABV 5.1%)
A sweet, malty, full-bodied amber ale with hops to balance in the taste and in the good, bittersweet finish.

Holland

Holland Brewery, 5 Browns Flats, Brewery Street, Kimberley, Nottinghamshire, NG16 2JU
☎ (0115) 938 2685
✉ hollandbrew@btopenworld.com

Len Holland, a keen home-brewer for 30 years, went commercial in 2000, in the shadow of now closed Hardys & Hansons. Seasonal beers: Holly Hop Gold (ABV 4.7%, Xmas), Dutch Courage (ABV 5%, winter), Glamour Puss (ABV 4.2%, spring), Blonde Belter (ABV 4.5%, summer).

Chocolate Clog (OG 1038, ABV 3.8%)

Golden Blond (OG 1040, ABV 4%)

Lipsmacker (OG 1040, ABV 4%)

Cloghopper (OG 1042, ABV 4.2%)

Double Dutch (OG 1045, ABV 4.5%)

Mad Jack Stout (OG 1045, ABV 4.5%)

Holt IFBB

Joseph Holt Ltd, The Brewery, Empire Street, Cheetham, Manchester, M3 1JD
☎ (0161) 834 3285 joseph-holt.com

The brewery was established in 1849 by Joseph Holt and his wife Catherine. It is still a family-run business in the hands of the great, great-grandson of the founder. Holt's supplies approximately 100 outlets as well as its own estate of 126 tied pubs. It still delivers beer to many of its tied houses in large 54-gallon hogsheads. A dedicated 30-barrel brew plant is used for seasonal beers: see website. Fewer and fewer Holts pubs are dispensing cask Mild since the introduction of Keg Black.

Mild (OG 1033, ABV 3.2%)
A dark brown/red beer with a fruity, malty nose. Roast, malt, fruit and hops in the taste, with strong bitterness for a mild, and a dry malt and hops finish.

Bitter (OG 1040, ABV 4%)
Copper-coloured beer with malt and hops in the aroma. Malt, hops and fruit in the taste with a bitter and hoppy finish.

Hook Norton IFBB

Hook Norton Brewery Co Ltd, The Brewery, Hook Norton, Banbury, Oxfordshire, OX15 5NY
☎ (01608) 737210 ✉ info@hook-norton-brewery.co.uk hooky.co.uk
Visitor Centre & Shop Mon-Sat 9.30am-4.30pm
Tours by arrangement (01608 730384)

Hook Norton was founded in 1849 by John Harris, a farmer and maltster. The current premises were built in 1900 and Hook Norton is one of the finest examples of a Victorian tower brewery, with a 25hp steam engine for most of its motive power. Hook Norton owns 47 pubs and supplies approximately 300 free trade accounts. Seasonal beers: see website. Bottle-conditioned beers are also available.

Hooky Dark (OG 1033, ABV 3.2%)
A chestnut brown, easy-drinking mild. A complex malt and hop aroma give way to a well-balanced taste, leading to a long, hoppy finish that is unusual for a mild.

Hooky Bitter (OG 1036, ABV 3.6%)
A classic golden session bitter. Hoppy and fruity aroma followed by a malt and hops taste and a continuing hoppy finish.

Hooky Gold (OG 1042, ABV 4.1%)
A golden, crisp beer with a citrus aroma and a fruity, rounded body.

Old Hooky (OG 1048, ABV 4.6%)
A strong bitter, tawny in colour. A well-rounded fruity taste with a balanced bitter finish.

Hop Back SIBA

Hop Back Brewery plc, Units 22-24, Batten Road Industrial Estate, Downton, Salisbury, Wiltshire, SP5 3HU
☎ (01725) 510986 ✉ info@hopback.co.uk
hopback.co.uk

Started by John Gilbert in 1987 at the Wyndham Arms in Salisbury, the brewery has expanded steadily ever since. It went public via a Business Expansion Scheme in 1993 and has enjoyed rapid continued growth. Summer Lightning has won many awards. The brewery has 11 tied houses and also sells to some 500 other outlets. Seasonal beers are produced on a monthly basis. Entire Stout is suitable for vegans. Bottle-conditioned beers are also produced.

GFB/Gilbert's First Brew (OG 1035, ABV 3.5%)
A golden beer, with a light, clean quality that makes it an ideal session ale. A hoppy aroma and taste lead to a good, dry finish.

Odyssey (OG 1040, ABV 4%)

THE BREWERIES

A darker bitter with toasted malty overtones from the use of three dark malts in the recipe.

Crop Circle (OG 1041, ABV 4.2%) ◆
A refreshingly sharp and hoppy summer beer. Gold coloured with a slight citrus taste. The crisp, dry aftertaste lingers.

Spring Zing (OG 1041, ABV 4.2%)
A dry-hopped version of Crop Circle which gives it a flowery, more rounded palate.

Taiphoon (OG 1041, ABV 4.2%)
A light gold speciality beer flavoured with lemongrass.

Entire Stout (OG 1043, ABV 4.5%) 🍷 ◆
A rich, dark stout with a strong roasted malt flavour and a long, sweet and malty aftertaste. A beer suitable for vegans.

Summer Lightning (OG 1048, ABV 5%) ◆
A pleasurable pale bitter with a good, fresh, hoppy aroma and a malty, hoppy flavour. Finely balanced, it has an intense bitterness leading to a long, dry finish.

Hopdaemon

Hopdaemon Brewery Co Ltd, Unit 1, Parsonage Farm, Seed Road, Newnham, Kent, ME9 0NA
☎ (01795) 892078 ✉ info@hopdaemon.com
⊕ hopdaemon.com
Tours by arrangement

⊗ Tonie Prins opened a 12-barrel plant in 2000 in Canterbury and within six months was supplying more than 30 pubs in the area with his cask ales and bottle-conditioned beers. In 2005 the brewery moved to bigger premises in Newnham and some 100 outlets are now supplied.

Golden Braid (OG 1039, ABV 3.7%) ◆
A refreshing golden session bitter with a good blend of bittering and aroma hops underpinned by pale malt.

Incubus (OG 1041, ABV 4%) ◆
A well-balanced, copper-hued best bitter. Pale malt and a hint of crystal malt are blended with bitter and slightly floral hops to give a lingering hoppy finish.

Skrimshander IPA (OG 1045, ABV 4.5%)

Green Daemon (OG 1048, ABV 5%)

Dominator (OG 1050, ABV 5.1%)

Leviathan (OG 1057, ABV 6%)

Hopshackle

Hopshackle Brewery Ltd, Unit F, Bentley Business Park, Blenheim Way, Northfields Industrial Estate, Market Deeping, Lincolnshire, PE6 8LD
☎ (01778) 348542
✉ nigel@hopshacklebrewery.co.uk
⊕ hopshacklebrewery.co.uk
Tours by arrangement

⊕ Hopshackle was established in 2006 on a five-barrel brew plant. Monthly seasonals are brewed providing variety in styles and ABVs. More than 40 outlets are supplied direct. Bottle-conditioned beers are also available.

Caskadia (OG 1040, ABV 4.3%)

Special Bitter (OG 1040, ABV 4.3%)

Hop and Spicy (OG 1045, ABV 4.5%)

Extra Special Bitter (OG 1045, ABV 4.8%)

Historic Porter (OG 1053, ABV 4.8%)

Shacklers Gold (OG 1048, ABV 5.2%)

Special No. 1 Bitter (OG 1048, ABV 5.2%)

Double Momentum (OG 1065, ABV 7%)

Resination (OG 1065, ABV 7%)

Hopstar SIBA

Hopstar Brewery, 11 Pole Lane, Darwen, Lancashire, BB3 3LD
☎ (01254) 703389 ☎ 07849 369798
✉ hopstarbrewery@hotmail.com
⊕ hopstarbrewery.co.uk
Tours by arrangement (for small groups)

⊕ Hopstar first brewed in 2004 on a 2.5-barrel kit. 20-50 outlets are supplied around Lancashire and Greater Manchester. Beer Festival organisers are offered a chance to brew beer for their own festival.

Dizzy Danny Ale (OG 1039, ABV 3.8%)

Dark Knight (OG 1041, ABV 4%)

J.C. (OG 1041, ABV 4%)

Lancashire Gold (OG 1041, ABV 4%)

Smokey Joe's Black Beer (OG 1041, ABV 4%)

Hornbeam

Hornbeam Brewery, 1-1c Grey Street, Denton, Manchester, M34 3RU
☎ (0161) 320 5627 ☎ 07984 443383
✉ kevin@hornbeambrewery.com
⊕ hornbeambrewery.com
Tours by arrangement

⊕ Hornbeam began brewing in 2007 on an eight-barrel plant. Regular monthly special beers are brewed and bottle-conditioned beers are planned. Seasonal beers: see website.

Lemon Blossom (OG 1037, ABV 3.7%)
Golden, citrussy and light in colour.

Bitter (OG 1038, ABV 3.8%)
A smooth, easy-drinking beer with a rich hop flavour.

Top Hop Best Bitter (OG 1041, ABV 4.2%)
Full-bodied with malt appeal and ample bitterness.

Black Coral Stout (OG 1043, ABV 4.5%)
A smooth, dry roast malt. Dark and full-bodied with a rich, creamy head. Satisfying with a subtle bitterness.

Hoskins

Hoskins Brothers Ales, The Ale Wagon, 27 Rutland Street, Leicester, LE1 1RE
☎ (0116) 262 3330 ✉ mail@alewagon.com
⊕ alewagon.co.uk

Hoskins brothers are not currently brewing pending the building of a new brewery at the Ale Wagon in Leicester. Their beers are currently contract brewed at Tower Brewery, Burton upon Trent. See Tower for beer list.

Houston SIBA

⧉ Houston Brewing Co, South Street, Houston, Renfrewshire, PA6 7EN
☎ (01505) 612620 ✉ ale@houston-brewing.co.uk
⊕ houston-brewing.co.uk
Shop open pub hours, daily
Tours by arrangement

Established by Carl Wengel in 1997, the brewery is attached to the Fox & Hounds pub and restaurant. Brewery tours include dinner and tastings. Houston deliver throughout Britain via a network of distributors and direct. Polypins, bottles and giftpacks are for sale via the website. Seasonal beers: see website.

Killellan Bitter (OG 1037, ABV 3.7%) ◆
A light session ale, with a floral hop and fruity taste. The finish of this amber beer is dry and quenching.

Blonde Bombshell (OG 1040, ABV 4%)
A gold-coloured ale with a fresh hop aroma and rounded maltiness.

Black & Tan (ABV 4.2%)

Peter's Well (OG 1042, ABV 4.2%) ◆
Well-balanced fruity taste with sweet hop, leading to an increasingly bittersweet finish.

Texas (ABV 4.3%)

Tartan Terror (ABV 4.5%)

Warlock Stout (ABV 4.7%)

Howard Town

Howard Town Brewery Ltd, Hawkshead Mill, Hope Street, Glossop, Derbyshire, SK13 7SS
☎ (01457) 869800
✉ beer@howardtownbrewery.co.uk
⊕ howardtownbrewery.co.uk
Tours by arrangement

Howard Town was established in 2005 and is the Midlands most northerly brewery. More than 100 outlets are supplied. Seasonal beers: Hope (ABV 4.1%, spring), Dragon's Nest (ABV 4.4%, St George's Day), Snake Ale (ABV 4%, autumn), Robins Nest (ABV 5.2%, winter), Sparrows Nest (ABV 3.6%, winter). Bottle-conditioned beers are also available.

Mill Town (OG 1036, ABV 3.5%)

Bleaklow (OG 1040, ABV 3.8%)

Longdendale Light (OG 1039, ABV 3.9%)

Monks Gold (OG 1041.5, ABV 4%)

Wrens Nest (OG 1043, ABV 4.2%)

Dinting Arches (OG 1045, ABV 4.5%)

Glotts Hop (OG 1049, ABV 5%)

Dark Peak (OG 1061, ABV 6.4%)

Sarah Hughes

⧉ Sarah Hughes Brewery, Beacon Hotel, 129 Bilston Street, Sedgley, Dudley, West Midlands, DY3 1JE
☎ (01902) 883381
Tours by arrangement

⊛ A traditional Black Country tower brewery, established in 1921. The original grist case and rare open-topped copper add to the ambience of the Victorian brewhouse and give a unique character to the brews. The Beacon Hotel is the brewery tap and the full range of beers is available there. Seasonal beer: Snowflake (ABV 8%, winter).

Pale Amber (OG 1038, ABV 4%)
A well-balanced beer, initially slightly sweet but with hops close behind.

Surprise (OG 1048, ABV 5%) ◆
A bittersweet, medium-bodied, hoppy ale with some malt.

Dark Ruby (OG 1058, ABV 6%) ⬚ ◆
A dark ruby strong ale with a good balance of fruit and hops, leading to a pleasant, lingering hops and malt finish.

Humpty Dumpty SIBA

Norfolk Broads Brewing LLP t/a Humpty Dumpty Brewery, Church Road, Reedham, Norfolk, NR13 3TZ
☎ (01493) 701818
✉ sales@humptydumptybrewery.co.uk
⊕ humptydumptybrewery.co.uk
Shop 12-5pm daily (Easter-end Oct); Sat-Sun 12.30-4pm (Nov-Xmas); Jan-Feb closed
Tours by arrangement

⊗ Established in 1998, the 11-barrel brewery moved to its present site in 2001. The brewers use local ingredients and many regional outlets are supplied. The on-site shop sells bottled and draught beer from the brewery as well as from other East Anglian micros. Seasonal beers: see website. Bottle-conditioned beers are also available.

Little Sharpie (OG 1040, ABV 3.8%) ⬚ ◆
A well-balanced golden beer with lemon and grapefruit notes. A light, hoppy nose introduces a lively initial taste with hops again to the fore. Citrus flavours mix well with malt to give depth.

Lemon & Ginger (OG 1041, ABV 4%)
An amber, crisp ale with a ginger and lemon tang.

Swallowtail (OG 1041, ABV 4%)
A pale amber ale with a lively hop finish.

Ale (OG 1043, ABV 4.1%) ◆
A hoppy vanilla fudge bouquet develops through the initial taste to become the signature flavour. Malt provides balance as a gentle bitterness quickly recedes. Long, sweet, sticky finish.

Bad Egg (OG 1043.5, ABV 4.1%)
A ruby-coloured ale with a full-bodied malty taste.

Swingbridge Stout (OG 1044, ABV 4.1%)
A robust black stout with a balance of roasty and hoppy notes and a pale brown rich, creamy head.

Broadland Sunrise (OG 1044, ABV 4.2%) ◆
Beautifully smooth almost vinous ale. Swirling malt, hop and fruit aroma. The sweet, hoppy, well-balanced first impression develops into a smooth malty finish.

Reedcutter (OG 1046, ABV 4.4%) ◆
A sweet, malty beer, golden hued with a gentle malt background. Smooth and full-bodied with a quick, gentle finish.

Cheltenham Flyer (OG 1048, ABV 4.6%) ◆
A full-flavoured golden, earthy bitter with a long, grainy finish. A strong hop bitterness dominates throughout. Little evidence of malt.

Norfolk Nectar (OG 1048, ABV 4.6%) ◆
A sweet honeyed note wraps around other flavours and aromas. Hops and caramel maintain a

THE BREWERIES

presence throughout to give a counterpoint to the rich, sweet base.

Railway Sleeper (OG 1051, ABV 5%)
A rich Christmas pudding aroma leads into a delightfully fruity brew. Malt mingles with sultanas and raisins against a bittersweet backdrop. A full-bodied, smooth finish.

Golden Gorse (OG 1054, ABV 5.4%)
A full-bodied, fruity beer. Hints of banana, rhubarb, vanilla, peaches and toffee throughout. Malt is also present and helps suppress a soft, bitter background. A surprisingly short finish.

Porter (OG 1054, ABV 5.4%)
A full-bodied, malty brew. Deeply red hued with a hint of liqourice in the taste. Roast notes come to the fore as the sweet fruitiness slowly diminishes.

Hunter's

Hunter's Brewery Ltd, Bulleigh Barton Farm, Ipplepen, Devon, TQ12 5UE
☎ (01803) 814399 ☎ 07540 657115

Office: Glebe Acres, Orley Road, Ipplepen, Devon, TQ12 5SA thehuntersbrewery.co.uk

Hunters began brewing in 2008 on a five-barrel brew plant. Expansion means the brewery now has six fermentors and is capable of a 60-barrel brew length. Seasonal beers: Hunny Bunny (ABV 4.5%), Dashers Dinkle (ABV 5.5%), Blood Bath (ABV 5%).

Crack Shot (ABV 3.8%)

Butchers Best (ABV 4%)

Half Bore (ABV 4%)

Albion Ale (ABV 4.2%)

Denbury Dreamer (ABV 4.2%)

Pheasant Plucker (ABV 4.3%)

Gold (ABV 4.8%)

Full Bore (ABV 8%)

Hurns

See Tomos Watkin

Hydes IFBB

Hydes Brewery Ltd, 46 Moss Lane West, Moss Side, Manchester, M15 5PH
☎ (0161) 226 1317 ✉ mail@hydesbrewery.com
hydesbrewery.com
Tours by arrangement (Mon-Thu 7.30-9.45pm)

Hydes has been a family-owned regional brewer since 1863 and is currently the biggest volume producer of cask ales in the north west, thanks in part to its contract brewing for InBev and others. The brewery has been on the same site for more than 120 years with the brewery building Grade II listed. Hydes owns over 70 tied pubs, all selling cask ale, and have more than 300 free trade accounts. In addition Hydes beers are supplied to Allgates and Greene King pubs. Six seasonal beers are also produced.

Light Mild/1863 (OG 1033.5, ABV 3.5%)
Lightly hopped, pale brown session beer with some hops, malt and fruit in the taste and a short, dry finish.

Owd Oak (OG 1033.5, ABV 3.5%)
Dark brown/red in colour, with a fruit and malt nose. Taste includes biscuity malt and green fruits, with a satisfying aftertaste.

Traditional Mild (OG 1033.5, ABV 3.5%)
A mid-brown beer with malt and citrus fruits in the aroma and taste. Dry, malty aftertaste.

Original Bitter (OG 1036.5, ABV 3.8%)
Pale brown beer with a malty nose, malt and an earthy hoppiness in the taste, and a good bitterness through to the finish.

Jekyll's Gold Premium (OG 1042, ABV 4.3%)
Pale gold in colour, with a fruity nose. A well-balanced beer with hops, fruit and malt in the taste and bitter finish.

XXXX (OG 1070, ABV 6.8%)
Auburn chestnut brown in colour with a sweet malt toffee nose. A strong robust winter ale with a rich toffee taste.

For InBev UK:

Boddingtons Bitter (OG 1038, ABV 4.1%)

Iceni SIBA EAB

Iceni Brewery, 3 Foulden Road, Ickburgh, Norfolk, IP26 5HB
☎ (01842) 878922 ✉ icenibrewe@aol.com
icenibrewery.co.uk
Shop Mon-Fri 8.30am-5pm; Sat 9am-3pm
Tours by arrangement

Iceni was launched in 1995 by Brendan Moore. The brewery has its own hop garden aimed at the many visitors that flock to the shop to buy the 28 different ales, stouts and lagers bottled on-site. 30 outlets are supplied as well as local farmers' markets and a tourist shop in nearby Thetford Forest. The brewery aims to malt its own barley. Special beers are brewed for festivals and many seasonal beers are available.

Elveden Forest Gold (OG 1040, ABV 3.9%)
Forest fruits on the nose give way to strong hop bitterness in the initial taste. Residual maltiness provides balance at first but is swamped by a long, dry, bitter finish.

Celtic Queen (OG 1038, ABV 4%)
A golden brew with a light hoppy nose giving way to distinctly bitter characteristics throughout. A shallow mix of malt and hops adds some depth. A long, lingering finish.

Fine Soft Day (OG 1038, ABV 4%)
Toffee tickles both the nostrils and tastebuds as it hovers over a creamy, lightly-hopped backdrop in this golden brew. A gentle mix of flavours softly sinks into a pleasant sweetness.

Fen Tiger (OG 1040, ABV 4.2%)

It's A Grand Day (OG 1044, ABV 4.5%)
Gentle hop and citrus aroma introduces this pale brown brew. An orange sweetness contrasts with the underlying hoppy bitterness. Long-lasting and creamy but undemanding.

Raspberry Wheat (OG 1048, ABV 5%)

Winter Lightning (ABV 5%)

Men of Norfolk (OG 1060, ABV 6.2%)
Chocolaty stout with roast overtones from initial aroma to strong finish. Malt and vine fruits counterbalance the initial roast character while a caramel undertone remains to the end.

For Brancaster Brewery:

Best (ABV 3.8%)

Malthouse Bitter (ABV 4.4%)

Idle

🍺 Idle Brewery, White Hart Inn, Main Street, West Stockwith, South Yorkshire, DN10 4EY
☎ (01427) 753226 ☎ 07949 137174
✉ theidlebrewery@btinternet.com
Tours by arrangement

☺ The brewery began production in 2007 and is situated in a converted stable at the back of the White Hart Inn alongside the River Idle. Seasonal beers: Idle B (ABV 4.1%, summer), Cricketer (ABV 4.6%, summer).

Boggin (ABV 3.8%)
Tawny with a bitter finish.

Bodger (ABV 4%)

Illusion (ABV 4%)

Dog (ABV 4.2%)
A copper-coloured ale, moderately hoppy with a good balance of malt and hops leading to a bitter finish.

Sod (ABV 4.2%)

Coopers (ABV 4.3%)

Grunter (ABV 4.4%)

Black Abbot (ABV 4.5%)

Landlord (ABV 4.6%)
A dark brown ale with plenty of body, a malty flavour and a caramel/coffee finish.

Ilkley

Ilkley Brewery Co Ltd, Unit 4, Lencia Industrial Estate, 52 East Parade, Ilkley, West Yorkshire, LS29 8JP
☎ (01943) 604604 ✉ info@ilkleybrewery.co.uk
🌐 ilkleybrewery.co.uk
Tours by arrangement

☺Ilkley began brewing in 2009 on an eight-barrel plant, bringing brewing back to the town after a gap of some 80 years. Beers are brewed traditionally using only the highest quality home-grown malted barley and whole hops with soft Yorkshire water. There are plans for expansion. Seasonal beers: Darwin's Tipple (ABV 4.5%), Ruby Cascade (ABV 3.8%). Bottle-conditioned beers are also available.

Mary Jane (OG 1035, ABV 3.5%)
A crisp, pale ale with citrus aromas.

Gold (OG 1039, ABV 3.9%)
A refreshing, light session golden ale with a floral citrus aroma and delicate bitter finish.

Best (OG 1040, ABV 4%)
A highly hopped golden ale with a strong, bitter finish.

Original (OG 1043, ABV 4.3%)
A full-bodied, chestnut-coloured Yorkshire ale with rich flavours and aroma.

Innis & Gunn

Innis & Gunn Brewing Co Ltd, Canning Street, Edinburgh, EH3 8EG

☎ (0131) 272 2782
✉ gregg.imlah@innisandgunn.com
🌐 innisandgunn.com

Innis & Gunn does not brew but Belhaven Brewery produces one regular bottled (not bottle-conditioned) beer for the company, Oak Aged Beer (ABV 6.6%). There are three further beers in their permanent range: Original (ABV 6.6%), Blonde (ABV 6%) and Rum Cask (ABV 7.4%). A range of limited edition beers are also produced each year.

Inveralmond SIBA

Inveralmond Brewery Ltd, 22 Inveralmond Place, Inveralmond, Perth, PH1 3TS
☎ (01738) 449448 ✉ info@inveralmond-brewery.co.uk 🌐 inveralmond-brewery.co.uk
Shop Mon-Fri 10am-7pm + online
Tours by arrangement

☺ Established in 1997, Inveralmond was the first brewery in Perth for more than 30 years. The brewery has expanded from a 10-barrel to a 30-barrel plant and there are plans for further growth. Around 250 outlets are supplied. Seasonal beers: see website.

Independence (OG 1040, ABV 3.8%) 🍷 ◆
A well-balanced Scottish ale with fruit and malt tones. Hop provides an increasing bitterness in the finish.

Ossian (OG 1042, ABV 4.1%) 🍴 ◆
Well-balanced best bitter with a dry finish. This full-bodied amber ale is dominated by fruit and hop with a bittersweet character although excessive caramel can distract from this.

Thrappledouser (OG 1043, ABV 4.3%) ◆
A refreshing amber beer with reddish hues. The crisp, hoppy aroma is finely balanced with a tangy but quenching taste.

Lia Fail (OG 1048, ABV 4.7%) 🍷 ◆
The Gaelic name means Stone of Destiny. A dark, robust, full-bodied beer with a deep malty taste. Smooth texture and balanced finish.

Sunburst Pilsner (ABV 4.8%)

Ironbridge

Ironbridge Brewery Ltd, Unit 7, Merrythought, The Wharfage, Ironbridge, Telford, Shropshire, TF8 7NJ
☎ (01952) 433910
✉ david@ironbridgebrewery.co.uk
🌐 ironbridgebrewery.co.uk
Shop & Bar Mon-Sat 12-6pm (closed winter Mon); Sun 12-4pm
Tours by arrangement

☺Ironbridge was established in spring 2008 and operates on a 12-barrel brewery in an old Victorian warehouse alongside the River Severn in the heart of the Ironbridge Gorge. A visitor centre and shop were opened in 2009. All regular beers are also available bottle conditioned.

Coracle Bitter (OG 1039, ABV 3.8%)

Ironbridge Pale Ale (IPA) (OG 1040, ABV 4%)

1779 (OG 1043, ABV 4.2%)

Foundry Gold (OG 1047, ABV 4.5%)

Steam (ABV 4.7%)

ISB (OG 1051, ABV 5%)

Heritage Ale (ABV 5.5%)

Irving SIBA

Irving & Co Brewers Ltd, Unit G1, Railway Triangle, Walton Road, Portsmouth, Hampshire, PO6 1TQ
☎ (023) 9238 9988 ✉ sales@irvingbrewers.co.uk
🌐 irvingbrewers.co.uk
Shop Thu & Fri 3-6pm
Tours by arrangement

Irving's was set up by former Gale's brewer Malcolm Irving and a small team of ex-Gales employees using a 15-barrel plant. Around 60 outlets are supplied direct. Seasonal beers: see website.

Frigate (OG 1039, ABV 3.8%)

Type42 (OG 1042, ABV 4.2%)

Invincible (OG 1048, ABV 4.6%)
A tawny-coloured strong bitter. Sweet and fruity with an underlying maltiness throughout and a dryness that increases gradually, contrasting well with the sweetness of the finish.

Isca SIBA

Isca Ales Ltd, Gargoyles Brewery, Court Farm, Holcombe Village, Dawlish, Devon, EX7 0JT
☎ 07773 444501 ✉ iscaales@yahoo.co.uk

Two CAMRA members took over Gargoyles Brewery in late 2009 under the name Isca Ales Ltd. The original brewery was established in 2005. The Gargoyles name will continue alongside Isca Ales. 10 outlets are supplied.

Golden Ale (ABV 3.8%)

Best Bitter (ABV 4.2%)
An amber-coloured beer with a fresh, hoppy aftertaste.

Porter (ABV 4.8%)

Humbug (ABV 5%)

Island (NEW)

Island Brewery (Isle of Wight Brewery Ltd), Dinglers Farm, Yarmouth Road, Newport, Isle of Wight, PO30 4LZ
☎ (01983) 821731 ✉ sales@islandales.co.uk
🌐 isleofwightbrewery.com
Tours by arrangement

Island Brewery is the realisation of Tom Mishull's ambition to brew real ales to complement the existing family-owned drinks distribution business called Island Ales. Brewing commenced in early 2010 using a 12-barrel brewery. 45 outlets are supplied direct.

Nipper Bitter (OG 1038, ABV 3.8%)
Straw-coloured, light and refreshing with a distinguishable balance of malt and hops and a satisfying afterbite.

Wight Gold (OG 1040, ABV 4%)
Golden brown in colour with rounded malt and hops throughout.

Yachtsman's Ale (OG 1042, ABV 4.2%)
Chestnut-coloured ale with a rich, malty mouthfeel and hop aroma.

Wight Knight (OG 1045, ABV 4.5%)
Strong, full-bodied beer.

Vectis Venom (OG 1048, ABV 4.8%)
Easy-drinking with an underlying smoothness.

Islay

Islay Ales Co Ltd, The Brewery, Islay House Square, Bridgend, Isle of Islay, PA44 7NZ
☎ (01496) 810014 ✉ info@islayales.com
🌐 islayales.com
Shop Mon-Sat 10.30am-5pm
Tours by arrangement

Brewing started on a four-barrel plant in a converted tractor shed in 2004. The brewery shop is next door. The island is more famous for its whisky, but the brewery has established itself as a must-see place for those visiting the eight working distilleries. Bottle-conditioned beers are available.

Finlaggan Ale (OG 1039, ABV 3.7%)
A mid brown beer with a gentle, rounded bitterness and a fresh, fruity and hoppy flavour.

Black Rock Ale (OG 1040, ABV 4.2%)
A reddish beer with a soft, nutty flavour, a robust body and a floral, grassy and herbal nose.

Dun Hogs Head Ale (OG 1044, ABV 4.4%)
A dark, dry stout with a fruity edge and dry bitterness.

Saligo Ale (OG 1044, ABV 4.4%)
A golden ale with a rounded bitterness and a refreshing citrussy, lemon and grapefruit nose and taste.

Angus Og Ale (OG 1045, ABV 4.5%)

Ardnave Ale (OG 1048, ABV 4.6%)
A dry, thirst-quenching, hoppy bitter.

Nerabus Ale (OG 1046, ABV 4.8%)
A deep ruby-coloured brew with a black treacle, spicy flavour balanced by the use of spicy and citrussy hops.

Single Malt Ale (OG 1050, ABV 5%)
A pale beer with a sweet edge and a long, bitter finish.

Isle of Arran

See Arran

Isle of Avalon SIBA (NEW)

Isle of Avalon Brewery, Stagman Lane, Ashcott, Somerset, TA7 9QW
☎ (01458) 210050 ✉ avalonwholesale@gmail.com
🌐 avalonwholesaleandbrewing.co.uk

Avalon opened in late 2009.

Isle Ale (OG 1038, ABV 3.8%)

Sunset (OG 1043, ABV 4.3%)

Sunrise (OG 1050, ABV 5%)

Isle of Mull

Isle of Mull Brewing Co Ltd, Ledaig, Tobermory, Isle of Mull, PA75 6NR
☎ (01688) 302821
✉ isleofmullbrewing@btinternet.com

Brewing started in 2005. Beers are contract brewed by an unnamed Scottish brewer.

Island Pale Ale (OG 1038, ABV 3.9%)

Galleon Gold (ABV 4.1%)

Royal Regiment of Scotland (ABV 4.1%)

McCaig's Folly (OG 1042, ABV 4.2%)

Terror of Tobermory (OG 1045, ABV 4.6%)

Isle of Purbeck

Isle of Purbeck Brewery, Manor Road, Studland, Dorset, BH19 3AU
☎ (01929) 450227
info@isleofpurbeckbrewery.com
isleofpurbeckbrewery.com
Tours by arrangement

The Isle of Purbeck Brewery was founded in 2002, bringing Dorset ales back to the Purbecks following the closure of Poole Brewery. The 10-barrel plant is situated in the grounds of the Bankes Arms Hotel, overlooking Studland Bay on the Jurassic Coast. The beers can be found all over Dorset and Hampshire and are now available in London and further afield. Further seasonal beers are planned and bottle-conditioned beers are available. Seasonal beers: Harry's Harvest Pale Ale (ABV 5%, autumn), Thermal Cheer (ABV 4.8%, winter).

Best Bitter (OG 1036, ABV 3.6%)
A classic malty best bitter with rich malt aroma and taste and smooth malty bitter finish.

Fossil Fuel (OG 1040, ABV 4.1%)
Amber bitter with complex aroma; hops and malt combine to provide a session ale with a smooth bitter finish.

Solar Power (OG 1043, ABV 4.3%)
Tawny mid-range ale brewed using Continental hops. Well-balanced flavours combine to provide a strong bitter taste but short, dry finish.

Studland Bay Wrecked (OG 1044, ABV 4.5%)
Deep red ale with slightly sweet aroma reflecting a mixture of caramel, malt and hops that lead to a dry, malty finish.

IPA (OG 1047, ABV 4.8%)
A novel twist on an old style of ale; golden-amber with a spicy hop aroma and well-balanced taste and aroma, leading to a dry bitter, hoppy finish.

Isle of Skye

Isle of Skye Brewing Co (Leann an Eilein) Ltd, The Pier, Uig, Isle of Skye, IV51 9XP
☎ (01470) 542477 info@skyebrewery.co.uk
skyebrewery.co.uk
Shop Mon-Sat 10am-6pm; Sun 12.30-4.30pm (Apr-Oct)
Tours by arrangement

The Isle of Skye Brewery was established in 1995, the first commercial brewery in the Hebrides. Originally a 10-barrel plant, it was upgraded to 20-barrels in 2004. Fermenting capacity now stands at 80 barrels, with plans to further increase this and upgrade bottling facilities. Seasonal beers: see website.

Skyelight (OG 1038, ABV 3.8%)
A slightly hoppy nose leads to a powerful hop and fruit taste and a sharp finish.

Young Pretender (OG 1039, ABV 4%)
A fruity, full-bodied golden ale, predominantly hoppy and fruity. The bitterness in the mouth is also balanced by summer fruits and hops, continuing into the lingering bitter finish.

Red Cuillin (OG 1041, ABV 4.2%)
A light, fruity nose with a hint of caramel leads to a full-bodied malty flavour and a long, dry, bittersweet finish.

Hebridean Gold (OG 1041.5, ABV 4.3%)
Porridge oats are used to produce this delicious speciality beer. Nicely balanced. it has a refreshingly soft fruity, bitter flavour.

Black Cuillin (OG 1044, ABV 4.5%)
A complex, tasty brew, full-bodied with a malty richness. Malt holds sway but there are plenty of hops and fruit to be discovered in its varied character. A delicious Scottish old ale.

Blaven (OG 1047, ABV 5%)
A well-balanced strong amber bitter with kiwi fruit and caramel in the nose and a lingering sharp bitterness.

Cuillin Beast (OG 1061.5, ABV 7%)
A winter warmer; sweet and fruity, and much more drinkable than the strength would suggest. Plenty of caramel throughout with a variety of fruit on the nose.

Itchen Valley SIBA

Itchen Valley Brewery Ltd, Unit 4, Prospect Commercial Park, Prospect Road, New Alresford, Hampshire, SO24 9QF
☎ (01962) 735111/736429
info@itchenvalley.com itchenvalley.com
Shop Mon-Fri 9am-5pm; Sat 9am-12pm
Tours by arrangement

Established in 1997, Itchen Valley moved to new premises in 2006. The brewery has a gift shop and offers brewery tours and mini conferencing facilities. More than 350 pubs are supplied, with wholesalers used for further distribution. Over 40 seasonal beers are available as are bottle-conditioned ales.

Godfathers (OG 1038, ABV 3.8%)
A citrus hop character with a malty taste and a light body, leading to an increasingly dry, bitter finish. Pale brown in colour.

Fagin's (OG 1041, ABV 4.1%)
Enjoyable copper-coloured best bitter with a hint of crystal malt and a pleasant bitter aftertaste.

Hampshire Rose (OG 1042, ABV 4.2%)
A golden amber ale. Fruit and hops dominate the taste throughout, with a good mouth feel.

Winchester Ale (OG 1042, ABV 4.2%)
Traditional English bitter, nut brown with a sweet, malty flavour and a good hoppy nose.

Pure Gold (OG 1046, ABV 4.8%)
An aromatic hoppy, golden bitter. Initial maltiness and grapefruit flavours lead to a dry finish.

Jacobi

Jacobi Brewery of Caio, Penlanwen Farm, Pumsaint, Carmarthenshire, SA19 8RR
☎ (01558) 650605 justin@jacobibrewery.co.uk
jacobibrewery.co.uk

Brewing started in 2006 on an eight-barrel plant in a converted barn. Brewer Justin Jacobi is also the owner of the Brunant Arms in Caio, which is a regular outlet for the beers. The brewery is located 50 yards from the Dolaucothi mines where the Romans dug for gold. A visitor centre and bottling line are planned.

Light Ale (OG 1040, ABV 3.8%)

Original (OG 1044, ABV 4%)

Dark Ale (OG 1052, ABV 5%)

Jarrow SIBA

Jarrow Brewery, The Maltings, 9 Claypath Lane, South Shields, Tyne & Wear, NE33 4PG
☎ (0191) 483 6792
✉ jarrowbrewery@btconnect.com
jarrowbrewing.co.uk
Tours by arrangement

Real ale enthusiasts Jess and Alison McConnell commenced brewing at the Robin Hood, Jarrow, in 2002. In 2008 all brewing was transferred to the Maltings in South Shields. Seasonal beers: Red Ellen (ABV 4.4%), Venerable Bede (ABV 4.5%), Old Cornelius (ABV 4.8%), Jarrow Brown Ale (ABV 5%).

Bitter (OG 1037.5, ABV 3.8%)
A light golden session bitter with a delicate hop aroma and a lingering fruity finish.

Rivet Catcher (OG 1039, ABV 4%)
A light, smooth, satisfying gold bitter. Subtle fruity hops give the taste profile on the tongue and nose.

Joblings Swinging Gibbet (OG 1041, ABV 4.1%)
A copper-coloured, evenly balanced beer with a good hop aroma and a fruity finish.

Caulker (OG 1040.5, ABV 4.2%)
A light, golden, hoppy ale with a lingering grapefruit zest finish.

Slake (OG 1041.5, ABV 4.3%)
A golden amber ale with a subtle floral taste.

McConnells Irish Stout (OG 1045, ABV 4.6%)
A rich, creamy stout with a long, lingering liquorice and pale chocolate finish.

Westoe IPA (OG 1044.5, ABV 4.6%)
A pale gold ale with a soft malt character and a refreshingly complex hop aroma.

Jennings

See Marston's in the New Nationals section

Jersey SIBA

Jersey Brewery, Tregear House, Longueville Road, St Saviour, Jersey, JE2 7WF
☎ (01534) 764089 ✉ paulhurley@victor-hugo-ltd.com liberationgroup.com
Tours by arrangement

Following the closure of the original brewery in Ann Street in 2004, the Jersey Brewery is now located in an old soft drinks factory. The brewery is owned by the Liberation Group. Distribution is only in the Channel Islands at present but export to the UK is planned. 66 pubs are owned with around half (and increasing) serving cask ale. Occasional ales: Mary Ann Best Bitter (ABV 3.6%), Mary Ann Special (ABV 4.5%).

Liberation Ale (OG 1039, ABV 4%)
Golden beer with a hint of citrus on the nose.

Jollyboat

Jollyboat Brewery (Bideford) Ltd, The Coach House, Buttgarden Street, Bideford, Devon, EX39 2AU
☎ (01237) 424343

Established in 1995, the brewery is named after a sailor's leave boat and all the beers have a nautical theme. Most outlets supplied are in Devon but a trade route to Bristol has been firmly established. Seasonal beers: Buccaneers (ABV 3.7%, summer), Contraband (ABV 5.8%, winter). Bottle-conditioned beers are also available.

Grenville's Renown (OG 1037, ABV 3.8%)

Freebooter (OG 1040, ABV 4%)

Mainbrace (OG 1042, ABV 4.2%)
Pale brown brew with a rich fruity aroma and a bitter taste and aftertaste.

Hart of Oak (OG 1044, ABV 4.4%)

Plunder (OG 1047, ABV 4.8%)

Jolly Brewer

Jolly Brewer, Kingston Villa, 27 Poplar Road, Wrexham, LL13 7DG
☎ (01978) 261884 ✉ pene@jollybrewer.co.uk
jollybrewer.co.uk
Tours by arrangement (small groups only)

Jolly Brewer is a well-established cottage industry. Penelope Coles now only brews bottle-conditioned ales as she is also the head brewster at Sandstone Brewery (qv). Her beers can be purchased at the Wrexham Farmer's Market on the third Friday of the month and at the Grosvenor Garden Centre Farmer's Market in Chester on the second Friday. All bottle-conditioned beers are suitable for vegetarians and vegans: Chwerw Cymreig (ABV 4%), Druid's Ale (ABV 4%), Festival Ale (ABV 4%), Taid's Garden (ABV 4%), Cwrw Du (ABV 4.2%), Lucinda's Lager (ABV 4.5%), Porter (Penelope's Secret) (ABV 4.5%), Suzanne's Stout (ABV 4.5%), Taffy's Tipple (ABV 4.5%), Y Ddraig Goch (ABV 4.5%), Ruddy Fox (ABV 4.7%), Dynes Dywyll (ABV 5%), Dark Lager (ABV 6%).

Joseph Herbert Smith

Joseph Herbert Smith Trad Brewers, Fox Inn, Hanley Broadheath, Nr Tenbury Wells, Worcestershire, WR15 8QS
☎ (01886) 853189 ☎ 07527 066474
✉ jhsbrewery@yahoo.co.uk
jhstraditionalbrewery.com
Tours by arrangement

The brewery was established in 2007 by Jonathan Smith on a 2.5-barrel plant from Danelaw Brewery. In 2008 it relocated from Wombourne in Staffordshire to barns adjacent to the Fox Inn in Tenbury Wells. All equipment is gas fired and ingredients are sourced locally where possible. Seasonal beer: Kinny's Port Stout (ABV 4.5%, Nov-Feb), Elm (ABV 3.9%). Monthly feature beers are also available.

Amy's Rose (OG 1040, ABV 4%)

Snooty Fox (OG 1042, ABV 4.1%)

Foxy Lady (OG 1043, ABV 4.3%)

Joules (NEW)

Joules Brewery, The Brewery, Great Hales Street, Market Drayton, Shropshire, TF9 1JP
☎ (01630) 654400 ✉ info@joulesbrewery.co.uk
⊕ joulesbrewery.co.uk
Tours by arrangement

⊠ The new Joules Brewery opened in 2010 after a break of 40 years. It is situated in Market Drayton in order to source the purest mineral water which, as before, is the essential foundation for Joule's ales.

Best Bitter (ABV 3.8%)

Original Pale Ale (ABV 4.1%)
Made from the original Joules' recipe from 1779.

Slumbering Monk (ABV 4.3%)

Kelburn SIBA

Kelburn Brewing Co Ltd, 10 Muriel Lane, Barrhead, East Renfrewshire, G78 1QB
☎ (0141) 881 2138 ✉ info@kelburnbrewery.com
⊕ kelburnbrewery.com
Tours by arrangement

⊠ Kelburn is a family business established in 2002. In the first seven years of business, the beers have won 29 awards. Beers are available bottled and in take-away polypins. Seasonal beers: Ca'Canny (ABV 5.2%, winter), Tartan Army (ABV 4.3%, when Scotland football team are playing), Kracker (ABV 6%, Xmas).

Goldihops (OG 1038, ABV 3.8%) ◆
Well-hopped session ale with a fruity taste and a bitter finish.

Pivo Estivo (ABV 3.9%)

Misty Law (ABV 4%)
A dry, hoppy amber ale with a long-lasting bitter finish.

Red Smiddy (OG 1040, ABV 4.1%) ◆
This bittersweet ale predominantly features an intense citrus hop character that assaults the nose and continues into the flavour, balanced perfectly with fruity malt.

Dark Moor (OG 1044, ABV 4.5%)
A dark, fruity ale with undertones of liquorice and blackcurrant.

Cart Blanche (OG 1048, ABV 5%) ◆
A golden, full-bodied ale. The assault of fruit and hop camouflages the strength of this easy-drinking ale.

Kelham Island SIBA

Kelham Island Brewery Ltd, 23 Alma Street, Sheffield, South Yorkshire, S3 8SA
☎ (0114) 249 4804 ✉ sales@kelhambrewery.co.uk
⊕ kelhambrewery.co.uk
Tours by arrangement

☺ The brewery opened in 1990 behind the Fat Cat public house. Due to its success, the brewery moved to new purpose-built premises in 1999 (adjacent to the pub), with five times the capacity of the original brewery. The old building is being converted into a visitor centre. Since surviving a flood in 2007, the brewery has gone from strength to strength, installing a new, larger brewhouse in 2009. Five regular beers are brewed as well as monthly themed specials and more than 200

outlets are supplied. Bottle-conditioned beers are also available and are suitable for vegetarians.

Kelham Best Bitter (OG 1038, ABV 3.8%) ◆
A clean, characterful, crisp, pale brown beer. The nose and palate are dominated by refreshing hoppiness and fruitiness, which, with a good bitter dryness, lasts in the aftertaste.

Pride of Sheffield (OG 1040.5, ABV 4%)
A full-flavoured amber coloured bitter.

Easy Rider (OG 1041.8, ABV 4.3%) ◆
A pale, straw-coloured beer with a sweetish flavour and delicate hints of citrus fruits. A beer with hints of flavour rather than full-bodied.

Riders on the Storm (OG 1045, ABV 4.5%)
A robust golden pale ale with berry notes and very slight roasted notes.

Pale Rider (OG 1050, ABV 5.2%) ◆
A full-bodied, straw pale ale, with a good fruity aroma and a strong fruit and hop taste. Its well-balanced sweetness and bitterness continue in the finish.

Keltek SIBA

OMC (UK) Ltd t/a Keltek Brewery, Candela House, Cardrew Way, Redruth, Cornwall, TR15 1SS
☎ (01209) 313620 ✉ sales@keltekbrewery.co.uk
⊕ keltekbrewery.co.uk
Shop Mon-Fri 9am-5pm

⊠ Keltek Brewery moved to Lostwithiel in 1999 and in 2006 moved again to Redruth and installed a new 25-barrel plant in addition to the original two-barrel plant, which is still used for specials and development. In 2009 the brewery expanded again with new bottling facilities, labelling equipment and five 50-barrel tanks. Keltek is now a major force in Cornwall with their beers available as far afield as Hong Kong. All ales are also available bottle conditioned. CAMRA members are welcome (by appointment) to try their hand at brewing.

4K Mild (OG 1038, ABV 3.8%)

Golden Lance (OG 1038, ABV 4%) ◆
Light fruity, flowery hops on the nose of this gold bitter leading to more hops, fruit and butterscotch in the mouth, balanced by gentle malt and sweetness, which linger on with a little dryness.

Magik (OG 1040, ABV 4.2%) ◆
A rounded, well-balanced and complex beer.

Mr Murdoch's Golden IPA (OG 1043, ABV 4.5%)

Trevithick's Revenge (OG 1043, ABV 4.5%)

King (OG 1049, ABV 5.1%)

Kemptown SIBA

🍺 Kemptown Brewery Co Ltd, 33 Upper St James's Street, Kemptown, Brighton, East Sussex, BN2 1JN
☎ (01273) 699595
Tours by arrangement

☺ Kemptown was established in 1989 and built in the tower tradition behind the Hand in Hand, which is possibly the smallest brewpub in England. It takes its name and logo from the former Charrington's Kemptown Brewery, which closed in 1964. Seasonal beers are available.

Kemptown (OG 1040, ABV 4%)

THE BREWERIES

A light session ale. Crisp and hoppy.

China (ABV 4.5%)
A full-bodied mid-brown ale with a fruity, floral aroma and a lingering, intense hoppy finish.

Ye Olde Trout (OG 1045, ABV 4.5%)
A golden brown beer with fruity aromas and a dry finish.

Kernel SIBA (NEW)

Kernel Brewery, 98 Druid Street, London, SE1 2HQ
☎ 07757 552636 ✉ evin@theknernalbrewery.com
🌐 thekernalbrewery.com
Shop Sat 9am-4pm
Tours by arrangement

Kernel was established in 2010 and produces bottle-conditioned beers on a four-barrel plant. All beers are suitable for vegetarians and vegans. Bottle-conditioned beers: Pale Ale (ABV 5.5%), Porter (ABV 6%), IPA (ABV 7.9%).

Keswick

Keswick Brewing Co, The Old Brewery, Brewery Lane, Keswick, Cumbria, CA12 5BY
☎ (01768) 780700 ✉ info@keswickbrewery.co.uk
🌐 keswickbrewery.co.uk
Shop – call for details (usually Mon-Fri 9am-5pm)
Tours by arrangement

Phil and Sue Harrison set up their 10-barrel brewery in 2006 with quality and environmental issues at its heart. It is located on the site of a brewery which closed in 1897. More than 70 outlets are supplied. Seasonal beers: see website.

Thirst Rescue (OG 1036, ABV 3.7%)

Thirst Pitch (OG 1037, ABV 3.8%)

Thirst Ascent (OG 1039, ABV 4%)

Thirst Run (OG 1041, ABV 4.2%)
A well-balanced golden beer that maintains its fruitiness from start to finish.

Thirst Fall (OG 1047, ABV 4.8%)

Thirst Celebration (OG 1065, ABV 7%)

Keystone SIBA

Keystone Brewery, Old Carpenters Workshop, Berwick St Leonard, Salisbury, Wiltshire, SP3 5SN
☎ (01747) 820426 ✉ info@keystonebrewery.co.uk
🌐 keystonebrewery.co.uk
Shop Mon, Tue & Fri 10am-5pm
Tours by arrangement

⊗ Keystone Brewery was set up in 2006 with a 10-barrel plant. The beers have low food miles to help support a sustainable local community. The brewery also use an award-winning solar heating system, which reduces carbon emissions. Around 150 outlets are supplied. Seasonal beers: see website. Bottle-conditioned beers are also available.

Bedrock (OG 1035, ABV 3.6%)

Gold Spice (OG 1039, ABV 4%)

Gold Standard (OG 1039, ABV 4%)

Large One (OG 1041, ABV 4.2%)

Very Pale Ale (OG 1045, ABV 4.6%)

Cornerstone (OG 1047, ABV 4.8%)

King SIBA

W J King & Co (Brewers), 3-5 Jubilee Estate, Foundry Lane, Horsham, West Sussex, RH13 5UE
☎ (01403) 272102 ✉ sales@kingbeer.co.uk
🌐 kingbeer.co.uk
Shop Sat 10am-2pm
Tours by arrangement (limited to 15)

⊗ Launched in 2001 on a 20-barrel plant, the brewery had expanded to a capacity of 50 barrels a week by mid-2004. In 2004 premises next door were added to give more cellar space and to enable room to stock more bottle-conditioned beers. Around 200 outlets are supplied. Seasonal beers: see website.

Horsham Best Bitter (OG 1038, ABV 3.8%)
A predominantly malty best bitter, brown in colour. The nutty flavours have some sweetness with a little bitterness that grows in the aftertaste.

Red River (OG 1048, ABV 4.8%)
A full-flavoured, mid-brown beer. It is malty with some berry fruitiness in the aroma and taste. The finish is reasonably balanced with a sharp bitterness coming through.

Kings Head

Kings Head Brewery, Kings Head, 132 High Street, Bildeston, Ipswich, Suffolk, IP7 7ED
☎ (01449) 741434
✉ kingshead.bildeston@tiscali.co.uk
🌐 bildestonkingshead.co.uk
Tours by arrangement

⊗ Kings Head has been brewing since 1996 in an old cart lodge at the back of the pub. Under new ownership since 2008, the three-barrel plant brews weekly. Local pubs and beer festivals are supplied. Seasonal beers: see website.

Bildeston Best (OG 1036, ABV 3.6%)
Traditional best. Well-hopped with a malty sweetness and dry finish.

Blondie (OG 1040, ABV 4%)
Cask lager.

Landlady (OG 1040, ABV 4%)
Pale ale, hoppy and fruity with a dry finish.

Crowdie (OG 1042, ABV 4.2%)
An oatmeal stout.

Bildeston Porter (OG 1045, ABV 4.4%)
Dark ale with complex maltiness and smooth, hoppy finish.

Brettvale Ale (OG 1044, ABV 4.4%)
Pale ale with balanced malty sweetness and hops.

Dark Vadar (OG 1051, ABV 5%)
A rich, dark ale.

Kingstone

Kingstone Brewery, Meadow Farm, Tintern, Monmouthshire, NP16 7NX
☎ (01291) 680111/680101
✉ shop@kingstonebrewery.co.uk
🌐 kingstonebrewery.co.uk

⊗ Kingstone Brewery is located in the Wye Valley where brewing began on a four-barrel plant in 2005. All cask ales are also available bottle conditioned.

Tewdric's Tipple (ABV 3.8%)

Challenger (ABV 4%)

Gold (ABV 4%)

No. 1 Stout (ABV 4.4%)

Classic (ABV 4.5%)

1503 (ABV 4.8%)

Abbey Ale (ABV 5.1%)

Humpty's Fuddle (ABV 5.8%)

Kinver SIBA

Kinver Brewery, Unit 2, Fairfield Drive, Kinver, Staffordshire, DY7 6EW
☎ **07715 842679/07906 146777**
✉ **kinvercave@aol.com** 🌐 **kinverbrewery.co.uk**
Tours by arrangement

Established in 2004 by two CAMRA members, Kinver Brewery consists of a five-barrel plant, producing six regular beers, seasonals and one-off brews. Kinver brews three times a week and supplies more than 30 pubs and clubs throughout the Midlands, including two in Kinver. Seasonal beers: Maybug (ABV 4.8%, May-Jun), Sunarise (ABV 4%, summer), Black Ram (ABV 5.2%, Oct-Jan), Holy Austin (ABV 5.3%, Dec), Over the Edge (ABV 7.6%, Nov-Mar).

Light Railway (OG 1038, ABV 3.8%)
Straw-coloured session beer. A malty start quickly gives way to well-hopped bitterness and lingering hoppy aftertaste.

Edge (OG 1041, ABV 4.2%)
Amber with a malty aroma. Sweet fruity start with a hint of citrus marmalade; lasting hoppy finish that is satisfyingly bitter.

Pail Ale (OG 1044, ABV 4.4%)
Gold with a hoppy aroma and malty background. Citrus hops dominate but are tempered with fruit for a bittersweet balance. Astringent note at the end.

Crystal (OG 1044, ABV 4.5%)
Pale premium bitter with a dry, citrus finish.

Caveman (OG 1046, ABV 4.8%)
A malt aroma leads into a malt and hop start that intensifies to a long hoppy aftertaste.

Half Centurion (OG 1048, ABV 5%)
A golden best bitter with American Chinook hop aroma and taste merging and balancing the malt towards the hoppy finish.

Khyber (OG 1054, ABV 5.8%)
Golden strong bitter with a Centennial hop bite that overwhelms the fleeting malty sweetness and drives through to the long dry finish.

Kirkby Lonsdale SIBA

Kirkby Lonsdale Brewery Co Ltd, Unit 2F, Old Station Yard, Kirkby Lonsdale, Lancashire, LA6 2HP
☎ **(01524) 272221** ☎ **07793 149999**
✉ **info@kirkbylonsdalebrewery.com**
🌐 **kirkbylonsdalebrewery.com**

Kirkby Lonsdale is a family-run business established in 2009 on a six-barrel plant. Seasonal and bottle-conditioned beers are available.

Ruskin's Bitter (OG 1039, ABV 3.9%)
A tawny bitter with a distinctive aroma of fruit and malt. The clean, hoppy flavour is well-balanced with fruity sweetness leading to a sustained bittersweet finish.

Radical Red (OG 1042, ABV 4.2%)
A sweet, malty, ruby-coloured beer.

Monumental Blonde (OG 1045, ABV 4.5%)
A floral golden ale.

Jubilee Stout (OG 1055, ABV 5.5%)
A smooth stout with hints of pale malt and liquorice.

Kissingate (NEW)

Kissingate Brewery, 2 Drury Close, Maidenbower, Crawley, West Sussex, RH10 7HF
☎ **(01293) 882198** ✉ **gary@kissingate.co.uk**
🌐 **kissingate.co.uk**

Kissingate began brewing commercially in 2010. Inspiration for the beers is drawn from the cottage brewing styles and cultures from the late middle ages. Local outlets and beer festivals are supplied.

Old Tale Porter (OG 1052, ABV 4.5%)

Moon (OG 1050, ABV 4.8%)

First Kiss (OG 1052, ABV 5.1%)

Warlock (OG 1056, ABV 5.2%)

Mary's Ruby Mild (OG 1072, ABV 6.5%)

Knops (NEW)

Knops Beer Co Ltd, c/o Abbotsford Court, Edinburgh, EH10 5EJ
☎ **(0131) 447 8104**
✉ **robert.knops@knopsbeer.co.uk**
🌐 **knopsbeer.co.uk**

Knops began brewing in 2010. Beer is brewed at Traditional Scottish Ales in Stirling. There are plans to extend the beer range. See Traditional Scottish Ales for beer list.

Lancaster SIBA

Lancaster Brewery Co Ltd, 19 Lansil Walk, Caton Road, Lancaster, LA1 3PQ
☎ **(01524) 848537** ✉ **info@lancasterbrewery.co.uk**
🌐 **lancasterbrewery.co.uk**
Tours by arrangement

Lancaster began brewing in 2005. In 2007 the brewery underwent a change in direction with new faciities installed and new brands launched. The brewery is soon to relocate to larger premises in Lancaster to facilitate continued growth. Seasonal beers: Redderer (ABV varies, Xmas), Slate (ABV 4.2%).

Amber (OG 1038, ABV 3.7%)
Dark gold session beer with a hoppy bouquet and subtle floral and citrus aromas.

Blonde (OG 1042, ABV 4.1%)
A crisp, hoppy flavour with a touch of caramel and a hint of citrus. Golden hued with a smooth, easy-drinking feel. Hops follow through to dominate in the aftertaste.

Black (OG 1046, ABV 4.6%)
Traditional stout; rich and full-bodied.

Red (OG 1048, ABV 4.9%)
Robust ale with a malt dominated body.

Langham

Langham Brewery, Old Granary, Langham Lane, Lodsworth, West Sussex, GU28 9BU
☎ (01798) 860861 ✉ office@langhambrewery.co.uk
langhambrewery.co.uk
Shop Tue & Sat 9am-5pm
Tours by arrangement

⊗ Langham Brewery was established in 2006 in an 18th-century granary barn and is set in the heart of West Sussex with fine views to the rolling South Downs. It is owned by Steve Mansley and James Berrow who both brew and run the business. The brewery is a 10-barrel steam heated plant and over 50 outlets are supplied.

Halfway to Heaven (OG 1035, ABV 3.5%)
A chestnut-coloured beer with a balanced biscuit maltiness and citrus and fruit hop character with a hint of spice.

Hip Hop (OG 1040, ABV 4%)
A blonde beer – clean and crisp. The nose is loaded with floral hop aroma while the pale malt flavour is overtaken by a dry and bitter finish.

Best (OG 1042, ABV 4.2%)
A tawny-coloured classic best with well-balanced malt flavours and bitterness.

Sundowner (OG 1042, ABV 4.2%)
A deep golden beer. The nose has tropical fruit, pineapple and citrus notes with a smooth maltiness in the background. There is a balanced dry and bitter finish with floral hop aroma.

Langham Special Draught/LSD (OG 1049, ABV 5.2%)
An auburn beer with rich, complex flavours and a deep red glow. The sweet maltiness is balanced with spicy hop aromas and a dry finish.

Langton

Langton Brewery, Grange Farm, Welham Road, Thorpe Langton, Leicestershire, LE16 7TU
☎ 07840 532826 langtonbrewery.co.uk
Tours by arrangement

⊗ The Langton Brewery started in 1999 in buildings behind the Bell Inn, East Langton. Due to demand, the brewery relocated in 2005 to a converted barn in Thorpe Langton, where a four-barrel plant was installed. Further expansion is planned due to increased demand. All beers are available to take away in casks, polypins or bottles. Seasonal beers: Welland Sunrise (ABV 4.5%, summer), Welland Fox (ABV 4.3%, autumn). Bottle-conditioned beers are also available.

Caudle Bitter (OG 1039, ABV 3.9%) ◆
Copper-coloured session bitter that is close to pale ale in style. Flavours are relatively well-balanced throughout with hops slightly to the fore.

Inclined Plane Bitter (OG 1042, ABV 4.2%)
A straw-coloured bitter with a citrus nose and long, hoppy finish.

Hop On (OG 1044, ABV 4.4%)
A premium bitter, deep chestnut colour with a good balance of flavours and aroma.

Bowler Strong Ale (OG 1048, ABV 4.8%)
A strong traditional ale with a deep red colour and a hoppy nose.

Larkins SIBA

Larkins Brewery Ltd, Larkins Farm, Hampkins Hill Road, Chiddingstone, Kent, TN8 7BB
☎ (01892) 870328
Tours by arrangement (Nov-Feb)

⊗ Larkins Brewery was founded in 1986 by the Dockerty family, who bought the Royal Tunbridge Wells Brewery. The company moved to Larkins Farm in 1987. Since then the production of three regular brews and Porter in the winter months has steadily increased. Larkins supplies around 70 free houses within a radius of 20 miles. Seasonal beer: Platinum Blonde (ABV 3.6%, summer).

Traditional Ale (OG 1035, ABV 3.4%)
Tawny in colour, a full-tasting hoppy ale with plenty of character for its strength.

Chiddingstone (OG 1040, ABV 4%)
Named after the village where the brewery is based, Chiddingstone is a mid-strength, hoppy, fruity ale with a long, bittersweet aftertaste.

Best (OG 1045, ABV 4.5%) ◆
Full-bodied, slightly fruity and unusually bitter for its gravity.

Porter (OG 1052, ABV 5.2%) ◆
Each taste and smell of this potent black winter beer (Nov-Apr) reveals another facet of its character. An explosion of roasted malt, bitter and fruity flavours leaves a bittersweet aftertaste.

Leadmill

Leadmill Brewery Ltd, Unit 1, Park Hall Farm, Park Hall Road, Denby, Derbyshire, DE5 8PX
☎ (01332) 883577 ☎ 07971 189915
✉ tlc@leadmill.fsnet.co.uk
Tours by arrangement

⊗ Originally set up in a pig sty in Selston, Leadmill moved to Denby in 2002 using a four-barrel plant. A sister brewery to Bottle Brook (qv), many of the brews are one-offs using rare hop varieties. There are plans to move the brewery across the yard to the Old Stables Bar site. The brewery tap is the Old Oak Inn in Horsley Woodhouse. Seasonal beers: Jersey City (ABV 5%, autumn), Ginger Spice (ABV 5%, summer), Autumn Goddess (ABV 4.2%), Get Stuffed (ABV 6.7%, Xmas), Mince Pied (ABV 4.8%, Xmas).

Mash Tun Bitter (OG 1036, ABV 3.6%)

Old Oak Bitter (OG 1037, ABV 3.7%)

Duchess (OG 1041, ABV 4.2%)

Old Mottled Cock (OG 1041, ABV 4.2%)

Dream Weaver (OG 1042, ABV 4.3%)

Frosted Hop (OG 1042, ABV 4.3%)

Strawberry Blonde (OG 1042, ABV 4.4%)

Rolling Thunder (OG 1043, ABV 4.5%)

Curly Blonde (OG 1044, ABV 4.6%)

Maple Porter (OG 1045, ABV 4.7%)

Snakeyes (OG 1045, ABV 4.8%)

Agent Orange (OG 1047, ABV 4.9%)

Born in the USA (OG 1048, ABV 5%)

Rampage (OG 1050, ABV 5.1%)

B52 (OG 1050, ABV 5.2%)

Destitution (OG 1051, ABV 5.3%)

Ghostrider (OG 1052, ABV 5.4%)

Beast (OG 1053, ABV 5.7%)

Slumdog (OG 1058, ABV 5.9%)

Leatherbritches

Leatherbritches Brewery, Green Man & Blacks Head Royal Hotel, St John Street, Ashbourne, Derbyshire, DE6 1GH
☎ 07976 279253 ✉ leatherbritches@btconnect.com
Shop: Opening times vary – please ring first (01335) 342374
Tours by arrangement

☺The brewery, founded in 1993 in Fenny Bentley, moved to Ashbourne in 2008 with a new, bigger brewing plant. The hotel and brewery business are separate but the hotel sells beers from the brewery. Seasonal beer: Porter (ABV 5%, winter). Bottle-conditioned beers are also available.

Goldings (OG 1036, ABV 3.6%)
A light golden beer with a flowery hoppy aroma and a bitter finish.

Ginger Spice (OG 1036, ABV 3.8%)
A light, highly-hopped bitter with the added zest of Chinese stem ginger.

Ashbourne Ale (OG 1040, ABV 4%)
A pale bitter brewed with Goldings hops for a crisp lasting taste.

Doctor Johnsons (ABV 4%)
A mid-brown ale, not heavily hopped but full-bodied with some caramel flavour.

Belt-n-Braces (OG 1040, ABV 4.4%)
Mid-brown, full-flavoured, dry-hopped bitter.

Belter (OG 1040, ABV 4.4%)
Maris Otter malt produces a pale but interesting beer.

Dovedale (OG 1044, ABV 4.4%)
A copper bitter with a crisp finish.

Ginger Helmet (OG 1047, ABV 4.7%)
As for Hairy Helmet but with a hint of China's most astringent herb.

Hairy Helmet (OG 1047, ABV 4.7%)
Pale bitter, well hopped but with a sweet finish.

Bespoke (OG 1050, ABV 5%)
Full-bodied, well-rounded premium bitter.

Leeds

Leeds Brewery Co Ltd, 3 Sydenham Road, Leeds, West Yorkshire, LS11 9RU
☎ (0113) 244 5866 ✉ sales@leedsbrewery.co.uk
⊕ leedsbrewery.co.uk

☺Leeds Brewery began production in 2007 using a 20-barrel plant. It is the largest independent brewer in the city and uses a unique strain of yeast originally used by another, now defunct, West Yorkshire brewery. Three pubs are owned in Leeds city centre: Pin, the Midnight Bell and the Brewery Tap. Around 300 outlets are supplied direct. Seasonal beers: see website.

Pale (OG 1037.5, ABV 3.8%) ◆
Well-balanced light ale, citrus in both aroma and flavour. Gold in colour with a refreshing bitter, hoppy finish.

Best (OG 1041, ABV 4.3%) ◆

A full flavoured, moderately hoppy beer, balanced with malt, leading to a slightly hoppy, lingering bitter aftertaste.

Midnight Bell (OG 1047.5, ABV 4.8%) 🍴 ◆
A malty, rich, fruity aroma carries through in the taste along with touches of chocolate and vanilla. Sweetness and roast malt flavours linger. Deep red, almost black in colour.

Leek

Staffordshire Brewing Co t/a Leek Brewery, 12 Churnet Court, Cheddleton, Staffordshire, ST13 7EF
☎ (01538) 361919 ☎ 07971 808370
✉ leekbrewery@hotmail.com
⊕ beersandcheese.co.uk
Tours by arrangement

⊠ Brewing started in 2002 with a 4.5-barrel plant located behind the owner's house, before moving to Cheddleton in 2004. The brewery upgraded to a six-barrel plant in 2007 and to a 20-barrel plant in 2010. In recent years the brewery has concentrated on producing bottle-conditioned beers but the new upgrade means that cask-conditioned beers will be regularly available again. A range of beer cheeses is made in the dairy, next door to the brewery.

Staffordshire Gold (ABV 3.8%) ◆
Light, straw-coloured with a pleasing hoppy aroma and a hint of malt. Bitter finish from the hops, making it easily drunk and thirst-quenching.

Danebridge IPA (ABV 4.1%) ◆
Full fruit and hop aroma. Flowery hop start with a bitter taste. Finish of hops and flowers.

Staffordshire Bitter (ABV 4.2%) ◆
Amber with a fruity aroma. Malty and hoppy start with the hoppy finish diminishing quickly.

Black Grouse (ABV 4.5%)

Hen Cloud (ABV 4.5%)

St Edwards (ABV 4.7%)

Rudyard Ruby (ABV 4.8%)

Double Sunset (ABV 5.2%)

Rocheberg Blonde (ABV 5.6%)

Cheddleton Steamer (ABV 6%)

Tittesworth Tipple (ABV 6.5%)

Lees IFBB

J W Lees & Co (Brewers) Ltd, Greengate Brewery, Middleton Junction, Manchester, M24 2AX
☎ (0161) 643 2487 ✉ mail@jwlees.co.uk
⊕ jwlees.co.uk
Tours by arrangement

☺ Lees is a family-owned brewery founded in 1828 by John Lees and run by the sixth generation of the family. Brewing takes place in the 1876 brewhouse designed and built by John Willie Lees, the grandson of the founder. The current head brewer is a family member. The brewhouse has been completely modernised in recent years to give greater flexibility. The company has a tied estate of around 180 pubs, mostly in North Manchester, with 30 in North Wales; almost all serve cask beer. Seasonal beers are brewed four times a year.

Brewer's Dark (OG 1032, ABV 3.5%) ◆

Formerly GB Mild, this is a dark brown beer with a malt and caramel aroma. Creamy mouthfeel, with malt, caramel and fruit flavours and a malty finish. Becoming rare.

Bitter (OG 1037, ABV 4%) ◆
Copper-coloured beer with malt and fruit in aroma, taste and finish.

Coronation Street (OG 1042, ABV 4.2%)
First brewed in 2009, the name is licensed to Lees by ITV.

John Willie's (OG 1041, ABV 4.5%)
A well-balanced, full-bodied premium bitter.

Moonraker (OG 1073, ABV 7.5%) ◆
A reddish-brown beer with a strong, malty, fruity aroma. The flavour is rich and sweet, with roast malt, and the finish is fruity yet dry. Available only in a handful of outlets.

Leila Cottage

▤ Leila Cottage Brewery, Countryman, Chapel Road, Ingoldmells, Skegness, Lincolnshire, PE25 1ND
☎ (01754) 872268
✉ countryman_inn@btconnect.com
⊕ countryman-ingoldmells.co.uk
Tours by arrangement

⊠ Leila Cottage started brewing in 2007 using a 0.5-barrel plant, which was upgraded in 2009 to a 2.5-barrel one. The brewery is situated at the Countryman pub – Leila Cottage was the original name of the building before it became a licensed club and more recently a pub. There are plans to start bottling using its own bottling plant. Only the Countryman is supplied at present.

Leila's Lazy Days (OG 1038, ABV 3.6%)

Ace Ale (OG 1040, ABV 3.8%)

Lincolnshire Life (OG 1042, ABV 4.2%)

Leith Hill

▤ Leith Hill Brewery, c/o Plough Inn, Coldharbour Lane, Coldharbour, Surrey, RH5 6HD
☎ (01306) 711793 ✉ theploughinn@btinternet.com
⊕ ploughinn.com
Tours by arrangement

⊠ Leith Hill was established in 1996 using home-made equipment to produce nine-gallon brews in a room at the front of the pub. The brewery moved to converted storerooms at the rear of the Plough Inn in 2001 and increased capacity to 2.5-barrels in 2005. All beers brewed are sold only on the premises.

Crooked Furrow (OG 1040, ABV 4%) ◆
A malty beer, with some balancing hop bitterness. Pale brown in colour with an earthy malty aroma and a long, dry and bittersweet aftertaste. Some fruit is also present throughout.

Tallywhacker (OG 1048, ABV 4.8%) ◆
Dark, sweet and fruity old ale with good roast malt character.

Leyden SIBA

▤ Leyden Brewing Ltd, Lord Raglan, Nangreaves, Bury, Greater Manchester, BL9 6SP
☎ (0161) 764 6680
Tours by arrangement

⊛ The brewery was built by Brian Farnworth and started production in 1999. Additional fermenting vessels have been installed, allowing a maximum production of 12 barrels a week. One pub is owned and 30 outlets are supplied. In addition to the permanent beers, a number of seasonal and occasional beers are brewed.

Balaclava (ABV 3.8%)

Black Pudding (ABV 3.8%)
A dark brown, creamy mild with a malty flavour, followed by a balanced finish.

Nanny Flyer (OG 1040, ABV 3.8%)
A drinkable session bitter with an initial dryness, and a hint of citrus, followed by a strong, malty finish.

Light Brigade (OG 1043, ABV 4.2%) ◆
Copper in colour with a citrus aroma. The flavour is a balance of malt, hops and fruit, with a bitter finish.

Rammy Rocket (ABV 4.2%)

Forever Bury (ABV 4.5%)

Raglan Sleeve (OG 1047, ABV 4.6%) ◆
Dark red/brown beer with a hoppy aroma and a dry, roasty, hoppy taste and finish.

Crowning Glory (OG 1069, ABV 6.8%)

Lichfield

Lichfield Brewery Co Ltd, Lichfield, Staffordshire
✉ robsondavidb@hotmail.com

Does not brew; beers mainly contracted by Tower Brewery (qv).

Linfit

▤ Linfit Brewery, Sair Inn, 139 Lane Top, Linthwaite, Huddersfield, West Yorkshire, HD7 5SG
☎ (01484) 842370

⊛ A 19th-century brew-pub that started brewing again in 1982. The beer is only available at the Sair Inn. Occasional beers: English Guineas Stout (ABV 5.3%), Leadboiler (ABV 6.6%).

Dark Mild (ABV 3.2%)

Bitter (OG 1035, ABV 3.7%) ◆
A refreshing session beer. A dry-hopped aroma leads to a clean-tasting, hoppy bitterness, then a long, bitter finish with a hint of malt.

Gold Medal (OG 1040, ABV 4.2%)
Very pale and hoppy. Use of the new dwarf variety of English hops, First Gold, gives an aromatic and fruity character.

Special (OG 1041, ABV 4.3%) ◆
Dry-hopping provides the aroma for this rich and mellow bitter, which has a very soft profile and character: it fills the mouth with texture rather than taste. Clean, rounded finish.

Swift (ABV 4.3%)

Autumn Gold (OG 1045, ABV 4.7%) ◆
Straw-coloured best bitter with hop and fruit aromas, then the bittersweetness of autumn fruit in the taste and the finish.

Old Eli (OG 1050, ABV 5.3%)
A well-balanced premium bitter with a dry-hop aroma and a fruity, bitter finish.

Lion's Tale SIBA

Lion's Tale Brewery, Red Lion, High Street, Cheswardine, Shropshire, TF9 2RS
☎ (01630) 661234 ✉ cheslion96@yahoo.co.uk

The building that houses the brewery was purpose-built in 2005 and houses a 2.5-barrel plant. Jon Morris and his wife have owned the Red Lion pub since 1996. Expansion is planned in the near future. Seasonal beer: Chesmas Bells (ABV 5.2%, Xmas).

Blooming Blonde (ABV 4.1%)

Lionbru (ABV 4.1%)

Chesbrewnette (ABV 4.5%)

Little Ale Cart

Little Ale Cart Brewing Co, c/o The Wellington, 1 Henry Street, Sheffield, South Yorkshire, S3 7EQ
☎ (0114) 249 2295

Brewing started in 2001, as Port Mahon, in a purpose-built brewery behind the Cask & Cutler. In 2007 the brewery and pub were taken over and the names of both changed to Little Ale Cart Brewing and the Wellington. Beer is only brewed for the Wellington and the Dragon pub in Worcester. The beer range varies as the brewer trials new recipes, but tends to include a 4%, 4.3% and a 5% ABV beer.

Little Valley SIBA

Little Valley Brewery Ltd, Unit 3, Turkey Lodge Farm, New Road, Cragg Vale, Hebden Bridge, West Yorkshire, HX7 5TT
☎ (01422) 883888
✉ info@littlevalleybrewery.co.uk
littlevalleybrewery.co.uk
Shop Mon-Fri 9am-5pm
Tours by arrangement

Little Valley Brewery opened in 2005 and is situated in the Upper Calder Valley, high above Cragg Vale in Hebden Bridge, West Yorkshire. The 10-barrel plant is in a converted turkey shed. It is a wholly organic brewery and is approved by the Soil Association. It does not use isinglass in the beers and is approved by the Vegan Society. The brewery is also a licensee of the Fairtrade Foundation for one of its beers, Ginger Pale Ale. All cask beers are also available in bottle-conditioned form. Around 100 outlets are supplied. Several beers are also contract brewed for Suma Wholefoods. A range of monthly specials was introduced in 2007.

Withens IPA (OG 1037, ABV 3.9%)
Creamy, gold-coloured, refreshingly light ale. Floral, spicy hop aroma, lightly-flavoured with hints of lemon and grapefruit. Clean, bitter aftertaste.

Fairtrade Ginger Pale Ale (OG 1037, ABV 4%)
Full-bodied speciality ale. Ginger predominates in the aroma and taste. It has a pleasantly powerful, fiery and spicy finish.

Cragg Vale Bitter (OG 1039, ABV 4.2%)
Grainy, pale brown session bitter, light on the palate with a delicate flavour of malt and fruit and a bitter finish.

Hebden's Wheat (OG 1043, ABV 4.5%)
A pale yellow, creamy wheat beer with a good balance of bitterness and fruit, a hint of sweetness but with a lasting, dry finish.

Stoodley Stout (OG 1044, ABV 4.8%)
Dark brown creamy stout with a rich roast aroma and luscious fruity, chocolate, roast flavours. Well-balanced with a clean bitter finish.

Tod's Blonde (OG 1045, ABV 5%)
Bright yellow, grainy, speciality beer with a citrus hop start and a dry finish. Fruity, with a hint of spice. Similar in style to a Belgian blonde beer.

Moor Ale (OG 1051, ABV 5.5%)
Tawny in colour with a full-bodied taste. It has a strong malty nose and palate with hints of heather and peat-smoked malt. Well-balanced with a bitter finish.

Python IPA (OG 1055, ABV 6%)
A straw-coloured beer with a powerful floral, minty and grassy aroma.

Litton

Litton Ale Brewery, Queens Arms, Litton, North Yorkshire, BD23 5QJ
☎ (01756) 770208 ✉ info@queensarmslitton.co.uk
queensarmslitton.co.uk

Brewing started in 2003 in a purpose-built stone extension at the rear of the pub. Brewing liquor is sourced from a spring that provides the pub with its own water supply. Around 20 outlets are supplied. All recipes were modified in 2009. Bespoke brewing is planned, allowing customers to have their own beer brewed for special occasions, either in bottles or casks.

Ale (OG 1038, ABV 3.8%)
An easy-drinking, traditional bitter with a good malt/hop balance and a bitter finish.

Leading Light (OG 1038, ABV 3.8%)
A long, bitter aftertaste follows a malty flavour with tart fruit and a rising hop bitterness in this light-coloured beer. Low aroma.

Gold Crest (OG 1039, ABV 3.9%)
A very pale beer with a smooth, creamy head. Heavy, fruity hoppiness with no lingering bitterness.

Dark Star (OG 1040, ABV 4%)
A smooth, creamy dark mild, full-bodied for its strength. The taste is quite bitter with roast coffee and tart dark fruit flavours, complemented by a bitter, roast finish.

Potts Beck (OG 1043, ABV 4.2%)
Malt and hops fight for control in this copper-coloured best bitter with a fruity aroma.

Liverpool One (NEW)

Liverpool One Brewery Ltd, 82-84 Vauxhall Road, Liverpool, Merseyside, L3 6DL
☎ 07948 918740
✉ info@liverpoolonebrewery.co.uk
liverpoolonebrewery.co.uk

Liverpool One started brewing in 2010 using a five-barrel plant. Seasonal beers are planned.

Session (ABV 3.4%)

Mersey Mist (ABV 4.1%)

Liverpool Light (ABV 4.2%)

Three Graces (ABV 4.2%)

Liverpool Dark (ABV 5%)

Liverpool Organic (NEW)

Liverpool Organic Brewery Ltd, 39 Brasenose Road, Liverpool, Merseyside, L20 8HL
☎ (0151) 933 9660
✉ info@liverpoolorganicbrewery.com
🌐 liverpoolorganicbrewery.com

Liverpool Organic started brewing in 2009. There are plans to start large-scale bottling. Around 40 outlets are supplied direct. Bottle-conditioned beers are available.

Founders Ale (OG 1040, ABV 3.7%)

King John Ale (OG 1037, ABV 3.9%)

Liverpool Pale Ale (OG 1042, ABV 4%)

Bier Head (OG 1042, ABV 4.1%)

24 Carat (OG 1041, ABV 4.2%)

Best Bitter (OG 1042, ABV 4.2%)

Port'er Liverpool (OG 1049, ABV 4.9%)

Shipwreck IPA (OG 1063, ABV 6.5%)

Lizard

Lizard Ales Ltd, The Old Nuclear Bunker, Pednavounder, nr Coverack, Cornwall, TR12 6SE
☎ (01326) 281135 ✉ lizardales@msn.com
🌐 lizardales.co.uk

Launched in 2004 Lizard Ales supplies mainly in west Cornwall. Bottle-conditioned beers are a speciality (suitable for vegetarians and vegans). The brewery moved in 2008 into a part of the former RAF Treleaver – a massive disused nuclear bunker in the depths of the Cornish countryside.

Kernow Gold (OG 1035, ABV 3.7%)

Bitter (OG 1041, ABV 4.2%)

Frenchman's Creek (OG 1042, ABV 4.8%)

An Gof (OG 1049, ABV 5.2%)

Llangollen

See Abbey Grange

Loch Leven

Loch Leven Brewery, Criochan House, Maryburgh, Blairadam, KY4 0JE
☎ (01383) 831751 ✉ neilwilkie64@yahoo.co.uk

Loch Leven was established in 2009 on a four-barrel brewery. More beers are planned.

Golden Goose (ABV 4.1%)

Loddon SIBA

Loddon Brewery Ltd, Dunsden Green Farm, Church Lane, Dunsden, Oxfordshire, RG4 9QD
☎ (0118) 948 1111 ✉ sales@loddonbrewery.com
🌐 loddonbrewery.com

⊗ Loddon was established in 2002 in a brick and flint barn that houses a 17-barrel brewery able to produce 85 barrels a week. 450 outlets are supplied. 2009 saw major building work to renovate extra barns for new offices, a malt store and bottled beer store. There are plans to increase capacity. Seasonal beers and monthly specials: see website. Bottle-conditioned beers are also available.

Hoppit (OG 1035.5, ABV 3.5%) ◆
Hops dominate the aroma of this drinkable, light-coloured session beer. Malt and hops create a balanced taste and a pleasant bitterness carries through to the aftertaste.

Hullabaloo (OG 1044, ABV 4.2%) ◆
A hint of fruit in the initial taste develops into a balance of hops and malt in this well-rounded, medium-bodied bitter with a bitter aftertaste.

Ferryman's Gold (OG 1045.5, ABV 4.4%) ◆
Golden coloured with a strong hoppy character throughout, accompanied by fruit in the taste and aftertaste.

Bamboozle (OG 1049.5, ABV 4.8%) ◆
Full-bodied and well balanced. Distinctive bittersweet flavour with hop and caramel to accompany.

For AVS Wholesale:

Gravesend Shrimpers (OG 1042.8, ABV 4.1%)

Loose Cannon (NEW)

Loose Cannon Brewery, Unit 6, Suffolk Way, Abingdon, Oxfordshire, OX14 5JX
☎ (01235) 531141 ✉ will@lcbeers.co.uk
🌐 lcbeers.co.uk

Loose Cannon began production in 2010 using a 15-barrel brew plant. Owner and Head Brewer Will Laithwaite previously worked at Rebellion Brewery.

Abingdon Bridge (ABV 4.1%)

Lord Conrad's (NEW)

Lord Conrad's Brewery, 23 Pheasant Rise, Bar Hill, Cambridge, CB23 8SA
☎ 07736 739700 🌐 lordconradsbrewery.co.uk

Lord Conrad's is a small 60-hectolitre brewery that began commercial brewing in 2010. Beer festivals and local outlets are supplied. Seasonal beers: see website.

Three Villages (ABV 3.8%)

Conkerwood (ABV 4.5%)

Pheasant Rise (ABV 5%)

Lovibonds

Lovibonds Brewery Ltd, Rear of 19-21 Market Place, Henley-on-Thames, Oxfordshire, RG9 2AA
☎ (01491) 576596 ✉ info@lovibonds.com
🌐 lovibonds.com
Shop Sat 11am-5pm; Sun 11am-4pm
Tours by arrangement

⊗ Lovibonds Brewery was founded by Jeff Rosenmeier in 2005 and is named after Joseph William Lovibond, who invented the Tintometer to measure beer colour. In addition to cask-conditioned ales, Lovibonds brews beers inspired by the traditions of other brewing nations. Around 50 outlets are supplied. Brewing also takes place on the Old Luxters Brewery plant (qv), 5 miles from Henley-on-Thames.

Henley Amber (OG 1035, ABV 3.4%)
An amber session bitter with a blend of roasted malts that gives a complex profile with a classic hop flavour and bitterness.

Henley Gold (OG 1045, ABV 4.6%)

Henley Dark (OG 1048, ABV 4.8%)

Loweswater

See Cumbrian Legendary Ales

Luckie

Luckie Ales, c/o 14 Kingsmill Drive, Kennoway, Fife, KY8 5LX
☎ (01333) 352801 ✉ info@luckie-ales.com
luckie-ales.com

Luckie Ales was established in 2009. Beer is brewed at an unnamed Scottish brewery.

Midnycht Myld (OG 1037, ABV 3.4%)

Amber Ale (OG 1040, ABV 3.7%)

80/- (OG 1056, ABV 5%)

19th Century IPA (ABV 6.5%)

Edinburgh Export Stout (ABV 7.5%)

Edinburgh 68/- (ABV 8.5%)

Ludlow SIBA

Ludlow Brewing Co Ltd, Kingsley Garage, 105 Corve Street, Ludlow, Shropshire, SY8 1DJ
☎ (01584) 873291
✉ gary@theludlowbrewingcompany.co.uk
theludlowbrewingcompany.co.uk
Shop Mon-Fri 10am-5pm; Sat 10am-1pm
Tours by arrangement

The brewery opened in 2006 in a renovated malthouse and operates locally-supplying pubs within a 40-mile radius. A move to larger premises, a former railway sidings shed on the same site, is underway. Bottle-conditioned beers are available.

Best (ABV 3.7%)

Gold (ABV 4.2%)

Black Knight (ABV 4.5%)

Boiling Well (ABV 4.7%)

Lymestone SIBA

Lymestone Brewery Ltd, The Old Brewery, Mount Road, Stone, Staffordshire, ST15 8LL
☎ (01785) 817796
✉ brad@lymestonebrewery.co.uk
lymestonebrewery.co.uk
Shop Mon-Fri 8am-5pm, Sat & Sun by arrangement
Tours by arrangement

Lymestone commenced brewing in 2008 on a 10-barrel brew plant. 200 outlets are supplied direct, with beer also being available via wholesalers.

Stone Cutter (ABV 3.7%)
Sulphurous aroma gives way to a caramel sweet start and pleasing hop and fruit balance. The mouth-watering hoppy promise is fulfilled in to the finish.

Stone Faced (ABV 4%)
Subtle citrus and toffee flavours balanced by a hoppy aroma and bitter finish.

Foundation Stone (OG 1047, ABV 4.5%)
An IPA-style beer with pale and crystal malts. Faint biscuit and chewy, juicy fruits burst on to the palate then the spicy Boadicea and Pilot hops pepper the taste buds to leave a dry bitter finish.

Ein Stein (OG 1052, ABV 5%)
A very pale, citrus, hoppy ale.

Stone The Crows (OG 1056, ABV 5.4%)
A rich dark beer from chocolate malts. Fruit, roasts and hops abound to leave a deep lingering bitterness from the Styrian Goldings and Millennium hop mix.

Lytham

Lytham Brewery Ltd, Unit 11, Lidun Park Industrial Estate, Boundary Road, Lytham, Lancashire, FY8 5HU
☎ (01253) 737707 ✉ info@LythamBrewery.co.uk
LythamBrewery.co.uk
Tours by arrangement

Lytham started brewing in 2008 at the Hastings Club in Lytham but moved to larger premises soon after due to demand.

Amber (OG 1037, ABV 3.6%)
A traditional malty beer using English hops.

Blonde (OG 1038, ABV 3.8%)
A pale golden beer with a subtle hop aroma and a smooth, dry finish.

Gold (OG 1042, ABV 4.2%)
A golden beer with a fruity aroma and lasting bitter finish.

Royal (OG 1044, ABV 4.4%)
A full-bodied English ale with a crisp fruity aroma and a smooth, dry finish.

Dark (OG 1047, ABV 5%)
Dark chocolate malt with a hint of vanilla and a smooth, dry finish.

IPA (OG 1054, ABV 5.6%)
A pale bitter with a fresh, sweet, hoppy flavour leading to a long, dry finish.

McGivern

McGivern Ales, c/o The Bridge End Inn, 5 Bridge Street, Ruabon, LL14 6DA
☎ (01978) 810881 ☎ 07891 676614
✉ mcgivernmatt@hotmail.com
mcgivernales.co.uk

The brewery was established in early 2008 and is based at the brewer's home in Wrexham but will move in 2011 to the Bridge End Inn in Ruabon. Bottle-conditioned beers are available occasionally.

Amber Ale (OG 1040, ABV 4%)

Cascade Pale Ale (ABV 4%)

Crest Pale (OG 1041, ABV 4%)

Stout (OG 1042, ABV 4.2%)

Porter (ABV 4.5%)

McGuinness

See Offa's Dyke

McLaughlin

See Camden

THE BREWERIES

McMullen IFBB

McMullen & Sons Ltd, 26 Old Cross, Hertford, Hertfordshire, SG14 1RD
☎ (01992) 584911 ✉ reception@mcmullens.co.uk
⊕ mcmullens.co.uk

⊗ McMullen is Hertfordshire's oldest independent brewery, celebrating 180 years of brewing in 2007. A new brewhouse opened in 2006, giving the company greater flexibility to produce its regular cask beers and up to eight seasonal beers a year. Cask beer is served in all 140 pubs.

AK (OG 1035, ABV 3.7%) ◆
A pleasant mix of malt and hops leads to a distinctive, dry aftertaste that isn't always as pronounced as it used to be.

Cask Ale (OG 1039, ABV 3.8%)
A light and refreshing beer marked by the use of Styrian Goldings and English Fuggle hops.

Country Bitter (OG 1042, ABV 4.3%) 🍺 ◆
A full-bodied beer with a well-balanced mix of malt, hops and fruit throughout.

Maclay

See Greene King in New Nationals section

Madcap (NEW)

John & Jason Maddison t/a Madcap Brewery, Greenknowe Avenue, Annan, Dumfriesshire, DG12 6ER
☎ (01461) 203495 ✉ john@madcapbrewery.com
⊕ madcapbrewery.com
Tours by arrangement

☺Madcap Brewery started production in 2009 and operates on a one-barrel plant in a small outbuilding at the rear of the family home. The brewery is mainly interested in producing a unique range of bottle-conditioned ales as well as Belgian and New World styles. There are plans to move and upgrade to a five-barrel plant. Seasonal beer: Annandale Black (ABV 4%, Oct-Mar).

Annandale Gold (ABV 4%)

Magpie

Magpie Brewery, Unit 4, Ashling Court, Ashling Street, Nottingham, Nottinghamshire, NG2 3JA
☎ 07738 762897 ✉ info@magpiebrewery.com
⊕ magpiebrewery.com

☺ Magpie is a six-barrel brewery launched in 2006 by three friends. It is located a few feet from the perimeter of the Meadow Lane Stadium, home of Notts County FC (the Magpies) from which the brewery name naturally derived. Seasonal and occasional beers: see website.

Fledgling (ABV 3.8%) ◆
A hoppy and bitter golden ale.

Best (ABV 4.2%) ◆
A malty traditional pale brown best bitter, with balancing hops giving a bitter finish.

Thieving Rogue (ABV 4.5%) ◆
A hoppy golden ale with a long-lasting, bitter finish.

Monty's Firkin (ABV 4.6%) ◆

A well-balanced premium amber best bitter. Originally brewed for the Queen Adelaide in Nottingham, and named after the pub dog.

Full Flight (ABV 4.8%)
A strong, dark winter beer.

Midnight Porter (ABV 5%)
A traditional porter.

Maldon

See Farmer's Ales

Mallard SIBA

Mallard Brewery, 15 Hartington Avenue, Carlton, Nottingham, NG4 3NR
☎ (0115) 952 1289
Tours by arrangement

⊗ Phil Mallard built and installed a two-barrel plant in a shed at his home and started brewing in 1995. The brewery is only nine square metres and contains a hot liquor tank, mash tun, copper, and three fermenters. Since 1995 production has risen from one barrel a week to between six or eight barrels, which is the plant's maximum. Around 12 outlets are supplied. Seasonal beers: Waddlers Mild (ABV 3.7%, spring), DA (ABV 5.8%, Jan-Mar), Quismas Quacker (ABV 6%, Dec), Owd Duck (ABV 4.8%, winter).

Duck 'n' Dive (OG 1039, ABV 3.7%) ◆
A bitter, pale golden beer, with a dry finish. Brewed with First Gold hops.

Quacker Jack (OG 1040, ABV 4%)

Feather Light (OG 1040, ABV 4.1%) ◆
A straw-coloured lager style beer with a hoppy taste and aroma.

Duckling (OG 1041, ABV 4.2%) ◆
A dry-hopped, golden ale. Very bitter; hops dominate in the aroma and aftertaste.

Webbed Wheat (OG 1043, ABV 4.3%)
A wheat beer with a fruity, hoppy nose and taste.

Spittin' Feathers (OG 1044, ABV 4.4%) ◆
A mellow, malty, reddish-brown bitter with a slightly sweet and fruity taste.

Drake (OG 1045, ABV 4.5%)
A full-bodied premium bitter, with malt and hops on the palate, and a fruity finish.

Duck 'n' Disorderly (OG 1050, ABV 5%)

Friar Duck (OG 1050, ABV 5%)
A pale, full malt beer, hoppy with a hint of blackcurrant flavour.

Mallinsons

Mallinsons Brewing Co, Plover Road Garage, Plover Road, Huddersfield, West Yorkshire, HD3 3HS
☎ (01484) 654301 ✉ info@drinkmallinsons.co.uk
⊕ drinkmallinsons.co.uk
Tours by arrangement

☺The brewery was set up in early 2008 on a six-barrel plant in a former garage by CAMRA member Tara Mallinson. Tara is Huddersfield's only brewster. A range of seasonal and one-off specials is planned as well as bottle-conditioned beers.

Emley Moor Mild (ABV 3.4%)

Black with a ruby hint. A full-bodied mild with a nutty taste and slightly bitter finish.

Stadium Bitter (ABV 3.8%)
Straw-coloured with a clean, bitter taste and dry, fruity finish.

Station Best Bitter (ABV 4.2%)
An amber-coloured best bitter with a balance of malt and fruity hops.

Castle Hill Premium (ABV 4.6%)
A golden-coloured premium bitter, hoppy with citrus tones.

Malt B

Malt B Brewing Co, Crown Inn, Beesby Road, Maltby le Marsh, Lincolnshire, LN13 0JJ
(01507) 450100 ✉ nigelwalpole007@o2.co.uk
thecrowninnmaltby.co.uk
Tours by arrangement

Malt B started brewing in early 2008. Until the 1970s the building that houses the brewery was an outside toilet, hence some beer names incorporate toilet humour. Seasonal beer: Tinkle Bells Christmas Beer (ABV 4.4%).

P.E.A. (Proper English Ale) (OG 1037, ABV 3.6%)

Old Reliable (OG 1042, ABV 4.2%)

Regal Flush (OG 1042, ABV 4.3%)

Smarty's Night Porter (OG 1045, ABV 4.5%)

Malvern Hills SIBA

Malvern Hills Brewery Ltd, 15 West Malvern Road, Malvern, Worcestershire, WR14 4ND
(01684) 560165 ✉ beer@tiscali.co.uk
malvernhillsbrewery.co.uk
Tours by arrangement

Founded in 1998 in an old quarrying dynamite store. Now an established presence in the Three Counties and Black Country, the brewery has around 80 regular outlets. Rationalisation of the product range in 2009 created a rolling programme of monthly specials to supplement the core permanent brews.

Santler (ABV 3.6%)

Feelgood (OG 1038, ABV 3.8%)

Swedish Nightingale (OG 1040, ABV 4%)

Priessnitz Plzen (OG 1043, ABV 4.3%)
A mix of soft fruit and citrus give this straw-coloured brew its quaffability, making it ideal for quenching summer thirsts.

Black Pear (OG 1044, ABV 4.4%)
A sharp citrus hoppiness is the main constituent of this golden brew that has a long, dry aftertaste.

Mansfield

See Marston's in New Nationals section

Marble SIBA

Marble Beers Ltd, 73 Rochdale Road, Manchester, M4 4HY
(0161) 819 2694
✉ thebrewers_marblebeers@msn.com
Tours by arrangement

Marble opened at the Marble Arch Inn in 1997 and produces organic and vegan beers as well as some non-organic ales. It is registered with the Soil Association and the Vegetarian Society. Marble currently owns two pubs and supplies around 10 outlets. In 2009 a second, 12-barrel plant was installed at Unit 41, Williamson Street, Manchester. A number of bottle-conditioned beers are available as well as regular seasonals such as Port Stout (ABV 4.7%, Xmas) and Festival (ABV 4.4%, Oct).

Pint (OG 1038.5, ABV 3.9%)
A pale, dry and extremely hoppy beer.

Manchester (OG 1042, ABV 4.2%)
Yellow beer with a fruity and hoppy aroma. Hops, fruit and bitterness on the palate and in the finish.

JP Best (OG 1043, ABV 4.3%)
Pale tawny in colour. Hoppy with a good malt balance, assertively bitter.

Ginger (OG 1046, ABV 4.5%)
Intense and complex. Full-bodied and fiery with a sharp, snappy bite.

Stouter Stout (OG 1048, ABV 4.7%)
Black in colour, with roast malt dominating the aroma. Roast malt and hops in the mouth, with a little fruit. Pleasant, dry, bitter aftertaste.

Lagonda IPA (OG 1047.5, ABV 5%)
Golden yellow beer with a spicy, fruity nose. Fruit, hops and malt in the mouth, with a dry fruitiness continuing into the bitter aftertaste.

Chocolate (OG 1054.5, ABV 5.5%)
A strong, stout-like ale.

Marlpool (NEW)

Marlpool Brewery, 5 Breach Road, Marlpool, Heanor, Derbyshire, DE75 7NJ
07963 511855
✉ enquiries@marlpoolbrewing.co.uk
marlpoolbrewing.co.uk

The brewery was set up in 2010 using a 2.5-barrel brewery and although situated in an old slaughterhouse next to the Queens Head pub, it is completely independent. The brewery operates on a part-time basis.

Stratty Ratty (ABV 4.4%)

Marston Moor

Marston Moor Brewery Ltd, PO Box 9, York, North Yorkshire, YO26 7XW
(01423) 359641
✉ info@marstonmoorbrewery.co.uk
rudgate-beers.co.uk

Established in 1983 in Kirk Hammerton, the brewery had a re-investment programme in 2005, moving brewing operations to nearby Tockwith, where it shares the site with Rudgate Brewery (qv). Two special beers are available each month. Around 250 outlets are supplied.

Cromwell's Pale (OG 1036, ABV 3.8%)
A golden beer with hops and fruit in strong evidence on the nose. Bitterness as well as fruit and hops dominate the taste and long aftertaste.

Matchlock Mild (OG 1038, ABV 4%)
Traditional, full-flavoured dark mild.

Mongrel (OG 1038, ABV 4%)
A balanced bitter with plenty of fruit character.

THE BREWERIES

Fairfax Special (OG 1039, ABV 4.2%)
A full-bodied premium bitter, pale in colour with a well-balanced slightly citrus aroma.

Merriemaker (OG 1042, ABV 4.5%)
A premium straw-coloured ale with a typical Yorkshire taste.

Brewers Droop (OG 1045.5, ABV 5%)
A powerful golden ale with a sweet taste.

Marston's

See Marston's in New Nationals section

Matthews

See Dawkins

Mauldons SIBA EAB

Mauldons Ltd, Black Adder Brewery, 13 Church Field Road, Sudbury, Suffolk, CO10 2YA
☎ (01787) 311055 ✉ sims@mauldons.co.uk
🌐 mauldons.co.uk
Shop Mon-Fri 9.30am-4pm
Tours by arrangement

⊗ The Mauldon family started brewing in Sudbury in 1795. The brewery with 26 pubs was bought by Greene King in the 1960s. The current business, established in 1982, was bought by Steve and Alison Sims – both former employees of Adnams – in 2000. They relocated to a new brewery in 2005, with a 30-barrel plant that has doubled production. The brewery tap was bought in 2008 and a second pub in 2010. Around 150 outlets are supplied. There is a rolling programme of seasonal beers: see website.

Micawber's Mild (OG 1035, ABV 3.5%) ◆
Fruit and roast flavours dominate the nose, with vine fruit and caramel on the tongue and a short, dry, coffeeish aftertaste. Full-bodied and satisfying.

Moletrap Bitter (OG 1038, ABV 3.8%) ◆
Easy-drinking session bitter. Crisp and refreshing, hoppy and fruity throughout.

Silver Adder (OG 1042, ABV 4.2%)
A light-coloured bitter with five hop and malt combinations giving a refreshing, crisp finish.

Suffolk Pride (OG 1048, ABV 4.8%) ◆
A full-bodied, copper-coloured beer with a good balance of malt, hops and fruit in the taste.

Black Adder (OG 1053, ABV 5.3%) ◆
Superbly balanced dark, sweet ale, but with rich vine fruit throughout. The brewery's flagship beer.

Mayfields

Mayfields Brewery, No. 8 Croft Business Park, Leominster, Herefordshire, HR6 0QF
☎ (01568) 611197 ✉ info@mayfieldsbrewery.co.uk
🌐 mayfieldsbrewery.co.uk

Established in 2005 Mayfields is a small family brewery located in the heart of one of England's major hop growing regions. 2008 saw a change of location and ownership. Since then the range of core beers have been changed and updated. Around 35 outlets are supplied. Seasonal beers are brewed on a monthly basis: see website. The brewery also distributes draught and bottled traditional local cider.

Copper Fox (ABV 3.8%)
A copper-coloured ale with a fresh malt body and lots of hop character.

Ducking Stool (ABV 4.2%)
A refreshing golden amber-coloured ale with plenty of hop character throughout.

Aunty Myrtle's (ABV 4.5%)
A dark copper-coloured ale with gentle malt flavours and strong hop finish.

Mayflower

Mayflower Brewery, Tower Hill Brewery, Wellcross Farm, Tower Hill Road, Up Holland, Lancashire, WN8 0DS
☎ 07984 404567 ✉ info@mayflowerbeer.co.uk
🌐 mayflowerbeer.co.uk

Mayflower was established in 2001 in Standish and relocated to the Royal Oak Hotel in Wigan in 2004 before moving to the current site in 2010. The original vessels and casks are still used. The Royal Oak is supplied as well as a number of other outlets in and around Lancashire including the Turks Head in St Helens. Seasonal beers: Autumn Gold (ABV 4.5%, autumn), Hic Bibi (ABV 5%, winter), Red Eye (ABV 5.2%, summer).

Black Diamond (OG 1033.5, ABV 3.4%)

Tower Hill (ABV 3.8%)

Douglas Valley Ale (OG 1044, ABV 4%)

Wigan Bier (OG 1039.5, ABV 4.2%)

Maypole

Maypole Brewery Ltd, North Laithes Farm, Wellow Road, Eakring, Newark, Nottinghamshire, NG22 0AN
☎ 07971 277598 ✉ maypolebrewery@aol.com
🌐 maypolebrewery.co.uk

◎ The brewery opened in 1995 in a converted 18th-century farm building. After changing hands in 2001 it was bought by the former head brewer, Rob Neil, in 2005. Seasonal beers can be ordered at any time for beer festivals: see website for details and list.

Little Weed (OG 1038, ABV 3.8%)

Mayfly Bitter (OG 1038, ABV 3.8%)

Gate Hopper (OG 1040, ABV 4%)

Mayfair (OG 1040, ABV 4.1%)

Maybee (OG 1041, ABV 4.3%)

Mae West/Wellow Gold (OG 1044, ABV 4.6%)

Kiwi IPA (OG 1046, ABV 4.8%)

Mayhem (OG 1048, ABV 5%)

Platinum Blonde (OG 1048, ABV 5%)

For Olde Red Lion, Wellow:

Olde Lions Ale (ABV 3.9%)

Meantime SIBA

Meantime Brewing Co Ltd, Blackwall Lane, London, SE10 0AR
☎ (020) 8853 3457 ✉ info@meantimebrewing.com
🌐 meantimebrewing.com
Tours by arrangement

Founded in 2000, Meantime brews a wide range of continental style beer and traditional English bottle-conditioned ales. Two pubs are owned. Bottle-conditioned beers: London Pale Ale (ABV 4.3%), London Stout (ABV 4.5%), Wheat (ABV 5%), Winter Time (ABV 5.4%), Coffee Porter (ABV 6%), Chocolate (ABV 6.5%), London Porter (ABV 6.5%), Raspberry Grand Cru (ABV 6.5%), IPA (ABV 7.5%). All beers are suitable for vegetarians and vegans. A six-barrel brewery is also owned at the Old Brewery, the Old Royal Naval College in Greenwich and is used to brew limited edition beers.

London Pale (ABV 4.3%) ◆
Citrus hops dominate this dry amber bitter, which is balanced by sweet malt that lingers in the aftertaste with a final hit of bitterness.

Meesons

See Old Bog

Melbourn

Melbourn Bros Brewery, All Saints Brewery, All Saints Street, Stamford, Lincolnshire, PE9 2PA
☎ **(01780) 752186**

A famous Stamford brewery that opened in 1825 and closed in 1974. It re-opened in 1994 and is owned by Samuel Smith of Tadcaster (qv). Melbourn brews three handcrafted, organic fruit beers (Cherry, Strawberry and Raspberry) using the antique steam-driven brewing equipment. The beers are all suitable for vegans and are organic.

Mersea Island

Mersea Island Brewery, Rewsalls Lane, East Mersea, Colchester, Essex, CO5 8SX
☎ **(01206) 385900** ✉ **beers@merseawine.com**
🌐 **merseawine.com**
Shop Wed-Sun 10.30am-4pm, closed Mon & Tue

The brewery was established at Mersea Island Vineyard in 2005, producing cask and bottle-conditioned beers. The brewery supplies several local pubs on a guest beer basis as well as most local beer festivals. The brewery holds its own festival of Essex-produced ales over the four-day Easter weekend.

Yo Boy Bitter (OG 1038, ABV 3.8%) ◆
Pale session beer. Peach and orange on the aroma and taste, leading to a pleasantly bitter finish.

Gold (OG 1043, ABV 4.5%)
A lager/Pilsner style.

Skippers Bitter (OG 1047, ABV 4.8%) ◆
Strong bitter, whose full character is dominated by pear drops and juicy malt. A raspberry tartness follows.

Oyster (OG 1048, ABV 5%)

Monkeys (OG 1049, ABV 5.1%)
A porter with deep and lasting malt and hop flavours.

Mighty Oak SIBA

Mighty Oak Brewing Co Ltd, 14b West Station Yard, Spital Road, Maldon, Essex, CM9 6TW
☎ **(01621) 843713**
✉ **sales@mightyoakbrewing.co.uk**
Tours by arrangement

⊗ Mighty Oak was formed in 1996 and moved in 2001 to Maldon, where capacity was increased. Around 200 outlets are supplied and a small number of wholesalers are used. Twelve monthly ales are brewed based on a theme; for 2010 the theme was 'Bars' including 'Barack Obama', 'Barking Mad' and 'Ilkley Moor Bar T'at'. 2011 is 'Cars' including 'Alfa Romeo' and 'Model T'.

IPA (OG 1031.5, ABV 3.5%) ◆
Light-bodied, pale session bitter, Hop notes are initially suppressed by a delicate sweetness but the aftertaste is more assertive.

Oscar Wilde (OG 1039.5, ABV 3.7%) ◆
Roasty dark mild with suggestions of forest fruits and dark chocolate. A sweet taste yields to a more bitter finish.

Maldon Gold (OG 1039.5, ABV 3.8%) ◆
Pale golden ale with a sharp citrus note moderated by honey and biscuity malt.

Burntwood Bitter (OG 1041, ABV 4%) ◆
Full-bodied bitter with an unusual blend of caramel, roast grain and grapefruit.

Simply The Best (OG 1044.1, ABV 4.4%) ◆
Well-balanced, mid-strength bitter with a sweet start and a dry, bitter finish.

English Oak (OG 1047.9, ABV 4.8%) ◆
Strong tawny, fruity bitter with caramel, butterscotch and vanilla. A gentle hop character is present throughout.

Milestone

Milestone Brewing Co Ltd, Great North Road, Cromwell, Newark, Nottinghamshire, NG23 6JE
☎ **(01636) 822255** ✉ **info@milestonebrewery.co.uk**
🌐 **milestonebrewery.co.uk**
Shop Mon-Fri 8am-5pm; Sat 9am-3pm
Tours by arrangement

◎ The brewery has been in production since 2005 on a 12-barrel plant. It was founded by Kenneth and Frances Munro with head brewer Dean Penney. Around 150 outlets are supplied. Seasonal beers: Cool Amber (ABV 6%, May-Aug), Donner & Blitzed/Xmas Cracker (ABV 5.4%, Nov-Dec). Bottle-conditioned beers are also available.

Lions Pride (ABV 3.8%)

Cromwell Gold (ABV 4%)

Old Oak (ABV 4%)

Shine On (ABV 4%)

Tucks Tipple (ABV 4%)

Loxley Ale (ABV 4.2%)

Black Pearl (ABV 4.3%)

Maid Marian (ABV 4.3%)

Crusader (ABV 4.4%)

Lion Heart (ABV 4.4%)

Rich Ruby (ABV 4.5%)

Imperial Pale Ale (ABV 4.8%)

Olde Home Wrecker (ABV 4.9%)

Little John (ABV 5%)

Raspberry Wheat Beer (ABV 5.6%)

Milk Street SIBA

Milk Street Brewery Ltd (MSB Ltd), The Griffin, 25 Milk Street, Frome, Somerset, BA11 3DL
(01373) 467766 rjlyall@hotmail.com
milkstreetbrewery.co.uk
Tours by arrangement

Milk Street was established in 1999 in a former pub and porn cinema. The cinema is long gone and now houses the brewery, which expanded in 2005 and is now capable of producing 30 barrels per week. It mainly produces for its own estate of three outlets with direct delivery to pubs in a 30-mile radius. Wholesalers are used to distribute the beers further afield.

Gulp (ABV 3.5%)
A session beer with a pleasant lemon and citrus aroma and a full mouthfeel with good hop balance. The finish has a clean bitterness with spicy and blackcurrant notes.

Funky Monkey (OG 1040, ABV 4%)
Copper-coloured summer ale with fruity flavours and aromas. A dry finish with developing bitterness and an undertone of citrus fruit.

Mermaid (OG 1041, ABV 4.1%)
Amber-coloured ale with a rich hop character on the nose, plenty of citrus fruit on the palate and a lasting bitter and hoppy finish.

Amarillo (OG 1043, ABV 4.3%)
Brewed with American hops to give the beer floral and spicy notes. Initially soft on the palate, the flavour develops to that of burnt oranges and a pleasant herbal taste.

Zig-Zag Stout (OG 1046, ABV 4.5%)
A dark ruby stout with characteristic roastiness and dryness with bitter chocolate and citrus fruit in the background.

Beer (OG 1049, ABV 5%)
A blonde beer with musky hoppiness and citrus fruit on the nose, while more fruit surges through on the palate before the bittersweet finish.

Mill Green SIBA

Mill Green Brewery, White Horse, Edwardstone, Sudbury, Suffolk, CO10 5PX
(01787) 211118
enquiries@millgreenbrewery.co.uk
millgreenbrewery.co.uk

Mill Green started brewing in 2008 as an eco brewery in a new build complex behind the White Horse pub. Brewing liquor is heated by solar panels, wood boiler and wind turbine. 20 outlets are supplied. Bottle-conditioned beers are available.

Mawkin Mild (OG 1028, ABV 2.9%)
A balanced sweetness and earthy bitterness with a chocolate coffee finish.

White Horse Bitter (ABV 3.6%)
A traditional session bitter with a spicy, bitter, lasting finish.

Green Goose (ABV 4%)
A dark bitter, rich in flavour with a hedgerow fruit aroma.

Loveleys Fair (OG 1039, ABV 4%)
A modern-style pale ale, golden in colour and heavily hopped with a tangy, citrus bite.

Good Ship Arbella (ABV 5.4%)
An American pale ale style, strong on hop.

Millis

Millis Brewing Co Ltd, St Margaret's Farm, St Margaret's Road, South Darenth, Dartford, Kent, DA4 9LB
(01322) 866233 millisbrewing.com

John and Miriam Millis started with a half-barrel plant at their home in Gravesend. Demand outstripped the facility and Millis moved in 2003 to a new site – a former farm cold store – with a 10-barrel plant. They now supply around 40 outlets within a 50-mile radius. Seasonal beer: Hopping Haze (ABV 4%), Kentish Gold (ABV 4%), Thieves 'n' Fakirs (ABV 4.3%), Old Kentish Ale (ABV 4.8%).

Kentish Dark (OG 1035, ABV 3.5%)
Well-balanced, easy-drinking dark mild.

Gravesend Guzzler (OG 1037, ABV 3.7%)
Pale, easy-drinking, fruity session beer.

Kentish Best (OG 1040, ABV 4%)
A copper-coloured best bitter; tangy, fruity and dry.

Dartford Wobbler (OG 1043, ABV 4.3%)
A tawny-coloured, full-bodied best bitter with complex malt and hop flavours and a long, clean, slightly roasted finish.

Kentish Red Ale (OG 1043, ABV 4.3%)
A traditional red ale with complex malt, hops and fruit notes.

Millstone SIBA

Millstone Brewery Ltd, Unit 4, Vale Mill, Micklehurst Road, Mossley, nr Oldham, OL5 9JL
(01457) 835835 info@millstonebrewery.co.uk
millstonebrewery.co.uk

Established in 2003 by Nick Boughton and Jon Hunt, the brewery is located in an 18th-century textile mill. The eight-barrel plant produces a range of pale, hoppy beers including five regular and seasonal/occasional beers (including the 'pub name' series). Over 50 outlets are supplied.

Vale Mill (OG 1039, ABV 3.9%)
A pale gold session bitter with a floral and spicy aroma building upon a crisp and refreshing taste.

Three Shires Bitter (OG 1040, ABV 4%)
Yellow beer with hop and fruit aroma. Fresh citrus fruit, hops and bitterness in the taste and aftertaste.

Tiger Rut (OG 1040, ABV 4%)
A pale, hoppy ale with a distinctive citrus/grapefruit aroma.

Grain Storm (OG 1042, ABV 4.2%)
Yellow/gold beer with a grainy mouthfeel and fresh fruit and hop aroma. Citrus peel and hops in the mouth, with a bitter finish.

True Grit (OG 1049, ABV 5%)
A well-hopped strong ale with a mellow bitterness and a citrus/grapefruit aroma.

Milton SIBA EAB

Milton Brewery Cambridge Ltd, 111 Cambridge Road, Milton, Cambridgeshire, CB24 6AT
(01223) 226198
enquiries@miltonbrewery.co.uk
miltonbrewery.co.uk

Tours by arrangement

⊗ The brewery has grown steadily since it was founded in 1999 and now operates pubs in Cambridge, London, Peterborough and Norwich through a sister company, Individual Pubs Ltd. Beers are available nationally via wholesalers. Regular seasonal beers are brewed including Mammon (ABV 7%, Dec-Feb). Nero is suitable for vegetarians and vegans.

Minotaur (OG 1035, ABV 3.3%) ◆
Red/brown mild with a defined malt and roast nose, then a sweetish malt and fruit balance with roast adding depth. The malt and sweetness remain in the aftertaste with little bitterness.

Jupiter (OG 1037, ABV 3.5%) ◆
A copper-coloured bitter with malt and hops in balance on nose and palate. Some caramel sweetness, but butterscotch lingers on in the aftertaste.

Neptune (OG 1039, ABV 3.8%) ◆
Delicious hop aromas introduce this well-balanced, nutty and refreshing copper-coloured ale. Good hoppy finish.

Pegasus (OG 1043, ABV 4.1%) ◆
This copper-coloured beer balances malty aroma and flavour with some kiwi fruit and faint toffee. Pleasing dry aftertaste.

Sparta (OG 1043, ABV 4.3%) ◆
A golden ale that is dominated by floral hops throughout with some citrus fruit on the palate. Refreshingly dry with a moderately bitter finish.

Nero (OG 1050, ABV 5%) ◆
A creamy black stout. Prunes and raisins on the nose lead in to flavours of sweet chocolate, malt and roast with layers of fruit. The aftertaste develops to chocolaty dryness.

Cyclops (OG 1055, ABV 5.3%)
Deep copper-coloured ale, with a rich hoppy aroma and full body; fruit and malt notes develop in the finish.

Mitchell Krause (NEW)

Mitchell Krause Brewing Ltd, PO Box 86, Workington, Cumbria, CA14 9BD
☎ 07825 580694 ✉ graeme@mkbrewing.co.uk
🌐 mkbrewing.co.uk

Mitchell Krause was set up in 2009 and produces three bottled beers, one of which (Bavarian Hefe Weiss No 3, ABV 5%) is bottle conditioned. Beers are contract brewed at Hepworth Brewery.

Mithril (NEW)

Mithril Ales, Mithril, Aldbrough St John, Richmond, North Yorkshire, DL11 7TL
☎ (01325) 374817 ✉ mithril58@btinternet.com
🌐 mithrilales.co.uk

Mithril started brewing in 2010 in an old stables on a 2.5-barrel plant. Owner/brewer Pete Fenwick is a well-known craft brewer who works at weekends to supply the local area of Darlington and Richmond. Monthly specials are available.

Local (Beer For Local People) (OG 1038, ABV 3.8%)

Route A66 (OG 1040, ABV 4%)

Flower Power (OG 1042, ABV 4.2%)

Moles SIBA

Moles Brewery (Cascade Drinks Ltd), 5 Merlin Way, Bowerhill, Melksham, Wiltshire, SN12 6TJ
☎ (01225) 704734/708842
✉ rogermole@molesbrewery.com
🌐 molesbrewery.com
Shop Mon-Fri 9am-5pm; Sat 9am-12pm
Tours by arrangement

⊗ Moles was established in 1982 by Roger Catte, a former Ushers brewer, using his nickname to name the brewery. 10 pubs are owned, all serving cask beer. Over 200 outlets are supplied direct. Seasonal beers: see website.

Tap Bitter (OG 1035, ABV 3.5%)
A session bitter with a smooth, malty flavour and clean bitter finish.

Double MM Mild (OG 1036, ABV 3.6%)

Best Bitter (OG 1040, ABV 4%)
A well-balanced, amber-coloured bitter, clean, dry and malty with some bitterness, and delicate floral hop flavour.

Elmo's Fire (OG 1044, ABV 4.4%)

Landlords Choice (OG 1045, ABV 4.5%)
A dark, strong, smooth porter, with a rich fruity palate and malty finish.

Rucking Mole (OG 1045, ABV 4.5%)
A chestnut-coloured premium ale, fruity and malty with a smooth bitter finish.

Mole Catcher (OG 1050, ABV 5%)
A copper-coloured ale with a delightfully spicy hop aroma and taste, and a long bitter finish.

Monty's SIBA

Monty's Brewery, Unit 1, Castle Works, Hendomen, Montgomery, Powys, SY15 6HA
☎ (01686) 668933 ✉ Pam@montysbrewery.co.uk
🌐 montysbrewery.co.uk
Tours by arrangement

Monty's is the first brewery to produce beer in Montgomeryshire since the closure of the Eagle Brewery in Newtown in 1988. It began brewing in 2009. Pump clips are available in English and Welsh. Seasonal beers: see website. Bottle-conditioned beers are also available.

Mojo (OG 1042, ABV 3.8%)
A golden, slightly toasty brew, with a hint of marmalade.

Midnight (OG 1043, ABV 4%)
A dark, smooth, creamy stout.

Moonrise (OG 1040, ABV 4%)
A copper-coloured, gently malty, well-balanced traditional brew.

Sunshine (OG 1041, ABV 4.2%)
A golden, hoppy, floral/citrus ale with a pleasantly dry finish.

Moodley's (NEW)

Moodley's Ltd, Office: 30 Erskine Park Road, Tunbridge Wells, Kent, TN4 8UR
☎ (01892) 821366 ✉ yudhistra@moodleys.co.uk
🌐 moodleys.co.uk
Tours by arrangement

⊗ Moodleys was established in 2008. The brewery itself is in Penshurst, Kent. At present only bottle-conditioned beers are produced, all vegan-friendly: Poundage Porter (ABV 4%), Original Mild (ABV 4%), Toad Rock Bitter (ABV 5%). Cask-conditioned ale is planned.

Moonstone

Moonstone Brewery (Gem Taverns Ltd), Ministry of Ale, 9 Trafalgar Street, Burnley, Lancashire, BB11 1TQ
☎ (01282) 830909 ✉ meet@ministryofale.co.uk
moonstonebrewery.co.uk
Tours by arrangement

A small, 2.5-barrel brewery, based in the Ministry of Ale pub. Brewing started in 2001 and beer is generally only available in the pub. Seasonal beer: Red Jasper (ABV 6%, winter).

Black Star (OG 1037, ABV 3.4%)

Blue John (ABV 3.6%)

Tigers Eye (OG 1037, ABV 3.8%)

White Sapphire (OG 1037, ABV 3.9%)

MPA (ABV 4%)

Moor SIBA

Moor Beer Co Ltd, c/o Chapel Court, Pitney, Somerset, TA10 9AE
☎ 07887 556521 ✉ justin@moorbeer.co.uk
moorbeer.co.uk
Tours by arrangement

Moor Beer was founded in 1996 and rescued from oblivion by award-winning brewer Justin Hawke in 2006. The beers are mostly found in Somerset and at select pubs and festivals across the UK via wholesalers. Specials and seasonal beers are available. Bottle-conditioned beers are also available.

Revival (OG 1038, ABV 3.8%)
An immensely hoppy and refreshing pale ale.

Merlin's Magic (OG 1045, ABV 4.3%)
Dark amber-coloured, complex, full-bodied beer, with fruity notes.

Peat Porter (OG 1047, ABV 4.5%)
Dark brown/black beer with an initially fruity taste leading to roast malt with a little bitterness. A slightly sweet malty finish.

Ported Peat Porter (OG 1049, ABV 4.7%)
Peat Porter with added Reserve Port.

Somerland Gold (OG 1052, ABV 5%)
Hoppy blonde ale with hints of honey and a long, hoppy finish.

Hoppiness (ABV 6.5%)

Old Freddy Walker (OG 1075, ABV 7.3%)
Rich, dark, strong ale with a fruity complex taste, leaving a fruitcake finish.

Grockle Grog (ABV 8%)

JJJ IPA (OG 1085, ABV 9%)
Copper-coloured, new world triple IPA. Immensely hoppy and malty.

Moorhouse's SIBA

Moorhouse's Brewery (Burnley) Ltd, The Brewery, Moorhouse Street, Burnley, Lancashire, BB11 5EN
☎ (01282) 422864/416004
✉ info@moorhouses.co.uk moorhouses.co.uk
Tours by arrangement

Established in 1865 as a drinks manufacturer, the brewery started producing cask-conditioned ale in 1978 and has achieved recognition by winning more international and CAMRA awards than any other brewery of its size. Two new additional 30-barrel fermenters were installed in 2004, taking production to 320 barrels a week maximum. A new brewhouse is planned that will increase production to 40,000 barrels a year. The company owns six pubs, all serving cask-conditioned beer, and supplies some 250 free trade outlets. There is a selection of seasonal ales throughout the year: see website.

Black Cat (OG 1036, ABV 3.4%)
A dark mild-style beer with delicate chocolate and coffee roast flavours and a crisp, bitter finish.

Premier Bitter (OG 1036, ABV 3.7%)
A clean and satisfying bitter aftertaste rounds off this well-balanced hoppy, amber session bitter.

Pride of Pendle (OG 1040, ABV 4.1%)
Well-balanced amber best bitter with a fresh initial hoppiness and a mellow, malt-driven body.

Blond Witch (OG 1045, ABV 4.5%)
A pale coloured ale with a crisp, delicate fruit flavour. Dry and refreshing with a smooth hop finish.

Pendle Witches Brew (OG 1050, ABV 5.1%)
Well-balanced, full-bodied, malty beer with a long, complex finish.

Moorview SIBA

Moorview Brewery, Upper Austby Farm, Nesfield, North Yorkshire, LS29 0EQ
☎ 07833 337289

Office: 1a Silverdale Close, Guiseley, Leeds, West Yorkshire, LS20 8BQ ☎ (01943) 878154
✉ eric.cusack@btopenworld.com
moorviewbrewery.co.uk

Moorview began brewing in 2008 using the old brew plant from the Turkey Inn at Goose Eye. Water is supplied from their own bore hole. Around 15 outlets are supplied direct.

First Born Bitter (ABV 3.4%)

Full Mashings (ABV 3.6%)

Golden Butts (ABV 3.7%)

Amber Gambler (ABV 3.8%)

Silicone Blonde (ABV 4.4%)

Cocker-Doodle-Brew (ABV 5.2%)

Mordue SIBA

Mordue Brewery, Units D1 & D2, Narvic Way, Tyne Tunnel Estate, North Shields, Tyne & Wear, NE29 7XJ
☎ (0191) 296 1879
✉ enquiries@morduebrewery.com
morduebrewery.com
Tours by arrangement

In 1995 the Fawson brothers revived the Mordue Brewery name (the original closed in 1879). High demand required moves to larger premises and replacing the original five-barrel plant with a 20-barrel one. The beers are distributed nationally and 200 outlets are supplied direct. Seasonal beers: see website.

Five Bridge Bitter (OG 1038, ABV 3.8%)

Crisp, golden beer with a good hint of hops, the bitterness carries on in the finish. A good session bitter.

Geordie Pride (OG 1042, ABV 4.2%) ◆
Well-balanced and hoppy copper-coloured brew with a long, bitter finish.

Workie Ticket (OG 1045, ABV 4.5%) ▣ ◆
Complex tasty bitter with plenty of malt and hops, long satisfying bitter finish.

Radgie Gadgie (OG 1048, ABV 4.8%) ▣ ◆
Strong, easy-drinking bitter with plenty of fruit and hops.

IPA (OG 1051, ABV 5.1%) ◆
Easy-drinking golden ale with plenty of hops, the bitterness carries on in the finish.

Morrissey Fox

Morrissey Fox Breweries Ltd, Tickton Hall, Tickton, Beverley, East Yorkshire, HU17 9RX

☺Morrissey Fox Breweries was developed in 2008 and filmed by Channel 4. The brewery was initially based at Ye Olde Punchbowl in Marton cum Grafton, North Yorkshire but the company left the pub in 2009. Beers are contract brewed elsewhere reportedly including Cropton Brewery and Celt Experience.

Bitter (OG 1040, ABV 3.9%)

Blonde (OG 1043, ABV 4.2%)

Morton

Morton Brewery, Unit 10, Essington Light Industrial Estate, Essington, Wolverhampton, Staffordshire, WV11 2BH
☎ 07988 069647

Office: 96 Brewood Road, Coven, Staffordshire, WV9 5EF ✉ mortonbrewery@aol.com
● mortonbrewery.co.uk
Tours by arrangement

Morton was established in 2007 on a three-barrel plant by Gary and Angela Morton, both CAMRA members. The brewery moved to Essington in 2008 to increase production. Essington Ale was introduced to celebrate the move and became so popular with the locals that a full range of 'Essington' beers is brewed regularly. 30 outlets are supplied direct plus various beer festivals. Seasonal and special beers: see website. Bottle-conditioned beers are also available.

Merry Mount (OG 1037, ABV 3.8%)

Essington Blonde (OG 1039, ABV 4%)

Essington Ale (OG 1041, ABV 4.2%)

Jelly Roll (OG 1041, ABV 4.2%)

Essington Gold (OG 1043, ABV 4.4%)

Essington Supreme (OG 1046, ABV 4.6%)

Scottish Maiden (OG 1045, ABV 4.6%)

Essington IPA (OG 1047, ABV 4.8%)

Essington Old Ale (OG 1051, ABV 5%)

Moulin

▤ **Moulin Hotel & Brewery, 2 Balemund Road, Moulin, Pitlochry, Perthshire, PH16 5EL**

☎ (01796) 472196 ✉ enquiries@moulinhotel.co.uk
● moulinhotel.co.uk
Shop 12-3pm daily
Tours by arrangement

☺ The brewery opened in 1995 to celebrate the Moulin Hotel's 300th anniversary. Two pubs are owned and four outlets are supplied. Bottle-conditioned beer is available.

Light (OG 1036, ABV 3.7%) ◆
Thirst-quenching, straw-coloured session beer, with a light, hoppy, fruity balance, ending with a gentle, hoppy sweetness.

Braveheart (OG 1039, ABV 4%) ◆
An amber bitter, with a delicate balance of malt and fruit and a Scottish-style sweetness.

Ale of Atholl (OG 1043.5, ABV 4.5%) ◆
A reddish, quaffable, malty ale, with a solid body and a mellow finish.

Old Remedial (OG 1050.5, ABV 5.2%) ◆
A distinctive and satisfying dark brown old ale, with roast malt to the fore and tannin in a robust taste.

Mr Grundys (NEW)

▤ **Mr Grundys Tavern & Brewery, Georgian House Hotel, Ashbourne Road, Derby, DE1 3SL**
☎ (01332) 349806 ✉ info@georgianhousehotel.info
● georgianhousehotel.info

The brewery opened in 2010 using a four-barrel plant. Beers are produced for the company's own tavern (Mr Grundys) and hotels.

Trench Foot (ABV 3.8%)

No Man's Land (ABV 4.5%)

Coffin Nail (ABV 5%)

Muirhouse

Muirhouse Brewery, Quantock Road, Long Eaton, Nottinghamshire, NG10 4FZ
☎ 07916 590525 ✉ rmuir@muirhousebrewery.co.uk
● muirhousebrewery.co.uk

▨ Muirhouse Brewery was established in 2009 by keen home brewer Richard Muir. The purpose-built 100-litre plant is situated in his garage and five regular beers are brewed, some being bottled for the Great Central Preserved Railway at Loughborough. Further expansion is planned due to popular demand. Seasonal beer: Master Brewer (ABV 5%, summer). All beers are also available bottle conditioned.

Shunters Pole (OG 1040, ABV 3.8%)
A pale, refreshing, hoppy beer with a Styrian hop finish and aroma.

Stout Fellow (OG 1040, ABV 3.8%)
A stout bursting with flavours of coffee, toffee and roasted barley.

Ruby Jewel (OG 1040, ABV 3.9%)
A ruby-coloured malty beer with tastes of toffee.

Fully Fitted Freight (OG 1041, ABV 4%)
A premium bitter with a fine blend of malt and hops and a distinctive finish.

Stumbling Around (OG 1050, ABV 5.2%)
A ruby-coloured beer.

Nailsworth

Nailsworth Brewery Ltd, Village Inn, The Cross, Nailsworth, Gloucestershire, GL6 0HH
☎ 07878 448377 ✉ jonk@nailsworth-brewery.co.uk
nailsworth-brewery.co.uk
Tours by arrangement

The original Nailsworth Brewery closed in 1908. In 2004, after a gap of 98 years, commercial brewing returned in the form of a six-barrel micro-brewery. This is the brainchild of Messrs Hawes and Kemp, whose aim is to make the town of Nailsworth once again synonymous with quality beer. Around 30 outlets are supplied direct. Seasonal beer: Winter Woolie (ABV 4.9%). Bottle-conditioned beer is also available.

Alestock (ABV 3.6%)

Artist's Ale (OG 1040, ABV 3.8%)
A light-coloured bitter full of citrus flavours.

Dudbridge Donkey (ABV 4%)

Mayor's Bitter (OG 1042, ABV 4.3%)
A best bitter with malt textures complemented by a long-lasting taste of blackcurrant.

Town Crier (OG 1046, ABV 4.5%)
A premium ale with delicate grassy and floral overtones.

Vicar's Stout (ABV 4.5%)

Nant

Bragdy'r Nant, Penrhwylfa, Maenan, Llanrwst, Conwy, LL26 0UA
☎ 07723 036862
✉ postmaster@jonesgw2.demon.co.uk
cwrwnant.co.uk

Nant commenced brewing in late 2007 with a plant purchased from the Yorkshire Dales Brewery. Capacity is currently 10-15 nine gallon firkins a week. Seasonal and one-off beers are also produced.

Mochyn Hapus (ABV 3.7%)

Cwrw Coryn (ABV 4.2%)

Pen Dafad (ABV 4.2%)

Chawden Aur (ABV 4.3%)

Grans's Lamb (ABV 4.5%)

Mwnci Nell (ABV 5.3%)

Naylor's

Naylor's Brewery, Midland Mills, Station Road, Cross Hills, Keighley, West Yorkshire, BD20 7DT
☎ (01535) 637451
✉ naylorsbrewery@btconnect.com
naylorsbrewery.com
Shop Mon-Fri 10am-5pm; Sat 10am-3pm
Tours by arrangement

Naylors started brewing early in 2005, based at the Old White Bear pub in Crosshills. Expansion required a move to the current site in 2006 and included a rebranding of the beers. Further expansion in 2009 gave better facilities for bottling as well as a shop and bar. Around 110 outlets are supplied. Bottle-conditioned ales are also produced. All bottled beers are suitable for vegetarians.

Pinnacle Mild (ABV 3.4%)
This dark brown, malty mild has complex roast flavours with chocolate and fruity undertones. A vine fruit aroma and a malty, bitter finish.

Pinnacle Pale Ale (ABV 3.6%)
A clean-tasting pale ale, which starts off sweet against a fruity background. A prickly hoppiness kicks in leading to a bitter, slightly astringent finish.

Pinnacle Bitter (ABV 3.9%)
Predominantly malty, this traditional mid-brown bitter also has subtle fruit and hops in the nose and taste and growing bitterness in the finish.

Pinnacle Blonde (ABV 4.3%)
This hoppy, fruity ale has hints of tropical fruit in the aroma and a bitter, astringent finish.

Pinnacle Porter (ABV 4.8%)
A roast bitterness characterises this full-bodied black beer. There are also hints of sweetness, chocolate and coffee against a fruity background. Roast and bitterness combine in the lingering aftertaste.

Neath (NEW)

Neath Ales, Endeavour Close, Baglan, SA12 8PT
✉ enquiries@neathales.co.uk neathales.co.uk

Neath Ales was established in 2009 and produces a range of unfiltered, unpasteurised, vegan-friendly bottle-conditioned beers with no added chemicals, additives, flavour enhancers or sulphates. Bottle-conditioned beers: Black (ABV 5.5%), Gold (ABV 5%), Firebrick (ABV 4.2%), Abbey Ale (ABV 4.2%), Reserve (ABV 7.5%).

Nelson SIBA

Nelson Brewing Co UK Ltd, Unit 2, Building 64, The Historic Dockyard, Chatham, Kent, ME4 4TE
☎ (01634) 832828
✉ sales@nelsonbrewingcompany.co.uk
nelsonbrewingcompany.co.uk
Shop Mon-Fri 9am-4.30pm
Tours by arrangement

Nelson started out in 1995 as the Flagship Brewery but changed its name in 2004. It was acquired by the current owner, Piers MacDonald, in 2006. The brewery is based in Chatham's preserved Georgian dockyard, where Nelson's flagship, HMS Victory, was built. 80 outlets are supplied direct. All cask beers are also available bottle conditioned. Seasonal and occasional beers: see website.

Master Mate Mild (OG 1038, ABV 3.7%)

Pieces of Eight (OG 1039, ABV 3.8%)

Jack Knife (OG 1040, ABV 4.1%)

Spanker (OG 1040, ABV 4.1%)

Trafalgar Bitter (OG 1039, ABV 4.1%)
A light, easy-drinking ale with balanced malt and hop flavour and hints of honey and nuts to finish.

Jammin' Jack (OG 1042, ABV 4.3%)

Powder Monkey (OG 1044, ABV 4.4%)

Dogwatch Stout (OG 1044, ABV 4.5%)

Friggin' in the Riggin' (OG 1048, ABV 4.7%)
Drinkable premium bitter with smooth malt flavour and bittersweet aftertaste.

Purser's Pussy Porter (OG 1049, ABV 5.1%)

Nethergate SIBA EAB

Nethergate Holdings Ltd, The Growler Brewery, The Street, Pentlow, Essex, CO10 7JJ
☎ (01787) 283220 ✉ orders@nethergate.co.uk
⊕ nethergatebrewery.co.uk
Tours by arrangement

⊗ Nethergate Brewery was established in 1986 at Clare, Suffolk. The plant was doubled in 1993 and the brewery moved over the border into Pentlow, Essex in 2005, where it doubled in size again. The brewery is still in the stewardship of one of its founders, Dick Burge, and has won many awards. A large range of individual monthly beers are brewed and most of the permanent and some monthly beers are also available bottle conditioned.

IPA (OG 1036, ABV 3.5%) ◆
Bitter-tasting session beer with some fruit and malt balancing the predominate hop character. Very dry aftertaste.

Priory Mild (OG 1036, ABV 3.5%) ◆
A 'black bitter' rather than a true mild. Strong roast and bitter tastes dominate throughout.

Umbel Ale (OG 1039, ABV 3.8%) ◆
Pleasant, easy-drinking bitter, infused with coriander, which dominates.

Three Point Nine (OG 1040, ABV 3.9%) ◆
Light tasting, sweetish and fruity session beer.

Suffolk County Best Bitter (OG 1041, ABV 4%) ◆
Dark bitter with roast grain tones off-setting biscuity malt and powerful hoppy, bitter notes.

Augustinian Ale (OG 1046, ABV 4.5%) ◆
A pale, refreshing, complex best bitter. A fruity aroma leads to a bittersweet flavour and aftertaste with a predominance of citrus tones.

Mary's Mild (OG 1046, ABV 4.5%)
A little stronger than the average mild, this dark ruby-red beer has a nutty, fruity aroma, light toffee, coffee and chocolate notes and a crisp, burnt roast finish.

Essex Border (OG 1049, ABV 4.8%)
A pale golden summer ale, fruity and spicy with a pleasant malty finish; a very easy drinking beer.

Old Growler (OG 1051, ABV 5%) ☐ ◆
Well-balanced porter in which roast grain is complemented by fruit and bubblegum.

Umbel Magna (OG 1051, ABV 5%) ☐ ◆
Old Growler flavoured with coriander. The spice is less dominant than in Umbel Ale, with some of the weight and body of the beer coming through.

Essex Beast (OG 1062, ABV 6.2%)
Strong, dark, complex and robust ale with chocolate and rich toffee flavours. Brewed in memory of Essex CAMRA stalwart Andrew Clifton.

For Truman's Beer Co:

Runner (ABV 4%)

Newby Wyke SIBA

Newby Wyke Brewery, Unit 24, Limesquare Business Park, Alma Park Road, Grantham, Lincolnshire, NG31 9SN
☎ (01476) 565682 ✉ sales@newbywyke.co.uk
⊕ newbywyke.co.uk
Tours by arrangement

⊗ The brewery is named after a Hull trawler skippered by brewer Rob March's grandfather. It

started life in 1998 as a 2.5-barrel plant in a converted garage then moved to premises behind the Willoughby Arms. In 2009 it moved back to Grantham with a brew length of 10 barrels. Seasonal beers: see website.

Kingston Topaz (OG 1037, ABV 4.2%)
A single-hopped ale with floral undertones.

Bear Island (OG 1044, ABV 4.6%)
A blonde beer with a hoppy aroma and a crisp, dry finish.

Marie Celeste (OG 1044, ABV 4.6%)
A fruity golden ale with a peach aroma.

White Squall (OG 1045, ABV 4.8%) ◆
Amber-hued with a hoppy aroma. Generous amounts of hop are well-supported by a solid malty undercurrent. An increasingly bittersweet tang makes itself known towards the finish.

HMS Warrior (OG 1047, ABV 5%)
A golden ale with a full fruit flavour and strong citrus aroma.

For Nobody Inn, Grantham:

Grantham Gold (OG 1037, ABV 4.2%)
A golden ale with a hoppy finish.

Newmans SIBA

T G Newman t/a Newmans Brewery, Unit 2E, Pontygwindy Industrial Estate, Pontygwindy Road, Caerphilly, CF83 3HU
☎ 0870 803 3876 ✉ sales@newmansbrewery.com
⊕ newmansbrewery.com
Tours by arrangement

⊗ Newmans opened on the day England won the Rugby World Cup in November 2003. It has since expanded from a five-barrel plant to a 20-barrel in 2005 and has re-located to a 40-barrel plant in South Wales, sharing the brewery with sister brewing company, The Celt Experience Ltd. Seasonal beers: see website.

Red Stag Bitter (OG 1039, ABV 3.6%) ◆
Dark red session ale, smooth, malty with soft fruit accents; dry fruit finish.

Wolvers Ale (OG 1042, ABV 4.1%) ◆
Well-rounded best bitter with good body for its strength. Initial sweetness with a fine malt flavour is balanced by a slightly astringent, hoppy finish.

Mammoth (ABV 4.3%)

Red Castle Cream (OG 1047, ABV 4.7%)

Last Lion of Britain (ABV 5%)

Nobby's

Nobby's Brewery, c/o Ward Arms, High Street, Guilsborough, Northamptonshire, NN6 8PY
☎ (01604) 740785 ✉ info@nobbysbrewery.co.uk
⊕ nobbysbrewery.co.uk
Shop Mon-Fri 9am-5pm; Sat 10am-1pm
Tours by arrangement

Paul 'Nobby' Mulliner started commercial brewing in 2004 on a 2.5-barrel plant at the rear of the Alexandra Arms in Kettering, which also served as the brewery tap. In 2007 a 14-barrel plant was also set up at the Ward Arms, Guilsborough. There are plans to install a bottling line. Seasonal beers: see website. The plant at the Alexandra was sold in 2009 and now brews as the Julian Church Brewery.

THE BREWERIES

Claridges Crystal (OG 1035, ABV 3.6%)

Best (OG 1039, ABV 3.8%)

Tressler XXX Mild (OG 1038, ABV 3.8%)

Guilsborough Gold (OG 1041, ABV 4%)

Wild West (OG 1046, ABV 4.6%)

Landlords Own (OG 1050, ABV 5%)

T'owd Navigation (OG 1061, ABV 6.1%)

Nook SIBA

The Nook Brewhouse, Riverside, 7b Victoria Square, Holmfirth, West Yorkshire, HD9 2DN
☎ (01484) 682373
office@thenookbrewhouse.co.uk
thenookbrewhouse.co.uk
Tours by arrangement

The Nook Brewhouse is the natural progression for the owners of the Nook public house, with a real ale pedigree including 30 consecutive years in the Good Beer Guide. It supplies two brewery taps and is built on the foundations of a previous brewhouse dating back to 1752, next to the River Ribble. A history room with renovated archives dating back to the 1700s and a brewery shop are planned once brewing is consolidated.

Yorks (OG 1037, ABV 3.7%)
A well-balanced bitter with light malt and hop aroma and hop and fruit in the taste, developing in strength. A good session beer.

Best (OG 1040.5, ABV 4.2%)
An easy-drinking best bitter with hints of malt and floral hops in the aroma. The taste has an abundance of hops and fruit and a pleasant, crisp, malty aftertaste.

Blond (OG 1042.5, ABV 4.5%)
A golden ale with intense fruit and hop tastes, which lessen in the aftertaste.

Red (OG 1044, ABV 4.5%)
Complex tastes of fruit and roasted malt throughout, enhanced by a strong, fruity aroma.

Norfolk Cottage SIBA

Norfolk Cottage Brewing, 98-100 Lawson Road, Norwich, Norfolk, NR3 4LF
☎ (01603) 788508/270520
norfolkcottagebeers@tiscali.co.uk

Launched in 2004 by Ray Ashworth, founder of Woodforde's, Norfolk Cottage undertakes consultancy brewing and pilot brews for the Fat Cat Brewing Co at the same address. Bespoke ales are available in small quantities to order.

Norfolk Square

Norfolk Square Brewery LLP, Unit 7, Estcourt Road, Great Yarmouth, Norfolk, NR30 4JQ
☎ (01493) 854484
beer@norfolksquarebrewery.co.uk
norfolksquarebrewery.co.uk

Norfolk Square began brewing in May 2008 on a 2.5-barrel plant. Bottle-conditioned beers are available. Seasonal beers: see website.

Pi (ABV 3.8%)

Scroby (ABV 4.2%)

Stiletto (ABV 4.5%)

North Cotswold SIBA

North Cotswold Brewery (Pilling Brewing Co), Unit 3, Ditchford Farm, Stretton-on-Fosse, Warwickshire, GL56 9RD
☎ (01608) 663947 ncb@pillingweb.co.uk
northcotswoldbrewery.co.uk
Shop Mon-Thu 9am-5pm; Fri 9am-12pm (Please ring first)
Tours by arrangement

North Cotswold started in 1999 as a 2.5-barrel plant, which was upgraded in 2000 to 10 barrels. A shop and visitor centre are on site. The brewery also distributes cider from Somerset and Hereford and owns the Happy Apple Cider Company, which produces real cider and perry from orchards on the estate of the farm. Over 200 outlets are supplied locally and nationally. Bottle-conditioned beer is available. Seasonal beers: see website.

Pig Brook (OG 1038, ABV 3.8%)
Full-flavoured session bitter.

Shag Weaver (OG 1045, ABV 4.5%)
A very pale bitter with New Zealand hops.

Hung, Drawn 'n' Portered (OG 1050, ABV 5%)
A black treacle porter.

North Curry SIBA

North Curry Brewery Co, The Old Coach House, Gwyon House, Church Road, North Curry, Somerset, TA3 6LH
☎ 07928 815053
thenorthcurrybreweryco@hotmail.co.uk
thenorthcurrybrewerycouk.com
Tours by arrangement

The brewery opened in summer 2006 and is attached to one of the oldest properties in North Curry where brewing last took place in the village in the 1920s. Two outlets are supplied direct. All beers are available bottle conditioned and are organic (but not suitable for vegetarians or vegans). Seasonal beer: Winter Warmer (ABV 5%, Dec).

Church Ale (OG 1038, ABV 3.9%)

Red Heron (OG 1041, ABV 4.3%)

The Withyman (OG 1042, ABV 4.6%)

Level Headed (OG 1043, ABV 4.7%)

Northern SIBA

Northern Brewing Ltd, Blakemere Brewery, Blakemere Craft Centre, Chester Road, Sandiway, Northwich, Cheshire, CW8 2EB
☎ (01606) 301000 sales@norbrew.co.uk
norbrew.co.uk
Tours by arrangement

Northern first brewed in 2003 on a five-barrel plant located in Runcorn. It relocated to a larger unit at Blakemere Craft Centre in 2005. A hospitality/bar area is available for brewery tours. Some beer names are Northern Soul themed and at least two specials per month are produced under both the Northern and Blakemere brand names. Specials: see website.

Navajo (ABV 3.9%)

Soul Rider (ABV 4%)

Dancer (ABV 4.2%)

Blakemere Gold (ABV 4.3%)

Blakemere Bronze (ABV 4.4%)

Hit & Run (ABV 4.5%)

One-Der-Ful Wheat (ABV 4.7%)

Soul Time (ABV 5%)

Deep, Dark Secret (ABV 5.2%)

Northumberland SIBA

Northumberland Brewery Ltd, Accessory House, Barrington Road, Bedlington, Northumberland, NE22 7AP
☎ (01670) 822112
✉ dave@northumberlandbrewery.co.uk
🌐 northumberlandbrewery.co.uk
Tours by arrangement

The brewery has been in operation for 11 years using a 10-barrel brew plant. More than 400 outlets are supplied. The Legends of the Tyne and Legends of the Wear series of beers are also produced as regulars. Seasonal beers: see website.

Pit Pony (ABV 3.8%)

Bucking Fastard (ABV 4%)

Fog on the Tyne (ABV 4.1%)

Brown Ale (ABV 4.6%)

Sheepdog (ABV 4.7%)
An old-fashioned tawny beer, with fruit and malt throughout and a hoppy finish.

North Wales SIBA

North Wales Brewery, Tan-y-Mynydd, Moelfre, Abergele, Conwy, LL22 9RF
☎ (0800) 083 4100
✉ northwalesbrewery@uwclub.net
🌐 northwalesbrewery.net

North Wales started brewing in June 2007 on a plant transferred from Paradise Brewery's former home in Wrenbury. Bottle-conditioned beers are available as are occasional seasonal brews.

Bodelwyddan Bitter (ABV 3.8%)

Farmers Ale (ABV 4%)

Llew Aur (Golden Lion) (ABV 4.5%)

Abergele Ale (ABV 5%)

Dragon's Wheat (ABV 5%)

Welsh Stout (ABV 5.2%)

North Yorkshire

North Yorkshire Brewing Co, Pinchinthorpe Hall, Pinchinthorpe, North Yorkshire, TS14 8HG
☎ (01287) 630200 ✉ sales@nybrewery.co.uk
🌐 nybrewery.co.uk
Shop 10am-5pm daily
Tours by arrangement (inc 3 course meal)

The brewery was founded in Middlesbrough in 1989 and moved in 1998 to Pinchinthorpe Hall, a moated and listed medieval estate near Guisborough that has its own spring water. The site also includes a hotel, restaurant and bistro. More than 100 free trade outlets are supplied. A special monthly beer is produced together with four beers in the Cosmic range. All beers are organic and bottle-conditioned beers are available.

Best (OG 1036, ABV 3.6%)

Golden Ginseng (ABV 3.6%)

Prior's Ale (OG 1036, ABV 3.6%)
Light, refreshing and surprisingly full-flavoured for a pale, low gravity beer, with a complex, bittersweet mixture of malt, hops and fruit carrying through into the aftertaste.

Archbishop Lee's Ruby Ale (OG 1040, ABV 4%)

Boro Best (OG 1040, ABV 4%)

Crystal Tips (OG 1040, ABV 4%)

Love Muscle (OG 1040, ABV 4%)

Honey Bunny (OG 1042, ABV 4.2%)

Mayhem (ABV 4.3%)

Cereal Killer (OG 1045, ABV 4.5%)

Blond (ABV 4.6%)

Fools Gold (OG 1046, ABV 4.6%)

Golden Ale (OG 1046, ABV 4.6%)
A well-hopped, lightly-malted, golden premium bitter, using Styrian Goldings and Goldings hops.

Flying Herbert (OG 1047, ABV 4.7%)

Lord Lee's (OG 1047, ABV 4.7%)
A refreshing, red/brown beer with a hoppy aroma. The flavour is a pleasant balance of roast malt and sweetness that predominates over hops. The malty, bitter finish develops slowly.

White Lady (OG 1047, ABV 4.7%)

Dizzy Duck (OG 1048, ABV 4.8%)

Rocket Fuel (OG 1050, ABV 5%)

Nottingham SIBA

Nottingham Brewing Co Ltd, Plough Inn, 17 St Peter's Street, Radford, Nottingham, NG7 3EN
☎ (0115) 942 2649 ☎ 07815 073447
✉ philip.darby@nottinghambrewery.com
🌐 nottinghambrewery.com
Tours by arrangement

The former owners of the Bramcote and Castle Rock Breweries re-established the Nottingham Brewery in 2000 in a purpose-built brewhouse behind the Plough Inn. Philip Darby and Niven Balfour set out to revive the brands of the original Nottingham Brewery, closed by Whitbread in the 1950s, with a view to supplying local outlets very much within the LocAle ethos.

Rock Ale Bitter Beer (OG 1038, ABV 3.8%)
A pale and bitter, thirst-quenching hoppy beer with a dry finish.

Rock Ale Mild Beer (OG 1038, ABV 3.8%)
A reddish-black malty mild with some refreshing bitterness in the finish.

Legend (OG 1040, ABV 4%)
A fruity and malty pale brown bitter with a touch of sweetness and bitterness.

Extra Pale Ale (OG 1042, ABV 4.2%)
A hoppy and fruity golden ale with a hint of sweetness and a long-lasting bitter finish.

Cock & Hoop (OG 1043, ABV 4.3%)
A fruity and bitter golden ale with citrus hops. Originally brewed for the Cock & Hoop pub in Nottingham.

THE BREWERIES

Dreadnought (OG 1045, ABV 4.5%)
Well-balanced best bitter. Blend of malt and hops give a rounded fruity finish.

Bullion (OG 1047, ABV 4.7%)
A refreshing premium golden ale. Brewed with a single malt variety, it is triple-hopped and exceptionally bitter.

Sooty Stout (OG 1048, ABV 4.8%)

Supreme Bitter (OG 1052, ABV 5.2%)
A strong amber fruity ale. A touch of malt in the taste is followed by a sweet and slightly hoppy finish.

Nutbrook

Nutbrook Brewery Ltd, 6 Hallam Way, West Hallam, Derbyshire, DE7 6LA
☎ 0800 458 2460 ✉ dean@nutbrookbrewery.com
nutbrookbrewery.com
Shop (by invite only) Mon-Fri 10am-6pm; Sat 10am-1pm
Tours by arrangement

Nutbrook was established in 2007 on a one-barrel brewery in the owner's garage. This was supplemented in 2010 with a six-barrel plant at Oakleaf Farm, Stanley Common. Beers are brewed to order for domestic and corporate clients, and customers can design their own recipes. All beers are available bottle conditioned and a range of organic beers is planned. Seasonal beer: Midnight (ABV 4.7%, Xmas).

Or8 (OG 1041.5, ABV 3.8%)

Squirrel (OG 1038.8, ABV 4.1%)

Bitlyke (OG 1040.6, ABV 4.2%)

Responsibly (OG 1044.1, ABV 4.4%)

Banter (OG 1040.9, ABV 4.5%)

Mongrel (OG 1046.9, ABV 4.5%)

More (OG 1047.2, ABV 4.8%)

For Seven Oaks:

Oak's Ale (OG 1039, ABV 4%)

O'Hanlon's SIBA

O'Hanlon's Brewing Co Ltd, Great Barton Farm, Whimple, Devon, EX5 2NY
☎ (01404) 822412 ✉ info@ohanlonsbrewery.com
ohanlonsbeer.com

Since moving to Whimple in 2000, O'Hanlon's has continued to expand to cope with ever-increasing demand. More than 100 outlets are regularly supplied, with wholesalers providing publicans nationwide with access to the cask products. A bottling plant has increased production and enabled O'Hanlon's to contract bottle for several other breweries. In 2009 the company stopped production of Thomas Hardy's Ale but has introduced two new beers, including a re-creation of one of their early brews, Red Ale. Bottle-conditioned ales are available. Seasonal beer: Goodwill Bitter (ABV 5%, Dec).

Firefly (OG 1035, ABV 3.7%)
Malty and fruity light bitter. Hints of orange in the taste.

Goldbade Wheat Beer (OG 1037, ABV 4%)
1999 and 2002 SIBA Champion Wheat Beer of Britain has a fine citrus taste.

Yellowhammer (OG 1041, ABV 4%)
A well-balanced, smooth pale yellow beer with a predominant hop and fruit nose and taste, leading to a dry, bitter finish.

Dry Stout (OG 1043, ABV 4.2%)
A dark malty, well-balanced stout with a dry, bitter finish and plenty of roast and fruit flavours up front.

Red Ale (OG 1044, ABV 4.5%)
Ruby red in colour with toffee, Ribena and roast barley in aroma. Gentle hop notes, fruity and soft mouthed.

Port Stout (OG 1046, ABV 4.8%)
A black beer with roast malt in the aroma that remains in the taste but gives way to hoppy bitterness in the aftertaste.

Stormstay (OG 1048, ABV 5%)
A ruby-coloured complex ale with a toffee and floral hop aroma and a surprisingly clean and citrussy finish after the malt toffee and biscuit flavours.

Oakham SIBA EAB

Oakham Ales, 2 Maxwell Road, Woodston, Peterborough, Cambridgeshire, PE2 7JB
☎ (01733) 370500 ✉ info@oakhamales.com
oakhamales.com
Tours by arrangement

The brewery started in 1993 in Oakham, Rutland and moved to Peterborough in 1998. The brewery's head office and main production site is a 75-barrel plant. An additional six-barrel plant is located at its brew pub central to the city, which allows special and one-off brews including beers made especially for its elite customers as members of the 'Oakademy of Excellence', which was launched in late 2008. Around 300 outlets are supplied and three pubs are owned. Seasonal beers: see website.

Jeffrey Hudson Bitter/JHB (OG 1038, ABV 3.8%)
Lemon, grapefruit and spicy hop notes abound on aroma and palate of this straw-coloured golden ale. Good bittersweet finish.

Inferno (OG 1039, ABV 4%)
Impressive golden ale with explosive fruity hop fumes. The palate comprises a powerful resiny and spicy hop character with complex fruit flavours and a satisfying bitterness. Strong, dry, hoppy finale.

White Dwarf (OG 1042, ABV 4.3%)
A speciality beer with fruit and hops on the aroma and in the taste. Dry and faintly astringent on the palate, leading to a strong, dry and moderately astringent finish.

Bishops Farewell (OG 1046, ABV 4.6%)
Citrus and grassy hops on the nose of this golden ale. A spirited spicy hop tang is coupled with strong bitterness and leads into an intense, dry, hoppy aftertaste.

Oakleaf SIBA

Oakleaf Brewing Co Ltd, Unit 7, Clarence Wharf Industrial Estate, Mumby Road, Gosport, Hampshire, PO12 1AJ
☎ (023) 9251 3222 ✉ info@oakleafbrewing.co.uk
oakleafbrewing.co.uk
Shop Mon-Fri 9am-5pm; Sat 10am-1pm
Tours by arrangement

⊠ Ed Anderson set up Oakleaf with his father-in-law, Dave Pickersgill, in 2000. The brewery stands on the side of Portsmouth Harbour. Some 350 outlets are supplied direct with national deliveries via wholesalers. Seasonal beers: see website/facebook. Bottle-conditioned beers are also available.

Bitter (OG 1038, ABV 3.8%) ◆
A copper-coloured beer with a hoppy and fruity aroma, which leads to an intensely hoppy and bitter flavour, with balancing lemon and grapefruit and some malt. A long dry finish. Full tasting for its strength.

Quercus Folium (OG 1040, ABV 4%)
A traditional mid-brown bitter with an inital malty flavour leading to a long hoppy finish.

Nuptu'ale (OG 1042, ABV 4.2%) ◆
A full-bodied pale ale, strongly hopped with an uncompromising bitterness. An intense hoppy, spicy, floral aroma leads to a complex hoppy taste. Well-balanced with malts and citrus flavours and a hint of sweetness making for a refreshing bitter.

Pompey Royal (ABV 4.5%)
A traditional mid-brown malty ale with a delicate hop balance.

Hole Hearted (OG 1048, ABV 4.7%) ◆
An amber-coloured strong bitter with strong floral hop and citrus notes in the aroma. These continue to dominate the flavour and lead to a long, bittersweet finish.

Blake's Gosport Bitter (OG 1053, ABV 5.2%) ◆
Packed with berry fruits and roastiness, this is a complex strong bitter. Malt, roast and caramel are prevalent as both bitterness and sweetness build at the same time to an uncompromising vinous finish. Warming, spicy, well-balanced and delicious.

For Suthwyk Ales:

Old Dick (ABV 3.8%) ◆
Formerly known as Bloomfield Bitter, this is a pleasant, clean-tasting pale brown bitter. Easy-drinking and well-balanced. Beer is brewed by Oakleaf for Suthwyk using ingredients grown on the farm.

Liberation (ABV 4.2%)

Skew Sunshine Ale (ABV 4.6%) ◆
An amber-coloured beer. Initial hoppiness leads to a fruity taste and finish. A slightly cloying mouthfeel. The beer is brewed by Oakleaf for Suthwyk using ingredients grown on the farm.

Palmerston's Folly (ABV 4.8%)

Oakwell SIBA

Oakwell Brewery, PO Box 87, Pontefract Road, Barnsley, South Yorkshire, S71 1EZ
☎ (01226) 296161
✉ jstancill@oakwellbrewery.co.uk

☺ Brewing started in 1997. Oakwell supplies around 30 outlets.

Old Tom Mild (OG 1033.5, ABV 3.4%) ◆
Fruit and malt in the aroma with fruit and roast malt in its flavour, these lead to a crisp finish. A good session mild.

Barnsley Bitter (OG 1036, ABV 3.8%) ◆
A sweet initial taste that quickly disappears and leads into a sustained fruity and malty flavour. A bitter and mellow finish.

Oban (NEW)

Oban Ales Ltd, Kilmelford Craft Brewery, Kilmelford, PA34 4XA
☎ (01852) 200731 ✉ sales@obanales.co.uk
⊕ obanales.co.uk
Shop Mon-Fri 10am-11pm
Tours by arrangement

☺Oban Ales was established in 2010 using the former Black Mountain Brewery plant. There are plans for expansion and to sell bottle-conditioned beers.

Rocky Pass (OG 1039, ABV 4%)

Oban Bay

⊟ **Oban Bay Brewery, Cuan Mor, 60 George Street, Oban, Argyll, PA34 5DS**
☎ (01631) 565078

Brewing began in 2009. 20 outlets are supplied. Bottle-conditioned beers are available.

Kilp Lifter (ABV 3.9%)

Skinny Blonde (ABV 4.1%)

Skelpt Lug (ABV 4.2%)

Fair Puggled (ABV 4.5%)

Odcombe

⊟ **Odcombe Brewery, Masons Arms, 41 Lower Odcombe, Odcombe, Somerset, BA22 8TX**
☎ (01935) 862591
✉ paula@masonsarmsodcombe.co.uk
⊕ masonsarmsodcombe.co.uk
Tours by arrangement

Odcombe Brewery opened in 2000 and closed a few years later. It re-opened in 2005 with assistance from Shepherd Neame. Brewing takes place once a week and beers are only available at the pub. Seasonal beers: Half Jack (ABV 3.8%), Winter's Tail (ABV 4.3%).

No 1 (OG 1040, ABV 4%)

Spring (OG 1041, ABV 4.1%)

Roly Poly (OG 1042, ABV 4.2%)

Offa's Dyke SIBA

⊟ **Offa's Dyke Brewery, Barley Mow Inn, Chapel Lane, Trefonen, Oswestry, Shropshire, SY10 9DX**
☎ (01691) 656889 ⊕ offasdykebrewery.com
Shop Mon-Fri 5-11pm; Sat & Sun 12-12
Tours by arrangement

Offa's Dyke was established in 2007. The brewery and adjoining pub straddle the old England/Wales border, Offa's Dyke. The owner grows barley locally and is experimenting with small-scale hop cultivation. Bottle-conditioned beers are available.

Barley Gold (OG 1038, ABV 3.6%)

Offa's Pride (OG 1040, ABV 3.8%)

Thirst Brew (OG 1042, ABV 4%)

Honey Blonde (OG 1045, ABV 4.2%)

Grim Reaper (OG 1050, ABV 5%)

Okells SIBA

Okell & Son Ltd, Kewaigue, Douglas, Isle of Man, IM2 1QG
☎ (01624) 699400 ✉ mac@okells.co.uk
🌐 okells.co.uk
Tours by arrangement

Founded in 1874 by Dr Okell and formerly trading as Isle of Man Breweries, this is the main brewery on the island, having taken over and closed the rival Castletown Brewery in 1986. The brewery moved in 1994 to a new, purpose-built plant at Kewaigue to replace the Falcon Brewery in Douglas. All the beers are produced under the Manx Brewers' Act 1874 (permitted ingredients: water, malt, sugar and hops only – amended in 1998 to allow the brewing of wheat and fruit beers). Approximately three quarters of the company's 48 Isle of Man pubs and four of the five in England and Wales sell cask beer and some 70 free trade outlets are also supplied. Seasonal beers: see website.

Mild (OG 1034, ABV 3.4%) ◆
A fine aroma of hops and crystal malt. Red-brown in colour, the beer has a full malt flavour with surprising bitter hop notes and a hint of blackcurrants and oranges.

Bitter (OG 1035, ABV 3.7%) ◆
A golden beer, malty and hoppy in aroma, with a hint of honey. Rich and malty on the tongue, it has a dry, malt and hop finish. A complex but rewarding beer.

Maclir (OG 1042, ABV 4.4%)
Beer with resiny hops and lemon fruit on the aroma, banana and lemon in the mouth and a big, bitter finish, dominated by hops, juicy malt and citrus fruit.

Dr Okell's IPA (OG 1044, ABV 4.5%)
A light-coloured beer with a full-bodied taste. The sweetness is offset by strong hopping that gives the beer an overall roundness with spicy lemon notes and a fine dry finish.

Old Brewery

See Meantime

Old Bear SIBA

Old Bear Brewery, Unit 1, Aireworth Mills, Aireworth Road, Keighley, West Yorkshire, BD21 4DH
☎ (01535) 601222 ✉ sales@oldbearbrewery.com
🌐 oldbearbrewery.co.uk
Shop Mon-Fri 9am-4pm, Sat 10am-1pm
Tours by arrangement

Old Bear is a family business founded in 1993 at the Old White Bear in Crosshills. The brewery moved to Keighley in 2004 to a purpose-built unit to cater for increased production. The original 10-barrel plant was retained and refurbished and there is now a one-barrel plant for special ales. Beers are supplied within a 60-mile radius of Keighley and are available nationally via wholesalers. All cask beers are also available bottle conditioned.

Bruin (OG 1035, ABV 3.5%)
The combination of hops gives off a sharp wild blackcurrant taste with a smoothness to follow.

Estivator (OG 1037, ABV 3.8%)
A light golden ale with a smooth, creamy, sweet lemon taste followed by buttery smoothness leading to a bitter, hoppy aftertaste.

Original (OG 1039, ABV 3.9%) ◆
The nose is fruity with a hint of hops and malt. Bitterness on the palate is balanced by malt, roast and sweetness. Bitterness increases in the malty finish.

Black Mari'a (OG 1043, ABV 4.2%)
A black stout, smooth on the palate with a strong roast malt flavour and fruity finish.

Honeypot (OG 1044, ABV 4.4%)
Straw-coloured beer enhanced with golden honey.

Goldilocks (OG 1047, ABV 4.5%) ◆
A fruity, straw-coloured golden ale, well-hopped and assertively bitter through to the finish.

Hibernator (OG 1055, ABV 5%) ◆
A complex rich dark ale dominated by roast and bitter flavours against a background sweetness. Look for roast coffee, hints of caramel and dark vine fruit on the nose. The finish is distinctly bitter and quite astringent.

Duke of Bronte (OG 1125, ABV 12.5%)
Caramel in colour and not too sweet with a distinctive nose giving hints of its strength, with a warming aftertaste.

Old Bog

Old Bog Brewery, Masons Arms, 2 Quarry School Place, Oxford, OX3 8LH
☎ (01865) 764579 ✉ theoldbog@hotmail.co.uk
🌐 masonsquarry.co.uk

Brewing started in 2005 on a one-barrel plant. At present Old Bog brews once a week. The beers, when available, are sold at the Masons Arms and occasionally at beer festivals. A number of one-off brews appear throughout the year.

Quarry Gold (OG 1041, ABV 4.1%)

Old Cannon

Old Cannon Brewery Ltd, 86 Cannon Street, Bury St Edmunds, Suffolk, IP33 1JR
☎ (01284) 768769
✉ drink@oldcannonbrewery.co.uk
🌐 oldcannonbrewery.co.uk
Tours by arrangement (small groups only)

The St Edmunds Head pub opened in 1845 with its own brewery. Brewing ceased in 1917, and Greene King closed the pub in 1995. It re-opened in 1999 as the Old Cannon Brewery complete with a unique state-of-the-art brewery housed in the bar area. A growing number of local outlets are supplied. Seasonal beers: Black Pig (ABV 4.2%), St Edmund's Head (ABV 5%, winter), Blonde Bombshell (ABV 4.2%), Bow Chaser (ABV 4%), Rusty Gun (ABV 4%).

Best Bitter (OG 1037, ABV 3.8%) ◆
Traditional East Anglian bitter. Rich hoppy aroma and bitterness dominate throughout with just a hint of sweetness in the aftertaste.

Gunner's Daughter (OG 1052, ABV 5.5%) ◆
A well-balanced strong ale with a complexity of hop, fruit, sweetness and bitterness in the flavour, and a lingering hoppy, bitter aftertaste.

Old Chimneys

Old Chimneys Brewery, Hopton End Farm, Church Road, Market Weston, Diss, Norfolk, IP22 2NX
☎ (01359) 221411/221013
oldchimneysbrewery.com
Shop Fri 2-7pm; Sat 11am-2pm
Tours by arrangement

Old Chimneys opened in 1995 and moved to larger premises in a converted farm building in 2001. Despite the postal address, the brewery is in Suffolk. The beers produced are mostly named after endangered local species. Seasonal beers: Red Clover (ABV 6%, winter), Ragged Robin (ABV 3.5%, summer). All cask ales are available bottle conditioned and are suitable for vegetarians and vegans except Black Rat and Hairy Canary.

Military Mild (OG 1035, ABV 3.3%)
A rich, dark mild with good body for its gravity. Sweetish toffee and light roast bitterness dominate, leading to a dry aftertaste.

Great Raft Bitter (OG 1040, ABV 4%)
Pale copper bitter bursting with fruit. Malt and hops add to the sweetish fruity flavour, which is rounded off with hoppy bitterness in the aftertaste.

Black Rat Stout (OG 1048, ABV 4.4%)

Golden Pheasant (OG 1044, ABV 4.5%)

Scarlet Tiger (OG 1046, ABV 4.7%)

Good King Henry (OG 1107, ABV 9%)

Old Cross

Old Cross Tavern Brewery, Old Cross Tavern, 8 St Andrew Street, Hertford, Hertfordshire, SG14 1JA
☎ (01992) 583133

The micro-brewery was set up in 2008 and is located within the pub. Owner Nigel Beviss brews solely for the Old Cross Tavern. There are currently two beers, with one usually available at the bar.

Laugh and Titter (ABV 3.7%)

OXT'ale (ABV 4%)

Old Dairy SIBA (NEW)

Old Dairy Brewery Ltd, The Old Parlour, Rawlinson Farm, Rolvenden, Kent, TN17 4JD
☎ (01580) 243185 ✉ fineale@olddairybrewery.com
olddairybrewery.com
Tours by arrangement

Old Dairy was founded in 2009. Sales expanded rapidly across pubs in Kent and new staff were taken on after only three months to help cope with the demand. 50 outlets are supplied direct. Bottle-conditioned beers are available.

Red Top (OG 1038, ABV 3.8%)

Gold Top (OG 1043, ABV 4.3%)

Blue Top (OG 1048, ABV 4.8%)

Oldershaw SIBA

Oldershaw Brewery, 12 Harrowby Hall Estate, Grantham, Lincolnshire, NG31 9HB
☎ (01476) 572135
✉ oldershawbrewery@btconnect.com
oldershawbrewery.com

Experienced home-brewer Gary Oldershaw and his wife Diane set up the brewery at their home in 1997. Grantham's first brewery for 30 years, Oldershaw now supplies 60 local free houses. The Oldershaws have introduced small-scale bottling and sell bottle-conditioned beer direct from the brewery. Seasonal beers: Sunnydaze (ABV 4%, May-Aug), Yuletide (ABV 5.2%, Nov-Dec), Grantham Dark (ABV 3.6%), Alma's Brew (ABV 4.1%).

Pearl (ABV 3%)

Mowbrays Mash (OG 1037, ABV 3.7%)

Harrowby Pale Ale (OG 1039, ABV 3.9%)

High Dyke (OG 1039, ABV 3.9%)
Golden and moderately bitter. A predominantly hoppy session beer.

OSB (OG 1040, ABV 4%)

Newton's Drop (OG 1041, ABV 4.1%)
Balanced malt and hops but with a strong bitter, lingering taste in this mid-brown beer.

Caskade (OG 1042, ABV 4.2%)
A gentle blend of flavours combine into a smooth, undemanding pint. Malt vies with a hoppy bitterness for initial recognition. Traces of caramel and sulphur appear before the short, sharp finish.

Ahtanum Gold (OG 1043, ABV 4.3%)
A gold-coloured, fruity, hoppy beer balanced with some maltiness. Moderately bitter.

Grantham Stout (OG 1043, ABV 4.3%)
Dark brown and smooth with rich roast malt flavour, supported by some fruit and bitterness. A long, moderately dry finish.

Regal Blonde (OG 1043, ABV 4.4%)
Straw-coloured, lager-style beer with a good malt/hop balance throughout; strong bitterness on the taste lingers.

Isaac's Gold (OG 1044, ABV 4.5%)

Old Boy (OG 1047, ABV 4.8%)
A full-bodied amber ale, fruity and bitter with a hop/fruit aroma. The malt that backs the taste dies in the long finish.

Alchemy (OG 1052, ABV 5.3%)
A golden, premium hoppy beer brewed with First Gold hops.

Olde Swan

Olde Swan Brewery, 89 Halesowen Road, Netherton, Dudley, West Midlands, DY2 9PY
☎ (01384) 253075
Tours by arrangement

A famous brew-pub best known as 'Ma Pardoe's' after the matriarch who ruled it for years. The pub has been licensed since 1835 and the present brewery and pub were built in 1863. Brewing continued until 1988 and restarted in 2001. The plant brews primarily for the on-site pub with some beer available to the trade. Seasonal beer: Black Widow (ABV 6.7%, winter). Monthly specials are available together with various commemorative beers for sporting events as well as bottle-conditioned beers from the brewery tap.

Original (OG 1034, ABV 3.5%)
Straw-coloured light mild, smooth but tangy, and sweetly refreshing with a faint hoppiness.

Dark Swan (OG 1041, ABV 4.2%)

Smooth, sweet dark mild with late roast malt in the finish.

Entire (OG 1043, ABV 4.4%)
Faintly hoppy, amber premium bitter with sweetness persistent throughout.

Bumble Hole Bitter (OG 1052, ABV 5.2%)
Sweet, smooth amber ale with hints of astringency in the finish.

Old Forge (NEW)

Old Forge Brewery, Radnor Arms, Coleshill, Oxfordshire, SN6 7PR
☎ (01793) 861575 oldforgebrewery.co.uk

Old Forge began brewing at the Radnor Arms in 2010 using a four-barrel plant. It is run by the owners of the nearby Halfpenny Brewery in Lechlade.

Anvil Ale (ABV 3.8%)

Blacksmiths Gold (ABV 4%)

Hammer & Tongs (ABV 4.2%)

Sledgehammer (ABV 5%)

Old Laxey

Old Laxey Brewing Co Ltd, Shore Hotel Brew Pub, Old Laxey, Isle of Man, IM4 7DA
☎ (01624) 863214 shore@mcb.net
shorehotel.im
Tours by arrangement

Beer brewed on the Isle of Man is brewed to a strict Beer Purity Act. Additives are not permitted to extend shelf life, nor are chemicals allowed to assist with head retention. Most of Old Laxey's beer is sold through the Shore Hotel alongside the brewery.

Bosun Bitter (OG 1038, ABV 3.8%)
Crisp and fresh with a hoppy aftertaste.

Old Luxters SIBA

Old Luxters Farm Brewery, Hambleden, Henley-on-Thames, Oxfordshire, RG9 6JW
☎ (01491) 638330 enquiries@chilternvalley.co.uk
chilternvalley.co.uk
Shop Mon-Fri 9am-6pm; Sat- Sun 11am-6pm (5pm winter)
Tours by arrangement

A traditional, full-mash farm brewery established in 1990 and now with the 'By Royal Appointment' accolade, is situated in a 17th-century barn alongside the Chiltern Valley Vineyard. The brewery is in Buckinghamshire despite the postal address. Several bottle-conditioned beers are brewed under contract. Three winter warmers are brewed for Xmas.

Barn Ale Bitter (OG 1038, ABV 4%)
A fruity, aromatic, fairly hoppy, bitter beer.

Barn Ale Special (OG 1042.5, ABV 4.5%)
Predominantly malty, fruity and hoppy in taste and nose, and tawny/amber in colour. Fairly strong in flavour: the initial, sharp, malty and fruity taste leaves a dry, bittersweet, fruity aftertaste. It can be slightly sulphurous.

Dark Roast Ale (OG 1048, ABV 5%)
The use of chocolate and crystal malts give this ale a nutty, roasty bitter flavour.

Old Mill SIBA

Old Mill Brewery, Mill Street, Snaith, East Yorkshire, DN14 9HU
☎ (01405) 861813 sales@oldmillbrewery.co.uk
oldmillbrewery.co.uk
Tours by arrangement to organisations and customers only

Old Mill is a craft brewery opened in 1983 in a 200-year-old former malt kiln and corn mill. The brew-length is 60 barrels. The brewery is building a tied estate, now standing at 19 houses. Beers can be found nationwide through wholesalers and around 80 free trade outlets are supplied direct. There is a rolling programme of seasonal beers (see website) and monthly specials.

Mild (OG 1034, ABV 3.4%)
A satisfying roast malt flavour dominates this easy-drinking, quality dark mild.

Bitter (OG 1038, ABV 3.9%)
A malty nose is carried through to the initial flavour. Bitterness runs throughout.

Blonde Bombshell (OG 1042, ABV 4%)

Yorkshire Porter (OG 1044, ABV 4.4%)

Old Curiosity (OG 1044, ABV 4.5%)
Slightly sweet amber brew, malty to start with. Malt flavours all the way through.

Bullion (OG 1047.5, ABV 4.7%)
The malty and hoppy aroma is followed by a neat mix of hop and fruit tastes within an enveloping maltiness. Dark brown/amber in colour.

Old Poet's

See Ashover

Old Spot

Old Spot Brewery Ltd, Manor Farm, Station Road, Cullingworth, Bradford, West Yorkshire, BD13 5HN
☎ (01535) 691144 sales@oldspotbrewery.co.uk
oldspotbrewery.co.uk
Tours by arrangement

Old Spot started brewing in 2005 and is named after a retired sheepdog on Manor Farm. The brewery targets the ever-changing guest ale market and creates new brews every 2-3 weeks, along with the stock beers. Around 35 outlets are supplied.

Darkside Pup (ABV 3.6%)
Full-bodied dark mild with a deep coffee taste with liquorice to finish.

Light But Dark (ABV 4%)
Chestnut-coloured bitter with a slight malty taste and pleasant bitter finish. An ideal session beer.

Spot Light (ABV 4.2%)
A light-coloured ale with a pleasant hoppy aftertaste.

Inn-Spired (ABV 4.3%)
Light-coloured bitter with a light, hoppy taste and a slight, fruity finish.

OSB (ABV 4.5%)
A golden-coloured, full-bodied bitter.

Spot O'Bother (ABV 5.5%)
Porter with a chocolate ice cream taste and slight liquorice bitterness to finish. A very complex brew.

Ole Slewfoot

Ole Slewfoot Brewing Co Ltd, 3 Pollard Road, Hainford, Norwich, NR10 3BE
☎ (01603) 279927 ☎ 07909 636966
✉ john@oleslewfootbrewery.co.uk
⊕ oleslewfootbrewery.co.uk

⊠ Ole Slewfoot was established in 2009. Five outlets are supplied direct.

White Dove (OG 1039, ABV 3.7%)

January 8th (OG 1040, ABV 4.2%)

Orange Blossom Special (OG 1042, ABV 4.4%)

Fox on the Run (OG 1045, ABV 4.8%)

Devils Dream (OG 1048, ABV 5%)

Friend of the Devil (OG 1077, ABV 8.4%)

Opa Hay's

Opa Hay's Brewery, Glencot, Wood Lane, Aldeby, NR34 0DA
☎ (01502) 679144 ☎ 07916 282729
✉ mail@engelfineales.com ⊕ engelfineales.com

Opa Hay's began brewing in late 2008. Seasonal beers: Engel's Porter (ABV 5.2%), Ether Party (ABV 5.2%).

Fruity Little Number (ABV 3.9%)

Engel's Best Bitter (ABV 4%)

Cliffhanger (ABV 4.3%)

Engel's Amber Ale (ABV 4.3%)

Engel's Pale Ale (ABV 4.6%)

6460 (ABV 6.4%)

For King's Head Hotel, Beccles:

Matilda's Revenge (ABV 4.3%)

Organic

See Chough

Orkney SIBA

Orkney Brewery, Sinclair Breweries Ltd, Quoyloo, Stromness, Orkney, KW16 3LT
☎ (01667) 404555 ✉ info@sinclairbreweries.co.uk
⊕ orkneybrewery.co.uk

⊛ Set up in 1988 in an old school building in the remote Orkney hamlet of Quoyloo. All beer is brewed along strict ecological lines from the brewery's own water supply with all waste water being treated through two lakes on its land, which in turn support fish and several dozen Mallard ducks. Development was completed in 2010 to double the capacity of the original brewery on an adjacent site with plans to convert the original building into a visitor centre with a shop and an events venue. After eight years based at Kinlochleven, 2010 saw the transfer of sister brewery Atlas (qv), part of Sinclair Breweries, to Quoyloo; the combined business distributes to some 600 outlets across Scotland and via wholesalers to the rest of Britain. Seasonal beers are available.

Raven (OG 1038, ABV 3.8%) 🍺 🍴 ◆

A well-balanced quaffable bitter. Malty fruitiness and bitter hops last through to the long, dry aftertaste.

Dragonhead Stout (OG 1040, ABV 4%) 🍴 ◆
A strong, dark malt aroma flows into the taste in this superb Scottish stout. The roast malt continues to dominate the aftertaste, and blends with chocolate to develop a strong, dry finish.

Northern Light (OG 1040, ABV 4%) ◆
A well-balanced golden ale with a real smack of fruit and hops in the taste and an increasing bitter aftertaste.

Red MacGregor (OG 1040, ABV 4%) 🍺 🍴 ◆
This tawny red ale has a powerful smack of fruit and a clean, fresh mouthfeel.

Dark Island (OG 1045, ABV 4.6%) 🍺 ◆
The roast malt and chocolate character varies, making the beer hard to categorise as a stout or an old ale. A sweetish roast malt taste leads to a long-lasting roasted, slightly bitter, dry finish.

Skull Splitter (OG 1080, ABV 8.5%) 🍴 ◆
An intense velvet malt nose with hints of apple, prune and plum. The hoppy taste is balanced by satiny smooth malt with fruity spicy edges, leading to a long, dry finish with a hint of nut.

For Atlas Brewery:

Latitude (OG 1036, ABV 3.6%) ◆
This golden ale has a light citrus taste with a smack of hops and grapefruit in the light bitter finish.

Three Sisters (OG 1043, ABV 4.2%) ◆
Malt, summer fruits and caramel in the nose and blackcurrant in the taste, followed by a short, hoppy, bitter finish.

Nimbus (OG 1050, ABV 5%) ◆
A full-bodied golden beer using some wheat malt and three types of hops. Sweet and fruity at the front, it becomes slightly astringent with lasting fruit and a pleasant, dry finish.

Ossett SIBA

Ossett Brewing Co Ltd, Kings Yard, Low Mill Road, Ossett, West Yorkshire, WF5 8ND
☎ (01924) 261333 ✉ brewery@ossett-brewery.co.uk ⊕ ossett-brewery.co.uk
Shop Mon-Fri 9am-4.30pm
Tours by arrangement

⊛ Brewing began in 1998 but the brewery soon outgrew the premises moving to a new site 50 metres away in 2005. A new 2,500 square feet cold store was added in 2008 and brewing capacity currently stands at 160 barrels per week. Ossett delivers between Newcastle and Peterborough and beer is available through wholesalers. The brewery owns 15 pubs, three restaurants and two micro-breweries. The Riverhead Brewery was purchased in 2006 and Fernandes Brewery in 2007. Seasonal and special beers: see website.

Pale Gold (OG 1038, ABV 3.8%)
A light, refreshing pale ale with a light, hoppy aroma.

Yorkshire Blonde (OG 1040, ABV 3.9%)
A very pale, full-bodied and well-rounded ale. Slightly sweet on the palate, with a generous late addition of Mount Hood hops for aroma.

Big Red Bitter (OG 1042, ABV 4%)
Deep red, malty Yorkshire bitter.

Silver King (OG 1041, ABV 4.3%) 🍺
A lager-style beer with a crisp, dry flavour and citrus fruity aroma.

Excelsior (OG 1051, ABV 5.2%)
A strong pale ale with a full, mellow flavour and a fresh, hoppy aroma with citrus/floral characteristics.

Otley

Otley Brewing Co Ltd, Unit 42, Albion Industrial Estate, Pontypridd, Mid Glamorgan, CF37 4NX
☎ (01443) 480555 ✉ info@otleybrewing.co.uk
⊕ otleybrewing.co.uk
Tours by arrangement

☺ Otley Brewing was set up during the summer of 2005. Since then the brewery has doubled in size and now supplies Mid, West, East Wales, Bristol and Bath. Seasonal beers: see website. Bottle-conditioned beers are also available.

Colombo (ABV 4%)

O1 (OG 1038, ABV 4%) ◆
A pale golden beer with a hoppy aroma. The taste has hops, malt, fruit and a thirst-quenching bitterness. A satisfying finish completes this beer.

Dark O (OG 1039.7, ABV 4.1%)
A medium bodied, easy-drinking mild/stout with chocolate and roasted barley flavours.

O2 (OG 1040.7, ABV 4.2%)
Golden-brown in colour, fruity with heavy floral aromas.

Boss (OG 1042.6, ABV 4.4%)

O-Garden (OG 1046.5, ABV 4.8%) 🍺

OG (OG 1052.3, ABV 5.4%) 🍺
A golden, honey-coloured ale, extremely smooth.

O8 (OG 1077.5, ABV 8%) 🍺🍺
A pale and strong ale, deceptively smooth.

Otter SIBA

Otter Brewery Ltd, Mathayes, Luppitt, Honiton, Devon, EX14 4SA
☎ (01404) 891285 ✉ info@otterbrewery.com
⊕ otterbrewery.com
Tours by arrangement

⊠ Otter Brewery was set up in 1990 by the McCaig family and has grown into one of the West Country's major producers of beers. The brewery is located in the Blackdown Hills, between Taunton and Honiton. 2009 saw the completion of Otter's 'eco cellar', partly underground and built with clay blocks and a grass roof. The beers are made from the brewery's own springs and are delivered to more than 500 pubs across the south-west including the family's first pub, the Holt, in Honiton. Seasonal beers: Mild (ABV 3.8%), Witch Otter/Otter Claus/McOtter/Cupid Otter (name varies) (ABV 5%).

Bitter (OG 1036, ABV 3.6%) ◆
Well-balanced amber session bitter with a fruity nose and bitter taste and aftertaste.

Amber (ABV 4%)
A finely balanced bitter with hints of tropical fruit and spice – sometimes with even an impression of ginger.

Bright (OG 1039, ABV 4.3%) ◆

Pale yellow/golden ale with a strong fruit aroma, sweet fruity taste and a bittersweet finish.

Ale (OG 1043, ABV 4.5%) ◆
A full-bodied best bitter. A malty aroma predominates with a fruity taste and finish.

Head (OG 1054, ABV 5.8%)
Fruity aroma and taste with a pleasant bitter finish. Dark brown and full-bodied.

Outlaw

See Roosters

Outstanding

Outstanding Brewing Co Ltd, Britannia Mill, Cobden Street, Bury, Lancashire, BL9 6AW
☎ (0161) 764 7723 ✉ info@outstandingbeers.co.uk
⊕ outstandingbeers.com

The brewery was set up as a collaboration between Paul Sandiford, Glen Woodcock and David Porter. The 15-barrel plant went into production in March 2008. Selective free trade accounts are supplied nationally. Lagers (Pilsner and Amber Bock) are also available as cask beer on request.

OSB (OG 1042, ABV 4.4%)
A mid range copper-coloured ale with a distinctive hop finish.

Blond (OG 1044, ABV 4.5%)
Pale and lightly bittered with citrus flavours and a floral nose.

Ginger (OG 1044, ABV 4.5%)
Light brown beer with a noticeable hint of ginger.

SOS (OG 1044, ABV 4.5%)
Light brown bitter, dry and intensely bitter.

Smoked Out (OG 1049, ABV 5%)
A brown ale brewed with traditional continental smoked lager malt.

White (OG 1048, ABV 5%)
A cloudy wheat beer with earthy, spicy, lemony flavours.

Standing Out (OG 1053, ABV 5.5%)
A pale golden ale, dry and bitter with lots of hop aroma.

Stout (OG 1057, ABV 5.5%)
Thick, jet black and bitter with liquorice overtones.

Pushing Out (OG 1065, ABV 7.4%)
A pale golden ale with a strong, distinctive dry, bitter flavour and a hop aroma.

Oxfordshire Ales

Bicester Beers & Minerals Ltd, 12 Pear Tree Farm Industrial Units, Bicester Road, Marsh Gibbon, Bicester, Oxfordshire, OX27 0GB
☎ (01869) 278765 ✉ bicesterbeers@tiscali.co.uk
⊕ oxfordshireales.co.uk
Tours by arrangement

⊠ The company first brewed in 2005. The five-barrel plant was previously at Picks Brewery but has now been upgraded to a 10-barrel plant with the purchase of a larger copper. It supplies 50-60 outlets as well as several wholesalers. Seasonal beers are produced.

Triple B (ABV 3.7%) ◆

This pale amber beer has a huge caramel aroma. The caramel diminishes in the initial taste, which changes to a fruit/bitter balance. This in turn leads to a long, refreshing, bitter aftertaste.

Pride of Oxfordshire (ABV 4.1%)
An amber beer, the aroma is butterscotch/caramel, which carries on into the initial taste. The taste then becomes bitter with sweetish/malty overtones. There is a long, dry, bitter finish.

Marshmellow (ABV 4.7%)
The slightly fruity aroma in this golden-amber beer leads to a hoppy but thin taste, with slight caramel notes. The aftertaste is short and bitter.

For Plough, Marsh Gibbon:

Ploughmans Pride (ABV 4.2%)

Palmer IFBB SIBA

JC & RH Palmer Ltd, The Old Brewery, West Bay Road, Bridport, Dorset, DT6 4JA
☎ (01308) 422396
✉ enquiries@palmersbrewery.com
palmersbrewery.com
Shop Mon-Sat 9am-6pm
Tours by arrangement (Please ring 01308 427500)

Palmers is Britain's only thatched brewery and dates from 1794. It is situated in Bridport, in the heart of the Jurassic Coast in south-west Dorset. The company continues to make substantial inventment in its 53 tenanted pubs, all serving cask ale. Around 400 outlets are supplied.

Copper Ale (OG 1036, ABV 3.7%)
Beautifully balanced, copper-coloured light bitter with a hoppy aroma.

Best Bitter (OG 1040, ABV 4.2%)
Hop aroma and bitterness stay in the background in this predominately malty best bitter, with some fruit on the aroma.

Dorset Gold (OG 1046, ABV 4.5%)
More complex than many golden ales thanks to a pleasant banana and mango fruitiness on the aroma that carries on into the taste and aftertaste.

200 (OG 1052, ABV 5%)
This is a big beer with a touch of caramel sweetness adding to a complex hoppy, fruit taste that lasts from the aroma well into the aftertaste.

Tally Ho! (OG 1057, ABV 5.5%)
A complex dark old ale. Roast malts and treacle toffee on the palate lead in to a long, lingering finish with more than a hint of coffee.

Paradise (NEW)

Paradise Coach House Ltd (Paradise Brewery), Bird in Hand, Trelissick Road, Hayle, Cornwall, TR27 4HY
☎ (01736) 753974
✉ birdinhand@paradisepark.org.uk
Tours by arrangement

Brewing first started in 1981 under the name Paradise Brewery, named after its location, the Paradise Bird Park. The name was changed to Wheal Ale in 1995. Brewing ceased in 2004 but re-started in 2009 under the original Paradise name.

IPA (OG 1035, ABV 3.3%)

Bitter (OG 1036, ABV 4.3%)

Artist Ale (OG 1048, ABV 5.6%)

Parish

Parish Brewery, 6 Main Street, Burrough on the Hill, Leicestershire, LE14 2JQ
☎ (01664) 454801 ☎ 07715 369410
✉ barrie@parishbrewery.orangehome.co.uk
Tours by arrangement

Parish began in 1983 and operates on a 20-barrel plant located in a 400-year-old building and former stables next to Grant's Freehouse, which is the main outlet for the full range of beers. In addition to the regular range, Poacher's Ale (ABV 6%), a blended ale comprising one part Baz's Bonce Blower and two parts PSB, is also available. Other local outlets are also supplied and special one-off brews are produced for beer festivals held across Leicestershire, Rutland and Cambridgeshire. Bottle-conditioned beers are also available.

PSB (OG 1039, ABV 3.9%)
Hoppy session beer with malty aftertaste.

Farm Gold (OG 1042, ABV 4.2%)
Light-coloured beer with distinctive hoppy taste and powerful aroma.

Burrough Bitter (OG 1048, ABV 4.8%)
Darker version of PSB with medium to strong bitterness and more pronounced malty aftertaste.

Baz's Bonce Blower (OG 1120, ABV 12%)
Strong, very dark beer with a very rich, malty character.

Patriot (NEW)

Patriot Brewery Ltd, Norman Knight, Whichford, Shipston-on-Stour, Warwickshire, CV36 5PE
☎ (01608) 684621 ✉ mwfindlay@btinternet.com

Patriot began in 2010 using a four-barrel brew plant. It is located next to the Norman Knight pub in the former Wizard Ales brewery building.

Missile (ABV 3.6%)

Heart of Oak (ABV 4%)

Bulldog (ABV 4.5%)

Peak Ales SIBA

Peak Ales, Barn Brewery, Chatsworth, Bakewell, Derbyshire, DE45 1EX
☎ (01246) 583737 ✉ info@peakales.co.uk
peakales.co.uk
Tours by arrangement

Peak Ales opened in 2005 in converted, former derelict farm buildings on the Chatsworth estate, with the aid of a DEFRA Rural Enterprise Scheme grant, with support from trustees of Chatsworth Settlement. The brewery supplies around 30 local outlets and selected distributors. Seasonal beer: Noggin Filler (ABV 5%, winter).

Swift Nick (OG 1038, ABV 3.8%)
Surprisingly complex for its strength. Easy-drinking, copper-coloured beer with initial flavours of caramel and malt, giving way to bitterness in the finish and aftertaste.

Bakewell Best Bitter (OG 1041, ABV 4.2%)
Full bodied, easy-drinking bitter. Well-balanced with an initial sweetness, which leads to a pleasantly dry finish.

Chatsworth Gold (ABV 4.6%)

THE BREWERIES

Interesting speciality beer made with honey, which comes through in the taste and aroma, giving a pleasant sweetness balanced by a hop and malt finish.

DPA (OG 1045, ABV 4.6%) ◆
Subtle best bitter that is deceptively strong. Flavours of fruit, hops and malt build slowly towards a well-balanced bittersweet finish.

Peakstones Rock

Peakstones Rock Brewery, Peakstones Farm, Cheadle Road, Alton, Staffordshire, ST10 4DH
☎ 07891 350908 🌐 peakstonesrock.co.uk
Tours by arrangement

⊗ Peakstones Rock was established in 2005 on a purpose-built, five-barrel plant in an old farm building. It was expanded to a 10-barrel plant in 2008 and added additional fermentation vessels to keep up with demand. 60-70 outlets are supplied direct.

Nemesis (OG 1042, ABV 3.8%) ◆
Gentle caramel and hop aroma from the pale brown body; sweet start then hops and a touch of roast. Gentle finish.

Chained Oak (OG 1045, ABV 4.2%)
A copper-coloured beer with a bitter finish and hop aroma.

Alton Abbey (OG 1051, ABV 4.5%)

Black Hole (OG 1048, ABV 4.8%)

Oblivion (OG 1055, ABV 5.5%)

Peerless

Peerless Brewing Co Ltd, The Brewery, 8 Pool Street, Birkenhead, Merseyside, CH41 3NL
☎ (0151) 647 7688
✉ brewer@peerlessbrewing.co.uk
🌐 peerlessbrewing.co.uk
Tours by arrangement (groups only)

Peerless began brewing in 2009 and is under the directorship of Steve Briscoe. Beers are sold through festivals, local pubs and the free trade. Seasonal beers are available.

Dark Arts (ABV 4.1%)
A complex black beer with hints of coffee and chocolate.

Hilbre Gold (ABV 4.5%)
A hoppy golden ale.

Storr Lager (OG 1048, ABV 4.8%)
A pale and hoppy cask lager.

Red Rocks (OG 1050, ABV 5%)
A strong ruby ale.

Full Whack (ABV 6%)
A strong pale ale with a fruity hop finish.

Penlon Cottage

Penlon Cottage Brewery, Penlon Farm, Pencae, Llanarth, Ceredigion, SA47 0QN
☎ (01545) 580022 ✉ beer@penlon.biz 🌐 penlon.biz

Penlon opened in 2004 and is located on a working smallholding in the Ceredigion coastal region of West Wales. Hops and malting barley are part of a programme of self-sufficiency, with grain, yeast and beer fed to pigs, sheep and chickens on the holding. It is the only Welsh brewery to have won the prestigious Wales True Taste awards twice for the best alcoholic drinks category. Bottle-conditioned beers: Lambs Gold Light Ale (ABV 3.2%), Tipsy Tup Pale Ale (ABV 3.8%), Heather Honey Ale (ABV 4.2%), Torddu Light Fruit Beer (ABV 4.2%), Chocolate Stout (ABV 4.5%), Torwen Dark Fruit Beer (ABV 4.5%), Stock Ram Stout (ABV 4.6%), Twin Ram IPA (ABV 4.8%), Ewes Frolic Lager (ABV 5.2%), Gimmers Mischief Premium Ale (ABV 5.2%), Ramnesia Strong Ale (ABV 5.6%). All bottled beers are suitable for vegetarians and vegans.

Cardi Bay Best Bitter (OG 1048, ABV 4%)

Pennine

See Rossendale

Penpont

Penpont Brewery, Inner Trenarrett, Altarnun, Launceston, Cornwall, PL15 7SY
☎ (01566) 86069 ✉ info@penpontbrewery.co.uk
🌐 penpontbrewery.co.uk
Tours by arrangement

⊗ Penpont opened in late 2008. Beers are available in outlets across Cornwall and at beer festivals. Seasonal beers: Silent Night (ABV 4.5%, winter), Blisland Gold (ABV 3.7%), Penpont Porter (ABV 5.8%, winter), Moorland IPA (ABV 6.3%). All beers are also available bottle conditioned.

St Nonna's (ABV 3.7%)

Cornish Arvor (ABV 4%)

Roughtor (ABV 4.7%)

Penzance

Penzance Brewing Company, Star Inn, Crowlas, Penzance, Cornwall, TR20 8DX
☎ (01736) 740375

Penzance began brewing in June 2008 on a five-barrel plant. The brewery is situated in the yard of the Star Inn. The beers are produced by owner Peter Elvin, who was head brewer for Cotleigh Brewery for 16 years. Beer is mostly produced for the pub but can be found at many beer festivals.

Crowlas Bitter (OG 1037, ABV 3.8%) ◆
Copper session bitter with good balance of malt, hops and citrus in the mouth. The aroma promises hops and malt, while the finish carries malt with dry bitterness.

Potion No 9 (OG 1039, ABV 4%) ◆
Citrus marmalade hops dominate the nose and taste of this smooth golden ale. Bitterness rises in taste and dominates the finish, which is balanced by sweetness and astringency.

Crows-an-Wra (OG 1041, ABV 4.3%) ◆
Rich aroma perfumed with citrus and elderflower. A golden ale well balanced with bitterness, grapefruit and a little malt in the mouth followed by a long, bitter finish.

Scilly Stout (OG 1067, ABV 7%)
Strong stout with a hint of chocolate.

Phipps NBC

See Grainstore

Phoenix

Oak Brewing Co Ltd t/a Phoenix Brewery, Green Lane, Heywood, Greater Manchester, OL10 2EP
☎ (01706) 627009 ✉ tony@phoenixbrewery.co.uk

⊕ A company established as Oak Brewery in 1982 at Ellesmere Port, it moved in 1991 to the old Phoenix Brewery and adopted the name. It now supplies 400-500 outlets with additional deliveries via wholesalers. Many seasonal beers are produced throughout the year. Restoration of the old brewery, built in 1897, is now complete.

Hopsack (OG 1038, ABV 3.8%)
A light-drinking, hoppy session beer.

Navvy (OG 1039, ABV 3.8%) ◆
Amber beer with a citrus fruit and malt nose. Good balance of citrus fruit, malt and hops with bitterness coming through in the aftertaste.

Monkeytown Mild (OG 1039, ABV 3.9%)

Arizona (OG 1040, ABV 4.1%) ◆
Yellow in colour with a fruity and hoppy aroma. A refreshing beer with citrus, hops and good bitterness, and a shortish dry aftertaste.

Spotland Gold (OG 1041, ABV 4.1%)
A pale, hoppy beer with a lingering bitter finish.

Pale Moonlight (OG 1042, ABV 4.2%)

Black Bee (OG 1045, ABV 4.5%)

White Monk (OG 1045, ABV 4.5%) ◆
Yellow beer with a citrus fruit aroma, plenty of fruit, hops and bitterness in the taste, and a hoppy, bitter finish.

Thirsty Moon (OG 1046, ABV 4.6%) ◆
Tawny beer with a fresh citrus aroma. Hoppy, fruity and malty with a dry, hoppy finish.

West Coast IPA (OG 1046, ABV 4.6%) ◆
Golden in colour with a hoppy, fruity nose. Strong hoppy and fruity taste and aftertaste with good bitterness throughout.

Double Gold (OG 1050, ABV 5%)

Wobbly Bob (OG 1060, ABV 6%) ⟐ ◆
A red/brown beer with malty, fruity aroma and creamy mouthfeel. Strongly malty and fruity in flavour, with hops and a hint of herbs. Both sweetness and bitterness are evident throughout.

Pictish

Pictish Brewing Co Ltd, Unit 9, Canalside Industrial Estate, Rochdale, Greater Manchester, OL16 5LB
☎ (01706) 522227 ✉ mail@pictish-brewing.co.uk
⊕ pictish-brewing.co.uk

⊕ The brewery was established in 2000 by Richard Sutton and supplies 60 free trade outlets in the north-west and west Yorkshire. Seasonal beers: see website.

Brewers Gold (OG 1038, ABV 3.8%) ◆
Yellow in colour, with a hoppy, fruity nose. Soft maltiness and a strong hop/citrus flavour lead to a dry, bitter finish.

Alchemists Ale (OG 1043, ABV 4.3%) ◆
Yellow beer with generous hop and fruit on the nose and palate. Good bitter hop finish.

Pilgrim SIBA

Pilgrim Brewery, 11 West Street, Reigate, Surrey, RH2 9BL
☎ (01737) 222651
✉ pilgrimbrewery@googlemail.com ⊕ pilgrim.co.uk

⊗ Pilgrim was set up in 1982 in Woldingham, Surrey, and moved to Reigate in 1985. The original owner, Dave Roberts, is still in charge. Beers are sold mostly in the Surrey area to around 30 outlets. Seasonal beers: see website. Other beers are also produced occasionally.

Surrey Bitter (OG 1037, ABV 3.7%) ◆
Pineapple, grapefruit and spicy aromas in this well-balanced quaffing beer. Initial biscuity maltiness with a hint of vanilla give way to a hoppy bitterness that becomes more pronounced in a refreshing bittersweet finish.

Weald Ale (ABV 3.7%)

Moild (ABV 3.8%)

Templar (ABV 3.8%) ◆
Smoked malt dominates throughout this amber brew but balancing hop is also present and grows in intensity. Smooth to the palate with a dry finish.

Porter (OG 1040, ABV 4%) ◆
Black beer with a good balance of dark malts plus berry fruit flavours. Roast character present throughout to give a bitter finish. Some balancing hop throughout.

Progress (OG 1040, ABV 4%) ◆
A well-rounded tawny-coloured bitter. Predominantly sweet and malty with an underlying fruitiness and a hint of toffee. The flavour is well-balanced overall with a subdued bitterness. Little aroma and the aftertaste dissipates quickly.

Pitfield

Pitfield Brewery, Ashlyns Farm, Epping Road, North Weald, Epping, Essex, CM16 6RZ
☎ (0845) 833 1492 ✉ sales@pitfieldbeershop.co.uk
⊕ pitfieldbeershop.co.uk
Shop daily 10am-4pm
Tours by arrangement

⊗ After 24 years in London, Pitfield Brewery left the capital in 2006 and moved to new premises in Essex. It has since moved again to an organic farm with 25 acres of organic barley for the brewery's use. The beers are sold at farmers' and organic markets in the south-east of England. Pitfield also produces organic wines, cider and perry. The beers are on sale in the brewery shop (at North Weald) but the brewery itself is located further afield on the farm. Seasonal beers: St George's Ale (ABV 4.3%), 1896 Stock Ale (ABV 10%, Nov). All beers are organically produced to Soil Association standards and are vegan-friendly. Two further beers are produced using non-organic ingredients under the Epping Brewery name.

Dark Mild (OG 1036, ABV 3.4%)

Bitter (OG 1036, ABV 3.7%)

Lager (OG 1036, ABV 3.7%)

Shoreditch Stout (OG 1038, ABV 4%) ◆
Chocolate and a raisin fruitiness on the nose lead to a fruity roast flavour and a sweetish finish with a little bitterness.

East Kent Goldings (OG 1040, ABV 4.2%) ◆

A dry, yellow beer with bitter notes throughout and a faint hint of honey on the palate.

Eco Warrior (OG 1043, ABV 4.5%) ◆
Golden ale with a vivid, citrus hop aroma. The hop character is balanced with a delicate sweetness in the taste, followed by an increasingly bitter finish.

Red Ale (OG 1046, ABV 4.8%) ◆
Complex beer with a full, malty body and strong hop character.

1850 London Porter (OG 1048, ABV 5%) ◆
Big-tasting dark ale dominated by coffee and forest fruits. The finish is dry but not acrid.

N1 Wheat Beer (OG 1048, ABV 5%)

1837 India Pale Ale (OG 1065, ABV 7%)

1792 Imperial Stout (OG 1085, ABV 9.3%)

For Duke of Cambridge, Islington:

SB Bitter (OG 1036, ABV 3.7%)

For Epping Brewery:

Dark (OG 1039, ABV 3.4%)

Forest Bitter (OG 1036, ABV 3.7%)

Pitstop

Pitstop Brewery, Bellingers, Station Road, Grove, Oxfordshire, OX12 0DH
☎ (01235) 770548 ✉ peterfowler@bellinger.co.uk
Shop Mon-Sat 8am-9pm; Sun 10am-8pm
Tours by arrangement

⊗ Pitstop was established in 2008 on a one-barrel plant to supply the existing off-licence (Bellingers). Demand was so great that the brewery expanded to a five-barrel plant in 2009. Seasonal beers: Penelope (ABV 5%), The Brickyard (ABV 6%), Last Lap (ABV 9%), Bitumen (ABV 10%).

Star (OG 1041, ABV 3.8%)

Pace Car (OG 1043, ABV 4%)

Grand Prix (OG 1046, ABV 4.5%)

Pole Position (OG 1053, ABV 5%)

Monaco (OG 1055, ABV 5.5%)

Sump (OG 1076, ABV 7%)

Plain Ales

Plain Ales Brewery, 17c Deverill Trading Estate, Sutton Veny, Wiltshire, BA12 7BZ
☎ (01985) 841481 ✉ james@plainales.co.uk
⊕ plainales.co.uk
Tours by arrangement

Plain Ales started production in 2008 on a 2.5-barrel plant and expanded in 2010 to a 10-barrel plant. More than 150 outlets are supplied direct.

Innocence (ABV 4%)
A straw-coloured, fragrant bitter.

Innspiration (ABV 4%)
A traditional, copper-coloured, easy-drinking bitter.

Inndulgence (ABV 4.5%)
A dark ruby porter with coffee, chocolate and a hint of smoke.

Plassey SIBA

Plassey Brewery, Eyton, Wrexham, LL13 0SP

☎ (01978) 781111 ☎ 07050 327127
✉ plassey@globalnet.co.uk ⊕ plasseybrewery.co.uk
Shop open office hours
Tours by arrangement

The brewery was founded in 1985 on the 250-acre Plassey Estate, which also incorporates a touring caravan park, craft centres, a golf course, three licensed outlets for Plassey's ales, and a brewery shop. Some 30 free trade outlets are also supplied. Seasonal beer: Ruddy Rudolph (ABV 4.5%, Xmas).

Original Border Mild (ABV 3.6%)

Welsh Border Exhibition Ale (OG 1036, ABV 3.8%)

Bitter (OG 1041, ABV 4%) ◆
Full-bodied and distinctive best bitter. Good balance of hops and fruit flavours with a lasting dry, bitter aftertaste.

Offa's Dyke Ale (OG 1043, ABV 4.3%) ◆
Sweetish and fruity refreshing best bitter with caramel undertones. Some bitterness in the finish.

Owain Glyndwr's Ale (OG 1043, ABV 4.3%)

Fusilier (OG 1046, ABV 4.5%)

Cwrw Tudno (OG 1048, ABV 5%) ◆
A mellow, sweetish premium beer with classic Plassey flavours of fruit and hops.

Dragon's Breath (OG 1060, ABV 6%)
A fruity, strong bitter, smooth and quite sweet, though not cloying, with an intense, fruity aroma.

Plockton

Plockton Brewery, 5 Bank Street, Plockton, Ross-shire, IV52 8TP
☎ (01599) 544276
✉ andy@theplocktonbrewery.com
⊕ theplocktonbrewery.com
Tours by arrangement

⊗ The brewery started trading in 2007 and expanded to a 2.5-barrel plant in 2009. Bottle-conditioned beers are available and are suitable for vegetarians.

Crags Ale (OG 1042, ABV 4.3%) ◆
Light fruit and hop notes are present in taste and nose.

Plockton Bay (OG 1044, ABV 4.6%)
A well-balanced, tawny-coloured best bitter with plenty of hops and malt which give a bittersweet fruity flavour.

Starboard! (OG 1049, ABV 5.1%) ◆
A fine fruity golden ale with a light citrus bitterness. Hop and spicy fruit feature in the nose with a smack of grapefruit in the taste. The bitterness holds well into the aftertaste.

Poachers

Poachers Brewery, 439 Newark Road, North Hykeham, Lincolnshire, LN6 9SP
☎ (01522) 807404 ☎ 07959 229638
⊕ poachersbrewery.co.uk
Tours by arrangement

Brewing started in 2001 on a five-barrel plant. In 2006 it was downsized to a 2.5-barrel plant and relocated by brewer George Batterbee at the rear of his house. Regular outlets are supplied throughout Lincolnshire and surrounding counties; outlets further afield are supplied via wholesalers. Seasonal beer: Santas Come (ABV 6.5%, Xmas).

Bottle-conditioned beers are also available.

Trembling Rabbit Mild (OG 1034, ABV 3.4%)
Rich, dark mild with a smooth malty flavour and a slightly bitter finish.

Shy Talk Bitter (OG 1037, ABV 3.7%)
Clean-tasting session beer, pale gold in colour; slightly bitter finish, dry hopped.

Poachers Pride (OG 1040, ABV 4%)
Amber bitter brewed using Cascade hops that produce a fine flavour and aroma that lingers.

Bog Trotter (OG 1042, ABV 4.2%)
A malty, earthy-tasting best bitter.

Poachers Trail (OG 1042, ABV 4.2%)
A flowery hop-nosed, mid-brown beer with a well-balanced but bitter taste that stays with the malt, becoming more apparent in the drying finish.

Billy Boy (OG 1044, ABV 4.4%)
A mid-brown beer hopped with Fuggles and Mount Hood.

Black Crow Stout (OG 1045, ABV 4.5%)
Dry stout with burnt toffee and caramel flavour.

Hare Repie (OG 1045, ABV 4.5%)
A golden-coloured, sweet smelling ale; dry in flavour.

Poachers Dick (OG 1045, ABV 4.5%)
Ruby-red bitter, smooth fruity flavour balanced by the bitterness of Goldings hops.

Jock's Trap (OG 1050, ABV 5%)
A strong, pale brown bitter; hoppy and well-balanced with a slightly dry fruit finish.

Trout Tickler (OG 1055, ABV 5.5%)
Ruby bitter with intense flavour and character, sweet undertones with a hint of chocolate.

Porter

See Outstanding

Port Mahon

See Little Ale Cart

Potbelly

Potbelly Brewery Ltd, Sydney Street Entrance, Kettering, Northamptonshire, NN16 0JA
☎ (01536) 410818 ☎ 07834 867825
✉ toni@potbelly-brewery.co.uk
potbelly-brewery.co.uk
Tours by arrangement

Potbelly started brewing in 2005 on a 10-barrel plant and supply some 200 outlets. The brewery has won more than 30 awards for its beers in only five years of brewing. Seasonal beers: see website. Bottle-conditioned beers are also available.

Best (OG 1036.5, ABV 3.8%)

Aisling (OG 1038.5, ABV 4.4%)

Beijing Black (OG 1045, ABV 4.4%)

Pigs Do Fly (OG 1041, ABV 4.4%)

Crazydaze (OG 1050, ABV 5.5%)

Potton SIBA

Potton Brewery Co Ltd, 10 Shannon Place, Potton, Bedfordshire, SG19 2SP
☎ (01767) 261042 ✉ info@potton-brewery.co.uk
potton-brewery.co.uk

Set up by the late Clive Towner and Bob Hearson in 1998, it was Potton's first brewery since 1922. The brewery expanded from 20 barrels a week to 50 in 2004 and further expansion is now taking place. Around 150 outlets are supplied. Seasonal beers: Bunny Hops (ABV 4.1%, Mar-Apr), Fallen Angel (ABV 4.8%, Nov-Dec). Bottle-conditioned beers are also available.

Shannon IPA (OG 1035, ABV 3.6%)
A well-balanced session bitter with good bitterness and fruity late-hop character.

Penny Bitter (ABV 4%)
A dark, malty bitter with a light, hoppy character.

Gold (OG 1040, ABV 4.1%)
Golden-coloured, refreshing beer with a spicy/ citrus late-hop character.

Shambles Bitter (OG 1043, ABV 4.3%)
A robust pale and heavily hopped beer with a subtle dry hop character imparted by Styrian Goldings.

Village Bike (OG 1042, ABV 4.3%)
Classic English premium bitter, amber in colour, heavily late-hopped.

Pride of Potton (OG 1057, ABV 6%)
Impressive, robust amber ale with a malty aroma, malt and ripe fruit in the mouth, and a fading sweetness.

Prescott

Prescott Brewery LLP, Unit 1, The Bramery Business Park, Alstone Lane, Cheltenham, Gloucestershire, GL51 8HE
☎ 07526 934866 ✉ info@prescottales.co.uk
prescottales.co.uk

Prescott started brewing in early 2009 on a 10-barrel plant.

Hill Climb (ABV 3.8%)

Track Record (ABV 4.4%)

Grand Prix (ABV 5.2%)

Preseli

Preseli Brewery, Unit 15, The Salterns, Tenby, Pembrokeshire, SA70 8EQ
☎ 07824 512103 ✉ preseli-brewery@hotmail.com
preseli-brewery.co.uk

Preseli began brewing in 2009 on a six-barrel plant.

Even Keel (OG 1038, ABV 3.8%)

Old Mariners (OG 1040, ABV 4%)

Rocky Bottom (OG 1040, ABV 4%)

Baggywrinkle (OG 1045, ABV 4.5%)

Prestonpans SIBA

Prestonpans Ales, 227-229 High Street, Prestonpans, East Lothian, EH32 9BE

☎ (01875) 819922 ☎ 07974 740248
✉ pans.ales@virginmedia.com
⊕ prestoungrange.org
Tours by arrangement

Prestonpans Ales opened as Fowler's in 2004 during the refurbishment of the Prestoungrange Gothenburg, the adjacent pub. After a period of inactivity, Roddy Beveridge, a member of the Scottish Craft Brewers, continued the range of beers left by the previous brewer with some twists. The Prestoungrange Gothenburg offers all the beers, which are also distributed to pubs in Edinburgh and the Lothians and throughout Britain. Seasonal beers are brewed.

Prestonpans IPA (OG 1041, ABV 4.1%)
Light, crisp, refreshing malt with complex hop bitterness and a dry hop aroma.

Prestonpans 80/- (OG 1042, ABV 4.2%)
Complex malt with marked caramel notes and solid bitterness with a green hoppy finish.

Gothenburg Porter (OG 1043, ABV 4.4%)
Pronounced roast barley character and a long, dark chocolate and espresso coffee finish.

Princetown

See Dartmoor

Prior's Well (NEW)

Prior's Well Brewery, The Old Kennels, Clumber Park, Hardwick Village, Nottinghamshire, S80 3PB
☎ 07971 277598

A sister brewery to Maypole, established in early 2010 on the Clumber Park Estate. Housed in the former estate kennels, built in 1891 for the then Duchess, which were abandoned in the mid-1960s and have now been sympathetically restored by the National Trust, who own the property. The 5.5-barrel plant was previously used at Tydd Steam and before that Oldershaws Brewery. Natural Clumber water from the estate is used in the brewing process. Bottle-conditioned beers are planned. The beer list was not finalised at the time of going to press.

Prospect SIBA

Prospect Brewery Ltd, Unit 11, Bradley Hall Trading Estate, Bradley Lane, Standish, Wigan, Lancashire, WN6 0XQ
☎ (01257) 421329 ✉ sales@prospectbrewery.com
⊕ prospectbrewery.com
Tours by arrangement

⊛Brewing commenced in 2007 on a five-barrel plant from Bank Top Brewery. The brewery was originally situated at the top of Prospect Hill – hence the name – but moved to new premises in 2010 using a 12-barrel plant. The beers are named along prospecting/mining themes. More than 150 outlets are supplied direct. Seasonal beers: Clementine (ABV 5%, late Nov-Jan), Pickaxe (ABV 5%, Oct-Jan). Bottle-conditioned beers are also available.

Silver Tally (OG 1037, ABV 3.7%)

Nutty Slack (OG 1039, ABV 3.9%) ◆
Dark brown mild ale with malt and fruit in the aroma. Creamy and chocolatey on the palate, with

both malt and fruit in evidence. Malty and moderately bitter finish.

Pioneer (OG 1040, ABV 4%)

Big Brew (OG 1041, ABV 4.1%)

Giants Hall (OG 1041, ABV 4.1%)

Blinding Light (OG 1042, ABV 4.2%)

Gold Rush (OG 1045, ABV 4.5%)

Purity

Purity Brewing Co Ltd, The Brewery, Upper Spernall Farm, Great Alne, Warwickshire, B49 6JF
☎ (01789) 488007 ✉ sales@puritybrewing.com
⊕ puritybrewing.com
Shop Mon-Fri 8am-5pm; Sat 10am-1pm
Tours by arrangement

⊛ Brewing began in 2005 in a purpose-designed plant housed in converted barns in the heart of Warwickshire. The brewery incorporates an environmentally-friendly effluent treatment system. It supplies the free trade within a 50-mile radius and delivers to over 300 outlets.

Pure Gold (OG 1039.5, ABV 3.8%) 🍺 🍺

Mad Goose (OG 1042.5, ABV 4.2%)

Pure Ubu (OG 1044.8, ABV 4.5%)

Purple Moose SIBA

Bragdy Mws Piws Cyf/Purple Moose Brewery Ltd, Madoc Street, Porthmadog, Gwynedd, LL49 9DB
☎ (01766) 515571 ✉ beer@purplemoose.co.uk
⊕ purplemoose.co.uk
Shop Mon-Fri 9am-5pm
Tours by arrangement

A 10-barrel plant opened in 2005 by Lawrence Washington in a former saw mill and farmers' warehouse in the coastal town of Porthmadog. The names of the beers reflect local history and geography. The brewery now supplies around 150 outlets. Seasonal and monthly special beers: see website.

**Cwrw Eryri/Snowdonia Ale
(OG 1035.3, ABV 3.6%)** 🍺 🍺 ◆
Golden, refreshing bitter with citrus fruit hoppiness in aroma and taste. The full mouthfeel leads to a long-lasting, dry, bitter finish.

**Cwrw Madog/Madog's Ale
(OG 1037, ABV 3.7%)** ◆
Full-bodied session bitter. Malty nose and an initial nutty flavour but bitterness dominates. Well balanced and refreshing with a dry roastiness on the taste and a good dry finish.

**Cwrw Glaslyn/Glaslyn Ale
(OG 1040.5, ABV 4.2%)** ◆
Refreshing light and malty amber-coloured ale. Plenty of hop in the aroma and taste. Good smooth mouthfeel leading to a slightly chewy finish.

**Ochr Tywyll y Mws/Dark Side of the Moose
(OG 1045, ABV 4.6%)**
A delicious dark ale with a deep malt flavour and a fruity bitterness.

Quantock

Quantock Brewery, Unit E, Monument View, Summerfield Avenue, Chelston Business Park, Wellington, Somerset, TA21 9ND
☎ (01823) 662669 ✉ rob@quantockbrewery.co.uk
🌐 quantockbrewery.co.uk

Quantock began brewing in 2008 on an eight-barrel plant. Bottle-conditioned beers are available.

Ale (ABV 3.8%)

Sunraker (ABV 4.2%)

Wills Neck (ABV 4.3%)

Stout (ABV 4.5%)

White Hind (ABV 4.5%)

Royal Stag IPA (ABV 6%)

UXB (ABV 9%)

Quartz

Quartz Brewing Ltd, Archers, Alrewas Road, Kings Bromley, Staffordshire, DE13 7HW
☎ (01543) 473965

2nd Brewery: Unit 18, Heart of the Country Village, London Road, Swinfen, Staffordshire, WS14 9QR
✉ scott@quartzbrewing.co.uk
🌐 quartzbrewing.co.uk
Shop Tue-Sun 10am-5pm (Fri 8pm, Apr-Dec)
Tours by arrangement

Quartz was established in 2005 by Scott and Julia Barnett and has two breweries near Lichfield. The brewery at Heart of the Country Craft Centre has a licensed visitor centre with a bar and shop. There are four regular beers produced in cask, bottle and mini-cask, supplemented with seasonal specials. Around 50 outlets are supplied direct.

Blonde (OG 1038, ABV 3.8%)
Little aroma, gentle hop and background malt. Sweet with unsophisticated sweetshop tastes.

Crystal (OG 1040, ABV 4.2%)
Sweet aroma with some fruit and yeasty Marmite hints. Hoppiness begins but dwindles to a bittersweet finish.

Extra Blonde (OG 1042, ABV 4.4%)
Sweet malty aroma with a touch of fruit. Sweet start, smooth with a hint of hops in the sugary finish.

Heart (OG 1045, ABV 4.6%)
Dark amber in colour with a spicy hop finish and a roasted character.

Quay

See Dorset

Quercus

Quercus Brewery & Beer House, Unit 2M, South Hams Business Park, Churchstow, Kingsbridge, Devon, TQ7 3QH
☎ (01548) 854888 ✉ info@quercusbrewery.com
🌐 quercusbrewery.com
Shop Wed-Thu 12-5pm, Fri 10am-5pm, Sat 10am-3pm

Quercus began trading in summer 2007 and is a small, family-run brewery and specialist beer shop. The brewery has an eight-barrel brew length. 80 outlets are supplied direct. Seasonal beer: Sunstorm (ABV 4.8%).

Origin (OG 1039, ABV 3.9%)
A smooth, easy-drinking amber ale with the sweetness of the malt balanced by the refreshing aroma and taste of Fuggles hops.

Prospect (OG 1039, ABV 4%)
Subtle bitterness and sweet malt flavour with a rich aroma and colour.

Shingle Bay (OG 1041, ABV 4.2%)
A light, golden, easy-drinking ale with fruity citrus aroma and taste giving a subtle, crisp bite to refresh the palate.

QB (Quercus Bitter) (OG 1044, ABV 4.5%)
A full-bodied best bitter with a hint of oak-smoked aroma and taste.

Stormbrew (OG 1050, ABV 5%)
A very dark ruby porter full of malty sweetness. The flavour of the roasted malts gives way to a smooth, lingering, bitter finish.

QPA (OG 1058, ABV 5.8%)
A strong, crisp, pale ale full of hops and bitterness, balanced by a subtle sweetness and a hint of vanilla toffee.

Rainbow

Rainbow Inn & Brewery, 73 Birmingham Road, Allesley Village, Coventry, West Midlands, CV5 9GT
☎ (02476) 402888
Tours by arrangement

Rainbow was launched in 1994. Output is through the pub although nine-gallon casks and polypins can be ordered for home use or beer festivals.

Piddlebrook (OG 1040, ABV 4%)

Ramsbury SIBA

Ramsbury Estates Ltd, Priory Farm, Axford, Marlborough, Wiltshire, SN8 2HA
☎ (01672) 520647/541407
✉ dgolding@ramsburyestates.com
🌐 ramsburybrewery.com
Tours by arrangement

Ramsbury started brewing in 2004. Ramsbury Estates is a farming company covering approximately 5,500 acres of the Marlborough Downs in Wiltshire. It grows malting barley for the brewing industry including Optic, which the brewery also uses. Additional fermenters have been purchased and contract bottling taken on. Around 90 outlets are supplied. Seasonal beer: Deerhunter (ABV 5%, winter).

Bitter (OG 1036, ABV 3.6%)
Amber-coloured beer with a smooth, delicate aroma and flavour.

Sunsplash (ABV 4%)

Kennet Valley (OG 1040, ABV 4.1%)
A light amber, hoppy bitter with a long, dry finish.

Flint Knapper (OG 1041, ABV 4.2%)
Rich amber in colour with a malty taste.

Gold (OG 1043, ABV 4.5%)
A rich golden-coloured beer with a light hoppy aroma and taste.

Chalk Stream (ABV 5%)

Rum Truffle (ABV 5.6%)

Ramsgate SIBA

Ramsgate Brewery Ltd, 1 Hornet Close, Pyson's Road Industrial Estate, Broadstairs, Kent, CT10 2YD
☎ (01843) 868453 ✉ info@ramsgatebrewery.co.uk
🌐 ramsgatebrewery.co.uk
Shop Mon-Fri 9am-5pm
Tours by arrangement

⊗ Ramsgate was established in 2002 in a derelict sea-front restaurant. In 2006 the brewery moved to its current location, allowing for increased capacity and bottling. Further expansion is planned for 2011 due to increased demand. Bottle-conditioned beers are available and are suitable for vegans. Seasonal and monthly specials: see website.

Gadds' No. 7 Bitter Ale (OG 1037, ABV 3.8%)

Gadds' Seasider (OG 1042, ABV 4.3%)

Gadds' No. 5 Best Bitter Ale (OG 1043, ABV 4.4%)

Gadds' No. 3 Kent Pale Ale (OG 1047, ABV 5%)

Gadds' Faithful Dogbolter Porter (OG 1054, ABV 5.6%)

Randalls SIBA

RW Randall Ltd, La Piette Brewery, St Georges Esplanade, St Peter Port, Guernsey, GY1 2BH
☎ (01481) 720134 ✉ tours@rwrandall.co.uk
🌐 randallsbrewery.co.uk
Tours by arrangement

Randalls has been brewing since 1868 and was bought in 2006 by a group of private investors. It moved a few years ago to new premises with a 36-barrel brewhouse. 18 pubs are owned and a further 50 outlets are supplied.

Patois (OG 1045, ABV 4.5%)

Raw (NEW)

Raw Brewing Co Ltd, Units 3 & 4, Silver House, Adelphi Way, Staveley, Derbyshire, S43 3LJ
☎ (01246) 475445 ✉ contact@rawbrew.com
🌐 rawbrew.com
Tours by arrangement

⊗ Raw began brewing in 2010 using a five-barrel plant from Prospect Brewery of Wigan. Three core beers are available with plans to extend the range and produce seasonal specials.

Blonde Pale (OG 1039, ABV 3.9%)

Dark Peak (OG 1045, ABV 4.5%)

Grey Ghost (OG 1058, ABV 5.9%)

RCH SIBA

RCH Brewery, West Hewish, Weston-Super-Mare, Somerset, BS24 6RR
☎ (01934) 834447 ✉ rchbrew@aol.com
🌐 rchbrewery.com

⊗ The brewery was originally installed in the early 1980s behind the Royal Clarence Hotel at Burnham-on-Sea. Since 1993 brewing has taken place in a former cider mill at West Hewish. A 30-barrel plant was installed in 2000. RCH supplies 150 outlets and the award-winning beers are available nationwide through its own wholesaling company, which also distributes beers from other small independent breweries. Seasonal beers: see website. Bottle-conditioned beers are also available.

Hewish IPA (OG 1036, ABV 3.6%)
Light, hoppy bitter with some malt and fruit, though slightly less fruit in the finish. Floral citrus hop aroma; pale/brown amber colour.

PG Steam (OG 1039, ABV 3.9%)
Amber-coloured, medium-bodied with a floral hop aroma. Bitter citrus taste with a hint of sweetness.

Pitchfork (OG 1043, ABV 4.3%)
Yellow, grapefruit-flavoured bitter bursting with citrus with underlying sweetness.

Old Slug Porter (OG 1046, ABV 4.5%)
Chocolate, coffee, roast malt and hops with lots of body and dark fruits. A complex, rich beer, dark brown in colour.

East Street Cream (OG 1050, ABV 5%)
Pale brown strong bitter. Flavours of roast malt and fruit with a bittersweet finish.

Double Header (OG 1053, ABV 5.3%)
Light brown, full-bodied strong bitter. Beautifully balanced flavours of malt, hops and tropical fruits are followed by a long, bittersweet finish. Refreshing and easy-drinking for its strength.

Firebox (OG 1060, ABV 6%)
An aroma and taste of citrus hops and pale crystal malt are followed by a strong, complex, full-bodied, mid-brown beer with a well-balanced flavour of malt and hops.

Reality (NEW)

Reality Brewery, 5b Factory Lane, Beeston, Nottingham, NG9 4AA
☎ 07801 539523

Reality began brewing in 2010 using a 2.5-barrel plant.

Virtuale Reality (ABV 3.8%)

Bitter Reality (ABV 4.4%)

Rebellion SIBA

Rebellion Beer Co, Marlow Brewery, Bencombe Farm, Marlow Bottom, Buckinghamshire, SL7 3LT
☎ (01628) 476594 ✉ info@rebellionbeer.co.uk
🌐 rebellionbeer.co.uk
Shop Mon-Fri 8am-6pm; Sat 9am-6pm
Tours by arrangement (1st Tue of the month 7.15pm – £10 per head)

⊗ Established in 1993, Rebellion has filled the void left when Wethereds ceased brewing in 1987 at Marlow. A steady growth in fortunes led to larger premises being sought and, following relocation in 1999, the brewery has gone from strength to strength and maximised output. Rebellion's nearby Three Horseshoes pub is the brewery tap. Rebellion Mild is exclusive to this pub. Around 200 other outlets are supplied. Seasonal beers: see website. Bottle-conditioned beer is also available.

Mild (OG 1035, ABV 3.5%)

IPA (OG 1039, ABV 3.7%) ◆
Copper-coloured bitter, sweet and malty, with resinous and red apple flavours. Caramel and fruit decline to leave a dry, bitter and malty finish.

Smuggler (OG 1042, ABV 4.1%) ◆
A red-brown beer, well-bodied and bitter with an uncompromisingly dry, bitter finish.

Mutiny (OG 1046, ABV 4.5%) ◆
Tawny in colour, this full-bodied best bitter is predominantly fruity and moderately bitter with crystal malt continuing to a dry finish.

Rectory SIBA

Rectory Ales Ltd, Streat Hill Farm, Streat Hill, Streat, Hassocks, East Sussex, BN6 8RP
☎ (01273) 890570 ✉ rectoryales@hotmail.com
Tours by arrangement (Easter-Sep)

⊗ Rectory was founded in 1995 by the Rector of Plumpton, the Rev Godfrey Broster, to generate funds for the maintenance of his three parish churches. 107 parishioners are shareholders. The brewing capacity is now 20 barrels a week. All outlets are supplied from the brewery. A different seasonal beer is produced each month – please ring for details.

Rector's Bitter (OG 1040, ABV 4%)

Rector's Light Relief (OG 1045, ABV 4.5%)

Parson's Porter (OG 1050, ABV 5%)

Rector's Old Ale (OG 1050, ABV 5%)

The Rector's Revenge (OG 1050, ABV 5%)

Redemption SIBA (NEW)

Redemption Brewing Co Ltd, Unit 2, Compass West Industrial Estate, 33 West Road, Tottenham, London, N17 0XL
☎ (020) 8885 5227
✉ andy.moffat@redemptionbrewing.co.uk
⊕ redemptionbrewing.co.uk

⊗ Redemption began brewing in 2010 on a 12-barrel plant.

Pale Ale (OG 1037.5, ABV 3.8%) ◆
Refreshing amber bitter, with sweetness on the palate balanced by floral hops and a bitterness that develops in the long aftertaste. Nose has citrus, peach and then hops.

Urban Dusk (OG 1044, ABV 4.6%) ◆
Mocha is present throughout in this full-flavoured, creamy, tawny-coloured beer. Strong fruit on the palate but this fades in the dry, bitter finish.

Red Fox

Red Fox Brewery Ltd, The Chicken Sheds, Upp Hall Farm, Salmons Lane, Coggeshall, Essex, CO6 1RY
☎ (01376) 563123 ✉ info@redfoxbrewery.co.uk
⊕ redfoxbrewery.co.uk
Tours by arrangement

⊗ Red Fox began brewing in 2008 on a five-barrel plant and has since taken on extra members of staff to cope with increased demand. Around 35 outlets are supplied direct. Bottle-conditioned beer is available as are seasonals including Arctic Fox (ABV 4.5%).

Mild (OG 1037, ABV 3.6%)
A dark, full-flavoured mild.

IPA (OG 1038, ABV 3.7%)
A copper-coloured ale with a dry aftertaste.

Bitter (OG 1039, ABV 3.8%)
A traditional-style beer.

Hunter's Gold (OG 1040, ABV 3.9%)
An aromatic golden beer.

Black Fox Porter (OG 1046, ABV 4.8%)
A rich-flavoured black beer.

Wily Ol' Fox (OG 1050, ABV 5.2%)
A very aromatic amber beer made from English hops and malt.

Red Rat

Red Rat Craft Brewery, c/o Denham Estate, Barrow Lane, Denham, Suffolk, IP29 5EQ
☎ (028) 481 1368 ☎ 07704 817632
✉ enquiries@redratcraftbrewery.co.uk
⊕ redratcraftbrewery.co.uk

Red Rat started brewing in 2007, and expanded in 2009 to a 10-barrel plant. Around 30 barrels are produced a week. The brewery also produces one-off customised brews on request. All beers are also available bottle conditioned.

Crazy Dog Blonde (ABV 4%)

Hadley's (ABV 4.2%)

Hot Stuff Chilli Beer (ABV 4.3%)

Crazy Dog IPA (ABV 5%)

Hadley's Gold (ABV 5%)

The Same Again (ABV 5.2%)

Crazy Dog Stout (ABV 6%)

Jimmy's Flying Pig (ABV 6%)

Jimmy's Large Black Pig (ABV 6%)

Red Rock

Red Rock Brewery Ltd, Higher Humber Farm, Bishopsteignton, Devon, TQ14 9TD
☎ (01626) 879738 ☎ 07894 035094
✉ john@redrockbrewery.co.uk
⊕ redrockbrewery.co.uk
Shop Mon-Fri 9am-4pm (phone for weekend hours)
Tours by arrangement

⊗ Red Rock first started brewing in 2006 with a four-barrel plant. It is based in a converted barn on a working farm using locally sourced malt, fresh hops and the farm's own spring water. All beers are also hand bottled (bottle conditioned) and labelled. Around 60 outlets are supplied. Seasonal beers: Christmas Cheer (ABV 5.2%, winter), Stocking Filler (ABV 4.5%, winter).

Humber Down (OG 1034, ABV 3.6%)

Back Beach (OG 1037, ABV 3.8%)

Lighthouse IPA (OG 1038, ABV 3.9%)

Red Rock (OG 1041, ABV 4.2%)

Drift Wood (OG 1042, ABV 4.3%)

Rushy Mede (OG 1043, ABV 4.4%)

Dark Ness (OG 1044, ABV 4.5%)

Break Water (OG 1045, ABV 4.6%)

Capstan (OG 1055, ABV 5.8%)

Red Rose

Red Rose Brewery, Royal Hotel, Station Road, Great Harwood, Lancashire, BB6 7BA
☎ (01254) 883541 ✉ beer@redrosebrewery.co.uk
redrosebrewery.co.uk
Tours by arrangement

Red Rose was launched in 2002 to supply the Royal Hotel, Great Harwood. Seasonal beers: Pissed Over Pendle Halloween Ale (ABV 4.4%, Oct-Nov), 34th Street Miracle Beer (ABV 4.5%, Dec-Jan), Cold Turkey (ABV 3.8%, Dec-Jan). Special beers are available throughout the year.

Bowley Best (ABV 3.7%)
Darkish northern bitter. Malty yet sharp with hoppy citrus finish.

Treacle Miners Tipple (ABV 3.9%)

Target (ABV 4%)

Festival Ale (ABV 4.1%)

Mel'n Collie (ABV 4.1%)

Felix (ABV 4.2%)
Dry, pale and remarkably hoppy with a keen nose, yet rounded and smooth with a lingering finish.

Old Ben (ABV 4.3%)
Pale, clean-tasting, crisp beer with a strong hop presence and no sweetness.

Lancashire & Yorkshire Aleway/ Steaming (ABV 4.5%)
Copper-coloured, strong beer. Initially sweet and malty, with a good hop aroma. Full and fruity.

Paddy O'Hackers Genuine Irish Stout (ABV 4.6%)

Older Empire (ABV 5.5%)

Caretaker of History (ABV 6%)
A dark, strong ale with a roast malt aroma. The taste is complex, rich and warming. Well-balanced and drinkable.

Redscar

Redscar Brewery Ltd, c/o The Cleveland Hotel, 9-11 High Street West, Redcar, TS10 1SQ
☎ 07828 855146 ✉ chris.appleby@ntlworld.com
redscar-brewery.co.uk
Tours by arrangement

Redscar first brewed in early 2008 on a 2.5-barrel plant. The brewery supplies the hotel, local pubs and beer festivals.

Sands (OG 1043, ABV 4.2%)

Pier (OG 1046, ABV 4.5%)

Rocks (OG 1045, ABV 4.5%)

Beach (OG 1050, ABV 5%)

Red Shoot

Red Shoot Inn & Brewery, Toms Lane, Linwood, Ringwood, Hampshire, BH24 3QT
☎ (01425) 475792 ✉ redshoot@wadworth.co.uk
redshoot.co.uk

The 2.5-barrel brewery, owned by Wadworth, was commissioned in 1998. In summer the brewery works to capacity, half the output going to the pub and half to other local outlets, being distributed by Wadworth. Seasonal beer: Forest Grump (ABV 3.6%, winter).

New Forest Gold (ABV 3.8%)

Muddy Boot (ABV 4.2%)

Tom's Tipple (ABV 4.8%)

Red Squirrel

Red Squirrel Brewery, 14b Mimram Road, Hertford, SG14 1NN
☎ (01992) 501100
✉ gary@redsquirrelbrewery.co.uk
redsquirrelbrewery.co.uk

Red Squirrel started brewing in 2004 using a 10-barrel plant. Seasonal and monthly specials are produced as are bottle-conditioned beers. Around 100 outlets are supplied in addition to the brewery's own pub, the Sportsman in Croxley Green.

RSX (OG 1038, ABV 3.9%)

Conservation Bitter (OG 1040, ABV 4.1%)

West Coast Stout (OG 1042, ABV 4.3%)

London Porter (OG 1048, ABV 5%)

Colorado American IPA (OG 1051, ABV 5.4%)

White Mountain American IPA (OG 1051, ABV 5.4%)

Rhymney

Rhymney Brewery Ltd, Unit A2, Valley Enterprise Centre, Pant Industrial Estate, Dowlais, Merthyr Tydfil, CF48 2SR
☎ (01685) 722253
✉ enquiries@rhymneybreweryltd.com
rhymneybreweryltd.com
Shop Sat 10am-2pm
Tours by arrangement

Rhymney first brewed in 2005. The 75-hl plant, sourced from Canada, is capable of producing both cask and keg beers. Around 220 outlets are supplied.

Best (OG 1037, ABV 3.7%)

Hobby Horse (OG 1038, ABV 3.8%)

Centenary Ale 1905 (OG 1039, ABV 3.9%)

Dark (OG 1040, ABV 4%)

Bevans Bitter (OG 1042, ABV 4.2%)

Bitter (OG 1043, ABV 4.3%)

General Picton (OG 1043, ABV 4.3%)

Premier Lager (OG 1044, ABV 4.4%)

Silver Drum (OG 1044, ABV 4.4%)

Export Ale (OG 1050, ABV 5%)

Richmond

Richmond Brewing Co Ltd, The Station Brewery, Richmond, North Yorkshire, DL10 4LD
☎ (01748) 828266 ✉ andy@richmondbrewing.co.uk
richmondbrewing.co.uk
Shop Tue-Sun 12-4pm (may be open outside these hours)
Tours by arrangement

Richmond opened in June 2008 and is situated in a multi million pound re-development of the listed Victorian station. The brewery concentrates on bottled ales with around 15% of the output cask conditioned. Richmond supplies the local area including Wetherspoons in Richmond and Harrogate.

Sw'Ale (OG 1035, ABV 3.7%)

Station Ale (OG 1039, ABV 4%)

Pale Ale (OG 1044, ABV 4.6%)

Stump Cross Ale (OG 1046, ABV 4.7%)

Ridgeside (NEW)

Ridgeside Brewing Co Ltd, Unit 24, Penraevon 2 Industrial Estate, Meanwood, Leeds, West Yorkshire, LS7 2AW
☎ 07595 380568
✉ simon.bolderson@ridgesidebrewery.co.uk
🌐 ridgesidebrewery.co.uk

Ridgeside began brewing in 2010 using a four-barrel plant. Seasonal special beers are produced each month.

Challenge (ABV 3.9%)

Best (ABV 4.5%)

Black Night (ABV 5%)

Ridgeway SIBA

Ridgeway Brewing, Beer Counter Ltd, South Stoke, Oxfordshire, RG8 0JW
☎ (01491) 873474
✉ peter.scholey@beercounter.co.uk

Ridgeway was set up by ex Brakspear head brewer Peter Scholey. It specialises in bottle-conditioned beers but equivalent cask beers are also available. At present Ridgeway beers are brewed by Peter using his own ingredients on a plant at Hepworth's of Horsham (qv) and occasionally elsewhere. All beers listed are available cask and bottle-conditioned. Six strong (ABV 6-9%) bottle-conditioned Christmas beers are produced annually, principally for export to the U.S.

Bitter (OG 1040, ABV 4%)

Organic Beer/ROB (OG 1043, ABV 4.3%)

Blue (OG 1049, ABV 5%)

Ivanhoe (OG 1050, ABV 5.2%)

IPA (OG 1055, ABV 5.5%)

Foreign Export Stout (OG 1078, ABV 8%)

For Coniston Brewing:

Coniston Bluebird (ABV 4.2%)

Coniston XB (ABV 4.4%)

Coniston Old Man (ABV 4.8%)

Ridleys

See Greene King in New Nationals section

Ringmore

Ringmore Craft Brewery Ltd, Higher Ringmore Road, Shaldon, Devon, TQ14 0HG
☎ (01626) 873114
✉ geoff@ringmorecraftbrewery.co.uk

❂ Ringmore was established in 2007 on a one-barrel plant and is the first brewery in Shaldon since 1920. It expanded to a 2.5-barrel plant in 2009 to keep up with demand. Bottle-conditioned beers are also available, including seasonals.

Holly Boo Ale (OG 1040, ABV 4%)

Rollocks (OG 1044, ABV 4.5%)

Oarsome Ale (OG 1046, ABV 4.6%)

Ringwood

See Marston's in New Nationals section

Riverhead

Riverhead Brewery Ltd, 2 Peel Street, Marsden, Huddersfield, West Yorkshire, HD7 6BR
☎ (01484) 841270 (Pub) ☎ (01924) 261333 (Brewery) ✉ brewery@ossett-brewery.co.uk
🌐 ossett-brewery.co.uk
Tours by arrangement (through Ossett Brewing Co)

❂ Riverhead is a brew-pub that opened in 1995 after conversion from an old grocery shop. Ossett Brewing Co Ltd purchased the site in 2006 but runs it as a separate brewery. It has since opened The Dining Room on the first floor, which uses Riverhead beers in its dishes. All original recipes have been retained with new beers also being added. The core range of beers are named after local reservoirs, with the height of the reservoir relating to the strength of the beer. Rotating beers: Leggers Lite (ABV 3.6%), Deer Hill Porter (ABV 4%), Wessenden Wheat (ABV 4%), Cupwith Special (ABV 4.2%), Marsden Best (ABV 4.2%), Black Moss Stout (ABV 4.3%), Premium Mild (ABV 4.7%). Seasonal beers: Ruffled Feathers (ABV 4.6%, Cuckoo Day), Bandsman's Bitter (ABV 4.5%, for Brass Band Competition), Jazz Bitter (ABV 3.8%, for Marsden Jazz Festival), Marsden Merrymaker (ABV 6.5%, Xmas).

Sparth Mild (ABV 3.6%)

Butterley Bitter (OG 1038, ABV 3.8%) ◆
A dry, amber-coloured, hoppy session beer.

March Haigh (OG 1046, ABV 4.6%)
A golden-brown premium bitter. Malty and full-bodied with moderate bitterness.

Redbrook Premium (ABV 5.5%)

Riverside

Riverside Brewery, Bee's Farm, Wainfleet, Lincolnshire, PE24 4LX
☎ (01754) 881288 ☎ 07779 280996

❂ Riverside started brewing in 2003, almost across the road from Bateman's, using a five-barrel plant. In 2008 the brewery moved to new premises. Eight barrels a week are produced, with some 15-20 outlets supplied. Seasonal beers: January's Ale (ABV 4.3%), Hoppy Easter (ABV 4.2%), Witches Wollop (ABV 4.4%), Dixon's Dynamite (ABV 4.5%), Autumn Ale (ABV 4.4%).

Dixon's Major (OG 1038, ABV 3.9%)

Dixon's Hoppy Daze (OG 1041, ABV 4.2%)

Dixon's Old Diabolical (OG 1043, ABV 4.4%)

John Roberts

See Three Tuns

THE BREWERIES

Robinson's IFBB

Frederic Robinson Ltd, Unicorn Brewery, Lower Hillgate, Stockport, Cheshire, SK1 1JJ
☎ (0161) 612 4061 ✉ brewery@frederic-robinson.co.uk 🌐 frederic-robinson.com
Tours by arrangement

Robinson's has been brewing since 1838 and the business is still owned and run by the family (fifth and sixth generations). It has an estate of just under 400 pubs. Contract beers are also brewed. Seasonal beers: see website.

Hatters (OG 1032, ABV 3.3%)
A light mild with a malty, fruity aroma. Biscuity malt with some hop and fruit in the taste and finish. (A darkened version is available in a handful of outlets and badged Dark Hatters.)

Old Stockport (OG 1034, ABV 3.5%)
A beer with a refreshing taste of malt, hops and citrus fruit, a fruity aroma, and a short, dry finish.

Dizzy Blonde (OG 1037, ABV 3.8%)
A straw-coloured summer ale with a distinctive hop aroma. A light, refreshing beer with a clean, zesty, hop-dominated palate complimented by a crisp, dry finish.

Hartleys XB (OG 1040, ABV 4%)
An overly sweet and malty bitter with a bitter citrus peel fruitiness and a hint of liquorice in the finish.

Cumbria Way (OG 1040, ABV 4.1%)
A pronounced malt aroma with rich fruit notes. Rounded malt and hops in the mouth, long dry finish with citrus fruit notes. Brewed for the Hartley's estate in Cumbria.

Unicorn (OG 1041, ABV 4.2%)
Amber beer with a fruity aroma. Malt, hops and fruit in the taste with a bitter, malty finish.

Double Hop (OG 1050, ABV 5%)
Pale brown beer with malt and fruit on the nose. Full hoppy taste with malt and fruit, leading to a hoppy, bitter finish.

Old Tom (OG 1079, ABV 8.5%)
A full-bodied, dark beer with malt, fruit and chocolate on the aroma. A complex range of flavours includes dark chocolate, full maltiness, port and fruits and lead to a long, bittersweet aftertaste.

Rockingham SIBA

Rockingham Ales, c/o 25 Wansford Road, Elton, Cambridgeshire, PE8 6RZ
☎ (01832) 280722 ✉ brian@rockinghamales.co.uk 🌐 rockinghamales.co.uk

A part-time brewery established in 1997 that operates from a converted farm building near Blatherwycke, Northamptonshire (business address as above). The two-barrel plant produces a prolific range of beers and supplies six local outlets. The regular beers are brewed on a rota basis, with special beers brewed to order. Seasonal beers: Fineshade (ABV 3.8%, autumn), Sanity Clause (ABV 4.3%, Dec), Old Herbaceous (ABV 4.5%, winter).

Forest Gold (OG 1039, ABV 3.9%)
A hoppy blonde ale with citrus flavours. Well-balanced and clean finishing.

Hop Devil (OG 1040, ABV 3.9%)
Six hop varieties give this golden ale a bitter start and spicy finish.

A1 Amber Ale (OG 1041, ABV 4%)
A hoppy session beer with fruit and blackcurrant undertones.

Saxon Cross (OG 1041, ABV 4.1%)
A golden-red ale with nut and coffee aromas. Citrus hop flavours predominate.

Fruits of the Forest (OG 1043, ABV 4.2%)
A multi-layered beer in which summer fruits and several spices compete with a big hop presence.

Dark Forest (OG 1050, ABV 5%)
A dark and complex beer, similar to a Belgian dubbel, with malty/smoky flavours that give way to a fruity bitter finish.

Rodham's

Rodham's Brewery, 74 Albion Street, Otley, West Yorkshire, LS21 1BZ
☎ (01943) 464530

Michael Rodham began brewing in 2005 on a one-barrel plant in the cellar of his house. Capacity has gradually increased and is now 2.5 barrels. All beers produced are malt-only, using whole hops. Occasional seasonal and bottle-conditioned beers are available.

Rubicon (OG 1039, ABV 4.1%)
Amber-coloured with a nutty, malt and light fruit taste. A dry, peppery and bitter aftertaste.

Wheat Beer (OG 1039, ABV 4.1%)
Naturally cloudy, sharp and refreshing.

Royale (OG 1042, ABV 4.4%)
A golden beer with a citrus, hoppy taste, underlying malt with a bitter finish.

Old Albion (OG 1048, ABV 5%)
Ruby black premium beer with a complex mix of roasted malt, liquorice and tart fruit with a balancing bitterness.

IPA (OG 1053, ABV 5.7%)
Rich malt combines with tart citrus hops giving a long, bitter finish.

Rooster's SIBA

Rooster's Brewing Co Ltd, Unit 3, Grimbald Park, Wetherby Road, Knaresborough, North Yorkshire, HG5 8LJ
☎ (01423) 865959 ✉ sean@roosters.co.uk 🌐 roosters.co.uk
Tours by arrangement

Rooster's was opened in 1993 by Sean and Alison Franklin. From 1996 beers were also brewed under the Outlaw Brewery Co label. The brewery moved to larger premises in 2001. Seasonal beer: Rooster's Nector (ABV 5.2%, autumn/winter). Bottle-conditioned beers are also available.

Special (OG 1038, ABV 3.9%)
Yellow in colour, a full-bodied, floral bitter with fruit and hop notes being carried over in to the long aftertaste. Hops and bitterness tend to increase in the finish.

Leghorn (ABV 4.3%)

Yankee (OG 1042, ABV 4.3%)
A straw-coloured beer with a delicate, fruity aroma leading to a well-balanced taste of malt and hops with a slight evidence of sweetness, followed by a refreshing, fruity/bitter finish.

YPA (OG 1042, ABV 4.3%)
A pale-coloured beer with pronounced raspberry and flower aromas.

Cream (ABV 4.7%)

Under Outlaw Brewery name:

Wrangler (ABV 3.7%)

Wild Mule (ABV 3.9%)

Dry Irish Stout (ABV 4.7%)

Dead or Alive (ABV 5%)

Roseland

Roseland Brewery, c/o Roseland Inn, Philleigh, nr St Mawes, Truro, Cornwall, TR2 5NB
☎ (01872) 580254

Roseland was established in 2009 by Phil Heslip at his pub, the Roseland Inn. The beers are named after local birds and are only available in the Roseland or its sister pub, the Victory at St Mawes.

Cornish Shag (OG 1037, ABV 3.8%)
A copper-coloured session bitter.

Choughed to Bits (OG 1042, ABV 4.2%)
A mid-brown hoppy bitter.

High as a Kite (OG 1047, ABV 4.8%)
A dark, hoppy bitter.

Rossendale

Rossendale Brewery Ltd, Griffin Inn, 84 Hud Rake, Haslingden, Lancashire, BB4 5AF
☎ (01706) 214021 rossendalebrewery.co.uk

Formerly known as Pennine Ales. The brewery acquired the brew plant previously used by Porter Brewing Co in November 2007 and is based in the cellar of the Griffin Inn in Haslingden. It produces six regular cask ales.

Floral Dance (OG 1035, ABV 3.6%)
A pale and fruity session beer.

Hameldon Bitter (OG 1037, ABV 3.8%)
A dark traditional bitter with a dry and assertive character that develops in the finish.

Ale (OG 1041, ABV 4.2%)
A malty aroma leads to a complex, malt dominated flavour, supported by a dry, increasingly bitter finish.

Railway Sleeper (OG 1040, ABV 4.2%)
An amber bitter.

Pitch Porter (OG 1050, ABV 5%)
A full-bodied, rich beer with a slightly sweet, malty start, counter balanced with sharp bitterness and a roast barley dominance.

Sunshine (OG 1050, ABV 5.3%)
A hoppy and bitter golden beer with a citrus character. The lingering finish is dry and spicy.

Rother Valley SIBA

Rother Valley Brewing Co, Gate Court Farm, Station Road, Northiam, East Sussex, TN31 6QT
☎ (01797) 252922 ☎ 07798 877551
Tours by arrangement

Rother Valley was established in Northiam in 1993 overlooking the Rother Levels. Hops grown on the farm and from Sandhurst are used. Brewing is split between cask and an ever-increasing range of filtered bottled beers. Around 100 outlets are supplied. A monthly seasonal ale is available.

Honeyfuzz (OG 1038, ABV 3.8%)
A pale bitter flavoured with Sussex honey, subtle but not sweet with a citrus twang on the finish.

Smild (OG 1038, ABV 3.8%)
A full-bodied, dark, creamy mild with hints of chocolate.

Level Best (OG 1040, ABV 4%)
Full-bodied tawny session bitter with a malt and fruit aroma, malty taste and a dry, hoppy finish.

Copper Ale (OG 1041, ABV 4.1%)
A copper-coloured ale with a good balance of malt and hops.

Hoppers Ale (OG 1044, ABV 4.4%)
A copper-coloured ale. The initial burst of hop is followed by a pleasant caramel taste.

Boadicea (OG 1045, ABV 4.5%)
A straw-coloured beer with a delicate, fruity flavour.

Blues (OG 1050, ABV 5%)
A dark brew full of complex tastes such as chocolate, raisins and a roast finish. Deceptively smooth.

Rotters (NEW)

Rotters Brewery, Tower Hotel, Talgarth, Powys, LD3 0BW
☎ (01874) 711253 rottersbrewery@gmail.com
rottersbrewery.co.uk
Tours by arrangement

Rotters Brewery opened in 2010. Seasonal beer: Whipping Tree (ABV 3.6%, summer). Rotters Stout is suitable for vegans.

Stout (OG 1046, ABV 4.5%)
A creamy stout with a roasted barley character.

Grounds For Divorce (OG 1048, ABV 4.7%)
A premium ruby ale.

Rowditch (NEW)

Rowditch Inn Brewery, Rowditch Inn, 246 Uttoxeter New Road, Derby, DE22 3LL
☎ (01332) 343123

Rowditch began brewing in 2010 using a three-barrel plant. Two regular beers will be available but the beer list was not finalised at the time of going to press.

Rowton

Rowton Brewery Ltd, Stone House, Rowton, Telford, Shropshire, TF6 6QX
☎ 07746 290995

Rowton was established in 2008 on a four-barrel plant in an old cow shed on the owner's farm. Water is from a borehole on site. Meteorite is named after a meteorite that landed on the farm in the 19th century and is now in a London museum. Seasonal beers: Rowton 33 (ABV 3.3%, summer), Rowton Rocket (ABV 5.5%, winter).

Bitter (ABV 3.9%)

Meteorite (ABV 4.7%)

Royal Tunbridge Wells SIBA (NEW)

Royal Tunbridge Wells Brewing Co Ltd, Spa Brewery, 18H Chapman Way, Royal Tunbridge Wells, Kent, TN2 3EF
☎ (01892) 618140
✉ info@royaltunbridgewellsbrewing.co.uk
🌐 royaltunbridgewellsbrewing.co.uk
Tours by arrangement

Brewing began in 2010 using a 10-barrel plant. Around 50 outlets are supplied direct. Seasonal beer: Sovereign (ABV 3.8%).

Royal (OG 1040, ABV 4.1%)

Rudgate SIBA

Rudgate Brewery Ltd, 2 Centre Park, Marston Moor Business Park, Tockwith, York, North Yorkshire, YO26 7QF
☎ (01423) 358382 ✉ sales@rudgatebrewery.co.uk
🌐 rudgatebrewery.co.uk

Rudgate Brewery was founded in 1992 and is located in an old armoury building on a disused World War II airfield. It has a 15-barrel plant and six open fermenting vessels, producing more than 70 barrels a week. Around 350 outlets are supplied direct. Seasonal beers: Rudolphs Ruin (ABV 4.6%, Xmas). Three seasonal beers are produced every month.

Jorvik Blonde (OG 1036, ABV 3.8%)
Flaxen blonde ale with a balanced hoppy bitterness and a crisp, fruity finish.

Viking (OG 1036, ABV 3.8%)
An initially warming and malty, full-bodied beer, with hops and fruit lingering into the aftertaste.

Battleaxe (OG 1040, ABV 4.2%)
A well-hopped bitter with slightly sweet initial taste and light bitterness. Complex fruit character gives a memorable aftertaste.

Ruby Mild (OG 1041, ABV 4.4%)
Nutty, rich ruby ale, stronger than usual for a mild.

Special (OG 1042, ABV 4.5%)
Moderately bitter leading to a citrus, hoppy finish.

Well Blathered (OG 1046, ABV 5%)
A premium bitter, golden-coloured with distinctive lemon on the nose.

Rugby

See Willey

Saddleworth

Church Inn & Saddleworth Brewery, Church Lane, Uppermill, Oldham, Greater Manchester, OL3 6LW
☎ (01457) 820902/872415
Tours by arrangement

Saddleworth started brewing in 1997 in a brewhouse that had been closed for around 120 years. Brewery and inn are set in a historic location at the top of a valley overlooking Saddleworth Moor and next to St Chads Church, which dates from 1215. Seasonal beers: Bert Corner (ABV 4%, Feb), St George's Bitter (ABV 4%, Apr), Ayrton's Ale (ABV 4.1%, Apr-May), Harvest Moon (ABV 4.1%, Aug-Sep), Robyn's Bitter (ABV 4.6%, Nov-Dec), Christmas Carol (ABV 6.6%, Dec-Jan).

Clog Dancer (ABV 3.6%)

Mild (ABV 3.8%)

More (ABV 3.8%)

Honey Smacker (ABV 4.1%)

Hop Smacker (ABV 4.1%)

Indya Pale Ale (ABV 4.1%)

Shaftbender (ABV 5.4%)

Sadler's

Sadler's Ales Brewery, 7 Stourbridge Road, Lye, Stourbridge, West Midlands, DY9 7DG
☎ (01384) 895230 ✉ enquiries@sadlersales.co.uk
🌐 sadlersales.co.uk
Tours by arrangement

Thomas Alexander Sadler founded the original brewery in 1900 adjacent to the Windsor Castle Inn, Oldbury. Fourth generation brewers John and Chris Sadler re-opened the brewery in its new location in 2004. The brewery tap house was built and opened in 2006 next to the brewery. Around 250 outlets are supplied. An extensive range of bottle-conditioned beers are available as well as beer-based cheeses and condiments.

Jack's Ale (OG 1037, ABV 3.8%)
A very pale, hoppy bitter with a crisp and zesty lemon undertone.

Green Man (ABV 4%)
A smooth pale ale, brewed with lager hops.

Mild Ale (OG 1039, ABV 4%)
A Black Country dark mild with hints of chocolate and a dry finish.

Worcester Sorcerer (OG 1043, ABV 4.3%)
Brewed with English hops and barley with hints of mint and lemon, creating a floral aroma and crisp bitterness.

Mellow Yellow (OG 1045, ABV 4.5%)
A pale ale brewed with plenty of hop and honey.

Thin Ice (OG 1045, ABV 4.5%)
A pale ale. Bitter but with an orange and lemon finish.

Stumbling Badger (OG 1049, ABV 4.9%)
A well-balanced strong ale, packed with flavour and aroma with hints of fruit and a hoppy finish.

Mud City Stout (OG 1066, ABV 6.6%)
Rich, full-bodied strong stout brewed with raw cocoa, fresh vanilla pods, oats, wheat and dark malts.

Saffron

Saffron Brewery, The Cartshed, Parsonage Farm, Henham, Essex, CM22 6AN
☎ (01279) 850923 ☎ 07747 696901
✉ tb@saffronbrewery.co.uk 🌐 saffronbrewery.co.uk
Tours by arrangement

Founded in 2005, Saffron is situated near the historic East Anglian town of Saffron Walden, famous for its malting industry in the 18th century. The brewery was upgraded to a 15-barrel plant in early 2008 and re-located to a converted barn at Parsonage Farm by Henham church, with a purpose-built reed bed for environmentally friendly disposal of waste products. 40 outlets are supplied direct. Seasonal beers: see website. Bottle-conditioned beers are also available.

Ramblers Tipple (OG 1040, ABV 3.9%)
A rich, copper-coloured bitter with toffee and caramel flavours.

Brewhouse Bell (OG 1041, ABV 4%)
Golden amber in colour with citrus and hop flavours balancing well for a clean, fresh finish.

Saffron Blonde (OG 1044, ABV 4.3%)
A light golden ale with a delicate balance of citrus and smooth, malty flavours and a crisp finish.

Squires Gamble (OG 1044, ABV 4.3%)
Traditional style copper ale; soft, mellow, full-flavoured and hoppy with citrus and biscuit hints.

Tiddly Vicar (OG 1051, ABV 5%)
Dark copper nutty beer with a light, spicy finish.

St Austell IFBB SIBA

St Austell Brewery Co Ltd, 63 Trevarthian Road, St Austell, Cornwall, PL25 4BY
☎ (01726) 74444 ✉ info@staustellbrewery.co.uk
⊕ staustellbrewery.co.uk
Shop Mon-Fri 9am-5pm; Sat 10am-4pm
Tours by arrangement

St Austell Brewery celebrated 150 years of brewing in 2001. Founded by Walter Hicks in 1851, the company is still family owned, with a powerful commitment to cask beer, available in all 169 licensed houses, as well as in the free trade throughout Cornwall, Devon and Somerset. A visitor centre offers guided tours and souvenirs from the brewery. Bottle-conditioned beers are available.

IPA (OG 1035, ABV 3.4%) ◆
Easy-drinking copper bitter with grainy palate. Hops are present from the start, balanced by light toffee malt in the mouth and a short, crisp, bitter finish.

Tinners (OG 1038, ABV 3.7%) ◆
Golden beer with an appetising malt aroma and a good balance of malt and hops in the flavour. Lasting finish.

Dartmoor Best Bitter (OG 1039, ABV 3.9%) ◆
Superbly balanced copper session bitter with a fruity malt nose. Full-bodied and grainy in the mouth but with a noticeable hoppy bite. Short finish of hops and malt.

Black Prince (OG 1041, ABV 4%) 🗄 🍷 ◆
Creamy dark mild with aroma of lightly roasted malt and caramel. Malt and sweetness dominate the flavour balanced by traces of bitterness and fruity hops, fading away.

Tribute (OG 1043, ABV 4.2%) 🗄 🍷 ◆
Medium-bodied, copper-bronze premium ale. Refreshingly bittersweet with a balance of malt and hops. Aroma of Oregon hops and malt with a trace of tangy ester. The finish is long, bitter and moderately dry.

Proper Job IPA (ABV 4.5%) 🗄 🍷 ◆
Floral aromatic hops greet the nose and persist in the mouth but are mellowed by a sweet, well-rounded and full-bodied palate that disappears in a bittersweet aftertaste.

Hicks Special Draught/HSD (OG 1052, ABV 5%) ◆
An aromatic, fruity, hoppy bitter that is initially sweet with an aftertaste of pronounced bitterness, but whose flavour is fully rounded.

St George's

St George's Brewery Ltd, Bush Lane, Callow End, Worcestershire, WR2 4TF
☎ (01905) 831316 ✉ info@stgeorgesbrewery.co.uk
⊕ stgeorgesbrewery.co.uk
Tours by arrangement

⊗ The brewery was established in 1998 in old village bakery premises. It was acquired in 2006 by Duncan Ironmonger. Andrew Sankey has been the brewer and brewery manager for a number of years. The brewery supplies local freehouses and wholesalers for a wider distribution. At least two monthly specials are usually available.

Order of the Garter (ABV 3.8%)
Light golden beer with a well-hopped, smooth taste.

Friar Tuck (OG 1040, ABV 4%)
A light, golden beer with a citrus fruity flavour.

Worcester Sauce (ABV 4%)
A well-balanced amber beer with a hoppy start and smooth, bitter finish.

Blues & Royals (OG 1043, ABV 4.3%)
Deep copper in colour with a biscuity, hoppy taste.

Charger (OG 1046, ABV 4.6%)
A light, refreshing beer.

Dragons Blood (OG 1048, ABV 4.8%)
A ruby red beer with a citrus flavour.

St Jude's

St Jude's Brewery Ltd, 2 Cardigan Street, Ipswich, Suffolk, IP1 3PF
☎ (01473) 413334 ☎ 07870 358834
⊕ stjudesbrewery.co.uk
Shop by prior appt Mon-Sat 10am-5pm
Tours by arrangement

⊗ St Jude's was established in 2006 on a seven-barrel plant. It bottles on site and supplies to many outlets in the UK. Bottle-conditioned beers are available. Seasonal beer: St Gabriels (ABV 6%, Xmas).

Brandon's Mild (OG 1034, ABV 3.4%)

Royal Tudor Honey Ale (ABV 4%)

St Francis (OG 1049, ABV 4%) ◆
Pale golden. Surprisingly malty aroma but the taste is all fruit and hops. Suitable for vegetarians and vegans.

Gainsborough Spring Ale (ABV 4.2%)

Gypeswic Bitter (OG 1048, ABV 4.4%) ◆
Fruity beer with a toffeish palate, elderflower and a clean aftertaste with lingering hop flavour.

Ipswich Bright (OG 1042, ABV 4.4%) ◆
A refreshing, golden bitter beer with a long, hoppy aftertaste.

Coachman's Whip (OG 1064, ABV 5.2%)
A well-balanced ale with a bitter, rich flavour.

Devereaux's Dark Porter (ABV 5.5%)

John Orford's Strong Brown Ale (ABV 5.5%) ◆
Strong caramel and malt aroma and taste.

St Mary's Stout (OG 1068, ABV 6.5%)

St Peter's EAB SIBA

St Peter's Brewery Co Ltd, St Peter's Hall, St Peter South Elmham, Suffolk, NR35 1NQ
☎ (01986) 782322 ✉ beers@stpetersbrewery.co.uk
stpetersbrewery.co.uk
Shop Mon-Fri 9am-5pm; Sat & Sun 11am-5pm
Tours Sat, Sun & bank holidays 12-4pm (groups of 20+ by arrangement)

St Peter's was launched in 1996 and concentrates in the main on bottled beer (90% of capacity) but has a rapidly increasing cask market. Two pubs are owned and 75 outlets are supplied. Seasonal beer: Suffolk Gold (ABV 4.9%).

Best Bitter (OG 1038, ABV 3.7%)
A complex but well-balanced hoppy brew. A gentle hop nose introduces a singular hoppiness with supporting malt notes and underlying bitterness. Other flavours fade to leave a long, dry, hoppy finish.

Mild (OG 1037, ABV 3.7%)
Sweetness balanced by bitter chocolate malt to produce a rare but much sought after traditional mild.

Organic Best (OG 1041, ABV 4.1%)
A very dry and bitter beer with a growing astringency. Pale brown in colour, it has a gentle hop aroma which makes the definitive bitterness surprising. One for the committed.

Ruby Red (ABV 4.3%)
A tawny red ale with subtle malt undertones and a distinctive spicy hop aroma.

Organic Ale (OG 1045, ABV 4.5%)
A rich toffee apple aroma and a smooth grainy feel. Malt and caramel initially match the dry hoppy bitterness. As the flavours mature, liqourice dryness develops. Full-bodied.

Golden Ale (OG 1047, ABV 4.7%)
Amber-coloured, full-bodied, robust ale. A strong hop bouquet leads to a mix of malt and hops combined with a dry, fruity hoppiness. The malt quickly subsides, leaving creamy bitterness.

Grapefruit Beer (OG 1047, ABV 4.7%)
With a very strong aroma and taste of grapefruit, this refreshing beer is exactly what it says on the tin. A superb example of a fruit beer.

IPA (OG 1055, ABV 5.5%)
A full-bodied, highly hopped pale ale with a zesty character.

Salamander

Salamander Brewing Co Ltd, 22 Harry Street, Bradford, West Yorkshire, BD4 9PH
☎ (01274) 652323
✉ salamanderbrewing@fsmail.net
salamanderbrewing.co.uk
Tours by arrangement

Salamander first brewed in 2000 in a former pork pie factory. Expansion in 2004 took the brewery to 40-barrel capacity. There are direct deliveries to more widespread areas such as Cumbria, East Yorkshire and Lancashire in addition to the established trade of about 100 outlets throughout Lancashire, Manchester, North Yorkshire and Derbyshire.

Axolotl (ABV 3.9%)

Mudpuppy (OG 1042, ABV 4.2%)
A well-balanced, copper-coloured best bitter with a fruity, hoppy nose and a bitter finish.

Golden Salamander (OG 1045, ABV 4.5%)
Citrus hops characterise the aroma and taste of this golden premium bitter, which has malt undertones throughout. The aftertaste is dry, hoppy and bitter.

Stout (OG 1045, ABV 4.5%)
Rich roast malts dominate the smooth coffee and chocolate flavour. Nicely balanced. A dry, roast, bitter finish develops over time.

Salopian SIBA

Salopian Brewing Co Ltd, 67 Mytton Oak Road, Shrewsbury, Shropshire, SY3 8UQ
☎ (01743) 248414
✉ enquiries@salopianbrewery.co.uk
salopianbrewery.co.uk
Shop Mon-Fri 9am-4pm
Tours by arrangement

The brewery was established in 1995 in an old dairy on the outskirts of Shrewsbury and, having grown steadily, now produces 60 barrels a week. Over 200 outlets are supplied. Salopian also brews under the Blackwater Brewery name.

Shropshire Gold (OG 1037, ABV 3.8%)
A light, copper-coloured ale with an unusual blend of body and dryness.

Oracle (OG 1040, ABV 4%)
A crisp golden ale with a striking hop profile. Dry and refreshing with a long-balanced aromatic finish.

Darwins Origin (OG 1042, ABV 4.3%)
A light copper ale with a striking hop profile.

Hop Twister (OG 1044, ABV 4.5%)
A premium bitter with a citrus flavour and complex hop finish. Refreshing and crisp.

Golden Thread (OG 1048, ABV 5%)
A bright gold ale. Strong and quite bitter but well-balanced.

Saltaire

Saltaire Brewery Ltd, Unit 6, County Works, Dockfield Road, Shipley, West Yorkshire, BD17 7AR
☎ (01274) 594959 ✉ info@saltairebrewery.co.uk
saltairebrewery.co.uk
Tours by arrangement

Launched in 2006, Saltaire Brewery is an award-winning 20-barrel brewery based in a Victorian industrial building that formerly generated electricity for the local tram system. A mezzanine bar gives visitors views of the brewing plant and the chance to taste the beers. More than 300 pubs are supplied across West Yorkshire and the north of England.

Rye Smile (OG 1038, ABV 3.8%)
Copper-coloured with silky toffee flavours.

Blonde (OG 1040, ABV 4%)
Straw-coloured light ale with soft malt flavours.

Raspberry Blonde (ABV 4%)
Refreshing blonde ale infused with a hint of raspberries.

Blackberry Cascade (ABV 4.8%)
Cascade hops infused with a hint of blackberries.

Cascade Pale Ale (OG 1047, ABV 4.8%)

American-style pale ale with floral aromas and strong bitterness.

Sambrook's

Sambrook's Brewery Limited, Units 1 & 2, Yelverton Road, Battersea, London, SW11 3QG
☎ (020) 7228 0598
✉ sales@sambrooksbrewery.co.uk
🌐 sambrooksbrewery.co.uk
Shop Mon-Fri 10am-6pm; Summer Sat 10am-1pm
Tours by arrangement

⊗ Sambrooks was established in 2008 by Duncan Sambrook and David Welsh using a 20-barrel plant. Bottle-conditioned beer is available.

Wandle Ale (OG 1038, ABV 3.8%) ◆
A touch of dryness balances the rounded sweetish malt flavour of this fruity, quaffable pale brown bitter. Some peach and citrus notes and hops are noticeable when fresh.

Junction Ale (OG 1044, ABV 4.5%) ◆
A traditional brown best bitter with an agreeable creamy mouthfeel and a sweetish malty toffee flavour, which is balanced by some bitterness, fruity and a trace of hops.

Sandstone SIBA

Sandstone Brewery LLP, Unit 5, Wrexham Enterprise Park, Preston Road, off Ash Road, North Wrexham Industrial Estate, Wrexham, LL13 9JT
☎ 07851 001118 ✉ info@sandstonebrewery.co.uk
🌐 sandstonebrewery.co.uk
Tours by arrangement

⊗ Sandstone Brewery was established in 2008 by three CAMRA members on a four-barrel brew plant. More than 60 regular outlets are supplied direct. Seasonal beer: Festive Fairy (ABV 5.3%, winter).

Edge (OG 1039, ABV 3.8%) ◆
A satisfying session ale, this pale, dry, bitter beer has a full mouthfeel and a lingering hoppy finish that belies its modest strength.

Sleeping Policeman (OG 1043, ABV 4.2%)
A traditional, copper-coloured premium bitter.

Post Mistress (OG 1046, ABV 4.4%) ◆
A full-bodied, smooth premium bitter, ruby-red in colour, with a rich, mellow taste. Good combination of malt, hops and fruit in aroma and initial taste leading to a lasting satisfying finish.

Buxom Barmaid (OG 1047, ABV 4.7%)
A rich, golden ale with fruity overtones.

Sarah Hughes

See under Hughes

Sawbridgeworth

▮ Sawbridgeworth Brewery, 81 London Road, Sawbridgeworth, Hertfordshire, CM21 9JJ
☎ (01279) 722313 ✉ thegatepub@talktalk.net
🌐 thegatepub.net
Tours by arrangement

Set up in 2000 by owners Tom and Gary Barnett, the brewery is situated behind the Gate Inn. Tom is a former professional footballer whose clubs included Crystal Palace. Brewing is carried out by ex-Nethergate brewer Bob Renvoise. Special or one-off beers are regularly brewed and all beers are available bottle conditioned.

Mead Mild (ABV 3.4%)

Selhurst Park Flyer (ABV 3.7%)

RACS (ABV 4%)

Is It Yourself (ABV 4.2%)

Dragon's Blood (ABV 4.3%)

Stout (ABV 4.3%)

Brooklands Express (ABV 4.6%)

Malt Shovel Porter (ABV 6%)

Scattor Rock

See Gidley's

Scottish Borders (NEW)

Scottish Borders Brewery, Lanton Mill, Jedburgh, TD8 6ST
☎ (01835) 830673 ✉ info@chestersestate.com
🌐 scottishbordersbrewery.com

Scottish Borders was established in 2010 and is a farm development using its own barley. No beer list available at present.

Severn Vale SIBA

Severn Vale Brewing Co, Woodend Lane, Cam, Dursley, Gloucestershire, GL11 5HS
☎ (01453) 547550 ☎ 07971 640244
✉ steve@severnvalebrewing.co.uk
🌐 severnvalebrewing.co.uk
Shop: Please ring first
Tours by arrangement

⊗ Severn Vale started brewing in 2005 in an old milking parlour using a new five-barrel plant. Warminster malted barley is used and mainly Herefordshire hops. Around 50 outlets are supplied. Seasonal beers: Severn Nations (ABV 4.4%, Feb-Mar), Severn Springs (ABV 4.4%, Mar-May), Monumentale (ABV 4.5%, May), Severn Bells (ABV 4.3%, Jun-Jul), Severn Swans a Swimming (ABV 4.7%. Xmas).

Session (OG 1035, ABV 3.4%)
A classic bitter that belies its low strength. It has a full-bodied malty flavour with a bitter, hoppy finish that lingers on the palate.

Vale Ale (OG 1039, ABV 3.8%)
A rich amber beer with full-bodied malt flavours and complex nose and taste.

Dursley Steam Bitter (OG 1043, ABV 4.2%)
A refreshing golden ale full of flowery hops.

Severn Sins (OG 1053, ABV 5.2%)
A jet-black stout with a dry roast malt flavour with hints of chocolate and liquorice.

Shalford

Shalford Brewery, c/o PO Box 10411, Braintree, Essex, CM7 5WP
☎ (01371) 850925 ☎ 07749 658512
✉ nigel@shalfordbrewery.co.uk
🌐 shalfordbrewery.co.uk

THE BREWERIES

⊗ Shalford began brewing in 2007 on a five-barrel plant at Hyde Farm in the Pant Valley in Essex. Over 20 outlets are supplied direct. Bottle-conditioned beers are available.

1319 Mild (ABV 3.7%)
Roast malt and chocolate sweetness with a slight bitter finish.

Barnfield Bitter (ABV 3.8%) ◆
Pale-coloured but full-flavoured, this is a traditional, hoppy bitter rather than a golden ale. Malt persists throughout, with bitterness becoming more dominant towards the end.

Braintree Market Ale (ABV 4%)
Traditional, easy-drinking session ale with a hoppy, lingering, dry finish.

Levelly Gold (ABV 4%)
Golden, summery bitter with a pleasant finish.

Stoneley Bitter (ABV 4.2%) ◆
Dark amber session beer whose vivid hop character is supported by a juicy, malty body. A dry finish makes this beer very drinkable.

Hyde Bitter (ABV 4.7%) ◆
Stronger version of Barnfield, with a similar but more assertive character.

Levelly Black (ABV 4.8%)
A winter stout; dark, malty and smooth.

Longfield Lager (ABV 5.5%)

Springfield Wheat Beer (ABV 6%)
A refreshing, crisp, clean bitter.

Rotten End (ABV 6.5%)
Strong beer with slightly sweet, nutty undertones and a bitter edge to finish.

Shardlow

Shardlow Brewing Co Ltd, The Old Brewery Stables, British Waterways Yard, Cavendish Bridge, Leicestershire, DE72 2HL
☎ **(01332) 799188** ✉ **nev@shardlowbrewing.co.uk**
Tours by arrangement

⊛ On a site associated with brewing since 1819, Shardlow delivers to more than 100 outlets throughout the East Midlands and is also a large cider distributor. Due to increased sales, two new fermenters have been added. Reverend Eaton is named after a scion of the Eaton brewing family, Rector of Shardlow for 40 years. The brewery tap is the Blue Bell Inn at Melbourne, Derbyshire. Seasonal beers: Frostbite (ABV 5.5%), Stedmans Tipple (ABV 5.1%), Six Bells (ABV 6%). Bottle-conditioned beers are also available.

Chancellors Revenge (OG 1036, ABV 3.6%)
A light-coloured, refreshing, full-flavoured and well-hopped session bitter.

Cavendish Dark (OG 1037, ABV 3.7%)

Special Bitter (OG 1039, ABV 3.9%)
A well-balanced, amber-coloured, quaffable bitter.

Golden Hop (OG 1041, ABV 4.1%)

Kiln House (ABV 4.1%)

Narrow Boat (OG 1043, ABV 4.3%)
A pale amber bitter, with a short, crisp hoppy aftertaste.

Cavendish Bridge (ABV 4.5%)

Cavendish Gold (ABV 4.5%)

Reverend Eaton (OG 1045, ABV 4.5%)
A smooth, medium-strong bitter, full of malt and hop flavours with a sweet aftertaste.

Mayfly (ABV 4.8%)

Five Bells (OG 1050, ABV 5%)

Whistlestop (OG 1050, ABV 5%)
Maris Otter pale malt and two hops produce this smooth and surprisingly strong pale beer.

Sharp's

Sharp's Brewery Ltd, Pityme Business Centre, Rock, Cornwall, PL27 6NU
☎ **(01208) 862121**
✉ **enquiries@sharpsbrewery.co.uk**
🌐 **sharpsbrewery.co.uk**
Shop Mon-Fri 9am-5pm
Tours by arrangement

⊗ Sharp's Brewery was founded in 1994. Within 15 years the brewery had grown from producing 1,500 barrels annually to selling 60,000. Sharp's has no pubs and delivers beer to more than 1,200 outlets across the south of England. All beer is produced at the brewery in Rock and is delivered via temperature controlled depots in Bristol and London. Seasonal beer: see website. Bottle-conditioned beer is also available.

Cornish Coaster (OG 1035.2, ABV 3.6%) ◆
A smooth, easy-drinking beer, golden in colour, with a fresh hop aroma and dry malt and hops in the mouth. The finish starts malty but becomes dry and hoppy.

Cornish Jack (OG 1037, ABV 3.8%)
Light candied fruit dominates the aroma, underpinned with fresh hop notes. The flavour is a delicate balance of light sweetness, fruity notes and fresh spicy hops. Subtle bitterness and dry fruit notes linger in the finish.

Doom Bar (OG 1038.5, ABV 4%) ◆
Flowery, spicy hop and berries on the nose lead to malt and fruit in the mouth with fresh bitterness running through into the long, sweet finish.

Own (OG 1042.5, ABV 4.4%) ◆
Full-bodied, deep golden brown beer rich in nutty malt and hops on the tongue. Bitterness develops, persisting in the finish together with some hoppy dryness and malt.

Special (OG 1048.5, ABV 5%) ◆
Deep golden brown with a fresh hop aroma. Dry malt and hops in the mouth; the finish is malty but becomes dry and hoppy.

Shaws

Shaws Brewery, The Old Stables, Park Road, Dukinfield, Greater Manchester, SK16 5LX
☎ **(0161) 330 5471** ✉ **sales@windsor-fabrications.co.uk**

⊛ The brewery is housed in the stables of William Shaws Brewery, established in 1856 and closed by John Smiths in 1941. Brewing re-started in 2002 with a five-barrel plant. Beer is supplied to more than 30 local free trade outlets and beer festivals. Monthly guest beers are produced.

Golden Globe (OG 1040, ABV 4.3%) ◆

Yellow beer with a modest hoppy/fruity aroma. Biscuity malt and tart fruits on the palate and in the bitter aftertaste.

Sheffield SIBA

Sheffield Brewery Co Ltd, Unit 111, JC Albyn Complex, Burton Road, Sheffield, South Yorkshire, S3 8BT
☎ (0114) 272 7256 ✉ sales@sheffieldbrewery.com
sheffieldbrewery.com
Tours by arrangement

Sheffield began brewing in 2007 in the former Blanco polish works on a 10-barrel plant. The brewery operates on a tower system and also acts as a venue for corporate or social gatherings, catering for up to 40 people. The brewery tap is the Gardeners Rest in Sheffield. More than 50 outlets are supplied direct. Seasonal beers: see website. Bottle-conditioned beers are also available.

Crucible Best (OG 1038, ABV 3.8%)
A complex traditional bitter.

Five Rivers (OG 1038, ABV 3.8%)
An easy-drinking, straw-coloured session ale with a hoppy aroma.

Blanco Blonde (OG 1041, ABV 4.1%)
A continental lager-style beer.

Paradise Pale (OG 1042, ABV 4.2%)
A hoppy best bitter with a light citrus aroma that carries through to the finish.

Porter (OG 1044, ABV 4.4%)
A rich, chocolaty, malty porter with caramel flavours.

Shepherd Neame IFBB

Shepherd Neame Ltd, 17 Court Street, Faversham, Kent, ME13 7AX
☎ (01795) 532206 shepherd-neame.co.uk
Shop Mon-Sat 10am-4.30pm
Tours by arrangement

Kent's major independent brewery is believed to be the oldest continuous brewer in the country (since 1698), but records show brewing began on the site as far back as the 12th century. The same water source is still used today and 1914 oak mash tuns are still operational. In 2004/2005 investment increased production to more than 200,000 barrels a year. The company has 370 tied houses in the South-east, nearly all selling cask ale. More than 2,000 other outlets are also supplied. All Shepherd Neame ales use locally sourced ingredients. The cask beers are made with Kentish hops, local malted barley and water from the brewery's own artesian well. In 2007 a new micro-plant was installed inside the main brewery to brew speciality ales in small quantities for special occasions. These brews are available for a limited time in selected pubs. In the first year over 50 beers were produced. A programme of monthly seasonal beers is available: see website for details. Bottle-conditioned beer is also available.

Canterbury Jack (OG 1033, ABV 3.5%)
A full-bodied, pale beer with a grapefruit aroma. Malty, citrus notes on the palate lead to a crisp, refreshing, bitter aftertaste.

Master Brew Bitter (OG 1032, ABV 3.7%) ◆
A distinctive bitter, mid-brown in colour, with a hoppy aroma. Well-balanced, with a nicely aggressive bitter taste from its hops, it leaves a hoppy/bitter finish, tinged with sweetness.

Kent's Best (OG 1036, ABV 4.1%)
A mellow bitter which merges the biscuity sweetness of English malt with the fruity, floral bitterness of locally grown hops.

Spitfire Premium Ale (OG 1036, ABV 4.2%)
A commemorative Battle of Britain brew for the RAF Benevolent Fund's appeal, now the brewery's flagship ale.

Late Red (OG 1042, ABV 4.3%)
A strong bitter with a deep sweetness, toffee and honey characteristics. The cascade hops give a resinous note reminiscent of autumn leaves.

Bishops Finger (OG 1046, ABV 5%)
A cask-conditioned version of a famous bottled beer. A strong ale with a complex hop aroma reminiscent of lemons, oranges and bananas combined with malt, molasses and toffee. Refreshing with a good malt character tinged with a lingering bitterness.

Sherborne

Sherborne Brewery Ltd, 257 Westbury, Sherborne, Dorset, DT9 3EH
☎ (01935) 812094 sherbornebrewery.co.uk

Sherborne Brewery started in late 2005 on a 2.5-barrel plant. It moved in 2006 to new premises at the rear of the brewery's pub, Docherty's Bar. Beer is supplied to the pub and to 15-20 other local outlets as a guest beer.

257 (OG 1039, ABV 3.9%)

Cheap Street (OG 1044, ABV 4.4%) ◆
Faint hop and fruit aromas lead to strong astringent flavours and lingering dry burnt aftertaste; reminiscent of German Rauch beer but with a thinner body and a straw colour.

Ship Inn

Ship Inn Brewery, Ship Inn, Newton Square, Low Newton by the Sea, Northumberland, NE66 3EL
☎ (01665) 576262 shipinnnewton.co.uk

The Ship Inn commenced brewing in 2008 on a 2.5-barrel plant designed and built by Michael Hegarty, formerly of Barefoot and Font Valley breweries. The beers are only available at the Ship Inn and may vary slightly in alcoholic strength as the brewer does not average out the ABV for duty payments as most microbrewers do; duty is paid on the actual ABV of each brew. Seasonal beer: Alelelujah (ABV 4.2%, Xmas).

Sandcastles at Dawn (ABV 3.8%)

Sea Coal (ABV 4%)

Sea Dog (ABV 4%)

Sea Wheat (ABV 4%)

Ship Hop Ale (ABV 4.2%)

Dolly Daydream (ABV 4.3%)

Indian Summer (ABV 4.4%)

Shires

Shires Brewery, All Nations Brewhouse, 20 Coalport Road, Madeley, Shropshire, TF7 5DP

THE BREWERIES

☎ (01952) 580570 (Brewery) ☎ (01746) 769606 (Office) ✉ info@shiresbrewery.co.uk
🌐 shiresbrewery.co.uk

Shires Brewery (formerly Worfield) was launched in 2009 and is based at the historic All Nations Brewhouse in Madeley near Telford, which has a brewing tradition stretching back to 1831. Mike Handley supervises the 10-barrel plant. The brewery supply the All Nations tap house next door as well as other outlets. Seasonal beers: see website.

Coalport Mild (OG 1034, ABV 3.5%)
Traditional dark mild, full of nutty flavour from dark malts and full-bodied for its strength.

Best Bitter (OG 1039, ABV 3.8%)
Pale in colour with fruity undertones and a hint of citrus. A tasty session beer. Sold in the All Nations as Dabley Ale.

Dabley Ale (OG 1039, ABV 3.8%)
Pale, fruit and citrus tasting session beer.

OBJ (Oh Be Joyful!) (OG 1043, ABV 4.2%) ◆
A light and sweet bitter; delicate flavour belies the strength.

Shropshire Pride (OG 1045, ABV 4.5%)
A mid-coloured bitter, very full-bodied and malty with a pleasant bittersweet balance.

Severn Gorgeous (OG 1048, ABV 4.8%)
A light-bodied ale with full hop bitterness accompanying pine and citrus aromas.

Dabley Gold (OG 1050, ABV 5%)
The big brother of Dabley Ale, produced from the same recipe but brewed to a higher gravity giving a sweeter, fuller flavour.

Shoes SIBA

Shoes Brewery, Three Horseshoes Inn, Norton Canon, Hereford, HR4 7BH
☎ (01544) 318375
Tours by arrangement

Landlord Frank Goodwin was a keen home brewer who decided in 1994 to brew on a commercial basis for his pub. The beers are brewed from malt extract and are normally only available at the Three Horseshoes. Each September Canon Bitter is brewed with 'green' hops fresh from the harvest. Bottle-conditioned beers are available.

Canon Bitter (OG 1038, ABV 3.6%)

Norton Ale (OG 1040, ABV 4.1%)

Peploe's Tipple (OG 1060, ABV 6%)

Farriers Ale (OG 1114, ABV 15.5%)

Shotover SIBA (NEW)

Shotover Brewing Co Ltd, Coopers Yard, Manor Farm Road, Horspath, Oxfordshire, OX33 1SD
☎ (01865) 876770 ☎ 07801 570444
✉ ed@shotoverbrewing.com
🌐 shotoverbrewing.com
Shop: please ring or email first
Tours by arrangement

Shotover is a family-run craft brewery four miles from Oxford city centre. It began brewing in 2009. 10 outlets are supplied direct. Bottle-conditioned beers are available and suitable for vegetarians and vegans. Vegetarian cask ale can be supplied on request.

Prospect (ABV 3.7%)
A pale copper, hoppy session bitter.

Scholar (ABV 4.5%)
A mid-copper classic English bitter.

Shropshire SIBA

Shropshire Brewery, The Brew House, Aston Park, Soulton Road, Wem, Shropshire, SY4 5SD

Sales & Administration: Suite 5, Victoria Square, Newport Road, Whitchurch, Shropshire, SY13 1QD
☎ (01948) 667947
✉ info@theshropshirebrewery.co.uk
🌐 theshropshirebrewery.co.uk

Originally set up in 1988 following the closure of Shrewsbury & Wem Brewery, the brewery moved to its present site in 1990. A new company was formed in 2008 (known as the Wem Brewery) following the purchase of Hanby Ales by locals Steven and Scott Woodland, thus continuing the 200 year old tradition of brewing in the area. Around 300 outlets are supplied direct. Bottle-conditioned beers are available. In 2010 the name changed to The Shropshire Brewery.

Drawwell Bitter (OG 1039, ABV 3.9%) ◆
A hoppy beer with excellent bitterness, both in taste and aftertaste. Beautiful amber colour.

Black Magic Mild (OG 1041, ABV 4%) ◆
A dark, reddish-brown mild, which is dry and bitter with a roast malt taste.

All Seasons (OG 1042, ABV 4.2%)
A light, hoppy bitter, well balanced and thirst quenching, brewed with a fine blend of Cascade and Fuggles hops.

Rainbow Chaser (OG 1043, ABV 4.3%)
A pale beer brewed with Styrian Goldings hops.

Wem Special (OG 1044, ABV 4.4%)
A pale, straw-coloured, smooth, hoppy bitter.

Cascade (OG 1045, ABV 4.5%)
A pale beer, brewed with American Cascade hops, producing a clean crisp flavour and a hoppy finish.

Golden Honey (OG 1045, ABV 4.5%)
A beer made with the addition of Australian honey. Not over sweet.

Scorpio Porter (OG 1045, ABV 4.5%)
A dark porter with a complex palate introducing hints of coffee and chocolate, contrasting and complementing the background hoppiness.

Stout (OG 1044, ABV 4.5%)
A full-bodied, rich ruby/black coloured stout. A blend of four malts produces a distinct chocolate malt dry flavour, with a mushroom-coloured head.

Premium (OG 1046, ABV 4.6%)
An amber-coloured beer that is sweeter and fruitier than most of the beers above. Slight malt and hop taste.

Old Wemian (OG 1049, ABV 4.9%)
Golden-brown colour with an aroma of malt and hops and a soft, malty palate.

Taverners (OG 1053, ABV 5.3%)
A smooth and fruity old ale, full of body.

Cherry Bomb (OG 1060, ABV 6%)
A splendid rich and fruity beer with maraschino cherry flavour.

Joy Bringer (OG 1060, ABV 6%)

Deceptively strong beer with a distinct ginger flavour.

Nutcracker (OG 1060, ABV 6%)
Tawny beer with a fine blend of malt and hops.

Shugborough

Shugborough Brewery, Shugborough Estate, Milford, Staffordshire, ST17 0XB
☎ (01782) 823447 ⊕ shugborough.org.uk
Tours daily Mar-Oct

Brewing in the original brewhouse at Shugborough, home of the Earls of Lichfield, restarted in 1990 but a lack of expertise led to the brewery being a static museum piece until Titanic Brewery of Stoke-on-Trent (qv) began helping in 1996. Brewing takes place every weekend during the visitor season with museum guides in period costume.

Miladys Fancy (OG 1048, ABV 4.6%)

Lordships Own (OG 1054, ABV 5%)

Silverstone

Silverstone Brewing Co Ltd, Kingshill Farm, Syresham, nr Silverstone, Northamptonshire, NN13 5TH
☎ (01280) 850629
✉ services@silverstonebrewingcompany.com
⊕ silverstonebrewingcompany.com
Tours by arrangement

⊠ The brewery, which is located near the celebrated motor racing circuit, opened in 2008. In keeping with its motor racing theme the brewery is the proud sponsor of Formula V10. 60 outlets are supplied direct.

Pitstop Bitter (OG 1038, ABV 3.8%)

On the Button (OG 1041, ABV 4%)

Chequered Flag (OG 1044, ABV 4.5%)

Sinclair

See Orkney

Six Bells SIBA

▤ **Six Bells Brewery, Church Street, Bishop's Castle, Shropshire, SY9 5AA**
☎ (01588) 638930 ⊕ sixbellsbrewery.co.uk
Tours by arrangement

⊠ Neville Richards – 'Big Nev' – started brewing in 1997 with a five-barrel plant and two fermenters. Alterations in 1999 included two more fermenters, a new grain store and mashing equipment. He supplies a number of customers both within the county and over the border in Wales. A new 12-barrel plant opened in 2007. In addition to the core beer range, 12 monthly specials are produced.

Big Nev's (OG 1037, ABV 3.8%)
A pale, fairly hoppy bitter.

Goldings BB (OG 1041, ABV 4%)
Made entirely with Goldings hops; moderately hoppy with a distinctive aroma.

Cloud Nine (OG 1043, ABV 4.2%)
Pale amber-colour with a slight citrus finish.

Skinner's SIBA

Skinner's Brewing Co Ltd, Riverside, Newham Road, Truro, Cornwall, TR1 2DP
☎ (01872) 271885 ✉ info@skinnersbrewery.com
⊕ skinnersbrewery.com
Shop Mon-Sat 10am-5pm
Tours by arrangement (ring 01872 245689)

⊠ Skinner's brewery was founded in 1997. To increase production the brewery moved to bigger premises in 2003, opening a brewery shop and visitor centre. The brewery is now a 25-barrel plant with production capacity of 375 barrels a week. Since opening, the brewery has won numerous awards. Merchandise and beer are available to purchase online. Seasonal beers: see website.

Ginger Tosser (OG 1038, ABV 3.8%)
Hoppy golden ale fused with Cornish honey. The rounded finish has a hint of ginger.

Spriggan Ale (OG 1038, ABV 3.8%) ◆
A light golden, hoppy bitter. Well-balanced with a smooth bitter finish.

Betty Stogs (OG 1040, ABV 4%) 🍴 ◆
Light hop perfume with underlying malt. Easy-drinking copper ale with balance of citrus and apple fruit, malt and bitterness, plus a hint of sulphur. Bitter finish is slow to develop but long to fade.

Heligan Honey (OG 1040, ABV 4%) 🍴 ◆
Creamy copper beer with malt and a hint of honey on the nose. Taste is dominated by sweetness balanced by bitterness and a little hop. The finish is fruity and bitter, fading slowly.

Keel Over (OG 1041, ABV 4.2%)
A classic Cornish bitter, amber in colour, beautifully balanced with a smooth finish.

Cornish Knocker Ale (OG 1044, ABV 4.5%) ◆
Refreshing, amber/gold beer full of life with hops all the way through. Spice and fruit in the mouth balanced by bitter and malt undertones, with a clean and lasting bittersweet finish.

Figgy's Brew (OG 1044, ABV 4.5%) ◆
A classic, dark, premium-strength bitter. Full-flavoured with a smooth finish.

Hunny Bunny (OG 1045, ABV 4.5%)

Cornish Blonde (OG 1048, ABV 5%)
A combination of wheat malt and English and American hops makes this light-coloured wheat beer deceptively easy to drink.

Slater's SIBA

Eccleshall Brewing Co Ltd, Slater's Brewery, St Albans Road, Common Road Industrial Estate, Stafford, ST16 3DR
☎ (01785) 257976 ✉ sales@slatersales.co.uk
⊕ slatersales.co.uk
Shop Mon-Fri 9am-5pm, Sat 10am-1pm
Tours by arrangement

⊛ The brewery was opened in 1995 and in 2006 moved to new, larger premises, resulting in a tripling of capacity. It has won numerous awards from CAMRA and SIBA and supplies more than 1,100 outlets. One pub is owned, the George at Eccleshall, which serves as the brewery tap.

Why Knot (ABV 3.6%)
A golden bitter with balanced malt and hops leading to a long, pleasant astringency.

THE BREWERIES

Original (OG 1040, ABV 4%) ◆
Amber bitter. Malty aroma with caramel notes, hoppy taste develops into a dry hoppy finish with a touch of sweetness.

Top Totty (OG 1040, ABV 4%) ◆
Great yellow colour with a fruit and hop nose. Hop and fruit balanced taste leads to citrus hints with mouth-watering edges. Dry finish with tangs of lemon.

Queen Bee (OG 1042, ABV 4.2%) ◆
Golden with a sweet and spicy aroma and hop background. Honey sweet taste followed by a gentle bitter finish on the tongue.

Premium (OG 1044, ABV 4.4%) ◆
Pale brown bitter with malt and caramel aroma. Malt and caramel taste supported by hops and some fruit provide a warming descent and satisfyingly bitter mouthfeel.

Slaughterhouse SIBA

Slaughterhouse Brewery Ltd, Bridge Street, Warwick, CV34 5PD
☎ (01926) 490986
✉ enquiries@slaughterhousebrewery.com
⊕ slaughterhousebrewery.com
Tours by arrangement

Production began in 2003 on a four-barrel plant in a former slaughterhouse. Due to its success, beer production now consists mainly of Saddleback, supplemented by monthly special and seasonal beers. Around 30 outlets are supplied. The brewery premises are licensed for off-sales direct to the public. Seasonal beers: see website.

Saddleback Best Bitter (OG 1038, ABV 3.8%)
Amber-coloured session bitter with a distinctive Challenger hop flavour.

Small Paul's

Small Paul's Brewery, 27 Briar Close, Gillingham, Dorset, SP8 4SS
☎ (01747) 823574 ✉ smallbrewer@aol.com
Tours by arrangement

⊠ The brewery was launched in 2006 by an enthusiastic home brewer on a half-barrel plant. There are usually two brews a month and half a dozen local free houses and clubs are supplied direct with beers being supplied to festivals further afield. Different beers can be designed and brewed to order.

Gylla's Gold (OG 1039, ABV 3.8%) ◆
Mild fruity hop aroma leads to bitter hop flavours and a lingering dry hop aftertaste.

Wyvern (OG 1044, ABV 4.4%) ◆
Red-brown, well-balanced best bitter with malt and caramel flavours and short, bittersweet finish.

Gillingham Pale (OG 1045, ABV 4.5%) ◆
Fruity, caramel aromas lead to complex bitter flavours and short, dry finish.

Samuel Smith

Samuel Smith Old Brewery (Tadcaster), High Street, Tadcaster, North Yorkshire, LS24 9SB
☎ (01937) 832225

☺ A fiercely independent, family-owned company. Tradition, quality and value are important, resulting in brewing without any artificial additives. All real ale is supplied in wooden casks, though nitrokeg has replaced cask beer in some pubs in recent years. An unfiltered draught wheat beer is a recent addition. Around 200 pubs are owned. A bottle-conditioned beer was introduced in 2008 (Yorkshire Stingo, ABV 8%) but is only available in specialist off-licences.

Old Brewery Bitter/OBB (OG 1040, ABV 4%) ◆
Malt dominates the aroma, with an initial burst of malt, hops and fruit in the taste, which is sustained in the aftertaste.

Snowdonia SIBA

▤ **Snowdonia Brewery, Snowdonia Parc Brewpub & Campsite, Waunfawr, Caernarfon, Gwynedd, LL55 4AQ**
☎ (01286) 650409 ✉ info@snowdonia-park.co.uk
⊕ snowdonia-park.co.uk

Snowdonia started brewing in 1998 in a two-barrel brewhouse. The brewing is now carried out by the owner, Carmen Pierce. The beer is brewed solely for the Snowdonia Park pub and campsite.

Snowdonia Gold (OG 1040, ABV 4%)

Carmen Sutra (OG 1043, ABV 4.4%)

Welsh Highland Bitter (OG 1048, ABV 5.2%)

Son of Sid

▤ **Son of Sid Brewery, The Chequers, 71 Main Road, Little Gransden, Bedfordshire, SG19 3DW**
☎ (01767) 677348
✉ chequersgransden@btinternet.com

⊠ Son of Sid was established in 2007 on a 2.5-barrel plant in a separate room of the pub. The brewery can be viewed from the lounge bar. It is named after the father of the current landlord, who ran the pub for 42 years. His son has carried the business on for the past 18 years as a family-run enterprise. Beer is sold in the pub and at local beer festivals.

Muckcart Mild (ABV 3.5%)

Golden Shower (ABV 3.9%)

South Hams SIBA

South Hams Brewery Ltd, Stokeley Barton, Stokenham, Kingsbridge, Devon, TQ7 2SE
☎ (01548) 581151
✉ info@southhamsbrewery.co.uk
⊕ southhamsbrewery.co.uk
Tours by arrangement

⊠ The brewery moved to its present site in 2003, with a 10-barrel plant and plenty of room to expand. It supplies more than 60 outlets in Plymouth and south Devon. Wholesalers are used to distribute to other areas. Two pubs are owned. Seasonal beers: see website. Bottle-conditioned beers are also available.

Devon Pride (OG 1039, ABV 3.8%)

Re'session Ale (ABV 4%)

XSB (OG 1043, ABV 4.2%) ◆
Amber nectar with a fruity nose and a bitter finish.

Wild Blonde (ABV 4.4%)

Eddystone (OG 1050, ABV 4.8%) ▤

Southport SIBA

Southport Brewery, Unit 3, Enterprise Business Park, Russell Road, Southport, Merseyside, PR9 7RF
☎ 07748 387652 ✉ southportbrewery@fsmail.net
⊕ southportbrewery.co.uk

☺ The Southport brewery opened in 2004 as a 2.5-barrel plant but moved to a five-barrel plant due to demand. Around 30 pubs are supplied in the North-west. It also supplies the free trade via Boggart Brewery (qv). Seasonal beers: see website.

Cyclone (OG 1039.5, ABV 3.8%)
A bronze-coloured bitter with a fruity blackcurrant aftertaste.

Sandgrounder Bitter (OG 1039.5, ABV 3.8%)
Pale, hoppy session bitter with a floral character.

Carousel (OG 1041.5, ABV 4%)
A refreshing, floral, hoppy best bitter.

Golden Sands (OG 1041.5, ABV 4%) 🍷
A golden-coloured, triple hopped bitter with citrus flavour.

Natterjack (OG 1043.5, ABV 4.3%)
A premium bitter with fruit notes and a hint of coffee.

For Southport Football Club:

Grandstand Gold (OG 1039.5, ABV 3.8%)
A gold-coloured bitter, available for all home matches.

Spectrum EAB SIBA

Spectrum Brewery, Unit 11, Wellington Road, Tharston, Norwich, NR15 2PE
☎ 07949 254383 ✉ info@spectrumbrewery.co.uk
⊕ spectrumbrewery.co.uk
Tours by arrangement

⊗ Proprietor and founder Andy Mitchell established Spectrum in 2002. The brewery moved premises in 2007 as well as increasing brew length and gaining organic certification for all beers. Seasonal beers: Spring Promise (ABV 4.5%, Jan-Feb), Autumn Beer (ABV 4.5%, Sep-Oct —names and formulations vary), Yule Fuel (ABV 7%). The beers are also available mail order via the website.

Light Fantastic (OG 1035.5, ABV 3.7%) ◆
Golden hued with a refreshing citrus character on nose and taste. Grapefruit notes add depth to the hoppy bitterness in the beginning. Initial malt background fades to a sharp, slightly astringent finish.

Dark Fantastic (OG 1041, ABV 3.8%) ◆
A rich vine fruit and roast aroma introduces this dark mild. Heavy chocolate notes permeate the malty sweetness, contrasting with the underlying bitterness. A long, rich, tapering ending.

Bezants (OG 1038, ABV 4%) ◆
Dry golden ale with a direct bitterness and a light hop flavour.

42 (OG 1039.5, ABV 4.2%) ◆
Sulphurous notes in the nose do not transfer to the taste. Although bitterness is the outstanding flavour there is more than a trace of both malt and soft fruits. A quick, crisp ending.

Black Buffle (OG 1047, ABV 4.5%) ◆
The deep roast backbone is softened by a blackcurrant fruitiness. Malt is in evidence but is

soon masked by a growing bitterness. A satisfying spectrum of aroma and taste.

XXXX (OG 1045.5, ABV 4.6%)
A deep copper strong bitter, first brewed for the proprietor's 40th birthday.

Wizzard (OG 1047.5, ABV 4.9%) ◆
Rich and fruity in nose and taste. A full-bodied, complex brew with raisin and cherry matching the heavy malt overtones. Well-balanced refreshing and creamy with an increasingly bitter finish.

Old Stoatwobbler (OG 1064.5, ABV 6%) ◆
Rich and creamy old ale with a dark chocolate digestive flavour. Roast and vine fruits with a touch of caramel mask a background hoppy bitterness. A long sustained finish.

Trip Hazard (OG 1061.5, ABV 6.5%) ◆
A sweet, fruity brew with bubblegum notes throughout. Smooth bodied and easy drinking. A bitter hop undertow lightens the sweet resinous maltiness towards the sustained end.

Solstice Blinder (OG 1079, ABV 8.5%)
Strong IPA. Brewed twice a year, dry-hopped and left to mature (unfined) for at least three months before release in time for the solstices.

Spinning Dog

See Hereford

Spire SIBA

Spire Brewery Ltd, Units 2-3 & 9, Gisborne Close, Ireland Business Park, Staveley, Chesterfield, Derbyshire, S43 3JT
☎ (01246) 476005 ✉ info@spirebrewery.co.uk
⊕ spirebrewery.co.uk
Shop Mon-Fri 9.30am-4.30pm
Tours by arrangement

☺ The brewery was set up by ex-Scots Guards musician and teacher David McLaren in 2006. The brewery continues to expand and produces a large range of both cask and bottle-conditioned beers. More than 100 outlets are supplied direct. Seasonal beers: see website.

Good As Gold (OG 1037, ABV 3.8%) ◆
Tasty golden session bitter with a surprising amount of body for its strength. Mildly fruity sweet start, leading to a short, yet dry aftertaste.

Overture (OG 1038, ABV 3.9%) 🍴 ◆
Traditional session beer with a little malt and hop aroma. Balanced malt flavours lead to a developing bitterness, ending in a malt finish and slight caramel aftertaste.

80/- Ale (OG 1043, ABV 4.3%) ◆
Good example of a Scottish 80/- style ale. Easy to drink, combining flavours of treacle and biscuit, leading to a slight bitter chocolate aftertaste.

Dark Side of the Moon (OG 1043, ABV 4.3%) 🍷 ◆
Complex and satisfying ruby mild with coffee aroma and toffee flavours. Dark and sweet but not too strong!

Chesterfield Best Bitter (OG 1044, ABV 4.5%) ◆
Classic brown strong bitter with malt and fruit flavours and a hint of caramel and chocolate in the finish. There is a little bitterness in the aftertaste.

Land of Hop & Glory (OG 1044, ABV 4.5%) ◆

An excellent example of a clean, crisp-tasting golden ale. Easy to drink with grapefruit and lemon flavours developing. These complex citrus hop flavours lead to a bitter, dry aftertaste.

Twist & Stout (OG 1044, ABV 4.5%) ◆
Creamy and dark with flavours of bitter chocolate and coffee. Easy drinking.

Sovereign IPA (OG 1051, ABV 5.2%)

Sgt Pepper Stout (OG 1053, ABV 5.5%) ⬜ ◆
Unique full-flavoured stout brewed with ground black pepper. Liquorice and pepper flavours dominate on both aroma and taste in this original, complex dark and delicious beer.

Britannia Cream Ale (OG 1062, ABV 6.4%) ◆
Strong, complex beer to be savoured and appreciated. Full bodied, with hints of marmalade tartness and fruit, leading to a dry, slightly bitter finish.

Spitting Feathers

Spitting Feathers Brewery, Common Farm, Waverton, Chester, CH3 7QT
☎ (01244) 332052 ✉ info@spittingfeathers.org
⊕ spittingfeathers.org
Tours by arrangement

Spitting Feathers was established in 2005 at Common Farm on the outskirts of Chester. The brewery and visitors' bar are in traditional sandstone buildings around a cobbled yard, which is also the setting for the West Cheshire Brewers' Beer Festival in July. Beehives provide honey for the brewery and spent grains are fed to livestock. The brewery opened its first pub in Chester in 2008. Around 200 outlets are supplied. Seasonal beers: see website. Bottle-conditioned beers are also available. All bottled beers are suitable for vegetarians and vegans.

Farmhouse Ale (OG 1035, ABV 3.6%)

Thirstquencher (OG 1038, ABV 3.9%) ◆
Powerful hop aroma leads into the taste. Bitterness and a fruity citrus hop flavour fight for attention. A sharp, clean golden beer with a long, dry, bitter aftertaste.

Special Ale (OG 1041, ABV 4.2%) ◆
Complex tawny-coloured beer with a sharp, grainy mouthfeel. Malty with good hop coming through in the aroma and taste. Hints of nuttiness and a touch of acidity. Dry, astringent finish.

Old Wavertonian (OG 1043, ABV 4.4%) ◆
Creamy and smooth stout. Full-flavoured with coffee notes in aroma and taste. Roast and nut flavours throughout, leading to a hoppy, bitter finish.

Basket Case (OG 1046, ABV 4.8%) ◆
Reddish, complex beer. Sweetness and fruit dominate taste, offset by hops and bitterness that follow through into the aftertaste.

Springhead SIBA

Springhead Fine Ales Ltd, Old Great North Road, Sutton-on-Trent, Newark, Nottinghamshire, NG23 6QS
☎ (01636) 821000 ✉ angie@springhead.co.uk
⊕ springhead.co.uk
Shop open daily 9am-6pm
Tours by arrangement

⊕ Springhead Brewery opened in 1990 moving to bigger premises three years later and, to meet increased demand, expanded to a brew length of 50 barrels. Around 500 outlets are supplied direct. Many of the beer names have a Civil War theme. Drop of the Black Stuff is suitable for vegans.

Liberty (OG 1036, ABV 3.8%)
A pale, straw-coloured beer with hints of lemon and a dry, biscuity finish.

Drop of the Black Stuff (OG 1041, ABV 4%)
Ominously dark but not heavy, smooth with the lingering finish of roasted barley.

Springhead (OG 1041, ABV 4%)
A clean-tasting, easy-drinking, hoppy bitter.

Rupert's Ruin (OG 1042, ABV 4.2%)
A caramel-coloured, easy-drinking bitter that combines a fruity aroma and a malty aftertaste.

The Bees Knees (OG 1042, ABV 4.2%)
A light golden beer made with local wildflower honey. Refreshing, mellow but not sweet.

Ginger Pig (OG 1044, ABV 4.4%)
A pale beer based on a 13th-century recipe that includes rosemary. It has a delicate flavour with a hint of ginger and a dry finish.

Oliver's Army (OG 1044, ABV 4.4%)
A ruby red beer with a fruity aroma and creamy head.

Charlie's Angel (OG 1045, ABV 4.5%)
A light, golden beer with a deeply fruity nose from the addition of oranges, well-balanced bitterness and a dry finish from the hint of coriander.

Sweetlips (OG 1046, ABV 4.6%)
A smooth, light, refreshing beer with hints of grapefruit.

The Leveller (OG 1047, ABV 4.8%)
A dark, smoky intense flavour with a toffee finish. Brewed in the style of Belgian Trappist ale.

Mulled Over (OG 1045, ABV 5%)
A tawny, smooth beer with a hint of juniper and cinnamon.

Newark Castle Brown (OG 1049, ABV 5%)
A rich, aromatic dark amber beer with a satisfying bitter finish.

Willy's Wheatbeer (OG 1051, ABV 5%)
A delicate, almost floral aroma with an initial fruitiness leading to a long, dry, biscuity finish. Brewed in the style of German white beers.

Roaring Meg (OG 1052, ABV 5.5%)
Smooth with a sweet, citrus honey aroma and a dry finish.

Stables

▤ **Stables Brewing Co, Beamish Hall Country House Hotel, Beamish, County Durham, DH9 0YB**
☎ (01207) 288750 ✉ stablejohn@hotmail.co.uk
⊕ beamish-hall.co.uk/stables
Tours by arrangement

⊕ Stables was established as part of a £1 million development of an old stable block, converting a disused building to a pub, restaurant and micro-brewery.

Old Miner Tommy (OG 1037, ABV 3.7%)

Beamish Hall Best Bitter (OG 1038, ABV 3.8%)

Bobby Dazzler (OG 1042, ABV 4.2%)

Coppy Lane (OG 1043, ABV 4.2%)

Silver Buckles (OG 1044, ABV 4.4%)

Beamish Burn (OG 1045, ABV 4.5%)

Bell Tower (OG 1052, ABV 5%)

Stanway

Stanway Brewery, Stanway, Cheltenham, Gloucestershire, GL54 5PQ
☎ (01386) 584320 stanwaybrewery.co.uk

Stanway is a small brewery founded in 1993 with a five-barrel plant that confines its sales to the Cotswolds area (15 to 20 outlets). The brewery is the only known plant in the country to use wood-fired coppers for all its production. Seasonal beers: see website.

Stanney Bitter (OG 1042, ABV 4.5%)
A light, refreshing, amber-coloured beer, dominated by hops in the aroma, with a bitter taste and a hoppy, bitter finish.

Stationhouse

See Frodsham

Steamin' Billy

Steamin' Billy Brewing Co Ltd, Registered Office: 5 The Oval, Oadby, Leicestershire, LE2 5JB
☎ (0116) 271 2616 enquiries@steamin-billy.co.uk steamin-billy.co.uk
Tours by arrangement

Steamin' Billy was formed in 1995 by licensee Barry Lount and brewer Bill Allingham. Bill originally brewed in Derbyshire but after outgrowing the plant the beers have since been contracted out. Bill is currently brewing at Tower Brewery (qv) in conjunction with John Mills. Four pubs are owned. The beers are named after the owners' Jack Russell dog, which is featured in cartoon form on the pump clips. Seasonal beers: see website. See Tower for regular beers.

Steel City (NEW)

Steel City Brewing Ltd, c/o The Wellington, 1 Henry Street, Sheffield, South Yorkshire, S3 7EQ
hops@steelcitybrewing.co.uk
steelcitybrewing.co.uk

Steel City was established in 2009 and makes use of the brewing facilities at the Little Ale Cart Brewery in Sheffield. Beer is brewed once a month, a different beer each time. A nine-gallon mini-plant is used to brew one-off beers, often extreme with an emphasis on very pale and very hoppy brews.

Stewart SIBA

Stewart Brewing Ltd, Unit 5, 42 Dryden Road, Bilston Glen Industrial Estate, Loanhead, Midlothian, EH20 9LZ
☎ (0131) 440 2442 stewartbrewing@gmail.com
stewartbrewing.co.uk
Shop Mon-Thu 10am-5pm, Fri 10am-6pm
Tours by arrangement

Established in 2004 by Steve Stewart, a qualified master brewer, and specialising in high-quality cask ales, all made from natural ingredients. The beers are widely available in South-east Scotland. Seasonal beers supplement the regular range. Beer in mini-casks can be purchased direct from the brewery for collection or delivery in the Edinburgh area. Bottle-conditioned beers are also available.

Pentland IPA (OG 1040, ABV 3.9%)
Pleasing, hoppy, golden session ale. The dry bitter taste is well balanced by sweetness from the malt and fruit flavours. The aftertaste is dry with a lingering bitterness.

Copper Cascade (OG 1041, ABV 4.1%)
A tawny-coloured beer born from American hops and Scottish malt. The hop character overlays a solid malt base. Hints of roast and substantial fruitiness give a complex character. A bittersweet taste leads to a dry bitter finish.

Edinburgh No.3 Premium Scotch Ale (OG 1043, ABV 4.3%)
A good example of a Scottish heavy ale. Full-bodied and dark with a predominantly malt character, fruit notes and a gentle infusion of hop. A bittersweet beer with a dry, moreish finish.

80/- (OG 1044, ABV 4.4%)
Superb traditional Scottish heavy. The complex profile is dominated by malt with fruit flavours giving a sweetish character typical of this beer style. Hops provide a gentle balancing bitterness that intensifies in the dry finish.

Edinburgh Gold (OG 1048, ABV 4.8%)
Full-bodied but easy-drinking Continental-style golden ale. Bitterness from the hop character is strong in the finish and complemented in the taste by a little sweetness from malt and fruit flavours.

Cauld Reekie (OG 1063, ABV 6.2%)
This strong, complex stout has dark malts and a little hop providing a pleasing bitterness, which is well balanced by sweeter fruit flavours.

Sticklegs

Sticklegs Brewery, Unit 7, Old Forge Court, Colchester Road, Elmstead Market, Essex, CO7 7EA
☎ 07962 012906 tom@sticklegs.co.uk
sticklegs.co.uk

Sticklegs was established in 2008 and expanded from a half-barrel to a two-barrel plant in 2009 serving pubs in north-east Essex. There are further plans for expansion to a five-barrel plant.

Malt Shovel Mild (OG 1032, ABV 3.4%)

MUA Bitter (OG 1034, ABV 3.4%)

Prizefighter (OG 1040, ABV 4.2%)

Stirling

See Traditional Scottish Ales

Stokesley (NEW)

Stokesley Brewing Co, Wainstones Brewery, Unit 9, Terry Dicken Industrial Estate, Station Road, Stokesley, TS9 7AE
☎ 07885 240226

Stokesley began brewing in 2010 using a 2.5-barrel plant.

THE BREWERIES

Amber (ABV 3.8%)

Sandstone (ABV 4%)

Ironstone (ABV 4.2%)

Jet (ABV 4.5%)

Stonehenge SIBA

Stonehenge Ales Ltd, The Old Mill, Mill Road, Netheravon, Salisbury, Wiltshire, SP4 9QB
☎ (01980) 670631 ✉ info@stonehengeales.co.uk
🌐 stonehengeales.co.uk
Tours by arrangement

The beer is brewed in a mill built in 1914 to generate electricity from the River Avon. The site was converted to a gravity-fed brewery in 1984 (Bunce's Brewery) and in 1994 the company was bought by Danish master brewer Stig Anker Andersen. More than 300 outlets in the south of England and several wholesalers are supplied. Seasonal beers: see website.

Spire Ale (OG 1037, ABV 3.8%)
A light, golden, hoppy bitter.

Pigswill (OG 1038, ABV 4%)
A full-bodied beer, rich in hop aroma, with a warm amber colour.

Heelstone (OG 1042, ABV 4.3%)
A crisp, clean, refreshing bitter, deep amber in colour, well balanced with a fruity blackcurrant nose.

Great Bustard (OG 1046, ABV 4.8%)
A strong, fruity, malty bitter.

Danish Dynamite (OG 1048, ABV 5%)
A strong, dry ale, slightly fruity with a well-balanced, bitter hop flavour.

Stonehouse

Stonehouse Brewery, Stonehouse, Weston, Oswestry, Shropshire, SY10 9ES
☎ (01691) 676457
✉ info@stonehousebrewery.co.uk
🌐 stonehousebrewery.co.uk
Shop Mon-Fri 9am-5pm
Tours by arrangement

Stonehouse was established early in 2007 by Shane Parr, on a 15-barrel plant. The brewery is based in former chicken sheds and is next to the old Cambrian railway line, hence the beer names. 120 outlets are supplied direct, mainly in mid and north Wales, Shropshire and South Cheshire. Bottle-conditioned beers are available.

Station Bitter (OG 1041, ABV 3.9%)

Cambrian Gold (OG 1042, ABV 4.2%)

Wheeltapper's Wheatbeer (OG 1045, ABV 4.5%)

KPA (OG 1047, ABV 4.6%)

Off the Rails (OG 1048, ABV 4.8%)

Storm SIBA

Storm Brewing Co Ltd, 2 Waterside, Macclesfield, Cheshire, SK11 7HJ
☎ (01625) 431234 ✉ stormbrewing@dsl.pipex.com
🌐 stormbrewing.co.uk

Storm Brewing was founded in 1998 and operated from an old ICI boiler room until 2001 when the brewing operation moved to the current location, which until 1937 was a public house known as the Mechanics Arms. More than 60 outlets are supplied in Cheshire, Manchester and the Peak District. Seasonal beers: Summer Breeze (ABV 3.8%), Looks Like Rain Dear (ABV 4.8%, Xmas). Bottle-conditioned beers are also available.

Beauforts Ale (OG 1038, ABV 3.8%)
Golden brown, full-flavoured session bitter with a lingering hoppy taste.

Desert Storm (OG 1039, ABV 3.9%)
Amber-coloured beer with a smoky flavour of fruit and malt.

Bitter Experience (OG 1040, ABV 4%)
A distinctive hop aroma draws you into this amber-coloured bitter. The palate has a mineral dryness that accentuates the crisp hop flavour and clean bitter finish.

Twister (OG 1041, ABV 4%)
A light golden bitter with a smooth fruity hop aroma complemented by a subtle bitter aftertaste.

Bosley Cloud (OG 1041, ABV 4.1%)
Dry, golden bitter with peppery hop notes throughout. Some initial sweetness and a mainly bitter aftertaste. Soft, well-balanced and quaffable.

Brainstorm (OG 1041, ABV 4.1%)
Light gold in colour and strong in citrus fruit flavours.

Ale Force (OG 1042, ABV 4.2%)
Amber, smooth-tasting, complex beer that balances malt, hop and fruit on the taste, leading to a roasty, slightly sweet aftertaste.

Downpour (OG 1043, ABV 4.3%)
A combination of Pearl and lager malts produces this pale ale with a full, fruity flavour with a hint of apple and sightly hoppy aftertaste.

PGA (OG 1044, ABV 4.4%)
Light, crisp, lager-style beer with a balance of malt, hops and fruit. Moderately bitter and slight dry aftertaste.

Tornado (OG 1044, ABV 4.4%)
Fruity premium bitter with some graininess. Dry, satisfying finish.

Hurricane Hubert (OG 1045, ABV 4.5%)
A dark beer with a refreshing full, fruity hop aroma and a subtle bitter aftertaste.

Windgather (OG 1045, ABV 4.5%)
A gold-coloured beer with a distinctive crisp, fruity flavour right through to the aftertaste.

Silk of Amnesia (OG 1047, ABV 4.7%)
Smooth premium, easy-drinking bitter. Fruit and hops dominate throughout. Not too sweet, with a good lasting finish.

Storm Damage (OG 1047, ABV 4.7%)
A light-coloured, well-hopped and fruity beer balanced by a clean bitterness and smooth full palate.

Typhoon (OG 1050, ABV 5%)
Copper-coloured, smooth strong bitter. Roasty overtones and a hint of caramel and marzipan.

Storyteller

Storyteller Brewery Ltd, Bay Horse Inn, Main Street, Terrington, York, YO60 6PP
☎ (01653) 648416
✉ storyteller@terringtonvillage.com
🌐 thestorytellerbrewery.co.uk

Storyteller was established in 2008. Originally it only brewed for the Bay Horse Inn in Terrington but now supplies other local pubs and festivals. In 2009 it doubled capacity. Seasonal beers: see website.

Full Moon (OG 1037, ABV 3.2%)
A traditional dark English mild.

R We (ABV 3.5%)

Genesis (OG 1039, ABV 3.8%)
A darker beer.

Telltale (OG 1039, ABV 3.8%)
A light-coloured session beer.

1402 (OG 1042, ABV 4.2%)
A golden, malty, hoppy ale.

Stowey

Stowey Brewery Ltd, Old Cider House, 25 Castle Street, Nether Stowey, Somerset, TA5 1LN
☎ (01278) 732228 ✉ info@stoweybrewery.co.uk
stoweybrewery.co.uk
Tours by arrangement (small groups only)

Stowey was established in 2006, primarily to supply the owners' guesthouse and to provide beer to participants on 'real ale walks' run from the accommodation. The brewery also runs brewery workshop courses and supplies seasonal brews to the village pubs on a guest beer basis.

Strands

Strands Brewery, Strands Inn, Nether Wasdale, Cumbria, CA20 1ET
☎ (019467) 26237 ✉ info@strandshotel.com
strandshotel.com
Tours by arrangement

Strands began brewing in early 2007 on a three-barrel plant with a 12-barrel fermenting capacity. The first beer produced was called Errmmm. . . as the owners couldn't think of a name for it.

Brown Bitter (OG 1042, ABV 3.8%)

Errmmm... (OG 1042, ABV 3.8%)

Corrsberg (ABV 4.1%)

Dafydd Ale (ABV 4.2%)

Bersteinale (OG 1047, ABV 4.5%)

Red Screes (OG 1047, ABV 4.5%)

T'Errmmm-inator (ABV 4.9%)

Strangford Lough

Strangford Lough Brewing Co, 22 Shore Road, Killyleagh, Downpatrick, Northern Ireland, BT30 9UE
☎ (028) 4482 1461 ✉ contact@slbc.ie slbc.ie

Beers for the company are contract-brewed by an unnamed brewery in England, though there are plans to build a plant in Northern Ireland. Bottle-conditioned beers: St Patrick's Best (ABV 3.8%), St Patrick's Gold (ABV 4.5%), St Patrick's Ale (ABV 6%), Barelegs Brew (ABV 4.5%), Legbiter (ABV 4.8%).

Strathaven

Strathaven Ales, Craigmill Brewery, Strathaven, ML10 6PB
☎ (01357) 520419 ✉ info@strathavenales.co.uk
strathavenales.co.uk
Shop Mon-Fri 9am-5pm (phone at weekend)
Tours by arrangement

Strathaven Ales is a 10-barrel brewery on the River Avon close to Strathaven and was converted from the remains of a 16th-century mill. The range is distributed throughout Scotland and the north of England. Seasonal beers: see website.

Clydesdale (OG 1038, ABV 3.8%)

Avondale (OG 1048, ABV 4%)

Old Mortality (OG 1046, ABV 4.2%)

Claverhouse (OG 1046, ABV 4.5%)

Stringers SIBA

Stringers Beer, Unit 3, Low Mill Business Park, Ulverston, Cumbria, LA12 9EE
☎ (01229) 581387 ✉ info@stringersbeer.co.uk
stringersbeer.co.uk

Stringers is a family-run, small craft brewery. Brewing started in 2008 on a five-barrel plant run on 100% renewable energy. A small number of seasonal beers are produced including Genuine Stunning (ABV 6.5%, Nov-Jan). No. 2 Stout and Dark Country are suitable for vegans.

Dark Country (OG 1036, ABV 3.5%)

Bitter (OG 1036, ABV 3.6%)
A straightforward old style darkish bitter with a lingering dry finish.

Golden (OG 1036, ABV 3.7%)
An easy-drinking, zingy, pale thirst quencher.

No. 2 Stout (OG 1041, ABV 4%)

Best Bitter (OG 1041, ABV 4.2%)
Well-crafted and well-balanced with a clean hoppy bitterness.

West Coast Blond (OG 1041, ABV 4.4%)

Stroud SIBA

Stroud Brewery Ltd, Unit 7, Phoenix Works, London Road, Thrupp, Stroud, Gloucestershire, GL5 2BU
☎ 07891 995878
Office: 141 Thrupp Lane, Thrupp, Stroud, Gloucestershire, GL5 2DQ
✉ greg@stroudbrewery.co.uk
stroudbrewery.co.uk
Tours by arrangement

The brewery was established in 2005 with production commencing in 2006 on a five-barrel plant. Stroud supports the local economy and does not sell any beer through supermarkets, delivering direct to around 50 pubs, independent retailers and direct to the public. A draught organic ale is produced and its full range of bottled beers are organic, all certified by the Soil Association. Seasonal beers: see website.

Tom Long (OG 1039, ABV 3.8%)
An amber-coloured bitter with a spicy citrus aroma.

Organic Ale (ABV 4%)
A fresh, hoppy, golden organic ale.

Budding (OG 1045, ABV 4.5%)
A pale ale with a grassy bitterness, sweet malt and floral aroma.

Stumpy's

See Yates'

Suddaby's SIBA

Suddaby's Ltd, Crown Hotel, 12 Wheelgate, Malton, North Yorkshire, YO17 7HP
☎ (01653) 692038 ✉ enquiries@suddabys.co.uk
suddabys.co.uk

Suddabys no longer brews on site. The beers are contract brewed by Brown Cow (qv) at Selby and are only sold in bottled form in the Malt'on Hops Beer & Wine Shop located within the Crown Hotel and a few other selected outlets. Suddabys draught beers are also available in the Crown Hotel.

Sulwath SIBA

Sulwath Brewers Ltd, The Brewery, 209 King Street, Castle Douglas, Dumfries & Galloway, DG7 1DT
☎ (01556) 504525 ✉ info@sulwathbrewers.co.uk
sulwathbrewers.co.uk
Tours daily at 1pm or by arrangement

Sulwath started brewing in 1995. The beers are supplied to markets as far away as Devon in the south and Aberdeen in the north. The brewery has a fully licensed brewery tap and off sales open 10am-5pm Mon-Sat. Cask ales are sold to around 100 outlets and four wholesalers. Seasonal beers: Rein Beer (ABV 4.5%, Nov-Dec), Tam O'Shanter (ABV 4.1%, Jan-Feb), Happy Hooker (ABV 4%, Feb), Woozy Wabbit (ABV 5%, Mar-Apr), Hells Bells (ABV 4.5%, May-Jun), Saltaire Cross (ABV 4.1%, Nov-Dec).

Cuil Hill (OG 1039, ABV 3.6%)
Distinctively fruity session ale with malt and hop undertones. The taste is bittersweet with a long-lasting dry finish.

John Paul Jones (ABV 4%)
A dark amber-coloured beer with a suggestion of sweetness in the aftertaste.

The Grace (OG 1044, ABV 4.3%)
A refreshing, rich ale with a full-bodied flavour that balances the caramel undertones.

Black Galloway (OG 1046, ABV 4.4%)
A robust porter/stout that derives its colour from the abundance of Maris Otter barley and chocolate malts used in the brewing process.

Criffel (OG 1044, ABV 4.6%)
Full-bodied beer with a distinctive bitterness. Fruit is to the fore of the taste with hops becoming increasingly dominant in the taste and finish.

Galloway Gold (OG 1049, ABV 5%)
A cask-conditioned lager that will be too sweet for many despite being heavily hopped.

Knockendoch (OG 1047, ABV 5%)
Dark, copper-coloured, reflecting a roast malt content, with bitterness from Challenger hops.

Solway Mist (OG 1052, ABV 5.5%)
A naturally cloudy wheat beer. Sweetish and fruity.

Summerskills SIBA

Summerskills Brewery, 15 Pomphlett Farm Industrial Estate, Broxton Drive, Billacombe, Plymouth, Devon, PL9 7BG
☎ (01752) 481283 ✉ info@summerskills.co.uk
summerskills.co.uk

Originally established in a vineyard in 1983 at Bigbury-on-Sea, Summerskills moved to its present site in 1985 and has expanded since then. National distribution is carried out by wholesalers. 20 outlets are supplied by the brewery. Seasonal beers: see website. Bottle-conditioned beers are also available.

Cellar Vee (OG 1037, ABV 3.7%)

Hopscotch (OG 1041, ABV 4.1%)

Best Bitter (OG 1043, ABV 4.3%)
A mid-brown beer, with plenty of malt and hops through the aroma, taste and finish. A good session beer.

Tamar (OG 1043, ABV 4.3%)
A tawny-coloured bitter with a fruity aroma and a hop taste and finish.

Menacing Dennis (OG 1045, ABV 4.5%)

Devon Dew (OG 1047, ABV 4.7%)

Summer Wine SIBA

Summer Wine Brewery Ltd, The Old Furnace, Unit 15, Crossley Mills, New Mill Road, Honley, Holmfirth, West Yorkshire, HD9 6QB
☎ (01484) 665466
✉ info@summerwinebrewery.co.uk
summerwinebrewery.co.uk

Brewing commenced in 2006 on a 10-gallon kit with an emphasis on bottle-conditioned beer. A 2007 upgrade saw a 0.5-barrel plant installed and in 2008 the brewery expanded to a six-barrel plant. Over 500 outlets are supplied direct. Bottle-conditioned beers are available. Two differing specials are available each month.

Dambusters Dark Mild (ABV 3.5%)

Elbow Grease (ABV 3.8%)

Helios (ABV 4%)

Tiberius (ABV 4.2%)

Houblon (ABV 4.4%)

Invictus (ABV 4.5%)

Treason Treacle Stout (ABV 4.8%)

Teleporter (ABV 5%)

Apache (ABV 5.2%)

Surrey Hills SIBA

Surrey Hills Brewery Ltd, Old Scotland Farm, Staple Lane, Shere, Guildford, Surrey, GU5 9TE
☎ (01483) 212812 ✉ info@surreyhills.co.uk
surreyhills.co.uk
Open for beer sales Thu-Fri 12-2pm, 4-5pm; Sat 10am-12pm
Tours by arrangement

Surrey Hills started in 2005 and is based in an old milking parlour, hidden away down country lanes in the Surrey Hills. More than 95% of production is sold in outlets less than 15 miles from the brewery. Seasonal beers: see website. The brewery plans to move in the near future to an address in Dorking – see website for details.

Ranmore Ale (ABV 3.8%)

A light session beer with plenty of flavour. An earthy hoppy nose leads into a grapefruit and hoppy taste and a clean, bitter finish.

Shere Drop (ABV 4.2%) ◆
A golden amber ale, hoppy with some balancing malt. There is a pleasant citrus aroma and a noticeable fruitiness in the taste. The finish is dry, hoppy and bitter.

Suthwyk

Suthwyk Ales, Offwell Farm, Southwick, Fareham, Hampshire, PO17 6DX
☎ (02392) 325252 ✉ mjbazeley@suthwykales.com
🌐 suthwykales.com/southwickbrewhouse.co.uk

Barley farmer Martin Bazeley does not brew himself. The beers are produced by Oakleaf Brewing (qv) in Gosport. For beer range please see Oakleaf entry.

Sutton

See South Hams

Swan

Swan Microbrewery, Swan on the Green, West Peckham, Maidstone, Kent, ME18 5JW
☎ (01622) 812271 ✉ info@swan-on-the-green.co.uk 🌐 swan-on-the-green.co.uk
Tours by arrangement

⊗ The brewery was established in 2000 to produce handcrafted beers. The beers are not filtered and no artificial ingredients are used. One pub is owned and other outlets and beer festivals are occasionally supplied. Seasonal beers are brewed including Ginger (ABV 3.6%, summer).

Fuggles Pale (OG 1037, ABV 3.6%)

Trumpeter Best (OG 1041, ABV 4%)

Cygnet (OG 1048, ABV 4.2%)

Bewick (OG 1052, ABV 5.3%)

Swansea SIBA

Swansea Brewing Co, Joiners Arms, 50 Bishopston Road, Bishopston, Swansea, SA3 3EJ
☎ (01792) 232658/290197 (Office)

Office: 74 Hawthorne Avenue, Uplands, Swansea, SA2 0LY ✉ rory@swansea_brewlng.co.uk
Tours by arrangement

◎ Opened in 1996, Swansea was the first commercial brewery in the area for almost 30 years and is the city's only brew-pub. It doubled its capacity within the first year and now produces four regular beers and occasional experimental ones. Four regular outlets are supplied along with other pubs in the South Wales area. Seasonal beers: St Teilo's Tipple (ABV 5.5%), Barland Strong (ABV 6%), Pwll Du XXXX (ABV 4.9%).

Deep Slade Dark (OG 1034, ABV 4%)

Bishopswood Bitter (OG 1038, ABV 4.3%) ◆
A delicate aroma of hops and malt in this pale brown colour. The taste is a balanced mix of hops and malt with a growing hoppy bitterness ending in a lasting bitter finish.

Three Cliffs Gold (OG 1042, ABV 4.7%) ◆
A golden beer with a hoppy and fruity aroma, a hoppy taste with fruit and malt, and a quenching bitterness. The pleasant finish has a good hop flavour and bitterness.

Original Wood (OG 1046, ABV 5.2%) ◆
A full-bodied, pale brown beer with an aroma of hops, fruit and malt. A complex blend of these flavours with a firm bitterness ends with increasing bitterness.

Swaton

Swaton Brewery, North End Farm, Swaton, Sleaford, Lincolnshire, NG34 0JP
☎ (01529) 421241
✉ swatonbrewery@hotmail.co.uk
🌐 swatonbrewery.com
Shop Tue-Sat 10am-5pm
Tours by arrangement

⊗ Swaton commenced brewing in 2007 on a five-barrel plant and is sited in the outbuildings of the owner's farm. It supplies beer festivals and local pubs. A visitor centre/cafe/shop is situated next to the brewery. All beers are also available bottle conditioned.

Happy Jack (OG 1040, ABV 4.2%)

Dozy Bull (OG 1041.8, ABV 4.5%)

Kiss Goodnight (OG 1041.8, ABV 4.5%)

Three Degrees (OG 1043.5, ABV 4.7%)

Sweet William

See Brodie's

Taddington

Taddington Brewery Ltd, Blackwell Hall, Blackwell, Buxton, SK17 9TQ
☎ (01298) 85734

No real ale. Taddington started brewing in 2007, and brews one Czech-style unpasteurised lager in two different strengths: Moravka (ABV 4.4% and 5%), which is available on draught.

Tatton SIBA (NEW)

Tatton Brewery Ltd, Unit 7, Longridge Trading Estate, Knutsford, Cheshire, WA16 8PR
☎ 07738 150898 ✉ beer@tattonbrewery.co.uk
🌐 tattonbrewery.co.uk
Shop Mon-Fri 8am-5pm (other times by arrangement)
Tours by arrangement

◎ Tatton is a family-run, 15-barrel brewery established in 2010. It supplies pubs throughout Cheshire as well as events such as the Cheshire Show and the Tatton Flower Show.

Ale (ABV 3.7%)
An easy-drinking session ale with a rich copper colour. It has a full malty/toffee flavour balanced by a soft bitterness and hoppy, fruity taste and aroma.

Best (ABV 4.2%)
A classic light amber-coloured best bitter with a clean malt flavour and fine hop character derived from a blend of aroma hops.

Gold (ABV 4.8%)

THE BREWERIES

A golden special ale with a maltiness backed by a robust hop character.

Taunton

Taunton Brewing Co Ltd, Unit 1F, Hillview Industrial Estate, West Bagbrough, Somerset, TA4 3EW
☎ (01823) 433999
✉ tauntonbrewingco@supanet.com
Tours by arrangement

Formerly Somerset Electric/Taunton Vale Brewery, established in 2003 in the cellar of the New Inn, Halse. Taunton Brewing Co took over in 2006, led by the former head brewer from Exmoor Ales, Colin Green. The brewery relocated in 2007 and now uses a 10-barrel plant. 140 outlets are supplied.

Phoenix (OG 1037, ABV 3.6%)

Ale (OG 1039.8, ABV 3.9%)

Braunton in Steam (OG 1042, ABV 4.2%)

Castle (OG 1043, ABV 4.3%)

Gold (OG 1045, ABV 4.5%)

Mayor (OG 1049, ABV 5%)

Timothy Taylor IFBB

Timothy Taylor & Co Ltd, Knowle Spring Brewery, Keighley, West Yorkshire, BD21 1AW
☎ (01535) 603139 ✉ timothy-taylor.co.uk

Timothy Taylor is an independent, family-owned company established in 1858. It moved to the site of the Knowle Spring in 1863. Its prize-winning ales, which use Pennine spring water, are served in the brewery's 29 tied pubs as well as more than 300 other outlets. A new distribution and warehouse facility has opened on nearby land, facilitating future brewery expansion on the main site.

Dark Mild (OG 1034, ABV 3.5%)
Malt and caramel dominate throughout in this sweetish beer with background hop and fruit notes.

Golden Best (OG 1033, ABV 3.5%)
This clean-tasting, refreshing, amber-coloured traditional Pennine light mild is malty throughout. A little fruit in the nose increases to complement the delicate hoppy taste.

Best Bitter (OG 1038, ABV 4%)
Hops and fruit combine well with a nutty malt character in this drinkable bitter. Bitterness increases down the glass and lingers in the aftertaste.

Landlord (OG 1042, ABV 4.3%)
A hoppy, increasingly bitter finish complements the background malt and citrus character of this full-flavoured and well-balanced amber beer.

Ram Tam (OG 1043, ABV 4.3%)
Caramel combines well with malt and hops to produce a well-balanced black beer with red hints and a coffee-coloured head.

Teignworthy SIBA

Teignworthy Brewery Ltd, The Maltings, Teignworthy, Newton Abbot, Devon, TQ12 4AA
☎ (01626) 332066
✉ sales@teignworthybreweryltd.co.uk
teignworthybrewery.com
Shop 10am-5pm weekdays at Tuckers Maltings
Tours available for trade customers only

Teignworthy Brewery was established in 1994 and is located in part of the historic Tuckers Maltings. The brewery is a 20-barrel plant and production is now up to 65 barrels a week, using malt from Tuckers. It supplies around 300 outlets in Devon and Somerset. A large range of seasonal ales is available: see website. Bottle-conditioned beers are also produced. Martha's Mild is suitable for vegans in bottle-conditioned form.

Neap Tide (OG 1038, ABV 3.8%)

Reel Ale (OG 1039.5, ABV 4%)
Clean, sharp-tasting bitter with lasting hoppiness; predominantly malty aroma.

Gun Dog (OG 1043.5, ABV 4.3%)

Springtide (OG 1043.5, ABV 4.3%)
An excellent, full and well-rounded, mid-brown beer with a dry, bitter taste and aftertaste.

Old Moggie (OG 1044.5, ABV 4.4%)
A golden, hoppy and fruity ale.

Beachcomber (OG 1045.5, ABV 4.5%)
A pale brown beer with a light, refreshing fruit and hop nose, grapefruit taste and a dry, hoppy finish.

Teme Valley SIBA

Teme Valley Brewery, The Talbot, Bromyard Road, Knightwick, Worcester, WR6 5PH
☎ (01886) 821235
✉ enquiries@temevalleybrewery.co.uk
temevalleybrewery.co.uk
Tours by arrangement

Teme Valley Brewery opened in 1997. In 2005, new investment enabled the brewery to expand to a 10-barrel brew-length. It maintains strong ties with local hop farming, using only Worcestershire-grown hops. Some 30 outlets are supplied. Seasonal beers: see website. Bottle-conditioned beers are also available. Occasional beer: Heartwarmer (ABV 6%).

T'Other (OG 1035, ABV 3.5%)
Refreshing amber beer offering an abundance of flavour in the fruity aroma, followed by a short, dry bitterness.

This (OG 1037, ABV 3.7%)
Dark gold brew with a mellow array of flavours in a malty balance.

That (OG 1041, ABV 4.1%)
A rich fruity nose and a wide range of hoppy and malty flavours in this copper-coloured best bitter.

Talbot Blond (OG 1042, ABV 4.4%)
A smooth, rich, pale beer.

Tempest (NEW)

Tempest Brewing Co, Winchester Row, Kelso, TD5 7DT
☎ (01573) 229664

Tempest began brewing in 2010 using a five-barrel plant. One pub is owned, the Cobbles Inn in Kelso, which acts as the brewery tap.

Into the Light Blonde (OG 1039, ABV 4.1%)

Emanation Pale Ale (OG 1043, ABV 4.5%)

Elemental Porter (OG 1049, ABV 5.1%)

Brave New World IPA (OG 1055, ABV 5.7%)

Thame (NEW)

Thame Brewery, 1 East Street, Thame, Oxfordshire, OX9 3HP
☎ (01844) 218202
✉ thamebrewery@btinternet.com
thamebrewery.co.uk
Tours by arrangement

The brewery was set up by Peter Lambert and Oak Taverns Ltd in the old stables at the rear of the Cross Keys in 2009. The one-barrel plant was the original brew plant of the Goldfinch Brewery in Dorchester. Beer is produced for the pub and local beer festivals. Further beers are planned.

Mr Splodge's Mild (OG 1040, ABV 4%)
A dark mild named after the pub cat.

Theakston

T&R Theakston Ltd, The Brewery, Masham, Ripon, North Yorkshire, HG4 4YD
☎ (01765) 680000 ✉ info@theakstons.co.uk
theakstons.co.uk
Tours available daily throughout the year

In July 2009 the brewery welcomed back the production of cask Best Bitter after a 35-year absence. The brewery's flagship brand had been brewed in Carlisle, Workington Tyne Brewery and then by John Smith's in Tadcaster. All Theakston's cask beers are now brewed at Masham. Theakstons returned to the independent sector in 2003 when the family bought the company back from S&N. It's now owned by four Theakston brothers. The brewery is one of the oldest in Yorkshire, built in 1875 by the brothers' great-grandfather, Thomas Theakston, the son of the company's founder. In 2004 a new fermentation room was added to provide additional flexibility and capacity. Further new capacity was added in 2006, with additional investment in 2009 to allow for the return of cask Best Bitter. Seasonal beers: see website.

Traditional Mild (OG 1035, ABV 3.5%)
A rich and smooth mild ale with a creamy body and a rounded liquorice taste. Dark ruby/amber in colour, with a mix of malt and fruit on the nose, and a dry, hoppy aftertaste.

Best Bitter (OG 1038, ABV 3.8%)
A golden-coloured beer with a full flavour that lingers pleasantly on the palate. With a good bitter/sweet balance, this beer has a robust hop character, citrus and spicy.

Black Bull Bitter (OG 1037, ABV 3.9%)
A distinctively hoppy aroma leads to a bitter, hoppy taste with some fruitiness and a short bitter finish.

XB (OG 1044, ABV 4.5%)
A sweet-tasting bitter with background fruit and spicy hop. Some caramel character gives this ale a malty dominance.

Old Peculier (OG 1057, ABV 5.6%)
A full-bodied, dark brown, strong ale. Slightly malty but with hints of roast coffee and liquorice. A smooth caramel overlay and a complex fruitiness leads to a bitter chocolate finish.

Abraham Thompson

Abraham Thompson's Brewing Co, Flass Lane, Barrow-in-Furness, Cumbria, LA13 0AD
☎ 07708 191437
✉ abraham.thompson@btinternet.com

Abraham Thompson was set up in 2004 to return Barrow-brewed beers to local pubs. This was achieved in 2005 after an absence of more than 30 years following the demise of Case's Brewery in 1972. With a half-barrel plant, this nano-brewery has concentrated almost exclusively on dark beers, reflecting the tastes of the brewer. As a result of the small output, finding the beers outside the Low Furness area is difficult. The only frequent stockist is the Black Dog Inn between Dalton and Ireleth.

Dark Mild (ABV 3.5%)

Lickerish Stout (ABV 3.8%)
A black, full-bodied stout with heavy roast flavours and good bitterness.

Oatmeal Stout (ABV 4.5%)

Porter (ABV 4.8%)
A deep, dark porter with good body and a smooth chocolate finish.

Letargion (ABV 9%)
Black, bitter and heavily roast but still very drinkable. A meal in a glass.

John Thompson

John Thompson Inn & Brewery, Ingleby, Melbourne, Derbyshire, DE73 7HW
☎ (01332) 862469 johnthompsoninn.com
Tours by arrangement

John Thompson set up the brewery in 1977. The pub and brewery are now run by his son, Nick. Seasonal beers: Rich Porter (ABV 4.5%, winter), St Nicks (ABV 5%, Xmas).

JTS XXX (OG 1041, ABV 4.1%)

Gold (OG 1045, ABV 4.5%)

Thornbridge SIBA

Thornbridge Brewery, Riverside Business Park, Buxton Road, Bakewell, Derbyshire, DE45 1GS
☎ (01629) 641000
✉ alex@thornbridgebrewery.co.uk
thornbridgebrewery.co.uk
Shop Mon-Fri 9am-5pm
Tours by arrangement

The first Thornbridge craft beers were produced in 2005 using a 10-barrel brewery, housed in the grounds of Thornbridge Hall. The beers have gained considerable success with over 100 CAMRA and SIBA awards being won. A 30-barrel brewery opened in Bakewell in 2009. The original site continues to develop new, seasonal and speciality beers. 150 outlets are supplied direct. Five pubs are owned. Bottle-conditioned beers are available.

Wild Swan (OG 1035, ABV 3.5%)
Extremely pale yet flavoursome and refreshing beer. Plenty of lemony citrus hop flavour, becoming increasingly dry and bitter in the finish and aftertaste.

Lord Marples (OG 1041, ABV 4%)
Smooth, traditional, easy-drinking bitter. Caramel, malt and coffee flavours fall away to leave a long, bitter finish.

Brock (OG 1040, ABV 4.1%)
A velvety dark, exceptionally smooth and creamy stout with soft treacle, smoky flavours and a full body.

Ashford (OG 1043, ABV 4.2%)
A brown ale with a floral hoppiness, a smooth, malty kick and a delicate coffee finish.

Kipling (OG 1050, ABV 5.2%) 🍺 ◆
Golden pale bitter with aromas of grapefruit and passion fruit. Intense fruit flavours continue throughout, leading to a long bitter aftertaste.

Jaipur IPA (OG 1055, ABV 5.9%) 🍺 ◆
Flavoursome IPA packed with citrus hoppiness that's nicely counterbalanced by malt and underlying sweetness and robust fruit flavours.

Saint Petersburg (Imperial Russian Stout) (OG 1072.4, ABV 7.7%) ◆
Good example of an imperial stout. Smooth and easy to drink with raisins, bitter chocolate and hops throughout, leading to a lingering coffee and chocolate aftertaste.

Thorne

Thorne Brewery CIC, Unit A2, Thorne Enterprise Park, King Edward Road, Thorne, South Yorkshire, DN8 4HU
☎ (01405) 741685 ✉ info@thornebrewery.com
⊕ thornebrewery.com
Tours by arrangement

⊕Thorne Brewery Community Interest Company was set up in 2008 to bring brewing back to Thorne. In early 2009 a 10-barrel brew plant was purchased and the first beers were available shortly after. Profits are re-invested in the local community to help improve the area.

Best Bitter (OG 1039, ABV 3.9%)
Malt dominates the taste with caramel, chocolate and fruitcake flavours. The hops complement this will a full-bodied bitterness and notes of orange peel, pepper and herbal aromas.

Pale Ale (OG 1041, ABV 4.2%)
English hops give a fruity flavour and a resinous, grassy aroma. Well-balanced bitterness gives a clean finish.

Three B's SIBA

Three B's Brewery, Laneside Works, Stockclough Lane, Feniscowles, Blackburn, Lancashire, BB2 5JR
☎ (01254) 207686 ✉ robert@threebsbrewery.co.uk
⊕ threebsbrewery.co.uk
Tours by arrangement

Robert Bell designed and began building his two-barrel brewery in 1998 and in 1999 he obtained premises in Blackburn to set up the equipment and complete the project. Now, after a move to larger premises, it is a 10-barrel brewery with up to 30-barrel production per week. More than 50 regular outlets are supplied. Seasonal beers: see website. Bottle-conditioned beers are also available.

Bee Thrifty (OG 1036, ABV 3.4%)
A light and refreshing amber-coloured beer.

Stoker's Slake (OG 1038, ABV 3.6%) ◆
Lightly roasted coffee flavours are in the aroma and the initial taste. A well-rounded, dark brown mild with dried fruit flavours in the long finish.

Honey Bee (OG 1039, ABV 3.7%)
A golden honey beer with honey apparent in both aroma and taste.

Bobbin's Bitter (OG 1040, ABV 3.8%)
A golden bitter with warm aromas of nutty grain and a full, fruity flavour with a light, dry finish.

Oatmeal Stout (OG 1040, ABV 3.8%)
A black roast beer with roast barley flavour and aroma and a complex hop taste.

Bee Blonde (OG 1041, ABV 4%)
A distinctive, pale bitter with a light, dry, balance of grain and hops and a delicate finish with citrus fruits.

Tackler's Tipple (OG 1044, ABV 4.3%)
A dark best bitter with full hop flavour, biscuit tones on the tongue and a deep, dry finish.

Doff Cocker (OG 1045, ABV 4.5%) ◆
Yellow with a hoppy aroma and initial taste giving way to subtle malt notes and orchard fruit flavours. Crisp, dry finish.

Pinch Noggin (OG 1046, ABV 4.6%)
A dark, strong best bitter with full hop flavour and a long aftertaste.

Knocker Up (OG 1047, ABV 4.8%) ◆
A smooth, rich, creamy porter. The roast flavour is foremost without dominating and is balanced by fruit and hop notes.

Shuttle Ale (OG 1050, ABV 5.2%)
A rustic-coloured traditional strong pale ale.

Three Castles SIBA

Three Castles Brewery Ltd, Unit 12, Salisbury Road Business Park, Pewsey, Wiltshire, SN9 5PZ
☎ (01672) 564433 ☎ 07725 148671
✉ sales@threecastlesbrewery.co.uk
⊕ threecastlesbrewery.co.uk
Shop Mon-Fri 9am-4pm; Sat 9am-1pm
Tours by arrangement

⊗ Three Castles is an independent, family-run brewery, established in 2006. Its location in the Vale of Pewsey has inspired the names for its range of ales. Seasonal beers: see website. Bottle-conditioned beers are also available and are suitable for vegetarians.

Barbury Castle (OG 1039, ABV 3.9%)
A balanced, easy-drinking pale ale with a hoppy, spicy palate.

Uffington Castle (OG 1042, ABV 4.2%)
Dark brown ale with a malty, nutty palate and a pleasant bitterness. The hop comes through well with a big spicy aroma.

Vale Ale (OG 1043, ABV 4.3%)
Golden-coloured with a fruity palate and strong floral aroma.

Tanked Up (OG 1050, ABV 5%)
Strong ale with a vibrant aroma.

Three Peaks

Three Peaks Brewery, 7 Craven Terrace, Settle, North Yorkshire, BD24 9DB
☎ (01729) 822939

⊗ Formed in 2006, Three Peaks is run by husband and wife team Colin and Susan Ashwell. The brewery is located in the cellar of their home. One beer is brewed at present on their 1.25-barrel plant but more are planned.

Pen-y-Ghent Bitter (OG 1040, ABV 3.8%) ◆
Malt and fruit flavours dominate this mid-brown session bitter, with some bitterness coming through afterwards.

Three Tuns SIBA

Three Tuns Brewery, 16 Market Square, Bishop's Castle, Shropshire, SY9 5BN
☎ (01588) 638392 ✉ tunsbrewery@aol.com
⊕ threetunsbrewery.co.uk
Shop Mon-Fri 9am-5pm
Tours by arrangement

⊗ Brewing started on the site sometime in the 16th century. The brewery was licensed in 1642 and is the oldest licensed brewery in the country. Brewing capacity was significantly increased in 2009. Seasonal beers: see website.

1642 Bitter (OG 1042, ABV 3.8%)
A golden ale with a light, nutty maltiness and spicy bitterness.

XXX (OG 1046, ABV 4.3%) ◆
A pale, sweetish bitter with a light hop aftertaste that has a honey finish.

Cleric's Cure (OG 1059, ABV 5%)
A light tan coloured ale with a malty sweetness. Strong and spicy with a floral bitterness.

Thwaites IFBB

Daniel Thwaites plc, Star Brewery, PO Box 50, Blackburn, Lancashire, BB1 5BU
☎ (01254) 686868 ✉ marketing@thwaites.co.uk
⊕ thwaites.co.uk
Tours by arrangement

☺ Established in 1807, Thwaites is still controlled by the Yerburgh family, descendants of the founder, Daniel Thwaites. The company owns around 400 pubs. Real ale is available in about 60% of these but Nutty Black is hard to find. Seasonal beers appear regularly throughout the year – see website for more information. One bottle-conditioned beer is produced.

Nutty Black (OG 1036, ABV 3.3%) ◆
A tasty traditional dark mild presenting a malty flavour with caramel notes and a slightly bitter finish.

Original (OG 1036, ABV 3.6%) ◆
Hop driven, yet well-balanced amber session bitter. Hops continue through to the long finish.

Wainwright (OG 1042, ABV 4.1%)
A straw-coloured bitter with soft fruit flavours and a hint of malty sweetness.

Lancaster Bomber (OG 1044, ABV 4.4%) ◆
Well-balanced, copper-coloured best bitter with firm malt flavours, a fruity background and a long, dry finish.

Tigertops SIBA

Tigertops Brewery, 22 Oakes Street, Flanshaw, Wakefield, West Yorkshire, WF2 9LN
☎ (01229) 716238 / (01924) 897728 ☎ 07951 812986 ✉ tigertopsbrewery@hotmail.com

☺ Tigertops was established in 1995 by Stuart Johnson and his wife Lynda. They own the brewery as well as running the Foxfield brew-pub in Cumbria (qv) but Tigertops is run on their behalf by Barry Smith. Five outlets are supplied. Seasonal beers: Billy Bock (ABV 7.9%, Nov-Feb), May Bock (ABV 6.2%, May-Jun), 8 Ace (ABV 8%, May).

Axeman's Block (OG 1036, ABV 3.6%)
A malty beer with a good hop finish.

Busy Lizzy (ABV 3.6%)

Dark Wheat Mild (OG 1036, ABV 3.6%)
An unusual mild made primarily with wheat malt.

Tom Tom Mild (ABV 3.7%)
Dark rye mild.

Thor Bitter (OG 1038, ABV 3.8%)
A light, hoppy bitter.

Blanche de Newland (OG 1044, ABV 4.5%)
A cloudy Belgian-style wheat beer.

Ginger Fix (OG 1044, ABV 4.6%)
A mid-amber ginger beer.

White Max (OG 1044, ABV 4.6%)
A light, German-style wheat beer.

Uber Weiss (OG 1046, ABV 4.8%)
A dark, German-style wheat beer.

Big Ginger (OG 1058, ABV 6%)
A strong, amber ginger beer.

Tinpot (NEW)

Tinpot Brewery, Allanwater Brewhouse, Queens Lane, Bridge of Allan, Stirlingshire, FK9 4NY
☎ (01786) 834555 ✉ tinpot@bridgeofallan.co.uk
⊕ tinpotbrewery.co.uk
Tours by arrangement

☺ Tinpot Brewery opened in 2009 using a one-barrel plant designed to brew speciality beers. Bottle-conditioned beers are available. The beer range varies depending on season and demand.

Tintagel

Tintagel Brewery Ltd, Condolden Farm, Tintagel, Cornwall, PL34 0HJ
☎ (01840) 213371 ✉ john@tintagelbrewery.co.uk
⊕ tintagelbrewery.co.uk

⊗ This 7.5-barrel brewery was established in 2009 in a redundant milking parlour on the highest farm in Cornwall. 70 outlets are supplied direct. Bottle-conditioned and seasonal beers are available.

Castle Gold (OG 1038, ABV 3.8%)

Gull Rock (OG 1042.6, ABV 4.2%)

Harbour Special (OG 1048.9, ABV 4.8%)

Tipples EAB

Tipples Brewery, Units 5 & 6, Damgate Lane Industrial Estate, Acle, Norwich, Norfolk, NR13 3DJ
☎ (01493) 741007 ✉ brewery@tipplesbrewery.com
⊕ tipplesbrewery.com

⊗ Tipples was established by Jason Tipple in 2004 on a six-barrel brew plant and produces both cask and bottle-conditioned ales. The brewery expanded in 2007 and opened a brewery shop on Elm Hill in Norwich the same year. There are plans for further expansion with an increase in the product range and diversity. Seasonal beers: Lazy

THE BREWERIES

Summer (ABV 4.3%, May-Sep), Crackle (ABV 6.5%, Nov-Feb).

Longshore (OG 1036, ABV 3.6%) ◆
Yellow hued with a soft, peachy aroma and creamy mouthfeel. The initial fruity apricot flavour quickly subsides to a long, dry bitterness.

Ginger (ABV 3.8%) ◆
A spicy aroma introduces this well-balanced yellow-gold brew. Ginger dominates but does not overwhelm the supporting malty bitterness. Quick ginger nut finish.

Hanged Monk (ABV 4%) ◆
Strong roast and malt notes dominate the aroma and follow through to the taste. A slightly grainy mouthfeel is softened by a hint of caramel and a growing vinous finish.

Lady Evelyn (OG 1041, ABV 4.1%) ◆
A crisp hoppy aroma introduces this lively pale ale. Bitterness and hop loom large in the taste throughout. Some malt and sweetness take the edge off as a background smoky flavour becomes apparent.

Redhead (OG 1042, ABV 4.2%) ◆
Malt and hops are well matched in both nose and palate. Toffee in the nose and initial taste soon gives way to an increasing bitterness. A fine finale retains the mix of flavours.

Topper (ABV 4.5%) ◆
Black-hued stout. Coffee and dark chocolate to the fore in all aspects. A roast-flavoured beer with just enough malt sweetness and bitterness to provide a counterpoint. Strong, big-hearted fiinish.

Brewers Progress (ABV 4.6%) ◆
A solid malty, tawny beer with strong caramel and vanilla support. The smooth creamy character is given added depth by a blackcurrant fruitiness. Some bitterness in the finish.

Moonrocket (ABV 5%) ◆
A complex golden brew with an earthy aroma. Malt hop bitterness and a fruity sweetness swirl round in an ever-changing kaleidoscope of flavours. A satisfying finish with hops finally emerging on top.

Jacks' Revenge (ABV 5.8%) ◆
An explosion of malt, chocolate, roast and plum pudding fruitiness. Full-bodied with a deep red hue and a strong solid finish that develops into a vinous fruitiness.

Tipsy Toad

See Jersey

Tirril SIBA

Tirril Brewery Ltd, Red House, Long Marton, Appleby-in-Westmorland, Cumbria, CA16 6BN
☎ (01768) 361846
Tours by arrangement

⊛ Tirril Brewery was established in 1999 in an abandoned toilet block behind the Queen's Head in Tirril. Since then it has relocated to the 1823 gothic brewing rooms at Brougham Hall and is now at the Red House Barn in Long Marton beneath the Pennines. Capacity has grown from 2.25 barrels to 20 barrels over the years. Around 70 outlets are supplied and one pub is owned. Seasonal beers:

Graduate (ABV 4.6%, Dec), Balls Up (ABV 3.9%, summer).

Bewsher's Bitter (OG 1038.5, ABV 3.8%)
A lightly-hopped, golden brown session beer, named after the landlord and brewer at the Queen's Head in the 1830s.

Nameless Ale (OG 1038.5, ABV 3.8%)
A golden, easy-drinking session beer.

Brougham Ale (OG 1039, ABV 3.9%)
A gently hopped, amber bitter.

Old Faithful (OG 1040, ABV 4%) ◆
Initially bitter, gold-coloured ale with an astringent finish.

1823 (OG 1041, ABV 4.1%)
A full-bodied session bitter with a gentle bitterness.

Academy Ale (OG 1041.5, ABV 4.2%)
A dark, full-bodied, traditional rich and malty ale.

Amber's Ale (OG 1041.5, ABV 4.2%)
Rosy golden ale. Light and hoppy.

Red Barn Ale (OG 1043, ABV 4.4%)
A ruby red ale with a strong hop finish.

Titanic SIBA

Titanic Brewery Co Ltd, Unit 5, Callender Place, Burslem, Stoke-on-Trent, Staffordshire, ST6 1JL
☎ (01782) 823447 ✉ titanic@titanicbrewery.co.uk
⊕ titanicbrewery.co.uk
Tours by arrangement

⊛ Founded in 1985, the brewery is named in honour of Captain Smith who hailed from the Potteries and had the misfortune to captain the Titanic. A monthly seasonal beer provides the opportunity to offer distinctive beers of many styles, each with a link to the liner. Titanic supplies 300 free trade outlets throughout the country. The brewery has a small, constantly expanding tied house estate. Bottle-conditioned beer is also available.

Mild (OG 1036, ABV 3.5%) ◆
Fruity plum aroma and sweet fruity start. Fruity throughout with roast leading to a dry bitterness.

Steerage (OG 1036, ABV 3.5%) ◆
Hoppy aroma with fruity hints. Gentle start then a developing zesty bitterness. Well balanced for a light session beer with a long, dry finish.

Lifeboat (OG 1040, ABV 4%) ◆
Tawny beer with a roast, caramel and fruity aroma, sweet fruity start with biscuity malt leading to a sweet finish with residual bitterness.

Anchor Bitter (OG 1042, ABV 4.1%) ◆
Spicy, peppery aroma, a sweet fruity start, a mouth-watering and spicy middle, and then a clean dry bitter finish.

Iceberg (OG 1042, ABV 4.1%) 🗇 🛢 ◆
Flowery and citrus aroma of lemon and grapefruit. Great raspy hop mouthfeel with refreshing hoppy bitterness and a lingering finish.

Stout (OG 1046, ABV 4.5%) ◆
Roasty, toasty with tobacco, autumn bonfires, chocolate and hints of liquorice; perfectly balanced with a bitter, dry finish reminiscent of real coffee.

White Star (OG 1050, ABV 4.8%) ◆

Honey and spice aroma belies the sharp, crisp and zesty taste leaving a satisfying hop bite and bitter finish.

Captain Smith's Strong Ale (OG 1054, ABV 5.2%) ◆
Lots of apple aroma with a hint of honey. Quite malty throughout but finishing on a bittersweet note.

Toad (NEW)

Toad Brewery, Stadium Way, Doncaster, South Yorkshire, DN4 5JB
☎ (01302) 365508 ✉ info@toadbrewery.co.uk
🌐 toadbrewery.co.uk

Toad began brewing in 2010 on a 10-barrel plant. Special and seasonal beers are available and bottle-conditioned beers are planned.

Tadpole (ABV 3.8%)

Golden Angel (ABV 4%)

Mature Toad (ABV 4.5%)

Toft (NEW)

Toft Brewing, 6 Tuscan Close, Cheadle, Staffordshire, ST10 1HS
☎ (01538) 755639 ✉ toftbrewing@yahoo.co.uk

Toft began brewing in 2009 in the owner's garage on a one-barrel plant. Several local pubs and beer festivals are supplied.

Full Toss (ABV 4%)

Nightwatchman (ABV 4.5%)

Stumped (ABV 4.5%)

Toll End

Toll End Brewery, c/o Waggon & Horses, 131 Toll End Road, Tipton, West Midlands, DY4 0ET
☎ 07903 725574
Tours by arrangement

The four-barrel brewery opened in 2004. With the exception of Phoebe's Ale, named after the brewer's daughter, all brews commemorate local landmarks, events and people. Toll End is brewing to full capacity and produces around 300 gallons a week. Four outlets are supplied. Several specials are also brewed throughout the year.

William Perry (OG 1043, ABV 4.3%)

Phoebe's Ale/PA (OG 1044, ABV 4.4%)

Polly Stevens (OG 1044, ABV 4.4%)

Black Bridge (OG 1046, ABV 4.6%)

Tipton Pride (OG 1046, ABV 4.6%)

Power Station (OG 1049, ABV 4.9%)
Cask-conditioned lager.

Tollgate SIBA

Tollgate Brewery, Unit 8, Viking Business Centre, High Street, Woodville, Swadlincote, Derbyshire, DE11 7EH
☎ (01283) 229194 ✉ tollgatebrewery@tiscali.co.uk
Tours by arrangement

Tollgate, a six-barrel brewery that opened in 2005, is on the site of the old Brunt & Bucknall Brewery, which was taken over by Salts Brewery in 1919 and then bought and closed by Bass in 1927. More than 100 outlets are supplied. Seasonal and bottle-conditioned beers are available.

Mellow Yellow (OG 1042, ABV 4%)

Mild (OG 1044, ABV 4.2%)

Bitter (OG 1045, ABV 4.3%)

High Street Bitter (OG 1046, ABV 4.4%)

Red Star IPA (OG 1047, ABV 4.5%)

Red McAdy (OG 1052, ABV 5%)

For Harrington Arms, Thulston:

Earl's Ale (OG 1042, ABV 4%)

Tomos Watkin

See under Watkin

Tonbridge SIBA (NEW)

Tonbridge Brewery, Whiteoaks, Tudeley Road, Tudeley, Kent, TN11 0NW
☎ (01732) 366770 ✉ mail@tonbridgebrewery.co.uk
🌐 tonbridgebrewery.co.uk
Tours by arrangement

Tonbridge Brewery was launched in 2010 using a four-barrel plant and is run by Paul and Lynne Bournazian. It produces cask-conditioned ales using only Kent-grown hops and supplies pubs within a 15-mile radius of Tonbridge.

Blonde Ambition (ABV 4.2%)
A crisp, clean blonde ale with a refreshing bitterness and slightly spicy aroma.

Topsham & Exminster

See Exeter

Tower SIBA

Tower Brewery, Old Water Tower, Walsitch Maltings, Glensyl Way, Burton upon Trent, Staffordshire, DE14 1LX ✉ **towerbrewery@aol.com**
Tours by arrangement

Tower was established in 2001 by John Mills, previously the brewer at Burton Bridge, in a converted derelict water tower of Thomas Salt's maltings. The conversion was given a Civic Society award for the restoration of a Historic Industrial Building in 2001. Tower has 20 regular outlets. Seasonal beers: Sundowner (ABV 4%, May-Aug), Spring Equinox (ABV 4.6%, Mar-May), Autumn Equinox (ABV 4.6%, Sep-Nov), Winter Spirit (ABV 5%).

Bitter (OG 1042, ABV 4.2%) ◆
Gold coloured with a malty, caramel and hoppy aroma. A full hop and fruit taste with the fruit lingering. A bitter and astringent finish.

Pale Ale (OG 1048, ABV 4.8%)

For Castle Rock, Nottingham:

Sheriff's Tipple (OG 1035, ABV 3.5%)
A light-tawny session bitter with distinctive hop character.

For George & Dragon, Belper:

East Mill (OG 1035, ABV 3.5%)

For Hoskins Brothers, Leicester:

THE BREWERIES

Hobs Best Mild (OG 1035, ABV 3.5%)

Brigadier Bitter (OG 1036, ABV 3.6%)

Hob Bitter (OG 1040, ABV 4%)

Tom Kelly's Stout (OG 1040, ABV 4%)

White Dolphin (OG 1040, ABV 4%)

EXS (OG 1050, ABV 5%)

For Malt & Hops, Fenton:

Bursley Bitter (OG 1040, ABV 4%)

For Steamin' Billy Brewing Co (qv):

Last Bark (OG 1038, ABV 3.8%)
A light, aromatic bitter.

Scrum Down (ABV 4%)
A dark mild with a bitter aftertaste.

Rat Tosser (ABV 4.1%)
A three-hop bitter.

Bitter (OG 1043, ABV 4.3%) ◆
Brown-coloured best bitter. Initial malt and hops aromas are superseded by fruit and hop taste and aftertaste, accompanied by a refreshing bitterness.

Skydiver (OG 1050, ABV 5%) ◆
Full-bodied, strong, mahogany-coloured beer in which an initial malty aroma is followed by a characteristic malty sweetness that is balanced by a hoppy bitterness.

Townes SIBA

Townes Brewery, Speedwell Inn, Lowgates, Staveley, Chesterfield, Derbyshire, S43 3TT
☎ **(01246) 472252**
✉ **curly@townes48.wanadoo.co.uk**
Tours by arrangement

Townes Brewery started in 1994 in an old bakery on the outskirts of Chesterfield using a five-barrel plant. It was the first brewery in the town for more than 40 years. In 1997, the Speedwell Inn at Staveley was bought and the plant was moved to the rear of the pub, becoming the first brew-pub in north Derbyshire in the 20th century. Seasonal beers: Stargazer (ABV 4.7%, Dec-Jan), Sunshine (ABV 3.7%, Jul-Aug). Bottle-conditioned beers are also available and are suitable for vegetarians and vegans.

Speedwell Bitter (OG 1039, ABV 3.9%) ◆
Straw-coloured session bitter with little aroma. Initially quite sweet leading to a bitterness developing in the long, slightly astringent aftertaste.

Lowgate Light (OG 1041, ABV 4.1%)

Staveley Cross (OG 1043, ABV 4.3%) ◆
Amber gold best bitter with a faint banana aroma. Hoppy with bitterness present throughout, culminating in a short, dry, slightly astringent aftertaste.

IPA (OG 1045, ABV 4.5%) ◆
Pleasant, hoppy bitter with little aroma and a good balanced flavour. This leads to a lingering bitter, hoppy aftertaste.

Pynot Porter (ABV 4.5%) ◆
Red-brown porter with a faint malt and roast coffee aroma. Roast malt flavours combine with vine fruit, becoming increasingly bitter towards the finish.

Staveleyan (OG 1049, ABV 4.9%)

Townhouse

Townhouse Brewery, Units 1-4, Townhouse Studios, Townhouse Farm, Alsager Road, Audley, Staffordshire, ST7 8JQ
☎ **07976 209437/07812 035143**
✉ **j.nixon2@btinternet.com**
Tours by arrangement

Townhouse was set up in 2002 with a 2.5-barrel plant. In 2004 the brewery scaled up to five-barrels. Demand is growing rapidly and in early 2006 two additional fermenting vessels were added. Bottling is planned. Some 30 outlets are supplied.

Audley Bitter (OG 1038, ABV 3.8%)
A pale, well-balanced session bitter with a citrus hop character.

Flowerdew (OG 1039, ABV 4%) ◆
Golden with a wonderful floral aroma. Fabulous flavour of flowery hops delivering a hoppy bite and presenting a lingering taste of flowery citrus waves.

Dark Horse (OG 1042, ABV 4.3%)
A dark ruby ale with malt character and late hoppy finish.

A'dleyweisse (OG 1043, ABV 4.5%)
An English-style wheat beer, full-bodied and golden with a strongly defined fruity hop character and a dry finish.

Audley Gold (OG 1043, ABV 4.5%) ◆
Straw colour with a flower hop aroma hinting at lime and grapefruit. A grassy hop start gives plenty of bitterness and a dry but not astringent finish.

Barney's Stout (OG 1043, ABV 4.5%) ◆
Roast chocolate and toffee nose atop this black stout. Sweet start becoming bitter at the end, with roast throughout.

Armstrong Ale (OG 1045, ABV 4.8%)
A rich, fruity ruby red beer with a hoppy, dry finish.

Monument Ale (OG 1048, ABV 5%)
A copper-coloured, well-balanced strong ale with a pronounced malt character.

Town Mill (NEW)

Town Mill Brewery, Mill Lane, Lyme Regis, Dorset, DT7 3PU
☎ **(01297) 444354** ✉ **jon@townmillbrewery.com**
🌐 **townmillbrewery.com**
Shop 11am-5pm Sat & Sun

Town Mill began brewing in 2010 using a four-barrel plant in a part of the town mill that at one time had been the home of Lyme Regis' electricity generation before the National Grid, although historic use of the building was as a brewer's malthouse.

Cobb (ABV 3.9%)

Traditional Scottish Ales

Traditional Scottish Ales Ltd, Unit 7c, Bandeath Industrial Estate, Throsk, Stirling, FK7 7NP
☎ **(01786) 817000**
✉ **info@traditionalscottishales.com**
🌐 **traditionalscottishales.co.uk**

A company set up in 2005 to develop and market the Bridge of Allan, Stirling and Trossach's Craft Brewery products. The brewery is located in a former torpedo factory. A large range of seasonal beers is available as are bottle-conditioned ales. All bottled ales are suitable for vegetarians and vegans.

Stirling Bitter (OG 1039, ABV 3.7%)

Ben Nevis Organic (OG 1042, ABV 4%)
A traditional Scottish 80/-, with a distinctive roast and caramel character. Bittersweet fruit throughout provides the sweetness typical of a Scottish Heavy.

Stirling Brig (OG 1042, ABV 4.1%)

Bannockburn Ale (OG 1044, ABV 4.2%)

Ruby Red IPA (ABV 4.2%)
A full-bodied malty IPA with a lightly-hopped aftertaste and a chilli bite due to the Scotch Bonnet chilli added to the mash.

Glencoe Wild Oat Stout Organic (OG 1048, ABV 4.5%)
A sweetish stout, surprisingly not dark in colour. Plenty of malt and roast balanced by fruit and finished with a hint of hop.

William Wallace (OG 1050, ABV 4.5%)

Double Espresso Wild Oat Stout (ABV 4.8%)
Stout brewed with double strength coffee beans.

Ginger Explosion (OG 1052, ABV 5%)

Lomond Gold Organic (OG 1052, ABV 5%)
A malty, bittersweet golden ale with plenty of fruity hop character.

Red Mist (OG 1052, ABV 5%)
A raspberry beer.

Black Velvet (ABV 5.5%)
A smooth, creamy and lightly-hopped champagne stout.

1488 (OG 1075, ABV 7%)

For Knops Beer Co Ltd:

California Common (OG 1048, ABV 4.6%)

For Trossach's Craft Brewery:

Waylade (OG 1040, ABV 3.9%)

LadeBack (OG 1048, ABV 4.5%)

LadeOut (OG 1055, ABV 5.1%)

Traquair SIBA

Traquair House Brewery, Traquair House, Innerleithen, Peeblesshire, EH44 6PW
☎ (01896) 830323 ✉ enquiries@traquair.co.uk
traquair.co.uk/brewery
Shop Easter-Oct 12-5pm daily (Jun-Aug 10.30am-5pm)
Tours by arrangement

The 18th-century brewhouse is based in one of the wings of the 1,000-year-old Traquair House, Scotland's oldest inhabited house. The brewhouse was rediscovered by the 20th Laird, the late Peter Maxwell Stuart, in 1965. He began brewing again using all the original equipment, which remained intact, despite having lain idle for more than 100 years. The brewery has been run by Peter's daughter, Catherine Maxwell Stuart, since his death in 1990. The Maxwell Stuarts are members of the Stuart clan, and the main Bear Gates will remain shut until a Stuart returns to the throne. All the beers are oak-fermented and 60 per cent of production is exported. Seasonal beer: Stuart Ale (ABV 4.5%, summer), Bear Ale (ABV 5%, winter).

Bear Ale (ABV 5%)

Laird's Liquor (ABV 6%)

Traquair House Ale (ABV 7%)

Jacobite Ale (ABV 8%)

Tring SIBA

Tring Brewery Co Ltd, Dunsley Farm, London Road, Tring, Hertfordshire, HP23 6HA
☎ (01442) 890721 ✉ info@tringbrewery.co.uk
tringbrewery.co.uk
Shop Mon-Tue 11am-5pm, Wed-Fri 9am-6pm, Sat 9am-1pm, closed Sun
Tours by arrangement

Founded in 1992, Tring Brewery brews 60 barrels a week. Most of the beers take their names from local myths and legends. In addition to the regular and seasonal ales it brews a selection of monthly specials. The brewery relocated to larger premises in 2010. Seasonal beers: see website.

Side Pocket for a Toad (OG 1035, ABV 3.6%)
Citrus notes from American Cascade hops balanced with a floral aroma and a crisp, dry finish in a straw-coloured ale.

Brock Bitter (ABV 3.7%)
A light brown session ale with hints of sweetness and caramel, gentle bitterness and a floral aroma from Styrian hops.

Mansion Mild (ABV 3.7%)
Smooth and creamy dark ruby mild with a fruity palate and gentle late hop.

Blonde (OG 1039, ABV 4%)
A refreshing blonde beer with a fruity palate, balanced with a lingering hop aroma.

Ridgeway (OG 1039, ABV 4%)
Balanced malt and hop flavours with a dry, flowery hop aftertaste.

Jack O'Legs (OG 1041, ABV 4.2%)
A combination of four types of malt and two types of aroma hops provide a copper-coloured premium ale with full fruit and a distinctive hoppy bitterness.

Tea Kettle Stout (OG 1047, ABV 4.7%)
Rich and complex traditional stout with a hint of liquorice and moderate bitterness.

Colley's Dog (OG 1051, ABV 5.2%)
Dark but not over-rich, strong yet drinkable, this premium ale has a long dry finish with overtones of malt and walnuts.

Death or Glory (ABV 7.2%)
A strong, dark, aromatic barley wine.

Trinity EAB (NEW)

Trinity Ales, Church Road, Gisleham, Suffolk, NR33 8DS
☎ (01502) 743121 ✉ graham@trinityales.co.uk
trinityales.co.uk

Trinity Ales was launched in 2009 using a four-barrel plant. Pure spring water is used from an ancient well along with Suffolk hops and barley from local farms. Outlets are supplied within a 30-mile radius of the brewery. Bottle-conditioned beers are available.

Wishing Well (OG 1039, ABV 3.8%)

High Light (OG 1040, ABV 4%)

THE BREWERIES

Black Street Smithy (OG 1050, ABV 4.5%)

Gisleham Gold (OG 1045, ABV 4.5%)

Triple fff SIBA

Triple fff Brewing Co, Magpie Works, Station Approach, Four Marks, Alton, Hampshire, GU34 5HN
☎ (01420) 561422 ✉ sales@triplefff.com
🌐 triplefff.com
Shop Mon-Fri 9am-5pm, Sat 10am-12pm
Tours by arrangement

The brewery was founded in 1997 with a five-barrel plant. Since then demand has rocketed with the brewery growing in size to a 50-barrel plant. The brewery has two of its own outlets, the Railway Arms in Alton and the White Lion in Aldershot, as well as supplying over 300 other outlets. Three core beers are available all year round, supplemented by some old favourites and occasional new brews: see website for details.

Alton's Pride (OG 1041, ABV 3.8%)
An excellent, clean-tasting brown session beer. Full-bodied for its strength with a glorious aroma of floral hops. An initially malty flavour fades as citrus notes and hoppiness take over, leading to a lasting hoppy/bitter finish.

Pressed Rat & Warthog (OG 1041, ABV 3.8%)
Complex hoppy and bitter mild, not in the classic style but nevertheless delicious. Ruby in colour, a toffee aroma with hints of blackcurrant and chocolate lead to a well-balanced flavour with roast, fruit and malt vying with the hoppy bitterness and a dry bitter finish.

Moondance (OG 1045, ABV 4.2%)
A golden ale, well-hopped, with an aromatic citrus hop nose, balanced by bitterness and a noticeable sweetness in the mouth. Bitterness increases in the finish as the fruit declines, leading to a bittersweet finish.

Trossach's Craft

See Traditional Scottish Ales

Truman's (NEW)

Truman's Beer Co, Top Floor, 8 Elder Street, London, E1 6BT
☎ (020) 7247 1147 ✉ trumans@trumansbeer.co.uk
🌐 trumansbeer.co.uk

Company set up to bring back the famous London brewery, Truman's, founded in 1666. The one beer is currently brewed by Nethergate (qv) but the company hopes to open its own brewery in the future.

Tryst SIBA

Tryst Brewery, Lorne Road, Larbert, Stirlingshire, FK5 4AT
☎ (01324) 554000 ✉ john@trystbrewery.co.uk
🌐 trystbrewery.co.uk
Shop Mon-Fri office hours; Sat am
Tours by arrangement

John McGarva, a member of Scottish Craft Brewers, started brewing in 2003 in an industrial unit near Larbert station. Around 100 outlets are supplied. All beers are also available bottle conditioned.

Brockville Dark (OG 1039, ABV 3.8%)
A full-tasting session ale with hints of liquorice and roasted grains.

Brockville Pale (OG 1039, ABV 3.9%)
A pale golden session ale, smooth on the palate.

Bla'than (OG 1041, ABV 4%)
A strong floral nose and refreshing taste enhanced with elderflower and pale malts.

Drovers 80/- (OG 1041, ABV 4%)
A traditional, well-malted 80/- with an element of sweetness. A gentle nose complements a smooth finish.

Carronade Pale Ale (OG 1043, ABV 4.2%)
A pale ale bursting with citrus flavours.

Zetland Wheatbier (OG 1046, ABV 4.5%)
Refreshing with a distinctive banana nose, a typical European cloudy wheat beer.

RAJ IPA (OG 1055, ABV 5.5%)
Exclusively English hopped with balanced flavours, with a hoppy aroma and palate.

Carron Oatmeal Stout (OG 1061, ABV 6.1%)
A strong, dark, silky ale bursting with flavour. Brewed from an old Scottish recipe dating from the early 19th century.

Tudor

Tudor Brewery, 1 Castle Meadow Park, Merthyr Road, Abergavenny, NP7 7RZ
☎ (01873) 735770 ☎ 07768 127242
✉ sales@tudorbrewery.co.uk 🌐 tudorbrewery.co.uk
Tours by arrangement

The Tudor Brewery was established in 2007 in the Kings Arms pub, Abergavenny. Around 60 outlets are supplied direct. Seasonal beer: Black Mountain Porter (ABV 5%, Nov-Jan).

Blorenge (ABV 3.8%)
A light summer ale with fresh scents and a clear, blonde appearance.

Skirrid (ABV 4.2%)
A robust, medium-strength, dark, hoppy beer.

Sugar Loaf (ABV 4.7%)
An amber medium-dry beer with a sweet aroma.

Tunnel SIBA

Tunnel Brewery Ltd, c/o Lord Nelson Inn, Birmingham Road, Ansley, Nuneaton, Warwickshire, CV10 9PQ
☎ (02476) 396450 ✉ info@tunnelbrewery.co.uk
🌐 tunnelbrewery.co.uk
Tours by arrangement

Bob Yates and Mike Walsh started brewing in 2005, taking the name from a rail tunnel that passes under the village. Pub and brewery are independent of one another but the beers are available in the pub as well as being supplied to more than 100 other outlets. Brewing more than doubled in 2008 and a new unit for storage and bottling has been established. Seasonal beers: see website. Tunnel also brews for Battlefield Brewery, which will take over production once the brewery is built at Bosworth Battlefield Visitor Centre in Leicestershire. Bottle-conditioned beers are also available and are suitable for vegans (for both Tunnel and Battlefield).

Linda Lear Beer (OG 1038, ABV 3.7%)
A dark amber, fruity beer with a strong hop finish.

Late Ott (OG 1040, ABV 4%)
Dark golden session bitter with a fruity nose and perfumed hop edge. The finish is dry and bitter.

Trade Winds (OG 1045, ABV 4.6%)
An aromatic, copper-coloured beer with an aroma of Cascade hops and a clean, crisp hint of citrus, followed by fruity malts and a dry finish full of scented hops.

Parish Ale (OG 1047, ABV 4.7%)
A reddish-amber, malty ale with a slight chocolate aroma enhanced by citrus notes. It becomes increasingly fruity as the English hops kick in. Smooth, gentle hop bitterness in the finish.

Shadow Weaver (OG 1046, ABV 4.7%)

Jean 'Cloudy' Van Damme (OG 1048, ABV 5%)

Stranger In The Mist (OG 1048, ABV 5%)

Nelson's Column (OG 1051, ABV 5.2%)
A ruby red, strong old English ale.

Boston Beer Party (OG 1056, ABV 5.6%)

For Battlefield Brewery:

Let Battle Commence (ABV 3.8%)

Richard III Plantagenet (ABV 4.2%)

Henry Tudor (ABV 5%)

Twickenham SIBA

Twickenham Fine Ales Ltd, Ryecroft Works, Edwin Road, Twickenham, Middlesex, TW2 6SP
☎ (020) 8241 1825 ✉ info@twickenham-fine-ales.co.uk ⊕ twickenham-fine-ales.co.uk
Tours by arrangement

The 10-barrel brewery was set up in 2004 and was the first brewery in Twickenham since the 1920s. The brewery supplies pubs and clubs within 25 miles of the brewery, including central London. It expanded into new premises in 2009 and is planning to increase brewing capacity and introduce bottled ales. Seasonal beers: see website.

Sundancer (OG 1037, ABV 3.7%) ◆
A dark gold beer with citrus fruit on the palate that lingers into the aftertaste. Bitterness grows on drinking. The aroma has a little perfumed hop.

Grandstand Bitter (OG 1037, ABV 3.8%) ◆
A classic, traditional brown bitter, well-balanced with citrus hops blending with the malt, leading to a slight dry finish. Some sulphur on the nose.

Original (OG 1042, ABV 4.2%) ◆
A fruity best bitter with a smooth mouthfeel. The beer has both a citrus and sweet malt character throughout. The aroma has a trace of blackcurrant.

Naked Ladies (OG 1044, ABV 4.4%) ◆
Pink grapefruit on nose, palate and aftertaste; well-balanced with some hoppy bitterness and a little caramel toffee. Smooth mouthfeel and a dry finish. Amber in colour.

Two Bridges SIBA (NEW)

Two Bridges Brewery, 37 Ardler Road, Caversham, Reading, Berkshire, RG4 5AE
☎ (0118) 947 0630
✉ kevin.durkan@twobridgesbrewery.co.uk
⊕ twobridgesbrewery.co.uk

⊠ Two Bridges Brewery was founded by husband and wife Kevin and Kerri Durkan in 2009. The Two Bridges are those over the Thames from Caversham to Reading and beer names all have a swan theme. The 2.5-barrel plant is already outgrowing its owners' garage. 30 outlets are supplied direct. Seasonal beer: Emerald Trumpeter (ABV 4.2%, Feb-Apr).

Blond Berkshire Bevy (OG 1039, ABV 3.9%)

Midnight Swan (OG 1041, ABV 4.4%)

Golden Cygnet (OG 1045, ABV 4.8%)

Two Towers (NEW)

Two Towers Brewery Ltd, Unit 1, Mott Street Industrial Estate, 51 Mott Street, Hockley, Birmingham, West Midlands, B19 3HE
☎ 07540 574032 ✉ trevor.r.harris@btinternet.com
Tours by arrangement (for parties of 5 or more)

Two Towers began brewing in 2010 and is run by two long-term friends, Trevor Harris and Mark Arnott-Job. Further beers are planned.

Chamberlain Pale Ale (OG 1037, ABV 4.3%)

Birmingham Special Ale (OG 1056, ABV 5.4%)

Tydd Steam SIBA

Tydd Steam Brewery, Manor Barn, Kirkgate, Tydd Saint Giles, Cambridgeshire, PE13 5NE
☎ (01945) 871020 ☎ 07932 726552
✉ info@tyddsteam.co.uk ⊕ tyddsteam.co.uk
Tours by arrangement

⊠ Tydd Steam opened in 2007 in a converted agricultural barn using a 5.5-barrel plant. A new eight-barrel plant was installed in 2009 to meet demand. The brewery is named after two farm steam engines which were formerly kept in the barn now used for brewing. The steam engines have now been moved to the Museum of Lincolnshire Life. 70 outlets are supplied direct. Seasonal/occasional beers are brewed and bottle-conditioned beers are available on an occasional basis.

Barn Ale (OG 1038, ABV 3.9%) ◆
A golden bitter that has good biscuity malt aroma and flavour, balanced by spicy hops. Long, dry, fairly astringent finish.

Piston Bob (OG 1044, ABV 4.6%) ◆
Malt and faint hops on the aroma progress through to a malty flavour complemented by a balance of hops and fruit. A long, dry finish rounds off this amber strong bitter.

Armageddon (OG 1049, ABV 5%)

Ufford

Ufford Ales Ltd, White Hart, Main Street, Ufford, Cambridgeshire, PE9 3BH
☎ (01780) 740250 ☎ 07855 666836
✉ info@uffordales.co.uk ⊕ uffordales.co.uk
Tours by arrangement

⊠ Opened in early 2005, the brewery has expanded to produce 120 firkins of beer per week. It supplies 15 local outlets, 30 further afield and beer festivals. Special beers are also brewed.

White Hart (ABV 3.8%)

THE BREWERIES

Union Jack (ABV 4%)

Golden Drop (ABV 4.3%)

Uley

Uley Brewery Ltd, The Old Brewery, 31 The Street, Uley, Gloucestershire, GL11 5TB
☎ (01453) 860120 ✉ chas@uleybrewery.com
⊕ uleybrewery.com

⊠ Brewing at Uley began in 1833 as Price's Brewery. After a long gap, the premises were restored and Uley Brewery opened in 1985. It has its own spring water, which is used to mash Tucker's Maris Otter malt and boiled with Herefordshire hops. Uley serves 40-50 free trade outlets in the Cotswold area and is brewing to capacity. Seasonal beer: Reverend Janet (ABV 4.3%, summer).

Hogshead Cotswold Pale Ale
(OG 1030, ABV 3.5%) ◆
A pale-coloured, hoppy session bitter with a good hop aroma and a full flavour for its strength, ending in a bittersweet aftertaste.

Bitter (OG 1040, ABV 4%) ◆
A copper-coloured beer with hops and fruit in the aroma and a malty, fruity taste, underscored by a hoppy bitterness. The finish is dry, with a balance of hops and malt.

Laurie Lee's Bitter (OG 1045, ABV 4.5%)
A copper-coloured, full-flavoured, hoppy bitter with some fruitiness and a smooth, long, balanced finish.

Old Ric (OG 1045, ABV 4.5%) ◆
A full-flavoured, hoppy bitter with some fruitiness and a smooth, balanced finish. Distinctively copper-coloured, this is the house beer for the Old Spot Inn, Dursley.

Old Spot Prize Strong Ale (OG 1050, ABV 5%) ◆
A distinctive full-bodied, red/brown ale with a fruity aroma, a malty, fruity taste, with a hoppy bitterness, and a strong, balanced aftertaste.

Pig's Ear Strong Beer (OG 1050, ABV 5%) ◆
A pale-coloured beer, deceptively strong. Notably bitter in flavour, with a hoppy, fruity aroma and a bitter finish.

Ulverston

Ulverston Brewing Co, Lightburn Road, Ulverston, Cumbria, LA12 0AX
☎ (01229) 584280 ☎ 07840 192022
✉ info.ubc@tiscali.co.uk ⊕ ulverstonbrewing.co.uk
Tours by arrangement

☺The brewery went into production in 2006 and was situated in the old engine house of the long extinct Lindal Moor Mining Company. In 2010 it moved to new premises with a bespoke 12-barrel plant also incorporating a shop, viewing area and educational facilities. Most of the beers are named using a Laurel & Hardy theme after Ulverston's most famous son, Stan Laurel. Seasonal beers: What the Dickens (ABV 4%, Nov), Stout Ollie (ABV 4.3%), Bad Medicine (ABV 6.3%).

Flying Elephants (OG 1037, ABV 3.7%) ◆
Clean, refreshing yellow bitter, sweet and fruity with a dry citrus finish.

Celebration Ale (OG 1039, ABV 3.9%) ◆

Yellow fruity bitter with hints of tangerine and a notably sustained dry finish.

Harvest Moon (OG 1039, ABV 3.9%)

Another Fine Mess (OG 1040, ABV 4%) ◆
A refreshing gold-coloured bitter. Initially fruity but with a rising bitterness.

Laughing Gravy (OG 1040, ABV 4%)

Lonesome Pine (OG 1042, ABV 4.2%) ◆
A fresh and fruity pale gold beer; honeyed, lemony and resiny with an increasingly bitter finish.

Uncle Stuarts

Uncle Stuarts Brewery, Wroxham Barns, Tunstead Road, Hoveton, Norwich, NR12 8QU
☎ (01603) 783888 ✉ stuartsbrewery@aol.com
⊕ wroxhambarns.co.uk
Shop open daily 10.30am-4.30pm
Tours by arrangement

The brewery started in 2002, selling bottle-conditioned beers and polypins direct to customers and by mail order. In 2009 the brewery moved to Wroxham Barns Craft Centre. The beers are also available in nine-gallon casks. Seasonal beer: Xmas (ABV 7%).

North Norfolk Beauty (ABV 3.8%)

Pack Lane (OG 1038, ABV 4%)

Excelsior (ABV 4.5%)

Local Hero (ABV 4.7%)

Wroxham Barns Bitter (ABV 4.8%)

Norwich Castle (ABV 5%)

Buckenham Woods (OG 1051, ABV 5.6%) ◆
Spicy with more than a hint of raisin and sultana. Heavy aroma translates into a richly-flavoured ale with a surprisingly light and creamy mouthfeel.

Strumpshaw Fen (ABV 5.7%)

Norwich Cathedral (ABV 6.5%)

Union

⊟ Union Brewery, Dartmoor Union, Fore Street, Holbeton, Devon, PL8 1NE
☎ (01752) 830460 ⊕ dartmoorunion.co.uk

⊠ The Union Brewery started as a pipe dream. It is now in the hands of very enthusiastic amateurs and is in full (although small) production.

Pride (OG 1037, ABV 3.9%)

Jacks (OG 1045, ABV 4.5%)

Untapped (NEW)

Untapped Brewing Co, Correspondence: 80 Carlisle Street, Cardiff, CF24 2PF
☎ 07988 199794 ✉ enquiries@untappedbrew.com
⊕ untappedbrew.com

The Untapped Brewing Company was established in 2009 and is owned and run by Owen Davies and Martyn Darby. They are currently brewing at Whittingtons Brewery in Newent, Gloucestershire, where they have an arrangement to use the equipment. No cask-conditioned ale is produced but there are plans to do so. All current production is bottle-conditioned and sold through farmer's markets in south Wales and in a small number of local outlets. Bottle-conditioned ales: Sundown

(ABV 4%), Eclipse (ABV 4.4%), U.P.A. (ABV 4.5%), Ember (ABV 5.2%).

Upham (NEW)

Upham Brewery llp, Stakes Farm, Cross Lane, Upham, Hampshire, SO32 1FL
☎ (01489) 861383 ✉ info@uphambrewery.co.uk
uphambrewery.co.uk

Upham began brewing in 2009 using a 3.5-barrel plant.

Ale (ABV 4%)
A well-balanced beer with a roasted malty nose, a hint of chocolate and a pronounced hoppy finish.

Ushers

See Wadworth and Wychwood

Vale SIBA

Vale Brewery Co, Tramway Business Park, Ludgershall Road, Brill, Buckinghamshire, HP18 9TY
☎ (01844) 239237 ✉ info@valebrewery.co.uk
valebrewery.co.uk

Established in 1994 and initially based in Haddenham, Vale moved to Brill in 2007. Capacity was expanded in 2009 and then doubled to 20 barrel length in 2010. Five pubs are owned, including a brewery tap, the Hop Pole in Aylesbury. There is a brewery shop open to the public. Seasonal and monthly specials: see website. A wide range of bottle-conditioned beers is available.

Best Bitter (OG 1036, ABV 3.7%)
This pale amber beer starts with a slight fruit aroma. This leads to a clean, bitter taste where hops and fruit dominate. The finish is long and bitter with a slight hop note.

Black Swan Mild (OG 1038, ABV 3.9%)
Dark and smooth with hints of chocolate and coffee on the nose and a malty, dry finish.

Wychert Ale (OG 1038, ABV 3.9%)
A traditional Thames Valley beer. Woody flavours are notable in this malty beer with a finish of port and berries on the nose.

VPA/Vale Pale Ale (OG 1042, ABV 4.2%)
An assertive, dry, hoppy ale with a citrus nose, combined with a pronounced malt background.

Black Beauty Porter (OG 1043, ABV 4.3%)
A very dark ale, the initial aroma is malty. Roast malt dominates initially and is followed by a rich fruitiness, with some sweetness. The finish is increasingly hoppy and dry.

Edgar's Golden Ale (OG 1043, ABV 4.3%)
A golden, hoppy best bitter with some sweetness and a dry, bittersweet finish. An unpretentious and well-crafted beer.

Special (OG 1046, ABV 4.5%)
Premium ale with a rich, complex and satisfying finish.

Grumpling Premium Ale (OG 1046, ABV 4.6%)
A rich, warming ruby brown traditional English bitter with mellow fruity malt flavours accompanied by a subtle dry, hoppy finish.

Gravitas (OG 1047, ABV 4.8%)
A strong pale ale packed with hop and citrus flavours, rounded off by a dry, malty, biscuit finish. A pronounced hop aroma throughout.

Vale of Glamorgan

Vale of Glamorgan Brewery Ltd, Unit 8a, Atlantic Trading Estate, Barry, Vale of Glamorgan, CF63 3RF
☎ (01446) 730757 ✉ info@vogbrewery.co.uk
vogbrewery.co.uk
Tours by arrangement (max. 15 people)

Vale of Glamorgan Brewery started brewing in 2005 on a 10-barrel plant. More than 40 local outlets are supplied. Occasional beer: Oggy VoG (ABV 4%). Seasonal beers are brewed and bottle-conditioned beers are available.

Grog Y VoG (OG 1043, ABV 4.3%)

VoG Best (OG 1040, ABV 4.3%)

For Mochyn Du, Cardiff:

Cwrw'r Mochyn (ABV 4%)

Valhalla

Valhalla Brewery, Shetland Refreshments Ltd, Baltasound, Unst, Shetland, ZE2 9DX
☎ (01957) 711658 ✉ mail@valhallabrewery.co.uk
valhallabrewery.co.uk
Tours by arrangement

The brewery started production in 1997, set up by husband and wife team Sonny and Sylvia Priest. A bottling plant was installed in 1999. One outlet is supplied direct.

White Wife (OG 1038, ABV 3.8%)
Predominantly malty aroma with hop and fruit, which remain on the palate. The aftertaste is increasingly bitter.

Old Scatness (OG 1038, ABV 4%)
A light bitter, named after an archaeological dig at the south end of Shetland where early evidence of malting and brewing was found. One of the ingredients is an ancient strain of barley called Bere which used to be common in Shetland until the middle of the last century.

Simmer Dim (OG 1039, ABV 4%)
A light golden ale, named after the long Shetland twilight. The sulphur features do not mask the fruits and hops of this well-balanced beer.

Island Bere (OG 1044, ABV 4.2%)

Auld Rock (OG 1043, ABV 4.5%)
A full-bodied, dark Scottish-style best bitter, it has a rich malty nose but does not lack bitterness in the long dry finish.

Sjolmet Stout (OG 1048, ABV 5%)
Full of malt and roast barley, especially in the taste. Smooth, creamy, fruity finish, not as dry as some stouts.

Verulam

Verulam Brewery, Farmers Boy, 134 London Road, St Albans, Hertfordshire, AL1 1PQ
☎ (01727) 860535 ☎ 07799 137395
✉ douglaskintu@yahoo.co.uk farmersboy.net
Tours by arrangement

Formerly Alehouse Brewery (since 2006), Verulam is situated at the back of the Farmer's Boy

THE BREWERIES

and reverted to its original name in 2010. It currently only brews for the Farmers Boy.

Clipper IPA (OG 1039, ABV 4%)

Farmers Joy (OG 1043, ABV 4.5%)

Village Brewer

See Hambleton

Wadworth IFBB SIBA

Wadworth & Co Ltd, Northgate Brewery, Devizes, Wiltshire, SN10 1JW
☎ **(01380) 723361** ✉ **sales@wadworth.co.uk**
🌐 **wadworth.co.uk**
Shop Mon-Fri 10am-5.30pm (4.30pm winter), Sat 10am-4pm
Tours by arrangement

A market town brewery set up in 1885 by Henry Wadworth, it is one of few remaining producers to sell beer locally in oak casks; the brewery still employs a cooper. Though solidly traditional, with its own dray horses, it continues to invest in the future and to expand, producing up to 2,000 barrels a week to supply a wide-ranging free trade, around 300 outlets in the south of England, as well as its own 255 pubs. All tied houses serve cask beer. Wadworth also has a 2.5-barrel micro-brewery used for brewing trials, speciality brews and the production of cask mild as well as a new environmentally-friendly brewhouse. Seasonal beers: see website.

Henry's IPA (OG 1035, ABV 3.6%)
A classic session beer with malt-led flavours.

Horizon (OG 1039, ABV 4%)
A pale gold beer with zesty citrus and hop aromas and a crisp, tangy finish on the palate.

Stronginthearm (ABV 4%)
A punchy, hoppy tang from Fuggles and Goldings hops.

6X (OG 1041, ABV 4.3%)
Copper-coloured ale with a malty and fruity nose, and some balancing hop character. The flavour is similar, with some bitterness and a lingering malty, but bitter finish.

Bishops Tipple (OG 1048, ABV 5%)
A golden brew giving well-balanced hop bitterness and a clean finish.

Waen

Waen Beer Co, The Waen Brewery, Unit 5, Penstrowed Enterprise Park, Penstrowed, SY17 5SG
☎ **(01686) 627042**
✉ **sue@thewaenbeercompany.co.uk**
🌐 **thewaenbrewery.co.uk**
Shop Fri-Sat 10am-5pm
Tours by arrangement

Waen Brewery began brewing in 2009 on a five-barrel plant. Special beers are brewed such as Blackberry Stout (ABV 3.8%). Bottle-conditioned beers are available and are suitable for vegetarians and vegans. 20 outlets are supplied direct.

Brewster's Waen (OG 1038, ABV 3.8%)
A dark, malty ale.

First of the Summer Waen (OG 1040, ABV 4%)
A medium-hopped beer with a touch of wheat.

Festival Landmark Waen (OG 1043, ABV 4.2%)
A golden, hoppy, citrus ale.

Landmark Waen (OG 1052, ABV 5.5%)
A rich, fruity and hoppy finish to this citrus, bitter ale.

Wagtail

Wagtail Brewery, New Barn Farm, Wilby Warrens, Old Buckenham, Norfolk, NR17 1PF
☎ **(01953) 887133**
✉ **wagtailbrewery@btinternet.com**
🌐 **wagtailbrewery.com**

Wagtail brewery went into full-time production in 2006. All cask-conditioned beers are also available bottle conditioned and are suitable for vegetarians and vegans.

Best Bittern (OG 1040, ABV 4%)

Gold Rush (OG 1040, ABV 4%)
A sulphurous peppery aroma. A rolling mix of hops and bitterness give a spicy taste to this golden ale. A quick finish leaves a fruity sulphurous taste.

King Tut (OG 1040, ABV 4%)
Golden hued with a grainy character. A gentle bittersweet introduction with grapefruit notes. Flavours rub gently together towards a dry, slightly astringent finish.

Royal Norfolk (OG 1040, ABV 4%)
A bitter beer with hops and malt giving depth. Pale brown with a slightly sulphurous nose. A softly receding finish with smoky overtones.

English Ale (OG 1042, ABV 4.2%)
Lots of malt and roast notes in the aroma. Chocolate and vine fruit are to the fore in the first taste. Background hop and bitter notes soon fade with the other flavours to leave a single raisin-like taste.

Black Beauty (OG 1044, ABV 4.5%)
Roast is well supported by malt and bitterness throughout. Background traces of hop, raisin and sweetness add character. A dry, bitter ending with roast and malt support.

Black Shuck (OG 1044, ABV 4.5%)
Black and brooding, as befits a Norfolk legend. Deep roast notes hold this classic stout together. A grainy mouthfeel is in keeping with the roast character. Malt and bitterness provide contrasting flavours.

Hornblower (OG 1044, ABV 4.5%)
Dominated by malt in both aroma and taste. Bitterness introduces a different perspective and gives balance. A grainy texture with caramel and soft fruit notes. A tapering, dry finish.

Jumping Jericho (OG 1050, ABV 5.2%)

Wainstones

See Stokesley

Wantsum SIBA (NEW)

Wantsum Brewery Ltd, Unit 22, Sparrow Way, Lakesview International Business Park, Hersden, Kent, CT3 4AL
☎ **(0845) 040 5980**
✉ **wantsumbrewery@googlemail.com**
🌐 **wantsumbrewery.co.uk**

Tours by arrangement

⊗ Wantsum Brewery is a six-barrel plant and was established in 2009. It is located about seven miles from the City of Canterbury and close to the Wantsum channel, from which it takes its name. The beers are named after historic events and people in Kent. Around 35 outlets are supplied direct. Bottle-conditioned beers are planned. Seasonal beer: Black Pig (ABV 4.8%, Oct-Mar).

More's Head (OG 1034, ABV 3.4%)
A chestnut-coloured bitter with malt and roasted grains balanced against fruit and floral hops with a hint of citrus.

1381 (OG 1038, ABV 3.8%)
A golden IPA with delicate citrus and herbal aromas.

Fortitude (OG 1041.5, ABV 4.2%)
Flagship best bitter with a smooth hop finish.

Turbulent Priest (OG 1042, ABV 4.4%)
Adapted from an original Imperial Russian Porter recipe, this beer is smooth with burnt chocolate and smoky malt notes mixed with delicate hop bitterness and floral hints.

Dynamo (OG 1043, ABV 4.6%)
A crisp, light, golden ale, fruity and floral with an orange citrus twist.

Hengist (OG 1046, ABV 5%)
A golden pale ale with hints of biscuit malt balancing a smooth, fruity hop profile.

Wapping

Wapping Beers Ltd, Baltic Fleet, 33a Wapping, Liverpool, Merseyside, L1 8DQ
☎ (0151) 709 3116 ✉ simon@wappingbeers.co.uk
wappingbeers.co.uk / balticfleet.co.uk
Merchandise available at bar
Tours by arrangement

Wapping Beers was established in 2002 in the cellars of the pub on the waterfront in Liverpool using the old Passageway Brewery plant. Around half a dozen regular house beers are produced with specials and seasonal brews appearing throughout the year including Winter Ale (ABV 6.5%). All cask beers are also available bottle conditioned.

Baltic Gold (OG 1039, ABV 3.9%)
Hoppy golden ale with plenty of citrus hop flavour. Refreshing with good body and mouthfeel.

Summer Ale (OG 1042, ABV 4.2%)
Refreshing golden beer with floral hops dominating the nose and taste. Some fruit also on the aroma and in the taste. Good bitterness throughout, leading to a dry, bitter aftertaste.

Blonde (OG 1045, ABV 4.5%)

Smoked Porter (OG 1050, ABV 5%)

Stout (OG 1050, ABV 5%)
Classic dry roasty stout with strong bitterness balanced by fruit and hop flavours. The flavours follow through to a pleasantly dry finish.

Warcop

Warcop Country Ales, c/o 9 Nellive Park, Saint Brides Wentlooge, Gwent, NP10 8SE
☎ (01633) 680058 ✉ wiliam.picton@tesco.net
warcopales.com

A small brewery at Newhouse Farm, Saint Brides Wentlooge, based in a converted milking parlour. Cask ales are also available bottle conditioned. The brewery has a portfolio of 28 beers which are made on a cyclical basis, with five to six beers normally in stock at any one time: see website for full range. Seasonal beers: see website.

Warwickshire

Warwickshire Beer Co Ltd, The Brewery, Queen Street, Cubbington, Warwickshire, CV32 7NA
☎ (01926) 450747 ✉ info@warwickshirebeer.co.uk
warwickshirebeer.co.uk
Shop open most days inc. Sat am (please ring first)

⊗ Warwickshire is a six-barrel brewery operating in a former village bakery since 1998. Brewing takes place four times a week. The cask beers are available in over 100 outlets as well as the brewery's four pubs. Bottle-conditioned and seasonal beers are available.

Shakespeare's County (OG 1034, ABV 3.4%)

Ffiagra (ABV 3.8%)

Best Bitter (OG 1039, ABV 3.9%)

Darling Buds (ABV 4%)

Duck Soup (ABV 4.2%)

Lady Godiva (OG 1042, ABV 4.2%)

Falstaff (OG 1044, ABV 4.4%)

Churchyard Bob (OG 1049, ABV 4.9%)

Golden Bear (OG 1049, ABV 4.9%)

Ball Stitcher (ABV 5%)

Kingmaker (OG 1055, ABV 5.5%)

Watermill SIBA

Watermill Brewing Co, Watermill Inn, Ings, nr Windermere, Cumbria, LA8 9PY
☎ (01539) 821309 ✉ info@lakelandpub.co.uk
lakelandpub.co.uk
Tours by arrangement

Watermill was established in 2006 in a purpose-built extension to the inn. The five-barrel plant and equipment were originally at the Hops Bar & Grill opposite Daytona International Speedway in Florida. The beers have a doggie theme; dogs are allowed in the main bar of the pub and usually get served with biscuits before their owners. The brewery was extended in 2008. A new brewery is planned within the grounds of the pub, which will double production.

Collie Wobbles (OG 1037.5, ABV 3.7%)
A pale gold bitter with a slight citrus taste. A good hop and malt balance gives way to a dry finish.

Black Beard (OG 1038, ABV 3.8%)
A dark mild with bags of fruit and malt flavours.

A Bit'er Ruff (OG 1041.5, ABV 4.1%)
Copper-coloured, balanced fruity beer with a lingering, bitter aftertaste.

Ruff Justice (OG 1041, ABV 4.2%)
A malty golden ale, well-balanced with caramel, light floral hops and a fresh, dry finish.

A Winters Tail (OG 1042, ABV 4.3%)
A warming, ruby-coloured bitter, smooth in the mouth with a subtle hint of ginger and orange.

THE BREWERIES

Well-balanced with a small amount of pale chocolate malt.

Isle of Dogs (OG 1044, ABV 4.5%)
A golden bitter with a fresh, malty aroma and a distinctive citrus fruity flavour with an intense, dry aftertaste.

Wruff Night (OG 1047.5, ABV 5%) ◆
Straw-coloured, sweet and fruity, uncomplicated beer with bitterness in a short-lived aftertaste.

Dog'th Vaider (OG 1050, ABV 5.1%)
A dark, hoppy ale with a refreshing, dry finish.

Tomos Watkin SIBA

Hurns Brewing Co Ltd t/a Tomos Watkin, Unit 3, Alberto Road, Century Park, Valley Way, Swansea Enterprise Park, Swansea, SA6 8RP
☎ (01792) 797300 ✉ phillparry@tomoswatkin.co.uk
⊕ hurns.co.uk
Shop Mon-Fri 9am-5pm
Tours by arrangement

☺Brewing started in 1995 in Llandeilo using a 10-barrel plant in converted garages. Tomos Watkin moved to bigger premises in Swansea in 2000 and the plant increased to a 50-barrel capacity. HBC Ltd was formed in 2002 when the brewery was purchased from Tomos Watkin. Over 60% of production is now bottled beers (not bottle conditioned). More than 400 outlets are supplied. Seasonal beers: see website.

Cwrw Braf (OG 1038, ABV 3.7%)
A clean-drinking, amber-coloured ale with a light bitterness and gentle hop aroma.

Chwarae Teg (OG 1041, ABV 4.1%)
A golden ale with malty, nutty flavours.

Cwrw Haf (ABV 4.2%)
A golden refreshing ale with citrus flavours and a floral aroma.

Old Style Bitter/OSB (OG 1046, ABV 4.5%) ◆
Amber-coloured with an inviting aroma of hops and malt. Full bodied; hops, fruit, malt and bitterness combine to give a balanced flavour continuing into the finish.

Waveney

▤ Waveney Brewing Co, Queen's Head, Station Road, Earsham, Norfolk, NR35 2TS
☎ (01986) 892623 ✉ lyndahamps@aol.com

Established at the Queens Head in 2004, the five-barrel brewery produces three beers, regularly available at the pub along with free trade outlets. Occasional beers are brewed. Seasonal beer: Raging Bullace (ABV 5.1%, Dec-Jan), Sugar Ray (ABV 4.4%, Mar-May), Great White Hope (ABV 4.8%).

East Coast Mild (OG 1037, ABV 3.8%) ◆
A traditional mild with distinctive roast malt aroma and red-brown colouring. A sweet, plummy malt beginning quickly fades as a dry roasted bitterness begins to make its presence felt.

Lightweight (OG 1039, ABV 3.9%) ◆
A gentle beer with a light but well-balanced hop and malt character. A light body is reflected in the quick, bitter finish. Golden hued with a distinctive strawberry and cream nose.

Welterweight (OG 1042, ABV 4.2%)

Wayland's Sixpenny SIBA

Wayland's Sixpenny Brewery, The Dairy Building, Manor Farm, Sixpenny Handley, Dorset, SP5 5NU
☎ (01725) 762006 ☎ 07956 531618
✉ mail@sixpennybrewery.co.uk
⊕ sixpennybrewery.co.uk
Shop Wed-Fri 11am-4pm, Sat 11am-12.30pm
Tours by arrangement

⊠ Established in 2007 and formerly known as Waylands Brewery, Wayland's Sixpenny relocated to Dorset from Surrey in 2009. Around 50 outlets are supplied direct. Seasonal beers: see website. Occasional beers: Addlestone Ale (ABV 4.2%), Special FX (ABV 4.8%).

Bitter (ABV 3.6%)
Refreshing, malty and well-hopped.

Best Bitter (ABV 4.2%)
A well-balanced ale with a rounded malt flavour that leads to a pleasantly bitter and hoppy finish.

Gold (ABV 4.2%)
A golden ale, slightly citrus flavoured with a distinct hoppy floral aroma.

Special (ABV 5%)
A traditional strong best bitter. Rich and full-bodied with a rounded malt flavour and long finish.

WC

WC Brewery, 3 Micklegate, Mickle Trafford, Chester, CH2 4TF ✉ thegents@wcbrewery.com
⊕ wcbrewery.com

☺Founded in 2003 by Ian Williams and Steve Carr, the WC Brewery is one of the smallest commercial breweries in the country. The Gents generally brew to order for local pubs and beer festivals. Seasonal beers are available.

IP Ale (ABV 3.8%)
A pale beer, heavily hopped for extra bitterness and a lingering citrus finish.

Kami-Khasi (ABV 3.8%)
Intensely hopped bitter.

Golden Cascade (ABV 4%)
A light and refreshing bitter with a distinct hoppy character.

Gypsy's Kiss (ABV 4.1%)
A copper-coloured ale, well-balanced with spicy citrus hops.

Lift a Buttercup (ABV 4.1%)
A refreshing pale ale with floral hop flavours.

Slow Motion Stout (ABV 4.5%)
Full of roast coffee and chocolate flavours.

Yank My Chain (ABV 4.5%)
Hugely-hopped American West Coast-style IPA.

Ivana Tinkle (ABV 4.6%)
Czech-style pale beer.

Le Chat Noir (ABV 5%)
Rich and complex porter.

SBD (ABV 5%)
A premium ale; rich, fruity and deceptively strong.

Weatheroak

Weatheroak Brewery Ltd, Unit 7, Victoria Works, Birmingham Road, Studley, Warwickshire, B80 7AP
☎ (0121) 445 4411 (eve) ☎ 07798 773894 (day)

Office: 25 Withybed Lane, Alvechurch, Birmingham, B48 7NX ✉ dave@weatheroakales.co.uk
⊕ weatheroakales.co.uk
Shop Fri & Sat 5.30-8.30pm

⊠ The brewery was set up in 1997 in an outhouse at the Coach & Horses, Weatheroak Hill. The first brew was produced in 1998. In 2008 it moved to Alvechurch (adjacent to the Weatheroak Ales Off-Licence – address to be used for correspondence) and then to a spacious factory unit in Studley. Weatheroak supplies 40 outlets. Seasonal beers are brewed on a regular basis.

Light Oak (ABV 3.6%) ◆
This straw-coloured quaffing ale has lots of hoppy notes on the tongue and nose, and a fleetingly sweet aftertaste.

Ale (ABV 4.1%) ◆
The aroma is dominated by hops in this golden-coloured brew. Hops also feature in the mouth and there is a rapidly fading dry aftertaste.

Keystone Hops (ABV 5%) ◆
A golden yellow beer that is surprisingly easy to quaff given the strength. Fruity hops are the dominant flavour without the commonly associated astringency.

For Weighbridge, Alvechurch:

Tillerman's Tipple (ABV 3.9%)
A pleasant, pale session beer with hops throughout.

Weatheroak Hill

⊟ Weatheroak Hill Brewery, Coach & Horses, Weatheroak Hill, Warwickshire, B48 7EA
☎ (01564) 823386 (pub)
Tours by arrangement

⊠ Weatheroak Hill started brewing in 2008. At present only the pub and beer festivals are supplied. Seasonal beers: Shires Ale (ABV 4.7%, summer), Radford Ale (ABV 4.7%, winter). There are plans to produce bottle-conditioned beers.

Icknield Pale Ale (OG 1038, ABV 3.8%)

Bitter (OG 1042, ABV 4.2%)

Weetwood

Weetwood Ales Ltd, Weetwood Grange, Weetwood, Tarporley, Cheshire, CW6 0NQ
☎ (01829) 752377 ✉ sales@weetwoodales.co.uk
⊕ weetwoodales.co.uk

☺The brewery was set up at an equestrian centre in 1993. In 1998, the five-barrel plant was replaced by a 10-barrel kit. Around 200 regular outlets are supplied.

Best Bitter (OG 1038.5, ABV 3.8%) ◆
Pale brown beer with an assertive bitterness and a lingering dry finish. Despite initial sweetness, peppery hops dominate throughout.

Mad Hatter (OG 1038.5, ABV 3.9%)
A red-brown beer with fruity and malty flavours throughout. Brewed with American Amarillo hops to give spicy and floral notes.

Cheshire Cat (ABV 4%) ◆
Pale, dry bitter with a spritzy lemon zest and a grapy aroma. Hoppy aroma leads through to the initial taste before fruitiness takes over. Smooth creamy mouthfeel and a short, dry finish.

Eastgate Ale (OG 1043.5, ABV 4.2%) ◆
Well-balanced and refreshing clean amber beer. Citrus fruit flavours predominate in the taste and there is a short, dry aftertaste.

Old Dog Bitter (OG 1045, ABV 4.5%) ◆
Robust, well-balanced amber beer with a slightly fruity aroma. Rich malt and fruit flavours are balanced by bitterness. Some sweetness and a hint of sulphur on nose and taste.

Ambush Ale (OG 1047.5, ABV 4.8%) ◆
Full-bodied malty, premium bitter with initial sweetness balanced by bitterness and leading to a long-lasting dry finish. Blackberries and bitterness predominate alongside the hops.

Oasthouse Gold (OG 1050, ABV 5%) ◆
Straw-coloured, crisp, full-bodied and fruity golden ale with a good dry finish.

Wellington

See Crown

Wells & Young's

See New Nationals section

Welton's SIBA

Welton's Brewery, 1 Mulberry Trading Estate, Foundry Lane, Horsham, West Sussex, RH13 5PX
☎ (01403) 242901/251873 ✉ sales@weltons.co.uk
⊕ weltonsbeer.com
Tours by arrangement

Ray Welton moved his brewery to a factory unit in Horsham in 2003, which has given him space to expand. Over 100 different beers were brewed during the past year. Around 400 outlets are supplied. Bottle-conditioned beers are available.

Pride 'n' Joy (ABV 2.8%) ◆
A light brown bitter with a slight malty and hoppy aroma. Fruity with a pleasant hoppiness and some sweetness in the flavour, leading to a short malty finish.

Horsham Bitter (ABV 3.8%)
Amber-coloured, bitter but with a huge aroma.

Old Cocky (OG 1043, ABV 4.3%)

Horsham Old (OG 1046, ABV 4.6%) ◆
Roast and toffee flavours predominate with some bitterness in this traditional old ale. Bittersweet with plenty of caramel and roast in a rather short finish.

Export Stout (ABV 4.7%)
Hints of burnt toast, balanced by good levels of hops with a long finish.

Old Harry (OG 1051, ABV 5.2%)

Wem

See Shropshire

Wensleydale

Wensleydale Brewery Ltd, Manor Road, Bellerby, Leyburn, North Yorkshire, DL8 5QH

THE BREWERIES

☎ (01969) 622463 ☎ 07939 751130
✉ enquiries@wensleydalebrewery.co.uk
🌐 wensleydalebrewery.co.uk
Shop Mon-Fri 9am-5pm
Tours by arrangement

⊗ Wensleydale Brewery (formerly Lidstone's) was set up in 2003 on a two-barrel plant in Yorkshire Dales National Park. A year later the brewery relocated to larger premises six miles away and is now operating on a four-barrel plant. Most beers are available in bottles – some bottle conditioned. Around 100 outlets are supplied. Seasonal beer: Beaters' Barley Wine (ABV 8.5%).

Lidstone's Rowley Mild (OG 1037, ABV 3.2%) ◆
Chocolate and toffee aromas lead into what, for its strength, is an impressively rich and flavoursome taste. The finish is pleasantly bittersweet.

Bitter (OG 1038, ABV 3.7%) ◆
Intensely aromatic, straw-coloured ale offering a superb balance of malt and hops on the tongue.

Semer Water (OG 1041, ABV 4.1%)
Golden ale with a hint of banana on the nose. The taste is clean, crisp and hoppy, with grapefruit flavours also present.

Coverdale Gamekeeper (OG 1042, ABV 4.3%)
A light copper best bitter with a spicy aroma and juicy malt leading to a bittersweet finish with citrus notes.

Black Dub Oat Stout (OG 1044, ABV 4.4%)
Black beer brimming with roasted chocolate taste and aroma.

Sheep Rustler's Nut Brown Ale (ABV 4.4%)
A dark, reddish brown beer with a sweetish roast malt taste leading to a long-lasting, roasted, slightly bitter finish.

Gold (ABV 4.5%)
A blonde ale with aromatic and spicy hops.

Coverdale Poacher IPA (OG 1049, ABV 5%) ◆
Citrus flavours dominate both aroma and taste in this pale, smooth, refreshing beer; the aftertaste is quite dry.

Porter (OG 1061, ABV 6.5%)
A rich ale brimming with roasted malt, raisins and molasses with a lingering hoppy bitterness.

Wentworth SIBA

Wentworth Brewery Ltd, Power House, Gun Park, Wentworth, South Yorkshire, S62 7TF
☎ (01226) 747070 ✉ info@wentworth-brewery.co.uk 🌐 wentworth-brewery.co.uk
Tours by arrangement

Brewing started at Wentworth in 1999. In 2006 custom-built brewing kit was installed, increasing production to 30 barrels a day. More than 300 outlets are supplied.

Imperial Ale (OG 1038, ABV 3.8%)
A tawny, bitter beer with a floral nose. There is a slight hint of sweetness on the aftertaste.

WPA (OG 1039.5, ABV 4%) ◆
An extremely well hopped IPA-style beer that leads to some astringency. A very bitter beer.

Best Bitter (OG 1040, ABV 4.1%) ◆
A hoppy, bitter beer with hints of citrus fruits. A bitter note dominates the aftertaste.

Bumble Beer (OG 1043, ABV 4.3%) ⎕
A pale golden beer, made with local honey, which gives it a unique and distinctive flavour throughout the year.

Black Zac (OG 1046, ABV 4.6%)
A mellow, dark ruby-red ale with chocolate and pale malts leading to a bitter taste, with a coffee finish.

Oatmeal Stout (OG 1050, ABV 4.8%) ◆
Black, smooth, with roast and chocolate malt and toffee overtones.

Rampant Gryphon (OG 1062, ABV 6.2%) ◆
A strong, well-balanced golden ale with hints of fruit and sweetness but which retains a hoppy character.

Wessex

CF Hobden t/a Wessex Brewery, Rye Hill Farm, Longbridge Deverill, Warminster, Wiltshire, BA12 7DE
☎ (01985) 844532
✉ wessexbrewery@tinyworld.co.uk
Tours by arrangement

⊗ The brewery went into production in 2001 and moved to its current location in 2004. 15 local outlets are supplied. Beers are also available through selected wholesalers. Seasonal beers: Burlington Bertie (ABV 3.33%, summer), Farmer's Tan (ABV 4.7%, autumn). Election years: Truth Decay Mild (ABV 4.3%), Electile Dysfunction (ABV 6.66%).

Potter's Ale (OG 1038, ABV 3.8%)
A classic bitter.

Longleat Pride (OG 1040, ABV 4%)
A pale, hoppy bitter.

Crockerton Classic (OG 1041, ABV 4.1%)
A full-bodied, tawny, full-flavoured bitter; fruity and malty.

Merrie Mink (OG 1041, ABV 4.2%)
A full-flavoured best with a strong hop aroma.

Deverill's Advocate (OG 1046, ABV 4.5%)
A well-balanced golden premium ale.

Warminster Warrior (OG 1045, ABV 4.5%)
Full-flavoured premium bitter.

Russian Stoat (OG 1080, ABV 9%)
Dark, strong and obvious.

West

West Brewery, Bar & Restaurant, Binnie Place, Glasgow Green, Glasgow, G40 1AW
☎ (0141) 550 0135 ✉ info@westbeer.com
🌐 westbeer.com
Tours by arrangement

No real ale. West opened in 2006 and produces a full range of European-style beers. The brewery's copper-clad system, visible from the 300-seat bar and restaurant, is a fully-automated German one with an annual capacity of 1.5 million litres. Brewing is in strict accordance with the Reinheitsgebot, the German purity law, importing all malt, hops and yeast from Germany. Five regular beers are produced along with a range of seasonals. Beers: Hefeweizen (ABV 4.9%), St Mungo (ABV 4.9%), Helles Light (ABV 3.9%), Dunkel (ABV 4.9%), Munich Red (ABV 4.9%).

West Berkshire SIBA

West Berkshire Brewery Co Ltd, Old Bakery, Yattendon, Thatcham, Berkshire, RG18 0UE
☎ (01635) 202968/202638 ✉ info@wbbrew.co.uk
wbbrew.com
Shop Mon-Fri 10am-4pm; Sat 10am-1pm
Tours by arrangement

The brewery, established in 1995, has since moved its main site to Yattendon. In 2006 the brewhouse was extended and a new plant installed; the original five-barrel plant at the Potkiln pub in Frilsham has now closed. Around 120 outlets are supplied and one pub is owned. A monthly beer is also brewed – the beer names follow an annual theme.

Old Father Thames (OG 1038, ABV 3.4%)
A traditional pale ale with a full flavour despite its low strength.

Mr Chubb's Lunchtime Bitter (OG 1040, ABV 3.7%)
A drinkable, balanced, session bitter. A malty caramel note dominates aroma and taste and is accompanied by a nutty bittersweetness and a hoppy aftertaste.

Maggs' Magnificent Mild (OG 1041, ABV 3.8%)
Silky, full-bodied, dark mild with a creamy head. Roast malt aroma is joined in the taste by caramel, sweetness and mild, fruity hoppiness. Aftertaste of roast malt with balancing bitterness.

Good Old Boy (OG 1043, ABV 4%)
Well-rounded, tawny bitter with malt and hops dominating throughout. A balancing bitterness accompanies the taste and aftertaste.

Dr Hexter's Wedding Ale (OG 1044, ABV 4.1%)
Fruit and hops dominate the aroma and are joined in the taste by a hint of malt. The aftertaste has a pleasant bitter hoppiness.

Full Circle (OG 1047, ABV 4.5%)
A golden ale with a pleasing aroma and taste of bitter hops with a hint of malt. The aftertaste is hoppy and bitter with a rounding note of malt.

Dr Hexter's Healer (OG 1052, ABV 5%)
An amber strong bitter with malt, caramel and hops in the aroma. Taste is a balance of malt, caramel, fruit, hops and bittersweetness. Caramel, fruit and bittersweetness dominate the aftertaste.

Westbury

See Wessex

Westerham SIBA

Westerham Brewery Co Ltd, Grange Farm, Pootings Road, Crockham Hill, Kent, TN8 6SA
☎ (01732) 864427
✉ sales@westerhambrewery.co.uk
westerhambrewery.co.uk
Shop Mon-Fri 9am-5pm
Tours by arrangement (min 30 people, charge made)

The brewery was established in 2004 and restored a brewing tradition to Westerham that was lost when the Black Eagle Brewery was taken over by Ind Coope in 1959 and closed in 1965. Two of Black Eagle's yeast strains were deposited at the National Collection of Yeast Cultures and are used to recreate the true flavour of Westerham beers. The new brewery is based at the National Trust's Grange Farm in a former dairy and uses the same water supply as Black Eagle. Around 200 outlets are supplied in Kent, Surrey, Sussex and South London. Single hop varietal beers and occasional brews: see website. Bottle-conditioned beers are also available.

Finchcocks Original (OG 1036.2, ABV 3.5%)
Mid-gold session beer. Citrus notes on the palate with a hint of biscuit and resiny hoppiness.

Grasshopper Kentish Bitter (OG 1039, ABV 3.8%)
A dark, malty bitter with nutty, roasted notes from the chocolate malt.

SPA (Special Pale Ale) (OG 1038.5, ABV 3.8%)

Summer Perle (OG 1038.5, ABV 3.8%)
Golden ale with a spicy, refreshing finish.

British Bulldog (OG 1043.5, ABV 4.3%)
A rich, full-bodied best bitter with a massive aroma and palate of jammy fruit, biscuity malt and bitter hop resins.

William Wilberforce Freedom Ale (OG 1042, ABV 4.3%)
Deep golden ale with a mellow bitterness and long, hoppy finish.

India Pale Ale (OG 1047, ABV 4.8%)
Traditional IPA with plum jam and blackcurrant aroma and palate, balanced by sappy malt and a long, lingering bitter, fruity finish.

1965 – Special Bitter Ale (OG 1047.5, ABV 4.9%)
A clean, refreshing bitter with a full-bodied flavour.

Whalebone

Whalebone Brewery, 163 Wincolmlee, Hull, East Yorkshire, HU2 0PA
☎ (01482) 226648
Tours by arrangement

The Whalebone pub, which dates from 1796, was bought by Hull CAMRA founding member Alex Craig in 2002. He opened the brewery the following year and his beers have names connected with the former whaling industry on the adjoining River Hull. Two or three outlets are supplied as well as the pub. Seasonal beers: Truelove Porter (ABV 4.7%), Joseph Allen (ABV 5%), Moby Dick (ABV 8%), Full Ship (ABV 8.4%).

Diana Mild (OG 1037, ABV 3.5%)

Neckoil Bitter (OG 1039, ABV 3.9%)

WharfeBank SIBA (NEW)

WharfeBank Brewery Ltd, Unit 4, Pool Business Park, Pool Road, Pool in Wharfedale, West Yorkshire, LS21 1EG
☎ (0113) 284 2392
✉ martin@wharfebankbrewery.com
wharfebankbrewery.com
Tours by arrangement

WharfeBank commenced brewing in 2010 on a 20-barrel plant with the capacity to brew 100 barrels per week. It is situated in a converted paper mill on the banks of the River Wharfe and was developed by Martin Kellaway, ex sales director of Caledonian Brewery. The brewing team is headed by Ian Smith, ex Tetley's head brewer. 50 outlets are supplied direct.

Slingers Gold (OG 1039, ABV 3.7%)

THE BREWERIES

Tether Blond (OG 1040, ABV 4.1%)

CamFell Flame (OG 1045, ABV 4.5%)

Wharfedale

See Dark Horse

Whim SIBA

Whim Ales Ltd, Whim Farm, Hartington, Derbyshire, SK17 0AX
☎ (01298) 84991 ✉ info@whimales.co.uk

A brewery opened in 1993 in outbuildings at Whim Farm. Whim's beers are available in 50-70 outlets and the brewery's tied house, the Wilkes Head in Leek, Staffs. Some one-off brews are produced. Occasional/seasonal beers: Kaskade (ABV 4.3%, lager), Snow White (ABV 4.5%, wheat beer), Easter Special (ABV 4.8%), Stout Jenny (ABV 4.7%), Black Xmas (ABV 6.5%).

Arbor Light (OG 1035, ABV 3.6%)
Light-coloured bitter, sharp and clean with lots of hop character and a delicate light aroma.

Hartington Bitter (OG 1039, ABV 4%)
A light, golden-coloured, well-hopped session beer. A dry finish with a spicy, floral aroma.

Hartington IPA (OG 1045, ABV 4.5%)
Pale and light-coloured, smooth on the palate allowing malt to predominate. Slightly sweet finish combined with distinctive light hop bitterness. Well rounded.

Flower Power (OG 1052, ABV 5.3%)
Light, golden coloured beer with a flowery hop aroma, citrus with mild spice on the palate and a dry, bitter finish.

White SIBA

White Brewing Co, 1066 Country Brewery, Pebsham Farm Industrial Estate, Pebsham Lane, Bexhill-on-Sea, East Sussex, TN40 2RZ
☎ (01424) 731066 ✉ whitebrewing@fsbdial.co.uk
🌐 white-brewing.co.uk
Tours by arrangement

The brewery was founded in 1995 to serve local free trade outlets and some wholesalers. White has expanded production threefold with the addition of seasonal and occasional beers. Around 30 outlets are supplied. Seasonal beers: White Gold (ABV 4.9%, summer), Old White Christmas (ABV 4%). Bottle-conditioned beers are also available.

1066 Country Bitter (OG 1040, ABV 4%)
Amber-gold in colour, a light, sweetish beer with good malt and hop balance, and a bitter, refreshing finish.

Dark (OG 1040, ABV 4%)

Heart of Rother (ABV 4.5%)

Chilly Willy (ABV 5.1%)

Whitehaven

Whitehaven Brewing Co Ltd, Croasdale Farm Barn, Ennerdale, Cleator, Cumbria, CA23 3AT
☎ (01946) 861755 ✉ info@twbcl.co.uk
🌐 twbcl.co.uk
Tours by arrangement

The brewery was established in late 2007 on a 10-barrel plant. Four regular beers are produced under the brand 'Real Ales' from Ennerdale. Seasonal beers: Ennerdale Spring (ABV 3.8%), Ennerdale Spice (ABV 4.2%), Ritsons Force (ABV 5.5%).

Ennerdale Bitter (ABV 3.6%) ◆
Mildly fruity and lightly-hopped amber beer.

Ennerdale Blonde (ABV 3.8%)

Ennerdale Copper (ABV 3.8%) ◆
Copper-coloured session bitter with an initially fruity taste and drying aftertaste.

Breeze (ABV 3.9%)

Darkest Ennerdale (ABV 4.2%)

White Horse

White Horse Brewery Co Ltd, 3 Ware Road, White Horse Business Park, Stanford-in-the-Vale, Oxfordshire, SN7 8NY
☎ (01367) 718700
Tours by arrangement

⊗ White Horse was founded on a modern industrial estate in 2004. The second-hand brewing plant was manufactured in Belgium and has a brew-length of 7.5 barrels. It uses the continental method of brewing with a lauter tun rather than an infusion mash tun. The brewery now has its own pub in Oxford as well as supplying more than 150 outlets. Seasonal beers: Dragon Hill (ABV 4.2%, autumn), Flibbertigibbet (ABV 4.3%, summer), Saracen IPA (ABV 4.5%, spring), Giant (ABV 4.3%, winter), Rudolf The Red Nosed White Horse (ABV 4.8%, Xmas).

Oxfordshire Bitter (OG 1039, ABV 3.7%)
Golden bitter, well-hopped with a clean, fruity finish.

Village Idiot (OG 1044.5, ABV 4.1%)
A blonde ale with a complex hop aroma and taste.

Wayland Smithy (OG 1049, ABV 4.4%)
A red-brown ale with a nice biscuit flavour that is balanced with a spicy hop finish.

Black Horse Porter (OG 1052, ABV 5%)
Dark red porter with a chocolate character and a fruity/berry hop aroma and taste.

The Guv'nor (OG 1066, ABV 6.5%)
A light golden strong ale with a fruity finish.

For Turf Tavern, Oxford:

Summer Ale (OG 1042, ABV 4.1%)
A golden ale with a dry aftertaste.

White Park

White Park Brewery, Perry Hill Farm, Bourne End Road, Cranfield, Beds, MK43 0BA
☎ (01223) 911357 ✉ info@whiteparkbrewery.co.uk
🌐 whiteparkbrewery.co.uk

White Park is a family business established in 2007 on a five-barrel plant. Spent malt is recycled as feed for rare breed cattle. 60 outlets are supplied direct. Seasonal beers: see website.

First Flight (OG 1036, ABV 3.7%)

White Gold (OG 1037, ABV 3.8%)

Bedford Best (OG 1040.5, ABV 4.1%)

Cranfield Bitter (OG 1042.5, ABV 4.4%)

GB (OG 1047, ABV 5%)

Moonshine (OG 1050, ABV 5.2%)

White Rose SIBA

White Rose Brewery Ltd, 119 Chapel Road, Burncross, Chapeltown, Sheffield, South Yorkshire, S35 1QL
☎ (0114) 297 6150
✉ whiterose.brewery@btinternet.com
Tours by arrangement

Gary Sheriff, former head brewer at Wentworth Brewery, set up White Rose in 2007. The brewery premises are behind the Wellington in Sheffield and are shared with Little Ale Cart Brewery. Some equipment is used jointly but White Rose uses its own fermenters. 70 outlets are supplied direct.

Honey Blonde (OG 1040, ABV 4%)

Original Blonde (OG 1040, ABV 4%)

Stairway to Heaven (OG 1044, ABV 4.3%)

Autumn Gold (OG 1046, ABV 4.4%)

Whitewater

Whitewater Brewing Co, 40 Tullyframe Road, Kilkeel, Co Down, Northern Ireland, BT34 4RZ
☎ (028) 4176 9449
✉ info@whitewaterbrewing.com
🌐 whitewaterbrewing.co.uk
Tours by arrangement

Set up in 1996, Whitewater is now the biggest brewery in Northern Ireland. Currently, Whitewater supplies 15 outlets and owns one pub, the White Horse, Saintfield, Co. Down. Seasonal beers: see website.

Crown & Glory (OG 1038, ABV 3.8%)

Belfast Black (OG 1042, ABV 4.2%)

Belfast Ale (OG 1046, ABV 4.5%)

Clotworthy Dobbin (OG 1050, ABV 5%)

Whitstable

Whitstable Brewery, Little Telpits Farm, Woodcock Lane, Grafty Green, Kent, ME17 2AY
☎ (01622) 851007
✉ whitstablebrewer@btconnect.com
🌐 whitstablebrewery.info

Whitstable was launched in 2003 when the Green family purchased the Swale and North Weald Brewery to supply their own outlets (a hotel and three restaurants) in Whitstable, and beer festival orders. In 2006 they opened a bar in East Quay. The brewery supplies over 75 outlets in Kent, Surrey and London. Seasonal beers: Winkle Picker (ABV 4.5%), Christmas Cake (ABV 4.6%).

Native Bitter (OG 1036, ABV 3.7%)
A deep amber beer with nutty notes and malt flavours.

East India Pale Ale (OG 1040, ABV 4.1%)
A pale-coloured, sharp, clean beer with well-balanced hop flavours leaving the palate on a bittersweet assertive finish.

Oyster Stout (OG 1045, ABV 4.5%)
Rich, dry deep chocolate and mocha flavours.

Pearl of Kent (OG 1043, ABV 4.5%)
A light-coloured, well-rounded premium beer with tropical fruit flavours.

Kentish Reserve (OG 1047, ABV 5%)
A copper ale with warm plum pudding flavours and a ruby port finish.

Whittington's SIBA

Whittington's Brewery, Three Choirs Vineyards Ltd, Newent, Gloucestershire, GL18 1LS
☎ (01531) 890555 ✉ brewery@threechoirs.com
🌐 whittingtonbrewery.co.uk
Shop 9am-5pm daily (later during summer)
Tours by arrangement (for a charge)

Whittington's started in 2003 using a purpose-built five-barrel plant. Dick Whittington came from nearby Pauntley, hence the name and feline theme. The beers are currently only available bottle conditioned from the onsite shop, online and from local outlets: Nine Lives (ABV 4%), Summer Pale Ale (ABV 4%), Cats Whiskers (ABV 4.6%), A Winter's Tail (ABV 5.1%).

Why Not

Why Not Brewery, 17 Cavalier Close, Thorpe St Andrew, Norwich, NR7 0TE
☎ (01603) 300786
✉ colin@thewhynotbrewery.co.uk
🌐 thewhynotbrewery.co.uk

Why Not opened in 2006 with equipment located in a shed and custom-made by Brendan Moore of Iceni Brewery. The brewery can produce up to two barrels per brew. All beers are available in bottle-conditioned form and are occasionally put into casks to order.

Wally's Revenge (OG 1040, ABV 4%) ◆
An overtly bitter beer with a hoppy background. The bitterness holds on to the end as an increasing astringent dryness develops.

Roundhead Porter (OG 1045, ABV 4.5%)
A traditional old style London porter.

Cavalier Red (OG 1047, ABV 4.7%) ◆
Explosive fruity nose belies the gentleness of the taste. The summer fruit aroma dominates this red-gold brew. A sweet, fruity start disappears under a quick, bitter ending.

Norfolk Honey Ale (OG 1050, ABV 5%)
A golden beer with a honey nose. A definite hop edge leaves a honey aftertaste.

Chocolate Nutter (OG 1056, ABV 5.5%)

Wibblers

Wibblers Brewery Ltd, Joyces Farm, Southminster Road, Mayland, Essex, CM3 6EB
☎ (01621) 772044 ✉ info@wibblers.com
🌐 wibblers.com
Tours by arrangement

Wibblers was established commercially in 2007 and expanded in 2009. All beers are available at the brewery tap, the Cap & Feathers in Tillingham, Essex. Seasonal and one-off beers are brewed every month. All beers are also available in bottle-conditioned form and are suitable for vegans. Seasonal beers: see website.

Dengie Best (OG 1036, ABV 3.6%)

Apprentice (OG 1039, ABV 3.9%)

Hoppy Helper (OG 1041, ABV 4%)

THE BREWERIES

Darker Mild (OG 1044, ABV 4.3%)

Crafty Stoat (OG 1056, ABV 5.3%)

Wicked Hathern

Wicked Hathern Brewery Ltd, 17 Nixon Walk, East Leake, Leicestershire, LE12 6HL
☎ (01509) 559308 ✉ sean.oneill@escapade-rs.com
🌐 wicked-hathern.co.uk

Opened in 2000, the brewery generally supplies beer on a guest basis to many local pubs and beer festivals, and brews commissioned beers for special occasions. All beers are available bottled from selected off-licences (see website) and from Hathern Stores. Special cask beer is brewed for the Albion Inn, Loughborough, and special bottled beers for Hathern Stores and Alexander Wines in Earlsdon. The brewery itself is not currently operating and the beers are being produced by the Wicked Hathern brewers at Leek Brewery (qv). Seasonal beer: Gladstone Tidings (ABV 5.1%, Xmas).

Dobles' Dog (OG 1035, ABV 3.5%)
A full-bodied, stout-like dark mild with fruit and nut flavours on the palate. Gently bitter, malty finish with a lingering hint of roasted malts.

Hathern Cross (OG 1037, ABV 3.7%)
A golden ale with spicy hops in the aroma. The taste is well-balanced and bittersweet with a lemon note from the hops contrasting with malt sweetness. A gently bitter and hoppy aftertaste. It is named after the cross in the middle of the village.

WHB/Wicked Hathern Bitter (OG 1038, ABV 3.8%)
A light-tasting session bitter with a dry palate and good hop aroma.

Cockfighter (OG 1043, ABV 4.2%)
A copper-coloured beer with an aroma of fruit, creamy malt and hop resins.

Hawthorn Gold (OG 1045, ABV 4.5%)
A pale golden ale with delicate malt and spicy hop in the aroma. The taste is hoppy and mostly bitter but with good malt support and body. Dry, malt and hops aftertaste.

Derby Porter (OG 1048, ABV 4.8%)
A deep ruby porter with a creamy nose of lightly smoky, chocolatey, nutty dark malts.

Soar Head (OG 1048, ABV 4.8%) ◆
A dark ruby-coloured strong bitter with a cocktail of distinctive flavours.

Swift 'Un (OG 1048, ABV 4.8%)
A light-golden mellow beer with fruity overtones.

For Albion, Canal Bank, Loughborough:

Albion Special (OG 1041, ABV 4%)
A light, copper-coloured bitter with a nutty aroma and smoky malt taste, hops leading through.

For Burleigh Court, Loughborough University Campus:

Burly Court Jester (OG 1038, ABV 3.8%)

Wickwar SIBA

Wickwar Brewing Co, Old Brewery, Station Road, Wickwar, Gloucestershire, GL12 8NB
☎ 0870 777 5671
✉ brew.crew@wickwarbrewing.com
🌐 wickwarbrewing.com

Shop Mon-Fri 8am-6pm, Sat 9am-5pm (Tel: 01454 299592)
Tours by arrangement

Wickwar was established as a 10-barrel brewery in 1990 in the cooper's shop of the former Arnold Perrett Brewery. In 2004 it was expanded to 50 barrels and moved into the original 19th-century brewery. 350 local outlets are supplied on a regular basis and the beers are available nationally through most distributors and SIBA. Seasonal beers are also brewed.

Coopers WPA (OG 1036.5, ABV 3.5%) ◆
Golden-coloured, this well-balanced beer is light and refreshing, with hops, citrus fruit, apple/pear flavour and notable pale malt character. Bitter, dry finish.

Banker$ Draft (OG 1040, ABV 4%)
An amber ale, well-hopped with a pleasant malt flavour.

Brand Oak Bitter (BOB) (OG 1039, ABV 4%) ◆
Amber-coloured, this has a distinctive blend of hop, malt and apple/pear citrus fruits. The slightly sweet taste turns into a fine, dry bitterness, with a similar malty-lasting finish.

Cotswold Way (OG 1043, ABV 4.2%) ◆
Amber-coloured, it has a pleasant aroma of pale malt, hop and fruit. Good dry bitterness in the taste with some sweetness. Similar though less sweet in the finish, with good hop content.

Rite Flanker (OG 1043, ABV 4.3%)
Amber in colour with a big malt taste and fruit notes and a hoppy finish.

IKB (OG 1045, ABV 4.5%)
A ruby-red ale with a complex hop aroma and flavour derived from the use of three hop varieties. Flowery but well balanced.

Station Porter (OG 1062, ABV 6.1%) ◆
This is a rich, smooth, dark ruby-brown ale. Starts with roast malt; coffee, chocolate and dark fruit then develops a complex, spicy, bittersweet taste and a long roast finish.

Wild Walker

See Buxton

Willey (NEW)

Willey Brewing Co Ltd, Wood Farm, Coalpit Lane, Willey, Warwickshire, CV23 0SL
☎ (01788) 833908
✉ dh.willeybrewing@hotmail.com

Willey was established in 2009 after the Rugby Brewing Co went into administration. There are plans to contract brew for other breweries and to brew one-off specials for individual pubs.

Best Bitter (ABV 4.2%)

Pale Ale (ABV 4.5%)

Warmer (ABV 5%)

Williams SIBA

Williams Brothers Brewing Co/Heather Ale Ltd, New Alloa Brewery, Kelliebank, Alloa, FK10 1NT
☎ (01259) 725511 ✉ fraoch@heatherale.co.uk
🌐 heatherale.co.uk
Tours by arrangement

Bruce and Scott Williams started brewing Heather Ale in the West Highlands in 1993. A range of indigenous, historic ales were added over the following 10 years before the brothers invested in a 40-barrel brewery and bottling line in 2003. New beers are branded as 'Williams Bros' of which there are many hoppy and esoteric styles to choose from. Around 50 regular cask ale outlets are supplied. Seasonal beers: Ebulum (ABV 6.5%, winter), Alba (ABV 7.5%, winter).

Gold (OG 1040, ABV 3.9%)

Harvest Sun (OG 1038, ABV 3.9%)

Fraoch Heather Ale (OG 1041, ABV 4.1%) ◆
The unique taste of heather flowers is noticeable in this beer. A fine floral aroma and spicy taste give character to this drinkable speciality beer.

Black (OG 1039, ABV 4.2%)

Roisin-Tayberry (OG 1040, ABV 4.2%)

Good Times (OG 1040, ABV 4.3%)

Red (OG 1045, ABV 4.5%)

Joker IPA (OG 1047, ABV 5%)

Seven Giraffes (OG 1047, ABV 5.1%)

Midnight Sun (OG 1056, ABV 5.6%)

Willoughby

Willoughby Brewing Co, Brockhampton Brewery, Whitbourne, Worcestershire, WR6 5SH
☎ (01885) 482359 ☎ 07974 371294
✉ wbc@mccallum66.fsnet.co.uk

Willoughby began brewing in 2008 on a six-barrel plant on part of the National Trust estate at Brockhampton. Bottle-conditioned beers are available.

Peace Keeper (ABV 3.8%)

Trust Gold (ABV 3.8%)

Tried & Trusted (ABV 4.2%)

Willy's SIBA

Willy's Wine Bar Ltd, 17 High Cliff Road, Cleethorpes, Lincolnshire, DN35 8RQ
☎ (01472) 602145
Tours by arrangement

The brewery opened in 1989 to provide beer for its two pubs in Grimsby and Cleethorpes. It has a five-barrel plant with maximum capacity of 15 barrels a week. The brewery can be viewed at any time from pub or street.

Original Bitter (OG 1038, ABV 3.8%) ◆
A light brown 'sea air' beer with a fruity, tangy hop on the nose and taste, giving a strong bitterness tempered by the underlying malt.

Burcom Bitter (OG 1044, ABV 4.2%) ◆
Sometimes known as Mariner's Gold, although the beer is dark ruby in colour. It is a smooth and creamy brew with a sweet chocolate-bar maltiness, giving way to an increasingly bitter finish.

Last Resort (OG 1044, ABV 4.3%)

Weiss Buoy (OG 1045, ABV 4.5%)
A cloudy wheat beer.

Coxswains Special (OG 1050, ABV 4.9%)

Old Groyne (OG 1060, ABV 6.2%) ◆
An initial sweet banana fruitiness blends with malt to give a vanilla quality to the taste and slightly bitter aftertaste. A copper-coloured beer reminiscent of a Belgian ale.

Wincle

Wincle Beer Co Ltd, Heaton House, Rushton Spencer, Cheshire, SK11 0RD
☎ (01260) 226166 ✉ sales@winclebeer.co.uk
🌐 winclebeer.co.uk
Tours by arrangement

Wincle was set up by publicans Giles Meadows and Neil Murphy in an old milking parlour. Brewing began in 2008 on a five-barrel plant purchased from Saffron Brewery. 120 outlets are supplied direct within a 25-mile radius. Bottle-conditioned beers are available.

Wincle Waller (OG 1038, ABV 3.8%)

Sir Phillip (OG 1041, ABV 4.2%)

Wibbly Wallaby (OG 1043, ABV 4.4%)

Undertaker (OG 1044, ABV 4.5%)

Mr Mullin's IPA (OG 1047, ABV 4.8%)

Windlestone (NEW)

Windlestone Brewery, Unit 1, Oakmill, Ironmasters Way, Stillington, TS21 1FD
🌐 windlestonebrewery.co.uk

The four-barrel plant was originally used by the former Wear Valley Brewery, at the Grand Hotel in Bishop Auckland, but was sold in 2009 and relocated to Coundon when the Windlestone name was adopted. It was sold to new owners in 2010 and relocated again to Stillington.

Eden Ale (ABV 4%)

Rushyford Red (ABV 4.2%)

Blackie Boy Stout (ABV 4.5%)

Windsor Castle

See Sadler's

Windsor & Eton (NEW)

Windsor & Eton Brewery, Duke Street, Windsor, Berkshire, SL4 1SE
☎ (01753) 854075 ✉ will.calvert@webrew.co.uk
🌐 webrew.co.uk

Windsor & Eton Brewery was established in 2010 bringing brewing back to Windsor 79 years after the closure of Burge's Brewery.

Guardsman (OG 1041, ABV 4.2%)

Winster Valley (NEW)

Winster Valley Brewery, Brown Horse Inn, Winster, Cumbria, LA23 3NR
☎ (01539) 443443
✉ steve@thebrownhorseinn.co.uk
🌐 thebrownhorseinn.co.uk
Tours by arrangement

Winster Valley was established in 2009 using a 2.5-barrel plant at the Brown Horse Inn in Winster. Six outlets are supplied direct. Both beers are also available bottle conditioned.

THE BREWERIES

Best Bitter (OG 1036, ABV 3.7%)

Old School (OG 1037, ABV 3.9%)

Winter's SIBA

Winter's Brewery, 8 Keelan Close, Norwich, NR6 6QZ
☎ (01603) 787820

⊗ David Winter, who had previous award-winning success as brewer for both Woodforde's and Chalk Hill breweries, decided to set up on his own in 2001. He purchased the brewing plant from the now defunct Scott's Brewery in Lowestoft. The local free trade is supplied.

Mild (OG 1036.5, ABV 3.6%) ◆
Classic dark mild, red-brown with a nutty roast character. A good balance of malt caramel and roast abetted by both sweetness and a light, hoppy bitterness. Lingering finish develops a plummy feel.

Bitter (OG 1039.5, ABV 3.8%) ◆
A well-balanced amber bitter. Hops and malt are balanced by a crisp citrus fruitiness. A pleasant hoppy nose with a hint of grapefruit. Long, sustained, dry, grapefruit finish.

Golden (ABV 4.1%) ◆
Just a hint of hops in the aroma. The initial taste combines a dry bitterness with a fruity apple buttress. The finish slowly subsides into a long, dry bitterness.

Revenge (OG 1047, ABV 4.7%) ◆
Blackcurrant notes give depth to the inherent maltiness of this pale brown beer. A bittersweet background becomes more pronounced as the fruitiness gently wanes.

Storm Force (OG 1053, ABV 5.3%) ◆
A well-defined, sweetish brew. Hops and vine fruit give depth to the malty backbone of this pale brown strong beer. All flavours hold up well as the finish develops a warming softness.

Wirksworth

Wirksworth Brewery, 25 St John Street, Wirksworth, Derbyshire, DE4 4DR
☎ (01629) 824011
✉ wirksworthbrewery@hotmail.co.uk
🌐 wirksworthbrewery.co.uk

◎ Jeff Green started brewing in 2007 with a 2.5-barrel plant in a converted stone workshop. Wirksworth supplies Derbyshire pubs with four core beers and supplements these with at least one seasonal offering. Every September there is a brew house open weekend giving visitors the opportunity to gain an insight into the brewing process and taste the real ales.

Cruckbeam (OG 1040, ABV 3.9%)

Sunbeam (OG 1040, ABV 4%)

First Brew (OG 1042, ABV 4.2%)

T'owd Man (OG 1050, ABV 4.9%)

Wissey Valley

Wissey Valley Brewery, 1 High Street, Downham Market, Norfolk, PE38 9DA
☎ (01366) 386658
✉ thehopandhog@btconnect.com
🌐 norfolkfoodanddrink.co.uk
Shop Wed-Sun 9am-5pm
Tours by arrangement

⊗ After several moves since starting up in 2002 (as Captain Grumpy's), the brewery is now located at the rear of the local produce store, team room and restaurant, the Hop & Hog.

Captain Grumpy's Best Bitter (OG 1039, ABV 3.9%)

Khaki Sargeant Strong Stout (OG 1059, ABV 6%)

Wizard SIBA

Wizard Ales, Unit 4, Lundy View, Mullacott Cross Industrial Estate, Ilfracombe, Devon, EX34 8PY
☎ (01271) 865350 ✉ mike@wizardales.co.uk
🌐 wizardales.co.uk
Tours by arrangement

⊗ Brewing started in 2003 on a 1.25-barrel plant, since upgraded to five barrels. The brewery moved from Warwickshire to Devon in 2007. Around 20 local outlets are supplied. Seasonal beer: Bah Humbug (ABV 5.8%, Xmas). Bottle-conditioned beers are also available.

Apprentice (OG 1038, ABV 3.6%)

Lundy Gold (OG 1042, ABV 4.1%)

Old Combe (OG 1043, ABV 4.2%)

Druid's Fluid (OG 1048, ABV 5%)

Wold Top SIBA

Wold Top Brewery, Hunmanby Grange, Wold Newton, Driffield, East Yorkshire, YO25 3HS
☎ (01723) 892222
✉ enquiries@woldtopbrewery.co.uk
🌐 woldtopbrewery.co.uk

◎ Wold Top commenced brewing in 2003 and is an integral part of Hunmanby Grange, a family farm. It uses home and Wold-grown malting barley and chalk-filtered water from the farm's borehole. The brewery installed a bottling line in 2008 and contract bottles for other breweries. Over 600 outlets are supplied. Seasonal beers: see website.

Bitter (OG 1037, ABV 3.7%)
A crisp, clean, aromatic session bitter. Full-flavoured with a long, hoppy finish.

Falling Stone Bitter (OG 1041, ABV 4.2%)
A full-bodied, smooth best bitter. Named after the first recorded UK meteorite, which fell in Wold Newton.

Mars Magic (OG 1044, ABV 4.6%)
An aromatic premium ale with a red glow and smooth, malty flavour.

Wold Gold (OG 1046, ABV 4.8%)
A light-coloured summer beer with a soft, fruity flavour with a hint of spice.

Wolf

WBC (Norfolk) Ltd t/a The Wolf Brewery, Rookery Farm, Silver Street, Besthorpe, Attleborough, Norfolk, NR17 2LD
☎ (01953) 457775 ✉ info@wolfbrewery.com
🌐 wolfbrewery.com
Shop Mon-Fri 9am-5pm (all year); Sat 10am-3pm (Dec only)
Tours by arrangement

⊗ The brewery was founded iin 1996 on a 20-barrel plant, which was upgraded to a 24-barrel one in 2006. Over 200 outlets are supplied. Seasonal beers: see website.

Golden Jackal (OG 1039, ABV 3.7%)
A hoppy, citrus nose carries through to the initial taste. The citrus notes remain right to the end as the initial hoppiness is replaced by a dry bitterness.

Wolf In Sheep's Clothing (OG 1039, ABV 3.7%)
A malty aroma with fruity undertones introduce this reddish-hued mild. Malt, with a bitter background that remains throughout, is the dominant flavour of this clean-tasting beer.

Coyote Bitter (OG 1044, ABV 4.3%)
A well-balanced golden brew with a hop and citrus aroma. The dominant hoppy bitterness is countered by a malty, slightly sweet backdrop. Complex flavours continue to mix as the dry, bitter ending slowly fades.

Straw Dog (ABV 4.5%)
A delicately flavoured brew with a fruity nuance. An aroma reminiscent of redcurrants gives way to a low key marmalade and hop beginning. A stronger finish with increasing bitterness.

Granny Wouldn't Like It (OG 1049, ABV 4.8%)
Red-brown with a pronounced malty bouquet. Bitterness increases throughout but is softened by a smoky malt background. Some roast notes and a gentle, fruity sweetness add depth.

Wolverhampton & Dudley

See Marston's in the New Nationals section

Wood SIBA

Wood Brewery Ltd, Wistanstow, Craven Arms, Shropshire, SY7 8DG
☎ (01588) 672523 ✉ mail@woodbrewery.co.uk
🌐 woodbrewery.co.uk
Tours by arrangement

The brewery opened in 1980 in buildings next to the Plough Inn, still the brewery's only tied house. Steady growth over the years included the acquisition of the Sam Powell Brewery and its beers in 1991. Around 200 outlets are supplied. Seasonal beers: see website. A monthly beer is also brewed.

Quaff (ABV 3.7%)
A pale and refreshing light bitter with a clean, hoppy finish.

Craven Ale (ABV 3.8%)
An attractively coloured beer with a pleasant hop aroma and a refreshing taste.

Parish Bitter (OG 1040, ABV 4%)
A blend of malt and hops with a bitter aftertaste. Pale brown in colour.

Shropshire Lass (OG 1041, ABV 4.1%)
A golden ale with zesty bitterness.

Special Bitter (OG 1042, ABV 4.2%)
A tawny brown bitter with malt, hops and some fruitiness.

Pot O' Gold (OG 1044, ABV 4.4%)

Shropshire Lad (OG 1045, ABV 4.5%)
A strong, well-rounded bitter, drawing flavour from a fine blend of selected English malted barley and Fuggles and Golding hops.

Old Sam (OG 1047, ABV 4.6%)
A dark copper ale with a ripe, rounded flavour and hop bitterness.

Wonderful (OG 1048, ABV 4.8%)
A mid-brown, fruity beer, with a roast and malt taste.

Tom Wood

See Highwood

Wooden Hand

Wooden Hand Brewery, Unit 3, Grampound Road Industrial Estate, Grampound Road, Truro, Cornwall, TR2 4TB
☎ (01726) 884596 ✉ chris@woodenhand.co.uk
🌐 woodenhand.co.uk

⊗ Wooden Hand was founded in 2004. The brewery is named after the Black Hand of John Carew of Penwarne, in the parish of Mevagissey – Carew lost his hand in fighting at the siege of Ostend in the reign of Elizabeth I. The brewery supplies around 50 outlets with a high percentage being sold further afield via wholesalers. A bottling line was installed in 2005, which also bottles for other breweries.

Pirates Gold (OG 1040.6, ABV 4%)
A slightly tart pale session bitter with hop aroma, light fruit yet malty underlying flavour and tangy fruit finish.

Cornish Buccaneer (OG 1043.6, ABV 4.3%)
A golden beer with full flavour hop character, good fruit and hop balance and a long, dry finish.

Black Pearl (OG 1050.6, ABV 4.5%)
A rich, nutty stout with good hop balance and dry chocolate finish.

Cornish Mutiny (OG 1048.6, ABV 4.8%)
Rich, full-bodied strong ale with distinctive full hop character. Slightly biscuity and complex flavour with full mouth finish.

Woodforde's SIBA

Woodforde's Norfolk Ales, Broadland Brewery, Woodbastwick, Norwich, NR13 6SW
☎ (01603) 720353 ✉ info@woodfordes.co.uk
🌐 woodfordes.co.uk
Shop Mon-Fri 10.30am-4.30pm; Sat & Sun 11.30am-4.30pm (01603 722218)
Tours by arrangement (Tue & Thu evenings)

Founded in 1981 in Drayton, Woodforde's moved to Erpingham in 1982, and then moved again to a converted farm complex in Woodbastwick, with greatly increased production capacity, in 1989. Major expansion took place in 2001 and 2008 to more than double production and included a new brewery shop and visitor centre. Woodforde's runs two tied houses with around 600 outlets supplied on a regular basis. Bottle-conditioned beers are available. The Woodforde's Club now has over 15,000 members and is free to join: see website for details. Occasional beer: Norfolk Nip (ABV 8.5%).

Mardler's (OG 1035, ABV 3.5%)
Chocolate and roast aromas introduce this well-balanced dark mild. Swathes of vanilla, caramel and malt boost the dominant roast and chocolate flavours. A fine, flavoursome finish.

Wherry (OG 1037.5, ABV 3.8%) 🍴 ◆
Amber-coloured with an orange citrus nose.
Complex, well-balanced but easy-drinking, the
swirling mix of malt, hops, citrus and bitterness
combine into a tangy marmalade dryness.

Sundew (OG 1039, ABV 4.1%) ◆
Hops emerge from a competing fusion of malt, fruit
and bitterness to provide a cutting edge to both
taste and aroma. Smooth-drinking with a long
ending.

Nelson's Revenge (OG 1045, ABV 4.5%) ◆
An infusion of vine fruit, malt and hops provide a
rich, rewarding experience. The aromas and
flavours bounce merrily along to a sweet, Madeira-
like finale.

Norfolk Nog (OG 1047, ABV 4.6%) ◆
Echoes of Pontefract cake in all aspects of this red-
hued, roast-dominated brew. A plummy sweetness
aided by a dry bitterness and a hint of caramel all
provide rallying points to counter the main roast
character.

Admiral's Reserve (OG 1049, ABV 5%) 🍴 ◆
Tawny-coloured strong ale with a gentle malty
aroma. A smooth sultana and malt introduction
with more than a hint of hop-induced bitterness.
Balanced finish with fruit making a noticeably quick
retreat.

Headcracker (OG 1069, ABV 7%) ◆
Malty, sweet-tasting tawny ale with a satisfyingly
sticky mouthfeel. Initially the malt matches the
heavy fruity aura. Initial traces of hop and caramel
soon disappear as the malty influence recedes.

Woodlands SIBA

Woodlands Brewing Co Ltd, Unit 3, Meadow Lane
Farm, London Road, Stapeley, Cheshire, CW5 7JU
☎ (01270) 841511

Office: Wayside, Dairy Lane, Nantwich, Cheshire,
CW5 6DS ☎ (01270) 620101
✉ woodlandsbrewery@btconnect.com
⊕ woodlandsbrewery.co.uk
Shop Mon-Fri 9am-4.30pm
Tours by arrangement

⊛The brewery opened in 2004 with a five-barrel
plant from the former Khean Brewery and moved
to larger premises in 2008. An extension in 2010
allows for increased production. The beers are
brewed using water from a spring that surfaces on
a nearby peat field at Woodlands Farm. More than
100 outlets are supplied including the brewery's
first tied house, the Globe in Nantwich. Bottle-
conditioned beers are available.

Mild (OG 1035, ABV 3.5%)
A dark mild ale.

Old Faithful (OG 1036, ABV 3.6%)
A pale session bitter.

Drummer (OG 1039, ABV 3.9%) ◆
Clean, malty session bitter with lasting dry finish
and increasing bitterness in the aftertaste.

Light Oak (OG 1040, ABV 4%)
A malty pale ale with a crisp, dry aftertaste.

Oak Beauty (OG 1042, ABV 4.2%) ◆
Malty, sweetish copper-coloured bitter with toffee
and caramel flavours. Long-lasting and satisfying
bitter finish.

Bitter (OG 1044, ABV 4.4%)

Midnight Stout (OG 1044, ABV 4.4%) ◆
Classic creamy dry stout with roast flavours to the
fore. Well-balanced with bitterness and good hops
on the taste and a good dry, roasty aftertaste.
Some sweetness.

Bees Knees (OG 1045, ABV 4.5%)
Tan-coloured bitter brewed with Acacia honey.

Redwood (OG 1049, ABV 4.9%)
A dark bitter with a sharp aftertaste.

Generals Tipple (OG 1055, ABV 5.5%)
A refreshing, medium-hopped IPA.

Super IPA (OG 1064, ABV 6.4%)

Worfield

See Shires

World's End (NEW)

🍺 World's End Ales, Crown Inn, 60 Wilcot Road,
Pewsey, Wiltshire, SN9 5EL
☎ (01672) 562653 ✉ vauni57@hotmail.com
⊕ thecrownatpewsey.com
Tours by arrangement

⊠ World's End Ales was established in 2009 on a
one-barrel plant at the rear of the Crown Inn in
Pewsey. 'World's End' is the 18th-century name for
the area in which the brewery is located.

Bitter End (ABV 4.2%)

Dark World (ABV 4.2%)

Gold Ale (ABV 4.4%)

George Wright

George Wright Brewing Co, Unit 11, Diamond
Business Park, Sandwash Close, Rainford, Merseyside,
WA11 8LY
☎ (01744) 886686
✉ sales@georgewrightbrewing.co.uk
⊕ georgewrightbrewing.co.uk
Shop Tue-Fri 10am-4pm
Tours by arrangement

George Wright started production in 2003. The
original 2.5-barrel plant was replaced by a five-
barrel one, which has since been upgraded again
to 25 barrels with production of 200 casks a week.

Black Swan (ABV 3.8%)
A dark, distinctive beer. Very creamy and full of
malty flavour.

Drunken Duck (ABV 3.9%) ◆
Fruity gold-coloured bitter beer with good hop and
a dry aftertaste. Some acidity.

Longboat (ABV 3.9%) ◆
Good hoppy bitter with grapefruit and an almost
tart bitterness throughout. Some astringency in the
aftertaste. Well-balanced, light and refreshing with
a good mouthfeel and long, dry finish.

Pipe Dream (ABV 4.3%) 🍴 ◆
Refreshing hoppy best bitter with a fruity nose and
grapefruit to the fore in the taste. Lasting dry, bitter
finish.

Pure Blonde (ABV 4.6%)
A premium blonde beer, very light in colour with a
herbal nose, floral taste and sweet finish.

Cheeky Pheasant (ABV 4.7%)

Strong, malty bitter. Highly hopped to give a distinctive dry aftertaste.

Roman Black (ABV 4.8%)
A black bitter. Strong, smooth and creamy.

Blue Moon (ABV 5%) ◆
Easy-drinking strong, gold-coloured beer. Good malt/bitter balance and well hopped.

Wychwood

See Marston's in New Nationals section

Wye Valley SIBA

Wye Valley Brewery, Stoke Lacy, Herefordshire, HR7 4HG
☎ **(01885) 490505**
✉ **sales@wyevalleybrewery.co.uk**
wyevalleybrewery.co.uk
Shop Mon-Fri 10am-4pm
Tours by arrangement

Founded in 1985 in Canon Pyon in Herefordshire, the brewery now occupies the historic Symonds Cider site at Stoke Lacy. Growth and investment continue and Wye Valley is now a successful regional brewery. Bottle-conditioned beers are available and are bottled on site.

Bitter (OG 1037, ABV 3.7%) ◆
A beer whose aroma gives little hint of the bitter hoppiness that follows right through to the aftertaste.

HPA (OG 1040, ABV 4%) ◆
A pale, hoppy, malty brew with a hint of sweetness before a dry finish.

Dorothy Goodbody's Golden Ale (OG 1042, ABV 4.2%)
A light, gold-coloured ale with a good hop character throughout.

Butty Bach (OG 1046, ABV 4.5%)
A burnished gold, full-bodied premium ale.

Dorothy Goodbody's Wholesome Stout (OG 1046, ABV 4.6%) ◆
A smooth and satisfying stout with a bitter edge to its roast flavours. The finish combines roast grain and malt.

Wylam SIBA

Wylam Brewery Ltd, South Houghton Farm, Heddon on the Wall, Northumberland, NE15 0EZ
☎ **(01661) 853377** ✉ **admin@wylambrewery.co.uk**
wylambrewery.co.uk
Tours by arrangement

Wylam started in 2000 on a 4.5-barrel plant, which increased to nine barrels in 2002. New premises and brew plant (20 barrel) were installed on the same site in 2006. The brewery delivers to more than 200 local outlets and beers are available through wholesalers around the country. Seasonal beers: see website.

Bitter (OG 1039, ABV 3.8%) ◆
A refreshing, copper-coloured, hoppy bitter with a clean, bitter finish.

Gold Tankard (OG 1040, ABV 4%) ◆
Fresh clean flavour, full of hops. This golden ale has a hint of citrus in the finish.

Magic (OG 1042, ABV 4.2%) ◆
Light, crisp and refreshing. Floral and spicy with a good bitter finish.

Angel (OG 1044, ABV 4.3%)

Northern Kite (OG 1046.5, ABV 4.5%)

Bohemia (OG 1046, ABV 4.6%) ◆
Czech-style Pilsner. Deep gold in colour with rich hop character.

Haugh (OG 1046, ABV 4.6%) ◆
A dark, satisfying porter, smooth, full of character and complex flavours —hints of chocolate, liquorice and malt.

Locomotion No. 1 (OG 1050, ABV 5%)

Rocket (OG 1048, ABV 5%) ◆
A pale, copper-coloured best bitter with a clean, bitter finish.

Wyre Piddle

Wyre Piddle Brewery Ltd, Highgrove Farm, Peopleton, nr Pershore, Worcestershire, WR10 2LF
☎ **(01905) 841853**
✉ **strongbow1@btopenworld.com**

Wyre Piddle was established in 1992. The brewery relocated and upgraded its equipment in 1997 and moved to its current location in 2002, where it has continued to expand. The beers can be found in pubs throughout the UK and around 100 pubs are supplied directly in the Midlands. It also brews for Green Dragon, Malvern: Dragon's Downfall (ABV 3.9%) and for Severn Valley Railway: Royal Piddle (ABV 4.2%). Seasonal beer: Yule Piddle (ABV 4.5%, Xmas).

Piddle in the Hole (OG 1039, ABV 3.9%) ◆
Copper-coloured and quite dry, with lots of hops and fruitiness throughout.

Piddle in the Dark (ABV 4.5%)
A rich ruby-red bitter with a smooth flavour.

Piddle in the Wind (ABV 4.5%) ◆
This drink has a superb mix of flavours. A hoppy nose continues through to a lasting aftertaste, making it a good, all-round beer.

Piddle in the Sun/Snow (ABV 5.2%) ◆
A dry, strong taste all the way through draws your attention to the balance between malt and hops in the brew. A glorious way to end an evening's drinking.

Yard of Ale SIBA

Yard of Ale Brewing Co Ltd, Surtees Arms, Chilton Lane, Ferryhill, County Durham, DL17 0DH
☎ **(01740) 655724** ✉ **surteesarms@btconnect.com**
thesurteesarms.co.uk
Tours by arrangement

Established in 2008, the 2.5-barrel micro supplies ales to its brewery tap, the Surtees Arms, beer festivals and to a growing number of pubs from North Tyne to South Tees. Seasonal specials are available as are bottle-conditioned beers.

First Yard (OG 1040, ABV 3.8%)
A copper-coloured session bitter with malty flavours and a mild roasted finish.

Yard Hopper (OG 1041, ABV 4%)
A pale ale, uniquely brewed using locally-grown hops resulting in delicate hop aromas and a bitter, zesty finish.

Black As Owt Stout (OG 1043, ABV 4.2%)
A traditional, bitter dark stout with distinctive roast coffee nose and smooth chocolate and coffee flavours.

Yard's Ahead IPA (OG 1045, ABV 4.2%)

One Foot In The Yard (OG 1044, ABV 4.5%)
Premium golden ale. Fruity on the nose and palate with a sweet finish.

Yates SIBA

Yates (Westnewton) Brewery Ltd, Ghyll Farm, Westnewton, Wigton, Cumbria, CA7 3NX
☎ (01697) 321081 ✉ enquiry@yatesbrewery.co.uk
yatesbrewery.co.uk
Tours by arrangement

Cumbria's oldest micro-brewery, established in 1986. The brewery was bought in 1998 by Graeme and Caroline Baxter, who had previously owned High Force Brewery in Teesdale. Deliveries are mainly to its Cumbrian stronghold and the A69 corridor as far as Hexham. A brewhouse and reed bed effluent system have been added on the same site. Around 40 outlets are supplied. Seasonal beers: see website.

Bitter (OG 1036, ABV 3.7%)
A well-balanced, full-bodied bitter, golden in colour with complex hop bitterness. Good aroma and distinctive flavour.

Golden Ale (OG 1038, ABV 3.9%)
Skilful use of lager malt and hops results in a pale beer with a light bitterness; melon fruit and a clean, refreshing finish.

Cumbrian Ale (OG 1041, ABV 4.2%)

Sun Goddess (OG 1041, ABV 4.2%)
A complex honeyed beer, packed with tropical fruit.

IPA (OG 1047, ABV 4.9%)

Yates' SIBA

Yates' Brewery, Unit 4C, Langbridge Business Centre, Newchurch, Isle of Wight, PO36 0NP
☎ (01983) 867878 ✉ info@yates-brewery.co.uk
yates-brewery.co.uk
Tours by arrangement

Brewing started in 2000 on a five-barrel plant at the Inn at St Lawrence. In 2009 the brewery moved to Newchurch and upgraded to a 10-barrel plant. Stumpy's Brewery was bought out by Yates' in 2009 and all beers are now produced by Yates'. Seasonal beers: Yule Be Sorry (ABV 7.6%, Xmas), Wight Winter (ABV 5%), St Lawrence Ale (ABV 5%, summer). Bottle-conditioned beers are also available.

Best Bitter (ABV 3.8%)
Initial sweetness is quickly balanced by subtle fruitiness and moderate hop bitterness. A full-flavoured beer with a bittersweet aftertaste.

Undercliff Experience (OG 1040, ABV 4.1%)
An amber ale with a bittersweet malt and hop taste with a dry, lemon edge that dominates the bitter finish.

Blonde Ale (OG 1045, ABV 4.5%)
A golden beer with a malty aroma, laced with floral, citrus hops. The taste is hoppy and bitter to start, with smooth malt support and light lemon notes. Dry, hoppy aftertaste.

Holy Joe (OG 1050, ABV 4.9%)
Strongly bittered golden ale with pronounced spice and citrus character, and underlying light hint of malt.

Special Draught (OG 1056, ABV 5.5%)
Easy-drinking strong, amber ale with pronounced tart bitterness and a refreshing bite in the aftertaste.

Wight Old Ale (ABV 6%)
A deep ruby ale with a smooth taste.

For Stumpy's Brewery:

Dog Daze (OG 1040, ABV 3.8%)
A light, golden summer beer with a strong, malty aroma. Tastes rather thin and sweet and lacking in bitterness. A sweet, malty finish.

Hop a Doodle Doo (OG 1040, ABV 4%)

Hot Dog (OG 1045, ABV 4.5%)

Old Ginger (OG 1045, ABV 4.5%)

Old Stumpy (OG 1045, ABV 4.5%)
Grassy best bitter with a strong hoppy and fruity aroma. Some malt and bitterness in the flavour lead to a harsh finish.

Bo'sun's Call (OG 1050, ABV 5%)

Haven (OG 1050, ABV 5%)

Tumbledown (OG 1050, ABV 5%)

Yeovil

Yeovil Ales Ltd, Unit 5, Bofors Park, Artillery Road, Lufton Trading Estate, Yeovil, Somerset, BA22 8YH
☎ (01935) 414888 ✉ rob@yeovilales.com
yeovilales.com
Sales counter Fri pm only until 5.30pm
Tours by arrangement

Yeovil Ales was established in 2006 using an 18-barrel plant. Production has steadily increased and up to 350 outlets are supplied across six counties in the south west. Seasonal beers: see website.

Glory (OG 1039, ABV 3.8%)
A well-balanced bitter with citrus hop notes.

Star Gazer (OG 1042, ABV 4%)
Dark copper bitter with late-hopped floral bouquet.

Summerset (OG 1043, ABV 4.1%)
Blonde ale with fruity hop finish.

Ruby (OG 1047, ABV 4.5%)
Red bitter with rich malt depth.

P.O.S.H. (OG 1054, ABV 5.4%)
A strong IPA with a fruity body and hoppy finish.

Yetman's

Yetman's Brewery, Bayfield Farm Barns, Bayfield Brecks Farm, Bayfield, Norfolk, BR25 7DZ
☎ 07774 809016 ✉ peter@yetmans.net
yetmans.net

A 2.5-barrel plant built by Moss Brew was installed in restored medieval barns in 2005. The brewery supplies local free trade outlets. Bottle-conditioned beers are available.

Red (OG 1036, ABV 3.8%)

Orange (OG 1040, ABV 4.2%)
Well-balanced and smooth-drinking. A light fruity aroma leads into a stirring mix of malt and hops

supported by a bittersweet background. A big finish combines malt and a vinous fruitiness.

Green (OG 1044, ABV 4.8%)

York SIBA

York Brewery Ltd, 12 Toft Green, York, North Yorkshire, YO1 6JT
☎ (01904) 621162 ✉ info@york-brewery.co.uk
⊕ york-brewery.co.uk
Shop Mon-Sat 12-6pm
Tours by arrangement (ring for daily tour times)

York started production in 1996, the first brewery in the city for 40 years. It has a visitor centre with bar and gift shop, and was designed as a show brewery, with a gallery above the 20-barrel plant and viewing panels to fermentation and conditioning rooms. The brewery owns several pubs and in 2006 additional space was acquired to increase production capacity. More than 400 outlets are supplied. Seasonal beers: see website. The brewery was bought by Mitchell's Hotels & Inns in 2008.

Guzzler (OG 1036, ABV 3.6%) 🍺 ◆
Refreshing golden ale with dominant hop and fruit flavours developing throughout.

Constantine (ABV 3.9%)

Yorkshire Terrier (OG 1041, ABV 4.2%) ◆
Refreshing and distinctive amber/gold brew where fruit and hops dominate the aroma and taste. Hoppy bitterness remains assertive in the aftertaste.

Centurion's Ghost Ale (OG 1051, ABV 5.4%) 🍺 ◆
Dark ruby in colour, full-tasting with mellow roast malt character balanced by light bitterness and autumn fruit flavours that linger into the aftertaste.

Yorkshire Dales

Yorkshire Dales Brewing Co Ltd, Seata Barn, Elm Hill, Askrigg, North Yorkshire, DL8 3HG
☎ (01969) 622027 ☎ 07818 035592
✉ rob@yorkshiredalesbrewery.com
⊕ yorkshiredalesbrewery.com

⊚Situated in the heart of the Yorkshire Dales, brewing started in 2005. Installation of a five-barrel plant and additional fermenters at the converted milking parlour increased capacity to 20 barrels a week. Over 150 pubs are supplied throughout the North of England. Four monthly special are always available, including a dark mild. Bottle-conditioned beers are also available.

Butter Tubs (OG 1037, ABV 3.7%)
A pale golden beer with a dry bitterness complemented by strong citrus flavours and aroma.

Leyburn Shawl (OG 1038, ABV 3.8%)
A crisp, dry, pale ale with an underlying sharpness.

Buckden Pike (OG 1040, ABV 3.9%)
A refreshing blonde beer with a crisp, fruity finish.

Kings' Arms Ale (OG 1041, ABV 4%)
A golden ale brewed with a trio of American hops for citrus and peach flavours throughout.

Muker Silver (OG 1041, ABV 4.1%)
A blonde lager-style ale, very crisp with a sharp, hoppy finish.

Askrigg Ale (OG 1043, ABV 4.3%)

A pale golden ale with intense aroma that generates a crisp, dry flavour with a long, bitter finish.

Yorkshire Penny (OG 1046, ABV 4.5%)
Classic dry stout with rich liquorice and chocolate malt flavours.

Garsdale Smokebox (OG 1057, ABV 5.6%)
A complex ale created by smoked and dark malts. Deep, rich chocolate and coffee flavours are complimented by the smokiness.

Young's

See Wells & Young's in New Nationals section

Zerodegrees SIBA

Blackheath: Zerodegrees Microbrewery, 29-31 Montpelier Vale, Blackheath, London, SE3 0TJ
☎ (020) 8852 5619

Bristol: Zerodegrees Microbrewery, 53 Colston Street, Bristol, BS1 5BA ☎ **(0117) 925 2706**

Cardiff: 27 Westgate Street, Cardiff, Berkshire, CF10 1DD ☎ **(029) 2022 9494**

Reading: 9 Bridge Street, Reading, RG1 2LR ☎ **(0118) 959 7959** ✉ **info@zerodegrees.co.uk**
⊕ zerodegrees.co.uk
Tours by arrangement

Brewing started in 2000 in London and incorporates a state-of-the-art, computer-controlled German plant, producing unfiltered and unfined ales and lagers, served from tanks using air pressure (not CO2). Four pubs are owned. All beers are suitable for vegetarians and vegans. All branches of Zerodegrees follow the same concept of beers with natural ingredients. There are regular seasonal specials including fruit beers.

Fruit Beer (OG 1040, ABV 4%)
The type of fruit used varies during the year.

Wheat Ale (OG 1045, ABV 4.2%) ◆
Refreshing wheat ale with spicy aroma; banana, vanilla and sweet flavours; dry, lasting finish.

Pale Ale (OG 1046, ABV 4.6%) ◆
American-style IPA with complex fruit aroma and peach flavours. Clean bitter finish with long aftertaste.

Black Lager (OG 1048, ABV 4.8%) ◆
Light, Eastern European-style black lager brewed with roasted malt. Refreshing coffee finish.

Pilsner (OG 1048, ABV 4.8%) ◆
Clean-tasting refreshing Pilsner with a malty aroma and taste, accompanied by delicate bitterness and citrus fruits.

REPUBLIC OF IRELAND BREWERIES
Arainn Mhor

Arainn Mhor Brewing Co, Airainn Mhor Island, Burtonport, Co Donegal 00353 87 630 6856
⊕ ambrewco.com

No cask beer but two bottle-conditioned ales, Ban and Rhua, plus keg lager and stout, all contract-brewed by Messrs Maguire in Dublin (qv).

THE BREWERIES

Beoir Chorca Dhuibhne/Dark Corner Beer

Beoir Chorca Dhuibhne/Dark Corner Beer, c/o Tig Bhric, nr Ballyferriter, Co Kerry 00353 66 915 6325 ✉ info@tigbhric.com 🌐 tigbhric.com

Beer is brewed on a 400-litre plant in a remote area where Erse/Gaelic is the main language.

Cul Dhorca (ABV 4.1%)

Carlow

Carlow Brewing Co, Muine Bhaeg Business Park, Royal Oak Road, Carlow, Co Carlow 00353 599 720509 ✉ info@carlowbrewing.com 🌐 carlowbrewing.com

One of the bigger Irish independents with a good range of cask beers.

O'Hara's Irish Stout (ABV 4.3%)

O'Hara's Red Ale (ABV 4.3%)

Druid's Brew Stout (ABV 4.7%)

Wheat Beer (ABV 4.7%)

Lann Follain Stout (ABV 6%)

Dungarvan

Dungarvan Brewing Co, Westgate Business Park, Dungarvan, Co Waterford 00353 58 24000 ✉ info@dungarvanbrewingcompany.com 🌐 dungarvanbrewingcompany.com

New brewery that produces three beers in bottle-conditioned format, occasionally available cask-conditioned.

Black Rock (ABV 4.3%)

Copper Coast (ABV 4.3%)

Helvick Gold (ABV 4.9%)

Franciscan Well

Franciscan Well Brewery, 14 North Mall, Cork City, Co Cork 00353 59 913 4356 ✉ info@franciscanwellbrewery.com 🌐 franciscanwellbrewery.com

Small brewery that brings choice to a city dominated by Beamish and Murphy, both owned by Heineken, which has closed Beamish. Franciscan Well brews Blarney Blond, Rebel Red, Shandon Stout and Friar Weisse, all keg beers that are occasionally produced in cask form for special events. The brewery hosts beer festivals that feature beers from other Irish cask brewers.

Galway Hooker

Galway Hooker Brewery, Roscommon Business Park, Racecourse Road, Roscommon, Co Galway 00353 87 77 62823 ✉ aidan@galwayhooker.ie 🌐 galwayhooker.ie

Galway Hooker produces filtered keg beer for the Irish market but provides it in cask form for beer festivals in Britain. It was available at the Great British Beer Festival in 2008 and 2009.

Irish Pale Ale (ABV 4.4%)

Messrs Maguire

Messrs Maguire Brewing Co, 1-2 Burgh Quay, Dublin 2 00353 16 705 7777 ✉ hickeygroupinfo@gmail.com 🌐 messrsmaguire.ie

Pub, brewery and restaurant in the historic O'Connell Bridge area of the city. It brews a range of keg beers, including stout, plain (porter) and wheat beer.

Best (ABV 4.3%)
Cask-conditioned best bitter.

Porterhouse

Porterhouse Brewing Co, Unit 6D, Rosemount, Park Road, Ballycoolin, Blanchardstown, Dublin 15 00353 18 227 417

The oldest surviving craft brewery in Ireland. It has three pubs in Dublin: 16-18 Parliament Street, Temple Bar, Dublin 2; Porterhouse North, Cross Guns Bridge, Glasnevin, Dublin 9; Porterhouse Central, 45-47 Nassau Street, City Centre South, Dublin 2; plus Porterhouse Bray, Strand Road, Co Wicklow. There's also a branch in Covent Garden, London. A range of keg stouts, porters and red ale is produced.

TSB (ABV 3.7%)
Cask-conditioned bitter.

Trouble

Trouble Brewing, Allenwood, Co Kildare 00353 87 908 6658 ✉ info@troublebrewing.ie 🌐 troublebrewing.ie

New small craft brewery producing one cask ale.

Or (ABV 4.3%)
A golden ale.

White Gypsy

White Gypsy, Shelta Beer Ltd, 14 Priory Place, Templemore, Co Tipperary 00353 86 17 24520 ✉ info@whitegypsy.ie 🌐 whitegypsy.ie

White Gypsy switched all production in 2010 to bottle-conditioned beer. The brewery is also experimenting with a vintage stout, Raven, that's matured for 10 month in oak casks.

Bock (ABV 7%)

Scottish Ale (ABV 7%)

Imperial Porter (ABV 7.5%)

India Pale Ale (ABV 7.5%)

> Where an entry states that some beers in a pub are served with the aid of cask breathers, this means that demand valves are connected to both casks and cylinders of gas; as beer is drawn off, it is replaced by applied gas (either carbon dioxide, nitrogen or both) to prevent oxidation. The method is not acceptable to CAMRA as it does not allow beer to condition and mature naturally. The Campaign believes brewers and publicans should use the size of casks best suited to the turnover of beer in order to avoid oxidation. If a pub in the Good Beer Guide uses cask breathers, we list only those beers that are free of the device.

R.I.P.

The following breweries have closed, gone out of business or suspended operations since the 2010 Guide was published:

3 Rivers, Reddish, Cheshire

Atlas (Sinclair Breweries Ltd), Kinlochleven, Highlands & Western Isles

Blue Bear, Kempsey, Worcestershire

Blue Moon, Barford, Norfolk

Bridge of Allan, Bridge of Allan, Loch Lomond, Stirling & The Trossachs

Bull Box, Downham Market, Norfolk

Cathedral, Lincoln, Lincolnshire

Cellar Rat, Reddish, Cheshire

Cwmbran, Upper Cwmbran, Gwent

Dane Town, Denton, Greater Manchester

Ffos y Ffin, Capel Dewi, West Wales

Highgate, Walsall, West Midlands

Kilderkin, Impington, Cambridgeshire

Loweswater, Loweswater, Cumbria

Old Foreigner, Glenkindie, Aberdeen & Grampian

Oyster, Easdale, Isle of Seil, Argyll & The Isles

Reepham, Reepham, Norfolk

Rugby, Willey, Warwickshire

Ryburn, Sowerby Bridge, West Yorkshire

Stumpy's, Newchurch, Isle of Wight

Tindall, Seething, Norfolk

Warrior, Redruth, Cornwall

Wild Walker, Derby, Derbyshire

Windie Goat, Failford, Ayrshire & Arran

Future breweries

The following new breweries have been notified to the Guide and will start to produce beer during 2010/2011. In a few cases, they were in production during the summer of 2010 but were too late for a full listing in the Guide:

4 T's, Warrington, Cheshire

Albion, Warrington, Cheshire

Brewery Tap, Leeds, West Yorkshire

Clun, Clun, Shropshire

Coppice Side, Heanor, Derbyshire

Cromarty, Davidston, Highlands & Western Isles

Dove Street, Ipswich, Suffolk

Grove, Huddersfield, West Yorkshire

Kent, Kent

Kinneil, Bo'ness, Edinburgh & The Lothians

Loch Ness, Drumnadrochit, Highlands & Western Isles

Merlin, Holmes Chapel, Cheshire

Mighty Hop, Lyme Regis, Dorset

Red Man, Braystones, Cumbria

Saints & Sinners, Walmer, Kent

Shenstone, Lichfield, Staffordshire

Tap House, Smisby, Leicestershire

Thorncombe, Thorncombe, Somerset

Tideswell, Tideswell, Derbyshire

Topsham, Topsham, Devon

Trent Navigation, Nottingham, Nottinghamshire

Trowel, Chesham, Buckinghamshire

Urban, Birmingham, West Midlands

Welbeck Abbey, Welbeck, Nottinghamshire

XT, Oxfordshire

New nationals

Greene King, Marston's and Wells & Young's are such a major force in British brewing that they have outstripped their status as 'super regionals' and become fully-fledged national producers. This is a result of the volumes of beer they produce and their national reach to consumers through their substantial pub estates and the free trade. These 'new nationals' do not match the size of the global brewers (see next section) but unlike the globals they have a powerful commitment to cask beer. Greene King's IPA, Marston's Pedigree and Wells & Young's Young's Bitter, Courage Best and Bombardier are among the best-selling cask beers in Britain. The nationals have reached their status by different routes: Greene King has a track record of buying and closing breweries, such as Ridley's and Hardy & Hanson and concentrating production at its Suffolk plant. Marston's, on the other hand, has bought the likes of Brakspear/Wychwood, Jennings and Ringwood and kept those breweries in operation; though it did close the Mansfield Brewery. Wells & Young's is a result of a merger in 2006 between Charles Wells of Bedford and Young's of Wandsworth in London, but Young's had signalled its intention to leave brewing and the merger was more of an arranged marriage. All production is now based at the Bedford brewery. As a result of the lack of interest in cask beer among the global producers, the nationals have picked up contracts to brew such once-revered brands as Draught Bass and Tetley Bitter. In the case of Wells & Young's, it is now the majority owner of the former S&N brands Courage Best and Directors.

GREENE KING
Greene King

Greene King plc, Westgate Brewery, Bury St Edmunds, Suffolk, IP33 1QT
☎ (01284) 763222 ✉ solutions@greeneking.co.uk
⊕ greeneking.co.uk
Shop Mon-Sat 10am-5pm; Sun 12-4pm
Tours 11am, 2pm and evening by arrangement

⊗ Greene King has been brewing in the market town of Bury St Edmunds since 1799. In the 1990s it bought the brands of the former Morland and Ruddles breweries and has given a massive promotion to Old Speckled Hen, which in bottled form is now the biggest ale brand in Britain. As a result of buying the former Morland pub estate, the company acquired a major presence in the Thames Valley region. But it has not confined itself to East Anglia or the Home Counties. Its tenanted and managed pubs, which include Old English Inns and Hungry Horse, total more than 2,100 while the assiduous development of its free trade sales, totalling more than 3,000 outlets, means its beers can be found as far from its home base as Wales and the north of England. In 2005 Greene King bought and rapidly closed Ridley's of Essex. Also in 2005, the group bought Belhaven of Dunbar in Scotland. Belhaven has a large pub estate that has enabled Greene King to build sales north of the border. In 2006 the group bought and closed Hardys & Hansons in Nottingham, taking its pub estate to close to 3,000. Seasonal beers change monthly with sporting or topical names. Bottle-conditioned beer: Hen's Tooth (ABV 6.5%).

XX Mild (OG 1035, ABV 3%) 🍺
A dark mild with a sweet and roast flavour.

IPA (OG 1036, ABV 3.6%) ◆
Hoppy bitter with a sweet aftertaste.

Ruddles Best Bitter (OG 1037, ABV 3.7%) ◆
An amber/brown beer, strong on bitterness but with some initial sweetness, fruit and subtle, distinctive Bramling Cross hop. Dryness lingers in the aftertaste.

H&H Bitter (OG 1038, ABV 3.9%)
A balance of sweetness and bitterness that combines with a subtle hop character. A distinctive beer with a full finish.

Morland Original Bitter (OG 1039, ABV 4%)
A subtle malt and fruit character and a pronounced bitter finish.

H&H Olde Trip (OG 1043, ABV 4.3%)
A rich toffee flavoured beer with a fruity character and a clean, bitter finish.

Ruddles County (OG 1048, ABV 4.3%) ◆
Sweet, malty and bitter, with a dry and bitter aftertaste.

Old Speckled Hen (OG 1045, ABV 4.5%) ◆
Smooth, malty and fruity, with a short finish.

Abbot Ale (OG 1049, ABV 5%)
A full-bodied, distinctive beer with a bittersweet aftertaste.

Belhaven

Belhaven Brewing Co, Spott Road, Dunbar, East Lothian, EH42 1RS
☎ (01368) 862734 ✉ info@belhaven.co.uk
⊕ belhaven.co.uk
Shop open during tours
Tours by arrangement

☺Belhaven is located in Dunbar, some 30 miles east of Edinburgh on the East Lothian coast. The company claimed to be the oldest independent brewery in Scotland but it lost that independence when Greene King bought it. Belhaven owns 275 tied pubs and has around 2,500 direct free trade accounts. Only 3% of production is cask beer: the company concentrates on its Belhaven Best keg beer. Seasonal beers: Fruit Beer (ABV 4.6%, Jul), Fruity Partridge (ABV 5.2%, Dec).

60/- Ale (OG 1030, ABV 2.9%) ◆
A fine but virtually unavailable example of a Scottish light. This bittersweet, reddish-brown beer is dominated by fruit and malt with a hint of roast and caramel, and increasing bitterness in the aftertaste.

70/- Ale (OG 1038, ABV 3.5%) 🍺 ◆
This pale brown beer has malt and fruit and some hop throughout, and is increasingly bittersweet in the aftertaste.

Sandy Hunter's Traditional Ale (OG 1038, ABV 3.6%) ◆
A distinctive, medium-bodied beer. An aroma of malt and hops greets the nose. A hint of roast combines with the malt and hops to give a bittersweet taste and finish.

80/- Ale (OG 1040, ABV 4.2%)
One of the last remaining original Scottish 80 Shillings, with malt the predominant flavour characteristic, though it is balanced by hop and fruit. Those used to hops as the leaders in a beer's taste may find this complex ale disconcerting.

St Andrew's Ale (OG 1046, ABV 4.9%)
A bittersweet beer with lots of body. The malt, fruit and roast mingle throughout with hints of hop and caramel.

For Edinburgh Brewing Co (qv):

Edinburgh Pale Ale (ABV 3.4%)

For Maclay pub group:

Signature (OG 1038, ABV 3.8%)
A pronounced malty note is followed by a digestive biscuit flavour. The beer has a late addition of Goldings and Styrian hops.

Kane's Amber Ale (ABV 4%)
A hoppy aroma gives way to a malty yet slightly bitter flavour.

Wallace IPA (ABV 4.5%)
A classic IPA in both colour and style, with a long, dry finish.

Golden Scotch Ale (ABV 5%)
Brewed to an original Maclay's recipe, the emphasis is firmly on malt.

MARSTON'S

Marston's plc, Marston's House, Wolverhampton, West Midlands, WV1 4JT
☎ (01902) 711811 ✉ enquiries@marstons.co.uk
marstons.co.uk

Marston's, formerly Wolverhampton & Dudley, has grown with spectacular speed in recent years. It became a 'super regional' in 1999 when it bought both Mansfield and Marston's breweries, though it quickly closed Mansfield. In 2005 it bought Jennings of Cockermouth and has invested £250,000 in Cumbria to expand fermenting and cask racking capacity. In total, Marston's owns 2,200 pubs and supplies some 3,000 free trade pubs and clubs throughout the country. It no longer has a stake in Burtonwood Brewery (qv) but brews Burtonwood Bitter for the pub estate, which is owned by Marston's. It added a further 70 pubs in 2006 when it bought Celtic Inns for £43.6 million. In January 2007 it paid £155 million for the 158-strong Eldridge Pope pub estate. In July 2007 it bought Ringwood in Hampshire and in the same year added Brakspear and Wychwood in Witney, Oxfordshire. It will brew Tetley Bitter at Wolverhampton when Carlsberg UK (qv) closes the Leeds brewery.

Banks's

Banks's Brewery, Park Brewery, Wolverhampton, West Midlands, WV1 4NY
☎ (01922) 711811 ✉ enquiries@marstons.co.uk
bankssbeer.co.uk
Shop Mon-Fri 10am-5pm; Sat 9.30am-12pm (excluding Bank Holidays)
Tours can be booked online or phone (01902) 329653

Banks's was formed in 1890 by the amalgamation of three local companies. Hanson's was acquired in 1943 but its Dudley brewery was closed in 1991. Hanson's beers are now brewed in Wolverhampton, though its pubs retain the Hanson's livery. Banks's Original, the biggest-selling brand, is a fine example of West Midlands mild ale and in 2010 the group decided to return to the traditional name of Mild to keep pace with growing demand for the style. Beers from the closed Mansfield Brewery are now brewed at Wolverhampton. Hanson's Mild has been discontinued.

Mild/Original (OG 1036, ABV 3.5%)
An amber-coloured, well-balanced, refreshing session beer.

Bitter (OG 1038, ABV 3.8%)
A pale brown bitter with a pleasant balance of hops and malt. Hops continue from the taste through to a bittersweet aftertaste.

Mansfield Cask Ale (OG 1038, ABV 3.9%)

Brakspear

Brakspear Brewing Co, Eagle Maltings, The Crofts, Witney, Oxfordshire, OX28 4DP
☎ (01993) 890800 ✉ info@brakspear-beers.co.uk
brakspear-beers.co.uk
Merchandise available online or in Brewery store Mon-Sat 10am-5pm (excluding Bank Holidays)
Tours by arrangement

Brakspear, along with Wychwood (see below) was bought by Marston's in 2007. Brakspear was originally based in Henley-on-Thames and is one of Britain's oldest breweries, founded before 1700 and run by the Brakspear family since 1779. In 2002, the brewery closed and became a pub company. Refresh UK, a company based in Witney and owners of Wychwood, bought the rights to the Brakspear brands and brewed them again from 2004 after moving the Henley equipment, including the famous 'double drop' fermenters, to Witney. NB Pubs that carry the Brakspear name belong to a separate company that has no connection with Brakspear Brewing Co, though the brewery does supply the pub company with beer. Bottle-conditioned beers are available.

Bitter (OG 1035, ABV 3.4%)
A classic copper-coloured pale ale with a big hop resins, juicy malt and orange fruit aroma, intense hop bitterness in the mouth and finish, and a firm maltiness and tangy fruitiness throughout.

Oxford Gold (OG 1040, ABV 4%)

Jennings

Jennings Bros plc, Castle Brewery, Cockermouth, Cumbria, CA13 9NE
☎ 0845 129 7185 jenningsbrewery.co.uk
Shop Mon-Sat 10am-4pm, Sun 10am-4pm (Jul & Aug)
Tours daily (except Sun); 7 days a week Jul & Aug. Booking advised. Other tours by arrangement. Book online or call 0845 129 7190

Jennings Brewery was established as a family concern in 1828 in the village of Lorton. The company moved to its present location in 1874. Pure Lakeland water is still used for brewing, drawn from the brewery's own well, along with Maris Otter barley malt and Fuggles and Goldings hops. The brewery was badly damaged in the Cumbrian floods of winter 2009 and was out of operation for three months. Marston's commitment to the plant was shown by the rapid repairs at a cost of several million pounds. Regular specials reflect the Cumbrian heritage of Jennings and include Sticklepike (ABV 3.8%), Crag Rat (ABV 4.3%), Golden Host (ABV 4.3%), Tom Fool (4%).

Dark Mild (OG 1031, ABV 3.1%)
A well-balanced, dark brown mild with a malty aroma, strong roast taste, not over-sweet, with some hops and a slightly bitter finish.

Bitter (OG 1035, ABV 3.5%)
A malty beer with a good mouthfeel that combines with roast flavour and a hoppy finish.

Cumberland Ale (OG 1039, ABV 4%)
A light, creamy, hoppy beer with a dry aftertaste.

Cocker Hoop (OG 1044, ABV 4.6%)
A rich, creamy, copper-coloured beer with raisiny maltiness balanced with a resiny hoppiness, with a developing bitterness towards the end.

Sneck Lifter (OG 1051, ABV 5.1%)
A strong, dark brown ale with a complex balance of fruit, malt and roast flavours through to the finish.

Marston's

Marston, Thompson & Evershed, Marston's Brewery, Shobnall Road, Burton upon Trent, Staffordshire, DE14 2BW
☎ (01283) 531131 ✉ enquiries@marstons.co.uk
marstons.co.uk
Shop Mon-Fri 10am-5pm; Sat 9.30am-12pm (excluding Bank Holidays)
Tours can be booked on (01283) 507391

Marston's has been brewing cask beer in Burton since 1834 and the current site is the home of the only working 'Burton Union' fermenters, housed in rooms known collectively as the 'Cathedral of Brewing'. Burton Unions were developed in the 19th century to cleanse the new pale ales of yeast. Only Pedigree is fermented in the unions but yeast from the system is used to ferment the other beers.

EPA (OG 1036, ABV 3.6%)
A new beer launched in spring 2010.

Burton Bitter (OG 1037, ABV 3.8%)
Overwhelming sulphurous aroma supports a scattering of hops and fruit with an easy-drinking sweetness. The taste develops from the sweet middle to a satisfyingly hoppy finish.

Pedigree (OG 1043, ABV 4.5%)
Pale brown with a gentle aroma of sweet malt and a dash of hops. Light in taste with no dominant flavours but a sweet aftertaste.

Old Empire (OG 1057, ABV 5.7%)
Sulphur dominates the aroma over malt. Malty and sweet to start but developing bitterness with fruit and a touch of sweetness. A balanced aftertaste of hops and fruit leads to a lingering bitterness.

For AB InBev:

Draught Bass (OG 1043, ABV 4.4%)
Pale brown with a fruity aroma and a hint of hops. Hoppy but sweet taste with malt, then a lingering hoppy bitterness.

Ringwood

Ringwood Brewery Ltd, Christchurch Road, Ringwood, Hampshire, BH24 3AP
☎ (01425) 471177
✉ enquiries@ringwoodbrewery.co.uk
ringwoodbrewery.co.uk
Shop Mon-Sat 9.30am-5pm
Tours Sat & Sun afternoon

Ringwood was bought in 2007 by Marston's for £19 million. The group plans to increase production to 50,000 barrels a year. Some 750 outlets are supplied and seven pubs are owned. Seasonal beers: Boondoggle (ABV 4%, summer), Showman's Tipple (ABV 3.8%, spring), Huffkin (ABV 4.4%, autumn), XXXX Porter (ABV 4.7%, winter).

Best Bitter (OG 1038, ABV 3.8%)
A malty session bitter with strong toffee notes in the aroma, leading to a short, bittersweet finish. Malt tends to dominate throughout.

Boondoggle (OG 1043, ABV 4.2%)

Fortyniner (OG 1049, ABV 4.9%)
Despite a change of ownership, this remains a beer with a fruity, biscuity aroma leading to a sweet but well-balanced taste with malt, fruit and hop flavours all present. The finish is bittersweet with some fruit.

Old Thumper (OG 1055, ABV 5.6%)
A powerful, sweet, copper-coloured beer. A fruity aroma preludes a strong, sweet, malty taste with soft fruit and caramel, which is not cloying and leads to a surprisingly bittersweet aftertaste.

SIBA Direct Delivery Scheme

In 2003 the Society of Independent Brewers (SIBA) launched a Direct Delivery Scheme (DDS) that enables its members to deliver beer to individual pubs rather than to the warehouses of pub companies. Before the scheme came into operation, small craft brewers could only sell beer to the national pubcos if they delivered beer to their depots. In one case, a brewer in Sheffield was told by Punch Taverns that the pubco would only take his beer if he delivered it to a warehouse in Liverpool and then returned to pick up the empty casks. In the time between delivery and pick-up, some of the beer would have been delivered by Punch to...Sheffield.

Now SIBA has struck agreements with Admiral Taverns, Edinburgh Woollen Mills, Enterprise Inns, New Century Inns, Orchard Pubs, and Punch, as well as off-licence chains Asda and Thresher to deliver direct to their pubs or shops. The scheme has been such a success that DDS is now a separate but wholly-owned subsidiary of SIBA. See **www.siba.co.uk/dds_site**

Wychwood

Wychwood Brewery Ltd, Eagle Maltings, The Crofts, Witney, Oxfordshire, OX28 4DP
☎ (01993) 890800 ✉ info@wychwood.co.uk
🌐 wychwood.co.uk
Shop Sat 2-6pm
Tours by arrangement

Wychwood Brewery is located on the fringes of the ancient medieval forest, the Wychwood. The brewery was founded in 1983 on a site dating back to the 1880s, which was once the original maltings for the town's brewery. A range of seasonal beers is produced.

Hobgoblin (OG 1045, ABV 4.5%)
The beer was reduced in strength early in 2008 by the previous owner, Refresh UK.

WELLS & YOUNG'S

Wells & Young's IFBB

Wells & Young's Brewing Co, Bedford Brewery, Havelock Street, Bedford, MK40 4LU
☎ (01234) 272766
✉ postmaster@wellsandyoungs.co.uk
🌐 wellsandyoungs.co.uk
Merchandise available online
Tours by arrangement

Wells & Young's was created in 2006 when Young's of Wandsworth, south London, announced it would close its brewery and transfer production to Bedford. The new company jointly owns the Bedford Brewery, which opened in 1976; the Wells family has been brewing in the town since 1876. Wells & Young's has a combined sales team that has expanded sales of such key brands as Wells Bombardier, the fastest-growing premium cask beer in Britain, and Young's Bitter, the fastest-growing standard cask bitter. Wells and Young's runs separate pub estates. In 2007, Scottish & Newcastle reached an agreement with W&Y to brew Courage beers at Bedford. A new company, Courage Brands Ltd, was created, with W&Y controlling 83% of the shares. The deal added a further 80,000 barrels a year at Bedford, taking volumes to more than 550,000-600,000 barrels and overtaking Greene King in size. The Courage beers are aimed primarily at the free trade. Some Wells' beers are now available in Young's pubs and vice-versa. Wells owns 257 pubs, of which 250 serve cask beer; Young's owns 222 pubs in London and the Home Counties, all selling real ale. Young's has invested heavily in estate improvement and expansion over the past two years. Seasonal beer: Young's Waggledance (ABV 4%). There are several occasional beers. Bottle-conditioned beers: Young's Bitter (ABV 4.5%). Young's London Gold (ABV 4.8%), Young's Special London Ale (ABV 6.4%).

Eagle IPA (OG 1035, ABV 3.6%) ◆
A refreshing, amber session bitter with pronounced citrus hop aroma and palate, faint malt in the mouth, and a lasting dry, bitter finish.

Young's Bitter (OG 1036, ABV 3.7%) ◆
This light drinking amber bitter has citrus initially on the palate with sweet malt and a hint of hops that linger into a slightly dry and bitter finish.

Wells Bombardier (OG 1042, ABV 4.3%) ◆
A heavy aroma of malt and raspberry jam. Traces of hops and bitterness are quickly submerged under a smooth, malty sweetness. A solid, rich finish.

Young's Special (OG 1044, ABV 4.5%) ◆
Pale brown in colour, this rounded best bitter has citrus throughout plus some slight creamy toffee, which balances the bitterness that grows in the aftertaste.

Young's Winter Warmer (OG 1055, ABV 5%) ◆
Dark ruby brown beer with roast coffee and raisin fruitiness on the nose and palate. Molasses are also present, lingering into the finish with a little burnt dryness.

For Courage Brands:

Courage Best Bitter (OG 1038.3, ABV 4%)
Malt and hops on the nose, with a full palate of malt, fruit and hops and a dry and bitter finish.

Courage Directors Bitter (OG 1045.5, ABV 4.8%)
A chestnut-coloured beer with a rich malty aroma, fruit and hops in the mouth and a long malty, fruity and hoppy finish.

Brewery organisations

There are three organisations mentioned in the Breweries section to which breweries can belong.

The Independent Families Brewers of Britain (IFBB) represents around 35 regional companies still owned by families. As many regional breweries closed in the 1990s, the IFBB represents the interests of the survivors, staging events such as the annual Cask Ale Week to emphasise the important role played by the independent sector.

The Society of Independent Brewers (SIBA) represents the growing number of small craft or micro brewers: some smaller regionals are also members. SIBA is an effective lobbying organisation and played a leading role in persuading the government to introduce Progressive Beer Duty. It has also campaigned to get large pub companies to take beers from smaller breweries and has had considerable success with Enterprise Inns, the biggest pubco.

The East Anglian Brewers' Co-operative (EAB) was the brainchild of Brendan Moore at Iceni Brewery. Finding it impossible to get their beers into pub companies and faced by the giant power of Greene King in the region, the co-op makes bulk deliveries to the genuine free trade and also sells beer at farmers' markets and specialist beer shops. EAB also buys malt and hops in bulk for its members, thus reducing costs.

Global giants

Eight out of ten pints of beer brewed in Britain come from the international groups listed below. Most of these huge companies have little or no interest in cask beer. Increasingly, their real ale brands are produced for them by smaller regional brewers. Their neglect of cask beer is remarkable, given that cask is the only growth sector of the beer market and sales of both the globals' lagers and keg ales are in decline. A-B InBev's response to the decline of its lagers has been to offer for sale its leading real ales, including Draught Bass; Carlsberg is closing the Tetley brewery in Leeds; and Heineken has axed the former Federation Clubs brewery in Gateshead.

A-B InBev

A-B InBev UK Ltd, Porter Tun House, 500 Capability Green, Luton, Bedfordshire, LU1 3LS
☎ (01582) 391166
✉ name.surname@interbrew.co.uk 🌐 inbev.com

The biggest merger in brewing history in 2008 created A-B InBev, when InBev of Belgium and Brazil bought American giant Anheuser-Busch, best-known for the world's biggest (but not best) beer brand, Budweiser. The giant is a major player in the European market with such lager brands as Stella Artois and Jupiler. It has a slight interest in ale brewing with the cask- and bottle-conditioned wheat beer, Hoegaarden, and the Abbey beer Leffe. It has a ruthless track record of closing plants and disposing of brands: it has already announced the closure of the historic Stag Brewery in Mortlake, London, formerly Watney's, where the British version of Budweiser is brewed. It's not known where the brand will be produced following the closure of the Mortlake plant but it's unlikely that many readers of the Good Beer Guide will care. In 2000 Interbrew, as it was then known, bought both Bass's and Whitbread's brewing operations, giving it a 32 per cent market share. The British government told Interbrew to dispose of parts of the Bass brewing group, which were bought by Coors (qv). Draught Bass has declined to around 60,000 barrels a year: it once sold more than two million barrels a year, but was sidelined by the Bass empire. It is now brewed under licence by Marston's (see New Nationals section). Only 30 per cent of draught Boddingtons is now in cask form and this is brewed under licence by Hydes of Manchester (qv Independents section).

Brewed for A-B InBev by Brain's of Cardiff:

Flowers IPA (ABV 3.6%)

Flowers Original (ABV 4.5%)
Along with Boddington's Bitter and Draught Bass, the Flowers' beers have been put up for sale by A-B InBev.

Carlsberg UK

Carlsberg Brewing Ltd, PO Box 142, The Brewery, Leeds, West Yorkshire, LS1 1QG
☎ (0113) 259 4594 🌐 carlsberg.co.uk/carlsberg.com

Tetley, the historic Leeds brewery, will close during the course of 2011. The two Tetley Milds are already produced by Marston's at its Burton-on-Trent site and cask Tetley Bitter will moved to Banks's Brewery in Wolverhampton. We leave it to the intellectual giants of the Carlsberg public relations department to explain how an iconic Yorkshire ale can be brewed in the West Midlands. Carlsberg UK is a wholly-owned subsidiary of Carlsberg Breweries of Copenhagen, Denmark, Carlsberg is an international lager giant. In Britain its lagers are brewed at a dedicated plant in Northampton.

Tetley Bitter (OG 1035, ABV 3.7%) ◆
A smooth, creamy bitter beer with a hoppy nose. Hops are joined by a good dose of balancing malt until both give way to the long, bitter finish.

Brewed for Carlsberg by JW Lees:

Ansells Mild (OG 1033, ABV 3.4%)

Ansells Best Bitter (OG 1035, ABV 3.7%)

Greenalls Bitter (ABV 3.8%)

Draught Burton Ale (OG 1047, ABV 4.8%) ◆
A beer with hops, fruit and malt present throughout, and a lingering complex aftertaste, but lacking some hoppiness compared to its Burton original.

Brewed for Carlsberg by Marston's:

Tetley Dark Mild (OG 1031, ABV 3.2%)

Tetley Mild (OG 1034, ABV 3.3%) ◆
A mid-brown beer with a light malt and caramel aroma. A well-balanced taste of malt and caramel follows, with good bitterness and a satisfying finish.

Molson Coors

Molson Coors Brewers Ltd, 137 High Street, Burton upon Trent, Staffordshire, DE14 1JZ
☎ (01283) 511000 🌐 molsoncoorsbrewers.com

Molson Coors is the result of a merger between Molson of Canada and Coors of Colorado, U.S. Coors established itself in Europe in 2002 by buying part of the former Bass brewing empire, when Interbrew (now A-B InBev) was instructed by the British government to divest itself of some of its interests in Bass. Coors owns several cask ale brands. It brews 110,000 barrels of cask beer a year (under licensing arrangements with other brewers) and also provides a further 50,000 barrels of cask beer from other breweries.

M&B Mild (OG 1034, ABV 3.2%)

Stones Bitter (OG 1037, ABV 3.7%)
The beer was brewed for Molson Coors by the Highgate Brewery in Walsall, which closed in June 2010. As the Good Beer Guide went to press, it was not known where Stones will now be produced.

Worthington's White Shield (ABV 5.6%)
Bottle-conditioned: Sweet aroma, woody tastes with angelica, nettles and sharp apples. Ever-changing tastes but a long hoppy finish. Due to the success of the beer since it returned to Burton, production has moved to the main Coors brewery where more than 100,000 barrels a year are produced. The beer has been a major success in Sainsbury's stores and increased production has

allowed the beer to go on sale in Asda, Morrisons and Waitrose outlets.

Brewed for Coors by Everards:

Hancock's HB (OG 1038, ABV 3.6%) ◆
A pale brown, slightly malty beer whose initial sweetness is balanced by bitterness but lacks a noticeable finish. A consistent if inoffensive Welsh beer.

Worthington's Bitter (OG 1038, ABV 3.6%)
A pale brown bitter of thin and unremarkable character.

M&B Brew XI (OG 1039.5, ABV 3.8%)
A sweet, malty beer with a hoppy, bitter aftertaste.

White Shield Brewery

White Shield Brewery, Horninglow Street, Burton upon Trent, Staffordshire, DE14 1YQ
☎ 0845 600 0598
Tours by arrangement

The White Shield Brewery, formerly the Museum Brewing Co, was based in part of the now-closed Museum of Brewing. The brewery opened in 1994 and recreated some of the older Bass beers that had been discontinued. The brewery's production is divided 50:50 between cask and bottled beers. Imperial Stout and No 1 Barley Wine are now brewed on an occasional basis and in bottle only, though draught versions are supplied to CAMRA festivals when supplies are available. NB: The brewery was due to move during 2010 to the re-opened National Brewery Centre. The range of beers may change.

Worthington's Red Shield (ABV 4.2%) ◆
Hay and straw bales aroma. Old corner sweetshop taste with malt, too. Sweet aftertaste with hints of fruit and hop bitterness for a perfect balance. A new cask beer due to be rolled out nationally during 2010/2011.

Worthington's St Modwen (OG 1038, ABV 4.2%) ◆
Hop and malt aroma. Delicate taste of hops and orange. Flowery citrus fruity finish.

Brewery Tap (OG 1042, ABV 4.5%)

Worthington E (OG 1044, ABV 4.8%) ◆
Grassy hop start with a bittersweet touch to follow. Bitterness grows with a dry edge and good hoppy finish.

Worthington's White Shield (ABV 5%) ◆
Sweet aroma and woody tastes with angelica, nettles and sharp apples. Ever-changing tastes but a long, hoppy finish. A new cask version of the bottled beer.

Czar's Imperial Stout (OG 1078, ABV 8%) ◆
A library of tastes, from a full roast, liquorice beginning, dark toffee, brown sugar, molasses, Christmas pudding, rum, dark chocolate to name but a few. Fruit emerges, blackberry changing to blackcurrant jam, then liquorice root.

No 1 Barley Wine (OG 1105, ABV 10.5%) ◆
Unbelievably fruity! Thick and chewy, with fruit and sugar going in to an amazing complex of bitter, fruity tastes. Brewed in summer and fermented in casks for 12 months.

Guinness

Guinness closed its London brewery in 2005. All Guinness keg and bottled products on sale in Britain are now brewed in Dublin.

Heineken UK

Heineken UK, 2-4 Broadway Park, South Gyle Broadway, Edinburgh, EH12 9JZ
☎ (0131) 528 1000 🌐 heineken.com

Heineken UK, formerly Scottish & Newcastle, is Britain's biggest brewing group with close to 30% of the market. Scottish & Newcastle was formed in 1960, a merger between Scottish Brewers (Younger and McEwan) and Newcastle Breweries. In 1995 it bought Courage from its Australian owners, Foster's/Carlton & United. Since the merger that formed Scottish Courage, the group rationalised by closing its breweries in Edinburgh, Newcastle, Nottingham, Halifax and the historic Courage (George's) Brewery in Bristol. The remaining beers were transferred to John Smith's in Tadcaster. It bought the financially stricken Bulmer's Cider group, which included the Beer Seller wholesalers, now part of WaverleyTBS. Heineken continues to own Bulmer's, WaverleyTBS and the S&N 2,000-strong pub estate (including the ex-Globe Pub Co), though the number of WaverleyTBS depots is being ruthlessly reduced and the pub estate is also being whittled down. In 2003, S&N sold the Theakston's Brewery in Yorkshire back to the original family (see Theakston's entry in Independents section). In February 2004, S&N entered into an arrangement with the Caledonian brewery in Edinburgh that gave S&N a 30% stake in Caledonian and 100% control of the brewery's assets but in March 2008 S&N bought the whole of the company, which is now a subsidiary of Heineken. S&N's sole Scottish cask beer, McEwan's 80/-, has been discontinued. The Courage brands are now brewed by Wells & Young's and owned by a new company, Courage Brands Ltd (see New Nationals section).

The closed brewery

To be sure, it was a deserted place, down to the pigeon-house in the brewery-yard, which had been blown crooked on its pole by some high wind, and would have made the pigeons think themselves at sea, if there had been any pigeons there to be rocked by it. But, there were no pigeons in the dove-cot, no horses in the stable, no pigs in the sty, no malt in the store-house, no smells of grains and beer in the copper or the vat. All the uses and scents of the brewery might have evaporated with its last reek of smoke. In a by-yard, there was a wilderness of empty casks, which had a certain sour remembrance of better days lingering about them; but it was too sour to be accepted as a sample of the beer that was gone. **Charles Dickens, Great Expectations**

Berkshire

Berkshire Brewery, Imperial Way, Reading, Berkshire, RG2 0PN
☎ (0118) 922 2988

No cask beer. Closed in April 2010.

Caledonian

Caledonian Brewing Co Ltd, 42 Slateford Road, Edinburgh, EH11 1PH
☎ (0131) 337 1286 ✉ info@caledonian-brewery.co.uk 🌐 caledonian-brewery.co.uk
Tours by arrangement

The brewery was founded by Lorimer & Clark in 1869 and was sold to Vaux of Sunderland in 1919. In 1987 the brewery was saved from closure by a management buy-out. The brewery site was purchased by S&N in 2004 and became a wholly-owned subsidiary of S&N/Heineken in 2008. A rolling programme of seasonal beers is produced. The Harviestoun Brewery (qv), which was a subsidiary of Caledonian, is now independent.

Deuchars IPA (OG 1039, ABV 3.8%) ◆
An extremely tasty and refreshing pale golden session beer. Hops and fruit are evident and are gently balanced by malt. The lingering aftertaste is delightfully bitter and hoppy.

80 (OG 1042, ABV 4.1%) ◆
A predominantly malty, tawny beer with caramel and roast notes throughout. Smooth and rounded with a sweet taste that dries in the finish.

XPA (ABV 4.3%)

Royal

Royal Brewery, 201 Denmark Road, Manchester, M15 6LD
☎ (0161) 220 4371

Massive brewery in Manchester capable of producing 1.3 million barrels of beer a year. No cask beer: concentrates on Foster's ('Drink Australian'!) and Kronenbourg.

Heineken UK Dunston

Brewery closed in 2010. Production (including Newcastle [sic] Brown Ale) has been transferred to John Smith's in Yorkshire.

Heineken UK Tadcaster

John Smith's Brewery, Tadcaster, North Yorkshire, LS24 9SA
☎ (01937) 832091 🌐 heineken.com
Tours by arrangement

The brewery was built in 1879 by a relative of Samuel Smith (qv). John Smith's became part of the Courage group in 1970 before being taken over by S&N. Major expansion has taken place, with 11 new fermenting vessels installed. Traditional Yorkshire Square fermenters have been replaced by conical vessels. John Smith's cask Magnet has been discontinued.

John Smith's Bitter (OG 1035.8, ABV 3.8%) ◆
A copper-coloured beer, well-balanced but with no dominating features. It has a short hoppy finish.

The importance of water to the brewing process is often overlooked. Most people know that barley malt and hops are the main ingredients used in beer making and that yeast turns malt sugars into alcohol. But 93% of even the strongest beer is made up of water – and the quality of the water is essential to the taste and character of the finished product.

Brewers call the water they use in the brewing process 'liquor' to distinguish it from cleaning water. Brewing liquor, whether it comes from natural wells or the public supply, will be filtered and cleaned to ensure its absolute purity. Care will be taken, however, to ensure that vital salts and irons are not removed during the filtering process, as they are essential to the production of cask beer.

The benchmark for brewing liquor is Burton-on-Trent in the English Midlands. The natural spring waters of the Trent Valley have rich deposits of calcium and magnesium sulphates – also known as gypsum and Epsom salts. Salt is a flavour-enhancer and the sulphates in Burton liquor bring out the finest flavours from malts and hops. Since the 19th century, ale brewers throughout Britain and other countries have added salts to 'Burtonise' their liquor.

It's fascinating to compare the levels of salts in the water of three famous brewing locations: Burton, London and Pilsen. Pilsen is the home of the first golden lager beer, Pilsner. Brewers of genuine lager beers want comparatively soft brewing liquor to balance the toasted malt and gentle, spicy hop nature of their beers. Pilsen water has total salts of 30 parts per milligram, with minute amounts of calcium and magnesium.

London, once celebrated as a dark beer region, famous for mild, porter and stout, has 463 total salts per milligram, with high levels of sodium and carbonate. (Dublin, another dark beer city, has similar water to London's). Burton liquor has an astonishing level of total salts of 1,226 per milligram. If this figure is further broken down, Burton liquor is rich in magnesium, calcium, other sulphates and carbonate.

The beers index

These beers refer to those in bold type in the breweries section (beers in regular production) and so therefore do not include seasonal, special or occasional beers that may be mentioned elsewhere in the text.

BEERS INDEX

BEERS INDEX

BEERS INDEX

E

BEERS INDEX

G

BEERS INDEX

H

I

J

M

BEERS INDEX

BEERS INDEX

Q

R

BEERS INDEX

S

T

BEERS INDEX

U

V

W

X

Y

Z

Readers' Feedback & Further Information

Pubs transport – 2011

Hop on a bus, train or tram

Using public transport is an excellent way to get to the pub, but many people use it irregularly, and systems can be slightly different from place to place. This Guide is designed to help you.

Information

First, you need to know the route and time. You should find information at the bus stop timetable case, which usually gives contact telephone numbers and text messaging services. You can also get information from information centres run nationally, regionally or locally. Remember that many operators will not tell you about other operators' services.

Information by phone

The national **Traveline** system (0871 200 22 33) gives information on all bus and local rail services throughout England, Scotland and Wales. Calls are put through to a local call centre and if necessary your call will be switched through to a more relevant centre. Mobile phone users will be given a series of menu options to locate the relevant centre. In London use Traveline or the **Transport for London** information line, 020 7222 1234. For **National Rail Enquiries** telephone 08457 48 49 50.

On the net

Try Transport Direct, **www.transportdirect.info**, or Traveline, **www.traveline.org.uk**. For London try **www.tfl.gov.uk**. National Rail Enquiries are at **www.nationalrail.co.uk/times_fares**. Scotland has its own planner at **www.travelinescotland.com**, with a link from Traveline. Just a tip – it can help to know the post code of the pub(s) you want to visit!

Coach

The two main UK coach sites are:
National Express, 08717 818181,
www.nationalexpress.com
Scottish Citylink, 08705 505050,
www.citylink.co.uk

Using the bus

Bus stops in towns and villages are clearly marked. If there is a number of stops in an area, make sure the service you want is listed on the bus stop plate or timetable case. If no services are listed then all buses should stop there, apart perhaps from some 'express' buses. Give a clear signal to the driver to stop the bus.

Some routes operate on a 'hail and ride' principle where the bus will stop anywhere it is safe to do so. Ask the enquiry service or operator, or, if you use a stop on the outward journey, ask the driver. If you don't know where to get off, ask the driver to let you know. It's often worth asking the driver where your return stop is, as sometimes it's not too obvious.

Some buses run 'on demand' so you'll have to telephone in advance. The information centre should know, and give you the contact number.

Paying your fare

You usually get on at the front and pay the driver. Have some small change ready as some companies operate a 'fast fare' system and don't give change. In central London and on many tram systems you need to buy a ticket in advance from a nearby machine.

The most economical and convenient way to travel around in London, on buses, trams, underground and most trains, is with an oyster card which can be obtained from oyster ticket shops, underground and some rail stations. There is a refundable £3 deposit for one.

Special fares

Where available, return tickets are often cheaper than two singles. Many operators, and some local authorities, offer 'network' tickets for a number of journeys. If buying an operator's multi-journey ticket check that you can use it on other operators' services – important if more than one company operates the route.

On trains, standard and 'saver' return tickets allow you to break your journey, so if you are visiting a number of pubs by train, book to the furthest station. This may not apply to other types of rail ticket – ask in advance.

Concessionary fares

There are concessionary fares schemes for seniors and people with certain disabilities. The English national concessionary fares scheme provides free travel for pass-holders on buses anywhere in England between 9.30am and 11pm, and at any time at weekends or on bank holidays. It does not provide free bus travel outside England, nor

is it generally valid on trains, trams or ferries. However, there are local exceptions where the scheme is enhanced, either for local residents or for everyone. It is worth checking locally.

The Scottish, Welsh and Northern Irish schemes are slightly different. Eligible people should enquire locally. As in England, there are local enhancements.

National Express offer half fare discounts for people over 60 or with certain disabilities on most of their services throughout the United Kingdom. If you think you are eligible, ask before you book. If you have a concessionary fares card, this will generally give proof of entitlement. Scottish passes are valid on long distance coaches within Scotland, such as those operated by Scottish CityLink. This entitlement is only for Scottish residents.

National Rail sell a range of rail cards, including ones for people over 60, with certain disabilities, or between the ages of 16 and 25. These give a discount of 34% on most tickets, and there can be other advantages. Either ask at your nearest staffed station, telephone National Rail Enquiries, or look on the National Rail web site

Complaints, problems and lost property

If you have any complaints, problems or lose anything when using public transport, please contact the operator running the service as soon as possible. Keep your ticket. The information is important. If you feel your complaint is not dealt with satisfactorily, contact the relevant Transport Authority who may be able to help. Service reliability is improving rapidly but occasionally things do go wrong and the bus doesn't turn up. If, because of this, you need get a taxi, ask for a receipt and send it in with your complaint. You may get reimbursed.

Outside Mainland UK, but within the area of this Guide, information services are:

NORTHERN IRELAND
Translink, 02890 666630,
www.translink.co.uk
or **www.traveline.org.uk**

ISLE OF MAN
Isle of Man Transport, 01624 662525,
www.iombusandrail.info

JERSEY
Telephone 01534 877772,
www.thisisjersey.com

GUERNSEY
Island Coachways 01481 720210,
www.buses.gg

NOTE: All information was correct at the time of writing, however CAMRA cannot be held responsible for any changes made since that date.

Award winning pubs

Local CAMRA Pubs of the Year

The Pub of the Year competition is judged by CAMRA members. Each of the CAMRA branches votes for its favourite pub. They are judged on criteria such as customer service, décor, clientele mix, value for money and, most importantly, the quality of the cask beer. The pubs listed below are the winners of the 2010 title; look out for the 🏆 symbol next to the entries in the Guide.

England

🏆 Bedfordshire
Wellington Arms, Bedford
Globe, Dunstable
Rising Sun, Potton

🏆 Berkshire
Bell, Aldworth
Jack o' Newbury, Binfield
Bird in Hand, Knowl Hill
Carpenters Arms, Windsor

🏆 Buckinghamshire
Red Lion, Fenny Stratford
Eight Bells, Long Crendon

🏆 Cambridgeshire
Empress, Cambridge
West End House, Ely
Chequers, Little Gransden
Hand & Heart, Peterborough

🏆 Cheshire
Bhurtpore Inn, Aston
Poachers Inn, Bollington
Brewery Tap, Chester
Red Bull, Kingsley

🏆 Cornwall
Driftwood Spars, Trevaunance Cove

🏆 Cumbria
Cumberland Inn, Alston
Brook House Inn, Boot
Black Dog Inn, Dalton-in-Furness
White Horse, Kings Meaburn

Bhurtpore Inn, Aston, Cheshire.

Woolpack, Chelmsford, Essex.

🏆 Derbyshire
Red Lion, Birchover
Chesterfield Arms, Chesterfield
Coach & Horses, Dronfield
Dead Poets Inn, Holbrook
Spanish Bar, Ilkeston
Bull's Head, Rosliston
Devonshire Arms, South Normanton
Old Hall, Whitehough

🏆 Devon
Teign House Inn, Christow
Old Market Inn, Holsworthy
Fortescue, Plymouth
Tom Cobley Tavern, Spreyton

🏆 Dorset
Cricketers Arms, Bournemouth
Nag's Head, Lyme Regis

🏆 Durham
Quakerhouse, Darlington
Surtees Arms, Ferryhill
Ship Inn, Middlestone Village

🏆 Essex
Bell, Castle Hedingham
Woolpack, Chelmsford
Odd One Out, Colchester
Haywain, Little Bromley
Traitor's Gate, Little Thurrock
Blue Boar Hotel, Maldon

🏆 Gloucestershire & Bristol
Seven Stars, Bristol (Central)
Ebrington Arms, Ebrington
Salutation, Ham

Hampshire
Eagle, Abbotts Ann
Prince of Wales, Farnborough
Leopold Tavern, Portsmouth
Guide Dog, Southampton

Herefordshire
Olde Tavern, Kington

Hertfordshire
Queens Head, Allens Green
Crown & Sceptre, Bridens Camp
Sportsman, Croxley Green
Half Moon, Hitchin
Six Bells, St Albans

Isle of Wight
Travellers Joy, Northwood

Kent
Haywain, Bramling
Halfway House, Brenchley
Elephant, Faversham
Bull, Horton Kirby
Bell Inn, Ivychurch
Flower Pot, Maidstone
Churchill Tavern, Ramsgate
Man of Kent, Rochester
Berry, Walmer

Lancashire
New Inn, Clitheroe
Ship Inn, Haskayne
Water Witch, Lancaster
Taps, Lytham

Leicestershire & Rutland
Black Horse, Grimston
Red Lion, Kegworth
Pub, Leicester
Grainstore, Oakham
Sample Cellar, Old Dalby
Elephant & Castle, Thurlaston

Lincolnshire
White Swan, Barrowby
No. 2 Refreshment Room, Cleethorpes
Strugglers, Lincoln

Dispensary, Liverpool, Merseyside.

Boars Head, Louth
Mama Liz's, Stamford
Half Moon, Willingham by Stow

Greater London
Olde Mitre, EC1: Hatton Garden
Pineapple, NW5: Kentish Town
Trafalgar, SW19: South Wimbledon
Harp, WC2: Covent Garden
Fox, W7: Hanwell
Hope, Carshalton
Five Bells, Chelsfield
Crayford Arms, Crayford
Olde Mitre, High Barnet
Red Lion, Isleworth
Woodies, New Malden
Traveller's Friend, Woodford Green

Greater Manchester
Pendle Witch, Atherton
Kings Head, Bolton
Angel, Manchester City Centre
Knott, Manchester City Centre
Ashton Arms, Oldham
Stalybridge Station Refreshment Rooms (Buffet Bar), Stalybridge
Crown Hotel, Worthington

Merseyside
Dispensary, Liverpool: City Centre
Wheatsheaf Inn, Raby
Ship Inn, Rainhill
Guest House, Southport

Mariners Tavern, Great Yarmouth, Norfolk.

Norfolk
Mariners Tavern, Great Yarmouth
Angel Inn, Larling

Northamptonshire
Malt Shovel Tavern, Northampton

Northumberland
Boathouse Inn, Wylam

Nottinghamshire
Crown, Beeston
Horse & Plough, Bingham
Hearty Goodfellow, Southwell
Corner Pin, Westwood

Horse & Groom, Caulcott, Oxfordshire.

Oxfordshire
Horse & Groom, Caulcott
Bird in Hand, Henley-on-Thames
Far from the Madding Crowd, Oxford
Royal Oak Inn, Wantage

Shropshire
Three Fishes, Shrewsbury
All Nations, Telford: Madeley

Somerset
Griffin Inn, Frome
Star Inn, Watchet

Staffordshire
Swan Hotel, Brewood
Burton Bridge Inn, Burton upon Trent
Duke of Wellington, Lichfield
Ivy House, Newtown
Coachmakers Arms, Stoke-on-Trent: Hanley
Swan Inn, Stone
Bell, Trysull

Suffolk
Dove, Bury St Edmunds
Cross Keys, Henley
Norman Warrior, Lowestoft
Royal Oak, Great Bookham
Surrey Oaks, Newdigate
Barley Mow, Shepperton
Herbert George Wells, Woking

East Sussex
Evening Star, Brighton
Hurst Arms, Eastbourne

Norman Warrior, Lowestoft, Suffolk.

West Sussex
Sportsman, Amberley
Horse & Groom, East Ashling
Royal Oak, Friday Street

Tyne & Wear
Steamboat, South Shields

Warwickshire
Boars Head, Hampton Lucy
Crown, Nuneaton
Raglan Arms, Rugby
Griffin Inn, Shustoke
Winged Spur, Ullenhall
Old Fourpenny Shop, Warwick

West Midlands
Wellington, Birmingham: City Centre
Greyhound Inn, Coventry
Beacon Hotel, Sedgley
Bishop Vesey, Sutton Coldfield
Plough & Harrow, Stourbridge
Black Country Arms, Walsall
Great Western, Wolverhampton

Boars Head, Hampton Lucy, Warwickshire.

Wiltshire
Red Lion Inn, Kilmington
Jolly Huntsman, Kington St Michael
Winchester Gate, Sailsbury
Carters Rest, Wroughton

Worcestershire
Weighbridge, Alvechurch
Fleece Inn, Bretforton
Bell, Pensax
Brewers Arms, West Malvern

East Yorkshire
Walters, Hull
Jemmy Hirst at the Rose & Crown, Rawcliffe

North Yorkshire
Birch Hall Inn, Beck Hole
Cover Bridge Inn, East Witton
Maypole Inn, Long Preston
One-Eyed Rat, Ripon
North Riding Hotel, Scarborough
Ferryboat Inn, Thorganby

South Yorkshire
Market Hotel, Elsecar
Bluecoat, Rotherham
Kelham Island Tavern, Sheffield: Central

West Yorkshire
Old Ship Inn, Brighouse
New Charnwood, Heckmondwike
Rat & Ratchet, Huddersfield
Arcadia Ale & Wine Bar, Leeds: Headingley
Reindeer, Overton
Fanny's Ale & Cider House, Saltaire

Wales

Glamorgan
Pen & Wig, Cardiff
Vale of Glamorgan Inn, Cowbridge
Potters Wheel, Swansea

Gwent
Crown, Pantygelli
Commercial, Risca

Mid-Wales
Ancient Briton, Pen-y-Cae
Severn Arms, Penybont
Star Inn, Talybont on Usk

North-East Wales
Bridge End Inn, Ruabon

North-West Wales
Bryntirion Inn, Llandderfel
Penrhyn Arms, Penrhynside

West Wales
Ship & Castle, Aberystwyth
Prince of Wales, Mynydd y Garreg
Ship, Solva

Marine Hotel, Stonehaven, Scotland.

Bridge House, Belfast, Northern Ireland.

Scotland

Aberdeen & Grampian
Marine Hotel, Stonehaven

Ayrshire & Arran
Geordie's Byre, Ayr

Borders
Border Hotel, Kirk Yetholm

Dumfries & Galloway
Cavens Arms, Dumfries

Edinburgh & The Lothians
Regent, Edinburgh
Volunteer Arms (Staggs), Musselburgh

Greater Glasgow & Clyde Valley
Fox & Hounds, Houston

Highlands & Western Isles
Castle Tavern, Inverness

Kingdom of Fife
Albert Tavern, Freuchie

Loch Lomond, Stirling & The Trossachs
Tappit Hen, Dunblane
Kilcreggan Hotel, Kilcreggan

Tayside
Ericht Ale House, Blairgowrie

Northern Ireland

Bridge House, Belfast

Channel Islands

Jersey
Lamplighter, St Helier

Isle of Man

White House Hotel, Peel

Readers' recommendations

Suggestions for pubs to be included or excluded

All pubs are surveyed by local branches of the Campaign for Real Ale. If you would like to comment on a pub already featured, or on any you think should be featured, please fill in the form below (or a copy of it), and send it to the address indicated. Alternatively, email **gbgeditor@camra.org.uk**. Your views will be passed on to the branch concerned. Please mark your envelope/email with the county where the pub is, which will help us to direct your comments efficiently.

Pub name:

Address:

Reason for recommendation/criticism:

Pub name:

Address:

Reason for recommendation/criticism:

Pub name:

Address:

Reason for recommendation/criticism:

Your name and address:

Please send to: [Name of county] Section, Good Beer Guide,
230 Hatfield Road, St Albans, Hertfordshire AL1 4LW

Pub name:

Address:

Reason for recommendation/criticism:

Pub name:

Address:

Reason for recommendation/criticism:

Pub name:

Address:

Reason for recommendation/criticism:

Pub name:

Address:

Reason for recommendation/criticism:

Your name and address:

Please send to: [Name of county] Section, Good Beer Guide,
230 Hatfield Road, St Albans, Hertfordshire AL1 4LW

Have your say

Feedback on the Good Beer Guide

We are always trying to improve the *Good Beer Guide* for our readers and we welcome your feedback. If you have any suggestions for how the *Good Beer Guide*, Good Beer Guide Mobile Edition or sat-nav POI could be improved, please let us know. Simply fill out the form below (or a copy of it) and send it to the address indicated, or make your comments on our website at: **www.camra.org.uk/gbgfeedback**. Thank you.

Colour section:

Pubs section:

Maps:

Brewery section:

Good Beer Guide Mobile Edition:

Good Beer Guide sat-nav POI:

What other suggestions do you have?

Please send to: Good Beer Guide – Have your say,
230 Hatfield Road, St Albans, Hertfordshire, AL1 4LW

Pub heritage

The National Inventory of Historic Pub Interiors

Victorian bar in the Holly Bush, Hampstead, London.

Pubs with a star (★ or ☆) in this Guide are among those identified by CAMRA as Britain's Real Heritage Pubs. Here, in addition to enjoying great real ale, you can do so in genuinely historic surroundings. It's a real irony that, although the pub is such a great traditional institution in our country, there are now very few which have not been radically altered in recent decades. A major CAMRA achievement over recent years has been to identify those that remain and campaign for their preservation.

The very best of our heritage pubs are now identified in the National Inventory of Historic Pub Interiors. This comes in two parts. Part One (★) lists pubs which are wholly or very largely intact since before the Second World War plus a few select examples built up to 1970. Part Two (☆) contains those which, although altered, have particular rooms or features of national historic significance.

Britain's real heritage pubs are an immensely varied bunch, ranging from small, unspoilt rural classics like the Birch Hall Inn at Beck Hole in North Yorkshire to the great palatial pubs built at the end of the Victorian era, represented most magnificently by the Philharmonic in Liverpool. To find Britain's real heritage pubs look up CAMRA's Heritage Pubs website highlighted at the end of this page. You will find interior photographs of the pubs and full descriptions that will tell you what to look out for.

In addition to these national treasures, there are other pubs which, perhaps not so complete or with such important features, still have genuine heritage to be savoured and saved. Examples in the *Good Beer Guide* include the Colpitts in Durham, a typical multi-room Victorian urban pub; the Bear in Faversham, Kent, a delightful town-centre pub with its Victorian fittings and layout; the Holly Bush, Hampstead, London NW3, also with much Victorian work; the Volunteer Arms, Musselburgh, Edinburgh & The Lothians, with its fine display of spirit casks mounted behind the bar; the Gate House, Norwich, an interwar roadhouse; and the Shakespeare's Head, Leicester, a now-rare survival from the early 1960s.

CAMRA has recently published *Real Heritage Pubs of Wales* which, along with *Scotland's True Heritage Pubs* and guides to London, East Anglia and the North East, can be purchased from CAMRA. In addition, you can find details on the CAMRA Pub Heritage website, where Scotland, London, East Anglia, North East and Northern Ireland real heritage-pubs guides are available for printing.

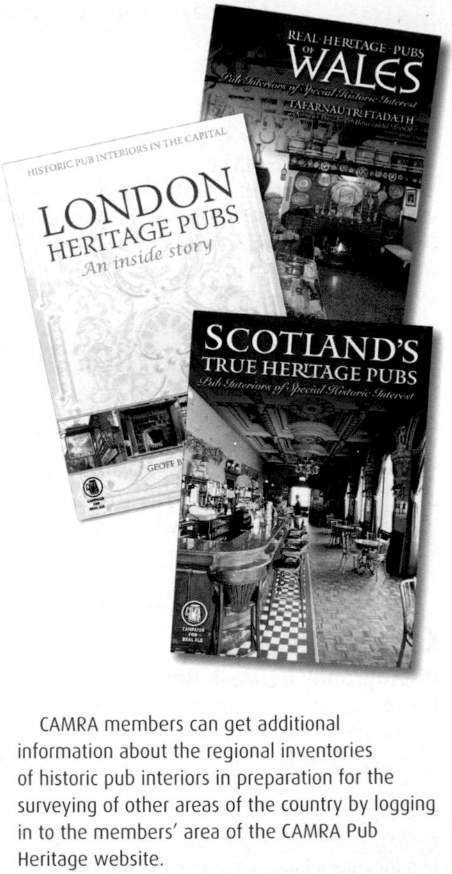

CAMRA members can get additional information about the regional inventories of historic pub interiors in preparation for the surveying of other areas of the country by logging in to the members' area of the CAMRA Pub Heritage website.

For further details of CAMRA's real heritage pubs, visit **www.heritagepubs.co.uk**. To buy heritage pubs guides, **visit www.camra.org.uk/books**.

Books for beer lovers

100 Belgian Beers to Try Before You Die!

Tim Webb & Joris Pattyn

100 Belgian Beers to Try Before You Die! showcases 100 of the best Belgian beers as chosen by internationally-known beer writers Tim Webb and Joris Pattyn. Lavishly illustrated throughout with images of the beers, breweries, Belgian beer bars and some of the characters involved in Belgian brewing, the book encourages both connoisseurs and newcomers to Belgian beer to sample them for themselves, both in Belgium and at home.

£8.50 ISBN 987-1-85249-248-9 Members' Price £7.50

300 Beers to Try Before You Die!

Roger Protz

300 beers from around the world, handpicked by award-winning journalist, author and broadcaster Roger Protz to try before you die! A comprehensive portfolio of top beers from the smallest microbreweries in the United States to family-run British breweries and the world's largest brands. This book is indispensible for both beer novices and aficionados.

£12.99 ISBN 978-1-85249-273-1 Members' Price £10.99

A Beer a Day

Jeff Evans

Written by leading beer writer Jeff Evans, *A Beer a Day* is a beer lover's almanac, crammed with beers from around the world to enjoy on every day and in every season, and celebrating beer's connections with history, sport, music film and television. Whether it's Christmas Eve, Midsummer's Day, Bonfire Night, or just a wet Wednesday in the middle of October, *A Beer a Day* has just the beer for you to savour and enjoy.

£9.00 ISBN 978-1-85249-235-9 Members' Price £8.00

Brew Your Own British Real Ale

Graham Wheeler

The perennial favourite of home-brewers, *Brew Your Own British Real Ale* is a CAMRA classic. This new edition is re-written, enhanced and updated with new recipes for contemporary and award-winning beers, as well as recipes for old favourites no longer brewed commercially. Written by home-brewing authority Graham Wheeler, *Brew Your Own British Real Ale* includes detailed brewing instructions for both novice and more advanced home-brewers, as well as comprehensive recipes for recreating some of Britain's best-loved beers at home.

£14.99 ISBN 978-1-85249-258-8 Members' Price £12.99

Cider

Photography by Mark Bolton

Proper cider and perry – made with apples and pears and nothing but, is a wonderful drink – but there's so much more to it than that. *Cider* is a lavishly illustrated celebration of real cider, and its close cousin perry, for anyone who wants to learn more about Britain's oldest drink. With features on the UK's most interesting and characterful cider and perry makers, how to make your own cider, foreign ciders, and the best places to drink cider – including unique dedicated cider houses, award-winning pubs and year-round CAMRA festivals all over the country – *Cider* is the essential book for any cider or perry lover.

£14.99 ISBN 978-1-85249-259-5 Members' Price £12.99

Good Bottled Beer Guide

Jeff Evans

A pocket-sized guide for discerning drinkers looking to buy bottled real ales and enjoy a fresh glass of their favourite beers at home. The 7th edition of the *Good Bottled Beer Guide* is completely revised, updated and redesigned to showcase the very best bottled British real ales now being produced, and detail where they can be bought. Everything you need to know about bottled beers; tasting notes, ingredients, brewery details, and a glossary to help the reader understand more about them.

£12.99 ISBN 978-1-85249-262-5 Members' Price £10.99

Good Beer Guide Belgium

Tim Webb

The completely revised and updated 6th edition of the guide so impressive that it is acknowledged as the standard work for Belgian beer lovers, even in Belgium itself. The *Good Beer Guide Belgium* includes comprehensive advice on getting there, being there, what to eat, where to stay and how to bring beers back home. Its outline of breweries, beers and bars makes this book indispensible for both leisure and business travellers a well as for armchair drinkers looking to enjoy a selection of Belgian brews from their local beer store.

£14.99 ISBN 978-1-85249-261-8 Members' Price £12.99

Edinburgh Pub Walks

Bob Steel

A practical, pocket-sized travellers' guide to the pubs in and around Scotland's capital city. Featuring 25 town, park and costal walks, Edinburgh Pub Walks enables you to explore the many faces of the city, while never straying too far from a decent pint. Featuring walks in the heart of Edinburgh, as well as routes through its historic suburbs and nearby towns along the Firth of Forth, all accessible by public transport, why not stray off the Royal Mile and explore the history, architecture and landscape of the city.

£9.99 ISBN 978-1-85249-274-8 Members' Price £7.99

London Pub Walks

Bob Steel

A practical, pocket-sized guide enabling you to explore the English capital while never being far away from a decent pint. The newly revised book includes 30 walks around more than 180 pubs serving fine real ale, from the heart of the City and bustling West End to majestic riverside routes and the leafy Wimbledon Common. Each pub is selected for its high-quality real ale, its location and its superb architectural heritage. The walks feature more pubs than any other London pub-walk guide.

£8.99 ISBN 978-1-85249-216-8 Members' Price £7.99

London Heritage Pubs – An inside story

Geoff Brandwood & Jane Jephcote

The definitive guidebook to London's most unspoilt pubs. Raging from gloriously rich Victorian extravaganzas to unspoilt community street-corner locals, the pubs not only have interiors of genuine heritage value, they also have fascinating stories to tell. *London Heritage Pubs – An inside story* is a must for anyone interested in visiting and learning about London's magnificent pubs.

£14.99 ISBN 978-1-85249-247-2 Members' Price £12.99

Order these and other CAMRA books online at **www.camra.org.uk/books**, ask your local bookstore, or contact: CAMRA, 230 Hatfield Road, St Albans, AL1 4LW. Telephone 01727 867201

An offer for CAMRA members

Good Beer Guide annual subscription

Being a CAMRA member brings many benefits, not least a big discount on the Good Beer Guide. Now you can take advantage of an even bigger discount on the Guide by taking out an annual subscription.

Simply fill in the form below and the Direct Debit form on p887 (photocopies will do if you don't want to spoil your book), and send them to CAMRA at 230 Hatfield Road, St Albans, Hertfordshire AL1 4LW.

You will then receive the **Good Beer Guide** automatically every year. It will be posted to you before the official publication date and before any other postal sales are processed.

You won't have to bother with filling in cheques every year and you will receive the book at a lower price than other CAMRA members (for instance, the **2011** Guide was sold to annual subscribers **for just £10** including postage & packing).

So sign up now and be sure of receiving your copy early every year.

Note: This offer is open only to CAMRA members and is only available through using a Direct Debit instruction to a UK bank. This offer applies to the **Good Beer Guide 2012** onwards.

Name ______________________________

CAMRA Membership No. ______________________________

Address and Postcode ______________________________

____

____

____

____

____

I wish to purchase the *Good Beer Guide* annually by Direct Debit and I have completed the Direct Debit instructions to my bank which are enclosed.

Signature ______________________ Date ______________

____

Find Good Beer Guide pubs on the move – any time, anywhere for just £5!

CAMRA is pleased to offer two hi-tech services for beer lovers – **Good Beer Guide Mobile** and the **Good Beer Guide POI** sat-nav file. Together, these offer the perfect solution to pub-finding on the move

Good Beer Guide Mobile

Available on the App Store

FREE 7 DAY TRIAL WITH NO OBLIGATION (Excludes iPhone/iPod Touch)

PACKED WITH USEFUL FEATURES FOR JUST £5 (£4.99 for iPhone/iPod Touch)

Good Beer Guide Mobile provides detailed information on local Good Beer Guide pubs, breweries and beers wherever you are or wherever you're going!

Simple to use, Good Beer Guide Mobile offers the following features:

- Search results with full pub and brewery descriptions and detailed visitor information.
- CAMRA tasting notes for hundreds of regular beers.
- Interactive maps help you find your way.
- Search from a postcode, place name or auto locate using GPS.
- Available on a wide range of mobile phones (please check the website for more information).

For iPhone/iPod Touch visit the **App Store**. For other phones, text **'camra'** to **07766 40 41 42** or visit **http://m.camra.org.uk**

(NOTE: Your standard network charges apply when using this service)

Find Good Beer Guide pubs using satellite navigation!

The Good Beer Guide POI (Points of Interest) file allows users of TomTom, Garmin and Navman sat-nav systems to see the locations of all the 4,500-plus current Good Beer Guide pubs and plan routes to them. So, now, wherever you are, there is no excuse for not finding your nearest Good Beer Guide pub!

The file is simple to install and use and full instructions are provided. Priced at just £5.00, it is the perfect tool for any serious pub explorer. No more wasting time thumbing through road atlases or getting lost down country lanes. Navigate your way easily, every time, and make the most of Britain's best pubs.

- To download the file vist: **www.camra.org.uk/gbgpoi**

Good Beer Guide e-book

The future of pub guides is about to arrive...

In early 2011, CAMRA Books will be launching the *Good Beer Guide* as an e-book in the widely compatible ePUB format. This further addition to CAMRA's digital *Good Beer Guide* products will present exciting new possibilities for users of the Guide. The e-book will provide all the benefits of searchable, adaptable and portable digital content while also making it readable in real size and fully interactive, using GPS, mobile and Internet connectivity (where the e-reader allows).

ePUB

Please check the CAMRA website **www.camra.org.uk/gbg** for the latest news and updates.

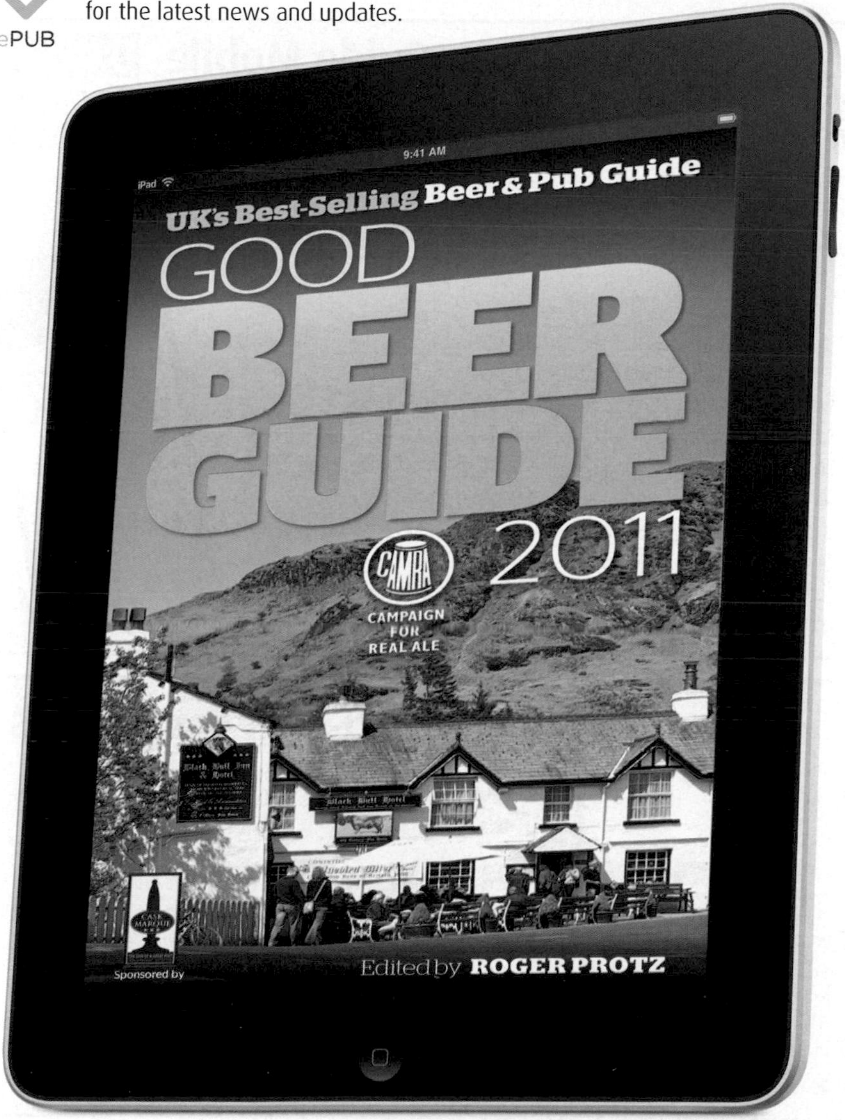

CAMPAIGN FOR REAL ALE

Instruction to your Bank or Building Society to pay by Direct Debit

DIRECT Debit

Please fill in the form and send to: Campaign for Real Ale Ltd. 230 Hatfield Road, St. Albans, Herts. AL1 4LW

Name and full postal address of your Bank or Building Society

To The Manager — Bank or Building Society

Address

Postcode

Name (s) of Account Holder (s)

Bank or Building Society account number

Branch Sort Code

Reference Number

Originator's Identification Number

9	2	6	1	2	9

FOR CAMRA OFFICIAL USE ONLY

This is not part of the instruction to your Bank or Building Society

Membership Number

Name

Postcode

Instruction to your Bank or Building Society

Please pay CAMRA Direct Debits from the account detailed on this Instruction subject to the safeguards assured by the Direct Debit Guarantee. I understand that this instruction may remain with CAMRA and, if so, will be passed electronically to my Bank/Building Society

Signature(s)

Date

Banks and Building Societies may not accept Direct Debit Instructions for some types of account

detached and retained this section

DIRECT Debit

This Guarantee should be detached and retained by the payer.

The Direct Debit Guarantee

- This Guarantee is offered by all Banks and Building Societies that take part in the Direct Debit Scheme. The efficiency and security of the Scheme is monitored and protected by your own Bank or Building Society.
- If the amounts to be paid or the payment dates change CAMRA will notify you 10 working days in advance of your account being debited or as otherwise agreed.
- If an error is made by CAMRA or your Bank or Building Society, you are guaranteed a full and immediate refund from your branch of the amount paid.
- You can cancel a Direct Debit at any time by writing to your Bank or Building Society. Please also send a copy of your letter to us.

It takes all sorts to Campaign for Real Ale

CAMRA, the Campaign for Real Ale, is an independent not-for-profit, volunteer-led consumer group. We promote good-quality real ale and pubs, as well as lobbying government to champion drinkers' rights and protect local pubs as centres of community life.

CAMRA has over 115,000 members from all ages and backgrounds, brought together by a common belief in the issues that CAMRA deals with and their love of good quality British beer. From just £20 a year – that's less than a pint a month – you can join CAMRA and enjoy the following benefits:

- A monthly colour newspaper and quarterly magazine informing you about beer and pub news and detailing events and beer festivals around the country.
- Free or reduced entry to over 150 national, regional and local beer festivals.
- Money off many of our publications including the *Good Beer Guide* and the *Good Bottled Beer Guide*.
- A 10% discount on all holidays booked with Cottages4you and a 8% discount on all holidays booked with Thomas Cook online.
- £20 worth of JD Wetherspoon real ale vouchers (40 x 50 pence off a pint).
- The opportunity to campaign to save pubs under threat of closure, for pubs to be open when people want to drink and a reduction in beer duty that will help Britain's brewing industry survive.

Do you feel passionately about your pint? Then why not join CAMRA

Just fill in the application form (or a photocopy of it) and the Direct Debit form on the previous page to receive 15 months membership for the price of 12!*

If you wish to join but do not want to pay by Direct Debit, please fill in the application form below and send a cheque, payable to CAMRA, to: CAMRA, 230 Hatfield Road, St Albans, Hertfordshire, AL1 4LW. Please note than non Direct Debit payments will incur a £2 surcharge. Figures are given below.

Please tick appropriate box	**Direct Debit**	**Non Direct Debit**
Single membership (UK & EU)	£20 ☐	£22 ☐
Concessionary membership (under 26 or 60 and over)	£14 ☐	£16 ☐
Joint membership	£25 ☐	£27 ☐
Concessionary joint membership	£17 ☐	£19 ☐

Life membership information is available on request.

Title ____________________ Surname ____________________

Forename(s) ____

Address ____

____________________ Postcode ____________________

Date of Birth ____________________ Email address ____________________

Signature ____

Partner's details (for Joint Membership)

Title ____________________ Surname ____________________

Forename(s) ____

Date of Birth ____________________ Email address ____________________

CAMRA will occasionally send you e-mails related to your membership. We will also allow your local branch access to your email. If you would like to opt-out of contact from your local branch please tick here ☐ (at no point will your details be released to a third party).

Find out more at **www.camra.org.uk/joinus** or telephone **01727 867201**

*15 months membership for the price of 12 is only available the first time a member pays by Direct Debit.

NOTE: Membership benefits are subject to change. REF: GBG2011